RELENTLESS

THE HARD-HITTING HISTORY OF BUFFALO BILLS FOOTBALL

Sal Maiorana

Quality Sports Publications

Dedication

To my girls, Christine and Taylor Marie. My world revolves around you
tighter than a Jim Kelly spiral. Thank you for your love, support and patience.
To mom, dad and Lisa: I ask you, now do you forgive me for all those
raucous Sunday afternoons spent screaming at the television?

Cover design by Mick McCay
Title page photograph by Scott Irwig

All photographs compliments of:
Buffalo Bills Archives
NFL Photos
Robert Smith
Michael Groll
Robert Skeoch
Tom Wolf
Rebecca Hooper
Joe Bongi

Quality Sports Publications
10841 Hauser Court
Lenexa, Kansas 66210
(913) 469-1961
(800) 464-1116

Duane Brown, Project Director
Melinda Brown, Designer
David Smale, Editor
Scott Irwig, Photographic Consultant

Printed in the U.S.A.
by
Walsworth Publishing Company

ISBN 1-885758-00-6

Contents

Acknowledgements

When you embark on a project of this magnitude, the list of people who must be thanked is enormous and very often, someone gets left out. With forewarned apologies to anyone whom I may have forgotten, here goes:

Without the help of the Buffalo Bills organization, this book never would have become a reality. First and foremost, I want to thank Ralph C. Wilson Jr., who brought the Bills to Buffalo 35 years ago. Can anyone imagine Buffalo without the Bills? I can't. Thanks, Ralph.

Next, thank you to General Manager John Butler, Vice President/ Administration Jerry Foran and Director of Marketing/Sales John Livsey for understanding the need for a 35th anniversary commemorative publication and allowing me the latitude to provide Bills fans with the most comprehensive history book ever written about a sports franchise.

Thank you to Director of Media Relations Scott Berchtold for his help in the selection of photos and his patience in answering all of my questions.

A special thanks to Director of Public and Community Relations Denny Lynch. It was Denny who first listened to my idea, liked it, and brought it to the attention of his superiors for their approval. Thanks, Denny, for your tireless dedication to detail, and your advice, encouragement and friendship.

And, of course, to the men who have worn the Buffalo Bills uniform, the men whose blood and sweat, laughter and tears, and victories and defeats are what this book is all about. Thanks to every one of you for 35 years of fun and excitement on the gridiron, but especially to Jack Kemp, O.J. Simpson, Fred Smerlas and Jim Kelly, who lent special help in the form of their recollections of their careers, their eras, and what it meant for them to be Buffalo Bills.

To all of the team's public relations directors – Chuck Burr, Jack Horrigan, Budd Thalman, Dave Senko. Denny Lynch and Scott Berchtold – thank you for your expert work on media guides and yearbooks, your maintaining of extensive statistical information and photo files, and most importantly, your diligence in establishing yearly newspaper scrapbooks dating back to 1959 which were the cornerstone of my research. Without those scrapbooks, this book probably would not have been published until the Bills' 40th anniversary.

In those scrapbooks are newspaper articles that chronicled the daily adventures of the Bills. They have been culled from a number of publications and wire services including *The Buffalo News*, the *Courier-Express*, the Rochester *Democrat and Chronicle*, the Rochester *Times-Union*, the Olean *Times-Herald*, the Jamestown *Post-Journal*, the *Batavia Daily News*, the *Toronto Sun*, the *Toronto Star*, the Erie *Times-News*, the *Tonawanda News*, the *Niagara Gazette*, the Dunkirk *Evening Observer*, the Lockport *Union, Sun & Journal*, The Associated Press and United Press International.

I would like to thank all of my fellow writers who have covered the Bills through the years and who filled those scrapbooks with wonderful, insightful, newsworthy prose including: Larry Felser, the dean of all Western New York sportswriters who has been on the Bills beat since Day One; Cy Kritzer, Jack Horrigan, Charley Bailey, Steve Weller, Charley Young, Jim Peters, Phil Ranallo, Mike Kanaley, George Beahon, Bill Cooke, Paul Pinckney, Keith Sheldon, Ralph Hymon, Dave Warner, Ken McKee, Jim Hunt, Jim Baker, Bob Powell, Chuck Ward, Brian Biggane, Marvin Pike, Chuck Pollock, Milt Northrop, Jack Polansky, Gene Cuneo, Warner Hessler, Chip Draper, Mike Dodd, Vic Carucci, Mark Gaughan, Alan Pergament, Russ White, Mike Billoni, Craig Stolze, Frank DeSantis, Larry Bump, Mel Reisner, Erik Brady, Ed McCullough, Bob Lowe, Peter Pascarelli, Bruno Sniders, Rick Woodson, Bill Wolcott, John Hoy, Scott Kindberg, Ed Plaisted, Donn Esmonde, Jerry Sullivan, Bob DiCesare, Jim Kelley, Scott Pitoniak, Mitch Lawrence, Frank LaGrotta, John Bonfatti, Dick Usiak, Jack Saunders, Jerry Reilly, Gary Fallesen, Leo Roth, Lisa Bell, Kyle Kubera, Mal VanValkenburg, Bob Matthews and Bob Salzman.

A hearty thanks to the people at Quality Sports Publications. To my editor, David Smale, who probably needs a new set of eyes after poring through this manuscript. To Melinda Brown, whose design and layout work was stupendous given the volume of materials she had to deal with, not to mention her patience in putting up with my perfectionist ways. To Scott Irwig, who was instrumental in choosing the photographs. And to my publisher, Duane Brown, who took on the project after just one phone conversation and before he ever had seen a paragraph of my writing. His belief in this book, his perseverance through some stretches of bumpy road along the way, and his willingness to let me, as the writer, dictate the style, content and length of the manuscript, made for a harmonious working relationship, the proof of which drips from every page.

Thanks to you, the fans, for your support of the Bills through the good times and the bad, through rain, sleet, wind, snow, hail and yes, once in a while sun. By leading the National Football League in attendance for six years in a row, you have made a name for yourselves nationwide as the greatest fans on earth. This book was written for you, to give you a lifelong keepsake of your favorite team.

And last, but certainly not least, thanks to my wife, Christine. During the writing of this book, she gave birth to our first child, Taylor Marie. Christine endured many long days and nights alone as I locked myself in my study churning out this material. I cannot begin to express how important her patience, love and support were.

Sal Maiorana

Sal Maiorana

*F*oreword

I was 26 years old and just starting to make a name for myself in athletic training while working full-time for the University of Detroit and part-time for the Detroit Lions when I got a phone call from Buster Ramsey, the Lions former defensive coordinator.

It was March of 1960 and Buster had been hired a few months earlier by Ralph Wilson to be head coach of the Buffalo Bills of the fledgling American Football League and he wanted me to come and be the head trainer. I didn't have to think twice. Having grown up in Erie, Pennsylvania, going to Buffalo would get me closer to home, plus, it would give me experience with a professional football team. I figured even if the AFL folded in a few years, working for the Bills would look good on my resume.

Thirty-five years later, I haven't needed to update my resume. Mr. Wilson and I are the only two people left who have been with the team since its inception, and together we have watched the Bills blossom from their humble beginnings into the only team in NFL history to appear in four consecutive Super Bowls.

When I think back on my 35 years with the Bills, what strikes me most is how things have changed. The game, the players, medical technology, the new stadiums, the fans, television. Everything, really. But for me, there has been one constant through it all – my love of my job.

My memories are endless and I cling to them fondly.

I'll never forget the night before training camp in 1961. The helmets arrived late at the old Roycroft Inn in East Aurora where we trained and our new equipment manager, Tony Marchitte, and I were up until four in the morning drilling holes and attaching the facemasks to get them ready for the first practice.

In those early years, Tony and I were virtually the entire behind-the-scenes operation. We would cut and fertilize the practice fields, erect the fences, do the laundry, paint the lockers, hammer 2-by-4s into the wall to make lockers, repair the players' equipment, and, take care of the players' medical needs. Those were long days, but they sure were fun.

I remember our days in War Memorial Stadium where I would set up garbage cans in the locker room to catch the water leaking from the roof, and where the training room was so small, I had to move out of the way while I was taping a player so that other players could walk by.

I remember Buster playing liar's poker on the airplanes, and Buster turning his cap around, getting down into a three-point stance and telling players to hit him so he could demonstrate how to do something.

I remember Lou Saban constantly bringing in new players and Tony having to find space for a new locker.

I remember how, when a player hurt his knee there wasn't much we could do for him. I wish the medical technology that allows us to get players ready within weeks today was available in the old days.

I remember how quietly great Billy Shaw and Tom Sestak were, how smart Jack Kemp was, how flamboyant Cookie Gilchrist was, how brilliant O.J. Simpson was, how classy Joe Ferguson was. I remember how strong Bruce Smith is, how determined Thurman Thomas is and how tough-minded Jim Kelly is.

To tell you the truth I remember an awful lot about the past 35 years.

I can only hope that when I retire, whoever succeeds me will have the same roller-coaster ride that I had because it's been a lot of fun and I've really enjoyed it. I've met a lot of good people over the years and I think my life has been enriched because of it. I hope you, the fans, will enjoy reliving the 35-year history of the Buffalo Bills as much as I have enjoyed being a part of it.

Eddie Abramoski

Ed Abramoski
Head Trainer

The Dream:
Professional Football in Buffalo

They were fools.

Nothing more, nothing less.

Fools.

How else can you describe eight very wealthy, very successful, very influential men who would risk portions of their fortunes and every ounce of their weighty reputations on a fledgling football league that was trying to take on the powerful National Football League starting in 1960, at a time when pro football was a distant, distant second in popularity and familiarity to Major League Baseball?

Wayne Valley, the majority leader of the Oakland Raiders, tabbed this group "The Foolish Club" and none of the other seven American Football League franchise owners – Ralph C. Wilson Jr., Lamar Hunt, Bud Adams, Bob Howsam, Barron Hilton, Billy Sullivan and Harry Wismer – could argue with the moniker.

"It was a foolish club," said Wilson, who after being turned down by Miami, placed his franchise in Buffalo. "It was like starting a new automobile company from scratch and bucking Ford and GM. The NFL was powerfully entrenched. In Detroit, my friends said 'You have a franchise in this honky-tonk AFL?' and they laughed at me at cocktail parties. I was a joke."

But while they may have been foolish, while they may have been laughingstocks in the eyes of men who wore crested blazers to dinner and washed down their caviar with martinis, they were, above all, visionaries. Unlike their innumerable critics, these eight men recognized that pro football had grown exponentially in the 1950s. Sure, the NFL

"The Foolish Club" The men who formed the American Football League: Seated, (left to right): K.S. "Bud" Adams Jr., Houston; Commissioner Joe Foss. Standing, (left to right): Bill Sullivan, Boston; Cal Kunz, who had bought the Denver franchise from Bob Howsam in 1961; Ralph C. Wilson Jr., Buffalo; Lamar Hunt, Dallas; Harry Wismer, New York; Wayne Valley, Oakland; Barron Hilton, San Diego. (Photo: Pro Football Hall of Fame/NFL Photos)

had survived three meek attempts – in 1926, 1936 and 1940, all of which were named the American Football League – to tap into its monopoly. And sure, the All-America Football Conference collapsed after only four seasons of operation in the late 40s.

Center Al Bemiller joined the Bills in 1961 and for the next nine years, he never missed a start, a streak of 126 that stood as the team record until Reggie McKenzie surpassed it in 1981.

But this was 1959. Sports had become an integral part of the American way of life, and 1959 was a great time to be an American. The country was free from war, free from recession, and Americans were about to enter into a new decade with a young, vibrant president in John F. Kennedy leading the way. There was room for more pro football on the sporting landscape, and these "fools" knew it.

Hunt believed in the American dream. Of course, being the youngest son of fabled millionaire Dallas oil tycoon H.L. Hunt, Lamar virtually could buy the American dream if he so chose. Eventually, that's exactly what he did.

Hunt had long been interested in owning a pro football team, but his repeated pleas to the NFL to allow him to enter an expansion team were denied. When he inquired about purchasing an existing franchise – namely the weak Chicago Cardinals – and moving it to his hometown of Dallas, again he was turned away. Fed up with the NFL, Hunt decided to start his own league.

Now the trick was, as Bob Carroll so aptly wrote in his book *When the Grass Was Real*, "to find seven other millionaires willing to buy cabins on the Titanic."

One of those millionaires was Wilson, an insurance and trucking magnate from Detroit.

Wilson was a great fan of the NFL's Detroit Lions, a team whose seeds were planted in Portsmouth, Ohio, before it moved to the Motor City in 1934. Wilson and his father, Ralph Sr., regularly attended Lions games at the University of Detroit stadium until Ralph Jr. went away in 1941 to spend five years in the Navy during World War II. When he returned home in 1946 to join his father in business, his hunger for pro football was ravenous.

Since 1940, the Lions had been owned by Fred Mandel of Chicago, but in 1948, a group of Detroit businessmen, headed by Edwin J. Anderson, felt the team should have local ownership and sought to buy the club from Mandel. Among those whom Anderson enlisted to help make the purchase were Wilson and his father. None of the stockholders owned more than four percent of the team because, as Wilson said, it was not a money-making venture; the goal was simply to get the Lions locally owned.

For the next 11 years, Wilson attended home games at Tiger Stadium and regularly watched the road games on television, but he never took an active role in the running of the club. However, as the years passed, he became more interested in the business and, knowing that the game was growing, he began exploring ways to get closer to the action.

"I saw the game of professional football becoming very popular," Wilson said. "Prior to TV, there were very few people in the country who knew anything about pro football. But then the games started getting on national TV and it started to get popular, although it was always popular with me.

"So I wanted to own a team. I inquired about buying an NFL franchise, but there weren't any for sale. The NFL wasn't interested in expanding at the time. And it wasn't just me. A lot of people wanted NFL franchises in their cities."

One of those people was Lamar Hunt.

"In August of 1959, I was in Saratoga for the racing season," Wilson said. "I picked up *The New York Times* and I read where a young man named Lamar Hunt, who had an oil business in Dallas, was starting a new pro football league and he wanted a franchise in Dallas. The NFL would not expand, so he decided to start his own league and he got hold of a friend of his in Houston, Bud Adams, and he talked to Barron Hilton, whose father owned the Hilton hotel chain, in Los Angeles.

Team owner Ralph C. Wilson Jr. has watched his team grow from its humble beginnings in the AFL in 1960 to the only team in NFL history to appear in four consecutive Super Bowls.

"And I saw that they were interested in establishing a franchise in Miami. I had a winter home in Miami, I wasn't a total stranger down there, I had been going to Miami since I was a youngster and spending a couple of months in the winter there."

Wilson telephoned Hunt and expressed his interest in financing the Miami franchise. Hunt alerted him to the fact that a couple of groups already had begun preliminary planning to tackle the Miami market, so if he wanted to get on board, he'd better get down to Miami.

Wilson flew to South Florida and met with the politicians to inform them of his plans and to try to work out a lease agreement for use of the Orange Bowl. To his surprise, Wilson received fierce opposition, not only from the political leaders, but from the University of Miami.

"Number one, Miami had a team in the old All-America Football Conference (in 1946) and it had failed," Wilson said. "So they weren't very interested in going into a new, fledgling football league because they had had one bad experience. They said they would rather wait for some time in the future to get an expansion franchise in the NFL. Secondly, the University of Miami opposed a pro franchise going into the Orange Bowl because it could possibly hurt their attendance. Well, if you couldn't lease the Orange Bowl, you had no place to play in Miami in those days. So I forgot about the whole thing."

Wilson returned to Detroit, disappointed that the deal had fallen through. Outside of Detroit, Miami was the only other city that he had strong ties to, so he figured his chances of owning an AFL franchise were nill.

A few days later, Hunt called Wilson and told him that the league had seven teams lined up and needed an eighth to balance out the two divisions. Hunt told Wilson that there were five cities – Buffalo, Louisville, Cincinnati, St. Louis and Atlanta – interested in coming on board and that he could have his choice as to where to place his franchise. Wilson was skeptical because he didn't know anyone in those cities, so he dismissed Hunt's request.

But before he totally divested himself from the AFL, he called Ed Hayes, then the sports editor of the now-defunct *Detroit Times*, and Nick Kerbawy, an executive with the Lions.

"I said to both of them, 'Even if you were goofy enough to go into a new speculative pro football league and buck the established NFL, which of these five cities would you pick?'" Wilson said. "They both said Buffalo and when I asked why, they said that Buffalo had good attendance in the All-America Conference, it was a good football city, an industrial city similar to Detroit on a smaller scale. And Buffalo had been without football for 10 years and wanted it back, so that was their choice.

"I still wasn't very interested, I didn't know anybody in Buffalo and I had never been to Buffalo. Ed Hayes said he knew the sports editor of the *Buffalo Evening News*, Paul Neville. He said 'Let me call him and you can go over and see him.' I said if I couldn't get Miami, I wasn't interested. Ed called me back and said he had made a luncheon appointment for me with Paul Neville the next day."

Reluctantly, Wilson flew to Buffalo and met with Neville.

"He was a rabid football fan," Wilson recalled. "He gave me a real sales pitch on how the franchise would do so well here. He told me people had stood in line to buy tickets for a potential NFL franchise (when the AAFC folded and there was talk the NFL would merge with the folding league) and that they were really disappointed that they didn't get one.

"He took me out to War Memorial, which had about 35,000 seats and had been built in the late 30s, and it was a functional stadium. But oh, those lockerrooms. I don't know if you could even call it a lockerroom. There were wooden stairs going up to it and it was so small, you could hardly get the team in there. Sometimes the hot water wouldn't work in the showers. It was an old dilapidated stadium, but in those days, people were just happy to have a football team. It sufficed for the crowds in the beginning with a new league and a new team.

"Anyway, I thought about it, so I jokingly said 'I'll tell you what Paul, if I should put a franchise in Buffalo, will your paper support me?' He said 'Ralph, we will support you 100 percent.' I said 'OK, I'll put one over here for three years and we'll see what happens.'"

On Monday, October 17, 1959, Neville wrote a story in the *Buffalo Evening News* – although he did not use his byline – with a headline that read: "Buffalo to Have Team in Pro Football League Next Fall."

"We didn't know if this league was going to go, the odds were certainly against it and everyone was laughing at me," Wilson said. "But after the three years were up, I decided to stay. I always say that after those three years, that was the last time the *News* ever supported me."

Wilson paid his $25,000 franchise fee, worked out a lease agreement for the stadium, chose Penn State all-America halfback Richie Lucas with his first draft choice, then began assembling his staff.

The first step was hiring a head coach and Wilson plucked Buster Ramsey off the Detroit Lions staff. The gregarious Ramsey had served as the Lions' defensive coordinator during three championship seasons in the 1950s, so Wilson knew of his credentials.

Next, Wilson chose Dick Gallagher, who had been Paul Brown's chief assistant with the NFL's Cleveland Browns, to be his general manager. Gallagher was considered a shrewd judge of talent and at Cleveland had set up a productive scouting network that continually provided the Browns with impressive new talent.

Bob Dove and Breezy Reid were hired in January of 1960 to be assistant coaches, Ed Abramoski came aboard in March as trainer, and the coaching staff was completed in May when Harvey Johnson was signed as an assistant coach and given the added duties of director of player personnel.

War Memorial Stadium (above) served as the home of the Bills for 13 years, from 1960 to 1972. Built in the 1930's on Best and Jefferson streets in the city, the rockpile also housed Buffalo's entry in the old All-America Football Conference in the 1940's as well as the baseball Bisons and numerous collegiate events.

Ron McDole (right) joined the Bills in 1963 and provided an immediate impact along the defensive line. Teaming with Tom Sestak, Tom Day and Jim Dunaway, the Bills front four was among the most feared in all of pro football in the 1960's.

With his staff in place, Wilson negotiated a deal to use Seymour H. Knox's East Aurora estate as a practice field for training camp and the team took up headquarters at the Roycroft Inn.

Given the amalgamation of players that were available to Ramsey in that first training camp – from impressive Elbert Dubenion and the all-American, Lucas, to mild-mannered future baseball umpire Ron Luciano and 310-pound Birtho Arnold – it didn't take long for Ramsey's effusive personality to bubble to the surface.

Ramsey was not a patient man, but that was the trait that he needed more than any other in the Bills initial season. It was tough for him to adjust from the championship-caliber play he had been associated with while coaching in Detroit to the ragtag style of the youthful Bills. If, for example, he saw that a defensive lineman wasn't mastering a technique, he didn't waste time trying to explain the problem, he'd try to solve it by jumping right into the fray and demonstrating how it was supposed to be done. Without any pads and giving away nearly 20 years, the 40-year-old bear of a man would line up across from the offensive lineman and execute the proper procedure, often driving the unsuspecting player 15 yards downfield.

"Buster was very dynamic," Wilson said. "When players didn't play well, they were scared of Buster. He'd threaten to beat 'em up, even though he never would. I know Dubenion was always scared of Buster."

Dubenion was not alone. Many of the players feared their coach because he spent a good part of that inaugural season looking furiously to the sky as the Bills bumbled and stumbled to a 5-8-1 record.

Luckily for Wilson, he can't recall much from that first season, but he did remember what used to take place before the games began.

"I used to arrive at the games 10 minutes before kickoff and I would go in the same entrance," Wilson said. "I remember there used to be five of the toughest looking fellas I've ever seen in my life always standing there near the gate. These were the kind of fellas you wanted on your side. They'd always have a big jug of red wine and when I'd show up, they'd recognize me and they'd yell at me 'Hey Wilson, come on over here and have a drink.' I was afraid not to go over and get a drink. So when I got to that old dilapidated box of ours, I always had a couple of wines under my belt."

Elbert Dubenion was a non-descript player from tiny Bluffton College in Ohio when he joined the Bills in their inaugural 1960 season. However, he made an immediate impression in the first training camp. He became known as "Golden Wheels" and went on to a brilliant AFL career. His 27.1 yards per catch average in 1964 stood up as the all-time AFL record.

If the wine didn't make the 41-year-old owner sleepy, watching his team play offense certainly did. The Bills finished No. 1 in defense in 1960, but dead last in offense, mainly because they lacked a competent quarterback. While the Los Angeles (later San Diego) Chargers had Jack Kemp, Houston had George Blanda and Denver possessed Frank Tripucka, the Bills began the season with aging Tommy O'Connell, a journeyman NFL veteran, directing the offense. He later was replaced by the inconsistent Johnny Green.

Things didn't improve in 1961. The team finished 6-8 as quarterbacks Green, Warren Rabb, M.C. Reynolds and Lucas failed to sustain the offensive attack. Defensive back Richie McCabe, upon retiring suddenly in November of 1961, summed up the Bills' plight when he said: "The trouble with the team is Ramsey doesn't have 22 football players. Some can't do the job."

Still, you can't fire all the players, so Ramsey paid the price for the team's failure when Wilson gave him the ax after the season.

"In those days I was too impetuous and I let Buster go after the first couple years and it's probably something I shouldn't have done," Wilson said. "As time went on, I learned more about the business. Changing coaches doesn't do a heckuva lot of good. You have to get better players."

That's what Wilson did in 1962.

Actually, Wilson already had begun assembling a stable of talented players. Rookie draft choices Billy Shaw, Stew Barber and Al Bemiller all moved into starting positions on the offensive line in 1961. Defensive lineman Tom Sestak and linebacker Mike Stratton then were drafted at the end of the year and after Lou Saban was hired to replace Ramsey, tight end Ernie Warlick and running back Cookie Gilchrist bolted the Canadian Football League to join the Bills before the 1962 season opener.

There was no question the Bills were a better outfit, but the continuing lack of leadership and production at the crucial quarterback position weighed down the Bills like an anchor. Buffalo lost its first three games of 1962, including an embarrassing 17-6 home defeat at the hands of the even weaker New York Titans, a loss that brought beer cans raining down on the field as the Bills exited to the lockerroom.

While that game was being played, though, the team's fortunes were secretly taking a turn for the better. Out in San Diego, quarterback Jack Kemp, hampered by a thumb injury, was unavailable for the Chargers' game against Houston. San Diego coach Sid

When you play football in Buffalo, snow is part of everyday life late in the season. But on this day, November 30, 1969, the weather was particularly atrocious. Veteran observers said it was the worst weather they had ever seen for a Buffalo sporting event as snow fell throughout Buffalo's 16-13 victory over Cincinnati.

Gillman tried to pull a fast one on the rest of the league by putting Kemp on the injured deferred list – exposing him to waivers – in an effort to create space on the roster to sign another quarterback for the Oilers' game. However, Gillman, who had intended to reclaim Kemp after the game, fouled up the paperwork and Kemp became fair game for the other seven teams. Five clubs put in a claim on him and because the Bills had the worst record of the five, they were awarded Kemp's services for the paltry sum of $100.

"I knew that Jack Kemp was a really good quarterback and we didn't have a quarterback of his caliber," Wilson said. "I had a friend in the league office and when Gillman put him on waivers over the weekend, I got wind of it and we claimed him, which was legal. Gillman was absolutely incensed and so was Kemp. He didn't want to come to Buffalo, that was the last place he wanted to be because he had been born and raised in California. I called him, introduced myself, and I remember it was a cool conversation – he wasn't too happy to be claimed by Buffalo.

He said he wanted a no-cut contract and I told him we didn't give any of those, so he hung up.

"We got back together on the phone, he relented and he came up and played for us. He was a great quarterback for us, a real leader of the team."

Kemp remembered his transfer from San Diego to Buffalo this way: "It wasn't Buffalo, it wasn't the team, it wasn't Ralph Wilson. I had a home, I had a son, Jeff, and I just didn't want to leave my home. I had a little business in San Diego and was a resident of San Diego. I was quarterback of the Chargers. And then I woke up one day and found out that I'd been placed on waivers. It had never happened before, at least in my day, that anyone had been picked up like that. But I

Jack Kemp (upper) joined the Bills in 1962, having been acquired off the waiver wire for a meager $100 from San Diego.

Lou Saban (lower) was known as a tough disciplinarian who kept his troops in line. He was also known as the team's winningest coach before Marv Levy dethroned him in the 1990's. Saban guided the Bills to AFL championships in 1964 and 1965.

was not at all upset with Ralph or Buffalo, I just loved San Diego. It was a shock more than anything else.

"But it turned out to be a blessing in disguise. My wife told me that one door closes in your life and another one opens. The door to the Buffalo Bills and politics and Congress really opened up that day when I realized I was going to go to Buffalo to play for Lou Saban and play for Ralph Wilson's team."

Kemp couldn't play right away because of his thumb injury and the Bills went on to lose two more games to fall to 0-5. But they finished with a flourish, going 7-1-1 in their final nine games to post the first winning record in franchise history. Kemp made his Buffalo debut in the second half of a 10-6 victory over the Raiders in Oakland. His first start came a week later – November 23 in Boston – and although he completed 14 of 22 passes for 194 yards and scored a touchdown, the Bills saw their six-game unbeaten streak and any realistic chances of a playoff spot come to a crashing halt in a 21-10 loss to the Patriots.

Defensive linemen Jim Dunaway and Ron McDole, safety George Saimes, quarterback Daryle Lamonica, linebacker Harry Jacobs, versatile Ed Rutkowski and wide receiver Bill Miller all joined the team for 1963. After going winless in their first four games, the Bills won seven of their final 10 – including a 45-14 rout of New York in which Cookie Gilchrist set what was then the single-game pro football rushing record with 243 yards – to tie Boston for first place in the Eastern Division with a 7-6-1 record.

The team's first postseason game in its history, the divisional playoff against the Patriots, was played on a bitterly cold December 28 afternoon at War Memorial Stadium and 33,044 watched Boston earn a 26-8 victory as Buffalo turned over the ball six times and rushed for just seven yards.

"That was a real downer," Kemp said of the Boston loss. "But I can remember Lou and I talking after the game. I told him `You know what coach, next year we're going to beat the Pats and we're going to win the championship and you and I are going to go off the field on the shoulders of the fans, not to the boos of the fans.' "

Even then, the 1996 Republican presidential candidate was prophetic. The Bills felt they were better than Boston at the end of 1963, and when San Diego throttled the Patriots, 51-10, in the AFL Championship Game, their suspicions were confirmed. So in the offseason, the players set a common goal for 1964 – winning the AFL title – and by the time training camp ended, there was little doubt that Saban had molded a quality outfit.

It took all of 12 minutes, 36 seconds on opening day to realize how good this team was. Buffalo scored 31 points in that span in the first quarter against Kansas City and went on to a 34-17 victory over the Chiefs. The Bills proceeded to win their next eight and often looked invincible.

But cracks started appearing in the foundation and Cookie Gilchrist was the man pecking away like a jackhammer. The Patriots ended the Bills winning streak at nine with a 36-28 victory at War Memorial. Two days after that game, Gilchrist was waived by Saban. The hard-line coach explained that he had grown tired of the enigmatic star's attitude and that the incident that pushed Saban over the brink was Gilchrist's refusal to take the field late in the first half against Boston.

"Cookie was just a character, he's difficult to describe," Wilson said. "Not his playing abilities, though. He could be an All-Pro today. He and Bronko Nagurski of the Bears were probably the two best fullbacks I ever saw. Cookie weighed about 260, but he could run like Thurman Thomas.

"He only had a high school education, but he could get up and speak extemporaneously on any subject. He could be very, very entertaining. He was smart, but he was hard to control. He gave us three years and he was very instrumental in our success back in those days."

Gilchrist had criticized Kemp's play-calling during the season in an interview with

Wide receiver J.D. Hill (left) was Buffalo's first-round draft choice in 1971. The fast-talking, fast-moving Arizona State product enjoyed his best season in 1972 when he caught 52 passes for 754 yards and five touchdowns.

Booker Edgerson (24, below) gets a hug from George Saimes after an interception against Denver. Edgerson finished his eight-year Buffalo career with 24 interceptions.

Owner Ralph C. Wilson Jr. (opposite page) shakes hands with Jack Kemp after a victory.

Sport magazine, saying he preferred the way Daryle Lamonica called a game. "Kemp passes too much and then we get in trouble and Lamonica has to come in and straighten us out," Gilchrist was quoted as saying. "The trouble with Kemp is he only uses me 18 to 20 times a game. Lamonica uses me, boom, boom, boom, three or four times in a row, 30 to 35 times a game and I stay hot. Kemp picks his plays out of a hat. Lamonica is smart."

Still, it was Kemp who coerced Gilchrist into apologizing to the team for his behavior, which in turn prompted Saban to reinstate the star fullback.

The Bills took an 11-2 record into the season finale at Boston, yet a loss to the 10-2-1 Patriots would have cost them the division title. With Kemp mired in a slump, Saban had started Lamonica the week before in a victory over Denver, but with the biggest game of the season on the horizon, Saban turned to his veteran.

"I had been hurt and there had been a controversy over the quarterbacks," Kemp recalled. "I had had some good games and we had had a good season. Daryle was also a good quarterback who went on to become a great quarterback with the Oakland Raiders. We were rivals and competitors and I can't say that we were as close as we are today, but it wasn't mean-spirited. It was certainly competitive and I think competitiveness brings out the best in everybody.

"But before that Boston game, I told Saban 'Coach, if you start me, I guarantee that I'll win this game for you.' He says that he told me that. It's apocryphal either way I guess."

Regardless of who said what, Kemp got the nod and was masterful in the snow at Fenway Park as he threw for 286 yards and one touchdown and ran for two other scores in a 24-14 victory that propelled the Bills into the AFL Championship Game against the mighty San Diego Chargers.

Cookie Gilchrist was one of the most enigmatic players to ever wear a Buffalo uniform. He led the AFL in rushing in 1962 and in 1963, his 243 yards gained against the New York Jets stood as the pro football single-game rushing record until 1971 when Willie Ellison of the Rams broke it.

"The Chargers were favored because they had won in '63 when they had killed the Pats," Kemp said. "They had Tobin Rote, John Hadl, Lance Alworth, Keith Lincoln, Earl Faison, Ernie Ladd, all my old buddies. But coming into Buffalo, I think they were surprised that we were as tough as we were."

And no Bill was tougher than Mike Stratton, who executed one of the greatest tackles in football history that day. The Chargers had scored just 3:11 into the game and after forcing a Buffalo punt, were poised to score again and take firm command. However, just as Lincoln was catching a short swing pass in the left flat, Stratton came up and leveled him with a vicious hit that broke a few ribs and knocked the star running back out of the game. The San Diego offense, already hampered with Alworth sidelined by a leg injury, never recovered from Stratton's hit.

The Bills scored the final 20 points and won their first championship, 20-7, as Gilchrist rushed for 122 yards, Kemp threw for 168 and the defense held San Diego to 179 yards over the final three-and-a-half quarters.

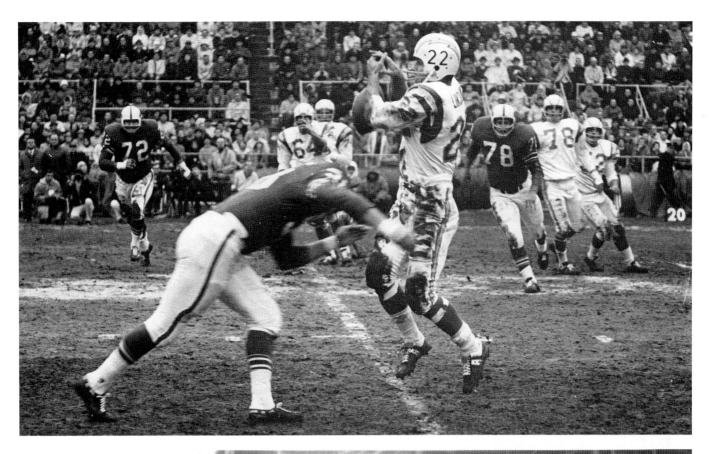

In the 1964 AFL Championship game (above), linebacker Mike Stratton authored "The Tackle" when he leveled San Diego's Keith Lincoln in the first quarter. Lincoln left the game with broken ribs and that play turned the tide in Buffalo's favor as the Bills went on to a 20-7 victory.

After the game (right), the fans tore down the goalposts at War Memorial Stadium in celebration of Buffalo's first championship.

"I think they got cocky after they scored in the first quarter and we were a tenacious team. No one ever gave up," Kemp said. "The scrapping and plugging and that trait of never giving up on ourselves gave us a quality that overcame the natural advantage the Chargers might have had on paper."

Never had Wilson been happier than on the day his Bills won their first championship. Except, perhaps, the afternoon of January 29, 1964, when NBC agreed to pay the AFL teams a total of $36 million for the rights to broadcast the league's games for five years.

So not only was Wilson the proud owner of a championship team, he also was rolling in dough. Buffalo had led the AFL in attendance in 1962 and '63 and finished a close second to the New York Jets in 1964, but only because new Jets owner Sonny Werblin had moved his team into the brand new 60,000-seat Shea Stadium. With gate revenues up, Wilson already had begun making a profit on his original $25,000 investment. Now, thanks to NBC, Wilson was pulling in an estimated $900,000 per year in television money.

There is no doubt in Wilson's mind that the AFL was saved by the NBC contract. Had it not been for that record TV payout, the league may have folded.

"When they gave us $900,000 per team, that made the AFL," he said. "That caused the NFL to merge with us. They (NFL teams) were getting a little more than $1 million per team (from CBS), but when we got our contract, they knew they were going to have fierce competition for players and that we were here to stay. It was bad enough for them before the NBC contract."

Werblin was the driving force behind the mega deal with NBC. He knew NBC was getting killed in the ratings on Sundays because CBS had the NFL and ABC was broadcasting AFL games (at a bargain-basement rate). But while Werblin got NBC to sign on,

Jim Dunaway (78, above) was a huge man who had the quickness of a fullback. Had he played in the NFL, he would have been recognized as one of the all-time best defensive tackles.

Lou Saban (opposite page) coached in Buffalo during two periods. His first stint lasted from 1962-1965 and he won two AFL Championships. He returned in 1972 and turned O.J. Simpson's career around. By using a ball-control running attack in 1973, he helped Simpson set an NFL rushing record with 2,003 yards. Saban quit during the 1976 season.

Billy Shaw (66, upper) leads Cookie Gilchrist (34) through a hole in a game against the Raiders.

Ernie Warlick (lower) joined the Bills in 1962 after playing in the Canadian Football League. Here, the big tight end makes a catch despite San Diego's Dich Harris climbing on his back.

it was Wilson who was responsible for the ultimate final sum of the contract.

"I went to Austria (in 1964) for the Innsbruck Olympics and Billy Sullivan phoned me over there," Wilson recalled. "Billy said 'Ralph, I've got some great news for you, NBC is going to give us $600,000 per team.' Billy was elated on the telephone, but I already knew the NFL had gotten just over $1 million. I told Billy that it wasn't enough. There was silence on the other end of the line. He was stunned and he said 'What do you mean that's not enough, it's six times more than we're getting now.' I said 'We still won't be able to compete if we're getting half of what the NFL is getting.' We went back and got the $900,000."

Chances of a championship repeat in 1965 for the Bills seemed dim when Gilchrist was traded to Denver before the season and starting receivers Elbert Dubenion and Glenn Bass were knocked out for the season by knee injuries before the fourth game had ended. But Kemp, gritty as ever, made do with what he had and turned in what he considers his finest season, leading the Bills to a 10-3-1 record and a return date with the Chargers in the title game, this time in San Diego.

Like the previous season, the Chargers were no match for the Bills as Buffalo rolled to a 23-0 victory. In the second quarter, Kemp, who was voted the game's MVP, fired a touchdown pass to Ernie Warlick and 2:30 later, Butch Byrd returned a punt 74 yards for a touchdown. Pete Gogolak kicked three second-half field goals.

"We had a lot of injuries, Cookie had left, and we were filling in a lot of gaps," Kemp recalled. "But we had a great defense again and '65 was, I guess, my best year. I was AP's player of the year. I was honored because I felt like I had to prove that the first championship was not a fluke, so winning it for the second straight time, particularly against the Chargers, was a great thrill. Again, on paper, they looked bigger and tougher and better, yet we overcame all those things plus all the injuries that we had, to win the championship. That was our greatest accomplishment."

Wilson will never forget an incident that occurred after that game.

"They had an elderly man on the field with a cannon and he fired it whenever the Chargers scored," Wilson said. "Well, this particular day, the Chargers didn't score. I was standing by our bench talking to someone, the players had left the field, and this old man was dragging the cannon back to the tunnel because he hadn't had much use for it that day. He got right in front of our bench and I guess he was so mad about the outcome of the game, he turned around and pointed the cannon toward our bench and fired it. He was gonna fire that cannon once during that day."

Armed with its NBC contract, its vastly improved play and its ability to fight toe-to-toe with the NFL in college player signings, merger talks heated up in the offseason. With Wilson playing a key role in the negotiations, NFL commissioner Pete Rozelle announced on June 8, 1966, that the two leagues would merge in time for the 1970 season and that a championship game would be played between the two leagues starting with the postseason of '66.

In Wilson's mind, the reason why the AFL was able to position itself for the merger was a simple one.

"What happened, as so frequently occurs in any venture, is that sometimes your competition takes you lightly and the NFL did that with the AFL," he said. "We were a joke. But we signed a lot of top college players and it took a lot away from the NFL. The NFL's reluctance to fight us for player talent gave us some momentum. We weren't just playing with bartenders and people who shouldn't have been on the field."

Wilson and Werblin had been appointed as the AFL representatives in preliminary merger talks with the NFL during 1964. The NFL countered with Los Angeles Rams owner Carroll Rosenbloom. Rosenbloom thought a merger would be great because it would cease the fighting over college players and would enable the NFL to expand into the AFL markets, all of which were either in big cities (Boston, New York) or in up-and-coming areas (Buffalo, Houston, Oakland, Denver, San Diego and Kansas City).

Werblin was against the merger, but he had a beautiful new stadium and his Jets were situated in the largest market in the country. Wilson tried to explain to Werblin that the other AFL owners wanted to merge because their smaller market teams would flourish, but Werblin held firm and plans were put off. Wilson tried to rekindle them on his own in 1965 when he met Rosenbloom and Dallas Cowboys' president Tex Schramm for lunch in Miami Beach. But when Wilson asked what it would cost the AFL to merge with the NFL, he was told $50 million. "Well fellas, forget it, we're not gonna pay $50 million," Wilson replied.

Lamar Hunt picked up the talks the following year and he finalized the merger with Schramm in Dallas. In the end, the AFL forked over $18 million, $2 million per team (Miami had become the AFL's ninth team in 1966). All of the money was given to the New York Giants ($10 million) and the San Francisco 49ers ($8 million) because both of those teams would be losing exclusivity to their territories (because of the New York Jets and Oakland Raiders).

That 1966 season was a difficult one for the Bills. Lou Saban had shocked the football world by resigning a couple of weeks after the 1965 champi-

Jack Kemp was one of the most well-spoken players of his generation and a favorite of the media.

onship victory, so Wilson promoted Joe Collier from defensive coordinator to head coach. The transition went fairly smoothly and the Bills overcame some tough stretches and managed to win their third straight division title. However, with a spot in the first Super Bowl on the line, they were crushed in the AFL Championship Game, 31-7, by a superb Kansas City team at War Memorial, and so began a decline that dragged the franchise to the depths of pro football.

The Bills slumped to 4-10 in 1967, and after a 48-6 loss to Oakland in the second game of the 1968 season, Collier was fired and replaced on an interim basis by Harvey Johnson. With Kemp out for the year thanks to a preseason knee injury, changing coaches meant little and the Bills finished with their worst record to date, 1-12-1.

Of course, by posting the worst mark in all of pro football, the Bills were able to make the first choice in the college draft and USC all-America Heisman Trophy winner O.J. Simpson was their man.

Born and raised in San Francisco and a devoted fan of the 49ers, Simpson had once bumped into Jim Brown in a soda shop a couple of blocks from Kezar Stadium where Brown's Cleveland Browns had just beaten the 49ers, 13-10, to conclude the 1962 season. While Brown was sucking on a milkshake, Simpson, then a 15-year-old street-wise kid, brazenly walked up to the star running back and told him "You're not so good. When I'm a pro, I'm gonna be better than you are."

Throughout his high school career, Simpson had set his sights on attending USC and playing football for the Trojans. However, while Simpson was brilliant on the football field at Galileo High, his work in the classroom was far from satisfactory and he was unable to go to USC.

He enrolled at City College of San Francisco, a two-year school that had a football team. In two years, he scored a national junior college record 54 touchdowns, but more importantly, improved his grades enough to gain admission to USC.

And from the moment he put on that crimson and gold uniform, the world of college football stood back and watched in awe at this marvel of a player. Simpson possessed blinding speed, head-spinning moves, an uncanny ability to change speeds instantly, great recognition of where daylight was, and a nose for the end zone.

O.J. Simpson came to Buffalo as the No. 1 overall choice in the 1969 draft, fresh off winning the 1968 Heisman Trophy. Here, he breaks a long run against the New York Jets, one of many that he would enjoy during his Hall of Fame career. (Photo: Melchior Di Giacomo/NFL Photos)

In 1967, his first year at USC under coach John McKay, he rushed for 1,543 yards, led the Trojans to a victory over Indiana in the Rose Bowl, and was runner-up in the Heisman Trophy balloting.

In 1968, he gained 1,880 yards – including four 200-yard games – won the Heisman Trophy and led the Trojans to their second straight Rose Bowl appearance, where they lost to eventual national champion Ohio State, 27-16, despite Simpson's 256 yards gained from scrimmage.

Simpson came out of USC as the highest-rated pro prospect in the history of BLESTO, the NFL's oldest and most respected scouting syndicate. He had become the first collegian ever named by *Sport* magazine as its Man of the Year. Every team in pro football salivated over the thought of Simpson wearing their uniform, but only one team – the moribund Buffalo Bills – would get the chance to draft him.

Tom Flores joined the Bills in 1967 when he was part of a trade that sent Daryle Lamonica to Oakland. Injuries hampered Flores' career in Buffalo. He later served as a Bills assistant coach in 1971 and eventually became the Raiders head coach and won two Super Bowls in the 1980's. He is currently the Seattle Seahawks head coach.

"It wasn't like a big surprise, I knew they had the first choice and I knew I wasn't going to have the opportunity to play in the National Football League, where I wanted to play, or out West where I lived," Simpson said of his draft-day feelings. "There was some disappointment, but I had already accepted the fact that Buffalo was going to draft me. And there was a certain amount of pride to be the first guy drafted.

"I had never been in Buffalo or the Buffalo area. And other than that one song about shuffling off to Buffalo and the other one about the Erie Canal, I had no real visual image of Buffalo. I just knew it snowed a lot."

New coach John Rauch, who had been hired to replace Harvey Johnson after a very successful stint with the Oakland Raiders, made the choice on draft day and wrote on a blackboard: "All the way with O.J."

"O.J. was extremely important to this franchise," Ralph Wilson said. "O.J. had a great, great name in college, he was a super player and a Heisman Trophy winner. For a great star like O.J. to come to Buffalo was a major plus for the city."

But once his rookie season started – following a lengthy holdout that didn't end until mid-August – Simpson mysteriously was de-emphasized. Rauch looked at the Bills' weak offensive line and concluded that even the great Simpson would have trouble running behind that group of blockers, so he favored the passing game and let Jack Kemp – who was playing his final season – try to win games through the air rather than fully utilize Simpson's brilliant skills. The Bills finished 4-10 in their final AFL campaign. Simpson managed 697 yards rushing, but never really was the awesome threat he had been in college.

In 1970, the AFL and NFL merged and the Bills were placed in the AFC East. It was a bright new beginning for pro football, but it was Simpson's darkest year as a football player. In the eighth game, he suffered a season-ending knee injury.

He termed his first two years in Buffalo as "very frustrating."

"I had been used to being the center of attention and to come into a situation where I was just one element, and what I thought was a very unused element, was hard to take," he said. "I was a runner, but with Rauch, I was probably running three pass

routes to every run. I wasn't getting the football, and the times I was getting it, they weren't in the most advantageous situations for me. I'd get it on third-and-one or other short-yardage situations. There weren't too many plays designed to go outside to get me the running room I needed. They put in a few I-formation plays, but they didn't have the concept of the I. That meant it was all window dressing. So the first couple of years in Buffalo were tough for me from an ego point of view.

"There was such a lack of communication from what was happening upstairs to what was happening on the field. You didn't always feel that everyone was in it for the same thing. And I attribute most of that to John Rauch. He wanted to win, but he wanted to win his way. He wasn't a people person and when you're in a rebuilding situation, you need a guy with real strong leadership qualities or a guy who for the most part is a people person, which wasn't the case.

"John was a very pleasant person in the offseason, but the major sense I got in my first couple of years was that I felt I was in the way. I felt that if he had his choice, I would not have been the guy he would have drafted. I didn't think I fit into the plan that he wanted. He came from the Oakland Raiders, a fullback-oriented offense. I had come out of maybe the greatest running program in the history of college football as a tailback. I just didn't fit the mold."

Rauch quit during training camp in 1971, which in most players' eyes was a stroke of luck. But then, according to Simpson, Wilson made a terrible mistake in naming Harvey Johnson as head coach on an interim basis for the second time in four years.

And just like in 1968, Johnson did not have the resources needed to compete and the Bills lost 13 of their 14 games, the worst record in franchise history. Simpson again muddled through a disappointing year, gaining 742 yards.

"Harvey Johnson, one of the nicest, funniest guys I've ever met, was a very capable head scout, but he was certainly not, in anybody's wildest dreams, capable of being a head coach," Simpson said. "It was the biggest joke of all time. We were running systems and he didn't have the foggiest idea of what was going on. Why they didn't elevate one of the assistants, nobody understood.

"We were losing every way there was to lose. It was a year that had absolutely no growth. It's one thing to be 1-13 and say we're working toward something. But we weren't learning anything because we knew whatever coach they brought in would change the system anyway."

In three years, Simpson had done nothing but disappoint Bills fans and whispers about him being a bust had become shouts. But to his credit, he never lashed out at his critics and he chose not to complain about the way he was being used in the Buffalo offense. At least not publicly. Privately, he had told the Bills former public relations director and later a vice-president, Jack Horrigan, that he wanted to get out of Buffalo after his contract expired.

"Jack Horrigan kept me sane those first few years," Simpson recalled. "I had reached the point where I didn't want to come back to Buffalo because the organization was in total disarray. Some very unpleasant things happened in 1971. It was real frustrating to know that after three years of being there and being three years into an admitted rebuilding program, we were no further along. We were still making changes. But Jack kept imploring me to keep a lid on it, and that something good was going to happen at the end of the year."

On December 23, 1971, Simpson's career got the boost it needed when Wilson rehired Lou Saban to be the team's head coach. Saban had bounced around the college and pro ranks since leaving Buffalo at the end of the 1965 season and he had expressed an interest in returning to the scene of his greatest coaching accomplishment. Wilson thought it was a great idea and soon enough, Simpson would beg to agree.

Saban knew all about Simpson and it didn't take him long to realize that the Bills had made a huge mistake in not exploiting Simpson's talent.

"I believe in running the ball-basic, hard-nosed football," Saban said. "We have a great runner, a gamebreaker, who is a big-play athlete. I intend to use him." You could almost hear Simpson saying "It's about time."

"That's why I had Lou present me in the Hall of Fame," Simpson said. "Sure he saved my career. Lou Saban came in and changed the focus and turned things around. I remember the first time we met, right off the top, you saw that this man was in charge. Lou was the kind of guy who said what was on his mind. Lou made it clear it was his way or the highway."

And Saban's way was to center the offense around Simpson.

Offensive guard Reggie McKenzie was drafted in 1972 and immediately became Simpson's personal bodyguard on the field, leading the Juice around the corner on sweeps or through the middle on traps and counters. Simpson called McKenzie his "main man" and the two became best buddies.

When the season ended, Simpson had amassed 1,251 yards on the ground, thus earning him the first of his four NFL rushing crowns. He also was selected to play in his first Pro Bowl and by running for 112 yards on 16 carries, he earned the game's MVP award.

Deacon Jones, the great defensive tackle of the Los Angeles Rams, once said that if

Paul Guidry (opposite page upper), shown here chasing down Cincinnati quarterback Virgil Carter, played seven years for Buffalo at linebacker.

Dennis Shaw (16, opposite page lower) was the NFL Rookie of the Year in 1970.

Simpson played for the Rams, he'd gain 2,000 yards.

In 1973, playing for the Buffalo Bills, Simpson did what Jones thought was possible, but very few others did – rush for 2,003 yards, a first in NFL history.

"Who would ever think about 2,000 yards?" Simpson said. "And to be honest, it didn't enter my mind until the last game of the year against the Jets. I had been focused on Jim Brown's record (of 1,863 yards), not 2,000 yards."

Even though Jones had implied that Simpson could do it and McKenzie vowed after the '72 season that Simpson would do it, 2,000 seemed a bit too much to ask. However, Simpson wasn't ready to rule out going after Brown's record, which would enable him to make good on that 1962 San Francisco soda shop boast he had made to the Cleveland Hall of Famer.

"If I could lead the league in rushing with the team that we had in 1972, I knew that if we improved the talent, I could do a lot better," he said. There were a lot of games (in 1972) where we were out of it and we had to throw. We also had a lot of injuries. Reggie was the only lineman who played every game and he was a rookie.

"There was a joke that year where I'd come into the huddle and I'd say 'Does everybody know everybody else?'"

Saban began assembling the necessary talent in the draft. In the first round, guard Joe DeLamielleure and tight end Paul Seymour were chosen while quarterback Joe Ferguson was selected in the third round.

DeLamielleure appeared to be a perfect compliment at guard to McKenzie because both were excellent at pulling and leading sweeps. The tackle positions had been solidified in 1972. Donnie Green had come into his own on the right side and Dave Foley had been acquired from the Jets on waivers and had moved into the starting lineup after Paul Costa had gotten hurt early in the year. At center there was Bruce Jarvis and his veteran backup, Mike Montler, who had come to the Bills from New England.

"By the time we got to camp in 1973, I saw an offense that I knew could be formidable," Simpson said. "We had no confidence in Dennis Shaw and we knew it would be only a matter of time before Ferguson would be the quarterback. We had to stop running into the strength of the defense. We needed a guy who could at least call audibles and we

O.J. Simpson (opposite page) is the only Bills player enshrined in the Pro Football Hall of Fame. (photo: Robert Shaver/NFL photos) In the inset, his main man, Reggie McKenzie, leads him around the corner on a sweep, Simpson's favorite play.

In Joe Ferguson's rookie year of 1973 (left), he often had to ask for quiet because O.J. Simpson was in the process of rushing for 2,003 yards and the Bills were playing in brand new 80,000-seat Rich Stadium.

31

knew Ferguson could do that. So even with a rookie quarterback and a few rookie line-men, it looked pretty good."

What also looked pretty good to O.J. and his teammates was 80,000-seat Rich Stadium, located in the well-scrubbed suburb of Orchard Park. After playing for 13 years in decaying War Memorial Stadium, Ralph Wilson's team was presented with a palatial new home by Erie County and State of New York. But it did not come without a fight.

Wilson had been talking about moving his Bills into a new stadium as far back as 1964 and throughout the second half of the decade of the 60s, he battled with Erie County politicians about how, what, why, when and where to build a new home for his team.

Some legislators wanted a downtown stadium, figuring that drawing people to the city's core would revitalize the sagging economy, but Wilson wondered aloud, "How is playing eight, nine or 10 games a year going to help downtown?"

Some political leaders wanted a domed stadium, others wanted it open air; some wanted it to seat 50,000, others preferred 60,000 seats; some wanted it in Lancaster, others wanted it in Lackawanna.

Wilson's battles with the city's Urban Development Committee became so frustrating, rumors abounded that he was going to pack up his Bills and move them, possibly to Seattle. Wilson denied that he ever intended to move the team, but he admitted there were times when he thought he'd never see a new stadium built.

Rich Stadium played host to its first *Monday Night Football* game on October 29, 1973 as the Bills beat the Kansas City Chiefs, 23-14.

"The team was committed to Buffalo," he said. "I never had any idea of not getting the best for Buffalo. The league said 'Hey, the stadium downtown is too small, you need at least 50,000 seats,' so in order to stay in the league, we had to get a new stadium.

"I spent a lot of personal time, mostly in dealing with the Urban Development Committee. I wanted a large open air stadium in the suburbs with easy access, like Kansas City had. I wanted it in a nice area, like where we are in Orchard Park. They wanted to build 60,000 seats and I wanted 80,000. Well, they thought it was ridiculous

and they said I'd never sell 80,000 seats. But my philosophy has always been 'If you're gonna take a trip, stay in the best places, don't go on the cheap.'

"It was a hard fight to get the stadium, but it was the right thing to do. I don't know anything about politics, but I knew something about sports. I knew this would be a great thing, having the biggest stadium in the country. Years later, we've got a great team and we've led the league in attendance for six straight years."

The night of August 16, 1973, was a memorable one for Wilson. On that balmy summer evening, the NFC champion Washington Redskins helped the Bills christen the shiny new park. Wilson hosted a gala party for his family, friends and politicians. Even though traffic congestion created a nightmare for thousands of fans and Washington's Herb Mul-key spoiled the fun by returning the opening kickoff 102 yards for a touchdown to start the Redskins on their way to a 37-21 victory, Wilson looks back on that night fondly because that was the moment his team had truly hit the big time.

"I knew this was the right thing for Buffalo," he said. "I didn't think we'd sell out as much as we have, because I didn't realize back in those days that this is a regional franchise. This is not just a Buffalo franchise. I didn't realize we were drawing 20-25 percent of our crowds from Rochester. I thought we'd occasionally get 80,000, but not consistently."

The Bills lost all six of their preseason games, and despite the beautiful new stadium, fans and media were down on the team and thought the progress that had been made during 1972 was a fluke. But, Simpson said, the reason for the dismal preseason was that Saban rested his regulars in order to give rookies like Ferguson, DeLamielleure and Seymour the playing time they needed to get acclimated to the Bills' system.

"All preseason long, the press was getting on us and I kept saying 'Don't worry about it, wait until the season starts, we'll be fine,'" Simpson said. "That first game, we had a whole running game in place and you saw what happened."

What happened on the afternoon of Sunday, September 16 at Schaefer Stadium in Foxboro, Massachusetts against the New England Patriots served as a precursor to what would become one of the greatest individual single-season accomplishments in sports history.

With the Bills trailing, 6-0, early in the game, Simpson broke an 80-yard touchdown run that gave the Bills the lead for good. But the outcome of the game, a 31-13 Buffalo victory which was the Bills' first in a season-opener since 1967, became an afterthought as Simpson went on to rush for a then NFL single-game record of 250 yards.

After a loss in San Diego, the Bills returned home to play the first regular-season game in Rich Stadium history.

There were nearly 80,000 fans on hand when the Jets came to town on September 30 with one thing on their minds – stopping Simpson. And although the Bills failed to score a touchdown, Simpson gained 123 yards and helped Buffalo to a 9-7 victory.

Simpson went on to top the 1,000-yard barrier in the seventh game against Kansas City, which was the Bills' first-ever appearance on *Monday Night Football*, and it was then that the rest of the nation began focusing on Buffalo and Simpson's chase for 2,000.

Lou Saban returned to the Buffalo sidelines in 1972 and turned a team that had been pro football's worst from 1968 to 1971 into a winner again.

O.J. Simpson surpassed the 1,000-yard mark in the 1973 season at the halfway point on his way to becoming the first player to top 2,000 yards rushing in one year. (photo: Malcom Emmons/NFL Photos)

Three times in the middle of the season – around the time *Sports Illustrated* splashed Simpson on its cover and when former Bills PR director Budd Thalman began calling the team's offensive line "The Electric Company" because it turned on the Juice – Simpson was held under 100 yards, by Miami, New Orleans and Cincinnati. Heading into the 12th game of the 14-game season at Atlanta, the opportunity to break Brown's record was starting to slip away.

"I knew the most vital game was the Atlanta game," Simpson said. "I knew if I didn't have a big game, I figured I'd have to gain about 400 yards in the last two games against New England and the Jets. Atlanta had a very formidable defense with Tommy Nobis and Claude Humphreys and they were on a winning streak (seven games), so it was going to be tough. But I had a good game (137 yards, bringing his total to 1,584 yards) and I knew I had a shot at Jim's record."

A blizzard hit Buffalo the day of the 13th game, against the Patriots, but Simpson shredded New England again, this time for 219 yards.

Patriots defensive lineman Dave Rowe, after hearing one of his coaches complain that Simpson was wearing special shoes which gave him better traction on the icy surface, turned around and said "Coach, it ain't the damned shoes. He could be running barefoot and he'd still be making the rest of us look like we were slipping on ice."

There was one game remaining, against the Jets at frigid Shea Stadium. The date was December 16, exactly three months after the odyssey had begun in New England. Simpson was 61 yards shy of breaking Brown's mark and 197 yards away from 2,000. The morning of the game, Simpson awoke nervous and said to his main man, McKenzie, "Reg, what if I only get 40 yards?" McKenzie broke out that enormous smile of his and reassured Simpson that there was "no way that's gonna happen."

"It was deadly cold for the Jets game and the ground was hard," Simpson remembered. "But if I had to carry the ball 61 times to get the 61 yards, we were going to do it to get Jim's record."

Before the first quarter ended, Simpson broke Brown's mark, the game was stopped, referee Bob Frederic presented him the ball and after a brief celebration, McKenzie turned to his pal and said "Job ain't done Juice. Got lots of work to do." With 5:56 left in the game, Simpson went off left tackle behind McKenzie and Foley for seven yards and the 2,000-yard mark, once thought to be unattainable, was surpassed.

"After '72, I knew I could be a star on this level, but what changed (after the 2,000-yard season) for me was my image of me, my satisfaction with myself," Simpson said.

Despite his record year, the Bills failed to qualify for the playoffs, but in 1974, the Bills made their first postseason appearance since the 1966 AFL Championship Game.

Simpson was slowed much of the season by an ankle injury suffered in the season-opening *Monday Night Football* victory over the Oakland Raiders, a game that saw Ahmad Rashad catch two touchdown passes in the final two minutes to give Buffalo one of its most exciting victories ever.

The Bills earned a wild-card berth and the right to meet the Pittsburgh Steelers in the first round at Three Rivers Stadium. Paul Seymour's 22-yard touchdown reception in the first quarter gave the Bills a 7-3 lead, but the Steelers erupted for 26 points in the second quarter and went on to a 32-14 victory. A few weeks later, Pittsburgh won the first of its four Super Bowl championships.

"The Steelers game, I hate to say it, but we were thoroughly outcoached," said Simpson, who was held to 49 yards rushing in what would be the only playoff game of his career. "I remember offensively we had an opportunity to make some big plays. I remember Jim Braxton breaking up the middle for 30 yards and fumbling, and Ahmad dropped a long pass down the sideline that would have been a touchdown.

"We had a draw package for them and everytime we'd run it, they'd hit me before the ball got to me. I think they had us figured out. But we ended up actually playing them

On this snowy December 9, 1973 day against New England at Rich Stadium, Joe Ferguson completed only two passes. However, O.J. Simpson ran for 219 yards in a 37-13 victory.

35

better than anyone else did in those playoffs. They annihilated everyone else."

Despite the loss, Simpson and his teammates were not fazed.

"We thought it was still all in front of us," he said. "Going into '75, I had no doubt in my mind that we were the best team in football. One day we took a picture after practice of the whole offense. We lounged on the field together and it turned out to be a great picture of this offensive unit. I remember us saying 'Remember this picture because we're going to be the best offense in football.' We had a great team."

But the march to the Super Bowl never got started. Linebackers Dave Washington and Jim Cheyunski were traded away, as was starting strong safety Neal Craig. Free safety Tony Greene, trying to bounce back from a knee injury, incurred a broken collarbone in preseason and was lost for a few months. Outstanding cornerback Robert James suffered what would turn out to be a career-ending knee injury and Ahmad Rashad saw his season end abruptly, also courtesy of a knee injury. And this was all before the season started.

"It was a tough luck year," Simpson said. "We lost some real vital people."

The Bills finished 8-6 and out of the playoffs despite a brilliant year from Simpson as he gained 1,817 yards, the third-best single-season performance in NFL history.

As it turned out, 1975 was only the beginning of the bitter disappointment for Simpson and the Bills. The events leading up to the start of the 1976 season so infuriated Simpson that he vowed never to return to Buffalo.

First, defensive end Pat Toomay was left unprotected in the expansion draft and the Tampa Bay Buccaneers grabbed him. Then, the other starting end, Earl Edwards, was traded to San Francisco. Rashad, one of Simpson's best friends, left the team in a salary dispute and signed with the expansion Seattle Seahawks. Another receiver, J.D. Hill, later was dealt to Detroit. Pushed to the edge, Simpson demanded a trade to a West coast team, saying he would "definitely not play in Buffalo again."

"I didn't hold out for more money, I held out because I wanted to be traded, I wanted out of Buffalo," he recalled. "They let Ahmad go, they let Earl Edwards go, people that no way we should have let go.

"I just saw us doing all the things we had done three years hence with management killing the team. Once that happened, I said 'Look, I've gone through my years of rebuilding and going through all the crap. From 1975-76, we were gutted. I was trying to be logical. I said I wasn't at a point where I can go through another two or three years of rebuilding, my career would be

Tony Greene (upper), who is about to hit Minnesota's John Gilliam, finished his Bills career with 37 interceptions, second on the all-time list behind Butch Byrd.

Nick Mike-Mayer (lower) stabilized Buffalo's kicking game from 1979-1982.

over. And the only way they'd get the players they needed to get this team back on track was by trading me. That was my logic to Ralph. We finally got a great team and we had a tough luck year in '75 and then they decided to gut the team. It was frustrating."

Wilson seemed willing to oblige Simpson's request, but a deal with the Los Angeles Rams never panned out. Finally, Wilson flew to Simpson's Southern California home armed with a can't-refuse three-year, $2.5 million contract. Sure enough, Simpson couldn't back away from that kind of money and re-signed.

"I had no doubt that wisdom would win out and they'd make the trade," Simpson said. "I thought they had it worked out with the Rams which would have put me on a team with a shot at the Super Bowl, it would have given me some financial security for years to come and at the same time, give the Bills some key players in key areas. It made all the sense in the world and when the deadline for inter-league trading passed, I was devastated.

"I said 'What in the world were they thinking? I'm going to go back to Buffalo and we'll win three or four games.' I wasn't going to do it. Roone Arledge had a job for me on *Monday Night Football* and I was going to retire. I couldn't go through this again. Ralph knew I didn't want to come back, but he knew I loved football and that I'd miss the guys. So, to be quite honest, Ralph gave me an offer that I couldn't refuse.

"But when Ralph came and talked me back, I knew this team was history. I knew there was nothing I could do that would make this team anywhere near Super Bowl contenders let alone get to the play-offs. We went as far south as a team could go. The biggest disappointment in my career was not going to Buffalo (originally), not missing the Super Bowl, not Ahmad being traded, it was that year that the Bills didn't trade me."

Four games into the season, Saban became fed up with the organization and quit and Jim Ringo replaced him. The Bills, hurt by the loss of Joe Ferguson at midseason, never won another game, losing their final 10 to finish 2-12. Simpson enjoyed one more shining moment as a Bill, rushing for a new NFL single-game record 273 yards against Detroit on Thanksgiving Day, and he finished the season with 1,503 yards to earn his fourth league rushing crown.

In 1977, Simpson was bothered by a knee injury from the start. On October 30, during one of the Bills most embarrassing losses ever, a 56-17 shellacking at the hands of the two-year-old Seattle Seahawks, Simpson reinjured the knee, ending his season, and ultimately his Buffalo career.

Before the '78 season, he was traded to his hometown team, the San Francisco 49ers, for five draft choices. His fabulous nine-year career in Buffalo included 10,183 rushing yards and 70 touchdowns and he remains Buffalo's only Hall of Famer, having been inducted in 1985.

"Had we had a better cast of characters, we would have done a lot better," said Wilson. "O.J. always gave 100 percent and he was a fine individual. Even when we were losing, he would sign autographs by the thousands. The players used to wait for him on the bus 45 minutes after the game. Even though we lost, people knew O.J. He meant a tremendous amount to the franchise and to the city of Buffalo. He was an exciting ballplayer. I'm sure a lot of people came just to see O.J."

Simpson played two years with terrible 49ers teams before retiring after the 1979 sea-

Joe Cribbs enjoyed two great years in 1980 and 1981 topping 1,000 yards rushing each season. However, contract squabbles with management short-circuited his career and he ended up leaving Buffalo to play in the U.S. Football League. He returned to the Bills in 1985, but was never a factor, and was eventually traded to San Francisco in 1986, one day after Jim Kelly arrived.

Trainer Ed Abramoski
has taped every player
who has ever come
through Buffalo. He
has been with the team
since its inception in
1960 and he counts Joe
Ferguson as one of his
all-time favorites.

son. He left the
game as the NFL's
second all-time
leading rusher,
behind only Jim
Brown, with 11,236
yards, a total that
now places him sev-
enth.

"I don't have any
bad memories, all
my memories are
good in Buffalo," he
said. "Those early
years in Buffalo
helped me become
who I am in terms
of what I am and
how I look at my
life. I had the good
fortune of having to
go through those
difficult years. It
breeds character, I
guess.

"When I think of
Buffalo, I think of
my friends like
Reggie McKenzie.
We had a reunion
last year (20th
anniversary of the

2,003-yard season) and it's mind-boggling to think that 20 years have gone by since '73.
We picked up right where we left off, everyone was right into character. We were the
boys again, the boys were back in town. We were as close as any team could be, that
offensive unit.

"A football team is unlike life. It's what you bring to that group, that's what you're
judged by. I don't care about your background or your politics, it's what you bring to the
group. We were all of the same mind and focus and no matter what the score was, we
had pride. When a game was over, we felt like winners. We knew our fans took pride in
us. We were a blue-collar town, a blue-collar team and we fought everybody."

A new era began in Buffalo in 1978. Simpson was gone and Chuck Knox became the
team's head coach. Knox had won five straight NFC West Division crowns as coach of
the Rams and his winning reputation and fresh approach virtually assured that the
Bills would be going in a different, more positive direction.

"Chuck was a solid coach," Wilson said. "Getting him gave us credibility, just like getting O.J. had."

In his first major move, Knox pulled the trigger on the Simpson trade to San
Francisco on March 24, 1978. In return he received five draft choices including a first-
rounder in 1979.

The fans seemed ambivalent about Knox and the team, though, as only 18,084 season
tickets were sold, the lowest total since 1963. However, the team showed improvement
and wound up 5-11 with six of the losses by a touchdown or a less. Terry Miller proved

to be one of the NFL's best rookies, rushing for 1,060 yards including 208 against the New York Giants.

Knox's rebuilding program really began to take shape in 1979. Knox and his scouting director, Norm Pollom, came up with a superb draft. Combined with the players who were left over from '78 who had had a year to digest Knox's system, the Bills became respectable.

Because the 49ers finished last in the NFL with a 2-14 record, they had the first pick in the draft. However, that pick belonged to the Bills courtesy of the Simpson trade and Knox used it to select Ohio State linebacker Tom Cousineau. Although Cousineau would spurn Buffalo for Montreal of the Canadian Football League, the Bills traded Cousineau's rights a few years later for valuable draft choices, so the No. 1 pick wasn't a total bust. In the meantime, the anger over Cousineau's defection was quelled by the unearthing of future stars Jerry Butler, Fred Smerlas and Jim Haslett plus solid performers in Jeff Nixon, Jon Borchardt, Rod Kush and Ken Johnson. Also, veteran linebacker Isiah Robertson was acquired from the Rams and wide receiver Frank Lewis came over from Pittsburgh.

Smerlas endeared himself to Knox right away and during that first year he began a decade-long love affair with the Bills and the city of Buffalo.

There had been numerous characters who had passed through Buffalo during the first two decades of the team's existence, but Smerlas — an off-the-wall nose tackle from Boston College — redefined lunacy. And what made Smerlas special was that unlike so many other free spirits, he actually could play.

Eugene Marve led the Bills in tackles in 1983 and 1984. His 200 stops in 1984 remains a team record.

Jim Haslett (opposite page) was one of the finest linebackers to ever play in Buffalo, but his fun-loving personality made him as popular with the fans as his hard-hitting tackles.

On the day of the draft, Smerlas had spoken to representatives of the Tampa Bay Buccaneers and he thought he was heading south. Meanwhile, the Bills had made contact with defensive end Mark Gastineau and seemed intent on choosing him. But Knox changed his mind and decided to take Smerlas.

"Chuck got on the phone and he said 'I heard you're a mean sucker, are you ready to come down here and kick some ass?'" Smerlas recalled. "I'm just coming out of Boston College and I'm like, 'Yeah, I guess so.' After I got there, I found out they had already called Gastineau and they were going to pick him, but I had more hair on my body so they figured I was more physically mature than he was."

A few picks later in the second round, Smerlas' soon-to-be partner in hijinks, Haslett, was chosen. As Knox later would say of the two youngsters, "There's a pair that can beat a full house."

"The first time I ever met Haslett, we were in a bar and he comes over to me and says 'Your girlfriend has a nice figure,'" Smerlas said. "That's the first thing he ever said to me. I thought he was a little odd. But we got to be good friends and that first year, it was like being in college. We'd go out, the whole team would hang together and party together, we'd drive our jeeps through the woods at two in the morning like a bunch of yahoos. It was perpetual adolescence.

"The team was just coming up, we were part of a resurgence and a new personality that ended up defining the early-80's Bills. We did what we wanted, we said what we wanted and we had fun."

And Knox didn't have a problem with their attitudes, as long as they performed on Sundays.

"Chuck would come in and look at you and he'd say 'I don't care what you do off the field, you just show up on time, you play the games and you play them good or you'll be looking for another job,'" Smerlas said. "It was black and white, right in front of you.

"Chuck had a lot of older players who weren't such great players, so Haz and I were kind of like veterans in our first year. We had a big impact and we played pretty well right away. It was almost like being thrown into a leadership role as rookies.

"I loved Chuck. He's the reason I became the player that I was. I was a big, strong, quick guy with some talent and I had killed people in college. But one day he came up to me and told me I had talent, but he said 'I made a mistake, you can't play football.' Later on, I found out he used different means to get the best out of people. Some guys he pampered, some guys he gave shock therapy to. I was one of the guys he gave shock therapy to. So I went out and did everything I could to develop myself and I was one of the best nose guards in the league by the end of my rookie year."

In the season opener against Miami, the Bills came within inches of ending their 18-game losing streak to the Dolphins when kicker Tom Dempsey's 34-yard field goal skidded just wide, enabling the Dolphins to escape Rich Stadium with a 9-7 victory.

The following week, Roland Hooks scored four touchdowns in a 51-24 rout of Cincinnati and in the fourth game, Jerry Butler caught 10 passes and set team records for touchdown receptions (four) and receiving yards (255) in a 46-31 rout of the Jets.

Late in the season following a 16-13 overtime win over New England, the Bills were 7-6 and in the playoff hunt, but the young team collapsed down the stretch, losing its final three to finish 7-9.

The Bills simply weren't ready to win in 1979, but that all changed in 1980. Knox continued to upgrade the squad with a mixture of promising rookies like offensive lineman Jim Ritcher, running back Joe Cribbs, tight end Mark Brammer and linebacker Ervin Parker and a few hard-bitten veterans like offensive guard Conrad Dobler and linebacker Phil Villapiano.

At the same time, quarterback Joe Ferguson's game had risen to a new level; Smerlas, Haslett and Butler now had NFL experience; and other young veterans like linebackers Shane Nelson and Lucius Sanford, offensive linemen Joe Devlin and Ken Jones, corner-

backs Charlie Romes and Mario Clark, defensive end Ben Williams and safety Steve Freeman had become seasoned, productive players.

"Chuck liked the mixture of crazy guys with normal guys and he liked mixing the old and young," said Smerlas. "We had such a great lockerroom. We had a ball.

"One day in training camp, we're warming up, it's hot and we're having a tough time and just as we're ready to start practice, Chuck calls us together and says 'Guys, you've been working your asses off, take it in.' We couldn't believe it. We had a couple of kegs of beer, we were hugging and singing. We were there five hours in the lockerroom, the whole team, just having a party.

"We weren't a super-talented team, we had some good players, but what we had was so much spirit and Chuck was like the wagon train leader. It was so much fun. He was a friend, but he was still your coach. You respected him because he told you the truth, but you were wary of him because he had the authority."

When camp ended at Niagara University, the Bills shared a special feeling about the upcoming season.

"You could tell by the spirit," Smerlas said. "When you have a guy like Conrad who's eating eyeballs before the games, you just knew that that mesh of guys in the lockerroom, with that coach, and the amount of energy we put

One of the most popular Bills of all-time was nose tackle Fred Smerlas. Always quick with a line, Smerlas' humor was backed up by his superb talent which got him elected to five Pro Bowls.

into games, you knew good things were going to happen. Of all the teams that I've been on, that team and the '88 team were the two that had that spirit that you could feel from the beginning to the end."

It had been a decade since the Bills had beaten Miami, a string of 20 consecutive losses that remains a National Football League record. But on a sun-splashed September day at soldout Rich Stadium, that ignominious streak came to a crashing halt as Buffalo opened the year with a 17-7 victory over the hated Dolphins.

"I remember the spirit going into that game," Smerlas said. "We walked out onto that field and it was like the new era had begun. The fans were pumped up, Chuck's boys were tough, we were kind of like the Raiders of the East. There was no question, no reservation in anyone's heart, that we were going to win that game. It was more like a college atmosphere. The fans were going crazy, we were going crazy. It was an electric atmosphere. When that final gun sounded and we beat them, there were no problems in the world that day. It was unbelievable."

The fans stormed the field, tore down both goal posts and passed one of the uprights all the way up to Ralph Wilson's luxury box. In the lockerroom, Wilson gushed "This is the biggest win in the history of the team, 20 years. Bigger than the AFL

Championships. I'll be happy to buy new goal posts."

Today, Wilson still remembers that game as if it were played yesterday.

"That was a great day," he said. "I remember them passing the upright all the way up to my box. I thought they were going to ram it right through the window. I'll never forget that day."

Neither will any of the players involved.

"It was so prideful to stand in the middle of the field and remember that event, knowing you were going to be part of a Buffalo Bills chapter," said Smerlas.

The Bills raced to a 5-0 record and were 9-4 at the end of November and enjoying a one-game lead in the AFC East over New England when the Los Angeles Rams came to town. It was a cold, damp, foggy day in Orchard Park and both teams' offenses emulated the weather for much of the game. After 60 minutes, both teams had managed just seven points, necessitating the first overtime game in Rich Stadium history.

The Rams won the coin toss, but failed to move and punted. Joe Ferguson then hit Frank Lewis with a 30-yard pass to set up Nick Mike-Mayer's game-winning 30-yard field goal, touching off another unforgettable celebration as the *Talkin' Proud* theme song blared over the public address system.

Tom Dempsey, the NFL record-holder for the longest field goal (63 yards) did not enjoy a stellar stint in Buffalo. His missed field goal on the final play of the 1979 season opener prevented the Bills from snapping their record losing streak against the Dolphins.

The sellout crowd refused to leave the park until the Bills returned to the field for a curtain call and most of the players responded.

"We were in the lockerroom and we were looking at each other saying 'Can you believe this?'" Smerlas recalled. "We were so fired up, so overwrought with emotions. It's such a great feeling when you win with a bunch of guys who really love each other. Then you hear the chanting, the ranting and raving outside asking us for a curtain call. We were really connected to the crowd. Buffalo fans have always been very into football and close to the team, it's a football-oriented town and when they wanted us out there, we gave them what they wanted. We were dancing, doing the high-kicking, it was unbelievable.

"Those are the memories that I have now that I'm retired from football. I remember putting my arm around Jim Ritcher and Benny (Williams) and Baby Johnson and Haz and dancing around doing the high step. I remember Baby Johnson singing 'Buffalo's going to the Super Bowl' that whole year. That made football special for me."

But the Super Bowl wasn't meant to be. The following week, Ferguson suffered a severely sprained ankle that would hamper him the rest of the year.

He gutted out the season-ending 18-13 victory over Joe Montana's up-and-coming San Francisco 49ers in the mud at Candlestick Park, enabling the Bills to clinch their first AFC East Division title. But in their first playoff game since 1974, a divisional round game at San Diego, Ferguson re-injured his ankle early in the first quarter. Though he gamely played on virtually one leg, the offense wasn't sharp and the Chargers eventually pulled out a 20-14 victory when Dan Fouts hit little-known Ron Smith with a heartbreaking, game-winning 50-yard touchdown pass with 2:08 left to play, ending Buffalo's magical season.

"As soon as Fergy got hurt, we were in trouble because we didn't have a backup," Smerlas said. "We didn't have Frank Reich, we had Dan Manucci. I remember Conrad sitting in the lockerroom saying 'Half of Ferguson is better than a whole Manucci.' Losing Fergy really hurt us and once we lost a little of our emotion, we lost our edge. Fergy was a really good quarterback. People didn't give him credit, but he didn't have the great weapons of the Jim Kelly era. He was a smart guy and the guys really liked him.

"I remember talking to players back then, like Matt Millen of the Raiders, and they said we were the team that year, nobody wanted to play us. We had great chemistry, but the head chemist got hurt. When that guy (Smith) caught that touchdown pass, my heart just fell to my feet. You just couldn't believe it. The low was so low because you had vented all your energy and spirit in that game. It took me months to recover from that. It was like a family loss."

Despite that gut-wrenching defeat, big things were expected from the Bills in 1981. However, Smerlas said the team got too cocky coming off the success of 1980 and it nearly ruined the year.

"We had been 11-5 and we thought we were pretty good and I think we lost a little concentration and thought we were better physically than we were," he said. "What we were was a decent team with a lot of emotion and I think we lost sight of that for awhile. Around the middle of the year we discussed it and we knew we had to outhustle, outhit, outwant everyone out there or we were not going to win.

Thousands of fans welcomed the Bills back to Buffalo after an 18-13 victory over San Francisco which clinched the team's first AFC East Division title in 1980.

"So we'd go to the Pierce Arrow every Monday night as a team. We hung together, we ate together and rekindled that spirit that we had had. We found what we had lost."

They made the playoffs as a wild-card team and disposed of the New York Jets in the first round at Shea Stadium, posting their first playoff victory since the 1965 AFL Championship Game.

The week after, they traveled to Cincinnati to take on the Bengals, but after battling evenly for three quarters, the Bills couldn't keep pace in the final quarter. Ken Anderson fired the go-ahead touchdown pass to Cris Collinsworth with 10:39 left and the Bengals held on for a 28-21 victory.

The Bills had driven to the Cincinnati 20 late in the game and were faced with fourth

down and three yards to go. Ferguson hit Lou Piccone for six yards and an apparent first down, but the 30-second play clock had expired a fraction of a second before Ferguson took the snap, thus wiping out the first down. On fourth and eight, Ferguson overthrew Roland Hooks in the end zone.

"I went up to see Chuck after the game and he was sitting there (in the film room) with a glass of scotch," Smerlas said. "All you could see was the giant clock, the back of the offensive line and Fergy. You could see the clock going from one to zero and Chuck said 'We pay that guy $600,000 a year and he can't tell time.' He kept flashing that film back and forth, back and forth. He knew we had a great chance, but to lose it like that ...

There have been many cold afternoons (upper) spent on the frozen grass at War Memorial or on the icy turf at Rich Stadium and without the portable heaters, those afternoons would have been much longer.

After a down period in the mid-80's (lower), the Bills began to turn things around in 1987. Here, from left, Jerry Butler, Robb Riddick, Chris Burkett and Andre Reed celebrate a touchdown.

"You stand on the sidelines, you're jumping around all excited after Lou catches it, then they blow the whistle and there's a flag and it's delay of game. My God, delay of game. It's like a jogger not running the marathon because he has a splinter. It was something so avoidable, the clock is right in front of you. But it wasn't just Fergy, the play didn't get in enough time and he had to check off.

"To go home and watch San Diego, a team we had beaten earlier in the season, play against Cincinnati (in the AFC Championship Game) and then see Cincinnati make it to the Super Bowl, that was tough."

The Bills could have gone all the way to No. 1 as Fred Smerlas is indicating in 1980 and 1981, but they didn't get the breaks they needed in the playoffs and saw two promising seasons come to unfulfilling ends.

As it turned out, that was as far as Knox could take this team that he had rebuilt so superbly. In 1982, after winning their first two games, the Bills joined the rest of the NFL players on strike and when they returned to work two months later, the chemistry and cohesiveness that meant so much to them was shattered. They lost five of their final seven games, missed the playoffs, and after the season Knox resigned and became the head coach of the Seattle Seahawks.

"That strike broke our focus and created some rifts within the ranks," Smerlas said. "The teams that did well were the teams that stuck together and we didn't stick together. We would call practices and guys wouldn't show up. It was a shame."

When Knox resigned, Smerlas was deeply hurt and his first inclination was to bolt Buffalo and follow his coach.

"I didn't want out of Buffalo, I just wanted to go with Chuck," he said. "Here was a guy who spoke our language, he talked football, it was no-nonsense. He took care of his players and he was a guy who I loved to play for. I wanted to win for him. He was a man's man and a players coach."

Ultimately, Smerlas let go of Knox and came back to the Bills, who were now under the leadership of young Kay Stephenson, Knox's former quarterbacks coach.

Stephenson's tenure as head coach appeared to get off to a great start when the Bills chose tight end Tony Hunter and quarterback Jim Kelly in the first round of the draft and tabbed linebacker Darryl Talley in the second.

Hunter and Kelly were going to do what Kellen Winslow and Dan Fouts did for the San Diego Chargers, at least that was what the Bills were hoping. But ultimately, Kelly – who groaned on draft day when he was selected by the Bills – refused to sign with the team and instead inked a contract to play for the Houston Gamblers of the U.S. Football League.

It was a crushing blow to the team because Joe Ferguson had just about come to the end of the line in Buffalo and Kelly was looked upon as the quarterback who would lead the Bills for at least the next decade.

In addition to losing Kelly, veteran defenders Isiah Robertson, Shane Nelson and Bill Simpson retired, Reggie McKenzie was traded to Seattle and Joe Devlin suffered an ankle injury before the season started, ending his year. And then there was enigmatic running back Joe Cribbs who announced that he would honor the final year of his contract and then join the Birmingham Stallions of the USFL in 1984, thus leaving him in a very strange limbo position throughout '83.

"A lot of things went wrong," Smerlas said of the 1983 season. "Kay was new at head coaching and I think he tried to do a lot of things. He tried to do what Washington and Dallas and Pittsburgh did, and he tired us out. His philosophy and his style didn't suit us at all. The combination of the wrong coach with the wrong players doesn't add up to a successful season."

Stephenson got all he could out of an injury-depleted, morale-whipped team and limped in with an 8-8 record, but the decline was in full swing and what followed were two of the worst years in Bills history.

In 1984 and '85, the Bills plummeted to the bottom of the NFL as they recorded back-to-back 2-14 seasons.

"The team was lost, there was no emotion, no spirit, we had lost the connection with the crowd," Smerlas said. "It was just the most miserable, disheartening thing I'd ever been through in my life. We were heading down the wrong track, and the more we lost, the harder we practiced and all that would do is get us exhausted before the games. We were still proud to play for Buffalo, but to go through that was very humiliating, both personally and professionally."

The Bills lost their first 11 games in 1984 before rookie Greg Bell's 85-yard touchdown run on the game's first play started Buffalo on its way to a stunning 14-3 victory over the Dallas Cowboys. The only other victory came against Indianapolis, with Joe Dufek starting at quarterback.

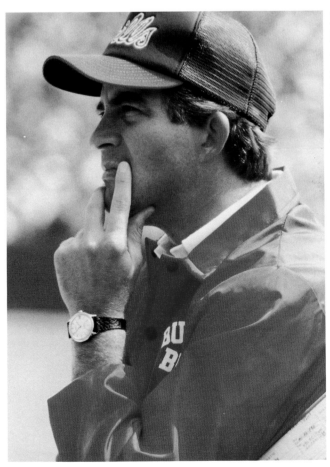

By the end of '84, Ferguson had been relegated to second string behind Dufek as Stephenson – with the season lost – began looking to the future knowing that Ferguson wasn't in the team's plans. It was a sad end to a career that was largely unspectacular, but at the same time, rather remarkable considering some of the woebegone teams he played on.

"Joe was a great quarterback, but he played without a supporting cast," Ralph Wilson said. "If he had had some of these players we have today, he probably would have taken us to the Super Bowl. You have to have a lot of good players, you can't just have two or three."

The man who began his career handing off to O.J. Simpson during the 2,003-yard season deserved a better fate, but on

Kay Stephenson took over as head coach in 1983, but he inherited a team that was on the downslide and he was unable to turn it around. The Bills finished 8-8 and 2-14 in his two full seasons.

47

draft day 1985, he was unceremoniously traded to Detroit, an event that was overshadowed by Buffalo's selection of Virginia Tech defensive end Bruce Smith with the No. 1 overall choice in the draft.

It's a good bet that when Jim Kelly's career as a Bill is complete, his name and number 12 will be added to Rich Stadium's Wall of Fame. Hopefully, Bills fans won't forget that Ferguson did that number proud before Kelly ever stepped foot in Buffalo.

Nothing improved for the Bills in 1985. Stephenson was fired early in the season and replaced by Hank Bullough, but a coaching change certainly wasn't the answer.

"Hank was, without a doubt, the worst coach I've ever been associated with," Smerlas said. "He was indecisive, talked out of both sides of his mouth, had no concept of what was going on, players were making fun of him, and he lost control of the team. Kay Stephenson tried, but Hank was something else. The guy was completely nuts. That was the lowest point in my career.

"But that also inspired me. It put the tough guys against the wall and we built character from that and that's why we became such good leaders after that. We were on the bottom of the mat and we could either stay there or get up and swing and we got up swinging."

Bill Polian, who had been the director of pro personnel since 1984, was promoted to general manager at the end of the '85 season and it was at that point that the Bills' fortunes began to turn for the better.

Polian understood football talent, and he also knew how to run an organization. Both of those qualities became evident immediately. A solid draft netted running back Ronnie Harmon and offensive tackle Will Wolford in the first round, and then Polian rolled up his sleeves and made the move that insured the Bills of a return to respectability and beyond – the signing, at long last, of Jim Kelly.

Kelly had enjoyed two brilliant seasons in the USFL, throwing for 9,842 yards and 83 touchdowns for the Gamblers. But when that league folded after it was awarded just $3 in its anti-trust suit against the NFL, the Bills, who still owned Kelly's NFL rights, were free to pursue him. And Polian, after a weekend of murderous negotiations with Kelly's representatives in a Houston hotel, consummated the deal on Aug. 18, 1986, touching off a celebration in Western New York that would have made visitors to the area think that a Super Bowl had been won that day.

"I thought Kelly was fabulous in college, unbelievable," Smerlas said. "When we drafted him, I thought it was going to be great, but then he went to Houston and that hurt us.

"But when he came to Buffalo, you knew they (the Bills' organization) were serious now. We had some guys already in place and we just needed a couple more players to put it together. When he came in, we knew we'd start turning it around. Of course they had to get rid of Hank before we could get anything going."

Kelly has experienced many great days in his life, on and off the football field, but August 18, 1986 is one he'll never forget. After stepping off Ralph Wilson's private jet at the Buffalo airport, Kelly was bombarded by TV cameras, photographers and reporters. He stepped into a black stretch limousine that was parked right on the tarmac, and he embarked on the ride of his life.

"I didn't know what the mood of the fans and the city of Buffalo would be because I had said I wouldn't be a Buffalo Bill," Kelly said, "but the reception I had at the airport and coming down the Thruway with all the banners and the people lined up on the overpasses waving to me, it was very exciting, unbelievable. I never thought I'd get that kind of reception.

"I remember at the stadium for my first game against the Jets, there was a banner that said 'Kelly is God' and it was like 'Hey, that's a little too much.' I guess it would have been different if the Bills had been winning, but they were coming off back-to-back 2-14 seasons, the fans needed something and they knew if the franchise was going to stay in Buffalo, they had to start getting some players and I was one of the stepping stones."

Lines formed at the Rich Stadium ticket office before the ink was dry on Kelly's signature and more than 1,000 season tickets were sold that day and about 3,000 were parceled out by the end of the week.

At the press conference to announce the signing, the main ballroom of the downtown Hilton was packed with reporters and fans. Local TV stations aired the event live. New York Governor Mario Cuomo called and spoke to Kelly and Kelly said, "Who knows, maybe I'll be able to take this team to the Super Bowl and get a call from the President next."

With Kelly at quarterback, the team and the city had renewed hope and even though the Bills won only four of 16 games that first year, it was obvious that they were a much better team.

In the second half of 1986, the inevitable firing of Hank Bullough occurred and Wilson brought in scholarly Marv Levy to replace him. It took about one day for the players to realize that Levy was the right man for the job.

"When they fired Hank, two guys came running up to me and said 'Ding dong,

When Jim Kelly arrived in Buffalo in August of 1986, the team and the city enjoyed a much-needed catharsis. He brought renewed hope to a team that had wallowed at the bottom of the NFL for two years. Here, at his first press conference, Kelly received a call from New York Governor Mario Cuomo and Kelly said perhaps someday the president would call to congratulate him on a Super Bowl victory.

the wicked witch is dead,'" Smerlas said. "It was so exciting to get Hank out of there, people were partying. It was like getting harmony with Russia. They brought in Marv and one thing about Marv is he knows how to prepare you for a game. He never burned you out, always gave you time to rest and be mentally prepared. We were so used to being so tired. After two weeks, we'd go into games not feeling tired and we started to play well. It was an unbelievable lift to have a guy come in like that."

Of all the coaches who have worked under Ralph Wilson, the owner says emphatically that Levy is his favorite.

"I called up (Kansas City Chiefs owner) Lamar Hunt because I knew Marv had coached there (from 1978-82)," Wilson said. "I said 'What about this Marv Levy, is he a pretty good coach?' and Lamar said 'I think we made a mistake in letting him go.' Right there I knew he was a good coach. Lamar is a very straight shooter, he'd tell me the truth. We've been friends for years.

"Marv has so many high qualities, so many attributes. He's a great organizer, he has the respect of his coaches, he lets them coach. He's just a top character.

"And he has a great sense of humor. To me, sense of humor is very important. I want to be with someone who is fun and can have some laughs. I can't say enough about Marv Levy. By far, not even close, he's the best coach we've ever had. He's No. 1."

Levy played out the '86 season with the existing coaching staff, but he assembled a new corps before '87, bringing in Walt Corey as his defensive coordinator and Ted Marchibroda as his quarterbacks coach and passing game-coordinator under offensive coordinator and line coach Jim Ringo. Levy also presided over – along with Polian – a stellar '87 draft as linebacker Shane Conlan, cornerback Nate Odomes, fullback Jamie Mueller, defensive end Leon Seals, tight end Keith McKeller and offensive tackle Howard Ballard all came aboard.

The team split their first two games before another NFL players strike interrupted the season. But unlike 1982 when the team got torn apart, the Bills went on strike as a team, remained close during the 24-day work stoppage, and came back eager to resume the season in mid-October.

"A lot of us had been around for the '82 strike," Smerlas said. "We knew Miami and Washington had stayed together during that strike (and wound up playing each other in the Super Bowl), so we knew we had to stay together and practice.

"Joe (Devlin) and I organized practices and it was very important to get Jim Kelly to come down because if he did, a lot of other guys would follow because he was the quarterback. And Kelly did come down. We had most of the team down there. We practiced religiously and it showed when we came back."

Said Kelly: "Joe and Fred came up to me and told me point blank that 'guys are going to do what you do. You're one of the leaders of the team and everyone is going to look at you because of your salary situation and if you cross the line, there will be tons of guys who will go with you and if you go to practice, they'll go with you to practice.' So I went to practice. Financially it wasn't the best thing for me to do, but I stayed together with the team and that's the only way I've ever played."

Andre Reed was a virtual unknown in college playing at tiny Kutztown (Pa.) State, but he has been one of the NFL's best receivers since entering the league in 1985. He owns almost every Bills receiving record.

Another major player acquisition occurred on Halloween night that year. The Bills participated in a three-team trade with the Los Angeles Rams and Indianapolis Colts that cost them running back Greg Bell, two first-round draft choices and a second-rounder, but netted them linebacker Cornelius Bennett.

Bennett proved to be an impact player on his first play as a Bill when he pressured Denver quarterback John Elway into an incompletion. The Bills stayed in the AFC East division race until the second-to-last week of the year when a loss to New England knocked them out, but, as Smerlas said, "That meshing together really propelled us into the '88 season."

Outside of 1980, Smerlas said 1988 was the most productive and enjoyable year he ever had playing football.

"We were playing with the emotion we had in the early 80s, but we also had some great talent, which we didn't have back then," he said. "We had a great defense

and we played with so much spirit. I could tell in preseason that we were meshing and that this was going to be something. It's just a feeling you get, a gut instinct. We were like machines, and it was a well-oiled machine. We were well-coached, well-conditioned and we wanted to win."

And win the Bills did, 11 times in their first 12 games. Rookie Thurman Thomas had been plugged into the halfback position after the Bills stole him in the second round of the draft. And led by Smerlas, Bruce Smith, Darryl Talley, Shane Conlan and Bennett, the defense dominated opponents.

"We knew we had the potential, it was just a matter of us putting it all together," Kelly said. "If you get the right players together and you stay healthy, anything can happen. I think we were a little surprised (by the great start). It was a matter of confidence because the team had been so used to losing close games at the end and all of a sudden things started changing and we started winning those games."

One of those games occurred on November 20, when the Bills clinched their second AFC East division crown in history, beating the New York Jets, 9-6, in overtime at Rich Stadium. Smerlas blocked a Pat Leahy field goal in the final seconds of the fourth quarter to force overtime and then Scott Norwood won the game with a field goal. Afterward, the fans flooded the field and tore down the goalposts.

"Coming out of the Hank era and living through it, then standing there in the tunnel and looking out on the field with 80,000 people chanting 'Fred-die', I had tears coming down my cheeks," Smerlas remembered. "Joe Devlin came up and gave me a kiss, Bruce, Kelly, Jim Ritcher, we were standing and watching and it was like 'Can you believe this? We've come a long way baby.' It was fandemonium. To climb all the way back up was really something special."

A late-season swoon cost Buffalo home-field advantage in the playoffs, though, and the Bills went on to lose the AFC Championship Game in Cincinnati, 21-10, denying them their first trip to the Super Bowl.

"Things didn't go our way that day," Smerlas said. "To blow that opportunity to go to the Super Bowl was a shame. It was frustrating because we had it right in the grasp of our hands and we knew we might not ever get that close again."

As it turned out, Smerlas would never get that close again, but the Bills would later make playing in the Super Bowl a record-breaking habit. Before that, though, came a learning experience that all at once ruined the 1989 season, but also enabled the Bills to

Even though the Bills didn't have a first-round draft choice in 1988, they managed to steal running back Thurman Thomas in the second round. He has become one of the greatest players in franchise history.

Cornelius Bennett came to the Bills in a Halloween night trade in 1987 that was one of the biggest in team history. He has gone on to play in five Pro Bowls.

grow up.

The team became known nationwide as the "Bickering Bills" because some players sniped at others using the local media as their sounding boards.

In the second game of the year, a Monday-nighter against Denver, Kelly and receiver Chris Burkett argued on the sidelines. Burkett was waived soon after.

Kelly suffered a shoulder separation in the fifth game at Indianapolis and the next day publicly singled out tackle Howard Ballard for allowing Jon Hand – the man who had hit Kelly – a clear path to the pocket.

Later in the season, Thurman Thomas took issue with Kelly for his arguing with Burkett and his comments about Ballard and when the national media picked up on the friction, the Bills were painted as a team divided.

"It was frustrating because I thought we had something very special (coming off of 1988)," Smerlas said. "Guys started whining, guys thought we were better than we were, we lost a little bit of that closeness. We lost what we had that was unique in '88."

Said Kelly of the bickering: "It was overblown. What hurt us more than anything was the way the media handled it. Every team has bad times and good times, and if the bad times are kept in the lockerroom, things smooth out a lot quicker. What happened that year was it got out into the public and the public perception started getting overblown.

"We had some problems, but they were problems that every sports team has. It's a matter of how you handle it and we were young and I think we let the media get the best of us."

Still, they managed to win their second straight division title when they crushed the Jets at the Meadowlands in the season finale, 37-0. That sent them off to a first-round playoff game at Cleveland, but one play after Ronnie Harmon dropped a sure game-winning touchdown pass, Kelly threw an interception at the goal line to Cleveland's Clay Matthews with two seconds left to play, and the Browns escaped with a 34-30 victory, ending Buffalo's tumultuous season.

"We should have beaten Cleveland, so it was a downer to lose with that much talent," said Smerlas. "When Ronnie dropped the pass, we just fell like dominoes on the field."

The Cleveland game proved to be Smerlas' swan song in Buffalo. After 11 hellacious years, the man in the middle wasn't protected during the Plan B free agency period in the off-season and, given no choice, signed a contract to play for the San Francisco 49ers.

It was a bittersweet day in the Smerlas household. He loved Buffalo and he loved the Bills, but with Jeff Wright set to move into the starting lineup, Smerlas wasn't needed and he knew it. The 49ers' offer was too good to pass up, plus, it gave Smerlas a chance to play for a team with a legitimate chance to go to the Super Bowl, the one thing he had not been able to accomplish. So with a tear in his eye, Smerlas bade Buffalo a fond farewell.

"I really loved playing football in Buffalo," he said. "Whether we were 2-14 or 14-2, I wanted to beat the guy in front of me. When I went to San Francisco, I lost that special pride of protecting my turf and my town. Then, when I came home to New England (he finished his career playing with the Patriots), I wouldn't accept bad talk about Buffalo.

"I became so entwined with the city, it was a pride thing for me. So there were nothing but good memories about playing for the Bills. It's something I cherish, those memories in Buffalo. Even though there was Hank Bullough and the losing seasons, you can never have a relationship with a town or a relationship with the players like I had in Buffalo. When I was playing for the Pats, I'd wear a Bills t-shirt underneath my uniform. Someone came up to me one day and said 'Fred, no matter what you wear on the outside, you'll always be a Buffalo Bill on the inside.'"

As disappointing as the Cleveland loss was, a lot of good came out of it. First, the players had held hands throughout the final, unsuccessful drive, a clear sign that this team wasn't nearly as divided as the rest of the country thought. Second, the no-huddle offense was born that day on the western shores of Lake Erie.

The Bills used the hurry-up, two-minute offense almost the entire second half against the Browns and Kelly enjoyed a huge day, throwing for an NFL career-high of 405 yards and four touchdowns. Ted Marchibroda, who had become offensive coordinator, filed that information away for use at a later time.

"We knew that our two-minute offense before the half and at the end of games was almost unstoppable," Kelly said. "I think from that point on, we realized 'Why don't we try this all the time?' The Cleveland game was a pivotal point for us as far as running the no-huddle."

Kelly, armed with a $20 million contract extension that tied him to the team for the rest of his career, started the season-opening drive of 1990 against Indianapolis in the no-huddle. He completed all nine of his passes and Scott Norwood capped the march with a field goal.

Interestingly, the Bills shunned the no-huddle as their primary offensive mode for much of the next three months. Instead, they attacked conventionally, and playing as well as they did, there was no reason to shift into the no-huddle. There was no more bickering, just one harmonious hum week after week as they tore through their schedule following a 30-7 loss at Miami in Week 2. They won eight in a row, then lost at Houston on a Monday night, before coming home to play Buddy Ryan's Philadelphia Eagles.

On that early-December day, Kelly used the no-huddle throughout the first quarter and the Bills decimated one of the best defenses in the NFL, scoring 24 points in

Kent Hull (67) joined the Bills on the same day in August of 1986 as Jim Kelly, albeit under far less fanfare. Not much has changed since then. Hull has quietly anchored the Bills offensive line for eight years and now ranks as one of the team's all-time best linemen.

the first 13 minutes. They went on to a 30-23 victory and from that day forward, the no-huddle became their main offensive philosophy.

Kelly suffered a knee sprain against the New York Giants, but backup Frank Reich came in and protected the lead Kelly had provided and the Bills came out of the Meadowlands with a huge 17-13 victory. The following week, Reich passed for 234 yards and two touchdowns to lead a 24-14 victory over the arch-rival Dolphins that clinched Buffalo's third consecutive AFC East crown.

During the 1988 season (upper), the Bills had the No.1 defense in the AFC. Nate Odomes (37) is congratulated by Darryl Talley (56) and Shane Conlan for an interception.

Fred Smerlas (below) points Buffalo's way after the Bills recovered a fumble.

Kelly returned in time for the play-offs and he was brilliant. In a 44-34 divisional round victory over the Dolphins, he threw for 339 yards and three touchdowns operating from the no-huddle.

And the week after, he passed for 300 yards and two scores while Thurman Thomas rushed for 138 yards. The defense forced seven turnovers in a mind-boggling 51-3 romp of the Los Angeles Raiders that gave the Bills their first AFC/AFL Championship since 1965 and sent them to their first Super Bowl against the Giants at Tampa Stadium.

"We caught a lot of teams by surprise with the no-huddle," Kelly said. "You have to have the players execut-

ing, the weapons to go to and the quarterback who can call the plays and we had it all. They left it in my hands and told me to take it from there and I took it.

"In the Raiders game, we couldn't do anything wrong. I'll never forget that, it was one of our best games ever and it was the game that put us in our first Super Bowl."

In their first trip to the Big Game, the Bills were installed as favorites and they should have been. Kelly was back in the groove, the offense virtually was unstoppable and the defense was playing well. Also, Giants starting quarterback Phil Simms was out for the season and untested Jeff Hostetler was at quarterback.

With the Persian Gulf War raging overseas, the nation's emotions were running wild and football seemed very inconsequential at the time. But the Bills and Giants provided the country, and the troops in the Gulf, an opportunity to forget about the world's problems for three hours.

"The war had an effect on everybody, but we had to concentrate on making it to our first Super Bowl," Kelly said. "You always have it in the back of your mind, the people who are fighting for you and your country, but on the other hand, I had an obligation to concentrate on what we had to do."

Obviously, every player on both sides felt the same way because the teams engaged in one of the best Super Bowls ever. Sadly for the Bills, Scott Norwood's 47-yard field goal with four seconds left to play sailed wide of the right upright and the Giants prevailed, 20-19.

"I don't think anyone in Buffalo will ever forget that," Kelly said of the vision of the ball failing to split the goal posts. "It was a heartbreak because we were the best team in the NFL that year and we were the best team that day."

The Bills weren't satisfied with just making the Super Bowl in 1990. They wanted to win one and throughout the '91 season, their mission was to repeat as AFC champs and make amends in Super Bowl XXVI in Minneapolis.

The fans went wild on the afternoon of November 20, 1988, when the Bills won the AFC East with an overtime victory over the New York Jets. Thousands stormed the field and tore down the goalposts. It was fandemonium!

The no-huddle was in full bloom and the team set single-season records for points scored (458), touchdowns (58), touchdown passes (39), first downs (360), total offense (6,252 yards), pass completions (332) and net yards passing (3,871).

Kelly and Thomas waged a personal race all season for league MVP honors with Thomas winning out, becoming the first Bill so honored since O.J. Simpson. While Kelly was setting personal highs for completions (304), yards passing (3,844) and touchdowns (33), Thomas was leading the NFL in yards gained from scrimmage for the third year in a row with 2,038 yards, the 12th-highest total in NFL history.

They won 10 of their first 11 games, clinched their fourth straight AFC East title on December 1 against the Jets and earned home-field advantage in the playoffs for the second year in a row.

In the divisional round, they crushed Kansas City, 37-14, thus avenging an embarrassing 33-6 loss on *Monday Night Football* earlier in the season.

After a decade of losing to Miami, the Bills began to play on even terms with the hated Dolphins in the 80's, then dominated them in the 90's. Here, Darryl Talley sacks Dan Marino.

A tough Denver squad came to Rich Stadium the following week for the AFC Championship Game, and the Broncos' defense found a way to slow down the no-huddle. But the Bills' defense was equal to the task and with the game scoreless in the third quarter, it was the defense – a unit that had been maligned all year as it finished 27th in the league in yards allowed – that made the game-breaking play. Jeff Wright tipped a John Elway pass at the line of scrimmage, linebacker Carlton Bailey caught the ball and rumbled 11 yards for a touchdown. The Bills went on to a 10-7 victory and set themselves up for a date with the powerful Washington Redskins in the Super Bowl.

Unlike the previous year when the Bills certainly seemed to be the more talented team, there was no question that the best team in the Metrodome during Super Bowl XXVI was the Redskins. They manhandled the Bills, racing to a 37-10 lead thanks to five Buffalo turnovers and the pinpoint accuracy of quarterback Mark Rypien, then held on for a convincing 37-24 victory.

"We had a great team again, but there was no doubt that the Redskins were the best team in football that year," Kelly conceded. "They had every aspect of the game – offense, defense, special teams. I got physically beat. I mean I didn't have time to take a snap. It came down to the better team prevailing that day. But we got back and we did it when no one thought we could repeat."

It had appeared that Denver and Washington had caught up to the magic of the no-huddle – of course Marv Levy will argue that "systems don't win, players do" – and the question entering 1992 was 'What can the Bills do to stay one step ahead of the competition?'

Well, during the first four weeks of 1992, the answer was nothing. The no-huddle went ballistic during September and the Bills won their first four games by a combined score of 153-45. During that torrid start, the Bills recorded a wild 34-31 victory in San Francisco in which neither team attempted a punt, a first in NFL history. The teams combined for 1,086 yards, the fourth-highest total in NFL history, and both quarterbacks, Kelly and Steve Young, surpassed 400 yards passing, only the third time that had happened.

Kelly and company could not keep up that pace and the team lost back-to-back games to Miami and the Raiders. A five-game winning streak was followed by shocking losses to Indianapolis and the Jets and then a season-ending defeat in Houston cost the Bills the division title as Miami took the honor.

Kelly had suffered a knee injury against the Oilers, so Frank Reich made his first playoff start against the Oilers the following week at Rich Stadium and for 32 minutes, it was a complete disaster. The Oilers stormed to a 28-3 halftime lead and less than two minutes into the third quarter, Bubba McDowell intercepted Reich and returned it 58 yards for a touchdown, giving Houston what appeared to be an insurmountable 35-3 lead.

But the Bills, relentless as ever, refused to quit. Kenneth Davis capped a 50-yard march with a touchdown plunge and after recovering an on-side kick, the Bills struck

Jim Kelly and Thurman Thomas have become one of the most lethal 1-2 offensive punches in the NFL. In 1991, both were considered for the league MVP award, with Thomas winning the honor.

again when Reich found Don Beebe on a 38-yard touchdown pass.

Before the quarter ended, Reich had fired two TD passes to Andre Reed and with a full 15 minutes remaining, the Bills were within 35-31, the Oilers were shaking their heads in disbelief and hundreds of fans in the crowd of 75,141 who had left in disgust were climbing the fences to get back into the stadium.

Reich hit Reed with another touchdown pass with 3:08 left to play to give the Bills the lead, but Warren Moon directed a 63-yard drive that produced Al Del Greco's game-tying field goal with 12 seconds remaining.

Houston won the coin toss in overtime, but Moon was intercepted by Nate Odomes and a few plays later, Steve Christie capped the greatest comeback in NFL history with a 32-yard field goal, giving the Bills a 41-38 triumph.

"This is one in a lifetime," Ralph Wilson said that day in the joyous lockerroom. "You never expect a team to come back the way the Bills did today. Anybody who does is dreaming."

"One thing about the Bills," Kelly said, "is we never give up."

But there was plenty of work to be done. Because they hadn't won the division, the Bills were forced to go on the road for the rest of the playoffs. The first stop was Pittsburgh's Three Rivers Stadium and no miracles were needed against the Steelers. Reich was efficient, Kenneth Davis rushed for 104 yards while subbing for banged up Thurman Thomas and the defense was stifling in a 24-3 victory.

So it was on to Miami for an AFC Championship showdown with the hated Dolphins. Steve Christie's five field goals and an inspired performance by the defense keyed a 29-10 victory, thus enabling the Bills to become just the second team in NFL history to make it to three Super Bowls in a row, Miami being the first (1971-73).

This time, the opponent was the Dallas Cowboys at the Rose Bowl in Pasadena, California. The Bills were under the national media spotlight all week because a loss would send them into the league record book as the first team to lose three Super Bowls in a row.

By the time the game was played, the players had grown weary of all the talk and it seemed to affect their performance once the ball was kicked off. Kelly suffered a knee injury in the second quarter and the Bills went on to turn over the ball a record nine times and lost a laugher, 52-17.

The scene in the locker room was reminiscent of a funeral, and for good reason. Most players never get the opportunity to play in a Super Bowl, yet here were the Bills, in the game three years in a row, and still without a ring. But as they had done following the previous two Super Bowl losses, the Bills' steadfastly vowed that they would be back to claim what had so despicably eluded them for three years.

Before the Bills could embark on their quest, a shocking development in the front office occurred. General manager Bill Polian was fired by Ralph Wilson just days after the loss to Dallas. Polian cited philosophical differences as the reason for his firing. The two-time NFL Executive of the Year took a job in the league office in New York and later, was hired to become the general manager of the expansion Carolina Panthers.

John Butler, one of the finest personnel men in pro football, was promoted to the general manager's office while Jerry Foran was named vice-president for administration, completing the front office shakeup.

There was also a big shakeup on the field in 1993. Free agency infiltrated the NFL and the Bills took heavy losses. Offensive tackle Will Wolford – one of the Bills' two transitional free agents whom they could have kept by matching another team's offer – went to Indianapolis when the Bills were unable to match the Colts' contract proposal due to a controversial escalator clause that would have thrown Buffalo's salary structure out of whack.

Linebacker Shane Conlan and wide

Steve Christie is mobbed by his teammates, including Mark Pike and Chris Mohr after his field goal in overtime which gave the Bills a 41-38 victory over Houston in the 1992 AFC wild-card round. Christie's kick capped Buffalo's rally from a 35-3 deficit making it the greatest comeback in NFL history.

receiver James Lofton took off for Hollywood, Conlan going to the Rams and Lofton to the Raiders; reserve offensive lineman Mitch Frerotte went to Seattle; punt returner Clifford Hicks went to the Jets; and linebacker Carlton Bailey accepted an enormous deal with the Giants. The Bills' only free agent signees were receiver Bill Brooks and defensive lineman Oliver Barnett.

Faced with a great challenge, Levy and his staff made the best of a trying situation. Brooks replaced Lofton, Marvcus Patton and Mark Maddox stepped in for Conlan and Bailey, rookie Russell Copeland proved to be an adequate punt returner in place of Hicks, and John Fina took over for Wolford at the difficult left tackle position and was surprisingly solid as a rock all year.

Meanwhile, Jim Kelly, Thurman Thomas, Andre Reed, Kent Hull, Bruce Smith, Cornelius Bennett, Darryl Talley, Nate Odomes and Henry Jones did typically marvelous jobs as the Bills won the AFC East for the fifth time in six years.

The year began with a mentally-soothing victory over the Cowboys in Dallas in Week 2, a huge psychological lift that in a small way, exacted some revenge for the embarrassing Super Bowl defeat. Later, victories over the Giants and Washington gave the Bills a three-game sweep of their Super Bowl conquerors.

There also were some down times, such as humbling defeats to Miami, Pittsburgh and Kansas City. After the loss to the Chiefs, the Bills came home to Rich and were beaten by the Raiders, 25-24. There was some unrest in Western New York as fans and media began to wonder if, finally, the Bills were going to succumb and allow another AFC team to rule the roost.

The Bills provided the answer to that probing question the next week with an inspired victory in Philadelphia. Reed, Maddox, Jeff Wright and Mark Kelso didn't dress for the game due to injuries and they were joined on the sidelines later by Kelly and Thomas. Still, the Bills rallied behind a group of reserves including Frank Reich and Davis and downed the Eagles, 10-7, scoring all their points in the final four min-

The Buffalo fans have poured into Rich Stadium in record numbers. In 1991, they set an all-time in-stadium **NFL** attendance record as **635,889** watched the team in person during eight home games. Buffalo has now led the league in attendance six years in a row.

59

Bruce Smith is the Bills all-time leading sack man with 106 and his 12 sacks in the playoffs are an NFL record.

utes.

Bennett delivered a rousing postgame speech in the lockerroom and termed the game one of the greatest victories he'd ever been a part of. John Butler called his team 'resilient' and Kelly said 'Don't count us out.'

It was the victory that turned around their season. The next week, Buffalo pummeled the Dolphins in Miami, 47-34, then finished with victories over the Jets at frigid Rich and over the Colts in the Hoosier Dome to assure that the AFC's road to the Super Bowl again would lead through snowy Buffalo.

First up were the Raiders, a team fresh off a big victory over Denver and a group of men who had recently come to Buffalo and beaten the Bills. Los Angeles, under the leadership of its new quarterback, Jeff Hostetler, knew it could beat Buffalo and entered the game very confident. But Mother Nature played a cruel trick on Al Davis' sunshine boys. The temperature dipped to minus-32 with the wind-chill, making it the coldest game in Bills history, and the Bills prevailed in the arctic conditions, 29-23.

In the AFC Championship Game, with seemingly everyone outside Western New York rooting against the Bills, the newly-dubbed "serial killers of the Super Bowl" routed Joe Montana and the Kansas City Chiefs, 30-13, to become the first team ever to win four straight AFC crowns.

Aside from not wanting the Bills in the Super Bowl, there was another reason why the nation's football fans were pining for a Buffalo loss: They wanted Montana to get back into the Big Game, which he had made his personal playground while winning four championships with the San Francisco 49ers in the 1980s.

The Bills would have none of that. Wright and Bruce Smith combined on a hard tackle of Montana early in the third quarter and he left the game with a concussion, barely able to say his name. And Thomas turned in one of the finest individual performances in team history, rushing for a Bills playoff record 186 yards and three touchdowns.

When the Bills got to Atlanta for Super Bowl XXVIII, the national perception of them had changed and it was as if casual observers were saying 'Now that the Bills are in the Super Bowl, we might as well root for them' and so Buffalo became the obvious sentimental favorite.

For a half, it looked as if the Bills would finally rid themselves of their Super Bowl inadequacies as they opened a 13-6 halftime lead. But Thomas fumbled on the third play of the third quarter and Dallas safety James Washington returned it 46 yards for the tying touchdown. A few minutes later, Emmitt Smith amassed 61 yards rushing on a 64-yard drive that ended with his 15-yard touchdown run and the Cowboys were on their way to a 30-13 victory.

"Nobody ever thought we could do it," Kelly said of returning to play in a fourth Super Bowl. "It was a season where we didn't give up. We had to fight through a very tough schedule, we kept coming back and we stayed focused. We're a team of resilience. We'll be back.

"When I look back on my eight years here, I remember the fans. Our fans continue to come out and push us and stay behind us. This city has the greatest fans in the world. We're going to keep going to the Super Bowl until we do it right."

For Ralph Wilson, it has been a magical 35-year run. Truthfully, there have been more bad seasons than good seasons, but the past four years have been among the greatest in his life. And while his team hasn't won the Super Bowl, the Bills have managed to provide him a brand of excitement he never had experienced.

"It's hard to put into words," Wilson said. "Everybody wants to win the Super Bowl, but that's really secondary to me. And I'm not just saying that because we haven't won one yet. Getting there is so difficult, let alone four consecutive times. It's been the greatest thrill I've ever had in my life, seeing this team go to four straight Super Bowls. It's going to be a long, long time before anybody does that again. Maybe in 75 years some-

In the 1993 AFC Championship Game, Cornelius Bennett and the Bills defense bottled up Kansas City's Marcus Allen and Buffalo defeated the Chiefs, 30-13, to advance to their record fourth consecutive Super Bowl.

one might do it again, but in the era of free agency, it's going to be tough. You can't keep a team together. And even if you could keep a team together, it would be tough.

"To be honest, the Super Bowl game, to me, is sort of a letdown. It may sound facetious, but it's sort of an aftermath because it's so difficult to win your conference. Every game is important, every play is important. Like I said,

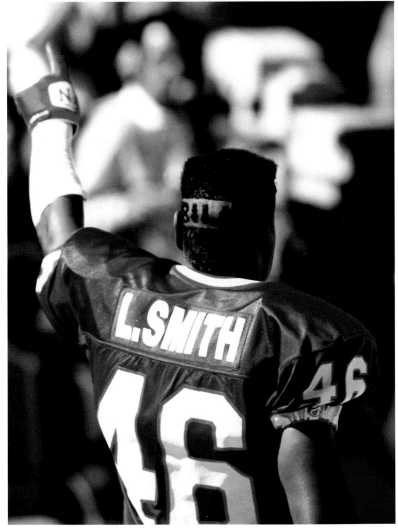

it's just a great thrill. Sure, I want to win a Super Bowl, I don't want to diminish that, but this has been the most fun I've ever had.

"We have 80,000 people coming to games, millions watching on television, it's what America is made of. This team is giving quality of life and enjoyment to a community. That's the great thing about sports. That's what I enjoy about it."

Let's go Buffalo!

As Jim Kelly and Leonard Smith indicate the Bills have been No. 1 in the AFC throughout the 1990's. Above, Marv Levy, Ralph Wilson and John Butler display the proof, the four Lamar Hunt Trophy's the team has won.

A<small>t</small> A G<small>lance</small>
1959 & 1960

Aug. 14, 1959 – The first organizational meeting of the American Football League was held in Chicago under the leadership of Lamar Hunt. Member teams named and their principal owners: New York, Harry Wismer; Dallas, Lamar Hunt; Los Angeles, Barron Hilton; Minneapolis, Max Winter and William Boyer; Denver, Bob Howsam; Houston, Bud Adams. Plans for a 1960 start of the league were announced.

Aug. 22 – American Football League was chosen as the name of the league.

Sept. 4 – Ralph Wilson, minority stockholder in the Detroit Lions of the NFL, said he was interested in bringing an AFL franchise to Miami.

Oct. 17 – Because Miami balked, Wilson turned to Buffalo and announced he would place his AFL franchise in Buffalo. "You can't get into this with the idea that you're going to make a lot of money. It's like owning horses. You pay a lot of feed bills and trainers fees and you have to be pretty darned lucky to get a Kentucky Derby winner. If you do, you might make some money."

Oct. 28 – In a meeting in New York, Buffalo officially was admitted as the league's seventh team.

Nov. 5 – It was projected that the AFL rosters would be about 40 players and the total payroll would run around $400,000.

Nov. 17 – Ralph Wilson said about 10 coaches had applied for the Bills head coaching position and he had narrowed the list to two or three candidates.

Nov. 20 – The Bills signed a War Memorial Stadium lease with the city.

Nov. 22 – In a meeting in Minneapolis, Boston was admitted as the eighth team with William H. Sullivan heading the 10-man ownership syndicate.

Nov. 23 – The AFL's first player draft was held and Penn State all-America back Richie Lucas was Buffalo's first choice. The Washington Redskins of the NFL also drafted him, but Lucas was said to be leaning toward the Bills because he would get a chance to play, and he had been offered an off-season job in a local accounting firm. The Bills drafted 33 players in all, including safety Larry Wilson (who later signed with the NFL Cardinals) and Tom Day.

Nov. 29 – Afraid that the NFL would lose SMU quarterback Don Meredith to the fledgling AFL, Bedford Wynne and Clint Murchison, the two men hoping to secure an NFL team for Dallas, signed Meredith to a $100,000 personal services contract, even though they didn't yet have a team.

Nov. 30 – The Buffalo franchise officially was named the Bills; Joe Foss was named as the AFL's first commissioner.

Dec. 2 – A secondary draft consisting of 20 rounds was held.

Dec. 5 – Tackle Joe Schaffer of Tennessee was the first player to sign with the Bills.

Dec. 9 – Syracuse coach Ben Schwartzwalder, whose Orangemen were ranked No. 1 in the nation and preparing for the Cotton Bowl and a possible national championship, was reported to be the No. 1 choice of the Boston franchise to become the head coach. "Money will not stand in our way," said William Sullivan. "We're prepared to go real high, doubling his Syracuse salary and giving him a long-term contract."

Dec. 10 – The Bills signed 310-pound tackle Birtho Arnold of Ohio State.

Dec. 16 – Buster Ramsey, a defensive assistant with the Detroit Lions, was hired as the Bills' first head coach. His salary was reported to be about $27,500 per season. George Wilson, the Lions head coach, reportedly was making about $18,000 a year.

Dec. 18 – Sammy Baugh signed to coach the New York Titans.

Dec. 22 – Dick Gallagher, a longtime aide of Cleveland head coach Paul Brown, was named general manager of the Bills. Gallagher predicted that within three years, the AFL and NFL would play a football world series. Upon hearing the appointment, former NFL passing champion Tommy O'Connell thought about a return to pro ball to become the Bills quarterback. O'Connell had quit the Browns to become an assistant coach at Illinois. He had just served as head coach at Drake in 1959.

Jan. 1, 1960 – Richie Lucas signed with the team for a reported $50,000 over three years.

Jan 4 – Bob Dove was the first assistant coach hired by Ramsey. The two worked together with the Lions.

Jan. 11 – Floyd "Breezy" Reid signed as backfield coach.

Jan. 26 – Lamar Hunt was named the first AFL president.

Jan. 27 – Minneapolis withdrew from the league because of stadium problems; a 14-game schedule was adopted.

Jan. 28 – The two-point conversion rule was passed.

Jan. 30 – Oakland was awarded Minneapolis' franchise with Chet Soda heading an eight-man ownership syndicate. Divisions were broken down into East (Buffalo, Boston, New York and Houston) and West (Dallas, Oakland, Denver and Los Angeles).

Feb. 5 – Buster Ramsey said he was not happy the AFL had adopted the two-point conversion. "It's a bad rule for pro football," Ramsey said. "Those (owners) who passed the rule seem to have forgotten that in pro football, we have the field goal. In college football, they need the two-point play to stir up interest."

Feb. 8 – Ticket sales for the Bills' games began and the team sold about 3,000 season tickets. A man named Arthur Diemer of Attica was first in line. "The early tremendous sale of tickets indicates that the fans of Buffalo, Western New York and the Niagara Frontier are hungry for professional football," general manager Dick Gallagher said.

Feb. 9 – A no-tampering verbal pact was announced between the AFL and NFL, referring to player contracts. Chuck Burr was named the Bills' director of public relations and also was given the role of administrative assistant to Dick Gallagher.

Feb. 17 – Jack Butler was hired as defensive assistant coach.

March 2 – Dick Gallagher flew to New York for a league meeting and said he would request the majority of the Bills home games be scheduled early in the year with only one home game in November to avoid any possible weather problems.

March 9 – AFL commissioner Joe Foss charged that the NFL – which had brought in a team to Dallas – had expanded "for the purpose of destroying, not competing with" the AFL. Newly appointed NFL commissioner Pete Rozelle responded by saying: "Inasmuch as they have sought competition by bringing AFL franchises into the NFL cities of New York, Los Angeles and San Francisco, the NFL sincerely hopes that competition between the AFL and its own member clubs will bring about a more highly skilled and entertaining brand of football for fans."

March 30 – Eddie Abramoski was hired as the Bills' trainer.

April 19 – ABC expressed interest in telecasting AFL games for $1.9 million per year.

April 21 – The Bills signed linebacker Laverne Torczon.

April 22 – Dick Gallagher said the AFL would be on a par with the NFL within three years.

May 4 – Harvey Johnson was hired as the final assistant coach. His duties also included serving as the director of player personnel.

June 9 – The league signed a five-year television contract with ABC, with the first-year revenue set at $1.785 million to be divided by the eight teams.

June 20 – Houston's first-round draft choice, Billy Cannon, won a court victory over the NFL team that drafted him, the Los Angeles Rams, enabling him to accept a $110,000 contract with the Oilers. The Oilers also gave Cannon a chain of five gas stations and a luxury car.

July 10 – Training camp opened at East Aurora.

July 11 – During the Bills' first practice, a wide receiver named Elbert Dubenion wowed the coaches with his speed.

July 17 – Buster Ramsey conducted the Bills' first scrimmage.

July 18 – Buster Ramsey made the first official roster cut, trimming the squad from 74 to 59.

July 29 – A crowd of 100,000 lined Main St. for a welcome parade for the team.

July 30 – A crowd of 16,474 at War Memorial Stadium watched Boston beat the Bills, 28-7, in the preseason opener which also served as the first game in AFL history. Maurice Bassett scored the Bills' only TD, as Buffalo was outgained, 430-316.

Aug. 2 – Maurice Bassett's TD didn't impress Buster Ramsey, as the coach cut the running back. Meanwhile, the team acquired running back Wray Carlton from Boston in a trade for defensive end Al Crow.

Aug. 13 – The Bills won their first preseason game, 31-14, over Denver in Rochester at Aquinas Stadium. Richie Lucas had an 88-yard kickoff return that set up a Buffalo TD.

Aug. 21 – Boston beat the Bills again, this time 21-7 in Worcester, Mass.

Aug. 24 – The Oakland Raiders spoiled the dedication of War Memorial Stadium, beating the Bills, 26-21, in front of 17,071. The Raiders scored 20 points in the first quarter.

Sept. 4 – The New York Titans scored six times on touchdown passes and routed the Bills, 52-31, before 6,281 at War Memorial Stadium in the preseason finale.

Sept. 9 – In the first regular-season AFL game, Denver beat Boston, 13-10, before 21,597 at Boston University.

Sept. 11 – The Bills lost their regular-season opener in New York, 27-3, at the Polo Grounds as Al Dorow rushed for two TDs. The Bills' offense was pathetic.

Sept. 18 – The Bills lost their regular-season home opener in front of 15,229 to Denver, 27-21, as Johnny Pyeatt returned a fourth-quarter interception 40 yards for a TD.

Sept. 23 – The Bills won their first game in franchise history by forcing five turnovers in a 13-0 win over the Patriots in Boston.

Oct. 2 – Los Angeles QB Jack Kemp missed the game and the Chargers gained only 159 yards, but still beat the Bills at War Memorial, 24-10.

Oct. 16 – Al Dorow scored the winning TD with 2:19 left as the Titans beat the Bills, 17-13, at War Memorial.

Oct. 23 – Johnny Green produced five TDs, including 263 yards passing and four TD passes, as the Bills rolled to a 38-9 victory over Oakland in front of 8,876 at War Memorial.

Oct. 30 – Billy Atkins kicked two fourth-quarter field goals to lift the Bills to a 25-24 victory over Houston in front of the largest crowd to see the Bills play thus far, 23,001 at War Memorial Stadium.

Nov. 6 – Abner Haynes gained 245 all-purpose yards as Dallas rolled past the Bills, 45-28.

Nov. 13 – In Buffalo's worst performance of the season, the running game produced only 42 yards in a 20-7 loss at Oakland.

Nov. 14 – In the early-round draft, the Bills chose and ultimately signed Auburn tackle Ken Rice (first round), Georgia Tech guard Billy Shaw (second), Syracuse fullback Art Baker (third) and Penn State offensive lineman Stew Barber (fourth). When the draft concluded on Dec. 5, the Bills had chosen 30 players.

Nov. 20 – In a stunning reversal from the week before, the Bills turned in their best performance. The defense held the Chargers to minus 11 yards rushing in a 32-3 rout at the Los Angeles Coliseum.

Nov. 27 – In the final game of a three-game West Coast trip, the Bills blew a 38-7 lead in the final 18 minutes and wound up with a 38-38 tie in snowy Denver. The Bills were outgained, 384-372. The Broncos scored 24 points in the fourth quarter including Gene Mingo's 19-yard field goal with four seconds left to play.

Dec. 4 – In the final home game of the season, the Bills limited Boston to 29 yards rushing in a 38-14 romp.

Dec. 11 – George Blanda set an AFL record with a 53-yard field goal as the Oilers topped the Bills, 31-23.

Dec. 12 – AFL Commissioner Joe Foss said the league would lose about $2 million in its first season, but league owners expressed satisfaction with the league's financial status.

Dec. 18 – The Bills closed the season with a 24-7 loss in Dallas. Buffalo finished No. 1 in total defense, dead last in total offense.

Dec. 19 – Ralph Wilson said the Bills would have to sell 25,000 season tickets by 1963 to insure the team's future in Buffalo. In 1960, the team sold 5,265 season tickets.

Dec. 24 – Laverne Torczon, Archie Matsos and Richie McCabe were named to the AFL's first All-Star team.

Jan. 1, 1961 – Houston won the first AFL Championship, beating Los Angeles, 24-16, in front of 32,183 in Houston. Each Oiler received $1,016.42 for winning.

BY THE NUMBERS — 1960

TEAM STATISTICS	BILLS	OPP
First downs	211	225
Rushing	77	103
Passing	109	109
Penalty	25	13
Total yards	3,900	3,854
Avg. game	278.6	275.3
Plays	909	903
Avg. play	4.3	4.3
Net rushing yds	1,211	1,393
Avg. game	86.5	99.5
Avg. play	2.6	2.9
Net passing yds	2,689	2,461
Comp/att	184/447	185/429
Interceptions	29	33
Percentage	41.2	43.1
Sacks not available		
Punts/avg	9-39.0	77-37.6
Fumbles/lost	30-15	27-16
Penalties/yds	57-615	62-608
Touchdowns	38	37
Extra points	28-34	37-37
Field goals	12-26	14-27
Safeties	0	1
Two-point conv	2-3	0-0
Kick ret./avg	47-20.1	55-25.4
Punt ret./avg	27-6.9	33-7.0

RUSHING	ATT	YDS	AVG	TD
Carlton	137	533	3.9	7
Fowler	93	370	4.0	1
Kulbacki	41	108	2.6	1
Dubenion	16	94	5.9	1
Lucas	46	90	2.0	2
Smith	19	61	3.2	0
Atkins	2	47	23.5	0
Brodhead	21	45	2.1	0
Ford	18	40	2.2	0
Harper	1	3	3.0	0
O'Connell	22	-24	-1.1	1
Green	46	-156	-3.4	2
TOTALS	**462**	**1211**	**2.6**	**15**

PASSING	COMP	ATT	INT	YDS	TD	COMP%
Green	89	228	10	1267	10	39.0
O'Connell	65	145	13	1033	7	44.8
Lucas	23	49	3	314	2	46.9
Brodhead	7	25	3	75	0	28.0
TOTALS	**184**	**447**	**29**	**2689**	**19**	**41.2**

KICKING	FG/ATT	PAT/ATT	PTS
Atkins	6-13	27-32	45
Harper	2-3	1-2	7
Yoho	2-5	0-0	6
Hergert	2-4	0-0	6
O'Connell	0-1	0-0	0
TOTALS	**12-26**	**28-34**	**64**

PUNTING	NO	AVG
Atkins	89	39.0

RECEIVING	CAT	YDS	AVG	TD
Rychlec	45	590	13.1	0
Dubenion	42	752	17.9	7
Carlton	29	477	16.4	4
Chamberlain	17	279	16.4	4
Crockett	14	173	12.4	1
Fowler	10	99	9.9	0
Smith	7	127	18.1	1
Brubaker	7	75	10.7	1
Lucas	5	58	11.6	1
Hoisington	4	45	11.3	0
Kulbacki	2	9	4.5	0
Ford	1	5	5.0	0
Green	1	0	0.0	0
TOTALS	**184**	**2689**	**14.6**	**19**

LEADERS

Punt returns: Kulbacki 12-100 yards, 8.3 avg, 0 TD; Kinard 2-24, 12.0, 0 TD

Interceptions: Matsos 8-142, 17.8, 1 TD

Non-kick scoring: Carlton 11 TDs, 66 pts
Dubenion 8 TDs, 56 pts

Kick returns: Kulbacki 13-226, 17.4, 0 TD

Richie Lucas (left) was the first draft pick in Bills history.

Tom Rychlec (opposite page) led the Bills with 45 receptions in their inaugural 1960 season.

Bills	3 0 0 0 - 3
Titans	0 17 3 7 - 27

Attendance at the Polo Grounds - 10,200

Buf: FG Harper 35, 7:00
NY: FG Shockley 15, 3:35
NY: Dorow 2 run (Shockley kick), 10:15
NY: Dorow 15 run (Shockley kick), 12:45
NY: FG Shockley 19, 7:36
NY: Powell 13 pass from Jamieson (Shockley kick), 14:55

	BUF	NY
First downs	9	20
Rushing yds	61	114
Passing yds	52	226
Punts-avg	3-39.0	3-32.3
Fumbles lost	1	0
Penalty yds	10	59

BILLS LEADERS: Rushing - Lucas 2-12, Carlton 7-13, Brodhead 6-29, O'Connell 2-5, Dubenion 3-5, Kulback 4- (-6), Harper 1-3; **Passing** - Brodhead 3-13-1 - 15, O'Connell 2-10-1 - 37; **Receiving** - Dubenion 1-22, Lucas 1-15, Brubaker 1-15, Rychlec 1-11, Carlton 1- (-11).

TITANS LEADERS: Rushing - Hart 11-66, Dorow 5-7, Shockley 3-11, Bohling 9-15, Martin 3-5, Mathis 3-9, Wegert 5-27, Jamieson 2- (-26); **Passing** - Jamieson 9-18-0 - 152, Dorow 6-12-1 - 74; **Receiving** - Powell 6-77, Maynard 4-116, Wegert 2-9, Hart 1-5, Bohling 1-15, Sapienza 1-4.

NOTES
• The Bills had lost their preseason finale to the Titans, 52-31.
• The game was played in intermittent rain on a muddy field and the Bills were inept on offense.
• Tommy O'Connell suffered an injured neck early, while recovering an Elbert Dubenion fumble, and did not return until the fourth quarter. Bob Brodhead replaced O'Connell. On the next play, first-round draft choice Richie Lucas suffered an arch injury and sat out the rest of the game. The Bills went on to score on that drive as Darrell Harper made a 35-yard field goal, but that was it for the day.
• Bill Shockley's first field goal was set up by a 57-yard Dick Jamieson-to-Don Maynard pass that carried to the 10. The Bills' defense stiffened and forced the field goal.
• Al Dorow, the balding reserve QB, then scored twice on improvised rollouts, the first on fourth down at the 2-yard line. Dorow had hit Maynard for 20 yards, then scrambled for 14 yards to the 14. Again, the Bills' defense rose up, but on fourth down, Dorow scored.
• Wray Carlton then fumbled at the Buffalo 45 and Maynard made 25- and 10-yard receptions before Dorow scored on a 15-yard run to make it 17-3 at the half.
• The Titans' last TD upset Bills coach Buster Ramsey. The score was 20-3 with less than a minute left and New York called timeout, then Jamieson hit Art Powell with a TD pass with five seconds left.
• The Bills roster had 34 players. The youngest were Lucas, Harper, Monte Crockett and Dennis Remmert at 21 and the oldest was O'Connell at 28.

QUOTES
• Buster Ramsey on the last TD: "They had us 20-3 and with less than a minute left they're still passing and even called timeout to make sure of the score. In 25 years of football that's the first time I've ever seen anything like that. Some day it'll come back to him (Titans coach Sammy Baugh)." (On defensive problems): "I've said it before, I'm going to keep making changes all over until I get someone who can do the job. On one play, I sent a man in specifically to stop the wide stuff. I set him two yards outside the offensive end where nobody could block him to the inside and told him all he had to do was keep Dorow from going outside. So he crashed inside and Dorow went around him. We had the right stuff set up to win this game. We spent a lot of time setting up a defense that will stop any rollout cold. But we made the same mistakes over and over again."
• Tommy O'Connell: "It should be remembered that we have 13 games to go. We have to get meaner and throw all caution to the wind."
• Jets quarterback Al Dorow: "When we came to camp, we didn't have any rollout plays. I started doing it on my own in practice. I'm only an average runner, but that's all you have to be to get away with it. When I roll out, the man I have to beat generally is a linebacker and there's a lot of pressure on him. I've got the edge because he does not know if I'm going to run or pass."

WEEK 1 GAMES	
LA 21, Dal 20	Hou 37, Oak 22
Den 13, Bos 10	

Broncos	0 6 14 7 - 27
Bills	0 13 8 0 - 21

Attendance at War Memorial Stadium - 15,229

Buf: Carlton 1 run (Harper kick), 4:53
Den: FG Mingo 31, 6:31
Den: FG Mingo 27, 14:07
Buf: Dubenion 53 pass from O'Connell (kick failed), 14:59
Den: Brodnax 9 pass from Tripucka (Mingo kick), 2:12
Den: Rolle 2 pass from Tripucka (Mingo kick), 9:42
Buf: Dubenion 56 pass from O'Connell (Brodhead run), 14:53
Den: Pyeatt 40 interception return (Mingo kick), 5:03

	BUF	DEN
First downs	14	17
Rushing yds	61	108
Passing yds	218	156
Punts-avg	4-39.8	5-36.8
Fumbles lost	0	0
Penalty yards	25	68

BILLS LEADERS: Rushing - Carlton 10-30, Ford 12-21, Kulbacki 9-14, Brodhead 2-(-5), O'Connell 1-1; **Passing** - O'Connell 13-23-5 - 218, Brodhead 0-2-1- 0; **Receiving** - Dubenion 3-112, Rychlec 6-78, Brubaker 2-16, Ford 1-5, Kulbacki 1-7.

BRONCOS LEADERS: Rushing - Bell 10-36, Carmichael 5-25, Brodnax 4-11, Rolle 9-20, Tripucka 5- (-11), Mingo 3- (-2), Stransky 5-21, McNamara 4-8; **Passing** - Tripucka 14-26-2 - 156, Mingo 0-1-0 - 0; **Receiving** - Carmichael 5-81, Greer 3-38, Mingo 1- (-5), Jessup 2-32, Brodnax 2-8, Rolle 1-2.

NOTES
• Johnny Pyeatt, a full-blooded Indian, picked off a Tommy O'Connell pass and returned it for the winning TD as the Bills lost their regular-season home opener at War Memorial Stadium.
• Goose Gonsoulin had four of Denver's six interceptions, including one in the final seconds. He was beaten by Monte Crockett for what would have been the winning TD, but O'Connell underthrew.
• Bills LB Archie Matsos was in on 14 tackles and made two interceptions.
• Elbert Dubenion produced the first 100-yard receiving game in team history.
• Wray Carlton gave the Bills the early lead after an interference penalty in the end zone on Tom Rychlec.
• Gene Mingo kicked two field goals, then O'Connell hit Dubenion with a 53-yard TD pass.
• Denver took the second-half kickoff and drove 73 yards to Frank Tripucka's nine-yard TD pass to J.W. Brodnax. The score was set up by a 53-yard Tripucka pass to Al Carmichael.
• Buddy Allison then intercepted O'Connell and returned it 65 yards to the Bills 20. Five plays later, Tripucka hit Dave Rolle for the TD and a 20-13 Denver lead.
• The Bills went ahead when Dubenion caught a 56-yard TD and Bob Brodhead rolled out and scored a two-point conversion to make it 21-20, but Pyeatt ruined the Bills' home debut.

QUOTES
• Tommy O'Connell on his performance: "As I see it, I was the goat of the game. I had that pass intercepted late in the game while we were leading and it led to the winning touchdown for the Broncos." (On the first TD to Dubenion): "When I faded back I took a look at Tom Rychlec and saw that he was covered. Then Dubenion came free deep in behind him. I threw it high and out in front of him and he did the rest. Our team is improving and I'm sure that before it's all over we will be a team that will make everyone proud."
• Archie Matsos: "I just hope the fans stay with us. We really wanted this one and I think we should have had it. I suppose it takes patience to stick with a losing team, but a football team is just like a baby growing into a man, it takes time."
• Buster Ramsey: "Our guys played their hearts out and should have won, but when you throw the ball in their hands, you lose. You can't defense against passes being intercepted. It's tough to lose anytime, but it's rough to do it when the plays you select and the defense you set up are what should do the job against the other team. Archie Matsos was great. They never really marched on us."
• Denver cornerback Johnny Pyeatt: "I thought to myself 'If anyone gets in my way, I'm going to run right over them.' Honest, that's just what I thought because we needed the points."
• Denver cornerback Goose Gonsoulin: "I think this club's strong point is that we all pull together. We know we aren't a great team, we aren't good enough to sweep through everybody, so we work together."

WEEK 2 GAMES	
Hou 38, LA 28	Bos 28, NY 24
Dal 34, Oak 16	

STANDINGS: SECOND WEEK

EAST	W	L	T	WEST	W	L	T
Houston	2	0	0	Denver	2	0	0
New York	1	1	0	Los Ang.	1	1	0
Boston	1	1	0	Dallas	1	1	0
Buffalo	0	2	0	Oakland	0	2	0

GAME 3 - Friday, Sept. 23, 1960 - BILLS 13, PATRIOTS 0

NOTES
• The Bills forced seven turnovers with three fumble recoveries and four interceptions to post their first regular-season AFL victory. Two of the interceptions, by Billy Atkins and Bill Kinard, were in the end zone.
• Tommy O'Connell's TD pass to Carl Smith was a screen on the third play of the game. Bob Brodhead started at quarterback and ran twice for 11 yards, then

O'Connell entered and flipped the screen to Smith. He got a block from Monte Crockett and went all the way. Billy Atkins' PAT was blocked.
• The Patriots got to the Bills 17 late in the first after a 39-yard halfback option pass from Dick Christy to Walt Beach, but Christy fumbled on the next play and Jim Wagstaff recovered.
• Christy fumbled a punt late in the first and Wagstaff again recovered at the Patriots 37. O'Connell hit Dan Chamberlain for 12 and Fred Ford carried twice for 10 yards and another first down. Two Boston offsides penalties moved the ball inside the 5 and Wray Carlton scored from the 2 early in the second.
• The Bills topped 100 yards rushing as a team for the first time.
• Mack Yoho and Laverne Torczon were the defensive stars.

QUOTES
• Buster Ramsey: "We'll still make changes whenever we feel we can strengthen the club. We were stronger against Boston." (On the screen to Smith): "I figured they'd be shooting their linebackers through at us. The movies of our games showed the other teams had stopped our running game by doing it. So my plan was to run a couple of rollouts, then throw a screen pass once they began laying back."
• Tommy O'Connell: "The victory belongs, of course, to our defense. This was the first time in our league a team was shut out, in exhibition or league play. The pressure our four defensive linemen kept on their passer was tremendous. And the work of Mack Yoho and Laverne Torczon was great. They forced Boston to play our type of game, which is the first time this has happened all season. Our team was alert and we played sharp football for 60 minutes."

Bills	6 7 0 0 -	13
Patriots	0 0 0 0 -	0

Attendance at Boston University - 20,723

Buf: Smith 58 pass from O'Connell (kick blocked), 1:53
Buf: Carlton 2 run (Atkins kick), :43

	BUF	BOS
First downs	14	18
Rushing yds	102	148
Passing yds	131	136
Punts-avg	7-41.2	3-41.3
Fumbles lost	0	3
Penalties-yds	7-83	7-55

BILLS LEADERS: Rushing - Carlton 12-41, Brodhead 4-21, Ford 6-19, Lucas 4-10, Smith 2-2, Kulbacki 5-15, O'Connell 4- (-6); **Passing** - O'Connell 6-16-1 - 131, Lucas 0-1-0 - 0; **Receiving** - Smith 1-58, Chamberlain 2-24, Dubenion 1-13, Carlton 1-25, Lucas 1-11.

PATRIOTS LEADERS: Rushing - Christy 9-93, Miller 9-35, Burton 5-8, Crawford 2-4, Greene 6-8; **Passing** - Songin 5-14-1 - 37, Greene 6-17-2 - 60, Christy 1-2-1 - 39; **Receiving** - Colclough 2-26, Beach 2-50, Atcheson 2-22, Burton 1-4, Christy 2-10, Crawford 1-6, Miller 2-18.

WEEK 3 GAMES
Oak 14, Hou 13   Dal 17, LA 0
NY 28, Den 24

GAME 4 - Sunday, Oct. 2, 1960 - CHARGERS 24, BILLS 10

NOTES
• Chargers QB Jack Kemp missed the game with a shoulder injury so Bobby Clatterbuck played.
• The Chargers started three rookies in the secondary, yet still managed four interceptions in rainy conditions.
• The Bills took a 3-0 lead on Darrell Harper's field goal that was set up by Billy Atkins' 36-yard run to the LA 14 off a fake punt.
• LA's longest scoring drive was just 59 yards, that coming after LA linebacker Paul Maguire intercepted a Tommy O'Connell pass. A pass interference call against Richie McCabe gave the Chargers a first down at the Bills 11 and Clatterbuck eventually hit Dave Kocourek for the TD.
• LA had just 67 yards at halftime, 159 for the game.
• Maguire's second interception and return of 37 yards led to Howard Ferguson's TD in the third.
• The Bills answered with their lone TD. They were faced with third-and-26, but an interference penalty gave them an automatic first down. Another interference call and an unsportsmanlike conduct penalty on Chargers coach Sid Gillman kept moving the ball in the right direction. Two plays later, Richie Lucas threw a 36-yard halfback-option TD pass to Elbert Dubenion and it was 14-10.
• Dick Harris' interception set up Flowers' TD run on the first play of the fourth quarter to wrap it up.
• Before the game, Lucas was presented the Phi Delta Theta Grantland Rice trophy for being the best college football player in the country in 1959 who was a member of the fraternity. Former Heisman Trophy winner Tom Harmon made the presentation.

QUOTES
• Buster Ramsey on the woeful QB situation: "We played well enough defensively to beat Los Angeles. If I sound like I'm repeating myself, forgive me. I'm going to make changes. I've been working Richie Lucas at quarterback and once he's completely well from the foot condition, I'll give him even more work. I'm dissatisfied with the number of interceptions and some of the calls we've had in our games. Our quarterbacks just haven't been able to move the club with any consistency." (On Dubenion): "One player has developed beyond my expectations for this stage of the season and that's Elbert Dubenion. He was green as a gourd when he came to camp and he was a disappointment in our first game against New York. But he didn't quit on himself and he's improved 100 percent. Duby is now a pro."
• Ralph Wilson: "We're either first or second in paid attendance right now. Sure we'd like to see attendance higher and we need to average around 25,000 fans a game to be major league. But so far we haven't shown the fans enough to make them come out in such numbers. Right now I'm sure of two things. We have good fans and a good coach. The rest is up to us. Today, the weather was a big factor (in low attendance). I think we would have had 18,000 or 20,000 if the weather hadn't been so bad. Naturally we're concerned about (NFL games on) television, too."

Chargers	0 7 7 10 –	24
Bills	0 3 7 0 –	10

Attendance at War Memorial Stadium - 15,821

Buf: FG Harper 35, 8:33
LA: Kocourek 4 pass from Clatterbuck (Agajanian kick), 13:45
LA: Ferguson 2 run (Agajanian kick), 8:26
Buf: Dubenion 36 pass from Lucas (Atkins kick), 11:48
LA: Flowers 7 run (Agajanian kick), :50
LA: FG Agajanian 15, 6:25

	BUF	LA
First downs	18	12
Rushing yds	89	89
Passing yds	149	70
Punts-avg	4-39.0	5-43.8
Fumbles lost	0	1
Penalties-yds	74	66

BILLS LEADERS: Rushing - Carlton 12-25, Kulbacki 8-35, Atkins 1-36, Brodhead 9-0, O'Connell 4- (-12), Dubenion 1-5, Lucas 3-0; **Passing** - O'Connell 8-14-3 - 53, Brodhead 4-10-1 - 60, Lucas 1-1-0 - 36; **Receiving** - Chamberlain 2-18, Dubenion 6-88, Rychlec 2-27, Carlton 2-8, Lucas 1-8.

CHARGERS LEADERS: Rushing - Flowers 10-60, Ferguson 15-40, Clatterbuck 3- (-6), Lowe 1- (-5); **Passing** - Clatterbuck 9-15-1 - 70; **Receiving** - Lowe 3-32, Flowers 3-8, Anderson 1-9, Kocourek 1-11, Ferguson 1-10.

WEEK 4 GAMES:
NY 37, Dal 35   Den 31, Oak 14

STANDINGS: FOURTH WEEK							
EAST	**W**	**L**	**T**	**WEST**	**W**	**L**	**T**
New York	3	1	0	Denver	3	1	0
Houston	2	1	0	Dallas	2	2	0
Boston	1	2	0	Los Ang.	2	2	0
Buffalo	1	3	0	Oakland	1	3	0

| Titans | 7 3 0 7 - 17 |
| Bills | 6 0 0 7 - 13 |

Attendance at War Memorial Stadium - 14,998

NY: Cooper 5 pass from Dorow (Shockley kick), 3:50
Buf: Carlton 54 run (kick failed), 14:29
NY: FG Shockley 44, 5:34
Buf: Dubenion 32 pass from Green (Atkins kick), 3:05
NY: Dorow 1 run (Shockley kick), 12:41

	BUF	NY
First downs	8	23
Rushing yds	77	133
Passing yds	127	158
Punts-avg	8-37.4	3-39.0
Fumbles lost	2	2
Penalties-yds	8-69	0-0

BILLS LEADERS: Rushing - Carlton 9-98, Fowler 7-28, Smith 2-9, Lucas 2- (-7), Green 6- (-51); **Passing** - Green 10-24-2 - 127; **Receiving** - Chamberlain 2-19, Dubenion 3-46, Rychlec 2-40, Crockett 1-10, Fowler 1-6, Smith 1-6.

TITANS LEADERS: Rushing - Dorow 21-48, Shockley 7-35, Mathis 8-22, Bohling 6-22, Paglee 1-6; **Passing** - Dorow 16-35-3 - 158, Jamieson 0-1-0 - 0; **Receiving** - Maynard 6-82, Ross 4-40, Powell 1-14, Bohling 2-9, Shockley 1-8, Cooper 1-3, Burton 1-2.

NOTES

• The Bills remained winless in three games at home. The Bills led, 13-10, and took possession at the NY 33 late in the game, but penalties pushed them out of scoring range.
• Later, Al Dorow directed an eight-play, 51-yard drive for the winning the TD with 2:19 left. He capped the drive with a one-yard run, his third against the Bills in two games. Dorow had 12- and 15-yard runs on the march.
• Newcomer Johnny Green played QB and drew ovations from the home crowd. He was picked up after being cut by the NFL's Pittsburgh Steelers. Also, running back Willmer Fowler, another newcomer, rushed well. However, Fowler dropped what could have been a 77-yard touchdown pass in the fourth.
• Leon Burton returned the opening kickoff to the Bills 41 and 11 plays later, Dorow hit Thurlow Cooper for a TD.
• Wray Carlton blew up the middle for a 54-yard TD on a draw later in the first, but Fred Julian broke through and blocked Billy Atkins' conversion, leaving the Bills behind 7-6.
• Bill Shockley's field goal made it 10-6 at the half and after a scoreless third, Atkins made a key play early in the fourth. He made the second of his three interceptions against Dorow and returned it to the Titans 34. Two plays later, Green fired a 32-yard TD pass to Elbert Dubenion.
• Green was intercepted twice by Julian. Bills QBs had now thrown 15 picks in five games.

QUOTES

• Buster Ramsey: "I really don't know what to think. Sure we should have won. These guys played their hearts out. I'd have to say each one of our boys gave to the best of their ability. We missed tackles at times and looked sloppy, but it was never because of lack of effort. We did just what we wanted to do, but it wasn't enough. They (the Titans) produced on some big third downs and got some good breaks. We contained Art Powell and Don Maynard, and we kept Dorow from going outside like he did in New York. But the guy has enough running ability that when he'd see where the pressure was coming from, he'd turn and scoot wherever a hole was open." (On Green and Fowler): "I was very pleased with Green and Fowler. They're going to help us. Green showed poise and he's only a rookie. He threw well and ate the ball as good quarterbacks do rather than turn it loose and get you in trouble."
• Ralph Wilson: "We're 0-6 at home (counting preseason) and the fans are still with us. Any time you hold the Titans to two touchdowns you should win, but we didn't."
• New York coach Sammy Baugh: "Buffalo played well enough to win. In fact, they should have won."
• New York quarterback Al Dorow: "Buffalo's pass defense did the best job of anybody on Art Powell. But when you double-team him, that leaves Don Maynard with a man-on-man situation. And nobody can cover Maynard like that."

WEEK 5 GAMES	
Bos 35, LA 0;	Oak 20, Dal 19
Hou 27, NY 21	
Buffalo and Denver had bye weeks	

WEEK 6 GAMES	
LA 23, Den 19	Oak 27, Bos 14;
Hou 20, Dal 10	

| Raiders | 0 7 0 2 - 9 |
| Bills | 14 14 3 7 - 38 |

Attendance at War Memorial Stadium - 8,876

Buf: Carlton 38 pass from Green (Atkins kick), :23
Buf: Carlton 23 pass from Green (Atkins kick), 12:50
Buf: Dubenion 55 pass from Green (Atkins kick), :16
Oak: Smith 1 run (Barnes kick), 4:28
Buf: Carlton 32 pass from Green (Atkins kick), 10:18
Buf: FG Hergert 26, 5:45
Buf: Green 2 run (Atkins kick), 5:03
Oak: Safety, ball snapped out of end zone, 9:38

	BUF	OAK
First downs	12	13
Rushing yds	79	85
Passing yds	260	134
Punts-avg	8-39.0	9-36.4
Fumbles lost	0	2
Penalties-yds	6-60	4-30

BILLS LEADERS: Rushing - Carlton 11-32, Fowler 7-39, Green 7-4, Kulbacki 3-4; **Passing** - Green 14-32-2 - 243, Lucas 1-2-1 - 17; **Receiving** - Carlton 5-110, Dubenion 2-65, Rychlec 3-52, Chamberlain 1-5, Fowler 3-11, Brubaker 1-17.

RAIDERS LEADERS: Rushing - Larscheid 8-30, McFarlane 1-17, Teresa 1-16, Parilli 1-16, Lott 2-4, Smith 6-6, Flores 2- (-4); **Passing** - Flores 7-14-1 - 42, Parilli 8-24-1 - 92, Teresa 1-2-1 - 0; **Receiving** - Prebola 4-25, Lott 1-28, Smith 2-5, Larscheid 3-2, Hardy 1-24, Asad 1-12, Hoisington 1-17, Teresa 1-4, Goldstein 1-17, Parilli 1-0.

NOTES

• The Bills won for the first time at home as quarterback Johnny Green threw for four TDs and rushed for another in the best quarterbacking performance to date.
• Wray Carlton produced the first three-TD game in team history on a muddy, rainy day.
• The Raiders had won three of four, but managed only 219 yards and lost five turnovers.
• Willmer Fowler ran 42 yards on the first play and Green hit Carlton on the next play for the first score just 23 seconds into the game.
• The score became 14-0 when the Bills went 70 yards in five plays to another Carlton TD reception. Tom Rychlec's 35-yard reception was the key play and Green had an 11-yard run.
• On their third TD drive, the Bills needed only two passes to Elbert Dubenion to travel 65 yards.
• The Bills made it 28-7 late in the first half as Jack Larscheid fumbled a punt and Don Chelf recovered at the Raiders 37. Three plays later, Carlton scored on a 32-yard screen pass.
• Because of the small crowd, Ralph Wilson figured he lost approximately $40,000.
• LB Archie Matsos had two interceptions for the second time this season.
• *Courier-Express* racing writer Phil Ranallo wrote "the Bills will get a superior mud rating" for their win on a rain-soaked field.

QUOTES

• Buster Ramsey on Green: "I have to thank my good friend Buddy Parker (Pittsburgh Steelers head coach) for Green. He was so sure of Johnny's potential that he kept him working with the Steelers even after he got Rudy Bukich to back up Bobby Layne. When I went looking for quarterback help, Buddy suggested I take a look at Johnny with the understanding he went back to Pittsburgh if I didn't think he could help us immediately. All Johnny needs is experience and it looks like he's going to get it from now on. I don't think Johnny played up to his potential; he'll get even better."
• Johnny Green: "I think the guys who ran with the ball after they caught it deserve the credit. It might have been the best day I ever had in football. It was certainly the best half. On most of my passes to Wray, he was the secondary target."
• Laverne Torczon on Green: "He can complete the money pass. He's tall enough to move back there and take a look. Last week we had some bad breaks on long passes, but today he showed what he can do. And he doesn't throw that interception."
• Raiders quarterback Babe Parilli on the Bills defense: "I never saw anything like it. The coaches kept telling us that they were tough. And we watched them in the game movies. They were tougher to move against than any team we've played."
• Raiders running back Wayne Crow: "I'm glad that's over. Everything happened like it was planned that way."

WEEK 7 GAMES	
Hou 42, NY 28	Den 31, Bos 24

STANDINGS: SEVENTH WEEK

EAST	W	L	T	WEST	W	L	T
Houston	5	1	0	Denver	4	2	0
New York	4	3	0	Los Ang.	3	3	0
Boston	2	4	0	Oakland	3	4	0
Buffalo	2	4	0	Dallas	2	4	0

NOTES

• The Bills produced their first two-game winning streak. Wray Carlton had the team's first back-to-back 100-yard receiving games. Johnny Green had the first 300-yard passing performance in team history.

• The Bills' defense, ranked No. 1 in the AFL, won the battle against the Oilers' No. 1 offense as George Blanda threw four interceptions.

• Billy Atkins took over field goal duties when Joe Hergert was hurt early and he made three, including two in the fourth quarter, which provided the winning points.

• Archie Matsos had his third two-interception game. His second pick halted the Oilers' final possession at the Houston 35.

• 1959 Heisman Trophy winner Billy Cannon had 148 total yards for Houston.

• Dave Smith produced the first 100-yard rushing game against the Bills.

• With 5:44 left and faced with fourth down at the 2, Buster Ramsey opted to kick a field goal. Atkins converted for a 25-24 lead and the defense held the rest of the way. That field goal was set up when a poor punt by Houston's Ken Hall gave the Bills the ball at the Oilers 39. Green hit Carlton with a screen pass that carried to the 3 and after three unsuccessful runs, Atkins kicked the winner after taking a deliberate delay-of-game penalty to get a better angle for the attempt.

• The Oilers drove 80 yards in four plays to the first score, but Carlton took a screen, which Houston struggled defensing all day, 70 yards for TD 1:37 later. A bad snap foiled the conversion attempt

• Hergert's field goal gave the Bills the lead, but Houston drove 64 yards to Blanda's TD pass to Cannon.

• Atkins' first field goal came after a Charlie Tolar fumble.

• Matsos had a 20-yard punt return that set up Green's 10-yard TD pass to Dick Brubaker, but the Oilers went ahead as Carlton fumbled and on the next play, Blanda hit Cannon with a 53-yard TD.

• Later in the third, Joe Kulbacki fumbled a punt that led to Blanda's only field goal and a 24-19 lead.

QUOTES

• Buster Ramsey on kicking a FG: "It was the right move. Houston's line is tough, but the big thing is that I had confidence our defense could hold a one-point lead, if we got it. Tommy O'Connell came over and told me it was a terrible angle. He suggested we draw an intentional penalty to give Atkins a better angle and I went along with him and it worked." (On offense): "I know we scored 63 points in our last two games and had only 60 before that, but we're still not taking advantage of our scoring opportunities."

• Archie Matsos: "I made more tackles against Denver, but I was more pass conscious against Houston. We had their offense down pat. They didn't do anything they hadn't done before. You can't get by on press clippings of your last game, though. It's the game that's coming up that's the big one"

WEEK 8 GAMES
Dal 17, Den 14   Oak 28, NY 27
LA 45, Bos 16

Oilers	7	7	10	0	- 24
Bills	9	10	0	6	- 25

Attendance at War Memorial Stadium - 23,001

Hou: Hennigan 8 pass from Blanda (Blanda kick), 8:26
Buf: Carlton 70 pass from Green (kick failed), 10:03
Buf: FG Hergert 36, 12:35
Hou: Cannon 21 pass from Blanda (Blanda kick), :43
Buf: FG Atkins 22, 5:32
Buf: Brubaker 10 pass from Green (Atkins kick), 12:07
Hou: Cannon 53 pass from Blanda (Blanda kick), 6:58
Hou: FG Blanda 51, 11:22
Buf: FG Atkins 45, 1:29
Buf: FG Atkins 18, 9:46

	BUF	HOU
First downs	17	13
Rushing yds	18	163
Passing yds	334	124
Punts-avg	7-39.0	9-36.4
Fumbles lost	2	1
Penalties-yds	6-55	6-52

BILLS LEADERS: Rushing - Carlton 6-25, Fowler 10-36, Kulbacki 2- (-1), Green 11- (-42); **Passing** - Green 18-49-1 - 334; **Receiving** - Carlton 6-177, Dubenion 5-76, Rychlec 2-19, Chamberlain 2-32, Brubaker 2-15, Fowler 1-15.
OILERS LEADERS: Rushing - Smith 12-107, Cannon 12-60, Tolar 5-4, Hall 1-0, Blanda 1- (-8); **Passing** - Blanda 9-32-4 - 124; **Receiving** - Cannon 3-88, Hennigan 2-17, Smith 2-2, Carson 1-15, Tolar 1-2.

NOTES

• The Bills turned over the ball seven times. The defense was given no chance yet still allowed just 214 yards.

• On the first play from scrimmage, Dave Webster intercepted Johnny Green's pitchout to Wray Carlton and scored a TD.

• Abner Haynes, who had 245 yards in total offense, returned a punt to Buffalo's 29 later in the first and then caught a six-yard TD pass from Cotton Davidson for a 14-0 lead.

• The Bills drove 44 yards in seven plays to Joe Kulbacki's TD run, but Texans' linebacker Walt Corey blocked a field goal attempt late in the second and returned it to Buffalo's 32, setting up Jack Spikes' field goal that made it 17-7 at the half.

• Haynes took the second-half kickoff back 82 yards, then caught a TD pass to make it 24-7. Two plays after the kickoff, Don Flynn intercepted a Green pass and ran 25 yards for a TD.

• Green hit Monte Crockett for a 41-yard score, but Haynes scored his third TD to nullify that. Green's 41-yard pass to Elbert Dubenion set up Wray Carlton's TD and then O'Connell passed to Dubenion for the final score, a 35-yard TD that capped a 77-yard drive.

• Green was benched for the first time; Tommy O'Connell looked sharp in his place.

• The Bills' defense remained No. 1 in the AFL at 257.3 yards per game, but the offense remained last at 263.8 and the running game had produced a paltry 516 yards in eight games.

QUOTES

• Buster Ramsey: "The score was not indicative of the way our defense played. They held the Texans to 214 yards and that shouldn't measure out to more than 17 points, at most. But when you give the ball away, your opponent doesn't have to do much on his own. We weren't a relaxed club. The tension was there just like our opener in New York. After that first Dallas TD, we never got untracked and the mistakes kept mounting." (On the pitchout that was intercepted and returned for a TD): "We've devoted considerable time to preparing for each game and devising a play or a sequence of plays designed to get us a quick touchdown. The play we called on our first try from scrimmage should have meant long yardage and instead it ended up in a Dallas touchdown. Johnny faked the pitchout to Carlton, but Webster stormed across. Johnny was committed, but his timing was off by a split second. Webster hit the ball with his arm and the ball came down to him in stride and he went into the end zone. The tenor of the game was set and we never recovered. We kept giving the ball to Dallas."

WEEK 9 GAMES
Bos 34, Oak 28   LA 12, NY 7
Hou 45, Den 25

Texans	14	3	21	7	- 45
Bills	0	7	7	14	- 28

Attendance at War Memorial Stadium - 19,610

Dal: Webster intercepted pitchout return (Spikes kick), 1:34
Dal: Haynes 6 pass from Davidson (Spikes kick), 4:49
Buf: Kulbacki 10 run (Atkins kick), 7:44
Dal: FG Spikes 40, 12:23
Dal: Haynes 8 pass from Davidson (Spikes kick), 1:20
Dal: Flynn 25 interception return (Spikes kick), 2:29
Buf: Crockett 41 pass from Green (Atkins kick), 5:06
Dal: Haynes 15 run (Spikes kick), 10:34
Dal: Robinson 11 run (Spikes kick), :05
Buf: Carlton 3 run (Atkins kick), 2:55
Buf: Dubenion 35 pass from O'Connell (Atkins kick), 8:04

	BUF	DAL
First downs	18	15
Rushing yds	29	145
Passing yds	323	69
Punts-avg	5-32.8	5-43.6
Fumbles lost	3	2
Penalty yds	26	39

BILLS LEADERS: Rushing - Carlton 8-23, Fowler 9-13, Kulbacki 2-14, Dubenion 1- (-1), Green 3- (-20); **Passing** - Green 9-26-4 - 153, O'Connell 8-16-0 - 170; **Receiving** - Dubenion 8-161, Crockett 2-67, Rychlec 5-52, Brubaker 1-12, Carlton 1-31.
TEXANS LEADERS: Rushing - Haynes 13-80, Robinson 14-43, Spikes 8-26, Dickerson 6-19, Johnson 1-1, Enis 1- (-7), Davidson 1- (-17); **Passing** - Davidson 9-23-0 - 57, Enis 1-1-0 - 12; **Receiving** - Haynes 4-25, Robinson 3-27, Bryant 3-17.

STANDINGS: NINTH WEEK

EAST	W	L	T	WEST	W	L	T
Houston	6	2	0	Los Ang.	5	3	0
New York	4	5	0	Denver	4	4	0
Buffalo	3	5	0	Dallas	4	4	0
Boston	3	5	0	Oakland	4	5	0

Bills	0	0	0	7 - 7
Raiders	10	3	7	0 - 20

Attendance at Kezar Stadium - 8,800

Oak: FG Barnes 20, 5:08
Oak: Lott 1 run (Barnes kick), 11:08
Oak: FG Barnes 40, 15:00
Oak: Teresa 87 run (Barnes kick), 14:59
Buf: O'Connell 1 run (Atkins kick), 14:46

	BUF	OAK
First downs	18	14
Rushing yds	42	150
Passing yds	240	186
Punts-avg	9-39.0	6-37.6
Fumbles lost	0	2
Penalty yds	62	52

BILLS LEADERS: Rushing - Carlton 6-61, Fowler 4-21, Lucas 5-9, Smith 2-13, Dubenion 1- (-7), O'Connell 4- (-15), Green 7- (-40); **Passing** - Green 14-32-1 - 133, O'Connell 7-10-0 - 87, Lucas 1-2-0 - 20; **Receiving** - Rychlec 10-123, Carlton 5-67, Crockett 5-42, Smith 1-7, Dubenion 1-1.

RAIDERS LEADERS: Rushing - Teresa 12-141, Lott 5-21, Larscheid 7-13, Goldstein 1-0, Smith 1-0, Parilli 2- (-5), Flores 2- (-6); **Passing** - Flores 7-9-0 - 94, Parilli 7-14-0 - 77, Teresa 1-1-0 - 15; **Receiving** - Lott 6-73, Goldstein 4-43, Hardy 2-31, Teresa 1-19, Asad 1-17, Smith 1-3.

WEEK 10 GAMES
LA 24, Hou 21   Dal 34, Den 7
Bos 38, NY 21

NOTES
• The Bills were bumbling, dropping passes, missing blocks, tackles and assignments, and dropped to the worst record in the AFL.
• Jetstream Smith of Oakland and Buffalo's Jack Laraway were ejected for fighting and numerous other scuffles broke out.
• Two Tom Flores-to-Billy Lott screen passes set up Larry Barnes' first field goal.
• Jack Larscheid's 31-yard punt return to the Bills 48 started the Raiders on their first TD drive, which culminated on Lott's one-yard run.
• Wray Carlton had a 49-yard run on a fourth-and-one play that carried to the Raiders 21. The drive stalled and Billy Atkins' 32-yard FG was nullified by an illegal-use-of-hands penalty on Eddie Meyer that pushed the Bills out of Atkins' range and he was forced to punt.
• At the end of the first half, the Raiders moved 54 yards in three plays to set up a 40-yard Barnes field goal. Tony Teresa's 87-yard run late in the third put a final touch on the victory.
• The Bills' only TD was set up by questionable pass-interference call against Oakland in the end zone, helping to avert a shutout with 14 seconds left.
• Johnny Green and Tommy O'Connell were sacked for losses totaling 117 yards in the last three games.

QUOTES
• Buster Ramsey: "They got one touchdown on us and we quit. When we beat them in Buffalo, a couple of breaks went against them right away and they quit. Today, one break went against us and we quit. We got second effort from nobody. There was no effort at all for the most part. Ordinarily you'd think your defense could hold them for 30 seconds (at the end of the half). But even though we punted to their 13, they still ended up with three points.

The way things have been going, I am afraid of what we face in Los Angeles (next week). I said before this trip that I'd decide from what our players did in these three games who would be coming back next season. From the Oakland game, I could forget 20 of them."
• Oakland coach Eddie Erdelatz: "It's (Buffalo) a tough outfit. Only this time our boys didn't sit back and take it, they gave it back. We were high all week and this was our best effort."
• Jack Laraway: "I made a tackle on him (Smith) and he started to punch me in the face. I know I should have kept my head, but I started to swing back when we were both on the ground."

Bills	6	13	0	13 - 32
Chargers	0	3	0	0 - 3

Attendance at Memorial Coliseum - 16,161

Buf: Lucas 17 pass from O'Connell (kick failed), 11:19
LA: FG Agajanian 31, 4:49
Buf: Carlton 1 run (Atkins kick), 11:43
Buf: Matsos 20 interception return (kick failed), 14:18
Buf: Carlton 7 pass from Green (Atkins kick), 1:02
Buf: Chamberlain 49 pass from Green (kick failed), 5:54

	BUF	LA
First downs	14	11
Rushing yds	69	-11
Passing yds	179	196
Punts-avg	8-39.0	5-44.0
Fumbles lost	1	2
Penalties-yds	3-28	1-3

BILLS LEADERS: Rushing - C. Smith 8-24, Dubenion 4-18, Fowler 7-14, Lucas 4-3, Carlton 3-9, O'Connell 3- (-6), Green 3- (-12), Kulbacki 2-19; **Passing** - Green 6-12-0 - 87, O'Connell 8-16-1 - 92; **Receiving** - C. Smith 3-40, Chamberlain 2-66, Crockett 2-7, Dubenion 1-7, Lucas 1-17, Hoisington 1-13, Fowler 1-12, Kulbacki 1-2, Green 1-0, Rychlec 1-15.

CHARGERS LEADERS: Rushing - Lowe 5-35, Ferguson 5-17, Martin 1-2, Ford 3-16, Laraba 2- (-6), Kemp 9 - (-75); **Passing** - Kemp 13-30-5 - 189, Laraba 1-4-1 - 7, Ford 0-1-0 - 0; **Receiving** - Anderson 4-109, Kocourek 3-53, Ferguson 1-26, Martin 1-7, Lowe 2-1.

NOTES
• The Bills picked off five of Jack Kemp's passes and he was sacked for losses totaling 87 yards.
• Tommy O'Connell was given the starting nod over Johnny Green and the Bills used a T-formation to offset the pass rush, putting Elbert Dubenion in the backfield.
• Archie Matsos had his fourth two-interception game and returned one for a TD. Jim Wagstaff also had two picks and had a great game in coverage and run support.
• The Bills missed three extra points.
• A fumbled punt forced and recovered by Chuck Muelhaupt led to O'Connell's TD pass to Richie Lucas, his first TD as a pro. The PAT was blocked.
• After LA got a Ben Agajanian field goal, Wray Carlton's plunge capped a 79-yard drive. O'Connell completed four passes along the way, including a 34-yarder to Carl Smith.
• On the ensuing series, Mack Yoho dropped Kemp for a 24-yard loss and on the next play, Matsos returned his pick for a TD to start the rout.
• A Wagstaff interception and return to the 22 set up Carlton's second TD and Green closed the scoring with a 49-yard TD pass to Dan Chamberlain who beat Maury Schlecher.
• Through 10 games, the Bills were still being outrushed by opponents, 1,119-627.

WEEK 11 GAMES
Bos 42, Dal 14   Hou 20, Den 10

QUOTES
• Buster Ramsey: "Makes you wonder, doesn't it? Why can't a team play well against a team it's capable of beating? Last week against Oakland we couldn't even run out on the field right. Then, we come back and wallop a team that should whomp us. I guess that's why I'm not sleeping at night. In this game, our overall execution was the best it's been all season. The boys didn't have those mental lapses that have hurt us so much. Using the three backs tight served its purpose. It kept the Chargers from bringing everybody up close. Our pass protection was better than it had been."
• Chargers coach Sid Gillman: "Our pass protection broke down, but maybe Kemp will learn something from this."

STANDINGS: ELEVENTH WEEK

EAST	W	L	T	WEST	W	L	T
Houston	7	3	0	Los Ang.	6	4	0
Boston	5	5	0	Dallas	5	5	0
New York	4	6	0	Oakland	5	5	0
Buffalo	4	6	0	Denver	4	6	0

NOTES

• It was a stunning reversal as the Bills raced to a 38-7 lead in a snowstorm, then collapsed and allowed Denver to score 31 unanswered points, 24 in the fourth quarter. Gene Mingo's game-tying 19-yard field goal came with nine seconds left.

• It was the Bills' best rushing day and Willmer Fowler recorded the team's first 100-yard rushing game.

• Fowler broke a 61-yard run to set up Billy Atkins' early field goal, then Jim Wagstaff's interception and 23-yard return to the Denver 31 set up Wray Carlton's TD and a 10-0 lead.

• In the second, Elbert Dubenion took a pass in the and raced 76 yards for TD, but the Broncos got that back when Mingo scored from the 1. That TD was set up when Ted Wegert picked up a Dave Rolle fumble and ran 38 yards to the Bills 17.

• In a 5:16 span in the third, Atkins kicked a field goal, Mack Yoho returned a Frank Tripucka interception 15 yards for a score, Fowler ran 19 yards for a TD one play after Richie McCabe's interception, and Atkins made another field goal to make it 38-7.

• But the Broncos then made their move. On the first play after the kickoff, Lionel Taylor went 80 yards with a short pass and in the first 6:39 of the fourth, he caught two more TD passes to make it 38-28. The Bills failed to move the ball twice in the final five minutes, allowing Denver to get the ball.

• A 17-yard punt by Atkins to the Buffalo 41 set up Denver for Don Allen's TD. Then, another punt pinned the Broncos back to their 33 with 1:14 left, but Tripucka completed three passes and was helped by an interference call on Archie Matsos that put the ball at the Buffalo 31. Denver eventually got to the 12 before calling on Mingo to tie it.

• Denver had rallied from 24-0 down to a 31-24 win over Boston and the Bills claimed the thin air in Denver had something to do with the Broncos' late-

game success. The Bills tried to prepare by practicing for five days in Denver.

QUOTES

• Buster Ramsey: "For the first three quarters I watched the greatest display of defensive football I've seen in the league this year. Every man had almost perfect execution on every play. Then, for reasons that I cannot put a finger on, the whole thing collapsed. We got to feeling a little too secure with that 38-7 lead and when Lionel Taylor broke loose on that 80-yard touchdown, everyone caved in. On that play, Jim Wagstaff tried for an interception and missed. A half dozen players had good shots at Taylor and they missed, too. If our players didn't realize there's no place for over-confidence in pro football, they know it now."

WEEK 12 GAMES

LA 52, Oak 28	NY 41, Dal 35
Hou 24, Bos 10	

Bills	10	7	21	0 -	38
Broncos	0	7	7	24 -	38

Attendance at Bears Stadium - 7,785

Buf: FG Atkins 20, 6:51
Buf: Carlton 1 run (Atkins kick), 14:44
Buf: Dubenion 76 pass from O'Connell (Atkins kick), 10:11
Den: Mingo 1 run (Mingo kick), 14:11
Buf: FG Atkins 13, 5:05
Buf: Yoho 15 interception return (O'Connell run), 6:53
Buf: Fowler 19 run (Atkins kick), 7:16
Buf: FG Atkins 31, 10:21
Den: Taylor 80 pass from Tripucka (Mingo kick), 10:44
Den: Taylor 24 pass from Tripucka (Mingo kick), 3:44
Den: Taylor 35 pass from Tripucka (Mingo kick), 6:39
Den: Allen 1 run (Mingo kick), 10:35
Den: FG Mingo 19, 14:56

	BUF	DEN
First downs	14	18
Rushing yds	206	56
Passing yds	167	328
Punts-avg	6-30.0	6-35.2
Fumbles lost	3	0
Penalties-yds	4-49	6-76

BILLS LEADERS: Rushing - Fowler 15-120, Carlton 20-66, Kulbacki 5-15, Green 3- (-3), O'Connell 2-2, Smith 4-6; **Passing** - Green 4-9-0 -33, O'Connell 6-15-0 - 134; **Receiving** - Dubenion 6-134, Hoisington 2-26, Lucas 1-7, Carlton 1-0.

BRONCOS LEADERS: Rushing - Wegert 5-37, Rolle 9-15, Mingo 3-8, Tripucka 4- (-25), Stransky 5-14, Brodnax 3-8, Allen 6- (-1); **Passing** - Tripucka 19-41-5 - 328; **Receiving** - Taylor 9-199, Carpenter 4-51, Greer 4-55, Brodnax 1-19, Rolle 1-4

NOTES

• An early-week snow was cleared in time and was not a factor.

• Richie Lucas saw the most extensive time at QB, and he threw the first TD pass of his career, but he hurt his ankle late in the game and came out.

• Al Hoisington recovered Billy Wells' fumbled punt at the 2 and Johnny Green scored from there, but Boston got that back in three plays as Ed Songin hit Tom Stephens for 53 yards to set up Songin's nine-yard pass to Dick Christy.

• Joe Hergert deflected a Songin pass that Wagstaff caught and ran 39 yards for a TD, but the Patriots again rallied to tie, moving 60 yards in eight plays to Songin's keeper.

• The Bills then romped in the second half. Joe Schaffer recovered a Christy fumble at the Boston 45 and Lucas later scored on an eight-yard run.

• Mack Yoho, normally the kickoff man, made his first field goal of the season and Elbert Dubenion scored on a reverse after taking a handoff from running back Joe Kulbacki early in the fourth to put the game out of reach.

• All that was left was Lucas' first TD pass, a 30-yarder to Dan Chamberlain. It came one play after a poor Boston punt from the end zone by Tom Greene rolled dead at the Patriots 30.

QUOTES

• Richie Lucas: "It felt really great. Being at quarterback means being such a big part of the game. I only hope this ankle doesn't become a chronic problem. Running as a quarterback is so much different than as a halfback. First, you don't take off unless there's an open field. So naturally, you've got a better chance of doing something."

• Buster Ramsey: "We had a fine team effort throughout the game, but what really pleased me most was the way every injured player who possibly could have stayed in the game did and did his best. I said at the start of the season we would give Buffalo's professional football fans some exciting afternoons. We won three of seven home games and even the ones we lost were worth the price of admission." (On playing Lucas at quarterback in the second half): "The team was up, you could feel it. I felt it was a good time to try Richie even though Tommy O'Connell had moved the team well when he was in there during the first half."

WEEK 13 GAMES

Dal 24, Hou 0	LA 41, Oak 17
NY 30, Den 27	

Patriots	7	7	0	0 -	14
Bills	7	7	10	14 -	38

Attendance at War Memorial Stadium - 14,335

Buf: Green 2 run (Atkins kick), 7:08
Bos: Christy 9 pass from Songin (Cappelletti kick), 13:04
Buf: Wagstaff 39 interception return (Atkins kick), 6:00
Bos: Songin 1 run (Cappelletti kick), 12:19
Buf: Lucas 8 run (Atkins kick), 8:39
Buf: FG Yoho 45, 12:42
Buf: Dubenion 66 run (Atkins kick), :55
Buf: Chamberlain 30 pass from Lucas (Atkins kicks), 9:11

	BUF	BOS
First downs	18	13
Rushing yds	133	29
Passing yds	138	138
Punts-avg	8-42.3	9-32.6
Fumbles lost	1	1
Penalty yds	63	56

BILLS LEADERS: Rushing - Fowler 15-32, Carlton 11-19, Dubenion 3-53, O'Connell 1-12, Lucas 6-9, Green 2-9, Kulbacki 1- (-1); **Passing** - Green 3-13-0 - 27, O'Connell 3-15-0 - 42, Lucas 5-9-0 - 69; **Receiving** - Dubenion 2-18, Rychlec 5-56, Hoisington 1-6, Carlton 2-28, Chamberlain 1-30.

PATRIOTS LEADERS: Rushing - Miller 11-35, Christy 5-19, Greene 2- (-16), Songin 5- (-7), Burton 1- (-2); **Passing** - Songin 8-29-1 - 111, Christy 1-2-0 - 15, Greene 1-2-0 - 12; **Receiving** - Stephens 2-63, Christy 3-28, Miller 2-4, Colclough 1-16, Lofton 2-27.

STANDINGS: THIRTEENTH WEEK

EAST	W	L	T	WEST	W	L	T
Houston	8	4	0	Los Ang.	8	4	0
New York	6	6	0	Dallas	6	6	0
Buffalo	5	6	1	Oakland	5	7	0
Boston	5	7	0	Denver	4	7	1

NOTES

• The Oilers clinched the East Division title with the victory, while the Chargers beat Denver later in the day to clinch the West.

• George Blanda hit Bill Groman for a 39-yard TD pass midway through the first, one play after he threw 35 yards to Charley Hennigan. Then Tommy O'Connell suffered an interception when his pass bounced out of Elbert Dubenion's hands and into the hands of Orville Trask at the Bills 33. A few plays later, Doug Cline scored to make it 14-0.

• The Bills struck back in the second as Mack Yoho made 48-yard field goal after a Billy Atkins interception. The Bills then drove 69 yards before Richie Lucas, who got the start at quarterback, lost a fumble. Johnny Green replaced Lucas and promptly hit Dan Chamberlain for a TD with 12 seconds left in the first half.

• Still trailing 14-10 in the third, Yoho faked a field goal. Holder Tommy O'Connell rolled right and had Tom Rychlec wide open for a TD, but underthrew. Two series later, George Blanda capped a nine-play, 64-yard drive with a six-yard TD pass to Charley Hennigan.

• Two plays after the kickoff, Bobby Gordon intercepted a Green pass to set up Blanda's AFL record 53-yard field goal that upped the count to 24-10.

• Dave Smith keyed Houston's final scoring drive. First, he threw a 32-yard option pass to Groman, then he caught a 21-yard TD pass from Blanda.

• The Bills scored twice within 1:05 in the fourth as O'Connell hit Chamberlain with a 33-yard TD pass and LB Joe Hergert returned an interception 29 yards for a TD. Here, O'Connell was stuffed on a two-point conversion and the Oilers were safe with an eight-point lead 3:38 from the finish.

QUOTES

• Buster Ramsey: "It was giveaway day for the Bills. We had two passes intercepted after the ball hit our intended receiver. First Tom Rychlec, then Elbert Dubenion let one get away. If O'Connell would have hit Rychlec (on the fake field goal) it would have been 17-14 and we would have had momentum. Despite everything, we still had several opportunities. Richie Lucas' fumble and failure to execute several key plays hurt. The defense lapsed badly in the first quarter but then adjusted pretty well."

• Oilers coach Lou Rymkus on Ramsey's pre-game talking: "Buster got us all fired up. He told everybody he was going to beat us and keep us from winning the title. Well, he didn't beat us and I'm delighted we won the title at Buster's expense."

Bills	0	10	0	13	- 23
Oilers	14	0	7	10	- 31

Attendance at Jeppesen Stadium - 25,247

Hou: Groman 39 pass from Blanda (Blanda kick), 7:01
Hou: Cline 1 run (Blanda kick), 10:03
Buf: FG Yoho 48, 4:35
Buf: Chamberlain 22 pass from Green (Atkins kick), 14:48
Hou: Hennigan 6 pass from Blanda (Blanda kick), 12:59
Hou: FG Blanda 53, :15
Hou: Smith 21 pass from Blanda (Blanda kick), 7:38
Buf: Chamberlain 33 pass from Green (Atkins kick), 10:07
Buf: Hergert 29 interception return (run failed), 11:22

	BUF	HOU
First downs	20	16
Rushing yds	156	112
Passing yds	184	206
Punts-avg	5-35.6	6-38.2
Fumbles lost	1	0
Penalties-yds	1-5	27

BILLS LEADERS: Rushing - Fowler 11-49, Carlton 16-53, Lucas 5-21, Dubenion 3-21, Green 3-1, Atkins 1-11; **Passing** - Green 4-12-0 - 55, O'Connell 2-8-2 - 47, Lucas 5-15-1 - 82; **Receiving** - Fowler 2-33, Rychlec 4-69, Chamberlain 4-73, Crockett 1-9.

OILERS LEADERS: Rushing - Cannon 19-57, Smith 11-42, Cline 9-14, Blanda 1- (-1); **Passing** - Blanda 7-20-3 - 175, Smith 1-1-0 - 31, Cannon 0-1-0 - 0; **Receiving** - Hennigan 3-70, Groman 3-101, Carson 1-14, Smith 1-21.

WEEK 14 GAMES

NY 31, Oak 28   LA 41, Den 33
Dal 34, Bos 0

NOTES

• Richie Lucas made his second straight start at quarterback and scored the first TD Dallas' defense had allowed in three games. He capped a 53-yard drive with a seven-yard TD run. The drive was kept alive when holder Tommy O'Connell faked a field goal and threw a 25-yard pass to Wray Carlton to the 11. Lucas scored three plays later.

• Lucas later was knocked from the game when tackled hard by Don Flynn in the third quarter.

• Dan Chamberlain was knocked out of the game on a bizarre play. Dallas defensive end Paul Miller forced a Buffalo runner out of bounds and the hurtling bodies crashed into Chamberlain who was kneeling on the sideline. The Bills players later confirmed that Miller punched Chamberlain in the mouth, knocking him out. Tom Rychlec had to take his place despite a knee injury.

• Dallas opened a 3-0 lead on Jack Spikes' field goal after Johnny Robinson's 42-yard pass reception from Cotton Davidson on a play that appeared to be offensive pass interference.

• The Bills' 7-3 lead held up as they stopped Dallas at the 1 as the half ended.

• Davidson's 33-yard TD pass to Chris Burford made it 10-7 in the third.

• Two plays after Lucas was knocked out of the game, O'Connell lost a fumble and Mel Branch recovered at the Bills 24. Eight plays later, Spikes plunged in from the 1.

• Robinson closed the scoring with a 74-yard TD reception.

QUOTES

• Buster Ramsey: "It's over; there are no more games to prepare for this season. I'd like to say that everyone has progressed as much as you'd look for them to in such a long season, but it just isn't true. Sunday against Dallas, we had some situations that were just as bad as they were in our first game. This tells a coach one thing, the personnel just isn't good enough. We'll have something to start with next season. This year we started from absolute scratch. There was no way to evaluate players, one against the other. It took time to find out which players belonged and which players belonged on offense or defense. If we're successful signing our draft choices, we should get the replacements we need in our club. That's the most important thing for our club as I see it. We'll improve ourselves, it's only natural that we will be better off with better players. Overall, considering all the injuries we had, I think the team improved a lot."

• Ralph Wilson on his thoughts of the initial season: "I think Buffalo is a fine pro football town. In my mind, Buffalo is better than a couple of towns in the other league right now. We lost a considerable amount of money, but it was just about what we anticipated in our initial phase of the operation. We became a little more optimistic after the preseason was played and we readjusted our expected losses to a lower figure. But television (of NFL games) hurt us more than we expected. We are still competing with TV when two National League games are shown while we're playing at home. I think we have the product to attract more fans. We didn't win many games this season, but you can't see any more exciting or spectacular football. Buster Ramsey went out of his way to give all our candidates a good chance to earn a job. As a result, our team was very slow in getting underway. When Buster decided on a set team, the play was much better."

Bills	0	7	0	0	- 7
Texans	0	3	7	14	- 24

Attendance at the Cotton Bowl - 18,000

Dal: FG Spikes 12, 6:53
Buf: Lucas 7 run (Atkins kick), 10:50
Dal: Burford 33 pass from Davidson (Spikes kick), 12:22
Dal: Spikes 1 run (Spikes kick), 2:51
Dal: Robinson 74 pass from Davidson (Spikes kick), 13:01

	BUF	DAL
First downs	17	22
Rushing yds	85	72
Passing yds	187	334
Punts-avg	6-45.3	3-48.0
Fumbles lost	1	0
Penalty yds	20	10

BILLS LEADERS: Rushing - Fowler 8-18, Carlton 6-38, Lucas 14-29, Smith 1-7, Green 1- -2, O'Connell 1- (-5); **Passing** - Lucas 10-19-1 - 90, Green 7-19-0 - 75, O'Connell 2-2-0 - 22; **Receiving** - Rychlec 3-39, Carlton 5-42, Fowler 2-22, Crockett 3-38, Smith 1-16, Chamberlain 1-12, Dubenion 3-9, Torczon 1-9.

TEXANS LEADERS: Rushing - Haynes 12-50, Spikes 10-18, Robinson 8-13, Davidson 1-3, Team -(-12); **Passing** - Davidson 18-37-0 - 334; **Receiving** - Burford 4-69, Boydston 3-57, Haynes 6-53, Robinson 4-130, Spikes 1-25.

WEEK 15 GAMES

Oak 48, Den 10   LA 50, NY 43
Hou 37, Bos 21

STANDINGS: FIFTEENTH WEEK

EAST	W	L	T	WEST	W	L	T
Houston	10	4	0	Los Ang.	10	4	0
New York	7	7	0	Dallas	8	6	0
Buffalo	5	8	1	Oakland	6	8	0
Boston	5	9	0	Denver	4	9	1

At A Glance
1961

Jan. 13 – Bud Adams was elected the new AFL president.

Jan. 14 – The AFL revised its projected losses from $2 million to $3.5 million in the first year of operation with Ralph Wilson estimating his losses at only $175,000. Los Angeles led the red-ink parade at about $900,000.

Jan. 22 – Rookie Billy Majors of Tennessee, the brother of Johnny Majors, signed with the Bills.

Feb. 2 – Tommy O'Connell retired as a player and became an assistant coach with the Bills.

Feb. 9 – Fullback Art Baker of Syracuse signed with the Bills.

Feb. 10 – The Los Angeles franchise was moved to San Diego.

Feb. 23 – Center Al Bemiller signed with the Bills.

March 23 – The Bills set a goal of selling 15,000 season tickets for 1961.

March 30 – Defensive back Billy Kinard quit the team and took a coaching position at Auburn University. He made six interceptions during the 1960 season.

April 13 – The General Tire Company purchased $14,000 worth of season tickets, the largest sale of season tickets in team history.

April 21 – First-round draft choice Ken Rice said he had been coaxed into signing an undated contract with the Bills. GM Dick Gallagher denied the charge.

May 21 – WBEN announced the Buffalo Bills Football Network would contain 20 stations. Van Miller was rehired as play-by-play man and Ralph Hubbell was added as a color commentator.

June 7 – For the first time in team history, the Bills gave up a future draft choice to secure a player, defensive end Jim O'Brien. The Bills obtained O'Brien from Oakland.

June 22 – The AFL held a two-day meeting in Buffalo at the Statler Hilton.

July 22 – The Bills opened training camp in East Aurora.

July 25 – Former Syracuse all-America tackle Ron Luciano was signed.

July 30 – The Bills conducted an intra-squad scrimmage at War Memorial Stadium before 11,191 fans and an autograph session called Meet the Bills Night.

Aug. 6 – The four Bills rookies who competed in the College All-Star game in Chicago - Billy Shaw, Stew Barber, Ken Rice and Art Baker - participated in their first Bills practice.

Aug. 8 – The Bills were embarrassed by a 38-21 loss to Hamilton of the CFL in an exhibition.

Aug. 18 – The Bills lost their preseason home opener, 35-26, to Dallas. Rookie Art Baker rushed for 73 yards.

Aug. 22 – Johnny Green injured his shoulder, so assistant coach Tommy O'Connell was re-activated out of retirement to the role of player-coach.

Aug. 25 – The Bills traveled to Providence and lost to Boston, 28-10, but Tommy O'Connell was impressive, completing 10 of 15 passes for 115 yards.

Aug. 26 – Buster Ramsey said that the competition was over and that O'Connell would be the Bills' quarterback.

Sept. 1 – Gino Cappelletti's third field goal with 1:50 left lifted the Patriots to a 15-12 victory over the Bills in the preseason finale before 9,022 at War Memorial Stadium.

Sept. 8 – Wide receiver Glenn Bass decided against a baseball career with either the Detroit Tigers or Baltimore Orioles organizations and signed as a free agent with the Bills.

Sept. 10 – The Bills dropped the season opener to the Broncos, 22-10, as two halfback-option TD passes from Gene Mingo keyed Denver's victory before 16,636 at War Memorial Stadium.

Sept. 14 – Trying to find a solution to their quarterback problem, the Bills signed Warren Rabb.

Sept. 17 – The Bills' first win over New York, a 41-31 thriller, was keyed by the defense despite the high score. The offense managed just nine first downs yet the Bills scored 41 points.

Sept. 18 – The Titans owner Harry Wismer, outraged by a sideline incident in his team's loss to Buffalo the day before, where Bills' coach Buster Ramsey battled with New York quarterback Al Dorow, demanded that the AFL "suspend or bar for life" Ramsey. "Coaches are supposed to stop trouble, not start it," Wismer said. "Ramsey's action yesterday in Buffalo could have incited a riot." Ramsey said he just grabbed Dorow, but Dorow said he got punched in the jaw by the coach.

Sept. 19 – Quarterback M.C. Reynolds was signed, giving the Bills more depth at the position.

Sept. 23 – The Bills managed only 175 yards in total offense in a 23-21 loss to Boston before 21,504 at War Memorial Stadium.

Sept. 30 – Joe Hergert missed four field goals in a 19-11 home loss to San Diego.

Oct. 5 – Houston coach Lou Rymkus told the Houston Touchdown Club, "If I can't beat Buffalo, I'll shoot myself. Buffalo always has been a rather punchless team." Buster Ramsey's response: "I'd rather let our players make their own reply Sunday in Houston. They may wish to furnish Mr. Rymkus with a gun since he thinks so little of our ability."

Al Bemiller was drafted out of Syracuse and became the Bills starting center in 1961. He was joined that year by Billy Shaw and Stew Barber. Those three would play together for nine years.

Oct. 8 – Warren Rabb made an impressive QB debut in relief of M.C. Reynolds in a 22-12 victory over the Oilers in Houston.

Oct. 15 – Richie Lucas returned a fumble 20 yards for the clinching TD in a 27-24 upset victory over Dallas at War Memorial Stadium. The Texans managed only 29 yards rushing.

Oct. 22 – The Bills suffered their worst loss ever, 52-21, in Boston. The game originally was scheduled for Oct. 20, but Pats owner Haywood Sullivan postponed it due to the threat of a hurricane which never did hit Boston.

Oct. 27 – Lou Saban, fired two weeks earlier as coach of the Patriots, was hired as director of player personnel by the Bills.

Oct. 29 – George Blanda threw for 464 yards and four TDs in Houston's 28-16 victory over the Bills in Buffalo.

Oct. 31 – The Bills first-ever draft choice, Richie Lucas, left the team to serve in the Army.

Nov. 5 – Oakland forced four turnovers and won just its second game of the season, 31-22 over the Bills at War Memorial Stadium.

Nov. 7 – Defensive back Richie McCabe suddenly announced his retirement. "The trouble with the team is Ramsey doesn't have 22 football players," McCabe said. "I mean real football players who love the game. Some can't do the job. Some of the boys are spoiled because of the money they're making. It's a shame, too, because with the weaknesses in our division this year, we could have taken it."

Nov. 8 – After saying he wouldn't draft Syracuse's Ernie Davis if he had the chance because he was sure Davis would sign with an NFL team, Ralph Wilson recanted and said he would.

Nov. 9 – Ralph Wilson said the Bills' performance during the final five games, all on the road, would determine Buster Ramsey's future.

Nov. 12 – The defense forced six turnovers and stuffe the dangerous Dallas ground game, holding it to 85 yards in a 30-20 victory in Dallas.

Nov. 19 – The Bills posted their first win over Denver, 23-10, as the defense forced nine turnovers.

Nov. 21 – It was announced that AFL owners secretly conducted a college player draft and that the Bills selected LSU's star back Wendell Davis in the first round. Wilson admitted he helped organize the draft. This touched off a feud between Titans owner Harry Wismer and AFL Commissioner Joe Foss. Foss cancelled the draft and Wismer erupted in anger because he had drafted Ernie Davis. He claimed he would try to sign Davis despite Foss' cancellation.

Nov. 23 – The Bills lost in New York to the Titans, 21-14, on Thanksgiving Day as Bills quarterbacks were sacked 10 times for 78 yards in losses.

Dec. 2 – The real AFL draft was held. Buffalo drafted Syracuse running back Ernie Davis (first round) and Titans owner Harry Wismer was outraged, claiming he had drafted Davis legally in the earlier draft that was cancelled by Joe Foss. Other draft choices included East Tennesee line-backer Mike Stratton (13th round), McNeese State defensive tackle Tom Sestak (17th), and Alabama defensive back Ray Abruzzese (23rd), who was Joe Namath's roommate.

Dec. 3 – Glenn Bass caught a team-record 12 passes in a 26-21 victory at Oakland.

Dec. 9 – The Bills closed the season with a lackluster 28-10 loss in San Diego. The Bills' season ended because they had a bye for the final week. Jack Kemp passed for 213 yards and one TD for the Chargers.

Dec. 10 – It was announced that Patrick J. McGroder would join the Bills front office.

Dec. 11 – Laverne Torczon and Billy Atkins were named to the UPI AFL All-Star team.

Dec. 12 – The Bills met with Ernie Davis and his attorney.

Dec. 15 – The Cleveland Browns traded Bobby Mitchell to Washington for the right to negotiate with Ernie Davis. Bills GM Dick Gallagher charged the Browns with tampering.

Dec. 21 – Ernie Davis signed with the Browns for reportedly $25,000 less than the Bills offered.

Dec. 22 – Billy Atkins was the lone Bill named to the AP AFL All-Star team.

Dec. 24 – Houston defeated San Diego for the AFL Championship for the second straight year, 10-3, before 29,556 in San Diego. Each Oiler received $1,792.79 for winning.

Jan. 7, 1962 – The first AFL All-Star Game was played in San Diego and the West won, 47-27. Dallas QB Cotton Davidson was named MVP.

BY THE NUMBERS - 1961

TEAM STATISTICS	BILLS	OPP
First downs	243	200
Rushing	92	61
Passing	128	124
Penalty	23	15
Total yards	3,950	4,264
Avg. game	282.1	304.6
Plays	940	815
Avg. play	4.2	5.2
Net rushing yds	1,606	1,377
Avg. game	114.7	98.4
Avg. play	3.7	3.9
Net passing yds	2,344	2,887
Comp/att	194/439	206/430
Interceptions	25	29
Percentage	44.2	47.9
Sacks/lost	63-442	36-350
Punts/avg	84-45.0	75-38.7
Fumbles/lost	32-17	20-15
Penalties/yds	65-549	76-693
Touchdowns	38	43
Extra points	29-31	41-42
Field goals	9-26	13-28
Two-point conv	4-7	1-1
Safeties	1	1
Kick ret./avg	57-21.2	54-20.6
Punt ret./avg	19-9.8	45-6.5

RUSHING	ATT	YDS	AVG	TD
Baker	152	498	3.3	3
Carlton	101	311	3.1	4
Brown	53	192	3.6	1
Dubenion	17	173	10.2	2
Reynolds	29	143	4.9	4
Bohling	42	134	3.2	2
Atkins	2	87	43.5	1
Rabb	13	47	3.6	0
Lucas	10	15	1.5	0
Green	14	15	1.1	1
Bass	2	8	4.0	0
Fowler	1	2	2.0	0
Mix	1	-1	-1.0	0
Rychlec	1	-18	-18.0	0
TOTALS	**438**	**1606**	**3.7**	**18**

PASSING	COMP	ATT	INT	YDS	TD	COMP%
Reynolds	83	181	13	1004	2	45.9
Green	56	126	5	903	6	44.4
Rabb	34	74	2	586	5	45.9
Lucas	20	50	4	282	2	40.0
O'Connell	1	5	1	11	0	20.0
Carlton	0	2	0	0	0	.000
Bohling	0	1	0	0	0	.000
TOTALS	**194**	**439**	**25**	**2786**	**15**	**44.2**

KICKING	FG/ATT	PAT/ATT	PTS
Atkins	2-6	29-31	35
Hergert	6-14	0-0	18
Shockley	1-2	0-0	3
Yoho	0-4	0-0	0
TOTALS	**9-26**	**29-31**	**56**

PUNTING	NO	AVG
Atkins	84	45.0

RECEIVING	CAT	YDS	AVG	TD
Bass	50	765	15.3	3
Rychlec	33	405	12.3	2
Dubenion	31	461	14.9	6
Crockett	20	325	16.3	0
Richards	19	285	15.0	3
Carlton	17	193	11.4	0
Bohling	10	183	18.3	1
Baker	6	73	12.2	0
Lucas	6	69	11.5	0
Chamberlain	1	16	16.0	0
Brown	1	11	11.0	0
TOTALS	**194**	**2786**	**14.3**	**15**

LEADERS

Kick returns: Dubenion 16-329 yards, 20.6 avg, 0 TD
Baker 12-281, 23.4, 0 TD

Punt returns: Bass 8-75, 9.4, 0 TD

Interceptions: Atkins 10-158, 15.8, 0 TD

Non-kick scoring: Dubenion 8 TDs, 48 pts

Ed Abramoski (right) has been the Bills trainer since day one. Tony Marchitte served as equipment manager from 1961-1979.

Despite problems at quarterback and a team that lost more than it won, the Bills continued to be a popular draw in the AFL (opposite page). They moved up to third in attendance with a count of 133,408 in 1961.

GAME 1 - Sunday, Sept. 10, 1961 - BRONCOS 22, BILLS 10

Broncos	7	8	7	0	-	22
Bills	8	0	0	2	-	10

Attendance at War Memorial Stadium - 16,636

Den: Taylor 50 pass from Mingo (Mingo kick), 6:49
Buf: Dubenion 65 run (Lucas run), 7:34
Den: Frazier 23 pass from Tripucka (Frazier run), 5:32
Den: Taylor 52 pass from Mingo (Mingo kick), 5:33

	BUF	DEN
First downs	13	12
Rushing yds	166	100
Passing yds	118	184
Punts-avg	8-41.5	8-41.4
Fumbles lost	1	1
Penalties-yds	2-10	3-35

BILLS LEADERS: Rushing - Carlton 10-59, Brown 8-29, Dubenion 2-57, Baker 7-28, Fowler 1-2, Lucas 3- (-9); **Passing** - Lucas 10-21-1 - 134, O'Connell 1-5-1 - 11, Carlton 0-1-0 - 0; **Receiving** - Dubenion 3-34, Rychlec 5-48, Bass 1-38, Carlton 1-14, Brown 1-11.

BRONCOS LEADERS: Rushing - Stone 10-22, Frazier 2-52, Mingo 5-7, Carmichael 6-9, Traynham 5-11, Bukaty 2-3, Allen 3- (-4); **Passing** - Tripucka 11-19-1 - 98, Mingo 2-2-0 - 102; **Receiving** - Taylor 6-132, Frazier 1-23, Mingo 2-25, Bukaty 1-5, Carmichael 1-10, Stone 1-6, Traynham 1- (-1).

NOTES

• The Bills coming off a woeful 0-4 preseason, continued their losing ways. Owner Ralph Wilson said that Coach Buster Ramsey's job was safe if the team shows improvement.
• Assistant coach Tommy O'Connell suited up because starting QB Johnny Green was out with an injury, but he was knocked out of the game in the second quarter and Richie Lucas took over and was ineffective.
• Gene Mingo threw two TD passes to Lionel Taylor, both on halfback options after taking laterals from Frank Tripucka. Mingo was the AFL's leading scorer in 1960.
• Elbert Dubenion went 65 yards for a TD on the first play after the kickoff following Mingo's first TD pass. Lucas scored on a two-point coversion to give the Bills an 8-7 lead.
• But Dubenion's fumble of a George Herring punt set up Denver's second TD, Al Frazier's 22-yard reception from Tripucka.
• Archie Matsos' interception went to waste in the third. One play after regaining possession after the Bills punt, Mingo threw his second TD pass.
• The Broncos took a safety late in the game when Herring ran out of the end zone.
• After the game, the Bills signed quarterback Warren Rabb.

WEEK 1 GAMES
NY 21, Bos 20   Hou 55, Oak 0
SD 26, Dal 0

QUOTES

• Ralph Wilson: "I have no thoughts at this time of making a coaching change. However, if we don't start playing the football this team is capable of playing, there will be changes in the future. I believe we have competent personnel with which to compete in the AFL. To date, the team simply has not played up to expectations. I'm not panicky or frantic, but it isn't easy to lose every week."
• Buster Ramsey on the option TD passes: "It's understandable that we make such a mistake once, but two mistakes in the same situation in pro football should cost you the game, and it did. We knew they had the play, we worked against it last week. (Billy) Majors was drawn in on the play when Mingo ran to his left. Majors is a rookie." (On the quarterback situation): "Let's face it, quarterback is the biggest part of your offense. No quarterback, no offense. We've lost our starting quarterback (O'Connell). The quarterback is the leader and when he went out, it demoralized the club. I'm going home and calling six National League coaches to see if I can round up some football players. I'm definitely in the market."

GAME 2 - Sunday, Sept. 17, 1961 - BILLS 41, TITANS 31

Titans	17	7	0	7	-	31
Bills	7	21	10	3	-	41

Attendance at War Memorial Stadium - 15,584

NY: Maynard 4 pass from Dorow (Guesman kick), 2:42
NY: FG Guesman 16, 5:51
NY: Maynard 14 pass from Dorow (Guesman kick), 14:40
Buf: Brown 93 kickoff return (Atkins kick), 14:59
Buf: Baker 1 run (Atkins kick), 7:30
NY: Cooper 2 pass from Dorow (Guesman kick), 11:16
Buf: Dubenion 72 run (Atkins kick), 13:16
Buf: Bass 45 pass from Lucas (Atkins kick), 14:56
Buf: Dubenion 33 pass from Lucas (Atkins kick), 7:01
Buf: FG Hergert 12, 12:16
NY: Powell 12 pass from Dorow (Guesman kick), 2:07
Buf: FG Hergert 27, 14:58

	BUF	NY
First downs	9	22
Rushing yds	168	66
Passing yds	120	250
Punts-avg	2-57.5	2-26.5
Fumbles lost	0	1
Penalties-yds	8-70	4-20

BILLS LEADERS: Rushing - Carlton 12-30, Brown 17-56, Dubenion 2-61, Lucas 4-18, Baker 3-3; **Passing** - Lucas 8-19-2 - 129; **Receiving** - Dubenion 1-33, Rychlec 1-15, Bass 2-57, Crockett 1-15, Carlton 2- (-7), Chamberlain 1-16.

TITANS LEADERS: Rushing - Mathis 9-15, Christy 7-32, Dorow 4-12, Bohling 3-7; **Passing** - Dorow 24-44-3 - 281; **Receiving** - Powell 8-125, Maynard 9-107, Cooper 3-27, Christy 1-13, Bohling 2-7, Mathis 1-2.

NOTES

• The Bills scored 41 points despite attaining just nine first downs.
• The Titans jumped to a 17-0 lead in the first quarter as Al Dorow hit Don Maynard with a pair of TD passes and Dick Guesman hit a field goal that was set up by Hubert Bobo's interception of a Richie Lucas pass.
• Rookie Fred Brown faked a reverse to Elbert Dubenion on the kickoff after Maynard's second score. It was the final play of the first quarter and Brown broke loose for a momentum-shifting 93-yard TD return.
• Dick Christy's fumble on a punt return set up Art Baker's TD that made it 17-14.
• The Titans drove 75 yards to Dorow's TD pass to Thurlow Cooper, but the Bills answered that with Dubenion's 73-yard TD run. The Bills then went ahead, 28-24, as Vern Valdez returned a punt 30 yards. One play later, Lucas fired a 45-yard TD pass to Glenn Bass.
• In the third, Dubenion scored on a 33-yard run after a Billy Atkins interception. Valdez intercepted a Dorow pass and returned it 50 yards to set up Joe Hergert's first field goal.
• With the Bills ahead, 38-31, and 2:07 left, Wray Carlton fumbled at the Buffalo 12. But the defense rose up, forced 13 yards in losses and Dick Guesman eventually missed a 42-yard field goal.
• Dorow was gang-tackled near the Bills sideline in the third quarter and got into a wrestling match with Buster Ramsey. After the game, the Titans charged the Bills with doctoring the game film and splicing out the incident.

WEEK 2 GAMES
Bos 45, Den 17   SD 44, Oak 0

QUOTES

• Buster Ramsey: "Richie ran the team well. He showed more know-how and didn't panic when we were behind and in pressure situations. The boy had confidence in himself and that's important. Show me a player who didn't do a job and I'll show you a player who didn't get in the game. Our defense was a little jittery at the start, but settled down and gave Mr. Dorow a busy afternoon."
• Trainer Ed Abramoski on the fight: "I got stepped on, elbowed and shoved and all I was trying to do was get away from those big guys."
• Richie Lucas: "I really wanted to win that game. But no more than the rest of the guys."
• Billy Atkins: "All Richie needs is experience. He'll get the confidence. I know we have confidence in him after today."
• Jim Sorey: "The type of football we played today is like rock 'n roll - it's here to stay."
• Elbert Dubenion: "We're going all the way now."

STANDINGS: SECOND WEEK

EAST	W	L	T	WEST	W	L	T
Houston	1	0	0	San Diego	2	0	0
New York	1	1	0	Denver	1	1	0
Buffalo	1	1	0	Dallas	0	1	0
Boston	1	1	0	Oakland	0	2	0

NOTES

• M.J. Reynolds replaced an ineffective Richie Lucas at quarterback in the second quarter.

• In the first quarter, Jim Wagstaff intercepted a pass and returned it 19 yards to the Pats 36. On the next play, a pass interference penalty in the end zone on Glenn Bass gave the Bills the ball at the 1. From there Wray Carlton scored to make it 7-3.

• Wagstaff returned a punt 35 yards to the Boston 10 on the final play of the first quarter, but a Lucas interception killed the threat.

• Gino Cappelletti's second field goal capped a 73-yard drive and made it 7-6 Bills at the half.

• In the first half, the Bills had the ball nine times and seven of the possessions were four plays or fewer.

• Larry Garron broke a 67-yard draw up the middle for the Pats' go-ahead score in the third.

• Boston's second TD came after the Bills refused an intentional delay of game penalty so that the Patriots wouldn't have a better angle on a field goal. After the decline, Pats coach Lou Saban opted to go for the TD and it worked.

• Reynolds capped an impressive drive with a one-yard TD to make it 20-14. The key plays were Carlton's 15- and 20-yard receptions.

• Cappelletti's third field goal put the game out of reach.

QUOTES

• Buster Ramsey: "Their defense was particularly effective against the rollout offense we put in for Lucas before the New York game. We adjusted our blocking assignments during the game, but it didn't do much good. Boston used a rushing defense and our offensive line didn't do a good job of picking up their rushers." (On declining the penalty): "It's a decision I'd make again. The defense held them three times, there was no reason to think they wouldn't again. We took a calculated risk, lost the gamble and it cost us the game. Our defense made a terrific stand for three downs, holding them to three yards. When we refused the penalty that almost certainly would have given Boston three points, we thought the defense would hold for one more play."

• Boston coach Lou Saban: "We knew this was going to be a tough game. The Bills are always tough, but we were doubling up at several positions due to injuries and the guys came through. What pleased me the most was the way our defense handled the Bills in the first half. Then Larry Garron gave us the big play to get us over the hump. His run in the third period was the lift we needed."

	WEEK 3 GAMES	
Dal 42, Oak 35		SD 34, Hou 24
NY 35, Den 28		

Patriots		3 3 14 3 - 23
Bills		7 0 7 7 - 21

Attendance at War Memorial Stadium - 21,504

Bos: FG Cappelletti 35, 3:16
Buf: Carlton 1 run (Atkins kick), 11:38
Bos: FG Cappelletti 35, 3:33
Bos: Garron 67 run (Cappelletti kick), 1:31
Bos: Stephens 1 pass from Songin (Cappelletti kick), 6:31
Buf: Reynolds 1 run (Atkins kick), 12:35
Bos: FG Cappelletti 46, 9:05
Buf: Dubenion 11 pass from Reynolds (Atkins kick), 14:00

	BUF	BOS
First downs	14	15
Rushing yds	63	156
Passing yds	112	163
Punts-avg	9-53.2	5-37.8
Fumbles lost	1	1
Penalties-yds	3-25	7-80

BILLS LEADERS: Rushing - Brown 7-32, Carlton 11-8, Reynolds 5-14, Bass 2-8, Baker 1-1; **Passing** - Lucas 2-10-1 - 19, Reynolds 12-22-0 - 129; **Receiving** - Dubenion 4-37, Rychlec 3-34, Bass 3-18, Carlton 2-40, Crockett 2-19.

PATRIOTS LEADERS: Rushing - West 7-49, Garron 7-90, Lott 3-15, Washington 1-3, Yewcic 2-3, Parilli 1-0, Burton 1- (-4); **Passing** - Songin 12-28-0 - 185, Parilli 1-8-1 - 7, Yewcic 0-1-0 - 0; **Receiving** - Colclough 3-69, Cappelletti 4-73, Garron 3-49, Stephens 1-1, West 1-5, Yewcic 1- (-5).

NOTES

• The Chargers won their fourth straight while the Bills fell to 1-3, as Joe Hergert missed field goals of 28, 47, 40 and 33 yards. The Chargers had topped 30 points in the previous three games.

• Dick Harris' interception return for a TD came just 1:37 into the game. The Chargers made it 13-0 late in the first when Paul Lowe broke a 30-yard TD run to cap a 78-yard drive that was kept alive by Jack Kemp's third-and-14 scramble for a first down.

• Art Baker returned the ensuing kickoff 36 yards and that led to Hergert's only successful field goal. The key play on the 41-yard march was M.C. Reynolds' 20-yard scramble.

• Elbert Dubenion's TD came one play after Richie McCabe intercepted a Kemp pass 28 seconds before halftime and returned it 17 yards to the San Diego 29.

• Reynolds ran and passed well in his debut as starting quarterback.

• The Bills were held to 54 yards in the second half.

• The Bills had possession for just four plays in the third quarter.

• Attendance for the league for the first four games was up 19,542 over 1960 at the same point.

QUOTES

• Buster Ramsey on the missed field goals: "He makes them in practice. What can you do about him missing in the game? There's not much to say about the game except that if we had made those field goals, we would have beaten them. I think we can beat any team in this league and that includes the Chargers who are the best team we've faced. We can win with this team. I won't make any more changes in personnel. I'm sick of changes. We played this game the way it was supposed to be played, except for the field goals."

• M.C. Reynolds: "This team is really coming along.

Coming from the outside, I can see it getting better with every workout and game. This is a young team and some of us have only been together a week or two. From now on, time will be in our favor as we get to know one another." (On Harris' interception return for a TD): "That was a huddle misunderstanding. I told Glenn to turn inside if he had double coverage on the play and outside if it was single. I threw as he reached the spot to make his break. When I saw him turn outside and Harris was going for the ball, I almost dropped."

• San Diego coach Sid Gillman: "This was our toughest game for 60 minutes. Just give that Reynolds a little time to adjust and Buffalo's attack will pick up. I know about Reynolds, I wanted him."

Chargers		13 0 6 0 - 19
Bills		0 11 0 0 - 11

Attendance at War Memorial Stadium - 20,472

SD: Harris 56 interception return (Blair kick), 1:37
SD: Lowe 30 run (kick failed), 12:55
Buf: FG Hergert 16, 2:12
Buf: Dubenion 29 pass from Reynolds (Lucas run), 14:32
SD: FG Blair 38, 4:00
SD: FG Blair 11, 14:41

	BUF	SD
First downs	15	15
Rushing yds	102	162
Passing yds	137	140
Punts-avg	3-41.3	4-43.8
Fumbles lost	1	0
Penalties-yds	3-25	6-50

BILLS LEADERS: Rushing - Brown 13-40, Reynolds 8-65, Baker 7- (-3); **Passing** - Reynolds 15-28-1 - 177; **Receiving** - Dubenion 4-52, Rychlec 5-57, Bass 3-36, Carlton 3-32.

CHARGERS LEADERS: Rushing - Lowe 22-128, Kemp 4-19, Flowers 3-17, Roberson 2- (-2); **Passing** - Kemp 14-26-1 - 146; **Receiving** - Hayes 4-49, Norton 3-35, Flowers 3-48, Lowe 3-6, Kocourek 1-8.

	WEEK 4 GAMES	
Dal 26, Hou 21		NY 37, Bos 30
Oak 33, Den 19		

STANDINGS: FOURTH WEEK

EAST	W	L	T	WEST	W	L	T
New York	3	1	0	San Diego	4	0	0
Boston	2	2	0	Dallas	2	1	0
Houston	1	2	0	Denver	1	3	0
Buffalo	1	3	0	Oakland	1	3	0

Bills	0	7	0	15	-	22
Oilers	0	10	2	0	-	12

Attendance at Jeppesen Stadium - 22,761

Buf: Brown 4 run (Atkins kick), :49
Hou: Groman 54 pass from Lee (Blanda kick), 8:58
Hou: FG Blanda 14, 13:45
Hou: Safety, Morris blocked Atkins punt out of end zone, 1:34
Buf: Richards 15 pass from Rabb (Lucas run), 8:32
Buf: Carlton 27 run (Atkins kick), 13:21

	BUF	HOU
First downs	18	8
Rushing yds	206	48
Passing yds	176	146
Punts-avg	7-33.9	7-46.4
Fumbles lost	3	1
Penalties-yds	3-23	3-15

BILLS LEADERS: Rushing - Carlton 10-87, Brown 8-35, Dubenion 5-35, Rabb 4-28, Baker 8-7, Reynolds 3-14; **Passing** - Reynolds 8-21-2 - 135, Rabb 2-5-0 - 47; **Receiving** - Crockett 4-102, Dubenion 1-16, Bass 1-32, Carlton 1- (-1), Baker 1- (-1), Lucas 1-19, Richards 1-15.

OILERS LEADERS: Rushing - Cannon 8-19, Tolar 11-23, Lee 2-6; **Passing** - Lee 10-26-2 - 196, Cannon 0-1-0 - 0; **Receiving** - Hennigan 4-109, Groman 3-79, McLeod 1-11, Tolar 1-1, Cannon 1-(-4).

WEEK 5 GAMES

Dal 19, Den 12   SD 38, Bos 27

NOTES

• M.C. Reynolds struggled, so Warren Rabb played for the first time in a regular-season game and he directed 4th-quarter TD drives of 77 and 50 yards that won the game.
• The 77-yard drive that put the Bills ahead was keyed by a 32-yard pass to Glenn Bass in which Rabb audibled at the line. On the next play, he hit Perry Richards for a 15-yard TD.
• Wray Carlton capped the second TD drive with a 27-yard scoring run up the middle.
• In the week before the game, Ramsey and Houston coach Lou Rymkus waged a war of words that was started the previous season.
• The Bills held Billy Cannon to 19 yards rushing and Rymkus indicated he would bench the former Heisman Trophy winner.
• The Bills had drives deep in Houston territory killed by fumbles by Carlton and Art Baker. In all, Buffalo turned the ball over five times.
• The Oilers' loss was just their second at home in 1 1/2 seasons.
• Monte Crockett caught four passes for 102 yards in the first quarter alone, but left the game with a knee injury.
• Fred Brown's second-quarter TD capped a 62-yard march, but he suffered a knee injury late in the game.

QUOTES

• Warren Rabb: "I wasn't nervous. The coach had told me earlier in the quarter that I might go in. I had just been mulling over what I might call."
• Buster Ramsey: "I put Rabb in because there was no consistency in our offense. Rabb called a pretty good game. We went right down to score and (Perry) Richards made a great effort on the touchdown pass that gave us the lead. Reynolds moved the team to

what should have been three touchdowns in the first quarter and that should have made our victory an easy one. Carlton had a hand in this fumbling, but by the end of the game he was our most consistent running threat."

Texans	3	0	0	21	-	24
Bills	3	7	7	10	-	27

Attendance at War Memorial Stadium - 20,678

Dal: FG Spikes 18, 5:33
Buf: FG Hergert 32, 11:06
Buf: Reynolds 1 run (Atkins kick), 11:51
Buf: Bass 87 pass from Rabb (Atkins kick), 2:21
Buf: FG Hergert 45, :09
Dal: Haynes 69 pass from Davidson (Spikes kick), :44
Dal: Haynes 3 run (Spikes kick), 9:45
Buf: Lucas 20 run with fumble recovery (Atkins kick), 12:28
Dal: Haynes 88 kickoff return (Spikes kick), 13:01

	BUF	DAL
First downs	5	11
Rushing yds	165	29
Passing yds	197	164
Punts-avg	5-45.8	6-39.5
Fumbles lost	2	1
Penalties-yds	9-76	3-28

BILLS LEADERS: Rushing - Carlton 20-48, Reynolds 5-19, Baker 11-46, Atkins 1-31, Lucas 3-6, Dubenion 4-3, Rabb 2-12; **Passing** - Reynolds 5-7-0 - 56, Rabb 5-8-1 - 164; **Receiving** - Bass 4-159, Rychlec 3-44, Carlton 2-13, Lucas 1-4.

TEXANS LEADERS: Rushing - Haynes 13-18, Spikes 4-11; **Passing** - Davidson 9-26-2 - 166, Duncan 1-2-0 - 7; **Receiving** - Haynes 3-73, Spikes 3-33, Boydston 2-32, Burford 1-13, Dickinson 1-22.

WEEK 6 GAMES

SD 25, NY 10   Den 27, Oak 24
Hou 31, Bos 31

NOTES

• M.C. Reynolds played the first half, Warren Rabb the second in an impressive victory.
• Abner Haynes scored three TDs, but his fumble of a punt with 2:31 left was returned 20 yards for a clinching TD by Richie Lucas. Haynes returned the ensuing kickoff 88 yards for a TD, and he also ran for a TD and caught a TD pass in a superb performance.
• The Texans had averaged 246 yards on the ground, including a 398-yard game two weeks before against Houston, but they managed only 29 against the Bills.
• Billy Atkins had two interceptions and punted four times for a 45.8 average. With the game tied 3-3, Atkins' first interception started the Bills on a 53-yard drive that Reynolds capped with a TD run. Art Baker had a 33-yard run to key the possession.
• Rabb started the second half and on his second play, he hit Glenn Bass over the middle. Bass outran the Texans to the end zone to complete an 87-yard TD for a 17-3 lead.
• Haynes then almost pulled out the game for Dallas. After Joe Hergert's second field goal, Haynes returned the kickoff 19 yards to the 31, then toted a short Cotton Davidson pass 69 yards for a TD. His three-yard TD run capped a 64-yard march. His fumbled punt then killed the rally.
• Big Jim Sorey brawled with Dallas' Al Reynolds and

Sherrill Headrick after the game.
• Tom Day made his first start at defensive tackle and played well.

QUOTES

• Buster Ramsey: "Heroes? Check the statistics. That team had rushed for an average of 246 yards. What did they get today? 29 yards. Everyone on that defensive team is a hero. We won and it was a good win, but if anyone ever told me I would have to win with three players (Monte Crockett, Fred Brown and Chuck McMurtry) hurting before we start and three players (Glenn Bass, Elbert Dubenion and Wray Carlton) knocked out of action during the game, I would never have thought it could be done."
• Richie Lucas on his fumble return: "Just lucky. I was in the right place at the right time."
• Jim Sorey on his post-game rumble: "It was just a nice little friendly get-together. Somebody hit me and I hit him back."
• Glenn Bass: "My foot's bothered me all week and today it really hurt, but I forgot about it a few times."
• Tom Day: "They used to say there was nothing in the line but brawn and all the brains were in the backfield. That won't go anymore. A defensive tackle has to watch the center, the guard and the tackle and when he gets through them, he has to play with the backs."

STANDINGS: SIXTH WEEK

EAST	W	L	T	WEST	W	L	T
New York	3	2	0	San Diego	6	0	0
Buffalo	3	3	0	Dallas	3	2	0
Boston	2	3	1	Denver	2	4	0
Houston	1	3	1	Oakland	1	4	0

NOTES
• The game was supposed to be played Friday, but Patriots owner Haywood Sullivan postponed it due to the threat of a hurricane. The weather turned out to be fine Friday and was much colder with rain and high winds Sunday. Thirty high school games were played Friday.
• Rychlec's TDs were his first despite having caught more than 60 passes in his 1 1/2 years with the Bills.
• Ron Hall intercepted an M.C. Reynolds pass that led to Babe Parilli's first of three TD passes to Billy Lott. Dick Klein partially blocked a Billy Atkins punt and that led to a Gino Cappelletti field goal that made it 10-0 very quickly. It became 17-0 when Ed Songin burned Vern Valdez with a 58-yard TD pass to Jimmy Colclough.

• In the second, the score rose to 38-0. Parilli hit Lott with a 43-yard TD pass and 3:35 later, Don Webb intercepted a pass that bounced off Richie Lucas' fingertips and went 26 yards for a TD.
• Warren Rabb replaced M.C. Reynolds in the second quarter and was knocked down at least 14 times. On his first series, he fumbled and Bob Dee ran 30 yards to the Bills 23. An interference penalty on Jim Wagstaff moved the ball to the 4 and Parilli hit Cappelletti for a TD.
• Lucas was knocked unconscious in the third quarter on a hit by Tom Addison.
• Rabb fired three TDs in the final quarter and passed for 261 yards.

QUOTES
• Buster Ramsey on his defense: "It went to sleep. The best illustration I can give is Billy Lott scored three touchdowns on rollout passes from Babe Parilli. This was a play we were waiting for. So what happened? We defensed each one differently and each time the man assigned to Lott blew his assignment and cost us a touchdown. Everything we did went wrong, now it's time for us to do everything right."
• M.C. Reynolds on the postponement: "It's no alibi, we played poorly. We were ready for them Friday and you can't hold that competitive edge under the circumstances we had. You could tell in the huddle right at the start of the game we didn't have the fire."
• Patriots coach Mike Holovak: "I favored the postponement. I knew it had to hurt the Bills. They were sitting in a hotel for two days while our players were at home. But our players were keyed up for this game, more than any we've ever played."

WEEK 7 GAMES	
SD 41, Oak 10	Den 27, NY 10
Hou 38, Dal 7	

Bills	0 0 0 21 - 21
Patriots	17 21 7 7 - 52

Attendance at Boston University - 9,398

Bos: Lott 14 pass from Songin (Cappelletti kick), 3:41
Bos: FG Cappelletti 12, 8:11
Bos: Colclough 58 pass from Songin (Cappelletti kick), 12:09
Bos: Lott 43 pass from Parilli (Cappelletti kick), 2:13
Bos: Webb 26 interception return (Cappelletti kick), 5:48
Bos: Cappelletti 5 pass from Songin (Cappelletti kick), 10:43
Bos: Lott 28 pass from Parilli (Cappelletti kick), 13:10
Buf: Richards 4 pass from Rabb (Atkins kick), 7:30
Buf: Rychlec 10 pass from Rabb (Atkins kick), 12:40
Bos: Garron 85 run (Cappelletti kick), 12:55
Buf: Rychlec 21 pass from Rabb (Atkins kick), 14:44

	BUF	BOS
First downs	23	18
Rushing yds	51	235
Passing yds	224	202
Punts-avg	6-48.6	2-37.5
Fumbles lost	3	0
Penalties-yds	5-54	8-86

BILLS LEADERS: Rushing - Carlton 8-20, Baker 11-25, Rabb 3-6; **Passing** - Rabb 19-33-0 - 261, Reynolds 1-7-2 - 16; **Receiving** - Richards 8-107, Rychlec 4-54, Lucas 4-46, Carlton 3-53, Crockett 1-17.
PATRIOTS LEADERS: Rushing - Garron 10-116, Lott 10-51, Crawford 8-45, Parilli 2-22, Songin 1-1, Burton 2-0; **Passing** - Parilli 8-11-0 - 117, Songin 5-11-2 - 85; **Receiving** - Lott 6-108, Cappelletti 3-29, Colclough 2-67, Johnson 2- (-2).

NOTES
• Wally Lemm had taken over as coach of the Oilers, so controversial Lou Rymkus wasn't around to stir any war of words. He also failed to get revenge on the Bills from the earlier loss.
• George Blanda hit Charley Hennigan for a TD on Houston's first offensive play of the game and went on to pass for an AFL record 464 yards.
• Joe Hergert intercepted a Blanda pass to set up his own 38-yard field goal late in the first.
• The Oilers made it 14-3 at the half as Blanda fired a 32-yard TD pass to Bill Groman after he had completed a 23-yard pass to John White on a third-and-18 play.
• Billy Atkins faked a punt and went 56 yards for his TD.
• Wray Carlton could have put the Bills ahead 17-14 in the third, but he dropped a 12-yard TD pass from M.C. Reynolds. Joe Hergert then missed a 15-yard field goal and three plays later, Blanda hit Hennigan for an 80-yard TD.
• Reynolds directed a 98-yard scoring drive in the fourth, but on Houston's next play from scrimmage, Blanda hit Groman with a 68-yard TD.
• The Bills had interceptions that stopped the Oilers' drives at the 30, 21 and 2.
• The Oilers had only 12 yards rushing in the second half, but Blanda was unstoppable.
• The Bills lost Richie Lucas for one year due to an Army commitment.

QUOTES
• Monte Crockett: "The fans always get on the coaches. It bothers me to hear the abuse they take because it's not deserved. When we win, it's the players who score the touchdowns, throw a pass or a block or make a spectacular play. When we lose, it's the coaches' fault. I believe in giving credit where credit is due and letting the fault go where's it's due, too. Coach Ramsey and the assistants had us prepared for Houston. We all want to win very badly, but something always seems to be happening over which the coaches have no control."
• Richie Lucas: "Now that I'm leaving, I realize just how much I've enjoyed Buffalo the past year and a half. While things didn't turn out exactly the way I would have liked, I've never really done anything to warrant the fine treatment I've had from Coach Ramsey and the rest of the team."
• Oilers quarterback George Blanda: "When you have the best pass protection in pro football and the best end (Hennigan), the rest is easy. With Charley Hennigan, you know he'll beat the defense more often than not, so you just keep throwing to him and eventually you have the big six. The Bills got to me only once all day. Even then I had time to see Hennigan and get the ball to him for a touchdown."
• Ralph Wilson on whether he was considering replacing Ramsey with Lou Saban: "When we hired Lou Saban it was with the single thought of getting the jump on other teams in what has become a highly competitive player market."

Oilers	7 7 7 7 - 28
Bills	0 3 7 6 - 16

Attendance at War Memorial Stadium - 21,237

Hou: Hennigan 56 pass from Blanda (Blanda kick), 2:42
Buf: FG Hergert 37, :21
Hou: Groman 32 pass from Blanda (Blanda kick), 13:22
Buf: Atkins 56 run (Atkins kick), 2:55
Hou: Hennigan 80 pass from Blanda (Blanda kick), 7:05
Buf: Reynolds 1 run (kick failed), 5:00
Hou: Groman 68 pass from Blanda (Blanda kick), 7:00

	BUF	HOU
First downs	22	17
Rushing yds	99	46
Passing yds	252	464
Punts-avg	5-41.6	4-44.0
Fumbles lost	0	0
Penalties-yds	3-30	6-70

BILLS LEADERS: Rushing - Baker 9-26, Atkins 1-56, Carlton 5-7, Bohling 2-3, Reynolds 2-5, Rabb 2-2; **Passing** - Rabb 8-25-1 - 114, Reynolds 11-26-3 - 160; **Receiving** - Bass 8-123, Richards 5-71, Crockett 3-43, Baker 3-37.
OILERS LEADERS: Rushing - Tolar 15-22, Cannon 13-5, Smith 3-12, Blanda 2-3, King 1-4; **Passing** - Blanda 18-32-4 - 464; **Receiving** - Hennigan 9-232, Groman 2-100, Tolar 3-56, White 1-23, Cannon 2-46, Smith 1-7.

WEEK 8 GAMES	
NY 14, Oak 6	Bos 18, Dal 17
SD 37, Den 0	

STANDINGS: EIGHTH WEEK

EAST	W	L	T	WEST	W	L	T
New York	4	3	0	San Diego	8	0	0
Boston	4	3	1	Dallas	3	4	0
Houston	3	3	1	Denver	3	5	0
Buffalo	3	5	0	Oakland	1	6	0

Raiders	14	0	14	3 - 31
Bills	0	15	0	7 - 22

Attendance at War Memorial Stadium- 17,027

Oak: Fuller 85 pass from Flores (Fleming kick), 3:05
Oak: Miller 1 run (Fleming kick), 8:01
Buf: Dubenion 63 pass from Green (Atkins kick), 2:23
Buf: Bohling 5 run (Rabb run), 13:17
Oak: Asad 30 pass from Flores (Fleming kick), 6:52
Oak: Miller 55 pass from Flores (Fleming kick), 13:35
Buf: Bass 9 pass from Green (Atkins kick), 3:22
Oak: FG Fleming 48, 10:33

	BUF	OAK
First downs	18	16
Rushing yds	124	125
Passing yds	241	256
Punts-avg	5-49.2	8-38.4
Fumbles lost	1	0
Penalties-yds	4-20	9-94

BILLS LEADERS: Rushing - Baker 12-68, Bohling 14-43, Dubenion 1-14, Green 3- (-1); **Passing** - Green 12-28-2 - 244, Bohling 0-1-0 - 0; **Receiving** - Bass 3-63, Bohling 4-71, Crockett 1-10, Dubenion 4-100.

RAIDERS LEADERS: Rushing - Crow 16-92, Papac 1-11, Miller 6-7, Flores 3-9, Daniels 2-1, Fuller 1-5, Fleming 1-0; **Passing** - Flores 14-24-0 - 271, Papac 1-3-0 - 6, Crow 0-1-0 - 0; **Receiving** - Fuller 1-85, Miller 4-64, Asad 3-64, Hardy 3-48, Coolbaugh 2-13, Crow 2-3.

NOTES

• In their last home game of the season, the Bills were terrible with four turnovers.
• Johnny Green made his first appearance of the regular season and played well.
• The Bills punted after their first possession and on Oakland's first offensive play, Tom Flores hit Charley Fuller for an 85-yard TD. Fuller got behind Richie McCabe.
• The Bills drove right back to the Oakland 24, but Dewey Bohling fumbled at the 16, Fred Williamson scooped up the ball and ran all the way to the Bills 9. Five plays later, Allen Miller scored.
• The Bills controlled the second quarter as Green hit

WEEK 9 GAMES

SD 48, NY 13   Bos 28, Dal 21
Hou 55, Den 13

Elbert Dubenion for a 63-yard TD, then he directed a scoring drive late in the half. A 39-yard pass to Glenn Bass led to Bohling's TD run and Warren Rabb's go-ahead two-point conversion for a 15-14 halftime lead.
• Flores' TD pass to Doug Asad in the third was set up by Riley Morris' interception.
• Art Baker fumbled at the Oakland 15 when the Bills were trailing just 21-15, then a 26-yard Green to Elbert Dubenion touchdown pass was wiped out by an illegal-motion penalty.
• Charley Hardy made a key reception in the fourth to set up the clinching field goal.

QUOTES

• Buster Ramsey: "Those three fumbles just killed us. Johnny Green moved the team well. I thought we would win decisively after Warren Rabb ran in the 2-point conversion. I thought making those two points would be the key. It was the edge I felt we needed to take it in from there in the second half."
• Ralph Wilson: "We can salvage this season by beating (Titans owner Harry) Wismer in New York and beating him good. If we win two or three games on the road now, I know everything will change. I'm going to stick with Buster, I have confidence in him. I've seen teams lose and there's an outcry which ends as soon as the team starts winning."
• Raiders coach Marty Feldman: "The turning point was Charley Hardy's catch of that slant pass. It put us in position (in the fourth quarter) for the field goal."
• Richie McCabe on getting beat on the first play: "Heck, I called the play when Oakland lined up. I knew Fuller was going to run a bend in the same manner as Charley Hennigan did the week before because they knew about my bum knee. But I couldn't cover and they scored."

Bills	3	7	0	20 - 30
Texans	3	14	0	3 - 20

Attendance at the Cotton Bowl - 15,000

Dal: FG Agajanian 22, 4:45
Buf: FG Atkins 37, 9:56
Dal: Robinson 14 pass from Davidson (Agajanian kick), 3:21
Buf: Green 1 run (Atkins kick), 8:53
Dal: Jackson 52 pass from Davidson (Agajanian kick), 13:25
Dal: FG Agajanian 51, 2:46
Buf: Bohling 2 run (run failed), 8:26
Buf: Carlton 3 run (Atkins kick), 11:47
Buf: Muelhaupt recovered fumble in end zone (Atkins kick), 14:08

	BUF	DAL
First downs	15	16
Rushing yds	100	85
Passing yds	69	195
Punts-avg	1-49.0	5-30.4
Fumbles lost	1	2
Penalties-yds	4-61	6-61

BILLS LEADERS: Rushing - Baker 10-29, Bohling 12-54, Dubenion 1-7, Carlton 4-10, Rabb 2- (-1), Nix 1- (-1), Green 3-2; **Passing** - Green 9-23-2 - 97, Reynolds 0-1-0 - 0, Rabb 0-3-0 - 0; **Receiving** - Bass 5-42, Crockett 2-35, Dubenion 1-8, Rychlec 1-12.

TEXANS LEADERS: Rushing - Haynes 9-62, Dickinson 9-31, Robinson 4-7, Burford 1- (-13), Davidson 1- (-2); **Passing** - Davidson 18-34-4 - 236; **Receiving** - Burford 9-107, Jackson 2-54, Robinson 3-36, Haynes 1-14, Dickinson 1-4, Barnes 1-13, Romeo 1-8.

NOTES

• The Bills snapped a three-game losing streak and extended Dallas' losing streak to five.
• The Bills again shut down the Texans running game, holding it to 85 yards including Abner Haynes 48-yard run on the first play.
• Johnny Green was ineffective at QB. Warren Rabb was lost for the season with a shoulder separation while running for a two-point conversion in the fourth quarter.
• Defensive back Jim Crotty was signed the day before the game from the Washington Redskins and helped immensely, even though he had never practiced with the team. Crotty hadn't been involved in a winning effort in nearly two years.
• A 27-yard pass to Monte Crockett set up Dewey Bohling's TD.
• Green's TD was set up by Billy Atkins' interception. Ralph Felton's interception and return to the Dallas 20 led to Wray Carlton's go-ahead score.
• On the final TD, Haynes fumbled a punt at the 7, Billy Shaw returned it to the goal line and fumbled and Chuck Muelhaupt recovered in the end zone.

WEEK 10 GAMES

Hou 27, Bos 15   NY 23, Oak 12
SD 19, Den 16

QUOTES

• Chuck Muelhaupt: "I've played 10 years of football and that's the first TD. My dad always said that the guard will get his gravy."
• Buster Ramsey: "That long pass (27-yarder) to Crockett changed the game. I never thought we were out of it. That play put us in scoring position and we went on to score three touchdowns." (On playing Crotty): "With Vern Valdez out and Richie McCabe retired, we had no choice but to try and get Crotty passably ready. And I think the way he responded might have given our defense a psychological lift it needed to battle when our offense couldn't get started. I know myself that when he came back after getting his nose stitched up (from a bad cleat cut suffered in the second quarter) and kept hitting hard, it helped me hang on when we were losing."
• Jim Crotty on the Bills' three-game losing streak: "If they want to see what real pressure and a low feeling is like, they should lose about 16 straight like the Redskins."
• Ralph Felton: "We should get a player a week from Washington and we'd never lose. A player coming from the Redskins hasn't won in so long, he'll die just for the smell of victory."
• Ralph Wilson, when questioned again about Ramsey's future: "In my opinion, Buster has done a good coaching job. We had some bad luck. We spent a lot of money signing rookies and we'll do it again next year."

STANDINGS: TENTH WEEK

EAST	W	L	T	WEST	W	L	T
Houston	5	3	1	San Diego	10	0	0
Boston	5	4	1	Dallas	3	6	0
New York	5	4	0	Denver	3	7	0
Buffalo	4	6	0	Oakland	2	7	0

GAME 11 - Sunday, Nov. 19, 1961 - BILLS 23, BRONCOS 10

NOTES

• The Bills beat Denver for the first time in four meetings and set a team record with six interceptions as Jim Crotty and Billy Atkins had two each, Ralph Felton and Stew Barber one each. Barber returned his 21 yards for the final TD. The defense also recovered three Al Frazier fumbles.

• Atkins' missed PAT, due to a bad snap, was his first of the year.

• The Bills burned Denver cornerback Phil Nugent on TD passes to Elbert Dubenion and Perry Richards. On Dubenion's TD, Duby caught a pass over the middle, then dazzled Nugent with a fake and ran the final 20 yards to the end zone 53 seconds before halftime. In the third, Johnny Green was faced with a third-and-11. He scrambled out of the pocket and when the safeties came up in run support, Nugent was left one-on-one with Richards. When Nugent slipped, Richards was all alone for the TD.

• On the first play after the kickoff, Barber picked off a George Herring pass and scored.

• Green was sacked nine times by a tough Denver pass rush

• The game was played in 29-degree weather with snow and ice on the field.

• The Bills double-teamed Lionel Taylor all day and the strategy worked.

QUOTES

• Buster Ramsey: "It was one of those days where it was up to the defense and the defense had its best game. The plan was to put interior pressure on Frank Tripucka by having a linebacker charge through. Our defense played a terrific game, but it was a badly played game from a spectator's standpoint. We didn't figure to run on this field, but had expected our passing attack to work better."

• Ralph Felton talking about Jim Crotty: "Having Jim Crotty has made us a whole unit again. We have our confidence back. He did a job on Taylor. He made him a bit leery the first time he ran a slant pattern, letting him know he was there."

• Art Baker: "Trying to cut around midfield, where they had spread sand was like playing at the beach. And other spots you'd just lose your footing and fall."

• Johnny Green: "There's no use in throwing when your receiver isn't open, so you just eat the ball."

• Billy Atkins: "It's a victory, that's about all you can say. But we played much better football in losing some of the games at home than we did in beating Dallas and Denver the last two weeks."

WEEK 11 GAMES

Hou 49, NY 13	Bos 20, Oak 17
SD 24, Dal 14	

Bills	0	10	0	13 - 23
Broncos	7	0	0	3 - 10

Attendance at Bears Stadium - 7,645

Den: Bukaty 43 run (Hill kick), 12:22
Buf: FG Atkins 39, 2:37
Buf: Dubenion 34 pass from Green (Atkins kick), 14:04
Den: FG Hill 13, 7:25
Buf: Richards 41 pass from Green (kick failed), 6:44
Buf: Barber 21 interception return (Atkins kick), 7:25

	BUF	DEN
First downs	13	11
Rushing yds	80	112
Passing yds	155	161
Punts-avg	9-42.0	7-31.9
Fumbles lost	0	3
Penalties-yds	7-55	3-28

BILLS LEADERS: Rushing - Baker 11-15, Bohling 10-13, Green 5-20, Carlton 9-22, Dubenion 1-10; **Passing** - Green 13-25-0 - 209, Reynolds 2-6-0 - 12; **Receiving** - Crockett 5-63, Dubenion 4-58, Rychlec 3-41, Richards 1-43, Bass 1-9, Bohling 1-7.

BRONCOS LEADERS: Rushing - Ames 9-52, Bukaty 8-60; **Passing** - Tripucka 11-25-4 - 69, Herring 3-16-2 - 102; **Receiving** - Prebola 4-46, Taylor 5-68, Frazier 3-49, Bukaty 1-5, Ames 1-3.

GAME 12 - Thursday, Nov. 23, 1961 - TITANS 21, BILLS 14

NOTES

• The Bills had a chance to tie or win in the final seconds. Aided by a personal foul penalty, M.C. Reynolds drove the Bills from their own 20 to the Titans 9, but then he threw three straight incompletions and on the fourth down, was sacked by Ed Cooke, the Titans' 10th sack of the day totaling 78 yards in losses. Reynolds replaced Johnny Green, who was mauled for seven of the sacks.

• The Bills took a 7-0 lead when Green hit Elbert Dubenion for a TD in the first quarter, but Jim Crotty's failed gamble at an interception resulted in Bob Renn's 67-yard TD.

• The Titans then went on a nine-play, 71-yard drive to the go-ahead TD, a two-yard run by Al Dorow. The key play was a 33-yard pass to Dick Christy which carried to the 2. Dorow scored on the next play.

• New York made it 21-7 in the third when Dick Felt picked off a Reynolds pass and went all the way. The Bills' second TD was set up when Titans guard Bob O'Neill caught a tipped pass and, thinking he was an ineligible receiver, purposely dropped the ball on the ground. Laverne Torczon recovered for the Bills at the New York 15 and four plays later, Reynolds scored from the 1.

• The Thanksgiving Day game attracted several hundred Buffalonians to the Polo Grounds.

• Buster Ramsey tried to procure a one-day pass for Richie Lucas to leave the Army camp because defensive back Jim Wagstaff couldn't play due to an injury suffered the day before the game. The Titans had linebacker Larry Grantham on a pass from his Army unit.

QUOTES

• Buster Ramsey: "I was disturbed by the effort we made, particularly on offense. Our defense did a fairly good job stopping their running game, but again, we beat ourselves with mistakes in key situations."

Bills	7	0	0	7 - 14
Titans	7	7	7	0 - 21

Attendance at the Polo Grounds - 12,023

Buf: Dubenion 8 pass from Green (Atkins kick), 9:48
NY: Renn 67 pass from Dorow (Guesman kick), 14:40
NY: Dorow 2 run (Guesman kick), 13:13
NY: Felt 55 interception return (Guesman kick), 14:25
Buf: Reynolds 1 run (Atkins kick), 7:30

	BUF	NY
First downs	22	12
Rushing yds	63	58
Passing yds	214	157
Punts-avg	6-42.3	7-37.7
Fumbles lost	1	2
Penalties-yds	2-10	5-40

BILLS LEADERS: Rushing - Baker 10-39, Carlton 5-12, Bohling 3-13, Dubenion 1- (-14), Green 2-9, Reynolds 2-4; **Passing** - Green 10-19-1 - 180, Reynolds 12-27-1 - 112; **Receiving** - Bass 5-57, Dubenion 5-53, Bohling 1-47, Rychlec 4-40, Richards 3-29, Baker 2-37, Carlton 2-29.

TITANS LEADERS: Rushing - Dorow 4-25, Mathis 11-20, Christy 7-12, West 1-1; **Passing** - Dorow 13-28-0 - 223; **Receiving** - Christy 3-60, Renn 4-117, Mathis 3-40, Powell 2-19, O'Neill 1- (-13).

WEEK 12 GAMES

Dal 43, Oak 11	Hou 45, Den 14

STANDINGS: TWELFTH WEEK

EAST	W	L	T	WEST	W	L	T
Houston	7	3	1	San Diego	11	0	0
Boston	6	4	1	Dallas	4	7	0
New York	6	5	0	Denver	3	9	0
Buffalo	5	7	0	Oakland	2	9	0

| Bills | 6 6 7 7 - 26 |
| Raiders | 0 7 7 7 - 21 |

Attendance at Candlestick Park - 8,011

Buf: Bohling 21 pass from Green (kick failed), 5:23
Oak: Miller 15 pass from Papac (Fleming kick), 12:19
Buf: Baker 1 run (run failed), 14:28
Buf: Carlton 3 run (Atkins kick), 7:38
Oak: Daniels 39 run (Fleming kick), 9:11
Buf: Baker 10 run (Atkins kick), 5:28
Oak: Miller 16 pass from Flores (Fleming kick), 6:31

	BUF	OAK
First downs	22	20
Rushing yds	120	97
Passing yds	149	220
Punts-avg	6-42.5	4-25.8
Fumbles lost	0	1
Penalties-yds	6-30	6-32

BILLS LEADERS: Rushing - Baker 21-97, Reynolds 4-22, Carlton 4- (-1), Bohling 1-2; **Passing** - Reynolds 15-27-1 - 146, Green 1-6-0 - 21, Carlton 0-1-0 - 0; **Receiving** - Bass 12-110, Bohling 1-21, Richards 1-20, Rychlec 1-15, Dubenion 1-1.

RAIDERS LEADERS: Rushing - Daniels 6-43, Miller 7-36, Fleming 7-19, Flores 2- (-1); **Passing** - Flores 19-36-1 - 253, Papac 1-1-0 - 15; **Receiving** - Miller 7-99, Coolbaugh 5-73, Burch 4-32, Asad 3-61, Daniels 1-3.

NOTES
• The Bills improved to 4-2 on the road, winning in Candlestick Park's mud.
• The field had been lined with lime and the moisture from the turf caused it to burn players.
• Ralph Wilson missed his first game as Bills owner when his flight connections failed to get him to San Francisco until 5 p.m.
• Glenn Bass, who was bothered by the flu, caught a Bills record 12 passes and also set a new team mark of 48 receptions for the year. Fellow rookie Art Baker had his best day with 97 yards and two TDs.
• With 2:30 left, Oakland had a first down at Buffalo's 44, but Laverne Torczon sacked Tom Flores on back-to-back plays for 21 yards in losses, securing the victory.
• Johnny Green started despite a back injury, but was replaced by M.C. Reynolds in the second quarter.
• Green's only completion was a 21-yard TD pass to Dewey Bohling. Mack Yoho had intercepted a Tom Flores pass on the previous play to set up the Bills.
• Reynolds completed five passes to Bass worth 56 yards on the drive that resulted in Baker's TD run late in the first half that gave the Bills a 12-7 halftime lead. Oakland had just taken a 7-6 lead on Nick Papac's 15-yard TD pass to Alan Miller 2:09 earlier.
• The Bills' third TD came after a six-yard punt by Gerald Burch gave the Bills possession at the Raiders 47. Baker carried three times for 34 yards before making the key block to allow Wray Carlton to score.
• After a 26-yard Flores-to-Miller pass, Lemen Daniels swept 39 yards for a TD that made it 19-14, but the Bills answered by driving to Baker's 10-yard TD run.
• The Raiders pulled to within 26-21 when Miller made a circus catch in the end zone.

QUOTES
• Buster Ramsey: "Baker really blossomed as a runner today. It was the first time we've been able to run out the clock in the last few minutes." (On the play of Glenn Bass): "A study of Oakland's films showed that their right cornerback, Bob Garner, was the most vulnerable. The consistency of our passing game and the running of Art Baker enabled us to control the ball. We lost to New York because a number of players lagged a bit at times. Against Oakland the boys never let up, enabling them to overcome their mechanical mistakes."

WEEK 13 GAMES	
Hou 33, SD 13	NY 28, Dal 7
Bos 28, Den 24	

| Bills | 10 0 0 0 - 10 |
| Chargers | 0 14 14 0 - 28 |

Attendance at Balboa Stadium - 24,486

Buf: FG Shockley 20, 4:37
Buf: McDonald 24 fumble return (Atkins kick), 10:20
SD: Lincoln 57 punt return (Blair kick), :18
SD: Hudson 4 interception return (Blair kick), 13:10
SD: Lowe 4 run (Blair kick), 8:52
SD: Kocourek 76 pass from Kemp (Blair kick), 12:52

	BUF	SD
First downs	18	7
Rushing yds	99	47
Passing yds	180	190
Punts-avg	6-46.8	6-47.8
Fumbles lost	1	2
Penalties-yds	2-25	7-54

BILLS LEADERS: Rushing - Baker 31-117, Carlton 3-9, Bohling 2-6, Green 1- (-15), Rychlec 1- (-18); **Passing** - Green 11-25-0 - 152, Reynolds 2-9-3 - 61; **Receiving** - Bass 2-21, Rychlec 3-45, Dubenion 3-69, Bohling 3-37, Crockett 1-21, Carlton 1-20.

CHARGERS LEADERS: Rushing - Lowe 14-57, Kemp 4-2, Enis 1- (-12); **Passing** - Kemp 11-21-2 - 213, Enis 0-4-0 - 0; **Receiving** - Kocourek 3-175, Norton 3-19, Lowe 2-17, Scarpitto 1-5, Flowers 2- (-3).

WEEK 14 GAMES	
Hou 48, NY 21	Bos 35, Oak 21
Dal 49, Den 21.	

NOTES
• The Bills took a stunning 10-0 first-quarter lead, keyed by Don McDonald's 24-yard TD return of a Paul Lowe fumble.
• But the Chargers fought back despite playing terribly on offense. Keith Lincoln returned a punt for a TD and Bill Hudson's interception return for a TD after Earl Faison had tipped M.C. Reynolds' pass gave them a 14-10 halftime lead. San Diego had just one first down in the first half.
• The Bills harrassed Jack Kemp all day, but he made just enough big plays, including a 76-yard TD pass to Dave Kocourek in the fourth period.
• The Bills could have made the game closer in the fourth, but failed on four straight plays from inside the 3-yard-line.
• Kicker Bill Shockley, who was signed in late November from the Titans, made his debut with the Bills and made a field goal in the first quarter.

QUOTES
• Buster Ramsey on injuries: "Johnny Green is calling his best game and we're controlling the ball. The next thing you know, he has a fractured finger. Wray Carlton, our most effective runner on screens and quick pitches gets clothes-lined and he's knocked out of the game on the final play of the first quarter. Glenn Bass gets clothes-lined in the first quarter and he's ineffective the rest of the day. I always thought clothes-lining was illegal, but there were no penalty calls." (On the season): "The season is over, there isn't much that can be done about what has happened except to hope we can profit from our errors and maybe figure that next year we'll be lucky enough to keep a healthy team on the field. We ended the season the same way we started - trying to put 11 healthy men on the field."
• Ralph Wilson: "We just haven't had the outstanding running or receiving in situations where we get up close, so the opposition has been able to stack up and stop us."

WEEK 15 GAMES	
Hou 47, Oak 16	Bos 41, SD 0
Dal 35, NY 24	
Buffalo and Denver had a bye week	

STANDINGS: FOURTEENTH WEEK

EAST	W	L	T	WEST	W	L	T
Houston	10	3	1	San Diego	12	2	0
Boston	9	4	1	Dallas	6	8	0
New York	7	7	0	Denver	3	11	0
Buffalo	6	8	0	Oakland	2	12	0

At A Glance
1962

Jan. 4 – Buster Ramsey was fired as head coach. "This came as a shock to me, so I haven't made any plans," Ramsey said. "I still think I can do the job as head coach under the right setup. I've felt that as far as nucleus, we have been behind most of the other teams. But we got six of the best young players available in the draft last year and then came up with two more good young ones in Tom Day and Glenn Bass. But even if the club comes up with six more good players from this year's draft, the team isn't going to reach it's potential until late next season or possibly in 1963."

Jan. 8 – Oakland's Wayne Valley was named league president; Commissioner Joe Foss was given a new five-year contract.

Jan. 18 – Lou Saban was hired as head coach and signed a one-year contract worth about $20,000. Patrick McGroder also was promoted to vice-president. "There are no big mysteries to coaching pro football," Saban said. "It's basically a game of blocking and tackling and working towards the goal of securing the best available talent together to get the job done. I don't feel that I have to prove myself as a coach. What happened in Boston is behind. It was the best I could do under the circumstances and I make no apology for our record or anything else."

Jan. 22 – Assistant coaches Red Miller, Jerry Smith, Joe Collier and John Mazur were hired.

Jan. 29 – The Bills' attempts to acquire Dallas Texans halfback Johnny Robinson hit a snag when it was revealed that Robinson's contract didn't contain an option clause for 1962.

Jan. 31 – The 17th-round draft choice, defensive end Tom Sestak, was signed. "My advisers consider the Bills one of the outstanding organizations in pro football and I feel I will have a good future with the Bills and in the AFL," Sestak said.

Feb. 7 – Despite all the quarterback problems the Bills had endured in their first two years, Lou Saban said he was confident Johnny Green, Warren Rabb or M.C. Reynolds could handle the position. "I'm convinced we're pretty fortified at the quarterback position," Saban said.

Feb. 12 – Ex-Bills head coach Buster Ramsey rejoined Buddy Parker's staff with the NFL's Pittsburgh Steelers. Ramsey worked under Parker with the Lions before coming to Buffalo.

March 6 – Ralph Wilson testified in the AFL's $10 million anti-trust suit against the NFL that his team was hurt when the NFL expanded into Minneapolis, forcing the AFL out of the area and into Oakland instead in 1960. Wilson said revenues were less in Oakland.

March 22 – Tight end Ernie Warlick left the Canadian Football League and joined the Bills.

March 30 – General Manager Dick Gallagher signed a contract extension through 1965.

May 21 – The AFL lost its anti-trust suit against the NFL when a federal judge in Baltimore ruled that the NFL did not have a monopoly power to

Lou Saban replaced Buster Ramsey to start the 1962 season. One of his prime running game weapons was fullback Wray Carlton.

restrict competition.

July 5 – Lou Saban made his first major trade as Bills coach, shipping quarterback M.C. Reynolds and defensive tackle Chuck McMurtry to Oakland for fullback Wayne Crow.

July 14 – Training camp opened in East Aurora with 96 players including 60 rookies. On the first day, Saban cut 11 of the rookies.

July 23 – Veterans reported to training camp, but Lou Saban wasn't talking about them. He was wowed by rookie defensive tackle Tom Sestak. "I like his speed and the way he moves," Saban said. "You never know he's out there. He knows his job and he just keeps working."

July 28 – At Meet the Bills Night at War Memorial Stadium, the Blue team won the intrasquad scrimmage, 14-0, with Warren Rabb making a strong bid for the quarterback position.

Aug. 4 – Cookie Gilchrist left the Toronto Argonauts of the CFL to sign with Buffalo. "I feel like a brand new person," Gilchrist said. "I'm a member of the Bills now, and I'll abide by all the rules and regulations." While Gilchrist was joining the fold, the Bills announced that right guard Ken Rice would be out at least 10 weeks with a knee injury suffered during a scrimmage.

Aug. 6 – With Ken Rice sidelined, Lou Saban shifted defensive end Tom Day to offensive right guard. "I played offensive guard and some offensive tackle in my rookie year with the St. Louis Cardinals," Day said, obviously not upset about the position switch. "To tell you the truth, I prefer offense."

Aug. 12 – The Bills beat the Titans in the preseason opener in New Haven, Connecticut, 20-10, as Wayne Crow debuted with 43 yards on seven carries.

Aug. 15 – Richie Lucas, the Bills' first draft choice in 1960, became a Denver Bronco in the equalization draft. "I'll always have a warm spot in my heart for Buffalo," Lucas said. The Bills lost to Boston, 12-7, at War Memorial in the home preseason opener, before a record crowd of 22,112.

Aug. 16 – The Bills traded Billy Atkins and Johnny Green to New York for QB Al Dorow. "We felt it was necessary to strengthen ourselves at quarterback," said Lou Saban.

Aug. 23 – The Bills traveled to Mobile, Ala. and defeated Houston, 21-14, as Warren Rabb threw two TD passes to Glenn Bass.

Sept. 1 – The Bills closed a successful 3-1 pre-

season with a 7-6 victory over Boston as Al Dorow completed 17 of 28 passes for 136 yards and appeared to claim the starting job.

Sept. 9 – The Bills lost the season opener at home to the Oilers, 28-23, in front of a record War Memorial Stadium gathering of 31,236, despite Art Baker's 100-yard kickoff return for a TD. Al Dorow made a terrible debut, completing four of 17 passes with three interceptions.

Sept. 15 – Denver escaped with a 23-20 victory with 13 fourth-quarter points. The Bills used a still camera to show the opponent formations during a game for the first time.

Sept. 22 – The Bills' record fell to 0-3 as the Titans beat the Bills at War Memorial, 17-6, bringing a shower of beer cans and boos.

Sept. 25 – Jack Kemp became a member of the Bills when the team claimed him on waivers from San Diego. Chargers' coach Sid Gillman waived Kemp with the intent of recalling him, but fouled up paperwork and three teams put in a claim. Kemp was awarded to the Bills due to their last-place standing. Kemp was unable to play right away, though, because of a broken finger. "Buffalo was within its rights," Gillman conced-

ed. "The Bills are getting a fine boy and a real good quarterback."

Sept. 30 – Dallas handed the Bills their fourth straight home loss, 41-21, as Len Dawson threw for 258 yards and three TDs.

Oct. 1 – After the Dallas game, five players were sent packing. Laverne Torczon, a team captain in 1960 and '61 and all-league both years, was traded to New York for an 11th-round draft choice, while four other players, most notably quarterback Al Dorow, were waived.

Oct. 7 – The Bills lost a controversial 17-14 decision in Houston as the officials were blamed for not giving a two-minute warning which cost the Bills possession and ultimately the game.

Oct. 11 – AFL commissioner Joe Foss admitted the officials blew it in the Oilers game, but nothing could be done.

Oct. 13 – The Bills crushed the Chargers, 35-10, for their first victory under Lou Saban as they rushed for a team-record 303 yards and gained a team-high 439 yards.

Oct. 20 – The Bills made it two wins in a row as the winless Raiders fell, 14-6. The Raiders had fired coach Eddie Erdelatz in the week prior to

the game and replaced him with Red Conkright, a former assistant with the Bills during their All-America Conference days in late 40s.

Oct. 27 – The Bills scored 22 fourth-quarter points to beat Denver, 45-38. Warren Rabb averaged 29 yards on his nine completions.

Oct. 29 – Ralph Wilson, who had signed Lou Saban to a one-year contract, admitted that he knew Saban would be his coach for more than 1962 after the Bills had lost their fifth game in a row at Houston. "I want Lou to stay on as coach until he builds us a championship team," Wilson said. "After that, it will be up to him."

Nov. 3 – The Patriots rallied for a 28-28 tie with 14 fourth-quarter points in front of 33,247 at War Memorial Stadium.

Nov. 4 – Ralph Wilson said he would need a stadium with 50,000 seats in a couple years because the AFL had grown to the point where rivalries had been established.

Nov. 11 – The Bills scored 37 first-half points and ripped the Chargers, 40-20, in San Diego. Afterward, Lou Saban claimed the Bills were the best team in the AFL.

Nov. 18 – The Bills completed a successful West coast swing, beating the winless Raiders, 10-6, as Jack Kemp made his Bills debut in the second half and directed the only touchdown drive of the game.

Nov. 23 – The Patriots ended the Bills six-game unbeaten streak in Jack Kemp's debut as the Bills starting quarterback with a 21-10 victory in Boston

Dec. 2 – A record War Memorial Stadium crowd of 35,261 saw the Bills defeat the eventual champion Dallas Texans, 23-14, in their most impressive performance of the season. Jack Kemp passed for 248 yards and two TDs.

Dec. 8 – The Bills completed their first winning season in history by beating the Titans, 20-3, as Cookie Gilchrist became the first AFL back to gain 1,000 yards.

Dec. 14 — The signing of Notre Dame QB Daryle Lamonica was announced as the Bills outbid the NFL's Green Bay Packers.

Dec. 18 – The Associated Press named Gilchrist the AFL player of the year while guard Billy Shaw and tackle Howard Olson made the first team.

Dec. 19 – The Bills signed all-America defensive back George Saimes.

Dec. 20 – Pro Football Illustrated named Tom Sestak its defensive rookie of the year and also named Sestak, Carl Charon, Booker Edgerson and Mike Stratton to its AFL all-rookie team.

Dec. 23 – Dallas edged Houston for the AFL Championship, 20-17, in the second overtime in what was, at the time, the longest game in pro football history; Each Dallas player received $2,261.80 for winning.

Dec. 26 – The AFL announced a 20.3 percent attendance increase for 1962 over 1961. The Bills finished second to Houston with a 27,922 average.

Jan. 13, 1963 – The West won its second straight AFL All-Star Game, 21-14, in San Diego. Jack Kemp was one-for-seven and fumbled three times; Archie Matsos led both teams with 13 tackles.

BY THE NUMBERS - 1962

TEAM STATISTICS	BILLS	OPP
First downs	238	229
Rushing	119	89
Passing	96	129
Penalty	23	11
Total yards	4,464	4,429
Avg. game	318.9	316.4
Plays	875	845
Avg. play	5.1	5.2
Net rushing yds	2,480	1,687
Avg. game	177.1	120.5
Avg. play	4.9	4.5
Net passing yds	1,984	2,742
Comp/att	150/351	215/440
Interceptions	26	36
Percentage	42.7	48.9
Sacks/lost	23-197	32-254
Punts/avg	76-38.8	70-38.1
Fumbles/lost	27-12	26-14
Penalties/yds	74-797	80-786
Touchdowns	41	35
Extra points	34-40	30-33
Field goals	9-23	10-20
Two-point conv.	1-1	1-2
Safeties	0	0
Kick ret./avg	52-22.6	56-21.0
Punt ret./avg	28-7.2	33-6.0

RUSHING	ATT	YDS	AVG	TD
Gilchrist	214	1096	5.1	13
Crow	110	589	5.4	1
Carlton	94	530	5.6	2
Rabb	37	77	2.1	3
Dorow	15	57	3.8	0
Kemp	12	56	4.7	1
Dubenion	7	40	5.7	0
Jones	4	17	4.3	0
Baker	2	9	4.5	0
Wheeler	3	7	2.3	0
Henley	3	2	0.7	0
TOTALS	**501**	**2480**	**5.0**	**20**

PASSING	COMP	ATT	INT	YDS	TD	COMP%
Rabb	67	177	14	1196	10	37.9
Kemp	51	94	4	636	3	54.3
Dorow	30	75	7	333	2	40.0
Crow	2	4	1	16	0	50.0
Taseff	0	1	0	0	0	.000
TOTALS	**150**	**351**	**26**	**2181**	**15**	**42.7**

KICKING	FG/ATT	PAT/ATT	PTS
Gilchrist	8-20	14-16	38
Yoho	1-3	20-24	23
TOTALS	**9-23**	**34-40**	**61**

PUNTING	NO	AVG
Crow	76	38.8

RECEIVING	CAT	YDS	AVG	TD
Warlick	35	482	13.8	2
Dubenion	33	571	17.3	5
Bass	32	555	17.3	4
Gilchrist	24	319	13.3	2
Crow	8	80	10.0	1
Carlton	7	54	7.7	0
Rychlec	6	66	11.0	1
Baker	3	12	4.0	0
Tracey	1	28	28.0	0
Crockett	1	14	14.0	0
TOTALS	**150**	**2181**	**14.5**	**15**

LEADERS

Punt returns:
West 14-112 yards, 8.0 avg, 0 TD
Rychlec 1-24, 24.0, 0 TD

Interceptions:
Charon 7-131, 18.7, 0 TD
Edgerson 6-111, 18.5, 0 TD
Stratton 6-99, 16.5, 0 TD
Matuszak 6-46, 7.7, 0 TD

Non-kick scoring:
Gilchrist 15 TDs, 90 pts
Bass 4 TDs, 24 pts

Kick returns:
Jones 14-287, 20.5, 0 TD
Dubenion 7-231, 33.0, 1 TD
Baker 7-220, 31.4, 1 TD

Former Canadian Football League star (right) Ernie Warlick, came to Buffalo in 1962 and in his first year led the team with 35 receptions.

Jack Kemp's arrival (opposite page) in 1962 ended the Bills search for a competent quarterback. Kemp was one of the keys to Buffalo's reversal of fortune.

Oilers	**7 14 7 0 - 28**	
Bills	**3 0 6 14 - 23**	

Attendance at War Memorial Stadium - 31,236

Hou: Tolar 19 run (Blanda kick), 9:29
Buf: FG Gilchrist 40, 13:31
Hou: Hennigan 9 pass from Blanda (Blanda kick), 11:17
Hou: Cannon 1 run (Blanda kick), 13:02
Hou: Hennigan 40 pass from Cannon (Blanda kick), 3:16
Buf: Baker 100 kickoff return (kick failed), 3:37
Buf: Dubenion 4 pass from Rabb (Yoho kick), 2:29
Buf: Rabb 1 run (Yoho kick), 9:35

	BUF	HOU
First downs	15	26
Rushing yds	134	204
Passing yds	86	216
Punts-avg	4-38.0	0-0
Fumbles-lost	3-2	1-0
Penalties-yds	3-16	5-68

BILLS LEADERS: Rushing - Carlton 6-84, Gilchrist 7-22, Dubenion 1-12, Rabb 4-7, Dorow 2-6, Crow 6-3; **Passing** - Dorow 4-17-3 - 44, Rabb 6-8-0 - 85, Crow 0-1-0 - 0; **Receiving** - Bass 4-85, Dubenion 2-20, Warlick 1-15, Crow 1-7, Gilchrist 1-2, Baker 1-0.

OILERS LEADERS: Rushing - Tolar 17-109, Cannon 20-80, Smith 4-15; **Passing** - Blanda 15-30-6 - 188, Cannon 1-1-0 - 40; **Receiving** - Hennigan 10-145, Frazier 3-46, McLeod 1-17, Cannon 1-11, Tolar 1-9.

NOTES
• A crowd of 31,236 was the largest to watch a Bills game, home or away.
• Al Dorow, supposedly the answer at QB after he was acquired in a trade with New York for popular Billy Atkins and QB Johnny Green, had a terrible debut.
• Marv Matuszak, Carl Taseff and Booker Edgerson each had two picks of George Blanda.
• On their second possession, the Oilers drove 65 yards in eight plays to Charley Tolar's TD, but the Bills answered with a Cookie Gilchrist field goal on the ensuing series.
• One play after Matuszak intercepted Blanda and returned it to the Oilers 13, Wray Carlton lost a fumble at the 9 with Doug Cline recovering. The Oilers then drove 91 yards in 10 plays to Blanda's TD pass to Charlie Hennigan. Then, two plays after the kickoff, Mark Johnston intercepted Dorow at the Bills 15 and Billy Cannon scored five plays later for a 21-3 lead.
• After Cannon's TD pass on the option play to Hennigan in the third, Art Baker returned the ensuing kickoff for a TD. Later in the third, Matuszak's second interception started the Bills on a 14-play, 70-yard drive with Warren Rabb at QB. Rabb was five-of-six for 37 yards including a TD pass to Elbert Dubenion on fourth down.
• Taseff's interception in the fourth gave the Bills the ball at their 38. Bobby Jancik was called for an interference penalty in the end zone, setting up Rabb's TD

sneak and Mack Yoho's PAT made it 28-23, but the Oilers ran out the remaining 5:25.

QUOTES
• Lou Saban: "It seems like someone was breaking down on each play, just enough to keep us from showing a cohesive attack. We donated a couple of touchdowns in the first half and you can't be too generous against a team like Houston. They are still the champs. If we had died in the second half when we were down 28-3, then I would have died, too. But the boys stayed right in there until the end and made it uncomfortable for Houston until the final gun. A guy like Blanda, when he was as hot as he was today, will make any player or team look bad. And it seems he can read Hennigan's mind."
• Al Dorow: "I played the worst game I've played in 10 years. I saw the receivers open, but I couldn't hit them. I never threw so poorly. I can't explain what happened. And this stadium is a place where I've always had pretty good games."
• Cookie Gilchrist: "There's nothing to worry about. This is a real good club and we'll get going."

WEEK 1 GAMES	
NY 28, Oak 17	Den 30, SD 21
Dal 42, Bos 28	

Broncos	**3 0 7 13 - 23**	
Bills	**6 14 0 0 - 20**	

Attendance at War Memorial Stadium - 30,557

Buf: Gilchrist 42 run (kick failed), 2:10
Den: FG Mingo 29, 9:35
Buf: Warlick 12 pass from Dorow (Yoho kick), 5:40
Buf: Gilchrist 18 pass from Dorow (Yoho kick), 13:21
Den: Scarpitto 10 pass from Tripucka (Mingo kick), 7:34
Den: FG Mingo 37, :27
Den: Frazier 96 pass from Tripucka (Mingo kick), 7:04
Den: FG Mingo 10, 14:29

	BUF	DEN
First downs	18	22
Rushing yds	211	27
Passing yds	174	428
Punts-avg	6-36.5	4-41.8
Fumbles-lost	2-0	1-1
Penalties-yds	8-76	9-93

BILLS LEADERS: Rushing - Carlton 7-29, Gilchrist 15-131, Dorow 9-40, Baker 2-9, Crow 2-5, Dubenion 1- (-3); **Passing** - Dorow 16-34-2 - 193; **Receiving** - Bass 3-32, Dubenion 3-54, Warlick 3-50, Gilchrist 4-48, Baker 2-12, Carlton 1- (-3).

BRONCOS LEADERS: Rushing - Frazier 4-10, Mingo 4-11, Stinnette 2-6; **Passing** - Tripucka 29-56-3 - 447; **Receiving** - Taylor 9-133, Frazier 4-125, Prebola 2-42, Stinnette 4-31, Scarpitto 6-90, Dickinson 2-20, Mingo 2-6.

NOTES
• Gene Mingo's field goal with 31 seconds left won it as the Broncos rallied from a 20-3 deficit.
• Frank Tripucka produced the third 400-yard passing game in AFL history, two coming against the Bills.
• Cookie Gilchrist set a team rushing record with 131 yards, but a pulled hamstring hampered his kicking and he missed two field goal attempts in the fourth quarter.
• Gilchrist returned the opening kickoff 34 yards, then on the third play, ran 42 yards for a TD, but Mack Yoho missed the PAT. A Carl Charon interception was wasted when Al Dorow was stopped on fourth-and-one.
• The Bills drove 48 yards in six plays to Dorow's TD pass to Ernie Warlick for a 13-3 lead. Then, after a Carl Taseff interception, Dorow hit Elbert Dubenion for 34 yards and capped the drive with an 18-yard TD pass to Gilchrist for the 20-3 halftime lead.
• Tripucka's 45-yard pass to Lionel Taylor set up a TD pass to Bob Scarpitto early in the third.
• Mingo's second field goal capped a 53-yard drive early in the fourth. Denver tied the score when, on third-and-36 from the 4, Tripucka hit Al Frazier at the 30 and he ran the final 70 yards to complete a 96-yard TD, the longest offensive scoring play in AFL history.
• Denver's drive to Mingo's winning field goal cov-

ered 68 yards and almost came to an end, but Sid Youngelman dropped an interception. The Broncos got the ball after Gilchrist missed a 48-yard field goal.

QUOTES
• Lou Saban: "I can't really complain. They paid the price and gave us honest effort all the way. What more can you ask of a team? I have not lost faith in this team. I still feel we can win and give a good accounting of ourselves before the AFL season is over. With one or two exceptions, the club that lost a 20-3 lead is the one I'm going with the rest of the season. I don't think anyone can debate that we were an improved club over what we were against Houston. I think Cookie Gilchrist showed he's going to be as tough a runner as there is in the league. On the play that tied the score at 20-20, Al Frazier made a great individual effort. We had the play properly defensed, but once a boy with Frazier's speed has some room to maneuver, it's good-bye. Nobody left War Memorial Stadium more downcast than me, but I still feel we can win."
• Denver coach Jack Faulkner on Gilchrist: "Our players said they've never tried to tackle anything like Cookie. The nicest thing I saw all night when Buffalo had the ball was Gilchrist going out of the game."
• Ralph Wilson: "I thought our boys played a whale of a game, but that one play by Tripucka for the long touchdown was one of the breaks of pro football."

WEEK 2 GAMES	
SD 40, NY 14	Bos 34, Hou 21

STANDINGS: SECOND WEEK

EAST	W	L	T	WEST	W	L	T
New York	1	1	0	Denver	2	0	0
Houston	1	1	0	Dallas	1	0	0
Boston	1	1	0	San Diego	1	1	0
Buffalo	0	2	0	Oakland	0	1	0

GAME 3 - Saturday, Sept. 22, 1962 - TITANS 17, BILLS 6

NOTES

• The Bills were pitiful and the rain-soaked crowd at War Memorial let them know as they booed and rained beer cans on the field.
• The Bills' front office distributed 5,000 rabbit's feet for good luck, but the ploy obviously failed.
• In 18 appearances in War Memorial Stadium, counting preseason, the Bills had lost 13.
• The Bills possessed the ball for the first 8:15 of the game but failed to score. Wayne Crow scored on an 11-yard run, but the play was nullified due to a penalty and Al Dorow then was intercepted by ex-Bill Billy Atkins in the end zone.
• Dick Christy's 41-yard run set up his two-yard TD run in the first.
• The Bills drove 83 yards in 10 plays to Elbert Dubenion's TD catch. Dorow was injured during a second-quarter drive and Warren Rabb took over and completed four straight passes for 53 yards.
• The Titans answered with an eight-play, 73-yard drive to Lee Grosscup's TD pass to Thurlow Cooper. Grosscup completed five of seven passes for 66 yards including a 30-yarder to Art Powell to the Bills 3.
• In the third quarter, Crow threw an interception in the end zone on a halfback option and later, Cookie Gilchrist lost a fumble at the New York 15.
• Gilchrist entered the game as the AFL's leading rusher, but the Titans stuffed him.

QUOTES

• Lou Saban: "It had to be my fault. But what am I doing wrong? I know we're a better team than New York and we were well prepared. We expect that mistakes will be made, this is a young team and is bound to pull a rock once in a while. But the fumbles, the interceptions and dropped passes really hurt. This club has reached a point where everyone is so tense that it seems nothing will ever go right. We moved the ball well in the first half and Warren Rabb got us our only touchdown, but we needed Al Dorow's experience in there. You can move the ball only so much on the ground, then you wear the players out and when that happens you make mistakes. It's going to cost a few players fines. There is no excuse for some of the things they did, missing blocks, missing signals, sloppy execution. I take responsibility for losing, but I can't be responsible for fumbles and interceptions and blown assignments."

WEEK 3 GAMES	
Hou 42, SD 17	Dal 26, Oak 16
Bos 41, Den 16	

Titans	7 7 3 0 - 17
Bills	0 6 0 0 - 6

Attendance at War Memorial Stadium - 24,024

NY: Christy 2 run (Shockley kick), 12:51
Buf: Dubenion 24 pass from Rabb (kick failed), 11:35
NY: Cooper 6 pass from Grosscup (Shockley kick), 13:55
NY: FG Shockley 35, 4:08

	BUF	NY
First downs	16	12
Rushing yds	172	84
Passing yds	155	157
Punts-avg	5-42.0	8-39.3
Fumbles-lost	5-3	2-1
Penalties-yds	3-33	10-77

BILLS LEADERS: Rushing - Crow 8-95, Carlton 9-54, Gilchrist 8-25, Dorow 2- (-2); **Passing** - Dorow 6-11-1 - 69, Rabb 8-23-2 - 107, Crow 0-1-1 - 0; **Receiving** - Bass 1-15, Dubenion 2-28, Warlick 6-89, Gilchrist 3-36, Carlton 2-8.

TITANS LEADERS: Rushing - Christy 10-47, Flowers 5-13, Grosscup 1-12, Johnson 3-10, West 5-2; **Passing** - Grosscup 17-26-1 - 169, Christy 0-1-0 - 0; **Receiving** - Richards 5-47, Powell 5-65, Cooper 2-16, Flowers 2-12, Christy 1-15, Maynard 1-13, West 1-1.

GAME 4 - Sunday, Sept. 30, 1962 - TEXANS 41, BILLS 21

NOTES

• Dallas came up four yards short of the AFL rushing record by gaining 320 yards in crushing the Bills.
• Sportswriter, Larry Felser, wrote "Compared to the Bills, the Three Stooges look organized."
• John Tracey played tight end on offense and linebacker on defense for the Bills.
• Abner Haynes went 71 yards for a TD on Dallas' first offensive play of the game. Haynes then capped a 91-yard drive with a 13-yard run for a 14-0 first-quarter lead. Haynes' 164 rushing yards were a Dallas record.
• In the second, Wayne Crow's punt pinned the Texans at the 3 and Mike Stratton then recovered a Len Dawson fumble. However, Warren Rabb was intercepted in the end zone by Dave Grayson, killing the threat.
• Dallas drove 62 yards in seven plays on its first series of the third to Chris Burford's TD reception.
• Laverne Torczon blocked an Eddie Wilson punt and Carl Charon recovered for a TD midway through the third to get the Bills to within 20-7. But Bobby Hunt's interception of Al Dorow and return to the Bills 23 set up Frank Jackson's TD run. After the Bills went three-and-out, Dawson scrambled out of the pocket and hit Jackson with a 62-yard TD for a 34-7 lead.
• The Bills then put together a 17-play, 74-yard drive with Rabb at QB, Gilchrist capping it with a TD run.
• Marv Matuszak then intercepted Dawson, the first against him in three games, and on the next play, Rabb hit Glenn Bass for a TD.
• The Texans then drove 77 yards in 11 plays to the final score, Dawson's TD pass to Tommy Brooker.

QUOTES

• Ralph Wilson: "You get to a point and you get philosophical. We know it now. We just don't have it. Why kid ourselves? We worked hard and improved, but as we improved, other teams did, too.

They still have that edge on us. We're going all the way with Lou Saban and the present staff. He's doing the best he can with what we've got. So are the players. Those pre-season game victories gave us false confidence. The players want to win for both themselves and for Lou, but they just can't seem to come through."
• Lou Saban: "We've just got to get better personnel if we're going to exist in this league. We feel we owe it to our fans not to stand still and accept defeat without trying to improve. But rebuilding takes time. More importantly, it takes patience. I hope Kemp's finger gets better, I'd like to get him some work in the Houston game."
• Texans coach Hank Stram: "That Dawson is making a great coach out of me. He's making the big plays himself and bringing them out in other players, too."

Bills	0 0 7 14 - 21
Texans	14 0 20 7 - 41

Attendance at the Cotton Bowl - 25,500

Dal: Haynes 71 run (Pennington kick), 9:19
Dal: Haynes 13 run (Pennington kick), 9:41
Dal: Burford 30 pass from Dawson (kick failed), 5:08
Buf: Charon 3 run with blocked punt (Yoho kick), 6:34
Dal: Jackson 10 run (Pennington kick), 10:23
Dal: Jackson 52 pass from Dawson (Pennington kick), 13:18
Buf: Gilchrist 6 run (Yoho kick), 3:27
Buf: Bass 31 pass from Rabb (Yoho kick), 5:12
Dal: Brooker 11 pass from Dawson (Pennington kick), 12:09

	BUF	DAL
First downs	14	24
Rushing yds	77	320
Passing yds	158	231
Punts-avg	8-43.4	4-22.0
Fumbles-lost	1-0	4-1
Penalties-yds	2-30	8-65

BILLS LEADERS: Rushing - Gilchrist 8-30, Rabb 4-24, Dorow 2-13, Carlton 3-6, Crow 5-5, Henley 3-2, Dubenion 1- (-3); **Passing** - Rabb 10-26-2 - 131, Dorow 4-13-1 - 27; **Receiving** - Bass 4-48, Dubenion 3-24, Warlick 3-21, Carlton 3-37, Tracey 1-28.

TEXANS LEADERS: Rushing - Haynes 16-164, Jackson 11-46, Dawson 5-59, Spikes 9-30, McClinton 2-12, Saxton 1-9; **Passing** - Dawson 12-19-1 - 258; **Receiving** - Jackson 2-67, Spikes 3-58, Haynes 3-27, Miller 1-39, Burford 1-30, Arbanas 1-26, Brooker 1-11.

WEEK 4 GAMES	
Den 32, NY 10	SD 42, Oak 33

STANDINGS: FOURTH WEEK

EAST	W	L	T	WEST	W	L	T
Boston	2	1	0	Dallas	3	0	0
Houston	2	1	0	Denver	3	1	0
New York	2	2	0	San Diego	2	2	0
Buffalo	0	4	0	Oakland	0	3	0

Bills	7	0	7	0 - 14
Oilers	3	0	0	14 - 17

Attendance at Jeppesen Stadium - 26,350

Hou: FG Blanda 16, 3:54
Buf: Charon 40 interception return (Yoho kick), 6:48
Buf: Gilchrist 1 run (Yoho kick), 8:16
Hou: Frazier 73 pass from Blanda (Blanda kick), 1:49
Hou: Groman 3 pass from Blanda (Blanda kick), 14:30

	BUF	HOU
First downs	13	12
Rushing yds	77	71
Passing yds	129	251
Punts-avg	7-41.9	4-45.0
Fumbles-lost	0-0	1-0
Penalties-yds	5-50	3-15

BILLS LEADERS: Rushing - Gilchrist 15-54, Carlton 9-30, Rabb 4-1, Crow 4- (-7); **Passing** - Rabb 11-29-3 - 150, Crow 1-1-0 - 6, Taseff 0-1-0 - 0; **Receiving** - Bass 6-94, Dubenion 1-9, Gilchrist 2-21, Carlton 1-12, Crockett 1-14, Crow 1-6.

OILERS LEADERS: Rushing - Smith 10-35, Tolar 11-38, Lee 1- (-2); **Passing** - Blanda 8-27-4 - 182, Lee 5-10-1 - 69; **Receiving** - Frazier 2-82, Groman 3-41, Smith 4-60, Hennigan 3-59, McLeod 1-9.

WEEK 5 GAMES

Bos 43, NY 14	Den 44, Oak 7
SD 32, Dal 28	

NOTES

• Houston drove 79 yards in eight plays in the final 1:55 to win the game and hand the Bills their fifth straight loss.
• The winning march began after a Warren Rabb pass was intercepted by Gary Cutsinger. On the play before the pick, Rabb was whistled for delay of game, nullifying what would have been a clinching TD run by Cookie Gilchrist. The Bills argued that the official never stopped the clock to give the two-minute warning and they were found to be right.
• Houston then benefited on the winning drive from a non-call on an obvious holding penalty. After the game, Ralph Wilson confronted the officials angrily on the field and demanded that they be suspended.
• The Bills deserved to win. They battled 93-degree heat and clearly outplayed the Oilers.
• A Rabb interception set up a George Blanda field goal early in the first quarter.
• The Bills' first TD came when Marv Matuszak intercepted a Blanda pass, then lateraled to Carl Charon, who went the final 40 yards for the TD, his second

score in two weeks.
• Interceptions by Matuszak and Mike Stratton were wasted as the offense failed to move.
• Jacky Lee replaced Blanda to start the second half and on the second play, Matuszak made his third interception at the Oilers 34. It took the Bills 13 plays before Gilchrist scored to make it 14-3.
• Houston got within 14-10 when Blanda returned and hit Charley Frazier for a 73-yard TD pass.
• In two games against Blanda, the Bills intercepted him an incredible 10 times.

QUOTES

• Warren Rabb on the delay penalty: "I looked at the clock going into the huddle and it said 2:18 remaining. So I figured I'd save one of my time-outs by waiting for the two-minute warning. We took our time, but still got our play started before someone blew a whistle. I figured it was for the two-minute warning, but then they penalized us for delay of game. Even then the clock said 1:55 so we still had two (actually seven) more seconds to get a play underway."
• Houston coach Pop Ivy: "We shouldn't have won it. The officials took the game away from them."
• Ralph Wilson: "I don't want this team playing under officiating like that. I want these officials suspended. I've never before said anything about officials, but this is different. They ruled in contradiction to the rule book. They took the game from us. As far as I'm concerned, we won this game. You can't expect our fellas to beat a championship club and the officials, too."
• Lou Saban: "I had just turned to Red Miller and said 'Well Redhead, I guess we're finally going to win one.' I tried to get an explanation after the game and I was ignored. One official kept telling me 'Get your hands off me, don't touch me.'"

Chargers	0	3	0	7 - 10
Bills	7	14	7	7 - 35

Attendance at War Memorial Stadium - 20,074

Buf: Dubenion 19 pass from Rabb (Yoho kick), 12:38
Buf: Bass 76 pass from Rabb (Yoho kick), 2:10
SD: FG Blair 27, 7:25
Buf: Gilchrist 1 run (Yoho kick), 14:27
Buf: Gilchrist 7 pass from Rabb (Yoho kick), 8:54
Buf: Crow 2 run (Yoho kick), 3:14
SD: Braxton 5 run (Blair kick), 11:34

	BUF	SD
First downs	13	7
Rushing yds	303	68
Passing yds	136	72
Punts-avg	5-39.0	4-45.6
Fumbles-lost	0-0	0-0
Penalties-yds	3-45	3-15

BILLS LEADERS: Rushing - Gilchrist 25-124, Crow 6-115, Carlton 11-43, Rabb 2-9, Wheeler 3-7, Jones 1-5; **Passing** - Rabb 5-12-1 - 144; **Receiving** - Bass 1-76, Dubenion 2-45, Gilchrist 2-23.

CHARGERS LEADERS: Rushing - Lincoln 10-32, Jackson 6-17, Braxton 2-11, MacKinnon 2-8; **Passing** - Hadl 2-12-2 - 17, Wood 8-20-2 - 70; **Receiving** - Kocourek 2-31, Lincoln 3-16, Robinson 1-18, Jackson 2-4, Norton 1-11, MacKinnon 1-7.

NOTES

• Lou Saban won his first game as the Bills head coach as the team snapped its five-game losing streak.
• The Bills set a team record with 303 rushing yards. Their previous best had been 210 against Denver in 1960. The 439 total yards also was a team record and the 12 passes, attempted by Warren Rabb, were the lowest in AFL history by one team.
• Carl Charon and Willie West each had two interceptions as the Bills shut down John Hadl, Lance Alworth and Keith Lincoln.
• Buffalo's first TD was set up by Wayne Crow, who faked a punt when the Chargers failed to rush him and ran 49 yards. Three plays later, Rabb hit Elbert Dubenion for the TD.
• West's first interception came at the Bills 10. Two plays later came Rabb's 76-yard TD connection with Glenn Bass to make it 14-0. The Chargers answered with a 58-yard march to a George Blair field goal.
• The Bills then drove 72 yards, all on the ground, with Cookie Gilchrist gaining 40 and eventually scoring the TD.
• Archie Matsos tackled San Diego punter Paul Maguire at the Chargers 10 after a bad center snap to set up the

Bills' fourth TD. Charon's second interception set up Crow's two-yard TD run in the fourth.
• The Chargers scored late in the game after Bob Mitinger recovered a Crow fumble at the Bills 13. It was the only time San Diego was in Buffalo territory in the second half.

QUOTES

• Lou Saban: "That (Crow's fake punt) was probably the key play in the game. Instead of giving up possession, we were in position to score. Our plan was to try and run against their weak side. We wanted to control the ball as much as possible. If they stopped our running game, we were prepared to go into a shotgun offense. The way the boys went to it, we can put aside the shotgun offense for another time. Give all the credit to those players. They really played their hearts out. A great many things contributed to the victory and that thing in Houston last week didn't hurt us. They knew we lost a game we never should have lost and they were determined that it wouldn't happen again."
• Ralph Wilson: "This was worth the wait. I'm happy for Lou and his staff and I'm thrilled for the players. I have felt right along that this is a good team, needing only a spark to get it going. This game certainly should be the spark."
• Chargers coach Sid Gillman: "No excuses, we just took a bad beating from a fired up team."
• Chargers defensive tackle Ron Mix: "They gave us a good going over."

WEEK 6 GAMES

Hou 56, NY 17	Den 23, Oak 6
Dal 27, Bos 7	

STANDINGS: SIXTH WEEK

EAST	W	L	T	WEST	W	L	T
Houston	4	1	0	Denver	5	1	0
Boston	3	2	0	Dallas	4	1	0
New York	2	4	0	San Diego	3	3	0
Buffalo	1	5	0	Oakland	0	5	0

NOTES

• Cookie Gilchrist broke his own record for rushing yards in a game and became the first Bill to have back-to-back 100-yard rushing games.

• Red Conkright made his coaching debut for the Raiders.

• The Bills went without a fumble for the third straight game.

• Carl Charon tied Marv Matuszak for the team and league lead with six interceptions. The Bills led the league in that department with 23 in just seven games.

• Warren Rabb attempted only 11 passes, breaking his week-old AFL record for fewest passes in a game. He completed a team-record low of three due to a steady rain that turned the field into a quagmire.

• Larry Felser wrote of the Titans impending loss to Dallas which would tie New York for last with Buffalo, "If the Titans win, you can expect the Japs to beat John Wayne on the late movie."

• The teams combined for seven punts in the first quarter before the Bills began a nine-play, 51-yard drive to Rabb's TD sneak early in the second quarter. Oakland's Jacki Simpson missed a 22-yard field goal at the end of the half.

• In the third, Wayne Crow's 54-yard punt rolled dead at the 3, but Oakland drove 97 yards in 11 plays to Bo Roberson's TD run, Simpson missed the PAT to leave the Raiders behind, 7-6.

• The Bills needed just seven plays to get that back as Gilchrist and Crow took turns covering 67 yards until Gilchrist scored early in the fourth and Mack Yoho's conversion made it 14-6.

• Ray Abruzzese intercepted Cotton Davidson at the Bills 39 late in the game to prevent a rally.

QUOTES

• Cookie Gilchrist: "The kind of blocking I got tonight and against San Diego, anybody could have gotten that yardage. Those guys up front opened up holes big enough for a truck."

• Lou Saban: "You like to balance your attack, but when you have a good thing going as we've had in our running game the last two games, you just keep hammering away. Besides I didn't want to throw in the rain. That's a good one to get out of the way and get in the win column because a muddy field is a great nullifier."

• Oakland owner Wayne Valley talking to Saban: "Your team is really good, but your fans are great. To turn out in a rain like that in the numbers they did to watch two teams that had only one victory between them, that's fantastic. This is a real pro city, believe me."

• Raiders defensive tackle Chuck McMurtry: "Cookie Gilchrist is the first runner who has ever really jarred me when I hit him."

Raiders	0	0	6	0 -	6
Bills	0	7	0	7 -	14

Attendance at War Memorial Stadium - 21,037

Buf: Rabb 1 run (Yoho kick), 3:27
Oak: Roberson 14 run (kick failed), 13:12
Buf: Gilchrist 7 run (Yoho kick), 7:04

	BUF	OAK
First downs	12	13
Rushing yds	201	147
Passing yds	51	143
Punts-avg	6-38.8	8-28.4
Fumbles-lost	0-0	0-0
Penalties-yds	8-91	11-107

BILLS LEADERS: Rushing - Gilchrist 19-143, Crow 6-34, Carlton 8-32, Rabb 6- (-8); **Passing** - Rabb 3-11-1 - 63; **Receiving** - Dubenion 1-37, Gilchrist 1-7, Warlick 1-19.

RAIDERS LEADERS: Rushing - Roberson 7-37, Daniels 15-89, Miller 4-11, Davidson 3-10; **Passing** - Davidson 9-28-2 - 143; **Receiving** - Roberson 3-43, Craig 2-31, Dorsey 3-43, Miller 1-

WEEK 7 GAMES

Den 20, Hou 10   Dal 20, NY 17
Bos 24, SD 20

NOTES

• After snapping a team-record five-game losing streak, the Bills established a team-best three-game winning streak.

• The Bills avenged a Week 2 loss when Denver rallied for 13 in the fourth to win, by scoring 22 in a row in the fourth. The Bills did it during a 10-minute span that took just 10 plays against the AFL's best defense.

• After falling behind 38-23 with 11:57 left, the Bills began their comeback when Warren Rabb hit Elbert Dubenion for a 75-yard TD pass on a third-and-10 play.

• After Denver's first punt, Rabb drove Buffalo 65 yards in four plays, hitting Glenn Bass with a 40-yard scoring pass. Rabb then went around right end for the

two-point conversion that tied the game.

• After Denver's second punt, Rabb tossed a short pass to Cookie Gilchrist and he raced 74 yards to the Denver 4, setting up Rabb's winning three-yard run behind a great block by guard Billy Shaw.

• Denver nearly tied the game in the final seconds, but John Yaccino knocked down Lionel Taylor's end-around option pass to an open Bob Scarpitto in the Bills' end zone.

• Gilchrist's field goal was the Bills' first since the opener against Houston.

• Tom Sestak's interception return came on a tipped pass by Mike Stratton.

• Denver then scored 24 in a row as Frank Tripucka threw three of his team-record five TD passes.

QUOTES

• Lou Saban: "It was the greatest thrill I've ever had in football, both as a player and a coach. I didn't think we played well in the first half. We got rough in the dressing room at halftime. We didn't make too many adjustments, I just told them to go out and play the way they're capable of playing. Warren did a great job, particularly on execution, and he passed well. And you can't say enough about Cookie. Cookie is in some respects a better all-around player than Jim Brown. He's a superior blocker, both on pass protection and run blocking. And I'd have to say he's just as strong a runner. What Brown has is greater moves in the open field. When I look back on the dark days at the start of the season, I can't help but be grateful for the way this team has refused to quit."

• Warren Rabb: "That was the best game I've ever played. I learned a lot of things in this one, most of all, you never give up."

• Broncos coach Jack Faulkner: "That Gilchrist is something else, and Rabb had his greatest day. You have to give them credit, they did a tremendous job. We couldn't stop the bomb and when you can't do that, you're in trouble."

Bills	7	6	10	22 -	45
Broncos	10	14	0	14 -	38

Attendance at Bears Stadium - 26,051

Buf: Sestak 6 interception return (Yoho kick), :43
Den: Taylor 7 pass from Tripucka (Mingo kick), 5:00
Den: FG Mingo 20, 13:00
Den: Dickinson 12 pass from Tripucka (Mingo kick), 1:19
Den: Prebola 55 pass from Tripucka (Mingo kick), 9:12
Buf: Gilchrist 2 run (kick failed), 14:15
Buf: Gilchrist 10 run (Yoho kick), 3:05
Buf: FG Gilchrist 33, 10:42
Den: Scarpitto 17 pass from Tripucka (Mingo kick), :50
Den: Olszewski 4 pass from Tripucka (Mingo kick), 3:03
Buf: Dubenion 75 pass from Rabb (Yoho kick), 3:48
Buf: Bass 40 pass from Rabb (Rabb run), 9:07
Buf: Rabb 3 run (Yoho kick), 12:28

	BUF	DEN
First downs	19	21
Rushing yds	199	196
Passing yds	253	167
Punts-avg	2-39.5	2-45.5
Fumbles-lost	1-1	1-1
Penalties-yds	4-51	3-30

BILLS LEADERS: Rushing - Gilchrist 17-89, Carlton 8-77, Crow 9-35, Rabb 5-10, Dubenion 1- (-12); **Passing** - Rabb 9-16-0 - 262; **Receiving** - Dubenion 2-87, Gilchrist 2-76, Bass 3-69, Crow 2-30.

BRONCOS LEADERS: Rushing - Stone 21-90, Olszewski 11-89, Dickinson 5-17; **Passing** - Tripucka 12-21-2 - 168, Shaw 2-2-0 - 32, Taylor 0-1-0 - 0; **Receiving** - Taylor 6-78, Olszewski 3-26, Prebola 1-55, Dickinson 3-23, Scarpitto 1-18.

WEEK 8 GAMES

Bos 26, Oak 16   Dal 31, Hou 7
NY 23, SD 3

STANDINGS: EIGHTH WEEK

EAST	W	L	T	WEST	W	L	T
Boston	5	2	0	Dallas	6	1	0
Houston	4	3	0	Denver	6	2	0
New York	3	5	0	San Diego	3	5	0
Buffalo	3	5	0	Oakland	0	7	0

Patriots	14	0	7	7 -	28
Bills	14	7	7	0 -	28

Attendance at War Memorial Stadium - 33,247

Buf: Gilchrist 2 run (Gilchrist kick), 3:46
Bos: Garron 95 kickoff return (Cappelletti kick), 4:03
Bos: Garron 29 pass from Parilli (Cappelletti kick), 10:48
Buf: Dubenion 93 kickoff return (Gilchrist kick), 11:08
Buf: Moore 4 interception return (Gilchrist kick), 5:02
Buf: Gilchrist 7 run (Gilchrist kick), 6:44
Bos: Cappelletti 6 pass from Parilli (Cappelletti kick), 14:20
Bos: Garron 23 pass from Parilli (Cappelletti kick), 4:44

	BUF	BOS
First downs	19	18
Rushing yds	194	88
Passing yds	46	287
Punts-avg	8-37.9	6-34.8
Fumbles-lost	0-0	2-2
Penalties-yds	4-22	4-47

BILLS LEADERS: Rushing - Gilchrist 23-107, Carlton 14-54, Rabb 4-26, Crow 4-7; **Passing** - Rabb 4-17-1 - 59; **Receiving** - Dubenion 2-41, Warlick 1-23, Gilchrist 1- (-5).

PATRIOTS LEADERS: Rushing - Garron 7-51, Lott 3-16, Burton 4-16, Parilli 3-10, Crawford 3- (-5); **Passing** - Parilli 20-33-1 - 296; **Receiving** - Cappelletti 7-103, Burton 4-46, Colcough 4-82, Garron 3-49, Crawford 1-15, Lott 1-1.

NOTES

• The largest crowd in team history produced the largest money gate for a sporting event in Buffalo.
• The Bills needed only five plays to score on their first possession, the key being a 27-yard Warren Rabb pass to Elbert Dubenion to the 2, which set up Cookie Gilchrist's first TD run. However, Larry Garron returned the ensuing kickoff 95 yards for a TD.
• After a Bills punt, the Patriots drove 86 yards in eight plays to Parilli's TD pass to Ron Burton. But Dubenion took a reverse on kickoff from Willie Jones and he sped 93 yards for the tying TD.
• Early in the second, Leroy Moore, released by the Patriots two weeks earlier, intercepted a Parilli screen pass and fell in the end zone to make it 21-14 Buffalo.
• Sid Youngelman recovered a Parilli fumble early in the third and the Bills drove 45 yards to Gilchrist's second TD to make it 28-14.
• Late in the third, the Patriots moved 52 yards in seven plays to Parilli's third-down TD pass to Gino Cappelletti.
• Rabb was intercepted by Ron Hall early in the fourth, leading to Parilli's tying TD pass to Garron.
• With 6:43 left, Archie Matsos had a 60-yard interception return for a TD called back when the referee ruled the play was blown dead because Parilli's

WEEK 9 GAMES

NY 31, Oak 21	Hou 14, Dal 6
Den 23, SD 20	

progress had been stopped. The Bills argued to no avail.
• The game ended in thrilling style. Marv Matuszak recovered a Garron fumble at the Bills 38 with less than a minute left. Rabb hit Ernie Warlick for 23, but Gilchrist was five yards short on a 46-yard field goal attempt and Boston's Ron Burton returned it to midfield before he was tackled.

QUOTES

• Warren Rabb: "I can't help but feel they'll put Kemp in as soon as he's ready and start getting him ready for next season. Jack's a better quarterback. He has the experience and he's smart. I've felt better-equipped to do a job each game I've played. I'm starting to recognize defenses better and some things are becoming more mechanical to me. But it's a hard job. There's so much to do and think about simultaneously."
• Lou Saban on Matsos' play: "I don't see how the official can blow the whistle when the man who has the ball is in motion and free enough to release a pass. But the call was made and the game is over so we'll have to forget about it. It's no disgrace to get a tie with Boston. That's a good club and Parilli is just great. It's the same as a defeat. I guess I'm not being fair. Actually we played a whale of an interesting game against a fine Boston team. I wanted this one so much for personal reasons."
• Mack Yoho on Matsos' play: "Tom Sestak and someone else had Parilli wrapped up, but he was struggling. I was just going to hit him when I saw him get rid of the ball and Archie take off. There was no whistle up to that time."

Bills	17	20	3	0 -	40
Chargers	0	0	6	14 -	20

Attendance at Balboa Stadium - 22,204

Buf: Gilchrist 22 run (Gilchrist kick), 5:56
Buf: FG Gilchrist 18, 12:39
Buf: Carlton 12 run (Gilchrist kick), 14:44
Buf: Carlton 14 run (Gilchrist kick), 3:03
Buf: Dubenion 68 pass from Rabb (Gilchrist kick), 7:06
Buf: Bass 12 pass from Rabb (kick blocked), 9:44
SD: Kocourek 15 pass from Hadl (kick failed), 6:35
Buf: FG Gilchrist 12, 11:28
SD: Jackson 1 run (run failed), 2:53
SD: Jackson 3 run (Braxton run), 13:06

	BUF	SD
First downs	20	21
Rushing yds	211	164
Passing yds	124	206
Punts-avg	3-43.6	2-37.5
Fumbles-lost	2-0	5-2
Penalties-yds	5-48	6-60

BILLS LEADERS: Rushing - Gilchrist 14-46, Carlton 12-90, Crow 6-66, Rabb 6-8, Jones 2-1; **Passing** - Rabb 6-16-2 - 124; **Receiving** - Dubenion 3-89, Warlick 1-9, Bass 1-13, Rychlec 1-13.

CHARGERS LEADERS: Rushing - MacKinnon 17-102, Jackson 10-37, Braxton 4-18, Gillett 2-8, Hadl 1- (-1); **Passing** - Hadl 15-28-3 - 217; **Receiving** - Kocourek 7-126, Robinson 3-20, Norton 3-43, Jackson 1-26, Braxton 1-2.

NOTES

• The Bills exploded for a 37-0 halftime lead, the largest in team history, and stayed unbeaten in five games.
• Jack Kemp was scheduled to play the second half, but Lou Saban decided against it due to the huge lead.
• Chargers QB John Hadl had three interceptions and three fumbles. Mike Stratton had two of the interceptions while Booker Edgerson had the other.
• During the 4-0-1 streak, the Bills became the AFL's top rushing team, averaging 221.6 yards per game during the stretch.
• The Bills drove 63 yards on their first possession, with Gilchrist capping the drive with a sweep for a TD.
• Dick Harris then fumbled a punt and Ray Abruzzese recovered, leading to a Gilchrist field goal.
• The Bills then made it 17-0 when Edgerson returned his pick 38 yards to the San Diego 11 to set up Wray Carlton's first TD.
• Stratton then made his first pick and lateraled to Edgerson who returned it 30 yards to the San Diego 39. Carlton broke a 25-yard run and on the next play, scored from the 14 to make it 24-0.
• The defense held on fourth down at the Bills 31, and two plays later, Warren Rabb hit Elbert Dubenion on a 68-yard TD pass. The final TD of the half was set up by Stratton's second interception.
• The Chargers drove 90 yards on their first possession of the third to Hadl's TD pass to Dave Kocourek, but Wayne Crow faked a punt on the next series and ran 52 yards to set up Gilchrist's field goal.

WEEK 10 GAMES

Dal 52, NY 31	Hou 28, Oak 20
Bos 33, Den 29	

QUOTES

• Lou Saban: "In the first half, we played as well as any team I've ever seen. We got a lot of early breaks on penalties and took advantage of them. I can't blame the boys for not being as sharp in the second half. They just made getting into that end zone a certainty every time we got the ball until the game was out of reach. I believe we are the strongest team in the league right now."
• Billy Shaw: "It's all the way now. We're rolling. And next year we'll beat Green Bay."
• Wayne Crow on his fake punt: "I didn't intend to run, but they rushed hard from the right. I started slow, figuring they'd have one guy covering the left and I'd kick on the run. When I saw there wasn't anyone there, I took off."

STANDINGS: TENTH WEEK

EAST	W	L	T	WEST	W	L	T
Boston	6	2	1	Dallas	7	2	0
Houston	6	3	0	Denver	7	3	0
Buffalo	4	5	1	San Diego	3	7	0
New York	4	6	0	Oakland	0	9	0

NOTES

• Jack Kemp made his debut with the Bills, and while his numbers weren't great, it was obvious Kemp gave the Bills a presence at QB as the team stretched its unbeaten streak to six games.

• Cookie Gilchrist rushed for 103 yards and remained the league's top back, but he had a horrible day with two fumbles, two dropped passes and three field goal misses, two of them chip shots.

• Wray Carlton was injured, but ex-Raider Wayne Crow stepped in and played well.

• Gilchrist missed a field goal from the 41 on the Bills first series of the game, then after Leroy Moore recovered Cotton Davidson's fumble at the Raiders 9, Gilchrist missed an 11-yarder.

• Ben Agajanian's 49-yard field goal gave the Raiders a 3-0 lead in the first.

• Gilchrist killed a drive at the Raiders 27 by fumbling, but after the defense forced a punt, the Bills got a break when Bob Garner was called for a 44-yard interference penalty, putting the ball at the 7. Two 15-yard penalties pushed them back to the 32, but after an 18-yard pass to Tom Rychlec, Gilchrist made his tying field goal.

• Jacki Simpson's interception of a Rabb pass set up Agajanian's second field goal in the third.

• On the next series, the Bills had to punt, but Garner fumbled Crow's kick and Monte Crockett recovered at the Oakland 33. On third-and-seven, Kemp passed 14 yards to Ernie Warlick for a first down, then hit Crow for the only TD of the game and the winning points.

QUOTES

• Coach Saban: "Without Kemp, I don't know what we would have done. He gave us the spark. He played very well for his first game. His hand was hurting him when he was on the sidelines. I think Kemp gave us that psychological lift I was hoping he would. He should have had a better completion percentage, as should have Warren, but our receivers dropped a lot of passes. This was our best defensive game of the season. We got banged up pretty good and looked ragged at times, but the boys - particularly the defense - hung in there against a hard-hitting club that was playing with nothing-to-lose abandon."

• Jack Kemp: "I was pretty rusty, but it felt good to be playing again. The finger? It hurts, but that doesn't matter because we won. That's what counts."

• Tom Sestak: "I'd have to say I feel pretty good about the game. I think I got my share of tackles (six)."

| Bills | 0 | 3 | 7 | 0 - 10 |
| Raiders | 3 | 0 | 3 | 0 - 6 |

Attendance at Frank Youell Field - 11,700

Oak: FG Agajanian 49, 14:49
Buf: FG Gilchrist 21, 11:19
Oak: FG Agajanian 36, 11:01
Buf: Crow 17 pass from Kemp (Gilchrist kick), 13:20

	BUF	OAK
First downs	17	6
Rushing yds	306	86
Passing yds	99	28
Punts-avg	6-41.3	7-44.3
Fumbles-lost	4-3	4-3
Penalties-yds	9-120	4-82

BILLS LEADERS: Rushing - Gilchrist 19-103, Crow 18-95, Carlton 7-31, Kemp 1-28, Dubenion 2-47, Rabb 1-2; **Passing** - Kemp 4-12-0-42, Rabb 4-14-1-46, Crow 1-1-0-10; **Receiving** - Dubenion 2-13, Warlick 2-24, Bass 2-25, Rychlec 2-21, Crow 1-16.

RAIDERS LEADERS: Rushing - Roberson 15-64, Lewis 7-17, Craig 1-8, Daniels 2-2, Davidson 2-(-5); **Passing** - Davidson 5-20-3 - 25, Enis 4-10-0 - 36, Roberson 0-1-0 - 0; **Receiving** - Lewis 4-25, Dorsey 2-9, Boydston 1-15, Daniels 1-7, Craig 1-5.

WEEK 11 GAMES	
Dal 24, Den 3	Hou 21, Bos 17

NOTES

• The Bills, the No. 1 rushing team in the AFL, struggled badly without injured Wray Carlton, then lost Cookie Gilchrist for stretches due to a sprained left ankle incurred in the second quarter.

• Patriots QB Babe Parilli missed the game, but Tom Yewcic was superb. Yewcic once played catcher for the Buffalo Bisons and had a brief stint with the 1960 Bills.

• The Bills also were without Booker Edgerson most of the game and Yewcic picked on rookie Tom Minter.

• Jack Kemp made his first start and on his first drive, the Bills went 88 yards in 12 plays to Kemp's six-yard TD run. Kemp was four-for-four for 62 yards, including a 49-yarder to Elbert Dubenion on that drive.

• The Pats tied it in the second on Yewcic's TD pass to Jim Colclough. On the next series, the Pats stuffed Kemp on a fourth-and-one at the Boston 12 and that turned the tide. Five plays later, Yewcic hit Ron Burton for a 69-yard TD pass while being tackled by Tom Sestak and Sid Youngelman.

• Gilchrist left for good early in the third and all Buffalo managed was Mack Yoho's 36-yard field goal late in the period. The score was set up by Kemp's 20-yard pass to Ernie Warlick.

• On the ensuing series, Yewcic completed a 15-yard pass to Ron Burton on third-and-six from the Pats 35 and that was the key play as they wound up scoring when Yewcic hit Gino Cappelletti for the clinching TD.

QUOTES

• Lou Saban: "Yewcic did a surprisingly good job. He deserves credit for it. But having both Cookie and Wray out of the lineup with injuries nullified the running game we've been winning with. I was pleased with the calls and yardage that Jack Kemp got us through the air, particularly in the face of the blitzing Boston did once Cookie was out." (On Kemp getting stopped on fourth-and-one): "That particular play was probably the only one we haven't gone over with Jack. He was supposed to hit over the guard."

• Jack Kemp on the fourth-and-one: "I didn't know I was supposed to call for a hole, I just ran the play the way I was accustomed to at San Diego. Unfortunately I didn't make it."

• Pats receiver Gino Cappelletti: "Yewcic took command in the huddle. He listened to his receivers, but he was the general, no mistaking it."

• Pats quarterback Tom Yewcic: "Parilli helped by talking to me on the sidelines. He's the one who called the first touchdown pass to Colclough."

• Ralph Wilson: "I wanted to see us win this game. I knew how much Lou wanted to beat Boston, but I was proud of our team. We had many key injuries and kept battling in a hard-hitting game. When you play as hard as they did and lose, there's nothing to be disgraced or discouraged about."

| Bills | 7 | 0 | 3 | 0 - 10 |
| Patriots | 0 | 14 | 0 | 7 - 21 |

Attendance at Boston University - 20,021

Buf: Kemp 6 run (Gilchrist kick), 10:50
Bos: Colclough 31 pass from Yewcic (Cappelletti kick), 8:27
Bos: Burton 69 pass from Yewcic (Cappelletti kick), 14:03
Buf: FG Yoho 36, 13:48
Bos: Cappelletti 18 pass from Yewcic (Cappelletti kick), 3:07

	BUF	BOS
First downs	11	15
Rushing yds	63	99
Passing yds	192	220
Punts-avg	6-36.6	5-38.2
Fumbles-lost	3-0	2-1
Penalties-yds	5-45	1-15

BILLS LEADERS: Rushing - Gilchrist 8-16, Crow 11-25, Kemp 3-11, Jones 1-11; **Passing** - Kemp 14-22-0 - 194, Rabb 1-4-1 - 25; **Receiving** - Dubenion 6-80, Warlick 3-58, Bass 2-39, Gilchrist 4-42.

PATRIOTS LEADERS: Rushing - Burton 9-36, Crawford 15-43, Yewcic 3-15, Lott 2-5, Garron 1-0; **Passing** - Yewcic 12-17-0 - 231; **Receiving** - Cappelletti 4-57, Colclough 4-72, Burton 3-97, Romeo 1-5.

WEEK 12 GAMES	
Hou 33, SD 27	Dal 35, Oak 7
NY 46, Den 45	

STANDINGS: TWELFTH WEEK

EAST	W	L	T	WEST	W	L	T
Houston	8	3	0	Dallas	9	2	0
Boston	7	3	1	Denver	7	5	0
Buffalo	5	6	1	San Diego	3	8	0
New York	5	6	0	Oakland	0	11	0

Texans	0	0 7	7 -	14
Bills	6	7 3	7 -	23

Attendance at War Memorial Stadium - 35,261

Buf: Rychlec 1 pass from Kemp (kick failed), 8:04
Buf: Warlick 1 pass from Kemp (Gilchrist kick), 11:26
Buf: FG Gilchrist 37, 5:21
Dal: Arbanas 13 pass from Dawson (Brooker kick), 8:10
Dal: Brooker 28 pass from Dawson (Brooker kick), 2:54
Buf: Gilchrist 2 run (Gilchrist kick), 6:38

	BUF	DAL
First downs	24	16
Rushing yds	91	131
Passing yds	230	162
Punts-avg	6-36.6	5-38.2
Fumbles-lost	1-1	2-2
Penalties-yds	3-45	4-30

BILLS LEADERS: Rushing - Gilchrist 19-63, Crow 6-18, Kemp 5-10; **Passing** - Kemp 21-35-0 - 248; **Receiving** - Dubenion 3-30, Warlick 9-117, Bass 3-23, Gilchrist 4-69, Crow 1-8, Rychlec 1-1.

TEXANS LEADERS: Rushing - Haynes 11-56, McClinton 5-49, Dawson 3-26; **Passing** - Dawson 18-33-2 - 186, Wilson 1-1-0 - 16; **Receiving** - Miller 6-46, Haynes 3-37, Arbanas 2-21, McClinton 5-52, Brooker 1-28, Robinson 1-16, Jackson 1-2.

WEEK 13 GAMES

Bos 24, NY 17	SD 31, Oak 21
Hou 34, Den 17	

NOTES

• A record crowd watched as Jack Kemp picked apart the eventual 1962 champions. Kemp was hoisted onto the shoulders of fans in the tunnel leading to the locker room after the game.
• The crowd was larger than four NFL games played that day.
• The day before, Kemp celebrated the birth of his daughter Jennifer.
• Kemp was given complete play-calling duty by Lou Saban.
• Cookie Gilchrist increased his rushing total to 953 yards, a new AFL record with one week to go. The Bills also broke an AFL team rushing record with a count of 2,196.
• Willie West picked off two Len Dawson passes to end scoring threats.
• The Bills had 17 first downs passing, only four rushing.
• The Bills drove 80 yards, taking 8:04, to score on their opening possession. In the second quarter, Mike Stratton recovered Curtis McClinton's fumble at the Texans 16, setting up Kemp's second one-yard TD pass.
• The Bills made it 16-0 when Gilchrist capped the opening possession of the third with a field goal.
• The Texans answered with Dawson's TD pass to Fred Arbanas after Dave Grayson had returned the kickoff 31 yards to the 40. On the play before the TD, Dawson fired a 16-yard pass to McClinton.
• Dallas pulled to within 16-14 early in the fourth with a four-play, 80-yard drive. McClinton ran for 40 and Dawson eventually hit Tommy Brooker with a 28-yard TD pass.
• But the Bills clinched it on the next series as Kemp hit Ernie Warlick for 17 and Gilchrist for 27. Then a pass interference penalty on Walt Corey gave the Bills first-and-goal from the 1 and Gilchrist scored.
• Gilchrist fumbled in the final minute inside the Buffalo 20, but the defense stiffened and West intercepted in the end zone. Gilchrist also missed two field goals and an extra point.

QUOTES

• Jack Kemp: "When guys come up with catches like the ones that Ernie and Cookie made, a quarterback just has to look good. But I thought we were just as good in Boston. Unfortunately they came up with the big bombs in that one and we didn't."
• Lou Saban: "I felt all week that we could win this one. These fellas come up for the big games now and this was no exception. We knew a few weaknesses existed in the Dallas defense and Jack just went out there and picked them apart. He's a great one for getting the quick picture and making the most of what he sees. Jack is providing us with the only thing we have needed from the start of the season - a field general in whom the players can place their complete confidence."
• Texan's quarterback Len Dawson: "I can't figure this situation out. Here's a team, the Bills, completely out of the championship race, yet they're up so high they beat us up physically as well as on the scoreboard. They're dead as far as title chances, yet 35,000 people come to cheer them on. That's amazing. I'd like to play in this city. This kind of fan support would inspire even the most calloused old pro."

Bills	3	3 7	7 -	20
Titans	3	0 0	0 -	3

Attendance at the Polo Grounds - 16,453

Buf: FG Gilchrist 42, 6:15
NY: FG Shockley 23, 14:10
Buf: FG Gilchrist 27, 14:59
Buf: Gilchrist 42 run (Gilchrist kick), 14:50
Buf: Gilchrist 30 run (Gilchrist kick), 1:14

	BUF	NY
First downs	23	11
Rushing yds	241	27
Passing yds	125	206
Punts-avg	5-29.2	9-43.3
Fumbles-lost	3-0	1-0
Penalties-yds	8-65	8-77

BILLS LEADERS: Rushing - Gilchrist 17-143, Crow 19-93, Kemp 3-7, Rabb 1- (-2); **Passing** - Kemp 12-25-4 - 151, Rabb 0-1-0 - 0; **Receiving** - Warlick 5-57, Bass 2-36, Rychlec 2-31, Crow 2-13, Dubenion 1-14.

TITANS LEADERS: Rushing - Mathis 7-10, Christy 7-16, Green 1-1; **Passing** - Green 20-39-3 - 206, Grosscup 0-4-0 - 0; **Receiving** - Maynard 7-83, Powell 8-80, Christy 5-43.

WEEK 14 GAMES

Bos 20, SD 14	Dal 17, Den 10
Hou 32, Oak 17	

WEEK 15 GAMES

Hou 44, NY 10	Dal 26, SD 17
Oak 20, Bos 0	
Buffalo and Denver had bye weeks	

NOTES

• The Bills finished on a 7-1-1 run to produce the first winning season in club history.
• Cookie Gilchrist finished with 1,096 yards, the first back in AFL history to top 1,000.
• Gilchrist scored all 20 Buffalo points to finish with a team-leading 128.
• Jack Kemp wasn't sharp, suffering four interceptions including three by former St. Bonaventure halfback Lee Riley.
• Ex-Buffalo QB Johnny Green hurt the Titans with his three interceptions and New York's running game was non-existent with 27 yards.
• Titans owner Harry Wismer announced the Polo Grounds crowd at 16,453 but later admitted at least 5,000 YMCA children were admitted free. Larry Felser wrote that the crowd number must have included "the inhabitants of the apartments that border Coogan's Bluff."
• The Bills drove 45 yards to a Gilchrist field goal on their first possession, but Green hit three-of-six passes for 29 yards to set up Bill Shockley's tying field goal late in the first.
• Late in the second, Crow was stopped on fourth-and-goal from the 1, but the Bills defense forced a punt and a personal foul penalty and two Kemp completions to Tom Rychlec (13 yards) and Ernie Warlick (16) positioned Gilchrist for a 27-yard field goal on the final play of the half.
• Kemp ended three straight possessions in the third by throwing interceptions, but late in the period after a Titans punt, Gilchrist broke a 42-yard TD run. Gilchrist busted another TD run on the next series.

QUOTES

• Ralph Wilson: "I think the franchise is so solidly established now that we needn't be as concerned with television (of NFL games) as we have been."
• Carl Taseff announcing his retirement: "I've had my kicks as a player, now I'd like to get a job in coaching." (On Jack Kemp): "The only young quarterback I've seen in the AFL who could really become a great one is Jack Kemp. He has the smartness, the quick release and ability to throw long that is necessary and he's able to move around when he's in trouble."
• Lou Saban: "Jim Brown is really something, but Cookie is just as great in the AFL – a league closer to parity with the NFL than people realize."

STANDINGS: FOURTEENTH WEEK

EAST	W	L	T	WEST	W	L	T
Houston	11	3	0	Dallas	11	3	0
Boston	9	4	1	Denver	7	7	0
Buffalo	7	6	1	San Diego	4	10	0
New York	5	9	0	Oakland	1	13	0

At A Glance
1963

Jan. 1 – Ralph Wilson was named Good Fellow of the Year by the *Courier-Express*.

Jan. 2 – The Bills signed defensive tackle Jim Dunaway, the No. 1 draft choice of the Minnesota Vikings and the first lineman chosen in the NFL draft. "He has the tools to have a long and possibly great pro career," Lou Saban said. "He's big, strong, quick. What more is there for a lineman to possess?"

Jan. 3 – Lou Saban was given a two-year contract and a pay raise. "The contract is a formality," Ralph Wilson said. "Lou knows how I feel about the job he's done and that I want him to stay on until the Bills win a championship. Lou did a tremendous job in bringing the club around after a poor start."

Jan. 6 – The Boston Patriots announced a move to Fenway Park from Boston University.

Jan. 10 – The AFL's guarantee for visiting teams was increased from $20,000 to $30,000.

Jan. 11 – The Bills obtained offensive guard Dick Hudson from San Diego in exchange for the negotiating rights to 34-year-old quarterback Tobin Rote.

Jan. 18 – Red Miller ended a six-year association with Lou Saban, quitting his position as offensive line coach to take a similar position with the Denver Broncos.

Jan. 22 – The Buffalo Common Council voted 12-3, approving the study of a controversial resolution for adding 14,000 seats to War Memorial Stadium.

Feb. 2 – Cookie Gilchrist filed for bankruptcy in federal court, listing more than $59,000 in debts with assets of just $7,400.

Feb. 5 – The Bills signed an agreement to move their training camp and regular-season workouts to the Camelot Motor Inn in Blasdell. The motel agreed to lay out two football fields, provide a 56-foot by 14-foot lockerroom, an equipment room, training room and a private dining room. "Having these fine facilities available all season will solve the problem of excessive use of War Memorial Stadium's field," Lou Saban said.

Feb. 8 – Lamar Hunt announced he would move his Dallas Texans to Kansas City and become the Chiefs. Herman Ball replaced Red Miller as the Bills' offensive line coach.

Feb. 9 – City planners proposed a $23 million stadium in the crossroads area of downtown Buffalo. The stadium would seat 55,000. This came two weeks after the Common Council approved a plan to study renovating War Memorial Stadium by adding 14,000 seats. Comparing the cost, planners pointed to the new stadium in Chavez Ravine outside Los Angeles ($22 million), Candlestick Park in San Francisco ($15 million) and the planned stadium in Flushing Park Meadow in New York ($18 million).

Feb. 15 – Bills PR director Chuck Burr was promoted to assistant general manager and John Walsh was named as an assistant to personnel director Harvey Johnson.

Feb. 24 – The AFL announced it would operate with seven teams, rather than allow Harry

Versatile halfback/receiver/punt returner Ed Rutkowski came to the team via Notre Dame in 1963. After he retired, he became the executive of Erie County.

Wismer to continue to own the New York Titans.

March 2 – *Buffalo News* reporter Jack Horrigan accepted position as AFL publicity director.

March 6 – The Common Council voted in favor of adding 14,000 seats to War Memorial Stadium at a cost of $1.5 million.

March 28 – A five-man syndicate headed by Sonny Werblin, bought the New York franchise from Harry Wismer for $1 million and changed the team nickname to the Jets.

May 13 – Cookie Gilchrist was arrested for striking a police officer. He had run a stop sign and was pulled over by police. When he refused to get into the patrol car, he struck the officer. He was released without bail 12 hours later and a court date was set.

May 14 – The Dallas Texans' move to Kansas City became official.

May 22 – The Bills signed back Ed Rutkowski.

June 18 – The Bills traded popular linebacker Archie Matsos to Oakland for three players.

June 29 – A crowd of 20,840 watched the West defeat the East, 22-21, in the third annual Coaches All-America game at War Memorial Stadium. Bills rookie Daryle Lamonica thrilled the crowd by throwing a fourth-quarter TD pass while another Bills rookie, George Saimes, rushed for 87 yards and scored once, but suffered

a rib injury and would likely miss the early portion of training camp.

July 19 – The Bills obtained linebacker Harry Jacobs in a straight cash deal from Boston, which enabled Lou Saban to leave Al Bemiller at center, rather than move him to middle linebacker.

July 21 – Training camp started at the new Camelot Motor Inn in Blasdell.

July 31 – About 6,000 fans watched the first intrasquad scrimmage.

Aug. 4 – A crowd of 12,749 attended the annual Meet the Bills night and intrasquad scrimmage. The White Team beat the Blue, 11-10, as rookie Lindy Infante starred with one interception.

Aug. 9 – The Bills made their first trip to Kansas City and lost the preseason opener to the Chiefs, 17-13.

Aug. 12 – Wide receiver Bill Miller was obtained in a cash deal from Kansas City.

Aug. 16 – The Bills beat the Jets, 23-8, before 19,142 in the home preseason opener.

Aug. 18 – QB Warren Rabb was waived as Lou Saban decided to stick with Jack Kemp and rookie Daryle Lamonica as his quarterbacks.

Aug. 24 – The Bills downed Boston at War Memorial, 24-14, but Cookie Gilchrist suffered a rib injury and his availability for the regular-season opener in San Diego was unknown.

Aug. 31 – The Bills traveled to Winston-Salem, N.C. and defeated Denver, 21-14, to close their second straight 3-1 exhibition season.

Sept. 8 – Jack Kemp threw three interceptions and injured Cookie Gilchrist saw very limited action as the Bills opened the regular season with a 14-10 loss at San Diego.

Sept. 15 – Bills went winless on the West Coast for the first time ever in one season as Oakland inflicted a 35-17 defeat.

Sept. 16 – Glenn Bass, the team's offensive MVP in 1961, and defensive end Leroy Moore were waived. Taking their places were two players cut by the NFL's Minnesota Vikings, receiver Charley Ferguson and defensive end Ron McDole. It also was announced that George Saimes would move to safety. Bass later was brought back.

Sept. 22 – Len Dawson rallied Kansas City from a 27-10 deficit to produce a 27-27 tie in the Bills home opener. Chris Burford caught a TD pass and a game-tying two-point conversion pass with 40 seconds left.

Sept. 28 – The Bills fell to 0-3-1 as Charley Hennigan caught three George Blanda TD passes to give the Oilers a 31-20 victory at War Memorial.

Sept. 30 – Lou Saban cut four players including running back Fred Brown; Billy Atkins rejoined the team after playing one season in New York. Atkins had been traded to New York along with QB Johnny Green for QB Al Dorow. He was the AFL's leading punter in 1961.

Oct. 2 – The Bills practiced using false numbers because Lou Saban suspected Al Davis of spying on his team. Davis wouldn't say if he was spying, but he did say: "I'm scared to death of Buffalo. The defense, particularly their line, is really tough. And I really like Booker Edgerson. I tried to trade for him the whole off-season because I

thought he was the best rookie defensive back in the league last year."

Oct. 5 – The Bills won their first game of the season, 12-0, over the Raiders, as the defense held Oakland to 143 yards. Jim Dunaway made the first start of his pro career.

Oct. 13 – Rookie Roger Kochman gained 166 total yards and Jack Kemp threw a clinching 89-yard TD pass to Elbert Dubenion with 1:40 left as the Bills beat the Chiefs in Kansas City, 35-26.

Oct. 16 – Wray Carlton was ruled out for the rest of the season with a severe groin injury. Wayne Crow was activated to take his place.

Oct. 20 – George Blanda passed for four TDs as the Oilers posted a 28-14 victory in Houston.

Oct. 26 – Little-used Charley Ferguson caught a 72-yard TD pass from Jack Kemp with 28 seconds left to play at War Memorial, giving the Bills a 28-21 victory over Boston.

Nov. 3 – Cookie Gilchrist overcame four fumbles with 125 yards rushing and two touchdowns as Buffalo edged the Broncos in Denver, 30-28. Lou Saban charged the Broncos with stealing one of the Bills' playbooks.

Nov. 9 – The Bills completed a back-to-back home-and-home series sweep of the Broncos with a 27-17 triumph at War Memorial as Jack Kemp passed for 273 yards, three TDs and rushed for the other TD.

Nov. 17 – In front of 38,592 at War Memorial Stadium, the largest crowd in AFL history to date, the Chargers beat the Bills, 23-13, as they rushed for 199 yards.

Nov. 22 – President John F. Kennedy was assassinated in Dallas and all AFL games for the weekend were postponed. The NFL decided to play its games and was criticized. Ralph Wilson was the first AFL owner to call off a game, and the rest of the league followed suit. "The assassination of President Kennedy is a tragic loss to the

United States and the world," Wilson said. "My heartfelt sympathies go out to Mrs. Kennedy and the Kennedy family. Out of deep respect to the President's memory, the Buffalo Bills' game with the Boston Patriots is definitely postponed and I am recommending postponement of all other games."

Nov. 29 – The Bills drafted defensive end Carl Eller, but he eventually would sign with Minnesota of the NFL. Also drafted were wide receiver Paul Warfield, but he later signed with Cleveland. Players who would sign with Buffalo were defensive back Butch Byrd and kicker Pete Gogolak.

Dec. 1 – Jack Kemp completed just 19 of 46 passes in a 17-7 loss at Boston. Lou Saban announced he would bench his starter for the final two games and go with Daryle Lamonica.

Dec. 8 – The Bills crushed the Jets, 45-14, at War Memorial for their largest margin of victory to date, as Cookie Gilchrist set the all-time pro football rushing record with 243 yards on 36 carries. He also scored five touchdowns to set a team and AFL record. Losses by Boston and Houston kept alive the Bills hopes for a division crown.

Dec. 14 – The Bills closed the regular season with a 19-10 victory over the Jets in New York, completing their second back-to-back home-and-home series sweep of the season. Jack Kemp came off the bench to lead a second-half rally.

Dec. 15 – San Diego clinched the AFL West with a 20-14 victory over Houston. But more importantly, the Oilers loss meant that the Bills and Patriots finished tied for first place in the East, necessitating a special divisional playoff game.

Dec. 17 – Cookie Gilchrist was left off the AFL All-Star team but Billy Shaw, Stew Barber and Tom Sestak made the first team. Oakland's Al Davis was named AFL coach of the year.

Dec. 28 – Boston won the Eastern Division title and the right to play San Diego in the AFL Championship Game with a 26-8 victory at bitter cold War Memorial Stadium. The Bills turned the ball over six times and rushed for just seven yards.

Jan. 5, 1964 – The Chargers destroyed the Patriots, 51-10, in the AFL Championship before 30,127 at San Diego's Balboa Stadium. Each Charger received $2,498.89 for the victory.

Jan. 19, 1964 – The West defeated the East for the third year in a row in the All-Star game at San Diego, 27-24. Ex-Bill Archie Matsos of Oakland was the defensive MVP.

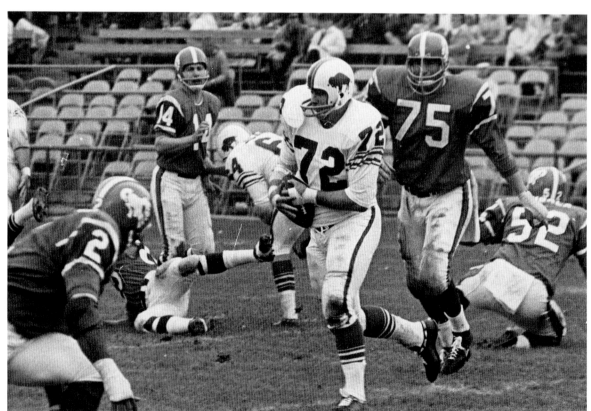

BY THE NUMBERS - 1963

TEAM STATISTICS	BILLS	OPP
First downs	272	224
Rushing	107	63
Passing	147	147
Penalty	18	14
Total yards	4,918	4,073
Avg. game	351.3	290.9
Plays	945	813
Avg. play	5.2	5.0
Net rushing yds	1,838	1,217
Avg. game	131.3	86.9
Avg. play	4.0	4.0
Net passing yds	3,080	2,856
Comp/att	228/457	218/472
Interceptions	24	21
Percentage	49.9	46.2
Sacks/lost	33-306	38-372
Punts/avg.	2-40.5	80-40.1
Fumbles/lost	25-16	19-12
Penalties/yds	63-532	55-507
Touchdowns	39	37
Extra points	32-37	35-35
Field goals	10-23	10-26
Two-point conv.	2-2	1-2
Safeties	2	1
Kick ret./avg	52-22.4	60-20.6
Punt ret./avg	37-8.5	21-6.9

RUSHING	ATT	YDS	AVG	TD
Gilchrist	232	979	4.2	12
Kochman	47	232	4.9	0
Kemp	52	226	4.3	8
Rutkowski	48	144	3.0	0
Carlton	29	125	4.3	0
Bass	14	59	4.2	0
Saimes	12	41	3.4	0
Brown	6	18	3.0	1
Lamonica	9	8	0.9	0
Crow	6	6	1.0	0
TOTALS	**455**	**1838**	**4.0**	**21**

PASSING	COMP	ATT	INT	YDS	TD	COMP%
Kemp	194	384	20	2914	13	50.5
Lamonica	33	71	4	437	3	46.5
Gilchrist	1	1	0	35	0	100.0
Rutkowski	0	1	0	0	0	00.0
TOTALS	**228**	**457**	**24**	**3386**	**16**	**49.9**

KICKING	FG/ATT	PAT/ATT	PTS
Yoho	10-23	32-37	62

PUNTING	NO	AVG
Lamonica	52	40.1
Crow	10	42.4

RECEIVING	CAT	YDS	AVG	TD
Miller	69	860	12.4	3
Dubenion	55	974	17.7	4
Warlick	24	479	19.9	1
Gilchrist	24	211	8.8	2
Rutkowski	19	264	13.8	1
Ferguson	9	181	20.0	3
Bass	9	153	17.0	1
Saimes	6	12	6.0	0
Crow	5	69	13.8	0
Kochman	4	148	37.0	1
Brown	2	7	3.5	0
Stratton	1	19	19.0	0
Carlton	1	9	9.0	0
TOTALS	**228**	**3386**	**14.9**	**16**

LEADERS

Kick returns: Rutkowski 13-396 yards, 30.5 avg, 0 TD
Dubenion 13-333, 25.6, 0 TD

Punt returns: Abruzzese 17-152, 8.9, 0 TD
West 11-86, 7.8, 0 TD

Interceptions: West 5-57, 11.4, 0 TD
Tracey 5-22, 4.4, 0 TD

Non-kick scoring: Gilchrist 14 TDs, 84 pts
Kemp 8 TDs, 48 pts

Lou Saban had a potent quarterback duo in 1963 when Daryle Lamonica (right) was drafted to back up Jack Kemp.

Ron McDole (opposite page), shown returning a fumble, was nicknamed the "Dancing Bear" because for his size he was very nimble.

GAME 1 - Sunday, Sept. 8, 1963 - CHARGERS 14, BILLS 10

NOTES

• Cookie Gilchrist, injured late in the preseason, saw limited duty and, as a result, the running game bogged down as San Diego earned the victory. Elbert Dubenion was poked in the eye early and never returned.

• George Saimes played running back and gained 40 yards on an 85-degree day.

• Chargers' defensive tackle Henry Schmidt was ejected for punching Billy Shaw.

• The night before the game, Lou Saban went to a race track and picked four winners. The morning of the game, Ralph Wilson played nine holes of golf and shot an impressive 38. Good luck ended at kickoff.

• Tobin Rote, whom the Bills rejected in the offseason, threw for 203 yards in the first half.

• The Chargers drove to the Bills 11 on the first series of the game, but George Blair missed a 19-yard field goal.

• Bob Mitinger's interception of a Jack Kemp pass at the Bills 48 launched San Diego's first scoring drive. Rote passed 26 yards to Bobby Jackson, and after a holding penalty, he hit Dave Kocourek for 31 yards to the Bills 1, setting up Jackson's one-yard TD plunge.

• Mack Yoho's field goal was set up when the Chargers were hit with three consecutive 15-yard penalties on the same play. Ernie Ladd was penalized for roughing Jack Kemp and when Schmidt and coach Sid Gillman argued, they were nailed for unsportsmanlike conduct, moving ball to the 11.

• Paul Lowe broke a 48-yard TD run in the third to make it 14-3.

• The Bills only TD came in fourth quarter as Fred Brown capped a 12-play, 90-yard drive. San Diego's

Paul Maguire had intercepted Kemp and returned it to the Bills 8, but Harry Jacobs intercepted Rote at the 2 and returned it to the 10. Kemp hit Ernie Warlick for 34, and also lateraled to Brown, who gained 17 on third-and-seven, putting the ball at the Chargers 18. Saban left himself open to second-guessing by not trying for the two-point conversion to possibly pull within three with 6:33 left.

QUOTES

• Lou Saban: "I don't know what it was. We played very poorly. We stunk. We had pinned our hopes on Cookie Gilchrist being ready for the game. He gave it a good try, but his injuries just bothered him too much. You can't blame the loss on his absence. Jack Kemp didn't have a good game for us and Tobin Rote played well for San Diego. The game-breaker was Paul Lowe's 48-yard run in the third quarter. That play broke our back. We missed two tackles on the play, but he's a good back and once in a while he's going to break one on you. We have no excuses, we just got beat." (On his decision not to go for the two-pointer): "If we had made it, we would have been down 14-11 and within a field goal and a tie. I never thought of it that way. We wanted to win and I never thought in terms of a tie."

• Jack Kemp: "I really wanted to win. Everybody has been so wonderful to me and I wanted to win for them. I feel awful. Give a lot of credit to Tobin Rote. He deserves it, he played wonderful."

• Chargers coach Sid Gillman: "It was a great team victory, one of the best and sweetest in a long time. Rote did a great job. Last week he was just a guy taking snaps from center."

| Bills | 0 3 0 7 - 10 |
| Chargers | 0 7 7 0 - 14 |

Attendance at Balboa Stadium - 22,344

SD: Jackson 1 run (Blair kick), 5:05
Buf: FG Yoho 17, 9:16
SD: Lowe 48 run (Blair kick), 13:37
Buf: Brown 4 run (Yoho kick), 3:27

	BUF	SD
First downs	19	17
Rushing yds	116	131
Passing yds	196	239
Punts-avg	3-48.0	4-41.0
Fumbles-lost	1-1	0-0
Penalties-yds	5-45	7-100

BILLS LEADERS: Rushing - Carlton 10-41, Gilchrist 2-4, Saimes 10-40, Kemp 2-19, Crow 2-0, Brown 1-12; **Passing** - Kemp 18-33-3 - 224; **Receiving** - Bass 4-54, Miller 5-60, Dubenion 1-17, Warlick 3-68, Carlton 1-9, Saimes 3-1, Moore 1-15.

CHARGERS LEADERS: Rushing - Lowe 10-96, Jackson 8-15, Lincoln 3-9, McDougall 1-6, Rote 1-5; **Passing** - Rote 18-29-1 - 260; **Receiving** - Jackson 6-56, Kocourek 2-60, Alworth 2-35, Lincoln 2-38, Robinson 2-45, Lowe 2-13, McDougall 2-13.

WEEK 1 GAMES

Bos 38, NY 14	KC 59, Den 7
Oak 24, Hou 13	

GAME 2 - Sunday, Sept. 15, 1963 - RAIDERS 35, BILLS 17

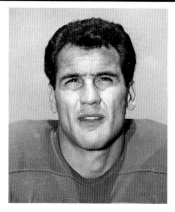

NOTES

• The Bills were sloppy, inept and disorganized, especially on pass defense, in falling to 0-2.

• For the first time in four years, the Bills failed to win on their West Coast trip.

• Mack Yoho's field goal made it 7-3 in the second, but Oakland QB Cotton Davidson escaped a heavy rush and flipped a pass to Clem Daniels, who took it 73 yards for a TD. Four plays after the ensuing kickoff, Jack Kemp fumbled. That led to Alan Miller's TD run and a 21-3 lead.

• Elbert Dubenion caught a Kemp TD pass on the final play of first half to get the Bills within 21-10. The Bills took the second-half kickoff and moved to the Raiders 45. However, ex-Bill Archie Matsos, who admitted before the game he wanted to beat the Bills more than anything, made a key third-down stop of Cookie Gilchrist and the Bills had to punt.

• Davidson fired 67-yard pass to Daniels, but then was

intercepted by John Tracey at the 12. That became moot when Kemp fumbled again and ex-Bill Chuck McMurtry recovered at the 5. Davidson scored on the next play to make it 28-10.

• Oakland's final score came when Joe Jelacic intercepted a deflected Kemp pass at the 1-yard-line and walked into the end zone.

• Daryle Lamonica made his pro debut late in the fourth.

• Starting offensive tackle Dick Hudson was lost for the season with a knee injury.

• The 752 yards passing was a new single-game two-team AFL record.

QUOTES

• Lou Saban: "Everyone has been picking us to win the AFL East, but maybe we aren't as good as some have been saying. But I'm not sure anyone could have beaten Oakland. We got the hell beat out of us. They played a great game, an aggressive game. We plan to make some changes to our squad, but not wholesale changes. We didn't hit very hard. Oakland came up with an inspired game. I don't know (where his team's inspiration was), but they'll get some from now on."

• Oakland coach Al Davis: "I know Buffalo isn't the same without Cookie Gilchrist and Wray Carlton, but we won the game; that's what counts. We figured there is only one way to defeat Jack Kemp and that's by destroying his security. He's the only quarterback I've ever seen who can get out of a tight situation by scrambling the way he does."

• Oakland linebacker Archie Matsos: "Those guys (the Bills) didn't want to play and we were all fired up."

| Bills | 0 10 7 0 - 17 |
| Raiders | 0 21 7 7 - 35 |

Attendance at Frank Youell Field - 17,568

Oak: Powell 5 pass from Davidson (Mercer kick), 4:41
Buf: FG Yoho 32, 10:43
Oak: Daniels 73 pass from Davidson (Mercer kick), 11:30
Oak: Miller 2 run (Mercer kick), 13:19
Buf: Dubenion 17 pass from Kemp (Yoho kick), 15:00
Oak: Davidson 5 run (Mercer kick), 7:45
Buf: Dubenion 58 pass from Kemp (Yoho kick), 12:07
Oak: Jelacic 1 interception return (Mercer kick), 6:44

	BUF	OAK
First downs	23	27
Rushing yds	84	102
Passing yds	355	397
Punts-avg	5-37.4	2-34.5
Fumbles-lost	3-3	2-2
Penalties-yds	4-30	3-25

BILLS LEADERS: Rushing - Carlton 6-24, Gilchrist 10-19, Brown 5-6, Kemp 7-34, Saimes 2-1, Lamonica 1-0; **Passing** - Kemp 19-36-1 - 284, Lamonica 6-11-1 - 36, Gilchrist 1-1-0 - 35; **Receiving** - Miller 7-108, Dubenion 6-131, Warlick 3-47, Crow 3-51, Saimes 3-11, Gilchrist 1-0, Brown 3-7.

RAIDERS LEADERS: Rushing - Daniels 13-76, Miller 5-26, Sommer 1-13, Shaw 1-3, Davidson 5-(-16); **Passing** - Davidson 14-29-1 - 315, Flores 3-6-1 - 82; **Receiving** - Daniels 3-172, Powell 8-91, Shaw 1-55, Roberson 3-45, Sommer 1-24, Mischak 1-10.

WEEK 2 GAMES

Hou 20, Den 14	SD 17, Bos 13

STANDINGS: SECOND WEEK

EAST	W	L	T	WEST	W	L	T
Boston	1	1	0	Oakland	2	0	0
Houston	1	1	0	San Diego	2	0	0
New York	0	1	0	Kan. City	1	0	0
Buffalo	0	2	0	Denver	0	2	0

GAME 3 - Sunday, Sept. 22, 1963 - CHIEFS 27, BILLS 27

Chiefs	10	0	9	8 - 27
Bills	6	14	7	0 - 27

Attendance at War Memorial Stadium - 33,487

KC: FG Brooker 31, 5:06
Buf: Stratton 26 interception return (kick blocked), 9:21
KC: Arbanas 31 pass from Dawson (Brooker kick), 11:25
Buf: Miller 20 pass from Kemp (kick blocked), 12:40
Buf: Kemp 2 run (Lamonica run), 13:01
Buf: Kemp 9 run (Yoho kick), 5:46
KC: Safety, West tackled in end zone, 7:27
KC: Burford 2 pass from Dawson (Brooker kick), 12:19
KC: Burford 19 pass from Dawson (Burford pass from Dawson), 14:20

	BUF	KC
First downs	17	20
Rushing yds	114	49
Passing yds	244	241
Punts-avg	4-43.5	4-31.5
Fumbles-lost	1-0	1-0
Penalties-yds	4-21	2-20

BILLS LEADERS: Rushing - Gilchrist 14-63, Kemp 7-32, Rutkowski 5-6, Crow 4-6, Kochman 2-7; **Passing** - Kemp 15-25-1 - 244, Lamonica 0-1-0 - 0; **Receiving** - Miller 5-87, Dubenion 5-100, Warlick 1-30, Crow 2-18, Gilchrist 2-9.

CHIEFS LEADERS: Rushing - Dawson 6-28, Haynes 9-14, McClinton 6-6, Spikes 1-1; **Passing** - Dawson 25-38-3 - 267; **Receiving** - Burford 11-106, Haynes 5-39, Jackson 5-76, Arbanas 2-31, McClinton 2-15.

NOTES

• The Bills blew a 27-10 third-quarter lead and tied their home opener.
• After a Buffalo punt, KC took over at the 50 with 1:39 left in the game. On third-and-seven, Len Dawson hit Chris Burford for a nine-yard gain. Dawson hit Burford on three more passes in a row, the final a 19-yard touchdown pass with 40 seconds left. The pair then combined for the fifth play in a row, the game-tying two-point conversion pass.
• The Chiefs took the lead on a Tommy Brooker field goal after a disputed interception by Duane Wood on Buffalo's first play of the game. Mike Stratton picked off a Dawson pass and ran 26 yards for a TD midway through the first, but the Chiefs recorded the first of two blocked extra points. Dave Grayson returned the ensuing kickoff to the 41 and three plays later, Dawson found Fred Arbanas for a TD.
• George Saimes' first pro interception stopped a KC march at the Bills 26. Eight plays later, Kemp fired a TD pass to Bill Miller. A two-point punt by Jerrol Wilson then gave the Bills the ball at the KC 23. Kemp scored three plays later and Daryle Lamonica added a two-pointer to make it 20-10 at the half.
• Kemp's nine-yard rollout TD on the opening drive of the third seemed to put the game away, but then the Bills crumbled. Willie West fielded a punt near his goal line and was tackled for a safety that turned the momentum in KC's favor. On the ensuing possession

after the free kick, Dawson passed two yards to Burford to make it 27-19. In the fourth, the defenses took over until KC's game-tying drive.
• Mack Yoho's 42-yard field goal in the fourth was nullified when the Bills had too many men on the field.
• Yoho missed a 45-yarder on the final play as Kemp had hit Miller for two passes worth 35 yards to give the Bills a last-ditch attempt at breaking the tie.

QUOTES

• Lou Saban: "We're not gonna die. We get another shot at them in three weeks and you can bet they will worry about that date as much as we will. These men know they are a better team. I'm proud of this team, I just wish we could have won it. We had this game won and gave it away. The blocked conversions were the difference; our blocking completely broke down on the first one. And on the key play of the game - the nine-pointer as it turned out - Willie West might have made a terrible mistake. On the 42-yard field goal Mack Yoho kicked that was nullified by the penalty, Ed Rutkowski didn't get off the field when he was supposed to so we had 12 men on the field. He's a rookie – a rookie who played a fine game – and that's a rookie mistake."
• Willie West: "I know I wasn't in the end zone, they pushed me in."
• Chiefs coach Hank Stram: "A tie means nothing. It's the same as if you didn't play the game, but today was different, this was a great comeback. A championship team has to withstand adversity and overcome it and we did that. We needed a big play to stimulate us when we were behind 27-10 and we got it on that safety. That meant not two points, but nine points for us. It was the turning point."

WEEK 3 GAMES	
NY 24, Hou 17	Bos 20, Oak 14

GAME 4 - Saturday, Sept. 28, 1963 - OILERS 31, BILLS 20

Oilers	14	14	3	0 - 31
Bills	17	3	0	0 - 20

Attendance at War Memorial Stadium - 32,340

Buf: FG Yoho 41, 7:24
Buf: Charon 23 fumble return (Yoho kick), 7:37
Hou: Tolar 1 run (Blanda kick), 10:23
Buf: Gilchrist 1 run (Yoho kick), 12:32
Hou: Hennigan 15 pass from Blanda (Blanda kick), 14:59
Buf: FG Yoho 34, 6:33
Hou: Hennigan 14 pass from Blanda (Blanda kick), 8:30
Hou: Hennigan 6 pass from Blanda (Blanda kick), 14:02
Hou: FG Blanda 28, 14:59

	BUF	HOU
First downs	19	23
Rushing yds	188	116
Passing yds	123	237
Punts-avg	3-43.5	3-48.3
Fumbles-lost	1-1	3-2
Penalties-yds	5-36	4-30

BILLS LEADERS: Rushing - Gilchrist 16-72, Kochman 19-99, Kemp 2-20, Lamonica 1-(-3); **Passing** - Kemp 6-10-0 - 119, Lamonica 5-17-2 - 49; **Receiving** - Miller 4-31, Kochman 1-68, Dubenion 3-45, Warlick 2-19, Gilchrist 1-5.

OILERS LEADERS: Rushing - Tolar 18-70, Smith 7-38, Cannon 3-10, Blanda 2-(-2); **Passing** - Blanda 18-25-1 - 242, Cannon 0-1-0 - 0; **Receiving** - Hennigan 8-123, Dewveall 4-51, Cannon 2-22, Tolar 2-10, Smith 1-22, McLeod 1-14.

NOTES

• For the third time in three weeks, the Bills fell victim to a superb pass receiving performance as Charley Hennigan scorched the Buffalo secondary for 123 yards and three TDs.
• Jack Kemp injured a finger on his throwing hand and didn't play in the second half.
• Roger Kochman, a rookie from Penn State, made his first start a memorable one gaining 167 yards of total offense.
• On the kickoff following Mack Yoho's first-quarter field goal, Billy Cannon fumbled. Carl Charon returned it 23 yards for a touchdown and a 10-0 lead 7:37 into the game.
• Bobby Jancik returned the ensuing kickoff to the Bills 33, setting up Charlie Tolar's scoring drive. On the first play after the kickoff, Kochman took a Kemp screen pass and raced 68 yards, setting up Cookie Gilchrist's one-yard run for a 17-7 lead. Then the bottom fell out.
• Hennigan caught his first TD pass on the next series to cap a six-play, 66-yard drive.
• The scoring barrage continued as the Bills drove 54 yards to Yoho's 34-yard field goal. But George Blanda answered with a six-play, 62-yard march to his go-ahead TD pass to Hennigan.
• After an exchange of fumbles, the Bills punted and Blanda moved the Oilers 57 yards to his third TD pass.
• The second half was dominated by defense as Daryle Lamonica couldn't move the Bills. Yoho missed a 22-

yard field goal early in the third. Late in the third, Blanda made a 28-yarder for the only score.
• Lamonica threw two fourth-quarter interceptions and threw incomplete on a fourth-down play at the Oilers 36.
• Fans were singing "Good Night Saban" and after the game, showered the field with beer cans.

QUOTES

• Houston coach Pop Ivy: "We are still the champs and the other teams will have a tough time with us from now on. Perhaps after two defeats our guys have realized they can't survive on last year's record. We had to open it up a little bit when the Bills got that early break. Blanda got better protection than he did in the last two games and it paid off. If everyone on the Bills had been hustling, they would have hurt us. But they weren't."
• Lou Saban: "The big thing was we couldn't get to Blanda. If you don't rush him, it doesn't matter what you use. The best secondary in the world can't cover if the line doesn't get to the passer. When we doubled our coverage on Hennigan, they went to Willard Dewveall. Our defensive backs are making their tackles at the target points, they're just not making the play on the ball. We didn't blitz in the first half because Blanda reads the blitz so well, but we switched to more blitzing in the second half and he wasn't as successful."

WEEK 4 GAMES	
SD 24, KC 10	Den 14, Bos 10
NY 10, Oak 7	

STANDINGS: FOURTH WEEK

EAST	W	L	T	WEST	W	L	T
New York	2	1	0	San Diego	3	0	0
Boston	2	2	0	Kan. City	1	1	1
Houston	2	2	0	Oakland	2	2	0
Buffalo	0	3	1	Denver	1	2	0

GAME 5 - Saturday, Oct. 5, 1963 - BILLS 12, RAIDERS 0

NOTES

• The Bills finally got a victory as the defense played superbly despite entering the game ranked last in the AFL. Jim Dunaway made his first pro start at defensive tackle.

• It was the first Buffalo shutout since the third game of the inaugural 1960 season (Boston).

• The loss was the Raiders' third straight since their victory over Buffalo in Week 2.

• Bill Miller tied a team record with 12 catches, giving him 33 in five games.

• Wray Carlton returned to action and the running game showed vast improvement. He suffered a groin injury late in the game that ultimately ended his season.

• The Bills sacked Raider QBs Cotton Davidson and Tom Flores seven times for 64 yards in losses.

• The Bills only scoring in the first half was Mack Yoho's field goal in the first quarter on the Bills' second possession.

• Willie West's interception in the first was wasted when Carlton lost a fumble two plays later. Cookie Gilchrist killed a drive at the Oakland 29 with a fumble, which was recovered by ex-Bill Archie Matsos.

• The turning point came in the third when Clem Daniels' fumble was recovered by George Saimes at the Oakland 25. Jack Kemp hit Miller for a 24-yard TD on a third-and-nine play for a 10-0 lead.

• With 12 seconds left in the third, Flores was sacked in the end zone by linebackers Mike Stratton and Harry Jacobs for a safety.

• Billy Atkins, who just had rejoined the team earlier in the week, suffered a dislocated shoulder.

• Ralph Wilson was delayed in London on business and missed only his second game in the team's 57-game history. He sent a telegram to Lou Saban, wishing him and the team good luck.

QUOTES

• Lou Saban: "Joe Collier and Jerry Smith put in a blitz system this week that kept the Raiders off guard all night. And our double flanker kept Oakland from doing the things to our offense that they did on their home grounds. But most of all, we got tremendous efforts from some of our young kids. You must give them credit, they have never let the bad games get them down. There's a long way to go, we had to win to stay alive, but there's still a lot of work ahead." (On Daniels' pivotal fumble): "Daniels fumbled all right, but only because Carl Charon lowered the boom on him as well as I have ever seen it lowered. And remember, a fumble is only good for you if you recover it and George Saimes was alert in grabbing the ball."

Raiders	0	0	0	0	-	0
Bills	3	0	9	0	-	12

Attendance at War Memorial Stadium - 24,846

Buf: FG Yoho 27, 10:06
Buf: Miller 24 pass from Kemp (Yoho kick), 10:42
Buf: Safety, Jacobs and Stratton tackled Flores in end zone, 14:29

	BUF	OAK
First downs	18	10
Rushing yds	135	24
Passing yds	140	119
Punts-avg	6-37.2	7-35.9
Fumbles-lost	2-2	1-1
Penalties-yds	4-40	5-38

BILLS LEADERS: Rushing - Gilchrist 16-48, Carlton 13-60, Kochman 5-14, Kemp 4-13; **Passing** - Kemp 15-33-1 - 177; **Receiving** - Miller 12-152, Dubenion 1-5, Warlick 1-9, Gilchrist. 1-11

RAIDERS LEADERS: Rushing - Daniels 6-21, Shaw 1-3; **Passing** - Davidson 7-24-2 - 113, Flores 5-13-0 - 70; **Receiving** - Powell 6-93, Roberson 3-26, Daniels 2-58, Miller 1-6.

WEEK 5 GAMES

Den 50, SD 34	KC 28, Hou 7
NY 31, Bos 24	

GAME 6 - Sunday, Oct. 13, 1963 - BILLS 35, CHIEFS 26

NOTES

• Leading 28-26 in the fourth, the Bills watched two Tommy Brooker field goal attempts hit the uprights. Then, Elbert Dubenion flew past cornerback Duane Wood and took in Jack Kemp's bomb. He raced 89 yards for the clinching score with 1:40 left.

• The Chiefs took an early 10-0 lead as Curtis McClinton capped the opening drive with a TD run. Brooker then made a field goal after Billspunter Daryle Lamonica tried to run for a first down and was stopped short at the KC 30.

• Roger Kochman broke a 48-yard run to set up Kemp's one-yard plunge. When Jack Spikes fumbled the ensuing kickoff, Cookie Gilchrist took advantage with a one-yard TD to make it 14-10 Buffalo.

• A Brooker field goal was followed by another Gilchrist score. It was set up when Dave Grayson was flagged for interference on Bill Miller in the end zone on a third-and-seven play.

• KC scored on its first series of the third quarter, but Harry Jacobs tackled Len Dawson before he could get off the two-point conversion pass, leaving the score 21-19 Bills.

• On the first play after the kickoff, Kochman took a Kemp pass over his shoulder and went 63 yards for a TD to make it 28-19.

• Sherrill Headrick then intercepted Kemp at the Bills 17 and Abner Haynes scored on a four-yard run. But 28-26 was as close as the Chiefs could get.

• Dawson attempted a KC record 46 passes. Burford caught 10, giving him 21 receptions for 206 yards in two games against the Bills this season.

• Tom Day was taken from the field by ambulance after experiencing numbness in his arms and legs after getting hit on the head. He was okay and released from a KC hospital.

QUOTES

• Jack Kemp: "The boss (Lou Saban) called the play (Dubenion's 89-yard TD). He figured they'd be blitz-

ing and the defensive backs would be in man-to-man coverage. He was right. Wood covered Duby and nobody ever covers Duby one-on-one."

• Elbert Dubenion: "I just gave him a little move to the right and then just tried to run away from him. He was only about six yards off me and I think he's a little too slow to cover that close."

• Lou Saban: "It was a great victory for us, a clutch victory. Our players hung in there when things couldn't have looked worse. Hot diggety, we're right back in it. Tom Sestak was outstanding on defense, Roger Kochman likewise on offense."

• Chiefs coach Hank Stram: "We were gambling on man-to-man coverage because we knew we had to get the ball back. Duby just beat our man and when that lad is in the clear, nobody is going to catch him."

Bills	7	14	7	7	-	35
Chiefs	10	3	13	0	-	26

Attendance at Municipal Stadium - 25,519

KC: McClinton 17 run (Brooker kick), 3:18
KC: FG Brooker 38, 8:57
Buf: Kemp 1 run (Yoho kick), 13:48
Buf: Gilchrist 1 run (Yoho kick), 2:03
KC: FG Brooker 27, 10:32
Buf: Gilchrist 1 run (Yoho kick), 11:24
KC: Burford 33 pass from Dawson (run failed), 7:04
Buf: Kochman 63 pass from Kemp (Yoho kick), 7:26
KC: Haynes 4 run (Brooker kick), 13:06
Buf: Dubenion 89 pass from Kemp (Yoho kick), 13:20

	BUF	KC
First downs	16	21
Rushing yds	97	123
Passing yds	300	176
Punts-avg	3-44.3	4-51.0
Fumbles-lost	1-1	2-1
Penalties-yds	3-27	1-6

BILLS LEADERS: Rushing - Gilchrist 12-14, Kochman 13-86, Kemp 2-2, Lamonica 1-5, Rutkowski 2-(-10); **Passing** - Kemp 12-24-2 - 300; **Receiving** - Miller 3-37, Dubenion 2-96, Warlick 2-47, Kochman 3-80, Rutkowski 1-30, Gilchrist 1-10.

CHIEFS LEADERS: Rushing - McClinton 13-71, Haynes 9-33, Spikes 5-9, Dawson 1-10; **Passing** - Dawson 23-46-1 - 210; **Receiving** - Burford 10-100, Arbanas 4-25, Jackson 3-25, Spikes 2-33, Haynes 3-28, McClinton 1-(-1).

WEEK 6 GAMES

SD 24, NY 20	Bos 20, Oak 14
Hou 33, Den 24	

STANDINGS: SIXTH WEEK

EAST	W	L	T	WEST	W	L	T
New York	3	2	0	San Diego	4	1	0
Boston	3	3	0	Kan. City	2	2	1
Houston	3	3	0	Denver	2	3	0
Buffalo	2	3	1	Oakland	2	4	0

Bills	0	7	0	7 - 14
Oilers	0	21	7	0 - 28

Attendance at Jeppesen Stadium - 23,948

Hou: Hennigan 3 pass from Blanda (Blanda kick), 4:36
Hou: McLeod 20 pass from Blanda (Blanda kick), 9:39
Hou: Tolar 1 run (Blanda kick), 13:08
Buf: Miller 4 pass from Kemp (Yoho kick), 14:59
Hou: Frazier 80 pass from Blanda (Blanda kick), 8:35
Buf: Warlick 55 pass from Kemp (Yoho kick), 10:44

	BUF	HOU
First downs	22	13
Rushing yds	140	82
Passing yds	241	205
Punts-avg	7-39.1	10-47.1
Fumbles-lost	2-1	0-0
Penalties-yds	3-25	6-30

BILLS LEADERS: Rushing - Gilchrist 11-49, Kochman 8-26, Rutkowski 6-47, Kemp 3-18; **Passing** - Kemp 18-43-4 - 252; **Receiving** - Miller 7-77, Dubenion 5-65, Warlick 3-98, Gilchrist 2-10, Rutkowski 1-2.

OILERS LEADERS: Rushing - Tolar 16-49, Tobin 9-33; **Passing** - Blanda 12-31-1 - 233, Lee 0-1-0 - 0; **Receiving** - Hennigan 3-41, Frazier 3-106, Tolar 2-39, McLeod 2-34, Dewveall 1-10, Smith 1-3.

NOTES
• The Oilers beat the Bills for the fifth straight time and snapped the Bills' two-game winning streak.
• Roger Kochman injured his knee and was thought to be out for the season. This came on the heels of the announcement that Wray Carlton was out for the year after getting hurt in practice.
• Jack Kemp threw four interceptions. Two other picks were nullified by penalties.
• The Bills forced the Oilers to punt 10 times, but Bill Norton kept Buffalo pinned back in its own territory. His 471 yards in punts were a league record.
• The Bills were two-for-15 on third downs. All 13 of Kemp's third-down passes failed.
• The Bills fell to 1-10 in their last 11 games against East Division rivals.
• The Oilers completed just one pass and had one first down in the second half.
• Houston went ahead 7-0 after Fred Glick intercepted a Kemp pass at the Bills 28. George Blanda hit Charley Hennigan for the TD on third-and-goal from the 3.
• After a punt, the Oilers drove 69 yards in nine plays to Blanda's TD pass to Bob McLeod. Blanda was five-of-eight for 68 yards on the march.
• Another Kemp interception moments later by Norton at the Houston 47 set up the Oilers' third score. Charley

Tolar caught a 33-yard pass, then scored on a one-yard plunge after Booker Edgerson was flagged for interference in the end zone.
• Buffalo scored on the last play of the first half as Kemp hit Bill Miller from four yards out. Miller had caught a 30-yard pass and Ernie Warlick a 22-yarder to set up the TD.
• After Charley Frazier's 80-yard TD midway through the third, the Bills killed themselves with mistakes. Elbert Dubenion dropped TD passes on back-to-back drives, the first on fourth down from the Oilers 19, the second on a bomb from the Oilers 45.
• Early in the fourth, Glick intercepted Kemp in the end zone., one play after Bill Miller's TD catch was nullified when he was called for offensive interference.
• On the final series, Kemp lost a fumble. The drive before, he hit Warlick for a 55-yard TD.

QUOTES
• Lou Saban: "We've had terrible luck with injuries. When we lost Kochman, that cut our offense by at least a third. All of the things we wanted to do with our attack went out the window when he was hurt. For instance, on our triple flanker, he averaged about seven yards per carry the first three times we ran it. Our big problem right now is personnel. We need two running backs and they're hard to find at this time of year."
• Bill Miller on the interference: "When I caught my first touchdown pass, Tony Banfield was holding me and I pushed off him. He complained to the officials and told them to watch me. I pushed off him again on that second one and they were watching me."

WEEK 7 GAMES	
SD 38, KC 17	Bos 40, Den 21
Oak 49, NY 26	

Patriots	0	0	7	14 - 21
Bills	0	7	7	14 - 28

Attendance at War Memorial Stadium- 27,243

Buf: Kemp 1 run (Yoho kick), 4:10
Bos: Romeo 6 pass from Parilli (Cappelletti kick), 3:04
Buf: Kemp 1 run (Yoho kick), 11:56
Buf: Kemp 1 run (Yoho kick), :02
Bos: Crump 2 run (Cappelletti kick), 6:20
Bos: Graham 77 pass from Parilli (Cappelletti kick), 9:11
Buf: Ferguson 72 pass from Kemp (Yoho kick), 14:32

	BUF	BOS
First downs	19	15
Rushing yds	83	104
Passing yds	267	201
Punts-avg	4-38.0	9-36.3
Fumbles-lost	1-0	3-1
Penalties-yds	4-40	3-45

BILLS LEADERS: Rushing - Gilchrist 13-49, Rutkowski 5-8, Kemp 9-26; **Passing** - Kemp 18-36-1 - 317; **Receiving** - Miller 5-97, Ferguson 3-109, Dubenion 5-58, Warlick 1-7, Gilchrist 4-36, Rutkowski 0-10 (lateral yards).

PATRIOTS LEADERS: Rushing - Crawford 7-43, Crump 3-25, Neumann 4-21, Garron 4-8, Parilli 3-7; **Passing** - Parilli 12-31-2 - 217; **Receiving** - Colclough 4-69, Graham 1-77, Romeo 5-30, Cappelletti 2-41.

WEEK 8 GAMES	
Hou 28, KC 7	Oak 34, SD 33
NY 35, Den 35	

NOTES
• Charley Ferguson, subbing for the injured Bill Miller, caught a 72-yard TD pass from Jack Kemp with just 28 seconds left to play to win the game.
• The Bills had driven to the Boston 11 with 2:20 left, but Kemp was sacked twice for losses totaling 29 yards and Mack Yoho's 47-yard field goal was no good. The defense held the Patriots, giving Kemp a chance to redeem himself and turn boos into cheers.
• Ferguson, who played for the Minnesota Vikings in 1962, was unimpressive in training camp, but stuck around. He had been active for just one game and had played one play before entering this game.
• Kemp scored on three one-yard plunges, but his fumble in the second quarter killed a scoring chance.
• The Bills drove 77 yards to Cookie Gilchrist's TD early in the second, the key play being a 17-yard pass to Elbert Dubenion on third-and-17 from the Patriots 30.
• Yoho missed two field goals later in the quarter to leave the score 7-0 at the half.
• After Boston tied it early in the third on Babe Parilli's TD pass to Tony Romeo, the Bills went ahead 21-7 on two more Kemp plunges. On the first, his 36-yard pass to Miller was the key; on the second, John Tracey intercepted a Parilli pass and returned it to the Boston 17.
• Tom Sestak then blocked a Gino Cappelletti field goal, but two plays later Ron Hall intercepted a Kemp pass and returned it to the Buffalo 25. Harry Crump scored three plays after that.
• After a Bills punt, Art Graham beat George Saimes for a 77-yard TD on the first play to tie it at 21.

QUOTES
• Lou Saban: "On the winning touchdown play, Ferguson just ran a regular post pattern, first faking to the outside. The idea was to split the two defensive backs. We thought Ferguson would help us. We just hadn't had much of a chance to use him with Bill Miller and Elbert Dubenion playing as well as they have. I think our success can be summed up by two things: we put heat on Parilli and kept it on, and we controlled the ball against the best defensive club in the league. We will be a pretty tough club from now on, even with all our ailments."
• Center Al Bemiller: "The play we used on those three touchdowns from in close was called quarterback-3 which means Kemp going between me and Billy Shaw. The blocking is just straight ahead. On the first score, we told (defensive tackle Houston) Antwine we were coming over him."
• Jack Kemp: "If we hadn't come up with that last one, I would have had to leave town. I had told the guys in the huddle I was going to use a phoney audible."
• Charley Ferguson: "I'd been in on only one play before tonight. Sure I get a little edgy not getting to play, but I know there's a problem being behind the top receiver (Bill Miller)."

STANDINGS: EIGHTH WEEK

EAST	W	L	T	WEST	W	L	T
Houston	5	3	0	San Diego	5	2	0
Boston	4	4	0	Oakland	4	4	0
New York	3	3	1	Kan. City	2	4	1
Buffalo	3	4	1	Denver	2	4	1

NOTES

• Cookie Gilchrist had his first 100-yard rushing day of the season, but he fumbled four times. His two fumbles late in the game nearly cost the Bills. After the first, the defense held and Gene Mingo missed a 53-yard field goal with 5:20 left. Four plays later, Gilchrist had the ball taken away by Wahoo McDaniel, but on the next play, Don Stone fumbled it back and Booker Edgerson recovered.

• Gilchrist's 26 carries were his most as a Bill and his four fumbles were a team record.

• Receiver Glenn Bass was activated off the taxi squad and played running back, and his 74-yard touchdown reception was the key play, putting the Bills ahead for good in the third.

• Jack Kemp suffered a pinched nerve in the second quarter. Daryle Lamonica led the team to victory with his first two pro TD passes; Even with Kemp out, the Bills set a team record with 459 total yards.

• Rookie Don Breaux replaced fellow rookie Mickey Slaughter at QB for Denver and fired four TD passes against the porous Buffalo secondary.

• After a Mack Yoho field goal was blocked, the Bills scored on their next possession as Kemp hit Charley Ferguson. Breaux's two TD passes to Bill Groman put Denver ahead at halftime, but the Bills scored 16 third-quarter points behind Lamonica.

• Gilchrist fumbled on Buffalo's first series of the third, but Denver's Goose Gonsoulin lateraled the ball to John McGeever and he fumbled it back with Elbert Dubenion recovering. The Bills went on to get Yoho's 22-yard field goal.

• One play after a Denver punt, Lamonica hit Bass on the 74-yard bomb. Charley Mitchell then fumbled the ensuing kickoff. Buffalo's Gene Sykes recovered and that led to Gilchrist's two-yard TD.

• Breaux hit Bob Scarpitto for a TD. But Lamonica retaliated with a 35-yard scoring toss to Gilchrist.

• Lou Saban charged a Bronco player with stealing defensive plays from Harry Jacobs' playbook before the game. Denver coach Jack Faulkner denied the allegation.

QUOTES

• Gilchrist on his last fumble: "I saw some daylight through the line. I wanted to open up some speed so I shifted the ball in my arm and he (McDaniel) just grabbed it."

• Linebacker Harry Jacobs: "I'd like to win a game 35-0. You'd have to say the people are getting their money's worth."

• Jack Faulkner on Saban's charge: "All pro defenses basically are the same. Besides, we know the Buffalo defensive setup. Saban apparently forgets we have Red Miller (former Bills offensive line coach) on my staff and Tom Rychlec (ex-Bills receiver). If he wants one of our playbooks, we'll send him one."

• Lou Saban: "If they had taken the whole book, we might not have been suspicious. But just taking some plays is obvious."

WEEK 9 GAMES		
Bos 45, Hou 3		SD 53, NY 7
Oak 10, KC 7		

Bills	7	0	16	7 -	30
Broncos	0	14	0	14 -	28

Attendance at Bears Stadium - 16,757

Buf: Ferguson 4 pass from Kemp (Yoho kick), 13:49
Den: Groman 45 pass from Breaux (Mingo kick), 5:10
Den: Groman 27 pass from Breaux (Mingo kick), 10:50
Buf: FG Yoho 22, 9:06
Buf: Bass 74 pass from Lamonica (Yoho kick), 9:48
Buf: Gilchrist 2 run (kick failed), 12:35
Den: Scarpitto 43 pass from Breaux (Mingo kick), :59
Buf: Gilchrist 35 pass from Lamonica (Yoho kick), 3:56
Den: Taylor 71 pass from Breaux (Mingo kick), 5:32

	BUF	DEN
First downs	20	11
Rushing yds	152	59
Passing yds	307	242
Punts-avg	2-51.5	5-43.8
Fumbles-lost	4-4	4-3
Penalties-yds	4-30	4-20

BILLS LEADERS: Rushing - Gilchrist 26-125, Bass 6-20, Lamonica 3-3, Kemp 2-3, Rutkowski 6-1; **Passing** - Kemp 7-11-0 - 121; Lamonica 9-17-0 - 211; **Receiving** - Ferguson 4-40, Dubenion 5-119, Warlick 2-40, Gilchrist 1-35, Bass 3-91, Rutkowski 1-7.

BRONCOS LEADERS: Rushing - Joe 5-28, Stone 6-19, Breaux 3-19, Mitchell 4-(-7); **Passing** - Breaux 10-23-0 - 239, Slaughter 1-4-1 - 34; **Receiving** - Taylor 3-85, Groman 2-72, Scarpitto 1-43, Prebola 1-34, Mingo 1-27, Joe 2-11, Stone 1-1.

NOTES

• The Bills completed a two-week home-and-home sweep of the Broncos, beating Denver for the first time in team history in Buffalo.

• Jack Kemp completed just five of 18 passes in the first half, but he rallied in the second half.

• Gene Mingo missed two long field goals in the first quarter.

• Kemp overcame a drive-killing interception in the first to hit Charley Ferguson with a TD pass in the second, but the extra point was blocked. The key play was a 42-yard pass to Cookie Gilchrist.

• Mingo made a 47-yard field goal late in the second. But early in the third, Kemp's short pass to Ed Rutkowski turned into a touchdown when Goose Gonsoulin tried for an interception and missed, leaving Rutkowski open field for the TD.

• Mike Stratton intercepted Mickey Slaughter on Denver's next play and Kemp drove the Bills 50 yards, capping the march with a TD pass to Gilchrist and a 20-3 lead.

• One play after a Bills punt, Slaughter hit Bill Groman for a 74-yard TD, but the Bills answered with a 63-yard march to Kemp's 14-yard keeper behind Billy Shaw for the clinching TD.

• The Broncos closed the scoring with Slaughter's late TD pass to Lionel Taylor.

• The Bills' defensive tackles Jim Dunaway and Tom Sestak played great games.

QUOTES

• Denver coach Jack Faulkner: "Those two guys (Sestak and Dunaway) are the best defensive tackle combination I've ever seen. Don't think for a moment that they can't play for any team in pro football. The red dogs didn't bother us too much, we just couldn't block those two big guys. They were picking up our guys and throwing them aside." (On Rutkowski's TD): "I thought Goose had a good shot at it and could have intercepted it, but he didn't and that was all she wrote."

• Lou Saban: "When Sestak doesn't play a great game, you start to think he's sick. The whole defense was outstanding and I'm particularly pleased with the rookies (Dunaway, Rutkowski and Gene Sykes) who keep looking better every day. It's a great feeling to watch them live up to the confidence the coaching staff has placed in them." (On the key play): "The turning point was when Goose Gonsoulin tried to intercept Kemp's pass to Ed Rutkowski in the third quarter."

WEEK 10 GAMES		
Oak 22, KC 7		SD 7, Bos 6
Hou 31, NY 27		

Broncos	0	3	0	14 -	17
Bills	0	6	14	7 -	27

Attendance at War Memorial Stadium - 30,989

Buf: Ferguson 21 pass from Kemp (kick blocked), 5:54
Den: FG Mingo 46, 14:57
Buf: Rutkowski 58 pass from Kemp (Yoho kick), 1:39
Buf: Gilchrist 7 pass from Kemp (Yoho kick), 6:00
Den: Groman 74 pass from Slaughter (Mingo kick), 9:50
Buf: Kemp 14 run (Yoho kick), 12:19
Den: Taylor 5 pass from Slaughter (Mingo kick), 14:31

	BUF	DEN
First downs	20	17
Rushing yds	94	77
Passing yds	267	168
Punts-avg	8-44.3	9-42.2
Fumbles-lost	3-1	1-0
Penalties-yds	4-35	3-25

BILLS LEADERS: Rushing - Gilchrist 16-47, Rutkowski 8-21, Kemp 6-23, Bass 1-3; **Passing** - Kemp 16-36-1 - 273; **Receiving** - Rutkowski 4-100, Miller 4-38, Ferguson 1-21, Dubenion 2-26, Gilchrist 3-58, Warlick 2-30.

BRONCOS LEADERS: Rushing - Joe 9-29, Stone 6-25, Slaughter 2-20, Mitchell 1-3; **Passing** - Breaux 9-17-1 - 62, Slaughter 12-25-0 - 181; **Receiving** - Taylor 9-84, Groman 3-95, Scarpitto 2-11, Prebola 2-24, Mitchell 2-24, Stone 2-10, Joe 1-(-5).

STANDINGS: TENTH WEEK							
EAST	**W**	**L**	**T**	**WEST**	**W**	**L**	**T**
Houston	6	4	0	San Diego	7	2	0
Buffalo	5	4	1	Oakland	6	4	0
Boston	5	5	0	Kan. City	2	6	1
New York	3	5	1	Denver	2	6	1

Chargers	10	0	7	6	-	23
Bills	7	3	3	0	-	13

Attendance at War Memorial Stadium - 38,592

Buf: Gilchrist 1 run (Yoho kick), 4:02
SD: Lincoln 46 run (Blair kick), 6:07
SD: FG Blair 39, 13:05
Buf: FG Yoho 27, 12:12
SD: Alworth 17 pass from Rote (Blair kick), 5:51
Buf: FG Yoho 9, 9:37
SD: FG Blair 15, 5:48
SD: FG Blair 41, 13:23

	BUF	SD
First downs	22	16
Rushing yds	119	199
Passing yds	239	156
Punts-avg	4-33.7	3-38.7
Fumbles-lost	1-0	0-0
Penalties-yds	6-50	5-38

BILLS LEADERS: Rushing - Gilchrist 17-95, Rutkowski 5-12, Kemp 1-12; **Passing** - Kemp 23-36-3 - 278, Rutkowski 0-1-0 - 0; **Receiving** - Rutkowski 7-49, Miller 4-52, Dubenion 6-112, Gilchrist 5-36, Warlick 1-29.

CHARGERS LEADERS: Rushing - Lincoln 10-101, Lowe 14-65, Rote 2-12; **Passing** - Rote 10-22-2 - 156; **Receiving** - Alworth 4-79, Lincoln 3-31, Norton 2-20, Kocourek 1-26.

WEEK 11 GAMES

NY 14, Den 9   KC 24, Bos 24

NOTES

• The Bills' three-game winning streak ended in front of a record AFL crowd.
• The Bills scored on their first possession as Cookie Gilchrist broke runs of 22 and 23 yards and later scored on a one-yard plunge.
• Three plays after the kickoff, Keith Lincoln broke free for a 46-yard TD run.
• The teams exchanged field goals to produce a 10-10 halftime tie. Jack Kemp's 29-yard pass to Ernie Warlick set up Mack Yoho's 27-yarder in the second quarter.
• Early in the third, Willie West intercepted Tobin Rote at the 1 to kill a drive. However, the Bills failed to move and then Daryle Lamonica's punt from his own end zone was blocked by Walt Sweeney and the ball rolled out of bounds at the 20. Rote then hit Lance Alworth with a 17-yard TD pass.
• On the next series, Elbert Dubenion went 56 yards with a short pass to the San Diego 5, but the Bills couldn't punch in the tying TD and settled for Yoho's second field goal. Gilchrist appeared to have the corner on second down, but slipped and fell for a two-yard loss. On third down, Kemp's pass to Dubenion went for only two yards. Saban's decision to kick a field goal was questioned by the media.
• George Blair's second and third field goals in the fourth locked it up for the Chargers.
• The Bills allowed a season-high 199 yards rushing and Rote never was sacked.

QUOTES

• Lou Saban on his decision to kick a field goal: "I felt we had to take what we could at the time. If I had to make the same decision, I'd do it again. I felt yardage was coming hard down there and the field goal was a certainty. I was confident we'd get another shot to score. As it turned out, we had two more chances, but could not get a touchdown. What convinced me to go for the field goal is when I saw Cookie slip and fall after he bounced off that pile and appeared certain to get the touchdown. I felt it wasn't in the cards at that time." (On the performance): "I'm not taking anything away from the Chargers, they have a very good team, but we didn't play our best game. A couple of breakdowns cost us two touchdowns (the blocked punt and a receiver who ran a wrong pattern that forced Dubenion to cut his route short before he reached the end zone on the series where Saban ordered the field goal). I had to watch the film to see if the high snap was the cause, but it wasn't. We missed one block and failed to sustain another. And one of our receivers, I won't say who, ran the wrong pattern and forced Duby inside. Kemp had no alternative. That mistake made it easier to cover and that's why the play gained only two yards."
• Chargers coach Sid Gillman: "We were the best team, it's as simple as that. Position by position, we have the better players and more of them. Rote was off on his throwing, but he has that great mind. He made the right calls at the right times."

Bills	0	7	0	0	-	7
Patriots	0	0	14	3	-	17

Attendance at Fenway Park - 16,981

Buf: Gilchrist 1 run (Yoho kick), 10:57
Bos: Garron 44 pass from Parilli (Cappelletti kick), 5:46
Bos: Parilli 2 run (Cappelletti kick), 9:50
Bos: FG Cappelletti 43, 3:49

	BUF	BOS
First downs	15	10
Rushing yds	73	64
Passing yds	166	177
Punts-avg	9-36.0	10-38.7
Fumbles-lost	0-0	0-0
Penalties-yds	4-41	4-18

BILLS LEADERS: Rushing - Gilchrist 12-37, Rutkowski 7-20, Kemp 4-16; **Passing** - Kemp 19-46-2 - 191; **Receiving** - Rutkowski 4-66, Miller 8-70, Dubenion 5-55, Gilchrist 2-0.

PATRIOTS LEADERS: Rushing - Crawford 14-27, Garron 5-15, Parilli 3-12, Yewcic 2-10, Crump 1-0; **Passing** - Parilli 12-31-0 - 184, Yewcic 1-6-0 - 13; **Receiving** - Colclough 4-56, Romeo 2-20, Garron 4-42, Graham 1-63, Cappelletti 1-13, Crawford 1-3.

WEEK 12 GAMES

SD 27, Hou 0   NY 17, KC 0
Oak 26, Den 10

NOTES

• In a game that was postponed by one week due to the assassination of President John F. Kennedy, the Bills were flat and damaged their East Division title hopes.
• Patriots coach Mike Holovak benched starting QB Babe Parilli in the second quarter but gave him another chance and he led Boston's second-half rally.
• After the game, Lou Saban declared that he was benching Jack Kemp in favor of Daryle Lamonica for the final two games, both against New York.
• The game was played in 10-degree cold with a biting wind that hampered both offenses.
• The Bills took a 7-0 lead with a 10-play, 80-yard drive, capped by Cookie Gilchrist's plunge in the second.
• The turning point in the game came in the third. The Bills roughed punter Tom Yewcic, giving Boston possession at its own 43. Five plays later, Parilli beat a safety blitz and hit Larry Garron for a 44-yard TD pass.
• After a Bills punt, the Pats drove to Parilli's go-ahead TD run. It was set up by his 63-yard pass to Art Graham.
• Gino Cappelletti put away the game early in the fourth with a field goal.
• Despite the chilling conditions, neither team fumbled and there was only one interception. But several passes were dropped, mostly by the Bills.

QUOTES

• Lou Saban when asked if he would stay with Kemp: "No, Lamonica will get a lot of work. So will the other rookies. We'll see what Lamonica can do, we haven't given him as much work as we would have liked." (On the roughing-the-kicker penalty): "That changed the whole complexion of the game. Our players say that Yewcic moved into them as they tried to avoid colliding with him on the slippery turf. He took a fall and the officials threw the flag. It was mostly a case of Boston

making the big play and our failing to make the big play. The Parilli-to-Graham pass, which covered 63 yards, was one of those plays. Our cornerback, Willie West, just didn't see the ball."
• Daryle Lamonica on being named starter: "Great. I believe I have the confidence now. Any athlete needs experience. A lot of questions remain to be answered and you can only get the answer on the field. I've learned so much. Playing for Notre Dame, I thought I knew football, but the coaches here have shown me how little I did know."

STANDINGS: TWELFTH WEEK							
EAST	**W**	**L**	**T**	**WEST**	**W**	**L**	**T**
Houston	6	5	0	San Diego	9	2	0
Boston	6	5	1	Oakland	7	4	0
New York	5	5	1	Kan. City	2	7	2
Buffalo	5	6	1	Denver	2	8	1

NOTES

• Cookie Gilchrist set an all-time pro football rushing record with 243 yards, topping the 237 yards Jim Brown had gained against the Los Angeles Rams in 1957 and the Philadelphia Eagles in 1961. His five TDs set an AFL record. He also had 50 yards in runs called back due to penalties. Gilchrist's total was one of only four 200-yard rushing games in AFL history.

• The Bills jumped into second place thanks to Boston's victory over Houston. But a win over the Jets and a Boston loss to Kansas City in their season finales still were needed to necessitate a playoff.

• Daryle Lamonica made his first pro start and called most of his own plays, although the game plan was obvious against the weak New York defense.

• New York starting QB Dick Wood was injured on the first play and didn't return. Backup Galen Hall was overmatched by Buffalo's defense.

• After Gilchrist's first TD, John Tracey recovered a fumble on the ensuing kickoff and that led to Mack Yoho's field goal and a quick 10-0 lead.

• The Jets pulled to within 10-7 with a 73-yard drive, but the Bills retaliated with a 59-yard drive highlighted by a fake field goal as Lamonica passed nine yards to Mike Stratton. Gilchrist eventually capped the march with a one-yard run.

• Late in the half, a Ray Abruzzese interception set up Lamonica's 23-yard TD pass to Elbert Dubenion.

• Gilchrist then scored three straight TDs in the second half, giving Buffalo its largest margin of victory in its AFL history.

• Captain Billy Shaw and New York's Bob McAdam were ejected for fighting in the second quarter.

QUOTES

• Cookie Gilchrist: "Lamonica called a fine game. It's nice to have the record, but here's how I feel: I like to play football and I like to play on a winning team. So if I block, play on defense or carry the water, that's fine with me."

• Daryle Lamonica: "Our game plan was to run Cookie and we stuck to it. I told him before the game, 'I'm going to put you to work' and he told me 'That's all right with me. If I get tired I'll yell for help.'"

• Lou Saban: "Cookie played a great game for us, but I was just as happy with Lamonica. He showed poise throughout, he followed the game plan and he threw the ball well. Basically, our game plan was to run Cookie, to stay on the ground because I figured the elements wouldn't be the best for passing. We haven't given up on Jack Kemp, he's still a good quarterback and we know that. Daryle did a good job and he'll start again Saturday (in season finale at New York). I'm not even going to think about who my quarterback is going to be for the playoff game, we have to win first Saturday or there won't be one."

WEEK 13 GAMES

KC 52, Den 21   Bos 46, Hou 28
Oak 41, SD 27

Jets	7	0	0	7	- 14
Bills	10	14	7	14	- 45

Attendance at War Memorial Stadium - 20,222

Buf: Gilchrist 4 run (Yoho kick), 3:00
Buf: FG Yoho 13, 6:52
NY: Smolinski 1 run (Guesman kick), 13:40
Buf: Gilchrist 1 run (Yoho kick), 3:40
Buf: Dubenion 23 pass from Lamonica (Yoho kick), 14:34
Buf: Gilchrist 1 run (Yoho kick), 12:03
Buf: Gilchrist 19 run (Yoho kick), :52
Buf: Gilchrist 6 run (Yoho kick), 8:18
NY: Maynard 23 pass from Hall (Guesman kick), 10:59

	BUF	NY
First downs	22	14
Rushing yds	285	38
Passing yds	85	130
Punts-avg	2-46.5	4-33.7
Fumbles-lost	2-0	3-2
Penalties-yds	6-37	2-27

BILLS LEADERS: Rushing - Gilchrist 36-243, Rutkowski 4-30, Bass 1-9, Lamonica 3-3; **Passing** - Lamonica 10-16-0 - 115; **Receiving** - Miller 3-33, Dubenion 3-53, Ferguson 1-11, Stratton 1-19, Rutkowski 1-0, Bass 1-(-1).

JETS LEADERS: Rushing - Smolinski 7-14, Maynard 1-8, Mathis 4-9, Hall 3-7; **Passing** - Hall 15-37-2 - 175; **Receiving** - Maynard 5-85, Mackey 2-12, Turner 5-71, Smolinski 2-9, Mathis 1-(-2).

NOTES

• With Boston losing to Kansas City, the Pats and Bills finished the regular season tied for first. The first division playoff in AFL history would become a reality if Houston lost one of its final two games. The Oilers went on to lose to San Diego the next day.

• The Bills completed their second back-to-back home-and-home series sweep of the season.

• Cookie Gilchrist had another big day. He also had a 44-yard run called back due to a penalty.

• The Bills trailed at the half, 10-3, as Galen Hall hit Don Maynard with a 73-yard TD pass despite fine coverage by Willie West, who tipped the ball.

• The Bills were charged with too many men on the field, allowing Dick Guesman to re-kick a field goal he had missed. He made it, making the score 10-3.

• Jack Kemp replaced an ineffective Daryle Lamonica in the second quarter. Kemp drove the Bills to the Jets 5, but after Ernie Warlick caught a pass, Buffalo had no time-outs and the clock ran out.

• After their first drive of the third ended in an interception at the goal line, the Bills drove 56 yards with Kemp scoring on a four-yard run. However, the Bills still trailed when Bob Watters blocked Mack Yoho's extra point.

• After Guesman missed a 34-yard field goal nine seconds into the fourth, the Bills marched 80 yards in 10 plays to the winning score with the key play a 32-yard Kemp-to-Elbert Dubenion pass. Lamonica faked the extra point and threw to John Tracey for two points and a 17-10 lead.

• On the next series, Yoho tackled Hall in the end zone for an insurance safety.

QUOTES

• Lou Saban: "I thought Jack Kemp's getting off the bench to give us a lift we needed was one of the biggest factors. Daryle sputtered a bit, but he's shown enough in

the last two games that we wouldn't hesitate to use him at any time. At halftime, I told our players it was the worst half of football we had played all year, even in our losses. We didn't play smart and we made stupid mistakes. This team never let up, even when it looked several times as if it would be eliminated. They could have quit two weeks ago in Boston after that loss, but they didn't. I'm very proud of them." (On why he did not go for two on the first TD and then Yoho's kick was blocked): "It wasn't a good time for a fake because we used it against them last week and they would be looking for it. I felt tying the score with so much time left would be a psychological factor and that we would come back and score some more. So many things had gone against us in the game, I felt it wouldn't be a good time to be behind."

Bills	3	0	6	10	- 19
Jets	7	3	0	0	- 10

Attendance at the Polo Grounds - 5,826

Buf: FG Yoho 13, 5:51
NY: Maynard 73 pass from Hall (Guesman kick), 11:04
NY: FG Guesman 17, 12:01
Buf: Kemp 4 run (kick blocked), 11:52
Buf: Gilchrist 2 run (Tracey pass from Kemp), 4:49
Buf: Safety, Yoho tackled Hall in end zone, 6:20

	BUF	NY
First downs	20	10
Rushing yds	158	49
Passing yds	150	168
Punts-avg	5-44.0	6-38.5
Fumbles-lost	1-1	1-1
Penalties-yds	7-75	6-65

BILLS LEADERS: Rushing - Gilchrist 31-114, Bass 6-27, Kemp 3-8, Rutkowski 1-9; **Passing** - Lamonica 3-9-1 - 26, Kemp 8-15-1 - 134; **Receiving** - Miller 2-18, Dubenion 4-77, Warlick 3-55, Bass 1-9, Gilchrist 1-1.

JETS LEADERS: Rushing - Smolinski 8-24, Mathis 9-18, Hall 3-7; **Passing** - Hall 11-33-2 - 175; **Receiving** - Maynard 3-98, Mackey 2-29, Turner 5-48, Mathis 1-0.

WEEK 14 GAMES

KC 35, Bos 3   SD 20, Hou 14
Oak 35, Den 31

WEEK 15 GAMES

Oak 52, Hou 49   KC 48, NY 0
SD 58, Den 20

Boston and Buffalo had bye weeks

STANDINGS: FIFTEENTH WEEK

EAST	W	L	T	WEST	W	L	T
Boston	7	6	1	San Diego	11	3	0
Buffalo	7	6	1	Oakland	10	4	0
Houston	6	8	0	Kan. City	5	7	2
New York	5	8	1	Denver	2	11	1

Patriots	10	6	0	10	- 26
Bills	0	0	8	0	- 8

Attendance at War Memorial Stadium - 33,044

Bos:	FG Cappelletti 28, 7:35
Bos:	Garron 59 pass from Parilli (Cappelletti kick), 10:04
Bos:	FG Cappelletti 12, :41
Bos:	FG Cappelletti 33, 8:22
Buf:	Dubenion 93 pass from Kemp (Tracey pass from Kemp), 13:29
Bos:	Garron 17 pass from Parilli (Cappelletti kick), 5:06
Bos:	FG Cappelletti 36, 7:06

	BUF	BOS
First downs	13	16
Rushing yds	7	83
Passing yds	279	292
Punts-avg	8-35.1	7-32.3
Fumbles-lost	3-2	0-0
Penalties-yds	9-100	7-65

BILLS LEADERS: Rushing - Gilchrist 8-7, Bass 2-4, Kemp 2- (-4); **Passing** - Kemp 10-21-1 - 133, Lamonica 9-24-3 - 168; **Receiving** - Dubenion 3-115, Bass 4-45, Warlick 3-33, Rutkowski 3-45, Ferguson 4-47, Gilchrist 1-11, Miller 1-5; **Kickoff returns** - Dubenion 5-136, Rutkowski 1-18, Murdock 1-3; **Punt returns** - Abruzzese 3-8.

PATRIOTS LEADERS: Rushing - Garron 19-44, Burton 8-12, Neumann 1-16, Crump 5-9, Lott 2-2, Parilli 1-0; **Passing** - Parilli 14-35-1 - 300; **Receiving** - Cappelletti 4-109, Garron 4-120, Colclough 3-22, Graham 1-22, Lott 1-18, Colclough 1-9; **Kickoff returns** - Suci 2-38; **Punt returns** - Graham 2-34.

NOTES

• The Patriots defense turned in a stunning performance, limiting Buffalo to seven yards rushing to win the East Division playoff and advance to the AFL title game against San Diego.

• The game was played in 24-degree weather on a snow-covered field.

• Elbert Dubenion fumbled the opening kickoff and Billy Lott recovered for Boston. Although the Pats did not score, as Ray Abruzzese intercepted a Babe Parilli pass, the Bills never got into the game.

• Boston went ahead 3-0 on Gino Cappelletti's field goal, then after the Bills went three-and-out, Larry Garron took a swing pass and raced 59 yards for a TD.

• After a Buffalo punt, Boston drove 75 yards to Cappelletti's second field goal early in the second quarter (which was partially blocked by Sid Youngelman but still made it through the uprights).

• Parilli had a TD pass to Billy Lott called back due to a penalty and had to settle for another Cappelletti field goal and a 16-0 lead midway through the second.

• Dubenion returned the kickoff 62 yards to the Pats 27. Jack Kemp, who had completed just three of 10 passes, was benched in favor of Daryle Lamonica, but he couldn't produce a first down and Cookie Gilchrist's 39-yard field goal missed.

• In the third, the Bills' offensive woes continued as they failed to move on three possessions. On the third, faced with fourth-and-one at their own 40, Lou Saban opted to punt, drawing a chorus of boos.

• The Bills finally scored when Lamonica heaved a bomb to Dubenion, who had beaten Dick Felt. Duby ran untouched for a 93-yard TD, the longest scoring play in team history. Lamonica passed to John Tracey for the two-point conversion to cut the deficit to 16-8 with 1:31 left in the third.

• However, the Patriots regained control as Parilli and Cappelletti combined on a 52-yard pass, then Parilli hit Garron with a 17-yard TD pass 5:06 into the fourth.

• A Lamonica interception set up Cappelletti's final field goal. Kemp was reinserted, but he failed to produce a score.

QUOTES

• Lou Saban: "They played an excellent game on offense and defense. We had a very poor day, that's about the game right there. We just didn't look good. But I want to thank every player personally. They did their best. We had a good season and we were very fortunate to get as far as we did. We lost some players like Wray Carlton, Dick Hudson and Roger Kochman who could have made us stronger. We had a lot of rookies come through and help us." (On the slow start): "We were in the hole immediately. Boston gets three points and then Garron breaks a couple of tackles and goes 59 yards. Ten points on that field was like a mountain. We intended to run a lot more, but on a field like that, you could run all day and not catch up. Boston knew we had to pass and they blitzed and blitzed and we couldn't get a drive going."

• Jack Kemp: "Blame it on the quarterbacks. We are either the heroes or the bums."

• Pats coach Mike Holovak: "You know those Chargers voted 31-2 that we would beat Buffalo and we didn't disappoint them."

The Bills lost their first playoff game on a snowy day in War Memorial Stadium as Boston won the AFL Eastern Division title with a 26-8 victory. Sid Youngelman (76) peers through the snow to watch the action.

At A Glance
1964

Jan. 14 – Boston's Tom Addison started the AFL Players' Association. Jack Kemp was named Buffalo's player rep.

Jan. 18 – William H. Sullivan was re-elected league president. Ralph Wilson said his Bills were worth $4 million, eight times his original investment. "It's the best thing we ever stumbled over," he said.

Jan. 20 – NFL executives said an NFL-AFL Championship Game wouldn't happen for at least five years.

Jan. 29 – The AFL signed a new five-year television contract with NBC for $36 million. A week earlier, CBS signed up the NFL for two years at $28 million. Wilson said he wouldn't sell his franchise for twice the $4 million figure.

Feb. 8 – Harvey Johnson, the Bills director of player personnel, turned down an offer to coach Edmonton of the Canadian Football League.

Feb. 25 – Fullback Wray Carlton announced that he would retire and concentrate on his burgeoning insurance business in North Carolina.

March 7 – Cookie Gilchrist mailed a letter to the Bills and to the *Courier-Express* asking that efforts be made to trade him. Ralph Wilson said he would listen to offers, but wouldn't give Gilchrist away. Gilchrist asked Raiders coach Al Davis to try and trade for him.

March 10 – Wilson told the Buffalo Common Council that his team had lost about $1 million in the four years of its existence.

March 31 – The Common Council approved a plan to add 7,725 sideline seats to War Memorial Stadium at a cost of $1.4 million. Wilson said the seats were needed to keep the Bills competitive in pro football. The expansion would increase seating to about 42,000.

April 6 – Assistant coach Herman Ball left the

Bills for a post with the NFL's Philadelphia Eagles.

April 12 – The Bills signed rookie placekicker Pete Gogolak, their 12th-round draft choice out of Cornell. "The most amazing kicker I have ever seen," raved Harvey Johnson.

April 16 – Elbert Dubenion asked to be traded because the Bills offered a $11,000 contract, their same offer from the previous season. Dubenion asked for $14,000.

April 17 – Dubenion recanted and said he was just "letting off some steam" and didn't want to be traded. "We are far apart on a contract, but I don't want to be traded. I've made a lot of friends in Buffalo and the fans have always been very good to me. But I do want a fair contract. I'm 29 years old now, which means my career is almost over. I have to make the money while I can."

May 9 – The Bills considered University of Buffalo assistant coach Buddy Ryan as the top candidate to replace offensive line coach Herman Ball.

May 11 – Ralph Wilson denied a report that his team was for sale. Alfred J. Roach, president of International Breweries Inc., said he was going to buy the team, but Wilson replied: "The Buffalo Bills have not been sold and they are not going to be sold at any price. This man's statements are, in my opinion, a publicity stunt and too ridiculous to be taken seriously."

May 13 – Wray Carlton announced that he was only considering retirement and when he sent "that letter to Dick Gallagher saying that I thought I'd retire, I didn't think they'd accept it just like that. I thought they might negotiate a little."

May 22 – Cookie Gilchrist was cleared of a second-degree assault charge stemming from his arrest in May of 1963 for traffic violations when he struck a police offer. The Appelate Division of the Supreme Court in Rochester dismissed the charges on grounds of double jeopardy.

May 27 – Coach Lou Saban heard criticism for trading Billy Atkins and Marv Matuszak to Denver for center Walt Cudzik. Later in the week, tackle Ken Rice was traded to Oakland for back Leroy Jackson, another controversial move, and

kicker/linebacker Mack Yoho was shipped to Boston for a draft choice, clearing the way for rookie Pete Gogolak to take over kicking chores.

June 3 – Cookie Gilchrist was supposed to sign his new contract, but he failed to show up.

June 11 – Gilchrist signed his $30,000 contract for 1964 and explained at a press conference that he was in the Canadian bush country staking claims on his new mining interests and that's why he failed to show up the previous week.

July 2 – Wray Carlton made it official and called off his retirement.

July 22 – Two days after being waived by San Diego, Paul Maguire was signed by the Bills.

July 23 – Training camp opened at the Camelot Motor Inn in Blasdell.

July 26 – Discussing his role as the team's "menu man" trainer Eddie Abramoski said the Bills would consume about 22,500 pounds of meat, 2 1/2 tons of vegetables and 2 1/2 tons of potatoes during training camp.

Aug. 4 – The offense beat the defense, 20-18, during the Meet the Bills Night scrimmage in front of 13,107 at War Memorial Stadium. Pete Gogolak's 10-yard field goal on the final play won it.

Aug. 8 – Pete Gogolak kicked a 57-yard field goal as the Bills won their preseason opener over the Jets, 26-13, in Tampa, Fla.

Aug. 14 – The Bills lost to the Chiefs, 24-21, in the preseason home opener.

Aug. 23 – Oakland scored the final 27 points to beat the Bills, 34-31.

Aug. 28 – The Bills beat Boston, 24-14 as the defense played superbly.

Sept. 5 – The Jets beat the Bills, 19-17, in the preseason finale in Kingston, Pa.

Sept. 8 – Wide receiver Bill Miller, who set a team record with 69 receptions in 1963, was traded to Oakland for a draft choice.

Sept. 12 – The New York Jets played their first game in new Shea Stadium, beating Denver, 30-6, before an AFL record crowd of 45,665. On the eve of the Bills opener, Cookie Gilchrist demanded a player vote to name a new captain. Although perturbed, Lou Saban agreed and incumbent Billy Shaw won easily as Gilchrist got one vote. Saban offered Gilchrist co-captaincy for the opener, but he turned it down.

Sept. 13 – The Bills ripped Kansas City in the season opener, 34-17, by scoring a team-record 31 points in the first quarter.

Sept. 20 – The Bllls beat the Broncos, 30-13, as Daryle Lamonica replaced the ineffective Jack Kemp and revved up the running game in the second half.

Sept. 26 – The Bills crushed San Diego, 30-3, in front of a War Memorial Stadium record crowd of 40,167.

Oct. 3 – The Bills edged the Raiders, 23-20, as Jack Kemp and Daryle Lamonica combined for 337 passing yards.

Oct. 11 – The Bills rolled up a team-record 565 yards of offense in a 48-17 romp over Houston.

Oct. 18 – The Bills won their sixth in a row, 35-22 over the Chiefs, despite nearly blowing a 28-0 lead.

Oct. 24 – The Bills scored the final 24 points to beat the Jets, 34-24. A sign hanging in War Memorial Stadium read: "Saban for President, Kemp for Vice-President."

Nov. 1 – Despite pro football records for completions (37) and attempts (68) by George Blanda, the

Jack Kemp led the Bills to nine straight victories to start the 1964 season. Later, he directed the team to a 20-7 victory in the AFL Championship Game.

Bills improved to 8-0 by beating Houston, 24-10. Their eight wins already were the most in team history.

Nov. 8 – In front of 60,300 at Shea Stadium, the largest crowd in AFL history, the Bills stopped the Jets, 20-7, as Glenn Bass caught eight passes for a team-record 231 yards.

Nov. 10 – Ralph Wilson abandoned an effort to have the upcoming Bills-Patriots game broadcast on closed-circuit TV because rental agreements were too expensive.

Nov. 13 – Sportswriter Tex Maule, a hard line NFL supporter who had gone out of his way to bad-mouth the AFL, predicted in *Sports Illustrated* that the NFL's top team, the Baltimore Colts, would pummel the Bills, 48-7, "or higher if coach Don Shula used his first-string units all the way" if the two teams played.

Nov. 14 – Two-time all-AFL receiver Bill Groman was added to the roster. He had been on the taxi squad all season. Ron Luciano, a former Syracuse star and briefly a Bill, was signed by the International League to become an umpire.

Nov. 15 – The Patriots snapped Buffalo's nine-game winning streak with a 36-28 victory in front of a record War Memorial Stadium crowd of 42,308.

Nov. 17 – Lou Saban waived star running back Cookie Gilchrist, citing "a combination of many things" which began May 14, 1963 when he was arrested for striking a police officer. Saban said he would like to trade Gilchrist to Oakland for Clem Daniels, Billy Cannon or Fred Williamson. The latest incident that prompted Saban's move occurred when Gilchrist refused to take the field with 24 seconds left in the first half of the loss to Boston. "His only concern is himself and how much yardage he gains," Saban said. "We've gotten 2 1/2 good seasons from him and we appreciate what he has done. But there is only so much you can take."

Nov. 18 – After Oakland, Boston and New York put in waiver claims for Gilchrist, Saban decided to reinstate the star running back. Oakland, with the worst record of the three teams, would have gotten Gilchrist. Oakland coach Al Davis was furious, saying the Bills reneged on a deal that was agreed

to. Davis called it a "publicity stunt" and thought the Bills' actions made the league look bad. Saban explained that because Gilchrist apologized to his teammates for his past problems, he decided to bring him back. "Because he asked for his teammates' forgiveness and admitted that he has been 100 percent wrong in incidents leading up to his dismissal, I have reconsidered and will give him a chance to prove he is part of the Buffalo Bills." Said Gilchrist: "I realize I had been somewhat of a headache during the season. I'm sorry for what I have done."

Nov. 23 – *Sport* magazine released an advance copy of an article slated for its January issue entitled "I Play for Pay, I Play for Me" in which Gilchrist took shots at Saban and his teammates. In the story, written by John Devaney, whom Gilchrist said he would sue for printing false statements, Gilchrist said: "Kemp passes too much and then we get in trouble when Lamonica has to come in and straighten us out. The trouble with Kemp is he only uses me 18-20 times a game. Lamonica uses me, boom, boom, boom, three or four times in a row, 30-35 times a game and I stay hot. Kemp picks his plays out of a hat, Lamonica is smart." About Saban, he said: "I heard this colored boy from the south on our taxi squad was making only $200 a week and everybody else was getting $300. I told Saban, 'Look, this kid has never talked back to white people before, he doesn't know how to ask for more money. But how can you pay him only $200 a week, that's a disgrace. Hell, Lou, it's not coming out of your pocket. Pay him $300 and he may have more respect for you. He may save your job someday.'"

Nov. 26 – Despite all the controversy, the Bills beat the Chargers, 27-24, on Pete Gogolak's 33-yard field goal with three seconds remaining in a Thanksgiving Day game in San Diego.

Nov. 27 – The AFL denied a report in the New York Daily News that it conducted a sneak draft two weeks before to get a jump on NFL teams in the signing wars. The Bills reportedly had drafted North Carolina fullback Ken Willard first and Ohio State offensive tackle Jim Davidson second.

Nov. 28 - In the actual draft, the Bills did select Davidson, but as their No.1 pick, and signed him

within two minutes. The New York Jets traded up to get the second overall pick and used it to select Alabama QB Joe Namath. Houston chose Baylor receiver Larry Elkins with the first pick. Other players chosen by the Bills: receiver Lance Rentzel (sixth round) who later signed with Dallas of the NFL and linebacker Marty Schottenheimer (seventh).

Dec. 6 – Art Powell caught a one-yard TD pass from Tom Flores on the final play of the game to give Oakland a 16-13 victory over the Bills in Oakland.

Dec. 7 – The AFL announced that if Denver tied Buffalo, giving the Bills an identical record with Boston, and then if the season finale between the Bills and Patriots ended in a tie, sudden death overtime would be utilized to decide the champion.

Dec. 13 – Daryle Lamonica got the start at quarterback and led the Bills to a 30-19 victory at Denver.

Dec. 15 – Ralph Wilson asked Bills fans to write letters to the team's draft choices in an effort to get them to sign with Buffalo. Fans were urged to talk about pluses of playing in Buffalo.

Dec. 17 – Billy Shaw, Stew Barber, Mike Stratton, Tom Sestak, Cookie Gilchrist and George Saimes were named to the AP All-AFL first team.

Dec. 20 – The Bills won their first AFL East Division title by beating the Patriots in Boston, 24-14. Jack Kemp threw for 286 yards and produced three TDs in snowy Fenway Park.

Dec. 22 – Lou Saban was named AFL Coach of the Year.

Dec. 26 – The Bills won their first AFL Championship, beating San Diego, 20-7, in front of 40,242 delirious fans at War Memorial Stadium.

Dec. 27 – Ralph Wilson denied that he offered his players illegal bonuses prior to the title game. "The story is pure fabrication," Wilson said. "The first I heard about it is when Sid Gillman called about it. I know it's against the rules and I did not pay bonuses." Commissioner Joe Foss immediately cleared Wilson.

Jan. 17, 1965 – The West won the All-Star game for the fourth straight year, 38-14, over Lou Saban's East squad.

BY THE NUMBERS - 1964

TEAM STATISTICS	BILLS	OPP
First downs	255	206
Rushing	114	48
Passing	130	145
Penalty	11	13
Total yards	5,206	3,878
Avg. game	371.9	277.0
Plays	924	867
Avg. play	5.6	4.5
Net rushing yds	2,040	913
Avg. game	145.7	65.2
Avg. play	4.1	3.0
Net passing yds	3,166	2,965
Comp/att	174/397	241/517
Interceptions	34	28
Percentage	43.8	46.6
Sacks/lost	35-256	50-396
Punts/avg	65-42.7	87-41.9
Fumbles/lost	32-18	24-15
Penalties/yds	62-521	54-577
Touchdowns	48	29
Extra points	45-46	22-23
Field goals	19-29	14-27
Two-point conv	2-2	2-5
Safeties	3	0
Kick ret./avg	48-21.2	59-23.5
Punt ret./avg	46-9.2	24-10.4

RUSHING	ATT	YDS	AVG	TD
Gilchrist	230	981	4.3	6
Smith	62	306	4.9	4
Lamonica	55	289	5.3	6
Auer	63	191	3.0	2
Kemp	37	124	3.4	5
Carlton	39	114	2.9	1
Dubenion	1	20	20.0	0
Ross	4	14	3.5	1
Hudson	1	1	1.0	0
TOTALS	**492**	**2040**	**4.1**	**25**

PASSING	COMP	ATT	INT	YDS	TD	COMP%
Kemp	119	269	26	2285	13	44.2
Lamonica	55	128	8	1137	6	43.0
TOTALS	**174**	**397**	**34**	**3422**	**19**	**43.8**

KICKING	FG/ATT	PAT/ATT	PTS
Gogolak	19-29	45-46	102

PUNTING	NO	AVG
Maguire	65	42.7

RECEIVING	CAT	YDS	AVG	TD
Bass	43	897	20.9	7
Dubenion	42	1139	27.1	10
Gilchrist	30	345	11.5	0
Warlick	23	478	20.8	0
Rutkowski	13	234	18.0	1
Auer	11	166	15.1	0
Smith	6	72	12.0	0
Groman	4	68	17.0	1
Carlton	2	23	11.5	0
TOTALS	**174**	**3422**	**19.7**	**19**

LEADERS

Kick returns: Rutkowski 21-498 yds, 23.7 avg, 0 TD
                       Clarke 16-330, 20.6, 0 TD

Punt returns: Clarke 33-317, 9.6, 1 TD
                       Rutkowski 8-45, 5.6, 0 TD

Interceptions: Byrd 7-178, 25.4, 1 TD
                       Saimes 6-56, 9.3, 0 TD

Non-kick scoring: Dubenion 10 TDs, 60 pts
                       Bass 7 TDs, 42 pts

Pete Gogolak was the first place-kicker in football history to kick soccer style. He honed his technique at Cornell and broke all Buffalo's kicking records in his rookie season of 1964.

NOTES

• The Bills erupted for 31 points in the first quarter and rolled to season-opening victory. Jack Kemp completed seven of 12 passes for 150 yards and two TDs in the first 15 minutes.

• The Bills took a 10-0 lead on Pete Gogolak's field goal and a 10-yard Kemp-to-Glenn Bass TD pass.

• Then, in a 56-second stretch, the Bills scored 21 points. Kemp hit Elbert Dubenion for a TD. Charley Warner fumbled the ensuing kickoff and Hatch Rosdahl recovered for Buffalo at the 18. Two plays later, Kemp fired 17 yards to Bass on a crossing route to make it 24-0. On the first play after the kickoff, Tom Sestak intercepted Len Dawson's screen pass to Jack Spikes and rumbled 15 yards untouched into the end zone.

• Linebackers John Tracey and Harry Jacobs and end Sestak were instrumental in shutting down the Chiefs' running game.

• Center Al Bemiller had his consecutive play streak snapped because Lou Saban alternated George Flint into the game. Bemiller had played on every offensive down since coming to the team in 1961.

• Hagood Clarke had a 40-yard punt return, which was the longest in team history.

QUOTES

• Tom Sestak on his interception: "I read their setup and smelled a screen pass so I drifted over to the right."

• Chiefs safety Johnny Robinson: "When Jack Kemp is right, nobody's better."

• Chiefs QB Len Dawson: "That ... Sestak."

• Lou Saban: "We won three of four preseason games in my two previous years here, yet we did a nose dive when the regular season opened. This year, we were pointing for Kansas City from the start and I didn't care if we lost every exhibition. We thought that if Jack had a good day

throwing the ball, our two speedy receivers (Dubenion and Bass) would beat somebody out there."

• Glenn Bass: "We knew from game movies that (Chiefs safety Dave) Grayson likes to take away the post pattern. On the first one I faked a post inside and went out. On the second, I gave him two moves outside and went inside."

• Denver assistant coach Red Miller, who scouted the game: "(Broncos head coach Jack Faulkner) would trade his coaching staff for Tom Sestak."

WEEK 1 GAMES
Bos 17, Oak 14	NY 30, Den 6
SD 27, Hou 21	

Chiefs	0	3	14	0	-	17
Bills	31	0	0	3	-	34

Attendance at War Memorial Stadium - 30,157

Buf:	FG Gogolak 13, 5:25
Buf:	Bass 10 pass from Kemp (Gogolak kick), 10:03
Buf:	Dubenion 6 pass from Kemp (Gogolak kick), 11:40
Buf:	Bass 17 pass from Kemp (Gogolak kick), 12:26
Buf:	Sestak 15 interception return (Gogolak kick), 12:36
KC:	FG Brooker 12, :03
KC:	Arbanas 5 pass from Dawson (Brooker kick), 5:45
KC:	Haynes 44 pass from Dawson (Brooker kick), 13:55
Buf:	FG Gogolak 13, 7:08

	BUF	KC
First downs	18	11
Rushing yds	123	70
Passing yds	208	234
Punts-avg	4-38.8	7-44.0
Fumbles-lost	0-0	5-4
Penalties-yds	1-15	5-75

BILLS LEADERS: Rushing - Gilchrist 14-52, Auer 7-21, Carlton 7-21, Kemp 5-24, Lamonica 3-5; **Passing** - Kemp 15-34-3 - 218; **Receiving** - Bass 5-98, Dubenion 6-84, Auer 2-11, Gilchrist 1-14, Rutkowski 1-11.

CHIEFS LEADERS: Rushing - McClinton 12-60, Spikes 4-7, Hill 1-3. Dawson 5-0; **Passing** - Dawson 16-25-1 - 253, Spikes 0-1-0 - 0; **Receiving** - Arbanas 6-113, Haynes 3-89, McClinton 3-22, Spikes 2-7, Jackson 1-11, Wilson 1-11.

NOTES

• For the first time in team history, the Bills moved two games above .500.

• Jack Kemp threw four interceptions in just over two quarters and was replaced by Daryle Lamonica. Lamonica threw only five passes as the running game produced 166 yards in the second half.

• The teams traded first-quarter field goals. Then the Bills took the lead after George Saimes' interception gave them possession at their own 49. Cookie Gilchrist capped the march with a 15-yard TD run.

• Kemp hit Elbert Dubenion for 29 and Ernie Warlick for 20 to set up Pete Gogolak's second field goal. The Broncos pulled to within 13-10 after Charley Mitchell returned a Paul Maguire punt 55 yards to the Buffalo 15. Jacky Lee's pass to Lionel Taylor was off the mark, but rookie Butch Byrd deflected it to Taylor, who made the grab in the end zone.

• Taylor beat Byrd for a 49-yard gain on the third play of the third quarter, leading to Gene Mingo's 49-yard field goal, but overall, Byrd was superb, holding the four-time AFL receiving champ to three catches.

• The Bills then took the lead with Lamonica at QB. He hit Dubenion for 38 yards and Gilchrist eventually scored from the 1.

• In the fourth quarter, after Mingo missed a 36-yarder, Joe Auer ran 21 yards and Gilchrist went 20 yards with a screen to set up Gogolak's third field goal. Later, Lamonica ran 28 yards and Gilchrist broke free for 25 to set up Lamonica's eight-yard TD run.

QUOTES

• Denver coach Jack Faulkner: "That Cookie Gilchrist just murdered us in the second half."

• Butch Byrd: "I'm beginning to feel more like I belong. It isn't that the players hold mistakes against a newcomer. I just think they're all good, experienced pros and I'm the rookie and I have to measure up."

• Assistant coach Johnny Mazur: "When we drafted Byrd high, everybody wanted to know 'Who's that guy?' I knew who he was, but nobody in the National League drafted him because we had him signed by midnight the day we drafted him. I had Butch when I was coaching at Boston U. and to show you how much he trusts me, he signed even though I didn't have a bonus check with me. I told him how much we'd give him and he took my word."

• Denver QB Jacky Lee: "What an improvement in that defense. They're really solid now."

WEEK 2 GAMES
Bos 33, SD 28	Hou 42, Oak 28

Broncos	3	7	3	0	-	13
Bills	3	10	7	10	-	30

Attendance at War Memorial Stadium - 28,501

Den:	FG Mingo 51, 3:14
Buf:	FG Gogolak 33, 5:29
Buf:	Gilchrist 15 run (Gogolak kick), :07
Buf:	FG Gogolak 21, 8:46
Den:	Taylor 16 pass from Lee (Mingo kick), 12:54
Den:	FG Mingo 49, 4:54
Buf:	Gilchrist 1 run (Gogolak kick), 13:08
Buf:	FG Gogolak 17, 7:22
Buf:	Lamonica 8 run (Gogolak kick), 11:30

	BUF	DEN
First downs	20	12
Rushing yds	230	69
Passing yds	177	157
Punts-avg	4-48.5	6-42.0
Fumbles-lost	4-1	0-0
Penalties-yds	1-15	7-64

BILLS LEADERS: Rushing - Gilchrist 20-92, Auer 10-44, Smith 3-39, Lamonica 6-47, Carlton 2-5, Kemp 3-2, Hudson 1-1; **Passing** - Kemp 8-18-4 - 136, Lamonica 2-5-0 - 58; **Receiving** - Dubenion 2-68, Bass 3-29, Auer 2-46, Gilchrist 2-30, Warlick 1-21.

BRONCOS LEADERS: Rushing - Dixon 11-34, Mingo 4-13, Mitchell 4-11, Lee 6-9, Slaughter 1-9, Odell 1- (-7); **Passing** - Lee 13-32-2 - 168, Slaughter 1-5-0 - 5; **Receiving** - Dixon 5-69, Taylor 3-70, Barry 3-18, Scarpitto 2-16, Mitchell 1-0.

STANDINGS: SECOND WEEK

EAST	W	L	T	WEST	W	L	T
Buffalo	2	0	0	San Diego	1	1	0
Boston	2	0	0	Kan. City	0	1	0
New York	1	0	0	Oakland	0	2	0
Houston	1	1	0	Denver	0	2	0

Chargers	0	3	0	0 -	3
Bills	7	7	3	13 -	30

Attendance at War Memorial Stadium - 40,167

Buf: Byrd 75 interception return (Gogolak kick), 5:45
SD: FG Blair 12, 1:28
Buf: Clarke 53 punt return (Gogolak kick), 12:43
Buf: FG Gogolak 13, 8:26
Buf: Auer 2 run (Gogolak kick), 8:41
Buf: Dubenion 40 pass from Lamonica (kick failed), 14:36

	BUF	SD
First downs	14	15
Rushing yds	109	128
Passing yds	163	118
Punts-avg	2-47.5	5-44.8
Fumbles-lost	2-1	2-1
Penalties-yds	1-15	2-25

BILLS LEADERS: Rushing - Gilchrist 23-81, Auer 6-16, Lamonica 3-21, Kemp 4- (-9); **Passing** - Kemp 8-19-1 - 95, Lamonica 2-2-0 - 68; **Receiving** - Dubenion 5-123, Gilchrist 3-15, Warlick 1-19, Auer 1-6.

CHARGERS LEADERS: Rushing - Lincoln 21-94, MacKinnon 7-32, McDougall 2-4, Rote 1- (-2); **Passing** - Hadl 4-12-1 - 50, Rote 9-21-1 - 137; **Receiving** - Norton 4-96, MacKinnon 4-39, Lincoln 2-21, Robinson 1-21, McDougall 1-14, Whitehead 1- (-4).

NOTES
• The crowd was the largest ever to see a Bills game. Several hundred fans were turned away when 2,000 standing-room tickets were sold.
• Prior to the game, a Larry Felser story revealed that fans in San Diego wrote a letter to GM and coach Sid Gillman protesting his waiving of Paul Maguire. The letter read, "Have you lost your senses?" and was signed "La Jolla Citizens for Paul Maguire."
• Lance Alworth and Paul Lowe didn't play for San Diego because of injuries.
• Joe Auer replaced the injured Wray Carlton at running back.
• San Diego moved downfield on its first possession, but Butch Byrd picked off Tobin Rote's sideline pass and went 75 yards for a touchdown 5:45 into the game.
• Auer's fumble set up George Blair's field goal in the second, but the Bills regained control when rookie Hagood Clarke returned John Hadl's punt 53 yards for a TD with 2:17 left in the half.
• In the fourth, Daryle Lamonica replaced Jack Kemp and hit Elbert Dubenion for 28 yards to set up Auer's TD run. Lamonica's only other pass attempt also was complete to Dubenion for 40 yards and a TD with 24 seconds left to play.
• The Bills had seven sacks totaling 69 yards as the move of Tom Day from offensive guard to defensive tackle in

WEEK 3 GAMES
Bos 33, NY 10   KC 21, Oak 9
Hou 38, Den 17

preseason began to take effect. Through three games, the Bills had 12 sacks.

QUOTES
• Chargers coach Sid Gillman: "I'm not going to come out and say that the Bills are the greatest defensive team going. Your club is really a good team. Buffalo has always had fine personnel, but it was one thing or another. I think they have a sound, well-balanced team now."
• Lou Saban: "We got great games from the rookies – Butch Byrd, Hagood Clarke and Joe Auer – and the defense did more than anyone could expect. Then Daryle Lamonica came in and broke the thing wide open. This was a tension game. I could feel it and I knew the players felt it. We tried to get them loosened up in the pre-game talk, but nothing worked. They stayed tense until they started to hit and get hit. Then Byrd really loosened them up with that touchdown run. Name a Buffalo player and I'll tell you he was one of the heroes. It was just a tremendous performance all around."
• San Diego QB Tobin Rote: "The difference in Buffalo's team now is they're playing as a unit."
• Harry Jacobs: "On a situation where maybe it's third-and-five, we have a defense we call 'Sloop' where Mike (Stratton) takes the swing man all by himself. That leaves George Saimes to help Butch. On that 75-yard run, Butch knew he could go for the ball because he knew George would be backing him up."
• Cookie Gilchrist: "We have a terrific chance to win it all now. We balanced off our running with our passing. The defense was just great. The guys are pulling together. We can do it."

Raiders	3	0	7	10 -	20
Bills	0	7	7	9 -	23

Attendance at War Memorial Stadium - 36,461

Oak: FG Mercer 25, 12:25
Buf: Kemp 9 run (Gogolak kick), 13:42
Oak: Davidson 6 run (Mercer kick), 6:48
Buf: Lamonica 1 run (Gogolak kick), 12:57
Oak: FG Mercer 19, :12
Buf: Dubenion 44 pass from Lamonica (Gogolak kick), 6:42
Buf: Safety, McDole tackled Davidson in end zone, 7:16
Oak: Barrett 4 pass from Davidson (Mercer kick), 12:33

	BUF	OAK
First downs	22	18
Rushing yds	113	90
Passing yds	299	160
Punts-avg	5-46.6	4-42.0
Fumbles-lost	1-0	0-0
Penalties-yds	4-31	4-40

BILLS LEADERS: Rushing - Gilchrist 20-91, Auer 4-6, Kemp 3-14, Lamonica 2-2; **Passing** - Kemp 10-26-2 - 173, Lamonica 7-10-0 - 164; **Receiving** - Dubenion 3-84, Bass 3-53, Auer 3-41, Gilchrist 4-87, Warlick 4-72.

RAIDERS LEADERS: Rushing - Daniels 14-58, C. Davidson 5-23, Cannon 3-9, Flores 1-0; **Passing** - C. Davidson 14-24-2 - 175, Flores 3-8-1 - 38; **Receiving** - Powell 6-98, Cannon 5-21, Roberson 3-62, Herock 2-22, Daniels 1-10.

WEEK 4 GAMES
Bos 39, Den 10   NY 17, SD 17
KC 28, Hou 17

NOTES
• It was a wild start as Tom Morrow ended Buffalo's first drive with an interception and 77-yard return to the Bills 16. Oakland had a TD nullified by a penalty, then Billy Cannon dropped a TD pass and the Raiders settled for a field goal.
• Booker Edgerson's interception started the Bills on a 73-yard TD drive that produced a 7-3 lead.
• The Raiders went ahead as Cotton Davidson capped an 85-yard march with a fourth-down TD run, but

Daryle Lamonica, on in relief of Jack Kemp for the third time, drove the Bills 80 yards to the go-ahead TD.
• After a Mike Mercer field goal, Lamonica hit Elbert Dubenion on a 44-yard scoring pass.
• Ron McDole sacked Davidson in the end zone for a safety to make it 23-13, enabling the Bills to withstand Davidson's TD pass to Jan Barrett late in the game. That score was set up when Ben Davidson blocked Pete Gogolak's 45-yard field goal attempt.
• The game ended with the Raiders on the Buffalo 32 and unable to stop the clock.
• Ernie Warlick, playing with a cast on his left hand to protect a broken bone, had four catches for 72 yards.
• The crowd was the largest ever to see the Raiders play.

QUOTES
• Lou Saban on who will be the starting QB: "I don't know. I have to mull this thing over. It's almost impossible for me to believe that this lad (Lamonica) has progressed so far in less than two seasons. With two quarterbacks like we have, it might just keep the opposition off balance. We might go along as we have."
• Ernie Warlick: "They're throwing to me more with the cast than they did without it. Maybe I better wear two casts."
• Oakland coach Al Davis: "One man is the difference in the Buffalo team. Cookie Gilchrist is the best all-around football player in America. Without him, the Bills are 0-4. Maybe they beat Kansas City without him, but nobody else. We'll catch up to them one of these years."
• Saban answering Davis: "How can he talk like that? It takes a lot of players to build a record like ours. We've had great defense, fine quarterbacking, excellent receiving, good blocking. Sure the big man has been great, but he's not the only one."

STANDINGS: FOURTH WEEK

EAST	W	L	T	WEST	W	L	T
Buffalo	4	0	0	Kan. City	2	1	0
Boston	4	0	0	San Diego	1	2	1
Houston	2	2	0	Oakland	0	4	0
New York	1	1	1	Denver	0	4	0

NOTES

• Jack Kemp set a Bills record and established his career-high with 378 passing yards. This time, Daryle Lamonica played only to mop up late in the game.
• The Bills finished with a team-record 565 yards on 58 offensive plays.
• Glenn Bass' 94-yard TD catch was the Bills' longest offensive scoring play ever.
• Kemp hit Elbert Dubenion for 55 yards on the game's second play, which led to Cookie Gilchrist's one-yard TD run.
• Hagood Clarke fumbled a punt at the Bills 12, but the defense stiffened and George Saimes blocked George Blanda's 16-yard field goal.
• A Kemp fumble gave the ball right back to the Oilers and they capitalized as Sid Blanks scored.
• But then the Bills erupted for 24 points to open a 31-10 halftime lead. Kemp passed 45 yards to Dubenion to set up his nine-yard TD pass to Bass.
• After two Kemp interceptions halted drives, Booker Edgerson stole a Blanda pass and returned it to the Houston 19. On the next play, Kemp passed to Dubenion for a 21-7 lead.
• After a Blanda field goal, Ed Rutkowski fumbled the kickoff and recovered it at the 4-yard-line. Two plays later, Kemp fired deep to Bass who made an over-the-shoulder catch and went the distance.
• John Tracey then blocked a punt and Buffalo took over at the Oilers 18. That resulted in Pete Gogolak's field goal.

QUOTES

• Former Houston head coach Lou Rymkus, who was in the press box spectating: "This club looks like a champion to me. That is the smoothest, most poised team I've seen in five years in this league. The Bills have what it takes. Fine passing, great receiving, gang tackling, running, pass defense, pass protection and depth. I've been watching Kemp for five years and I've never seen him play this well."
• Lou Saban: "The game plan was to pass. We figured on passing as many as 30 or 40 times because we wanted to pick on those rookies (Houston DBs W.K. Hicks, Pete Jacquess and Ben Nelson)."

Bills	14	17	7	10	-	48
Oilers	7	3	7	0	-	17

Attendance at Jeppesen Stadium - 26,218

Buf: Gilchrist 1 run (Gogolak kick), 3:55
Hou: Blanks 4 run (Blanda kick), 9:11
Buf: Bass 9 pass from Kemp (Gogolak kick), 10:57
Buf: Dubenion 19 pass from Kemp (Gogolak kick), 6:32
Hou: FG Blanda 47, 12:36
Buf: Bass 94 pass from Kemp (Gogolak kick), 13:47
Buf: FG Gogolak 18, 14:47
Hou: Hennigan 53 pass from Blanda (Blanda kick), :53
Buf: Gilchrist 3 run (Gogolak kick), 4:42
Buf: FG Gogolak 26, 4:19
Buf: Ross 1 run (Gogolak kick), 14:46

	BUF	HOU
First downs	22	8
Rushing yds	160	44
Passing yds	405	93
Punts-avg	3-37.3	10-39.5
Fumbles-lost	4-2	1-0
Penalties-yds	7-84	5-43

BILLS LEADERS: Rushing - Gilchrist 18-92, Smith 7-22, Kemp 5-22, Auer 1-4, Ross 4-14, Lamonica 2-6; **Passing** - Kemp 14-26-3 - 378, Lamonica 2-3-0 - 27; **Receiving** - Dubenion 5-183, Bass 5-147, Gilchrist 4-48, Warlick 2-27.

OILERS LEADERS: Rushing - Blanks 11-30, Tolar 4-16, Trull 1- (-2); **Passing** - Blanda 7-18-2 - 55, Trull 3-14-0 - 49; **Receiving** - Hennigan 2-80, Blanks 4-9, McLeod 1-20, Tolar 3- (-5).

WEEK 5 GAMES

SD 26, Bos 17	NY 35, Oak 13
Den 33, KC 27	

NOTES

• The Bills rolled to a 28-0 lead in the third quarter, then were stunned as KC scored 22 points in a row.
• Jack Kemp completed 10 of 12 passes for 195 yards and two TDs in the first half, but he slumped, throwing three interceptions and was replaced by Daryle Lamonica with 10:36 left in the game.
• Len Dawson was benched in the second quarter in favor of Eddie Wilson. Dawson had sore ribs.
• Kemp capped an 80-yard march with a one-yard TD sneak on third down midway through the first.
• After a short Jerrol Wilson punt, the Bills quickly made it 14-0, as Kemp fired 55 yards to Elbert Dubenion. After Tommy Brooker missed a field goal, the Bills went 72 yards to score on Kemp's TD pass to Glenn Bass.
• The Bills made it 28-0 as Al Bemiller recovered a fumbled punt at the KC 22 to set up Kemp's TD pass to Dubenion 2:16 into the third period.
• The Chiefs scored on Mack Lee Hill's 53-yard run. Then Cookie Gilchrist fumbled at the Bills 11. Bobby Bell recovered and ran it in for a TD and although a second straight two-point conversion failed, it was 28-12.
• Wilson's 55-yard strike to Curtis McClinton and a 25-yarder to Fred Arbanas set up Wilson's one-yard sneak. Bobby Hunt then intercepted a Kemp pass and returned it 21 yards to the Bills 14. Here, the defense held and Brooker kicked a field goal to make it 28-22.
• With 7:34 left in the game, the Chiefs were faced with fourth-and-inches at their own 35. Coach Hank Stram gambled and lost as Gene Sykes and George Saimes dumped Wilson for a loss as he tried to roll right. Lamonica then drove the Bills to the clinching TD.
• About 5,000 cheering fans welcomed the team home at 11 p.m. at the Buffalo airport.
• Head scout Harvey Johnson observed the Alabama-Tennessee game the day before the Bills game and reported that Joe Namath "is an outstanding prospect."

QUOTES

• Chiefs coach Hank Stram: "If you can't make half a yard in pro football, you deserve to get beat. Our failure to do that blew us out of the box. There was a broken assignment on the part of one of our backs on the play, a weak-side sweep which normally would have been good for first down and 10. We came out very, very flat in the first half. I don't know why. I thought we would do much better today because of the boys' resentment over the beating we took in Buffalo in the opening game. It's a game of four quarters and we only played two."
• Lou Saban: "The Chiefs had momentum going for them after scoring 22 points in the third quarter. And when they missed that first down, they seemed to lose that momentum. One thing I am pleased about is that after they scored those 22 points, our guys maintained poise and came on to win. We could have crumbled."

Bills	7	14	7	7	-	35
Chiefs	0	0	22	0	-	22

Attendance at Municipal Stadium - 20,904

Buf: Kemp 1 run (Gogolak kick), 7:51
Buf: Dubenion 55 pass from Kemp (Gogolak kick), :46
Buf: Bass 15 pass from Kemp (Gogolak kick), 14:08
Buf: Dubenion 22 pass from Kemp (Gogolak kick), 2:16
KC: Hill 53 run (pass failed), 5:46
KC: Bell 11 fumble return (pass failed), 5:59
KC: Wilson 1 run (Brooker kick), 11:51
KC: FG Brooker 31, 13:51
Buf: Smith 3 run (Gogolak kick), 10:27

	BUF	KC
First downs	20	15
Rushing yds	121	130
Passing yds	274	168
Punts-avg	3-50.0	5-51.0
Fumbles-lost	2-1	2-1
Penalties-yds	2-10	3-35

BILLS LEADERS: Rushing - Gilchrist 17-47, Auer 6-20, Lamonica 7-48, Smith 2-5, Kemp 3-1; **Passing** - Kemp 14-23-3 - 256, Lamonica 1-2-1 - 20; **Receiving** - Dubenion 5-122, Bass 3-41, Auer 1-43, Gilchrist 3-10, Warlick 2-40, Smith 1-20.

CHIEFS LEADERS: Rushing - Hill 10-79, McClinton 6-20, Haynes 9-33, Wilson 3-9, Dawson 1- (-10), Spikes 1- (-1); **Passing** - Dawson 5-9-1 - 46, Wilson 9-15-0 - 162; **Receiving** - Arbanas 3-58, McClinton 1-55, Jackson 6-70, Burford 3-27, Haynes 1- (-2).

WEEK 6 GAMES

Oak 43, Bos 43	NY 24, Hou 21
SD 42, Den 14	

STANDINGS: SIXTH WEEK

EAST	W	L	T	WEST	W	L	T
Buffalo	6	0	0	San Diego	3	2	1
Boston	4	1	1	Kan. City	2	3	0
New York	3	1	1	Denver	1	5	0
Houston	2	4	0	Oakland	0	5	1

GAME 7 - Saturday, Oct. 24, 1964 - BILLS 34, JETS 24

Jets	7	7	10	0	- 24
Bills	0	10	7	17	- 34

Attendance at War Memorial Stadium - 39,621

NY: B. Turner 7 pass from Wood (J. Turner kick), 9:42
Buf: FG Gogolak 12, 4:24
NY: Maynard 12 pass from Wood (J. Turner kick), 11:24
Buf: Dubenion 44 pass from Kemp (Gogolak kick), 13:24
NY: Maynard 15 pass from Wood (J. Turner kick), 1:49
NY: FG J. Turner 9, 7:20
Buf: Smith 13 run (Gogolak kick), 15:00
Buf: Dubenion 44 pass from Lamonica (Gogolak kick), 7:16
Buf: Lamonica 3 run (Gogolak kick), 10:41
Buf: FG Gogolak 31, 14:37

	BUF	NY
First downs	20	15
Rushing yds	180	66
Passing yds	347	179
Punts-avg	4-42.5	7-47.0
Fumbles-lost	1-1	0-0
Penalties-yds	4-45	4-48

BILLS LEADERS: Rushing - Gilchrist 15-27, Smith 12-98, Kemp 3-34, Auer 3-7, Lamonica 4-14; **Passing** - Kemp 8-16-1 - 220, Lamonica 4-11-1 - 127; **Receiving** - Dubenion 5-218, Bass 3-40, Gilchrist 3-59, Warlick 1-30.

JETS LEADERS: Rushing - Mathis 12-34, Snell 12-28, Maynard 1-3, Smolinski 4-1; **Passing** - Wood 16-40-0 - 183, Johnson 0-1-0 - 0; **Receiving** - Snell 6-48, B. Turner 5-74, Maynard 4-53, Heeter 1-8.

NOTES
• The Bills matched their previous high win total and remained the only unbeaten team in pro football.
• The Bills needed a 17-point fourth quarter to subdue the Jets and it was Daryle Lamonica who provided the spark with a 56-yard TD pass to Elbert Dubenion and a three-yard scoring run.
• Jack Kemp saw three scoring chances wiped out in the first half by penalties and turnovers.
• The Jets shut down Cookie Gilchrist, but Bobby Smith produced a big game (all his yards came in the second half) as the Bills rushed for 180 yards and totaled 527 yards.
• After partially blocking a Paul Maguire punt, the Jets scored first. They were helped out by an interference call on Butch Byrd at the Buffalo 11.
• After Wahoo McDaniel blocked a Pete Gogolak field goal, Gene Sykes' 72-yard TD run with a Matt Snell fumble was nullified by a penalty.
• The Bills' first score was set up by Dubenion's 72-yard catch-and-run with a Kemp pass.
• Bake Turner's second TD reception made it 14-3. But on the ensuing possession, Kemp scrambled three times for 34 yards, then hit Dubenion with a 44-yard TD pass to make it 14-10.
• A Kemp interception led to Dick Wood's TD pass to Don Maynard in the third and McDaniel's interception of a Lamonica pass set up Jim Turner's nine-yard field

WEEK 7 GAMES
Bos 24, KC 7
Oak 40, Den 7
SD 20, Hou 17

goal that gave New York a 24-10 lead with 7:40 left in the third.
• The Bills then scored the final 24 points. Smith capped an 80-yard drive that was keyed by Lamonica passes to Dubenion (27 yards) and Ernie Warlick (30). With 7:44 left in the game, Dubenion hauled in Lamonica's 56-yard TD pass behind Bill Pashe to tie it at 24. The defense forced a punt and the Bills started at the Jets 35. They drove to the winning score with 4:19 left.
• Dubenion already had 882 receiving yards, tops in the AFL, and an incredible 28.7 per catch average.

QUOTES
• Lou Saban: "You have to expect that kind of a half after a team wins six straight. It seemed that everything went to pieces. Blocked kicks, failing to capitalize on good opportunities, costly penalties, but the guys came back with the necessary big effort. You must realize that the Jets have a fine team, they're much improved over last year."
• Jets coach Weeb Ewbank: "We stopped Cookie but that rookie, Bobby Smith, turned the game against us. The Bills are an outstanding team. We played a good game but we couldn't match them."
• Joe Cahill, assistant to Jets president Sonny Werblin: "(Bills GM) Dick Gallagher was telling me that he rates this Buffalo team on a par with the great Cleveland NFL champion Browns of the Otto Graham era."
• Werblin: "We'd go the limit to buy a quarterback like Kemp or Lamonica. But nobody helps you in this game and money won't. We need six or seven more top men to match the Bills."

GAME 8 - Sunday, Nov. 1, 1964 - BILLS 24, OILERS 10

Oilers	10	0	0	0	- 10
Bills	7	0	0	17	- 24

Attendance at War Memorial Stadium - 40,119

Hou: Dewveall 11 pass from Blanda (Blanda kick), 8:58
Buf: Smith 37 run (Gogolak kick), 12:46
Hou: FG Blanda 49, 13:54
Buf: Smith 3 run (Gogolak kick), 2:37
Buf: Gilchrist 60 run (Gogolak kick), 7:33
Buf: FG Gogolak 17, 13:22

	BUF	HOU
First downs	18	27
Rushing yds	290	35
Passing yds	107	393
Punts-avg	3-38.7	2-44.0
Fumbles-lost	1-1	1-1
Penalties-yds	3-28	0-0

BILLS LEADERS: Rushing - Gilchrist 15-139, Smith 14-88, Lamonica 8-61, Kemp 1-2; **Passing** - Kemp 2-7-1 - 43, Lamonica 5-11-2 - 69; **Receiving** - Dubenion 1-15, Gilchrist 2-13, Warlick 3-59, Smith 1-25.

OILERS LEADERS: Rushing - Blanks 8-3, Tolar 13-32; **Passing** - Blanda 37-68-3 - 393; **Receiving** - Hennigan 12-160, Dewveall 5-63, Frazier 8-82, Tolar 7-51, Blanks 2-17, Baker 2-18, Smith 1-2.

WEEK 8 GAMES
NY 35, Bos 14
KC 49, Den 39
SD 31, Oak 17

NOTES
• The Bills struggled to get to 8-0 as George Blanda set pro records for completions and attempts.
• The Oilers ran 93 plays, gained 428 yards, but scored only 10 points, all in the first quarter.
• The Oilers were determined to stop the Bills' passing game and did, so the Bills' running game rolled up 290 yards.
• Jack Kemp left in the second quarter with a back injury and Daryle Lamonica played the rest of the game.
• After Ron McDole blocked a Blanda field goal on the first series, Bobby Smith fumbled and the Oilers recovered at the Buffalo 36. Blanda later hit Willard Dewveall for the score.
• The Bills responded with an 80-yard TD drive as Smith scored on a 37-yard run.
• Blanda made a 49-yard field goal after Ode Burrell returned Pete Gogolak's kickoff to midfield.
• The second and third quarters were scoreless. George Saimes' interception halted one Oilers march at the Bills 5. Saimes also recovered a fumble at the Bills 3 and Blanda missed two field goals.
• The Bills finally took the lead 2:37 into the fourth as Smith capped an 80-yard drive. Elbert Dubenion's only catch of the day went for 15 yards and Ernie Warlick had a 22-yard reception.
• The Oilers drove to the Bills 26, but Dewveall couldn't hold a fourth-down pass at the goal line killing the threat. Three plays later, Gilchrist broke his 60-yard TD run to clinch it.
• Again the Oilers moved downfield, but Booker Edgerson intercepted a Blanda pass and raced 91 yards to the 8, setting up Gogolak's 17-yard field goal.

QUOTES
• Daryle Lamonica: "They were double-teaming Duby and Glenn Bass most of the game. The linebackers were doing a good job covering in the flat and holding up Ernie Warlick at the line of scrimmage. But that made them vulnerable to running up the middle. We were getting five and six yards with each run. You can't turn your back on yardage like that."
• Cookie Gilchrist on his 60-yard TD run: "I got a big block from Walt Cudzik at the line. I cut back and saw the flow of tacklers going the other way. Bobby Smith got out in front of me and gave me a screen down the sideline. Having Bobby in there really helps me."
• Houston coach Sammy Baugh: "Well, that touchdown pass that Dewveall dropped going over the goal line certainly hurt us."
• Oilers quarterback George Blanda, explaining why he threw his helmet when Dewveall dropped the ball: "Well, why not? That with the conversion would have made it 17-14 in our favor and put the Bills in a hole. Charley Hennigan was the first choice, but he was double-teamed so I had to go to Dewveall."
• Lou Saban: "When that guy (Blanda) is right, he's just too tough. I'm sure glad we don't have to look at him again this season. We expected George would be doing a lot of throwing against us, but not that much. The difference was we got the big plays when we needed them and they didn't."
• Oilers receiver Charley Hennigan: "I hope the Bills go all the way. You know you've been hit when they hit you, but they're one of the cleanest teams in the league. You don't mind seeing a bunch of guys like that have success."

STANDINGS: EIGHTH WEEK

EAST	W	L	T	WEST	W	L	T
Buffalo	8	0	0	San Diego	5	2	1
Boston	5	2	1	Kan. City	3	4	0
New York	4	2	1	Oakland	1	6	1
Houston	2	6	0	Denver	1	7	0

NOTES

• The largest crowd in AFL history attended the game and on the same day, 63,031 watched the New York Giants lose to Dallas, 31-21, at Yankee Stadium. It was the first time both New York teams were at home on the same day since the Jets moved into Shea Stadium.

• Glenn Bass set a team record with 231 receiving yards.

• Dick Wood stunned the Bills with a TD pass to Bake Turner late in the first following a Kemp interception.

• The Jets dominated much of the first half. Booker Edgerson's interception killed a New York march at the Bills 11. Butch Byrd intercepted Wood in the end zone to halt another drive and following a 45-yard Wood-to-Turner pass to the Bills' 30, Matt Snell dropped a TD pass. Jim Turner eventually had a 36-yard field goal blocked giving the Bills the ball at the 20.

• Daryle Lamonica, replacing the ineffective Jack Kemp, promptly fired an 80-yard TD pass to Bass, who beat former-Bill Willie West. West had just joined the Jets earlier in the week.

• In the third, Pete Gogolak kicked a 47-yard field goal after Lamonica hit Ed Rutkowski for 27.

• After Lamonica threw an interception which Larry Grantham returned to the Bills 27, Tom Sestak and Mike Stratton combined for two sacks worth 21 yards to force a punt.

• Lamonica then hit Bass for 52 yards to set up Gogolak's 33-yard field goal.

• Cookie Gilchrist then broke a 67-yard TD run with 43 seconds left to play.

• A New York paper quoted Lamonica as saying: "I think I became a first-string quarterback today." Lamonica denied it, saying: "I couldn't have said it because I never talked to the sportswriter who wrote

the story. And besides, I don't think I played a good enough game."

QUOTES

• Glenn Bass: "We wanted to take advantage of the hook zone, but they might have been a little too cocky. Willie West did a good job on me earlier in the year when he was with Denver and I guess he figured he could play me tight. That gave me a chance to go deep."

• Daryle Lamonica: "We figured West might be a little strange to things here and when we saw him come in and there was a one-on-one situation with Glenn, we worked on it."

• Lou Saban: "We always seemed to be going backwards, but then we'd come back with a big play. I don't know how to describe this game. Certainly it wasn't our best. Glenn supplied the difference for us today. He not only made a lot of catches, but he was making the vital ones to get us out of the holes we were digging for ourselves." (On changing quarterbacks again): "We thought it was time for a change. Jack looked really good on the first drive before the fumble, but after that he didn't get the club moving."

• Jets owner Sonny Werblin: "Football is show business and you gotta have stars. Did you hear them cheer the crowd announcement? Wasn't that something? I'm really pleased. I don't regard this as a conquest of anybody, but we had a good attraction and we now have a core of our own fans. I thought it would be four years before we drew like this."

• Jets coach Weeb Ewbank: "This game was a tribute to the crowd. I'm sorry we didn't win it for them. I was proud of my team's effort today. We lost to a really good football team, but we were in the game all the way."

Bills	0 7 3 10 - 20
Jets	7 0 0 0 - 7

Attendance at Shea Stadium - 60,300

NY: B. Turner 71 pass from Wood (J. Turner kick), 12:31
Buf: Bass 80 pass from Lamonica (Gogolak kick), 13:33
Buf: FG Gogolak 47, 9:49
Buf: FG Gogolak 33, 6:39
Buf: Gilchrist 67 run (Gogolak kick), 14:17

	BUF	NY
First downs	13	15
Rushing yds	140	31
Passing yds	228	338
Punts-avg	6-47.0	5-41.0
Fumbles-lost	1-1	0-0
Penalties-yds	9-76	4-54

BILLS LEADERS: Rushing - Gilchrist 9-99, Smith 12-20, Dubenion 1-20, Kemp 1-3, Lamonica 2- (-2); **Passing** - Kemp 2-7-1 - 26, Lamonica 11-24-1 - 267; **Receiving** - Bass 8-231, Warlick 2-23, Rutkowski 1-27, Smith 2-12.

JETS LEADERS: Rushing - Mathis 7-16, Snell 6-15; **Passing** - Wood 23-49-5 - 367; **Receiving** - Snell 6-46, B. Turner 5-165, Maynard 5-100, Mackey 2-23, Baker 2-15, Mathis 2-16, Smolinski 1-2.

WEEK 9 GAMES

Bos 25, Hou 24	KC 42, Oak 7
SD 31, Den 20	

NOTES

• In the Bills' final home game of the regular-season, the Patriots rallied for 15 fourth-quarter points to spoil Buffalo's perfect home season. The Bills turned over the ball six times.

• With the Bills leading 28-14 in the third, Lou Saban yanked Jack Kemp in favor of Daryle Lamonica. Three plays later, Lamonica lost a fumble and the Patriots began their comeback.

• Penalties nullified two long gains into Boston territory and an interception by John Tracey stopped Buffalo at the Boston 30 with Buffalo still ahead 28-21.

• Elbert Dubenion didn't play because of a knee injury and Glenn Bass had to leave with a hamstring injury after catching six passes for 141 yards.

• The Bills trailed 14-13 at the half, but then scored twice in 12 seconds as Kemp hit Bill Groman on a 22-yard TD pass and Lamonica faked the extra point and ran in for two points. Hagood Clarke then forced Larry Garron to fumble the kickoff. Joe Auer ran 18 yards for a TD and a 28-14 lead.

• After an exchange of interceptions, Lamonica replaced Kemp and fumbled at his own 5. Babe Parilli hit Gino Cappelletti for a TD on the next play.

• Kemp returned and moved the Bills downfield, but Pete Gogolak missed a 36-yard field goal.

• Midway through the fourth, Boston went ahead when Parilli passed six yards to Garron to climax a 49-yard drive. Booker Edgerson was hurt on the play and his replacement, rookie Oliver Dobbins, was victimized by Parilli on the go-ahead two-point conversion toss to Cappelletti.

• Kemp fumbled right after the kickoff and Cappelletti again beat Dobbins for a 34-yard clinching TD with

6:02 left.

• In the closing minutes, Lamonica hit Ed Rutkowski for gains of 23, 20 and 21 yards to move the team to the Boston 16, but his third-down pass into the end zone with 47 seconds left was intercepted by Ron Hall.

• Kemp and Lamonica combined for a team-record 53 pass attempts and Kemp admitted it was the worst beating he ever had taken as Boston registered seven sacks worth 56 yards.

QUOTES

• Lou Saban explaining the QB switch: "When Jack throws one away, we like to get him out of there and then put him back in. We made some mistakes and you can't do that in a tough game. It's just too bad we had to make unfortunate mistakes against that club. Now we can get back to work and stop worrying about keeping winning streaks alive. In pro football, you can't keep winning week after week."

• Babe Parilli: "It's going to go down to the final day of the race when the Bills play at Boston and we'll win that one for the title."

Patriots	0 14 7 15 - 36
Bills	10 3 15 0 - 28

Attendance at War Memorial Staduim - 42,308

Buf: Bass 29 pass from Kemp (Gogolak kick), 7:05
Buf: FG Gogolak 41, 12:18
Bos: Romeo 15 pass from Parilli (Cappelletti kick), 5:24
Bos: Cappelletti 35 pass from Parilli (Cappelletti kick), 6:34
Buf: FG Gogolak 33, 13:04
Buf: Groman 22 pass from Kemp (Lamonica run), 3:07
Buf: Auer 18 fumble return (Gogolak kick), 3:19
Bos: Cappelletti 5 pass from Parilli (Cappelletti kick), 8:18
Bos: Garron 6 pass from Parilli (Cappelletti pass from Parilli), 7:28
Bos: Cappelletti 34 pass from Parilli (Cappelletti kick), 8:48

	BUF	BOS
First downs	20	14
Rushing yds	70	44
Passing yds	316	208
Punts-avg	6-44.2	10-41.0
Fumbles-lost	5-3	1-1
Penalties-yds	8-50	1-15

BILLS LEADERS: Rushing - Gilchrist 11-31, Smith 5-17, Kemp 3-10, Auer 2-12; **Passing** - Kemp 16-41-2 - 295, Lamonica 4-12-1 - 77; **Receiving** - Bass 6-141, Warlick 1-21, Rutkowski 7-127, Groman 4-68, Smith 2-15.

PATRIOTS LEADERS: Rushing - Garron 10-21, Burton 5-18, J.D. Garrett 2-5, Parilli 4-0; **Passing** - Parilli 18-35-3 - 240; **Receiving** - Cappelletti 4-90, Garron 5-50, Colclough 3-38, Romeo 3-34, Graham 2-26, Burton 1-2

WEEK 10 GAMES

Oak 20, Hou 10	Den 20, NY 16
SD 28, KC 14	

STANDINGS: TENTH WEEK

EAST	W	L	T	WEST	W	L	T
Buffalo	9	1	0	San Diego	7	2	1
Boston	7	2	1	Kan. City	4	5	0
New York	4	4	1	Oakland	2	7	1
Houston	2	8	0	Denver	2	8	0

Bills	0	14	0	13 - 27
Chargers	10	0	7	7 - 24

Attendance at Balboa Stadium - 34,865

SD: FG Lincoln 27, 7:04
SD: Alworth 63 pass from Hadl (Lincoln kick), 11:40
Buf: Auer 1 run (Gogolak kick), 12:11
Buf: Kemp 1 run (Gogolak kick), 13:04
SD: Norton 17 pass from Hadl (Lincoln kick), 13:06
SD: Alworth 53 pass from Lincoln (Lincoln kick), :07
Buf: Safety, Stratton tackled Hadl in end zone, 8:10
Buf: Lamonica 1 run (Lamonica run), 11:36
Buf: FG Gogolak 33, 14:57

	BUF	SD
First downs	18	11
Rushing yds	140	52
Passing yds	133	282
Punts-avg	6-42.7	4-50.0
Fumbles-lost	2-1	3-2
Penalties-yds	5-50	6-37

BILLS LEADERS: Rushing - Gilchrist 21-87, Auer 15-46, Lamonica 6-6, Kemp 2-1; **Passing** - Kemp 8-20-1 - 136, Lamonica 4-7-0 - 40; **Receiving** - Dubenion 3-55, Bass 1-14, Warlick 3-79, Auer 2-19, Gilchrist 3-9.

CHARGERS LEADERS: Rushing - Lincoln 8-34, Lowe 9-5, Hadl 2-13; **Passing** - Hadl 10-20-3 - 209, Rote 1-3-2 - 20, Lincoln 1-1-0 - 53; **Receiving** - Alworth 4-185, Norton 5-65, Lincoln 3-32.

NOTES

• Pete Gogolak won the Thanksgiving Day game with a 33-yard field goal with three seconds left.
• Lou Saban said the key to the game was the double-wing offense that the Bills employed.
• Trailing 24-14, the Bills were stopped at the San Diego 2 and the game appeared to be lost with 6:50 left. But Mike Stratton tackled John Hadl for a safety, then Charley Warner returned the free kick back to the San Diego 18.
• Charger safety Ken Graham was called for interfering with Ernie Warlick at the 5, setting up Daryle Lamonica's sneak with 3:24 left. Lamonica was stopped on the two-point conversion, but a holding penalty gave the Bills another chance and Lamonica snuck in from the 1 to tie it.
• Tom Day then tipped a Hadl pass and Stratton intercepted at the Bills 44.
• Gilchrist ripped off runs of 18 and 11 yards, thanks to key blocks by Joe Auer in the double-wing formation. Lamonica then ran three plays to the middle of the field to put Gogolak in position for the winning kick.

WEEK 11 GAMES

Bos 12, Den 7	Oak 35, NY 26
KC 28, Hou 19	
Buffalo and San Diego had bye weeks.	

WEEK 12 GAMES

Oak 20, Den 10	Bos 34, Hou 17
NY 27, KC 14	

• The Chargers led 10-0 late in the second quarter because Gilchrist had lost a fumble at the San Diego 4 and Gogolak had missed a 23-yard field goal. But Buffalo went ahead with two quick TDs.
• John Tracey's interception at the Chargers 16 set up Auer's TD run. Gene Sykes picked off a Tobin Rote pass and returned it to the 1, from where Jack Kemp snuck in.
• On the first play of the fourth quarter, Keith Lincoln hit Lance Alworth on a halfback option pass for a 53-yard TD for San Diego.
• The crowd was the largest ever in San Diego for a Chargers game. Ralph Wilson hosted a party after the game.

QUOTES

• Pete Gogolak: "I was shaking like a leaf on the sidelines. But everything was OK once I got in there."
• Lou Saban: "That'll be the damndest turkey you ever see. I never had a more satisfying win. This was a big one. We had to have it with Boston breathing down our necks. Gee, Gogo really hit one when we needed it, didn't he? These guys just never quit, never lost their poise when things looked tough in the fourth quarter."
• Tom Day: "Jack told me that Hadl threw a low ball, but I was surprised when I tipped it. My man put an aggressive block on me, but I just whipped his head to the side and reached up."
• Mike Stratton: "With the horses we have on the line, it's easy playing linebacker because we don't have to worry about getting killed inside."

Bills	0	0	7	6 - 13
Raiders	0	7	3	6 - 16

Attendance at Frank Youell Field - 18,134

Oak: Daniels 35 pass from Flores (Mercer kick), 13:25
Oak: FG Mercer 40, 2:53
Buf: Dubenion 38 pass from Lamonica (Gogolak kick), 14:27
Buf: FG Gogolak 12, 10:48
Buf: FG Gogolak 24, 12:40
Oak: Powell 1 pass from Flores (No PAT attempt), 15:00

	BUF	OAK
First downs	12	18
Rushing yds	112	79
Passing yds	133	261
Punts-avg	7-45.9	6-42.0
Fumbles-lost	1-1	2-2
Penalties-yds	7-36	6-68

BILLS LEADERS: Rushing - Gilchrist 10-24, Auer 9-15, Smith 7-23, Lamonica 6-48, Kemp 6-48; **Passing** - Kemp 2-6-1 - 23, Lamonica 7-18-1 - 131; **Receiving** - Dubenion 3-57, Warlick 2-42, Gilchrist 4-55.

RAIDERS LEADERS: Rushing - Daniels 13-56, Davidson 1-19, Cannon 1-4; **Passing** - Davidson 4-11-0 - 48, Flores 16-32-1 - 244; **Receiving** - Powell 9-106, Roberson 5-89, Daniels 3-62, Herock 2-29, Cannon 1-6.

WEEK 13 GAMES

Bos 31, KC 24	SD 38, NY 3

NOTES

• This time, the final play went against Buffalo. Art Powell caught Tom Flores' one-yard pass in the front left corner of the end zone, with Butch Byrd all over him as time ran out.
• The loss dropped the Bills into a virtual tie for first with Boston, setting up a season-ending showdown.
• The winning score, which climaxed an 11-play, 75-yard drive, was set up when Charley Warner was penalized for interference at the goal line on Bo Roberson with four seconds left. Al Davis then bypassed a tying field goal and went for the win.
• Elbert Dubenion and Bobby Smith each dropped a TD pass. Smith also had a four-yard TD run that was nullified by a penalty as the Bills played their sloppiest game of the season.
• Daryle Lamonica took over for Jack Kemp in the second quarter. Dubenion dropped a TD bomb, and Oakland proceeded to drive 74 yards to the game's first score, Clem Daniels' 35-yard TD reception.
• Mike Mercer's 40-yard field goal 2:53 into the third made it 10-0. But then the Bills took charge as Lamonica hit Dubenion for a TD late in the third.
• Gogolak then kicked a 12-yard field goal with 4:12 left after Smith's TD had been called back.
• The Bills recovered an onside kick, but Lamonica was intercepted at the Oakland 6 by Warren Powers. The defense forced a punt. Lamonica drove the Bills to the Oakland 17 with the key play a 19-yard pass to Cookie Gilchrist and a subsequent personal foul penalty that was tacked on.
• Gogolak then kicked a 24-yard field goal with 2:20 left.

QUOTES

• Lou Saban: "I didn't think we'd lose after we kicked that field goal. But I don't think we played well at all. We lost the game in the first half. We had a lot of opportunities and didn't make the most of them. The defense did a fine job, but our offense looked bad. I've been worried something like this might happen, although I thought after we won such a big game in San Diego that it wouldn't happen today. All these guys can think of is 'Get Boston.' Our job will be to make sure they aren't looking past Denver (even though the game means nothing). It seems funny that you play the whole season and the championship boils down to one game. I guess that's as it should be."
• Raiders receiver Art Powell: "When you're that close, they have to play man-to-man. I gave Byrd two moves, one right at him, hitting him, because I knew he was going to hit me. Then I broke hard to the left and the ball was right there with me between the ball and Byrd."
• Raiders coach Al Davis: "The Bills were coming off a big victory and obviously they were pretty flat. They didn't hit as well as they've hit in other games. I had our guys ready. The Bills will win it (the showdown with Boston). That is, they'll win it if they don't panic. When Boston beat the Bills in Buffalo, the Bills didn't have Elbert Dubenion and Bass got hurt in that game. I'd make sure both of them stayed healthy in the Denver game next Sunday. Besides, Buffalo has a better team than Boston."

STANDINGS: THIRTEENTH WEEK

EAST	W	L	T	WEST	W	L	T
Buffalo	10	2	0	San Diego	8	3	1
Boston	10	2	1	Kan. City	5	7	0
New York	5	6	1	Oakland	4	7	2
Houston	2	10	0	Denver	2	9	1

GAME 13 - Sunday, Dec. 13, 1964 - BILLS 30, BRONCOS 19

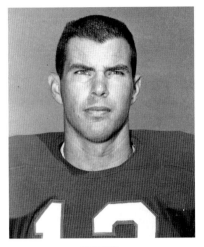

NOTES

• Daryle Lamonica started ahead of Jack Kemp and directed a victory to set up the season finale in Boston. Lamonica wasn't overly sharp, fumbling three times and completing just seven of 20 passes.

• The Bills were sloppy, turning over the ball six times in windy, cold conditions. The teams combined for 18 punts.

• George Saimes was used on many safety blitzes and the Bills recorded 11 sacks for 84 yards.

• The Bills got off to a fast start as Lamonica hit Ed Rutkowski with a 46-yard TD pass, then Ron McDole trapped Billy Joe for a safety and a 9-0 lead.

• Wray Carlton, playing for the first time in three months, scored on a five-yard run after McDole forced Charley Mitchell to fumble and McDole recovered the loose ball.

• Late in the half, Lamonica broke free from a near sack for a 23-yard TD as the Bills opened a 23-3 halftime lead.

• Denver rallied with 16 straight points to pull within 23-19. Jacky Lee threw a TD pass to Lionel Taylor and Mickey Slaughter's only pass attempt went for a TD to Bob Scarpitto. Dick Guesman also kicked his second field goal of the day.

• The Bills put away the game with an impressive 10-play running drive. The key play was Carlton gaining 11 yards on a fourth-and-two play at the Denver 19. Lamonica eventually scored on a one-yard sneak.

QUOTES

• Lou Saban: "Everything we did was to get us ready for Boston next Sunday. We got by with as little as possible on offense. I can't explain our seven fumbles, but the way Denver was hitting might have had something to do with it." (On why he started Lamonica): "We wanted to know what he could do when he had to take control of the club from the start. Now we know." (On why he started Carlton and Rutkowski): "We want to have a man ready for every possible situation that can develop against Boston. We might need a strong, tough short receiver. We wanted to get Rutkowski ready for that job. And Carlton needed the game. Outside of that first fumble, he played pretty well. Now he has the feel of things again."

WEEK 14 GAMES	
KC 49, SD 6	Hou 33, NY 17

Bills	9 14 0 7 - 30
Broncos	0 3 13 3 - 19

Attendance at Bears Stadium - 14,431

Buf: Rutkowski 46 pass from Lamonica (Gogolak kick), 11:03
Buf: Safety, McDole tackled Joe in end zone, 14:23
Den: FG Guesman 30, 1:59
Buf: Carlton 5 run (Gogolak kick), 4:57
Buf: Lamonica 23 run (Gogolak kick), 12:32
Den: Taylor 30 pass from Lee (Guesman kick), 7:09
Den: Scarpitto 37 pass from Slaughter (kick blocked), 14:16
Den: FG Guesman 45, 7:43
Buf: Lamonica 1 run (Gogolak kick), 12:53

	BUF	DEN
First downs	13	7
Rushing yds	157	47
Passing yds	64	70
Punts-avg	8-34.8	10-37.0
Fumbles-lost	7-5	5-1
Penalties-yds	4-26	5-53

BILLS LEADERS: Rushing - Gilchrist 17-67, Carlton 15-57, Lamonica 6-33; **Passing** - Lamonica 6-21-1 - 89; **Receiving** - Dubenion 1-3, Rutkowski 4-69, Carlton 1-17.

BRONCOS LEADERS: Rushing - Mitchell 9-14, Joe 7-18, Slaughter 3-12, Lee 1-3; **Passing** - Slaughter 11-30-0 - 124, Lee 1-1-0 - 30; **Receiving** - Taylor 4-63, Scarpitto 3-59, Mitchell 3-19, Dixon 2-13.

GAME 14 - Sunday, Dec. 20, 1964 - BILLS 24, PATRIOTS 14

NOTES

• The Bills were spurred on by trash-talking by the Pats during the week. Pats players continually expressed confidence that they would win the game.

• Jack Kemp went all the way at QB for the first time since the season opener as Lou Saban gained revenge against the team he once coached.

• The Patriots managed just 33 yards rushing, the seventh time this season the Bills allowed 52 yards or fewer.

• Just 5:37 into the game, Kemp hit Elbert Dubenion with a 57-yard TD pass as Dubenion beat Chuck Shonta cleanly.

• Boston answered with a 72-yard TD drive. Tony Romeo found a seam in the Buffalo defense and was all alone to haul in Babe Parilli's 37-yard pass. Parilli's two-point conversion pass went incomplete as wide-open Gino Cappelletti fell down on the slick turf.

• The Bills fired right back after the kickoff as Kemp and Dubenion hooked up for a 52-yard gain to the Boston 20. But Ron Hall intercepted a Kemp pass in the end zone. On the next series, though, Kemp passed 45 yards to Ernie Warlick. Kemp eventually scored on a one-yard run.

• A 33-yard Kemp-to-Glenn Bass pass was the key to setting up Pete Gogolak's 12-yard field goal with 24 seconds left in the first half. That made it 17-6.

• Early in the fourth, after a Charley Warner interception and 38-yard return to the Patriot 17, Wray Carlton gained 14 yards on third down. Kemp snuck in from the 1 again.

• Buffalo's 12 wins tied San Diego's league mark set in 1961.

QUOTES

• Lou Saban: "It's taken us a long time to reach this pinnacle. Now that we're there, we're going to be there for a long, long time. This is a fine football team. We don't have to do too much to stay on top, just a little green grass (rookies) every year and we're set. This was the big one for us, we're over the hump. We had a mental block about beating Boston. If we could get this one thing out of our system, then we knew we'd be OK and we did. It's downhill from here. We'll take San Diego for sure. This is the greatest victory I've ever had, especially after all the nonsense from this city. There will never be another victory like this for me. We've had to sit back and take a lot of stuff, but that's all immaterial. My everlasting thanks to you (the players) for beating Boston."

• Jack Kemp: "We didn't do anything new or unusual. We knew the plays would go if we kept our mistakes to a minimum. I made some, but fortunately they didn't hurt us. The big thing was the blocking. Boston's blitzers were being picked up so quickly and I had plenty of time for Bass and Dubenion to get open downfield. After we stung them with a couple of long ones, I knew we'd be in good shape."

• Boston coach Mike Holovak: "I don't want to make excuses, but I think the weather hurt us and helped them. With two big backs like Gilchrist and Carlton, they can move the ball a lot better on the ground. The footing was tough on our receivers and it took a lot out of our blitzing. But the Bills played well, they deserved it."

Bills	7 10 0 7 - 24
Patriots	6 0 0 8 - 14

Attendance at Fenway Park - 38,021

Buf: Dubenion 57 pass from Kemp (Gogolak kick), 5:37
Bos: Romeo 37 pass from Parilli (pass failed), 9:11
Buf: Kemp 1 run (Gogolak kick), 3:23
Buf: FG Gogolak 12, 14:36
Buf: Kemp 1 run (Gogolak kick), 4:41
Bos: Romeo 15 pass from Parilli (Colclough pass from Parilli), 12:44

	BUF	BOS
First downs	17	15
Rushing yds	94	33
Passing yds	286	294
Punts-avg	5-38.0	5-30.0
Fumbles-lost	1-0	2-1
Penalties-yds	6-40	2-20

BILLS LEADERS: Rushing - Gilchrist 20-52, Carlton 15-31, Kemp 6-11; **Passing** - Kemp 12-24-3 - 286; **Receiving** - Dubenion 3-127, Bass 6-103, Warlick 1-45, Carlton 1-6, Gilchrist 1-5.

PATRIOTS LEADERS: Rushing - Garron 8-26, J.D. Garrett 2-3, Parilli 1-4; **Passing** - Parilli 19-39-2 - 294, Garron 0-1-0 - 0; **Receiving** - Colclough 6-134, Romeo 3-60, Garrett 3-30, Garron 4-25, Cappelletti 3-45.

WEEK 15 GAMES	
Oak 21, SD 20	KC 24, NY 7
Hou 34, Den 15	

STANDINGS: FIFTEENTH WEEK

EAST	W	L	T	WEST	W	L	T
Buffalo	12	2	0	San Diego	8	5	1
Boston	10	3	1	Kan. City	7	7	0
New York	5	8	1	Oakland	5	7	2
Houston	4	10	0	Denver	2	11	1

Chargers	7	0	0	0	- 7
Bills	3	10	0	7	- 20

Attendance at War Memorial Stadium - 40,242

SD : Kocourek 26 pass from Rote (Lincoln kick), 3:11
Buf: FG Gogolak 12, 10:40
Buf: Carlton 4 run (Gogolak kick), 7:49
Buf: FG Gogolak 17, 12:32
Buf: Kemp 1 run (Gogolak kick), 5:48

	BUF	SD
First downs	21	15
Rushing yds	219	124
Passing yds	168	135
Punts-avg	5-46.8	5-36.4
Fumbles-lost	0-0	1-0
Penalties-yds	3-45	3-20

BILLS LEADERS: Rushing - Gilchrist 16-122, Carlton 18-70, Kemp 5-16, Dubenion 1-9, Lamonica 1-2; **Passing** - Kemp 10-20-0 - 168; **Receiving** - Dubenion 3-36, Bass 2-70, Warlick 2-41, Gilchrist 2-22, Ross 1- (-1); **Punt returns** - Clarke 1-6; **Kickoff returns** - Rutkowski 1-27, Warner 1-17.

CHARGERS LEADERS: Rushing - Lincoln 3-47, Lowe 7-34, MacKinnon 1-17, Kinderman 4-14, Hadl 1-13, Rote 1-6, Norton 1- (-7); **Passing** - Hadl 3-10-1 - 31, Rote 10-26-2 - 118; **Receiving** - Kocourek 2-52, Kinderman 4-52, MacKinnon 3-12, Lowe 2-9, Norton 1-13, Lincoln 1-11; **Punt returns** - Robinson 1-30, Duncan 1-28; **Kickoff returns** - Duncan 3-147, Warren 1-28.

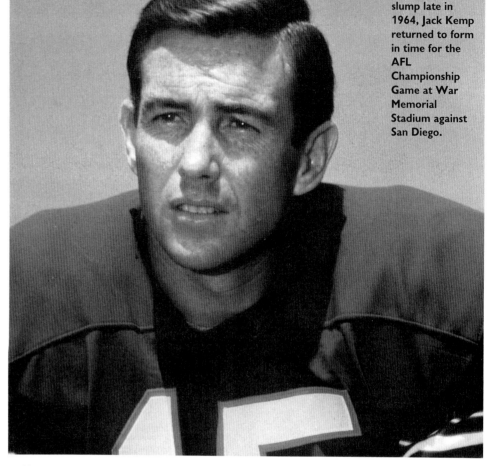

After suffering through a mini-slump late in 1964, Jack Kemp returned to form in time for the AFL Championship Game at War Memorial Stadium against San Diego.

NOTES

• The Bills defense was superb, limiting the Chargers to 179 yards of total offense after San Diego opened the game with an 80-yard TD drive.
• The Buffalo ground game piled up 219 yards, the third-best total of the season.
• Champagne was not allowed in the winning dressing room because the AFL was flooded with calls the previous year when the Chargers celebrated with the bubbly. This had Ralph Wilson angered.
• Because this was ABC's final year of broadcasting the AFL, the network didn't aggressively sell advertising for the game and thus, the player's shares were far less than expected. Each Buffalo player received $2,668, only about $200 more than the victorious Chargers received in 1963. With NBC taking over the telecasts in 1965, shares were expected to at least double, but that was no consolation to the Bills. "How can they do this to us?" asked Paul Maguire.
• The Chargers struck first as Keith Lincoln raced 38 yards on the first play. Tobin Rote then fired over the middle to Dave Kocourek for a 26-yard TD three plays later.
• After a Buffalo punt, San Diego gained possession, but not for long. Lincoln couldn't hold on to a swing pass in the left flat because he was crushed by linebacker Mike Stratton, one of the most famous tackles in AFL history. Lincoln lay on the ground for five minutes, suffering from broken ribs. With star receiver Lance Alworth unable to play because of a leg injury, the Chargers' offense was greatly hampered.
• The Bills started a drive from their own 36. With the aid of a facemask penalty on Ernie Ladd and Jack Kemp completions of 20 yards to Glenn Bass and 11 to Ernie Warlick, they moved to the Chargers 3. However, Kemp's third-down pass went incomplete and Pete Gogolak kicked a 12-yard field goal.
• Leslie Duncan returned the ensuing kickoff 70 yards to the Buffalo 35, but Charley Warner intercepted a Rote pass.
• The Bills drove quickly as Gilchrist ran for 32 yards and Kemp hit Warlick for 27 yards to the San Diego 14. When the possession stalled, Gogolak lined up for a field goal attempt. Holder Daryle Lamonica audibled to a fake, but because of crowd noise, Warlick and John Tracey couldn't hear the audible and didn't run pass routes. Lamonica was left to run for the first down

and he was stopped short.
• After forcing another punt, the Bills drove 56 yards in eight plays to take the lead for good. Kemp passed 18 yards to Dubenion, then Gilchrist and Wray Carlton alternated for three runs to the Chargers 27. Dubenion gained eight on a reverse, then Kemp passed 15 yards to Carlton while being tackled. Carlton scored on the next play and it was 10-7 midway through the second.
• Buffalo's next possession resulted in a field goal by Gogolak. Gilchrist ripped off a 39-yard run and Kemp scrambled for 12, but from the 3-yard-line, Kemp dropped back to pass on third down and slipped at the 10, necessitating the field goal and a 13-7 halftime lead.
• Stratton stopped a late second-half drive at the Bills 15 with an interception, a play in which Rote was just trying to throw the ball out of bounds.
• After a scoreless third quarter, the Bills added an insurance touchdown in the final quarter. John Hadl's 27-yard punt gave the Bills possession at their own 48. On the first play, Kemp threw to Bass at the Chargers 35; he broke a tackle and went all the way to the 1. Two plays later, Kemp scored on a sneak.
• Former Chargers Kemp and Maguire were stars. Maguire averaged 46.8 on five punts and dropped two inside the San Diego 10.
• The 38-year-old Rote retired after the game.

QUOTES

• Mike Stratton explaining his jolting tackle of Lincoln: "I keyed on Rote and I could see he was looking for a receiver downfield and couldn't find one. As soon as I saw that, I sprinted for Lincoln. One second earlier and it's pass interference and one second later it's a missed tackle. He rolled over and I heard him groan. I thought he had the wind knocked out of him, but then he didn't get up. I knew he was really hurt."
• Chargers running back Keith Lincoln: "It was a fine

tackle by a fine football player. I'm disappointed that we lost and also that I couldn't play the whole game."
• Jack Kemp on the success of the running game: "They were using double coverage on Duby and Bass so that meant their linebacker had to drop back to cover in the middle which invited us to run. They used zone defense most of the game and you beat that by throwing at the seams. The big thing for us was control and we had it. Our whole offensive line did a great job. Our defense gave us the ball and we kept it."
• Glenn Bass on his 50-yard reception in the fourth quarter: "Jack called a post pattern. I told him I was going to run it a little deeper than usual to get behind the linebacker. It worked pretty well."
• San Diego coach Sid Gillman on the Stratton tackle: "That was one of the most beautiful tackles I have ever seen in my life. That is the name of the game. They just beat us. Cookie hurt us for the first time. Buffalo has great balance. They are great champs. We have to have Alworth and Lincoln. But our kids have gone well. They've won the West Division championship four out of five years."
• Lou Saban: "Well, what do we do for an encore. Ralph Wilson should keep me around for the start of next season, anyway. Jack had a good day and Cookie had a great day. We gave him running room and he ran like he never ran before. He is just a great football player."
• Tobin Rote on his interception late in the first half: "I made one awful mistake. I wanted to throw what we call a 'clutch' when we run up to the line and I throw the ball out of bounds. I would have thrown the ball 40 yards into the stands, but I threw it too low. I didn't even see (Stratton). Our defense played good, but we just didn't score. I really thought we had these guys. The way we started, I thought we could do the job. But then Lincoln got hurt and he's a helluva player."

At A Glance
1965

Jan. 2 – The Jets signed Alabama quarterback Joe Namath to a reported $400,000 contract, the largest ever paid to a graduating collegian. Ray Abruzzese, Buffalo's veteran safety and a former roommate of Namath's, helped the Jets persuade Namath to sign with the AFL team. The Bills signed LSU All-America offensive lineman Remi Prudhomme. Prudhomme had been Buffalo's No. 1 choice in the 1963 redshirt draft.

Jan. 10 – The 22 black players slated to play in the annual AFL all-star game announced they wouldn't play because of racial incidents that occurred in New Orleans, the site of the game. Buffalo's Ernie Warlick served as spokesman for the black players. The players said they were refused cab service, refused entrance into certain restaurants and endured racial slurs.

Jan. 11 – The University of Georgia announced that the Bills were banned from campus. Georgia officials were upset because tackle Ray Rismiller, Buffalo's eighth-round draft choice, said that the Bills pressured him into signing an undated contract worth $18,000 before the Bulldogs' season was complete. Rismiller eventually signed with Philadelphia of the NFL. The all-star game was shifted from New Orleans to Houston. Tom Addison, president of the AFL Players Association, said the switch "rescued the pension plan. If the game had been canceled, all players would have suffered."

Jan. 14 – Ralph Wilson proposed a common draft between the AFL and NFL. "I think the two leagues must have some sort of an understanding on the draft before too many years roll by, or I see some very serious storm clouds on the horizon for pro football. The AFL came of age this year, we're here to stay. The television contract (with NBC) was the big bomb."

Jan. 15 – Commissioner Joe Foss said that to date, he had received applications from 38 groups representing 11 cities for possible expansion. NBC purchased the rights to the AFL championship and all-star games for more than $7 million, bringing its TV package with the league up to $43 million.

Jan. 20 – Lou Saban turned down a trade for Kansas City's Abner Haynes. It was believed KC coach Hank Stram wanted Jim Dunaway, Mike Stratton and Dave Behrman.

Jan. 26 – Cookie Gilchrist lashed out at Boston linebacker Nick Buoniconti, who had termed the black players walkout at the all-star game "a raw deal." Gilchrist said, "In my 11 years of playing pro football, the players have all stuck together, on and off the field."

Feb. 24 – Cookie Gilchrist was traded to Denver for running back Billy Joe, the AFL's rookie of the year in 1963. "It had to come," Lou Saban said. "The situation between Cookie and the Bills had become impossible. I felt a change was necessary. He has been a great player, I wish him well in Denver, but we believe we got ourselves a fine football player in return."

Feb. 25 – Guard Billy Shaw said of the Gilchrist trade, "Sure we can win without Gilchrist. He wasn't a one-man team. If we keep unity as a team, we can win again. I don't think we'll have anything to worry about." Said Al Bemiller: "When that incident occurred last November, I thought we could

win without him and I still do."

June 7 – Commissioner Joe Foss announced that the owners had voted to expand the AFL by two teams for the 1966 season. Also, an increase of the active roster to 40 was approved. Atlanta was rumored to have the inside track on one of the new franchises.

June 30 – The NFL outfoxed the AFL and convinced Atlanta to join its league.

July 1 – The Bills' season ticket sales reached a record 26,000 thanks to the completion of the stadium expansion which added 7,725 seats.

July 3 – The AFL announced it was looking at Miami with Atlanta out of the picture.

July 23 – The Bills opened training camp at the Camelot-Voyager in Blasdell.

Aug. 8 – The Bills blanked the Patriots, 23-0, in the preseason opener at Boston College's Alumni Stadium. Billy Joe gained 61 yards on six carries in his debut.

Aug. 14 – For the first time, Meet the Bills Night was more than an intrasquad scrimmage. The Bills lost to Houston, 29-7, in front of 14,287.

Aug. 16 – Miami officially was awarded a franchise for the 1966 season with Minneapolis attorney Joe Robbie and entertainer Danny Thomas in partnership. The cost of the team was $7.5 million. Commissioner Joe Foss announced rosters would be 38 active players and two for the unclaimable injured-deferred list for 1965. The eight existing teams would be able to protect 23 players with Miami able to draft other players.

Aug. 21 – The Bills ripped the Jets, 30-14, at Rutgers University as Joe Namath completed just six of 24 passes for 72 yards with two interceptions.

Aug. 28 – Kansas City beat the Bills, 18-16, in Wichita, Kan.

Sept. 2 – The Bills whipped the Jets, 31-10, at home in the preseason finale as Joe Namath completed four of 17.

Sept. 11 – Before a record crowd of 45,502 at War Memorial Stadium in the regular-season opener, the Bills handled Boston, 24-7, as the defense held the Pats to 215 yards.

Sept. 13 – The format of the AFL all-star game was changed so that the defending champions would play the all-stars of the other seven teams.

Sept. 19 – Ex-Bill Cookie Gilchrist was held to 26 yards on 12 carries while Billy Joe gained 48 on 14 attempts as the Bills beat Denver, 30-15.

Sept. 26 – Joe Namath made his first regular-season start, but was overshadowed by a season-ending knee injury suffered by Elbert Dubenion in Buffalo's 33-21 victory over the Jets.

Oct. 3 – Buffalo limited Oakland to seven pass completions, a new defensive record, and went on to defeat Oakland, 17-12.

Oct. 10 – Buffalo was held without a touchdown for the first time since its inaugural game against the New York Titans in 1960, during a 34-3 pasting at the hands of San Diego.

Oct. 18 – The Bills acquired receiver Bo Roberson from the Raiders for two players to be named later. Al Davis felt it was time to go with rookie Fred Biletnikoff, who hadn't yet played in a regular-season game.

Oct. 24 – Jack Kemp passed for 280 yards as the Bills downed Denver, 31-13. Cookie Gilchrist

gained 87 yards in his return to War Memorial Stadium.

Oct. 31 – Houston edged the Bills, 19-17, as Lou Saban's gamble backfired. Late in the game, Saban opted to try for a TD from the 1-yard-line rather than kick a field goal and Jack Kemp was stuffed for no gain.

Nov. 4 – The AFL considered going to a 16-game schedule with Miami joining the league in 1966.

Nov. 7 – Charley Warner returned a kickoff 102 yards for a TD in Buffalo's 23-7 victory at Boston.

Nov. 11 – Kicker Pete Gogolak's future with the team became cloudy. Gogolak said he was playing out his option because his agent hadn't come to new terms with the Bills. "I've got to look out for myself," Gogolak said, sounding a lot like Cookie Gilchrist. "I know I can get what I want elsewhere."

Nov. 14 – Billy Joe capped a 62-yard drive with a one-yard run with seven seconds left to play to give the Bills a 17-14 victory over Oakland.

Nov. 25 – Pete Gogolak kicked a 22-yard field goal with six seconds left, capping a last-minute drive engineered by Jack Kemp that lifted the Bills into a 20-20 tie at San Diego.

Nov. 26 – Chargers star running back Keith Lincoln, who was benched for the Bills game the day before, asked the Chargers to trade him, preferably to the Bills or Raiders. "I'd give my right arm to play in Buffalo," he said.

Nov. 27 – The college draft began and the Bills selected Mississippi running back Mike Dennis with its first choice. Others drafted included Arkansas running back Bobby Burnett (fourth) and McNeese State linebacker Paul Guidry (eighth). Guidry signed immediately.

Dec. 5 – Pete Gogolak attempted a league-record seven field goals and made a team record five as the Bills downed Houston, 29-14.

Dec. 12 – Jack Kemp passed for 295 yards as the Bills stopped Kansas City, 34-25.

Dec. 14 – Chiefs running back Mack Lee Hill, who suffered torn knee ligaments against the Bills two days earlier, died of a massive blood clot during his knee surgery in Kansas City.

Dec. 15 – Billy Shaw, Jack Kemp, Mike Stratton, Tom Sestak, George Saimes and Butch Byrd were named to the AP's AFL all-star first team. Kemp was named MVP.

Dec. 16 – Lou Saban was named coach of the year by the AP. Saban denied a report in a New York paper that QB Daryle Lamonica would be one of the players going to Oakland in the trade that brought Bo Roberson to Buffalo.

Dec. 18 – Buffalo's first-round draft choice, Mike Dennis, signed with the NFL's LA Rams.

Dec. 19 – The Bills closed the season with a meaningless 14-12 loss to the Jets before 57,396 at Shea.

Dec. 21 – The Bills flew to San Diego to begin preparations for the championship game.

Dec. 26 – The Bills won their second straight AFL championship, throttling the Chargers, 23-0, in San Diego. It was the first title game shutout in league history. Each Bill received a winners share of $5,189.92.

Jan. 15, 1966 – The AFL all-stars beat the champion Bills, 30-19, in the new format all-star game at Houston's Rice Stadium. New York's Joe Namath threw three TD passes. George Saimes returned a botched field goal attempt 61 yards for a TD and Daryle Lamonica hit Wray Carlton with a 34-yard TD pass for Buffalo.

BY THE NUMBERS – 1965

TEAM STATISTICS	BILLS	OPP
First downs	206	226
Rushing	69	65
Passing	119	141
Penalty	18	20
Total yards	3,749	4,284
Avg. per game	267.8	306.0
Plays	882	890
Avg. per play	4.3	4.8
Net rushing yds	1,288	1,114
Avg. per game	92.0	79.6
Avg. per play	3.3	3.1
Net passing yds	2,461	3,170
Comp/att	208/461	227/502
Sacks/lost	29-283	28-246
Interceptions	24	32
Percentage	45.1	45.2
Punts/avg	80-43.0	76-40.2
Fumbles/lost	28-14	33-25
Penalties/yds	78-685	69-832
Touchdowns	33	25
Extra points	31-31	21-21
Field goals	28-46	15-30
Two-point conv	0-2	4-4
Safeties	0	1
Kick ret./avg	45-22.7	60-24.2
Punt ret./avg	36-10.8	30-7.4

RUSHING	ATT	YDS	AVG	TD
Carlton	156	592	3.8	6
Joe	123	377	3.1	4
Smith	43	137	3.2	1
Stone	19	61	3.2	0
Kemp	36	49	1.4	4
Lamonica	10	30	3.0	1
Maguire	1	21	21.0	0
Auer	3	19	6.3	0
Warner	1	2	2.0	0
TOTALS	**392**	**1288**	**3.3**	**16**

PASSING	COMP	ATT	INT	YDS	TD	COMP%
Kemp	179	391	18	2368	10	45.8
Lamonica	29	70	6	376	3	41.4
TOTALS	**208**	**461**	**24**	**2744**	**13**	**45.1**

PUNTING	NO	AVG
Maguire	80	43.0

KICKING	FG/ATT	PAT/ATT	PTS
Gogolak	28-46	31-31	115

RECEIVING	CAT	YDS	AVG	TD
Roberson	31	483	15.5	3
Joe	27	271	10.0	2
Carlton	24	196	8.2	1
Costa	21	401	19.1	0
Ferguson	21	262	12.5	2
Bass	18	299	16.6	1
Dubenion	18	281	15.6	1
Rutkowski	18	247	13.7	1
Smith	12	116	9.7	0
Warlick	8	112	14.0	1
Stone	6	29	4.8	0
Mills	1	43	43.0	0
Warner	1	11	11.0	1
Tracy	1	2	2.0	0
Kemp	1	-9	-9.0	0
TOTALS	**208**	**2744**	**13.2**	**13**

LEADERS

Punt returns:
Byrd 21-201 yds, 9.6 avg, 0 TD
Rutkowski 11-127, 11.5, 0 TD

Kick returns:
Warner 32-825, 25.8, 2 TD
Rutkowski 5-97, 19.4, 0 TD

Interceptions:
Clarke 7-60, 8.6, 0 TD
Byrd 5-119, 23.8, 0 TD
Warner 5-84, 16.8, 1 TD
Edgerson 5-55, 11.0, 0 TD

Non-kick scoring:
Carlton 7 TD, 42 pts
Joe 6 TDs, 42 pts

Jack Kemp enjoys a quiet moment with defensive tackle Tom Sestak. One of the greatest Bills, Sestak died of a heart attack in March of 1986.

GAME 1 - Saturday, Sept. 11, 1965 - BILLS 24, PATRIOTS 7

Patriots	0	7	0	0	- 7
Bills	0	7	10	7	- 24

Attendance at War Memorial Stadium - 45,502

Bos: Cappelletti 11 pass from Parilli (Cappelletti kick), 3:55
Buf: Bass 26 pass from Kemp (Gogolak kick), 12:46
Buf: Warner 22 interception return (Gogolak kick), 5:00
Buf: FG Gogolak 36, 6:51
Buf: Kemp 1 run (Gogolak kick), 9:18

	BUF	BOS
First downs	17	13
Rushing yds	77	104
Passing yds	271	111
Punts-avg	8-41.3	8-41.6
Fumbles-lost	0-0	2-0
Penalties-yds	6-51	7-97

BILLS LEADERS: Rushing - Carlton 11-28, Joe 9-34, Auer 2-15, Kemp 4-(-8), Stone 1-8; **Passing** - Kemp 19-40-2 - 280, Lamonica 0-2-0 - 0; **Receiving** - Carlton 2-27, Joe 3-33, Bass 4-78, Warlick 4-59, Dubenion 6-83.

PATRIOTS LEADERS: Rushing - Nance 9-17, Parilli 7-71, Johnson 5-10, J.D. Garrett 3-6; **Passing** - Parilli 10-35-5 - 151; **Receiving** - Cappelletti 3-45, Graham 2-44, Johnson 1-23, Colclough 1-16, Nance 1-7, Romeo 1-9, J.D. Garrett 1-7.

NOTES

• The Bills had trouble handling blitzes in the preseason, but in the opener, they handled Boston's rush tactics easily. Jack Kemp passed for 280 yards and was sacked just twice for nine yards.
• Boston used a four-receiver offense with only Jim Nance in the backfield, but Babe Parilli had a miserable day with five interceptions. All 24 Buffalo points were a result of interceptions. The other pick, by Harry Jacobs, killed a Boston drive at the Buffalo 5. Parilli was sacked five times for 40 yards, all in the second half.
• Parilli's perfect play-action fake fooled cornerback Charley Warner, allowing Gino Cappelletti to catch an 11-yard TD pass in the second quarter.
• The Bills came back after a George Saimes interception as Kemp passed 26 yards to Glenn Bass.
• Early in the third, Warner got redemption by picking off a Parilli pass intended for Jim Colclough on the sideline and running 22 yards for the go-ahead TD.
• Saimes intercepted Parilli later in the third when Ron McDole hit the Boston QB as he was throwing. That set up Pete Gogolak's 30-yard field goal.
• Warner then got his second pick in the fourth and Kemp directed a 77-yard drive that ended with his one-yard sneak.
• Stew Barber and Boston's Larry Eisenhaur were ejected for fighting in the first quarter. The two all-league players almost got into a fight during all-star practice the previous January, and they were on the same team.
• Gogolak, who had held out for part of training camp, missed two field goals and had another blocked.
• The crowd of 45,502 was the largest in Buffalo sports history.

QUOTES

• Charley Warner: "Old quarterbacks will keep picking at a guy they think they can beat. Parilli fooled me with the play-action pass on the touchdown to Cappelletti. I came up to force what looked like a run and Cappelletti slipped behind me."
• Billy Joe: "The atmosphere here is the big difference. When these guys step on the field, they know they're going to win. Everybody feels it. I didn't know I could catch (he had a reputation for being a bad pass receiver) until I was traded. Then all at once I couldn't do anything, run, catch or block. I wasn't even a football player according to Denver."
• Lou Saban: "He's (Joe) a pretty good horse, isn't he? He did a tremendous job of picking up the blitzes and in general blocking. (On Gogolak): It was just a bad night, we know he's a better kicker."
• Boston coach Mike Holovak: "I'm very disappointed in our offense. If we had our offense working, we could have blown the game wide open."

WEEK 1 GAMES
SD 34, Den 31	Oak 37, KC 10
Hou 27, NY 21	

GAME 2 - Sunday, Sept. 19, 1965 - BILLS 30, BRONCOS 15

Bills	3	10	7	10	- 30
Broncos	0	0	7	8	- 15

Attendance at Bears Stadium - 30,682

Buf: FG Gogolak 28, 5:55
Buf: Carlton 1 run (Gogolak kick), :02
Buf: FG Gogolak 18, 13:13
Buf: Joe 7 pass from Kemp (Gogolak kick), 5:39
Den: Dixon 15 pass from Slaughter (Kroner kick), 7:45
Buf: Kemp 1 run (Gogolak kick), 1:27
Buf: FG Gogolak 18, 7:59
Den: Taylor 25 pass from Slaughter (Gonsoulin pass from Slaughter), 14:53

	BUF	DEN
First downs	20	17
Rushing yds	88	69
Passing yds	276	291
Punts-avg	5-40.2	4-49.0
Fumbles-lost	3-0	3-3
Penalties-yds	5-72	2-33

BILLS LEADERS: Rushing - Carlton 7-25, Joe 14-48, Kemp 4-(-1), Lamonica 1-1, Smith 1-4, Stone 1-11; **Passing** - Kemp 20-49-2 - 280, Lamonica 1-3-0 - 17; **Receiving** - Carlton 5-68, Joe 4-36, Bass 6-73, Dubenion 5-103, Rutkowski 1-17.

BRONCOS LEADERS: Rushing - Gilchrist 12-26, Slaughter 4-26, Haynes 4-19, Hayes 4-(-2); **Passing** - Slaughter 22-42-5 - 291; **Receiving** - Taylor 9-172, Scarpitto 4-74, Haynes 6-27, Dixon 3-18.

WEEK 2 GAMES
KC 14, NY 10	SD 17, Oak 6
Hou 31, Bos 10	

NOTES

• The Bills stuffed Cookie Gilchrist in his first game against Buffalo.
• The Bills stole five interceptions – three by Charley Warner – for the second week in a row and also recovered three fumbles – two by Ron McDole.
• Already ahead 3-0, the Bills drove 70 yards in 10 plays with Elbert Dubenion making a 48-yard reception to set up Wray Carlton's fourth-down one yard TD plunge.
• McDole's interception stopped a Denver threat and that led to Pete Gogolak's second field goal and a 13-0 halftime lead.
• The Bills made it 20-0 as Billy Joe caught a seven-yard TD pass from Jack Kemp. The drive was aided by 15- and 24-yard catches by Dubenion.
• Denver broke the shutout when Mickey Slaughter underhanded a pass to Hewritt Dixon and Dixon eluded two Bills to score on the broken play. The Broncos then got a jolt of momentum when Goose Gonsoulin picked off a Kemp pass and returned it 29 yards to the Buffalo 17. However, Slaughter overthrew a wide-open Bob Scarpitto in the end zone on fourth down.
• In the fourth, Marty Schottenheimer recovered a fumbled punt, starting the Bills on a 51-yard TD drive that ended on Kemp's two-yard run that put away the game.
• Kemp's 49 passes attempted tied a team record.
• Incredibly, Dubenion and Glenn Bass dropped eight passes between them, including two TDs.
• It was reported that Denver players were angry because Gilchrist and Abner Haynes were traveling to road games via jet while the rest of the team flew on slower, propeller-driven craft.

QUOTES

• Lou Saban: "We needed this game for psychological reasons. The defense had to prove something and it did. Billy Joe showed everybody he is the fullback we need. The whole team saw that decisions are made for the good (trading Gilchrist). Jack threw beautifully, but I can't explain our dropping so many, though the ball may have been slick because of the rain. Our defense gave us additional opportunities. We were in control at all times."
• Jack Kemp on the dropped passes: "Look, they have given us so much in other games, who would expect that Duby and Glenn would have off days on the same day? You can't be happy, but you can't be mad either. I've had my share of bad days."
• Billy Joe: "The big difference (between Buffalo and Denver) is the line. A fullback can't do a thing without a good line in front of him. Cookie's going to find out there's a big difference in the line in Denver and the one in Buffalo."
• Denver coach Mac Speedie: "They're the best team in pro football, bar none. I just wish the NFL would try to prove me wrong. The Bills have it all."

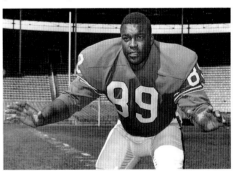

STANDINGS: SECOND WEEK

EAST	W	L	T		WEST	W	L	T
Buffalo	2	0	0		San Diego	2	0	0
Houston	2	0	0		Oakland	1	1	0
Boston	0	2	0		Kan. City	1	1	0
New York	0	2	0		Denver	0	2	0

NOTES

• Joe Namath's first regular-season start of his career was overshadowed by the season-ending injury to star receiver Elbert Dubenion. Duby tore a ligament in his left knee and underwent surgery after the game. The injury occurred when he caught an 11-yard TD pass from Jack Kemp in the third quarter and ex-Bill Willie West fell on his leg.

• Jack Kemp also was knocked out of the game in the fourth quarter, and defensive end Tom Sestak and safety Gene Sykes didn't play at all as the Bills subs turned in big efforts.

• The Bills jumped to a 13-0 lead, then saw the Jets rally to within 13-10 by halftime. In the third, Kemp completed 13 of 17 passes for 131 yards and led the Bills to 10 points on his TD pass to Dubenion and Pete Gogolak's 27-yard field goal.

• Following a Tom Day interception of a Namath pass that was tipped by Mike Stratton, Kemp directed a march to the Jets 2. On third down, he rolled out and was knocked unconscious. Gogolak kicked a nine-yard field goal to make it 26-10.

• The Jets went 69 yards for a TD as Namath hit Del Mackey from nine yards out, then passed to Mackey for the two-point conversion.

• Daryle Lamonica's first series ended in a punt and the Jets quickly drove into scoring territory. However, they had to settle for Jim Turner's 23-yard field goal when Butch Byrd broke up Namath's pass to Mackey in the end zone.

• Lamonica then iced the game by leading a long TD march that climaxed when Wray Carlton bulled over from the 1 with 11 seconds left. Billy Joe had runs of 19 and 12 yards along the way.

QUOTES

• Lou Saban: "I told you before the game this was going to be a helluva ballgame. We're the champions and every game is going to be like this (hard-hitting). I want to commend the quarterbacks. Daryle had to go in when Jack got hurt and he did an excellent job. Daryle made several excellent calls in crucial situations."

• Tom Day on Namath's play: "He's going to be one of the greats, no question about it. To me he's worth the $400,000. There are a lot of clubs in the league that would like to have him. I'm going to hate to see him when we get to Shea Stadium, he'll be well-seasoned by then."

• Jack Kemp: "It was inconsequential, but I was getting a little tired watching our guys pick up Namath after they had knocked him down. I told them none of their guys picked me up."

• New York coach Weeb Ewbank: "Kemp was tremendous. If he were my quarterback, we'd never run."

Jets	0	10	0	11	- 21
Bills	7	6	10	10	- 33

Attendance at War Memorial Stadium - 45,056

Buf: Kemp 4 run (Gogolak kick), 5:55
Buf: FG Gogolak 33, 5:30
Buf: FG Gogolak 22, 10:39
NY: FG J. Turner 24, 13:57
NY: Mathis 3 pass from Namath (J. Turner kick), 14:37
Buf: Dubenion 11 pass from Kemp (Gogolak kick), 5:21
Buf: FG Gogolak 27, 13:42
Buf: FG Gogolak 9, 1:29
NY: Mackey 9 pass from Namath (Mackey pass from Namath), 3:48
NY: FG J. Turner 23, 10:44
Buf: Carlton 1 run (Gogolak kick), 14:49

	BUF	NY
First downs	27	18
Rushing yds	104	44
Passing yds	304	258
Punts-avg	1-51.0	4-29.0
Fumbles-lost	1-1	0-0
Penalties-yds	5-44	5-63

BILLS LEADERS: Rushing - Carlton 14-36, Joe 13-61, Kemp 6-5, Lamonica 2-2; **Passing** - Kemp 22-37-0 - 292, Lamonica 3-5-0 - 30; **Receiving** - Carlton 2-28, Joe 5-40, Bass 6-86, Dubenion 7-95, Warlick 3-50, Rutkowski 2-23.

JETS LEADERS: Rushing - Snell 7-31, Mathis 5-13; **Passing** - Namath 19-40-2 - 282; **Receiving** - Maynard 4-81, B. Turner 6-55, Snell 3-64, Mathis 4-58, Mackey 2-24.

WEEK 3 GAMES

SD 10, KC 10   Oak 21, Hou 17
Den 27, Bos 10

NOTES

• For the second week in a row, a starting receiver was lost for the season as Glenn Bass tore ligaments in his left ankle. Ed Rutkowski started for Dubenion and Charley Ferguson replaced Bass.

• In the third, Kemp fired a three-yard TD pass to Ernie Warlick. Before the snap, Kemp faked the Raiders out by appearing to tell Billy Joe he was going to him. Two Raider defenders went after Joe when the ball was snapped and Warlick was alone in the end zone.

• By limiting the Raiders to seven pass completions, the Bills set a new team record. The previous low was eight by Houston in a 1960 game.

• Attendance for the first three home games of 131,804 was more than the team drew in seven home games in 1960. The game was the team's ninth straight sellout.

• For the fourth game in a row, the Bills blanked the opposition in the first quarter.

• With the passing game seriously hampered, Wray Carlton had his best game since gaining 90 yards against San Diego on Nov. 11, 1962.

• Coach Lou Saban placed Dubenion and Bass on the reserve list, meaning they were officially out for the season. Former Oilers receiver Bill Groman was placed on the active roster before the game.

QUOTES

• Raiders linebacker and ex-Bill Archie Matsos: "Well, I hope people realize something from this game. I hope they finally realize that Wray Carlton is a fine football player. For some reason, everyone underrates him."

• Jack Kemp: "Wray is a tremendous blocker. I really have confidence in him, Billy Joe and our line protecting me. I'm another person who thinks he's tremendously underrated. Last year it gave us a big lift when he came back for the last few games. Some of the pressure they put on me was my fault. Oakland gave us some new designs on defense and I was misreading some of them. I didn't realize they'd be sending so many people."

• Lou Saban on declaring Bass and Dubenion out for the year: "I have no choice. Maybe Glenn and Duby might be able to play 10 weeks from now and maybe not. I can't afford to wait and find out. We have 10 games to play. Chances are they'll both be in casts all that time. I'm just thankful that we have the taxi squad that we do, or we'd really be in the tank."

• Al Bemiller on the Raiders physical style: "They hit. They always are tough on us."

• Dick Hudson: "That front four of theirs is rough. That Ike Lassiter makes a difference. He was throwing me around like a rag doll."

• Raiders coach Al Davis: "There are three teams in this league who are capable of playing anyone who walks - the Bills, Chargers and Chiefs. The most characteristic thing about all three – in addition to size and balance – is that they're built from the ground up. We're closing the gap on size and talent. We're starting to see hope."

Raiders	0	10	2	0	- 12
Bills	3	7	7	0	- 17

Attendance at War Memorial Stadium - 41,256

Buf: FG Gogolak 20, 7:35
Buf: Joe 1 run (Gogolak kick), 4:49
Oak: Miller 5 pass from Flores (Mercer kick), 8:31
Oak: FG Mingo 33, 14:49
Buf: Warlick 3 pass from Kemp (Gogolak kick), 6:49
Oak: Safety, Lassiter forced Kemp out of end zone, 13:26

	BUF	OAK
First downs	14	12
Rushing yds	140	93
Passing yds	123	69
Punts-yds	6-49.5	6-37.8
Fumbles-lost	2-1	2-2
Penalties-yds	5-30	3-29

BILLS LEADERS: Rushing - Carlton 21-79, Joe 14-58, Kemp 3-3; **Passing** - Kemp 10-21-2 - 154; **Receiving** - Carlton 2-22, Bass 2-62, Warlick 1-3, Rutkowski 3-64, Joe 1-(-4), Stone 1-7.

RAIDERS LEADERS: Rushing - Daniels 16-55, Miller 7-36, Flores 1-2; **Passing** - Flores 6-25-1 - 66, Daniels 1-1-0 - 42; **Receiving** - Roberson 3-69, Miller 2-17, Powell 1-14, Herock 1-8.

WEEK 4 GAMES

KC 27, Bos 17   SD 31, Hou 14
Den 16, NY 13

STANDINGS: FOURTH WEEK

EAST	W	L	T		WEST	W	L	T
Buffalo	4	0	0		San Diego	3	0	1
Houston	2	2	0		Kan. City	2	1	1
New York	0	4	0		Denver	2	2	0
Boston	0	4	0		Oakland	2	2	0

Chargers	0 14 17 3 - 34
Bills	3 0 0 0 - 3

Attendance at War Memorial Stadium - 45,260

Buf: FG Gogolak 38, 4:02
SD: Alworth 14 pass from Hadl (Travenio kick), 7:13
SD: Lincoln 8 pass from Hadl (Travenio kick), 8:11
SD: FG Travenio 15, 5:09
SD: Alworth 52 pass from Hadl (Travenio kick), 8:10
SD: Whitehead 35 interception return (Travenio kick), 9:00
SD: FG Travenio 19, 6:41

	BUF	SD
First downs	8	18
Rushing yds	57	89
Passing yds	193	369
Punts-avg	6-45.0	3-35.0
Fumbles-lost	2-2	1-1
Penalties-yds	5-48	8-90

BILLS LEADERS: Rushing - Carlton 6-11, Joe 4-22, Kemp 2-14, Auer 1-4, Stone 2-6; **Passing** - Kemp 7-23-2 - 48, Lamonica 8-14-0 - 60; **Receiving** - Carlton 1-6, Joe 2-10, Rutkowski 4-44, Ferguson 3-37, Costa 2-15, Stone 2-5, Kemp 1-(-9).

CHARGERS LEADERS: Rushing - Lowe 19-37, Foster 9-27, Lincoln 4-21, Hadl 1-5, Allison 1-(-1); **Passing** - Hadl 18-29-1 - 314, Breaux 1-1-0 - 7, Lincoln 1-1-0 - 31, Lowe 1-1-0 - 17; **Receiving** - Norton 6-107, Alworth 8-168, Kocourek 3-54, Lincoln 2-16, Foster 2-24.

NOTES
• In a rematch of the 1964 AFL title game, the Chargers dominated. The Bills' beleaguered offense managed just 150 net yards, its lowest production since Oct. 13, 1962, when the Chargers held them to 140.
• The Bills committed six turnovers.
• Buffalo led briefly after scoring on its first possession, but the Chargers took a 14-3 halftime lead. On the first TD march, Paul Lowe and Keith Lincoln each completed a halfback-option pass totaling 48 yards. The TD also was a crazy play. Lowe began a sweep to the right, but was trapped so he lateraled back to QB John Hadl, who passed to Lance Alworth for the TD. The Bills argued to no avail that San Diego had ineligible men downfield. They seemed to be right.
• Leslie Duncan's 26-yard punt return set up the next TD as Hadl passed eight yards to Lincoln.
• Charley Ferguson, starting for Glenn Bass, dropped two long Jack Kemp passes that could have given the Bills the lead.
• The Chargers turned the game into a rout with 17 points in a nine-minute span of the third quarter. A 34-yard Hadl pass to Don Norton set up Herb Travenio's 15-yard field goal. On their next possession, Hadl threw deep to Alworth, who got behind Booker Edgerson for a 52-yard score. On Buffalo's first play after the kickoff, Kemp's pass bounced off Ed Rutkowski's hands and into Bud Whitehead's and he went 35 yards for a killing TD.
• The Bills failed to score a TD for the first time since the team's inaugural game in 1960, a 27-3 loss to the New York Titans, a span of 76 games counting playoffs.
• The halfback option plays were designed to take advantage of George Saimes' aggressive run support and they worked perfectly.

QUOTES
• Billy Shaw: "We've got to get it out of our minds and get back to work for Kansas City. We'll do it."
• Chargers running back Keith Lincoln: "I think the Bills still have to be favored in the East. But you don't lose two receivers like Dubenion and Bass without it hurting you. If we lost Alworth and Norton or Oakland lost Art Powell and Bo Roberson, it would hurt, too. The Bills are a different club without those two guys."
• Lou Saban: "If Fergy had caught those two passes, it would have changed the complexion of the game. We were lousy. We were up, but we had no guns. Our offense put too much pressure on our defense. We wanted to control the ball and we didn't. You can't give a team like the Chargers the ball that much and expect to win. Our passing game was shot. Anytime you put two new receivers in there, you automatically make it tough on your quarterback because it takes time before they work together properly. I don't like to say we have to reorganize our passing game, but we have to sharpen it. With Duby and Bass, our offense was accustomed to big plays."

Bills	0 3 0 20 - 23
Chiefs	7 0 0 0 - 7

Attendance at Municipal Stadium - 26,941

KC: Arbanas 18 pass from Dawson (Brooker kick), 14:42
Buf: FG Gogolak 14, 4:05
Buf: Ferguson 30 pass from Lamonica (Gogolak kick), 3:58
Buf: Saimes 18 fumble return (Gogolak kick), 8:25
Buf: FG Gogolak 13, 11:59
Buf: FG Gogolak 34, 13:45

	BUF	KC
First downs	7	12
Rushing yds	47	70
Passing yds	80	161
Punts-avg	8-50.0	6-43.0
Fumbles-lost	3-3	6-5
Penalties-yds	6-44	5-60

BILLS LEADERS: Rushing - Joe 11-18, Kemp 2-10, Stone 7-10, Smith 2-10, Carlton 3-0, Lamonica 2-(-1); **Passing** - Kemp 13-25-1 - 71, Lamonica 1-4-1 - 30; **Receiving** - Carlton 3-13, Joe 4-(-11), Rutkowski 1-6, Ferguson 3-52, Costa 2-33, Stone 1-8.

CHIEFS LEADERS: Rushing - McClinton 10-28, Hill 8-36, Beathard 2-10, Coan 2-6, Taylor 1-2, Dawson 4-(-12); **Passing** - Dawson 15-25-2 - 154, Beathard 3-9-2 - 39; **Receiving** - Hill 3-21, Jackson 5-49, Burford 4-39, Arbanas 3-43, McClinton 1-25, Taylor 1-15, Coan 1-1.

NOTES
• The Bills produced their lowest offensive yardage total since the first game in team history when they managed just 113 against the New York Titans.
• The Bills trailed 7-3 in the third when they stopped the Chiefs at the Buffalo 5. Ron McDole recovered a Curtis McClinton fumble.
• Early in the fourth, Johnny Robinson intercepted a Jack Kemp pass and returned it to the Buffalo 7. But the defense held again. Tom Brooker's 10-yard field goal was nullified by a procedure penalty and his 15-yarder was wide to the left.
• When the Bills couldn't move, Paul Maguire punted 55 yards and Stew Barber forced Willie Mitchell to fumble at the KC 30. Tom Janik recovered. On the next play, Daryle Lamonica hit Charley Ferguson for a TD as Fergy beat Fred Williamson 3:58 into the fourth.
• After an exchange of interceptions left the Chiefs with the ball deep in their own territory, George Saimes blitzed backup QB Pete Beathard. Beathard fumbled and Saimes returned it 18 yards for the clinching score.
• Hagood Clarke then intercepted a Beathard pass and returned it 40 yards to set up Pete Gogolak's 13-yard field goal. On the next series, Butch Byrd forced Otis Taylor to fumble and Clarke recovered at the 30. Gogolak eventually kicked a 34-yard field goal.
• Tight end Paul Costa was inserted into the lineup ahead of Ernie Warlick.
• Lamonica suffered a broken nose.

QUOTES
• Lou Saban: "They knew we couldn't do much effective throwing. I said all week I felt if we could get by this game, we could get our offense straightened out. We needed this one to prove we could bounce back. They didn't lose a bit of poise. We never panicked when things got tough. Our defense played well and I was sure if we could stay close we would get some points. Stamina had a lot to do with it. We got stronger in the fourth quarter. The boys complain about the wind sprints in practice, but that's what kept them going in that fourth quarter."
• George Saimes: "Don't know a better way to celebrate the arrival of little Carolyn Elizabeth than that (his wife had delivered their first child in the week before the game). She's our first baby and the touchdown today was my first in three years as a pro. Maybe firsts like these go together."
• Chiefs coach Hank Stram: "Defensively we played well enough to win, but our failure to cash in on scoring opportunities proved too costly, and our fumbles and interceptions were fatal. Our defense certainly deserved a different fate."

STANDINGS: SIXTH WEEK

EAST	W	L	T	WEST	W	L	T
Buffalo	5	1	0	San Diego	4	0	2
Houston	2	3	0	Kan. City	3	2	1
New York	0	4	1	Oakland	3	2	1
Boston	0	5	1	Denver	3	3	0

NOTES

• Despite being banged up with knee, elbow and shoulder ailments, Jack Kemp passed for 280 yards and two TDs to offset Cookie Gilchrist's 87-yard effort in his return to War Memorial Stadium.

• Gilchrist again was outplayed by the man for whom he was traded, Billy Joe. Although Joe gained only 11 yards rushing, he caught six passes for 156 yards including a 78-yard catch and run for the first TD. Kemp admitted the pass was intended for Paul Costa and that Joe wasn't even supposed to be downfield.

• After that TD, a promising Denver drive died as Tom Sestak blocked Gary Kroner's field goal try.

• Kroner later made a 33-yarder, but the Bills quickly established a 14-3 lead when Kemp passed eight yards to Charley Ferguson for a TD after completing a 46-yarder to Costa on a play that appeared to be broken down. Kemp appeared to be trapped, but he scrambled away and he heaved a bomb downfield on which Costa made a spectacular catch.

• On their next possession, the Bills went 61 yards. Carlton scored from the 1 and the game was effectively decided.

• Sestak's field goal block gave the Bills a string of four straight games in which they had blocked a field goal.

• Ernie Warlick again sat on the bench and was used sparingly. Apparently he was going to stay there for the rest of the year.

QUOTES

• Jack Kemp: "This is the guy (trainer Eddie Abramoski) who got me ready to play." (On the acquisition of receiver Bo Roberson): "He gives us the needed speed on the outside. He did a great job for having been with us only a few days."

• Denver coach Mac Speedie: "We played our worst game of the season against the best team in the league. Buffalo's big four is a great unit up front, as good as San Diego's. Edgerson's interception and Costa's catch hurt us the most. And Kemp did a great job. We expected to be screened, but our defense broke down."

• Denver running back Cookie Gilchrist on the favorable ovation he got from the crowd before the game: "It made me think of my days when I was a Bill. That showed me the fans appreciate my ability and my performances. I think it was a great tribute to me and I truly appreciated it."

• Lou Saban: "Kemp was superb. He read his keys perfectly and really burned Denver with the screens. Fergy just needed some time and Bo Roberson is an established receiver. They'll both help us. And I'd have to say Costa is coming along, too. With this boost in our passing game, the rest of our game is opened up. After we made these decisions, I had forebodings. But I determined not to second-guess myself and the staff and stick with the decisions. I'm glad I did."

WEEK 7 GAMES

Hou 38, KC 36	SD 34, NY 9
Oak 30, Bos 21	

Broncos	0	6	0	7 - 13
Bills	7	14	10	0 - 31

Attendance at War Memorial Stadium - 45,046

Buf: Joe 78 pass from Kemp (Gogolak kick), 9:21
Den: FG Kroner 33, 3:16
Buf: Ferguson 8 pass from Kemp (Gogolak kick), 6:25
Buf: Carlton 1 run (Gogolak kick), 12:03
Den: FG Kroner 20, 14:26
Buf: Carlton 1 run (Gogolak kick), 4:05
Buf: FG Gogolak 22, 13:54
Den: Haynes 30 pass from Slaughter (Kroner kick), 11:18

	BUF	DEN
First downs	21	19
Rushing yds	76	95
Passing yds	262	264
Punts -avg	4-43.8	4-36.0
Fumbles-lost	3-1	0-0
Penalties-yds	11-95	10-97

BILLS LEADERS: Rushing - Carlton 12-48, Joe 6-11, Stone 2-14, Smith 3-3; **Passing** - Kemp 14-22-0 - 280, Lamonica 2-5-0 - 16; **Receiving** - Joe 6-156, Ferguson 4-36, Costa 2-64, Roberson 3-35, Stone 1-5.

BRONCOS LEADERS: Rushing - Gilchrist 21-87, Hayes 6-9, Haynes 1-1, Slaughter 1-(-2); **Passing** - McCormack 10-23-1 - 138, Slaughter 10-17-0 - 137; **Receiving** - Haynes 6-63, Taylor 6-86, Gilchrist 3-55, Scarpitto 3-34, Dixon 2-37.

NOTES

• Lou Saban elected to try for a TD from the 1-yard-line late in the game rather than kick a field goal. The gamble backfired when Jack Kemp was stopped for no gain. The Bills were lucky to be there in the first place because Oilers cornerback Tony Banfield was penalized for a very questionable pass interference on Bo Roberson at the Houston 6.

• The Bills defense forced a punt from the end zone and the offense took over at the Oiler's 34. However, a holding penalty wiped out a 10-yard Wray Carlton run and Pete Gogolak's desperation 55-yard field goal attempt was short with 2:09 left.

• The Bills offense was hurt because Kemp lost his voice. Failure to hear a Kemp audible in the third quarter cost them a scoring chance. He eventually took himself out of the game, but later returned.

• Houston was penalized for 189 yards, a new AFL record.

• Gogolak missed a 45-yard field goal on the first possession, but Mike Stratton's interception gave the Bills the ball back at the Oilers 30. Kemp hit Paul Costa for 28 and Billy Joe scored from the 4.

• Houston drove 80 yards to tie it up, but Buffalo regained the lead when W.K. Hicks, who later redeemed himself with three interceptions, was called for pass interference at the Houston 2 and Carlton took it in from there.

• George Blanda, who was playing with a sore knee, then kicked four field goals and Houston's defense frustrated the Bills the rest of the way. Jack Spikes had missed a field goal early and Blanda told coach Bones Taylor that he felt well enough to kick.

QUOTES

• Lou Saban on his gamble: "I never thought of not making it. A touchdown meant they couldn't beat us with a field goal. It would have forced them to go for the big play which we had been stopping. And with that ball on the hashmark, Pete Gogolak would have had a very rough angle for a field goal. We had gone off tackle three straight times, which was another reason for the quarterback sneak. We had only six inches to go. I thought we could have rooted them out of there. If I had to do it over, I'd still go for the touchdown." (On why he didn't take Kemp out with his voice strained): "When Daryle comes into the game it takes our offense two or three plays to get used to his cadence. We couldn't risk a penalty."

• Oilers cornerback W.K. Hicks: "This was my greatest day. When you have a day like this, someone against you has to have a bad day. Ferguson was playing banana style and he was easy to cover."

• Oilers coach Bones Taylor: "Where would we be if Blanda hadn't decided to kick? Our senior citizen is still a proud pro."

Oilers	7	6	3	3 - 19
Bills	14	0	0	3 - 17

Attendance at War Memorial Stadium - 44,267

Buf: Joe 4 run (Gogolak kick), 7:04
Hou: Burrell 10 pass from Blanda (Spikes kick), 10:36
Buf: Carlton 2 run (Gogolak kick), 14:19
Hou: FG Blanda 31, 12:05
Hou: FG Blanda 30, 14:59
Hou: FG Blanda 13, 8:16
Buf: FG Gogolak 39, 2:03
Hou: FG Blanda 7, 6:39

	BUF	HOU
First downs	19	16
Rushing yds	121	124
Passing yds	121	148
Punts-avg	3-32.0	0-0
Fumbles-lost	2-0	0-0
Penalties-yds	9-72	11-189

BILLS LEADERS: Rushing - Carlton 13-57, Joe 19-58, Lamonica 1-10, Kemp 4-(-4); **Passing** - Kemp 10-22-2 - 148, Lamonica 2-5-2 - 14; **Receiving** - Ferguson 3-22, Costa 3-46, Roberson 6-94.

OILERS LEADERS: Rushing - Burrell 10-72, Tolar 7-30, Jackson 6-15, Spikes 1-8, Blanda 2-(-1); **Passing** - Blanda 13-35-1 - 158; **Receiving** - Burrell 5-66, Hennigan 3-47, Frazier 2-34, Tolar 2-2, Spikes 1-9.

WEEK 8 GAMES

KC 14, Oak 7	NY 45, Den 10
Bos 22, SD 6	

STANDINGS: EIGHTH WEEK

EAST	W	L	T	WEST	W	L	T
Buffalo	6	2	0	San Diego	5	1	2
Houston	4	3	0	Kan. City	4	3	1
New York	1	5	1	Oakland	4	3	1
Boston	1	6	1	Denver	3	5	0

Bills	3 17 3 0 - 23
Patriots	0 7 0 0 - 7

Attendance at Fenway Park - 24,415

Buf: FG Gogolak 28, 13:14
Buf: Kemp 3 run (Gogolak kick), 5:54
Buf: FG Gogolak 16, 9:05
Bos: Garrett 1 run (Cappelletti kick), 13:00
Buf: Warner 102 kickoff return (Gogolak kick), 13:17
Buf: FG Gogolak 32, 14:55

	BUF	BOS
First downs	9	15
Rushing yds	62	28
Passing yds	99	236
Punts-avg	9-38.2	6-30.0
Fumbles-lost	0-0	2-2
Penalties-yds	5-36	3-25

BILLS LEADERS: Rushing - Carlton 16-43, Joe 8-19, Kemp 3-0; **Passing** - Kemp 7-23-0 - 99; **Receiving** - Ferguson 3-42, Costa 2-46, Roberson 2-11.

PATRIOTS LEADERS: Rushing - Garron 12-26, Parilli 7-16, Wilson 3-(-16), J.D. Garrett 1-1, Burton 5-1; **Passing** - Parilli 15-35-2 - 206, Wilson 3-5-0 - 39; **Receiving** - Colclough 4-114, Cappelletti 3-51, Nance 2-17, Whalen 3-27, Garron 3-9, Johnson 1-14, Garrett 1-5, Burton 1-8.

NOTES

• Leading 3-0, the Bills took advantage of a fumble to make it 10-0 in the second. Ron Burton was knocked unconscious on a hit by Tom Day and George Saimes. Burton fumbled with Butch Byrd recovering at the Boston 18. Two plays later Jack Kemp scored on a three-yard run.
• A few plays later, Bill Laskey blocked Tom Yewcic's punt and Dudley Meredith recovered at the Boston 8 leading to Pete Gogolak's second field goal.
• The Bills allowed their first rushing TD in 17 games and it was a gift. Hagood Clarke had intercepted a Babe Parilli pass at the 10, but Booker Edgerson was flagged for interference on Gino Cappelletti in the end zone, giving Boston a first-and-goal at the 1. J.D. Garrett scored.
• Charley Warner then returned the ensuing kickoff 102 yards for the TD that broke Boston's spirit.
• Gogolak's final field goal was set up when Stew Barber recovered a muffed punt by Burton at the Boston 31.
• The game was played in intermittent rain. The Bills managed only 169 yards of total offense.

WEEK 9 GAMES	
NY 13, KC 10	SD 35, Den 21
Oak 33, Hou 21	

• Kemp used a longer cadence to keep the Patriots' blitzing defense guessing.

QUOTES
• Lou Saban: "We were using longer calls. That and the slower signals had the Patriots afraid of jumping off-sides or revealing their blitzes. The constant rain made the field a mess and the conditions very bad so I decided to take the three points whenever I could (unlike last week against Houston). I also told Kemp that if he wasn't positive his targets were completely clear, he was to throw the ball away. Under those conditions, I thought we could punt them into trouble." (On the play of the defense): "We're allowing yardage between the 30s and then we get tough from the 30 on. Our offense hasn't helped the defense much. The defensive unit has been on the field much more than it should be."
• Charley Warner on his return: "I just followed that wedge. A couple hands hit my shoulders, but it didn't slow me down."
• Boston coach Mike Holovak: "They'll never get any more given to them than we gave them today. That blocked punt gave them a field goal, the muffed punt another field goal and Burton's fumble a touchdown."

Bills	0 7 0 10 - 17
Raiders	7 0 0 7 - 14

Attendance at Frank Youell Field - 19,352

Oak: Daniels 41 run (Mercer kick), 11:41
Buf: Joe 1 run (Gogolak kick), 3:41
Oak: Wood 25 pass from Daniels (Mingo kick), 1:14
Buf: FG Gogolak 37, 7:27
Buf: Joe 1 run (Gogolak kick), 14:53

	BUF	OAK
First downs	11	10
Rushing yds	94	137
Passing yds	129	158
Punts-avg	6-37.5	8-33.0
Fumbles-lost	2-2	2-0
Penalties-yds	2-20	1-50

BILLS LEADERS: Rushing - Carlton 9-30, Joe 11-23, Kemp 4-20, Smith 4-17, Stone 2-2, Warner 1-2; **Passing** - Kemp 11-31-2 - 142; **Receiving** - Ferguson 2-34, Costa 1-20, Roberson 5-43, Smith 2-41, Stone 1-4.

RAIDERS LEADERS: Rushing - Daniels 14-91, Miller 4-37, Todd 8-14, Wood 1-(-5); **Passing** - Wood 10-26-3 - 186; **Receiving** - Biletnikoff 3-30, Miller 2-40, Herock 2-22, Daniels 2-51, Todd 1-43.

WEEK 10 GAMES	
KC 31, SD 7	NY 30, Bos 20
Den 31, Hou 21	

NOTES
• The Bills trailed 14-7 in the fourth after Clem Daniels caught a 25-yard TD pass from Dick Wood. But Buffalo rallied for 10 points and won the game when Billy Joe scored on a one-yard plunge with seven seconds left to play, capping a 12-play, 62-yard drive.
• It was Buffalo's first win at Oakland since 1962 and

avenged their 1964 defeat when Art Powell caught a game-winning one yard TD pass on the final play.
• The game was played in the mud after two days of steady rain and it affected both teams on offense.
• Daniels broke free for a 41-yard TD run in the first and the Bills answered in the second following Butch Byrd's interception and 61-yard return to the Oakland 20. Five plays later, Joe scored from the 1-yard-line.
• Byrd's second interception in the fourth halted an Oakland drive at the Bills 16, but Don Stone fumbled a couple of plays later and Dan Conners recovered for the Raiders at the 20. After Wood lost five yards recovering his own fumble, he hit Daniels in the end zone for the go-ahead score.
• Two series later, a pair of 20-yard Kemp completions set up Bobby Smith set up Pete Gogolak's fourth field goal attempt. After missing his first three, he made a 37-yarder to make it 14-10 with 7:33 left to play.
• The defense forced a punt and the winning drive began at the Bills 38. Kemp hit Charley Ferguson for 21 and later, on fourth-and-six from the Oakland 34, Kemp threw cross-field to Paul Costa who juggled the pass before latching on for a 20-yard gain. Four plays later, Joe scored.
• The Raiders' 137 rushing yards was almost double what the Bills had been allowing, but Oakland gained just eight in the second half as Lou Saban adjusted his defense perfectly.

QUOTES
• Lou Saban: "This was the big one for us. It's not just that it enhanced our chances for the title but to come back as we did was just great." (On why he rested starting backs Billy Joe and Wray Carlton during the game): "For big men to carry all that mud around is tiring and the extra speed we got from Bobby Smith and Don Stone really helped. And it paid off in the end when Billy and Wray went back in. They were fresh then, and got us tough yards when we needed them."
• Jack Kemp on the fourth-down pass to Costa: "I had

rolled to the right, then I spotted Paul on the other side of the field. Just after I threw the ball, I got knocked down in front of the Oakland bench. I heard Al Davis swear, so I figured Paul must have caught it."
• Paul Costa: "I thought the play had broken down. I finished my pattern, then I just tried to get free and hoped that Jack would see me."
• Raiders coach Al Davis expressing displeasure over Dick Wood's play-calling in the second half: "He called six straight runs. I never had a quarterback who called six straight runs in my career. New York's offense, he's used to New York's offense. He called three straight traps (midway through the fourth quarter) and I hate traps."

STANDINGS: TENTH WEEK							
EAST	W	L	T	WEST	W	L	T
Buffalo	8	2	0	San Diego	6	2	2
Houston	4	5	0	Oakland	5	4	1
New York	3	5	1	Kan. City	5	4	1
Boston	1	8	1	Denver	4	6	0

NOTES

• The Bills clinched at least a tie for the East Division title as Jack Kemp directed his second straight last-second drive to avert a loss. The Bills clinched the division later that weekend as the Jets lost to the Patriots.

• The Bills began the final drive at their 25 with 1:16 left. Kemp hit Paul Costa for a 35-yard gain on third-and-10. Then he threw 16 yards to Bo Roberson. With 18 seconds left, Kemp was forced to scramble for nine to the 15 before stepping out of bounds. Pete Gogolak kicked the tying field goal with six seconds left.

• The Bills had blown a 17-10 lead in the fourth. After a 36-yard Gogolak miss, John Hadl and Lance Alworth combined on a 66-yard gain to the Bills 10. Buffalo held and Herb Travenio kicked a 14-yard field goal.

• Three plays later, Dick Westmoreland intercepted a Kemp pass and returned it 28 yards to the Bills 15. On third-and-six, Hadl scrambled to the 3, fumbled, and Paul Lowe recovered in the end zone to give San Diego a 20-17 lead.

• The Bills took a 7-0 lead after John Tracey forced Gene Foster to fumble at the Bills 45. Three Kemp passes, including the TD pass to Wray Carlton, keyed the drive.

• San Diego took a 10-7 lead at halftime, but the Bills went ahead 17-10 in the third. A 79-yard drive, in which Kemp completed six of seven passes for 76 yards before suffering a shoulder injury, ended when Daryle Lamonica came in and snuck over from the 1.

• Alworth caught a 65-yard pass on the next series, but Booker Edgerson did the unthinkable and caught him from behind, forced him to fumble and Tracey recovered in the end zone.

• Gogolak's 12-yard field goal was set up when long snapper Sam Grueisen's snap flew over punter Hadl's head and by the time he recovered, Hadl had lost 42 yards to his own 6. The Chargers defense held, forcing the field goal.

QUOTES

• Lou Saban: "That's all right, the players said they'd rather drink champagne in Houston. We played the percentages punting with less than two minutes to go. We figured we could get the ball back again. That (the final drive) was one of the finest efforts an offensive club of mine ever made. We went from our own 25 with no timeouts. Sure we wanted to win it, but I'm not complaining. Besides, the tie eliminates Houston."

• Jack Kemp: "I almost lost it (referring to Westmoreland's pick). I had to do something to get it back. I felt we should have won, I'm not satisfied with a tie."

• Chargers coach Sid Gillman on the pass play to Costa: "Our safety man, Dick Harris, fell down. You can't cover someone on your hands and knees."

WEEK 11 GAMES	
KC 10, Bos 10	NY 41, Hou 14
Oak 28, Den 20	
Buffalo and San Diego had bye weeks.	

WEEK 12 GAMES	
KC 52, Hou 21	Bos 27, NY 23

Bills	7	0	10	3	- 20
Chargers	0	10	0	10	- 20

Attendance at Balboa Stadium - 27,473

Buf: Carlton 6 pass from Kemp (Gogolak kick), 9:42
SD: Lowe 6 run (Travenio kick), 9:27
SD: FG Travenio 9, 14:42
Buf: Lamonica 1 run (Gogolak kick), 4:39
Buf: FG Gogolak 12, 9:54
SD: FG Travenio 14, 6:43
SD: Lowe recovered fumble in end zone(Travenio kick), 8:37
Buf: FG Gogolak 22, 14:54

	BUF	SD
First downs	13	23
Rushing yds	47	52
Passing yds	184	309
Punts-avg	8-43.1	5-36.0
Fumbles-lost	3-2	5-3
Penalties-yds	8-78	5-37

BILLS LEADERS: Rushing - Carlton 6-14, Joe 7-11, Kemp 2-11, Smith 2-10, Lamonica 1-1; **Passing** - Kemp 17-35-1 - 201, Lamonica 1-2-0 - 4; **Receiving** - Carlton 3-15, Joe 2-11, Ferguson 3-39, Costa 3-70, Roberson 5-59, Smith 2-11.

CHARGERS LEADERS: Rushing - Lowe 20-69, Foster 8-10, Hadl 5-12, Lincoln 1-3, TEAM (bad punt snap) 1-(-42); **Passing** - Hadl 18-37-2 - 315; **Receiving** - Foster 3-39, Alworth 7-127, Lincoln 2-68, Norton 3-42, MacKinnon 3-39.

NOTES

• Pete Gogolak attempted a league-record seven field goals and made a team-record five (both misses were from the 50).

• The game featured nine turnovers as neither team was very sharp.

• Wray Carlton's 80-yard TD run was the longest run from scrimmage in Bills history. He gained a career-high 148 yards.

• A 91-yard Jack Kemp to Ed Rutkowski TD pass was nullified by a penalty on Paul Costa.

• The Bills' five pass completions tied their all-time low, set in their inaugural game against the New York Titans in 1960.

• Ralph Wilson was home sick with the flu and missed only his third game in six years.

• The Bills trailed 7-3 in the first when Daryle Lamonica, who got the start, connected with Bo Roberson after Gary Cutsinger had deflected the pass. Roberson went 74 yards for the TD.

• Tom Janik recovered a fumble on the next Oilers series leading to Gogolak's second field goal.

• After an exchange of field goals made it 16-10 starting the fourth, Carlton followed guard Billy Shaw around right end and went the distance and it was 23-10 just 29 seconds into the period.

• Two more Gogolak field goals offset George Blanda's 95-yard TD pass to Dick Compton, the longest pass play in the AFL since 1962.

• Another injury occurred in the receiving corps as Charley Ferguson suffered a pulled hamstring.

QUOTES

• Pete Gogolak: "My leg felt really good today. I really felt I could get into the ball because of the warm weather and the dry field."

• Lou Saban: "I'm not alarmed (by the ragged play). I used a lot of new men and substituted heavily. We didn't use Tom Sestak until the second half and had two rookie linebackers in there at one time. But I wanted to win this one, even if it wasn't neat. It meant that we beat every team in our division at least once and it showed the Oilers they couldn't beat us merely by throwing their helmets out there on the field. If they couldn't beat us today, they should never beat us. I wanted to beat them. They're always popping off about how they can beat us."

• Wray Carlton: "Billy (Shaw) had me hemmed in on the sideline so I stayed there all the way. I thought I stepped out of bounds at about the 50. I haven't run that far in a long time. I felt all right when I came out, but then I got off the bench and I started to see spots in front of my eyes. I thought I was going to pass out."

Bills	13	0	3	13	- 29
Oilers	7	3	0	8	- 18

Attendance at Rice Stadium - 23,087

Buf: FG Gogolak 12, 6:00
Hou: Spikes 4 run (Blanda kick), 9:20
Buf: Roberson 74 pass from Lamonica (Gogolak kick), 10:54
Buf: FG Gogolak 12, 13:29
Hou: FG Blanda 41, 4:26
Buf: FG Gogolak 47, 10:34
Buf: Carlton 80 run (Gogolak kick), :29
Buf: FG Gogolak 34, 4:56
Hou: Compton 95 pass from Blanda (Burrell pass from Blanda), 11:05
Buf: FG Gogolak 19, 14:49

	BUF	HOU
First downs	11	15
Rushing yds	201	86
Passing yds	82	214
Punts-avg	4-49.8	4-51.0
Fumbles-lost	3-1	4-3
Penalties-yds	2-21	5-54

BILLS LEADERS: Rushing - Carlton 11-148, Joe 6-14, Stone 3-9, Smith 8-23, Lamonica 2-8, Kemp 2- (-1); **Passing** - Kemp 1-10-1 - 25, Lamonica 3-14-1 - 83; **Receiving** - Roberson 3-106, Rutkowski 1-4, Smith 1- (-2).

OILERS LEADERS: Rushing - Burrell 12-45, Jackson 8-23, Spikes 7-17, Trull 1-1; **Passing** - Blanda 10-24-1 - 209, Trull 2-10-1 - 43; **Receiving** - Hennigan 4-61, Burrell 3-25, Frazier 3-65, Compton 1-95, Spikes 1-6.

WEEK 13 GAMES	
Oak 24, Den 13	SD 38, NY 7

STANDINGS: THIRTEENTH WEEK

EAST	W	L	T	WEST	W	L	T
Buffalo	9	2	1	San Diego	7	2	3
New York	4	7	1	Oakland	7	4	1
Houston	4	8	0	Kan. City	6	4	2
Boston	2	8	2	Denver	4	8	0

GAME 13 - Sunday, Dec. 12, 1965 - BILLS 34, CHIEFS 25

Chiefs	7	0	3	15 -	25
Bills	10	10	0	14 -	34

Attendance at War Memorial Stadium - 40,298

Buf: Roberson 66 pass from Kemp (Gogolak kick), 3:34
Buf: FG Gogolak 30, 6:14
KC: Arbanas 67 pass from Dawson (Brooker kick), 8:30
Buf: FG Gogolak 22, :51
Buf: Roberson 13 pass from Kemp (Gogolak kick), 9:56
KC: FG Brooker 21, 4:08
KC: Taylor 19 pass from Dawson (Brooker kick), 1:11
Buf: Smith 1 run (Gogolak kick), 8:38
KC: Coan 22 pass from Dawson (Carolan pass from Dawson), 9:30
Buf: Rutkowski 47 pass from Kemp (Gogolak kick), 11:36

	BUF	KC
First downs	19	18
Rushing yds	74	63
Passing yds	264	347
Punts-avg	4-42.3	1-45.0
Fumbles-lost	1-0	3-3
Penalties-yds	3-26	1-15

BILLS LEADERS: Rushing - Carlton 12-25, Smith 9-27, Maguire 1-21, Stone 1-1; **Passing** - Kemp 22-34-2 - 295; **Receiving** - Carlton 3-4, Rutkowski 5-83, Costa 3-44, Roberson 6-127, Smith 5-37.

CHIEFS LEADERS: Rushing - Hill 8-22, Dawson 5-23, McClinton 3-14, Coan 1-4; **Passing** - Dawson 23-37-1 - 356; **Receiving** - Taylor 5-85, Hill 4-39, McClinton 4-28, Coan 4-60, Jackson 4-50, Arbanas 3-94.

NOTES

• With nothing to play for, and going against a team that was still alive in the West Division race, the Bills pulled out a victory despite a brilliant performance by Len Dawson. San Diego's victory over Houston set up an AFL title-game rematch between the Bills and the Chargers, this time in San Diego.
• Pete Gogolak's two field goals gave him 28, an all-time pro football record, breaking the mark of Gene Mingo (27), then with Denver, set in the 1962 AFL season. Gogolak also broke the record of Lou Michaels for most attempts in one season. Michaels attempted 42 for Pittsburgh of the NFL in 1962.
• The Bills raced to a 20-7 halftime lead. Jack Kemp hit Bo Roberson on a 66-yard TD pass 3:34 into the game. Moments later, Tom Sestak sacked Dawson, forced him to fumble and Sestak recovered at the KC 13. That led to Gogolak's 30-yard field goal.
• After Dawson and Fred Arbanas hooked up on a 67-yard TD, Kemp completed five straight passes, but the march stalled at the KC 41. Punter Paul Maguire, taking advantage of a token rush, ran 21 yards for a first down. Gogolak then kicked a 22-yarder to make it 13-7.
• Hagood Clarke killed a KC drive with an interception and the Bills went 80 yards with Kemp completing five passes including a 13-yarder for the TD to Roberson.
• KC got to within 20-17 early in the fourth when Dawson capped a 71-yard march with a 19-yard TD pass to Otis Taylor.
• Stew Barber recovered a muffed punt by Willie Mitchell at the KC 18, leading to Bobby Smith's one-yard run. After Dawson passed 23 yards to Bert Coan and then hit Reg Carolan for the two-point conversion, the Chiefs were within 27-25 with 5:30 left. However, Ed Rutkowski caught a sideline pass and after Mitchell dove and failed to intercept, Rutkowski had clear sailing to the end zone.

QUOTES

• Lou Saban: "This is great, I am thoroughly enjoying this. These guys just don't know what it means to quit. That's wonderful. Someone gets close and they just zoom away. You know the amazing thing, we had the division two games ago and we've won twice since. I can describe this team best in the words of my favorite trainer, Eddie Abramoski: It's got a heart like a blow-torch."
• Chiefs coach Hank Stram: "Jack Kemp is just unbelievable. And I've always maintained that Roberson is the most underrated flanker in the game."
• Paul Maguire: "I never ran before on fourth down, and I'll never do it again. Sestak said it took me 41 seconds to go 25 yards. I was running scared. You say the crowd was roaring – I didn't hear a thing."
• Bo Roberson: "This team plays as hard as it has to do to win."

WEEK 14 GAMES

SD 37, Hou 26   Oak 24, NY 14
Bos 28, Den 20

GAME 14 - Sunday, Dec. 19, 1965 - JETS 14, BILLS 12

Bills	6	0	0	6 -	12
Jets	7	0	7	0 -	14

Attendance at Shea Stadium - 57,396

NY: Maynard 19 pass from Namath (J. Turner kick), 12:23
Buf: Warner 87 kickoff return (pass failed), 12:39
NY: Maynard 36 pass from Namath (J. Turner kick), 9:37
Buf: Warner 11 pass from Lamonica (run failed), :47

	BUF	NY
First downs	11	14
Rushing yds	99	60
Passing yds	137	239
Punts-avg	8-39.1	10-41.0
Fumbles-lost	4-2	1-1
Penalties-yds	6-48	3-38

BILLS LEADERS: Rushing - Carlton 15-48, Smith 13-42, Lamonica 1-9; **Passing** - Kemp 5-16-1 - 43, Lamonica 8-16-0 - 122; **Receiving** - Carlton 3-13, Rutkowski 1-6, Costa 3-53, Roberson 1-8, Smith 2-29, Warner 1-11, Mills 1-43, Tracey 1-2.

JETS LEADERS: Rushing - Mathis 11-21, Smolinski 11-26, McDaniel 1-13; **Passing** - Namath 17-44-2 - 239; **Receiving** - Maynard 9-180, Smolinski 4-20, Sauer 2-24, B. Turner 2-15.

WEEK 15 GAMES

KC 45, Den 35   SD 24, Oak 14
Bos 42, Hou 14

NOTES

• Both teams were sloppy. The Bills' long snapper, Al Bemiller, flubbed two snaps, his first in five years handling those duties. One came on a conversion and the other in the fourth quarter prevented Pete Gogolak from attempting a go-ahead 12-yard field goal with four minutes left. Holder Daryle Lamonica scrambled away from the rush and hit John Tracey with a pass, but Tracey wound up one yard shy of a first down. The Jets then ran out most of the clock.
• New York took a 7-0 lead when AFL Rookie of the Year Joe Namath hit Don Maynard with a 19-yard TD pass, one play after Bert Wilder recovered Bobby Smith's fumble.
• Charley Warner returned the ensuing kickoff 87 yards for a TD, his second of the season. But Bemiller's high snap forced Lamonica to throw to Tracey and he was short of the end zone on the PAT.
• Before the first half ended, Gogolak, who was shut out for the first time in his pro career, had 40- and 42-yard field goal attempts blocked.
• Namath and Maynard combined again on a 36-yard TD pass in the third, but 47 seconds into the fourth, Lamonica play-faked beautifully to Smith and hit Warner - a cornerback who was used at split end - for an 11-yard TD. The two-point conversion failed, leaving it 14-12.
• The botched field goal attempt at the end was set up when rookie Pete Mills – another cornerback who was playing offense – caught a 43-yard pass from Lamonica.
• The loss was the first for the Bills on the road and snapped their six-game winning streak against the Jets.
• The 18 punts were one short of the league record for two teams.

QUOTES

• Lou Saban: "Better this week than next Sunday. I expected them to be looking a week ahead. The kicker can't kick until the ball's placed down. He can't do his own blocking against the defensive rush."
• Joe Namath: "They're (the Bills defense) the toughest, man."
• Bills assistant coach Joe Collier: "That had to be the craziest game for the kicking teams I've ever seen."
• Al Bemiller: "I don't remember ever having snapped one high for either a conversion or a field goal."

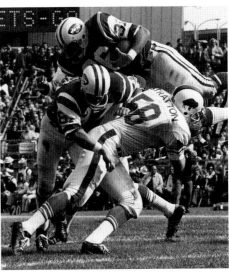

STANDINGS: FIFTEENTH WEEK

EAST	W	L	T	WEST	W	L	T
Buffalo	10	3	1	San Diego	9	2	3
New York	5	8	1	Oakland	8	5	1
Boston	4	8	2	Kan. City	7	5	2
Houston	4	10	0	Denver	4	10	0

Bills	0	14	6	3 - 23
Chargers	0	0	0	0 - 0

Attendance at Balboa Stadium - 30,361

Buf: Warlick 18 pass from Kemp (Gogolak kick), 10:01
Buf: Byrd 74 punt return (Gogolak kick), 12:31
Buf: FG Gogolak 11, 5:39
Buf: FG Gogolak 39, 14:15
Buf: FG Gogolak 32, 3:15

	BUF	SD
First downs	23	12
Rushing yds	108	104
Passing yds	152	119
Punts-avg	4-46.3	7-40.7
Fumbles-lost	0-0	0-0
Penalties-yds	2-21	3-41

BILLS LEADERS: Rushing - Carlton 16-63, Joe 16-35, Stone 3-5, Smith 1-5; **Passing** - Kemp 8-19-1 - 155, Lamonica 1-1-0 - 12; **Receiving** - Roberson 3-88, Warlick 3-35, Costa 2-32, Tracy 1-12; **Punt returns** - Byrd 3-87; **Kickoff returns** - Warner 1-17.

CHARGERS LEADERS: Rushing - Lowe 12-57, Hadl 8-24, Lincoln 4-16, Foster 2-9, Breaux 1-(-2); **Passing** - Hadl 11-23-2 - 140, Breaux 1-2-0 - 24; **Receiving** - Alworth 4-82, Norton 1-35, Farr 1-24, MacKinnon 1-10, Lincoln 1-7, Lowe 3-3, Kocourek 1-3; **Punt returns** - Duncan 1-12; **Kickoff returns** - Duncan 2-62, Farr 1-35.

Jack Kemp was named the Associated Press AFL Player of the Year after guiding the Bills to their second straight AFL Championship.

NOTES

• The game was played exactly one year after the Bills' first championship victory over the Chargers, only this time the temperature was 59 degrees and the wind was mild.

• The shutout was the first in AFL Championship Game history and it was the first time the Chargers had been blanked since a 41-0 loss to Boston on Dec. 17, 1961.

• Butch Byrd's 74-yard punt return was the longest in AFL title-game history.

• The Chargers never got inside Buffalo's 24-yard-line.

• The Chargers suffered their fourth loss in five appearances in the AFL Championship Game.

• Tight end Ernie Warlick, who was banished to the bench for the final nine games and did not catch a pass during that stretch, started and caught three passes, including the first touchdown.

• Center Dave Behrman didn't make the trip because of a back injury and all-league guard Billy Shaw was injured on the opening kickoff and didn't play the rest of the day. Joe O'Donnell and George Flint stepped in admirably at the guard spots and Al Bemiller moved to center.

• San Diego drove to the Bills 28 early in the game, but Herb Travenio's 35-yard field goal attempt was blocked by Jim Dunaway.

• QB John Hadl took over the punting chores in the second quarter after rookie Jim Allison kicked two wobblers in the first quarter. Hadl nailed a 69-yarder from his own end zone that Byrd returned 12 yards to the Buffalo 40. From there, the Bills drove 60 yards for the first score of the game. Two eight-yard runs by Wray Carlton and a 22-yard Kemp-to-Paul Costa pass moved the ball to the San Diego 22. On third down, Kemp, who was named the game's MVP, rifled a bullet between the goal posts, past San Diego defender Leslie Duncan and into the hands of Warlick.

• The Chargers failed to move on their next possession and Byrd took Hadl's punt, started up the right sideline and needed only Paul Maguire's final clearing block at the Charger 20 before getting into the end zone for a 14-0 advantage with 2:29 left in the first half.

• The game almost became a rout on the next play when Harry Jacobs picked off a Hadl pass and returned it 12 yards to the Chargers 20, but San Diego held and Duncan sliced through to block Pete Gogolak's 24-yard field goal attempt.

• San Diego set off on its deepest penetration, but the drive ended when Travenio's hurried 31-yard field goal as time ran out missed to the left.

• On Buffalo's first offensive play of the third, Bo

Roberson beat Jim Warren and caught a 49-yard Kemp pass which set up Gogolak's 11-yard field goal.

• The Bills defense stopped the next two San Diego advances, first when Tom Sestak and John Tracey sacked Hadl on fourth down from the Bills 29. After Paul Maguire punted to the 1-yard line, Hadl was intercepted by Byrd who returned 24 yards to the San Diego 23. That led to Gogolak's 39-yard field goal with 45 seconds left in the third.

• After stopping Paul Lowe on a fourth-down run at the San Diego 30, the Bills moved into position for Gogolak's third field goal, a 32-yarder, which ended the scoring.

• The Bills were rated a seven-point underdog before the game but Daryle Lamonica proclaimed: "We know we can beat them. And they know it."

• Because of the TV contract with NBC, the Bills' per-player share was $5,189.92, the largest in league history. San Diego's per player share of $3,447.85 was higher than any winning team ever had received.

QUOTES

• Ralph Wilson: "I've seen the Bills play some great games, but this one tops them all." New York governor Nelson Rockerfeller and California governor Edmund Brown wagered a basket of fruit on the winner and Wilson wired Rockefeller a message that read: "On behalf of the Buffalo Bills, I hope you enjoy the California fruit."

• Buffalo mayor-elect Frank Sedita: "The Buffalo Bills are a credit to our city."

• Jack Kemp: "We are established. Congratulations to

Lou on a great job today. That was the greatest game plan we've ever had. Look at this (spotless) uniform. I can't say enough about our line, especially Al Bemiller, George Flint and Joe O'Donnell. They came through in the clutch." When asked what he would do with his winner's share, Kemp said: "You can't play football forever. You gotta look to the future, so I'm putting all my money in securities. I hope."

• Paul Maguire: "I'm so happy I could kiss Tippy Day (Day overheard him and came over and kissed Maguire)."

• Ron McDole: "We've got something the Chargers will never have. We hang together no matter what."

• Ernie Warlick: "I'm just glad he (Saban) thought enough of me to give me the opportunity. I didn't know until just before we took the field, but I was fired up anyway. It's unbelievable. I can't wait to see the morning paper in Buffalo tomorrow and find out it's all true. The Chargers have so many guns, but they don't know which one to use."

• Chargers coach Sid Gillman: "We lost to an excellent football team, that's all. I have no alibis. There was no single factor, they just beat us. They are a beautiful team and beautifully coached. I don't know why, it was just their day and they beat the hell out of us."

• Chargers running back Paul Lowe: "When I got that long run (his 47-yarder in the first quarter), I felt like we were winning. But mistakes killed us. We just couldn't get the ball rolling. I hate to say look to next year, but that's what it is."

• Chargers wide receiver Lance Alworth: "We'll get 'em next year."

At A Glance
1966

Jan. 2 – Lou Saban, the 1965 Coach of the Year who coached the Bills to back-to-back AFL championships, resigned his position to take the head coaching job at the University of Maryland. "I will cherish my four years in Buffalo for the rest of my life," Saban said. "I've had a wonderful time here, an unforgettable time. I owe a great deal to a lot of young men on that football team. But the most important thing about my association with Buffalo has been the lasting friends I've made. Pro football is strictly business, nothing outside of it." Saban turned down "one of the longest-term contracts with one of the biggest salaries in professional coaching," according to Ralph Wilson. "I think Lou made a courageous decision. The thing he emphasized most of all in our discussion was his desire to get out from under the tremendous pressure of being a professional coach."

Jan. 6 – Defensive coordinator Joe Collier was hired as Lou Saban's replacement. At the age of 33, he became the youngest head coach in pro football. Collier said that Harvey Johnson would remain as personnel director, Jerry Smith would remain as running offense coach and Johnny Mazur would handle the passing game. "I had applications from three or four other candidates, but I talked to several of my associates in the Bills' organization before I decided on Joe Collier," Ralph Wilson said. "One of the things that prompted my decision was the job Joe had done for us as defensive coach the last several seasons. I believe that the defensive phase of the game is becoming more important every year in pro football."

Jan. 11 – Richie McCabe, a member of the original 1960 Bills, was named defensive backfield coach by Joe Collier.

Jan. 17 – Fullback Billy Joe, flanker Bo Roberson, 1965 No. 1 draft choice Jim Davidson and defensive end Howard Simpson were plucked off the Bills' roster by the Miami Dolphins in the expansion draft. The Dolphins also selected all-star guard Billy Neighbors from Boston, tackle Norm Evans from Houston, linebacker Wahoo McDaniel and defensive end Laverne Torczon from the Jets, quarterback Dick Wood and kicker Gene Mingo from Oakland, tight end Dave Kocourek and cornerback Dick Westmoreland from San Diego. Also, in completing the trade that brought Roberson to Buffalo in mid-1965, the Raiders took offensive lineman George Flint and defensive tackle Tom Keating.

March 10 – Jack Horrigan, a former Bills beat writer for the *Buffalo News* who left to become PR director for the NFL, was named vice-president of the Bills.

April 7 – Joe Foss, commissioner of the AFL since its inception, announced his resignation.

April 8 – Al Davis, general manager and coach of the Oakland Raiders, was named to succeed Foss as commissioner.

May 17 – The New York Giants announced they had signed Pete Gogolak. The Bills placekicker had played out his option and had not signed a new contract with Buffalo.

June 8 – The AFL and the NFL announced plans to merge into one professional football league in time for the 1970 season. In the meantime, the

Joe Collier became the Bills head coach in 1966 after Lou Saban resigned suddenly. Here he poses with captains Jack Kemp and Ron McDole.

leagues would participate in a common college player draft in January and the champions of each league would play in a world championship game starting with the 1966 season. NFL commissioner Pete Rozelle was named commissioner of the merging leagues. Kansas City owner Lamar Hunt negotiated primarily with NFL president Tex Schramm. Ralph Wilson and Patriots owner William Sullivan backed Hunt in the talks. "I think it's great for both leagues and particularly for the fans," Wilson said.

July 16 – The Bills opened training camp at the Camelot-Voyager.

July 25 – Refusing to serve as AFL president under the reign of Pete Rozelle, Al Davis quit as commissioner. Milt Woodard was named league president.

Aug. 7 – Pete Gogolak's replacement, Booth Lusteg, kicked four field goals as the Bills opened the preseason with a 19-13 victory over the Patriots at Boston College.

Aug. 12 – The Bills beat Denver, 25-3, in front of 28,144 at War Memorial in the home preseason opener as Booth Lusteg again kicked four field goals and Daryle Lamonica passed for 314 yards.

Aug. 16 – Tight end Ernie Warlick and running back Bobby Smith were cut.

Aug. 20 – The Bills improved to 3-0 with a 28-16 victory over Houston in Little Rock, Ark.

Aug. 25 – Gene Klein bought the Chargers from Barron Hilton for approximately $10 million.

Aug. 27 – The Jets whipped the Bills, 34-17, at Allentown, Pa. in the preseason finale.

Aug. 30 – Six-year AFL veteran running back Jack Spikes was acquired from Miami for a draft choice.

Sept. 2 – Miami began its history in dazzling

fashion as ex-Bill Joe Auer returned the opening kickoff at the Orange Bowl 95 yards for a TD. However, the Dolphins lost to Oakland, 23-14.

Sept. 4 – The Bills were awful in the season opener at San Diego, losing 27-7. Jack Kemp completed only four of 20 passes with three interceptions that led to Charger TDs.

Sept. 11 – The Bills fell to 0-2 as Kansas City routed them, 42-20, on the strength of a 21-point first quarter and a 79-yard Mike Garrett punt return for a TD.

Sept. 18 – The Bills crushed Miami, 58-24, in the Dolphins' first appearance at War Memorial Stadium. The Bills set team scoring and margin of victory records.

Sept. 25 – Hagood Clarke intercepted a George Blanda pass and returned it 66 yards for the winning TD with 27 seconds left to give Buffalo a 27-20 victory over Houston.

Oct. 2 – The Bills downed the Chiefs, 29-14, before 43,885 at Municipal Stadium, the largest crowd ever to see a sporting event in Kansas City.

Oct. 8 – Booth Lusteg missed four field goals, disappointing a record crowd of 45,542 during the Bills 20-10 loss to Boston.

Oct. 14 – Booth Lusteg missed a 23-yard field goal with six seconds left and the Bills and Chargers ended in a 17-17 draw. Ralph Wilson, trying to console his kicker, said: "You'll make them forget that miss." Said Lusteg: "Contrary to what people think, I still think I'm a good kicker. Sure I'm disappointed. I hate to miss, I hate to lose. But (Pete) Gogolak missed a couple, too. I wasn't nervous before that kick, I was confident. I felt good, I hit it good, I didn't choke, I just missed it."

Oct. 17 – Lusteg refused to sign a complaint against the "over-wrought, irresponsible and

youthful punks" he said attacked him following the Chargers game. "I consider it an unfortunate incident that does not represent the true spirit of Buffalonians."

Oct. 28 – After a bye week, the Bills bounced back and topped the Jets at Shea, 33-23, as Lusteg made four field goals. "They have people in Buffalo who know how to build a football team," said Jets coach Weeb Ewbank. "They went out and got themselves a bunch of brutes for those lines. That's what wins games. Guys like Tom Sestak and Jim Dunaway can make anybody look good."

Nov. 2 – Joe Namath, intercepted five times by the Bills, flew to San Juan, Puerto Rico on the Jets' off week for some relaxation

Nov. 6 – The Bills blanked the Dolphins, 29-0, as they limited Miami to 171 total yards.

Nov. 13 – In front of another record crowd at War Memorial Stadium (45,738), the Bills downed the Jets, 14-3, with a 14-point fourth quarter keyed by Jim Dunaway's 72-yard TD run with a blocked field goal.

Nov. 20 – The Bills crushed Houston, 42-20, with a 508-yard offensive outburst.

Nov. 24 – With another huge day from its offense in the form of 465 yards, the Bills beat the Raiders in Oakland on Thanksgiving Day, 31-10.

Nov. 25 – Daryle Lamonica denied that he had requested a trade, but admitted he wanted to have a talk with coach Joe Collier at the end of the season. "It would kill me to sit on the bench much longer," he said. "But I wouldn't do anything rash. I want to stay in Buffalo, but I want a chance to win a regular job. I think Jack Kemp is a better quarterback because I've pushed him. The competition has been good for me, too."

Nov. 30 – Ted Barron, a Boston businessman and owner of the minor league team Booth Lusteg kicked for in 1965, said he would try to prevent the Bills kicker from playing in the showdown against the Patriots in Fenway Park. Barron said Lusteg still was bound to an option clause in his contract with the New Bedford Sweepers of the Atlantic Coast League. It also was revealed that Barron was

suing the Patriots, whom he said promised to supply his team with four to six players for the 1966 season, then reneged on the deal. Barron said the failure of the Patriots to give him some players facilitated the demise of his team at a loss of about $100,000 to Barron and his partner, Manny Mello. Barron said he offered Lusteg to the Patriots, but they declined, and Lusteg then made his own deal with the Bills after Pete Gogolak joined the New York Giants of the NFL. Barron said the Bills offered him $500 for Lusteg's services after Lusteg had agreed to join the Bills. The Bills denied ever having made an offer for Lusteg.

Dec. 1 – New pro football commissioner Pete Rozelle announced that Los Angeles had been awarded the first Super Bowl game, to be played either Jan. 7, 8 or 15 at the Coliseum. Winners shares were set at $15,000 and losers at $7,500.

Dec. 2 – A story in the Boston Traveler revealed that Booth Lusteg had lied about his age (he was 27, not 25) and that he wasn't a graduate of Boston College as he had said, but actually was a 1960 cum laude graduate of the University of Connecticut. Lusteg reportedly pretended to be his brother, Wally, who did attend Boston College, but quit the football team after one day. The reason for taking on Wally's identity was that Wally was only 25. "Who ever heard of a 27-year old rookie in pro football?" Lusteg said when asked why he lied. "I feel bad about this, though I never expected to keep it a secret forever. I did it to play football and hoped I could keep it quiet until I became established. I was afraid the Bills wouldn't give me a chance if they knew I was a 27-year-old rookie." Said Joe Collier: "I don't care if he's Brand X, as long as he keeps kicking field goals."

Dec. 3 – The Bills arrived in Boston for the big game with the Patriots and found a pair of $50,000 lawsuits waiting for them, one for the team, one for Lusteg. The suits were for breach of contract, arising from Ted Barron's contention that the Bills did not pay him after signing Lusteg. Barron, however, did back off on trying to get Lusteg banned from the game, saying "it would be unsportsmanlike and

many fans have already purchased tickets expecting to see him play."

Dec. 4 – Jim Nance broke a 65-yard TD run and Boston's defense dominated the Bills in a 14-3 victory that put the Patriots in first place.

Dec. 11 – The Patriots beat the Oilers in Houston, 38-14, meaning a victory or tie in their final game would lock up the East Division. The Bills were off this week and watched solemnly on TV.

Dec. 15 – The Denver Broncos announced that ex-Bills coach Lou Saban would be their new coach and general manager. Saban's contract was reportedly for 10 years at about $50,000 per season.

Dec. 17 – The Jets shocked the Patriots, 38-28, at Shea Stadium, to open the door for the Bills to win the East Division. Joe Namath passed for 287 yards and three TDs.

Dec. 18 – The Bills jumped to a 24-7 lead and went on to beat the Broncos, 38-21, to clinch the East Division title for the third year in a row. After the game, fans stormed the field and tore down the goal posts. It was an ugly scene as special security guards clubbed fans, sending six to the hospital.

Dec. 20 – Rookie Bobby Burnett was voted by his teammates as the Bills' MVP.

Dec. 23 – Bobby Burnett was named AFL Rookie of the Year, beating out Kansas City's Mike Garrett.

Dec. 26 – Billy Shaw, Jim Dunaway, Mike Stratton, Ron McDole and Butch Byrd were named to the AFL all-star first team by the AP; the Bills left snowy Buffalo for the warmth of Winston-Salem, N.C. to begin practicing for the AFL Championship Game.

Dec. 28 – The Bills moved their workouts from Wake Forest University to a city stadium in Winston-Salem in order to work on a secret offensive drill behind locked gates.

Dec. 30 – The team returned from North Carolina and were greeted by about 3,000 fans at the airport. "And all we're doing is coming back from practice," Tom Day said.

Jan. 1, 1967 – Kansas City cruised to a 31-7 rout of the Bills before 42,080 fans at War Memorial Stadium – the largest crowd to see an AFL Championship Game – and earned the right to play the Green Bay Packers in the first Super Bowl. The Packers defeated Dallas, 34-27, later in the day. The Bills managed just 40 yards rushing and turned over the ball four times.

Jan. 15, 1967 – Green Bay routed Kansas City, 35-10, in Super Bowl I before a non-sellout crowd of 63,036 at the Los Angeles Coliseum. Both CBS and NBC televised the game. Asked if the Bills would have done any better against the Packers, Joe Collier said: "The Chiefs beat us, 31-7. That's not a very strong argument for us doing better." Green Bay coach Vince Lombardi said that the top six teams in the NFL were better than the Chiefs.

Jan. 21, 1967 – The AFL all-star game, returning to the traditional East vs. West format with the advent of the Super Bowl, was won for the first time by the East, 30-28. Bobby Burnett scored on a 12-yard run in the fourth quarter and after a Mike Stratton interception, Babe Parilli threw the game-winning TD pass.

BY THE NUMBERS - 1966

TEAM STATISTICS	BILLS	OPP
First downs	255	192
Rushing	110	49
Passing	126	131
Penalty	19	12
Total yards	4,748	4,109
Avg. game	339.1	293.5
Plays	944	842
Avg. play	5.0	4.9
Net rushing yds	1,892	1,051
Avg. game	135.1	75.1
Avg. play	4.1	3.1
Net passing yds	2,856	3,058
Comp/att	199/473	205/466
Sacks/lost	16-144	32-249
Interceptions	21	29
Percentage	42.1	44.0
Punts/avg	69-41.2	84-39.6
Fumbles/lost	27-15	19-9
Penalties/yds	62-637	55-546
Touchdowns	43	31
Extra points	41-42	28-28
Field goals	19-38	13-22
Two-point conv	0-1	1-3
Safeties	1	0
Kick ret./avg	51-21.9	65-20.4
Punt ret./avg	43-9.6	20-15.1

RUSHING	ATT	YDS	AVG	TD
Burnett	187	766	4.1	4
Carlton	156	696	4.5	6
A. Smith	31	148	4.8	0
Kemp	40	130	3.3	5
Spikes	28	119	4.3	3
Dubenion	3	16	5.3	0
Rutkowski	1	10	10.0	0
Lamonica	9	6	0.7	1
Costa	0	1	0.0	0
TOTALS	**455**	**1892**	**4.2**	**19**

PASSING	COMP	ATT	INT	YDS	TD	COMP%
Kemp	166	389	16	2451	11	42.7
Lamonica	33	84	5	549	4	39.3
TOTALS	**199**	**473**	**21**	**3000**	**15**	**42.1**

KICKING	FG/ATT	PAT/ATT	PTS
Lusteg	19-38	41-42	98

PUNTING	NO	AVG
Maguire	69	41.2

RECEIVING	CAT	YDS	AVG	TD
Dubenion	50	747	14.9	2
Burnett	34	419	12.3	4
Crockett	31	533	17.2	3
P. Costa	27	400	14.8	3
Carlton	21	280	13.3	0
Ferguson	16	293	18.3	1
Bass	10	130	13.0	0
Rutkowski	6	150	25.0	1
Spikes	2	45	22.5	1
O'Donnell	1	2	2.0	0
A. Smith	1	1	1.0	0
TOTALS	**199**	**3000**	**15.1**	**15**

LEADERS

Kick returns: Warner 33-846 yds, 25.6 avg, 1 TD
Rutkowski 6-121, 20.2, 0 TD

Punt returns: Rutkowski 18-209, 11.6, 1 TD
Byrd 23-186, 8.1, 1 TD

Interceptions: Janik 8-136, 17.0, 2 TD
Byrd 6-110, 18.3, 1 TD

Non-kick scoring: Burnett 8 TDs, 48 pts
Carlton 6 TDs, 36 pts

Paul Maguire (right) was the Bills punter from 1964-70. His career average of 42.12 yards per punt remains a Buffalo record, as does his 130 punts downed inside the 20-yard line.

Bobby Burnett (opposite page) amassed 1,185 yards from scrimmage in 1966 and was voted the most valuable player of the Bills by his teammates as well as the AFL's rookie of the year.

GAME 1 - Sunday, Sept. 4, 1966 - CHARGERS 27, BILLS 7

NOTES

• The Chargers avenged the 1965 championship loss by dominating the Bills and frustrating Jack Kemp into one of his worst performances. His three interceptions all led to San Diego TDs.

• Bobby Burnett's TD run with 1:27 left enabled the Bills to avoid being shutout for the first time in club history.

• New coach Joe Collier hesitated in lifting Kemp, mainly because he didn't want to seem to be panicking in his first game. Also, Daryle Lamonica hadn't played well in preseason.

• Kemp was penalized three times for delay of game, twice on third-and-one situations.

• The Bills threatened on their first two possessions, but the delay penalty forced Booth Lusteg to try a 44-yard field goal, which he missed. Kemp then was picked off by Ken Graham on the second series. From there, the Chargers drove to their first score, a 10-play, 73-yard drive, capped by John Hadl's TD pass to Lance Alworth.

• San Diego held the ball for all but three plays in the third quarter, but managed only a field goal by Dick Van Raaphorst.

• In the fourth, Miller Farr's interception of Kemp was followed by a 42-yard Hadl pass to Jacque MacKinnon, which led to another Van Raaphorst field goal and a 13-0 lead.

• Bud Whitehead intercepted Kemp a few minutes later and returned it 61 yards to the Buffalo 31, setting up Hadl's TD pass to MacKinnon. Leslie Duncan then returned a Paul Maguire punt 81 yards for a TD on the ensuing series.

• Lamonica drove the Bills to their only TD, hitting Charley Ferguson for completions of 19, 27 and 31 yards along the way.

QUOTES

• Jack Kemp: "I was unbelievably bad. I just smelled up the stadium. The rest of the team was fine, But I was just terrible. Look, I just haven't had enough work. When my arm was sore (in training camp), I missed all kinds of work and I needed it. I had a horrible training camp. What I need now is more work, not more rest."

• Billy Shaw: "That was the most frustrating game I've ever played in. Everything was going good up front, but we just weren't getting anywhere. This game was perfectly plotted by the coaches."

• Joe Collier: "I thought we could have won the game with better quarterbacking. We went into the game with the idea of using long counts. San Diego is blitzing a lot now and they change defenses quickly to prevent the quarterback from calling a checkoff. The long count was to keep them from disguising what they wanted to do." (On why he didn't go to Lamonica earlier): "The main reason is that a quarterback on the field can learn more than he can on the bench. The view from the bench is poor. In order to keep continuity in the attack, one quarterback should remain in there."

WEEK 1 GAMES

Oak 23, Miami 14	Hou 45, Den 7

Bills	0	0	7	-	7
Chargers	0	7	3	17	- 27

Attendance at Balboa Stadium - 27,572

SD: Alworth 7 pass from Hadl (Van Raaphorst kick), :56
SD: FG Van Raaphorst 30, 9:07
SD: FG Van Raaphorst 10, :02
SD: MacKinnon 3 pass from Hadl (Van Raaphorst kick), 9:38
SD: Duncan 81 punt return (Van Raaphorst kick), 10:55
Buf: Burnett 2 run (Lusteg kick), 13:33

	BUF	SD
First downs	15	15
Rushing yds	117	137
Passing yds	150	153
Punts-avg	4-51.2	4-30.8
Fumbles-lost	0-0	1-1
Penalties-yds	3-15	3-38

BILLS LEADERS: Rushing - Burnett 9-22, Carlton 16-87, Rutkowski 1-10, Spikes 1-(-2); **Passing** - Kemp 4-20-3 - 74, Lamonica 5-7-0 - 76; **Receiving** - Dubenion 1-14, Ferguson 3-77, Costa 2-44, Carlton 1-16, O'Donnell 1-2, Burnett 1-(-3).

CHARGERS LEADERS: Rushing - Foster 12-58, Lowe 15-36, Allison 5-37, Hadl 4-6; **Passing** - Hadl 14-19-0 - 160; **Receiving** - Alworth 5-46, MacKinnon 3-56, Lowe 3-7, Garrison 2-47, Hadl 1-4.

GAME 2 - Sunday, Sept. 11, 1966 - CHIEFS 42, BILLS 20

NOTES

• The Chiefs beat the Bills for the first time since Sept. 30, 1962 when the franchise was in Dallas.

• Bobby Crockett was ejected for throwing the ball in anger at Fred Williamson.

• Glenn Bass fumbled on Buffalo's fourth play of the game. The Chiefs went on to score 21 points in the first quarter.

• The first TD came when Len Dawson passed to Bert Coan for 12 yards. After a Buffalo punt, KC went 76 yards in six plays as Dawson hit Fred Arbanas for 31 and Coan broke a 22-yard run to set up his four-yard TD.

• Garrett had a 64-yard punt return for a TD nullified because of an illegal lateral he received from Emmitt Thomas. The Chiefs still wound up scoring, going 69 yards with Dawson hitting Otis Taylor from 14 yards to make it 21-0.

• Booth Lusteg kicked a field goal early in the second and the Bills got to within 21-10 by halftime as Jack Kemp snuck in from the 1. The drive capped a 56-yard drive that was aided by pass interference and defensive holding penalties against the Chiefs.

• A low snap from center forced KC punter Jerrol Wilson to eat the ball at the KC 21 early in the third, but the Bills could manage only a field goal.

• KC then put it away. Coan broke a 32-yard run and Pete Beathard, in for Dawson, passed 17 yards to Curtis McClinton for a score. Garrett then busted a 79-yard punt return late in the third that counted.

• Beathard's 68-yard pass to McClinton set up McClinton's TD in the fourth to make it 42-13. Ed Rutkowski closed the scoring with a 73-yard punt return.

QUOTES

• Chiefs running back Mike Garrett: (On his nullified punt return): "I wanted that one, but I had a feeling it might be a forward lateral, but I ran anyway." (On whether he thought KC was title-bound): "I don't believe in predictions. I made too many in college (at USC) and we never went to the Rose Bowl."

• Joe Collier: "I'm admittedly disappointed, but not discouraged. They beat us every way a team can be beaten - defense, offense and the special units, too." (On Kemp): "I don't think his arm is ailing, we just haven't been getting good catching. We have the club that can beat the Chiefs and we can beat them out there (in KC). But they ran over us and I didn't think any team could do that. We're the champions and everyone is gunning for us. We must expect that. In these first two games, I never saw the opposition make so few mistakes."

• Chiefs coach Hank Stram: "The Bills won for two years by letting the other team make mistakes, by playing defense and on Pete Gogolak's kicking. Now the Bills are making mistakes, that's the biggest single difference."

Chiefs	21	0	14	7	-	42
Bills	0	10	3	7	-	20

Attendance at War Memorial Stadium - 42,572

KC: Coan 12 pass from Dawson (Brooker kick), 5:13
KC: Coan 4 run (Brooker kick), 10:37
KC: Taylor 14 pass from Dawson (Brooker kick), 13:57
Buf: FG Lusteg 22, 1:56
Buf: Kemp 1 run (Lusteg kick), 13:45
Buf: FG Lusteg 9, 5:43
KC: McClinton 17 pass from Beathard (Brooker kick), 8:02
KC: Garrett 79 punt return (Brooker kick), 13:02
KC: McClinton 1 run (Brooker kick), 6:47
Buf: Rutkowski 73 punt return (Lusteg kick), 11:39

	BUF	KC
First downs	15	17
Rushing yds	79	165
Passing yds	136	223
Punts-avg	7-45.0	5-39.8
Fumbles-lost	1-1	1-1
Penalties-yds	3-25	7-70

BILLS LEADERS: Rushing - Burnett 12-40, Carlton 11-42, Kemp 4-(-3); **Passing** - Kemp 6-21-0 - 102, Lamonica 5-17-0 - 43; **Receiving** - Dubenion 3-63, Ferguson 1-5, Costa 2-21, Crockett 3-39, Bass 1-12, Burnett 1-5.

CHIEFS LEADERS: Rushing - Coan 11-101, McClinton 14-39, Garrett 7-10, Beathard 3-10, Wilson 1-5, Thomas 1-0; **Passing** - Dawson 8-11-0 - 129, Beathard 3-6-0 - 98; **Receiving** - McClinton 4-96, Taylor 4-80, Arbanas 1-31, Coan 1-12, Burford 1-8.

WEEK 2 GAMES

NY 19, Miami 14	SD 24, Bos 0
Hou 31, Oak 0	

STANDINGS: SECOND WEEK

EAST	W	L	T	WEST	W	L	T
Houston	2	0	0	San Diego	2	0	0
New York	1	0	0	Kan. City	1	0	0
Boston	0	1	0	Oakland	1	1	0
Buffalo	0	2	0	Denver	0	1	0
Miami	0	2	0				

GAME 3 - Sunday, Sept. 18, 1966 - BILLS 58, DOLPHINS 24

Dolphins	3	7	0	14 -	24
Bills	21	27	3	7 -	58

Attendance at War Memorial Stadium - 37,546

Buf:	Kemp 1 run (Lusteg kick), 6:54
Buf:	Byrd 60 interception return (Lusteg kick), 7:22
Buf:	Byrd 72 punt return (Lusteg kick), 9:48
Mia:	FG Mingo 24, 13:22
Buf:	Crockett 26 pass from Kemp (Lusteg kick), 1:15
Buf:	Burnett 1 run (Lusteg kick), 2:41
Buf:	Burnett 3 run (kick blocked), 4:08
Mia:	Roderick 4 pass from Wilson (Mingo kick), 12:53
Buf:	Spikes 11 run (Lusteg kick), 14:07
Buf:	FG Lusteg 13, 13:00
Mia:	Roberson 66 pass from Wilson (Mingo kick), 6:37
Buf:	Spikes 18 pass from Lamonica (Lusteg kick), 9:06
Mia:	Kocourek 13 pass from Wilson (Mingo kick), 13:09

	BUF	MIA
First downs	25	17
Rushing yds	179	111
Passing yds	329	202
Punts-avg	4-43.8	6-44.2
Fumbles-lost	2-1	1-0
Penalties-yds	8-109	4-30

BILLS LEADERS: Rushing - Burnett 14-64, Carlton 10-19, A. Smith 4-29, Spikes 3-53, Kemp 3-14; **Passing** - Kemp 13-26-1 - 226, Lamonica 4-7-1 - 103; **Receiving** - Dubenion 5-101, Ferguson 2-53, Costa 3-36, Burnett 2-21, Crockett 2-70, Spikes 1-18, Carlton 1-(-2), Rutkowski 1-32.
DOLPHINS LEADERS: Rushing - Joe 10-36, Auer 8-35, Chesser 9-18, Price 1-14, Wilson 3-10, Norton 1-(-2); **Passing** - Wilson 10-30-1 - 185, Norton 3-10-3 - 17; **Receiving** - Roberson 5-128, Roderick 2-12, Joe 2-6, Twilley 1-20, Kocourek 1-13, Matthews 1-20, Auer 1-3.

NOTES

• The Bills won their first game and set team records for scoring (58), touchdowns (8), margin of victory (34) and interception-return yards (112). The 48-10 halftime spread was an AFL record for most points in a half and largest halftime lead.
• Four Miami interceptions led to Buffalo touchdowns including Butch Byrd's 60-yard return in the first quarter. Byrd also had a 72-yard punt return later in the opening quarter.
• George Wilson Jr., son of Dolphins coach George Wilson Sr., threw three TD passes.
• The Bills drove 56 yards on their first possession to score, then Byrd picked off Rick Norton's sideline pass and went all the way. On the next series, Byrd returned Wilson's punt for a TD and a 21-0 lead.
• Miami got a field goal from Gene Mingo, but the Bills responded with Jack Kemp's TD pass to Bobby Crockett and back-to-back short TD runs by Bobby Burnett. Burnett's first score was set up when Mike Stratton returned an interception to the 1. The second was the result of Stratton's interception and return to the 6.
• After Miami scored, the Bills drove 74 yards in 11 plays to Jack Spikes' TD for a 48-10 lead at the half.
• Joe Collier eased up in the second half. Miami's second TD was aided by a 15-yard unsportsmanlike conduct penalty assessed against the Bills because of excessive crowd booing with 8:35 left. The crowd was angry for a penalty that was called against Billy Shaw and booed for 10 minutes, making it difficult for the Dolphins' to call offensive plays. The score was 58-17 at the time.

WEEK 3 GAMES

Bos 24, Den 10	KC 32, Oak 10
NY 52, Hou 13	

QUOTES

• Joe Collier: "I think Jack's throwing pleased me the most. The reason we left him in so long was because he needed the work. We've been saying that all along." (He also pointed to three other areas that impressed him): "The fact that we were very aggressive and our execution was good; the work of the special units; and defensively we improved. With Houston losing to the Jets and the Oilers coming here next week, we're right back in the thick of it, but we have a long way to go."
• Jack Kemp on the fans' booing: "I doubt booing the officials' decision and booing until it upset us enough to let Miami score on that long pass will cure those fans who boo just about everybody and everything."
• Butch Byrd: "I anticipated a sideline pass to Bo Roberson and I won a gamble."

GAME 4 - Sunday, Sept. 25, 1966 - BILLS 27, OILERS 20

Oilers	0	6	0	14 -	20
Bills	3	17	0	7 -	27

Attendance at War Memorial Stadium - 42,526

Buf:	FG Lusteg 47, 11:21
Buf:	Carlton 8 run (Lusteg kick), :45
Hou:	FG Blanda 47, 5:13
Buf:	FG Lusteg 32, 6:54
Buf:	Burnett 15 pass from Kemp (Lusteg kick), 9:45
Hou:	FG Blanda 35, 13:56
Hou:	Burrell 11 pass from Blanda (Blanda kick), 4:00
Hou:	Frazier 62 pass from Blanda (Blanda kick), 6:27
Buf:	Clarke 66 interception return (Lusteg kick), 14:33

	BUF	HOU
First downs	14	15
Rushing yds	136	24
Passing yds	140	276
Punts-avg	5-34.8	5-34.8
Fumbles-lost	2-1	1-0
Penalties-yds	3-25	2-20

BILLS LEADERS: Rushing - Burnett 13-70, Carlton 13-44, Dubenion 1-17, Kemp 2-2, Smith 1-(-4), Lamonica 3-7; **Passing** - Kemp 11-26-2 - 172; **Receiving** - Dubenion 2-33, Costa 2-75, Carlton 3-19, Burnett 1-15, Crockett 3-30.
OILERS LEADERS: Rushing - Blanks 6-16, Tolar 5-5, Burrell 8-3, Blanda 1-0, Stone 1-0; **Passing** - Blanda 23-54-5 - 303; **Receiving** - Hennigan 9-93, Frazier 6-128, Burrell 3-44, McLeod 3-27, Blanks 1-11, Tolar 1-0.

NOTES

• The Bills blew a 20-6 lead, but recovered and won when Hagood Clarke intercepted a George Blanda pass and returned it 66 yards for the winning TD with 27 seconds to play.
• The sequence unfolded this way: Paul Maguire shanked a 19-yard punt to the Oilers 42 with 1:52 left to play. After two incompletions, Blanda hit Charley Frazier for 19 yards. Harry Jacobs sacked Blanda for a loss of eight, then Blanda passed seven yards to Charley Hennigan. On third down, Blanda tried to hit Bob McLeod on the far sideline and Clarke stepped in front. He took off down the sideline, Ron McDole cleared out Blanda and Clarke broke a tackle before getting to the end zone as the crowd went wild. It was Blanda's fifth interception of the game.
• Jack Kemp completed eight of 13 for 137 yards in the first half, but Houston coach Wally Lemm told his corners to jam the Bills receivers. He also used a nickel defense and Buffalo's offense sputtered.
• After a Booth Lusteg field goal, Butch Byrd picked off a pass at the Oilers 37 that led to Wray Carlton's TD.
• The teams traded field goals, then Tom Janik intercepted Blanda and returned it to the Houston 33 to set up Kemp's 15-yard screen pass TD to Bobby Burnett.

WEEK 4 GAMES

KC 43, Bos 24	SD 29, Oak 20
NY 16, Den 7	

• Down 20-6 after a scoreless third quarter, the Oilers tied the game. Doug Cline picked off a Kemp pass and returned it 23 yards to the Bills 11. Two plays later, Blanda hit Ode Burrell to make it 20-13. Bernie Parrish, playing his first AFL game, then intercepted a deep Kemp pass. Blanda took advantage, hooking up with Frazier on a 62-yard TD with 8:33 left.

QUOTES

• Hagood Clarke: "I was just trying to cover my man. I really didn't think he would throw. Ron McDole got us the six points. He took out Blanda downfield and I cut off his block."
• Joe Collier: "I never saw the finish of Clarke's run, I was too busy looking for flags. When I saw Hagood intercept, I figured we'd be in position for a field goal and the way Booth Lusteg kicked today, I felt sure we'd get those points."
• Houston coach Wally Lemm: "What can I say? We were just trying to get closer for field goal position. Clarke made a good move. Blanda called the pass and no, I don't think it was a bad call. I thought he called a good game."
• Oilers QB George Blanda: "I've had better days. But things were looking up until that interception. The ball didn't slip and no, I don't think it was a poor pass or call. He just made a good play."
• Booth Lusteg: "Saturday I studied movies of myself and how Blanda kicks and I learned from him. The fast start towards the ball, the slowdown and the dip before you boot the ball for elevation."

STANDINGS: FOURTH WEEK

EAST	W	L	T	WEST	W	L	T
New York	3	0	0	San Diego	3	0	0
Houston	2	2	0	Kan. City	3	0	0
Buffalo	2	2	0	Oakland	1	3	0
Boston	1	2	0	Denver	0	3	0
Miami	0	3	0				

131

NOTES

• The Bills avenged their defeat at Buffalo and dealt KC its first loss of the year.

• The Chiefs went ahead, 7-0, less than two minutes into the game as Len Dawson hit Otis Taylor for 71 yards. Tom Janik was hurt the play before and Charley Warner replaced him. Dawson took advantage immediately.

• Mike Stratton forced Curtis McClinton to fumble and Harry Jacobs recovered at the KC 41 to set up Booth Lusteg's 27-yard field goal. Janik, back in the game, intercepted a Dawson pass and returned it 19 yards to the KC 9, and Lusteg kicked a 16-yarder.

• KC made it 14-6 late in the first after Bobby Bell intercepted Kemp and returned it to the Buffalo 18. Dawson passed 15 yards to McClinton on third down.

• Buffalo came right back as Kemp went five-for-five for 55 yards during a 13-play, 89-yard TD march. After the TD pass to Elbert Dubenion, the Bills faked the conversion, but Daryle Lamonica overthrew John Tracey on the two-point try.

• The Bills ruled the second half. Kemp's 32-yard pass to Bobby Burnett led to Lusteg's go-ahead 20-yard field goal.

• Early in the fourth, after KC failed on a fake field goal, the Bills drove 75 yards to Kemp's 24-yard TD pass to Ed Rutkowski, who beat Fred Williamson.

• A 72-yard drive wrapped up the game with Dubenion catching 15- and 17-yard passes before Wray Carlton bulled in from the 10.

QUOTES

• Hagood Clarke: "It was the front four that did it for us. They took away Kansas City's running. They allowed us to play our type of defense, not the defense they wanted us to play. We played normal pass defenses and used blitzes because they shut down the Chiefs."

• Butch Byrd: "They (the front four) took the pressure off us, gave us more time by making the Kansas City quarterbacks get rid of the ball faster. Give them credit."

• Joe Collier: "We had practically the same game plan we had when we played them in Buffalo. The difference was in our execution. Where the game is decided, especially against a team as strong physically as Kansas City, is in the lines. Our offensive and defensive lines beat theirs, and that's what they had to do for us to win. We contained their ground game, which hurt their usual success with the play-action pass. On the other hand, we ran well and consequently went to the play-action pass more ourselves. This was our best effort to date. We beat a very fine football team."

• Chiefs safety Dave Grayson talking about Jack Kemp: "You can feel those eyes of his staring at you and all you can do is stand there and hope he doesn't throw anything in your direction."

WEEK 5 GAMES
Bos 24, NY 24	SD 44, Miami 10
Den 40, Hou 38	

Bills   6   6   3   14 - 29
Chiefs   14   0   0   0 - 14

Attendance at Municipal Stadium - 43,885

KC: Taylor 71 pass from Dawson (Brooker kick), 1:29
Buf: FG Lusteg 27, 6:33
Buf: FG Lusteg 16, 9:19
KC: McClinton 15 pass from Dawson (Brooker kick), 13:53
Buf: Dubenion 10 pass from Kemp (pass failed), 6:36
Buf: FG Lusteg 20, 7:59
Buf: Rutkowski 24 pass from Kemp (Lusteg kick), :44
Buf: Carlton 10 run (Lusteg kick), 7:06

	BUF	KC
First downs	20	11
Rushing yds	147	51
Passing yds	214	214
Punts-avg	6-48.3	7-50.4
Fumbles-lost	1-0	2-1
Penalties-yds	1-12	0-0

BILLS LEADERS: Rushing - Burnett 15-46, Carlton 15-92, Kemp 3-8, Costa 0-1; **Passing** - Kemp 19-36-1 - 214; **Receiving** - Dubenion 6-82, Costa 2-17, Burnett 3-39, Bass 2-32, Crockett 3-25, Rutkowski 1-24, Carlton 2-(-5).

CHIEFS LEADERS: Rushing - Garrett 3-10, Beathard 3-23, Dawson 1-12, McClinton 7-2, Coan 6-4; **Passing** - Dawson 5-15-1 - 143, Beathard 7-19-1 - 96; **Receiving** - Taylor 4-125, Burford 4-60, Arbanas 2-34, McClinton 1-15, Coan 1-5.

NOTES

• The Bills fumbled six times, losing three, and Booth Lusteg missed four of five field goals. Boston took advantage in front of a new War Memorial Stadium record crowd.

• Paul Maguire's poor punt enabled Boston to drive for its first score, a 10-yard Gino Cappelletti field goal. Moments later, Wray Carlton fumbled (the first of three) and Bob Dee recovered for Boston at the Bills 19. On the next play, Jim Nance broke three tackles and plowed into the end zone for a 10-0 lead six minutes in.

• Cappelletti missed a 47-yard field goal, then John Tracey recovered a Nance fumble at the Patriots 44, but the Bills failed to score when Lusteg missed a 33-yard field goal. Lusteg later missed a 36-yarder before the half ended.

• Buffalo's next possession died when Kemp tripped over referee Jack Vest and lost 20 yards.

• With 44 seconds left in the half, Cappelletti nailed a 44-yarder to make it 13-0. Just before the half ended, Carlton raced 55 yards with a short Kemp pass, but fumbled at the Boston 29.

• Another Carlton fumble to open the second half stopped the first Bills' possession, but Kemp passed them downfield on their next series. Lusteg missed a 42-yarder, but the Pats were offsides and Lusteg converted from 37.

• However, Boston's ensuing 75-yard TD drive put it away. Carlton's one-yard run early in the fourth, after Elbert Dubenion caught a 46-yard pass, wasn't enough.

• Joe Collier said that Boston's use of a three-man line on defense was a key, as was the blitzing.

QUOTES

• Patriots coach Mike Holovak: "New York is going to lose. Buffalo is going to beat them twice. Just put that in your memory that I said it. I still think the Bills are the best team in the league. We blitzed more than we have all season, but it wasn't just to stop the running. You have to defense everything to stop Buffalo."

• Joe Collier: "We played fair football and as I told them after the game, fair football is about a 7-7 won-lost record. Now we'll have to see what kind of football players we have, what they're made of. We'll see what kind of coaches we have, too. Beat New York twice? We can't afford to lose to New York or San Diego or Miami or Denver or anyone." (On whether he was considering going with Daryle Lamonica): "The circumstances under which we would make a change at quarterback would be if Jack Kemp wasn't doing his job. I see no reason why we should make a change now."

• Elbert Dubenion on the slow start: "Training camp is a most important time for a pro football player and I feel part of our early-season problems stem from the fact that we had such a poor training camp. With Jack not working because of his sore elbow, our timing was off when we opened the season. But things are getting better, Jack is throwing better. I thought Jack called a real good game but people kept booing him. It wasn't his fault, he didn't fumble, he didn't drop any passes."

Patriots   10   3   7   0 - 20
Bills   0   0   3   7 - 10

Attendance at War Memorial Stadium - 45,542

Bos: FG Cappelletti 10, 4:31
Bos: Nance 19 run (Cappelletti kick), 6:00
Bos: FG Cappelletti 31, 14:16
Buf: FG Lusteg 37, 7:32
Bos: Bellino 25 pass from Parilli (Cappelletti kick), 13:26
Buf: Carlton 1 run (Lusteg kick), :02

	BUF	BOS
First downs	15	12
Rushing yds	52	109
Passing yds	269	177
Punts-avg	7-40.6	8-36.4
Fumbles-lost	6-3	1-1
Penalties-yds	2-20	3-36

BILLS LEADERS: Rushing - Carlton 16-53, Kemp 4-8, Burnett 3-(-3), Dubenion 1-(-6); **Passing** - Kemp 18-38-0 - 298; **Receiving** - Dubenion 7-104, Ferguson 2-20, Carlton 2-81, Burnett 5-54, Crockett 2-39.

PATRIOTS LEADERS: Rushing - Nance 23-88, Parilli 1-17, Garron 9-4; **Passing** - Parilli 12-26-0 - 177; **Receiving** - Cappelletti 6-99, Bellino 2-33, Colclough 2-23, Graham 2-22.

WEEK 6 GAMES
KC 37, Den 10	NY 17, SD 16
Oak 21, Miami 10	

STANDINGS: SIXTH WEEK

EAST	W	L	T	WEST	W	L	T
New York	4	0	1	San Diego	4	1	0
Buffalo	3	3	0	Kan. City	4	1	0
Boston	2	2	1	Oakland	2	3	0
Houston	2	3	0	Denver	1	4	0
Miami	0	5	0				

GAME 7 - Sunday, Oct. 16, 1966 - BILLS 17, CHARGERS 17

Chargers	7	10	0	0	- 17
Bills	0	3	7	7	- 17

Attendance at War Memorial Stadium - 45,169

SD: Frazier 6 pass from Hadl (Van Raaphorst kick), 13:55
SD: FG Van Raaphorst 23, 13:07
SD: Lincoln 21 pass from Hadl (Van Raaphorst kick), 14:25
Buf: FG Lusteg 41, 14:58
Buf: Burnett 3 pass from Lamonica (Lusteg kick), 10:47
Buf: Lamonica 1 run (Lusteg kick), 11:13

	BUF	SD
First downs	22	12
Rushing yds	213	50
Passing yds	107	169
Punts-avg	3-36.7	5-38.2
Fumbles-lost	3-0	0-0
Penalties-yds	3-25	4-53

BILLS LEADERS: Rushing - Burnett 27-138, Carlton 12-61, Lamonica 2-11, Spikes 1-3; **Passing** - Kemp 6-18-2 - 75, Lamonica 5-8-0 - 49; **Receiving** - Dubenion 3-22, Costa 2-42, Carlton 2-13, Burnett 2-13, Crockett 2-34.

CHARGERS LEADERS: Rushing - Lowe 15-33, Hadl 2-7, Lincoln 4-1, Hibson 2-9; **Passing** - Hadl 11-20-0 - 185, Lincoln 1-1-0 - 35; **Receiving** - Alworth 3-56, Lincoln 5-123, Frazier 3-36, Garrison 1-5.

NOTES

• The Bills battled back from a 17-0 deficit, only to settle for a tie when Booth Lusteg was wide right on a 23-yard field goal attempt with six seconds left. It was his third miss in four attempts.
• The Bills' defense was brilliant in the second half, allowing zero yards. It had six sacks for 51 yards.
• San Diego went up 7-0 with a 17-play, 95-yard drive that ate up nine minutes.
• Lusteg missed 42- and 34-yard attempts on Buffalo's next two possessions.
• Dick Van Raaphorst made a 31-yarder following a 35-yard Keith Lincoln option pass to Lance Alworth.
• San Diego drove 63 yards in four plays to make it 17-0, as John Hadl hit Lincoln on a 41-yard pass, then threw to Lincoln for the 21-yard TD. The Bills got on the board with two seconds left, as Jack Kemp passed 29 yards to Paul Costa to set up Lusteg's 41-yard field goal.
• Kemp drove to the San Diego 20 on Buffalo's first possession of the second half, but he was intercepted by Howard Kindig. The Bills began their comeback when Joe Collier yanked Kemp in favor of Daryle Lamonica with 6:20 left in the third.
• The Chargers had to punt from their own end zone. Ed Rutkowski returned it 33 yards to the 4 and Lamonica hit Bobby Burnett with a three-yard TD pass to make it 17-10.
• Lamonica engineered a 61-yard tying TD drive, capping it with a one-yard run. The march was helped by a pass-

WEEK 7 GAMES

Oak 34, KC 13	Hou 24, NY 0
Miami 24, Den 7	

interference penalty on Elbert Dubenion by Leslie Duncan.
• The Bills' final drive began from their own 45 with 2:35 left. Burnett carried four straight times for 19 yards. Four more runs put the ball at the 16, setting the stage for Lusteg's miss.
• After the game, it was reported that Lusteg was attacked on Delaware Ave. by three men. "They pulled over to the curb and started yelling 'You bum' and cursing me," Lusteg said. "One hit me and the other ripped my shirt. It was still broad daylight and people were around, so they jumped back in their car and drove away."

QUOTES

• Joe Collier: "Frustrating. To miss when you're so close in the closing seconds is frustrating." (On whether he would change QBs for the next game): "If we let the fans make our decisions for us, we wouldn't be very good coaches, would we? They're both good quarterbacks."
• Chargers coach Sid Gillman: "We're only human beings. We've missed easy field goals, so did Green Bay last week. Everyone does."
• Chargers running back Paul Lowe: "I think I can run against any team, but that defense really got keyed up in the second half and plugged the openings."
• Daryle Lamonica: "Well, naturally I was anxious at the start. My timing was off, too. But after the first couple of plays, I felt all right. I had confidence we could come back, we've done it so often."
• An unidentified Bill talking about Lusteg: "Everyone blows one at one time or another, but this guy will never be a real pro if he's going to sulk like that. He felt sorry for himself all week after the Boston game. He better discipline himself and pull out of it."

GAME 8 - Sunday, Oct. 30, 1966 - BILLS 33, JETS 23

Bills	0	13	17	3	- 33
Jets	3	0	0	20	- 23

Attendance at Shea Stadium - 61,552

NY: FG J. Turner 28, 4:07
Buf: Kemp 1 run (Lusteg kick), 2:10
Buf: FG Lusteg 36, 8:32
Buf: FG Lusteg 10, 14:50
Buf: Warner 95 kickoff return (Lusteg kick), :16
Buf: Kemp 1 run (Lusteg kick), 8:48
Buf: FG Lusteg 38, 12:35
NY: Lammons 34 pass from Namath (J. Turner kick), :07
NY: Baird 39 interception return (J. Turner kick), 1:02
Buf: FG Lusteg 17, 8:13
NY: Maynard 19 pass from Namath (pass failed), 11:29

	BUF	NY
First downs	17	17
Rushing yds	134	5
Passing yds	134	323
Punts-avg	3-42.0	4-44.0
Fumbles-lost	3-2	3-1
Penalties-yds	7-66	5-63

BILLS LEADERS: Rushing - Burnett 17-84, Carlton 6-20, Spikes 6-28, Kemp 2-2; **Passing** - Kemp 16-40-3 - 152; **Receiving** - Dubenion 4-75, Ferguson 2-29, Burnett 5-25, Crockett 2-13, Costa 2-7, Carlton 1-3.

JETS LEADERS: Rushing - Snell 3-4, Mathis 5-1, Boozer 1-0; **Passing** - Namath 24-53-5 - 343; **Receiving** - Sauer 7-114, Lammons 7-95, Mathis 4-34, Maynard 2-69, Snell 4-31.

WEEK 8 GAMES

Bos 35, SD 17	KC 56, Den 10
Oak 24, NY 21	Miami 20, Hou 13

Buffalo had a bye week.

WEEK 9 GAMES

Bos 24, Oak 21	KC 48, Hou 23
SD 24, Den 17	

NOTES

• Booth Lusteg gained a measure of redemption as he kicked four field goals and the Bills beat first-place New York. Lusteg's teammates awarded him the game ball.
• Larry Felser wrote of Joe Namath, who threw five interceptions: "(The Bills) exposed the Jets' glaring weakness: Utter dependency upon a gifted, but inexperienced quarterback who has a lot – an awful lot – to learn."
• The Jets took a 3-0 lead in the first quarter, but the Bills took control in the second. After Tom Day dropped an interception that would have been a TD, the Jets punted from their own end zone. Buffalo started at the NY 39 and Jack Kemp eventually scored on a one-yard run.
• A Hagood Clarke interception led to Lusteg's first field goal and he later made a 10-yarder.
• After Charley Warner's TD, The Jets drove to the Buffalo 15, but Ron McDole made an interception and the Bills turned around and marched 78 yards to another Kemp one-yard plunge and a 27-3 advantage.
• Lusteg's third field goal made it 30-3, but then the Jets started a superb comeback. Namath directed a 95-yard TD march, hitting Pete Lammons for the score. Moments later Billy Baird intercepted a Kemp pass and went 39 yards for a TD.
• Ex-University of Buffalo star Gerry Philbin then forced Kemp to fumble and Paul Rochester ran it back to the Bills 11. However, the Bills defense rose up when John Tracey intercepted Namath's fourth-down pass in the end zone. Later, Butch Byrd picked off Namath and returned 27 yards to the Jet 11 and Lusteg kicked his final field goal.

QUOTES

• Booth Lusteg: "In one way, I benefited from that missed kick against the Chargers. I studied the films over and over and spotted a minor flaw. I corrected it and I think the correction helped. It has been a long two weeks."
• Jets quarterback Joe Namath: "The five interceptions were the ball game. Their rush was good, but I wasn't pressured that much. The ball was going where I wanted it to go."
• Jets coach Weeb Ewbank: "He's (Namath) like any other second-year QB. He has to learn when not to throw the ball. You writers expected him to throw a TD pass every time."

STANDINGS: NINTH WEEK

EAST	W	L	T	WEST	W	L	T
Boston	4	2	1	Kan. City	6	2	0
Buffalo	4	3	1	San Diego	5	2	1
New York	4	3	1	Oakland	4	4	0
Houston	3	5	0	Denver	1	7	0
Miami	2	5	0				

NOTES

• The Bills moved into first place, thanks to the victory and Boston's loss to Denver. Broncos rookie QB Max Choboian hit Al Denson with a 64-yard TD pass with two seconds remaining to win, 17-10.

• Marty Schottenheimer, inserted into the game when Harry Jacobs sprained his elbow, threw ex-Bill Joe Auer for a 13-yard loss, sacked Miami QB George Wilson for nine yards, intercepted a pass and blocked a punt that resulted in a safety.

• The Bills offense was sloppy with two fumbles, three interceptions and five dropped passes.

• The Bills led 13-0 in the third when Butch Byrd intercepted a Wilson pass and returned it 17 yards to the Miami 15. Two runs by Bobby Burnett and the Bills were ahead 20-0.

• Auer had a 68-yard punt return nullified by a clipping penalty. After the Bills' defense forced a punt, Kemp drove Buffalo 75 yards to make it 27-0, hitting Paul Costa for 46 yards before throwing the four-yard TD pass to Costa.

• Miami's Jim Warren stopped a Buffalo drive at the 6 with an interception, but when the Dolphins couldn't move, Wahoo McDaniel had to punt from the end zone and Schottenheimer broke through.

• In addition to Auer, ex-Bills backs Billy Joe and Cookie Gilchrist also played for Miami.

• Running back Jack Spikes had a solid day blocking on the blitz pickup for Buffalo.

QUOTES

• Billy Shaw: "He (Schottenheimer) said he was going to lead the Bills to a championship when he signed with us and it looks like he's producing." (Shaw's remark was in reference to a magazine story about the former Pitt all-America being brash and boastful when he signed with the Bills in 1965).

• Joe Collier: "Considering that Schottenheimer has hardly played, I'd say he did a whale of a job. The big thing about Marty is his intelligence. He prepares for every game as though he were starting. He's thinking all the time and it paid off. His play-calling was good. As for being in first place, that's nice, but we have a long way to go."

• Miami coach George Wilson: "The Bills have a fine defensive unit. The pass rush was the toughest we've seen all season. And their success with third-down passes to their tight ends was the key to their offense today."

• Marty Schottenheimer: "Coming in for Harry was tougher on me from a physical standpoint than mentally. I hadn't had any real contact in about 10 weeks. But I've tried to keep up on everything defensively just in case. Harry and I have become buddies and he's helped me all he could and so has Richie McCabe. I decided to stick to man-to-man coverages, which is our bread-and-butter defense. The guys were all great when I came into the game. Jim Dunaway said just to call my own game and they'd execute as best they could. Mike Stratton said all our defenses are designed to work, so we'd stop them with whatever I called. All in all, the day was just unreal. It's a privilege even to play on this club."

Bills	0 10 10 9 - 29
Dolphins	0 0 0 0 - 0

Attendance at The Orange Bowl - 37,177

Buf:	Burnett 16 pass from Kemp (Lusteg kick), 1:20
Buf:	FG Lusteg 44, 14:50
Buf:	FG Lusteg 44, 1:54
Buf:	Burnett 3 run (Lusteg kick), 4:00
Buf:	Costa 4 pass from Kemp (Lusteg kick), :21
Buf:	Safety, Schottenheimer blocked punt out of end zone, 6:24

	BUF	MIA
First downs	18	11
Rushing yds	114	48
Passing yds	271	123
Punts-avg	1-46.0	7-31.7
Fumbles-lost	2-2	3-1
Penalties-yds	6-80	5-46

BILLS LEADERS: Rushing - Burnett 13-52, A. Smith 5-33, Spikes 8-23, Kemp 1-6; **Passing** - Kemp 13-33-1 - 207, Lamonica 3-13-2 - 64; **Receiving** - Dubenion 2-33, Ferguson 2-45, Costa 4-84, Burnett 4-60, Bass 2-22, Rutkowski 1-19, Crockett 1-8.

DOLPHINS LEADERS: Rushing - Gilchrist 6-10, Joe 4-6, Jackson 1-24, Price 2-9, Auer 6- (-3), Wilson 1-2; **Passing** - Wilson 3-13-3 - 28, Wood 12-26-0 - 132; **Receiving** - Noonan 4-30, Jackson 3-31, Twilley 2-27, Kocourek 3-41, Roberson 1-10, Cronin 1-9, Joe 1-12.

WEEK 10 GAMES

Den 17, Bos 10	KC 24, SD 14
Oak 38, Hou 23	

NOTES

• The experienced Bills defeated the youthful Jets again thanks to a 14-point fourth-quarter rally and a superb defensive effort in front of another record crowd of 45,738.

• Leading 7-3 in the fourth, the Bills got the clinching score when 285-pound defensive tackle Jim Dunaway blocked Jim Turner's 38-yard field goal attempt, picked up the loose ball and rumbled 72 yards for a touchdown.

• George Sauer caught 12 passes for 248 yards in two games against the Bills, but in the two games between the teams, the Jets managed just 60 yards rushing, including 55 in this game.

• After Joe Namath beat a safety blitz late in the first half with a 54-yard strike to Pete Lammons to the Bills 8, the defense stymied three running plays. Then Jets holder Jim Hudson faked the field goal attempt and threw incomplete into the end zone, leaving it 0-0 at the half.

• Turner's 43-yard field goal late in the third gave the Jets the lead, but seemed to wake up the slumbering Buffalo offense.

• On the first play after the kickoff, Jack Kemp play-faked to Wray Carlton, then threw to Carlton for a 32-yard gain. Carlton caught a 14-yard pass, then Kemp zipped a 14-yard bullet over the middle to Elbert Dubenion for the go-ahead score.

• The Jets drove downfield after that, but on fourth and a foot, Weeb Ewbank elected to kick the field goal. Dunaway then made the biggest play of the cold day.

QUOTES

• Jets coach Weeb Ewbank: "There were 10 minutes,

30 seconds to play. We decided to go for the field goal because there was still plenty of time to score a touchdown later. That was the turning point." (On the fake field goal): "We've missed those angled field goals and this was a difficult angle. On such a field goal, the Bills always overload the defense to the right, leaving the left weak. The pass was intended for Matt Snell, but Stratton came up and creamed him and then the pass was low to our secondary receiver (Pete Lammons). If it had worked, you guys would be telling me how smart we were."

• Elbert Dubenion on his TD reception: "Jack called it in the huddle. He said 'Get out wide, I'm going to throw it right between the goal posts.' I couldn't have dropped it if I wanted to. It was a perfect pass."

• Jim Dunaway: "This was my greatest thrill. I can't tell you how I did it. I broke through between the center and their left guard. I put my hands up high, I didn't leap. On every stride I took, I thought somebody was going to get me from behind, one of their speed backs. For a long while—for these four seasons I've been with the Bills—I wanted to get a game ball and now I have it. I checked in today at 285 pounds. Those 30 or 40 wind sprints we do every day got me down there and that's my best weight. But I'm not slow. I ran the 100 in 10.6 in high school (while he weighed 271)."

• Jets quarterback Joe Namath: "Any one guy bother me? Yeah, that Tommy Janik is outstanding. Finger nails is the word. We miss two touchdowns by his finger nails. I believe he's the tallest defensive back in the league and only he probably could have made those plays (Janik made two diving deflections of passes intended for Don Maynard)."

Jets	0 0 3 0 - 3
Bills	0 0 0 14 - 14

Attendance at War Memorial Stadium - 45,738

NY:	FG J. Turner 43, 12:55
Buf:	Dubenion 14 pass from Kemp (Lusteg kick), :30
Buf:	Dunaway 72 blocked field goal return (Lusteg kick), 4:44

	BUF	NY
First downs	10	15
Rushing yds	92	55
Passing yds	132	274
Punts-avg	9-39.3	6-38.7
Fumbles-lost	0-0	0-0
Penalties-yds	4-60	4-20

BILLS LEADERS: Rushing - Burnett 15-40, Carlton 13-44, Kemp 4-8; **Passing** - Kemp 10-23-0 - 132; **Receiving** - Dubenion 2-42, Costa 4-35, Carlton 3-50, Burnett 1-5.

JETS LEADERS: Rushing - Snell 12-19, Mathis 6-11, Boozer 9-25; **Passing** - Namath 19-36-1 - 286, Hudson 0-1-0 - 0; **Receiving** - Sauer 5-134, Maynard 2-39, Boozer 4-68, Snell 5-16, Lammons 2-11, Mathis 1-18.

WEEK 11 GAMES

Bos 27, Hou 21	KC 34, Miami 16
Oak 41, SD 19	

STANDINGS: ELEVENTH WEEK

EAST	W	L	T	WEST	W	L	T
Buffalo	6	3	1	Kan. City	8	2	0
Boston	5	3	1	Oakland	6	4	0
New York	4	4	1	San Diego	5	4	1
Houston	3	7	0	Denver	2	7	0
Miami	2	7	0				

Bills	0	14	14	14	-	42
Oilers	3	10	0	7	-	20

Attendance at Rice Stadium - 27,312

Hou: FG Blanda 49, 3:42
Hou: Trull 1 run (Blanda kick), 6:41
Buf: Costa 10 pass from Lamonica (Lusteg kick), 11:02
Buf: Crockett 53 pass from Kemp (Lusteg kick), 13:19
Hou: FG Blanda 35, 14:49
Buf: Kemp 26 run (Lusteg kick), 4:45
Buf: Janik 37 interception return (Lusteg kick), 8:43
Buf: Costa 3 pass from Kemp (Lusteg kick), 4:28
Hou: Frazier 40 pass from Blanda (Blanda kick), 6:07
Buf: Ferguson 12 pass from Lamonica (Lusteg kick), 8:12

	BUF	HOU
First downs	23	11
Rushing yds	156	87
Passing yds	352	228
Punts-avg	5-42.2	7-50.9
Fumbles-lost	1-0	0-0
Penalties-yds	4-30	6-60

BILLS LEADERS: Rushing - Burnett 14-49, Carlton 10-46, A. Smith 8-25, Kemp 2-26, Spikes 3-5, Dubenion 1-5; **Passing** - Kemp 14-31-0 - 248, Lamonica 4-7-0 - 104; **Receiving** - Dubenion 4-57, Costa 2-13, Carlton 2-77, Bass 3-29, Spikes 1-27, Rutkowski 2-60, Crockett 2-74, Ferguson 1-12, Burnett 1-3.

OILERS LEADERS: Rushing - Trull 5-43, Granger 4-24, Burrell 4-13, Tolar 3-7; **Passing** - Trull 6-25-2 - 123, Blanda 4-10-1 - 119; **Receiving** - Frazier 4-119, Poole 3-40, Elkins 2-69, Granger 1-14.

NOTES
• The Bills were shocked into a 10-0 hole, but regrouped and crushed the Oilers with 508 total yards.
• George Blanda, who was replaced by Don Trull at QB but later appeared in relief, kicked a 47-yard field goal in the first. After two Booth Lusteg field goals missed, the Oilers put together a 78-yard TD drive, the big play a 62-yard Trull pass to Larry Elkins.
• The Bills got within 10-7 when Daryle Lamonica passed 10 yards to Paul Costa on a fake field goal, then went ahead 14-10 as Jack Kemp fired a 53-yard TD pass to Bobby Crockett.
• Blanda made a 35-yard field goal with 11 seconds left in the half, but that was as close as the Oilers could get. Two plays into the second half, Tom Janik intercepted a Trull pass and the Bills set off on a 76-yard march that ended when Kemp scrambled for a 26-yard TD.
• Janik's second pick came four minutes later and he went 37 yards for a TD to make it 28-13.
• The Bills increased the lead to 35-13 when Kemp and Carlton connected for 54 yards and Kemp tossed three yards to Costa for the TD.
• Blanda drove the Oilers to a TD, but that was offset by Lamonica's second TD pass late in the game.

WEEK 12 GAMES
Bos 27, KC 27	NY 30, Miami 13
Oak 17, Den 3	

QUOTES
• Jack Kemp: "The story of our season is that we've improved every week. We fell behind 10-0, but we all felt we'd come back to win. Everyone knows the trouble (on offense) we had earlier, but I feel completely well now and our passing game is getting better. It has to if we're going to win the title again. The Oilers blitzed more than we expected and they disguised them well and it took us a quarter or so to read them properly. Both of my touchdown passes were against blitzes. About that dive I took into the end zone at the end of the 26-yard run, you can hurt a shoulder diving like that, but as I dove, I turned so I hit on my back. All the falls I've taken skiing have helped me learn how to avoid getting hurt."
• Daryle Lamonica on the fake field goal: "I took a peek to the right when we broke out of the huddle. They were wide open. I had a hard time keeping myself from looking over there. John Tracey was open, too, and I could have run it in myself. After I called the fake, all I could think of was (Jets coach Weeb Ewbank). If it had failed, I never would have heard the end of it."
• Joe Collier on Janik's TD return: "We had a blitz on, so Tommy probably figured if he didn't get to the ball in time, the blitzers might get to the quarterback. I gambled and Tommy gambled and we both won. That was the big play of the game. I don't know if Tommy gambles now and then because I know the opposing quarterbacks think about it. They have to say to themselves, 'Can I risk throwing his way?'"

Bills	0	17	7	7	-	31
Raiders	7	3	0	0	-	10

Attendance at Oakland-Alameda County Coliseum - 36,781

Oak: Cannon 16 pass from Flores (Eischeid kick), 9:52
Buf: Burnett 26 pass from Kemp (Lusteg kick), :06
Oak: FG Eischeid 8, 6:00
Buf: FG Lusteg 19, 12:12
Buf: Carlton 11 run (Lusteg kick), 14:29
Buf: Carlton 2 run (Lusteg kick), 10:17
Buf: Spikes 1 run (Lusteg kick), 3:25

	BUF	OAK
First downs	25	11
Rushing yds	226	58
Passing yds	239	257
Punts-avg	5-37.8	7-42.6
Fumbles-lost	2-2	2-0
Penalties-yds	3-45	1-3

BILLS LEADERS: Rushing - Burnett 16-59, Carlton 19-97, A. Smith 3-20, Kemp 6-45, Spikes 2-5; **Passing** - Kemp 14-29-0 - 241, Lamonica 0-3-0 - 0; **Receiving** - Dubenion 4-56, Carlton 2-10, Burnett 3-82, Crockett 4-84, Costa 1-9.

RAIDERS LEADERS: Rushing - Daniels 13-36, Hagberg 4-14, Dixon 1-8; **Passing** - Flores 17-30-2 - 286; **Receiving** - Powell 4-116, Hagberg 3-49, Mitchell 3-25, Daniels 2-45, Cannon 2-25, Todd 2-21, Dixon 1-5.

WEEK 13 GAMES
Bos 20, Miami 14	KC 32, NY 24
Den 20, SD 17	

NOTES
• Playing on Thanksgiving Day for the fifth time in six years, the Bills came up with a huge effort in trouncing the Raiders behind a 465-yard offensive outburst for their fifth straight victory.
• Oakland drove 80 yards to take an early 7-0 lead, the key play a 41-yard Tom Flores pass to Art Powell. But the Bills tied it on the first play of the second quarter as Jack Kemp hit Bobby Burnett to cap an 80-yard drive.
• The Raiders, helped by a 35-yard Flores-to-Powell pass, drove to the Bills' 1, but couldn't punch it in and had to settle for Mike Eischeid's eight-yard field goal. Booth Lusteg matched that six minutes later after a Hagood Clarke interception.
• The Bills then took the lead for good. Butch Byrd returned a punt 27 yards to the Oakland 40. Wray Carlton eventually scored on an 11-yard run with 29 seconds left in the half.
• In the third, Mike Stratton forced Clem Daniels to fumble and Harry Jacobs recovered at midfield. Eight plays later, following a 22-yard Kemp scramble, Carlton scored.
• In the fourth, a 59-yard drive highlighted by Kemp's 52-yard pass to Bobby Crockett culminated in Jack Spikes' one-yard run.
• The 226 yards rushing was a season-high.
• The night before the game, trainer Eddie Abramoski said: "Don't worry about a thing, this isn't going to be as close as everyone thinks."

QUOTES
• Joe Collier: "What a job Johnny (Mazur) and Jerry (Smith) did in the short time we had to prepare for this game. Not just in getting our offensive game plan ready, but in getting it across to the players. The execution matched anything we've done this year. It was the result of a lot of extra hours' work for the coaches and the players, but the effort was worthwhile. Bobby Burnett had a real fine game and Wray was real sharp. Jack has been tremendous the last two games. He's getting the job done the way we knew he could once he got his timing down. And our defense in general was its usual tough self."
• Harry Jacobs: "I'll bet there weren't too many people who thought after those two opening losses we'd be where we are today."
• Billy Shaw: "(Offensive line coach) Jerry Smith had the Raiders defense plotted perfectly. Tom Keating (the ex-Bill) did just about everything on each given play that Jerry said he would do."
• Tom Sestak: "I can hardly wait for that game (the upcoming battle with Boston)."

STANDINGS: THIRTEENTH WEEK

EAST	W	L	T	WEST	W	L	T
Buffalo	8	3	1	Kan. City	9	2	1
Boston	6	3	2	Oakland	7	5	0
New York	5	5	1	San Diego	5	5	1
Houston	3	8	0	Denver	3	8	0
Miami	2	9	0				

NOTES

• The Patriots prevented Buffalo from locking up its third straight East Division title and moved into the driver's seat of the race.

• With two games left (the Bills had one plus a bye week), the Patriots put themselves in position to win the East with victories over Houston and New York.

• Boston's three-man defensive line was the key, limiting the Bills to 40 rushing yards and forcing four turnovers.

• During a stretch from early in the second quarter to midway through the fourth, the Bills never advanced past their own 44.

• On their first possession, the Bills drove to the Boston 13, but a third-down Jack Kemp pass in the end zone was picked off by Tom Hennessey. On their next series, the Bills got to the Boston 5 after Kemp's 48-yard pass to Bobby Burnett. However, the Bills settled for an 11-yard Booth Lusteg field goal.

• Jim Nance then put the Pats ahead for good three plays later when he broke a 65-yard TD run.

• In the second quarter, Glenn Bass caught a 56-yard TD pass, but he was penalized for offensive interference and the play was nullified.

• The Patriots made it 14-3 with a 60-yard drive that culminated on Babe Parilli's three-yard run 4:41 into the third quarter. Parilli's 37-yard pass to Art Graham was the key play.

• Kemp was knocked out of the game late in the third, as was Bobby Burnett.

• In the fourth, Daryle Lamonica lost a fumble at the Boston 36. Ron McDole blocked a Gino Cappelletti field

goal, John Tracey picked it up and appeared headed for a TD, but stumbled and fell. The game then ended with Allen Smith being stopped at the Boston 1.

QUOTES

• Pats quarterback Babe Parilli: "We (the offense) weren't sharp at all, but those guys on the defensive line, they did it."

• Pats defensive end Larry Esenhauer: "We beat Buffalo with the same defense they used to beat us twice last year."

• Pats linebacker Nick Buoniconti: "We're in the driver's seat now and does it ever feel good for a change. We've had to stand by in the shadows for weeks while Buffalo kept winning, but it's all up to us now. How did we do it? It's very simple, we contained Kemp."

• Jim Dunaway: "We should have beaten them both times, but should and did are different things."

• Ron McDole, who had 15 tackles: "The one big play was Nance's 65-yard TD run. That really hurt us because we stopped him on 23 other carries. We were in a 51 defense on that play which means the front men were shooting low for a short-yardage play. Getting to Parilli was a problem because he threw pretty quick and he was hitting spot passes."

• Joe Collier: "If Houston and New York play like we did, then Boston won't have any problems. If Houston or New York plays top football, they can beat Boston."

• Chiefs coach Hank Stram: "I still think we'll end up playing the Bills, but I have to admit that I never saw Buffalo's offensive line handled like Boston handled it."

| Bills | 3 | 0 | 0 | 0 - | 3 |
| Patriots | 7 | 0 | 7 | 0 - | 14 |

Attendance at Fenway Park - 39,350

Buf: FG Lusteg 11, 12:08
Bos: Nance 65 run (Cappelletti kick), 14:08
Bos: Parilli 3 run (Cappelletti kick), 4:41

	BUF	BOS
First downs	17	11
Rushing yds	40	107
Passing yds	274	119
Punts-avg	7-35.7	8-33.1
Fumbles-lost	3-2	0-0
Penalties-yds	8-70	3-38

BILLS LEADERS: Rushing - Burnett 6-29, Carlton 7-36, Kemp 7-(-15), Smith 2-2, Lamonica 4-(-12); **Passing** - Kemp 13-25-2 - 183, Lamonica 6-15-0 - 91; **Receiving** - Dubenion 3-30, Ferguson 2-33, Burnett 3-78, Crockett 4-47, Bass 2-35, Carlton 2-18, Costa 1-17, Rutkowski 1-15, Smith 1-1.

PATRIOTS LEADERS: Rushing - Nance 24-109, Garron 4-5, Parilli 5-(-7); **Passing** - Parilli 9-22-0 - 119; **Receiving** - Graham 5-79, Bellino 1-20, Whalen 1-12, Garron 2-8.

WEEK 14 GAMES
SD 28, Hou 22	Oak 28, NY 28
Den 17, Miami 7	

NOTES

• The day before the game, Boston lost to New York, meaning the Bills could win the division with a victory. And they did it, jumping on the overmatched Broncos quickly, then holding on.

• Before the game, it was announced that ex-Bills coach Lou Saban would replace Ray Malavasi as Denver's coach.

• The Broncos opened the game with an on-side kick and tried four more. The first kick didn't travel 10 yards so the re-kick was sent deep and Charley Warner returned it to the Bills 49. Seven plays later, it was 7-0 as Wray Carlton scored after Jack Kemp's 26-yard run put the Bills into position.

• After a 16-yard Bob Scarpitto punt gave the Bills possession at the Denver 28, a pair of Kemp to Elbert Dubenion passes set up Jack Spikes' TD and a 14-0 lead.

• Tom Janik's first interception set up a Booth Lusteg field goal. After Denver scored midway through the second, the Bills put the game away with 22 seconds left in the first half as Paul Maguire recovered an on-side kick at the 49. Kemp eventually hit Bobby Crockett for a 38-

yard TD.

• On the first play of the second half, Janik picked off a John McCormick pass and scored. Early in the fourth, George Saimes blitzed and forced McCormick to fumble. Mike Stratton raced 22 yards for the TD that made it 38-7. Two Denver TDs only made the score a little closer.

QUOTES

• Joe Collier: "I told the players before the game that Denver was likely to blitz half the time so don't get discouraged if you play sloppy. I think that when you play a team that blitzes a lot, no one looks good. You won't get anything sustained, but you'll break a big play once in a while. I've only been nervous before three games, both Miami games and this one. I didn't feel sure about this one until Janik's touchdown." (Addressing the team): "Men, we've got two games left and we'll go all the way, but we have to be a lot sharper against Kansas City."

• Tom Janik: "I gambled on the (second) interception and won. He threw the same type of pass on first down in an earlier situation. John Tracey tipped the pass right into my arms. Then McDole was right there and he yelled 'Run, Tom, run.' For a bewildered moment, I thought they were Denver players and I was wondering how I would get by them. Then I started running for the easiest, sweetest TD of my life. My game is gambling. Sometimes you win, sometimes you lose."

| Broncos | 0 | 7 | 0 | 14 - | 21 |
| Bills | 14 | 10 | 7 | 7 - | 38 |

Attendance at War Memorial Stadium - 40,583

Buf: Carlton 6 run (Lusteg kick), 7:30
Buf: Spikes 1 run (Lusteg kick), 12:39
Buf: FG Lusteg 16, 6:22
Den: Scarpitto 62 pass from McCormick (Kroner kick), 13:35
Buf: Crockett 38 pass from Kemp (Lusteg kick), 14:38
Buf: Janik 25 interception return (Lusteg kick), :12
Buf: Stratton 22 fumble return (Lusteg kick), 3:59
Den: Scarpitto 28 pass from McCormick (pass failed), 8:43
Den: Scarpitto 11 pass from McCormick (Scarpitto pass from McCormick), 10:51

	BUF	DEN
First downs	19	16
Rushing yds	207	44
Passing yds	129	320
Punts-avg	2-37.0	5-35.8
Fumbles-lost	1-1	4-2
Penalties yds	7-55	8-79

BILLS LEADERS: Rushing - Burnett 13-76, Carlton 8-55, A. Smith 8-43, Kemp 2-29, Spikes 4-4; **Passing** - Kemp 9-23-1 - 147, Lamonica 1-7-2 - 19; **Receiving** - Dubenion 4-55, Burnett 2-22, Crockett 3-70, Ferguson 1-19.

BRONCOS LEADERS: Rushing - Haynes 10-24, Hayes 6-21, Glackson 2-(-1); **Passing** - McCormick 13-37-3 - 328, Glacken 1-3-0 - 15; **Receiving** - Scarpitto 5-123, Taylor 4-61, Haynes 2-86, Denson 2-44, Hayes 1-29.

WEEK 15 GAMES
Bos 38, Hou 14	KC 19, Miami 18
SD 42, NY 27	Oak 28, Den 10
Buffalo had a bye week.	

WEEK 16 GAMES
NY 38, Bos 28	KC 27, SD 17
Hou 38, Miami 29	

STANDINGS: SIXTEENTH WEEK

EAST	W	L	T		WEST	W	L	T
Buffalo	9	4	1		Kan. City	11	2	1
Boston	8	4	2		Oakland	8	5	1
New York	6	6	2		San Diego	7	6	1
Houston	4	10	0		Denver	4	10	0
Miami	2	12	0					

Chiefs	7	10	0	14	-	31
Bills	7	0	0	0	-	7

Attendance at War Memorial Stadium - 42,080

KC: Arbanas 29 pass from Dawson (Mercer kick), 1:43
Buf: Dubenion 69 pass from Kemp (Lusteg kick), 6:22
KC: Taylor 29 pass from Dawson (Mercer kick), 4:31
KC: FG Mercer 32, 14:57
KC: Garrett 1 run (Mercer kick), 6:16
KC: Garrett 18 run (Mercer kick), 7:47

	BUF	KC
First downs	9	14
Rushing yds	40	113
Passing yds	215	164
Punts-avg	8-39.3	6-42.3
Fumbles-lost	3-2	1-0
Penalties-yds	3-23	4-40

BILLS LEADERS: Rushing - Burnett 3-6, Carlton 9-31, Kemp 1-3; **Passing** - Kemp 12-27-2 - 253; **Receiving** - Dubenion 2-79, Burnett 6-127, Carlton 1-5, Bass 2-26, Crockett 1-16; **Kickoff returns** - Warner 5-91, Meredith 1-8; **Punt returns** - Rutkowski 2-16, Byrd 3-0.

CHIEFS LEADERS: Rushing - McClinton 11-38, Garrett 13-39, Dawson 5-28, Coan 2-6, E. Thomas 2-2; **Passing** - Dawson 16-24-0 - 227; **Receiving** - Taylor 5-78, Arbanas 2-44, Garrett 4-16, Burford 4-76, McClinton 1-13; **Kickoff returns** - Coan 1-35, Garrett 1-3; **Punt returns** - Garrett 3-37.

John Tracey chases down Kansas City running back Curtis McClinton during the Chiefs' 31-7 victory at War Memorial Stadium in the AFL Championship Game. The loss prevented the Bills from playing in the first Super Bowl against Green Bay.

NOTES

• Kansas City earned the right to play in Super Bowl I, ending the Bills' two-year reign in the AFL with a methodical romp.

• The Bills defense put good pressure on Len Dawson, sacking him for losses totaling 63 yards, but he continually made the big plays when he needed them.

• Dudley Meredith fumbled the opening kickoff and Jerrol Wilson recovered for KC at the Bills 31. Three plays later, Dawson faked a draw play and hit a wide-open Fred Arbanas with a 29-yard TD pass 1:43 into the game.

• The Bills struck back quickly as five plays later, Jack Kemp beat a blitz and hit Elbert Dubenion for a 69-yard TD. Fred Williamson had slipped, leaving Dubenion wide open.

• Early in the second, Mike Garrett returned a punt 42 yards. Although a clipping penalty set the Chiefs back to the Bills 45, they scored six plays later. Dawson scrambled for 11, then was sacked for a 10-yard loss by John Tracey. A 15-yard pass to Arbanas left the Chiefs with third-and-five. Here, Dawson fired a strike to Otis Taylor who beat Butch Byrd for the TD 4:31 into the second.

• Late in the half, the Bills drove to what appeared would be the tying touchdown. Kemp hit Bobby Burnett for gains of 18 and 33 yards. Then, from the 11-yard-line, Kemp tried to hit Bobby Crockett – who had beaten Willie Mitchell – at the goal line, but safety Johnny Robinson cut in front and intercepted and returned it 72 yards. Mike Mercer then kicked a 32-yard field goal with three seconds left in the half and the Bills were doomed.

• The third quarter was ruled by the Chiefs, who used short passes to offset the Buffalo rush. Although they didn't score – Mercer missed a 49-yard field goal – they successfully chewed up time.

• In the fourth, Dawson directed a 63-yard TD drive keyed by his 45-yard pass to Chris Burford, who beat Byrd. The play carried to the 4-yard-line, and it took four straight Garrett runs to get the TD. On the scoring run, from the 1-foot line, Ron McDole had him stopped, but his second effort enabled him to get into the end zone for an insurmountable 24-7 lead with 8:44 left.

• On the ensuing series, Kemp was sacked and knocked out. He lost the ball and Bobby Hunt returned it to the Bills 21. Three plays later, Garrett ran left, was cut off by Tracey, reversed his field and retreated all the way back to the 35 before turning the corner and outrunning the Bills defense to the end zone for the final score.

• The Chiefs pocketed $5,308.39 each for winning while the Bills took home $3,799.98 per man.

QUOTES

• Chiefs safety Johnny Robinson on his interception: "I was keying on Jack Spikes, but when I saw him block E.J. Holub, I eased off and watched Kemp. He looked to the strong side, then when he pumped to the weak side, I saw Crockett cutting toward the middle and I gambled. I read Kemp's eyes and I got lucky. I stretched to the limit and just got the ball. It was my 11th of the year, but believe me, it was my biggest. If we had been in any other defense, we would have been in trouble. Mitchell told me he slipped on the play and Crockett would have caught the pass for the touchdown."

• Jack Kemp on Robinson's interception: "He made a great individual play. I thought we had him occupied but he came in on a free lance to get between Bobby and the ball. I put everything I had on that pass. It was as hard as I can throw."

• Chiefs quarterback Len Dawson: "I felt like an old man. I've never felt such tremendous pressure. I'm bruised all over and I'm ready to lie down and rest for about three days. Buffalo is a great team at reading the regular formations. They seem to know where each play is headed and this can kill you. We showed them variety and we fooled them."

• Chiefs coach Hank Stram on why the Chiefs used such a diversified offense: "We changed the makeup, but the face was the same. We used 10 or 12 different formations with one purpose and that was to shrink the reaction time for the Buffalo defense, to reduce their recognition of what we were trying to do. I think we achieved what we planned to do two weeks ago when we made our game plan for the Bills." (On his defense): "Our defensive team was fantastic. It was their best game of the year. Johnny Robinson gave us the big play with his interception of Kemp under the goal posts, but we didn't need anything more than Dawson's direction and leadership. There isn't a finer quarterback or more accurate passer in the game, and that includes Johnny Unitas. We got control early with that touchdown, that's what started us, and we never stopped."

• Joe Collier, speaking to Stram: "If you play in the Super Bowl the way you played today, you'll give them (the Green Bay Packers) all they can handle. Your execution was nearly perfect." (On his team's performance): "We fumbled on the opening kickoff and got progressively worse. They simply played much better than we did. We had no interceptions, no fumble recoveries, they executed everything well. The Chiefs played opportunistic football and when they don't make mistakes, they're tough to contain. We lost to a good team. I think we have a good, young team which should be in the thick of it again next season, but I hate to end one like this."

• Tom Janik: "The Packers have never defended against a receiver with the moves of Otis Taylor. Next season, Taylor will be recognized as a better receiver than Lance Alworth. It takes time for such recognition. I've never played against a receiver with such a long, deceptive stride. He's past you before you know it."

• Hagood Clarke: "The Chiefs have the best 1-2 receiving combination in pro football in Taylor and Chris Burford. The Packers won't stop them."

• Tom Sestak: "They capitalized on every break and we didn't. At their best, like they were today, they can beat anybody."

• Elbert Dubenion on his touchdown: "We could have used a few more plays like that. We tried it once, only once."

A_t A G_{lance}
1967

Jan. 3 – Joe Collier said the Bills would be "very interested" in trading for San Diego's Keith Lincoln, but doubted the team would go after Oakland receiver Art Powell.

Jan. 4 – Ten Bills were named to the AFL all-star squad.

Jan. 7 – Jack Kemp, president of the AFL Players' Association, met with NFLPA president Mike Pyle of the Chicago Bears. The two announced that they wanted to see an all-star game between the two leagues starting in 1968 with the proceeds going to charity and player pensions. With the new common draft in place, the Bills were awarded the 22nd choice out of 25.

Jan. 19 – Mike Mercer, the most accurate kicker in 1966 while with the Chiefs, was acquired for a fifth-round choice in the 1968 draft. Mercer had joined the Bills developmental squad after being waived by Oakland early in the '66 season. However, satisfied with Booth Lusteg, Joe Collier released him and the Chiefs picked him up on the condition that Collier could take him back at the end of the season. Surprisingly, the Chiefs and the league went along with the demand.

Feb. 13 – AFL president Milt Woodard was given a new three-year contract.

Feb. 14 – Rumors at the annual AFL meetings had the Bills using quarterback Jack Kemp as trade bait, but the Bills denied it. New Detroit Lions head coach Joe Schmidt lured New York Jets offensive line coach Chuck Knox to the motor city to be his line coach.

Feb. 15 – With the inception of a ninth team, Miami, the AFL announced a 16-week regular-season schedule where one team would be off every week; The AFL also announced it was boosting the players' pension plan almost fourfold, therefore bringing it up to par with the NFL and paving the way for interleague player trading.

Feb. 19 – The Bills' first game against an NFL team became official when it was announced the Bills would play the Lions in Detroit in the preseason on Aug. 14.

Feb. 20 – Jack Kemp accepted a "permanent off-season job" on California governor Ronald Reagan's staff. "This won't conflict with football," Kemp said. "I've always enjoyed politics."

March 13 – The Bills traded defensive end Tom Day and their second-round choice in the upcoming draft to San Diego for running back Keith Lincoln.

March 14 – The Bills traded quarterback Daryle Lamonica and wide receiver Glenn Bass to Oakland for quarterback Tom Flores and receiver Art Powell. Said Lamonica: "I can hardly wait to come into Buffalo against the Bills. I've got a lot to prove." Said Al Davis: "I don't know that I would have made the deal (coach Johnny Rauch did). Rauch and Powell had a communication problem and Rauch wanted to get his own quarterback in here, and Lamonica may be something special."

March 15 – The Bills' first draft choice in the inaugural common draft was split end John Pitts of Arizona State. The Baltimore Colts acquired expansion New Orleans' top pick and used it to select Michigan State defensive tackle Bubba Smith.

March 20 – The Oilers announced they were releasing veteran quarterback/kicker George Blanda.

March 29 – It was announced that the Philadelphia Eagles would be the first NFL team to play the Bills at War Memorial Stadium as an Aug. 25 exhibition game was scheduled.

May 12 – First-round draft choice John Pitts signed his contract.

May 22 – The future of the Bills was thrust into doubt because the city and the team were unable to come to terms on a new lease for War Memorial Stadium. Mayor Frank Sedita presented two proposals to Ralph Wilson. One had the city getting 10 percent of gross revenues from all games and in turn would assume stadium maintenance costs. The other called for six percent of gross revenues, with the Bills taking care of maintenance costs. Wilson's original proposal called for the Bills to pay four percent of their revenues to the city with the city paying for maintenance.

May 24 – The AFL awarded its 10th franchise to Cincinnati with plans for it to start play in 1968.

May 25 – The citizens committee to keep big league football in Buffalo ran an ad in the *Buffalo Evening News* that read: "To the mayor and every red-blooded football fan in Western New York – If we don't act now, we may lose the Buffalo Bills." The ad urged fans to let Mayor Frank Sedita know they wanted him to reach an accord with Wilson on the new stadium lease.

May 26 – Jack Kemp, representing the AFL players association at the AFL meetings in New York, said the Bills would be the league's next Super Bowl representative. "I think we have the team to go to the Super Bowl. I think we can go all the way."

June 7 – The Chamber of Commerce recommended that a two-stadium complex - one for football seating 65,000 and another seating 15,000 for baseball - be built on Millersport Highway in Amherst at a cost of $20 million.

June 9 – Mayor Frank Sedita and Ralph Wilson agreed on a new three-year lease for War Memorial Stadium with the Bills paying the city four percent of its gate revenues and the city taking over stadi-

um maintenance. The agreement was made "in contemplation of a new stadium" according to both parties.

July 17 – Training camp opened at the Sheraton-Camelot Motor Inn in Blasdell.

July 20 – Unsigned veterans Keith Lincoln, Art Powell, Marty Schottenheimer, Tom Flores, Bobby Burnett, Elbert Dubenion and Booker Edgerson all skipped practice because they were dissatisfied with their contracts.

July 21 – All-Pro guard and offensive team captain Billy Shaw tore a knee ligament and underwent surgery. It was announced he would be out at least three months.

Aug. 5 – Former University of Buffalo QB John Stofa threw a 16-yard TD pass to lead Miami past the Bills, 10-7, in the preseason opener at Memphis, Tenn. In Denver, Lou Saban's return to the pros was a success as the Broncos beat the NFL's Detroit Lions, 13-7, in the first preseason game played between the two leagues.

Aug. 14 – The Bills lost their first encounter with the NFL as Detroit won, 19-17, before 43,503 at Tiger Stadium – the largest preseason crowd in front of which the Bills ever had played.

Aug. 20 – Boston handed the Bills a 13-10 defeat before 15,300 at Rochester's Aquinas Stadium. In San Diego, the Chargers lost to the NFL's Lions, 38-17, before 45,988 in brand new $28 million San Diego Stadium.

Aug. 25 – The Philadelphia Eagles became the first NFL team to play the Bills at War Memorial and came away with a wild 38-30 victory before 41,488. Fans greeted Jack Kemp with boos when he entered the game and Kemp's teammates were angered by the display. Commissioner Pete Rozelle was on hand for the game.

Aug. 31 – The Bills avoided their first winless preseason by beating the Jets, 31-23, at the Senior Bowl in Mobile, Ala. in the preseason finale.

Sept. 10 – The Bills performed the best comeback in team history, rallying for 20 fourth-quarter points to upset the Jets, 20-17, in front of a War Memorial Stadium record crowd of 45,748. For the first time in his career, Jack Kemp was not the starting quarterback: "Two weeks ago, I was feeling

sorry for myself, but then I reasoned it out. Tom (Flores) had a better training camp than I did and he knew our new receivers (Art Powell and Keith Lincoln) better."

Sept. 17 – Buffalo held Houston to 26 net passing yards yet still lost, 20-3.

Sept. 24 – After 142 games counting playoffs, Buffalo suffered its first shutout loss, 23-0 to Boston. The 10 millionth fan to attend an AFL game passed through the turnstiles at War Memorial Stadium.

Sept. 27 – The Cincinnati expansion franchise was awarded to Cleveland Browns founder Paul Brown and the nickname Bengals was chosen.

Oct. 1 – San Diego rolled up 484 total yards, the most Buffalo had allowed since Oakland gained 499 in a 1963 game, in a 37-17 romp over the Bills.

Oct. 8 – The Bills snapped a three-game losing streak with a come-from-behind 17-16 victory at Denver in their first game against former coach Lou Saban.

Oct. 15 – Daryle Lamonica returned to War Memorial Stadium and despite throwing four interceptions, he led the Raiders to a 24-20 victory in front of a record crowd of 45,758.

Oct. 24 – Art Powell underwent season-ending knee surgery.

Oct. 29 – The Bills limited Houston to 181 total yards, but lost in a rainstorm at Rice Stadium, 10-3.

Nov. 5 – The Bills held Miami to 127 total yards in a 35-13 victory.

Nov. 12 – Johnny Sample's 41-yard interception return for a TD clinched the Jets' 20-10 win over the Bills at Shea Stadium in front of 62,671. Running back Jack Spikes suffered a concussion and went into convulsions on the field. He spent the night in a New York hospital, but was pronounced okay.

Nov. 16 – Pete Rozelle said he was concerned about television saturation of pro football: "We are concerned about the televising of doubleheaders, although we can't stop the networks from doing it if they want to schedule games in the different time zones to reach the largest possible audience. What we'd like to do is expand our Monday night telecasts. There's a possibility of a regular Monday night game in the future."

Nov. 19 – Lou Saban returned to War Memorial Stadium and beat the Bills, 21-20, as Mike Mercer missed a 24-yard field goal with 16 seconds left.

Nov. 25 – Joe Collier announced that he was benching Marty Schottenheimer because he "hasn't played as well as we expected" since taking over for injured Harry Jacobs. Paul Guidry was inserted into the starting lineup for the Miami game.

Nov. 26 – Miami posted its first victory over the Bills, 17-14, at the Orange Bowl.

Dec. 3 – The Chiefs held the Bills to eight first downs in a 23-13 victory.

Dec. 9 – The Bills exploded for a season-best

offensive performance in a 44-16 rout of Boston at Fenway Park. Tommy Janik had three of Buffalo's six interceptions.

Dec. 16 – Keith Lincoln was selected as the Bills MVP.

Dec. 20 - Keith Lincoln, Billy Shaw, Ron McDole, Jim Dunaway, Mike Stratton and George Saimes were selected to the AFL East Division all-star team, coached by Joe Collier. Meanwhile, Saimes, McDole and Stratton were voted to the all-AFL first team by the league's coaches.

Dec. 24 – Oakland dealt the Bills their 10th loss, 28-21, in the season finale. In the process, the Raiders finished with an AFL record 13 regular-season victories.

Dec. 28 – Speculation that Weeb Ewbank would move upstairs into the Jets front office surfaced, and Penn State coach Joe Paterno was rumored to be a possible successor as head coach.

Dec. 31 – Oakland won its first league championship, crushing Houston, 40-7, in front of a Championship Game record crowd of 53,330 at Oakland-Alameda County Stadium. Hewritt Dixon (144 yards) and Pete Banaszak (116) led a punishing ground attack as Daryle Lamonica passed for just 111 yards. Each Raider received $6,321 for winning, a record AFL payoff.

Jan. 14, 1968 – Green Bay won its second straight Super Bowl, ripping the Raiders, 33-14, in front of 75,546 at Miami's Orange Bowl. MVP Bart Starr threw for 202 yards and one TD.

Jan. 21, 1968 – The East beat the West, 25-24, in the AFL all-star game as Joe Namath snuck in from the 1 with 58 seconds left behind a block by Buffalo's Billy Shaw.

Former San Diego star running back Keith Lincoln (above), who is best known for getting his ribs broken on a tackle by Mike Stratton in the 1964 AFL Championship Game, joined the Bills in 1967 and led the team in rushing that year.

Tom Janik (opposite page) intercepted 10 passes in 1967, which tied the team record for one season also held by Billy Atkins in 1961.

BY THE NUMBERS - 1967

TEAM STATISTICS	BILLS	OPP
First downs	203	201
Rushing	65	73
Passing	119	106
Penalty	19	22
Total yards	3,588	3,447
Avg. game	256.3	246.2
Plays	850	857
Avg. play	4.2	4.0
Net rushing yds	1,271	1,622
Avg. game	90.8	115.8
Avg. play	3.4	3.7
Net passing yds	2,317	1,825
Comp/att	183/434	162/377
Sacks/lost	45-446	43-366
Interceptions	34	27
Percentage	42.2	43.0
Punts/avg	77-43.1	74-41.0
Fumbles/lost	32-13	26-9
Penalties/yds	74-828	51-507
Touchdowns	27	33
Extra points	25-26	32-33
Field goals	16-27	17-38
Two-point conv	1-1	0-0
Safeties	0	2
Kick ret./avg	51-21.8	56-23.1
Punt ret./avg	47-4.2	33-9.1

RUSHING	ATT	YDS	AVG	TD
Lincoln	159	601	3.8	4
Carlton	107	467	4.4	3
Burnett	45	96	2.1	0
Bivins	15	58	3.9	0
Stone	36	58	1.6	2
Spikes	4	9	2.3	0
Donaldson	3	-1	-0.3	0
Dubenion	2	-17	-8.5	0
TOTALS	**371**	**1271**	**3.4**	**9**

PASSING	COMP	ATT	INT	YDS	TD	COMP%
Kemp	161	369	26	2503	14	43.6
Flores	22	64	8	260	0	34.4
Rutkowski	0	1	0	0	0	.000
TOTALS	**183**	**434**	**34**	**2763**	**14**	**42.2**

KICKING	FG/ATT	PAT/ATT	PTS
Mercer	16-27	25-26	73

PUNTING	NO	AVG
Maguire	77	43.1

RECEIVING	CAT	YDS	AVG	TD
Lincoln	41	558	13.6	5
P. Costa	39	726	18.6	2
Dubenion	25	384	15.4	0
Powell	20	346	17.3	4
Masters	20	274	13.7	2
Burnett	11	114	10.4	0
Ledbetter	9	161	17.9	1
Carlton	9	97	10.8	0
Rutkowski	6	59	9.8	0
Donaldson	1	20	20.0	0
Tracey	1	15	15.0	0
Spikes	1	9	9.0	0
TOTALS	**183**	**2763**	**15.1**	**14**

LEADERS

Kick returns:
Bivins 16-380 yds, 23.8 avg, 0 TD
Smith 16-346, 21.6, 0 TD

Punt returns:
Byrd 30-142, 4.7, 0 TD
Rutkowski 15-43, 2.9, 0 TD

Interceptions:
Janik 10-222, 22.0, 2 TD
Byrd 5-25, 5.0, 0 TD

Non-kick scoring:
Lincoln 9 TDs, 54 pts
Powell 4 TDs, 24 pts

Tom Flores came to the Bills in 1967, but his playing time was curtailed by injuries. He went on to coach the Oakland Raiders to two Super Bowl titles.

GAME 1 - Sunday, Sept. 10, 1967 - BILLS 20, JETS 17

Jets	0	14	3	0 -	17
Bills	0	0	0	20 -	20

Attendance at War Memorial Stadium - 45,748

NY: Maynard 19 pass from Namath (J. Turner kick), 8:40
NY: Maynard 56 pass from Namath (J. Turner kick), 14:39
NY: FG J. Turner 32, 4:37
Buf: Powell 24 pass from Kemp (Mercer kick), 2:01
Buf: Powell 37 pass from Kemp (Mercer kick), 4:39
Buf: FG Mercer 51, 12:33
Buf: FG Mercer 43, 14:56

	BUF	NY
First downs	15	14
Rushing yds	89	152
Passing yds	159	135
Punts-avg	5-48.4	6-35.0
Fumbles-lost	0-0	0-0
Penalties-yds	7-67	4-40

BILLS LEADERS: Rushing - Lincoln 13-81, Burnett 7-9, Kemp 1-0, Dubenion 1-(-1); **Passing** - Kemp 12-23-2 - 167, Flores 6-11-0 - 40; **Receiving** - Lincoln 3-23, Costa 3-37, Dubenion 6-54, Powell 5-91, Burnett 1-2.

JETS LEADERS: Rushing - Snell 19-95, Boozer 16-53, Mathis 1-4; **Passing** - Namath 11-23-0 - 153; **Receiving** - Maynard 5-106, Sauer 4-35, Lammons 1-13, Snell 1-(-1).

WEEK 1 GAMES
Den 26, Bos 21

WEEK 2 GAMES
SD 28, Bos 24   KC 25, Hou 20
Oak 51, Den 0

NOTES

• The Bills pulled off the greatest comeback in team history with 20 fourth-quarter points, the final three coming from kicker Mike Mercer with four seconds left. Earlier, Mercer's club-record 51-yarder had tied the game. Tom Flores started the game but suffered a twisted knee and was replaced by Jack Kemp.
• The Jets took a 14-0 lead in the second on a pair of Joe Namath-to-Don Maynard TD passes. The first one capped a 57-yard drive, keyed by an interference penalty on John Tracey. The second capped a quick 74-yard march. Maynard beat Booker Edgerson on a streak pattern with 21 seconds left in the half.
• Jim Hudson's interception of a Kemp pass set up Jim Turner's 32-yard field goal 4:37 into the third, and when Kemp was picked off again, this time by Cornell Gordon, it appeared the Bills were dead. However, on that play, Elbert Dubenion made a crushing tackle on Gordon, knocking him out of the game and that later hurt the Jets.
• On Buffalo's next possession, Gordon's replacement, Solomon Brannan, dropped an interception in the end zone. On the next play, Kemp hit Art Powell with a 24-yard TD pass.
• The Jets punted on the ensuing series and Butch Byrd returned it 29 yards to the Jets 37. On first down, Kemp hit Powell, who had beaten Brannan, with a TD pass and it was 17-14.
• Jim Turner missed a 35-yard field goal. Then following a Jets punt, Mercer kicked his game-tying 51-yarder with 2:27 left.
• The defense rose again and forced New York to punt. The Bills began their final drive from their own 18 with 1:20 left. Keith Lincoln took a Kemp swing pass 24 yards, then Paul Costa made a leaping grab on third down for 21 yards to the 35. One play later, Mercer kicked the winner.

QUOTES

• Joe Collier: "We picked up some momentum with Jack's touchdown pass to Powell and added to the momentum as we went along. Our defense helped in the second half and Paul Maguire's kicking was good. We made the decision to switch to Jack when the doctor told us it would be too risky to use Tom anymore."
• Elbert Dubenion on his hit on Cornell Gordon: "That was the hardest tackle I've ever made. I sort of sneaked up on him, he didn't see me coming."
• Art Powell: "I was running poor patterns in the first half. I think I can beat anyone if I'm running patterns right. I think I ran them right in the second half."
• Mike Mercer on the winning kick: "I never even thought about it. When you've played the game this long, you don't think about it (the pressure). That was the longest one I ever tried. I checked the wind before the game and knew it could go 50 yards in that direction. Fortunately I had the wind with me on both kicks."

GAME 2 - Sunday, Sept. 17, 1967 - OILERS 20, BILLS 3

Oilers	0	10	0	10 -	20
Bills	3	0	0	0 -	3

Attendance at War Memorial Stadium - 41,384

Buf: FG Mercer 47, 4:01
Hou: FG Wittenborn 22, 6:49
Hou: Frazier 4 pass from Lee (Wittenborn kick), 14:28
Hou: FG Wittenborn 42, 10:35
Hou: Granger 1 run (Wittenborn kick), 14:00

	BUF	HOU
First downs	9	9
Rushing yds	43	113
Passing yds	150	26
Punts-avg	6-47.3	7-42.8
Fumbles-lost	2-2	2-2
Penalties-yds	4-47	4-47

BILLS LEADERS: Rushing - Lincoln 12-47, Kemp 3-7, Burnett 4-(-11); **Passing** - Kemp 14-30-2 - 177, Flores 0-1-0 - 0; **Receiving** - Lincoln 5-26, Costa 5-68, Dubenion 2-31, Burnett 1-38, Carlton 1-14.

OILERS LEADERS: Rushing - Granger 17-55, Blanks 16-42, Elkins 1-14, Lee 3-2; **Passing** - Lee 8-18-2 - 31; **Receiving** - Frazier 4-31, Blanks 2-(-1), Granger 1-2, Lee 1-(-1).

NOTES

• Dating back to 1966, the Oilers had lost 11 straight games.
• The Bills were anemic on offense. During one stretch, they failed on 11 straight third-down plays.
• Jack Kemp started at QB and was sacked five times for 27 yards in losses.
• The defense allowed a team-record low of 26 net passing yards to new Houston starting QB Jacky Lee.
• The Bills scored on their first possession as Mike Mercer kicked a 47-yard field goal, but then saw 12 straight possessions fizzle.
• A Bobby Burnett fumble at the Bills 27 didn't hurt as Houston failed to score, but Kemp was intercepted by Jim Norton who returned it 23 yards to the Bills 20. That led to John Wittenborn's first field goal.
• Later in the second, Zeke Moore returned a Paul Maguire punt 45 yards to the Bills 7. Two plays later, Lee threw to Charlie Frazier for a TD.
• Another Wittenborn field goal, set up by Moore's 34-yard punt return to the Buffalo 43, made it 13-3. The clincher for Houston came in the fourth when W.K. Hicks picked off a Kemp pass and returned it 62 yards to the Bills 6. Hoyle Granger then scored on a one-yard plunge.

QUOTES

• Joe Collier: "I can't remember a game where we made so many mental mistakes. If our offense can't play any better than that, we're not going to do much winning this year. We had poor practices all week long. We made the same mental mistakes during the week that we made during the game. We chewed them out all week, but it didn't do any good. Whether or not the club comes back isn't up to me or the coaches, it's up to the players. Anyone who isn't playing up to his capabilities is in danger of being removed if there is an adequate replacement."
• Elbert Dubenion: "We lose one game and everyone is pushing the panic button. Sure, we looked bad against Houston, but it was one game, not the whole season. We lost the first two games last year and won the division championship. We've had bad starts before and we've always come back. This is a good club, we're going to be okay."

WEEK 3 GAMES
Oak 35, Bos 7   Mia 35, Den 21

STANDINGS: THIRD WEEK

EAST	W	L	T	WEST	W	L	T
Miami	1	0	0	Oakland	2	0	0
Buffalo	1	1	0	San Diego	1	0	0
Houston	1	1	0	Kan. City	1	0	0
New York	0	1	0	Denver	1	2	0
Boston	0	3	0				

NOTES

• The Bills were shut out for the first time in their history, a span of 142 games counting playoffs, and their scoreless streak for this season reached 7 1/2 quarters.

• Jim Nance rushed for 185 yards, the most the Bills ever had allowed to a single runner. Through three games, the Bills had only 174 rushing yards.

• Tom Flores started and played most of the game and was awful, throwing a team record-tying five interceptions. Jack Kemp replaced him in the second quarter, but jammed his right thumb and Flores had to go back in.

• The offensive line didn't give the quarterbacks much help. With Billy Shaw and Dick Hudson out, Al Bemiller was playing right tackle, rookie Dick Cunningham had to play left tackle, Stew Barber moved to left guard and newly acquired Wayne Frazier was at center.

• Gino Cappelletti attempted an AFL record-tying seven field goals and made three while Mike Mercer was 0-for-3, including a miss from 20 yards.

• Bobby Burnett fumbled on the fifth play of the game and Jim Hunt recovered at the Bills 40. That led to Cappelletti's first field goal. On the ensuing series, Flores was intercepted by Nick Buoniconti and that led to another Cappelletti field goal.

• Nance broke free for a 53-yard run, then scored from the 3 on the next play for a 13-0 lead.

• After a scoreless third, Boston added 10 points in the fourth. Don Webb's interception and return to the Bills 27 led to Babe Parilli's TD pass to Larry Garron. Leroy Mitchell's interception resulted in Cappelletti's final field goal.

QUOTES

• Ralph Wilson: "I've been disturbed all season long."

• Joe Collier: "We just have to keep working. We had our best week of practice all season, we were prepared for the game and as up for it as we would get for a championship game. Then we just got outplayed. I can think of nothing positive to say. "

• Patriots coach Mike Holovak: "This was our best game. We had no fumbles, no interceptions. The Bills are still the toughest club in our league defensively. But we know what it's like to play well and lose, or to play badly and win."

• Jim Nance: "Buffalo is stronger than Oakland and any of the three clubs we've already played. The Buffalo game here last year was a springboard for us, too. It's too early to pick a team in the Eastern Division."

• Babe Parilli: "I only checked off once all day. We played it conservatively. When Jim Nance makes our running game go, everything else falls into pattern."

Patriots	6	7	0	10	- 23
Bills	0	0	0	0	- 0

Attendance at War Memorial Stadium - 45,748

Bos:	FG Cappelletti 33, 6:54
Bos:	FG Cappelletti 23, 9:09
Bos:	Nance 3 run (Cappelletti kick), 7:18
Bos:	Garron 11 pass from Parilli (Cappelletti kick), 7:55
Bos:	FG Cappelletti 45, 13:04

	BUF	BOS
First downs	11	13
Rushing yds	42	183
Passing yds	199	82
Punts-avg	5-40.1	5-42.4
Fumbles-lost	4-1	2-0
Penalties-yds	4-37	3-20

BILLS LEADERS: Rushing - Lincoln 13-41, Burnett 5-6, Kemp 2-(-6), Spikes 1-1; **Passing** - Kemp 2-3-0 - 58, Flores 11-30-5 - 159; **Receiving** - Lincoln 2-58, Costa 2-25, Dubenion 2-42, Powell 4-76, Burnett 3-16.

PATRIOTS LEADERS: Rushing - Nance 34-185, Garron 4-8, Parilli 1- (-5), J.D. Garrett 3-(-5); **Passing** - Parilli 9-24-0 - 94; **Receiving** - Garron 4-48, Whalen 2-22, Cappelletti 1-22, Graham 1-10, Nance 1-(-8).

NOTES

• The Chargers ripped through the AFL's best defense for 484 total yards, the most the Bills had allowed since 1963 when Oakland gained 499. San Diego had 311 yards at halftime.

• The Bills were zero-for-seven on third-down conversions.

• Allen Smith returned the opening kickoff 64 yards and that led to a Mike Mercer field goal.

• The Chargers then took control and raced to a 21-3 lead. Strong safety Hagood Clarke left the game with a knee injury and when Tom Janik moved over from free safety, John Hadl went right at him. Hadl threw four passes to tight end Willie Frazier for 86 yards during an 83-yard scoring drive (there was a five-yard penalty against San Diego) that was capped by Dick Post's one-yard run.

• In the second quarter, Frazier and another tight end, Jacque MacKinnon, caught TD passes from Hadl.

• Two field goals by Dick Van Raaphorst and Scott Appleton's two-yard return of a fumble made it 34-3. The Bills finally broke their TD drought at 11 quarters when Keith Lincoln raced 60 yards after catching a Jack Kemp screen pass in the third. And on the last play of the game, Kemp scrambled, then lateraled to Lincoln who dove into the end zone on the broken play.

QUOTES

• Joe Collier: "We'll be back. That's right, we'll be back." (On who would be his quarterback): "As soon as he's physically whole, Jack Kemp will be our quarterback. Off what he's shown in the last two or three games, I think he deserves it. But anytime you say the quarterback is completely at fault, you're lying."

• Chargers defensive end and ex-Bill Tom Day: "We lost some in past years, but nothing like this. We never played so poorly. I asked the guys (Buffalo players) and they all said they didn't know what was the matter."

• Chargers running back Dick Post: "It was just like running in practice, like no one was out there."

• Keith Lincoln: "Like everyone else on the team, I'm lost trying to figure out what's wrong. The thing that bothers me most is that I feel we're better than any team we've played. Losing is bad enough, but our poor showings are what really hurt."

Chargers	7	14	13	3	- 37
Bills	3	0	7	7	- 17

Attendance at War Memorial Stadium - 39,310

Buf:	FG Mercer 26, 2:22
SD:	Post 1 run (Van Raaphorst kick), 12:50
SD:	Frazier 21 pass from Hadl (Van Raaphorst kick), 5:26
SD:	MacKinnon 3 pass from Hadl (Van Raaphorst kick), 12:46
SD:	FG Van Raaphorst 32, 6:01
SD:	FG Van Raaphorst 30, 10:20
SD:	Appleton 2 fumble return (Van Raaphorst kick), 12:48
Buf:	Lincoln 60 pass from Kemp (Mercer kick), 14:55
SD:	FG Van Raaphorst 25, 13:55
Buf:	Lincoln 10 lateral from Kemp (Mercer kick), 14:59

	BUF	SD
First downs	12	26
Rushing yds	54	202
Passing yds	193	282
Punts-avg	5-45.4	1-38.0
Fumbles-lost	1-1	0-0
Penalties-yds	6-64	5-67

BILLS LEADERS: Rushing - Lincoln 8-34, Kemp 2-12, Spikes 3-8; **Passing** - Kemp 7-18-1 - 198, Flores 3-12-1 - 26; **Receiving** - Lincoln 3-90, Dubenion 1-42, Powell 4-68, Masters 1-15, Spikes 1-9.

CHARGERS LEADERS: Rushing - Post 20-121, Hubbert 17-57, Smith 3-14, Hadl 3-10; **Passing** - Hadl 18-31-0 - 282, Alworth 0-1-0 - 0; **Receiving** - Frazier 5-106, Garrison 4-50, Alworth 4-99, Post 3-20, MacKinnon 1-3, Hubbert 1-4.

STANDINGS: FIFTH WEEK

EAST	W	L	T	WEST	W	L	T
New York	2	1	0	Oakland	3	0	0
Houston	2	2	0	San Diego	3	0	0
Miami	1	2	0	Kan. City	2	1	0
Buffalo	1	3	0	Denver	1	4	0
Boston	1	3	0				

Bills	0	3	0	14	-	17
Broncos	0	2	7	7	-	16

Attendance at Bears Stadium - 35,188

Den: Safety, Jackson tackled Kemp in end zone, :14
Buf: FG Mercer 32, 13:54
Den: Hayes 1 run (LeClerc kick), 13:35
Den: Denson 12 pass from LeClair (LeClerc kick), :05
Buf: Powell 5 pass from Kemp (Mercer kick), 7:51
Buf: Lincoln 4 run (Mercer kick), 11:23

	BUF	DEN
First downs	21	13
Rushing yds	87	83
Passing yds	210	107
Punts-avg	5-43.0	5-48.4
Fumbles-lost	5-1	2-1
Penalties-yds	8-89	7-66

BILLS LEADERS: Rushing - Lincoln 9-55, Burnett 9-26, Kemp 6-6; **Passing** - Kemp 15-39-3 - 224; **Receiving** - Lincoln 2-39, Dubenion 4-90, Powell 4-42, Burnett 4-41, Rutkowski 1-12.

BRONCOS LEADERS: Rushing - Mitchell 17-55, Hickey 7-0, Little 4-16, LeClair 5-8, Scarpitto 1-5, Hayes 5-(-1); **Passing** - LeClair 9-17-0 - 114, Tensi 2-2-0 - 45; **Receiving** - Denson 5-87, Crabtree 3-57, Hickey 2-8, Hayes 1-7

WEEK 6 GAMES

NY 27, Oak 14	Bos 31, SD 31
KC 41, Mia 0	

NOTES

• Rookie quarterback John LeClair made his pro debut and would have won the game had it not been for kicker John LeClerc's five field goal misses.
• The Bills' defense had seven sacks for 52 yards in losses. Harry Jacobs had 20 tackles and three of the sacks.
• The Bills' first drive halted when Keith Lincoln fumbled and John Huard recovered at the Denver 10.
• Early in the second quarter, Dave Costa sacked Jack Kemp for a safety. When Fran Lynch returned the free kick 27 yards and 15 more were tacked on for a personal foul, the Broncos were on the Bills 31. They couldn't move, and LeClerc began his folly, missing a 48-yarder.
• Huard's interception of a Kemp pass and return to the Bills 6 was wasted when LeClerc's 13-yard attempt was blocked and shortly thereafter, he blew a 42-yarder. Following that miss, the Bills drove 40 yards to Mike Mercer's 32-yard field goal which gave Buffalo a 3-2 halftime lead.
• Jim Summers picked off a Kemp pass in the end zone early in the third, and that began Denver's 80-yard march to its first TD. The drive was aided by a roughing penalty on Paul Maguire which gave Denver a first down. Steve Tensi replaced LeClair at QB and hit Eric Crabtree for 40 yards to the 16. After a pass interference penalty on Butch Byrd, Wendell Hayes scored from the 1.
• Carl Cunningham intercepted Kemp two plays later and returned it to the Bills 15. Then, on the first play of the fourth quarter, Booker Edgerson picked off LeClair in the end zone, but because Edgerson didn't down the ball, the play was still alive and Al Denson stole the ball from the Bills' cornerback and was awarded a TD.
• The Bills then performed their second fourth-quarter rally of the season. Art Powell's TD reception came after a Hayes fumble was recovered by Byrd.
• Then, Denver punter Bob Scarpitto faked a punt and was stopped short of the first down by Marty Schottenheimer. From there, Kemp drove the Bills into the end zone. He hit Elbert Dubenion for 13 yards and Bobby Burnett for 14 before Lincoln scored on a four yard run.

QUOTES

• Joe Collier: "It's just a win, that's all I can say of this one. It was a game of breaks. We haven't been getting many breaks, except of bones, this season. I'd say Scarpitto's gamble gave us the break we needed. He could have kicked us into a hole as he had been doing all day. Our defense was up to protect against a pass or a run on that one."
• Lou Saban: "What a way to lose. It seems one guy breaks down every week. We knew Tensi had a bad right arm, but we didn't want Buffalo to know we were going with LeClair. Then LeClair jammed his thumb and we put Tensi in and you know what happened, Tensi hurt his left arm."
• Harry Jacobs: "There seemed to be a lot of concern over what was wrong with our defense after the San Diego game. I didn't think anything was wrong, even then. Teams had been moving the ball because they had been coming up with the right play at the right time. But I felt maybe some of the guys on the defensive unit were starting to wonder, too, so it was my theory to go back to basic stuff against Denver. We stayed in the 41 (four-man line, Jacobs over center) all day. We bottled up their running game and put pressure on their quarterbacks."

Raiders	0	17	0	7	-	24
Bills	7	0	7	6	-	20

Attendance at War Memorial Stadium - 45,758

Buf: Costa 30 pass from Kemp (Mercer kick), 4:42
Oak: FG Blanda 31, 10:09
Oak: Biletnikoff 41 pass from Lamonica (Blanda kick), 11:37
Oak: Conners 30 interception return (Blanda kick), 13:12
Buf: Lincoln 3 run (Mercer kick), 9:46
Oak: Cannon 3 pass from Lamonica (Blanda kick), 11:20
Buf: Powell 26 pass from Kemp (kick failed), 13:05

	BUF	OAK
First downs	10	13
Rushing yds	38	144
Passing yds	120	79
Punts-avg	11-45.3	5-47.2
Fumbles-lost	3-0	1-1
Penalties-yds	3-35	2-10

BILLS LEADERS: Rushing - Lincoln 7-15, Carlton 5-33, Bivins 2-4, Kemp 1-2, Dubenion 1-(-16); **Passing** - Kemp 13-33-2 - 216; **Receiving** - Lincoln 4-29, Costa 2-67, Powell 3-69, Burnett 1-9, Rutkowski 2-14, Masters 1-28.

RAIDERS LEADERS: Rushing - Daniels 18-75, Dixon 11-68, Lamonica 1-1; **Passing** - Lamonica 9-23-4 - 129; **Receiving** - Dixon 4-22, Biletnikoff 2-68, Miller 2-36, Cannon 1-3.

NOTES

• The long-awaited return of Daryle Lamonica and his duel with Jack Kemp was tempered as the two quarterbacks combined to throw six interceptions in front of a record crowd.
• Oakland won in Buffalo for the first time since 1961 as it sacked Kemp 11 times for 96 yards despite the return of Billy Shaw to the lineup.
• Tommy Janik's interception and 33-yard return to the Raiders 22 led to Kemp's 30-yard TD pass to Paul Costa 4:42 into the game.
• In the second, after a George Blanda field goal, the Raiders went ahead 10-7. Rodger Bird's 34-yard punt return set up Lamonica's 41-yard TD to Fred Biletnikoff. Three plays later, Kemp threw an ill-advised pass while under pressure and Dan Conners intercepted and scored easily.
• The Bills got back into it early in the third when Ron McDole tipped a pass, Jim Dunaway intercepted and rumbled to the 3, from where Keith Lincoln scored.
• McDole then intercepted a pass on the next series and the Bills started from the Oakland 35. But Elbert Dubenion lost 16 yards on a reverse and the threat died.
• On the Bills' next possession, Kemp's long pass was intercepted by Howie Williams and returned 36 yards to the Bills 32. Lamonica hit Billy Cannon with a perfect play-action-fake TD pass and it was 24-14 with 3:40 left.
• The Bills pulled within 24-20 as Kemp hit Billy Masters for 28 and Art Powell for 29, then threw a 26-yard TD pass to Powell with 1:55 left. The Bills got the ball back one more time with 35 seconds left and no timeouts, yet Kemp drove them 48 yards to the Oakland 30 before the clock ran out.

QUOTES

• Raiders quarterback Daryle Lamonica: "I still say the Bills are the best team, man-for-man, in the East Division. I know they gave me a lot of trouble early in the game with their safety blitz. I was quite shaky at the start. It seemed I wasn't getting the feel of the game. But then in the second quarter I started reading the defenses better and that calmed me down. I've always had the feeling I could be a good quarterback and now that I'm a starter, I have to prove that feeling. Today's game helped a lot."
• Raiders linebacker Dan Conners on his interception: "I didn't think Kemp would throw it. He just threw it away."
• Joe Collier on Williams' interception which led to the winning score: "That was Oakland's biggest play. I wish Jack would have thrown it away. Everything was perfect on that play. If that pass had been complete, we would have had a first down at their 30. If we had gotten just a field goal, the score would have been tied. Then they ended up getting a touchdown."
• Ron McDole: "The game was both disappointing and encouraging. It actually went well as far as building confidence, even though we lost. We were in it all the way. Take away a couple mental mistakes and we could have won. My feeling is we can beat anyone, it's just a matter of getting things to click."

WEEK 7 GAMES

Hou 28, NY 28	SD 45, KC 31
Bos 41, Mia 10	

STANDINGS: SEVENTH WEEK

EAST	W	L	T	WEST	W	L	T
New York	3	1	1	San Diego	4	0	1
Houston	2	2	1	Oakland	4	1	0
Boston	2	3	1	Kan. City	3	2	0
Buffalo	2	4	0	Denver	1	5	0
Miami	1	4	0				

NOTES

- A driving rainstorm hindered both offenses. The Bills turned over the ball four times.
- Harry Jacobs suffered a season-ending broken collarbone and was replaced by Marty Schottenheimer at middle linebacker. Jacobs had started his 80th game in a row.
- The Oilers held the Bills without a TD for the second time this season.
- The Bills had a chance to tie or win late in the game after Dudley Meredith blocked an Oiler punt and Paul Maguire recovered at the Houston 36. They moved to the 7, mainly on the ground with Keith Lincoln converting twice on two short fourth-down plunges, and called their final timeout with 58 seconds left. Jack Kemp's swing pass to Wray Carlton was broken up by Garland Boyette. On fourth down, he overthrew Elbert Dubenion at the 4, killing the threat.
- Mike Stratton's interception ended Houston's first possession and the Bills proceeded to drive to their only score, Mike Mercer's 47-yard field goal.
- A fumbled punt snap by Jim Norton was recovered by Paul Guidry at the Oilers 27, but Kemp was intercepted by Miller Farr.
- Kemp lost a fumble at his own 27 and John Wittenborn kicked a 25-yard field goal to tie it.
- With 20 seconds left in the half, Mercer made a field goal, but a roughing penalty gave the Bills a first down at the 9 and Joe Collier took the points off the board. After three incompletions, Mercer came back, but this time he missed from the 22.

- Houston's winning score came after Maguire's punt from his own end zone traveled only to the Bills 34. Houston QB Pete Beathard scrambled to the 13 and fumbled, but Bobby Maples recovered at the 1. Two plays later, Beathard plunged in.
- Houston's 127 yards were the fewest the Bills had allowed since holding Denver to 117 on Dec. 13, 1964.

QUOTES

- Harry Jacobs: "I feel worse about breaking the streak than I do about the injury."
- Joe Collier on his decision to nullify Mercer's field goal: "We had timeouts left and felt we had a chance for the touchdown. As it turned out, we got nothing, but I'd do the same thing again. In coaching, it's not always the decision you make, but how the execution goes that makes you appear right or wrong."
- Houston coach Wally Lemm: "I was surprised they didn't take the field goal. I've seen the same thing happen many times where you give up the three you have to try for six, then miss the second chance."
- Marty Schottenheimer on becoming a starter: "The only thing I feel bad about is that Harry Jacobs got hurt. He worked like a dog for eight years and finally got some deserved recognition this year. This is a time for action, not words. I still have my confidence."

| Bills | 3 | 0 | 0 | 0 | - | 3 |
| Oilers | 0 | 3 | 7 | 0 | - | 10 |

Attendance at Rice Stadium - 30,060

Buf: FG Mercer 47, 9:08
Hou: FG Wittenborn 25, 11:29
Hou: Beathard 1 run (Wittenborn kick), 12:24

	BUF	HOU
First downs	14	10
Rushing yds	115	120
Passing yds	100	61
Punts-avg	4-40.8	4-32.5
Fumbles-lost	7-2	2-0
Penalties-yds	3-15	4-34

BILLS LEADERS: Rushing - Lincoln 14-77, Carlton 10-24, Burnett 6-15, Kemp 9-(-1); **Passing** - Kemp 10-22-2 - 106, Flores 0-1-0 - 0; **Receiving** - Lincoln 5-53, Costa 1-5, Dubenion 1-6, Masters 3-42.

OILERS LEADERS: Rushing - Campbell 11-44, Hopkins 8-39, Beathard 9-32, Granger 2-12, Norton 1- (-7); **Passing** - Beathard 6-13-3 - 77, Campbell 0-1-0 - 0; **Receiving** - Burrell 3-41, Taylor 2-29, Hopkins 1-7.

WEEK 8 GAMES
Hou 24, KC 19   Oak 48, Bos 14
NY 33, Mia 14   SD 38, Den 21
Buffalo had a bye week.

WEEK 9 GAMES
Oak 51, SD 10   NY 30, Bos 23
KC 52, Den 9

NOTES

- The Bills snapped out of their offensive doldrums in front of the smallest crowd since the second game of 1964.
- After failing to gain 100 yards rushing in the first six games, the Bills topped 100 for the second game in a row. The key was a two-tight end formation that helped the blocking.
- With snow falling and covering the field, former Bill Joe Auer fumbled the opening kickoff. Tony King recovered at the Miami 26 and four running plays later, Wray Carlton scored.
- On their second possession, the Bills drove 80 yards as Jack Kemp threw 22 yards to Billy Masters, 19 to Paul Costa and then 19 to Masters for the TD.
- After stopping a Miami drive to the 6 on downs, the defense came up with another big play as Tommy Janik picked off a Bob Griese pass and went 19 yards for the TD.
- Miami made it 21-7 with the help of a 39-yard interference call on Booker Edgerson and a personal foul on John Tracey that wiped out Marty Schottenheimer's interception. Eventually, Griese passed 13 yards to Doug Moreau

for the score.
- Kemp drove the Bills into position for another score, but missed three plays when he hurt his knee. Tom Flores entered and threw an interception in the end zone.
- After Paul Maguire pinned Miami at the 1 with a punt, the defense held and forced the Dolphins to punt. Starting from the Miami 38, Wray Carlton scored four plays later.
- Masters' TD capped a 40-yard drive. Auer scored with 45 seconds left for Miami.

QUOTES

- Joe Collier on the two-tight end look: "It's been good for us so far. When your running game is going well, everything else seems to go well. It is designed to help your running game and it narrows the number of defenses a team can use and should eliminate some of the stunting teams do. If they try to stunt anyway, you can hurt a team. Miami tried it early, and we hurt them. It would have worked last week against Houston, if the rain hadn't ruined everything. Had we won that one, we'd be right in the race. Bob Griese is the best quarterback to come into the league since Joe Namath."
- Miami quarterback Bob Griese on Janik's interception TD: "I squeezed the ball too tight and didn't control it well enough for that type of pass. I should have thrown it harder. The pressure made it float. Janik's touchdown took us out of the game. I've never been up against such a great front four. They had the pressure on me all day, never let up."
- Miami coach George Wilson: "From our scouting reports and study of the films, that had to be Buffalo's best game of the year. We couldn't stop them in third-down situations. Maybe the Bills looked so good because they were playing against us."
- Marty Schottenheimer: "Mike (Stratton) and John (Tracey) kept talking me through it, so I wasn't worried about the job at all."

| Dolphins | 0 | 7 | 0 | 6 | - | 13 |
| Bills | 14 | 7 | 7 | 7 | - | 35 |

Attendance at War Memorial Stadium - 31,622

Buf: Carlton 6 run (Mercer kick), 1:57
Buf: Masters 19 pass from Kemp (Mercer kick), 7:52
Buf: Janik 19 interception return (Mercer kick), 7:01
Mia: Moreau 13 pass from Griese (Lusteg kick), 10:18
Buf: Carlton 14 run (Mercer kick), 11:08
Buf: Masters 5 pass from Kemp (Mercer kick), 11:35
Mia: Auer 2 run (kick failed), 14:15

	BUF	MIA
First downs	18	16
Rushing yds	182	47
Passing yds	128	80
Punts-avg	5-44.2	7-36.7
Fumbles-lost	2-1	3-1
Penalties-yds	10-144	2-30

BILLS LEADERS: Rushing - Lincoln 17-65, Carlton 15-97, Burnett 4-19, Kemp 1-1; **Passing** - Kemp 9-18-1 - 150, Flores 0-1-0 - 0; **Receiving** - Lincoln 1-19, Costa 2-38, Dubenion 1-31, Burnett 1-8, Masters 4-54.

DOLPHINS LEADERS: Rushing - Price 9-23, Griese 3-17, Haynes 3-6, Auer 4-1, Mitchell 1-0; **Passing** - Griese 16-37-1 - 107; **Receiving** - Moreau 5-36, Clancy 4-40, Auer 4-16, Price 1-8, Haynes 1-5, Jackson 1-2.

WEEK 10 GAMES
KC 42, NY 18   Bos 18, Hou 7
Oak 21, Den 17

STANDINGS: TENTH WEEK

EAST	W	L	T	WEST	W	L	T
New York	5	2	1	Oakland	7	1	0
Houston	4	3	1	San Diego	5	1	1
Boston	3	5	1	Kan. City	5	3	0
Buffalo	3	5	0	Denver	1	8	0
Miami	1	6	0				

Bills	0	10	0	0	-	10
Jets	10	0	3	7	-	20

Attendance at Shea Stadium - 62,671

NY: FG J. Turner 48, 4:40
NY: Sauer 47 pass from Namath (J. Turner kick), 8:02
Buf: Lincoln 2 run (Mercer kick), 8:16
Buf: FG Mercer 17, 8:47
NY: FG J. Turner 14, 8:47
NY: Sample 41 interception return (J. Turner kick), 5:06

	BUF	NY
First downs	16	15
Rushing yds	121	67
Passing yds	136	293
Punts-avg	6-45.0	4-47.0
Fumbles-lost	1-0	2-1
Penalties-yds	3-47	3-45

BILLS LEADERS: Rushing - Lincoln 12-30, Carlton 9-59, Burnett 10-32, Kemp 1-0; **Passing** - Kemp 10-30-2 - 172; **Receiving** - Lincoln 1-0, Costa 1-30, Dubenion 3-43, Carlton 1-7, Masters 1-24, Rutkowski 2-26, Ledbetter 1-42.

JETS LEADERS: Rushing - Snell 6-12, Mathis 5-32, Joe 4-11, Smolinski 8-13, Maynard 1-(-1); **Passing** - Namath 13-37-2 - 338; **Receiving** - Maynard 4-103, Sauer 6-170, Mathis 2-51, Joe 1-14.

WEEK 11 GAMES

Hou 20, Den 18	SD 24, Mia 0
KC 33, Bos 10	

NOTES

• The Bills' hopes of a fourth straight division title were just about killed as Johnny Sample returned an interception 41 yards for the clinching score in the fourth quarter.
• The Bills fell behind 10-0 in the first quarter. Jim Turner kicked a 48-yard field goal on the opening series after key passes from Joe Namath to Don Maynard (16) and George Sauer (27). After a Buffalo punt, Namath drove the Jets 73 yards, hitting Sauer with a 47-yard TD pass 8:02 into the game. Sauer reached back for the underthrown pass, then side-stepped Butch Byrd.
• Sauer caught a 38-yard pass early in the second, but Byrd forced him to fumble and Mike Stratton recovered. That threat died when Verlon Biggs blocked Mike Mercer's 48-yard field goal attempt.
• Two roughing-the-kicker penalties aided the Bills on a 74-yard TD march later. After the second penalty, Jack Kemp passed 32 yards to Paul Costa to the 2, from where Keith Lincoln scored.
• Two plays after the kickoff, George Saimes intercepted a Namath pass which led to Mercer's 17-yard field goal and a 10-10 tie at halftime.
• The Jets went ahead 13-10 early in the third. Three Namath passes to Sauer (19), Bill Mathis (31) and Maynard (11) and a pass-interference call on Byrd moved the ball to the 7. The Bills stiffened and Turner kicked a 14-yard field goal.
• After a Ron McDole interception, the Bills drove to the Jets 29, but Elbert Dubenion dropped a potential TD pass and Mercer then missed a 36-yard field goal attempt.

• Sample's interception came when Bobby Burnett had Kemp's pass glance off his hands over the middle. The ball was batted into the air by Jets linebacker Ralph Baker and into Sample's hands. The Jets safety then made a superb dash to the end zone.
• Tom Janik picked off a pass and returned it to the New York 39, but Costa dropped a TD pass with three minutes left to seal the Bills' fate.

QUOTES

• Tommy Janik: "We're a pretty downhearted group. We had a chance to get back in the race and we played our hearts out, but we lost. It's the first time I've been with a club that has had so many injuries. No matter what we do, there seems to be a black cloud hanging over us. We've had enough things happen to us this season to last us for a couple years. I hope."
• Joe Collier: "I thought we gave it away. We had no consistency on offense due to one thing or another, but those dropped passes hurt us more than anything. We were up for the game. They had worked hard all week and were in the proper frame of mind and I told them all that could beat them was their own mistakes. And that's what happened."
• Jets linebacker Ralph Baker: "If it had been a good pass, Burnett would have gotten some pretty good yardage because there was no one in front of him. I was just there to make the tackle. When the ball bounced off his shoulder, I just got a hand on it."

Broncos	7	14	0	0	-	21
Bills	0	7	13	0	-	20

Attendance at War Memorial Stadium - 30,891

Den: Little 13 run (Humphreys kick), 13:13
Buf: Lincoln 3 pass from Kemp (Mercer kick), :57
Den: Denson 14 pass from Tensi (Humphreys kick), 14:13
Den: Denson 2 pass from Tensi (Humphreys kick), 14:49
Buf: Lincoln 19 pass from Kemp (Mercer kick), 3:52
Buf: FG Mercer 43, 7:20
Buf: FG Mercer 21, 13:21

	BUF	DEN
First downs	21	13
Rushing yds	138	40
Passing yds	229	154
Punts-avg	5-37.2	10-41.8
Fumbles-lost	2-2	3-1
Penalties-yds	3-43	3-41

BILLS LEADERS: Rushing - Lincoln 16-72, Carlton 13-51, Kemp 3-15; **Passing** - Kemp 19-37-1 - 249; **Receiving** - Lincoln 6-59, Costa 7-138, Dubenion 3-29, Carlton 2-16, Rutkowski 1-7.

BRONCOS LEADERS: Rushing - Mitchell 1-2, Hickey 6-17, Little 11-25, Tensi 3-(-4); **Passing** - Tensi 14-33-2 - 190; **Receiving** - Denson 7-102, Crabtree 2-21, Beer 4-62, Little 1-5.

WEEK 12 GAMES

Oak 31, Mia 17	SD 17, KC 16
NY 29, Bos 24	

NOTES

• Mike Mercer missed a 24-yard field goal with 16 seconds left, his third miss of the day, to hand Denver the victory in Lou Saban's return to War Memorial Stadium. The loss officially eliminated the Bills from the division title chase and snapped Denver's nine-game losing streak.
• The Bills botched their clock management at the end of the game. Jack Kemp hit Paul Costa with a pass to the 17 on the right sideline and it appeared Costa got out of bounds with 32 seconds left. However, the side judge ruled he was still in, so the clock wound down to 19 seconds before Kemp called his final timeout. That left Mercer at an angle for the winning kick. Kemp should have run a play to the middle, then called his final timeout.
• The game was tied 7-7, late in the first half when the Bills collapsed. Kemp's pass to Elbert Dubenion was intercepted by Frank Richter and returned six yards to the Bills 14. On the next play, Steve Tensi hit Al Denson for the score with 47 seconds left. The ensuing kickoff was botched by the Bills and Henry Sorell recovered for Denver at the 27. Tensi completed three passes in a row, the last to Denson for the TD with 11 seconds left.
• Butch Byrd intercepted Tensi and Buffalo drew to within 21-14, 3:52 into the third when Kemp hit Costa for 18 yards on a third down, then flipped a screen to Keith Lincoln who scored from 19 yards out.
• On their next series, Lincoln's 28-yard run, the Bills longest of the season to date, set up Mercer's 43-yard field goal. On the next possession, a 35-yard reception by Costa led to Buffalo's final points. In the fourth, Mercer was short on a 44-yard attempt.
• The Bills' last-ditch drive was set up when John Tracey recovered Bo Hickey's fumble at the Bills 47.

Lincoln kept it alive with a fourth-down conversion and Kemp hit Costa for 12 to the 26, where the Bills called their second timeout. Wray Carlton gained three and Costa six to the 17 before Mercer's miss.
• Syracuse grad Floyd Little's TD in the first quarter was his first as a pro.

QUOTES

• Joe Collier: "I shouldn't have had Jack passing in that area (deep in Bills territory late in the first half). Nobody to blame but myself, I gave them 14 points. We should have gone off the field tied at 7-7. (On the last field goal): "If the clock had been stopped, we could have run a play for better position for the kick. As it was, we had time only for Mercer's kick from the angle. However, we shouldn't have been in that predicament late in the game. We should have had the advantage by then."
• Broncos coach Lou Saban: "Believe me, winning anywhere has satisfaction for me at this stage of the game. I was very happy the way we quickly capitalized on Richter's interception. When breaks come your way and you take advantage of them, you're playing good ball. We lost a few games by missing field goals like they did today."

STANDINGS: TWELFTH WEEK

EAST	W	L	T	WEST	W	L	T
New York	7	2	1	Oakland	8	1	0
Houston	5	3	1	San Diego	7	1	1
Boston	3	7	1	Kan. City	6	4	0
Buffalo	3	7	0	Denver	2	9	0
Miami	1	8	0				

NOTES

• Joe Collier hung the goat's tag on Jack Kemp. Dick Westmoreland's third interception of the day with 2:23 left enabled Miami to drive to the winning TD. Bob Griese's pass to Howard Twilley with 1:01 left won it.

• The victory snapped Miami's eight-game losing streak.

• Defensive assistant Richie McCabe shattered a glass door in the press box with his foot when Twilley caught the winning pass.

• Ron McDole blocked a Booth Lusteg field goal on Miami's first possession. But the Dolphins got the ball right back on Bob Petrella's interception, which led to Stan Mitchell's TD.

• Frank Jackson's 57-yard run on a reverse set up Lusteg's field goal and a 10-0 Miami lead.

• The Bills then got their act together and took a 14-10 halftime lead. Three plays after the kickoff, Kemp hit rookie Monte Ledbetter with a 60-yard TD pass. On their next possession, they drove 80 yards to Kemp's one-yard plunge.

• Tommy Janik's interception at the Bills 4 killed a Miami drive in the third.

• After a long drive late in the third, holder Tom Flores faked a field goal attempt, but his 15-yard pass to John Tracey was two yards shy of a first down.

• Tracey then intercepted Griese and the Bills drove to what appeared to be the clinching score. But Kemp's 12-yard TD pass to Wray Carlton was nullified when Carlton was called for offensive interference. Three plays later, Westmoreland intercepted Kemp in the end zone.

• Miami drove to the 10, but George Saimes broke up a fourth-down pass with 4:36 left and the Bills seemed safe. But on second-and-nine, Westmoreland struck again, picking off a bomb intended for Ledbetter at the 50 and returning it to the Bills 22.

• Tom Sestak sacked Griese at the 31, but on third down Griese found Twilley for the winner.

• Ralph Wilson said after the game that Joe Collier would remain as coach in 1968.

QUOTES

• Jack Kemp on his last interception: "We had a long way to go (in time). We needed a first down and I thought we could get it with a pass. Did I see something? Yes, they were blitzing." Kemp said he was trying to throw the ball away when he realized the play wouldn't work, "but I didn't throw that one far enough."

• Joe Collier: "You tell me why he threw it and we'll both know. It was a mistake in judgement. He's human, but it cost us the ballgame. It was the same as last week against Denver. The defense played a good game and didn't deserve to be put under pressure like they were at the end of the game."

• Ralph Wilson: "Joe Collier will be the coach of the Buffalo Bills next year with whatever staff he wants. I think in the face of all the injuries we had, he and his staff have done a good job."

Bills	0	14	0	0	-	14
Dolphins	7	3	0	7	-	17

Attendance at the Orange Bowl - 27,050

Mia: Mitchell 1 run (Lusteg kick), 11:46
Mia: FG Lusteg 17, 4:02
Buf: Ledbetter 60 pass from Kemp (Mercer kick), 5:21
Buf: Kemp 1 run (Mercer kick), 14:26
Mia: Twilley 31 pass from Griese (Lusteg kick), 13:59

	BUF	MIA
First downs	19	18
Rushing yds	106	116
Passing yds	245	202
Punts-avg	3-37.3	3-36.0
Fumbles-lost	0-0	1-0
Penalties-yds	5-65	2-27

BILLS LEADERS: Rushing - Lincoln 14-54, Carlton 14-43, Kemp 2-9; **Passing** - Kemp 16-30-4 - 252, Flores 1-1-0 - 15; **Receiving** - Lincoln 1-23, Costa 6-92, Dubenion 2-16, Carlton 2-17, Masters 3-37, Ledbetter 2-67, Tracey 1-15.

DOLPHINS LEADERS: Rushing - Haynes 4-16, Auer 4-18, Mitchell 9-19, Jackson 1-48, Harper 4-16, Griese 1-0, Clancy 1-(-1); **Passing** - Griese 17-33-3 - 222; **Receiving** - Twilley 5-92, Clancy 2-34, Auer 2-33, Mitchell 3-25, Price 2-18, Haynes 2-13, Moreau 1-7.

WEEK 13 GAMES

Oak 44, KC 22   SD 24, Den 20
Hou 27, Bos 6

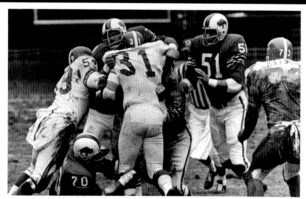

NOTES

• Buffalo dropped its fourth in a row and ensured its worst record in its AFL history.

• In the first, the Bills offset two Jan Stenerud field goals with Jack Kemp's 18-yard TD pass to Keith Lincoln. Kemp was four-for-four on the 57-yard drive.

• Jim Lynch's interception and return to the Bills 14 was washed out when Tommy Janik intercepted Len Dawson at the 1 and went 99 yards for an apparent TD. However, he was ruled out of bounds at the Bills 47. The Bills drove to the 30 when Kemp's TD pass to Monte Ledbetter was dropped, so Mike Mercer kicked a 35-yard field goal. Mercer added a 40-yarder with 15 seconds left in the half.

• The Chiefs tied it early in the third. Paul Costa fumbled at midfield and Bud Abell returned it 19 yards to the Bills 31. Dawson hit Otis Taylor with a third-down pass to the 5 before Gene Thomas scored from the 2.

• The Chiefs' go-ahead TD typified the Bills season. The drive began with Dawson getting sacked and fumbling, but ex-Bill Willie Frazier recovered at the KC 20. On third-and-14, Dawson hit Mike Garrett for 19 yards.

Eight plays later, he hit Otis Taylor for the winning score. On the play, Janik had excellent coverage, but the ball was underthrown and Taylor made a good adjustment. Janik couldn't control his body and Taylor got past him and went into the end zone.

• Kemp then threw a bomb to Ed Rutkowski, but Fletcher Smith intercepted and returned it to the Bills 46. Stenerud then tacked on his 20-yard field goal.

QUOTES

• Chiefs receiver Otis Taylor: "Dawson underthrew the pass. Janik had me played perfectly, but I came back for the ball and got in front of him."

• Chiefs coach Hank Stram: "Otis just made a great play. Janik was right with him. We have quite a bit of respect for Janik."

• Joe Collier: "We had the usual dropped passes, penalties, interceptions, etcetera. It was typical of our season. We did everything well, to a point, and then we didn't make the plays we needed to come out on top."

• Keith Lincoln: "It probably was my worst day in football. Seven carries for seven yards."

Bills	7	6	0	0	-	13
Chiefs	6	0	7	10	-	23

Attendance at Municipal Stadium - 41,948

KC: FG Stenerud 17, 6:52
Buf: Lincoln 18 pass from Kemp (Mercer kick), 13:56
KC: FG Stenerud 25, 14:55
Buf: FG Mercer 35, 13:09
Buf: FG Mercer 40, 14:45
KC: G. Thomas 3 run (Stenerud kick), 7:07
KC: Taylor 34 pass from Dawson (Stenerud kick), 2:00
KC: FG Stenerud 20, 9:06

	BUF	KC
First downs	8	18
Rushing yds	31	129
Passing yds	211	128
Punts-avg	6-49.0	6-39.3
Fumbles-lost	1-1	5-0
Penalties-yds	6-50	2-10

BILLS LEADERS: Rushing - Lincoln 7-7, Carlton 9-24; **Passing** - Kemp 16-37-3 - 223; **Receiving** - Lincoln 4-78, Costa 3-46, Carlton 2-29, Masters 3-27, Ledbetter 4-43.

CHIEFS LEADERS: Rushing - Garrett 15-46, Thomas 9-45, Dawson 3-17, Coan 4-6, McClinton 4-11, Taylor 1-13, Lee 1-(-3), Pitts 1-(-6); **Passing** - Dawson 15-29-1 - 159; **Receiving** - Taylor 6-86, Arbanas 4-42, Garrett 2-20, McClinton 1-11.

WEEK 14 GAMES

Oak 41, SD 21   Hou 17, Mia 14
Den 33, NY 24

STANDINGS: FOURTEENTH WEEK

EAST	W	L	T	WEST	W	L	T
New York	7	3	1	Oakland	10	1	0
Houston	7	3	1	San Diego	8	2	1
Boston	3	8	1	Kan. City	7	5	0
Buffalo	3	9	0	Denver	3	10	0
Miami	2	9	0				

Bills	14	14	10	6	-	44
Patriots	0	7	2	7	-	16

Attendance at Fenway Park - 20,627

Buf: Lincoln 8 pass from Kemp (Mercer kick), 3:59
Buf: Carlton 5 run (Mercer kick), 13:13
Buf: Kemp 3 run (Mercer kick), 4:03
Buf: Janik 38 interception return (Mercer kick), 6:27
Bos: Trull 7 run (Cappelletti kick), 12:24
Bos: Safety, Hunt tackled Kemp in end zone, 1:48
Buf: Schottenheimer 45 interception return (Mercer kick), 3:02
Buf: FG Mercer 12, 14:16
Buf: FG Mercer 11, 1:31
Buf: FG Mercer 23, 6:18
Bos: Leo 25 pass from Parilli (Cappelletti kick), 14:55

	BUF	BOS
First downs	17	9
Rushing yds	133	53
Passing yds	119	97
Punts-avg	2-44.0	5-39.6
Fumbles-lost	0-0	2-1
Penalties-yds	6-50	6-50

BILLS LEADERS: Rushing - Lincoln 8-12, Carlton 13-57, Bivins 13-54, Kemp 2-11, Donaldson 3-(-1); **Passing** - Kemp 9-16-1 - 122, Flores 1-7-1 - 20; **Receiving** - Lincoln 3-51, Costa 1-17, Carlton 1-14, Masters 3-35, Donaldson 1-20, Ledbetter 1-5.

PATRIOTS LEADERS: Rushing - Nance 13-35, Trull 5-11, Leo 1-7; **Passing** - Parilli 2-9-3 - 67, Trull 5-20-3 - 57; **Receiving** - Whalen 2-20, Cappadona 1-42, Leo 1-25, Nance 1-13, Garron 1-11, Colclough 1-13.

NOTES

• The Bills enjoyed their biggest offensive scoring output of the season against a team they had scored 13 points on in their previous three meetings.
• Linebacker John Tracey's streak of 100 straight starts ended when he missed the game due to a pulled leg muscle. Tracey's streak had begun on Nov. 18, 1962, the same day Jack Kemp made his Buffalo debut against the Oakland Raiders. Marty Schottenheimer started for Tracey.
• Tommy Janik had three of Buffalo's six interceptions. The six picks resulted in 173 return yards.
• Schottenheimer intercepted Don Trull and returned it 33 yards to the 8 to set up Kemp's TD pass to Keith Lincoln.
• Jim Dunaway recovered a Trull fumble on the next series and Kemp passed 32 yards to Lincoln, setting up Wray Carlton's TD run and a 14-0 lead.
• It became 21-0 when Kemp hit four of five passes for 50 yards, then capped a 60-yard drive with a three-yard TD run. Moments later, Janik picked off Trull and raced 38 yards for a score.
• Trull scored on a short run late in the half, then Kemp was tackled for a safety by Jim Hunt early in the third, but Schottenheimer stole their momentum when he intercepted a Trull pass and raced 45 yards for his first pro TD.
• Mike Mercer kicked three field goals before Babe

WEEK 15 GAMES	
Oak 19, Hou 7	KC 21, NY 7
Mia 41, SD 24	

Parilli hit Bobby Leo for Boston's final score with five seconds left to play in the game.

QUOTES

• Tommy Janik: "How do I explain our whipping Boston and looking so good after such a disappointing season? I think everyone got tired of losing and decided to just go out there and play tough football. Just throw caution to the wind. This time the breaks went with us."
• Joe Collier: "Janik is an offensive player on defense. He breaks up ballgames. He's not a crushing tackler, but he is so quick and gets into a play so fast that the runner or pass receiver doesn't have a chance to make his move." (On stopping Jim Nance): "Getting a quick lead as we did was part of the answer. It forced Boston to throw the ball more and that's as effective a way as you'll find to stop Nance."

Bills	10	0	3	8	-	21
Raiders	7	7	7	7	-	28

Attendance at Oakland-Alameda County Stadium - 30,738

Buf: FG Mercer 30, 5:32
Buf: Sestak fumble recovery in end zone (Mercer kick), 6:49
Oak: Cannon 23 pass from Lamonica (Blanda kick), 10:30
Oak: Conners 21 fumble return (Blanda kick), 14:53
Buf: FG Mercer 39, 8:07
Oak: Oats 11 fumble return (Blanda kick), 13:14
Buf: Costa 63 pass from Kemp (Kemp run), 4:29
Oak: Dixon 1 run (Blanda kick), 12:47

	BUF	OAK
First downs	12	14
Rushing yds	92	173
Passing yds	118	99
Punts-avg	9-38.1	6-43.0
Fumbles-lost	3-1	4-1
Penalties-yds	6-78	4-20

BILLS LEADERS: Rushing - Lincoln 9-11, Carlton 19-79, Kemp 3-2; **Passing** - Kemp 9-33-2 - 189; **Receiving** - Lincoln 1-10, Costa 6-163, Masters 1-12, Ledbetter 1-4.

RAIDERS LEADERS: Rushing - Dixon 7-31, Banaszak 12-74, Lamonica 1-23, Hagberg 6-24, Todd 6-21; **Passing** - Lamonica 5-12-1 - 51, Blanda 3-13-2 - 75; **Receiving** - Biletnikoff 4-85, Cannon 2-25, Banaszak 1-14, Dixon 1-2.

NOTES

• The season ended in a typical fashion of the way the Bills played in 1967. There was some good defense, an erratic offensive showing, some bonehead plays that ruined any momentum they may have built up and an unhappy ending for the 10th time in 14 games.
• Oakland set an AFL record with its 13th victory, breaking the mark of 12 shared by the 1964 Bills and 1961 San Diego Chargers.
• The Bills blew a scoring chance after Marty Schottenheimer blocked a Mike Eischeid punt and gave the Bills the ball at Oakland's 23. Buffalo wound up punting from its own territory.
• Jack Kemp suffered a 31-yard sack that forced a Paul Maguire punt which traveled only four yards into a stiff breeze. The Raiders failed to take advantage, though.
• The Bills jumped to a 10-0 first-quarter lead as Mike Mercer kicked a field goal to cap the opening series. Then Jim Dunaway sacked Daryle Lamonica forcing a fumble that Tom Sestak fell on in the end zone.
• Oakland pulled to within 10-7 when Lamonica hit Billy Cannon with a 23-yard TD pass. On the play before, Hewritt Dixon appeared to be stopped for a two-yard loss, but the officials never blew the whistle, the Bills let up, and Dixon ran for 20 yards. The Bills bench argued and was hit with a 15-yard unsportsmanlike penalty which moved the ball to the 23.
• While the Bills were trying to run out the clock with

seven seconds left in the first half, Dan Conners stole the ball from Wray Carlton and ran 21 yards for a touchdown.
• After Mercer kicked a field goal to make it 14-13, late in the third, Ben Davidson nailed Kemp and forced him to fumble. Carlton Oats picked it up and ran 11 yards for a score.
• The Bills tied the game with 10:31 left as Kemp uncorked Buffalo's longest TD pass of the season, a 62-yard strike to Paul Costa. Kemp then followed Billy Shaw's block for the tying two pointer.
• However, the Raiders won it when Dixon plunged in from the 1 with 2:13 left. The TD was set up when Booker Edgerson was called for pass interference in the end zone against Fred Biletnikoff.

QUOTES

• Joe Collier: "We played a pretty good game physically. I can't say the same for the mental part. We should have won the football game." (On the upcoming AFL title game): "It's not for me to decide whether New York or Houston would have been the tougher opponent (for Oakland). I just wish we were playing. Oakland's outstanding defensively and will be a good representative if it gets to the Super Bowl."

WEEK 16 GAMES	
Hou 24, SD 17	Oak 38, NY 29
KC 38, Den 24	Mia 41, Bos 32
Buffalo had a bye week.	

WEEK 17 GAMES	
Hou 41, Mia 10	NY 42, SD 31

STANDINGS: SEVENTEENTH WEEK

EAST	W	L	T	WEST	W	L	T
Houston	9	4	1	Oakland	13	1	0
New York	8	5	1	Kan. City	9	5	0
Buffalo	4	10	0	San Diego	8	5	1
Miami	4	10	0	Denver	3	11	0
Boston	3	10	1				

At A Glance
1968

Jan. 16 – The Cincinnati Bengals selected five players from each team except Miami in the stock draft. The first player they picked was former University of Buffalo quarterback John Stofa of Miami. The Bills lost Bobby Burnett, Gary Bugenhagen, Charley King, Bob Schmidt and Rich Zecher.

Jan. 30 – The Bills chose wide receiver Haven Moses of San Diego State with their No. 1 draft pick. The Minnesota Vikings chose USC tackle Ron Yary No. 1 overall while Heisman Trophy winner Gary Beban of UCLA wasn't chosen until the second round by the Rams. The Bills also selected receiver Richard Trapp (third round), linebacker Edgar Chandler (fourth), running backs Ben Gregory (fifth), Max Anderson (fifth) and Gary McDermott (ninth) and quarterback Dan Darragh (13th).

Feb. 7 – Tony Sardisco was hired to coach the defensive line. It was the first time the Bills had five full-time assistant coaches since Herman Ball left before the 1964 season.

Feb. 27 – The Erie County legislature approved by an 18-1 vote a resolution to build a major league sports stadium. Ralph Wilson said he was opposed to the Crossroads site, and also indicated the stadium would have to have at least 70,000 seats.

March 20 – Jack Kemp talked of his recent visit to Vietnam with a group of other players including Kansas City's Bobby Bell, Pittsburgh's Andy Russell, San Francisco's John David Crow and Minnesota's Bill Brown. The group was trapped in Saigon for six days as air traffic came to a halt when the Tet offensive began. Eventually, they were able to visit the Demilitarized Zone and showed football films and answered questions from the GIs. They also flew to Thailand and spent two weeks visiting troops. "We all went over there a little naive," Kemp said. "We thought we were going to be able to shop, take pictures, stroll along the street and so on. Our motives are right for being there, I think. It was the greatest thrill of my life. I would go back tomorrow."

April 3 – Ralph Wilson on the rising costs of owning a pro team: "Considering the financial problems we are facing with players today, a guy would have to be nuts to buy a franchise at these inflated prices. Your profit prospects are growing dimmer. You have to come into this thing for fun or for the laughable thing called prestige. Owning a sports franchise isn't as much fun as it used to be."

April 18 – Oklahoma tackle Bob Kalsu, the Bills eighth-round draft choice, signed his contract.

May 10 – An eight-member economic development committee recommended that the full 20-member Erie County legislature authorize a bond issue of up to $50 million to build a domed stadium at the Crossroads site. Ralph Wilson reiterated his feeling that the Crossroads site would be a mistake and that a suburban area would be better suited.

May 15 – Clubs from both leagues voted to experiment running or passing for a one-point conversion during the scheduled 23 inter-league preseason games, thus eliminating the conversion kick.

May 16 – The $50 million stadium bond issue was approved by a vote of 19-1.

May 20 – Jets president Sonny Werblin was bought out for $1.6 million by four partners, including Leon Hess.

June 1 – Jack Kemp, head of the AFL Players' Association, released the results of a survey he conducted on player salaries. The average salary for all AFL quarterbacks, starters and reserves, was $25,052. About 350 of the 400 players Kemp polled, answered. The Bills' average salary was $18,567.

July 3 – The Bills signed a contract with Niagara University to move its training camp base there from the Camelot-Voyager in Blasdell, where they had been for five years.

July 10 – While the NFL players were on strike, the AFL and the AFL Players' Association agreed to a two-year contract that increased the pension plan as well as pay for players during preseason games. Jack Kemp called it "a tremendous step forward. It's a historic and very progressive agreement."

July 22 – The Bills opened their first training camp at Niagara University.

Aug. 2 – Holdout linebacker Marty Schottenheimer signed a new contract and joined the team at camp. "After looking around and talking to other clubs, I made the choice I felt was best for Marty Schottenheimer in returning to Buffalo."

Aug. 5 – The Bills beat an NFL opponent for the first time in their 13-9 preseason-opening victory over the Detroit Lions in front of 40,412 soggy fans at War Memorial. Keith Lincoln suffered cracked ribs on the first series and was ruled out for the rest of the preseason.

Aug. 11 – Guard Joe O'Donnell was lost for the year with a knee injury as the Bills tied Miami, 28-28, at Rochester's Aquinas Stadium. In his first pro game, rookie Larry Csonka of Syracuse gained 31 yards for the Dolphins.

Aug. 17 – The Bills played badly, but still beat the expansion Bengals, 10-6, in their first visit to Cincinnati.

Aug. 23 – Joe Collier was furious after Houston whipped the Bills, 37-7, in Tulsa, Okla.

Aug. 26 – After the embarrassing loss to Houston, Collier put the team through a rugged 40-play scrimmage and disaster struck as quarterback Jack Kemp suffered a knee injury and was ruled out for the season. Defensive end Ron McDole fell on Kemp's right knee.

Aug. 27 – After getting cut by San Diego, Tom Day returned to the Bills. Also, quarterback Kay Stephenson was acquired in a trade with San Diego for a draft choice. Joe Collier announced that rookie Dan Darragh would be the team's No. 1 quarterback.

Aug. 30 – The Bills lost their preseason finale to the Cleveland Browns, 22-12, as Dan Darragh threw for 185 yards.

Sept. 2 – The team's all-time leading rusher, Wray Carlton, was cut along with Ed Rutkowski. Rutkowski was re-signed a few days later.

Sept. 8 – The Bills started six rookies and lost to Boston, 16-7, in the season opener at War Memorial Stadium.

Sept. 15 – Oakland dealt the Bills their worst loss in team history, 48-6, as George Atkinson set an AFL record with 205 yards on five punt returns. After the game, Joe Collier was fired as head coach and replaced by personnel director Harvey Johnson.

Sept. 16 – Offensive line coach Jerry Smith, who

had hoped to be promoted to head coach, resigned. Johnny Mazur, Richie McCabe and Tony Sardisco elected to remain with Johnson.

Sept. 17 – Johnson hired Marvin Bass to coach the offensive line and Bob Celeri to coach the receivers, assisting Johnny Mazur.

Sept. 18 – The Bills were put through a spirited workout which was influenced heavily by Bass. "I felt like I was a freshman at Arkansas," said veteran offensive lineman Dick Cunningham.

Sept. 22 – The Bills suffered the indignity of losing to the first-year Cincinnati Bengals, 34-23, at Nippert Stadium. Fortunately for the Bills, Lou Saban's Denver Broncos were the first team to lose to Cincinnati the week before.

Sept 24 – An article written by San Francisco Chronicle reporter Glenn Dickey was reprinted in The Buffalo Evening News. Dickey wrote that Joe Collier should be smiling because he was fired by the Bills, thus enabling him to get out of Buffalo. In calling Buffalo the armpit of the East, Dickey wondered why the title wasn't extended to include the whole country. "It's a town that seems to take pride in its ugliness. Women still wear long skirts and men are wearing wide-lapel jackets. People here take their football seriously. After all, what else is there?" Dickey also said that a Buffalo writer told him, "Putting the Bills in a new stadium would be like putting Tiny Tim in the Met."

Sept. 29 – The Bills shocked the Jets, 37-35, as Tom Janik, Butch Byrd and Booker Edgerson all returned interceptions for touchdowns. Also, in his first game with the Bills, kicker Bruce Alford made three field goals and four extra points.

Oct. 5 – Jan Stenerud kicked four field goals to lead the Chiefs past the Bills, 18-7.

Oct. 12 – Dan Darragh passed three yards to Gary

Haven Moses was Buffalo's first-round draft choice in 1968 and he played less than five years with the Bills before being traded to Denver in 1972.

McDermott with 18 seconds left, then Ed Rutkowski hit McDermott for the two-point conversion to give the Bills a 14-14 tie with Miami.

Oct. 16 – Elbert Dubenion, an original member of the Bills, retired. Dubenion had started only the Boston and Cincinnati games and had no receptions in his ninth season with the team. Harvey Johnson announced that Dubenion was hired as a full-time scout for the team. He ended his career owning eight Bills records and the AFL record for highest season average per catch (27.1 in 1964).

Oct. 20 – Nick Buoniconti intercepted three Dan Darragh passes as the Patriots beat the Bills, 23-6.

Oct. 28 – Buffalo's offense was futile, tying the all-time team record for fewest yards gained (113) in a 30-7 loss to the Oilers. The mark was set in Buffalo's first AFL game, Sept. 11, 1960, against the New York Titans.

Oct. 29 – Realizing his team may be doomed for the worst record in pro football, Harvey Johnson began evaluating quarterback talent in the draft. He rated Kansas' Bobby Douglass as the best of the collegiate lot, ahead of Notre Dame's Terry Hanratty. However, O.J. Simpson of USC, it was admitted, was the prize every pro team coveted.

Oct. 30 – Running back Keith Lincoln, who had played sparingly in four games, was waived and reclaimed by the San Diego Chargers, his original team.

Nov. 3 – New York's Jim Turner set an AFL record by attempting eight field goals. He tied the league mark by making six in a 25-21 Jets victory over the Bills at Shea Stadium.

Nov. 10 – Kay Stephenson suffered a separated shoulder and the Bills blew a 17-0 lead in losing to Miami, 21-17.

Nov. 11 – Harvey Johnson wanted to ask com-

missioner Pete Rozelle for special permission to activate quarterback Jack Kemp, who was made ineligible for the season when he was injured in the preseason. However, Ralph Wilson squelched the idea, knowing he wouldn't get the needed approval of the other owners. "I seriously doubt Al Davis would okay it. His team's in the race. We have to play them Thanksgiving Day and heck, Jack just might come in and beat them. Besides, I'm not sure we should go asking other teams to do us a favor."

Nov. 12 – San Diego coach Sid Gillman suggested that if stadiums began installing artificial turf, injuries would decrease. "From what I understand, injuries have been reduced where the astroturf has been installed."

Nov. 13 – Quarterback Ben Russell was granted a 17-day military leave from the Air Force to rejoin the Bills and help with the quarterback shortage. He had spent the entire 1967 season on the taxi squad and knew most of the system and personnel.

Nov. 17 – In horrible, muddy conditions at War Memorial, San Diego topped the Bills, 21-6. And while the Oakland Raiders were rallying in the final minute to beat the Jets, 43-32, NBC-TV switched from the game at 7 p.m. EST to the movie *Heidi* in one of the great television gaffes.

Nov. 18 – Ralph Wilson said the Bills would be playing in Buffalo in 1969 if he received concrete evidence that a new stadium would be in the planning stages by then.

Nov. 24 – A superb rally was killed in heartbreaking fashion as the Broncos beat the Bills, 34-32, in snowy Denver. Broncos QB Marlin Briscoe threw for 335 yards and four TDs and hit Floyd Little for a 59-yard gain that set up Bobby Howfield's 12-yard field goal with seven seconds left.

Nov. 28 – The Bills put up quite a fight on Thanksgiving Day, but still lost to the powerful Raiders, 13-10. Harvey Johnson said after the game: "They're talking about the Bills being in contention with the Philadelphia Eagles for O.J. Simpson. I would have traded Simpson or anyone else for a victory over the Oakland Raiders. Our players outhit, outhustled and outplayed the Raiders on offense and defense. The only thing the Raiders did was outluck us."

Nov. 30 – While on the west coast, the Bills brass scouted O.J. Simpson first-hand as USC played host to Notre Dame. The Irish held O.J. in check, but that didn't sour the Bills: "He had a bad day," Harvey Johnson said. "Notre Dame did a good job defensing him. But there's no doubt he's a great runner. I've seen him before when he's had good days and I know his ability. Besides, the way our luck is going this season, we'll probably tie with Philadelphia, then lose O.J. on the coin flip."

Dec. 7 – The Bills closed their worst season by losing for the eighth straight time, 35-6, in Houston's Astrodome.

Dec. 8 – The Philadelphia Eagles beat the New Orleans Saints, 12-0, thus assuring the Bills of the worst record in both pro football leagues. That gave the Bills the first choice in the draft and the opportunity to pick O.J. Simpson.

Dec. 18 – Defensive end Ron McDole was named the team's MVP at the annual Third Down Award presentations. McDole was also the lone Bill named to the AFL all-star team.

Dec. 20 – General manager Bob Lustig denied a published report that the Bills were interested in hiring fired Los Angeles Rams coach George Allen to be their coach and general manager.

Dec. 22 – In the first West Division playoff ever, Oakland routed Kansas City, 41-6, to earn a spot in the AFL Championship Game against the New York Jets.

Dec. 24 – Harvey Johnson made it official that he did not want to return as the Bills head coach but rather in the personnel department. "I feel that I am a good personnel man. I do not think I am that good a coach," he said.

Dec. 27 – The George Allen to Buffalo rumor heated up as Ralph Wilson said "He is one of the few we're considering."

Dec. 29 – The New York Jets won their first AFL Championship, beating the Raiders, 27-23. Joe Namath passed for 266 yards and three TDs including the game-winner to Don Maynard in the fourth quarter after the Raiders had rallied to go ahead, 23-20. The Jets pocketed $7,007.91 each for winning. Weeb Ewbank became the first coach to win titles in both leagues. Later, the Baltimore Colts routed the Cleveland Browns, 34-0, to win the NFL championship.

Jan. 12, 1969 – Joe Namath, backing up his bold prediction of victory earlier in the week, led the Jets to a stunning 16-7 victory over the Colts in Super Bowl III at Miami's Orange Bowl. It was the first victory for the AFL in the world championship game, which was recognized as the Super Bowl for the first time by the NFL. Namath threw for 206 yards, Matt Snell rushed for 121 and Jim Turner kicked three field goals for New York.

Jan. 19, 1969 – Kansas City's Len Dawson engineered a 25-point fourth quarter and the West beat the East, 38-25, in the AFL All-Star Game at the Gator Bowl in Jacksonville, Fla.

BY THE NUMBERS - 1968

TEAM STATISTICS	BILLS	OPP
First downs	159	210
Rushing	71	85
Passing	72	103
Penalty	16	22
Total yards	2,870	4,225
Avg. game	205.0	301.8
Plays	844	876
Avg. play	3.4	4.8
Net rushing yds	1,527	2,021
Avg. game	109.1	144.4
Avg. play	3.8	4.0
Net passing yds	1,343	2,204
Comp/att	168/405	143/340
Sacks/lost	39-371	31-273
Interceptions	28	22
Percentage	41.5	42.1
Punts/avg	100-41.8	75-39.7
Fumbles/lost	23-14	24-13
Penalties/yds	67-687	66-540
Touchdowns	22	41
Extra points	19-19	40-41
Field goals	14-28	27-48
Two-point conv.	2-3	0-0
Safeties	1	0
Kick ret./avg	69-22.3	49-21.7
Punt ret./avg	44-6.8	45-11.6

RUSHING	ATT	YDS	AVG	TD
Anderson	147	525	3.6	2
Gregory	52	283	5.4	1
Cappadona	73	272	3.7	1
McDermott	47	102	2.2	3
Rutkowski	20	96	4.8	1
Lincoln	26	84	3.2	0
Masters	6	70	11.7	0
Brown	3	39	13.0	0
Stephenson	4	30	7.5	0
Costa	2	11	5.5	0
Darragh	13	11	0.8	0
Maguire	1	6	6.0	0
Patrick	1	2	2.0	0
Moses	5	-4	-0.8	0
TOTALS	**400**	**1527**	**3.8**	**8**

PASSING	COMP	ATT	INT	YDS	TD	COMP%
Darragh	92	215	14	917	3	42.8
Rutkowski	41	100	6	380	0	41.0
Stephenson	29	79	7	364	4	36.7
Flores	3	5	1	15	0	60.0
McDermott	2	3	0	35	0	66.6
Russell	1	2	0	3	0	50.0
Anderson	0	1	0	0	0	00.0
TOTALS	**168**	**405**	**28**	**1714**	**7**	**41.5**

KICKING	FG/ATT	PAT/ATT	PTS
Alford	14-24	15-15	57
Mercer	0-4	4-4	4
TOTALS	**14-28**	**19-19**	**61**

PUNTING	NO	AVG
Maguire	100	41.8

RECEIVING	CAT	YDS	AVG	TD
Moses	42	633	15.1	2
Trapp	24	235	9.8	0
Anderson	22	140	6.4	0
McDermott	20	115	5.8	1
Cappadona	18	92	5.1	2
Costa	15	172	11.5	1
Masters	8	101	12.6	0
Crockett	6	76	12.7	0
Gregory	5	21	4.2	0
Ledbetter	4	94	23.5	1
Rutkowski	1	27	27.0	0
Patrick	1	5	5.0	0
Lincoln	1	3	3.0	0
Bemiller	1	0	0.0	0
TOTALS	**168**	**1714**	**10.2**	**7**

LEADERS

Kick returns: Anderson 39-971 yds, 24.9 avg, 1 TD
Brown 12-274, 22.8, 0 TD

Punt returns: Clarke 29-241, 8.3, 1 TD
Trapp 5-26, 5.2, 0 TD

Interceptions: Byrd 6-76, 12.7, 1 TD
Edgerson 4-100, 25.0, 2 TD

Non-kick scoring: McDermott 4 TDs, 1 2-pt conv., 26 pts
Cappadona 3 TDs, 1 2-pt conv., 20 pts

Kay Stephenson played briefly for the Bills in 1968, then returned to Buffalo as an assistant coach in 1978 and eventually served as head coach during 1983 and 1984.

NOTES

• Despite attaining just nine first downs, the Patriots topped the Bills as rookie quarterback Dan Darragh threw two interceptions and was confused on some play calls.

• The Bills started six rookies, including Darragh, first-round draft choice Haven Moses and guard Bob Kalsu.

• The Patriots were without Jim Nance, out with an ankle injury, but R.C. Gamble had a big game.

• The Bills scored on their opening possession. Ben Gregory broke a 35-yard run and Darragh hit Moses with a 21-yard pass to the Boston 12. After reaching the 1, an illegal motion penalty moved them back to the 6, from where Paul Costa scored on a reverse.

• Trailing 7-3 at halftime, the Patriots scored 10 in the third to take control. Willie Porter returned the second-half kickoff 45 yards to the Buffalo 45 and on the first play, Gamble broke free for a 45-yard TD.

• Mike Mercer, who made his final seven field goals in 1967, missed his first attempt in the second quarter, thus failing to set an AFL record for most consecutive field goals made. He also missed in the third. A Bills drive also was ruined when Leroy Mitchell intercepted a pass intended for Moses in the end zone.

• Richard Trapp fumbled a punt, Boston recovered at the Bills 28 and Gino Cappelletti kicked a 28-yard field goal. An interception of Darragh by Daryl Johnson resulted in Cappelletti's final field goal.

QUOTES

• Joe Collier on the rookies who started: "They're not rookies anymore. They're professional football players and they have to play. To hell with this rookie business. (Overall) It was just a poor performance. Some of the rookies made mistakes and some of the veterans didn't perform. It was a case of poor execution by all concerned. It looked like our outside receivers did well, but there will be no credits until we review the film."

• Dan Darragh: "I can think of a better way to start the season. It looked to me as though the Patriots changed their defensive philosophy after we scored on the first series. I was forced out of the pocket a lot. Many times I would see a receiver open but I was running the other way. Mistakes? Yes, I made plenty. The worst one was when I tossed that sideline pass for Moses in the end zone and it was intercepted. That was the worst call of the game."

• Haven Moses: "The one play that probably hurt us the most was the interception Mitchell made in the end zone. I had the wide side of the field and I felt I could beat him, so I suggested we try it. I'm afraid I just wasn't thinking. At San Diego State, we could go back to the huddle and suggest a play. Inexperience, at least on my part, hurt us so much. We made a lot of mental mistakes which, as games go by, we'll remember not to repeat. I tried to adapt myself before the game. I tried to think of it as just another game, but when we started to dress, my stomach got a few butterflies. When we started the game, though, I didn't see anything I didn't expect."

• Gary McDermott: "We're not dead yet. We've got to buckle down and work hard, that's all."

Patriots	0	3 10	3 -	16
Bills	7	0 0	0 -	7

Attendance at War Memorial Stadium - 38,865

Buf: Costa 6 run (Mercer kick), 6:47
Bos: FG Cappelletti 10, 1:30
Bos: Gamble 45 run (Cappelletti kick), :29
Bos: FG Cappelletti 28, 9:01
Bos: FG Cappellettli 30, 10:13

	BUF	BOS
First downs	11	9
Rushing yds	76	150
Passing yds	115	45
Punts-avg	6-46.8	8-42.7
Fumbles-lost	3-2	3-2
Penalties-yds	6-45	5-26

BILLS LEADERS: Rushing - Gregory 7-42, Cappadona 6-18, Anderson 9-5, Darragh 5-9, Costa 1-6, McDermott 2-(-4); **Passing** - Darragh 13-25-2 - 150; **Receiving** - Moses 6-82, Trapp 2-38, Costa 2-32, McDermott 1-7, Anderson 2- (-9).

PATRIOTS LEADERS: Rushing - Gamble 16-90, Garron 14-61, Thomas 11-18, Marsh 1-(-7), Sherman 1-(-7); **Passing** - Taliaferro 5-13-1 - 60; **Receiving** - Whalen 2-33, Marsh 2-15, Cappelletti 1-12.

WEEK 1 GAMES

SD 29, Cinc 13   KC 26, Hou 21

NOTES

• A banner hanging in War Memorial Stadium said "Goodbye Collier." Sure enough, after the game, Joe Collier was fired as head coach. Personnel director Harvey Johnson, who was celebrating his 23rd wedding anniversary, was elevated to head coach.

• Johnson was summoned to Ralph Wilson's private box early in the second half by a messenger who was sent to the press box. After the game, Johnson and Collier were told to go to Wilson's suite at the Statler Hilton to discuss the change.

• The loss was the worst in team history, as was the net passing yardage of minus-19, as Oakland had eight sacks for 94 yards in losses.

• George Atkinson returned five punts for an AFL record of 205 yards. He scored the game's first TD on an 86-yard return, then went 54 yards to the Bills 9 with the next punt before Pete Banaszak scored.

• On Oakland's next possession, Warren Wells beat

Butch Byrd for a 57-yard TD and the Bills were through. Thanks to Atkinson, at that point, not counting their first series on which they didn't score, the Raiders had run four offensive plays and were ahead 21-0.

QUOTES

• Ralph Wilson: "I make this move regretting its necessity as I have personal admiration for Joe Collier as a person and a coach. You don't like to ever hurt a man of his caliber and quality, but a change had to be made. I know that I'm asking Harvey to assume a difficult responsibility since the season is already underway. I don't envy him, but I think he can get the best out of our squad."

• Joe Collier: "I know such things happen in sports. I appreciate the opportunity Mr. Wilson gave me. I leave the Bills fully intending to continue in the coaching profession."

• Harvey Johnson: "I could give you a bunch of baloney about changes we're going to make and things we're going to do, but there isn't much we can do. This thing is going to take time. I don't want to bring guys in just to make changes, I want good men."

• Unidentified Raider who was a former Bill: "I don't know what has happened to the Bills, but they're not the same team. If our whole team had walked off the field after halftime and hadn't returned, I still don't think Buffalo would have scored."

• Raiders quarterback Daryle Lamonica: "It's always an extra incentive to come back and play against your old team. It's a psychological factor no matter how much you try to treat it as just another game. But don't underestimate the Bills. Their defense is feared by every quarterback in the league."

• Raiders owner Al Davis: "We have a tremendous amount of respect for the Bills."

Raiders	21	10 3	14 -	48
Bills	0	0 0	6 -	6

Attendance at War Memorial Stadium - 43,056

Oak: Atkinson 86 punt return (Blanda kick), 6:18
Oak: Banaszak 9 run (Blanda kick), 9:12
Oak: Wells 57 pass from Lamonica (Blanda kick), 11:23
Oak: FG Blanda 22, 3:02
Oak: Dixon 17 run (Blanda kick), 9:58
Oak: FG Blanda 9, 5:07
Buf: Cappadona 7 pass from Darragh (run failed), 11:39
Oak: Todd 11 run (Blanda kick), 3:45
Oak: Todd 31 run (Blanda kick), 9:34

	BUF	OAK
First downs	14	20
Rushing yds	210	210
Passing yds	-19	201
Punts-avg	10-44.1	5-37.2
Fumbles-lost	4-1	1-1
Penalties-yds	4-48	6-59

BILLS LEADERS: Rushing - Anderson 11-88, Gregory 15-57, Cappadona 4-25, Masters 1-35, Costa 1-5, McDermott 5-2; **Passing** - Darragh 4-20-0 - 48, Stephenson 0-5-0 - 0, McDermott 1-1-0 - 27; **Receiving** - Moses 1-18, Cappadona 2-25, Rutkowski 1-27, Trapp 1-5.

RAIDERS LEADERS: Rushing - Dixon 16-104, Todd 6-61, Banaszak 7-28, Smith 3-11, Hagberg 1-3, Lamonica 2-3; **Passing** - Lamonica 10-30-0 - 167, Blanda 1-2-0 - 34; **Receiving** - Biletnikoff 4-47, Wells 3-92, Todd 2-14, Dickey 1-34, Banaszak 1-14.

WEEK 2 GAMES

Hou 24, Mia 10   Cinc 24, Den 10
NY 20, KC 19

STANDINGS: SECOND WEEK

EAST	W	L	T	WEST	W	L	T
Boston	1	0	0	Oakland	1	0	0
New York	1	0	0	San Diego	1	0	0
Houston	1	1	0	Kan. City	1	1	0
Miami	0	1	0	Cincinnati	1	1	0
Buffalo	0	2	0	Denver	0	1	0

Bills	0	7	7	9 - 23
Bengals	10	0	10	14 - 34

Attendance at Nippert Stadium - 24,405

Cin: FG Livingston 11, 7:51
Cin: McVea 80 run (Livingston kick), 12:51
Buf: Anderson 14 run (Mercer kick), 7:34
Buf: McDermott 5 run (Mercer kick), 4:39
Cin: FG Livingston 39, 6:39
Cin: King 32 interception return (Livingston kick), 14:56
Cin: Beauchamp 17 interception return (Livingston kick), :12
Buf: Anderson 100 kickoff return (Mercer kick), :29
Buf: Safety, Robinson tackled in end zone by Pitts and Guidry, 13:06
Cin: Smiley 1 run (Livingston kick), 14:59

	BUF	CIN
First downs	17	9
Rushing yds	92	162
Passing yds	123	52
Punts-avg	6-39.0	5-40.0
Fumbles-lost	1-0	1-0
Penalties-yds	5-65	6-34

BILLS LEADERS: Rushing - Anderson 13-45, Gregory 7-34, Darragh 1-8, Cappadona 1-2, McDermott 2-3; **Passing** - Darragh 14-35-1 - 152, Stephenson 0-2-1 - 0, McDermott 1-1-0 - 8; **Receiving** - Moses 6-56, Trapp 2-28, Cappadona 2-9, Masters 4-62, McDermott 1-5.

BENGALS LEADERS: Rushing - Robinson 9-25, Smiley 13-42, Stofa 3-5, McVea 1-80, Livingston 1-11, Johnson 1-(-1); **Passing** - Stofa 8-19-1 - 68; **Receiving** - Sherman 3-65, Smiley 2-2, Trumpy 1-4, McVea 1-5, Robinson 1-(-8).

NOTES

• Trailing 27-23 with 1:02 left, Dan Darragh's 42-yard completion to Haven Moses to the Bengals 12 on fourth down was nullified by a holding penalty on Dick Cunningham. The Bills lost 66 yards on the play and when they failed to make the first down, Cincinnati scored an insurance TD with one second remaining.
• Darragh suffered a right foot injury in the third with the Bills ahead 14-13. Kay Stephenson entered and his first pass was intercepted by Charley King and returned for a TD.
• Darragh came back hobbling, but he threw an interception to Al Beauchamp, which also went for a TD.
• Max Anderson returned the ensuing kickoff 100 yards for a TD and later in the fourth, after Paul Maguire pinned the Bengals back to their 1, John Pitts and Paul Guidry combined to tackle Paul Robinson for a safety to make it 27-23.
• The Bills botched several good opportunities: Bob Cappadona dropped a sure TD pass. Bengals punter Mike Livingston bobbled a snap, was hit by three Bills and still escaped for a first down. A Ron McDole fumble recovery at the Bengals 13 was wasted when Mike Mercer missed a field goal. And a George Saimes interception and return to the Bengals 38 resulted in no points.
• The Bengals first score was set up when Estes Banks blocked a Maguire punt. Later in the first, Warren McVea broke free on an 80-yard reverse for a 10-0 lead.
• Darragh directed an 80-yard TD drive before half-time, and early in the third, three completions to Billy Masters led to Gary McDermott's TD run.

QUOTES

• Harvey Johnson on the defense: "They played about as well as you could ask them to play. Give them the field goals and the reverse even though we worked on that in practice, but other than that, they didn't do anything on offense. I'm just terribly disappointed. We worked on every phase of the game this week and the kids played their hearts out. We earned our points but we gave them some of theirs." (On Cunningham's holding penalty): "I want to see the films on that call. Dick's not a holder and he told me he wasn't holding."
• Dick Cunningham: "The official has his job to do. I'm just sorry we couldn't win it for Coach Johnson. I want to apologize for losing my poise and throwing my helmet. I'm not that kind of player and I'm sorry I did it."

WEEK 3 GAMES	
SD 30, Hou 14	Oak 47, Mia 21
KC 34, Den 2	NY 47, Bos 31

Jets	7	14	0	14 - 35
Bills	10	10	3	14 - 37

Attendance at War Memorial Stadium - 38,044

NY: Sauer 4 pass from Namath (J. Turner kick), 2:11
Buf: FG Alford 35, 7:01
Buf: Gregory 2 run (Alford kick), 14:56
Buf: Janik 100 interception return (Alford kick), 10:30
NY: Boozer 1 run (J. Turner kick), 12:46
Buf: FG Alford 41, 13:59
NY: Maynard 55 pass from Namath (J. Turner kick), 14:39
Buf: FG Alford 37, 8:26
Buf: Byrd 53 interception return (Alford kick), 2:34
Buf: Edgerson 45 interception return (Alford kick), 3:36
NY: Snell 3 pass from Namath (J. Turner kick), 5:36
NY: Sauer 10 pass from Namath (J. Turner kick), 13:56

	BUF	NY
First downs	10	17
Rushing yds	140	170
Passing yds	57	257
Punts-avg	6-32.5	5-38.2
Fumbles-lost	3-1	3-1
Penalties-yds	3-25	3-38

BILLS LEADERS: Rushing - Anderson 13-17, Gregory 12-87, Cappadona 3-15, Darragh 5-0, Masters 1-3, Moses 1-19, Lincoln 4-(-1); **Passing** - Darragh 8-18-1 - 79, Anderson 0-1-0 - 0; **Receiving** - Moses 2-23, Trapp 3-37, Anderson 1-7, Gregory 2-12.

JETS LEADERS: Rushing - Snell 12-124, Boozer 9-43, Namath 1-3; **Passing** - Namath 19-43-5 - 280; **Receiving** - Sauer 7-113, Maynard 3-114, Snell 4-20, Johnson 2-31, Boozer 2-10, Lammons 1-(-8).

NOTES

• The Bills shocked the previously unbeaten Jets with five interceptions, three of which were returned for TDs.
• Buffalo led 10-7 in the second when the Jets recovered a Dan Darragh fumble at the Bills 10. After two incompletions, Joe Namath's pass to Curley Johnson at the goal line was picked off by Tom Janik, who went 100 yards untouched for a TD. Namath's next pass was intercepted and returned 52 yards for a TD by Butch Byrd, but the play was nullified because Tom Day had jumped offsides.
• The Jets took the lead by halftime. Matt Snell's 60-yard run set up Emerson Boozer's one-yard TD. After Bruce Alford, who replaced the injured Mike Mercer, kicked a 41-yard field goal that was set up by Max Anderson's 63-yard kickoff return, Namath hit Don Maynard with a 55-yard TD for a 21-20 lead.
• A Namath fumble led to Alford's 37-yard field goal in the third. Then Byrd and Edgerson returned picks for TDs 1:02 apart to make it 37-21 with 11:24 remaining.
• A 65-yard Jets drive, aided by Snell's 39-yard run, culminated on Snell's TD reception. Another Jets march was halted when Byrd intercepted Namath's bomb to George Sauer at the Bills 5. But when the Bills couldn't move and Paul Crane blocked Paul Maguire's punt at the Bills 11, Namath took advantage with a TD pass to Sauer to cut the Bills' lead to 37-35 with 1:04 left.

QUOTES

• Jets QB Joe Namath: "I didn't throw very well and they had great coverages. Somebody asked if we took the Bills lightly, that we weren't up for the game. Not true. We were up. We've never had an easy game in Buffalo. What won it for them was their five interceptions and that's my fault."
• Tom Janik: "I was covering Curley Johnson all the way. The ball was perfectly thrown. I hesitated for a split second, then stepped inside my man. All I saw was daylight. Namath came up on the play downfield and I was getting tired, but I knew he was, too, and that knee of his had to be bothering him, so I just kept going."
• Harvey Johnson: "I'm going to touch you for a few drinks, Ralph. Maybe there won't be many more opportunities so I'm going to get you now. I didn't think we had maximum effort in Cincinnati, but I'd have to guess we had 100 percent effort from everybody today."
• Jets coach Weeb Ewbank: "I thought the Bills front four rushed Joe very hard. They knocked the tar out of Namath so much that I thought of putting Babe Parilli in. We met a fired up team and didn't meet the challenge. If they can get together, they can beat anybody in the league."

WEEK 4 GAMES	
KC 48, Mia 3	Bos 20, Den 17
Oak 24, Hou 15	SD 31, Cinc 10

STANDINGS: FOURTH WEEK

EAST	W	L	T	WEST	W	L	T
New York	2	1	0	Oakland	3	0	0
Boston	2	1	0	San Diego	3	0	0
Houston	1	3	0	Kan. City	3	1	0
Buffalo	1	3	0	Cincinnati	2	2	0
Miami	0	3	0	Denver	0	3	0

NOTES

• Five turnovers and seven penalties doomed the Bills, as did Jan Stenerud's leg.

• After Tom Sestak blocked Stenerud's 52-yard field goal attempt, the Bills drove 54 yards to Dan Darragh's five-yard TD pass to Haven Moses. It was Moses' first pro TD and he had his initial 100-yard receiving game.

• Two series later, the Chiefs responded with a 65-yard march that was climaxed by Len Dawson's TD pass to Gloster Richardson. Dawson had thrown 48 yards to Fred Arbanas to key the drive. Stenerud missed the conversion, his first failure in 59 pro attempts.

• The Chiefs took the lead in the second after Buck Buchanan recovered Bob Cappadona's fumble at the Bills 25. Stenerud made an 18-yard field goal.

• Following a Buffalo punt, the Chiefs were awarded three first downs via penalties on their way to another Stenerud field goal and a 12-7 lead.

• The Chiefs tried an on-side kick that Stew Barber recovered at midfield. However, the Bills botched the chance. With 27 seconds and three timeouts left, the Bills used none of their timeouts. A 41-yard pass to Haven Moses came as the half was ending.

• In the third, a Willie Mitchell interception led to another Stenerud field goal. In the fourth, Dawson directed a spectacular 16-play drive that ate up nearly 10 minutes. It resulted in Stenerud's final field goal.

QUOTES

• Harvey Johnson: "Our three fumbles hurt us more than the interceptions. You just can't cough the ball up against a powerful club like Kansas City." (On the botched first-half drive): "We intended on using our two-minute offense. Maybe the pressure of carrying the whole load was getting to the kid (Darragh) because we were in a desperate situation. But we should have called a timeout. Our offensive line play has improved each week; you can see it. The kid had pretty fair protection and we ran on them. Kansas City is a fine team, but we could have beaten them with a little more continuity."

• Chiefs coach Hank Stram: "You don't score on the Buffalo defense, you score on its offense. I really think the Bills defense is better than when the team was winning championships. I felt our defense could control their offense, but we felt we couldn't let their defense make the big plays like they made against New York."

• Tom Sestak: "Except for that last 10-minute drive, which was really frustrating because they rammed the ball down our throats, I think we stopped their running game enough to win the game. Our pass rush is getting better and the reason is because Coach Sardisco, instead of having us reading and then reacting, is having us react, period."

Chiefs	6 6 3 3 -	**18**
Bills	7 0 0 0 -	**7**

Attendance at War Memorial Stadium - 40,748

Buf: Moses 5 pass from Darragh (Alford kick), 9:20
KC: Richardson 15 pass from Dawson (kick failed), 13:58
KC: FG Stenerud 18, 5:28
KC: FG Stenerud 12, 14:30
KC: FG Stenerud 16, 14:26
KC: FG Stenerud 15, 13:03

	BUF	KC
First downs	11	20
Rushing yds	115	212
Passing yds	136	141
Punts-avg	5-39.6	2-54.5
Fumbles-lost	3-3	2-0
Penalties-yds	7-59	6-41

BILLS LEADERS: Rushing - Gregory 10-58, Anderson 3-14, Lincoln 8-43, Cappadona 1-1, McDermott 1-(-1); **Passing** - Darragh 8-20-2 - 136; **Receiving** - Moses 5-108, Anderson 1-19, Gregory 2-9.

CHIEFS LEADERS: Rushing - Holmes 15-91, Garrett 22-39, Hayes 7-29, Pitts 2-30, Dawson 3-23; **Passing** - Dawson 9-17-2 - 149, Garrett 0-1-0 - 0; **Receiving** - Richardson 4-50, Garrett 2-20, Arbanas 1-48, Pitts 1-23, Hayes 1-8.

WEEK 5 GAMES

NY 23, SD 20	Den 10, Cinc 7
Mia 24, Hou 7	Oak 41, Bos 10

NOTES

• The Bills may have set a record when they used four quarterbacks, including Ed Rutkowski, who threw the game-tying two-point conversion pass to Gary McDermott with 18 seconds left. Tom Flores started, but his first appearance since Oct. 1, 1967, ended in the second quarter when his sore shoulder tightened up; Kay Stephenson came in and was as ineffective as he had been all year. Hobbling Dan Darragh finished the game and he directed a 12-play, 80-yard drive that began with 2:15 left to play.

• Darragh completed seven of 10 passes on the final march, including four to Paul Costa and then a three-yarder to McDermott for the score on a third-down play.

• Bruce Alford tied a team-record with a 51-yard field goal in the first quarter.

• Miami came back with a 13-play, 63-yard march in which Bob Griese completed three third-down passes before Jim Kiick swept in from the 1 to make it 7-3.

• After Ron McDole's interception and 42-yard return, the Bills drove to Alford's second field goal.

• A missed field goal, a Max Anderson fumble and a Stephenson pass that was intercepted by Willie West killed three scoring threats in the second half. After West's interception and return to the Bills 40, Miami drove to a 14-6 lead when Stan Mitchell scored with 6:59 left to play.

• After tying the game, the Bills tried an on-side kick, but Miami recovered. Booker Edgerson preserved the tie by intercepting a Griese pass at the Bills 20.

• Flores (shoulder) and running back Ben Gregory (knee) were lost for the season.

QUOTES

• Harvey Johnson on the quarterback situation: "I can't say enough about his (Darragh) courage. He was so hobbled, he had trouble trotting to the sidelines. We don't contemplate making Rutkowski a quarterback, but in Stephenson's behalf, he really hasn't had a good shot. Kay was very limited in the third quarter when the wind was such a factor and we felt we had to control the ball. Everyone's going to throw an interception, plus we had some penalties and dropped passes. He came up with some good calls in the fourth period." (On why he tried the on-side kick): "Because the boys battled back so successfully under the gun, I decided to take a shot at winning the game, while also risking a defeat. If we had recovered, we would have been in field goal range with a stiff wind at Bruce Alford's back. The defense saved me from looking bad by stopping Bob Griese cold on three plays."

• Dan Darragh: "When we went on the field for the final drive, I really think we felt we could score. I realize we're not scoring a lot of points, but we're all getting more confidence in ourselves as an offensive team and this is very important. On the touchdown play, we sent Haven (Moses) and Paul (Costa) to the inside and McDermott to the outside to try to cause a traffic jam. Their safety, Dick Anderson, in trying to cover Gary, had to step around Costa and the back covering him and that gave me just enough time to get the ball to Gary."

Bills	3 3 0 8 -	**14**
Dolphins	0 7 0 7 -	**14**

Attendance at the Orange Bowl - 28,559

Buf: FG Alford 51, 10:47
Mia: Kiick 1 run (Keyes kick), 2:59
Buf: FG Alford 20, 12:13
Mia: Mitchell 1 run (Keyes kick), 8:01
Buf: McDermott 3 pass from Darragh (McDermott pass from Darragh), 14:42

	BUF	MIA
First downs	12	14
Rushing yds	144	112
Passing yds	93	59
Punts-avg	5-40.4	8-43.1
Fumbles-lost	1-1	0-0
Penalties-yds	4-44	4-32

BILLS LEADERS: Rushing - Lincoln 10-29, Anderson 10-72, Cappadona 4-19, Gregory 2-15, Rutkowski 1-5, Moses 1-4; **Passing** - Darragh 8-14-0 - 79, Stephenson 3-8-1 - 11, Flores 3-5-1 - 15; **Receiving** - Moses 1-9, Trapp 2-14, Costa 6-63, Masters 1-12, McDermott 1-3, Lincoln 1-3, Anderson 1-1, Gregory 1-0.

DOLPHINS LEADERS: Rushing - Csonka 17-50, Kiick 10-29, Griese 6-29, Mitchell 4-4; **Passing** - Griese 9-22-2 - 97; **Receiving** - Moreau 4-44, Noonan 3-21, Csonka 1-21, Kiick 1-11.

WEEK 6 GAMES

KC 13, Cinc 3	Den 21, NY 13
Hou 16, Bos 0	SD 23, Oak 14

STANDINGS: SIXTH WEEK

EAST	W	L	T	WEST	W	L	T
New York	3	2	0	Kan. City	5	1	0
Boston	2	3	0	Oakland	4	1	0
Houston	2	4	0	San Diego	4	1	0
Miami	1	3	1	Denver	2	3	0
Buffalo	1	4	1	Cincinnati	2	4	0

Bills	3	3	0	0 -	6
Patriots	3	3	17	0 -	23

Attendance at Fenway Park - 21,082

Bos: FG Cappelletti 39, 3:03
Buf: FG Alford 16, 10:37
Bos: FG Cappelletti 20, 1:15
Buf: FG Alford 11, 7:46
Bos: Whalen 40 pass from Taliaferro (Cappelletti kick), 6:19
Bos: FG Cappelletti 16, 8:28
Bos: Whalen 18 pass from Taliaferro (Cappelletti kick), 14:59

	BUF	BOS
First downs	9	11
Rushing yds	49	203
Passing yds	154	96
Punts-avg	7-44.4	4-43.3
Fumbles-lost	1-1	1-1
Penalties-yds	4-54	6-52

BILLS LEADERS: Rushing - Anderson 11-14, Cappadona 4-16, McDermott 4-6, Lincoln 4-13; **Passing** - Darragh 15-30-4 - 153, Stephenson 1-2-0 - 6, McDermott 0-1-0 -0; **Receiving** - Moses 6-93, Trapp 3-24, Anderson 1-12, Masters 2-16, Costa 1-9, McDermott 1-4, Cappadona 2-1.

PATRIOTS LEADERS: Rushing - Nance 24-82, Thomas 18-76, Taliaferro 2-27, Gamble 2-18; **Passing** - Taliaferro 4-12-1 - 96; **Receiving** - Whalen 3-78, Graham 1-18.

NOTES

• Linebacker Nick Buoniconti intercepted three Dan Darragh passes in the second half, two of which resulted in 10 Boston points.
• The teams exchanged two field goals in the first half, but the Patriots scored 17 points in the third to win it.
• Billy Johnson returned the opening kickoff 49 yards for Boston, leading to Gino Cappelletti's first field goal. The Bills tied it when George Flint forced Johnson to fumble a punt and Al Bemiller recovered at the Boston 39, leading to a Bruce Alford field goal.
• Leroy Mitchell's interception and return to the Bills 25 set up Cappelletti's second field goal, but Darragh's 35-yard pass to Haven Moses keyed a drive that ended on Alford's second kick.
• Three plays after Buoniconti's first pick, Mike Taliaferro hit Jim Whalen, who had beaten Hagood Clarke, for a 40-yard TD.
• Max Anderson fumbled the ensuing kickoff at the 18 and Cappelletti kicked a field goal to make it 16-6.
• Two plays after the kickoff, Buoniconti intercepted Darragh and returned it to the Bills 37. From there, Taliaferro hit Whalen with an 18-yard TD pass.

WEEK 7 GAMES	
SD 55, Den 24	Mia 24, Cinc 22
NY 20, Hou 14	KC 24, Oak 10

QUOTES

• Patriots linebacker Nick Buoniconti: "I made those three interceptions by reading the quarterback. He gives you a little tip-off as to where he's going to throw."
• Harvey Johnson: "It's a shame because no one in the East Division is that much stronger than anyone else. If we had an experienced quarterback, we'd be as good as any club in our division. But we don't, so we're not. I think we have as good a football team as Boston, but look where they are, only a game out of first place. The way our division is, either (Jack) Kemp or (Tom) Flores could have put us right up there. Our pass protection was remarkably good, we had enough receivers open, too, but what are you going to do? We were either late throwing the ball or we were throwing into the thick of their coverage. Was Bouniconti reading Darragh? He merely reacted and managed to get to the ball once it was thrown. They got the breaks and we didn't. We're concerned about the players getting totally demoralized, I'll admit that. Dan's a rookie quarterback and that's how it is with rookie quarterbacks. One week they're up and you're convinced they're going to make it and the next week they're down and you're not so sure. Joe Namath didn't win many games when he was a rookie, Bob Griese didn't win many when he was a rookie. Our guy isn't any different."
• Patriots receiver Jim Whalen: "I'd be all-league if I played against Buffalo every week."

Oilers	10	0	10	10 -	30
Bills	0	7	0	0 -	7

Attendance at War Memorial Stadium - 34,339

Hou: Campbell 2 run (Walker kick), 6:28
Hou: FG Walker 39, 12:30
Buf: Ledbetter 36 pass from Stephenson (Alford kick), 14:00
Hou: FG Walker 22, 5:35
Hou: Reed 23 pass from Trull (Walker kick), 14:39
Hou: Reed 42 pass from Trull (Walker kick), 3:01
Hou: FG Walker 19, 9:56

	BUF	HOU
First downs	8	13
Rushing yds	50	133
Passing yds	63	199
Punts-avg	9-49.7	5-44.6
Fumbles-lost	0-0	1-0
Penalties-yds	5-68	5-45

BILLS LEADERS: Rushing - Anderson 14-32, McDermott 5-14, Stephenson 2-18, Cappadona 1-0, Moses 1-(-14); **Passing** - Darragh 3-8-1 - 0, Stephenson 6-20-1 - 63, Rutkowski 0-4-1 - 0; **Receiving** - Anderson 2-13, McDermott 3-(-10), Crockett 2-20, Ledbetter 1-36, Trapp 1-4.

OILERS LEADERS: Rushing - Campbell 23-75, Granger 9-25, Norton 1-20, Hopkins 8-9, Beirne 1-3, Trull 3-1; **Passing** - Trull 8-17-0 - 224, Davis 1-1-0 - 10; **Receiving** - Reed 4-132, Haik 2-21, Campbell 1-39, Granger 1-32, Frazier 1-10.

WEEK 8 GAMES	
NY 48, Bos 14	Oak 31, Cinc 10
Den 21, Mia 14	KC 27, SD 20

NOTES

• Buffalo's 113 net yards of offense tied the all-time team low, set in the first game the team ever played on Sept. 11, 1960, against the New York Titans.
• Oilers quarterback Don Trull won for the first time as a starter in his five-year career.
• The key were his two TD passes to Alvin Reed within seven plays in the second half. Leading 13-7, the Oilers were faced with third-and-goal from the 23. Trull threw a pass down the middle that both Hagood Clarke and George Saimes should have knocked down, but the ball somehow found its way into Reed's hands for a score.
• Then, on another third-down play from the Bills 42, Trull lofted a short pass to Reed who faked John Pitts beautifully and scooted all the way for the killing TD.
• The Bills averaged 1.9 yards per pass attempt.
• Kay Stephenson started for the first time as a pro and was lifted in favor of Dan Darragh who was equally inept. Things were so bad, Harvey Johnson turned to disaster QB Ed Rutkowski whose first pass was picked off by W.K. Hicks, setting up Houston's final points.
• Stephenson's TD pass to Monte Ledbetter was Buffalo's first TD against Houston since 1966.
• That streak would have ended in the first quarter, but Haven Moses dropped a sure TD pass.

QUOTES

• Harvey Johnson on the turning point: "It came in the third quarter when the game was 13-7. That middle alley touchdown pass to Reed wrecked us. Someone should have picked off that pass or deflected it. There's no way Reed should have scored on that play." (On the overall performance): "I'm sorry I used Eddie. It was embarrassing for him. We worked him a lot during the week, but he just hasn't had enough experience at the position to do much. We were a poor football team. Our defense played a good second quarter and were up for a portion of the third, but their day ended right there. Ron McDole had his usual strong effort and our cornerbacks, Booker Edgerson and Butch Byrd, covered well the few times they were tested. Outside of that, nobody was above an average performance. Anybody who thinks we'll tolerate just going through the motions the last six games is in for a rude awakening. I know the fans in the stands couldn't help but wonder what kind of plan we had to beat the Oilers. It was sound, believe me, but if you don't execute, the best plan in the world is worthless. And our offensive execution, rather lack of it, made the day worthless."
• Offensive line coach Marvin Bass: "You don't move the ball if you don't block and we didn't block anyone."

STANDINGS: EIGHTH WEEK							
EAST	W	L	T	WEST	W	L	T
New York	5	2	0	Kan. City	7	1	0
Boston	3	4	0	San Diego	5	2	0
Houston	3	5	0	Oakland	5	2	0
Miami	2	4	1	Denver	3	4	0
Buffalo	1	6	1	Cincinnati	2	6	0

GAME 9 - Sunday, Nov. 3, 1968 - JETS 25, BILLS 21

NOTES

• The Bills lost a heartbreaker as Jim Turner attempted an AFL record eight field goals and tied the league mark by making six, including two in the final 3:26 that won the game.

• The defense turned in a superb effort, holding the potent Jets offense without a TD and extended Joe Namath's streak of not throwing a TD pass to five games.

• After Ron McDole blocked a Turner field goal, Kay Stephenson hit Haven Moses with a 55-yard TD pass, but minutes later a fumbled punt by Richard Trapp set up Turner's first field goal.

• Johnny Sample picked off Stephenson's quick pitch for Trapp and scored untouched. Turner added two more field goals before the half ended for a 16-7 lead and Turner's fourth field goal made it 19-7 after three quarters.

• The Bills then stunned the Jets with two quick scores. After Bruce Alford missed a 32-yard field goal, the Bills' big rush forced punter Curley Johnson to run and he was stopped at the Jets 25. Stephenson completed three passes to Trapp for 15 yards, then found Paul Costa for a TD with 7:58 left. On the ensuing series, Johnson's punt was returned 82 yards for a TD by Hagood Clarke. Here, Harvey Johnson made a tactical mistake by not going for two points. He settled for the conversion and a 21-19 lead with 6:18 left. Assistant coach Richie McCabe was screaming to go for two from the coaches box in the press box, but no one was wearing the headsets in all the excitement over Clarke's return.

• The Jets then drove to the go-ahead field goal, aided along the way by a 25-yard Namath to Pete Lammons pass and a pass-interference penalty on Marty Schottenheimer.

• Al Atkinson's interception allowed Turner to kick an insurance field goal, and the clock finally ran out with the Bills threatening at the Jets 20. A successful two-pointer might have provided the Bills an opportunity to kick a tying field goal at the end.

QUOTES

• Harvey Johnson on not going for the two-pointer: "You're damn right I regret it. I'm a dumb guy for not going for two points. One point didn't help us at all. The truth is I got too excited because we were ahead in a big ballgame. I never even gave any thought to a two-pointer. I apologized to the players for not going for two. For our defense, it was their best effort in a long time. Offensively we sputtered against what amounted to an eight-man line in the first half. We made some blocking adjustments and did some fair running up the middle after that."

• Jets kicker Jim Turner: "The last time I kicked six field goals was in a squad scrimmage when I was kicking for both teams. You bet I felt pressure (on the go-ahead kick)."

• Jets quarterback Joe Namath: "It's still a victory."

WEEK 9 GAMES

Den 35, Bos 14	Hou 27, Cinc 17
Oak 38, KC 21	SD 34, Mia 28

Bills	7	0	0	14	-	21
Jets	3	13	3	6	-	25

Attendance at Shea Stadium- 61,452

Buf: Moses 55 pass from Stephenson (Alford kick), 8:54
NY: FG J. Turner 32, 12:33
NY: Sample 36 interception return (J. Turner kick), 5:18
NY: FG J. Turner 9, 10:33
NY: FG J. Turner 32, 14:32
NY: FG J. Turner 27, 5:38
Buf: Costa 10 pass from Stephenson (Alford kick), 7:02
Buf: Clarke 82 punt return (Alford kick), 8:42
NY: FG J. Turner 35, 11:34
NY: FG J. Turner 27, 14:08

	BUF	NY
First downs	10	11
Rushing yds	62	110
Passing yds	134	164
Punts-avg	8-38.3	6-39.8
Fumbles-lost	3-2	0-0
Penalties-yds	2-19	4-30

BILLS LEADERS: Rushing - Cappadona 11-30, Anderson 13-32; **Passing** - Stephenson 12-29-3 - 155; **Receiving** - Moses 1-55, Trapp 4-41, Costa 2-25, Anderson 1-15, Ledbetter 1-9, Cappadona 1-4, Crockett 1-6, Bemiller 1-0.

JETS LEADERS: Rushing - Snell 14-49, Boozer 9-16, Joe 9-33, Mathis 3-12, Johnson 1-0; **Passing** - Namath 10-28-1 - 164; **Receiving** - Sauer 4-88, Maynard 2-29, Lammons 2-34, Snell 1-8, Boozer 1-5.

GAME 10 - Sunday, Nov. 10, 1968 - DOLPHINS 21, BILLS 17

NOTES

• Kay Stephenson, just starting to find his way in the Buffalo offense, suffered a season-ending broken collarbone. The Bills blew a 17-0 lead and fell to the Dolphins in front of the smallest War Memorial crowd since Sept. 20, 1964.

• The Bills scored 17 points in the second quarter. Bob Cappadona broke loose on a 33-yard TD run. George Saimes then picked off a Bob Griese pass and after Stephenson hit Monte Ledbetter for 43 yards, Bruce Alford kicked a 22-yard field goal. And to close the half, the Bills needed just 1:10 to go 84 yards. Max Anderson sprinted for 30 and on the next play, Stephenson beat a blitz by hitting Cappadona over the middle for a 21-yard TD.

• But Stephenson was hurt on the second play of the second half and Buffalo's offense died under the direction of Dan Darragh.

• Cappadona's fumble started the Dolphins on their first scoring drive, which Griese capped with a 13-yard scramble.

• Early in the fourth, Griese ran for 22, hit Karl Noonan for 19 and eventually passed five yards to Noonan to make it 17-14 with 11:10 left. Three plays later, Randall Edmunds intercepted Darragh at the Bills 44 and that set up the winning score, Jim Kiick's four-yard run.

QUOTES

• Billy Shaw: "You (a reporter) better get out of here, the roof is going to collapse on us any minute (referring to the rash of injuries)."

• Booker Edgerson: "Buzzard's luck, that's what we have."

• Harvey Johnson: "We were just starting to look like a ballclub, the best we've looked all year. Kay did a fine job in there. He had just gotten his confidence. What did we get after he left, one first down? Would someone please tell me how we're going to face San Diego? (with only Darragh and Ed Rutkowski available at QB). I can't fault our defense. You can't play all day against Griese as we had to do in the second half, without him putting points on the board. Even when we had them down, 17-0, he never panicked, never tried to bomb us with long passes."

• Ralph Wilson: "If I offered Harvey a five-year contract right now, I don't know if he'd accept. He might want an escape clause. The defeat brings me back to our struggles the first year when General Motors was supporting the team and our heavy losses. I had to smile then because I knew you couldn't have a long face the next day when talking contract or business with the GM people."

• Miami coach George Wilson: "Stephenson's injury had no affect on our attitude, but when anything like that happens to you, your team goes downhill."

Dolphins	0	0	7	14	-	21
Bills	0	17	0	0	-	17

Attendance at War Memorial Stadium - 28,759

Buf: Cappadona 33 run (Alford kick), 2:19
Buf: FG Alford 22, 9:19
Buf: Cappadona 21 pass from Stephenson (Alford kick), 14:10
Mia: Griese 13 run (Keyes kick), 7:48
Mia: Noonan 5 pass from Griese (Keyes kick), 3:50
Mia: Twilley 4 pass from Griese (Keyes kick), 7:40

	BUF	MIA
First downs	12	22
Rushing yds	133	149
Passing yds	141	156
Punts-avg	4-46.5	4-37.7
Fumbles-lost	1-1	3-1
Penalties-yds	5-44	2-20

BILLS LEADERS: Rushing - Cappadona 11-63, Anderson 11-54, Stephenson 2-12, Masters 1-13, Moses 1-(-9); **Passing** - Stephenson 7-13-1 - 129, Darragh 5-12-1 - 36; **Receiving** - Moses 3-53, Trapp 2-13, Cappadona 2-21, McDermott 2-11, Anderson 1-13, Masters 1-11, Ledbetter 1-43.

DOLPHINS LEADERS: Rushing - Kiick 23-111, Griese 5-32, Mitchell 8-6; **Passing** - Griese 13-28-1 - 188; **Receiving** - Moreau 4-69, Noonan 5-71, Twilley 2-32, Mitchell 1-11, Kiick 1-5.

WEEK 10 GAMES

NY 26, Hou 7	KC 16, Cinc 9
Oak 45, Den 7	SD 27, Bos 17

STANDINGS: TENTH WEEK

EAST	W	L	T	WEST	W	L	T
New York	7	2	0	Kan. City	8	2	0
Houston	4	6	0	San Diego	7	2	0
Miami	3	5	1	Oakland	7	2	0
Boston	3	6	0	Denver	4	5	0
Buffalo	1	8	1	Cincinnati	2	8	0

Chargers	7	14	0	0 - 21
Bills	3	0	3	0 - 6

Attendance at War Memorial Stadium - 27,993

SD: MacKinnon 18 pass from Hadl (Partee kick), 6:59
Buf: FG Alford 25, 12:52
SD: MacKinnon 62 pass from Hadl (Partee kick), 9:48
SD: Post 12 run (Partee kick), 13:06
Buf: FG Alford 16, 5:51

	BUF	SD
First downs	7	15
Rushing yds	90	76
Passing yds	61	206
Punts-avg	10-34.3	5-35.8
Fumbles-lost	0-0	2-2
Penalties-yds	1-13	3-25

BILLS LEADERS: Rushing - Cappadona 6-21, Anderson 12-40, Rutkowski 4-24, McDermott 1-1, Masters 1-4; **Passing** - Darragh 8-21-0 - 38, Rutkowski 7-15-1 - 35, Russell 1-2-0 - 3; **Receiving** - Moses 3-18, Anderson 5-13, Cappadona 4-12, Crockett 1-20, Trapp 1-4, McDermott 2-9.

CHARGERS LEADERS: Rushing - Post 15-67, Smith 12-9, Hadl 1-0; **Passing** - Hadl 11-22-3 - 223, Smith 0-1-0 - 0; **Receiving** - MacKinnon 3-103, Garrison 3-74, Alworth 2-29, Post 2-13, Smith 1-4.

NOTES

• The Bills offense was helpless in horribly muddy conditions at War Memorial, even with the help of five San Diego turnovers.
• Injuries again killed the Bills as Dan Darragh suffered bruised ribs, disaster QB Ed Rutkowski left the game twice because of a back injury and Ben Russell had to play briefly.
• The Bills had a chance to get back into the game midway through the fourth when Marty Schottenheimer recovered a Russ Smith fumble and returned it 16 yards to the San Diego 4. He would have scored had he not tripped over teammate Paul Guidry. The scoring threat died when Rutkowski was sacked and injured on third down and Russell threw incomplete on fourth down.
• Bruce Alford's first field goal was set up by a John Pitts interception. His second came after Paul Costa returned a kickoff to the San Diego 48.
• John Hadl hit tight end Jacque MacKinnon twice for TDs. On the first, MacKinnon scored when George Saimes slipped and failed to tackle him.
• Guard Billy Shaw left the game in the second half with an ankle injury, but x-rays were negative.
• During a halftime TV interview, referee John McDonough was pelted with snowballs. Bills guard Joe O'Donnell took it upon himself to shield the referee. "I didn't want to see Buffalo disgraced any more than it has been."

WEEK 11 GAMES

KC 31, Bos 17	Cinc 38, Mia 21
Hou 38, Den 17	Oak 43, NY 32

QUOTES

• Chargers coach Sid Gillman on the condition of the field: "I've been coaching for 34 years and I've never seen a field worse than this one. It was disgraceful. When a man pays six or seven bucks for a seat he shouldn't have to watch a mud fight in a garbage pit. If the man in charge of taking care of that field worked for me, I'd fire him on the spot. They say they had a tarp on the field, but when I came out there was snow all over it."
• Harvey Johnson on the quarterback situation after learning that Darragh's ribs weren't broken and Rutkowski's back injury wasn't serious: "We're not looking for another candidate. If I could get a quarterback who would give us immediate respectability, I'd get him. I don't feel good standing on the sideline getting beat. But let's face it, where are we going this year? I'm certainly not going to give up a high draft choice for anyone at this point. And the guys who would be available couldn't help us win anyway." (On the field condition): "I can't help but smile – and that's not too easy for me to do these days – when I'm told that mud is a great equalizer. A sloppy field can put a crimp in the running game, but it won't stop the passing game and who was it who had the experienced quarterback? San Diego with John Hadl."
• Ralph Wilson on the race for drafting rights to O.J. Simpson: "I'm not sure we can beat the Eagles, but I still have given a lot of thought to Simpson. He would be a great draw and we must assume that he will be a great pro."

Bills	0	7	7	18 - 32
Broncos	0	21	7	6 - 34

Attendance at Bears Stadium - 35,142

Den: McCarthy 40 pass from Briscoe (Howfield kick), :13
Den: Crabtree 15 pass from Briscoe (Howfield kick), 2:27
Buf: Rutkowski 1 run (Alford kick), 10:31
Den: Little 66 pass from Briscoe (Howfield kick), 14:30
Buf: Edgerson 35 interception return (Alford kick), 8:59
Den: Denson 15 pass from Briscoe (Howfield kick), 13:30
Buf: McDermott 2 run (Cappadona pass from Rutkowski), 2:59
Den: FG Howfield 42, 8:43
Buf: McDermott 3 run (Alford kick), 13:27
Buf: FG Alford 18, 14:34
Den: FG Howfield 12, 14:53

	BUF	DEN
First downs	14	15
Rushing yds	88	84
Passing yds	132	302
Punts-avg	8-41.1	8-30.3
Fumbles-lost	0-0	1-1
Penalties-yds	7-60	9-86

BILLS LEADERS: Rushing - McDermott 8-25, Anderson 9-3, Cappadona 3-6, Rutkowski 5-48, Maguire 1-6; **Passing** - Rutkowski 17-38-2 - 161; **Receiving** - Moses 2-24, Trapp 2-15, Costa 2-23, Anderson 4-17, McDermott 6-78, Cappadona 1-4.

BRONCOS LEADERS: Rushing - Little 27-71, McCarthy 3-16, Jones 1-(-1), Briscoe 2-(-2); **Passing** - Briscoe 12-29-2 - 335; **Receiving** - Denson 5-107, Little 4-165, McCarthy 2-48, Crabtree 1-15.

NOTES

• The Bills lost a heartbreaker as Bobby Howfield kicked a 12-yard field goal with seven seconds left.
• Bruce Alford had completed an 18-point fourth quarter for the Bills with a 17-yard field goal with 26 seconds left, but after the kickoff, Marlin Briscoe hit Floyd Little with a 59-yard pass and a 15-yard facemask penalty moved the ball to the 5 from where Howfield attempted his kick.
• Briscoe hit Brendan McCarthy for a TD in the second, then two minutes later he found Eric Crabtree for a TD.
• Butch Byrd picked off a Briscoe pass and returned it to the Denver 31 from where Ed Rutkowski, in his first start as a quarterback since his sophomore year at Notre Dame nine years earlier, capped the short drive with a one-yard plunge.
• Denver took a 21-7 halftime lead when Briscoe threw a screen to Floyd Little and the ex-Syracuse star turned it into a 66-yard TD with 30 seconds left. The Broncos had gotten the ball when Rex Mirich blocked an Alford field goal.
• The teams traded third-quarter TDs with Booker Edgerson scoring on an interception return. Then the Bills made a push for victory.
• Gary McDermott's TD with 12:01 left was set up by a 38-yard pass-interference penalty on Charley Greer. Rutkowski then passed to Bob Cappadona for the two-point conversion to make it 28-22. Gus Holloman's interception set up Howfield's 42-yard field goal, but the Bills came right back when Howard Kindig blocked a punt and Paul Guidry returned it to the Denver 3. McDermott scored from there to make it 31-29 with 1:33 left.

WEEK 12 GAMES

Mia 34, Bos 10	NY 37, SD 15
Oak 34, Cinc 0	

• Three plays later, Byrd forced Little to fumble and George Saimes returned 29 yards to the 10, setting up Alford's go-ahead kick.

QUOTES

• Harvey Johnson: "I don't believe it, I just don't believe it. The kid (Edgerson) just fell down (covering Little on the 59-yard pass). We were double covering both sides of the field and there is no way they can get deep. But what are you going to do?"
• Broncos coach Lou Saban: "I've been in a lot of close ones, but never one like this. I guess I shouldn't feel so bad, I just won a game. I guess it's better to be lucky than good."
• Broncos running back Floyd Little, on what he said to Briscoe after his fumble: "I said 'Marlin, you've got to throw to me. I've got to atone. Call an up-and-out to the flag. I don't care who's there, I'll catch it.' I didn't see the coach when I came off the field (after the fumble). I knew I had to redeem myself before I saw him again."

STANDINGS: TWELFTH WEEK

EAST	W	L	T	WEST	W	L	T
New York	8	3	0	Kan. City	9	2	0
Houston	5	6	0	Oakland	9	2	0
Miami	4	6	1	San Diego	8	3	0
Boston	3	8	0	Denver	5	6	0
Buffalo	1	10	1	Cincinnati	3	9	0

GAME 13 - Thursday, Nov. 28, 1968 - RAIDERS 13, BILLS 10

NOTES

• In perhaps their best performance of the year, Bruce Alford's 48-yard field goal fell two feet short with 48 seconds left, costing Buffalo a tie with the team that had beaten it, 48-6, earlier in the year and cost Joe Collier his job. The Bills were 24-point underdogs.

• Three minutes earlier, the Bills were in a position to win, but Ed Rutkowski fumbled at the Oakland goal line and Warren Powers recovered for the Raiders.

• The Raiders' league-leading offense didn't score a TD and managed only 186 yards.

• The game was tied, 3-3, at halftime, but Oakland got 10 quick points in the third when George Blanda kicked a 33-yard field goal following a George Atkinson interception. And 1:07 later, Atkinson intercepted another Rutkowski pass and returned it 33 yards for a TD and a 13-3 lead.

• The Bills refused to quit. Rutkowski marched them 81 yards in 10 plays, hitting Haven Moses for 41 yards along the way. Max Anderson contributed a 17-yard run and he eventually scored off right tackle to cut the deficit to 13-10.

• Buffalo forced an Oakland punt and promptly moved – mostly on the ground – from their own 21 to the Raider 38. Rutkowski was shaken up and left briefly. Dan Darragh entered, threw a pass to Monte Ledbetter and Willie Brown interfered at the 18. Rutkowski returned and five plays later he rolled around right end, was hit by Atkinson and Powers recovered the fumble.

QUOTES

• Raiders owner Al Davis: "If the Bills could play defense only, they'd win the American Football League championship."

• Raiders coach John Rauch: "They came to play and they got some offense to go with their great defense."

• Harvey Johnson: "That's one helluva team to shut out without its offense scoring a touchdown. But our team always has played good football against strong teams. Our defense was just great and our offense was really taking it to them, especially when we got 10 points down. And we were using nothing but straight power stuff all the while. We were going for the win. If Eddie hadn't fumbled, we would have gone for the touchdown on fourth down, not the field goal. And on our last drive, we could have stayed on the ground to get closer for Alford's kick, but we passed twice because we wanted to win."

• Raiders cornerback George Atkinson on Rutkowski's fumble: "I went for the ball. He was struggling and I tried to slide my hands down his arms. I felt the ball slip away and the next thing I knew the official was signaling our way."

• Raiders quarterback Daryle Lamonica: "That's the best defense I've played against all year."

WEEK 13 GAMES

KC 26, Hou 10	Bos 33, Cinc 14
NY 35, Mia 17	SD 47, Den 23

Bills	0 3 0 7 - 10
Raiders	0 3 10 0 - 13

Attendance at Oakland-Alameda County Coliseum - 39,883

Oak: FG Blanda 39, :32
Buf: FG Alford 26, 8:52
Oak: FG Blanda 33, 12:52
Oak: Atkinson 33 interception return (Blanda kick), 14:09
Buf: Anderson 5 run (Alford kick), 2:43

	BUF	OAK
First downs	17	11
Rushing yds	199	75
Passing yds	144	111
Punts-avg	5-41.8	6-46.8
Fumbles-lost	2-2	2-1
Penalties-yds	6-60	6-52

BILLS LEADERS: Rushing - Cappadona 10-30, Anderson 11-60, McDermott 15-59, Rutkowski 5-39, Masters 2-15, Moses 1-(-4) **Passing** - Rutkowski 10-25-2 - 160; **Receiving** - Moses 5-89, Anderson 2-31, Costa 1-11, Crockett 1-23, Cappadona 1-6.

RAIDERS LEADERS: Rushing - Dixon 9-21, Smith 12-54, Hagberg 2-1, Lamonica 2-(-1); **Passing** - Lamonica 12-32-1 - 145; **Receiving** - Biletnikoff 3-41, Wells 3-61, Cannon 2-17, Hagberg 2-18, Dixon 2-8.

GAME 14 - Saturday, Dec. 7, 1968 - OILERS 35, BILLS 6

and John Pitts recovered at the Oilers 2. An illegal procedure penalty nullified Bob Cappadona's TD run and Buffalo settled for Bruce Alford's first field goal.

• Marty Schottenheimer then intercepted a Pete Beathard pass and returned it 22 yards to the Oilers 22. Again, the offense lost yardage and Alford kicked a 36-yard field goal.

• That was it for the Bills. Houston's first threat ended when Paul Guidry recovered a fumble, but Beathard took them 63 yards to Woodie Campbell's one-yard run early in the second to get the lead for good.

• Beathard's day ended when Pitts intercepted his first pass of the second half. The Bills failed to capitalize and Don Trull, who earned his first victory as a starting QB against the Bills earlier in the season, hit Mac Haik on a 40-yard scoring pass.

• In the fourth, Trull's 29-yard TD pass to Alvin Reed was sandwiched between 52- and 40-yard interception returns for TDs by cornerback Miller Farr.

• In two games against the Bills, the Oilers held Buffalo to 212 total yards.

QUOTES

• Butch Byrd: "None of us is proud of the season we had or the way it ended in Houston. When you lose 12 games, it probably sounds foolish to dwell on the last one and say we weren't up for that one, but I do not feel we were. I feel the drive it takes to win was lacking somewhat. I'd have to blame it on the combination of the losing season as a whole and the fact that we lost many close ones. We played pretty well in the first half, but there was a noticeable letdown in the second half. Some of us feel we had pretty good individual seasons. The ones who had a good year will have to do it again next year and the ones who didn't will have to come back with a good year."

• Ralph Wilson: "I am very embarrassed and no one player we can draft can compensate for our poor record this year."

NOTES

• The Bills put on a classic run-for-the-bus performance in their season finale, and the players knew it.

• The Bills set an all-time low for total offense with 89 yards, including 10 net yards passing as Houston sacked Ed Rutkowski and Dan Darragh for losses totaling 60 yards.

• The Bills actually led, 6-0, without the benefit of a first down. Larry Carwell fumbled the opening kickoff

Bills	6 0 0 0 - 6
Oilers	0 7 7 21 - 35

Attendance at the Astrodome - 34,110

Buf: FG Alford 28, 2:13
Buf: FG Alford 36, 10:35
Hou: Campbell 1 run (Walker kick), 3:23
Hou: Haik 40 pass from Trull (Walker kick), 8:39
Hou: Farr 52 interception return (Walker kick), 1:26
Hou: Reed 29 pass from Trull (Walker kick), 7:52
Hou: Farr 40 interception return (Walker kick), 8:23

	BUF	HOU
First downs	7	23
Rushing yds	79	188
Passing yds	10	215
Punts-avg	11-44.8	4-43.5
Fumbles-lost	1-0	3-2
Penalties-yds	5-55	3-15

BILLS LEADERS: Rushing - Anderson 7-49, Cappadona 7-16, Brown 3-39, Patrick 1-2, Darragh 1-(-4), McDermott 4-(-3), Rutkowski 5-(-20); **Passing** - Rutkowski 7-18-0 - 24, Darragh 6-14-2 - 46; **Receiving** - Moses 1-5, Cappadona 3-10, McDermott 3-8, Costa 1-9, Trapp 1-12, Anderson 1-8, Crockett 1-7, Ledbetter 1-6, Patrick 1-5.

OILERS LEADERS: Rushing - Campbell 15-41, Granger 15-96, Hopkins 4-37, Trull 1-12, Haik 1-5, Blanks 2-4, Beathard 3-(-7); **Passing** - Trull 6-11-0 - 117, Beathard 5-13-2 - 120; **Receiving** - Haik 6-129, Reed 3-58, Beirne 1-35, Granger 1-15.

WEEK 14 GAMES

Mia 38, Bos 7	NY 27, Cinc 14
Oak 33, Den 27	KC 40, SD 3

WEEK 15 GAMES

KC 30, Den 7	Hou 45, Bos 17
NY 31, Mia 7	Oak 34, SD 27
Buffalo and Cincinnati had bye weeks.	

STANDINGS: FIFTEENTH WEEK

EAST	W	L	T	WEST	W	L	T
New York	11	3	0	Kan. City	12	2	0
Houston	7	7	0	Oakland	12	2	0
Miami	5	8	1	San Diego	9	5	0
Boston	4	10	0	Denver	5	9	0
Buffalo	1	12	1	Cincinnati	3	11	0

At A Glance
1969

Jan. 1 – O.J. Simpson gained 171 yards on 28 carries and caught eight passes for 85 yards in a brilliant performance, but it wasn't enough as Ohio State defeated USC in the Rose Bowl. The 1968 Heisman Trophy winner finished his two-year USC career with 3,423 yards and 36 touchdowns in 21 games.

Jan. 2 – Ralph Wilson said he had no intention of trading the draft rights for O.J. Simpson and sources indicated he was ready to make a record contract offer to the USC star, topping the package Sonny Werblin bestowed upon Joe Namath in 1965.

Jan. 3 – A report in a Pasadena newspaper said Simpson preferred to play for an NFL team rather than the Bills. "I just prefer an NFL city," Simpson was quoted as saying. "I'm from an NFL city (San Francisco) and I grew up following the NFL. However, if I'm happy financially, I'm happy."

Jan. 4 – A report in Los Angeles indicated that Ralph Wilson had offered former Rams coach George Allen a $75,000 per year contract. The story, by Mel Durslag, quoted Wilson as saying: "Allen and I had never met before. I told him frankly that what we have in Buffalo today isn't a paradise for football teams. We have a bad stadium and in as much as we practice in the stadium, our training facilities are bad, too. And our locker room won't remind him of the Ritz. But I also told him we wouldn't be putting up with those facilities much longer. Either we get a new stadium in Buffalo or we're off to Seattle."

Jan. 9 – O.J. Simpson announced he would demand $1 million over a 10-year period with a $50,000 signing bonus.

Jan. 11 – The AFL voted to include special play-offs for the 1969 season with the division winners playing the second-place finishers in the other divisions with the two survivors meeting in the AFL Championship Game.

Jan. 14 – The *Courier-Express* reported that Baltimore defensive backfield coach Chuck Noll would become the new Bills head coach.

Jan. 17 – The search for a coach ended when John Rauch quit his post with Oakland and agreed to take over the Bills. Rauch, who had an .805 winning percentage in three years with the Raiders, agreed to a four-year pact, the longest ever given to a Buffalo coach. "I feel there is an excellent nucleus of playing talent in Buffalo, that the organization is a good one and that Ralph Wilson is a fine person to work for. That means the opportunity is there." Rauch's appointment sent Harvey Johnson back to the scouting department as director of player personnel, which is where he wanted to be anyway.

Jan. 24 – Former star receiver Elbert Dubenion and assistant coach Bob Celeri were named full-time scouts and John Rauch also indicated they would serve as coaches in training camp.

Jan. 25 – Former Bills coach Joe Collier joined another former Bills coach, Lou Saban, in Denver. Collier was signed to be a defensive assistant.

Jan. 26 – During a visit to Japan, Jets Super Bowl hero Joe Namath predicted that the Bills could be among the best teams in the AFL in 1969. "The Bills give me the most trouble of any pro team,"

O.J. Simpson's rookie year was frustrating because after being the main weapon throughout his collegiate career, Simpson didn't see the ball nearly as much with the Bills.

Namath said. "I really have a rough time reading their defenses. With O.J. Simpson and a quarterback, the Bills could make trouble."

Jan. 28 – The Bills made O.J. Simpson the first player selected in the college draft. Said Ralph Wilson: "I think we'll be able to sign him all right." Said Simpson: "They want to get this settled quickly and that's how I feel. I know they have a real good defense and an offense with a future." With their second choice, the Bills chose Oregon State fullback Bill Enyart and in the eighth round, they selected James Harris, a black quarterback from Grambling. A *Buffalo Evening News* headline read: "A 6-4 Negro QB, Harris, drafted 8th by the Bills." The story said Harris "is a negro, one of the few of his race to be drafted as a quarterback in pro football."

Jan. 29 – Assistant coaches Richie McCabe and Marvin Bass were retained and ex-Buffalo receiver Bill Miller and Bugsy Engelberg were added. Miller, retiring as a player with the Raiders, was hired to coach receivers and Engelberg was hired to coach kickers and punters.

Feb. 3 – Ray Malavasi was hired as the defensive line coach.

Feb. 4 – With the departure of John Rauch to Buffalo, Al Davis filled his head coaching void by promoting John Madden to the top position. At 33, Madden was the youngest head coach in pro football. Despite a 1-12-1 record, the Bills raised ticket prices by $1 across the board. It was only the second increase in team history.

Feb. 6 – After six hours of negotiating, Ralph Wilson said that the Bills and O.J. Simpson's representatives were "miles apart." Johnny Mazur, who served as Buffalo's backfield coach since 1962, but was not retained by John Rauch, signed on with the Boston Patriots.

Feb. 10 – The Bills ticket office at 69 W. Mohawk St. was burglarized and about $1,000 in cash was taken.

Feb. 11 – John Rauch completed his coaching

staff by hiring Ralph Hawkins to coach the linebackers.

Feb. 12 – Bills ticket director Duncan Lectka died of a heart attack at the Buffalo Athletic Club. He had been with the club since 1965.

March 3 – Richie McCabe quit the coaching staff to join John Madden in Oakland.

March 4 – Claude Gibson, who coached Boston's secondary in 1968, was hired to replace Richie McCabe.

March 5 – Ralph Wilson called O.J. Simpson's contract demands "Outrageous. I'm not sure anyone short of Howard Hughes can handle the package." It was reported that Simpson now wanted $600,000 in salary and bonuses over five years, plus a $500,000 loan for investment purposes.

March 24 – Linebacker Nick Buoniconti was traded by Boston to Miami for quarterback Kim Hammond and linebacker Ron Caveness.

March 28 – Talks again were fruitless between Ralph Wilson and O.J. Simpson's representatives. "It's beginning to look more and more like we're not going to get together," said Simpson's agent Chuck Barnes.

March 29 – Offensive lineman Bob Kalsu was inducted into the Army and lost to the team.

April 1 – Simpson's representatives told Ralph Wilson to pay their client what he wants or sell the team to a group of prospective buyers it had lined up. "I am gratified they are allowing me to keep my other businesses," Wilson said.

April 14 – Simpson rejected an offer to play minor league football for Indianapolis of the Continental Football League. The Capitols had offered $150,000 per year plus a $250,000 loan for investment purposes.

May 10 – Commissioner Pete Rozelle announced that Cleveland, Baltimore and Pittsburgh of the NFL would switch allegiances to the new American Football Conference for the 1970 season. That put 13 teams in the AFC and 13 in the National Football Conference under the new

National Football League.

May 26 – ABC signed a landmark three-year deal to telecast Monday night games in prime time starting in 1970, the first regularly scheduled series of sports telecasts in history.

May 29 – O.J. Simpson took a "pay me or trade me" approach to his negotiations with Ralph Wilson and threatened to sit out the 1969 season.

June 14 – The Bills disclosed that quarterback Dan Darragh reported to basic training in Fort Gordon, Ga. with his Army National Guard unit and would not be available to the team until late September.

July 9 – The Bills opened training camp at Niagara University without O.J. Simpson. Also, John Rauch closed practice to the fans, allowing only media to watch. Rauch explained that other teams send scouts to watch practices and he didn't want that occurring. "All I know is when I was with the Raiders, we benefited from the Bills being watched," Rauch said. "We got a lot of information out of Buffalo. In fact, it was common knowledge around the league what Buffalo was doing and what it had."

July 10 – Safety Hagood Clarke announced his retirement to concentrate full-time on his job as a stockbroker in Miami.

July 25 – About 5,000 fans got their first chance to see the team at Family Day at Niagara. The team held a scrimmage in the morning, then gave the crowd a clinic in the afternoon followed by an autograph session.

Aug. 2 – The Bills dropped their preseason opener in Houston, 24-7, but Jack Kemp, returning after missing 1968 with a knee injury, looked sharp.

Aug. 4 – With Kemp apparently healed, John Rauch released quarterback Kay Stephenson.

Aug. 8 – The Bills defeated the Washington Redskins and coach Vince Lombardi, 21-17, before 37,012 at War Memorial Stadium. Tom Flores threw the winning TD pass to Haven Moses.

Aug. 9 – The Bills and O.J. Simpson finally came to terms and Simpson signed with the Bills. Speculation was that the four-year, no-cut pact was for about $215,000 in salary with a $100,000 loan. Bonus incentive clauses also were included.

Aug. 11 – Simpson was greeted at the Buffalo airport by about 2,500 fans and was presented the key to the city by Mayor Frank Sedita. "I hope the game in Detroit (later in the week) isn't going to be as rough as the reception here," Simpson said. "I've had good-sized crowds greet us before like when we came back from South Bend after beating Notre Dame, but never for doing nothing. I'm glad I was finally able to get here."

Aug. 12 – Simpson reported for his first day of training camp at Niagara. He dropped a pitchout from James Harris and veteran Tom Day teased, "Do I have to put handles on the ball for you, young man?" Said Jack Kemp: "There's always going to be a little resentment, but no one can resent anybody when they contribute to a team's success, which ultimately puts money in everyone's pocket. There's also no doubt that O.J. adds glamour to the team. He's an attraction and this is also going to put money in our pockets." As for the number 32 he made famous in college, that number was taken by Gary McDermott who said he didn't want to relinquish it. Thus, Simpson was issued No. 36.

Aug. 15 – Simpson played 19 plays and rushed four times for 19 yards in his pro debut during Buffalo's 24-12 loss to the Detroit Lions at Tiger Stadium.

Aug. 20 – Unwanted in Denver as a quarterback, Marlin Briscoe signed with the Bills as a wide receiver.

Aug. 22 – Johnny Unitas led the Baltimore Colts to a 20-7 victory at War Memorial Stadium.

Aug. 25 – Tom Sestak, a five-time AFL all-star and one of the most dominating defensive players in Bills history, announced his retirement, as did guard George Flint. In addition, veteran Ed Rutkowski, the team's 1968 MVP, was released.

Aug. 27 – Safety Tom Janik, the Bills leading career pass interceptor with 21, was traded to Boston for a future draft choice as John Rauch's restructuring of the team continued.

Aug. 30 – The Bills played the first game of a Municipal Stadium doubleheader in Cleveland and lost to the Chicago Bears, 23-16. In the second game, Green Bay beat the Browns, 27-17. The crowd of 85,532 was the largest in Cleveland's pro football history.

Sept. 6 – The Bills concluded the preseason with a horrendous 50-20 loss to the Los Angeles Rams at The Coliseum. O.J. Simpson's return to Los Angeles and USC's home field was a bust as he carried seven times for 20 yards.

Sept. 8 – Veteran defensive players Marty Schottenheimer and Tom Day were cut.

Sept. 14 – The Super Bowl champion New York Jets spoiled O.J. Simpson's pro debut, 33-17, before a record crowd of 46,165 at War Memorial Stadium. Simpson gained 35 yards rushing, 64 on pass receptions and scored a touchdown.

Sept. 21 – Houston beat the Bills, 17-3, stretching its dominance over Buffalo to five games.

Sept. 23 – With Dan Darragh back from his National Guard duty, quarterback Tom Flores was waived.

Sept. 28 – The Bills won for the first time in almost one year as O.J. Simpson enjoyed his first 100-yard rushing game in a 41-28 victory over Denver.

Sept. 29 – A model of a proposed $39.7 million domed stadium in Lancaster was revealed. New York Governor Nelson Rockefeller promised the state's cooperation in assuring prompt realization of the stadium, plus aid in paying for $50 million in road construction around the site.

Oct. 5 – The Bills turned the ball over seven times and lost to Houston for the sixth straight time, 28-14.

Oct. 11 – Preston Ridlehuber's halfback-option TD pass to Haven Moses with 5:02 left lifted the Bills over the Patriots, 23-16, before another record War Memorial crowd of 46,201.

Oct. 19 – Oakland routed the Bills, 50-21, as Daryle Lamonica threw for six TDs in the first half. NBC waited eight minutes to start its yearly showing of the movie *Heidi*, unlike 1968 when it cut away from the Raiders-Jets game, missing Oakland's last-minute rally.

Oct. 26 – Miami won its first game of the year, whipping the Bills, 24-6, as O.J. Simpson gained a mere 12 yards on 10 carries, giving him just 292 yards in the six games he had played.

Nov. 2 – The Bills committed six turnovers and allowed Kansas City to score 23 fourth-quarter points in a 29-7 victory. Chiefs coach Hank Stram was charged with running up the score by calling timeout with three seconds left. Mike Garrett scored on the final play.

Nov. 9 – The Bills outplayed the Jets, but lost at Shea Stadium, 16-6.

Nov. 10 – Sid Gillman stepped down as head coach of the Chargers because of health reasons and assistant Charlie Waller took over. Gillman remained the team's general manager.

Nov. 16 – O.J. Simpson gained 226 all-purpose yards, including a 73-yard gallop with the opening kickoff, as the Bills ripped Miami, 28-3.

Nov. 19 – Ralph Wilson said that when the merger occurred for the 1970 season, rookies would no longer be able to command six-figure salaries. "The high salaries must be saved for the proven players. If anyone accuses me of skimping, just give me Roman Gabriel and I'll show you what a good sport and big tipper I am. If I had permitted myself to get all excited over all the wild talk about Simpson, I could have made a spectacular mistake (paying him his original $1.1 million demand)."

Nov. 23 – The Bills lost their 13th straight road game as the Patriots won at Boston College Field, 35-21, behind three Mike Taliaferro TD passes.

Nov. 30 – In a snowstorm, the Bills outlasted Cincinnati, 16-13, as the Bengals lost seven fumbles in Jack Kemp's final game at War Memorial Stadium.

Dec. 7 – For the second time in a month, Jan Stenerud kicked five field goals, including the game-winner with 1:59 to play, to beat the Bills, 22-19. In the process, he set a pro football record with 16 straight field goals made.

Dec. 9 – Butch Byrd was named to the all-AFL team.

Dec. 14 – The Bills got outclassed by San Diego, 45-6, in a run-for-the-bus performance. San Diego rolled up 547 yards and Lance Alworth extended his streak of consecutive games catching a pass to 96, breaking Don Hutson's pro football record set from 1937-45.

Dec. 15 – Al Bemiller, who never missed a game – regular season or exhibition since joining the team in 1961 – underwent surgery to repair a torn knee ligament which he suffered on the first play of the San Diego game.

Dec. 17 – Ralph Wilson predicted that his team would return to the top within three years, which was the length remaining on John Rauch's contract. "It wasn't a very satisfactory season, but I liked one thing about the season. I think we now have a good coach in John Rauch. I think he's tough and he'll get rid of the fellows who don't want to play his kind of football. I think it could take three years for us to come back, but I think we can be 7-7 next year."

Dec. 20 – In the first interdivisional playoff game, Kansas City edged the Jets, 13-6.

Dec. 21 – In the other playoff game, Oakland embarrassed Houston, 56-7.

Jan. 4, 1970 – Kansas City defeated Oakland, 17-7, to win the final AFL Championship Game, in front of 54,544 at Oakland-Alameda County Coliseum. The Chiefs received a record $7,775 per man as the winners. In the NFL Championship, Minnesota defeated Cleveland, 27-7.

Jan. 11, 1970 – Kansas City made it two Super Bowl victories in a row for the AFL as it whipped Minnesota, 23-7, before 80,998 at Tulane Stadium in New Orleans.

Jan. 17, 1970 – The West routed the East, 26-3, in the final AFL All-Star Game. John Hadl keyed the victory at the Astrodome.

BY THE NUMBERS - 1969

TEAM STATISTICS	BILLS	OPP
First downs	224	236
Rushing	83	106
Passing	122	118
Penalty	19	12
Total yards	3,867	4,334
Avg. game	276.2	309.6
Plays	868	853
Avg. play	4.5	5.1
Net rushing yds	1,522	1,858
Avg. game	108.7	132.7
Avg. play	4.0	4.1
Net passing yds	2,345	2,476
Comp/att	215/442	175/368
Sacks/lost	42-371	31-296
Interceptions	30	19
Percentage	48.6	47.6
Punts/avg	78-44.5	62-42.7
Fumbles/lost	35-21	25-19
Penalties/yds	67-632	71-719
Touchdowns	26	40
Extra points	23-24	39-40
Field goals	17-26	26-41
Two-point conv.	0-2	0-0
Safeties	0	1
Kick ret./avg	62-23.8	55-24.0
Punt ret./avg	31-6.0	45-10.4

RUSHING	ATT	YDS	AVG	TD
Simpson	181	697	3.9	2
Patrick	83	361	4.3	3
Enyart	47	191	4.1	1
Kemp	37	124	3.4	0
Anderson	13	74	5.7	1
Ridlehuber	4	25	6.3	0
Harris	10	25	2.5	0
Sherman	2	14	7.0	0
Darragh	6	14	2.3	0
Masters	1	-3	-3.0	0
TOTALS	**384**	**1522**	**4.0**	**7**

PASSING	COMP	ATT	INT	YDS	TD	COMP%
Kemp	170	344	22	1981	13	49.4
Darragh	24	52	6	365	1	46.2
Harris	15	36	1	270	1	41.7
Ridlehuber	1	1	0	45	1	100.0
Sherman	2	2	0	20	1	100.0
Maguire	1	1	0	19	0	100.0
Flores	2	5	0	16	0	40.0
Briscoe	0	1	1	0	0	00.0
TOTALS	**215**	**442**	**30**	**2716**	**17**	**48.6**

KICKING	FG/ATT	PAT/ATT	PTS
Alford	17-26	23-24	74

PUNTING	NO	AVG
Maguire	78	44.5

RECEIVING	CAT	YDS	AVG	TD
Moses	39	752	19.3	5
Patrick	35	229	6.5	0
Masters	33	387	11.7	1
Briscoe	32	532	16.6	5
Simpson	30	343	11.4	3
Enyart	19	186	9.8	2
Thornton	14	134	9.6	0
Anderson	7	65	9.3	0
Crockett	4	50	12.5	0
Grate	1	19	19.0	1
James	1	19	19.0	0
TOTALS	**215**	**2716**	**12.6**	**17**

LEADERS

Kick returns: Simpson 21-529 yds, 25.2 avg, 0 TD
Thornton 30-749, 25.0, 0 TD

Punt returns: Anderson 19-142, 7.5, 0 TD
Byrd 7-37, 5.3, 0 TD

Interceptions: Byrd 7-95, 13.6, 1 TD
Saimes 3-47, 15.7, 0 TD

Non-kick scoring: Simpson 5 TDs, 30 pts
Moses 5 TDs, 30 pts
Briscoe 5 TDs, 30 pts

Jack Kemp, after missing all of 1968 with a knee injury, returned to play his final season in 1969. He finished his Bills career with 77 touchdown passes, which ranks him third behind Jim Kelly and Joe Ferguson.

NOTES
• The Super Bowl-champion Jets spoiled O.J. Simpson's pro debut in front of a record War Memorial Stadium crowd.
• Rookie quarterback James Harris started, but pulled a groin and Tom Flores and Jack Kemp finished. Kemp played for the first time since 1967 and rallied the Bills from 19-3 down to a tie before the Jets scored twice in the fourth to put it away.
• With the score 19-19, Mike Battle returned the kickoff to the Jets 42. Matt Snell burst free for 34 yards to the Bills 24 and he eventually scored the winning TD from 11 yards out.
• Kemp was intercepted by Cornell Gordon on the ensuing series and after the Bills held, Kemp was picked off by Paul Crane who ran 23 yards for the clinching TD.
• Already ahead 9-3 in the second quarter, the Jets got a scare when Joe Namath appeared to suffer a serious knee injury. But after a lengthy on-field exam, he was deemed OK. One play later, he hit Don Maynard on a 60-yard TD pass.
• Trailing 19-3, the Bills began their comeback when John Pitts returned Snell's fumble to the 8. Two plays later, rookie Bill Enyart scored.
• George Saimes then intercepted Namath and returned it to the 16. After a Jet penalty, Simpson scored on an eight-yard run.
• On the next series, Paul Guidry picked off Namath and returned it 39 yards to the 4. However, NY held and Bruce Alford kicked a 10-yard field goal.

QUOTES
• John Rauch: "It will be quite a while before the rough spots are smoothed out. It all depends on our morale. If we can stay up – and I think we have the kind of guys who will – we can play good football eventually. We stressed throwing in our game plan with the Jets record against the run (AFL-best in 1968). We have to be more consistent and you have to give the Jets credit for coming back. I can't say I'm satisfied, but I'm not discouraged."
• O.J. Simpson: "He (Namath) wished me good luck and told me not to let the press bother me."
• Jets coach Weeb Ewbank: "We blew a lot of our plays because our receivers couldn't hear Joe's audible signals. I've tried to get electronic amplifier aids from Japan to beat the noise in this stadium, but I haven't come up with anything yet."

Jets	6	10	3	14 -	33
Bills	3	0	6	10 -	19

Attendance at War Memorial Stadium - 46,165

NY: FG J. Turner 9, 6:34
Buf: FG Alford 35, 10:23
NY: FG J. Turner 26, 14:06
NY: FG J. Turner 41, 2:00
NY: Maynard 60 pass from Namath (J. Turner kick), 9:14
NY: FG J. Turner 21, 11:42
Buf: Enyart 5 pass from Kemp (pass failed), 14:46
Buf: Simpson 8 run (Alford kick), :59
Buf: FG Alford 10, 4:05
NY: Snell 11 run (J. Turner kick), 7:29
NY: Crane 23 interception return (J. Turner kick), 12:47

	BUF	NY
First downs	13	15
Rushing yds	59	178
Passing yds	122	146
Punts-avg	5-45.2	2-55.5
Fumbles-lost	2-2	2-1
Penalties-yds	3-33	6-88

BILLS LEADERS: Rushing - Simpson 10-35, Enyart 9-18, Harris 1-6; **Passing** - Kemp 7-13-3 - 72, Harris 3-12-1 - 74, Flores 2-5-0 - 16; **Receiving** - Moses 1-14, Simpson 2-64, Enyart 2-7, Patrick 1-7, Masters 1-3, Thornton 3-35, Anderson 2-32.

JETS LEADERS: Rushing - Snell 26-106, Boozer 11-55, Mathis 2-9, Namath 2-8; **Passing** - Namath 7-19-3 - 157; **Receiving** - Maynard 3-118, Lammons 3-35, Boozer 1-4.

WEEK 1 GAMES
Den 35, Bos 7	Oak 21, Hou 17
KC 27, SD 9	Cinc 27, Mia 21

NOTES
• The Bills lost to the Oilers for the fifth straight time. It was the fourth time in those games that they failed to score a TD. Counting preseason, they had lost seven in a row to Houston.
• In their last three games against Houston, the Bills totaled 335 yards and 16 points. In the second half, Jack Kemp was minus-23 net yards passing as he was sacked four times.
• In the second quarter, the Bills drove into Houston territory three times, but Kemp threw two interceptions, both by Ken Houston, and Billy Masters lost a fumble.
• The Oilers had only 43 yards at halftime, but led 7-3, because Jerry Levias returned a punt 58 yards to the Bills 35, setting up Pete Beathard's TD pass to Alvin Reed.
• Houston's second TD was the result of Beathard's 56-yard pass to Roy Hopkins that put the ball on the 1. Hoyle Granger scored from there.
• Newly converted tackle Paul Costa and All-Pro guard Billy Shaw were injured and didn't play in the second half.

QUOTES
• John Rauch: "Jinx? I can't say it's a matter of being jinxed. We had opportunities, but we're not at the stage where we can cash in on them. The big play, the opportunistic play, that's what we need to get on the winning track. Houston did nothing that surprised us on offense or defense. The interceptions Kemp threw were not, contrary to what I hear being whispered, due to a lack of strength in his passing arm. Kemp is still capable of throwing long and hard. If this wasn't fact, he wouldn't be in the lineup, it's that simple. We dropped too many passes and there were a lot of people in there who he's not too familiar with. Our own defense played as fine a game as it could be expected against a club with Houston's talent. I'd be less than candid if I didn't say we're making strides towards becoming a respectable football team. We're looking forward to our future games."
• Houston coach Wally Lemm: "The Bills have become a lot tougher in just a month. Our quarterback ran at the right side of the line because it's a waste of time to keep testing that Jim Dunaway. Of course you don't win too many prizes running at that (Mike) Stratton. On defense, we didn't especially key on O.J. Our linebackers kept stunting to give Kemp something to worry about."

Oilers	0	7	3	7 -	17
Bills	3	0	0	0 -	3

Attendance at War Memorial Stadium - 40,146

Buf: FG Alford 14, 7:36
Hou: Reed 12 pass from Beathard (Gerela kick), :06
Hou: FG Gerela 21, 7:49
Hou: Granger 1 run (Gerela kick), 1:53

	BUF	HOU
First downs	10	15
Rushing yds	93	123
Passing yds	40	122
Punts-avg	7-55.1	2-44.1
Fumbles-lost	1-0	0-0
Penalties-yds	4-27	4-30

BILLS LEADERS: Rushing - Simpson 19-58, Enyart 1-2, Patrick 3-8, Kemp 4-25; **Passing** - Kemp 12-21-3 - 99; **Receiving** - Moses 2-24, Simpson 1-5, Patrick 2-6, Masters 4-47, Thornton 3-17.

OILERS LEADERS: Rushing - Hopkins 15-66, Granger 13-25, Burrell 4-17, Johnson 3-9, Beathard 1-6; **Passing** - Beathard 10-20-0 - 140; **Receiving** - Beirne 3-30, Reed 2-22, Granger 2-12, Hopkins 1-56, Haik 1-11, Joiner 1-9.

WEEK 2 GAMES
Oak 20, Mia 17	KC 31, Bos 0
Den 21, NY 19	Cinc 34, SD 20

STANDINGS: SECOND WEEK

EAST	W	L	T	WEST	W	L	T
New York	1	1	0	Oakland	2	0	0
Houston	1	1	0	Kan. City	2	0	0
Buffalo	0	2	0	Denver	2	0	0
Boston	0	2	0	Cincinnati	2	0	0
Miami	0	2	0	San Diego	0	2	0

Broncos	14	0	7	7 -	28
Bills	3	17	21	0 -	41

Attendance at War Memorial Stadium - 40,302

Den: Smiley 1 run (Howfield kick), 4:05
Buf: FG Alford 27, 10:02
Den: Haffner 11 pass from Liske (Howfield kick), 14:11
Buf: Simpson 3 pass from Kemp (Alford kick), 2:54
Buf: FG Alford 30, 5:5
Buf: Moses 55 pass from Kemp (Alford kick), 12:33
Den: Denson 62 pass from Liske (Howfield kick), 1:54
Buf: Patrick 4 run (Alford kick), 5:10
Buf: Byrd 12 interception return (Alford kick), 5:46
Buf: Masters 6 pass from Kemp (Alford kick), 12:27
Den: Haffner 15 pass from Liske (Howfield kick), 4:33

	BUF	DEN
First downs	28	20
Rushing yds	159	69
Passing yds	247	233
Punts-avg	6-43.5	4-36.0
Fumbles-lost	2-1	1-0
Penalties-yds	7-72	9-77

BILLS LEADERS: Rushing - Simpson 24-110, Enyart 3-15, Patrick 4-7, Kemp 2-16, Harris 2-11; **Passing** - Kemp 19-38-0 - 249, Harris 2-4-0 - 17; **Receiving** - Moses 4-80, Simpson 5-45, Patrick 2-21, Masters 5-63, Briscoe 1-17, Thornton 3-29, Enyart 1-11.

BRONCOS LEADERS: Rushing - Liske 3-32, Quayle 9-27, Smiley 5-10; **Passing** - Liske 17-45-5 - 289; **Receiving** - Denson 6-138, Haffner 4-48, Quayle 4-40, Beer 3-63.

NOTES

• O.J. Simpson gave a glimpse of the future and Jack Kemp provided a look at the past in Buffalo's first victory. Simpson had his first 100-yard rushing game and Kemp threw for 249 yards and three TDs before jamming his thumb late in the game.
• The win was the Bills' first since Sept. 29, 1968, almost exactly one year ago.
• Denver was without starting QB Steve Tensi and star running back Floyd Little.
• The 28 first downs was a team record as Simpson picked up 12 either running or receiving.
• The Bills intercepted Pete Liske five times, which resulted in three touchdowns.
• Denver took a 7-0 lead after Carl Cunningham returned a blocked field goal 46 yards to the 1.
• A Harry Jacobs interception led to a Buffalo field goal (after a Billy Masters TD reception was nullified because Paul Costa was holding). The Bills fell behind 14-3, then turned the game around. Kemp capped an 80-yard drive with a TD pass to Simpson. The Bills got a field goal and later a 55-yard Kemp-to-Haven Moses TD for a 20-14 halftime lead.
• Booker Edgerson was beaten by Al Denson for a 62-yard score early in the third, but Simpson's 28-yard run highlighted another 80-yard drive that ended in Wayne Patrick's score.
• Just 36 seconds later, Butch Byrd picked off a Liske pass and went 12 yards for the clinching TD. John Pitts' superb interception at the Bills 1 and 39-yard return started the Bills on their way to their final TD.

QUOTES

• Broncos coach Lou Saban: "Hats off to Jack Kemp, he did the job for them. What's more, Jack got off the deck to do the job. He was out all last year with an injury, yet he has come back this season in fine form, especially today. Without Jack today, the Bills have to be in trouble. With him, they were great. We played poorly and those interceptions really hurt us. The one Butch Byrd intercepted was especially damaging."
• John Rauch: "Give him (Kemp) credit. So many people played big parts in this win, but give Jack a lot of credit. He did a tremendous job."
• Jack Kemp: "You've seen me in practice, you know I can throw. I didn't expect to be passing that much today, but the passing game was working so I stuck with it."
• O.J. Simpson: "I got tired at the beginning today until I got into the groove. But it wasn't only the good running day that I had that I'm happy about, it's the fact that we won. Naturally I was glad to go over 100 yards for the first time, but I'm happy about my blocking."

WEEK 3 GAMES

SD 34, NY 27	Oak 38, Bos 23
Hou 22, Mia 10	Cinc 24, KC 19

Bills	0	0	7	7 -	14
Oilers	7	7	7	7 -	28

Attendance at The Astrodome - 46,485

Hou: Hopkins 3 pass from Beathard (Gerela kick), 10:05
Hou: Beathard 3 run (Gerela kick), 8:13
Hou: Houston 51 interception return (Gerela kick), 7:19
Buf: Anderson 6 run (Alford kick), 10:07
Hou: Granger 1 run (Gerela kick), 2:58
Buf: Briscoe 26 pass from Kemp (Alford kick), 3:56

	BUF	HOU
First downs	12	15
Rushing yds	44	113
Passing yds	237	139
Punts-avg	6-48.2	5-44.0
Fumbles-lost	3-3	1-1
Penalties-yds	3-30	4-64

BILLS LEADERS: Rushing - Simpson 13-27, Kemp 2-12, Anderson 1-6, Patrick 2-2, Masters 1-(-3); **Passing** - Kemp 20-46-4 - 223, Maguire 1-1-0 - 19; **Receiving** - Moses 2-32, Simpson 3-32, Patrick 2-23, Masters 3-21, Briscoe 3-59, Thornton 3-19, Anderson 3-34, James 1-19, Enyart 1-3.

OILERS LEADERS: Rushing - Granger 22-62, Hopkins 12-32, Beathard 3-8, Haik 1-11; **Passing** - Beathard 10-28-3 - 139; **Receiving** - Reed 4-48, Hopkins 3-35, Granger 1-17, LeVias 1-29, Haik 1-10.

WEEK 4 GAMES

NY 23, Bos 14	Oak 20, Mia 20
SD 21, Cinc 14	KC 26, Den 13

NOTES

• The Bills finally enjoyed some offensive success against the Oilers, but lost for the sixth straight time, thanks to four Jack Kemp interceptions and three Wayne Patrick fumbles.
• W.K. Hicks' interception and return to the Bills 21 set up Houston's first TD. Patrick's first fumble at the Buffalo 37 preceded the second TD, which gave Houston a 14-0 halftime lead.
• Ken Houston then returned a Kemp interception 51 yards for a TD in the third.
• The Bills almost made a game of it at this point. Bubba Thornton returned the kickoff 51 yards to the Houston 46 and Max Anderson eventually scored on a six-yard sweep. An unsportsmanlike conduct penalty was assessed on the kickoff, so the Bills tried an onside kick and Robert James recovered it at the Oilers 36. Miller Farr was called for interfering with Haven Moses at the 7 and Simpson ran six yards to the 1. However, Simpson lost a yard, Kemp was sacked and then Kemp's fourth-down pass in the end zone fell incomplete.
• Houston then marched 80 yards with the help of a 31-yard Pete Beathard-to-Roy Hopkins pass, which led to Hoyle Granger's clinching TD.
• Butch Byrd's club record-tying third interception and 24-yard return to the Oilers 26 set up Kemp's TD pass to Marlin Briscoe on the next play with 11:04 remaining. But the Bills never threatened to score again.

QUOTES

• John Rauch: "Football is a game of blocking, tackling, hitting and hustling. We didn't lose to Houston because they're our jinx team, we lost because we didn't put the blocking, tackling, hitting and hustling together. One of the things that upsets me is the difference between the two teams isn't great. We should have taken them, but obviously the interceptions and fumbles hurt us. Our pass protection by and large was favorable, but there was one sufficient breakdown (Kemp getting sacked on third-and-goal from the 2) when a touchdown would have pulled us within 21-14. I didn't even consider a field goal there; we needed touchdowns. We are not as aggressive offensively as we are defensively. And I don't know if it's because they're unsure of themselves."
• O.J. Simpson on the Oilers rough style of play: "They just played aggressively. Some of our guys were hollering about it from the bench, but yelling isn't going to get us anyplace. We gave them a lot of points."

STANDINGS: FOURTH WEEK

EAST	W	L	T	WEST	W	L	T
Houston	3	1	0	Oakland	3	0	1
New York	2	2	0	Cincinnati	3	1	0
Buffalo	1	3	0	Kan. City	3	1	0
Miami	0	3	1	Denver	2	2	0
Boston	0	4	0	San Diego	2	2	0

NOTES

• Newly activated Preston Ridlehuber became a hero when he threw a 45-yard halfback option TD pass to Haven Moses with 5:02 left. Ridlehuber was the man who scored the clinching TD for Oakland on a fumble recovery in the historic 1968 *Heidi* game between the Raiders and the Jets.

• O.J. Simpson was held out of the game as a precautionary measure due to a head injury he had suffered the previous week against Houston.

• Wayne Patrick recorded his first 100-yard game as the Bills rushed for 204 yards without Simpson.

• Controversial Boston coach Clive Rush pulled his defense off the field in the second quarter while arguing with referee Ben Dreith.

• Ex-Bill Marty Schottenheimer's interception set up Boston's first TD.

• Patrick's 72-yard run led to Bruce Alford's first field goal and a 10-6 Buffalo lead.

• Butch Byrd's interception and 21-yard return to the Pats 19 set up another Alford field goal.

• Carl Garrett returned the ensuing kickoff 57 yards. Three plays later, Mike Taliaferro hit Charley Frazier with a 29-yard TD pass on a third-and-one play, tying the game at 13-13.

• Byrd stole the ball from Garrett after a 39-yard run and returned it 42 yards to the Pats 16. Buffalo settled for another Alford field goal, and Gino Cappelletti tied it later.

• Buffalo's winning score came on a wild series. While being tackled, James Harris passed 19 yards to Billy Masters on third-and-nine. Then, Max Anderson fumbled, but the officials ruled the play dead, enraging the Patriots. On the next play, Anderson had two teeth knocked out and six others broken on a tackle by John Bramlett. In came Ridlehuber. He took a handoff, rolled left and hit Moses for the score on a play that Simpson, had he been playing, or Anderson would have been throwing.

• Boston head coach Clive Rush and Buffalo assistant Hoot Gibson got into a heated shouting match after the game. Gibson, a former Boston assistant, had visited the Patriots hotel the night before and Rush was angered. Gibson said Rush called him names prior to the game and accused him of tampering with his players.

QUOTES

• Preston Ridlehuber: "I would have rather had Harris run the play to the other side of the field. This time, I had to run to my left while I sought the receiver. I saw Haven downfield, but I didn't know if I could get the ball to him. I had a little trouble getting into throwing position, but I made it all right. I didn't practice that play at all."

WEEK 5 GAMES	
NY 21, Cinc 7	SD 21, Mia 14
KC 24, Hou 0	Oak 24, Den 14

Patriots	6	0	7	3 - 16
Bills	7	3	3	10 - 23

Attendance at War Memorial Stadium - 46,201

Buf: Patrick 2 run (Alford kick), 6:48
Bos: Garrett 1 run (kick failed), 12:03
Buf: FG Alford 24, 8:37
Buf: FG Alford 22, 11:58
Bos: Frazier 29 pass from Taliaferro (Cappelletti kick), 13:47
Buf: FG Alford 22, 3:26
Bos: FG Cappelletti 32, 6:21
Buf: Moses 45 pass from Ridlehuber (Alford kick), 9:58

	BUF	BOS
First downs	20	14
Rushing yds	204	100
Passing yds	160	148
Punts-avg	3-48.7	4-45.0
Fumbles-lost	2-0	1-1
Penalties-yds	8-76	9-67

BILLS LEADERS: Rushing - Patrick 17-131, Anderson 10-46, Harris 3-2, Ridlehuber 4-25; **Passing** - Kemp 10-21-2 - 102, Harris 2-4-0 - 23, Ridlehuber 1-1-0 - 45; **Receiving** - Moses 3-89, Patrick 5-20, Masters 3-41, Thornton 1-21, Anderson 1-(-1).
PATRIOTS LEADERS: Rushing - Nance 12-35, Garrett 10-61, Gamble 2-4; **Passing** - Taliaferro 13-31-1 - 162; **Receiving** - Marsh 3-41, Frazier 2-43, Rademacher 2-23, Nance 2-22, Garrett 2-15, Whalen 1-12, Sellers 1-6.

NOTES

• In John Rauch's first game against his old team, John Madden's Raiders crushed the Bills.

• Ex-Bill Daryle Lamonica thrilled an Oakland football record crowd with six first-half TD passes.

• The Bills turned over the ball seven times, yet were only outgained by 12 yards.

• QB James Harris was lost for the season with a knee injury.

• On the first play of the game, Butch Byrd dropped an interception. Five plays later, Lamonica and Billy Cannon combined on a 53-yard TD pass.

• Lamonica completed six straight passes during a 65-yard march to the second TD.

• In the second quarter, Ike Lassiter returned a Jack Kemp fumble to the Bills 4 to set up the third TD. Bubba Thornton fumbled the ensuing kickoff and on the next play, Lamonica had his fourth TD pass.

• Kemp promptly was intercepted by Bill Laskey and on the next play, Lamonica hit Fred Biletnikoff for a 35-0 lead, capping a three-TD spurt in 3:48.

• The Raiders' sixth TD was set up when a punt bounced off Byrd's rear end and was recovered by the Raiders.

• Ironically, NBC aired the children's movie *Heidi* after the game. Only this time, the network delayed the start of the movie when the game ran eight minutes long. *Buffalo Evening News* writer Steve Weller wrote "The Sunday afternoon fright show had millions of television viewers crying out for the early arrival of *Heidi.*

QUOTES

• John Rauch: "When a team is beaten that soundly, any explanation sounds like sour grapes. I felt confident we could win. We worked a little extra hard and I'm sure the Raiders did, too. So you had two teams anxious for the game, but as sometimes happens, the Raiders got that first quick touchdown, their impetus

then increased and we added a lot of fuel to their fire with our rash of fumbles. I'll take my lumps. Maybe someday the shoe will be on the other foot."

• Raiders quarterback Daryle Lamonica: "I have the same feeling now against the Bills that I have against every other club. Much of the resentment I had early in the wake of the trade has rubbed off. I want to beat them as much as I want to beat any other team. Of course, we all naturally gave a lot of thought to the fact that we didn't want to be beat by our former coach, handling a team that we felt we never should be beaten by."

WEEK 6 GAMES	
Den 30, Cinc 23	NY 26, Hou 17
KC 17, Mia 10	SD 13, Bos 10

Bills	0	7	0	14 - 21
Raiders	14	28	6	2 - 50

Attendance at Oakland-Alameda County Stadium - 54,418

Oak: Cannon 53 pass from Lamonica (Blanda kick), 2:07
Oak: Banaszak 10 pass from Lamonica (Blanda kick), 14:14
Oak: Banaszak 1 pass from Lamonica (Blanda kick), 2:08
Oak: Wells 13 pass from Lamonica (Blanda kick), 2:43
Oak: Biletnikoff 16 pass from Lamonica (Blanda kick), 5:56
Oak: Biletnikoff 23 pass from Lamonica (Blanda kick), 10:27
Buf: Moses 39 pass from Harris (Alford kick), 12:12
Oak: FG Blanda 20, 8:50
Oak: FG Blanda 36, 11:16
Buf: Enyart 30 pass from Kemp (Alford kick), :08
Buf: Briscoe 50 pass from Kemp (Alford kick), 3:53
Oak: Safety, Kemp tackled in end zone by Dotson, 14:26

	BUF	OAK
First downs	19	20
Rushing yds	146	84
Passing yds	246	320
Punts-avg	6-35.5	7-45.1
Fumbles-lost	7-5	1-0
Penalties-yds	5-40	7-65

BILLS LEADERS: Rushing - Simpson 6-50, Enyart 10-68, Kemp 3-19, Patrick 4-3, Harris 4-6; **Passing** - Kemp 8-26-2 - 155, Harris 8-16-0 - 156; **Receiving** - Moses 2-56, Simpson 1-11, Patrick 2-14, Briscoe 6-119, Masters 2-42, Enyart 3-69.
RAIDERS LEADERS: Rushing - Banaszak 6-20, Hubbard 4-22, Smith 7-12, Todd 7-18, Lamonica 1-12; **Passing** - Lamonica 21-36-1 - 313, Blanda 3-5-1 - 26; **Receiving** - Smith 5-45, Wells 4-84, Todd 4-33, Banaszak 4-20, Cannon 3-64, Biletnikoff 3-56, Buie 1-37.

STANDINGS: SIXTH WEEK

EAST	W	L	T	WEST	W	L	T
New York	4	2	0	Oakland	5	0	1
Houston	3	3	0	Kan. City	5	1	0
Buffalo	2	4	0	San Diego	4	2	0
Miami	0	5	1	Cincinnati	3	3	0
Boston	0	6	0	Denver	3	3	0

GAME 7 - Sunday, Oct. 26, 1969 - DOLPHINS 24, BILLS 6

Bills	3	0	3	0	-	6
Dolphins	0	14	3	7	-	24

Attendance at The Orange Bowl - 39,837

Buf: FG Alford 14, 3:17
Mia: Seiple 41 pass from Griese (Kremser kick), 1:02
Mia: Kiick 53 pass from Griese (Kremser kick), 12:32
Buf: FG Alford 9, 4:51
Mia: FG Kremser 12, 12:01
Mia: Kiick 1 run (Kremser kick), 12:00

	BUF	MIA
First downs	13	17
Rushing yds	56	136
Passing yds	220	217
Punts-avg	5-48.0	3-43.0
Fumbles-lost	3-1	3-2
Penalties-yds	5-50	5-40

BILLS LEADERS: Rushing - Simpson 10-12, Patrick 5-11, Kemp 7-16, Darragh 4-16, Enyart 1-1; **Passing** - Kemp 14-19-1 - 156, Darragh 6-17-2 - 81; **Receiving** - Moses 4-47, Simpson 4-60, Patrick 4-32, Masters 4-38, Briscoe 1-38, Enyart 3-22.

DOLPHINS LEADERS: Rushing - Csonka 12-54, Kiick 12-32, Morris 6-28, Griese 4-14, Milton 1-19, Noonan 1-(-11); **Passing** - Griese 9-18-2 - 232; **Receiving** - Kiick 3-109, Seiple 3-66, Clancy 1-32, Milton 1-15, Noonan 1-10.

NOTES

• It was one of the most frustrating losses for the Bills as they scored six points on four opportunities inside the Miami 10.
• George Saimes intercepted Bob Griese on the first play of the game and returned it 14 yards to the 27. But after a 19-yard pass to Wayne Patrick, the Bills settled for Bruce Alford's field goal.
• Mercury Morris fumbled the ensuing kickoff and Pete Richardson recovered at the 25, but the threat died when Nick Buoniconti intercepted a Jack Kemp pass on the 2.
• Miami drove all the way to the Bills' 4, but Robert James foiled a fake field goal. However, the Dolphins struck on their next possession when Larry Seiple beat John Pitts for his TD.
• Kemp lost a fumble at the Miami 36 and four plays later, Griese hit Jim Kiick for a 53-yard TD.
• Late in the half, the Bills drove to the Miami 9, but Alford missed a field goal.
• Kemp was benched in favor of Dan Darragh in the second half. Bubba Thornton returned the second-half kickoff to the 50 and Darragh hit O.J. Simpson for 33 yards. They eventually moved to the 2 before Alford had to come in and kick a field goal.

WEEK 7 GAMES	
KC 42, Cinc 22	Hou 24, Den 21
NY 23, Bos 17	Oak 24, SD 12

• After Pitts dropped an interception, Karl Kremser kicked a field goal and after Dick Anderson intercepted Darragh, Miami scored its final TD.
• Through seven games, the Bills had penetrated the opponents' 25-yard-line on 24 occasions and scored seven TDs and 10 field goals.

QUOTES

• John Rauch: "It's our offense that is lacking and I'll be the first one to take the blame. We're making far too many mistakes and penalties. The defense can hold up just so long. It's frustrating for them. Reading, saying or just hearing it, the sound of a 2-5 record is like the clash of cymbals in a telephone booth. The facts are loud, the reverberations too loud. I'll buy the uphill fight. I'll only admit to a team being a loser when it quits on itself and that, the Bills haven't done, nor intend to do. There's two ways to go – keep working or lay down. I intend to keep battling and I hope the players do, too. This was probably the most disheartening loss for the players and it should have been. The game was ours to take command in the first few minutes. If we had come out of those first two sequences with 14 points, the momentum would have been ours. Instead, we were down 14-3 at the half."
• O.J. Simpson: "We get behind so fast and often that we have to throw to establish a ground attack. Buffalo has a long way to go and was going to take some knocks. But I thought it would be better by now. I have a long-term contract and maybe that's a good thing the way I'm coming along."

GAME 8 - Sunday, Nov. 2, 1969 - CHIEFS 29, BILLS 7

Chiefs	0	3	3	23	-	29
Bills	7	0	0	0	-	7

Attendance at War Memorial Stadium - 45,844

Buf: Briscoe 14 pass from Darragh (Alford kick), 9:18
KC: FG Stenerud 47, 2:35
KC: FG Stenerud 34, 14:24
KC: FG Stenerud 37, :51
KC: FG Stenerud 44, 9:36
KC: FG Stenerud 18, 13:03
KC: Garrett 34 run (Stenerud kick), 13:44
KC: Garrett 5 run (Stenerud kick), 14:59

	BUF	KC
First downs	14	14
Rushing yds	105	147
Passing yds	39	98
Punts-avg	5-42.0	3-46.0
Fumbles-lost	3-2	2-2
Penalties-yds	2-30	4-60

BILLS LEADERS: Rushing - Simpson 16-41, Patrick 12-66, Darragh 2-(-2); **Passing** - Darragh 10-25-4 - 132; **Receiving** - Moses 2-43, Simpson 2-32, Patrick 1-6, Masters 2-18, Briscoe 2-27, Enyart 1-6.

CHIEFS LEADERS: Rushing - Garrett 14-71, Holmes 7-33, McVea 7-23, Hayes 2-13, Pitts 1-7; **Passing** - Dawson 7-14-0 - 94, Livingston 2-8-1 - 15; **Receiving** - Pitts 4-70, Richardson 2-38, Arbanas 1-9, Garrett 1-1, Holmes 1-(-9).

WEEK 8 GAMES	
Bos 24, Hou 0	NY 33, Mia 31
Cinc 31, Oak 17	Den 13, SD 0

NOTES

• Len Dawson came back from a six-week layoff, relieved rookie Mike Livingston and helped the Chiefs to victory, but it was Jan Stenerud who killed Buffalo with a Chiefs' record five field goals.
• Chiefs coach Hank Stram was charged with rubbing it in when he called timeout with three seconds left to set up Mike Garrett's five-yard TD run on the game's final play. It capped a 23-point fourth-quarter rally.
• George Saimes (knee) and Paul Guidry (shoulder) were lost for the season due to injuries.
• The Chiefs recorded nine sacks for 93 yards, four each by Aaron Brown and Curley Culp.
• The Bills took a 7-0 lead when Dan Darragh hit Marlin Briscoe with a 14-yard TD pass 9:18 into the game. The Chiefs only could retaliate with two Stenerud field goals through three quarters.
• But after the second field goal, Bubba Thornton fumbled the kickoff and Ceasar Belser recovered for KC at the Bills 22. Stenerud kicked his third field goal for a 9-7 lead.
• Two more three-pointers made it 15-7 with less than two minutes left before Stram poured it on.
• Darragh overthrew O.J. Simpson and Johnny Robinson intercepted at the Bills 34. On the next play, Garrett raced in for a TD.
• Another Robinson interception set the stage for the final insulting Garrett TD.

QUOTES

• Chiefs coach Hank Stram: "Really, I didn't know how much time remained when I called timeout. I just called it to send in a play. It wasn't meant to run up the score, really." (On the return of Len Dawson): "He really pulled us out of some holes. I wanted Lenny in there because he stabilizes the team. The players have a great deal of confidence in him. Buffalo used a lot of defenses and he reads them a lot better than Mike."

• John Rauch on Stram: "I wasn't surprised that he called time like that. The shoe has been on the other foot with him before. Oakland (with Rauch as coach) beat him, 41-6, in the West Division playoff last year, although I can't recall calling timeout with three seconds left. He's that type of person. He wants to get as many points as he can because he's interested in records." (On not replacing Darragh with Jack Kemp): "I didn't consider playing Kemp in the fourth quarter. By and large, he (Darragh) directed the club well. What happened to him in the fourth quarter (a lost fumble and two interceptions that led to 17 points) was just unfortunate."
• Chiefs QB Len Dawson: "I just wanted to let the clock run out. The game was over at that point so why insult the other team? Of course you've always got guys who want to score more."
• Harry Jacobs: "Thanks to Stram, the score doesn't indicate how close the game was."
• O.J. Simpson: "We're beating ourselves by taking ourselves out of position too much. But the line did a helluva job and we're coming together as a team."

STANDINGS: EIGHTH WEEK

EAST	W	L	T	WEST	W	L	T
New York	6	2	0	Kan. City	7	1	0
Houston	4	4	0	Oakland	6	1	1
Buffalo	2	6	0	San Diego	4	4	0
Miami	1	6	1	Cincinnati	4	4	0
Boston	1	7	0	Denver	4	4	0

NOTES

• QB Dan Darragh suffered a shoulder separation late in the first half after playing superbly and was ruled out for the season.

• Once again, trouble in enemy territory killed the Bills. In the first half, they reached New York's 6, 15, 18, 36 and 13, but managed only three points.

• Early in the first quarter, O.J. Simpson's three-yard TD run was nullified when it was ruled he moved before the snap. The Bills wound up turning over the ball on downs and didn't score.

• The Jets' first TD came as a result of a very questionable pass-interference penalty in the end zone on Booker Edgerson against Don Maynard. That put the ball on the 1 from where Bill Mathis scored in the second quarter.

• After Darragh's injury, Kemp drove the Bills to the Jets 36, but was knocked cold on a tackle by Larry Grantham. Emergency QB Marlin Briscoe threw an interception on his first play.

• Bruce Alford's partially blocked 20-yard field goal on the final play of the first half still cleared the goal posts to cut the Jets' lead to 7-3.

• In the third, Alford added a 29-yarder after Kemp was sacked on third down.

• Jim Turner kicked two field goals to make it 13-6 and then O.J. Simpson lost a fumble with less than four minutes remaining. John Neidert recovered and it led to Turner's clinching 47-yard field goal in the final minute.

QUOTES

• John Rauch: "There's no doubt that two penalty calls against us affected the Jets win (Simpson's nullified TD and Edgerson's interference call). The call against Booker could have been the difference between losing and winning. I'm neither seeking an alibi nor questioning the calls, but merely pointing out that the big plays went against us because of penalties. Again, and I don't want to sound like a broken record, this was a game we should have won."

• Booker Edgerson: "We have buzzard's luck. We can't find anything and we can't kill anything. The ball was overthrown (on the interference penalty). I pushed him as the ball hit his fingertips. I wish I hadn't been there at all."

• Jets receiver Don Maynard: "I don't think he (Edgerson) pushed me. I think he might have held me so I couldn't reach the ball."

• Billy Shaw on the play where Darragh was injured: "Dan told me he had released the ball when (Gerry) Philbin hit him and he just kept driving him back. He must have taken him six or seven yards before he drove him into the ground. After Dan got hurt, we were a little cautious."

• O.J. Simpson on his nullified TD: "When I saw the flag, I thought it was holding or something. I couldn't believe they called motion on me. We had gone through an audible, but I had adjusted and was set in plenty of time."

Bills	0	3	3	0	-	6
Jets	0	7	3	6	-	16

Attendance at Shea Stadium - 62,680

NY:	Mathis 1 run (J. Turner kick), 5:00
Buf:	FG Alford 20, 15:00
Buf:	FG Alford 29, 9:41
NY:	FG J. Turner 37, 12:33
NY:	FG J. Turner 25, 3:40
NY:	FG J. Turner 47, 14:37

	BUF	NY
First downs	13	16
Rushing yds	106	104
Passing yds	191	169
Punts-avg	5-45.6	6-38.5
Fumbles-lost	1-1	0-0
Penalties-yds	9-69	6-52

BILLS LEADERS: Rushing - Simpson 14-70, Enyart 5-17, Kemp 2-16, Patrick 3-3; **Passing** - Kemp 6-13-0 - 68, Darragh 8-10-0 - 152, Briscoe 0-1-1 - 0; **Receiving** - Moses 6-147, Simpson 2-(-11), Masters 2-30, Briscoe 2-49, Enyart 2-5.

JETS LEADERS: Rushing - Boozer 9-24, Mathis 9-29, Snell 18-52, Sauer 1-5, White 1-(-6); **Passing** - Namath 10-22-1 - 169; **Receiving** - Maynard 2-38, Lammons 3-56, Boozer 2-18, Snell 2-24, Sauer 1-33.

WEEK 9 GAMES

Mia 17, Bos 16	Cinc 31, Hou 31
Oak 41, Den 10	KC 27, SD 3

NOTES

• With starting QB Bob Griese and LB Nick Buoniconti sidelined with injuries, the Dolphins were no match for the Bills at War Memorial as backup quarterback Rick Norton was sacked eight times for 83 yards.

• O.J. Simpson had 153 yards from scrimmage and a 73-yard return of the game's opening kickoff.

• After the kickoff return, Jack Kemp hit Simpson for 18 yards, then eight yards for the TD.

• Buffalo's second TD came when a roughing-the-kicker penalty by Dale McCullers on Paul Maguire kept a drive alive. On third down, Kemp hit Marlin Briscoe for the TD.

• Trailing 14-3 in the second quarter, a Miami gamble backfired when, on fourth-and-goal from the 6, Norton was sacked for a 14-yard loss by Mike McBath, who had run a stunt rush with Mike Stratton.

• In the third quarter, Edgar Chandler forced Mercury Morris to fumble. Booker Edgerson returned it 20 yards to the Miami 29, setting up Bill Enyart's (playing for injured Wayne Patrick) one-yard TD.

• The final Buffalo TD came when Simpson made some much-advertised moves on his way to a 55-yard score after catching a short Kemp pass.

• Chandler, playing for Paul Guidry, and Pete Richardson, in for George Saimes, played very well.

• Miami had a sure TD wiped out when a pass for Larry Seiple bounced off the goal post. Seiple went on to set a Miami record with eight pass receptions.

• Nearly seven inches of snow fell Saturday and early morning Sunday, but the field was in decent shape as the field crew began working at 3:30 a.m. to get it ready.

QUOTES

• O.J. Simpson: "All of us were pretty disappointed (after losing to Miami previously). The next time we practiced, we all got to the stadium a half-hour early and had a meeting to talk over what was wrong with us. Marlin got up and said maybe we don't know each other well enough, that we don't see each other much after practice. There are a lot of older guys and a lot of younger guys and we just weren't communicating. It was a good bull session and for the last two weeks we've been more comfortable with one another. It's made us a better team." (On the dotted-I formation the Bills used): "The way we were working out of the new dotted-I formation, I think we could have run well even with Nick (Buoniconti) in there. I would have preferred he was; I'd feel better about this victory. From the I formation, I can use my stutter-step style more effectively and go where I see running room. That you can't do in a regular formation. You have to go where the play is designed. I think we can win the rest of our games."

• Jack Kemp: "Miami uses a lot of shifts in its defense. The dotted-I forces them out of those defenses and also forces them into more normal coverages."

• Miami coach George Wilson: "Well, I've been saying all along that he'd (Simpson) explode pretty good on someone, but why, oh why, did he have to pick the game with us?"

• John Rauch: "Kemp directed the team very well, O.J. had a fine game, but you can't single out one or two players. It was just a tremendous team effort."

• Mike Stratton: "We didn't have to blitz too much, not the way our front four was rushing. They had to keep both backs in most of the time to try and handle our linemen."

Dolphins	3	0	0	0	-	3
Bills	7	7	7	7	-	28

Attendance at War Memorial Stadium - 32,868

Buf:	Simpson 8 pass from Kemp (Alford kick), 1:42
Mia:	FG Kremser 21, 4:15
Buf:	Briscoe 12 pass from Kemp (Alford kick), 5:59
Buf:	Enyart 1 run (Alford kick), 12:13
Buf:	Simpson 55 pass from Kemp (Alford kick), 1:05

	BUF	MIA
First downs	18	16
Rushing yds	122	50
Passing yds	187	198
Punts-avg	7-40.3	6-44.3
Fumbles-lost	2-1	2-1
Penalties-yds	2-29	1-15

BILLS LEADERS: Rushing - Simpson 21-72, Enyart 8-35, Kemp 3-9, Anderson 1-6; **Passing** - Kemp 12-24-0 - 189; **Receiving** - Moses 3-45, Briscoe 5-61, Simpson 3-81, Enyart 1-2.

DOLPHINS LEADERS: Rushing - Kiick 7-8, Csonka 10-41, Morris 1-1; **Passing** - Norton 20-41-0 - 281; **Receiving** - Seiple 8-106, Csonka 4-34, Morris 1-29, Noonan 2-29, Kiick 2-29, Hines 1-22, Mertens 1-15, Milton 1-17.

WEEK 10 GAMES

Bos 25, Cinc 14	Hou 20, Den 20
KC 34, NY 16	Oak 21, SD 16

STANDINGS: TENTH WEEK

EAST	W	L	T	WEST	W	L	T
New York	7	3	0	Kan. City	9	1	0
Houston	4	4	2	Oakland	8	1	1
Buffalo	3	7	0	Cincinnati	4	5	1
Miami	2	7	1	Denver	4	5	1
Boston	2	8	0	San Diego	4	6	0

Bills	7	7	7	0	-	21
Patriots	14	7	0	14	-	35

Attendance at Boston College Field - 25,584

Bos: Frazier 34 pass from Taliaferro (Cappelletti kick), 1:26
Buf: Patrick 1 run (Alford kick), 4:10
Bos: Frazier 24 pass from Taliaferro (Cappelletti kick), 9:13
Bos: Sellers 35 pass from Taliaferro (Cappelletti kick), 8:05
Buf: Moses 48 pass from Kemp (Alford kick), 9:38
Buf: Moses 2 pass from Kemp (Alford kick), 12:34
Bos: Nance 2 run (Cappelletti kick), :06
Bos: Garrett 44 run (Cappelletti kick), 14:10

	BUF	BOS
First downs	24	16
Rushing yds	177	139
Passing yds	248	234
Punts-avg	2-49.0	4-39.5
Fumbles-lost	1-0	1-0
Penalties-yds	6-56	7-91

BILLS LEADERS: Rushing - Simpson 17-98, Enyart 3-15, Patrick 13-39, Kemp 3-25; **Passing** - Kemp 18-32-4 - 255; **Receiving** - Moses 6-130, Patrick 8-59, Masters 2-24, Briscoe 1-19, Enyart 1-23.

PATRIOTS LEADERS: Rushing - Nance 17-43, Garrett 13-96; **Passing** - Taliaferro 12-19-1 - 244; **Receiving** - Frazier 2-58, Sellers 5-102, Nance 2-43, Garrett 2-26, Brown 1-15.

NOTES

• Jack Kemp was intercepted on the game's first play by Ed Philpott. On the next play, Mike Taliaferro hit Charley Frazier with a 34-yard TD pass.
• The Bills drew even when Wayne Patrick plunged in from the 1 after a 40-yard Kemp-to-Haven Moses pass. But the Pats answered with a 69-yard march as Frazier beat Butch Byrd for the TD.
• Philpott intercepted Kemp again, killing an advance to the Boston 13. Later, Carl Garrett went 41 yards with a punt return and five plays later, Ron Sellers got behind Booker Edgerson and caught Taliaferro's third TD pass.
• Again, the Bills struck back quickly when Moses caught Kemp's bomb for a 48-yard score.
• The Bills tied it in the third. A personal foul penalty after a punt set them up at the Boston 34. Eventually, Moses got free in the end zone for a two-yard TD reception on fourth-and-two.
• Boston then went 71 yards, with Jim Nance breaking a 27-yard run before scoring from the 2.
• With less than six minutes left, faced with second-and-one at his own 43, Kemp tried to throw deep to Moses, but John Charles intercepted at the Boston 29.

WEEK 11 GAMES

SD 45, Den 24	Hou 32, Mia 7
NY 40, Cinc 7	Oak 27, KC 24

A little earlier, O.J. Simpson was stopped on fourth-and-one from the Boston 39.
• With three minutes left, the Bills began a potential tying TD drive at the Boston 46, but Kemp threw three incomplete passes and was sacked for a seven-yard loss. Garrett then ripped off a 44-yard run to score the clincher with 50 seconds left.

QUOTES

• John Rauch: "We just didn't play good football. We had opportunities but didn't capitalize on them. We bogged down. We had chances for first downs with short yardage, but our percentage in these situations hasn't been good all season." (On Charles' interception): "That helped them a lot. I've never heard of an interception helping you (on offense). That first play interception was another big break for Boston. Any time a team scores 35 points on you, you have to be disappointed. But our defense has played exceptionally well under extreme pressure the last few weeks, so it was probably inevitable that we'd have a day like this."
• Pats safety John Charles on his interception: "We were reading Kemp all day. He was looking at the receiver he would throw to when he came to the line of scrimmage. He looked at Moses before that pass."
• Haven Moses: "Things are starting to go a little more smoothly. I think we've digested the system and we're on our way to being a fine team."

Bengals	3	3	0	7	-	13
Bills	3	3	10	0	-	16

Attendance at War Memorial Stadium - 35,122

Cin: FG Muhlmann 16, 8:47
Buf: FG Alford 33, 14:31
Buf: FG Alford 24, 7:05
Cin: FG Muhlmann 26, 14:35
Buf: FG Alford 35, 8:54
Buf: Edgerson 10 fumble return (Alford kick), 11:20
Cin: Wyche 9 run (Muhlmann kick), :17

	BUF	CIN
First downs	8	11
Rushing yds	100	227
Passing yds	84	26
Punts-avg	6-38.8	4-22.5
Fumbles-lost	3-2	7-7
Penalties-yds	4-28	5-39

BILLS LEADERS: Rushing - Simpson 13-35, Enyart 5-14, Patrick 8-44, Kemp 6-7; **Passing** - Kemp 10-26-1 - 84; **Receiving** - Moses 1-8, Patrick 3-10, Masters 2-24, Briscoe 2-16, Simpson 1-24, Enyart 1-2.

BENGALS LEADERS: Rushing - Robinson 24-117, Wyche 3-43, Turner 5-40, Cook 4-21, Phillips 1-6; **Passing** - Wyche 2-4-0 - 48, Cook 0-3-0 - 0; **Receiving** - Robinson 1-25, Myers 1-23.

WEEK 12 GAMES

KC 31, Den 17	SD 21, Hou 17
Bos 38, Mia 23	Oak 27, NY 14

NOTES

• Veteran observers said they never had seen worse conditions for a Buffalo game. Heavy snow fell throughout and the field was obliterated. Clearly, the Bills were better-suited as Cincinnati lost seven fumbles.
• Jack Kemp's fumble and Al Beauchamp's return to the Bills 32 set up Horst Muhlmann's first field goal, which the Bengals settled for when a penalty set them back after reaching the 2.
• Paul Robinson, who was brilliant in gaining 117 yards, lost a fumble and Booker Edgerson recovered, setting up Bruce Alford's first field goal.
• In the second quarter, Paul Maguire deadened a punt at the Bengals 2 and when they couldn't move, coach Paul Brown ordered a third-down punt. Dale Livingston shanked it 13 yards to the 20. That led to another Alford field goal.
• Chip Myers blocked a Maguire punt late in the half and Muhlmann capitalized to tie it at 6-6.
• Cincinnati's second fumble of the third quarter was recovered at the Bengals 43 by Mike McBath. That led to Alford's third field goal after Kemp had passed 13 yards to Billy Masters.
• The Bengals then lost three more fumbles within three minutes, but all the Bills could manage was Edgerson's 10-yard TD return with one of them and a 16-6 lead. On the others, Kemp was intercepted and O.J. Simpson fumbled at the goal line.
• Greg Cook, who never completed a pass, was benched in the third and Sam Wyche took over. He directed an 80-yard drive, highlighted by his 25-yard pass to Robinson, a 40-yard run by Clem Turner and Wyche's nine-yard bootleg for the TD with 14:43 left.
• A long Buffalo drive killed much of the clock, but the Bengals, on their final possession, reached the Bills 40

before Edgar Chandler sacked Wyche for a 12-yard loss.

QUOTES

• Booker Edgerson: "It was petty larceny, that ball's only worth $25. It was a lucky play on Cook. But I've had receivers score touchdowns on me this year when I fell down or when the ball was underthrown. It's about time some luck came my way. When I saw my man block down on the linebacker, I knew it was a run. When I went after the ball carrier, the halfback blocked me into Cook. I was trying to reach around to jostle the ball away and when I saw it, I just grabbed it."
• Bengals coach Paul Brown: "The worst conditions I've ever seen. On a day like today, the team that makes the fewest mistakes wins the game. We fumble seven times and they recover all of them. Let's just say that today we got a very interesting study of some of our people. Under these conditions, the hard-bitten pro produces."
• John Rauch: "That was some scene. All things considered, the teams put on a pretty fair performance, but I must admit I was more impressed by the fans. I was told the Bills had great fans and they sure proved it to me. You had to be a real fan to sit through that weather."

STANDINGS: TWELFTH WEEK

EAST	W	L	T	WEST	W	L	T
New York	8	4	0	Oakland	10	1	1
Houston	5	5	2	Kan. City	10	2	0
Buffalo	4	8	0	San Diego	6	6	0
Boston	4	8	0	Denver	4	7	1
Miami	2	9	1	Cincinnati	4	7	1

NOTES

• The Bills caught a break when Len Dawson couldn't play, but for the second time this season, Jan Stenerud beat them with five field goals, including the winner with 1:59 left. That gave him a pro football-record 16 consecutive successes. In four career games against Buffalo, Stenerud had made 17 field goals.

• The Bills tied it at 19-19 with 8:04 left when O.J. Simpson ran 32 yards for a TD, his longest run from scrimmage thus far. However, Al Bemiller's high snap forced holder Marlin Briscoe to try a two-point pass to Wayne Patrick. Patrick dropped it, leaving the score tied.

• The Chiefs then drove to the 17 and after Mike Livingston fell on Mike Garrett's fumble, Stenerud kicked the winning field goal.

• The Bills took a 3-0 lead when Robert Holmes fumbled on the second play of the game and Edgar Chandler recovered, setting up Bruce Alford's first field goal.

• Holmes atoned later in the first, catching a 29-yard pass to set up his three-yard TD run.

• Stenerud made a 52-yarder, then after Simpson fumbled the kickoff, he hit an eight-yarder which broke Lou Groza's record of 12 successful kicks in a row, set with Cleveland in 1953.

• The teams traded field goals early in the third and after Ed Podolak fumbled a punt and Bemiller recovered, the Bills drove 51 yards to Jack Kemp's 17-yard TD pass to Briscoe.

• Stenerud's fourth field goal came after Patrick's fumble at the Bills 20.

QUOTES

• Marlin Briscoe on the two-point attempt: "The snap was high and Bruce stopped his approach. I took a look and decided it was too late to try the kick so I yelled 'fire.' Billy Masters was open but I would have had to loft the ball over Wayne Patrick and the man covering him. I decided not to risk the interception so I threw to Patrick."

• John Rauch: "Briscoe did it the way we told him to in a case like that. He yelled 'fire' and both Patrick and Masters broke out as receivers like they're supposed to. Patrick had it in his hands and he dropped it." (On why he didn't go for two after Briscoe's TD): "I thought there was too much time left to play, a whole quarter."

• Chiefs coach Hank Stram: "Let's say I was happy Buffalo decided to go for the one point there."

• Ron McDole: "If Lenny Dawson had been at quarterback, we would have won for sure. Dawson couldn't scramble with that bad knee and Livingston scrambled just enough to get them out of some tough spots. I don't see how Kansas City ever loses a game."

WEEK 13 GAMES	
NY 34, Hou 26	SD 28, Bos 18
Oak 37, Cinc 17	Mia 27, Den 24

Bills	3 0 10 6 - 19
Chiefs	7 6 3 6 - 22

Attendance at Municipal Stadium - 47,112

Buf: FG Alford 16, 5:23
KC: Holmes 3 run (Stenerud kick), 15:00
KC: FG Stenerud 52, 3:55
KC: FG Stenerud 8, 6:46
Buf: FG Alford 34, 5:50
KC: FG Stenerud 47, 8:13
Buf: Briscoe 17 pass from Kemp (Alford kick), 13:28
KC: FG Stenerud 20, 5:39
Buf: Simpson 32 run (pass failed), 6:55
KC: FG Stenerud 25, 13:01

	BUF	KC
First downs	17	17
Rushing yds	93	146
Passing yds	144	131
Punts-avg	6-49.5	4-51.0
Fumbles-lost	4-2	4-3
Penalties-yds	3-26	2-10

BILLS LEADERS: Rushing - Simpson 11-62, Patrick 8-38, Kemp 4-(-7); **Passing** - Kemp 18-32-0 - 165; **Receiving** - Moses 2-29, Simpson 3-8, Patrick 4-25, Masters 2-20, Briscoe 3-33, Crockett 4-50.

CHIEFS LEADERS: Rushing - Garrett 18-67, Holmes 8-23, McVea 6-13, Livingston 3-17, Hayes 1-5, Pitts 1-11, Taylor 1-10; **Passing** - Livingston 13-23-0 - 142; **Receiving** - Garrett 4-43, Taylor 4-20, Pitts 2-22, Holmes 1-29, McVea 1-9, Arbanas 1-19.

NOTES

• For the second year in a row, the Bills were pathetic in the season finale as San Diego gained 547 yards, the most ever against the Bills. It was both teams' last official AFL game.

• Speedy Duncan returned Paul Maguire's first punt 38 yards to the Bills 41 and on their first offensive play, the Chargers scored when John Hadl hit Gary Garrison for a TD.

• On the next possession, Lance Alworth, who finished with 122 yards thus allowing him to top 1,000 yards receiving for the seventh year in a row, made a catch that gave him at least one in 96 straight games, breaking the old mark set by Don Hutson from 1937-45. The Chargers eventually got a field goal on that series.

• Gene Foster threw a 30-yard TD to Rick Eber on a halfback-option pass to make it 17-0 and the count rose to 24-0 by halftime when Hadl capped a 15-play, 73-yard march with a TD toss to Alworth.

• Dick Post, who locked up the AFL rushing title by gaining 106 yards, scored a pair of TDs. San Diego made it 45-0 in the fourth when backup QB Marty Domres scored on a scramble.

• The Bills avoided being shut out for only the second time in their history and also avoided their worst loss ever when backup QB Tom Sherman hit equally little-used Willie Grate with a 19-yard TD pass with 1:26 remaining.

• In two games on the west coast, the Bills were outscored 95-27. It also kept the Bills winless on the left side of the country since 1966.

• The loss gave the Bills an all-time regular-season AFL record of 65-69-6. They were 2-2 in the playoffs, including 2-1 in AFL Championship games.

QUOTES

• John Rauch: "A game like this you can't ever write off. To be a good team you don't ever come up flat like this. You can lead a horse to water, but what if he isn't thirsty? It was embarrassing to lose our last game of the season like this. We have to keep confident that we are a good football team, but you have to have dedication. I feel we played good football this season and we are looking forward to more improvement."

• Chargers receiver Lance Alworth: "In this day and age of football, I don't think it's asking too much to catch a pass in every game."

• San Diego sports writer Jack Murphy: "Tell me, did the Bills get any sleep this week? How would you like to be Ralph Wilson who had to pay the hotel tab for a week's stay, then have to watch this thing?"

WEEK 14 GAMES	
Oak 10, KC 6	Den 27, Cinc 16
NY 27, Mia 9	Hou 27, Bos 23

Bills	0 0 0 6 - 6
Chargers	10 14 7 14 - 45

Attendance at San Diego Stadium - 47,582

SD: Garrison 41 pass from Hadl (Partee kick), 2:05
SD: FG Partee 33, 13:20
SD: Eber 30 pass from Foster (Partee kick), 5:27
SD: Alworth 41 pass from Hadl (Partee kick), 12:18
SD: Post 34 run (Partee kick), 7:53
SD: Post 2 run (Partee kick), :03
SD: Domres 9 run (Partee kick), 6:52
Buf: Grate 19 pass from Sherman (kick failed), 13:34

	BUF	SD
First downs	15	30
Rushing yds	58	242
Passing yds	180	305
Punts-avg	8-45.2	2-54.0
Fumbles-lost	1-0	2-1
Penalties-yds	5-55	3-21

BILLS LEADERS: Rushing - Simpson 7-27, Enyart 2-6, Patrick 4-9, Anderson 1-16, Sherman 2-14, Kemp 1-(-14); **Passing** - Kemp 16-33-2 - 164, Sherman 2-2-0 - 20; **Receiving** - Moses 1-8, Simpson 3-(-8), Patrick 1-6, Masters 1-16, Briscoe 6-94, Enyart 3-36, Thornton 1-13, Grate 1-19, Anderson 1-0.

CHARGERS LEADERS: Rushing - Post 19-106, Hubbert 13-61, Foster 5-34, Sayers 6-22, Domres 1-9, Smith 1-10; **Passing** - Hadl 16-29-0 - 262, Post 1-1-0 - 4, Domres 1-1-0 - 25, Foster 1-1-0 - 30; **Receiving** - Alworth 7-122, Post 3-77, Eber 2-42, Queen 3-19, Garrison 1-41, Foster 1-6, Frazier 2-14.

STANDINGS: FOURTEENTH WEEK							
EAST	**W**	**L**	**T**	**WEST**	**W**	**L**	**T**
New York	10	4	0	Oakland	12	1	1
Houston	6	6	2	Kan. City	11	3	0
Buffalo	4	10	0	San Diego	8	6	0
Boston	4	10	0	Denver	5	8	1
Miami	3	10	1	Cincinnati	4	9	1

At A Glance
1970

Jan. 4 – Stew Barber, who signed his first pro contract with the Bills on this date in 1961, announced his retirement. He was an AFL all-star five times.

Jan. 13 – Mel Durslag reported in the *Los Angeles Herald-Examiner* that Ralph Wilson was willing to trade O.J. Simpson to the Los Angeles Rams for quarterback Roman Gabriel as soon as the inter-league trading barrier was lifted. Durslag quoted Wilson as saying: "This is the perfect trade. The Rams have had their eye on O.J. for years and he has had an eye on them. I have had my eye on Gabriel. We are desperate for a top quarterback."

Jan. 14 – Three Bills – Billy Shaw, Tom Sestak and George Saimes – were named to the all-time AFL all-star team, which was announced by the Pro Football Hall of Fame. Los Angeles Rams coach George Allen halted any speculation about a Simpson-for-Gabriel trade. "I wouldn't trade Gabriel for anyone in either league," Allen said.

Jan. 16 – The realignment of the new NFL was completed when commissioner Pete Rozelle came up with five possible divisional alignments for the NFC and placed them in a flower vase. His secretary, Thelma Elkjer, then performed a blind draw and picked the plan that put Dallas, Philadelphia, the Giants, Washington and St. Louis in the East. Chicago, Minnesota, Detroit and Green Bay were placed in the Central; and Los Angeles, San Francisco, Atlanta and New Orleans were placed in the West.

Jan. 26 – Four-year TV contracts were signed with NBC televising AFC games and CBS televising NFC games. ABC had already agreed to house Monday Night Football.

Jan. 27 – The Bills chose Al Cowlings, a USC defensive tackle, as their No. 1 pick in the draft. In the second round, they grabbed San Diego State quarterback Dennis Shaw. The Pittsburgh Steelers chose quarterback Terry Bradshaw with the No. 1 overall selection.

Feb. 3 – Receivers coach Bill Miller quit John Rauch's staff.

Feb. 9 – Defensive backfield coach Hoot Gibson quit the staff to become offensive coordinator at the University of Tulsa.

March 3 – Butch Byrd was quoted as saying of O.J. Simpson: "He's going to be a great running back, but he's going to have to decide whether he wants to be flying to Chicago and Detroit all the time to be on television or play football. You have to dedicate yourself to this game. I think he'll be a better player this year."

March 5 – A story in the *Buffalo Evening News* said that Jack Kemp was going to retire from pro football and enter the world of politics.

March 6 – Bobby Hunt retired as a player and joined the Bills coaching staff as the defensive backfield tutor, replacing Hoot Gibson.

March 12 – Baltimore's John Mackey met with Jack Kemp in Buffalo and Mackey assumed command of the Pro Football Players' Association. Kemp had been head of the AFLPA and he relinquished his duties to Mackey; Art Modell resigned as president of the NFL and was

1st Lt. James Robert (Bob) Kalsu

BORN: APRIL 13, 1945 IN OKLAHOMA CITY, OKLAHOMA
DIED: JULY 21, 1970 AT RIPCORD BASE, SOUTH VIETNAM

IN MEMORY

BOB KALSU, OFFENSIVE GUARD FROM THE UNIVERSITY OF OKLAHOMA, MEMBER OF THE AMERICAN FOOTBALL LEAGUE BUFFALO BILLS IN 1968. THE ONLY FOOTBALL PLAYER OF THE AMERICAN OR NATIONAL FOOTBALL LEAGUE TO BE KILLED IN ACTION IN VIETNAM. "NO ONE WILL EVER KNOW HOW GREAT A FOOTBALL PLAYER BOB MIGHT HAVE BEEN, BUT WE DO KNOW HOW GREAT A MAN HE WAS TO GIVE UP HIS LIFE FOR HIS COUNTRY."

This memorial plaque hangs in the entrance way to the Bills administrative offices at Rich Stadium. It honors ex-Bill Bob Kalsu, who was the only pro football player killed in Vietnam.

replaced by George Halas.

March 13 – Milt Woodall resigned as president of the AFL and was replaced by Lamar Hunt.

March 18 – The newly merged NFL adopted rule changes to make conversions worth one point, to have players' names on the backs of their jerseys, and to make the stadium scoreboards the official timing device.

March 21 – Jack Kemp announced his intention to run for Congress in Erie County's 39th district. Kemp vowed to "be my own man. I feel strongly, and always have, about making the American dream applicable to as many people as possible."

June 1 – Ralph Wilson Sr., the father of Bills owner Ralph Wilson Jr., died.

June 11 – Billy Shaw, one of the all-time great Bills, announced his retirement ending a brilliant nine-year career in which he was named to the all-time AFL team.

June 13 – A retirement dinner was held in honor of Jack Kemp at the Hearthstone Manor. Among the guests were Pete Rozelle, Cookie Gilchrist, Daryle Lamonica, Lou Saban and O.J. Simpson.

June 17 – O.J. Simpson was voted the outstanding college football player of the 1960s by writers and broadcasters from across the country.

June 27 – Buffalo's second-round draft choice, Dennis Shaw, set a record for completions (25) and yards passing (384), but it wasn't enough as his West all-stars lost to the East, 37-34, in the annual Coaches All-America game in Lubbock, Texas.

June 30 – No. 1 draft choice Al Cowlings

agreed to terms.

July 13 – It was reported that Dennis Shaw was demanding a no-cut contract worth $350,000 over three years.

July 18 – The Bills' rookies opened training camp at Niagara University, but the chances of the veterans being in on time began to look remote. It was announced that the NFLPA and the owners were about $7.8 million apart on the issue of pension benefits.

July 20 – After conducting a scrimmage the day before, John Rauch cut 14 players from the squad, indicating he was serious about finding the right types of players for his system.

July 21 – Bob Kalsu, Buffalo's eighth-round draft choice in 1968 and an offensive line starter in nine games that year, was killed by mortar fire in Vietnam. He was the first pro football player killed in the war.

July 25 – Nineteen veteran Bills began working out together at Hamburg High School as the impasse between the NFLPA and the owners continued.

July 30 – The NFLPA officially went on strike; Quarterback Dan Darragh decided to report to the Bills training camp, the first veteran Bill to do so, and it prompted a question as to whether his teammates may resent him for breaking up their united chapter.

July 31 – Dennis Shaw started at quarterback for the collegians in their 24-3 loss to the Kansas City Chiefs in the annual College All-Star game in Chicago.

Aug. 3 – The players' strike ended when it was agreed that $4.5 million would be put into the players' pension fund and insurance benefits on an annual basis. The agreement also provided increased preseason and per diem payments. The owners also agreed to contribute $250,000 annually to implement or improve disability payments, widow's benefits, maternity benefits and dental benefits.

Aug. 4 – Most of the Bills were in camp, 18 days after it had opened, and began two-a-day work immediately.

Aug. 8 – The Jets rolled to a 33-10 victory over the Bills in the preseason opener at Legion Field in Birmingham, Ala.

Aug. 14 – Detroit handed the Bills a 22-6 loss in Buffalo's home preseason opener as Errol Mann kicked five field goals.

Aug. 19 – Second-round draft choice Dennis Shaw, the most stubborn holdout in team history, signed his contract, believed to be worth more than $100,000 over three years including salary and bonuses. Shaw's signing came one day later than O.J. Simpson's signing in 1969.

Aug. 20 – Veteran safety George Saimes, who had become a free agent on May 1 but was unable to sell his services to anyone because no one was willing to pay the Bills draft choice compensation, re-signed with the Bills.

Aug. 21 – The Bills downed the Philadelphia Eagles at War Memorial, 35-20, but after gaining 77 yards rushing, O.J. Simpson suffered an ankle injury.

Aug. 28 – Despite possessing one of the weakest defenses in the NFL, Washington blanked the Bills at RFK, 27-0.

Aug. 31 – Cornerback Booker Edgerson, a starter since 1962, was traded to Denver for an

undisclosed draft choice.

Sept. 4 – Dennis Shaw made his debut and threw for 150 yards in a 10-7 home loss to Atlanta. Shaw was cheered lustily by the home crowd.

Sept. 7 – John Rauch took a deep cut out of the Bills' past as he cut veterans Al Bemiller, George Saimes and Harry Jacobs. Bemiller had started every game since 1961, a streak of 173; Saimes and Jacobs had been starters since 1963.

Sept. 9 – After being placed on waivers, QB James Harris left camp. He was free to join any other team, but only for 1970 because he already had a 1971 contract with the Bills. No one claimed Harris and he rejoined the team before the third game of the season against the Jets.

Sept. 12 – Green Bay routed the Bills, 34-0, in the preseason finale. After final cuts, the Bills had 12 rookies on their roster and seven players with one year or less of pro experience.

Sept. 20 – In front of the smallest opening-day crowd (34,882) at War Memorial since 1964, the Bills lost their inaugural game in the new NFL, 25-10, to Lou Saban's Denver Broncos.

Sept. 27 – The Los Angeles Rams came to Buffalo and disappointed a record crowd of 46,206 by blanking the Bills, 19-0. It was Buffalo's first regular-season game against an old NFL team.

Oct. 4 – O.J. Simpson returned a kickoff 95 yards for a touchdown, rushed for 99 yards and caught three passes for 63 yards as the Bills beat the New York Jets, 34-31.

Oct. 6 – Dennis Shaw was named the NFL's offensive player of the week, the first Bill so honored since the merger.

Oct. 11 – The Bills turned the ball over five times and even though rookie Terry Bradshaw completed only three of 12 passes for 24 yards, Pittsburgh won easily, 23-10, at brand new Three Rivers Stadium.

Oct. 18 – In Don Shula's first visit to Buffalo as coach of the Dolphins, Miami crushed the Bills, 33-14, despite 349 yards passing by Dennis Shaw.

Oct. 25 – The Bills snapped their 14-game regular-season road losing streak by upsetting the Jets at Shea Stadium, 10-6. New York played without injured quarterback Joe Namath.

Nov. 1 – The Bills won back-to-back games for the first time since 1966 as they routed the Patriots, 45-10, also on the road. They opened a 31-0 halftime lead.

Nov. 8 – O.J. Simpson suffered a season-ending knee injury that did not require surgery and the Bills were crushed by the Cincinnati Bengals, 43-14. Rookie Lemar Parrish returned a kickoff 95 yards for a TD and returned a blocked field goal 83 yards for a TD.

Nov. 15 – Buffalo traveled to first-place Baltimore and stunned the Colts by playing them to a 17-17 tie. Wayne Patrick and Mike Stratton suffered season-ending injuries, though. Grant

Guthrie's 36-yard field goal with 1:09 left tied the game for Buffalo.

Nov. 22 – Five turnovers doomed the Bills in a 31-13 loss to the Chicago Bears at Wrigley Field. Bobby Douglass completed only eight passes, but they went for 196 yards and four TDs.

Nov. 29 – With ex-Bills assistant coach Johnny Mazur now the head coach in Boston, after Clive Rush was fired, the Patriots knocked off the Bills at War Memorial, 14-10, despite gaining only 167 yards on offense.

Dec. 6 – The Giants beat the Bills, 20-6, at Yankee Stadium, on the strength of two Fran Tarkenton TD passes in the fourth quarter.

Dec. 9 – O.J. Simpson, home in California recuperating from his knee injury, reflected on his first two years in pro football: "The whole thing was like a fairy tale. It's just now that I'm getting back to living like a normal person. More important, I'm starting to understand what pro football is all about. In my rookie year, I couldn't see the picture, all I wanted to do was run the ball."

Dec. 13 – Baltimore didn't lapse this time as it beat the Bills, 20-14, to clinch the AFC East title.

Dec. 20 – Miami clinched its first playoff berth in Don Shula's initial season as coach by blasting the Bills, 45-7, at the Orange Bowl. The Bills held a closed-door, players-only meeting after the game pledging their support for coach John Rauch. Before the meeting, punter Paul Maguire told his teammates he had played his last game as a Bill. Maguire and Rauch had not seen eye-to-eye and the 11-year veteran said: "He doesn't want me back, he knows it, I know it, we all know it. But I wanted to tell the guys that they better pull together behind him if they expect to come back next year with the right attitude."

Dec. 26 – In the start of the divisional playoffs, Baltimore blanked Cincinnati, 17-0, and Dallas matched that shutout with a 5-0 victory over Detroit.

Dec. 27 – San Francisco defeated Minnesota, 17-14, and Oakland topped Miami, 21-14, in the second day of divisional playoffs.

Jan. 3, 1971 – Baltimore edged Oakland, 27-17, in the AFC Championship Game; Dallas defeated San Francisco, 17-10, in the NFC Championship Game.

Jan. 17, 1971 – Baltimore defeated Dallas, 16-13, in Super Bowl V at Miami's Orange Bowl as Jim O'Brien kicked a 32-yard field goal with five seconds remaining. The estimated television viewing audience for NBC's telecast was about 24 million, making it the largest viewership ever for a one-day sporting event.

Jan. 24, 1971 – The NFC defeated the AFC, 27-6, in the first Pro Bowl at the Los Angeles Coliseum.

Haven Moses was Buffalo's second leading receiver in 1970, the Bills first in the NFL following the pro football merger.

BY THE NUMBERS - 1970

TEAM STATISTICS	BILLS	OPP
First downs	203	213
Rushing	71	87
Passing	120	103
Penalty	12	23
Total yards	3,895	3,806
Avg. game	278.2	271.9
Plays	822	853
Avg. play	4.7	4.5
Net rushing yds	1,465	1,718
Avg. game	104.6	122.7
Avg. play	4.0	3.5
Net passing yds	2,430	2,088
Comp/att	213/402	157/338
Sacks/lost	53-486	31-246
Interceptions	26	11
Percentage	53.0	46.4
Punts/avg	83-38.9	76-44.0
Fumbles/lost	37-26	23-15
Penalties/yds	99-1108	73-814
Touchdowns	25	34
Extra points	24-25	35-35
Field goals	10-19	30-46
Safeties	0	1
Kick ret./avg	62-20.1	46-24.2
Punt ret./avg	45-6.6	42-6.9

RUSHING	ATT	YDS	AVG	TD
Simpson	120	488	4.1	5
Patrick	66	259	3.9	1
Shaw	39	210	5.4	0
Enyart	58	196	3.4	0
Pate	46	162	3.5	1
Jones	31	113	3.6	1
Darragh	1	26	26.0	0
Briscoe	3	19	6.3	0
Harris	3	-8	-2.7	0
TOTALS	**367**	**1465**	**4.0**	**8**

PASSING	COMP	ATT	INT	YDS	TD	COMP%
Shaw	178	321	20	2507	10	55.5
Harris	24	50	4	338	3	48.0
Darragh	11	29	2	71	0	37.9
Simpson	0	2	0	0	0	00.0
TOTALS	**213**	**402**	**26**	**2916**	**13**	**53.0**

RECEIVING	CAT	YDS	AVG	TD
Briscoe	57	1036	18.2	8
Moses	39	726	18.6	2
Enyart	35	235	6.7	1
Pate	19	103	5.4	0
Patrick	16	142	8.9	0
Denney	14	201	14.4	0
Simpson	10	139	13.9	0
Jones	8	89	11.1	0
Grate	7	147	21.0	2
Alexander	4	51	12.8	0
Moss	2	31	15.5	0
Glosson	2	16	8.0	0
TOTALS	**213**	**2916**	**13.7**	**13**

KICKING	1-19	20-29	30-39	40-49	50+	TOT	PAT	PTS
Guthrie	3-3	3-4	2-3	1-4	1-5	10-19	24-25	54

PUNTING	NO	AVG	LG	BL
Maguire	83	38.9	58	1

LEADERS

Kick returns: Alexander 12-204 yds, 17.0 avg, 0 TD
Simpson 7-333, 47.6, 1 TD

Punt returns: Pharr 23-184, 8.0, 0 TD
Hill 19-102, 5.4, 0 TD

Interceptions: Richardson 5-46, 9.2, 0 TD
Byrd 4-63, 12.8, 1 TD

SCORE BY QUARTERS

BILLS	54	70	21	59 -	204
OPP	67	96	84	90 -	337

Marlin Briscoe failed as a quarterback with Denver, so he joined the Bills as a receiver and in 1970, led the team in receptions, yards and touchdowns, earning him the nickname "Marlin the Magician."

GAME 1 - Sunday, Sept. 20, 1970 - BRONCOS 25, BILLS 10

NOTES

• The Bills lost their inaugural game in the new NFL as Denver rallied for 20 unanswered second-half points in front of the smallest opening-day crowd in Buffalo since 1964.

• The Bills opened strongly. Butch Byrd intercepted Pete Liske on the second play of the game and the offense proceeded to drive 40 yards in seven plays with O.J. Simpson capping the march with a TD run. That was as effective as the offense would be the rest of the day.

• After an exchange of fumbles, Denver got a safety when Howard Kindig's high snap went through punter Paul Maguire's hands and through the end zone.

• Floyd Little's fumble, recovered by John Pitts at the Denver 28, led to rookie Grant Guthrie's field goal, but that was Buffalo's final score. Guthrie had been activated the day before.

• Trailing 10-5, Little returned a punt 24 yards, then carried eight plays in a row (seven times to Denver's left side) for 54 yards, getting the ball to the 3. From there, Steve Tensi, who replaced the ineffective Liske, hit Al Denson with a TD pass and the Broncos were ahead for good, 12-10.

• In the fourth, a 42-yard Tensi-to-Denson pass set up Bobby Anderson's 27-yard TD run and Bobby Howfield kicked two field goals to close the scoring.

• Howfield shanked six kickoffs out of bounds for a total of 30 yards in penalties.

QUOTES

• John Rauch: "We came out so flat in the second half. Our defense was respectable until they took it to us. They went right at us, manhandled us. We knew after the exhibition season that we had a problem with our passing game. We led at the half, but we didn't know how to open up the lead considering our passing problems. We tried to utilize our running game as best we could, but we simply aren't getting the big gains we should from some of the plays."

• Broncos running back Floyd Little: "We ran toward our weak side because we often run that way. Why run against their strength? McDole and Dunaway are Buffalo's strongest men against the run or pass, so we felt it was logical to run away from their strength."

• Ex-Bill Booker Edgerson: "It's great to be back with Lou Saban. Football is fun again. If you mess up, he's on you, but nobody is really uptight. With John (Rauch), everyone is uptight. There's enough pressure in this game without putting more on the players when it's not necessary. Rauch doesn't seem to believe in fun for the players. Whenever they have any, he takes it away from them. I don't think anyone can play well when they're uptight."

WEEK 1 GAMES

LA 34, St. L 13	Chi 24, NYG 16
Bos 27, Mia 14	SF 26, Wash 17
Atl 14, NO 3	Det 40, GB 0
Dal 17, Phil 7	Balt 16, SD 14
Min 27, KC 10	Hou 19, Pitt 7
Cin 31, Oak 21	Clev 31, NYJ 21

Broncos	0	5	7	13 -	25
Bills	7	3	0	0 -	10

Attendance at War Memorial Stadium - 34,882

Buf: Simpson 2 run (Guthrie kick), 4:34
Den: Safety, ball snapped through end zone, :58
Buf: FG Guthrie 16, 8:06
Den: FG Howfield 27, 13:15
Den: Denson 3 pass from Tensi (Howfield kick), 6:56
Den: Anderson 27 run (Howfield kick), 1:12
Den: FG Howfield 48, 4:37
Den: FG Howfield 31, 12:59

	BUF	DEN
First downs	8	11
Rushing yds	93	136
Passing yds	56	146
Punts-avg	10-48.0	7-43.9
Fumbles-lost	3-3	2-2
Penalties yds	5-65	11-85

BILLS LEADERS: Rushing - Simpson 18-52, Enyart 5-5, Patrick 4-9, Darragh 1-26, Shaw 2-1; **Passing** - Darragh 6-15-1 - 40, Shaw 4-7-0 - 52, Simpson 0-1-0 - 0; **Receiving** - Simpson 3-49, Enyart 1-8, Briscoe 4-35, Patrick 1-2, Pate 1- (-2).

BRONCOS LEADERS: Rushing - Little 18-82, Anderson 8-49, Tensi 1-3, Crenshaw 5-2; **Passing** - Tensi 4-14-0 - 108, Liske 4-11-1 - 52, Little 0-1-0 - 0; **Receiving** - Denson 3-74, Whalen 3-62, Haffner 1-24, Little 1-0.

GAME 2 - Sunday, Sept. 27, 1970 - RAMS 19, BILLS 0

NOTES

• In their first regular-season game against an established NFL team, the Bills weren't horrible, but they proved they have a long, long way to go in losing to the Rams. They managed a mere 177 net yards on offense in front of a record home crowd.

• The Rams' fearsome pass rush was neutralized for the most part. Paul Costa, often in one-on-one blocking, held Deacon Jones without a sack.

• On the other side, Paul Guidry recorded two sacks of Roman Gabriel. Two other times, he was tackled at the line to avoid sacks. Gabriel, the NFL's MVP in 1969, threw for 202 yards but wasn't overly impressive.

• Trailing 3-0 in the first quarter, starting QB Dan Darragh moved the Bills to the Rams 29, then overthrew Haven Moses in the end zone. He was intercepted by Clancy Williams on the next play, killing the drive. Williams wound up with three interceptions.

• With the score 6-0, defensive linemen Ron McDole and Bob Tatarek both were hurt and the Rams went right at them. Willie Ellison carried six straight times during a 49-yard drive that culminated with his four-yard TD run.

• David Ray matched his first-half output with two more field goals in the second half. One of those was set up by a 71-yard catch-and-run by Jack Snow, who was caught from behind by John Pitts.

• Darragh was replaced at the start of the second half by Dennis Shaw and Shaw had success throwing the ball, but couldn't produce any points.

QUOTES

• John Rauch: "I feel that if we get this kind of overall effort from our team in the future, we're going to win some games." (On Darragh's overthrow in the end zone): "Moses ran a corner pattern. The cornerback (Kermit Alexander) laid off so deep that Haven made his break in front of him. Dan laid the ball deep instead of shallow. A touchdown very well could have made it a different game. It would have been a morale boost for us."

• Rams coach George Allen: "We started to red dog more in the third quarter and Shaw did a good job. We had a good rush on him and he got off the passes."

• O.J. Simpson: "We wanted to run traps on them, but they seemed to know where we were going on every play. Wherever I went, Merlin Olsen was there. The Rams' front four is the best I've ever played against. They have great pursuit. We gained some yardage with our quick toss play the first time we used it (18 yards), but when we tried it again, Olsen just floated over to that side and I had to reverse my field."

Rams	3	13	0	3 -	19
Bills	0	0	0	0 -	0

Attendance at War Memorial Stadium - 46,206

LA: FG Ray 21, 7:36
LA: FG Ray 19, 6:42
LA: Ellison 4 run (Ray kick), 12:09
LA: FG Ray 46, 14:55
LA: FG Ray 21, 1:08

	BUF	LA
First downs	12	21
Rushing yds	52	169
Passing yds	125	193
Punts-avg	7-35.4	2-44.0
Fumbles-lost	1-1	3-2
Penalties-yds	7-90	4-64

BILLS LEADERS: Rushing - Simpson 14-24, Enyart 3-19, Briscoe 1-11, Shaw 2- (-2); **Passing** - Darragh 4-13-1 - 29, Shaw 13-18-2 - 143; **Receiving** - Enyart 5-18, Briscoe 3-61, Moses 4-50, Alexander 1-16, Denney 1-15, Glosson 1-14, Pate 1-0, Patrick 1- (-2).

RAMS LEADERS: Rushing - Ellison 16-90, Curran 22-78, Gabriel 1-1; **Passing** - Gabriel 15-28-0 - 202, Curran 0-1-0 - 0; **Receiving** - Snow 7-138, Curran 3-25, Ellison 2-17, Studstill 1-11, Tucker 1-8, Truax 1-3.

WEEK 2 GAMES

SF 34, Clev 31	GB 27, Atl 24
Oak 27, SD 27	KC 44, Balt 24
Dal 28, NYG 10	Den 16, Pitt 13
Chi 20, Phil 16	St.L 27, Wash 17
Det 38, Cinc 3	Minn 26, NO 0
Mia 20, Hou 10	NYJ 31, Bos 21

STANDINGS: SECOND WEEK

AFC EAST	W	L	T	CENTRAL	W	L	T	WEST	W	L	T	NFC EAST	W	L	T	CENTRAL	W	L	T	WEST	W	L	T
Baltimore	1	1	0	Houston	1	1	0	Denver	2	0	0	Dallas	2	0	0	Chicago	2	0	0	San Fran	2	0	0
Boston	1	1	0	Cleveland	1	1	0	Kan. City	1	1	0	St. Louis	1	1	0	Detroit	2	0	0	LA Rams	2	0	0
Miami	1	1	0	Cincinnati	1	1	0	Oakland	0	1	1	Washington	0	2	0	Minnesota	2	0	0	Atlanta	1	1	0
NY Jets	1	1	0	Pittsburgh	0	2	0	San Diego	0	1	1	Philadelphia	0	2	0	Green Bay	1	1	0	N. Orleans	0	2	0
Buffalo	0	2	0									NY Giants	0	2	0								

Jets	17	7	7	0	-	31
Bills	7	6	7	14	-	34

Attendance at War Memorial Stadium - 46,206

NY: Tannen 41 blocked punt return (Turner kick), 3:01
Buf: Simpson 95 kickoff return (Guthrie kick), 3:20
NY: Caster 72 pass from Namath (Turner kick), 4:48
NY: FG Turner 22, 7:48
Buf: FG Guthrie 10, 7:44
NY: Sauer 25 pass from Namath (Turner kick), 14:29
Buf: FG Guthrie 10, 7:44
Buf: Briscoe 19 pass from Shaw (Guthrie kick), 4:15
NY: Boozer 6 run (Turner kick), 6:45
Buf: Simpson 1 run (Guthrie kick), 5:20
Buf: Briscoe 25 pass from Shaw (Guthrie kick), 7:40

	BUF	NY
First downs	20	11
Rushing yds	149	109
Passing yds	252	228
Punts-avg	5-39.6	5-36.0
Fumbles-lost	4-3	0-0
Penalties-yds	7-46	7-97

BILLS LEADERS: Rushing - Simpson 21-99, Shaw 6-23, Patrick 8-19, Enyart 1-8; **Passing** - Shaw 12-21-2 - 317; **Receiving** - Briscoe 4-120, Moses 4-118, Simpson 3-63, Denney 1-16.

JETS LEADERS: Rushing - Snell 22-88, Boozer 8-11, White 2-10; **Passing** - Namath 12-26-0 - 228; **Receiving** - Boozer 4-40, Caster 4-138, Lammons 2-26, Sauer 1-25, Snell 1- (-1).

NOTES

• Dennis Shaw's first start as a pro was memorable as he passed for 317 yards and two TDs and got a huge assist from O.J. Simpson, who had his finest day as a pro in terms of total yards.

• The winning TD came when Marlin Briscoe beat Steve Tannen on a corner route and caught Shaw's perfect pass with 7:20 left to play.

• The Bills entered the fourth trailing 31-20. But after Jim Turner missed a field goal, Briscoe made a 45-yard catch to set up Simpson's one-yard TD. With nearly 10 minutes left, John Rauch ordered an on-side kick and the Bills' Jackie Allen recovered, setting the stage for Briscoe's game-winning TD.

• After that, Turner missed two more field-goal attempts that could have tied and won the game.

• The Jets scored first when Tannen blocked a Paul Maguire punt and ran it in for a TD.

• Simpson fumbled the ensuing kickoff at the 5, picked it up and weaved his way 95 yards for a TD.

• Moments later, Joe Namath fired a 72-yard bomb to rookie Rich Caster.

• After an exchange of field goals, Namath hit George Sauer for a 25-yard TD, but 30 seconds later, and one second before the end of the half, Briscoe made a good catch of a high snap and Grant Guthrie made a 40-yard

field goal to make it 24-13.

• Moses' 45-yard reception set up Briscoe's 19-yard TD catch in the third.

QUOTES

• Dennis Shaw: "I was nervous until I reached the stadium. After our pre-game meal, I called home and talked to my mom and dad and brothers and it made me feel better. As far as gambling, I played this way in college. We tried for big plays and while they require a certain amount of luck, we hit on 50 percent of them. My feeling is we have players who can make big plays, so why not keep using them." (On the winning TD): "I was looking for Haven on the play, but Haven was covered and Briscoe had given Tannen a good move to get open."

• John Rauch: "We told Dennis to lay the ball out there and let the receivers battle for it. We improved, we won, but we're not there yet by any means."

• O.J. Simpson: "This is the first time since I've been here that we beat a good team. Last year we beat Denver when it didn't have Steve Tensi and Floyd Little and we beat Miami when Bob Griese and Nick Buoniconti were hurt. This wasn't like that, it was us playing against one of the best teams in football." (On fumbling the kickoff before scoring): "All I heard were those boos."

WEEK 3 GAMES

LA 37, SD 10	Atl 21, SF 20
NO 14, NYG 10	Balt 14, Bos 6
St.L 20, Dal 7	GB 13, Minn 10
Den 26, KC 13	Hou 24, Cin 13
Clev 15, Pitt 7	Mia 20, Oak 13
Wash 33, Phil 21	Det 28, Chi 14

Bills	3	0	7	0	-	10
Steelers	3	7	3	10	-	23

Attendance at War Memorial Stadium - 41,312

Pitt: FG Mingo 28, 4:02
Buf: FG Guthrie 52, 10:52
Pitt: Smith 6 pass from Hanratty (Mingo kick), 3:09
Buf: Simpson 4 run (Guthrie kick), 8:03
Pitt: FG Mingo 49, 11:11
Pitt: Pearson 2 run (Mingo kick), 4:28
Pitt: FG Mingo 42, 7:06

	BUF	PITT
First downs	16	12
Rushing yds	85	171
Passing yds	200	38
Punts-avg	6-42.5	8-45.6
Fumbles-lost	5-2	1-0
Penalties-yds	8-82	5-62

BILLS LEADERS: Rushing - Simpson 14-60, Shaw 3-12, Patrick 6-12, Harris 1-1; **Passing** - Shaw 12-26-1 - 203, Harris 4-9-2 - 52, Darragh 1-1-0 - 2, Simpson 0-1-0 - 0; **Receiving** - Briscoe 4-73, Moses 4-122, Patrick 4-29, Enyart 5-33.

STEELERS LEADERS: Rushing - Pearson 20-86, Fuqua 11-62, Hoak 2-6, Bradshaw 2-18, Hanratty 1-0, Bryant 1-0, Cole 3- (-1); **Passing** - Hanratty 4-10-0 - 26, Bradshaw 3-12-0 - 24; **Receiving** - Shanklin 2-20, Hughes 2-14, Smith 2-6, Hoak 1-10.

NOTES

• The Bills' road woes continued as they remained winless away from Buffalo for the 16th straight time, including 13 losses in a row, dating back to Dec. 9, 1967.

• The Bills had five turnovers, eight penalties and numerous dropped passes as Pittsburgh snapped a 16-game regular-season losing streak.

• The victory was the first of rookie Terry Bradshaw's career, although he had a poor day passing and he was benched for half the game in favor of Terry Hanratty.

• The Steelers took the lead as Frenchy Fuqua ran 23 yards to set up the first of three Gene Mingo field goals.

• Marlin Briscoe then made a 36-yard reception to set up Grant Guthrie's 52-yard field goal, which was the longest in team history.

• Andy Russell recovered an O.J. Simpson fumble at the Bills 17 and Hanratty hit Dave Smith for a TD to make it 10-3.

• The Bills tied it midway through the third as Simpson scored after Haven Moses' 35-yard reception got them in position.

• Mingo put Pittsburgh ahead for good when he made a 49-yard field goal.. The Bills were called for offsides

when the Steelers tried to fake the field goal.

• Preston Pearson scored the clincher, capping a 47-yard drive after a Bills punt.

• Before the game, Steelers owner Art Rooney gave Bills' officials a tour of new Three Rivers Stadium. Of particular interest were the private boxes that sold for $37,500 for five years.

• In four games, the Bills had recorded only five sacks while the opponents had registered 19.

QUOTES

• John Rauch: "We killed our own opportunities. It seemed like every time we had something going we were hit with all kinds of penalties. They (the Steelers) didn't play that well, we just gave it away. This isn't a business designed for such charitable contributions. The Steelers did play well on defense, particularly in the line, but we expected that. We knew we'd have trouble running on them. Dennis Shaw took some pretty good cracks and came out several times pretty woozy. We thought that he had been physically shaken up to the extent that he was getting away from the game plan. I was disturbed by the mistakes, but I couldn't fault the effort and that always gives you reason for optimism. Joe O'Donnell had the most difficult assignment going against Pittsburgh's highly-rated – and deservedly so – defensive tackle Joe Greene. O'Donnell did an excellent job making Greene less of a factor than he was in any of the previous Steelers games we had seen on film." (On Terry Bradshaw): "It struck me that he seemed to be pressing too hard to be the hub in their wheel. But I also had the feeling that he's capable of making a big play at any time."

WEEK 4 GAMES

Mia 20, NYJ 6	Dal 13, Atl 0
SF 20, LA 6	KC 23, Bos 10
St.L 24, NO 17	Balt 24, Hou 20
Wash 31, Det 10	Clev 30, Cin 27
Oak 35, Den 23	NYG 30, Phil 23
Minn 24, Chi 0	GB 22, SD 20

STANDINGS: FOURTH WEEK

AFC EAST	W	L	T	CENTRAL	W	L	T	WEST	W	L	T	NFC EAST	W	L	T	CENTRAL	W	L	T	WEST	W	L	T
Baltimore	3	1	0	Cleveland	3	1	0	Denver	3	1	0	Dallas	3	1	0	Detroit	3	1	0	LA Rams	3	1	0
Miami	3	1	0	Houston	2	2	0	Kan. City	2	2	0	St. Louis	3	1	0	Minnesota	3	1	0	San Fran	3	1	0
Boston	1	3	0	Cincinnati	1	3	0	Oakland	1	2	1	Washington	2	2	0	Green Bay	3	1	0	Atlanta	2	2	0
NY Jets	1	3	0	Pittsburgh	1	3	0	San Diego	0	3	1	NY Giants	1	3	0	Chicago	2	2	0	N. Orleans	1	3	0
Buffalo	1	3	0									Philadelphia	0	4	0								

NOTES

• It was another sour effort as six turnovers and eight penalties helped Miami to win easily in new coach Don Shula's first visit to Buffalo with his Dolphins. Dennis Shaw set a Bills record with 348 passing yards, breaking the old mark set by Johnny Green (334) in 1960.

• Miami began the game with a 53-yard TD march, then O.J. Simpson lost a fumble at the Miami 39 and the Dolphins came back to get a field goal by Garo Yepremian.

• The count soared to 13-0 when Yepremian made another field goal before Shaw hit Marlin Briscoe with an 18-yard TD pass with 1:30 left in the first half.

• The Bills answered Larry Csonka's second TD run of the game with Briscoe's second TD catch to make it 20-14 entering the fourth quarter. Buffalo then began moving toward a potential go-ahead touchdown. From the 26, Shaw tried to hit Haven Moses, but safety Dick Anderson intercepted and returned it out to the Miami 36. Five plays later, Bob Griese hit Paul Warfield with a game-breaking 42-yard TD pass on a third-and-one-inch play.

• Yepremian, who finished with four field goals, claimed he had written to the Bills several times in the offseason requesting a tryout, but was denied.

• Briscoe had a huge game, catching most of his passes against Dolphins rookie CB Curtis Johnson.

QUOTES

• Dolphins quarterback Bob Griese: "Paul Warfield wasn't thrown to very often early in the game, but eventually we always get around to him."

• Dolphins Coach Don Shula on Warfield's TD: "The Bills had shown us their short yardage defense four or five times earlier in the game. We felt we could work the Warfield play when we saw it again."

• Dolphins receiver Paul Warfield: "It's a play-action pass and Griese executed it perfectly. The Bills were drawn up for a run and Griese's fake froze the safety (John Pitts) and the cornerback (Robert James) and enabled me to get free. As soon as I was released, I ran straight ahead and turned and the ball was right there."

• Butch Byrd on the play of Marlin Briscoe: "Marlin is playing better than any receiver we've ever had here. If we were winning, he'd be rated better than Paul Warfield."

• Dolphins safety Dick Anderson: "I was alone in a weak deep zone and I was just trying to play the defense that was called for in that situation and I reacted to the ball. I just rolled to my right and the quarterback threw it right to me."

• John Rauch on Simpson's fumbling: "Sure I'm concerned about it, but I never want to overly stress it. The harder a back tries to overcome something like this, the worse it becomes."

Dolphins	10	3	7	13 - 33
Bills	0	7	7	0 - 14

Attendance at War Memorial Stadium - 41.312

Mia: Csonka 4 run (Yepremian kick), 5:55
Mia: FG Yepremian 46, 11:16
Mia: FG Yepremian 42, :05
Buf: Briscoe 18 pass from Shaw (Guthrie kick), 13:30
Mia: Csonka 5 run (Yepremian kick), 6:43
Buf: Briscoe 16 pass from Shaw (Guthrie kick), 9:49
Mia: Warfield 43 pass from Griese (Yepremian kick), 5:02
Mia: FG Yepremian 47, 9:09
Mia: FG Yepremian 30, 13:11

	BUF	MIA
First downs	14	20
Rushing yds	53	147
Passing yds	337	154
Punts-avg	2-28.0	3-48.3
Fumbles-lost	4-4	0-0
Penalties-yds	8-74	3-43

BILLS LEADERS: Rushing - Simpson 11-35, Shaw 2-12, Patrick 9-6; **Passing** - Shaw 24-32-2 - 348; **Receiving** - Briscoe 7-145, Moses 1-15, Patrick 6-111, Enyart 3-26, Simpson 3-24, Alexander 1-13, Jones 1-9, Denney 1-3, Grate 1-2.

DOLPHINS LEADERS: Rushing - Csonka 16-60, Kiick 13-49, Griese 2-13, Warfield 1-16, Morris 2-7, Mitchell 1-2; **Passing** - Griese 15-22-1 - 196, Stofa 0-1-0 - 0; **Receiving** - Kiick 6-49, Warfield 4-89, Fleming 4-37, Csonka 1-21.

WEEK 5 GAMES	
Balt 29, NYJ 22	SD 20, Chi 7
KC 27, Cinc 17	NO 20, SF 20
LA 31, GB 21	Pitt 7, Hou 3
Det 41, Clev 24	NYG 16, Bos 0
St.L 35, Phil 20	Den 24, Atl 10
Minn 34, Dal 13	Oak 34, Was 20

NOTES

• The Bills snapped their 14-game regular-season losing streak on the road. It also was their first win on the road (counting playoffs) in 23 games.

• The Jets played without Joe Namath, out with a broken wrist. He watched the game from the sidelines wearing wild Indian print bell bottoms.

• Marlin Briscoe enjoyed his third 100-yard receiving day.

• Trailing 6-3 with 8:30 left to play, the Bills made a big play, then received a big break en route to the winning touchdown. First, Dennis Shaw hit Haven Moses with a 40-yard pass that carried to the Jets' 6-yard-line after he had audibled out of a running play. Shaw was nailed on the play and never saw the final result.

• Then, his pass in the end zone was intercepted by Al Atkinson, but the Jets' Steve Tannen was penalized for defensive holding on Briscoe. That put the ball on the 3 and Wayne Patrick scored from there with 6:23 left.

• Two Buffalo drives in the first half ended when Shaw threw interceptions.

• The Bills also had a TD nullified in the second quarter when Haven Moses' reception was wiped out when Moses was detected for offensive interference. The Bills settled for Grant Guthrie's nine-yard field goal.

QUOTES

• Dennis Shaw on the pass to Moses: "I went up there with a running play, but when I saw that we could get W.K. Hicks (the Jets safety) on Haven with single coverage, I changed the play."

• Haven Moses: "Dennis threw the ball even before my last break on the pattern. It was an excellent pass."

• John Rauch: "All we needed to do was connect on one or two of those situations and we would get some long gains. I expected the Jets to continue blitzing Shaw heavily and leaving themselves dangerously exposed as the line picked up the blitzers and gave him some time."

• O.J. Simpson: "You can't play much worse and still win, can you?"

• Jets cornerback Steve Tannen: "The official walked over, smiled and pointed at me."

• Jets coach Weeb Ewbank: "If that's a penalty, the guy's going to have some busy back pockets."

• Edgar Chandler: "This game was both surprising and encouraging. It was encouraging because we were able to stick pretty much to basic defenses and hold the Jets to 119 yards. What's surprising is that we could stick to these basic defenses. We aren't talking division title yet, but we aren't dismissing the possibility. All we have to do is win, which we should have been doing all along."

Bills	0	3	0	7 - 10
Jets	0	0	6	0 - 6

Attendance at Shea Stadium - 62,712

Buf: FG Guthrie 9, 7:04
NYJ: FG Turner 29, 6:02
NYJ: FG Turner 33, 12:09
Buf: Patrick 3 run (Guthrie kick), 8:37

	BUF	NYJ
First downs	15	10
Rushing yds	89	86
Passing yds	104	33
Punts-avg	6-40.8	8-45.3
Fumbles-lost	1-0	2-1
Penalties-yds	9-97	7-68

BILLS LEADERS: Rushing - Simpson 15-55, Shaw 4-6, Patrick 6-28; **Passing** - Shaw 10-24-2 - 163; **Receiving** - Briscoe 5-100, Moses 2-60, Patrick 1- (-4), Enyart 1-4, Simpson 1-3.

JETS LEADERS: Rushing - Boozer 13-65, White 13-26, Nock 4-10, Woodall 3-(-5), Bell 1-(-7), Mercein 1-(-3); **Passing** - Woodall 7-16-1 - 63; **Receiving** - Maynard 3-29, Bell 2-19, Lammons 1-8, White 1-7.

WEEK 6 GAMES	
Det 16, Chi 10	Wash 20, Cinc 0
GB 30, Phil 17	Dal 27, KC 16
NYG 35, St.L 17	SF 19, Den 14
Hou 31, SD 31	Atl 32, NO 14
Clev 28, Mia 0	Balt 27, Bos 3
Oak 31, Pitt 14	Minn 13, LA 3

STANDINGS: SIXTH WEEK

AFC EAST	W	L	T	CENTRAL	W	L	T	WEST	W	L	T	NFC EAST	W	L	T	CENTRAL	W	L	T	WEST	W	L	T
Baltimore	5	1	0	Cleveland	4	2	0	Denver	4	2	0	St. Louis	4	2	0	Detroit	5	1	0	San Fran	4	1	1
Miami	4	2	0	Houston	2	3	1	Oakland	3	2	1	Dallas	4	2	0	Minnesota	5	1	0	LA Rams	4	2	0
Buffalo	2	4	0	Pittsburgh	2	4	0	Kan. City	3	3	0	Washington	3	3	0	Green Bay	4	2	0	Atlanta	3	3	0
NY Jets	1	5	0	Cincinnati	1	5	0	San Diego	1	3	2	NY Giants	3	3	0	Chicago	2	4	0	N. Orleans	1	4	1
Boston	1	5	0									Philadelphia	0	6	0								

Bills	10 21 0 14 - 45
Patriots	0 0 3 7 - 10

Attendance at Harvard Stadium - 31,148

Buf: FG Guthrie 20, 3:01
Buf: Jones 2 run (Guthrie kick), 9:55
Buf: Simpson 56 run (Guthrie kick), 3:17
Buf: Chandler 59 interception return (Guthrie kick), 5:22
Buf: Enyart 37 pass from Shaw (Guthrie kick), 14:43
Bos: FG Gogolak 32, 14:14
Buf: Moses 13 pass from Harris (Guthrie kick), 5:09
Bos: Nance 19 run (Gogolak kick), 11:05
Buf: Jones 52 kickoff return (Guthrie kick), 11:15

	BUF	BOS
First downs	18	19
Rushing yds	215	100
Passing yds	149	151
Punts-avg	4-39.3	6-38.2
Fumbles-lost	3-2	4-3
Penalties-yds	10-108	8-60

BILLS LEADERS: Rushing - Simpson 17-123, Patrick 10-65, Jones 5-16, Enyart 1-11, Shaw 1-0; **Passing** - Shaw 9-14-0 -140, Harris 2-3-0 - 30; **Receiving** - Briscoe 2-47, Moses 4-66, Jones 1-11, Grate 1-17, Patrick 1- -5, Enyart 2-34.

PATRIOTS LEADERS: Rushing - Nance 16-76, Garrett 9-26, Blanks 1-(-2); **Passing:** Kapp 7-18-2 - 75, Taliaferro 11-20-0 - 106; **Receiving** - Sellers 5-53, Brown 3-46, Garrett 4-40, Frazier 2-18, Nance 2-8, Turner 1-11, Lawson 1-5.

NOTES
• Boston coach Clive Rush was taken to a nearby motel and attended to by his personal physician before the game, due to a fast heartbeat. By the time he returned, the score was 24-0.
• This was the Bills' first two-game winning streak since 1966.
• O.J. Simpson was weakened by a virus, but still produced 121 rushing yards.
• The Bills opened the game with an impressive drive as Simpson gained 41 yards, but they settled for a Grant Guthrie field goal.
• After ex-Bill Tom Janik shanked a punt, the Bills drove 47 yards in nine plays to Greg Jones' TD.
• Early in the second quarter, Simpson took a pitchout, put a brilliant move on cornerback Daryl Johnson and sped 56 yards for his longest TD from scrimmage as a pro.
• Two minutes later, Joe Kapp's pass was intercepted by Edgar Chandler and he took it 59 yards for the TD that made it 24-0.
• Boston's Jim Nance fumbled to kill two Patriots drives, the second at the Bills 15. Shaw then directed Buffalo 85 yards in eight plays, the TD coming on his pass to Bill Enyart.
• In the third, Tommy Pharr's 54-yard punt return led to Haven Moses' 13-yard TD reception.
• After a Nance TD, Boston tried an on-side kick and Jones took the ball on the hop and dashed past the hard-charging Boston kickoff team for a stunning 52-yard kickoff return TD.
• The Bills finished the game with 242 return yards.

QUOTES
• Boston quarterback Joe Kapp: "That wasn't a game plan, that was a disaster plan. In all my years of football, I've never seen so many things go wrong for one team in a game."
• O.J. Simpson on his illness: "A couple of hours before the game I told the coaches I was still weak but that I could play. They told me to give them a signal when I didn't feel well and they would send in Greg (Jones)."
• John Rauch: "We grew up quite a bit today. We're just a young club prone to making mistakes, but we avoided those mistakes today and moved the ball against what I consider a very decent defense."
• Boston coach Clive Rush: "I said a week or so ago that our team hadn't played a bad game. Well, we've had it now."
• Dennis Shaw: "I feel real good about this one. We played better as a unit today than we did against New York. But of course, it's always nice to win."
• Edgar Chandler: "I've never scored a touchdown in any football game in my life. When I saw those two ones on that red jersey (Kapp), I just wanted to make sure he didn't nail me."

WEEK 7 GAMES	
Balt 35, Mia 0	St.L 44, Hou 0
Chi 23, Atl 14	SD 27, Clev 10
Oak 17, KC 17	Pitt 21, Cin 10
LA 30, NO 17	SF 26, GB 10
NYG 22, NYJ 10	Minn 30, Det 17
Wash 19, Den 3	Dal 21, Phil 17

Bengals	3 20 13 7 - 43
Bills	7 7 0 0 - 14

Attendance at War Memorial Stadium - 43,587

Buf: Briscoe 29 pass from Shaw (Guthrie kick), 9:04
Cin: FG Muhlmann 22, 12:49
Cin: Phillips 1 run (Muhlmann kick), 6:42
Cin: FG Muhlmann 30, 8:18
Buf: Simpson 1 run (Guthrie kick), 10:05
Cin: Parrish 95 kickoff return (Muhlmann kick), 10:22
Cin: FG Muhlmann 13, 14:49
Cin: FG Muhlmann 36, 3:16
Cin: Berry 8 fumble return (Muhlmann kick), 4:24
Cin: FG Muhlmann 43, 12:49
Cin: Parrish 83 blocked field goal return (Muhlmann kick), 1:27

	BUF	CIN
First downs	17	17
Rushing yds	103	156
Passing yds	274	164
Punts-avg	5-39.4	4-46.3
Fumbles-lost	5-4	1-0
Penalties-yds	7-41	2-30

BILLS LEADERS: Rushing - Simpson 10-40, Patrick 8-36, Jones 3-24, Enyart 1-5, Shaw 1- (-2); **Passing** - Shaw 11-23-1 - 251, Harris 4-8-1 - 39; **Receiving** - Briscoe 5-109, Moses 4-77, Denney 4-66, Jones 1-34, Patrick 1-4.

BENGALS LEADERS: Rushing - Robinson 13-49, Phillips 13-35, Carter 5-31, Dressler 6-23, Thomas 1-13, Johnson 2-4, Lewis 1-1; **Passing** - Carter 12-24-0 - 164; **Receiving** - Trumpy 4-96, Crabtree 2-17, Robinson 3-15, Phillips 2-23, Meyers 1-13.

NOTES
• O.J. Simpson's season came to an end when he suffered a knee injury. The good news for him and the team, though, was that surgery was not required to repair the damage. Simpson was hurt returning a kickoff on the final play of the first half.
• Safety Pete Richardson was ejected for getting into a scuffle with Bengals tight end Bob Trumpy.
• The Bengals snapped a six-game losing streak and set a team record for scoring.
• Marlin Briscoe caught a 48-yard pass early in the game, but fumbled it away at the Bengals 5. He redeemed himself on the next series, beating rookie Lemar Parrish and catching a 29-yard TD pass.
• Parrish got his revenge, and then some. He returned the ensuing kickoff 49 yards to set up the first of five Horst Muhlmann field goals.
• Trailing 13-7, the Bills regained the lead. Simpson returned a kickoff 51 yards and after Austin Denney made a 24-yard reception, Simpson scored on a one-yard run to make it 14-13.
• However, Parrish returned the kickoff 95 yards for a TD.
• Later, Bob Trumpy's 46-yard reception set up a Muhlmann field goal 14 seconds before halftime.
• In the third, the Bills got a bad break. Royce Berry broke through the line and hit Dennis Shaw as he was dropping to pass. Shaw's arm appeared to be in motion,

but the officials ruled fumble, Berry scooped it up and scored to make the score 33-14.
• Early in the fourth, Ken Riley blocked a Grant Guthrie field goal and Parrish concluded his brilliant day by taking it back 83 yards for the final score.

QUOTES
• Bengals cornerback Ken Riley on Cincinnati's defense after Simpson went out: "We started playing more for the pass. When O.J. went out, we knew we didn't have to worry too much about the run anymore."
• Austin Denney: "We gave the Bengals 21 points on plays which weren't even from scrimmage. That's tough to overcome. It's hard to believe you can gain close to 400 yards and still get walloped."
• Bengals coach Paul Brown: "Maybe the Bills weren't up for this game because we had lost six in a row. Anyway, the turning point was Parrish's kickoff return for the touchdown."
• John Rauch: "I thought we were still in the game until the blocked field goal."

WEEK 8 GAMES	
SF 37, Chi 16	Pit 21, NYJ 17
KC 24, Hou 9	SD 24, Den 21
Min 19, Was 10	LA 10, Atl 10
Phil 24, Mia 17	St.L 31, Bos 0
Oak 23, Cle 20	NYG 23, Dal 20
Balt 13, GB 10	NO 19, Det 17

STANDINGS: EIGHTH WEEK

AFC EAST	W	L	T	CENTRAL	W	L	T	WEST	W	L	T	NFC EAST	W	L	T	CENTRAL	W	L	T	WEST	W	L	T
Baltimore	7	1	0	Cleveland	4	4	0	Oakland	4	2	2	St. Louis	6	2	0	Minnesota	7	1	0	San Fran	6	1	1
Miami	4	4	0	Pittsburgh	4	4	0	Kan. City	4	3	1	Dallas	5	3	0	Detroit	5	3	0	LA Rams	5	2	1
Buffalo	3	5	0	Houston	2	5	1	Denver	4	4	0	NY Giants	5	3	0	Green Bay	4	4	0	Atlanta	3	4	1
NY Jets	1	7	0	Cincinnati	2	6	0	San Diego	3	3	2	Washington	4	4	0	Chicago	3	5	0	N. Orleans	2	5	1
Boston	1	7	0									Philadelphia	1	7	0								

GAME 9 - Sunday, Nov. 15, 1970 - BILLS 17, COLTS 17

NOTES

• The Bills went to Baltimore for the first time and shocked the AFC East-leading Colts with the tie. It probably was the best the Bills had played since 1966.

• Linebacker Mike Stratton was lost for the season with an Achilles tendon tear. Wayne Patrick was lost with a shoulder separation.

• The Bills took the lead on their first possession when Dennis Shaw led a 16-play, 71-yard drive that ended with his four-yard TD pass to Haven Moses.

• After Jim O'Brien missed a 28-yard field goal, the Bills went 80 yards in nine plays. Wayne Patrick gained 20 yards on one play and Shaw scrambled 20 on another before passing 20 yards to Marlin Briscoe for a stunning 14-0 lead.

• Johnny Unitas drove the Colts right back 80 yards, hitting John Mackey for the score.

• Baltimore opened the second half with another 80-yard drive and Eddie Hinton scored on a 16-yard reverse.

• O'Brien missed a 37-yarder late in the third, but made an 18-yarder early in the fourth.

• Buffalo started its tying drive with 5:11 left. The Bills advanced into Colts territory for the first time in the second half and reached the 28 and on fourth-and-one, John Rauch called on Grant Guthrie to tie it and he did, but Rauch was second-guessed for not going for the first down and trying for the win.

• Pete Richardson intercepted a Unitas pass with six seconds left, but Guthrie's 58-yard field goal with a crosswind fell about 30 yards short.

QUOTES

• John Rauch: "I thought the tie would give our club a lift, especially the younger members. We gave some thought to going for the first down and trying to keep the drive alive for a touchdown. Some of the players wanted to go for it. However, I thought it was best to go for the tie at that time. One factor that entered into the decision was the time."

• Wayne Patrick: "We played well enough to win, but I guess a tie against as good a team as Baltimore is something to be happy about. When O.J. isn't in the lineup, it puts more of the running load on me. With O.J. not playing, the Colts didn't think we could run the ball so well. We certainly miss O.J., but Greg Jones did a fine job replacing him. I think the Colts might have taken us too lightly."

• Colts quarterback Johnny Unitas on the play of Dennis Shaw: "He got them the tie, he did what he had to do. He's got to stop trying to force the ball (into double coverage) and trying to throw deep when he shouldn't. But he looks like he can do it to me."

WEEK 9 GAMES

Atl 13, Phil 13	Minn 24, Det 20
KC 31, Pitt 14	Cin 14, Clev 10
SD 16, Bos 14	GB 20, Chi 19
SF 30, Hou 20	Mia 21, NO 10
NYG 35, Wash 33	Oak 24, Den 19
NYJ 31, LA 20	St.L 38, Dal 0

Bills	7	7	0	3 - 17
Colts	0	7	7	3 - 17

Attendance at Memorial Stadium - 60,240

Buf: Moses 4 pass from Shaw (Guthrie kick), 8:56
Buf: Briscoe 20 pass from Shaw (Guthrie kick), 9:58
Bal: Mackey 25 pass from Unitas (O'Brien kick), 13:12
Bal: Hinton 16 run (O'Brien kick), 5:05
Bal: FG O'Brien 18, 2:32
Buf: FG Guthrie 26, 13:51

	BUF	BAL
First downs	16	21
Rushing yds	181	136
Passing yds	90	209
Punts-avg	4-43.0	4-47.2
Fumbles-lost	0-0	0-0
Penalties-yds	4-43	3-26

BILLS LEADERS: Rushing - Patrick 15-84, Jones 14-46, Shaw 4-36, Enyart 1-10, Briscoe 1-5; **Passing** - Shaw 10-20-2 - 94; **Receiving** - Briscoe 4-50, Moses 2-12, Alexander 1-14, Jones 2-11, Patrick 1-7.

COLTS LEADERS: Rushing - Bulaich 22-86, Hill 3-7, Jefferson 1-19, Hinton 1-16, Nowatzke 2-6, Perkins 1-2; **Passing** - Unitas 15-29-1 - 221; **Receiving** - Mitchell 5-69, Mackey 3-54, Hinton 3-44, Jefferson 1-22, Perkins 1-14, Bulaich 1-9, Hill 1-9.

GAME 10 - Sunday, Nov. 22, 1970 - BEARS 31, BILLS 13

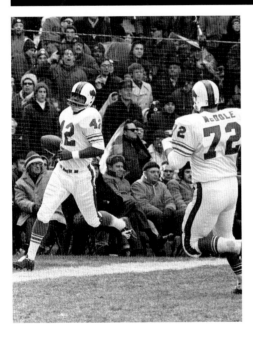

NOTES

• The up-and-down play continued and in this game, the Bills were way down, beaten by a bad Bears team thanks to five turnovers and four Bobby Douglass TD passes.

• Butch Byrd intercepted Douglass' first pass and raced 26 yards for a TD.

• Tommy Pharr had a 52-yard punt return nullified by a penalty early in the second quarter and moments later, Bill Enyart fumbled at midfield. Byrd nearly picked off another pass and he would have scored, but he dropped the ball. The Bills defense held, but Bobby

Joe Green faked a punt and ran for a first down. On the next play, Douglass threw 36 yards to Dick Gordon for his first TD.

• Four plays after the kickoff, Doug Buffone intercepted Shaw and that led to Jim Seymour's first TD reception.

• The Bills drove back to the Bears' 13 and Grant Guthrie was going to kick a field goal, but the snap went through Marlin Briscoe's hands, killing the threat. Later in the half, Shaw lost a fumble at the Bears 29 to Dick Butkus.

• The Bears made it 21-6 on Seymour's second TD, but Al Cowlings sacked Douglass, forcing him to fumble, and Jim Dunaway recovered at the Bears 17, leading to Briscoe's TD reception.

• A Butkus interception set up Max Percival's field goal and Douglass completed the rout with a TD pass to Gordon with :51 left.

• Despite his heroics, it wasn't such a good day for Douglass because he suffered a season-ending wrist injury.

QUOTES

• John Rauch: "We have so many inexperienced guys, you never know when the roof is going to fall in on us. If we make a couple of mistakes, it's disastrous. We can't say we didn't have enough breaks against the Bears. We had them, particularly early in the game, and we didn't cash in on them. The cold fact is we had the opportunity to win the game. We had the momentum, but we defeated ourselves, first by allowing Bobby Douglass time to complete touchdown passes and secondly, by mistakes of commission. That includes fumbles, interceptions, a blocked conversion and a field goal fumble."

• Al Cowlings: "The team that makes the most mistakes loses and we had them all. Until we stop hurting ourselves and start causing our opponents to be guilty of them, we're not going to win consistently."

Bills	6	0	0	7 - 13
Bears	0	14	7	10 - 31

Attendance at Wrigley Field - 43,332

Buf: Byrd 26 interception return (kick failed), 4:14
Chi: Gordon 36 pass from Douglass (Percival kick), 3:41
Chi: Seymour 36 pass from Douglass (Percival kick), 6:38
Chi: Seymour 53 pass from Douglass (Percival kick), 5:23
Buf: Briscoe 17 pass from Shaw (Guthrie kick), 5:16
Chi: FG Percival 37, 12:33
Chi: Gordon 28 pass from Douglass (Percival kick), 14:09

	BUF	CHI
First downs	14	12
Rushing yds	134	91
Passing yds	119	150
Punts-avg	5-37.2	7-47.7
Fumbles-lost	5-3	2-1
Penalties-yds	5-52	6-82

BILLS LEADERS: Rushing - Enyart 12-44, Jones 9-27, Shaw 5-48, Pate 2-19, Harris 1-(-4); **Passing** - Shaw 13-18-2 - 147, Harris 1-4-0 - 5; **Receiving** - Briscoe 4-49, Moses 2-44, Enyart 3-14, Jones 3-24, Denney 1-16, Pate 1-5.

BEARS LEADERS: Rushing - Shy 16-46, Bull 8-19, Douglass 5-12, Green 1-7, Gordon 1-7, Montgomery 1-3, Turner 1-(-3); **Passing** - Douglass 8-20-1 - 196; **Receiving** - Gordon 6-107, Seymour 2-89.

WEEK 10 GAMES

Minn 10, GB 3	NYJ 17, Bos 3
Mia 34, Balt 17	Den 31, NO 6
St.L 6, KC 6	Det 28, SF 7
Dal 45, Wash 21	LA 17, Atl 7
Cinc 34, Pitt 7	Oak 20, SD 17
Clev 28, Hou 14	Phil 23, NYG 20

STANDINGS: TENTH WEEK

AFC EAST	W	L	T	CENTRAL	W	L	T	WEST	W	L	T	NFC EAST	W	L	T	CENTRAL	W	L	T	WEST	W	L	T
Baltimore	7	2	1	Cleveland	5	5	0	Oakland	6	2	2	St. Louis	7	2	1	Minnesota	9	1	0	San Fran	7	2	1
Miami	6	4	0	Pittsburgh	4	6	0	Kan. City	5	3	2	NY Giants	6	4	0	Detroit	6	4	0	LA Rams	6	3	1
Buffalo	3	6	1	Cincinnati	4	6	0	San Diego	4	4	2	Dallas	6	4	0	Green Bay	5	5	0	Atlanta	3	5	2
NY Jets	3	7	0	Houston	2	7	1	Denver	5	5	0	Washington	4	6	0	Chicago	4	6	0	N. Orleans	2	7	1
Boston	1	9	0									Philadelphia	2	7	1								

Patriots	0	7	7	0 - 14
Bills	0	3	0	7 - 10

Attendance at War Memorial Stadium - 31,427

Bos: Sellers 10 pass from Taliaferro (Cappelletti kick), 3:15
Buf: FG Guthrie 37, 7:05
Bos: Nance 1 run (Cappelletti kick), 11:34
Buf: Grate 28 pass from Harris (Guthrie kick), 13:02

	BUF	BOS
First downs	12	10
Rushing yds	95	58
Passing yds	230	109
Punts-avg	7-43.4	7-43.9
Fumbles-lost	2-1	1-1
Penalties-yds	10-159	6-56

BILLS LEADERS: Rushing - Enyart 11-37, Shaw 4-36, Pate 8-22; **Passing** - Shaw 15-31-1 - 163, Harris 3-6-0 - 92; **Receiving** - Briscoe 3-73, Enyart 6-38, Pate 5-42, Denney 2-42, Grate 2-60.

PATRIOTS LEADERS: Rushing - Nance 21-54, Lawson 12-4; **Passing** - Taliaferro 4-9-1 - 34, Kapp 4-9-2 - 83; **Receiving** - Lawson 5-49, Turner 2-58, Sellers 1-10.

WEEK 11 GAMES

Det 28, Oak 14	Dal 16, GB 3
NYJ 20, Minn 10	Cinc 26, NO 6
NYG 27, Wash 24	KC 26, SD 14
LA 30, SF 13	Hou 31, Den 21
St.L 23, Phi 14	Bal 21, Chi 20
Pitt 28, Clev 9	Mia 20, Atl 7

NOTES

• Dennis Shaw suffered a pulled groin and James Harris replaced him and rallied the Bills back into the game. However, Shaw took over for Harris on the final play and he threw an incomplete pass at the goal line to Marlin Briscoe that ended the game.
• Bills players were furious over Rauch's decision to replace Harris. Off the record, one player said it was "the worst thing I've ever seen in football. It was Harris' game to win at that point." Another said "This is a sure way to create dissension between the players and the coaches."
• Shaw came out with two minutes left and the Bills trailing 14-3. Harris went in and on his first play, threw a 28-yard TD pass to Willie Grate.
• On the ensuing series, the defense held and Tom Janik punted to the Bills 21. Harris hit Briscoe for 32 yards to the Pats 47 with 30 seconds left. After a deliberate incompletion, he found Grate for 32 yards to the 15 with 19 seconds left. When the officials didn't stop the clock because the Patriots were slow getting to the line, the clock dwindled to six seconds before Shaw, who had sprinted onto the field, was able to get the ball snapped. He tried to hit Briscoe on the right side and Randy Beverly knocked the pass away to preserve Boston's win.
• Early in the game, Jim Nance appeared to fumble and Paul Guidry ran 96 yards for a TD, but the play had been ruled dead by the officials. The Patriots did not score, though.
• Shaw lost a fumble in the second quarter, recovered by Houston Antwine, and that set up Mike Taliaferro's TD pass to Ron Sellers. Taliaferro replaced ineffective Joe Kapp.
• Robert James' 45-yard pass-interference penalty led to Nance's one-yard TD run in the third.

QUOTES

• James Harris describing the final play fiasco: "I probably would have thrown to Willie Grate again on a play something like the one that got us the touchdown or the one that got us to the 15. They were different plays, but Willie ran the same pattern on both of them. They were in a prevent and Willie was being covered by a linebacker. You never want to come out of a game. I might have felt really bad (about coming out) but Dennis threw a strike."
• Dennis Shaw: "I suggested the play and coach Rauch said 'OK, go in and run it.'"
• John Rauch: "I had a play I wanted to get in and I was afraid if I sent someone else, he would have had to shove people out of the way to get it across to everyone. I knew Dennis would call it correctly. The thought was to eliminate any possible error in transmitting it. I had no idea the reaction would be as it was. It was no more a reflection upon Jim Harris' ability to execute the same play than it would have been if the situation between him and Dennis were reversed."
• Marlin Briscoe: "I don't think I was in the end zone anyway. It would have gone for naught even if I had caught it."

Bills	0	6	0	0 - 6
Giants	0	3	3	14 - 20

Attendance at Yankee Stadium - 62,870

NYG: FG Gogolak 25, :26
Buf: FG Guthrie 23, 9:47
Buf: FG Guthrie 28, 14:56
NYG: FG Gogolak 15, 3:07
NYG: McNeil 9 pass from Tarkenton (Gogolak kick), 2:21
NYG: Frederickson 4 pass from Tarkenton (Gogolak kick), 8:29

	BUF	NYG
First downs	13	15
Rushing yds	73	151
Passing yds	107	119
Punts-avg	6-37.0	3-45.0
Fumbles-lost	2-1	3-3
Penalties-yds	5-70	5-40

BILLS LEADERS: Rushing - Enyart 9-22, Pate 13-53, Briscoe 1-3, Harris 1-(-5); **Passing** - Shaw 14-28-1 - 163, Harris 1-3-0 - 11; **Receiving** - Briscoe 4-88, Enyart 4-18, Moses 5-54, Pate 1-4, Denney 1-10.

GIANTS LEADERS: Rushing - Johnson 21-100, Frederickson 12-39, Duhan 1-13, Tarkenton 1-(-1); **Passing** - Tarkenton 11-19-0 - 141; **Receiving** - Tucker 5-82, McNeil 3-46, Frederickson 2-8, Johnson 1-5.

WEEK 12 GAMES

Minn 16, Chi 13	Mia 37, Bos 20
LA 34, NO 16	KC 16, Den 0
Det 16, St.L 3	GB 20, Pitt 12
Dal 34, Wash 0	Oak 14, NYJ 13
Balt 29, Phil 10	SF 24, Atl 20
Clev 21, Hou 10	Cinc 17, SD 14

NOTES

• In their first meeting with the New York Giants, the Bills allowed 14 fourth-quarter points to squander away the game.
• With the game tied at 6-6 late in the third quarter, Marlin Briscoe made a crucial error. The Bills were about to attempt a 33-yard field goal, but Briscoe took the snap and decided to try for the first down, even though 14 yards were needed. He originally wanted to throw a pass, but nothing was open so he ran and gained only three yards to the 23.
• Fran Tarkenton then drove the Giants 77 yards for the go-ahead TD, his nine-yard pass to Clifton McNeil.
• The Giants put the game away six minutes later when Willie Williams intercepted Dennis Shaw and the Giants drove 64 yards in seven plays to Tarkenton's four-yard TD pass to Tucker Frederickson.
• Pete Gogolak missed two field goals in the first quarter, but he connected from 25 yards in the second to make it 3-0. It was his 21st of the season, a Giants record.
• The Bills took advantage of Frederickson's fumble, recovered by Pete Richardson, and drove to Grant Guthrie's first field goal. Late in the half, Paul Guidry forced Tarkenton to fumble and Julian Nunamaker recovered. Shaw hit Briscoe for 38 yards to the Giants 21 with eight seconds left and Guthrie came on to kick a 28-yard field goal.
• New York tied it quickly in the third as Tes Shy returned the kickoff 62 yards and Gogolak eventually made a 15-yarder.
• The team bus arrived almost an hour late when the driver got lost.
• The Giants used the safety blitz to disrupt the Bills' passing game. Spider Lockhart sacked Shaw four times for 39 yards in losses.

QUOTES

• Marlin Briscoe: "I'm supposed to be a leader on this team and I do a fool thing like that. I take the entire blame for losing the game. It was my own idea. I thought I could hit J.C. Collins with a pass, but I guess he didn't hear me call the play. It was strictly impulsive. I thought I saw something, but it turned out not to be there. It changed the tempo of the entire game. I guess when you're going bad, as we are, the breaks generally go against you."
• John Rauch: "Marlin has the option of calling the play and he did. I can't see the play as the turning point of the game in New York's favor, but it did, of course, give the Giants a lift. We saw things in the movies and we practiced the fake field goal several times last week"
• Giants safety Spider Lockhart: "We usually don't blitz that much, but we'll try it on young quarterbacks like Shaw. They might have trouble reading it correctly."
• Giants coach Alex Webster in reference to his halftime speech: "I hollered a little. I told them if they played the same way in the second half they'd lose the whole season. I had to get a little emotional to have it rub off."

STANDINGS: TWELFTH WEEK

AFC EAST	W	L	T	CENTRAL	W	L	T	WEST	W	L	T	NFC EAST	W	L	T	CENTRAL	W	L	T	WEST	W	L	T
Baltimore	9	2	1	Cleveland	6	6	0	Oakland	7	3	2	St. Louis	8	3	1	Minnesota	10	2	0	San Fran	8	3	1
Miami	8	4	0	Cincinnati	6	6	0	Kan. City	7	3	2	NY Giants	8	4	0	Detroit	8	4	0	LA Rams	8	3	1
NY Jets	4	8	0	Pittsburgh	5	7	0	San Diego	4	6	2	Dallas	8	4	0	Green Bay	6	6	0	Atlanta	3	7	2
Buffalo	3	8	1	Houston	3	8	1	Denver	5	7	0	Washington	4	8	0	Chicago	4	8	0	N. Orleans	2	9	1
Boston	2	10	0									Philadelphia	2	9	1								

NOTES

• The Colts clinched the first AFC East division title by rallying from a 14-10 halftime deficit to win on a snowy day at War Memorial.

• The Colts took the early lead when Johnny Unitas' 30-yard pass to Roy Jefferson set up Jim O'Brien's first field goal.

• The Bills went ahead when Roland Moss, making his Bills' debut, returned the kickoff 56 yards to the Baltimore 41. Dennis Shaw threw six straight passes, leading to Lloyd Pate's one-yard plunge.

• The Colts got plenty of help from the officials on their next sequence. First, a Paul Guidry sack was wiped out when Robert James was flagged for lining up offsides; a bad first-down measurement kept them moving and finally, an interference penalty on John Pitts moved the ball to the Bills 24. Nine runs later and the Colts were ahead, 10-7.

• In the second quarter, the Bills went 78 yards with Haven Moses making a fingertip catch for 33 yards to the Colts 14, leading to Shaw's TD pass to Marlin Briscoe.

• Another questionable penalty went against the Bills in the third when Howard Kindig was flagged for interfering with Ron Gardin's fair catch of a punt. The 15-yarder gave the Colts a drive start at the Bills 33 and Norm Bulaich eventually scored.

• O'Brien made a 38-yard field goal, but the Bills had chances to win. Charlie Stukes' interception killed one, then with 4:30 left, the Bills began a drive at their own 38 and moved to the Colts 30 only to have Rick Volk recover a Pate fumble. And in the waning seconds, they reached the Colts 35 before Stukes made another interception on the game's final play.

QUOTES

• Colts coach Don McCafferty: "I was scared all the way. The Bills were in it all the way. They played it tough and made it a struggle. It typified our season as a whole for we've been struggling game after game."

• Colts quarterback Johnny Unitas: "I was unhappy with our play defensively and offensively."

• Butch Byrd: "It's frustrating. The field is covered with snow and they call Robert James for lining up off-sides. That wiped out a big loss on a blitz and kept their first touchdown drive going. And on the measurement, it was close, but you could see daylight between the stick and the ball."

• John Rauch: "I'm tremendously proud of the effort and the performance. We were a team out of contention, hurt by several key injuries, and we were playing a team that felt it was a fluke when we tied them five weeks ago. If there was any doubt that Shaw could quarterback a pro team, he answered it. And I can only say that Baltimore's two touchdown drives included key plays centered around judgement calls. That's really doing a job defensively against a quarterback like Johnny Unitas."

Colts	10	0	7	3	-	20
Bills	7	7	0	0	-	14

Attendance at War Memorial Stadium - 34,346

Bal: FG O'Brien 32, 5:54
Buf: Pate 1 run (Guthrie kick), 9:01
Bal: Nowatzke 1 run (O'Brien kick), 14:53
Buf: Briscoe 10 pass from Shaw (Guthrie kick), 4:34
Bal: Bulaich 2 run (O'Brien kick), 6:21
Bal: FG O'Brien 38, 4:34

	BUF	BAL
First downs	18	15
Rushing yds	97	49
Passing yds	236	226
Punts-avg	8-32.9	7-44.6
Fumbles-lost	1-1	1-1
Penalties-yds	7-103	1-5

BILLS LEADERS: Rushing - Enyart 10-36, Pate 15-49, Shaw 2-12; **Passing** - Shaw 23-43-2 - 252; **Receiving** - Briscoe 7-78, Moses 6-100, Pate 6-29, Enyart 2-18, Grate 1-25, Denney 1-2.

COLTS LEADERS: Rushing - Bulaich 15-18, Nowatzke 9-20, Maitland 5-11; **Passing** - Unitas 13-31-0 - 236; **Receiving** - Jefferson 5-125, Orr 3-70, Perkins 2-22, Mackey 1-17, Nowatzke 2-2.

WEEK 13 GAMES

Oak 20, KC 6	SF 38, NO 27
Wash 24, Phil 6	Dal 6, Clev 2
NYG 34, St.L 17	Atl 27, Pit 16
Cinc 30, Hou 20	SD 17, Den 17
Mia 16, NYJ 10	Chi 35, GB 17
Minn 35, Bos 14	Det 28, LA 23

NOTES

• Don Shula, in his first season as coach of the Dolphins, got the team into the playoffs as a wild-card entry, Miami's first playoff appearance, by beating up on the Bills.

• Miami went from 3-10-1 in 1969 to 10-4, thanks to a six-game season-ending winning streak.

• Buffalo closed with its third straight season-ending debacle. The combined score of its last three year-enders was 125-20.

• After the game, the players held a closed-door meeting pledging to stick together for next year and also said they wanted John Rauch back as coach.

• Marlin Briscoe caught only one pass, but he finished with an AFC-best 57.

• Miami ate up the first 7:02 of the clock to score and the Bills never recovered.

• Dennis Shaw was picked off by Lloyd Mumphord at the Bills 35, leading to Bob Griese's TD pass to Howard Twilley. On its next series, Miami scored after Larry Csonka went 54 yards to the 4 with a screen pass.

• In the second quarter, Csonka broke free for a 53-yard gain and Jim Kiick eventually capped the 81-yard march with a two-yard TD; Garo Yepremian added a field goal and it was 31-0 at the half.

• The Bills lone TD came when they were down 45-0, as James Harris hit Willie Grate with 4:32 left.

QUOTES

• Miami quarterback Bob Griese: "To tell you the truth, it gets boring when you get so far ahead. But you can accept a boring, lopsided game when you're winning. We had tough, consistent scoring drives and after you get so far ahead, it begins to compound. Toward the end, I looked across the field at the Buffalo bench. I could see those Bills aching to get it all over with and clear out. That's about the way it's been for us until this year."

• Miami coach Don Shula: "It's a happy day. We fought back after losing three in a row and now we've won six in a row."

• Miami linebacker Nick Buoniconti: "This is just another stepping stone toward bigger things."

• Edgard Chandler talking about the difficulties with coach John Rauch: "We've got to get together next year or have no football team. If we had given him a better effort at times, he may have given us a better side of himself. You can't pat a losing team on the back too much. I certainly hope he's back, he has a tremendous knowledge of the game."

• Butch Byrd: "I'm confident a large majority of us are with John and finally realizing what it takes if you want to be a winning team."

Bills	0	0	0	7	-	7
Dolphins	21	10	7	7	-	45

Attendance at the Orange Bowl - 70,990

Mia: Kiick 4 run (Yepremian Kick), 7:02
Mia: Twilley 21 pass from Griese (Yepremian), 10:34
Mia: Csonka 2 run (Yepremian kick), 14:57
Mia: Kiick 2 run (Yepremian kick), 5:45
Mia: FG Yepremian 43, 8:44
Mia: Kiick 2 run (Yepremian kick), 11:37
Mia: Mitchell 36 pass from Stofa (Yepremian kick), :55
Buf: Grate 30 pass from Harris (Guthrie kick), 10:28

	BUF	MIA
First downs	10	19
Rushing yds	46	159
Passing yds	151	166
Punts-avg	8-36.9	5-41.0
Fumbles-lost	1-1	3-1
Penalties-yds	7-78	5-96

BILLS LEADERS: Rushing - Pate 8-19, Enyart 4-(-1), Shaw 4-28; **Passing** - Shaw 8-16-2 - 71, Harris 9-17-1 - 109; **Receiving** - Briscoe 1-8, Moses 1-8, Pate 4-25, Enyart 3-49, Grate 2-43, Denney 2-31, Glosson 1-2, Alexander 1-8, Moss 2-31.

DOLPHINS LEADERS: Rushing - Csonka 14-89, Kiick 11-24, Morris 7-19, Mitchell 5-19, Stofa 2-5, Ginn 3-7, Griese 2-(-4); **Passing** - Griese 7-10-0 - 143, Stofa 1-7-0 - 36; **Receiving** - Csonka 1-54, Kiick 2-25, Mitchell 1-36, Twilley 2-29, Fleming 1-36, Morris 1-(-1).

WEEK 14 GAMES

Balt 35, NYJ 20	Det 20, GB 0
Chi 24, NO 3	Clev 27, Den 13
SF 30, Oak 7	Minn 37, Atl 7
SD 31, KC 13	Cinc 45, Bos 7
Phil 30, Pitt 20	Dal 52, Hou 10
Wash 28, St.L 27	LA 31, NYG 3

STANDINGS: FOURTEENTH WEEK

AFC EAST	W	L	T	CENTRAL	W	L	T	WEST	W	L	T	NFC EAST	W	L	T	CENTRAL	W	L	T	WEST	W	L	T
Baltimore	11	2	1	Cincinnati	8	6	0	Oakland	8	4	2	Dallas	10	4	0	Minnesota	12	2	0	San Fran	10	3	1
Miami	10	4	0	Cleveland	7	7	0	Kan. City	7	5	2	NY Giants	9	5	0	Detroit	10	4	0	LA Rams	9	4	1
NY Jets	4	10	0	Pittsburgh	5	9	0	San Diego	5	6	3	St. Louis	8	5	1	Green Bay	6	8	0	Atlanta	4	8	2
Buffalo	3	10	1	Houston	3	10	1	Denver	5	8	1	Washington	6	8	0	Chicago	6	8	0	N. Orleans	2	11	1
Boston	2	12	0									Philadelphia	3	10	1								

At A Glance
1971

Jan. 5 – Dennis Shaw was named the consensus NFL rookie of the year for 1970, outpolling Dallas' Duane Thomas and Oakland's Raymond Chester.

Jan. 6 – Eleven legislators proposed that Erie County drop plans to build a domed stadium in Lancaster and seek an alternate site; NBC's Curt Gowdy said he was interested in getting Paul Maguire into the broadcast booth.

Jan. 28 – The Bills began the draft by selecting Arizona State wide receiver J.D. Hill with the fourth pick of the first round; The Bills also selected tight end Jan White, center Bruce Jarvis, fullback Jim Braxton, offensive tackle Donnie Green and wide receiver Bob Chandler on the first day. In addition, they traded fullback Bill Enyart to Oakland for cornerback Alvin Wyatt; Boston selected Stanford quarterback Jim Plunkett No. 1.

Feb. 23 – Butch Byrd, who was one of six NFL players on a tour of Vietnam, said the experience was not a good one for him. "I didn't like it, it was depressing," Byrd said. "I wouldn't want to go back there. I consider myself very fortunate to be home. The most surprising thing to me was finding the morale of our troops is pretty high."

Feb. 24 – Defensive line coach Ray Malavasi resigned to become the Oakland Raiders' linebackers coach.

March 6 – Coach John Rauch defended O.J. Simpson's decision to leave the team and return to his Los Angeles home with one month left in the 1970 season after he learned he was through for the year. "I don't think his leaving had all that much to do with the team's spirit," Rauch said. "I had set a policy that any injured player could go home under those circumstances."

March 25 – The Boston Patriots changed their name to the New England Patriots; The NFL owners, at their annual meetings in Palm Beach, Fla., rejected a proposal to bring back the old AFL's two-point conversion rule. "It wasn't even close," said Miami coach Don Shula who was in favor of the change.

May 11 – Defensive end Ron McDole, a starter since 1963, was traded to the Washington Redskins for undisclosed draft choices. "I know I'm not going to end up looking like a good guy and the older players will try to make it appear that the purge is on, but from the organization's standpoint, I felt it was a logical thing to do for the future," said John Rauch. Said McDole: "I don't relish leaving Buffalo, but it's obvious that Al Cowlings isn't going to sit on the bench. I'm aware that George Allen likes older guys, so I should fit in."

May 25 – Commissioner Pete Rozelle said he was concerned that Off-Track Betting might expand to pro football.

May 29 – Tom Day, the longtime Bills star, was hired by John Rauch to be the team's defensive line coach, thus becoming the first black assistant coach in team history.

June 1 – A three-day rookie camp opened and all rookies except the top two draft choices, J.D. Hill and Jan White, were present.

June 11 – J.D. Hill avoided a holdout by agreeing to terms well before training camp.

June 26 – Paul Maguire officially announced his retirement and said he would pursue a television broadcasting career.

June 27 – J.D. Hill returned a punt 73 yards for a touchdown and also caught six passes to help the West beat the East, 33-28, in the Coaches All-America game in Lubbock, Tex.

July 11 – Appearing on WBEN's *Let's Talk Sports*, John Rauch made some disparaging remarks about two former Bills. Of Ron McDole he said: "He has not played what I would call winning football for the last three years." And he called Paul Maguire "the clown of the team" who was more interested in "how we can get out of work or where's the party?" McDole responded a few days later by saying "The man is strange. What he said made me mad. It was tactless. If I was as bad as he says, why didn't he trade me two years ago?"

July 15 – Training camp opened at Niagara University for rookies and a few veteran players.

July 16 – Rookie offensive tackle Donnie Green went AWOL.

July 20 – John Rauch quit as head coach and was replaced by personnel director Harvey Johnson. Rauch met with Ralph Wilson and Wilson told the coach that he was going to publicly defend Ron McDole and Paul Maguire, the two players Rauch criticized in his TV appearance. When he heard this, Rauch tendered his resignation. "I told John that I was going to make a statement to the media in defense of McDole and Maguire as I felt they gave the Bills' organization several years of outstanding service," Wilson said. "He told me if I did so, I would have to look for a new head coach. I regret John's decision as I respect his knowledge of football and the willingness the last two years to go with younger players."

July 21 – Former quarterback Tom Flores was hired by new coach Harvey Johnson to tutor the team's quarterbacks. Flores had been with the Kansas City Chiefs the previous two years; The remainder of the veterans reported to camp, some unaware that Rauch had quit.

July 22 – John Rauch fired back at the Bills organization, saying the Ron McDole trade was instigated by the organization, primarily owner Ralph Wilson. He also charged that vice presidents Pat McGroder and Jack Horrigan put Wilson "up" to making his statement in defense of McDole and Paul Maguire.

July 24 – Rookie Jim Braxton ended his holdout and signed his contract.

July 30 – Donnie Green, with his wife and child in tow, returned to training camp.

July 31 – The Bills conducted an intrasquad scrimmage at Niagara in front of about 9,000 fans and O.J. Simpson thrilled everyone with some dazzling plays.

Aug. 4 – John Rauch took a job as a scout for the Green Bay Packers.

Aug. 6 – The Bills opened the preseason with a 14-10 victory over New Orleans before 35,758 at War Memorial Stadium. Alvin Wyatt returned a kickoff 92 yards for a score. Rookie Jim Braxton fractured an ankle and was lost to the team until mid-season.

Aug. 13 – Former University of Buffalo head coach Doc Urich joined the Bills staff and was given the defensive line responsibilities. Tom Day, hired by John Rauch in late May, was moved to the scouting department in the newly created position of pro talent scout. In the past, the Bills scouts only watched for college prospects.

Aug. 14 – Mayor Frank Sedita said he would endorse "the construction of a county stadium on the proposed Orchard Park site."

Aug. 15 – Incredible traffic jams spoiled the night for many Patriots fans as New England played its first game in new Schaefer Stadium in suburban Foxboro, beating the New York Giants, 20-14.

Aug. 16 – Philadelphia rallied from a 28-10 deficit and beat the Bills, 34-28, in the first football game ever played at new Veterans Stadium.

Aug. 22 – The Bills beat New England, 28-14, as they intercepted rookie Jim Plunkett four times.

Aug. 29 – Atlanta rushed for 210 yards in whipping the Bills, 35-24.

Aug. 31 – Cornerback Butch Byrd, a Bill for seven years, was traded to Denver for a future draft choice. Byrd had started 143 straight games counting preseason since joining the team in 1964. The five-time all-AFL selection was the Bills career leader with 40 interceptions.

Sept. 1 – A story in *Newsweek* indicated that New York City Mayor John Lindsay had begun discussions with the Bills on moving the team to Yankee Stadium because the Giants had announced their intention to move to New Jersey in 1975. The speculation was fueled by the ongoing difficulties in Buffalo over the building of the new county stadium.

Sept. 4 – The Bills defeated the Detroit Lions, 31-17, as Dennis Shaw passed for 234 yards. No. 1 draft choice J.D. Hill suffered a knee injury. He underwent surgery a few days later and was not expected back until late in the season.

Sept. 11 – Green Bay downed the Bills, 20-14, in the preseason finale at War Memorial Stadium.

Sept. 17 – Cookie Gilchrist became the first member inducted into the new Bills Hall of Fame.

Sept. 19 – The Bills played a thriller with the defending NFC champion Dallas Cowboys, but fell at War Memorial Stadium, 49-37, in the season opener.

Sept. 23 – The Bills claimed punter Spike Jones and released running back Max Anderson. The Erie County legislature approved a $23.5 million bond resolution to build a new 80,000 seat stadium in Orchard Park, and it also agreed to a lease with the Bills.

Sept. 26 – Miami, behind 100-yard rushing games by Larry Csonka and Jim Kiick, manhandled the Bills, 29-14, at War Memorial Stadium.

Sept. 29 – A revised timetable was announced that would have the new stadium in Orchard Park completed by July of 1973 and in time for the '73 season. It also was announced that construction would begin in April of 1972.

Oct. 3 – Minnesota held the Bills to a team-record low of 64 net offensive yards in a 19-0 shutout at Metropolitan Stadium.

Oct. 5 – O.J. Simpson spoke out in a national magazine about the way the Bills were using him. "I want to lead the league in rushing and I'm not just talking about the conference, I want to lead the whole National Football League." However, in three games he had just 152 yards and he said, "I'm gonna really have to get some in bunches and I think I will once we develop a scheme and stick to it. By that I mean we have to attack with what's working for us and continue to attack and force the other team to loosen up somewhere else. We haven't been doing that. I thought we could have run more on Minnesota. Their front four penetrated so much that they committed themselves and it was easy to hit inside, then bounce outside."

Oct. 10 – For the second week in a row, the Bills were shut out as Baltimore humbled them, 43-0. Buffalo's 49 total yards was a new record, lowering the mark set the previous week.

Oct. 11 – After watching film of the 43-0 loss to Baltimore, Harvey Johnson said he had "never seen

a team so inept. We're at the point now where everyone is blaming everyone else. We have to shake this thing off. We either have to play up to potential or something will have to be done like hold up some paychecks and alter some others."

Oct. 12 – Bob Celeri was promoted from scout to director of player personnel, meaning Harvey Johnson would remain as head coach and not take back his old player personnel position.

Oct. 13 – Ralph Wilson was suspended for 30 days by the New York Racing Commission for charges of concealing the ownership of horses by an unlicensed person.

Oct. 15 – Ralph Wilson and Erie County executive John Tutuska officially signed a 25-year lease granting the Bills use of the new stadium in Orchard Park. Wilson guaranteed the county $17.5 million in revenue.

Oct. 17 – The Bills finally scored on offense, but it wasn't enough as the New York Jets - without Joe Namath and Matt Snell - beat them 28-17.

Oct. 19 – Harvey Johnson announced the benching of four starters – fullback Wayne Patrick, defensive tackle Jim Dunaway, outside linebacker Mike Stratton and strong safety John Pitts – and replaced them with Greg Jones, Mike McBath, Al Andrews and Tim Beamer respectively. It was the lineup shuffle Johnson had been threatening due to the horrendous play.

Oct. 23 – Dennis Shaw, playing with a sore throwing arm, admitted he shouldn't have been playing and he was terrible in a 20-3 loss at San Diego in a Saturday night game.

Oct. 28 – Kicker Grant Guthrie was put on waivers and the Bills signed rookie John Leypoldt, whom Guthrie had beaten out during training camp. "I cut Grant because he was missing too many field goals and his kickoffs weren't going far enough," coach Harvey Johnson said.

Oct. 31 – The losing streak reached seven as St. Louis downed the Bills, 28-23.

Nov. 1 – Harvey Johnson said he planned to remain as coach of the team in 1972. "I'm out there now with 34 kids and I'll be a son of a bitch if I don't want to be around when they start winning," he said.

Nov. 7 – Miami recorded its first shutout in team history, blanking the Bills, 34-0, at the Orange Bowl.

Nov. 14 – Special teams blunders killed the Bills in a 38-33 loss at New England.

Nov. 17 – Lou Saban unexpectedly resigned as coach of the Denver Broncos, fueling speculation that he might return to coach the Bills in 1972.

Nov. 21 – Still without Joe Namath, the Jets dealt the Bills a 20-7 loss by intercepting five Buffalo passes.

Nov. 22 – Ralph Wilson said that he felt his team "went too far in our rebuilding program" and is now two or three years away from being a contender in the NFL. "We have so many inexperienced players that we play like the college all-stars. We're just disorganized. There is only so much the coaches can do, then it's up to the players themselves."

Nov. 23 – Ralph Wilson repeated that if Harvey Johnson wanted to continue as coach in 1972, he was more than welcome to. "If he wants to come back, I gave him my word that he can. I'm not going to break my word. I haven't in the past and I won't start with Harvey."

Nov. 28 – J.D. Hill made his NFL debut a memorable one, catching two TD passes to lead the Bills to their first win of the season, a 27-20 victory over New England before only 27,166 at War Memorial Stadium. Hill had been sidelined since the preseason with a knee injury.

Dec. 5 – Baltimore completed a two-game series shutout sweep, beating the Bills, 24-0. Willie Ellison of the Los Angeles Rams rushed for 247 yards on 36 carries to break ex-Bill Cookie Gilchrist's record for rushing yards in a single game, set on Dec. 8, 1963, against the Jets.

Dec. 7 – Frustration over the pitiful 1-11 record began overrunning the team. *Buffalo Evening News* sportswriter Larry Felser wrote of the O.J. Simpson-Jim Braxton argument on the sidelines during the Colts game. Simpson said they were arguing over who was supposed to block whom. Also, Felser revealed that Harvey Johnson told his players after the game, "We might win a few more games if we stopped fighting among ourselves." Simpson responded to that by saying: "We're just doing for ourselves what someone else should be doing for us," a statement that clearly indicated Juice thought very little of the coaching staff.

Dec. 8 – Larry Felser took Ralph Wilson to task on his statement that the head coaching job was Harvey Johnson's in 1972 if he wanted it. Felser opined that Johnson never volunteered for the job either time he was asked to take over (after the firing of Joe Collier in 1968 and after John Rauch's resignation earlier this year) and that he is clearly not suited to head coaching. "Wilson is the Bill most on the spot for 1972."

Dec. 12 – Houston, sporting a 2-9-1 record,

downed the Bills at War Memorial, 20-14, as Robert Holmes scored on a two-yard run with 24 seconds left to play.

Dec. 14 – Ralph Wilson said he would sit down with Harvey Johnson and discuss what the best coaching situation would be for the fans, the organization and the team. "We have to stabilize our coaching situation," Wilson said. "I'm not an eternal optimist, I'm more of a realist and I think things will turn around for us to what they were in the mid-60s."

Dec. 19 – The worst season in Bills history came to an end when Kansas City beat them, 22-9, as Bills-killer Jan Stenerud kicked five field goals.

Dec. 20 – Lou Saban denied he had discussed the Bills' coaching job. "I haven't given much thought to my situation," said Saban, who resigned as Denver's coach at midseason but maintained general manager duties. "I haven't spoken to anyone about another job."

Dec. 21 – The Broncos announced that Saban had severed all connections with the team.

Dec. 22 – Saban flew into Buffalo at 10:30 p.m., presumably to meet with Ralph Wilson.

Dec. 23 – As expected, Saban was named the Bills head coach and also assumed the title of vice-president. Harvey Johnson amicably resigned the head coaching position and was put back into his preferred role as director of player personnel. General manager Bob Lustig was retained, but his vice-president's role was diminished. "I have no intention of moving again," Saban said. "Actually there never was any problem between Ralph and myself. What I did six years ago, I did on my own."

Dec. 24 – Saban cleaned house, firing all of Harvey Johnson's assistant coaches including Marvin Bass, Ralph Hawkins, Bobby Hunt, Chuck Gottfried, Tom Flores and Doc Urich.

Dec. 25 – O.J. Simpson expressed his glee over the hiring of Saban. "It's a tough thing to say without sounding disrespectful to Harvey Johnson because I like Harvey, but I'm delighted," Simpson said. "Coach Saban seems to be a take-charge guy. That alone should help the team a lot." In the divisional playoffs, Garo Yepremian kicked a 37-yard field goal to end the longest game in pro football history, a 27-24 Miami victory over Kansas City in the final game at Kansas City's Municipal Stadium. The game ended at 7:40 of the second overtime on Christmas Day. Earlier in the day, Dallas defeated Minnesota, 20-12.

Dec. 26 – San Francisco downed Washington, 24-12, and Baltimore beat Cleveland, 20-3, in the second day of divisional playoffs.

Jan. 2, 1972 – Miami blanked Baltimore, 21-0, in the AFC Championship Game; for the second year in a row, Dallas stopped San Francisco, 14-3, in the NFC Championship Game.

Jan. 16, 1972 – Dallas amassed a Super Bowl-record 252 rushing yards and crushed Miami, 24-3, to win Super Bowl VI at Tulane Stadium in New Orleans.

Jan. 23, 1972 – The AFC beat the NFC, 26-13, in the Pro Bowl at the Los Angeles Coliseum as Jan Stenerud of Kansas City kicked four field goals.

Tom Flores began his coaching career as an assistant coach in Buffalo. He later became head coach of the Oakland Raiders and Seattle Seahawks.

BY THE NUMBERS - 1971

TEAM STATISTICS	BILLS	OPP
First downs	185	250
Rushing	68	135
Passing	96	101
Penalty	21	14
Total yards	3,326	4,604
Avg. game	237.6	328.9
Plays	770	895
Avg. play	4.3	5.1
Net rushing yds	1,337	2,496
Avg. game	95.5	178.3
Avg. play	4.2	4.4
Net passing yds	1,989	2,108
Comp/att	202/401	157/303
Sacks/lost	49-421	30-225
Interceptions	32	11
Percentage	50.4	51.8
Punts/avg	75-40.9	66-39.0
Fumbles/lost	33-16	17-11
Penalties/yds	74-691	89-883
Touchdowns	21	45
Extra points	20-21	45-45
Field goals	12-25	25-38
Safeties	1	2
Kick ret./avg	74-22.6	42-23.1
Punt ret./avg	44-7.8	40-11.2

RUSHING	ATT	YDS	AVG	TD
Simpson	183	742	4.1	5
Patrick	79	332	4.2	1
Braxton	21	84	4.0	0
Shaw	14	82	5.9	0
G. Jones	16	53	3.3	0
Harris	6	42	7.0	0
J.D. Hill	1	2	2.0	0
TOTALS	**320**	**1337**	**4.2**	**6**

PASSING	COMP	ATT	INT	YDS	TD	COMP%
Shaw	149	291	26	1813	11	51.2
Harris	51	103	6	512	1	49.5
Braxton	1	3	0	49	0	33.3
Briscoe	1	2	0	36	0	50.0
Simpson	0	2	0	0	0	00.0
TOTALS	**202**	**401**	**32**	**2410**	**12**	**50.4**

KICKING	1-19	20-29	30-39	40-49	50+	TOT	PAT	PTS
Leypoldt	3-3	0-2	1-1	5-6	0-3	9-15	12-12	39
Guthrie	0-0	0-1	1-2	1-5	1-2	3-10	8-9	17
TOTALS	**3-3**	**0-3**	**2-3**	**6-11**	**1-5**	**12-25**	**20-21**	**56**

PUNTING	NO	AVG	LG	BL
S. Jones	72	42.1	62	0
Chapple	3	33.7	47	0
TOTALS	**75**	**40.9**	**62**	**0**

RECEIVING	CAT	YDS	AVG	TD
Briscoe	44	603	13.7	5
Patrick	36	327	9.1	0
Moses	23	470	20.4	2
Simpson	21	162	7.7	0
Braxton	18	141	7.8	0
G. Jones	16	113	7.1	1
White	13	130	10.0	0
J.D. Hill	11	216	19.6	2
Koy	10	133	13.3	1
Chandler	5	60	12.0	0
I. Hill	5	55	11.0	1
TOTALS	**202**	**2410**	**11.9**	**12**

LEADERS

Kick returns: Wyatt 30-762 yds, 25.4 avg, 0 TD
Beamer 20-394, 19.7, 0 TD

Punt returns: Wyatt 23-188, 8.2, 1 TD
I. Hill 14-133, 9.5, 1 TD

Interceptions: R. James 4-25, 6.3, 0 TD
Pitts 2-12, 6.0, 0 TD

SCORE BY QUARTERS

BILLS	38	62	43	41	- 184
OPP	82	110	83	119	- 394

After being named Rookie of the Year in 1970, Dennis Shaw (16) never panned out as the top-notch quarterback the Bills thought he would become. He was traded for Ahmad Rashad in 1974.

NOTES

• A rain-soaked sellout crowd gave the Bills a standing ovation after they took the defending NFC champs to the wire in the highest scoring game in team history (86 combined points).

• One fan on-hand was ex-Bill Paul Maguire who said: "When you play football like that, you can sell tickets for $14 apiece."

• It was the first time the Bills had scored 37 points and lost in team history.

• Four of Dallas' five TD drives started inside Buffalo territory as a result of two shanked punts, a fumble and an interception.

• Dennis Shaw threw for 353 yards, the second-highest total in team history and his four TD passes tied the record set by Johnny Green in 1960.

• Buffalo rookie Dave Chapple's first punt went 23 yards to the Bills 44 and Dallas capitalized for a 7-0 lead. Less than a minute later, Haven Moses hauled in a 73-yard TD pass as Mel Renfro and Charlie Waters collided, leaving him open.

• One play after the kickoff, Walt Garrison fumbled and Pete Richardson returned 24 yards to the 15, leading to O.J. Simpson's TD.

• Dallas roared back when Bob Hayes scored on the first play of the second quarter and 1:34 later, Chuck Howley intercepted a Shaw pass and returned 53 yards to the 3 setting up Calvin Hill's second of four TD runs.

• The Bills led 30-28 in the third, but Dallas scored 21 straight points. The go-ahead score came after Waters returned a punt 52 yards to the Bills 28.

QUOTES

• Harvey Johnson: "We got a lot of help, but they got their help when they needed it. We're just not strong enough to handle a good team if they're getting the best of the breaks. Just give us three more studs and we'll be

a helluva football team. Nobody is going to stop us from scoring, our problem now is to stop them."

• O.J. Simpson: "The defense is apologizing to us all over the place, but this was a team defeat. We gave them three touchdowns."

• Cowboys DT Bob Lilly: "We knew Buffalo could score with Shaw. I'd have to say he's the best young quarterback I've ever faced."

WEEK 1 GAMES

Balt 22, NYJ 0	Cinc 37, Phil 14
Mia 10, Den 10	Clev 31, Hou 0
SD 21, KC 14	NE 20, Oak 6
Chi 17, Pitt 15	Atl 20, SF 17
Minn 16, Det 13	NYG 42, GB 40
NO 24, LA 20	Wash 24, St.L 17

Cowboys	7	21	7	14	-	49
Bills	14	10	6	7	-	37

Attendance at War Memorial Stadium - 46,206

Dal: Hill 2 run (Clark kick), 6:21
Buf: Moses 73 pass from Shaw (Guthrie kick), 7:33
Buf: Simpson 6 run (Guthrie kick), 9:38
Dal: Hayes 76 pass from Morton (Clark kick), :10
Dal: Garrison 3 run (Clark kick), 1:44
Buf: FG Guthrie 40, 5:34
Buf: Briscoe 76 pass from Shaw (Guthrie kick), 8:05
Dal: Hill 3 run (Clark kick), 13:03
Buf: Briscoe 23 pass from Shaw (kick blocked), 5:01
Dal: Rucker 19 pass from Morton (Clark kick), 14:48
Dal: Hill 1 run (Clark kick), 6:14
Buf: I. Hill 26 pass from Shaw (Guthrie kick), 14:32
Dal: Hill 1 run (Clark kick), 12:52

	BUF	DAL
First downs	18	19
Rushing yds	66	160
Passing yds	335	211
Punts-avg	3-33.7	6-40.2
Fumbles-lost	1-1	2-1
Penalties-yds	8-95	13-129

BILLS LEADERS: Rushing - Simpson 14-25, Patrick 7-30, Shaw 1-11; **Passing** - Shaw 18-30-3 - 353; **Receiving** - Briscoe 3-113, White 3-52, Jones 5-58, Moses 1-73, Simpson 1-4, Patrick 2-11, Chandler 2-16, I. Hill 1-26.

COWBOYS LEADERS: Rushing - Hill 22-84, Garrison 16-78, Reeves 1-7, Ditka 1-(-9); **Passing** - Morton 10-14-0 - 221; **Receiving** - Hill 4-43, Garrison 1-33, Ditka 2-35, Hayes 2-91, Rucker 1-19.

NOTES

• A punishing Miami ground game killed the Bills, as did Garo Yepremian's five field goals.

• Larry Csonka and Jim Kiick each topped 100 yards. Kiick produced 11 first downs and Csonka six.

• The Dolphins controlled the ball for 26 more plays than Buffalo.

• Bills QB Dennis Shaw had difficulty solving Miami's zone defense. Only two of his 17 completions went to wide receivers, both to Marlin Briscoe.

• The Bills stopped Miami three times after the Dolphins drove inside the 10 in the first half, but Yepremian gave the Dolphins points each time and also made a 46-yarder.

• Buffalo put together a 66-yard scoring march that produced a 7-3 lead. O.J. Simpson broke a 22-yard run and Wayne Patrick ran 25 yards to the 1, then scored on the next play.

• Mercury Morris returned the second-half kickoff 60 yards to the Buffalo 44 and eight runs later, Larry Csonka bulled in from the 1 on fourth down.

• The Bills drew within 19-14 a few plays later when Simpson broke free for a 46-yard TD run.

• In the fourth, Dick Anderson intercepted a Dennis Shaw pass and returned it to the Buffalo 47. All it took was a 17-yard run by Csonka, a seven-yard Jim Kiick run and a 23-yard Bob Griese-to-Paul Warfield TD pass to make it 26-14.

QUOTES

• Harvey Johnson: "When you get blown out of the tub, and that's what Miami's running game did to us, all you can do is face facts. They had 26 more plays than we did and they did what we feared most, keep control of the ball. They kept our offense in drydock. They just took the play away from us. Those two bulls (Csonka and Kiick) ran over, around and through our defense."

• Miami coach Don Shula: "Buffalo couldn't stop them (Csonka and Kiick) all day. That's the strength of our football team." (On failure to score TDs early in the game): "Those things sometimes come back to haunt you later in the game. I was afraid we wouldn't get those scoring opportunities in the second half and I was afraid Shaw would get hot."

• Marlin Briscoe on the failure of the passing game: "We were finding the seams in the zone, but probably a split second later than normal because of the double coverage. By then, I guess, Dennis had looked away and gone to the backs."

WEEK 2 GAMES

Clev 14, Balt 13	GB 34, Den 13
Pitt 21, Cinc 10	KC 20, Hou 16
St.L 17, NYJ 10	Det 34, NE 7
Atl 20, LA 20	Oak 34, SD 0
Chi 20, Minn 17	SF 38, NO 20
Wash 30, NYG 3	Dal 42, Phil 7

Dolphins	3	9	7	10	-	29
Bills	7	0	7	0	-	14

Attendance at War Memorial Stadium - 45,139

Mia: FG Yepremian 15, 9:54
Buf: Patrick 1 run (Guthrie kick), 13:44
Mia: FG Yepremian 46, 2:35
Mia: FG Yepremian 13, 9:49
Mia: FG Yepremian 9, 14:36
Mia: Csonka 1 run (Yepremian kick), 5:05
Buf: Simpson 46 run (Guthrie kick), 6:04
Mia: Warfield 23 pass from Griese (Yepremian kick), 1:25
Mia: FG Yepremian 48, 8:06

	BUF	MIA
First downs	14	20
Rushing yds	118	226
Passing yds	154	150
Punts-avg	5-40.8	2-34.5
Fumbles-lost	2-1	0-0
Penalties-yds	1-13	4-40

BILLS LEADERS: Rushing - Simpson 9-82, Patrick 7-41, Shaw 2-(-5); **Passing** - Shaw 17-23-2 - 154; **Receiving** - Briscoe 2-34, White 1-2, Simpson 5-31, Patrick 6-53, Koy 2-29, Braxton 1-5.

DOLPHINS LEADERS: Rushing - Kiick 20-108, Csonka 20-103, Morris 3-9, Griese 2-6; **Passing** - Griese 10-18-0 - 159; **Receiving** - Kiick 3-48, Csonka 2-34, Warfield 4-65, Twilley 1-12.

STANDINGS: SECOND WEEK

AFC EAST	W	L	T	CENTRAL	W	L	T	WEST	W	L	T	NFC EAST	W	L	T	CENTRAL	W	L	T	WEST	W	L	T
Miami	1	0	1	Cleveland	2	0	0	San Diego	1	1	0	Dallas	2	0	0	Chicago	2	0	0	Atlanta	1	0	1
N. England	1	1	0	Cincinnati	1	1	0	Oakland	1	1	0	Washington	2	0	0	Minnesota	1	1	0	N. Orleans	1	1	0
Baltimore	1	1	0	Pittsburgh	1	1	0	Kan. City	1	1	0	NY Giants	1	1	0	Detroit	1	1	0	San Fran	1	1	0
NY Jets	0	2	0	Houston	0	2	0	Denver	0	1	1	St. Louis	1	1	0	Green Bay	1	1	0	LA Rams	0	1	1
Buffalo	0	2	0									Philadelphia	0	2	0								

GAME 3 - Sunday, Oct. 3, 1971 - VIKINGS 19, BILLS 0

Bills	0	0	0	0 -	0
Vikings	0	12	0	7 -	19

Attendance at Metropolitan Stadium - 47,900

Min: Osborn 1 run (Cox kick), 5:58
Min: FG Cox 40, 7:17
Min: Safety, Page tackled Shaw in end zone, 13:45
Min: Snead 1 run (Cox kick), 4:23

	BUF	MIN
First downs	7	23
Rushing yds	56	193
Passing yds	8	133
Punts-avg	5-41.6	4-30.8
Fumbles-lost	5-1	1-1
Penalties-yds	2-8	6-47

BILLS LEADERS: Rushing - Simpson 12-45, Patrick 3-(-7), Jones 1-11, Shaw 2-7; **Passing** - Shaw 12-20-2 - 67; **Receiving** - Briscoe 2-14, Moses 1-4, White 2-10, Simpson 3-9, Koy 1-7, Braxton 3-23.

VIKINGS LEADERS: Rushing - Osborn 19-93, C. Jones 27-71, Grim 1-25, Snead 2-4, Brown 3-0; **Passing** - Snead 12-21-2 - 150; **Receiving** - Osborn 5-65, C. Jones 4-46, Grim 1-16, Voigt 2-23.

WEEK 3 GAMES

Balt 23, NE 3	GB 20, Cinc 17
Oak 34, Clev 20	KC 16, Den 3
NYJ 14, Mia 10	Hou 13, NO 13
Pitt 21, SD 17	Det 41, Atl 38
LA 17, Chi 3	Wash 20, Dal 16
SF 31, Phil 3	NYG 21, St.L 20

NOTES

• It was a complete domination by the Vikings as they held a 75-45 advantage in plays (47-19 in the first half alone), held the Bills to eight net passing yards and 64 yards overall. It was the lowest total in team history and also the best Minnesota defensive effort in its history.

• The Bills never got past the Minnesota 33 and didn't get a first down passing until 4:15 remained in the game. The Vikings' front four of Alan Page, Jim Marshall, Carl Eller and Gary Larsen, known as the "Purple People Eaters," recorded seven sacks for 59 yards in losses.

• Dennis Shaw's overthrown interception to Charlie West set up the Vikings first TD as Dave Osborn capped a 47-yard drive in the second quarter.

• Rookie Tim Beamer fumbled the ensuing kickoff and Fred Cox made a 40-yard field goal.

• Shaw was intercepted by Wally Hilgenberg a few plays later and the Vikings started from the Bills 30. The Buffalo defense stopped a fourth-and-goal run by Clinton Jones at the 1, but a couple of plays later, Shaw tried to pass from his own end zone, was hit by Alan Page and fumbled out of the end zone for a safety.

• After a Grant Guthrie field goal miss, Minnesota drove 76 yards to its final score, aided by a 25-yard run on a reverse by Bob Grim.

QUOTES

• Harvey Johnson: "I thought we were ready for Minnesota. I was mistaken. Dennis' biggest problem was he didn't have time to raise his passing arm. We just never were able to get untracked. That front four of theirs has to be the best in football. When we did appear to get started, we dropped passes and then when we got behind by 12 points, that front four really came. I think our defense did a pretty good job, we gave them a battle all day long. We expected them to score 17 points and we held them to that."

• Dennis Shaw: "I had trouble getting the ball over them; they've got all that size and speed. Lets face it, we're still a young team and an experienced one like Minnesota with that pass rush is hard for us to handle. I know I was on the turf an awful lot."

• O.J. Simpson: "This was a learning day. Every time I turned around, Dennis, was on the ground. It wasn't a case of not being open, it was that he didn't have time to throw."

• Vikings coach Bud Grant: (The front four) didn't give him much of a chance back there. That was probably the difference in the game. Buffalo's young, but they have some good personnel and are going to be tough when they mature a little. We were very much aware where O.J. lined up. He's quite a runner."

GAME 4 - Sunday, Oct. 10, 1971 - COLTS 43, BILLS 0

Colts	14	8	0	21 -	43
Bills	0	0	0	0 -	0

Attendance at War Memorial Stadium - 46,206

Bal: Bulaich 30 pass from Morrall (O'Brien kick), 6:17
Bal: Bulaich 1 run (O'Brien kick), 8:14
Bal: FG O'Brien 42, 4:53
Bal: Safety, Bills holding in end zone, 11:44
Bal: FG O'Brien 28, 13:54
Bal: Nottingham 36 run (O'Brien kick), 1:11
Bal: McCauley 1 run (O'Brien kick), 4:22
Bal: McCauley 3 run (O'Brien kick), 8:13

	BUF	BAL
First downs	4	19
Rushing yards	4	214
Passing yards	45	187
Punts-avg	7-40.1	4-44.3
Fumbles-lost	4-2	2-1
Penalties-yds	8-67	6-71

BILLS LEADERS: Rushing - Simpson 7-(-10), Patrick 2-2, Harris 1-10, G. Jones 1-2; **Passing** - Shaw 9-23 - 30, Harris 8-12-1 - 91; **Receiving** - Briscoe 1-15, Moses 1-13, Koy 2-24, Patrick 4-55, Simpson 2-14.

COLTS LEADERS: Rushing - Nottingham 13-69, McCauley 12-53, Bulaich 11-51, Matte 6-11, Hinton 1-30; **Passing** - Morrall 10-17-1 - 133, Unitas 3-9-1 - 60; **Receiving** - Bulaich 2-37, Matte 3-28, Mitchell 6-111, Hinton 1-10, Mackey 1-7.

WEEK 4 GAMES

Mia 23, Cinc 13	Oak 27, Den 16
Clev 27, Pitt 17	Wash 22, Hou 13
NE 20, NYJ 0	KC 31, SD 10
St.L 26, Atl 9	Chi 35, NO 14
Dal 20, NYG 13	Det 31, GB 28
LA 20, SF 13	Minn 13, Phil 0

NOTES

• It didn't seem possible after what happened in Minnesota, but the Bills' offense was worse against defending Super Bowl champion Baltimore, managing 49 net yards, an all-time low for the second game in a row.

• The Bills suffered back-to-back shutouts for the first time in club history.

• A sellout crowd at War Memorial Stadium booed lustily and even cheered the Colts at times.

• The Colts recorded nine sacks for 76 yards and forced six Buffalo turnovers.

• Dennis Shaw admitted that he asked to be taken out of the game because of anger and frustration. Harvey Johnson complied, sending in James Harris and he fared even worse.

• The four yards rushing was an all-time team low as O.J. Simpson had a minus-10.

• Norm Bulaich scored on a 30-yard screen pass on Baltimore's first possession, then Mike Curtis intercepted a Shaw pass and returned it 31 yards to the 1 from where Bulaich plunged in.

• Jim O'Brien kicked a field goal, then Curtis intercepted another pass and Baltimore drove to the 2. The Bills defense held, but a couple plays later, Paul Costa was penalized for holding in the end zone, an automatic safety. O'Brien added another field goal for a 22-0 halftime lead.

• With Johnny Unitas replacing Earl Morral, Baltimore scored 21 points in the fourth.

QUOTES

• Harvey Johnson: "Baltimore is either a great team, or we're pretty bad. We just started bad and then we got worse. They beat the hell out of us. We've only got 47 guys here and we're going to have to go with them. I thought the defense at least tried until it got to the point where the game was lost." (On Shaw coming out of the game): "I'm sticking with Dennis. He's a fine young quarterback and a fine young man. He's an intense competitor. He gets (as) angry at himself as he does with the guys he's playing with who make mistakes."

• Marlin Briscoe: "We're disgusted with ourselves. We've still got 10 games left and the thing we have to do now is stop trying to make excuses. It isn't just a few players to blame, it's all of us."

• Dennis Shaw: "We can't even do anything right that's merely fundamental. I'm not usually one who pops off at my own teammates, but I was yelling at all of them. I was calling audibles at the line of scrimmage and they weren't hearing them. I don't know if it was lack of concentration or what, but I got frustrated. It just built up to where I couldn't take it any longer so I told them to put Harris in there."

• Joe O'Donnell: "He (Shaw) should have been yelling."

STANDINGS: FOURTH WEEK

AFC EAST	W	L	T	CENTRAL	W	L	T	WEST	W	L	T	NFC EAST	W	L	T	CENTRAL	W	L	T	WEST	W	L	T
Baltimore	3	1	0	Cleveland	3	1	0	Oakland	3	1	0	Washington	4	0	0	Chicago	3	1	0	LA Rams	2	1	1
Miami	2	1	1	Pittsburgh	2	2	0	Kan. City	3	1	0	Dallas	3	1	0	Minnesota	3	1	0	San Fran	2	2	0
N. England	2	2	0	Cincinnati	1	3	0	San Diego	1	3	0	NY Giants	2	2	0	Detroit	3	1	0	Atlanta	1	2	1
NY Jets	1	3	0	Houston	0	3	1	Denver	0	3	1	St. Louis	2	2	0	Green Bay	2	2	0	N. Orleans	1	2	1
Buffalo	0	4	0									Philadelphia	0	4	0								

GAME 5 - Sunday, Oct. 17, 1971 - JETS 28, BILLS 17

NOTES

• The Bills lost their fifth in a row and 10th straight dating to 1970, but snapped their scoreless drought at 10 quarters.

• The Jets, playing without injured stars Joe Namath and Matt Snell, had scored only 24 points in their previous three games.

• New York scored on its first possession, aided by three offsides penalties against the Bills.

• Phil Wise then intercepted a Dennis Shaw pass and returned it 33 yards to the 11. On the first play, Bob Davis hit Rich Caster in the end zone for a 14-0 lead.

• In the second quarter, Buffalo drove 83 yards in seven plays to break its scoring drought. O.J. Simpson had a 29-yard run and Haven Moses made a 40-yard reception along the way.

• Grant Guthrie's field goal made it 14-10, but the Jets took control when Davis hit Don Maynard with a 44-yard bomb to the 15 to set up Clifford McClain's short TD run.

• The Bills retaliated when Tim Beamer returned the kickoff 44 yards and Moses made a 25-yard reception that led to Simpson's three-yard TD.

• But the Jets came right back as five runs moved them to the Bills 32, then Davis dumped a short pass to John Riggins, who ran over Mike Stratton on his way to a 32-yard clinching TD.

QUOTES

• O.J. Simpson: "The guys that are playing aren't doing it. We should have put 30 points on the board against this team. They had a makeshift defensive line and quarterback who had thrown only a few passes. We need a few more ballplayers to be a contender. We also need total dedication and we haven't been getting it. When we fell behind 14-0 at the start, some of the guys said 'Heck, it's another one of those games.' Then we scored and they got some life. Ever since the Miami game, we've been playing terrible football. We have to

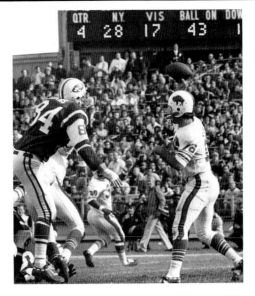

do something this week or San Diego will blow us right out of Southern California."

• Harvey Johnson: "We have a lot of young kids and they have to get better. We had about 10 guys out there playing football. We played defense with about five guys. We're too placid offensively and defensively. We didn't attack people, we didn't knock anybody down, we didn't hit people." (On the 44-yard Maynard pass): "It was a perfect play. The ball was well thrown, there was a good catch and we had good coverage (Alvin Wyatt). It hurt us a lot."

• Linebackers coach Ralph Hawkins: "The problem is we have too many eat, ride and warm-up guys. They want to be associated with a pro football team, but they don't want to pay the price you have to pay to be a winner."

Bills	0	7	10	0	-	17
Jets	14	0	7	7	-	28

Attendance at Shea Stadium - 61,498

NYJ: Boozer 2 run (Howfield kick), 10:19
NYJ: Caster 11 pass from Davis (Howfield kick), 12:03
Buf: Briscoe 12 pass from Shaw (Guthrie kick), 11:02
Buf: FG Guthrie 51, 6:14
NYJ: McClain 1 run (Howfield kick), 9:27
Buf: Simpson 3 run (Guthrie kick), 12:32
NYJ: Riggins 32 pass from Davis (Howfield kick), 4:25

	BUF	NYJ
First downs	14	20
Rushing yds	83	191
Passing yds	188	140
Punts-avg	4-47.8	5-34.0
Fumbles-lost	1-0	1-0
Penalties-yds	7-43	5-35

BILLS LEADERS: Rushing - Simpson 18-69, Patrick 4-12, Braxton 1-2; **Passing** - Shaw 10-29-1 - 162, Harris 0-3-1 - 0, Briscoe 1-1-0 - 36; **Receiving** - Moses 6-151, Briscoe 1-12, Patrick 3-15, Chandler 1-20.

JETS LEADERS: Rushing - Boozer 31-116, Riggins 9-32, McClain 7-26, Davis 2-7, Harkey 3-10; **Passing** - Davis 7-12-0 - 140; **Receiving** - Riggins 4-72, Maynard 1-44, Lammons 1-13, Caster 1-11.

WEEK 5 GAMES

Balt 31, NYG 7	Den 20, SD 16
Clev 27, Cinc 24	Det 31, Hou 7
KC 38, Pitt 16	Mia 21, NE 3
LA 24, Atl 16	SF 13, Chi 0
Wash 20, St.L 0	Min 24, GB 13
Oak 34, Phil 10	NO 24, Dal 14

GAME 6 - Saturday, Oct. 23, 1971 - CHARGERS 20, BILLS 3

NOTES

• For the third time, the Bills were held without a touchdown and they set a new team record for consecutive losses over two seasons at 11.

• Dennis Shaw was bothered by a very sore throwing arm, but Harvey Johnson started him and played him for more than three quarters, even though he was terribly ineffective.

• The Bills defense allowed 446 yards, but had five takeaways. Unfortunately, the offense did nothing with them.

• O. J. Simpson gained 91 of his 106 yards in the first half, before injuring his left foot.

• In the first quarter, Mike McBath recovered a Mike Garrett fumble at the Chargers 32, but Grant Guthrie missed a 35-yard field goal. Later in the quarter, Guthrie had a 26-yarder blocked.

• John Hadl hit Billy Parks on a 56-yard TD pass on a play when Alvin Wyatt and Tim Beamer thought Parks was down when he caught the ball, then watched him get up and run in untouched. The TD was set up when Jackie Allen's interception was nullified by a defensive-holding penalty.

• Dennis Partee's second field goal was set up when Garrett hit Gary Garrison with a 53-yard halfback-option pass that Robert James should have knocked down, but mistimed.

• After that, the Bills had a chance to get back into the game when Al Cowlings recovered a Leon Burns fumble at the San Diego 41. But Shaw missed on three straight

passes and Guthrie missed a 48-yard field goal.

QUOTES

• Dennis Shaw: "My right arm has been hurting – from the shoulder to the wrist – for more than seven weeks now. I shouldn't have played. I can't grip the ball and I can't get anything on my passes." (On Haven Moses dropping a pass): "Haven couldn't catch a cold."

• Harvey Johnson: "He threw all right in the pre-game warmup, which is when I decided to go with him. I told him Friday if he wasn't right, I wasn't going to start him. I watched him closely in the warmup and after we went into the dressing room, I double checked with Eddie (Abramoski). I guess his arm would have felt all right if he had hit a couple of those guys in the end zone, wouldn't it?"

• Eddie Abramoski: "I asked him before the game how he felt. In fact I told him I didn't want to see any of those quails. He said he wanted to play. I asked him at halftime and he said he was fine."

Bills	0	0	3	0	-	3
Chargers	7	3	3	7	-	20

Attendance at San Diego Stadium - 49,261

SD: Parks 56 pass from Hadl (Partee kick), 5:09
SD: FG Partee 9, 10:47
Buf: FG Guthrie 36, 5:29
SD: FG Partee 10, 8:29
SD: Parks 12 pass from Hadl (Partee kick), 12:23

	BUF	SD
First downs	11	22
Rushing yds	152	198
Passing yds	37	248
Punts-avg	6-44.3	3-36.3
Fumbles-lost	1-0	4-4
Penalties-yds	5-33	6-50

BILLS LEADERS: Rushing - Simpson 18-106, Patrick 2-5, G. Jones 5-21, Harris 1-13, Shaw 1-7; **Passing** - Shaw 4-16-1 - 20, Harris 4-8-1 - 36; **Receiving** - Moses 1-5, Briscoe 1-12, White 2-14, I. Hill 2-20, G. Jones 2-5.

CHARGERS LEADERS: Rushing - Garrett 19-94, Burns 18-87, Parks 1-11, Montgomery 4-6; **Passing** - Hadl 14-28-1 - 215, Garrett 1-1-0 - 53; **Receiving** - Garrison 4-106, Parks 4-86, Norman 3-47, Garrett 3-14, Gillette 1-15.

WEEK 6 GAMES

Minn 10, Balt 3	Oak 31, Cinc 27
Den 27, Clev 0	Pitt 23, Hou 16
Mia 30, NYJ 14	Atl 28, NO 6
Chi 28, Det 23	Dal 44, NE 21
LA 30, GB 13	Phil 23, NYG 7
SF 26, St.L 14	KC 27, Wash 20

STANDINGS: SIXTH WEEK

AFC EAST	W	L	T	CENTRAL	W	L	T	WEST	W	L	T	NFC EAST	W	L	T	CENTRAL	W	L	T	WEST	W	L	T
Miami	4	1	1	Cleveland	4	2	0	Oakland	5	1	0	Washington	5	1	0	Minnesota	5	1	0	LA Rams	4	1	1
Baltimore	4	2	0	Pittsburgh	3	3	0	Kan. City	5	1	0	Dallas	4	2	0	Detroit	4	2	0	San Fran	4	2	0
N. England	2	4	0	Cincinnati	1	5	0	Denver	2	3	1	NY Giants	2	4	0	Chicago	4	2	0	N. Orleans	2	3	1
NY Jets	2	4	0	Houston	0	5	1	San Diego	2	4	0	St. Louis	2	4	0	Green Bay	2	4	0	Atlanta	2	3	1
Buffalo	0	6	0									Philadelphia	1	5	0								

Cardinals	14	0	7	7 - 28
Bills	0	9	7	7 - 23

Attendance at War Memorial Stadium - 40,040

St.L: Lane 1 run (Bakken kick), 5:46
St.L: Edwards 1 run (Bakken kick), 13:36
Buf: Safety, Chandler tackled Edwards, 2:20
Buf: Koy 20 pass from Shaw (Leypoldt kick), 13:07
St.L: Smith 10 pass from Hart (Bakken kick), 1:35
Buf: G. Jones 7 pass from Shaw (Leypoldt kick), 6:34
St.L: McFarland 5 pass from Hart (Bakken kick), 3:47
Buf: Wyatt 61 punt return (Leypoldt kick), 13:27

	BUF	ST.L
First downs	19	24
Rushing yds	62	142
Passing yds	247	163
Punts-avg	5-44.6	5-37.4
Fumbles-lost	1-1	1-0
Penalties-yds	10-75	8-78

BILLS LEADERS: Rushing - Simpson 16-42, G. Jones 5-16, Braxton 2-4; **Passing** - Shaw 17-33-2 - 220, Braxton 1-1-0 - 49; **Receiving** - Moses 5-92, Briscoe 3-56, G. Jones 4-17, Simpson 2-42, Braxton 2-20, Koy 2-42.

CARDINALS LEADERS: Rushing - Lane 14-54, Edwards 17-52, Shivers 5-16, Gray 1-18, Hart 4-2; **Passing** - Hart 15-27-0 - 171; **Receiving** - Smith 3-37, D. Williams 2-23, Lane 4-38, Edwards 2-43, Shivers 2-17, Gilliam 1-8, McFarland 1-5.

WEEK 7 GAMES

Balt 34, Pitt 21	Hou 10, Cin 6
Atl 31, Clev 14	Mia 20, LA 14
Phil 17, Den 16	KC 20, Oak 20
SD 49, NYJ 21	SF 27, NE 10
Chi 23, Dal 19	Det 14, GB 14
Minn 17, NYG 10	Wash 24, NO 14

NOTES

• Key mistakes doomed the Bills again as they lost their seventh in a row and 12th straight over two years.
• Trailing 14-9 in the third, Tim Beamer fumbled the second-half kickoff and three plays later, Jim Hart hit Jackie Smith with a TD pass.
• The Bills got within 21-16 in the third, then blocked a Jim Bakken field goal, but the play was nullified when Louis Ross couldn't get off the field in time and the penalty gave St. Louis a first down. Eventually, Hart passed five yards to Jim McFarland for the clinching TD.
• The Cards opened a 14-0 first-quarter lead. Larry Willingham took the opening kickoff 56 yards to the Bills 44 and MacArthur Lane scored nine plays later. Two Buffalo penalties assisted a 55-yard march on St. Louis' next possession.
• Buffalo got back in it when a Spike Jones punt was downed at the 1 and Cid Edwards was trapped for a safety by Edgar Chandler. Alvin Wyatt then returned the free kick 30 yards to the St. Louis 37, but the Bills stalled at the 18 when O.J. Simpson was stopped on a fourth-down run.
• The Bills drove 81 yards to make it 14-9 late in the half as a 23-yard pass to Marlin Briscoe and an additional 15-yard roughness penalty set up Ted Koy's 20-yard TD catch.
• Down 21-9, the Bills marched 93 yards, the key play a 38-yard pass to Simpson.
• And trailing 28-16, Wyatt returned a punt 61 yards for a score, but the Bills failed to recover an on-side kick and that was the game.

QUOTES

• Harvey Johnson: "You talk about playing young guys, but this is what happens. Penalties and our special teams cost us the game. Ross, for example, was sent in the play before to rush the passer. He isn't on our field goal team. If we don't get all those penalties and the special teams play well, I think we would have won the game. The Cardinals certainly did not outplay us." (On not kicking the field goal in the second quarter): "We were down 14-2 and we hadn't been moving the ball. I thought we had to go for it to give ourselves a lift. I knew I was gambling."
• O.J. Simpson: "We thought we could run outside on them and that was the plan. But they covered so well on our sweeps that we had to go inside."

Bills	0	0	0	0 - 0
Dolphins	7	7	7	13 - 34

Attendance at the Orange Bowl - 61,016

Mia: Csonka 12 run (Yepremian kick), 4:52
Mia: Warfield 3 pass from Griese (Yepremian kick), 2:38
Mia: Mandich 10 pass from Griese (Yepremian kick), 4:59
Mia: Morris 45 run (Yepremian kick), :59
Mia: FG Yepremian 38, 6:48
Mia: FG Yepremian 24, 11:37

	BUF	MIA
First downs	19	23
Rushing yds	206	302
Passing yds	158	89
Punts-avg	2-36.5	3-41.7
Fumbles-lost	7-3	0-0
Penalties-yds	3-41	7-48

BILLS LEADERS: Rushing - Simpson 10-90, Patrick 7-69, Braxton 6-28, Harris 3-15, G. Jones 3-4; **Passing** - Harris 18-30-2 - 165; **Receiving** - Moses 2-21, Briscoe 7-68, G. Jones 3-8, Simpson 1-9, Braxton 2-36, Koy 1-6, White 1-15, Patrick 1-2.

DOLPHINS LEADERS: Rushing - Morris 13-116, Csonka 12-88, Ginn 8-29, Warfield 1-39, Griese 1-21, Leigh 3-9; **Passing** - Griese 7-14-0 - 68, Mira 2-5-0 - 27; **Receiving** - Warfield 2-12, Morris 1-11, Csonka 1-16, Noonan 2-27, Mandich 2-13, Twilley 1-16.

WEEK 8 GAMES

Balt 24, LA 17	Atl 9, Cinc 6
Pitt 26, Clev 9	Det 24, Den 20
NE 28, Hou 20	NYJ 13, KC 10
NYG 35, SD 17	GB 17, Chi 14
Dal 16, St.L 13	SF 13, Minn 9
NO 21, Oak 21	Phil 7, Wash 7

NOTES

• The Bills gained 364 yards on offense, but turned it over five times and became the first shutout victim in Miami's history. Also, it was the Bills' third blanking of the year.
• The Bills lost three fumbles in Miami territory in the first half. On their first series, Wayne Patrick ran 41 yards to the 33, but Jim Braxton lost the ball on the next play. Miami promptly went in to score.
• O.J. Simpson broke a 24-yard run, then fumbled on the next play at the Miami 45 and later, James Harris, who started for Dennis Shaw, fumbled on a QB sneak and that resulted in a missed 50-yard field goal by John Leypoldt.
• Miami made it 14-0 in the second when Tony Greene was called for a 31-yard interference penalty against Paul Warfield that led to Warfield's three-yard TD catch.
• Late in the half, a bad handoff by Harris resulted in a lost fumble at the Miami 1.
• Miami took the second-half kickoff and marched 74 yards to Bob Griese's 10-yard TD pass to Jim Mandich. Warfield's 39-yard run on a reverse was the key play.
• Another Buffalo drive into Miami territory ended in a Harris interception in the end zone and Miami went on to score 13 fourth-quarter points.

QUOTES

• O.J. Simpson: "It seems that each week we find a way to lose. This week it was fumbles, who knows what it will be next week? We moved the ball great today, but the fumbles kept us from scoring and you can't do that against Miami and expect to win. Before the season is over, I know we're going to win a few. Sooner or later we're going to stop making the mistakes that have been holding us back. Anyway, with the way we're going, we should get plenty of help in the draft."
• Harvey Johnson: "It's kind of hard to say anything after a game like this. Miami has a real fine ballclub and we just gave them too much help today. It seems that every fumble or penalty we had was at an opportune time for them, especially the one at the 1-yard-line. If we could have gotten in then, it would have been a new ballgame." (On the quarterback situation): "I really don't want to get into any quarterback controversy. We moved the ball very well, especially considering the young and inexperienced offensive line that we had."
• James Harris: "You're never satisfied when you lose, but I thought we moved the ball well. I think one of the most important things for us is to score early. We're always trying to come from behind. Just once I'd like to get ahead and have someone chasing us."

STANDINGS: EIGHTH WEEK

AFC EAST	W	L	T	CENTRAL	W	L	T	WEST	W	L	T	NFC EAST	W	L	T	CENTRAL	W	L	T	WEST	W	L	T
Miami	6	1	1	Cleveland	4	4	0	Oakland	5	1	2	Washington	6	1	1	Minnesota	6	2	0	San Fran	6	2	0
Baltimore	6	2	0	Pittsburgh	4	4	0	Kan. City	5	2	1	Dallas	5	3	0	Detroit	5	2	1	LA Rams	4	3	1
N. England	3	5	0	Houston	1	6	1	San Diego	3	5	0	St. Louis	3	5	0	Chicago	5	3	0	Atlanta	4	3	1
NY Jets	3	5	0	Cincinnati	1	7	0	Denver	2	5	1	NY Giants	3	5	0	Green Bay	3	4	1	N. Orleans	2	4	2
Buffalo	0	8	0									Philadelphia	2	5	1								

NOTES

• The Bills scored first, taking their first lead in 26 quarters, but they still lost their ninth in a row this season as they continued to make game-losing mistakes.

• With the Pats trailing 17-14 late in the second quarter, Carl Garrett took a short Jim Plunkett pass and went 80 yards for a TD. Twenty-three seconds later, ex-Bill Roland Moss rushed unblocked to block a Spike Jones punt and he returned the loose ball 10 yards for a TD and a 28-17 lead.

• The Bills had taken the early lead when Ike Hill went 68 yards with a punt. But the Pats went ahead when Plunkett's 44-yard pass to Randy Vataha set up his 16-yarder to Vataha and Garrett's 46-yard punt return led to Plunkett's TD pass to Tom Beer.

• Buffalo tied it when Wayne Patrick went 62 yards with

a short James Harris pass to the 15 and Harris then hit Marlin Briscoe for the TD. John Leypoldt later made a field goal to make it 17-14.

• Hill fumbled a punt early in the third at the Bills 31 and that resulted in Eric Crabtree's TD that gave New England a 35-20 lead. But the Bills got back in the game when Leypoldt made a field goal, then Al Cowlings forced Garrett to fumble in his end zone and Robert James recovered to make it 35-30.

• Two plays after the kickoff, Cal Snowden sacked Plunkett and forced him to fumble with Cowlings recovering at the 10. But the Bills failed to get the TD and settled for a field goal.

• Charley Gogolak's field goal with 4:39 left made it 38-33 and the Bills didn't threaten.

QUOTES

• Harvey Johnson: "The special teams hurt us again. A blocked punt, a few poor tackles and we got hurt. At least we tried and kept trying, but we just couldn't get the big one."

• Patriots cornerback Roland Moss on his blocked punt and TD: "No one touched me. I just took a step outside the man who was supposed to block me, then I went right into the kicker. It was all the sweeter because Buffalo released me after I finished last season with them."

• Spike Jones on the block: "Those things wouldn't happen if we worked on it more in practice. That's the second blocked punt in two weeks."

WEEK 9 GAMES	
Balt 14, NYJ 13	KC 13, Clev 7
Cinc 24, Den 10	Oak 41, Hou 21
Mia 24, Pitt 21	SD 20, St.L 17
Chi 16, Wash 15	NYG 21, Atl 17
Dal 20, Phil 7	LA 21, Det 13
Minn 3, GB 0	NO 26, SF 20

Bills	7	13	10	3	-	33
Patriots	7	21	7	3	-	38

Attendance at Schaefer Stadium - 57,446

Buf:	I. Hill 68 punt return (Leypoldt kick), 11:28
NE:	Vataha 16 pass from Plunkett (Gogolak kick), 15:00
NE:	Beer 10 pass from Plunkett (Gogolak kick), 3:35
Buf:	Briscoe 15 pass from Harris (Leypoldt kick), 5:51
Buf:	FG Leypoldt 17, 12:14
NE:	Garrett 80 pass from Plunkett (Gogolak kick), 12:32
NE:	Moss 10 blocked punt return (Gogolak kick), 13:55
Buf:	FG Leypoldt 48, 14:55
NE:	Crabtree 31 pass from Plunkett (Gogolak kick), 3:12
Buf:	FG Leypoldt 17, 11:54
Buf:	James 2 fumble return (Leypoldt kick), 12:40
Buf:	FG Leypoldt 12, :08
NE:	FG Gogolak 38, 10:21

	BUF	NE
First downs	15	9
Rushing yds	89	119
Passing yds	128	180
Punts-avg	9-35.3	7-39.7
Fumbles-lost	2-1	2-2
Penalties-yds	2-10	6-71

BILLS LEADERS: Rushing - Simpson 16-61, Patrick 6-21, Braxton 2-7; **Passing** - Harris 13-32-0 - 160, Shaw 2-4-0 - 14; **Receiving** - Moses 2-31, Briscoe 6-44, Patrick 2-72, Braxton 3-9, White 1-13, I. Hill 1-5.
PATRIOTS LEADERS: Rushing - Gladieux 4-48, Nance 8-26, Garrett 8-21, Crabtree 1-18, Maitland 4-5, Plunkett 2-1; **Passing** - Plunkett 9-16-1 - 218; **Receiving** - Garrett 2-97, Crabtree 2-38, Vataha 3-63, Beer 1-10, Gladieux 1-10.

NOTES

• A power failure knocked out the lights for more than an hour, a fitting thing to happen to the powerless Bills as they lost their 10th in a row, 15th over two seasons.

• Dennis Shaw and James Harris suffered five interceptions and were outplayed by Bob Davis for the second time this year as Joe Namath remained sidelined.

• The Bills scored on their first possession as Shaw hit Marlin Briscoe with a 41-yard TD pass.

• W.K. Hicks' 33-yard interception TD return was nullified by a penalty, but the Jets later drew even on Davis' TD pass to Don Maynard, then went ahead when Bobby Howfield kicked a field goal following Shaw's second interception.

• Another Shaw interception led to Davis' TD pass to George Nock and a 17-7 lead for the Jets.

• With 24 seconds left in the half, Shaw tried to hit Greg Jones in the end zone but John Dockery intercepted, which probably was the fatal blow.

• John Pitts' interception of a Davis pass was wasted in the third when John Leypoldt missed a 28-yard field goal and he also missed a 49-yarder later.

• Howfield's field goal in the fourth was preceded by a drive in which the Jets ran 13 times, consuming more than eight minutes.

QUOTES

• Jets quarterback Bob Davis on Shaw's late interception in the first half: "I thought Shaw made an awful mistake. If the Bills even got three points out of that

scoring opportunity they're right back in the ballgame. But Dennis threw it up for grabs and when we intercepted, the Bills were dead. They had much better field position than we did. Inside the 10-yard-line, a quarterback must take his team in for the score and Shaw didn't. That changed the whole game."

• O.J. Simpson: "All last week we agreed you couldn't run a sweep against the Jets 4-4 defense. So sweeps weren't even in our gameplan. It's too tough to sweep that kind of defense and the Jets players are way too quick for it. Yet we ran five weakside sweeps. I don't call the plays and I don't work the gameplan."

• Dennis Shaw on his last interception: "Greg Jones was free in the end zone. I thought I might as well throw it. But I couldn't put enough on the ball to get it to him and all of a sudden Dockery came out of nowhere to intercept it. It probably was a bad play on my part."

• Harvey Johnson: "We had our troubles moving against the Jets, but some of the better teams in the league have had the same problem. Obviously the key situation was late in the second quarter. Seven points or three points at that juncture could have been a turning point. But our players didn't quit on themselves. Regardless of our record, the way our club has given good effort in the last five games shows they have pride."

Jets	0	17	0	3	-	20
Bills	7	0	0	0	-	7

Attendance at War Memorial Stadium - 41,577

Buf:	Briscoe 41 pass from Shaw (Leypoldt kick), 6:42
NYJ:	Maynard 33 pass from Davis (Howfield kick), :34
NYJ:	FG Howfield 37, 12:23
NYJ:	Nock 19 pass from Davis (Howfield kick), 14:05
NYJ:	FG Howfield 31, 13:58

	BUF	NYJ
First downs	12	10
Rushing yds	78	153
Passing yds	119	78
Punts-avg	6-39.0	7-40.7
Fumbles-lost	2-1	1-0
Penalties-yds	4-30	7-73

BILLS LEADERS: Rushing - Simpson 14-48, Patrick 7-15, Shaw 1-11, Harris 1-4; **Passing** - Shaw 7-18-4 - 109, Harris 6-15-1 - 41; **Receiving** - Patrick 8-70, I. Hill 1-4, Briscoe 4-76.
JETS LEADERS: Rushing - Riggins 17-74, Boozer 20-61, Davis 2-12, Nock 2-4, Maynard 1-2; **Passing** - Davis 6-14-1 - 81; **Receiving** - Nock 1-19, Maynard 2-49, Riggins 3-13.

WEEK 10 GAMES	
Mia 17, Balt 14	Cinc 28, Hou 13
Clev 28, NE 7	KC 28, Den 10
Oak 34, SD 33	Pitt 17, NYG 13
Atl 28, GB 21	Det 28, Chi 3
Dal 13, Wash 0	LA 17, SF 6
Phil 37, St.L 20	Minn 23, NO 10

STANDINGS: TENTH WEEK

AFC EAST	W	L	T	CENTRAL	W	L	T	WEST	W	L	T	NFC EAST	W	L	T	CENTRAL	W	L	T	WEST	W	L	T
Miami	8	1	1	Cleveland	5	5	0	Oakland	7	1	2	Dallas	7	3	0	Minnesota	8	2	0	LA Rams	6	3	1
Baltimore	7	3	0	Pittsburgh	5	5	0	Kan. City	7	2	1	Washington	6	3	1	Detroit	6	3	1	San Fran	6	4	0
N. England	4	6	0	Cincinnati	3	7	0	San Diego	4	6	0	NY Giants	4	6	0	Chicago	6	4	0	Atlanta	5	4	1
NY Jets	4	6	0	Houston	1	8	1	Denver	2	7	1	Philadelphia	3	6	1	Green Bay	3	6	1	N. Orleans	3	5	2
Buffalo	0	10	0									St. Louis	3	7	0								

Patriots	3	3	7	7 - 20
Bills	0	17	0	10 - 27

Attendance at War Memorial Stadium - 27,166

NE: FG Gogolak 40, 11:05
Buf: J.D. Hill 11 pass from Shaw (Leypoldt kick), 7:26
NE: FG Gogolak 17, 11:36
Buf: J.D. Hill 47 pass from Shaw (Leypoldt kick), 13:11
Buf: FG Leypoldt 48, 14:58
NE: Nance 1 run (Gogolak kick), 12:29
Buf: Simpson 7 run (Leypoldt kick), 2:41
NE: Sellers 12 pass from Plunkett (Gogolak kick), 7:55
Buf: FG Leypoldt 41, 10:31

	BUF	NE
First downs	15	15
Rushing yds	147	189
Passing yds	117	105
Punts-avg	4-41.4	4-34.8
Fumbles-lost	3-1	0-0
Penalties-yds	4-45	4-30

BILLS LEADERS: Rushing - Simpson 14-61, Patrick 17-76, Braxton 1-11, G. Jones 1-(-1), Shaw 1-0; **Passing** - Shaw 9-17-0 - 154; **Receiving** - Patrick 2-7, J.D. Hill 3-82, Briscoe 3-46, G. Jones 1-19.

PATRIOTS LEADERS: Rushing - Garrett 21-127, Nance 8-18, Plunkett 4-33, Maitland 1-6, Gladiuex 1-4, Bryant 1-1; **Passing** - Plunkett 10-22-3 - 138; **Receiving** - Sellers 2-36, Beer 2-24, Vataha 2-26, Garrett 2-35, Nance 1-8, Bryant 1-9.

WEEK 11 GAMES

Balt 37, Oak 14	Cinc 31, SD 0
Clev 37, Hou 24	Den 22, Pit 10
Det 32, KC 21	Mia 34, Chi 3
SF 24, NYJ 21	Minn 24, Atl 7
Dal 28, LA 21	NO 29, GB 21
Wash 20, Phil 13	St.L 24, NYG 7

NOTES

• The Bills snapped their two-year, 15-game losing streak as rookie first-round draft choice J.D. Hill made a spectacular NFL debut with two TD receptions. A crowd of 27,166 was the smallest since 1963. On that day Cookie Gilchrist rushed for a then pro football record 243 yards.
• Tim Beamer's fumbled punt led to Charley Gogolak's 40-yard field goal and a 3-0 Pats lead.
• But the Bills then played fairly error-free football the rest of the way.
• The Bills went ahead 7-3 when Hill beat John Outlaw for his first TD, which was set up by a 19-yard run by O.J. Simpson.
• Gogolak drew New England within 7-6 after Carl Garrett broke a 38-yard run, but the Bills answered three plays after the kickoff when Hill beat Outlaw down the sideline and caught a 47-yard TD pass. Later John Leypoldt made a 48-yard field goal for a 17-6 halftime lead, the first time all year the Bills led at the break.
• Garrett's 50-yard punt return and a 24-yard Jim Plunkett-to-Ron Sellers pass led to Jim Nance's TD run late in the third, but the Bills retaliated with an 80-yard drive capped by Simpson's TD.
• A 24-yard Garrett run ignited a TD march that ended on Sellers' 12-yard catch, but Leypoldt boosted the Bills lead to 27-20 with a 41-yard field goal.
• The Bills defense then held after the Pats drove to the Buffalo 29 in the final two minutes as Paul Guidry knocked down three straight passes to secure the victory.

QUOTES

• J.D. Hill: "We're here, we have arrived and we're going to be tough. Catching my first touchdown pass was a real thrill. I gave the "soul" shake to every guy on the squad. I want to get better and do more, score more. I want to be the best. I've been dying standing on the sidelines watching us lose. All I wanted us to do was get me the ball. Football is supposed to be fun and losing takes all the fun out of it."
• Harvey Johnson: "The Patriots play bump and run without the bump. Their defensive backs weren't going to keep up with J.D. so I knew he'd be getting open. I'll take a bow on two counts. I said we'd win and I said J.D. would have a big game. I can single out a lot of players who contributed outstanding efforts, but what pleased me most was we minimized our mental errors. And I thought Dennis Shaw did well. He not only did a good job of play-calling, but he virtually eliminated the interception by eating the ball when he couldn't throw it."
• O.J. Simpson on Hill: "Sure he's a cocky cat and he never stops talking, but he won't let anyone think there isn't a team we can't beat. J.D. makes you think about winning."

Bills	0	0	0	0 - 0
Colts	0	0	14	10 - 24

Attendance at Memorial Stadium - 58,476

Bal: Bulaich 1 run (O'Brien kick), 10:14
Bal: Perkins 5 pass from Unitas (O'Brien kick), 14:50
Bal: FG O'Brien 13, 11:18
Bal: Newsome 19 interception return (O'Brien kick), 11:50

	BUF	BAL
First downs	8	16
Rushing yds	76	179
Passing yds	106	130
Punts-avg	7-42.0	6-44.3
Fumbles-lost	2-2	2-1
Penalties-yds	7-70	5-75

BILLS LEADERS: Rushing - Simpson 9-26, Patrick 6-19, Braxton 4-12, Shaw 2-19; **Passing** - Shaw 14-29-4 - 101; **Passing** - Harris 2-3-0 - 19; **Receiving** - Simpson 5-26, Patrick 2-17, Briscoe 4-35, J.D. Hill 2-18, G. Jones 1-6, Koy 1-22, Braxton 1-(-4).

COLTS LEADERS: Rushing - Matte 14-57, Nottingham 5-47, Bulaich 13-43, McCauley 5-22, Hinton 1-11, Pittman 2-3, Unitas 1-0, Mitchell 1-(-4); **Passing** - Unitas 11-21-1 - 134; **Receiving** - Bulaich 4-26, Hinton 3-62, Perkins 2-14, Matte 1-28, Mitchell 1-4.

WEEK 12 GAMES

Clev 31, Cinc 27	Den 6, Chi 3
Hou 29, Pitt 3	KC 26, SF 17
Dal 52, NYJ 10	NE 34, Mia 13
Wash 23, NYG 7	SD 30, Min 14
Phil 23, Det 20	LA 45, NO 28
St.L 16, GB 16	Atl 24, Oak 13

NOTES

• The Colts completed a two-game shutout sweep of the Bills by an aggregate score of 67-0.
• It was the Bills fourth shutout of the year and the fifth time they had been held without a TD.
• Rookie Donnie Green fought with Mike Curtis and Ted Hendricks and all three were ejected with 7:20 left. At that point, Buffalo trailed 14-0 and momentum could have shifted, but the Colts went on to add 10 points as the Bills final four possessions ended in turnovers.
• The game was scoreless for 40 minutes. Baltimore didn't get a first down until 6:57 was left in the first half.
• Paul Guidry intercepted Johnny Unitas' first pass, but John Leypoldt missed a 22-yard field goal. The Colts also blew a chance when Charlie Stukes' first-quarter interception was wasted when Jim O'Brien missed a 40-yard field goal.
• The Colts' first scoring drive was highlighted by a 21-yard pass to Ed Hinton and Norm Bulaich's 14-yard run. Bulaich later scored from the 1. On their next series, they went 62 yards to make it 14-0 as Unitas' 28-yard pass to Tom Matte and Don Nottingham's 12-yard run were key plays before Unitas' first TD pass of the season, a five-yarder to Ray Perkins.
• After the fight, Greg Jones lost a fumble and the Colts moved to O'Brien's 13-yard field goal.
• On the first play after the kickoff, Dennis Shaw threw a terrible pass that was intercepted by Billy Newsome and returned 19 yards for the final score.
• O'Brien missed three field goals inside 40 yards. He hadn't missed from that range all year.
• O.J. Simpson and Jim Braxton got into a heated argument on the sidelines and Alvin Wyatt was so frustrated, he began to cry on the bench.

QUOTES

• O.J. Simpson: "We're confused. We've lost a lot of games this year that we should have won because we get confused. We're a young team, I know that's part of it. I was as good a back as a rookie as I am now, but you can't do it if you don't have the stuff with you. I look around the league at Miami and Baltimore and I see backs like Norm Bulaich and Larry Csonka getting all kinds of yardage and it hurts me because I think I'm better than they are. But I see the kind of blockers they have and I understand why their statistics are so good compared to mine."
• Harvey Johnson when told of Simpson's comments: "I'd like to get some defensive help first in the draft. He's a great runner and when our linemen mature, he'll be a lot better." (On the game): "We played well enough defensively in the first half, but we didn't do much offensively. But I thought we'd stay in the ballgame instead of losing as bad as we did."
• Dennis Shaw: "We're all disappointed (with the 1-11 record), but what we've got to do is stop fighting among ourselves."
• Ex-Eagles coach Joe Kuharich, who observed the game from the press box: "Shaw could be a good quarterback, but he's got to develop some mental discipline."

STANDINGS: TWELFTH WEEK

NFC EAST	W	L	T	CENTRAL	W	L	T	WEST	W	L	T	AFC EAST	W	L	T	CENTRAL	W	L	T	WEST	W	L	T
Miami	9	2	1	Cleveland	7	5	0	Kan. City	8	3	1	Dallas	9	3	0	Minnesota	9	3	0	LA Rams	7	4	1
Baltimore	9	3	0	Pittsburgh	5	7	0	Oakland	7	3	2	Washington	8	3	1	Detroit	7	4	1	San Fran	7	5	0
N. England	5	7	0	Cincinnati	4	8	0	San Diego	5	7	0	St. Louis	4	7	1	Chicago	6	6	0	Atlanta	6	5	1
NY Jets	4	8	0	Houston	2	9	1	Denver	4	7	1	Philadelphia	4	7	1	Green Bay	3	7	2	N. Orleans	4	6	2
Buffalo	1	11	0									NY Giants	4	8	0								

NOTES

• The Bills were at their absolute worst for 50 minutes, then stunned their fans with a brief rally before failing at the end to hold on.

• The Bills trailed 13-0 in the fourth, when Haven Moses made a diving catch for 39 yards. Dennis Shaw hit J.D. Hill for 29 yards to set up O.J. Simpson's dazzling TD run.

• Houston punted on its next series and Alvin Wyatt returned it 18 yards to the Bills 38. Shaw then completed three passes to the Houston 24. On fourth-and-seven, he hit Wayne Patrick for a first down, then threw to Moses for the go-ahead TD with 1:55 left.

• The Oilers came back to win, though, as Dan Pastorini made two big plays. First, he hit Charlie Joiner for 26 yards on third down to the Bills 47. He then made a miraculous throw to Jim Bierne on fourth-and-10 from that point with 47 seconds left. He scrambled out of the pocket and as he was being sacked by Bob Tatarek, got the ball away to Bierne who was at the 30. Bierne made the catch and raced to the 6 before Robert James pushed him out of bounds. Robert Holmes scored two plays later.

• Buster Ramsey, the first head coach in Bills history, attended the game and tried to cheer up Harvey Johnson afterwards. Rumors were started that Ramsey would be hired as defensive coordinator in the offseason.

• Fans serenaded Johnson for much of the game with the chant "Goodbye, Harvey." Said Johnson: "I thought they were in tune."

• Ken Houston's interception TD return in the third was the seventh of his career, which tied the NFL record held by Herb Adderly and Erich Barnes.

QUOTES

• Harvey Johnson: "There is no way you can plan for a broken play. It was fourth-and-10 and we had a good rush on Pastorini, despite the fact that Cal Snowden obviously was held on the play. Pastorini felt the pressure, started out of the pocket with Bob Tatarek in pursuit and everything was great from our standpoint. All the receivers were covered so he ran faster and that's when he got the break. John Pitts began to move forward to prevent Pastorini from running for the first down. Just then, Pastorini stopped about a half yard from the line of scrimmage and Pitts' man, Jim Bierne, was alone and that was the ball game right there."

• Oilers receiver Jim Bierne: "I thought Pastorini was scrambling beyond the line of scrimmage. I thought it had become a running play. I felt there was nothing I could do to help him so I just moved upfield a little bit."

• Oilers quarterback Dan Pastorini: "His eyes were as big as saucers when I threw it to him. I was hit, but I still had enough balance and I knew where the line of scrimmage was."

• Ralph Wilson: "That's the picture of the whole season. Nothing else could happen."

WEEK 13 GAMES	
NYJ 16, NE 13	SD 45, Den 17
KC 16, Oak 14	Pitt 21, Cinc 13
Balt 14, Mia 3	Clev 21, NO 17
SF 24, Atl 3	GB 31, Chi 10
Minn 29, Det 10	Dal 42, NYG 14
Phil 19, St.L 7	Wash 38, LA 24

Oilers	3	3	7	7 -	20
Bills	0	0	0	14 -	14

Attendance at War Memorial Stadium - 28,107

Hou: FG Moseley 44, 2:06
Hou: FG Moseley 44, 2:36
Hou: Houston 17 interception return (Moseley kick), 7:47
Buf: Simpson 6 run (Leypoldt kick), 5:57
Buf: Moses 14 pass from Shaw (Leypoldt kick), 13:05
Hou: Holmes 2 run (Moseley kick), 14:36

	BUF	HOU
First downs	14	16
Rushing yds	85	92
Passing yds	207	176
Punts-avg	7-42.9	5-45.0
Fumbles-lost	1-1	1-1
Penalties-yds	4-66	4-50

BILLS LEADERS: Rushing - Simpson 12-29, Patrick 7-32, Shaw 3-21, J.D. Hill 1-2, Braxton 1-1; **Passing** - Shaw 20-29-2 - 233; **Receiving** - Simpson 1-14, Patrick 4-15, Briscoe 4-38, J.D. Hill 4-76, Braxton 3-22, Chandler 1-12, Koy 1-3, Moses 2-53.

OILERS LEADERS: Rushing - Walsh 11-56, Campbell 9-19, Holmes 5-12, Pastorini 1-7, Post 1-(-2); **Passing** - Pastorini 17-33-0 - 211; **Receiving** - Campbell 6-45, Beirne 4-78, Reed 2-28, Burrough 2-19, Joiner 1-26, Holmes 2-15.

NOTES

• The worst season in team history ended as Jan Stenerud had his third five-field goal game against the Bills, raising his total to 22 field goals in five career games against Buffalo.

• The 1-13 record made the Bills only the fourth team in history to record such a lowly mark, matched by the Oakland Raiders in 1962 and the Pittsburgh Steelers and Chicago Bears in 1969.

• It was the last regular-season game played at Municipal Stadium with brand new Arrowhead Stadium scheduled to be opened in 1972.

• The teams traded three field goals each to produce a 9-9 tie at halftime before Bobby Bell broke it open with a 26-yard interception return for a TD in the third.

• Dennis Shaw was intercepted twice, giving him 26 for the season and tying Jack Kemp's team record set in 1964.

• Lenny Dawson was held out to rest a sore ankle and Mike Livingston played QB for KC. The Chiefs failed to score an offensive TD for only the second time all season.

• The Bills were one-for-14 on third- and fourth-down conversions.

• Stenerud's fourth field goal made it 12-9 in the third. It came after Johnny Robinson's 29-yard return of a Shaw interception. Ten minutes later, Bell stepped in front of J.D. Hill and picked off Shaw's pass and the game, and the season were over.

QUOTES

• Chiefs kicker Jan Stenerud: "I really don't have anything against Buffalo. In fact, I like Buffalo, I've spent a lot of time there, saw my first pro football game there. It's just that everything goes right for me against the Bills. I think the reason I get so many chances against the Bills is because their defense stops our offense short of touchdowns."

• Harvey Johnson: "This time we gave an honest effort (in a season finale). There was some hitting out there, not like the season before when the guys didn't give it everything (in a 45-7 loss to Miami). There is no question this club can be respectable next season. I don't mean Super Bowl, though. We could have won five or six games this year. The team is developing."

• O.J. Simpson capsulizing the season: "We thought we'd do seven times as good."

WEEK 14 GAMES	
Mia 27, GB 6	LA 23, Pitt 14
Clev 20, Wash 13	NE 21, Balt 17
NYJ 35, Cinc 21	Oak 21, Den 13
Hou 49, SD 33	Phil 41, NYG 28
SF 31, Det 27	Minn 27, Chi 10
Atl 24, NO 20	Dal 31, St.L 12

Bills	3	6	0	0 -	9
Chiefs	3	6	10	3 -	22

Attendance at Municipal Stadium - 48,121

Buf: FG Leypoldt 45, 5:31
KC: FG Stenerud 48, 12:21
Buf: FG Leypoldt 31, 1:40
KC: FG Stenerud 23, 6:13
Buf: FG Leypoldt 49, 13:45
KC: FG Stenerud 48, 14:57
KC: FG Stenerud 45, 2:27
KC: Bell 26 interception return (Stenerud kick), 12:27
KC: FG Stenerud 34, 11:10

	BUF	KC
First downs	15	14
Rushing yds	102	137
Passing yds	158	118
Punts-avg	4-41.7	5-36.2
Fumbles-lost	1-1	0-0
Penalties-yds	9-95	8-86

BILLS LEADERS: Rushing - Simpson 14-68, Patrick 4-17, Braxton 4-19, Shaw 1-(-2); **Passing** - Shaw 17-34-2 - 196, Braxton 0-1-0 - 0; **Receiving** - Simpson 1-13, Braxton 3-30, Patrick 2-10, Briscoe 3-40, J.D. Hill 2-40, White 3-24, Moses 2-27, Chandler 1-12.

CHIEFS LEADERS: Rushing - McVea 5-40, Adamle 9-39, Otis 8-31, Podolak 5-10, Hayes 3-9, Livingston 3-8; **Passing** - Livingston 11-25-0 - 136, Huarte 2-6-0 - 18; **Receiving** - Otis 4-43, Wright 1-36, Taylor 4-55, Frazier 1-18, Podolak 2-6, McVea 1-(-4).

STANDINGS: FOURTEENTH WEEK

NFC EAST	W	L	T	CENTRAL	W	L	T	WEST	W	L	T	AFC EAST	W	L	T	CENTRAL	W	L	T	WEST	W	L	T
Miami	10	3	1	Cleveland	9	5	0	Kan. City	10	3	1	Dallas	11	3	0	Minnesota	11	3	0	San Fran	9	5	0
Baltimore	10	4	0	Pittsburgh	6	8	0	Oakland	8	4	2	Washington	9	4	1	Detroit	7	6	1	LA Rams	8	5	1
N. England	6	8	0	Houston	4	9	1	San Diego	6	8	0	Philadelphia	6	7	1	Chicago	6	8	0	Atlanta	7	6	1
NY Jets	6	8	0	Cincinnati	4	10	0	Denver	4	9	1	St. Louis	4	9	1	Green Bay	4	8	2	N. Orleans	4	8	2
Buffalo	1	13	0									NY Giants	4	10	0								

A<small>t</small> A G<small>lance</small>
1972

Jan. 6 – Floyd Little, the former Syracuse star and 1971 NFL rushing champion, indicated he wanted Denver to trade him to Buffalo so he could rejoin coach Lou Saban. "I'm a Lou Saban man," Little said. "There are very few coaches left like him. I'd like him to be my coach for the rest of my time in football."

Jan. 7 – Saban began constructing his new staff in Buffalo by hiring two assistants he had in Denver, Hunter Enis (offensive backfield) and Stan Jones (defensive line).

Jan. 8 – While watching the Hula Bowl in Hawaii, Saban took ill and had to be rushed to a hospital where he remained for 11 days. His problem was diagnosed as a gall-bladder ailment.

Jan. 26 – Lou Saban indicated that the Bills would demand a great deal for the rights to the No. 1 draft choice, which they held. Meanwhile, it became more evident that the Bills were leaning toward drafting Notre Dame defensive end Walt Patulski if they kept the top pick.

Jan. 29 – Saban added ex-Bill Billy Atkins to his staff as the defensive backfield coach.

Feb. 1 – The Bills made Walt Patulski the first pick in the college draft. In the second round, the Bills chose Michigan guard Reggie McKenzie. "I made it clear this is where I wanted to play from the start," Patulski, a resident of Liverpool, a suburb of Syracuse, said. "I think I can add something to the play of the Bills. I know they have a lot of good offensive players, but they're a little weak defensively." Later in the first round, Pittsburgh chose running back Franco Harris and St. Louis grabbed running back Bobby Moore.

Feb. 9 – Lou Saban completed his five-man coaching staff by hiring Jim Ringo to coach the offensive line and Jim Dooley to tutor the linebackers.

Feb. 11 – Saban underwent surgery to remove his gall bladder in Denver.

Feb. 16 – Ex-Buffalo quarterback and quarterbacks coach Tom Flores was hired by John Madden to become Oakland's receivers coach.

March 14 – Veteran guard Joe O'Donnell was traded to St. Louis for lineman Irv Goode.

March 24 – In a rule change that was deemed excellent by most NFL coaches, the league owners decided to move the hash marks 3.5 yards closer to the center of the field, thus giving offenses more room to maneuver on the short side.

March 28 – The Bills failed to reach an agreement with WBEN radio, the station that had broadcast the teams games since 1960, and instead signed with WKBW. The agreement ended Van Miller's reign as "Voice of the Bills."

March 30 – Hunter Enis, in a surprise move, quit the Bills' staff to take a job in the construction business.

April 4 – Ground-breaking ceremonies were held in Orchard Park, site of the new 80,000 seat stadium. The first shovel full of dirt was turned jointly by Erie County Legislature Chairman Richard J. Keane and Ralph Wilson.

April 8 – Lou Saban filled the coaching vacancy by hiring Bob Shaw to coach the receivers.

May 24 – Al Meltzer was named the new play-by-play announcer for the Bills with Rick Azar and former-Bill Ed Rutkowski providing analysis and color commentary. The trio replaced WBEN's Van Miller and Stan Barron.

June 6 – First-round draft choice Walt Patulski signed his contract.

June 7 – Wide receiver Marlin Briscoe and defensive lineman Jim Dunaway were traded to Miami for the Dolphins No. 1 draft choice in the 1973 draft plus linebacker Dale Farley.

June 20 – With Walt Patulski signed, the Bills traded starting defensive end Cal Snowden to San Diego for a conditional draft pick.

June 23 – Second-round draft choice Reggie McKenzie signed his contract; Lou Saban, in talking about what kind of offense he would try to run, said: "You win by passing, but you have to make them respect your running in order for your passing game to work. I'm not saying O.J. will get the ball as much as Floyd (Little) did last year because Denver didn't have a thrower, but he'll be getting it a lot more than he has been."

June 28 – Jack Kemp, the ex-Bills quarterback and now a congressman, told Congress that the Federal government should stay out of labor-management relations in pro sports.

July 14 – The Bills reported to training camp at Niagara University and Lou Saban held the first formal meeting with the team.

July 20 – Ralph Wilson said he was confident that at least half of the 1973 schedule could be salvaged at the new stadium in Orchard Park. A strike delayed construction during the late spring and early summer.

July 23 – No.1 pick Walt Patulski injured his knee while practicing in Chicago for the College All-Star Game.

July 28 – With one year still remaining on his original four-year deal with the Bills, O.J. Simpson signed a new multi-year contract that

Ralph Wilson said was "for lots of years for lots of money."

Aug. 4 – The Bills dropped their preseason opener, 27-10, to the St. Louis Cardinals.

Aug. 9 – Walt Patulski participated in his first workout with the team since hurting his knee. He was unimpressive in the morning workout, but rebounded well in the afternoon.

Aug. 12 – The Bills traveled to New Orleans and beat the Saints, 24-21, on John Leypoldt's final-play 38-yard field goal.

Aug. 18 – The Bills downed Minnesota, 21-10, behind three TD passes by Dennis Shaw.

Aug. 26 – Despite Al Davis' concerns about the Bills – "Buffalo's gonna kill us" – the Oakland Raiders ripped Buffalo, 31-13.

Sept. 3 – Buffalo blew a 24-0 halftime lead and settled for a 24-24 tie at Chicago.

Sept. 8 – The Bills closed the preseason with a 3-2-1 record after a 34-17 victory over Philadelphia at War Memorial. Kicker John Leypoldt was placed on waivers and Mike Clark was signed from Dallas.

Sept. 9 – It was learned that Mike Clark suffered a broken arm in the Eagles game and John Leypoldt was re-signed.

Sept. 12 – The Bills signed offensive tackle Dave Foley off waivers from the Jets.

Sept. 17 – The Bills regular-season opener, the final one at War Memorial Stadium, was spoiled by the Jets, 41-24, even though Joe Namath completed only five passes.

Sept. 19 – With Irv Goode and now Bruce Jarvis out for the season, the Bills needed a center and Lou Saban thought he had one in a trade with Miami for Bob DeMarco, but DeMarco said he couldn't come to Buffalo because of "family problems."

Sept. 21 – Saban waived quarterback James Harris and signed Mike Taliaferro off waivers. Taliaferro, formerly of New England, was signed during training camp, then released a week later because Saban felt he should go with Dennis Shaw and Harris, but Harris continued to be unimpressive, so Saban made the move.

Sept. 24 – O.J. Simpson, playing against "football men I idolized as a teenager," rushed for 138 yards and the Bills rallied for two touchdowns in the final 4:08 to shock San Francisco, 27-20, at War Memorial.

Oct. 1 – Baltimore recorded its third straight shutout of the Bills with a 17-0 victory.

Oct. 8 – The Bills evened their record at 2-2 by ripping New England, 38-14, thanks to a 28-point eruption in the second quarter.

Oct. 12 – Due to a heavy rainstorm, the Bills practice field at the Regency Motor Hotel in Blasdell was a quagmire, so the players donned sneakers and practiced in the parking lot.

Oct. 15 – The Bills' West Coast woes continued as they fell to the Oakland Raiders, 28-16, blowing a 13-0 halftime lead. The Bills hadn't won on the left coast since Nov. 24, 1966 against the Raiders. They had lost in their last seven trips to California to play Oakland or San Diego.

Oct. 16 – The Bills traded Haven Moses to Denver for receiver Dwight Harrison. Moses had been riding the bench behind Bob Chandler since the start of the season. "I knew the trade was coming," Moses said. "There was a misunderstanding about my attitude. He (Lou Saban) wants to control people completely. He wants the gung-ho type who is always yelling. He doesn't think you're giving 100 percent if you're not doing that. I've never been that type, but my attitude this year has been the same as always."

Oct. 17 – Erie County legislator Richard Gallagher of Lackawanna proposed that the Bills be renamed the Erie County Bills so that Erie County could become a "national byword." Also, in a letter to Ralph Wilson, Gallagher said he favored accepting the offer of Rich Products Corp. to pay $1 million to name the stadium Rich Stadium.

Oct. 22 – Miami remained unbeaten at 6-0 by edging the Bills, 24-23, before 80,010 at the Orange Bowl. It was Buffalo's 12th straight road loss.

Oct. 29 – O.J. Simpson's 94-yard TD run, the longest in team history, and his 189 rushing yards weren't enough as Pittsburgh dealt the Bills a frustrating 38-21 loss.

Nov. 5 – Miami's bid to become the only undefeated team in pro football history remained on track as the Dolphins rushed for 254 yards and beat the Bills, 30-16.

Nov. 7 – The Erie County legislature approved by a 16-4 vote to accept $1.5 million in naming rights from Rich Products Corp. and thus the new stadium was deemed Rich Stadium.

Nov. 12 – In a truly awful performance, the Bills were slugged by the Jets at Shea Stadium, 41-3, for their 13th straight road loss.

Nov. 18 – Mike Taliaferro, who had battled with starting QB Dennis Shaw for playing time and caused a weekly quarterback controversy, was released and recently-signed Leo Hart was promoted to second-string.

Nov. 19 – John Leypoldt kicked a 45-yard field goal with five seconds remaining to lift the Bills to a 27-24 victory over New England, snapping their five-game losing streak and a 13-game road

losing streak.

Nov. 23 – A rumor heated up that Lou Saban wanted to trade for Houston second-year quarterback Dan Pastorini at the end of the season.

Nov. 26 – O.J. Simpson topped the 1,000-yard mark for the first time in his career, but the Bills blew a 10-0 lead and lost at Cleveland, 27-10.

Dec. 3 – The Bills scored their first points against the Colts in nearly 18 quarters when O.J. Simpson scored with 30 seconds left, averting a fourth straight shutout loss to Baltimore, but the 35-7 final dropped the Bills to 3-9.

Dec. 10 – Playing the final pro football game in War Memorial Stadium, the Bills knocked the Detroit Lions out of the NFC playoff hunt with a 21-21 tie before 41,583 rain-soaked fans. O.J. Simpson surpassed Cookie Gilchrist's team rushing record of 1,096 yards set in 1962.

Dec. 16 – The Miami Dolphins concluded the first perfect regular season in NFL history with a 16-0 victory over Baltimore.

Dec. 17 – O.J. Simpson won his first NFL rushing title with a team-record 1,251 yards on a team-record 292 carries as the Bills stunned the Washington Redskins at RFK Stadium, 24-17, thanks to two fourth-quarter touchdowns.

Dec. 23 – Franco Harris made the "Immaculate Reception" to give Pittsburgh a 13-7 victory over Oakland and for the third year in a row, Dallas knocked San Francisco out of the post-season, 30-28, in divisional-round play.

Dec. 24 – Washington beat Green Bay, 16-3, and Miami edged Cleveland, 20-14, in the second day of divisional play.

Dec. 27 – O.J. Simpson was named the AFC's player of the year by UPI.

Dec. 31 – Miami defended its AFC Championship by edging Pittsburgh, 21-17, while Washington ended Dallas' two-year run as NFC champs with a 26-3 rout.

Jan. 14, 1973 – Miami completed the first perfect season in NFL history at 17-0 with a 14-7 victory over Washington in Super Bowl VII at the Los Angeles Coliseum.

Jan. 22, 1973 – O.J. Simpson gained 112 yards and was named the MVP of the Pro Bowl as the AFC defeated the NFC, 33-28, at Texas Stadium.

After a long and arduous fight (opposite page), Ralph Wilson finally convinced Erie County politicians to build the team a new home. Construction of Rich Stadium began in 1972.

Lou Saban (below) returned to Buffalo as head coach in 1972 and guided the Bills into the 1974 playoffs. His career record in Buffalo was 70-47-4, a winning percentage of .600, second only to Marv Levy.

By the Numbers - 1972

TEAM STATISTICS	BILLS	OPP
First downs	221	249
Rushing	104	125
Passing	98	95
Penalty	19	29
Total yards	3,733	4,192
Avg. game	266.6	299.4
Plays	877	862
Avg. play	4.3	4.9
Net rushing yds	2,132	2,241
Avg. game	152.3	160.1
Avg. play	4.2	4.2
Net passing yds	1,601	1,951
Comp/att	164/316	131/308
Sacks/lost	49-411	22-197
Interceptions	24	23
Percentage	51.9	42.5
Punts/avg	80-38.8	65-39.5
Fumbles/lost	29-15	20-8
Penalties/yds	87-900	72-685
Touchdowns	30	47
Extra points	29-30	47-47
Field goals	16-24	16-27
Safeties	0	0
Kick ret./avg	60-23.2	29-22.2
Punt ret./avg	25-6.6	39-8.4

RUSHING	ATT	YDS	AVG	TD
Simpson	292	1251	4.3	6
Braxton	116	453	3.9	5
Shaw	35	138	3.9	0
Patrick	35	130	3.7	0
Jackson	17	57	3.4	0
Chandler	3	27	9.0	0
Hart	5	19	3.8	0
Taliaferro	5	19	3.8	0
S. Jones	2	18	9.0	0
J.D. Hill	1	11	11.0	0
Koy	1	9	9.0	0
TOTALS	512	2132	4.2	11

PASSING	COMP	ATT	INT	YDS	TD	COMP%
Shaw	136	258	17	1666	14	52.7
Taliaferro	16	33	4	176	1	48.5
Simpson	5	8	0	113	1	62.5
Hart	6	15	3	53	0	40.0
Jones	1	2	0	4	0	50.0
TOTALS	164	316	24	2012	16	51.9

KICKING	1-19	20-29	30-39	40-49	50+	TOT	PAT	PTS
Leypoldt	2-2	4-5	6-7	4-9	0-1	16-24	29-30	77

PUNTING	NO	AVG	LG	BL
S. Jones	80	38.8	67	1

RECEIVING	CAT	YDS	AVG	TD
J.D. Hill	52	754	14.5	5
Chandler	33	528	16.0	5
Simpson	27	198	7.3	0
Braxton	24	232	9.7	1
White	12	148	12.3	2
Patrick	8	42	5.3	1
Moses	3	60	20.0	1
Jackson	2	21	10.5	1
Harrison	1	16	16.0	0
Koy	1	9	9.0	0
Washington	1	4	4.0	0
TOTALS	164	2012	12.3	16

LEADERS

Kick returns:	Wyatt 17-432 yds, 25.4 avg, 0 TD
	Cole 16-415, 25.9, 0 TD
Punt returns:	Wyatt 11-85, 7.7, 0 TD
	Cole 7-35, 5.0, 0 TD
Interceptions:	Lee 6-155, 25.8, 1 TD
	Tyler 4-61, 15.3, 0 TD
	Wyatt 4-52, 13.0, 1 TD

SCORE BY QUARTERS

BILLS	35	95	38	89 -	257
OPP	79	92	89	117 -	377

Jim Braxton served as the blocking fullback for O.J. Simpson and he helped Simpson to his first 1,000-yard rushing season in 1972.

GAME 1 - Sunday, Sept. 17, 1972 - JETS 41, BILLS 24

NOTES

• The Bills opened their final season at War Memorial Stadium with a poor opening-day performance as Dennis Shaw threw four interceptions and was sacked four times. The running game netted only 80 yards.
• Down 21-0, Shaw hit J.D. Hill with a 38-yard TD pass, then Alvin Wyatt intercepted a Joe Namath pass and returned it to the Jets 38 and the Bills seemed to have stolen the momentum. But on the next play, Shaw was intercepted by Al Atkinson and the Jets promptly drove 64 yards, capped by Emerson Boozer's 15-yard TD, and the Bills were done.
• The Jets first TD was set up by Steve Tannen's interception and their third TD was the result of a 41-yard pass to Eddie Bell and an interference call on Wyatt that put the ball at the 19.
• O.J. Simpson completed two passes, including a 21-yard TD pass to Hill in the third.
• Chris Farasopoulos' punt-return TD was the first for the Jets since 1963.
• Edgar Chandler and Bruce Jarvis were lost for the season with knee injuries.

QUOTES

• Lou Saban: "We became unraveled. I'd have to say the best description would be a shambles. We now know we have several areas we must upgrade. Maybe we overestimated the ability of some of our players. We're a very conservative team, we have to hang onto the ball. If we do the things that we did today, we'll be 1-13 again and I don't think the fans could stand that. I know I couldn't. Shaw has to learn he has to be able to carry this team. I'm not sure why Denny had such a bad day."
• Dennis Shaw on the Atkinson interception: "I got greedy there. To me that was the big play of the game. I thought Atkinson would bite for the play-action and come up on the play. But he didn't, he was right there in the path of the ball. I wanted to get it all at once, I should have been more patient."
• Jets linebacker Gerry Philbin: "It was the easiest time we've ever had beating the Bills. We've had big leads on them, but then blown them. I expected a tougher ballgame and if they hadn't been so unlucky in the early going I'm sure it would have been. Besides, we were overdue in War Memorial. We still have a lot of catching up to do."
• Jets assistant Buddy Ryan: "That team (the 1968 Super Bowl champs) had about 16 players that were very ordinary. This one has a helluva lot more talent and with Namath healthy, we're going to be tough."

WEEK 1 GAMES

St.L 10, Balt 3	Cinc 31, NE 7
GB 26, Clev 10	Mia 20, KC 10
Den 30, Hou 17	Pitt 34, Oak 28
SF 34, SD 3	Atl 37, Chi 21
Dal 28, Phil 6	Det 30, NYG 16
Wash 24, Minn 21	LA 34, NO 14

Jets	14	14	3	10	-	41
Bills	0	7	7	10	-	24

Attendance at War Memorial Stadium - 46,206

NYJ: Riggins 16 run (Howfield kick), 6:31
NYJ: Farasopolous 65 punt return (Howfield kick), 8:20
NYJ: Boozer 12 pass from Namath (Howfield kick), :05
Buf: J.D. Hill 38 pass from Shaw (Leypoldt kick), 6:44
NYJ: Boozer 15 run (Howfield kick), 14:18
NYJ: FG Howfield 35, 4:37
Buf: J.D. Hill 21 pass from Simpson (Leypoldt kick), 11:28
NYJ: Boozer 2 run (Howfield kick), 2:09
NYJ: FG Howfield 11, 5:04
Buf: FG Leypoldt 48, 7:23
Buf: Moses 25 pass from Shaw (Leypoldt kick), 13:44

	BUF	NYJ
First downs	16	19
Rushing yds	80	191
Passing yds	207	102
Punts-avg	4-42.0	3-35.6
Fumbles-lost	0-0	0-0
Penalties-yds	8-78	3-35

BILLS LEADERS: Rushing - Simpson 14-41, Braxton 5-20, Patrick 3-3, Shaw 3-16; **Passing** - Shaw 14-24-4 - 190, Simpson 2-2-0 - 46; **Receiving** - J.D. Hill 6-95, Moses 2-43, Chandler 1-15, White 2-33, Simpson 2-10, Braxton 3-40.

JETS LEADERS: Rushing - Riggins 26-125, Boozer 13-50, Harkey 7-16, McClain 1-0; **Passing** - Namath 5-14-1 - 113, Davis 1-2-0 - 7; **Receiving** - Bell 2-43, Stewart 1-22, Caster 1-36, Boozer 1-12, McClain 1-7.

GAME 2 - Sunday, Sept. 24, 1972 - BILLS 27, 49ERS 20

NOTES

• San Francisco QB John Brodie was knocked out of the game in the second quarter. The 49ers couldn't overcome his loss and lost a shocker to the Bills.
• The patched-up Bills defense stuffed the 49ers for 33 rushing yards and one first down attained via the ground.
• The Bills trailed 20-13 in the fourth, but rallied to score the final 14 points.
• They drove 58 yards to score the tying TD. Haven Moses made a 17-yard reception for a first down, then on second-and-23 from the Bills 47, Simpson took a screen pass and went 25 yards. Dennis Shaw hit J.D. Hill for three, then Simpson ran 11 yards before Jim Braxton scored his first NFL TD.
• Moments later, Steve Spurrier was intercepted by John Pitts who returned it 10 yards to the 49ers 18. Simpson carried three times for 12 yards and Braxton went the final six in two carries to score with 1:13 left.
• Shaw completed only one pass in the first half and endured the crowd's wrath. But after the 49ers went ahead 13-6 early in the third, Shaw began to find his groove. He hit Hill for 20 yards and Jan White for 17 before throwing 20 yards to White for the tying TD.
• The Bills controlled the ball for 17 more plays (69-52).
• The Bills' defensive line consisted of three rookies (Walt Patulski, Jerry Patton and Don Croft).

QUOTES

• Lou Saban: "It's been a fantastic, almost unbelievable week. We've been in constant turmoil just trying to get bodies in here, and now this."
• O.J. Simpson: "This game was won by attitude. We still made a lot of mistakes, still got behind, but we didn't give up and that was the difference. Maybe we caught them off-balance looking at their press clippings. I'm as happy about this game as any I've ever played."
• 49ers linebacker Skip Vanderbunt: "I was on the Oregon State team that upset Southern Cal when O.J. was there. I said it then and I'll say it today, O.J. is the best I've ever seen."
• Paul Guidry: "I wasn't surprised because of the mounting enthusiasm in every player all last week."
• John Pitts on his interception: "Paul (Guidry) forced Ted Kwalick to the middle and when he kept him there, I just took off for that area. I said to myself I better catch it because I couldn't afford to tip it and have Kwalick catch it."
• Walt Patulski on the young defensive line: "We hardly know each other, much less know about playing together. We've only been together three days."

WEEK 2 GAMES

NYJ 44, Balt 34	Cinc 15, Pitt 10
Clev 27, Phil 17	SD 37, Den 14
Mia 34, Hou 13	KC 20, NO 17
NE 21, Atl 20	Oak 20, GB 14
Chi 13, LA 13	Dal 23, NYG 14
Minn 34, Det 10	Wash 24, St.L 10

49ers	3	7	3	7	-	20
Bills	0	6	7	14	-	27

Attendance at War Memorial Stadium - 45,845

SF: FG Gossett 47, 4:37
Buf: FG Leypoldt 32, :03
Buf: FG Leypoldt 22, 4:54
SF: Kwalick 20 pass from Spurrier (Gossett kick), 13:58
SF: FG Gossett 20, 1:49
Buf: White 17 pass from Shaw (Leypoldt kick), 12:38
SF: Schreiber 2 run (Gossett kick), :03
Buf: Braxton 2 run (Leypoldt kick), 10:52
Buf: Braxton 1 run (Leypoldt kick), 13:47

	BUF	SF
First downs	17	10
Rushing yds	177	33
Passing yds	56	169
Punts-avg	8-46.5	6-43.0
Fumbles-lost	0-0	2-1
Penalties-yds	8-98	10-101

BILLS LEADERS: Rushing - Simpson 29-138, Braxton 8-25, Shaw 6-14; **Passing** - Shaw 8-20-1 - 105, Simpson 0-1-0 - 0; **Receiving** - J.D. Hill 2-33, Moses 1-17, Chandler 1-15, White 1-17, Simpson 2-20, Braxton 1-3.

49ERS LEADERS: Rushing - V. Washington 9-18, Schreiber 8-12, Willard 2-5, Thomas 2-(-2); **Passing** - Spurrier 10-25-2 - 171, Brodie 1-5-1 - 18; **Receiving** - Schreiber 3-24, G. Washington 3-89, Kwalick 3-66, Willard 2-10.

STANDINGS: SECOND WEEK

AFC EAST	W	L	T	CENTRAL	W	L	T	WEST	W	L	T	NFC EAST	W	L	T	CENTRAL	W	L	T	WEST	W	L	T
NY Jets	2	0	0	Cincinnati	2	0	0	Denver	1	1	0	Dallas	2	0	0	Green Bay	1	1	0	LA Rams	1	0	1
Miami	2	0	0	Pittsburgh	1	1	0	Oakland	1	1	0	Washington	2	0	0	Detroit	1	1	0	Atlanta	1	1	0
New England	1	1	0	Cleveland	1	1	0	Kan. City	1	1	0	St. Louis	1	1	0	Minnesota	1	1	0	San Fran	1	1	0
Baltimore	0	2	0	Houston	0	2	0	San Diego	1	1	0	Philadelphia	0	2	0	Chicago	0	1	1	N. Orleans	0	2	0
Buffalo	1	1	0									NY Giants	0	2	0								

Colts	10	7	0	0 - 17
Bills	0	0	0	0 - 0

Attendance at War Memorial Stadium - 46,206

Bal: Mitchell 27 pass from Unitas (O'Brien kick), 8:51
Bal: FG O'Brien 30, 14:57
Bal: Havrilak 12 run (O'Brien kick), 12:08

	BUF	BAL
First downs	11	17
Rushing yds	118	159
Passing yds	111	180
Punts-avg	9-38.3	5-42.2
Fumbles-lost	2-2	2-2
Penalties-yds	10-74	1-5

BILLS LEADERS: Rushing - Simpson 21-78, Braxton 3-15, Patrick 8-25; **Passing** - Shaw 6-21-2 - 79, Taliaferro 5-7-1 - 67; **Receiving** - J.D. Hill 8-115, Simpson 2-21, Patrick 1-10.

COLTS LEADERS: Rushing - Nottingham 18-78, McCauley 13-43, Matte 7-30, Havrilak 2-8, Nowatzke 1-0; **Passing** - Unitas 12-28-2 - 184, Havrilak 0-1-0 - 0; **Receiving** - Nottingham 5-63, McCauley 2-37, Mitchell 2-44, Matte 1-20, Spreyer 1-9, Havrilak 1-11.

WEEK 3 GAMES

Clev 27, Cinc 6	KC 45, Den 24
Hou 26, NYJ 20	Mia 16, Minn 14
NE 24, Wash 23	Oak 17, SD 17
Pitt 25, St.L 19	Atl 31, LA 3
Det 38, Chi 24	GB 16, Dal 13
SF 37, NO 2	NYG 27, Phil 12

NOTES

• The Colts posted their third straight shutout over the Bills and stretched Buffalo's scoreless streak against Baltimore to 14 quarters dating back to the teams' second meeting in 1970.
• The Bills didn't achieve a first down in the first half as Dennis Shaw, for the second week in a row, had only one pass completion at the break. The Colts outgained the Bills, 212-13, in the first half.
• A short Spike Jones punt set up the Colts at the Bills 29 on their second possession and Johnny Unitas hit Tom Mitchell with a 27-yard TD pass as Mitchell beat Maurice Tyler on a post.
• On their next drive, the Colts moved to Jim O'Brien's only successful field goal in four tries. Unitas hit Mitchell for 17 yards and Tom Matte for 20 to get O'Brien in position.
• Early in the second quarter, the Colts drove to the Bills 11, but the defense stiffened and stopped Don McCauley on fourth-and-one. However, the offense failed to get a first down and had to punt, killing the momentum.
• Moments later, Ken Lee intercepted Unitas at the Colts 35, but O.J. Simpson fumbled it back on the next play.
• Two fumbled punts allowed the Bills to blow two more scoring chances. The first glanced off Jerry Logan and was recovered by Buffalo's Dave Washington at the Bills 49 with 1:45 left in the first half. But the offense stumbled and Spike Jones punted. Again, the Colts fumbled and Dale Farley recovered at the Colts 29 with 1:16 left. This time, Shaw was intercepted by Charlie Stukes.
• The second half was more productive in terms of yardage, but the Bills never scored, even though Mike Taliaferro replaced Shaw.
• Robert Irsay, who bought the Colts before the season for $16 million, was presented a game ball.

QUOTES

• Lou Saban: "Dennis had a very bad day. I'm not quitting on Dennis, I don't think I'll ever quit on the young man. I still feel he is a promising quarterback. We played horrible football on offense, but I thought the defense played pretty well. As well as we played on offense last week, we played as poorly this week."
• Dennis Shaw: "I can't believe this. I don't want to talk about this game."
• Paul Guidry: "We can't give up on the offense. I keep telling the guys things will pick up and we've got to work to get the turnovers for the offense. You won't find us giving up."
• Colts quarterback Johnny Unitas: "I wasn't throwing well. I was over-shooting receivers, throwing too often to the wrong man and missing the open man. And we folded too many times in third-down situations. You can't do that against the good defensive teams we have to face and expect to win."

Patriots	7	0	0	7 - 14
Bills	3	28	7	0 - 38

Attendance at War Memorial Stadium - 41,749

NE: Ashton 1 run (Gogolak kick), 7:29
Buf: FG Leypoldt 11, 13:16
Buf: Braxton 1 run (Leypoldt kick), 3:15
Buf: J.D. Hill 36 pass from Shaw (Leypoldt kick), 4:56
Buf: Braxton 1 run (Leypoldt kick), 9:58
Buf: Simpson 11 run (Leypoldt kick), 14:30
Buf: Chandler 43 pass from Shaw (Leypoldt kick), 2:03
NE: Dowling 1 run (Gogolak kick), 9:51

	BUF	NE
First downs	19	23
Rushing yds	145	110
Passing yds	160	224
Punts-avg	4-32.5	4-29.6
Fumbles-lost	2-2	2-1
Penalties-yds	4-35	4-34

BILLS LEADERS: Rushing - Simpson 13-31, Braxton 15-58, Patrick 9-21, Jackson 5-14, Shaw 2-12, Koy 1-9; **Passing** - Shaw 7-10-0 - 125, Simpson 2-3-0 - 53; **Receiving** - J.D. Hill 2-47, Chandler 3-88, Braxton 3-34, Patrick 1-9.

PATRIOTS LEADERS: Rushing - Garrett 15-45, Ashton 13-45, Maitland 4-13, Dowling 1-1, Plunkett 1-6; **Passing** - Plunkett 13-30-3 - 198, Dowling 4-8-0 - 70, Studstill 0-1-0 - 0; **Receiving** - Garrett 2-61, Rucker 7-103, Beer 2-40, Vataha 3-29, Gladieux 1-22, Maitland 1-8, Ashton 1-5.

WEEK 4 GAMES

SD 23, Balt 20	Cinc 21, Den 10
KC 31, Clev 7	Oak 34, Hou 0
Mia 27, NYJ 17	Dal 17, Pitt 13
Det 26, Atl 23	GB 20, Chi 17
St.L 19, Min 17	LA 31, SF 7
NYG 45, NO 21	Wash 14, Phil 0

NOTES

• The Pats took an early lead on Josh Ashton's one-yard plunge, but then the Bills took control of the game. Ex-Bill Bob Gladieux fumbled a punt and Ted Koy returned it to the Pats 2. The Bills failed to get into the end zone, but John Leypoldt kicked a field goal to make it 7-3.
• With the wind at their backs, the Bills then scored 28 second-quarter points. After a short punt, the Bills drove 53 yards in seven plays to take the lead.
• New England drove to the Bills 9, but Al Cowlings hit Jim Plunkett and forced an ill-advised pass that Ken Lee intercepted and returned 61 yards to the Pats 36. On the next play, Dennis Shaw hit J.D. Hill for a TD and a 17-7 lead.
• On their next possession, the Bills drove 55 yards in seven plays to Jim Braxton's second TD, the key play being O.J. Simpson's 34-yard option pass to Bob Chandler.
• Lee then intercepted his second pass and returned it 41 yards to the 11 and Simpson scored on the next play to make it 31-7 at the half.
• Plunkett, the 1971 Rookie of the Year who had thrown 10 interceptions in three career games against the Bills, was benched in the fourth quarter for the first time in his brief pro career.

QUOTES

• Lou Saban on Ken Lee: "Lee got us the ball twice and has been a big help to us. I don't know why he was ever put on waivers." (On Dennis Shaw): "He did the job with everybody staring him in the eye."
• Pats coach Johnny Mazur: "Mistakes, that's what did it. Two interceptions and a fumble led to 17 points and we were in a hole we couldn't get out of. As far as Plunkett is concerned, all the great ones go through those kinds of bad days."
• Robert James on Lee's first interception followed by Hill's TD: "Those two plays turned the game around. If New England had gone in to score that touchdown, it would have been a much tougher game for us. We wanted to force him (Plunkett) into making mistakes, into throwing the kinds of passes he was throwing."
• Al Cowlings on hitting Plunkett: "When that happened, Plunkett shouldn't have thrown the ball. I think Jim is a great quarterback, but he did the same thing when he was at Stanford that he does as a pro - he throws the ball at times when he should eat it."
• Dennis Shaw: "Coach Saban had a perfect game plan. He sent us into a quick cadence offense, no five and six counts. We didn't give them time to make defensive adjustments."

STANDINGS: FOURTH WEEK

AFC EAST	W	L	T	CENTRAL	W	L	T	WEST	W	L	T	NFC EAST	W	L	T	CENTRAL	W	L	T	WEST	W	L	T
Miami	4	0	0	Cincinnati	3	1	0	Kan. City	3	1	0	Dallas	3	1	0	Green Bay	3	1	0	LA Rams	2	1	1
NY Jets	2	2	0	Pittsburgh	2	2	0	Oakland	2	1	1	Washington	3	1	0	Detroit	3	1	0	Atlanta	2	2	0
Buffalo	2	2	0	Cleveland	2	2	0	San Diego	2	1	1	NY Giants	2	2	0	Minnesota	1	3	0	San Fran	2	2	0
New England	2	2	0	Houston	1	3	0	Denver	1	3	0	St. Louis	2	2	0	Chicago	0	3	1	N. Orleans	0	4	0
Baltimore	1	3	0									Philadelphia	0	4	0								

NOTES

• The Bills remained winless in California since Nov. 24, 1966, as the Raiders rolled to victory. Overall, it was Oakland's sixth straight win over the Bills, all with ex-Bill QB Daryle Lamonica.

• The Bills owned a 13-0 halftime lead and led 16-7 after three quarters, but mistakes killed them.

• Lamonica hit Charlie Smith for 43 yards and Raymond Chester for 23 to set up Marv Hubbard's one-yard plunge early in the fourth that made it 16-14.

• The Bills then failed to get a first down when O.J. Simpson was stuffed on third-and-one, and the Bills punted. Three plays later, Robert James was penalized for interfering with Fred Biletnikoff and the 33-yard penalty helped the Raiders drive to the go-ahead score, Clarence Davis' seven-yard run with 2:57 left.

• Trying to rally, the Bills had an apparent first down on a pass to Wayne Patrick, but a clipping penalty on J.D. Hill set them back into a hole and they couldn't climb out. They turned the ball over on downs and Davis broke a 20-yard TD run with 52 seconds left to clinch the win.

• Lamonica completed only two of his first 14 passes and Biletnikoff was held without a reception.

• Down 13-0, the Raiders got a huge break when Cliff Branch fumbled a punt, but Dan Conners recovered at the 45. On the next play, Lamonica hit Chester for a 55-yard TD as Chester beat Alvin Wyatt.

QUOTES

• O.J. Simpson: "They didn't deserve to win the game. Oakland is an excellent team, maybe the most balanced team in football. But when their defensive line gets pushed around like our offensive line pushed them, they just don't deserve to win. I thought the Raiders were ripe for us. We had them down, but we couldn't knock them out."

• Raiders coach John Madden: "We were mad at ourselves at halftime and came out and did something about it."

• Raiders owner Al Davis: "This is the most disciplined offense a Buffalo team has had in years. And their defense was forcing us into mistakes for three quarters of the game. They are going to be a good football team pretty soon, if they don't get down over this loss and they hold themselves together. They're going to be a good team before a lot of people expect them to be."

• John Leypoldt: "I was standing right at the sideline when Lamonica threw that pass to Biletnikoff. When he threw it, Robert (James) looked back and dove for the ball. The only contact he made was his right hand hit Biletnikoff's shoulder, but it just grazed him. The pass was overthrown and neither Robert or Biletnikoff would have caught it."

WEEK 5 GAMES

Dal 21, Balt 0	Cinc 23, KC 16
Chi 17, Clev 0	Minn 23, Den 20
Pitt 24, Hou 7	Mia 24, SD 10
NYJ 41, NE 13	Atl 21, NO 14
GB 24, Det 23	LA 34, Phil 3
NYG 23, SF 17	Wash 33, St.L 3

Bills	3	10	0	3	-	16
Raiders	0	0	7	21	-	28

Attendance at Oakland-Alameda County Coliseum - 53,501

Buf: FG Leypoldt 32, 12:36
Buf: FG Leypoldt 31, 5:44
Buf: J.D. Hill 39 pass from Shaw (Leypoldt kick), 8:36
Oak: Chester 55 pass from Lamonica (Blanda kick), 10:51
Buf: FG Leypoldt 2, 2:06
Oak: Hubbard 1 run (Blanda kick), 4:18
Oak: Davis 7 run (Blanda kick), 12:03
Oak: Davis 20 run (Blanda kick), 14:08

	BUF	OAK
First downs	16	22
Rushing yds	181	215
Passing yds	114	181
Punts-avg	5-38.4	6-42.0
Fumbles-lost	0-0	1-0
Penalties-yds	7-77	7-67

BILLS LEADERS: Rushing - Simpson 28-144, Braxton 13-30, Shaw 4-7; **Passing** - Shaw 14-21-1 - 125, Simpson 1-1-0 - 14, Jones 0-1-0 - 0; **Receiving** - J.D. Hill 3-52, Chandler 2-21, Braxton 6-49, Simpson 2-9, Patrick 2-8.

RAIDERS LEADERS: Rushing - Hubbard 20-122, Davis 6-56, Smith 5-20, Banaszak 3-17; **Passing** - Lamonica 10-26-2 - 192; **Receiving** - Chester 4-84, Siani 2-30, Davis 2-30, Smith 1-43, Hubbard 1-5.

NOTES

• The Bills lost their 12th straight road game and enabled Miami to remain unbeaten at 6-0.

• The Bills did not get a first down in the first half for the second time this season, yet they led, 13-7, at the break.

• Dennis Shaw was benched in the third quarter in favor of Mike Taliaferro. Earl Morrall, 38, made his first start for Miami with Bob Griese out for the rest of the regular season with a knee injury.

• The Dolphins led 7-0 and gambled on fourth-and-goal from the 1 in the first, but the Bills held and then drove to their first score, a 35-yard John Leypoldt field goal.

• In the second quarter, two holding penalties in a row forced a second-and-36 for Miami and Morrall was intercepted by Ken Lee who returned it 16 yards for a TD and a 10-7 Buffalo lead.

• Another break led to Leypoldt's 34-yard field goal 44 seconds before halftime. Dave Washington tipped a pass intended for Mercury Morris and the ball fell to the ground incomplete. Morris ignored it, but the officials ruled the pass a lateral and Don Croft recovered for the Bills. When Miami coach Don Shula grabbed one of the officials, a 15-yard penalty was tacked on, setting up Leypoldt for the field goal.

• Early in the third, Manny Fernandez stole a handoff from Shaw and that led to Larry Csonka's TD. Midway through the quarter, the Dolphins blocked a punt and recovered at the Bills 26, but because of penalties, were pushed back to the 47, so Garo Yepremian kicked a 54-yard field goal, the longest in Miami history.

• Mercury Morris' winning TD run stood up despite an obvious hold by tackle Norm Evans.

• The Bills drew within 24-23 when they drove 64 yards in 11 plays with Taliaferro at QB. Jim Braxton converted a fourth-down play, then took Taliaferro's TD pass, but it wasn't enough.

QUOTES

• Lou Saban on benching Shaw: "I made the switch because I thought a change just might get us going. Shaw will start next week. Two plays and we could be 4-2 instead of 2-4. All it takes is a little guts, a little courage, a little talent. (The two plays were a holding penalty on Robert James that kept alive Miami's winning TD drive and James' interference on Fred Biletnikoff the week before in Oakland)."

• Dolphins coach Don Shula: "Buffalo is a far, far better team than it has been the last couple of years. One of the reasons is Lou made some excellent claims off the waiver wire."

WEEK 6 GAMES

NYJ 24, Balt 20	LA 15, Cinc 12
Clev 23, Hou 17	Den 30, Oak 23
Phil 21, KC 20	Pitt 33, NE 3
NYG 27, St.L 21	Atl 10, GB 9
Chi 13, Minn 10	SF 20, NO 20
Wash 24, Dal 20	Det 34, SD 20

Bills	0	13	0	10	-	23
Dolphins	7	0	10	7	-	24

Attendance at the Orange Bowl - 80,010

Mia: Morris 5 run (Yepremian kick), 7:28
Buf: FG Leypoldt 35, 2:36
Buf: Lee 16 interception return (Leypoldt kick), 5:44
Buf: FG Leypoldt 34, 14:16
Mia: Csonka 10 run (Yepremian kick), 1:54
Buf: FG Leypoldt 45, :16
Mia: Yepremian 54, 8:14
Mia: Morris 15 run (Yepremian kick), 5:42
Buf: Braxton 6 pass from Taliaferro (Leypoldt kick), 13:53

	BUF	MIA
First downs	11	20
Rushing yds	153	230
Passing yds	24	80
Punts-avg	6-37.5	2-37.0
Fumbles-lost	2-1	3-3
Penalties-yds	6-66	5-91

BILLS LEADERS: Rushing - Simpson 16-57, Braxton 9-75, Taliaferro 1-14, Jones 1-8, Patrick 2-6, Shaw 3-(-7); **Passing** - Shaw 3-6-0 - 29, Taliaferro 4-12-0 - 16; **Receiving** - J.D. Hill 2-17, Chandler 2-9, Braxton 2-18, Simpson 1-1.

DOLPHINS LEADERS: Rushing - Csonka 18-107, Kiick 25-81, Morris 5-35, Morrall 3-7; **Passing** - Morrall 6-10-1 - 91; **Receiving** - Twilley 2-41, Warfield 2-33, Kiick 2-17.

STANDINGS: SIXTH WEEK

AFC EAST	W	L	T	CENTRAL	W	L	T	WEST	W	L	T	NFC EAST	W	L	T	CENTRAL	W	L	T	WEST	W	L	T
Miami	6	0	0	Cincinnati	4	2	0	Oakland	3	2	1	Washington	5	1	0	Green Bay	4	2	0	LA Rams	4	1	1
NY Jets	4	2	0	Pittsburgh	4	2	0	Kan. City	3	3	0	Dallas	4	2	0	Detroit	4	2	0	Atlanta	4	2	0
Buffalo	2	4	0	Cleveland	3	3	0	San Diego	2	3	1	NY Giants	4	2	0	Chicago	2	3	1	San Fran	2	3	1
New England	2	4	0	Houston	1	5	0	Denver	2	4	0	St. Louis	2	4	0	Minnesota	2	4	0	N. Orleans	0	5	1
Baltimore	1	5	0									Philadelphia	1	5	0								

Steelers	0	17	7	14 - 38
Bills	0	0	7	14 - 21

Attendance at War Memorial Stadium - 45,882

Pit: Harris 2 run (Gerela kick), 3:33
Pit: Bradshaw 1 run (Gerela kick), 7:19
Pit: FG Gerela 29, 14:26
Buf: Simpson 94 run (Leypoldt kick), 8:32
Pit: Harris 18 run (Gerela kick), 14:06
Buf: Chandler 11 pass from Shaw (Leypoldt kick), 5:44
Pit: Harris 17 pass from Bradshaw (Gerela kick), 6:06
Buf: Chandler 4 pass from Shaw (Leypoldt kick), 9:29
Pit: Fuqua 4 run (Gerela kick), 13:02

	BUF	PIT
First downs	24	18
Rushing yds	249	207
Passing yds	164	93
Punts-avg	2-36.5	3-43.3
Fumbles-lost	1-0	1-0
Penalties-yds	3-23	6-64

BILLS LEADERS: Rushing - Simpson 22-189, Braxton 9-28, Chandler 3-27, Shaw 1-6, Taliaferro 3-(-1); **Passing** - Shaw 12-17-2 - 102, Taliaferro 5-10-2 - 62, Jones 1-1-0 - 4, Simpson 0-1-0 - 0; **Receiving** - J.D. Hill 6-52, Chandler 7-94, White 1-11, Simpson 3-7, Washington 1-4.

STEELERS LEADERS: Rushing - Harris 15-131, Fuqua 10-61, Davis 5-9, Bradshaw 2-6; **Passing** - Bradshaw 9-17-1 - 93; **Receiving** - Fuqua 3-21, Harris 1-17, Lewis 2-23, McMakin 1-13, Shanklin 1-14, Davis 1-5.

NOTES

• Despite not even starting, rookie Franco Harris rushed for 131 yards and scored three TDs, which proved more important than O.J. Simpson's 189 yards and team-record 94-yard TD run. Simpson's run was the longest in pro football since 1950 and his yardage total ranked second in team history to Cookie Gilchrist's 243-yard output in a 1963 game against the New York Jets.

• The Steelers led 17-0 at the half, due largely to Buffalo mistakes. Jack Ham intercepted a Dennis Shaw pass at the Bills 18 and that led to Terry Bradshaw's one-yard sneak. Late in the half, Spike Jones faked a punt, but his pass to Dave Washington came up four yards shy of the first down and the Steelers wound up getting a 29-yard field goal by Roy Gerela 36 seconds before halftime.

• Early in the third, a Steeler punt was downed at the 1. But Simpson electrified the crowd with his run and the Bills were back in it, but only briefly.

• On the Bills' next series, backup QB Mike Taliaferro's pass to Simpson was intercepted by Mel Blount and returned 34 yards to the Bills 18. Harris scored on the next play.

• Buffalo got within 24-14 when Dennis Shaw, who was reinserted, hit Bob Chandler for a TD to cap an 80-yard drive, but Steve Davis returned the ensuing kickoff 82 yards and on the next play, Terry Bradshaw threw to Harris for the TD and a 31-14 lead.

• Saban used an unbalanced line with three tackles and it worked very well for a season-high 413 yards.

• The 38 points was Pittsburgh's highest total since Chuck Noll took over as coach in 1969.

QUOTES

• Steelers owner Art Rooney: "Next to "Whizzer" White (now a Supreme Court Justice), Harris looks like he'll be our best No. 1 draftee in history."

• Steelers coach Chuck Noll: "The crowd really picked the Bills up after O.J.'s great run, but each time they took the momentum, we took it away like on Davis' kickoff return. The score then was 24-14 and Steve's play was a tremendous one for us."

• Steelers running back Franco Harris: "I wasn't disappointed and I won't be disappointed if I don't start next week."

• Lou Saban on the quarterback situation: "I have no thoughts about making any changes. The players don't have a bad attitude toward Dennis. They were all at his house for a Halloween party a couple nights ago. Dennis was having a rough go and I hoped a change would get things going as it sometimes has in the past. I wasn't happy with the quarterbacking. He realizes he makes mistakes and why certain moves are made. Defensively, this was our worst game since the opener."

WEEK 7 GAMES

Mia 23, Balt 0	Cinc 30, Hou 7
Clev 27, Den 20	KC 26, SD 14
NYJ 34, NE 10	Oak 45, LA 17
SF 49, Atl 14	Chi 27, St.L 10
Dal 28, Det 24	Minn 27, GB 13
NO 21, Phil 3	Wash 23, NYG 16

Dolphins	10	6	7	7 - 30
Bills	6	7	3	0 - 16

Attendance at War Memorial Stadium - 46,206

Mia: FG Yepremian 33, 4:44
Buf: Jackson 13 pass from Shaw (kick blocked), 11:08
Mia: Morris 22 run (Yepremian kick), 14:50
Mia: FG Yepremian 17, 3:51
Mia: FG Yepremian 16, 8:12
Buf: Greene 39 interception return (Leypoldt kick), 12:59
Mia: Fleming 7 pass from Morrall (Yepremian kick), 6:41
Buf: FG Leypoldt 28, 10:24
Mia: Morris 4 run (Yepremian kick), 11:05

	BUF	MIA
First downs	12	21
Rushing yds	73	254
Passing yds	99	73
Punts-avg	5-28.8	3-44.0
Fumbles-lost	0-0	0-0
Penalties-yds	3-35	5-35

BILLS LEADERS: Rushing - Simpson 13-45, Braxton 7-20, Shaw 2-4, Jackson 2-3, Patrick 1-1; **Passing** - Shaw 12-23-2 - 125; **Receiving** - J.D. Hill 4-55, Simpson 3-20, Chandler 2-13, Harrison 1-16, Jackson 1-13, Braxton 1-8.

DOLPHINS LEADERS: Rushing - Csonka 17-72, Kiick 12-63, Morris 11-106, Ginn 3-19, Morrall 1-4, Warfield 1-(-10); **Passing** - Morrall 5-14-1 - 89; **Receiving** - Twilley 1-12, Fleming 2-38, Mandich 1-13, Morris 1-26.

NOTES

• The Dolphins improved to 8-0 by beating the Bills for the sixth time in a row.

• The Bills tried a 3-4 defense to contain Miami's running game, but poor tackling and great running enabled the Dolphins to gain 254 yards on the ground.

• The Bills managed only one first down in the fourth quarter.

• Mercury Morris' 33-yard run led to Miami's first score, a 33-yard Garo Yepremian field goal. After the Bills got a TD pass from Dennis Shaw to Randy Jackson, Morris broke three tackles on his way to a 22-yard TD run with 10 seconds left in the first quarter.

• After two more Yepremian field goals, Tony Greene picked off an Earl Morrall pass and went 39 yards for a TD to cut the Bills deficit to 16-13 just before halftime.

• The Bills would have been in the lead, but holder Bob Chandler mishandled a snap after Jackson's TD and later, new center Remi Prudhomme's bad snap aborted a 27-yard John Leypoldt field goal. Also, with 13 seconds left in the half, the Bills got to the Miami 20 and Lou Saban tried to get the touchdown, but Shaw was picked off by Tim Foley, killing the threat.

• Early in the third, a key sequence doomed the Bills. On third-and-two, John Pitts appeared to stop Larry Csonka short of the first down. A poor mark by the officials angered defensive lineman Jerry Patton who used a curse word while venting his anger to the official and a 15-yard unsportsmanlike penalty moved the ball to the Buffalo 30. Four plays later, Earl Morrall hit Marv Fleming for a TD to make it 23-13.

• The Dolphins put away the game when Jake Scott intercepted Shaw and returned it to the Bills 47. Then Morris made a 26-yard pass reception and eventually scored on a four-yard run.

QUOTES

• Dolphins running back Mercury Morris on his preference for natural grass: "I love it. To me, there's nothing like it for cutting, holding your balance, doing all the things a runner has to do."

• Lou Saban on Patton's penalty: "His (the official's) explanation to me was that obscene language was used. Well, he's going to hear a lot of that in the heat of a tough football game. I asked Jerry and he said 'the so-and-so didn't make it.' I expect to get the truth from my players and I believe Jerry. As far as I'm concerned, that was the ballgame, and the great running of Mercury Morris. But one of the things I'm proud about is Morrall thought he could beat our secondary and he found out he couldn't."

WEEK 8 GAMES

Balt 24, NE 17	Clev 20, Hou 0
Pitt 40, Cinc 17	NYG 29, Den 17
KC 27, Oak 14	Wash 35, NYJ 17
Dal 34, SD 28	LA 20, Atl 7
Det 14, Chi 0	GB 34, SF 24
Minn 37, NO 6	Phil 6, St.L 6

STANDINGS: EIGHTH WEEK

AFC EAST	W	L	T	CENTRAL	W	L	T	WEST	W	L	T	NFC EAST	W	L	T	CENTRAL	W	L	T	WEST	W	L	T
Miami	8	0	0	Pittsburgh	6	2	0	Kan. City	5	3	0	Washington	7	1	0	Green Bay	5	3	0	LA Rams	5	2	1
NY Jets	5	3	0	Cincinnati	5	3	0	Oakland	4	3	1	Dallas	6	2	0	Detroit	5	3	0	Atlanta	4	4	0
Baltimore	2	6	0	Cleveland	5	3	0	San Diego	2	5	1	NY Giants	5	3	0	Minnesota	4	4	0	San Fran	3	4	1
New England	2	6	0	Houston	1	7	0	Denver	2	6	0	St. Louis	2	5	1	Chicago	3	4	1	N. Orleans	1	6	1
Buffalo	2	6	0									Philadelphia	1	6	1								

GAME 9 - Sunday, Nov. 12, 1972 - JETS 41, BILLS 3

NOTES

• The Bills lost their fifth in a row and also their 13th straight on the road.

• Before the game during warm-ups, New York's Ed Bell and Buffalo's Linzy Cole collided. Bell was carried off on a stretcher with a concussion. Jerome Barkum replaced him and had a big game.

• Again, ineffective Dennis Shaw was benched in favor of Mike Taliaferro in the second half.

• O.J. Simpson fumbled on the first play of the game, leading to the Jets' first TD.

• The Bills only decent drive of the day, a 15-play, 78-yard march on which Simpson gained 54 yards, ended at the 2 when Simpson was stopped on third down and John Leypoldt had to kick a nine-yard field goal.

• Chris Farasopoulos' 34-yard punt return to the 25 set up Emerson Boozer's one-yard run, a TD that never should have occurred as three Bills failed to recover a Boozer fumble at the 6.

• A Spike Jones punt that was returned to the Bills 30 was nullified when the Bills accepted an offside penalty against the Jets. On the re-kick, Jones shanked it 10 yards to the 16. The defense forced a field goal attempt, but Jerry Patton was penalized for holding, giving the Jets the chance to take the points off and go for a TD, which they got when Joe Namath passed to Boozer.

• Farasopoulos' interception led to Bobby Howfield's field goal with 25 seconds left in the half.

• The Jets surprised the Bills with an on-side kick, which they recovered, to start the second half. Four plays later, Namath hit Rich Caster for a TD.

QUOTES

• O.J. Simpson: "I've cried with these guys, I want to drink champagne with them. I could have made a lot of a hullabaloo about getting out of Buffalo, but a lot of other guys are stuck here, if that's the word, and they can't get out."

• Lou Saban: "We don't have an offensive line. We haven't had one since the beginning of the season. I'm not worried about morale, I think these guys are still fighting for their lives. Anyway, they can't afford to slack off because they know their status next season depends on what they do now."

• Don Croft: "We had some breakdowns (in the defensive line) but we came on in bad field position several times. When we play at our best, we're not that bad of a team."

WEEK 9 GAMES

SF 24, Balt 21	Oak 20, Cinc 14
Clev 21, SD 17	Den 16, LA 10
Phil 18, Hou 7	Pitt 16, KC 7
Mia 52, NE 0	Atl 36, NO 20
GB 23, Chi 17	Dal 33, St.L 24
Minn 16, Det 14	Wash 27, NYG 13

Bills	3	0	0	0 -	3
Jets	7	17	7	10 -	41

Attendance at Shea Stadium - 62,853

NYJ: Riggins 1 run (Howfield kick), 4:26
Buf: FG Leypoldt 9, 12:49
NYJ: Boozer 1 run (Howfield kick), 6:10
NYJ: Boozer 4 pass from Namath (Howfield kick), 11:09
NYJ: FG Howfield 26, 14:35
NYJ: Caster 26 pass from Namath (Howfield kick), 2:43
NYJ: FG Howfield 25, 6:52
NYJ: Barkum 9 pass from Davis (Howfield kick), 10:05

	BUF	NYJ
First downs	11	17
Rushing yds	143	148
Passing yds	67	141
Punts-avg	3-33.3	3-30.3
Fumbles-lost	2-1	1-0
Penalties-yds	8-69	5-45

BILLS LEADERS: Rushing - Simpson 20-89, Braxton 5-15, Shaw 3-24, Hill 1-11, Taliaferro 1-1, Jackson 1-3; **Passing** - Shaw 7-16-2 - 113, Taliaferro 2-4-1 - 31; **Receiving** - J.D. Hill 2-23, Chandler 4-78, Braxton 2-25, White 1-18.

JETS LEADERS: Rushing - Riggins 14-64, Boozer 16-54, Bjorkland 6-14, McClain 3-9, Davis 2-7; **Passing** - Namath 6-12-1 - 106, Davis 3-4-0 - 49; **Receiving** - Barkum 4-67, Maynard 1-18, Caster 1-26, Riggins 1-5, Boozer 1-4, Bjorkland 1-35.

GAME 10 - Sunday, Nov. 19, 1972 - BILLS 27, PATRIOTS 24

NOTES

• The Bills put on a miraculous rally to score 10 points in the final 46 seconds to pull out the victory and snap their 13-game road losing streak and five-game winless skein this season.

• Earlier in the week, Patriots coach Johnny Mazur, the ex-Bills assistant, quit and was replaced by Phil Bengston.

• Mike Walker's 36-yard field goal with 1:55 left gave the Pats a 24-17 lead, but Linzy Cole returned the ensuing kickoff 51 yards to the New England 47. Three plays later, Dennis Shaw hit Bob Chandler with a 42-yard TD pass that tied the game with 51 seconds left.

• Jim Plunkett then threw two incompletions and his third pass was picked off by Maurice Tyler who

returned it 29 yards to the Pats 37 before going out of bounds with 10 seconds left.

• Lou Saban opted not to risk a play, so he sent in John Leypoldt and he made a game-winning 45-yard field goal.

• The Pats took a 7-0 lead on Plunkett's only first-half completion in 11 attempts, an 18-yard TD to Randy Vataha. It was set up when punter Pat Studstill turned a bad snap into an ad-libbed run for a first down.

• The Bills responded with 17 second-quarter points, but the Pats regained the lead at 21-17 when Plunkett hit Bob Windsor for 20 yards to set up their two-yard connection on the first series of the second half. Later, O.J. Simpson's fumble resulted in Plunkett's one-yard TD pass to John Tarver.

QUOTES

• John Leypoldt: "I was determined to take enough time and not rush it and I really took my time on it. The line has been giving me great protection all season, I haven't been close to having a kick blocked. So I said to myself 'take all the time you need.' Wow, that felt good. I had that 38-yarder in the preseason against New Orleans, but that doesn't come close to this. I mean this one counted and we needed it. I was roughed after I kicked it, I don't know who hit me, but we were lying side by side and he asked me 'Is it good?' and I said 'I don't know. But I soon found out it was good. That was the most important kick I've ever made."

• O.J. Simpson: "My longest gain was 13 yards, so it was the offensive line that was getting that yardage for me."

• Maurice Tyler: "We were playing a prevent defense with double coverage on the outside receivers on my second interception. When I intercepted, there was a whole bunch of open field so I tried to jitter-bug and run and get us into field goal range."

Bills	0	17	0	10 -	27
Patriots	7	0	14	3 -	24

Attendance at Schaefer Stadium - 60,999

NE: Vataha 32 pass from Plunkett (Walker kick), 14:08
Buf: Simpson 13 run (Leypoldt kick), 4:44
Buf: FG Leypoldt 44, 9:56
Buf: Patrick 7 pass from Shaw (Leypoldt kick), 14:41
NE: Windsor 2 pass from Plunkett (Walker kick), 2:34
NE: Tarver 1 run (Walker kick), 10:13
NE: FG Walker 36, 13:05
Buf: Chandler 42 pass from Shaw (Leypoldt kick), 14:09
Buf: FG Leypoldt 45, 14:55

	BUF	NE
First downs	19	15
Rushing yds	179	104
Passing yds	105	183
Punts-avg	8-41.3	7-40.1
Fumbles-lost	5-4	2-1
Penalties-yds	8-60	6-59

BILLS LEADERS: Rushing - Simpson 22-103, Braxton 6-43, Patrick 7-33; **Passing** - Shaw 11-25-0 - 132; **Receiving** - J.D. Hill 2-25, Chandler 4-71, Braxton 1-16, White 1-12, Patrick 3-8.

PATRIOTS LEADERS: Rushing - Ashton 24-66, Plunkett 4-29, Tarver 7-16, Gladieux 2-1, Rucker 1-(-8); **Passing** - Plunkett 9-23-2 - 208; **Receiving** - Rucker 2-77, Vataha 1-32, Windsor 5-72, Reynolds 1-27.

WEEK 10 GAMES

Balt 20, Cinc 19	Oak 37, Den 20
Clev 26, Pitt 24	GB 23, Hou 10
SD 27, KC 17	Mia 28, NYJ 24
Wash 24, Atl 13	SF 34, Chi 21
Dal 28, Phil 7	Det 27, NO 14
Minn 45, LA 41	NYG 13, St.L 7

STANDINGS: TENTH WEEK

AFC EAST	W	L	T	CENTRAL	W	L	T	WEST	W	L	T	NFC EAST	W	L	T	CENTRAL	W	L	T	WEST	W	L	T
Miami	10	0	0	Pittsburgh	7	3	0	Oakland	6	3	1	Washington	9	1	0	Green Bay	7	3	0	LA Rams	5	4	1
NY Jets	6	4	0	Cleveland	7	3	0	Kan. City	5	5	0	Dallas	8	2	0	Detroit	6	4	0	San Fran	5	4	1
Baltimore	3	7	0	Cincinnati	5	5	0	San Diego	3	6	1	NY Giants	6	4	0	Minnesota	6	4	0	Atlanta	5	5	0
Buffalo	3	7	0	Houston	1	9	0	Denver	3	7	0	Philadelphia	2	7	1	Chicago	3	6	1	N. Orleans	1	8	1
New England	2	8	0									St. Louis	2	7	1								

GAME 11 - Sunday, Nov. 26, 1972 - BROWNS 27, BILLS 10

Bills	10	0	0	0	- 10
Browns	0	10	7	10	- 27

Attendance at Cleveland Stadium - 70,104

Buf: Simpson 6 run (Leypoldt kick), 1:30
Buf: FG Leypoldt 38, 5:22
Cle: FG Cockroft 33, 8:19
Cle: Kelly 13 pass from Phipps (Cockroft kick), 14:16
Cle: Brown 1 run (Cockroft kick), 8:18
Cle: Roman 36 interception return (Cockroft kick), 1:12
Cle: FG Cockroft 49, 9:19

	BUF	CLE
First downs	12	16
Rushing yds	147	132
Passing yds	28	121
Punts-avg	9-37.0	6-39.2
Fumbles-lost	7-1	1-0
Penalties-yds	2-20	3-22

BILLS LEADERS: Rushing - Simpson 27-93, Braxton 10-34, Shaw 3-17, Patrick 1-2, Hart 3-1; **Passing** - Shaw 3-6-0 - 34, Hart 2-6-1 - 22; **Receiving** - Chandler 1-13, Simpson 2-25, Braxton 1-9, Koy 1-9.

BROWNS LEADERS: Rushing - Kelly 18-58, Scott 8-40, Brown 5-25, Cornell 2-5, Lefear 1-3, Phipps 2-1; **Passing** - Phipps 11-22-2 - 145; **Receiving** - Scott 6-62, Kelly 1-13, Pitts 2-36, Glass 1-16, Morin 1-18.

WEEK 11 GAMES

Det 37, NYJ 20	SF 31, Dal 10
Balt 31, NE 0	Cinc 13, Chi 3
Atl 23, Den 20	SD 34, Hou 20
Oak 26, KC 3	Mia 31, St.L 10
Pitt 23, Min 10	Wash 21, GB 16
NO 19, LA 16	NYG 62, Phil 10

NOTES

• O.J. Simpson topped the 1,000-yard mark in rushing for the first time in his career, but the Bills fell to Cleveland, the Browns' sixth straight win.

• Dennis Shaw was knocked cold on the first play of the fourth quarter with the Bills trailing only 17-10. Leo Hart came in and his first pass was deflected by Dale Lindsey, the man who knocked out Shaw, and caromed into the hands of Nick Roman who raced 36 yards for a TD.

• Tony Greene returned the opening kickoff 66 yards and Simpson eventually scored on a six-yard run to give the Bills an early 7-0 lead, but Greene killed the Bills later on.

• After a John Leypoldt field goal on their second series made it 10-0, things began collapsing. Greene fumbled a second-quarter kickoff out of bounds at the 7 and when the Bills failed to move, they punted. Cleveland had great field position and it led to Mike Phipps' game-tying TD pass to Leroy Kelly.

• In the third, Simpson's fumble at the Bills 28 set up Ken Brown's one-yard TD for a 17-10 Browns lead and on the ensuing kickoff, Greene bobbled the ball in the end zone, tried to run out and was tackled at the 4, preventing the Bills from opening up their offense.

• Roman's play then broke open the game and Don Cockroft added a field goal later in the fourth.

• J.D. Hill, the Bills leading receiver, was held without a catch.

QUOTES

• Browns lineman Dale Lindsey: "I'm not the kind of tackler who knocks guys out. There's no threat of bodily harm when I hit you, so I was surprised when I looked back and Dennis Shaw was out cold." (On Roman's interception): "I wasn't really that close to Hart, I just threw up my arms when I saw I wasn't going to get to him. The ball hit my hands and somehow ended up in Nick's hands. We didn't plan it that way. Hart's first pass for Buffalo might not have been memorable for him, but it was for me."

• O.J. Simpson: "I'm certainly happy to get 1,000 yards, I just wish I could have gained some more pertinent yards early in the game. I was pleased that the guys wanted me to get it, but I would rather have a shot at winning the game. I'm not running any differently, I just have better blockers this year and a coach with a system geared to running."

• J.D. Hill: "I just don't understand it. I'm not getting the ball, man. They threw to me once today. Catching passes makes me go, it's my game and they're not letting me play it. In that Jets game, they didn't start throwing to me until the fourth quarter. Last week they were trying to throw bombs all day to me when they threw to me. Today it was run, run, run to get O.J. his 1,000 yards."

GAME 12 - Sunday, Dec. 3, 1972 - COLTS 35, BILLS 7

Bills	0	0	0	7	- 7
Colts	14	0	7	14	- 35

Attendance at Memorial Stadium - 55,390

Bal: McCauley 29 pass from Domres (O'Brien kick), 8:16
Bal: L. Mitchell 17 pass from Domres (O'Brien kick), 12:06
Bal: McCauley 9 pass from Domres (O'Brien kick), 14:59
Bal: Domres 15 run (O'Brien kick), 5:41
Bal: Hinton 63 pass from Unitas (O'Brien kick), 9:48
Buf: Simpson 1 run (Leypoldt kick), 14:30

	BUF	BAL
First downs	13	22
Rushing yds	100	189
Passing yds	144	202
Punts-avg	8-45.8	6-44.5
Fumbles-lost	1-1	4-0
Penalties-yds	6-82	4-57

BILLS LEADERS: Rushing - Simpson 14-26, Jackson 9-37, Braxton 4-19, Hart 2-18; **Passing** - Shaw 10-15-1 - 150, Hart 4-9-2 - 31; **Receiving** - J.D. Hill 4-78, Simpson 6-62, Chandler 1-17, Braxton 2-16, Jackson 1-8.

COLTS LEADERS: Rushing - McCauley 17-68, L. Mitchell 10-45, Domres 7-40, Nottingham 6-25, Mildren 3-8, Havrilak 1-3; **Passing** - Domres 12-24-0 - 138, Unitas 2-2-0 - 64; **Receiving** - L. Mitchell 7-69, Hinton 1-63, McCauley 5-61, T. Mitchell 1-9.

NOTES

• Leo Hart started in place of Dennis Shaw and his first pass was picked off by Rick Volk, but the Colts failed to score.

• Baltimore already had a 7-0 lead as it scored on its first possession when Don McCauley went 29 yards into the end zone with a swing pass. The drive was aided by an interference penalty on Maurice Tyler, followed by a 15-yard unsportsmanlike penalty on Lou Saban for arguing the call.

• On the second Bills series, Hart was picked off by Jerry Logan who returned it to the Bills 14. Marty Domres hit Lydell Mitchell for a 17-yard TD and a 14-0 lead. Domres completed 11 of his 12 passes to backs and despite throwing three TDs, wasn't particularly sharp.

• Baltimore didn't score again until the third when Domres kept a drive alive by scrambling for 11 yards on third-and-nine, then Tyler was nailed again for pass interference and Ken Lee was hit with a personal foul. Domres eventually hit McCauley with a nine-yard dump pass for the TD.

• In the fourth, Domres ran 15 yards for a score and was hurt on the play. Johnny Unitas, making his final appearance as a Colt in Baltimore, hit Ed Hinton on a 63-yard TD pass.

QUOTES

• Lou Saban: "At least we scored. We had to do that. We hadn't scored on this team in 17 quarters and you can't have something like that hanging over your head. We couldn't get much lower. But I felt we came up with a great many answers as to what's wrong with this team. I'm tired of looking at some of the faces we've seen the last 12 games and I despise lack of effort. I guess we were lucky to win three games. When we were down 35-0, I looked at some of the members of our squad and they seemed to be enjoying it. We've just got to make changes. I want new players. We'll put up with this for another two weeks and that will be it. At this stage, the Bills have a long way to go. It looks like a long two or three years ahead unless we get lucky. The Bills have played like this the last four years, but the fans won't have to put up with it in the future; we're going to make changes."

• Colts linebacker Mike Curtis: "I don't think we intimidate them, I just think we've executed in the last four games we've played against Buffalo."

• Colts cornerback Charlie Stukes: "It isn't that we've got their number. The way we've played this year, we don't have anybody's number."

• O.J. Simpson: "No, it (scoring) didn't feel good because it didn't mean anything. Baltimore is a very aggressive team, more aggressive than we are."

WEEK 12 GAMES

Cinc 13, NYG 10	Pitt 30, Clev 0
KC 24, Den 21	Atl 20, Hou 10
Mia 37, NE 21	NYJ 18, NO 17
Oak 21, SD 19	Minn 23, Chi 10
Dal 27, St.L 6	GB 33, Det 7
LA 26, SF 16	Wash 23, Phil 7

STANDING: TWELFTH WEEK

AFC EAST	W	L	T	CENTRAL	W	L	T	WEST	W	L	T	NFC EAST	W	L	T	CENTRAL	W	L	T	WEST	W	L	T
Miami	12	0	0	Pittsburgh	9	3	0	Oakland	8	3	1	Washington	11	1	0	Green Bay	8	4	0	Atlanta	7	5	0
NY Jets	7	5	0	Cleveland	8	4	0	Kan. City	6	6	0	Dallas	9	3	0	Detroit	7	5	0	San Fran	6	5	1
Baltimore	5	7	0	Cincinnati	7	5	0	San Diego	4	7	1	NY Giants	7	5	0	Minnesota	7	5	0	LA Rams	6	5	1
Buffalo	3	9	0	Houston	1	11	0	Denver	3	9	0	Philadelphia	2	9	1	Chicago	3	8	1	N. Orleans	2	9	1
New England	2	10	0									St. Louis	2	9	1								

NOTES

• In the final pro football game ever played at War Memorial Stadium, the Bills played an inspired tie with the Lions which helped knock Detroit out of the NFC playoff picture.

• The Bills dominated statistically in the rain and mud, but lost three fumbles and made enough mistakes to prevent victory.

• O.J. Simpson set a new team record for rushing yards (1,150 through 13 games) in a season, breaking Cookie Gilchrist's mark of 1,096 in 1962.

• The Lions took a 7-0 lead after Dennis Shaw's fumble gave them possession at the Bills 41 as Greg Landry hit Earl McCollough for a score.

• The Bills answered two minutes later when J.D. Hill beat Rudy Redmond and caught a 58-yard TD. They would have led at the half, but Simpson later lost a fumble at the 1.

• Buffalo went ahead 14-7 on its first possession in the third as six runs moved the ball to the 39 where Chandler made the catch of the year for a 39-yard TD.

• Detroit tied it when Linzy Cole fumbled a punt at the Bills 36 and on the next play, Landry hit Nick Eddy with a TD pass.

• The Bills regained the lead in the fourth with a 78-yard drive that culminated in Shaw's TD pass to Jan White, but the Lions tied it with 2:01 left when Ron Jessie beat Robert James one-on-one on a third-and-11 and hauled in a 37-yard TD pass.

• A holding penalty against Bobby Penchion forced the Bills into a first-and-25 at their own 26 after the kickoff, and Saban kept the ball on the ground and the Bills had to punt with 1:09 left. Detroit was unable to move and the game ended in a tie.

QUOTES

• Lou Saban on not going for the win: "They were looking for the pass with the extra linebacker. It was a 3-8 ratio and if you throw into that, you have a good chance of throwing an interception and I wasn't about to do it." (On the effort of his players): "They knew I was down about the way we played in Baltimore. They all kept saying 'Don't give up on us coach, we're not giving up on ourselves.' They've got to know what it feels like to play it all the way, to pay the price. I think they got the idea today. It's a strange feeling to get a tie and still be unhappy, but it was a great ballgame and they tied us, we didn't tie them."

• O.J. Simpson: "We should have beaten them easily."

• J.D. Hill: "This was my best day here and it sure feels good."

• Dennis Shaw: "The offense as a whole looked better. The going was so sluggish out there, it cut down on the running game."

Lions	0 7 7 7 - 21
Bills	0 7 7 7 - 21

Attendance at War Memorial Stadium - 41,583

Det:	McCollough 9 pass from Landry (Mann kick), 6:48
Buf:	J.D. Hill 58 pass from Shaw (Leypoldt kick), 8:45
Buf:	Chandler 39 pass from Shaw (Leypoldt kick), 5:07
Det:	Eddy 36 pass from Landry (Mann kick), 7:58
Buf:	White 2 pass from Shaw (Leypoldt kick), 8:22
Det:	Jessie 37 pass from Landry (Mann kick), 12:59

	BUF	DET
First downs	23	14
Rushing yds	187	116
Passing yds	231	144
Punts-avg	3-37.6	5-40.2
Fumbles-lost	5-3	0-0
Penalties-yds	5-61	2-20

BILLS LEADERS: Rushing - Simpson 27-116, Braxton 9-31, Patrick 3-21, Shaw 3-9, Jones 1-10; **Passing** - Shaw 18-32-0 - 239; **Receiving** - J.D. Hill 8-129, Simpson 3-17, Chandler 3-71, Braxton 2-14, White 2-8.

LIONS LEADERS: Rushing - Landry 9-46, Farr 9-22, Zofko 6-21, Triplett 4-13, Eddy 3-14; **Passing** - Landry 8-25-0 - 150; **Receiving** - Farr 4-54, Jessie 2-51, Eddy 1-36, McCullough 1-9.

WEEK 13 GAMES

Clev 27, Cinc 24	Dal 34, Wash 24
Den 38, SD 13	Mia 23, NYG 13
Chi 21, Phil 12	GB 23, Minn 7
SF 20, Atl 0	St.L 24, LA 14
NE 17, NO 10	Pitt 9, Hou 3
KC 24, Balt 10	Oak 24, NYJ 16

NOTES

• The Bills ended the season on a high note, pulling a stunning upset of the Redskins with two fourth-quarter touchdowns.

• With Washington's Larry Brown held out of the game because of an injury that coach George Allen wanted to rest for the playoffs, O.J. Simpson won the NFL rushing title by finishing with a team-record 1,251 yards on a team-record 292 carries.

• It was the Bills first victory in a season finale since 1966 when they beat Denver to win the AFL East Division title before losing to Kansas City in the AFL Championship Game.

• The Bills trailed 17-10 entering the fourth, but Simpson capped a scoring drive by sweeping 21 yards around right end for the tying TD with 11:17 left. Three plays before the score, Wayne Patrick covered Bob Chandler's fumble to keep the drive alive.

• Both teams sputtered on offense the rest of the way and the Redskins made the vital mistake. Billy Kilmer's pass went off Herb Mul-key's hands near midfield and Dale Farley intercepted the carom and raced 42 yards to the 3. Two plays later, Jim Braxton scored on a four-yard run with 46 seconds left to play.

• The Bills opened a 10-0 first-quarter lead when Alvin Wyatt intercepted a pass intended for Mul-key and raced untouched for a TD. John Leypoldt added a field goal later in the first.

• Washington then scored 17 points in a row before the Bills rallied to win.

QUOTES

• O.J. Simpson: "I'm going to be ready in February and I hope you guys (his teammates) are, too."

• Redskins coach George Allen: "I have been telling everyone that Buffalo was a much better team than anyone thought. You saw what happened. Lou Saban has done a fine coaching job with them. They outplayed us. Losing a game like that is like a death in the family. There's only one thing to do after a game like that and that's hide."

• Ex-Bill Ron McDole: "You think George Allen is upset now? You should be here next week with him like we have to be. The Bills are going to be a real good team. You can tell that Lou Saban is back."

• Dale Farley: "I didn't touch him (Mul-key), he just fumbled the ball away. I saw him looking at me and trying to turn the corner, then the ball just popped into the air."

• Lou Saban: "We've been known as the run-for-the-bus-gang and now I think we're over that. When you consider all the problems we've had with our offensive line, it's remarkable we could get O.J. over 1,000 yards. And I don't think he's even scratched the surface yet, I think he can do so many outstanding things."

Bills	10 0 0 14 - 24
Redskins	0 7 10 0 - 17

Attendance at RFK Stadium - 53,039

Buf:	Wyatt 49 interception return (Leypoldt kick), 5:32
Buf:	FG Leypoldt 23, 11:13
Was:	Mul-key 8 run (Knight kick), 8:00
Was:	Brunet 2 run (Knight kick), 7:49
Was:	FG Knight 35, 12:49
Buf:	Simpson 21 run (Leypoldt kick), 3:43
Buf:	Braxton 4 run (Leypoldt kick), 14:14

	BUF	WAS
First downs	17	15
Rushing yds	184	133
Passing yds	80	38
Punts-avg	6-34.0	6-37.1
Fumbles-lost	2-0	1-0
Penalties-yds	9-122	6-40

BILLS LEADERS: Rushing - Simpson 26-101, Braxton 8-30, Patrick 6-28, Shaw 5-25; **Passing** - Shaw 10-21-2 - 107; **Receiving** - J.D. Hill 2-22, Simpson 1-6, Chandler 2-23, White 4-49, Patrick 1-7.

REDSKINS LEADERS: Rushing - Mul-key 25-95, Taylor 1-17, Harraway 6-13, Brunet 3-8; **Passing** - Kilmer 4-15-3 - 62; **Receiving** - Mul-key 2-28, Jefferson 1-17, Alston 1-17.

WEEK 14 GAMES

Mia 16, Balt 0	SF 20, Minn 17
NYG 23, Dal 3	KC 17, Atl 14
Clev 26, NYJ 10	Den 45, NE 21
Det 34, LA 17	Pitt 24, SD 2
Cinc 61, Hou 17	Oak 28, Chi 21
St.L 24, Phil 23	GB 30, NO 20

STANDINGS: FOURTEENTH WEEK

AFC EAST	W	L	T	CENTRAL	W	L	T	WEST	W	L	T	NFC EAST	W	L	T	CENTRAL	W	L	T	WEST	W	L	T
Miami	14	0	0	Pittsburgh	11	3	0	Oakland	10	3	1	Washington	11	3	0	Green Bay	10	4	0	San Fran	8	5	1
NY Jets	7	7	0	Cleveland	10	4	0	Kan. City	8	6	0	Dallas	10	4	0	Detroit	8	5	1	Atlanta	7	7	0
Baltimore	5	9	0	Cincinnati	8	6	0	Denver	5	9	0	NY Giants	8	6	0	Minnesota	7	7	0	LA Rams	6	7	1
Buffalo	4	9	1	Houston	1	13	0	San Diego	4	9	1	St. Louis	4	9	1	Chicago	4	9	1	N. Orleans	2	11	1
New England	3	11	0									Philadelphia	2	11	1								

Rich Stadium became the new home of the Bills in 1973. At the time, it possessed "the most advanced scoreboard in the country."

At A Glance
1973

Jan. 12 – Defensive coordinator Jim Dooley unexpectedly resigned.

Jan. 16 – J.D. Hill was named to the AFC Pro Bowl team, joining teammates O.J. Simpson and Robert James, when Miami's Paul Warfield was forced to pull out.

Jan. 20 – It was determined by a draw of straws that the Bills would pick seventh in the upcoming draft.

Jan. 30 – The Bills selected Michigan offensive tackle Paul Seymour in the first round of the draft with the seventh pick overall, then used the first-round choice obtained in the trade that sent Marlin Briscoe to Miami to select Michigan State guard Joe DeLamielleure. They took USC defensive tackle Jeff Winans in the second round and Arkansas quarterback Joe Ferguson in the third round. They later chose defensive linemen Bob Kampa (third) and Jeff Yeates (fourth), wide receiver Wallace Francis (fifth), linebacker John Skorupan (sixth) and linebacker Merv Krakau (14th); Other first round choices included John Matuszak (Houston), Bert Jones (Baltimore), John Hannah and Darryl Stingley (New England), Chuck Foreman (Minnesota), Ray Guy (Oakland) and Johnny Rodgers (San Diego).

Feb. 14 – Veteran linebacker Paul Guidry was traded to Houston for defensive end Allen Aldridge.

Feb. 16 – Johnny Ray was hired to replace Jim Dooley and was given the responsibility of coaching the linebackers. WKBW was given another one-year contract to broadcast Bills games.

Feb. 28 – Rich Parinnello, a wide receiver who held three University of Rochester records, signed a free-agent contract with the Bills.

March 11 – At the conclusion of a three-day mini-camp at the Regency Motor Hotel in Blasdell, Lou Saban said that Dennis Shaw would be his quarterback for the 1973 season.

March 24 – Joe DeLamielleure was found to have a heart problem during his examination by team doctors and was told he would never play football or any strenuous sport again. "I wanted to play pro football for as long as I can remember," DeLamielleure said. "This is a shock, but health is something you can't buy. I have decided not to play pro football."

March 28 – Another offensive lineman, Jim Reilly, was informed that a kidney ailment would prevent him from playing football again. He missed all of the 1972 season with the problem.

March 29 – Kenneth Souliske purchased the 46,207th season ticket for the 1973 season, assuring the Bills of their largest home attendance ever. War Memorial Stadium's capacity was 46,206. Souliske was presented an official NFL ball with the number 46,207 printed on it by general manager Bob Lustig and ticket director Jim Cipriano.

April 10 – After a visit to Cleveland Clinic, where a heart catharization was performed, Joe DeLamielleure's condition was re-evaluated and the possibility of his playing football wasn't ruled out.

April 19 – The Bills traded linebackers Edgar Chandler and Jeff Lyman and fullback Wayne Patrick to New England for linebacker Jim Cheyunski, defensive lineman Halvor Hagen and center Mike Montler.

April 26 – The NFL released its 1973 schedule and the Bills were slated for their first *Monday Night Football* appearance, an October 29 game at Rich Stadium against the Kansas City Chiefs. "The image of Western New York and the Bills hasn't been that good throughout the country, but we will get a chance October 29 to show the people of the country that our image has changed for the better," Ralph

Wilson said.

April 30 – Al Cowlings, who found his way into Lou Saban's doghouse in 1972, was traded to Houston for a second-round draft choice and the No. 1 draft choice in 1970 responded bitterly. "Tell Lou Saban I'm going to come back and whup him," he said. "It's no secret I had a bad season last year and it's no secret that Saban wanted to trade me. I'm going to miss a lot of my friends in Buffalo and my dear friend, O.J. Simpson, but I'm not going to miss Saban. That man speaks with a forked-tongue and I have lost all respect for the man."

May 10 – Joe DeLamielleure was given the medical okay to resume his football career when results from the tests he underwent at Cleveland Clinic were released and showed that his heart was functional.

June 2 – Jack Horrigan, vice-president in charge of public relations the previous seven years, died after a lengthy bout with cancer at the age of 47.

June 8 – Joe DeLamielleure, the Bills' second first-round draft choice, signed his first pro contract. "Joe D reminds me in so many ways, physically and mentally, of Billy Shaw," Lou Saban said. "And he can be another Billy Shaw."

June 9 – The other first-round draft choice, Paul Seymour, signed his contract.

June 19 – L. Budd Thalman, for the past 11 years the sports information director at the Naval Academy, was hired to replace the late Jack Horrigan as vice-president of public relations.

July 17 – The Bills opened training camp at Niagara University.

July 25 – Jan White, the starting tight end the previous two years, left camp to ponder retirement.

July 26 – Third-round draft choice Joe Ferguson became the final rookie to sign his contract. He mailed the pact to the Bills because he was in Chicago preparing for the College All-Star game against the world champion Miami Dolphins.

July 28 – Joe Ferguson arrived at training camp and took part in his first drills, looking very impressive.

Aug. 4 – The Bills lost their preseason opener to Philadelphia, 13-6, at the Gator Bowl in Jacksonville, despite 95 rushing yards in 10 carries by O.J. Simpson.

Aug. 11 – Host Green Bay beat the Bills, 10-3, as the offense was punchless.

Aug. 16 – Middle linebacker Dick Cunningham was traded to Philadelphia for fullback Larry Watkins.

Aug. 17 – Rich Stadium was opened officially as the Bills played host to Washington in front of a sell-out crowd of 80,020. Herb Mul-key of the Redskins returned the opening kickoff 102 yards for a touchdown. Duane Thomas, the enigmatic former Dallas Cowboy who joined the Redskins earlier in the year, charged into the stands behind the Redskins bench after allegedly being taunted by fans for being disrespectful during the playing of the national anthem. Thomas allegedly threw his helmet into the crowd and also wielded a thermos at the fans as he climbed over the retaining wall. Because of incredible traffic jams, some fans didn't arrive until near halftime.

Aug. 26 – The Bills fell to 0-4 in the preseason with a 13-10 loss to Chicago before 61,165 at Rich Stadium.

Aug. 28 – The Bills traded guard Irv Goode to Miami for defensive tackle Mike Kadish.

Aug. 31 – The Bills fell to 0-5 as Denver beat them, 16-14.

Sept. 3 – Mike Stratton, an 11-year member of the Bills, was traded to San Diego for a draft choice.

Sept. 8 – The Bills completed the second winless preseason in team history (the first was 1961) as Oakland downed them, 17-7, before 70,128 at Rich Stadium.

Sept. 10 – Defensive end Earl Edwards was acquired in a trade for running back Randy Jackson and a future draft choice.

Sept. 14 – Congress adopted experimental legislation (for three years) requiring any NFL game that had been sold out 72 hours prior to kickoff be made available for local television broadcast.

Sept. 16 – O.J. Simpson set a new NFL record for rushing yards in a single game, totaling 250 on 29 carries as the Bills set a team record of 360 rushing yards and routed New England, 31-13, in the season opener at Schaefer Stadium.

Sept. 17 – No surprise as Simpson was named NFL player of the week. "I'll probably relish what happened Sunday more at the end of the season than now," Simpson said. "I've got no time to think about it now, San Diego is coming up Sunday and we can't go there thinking about this or we'll get blown out of the stadium."

Sept. 23 – Recently traded Mike Stratton, one of the finest players in Bills history, exacted revenge against his former team by intercepting two passes for San Diego as the Chargers routed the Bills, 34-7. Johnny Unitas, who joined the Chargers after a Hall of Fame career in Baltimore, crept to within two yards of the 40,000-yard mark in career passing and he threw his first two TD passes as a Charger.

Sept. 30 – In the first regular-season game played at Rich Stadium, a sellout crowd watched the Bills' defense turn in one of their best efforts in years in a 9-7 victory over the New York Jets.

Oct. 2 – The World Football League announced that it was in operation and would begin play in 1974.

Oct. 3 – Former first-round draft choice John Pitts (1967) was traded to Denver for veteran middle linebacker Fred Forsberg. Pitts became the third former top draft choice to be traded since Lou Saban returned as coach (Al Cowlings and Haven Moses were the others).

Oct. 7 – Tom Dempsey missed a 26-yard field goal on the game's final play and the Bills escaped with a 27-26 victory over the Eagles at Rich Stadium to improve to 3-1.

Oct. 11 – Reggie McKenzie said he not only wanted to make All-Pro this season, he wanted to eventually make the Hall of Fame and be known as the best blocker of the 1970s.

Oct. 14 – The Bills improved to 4-1 and stayed tied with Miami for first in the AFC East as O.J. Simpson rolled up 166 yards in a 31-13 rout of Baltimore before a sellout crowd at Rich Stadium.

Oct. 15 – O.J. Simpson was asked if he knew Jim Brown and he said: "I've known him ever since my USC days. We're friends. My first year there, he came to school one day and talked to me. I even met him when I was 14. A group of us kids were in an ice cream shop and he came in after a game and we started teasing him like, 'Hey man, you're not so good.' But he was. The comparison (to Brown) gives us an offensive goal to shoot at, but the linemen talk about it more than I do. We're a ball-control team and we've got to get yards rushing in order to win games. That's our goal. The pressure isn't getting 100 or 150 yards, it's getting first downs and winning."

Oct. 19 – Jimmy "The Greek" Snyder predicted the Dolphins would win by at least 15 points and laid 2-1 odds that O.J. Simpson wouldn't gain 100 yards rushing in the team's upcoming game.

Oct. 21 – Playing in their first truly big game since 1966, the Bills were no match for the defending Super Bowl champion Dolphins at the Orange Bowl, losing 27-6. O.J. Simpson was held to 55 yards and suffered an ankle sprain which ended his day early in the fourth quarter.

Oct. 28 – Making their *Monday Night Football* debut, the Bills ripped Kansas City, 23-14, as O.J. Simpson set an NFL record with 39 carries. He also went over the 1,000-yard mark in just his seventh game. Jim Brown had 971 after seven games in 1963 when he rushed for the record 1,863 yards.

Nov. 3 – The Bills' chartered plane to New Orleans had to make an emergency landing in Cleveland because of a rupture in the hydraulic line at takeoff from the Buffalo airport. Landing gear had to be brought down manually and everyone on board was told to get into the crash position. O.J. Simpson stood up after the announcement was made on the plane and said, "Can I get out the back door?"

Nov. 4 – The Bills became the Saints' first shutout victim in team history (92 games) as New Orleans held O.J. Simpson to 79 yards and won at Tulane Stadium, 13-0.

Nov. 11 – Horst Muhlmann's 33-yard field goal with one second left lifted Cincinnati past the Bills at cold, windy Rich Stadium, 16-13.

Nov. 13 – O.J. Simpson hinted that his playing career may be very short if he wins a Super Bowl. "My goal is to go to the Super Bowl and if I do and then I can find something nearly as lucrative, I will go into it," he said. "My contract with the Bills has two years to run on it and right now I see that as the end of it. However, if at the end of that time I see our team is close to the Super Bowl and I still enjoy playing, I will stay on."

Nov. 18 – Miami dealt the Bills their third straight loss, 17-0, at Rich Stadium. It was their eighth win in a row over Buffalo since the decade of the 70s began.

Nov. 25 – Dwight Harrison's 31-yard interception return for a TD lifted the Bills to a wild 24-17 victory over Baltimore. Only 23 seconds earlier, Bob Chandler had tied the game with a 37-yard TD reception. The win snapped Buffalo's three-game losing streak.

Nov. 27 – Atlanta coach Norm Van Brocklin, who earlier in the season had called Minnesota quarterback Fran Tarkenton selfish, said of O.J. Simpson: "Simpson could never play for me because he won't put his nose in there. He doesn't like contact."

Dec. 2 – The Bills went to Atlanta and outmuscled a Falcons team that prided itself on toughness and intimidation. O.J. Simpson gained 137 yards in the 17-6 victory.

Dec. 7 – Budd Thalman, the vice-president of public relations for the Bills, offered "The Electric Company" as a nickname for the team's offensive line. Asked why he chose that name, Thalman said: "Because they turn on the Juice." Thalman's two small sons regularly watched the children's television show "The Electric Company" and that's how he came up with the moniker. When they first heard of the nickname, the linemen hated it, especially line coach Jim Ringo, but they came to love it.

Dec. 9 – Despite a snow-covered slippery Rich Stadium field, O.J. Simpson tore through the Patriots for 219 yards in a 37-13 romp. Simpson totaled 469 yards in two games against New England.

Dec. 10 – Steve Sabol, executive vice-president of NFL Films Inc., said he was assigning his four best cameramen to the Bills-Jets game in Shea Stadium to capture O.J. Simpson breaking Jim Brown's rushing record.

Dec. 11 – Simpson became the first player in NFL history to win player of the week honors for the third time in one season.

Dec. 12 – Former Bill Al Cowlings joked that if Simpson took up a collection and sent the Oilers $1,000, they'd beat Cincinnati for him. In order to make the playoffs, the Bills needed to beat the Jets and hope 1-12 Houston upset the Bengals and Cleveland defeated the Los Angeles Rams.

Dec. 16 – O.J. Simpson broke Jim Brown's NFL rushing record in the first quarter, then went on to gain 200 yards to become the first player in NFL history to gain 2,000 rushing yards in a season. The Bills cruised to a 34-14 victory over the Jets at Shea Stadium, and they also set a new team rushing record of 3,088 yards, but they failed to make the playoffs because Cincinnati beat Houston, the Rams beat Cleveland and Pittsburgh downed San Francisco. After the game, in a special interview room, Simpson brought the entire offensive unit with him to meet the press. "Gentlemen, I'd like you to meet some friends of mine," Simpson said. He went on to introduce every member.

Dec. 17 – Budd Thalman revealed that he got the scare of his life upon arriving home from New York the night before. The Elias Sports Bureau informed him that Simpson originally hadbeen credited with 198 yards in the game, not 200, and thus his total for the season was 2,003, not 2,001. When Thalman took the call, he thought Elias was going to tell him Simpson hadn't reached 2,000 yards and he was trying to figure out a way to break the news to Simpson, the Electric Company and coach Lou Saban. He was gratefully relieved when yardage was added.

Dec. 19 – O.J. Simpson and the entire Bills offensive line were named co-players of the week by the AP. It was the fourth time Simpson had been named, an NFL record.

Dec. 20 – O.J. Simpson and Robert James were named to the AFC Pro Bowl squad, but guard Reggie McKenzie was overlooked. Simpson had vowed two months before that he wouldn't play in the game if McKenzie wasn't named to the team. "He's the guy opening the holes for me and I won't play without him because I know his worth," Simpson had said. Oakland's Gene Upshaw, Miami's Larry Little and Pittsburgh's Bruce Van Dyke were selected ahead of McKenzie. McKenzie received some solace when he made the AFC first-team all-UPI squad.

Dec. 22 – Oakland ripped Pittsburgh, 33-14, and Minnesota overcame Washington, 27-20, in the first day of divisional-round playoffs.

Dec. 23 – Miami stopped Cincinnati, 34-16, and Dallas beat Los Angeles, 27-16, in the second day of divisional round playoffs.

Dec. 30 – Miami whipped Oakland, 27-10, in the AFC Championship Game, as Larry Csonka ran for 117 yards and three TDs. Minnesota beat Dallas by the identical 27-10 score, in the NFC Championship Game, as the Vikings defense limited the Cowboys to 153 yards of total offense.

Jan. 13, 1974 – Larry Csonka rushed for a Super Bowl record 145 yards on 33 attempts and scored two TDs to lead the Dolphins to their second straight NFL championship, 24-7, over Minnesota at Rice Stadium.

Jan. 20, 1974 – The AFC got five field goals from Garo Yepremian and beat the NFC, 15-13, in Kansas City's Arrowhead Stadium, in the Pro Bowl.

BY THE NUMBERS - 1973

TEAM STATISTICS	BILLS	OPP
First downs	219	231
Rushing	152	101
Passing	60	112
Penalty	7	18
Total yards	4,085	3,915
Avg. game	291.8	279.6
Plays	849	855
Avg. play	4.8	4.6
Net rushing yds	3,088	1,797
Avg. game	220.6	128.4
Avg. play	5.1	3.9
Net passing yds	997	2,118
Comp/att	96/213	166/368
Sacks/lost	31-239	32-276
Interceptions	14	14
Percentage	45.1	45.1
Punts/avg	66-40.3	63-39.8
Fumbles/lost	27-13	30-19
Penalties/yds	75-744	53-485
Touchdowns	28	25
Extra points	28-28	23-25
Field goals	21-30	19-34
Safeties	0	0
Kick ret./avg	42-23.1	44-21.2
Punt ret./avg	32-8.7	34-9.2

RUSHING	ATT	YDS	AVG	TD
Simpson	332	2003	6.0	12
Braxton	108	494	4.6	4
Watkins	98	414	4.2	2
Ferguson	48	147	3.1	2
Vanvalkenburg	2	20	10.0	0
Cornell	4	13	3.3	0
St. Jones	3	9	3.0	0
Shaw	4	2	0.5	0
Sp. Jones	1	0	0.0	0
Chandler	5	-14	-2.8	0
TOTALS	**605**	**3088**	**5.1**	**20**

PASSING	COMP	ATT	INT	YDS	TD	COMP%
Ferguson	73	164	10	939	4	44.5
Shaw	22	46	4	300	0	47.8
Simpson	1	2	0	-3	0	50.0
Chandler	0	1	0	0	0	00.0
TOTALS	**96**	**213**	**14**	**1236**	**4**	**45.1**

KICKING	1-19	20-29	30-39	40-49	50+	TOT	PAT	PTS
Leypoldt	7-7	3-5	5-6	4-8	2-4	21-30	27-27	90
Chandler	0-0	0-0	0-0	0-0	0-0	0-0	1-1	1
TOTALS	**7-7**	**3-5**	**5-6**	**4-8**	**2-4**	**21-30**	**28-28**	**91**

PUNTING	NO	AVG	LG	BL
Sp. Jones	66	40.3	62	0

RECEIVING	CAT	YDS	AVG	TD
Chandler	30	427	14.2	3
J.D. Hill	29	422	14.6	0
Watkins	12	86	7.2	1
Seymour	10	114	11.4	0
Braxton	6	101	16.8	0
Simpson	6	70	11.7	0
R. Jarvis	1	12	12.0	0
Vanvalkenburg	1	7	7.0	0
Ferguson	1	-3	-3.0	0
TOTALS	**96**	**1236**	**12.9**	**4**

LEADERS

| Kick returns: | Francis 23-687 yds, 29.2 avg, 2 TD |
| | St. Jones 6-115, 19.3, 0 TD |

| Punt returns: | Walker 25-210, 8.4, 0 TD |
| | Cahill 4-71, 17.8, 1 TD |

Interceptions:	Harrison 5-117, 23.4, 1 TD
	Cheyunski 3-31, 10.3, 0 TD
	Kellerman 2-23, 11.5, 0 TD

SCORE BY QUARTERS

BILLS	64	71	61	63	-	259
OPP	58	84	38	50	-	230

O.J. Simpson receives congratulations for breaking Jim Brown's single-season rushing record on December 16, 1973. Later in the game, Simpson became the first player to surpass 2,000 yards rushing.

GAME 1 - Sunday, Sept. 16, 1973 - BILLS 31, PATRIOTS 13

NOTES

• The winless preseason quickly was forgotten as the Bills opened the regular season in record-shattering fashion. O.J. Simpson rushed for an NFL record 250 yards on 29 carries and Larry Watkins also topped 100 yards.

• The team set records for rushing yards (360), attempts (51) and rushing first downs (18).

• The Bills opened the season on the road for only the fourth time in club history and this was their first win in such games. It also was the first opening-day victory since 1967.

• After doing a TV interview, Simpson entered the lockerroom to a standing ovation from teammates. Simpson became the team's all-time leading career rusher, topping Wray Carlton's total of 3,368.

• Rookie Joe Ferguson started, but was knocked out in the second quarter and Dennis Shaw finished at QB.

• Sam Cunningam gave the Pats a 6-0 lead, but on the first play after the ensuing kickoff, Simpson swept around right end for an 80-yard TD.

• After Shaw replaced Ferguson, he killed a drive with an interception, but he drove the Bills into position for John Leypoldt's 48-yard field goal with one second left in the half.

• Cunningham's fumble at the Bills 29 stopped the Pats opening march of the second half and Buffalo drove 71 yards to a 17-6 lead as Simpson had a 22-yard run and Larry Watkins a 28-yard pass reception.

• The Pats answered with an 80-yard TD drive, but the Bills came right back as Simpson scored on the first play of the fourth quarter.

QUOTES

• O.J. Simpson: "I've been telling people we're a much better club than anyone thinks. We didn't win a game in the preseason, but you have to remember Coach Saban was looking at our young guys. We knew when we got together we'd be a good team. I'm ecstatic about (the record); it's a great thrill. I don't think anyone will bad-mouth our offensive line this year. Larry also went over 100 yards; that's a tribute to the line. Our guys up front really did a job blowing people out of there."

• Pats coach Chuck Fairbanks: "O.J. looked like General Grant going through Richmond. We were helpless. It looked like a track meet out there."

• Pats linebacker and ex-Bill Edgar Chandler: "O.J. had more yardage than Secretariat."

• Lou Saban: "I didn't know about the record until late in the game when somebody on the bench said he needed 15 yards. I was reluctant to risk injury, but I put him back in and he got the record and I'm glad he did. He's a great man, and he's a great team man."

• Reggie McKenzie on his preseason prediction that Simpson would gain 2,000 yards this year: "Did I lie? I'm telling you, Juice is the greatest."

WEEK 1 GAMES

Atl 62, NO 7	St.L 34, Phil 23
LA 23, KC 13	Den 28, Cinc 10
Wash 38, SD 0	Mia 21, SF 13
NYG 34, Hou 13	Minn 24, Oak 16
Clev 24, Balt 14	Pitt 24, Det 10
Dal 20, Chi 17	GB 23, NYJ 7

Bills	7	3	7	14	-	31
Patriots	6	0	7	0	-	13

Attendance at Schaefer Stadium - 56,119

NE: Cunningham 7 run (kick failed), 12:31
Buf: Simpson 80 run (Leypoldt kick), 12:49
Buf: FG Leypoldt 48, 14:59
Buf: Watkins 4 run (Leypoldt kick), 6:27
NE: Herron 10 run (Bell kick), 11:53
Buf: Simpson 22 run (Leypoldt kick), :07
Buf: Watkins 15 run (Leypoldt kick), 9:05

	BUF	NE
First downs	23	17
Rushing yds	360	107
Passing yds	99	190
Punts-avg	2-42.5	2-39.5
Fumbles-lost	1-1	3-3
Penalties-yds	11-95	4-40

BILLS LEADERS: Rushing - Simpson 29-250, Watkins 18-105, Ferguson 2-4, Shaw 2-1; **Passing** - Shaw 7-9-1 - 109, Ferguson 1-2-0 - 10, Simpson 1-1-0-(-3); **Receiving** - Chandler 3-44, Hill 3-37, Watkins 2-38, Ferguson 1-(-3).

PATRIOTS LEADERS: Rushing - Cunningham 12-53, Ashton 9-33, Plunkett 2-12, Herron 2-8, Stingley 1-1; **Passing** - Plunkett 16-27-1 - 226; **Receiving** - Rucker 3-26, Stingley 2-26, Windsor 2-26, Adams 3-35, Cunningham 3-29, Ashton 2-55, Herron 1-29.

GAME 2 - Sunday, Sept. 23, 1973 - CHARGERS 34, BILLS 7

NOTES

• The Bills were brought quickly back down to earth as they were routed in San Diego. Ex-Bill Mike Stratton intercepted two passes and ex-Colts great Johnny Unitas threw two TD passes.

• Ron Smith's 72-yard punt return for a TD got things started for the Chargers. The Bills tied when Simpson scored after San Diego's Reggie Berry had roughed John Leypoldt on a field-goal attempt. Lou Saban took the points off the board and it paid off.

• Robert Holmes' first TD made it 14-7 and preceded a key play in the game. Late in the half the Bills drove to the Chargers 23, but Dennis Shaw, who had relieved ineffective Joe Ferguson, tried to hit well-covered Paul Seymour at the 7, but Stratton intercepted.

• Unitas threw a pair of TD passes in the third, the first coming after Tim Rossovich's interception of a poorly thrown Shaw pass on the third play of the second half. The second capped an 80-yard drive in which Unitas was brilliant, especially on third down.

• The final TD was a result of a Ferguson pass inter-cepted by Bob Howard.

• Saban benched Walt Patulski and replaced him with Steve Okoniewski.

QUOTES

• Chargers linebacker Mike Stratton: "I told all that I knew about Buffalo, but I don't know how much it helped. I think it's pretty obvious what the Bills do best on offense and they like to run through the six and eight holes (where he was playing)." Asked whether he was surprised Shaw tried to hit Seymour in the second quarter, Stratton laughed and said: "I don't even want to get into that," an obvious rap on Shaw who often tried to throw into coverage.

• Lou Saban: "We were very, very poor in the second half. No one was outstanding, there were many who were very poor. The receivers were open, we just didn't get the ball to them. That interception by Stratton was a terrible error (which he called the turning point in the game)." (On why he yanked Ferguson early): "Joe was shaken up. Further, we were down by seven points and I thought experience (with Shaw) was more important. It didn't work out that way."

• J.D. Hill: "We probably should have passed more in the beginning. The run usually opens up the passing game, but this game was just the opposite, we needed the pass to open up the run. They were keying on O.J. The coaches get a lot of criticism, but all they can do is prepare us. It's up to us, the players, and if we don't do what they tell us, it's our own fault. We have no one to blame but ourselves. And I'm tired of being a loser. We've got too much of this friendship stuff going on, things like, 'He's my friend, don't criticize.' I say do your job and I'll do mine. That's my attitude. I don't care if you like it or not. Do your job, that's the way it has to be."

Bills	0	7	0	0	-	7
Chargers	7	7	14	6	-	34

Attendance at San Diego Stadium - 49,124

SD: Smith 72 punt return (Wersching kick), 9:51
Buf: Simpson 6 run (Leypoldt kick), 5:10
SD: Holmes 1 run (Wersching kick), 8:27
SD: Garrison 26 pass from Unitas (Wersching kick), 2:29
SD: Thaxton 12 pass from Unitas (Wersching kick), 14:49
SD: Holmes 4 run (kick blocked), 6:54

	BUF	SD
First downs	16	17
Rushing yds	148	105
Passing yds	139	249
Punts-avg	6-35.6	4-49.9
Fumbles-lost	1-0	1-0
Penalties-yds	4-48	7-70

BILLS LEADERS: Rushing - Simpson 22-103, Watkins 11-25, Ferguson 1-(-5), Chandler 1-18, S. Jones 1-7; **Passing** - Shaw 7-15-2 - 106, Ferguson 5-17-2 - 53; **Receiving** - Hill 7-118, Seymour 2-34, Watkins 2-(-5), R. Jarvis 1-12.

CHARGERS LEADERS: Rushing - Holmes 12-29, Jones 7-42, Edwards 2-17, Thomas 9-17; **Passing** - Unitas 10-18-0 - 175, Clark 4-5-1 - 88; **Receiving** - Williams 5-86, Garrison 3-67, Holmes 2-14, Thomas 1-37, Thaxton 2-43, Norman 1-16.

WEEK 2 GAMES

Pitt 33, Clev 6	LA 31, Atl 0
Cinc 24, Hou 10	KC 10, NE 7
NYG 23, Phil 23	GB 13, Det 13
NYJ 34, Balt 10	SF 36, Den 34
Minn 22, Chi 13	Oak 12, Mia 7
St.L 34, Wash 27	Dal 40, NO 3

STANDINGS: SECOND WEEK

AFC EAST	W	L	T	CENTRAL	W	L	T	WEST	W	L	T	NFC EAST	W	L	T	CENTRAL	W	L	T	WEST	W	L	T
Miami	1	1	0	Pittsburgh	2	0	0	Denver	1	1	0	Dallas	2	0	0	Minnesota	2	0	0	LA Rams	2	0	0
Buffalo	1	1	0	Cleveland	1	1	0	Oakland	1	1	0	St. Louis	2	0	0	Green Bay	1	0	1	Atlanta	1	1	0
NY Jets	1	1	0	Cincinnati	1	1	0	Kan. City	1	1	0	NY Giants	1	0	1	Detroit	0	1	1	San Fran	1	1	0
Baltimore	0	2	0	Houston	0	2	0	San Diego	1	1	0	Washington	1	1	0	Chicago	0	2	0	N.Orleans	0	2	0
New England	0	2	0									Philadelphia	0	1	1								

Jets	0	0	7	-	7
Bills	3	0	6	-	9

Attendance at Rich Stadium - 77,425

Buf: FG Leypoldt 42, 4:41
Buf: FG Leypoldt 20, 4:07
Buf: FG Leypoldt 42, 13:06
NYJ: Barkum 34 pass from Woodall (Howfield kick), 14:58

	BUF	NYJ
First downs	15	17
Rushing yds	208	102
Passing yds	64	148
Punts-avg	3-41.7	8-37.6
Fumbles-lost	2-0	2-1
Penalties-yds	6-61	7-68

BILLS LEADERS: Rushing - Simpson 24-123, Watkins 13-78, Ferguson 4-13, Cornell 2-4, Chandler 1-(-10); **Passing** - Ferguson 7-17-1 - 74; **Receiving** - Chandler 2-28, Hill 1-8, Seymour 1-16, Watkins 1-7, Simpson 2-15.

JETS LEADERS: Rushing - Boozer 9-43, Riggins 12-43, Woodall 4-18, McClain 1-(-2); **Passing** - Woodall 12-31-0 - 186; **Receiving** - Barkum 3-57, Caster 4-99, Bell 2-26, McClain 1-11, Riggins 1-0, Boozer 1-(-7).

WEEK 3 GAMES

Clev 12, NYG 10	Mia 44, NE 23
Wash 28, Phil 7	KC 16, Oak 3
Balt 14, NO 10	Cin 20, SD 13
Dal 45, St.L 10	Minn 11, GB 3
Pitt 36, Hou 7	LA 40, SF 20
Chi 33, Den 14	Det 31, Atl 6

NOTES

• The Bills opened the regular season portion of Rich Stadium's existence with a superb defensive effort in beating the Jets, minus Joe Namath, in front of 77,425 fans and a local and regional TV audience thanks to the blackout ban being lifted.
• The Bills started the game with three new defensive backfield starters – Ken Stone, converted wide receiver Dwight Harrison and Donnie Walker. The defense held the Jets to 250 yards, but the shutout was ruined with two seconds to play when Al Woodall hit Jerome Barkum on a 34-yard TD. The Bills hadn't shut out an opponent since the 1965 AFL Championship Game when they beat San Diego, 23-0.
• Defensive end Earl Edwards recorded three sacks for 29 yards in losses.
• John Leypoldt provided the offense with three field goals. The first came after a short Julian Fagan punt gave the Bills good field position, and O.J. Simpson bettered it with a 15-yard run.
• Simpson killed a threat with a fumble in the second. Early in the third, a holding call on Donnie Green thwarted another drive, and a Joe Ferguson interception halted another advance.
• However, Emerson Boozer gave the ball right back after the pick with a fumble that was recovered by John Skorupan at the Jets 18 and that led to the second FG.
• Walt Patulski blocked a punt in the fourth and that led to Leypoldt's final kick.

QUOTES

• Jets coach Weeb Ewbank: "Buffalo was keyed up and we thought we were ready for a big game ourselves. The key was Buffalo never fell behind and had to pass. They led all the way, controlled the game with their running and passed only when they felt like it. They were blocking when they had the ball and we were holding when we had it."
• O.J. Simpson: "Joe Ferguson was smooth and in control all the way. Here's a rookie going all the way for the first time, but he kept coming into the huddle and telling us to relax, that we were going to score. He was our quarterback, he took charge. It was nice."
• Lou Saban: "That's the kind of game that will keep you on your toes. We took three wild shots in our defensive backfield and they played well. Only time will tell how good they'll be, but it seems we have some life and energy back there. We accomplished something today and I think we're establishing a good base to work from."
• Earl Edwards: "Basically I'd say I had a pretty good game with three sacks and I must have knocked him down five other times after he passed. The big thing for me was to be able to make big plays when they counted. I felt terrible before the game, had a bad case of indigestion, but I felt better when I started tackling people."
• Jets linebacker Al Atkinson: "A new stadium, but the same old jinx (New York is 5-9 all time in Buffalo)."

Eagles	6	10	7	3 -	26
Bills	10	14	0	3 -	27

Attendance at Rich Stadium - 72,364

Phi: FG Dempsey 51, 3:48
Buf: FG Leypoldt 12, 7:10
Phi: FG Dempsey 22, 10:46
Buf: Francis 101 kickoff return (Leypoldt kick), 11:03
Buf: Ferguson 1 run (Leypoldt kick), 1:48
Phi: Bulaich 7 pass from Gabriel (Dempsey kick), 6:17
Buf: Simpson 2 run (Leypoldt kick), 14:04
Phi: FG Dempsey 14, 14:58
Phi: Young 9 pass from Gabriel (Dempsey kick), 13:26
Phi: FG Dempsey 19, 7:19
Buf: FG Leypoldt 47, 11:09

	BUF	PHIL
First downs	16	28
Rushing yds	229	275
Passing yds	47	176
Punts-avg	3-43.3	1-37.0
Fumbles-lost	1-1	2-1
Penalties-yds	5-52	3-25

BILLS LEADERS: Rushing - Simpson 27-171, Watkins 5-33, Ferguson 4-25; **Passing** - Ferguson 6-9-0 - 63; **Receiving** - Chandler 1-14, Hill 1-7, Watkins 1-9, Simpson 3-33.

EAGLES LEADERS: Rushing - Sullivan 26-155, Bulaich 13-104, James 2-13, Bailey 3-3; **Passing** - Gabriel 16-29-0 - 182; **Receiving** - Sullivan 4-29, Young 6-58, Carmichael 2-49, Bulaich 2-16, Hawkins 2-30.

NOTES

• Tom Dempsey missed a 26-yard field goal on the game's final play, giving the Bills the victory.
• John Leypoldt kicked a go-ahead 47-yard field goal with 3:51 left after Lou Saban elected not to go for a fourth-and-inches play at the 40.
• Roman Gabriel then directed the Eagles from their own 20 to the Bills 19. Along the way, he hit tight end Charley Young for a first down on third-and-six. Later, after Jerry Patton had sacked Gabriel to force a fourth-and-13 at the Eagles 27, Gabriel hit Young for the first down. Tom Sullivan added runs of 11 and 10 yards and Po James had a 10-yarder to get Dempsey into position.
• The Eagles outrushed the Bills despite O.J. Simpson's huge day.
• The Bills tied the game at 3-3 after John Skorupan recovered Bill Bradley's muffed punt at the 8.
• After the Eagles went ahead 6-3, Wallace Francis returned the kickoff 101 yards for a TD.
• Simpson gained 47 yards on two plays to set up Joe Ferguson's TD and a 17-6 lead. After the Eagles pulled within 17-13, the Bills drove 80 yards to Simpson's three-yard TD.
• Philadelphia got within 24-23 in the third when Gabriel hit Young for a TD despite double coverage and Dempsey made a 19-yarder in the fourth after a Simpson fumble to give the Eagles a 26-24 lead.

• Simpson ran five times for 22 yards on the ensuing possession, but was short of a first down at the 40 and Saban went for the field goal and it paid off.

QUOTES

• Eagles kicker Tom Dempsey: "I knew as soon as I kicked it that it was off. I didn't bother to look."
• John Leypoldt: "As a Buffalo Bill, I was glad to see him miss, of course. But as a fellow place-kicker, I was sorry for him. I never like to see a place-kicker miss." (On the winning 47-yarder): "I'm glad he (Saban) has confidence in me, but he knows I haven't missed too many this season."
• Joe Ferguson: "I wouldn't trade O.J. for any five backs in the game. Just having him in our backfield gives me confidence. I feel the rookie pressure, but I don't go out there tight or scared because I know O.J. is on my side."
• Wallace Francis: "I usually go up the middle on that return, but this time I looked up the sideline and saw room. When I got to midfield, I saw Dempsey and I knew I could get by him."
• O.J. Simpson: "The guys on the offensive line tell me how much I've got and they say 'Let's get more,' We have a real cocky offensive line. If it isn't Reggie, then it's Donnie or some of the others saying to run the next play their way."

WEEK 4 GAMES

Clev 17, Cin 10	NE 24, Balt 16
Mia 31, NYJ 3	SF 13, Atl 9
Pitt 38, SD 21	KC 16, Den 14
Minn 23, Det 9	LA 31, Hou 26
Oak 17, St.L 10	GB 16, NYG 14
NO 21, Chi 16	Wash 14, Dal 7

STANDINGS: FOURTH WEEK

AFC EAST	W	L	T	CENTRAL	W	L	T	WEST	W	L	T	NFC EAST	W	L	T	CENTRAL	W	L	T	WEST	W	L	T
Buffalo	3	1	0	Pittsburgh	4	0	0	Kan. City	3	1	0	Dallas	3	1	0	Minnesota	4	0	0	LA Rams	4	0	0
Miami	3	1	0	Cleveland	3	1	0	Oakland	2	2	0	Washington	3	1	0	Green Bay	2	1	1	San Fran	2	2	0
Baltimore	1	3	0	Cincinnati	2	2	0	Denver	1	3	0	St. Louis	2	2	0	Detroit	1	2	1	Atlanta	1	3	0
NY Jets	1	3	0	Houston	0	4	0	San Diego	1	3	0	NY Giants	1	2	1	Chicago	1	3	0	N.Orleans	1	3	0
New England	1	3	0									Philadelphia	0	3	1								

NOTES

• After having scored just seven points in the previous 19 quarters against the Colts, the Bills erupted in the final three quarters and rolled to their third straight victory and first ever against Baltimore. It was Buffalo's first three-game winning streak since 1966.

• O.J. Simpson enjoyed his fifth straight 100-yard rushing game after being held to 26 yards in the first half. Counting 1972, he had a string of seven 100-yard games in a row, a two-season NFL record.

• Joe Ferguson threw his first pro TD pass, a 10-yarder to Larry Watkins that gave the Bills a 7-3 lead. The TD was set up when punter David Lee dropped a snap and the Bills took over at the Colts 35.

• John Leypoldt's 52-yard field goal tied the Bills record set by Grant Guthrie in 1970.

• The Bills wasted two scoring chances in the second quarter as Watkins fumbled and Ferguson threw an interception, but in the third, they took control.

• Walt Patulski's partial block of a punt gave the Bills the ball at the Colts 40 early in the third and they drove to Simpson's three-yard TD run.

• On the next series, Bert Jones was intercepted by Dwight Harrison who lateraled to Ken Stone and Stone ran 31 yards to the Colts 39. Ferguson snuck in from the 1.

• Simpson then broke his gorgeous 78-yard TD run to ice the game.

• The Colts lost starting linebackers Mike Curtis and Ted Hendricks to injuries during the game.

• Five of Ferguson's seven pass completions went for first downs, including three to Paul Seymour.

QUOTES

• Colts coach Howard Schnellenberger: "In addition to all the other things that make him a great athlete, O.J. seems able to see everything that is happening all over the field. It's just like he's looking at game film. When it's time to make a decision, he never makes a mistake."

• O.J. Simpson: "I said we would win 10 games because I felt it would take 10 to make the playoffs. We could get in with only nine, but we're going after 10." (On his long TD run): "It's a great feeling to break into the clear and know you have 80,000 fans and a television camera with you."

• Colts linebacker Mike Curtis when asked if he was hurt tackling Simpson: "He couldn't hurt anybody."

• Dwight Harrison on next week's showdown in Miami: "I'm going to start thinking about Miami right now. Some of us were thinking about Miami last week and I was hoping it wouldn't hurt us today."

• Colts linebacker Ted Hendricks: "The biggest difference in Buffalo is that offensive line. They have never done to us what they did today. O.J. is the same, but now he has some help."

WEEK 5 GAMES

Den 48, Hou 20	NO 20, Det 13
Cin 19, Pitt 7	LA 37, Dal 31
Phil 27, St.L 24	NYJ 9, NE 7
Minn 17, SF 13	KC 10, GB 10
Mia 17, Clev 9	Oak 27, SD 17
Wash 21, NYG 3	Atl 46, Chi 6

Colts	3	3	0	7	-	13
Bills	0	10	7	14	-	31

Attendance at Rich Stadium - 78,875

Bal:	FG Hunt 19, 5:05
Buf:	Watkins 10 pass from Ferguson (Leypoldt kick), 2:25
Bal:	FG Hunt 22, 13:23
Buf:	FG Leypoldt 52, 14:25
Buf:	Simpson 3 run (Leypoldt kick), 7:38
Buf:	Ferguson 1 run (Leypoldt kick), :34
Buf:	Simpson 78 run (Leypoldt kick), 2:54
Bal:	Olds 2 run (Hunt kick), 12:11

	BUF	BAL
First downs	18	13
Rushing yds	259	143
Passing yds	52	60
Punts-avg	3-31.0	4-30.5
Fumbles-lost	2-2	3-2
Penalties-yds	4-53	2-10

BILLS LEADERS: Rushing - Simpson 22-166, Watkins 10-39, Ferguson 9-37, VanValkenburg 1-8, Cornell 2-9; **Passing** - Ferguson 7-13-1 - 57; **Receiving** - Chandler 2-13, Watkins 1-10, Seymour 4-34.

COLTS LEADERS: Rushing - L. Mitchell 16-56, McCauley 13-58, Jones 3-7, Ginn 5-11, Olds 2-14, Lee 1-0, Smith 1- -3; **Passing** - Jones 7-15-2 - 71; **Receiving** - T. Mitchell 5-59, McCauley 1-15, Olds 1-(-3).

NOTES

• The Bills were no match for the powerful Dolphins as they lost their AFC East showdown and dropped out of a tie for first place.

• O.J. Simpson was held to 55 yards rushing, snapping his seven-game streak of 100-yard games. He suffered a sprained ankle, ending his day early in the fourth quarter.

• The victory was Miami's 19th straight at home and seventh in a row over the Bills.

• The Bills had no first downs at halftime. Buffalo QBs were sacked nine times, eight in the second half, and six were against Dennis Shaw, resulting in a net passing total of one yard.

• Jim Mandich, who had complained about not playing regularly, caught two TD passes.

• Walt Patulski recovered a Bob Griese fumble at the Dolphins 7 on the third play of the game, but the Bills managed only a field goal. Moments later, Fred Forsberg recovered a Jim Kiick fumble at the 35, but Joe Ferguson was intercepted.

• J.D. Hill muffed a punt at the Bills 31 and that led to Garo Yepremian's first field goal.

• Miami took the lead for good with an 18-play, 75-yard drive that ended with Mandich's first TD.

• The Dolphins also scored on the next series behind the running of Mercury Morris and Mandich's 25-yard TD.

• Miami made it 24-3 before the half ended as Jake Scott's 22-yard punt return to the Bills 33 set up a short drive that culminated in Morris' TD run.

QUOTES

• Dolphins coach Don Shula: "If the Bills had gone in for the touchdown (on the first turnover), there's no telling what might have happened for a young club like that. Our defense made the big plays for us."

• Lou Saban: "That was a horrible show we put on. They're the Super Bowl champs and they showed why. We had a couple of opportunities, but we couldn't capitalize. There are so many unanswered questions about our defense. This was something we thought could happen. Our youth showed up today. That and the inability to stand the heat (it was 83 degrees). Here and in San Diego, we were awfully bad."

• Dwight Harrison: "You can't make mistakes against them. It wasn't any one person who slipped up. This was not a true indication of how we can play."

• O.J. Simpson: "I thought we could run on them. In the second half we were doing the things we do well, but by then the game was all but out of reach. When the game was tight, they were playing football."

• Reggie McKenzie: "What can you say? We'll find out what we're made of now."

WEEK 6 GAMES

Dal 45, NYG 28	Cin 14, KC 6
Wash 31, St.L 13	Atl 41, SD 0
Pit 26, NYJ 14	NE 13, Chi 10
Balt 29, Det 27	Den 23, Oak 23
Min 28, Phil 21	LA 24, GB 7
Clev 42, Hou 13	SF 40, NO 0

Bills	3	0	0	3	-	6
Dolphins	3	21	3	0	-	27

Attendance at the Orange Bowl - 65,241

Buf:	FG Leypoldt 11, 3:05
Mia:	FG Yepremian 28, 8:53
Mia:	Mandich 2 pass from Griese (Yepremian kick), 2:14
Mia:	Mandich 25 pass from Griese (Yepremian kick), 9:02
Mia:	Morris 4 run (Yepremian kick), 14:32
Mia:	FG Yepremian 47, 9:01
Buf:	FG Leypoldt 50, 4:40

	BUF	MIA
First downs	8	18
Rushing yds	75	183
Passing yds	1	127
Punts-avg	5-45.0	2-44.0
Fumbles-lost	4-1	3-3
Penalties-yds	1-10	4-40

BILLS LEADERS: Rushing - Simpson 14-55, Watkins 10-17, Ferguson 4-6, VanValkenburg 1-12, Jones 2-2, Chandler 1-(-17); **Passing** - Ferguson 3-9-1 - 25, Shaw 3-9-0 - 35; **Receiving** - Chandler 1-10, Hill 3-38, Seymour 1-5, VanValkenburg 1-7.

DOLPHINS LEADERS: Rushing - Csonka 17-79, Morris 15-61, Kiick 2-4, Warfield 1-15, Nottingham 3-19, Leigh 1-5, Griese 1-0; **Passing** - Griese 10-20-1 - 136, Morrall 0-1-1 - 0; **Receiving** - Mandich 4-71, Kiick 2-8, Briscoe 1-12, Warfield 2-50, Csonka 1-(-5).

STANDINGS: SIXTH WEEK

AFC EAST	W	L	T	CENTRAL	W	L	T	WEST	W	L	T	NFC EAST	W	L	T	CENTRAL	W	L	T	WEST	W	L	T
Miami	5	1	0	Pittsburgh	5	1	0	Kan. City	3	2	1	Washington	5	1	0	Minnesota	6	0	0	LA Rams	6	0	0
Buffalo	4	2	0	Cleveland	4	2	0	Oakland	3	2	1	Dallas	4	2	0	Green Bay	2	2	2	San Fran	3	3	0
Baltimore	2	4	0	Cincinnati	4	2	0	Denver	2	3	1	St. Louis	2	4	0	Detroit	1	4	1	Atlanta	3	3	0
NY Jets	2	4	0	Houston	0	6	0	San Diego	1	5	0	NY Giants	1	4	1	Chicago	1	5	0	N.Orleans	2	4	0
New England	2	4	0									Philadelphia	1	4	1								

Chiefs	0	7	0	7	-	14
Bills	14	0	9	0	-	23

Attendance at Rich Stadium - 76,071

Buf: Simpson 1 run (Leypoldt kick), 2:33
Buf: Simpson 4 run (Chandler run), 3:37
KC: Hayes 1 run (Stenerud kick), 13:10
Buf: FG Leypoldt 31, 6:42
Buf: FG Leypoldt 17, 8:28
Buf: FG Leypoldt 8, 11:30
KC: Beathard 2 run (Stenerud kick), :02

	BUF	KC
First downs	21	8
Rushing yds	246	37
Passing yds	63	67
Punts-avg	3-34.7	9-41.1
Fumbles-lost	3-2	2-2
Penalties-yds	8-88	4-60

BILLS LEADERS: Rushing - Simpson 39-157, Watkins 19-81, Ferguson 5-11, Jones 1-0, Chandler 1-(-3); **Passing** - Ferguson 6-11-1 - 63, Chandler 0-1-0 - 0; **Receiving** - Chandler 3-35, Hill 3-28.

CHIEFS LEADERS: Rushing - Podolak 7-28, Hayes 7-5, Beathard 2-4, Dawson 1-0; **Passing** - Beathard 6-23-0 - 73, Dawson 2-6-2 - 26; **Receiving** - Hayes 2-33, Podolak 3-27, Kinney 1-13, Stroud 1-13, Taylor 1-13.

WEEK 7 GAMES
NO 19, Wash 3	Oak 34, Balt 21
Den 40, NYJ 28	Chi 35, Hou 14
Phil 30, Dal 16	Atl 17, SF 3
Clev 16, SD 16	Mia 30, NE 14
Pitt 20, Cin 13	Det 34, GB 0
St.L 35, NYG 27	Minn 10, LA 9

NOTES
• In the Bills' *Monday Night Football* debut, O.J. Simpson went over the 1,000-yard mark just seven games into the season. He also set an NFL record with 39 carries, breaking the mark of 38 set by Harry Newman of the Giants in 1934 and Jim Nance of the Patriots in 1966. The team also set a new record with 65 rushing attempts, breaking the mark of 51 set in the season opener.

• Rich Stadium fans went wild for the MNF cameras and the stadium was plastered with signs.

• Some fans gave Howard Cosell fits while he was taping his opening segment from the photo deck in front of the press box. Confetti was dumped on him and a picture of a naked baby with Cosell's picture superimposed was held up behind him. Don Meredith couldn't contain his laughter.

• Lou Saban opted to take the wind and kick off after winning the opening coin toss. It paid dividends in the third quarter when John Leypoldt kicked three field goals with the wind.

• Jim Cheyunski recovered a Len Dawson fumble at the KC 15 setting up Simpson's first TD, then intercepted a Dawson pass and returned it 31 yards to the 4, setting up Simpson's second TD. Holder Bob Chandler ran for the extra point on that TD when he misplayed the snap.

• A Joe Ferguson fumble at the Bills 43 led to the Chiefs' first TD, a drive directed by backup Pete Beathard who replaced the benched Dawson. Dawson returned, but then injured his ankle.

• After Leypoldt's first field goal, Warren McVea fumbled the kickoff and Bo Cornell recovered at the 15 and Leypoldt made another field goal for a 20-7 lead.

QUOTES
• Howard Cosell: "O.J. is the most powerful offensive force in football today."

• Walt Patulski: "This was definitely a turning point in our season. If we were to have any kind of year, we had to beat Kansas City." (On his recent four-game benching): "Maybe this was a psychological ploy by the coach. It changed my whole game. I realized I could be out on the street just like anybody else. Believe me, sitting on the bench was a sobering experience. My career up to this point has been pretty blasé and I wanted to prove what I could do."

• Joe Ferguson: "When O.J. got close to 1,000, the guys in the huddle got real excited. With his ability and if our offensive line keeps blocking, he can get 2,000 yards."

• Lou Saban: "Our young guys are really something. This was a big game and we had to win one pretty quick to go anywhere. If we can just keep playing this way, there's no telling where we'll finish. We played inspired football, it was our biggest victory to date."

• Chiefs coach Hank Stram: "Those three field goals took us out of it. We found it especially tough going into the wind. I can't remember when it had so much to do with the final result. It was difficult to get anything established, especially after those early breaks went against us. You can't reduce the size of the field to 15 yards, and then to four yards."

Bills	0	0	0	0	-	0
Saints	3	10	0	0	-	13

Attendance at Tulane Stadium - 74,770

NO: FG McClard 42, 14:53
NO: Newland 9 pass from Manning (McClard kick), 13:09
NO: FG McClard 24, 14:47

	BUF	NO
First downs	10	19
Rushing yds	124	115
Passing yds	66	166
Punts-avg	8-47.1	6-40.7
Fumbles-lost	4-1	1-0
Penalties-yds	4-49	3-28

BILLS LEADERS: Rushing - Simpson 20-79, Watkins 8-22, Ferguson 3-23; **Passing** - Ferguson 9-19-0 - 87; **Receiving** - Chandler 2-23, Hill 3-40, Watkins 4-24.

SAINTS LEADERS: Rushing - Phillips 18-52, Manning 4-23, Profit 6-21, Butler 5-19, Stevens 1-0; **Passing** - Manning 16-33-0 - 188; **Receiving** - Beasley 6-47, Newland 3-44, Profit 2-33, Winslow 3-33, Phillips 1-20, Dunbar 1-11.

WEEK 8 GAMES
Minn 26, Clev 3	KC 19, SD 0
Dal 38, Cinc 10	Phil 24, NE 23
St.L 17, Den 17	Hou 31, Balt 27
Chi 31, GB 13	Atl 15, LA 13
Det 30, SF 20	Oak 42, NYG 0
Mia 24, NYJ 14	Pitt 21, Wash 16

NOTES
• The Saints stopped O.J. Simpson, holding him under 100 yards for only the second time this season.

• Simpson was stopped on fourth-and-one from the Saints 11 early in the fourth quarter and that killed the Bills, who were trailing, 13-0, and needed to score a touchdown at that point.

• The Saints toyed with a four-linebacker alignment, but reverted to a seven-man line and it worked.

• The shutout was the first in New Orleans history, a span of 92 games, and it was the first time a Saints team had reached .500 this late in a season.

• The Bills had two first downs in the first half, the Saints had 15.

• Joe Ferguson played his first game as a pro in his home state of Louisiana and he struggled.

• Walt Patulski was in on 10 tackles and sacked Archie Manning three times.

• On the only TD of the game, Manning's nine-yard TD pass to Bob Newland, Dwight Harrison was beaten on the play.

QUOTES
• Lou Saban: "I'm not going to give New Orleans any credit. We just didn't go out and do the job. We did feel just before the game that we'd have trouble. It's strictly a coach's feeling. When we get the ball on the road, it gets very quiet (on offense). Maybe this bothers us in comparison to the noise at home." (On the fourth-down failure by Simpson): "I felt we needed a touchdown for emotional reasons. I would have bet my life we would make that first down. We didn't hit in the first half, we didn't attack. We weren't the same club that we were against Kansas City." (On whether he would stick with Joe

Ferguson): "This young man has done a fine job for us. Joe needs the experience. The kid was wound pretty tight playing in his home territory for the first time as a pro. Plus, our pass protection wasn't good and we ran our routes pretty poorly."

• Saints safety Tommy Myers: "We (his defensive teammates) would practice making moves on each other every day. No one can duplicate O.J.'s moves, but we did the best we could. And we practiced tackling him high, too, enough to hold him up until two or three others came up to help out. O.J.'s greatness was our motivation."

• Saints linebacker Wayne Coleman: "For five days all we saw were movies of O.J. We saw him get his 250 yards against New England, we saw him tear up Baltimore, we saw him in the Bills' Monday night victory over Kansas City. We all agreed he was the greatest we had ever seen. We also agreed we were going to stop him. He's so good, he challenges your pride."

STANDINGS: EIGHTH WEEK

AFC EAST	W	L	T	CENTRAL	W	L	T	WEST	W	L	T	NFC EAST	W	L	T	CENTRAL	W	L	T	WEST	W	L	T
Miami	7	1	0	Pittsburgh	7	1	0	Oakland	5	2	1	Washington	5	3	0	Minnesota	8	0	0	LA Rams	6	2	0
Buffalo	5	3	0	Cleveland	4	3	1	Kan. City	4	3	1	Dallas	5	3	0	Detroit	3	4	1	Atlanta	5	3	0
Baltimore	2	6	0	Cincinnati	4	4	0	Denver	3	3	2	Philadelphia	3	4	1	Chicago	3	5	0	N.Orleans	4	4	0
NY Jets	2	6	0	Houston	1	7	0	San Diego	1	6	1	St. Louis	3	4	1	Green Bay	2	4	2	San Fran	3	5	0
New England	2	6	0									NY Giants	1	6	1								

NOTES

• Horst Muhlmann's 33-yard field goal with one second left sent the Bills to their second straight loss. In the process, Joe Ferguson jammed his right thumb and missed most of the game.
• For the second week in a row, O.J. Simpson was held under 100 yards, although barely at 99.
• Even with the Bengals keying heavily on Simpson, the passing was miserable, producing a net 30 yards as Ferguson and Dennis Shaw struggled badly.
• The Bills tied the game at 13-13 when Simpson swept in from 32 yards following Dwight Harrison's second interception of the game.
• Moments later, John Leypoldt was roughed on a field goal attempt and the Bills were in business at the Bengals 33, but Shaw threw an interception and the Bills never threatened again.
• The winning field goal was set up by Buffalo blunders. Simpson gained seven yards and a first down to the 35, but it was wiped out by a clipping penalty against Bob Chandler. The Bills were pushed back to their 14 and never got out, then Spike Jones shanked a punt 30 yards and Cincinnati took over at the Bills 44 with 2:30 left.
• Earl Edwards' offside gave Cincinnati one first down and eventually, they got to the 26 and lined up for Muhlmann's winner after winding the clock down to three seconds.

QUOTES

• O.J. Simpson: "We've just got to get more out of our passing game."
• Reggie McKenzie: "I know people are saying that if you stop O.J., you beat the Bills, but I'm not ready to concede that point yet. Not being able to pass the ball is part of the game, but I have to keep believing that Dennis and Joe can throw the ball. I don't want to believe otherwise. O.J. can't do it all and we just have to compensate with the pass. we've lost two straight games and now you can assume a lot of things are wrong with the team. We're going to find out what kind of team we have."
• Lou Saban: "Our passing game is in tough straits right now and I'm not satisfied with it at all. We work hard on it all week in practice and there's no consistency in it. I just don't understand. Ferguson is our starter and there is only so much time we can give Dennis in practice. If Ferguson's jammed thumb is OK, he's still going to be our starter."
• Bengals coach Paul Brown: "The Bills can really kill you. They're one of the best defensive teams in the game. And we had to do more than just stop O.J."
• Dwight Harrison: "We've had two disappointments in a row, but now if we can just beat Miami, it would make the whole year worthwhile."

Bengals	6	7	0	3 - 16
Bills	3	3	7	0 - 13

Attendance at Rich Stadium - 76,927

Cin: FG Muhlmann 35, 6:13
Buf: FG Leypoldt 21, 12:28
Cin: FG Muhlmann 36, 14:50
Cin: Clark 1 run (Muhlmann kick), 6:57
Buf: FG Leypoldt 39, 14:52
Buf: Simpson 32 run (Leypoldt kick), 2:35
Cin: FG Muhlmann 33, 14:59

	BUF	CIN
First downs	10	18
Rushing yds	150	161
Passing yds	30	120
Punts-avg	9-36.2	4-40.0
Fumbles-lost	1-0	3-2
Penalties-yds	7-54	9-85

BILLS LEADERS: Rushing - Simpson 20-99, Watkins 1-6, Braxton 11-44, Shaw 2-1; **Passing** - Ferguson 0-3-1 - 0, Shaw 5-13-1 - 50; **Receiving** - Chandler 3-24, Hill 1-23, Watkins 1-3.

BENGALS LEADERS: Rushing - Clark 24-98, Johnson 15-49, Anderson 6-26, Curtis 1-(-12); **Passing** - Anderson 9-22-1 - 141; **Receiving** - Curtis 5-94, Trumpy 2-23, Coslet 1-15, Johnson 1-9.

WEEK 9 GAMES

GB 25, St.L 21	Mia 44, Balt 0
Dal 23, NYG 10	NYJ 33, NE 13
Pitt 17, Oak 9	Atl 44, Phil 27
Clev 23, Hou 13	Minn 28, Det 7
Den 30, SD 19	LA 29, NO 7
KC 19, Chi 7	Wash 33, SF 9

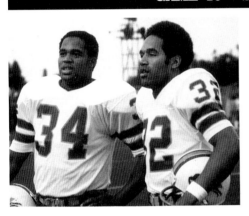

NOTES

• The Bills enjoyed a great day running as O.J. Simpson and Jim Braxton each topped 100 yards, but the offense failed to score as Miami dealt Buffalo it's third loss in a row. The Dolphins also clinched the AFC East title.
• The Miami defense hadn't allowed an opposing runner to top 100 yards in 45 games.
• The Dolphins used up the first 8:55 of the game on an 18-play, 80-yard TD drive with Larry Csonka scoring.
• Buffalo came back as Joe Ferguson hit J.D. Hill for 42 yards and advanced the ball to the 16, but John Leypoldt missed a 23-yard field goal.
• On the next play, Mercury Morris zipped 45 yards to set up Garo Yepremian's field goal.
• Again the Bills came back, driving to the 4, but Braxton was stopped on fourth-and-goal at the 1. Linebacker Mike Kolen made three tackles during the goal-line stand.
• A pass intended for Simpson bounced off his hands and Kolen intercepted and returned 25 yards to the Bills 40. Bob Griese then threw 23 yards to Jim Mandich and then hit Paul Warfield with a 17-yard TD pass to make it 17-0.
• On the Bills' final drive, they went from their 16 to the Miami 17 before a fourth-down incomplete pass.
• Robert James held ex-teammate Marlin Briscoe to one catch for six yards.

QUOTES

• Robert James: "I think we showed in the second half that we aren't a team that gives up. I don't think we're down. I think we'll come back in the last four games."
• O.J. Simpson: "What the defense did in the second half and what we did on that last drive, that tells a lot about us. We could have put our heads down by then, but the guys kept yelling 'Let's remind 'em they have to play us next year, show 'em what to expect next year.' The threat of Joe's passes opened up the defense for Jim and me. The first ball Joe threw (the 42-yarder to Hill) had Shula pacing up and down the sidelines."
• Dolphins coach Don Shula on the opening TD drive: "That kind of control has to be demoralizing to the opposition. I'm happy I wasn't on the other side, for I know what such a touchdown drive can do for morale. That was a great demonstration by Braxton. Sure we have keys on O.J. and we're always aware of where he is."
• Dolphins receiver Marlin Briscoe: "Buffalo will never be a title contender as long as Saban is coaching them. Saban has a history of giving up good players because they may not always agree with his coaching methods. He lets personal differences enter into it. It happened with me and a lot of other players. To be a winner, you have to have experienced players and he will never have an experienced team because older players may disagree with him. Lou can't stand that, so he trades a good player even though the team may suffer. The Bills would be better without him."
• Lou Saban: "I've never said anything to hurt Marlin and I'm not going to now."

Dolphins	7	10	0	0 - 17
Bills	0	0	0	0 - 0

Attendance at Rich Stadium - 77,138

Mia: Csonka 1 run (Yepremian kick), 8:55
Mia: FG Yepemian 39, :10
Mia: Warfield 17 pass from Griese (Yepremian kick), 13:44

	BUF	MIA
First downs	15	17
Rushing yds	238	154
Passing yds	71	123
Punts-avg	6-35.8	4-39.5
Fumbles-lost	2-1	3-0
Penalties-yds	7-65	3-14

BILLS LEADERS: Rushing - Simpson 20-120, Braxton 17-119, Ferguson 1-1, Chandler 1-(-2); **Passing** - Ferguson 6-21-1 - 98, Simpson 0-1-0 - 0; **Receiving** - Hill 3-57, Braxton 1-16, Seymour 1-3, Simpson 1-22.

DOLPHINS LEADERS: Rushing - Morris 13-79, Csonka 15-56, Kiick 11-13, Nottingham 1-5, Griese 2-1; **Passing** - Griese 11-20-0 - 123; **Receiving** - Warfield 4-59, Mandich 4-52, Briscoe 1-6, Kiick 1-4, Morris 1-2.

WEEK 10 GAMES

Cin 20, NYJ 14	LA 31, SF 13
NYG 24, St.L 13	KC 38, Hou 14
Atl 20, Minn 14	NE 33, GB 24
Dal 31, Phil 10	Det 30, Chi 7
Den 23, Pitt 13	SD 17, NO 14
Wash 22, Balt 14	Clev 7, Oak 3

STANDINGS: TENTH WEEK

AFC EAST	W	L	T	CENTRAL	W	L	T	WEST	W	L	T	NFC EAST	W	L	T	CENTRAL	W	L	T	WEST	W	L	T
Miami	9	1	0	Pittsburgh	8	2	0	Kan. City	6	3	1	Washington	7	3	0	Minnesota	9	1	0	LA Rams	8	2	0
Buffalo	5	5	0	Cleveland	6	3	1	Oakland	5	4	1	Dallas	7	3	0	Detroit	4	5	1	Atlanta	7	3	0
New England	3	7	0	Cincinnati	6	4	0	Denver	5	3	2	Philadelphia	3	6	1	Green Bay	3	5	2	N.Orleans	4	6	0
NY Jets	3	7	0	Houston	1	9	0	San Diego	2	7	1	St. Louis	3	6	1	Chicago	3	7	0	San Fran	3	7	0
Baltimore	2	8	0									NY Giants	2	7	1								

GAME 11 - Sunday, Nov. 25, 1973 - BILLS 24, COLTS 17

Bills	3	7	0	14 - 24
Colts	7	0	0	10 - 17

Attendance at Memorial Stadium - 52,250

Buf: FG Leypoldt 36, 10:45
Bal: Speyrer 101 kickoff return (Hunt kick), 11:03
Buf: Simpson 57 run (Leypoldt kick), 12:09
Bal: T. Mitchell 11 pass from Domres (Hunt kick), 6:11
Bal: FG Hunt 27, 8:32
Buf: Chandler 37 pass from Ferguson (Leypoldt kick), 13:26
Buf: Harrison 31 interception return (Leypoldt kick), 13:49

	BUF	BAL
First downs	16	15
Rushing yds	215	152
Passing yds	169	69
Punts-avg	7-41.0	5-38.6
Fumbles-lost	1-1	0-0
Penalties-yds	6-73	1-5

BILLS LEADERS: Rushing - Simpson 15-124, Braxton 18-83, Ferguson 4-8; **Passing** - Ferguson 11-19-1 - 201; **Receiving** - Chandler 5-97, Hill 1-12, Seymour 1-22, Braxton 4-70.

COLTS LEADERS: Rushing - L. Mitchell 22-67, McCauley 9-36, Doughty 1-30, Domres 4-19; **Passing** - Domres 8-25-2 - 86; **Receiving** - T. Mitchell 2-44, Speyrer 2-22, McCauley 2-1, Doughty 1-15, L. Mitchell 1-4.

NOTES

• The Bills pulled out a great victory as Bob Chandler's TD reception tied the game with 1:34 left and 23 seconds later, Dwight Harrison returned an interception 31 yards for the winning score.
• It was third-and-10 from the 24 when Marty Domres tried to pass. Harrison actually had been in the wrong coverage and was running from right to left to try and get over to guard Glenn Doughty. Doughty was open, Domres didn't see him and instead tried to hit Sam Havrilak. Walt Patulski tipped the pass and Harrison caught it and raced in untouched for the score.
• Patulski continued his strong play. He had three pass deflections, a sack and seven tackles and was named defensive player of the week in the NFL.
• The Colts had taken a 17-10 lead with two scores within 2:21 in the fourth. However, Fred Hoaglin long-snapped the ball over punter David Lee's head, it hit the crossbar of the goal posts, came back to Lee and he managed to punt to the Colts 37. But on the first play, Joe Ferguson threw only the second TD pass of his career to Chandler, who had beaten Rex Kern.
• Robert James' interception ended Baltimore's final possession.
• The Bills outgained the Colts 240-46 in the first half

with O.J. Simpson's 58-yard TD run the highlight.
• John Leypoldt ruined an excellent first-half drive by missing a 25-yard field goal.
• Ferguson enjoyed his finest day as a pro, his first 200-yard passing game.

QUOTES

• Dwight Harrison: "What I was about to do was make a mistake in pass coverage. They had three wide receivers in with a slot formation and I didn't see it. (Safety) Ernie Kellerman yelled for me to get into the right coverage quick."
• Lou Saban: "This was a real big win for us. It must really be tough for the Colts, but then we've had a few tough ones ourselves. It's funny, we didn't make nearly as many mistakes in our three previous games as we did against Baltimore, yet we didn't win any of those games."
• O.J. Simpson: "Today we played more like the Dolphins than we ever have. When you play like the Dolphins, there's always Csonka popping you and Morris popping you and I think that's the way we played today."
• Colts tackle Joe Ehrmann: "The guy who hurt us was Ferguson. We had them typed pretty good, then here comes a quarterback having a good game against us, a guy who's never done that before. This was the most frustrating loss I've ever been associated with, and we had some ridiculous things happen at Syracuse."
• Bob Chandler: "If I had missed that touchdown pass I would have kept running out of the stadium and boarded a plane for California. Joe laid it right in there beautifully."

WEEK 11 GAMES	
Wash 20, Det 0	Mia 14, Dal 7
Oak 31, SD 3	NE 32, Hou 0
Cinc 42, St.L 24	Atl 28, NYJ 20
Phil 20, NYG 16	Min 31, Chi 13
Clev 21, Pitt 16	LA 24, NO 13
Den 14, KC 10	SF 20, GB 6

GAME 12 - Sunday, Dec. 2, 1973 - BILLS 17, FALCONS 6

Bills	7	3	7	0 - 17
Falcons	0	6	0	0 - 6

Attendance at Atlanta- Fulton County Stadium - 58,850

Buf: Braxton 1 run (Leypoldt kick), 10:49
Atl: FG Mike-Mayer 26, 9:55
Atl: FG Mike-Mayer 16, 13:08
Buf: FG Leypoldt 20, 14:55
Buf: Braxton 1 run (Leypoldt kick), 7:23

	BUF	ATL
First downs	17	12
Rushing yds	239	125
Passing yds	95	147
Punts-avg	7-41.0	5-48.8
Fumbles-lost	1-0	3-3
Penalties-yds	3-41	4-20

BILLS LEADERS: Rushing - Simpson 24-137, Braxton 23-80, Ferguson 7-22; **Passing** - Ferguson 7-12-1 - 95; **Receiving** - Chandler 4-41, Hill 3-54.

FALCONS LEADERS: Rushing - Ray 13-61, Hampton 16-49, Lee 3-15; **Passing** - Lee 9-22-0 - 195; **Receiving** - J. Mitchell 4-71, Neal 1-50, Geredine 1-46, Ray 3-28.

WEEK 12 GAMES	
Clev 20, KC 20	SF 38, Phil 28
Dal 22, Den 10	Wash 27, NYG 24
Cinc 27, Minn 0	LA 26, Chi 0
NYJ 20, Balt 17	NE 30, SD 14
Oak 17, Hou 6	GB 30, NO 10
Det 20, St.L 16	Mia 30, Pitt 26

NOTES

• The Bills snapped Atlanta's seven-game winning streak and kept alive their own wild-card playoff hopes
• The Bills' defense sacked Bob Lee four times and also stopped Atlanta in fourth-and-one situations in the third and fourth quarters.
• Buffalo neutralized Atlanta's outstanding defensive ends, Claude Humphrey and John Zook, with double-team blocking and the Bills rushed for 239 yards.
• O.J. Simpson recorded his ninth 100-yard game of the season, tying Jim Brown's single-season record.
• The Bills took a 7-0 lead on Jim Braxton's first TD of the season. Ray Brown fumbled Spike Jones' 52-yard punt at the 27. Fred Forsberg recovered and the Bills took it in from there.
• Nick Mike-Mayer kicked a pair of second-quarter field goals, the second one coming after Humphrey intercepted a screen pass and returned it to the Bills 14.
• The Bills answered before the half ended as Joe Ferguson hit J.D. Hill for 34 yards and Bob Chandler for 11 to position John Leypoldt for a 20-yard field goal with five seconds left.
• The Bills drove 54 yards for their final TD, helped by Hill's recovery of a Simpson fumble after an 18-yard run. Ferguson also hit Chandler for 16 yards and Braxton gained the final 17 yards on five carries until he scored for a 17-6 lead.

QUOTES

• O.J. Simpson: "Braxton's a lot like Larry Csonka of Miami. Look at what Csonka does for Mercury Morris. With Jim going inside, it helps me going outside. I can do more things. We lost to New Orleans because we ran all day. We've won the last two with Joe throwing the ball. Joe's coming into his own now. We had to keep the reigns on him early in the year, but he's starting to throw well now. We can run and beat anyone if we can play them straight up. The Falcons thought they were going to intimidate our linemen. They're crazy, no one intimidates our guys."
• Falcons defensive end John Zook: "This isn't hockey or basketball, we only play 14 games, so it's hard for me to believe you can let down with what we have at stake."
• Lou Saban: "Zook and Humphrey were really bothered. It looked like in the second half like they forgot how to play."
• Joe Ferguson: "I knew our offensive line was ready. We watched movies of the Falcons beating the Jets and every time one of their defensive players would give somebody one of those 'extras' Reggie McKenzie or Joe DeLamielleure or one of the others would say 'hot dog' or 'we'll put a stop to that.'"
• Jerry Patton on Bob Lee, whom Falcons fans refer to as General Lee: "General Lee met General Patton today."
• Reggie McKenzie: "Around the country, people know who the Buffalo Bills are now."

STANDINGS: TWELFTH WEEK

AFC EAST	W	L	T	CENTRAL	W	L	T	WEST	W	L	T	NFC EAST	W	L	T	CENTRAL	W	L	T	WEST	W	L	T
Miami	11	1	0	Cincinnati	8	4	0	Oakland	7	4	1	Washington	9	3	0	Minnesota	10	2	0	LA Rams	10	2	0
Buffalo	7	5	0	Pittsburgh	8	4	0	Denver	6	4	2	Dallas	8	4	0	Detroit	5	6	1	Atlanta	8	4	0
New England	5	7	0	Cleveland	7	3	2	Kan. City	6	4	2	Philadelphia	4	7	1	Green Bay	4	6	2	San Fran	5	7	0
NY Jets	4	8	0	Houston	1	11	0	San Diego	2	9	1	St. Louis	3	8	1	Chicago	3	9	0	N. Orleans	4	8	0
Baltimore	2	10	0									NY Giants	2	9	1								

NOTES

• The Bills stayed alive in the AFC wild-card race and O.J. Simpson got to the brink of NFL immortality by rushing for 219 yards, leaving him 61 yards shy of Jim Brown's all-time rushing record. Simpson totaled 469 yards in two games against the Pats.

• Despite the snow-covered field, Simpson recorded his 10th 100-yard game, a single-season record.

• Joe Ferguson's only two pass completions went for TDs to Bob Chandler.

• Wallace Francis' 90-yard kickoff return that gave the Bills the lead for good in the first quarter enabled him to take over the No. 1 spot in the AFC in that category.

• Jim Braxton's fourth-down conversion run helped the Bills drive to Simpson's six-yard TD run.

• Bob McCall fumbled the ensuing kickoff and the Bills turned the miscue into John Leypoldt's 34-yard field goal, but Jeff White's second field goal made it 17-6 just before halftime.

• Simpson's 25-yard burst led to Ferguson's 37-yard TD pass to Chandler and Donnie Walker's interception and 16-yard return to the Pats 33 resulted in another Leypoldt field goal.

• After the Pats scored, Simpson ripped off right tackle and went 71 yards to the 9. Ferguson hit Chandler with a TD pass.

• Fans wanted Lou Saban to leave Simpson in the game and shoot for the record, but he feared injury and pulled Simpson.

QUOTES

• O.J. Simpson: "These fans in Buffalo have been great to us all year and I wanted to do something special for them in our last home game. I wanted to break Jim Brown's rushing record right here in Buffalo. Next week, if I can break the individual record and the team can break Miami's record, it'll be the biggest day of my life." (About playing in snow): "I always played well in the mud in California, but I never played in snow until today. I tried out three different pairs of shoes in the pre-game practice and I finally went back to the ones I've been wearing all season. In the snow, I had the advantage for the most part. I knew where I was going, they didn't. I didn't mind the snow. Once we started playing, I found the traction wasn't bad."

• Bob Chandler: "O.J. is so good he makes a small guy like me look like a good crackback blocker. The better our passing game is, the easier it is for O.J. and Braxton."

• Pats coach Chuck Fairbanks was asked if the Jets could stop Simpson next week: "Sure, if they break both his ankles."

Patriots	3	3	7	0 -	13
Bills	7	10	17	3 -	37

Attendance at Rich Stadium - 72,470

NE: FG White 14, 5:11
Buf: Francis 90 kickoff return (Leypoldt kick), 5:26
Buf: Simpson 6 run (Leypoldt kick), 5:02
Buf: FG Leypoldt 34, 7:03
NE: FG White 12, 14:17
Buf: Chandler 37 pass from Ferguson (Leypoldt kick), 3:42
Buf: FG Leypoldt 34, 8:38
NE: Plunkett 5 run (White kick), 9:53
Buf: Chandler 6 pass from Ferguson (Leypoldt kick), 12:33
Buf: FG Leypoldt 19, 6:58

	BUF	NE
First downs	13	20
Rushing yds	293	98
Passing yds	31	292
Punts-avg	2-38.5	2-42.0
Fumbles-lost	1-0	3-2
Penalties-yds	7-45	2-20

BILLS LEADERS: Rushing - Simpson 22-219, Braxton 15-70, Watkins 1-2, Ferguson 2-2; **Passing** - Ferguson 2-7-0 - 43; **Receiving** - Chandler 2-43.

PATRIOTS LEADERS: Rushing - Tarver 11-52, Cunningham 14-30, Plunkett 5-16; **Passing** - Plunkett 17-41-2 - 292; **Receiving** - B. Adams 6-100, Rucker 4-79, Vataha 1-48, Herron 2-38, Stingley 2-31, Cunningham 2-(-4).

WEEK 13 GAMES	
Dal 27, Wash 7	Oak 37, KC 7
Balt 16, Mia 3	Det 40, Chi 7
Cinc 34, Clev 17	NO 16, SF 10
St.L 32, Atl 10	Den 42, SD 28
Pitt 33, Hou 7	Minn 31, GB 7
Phil 24, NYJ 23	LA 40, NYG 6

NOTES

• O.J. Simpson became the first man to gain 2,000 yards rushing in a single season and the Bills also set an NFL record for team rushing with 3,088 yards in whipping the Jets to close the season with their fourth straight victory.

• Simpson gained 57 yards on the first series, which ended with Jim Braxton's TD run. On the first play of the next series, he surpassed Jim Brown's record of 1,863 yards with a six-yard gain off the left side. After being mobbed by him teammates, Simpson fumbled on the next play and the Jets went on to tie the score, but after that, Buffalo dominated.

• Simpson capped a 70-yard drive with a 13-yard TD run, and rookie Bill Cahill returned a punt 51 yards for a TD 51 seconds later to make it 21-7 and all that was left was the run for 2,000.

• Joe Ferguson entered the huddle with about seven minutes to go and informed the unit that Simpson was 60 yards shy of 2,000. They immediately got excited

and they got Simpson the milestone.

QUOTES

• O.J. Simpson: "We're the youngest team in pro football. We average only 24.3 years. We're going to be good for a long time. Our goal is the Super Bowl and we're going to make it. Our gameplan, as you could tell, was to go after the record from the beginning, get it out of the way, then settle down and win the game. Getting the record meant a lot to me, personally. Just two years ago, I was as low as I could be, so you will never realize just how much this means to me. All season long people talked about the record, but I tried to keep it out of my mind so I could concentrate on playing football. I was able to do that pretty well until last week when the record drew very near. Every team has been playing us for the run, but these guys have been knocking them out."

• Reggie McKenzie: "I told O.J. during the summer 'Let's shoot for two grand and really set the world on fire' and we did. O.J. is always talking about his offensive line and you have to feel something special for a man like that. I love him."

• Joe Ferguson describing the play that broke Brown's record: "It was a 27 play. I fake to the fullback up the middle. Reggie McKenzie leads the way and the center guard, Joe D, pulls in front of him into the hole. It's O.J.'s favorite play."

• Jets safety Phil Wise: "He just used me up all day. You know how a streetcar conductor punches your ticket? He just punched my ticket and waved to me in the end zone. All my life I thought Jim Brown was the greatest runner, but O.J. broke his record. I don't see how anybody could be better, even Jim Brown."

• Mike Montler: "Just think, I'll be sitting in some bar 20 years from now and I'll be telling 'em I blocked on that line."

Bills	7	14	7	6 -	34
Jets	7	0	0	7 -	14

Attendance at Shea Stadium - 47,740

Buf: Braxton 1 run (Leypoldt kick), 8:52
NYJ: Barkum 48 pass from Namath (Howfield kick), 11:52
Buf: Simpson 13 run (Leypoldt kick), 13:48
Buf: Cahill 51 punt return (Leypoldt kick), 14:38
Buf: Braxton 1 run (Leypoldt kick), 8:35
Buf: FG Leypoldt 12, 4:02
Buf: FG Leypoldt 11, 11:49
NYJ: Caster 16 pass from Namath (Howfield kick), 14:34

	BUF	NYJ
First downs	21	12
Rushing yds	304	39
Passing yds	70	184
Punts-avg	2-34.5	7-32.5
Fumbles-lost	3-1	1-0
Penalties-yds	2-10	0-0

BILLS LEADERS: Rushing - Simpson 34-200, Braxton 24-98, Watkins 2-6, Ferguson 2-0; **Passing** - Ferguson 3-5-0 - 70; **Receiving** - Chandler 2-55, Braxton 1-15.

JETS LEADERS: Rushing - Boozer 7-32, Adamle 3-6, Bjorklund 1-1; **Passing** - Namath 13-30-0 - 206; **Receiving** - Barkum 4-102, Caster 3-58, Knight 2-23, Boozer 2-12, Bell 1-11, Adamle 1-0.

WEEK 14 GAMES	
Pitt 37, SF 14	Mia 34, Det 7
Balt 18, NE 13	LA 30, Clev 17
Dal 30, St.L 3	Cinc 27, Hou 24
Atl 14, NO 10	Minn 31, NYG 7
Wash 38, Phil 20	GB 21, Chi 0
KC 33, SD 6	Oak 21, Den 17

STANDINGS: FOURTEENTH WEEK

AFC EAST	W	L	T	CENTRAL	W	L	T	WEST	W	L	T	NFC EAST	W	L	T	CENTRAL	W	L	T	WEST	W	L	T
Miami	12	2	0	Cincinnati	10	4	0	Oakland	9	4	1	Dallas	10	4	0	Minnesota	12	2	0	LA Rams	12	2	0
Buffalo	9	5	0	Pittsburgh	10	4	0	Denver	7	5	2	Washington	10	4	0	Detroit	6	7	1	Atlanta	9	5	0
New England	5	9	0	Cleveland	7	5	2	Kan. City	7	5	2	Philadelphia	5	8	1	Green Bay	5	7	2	San Fran	5	9	0
Baltimore	4	10	0	Houston	1	13	0	San Diego	2	11	1	St. Louis	4	9	1	Chicago	3	11	0	N. Orleans	5	9	0
NY Jets	4	10	0									NY Giants	2	11	1								

At A Glance
1974

Jan. 4 – O.J. Simpson was named the NFL's player of the year by the AP. He was philosophical about his record-shattering 1973 season, saying: "Someone will break the record, but I'll always be the first one to get 2,000 yards."

Jan. 12 – With the fledgling World Football League looking to sign NFL players, Ralph Wilson extended O.J. Simpson's contract to assure the star running back would remain with the team "for the rest of his career." But only one year was added to Simpson's original deal, which was to run out after 1976.

Jan. 14 – A *Courier-Express* story reported that the WFL was willing to pay O.J. Simpson $2 million per year to join its league. One of the keys to the offer was that Simpson would get to choose what team he wanted to play for. Simpson declined the offer.

Jan. 16 – Offensive tackle Dave Foley was added to the AFC Pro Bowl roster when Miami's Wayne Moore had to pull out. Simpson backed off on his threat not to play in the game because one of his linemen was going to be there with him, although he still preferred it was Reggie McKenzie.

Jan. 21 – O.J. Simpson received the Maxwell Award as pro football player of the year. Penn State's John Cappelletti won the collegiate award.

Jan. 26 – Quarterback Dennis Shaw was traded to St. Louis for wide receiver Ahmad Rashad.

Jan. 29 – The Bills selected Oklahoma State tight end Reuben Gant with their No.1 pick in the draft, the 18th pick overall. Dallas, having obtained the No. 1 overall pick in a trade with Houston in 1973, chose defensive end Ed "Too Tall" Jones. Other first-round choices included defensive end John Dutton (Baltimore), running back John Cappelletti (Los Angeles), linebacker Randy Gradishar (Denver) and wide receiver Lynn Swann (Pittsburgh). Other Bills choices included Penn State linebacker Doug Allen (second), Boston College quarterback Gary Marangi (third), East Carolina running back Carlester Crumpler (fourth), Penn State running back Gary Hayman (fifth) and Kansas State running back Don Calhoun (10th).

Feb. 2 – O.J. Simpson was the landslide winner of the S. Rae Hickok Professional Athlete of the Year award.

Feb. 5 – Simpson and UCLA basketball star Bill Walton were presented pro and amateur athlete of the year awards at the annual Dunlop dinner in Buffalo.

Feb. 23 – After being courted by the Boston Bulls of the WFL, Gary Marangi came to Buffalo and signed a contract.

Feb. 26 – O.J. Simpson predicted that a player strike before the upcoming season was "unavoidable." He said the players' greatest objection was the Rozelle Rule which made free agency virtually impossible. After a player played out his contract, he couldn't sign with another team unless the new team compensated the old team. "The players should be given greater freedom," Simpson said.

Feb. 27 – The NFL owners gave commissioner Pete Rozelle a new 10-year contract and a substantial pay hike, raising his salary to about $200,000 a year.

March 22 – The Bills opened a three-day minicamp and newcomer Ahmad Rashad said he was thrilled to be a Bill after two miserable years in St. Louis. "I think the trade to Buffalo is fantastic," Rashad said.

March 26 – No. 1 draft choice Reuben Gant signed his contract.

March 31 – The WFL made its biggest move to date as the Toronto Northmen signed Miami Dolphins stars Larry Csonka, Jim Kiick and Paul Warfield to a combined $3.5 million deal starting with the 1975 season. "I am disappointed, sick, whatever," Dolphins owner Joe Robbie said.

April 3 – Oakland quarterback Ken Stabler signed a contract to play with Birmingham of the WFL starting in 1976.

April 12 – Reggie McKenzie turned down an offer to play for Washington of the WFL saying that he wanted to play in the Super Bowl with the Bills.

April 24 – The NFL owners awarded Tampa Bay an expansion team to begin play in the 1976 season.

Ralph Wilson was opposed to Tampa Bay and preferred Phoenix or Seattle.

April 25 – The league meetings continued and big changes were approved. One sudden-death overtime period would be played in an effort to rid the league of ties; the goal posts were pushed back to the end line to discourage so many field goals being kicked, plus, on any field goal missed from outside the 20, the ball would be returned to the line of scrimmage; the kickoff was moved back to the 35; restrictions were made on punt coverage teams to open up the return game; roll blocking and cutting of wide receivers was eliminated; the penalties for holding, tripping, and illegal use of hands were reduced from 15 to 10 yards; wide receivers were prohibited from blocking below the waist.

May 6 – The Memphis City Park Commission voted to lease Memphis Stadium to the Toronto franchise of the WFL, assuring the city of a pro football team and meaning Larry Csonka, Jim Kiick and Paul Warfield would play in Memphis in 1975.

June 1 – The Bills held a free-agent tryout camp at Rich Stadium and 22 of 110 men were invited to join the team at the start of their training camp on July 12 at Niagara University.

June 4 – The NFL owners awarded Seattle its second expansion franchise with 1976 as the start-up season. Both Tampa Bay and Seattle paid $16 million expansion fees to join the NFL.

June 6 – With Ralph Wilson leading the charge, the NFL modified the punt coverage rule to allow two outside linemen to run downfield before the kick. Wilson was opposed to the rule change that would force all players to stay on the line of scrimmage until the punt was away, so Wilson won a minor battle.

June 14 – Talks between the Management Council and the Players Association were terminated and a strike seemed imminent; Former Bills GM Dick Gallagher, the director of the Pro Football Hall of Fame in Canton, Ohio, said the Hall of Fame game between Buffalo and St. Louis on July 27 would go on even if a strike occured and rookies and free agents were left to play.

June 25 – With the help of a federal mediator, talks resumed between the two sides.

June 30 – The players officially went on strike.

July 2 – When asked if violence may erupt if rookies and free agents crossed the players' picket line at Niagara when the Bills were due to open training camp, player rep Reggie McKenzie said: "It could get what I call 'funky.' I've never seen a nice strike in any business and I don't expect this one to be any different."

July 3 – The San Diego Chargers' training camp was the first to open in the NFL and 53 rookies and free agents ignored the veterans' picket line and reported without incident.

July 6 – The Band and Eric Clapton highlighted the first concert in Rich Stadium history and more than 47,000 fans attended.

July 9 – Second-round draft choice Doug Allen, who put his Penn State degree in labor relations to use by working for the AFL-CIO in Harrisburg, Pa. since graduating in December, admitted he didn't understand the NFL players' strike. "To me, the Players' Association is caught in a bind," he said. "They're trying to come up with an individual solution to a fantasy world problem. Most pro sports are more or less a diversion to most of the guys. The average career is four or five years."

July 10 – The WFL began its first season of play.

July 11 – The College All-Star game was canceled because of the players' strike.

July 12 – Ralph Wilson crossed his players' picket line, which was formed by Reggie McKenzie and O.J. Simpson at Niagara University. Sixty-five rookies and free agents crossed the line and reported to coach Lou Saban.

July 19 – The Management Council offered a $12.5 million deal to the Players' Association that would cover preseason salaries, pensions, insurance and Pro Bowl pay. In Buffalo, every veteran remained unified for the cause and none had crossed the picket line.

July 20 – Quarterback Joe Ferguson said that if progress wasn't made within the week, he would report to camp. "I'm having second thoughts about this strike every day," he said from his parents' home in Shreveport, La.

July 22 – Fourteen striking veterans held their own workout at Frontier High School, the first formal get-together practice.

July 27 – The "counterfeit" Bills opened the preseason with a 21-13 loss to St. Louis in the Hall of Fame game in Canton, Ohio. First-round draft choice Reuben Gant suffered a shoulder sprain while making his only catch of the game and did not return to action. NFL players picketed outside the stadium and it put a damper on the enshrinement of Lou Groza, Night Train Lane, Bill George and Tony Canadeo into the Hall of Fame.

Aug. 2 – After refunding nearly 25,000 tickets, the Bills played their first exhibition game of the season at Rich Stadium and lost to Green Bay, 16-13. The club announced it had sold a team record 54,146 season tickets.

Aug. 5 – Bo Cornell became the first veteran Bill to cross the picket line. The Bills were the last team to have 100 percent unification. Around the league, star quarterbacks Bob Griese, John Hadl and Terry Bradshaw reported to their respective camps.

Aug. 12 – With the players' strike crumbling because scores of veterans began reporting to camps, the Bills beat Kansas City, 35-21, at Arrowhead Stadium. Quarterback Joe Ferguson was one of 12 vets who saw their first game action. A federal mediator said that all veterans would report to their teams' camps for a 14-day cooling-off period while the negotiators tried to reach an agreement.

Aug. 13 – O.J. Simpson reported to camp, and the rest of the team followed him in. "There is no longer a strike," Simpson said. "I hope they can get the negotiations over in the next two weeks."

Aug. 18 – John Leypoldt kicked a 52-yard field goal on the final play as Buffalo defeated Washington, 16-15, at RFK Stadium.

Aug. 25 – In their worst showing to date, the Bills were trounced by Minnesota, 32-13.

Aug. 27 – The players rejected the owners' latest offer, but voted to remain in training camp.

Aug. 30 – The Bills routed Detroit, 28-7, at Rich Stadium as O.J. Simpson rushed for 116 yards.

Sept. 6 – The longest preseason in team history came to an end as the Bills beat the Giants at Rich, 23-17, in the first overtime game in team history. Wayne Mosley's four-yard TD run decided the issue 8:14 into the extra period.

Sept. 16 – In their second *Monday Night Football* appearance, the Bills stunned the Oakland Raiders, 21-20, in one of the most exciting games in team history. Ahmad Rashad caught two TD passes in the final two minutes to give the Bills the victory. It was Oakland's first loss on Monday night.

Sept. 22 – Miami beat Buffalo, 24-16, at Rich Stadium, for its ninth straight victory over the Bills. O.J. Simpson was slowed by the ankle injury he suffered against the Raiders.

Sept. 29 – With winds gusting to 40 mph, the Bills failed to complete a pass for the first time in team history, yet still defeated the Jets at Rich Stadium, 16-12.

Oct. 6 – The Green Bay Packers became the last team to play the Bills since the 1970 merger, and the Bills went to Lambeau Field and ripped them, 27-7.

Oct. 13 – The Bills sleepwalked through a 27-14 victory over Baltimore as Neal Craig returned a Bert Jones interception 55 yards for a key touchdown.

Oct. 20 – In a showdown for first place in the AFC East, the Bills scored 20 first-quarter points and held on for a 30-28 victory over New England at soldout Rich Stadium. The win enabled the Bills to tie the Patriots for first place at 5-1.

Oct. 27 – The Bills' defense held the Bears without a touchdown in a 16-6 victory at Rich Stadium.

Oct. 28 – At his weekly press conference in Chicago, Bears coach Abe Gibron denied saying that O.J. Simpson ordered that Jim Braxton replace Larry Watkins in the third quarter. Gibron said those comments were made by one or two of his players and that he never said anything "bad about O.J." Said Simpson: "I should have been mad that somebody would even suggest that I would call for a substitution, but it was so ridiculous I couldn't even get mad."

Nov. 3 – For the second time in two weeks, the Bills beat the Patriots with first place on the line in the AFC East. This time, the 29-28 win at Schaefer Stadium gave Buffalo sole possession of the top spot in the division. About 5,000 fans attempted to meet the team at the airport upon arrival from Boston, but the chartered plane taxied to a Prior Aviation gate because the crowd was too large.

Nov. 10 – Houston defeated the Bills for the eighth time in a row as O.J. Simpson was held to 57 yards and the offense failed to score a touchdown in a 21-9 loss at Rich Stadium. Joe Ferguson tied a team record by throwing six interceptions. The mark originally was set by Tommy O'Connell in the team's second game of 1960, the first regular-season game ever played at old War Memorial Stadium.

Nov. 13 – Punter Spike Jones was waived and Marv Bateman was signed.

Nov. 15 – With their huge game against Miami just two days away, the Bills got an unneeded distraction when a blizzard swept through Western New York. Seven players, including O.J. Simpson, failed to make it to Rich Stadium for practice; Linebacker Rich Lewis, who had started 13 straight games from mid-1973 until he was hurt in the first New England game, was claimed on waivers by the Jets. Lou Saban was trying to sneak him through waivers, but failed.

Nov. 17 – For the third time this season, the Bills played with first place in the AFC East on the line and for the first time, they lost, 35-28, at Miami. It was the Dolphins 10th win in a row over Buffalo.

Nov. 24 – The Bills got past Cleveland in the mud at Municipal Stadium, 15-10, and Miami lost to the Jets, creating a first-place tie in the AFC East.

Dec. 1 – On a bitterly cold day at Rich Stadium, the Bills blanked Baltimore, 6-0, recording their first shutout since Nov. 6, 1966, a 29-0 whitewash of Miami, a span of 115 games. The chartered jet that was flying to pick up the Colts after the game, crashed, killing the three crew members aboard.

Dec. 2 – Miami defeated Cincinnati, 24-3, thus assuring the Bills of at least a wild-card playoff spot, their first playoff appearance since the 1966 AFL Championship Game.

Dec. 5 – The Bills learned that they would be without free safety Tony Greene for the rest of the season because of a knee injury suffered against Baltimore.

Dec. 8 – The Jets crushed the Bills' slim hopes of a division title by upsetting them, 20-10, at half-empty Shea Stadium. Miami beat Baltimore, 17-16, to secure the AFC East title again. It was rumored to be Joe Namath's final game at Shea Stadium as the Jets quarterback and he threw two TD passes.

Dec. 12 – Reggie McKenzie, O.J. Simpson, Tony Greene and Robert James were first-team all-AFC selections by the UPI.

Dec. 13 – O.J. Simpson said in an interview that the Bills organization didn't give former quarterback James Harris "an up-and-up deal. If I had to write a book and there was a chapter about a guy being kind of cheated, Jim would be it." Harris responded by saying, "Basically, I was attacked (in Buffalo). The press hurt me a lot. You (media) are the reason I was let go and nobody wanted me. All I read back there was how bad I was. You people didn't like me for some reason. You always brought out the worst in me. And they (the fans) kept booing me and never gave me a chance."

Dec. 15 – A crowd of 84,324 was onhand at the Los Angeles Coliseum to watch former USC star O.J. Simpson get held to 73 yards in Buffalo's 19-14 loss to the Rams in a disappointing season finale for the Bills.

Dec. 21 – In one of the most exciting playoff games in history, Oakland prevented Miami from defending its Super Bowl title by edging the Dolphins, 28-26, on Ken Stabler's miraculous TD pass to Clarence Davis with 26 seconds left to play. In the NFC, Minnesota beat St. Louis, 30-14.

Dec. 22 – Pittsburgh erupted for four second-quarter TDs and ripped the Bills, 32-14, to win the AFC divisional playoff game, Buffalo's first post-season game since the 1966 AFL Championship Game. In the NFC, Los Angeles topped Washington, 19-10

Dec. 29 – Pittsburgh beat Oakland, 24-13, to win the AFC Championship as Franco Harris ran for 111 yards and two TDs. Minnesota clipped Los Angeles, 14-10, to win the NFC Championship, as the Vikings forced five turnovers.

Jan. 12, 1975 – After 42 years of owning the Pittsburgh Steelers, Art Rooney finally celebrated a championship as his Steelers bludgeoned Minnesota, 16-6, to win Super Bowl IX at blustery Tulane Stadium. The Steelers defense limited the Vikings to 119 total yards.

Jan. 19, 1975 – Ex-Bills quarterback James Harris passed for 119 yards and two TDs to lead the NFC to a 17-10 win over the AFC in the Pro Bowl at Miami's Orange Bowl.

Ahmad Rashad (opposite page), playing his first game as a Bill, catches the first of his two touchdowns in the final two minutes, as the Bills defeated Oakland in the 1974 season-opener.

BY THE NUMBERS - 1974

TEAM STATISTICS	BILLS	OPP
First downs	220	219
Rushing	118	96
Passing	85	97
Penalty	17	26
Total yards	3,591	3,470
Avg. game	256.5	247.9
Plays	829	832
Avg. play	4.3	4.2
Net rushing yds	2,099	1,859
Avg. game	149.9	132.8
Avg. play	3.8	3.8
Net passing yds	1,492	1,611
Comp/att	128/251	146/311
Sacks/lost	33-236	32-287
Interceptions	15	20
Percentage	51.0	46.9
Punts/avg	69-40.6	77-37.1
Fumbles/lost	32-14	26-11
Penalties/yds	79-706	73-597
Touchdowns	30	32
Extra points	25-30	28-32
Field goals	19-33	8-15
Safeties	1	0
Kick ret./avg	50-22.6	58-23.2
Punt ret./avg	56-8.2	45-9.2

RUSHING	ATT	YDS	AVG	TD
Simpson	270	1125	4.2	3
Braxton	146	543	3.7	4
Watkins	41	170	4.1	2
Ferguson	54	116	2.1	2
Calhoun	21	88	4.2	0
Hayman	7	31	4.4	0
Marangi	4	20	5.0	0
Mosley	2	6	3.0	0
TOTALS	**545**	**2099**	**3.9**	**11**

PASSING	COMP	ATT	INT	YDS	TD	COMP%	SACKS	RATE
Ferguson	119	232	12	1588	12	51.3	32-235	69.0
Marangi	9	18	3	140	2	50.0	1-1	73.6
Simpson	0	1	0	0	0	0.0	0-0	39.6
TOTALS	**128**	**251**	**15**	**1728**	**14**	**51.0**	**33-236**	**67.3**

KICKING	1-19	20-29	30-39	40-49	50+	TOT	PAT	PTS
Leypoldt	0-0	8-10	6-9	5-12	0-2	19-33	25-29	82
TEAM	0-0	0-0	0-0	0-0	0-0	0-0	0-1	0
TOTALS	**0-0**	**8-10**	**6-9**	**5-12**	**0-2**	**19-33**	**25-30**	**82**

PUNTING	NO	AVG	LG	BL
Bateman	34	43.9	66	0
Jones	35	37.3	56	0
TOTALS	**69**	**40.6**	**66**	**0**

RECEIVING	CAT	YDS	AVG	TD
Rashad	36	433	12.0	4
J.D. Hill	32	572	17.9	6
Braxton	18	171	9.5	0
Seymour	15	246	16.4	2
Simpson	15	189	12.6	1
Chandler	7	88	12.6	1
Calhoun	2	10	5.0	0
Jenkins	1	12	12.0	0
Watkins	1	7	7.0	0
Green	1	0	0.0	0
TOTALS	**128**	**1728**	**13.5**	**14**

LEADERS

Kick returns: Francis 37-947 yards, 25.6 avg, 0 TD
Calhoun 6-90, 15.0, 0 TD

Punt returns: Walker 43-384, 8.9, 0 TD
Cahill 10-62, 6.2, 0 TD

Interceptions: Greene 9-157, 17.4, 0 TD
James 3-13, 4.3, 0 TD
Washington 2-72, 36.0, 1 TD

SCORE BY QUARTERS

BILLS	53	84	37	90 -	264
OPP	28	64	77	75 -	244

Reuben Gant was the Bills first-round draft pick in 1974, but in seven years with the Bills, he caught only 127 passes and scored just 15 touchdowns.

Raiders	0	3	10	7 - 20
Bills	0	7	0	14 - 21

Attendance at Rich Stadium - 79,876

Buf: Hill 4 pass from Ferguson (Leypoldt kick), 4:25
Oak: FG Blanda 34, 13:49
Oak: Davis 15 run (Blanda kick), 4:25
Oak: FG Blanda 41, 11:25
Buf: Rashad 8 pass from Ferguson (Leypoldt kick), 13:04
Oak: Thoms 29 fumble return (Blanda kick), 13:45
Buf: Rashad 13 pass from Ferguson (Leypoldt kick), 14:34

	BUF	OAK
First downs	22	18
Rushing yds	200	152
Passing yds	106	100
Punts-avg	4-35.3	4-40.5
Fumbles-lost	2-1	2-1
Penalties-yds	6-44	10-104

BILLS LEADERS: Rushing - Simpson 12-78, Braxton 19-69, Ferguson 5-16, Hayman 7-31, Mosley 2-6; **Passing** - Ferguson 10-20-0 - 122; **Receiving** - Rashad 5-68, Hill 3-31, Braxton 1-10, Seymour 1-13.

RAIDERS LEADERS: Rushing - C. Smith 14-64, Davis 10-61, Hubbard 10-27, Stabler 1-0; **Passing** - Stabler 9-22-1 - 122; **Receiving** - Branch 4-60, Biletnikoff 3-34, Hubbard 1-15, C. Smith 1-13.

NOTES

• In one of the most exciting games in team history, the Bills upset the Raiders in their second appearance on *Monday Night Football*.
• Ahmad Rashad caught two TD passes in the final two minutes to give the Bills the victory.
• O.J. Simpson sprained his right ankle and sat out the second half. His replacement, rookie Gary Hayman, was lost for the season due to a broken leg.
• Trailing 13-7, the Bills were given life when John Skorupan recovered Marv Hubbard's fumble at the Raiders 33. Rashad then beat Skip Thomas on a slant pattern in the end zone and caught Joe Ferguson's low pass for the go-ahead score with 1:56 left.
• Oakland tried to rally, but Cliff Branch dropped a perfectly thrown Ken Stabler bomb at the Bills 20. The Raiders punted with 1:33 left and Donnie Walker returned it to the Bills 31.
• On the first play, Jim Braxton fumbled, Art Thoms picked up the ball and ran 29 yards for a TD, silencing the sellout crowd.
• Wallace Francis returned the kickoff to the 28 and Ferguson went to work with 1:08 left. He hit Braxton for 10 and a 15-yard roughing-the-passer penalty against Horace Jones was tacked on. After an incompletion, Ferguson hit Rashad for 20 to the Oakland 27. Next came a 10-yard pass to J.D. Hill and then a four-

WEEK 1 GAMES	
Pitt 30, Balt 0	LA 17, Den 10
Cinc 33, Clev 7	Hou 21, SD 14
KC 24, NYJ 16	NE 34, Mia 24
Dal 24, Atl 0	Chi 17, Det 9
Minn 32, GB 17	SF 17, NO 13
Wash 13, NYG 10	St.L 7, Phil 3

yard interference penalty against Thomas with 35 seconds left. After an incompletion, Rashad beat Willie Brown to the inside and caught the winning TD with 26 seconds left. The Raiders nearly won it on the final play, but 47-year-old George Blanda's 50-yard field goal was no good.

QUOTES
• Joe Ferguson: "I just told our linemen in the huddle (before the first TD drive), 'You know what we have to do, they know what we have to do, all I want is a little extra time.' I've never been so tired or as excited in my life."
• Ahmad Rashad: "Nothing was said in the huddle (before the final TD drive). We knew we could get back into it. In that situation, I think I can get open any time. Joe was right on the money, both times. No way I wasn't going to catch them. I'm emotionally drained. We had to regroup twice, the first time after O.J. went out and the second time after Oakland went ahead."
• Lou Saban: "They learned tonight that they can win without him (Simpson) when they have to. Ferguson came through under tremendous pressure, but heck, they all came through."
• Walt Patulski: "That was the hardest-hitting game I've ever played in."
• Mike Montler: "On that last drive we knew Joe could take us in if we kept everybody off him. We just had our tails nailed to the ground. Oakland is always physical and they try to intimidate you, get you to worry about your health."
• O.J. Simpson: "This may be a blessing in disguise (his injury) because the guys found out they could win against a good team without me."

Dolphins	0	7	7	10 - 24
Bills	3	0	6	7 - 16

Attendance at Rich Stadium - 78,990

Buf: FG Leypoldt 22, 13:10
Mia: Mandich 1 pass from Griese (Yepremian kick), 6:42
Mia: Fleming 3 pass from Griese (Yepremian kick), 2:27
Buf: Rashad fumble recovery in end zone (kick failed), 9:41
Mia: Morris 17 run (Yepremian kick), 3:12
Buf: Hill 25 pass from Ferguson (Leypoldt kick), 6:52
Mia: FG Yepremian 22, 13:44

	BUF	MIA
First downs	16	16
Rushing yds	107	176
Passing yds	157	72
Punts-avg	4-39.3	4-36.0
Fumbles-lost	4-3	3-2
Penalties-yds	3-35	3-15

BILLS LEADERS: Rushing - Simpson 15-63, Braxton 11-30, Ferguson 4-14; **Passing** - Ferguson 17-22-0 - 188; **Receiving** - Rashad 2-24, Hill 5-75, Braxton 7-67, Seymour 2-22, Green 1-0.

DOLPHINS LEADERS: Rushing - Morris 13-88, Csonka 19-68, Kiick 4-17, Griese 2-5, Malone 1-(-2); **Passing** - Griese 10-13-2 - 84; **Receiving** - Warfield 5-52, Twilley 2-20, Mandich 2-9, Fleming 1-3.

NOTES
• The two-time defending Super Bowl champion Dolphins beat Buffalo for the ninth straight time.
• The Bills led 3-0 in the second and they stopped Miami at the 6 when Jim Cheyunski recovered a Mercury Morris fumble. On the next play, O.J. Simpson fumbled it back and Doug Swift recovered at the 1, leading to Bob Griese's TD pass to Jim Mandich.
• The Bills drove to Miami's 6 late in the half, but Ahmad Rashad dropped a TD pass and John Leypoldt then missed a 27-yard field goal.
• Jim Braxton fumbled on the second play of the second half and Jake Scott returned it to the 9. The Dolphins converted that into another easy TD as Griese hit Marv Fleming for a three-yard score.
• After a Dwight Harrison interception, the Bills marched 66 yards to a score. Simpson ran 22 yards, but fumbled into the end zone. However, Rashad fell on the ball for the TD. A bad snap aborted the extra point.
• A roughing penalty on Harrison against Paul Warfield gave the Dolphins a first down at the 20 early in the fourth and two plays later, Morris swept in from the 17.
• After J.D. Hill's TD catch, Harrison hurt the Bills with another penalty, a personal foul on the ensuing kickoff, that moved the ball all the way to the Bills 48. Miami drove 43 yards to Garo Yepremian's game-clinching field goal.

WEEK 2 GAMES	
GB 20, Balt 13	SD 20, Cinc 17
Clev 20, Hou 7	Oak 27, KC 7
Pitt 35, Den 35	NE 28, NYG 20
NYJ 23, Chi 21	SF 16, Atl 10
Phil 13, Dal 10	Minn 7, Det 6
St.L 17, Wash 10	LA 24, NO 0

QUOTES
• Dolphins receiver Paul Warfield: "I was complaining about Harrison from the first play of the game. He was aiming haymakers at me all afternoon. The official didn't call anything for a long time, but when he finally did, it hurt Buffalo badly. He's aggressive, but the new rules make it difficult for him. He's allowed only one chuck."
• Lou Saban: "It was a poor game for us. Those errors are too costly against a team like Miami. We threw well enough, but we couldn't run. Someday we're going to get them. There was no change in offensive approach against Miami. If the calls work, they seem imaginative. If they don't, we open ourselves up for the second guess. "
• Dolphins guard Bob Kuechenberg: "Buffalo is a good team. They came after us, but once again we proved we're a better team. Last year, the Bills were ridiculous. They ran even when they were losing, but this year they put the pass in their offense and they've improved. They're going to be good for years to come, but we're still the best."
• Joe Ferguson: "I'd be lying if I said I wasn't pleased with the way our passing game has come around. It's taking the pressure off the backs. The difference today was our mistakes. We should have won. Miami is a great team, but we played the heck out of them. One day it's going to be our turn and they know it."

STANDINGS: SECOND WEEK

AFC EAST	W	L	T	CENTRAL	W	L	T	WEST	W	L	T	NFC EAST	W	L	T	CENTRAL	W	L	T	WEST	W	L	T
New England	2	0	0	Pittsburgh	1	0	1	Kan. City	1	1	0	St. Louis	2	0	0	Minnesota	2	0	0	LA Rams	2	0	0
Buffalo	1	1	0	Cincinnati	1	1	0	Oakland	1	1	0	Washington	1	1	0	Chicago	1	1	0	San Fran	2	0	0
Miami	1	1	0	Houston	1	1	0	San Diego	1	1	0	Dallas	1	1	0	Green Bay	1	1	0	Atlanta	0	2	0
NY Jets	1	1	0	Cleveland	1	1	0	Denver	0	1	1	Philadelphia	1	1	0	Detroit	0	2	0	N.Orleans	0	2	0
Baltimore	0	2	0									NY Giants	0	2	0								

NOTES

• With winds gusting to 40 mph and rain pouring down, the Bills, for the first time in team history, failed to complete a pass, but they didn't need to, rushing 61 times for 223 yards.

• The stadium was half-empty by game's end as many fans went home and watched the second half on TV.

• Joe Namath had more interceptions (three) than completions (two). Both his completions came in the final two minutes as the game nearly became the first in the 55-year history of the NFL to be played without a completion. As it was, the two completions were the fewest by two teams in a game since Brooklyn and Pittsburgh combined for one completion in a 1942 contest.

• Tony Greene's interception and 20-yard return to the 5 set up Joe Ferguson's one-yard TD run.

• The Bills consumed 9:43 on an 89-yard drive that culminated in John Leypoldt's first field goal.

• Jim Braxton's fumble and Richard Neal's recovery at the Bills 22 led to John Riggins' TD midway through the second, but the PAT failed when the wind forced a bad snap.

• The Jets took the wind to start the second half and it resulted in two Bobby Howfield field goals.

• The Bills' winning drive began at midfield after Jets punter Greg Gantt got off a 26-yarder into the wind. O.J. Simpson and Braxton took turns moving the ball to the 21, then Braxton broke free for a 21-yard TD run to win the game.

• Leypoldt became the Bills all-time leading field goal kicker with 48 successes, passing Pete Gogolak.

QUOTES

• Jim Braxton: "You never make up for a fumble. Besides, that touchdown was scored by the offensive line. Joe DeLamielleure pulled and drove their left end right out of the play. There was no one to stop me."

• Lou Saban: "You reporters sit up in that press box eating hot dogs and drinking coffee and then you come down here and ask how was the weather. You won't ever find worse conditions than today. I'm just glad we won. We tried a few passes in the first half, but when we saw how the wind and rain was affecting the ball, we just said the devil with it and stuck with our running game." (On Braxton's recent fumbling): "No one feels worse about those fumbles, and as a result will work harder to correct that, than Jim Braxton."

• Robert James: "I felt that the first team that had to pass was going to be in trouble."

• O.J. Simpson: "The weather wasn't an advantage to anybody, but it hindered the Jets more than us because we're a running team. The field condition didn't bother my running. The only thing that made trouble was the wet ball."

• Jets quarterback Joe Namath: "If this were a golf tournament, they would have called it off, but the conditions were the same for both teams and the Bills won. Sure it was frustrating when you can't perform to the best of your abilities."

Jets	0	6	6	0	-	12
Bills	7	3	0	6	-	16

Attendance at Rich Stadium - 76,978

Buf: Ferguson 1 run (Leypoldt kick), 6:11
Buf: FG Leypoldt 21, 7:08
NYJ: Riggins 13 run (kick failed), 9:54
NYJ: FG Howfield 31, 6:32
NYJ: FG Howfield 40, 13:54
Buf: Braxton 21 run (kick failed), 8:01

	BUF	NYJ
First downs	17	7
Rushing yds	223	106
Passing yds	0	33
Punts-avg	7-31.4	7-33.4
Fumbles-lost	4-2	1-0
Penalties-yds	4-36	6-42

BILLS LEADERS: Rushing - Simpson 31-117, Braxton 17-84, Watkins 3-8, Ferguson 10-14; **Passing** - Ferguson 0-2-0 - 0; **Receiving** - None.

JETS LEADERS: Rushing - Boozer 17-69, Riggins 15-37, Namath 1-0; **Passing** - Namath 2-8-3 - 33; **Receiving** - Brister 1-21, Knight 1-12.

WEEK 3 GAMES

Phil 30, Balt 10	Cinc 21, SF 3
St.L 29, Clev 7	Wash 30, Den 3
KC 14, Hou 7	Mia 28, SD 21
NE 20, LA 14	Oak 17, Pitt 0
NO 14, Atl 13	Minn 11, Chi 7
NYG 14, Dal 6	GB 21, Det 19

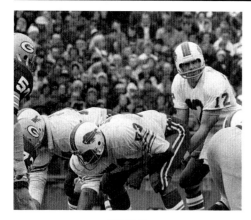

NOTES

• By playing Green Bay, the Bills finally had played every team in the NFL in the regular season.

• The Bills employed eight-, nine- and 10-man defensive lines to harass Packers QB Jerry Tagge.

• The Bills outgained Green Bay, 118-17, in the first quarter, but Jim Braxton's fumble at the Packers 28 killed one scoring threat and John Leypoldt missed a 48-yard field goal. Late in the quarter, Ahmad Rashad capped an 87-yard scoring drive with a nine-yard TD reception.

• A 48-yard drive early in the second made it 13-0, but Leypoldt missed the extra point and another Leypoldt field goal miss from 48 prevented the score from mounting.

• Tony Greene's interception and 38-yard return to the Packers 22 led to Braxton's second TD. On the play before, O.J. Simpson nearly had his first receiving TD since 1969, but he was pushed out of bounds at the 1.

• Braxton's third TD came after Robert James' interception at the Bills 45.

• Braxton had fumbled in four straight games, but for the first time, opponents didn't score after one of his giveaways.

• Ferguson's interception was his first since Week 12 in 1973, a span of nearly six games.

• A game ball went to offensive line coach Jim Ringo, a former Packers great.

• The win was Buffalo's fourth straight on the road dating back to 1973.

QUOTES

• Green Bay quarterback Jerry Tagge: "They were meeting our backs at the line and knocking them off their paths. The beating I took wasn't any worse than normal. What is normal, anyway? They were coming at us pretty good, especially when they had us where we had to throw."

• Bills linebackers coach John Ray talking about his three starters, Jim Cheyunski, Rich Lewis and John Skorupan: "We want our linebackers knocking those receivers around and we probably do it more than most teams. Quickness and courage is what they have most of. They aren't big, but they listen. Some linebackers are afraid to do the things ours do because it's easy to get beat when you're trying to bump guys at the line. Every week they rise to the challenge."

• Green Bay running back John Brockington: "I thought we could run on this team, but nothing went right."

• Joe Ferguson: "Our aim is to win, not to prove whether we can run or pass. All of us will be happy if we make the playoffs, no matter how we get there."

• Lou Saban: "We expect teams to try to control our running game, so consequently we featured our passing more. Ferguson was 13 of 16 and he threw one away. I'd say that's a pretty good performance."

Bills	7	6	7	7	-	27
Packers	0	0	0	7	-	7

Attendance at Lambeau Field - 56,267

Buf: Rashad 9 pass from Ferguson (Leypoldt kick), 14:56
Buf: Braxton 1 run (kick failed), 5:51
Buf: Braxton 1 run (Leypoldt kick), 5:31
GB: Lane 3 run (Marcol kick), 3:13
Buf: Braxton 1 run (Leypoldt kick), 9:33

	BUF	GB
First downs	22	18
Rushing yds	148	100
Passing yds	157	131
Punts-avg	2-35.5	4-32.5
Fumbles-lost	1-1	1-1
Penalties-yds	10-73	7-51

BILLS LEADERS: Rushing - Simpson 16-62, Braxton 25-86; **Passing** - Ferguson 13-16-1 - 175; **Receiving** - Rashad 7-79, Hill 2-48, Braxton 1-12, Seymour 1-23, Simpson 2-13.

PACKERS LEADERS: Rushing - Brockington 14-56, Lane 11-44; **Passing** - Tagge 17-31-2 - 141; **Receiving** - B. Smith 4-66, McGeorge 4-32, Lane 5-30, Payne 1-8, Brockington 3-5.

WEEK 4 GAMES

NE 42, Balt 3	Oak 40, Clev 24
Cinc 28, Wash 17	Den 17, KC 14
Pitt 13, Hou 7	Mia 21, NYJ 17
Phil 13, SD 6	Atl 14, NYG 7
Chi 24, NO 10	Minn 23, Dal 21
LA 16, Det 13	St.L 34, SF 9

STANDINGS: FOURTH WEEK

AFC EAST	W	L	T	CENTRAL	W	L	T	WEST	W	L	T	NFC EAST	W	L	T	CENTRAL	W	L	T	WEST	W	L	T
New England	4	0	0	Cincinnati	3	1	0	Oakland	3	1	0	St. Louis	4	0	0	Minnesota	4	0	0	LA Rams	3	1	0
Buffalo	3	1	0	Pittsburgh	2	1	1	Kan. City	2	2	0	Philadelphia	3	1	0	Chicago	2	2	0	San Fran	2	2	0
Miami	3	1	0	Houston	1	3	0	Denver	1	2	1	Washington	2	2	0	Green Bay	2	2	0	N.Orleans	1	3	0
NY Jets	1	3	0	Cleveland	1	3	0	San Diego	1	3	0	Dallas	1	3	0	Detroit	0	4	0	Atlanta	1	3	0
Baltimore	0	4	0									NY Giants	1	3	0								

Bills	0	17	0	10	-	27
Colts	0	7	7	0	-	14

Attendance at Memorial Stadium - 40,626

Buf: FG Leypoldt 28, 3:11
Bal: Jones 9 run (Linhart kick), 8:38
Buf: Craig 55 interception return (Leypoldt kick), 11:50
Buf: Hill 47 pass from Ferguson (Leypoldt kick), 14:55
Bal: L. Mitchell 6 run (Linhart kick), 6:00
Buf: FG Leypoldt 33, 4:46
Buf: Watkins 1 run (Leypoldt kick), 13:57

	BUF	BAL
First downs	15	11
Rushing yds	181	161
Passing yds	125	1
Punts-avg	6-41.2	8-40.6
Fumbles-lost	2-1	2-1
Penalties-yds	7-73	2-30

BILLS LEADERS: Rushing - Simpson 23-127, Braxton 6-17, Watkins 6-34, Ferguson 1-3; **Passing** - Ferguson 11-27-1 - 155; **Receiving** - Rashad 3-21, Hill 3-74, Braxton 2-15, Seymour 2-37, Simpson 1-8.

COLTS LEADERS: Rushing - L. Mitchell 20-81, Olds 18-70, Jones 2-9, McCauley 2-1; **Passing** - Jones 6-16-1 - 44; **Receiving** - Chester 2-21, L. Mitchell 3-13, Carr 1-10.

NOTES

• Baltimore remained winless and the Bills set up a first-place showdown with New England with the win.
• Lou Saban won his 53rd regular-season game as Bills coach and celebrated his 53rd birthday.
• The Bills led 10-7 late in the first half when John Leypoldt missed a 29-yard field goal. Saban used time-outs on defense in an effort to get the ball back and it worked. Then, J.D. Hill made a spectacular 47-yard TD catch, beating Nelson Munsey with five seconds left for a 17-7 lead.
• Three minutes earlier, Neal Craig put the Bills ahead when he stepped in front of Raymond Chester, picked off Bert Jones' pass and ran 55 yards for a TD.
• After the Colts pulled to within 17-14 in the third, Spike Jones' punt to the Colts 10 wound up resulting in a field goal by Leypoldt as the Bills defense held and forced an end zone punt by David Lee that carried to the Colts 44.
• With a chance to ice the game, Leypoldt missed a 35-yard field goal, leaving the Colts in contention. But Jones was sacked by Mike Kadish and Earl Edwards on fourth down at his own 11 with 1:44 left. Larry Watkins, in for Jim Braxton who hurt his knee, scored an insurance TD with 1:03 left.

WEEK 5 GAMES
Cinc 34, Clev 24	Den 33, NO 17
Minn 51, Hou 10	Pitt 34, KC 24
Wash 20, Mia 17	NE 24, NYJ 0
Oak 14, SD 10	Atl 13, Chi 10
St.L 31, Dal 28	Det 17, SF 13
GB 17, LA 6	Phil 35, NYG 7

QUOTES

• J.D. Hill: "Joe told me to run a streak to get behind the coverage. It was the kind of catch I've been dreaming about making all my life. Joe got perfect pass protection from the line and I dove for the ball. In the past, I seemed to get the Bill of the Week honor in games we had lost. It's beautiful to get it when we win. The only thing is we kind of got lackadaisical. We took the Colts too soft. They're a far better team than they showed on film."
• Lou Saban: "I don't think the Colts are far from being a good team and I'm not just saying that to be nice, I mean it."
• Neal Craig: "Jones' ball was well thrown. In 99 percent of the cases it would have been complete, but I read the play and we were in a coverage which had me playing wide anyway. Experience is what enabled me to make that play. It wasn't Jones' fault, I just knew he was going to throw it. Chester introduced me to pro football when I was a rookie, catching a couple of touchdown passes off me when he was with Oakland. I've been battling him ever since."
• Reggie McKenzie: "I'll tell you this, I'll never underestimate Baltimore again. Baltimore was 0-4 and lost 43-0 last week. what would you do? But we should have realized they'd be fired up. We were in the same situation not too long ago."
• Joe Ferguson: "I felt lackadaisical out there. I had trouble getting my mind on the game early."

Patriots	7	7	7	7	-	28
Bills	20	7	0	3	-	30

Attendance at Rich Stadium - 78,935

NE: Cunningham 75 run (Smith kick), :21
Buf: Seymour 10 pass from Ferguson (Leypoldt kick), 5:57
Buf: Simpson 29 pass from Ferguson (kick blocked), 11:06
Buf: Simpson 1 run (Leypoldt kick), 12:45
NE: Cunningham 12 run (Smith kick), 5:57
Buf: Seymour 40 pass from Ferguson (Leypoldt kick), 10:04
NE: Cunningham 1 run (Smith kick), 6:05
Buf: FG Leypoldt 35, 1:24
NE: Rucker 12 pass from Plunkett (Smith kick), 14:55

	BUF	NE
First downs	19	19
Rushing yds	180	189
Passing yds	135	131
Punts-avg	5-43.8	5-29.2
Fumbles-lost	0-0	1-1
Penalties-yds	8-57	6-47

BILLS LEADERS: Rushing - Simpson 32-122, Braxton 12-39, Ferguson 8-19; **Passing** - Ferguson 8-12-0 - 153; **Receiving** - Rashad 2-36, Braxton 2-24, Seymour 3-64, Simpson 1-29.

PATRIOTS LEADERS: Rushing - Cunningham 11-125, Herron 14-50, Plunkett 1-9, Ashton 2-5; **Passing** - Plunkett 11-21-1 - 150; **Receiving** - Rucker 5-78, Windsor 3-34, Cunningham 2-21, Herron 1-17.

NOTES

• The Bills pulled into a first-place tie with the Patriots.
• Tight end Paul Seymour scored the first two TDs of his career.
• The Patriots hadn't allowed a TD in their previous nine quarters before the Bills struck for three in the first.
• Sam Cunningham went 75 yards for a TD on the first play of the game, but Wallace Francis returned the ensuing kickoff to the 43 and the Bills drove to Seymour's first TD.
• After a short Patriots punt, the Bills drove 54 yards with Simpson catching his first TD pass since 1969. John Leypoldt missed his fourth extra point of the year, leaving the score 13-7.
• Tony Greene picked off a poor Jim Plunkett pass and returned it 23 yards to the 4 from where Simpson scored. Greene recovered a fumble on the next series, but the Bills had to punt.
• The Pats then marched 80 yards to Cunningham's second TD to make it 20-14, but back came Buffalo when Ferguson hit Seymour all alone on the right sideline for a 40-yard score.
• Mack Herron's 48-yard punt return led to Cunningham's third TD, but Leypoldt's fourth-quarter field goal put it out of reach and made Reggie Rucker's TD with five seconds to play meaningless.

WEEK 6 GAMES
Balt 35, NYJ 20	Den 27, SD 7
Oak 30, Cinc 27	Mia 9, KC 3
Pitt 20, Clev 16	NO 13, Atl 3
St.L 31, Hou 27	Chi 10, GB 9
Dal 31, Phil 24	LA 37, SF 14
Det 20, Minn 16	Was 24, NYG 3

QUOTES

• Jim Cheyunski: "We still felt we were going to beat them, even after Cunningham's run. There was no way they could stop our offense, so our job was to keep getting the ball back for the offense."
• Paul Seymour: "I don't think anyone thought of me as a devastating threat as a pass catcher. I was drafted as a tackle, but I'd rather play tight end, that's where I've played most of my life. I think I'm catching the ball better this season because I'm concentrating better."
• Joe Ferguson: "They were doubling on J.D. and Ahmad on the outside. I really don't know what happened to the coverage on Paul."
• O.J. Simpson on the Bills' plan of attack against the Pats' 3-4 defense: "We had our two guards (Joe DeLamielleure and Reggie McKenzie) matched up with their two linebackers. I don't care how good the linebackers are, you can't expect them to come out on top against two guards like ours."
• Pats running back Mack Herron: "I wouldn't say Buffalo played a dirty game, but then I wouldn't exactly say Buffalo played a clean game, either. Some of the Bills took cheap shots when they had them and some took cheap shots when they didn't have them."
• Earl Edwards: "Nobody got paid for playing nice today. The Patriots were complaining to the refs all day but heck, I could cry to the officials every play because somebody's always holding. So much was at stake, you couldn't talk a good game, you had to play a good game. So let them do all the talking, we won the game and that's what matters."

STANDINGS: SIXTH WEEK

AFC EAST	W	L	T	CENTRAL	W	L	T	WEST	W	L	T	NFC EAST	W	L	T	CENTRAL	W	L	T	WEST	W	L	T
New England	5	1	0	Pittsburgh	4	1	1	Oakland	5	1	0	St. Louis	6	0	0	Minnesota	5	1	0	LA Rams	4	2	0
Buffalo	5	1	0	Cincinnati	4	2	0	Denver	3	2	1	Philadelphia	4	2	0	Chicago	3	3	0	San Fran	2	4	0
Miami	4	2	0	Houston	1	5	0	Kan. City	2	4	0	Washington	4	2	0	Green Bay	3	3	0	Atlanta	2	4	0
NY Jets	1	5	0	Cleveland	1	5	0	San Diego	1	5	0	Dallas	2	4	0	Detroit	2	4	0	N.Orleans	2	4	0
Baltimore	1	5	0									NY Giants	1	5	0								

NOTES

• The Buffalo defense turned in a gritty effort and out-muscled the Bears despite playing without Dwight Harrison, John Skorupan (out for the season) and Rich Lewis.

• Mike Kadish made two huge plays, sacking Bears QB Gary Huff for a 17-yard loss that cost Chicago a chance for a field goal late in the third. Midway through the fourth, he sacked Huff for an 11-yard loss forcing a punt that led to Buffalo's final, clinching points.

• The Bills scored on their opening possession when John Leypoldt made a 47-yard field goal. Tony Greene, playing cornerback in place of Harrison, intercepted Huff's first pass of the game and returned it 15 yards to the Bears 26 and a personal foul on the play moved the ball to the 13. Larry Watkins scored three plays later for a 10-0 lead.

• The Bears were foiled on fourth-and-one in the second quarter at the Bills 17.

• In the third, the Bears faked a punt at the Bills 44, but punter Bob Parsons' pass was dropped by Bill Knox.

• The 6-1 record was Buffalo's second-best first half of a season since 1964 when it opened with nine straight wins.

QUOTES

• Bears safety Gary Lyle: "O.J. didn't want to run in the second half. He caught a pass, then he ran for nine yards on the next play and somebody hit him. He didn't run the rest of the game. He carried the ball, but he didn't run."

• O.J. Simpson: "Those comments remind me of what I used to hear at USC. Everyone used to claim they could beat us on Tuesday and Wednesday, but they hadn't done too well the Saturday before. Every week you hear about how such and such team should have beaten the Dolphins, that Miami is no good and so on, but Miami just goes on winning no matter what's said. I think that's the case here. What have the Bears won, three games? They must be getting dizzy from all that winning."

• Lou Saban: "This was one of the longest afternoons I've spent in a long time. The defense had its good points and the offense did enough to keep us from losing."

• John Leypoldt: "My missed field goals haven't been by much. I think I'm better in pressure situations. I'm calmer. I'm glad to be in position where games are won or lost by my field goals."

• Bears coach Abe Gibron: "What burned me up were some of the comments made by Mike Kadish knocking our division and I didn't like that. When a reporter asked me if I'd like to play Buffalo every week, I said 'Sure.' What was I supposed to say, that I was scared to play Buffalo every week?"

Bears	0	3	0	3 - 6
Bills	10	0	0	6 - 16

Attendance at Rich Stadium - 77,910

Buf:	FG Leypoldt 47, 4:53
Buf:	Watkins 1 run (Leypoldt kick), 7:17
Chi:	FG Roder 42, 13:44
Buf:	FG Leypoldt 25, :43
Chi:	FG Roder 28, 7:37
Buf:	FG Leypoldt 36, 13:00

	BUF	CHI
First downs	16	17
Rushing yds	126	99
Passing yds	100	159
Punts-avg	4-41.3	4-40.8
Fumbles-lost	2-0	0-0
Penalties-yds	5-40	7-63

BILLS LEADERS: Rushing - Simpson 17-62, Braxton 6-21, Watkins 10-40, Ferguson 4-3; **Passing** - Ferguson 8-17-0 - 103; **Receiving** - Rashad 1-11, Hill 5-57, Simpson 1-28, Watkins 1-7.

BEARS LEADERS: Rushing - Garrett 15-70, Williams 7-13, Harrison 1-6, Grandberry 2-6, Huff 3-4; **Passing** - Huff 16-36-1 - 204, Parsons 0-1-0 - 0; **Receiving** - Wade 6-79, Garrett 6-58, Rather 3-53, Kelly 1-14.

WEEK 7 GAMES	
Mia 17, Balt 7	Hou 34, Cinc 21
Clev 23, Den 21	KC 24, SD 14
NE 17, Minn 14	LA 20, NYJ 13
Oak 35, SF 24	Pitt 24, Atl 17
Dal 21, NYG 7	Det 19, GB 17
NO 14, Phil 10	St.L 23, Wash 20

NOTES

• Tonawanda native Jeff Yeates blocked John Smith's 46-yard field goal attempt with 56 seconds left after O.J. Simpson's fumble had given the Pats the chance to win.

• The win lifted the Bills into sole possession of first place in the AFC East.

• The win was Buffalo's sixth in a row this year, sixth straight on the road and seventh straight over the Pats.

• John Leypoldt became the Bills all-time leading scorer, raising his career total to 256.

• For the first time in team history, the Bills were not forced to punt.

• Leypoldt gave the Bills the early lead, but the Pats replied with Jim Plunkett's TD pass to Mack Herron.

• Wallace Francis returned the kickoff 74 yards to set up Leypoldt's second field goal.

• Joe Ferguson lost a fumble at the Bills 31 in the second and Plunkett converted with another TD pass to Herron, who beat linebacker Dave Washington.

• Ferguson came back and drove the Bills to a TD, hitting Ahmad Rashad, but the PAT was blocked.

• Ferguson then was intercepted by Ron Bolton at the Bills 37 and that led to Sam Cunningham's TD. When Ferguson was intercepted again, by Sam Hunt who returned it to the 15, the Bills appeared to be in big trouble. But Merv Krakau intercepted Plunkett and returned it out to the 37, Ferguson hit Rashad for 20- and 10-yard gains and J.D. Hill for 27 to the 1, from where Simpson scored to make it 21-19 at the half.

• Washington then made the play of the game in the third, intercepting a fourth-and-inches pass intended for Cunningham and running 72 yards for the go-ahead score.

• Eddie Hinton brought back the kickoff 53 yards and the Pats eventually regained the lead on Herron's run, but Ferguson moved the Bills to Leypoldt's game-winning field goal on the first play of the fourth quarter and the defense held firm the rest of the way.

QUOTES

• Mike Montler: "That's the rare game where neither team leaves with its heads down."

• O.J. Simpson: "Yeates saved my life. I felt so terrible when I fumbled that ball. The guys look to me for leadership and here we were in the biggest game of the year and I give the ball away when we have the game under control."

• Jeff Yeates: "I just said to myself before the ball was snapped, 'This is it' and I went hard. I was able to slip between (Leon) Gray and (John) Hannah. It was just one of those things. You might try it 100 times and it may work only once, and it did this time."

Bills	6	13	7	3 - 29
Patriots	7	14	7	0 - 28

Attendance at Schaefer Stadium - 58,932

Buf:	FG Leypoldt 45, 4:50
NE:	Herron 43 pass from Plunkett (Smith kick), 8:55
Buf:	FG Leypoldt 20, 11:43
NE:	Herron 20 pass from Plunkett (Smith kick), 1:47
Buf:	Rashad 25 pass from Ferguson (kick blocked), 7:08
NE:	Cunningham 31 run (Smith kick), 13:09
Buf:	Simpson 1 run (Leypoldt kick), 14:21
Buf:	Washington 72 interception return (Leypoldt kick), 6:23
NE:	Herron 2 run (Smith kick), 11:20
Buf:	FG Leypoldt 47, :05

	BUF	NE
First downs	22	20
Rushing yds	103	155
Passing yds	219	200
Punts-avg	0-0	2-38.0
Fumbles-lost	2-2	1-0
Penalties-yds	5-37	6-40

BILLS LEADERS: Rushing - Simpson 19-74, Braxton 7-14, Ferguson 1-15; **Passing** - Ferguson 16-24-2 - 247; **Receiving** - Rashad 8-115, Hill 4-67, Seymour 2-35, Simpson 2-30.

PATRIOTS LEADERS: Rushing - Cunningham 18-85, Herron 17-69, Plunkett 2-9. Vataha 1-(-8); **Passing** - Plunkett 12-28-3 - 204; **Receiving** - Herron 4-77, Vataha 2-40, Rucker 2-34, B. Adams 1-24, Tanner 1-21, Cunningham 1-6, Tarver 1-2.

WEEK 8 GAMES	
Cinc 24, Balt 14	Oak 28, Den 17
SD 36, Clev 35	Hou 27, NYJ 22
NYG 33, KC 27	Mia 42, Atl 7
Pitt 27, Phil 0	Minn 17, Chi 0
Dal 17, St.L 14	Det 19, NO 16
Wash 17, GB 6	LA 15, SF 13

STANDINGS: EIGHTH WEEK

AFC EAST	W	L	T	CENTRAL	W	L	T	WEST	W	L	T	NFC EAST	W	L	T	CENTRAL	W	L	T	WEST	W	L	T
Buffalo	7	1	0	Pittsburgh	6	1	1	Oakland	7	1	0	St. Louis	7	1	0	Minnesota	6	2	0	LA Rams	6	2	0
New England	6	2	0	Cincinnati	5	3	0	Denver	3	4	1	Washington	5	3	0	Detroit	4	4	0	N.Orleans	3	5	0
Miami	6	2	0	Houston	3	5	0	Kan. City	3	5	0	Philadelphia	4	4	0	Chicago	3	5	0	San Fran	2	6	0
NY Jets	1	7	0	Cleveland	2	6	0	San Diego	2	6	0	Dallas	4	4	0	Green Bay	3	5	0	Atlanta	2	6	0
Baltimore	1	7	0									NY Giants	2	6	0								

Oilers	14 0 7 0 - 21
Bills	**0 6 3 0 - 9**

Attendance at Rich Stadium - 79,223

Hou: Rodgers 13 run (Butler kick), 3:03
Hou: Alston 25 pass from Pastorini (Butler kick), 10:12
Buf: FG Leypoldt 32, 3:57
Buf: FG Leypoldt 28, 13:57
Buf: FG Leypoldt 22, 9:28
Hou: V. Washington 9 run (Butler kick), 11:58

	BUF	HOU
First downs	16	10
Rushing yds	133	115
Passing yds	91	59
Punts-avg	3-28.3	6-43.0
Fumbles-lost	2-0	2-2
Penalties-yds	8-98	8-64

BILLS LEADERS: Rushing - Simpson 17-57, Braxton 19-71, Ferguson 4-5; **Passing** - Ferguson 10-28-6 - 110; **Receiving** - Rashad 2-14, Braxton 2-22, Chandler 5-62, Jenkins 1-12.

OILERS LEADERS: Rushing - V. Washington 18-58, Anderson 7-32, Rodgers 7-31, Pastorini 5-(-6); **Passing** - Pastorini 6-10-2 - 59, Amundson 0-1-0 - 0; **Receiving** - Alston 2-28, Washington 2-16, Burrough 1-13, Rodgers 1-2.

WEEK 9 GAMES

Den 17, Balt 6	Cinc 17, Pitt 10
Clev 21, NE 14	SD 14, KC 7
Mia 21, NO 0	NYJ 26, NYG 20
Oak 35, Det 13	Wash 27, Phil 20
GB 20, Chi 3	Dal 20, SF 14
LA 21, Atl 0	Minn 28, St.L 24

NOTES

• The Bills' six-game winning streak came to a halt and they slipped into a tie for first with Miami.

• The Bills' defense held Houston to a paltry 174 yards of total offense, but Joe Ferguson, playing against the AFC's worst defense, had his worst day as a pro with six interceptions. That tied the Bills all-time record held by Tommy O'Connell, who threw six in the Bills first regular-season game in 1960 at War Memorial Stadium.

• Ferguson was intercepted by Gregg Bingham on the second play and four plays later, Willie Rodgers scored on a 13-yard run.

• Midway through the quarter, Billy Johnson returned a poor Spike Jones punt to the Bills 34. Faced with fourth-and-one at the 25, Dan Pastorini play-faked masterfully and hit wide-open Mack Alston with the TD pass that made it 14-0.

• Buffalo got three straight field goals from John Leypoldt to pull within 14-9, but Houston put it away late in the third on Vic Washington's TD. The drive was helped by a 29-yard pass-interference penalty on Dwight Harrison that put the ball on the 9.

• A 15-year-old Lackawanna boy sprayed white paint on Ferguson and O.J. Simpson after the game as they were walking through the tunnel on the way to the lockerroom.

• Wide receiver Bob Chandler caught his first five passes of the season. He had offseason knee surgery, lost his starting job to Ahmad Rashad and had been used only as the placement holder.

QUOTES

• Oilers quarterback Dan Pastorini: "We felt like the Christians being led to the Lions when we heard those people (the fans roared during pre-game introductions)." (On the TD pass to Alston): "They never expected a pass. You could tell by their faces. They had to play for the run because we had been going right at them. They had their strong safety right up on the line. If he hadn't been there, I would have audibled out of the pass play."

• Joe Ferguson: "It's hard to get a game like this out of your system and it's going to be harder because I'll be hearing about it all week. We'll come back, though, I guarantee it. Maybe we need a game like this to see if we can come back."

• O.J. Simpson: "It's impossible for a team to get up as high as we were last week, but every time we went out there on the field, I thought we would get it going. Hey, give Houston credit, they made the most out of everything we gave them. I won't speculate as to how many times we should beat them if we played 10 times, because we only play them once and on this day, they were the better team."

• Lou Saban: "We sure are great when we play a good game, but we sure were bad in this one. When you get beat like that, there isn't much to say. But it wasn't just Joe. I never had any intention of taking Joe out. I don't want him looking over his shoulder when he makes a mistake."

Bills	0 0 7 21 - 28
Dolphins	**0 14 7 14 - 35**

Attendance at the Orange Bowl - 69,313

Mia: Csonka 2 run (Yepremian kick), 6:44
Mia: Warfield 49 pass from Griese (Yepremian kick), 14:34
Buf: Ferguson 1 run (Leypoldt kick), 8:44
Mia: Csonka 6 run (Yepremian kick), 13:12
Buf: Washington 42 fumble return (Leypoldt kick), 1:02
Buf: Hill 44 pass from Marangi (Leypoldt kick), 3:50
Mia: Nottingham 11 run (Yepremian kick), 9:59
Buf: Chandler 5 pass from Marangi (Leypoldt kick), 14:04
Mia: Nottingham 23 run (Yepremian kick), 14:41

	BUF	MIA
First downs	16	21
Rushing yds	132	155
Passing yds	139	223
Punts-avg	7-46.0	6-38.0
Fumbles-lost	5-1	4-2
Penalties-yds	5-49	4-36

BILLS LEADERS: Rushing - Simpson 14-60, Braxton 11-44, Ferguson 2-8, Marangi 4-20; **Passing** - Ferguson 7-14-0 - 83, Marangi 6-9-1 - 98; **Receiving** - Rashad 1-14, Hill 3-60, Braxton 2-14, Chandler 2-26, Seymour 2-32, Simpson 3-35.

DOLPHINS LEADERS: Rushing - Nottingham 6-41, Malone 12-36, Kiick 3-34, Csonka 8-30, Griese 4-7, Morris 7-7; **Passing** - Griese 11-18-0 - 237; **Receiving** - Warfield 4-139, Moore 3-73, Kiick 2-20, Csonka 1-3, Mandich 1-2.

NOTES

• The Bills lost their showdown for first place in the AFC East as Don Nottingham ran 23 yards for the winning TD with 19 seconds remaining, the Dolphins' 10th win in a row over Buffalo.

• Rookie Gary Marangi replaced the injured Joe Ferguson and led the Bills to two fourth-quarter TDs.

• The Dolphins went from down 7-0 to up 7-0 in a blink as Tony Greene's 105-yard interception return for a TD was nullified when Robert James was detected for holding Howard Twilley, giving Miami a first down. Larry Csonka scored on the next play. Miami made it 14-0 when Bob Griese hit Paul Warfield with a 49-yard TD pass 26 seconds before halftime.

• Ferguson engineered a 55-yard scoring drive and scored on a one-yard run, but the Dolphins got that back when Griese hit Warfield for 54 yards and a roughing penalty moved the ball to the 6. Csonka scored two plays later for a 21-7 lead.

• Ferguson suffered a badly bruised knee late in the third, but the Bills got back into the game when Dave Washington scooped up Mercury Morris' fumble and went 42 yards for a TD.

• Greene then forced Warfield to fumble and Washington recovered at the Bills 44. Three plays later, Marangi's first pass as a pro was caught by J.D. Hill for a 44-yard TD that tied the game.

• James' interference penalty on Nat Moore kept alive Miami's 81-yard ensuing drive that resulted in a Nottingham TD, but the Bills rallied to tie when Marangi directed a gutty eight-play, 71-yard drive. He scrambled three times for 20 yards and completed five passes including the tying TD with 56 seconds left.

• But Miami won it when Griese took his team 81 yards in four plays, calling an audible when he recognized a blitz coming on Nottingham's winning TD run through a gaping hole up the middle.

QUOTES

• Dolphins running back Jim Kiick: "What sets us apart from a good team like Buffalo is depth and poise. That's why we are Super Bowl champions."

• Mike Kadish: "I knew they were going to run (on the winning TD). All they had to do was keep the ball on the ground and kick a field goal. I don't know why in the world we were in a blitz."

• Jim Cheyunski: "We gambled and it didn't pay off. If the blitz had worked it would have been a great play. It didn't, so it was a bust."

• Dolphins coach Don Shula: "We were thinking field goal and if Nottingham hadn't scored, Griese had already been told to let the clock run down to four seconds and then we'd kick."

WEEK 10 GAMES

NO 20, LA 7	St.L 13, Phil 3
Balt 17, Atl 7	Hou 20, Cinc 3
KC 42, Den 34	Pitt 26, Clev 16
NYJ 21, NE 16	Oak 17, SD 10
SF 34, Chi 0	Wash 28, Dal 21
Det 20, NYG 19	GB 19, Minn 7

STANDINGS: TENTH WEEK

AFC EAST	W	L	T	CENTRAL	W	L	T	WEST	W	L	T	NFC EAST	W	L	T	CENTRAL	W	L	T	WEST	W	L	T
Miami	8	2	0	Pittsburgh	7	2	1	Oakland	9	1	0	St. Louis	8	2	0	Minnesota	7	3	0	LA Rams	7	3	0
Buffalo	7	3	0	Cincinnati	6	4	0	Denver	4	5	1	Washington	7	3	0	Detroit	5	5	0	N.Orleans	4	6	0
New England	6	4	0	Houston	5	5	0	Kan. City	4	6	0	Dallas	5	5	0	Green Bay	5	5	0	San Fran	3	7	0
NY Jets	3	7	0	Cleveland	3	7	0	San Diego	3	7	0	Philadelphia	4	6	0	Chicago	3	7	0	Atlanta	2	8	0
Baltimore	2	8	0									NY Giants	2	8	0								

NOTES

- Thanks to a workmanlike effort by O.J. Simpson and the Jets' shocking upset over Miami, the Bills were back in a first-place tie with the Dolphins in the AFC East.
- The victory was the first for any Buffalo team over a Cleveland team, dating back to the All-America Conference days from 1946-49.
- Joe Ferguson started at quarterback, but played in slight pain due to his contused knee. He completed only one pass, which enabled Cleveland to set a team defensive record for fewest completions allowed in a single game.
- The Browns had a remarkable 24-play drive that moved 85 yards in nearly 13 minutes, but it resulted in only a 3-0 lead as the Bills defense stiffened. Buffalo then needed one minute to go ahead as Simpson raced 41 yards for a TD after Wallace Francis' 46-yard kickoff return.
- After a field goal, the Bills got a break when Greg Pruitt was stopped at the 18 on the kickoff return. A penalty set the Browns back to the 9. On the first play, Mike Kadish smashed through and sacked Brian Sipe for a safety and a 12-3 lead. Sipe was benched in favor of Mike Phipps, but Phipps went on to throw three interceptions, two by Tony Greene.
- Simpson's running led the Bills to their final points in the fourth quarter, rendering meaningless Phipps' TD pass to Ken Brown with four seconds left.

QUOTES

- O.J. Simpson: "I didn't sleep at all. I came over to the stadium at 9:30 this morning and Bob Reese, our assistant trainer, told me to go into the trainer's room and get some sleep. Then he and J.D. Hill reminded me that whenever I've played when I was sick, I've always had a big game. Also, some of the best games I've had have been in the mud."
- Lou Saban: "To me, the safety was the big play. The safety meant they would have needed two touchdowns to go ahead (when the Bills led 15-3)."
- Joe Ferguson on completing only one pass: "We won the game, that's all that matters. And I had a few dropped (J.D. Hill dropped a sure TD and Simpson dropped what could have been a TD)."

Bills	0	12	0	3 -	15
Browns	0	3	0	7 -	10

Attendance at Municipal Stadium - 66,504

Cle: FG Cockroft 21, 1:00
Buf: Simpson 41 run (Leypoldt kick), 2:00
Buf: FG Leypoldt 41, 6:54
Buf: Safety, Kadish tackled Sipe in end zone, 7:21
Buf: FG Leypoldt 42, :58
Cle: K. Brown 3 pass from Phipps (Cockroft kick), 14:56

	BUF	CLE
First downs	10	19
Rushing yds	188	147
Passing yds	9	130
Punts-avg	5-42.2	4-39.8
Fumbles-lost	1-0	2-0
Penalties-yds	4-19	4-47

BILLS LEADERS: Rushing - Simpson 22-115, Braxton 10-49, Watkins 6-24, Ferguson 2-0; **Passing** - Ferguson 1-7-0 - 9; **Receiving** - Rashad 1-9.

BROWNS LEADERS: Rushing - K. Brown 15-73, McKinnis 16-49, Phipps 3-17, Pruitt 1-4, Sipe 2-4; **Passing** - Phipps 10-19-3 - 102, Sipe 6-10-0 - 37; **Receiving** - Morin 4-46, Hooker 2-34, Holden 3-24, K. Brown 3-21, McKinnis 3-10, Pruitt 1-4.

WEEK 11 GAMES

NE 27, Balt 17	Cinc 33, KC 6
Den 20, Oak 17	Dal 10, Hou 0
NYJ 17, Mia 14	Pitt 28, NO 7
GB 34, SD 0	SF 27, Atl 0
Det 34, Chi 17	LA 20, Minn 17
St.L 23, NYG 21	Wash 26, Phil 7

NOTES

- The Bills recorded their first shutout since blanking Miami, 29-0, in 1966, a span of 115 games. Also, it was the first shutout at home since a 12-0 win over Oakland in 1963, a span of 82 games.
- Bitter wind and cold produced a windchill of minus-four degrees and made the passing game difficult. The Colts also failed to run well.
- The Bills sacked Bert Jones eight times for 72 yards in losses.
- The Colts nearly pulled out the game though, driving to the Bills 8 with eight minutes left to play. But Lydell Mitchell was stopped on first and second down, then Jones threw incomplete into the end zone on third down. Mitchell then took a pitch to the right on fourth down but was nailed by Walt Patulski and Jim Cheyunski at the 2, ending the threat.
- The Bills' offense then made its most important drive of the game as it chewed up nearly six minutes with O.J. Simpson converting two crucial third-down plays.
- With the wind at his back in the second quarter, John Leypoldt made field goals of 20 and 31 yards. The first was set up when Marv Bateman punted to the 1-yard-line and when the Colts couldn't move, David Lee got off a weak 15-yarder into the wind to the Bills 24.
- The second field goal came after Doug Allen sacked Jones and forced Lee to punt, this time a meak 28-yarder to the Colts 34.
- The Colts were 0-for-13 on third-down conversions.

QUOTES

- Earl Edwards on the fourth-down stop of Mitchell: "Normally we submarine our defensive line on a play like that, but we changed our goal line defense for this game since we know the Colts like to run in a situation like that."
- Lou Saban: "We had our choice as to which goal to defend in the second half after Baltimore elected to receive. We elected to kick into the wind. Our reasoning was that we felt we could hold them in the third

quarter and then we'd have the wind at our back at the end. When we got those six points in the second quarter, we weren't going to take any unnecessary chances. Even on the short passes the ball was curving a couple of feet."
- Colts quarterback Bert Jones joking about getting

bounced around by Mike Kadish: "Mike and I were engaging in a normal conversation. I told Mike if he hurts me again, I'm going to kill him. I know I have the height and weight to hurt that little guy. Sure the rush was tough, I was just trying to get rid of the ball sometimes."

Colts	0	0	0 -	0
Bills	0	6	0 -	6

Attendance at Rich Stadium - 75,325

Buf: FG Leypoldt 20, 7:36
Buf: FG Leypoldt 31, 13:07

	BUF	BAL
First downs	9	10
Rushing yds	138	46
Passing yds	46	98
Punts-avg	9-37.6	10-33.8
Fumbles-lost	1-1	0-0
Penalties-yds	3-30	1-15

BILLS LEADERS: Rushing - Simpson 24-67, Watkins 16-64, Ferguson 6-7; **Passing** - Ferguson 5-13-0 - 46; **Receiving** - Rashad 2-18, Hill 1-10, Seymour 1-12, Simpson 1-6.

COLTS LEADERS: Rushing - L. Mitchell 11-30, Olds 8-12, Scott 1-3, Jones 1-1; **Passing** - Jones 11-27-1 - 170; **Receiving** - Chester 2-57, Scott 3-55, Carr 2-33, Mitchell 3-20, Olds 1-5.

WEEK 12 GAMES

Dal 24, Wash 23	Den 31, Det 27
Minn 29, NO 0	Phil 36, GB 14
Clev 7, SF 0	NYJ 27, SD 14
Chi 16, NYG 13	Oak 41, NE 26
KC 17, St.L 13	LA 30, Atl 7
Hou 13, Pitt 10	Mia 24, Cinc 3

STANDINGS: TWELFTH WEEK

AFC EAST	W	L	T	CENTRAL	W	L	T	WEST	W	L	T	NFC EAST	W	L	T	CENTRAL	W	L	T	WEST	W	L	T
Miami	9	3	0	Pittsburgh	8	3	1	Oakland	10	2	0	St. Louis	9	3	0	Minnesota	8	4	0	LA Rams	9	3	0
Buffalo	9	3	0	Cincinnati	7	5	0	Denver	6	5	1	Washington	8	4	0	Detroit	6	6	0	N.Orleans	4	8	0
New England	7	5	0	Houston	6	6	0	Kan. City	5	7	0	Dallas	7	5	0	Green Bay	6	6	0	San Fran	4	8	0
NY Jets	5	7	0	Cleveland	4	8	0	San Diego	3	9	0	Philadelphia	5	7	0	Chicago	4	8	0	Atlanta	2	10	0
Baltimore	2	10	0									NY Giants	2	10	0								

Bills	0	0	7	3 - 10
Jets	0	0	6	14 - 20

Attendance at Shea Stadium - 32,805

Buf: Hill 41 pass from Ferguson (Leypoldt kick), 4:59
NYJ: Caster 19 pass from Namath (kick blocked), 8:34
Buf: FG Leypoldt 36, 8:35
NYJ: Barkum 36 pass from Namath (Leahy kick), 11:00
NYJ: Baker 67 interception return (Leahy kick), 12:55

	BUF	NYJ
First downs	12	12
Rushing yds	131	90
Passing yds	87	131
Punts-avg	6-43.3	6-36.0
Fumbles-lost	5-2	4-1
Penalties-avg	6-35	5-25

BILLS LEADERS: Rushing - Simpson 15-48, Calhoun 18-71, Ferguson 4-12; **Passing** - Ferguson 5-16-1 - 76, Marangi 2-3-0 - 27; **Receiving** - Rashad 1-20, Hill 2-54, Simpson 2-19, Calhoun 2-10.

JETS LEADERS: Rushing - Bjorkland 14-41, Riggins 14-41, Adamle 2-9, Boozer 1-4, Jackson 1-0, Namath 1-(-4), Gantt 1-(-1); **Passing** - Namath 8-19-0 - 131; **Receiving** - Barkum 2-58, Caster 2-32, Riggins 2-13, Knight 1-20, Bjorkland 1-8.

WEEK 13 GAMES

Dal 41, Clev 17	Minn 23, Atl 10
Mia 17, Balt 16	Phil 20, NYG 7
NO 14, St.L 0	SF 7, GB 6
Det 23, Cinc 19	SD 28, Chi 21
Pitt 21, NE 17	Den 37, Hou 14
Oak 7, KC 6	Wash 23, LA 17

NOTES

• The Bills saw their chances of a division title slip away in the mud as the Jets pulled the upset, which, coupled with Miami's win over Baltimore, gave the Dolphins the AFC East crown and assured the Bills of a playoff date in Pittsburgh, the AFC Central champ.
• Playing without free safety Tony Greene, the Bills lost tackle Mike Kadish to a knee injury.
• After a scoreless first half, the Bills took the lead on their first possession of the third quarter when J.D. Hill beat Rich Sowells on a slant and Joe Ferguson hit him for a TD.
• But then the Bills began making costly mistakes. Ferguson slipped in the mud, fumbled, and Al Atkinson recovered at the Buffalo 19. On the next play, Joe Namath hit Rich Caster for a TD, beating Neal Craig, who had turned the wrong way and slipped trying to recover. Robert James blocked Pat Leahy's conversion, leaving the Bills ahead 7-6.
• John Leypoldt made it 10-6 with a fourth-quarter field goal, but the Jets roared back to win.
• On third-and-10 from the Bills 36, Namath lofted a jump ball type of pass into the end zone and Jerome Barkum came down with it for the winning TD, taking it away from Dwight Harrison and Donnie Walker.
• Ferguson hit Hill and O.J. Simpson for back-to-back first downs to the Jet 39. On the next play, a pass bounced off Simpson and into Ralph Baker's arms and he ran 67 yards for the clinching TD.

QUOTES

• Donnie Walker describing the Barkum TD: "I thought I got my hands on the ball and could intercept it. But I couldn't squeeze it. I thought I had the inside on Barkum."
• O.J. Simpson on the interception TD by Baker: "When I got my face out of the mud, I asked Al Atkinson what happened. He told me the ball bounced off my knee up into the air and Baker picked it off. Sure enough, I looked downfield and there was Baker running for a touchdown. I thought we had the game under control and were doing pretty good. We didn't expect to score a lot in that mud and rain and the fact that they were playing us to run. It's weird. I was having fun out there and suddenly we lose."
• Lou Saban: "It wasn't a case of them containing Simpson. The conditions were bad and that hurt, but we had opportunities and we blew them. They got all their points on our mistakes, fumbles, interceptions and that jump ball in the end zone. I hate to see us lose like that.
• Neal Craig: "If that's Joe Willie's last game as a Jet (at Shea), I guess you can say he went out in style. I hope he doesn't leave the Jets. I don't like him throwing touchdown passes against me and getting away with it."

Bills	0	7	0	7 - 14
Rams	0	0	13	6 - 19

Attendance at the Coliseum - 84,324

Buf: Rashad fumble recovery in end zone (Leypoldt kick), 6:42
LA: Scribner 14 pass from Harris (Burke kick), 7:20
LA: Harris 1 run (kick blocked), 12:39
LA: Jaworski 1 run (kick blocked), 1:10
Buf: Hill 55 pass from Ferguson (Leypoldt kick), 7:44

	BUF	LA
First downs	9	19
Rushing yds	109	168
Passing yds	109	153
Punts-avg	7-51.8	7-37.3
Fumbles-lost	1-0	1-1
Penalties-yds	5-80	3-18

BILLS LEADERS: Rushing - Simpson 13-73, Braxton 3-19, Calhoun 3-17, Ferguson 2-0; **Passing** - Ferguson 8-14-1 - 121, Marangi 1-6-2 - 15; **Receiving** - Rashad 1-4, Hill 4-96, Simpson 2-21, Braxton 1-7, Seymour 1-8.

RAMS LEADERS: Rushing - Baker 24-71, McCutcheon 7-45, Josephson 7-20, Jaworski 4-18, Scribner 6-14, Cappelletti 4-7, Harris 3-(-7); **Passing** - Harris 9-17-0 - 170, Jaworski 2-4-0 - 10; **Receiving** - Rentzel 3-75, Baker 4-65, Scribner 2-28, McCutcheon 1-9, Klein 1-3.

WEEK 14 GAMES

Oak 27, Dal 23	Minn 35, KC 15
Pitt 27, Cinc 3	SF 35, NO 21
Hou 28, Clev 24	SD 17, Den 0
St.L 26, NYG 14	Atl 10, GB 3
Phil 28, Det 17	Wash 42, Chi 0
NYJ 45, Balt 38	Mia 34, NE 27

NOTES

• The Bills ended the season on a two-game losing streak and with a struggling offense that produced just four TDs in the last four games.
• The Bills were lucky to be up 7-0 at the half as O.J. Simpson, making his return to the stadium where he starred for two years at USC, fumbled into the end zone and Ahmad Rashad recovered for a TD. It was the second time this season Rashad had recovered a Simpson fumble for a TD.
• The NFC West champion Rams pulled even in the third when ex-Bills quarterback James Harris, coming off a horrible first half, hit Rob Scribner with a TD pass as the Bills secondary blew the coverage and left Scribner all alone.
• Later in the third, on a third-down incompletion, Dave Washington was penalized for an illegal chuck, giving the Rams a first down at the 5 and Harris eventually scored. The extra point attempt by punter Mike Burke was blocked. Burke had replaced kicker David Ray, who was taken to the hospital before the game because of back spasms.
• In the fourth, Donnie Walker's interception at the 2 was turned into a 47-yard penalty when it was ruled he interfered with Harold Jackson. Lackawanna native Ron Jaworski, who had replaced Harris, ran in from the 1 and after Washington blocked his second conversion, it was 19-7.
• Joe Ferguson hit J.D. Hill with a brilliant 55-yard TD pass, but the Bills couldn't get closer as the defense permitted a six-minute drive that nearly ran out the clock.

QUOTES

• Lou Saban: "I was disappointed. We've had our troubles and there's no question in my mind that it's execution. We're just making too many errors. We've looked terrible, we've busted play after play and we simply can't do that. We're even missing audibles. It's a completely new season now, if you don't win, you're out."
• Ralph Wilson, who was angered by the official on Walker's interference: "This is no excuse for the loss, but I'm going to bring it up at our next league meeting that unless a pass-interference call is flagrant and the pass catchable, interference should be a 10- or 15-yard penalty. Too many games are decided by the yellow flag."
• Rams quarterback Ron Jaworski: "I feel great about winning the game, but I feel terrible about beating Buffalo."

STANDINGS: FOURTEENTH WEEK

AFC EAST	W	L	T	CENTRAL	W	L	T	WEST	W	L	T	NFC EAST	W	L	T	CENTRAL	W	L	T	WEST	W	L	T
Miami	11	3	0	Pittsburgh	10	3	1	Oakland	12	2	0	St. Louis	10	4	0	Minnesota	10	4	0	LA Rams	10	4	0
Buffalo	9	5	0	Cincinnati	7	7	0	Denver	7	6	1	Washington	10	4	0	Detroit	7	7	0	San Fran	6	8	0
New England	7	7	0	Houston	7	7	0	Kan. City	5	9	0	Dallas	8	6	0	Green Bay	6	8	0	N.Orleans	5	9	0
NY Jets	7	7	0	Cleveland	4	10	0	San Diego	5	9	0	Philadelphia	7	7	0	Chicago	4	10	0	Atlanta	3	11	0
Baltimore	2	12	0									NY Giants	2	12	0								

Bills	7	0	7	0 -	**14**
Steelers	3	26	0	3 -	**32**

Attendance at Three Rivers Stadium - 48,321

Pit:	FG Gerela 21, 6:09
Buf:	Seymour 22 pass from Ferguson (Leypoldt kick), 13:34
Pit:	Bleier 27 pass from Bradshaw (kick failed), 3:09
Pit:	Harris 1 run (Gerela kick), 9:52
Pit:	Harris 1 run (kick failed), 11:51
Pit:	Harris 1 run (Gerela kick), 14:44
Buf:	Simpson 3 pass from Ferguson (Leypoldt kick), 9:36
Pit:	FG Gerela 22, 2:39

	BUF	PIT
First downs	15	29
Rushing yds	100	235
Passing yds	164	203
Punts-avg	5-39.4	3-38.7
Fumbles-lost	2-1	2-0
Penalties-yds	3-15	2-10

BILLS LEADERS: Rushing - Simpson 15-49, Braxton 5-48, Ferguson 1-3; **Passing** - Ferguson 11-26-0 - 164; **Receiving** - Hill 4-59, Rashad 1-25, Simpson 3-37, Braxton 1-8, Seymour 2-35; **Punt returns** - Walker 2-11; **Kickoff returns** - Francis 6-118.

STEELERS LEADERS: Rushing - Harris 24-74, Bleier 14-45, Bradshaw 5-48, Davis 5-32, Swann 2-24, Gilliam 1-12; **Passing** - Bradshaw 12-19-0 - 203, Gilliam 0-2-0 - 0; **Receiving** - Swann 3-60, Bleier 3-54, Brown 1-29, McMakin 1-22, Lewis 2-18, Shanklin 1-15, Harris 1-5; **Punt returns** - Swann 2-12, Edwards 2-13; **Kickoff returns** - Blount 2-56, Davis 1-30.

NOTES

• The Bills' first playoff appearance since the 1966 AFL Championship Game was a bust as Pittsburgh dominated them.

• Terry Bradshaw, who endured a rough season in which his marriage to figure skater Jo Jo Starbuck ended in divorce and his hold on the starting quarterback job was broken by Joe Gilliam, rebounded with a superb performance.

• Franco Harris' three TDs tied a playoff record.

• The Steelers struck first, but the Bills were feeling pretty good because after driving to the Bills 4, the Steelers couldn't punch it in and had to settle for Roy Gerela's first field goal.

• Late in the first quarter, the Bills marched 66 yards to Joe Ferguson's 22-yard TD pass to Paul Seymour and an upset seemed possible.

• But then the second quarter began and the Bills were blown out of Three Rivers Stadium under a 26-point barrage.

• Bradshaw scrambled for a pair of first downs, then was given great protection while hitting Rocky Bleier on a 27-yard TD pass down the sideline. Bleier had beaten Dave Washington. Clint Haselrig blocked Gerela's extra point, leaving the score 9-7.

• The Bills saw a scoring chance fall by the wayside when Ferguson's bomb to Ahmad Rashad was knocked away at the last second by J.T. Thomas.

• After a 28-yard Marv Bateman punt, the Steelers went 66 yards in seven plays with Lynn Swann racing 25 yards on a reverse to the Bills 38. Then, three straight first-down plays resulted in first-down yardage and Harris capped the drive with a one-yard plunge.

• On the first play after the kickoff, Jim Braxton broke a 30-yard run but Mel Blount forced him to fumble and Jack Ham recovered at the Steelers 42.

• Bradshaw hit Bleier for 19, then Swann made a brilliant 35-yard reception over Robert James to set up Harris' second one-yard plunge. Doug Allen blocked the PAT, so it was 22-7.

• After another punt, the Steelers went 56 yards with the key play being Bradshaw's 28-yard pass to tight end Larry Brown to the 1 with 18 seconds left. Harris scored on the next play.

• The Bills got within 29-14 in the third when Ferguson, while being hammered by Jack Lambert, threw a three-yard TD pass to O.J. Simpson, but Gerela's 22-yard field

goal in the fourth ended any hopes of a miracle rally.

QUOTES

• Lou Saban: "I just don't think we played very good football. I don't have a Super Bowl pick. Football is over for me this year. We have to do many things if we're going to maintain the growth of the last three years. We have our problems and we couldn't hide them today. I take my hat off to Bradshaw, the man played a fine game. He really hurt us."

• Ahmad Rashad: "I enjoyed my first season in Buffalo and I think I'm going to have some more good years here. We set a standard this year to live up to and improve on and there can't be any letting up."

• Earl Edwards: "I'm still confused. We just didn't play our best. Whatever defense we came out with, they were ready for it. Whether it's a case of them being smarter, I don't know, but Terry Bradshaw is no genius. I feel we can come back to this playoff scene and win. We are making some progress, though. Last year, the season was over one week earlier than it was this year."

• Neal Craig: "We folded or tightened up. We made a lot of mistakes. Nothing they did surprised us, but we just couldn't handle them. They kept calling the right play at the right time in the second quarter. They had a super gameplan, but we made two or three mistakes that really hurt us. Maturity might be the best choice of a word to describe today. This was our first trip to the playoffs and we learned a lot."

• O.J. Simpson: "Everyone set their goal at wanting to make the playoffs and it's possible that once we made it, we may have become a little satisfied at doing that and lost our edge. Next year, we're all coming back with the goal of making it all the way. It's hard to single out any one thing as the turning point out there. The entire second period was the turning point. When a good team gets hot like that, they can put a lot of points on the board. We outscored them 14-6 in the other three periods, but they scored 26 in the second."

• Steelers quarterback Terry Bradshaw: "The thing I pride myself most on is the fact that I've been able to come back this year. It's just a great feeling to face adversity, overcome it, and rise to the top. This is probably the best game I've played since I've been here. I had all the time in the world and it made it so easy. I have just gotten so confident in my game the last few weeks and confidence is the

key to winning. We concentrated running at one member of the Bills front line (Walt Patulski). We didn't run at him because we thought he was a weak link, though. We ran a series of off-tackle plays at him to set up some of our wide stuff and passes. When you're a good team, you don't have to just pick on one player to find success."

• Steelers coach Chuck Noll: "It's no deep, dark mystery as to why we scored a lot of points in the second quarter. We made a couple of minor adjustments in the first period, but that's all. The offense just did some super executing and we wound up with our best offensive showing of the season. I'd like to take credit for masterminding what happened in the second period, but I can't. The men just executed."

• Steelers running back Franco Harris: "After that (when the Bills went ahead 7-3), you could feel the whole team say 'Hey, let's get going.' The adrenaline really started flowing because we realized that we might get beat. Then we took it to them."

• Steelers running back Rocky Bleier on his TD: "I was supposed to pick up the blitzing linebacker on the play, but there was no blitzing linebacker so I ran a pass pattern along the sideline into the end zone. The trouble was that it was the wrong thing for me to do because Franco was running the same kind of pattern a few yards away. They had us a little confused on the first series or two. Then we just decided to attack them straight ahead rather than trap and finesse them."

• Steelers wide receiver Lynn Swann: "When USC was trying to recruit me, I got a call from O.J., but I know that's all you usually hear from famous alumni, one call for recruiting purposes, so I forgot about it. Then I was in O'Hare Airport on my way to visit Notre Dame which was also trying to recruit me, and I spotted O.J. in the terminal. I went up to him and introduced myself as Lynn Swann and asked if he remembered me. He said 'Sure, you're the flanker back from Foster City.' I almost fell over when he said it. We got to be friends and when I was at USC, I used to go up to his house to baby-sit while he and Marguerite went out. My last year in school, he asked me if I'd like to live in his California house to take care of it while he was in Buffalo for the season. I jumped at the chance."

At A Glance
1975

Jan. 8 – O.J. Simpson, Tony Greene and Robert James were named to the Associated Press All-Pro first team. Pro Football Weekly named the same three players to its All-Pro team.

Jan. 27 – The Bills raised tickets $1 across the board. Erie County Legislature chairman Richard Keane called it "a callous slap in the face to the most loyal football fans in the country." The Bills led the NFL in attendance in 1973 and 1974 and in paid attendance in 1974.

Jan. 28 – Nebraska linebacker Tom Ruud was the Bills' first-round draft choice, the 19th player picked. Also chosen were Ruud's Cornhusker teammate, linebacker Bob Nelson (second) and running back Roland Hooks from North Carolina State (10th). Other first-round picks included quarterback Steve Bartkowski by Atlanta (first), defensive lineman Randy White to Dallas (second), running back Walter Payton to Chicago (fourth), tight end Russ Francis to New England (16th) and Thomas "Hollywood" Henderson to Dallas (18th).

Feb. 19 – O.J. Simpson won The Superstars competition in Rotunda, Fla.

March 9 – Top talent scout Bob Celeri died of a heart attack at his home.

March 11 – Wallace Francis, the top kickoff returner in the NFL in 1973, was traded to Atlanta for two draft choices.

March 29 – Receivers coach Bob Shaw was named director of pro personnel, replacing the deceased Bob Celeri.

April 5 – The NFL Players' Association, which just signed a new collective bargaining agreement after going on strike for 42 days before the 1974 season, outlined a plan to go on strike again if its demand for a $25,000 minimum salary for veterans wasn't granted. Reggie McKenzie, the Bills player rep, said the union was falling apart and only about 16 Bills were members.

April 18 – Fullback Larry Watkins was traded to the New York Giants for a 1976 draft choice. It was Lou Saban's 50th trade since taking over the team after the 1971 season.

May 28 – Bob Shaw returned to his former position of receivers coach because Lou Saban said he wasn't able to find a suitable replacement. Shaw's return to the field left open the pro personnel director position.

June 11 – NFLPA executive director Ed Garvey, under fire by his own troops, announced that the union would not strike, even if their newest demands were not met.

June 13 – Don Shula said if the NFL eliminates the Rozelle Rule, other teams could suffer what happened to the Dolphins when Larry Csonka, Jim Kiick and Paul Warfield fled to the World Football League. The Rozelle Rule stipulates that compensation must be awarded for a player who leaves his team as a free agent. It prevents player movement, which in Shula's mind is good. "It (excessive player movement) would be bad for the game overall - for the fans, the league and the players. When you have to buy a program to see who you're going to root for, I don't think you have the type of fan support you had previously.

June 26 – NFL owners voted to award home-field advantage in the playoffs to the teams with the best record. Previously, playoff sites were rotated. The owners also voted to allow stadiums that have scoreboards capable of showing instant replays to show replays during games. Only Buffalo, Kansas City, Los Angeles, Dallas and New Orleans had scoreboards capable of displaying replays.

June 27 – The owners voted to reduce the player roster limit to 43, down from 47.

July 18 – Former Bills offensive tackle Stew Barber rejoined the organization as a talent scout. Barber last worked for the Bills as a part-time scout in 1973. Barber assumed many of the duties held by Bob Celeri. The Bills traded linebacker Jim Cheyunski to Baltimore for a draft choice.

July 19 – The Bills opened training camp at Niagara University, but the top two draft picks, Tom Ruud and Bob Nelson, remained unsigned and did not report.

July 20 – Defensive end Pat Toomay was acquired from the Dallas Cowboys. "When we heard the news about Toomay signing," said O.J. Simpson, "everybody thought 'we're now a much better football team.' It was just like when Earl Edwards came to us, you knew we were going to be upgraded. That cat Toomay is a player."

July 21 – The Bills learned that rookie Roland Hooks had contracted hepatitis and would miss the entire season. However, he returned to the team on Aug. 11.

July 22 – Linebacker Dave Washington was traded to San Francisco for a draft choice.

July 23 – Center Bruce Jarvis walked out of camp because of a contract dispute.

Aug. 1 – Joe Namath signed a $400,000 per year contract with the Jets and upon hearing the news, O.J. Simpson jokingly said: "Where are you Ralph?" Then he said he would not ask Wilson to renegotiate his contract on any basis other than his performance in the upcoming season.

Aug. 6 - Tom Ruud and Bob Nelson and their agent, Howard Slusher, came to Rich Stadium to talk contract in an apparent break in the stalemate, but talks broke off without an agreement and the Bills began to think they would lose their top two draft choices to the WFL.

Aug. 8 – The Rolling Stones rocked Rich Stadium as more than 70,000 fans attended despite heated protests by Orchard Park residents who fought to have concerts banned from the stadium.

Aug. 9 – Green Bay downed the Bills, 23-6, in the preseason opener at Lambeau Field. Safety Tony Greene, coming back from offseason knee surgery, fractured his collarbone and was lost to the team for at least six weeks.

Aug. 15 – Cincinnati drubbed the Bills, 38-28, before 48,247 at Rich Stadium as the defense allowed 442 yards. The team announced the final season ticket count of 43,184, down 10,998 from 1974. Western New York's 13.5 percent unemployment rate and not the $1 ticket price hike was blamed for the decline by general manager Bob Lustig.

Aug. 17 – Angered by his team's lackluster start to the preseason schedule, Lou Saban put the Bills through a 45-minute scrimmage at Niagara University.

Aug. 21 – Safety Steve Freeman was acquired from New England after the Patriots put their fifth-round draft choice on waivers.

Aug. 22 – International Cable of West Seneca tried to buck the NFL's blackout rule and broadcast the Bills preseason game against the Los Angeles Rams, who were going to be playing West Seneca native Ron Jaworski at quarterback. The FCC ordered International Cable to pull the plug on its plan to show the game on an illegal feed from Syracuse.

Aug. 23 – A national TV audience that excluded western New York saw the Bills upset the Rams, 31-24, in rainy Rich Stadium. Gary Marangi was given a surprise start and he passed for 148 yards. Ron Jaworski returned home and passed for 168 yards in an impressive performance. The Bills did receive bad news as All-Pro cornerback Robert James suffered a season-ending knee injury.

Aug. 28 – Tom Ruud and Bob Nelson finally agreed to contract terms and were in Buffalo to sign the deals. However, only Ruud, who became the final first-round choice in the 1975 draft to sign, put his name on a contract. Nelson had trouble with his physical and also wanted a waiver clause ironed out before signing. "I haven't even been thinking about this," said quarterback Joe Ferguson. "We need help at linebacker. Now they have to prove they can play."

Sept. 1 – In a Labor Day special, the Bills ripped Cleveland at Municipal Stadium, 34-20, as Joe Ferguson reclaimed his position as the undisputed No. 1 quarterback with 174 passing yards.

Sept. 2 – Bob Nelson finally signed his contract.

Sept. 7 - Buffalo edged Atlanta, 16-14, in Tampa Stadium, the future home of the Tampa Bay Buccaneers. Steve Bartkowski, the NFL's No.1 overall draft choice, completed only three passes for 41 yards against the Bills' depleted secondary. The teams combined for 13 fumbles (losing eight), eight interceptions and 16 penalties.

Sept. 8 - Despite the inexperience piercing his secondary, Lou Saban traded Neal Craig, the starting strong safety in 1974, to Cleveland for a draft choice as he pared the roster to 49.

Sept. 9 – Doug Jones, the man whom Saban figured would play strong safety, underwent knee surgery and was lost for the season.

Sept 10 - Second-round draft choice Glenn Lott was cut and Saban admitted he made a mistake by choosing Lott with the 50th pick overall in the draft. Newcomer Charlie Ford, acquired on waivers from Houston, moved ahead of Lott on the depth chart and Lott was disappointed. His reaction was another reason Saban cut him. "Lott was ticked off when Charlie went ahead of him, but better him ticked off than the rest of us when Richard Caster would be spiking all those balls after burning him for touchdowns in our opener against the Jets."

Sept. 12 – The preseason schedule mercifully came to an end, but not before another star player was felled by a knee injury. Wide receiver Ahmad Rashad was lost for the year during the Bills 9-7 loss to Kansas City at Rich Stadium.

Sept. 13 – The New England Patriots went on strike to protest the collective bargaining agreement that was signed in 1974. The strike forced postponement of New England's preseason game against the New York Jets and also threatened the season opener against Houston.

Sept. 16 – The New York Jets, Washington Redskins, New York Giants and Detroit Lions joined the Patriots on strike and put the start of the NFL season in jeopardy. However, the league said it would press forward.

Sept 17 – The Bills voted 43-0 not to strike and

The Electric Company, led by Reggie McKenzie (67) and Joe DeLamielleure (68) paved the way for O.J. Simpson. In 1975, Simpson won his third NFL rushing title with 1,817 yards.

player rep Reggie McKenzie called for the ouster of NFLPA director Ed Garvey. Meanwhile, Ralph Wilson, a member of the Management Council's six-man executive committee, said the league planned to open its season.

Sept. 18 – The striking teams returned to work as federal mediator W.J. Usery convinced them to play ball and wait for a new contract offer from the Management Council, which was due the day after the Sunday season openers. The NFLPA signed a two-week no-strike pledge. A number of Jets players vowed their game against the Bills would be a blood bath because they were upset that the Bills' players refused to back the strike. "It's going to be a blood match," said Jets player rep Richard Neal. "They are trying to get something for nothing. That statement of theirs that they won't support the teams on strike was damn lousy. They're just a lousy bunch, trying for an easy win, a forfeit. Last year, they were one of the strong teams for the strike. Then they got to the playoffs and it changed them, they got greedy." Said safety Phil Wise: "Look at it this way, don't you think we won't be ready to kick some ass when we play those guys. I could play forever and never get tired against a team like that." Reggie McKenzie responded by saying: "We'll be ready to play football Sunday. The time to get mad about a strike was last year."

Sept. 21 – The Bills crushed the Jets, 42-14, in the season opener before 77,895 at Rich Stadium. O.J. Simpson rushed for 173 yards and he had 71 yards in runs called back due to penalties. Afterwards, Ralph Wilson took a shot at the Jets when he told his team: "You fellows played pretty well for a lousy bunch." He was mocking Richard Neal's statement earlier in the week.

Sept. 22 – Negotiations between the players and owners began again in Chicago and the owners' proposed modification of the Rozelle Rule didn't satisfy the players.

Sept. 24 – The players rejected ownership's newest contract offer. The Bills voted 43-0 not to accept the offer and 14 other teams, more than half

the league, voted no. But none of the clubs said they would strike. The players played without a contract throughout the 1974 season and Mike Montler, who represented the Bills in Chicago, said that he expected the season to be played without a contract again.

Sept. 28 – O.J. Simpson rushed for 227 yards, including an 88-yard TD run, as the Bills got revenge on the Pittsburgh Steelers for their 1974 playoff loss with a 30-21 victory at Three Rivers Stadium over the defending Super Bowl champions.

Oct. 5 – O.J. Simpson gained 138 yards and moved into fifth place on the NFL's all-time rushing list as the Bills routed Denver, 38-14 to record their best start (3-0) since 1964 when they won their first nine games.

Oct. 6 – Despite three lopsided victories, second-round draft choice Bob Nelson hadn't seen any action and Lou Saban began to wonder if the Bills made a draft-day mistake. Asked if Nelson was a disappointment and whether he would consider trading him, Saban said: "That (not playing yet) should tell you something. A lot of teams are seeking linebackers."

Oct 9 – Wide receiver Dan Abramowicz joined the Bills as a free agent. His NFL record of 105 consecutive games with a catch dating back to 1967 was still alive because he hadn't played in a game in 1975 after being cut by Washington in the preseason.

Oct. 12 – The Bills rallied to defeat Baltimore, 38-31, as O.J. Simpson rushed for 159 yards and unknown John Holland caught six passes for 121 yards.

Oct. 20 – In a bizarre Monday night affair at Rich Stadium, the Bills were beaten by the New York Giants, 17-14, their first loss of the season. Fans acted atrociously in front of Frank Gifford, Howard Cosell and Alex Karras. One fan dangled high above the stadium on a cable that is used to support the net behind the goal posts, many were involved in numerous brawls and others took their clothes

off and mugged for the national TV cameras.

Oct. 21 – International Cable of West Seneca illegally broadcast about half the Oct. 20 game, which was blacked out in Western New York, by accepting a feed from WNYS, the ABC affiliate in Syracuse. International Cable fully expected trouble, but went ahead and aired the game to about 27,000 customers. The move paid off because the FCC couldn't find fault with what the cable company did, it just took advantage of a loophole in the blackout rule.

Oct. 22 – The World Football League officially folded, sending hundreds of players on the hunt for jobs. While many NFL teams expected to sign players, the Bills had no plans because only two WFL players had ties to the Bills – Chris Kupec and Tim Guy – and Lou Saban said the team wasn't interested in either player.

Oct. 23 – Just two weeks after being signed, wide receiver Dan Abramowicz was waived. Also, cornerback Charlie Ford was cut to make room for running back Don Calhoun.

Oct. 24 – NFL Commissioner Pete Rozelle banned teams from signing wayward WFL players for the rest of the 1975 season. "I'm not really surprised by the ruling," said Miami coach Don Shula, who had hoped Larry Csonka, Jim Kiick and Paul Warfield could rejoin his team. "It was predominantly a ruling on the Dolphins."

Oct. 26 – Miami rallied for 14 points in the final 3:18 and knocked off the Bills, 35-30, for its 11th straight victory over Buffalo. The loss dropped the Bills into second place in the AFC East behind the Dolphins.

Nov. 2 – O.J. Simpson caught a 64-yard pass from Joe Ferguson for the winning touchdown with 3:46 left to play as the Bills edged the Jets at Shea Stadium, 24-23.

Nov. 6 – A federal judge in St. Paul, Minn. ruled that WFL players could seek employment in the NFL this season with the teams that own their rights, but NFL Commissioner Pete Rozelle estimated that fewer than 20 players would be signed.

He then imposed a deadline for signing players of Nov. 26.

Nov. 9 – The Bills blew a 28-7 lead and lost to Baltimore, 42-35, before 77,320 stunned fans at Rich Stadium. The loss snapped Buffalo's five-game winning streak over the Colts.

Nov. 10 – After suffering a concussion the day before, Joe Ferguson was released from Mercy Hospital. Ferguson said he did not remember the hit on him by Buffalo native Joe Ehrmann, the Colts defensive tackle.

Nov. 17 – The Bills lost for the second time on Monday night, 33-24, in Cincinnati as Ken Anderson passed for 447 yards, a Cincinnati record. The Bengals never punted in the game and rolled up 34 first downs, the most ever allowed by the Bills.

Nov. 19 – The NFL announced that it would allow teams to protect 30 active players and two from their injured reserve list in preparation for the expansion draft for Seattle and Tampa Bay. The new clubs also were awarded the first two picks in each round of the college draft. "We have created the largest pool of quality players ever available in football expansion," Commissioner Pete Rozelle said.

Nov. 21 – Speculation arose over possible friction between Lou Saban and Ralph Wilson. It was rumored that Saban was angry because a number of trades for defensive help that he had set up were nixed by the front office. "Lou and I get along very well," Wilson said. "I call him four times a week and we meet every Friday. When Lou took this job, I said he could have it as long as he wants, for the rest of his life. That's the way I feel now."

Nov. 23 – O.J. Simpson enjoyed the first four-touchdown game of his career and stretched his streak of scoring a rushing TD to a team-record 10 games as the Bills routed New England, 45-31.

Nov. 24 – Lou Saban brushed off an NBC report that said he would resign if his team lost to New England. "My rapport, my relationship with Ralph is just fine. I'm running this football team." Said O.J. Simpson: "I consider Ralph a friend of mine and you know how much I love coach Saban. A little communication was all that was needed. I don't think there was anything to that (the TV report). Coach told us he wouldn't let us down, that he would give us everything he had. He wouldn't leave us now. Lou has meant a lot to me, he understands me more than any coach I've ever played for."

Nov. 25 – Pat Toomay, who battled St. Louis' Conrad Dobler when he played for Dallas, said that everything anyone had ever heard about Dobler was true. "You've got to keep your head on a swivel when Dobler is around," Toomay said. "You have to watch him closely, especially when the play is over. He's not what you would call an endearing player. And (Dan) Dierdorf is good at leg-whipping, too. His legs are like two stumps. Walt Patulski will be opposite Dierdorf and he can have him."

Nov. 26 – The Bills were forced to land in Chicago on their way to St. Louis and were stranded there overnight due to a snowstorm.

Nov. 27 – The Bills didn't arrive in St. Louis until two hours before gametime, but they got off the bus, went onto the field and pummeled the Cardinals, 32-14, on Thanksgiving Day at Busch Stadium. "I told the players there's nothing you can do about the situation, so just do the best you can,"

said Lou Saban. Jim Braxton set career highs with 34 carries for 160 yards.

Dec. 2 – With Bob Griese out with a toe injury and Earl Morrall sidelined the night before by a knee injury, Don Shula said he would go with third-string quarterback Don Strock for the show-down against the Bills at the Orange Bowl. Strock had one pass completion in his three-year career as a pro.

Dec. 7 – The Bills' playoff hopes officially were dashed when Miami posted its 12th consecutive victory over Buffalo, 31-21, at the Orange Bowl. Third-string QB Don Strock ran for one TD and passed for two in building a 21-0 halftime lead. Then the Dolphins got a huge break when they retained possession after it appeared Mercury Morris had fumbled at his own 28 in the fourth quarter. Pat Toomay was then hit with a 15-yard penalty for brushing linesman Jerry Bergman and two plays later, the Dolphins scored the clinching TD.

Dec. 8 – Ralph Wilson, still fuming over the non-fumble call in the Miami game, stepped up his attack on official Jerry Bergman, the man who called the 15-yard penalty on Pat Toomay. "He should be fired from his job and never allowed to work another game," Wilson fumed. "I will not again send my team out to play a game that he's working. It was a rotten call that cost my team a shot at the Super Bowl. I haven't protested a call since 1962, but I'm protesting this one."

Dec. 9 – Asked about the possibility of using television cameras for instant replays to aid officials in the wake of Wilson's statements, Pete Rozelle said: "If there is a practical way, if the mechanics can be worked out, we are not opposed to it." Rozelle said he would instruct the Competition Committee to look into the matter at the next league meetings.

Dec. 10 – Los Angeles Rams owner Carroll Rosenbloom pledged his support of Wilson and offered to pay half of Wilson's fine, if he is fined. "When a man gets robbed like that, he must give me part of the action," Rosenbloom said. "I know the feeling, I've lost two playoff games because of bad officiating.

Dec. 14 – The Bills amassed 26 first downs to set an all-time NFL record for first downs in a season with 298, and they still had one game left to play. O.J. Simpson rushed for 185 yards in the 34-14 victory at New England, their ninth win in a row over the Patriots.

Dec. 19 – Hounded by reports that he would be retiring from football, O.J. Simpson said: "If I can work it out to play football, I will. I just don't want to be in a situation where I'm appearing to use my movie career to get more money from Ralph Wilson." Simpson said his quest for a role in the film *Ragtime* which would be filmed in September presented a possible conflict to continuing his football career. "As far as attitude goes, it's no problem for me to come back and play. But I've geared myself to not playing next year. My family is out west, I'm here, we've been apart since July and none of us likes it."

Dec. 20 – The Bills closed the season on a snowy day in Rich Stadium, losing to the Vikings, 35-13. The smallest regular-season crowd in stadium history, 54,993, witnessed history as O.J. Simpson set an NFL record for touchdowns in a season with 23, breaking Gale Sayers' mark of 22 established in 1965. Minnesota QB Fran Tarkenton set a new NFL record for career TD passes with 291, break-

ing John Unitas' mark of 290. On the negative side, some unruly fans rained snowballs at the Viking players and one snowball struck Chuck Foreman in the eye, causing blurred vision and making him questionable for the Vikings upcoming playoff run. "The snowball barrage was the most ridiculous thing I've seen in 19 years of football," Tarkenton said. "The people of Buffalo ought not to be proud of what happened here today."

Dec. 21 – Joe Ferguson finished the season without a signed contract for 1976 and he expressed reservations about signing with the Bills. "Next season is my option year and my lawyer will do the talking for me," Ferguson said. "I really don't know what is going to happen. I want to see how things go here this winter on a couple of things. I think everybody realizes we're going to have to make some changes. The differences between Mr. Wilson and Coach Saban bothered me, too. They say the problems are solved, but I'd like to wait and see about that, too."

Dec. 22 – Backup quarterback Gary Marangi said he was frustrated all season about his lack of playing time. "I thought I played well enough last summer to win the job, then I didn't even get to play when we beat the Jets, 42-14," he said. "I didn't mind sitting on the bench last year when I was a rookie, but I minded this year. Do I think the quarterback job will be thrown open next summer in training camp? How can I think that when it wasn't thrown open last summer when I was led to believe that it would be."

Dec. 23 – O.J. Simpson and Joe DeLamielleuere were named to the UPI first-team all-star squad. They were later both named to the Pro Bowl squad.

Dec. 24 – It was reported that Ralph Wilson was fined $5,000 by Pete Rozelle for his remarks concerning official Jerry Bergman after the game in Miami. And because he sided with Wilson, Rams owner Carroll Rosenbloom was fined the same amount. "I don't mind paying the fine, but I do resent the league trying to make a fool of me by stating, beyond any shadow of a doubt, that both calls by the official were right," Wilson said. "Too many people who saw the game know otherwise."

Dec. 27 – Pittsburgh topped Baltimore, 28-10, and Los Angeles beat St. Louis, 35-23, on day one of the divisional playoffs.

Dec. 28 – Oakland got past Cincinnati, 31-28, and Roger Staubach's "Hail Mary" controversial TD pass to Drew Pearson with 24 seconds left gave Dallas a 17-14 victory over the Vikings in Minnesota on the second day of divisional play-offs.

Jan. 4, 1976 – Dallas routed Los Angeles, 37-7, in the NFC Championship Game as Roger Staubach passed for 220 yards and four TDs, three to Preston Pearson, while the defense held the Rams to 118 yards of total offense. Pittsburgh won its second straight AFC Championship 16-10, over Oakland, as the Steelers outscored the Raiders, 13-10, in the final quarter.

Jan. 18, 1976 – Lynn Swann caught four passes for 161 yards and one TD as the Steelers won their second consecutive Super Bowl, 21-17 over Dallas before 80,187 fans in Miami's Orange Bowl.

Jan. 26, 1976 – Mike Boryla hit Mel Gray with the winning TD pass with 1:09 left as the NFC edged the AFC, 23-20, in the Pro Bowl at the Superdome in New Orleans.

BY THE NUMBERS - 1975

TEAM STATISTICS	BILLS	OPP
First downs	318	300
Rushing	162	124
Passing	132	151
Penalty	24	25
Total yards	5,467	5,073
Avg. game	390.5	362.4
Plays	964	941
Avg. play	5.7	5.4
Net rushing yds	2,974	1,993
Avg. game	212.4	142.4
Avg. play	5.1	4.2
Net passing yds	2,493	3,080
Comp/att	182/354	237/431
Sacks/lost	22-168	30-275
Interceptions	19	25
Percentage	51.4	55.0
Punts/avg	61-41.6	59-40.5
Fumbles/lost	24-15	42-20
Penalties/yds	90-748	82-651
Touchdowns	57	47
Extra points	51-57	46-47
Field goals	9-16	9-16
Safeties	0	0
Kick ret./avg	62-23.5	64-23.4
Punt ret./avg	33-8.4	29-6.2

RUSHING	ATT	YDS	AVG	TD
Simpson	329	1817	5.5	16
Braxton	186	823	4.4	9
Ferguson	23	82	3.6	1
Calhoun	19	80	4.2	0
Marangi	7	78	11.1	0
Washington	9	49	5.4	0
Hayman	10	30	3.0	0
Haselrig	2	9	4.5	0
Chandler	2	5	2 5	0
Hill	1	1	1.0	0
TOTALS	**588**	**2974**	**5.1**	**26**

PASSING	COMP	ATT	INT	YDS	TD	COMP%	SACKS	RATE
Ferguson	169	321	17	2426	25	52.6	20-153	81.4
Marangi	13	33	2	235	3	39.4	2-15	69.5
TOTALS	**182**	**354**	**19**	**2661**	**28**	**51.4**	**22-168**	**80.1**

KICKING	1-19	20-29	30-39	40-49	50+	TOT	PAT	PTS
Leypoldt	0-1	2-2	4-5	3-7	0-1	9-16	51-57	78

PUNTING	NO	AVG	LG	BL
Bateman	61	41.6	74	2

RECEIVING	CAT	YDS	AVG	TD
Chandler	55	746	13.6	6
J.D. Hill	36	667	18.5	7
Simpson	28	426	15.2	7
Braxton	26	282	10.8	4
Seymour	19	268	14.1	1
Gant	9	107	11.9	2
Holland	7	144	20.6	1
Washington	2	21	10.5	0
TOTALS	**182**	**2661**	**14.6**	**28**

LEADERS

Kick returns: Washington 35-923 yards, 26.4 avg, 0 TD
Hayman 8-179, 22.4, 0 TD

Punt returns: Hayman 25-216, 8.6, 0 TD
Holland 7-53, 7.6, 0 TD

Interceptions: Harrison 8-99, 12.4, 0 TD
Greene 6-81, 13.5, 0 TD
Jones 3-13, 4.3, 0 TD

SCORE BY QUARTERS

BILLS   97 121 112 90 - 420
OPP   65 132 62 96 - 355

Steve Freeman joined the Bills in 1975 and wound up playing for 12 years. He finished his Buffalo career as the all-time leader in games played with 181, a total that now ranks him fourth.

GAME 1 - Sunday, Sept. 21, 1975 - BILLS 42, JETS 14

Jets	7	7	0	0 -	14
Bills	14	7	14	7 -	42

Attendance at Rich Stadium - 77,895

Buf: Simpson 1 run (Leypoldt kick), 3:41
Buf: Braxton 3 pass from Ferguson (Leypoldt kick), 8:33
NYJ: Caster 28 pass from Namath (Leahy kick), 14:39
Buf: Simpson 5 run (Leypoldt kick), 1:04
NYJ: Bell 12 pass from Namath (Leahy kick), 7:34
Buf: Seymour 2 pass from Ferguson (Leypoldt kick), 6:46
Buf: Ferguson 1 run (Leypoldt kick), 10:24
Buf: Toomay 44 interception return (Leypoldt kick), 1:47

	BUF	NYJ
First downs	26	17
Rushing yds	309	111
Passing yds	52	150
Punts-avg	7-37.4	6-40.3
Fumbles-lost	0-0	1-1
Penalties-yds	9-89	7-58

BILLS LEADERS: Rushing - Simpson 32-173, Braxton 15-61, Calhoun 11-58, Ferguson 2-2, Haselrig 2-9, Chandler 1-5, Hayman 1-1; **Passing** - Ferguson 7-13-0 - 67; **Receiving** - Chandler 3-34, Simpson 1-5, Braxton 1-3, Holland 1-23.
JETS LEADERS: Rushing - Riggins 10-61, Garrett 5-38, Gresham 5-13, Namath 1-(-1); **Passing** - Namath 14-36-4 - 173; **Receiving** - Caster 6-103, Garrett 2-24, Barkum 3-21, Riggins 2-13, Bell 1-12.

WEEK 1 GAMES

Balt 35, Chi 7	Den 37, KC 33
Cinc 24, Clev 17	Hou 7, NE 0
Oak 31, Mia 21	Pitt 37, SD 0
St.L 23, Atl 20	Dal 18, LA 7
Det 30, GB 16	Minn 27, SF 17
NYG 23, Phil 14	Wash 41, NO 3

NOTES
• The Bills opened the season with an impressive rout of the Jets as O.J. Simpson rushed for 173 yards. Simpson's two TDs enabled him to set a new team record with 40, surpassing Elbert Dubenion.
• The team record of 65 rushing attempts, set against Kansas City in 1973, nearly fell as well as windy conditions hurt the passing game.
• Newcomer Pat Toomay's debut was superb as he returned an interception 44 yards for a TD, his first score since high school.
• Steve Freeman's fumble recovery at the Jets 28 set up the first score, which was helped by two Jets offsides penalties, including one on third-and-one at the 8.
• Another third-down offsides by New York gave the Bills a second third-down chance and Ferguson converted it with a TD pass to Jim Braxton.

• After Walt Patulski was nailed for roughing punter Greg Gantt, Joe Namath hit Richard Caster for a 28-yard TD, but the Bills retaliated with Simpson's second TD.
• A 13-yard Marv Bateman punt into the wind set up the Jets next TD, but the Bills took charge by moving into the wind 77 yards in 14 plays to score after the second-half kickoff. Paul Seymour, who dropped a TD pass late in the first half, atoned for his error.
• Ferguson's TD run came after a mix-up when Simpson wasn't there to receive the hand off.

QUOTES
• Jets safety Phil Wise: "We played bad, that's the talk right there. Words can't help you when they're running the 38 sweep with O.J. O.J. said to me 'Why don't you let me break one?' and I said 'You're chewing us up. Why don't you let me tackle you solo three or four times. I'd rather play against a big back. I can find a big back. With him it's like letting a rabbit out of a box."
• Pat Toomay: "I felt it was the right time for a screen and Namath threw it right into my arms. I've got a no-hit contract when I've got the ball, so I was looking around. Then I used my false spike that I've been working on for years – you know, make like you're going to spike the ball and then just let it down."
• Jets quarterback Joe Namath: "Look, Toomay's supposed to be on the ground, not in a position to steal the ball. He made a helluva play. Sometimes you get your ass whipped."
• Bob Chandler: "I'll say this, the Jets helped us get ready for this game, but they played fair, no cheap shots."
• Lou Saban: "Of all the teams I've been associated with over the years, this one in this game will stick out in my mind. It's been a long time since a team with so much going against it gave so much effort to win."

GAME 2 - Sunday, Sept. 28, 1975 - BILLS 30, STEELERS 21

Bills	0	10	13	7 -	30
Steelers	0	0	7	14 -	21

Attendance at Three Rivers Stadium - 49,348

Buf: FG Leypoldt 37, :08
Buf: Kadish 26 fumble return (Leypoldt kick), 8:54
Buf: Gant 7 pass from Ferguson (Leypoldt kick), 5:18
Buf: Simpson 88 run (kick failed), 7:57
Pit: Harris 2 run (Gerela kick), 14:30
Buf: Chandler 28 pass from Ferguson (Leypoldt kick), 2:17
Pit: Grossman 20 pass from Gilliam (Gerela kick), 5:31
Pit: Harris 1 run (Gerela kick), 13:12

	BUF	PIT
First downs	21	19
Rushing yds	310	122
Passing yds	124	231
Punts-avg	8-34.4	5-42.0
Fumbles-lost	3-1	3-3
Penalties-yds	7-47	3-30

BILLS LEADERS: Rushing - Simpson 28-227, Braxton 14-80, Ferguson 2-1, Calhoun 2-2; **Passing** - Ferguson 9-20-0 - 129; **Receiving** - Chandler 3-59, Braxton 1-2, Seymour 2-33, Gant 3-35.

STEELERS LEADERS: Rushing - Harris 18-84, Bleier 7-18, Fuqua 2-13, Bradshaw 3-7; **Passing** - Gilliam 11-21-1 - 200, Bradshaw 3-8-1 - 69; **Receiving** - Stallworth 3-103, Lewis 2-63, Swann 3-51, Grossman 1-20, Fuqua 1-13, Harris 3-10, Bleier 1-9.

NOTES
• The Bills avenged their playoff defeat of a year before as O.J. Simpson ran for 227 yards, the fourth 200-yard game of his career, which tied the NFL record set by Jim Brown.
• It was the first time since 1965 that the Bills opened a season 2-0.
• Merv Krakau had 11 tackles and made an interception.
• The Bills had four sacks against a Steelers line that allowed only 18 in 1974. The Steelers had one sack.
• Pittsburgh's first series ended when Terry Bradshaw lost a fumble at the Bills 26 to Earl Edwards. Krakau's interception killed their second possession at the Steelers 24, which led to John Leypoldt's field goal.
• Midway through the second, Bradshaw lost another fumble to Edwards who lateraled to Mike Kadish and he rambled in for a TD that made it 10-0.
• Early in the third, Bo Cornell sacked Bradshaw at the 5 to force a punt. The Bills had to drive only 51 yards to make it 17-0 as Reuben Gant caught the first TD pass of his career.
• After a Bobby Walden punt rolled out of bounds at the 3, Simpson iced the game three plays later when he broke off right tackle and raced 88 yards for a TD

behind a block by Jim Braxton on Jack Ham.
• Marv Kellum blocked a Marv Bateman punt and Loren Toews returned it 30 yards to the 6 to set up Pittsburgh's first score, but the Bills responded with Bob Chandler's TD and the game was over.

QUOTES
• O.J. Simpson: "There were two great things about this game. First of all, it came against the Steelers, which I regard as the best defensive team in football, by far. Secondly, I got a chance to do something I've never done before. I won what amounted to a 100-yard dash on a football field. My teammates keep telling me they can beat me in a sprint. Reggie McKenzie thinks he can beat me, but he's too slow. Nobody can beat me if I'm healthy and fresh. But as much as we wanted this win, as great a win as it was, I'd swap it for a win here last December in the playoffs. We know now that we can beat anybody."
• Steelers coach Chuck Noll: "Most backs wouldn't have gained a yard on the play he gained 88. O.J. is something special."
• Steelers defensive tackle Joe Greene: "They talk a lot about Buffalo's offensive line, but it's the Juice who makes the difference, not the line."
• Lou Saban: "It was a great victory, one of the most important games we've ever played. But remember those championship games against San Diego. A championship game is still a championship game."
• Steelers defensive end Dwight White: "I never played against Jim Brown, but it's beyond my wildest imagination to think he could be better than Juice."

WEEK 2 GAMES

Oak 31, Balt 20	Cinc 21, NO 0
Minn 42, Clev 10	Den 23, GB 13
Hou 33, SD 17	NYJ 30, KC 24
Wash 49, NYG 13	Det 17, Atl 14
Chi 15, Phil 13	LA 23, SF 14
Dal 37, St.L 31	Mia 22, NE 14

STANDINGS: SECOND WEEK

AFC EAST	W	L	T	CENTRAL	W	L	T	WEST	W	L	T	NFC EAST	W	L	T	CENTRAL	W	L	T	WEST	W	L	T
Buffalo	2	0	0	Cincinnati	2	0	0	Oakland	2	0	0	Dallas	2	0	0	Minnesota	2	0	0	LA Rams	1	1	0
Baltimore	1	1	0	Houston	2	0	0	Denver	2	0	0	Washington	2	0	0	Detroit	2	0	0	San Fran	0	2	0
Miami	1	1	0	Pittsburgh	1	1	0	Kan. City	0	2	0	St. Louis	1	1	0	Chicago	1	1	0	Atlanta	0	2	0
NY Jets	1	1	0	Cleveland	0	2	0	San Diego	0	2	0	NY Giants	1	1	0	Green Bay	0	2	0	N.Orleans	0	2	0
New England	0	2	0									Philadelphia	0	2	0								

NOTES
• O.J. Simpson moved into fifth place on the NFL's all-time rushing list as the Bills improved to 3-0.
• Simpson also moved into second place on the Bills' all-time scoring list behind John Leypoldt, passing Cookie Gilchrist. His total of 538 yards rushing was the largest ever amassed in three consecutive games in NFL history.
• The Bills set team records with 29 first downs and 20 rushing first downs and their 110 points were the most they'd ever scored in a three-game stretch.
• The Bills possessed the ball for more than 41 minutes.
• The Broncos cut the deficit to 17-7 with 1:34 left in the first half on Charley Johnson's TD pass to Floyd Little, but the Bills drove 82 yards in five plays for a backbreaking TD. Joe Ferguson hit J.D. Hill for 15 yards and Bob Chandler with a 35-yard pass to the Denver 16 with nine seconds left. Rather than kick the field goal, the Bills went for the TD and Ferguson hit Hill, who had beaten Calvin Jones to the left side.
• Jim Braxton scored three TDs. His first came after Dwight Harrison forced a fumble that was recovered by Tony Greene and returned 32 yards to the 3. The second made it 17-0 as he was wide open for a 19-yard pass reception and the third came after a Harrison interception and return to the Denver 13.

QUOTES
• Bronco's linebacker Tom Jackson: "The Bills beat us and they beat us good."
• Jim Braxton: "I guess it was my day today. I try to be a complete player, so keeping that in mind, this was not my best day as a pro. If I had blocked well, it might have been. The touchdowns were team touchdowns because we were in close and anybody could have scored them. But the ball happened to go to me."
• Lou Saban: "You've got to give Braxton credit, he's playing with a sore leg, yet he didn't want to come out. He wanted that 100 yards."
• J.D. Hill: "I knew that one of these days I was going to catch a pass. I'm just glad I was able to come through on a big play like that. Calvin Jones tried bump and run at the line, but that's what I want to see, bump and run."
• Broncos coach John Ralston: "We made enough mistakes to lose, but if any one play can be singled out as a crucial one, the touchdown pass to Hill was the one."
• Joe Ferguson: "Most of our pass patterns were to the strong side and J.D. plays on the weak side. Today we passed to both sides of the field. Our offense has been so varied in the first three games that I honestly think the defenses are confused. We all had a good feeling about this back in training camp. Everybody came back very concerned about football and having a good season, moreso than in past years. If we keep it up, we can go all the way."

WEEK 3 GAMES	
LA 24, Balt 13	Cinc 21, Hou 19
Pitt 42, Clev 6	SF 20, KC 3
Mia 31, GB 7	NYJ 36, NE 7
Phil 26, Wash 10	Atl 14, NO 7
Minn 28, Chi 3	Dal 36, Det 10
St.L 26, NYG 14	Oak 6, SD 0

Broncos	0	7	7	0	- 14
Bills	10	14	14	0	- 38

Attendance at Rich Stadium - 79,864

Buf: FG Leypoldt 39, 9:38
Buf: Braxton 3 run (Leypoldt kick), 10:08
Buf: Braxton 19 pass from Ferguson (Leypoldt kick), 11:09
Den: Little 35 pass from Johnson (Turner kick), 13:26
Buf: Hill 16 pass from Ferguson (Leypoldt kick), 14:56
Buf: Simpson 16 run (Leypoldt kick), 8:38
Buf: Braxton 4 run (Leypoldt kick), 9:14
Den: Upchurch 80 pass from Hufnagel (Turner kick), 12:56

	BUF	DEN
First downs	29	13
Rushing yds	293	47
Passing yds	143	258
Punts-avg	4-49.3	4-40.8
Fumbles-lost	3-1	3-1
Penalties-yds	6-46	4-31

BILLS LEADERS: Rushing - Simpson 26-138, Braxton 17-102, Calhoun 6-20, Ferguson 3-6, Washington 2-13, Hayman 4-6, Marangi 1-7, Hill 1-1; **Passing** - Ferguson 9-18-0 - 143; **Receiving** - Chandler 4-69, Hill 3-41, Braxton 1-19, Seymour 1-14.

BRONCOS LEADERS: Rushing - Little 6-21, Ross 5-15, Hufnagel 1-8, Keyworth 2-3, Armstrong 1-0; **Passing** - Hufnagel 5-14-1 - 135, Johnson 10-22-2 - 131; **Receiving** - Upchurch 1-80, Van Heusen 3-48, Moses 3-47, Little 3-39, Odoms 3-38, Dolbin 1-12, Keyworth 1-2.

NOTES
• The Bills' offense continued its incredible pace with 424 yards in a come-from-behind victory.
• Joe Ferguson had his best yardage day as a pro, passing for 253 yards.
• Lydell Mitchell had 160 total yards and tied a Colts record with four touchdowns.
• O.J. Simpson recorded his 28th 100-yard game, moving into second place on the all-time NFL list ahead of Leroy Kelly. He still trailed Jim Brown, who had 58.
• The Bills possessed the ball for 11:25 in the pivotal fourth quarter and they converted 11 of 14 third downs. Baltimore was seven-of-12 on third down.
• John Holland, a second-round choice of Minnesota in 1974, started in place of injured Bob Chandler and was presented a game ball for his efforts.
• Trailing 21-17 late in the first half, Holland caught a 15-yard slant-in for a TD.
• The Colts regained the lead early in the third, but the Bills got it back when Holland made a 63-yard reception to the 2, which set up Ferguson's five-yard TD pass to Jim Braxton that made it 31-28 Buffalo.

• Toni Linhart's field goal tied the game early in the fourth, but the Bills got the winning points when Braxton's third TD of the game capped an 80-yard march that consumed 7:31.

QUOTES
• John Holland: "I knew all along, even when I was in Minnesota, that I could play. Coach told me, 'I'm going to give you your chance, now show me what you can do.'"
• O.J. Simpson: "When a young team plays good against a good team, experience is going to be the determining factor. Youth is the only thing against the Colts. All they have to do is win a few. They seem to be believing that they can win. They're just like we were a few years ago. No one in this locker room is surprised by what we ran into out there. If they move the ball the way they did against us, they're going to win this year."
• Colts coach Ted Marchibroda: "O.J. played his game. His mere presence in there makes their offense more effective. What hurt was that he (Ferguson) managed to complete passes. He made some big plays."
• Lou Saban: "This may sound strange, but I felt better when we were 14 points down than before the game. All week long I felt we were going to have a rough afternoon in Baltimore. We've just played three big games against strong teams and I felt we might be flat against the Colts. For the first time, we proved we could fall behind by as many as 14 points and strike back and win. We're going to be down again and now the guys can think back to Baltimore."

WEEK 4 GAMES	
Cinc 27, NE 10	Hou 40, Clev 10
Pitt 20, Den 9	KC 42, Oak 10
Mia 24, Phil 16	Minn 29, NYJ 21
LA 13, SD 10	Atl 17, SF 3
Det 27, Chi 7	Dal 13, NYG 7
Wash 27, St.L 17	NO 20, GB 19

Bills	10	14	7	7	- 38
Colts	14	7	7	3	- 31

Attendance at Memorial Stadium - 43,907

Bal: Mitchell 6 run (Linhart kick), 2:50
Bal: Mitchell 11 run (Linhart kick), 6:49
Buf: FG Leypoldt 44, 10:33
Buf: Simpson 12 run (Leypoldt kick), 13:20
Bal: Mitchell 25 pass from Jones (Linhart kick), 2:35
Buf: Braxton 1 run (Leypoldt kick), 10:55
Buf: Holland 15 pass from Ferguson (Leypoldt kick), 13:26
Bal: Mitchell 23 pass from Jones (Linhart kick), 7:21
Buf: Braxton 5 pass from Ferguson (Leypoldt kick), 9:00
Bal: FG Linhart 19, 1:28
Buf: Braxton 3 run (Leypoldt kick), 8:56

	BUF	BAL
First downs	26	19
Rushing yds	178	196
Passing yds	246	153
Punts-avg	2-23.0	4-40.8
Fumbles-lost	3-1	0-0
Penalties-yds	5-35	8-62

BILLS LEADERS: Rushing - Simpson 32-159, Braxton 9-13, Ferguson 2-6; **Passing** - Ferguson 14-26-1 - 253; **Receiving** - Holland 6-121, Hill 2-42, Simpson 1-14, Braxton 3-27, Seymour 2-49.

COLTS LEADERS: Rushing - Mitchell 19-107, Jones 4-46, Olds 10-28, McCauley 3-15; **Passing** - Jones 11-23-1 - 155; **Receiving** - Doughty 6-83, Mitchell 3-53, Chester 2-19.

STANDINGS: FOURTH WEEK

AFC EAST	W	L	T	CENTRAL	W	L	T	WEST	W	L	T	NFC EAST	W	L	T	CENTRAL	W	L	T	WEST	W	L	T
Buffalo	4	0	0	Cincinnati	4	0	0	Oakland	3	1	0	Dallas	4	0	0	Minnesota	4	0	0	LA Rams	3	1	0
Miami	3	1	0	Houston	3	1	0	Denver	2	2	0	Washington	3	1	0	Detroit	3	1	0	Atlanta	2	2	0
NY Jets	2	2	0	Pittsburgh	3	1	0	Kan. City	1	3	0	St. Louis	2	2	0	Chicago	1	3	0	San Fran	1	3	0
Baltimore	1	3	0	Cleveland	0	4	0	San Diego	0	4	0	NY Giants	1	3	0	Green Bay	0	4	0	N.Orleans	1	3	0
New England	0	4	0									Philadelphia	1	3	0								

GAME 5 - Monday, Oct. 20, 1975 - GIANTS 17, BILLS 14

Giants	0	7	0	10	- 17
Bills	7	7	0	0	- 14

Attendance at Rich Stadium - 79,518

Buf: Simpson 1 run (Leypoldt kick), 13:00
Buf: Hill 13 pass from Ferguson (Leypoldt kick), 2:56
NYG: Rhodes 20 pass from Morton (Hunt kick), 13:00
NYG: Johnson 13 run (Hunt kick), 6:31
NYG: FG Hunt 37, 14:54

	BUF	NYG
First downs	18	16
Rushing yds	171	135
Passing yds	138	214
Punts-avg	4-41.3	3-43.0
Fumbles-lost	1-1	6-2
Penalties-yds	5-30	3-20

BILLS LEADERS: Rushing - Simpson 34-126, Braxton 11-41, Ferguson 1-1, Washington 1-3; **Passing** - Ferguson 11-19-2 - 147; **Receiving** - Chandler 3-51, Hill 4-51, Braxton 2-23, Seymour 2-22.

GIANTS LEADERS: Rushing - Johnson 13-77, Dawkins 17-55, Kotar 5-11, Morton 4-5, Watkins 1-4, Rhodes 1-(-17); **Passing** - Morton 15-21-1 - 220; **Receiving** - Rhodes 5-83, Dawkins 4-63, Gillette 2-43, Johnson 2-20, Tucker 1-6, Hicks 1-5.

WEEK 5 GAMES

NE 21, Balt 10	Cinc 14, Oak 10
Den 16, Clev 15	Hou 13, Wash 10
KC 12, SD 10	Mia 43, NYJ 0
Pitt 34, Chi 3	LA 22, Atl 7
GB 19, Dal 17	Minn 25, Det 19
St.L 31, Phil 20	SF 35, NO 21

NOTES

• George Hunt's 37-yard field goal with six seconds left dealt Buffalo its first loss of the season.
• John Leypoldt's 50-yard attempt with 1:02 left was blocked by Spider Lockhart and gave the Giants possession at their own 32. Ron Johnson ran 18 yards, Craig Morton hit Ray Rhodes for 22 yards and Johnson gained eight on a run to the 20 to set up Hunt's winning kick.
• Hunt had missed field goals of 40 and 47 in the third quarter.
• The Bills jumped to a quick 14-0 lead. O.J. Simpson scored on a one-yard run and 4:56 later, after Merv Krakau recovered a Doug Kotar fumble at the Giants 26, Joe Ferguson hit J.D. Hill with a 13-yard TD pass.
• The Giants pulled within 14-7 when Morton directed a 91-yard TD drive that culminated in his 20-yard TD pass to Rhodes. They had been stuck in that hole when Danny Buggs misplayed a punt, but the Bills failed to hold the Giants and they allowed the visitors to gain the momentum.
• Johnson capped a 90-yard drive to tie the game at 14-14 in the fourth.
• The Bills then had two chances to win. They drove to the 2 and Leypoldt blew a 19-yard field goal.
• Then Rhodes fumbled and Charlie Ford recovered at the Giants 37 and the Bills were in business again. But after moving only four yards, Leypoldt's kick was blocked.

QUOTES

• Pat Toomay: "This was a night when we were knocked off our high horse."
• Lou Saban: "We've got some holes in our defense and they took advantage of it. I was afraid something like this would happen. We expected the Giants to be up and we got just what we expected. Hand it to them, they just beat us. It was a beautiful four weeks, but now we have to get back to work."
• O.J. Simpson: "Teams that play the way we did tonight don't win football games. We turned the ball over three times, had several nice gains nullified by penalties and they hung in there well enough to win."
• John Leypoldt on his 19-yard miss: "It was a good snap, a good hold, I just missed it. I usually don't miss those. Oh well, that's the way it goes."
• Giants kicker George Hunt: "I never had a win-the-game type of field goal in the pros before. I hit it great. It could have been good from 60 yards."
• J.D. Hill: "One thing that bothered me was that there was too much talking and advice-giving on our sideline. You've got to be out there playing ball, man, not running your mouth off telling other players what to do. We just didn't play the way we know how. Maybe this is a lesson for us. We'd talked about upsets and how we weren't going to let it happen to us, but it did. I still feel we're the best team in the league, we just have to keep our heads together. Now that we've lost, maybe all the news media will leave us alone and let us play ball."

GAME 6 - Sunday, Oct. 26, 1975 - DOLPHINS 35, BILLS 30

Dolphins	0	14	7	14	- 35
Bills	13	10	0	7	- 30

Attendance at Rich Stadium - 79,141

Buf: Freeman 30 interception return (Leypoldt kick), 1:23
Buf: Simpson 26 run (kick failed), 10:24
Mia: Nottingham 1 run (Yepremian kick), 5:51
Buf: Chandler 4 pass from Ferguson (Leypoldt kick), 13:00
Mia: Moore 13 pass from Griese (Yepremian kick), 14:31
Buf: FG Leypoldt 45, 14:57
Mia: Nottingham 1 run (Yepremian kick), 9:12
Buf: Chandler 5 pass from Ferguson (Leypoldt kick), 7:42
Mia: Mandich 5 pass from Griese (Yepremian kick), 11:42
Mia: Nottingham 1 run (Yepremian kick), 13:35

	BUF	MIA
First downs	21	25
Rushing yds	128	245
Passing yds	217	132
Punts-avg	3-48.7	5-35.8
Fumbles-lost	2-2	2-0
Penalties-yds	6-37	3-13

BILLS LEADERS: Rushing - Simpson 19-88, Braxton 10-35, Ferguson 3-5, Chandler 1-0; **Passing** - Ferguson 20-29-2 - 221; **Receiving** - Chandler 8-96, Hill 2-22, Simpson 2-16, Braxton 3-19, Seymour 4-57, Gant 1-11.

DOLPHINS LEADERS: Rushing - Morris 20-124, Nottingham 15-61, Bulaich 4-43, Griese 2-19, Ginn 2-(-2); **Passing** - Griese 13-21-2 - 151; **Receiving** - Solomon 5-61, Moore 5-57, Bulaich 1-22, Seiple 1-6, Mandich 1-5.

NOTES

• In a showdown for AFC East supremacy, the Dolphins, as usual, came out on top.
• Joe Ferguson completed a career-high 20 passes, but his interception to Jake Scott with 3:04 remaining set up Don Nottingham's winning TD.
• Miami had just pulled to within 30-28 on Jim Mandich's TD reception and the Bills were pushed back to their own 12. Saban had Ferguson throw a pass and Ferguson misread the Dolphins defense which was man-to-man, not zone. His pass for J.D. Hill was picked off by Scott at the 22 and six plays later, Nottingham scored the winning points with 1:25 left. The Bills' final possession ended when Vern Den Herder sacked Ferguson, forcing him to fumble, and then recovered the loose ball.
• The Bills began the game superbly as Steve Freeman intercepted Bob Griese's first pass and returned it 30 yards for a TD. Later in the first, O.J. Simpson, who was held under 100 yards for the first time this season, jaunted 26 yards for a TD to make it 13-0 as John Leypoldt missed the PAT.
• Nottingham made it 13-7 early in the second, then a late flurry in the period produced a 23-14 Buffalo halftime lead. Tony Greene's interception and return to the Miami 34 led to Bob Chandler's TD, but the Dolphins answered when Greiese hit Nat Moore for a TD. The Bills got the ball back with 25 seconds left and three Ferguson com-

pletions moved them into position for Leypoldt to make a 45-yard field goal.

QUOTES

• Miami safety Jake Scott: "Ferguson misread the coverage, he thought we were still in a zone. The call was a good one on his part. If he hadn't executed it wrong, it would have been a fine play to move the ball upfield out of trouble."
• Lou Saban: "The score is 30-28, I'm back on my own 12. If they stop me, they can beat me with a field goal or a touchdown. If they stop the running game, we have to punt. We had a tough time running all day and I felt like if we were going to throw, it should be on first-and-10, rather than third-and-long. Miami was playing that 50 defense which is tough to run against. I can't say let's try it again, I don't have that luxury. This game is brutal, just brutal."
• Joe Ferguson: "I don't know if Scott read my checkoff. But my key wasn't him. I audibled out of the bootleg pass because it's a hard pass for the offensive line to block for against that defense. If it had been a running play, I wouldn't have checked off. When coach Saban calls a run, I stay with it."
• Bob Chandler: "If we had run two or three times and had to punt, the fans would have asked why didn't we throw. So we passed and they're probably second-guessing that."

WEEK 6 GAMES

Balt 45, NYJ 28	Cinc 21, Atl 14
Wash 23, Clev 7	KC 26, Den 13
Hou 24, Det 6	NE 24, SF 16
Oak 25, SD 0	Pitt 16, GB 13
Minn 13, Chi 9	Dal 20, Phil 17
LA 38, NO 14	St.L 20, NYG 13

STANDINGS: SIXTH WEEK

AFC EAST	W	L	T	CENTRAL	W	L	T	WEST	W	L	T	NFC EAST	W	L	T	CENTRAL	W	L	T	WEST	W	L	T
Miami	5	1	0	Cincinnati	6	0	0	Oakland	4	2	0	Dallas	5	1	0	Minnesota	6	0	0	LA Rams	5	1	0
Buffalo	4	2	0	Houston	5	1	0	Denver	3	3	0	Washington	4	2	0	Detroit	3	3	0	Atlanta	2	4	0
NY Jets	2	4	0	Pittsburgh	5	1	0	Kan. City	3	3	0	St. Louis	4	2	0	Chicago	1	5	0	San Fran	2	4	0
Baltimore	2	4	0	Cleveland	0	6	0	San Diego	0	6	0	NY Giants	2	4	0	Green Bay	1	5	0	N.Orleans	1	5	0
New England	2	4	0									Philadelphia	1	5	0								

225

GAME 7 - Sunday, Nov. 2, 1975 - BILLS 24, JETS 23

NOTES

• Leading 23-17 with 5:19 left, Jets coach Charley Winner elected to go for a fourth-and-one at the Bills 20 rather than kick a game-clinching field goal and Earl Edwards stopped John Riggins shy of the first down.

• Joe Ferguson then hit O.J. Simpson with a short pass over the middle as linebacker Richard Wood was caught in one-on-one coverage. Simpson deked Wood, then rambled through the secondary to complete a 64-yard TD pass with 3:46 remaining. It was the longest TD pass for Ferguson since high school and Simpson's longest reception as a pro.

• With the Jets trying to come back, Pat Toomay, Walt Patulski and Don Croft all recorded sacks of Joe Namath to prevent the Jets from getting into scoring position in their final two possessions.

• Simpson moved into fourth place on the all-time NFL rushing list and he topped the 1,000-yard mark for the season in the seventh game, the same thing he did in 1973 when he rushed for 2,003 yards.

• Ferguson's 296 yards passing were a new career high.

• Lou Saban benched linebackers Merv Krakau and Bo Cornell and replaced them with Tom Ruud and John McCrumbley, but the two youngsters were on the bench by the second quarter.

• The Bills drove 74 yards to score on their first possession, then saw the Jets score 23 straight points.

• Buffalo had three TDs called back due to penalties, committing three holding penalties, and Bob Chandler dropped a sure TD pass.

QUOTES

• Jets coach Charley Winner: "It was a calculated risk, but a good one. Our aim was to try and gain longer possession of the ball. The Bills are a quick-striking team. We had to believe they were capable of scoring twice in the final five minutes. I went for it because I thought we could make it. Our guys thought they could get it."

• Lou Saban: "You're not going to get me to talk about that decision. I was looking for the field goal unit and I was happy to see they didn't come in. It would have been tough for us to score twice."

• O.J. Simpson: "I gave Wood a move to the outside and he went for it which gave me room, enough room so that I know a linebacker isn't going to recover in time to get me. Once I was by him, I ran right at the safety, Delles Howell, and when he committed himself, I knew I had six points. How did I feel when the Jets went for it? Happy."

• Joe Ferguson on the TD to Simpson: "It's a play designed to get a first down, but whenever you give the Juice room, he can do anything. I never saw him run so fast. I think for me it's just a matter of growing up and realizing what my responsibilities are."

Bills	7	0	10	7	-	24
Jets	3	13	7	0	-	23

Attendance at Shea Stadium - 58,343

Buf: Braxton 11 pass from Ferguson (Leypoldt kick), 4:33
NYJ: FG Leahy 42, 14:06
NYJ: FG Leahy 41, 10:01
NYJ: FG Leahy 31, 14:29
NYJ: Boozer 16 pass from Namath (Leahy kick), 14:46
NYJ: Bell 31 pass from Namath (Leahy kick), 3:06
Buf: FG Leypoldt 40, 7:06
Buf: Hill 28 pass from Ferguson (Leypoldt kick), 12:53
Buf: Simpson 64 pass from Ferguson (Leypoldt kick), 11:14

	BUF	NYJ
First downs	22	25
Rushing yds	148	199
Passing yds	287	167
Punts-avg	3-35.0	3-48.7
Fumbles-lost	2-1	2-0
Penalties-yds	6-47	6-50

BILLS LEADERS: Rushing - Simpson 21-94, Braxton 10-43, Ferguson 2-11; **Passing** - Ferguson 15-29-2 - 296; **Receiving** - Chandler 5-75, Hill 4-88, Simpson 2-66, Braxton 4-67.

JETS LEADERS: Rushing - Riggins 24-108, Boozer 10-37, Davis 2-33, Garrett 5-21; **Passing** - Namath 16-31-1 - 208; **Receiving** - Bell 3-60, Caster 4-56, Barkum 5-44, Riggins 2-23, Boozer 1-16, Piccone 1-9.

GAME 8 - Sunday, Nov. 9, 1975 - COLTS 42, BILLS 35

NOTES

• The Bills blew a 28-7 second-quarter lead as Bert Jones beat the Bills for the first time in his career with a 306-yard passing day.

• Joe Ferguson's three TD passes enabled him to set a new team record for TD passes in a season (17).

• Lydell Mitchell increased his TD total against the Bills to seven this season.

• O.J. Simpson scored the first three TDs to make it 21-0. His 44-yard run came on a reverse from a double wing, the 22-yard pass came when he beat ex-Bill Jim Cheyunski and the 32-yard pass when he beat safety Jackie Wallace.

• Down 28-7, the Colts turned the game around when they faked a field goal and Marty Domres hit Bill Olds with a 15-yard TD pass. The Bills had stopped the Colts on third down at the 49, but Pat Toomay was penalized for a head slap that gave Baltimore a first down. Six plays later, they were stopped again, but Ted Marchibroda called for the fake.

• Less than a minute later, after a Buffalo punt, Roger Carr got behind Frank Oliver for an 89-yard TD. Oliver had replaced injured Dwight Harrison in the first quarter.

• After a scoreless third, the Colts attacked for 21 more points in the fourth. The tying score came after Jones hit Carr for 47 yards to the Bills 11. On the Bills' next possession Joe Ferguson was intercepted by Stan White, who returned it to the Bills 23 and two plays later, Jones scrambled 19 yards for the go-ahead TD.

QUOTES

• Lou Saban: "We were trying to play pass defense with some guys who just aren't ready. We were hoping to patch up and get by in spots where we were hurt by injuries, but we're not and it's showing more and more every week. We've known we've had this problem all year, we've tried everything we could to cover it up. These players are all I've got this year."

• Pat Toomay: "I barely hit him (tackle Ed George) on top of the head. But with all the holding going on, what are you supposed to do? I've been doing the same thing for six years. I did the same thing in the fourth quarter and Baltimore was called for holding."

• Colts quarterback Bert Jones: "We saw in the films that Buffalo was set up for a fake field goal. We practiced the fake all week. Even when we were down 28-7, we knew we could score on Buffalo and get back into the game. This is the biggest comeback I've ever been involved in."

• O.J. Simpson: "We have some youngsters back there (in the secondary) who we feel will develop into good players. I just hope they do it while I'm still playing."

Colts	0	21	0	21	-	42
Bills	7	21	0	7	-	35

Attendance at Rich Stadium - 77,320

Buf: Simpson 44 run (Leypoldt kick), 2:32
Buf: Simpson 22 pass from Ferguson (Leypoldt kick), :48
Buf: Simpson 32 pass from Ferguson (Leypoldt kick), 1:43
Bal: Mitchell 9 pass from Jones (Linhart kick), 3:04
Buf: Chandler 19 pass from Ferguson (Leypoldt kick), 6:30
Bal: Olds 15 pass from Domres (Linhart kick), 12:32
Bal: Carr 89 pass from Jones (Linhart kick), 13:24
Bal: Mitchell 11 run (Linhart kick), 1:44
Bal: Jones 19 run (Linhart kick), 3:48
Bal: Mitchell 12 run (Linhart kick), 11:50
Buf: Chandler 18 pass from Marangi (Leypoldt kick), 13:22

	BUF	BAL
First downs	20	25
Rushing yds	179	199
Passing yds	239	299
Punts-avg	6-48.5	4-44.8
Fumbles-lost	1-1	2-2
Penalties-yds	7-55	7-60

BILLS LEADERS: Rushing - Simpson 19-123, Braxton 4-6, Ferguson 1-4, Marangi 3-46; **Passing** - Ferguson 12-21-1 - 234, Marangi 2-10-1 - 33; **Receiving** - Chandler 7-118, Hill 2-34, Simpson 3-71, Braxton 1-32, Seymour 1-12.

COLTS LEADERS: Rushing - Mitchell 27-112, Jones 9-59, Olds 7-17, McCauley 2-7, Leaks 1-4; **Passing** - Jones 14-22-1 - 306, Domres 1-1-0 - 15; **Receiving** - Carr 2-136, Doughty 3-102, Chester 3-31, Olds 3-27, Mitchell 4-25.

GAME 9 - Monday, Nov. 17, 1975 - BENGALS 33, BILLS 24

Bills	3	7	7	7	-	24
Bengals	6	14	3	10	-	33

Attendance at Riverfront Stadium - 56,666

Cin: Elliott 5 pass from Anderson (kick failed), 8:36
Buf: FG Leypoldt 28, 10:39
Cin: Fritts 1 run (Green kick), 6:42
Buf: Simpson 2 run (Leypoldt kick), 10:42
Cin: Joiner 20 pass from Anderson (Green kick), 13:47
Buf: Simpson 1 run (Leypoldt kick), 3:49
Cin: FG Green 28, 12:10
Cin: Fritts 1 run (Green kick), 2:30
Buf: Hill 10 pass from Ferguson (Leypoldt kick), 6:58
Cin: FG Green 18, 13:03

	BUF	CIN
First downs	20	34
Rushing yds	242	108
Passing yds	93	441
Punts-avg	4-46.3	0-0
Fumbles-lost	2-2	1-1
Penalties-yds	7-78	4-51

BILLS LEADERS: Rushing - Simpson 17-197, Braxton 10-40, Ferguson 1-5; **Passing** - Ferguson 9-18-0 - 106; **Receiving** - Chandler 1-19, Hill 3-33, Simpson 2-21, Braxton 2-14, Seymour 1-19.

BENGALS LEADERS: Rushing - Clark 15-56, Elliott 9-29, Fritts 5-10, Anderson 6-8, Williams 2-5; **Passing** - Anderson 30-46-0 - 447; **Receiving** - Curtis 7-139, Myers 7-108, Joiner 5-90, Clark 6-64, Trumpy 1-18, Coslet 1-18, Elliott 3-10.

NOTES

• Ken Anderson set Bengals records with 447 passing yards and 22 passing first downs.
• Cincinnati never punted in the game, a first in Bills history.
• O.J. Simpson scored a rushing TD for the ninth straight game, tying a team record. Simpson had 113 yards on his first four carries and had 154 yards on nine carries by halftime.
• Simpson's 59-yard run led to John Leypoldt's first-quarter field goal. His 44-yard run was wasted when Jim Braxton lost a fumble early in the second and from there, Anderson hit Isaac Curtis for 47 yards to set up Stan Fritts' one-yard plunge and a 13-3 Bengals lead.
• Vic Washington returned the ensuing kickoff 42 yards and Simpson eventually scored, but the Bengals answered when Buffalo's third interference penalty of the night helped lead to Charlie Joiner's 20-yard TD reception over Tony Greene.
• Greene's 32-yard return of a Curtis fumble led to Simpson's second TD. The Bills got a break when Lenvil Elliott's 101-yard kickoff return was nullified by a clip.
• Leading 23-17, the Bengals drove 80 yards with

WEEK 9 GAMES

Balt 52, NYJ 19	Oak 38, Clev 17
Den 27, SD 17	Hou 20, Mia 19
Pitt 28, KC 3	Dal 34, NE 31
LA 16, Atl 7	SF 31, Chi 3
Det 13, GB 10	Minn 20, NO 7
Phil 13, NYG 10	St.L 20, Wash 17

Joiner's 33-yard reception the key.
• The Bills fought back to 30-24 as Ferguson hit J.D. Hill for a score, but that was it for the Bills.
• Dave Green's clinching field goal came moments after Dwight Harrison dropped an interception.
• The Bengals ran 84 plays compared to 47 for the Bills. Buffalo tried a 3-4 defense with Tom Ruud, Mark Johnson and Doug Allen joining John Skorupan at linebacker in the formation.
• After the game, Bengals linebacker Al Beauchamp spit in Braxton's face, then ran off the field.

QUOTES

• O.J. Simpson: "They won because they're better than we are. They simply beat our butts. We figured we could move the ball on them and we did, but we didn't move it enough."
• Jim Braxton: "If we ever play Cincinnati again, Beauchamp won't finish the game, I promise. And you can print that. It won't be anything dirty, I don't play that way. But I'll get him and it'll be clean. He's the worst linebacker I ever played against. I beat his butt off the whole game and he couldn't take it."
• Bengals linebacker Al Beauchamp: "Yeah, he opened his mouth and I spit in it. I feel the same way about him the next time we play."
• Lou Saban: "We used the 30 defense to give our secondary more help in coverage. We used zones, man-to-man, but neither tactic worked very well. We've lost our depth. When we were 4-0, our opponents hadn't caught up to our weaknesses. Now they have."

GAME 10 - Sunday, Nov. 23, 1975 - BILLS 45, PATRIOTS 31

Patriots	7	14	7	3	-	31
Bills	14	10	7	14	-	45

Attendance at Rich Stadium - 65,655

Buf: Gant 19 pass from Ferguson (Leypoldt kick), 2:31
Buf: Hill 77 pass from Ferguson (Leypoldt kick), 10:02
NE: Cunningham 10 run (Smith kick), 13:02
NE: Cunningham 11 pass from Grogan (Smith kick), 4:51
Buf: Simpson 2 run (Leypoldt kick), 9:57
Buf: FG Leypoldt 28, 11:36
NE: Francis 21 pass from Grogan (Smith kick), 13:28
NE: Cunningham 1 run (Smith kick), 3:17
Buf: Simpson 3 pass from Ferguson (Leypoldt kick), 14:08
NE: FG Smith 34, 9:33
Buf: Simpson 1 run (Leypoldt kick), 10:51
Buf: Simpson 3 pass from Ferguson (Leypoldt kick), 13:03

	BUF	NE
First downs	23	28
Rushing yds	153	138
Passing yds	263	360
Punts-avg	4-41.3	4-41.0
Fumbles-lost	2-0	2-0
Penalties-yds	8-65	11-67

BILLS LEADERS: Rushing - Simpson 27-69, Braxton 13-84; **Passing** - Ferguson 16-32-1 - 276; **Receiving** - Chandler 6-78, Hill 4-147, Simpson 4-22, Braxton 1-10, Gant 1-19.

PATRIOTS LEADERS: Rushing - Cunningham 19-100, Grogan 5-22, Johnson 7-16; **Passing** - Grogan 25-46-3 - 365; **Receiving** - Francis 7-125, Vataha 5-96, Stingley 3-47, Wright 4-46, Johnson 4-37, Cunningham 2-14.

NOTES

• Although he was held to a season-low 69 yards rushing, O.J. Simpson scored four TDs in one game for the first time in his career, and he set a new team record by scoring a rushing TD for the 10th game in a row. He also set the team record for TDs in a season, breaking Cookie Gilchrist's mark of 15 set in 1962. However, the smallest regular-season crowd in Rich Stadium history saw the feat.
• Joe Ferguson's four TD passes tied the club record set by Johnny Green in 1960.
• Before the game, an NBC report said that Lou Saban would resign if the Bills lost.
• WFL refugee Ike Thomas intercepted a Steve Grogan

WEEK 10 GAMES

Balt 33, Mia 17	Pitt 32, Hou 9
Clev 35, Cinc 23	Atl 35, Den 21
KC 24, Det 21	St.L 37, NYJ 6
Oak 26, Wash 23	Minn 28, SD 13
LA 38, Chi 10	GB 40, NYG 14
Dal 27, Phil 17	SF 16, NO 6

pass with 2:30 left and returned it 58 yards to the Pats 11, setting up Joe Ferguson's clinching TD pass to Simpson with 1:57 left.
• The Bills drove 66 yards to score on their first possession, then later in the first, Ferguson threw the longest TD pass of his career, a 77-yarder to J.D. Hill.
• New England tied it early in the second quarter, but Steve Freeman's interception set up Simpson's first TD. After a John Leypoldt field goal, the Patriots raced 85 yards in less than two minutes to get within 24-21 at halftime, then took the lead early in the third on Sam Cunningham's third TD of the day.
• With the game tied at 31-31, Vic Washington returned a kickoff 56 yards and two plays later, Ferguson hit Hill for 44 yards to the 1 and Simpson scored from there.

QUOTES

• O.J. Simpson: "My teammates started calling me 'knuckles' last year because I was never a big part of the passing game. I'm more into it this year and I don't think I'll be hearing them calling me 'knuckles' anymore."
• Joe Ferguson: "I guess we should have been using Juice more in the passing game. His first touchdown was probably the toughest catch he's made all year. He catches the ball well in clutch situations. In practice he drops a few, but you know how he is."
• Lou Saban on Ike Thomas: "We didn't even know if he could play until today."
• Ike Thomas: "I got a call from Stew Barber who was a coach for Charlotte (in the WFL) the year before. I had a lot of offers from the NFL, but most of them were for 1976. I wanted to play this year. Only two teams, Buffalo and New England, said I would play this year."
• J.D. Hill on his 44-yard reception: "It was a play we put in this week. But it was designed for Bobby Chandler on the other side. Joe saw me get open and threw a perfect pass."

STANDINGS: TENTH WEEK

AFC EAST	W	L	T	CENTRAL	W	L	T	WEST	W	L	T	NFC EAST	W	L	T	CENTRAL	W	L	T	WEST	W	L	T
Miami	7	3	0	Pittsburgh	9	1	0	Oakland	8	2	0	St. Louis	8	2	0	Minnesota	10	0	0	LA Rams	8	2	0
Buffalo	6	4	0	Cincinnati	8	2	0	Kan. City	5	5	0	Dallas	7	3	0	Detroit	6	4	0	San Fran	5	5	0
Baltimore	6	4	0	Houston	7	3	0	Denver	4	6	0	Washington	6	4	0	Chicago	2	8	0	Atlanta	3	7	0
New England	3	7	0	Cleveland	1	9	0	San Diego	0	10	0	NY Giants	3	7	0	Green Bay	2	8	0	N.Orleans	2	8	0
NY Jets	2	8	0									Philadelphia	2	8	0								

NOTES

• Despite arriving in St. Louis just two hours before the game, due to a snowstorm, the Bills ripped the NFC East's first-place team and snapped the Cardinals six-game winning streak as Jim Braxton set career-highs with 34 carries for 160 yards and scored three TDs.

• O.J. Simpson tied the NFL record for consecutive games with a rushing TD with 11. The Cards hadn't allowed a rushing TD during their winning streak.

• The Bills intercepted Jim Hart four times, forced him to fumble three times and sacked him twice.

• The Bills had the ball for 27 more plays and had a possession time of 39:25.

• St. Louis took a 7-0 lead, driving for a TD after blocking a John Leypoldt field goal.

• The Bills trailed, 7-6, thanks to Leypoldt's missed extra point, but they took the lead for good in the second quarter after Jeff Winans recovered a fumble by ex-Bill Steve Jones at the Cards 37 with 52 seconds left in the half. Three plays and 25 seconds later, Simpson scored for a 13-7 lead.

• In the first half, the Bills committed three turnovers to waste scoring chances.

• Dwight Harrison's interception on the second play of the third and Don Croft's recovery of a Hart fumble led to a pair of Leypoldt field goals.

• Harrison's second interception in the fourth resulted in Braxton's second TD, and Tony Greene's interception and 37-yard return to the 2 set up Braxton's final TD.

QUOTES

• Walt Patulski on the defense: "We just got tired of hearing how bad we were. For once we were relaxed. We were so pressed for time getting to the stadium, we didn't have time to get nervous. I'd have to say this was our biggest win of the year, even bigger than Pittsburgh, especially for the defense. We had a major part in the victory today."

• Dwight Harrison: "To begin with, we were lucky. Just about the time St. Louis would try something tricky, we were in the right defense. When they were going to Mel Gray, we had him double-teamed. When they tried to go down the middle, we had a zone called to the middle. I really don't know why we contained them as well as we did."

• Cardinals quarterback Jim Hart: "Their pass rush was a little greater than I had seen in the films. It was the hardest rush I've seen in a long time."

• Jim Braxton: "I don't know about the spotlight, I'm still the blocking back on this team. They just keyed on O.J. and I had to be open sooner or later."

• Cardinals running back Terry Metcalf: "I talked to Ahmad Rashad and he told me we were going to kill 'em (the Bills) because they've got no defense. I said 'No way.' On any given day."

• Lou Saban: "It's the best defensive game we've had. When you get some confidence in the secondary, you're much better up front and that's what happened today."

Bills	6	7	6	13 -	32
Cardinals	7	0	0	7 -	14

Attendance at Busch Memorial Stadium - 41,899

St.L: Metcalf 1 run (Bakken kick), 6:51
Buf: Braxton 1 run (kick failed), 13:45
Buf: Simpson 3 run (Leypoldt kick), 14:33
Buf: FG Leypoldt 30, 4:52
Buf: FG Leypoldt 33, 13:55
Buf: Braxton 5 run (Leypoldt kick), 2:19
Buf: Braxton 1 run (kick failed), 3:22
St.L: Metcalf 4 pass from Hart (Bakken kick), 5:41

	BUF	ST.L
First downs	25	16
Rushing yds	264	54
Passing yds	128	156
Punts-avg	3-41.7	3-37.3
Fumbles-lost	1-1	6-3
Penalties-yds	6-40	4-17

BILLS LEADERS: Rushing - Simpson 23-85, Braxton 34-160, Ferguson 2-19; **Passing** - Ferguson 11-22-2 - 128; **Receiving** - Chandler 3-29, Hill 5-66, Braxton 3-33.

CARDINALS LEADERS: Rushing - Otis 13-50, Metcalf 5-7, Jones 2-1, Hart 1-(-4); **Passing** - Hart 13-31-4 - 167; **Receiving** - Metcalf 4-52, Gray 2-45, Jones 5-39, Harris 2-31.

WEEK 11 GAMES

LA 20, Det 0	Balt 28, KC 14
Cinc 23, Hou 19	Clev 17, NO 16
Den 13, SD 10	Mia 20, NE 7
Oak 37, Atl 34	GB 28, Chi 7
Dal 14, NYG 3	Wash 31, Minn 30
Phil 27, SF 17	Pitt 20, NYJ 7

NOTES

• The Bills saw their playoff hopes officially dashed as Miami posted its 12th straight win over them.

• O.J. Simpson set an NFL record by scoring a rushing TD for the 12th game in a row, breaking former Colts star Lenny Moore's record. Simpson also set career highs for receptions (8) and yards (117).

• The Bills were the victims of a poor official's call. Trailing 24-21, the Bills' John Skorupan appeared to recover a Mercury Morris fumble at the Miami 28 with nine minutes remaining, but referee Gene Barth ruled it wasn't a fumble. The Bills argued vehemently and Pat Toomay was penalized 15 yards for brushing an official. On the next play, Don Nottingham broke a 56-yard run to the 1 and on the next play, Norm Bulaich scored the clinching TD.

• Third-string QB Don Strock completed 11 passes in a row in the first half of his first NFL start as Miami jumped to a 21-0 lead. On the Dolphins second possession, he scrambled four yards for a TD, then in the second quarter, he threw two TD strikes to Howard Twilley. The second TD pass was set up when Dwight Harrison interfered with Nat Moore in the end zone on a flanker reverse pass thrown by Freddie Solomon.

• The Bills converted four third downs on the way to their first TD on the first possession of the third quarter.

• The Bills pulled to within 24-14 when Joe Ferguson hit J.D. Hill for a 31-yard score, and with 9:23 left, Simpson took a short pass and raced 62 yards for a TD. And then the officials short-circuited the rally.

QUOTES

• Ralph Wilson: "The official who made that call (on the non-fumble) should be barred from football. Anyone that incompetent shouldn't be allowed to officiate. I don't care if Commissioner Rozelle fines me $10,000 or $15,000 for my remarks."

• Pat Toomay: "I saw the fumble and I ran over there and pushed the official out of the way to get at the ball. It was an unbelievable call (his penalty). Even if it wasn't a fumble, which I think it was, it would have been third-and-seven and we could have gotten the ball back. And we had the momentum at the time."

• Lou Saban: "We saw the fumble, but there must have been a whistle we didn't hear. And the next thing you know, they're marching 15 yards off. It was a crucial call, I couldn't believe they could make a call like that. We didn't play ball in the first half, but we had the game under control when that call was made."

• O.J. Simpson on the slow start: "We hadn't played in 10 days. We hadn't been able to go all out in practice because we were in cold weather gear. I don't think we were right in the first half. I think the explanation was we were rusty."

WEEK 12 GAMES

Balt 21, NYG 0	Hou 27, SF 13
Pitt 31, Clev 17	Oak 17, Den 10
Cinc 31, Phil 0	SD 28, KC 20
NYJ 30, NE 28	Wash 30, Atl 27
Chi 25, Det 21	St.L 31, Dal 17
Minn 24, GB 3	LA 14, NO 7

Bills	0	0	14	7 -	21
Dolphins	7	14	3	7 -	31

Attendance at the Orange Bowl - 78,701

Mia: Strock 4 run (Yepremian kick), 13:56
Mia: Twilley 8 pass from Strock (Yepremian kick), 3:32
Mia: Twilley 1 pass from Strock (Yepremian kick), 12:43
Buf: Simpson 14 run (Leypoldt kick), 7:40
Mia: FG Yepremian 20, 11:39
Buf: Hill 31 pass from Ferguson (Leypoldt kick), 14:11
Buf: Simpson 62 pass from Ferguson (Leypoldt kick), 5:37
Mia: Bulaich 1 run (Yepremian kick), 6:48

	BUF	MIA
First downs	21	19
Rushing yds	130	197
Passing yds	255	99
Punts-avg	6-42.3	7-39.7
Fumbles-lost	0-0	0-0
Penalties-yds	7-99	7-75

BILLS LEADERS: Rushing - Simpson 18-96, Braxton 9-31, Ferguson 2-3; **Passing** - Ferguson 20-41-2 - 279; **Receiving** - Chandler 5-63, Hill 3-57, Simpson 8-117, Braxton 1-11, Seymour 2-22, Gant 1-9.

DOLPHINS LEADERS: Rushing - Morris 21-93, Nottingham 9-87, Strock 3-15, Malone 5-1, Bulaich 6-1; **Passing** - Strock 12-15-0 - 99; **Receiving** - Twilley 3-26, Nottingham 2-22, Solomon 3-17, Tillman 1-16, Moore 1-11, Bulaich 2-7.

STANDINGS: TWELFTH WEEK

AFC EAST	W	L	T	CENTRAL	W	L	T	WEST	W	L	T	NFC EAST	W	L	T	CENTRAL	W	L	T	WEST	W	L	T
Miami	9	3	0	Pittsburgh	11	1	0	Oakland	10	2	0	St. Louis	9	3	0	Minnesota	11	1	0	LA Rams	10	2	0
Baltimore	8	4	0	Cincinnati	10	2	0	Kan. City	5	7	0	Dallas	8	4	0	Detroit	6	6	0	San Fran	5	7	0
Buffalo	7	5	0	Houston	8	4	0	Denver	5	7	0	Washington	8	4	0	Green Bay	3	9	0	Atlanta	3	9	0
New England	3	9	0	Cleveland	2	10	0	San Diego	1	11	0	NY Giants	3	9	0	Chicago	3	9	0	N.Orleans	2	10	0
NY Jets	3	9	0									Philadelphia	3	9	0								

Bills	6	7	14	7	-	34
Patriots	0	7	0	7	-	14

Attendance at Schaefer Stadium - 58,393

Buf: Braxton 1 run (kick blocked), 14:49
NE: Calhoun 62 pass from Grogan (Smith kick), 13:13
Buf: Chandler 5 pass from Ferguson (Leypoldt kick), 14:37
Buf: Braxton 1 run (Leypoldt kick), 10:59
Buf: Simpson 63 run (Leypoldt kick), 13:48
Buf: Hill 41 pass from Marangi (Leypoldt kick), 1:49
NE: Johnson 20 run (Smith kick), 13:17

	BUF	NE
First downs	26	16
Rushing yds	349	86
Passing yds	119	185
Punts-avg	4-50.3	6-37.1
Fumbles-lost	3-3	5-4
Penalties-yds	6-45	5-56

BILLS LEADERS: Rushing - Simpson 21-185, Braxton 23-101, Ferguson 1-13, Washington 4-30, Hayman 4-20; **Passing** - Ferguson 10-17-1 - 96, Marangi 1-2-0 - 41; **Receiving** - Chandler 3-22, Hill 3-60, Simpson 2-28, Seymour 2-20, Braxton 1-7.

PATRIOTS LEADERS: Rushing - Johnson 13-65, Cunningham 4-10, Grogan 3-7, McQuay 3-4, Calhoun 7-0; **Passing** - Grogan 17-30-2 - 272; **Receiving** - Calhoun 3-100, Stingley 3-59, Francis 2-46, Windsor 3-25, Cunningham 1-16, Johnson 2-16, Vataha 1-12, McQuay 2-(-2).

NOTES

• The Bills beat the Patriots for the ninth time in a row as they amassed 26 first downs and set an NFL record for most first downs in a season with 298, one more than Dallas had in 1968 and the Raiders had in 1972.
• O.J. Simpson enjoyed his 32nd 100-yard game. It was the fourth time in three years that two Bills runners topped 100 yards in the same game.
• The Bills set a team scoring record with 407 points, the old mark being 400 in 1964.
• The Bills sacked Steve Grogan eight times for 87 yards and forced six Patriots turnovers.
• Three times in the first 20 minutes, the Bills drove inside the 20, yet scored only once on Braxton's run. Ex-Bill Jerry Patton blocked the conversion.
• Ex-Bill Don Calhoun then lugged a Grogan pass 62 yards for a TD and a 7-6 New England lead, but late in the half, Ed Jones forced Calhoun to fumble and Pat Toomay recovered at the Pats 21. Jim Braxton gained 16, then Ferguson hit Bob Chandler for the go-ahead TD with 23 seconds left.
• Braxton capped a 79-yard march in the third, then Jones recovered a fumble and Simpson broke his 63-yard TD run for a 27-7 lead. On their next possession, the Bills scored again as backup QB Gary Marangi's

WEEK 13 GAMES

Balt 10, Mia 7	Clev 40, KC 14
Pitt 35, Cinc 14	Hou 27, Oak 26
Den 25, Phil 10	SD 24, NYJ 16
St.L 34, Chi 20	Atl 31, SF 9
Dal 31, Wash 10	LA 22, GB 5
Det 17, Minn 10	NYG 28, NO 14

first pass went for a 41-yard TD to J.D. Hill.
• Simpson voluntarily took himself out with nine minutes to play, even though he was only 15 yards shy of an NFL record fifth 200-yard game.
• The victory gave the Bills a 5-2 road record, their best since 1966.

QUOTES

• Lou Saban: "I feel especially good about this victory because we hadn't played a game this late in the season without a playoff berth at stake in three years. I was curious to see how the team would react. We went into this game hoping to get O.J. 200 yards. I talked to him at the close of the third period and he only needed 15 yards, but I didn't want to risk an injury and he told me to do what I thought was best."
• O.J. Simpson on why he took himself out: "They were playing for the run, the guys and I were tired and we're playing a tough team next week, the Minnesota Vikings. I told Jim Braxton before the game what a strange feeling it was going into a game that doesn't mean anything. I told him we should just go out and have fun. I think I was a little too lackadaisical because I fumbled twice and dropped a pass."
• Pat Toomay on the difference in the better defensive play: "Our defensive backfield is healthy again. We're playing now the way we knew we could have when we had everyone healthy. We seemed to confuse Grogan and we kept the pressure on him all day."
• Patriots linebacker Sam Hunt on the rumors that Simpson would retire: "I hope not."

Vikings	14	7	14	0	-	35
Bills	0	7	6	0	-	13

Attendance at Rich Stadium - 54,993

Min: Foreman 4 run (Cox kick), 5:54
Min: Lash fumble recovery in end zone (Cox kick), 12:08
Min: Foreman 1 run (Cox kick), 11:46
Buf: Simpson 24 run (Leypoldt kick), 13:05
Min: Foreman 1 pass from Tarkenton (Cox kick), 10:39
Min: Foreman 6 pass from Tarkenton (Cox kick), 13:49
Buf: Simpson 64 pass from Marangi (kick failed), 14:18

	BUF	MIN
First downs	20	28
Rushing yds	120	168
Passing yds	189	219
Punts-avg	3-39.7	5-40.8
Fumbles-lost	1-1	5-1
Penalties-yds	5-35	8-44

BILLS LEADERS: Rushing - Simpson 12-57, Braxton 7-26, Ferguson 1-6, Marangi 3-25, Washington 2-3, Hayman 1-3; **Passing** - Ferguson 6-16-3 - 51, Marangi 10-19-1 - 161; **Receiving** - Chandler 4-33, Hill 1-26, Simpson 3-66, Braxton 2-15, Seymour 1-18, Gant 3-33, Washington 2-21.

VIKINGS LEADERS: Rushing - Foreman 19-85, Osborn 6-20, McClanahan 12-47, Marinaro 3-16, Lee 1-0; **Passing** - Tarkenton 25-36-0 - 216, Lee 2-7-1 - 26; **Receiving** - Foreman 10-87, Lane 4-61, Voight 3-36, Gilliam 4-35, Marinaro 3-15, McClanahan 3-8.

NOTES

• The Bills played poorly as snow covered the field, but O.J. Simpson set a new NFL record with 23 TDs, breaking Gale Sayers' mark of 22 set in 1965. Vikings QB Fran Tarkenton set the NFL record for career TD passes with 291, one more than John Unitas. Chuck Foreman's four TDs gave him 22 for the season, but he didn't get a chance to tie Simpson because he came out of the game after being hit in the eye by a snowball in the third quarter.
• Simpson fell shy of breaking his own 1973 record for carries in a season and he finished with the third-best single-season rushing total in NFL history of 1,817 yards, giving him his third rushing title.
• A Bobby Bryant interception set up Foreman's first TD, and after a 67-yard march on their next possession, the Vikings made it 14-0 when Foreman fumbled into the end zone and Jim Lash recovered.
• Another interception of Joe Ferguson started the Vikings on their third TD drive, but less than two minutes after Foreman scored, Simpson scored his record-tying TD on a 24-yard run.
• Tarkenton set his record in the third with a pair of TD tosses to Foreman, then Simpson entered the record book when he caught Gary Marangi's short pass and whirled his way 64 yards to the end zone as the fans went wild in the stands.
• The Bills wound up setting team records for total

WEEK 14 GAMES

LA 10, Pitt 3	Mia 14, Den 13
Oak 28, KC 20	Hou 21, Clev 10
Cinc 47, SD 17	Balt 34, NE 21
Dal 31, NYJ 21	NYG 26, SF 23
GB 22, Atl 13	St.L 24, Det 13
Chi 42, NO 17	Phil 26, Wash 3

offense (5,467 yards), first downs (318), rushing first downs (162), touchdowns (57), passing TDs (28), PATs (51) and points (420).

QUOTES

• Lou Saban: "We didn't have any goals to shoot for today, but there was no excuse to play as poorly as we did. Our problems all year have been on defense and they were again today."
• Minnesota coach Bud Grant: "Why don't you get Miami up here on a day like today? Our players were being subjected to a barrage (of snowballs) and nobody was doing anything about it. Buffalo has some of the best fans in the league, but there are a few who spoil it for everybody."
• O.J. Simpson: "I'm planning on playing next year, I'm really going to try and work it out. If a good acting opportunity comes up, I'll have to grab it, but I have reason to believe I can work both careers together next year. A lot has been made about me saying I want a role in the movie *Ragtime* and I do want a role. I'm campaigning and politicking for it. Muhammad Ali and Redd Foxx have also come out saying they want a role. Acting is what I want to do, it's where my future is, but I also want to play some football."
• Jim Braxton: "I've given some thought to playing next year without Juice next to me, but you have to take life as it comes. If he doesn't come back, I wish him all the best."

STANDINGS: FOURTEENTH WEEK

AFC EAST	W	L	T	CENTRAL	W	L	T	WEST	W	L	T	NFC EAST	W	L	T	CENTRAL	W	L	T	WEST	W	L	T
Baltimore	10	4	0	Pittsburgh	12	2	0	Oakland	11	3	0	St. Louis	11	3	0	Minnesota	12	2	0	LA Rams	12	2	0
Miami	10	4	0	Cincinnati	11	3	0	Denver	6	8	0	Dallas	10	4	0	Detroit	7	7	0	San Fran	5	9	0
Buffalo	8	6	0	Houston	10	4	0	Kan. City	5	9	0	Washington	8	6	0	Green Bay	4	10	0	Atlanta	4	10	0
New England	3	11	0	Cleveland	3	11	0	San Diego	2	12	0	NY Giants	5	9	0	Chicago	4	10	0	N.Orleans	2	12	0
NY Jets	3	11	0									Philadelphia	4	10	0								

At A Glance 1976

Jan. 1 – O.J. Simpson was named the AFC player of the year for 1975 by UPI.

Jan. 3 – Dave Anderson wrote in *The New York Times* that the use of instant replay would cut down on officials' errors.

Jan. 8 – Receivers coach Bob Shaw resigned to become the general manager of the Hamilton Tiger Cats of the Canadian Football League.

Jan. 12 – Minnesota quarterback Fran Tarkenton outpolled O.J. Simpson in the Associated Press voting for MVP and offensive player of the year.

Jan. 14 – O.J. Simpson said he would "love" to have Ralph Wilson agree to salary arbitration, similar to what Joe Namath did in 1975 with the Jets. "I'm grateful to Namath for raising the standard for all of us, but when I read his salary was six figures higher than mine, I wonder if he's that much better or that much bigger an attraction," Simpson said.

"Six figures is a lot of money and his $450,000 is a lot more than that above me."

Jan. 15 – The owners of the Tampa Bay and Seattle expansion franchises filed a lawsuit against the players' union, delaying the expansion and college drafts.

Jan. 28 – Secondary coach Billy Atkins resigned to take a similar position with the San Francisco 49ers under their new head coach, Monte Clark.

Jan. 30 – Stan Jones became the third Bills assistant to quit when he took a job with Denver. One of the three coaches wives remarked: "Why are we leaving? This is survival we're talking about. Everything seems so unstable here and we have to think about our future."

Feb. 7 – Richie McCabe rejoined the Bills coaching staff as the secondary coach, assuming a position he held with the team from 1966-68.

Feb. 8 – Jerry Wampfler was hired to coach the defensive line as he resigned his post with the Philadelphia Eagles.

Feb. 23 – Jim Larue was hired as receivers coach and special teams coach Ed Cavanaugh was promoted to director of pro personnel.

Feb. 27 – O.J. Simpson said he wanted to play football in 1976 and that he was confident his contract would be renegotiated. He spoke via telephone from Italy where he was filming *Cassandra's Crossing*, a movie with Richard Harris and Sophia Loren.

March 15 – John Bassett, a Toronto tycoon who owned the Memphis franchise of the defunct WFL, tried to muscle his way into the NFL, but the league's owners turned down Memphis and Birmingham for the 1976 season. With the draft delayed for more than a month, the owners voted to hold the expansion draft March 30-31 and the college draft April 8-9.

March 16 – The owners approved the use of 30-second clocks so fans could see how close teams were to getting plays off in time. Previously, an on-field official kept time.

March 17 – Ralph Wilson said he expected O.J. Simpson to ask for $500,000 per year, but he said he wouldn't pay it. "I won't resent it, but of course, I won't give it to him, either," Wilson said. "O.J. is definitely a gate attraction and a great asset to our franchise, but the risk factor is worse in football than basketball or baseball. If O.J. got clobbered, all that money goes down the drain. The way profits are sliding in the league today, you can't take losses like that very long. I like O.J., I've been closer to him than any player in the 16 years I've been in football. All of us are record-conscious in sports, but this is one record (having the highest-paid player in football) I'm not anxious to hold."

March 30 – In a surprise move, Lou Saban left defensive end Pat Toomay unprotected in the expansion draft and Toomay was taken by Tampa Bay. The Bucs also chose defensive back Frank Oliver while Seattle grabbed running back Gary Hayman.

April 2 – Walt Patulski was traded to St. Louis for the Cardinals second-round choice in the upcoming draft. "I'm going to miss the chicken wings and the Genesee beer, but it's like being a corporate executive, you have to move every three or four years," Patulski said.

April 8 – The Bills selected Oregon cornerback Mario Clark in the first round of the college draft. They grabbed Arkansas State guard Ken Jones in the second round, then used the second-round choice they obtained for Walt Patulski to choose Iowa offensive tackle Joe Devlin. Other players chosen were Mississippi defensive tackle Ben Williams (third round), Michigan linebacker Dan Jilek (fourth) and Syracuse defensive back Keith Moody (10th). Tampa Bay made Oklahoma defensive end Leroy Selmon the No. 1 overall pick and Seattle took offensive lineman Steve Niehaus second. Other players chosen in the first round included running backs Chuck Muncie by New Orleans (third), Joe Washington by San Diego (fourth), Mike Pruitt by Cleveland (seventh) and two-time Heisman Trophy winner Archie Griffin by Cincinnati (24th). Also, the Jets chose quarterback Richard Todd (sixth), New England grabbed defensive back Mike Haynes (fifth), Miami selected linebacker Kim Bokamper (18th) and Baltimore tabbed defensive tackle Ken Novak (21st).

April 9 – Ralph Wilson and Lou Saban reportedly cleared the air in a long discussion about their past problems and the team's future. "It has all been squared away," Saban said. "I am very optimistic about the future. We know what has to be done to become a winner."

April 10 – Errol Prisby was hired to coach the spe-

The Bills began rebuilding their offensive line in the 1976 draft when they chose Joe Devlin (upper) and Ken Jones (lower), both in the second round.

cial teams, completing Lou Saban's staff. Also, Ed Cavanaugh was put in charge of player signings. "We weren't too organized in the draft the past two years," Ralph Wilson said, "but I guarantee you we will be organized in the future. We will have a man in charge of player signing." However, it was clear that Wilson would deal with O.J. Simpson himself and the contracts of Ahmad Rashad and Joe Ferguson would be dealt with by general manager Bob Lustig.

April 20 – Ahmad Rashad told Lou Saban he wanted to play in Buffalo, but the bottom line was money.

April 29 – O.J. Simpson parted ways amicably with his former agents, Sports Headliners, Inc., and said he would represent himself in future business dealings under O.J. Simpson Enterprises, Inc.

May 7 – Mini-camp opened and the Bills announced the signing of second-round pick Ken Jones.

May 28 – Ahmad Rashad signed a contract with the expansion Seattle Seahawks, thus leaving the Bills as a free agent without compensation. "It was strictly a business decision," Rashad said. "I just reached a financial impasse with Buffalo and money was the only real difference."

May 30 – With O.J. Simpson as his best man, guard Reggie McKenzie was married in Buffalo.

June 2 – Joe Ferguson reacted angrily from his home in Louisiana to the loss of Rashad and to his own lack of contract negotiations. "There has been no contact whatsoever since mid-February when Bob Lustig and Harvey Johnson came down to Shreveport," Ferguson said. "We're far apart. The way I feel is if they want to talk, fine. If not, then I'll come to camp, play out my option and everyone will be happy. Mr. Wilson has established himself around the league as one who doesn't want to pay well. Maybe that's his way of doing business. If Bert (Jones) is making $200,000, more power to him. If he is, that's out of reach for me. Maybe with other teams it wouldn't be, but for Buffalo it's completely out of reach. If Gary (Marangi) beats me out because of my contract, then the Buffalo Bills can go jump in a lake."

June 12 – O.J. Simpson asked the Bills to trade him to a West Coast team so that he could be closer to his family. "I definitely will not play in Buffalo again," Simpson said. "It has nothing to do with money or a new contract. It has to do with a number of things, mainly wanting to stay near my family and not being separated from them for another football season." Simpson also insinuated that he did not feel the Bills were making a sincere effort to field a championship team with the losses of Pat Toomay and Ahmad Rashad. The Bills were rumored to be asking the Los Angeles Rams for running back Lawrence McCutcheon, two top defensive players and cash in a deal for Simpson.

June 17 – Ralph Wilson granted Rams owner Carroll Rosenbloom permission to meet with Simpson, but he said no matter what is discussed, Wilson would demand three quality veteran players in exchange for the star running back. "I don't care if O.J. plays four weeks or two years, the Bills must get equal value in any deal for him," Wilson said. "We are not giving him away. We are putting our team back together and I need players, not draft choices."

June 22 – Lou Saban began earnest trade talks with Oakland coach John Madden and Rams coach Chuck Knox concerning O.J. Simpson.

July 1 – Rookie offensive lineman Joe Devlin signed his first pro contract.

July 9 – Training camp opened at Niagara University with rookies reporting.

July 10 – On his 29th birthday, O.J. Simpson came to Niagara and said good-bye to coach Lou Saban. "There is absolutely no chance I'll ever play here again," Simpson re-affirmed. "My family situation, my outside interests, my future all center around the West Coast and I can't afford to be away from them. The Buffalo Bills are going to have a strong offense, with or without me. We need a couple of defensive starters in a trade for me. I think if a trade is made, the Bills will deal themselves right into a division championship."

July 12 – Defensive end Earl Edwards was traded to Cleveland for two draft choices.

July 14 – Ralph Wilson asked O.J. Simpson if he could expand trade horizons to include teams not on the West Coast and Simpson denied him. "They're missing the gist of why I want to be traded," Simpson said. "If I wanted to play for any other team not on the West Coast, it would be Buffalo. I cannot play back East. I have to be here with my family."

July 16 – Wide receiver J.D. Hill and tackle Donnie Green missed the veterans reporting date to camp and indicated that they would hold out. "This hurts us, this hurts us a lot," Lou Saban said of their absences.

July 20 – Discouraged by trade talks, Ralph Wilson predicted that O.J. Simpson would retire from football and the Bills would get nothing in return for him. However, a report said the Rams were interested in trading Lawrence McCutcheon, Jack Snow, Steve Preece and Bill Nelson for Simpson.

July 22 – The Bills traded J.D. Hill to Detroit for the Lions No.1 draft choice in 1977. The Bills then dealt their own top draft selection in 1977 to Cincinnati for defensive end Sherman White.

July 23 – Ralph Wilson said the key to any trade with the Rams for O.J. Simpson would be the inclusion of All-Pro defensive end Jack Youngblood. "If there is to be any kind of trade, Jack Youngblood must be in the package," Wilson said. "But the Rams have said he is untouchable." Rams owner Carroll Rosenbloom then said that the Simpson trade talks were "dead."

July 24 – No. 1 draft choice Mario Clark signed his first contract and reported to camp.

July 27 – Sherman White reported to camp, five days after being acquired in a trade.

July 31 – The Bills opened the preseason in Detroit and lost to the Lions, 20-17. Unsigned Joe Ferguson was given the starting nod, but was ineffective.

Aug. 3 – Disillusioned by Ralph Wilson's inability to trade him, O.J. Simpson said: "I always felt I was a friend of Ralph's, but it seems that all I am to him is a piece of meat, just a piece of property that he owns."

Aug. 7 – Cincinnati drubbed the Bills, 31-10, as Gary Marangi was the starter at QB and he and Joe Ferguson were ineffective.

Aug. 8 – O.J. Simpson said: "As far as I'm concerned, I'm retired. But I'm working out just in case I come out of retirement."

Aug. 13 – With only 36,110 in attendance, the Bills lost their preseason home opener to New Orleans, 21-14. The club announced that only 33,308 season tickets were sold, a drop of more than 21,000 in two years. The Bills' three-year reign as attendance kings

in the NFL would be in serious jeopardy.

Aug. 20 – The Bills won their first exhibition of the summer, routing Green Bay, 37-0, as Jim Braxton rushed for 84 yards and one TD.

Aug. 28 – While the overriding theme of Buffalo's trip to Los Angeles concerned Ralph Wilson's meeting with Carroll Rosenbloom, nothing happened on the O.J. Simpson front and the Bills were whipped by the Rams, 31-17.

Sept. 3 – The Bills evened their preseason record at 3-3 with a 28-10 victory over Cleveland.

Sept. 6 – With the interconference trading deadline two days away, the Rams rejected Ralph Wilson's proposal for an O.J. Simpson trade. He immediately turned his attention to the San Francisco 49ers.

Sept. 7 – Ralph Wilson tried to convince O.J. Simpson to return to Buffalo. "I told O.J. I was sorry we couldn't make a deal for him, but we could never get together with the Rams on a satisfactory deal. I told him I drove a hard bargain because we needed defensive help to make up for his loss."

Sept. 8 – A federal judge in Washington ruled that the NFL's college draft was illegal because it violated federal anti-trust laws. The NFL promised an appeal.

Sept. 10 – Ralph Wilson flew to Los Angeles to meet with O.J. Simpson in hopes of getting him to return to the Bills.

Sept. 11 – Offensive tackle Donnie Green ended his holdout and reported to the Bills. Green reportedly owed about $9,000 in fines for missing camp. Lou Saban said that Joe Ferguson had won the training camp battle and would start at quarterback in the Monday night season opener against Miami at Rich Stadium.

Sept. 12 – After promising that he would never play in Buffalo again, O.J. Simpson agreed to return after Ralph Wilson offered him a three-year contract worth a reported $2.5 million, making him the highest-paid player in pro football. "When it became apparent that I might not be playing football, well, I felt really depressed," Simpson said. "Marguerite realized how much it hurt me. She will commute here every week or so, but we aren't going to move the kids. They're in school and they'll stay on the coast. What it came down to was financial security for Marguerite and the kids. We both realized it was something we couldn't say no to." On opening day in the NFL, Tampa Bay lost to Houston, 20-0, and Seattle fell to St. Louis, 30-24, in their inaugural games.

Sept. 13 – Simpson played sparingly and the Bills opened their season on *Monday Night Football* with a 30-21 loss to Miami before 77,683 at Rich Stadium. The Dolphins beat the Bills for the 13th straight time as Simpson gained 28 yards on five carries and caught a 43-yard pass. John Leypoldt missed three field goals.

Sept. 14 – After missing three field goals in the opener, John Leypoldt, the Bills all-time leading scorer, was waived and Benny Ricardo was signed.

Sept. 15 – With Jim Braxton out for the season after suffering a knee injury against the Dolphins, fullback Jeff Kinney was picked up on waivers from Kansas City.

Sept. 19 – A lackluster offensive performance doomed the Bills in a 13-3 loss to Houston.

Sept. 24 – Fullback Vic Washington was waived and Jeff Kinney was promoted to the starting lineup as O.J. Simpson's blocker.

Sept. 26 – The Bills avoided a terrible embarrassment by edging the expansion Tampa Bay

Buccaneers, 14-9, on Reuben Gant's fourth-quarter TD reception. The Bucs 3-4 defense held O.J. Simpson to 39 yards on 20 attempts as he failed to have a big game in front of his old college coach, John McKay.

Sept. 28 – Defensive lineman Jeff Yeates, a Buffalo native and a member of the Bills for three years, new kicker Benny Ricardo and cornerback Roscoe Word were cut.

Oct. 1 – After a week of auditioning kickers, Lou Saban settled on George Jakowenko.

Oct. 3 – Joe Ferguson and Bob Chandler hooked up for three TDs, Tony Greene set a team record with a 101-yard interception return for a TD and the Bills topped 50 points for only the second time in team history as they ripped hapless and winless Kansas City, 50-17, at Rich Stadium.

Oct. 4 – Angered at the media for reporting that the offense is inconsistent and not up to its usual standards and that there is dissension on the team, Joe DeLamielleure said: "I'm mad at all you guys in the press. The stuff about us not working is so much crap, but you'll believe what you want to believe. We didn't work any harder yesterday than we had in the first three weeks. We just started coming together. It just takes time with all the changes we've made." Said O.J. Simpson: "Look, the offense has been the goat the past three weeks and I can buy that, and I'm not in shape and I've played lousy. But there is no way anyone can start making up things about dissension."

Oct. 10 – Pat Leahy's 38-yard field goal with 48 seconds left gave the Jets a 17-14 victory over the Bills, giving Lou Holtz his first victory in the NFL. Across the river in East Rutherford, N.J., the New York Giants lost to Dallas, 24-14, in the first regular-season game played at Giants Stadium.

Oct. 15 – Lou Saban suddenly resigned as head coach, the second time he had done this to owner Ralph Wilson. "My reasons are my own and now I'm history," Saban said after meeting with Wilson. "I felt it was something I had to do for myself and for the good of the team. I've been thinking about this for quite a while. But I just put the facts together and realized that to continue the way I was going would destroy everything we had built up here. I had taken this team and this situation as far as I could. The situation needs a new face. This was the most difficult decision of my life." Jim Ringo, the offensive line coach, was named as Saban's successor. "We wanted a man we could build a future upon and we feel Jim is such a man," Wilson said. "I didn't want to go outside the organization for Lou's successor and Jim has the most tenure among the assistants. It was obvious to me that Lou had made his mind up. I regret it came to an end like this because I wanted to extend his 10-year contract." Ed Cavanaugh was brought down from the front office to replace Ringo as offensive line coach.

Oct. 16 – O.J. Simpson addressed the coaching change: "I'm surprised like everyone else. There was very little conversation and I can't say there was anger among the players. Lou came here when we were a rag-tag team and he salvaged my career. I guess he reached a point in his career, as I will with my career, where the end has to come. I hate to see Lou Saban leave, but I can't think of a better man under any circumstances than Jim Ringo."

Oct. 17 – Baltimore came to Rich Stadium and spoiled the head coaching debut of Jim Ringo with a 31-13 victory as the Bills were assessed a team-record 14 penalties.

Oct. 18 – Newly promoted offensive line coach Ed Cavanaugh was resting comfortably at Mercy Hospital after being taken there after the Colts game and spending the night because he had chest pains.

Oct. 19 – Kicker George Jakowenko said he felt far less pressure under new coach Jim Ringo than he had with Lou Saban. "What made a big difference to me was coach Ringo's attitude starting with our drills on Saturday," Jakowenko said. "If I missed a kick he'd say 'Don't worry about it.' There was less pressure. Before, there was a new kicker trying out all the time. Coach Saban always wanted to know what kickers were available. For me, it was hard pressure to perform."

Oct. 24 – Joe Ferguson suffered a back injury and was lost for the season. New England snapped a nine-game losing streak to the Bills by winning at Rich Stadium, 26-22, in front of only 45,144, the smallest crowd in the facility's 3 1/2-year history.

Oct. 26 – The Bills signed Sam Wyche to serve as Gary Marangi's backup.

Oct. 30 – Lou Saban met with Ralph Wilson and was officially declared free from the team and able to pursue other career ventures.

Oct. 31 – The Bills lost their fourth game in a row, 19-14 to the Jets, as Richard Todd started at QB in place of Joe Namath. The Bills turned over the ball five times.

Nov. 1 – Lou Saban accepted the position of athletic director at the University of Cincinatti and he said: "I don't have any $2 1/2 million halfbacks here. Thank God I don't have to contend with that."

Nov. 2 – Ralph Wilson defended personnel director Harvey Johnson and said that Lou Saban initiated every trade that was made. "The exodus of quality players is the cause of our present situation," Wilson said. "Maybe we didn't have all the quality players we needed to get to the Super Bowl (in 1974), but you don't trade players until you have adequate replacements."

Nov. 5 – Ralph Wilson lifted the interim tag off Jim Ringo and said he would coach the team in 1977.

Nov. 7 – O.J. Simpson was ejected for the first time in his career for fighting and the Bills lost their fifth straight, 20-10, at New England.

Nov. 10 – Dallas coach Tom Landry said that O.J. Simpson "has to rank as the greatest back I've ever seen. I played against Brown and he was gifted and big, but Brown played on some great teams. O.J. has not been on great teams. Considering all that, his record is phenomenal."

Nov. 15 – Dallas improved to 9-1 with an uninspired 17-10 victory over the Bills on *Monday Night Football* as Drew Pearson caught nine passes for 135 yards.

Nov. 21 – In one of the worst quarterback performances in team history, Gary Marangi completed eight of 30 passes and the Bills lost their seventh straight, 34-13, to San Diego, before another record small crowd of 36,539 at Rich Stadium.

Nov. 25 – On Thanksgiving Day in Detroit, O.J. Simpson thrilled a Silverdome crowd of 66,875 and a national TV audience by rushing for 273 yards on 29 carries, breaking his own single-game rushing record. Also, his fifth career 200-yard game broke Jim Brown's record and it came against a defense that was No. 1 in the NFC. Despite his heroics, the Bills still lost their eighth straight game, 27-14.

Dec. 3 – Thanks to a snowstorm that dumped about 34 inches on Rich Stadium, the Bills decided to fly to Miami a day early and avoid the risk of traveling the day before the game.

Dec. 4 – Jim Ringo announced that rookie Joe Devlin would replace Donnie Green in the starting lineup, giving Devlin his first start. "Joe has been coming along very well and this will give him a test against one of the league's best defensive ends in Vern Den Herder," Ringo said. Green is the only member of the Electric Company to miss a game since 1973.

Dec. 5 – Miami beat the Bills for the 14th straight time, 45-27, despite O.J. Simpson's second consecutive 200-yard rushing performance. Freddie Solomon scored on a run, a pass and a punt return as he rolled up 252 all-purpose yards.

Dec. 12 – The Bills closed perhaps their most disappointing season with their 10th consecutive loss and ninth in a row under Jim Ringo as the Colts clobbered them, 58-20. It was the most points ever scored against Buffalo. The silver lining was O.J. Simpson wrapped up his fourth league rushing title in the past five years as he gained 173 yards to finish with 1,503. Walter Payton got hurt in the Chicago Bears' finale against Denver and finished with 1,390.

Dec. 13 – Ralph Wilson absolved Jim Ringo of the blame for the 2-12 season saying: "Houdini couldn't have won with that defense. I don't think any coach in the business could have done anything more. As far as I'm concerned, Jim Ringo is not responsible for these defeats." Wilson quashed any rumors about Ringo not returning as coach when he announced Ringo was signed "for longer than one year."

Dec. 14 – Jim Braxton, upset over a salary increase offer of just $8,500 for the 1977 season, asked to be traded. "It was so embarrassing a figure, I was afraid to tell Jim," said Braxton's agent, John Dobbertin. "It's that degrading." It was later learned that Braxton wanted $550,000 spread over three years and other clauses, deferred payments and trust funds for his children that added up to approximately a $960,000 package. Dobbertin denied the figures.

Dec. 18 – Stew Barber was elevated to assistant general manager and absorbed many of the duties of Harvey Johnson. Johnson was demoted to what Ralph Wilson called a "Superscout." Oakland beat New England, 24-21, and Minnesota romped past Washington, 35-20, on the first day of divisional round playoff games.

Dec. 19 – Pittsburgh crushed Baltimore and league MVP Bert Jones, 40-14, and Los Angeles shocked the Cowboys in Dallas, 14-12, on the second day of divisional playoff action.

Dec. 25 – O.J. Simpson and Joe DeLamielleure were named to the Pro Football Writers Association of America All-Pro team. They also were selected to The Associated Press' first team.

Dec. 26 – Oakland stretched its winning streak to 12 games as it downed two-time defending Super Bowl champion Pittsburgh, 24-7, in the AFC Championship Game. Chuck Foreman rushed for 118 yards and a TD as Minnesota stopped Los Angeles, 24-13, in the NFC Championship Game.

Jan. 9, 1977 – Oakland won its first Super Bowl title, 32-14, over Minnesota before a record crowd of 103,438 at the Rose Bowl. Willie Brown returned an interception 75 yards for a TD and the Raiders offense rolled up a Super Bowl-record 429 yards.

Jan. 16, 1977 – MVP Mel Blount intercepted two passes to help the AFC beat the NFC, 24-14, in the Pro Bowl at the Kingdome in Seattle.

BY THE NUMBERS - 1976

TEAM STATISTICS	BILLS	OPP
First downs	250	262
Rushing	135	128
Passing	102	110
Penalty	13	24
Total yards	4,404	4,730
Avg. game	314.6	337.9
Plays	964	898
Avg. play	4.6	5.3
Net rushing yds	2,566	2,476
Avg. game	183.3	176.9
Avg. play	4.7	4.6
Net passing yds	1,838	2,254
Comp/att	156/383	163/337
Sacks/lost	33-246	28-210
Interceptions	17	19
Percentage	40.7	48.4
Punts/avg	87-42.3	72-38.5
Fumbles/lost	45-26	37-23
Penalties/yds	91-797	92-704
Touchdowns	30	41
Extra points	26-30	39-41
Field goals	13-24	26-30
Safeties	0	0
Kick ret./avg	75-21.3	48-25.1
Punt ret./avg	33-6.7	52-16.9

RUSHING	ATT	YDS	AVG	TD
Simpson	290	1503	5.2	8
Kinney	116	475	4.1	1
Marangi	39	230	5.9	2
Hooks	25	116	4.6	0
Ferguson	18	81	4.5	0
Washington	22	65	3.0	0
Ray	24	56	2.3	0
Powell	11	40	3.6	0
Chandler	1	0	0.0	0
Braxton	1	0	0.0	0
Edwards	1	0	0.0	0
TOTALS	**548**	**2566**	**4.7**	**11**

RECEIVING	CAT	YDS	AVG	TD
Chandler	61	824	13.5	10
Simpson	22	259	11.8	1
Seymour	16	169	10.6	0
Holland	15	299	19.9	2
Kinney	14	78	5.6	0
Gant	12	263	21.9	3
Hooks	6	72	12.0	0
Washington	3	29	9.7	0
Ray	3	26	8.7	0
Edwards	2	53	26.5	0
Montler	1	6	6.0	0
Powell	1	6	6.0	0
TOTALS	**156**	**2084**	**13.4**	**16**

PASSING	COMP	ATT	INT	YDS	TD	COMP%	SACKS	RATE
Ferguson	74	151	1	1086	9	49.0	11-80	90.0
Marangi	82	232	16	998	7	35.3	22-166	30.7
TOTALS	**156**	**383**	**17**	**2084**	**16**	**40.7**	**33-246**	**54.0**

KICKING	1-19	20-29	30-39	40-49	50+	TOT	PAT	PTS
Jakowenko	0-0	5-5	3-5	4-7	0-0	12-17	21-24	57
Leypoldt	0-0	0-0	0-3	0-0	0-0	0-3	3-3	3
Ricardo	0-0	1-3	0-0	0-0	0-1	1-4	2-2	5
TOTAL	**0-0**	**6-8**	**3-8**	**4-7**	**0-1**	**13-24**	**26-29**	**65**

PUNTING	NO	AVG	LG	In 20	BL
Bateman	86	42.7	78	17	1

LEADERS

Kick returns: Moody 26-605 yards, 23.3 avg, 0 TD

Punt returns: Moody 16-166, 10.4, 1 TD
Hooks 11-45, 4.1, 0 TD

Interceptions: Greene 5-135, 27.0, 1 TD
Moody 3-63, 21.0, 0 TD
D. Jones 3-5, 1.7, 0 TD

SCORE BY QUARTERS

BILLS	35	67	58	85 -	245
OPP	50	140	96	77 -	363

Jim Ringo took over as head coach early in 1976 when Lou Saban resigned suddenly. The Bills lost all nine games with Ringo as their leader that year, but he returned for the 1977 season.

GAME 1 - Monday, Sept. 13, 1976 - DOLPHINS 30, BILLS 21

Dolphins	7	10	10	3	- 30
Bills	0	14	0	7	- 21

Attendance at Rich Stadium - 77,683

Mia: Malone 5 run (Yepremian kick), 12:23
Buf: Holland 55 pass from Ferguson (Leypoldt kick), :53
Mia: Nottingham 1 run (Yepremian kick), 4:42
Buf: Holland 58 pass from Ferguson (Leypoldt kick), 7:42
Mia: FG Yepremian 25, 14:42
Mia: Moore 30 pass from Griese (Yepremian kick), 1:03
Mia: FG Yepremian 20, 9:53
Buf: Chandler 12 pass from Ferguson (Leypoldt kick), 4:19
Mia: FG Yepremian 30, 9:18

	BUF	MIA
First downs	16	25
Rushing yds	108	204
Passing yds	275	197
Punts-avg	4-38.3	2-38.5
Fumbles-lost	2-0	2-2
Penalties-yds	6-26	6-35

BILLS LEADERS: Rushing - Simpson 5-28, Braxton 1-0, Washington 19-56, Ferguson 2-19, Hooks 3-5; **Passing** - Ferguson 13-28-0 - 282, Marangi 0-2-0 - 0; **Receiving** - Chandler 3-50, Holland 2-111, Washington 3-29, Seymour 2-26, Hooks 1-8, Gant 1-15, Simpson 1-43.

DOLPHINS LEADERS: Rushing - Bulaich 19-107, Malone 10-31, Nottingham 10-29, Winfrey 7-34, Griese 2-3; **Passing** - Griese 13-21-1 - 199; **Receiving** - Moore 6-94, Twilley 4-53, Nottingham 1-29, Harris 2-23.

NOTES

• Having signed the day before after a long holdout, O.J. Simpson did not start, but he entered the lineup when Jim Braxton suffered a season-ending knee injury on the first play.

• Miami beat Buffalo for the 13th straight time; it was the Bills' third straight loss on Monday.

• John Leypoldt missed three field goals and was booed loudly.

• The Dolphins drove 79 yards to the opening TD and 74 yards for their second score, but the Bills answered each time with a long Joe Ferguson-to-John Holland TD pass.

• Miami took the lead for good late in the second quarter on Garo Yepremian's field goal. Then Duriel Harris returned the second-half kickoff 62 yards. Two plays later, Bob Griese hit Nat Moore for a TD on a pass that should have been intercepted by Mario Clark or Tony Greene, but both misplayed it.

• The Bills trailed 27-14 when Leypoldt missed a 39-yarder, but Doug Jones intercepted Griese at the Miami 30 to set up Bob Chandler's TD reception and the Bills were back in it.

• After a Yepremian field goal, the Bills drove to the Miami 11 and with 3:36 left, Lou Saban figured he'd

WEEK 1 GAMES

LA 30, Atl 14	Hou 20, TB 0
Oak 31, Pitt 28	Chi 10, Det 3
St.L 30, Sea 24	Minn 40, NO 9
Wash 19, NYG 17	Dal 27, Phil 7
Cinc 17, Den 7	SF 26, GB 14
SD 30, KC 16	Balt 27, NE 13
Clev 38, NYJ 17	

take the easy field goal and try to get the ball back later. But Leypoldt, who had a second-quarter field goal blocked, missed a 28-yarder.

QUOTES

• Lou Saban: "No question about it, the three missed field goals did it. The first one was a case of a man blowing in without being blocked, but the other two, there was nothing wrong with them except the guy kicking them. On the first one, ordinarily Bubbie (Jim Braxton) would have been the blocker but he was injured – he tore up his knee and he'll be out the rest of the season – and Merv Krakau was in his place. Krakau missed the block. Our special teams were terrible. Their play makes the coach (Errol Prisby) look like an idiot. The loss of Braxton killed us. The whole offense was centered around him in the preseason and when you lose a man like that, you lose a lot. It was an upsetting game and it has been tough around here the last two days. It (all the uproar over Simpson's new contract and Donnie Green's return) bothers me. It's a tough way to coach, not really worth it."

• O.J. Simpson: "It felt good to play again, but I'm not in playing shape. When I'm in playing shape, I get cocky. I'm not cocky yet." (On hearing boos before game): "It's not the first time I've been booed in Buffalo."

• John Leypoldt: "I'm pressing now and I don't know why."

• Dolphins kicker Garo Yepremian: "I feel bad for him (Leypoldt). Now he has to keep his cool, forget about the misses and think about next week. One day doesn't make or break a person."

GAME 2 - Sunday, Sept. 19, 1976 - OILERS 13, BILLS 3

Oilers	0	3	0	10	- 13
Bills	0	3	0	0	- 3

Attendance at Rich Stadium - 61,364

Hou: FG Butler 54, 2:44
Buf: FG Ricardo 27, 13:45
Hou: FG Butler 28, 5:32
Hou: Hardeman 19 run (Butler kick), 10:59

	BUF	HOU
First downs	13	11
Rushing yds	89	208
Passing yds	79	52
Punts-avg	9-42.7	9-36.0
Fumbles-lost	3-2	2-0
Penalties-yds	7-58	8-51

BILLS LEADERS: Rushing - Simpson 16-38, Washington 3-9, Powell 9-32, Ferguson 3-6, Hooks 1-0, Marangi 1-4; **Passing** - Ferguson 9-24-0 - 90, Marangi 2-6-0 - 21; **Receiving** - Chandler 3-34, Seymour 3-38, Simpson 3-25, Powell 1-6, Hooks 1-8.

OILERS LEADERS: Rushing - Willis 16-96, Coleman 16-74, Pastorini 2-14, Hardeman 2-21, Dawkins 2-5, Johnson 1- (-2); **Passing** - Pastorini 9-24-1 - 80; **Receiving** - B. Johnson 2-8, Alston 1-29, Burrough 3-20, Willis 3-23.

WEEK 2 GAMES

Chi 19, SF 12	NE 30, Mia 14
St.L 29, GB 0	Balt 28, Cinc 27
LA 10, Minn 10	Det 24, Atl 10
SD 23, TB 0	Phil 20, NYG 7
Dal 24, NO 6	Den 46, NYJ 3
Wash 31, Sea 7	Pitt 31, Clev 14
Oak 24, KC 21	

NOTES

• Benny Ricardo, who replaced the waived John Leypoldt, missed two field goals and the offense sputtered badly against the Oilers in windy Rich Stadium.

• After Ken Jones blocked a Skip Butler field goal in the second, Ricardo made a 27-yarder to tie the game. Butler had boomed a windblown 54-yarder earlier in the quarter.

• The Bills blew a chance to take the lead in the third when Dan Pastorini's 23-yard punt into the wind left them at the Oilers 43. However, after moving to the 8, Willie Parker's low snap foiled Ricardo's 27-yard field goal attempt.

• After Butler's 28-yard field goal in the fourth, struggling Joe Ferguson was replaced by Gary Marangi. Marangi was sacked by Elvin Bethea and fumbled and Curley Culp recovered. On the next play, Don Hardeman burst up the middle for a 19-yard TD to clinch the game.

QUOTES

• Lou Saban: "I thought a change of pace (at quarterback) would work, but it didn't. We played as well as we know how today. We lost to a very good team. I don't know how far we are from the offense we had last season. We are making too many errors and Juice isn't in shape yet. The kids don't have enough experience to handle a defense like Houston's, one of the best in the league. We need a win and I'm not choosy about who we beat, we need one."

• O.J. Simpson: "I didn't feel good out there all day. I've been listless all week and I was listless in the game. I'm not as sharp as I want to be. I expected to have a couple of bad weeks after getting back and I sure had one today. To tell you the truth, I thought we would lose the first two games because of our defensive problems. But that was before I got here and saw guys like Ken Jones and Dan Jilek and Mario Clark. I had no idea they were as good as they are."

• Oilers coach Bum Phillips: "I thought O.J.'s lack of practice showed. He had just enough work during the week to get his legs dead. That's what a guy usually goes through in his first week. O.J. is usually too good a back to contain that way. Buffalo's offense is built around him and he came out with dead legs. I felt bad for Ferguson. He had a lot of his passes dropped, yet the fans thought it was his fault. Buffalo played well enough to beat us and anyone else. Their defense has been bad-mouthed, but you won't catch me doing it. They are as aggressive as the devil. They are definitely going to get better and their offense won't always get shut down like it did today. I'm glad we played the Bills early in the season, sincerely glad."

• Mike Kadish: "I suppose some people probably felt Houston's offense was sluggish, but I'd like to think we made it that way."

STANDINGS: SECOND WEEK

AFC EAST	W	L	T	CENTRAL	W	L	T	WEST	W	L	T	NFC EAST	W	L	T	CENTRAL	W	L	T	WEST	W	L	T
Baltimore	2	0	0	Houston	2	0	0	Oakland	2	0	0	St. Louis	2	0	0	Chicago	2	0	0	LA Rams	1	0	1
Miami	1	1	0	Cleveland	1	1	0	San Diego	2	0	0	Dallas	2	0	0	Minnesota	1	0	1	San Fran	1	1	0
New England	1	1	0	Cincinnati	1	1	0	Denver	1	1	0	Washington	2	0	0	Detroit	1	1	0	Atlanta	0	2	0
Buffalo	0	2	0	Pittsburgh	1	1	0	Kan. City	0	2	0	Philadelphia	1	1	0	Green Bay	0	2	0	N.Orleans	0	2	0
NY Jets	0	2	0					Tampa Bay	0	2	0	NY Giants	0	2	0					Seattle	0	2	0

NOTES

• O.J. Simpson moved into second place on the all-time NFL rushing list, going past Green Bay's Jim Taylor on a rainy day at Rich Stadium. Simpson increased his career total to 8,609 yards.

• Joe Ferguson was lost for the season when he fractured four vertebrae in his lower back.

• It was 6-3 at the half when the Patriots took charge in the third quarter. On their second series, Sam Cunningham ripped off runs of 19 and 22 yards and eventually, Steve Grogan hit Russ Francis for a TD. John Smith's extra point missed, leaving the score 12-3.

• After an exchange of fumbles, Bob Chandler made a brilliant catch for 38 yards and the Bills appeared to be poised to get back in the game. But Eddie Ray fumbled at the Patriots 31 and five plays later, Cunningham scored from the 1 and it was 19-3.

• Simpson broke a 32-yard TD run, but Chandler dropped the PAT snap. Then, Jess Phillips returned the ensuing kickoff 71 yards, setting up a 10-yard TD run by Grogan.

• Buffalo rallied in the fourth. Marangi scrambled for gains of 16 and 14 yards, then got nine on fourth-and-three from the 13 before hitting Chandler for a TD with 6:05 left.

• Two plays later, Merv Krakau recovered Phillips' fumble at the Patriots 28, but the threat died when George Jakowenko missed a 34-yard field goal. Keith Moody's interception and 44-yard return to the 19 set up Simpson's two-yard TD run, but Jakowenko missed the PAT, leaving the Bills more than a field goal behind.

QUOTES

• Jim Ringo on the hit on Ferguson: "I'm not saying it was a cheap shot, but I do know that I have to find another quarterback. I was worried about Marangi running so much."

• Gary Marangi: "I was right there on the sideline and I thought it was a late hit. Sam Hunt told me he didn't mean to hit Fergy like that and he sounded like he was guilty. Coach Ringo told me not to run because if I got hurt, all we had left to put in was Bobby Chandler. But when you get in the middle of the game, you have to do what you have to do. I feel bad that Joe got hurt, but I want to play and that's the way this game is."

• O.J. Simpson on the possibility of passing Jim Brown: "Being No. 2 doesn't excite me too much, but being No. 1 does. It's going to take at least three years and I don't know what's going to happen by then. If I do it, it'll be in a Buffalo uniform. I'll never go in again and ask for a trade to another team. Whether I'll be back next year depends strictly on what happens upstairs (in the front office) and in Hollywood." (On Ferguson's injury): "Gary doesn't have the arm Joe has and losing Fergy has got to hurt us. When they gang up on our running, Fergy can pick them apart with his throwing."

WEEK 7 GAMES

SF 15, Atl 0	Dal 31, Chi 21
Det 41, Sea 14	Cinc 27, Hou 7
Mia 23, TB 20	Oak 18, GB 14
Clev 21, SD 17	Balt 20, NYJ 0
LA 16, NO 10	Pitt 27, NYG 0
Minn 27, Phil 12	Den 35, KC 26
Wash 20, St.L 10	

Patriots	0	6	13	7	-	26
Bills	0	3	6	13	-	22

Attendance at Rich Stadium - 45,144

NE: FG Smith 44, 2:36
Buf: FG Jakowenko 46, 9:30
NE: FG Smith 32, 14:44
NE: Francis 9 pass from Grogan (kick failed), 5:22
NE: Cunningham 3 run (Smith kick), 10:57
Buf: Simpson 32 run (kick failed), 14:58
NE: Grogan 10 run (Smith kick), 1:16
Buf: Chandler 4 pass from Marangi (Jakowenko kick), 6:05
Buf: Simpson 2 run (kick failed), 14:13

	BUF	NE
First downs	21	18
Rushing yds	209	184
Passing yds	100	93
Punts-avg	3-45.0	4-38.5
Fumbles-lost	6-4	5-3
Penalties-yds	6-68	8-57

BILLS LEADERS: Rushing - Simpson 25-110, Marangi 8-74, Ferguson 3-10, Ray 6-15; **Passing** - Ferguson 5-7-0 - 39, Marangi 6-22-1 - 61; **Receiving** - Chandler 3-46, Holland 3-34, Ray 2-11, Kinney 2-0, Simpson 1-9.

PATRIOTS LEADERS: Rushing - Cunningham 22-118, Johnson 11-40, Grogan 5-34, Phillips 2-8, Patrick 1- (-16); **Passing** - Grogan 8-21-1 - 122; **Receiving** - Cunningham 3-43, Francis 3-41, Stingley 1-27, Briscoe 1-11.

NOTES

• Gary Marangi made the first regular-season start of his career, as did New York's Richard Todd, and while neither played well, Marangi was the loser, completing only two of 16 in the first half.

• The victory was Lou Holtz's second in the NFL, both against the Bills. The Bills ran 81 plays and the Jets 54.

• Bob Chandler moved into second place on the team's all-time reception list with 164.

• Linebacker Larry Keller played a huge role for the Jets. His interception and 30-yard return in the second quarter led to Todd's TD pass to David Knight. Just 1:08 later, Keller blocked a Marv Bateman punt and Larry Poole picked the ball up and ran in for a TD. That PAT was blocked.

• Down 16-0 at the half, Jim Ringo and O.J. Simpson delivered lectures at halftime and the Bills came out fired up. They began a comeback as Joe Devlin forced Keith Benson to fumble the second-half kickoff and Bo Cornell recovered at the 16. Three plays later, Bob Chandler made a great 11-yard TD catch in the corner of the end zone.

• After a punt, the Bills drove 75 yards in 11 plays. O.J. Simpson, who had a season-high rushing total, went 21 yards on one burst and Marangi snuck for a first down on fourth-and-one. Two plays after that, Chandler made a diving catch for a TD and it was 16-14.

• On the next series, Simpson broke a 40-yard run to the Jets 7 and the Bills seemed poised to go ahead, but Simpson lost a fumble and the Bills' momentum died.

• Paul Seymour's fumble after a reception at the Jets 16 led to Pat Leahy's field goal.

QUOTES

• O.J. Simpson: "I came in and got a little upset with all the guys (at halftime). You can't do it all by yourself. Today I got to the point where I was trying to run over everybody in the second half. I'm very depressed, I'm very down. I felt we shouldn't have been that many points down. I'm frustrated. We're not the football team that we were. I got upset because it seemed like we weren't going after them. I thought we'd be a contender for the rest of my career here. Two years ago we were in the playoffs and now we're right back in the same old house we were in when I first came here." (On his costly fumble): "I was tired on that play and when I tried to get outside I got stripped from behind."

• Gary Marangi: "We should never have had a first half like we had, or I had. We lost the game in the first half. I was trying to steer the ball, not throw it. Nobody tells me not to run, nobody tells me what to do." (On Seymour's controversial fumble): "He never had that ball. They have seven officials out there and only one guy saw it and he wasn't sure. He told the ref 'I think it was a fumble.'"

• Jets safety Phil Wise: "They've lost a lot of good people like Ahmad Rashad, J.D. Hill, Earl Edwards. They knew what they were doing (when they traded them). They made their bed."

WEEK 8 GAMES

Balt 38, Hou 14	Oak 19, Den 6
Chi 14, Minn 13	Atl 23, NO 20
Phil 10, NYG 0	LA 45, Sea 6
Dal 20, Wash 7	Det 27, GB 6
Pitt 23, SD 0	KC 28, TB 19
Cinc 23, Clev 6	Mia 10, NE 3
St.L 23, SF 20 (OT)	

Jets	0	16	0	3	-	19
Bills	0	0	14	0	-	14

Attendance at Rich Stadium - 41,285

NYJ: Knight 20 pass from Todd (Leahy kick), 6:59
NYJ: Poole 7 blocked punt return (kick failed), 8:07
NYJ: FG Leahy 20, 13:40
Buf: Chandler 11 pass from Marangi (Jakowenko kick), 1:21
Buf: Chandler 9 pass from Marangi (Jakowenko kick), 7:45
NYJ: FG Leahy 35, 2:54

	BUF	NYJ
First downs	17	16
Rushing yds	224	155
Passing yds	87	79
Punts-avg	8-37.4	6-38.5
Fumbles-lost	3-2	5-2
Penalties-yds	7-68	4-35

BILLS LEADERS: Rushing - Simpson 29-166, Kinney 9-33, Marangi 4-7, Hooks 2-7, Ray 4-11; **Passing** - Marangi 10-30-3 - 116; **Receiving** - Chandler 7-58, Holland 1-31, Hooks 1-28, Seymour 1- (-1).

JETS LEADERS: Rushing - Gaines 24-119, Gresham 2-28, Todd 3-7, Giammona 4-1; **Passing** - Todd 6-20-2 - 87; **Receiving** - Gaines 2-14, Giammona 2-44, Knight 1-20, Piccone 1-9.

STANDINGS: EIGHTH WEEK

AFC EAST	W	L	T	CENTRAL	W	L	T	WEST	W	L	T	NFC EAST	W	L	T	CENTRAL	W	L	T	WEST	W	L	T
Baltimore	7	1	0	Cincinnati	6	2	0	Oakland	7	1	0	Dallas	7	1	0	Minnesota	6	1	1	LA Rams	6	1	1
New England	5	3	0	Houston	4	4	0	San Diego	4	4	0	St. Louis	6	2	0	Chicago	4	4	0	San Fran	6	2	0
Miami	4	4	0	Cleveland	4	4	0	Denver	4	4	0	Washington	5	3	0	Detroit	4	4	0	N.Orleans	2	6	0
Buffalo	2	6	0	Pittsburgh	4	4	0	Kan. City	3	5	0	Philadelphia	3	5	0	Green Bay	3	5	0	Atlanta	2	6	0
NY Jets	2	6	0					Tampa Bay	0	8	0	NY Giants	0	8	0					Seattle	1	7	0

Bills	0	3	0	7 -	10
Patriots	3	10	7	0 -	20

Attendance at Schaefer Stadium - 61,157

NE: FG Smith 46, 4:18
NE: FG Smith 33, 7:14
NE: Haynes 89 punt return (Smith kick), 13:11
Buf: FG Jakowenko 31, 14:59
NE: Cunningham 8 run (Smith kick), 2:17
Buf: Marangi 6 run (Jakowenko kick), 12:41

	BUF	NE
First downs	20	16
Rushing yds	149	177
Passing yds	224	121
Punts-avg	5-46.8	5-35.4
Fumbles-lost	5-4	4-3
Penalties-yds	5-45	6-60

BILLS LEADERS: Rushing - Simpson 6-8, Ray 13-32, Hooks 18-80, Marangi 4-26, Kinney 1-3; **Passing** - Marangi 15-34-4 - 241; **Receiving** - Chandler 7-104, Holland 1-13, Hooks 3-28, Seymour 1-12, Gant 2-69, Ray 1-15.

PATRIOTS LEADERS: Rushing - Cunningham 25-141, Johnson 7-9, Grogan 3-19, Calhoun 1-0, Forte 2-8; **Passing** - Grogan 8-18-2 - 137; **Receiving** - Johnson 3-35, Vataha 2-50, Stingley 2-36, Briscoe 1-16.

WEEK 9 GAMES

St.L 17, Phil 14	Sea 30, Atl 13
Wash 24, SF 21	Minn 31, Det 23
Den 48, TB 13	Dal 9, NYG 3
GB 32, NO 27	Clev 21, Hou 7
Mia 27, NYJ 7	Balt 37, SD 21
Pitt 45, KC 0	Oak 28, Chi 27
Cinc 20, LA 12	

NOTES

• O.J. Simpson was ejected from a game for the first time in his career as he got into a fight with Mel Lunsford and referee Gordon McCarter tossed him with 5:51 left in the first quarter. Without Simpson, the Bills went on to their fifth straight loss and fourth in a row under Jim Ringo.
• Mike Haynes' punt return for a TD was the Patriots first in their 17-year history.
• Sam Cunningham's 141 rushing yards were a career-high.
• The Bills dominated the stat sheet, but committed eight turnovers.
• Gary Marangi's first interception, by Tim Fox, led to John Smith's first field goal.
• Haynes fumbled a punt at the Bills 36, but the Bills failed to take advantage and when they punted back, Haynes went 89 yards for a TD.
• George Jakowenko's field goal one second before half-time came after John Skorupan intercepted an ill-advised Steve Grogan pass and returned 13 yards to the 13.
• However, a second-half-opening 64-yard drive, which began with ex-Bill Don Calhoun's 33-yard kickoff return, gave the Patriots control. Cunningham gained the final 50 yards on four runs.
• The Bills could have gotten back in it after Bob Chandler's brilliant 30-yard reception to the 1, but Marangi fumbled and Ray Hamilton recovered. With 6:09 left, Roland Hooks lost a fumble at the Patriots 13.

QUOTES

• O.J. Simpson: "I swept right and three guys grabbed me. I heard the whistle blow and I felt two of the guys let me go, but the third guy (Lunsford) kept holding me and then flipped me onto my head. So I got up and hit the guy. I get hit on every play, I take all the shots and I never complain, but when it's unnecessary, I'm going to do something about it. I'm not going to take illegal shots, I get hit enough illegally as it is. And I still can't understand why I was the only one thrown out. Lunsford went after me and threw a few punches. I think the referees panicked, they didn't handle it very diplomatically."
• Reggie McKenzie: "O.J. is my main man and I saw him in trouble so I went to help him. They throw the Juice out; how the hell can they do that? He takes our damn meal ticket, the pride and joy of the Buffalo Bills and puts him on the sidelines. All I know is Lunsford kept his eyes open the rest of the day. Our line was looking to give him a shot."
• Gary Marangi: "We didn't change anything (with Simpson out). Roland Hooks did a heckuva job. We just killed ourselves and I took too long to get going."
• Jim Ringo: "We are not a good enough team to make that many mistakes. And it wasn't just the turnovers. The special teams broke down badly on several occasions. And it hurts even more because our defense played a strong game. To waste that effort really hurts."

Bills	0	7	0	3 -	10
Cowboys	0	14	0	3 -	17

Attendance at Texas Stadium - 51,779

Dal: P. Pearson 2 run (Herrera kick), 7:19
Buf: Gant 27 pass from Marangi (Jakowenko kick), 10:09
Dal: D. Pearson 21 pass from Staubach (Herrera kick), 14:47
Dal: FG Herrera 43, 3:23
Buf: FG Jakowenko 22, 13:03

	BUF	DAL
First downs	19	14
Rushing yds	161	63
Passing yds	103	165
Punts-avg	11-44.1	10-39.9
Fumbles-lost	4-0	3-1
Penalties-yds	4-21	7-65

BILLS LEADERS: Rushing - Simpson 24-78, Kinney 15-77, Marangi 3-6; **Passing** - Marangi 10-28-1 - 132; **Receiving** - Chandler 5-63, Gant 2-51, Simpson 2-10, Seymour 1-8.

COWBOYS LEADERS: Rushing - P. Pearson 7-29, Laidlaw 7-21, Dennison 7-9, Staubach 4-4, Young 1-0; **Passing** - Staubach 15-34-0 - 202; **Receiving** - D. Pearson 9-135, Laidlaw 2-17, P. Pearson 1-25, Richards 1-17, Dupree 1-6, Young 1-2.

WEEK 10 GAMES

NO 17, Det 16	NYJ 34, TB 0
Den 17, SD 0	Atl 21, SF 16
NE 21, Balt 14	Chi 24, GB 13
Pitt 14, Mia 3	NYG 12, Was 9
Minn 27, Sea 21	Oak 21, KC 10
Clev 24, Phil 3	St.L 30, LA 21
Cinc 31, Hou 27	

NOTES

• The Bills lost their fourth straight on *Monday Night Football* and their sixth straight this season.
• Marv Bateman's 11 punts tied a club record set twice by Paul Maguire.
• The Bills held the ball for the first 6:11 of the game but the drive was wasted when George Jakowenko missed the field goal.
• The Cowboys took the lead in the second when Preston Pearson caught a 25-yard pass and Golden Richards a 17-yarder to set up Pearson's two-yard run.
• Butch Johnson fumbled a punt and Dan Jilek recovered at the Dallas 42 and the Bills went on to tie the game. Gary Marangi, working out of a two-tight end formation, hit Reuben Gant over the middle for a TD with Gant beating Mel Renfro.
• After a Bills punt, Dallas got the ball with 26 seconds left in the first half, but two plays and 13 seconds later, it was 14-7. Roger Staubach hit Drew Pearson for 40 yards, then threw to him for a 21-yard TD on the next play.
• Efren Herrera's 43-yard field goal early in the fourth made it 17-7. The Bills reached the Dallas 33 later in the fourth, but Jim Ringo, rather than try a long field goal or go for the first down on fourth-and-one, punted into the end zone.
• Gant made a dazzling 24-yard catch to the Dallas 8 with three minutes left, but Marangi threw two incomplete passes, then ran for three yards and Jakowenko had to kick a field goal.

QUOTES

• Jim Ringo: "It's an easy word to use, but patience really is a virtue. The men believe in what they're doing and they depend on each other. They're well coordinated now. How many defensive linemen do you see who were here last year? The answer is one, Mike Kadish. Look at the young linebackers and three of the four defensive backs who played most of the way weren't here last year. You have to have patience. We've improved vastly on defense. We really came off the line. So many played well. Ben Williams, Kadish, John Skorupan to name a few."
• Cowboys tackle Ralph Neely: "This was an embarrassing game for us and me personally."
• O.J. Simpson: "I think the Cowboys have some offensive problems to work out before they go to the Super Bowl."
• Donnie Green: "We're looser now, even though we're losing. It's a happy bunch. We're not just hoping the season ends so we can get a fresh start. We want to play well and I think we will. Maybe it's because I know Ringo so well as an offensive line coach, but I think he'll be a really good head coach. How tough was Too Tall Jones? Well, did you hear much about him on TV? I guess that answers it."
• Reuben Gant: "I feel good having the opportunity to play and show what I can really do. I've been here three years and I've hardly played. I feel more comfortable now."

STANDINGS: TENTH WEEK

AFC EAST	W	L	T	CENTRAL	W	L	T	WEST	W	L	T	NFC EAST	W	L	T	CENTRAL	W	L	T	WEST	W	L	T
Baltimore	8	2	0	Cincinnati	8	2	0	Oakland	9	1	0	Dallas	9	1	0	Minnesota	8	1	1	LA Rams	6	3	1
New England	7	3	0	Pittsburgh	6	4	0	Denver	6	4	0	St. Louis	8	2	0	Chicago	5	5	0	San Fran	6	4	0
Miami	5	5	0	Cleveland	6	4	0	San Diego	4	6	0	Washington	6	4	0	Detroit	4	6	0	N.Orleans	3	7	0
NY Jets	3	7	0	Houston	4	6	0	Kan. City	3	7	0	Philadelphia	3	7	0	Green Bay	4	6	0	Atlanta	3	7	0
Buffalo	2	8	0					Tampa Bay	0	10	0	NY Giants	1	9	0					Seattle	2	8	0

NOTES

• For the third home game in a row, the Bills set a Rich Stadium record for smallest crowd as they dropped their seventh straight game.
• Dan Fouts completed 14 of 19 passes for 172 yards in the first half as the Chargers led, 27-10.
• Meanwhile, fans began wondering why they ever clamored for Gary Marangi at quarterback. He suffered through a brutal day. In the second half, he was zero-for-seven with two interceptions before finally completing a pass with 5:37 left in the game.
• Charlie Joiner caught all of his passes in the first half as Buffalo's secondary was overmatched by San Diego offensive coordinator Bill Walsh's attack.
• San Diego scored on the fourth play of the game after Fouts had thrown 39 yards to Pat Curran on the first

play.
• Buffalo retaliated with a George Jakowenko field goal after Marangi missed a wide-open O.J. Simpson with what would have been a sure TD pass.
• Joiner caught three passes including the TD toss on San Diego's next drive and Mike Fuller's 43-yard punt return set up Joiner's 31-yard TD reception.
• Buffalo pulled within 21-10 when John Holland recovered a bad punt snap in the end zone.
• Rickey Young's 44-yard run set up a Ray Wersching field goal and then Wersching made a 45-yard free kick to close the first half. San Diego took advantage of an obscure rule that noted if a punt is fair caught as time elapses, a free kick could be attempted.

QUOTES

• O.J. Simpson: "I just want to get this season over with. I want to stay alive and be able to go home in one piece. It's been a very frustrating season. I think I'll prove one thing – that gaining 1,000 yards doesn't mean a productive year. I think this has been my least productive year in football. They used to boo me like they booed Gary today. I know what he's going through. One thing's for sure, Gary will never have to worry about having a day as bad as this."
• Jim Ringo: "Losing (defensive ends) Sherm White and Ben Williams hurt a lot, that made a helluva difference, but really, the entire team came up with an awful performance – easily the worst of the season. Gary has to learn to work himself out of situations. He was prepared to play, but he had a bad afternoon."
• Gary Marangi: "My problem is not confidence. Maybe I'm forcing the ball, maybe I'm aiming it. I like to think I can throw myself out of days like this, but I couldn't. I'm better than what I've been showing. I've been throwing a ball all my life, I'm not doing anything differently."

Chargers	14	13	7	0	-	34
Bills	3	7	3	0	-	13

Attendance at Rich Stadium - 41,701

SD: Woods 13 run (Wersching kick), 1:39
Buf: FG Jakowenko 29, 7:29
SD: Joiner 5 pass from Fouts (Wersching kick), 11:59
SD: Joiner 30 pass from Fouts (Wersching kick), 3:45
Buf: Holland fumble recovery in end zone (Jakowenko kick), 7:09
SD: FG Wersching 35, 12:42
SD: FG Wersching 45, 15:00
Buf: FG Jakowenko 42, 7:55
SD: Young 13 run (Wersching kick), 14:01

	BUF	SD
First downs	14	20
Rushing yds	148	184
Passing yds	71	198
Punts-avg	8-45.9	6-38.3
Fumbles-lost	1-0	1-1
Penalties-yds	4-81	8-65

BILLS LEADERS: Rushing - Simpson 25-118, Kinney 9-20, Marangi 4-10; **Passing** - Marangi 8-30-3 - 83; **Receiving** - Chandler 3-40, Kinney 2-17, Montler 1-6, Simpson 2-20.
CHARGERS LEADERS: Rushing - Woods 14-48, Young 11-82, Morris 6-51, Matthews 2-6, West 1-0, Fouts 1- (-3); **Passing** - Fouts 19-29-3 - 200; **Receiving** - Joiner 6-97, Young 4-20, Curran 2-43, Woods 5-31, McDonald 1-7, Matthews 1-2.

WEEK 11 GAMES

Minn 17, GB 10	Pit 32, Hou 16
Wash 16, St.L 10	Cinc 27, KC 24
Clev 24, TB 7	Den 14, NYG 13
NE 38, NYJ 24	LA 23, SF 3
Atl 17, Dal 10	Det 14, Chi 10
NO 51, Sea 27	Oak 26, Phil 7
Balt 17, Mia 16	

NOTES

• O.J. Simpson broke his own NFL record for yards rushing in a game, ripping for 273, but the Bills dropped the Thanksgiving Day game, their eighth straight loss.
• The Bills managed only 49 yards of offense outside of Simpson's rushing total.
• Simpson went over 1,000 yards for the fifth time in his career and his fifth 200-yard game broke Jim Brown's all-time record.
• Another horrific day was turned in by Gary Marangi. In his last two games, Marangi had completed 12 of 51 passes for 112 yards and four interceptions.
• George Jakowenko missed two field goals in the first quarter. Detroit then went ahead 10-0 as Greg Landry hit David Hill for a TD and Benny Ricardo, who played two games for the Bills before being replaced by Jakowenko, kicked his first field goal which was set up by Keith Moody's muffed punt.
• Another Ricardo field goal and Hill's second TD catch made it 20-0 in the third.
• After an exchange of fumbles, Simpson broke a 48-yard TD run, but the Lions answered that when Landry passed 25 yards to Charlie Sanders, then scrambled 28 yards to the 3 to set up Dexter Bussey's TD run early in the fourth.
• Simpson then accounted for all 58 yards in the final Buffalo scoring drive. He gained 16 yards to the Lions 15 and that carry gave him the new record. He then capped his day with a 12-yard TD run on a fourth-and-seven draw call.

QUOTES

• O.J. Simpson: "The purpose of coming in was to win, not to set a record. If it occurs, it occurs. Going into the game I felt like I hadn't helped the team like I feel I can. It's something that when your career is over, you can look back on with fond memories. But the things I'm proudest about were still in college." (On the possibility of breaking Jim Brown's career rushing record): "Like everyone else, I'd like to be No. 1. Jim Brown set the standard. If I stay in football long enough, I'd like the chance to pass Brown. It's incentive for me, for all runners. This year I missed camp and this was the first week where I felt 100 percent in shape. What I mean is this was the first week I was able to do things downfield like juke a guy. Next year I'll be in camp in the best shape of my life and I'll be with the Bills unless Ralph Wilson trades me." (On what he said to Jim Ringo after he broke the record): "I just thanked him when I came over to the sideline. Jim has been part of every success I've had in pro football. He's been as responsible as anyone I've known because he coached the offensive line that did the great blocking for me."
• Lions coach Tommy Hudspeth: "O.J. is one hellacious player. There's only one O.J., he's in a class by himself, no doubt about it, but I'll take a win over a record any day."
• Reggie McKenzie: "This gives us something positive, but it still doesn't solve our problems. And you can't assume anything about what might happen in the off-season."

Bills	0	0	7	7	-	14
Lions	0	10	10	7	-	27

Attendance at The Silverdome - 66,875

Det: Hill 21 pass from Landry (Ricardo kick), 7:42
Det: FG Ricardo 22, 12:25
Det: FG Ricardo 35, 6:12
Det: Hill 24 pass from Landry (Ricardo kick), 10:34
Buf: Simpson 48 run (Jakowenko kick), 13:38
Det: Bussey 4 run (Ricardo kick), 1:24
Buf: Simpson 12 run (Jakowenko kick), 11:30

	BUF	DET
First downs	19	17
Rushing yds	307	193
Passing yds	15	111
Punts-avg	6-46.5	5-45.4
Fumbles-lost	4-2	3-2
Penalties-yds	8-75	6-45

BILLS LEADERS: Rushing - Simpson 29-273, Kinney 9-21, Marangi 3-13; **Passing** - Marangi 4-21-1 - 29; **Receiving** - Chandler 3-22, Kinney 1-7.

LIONS LEADERS: Rushing - Bussey 17-137, Gaines 12-24, Landry 2-32; **Passing** - Landry 8-20-1 - 143; **Receiving** - Hill 4-74, Sanders 4-69.

WEEK 12 GAMES

Dal 19, St.L 14	SF 20, Minn 16
Pitt 7, Cinc 3	Oak 49, TB 16
Chi 16, GB 10	NE 38, Den 14
KC 23, SD 20	NYG 28, Sea 16
Balt 33, NYJ 16	Hou 20, Atl 14
Clev 17, Mia 13	LA 33, NO 14
Wash 24, Phil 0	

STANDINGS: TWELFTH WEEK

AFC EAST	W	L	T	CENTRAL	W	L	T	WEST	W	L	T	NFC EAST	W	L	T	CENTRAL	W	L	T	WEST	W	L	T
Baltimore	10	2	0	Cincinnati	9	3	0	Oakland	11	1	0	Dallas	10	2	0	Minnesota	9	2	1	LA Rams	8	3	1
New England	9	3	0	Pittsburgh	8	4	0	Denver	7	5	0	St. Louis	8	4	0	Chicago	6	6	0	San Fran	7	5	0
Miami	5	7	0	Cleveland	8	4	0	San Diego	5	7	0	Washington	8	4	0	Detroit	6	6	0	N.Orleans	4	8	0
NY Jets	3	9	0	Houston	5	7	0	Kan. City	4	8	0	Philadelphia	3	9	0	Green Bay	4	8	0	Atlanta	4	8	0
Buffalo	2	10	0					Tampa Bay	0	12	0	NY Giants	2	10	0					Seattle	2	10	0

Bills	10	3	7	7 - 27
Dolphins	3	14	14	14 - 45

Attendance at the Orange Bowl - 43,475

Buf: FG Jakowenko 28, 2:19
Mia: FG Yepremian 52, 3:26
Buf: Simpson 75 run (Jakowenko kick), 3:49
Mia: Harris 37 pass from Strock (Yepremian kick), 1:52
Mia: Solomon 79 punt return (Yepremian kick), 13:12
Buf: FG Jakowenko 49, 14:46
Mia: Solomon 53 pass from Strock (Yepremian kick), 1:18
Mia: Strock 2 run (Yepremian kick), 8:32
Buf: Gant 11 pass from Marangi (Jakowenko kick), 13:48
Mia: Solomon 59 run (Yepremian kick), 3:18
Buf: Chandler 15 pass from Marangi (Jakowenko kick), 6:07
Mia: Nottingham 1 run (Yepremian kick), 9:16

	BUF	MIA
First downs	23	19
Rushing yds	269	218
Passing yds	155	207
Punts-avg	5-46.0	3-35.7
Fumbles-lost	0-0	0-0
Penalties yds	7-38	6-50

BILLS LEADERS: Rushing - Simpson 24-203, Kinney 12-40, Marangi 5-28, Ray 1- (-2); **Passing** - Marangi 13-29-2 - 155; **Receiving** - Chandler 4-68, Kinney 3-26, Gant 2-26, Simpson 2-12, Holland 1-13, Seymour 1-10.
DOLPHINS LEADERS: Rushing - Davis 7-79, Solomon 1-59, Bulaich 6-33, Winfrey 4-25, Malone 5-10, Nottingham 4-10, Strock 1-2, Heath 1-0; **Passing** - Strock 11-22-1 - 219; **Receiving** - Solomon 5-114, Harris 2-66, Seiple 1-25, Tillman 1-10, Davis 1-6, Nottingham 1- (-2).

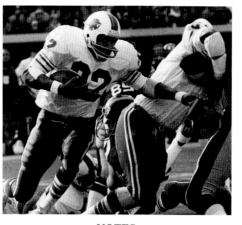

NOTES

• Miami recorded its 14th straight victory over the Bills as Freddie Solomon amassed 252 all-purpose yards and scored TDs on a run, a pass and a punt return.
• O.J. Simpson gained more than 200 yards for the second week in a row, the second time he had done that in his career. After 13 games, he was only nine yards behind Walter Payton for the league rushing title despite starting the season with 105 yards in the first three games.

WEEK 13 GAMES	
St.L 24, Bal 17	LA 59, Atl 0
Minn 20, GB 9	NE 27, NO 6
Clev 13, Hou 10	Dal 26, Phil 7
Wash 37, NYJ 16	Chi 34, Sea 7
Den 17, KC 16	Pitt 42, TB 0
Oak 35, Cinc 20	NYG 24, Det 10
SD 13, SF 7 (OT)	

• Don Strock started in place of veteran Miami QB Bob Griese. Also, rookie Joe Devlin started at tackle for the Bills in place of Donnie Green, the first start of Devlin's career.
• Counting all returns, Miami outgained Buffalo, 739-602.
• After trading field goals, Simpson followed a Reggie McKenzie block for a 75-yard TD run.
• Strock tied the game when he hit Duriel Harris on a 37-yard TD after a holding penalty on John Skorupan had nullified a third-down incompletion.
• Late in the half, Solomon returned a Marv Bateman punt 79 yards for a TD. The Bills managed to score on George Jakowenko's longest field goal of the season just before the half ended.
• However, the Dolphins put it away in the third as an off-sides penalty against the Bills gave Miami a first down. It cost them as Solomon made a great catch for a 53-yard TD. Later, Strock fooled the Bills on a naked bootleg to score. Buffalo was fooled badly again on Solomon's 59-yard TD run on a reverse.

QUOTES

• O.J. Simpson: "It means so little to me right now to be gaining all these yards. There is personal satisfaction and when I look back on it years from now I know it will be meaningful, but we just can't win a football game. Last week when we set that record was a thrill, but going over 200 today really didn't mean much to me."
• Jim Ringo: "We can't expect to win when we keep making stupid, asinine mistakes."
• Dolphins receiver Freddie Solomon: "It's been a long road for me. I feel the way I played today is the way I could have played all year if I didn't have that (kidney) surgery. Big plays are in me."

NOTES

• The Bills closed a miserable season losing their 10th game in a row and ninth straight under Jim Ringo. The 58 points were the most ever allowed by the Bills in their 17-year history, the previous being 52 by the Patriots on Oct. 22, 1961, and the 38-point margin of defeat was second-worst behind a 48-6 shellacking against Oakland in 1968 that cost Joe Collier his job.
• The 58 points was a Colts team record.
• O.J. Simpson salvaged something from the season, winning his fourth NFL rushing title.
• The Colts clinched the AFC East title under Ted Marchibroda for the second year in a row.
• Bob Chandler's TD reception was his 10th of the year, tying Elbert Dubenion's team mark set in '64. Chandler dropped a TD pass on the final play of the game that would have set a new record
• The team finished with records for most kickoff returns in one season (75), including a single-game record 10 for a record 208 yards against Baltimore.
• Marv Bateman, despite a blocked punt against the Colts, finished as the league's top punter.
• After the game, O.J. Simpson told his teammates: "I'd like some of you guys to know that this game is played for 60 minutes." Reggie McKenzie added: "If you don't want to play when you come back next year, then don't bother to come back."

QUOTES

• Reggie McKenzie: "Once we saw that the season was going to be one long struggle, we turned our goals to O.J. winning the AFC rushing title and maybe the league title. We feel we salvaged something. In the five years I've been here, Juice has gone over 1,000 yards each time. It gives you pride as an offensive line. I feel we will be a much-improved team next year with Joe Ferguson and Jim Braxton back."
• Jim Ringo: "It was the longest game of my life. It was embarrassing as hell to stand out there all day."
• O.J. Simpson on winning the rushing title: "It's some consolation, but not much. I'd trade it all for a chance to play in the Super Bowl. I've won rushing titles before in years when we were a contender and it meant a lot more. I just hope that management gets us a few players."

WEEK 14 GAMES	
Minn 29, Mia 7	LA 20, Det 17
Pitt 21, Hou 0	SF 27, NO 7
Wash 27, Dal 14	Cin 42, NYJ 3
St.L 17, NYG 14	NE 31, TB 14
Phil 27, Sea 10	KC 39, Cle 14
Oak 24, SD 0	GB 24, Atl 20
Den 28, Chi 14	

Bills	3	3	7	7 - 20
Colts	7	13	28	10 - 58

Attendance at Memorial Stadium - 50,451

Bal: Mitchell 5 run (Linhart kick), 2:56
Buf: FG Jakowenko 28, 13:19
Bal: FG Linhart 24, 6:47
Bal: Doughty 7 pass from Jones (Linhart kick), 9:12
Buf: FG Jakowenko 34, 13:49
Bal: FG Linhart 22, 14:59
Bal: Carr 36 pass from Jones (Linhart kick), 2:32
Bal: Chester 26 pass from Jones (Linhart kick), 5:41
Bal: Luce 21 fumble return (Linhart kick), 7:18
Buf: Simpson 44 run (Jakowenko kick), 11:18
Bal: Stevens 3 run (Linhart kick), 14:15
Bal: Leaks 1 run (Linhart kick), 1:30
Bal: FG Linhart 36, 3:21
Buf: Chandler 14 pass from Marangi (Jakowenko kick), 10:05

	BUF	BAL
First downs	21	25
Rushing yds	271	139
Passing yds	84	257
Punts-avg	4-39.3	2-45.0
Fumbles-lost	5-4	0-0
Penalties-yds	9-94	5-26

BILLS LEADERS: Rushing - Simpson 28-171, Kinney 12-37, Marangi 4-39, Hooks 1-24, Chandler 1-0; **Passing** - Marangi 11-24-1 - 120; **Receiving** - Chandler 5-67, Seymour 3-20, Gant 1-13, Kinney 1-2, Simpson 1-18.

COLTS LEADERS: Rushing - Mitchell 11-34, Leaks 5-15, Jones 2-4, R. Lee 18-83, Stevens 1-3; **Passing** - Jones 13-20-1 - 248, Troup 2-3-1 - 19; **Receiving** - Carr 4-114, Doughty 4-74, Chester 2-51, Mitchell 3-29, Leaks 1-8, R. Lee 1- (-9).

STANDINGS: FOURTEENTH WEEK

AFC EAST	W	L	T	CENTRAL	W	L	T	WEST	W	L	T	NFC EAST	W	L	T	CENTRAL	W	L	T	WEST	W	L	T
Baltimore	11	3	0	Pittsburgh	10	4	0	Oakland	13	1	0	Dallas	11	3	0	Minnesota	11	2	1	LA Rams	10	3	1
New England	11	3	0	Cincinnati	10	4	0	Denver	9	5	0	Washington	10	4	0	Chicago	7	7	0	San Fran	8	6	0
Miami	6	8	0	Cleveland	9	5	0	San Diego	6	8	0	St. Louis	10	4	0	Detroit	6	8	0	Orleans	4	10	0
NY Jets	3	11	0	Houston	5	9	0	Kan. City	5	9	0	Philadelphia	4	10	0	Green Bay	5	9	0	Atlanta	4	10	0
Buffalo	2	12	0					Tampa Bay	0	14	0	NY Giants	3	11	0					Seattle	2	12	0

O.J. Simpson's brilliant career in Buffalo came to an end in 1977 when he suffered a season-ending knee injury that even trainer Ed Abramoski could do nothing about.

At A Glance
1977

Jan. 1 – Former Bills coach Lou Saban hired Ed Cavanaugh to coach his offensive line at the University of Miami, the latest stop on his coaching tour. Cavanaugh had been with the Bills since 1972, but he suffered a heart attack on Oct. 17, 1976, and never returned to the team.

Jan. 12 – Linebackers coach John Ray resigned to join his brother in a private business in Indianapolis.

Jan. 28 – The famous Blizzard of '77 began in Buffalo and Rich Stadium wound up being home to a number of stranded motorists. Head coach Jim Ringo and a couple of assistants already were stranded at the administration building, so they ventured out to see if anyone needed help. More than two dozen spent the night at the stadium.

Feb. 6 – Jim Wietcha was hired to coach the offensive line, relieving head coach Jim Ringo of those duties. Ringo assumed the line duties after he was promoted to head coach last October when Ed Cavanaugh suffered a heart attack.

Feb. 7 – Jimmy Carr was hired to replace John Ray as linebackers coach.

Feb. 11 – Richie McCabe was named defensive coordinator, the first time that position had been filled in five years. He also retained his duties as secondary coach. Jim LaRue was reassigned from receivers to offensive backfield and Marvin Bass was given a pro personnel scouting job.

Feb. 14 – Kay Dalton was hired as receivers coach.

Feb. 25 – After three years of bickering and heated negotiations, the NFLPA and the NFL Management Council finally reached a peaceable solution and agreed to a five-year basic agreement. Included in the deal was a modified 12-round draft and a modification of the controversial Rozelle Rule, softening compensation for free agents.

March 22 – Bruce Beatty was hired as special teams coach, thus completing the coaching staff. Errol Prisby, the former special teams coach, resigned to enter private business.

March 29 – The owners voted to expand the regular season to 16 games and add one wild card playoff team in each conference starting in 1978. Also, the preseason was cut to four games.

March 31 – Tampa Bay and Seattle were permanently aligned in the NFC Central and AFC West, respectively.

May 3 – Oklahoma State defensive end Phil Dokes was chosen in the first round by the Bills, the No. 12 overall choice. The Bills also selected running back Curtis Brown of Missouri (third round), St. Cloud State wide receiver John Kimbrough (third), quarterback Fred Besena of California (fifth), kicker Neil O'Donoghue of Auburn (fifth) and cornerback Charlie Romes of N.C. Central (12th). The big news on draft day was the selection of Pitt running back Tony Dorsett by Seattle and his trade to Dallas for a host of draft picks. Tampa Bay selected USC running back Rickey Bell No.1 overall.

May 11 – Fullback Jim Braxton signed a new contract, avoiding a holdout.

June 3 – The Bills opened their three-day mini-camp at Rich Stadium. "The attitude is like we jumped over a year and went back to the '75 season," O.J. Simpson said. "It's an up attitude."

June 25 – Veteran backup quarterback Sam Wyche announced his retirement from the Bills.

July 14 – On the eve of the opening of training camp at Niagara University, center Mike Montler quit the team, blasting the Bills management in the process. "I feel my heart has been cut out by the Buffalo Bills," said Montler, who claimed he was denied a three-year contract by the team. "I paid my dues in Buffalo. I've been working out four hours a day since January."

July 15 – The only no-shows at the Bills first drill were first-round draft choice Phil Dokes and fifth-round pick Neil O'Donoghue.

July 22 – The Bills traded center Mike Montler to Denver, which is where he wanted to go, for the Broncos' second-round choice in the 1979 draft, thus salvaging something from his retirement. Veterans reported to training camp, including O.J. Simpson.

July 25 – Veteran cornerback Robert James, out with an injured knee since the preseason of 1974, was placed on waivers. Also, offensive tackle Donnie Green walked out of camp.

July 26 – O.J. Simpson expressed displeasure at what he had been seeing in the first few days of camp. "I'm frustrated as hell," Simpson said. "We look like we're gearing up for another rebuilding. If we had kept people like Earl Edwards, Ahmad Rashad, Pat Toomay and Mike Montler, we'd be playoff contenders right now. What's frustrating is I can't do anything about this. Management must do it."

July 29 – First-round choice Phil Dokes agreed to his first pro contract.

Aug. 6 – O.J. Simpson sat out because of blurred vision and the Bills dropped their preseason opener to the Steelers, 28-24, in Pittsburgh.

Aug. 9 – It was disclosed that O.J. Simpson's eye ailment was minor and that surgery would not be required.

Aug. 13 – It was only a preseason game, but Jim Ringo got his first victory as a head coach as the Bills beat Detroit, 17-10, at Rich Stadium.

Aug. 20 – New Orleans edged the Bills, 20-17, at the Superdome as the Bills committed five turnovers.

Aug. 23 – Disgruntled offensive tackle Donnie Green was traded to Philadelphia for a sixth-round draft choice in 1978. "Philadelphia did me a tremendous favor," Green said.

Aug. 25 – Placekicker George Jakowenko was cut and kicker Carson Long was signed as the Bills awaited the outcome of Neil O'Donoghue's holdout.

Aug. 29 – Joe Danelo's 30-yard field goal in overtime lifted the Giants to a 24-21 victory over the Bills at Giants Stadium.

Aug. 31 – Backup quarterback Gary Marangi was traded to Green Bay for an undisclosed draft choice and wide receiver Lou Piccone was acquired from the New York Jets for a draft choice.

Sept. 1 – Gary Marangi failed his physical with the Packers and the trade was voided by the league, so Marangi returned to Niagara University.

Sept. 3 – Buffalo defeated Tampa Bay, 17-6, as O.J. Simpson gained 127 yards on 12 carries.

Sept. 7 – Neil O'Donoghue ended one of the longest holdouts in team history by signing a three-year contract.

Sept. 10 – The Bills looked terrible in their final preseason test, losing to Minnesota, 30-6.

Sept. 18 – The Bills opened the regular season in front of 76,097 rain-soaked fans at Rich Stadium and were shutout by Miami, 13-0, the Dolphins' 15th straight victory in the series.

Sept. 21 – A story in the *Buffalo Evening News*, written by Milt Northrop, chronicled the latest rage in armchair quarterbacking. Northrop wrote about his friends and himself and their fantasy football league. Baltimore QB Bert Jones was the first player drafted in Northrop's league while Milt picked Minnesota's Fran Tarkenton in the first round, No. 4 overall.

Sept. 25 – Denver's Orange Crush defense limited the Bills to 129 yards in a 26-6 victory at Mile High Stadium.

Oct. 2 – The Bills' losing streak reached 13 regular-season games as a staunch effort in Baltimore fell short, 17-14.

Oct. 6 – The NFL admitted that umpire Gerry Hart was in error when he refused to stop the clock at the end of the Bills-Colts game. Hart was suspended for two weeks.

Oct. 9 – Joe Ferguson fumbled at his own 22 with 2:48 remaining, setting up New York's game-winning score in a 24-19 Jets victory before 32,046 rain-soaked fans, the smallest regular-season crowd in Rich Stadium history.

Oct. 10 – Ralph Wilson ended speculation that Jim Ringo was about to be fired when he said: "Jim Ringo is going to coach the team this year. This is no day-to-day, week-to-week thing. He's going to coach for the season and we're going to win some games."

Oct. 16 – In the lowest-scoring game in team history, the Bills blanked Atlanta, 3-0, as Neil O'Donoghue's second-quarter field goal was the only score. A new low was established at Rich Stadium as only 27,348 were onhand in the rain.

Oct. 19 – Neil O'Donoghue was cut and Carson Long, who was with the team in training camp, was re-signed.

Oct. 23 – Mistakes derailed the Bills as Cleveland came into Rich Stadium and handed Buffalo a frustrating 27-16 loss as the Browns possessed the ball for more than 38 minutes.

Oct. 27 – Seattle kicker John Leypoldt, the Bills second-leading all-time scorer now kicking for Seattle, expressed excitement over playing his ex-teammates. "One bad game (the 1976 season opener against Miami) got me fired," he said. "So this game means a lot to me. Not because I have sour grapes, but because I want to prove that they made a mistake."

Oct. 30 – O.J. Simpson's marvelous career as a Bill came to a crashing end as he suffered a season-ending knee injury and the Bills absorbed perhaps the most embarrassing loss in team history, a 56-17 laugher to the 1 1/2-year-old Seattle Seahawks at the Kingdome.

Oct. 31 – Jim Ringo said he won't quit as head coach. "It's going to take a helluva lot worse than that for me to quit, and I can't foresee anything worse than that," he said. "We're way down, so there's no sense being tight anymore."

Nov. 1 – It was officially announced that O.J. Simpson would need surgery on his left knee, the first time in his nine-year career that his body would need to be operated on, and that his season and likely his Bills career was over. "This might be it," said Reggie McKenzie, Simpson's closest friend on the team. "After the game in Seattle he was going around asking for our jerseys. I sort of looked at him funny and then it dawned on me that the chapter was closing. At the airport, he was on his way to Los Angeles and we were ready to get back on our flight to Buffalo and I looked over at him and he looked back and I think we both knew this was the end."

Nov. 6 – The Bills rebounded from their catastrophic loss to Seattle and the departure of O.J. Simpson with an emotional 24-14 victory over the Patriots at Schaefer Stadium as Roland Hooks, in his first start, rushed for 155 yards.

Nov. 7 – O.J. Simpson held a press conference at Rich Stadium and indicated he wanted to play one more year of football. He said he wanted to end his career on a positive note. "I've had a ton of thrills here and the only thing I haven't had is a championship," he said. "That's the only thing I want out of football now. I would play for any championship team, and for a lot less money."

Nov. 9 – O.J. Simpson underwent successful left knee surgery, performed by team doctor Joseph Godfrey at Mercy Hospital.

Nov. 13 – Baltimore sacked Joe Ferguson 10 times for 68 yards and the Colts ripped the Bills, 31-13, at Rich Stadium.

Nov. 20 – It was a doubly bad day for the Bills as New England beat them, 20-7, in front of a sparse turnout of 27,598 at Rich Stadium. And in Chicago, Walter Payton gained 275 yards against the Minnesota Vikings, breaking O.J. Simpson's single-game rushing record of 273 yards set on Thanksgiving Day 1976 against Detroit.

Nov. 27 – It was revealed that of all the teams that have been playing football since 1960, when the AFL was born, the Bills possessed the third-worst record. At 103-137-8, a winning percentage of 42.9, only Denver and Philadelphia were worse. Atlanta and New Orleans, expansion teams in 1967, and the 1976 additions, Seattle and Tampa Bay were worse as well. The Oakland Raiders, with a record of 156-81-11, were No. 1 at 65.8 percent. Another study showed 17 former Bills starting for other teams around the league including wide receivers Haven Moses, J.D. Hill and Ahmad Rashad, defensive linemen Earl Edwards, Ron McDole and Billy Newsome and running back Don Calhoun.

Nov. 28 – O.J. Simpson joined Howard Cosell and Frank Gifford in the *Monday Night Football* broadcast booth and said before the game, "The Bills aren't as bad as their record, so this game might not be that bad." Simpson was wrong as the Raiders pummeled Buffalo, 34-13. Mark van Eeghen rushed for 143 yards and Ken Stabler passed for three TDs.

Dec. 3 – Larry Felser of the *Buffalo Evening News* listed a number of candidates for the Bills head coaching job, which he speculated would be open once the season ended. One name he listed was that of Marv Levy, who just had won the Grey Cup coaching the Montreal Alouettes of the CFL. On the positive side, Felser said: "A PhD, Levy is a bright, ambitious man who had the inner strength to get rid of Johnny Rodgers after a confrontation last season. Then he won the title without the best player in the league." On the negative side, Felser said: "Some of his ex-players feel he has such trouble communicating on a lower plane that he sometimes treats the stars as rivals."

Dec. 4 – In a truly listless performance, the Bills lost to Washington, 10-0, in front of a new record low crowd of 22,975 at Rich Stadium. Joe Theismann passed for 150 yards and a TD.

Dec. 5 – Ralph Wilson absolved himself of blame for the Bills' sorry state and took out his frustrations on the Buffalo papers. "I'm not to blame," Wilson told the Associated Press. "I'm not out there making the passes and the blocks and the tackles. I didn't make the lousy trades and the lousy draft picks. All this is a personal vendetta against me. All the Buffalo newspapers are interested in is selling papers. All these personal attacks really hurt me. But I'm willing to take it because I don't want to hurt the players or the people who work for me."

Dec. 6 – O.J. Simpson's knee looked fine as he danced the night away at New York City's famous disco, Studio 54. He was in New York to act as host for the presentation of the Heisman Trophy later in the week.

Dec. 8 – Former San Francisco head coach Monte Clark was rumored to be the choice to succeed Jim Ringo at the end of the season. Ralph Wilson denied having spoken to Clark, though.

Dec. 11 – The Bills showed some life in Shea Stadium, rallying in the final two minutes to defeat the Jets, 14-10, on Joe Ferguson's 11-yard TD pass to Bob Chandler with 40 seconds left. The play capped a brilliant nine-play, 92-yard drive in just 1:13. Tampa Bay ended an NFL record 26-game losing streak with a 33-14 victory over New Orleans. It was the first victory in franchise history.

Dec. 15 – Joe DeLamielleure and Tony Greene were voted to the AFC's Pro Bowl squad. Bob Chandler, who was leading all wide receivers in pass receptions with 53 with one game to go, expressed anger when he was left off the team. "At this minute, I'd just as soon quit football," he said. "It all seems so worthless. I'd never do anything to take away from the people who made the team and

I'm not blaming our organization. It just gets old. I defy anybody to come to Buffalo and match my statistics. You can't practice in Buffalo, you have no feeling for the ball, no timing (because of the cold weather). You're just going through the motions. I haven't given up on being traded. After this happening, I feel stronger about it than ever. How I'm going to get myself up for Miami the way I feel right now is something I just don't know." Miami's Nat Moore, Oakland's Cliff Branch, Pittsburgh's Lynn Swann and Houston's Ken Burrough made the team.

Dec. 17 – The Bills closed a miserable season with a 31-14 defeat in Miami, their 16th loss in a row to the hated Dolphins in a nationally televised Saturday game.

Dec. 22 – To the surprise of no one, Jim Ringo was fired as the Bills head coach. "We feel a new approach is needed to improve the overall football situation," Ralph Wilson said. "At this time, a change seems to be in everyone's best interest. This was a difficult decision to make because of the great respect I have for Jim Ringo."

Dec. 24 – Ken Stabler's 10-yard TD pass to Dave Casper 53 seconds into the second overtime lifted Oakland past Baltimore, 37-31, while Denver downed Pittsburgh, 34-21, on the first day of divisional round playoffs.

Dec. 26 – The NFL took the Christmas holiday off and resumed divisional playoffs on a Monday and Minnesota edged Los Angeles, 14-7, while Dallas routed Chicago, 37-7.

Dec. 27 – Former 49ers coach Monte Clark said he was very interested in the Bills' job, saying that former Bills assistant Billy Atkins, who worked with Clark in San Francisco, had filled his ears with positive things about Buffalo.

Dec. 29 – Ralph Wilson said he had narrowed his list of candidates for the head coaching job to three: Monte Clark, Stanford coach Bill Walsh and New Orleans assistant Dick Nolan.

Dec. 30 – Monte Clark was rumored to be going to Detroit to take the Lions head coaching job. Meanwhile, Jim Ringo was hired by New England to be the Patriots' offensive line coach.

Jan. 1, 1978 – Denver qualified for its first Super Bowl by edging arch-rival Oakland, 20-17, in the AFC Championship Game behind Craig Morton's two TD passes to ex-Bill Haven Moses. In the NFC Championship Game, Dallas limited Minnesota to 214 total yards and ran away with a 23-6 victory.

Jan. 15, 1978 – Dallas' Doomsday defense forced a Super Bowl record eight turnovers as the Cowboys routed Denver, 27-10, before 76,400 fans at the New Orleans Superdome. Dallas' victory was the first for the NFC in the Super Bowl since Dallas downed Miami following the 1971 season.

Jan. 23, 1978 – The NFC edged the AFC, 14-13, on Walter Payton's TD run with 7:37 left. Payton was named the game's MVP for gaining 77 yards at Tampa Stadium.

Tony Greene's 37 interceptions (upper) are the second-most in Bills history behind Butch Byrd (40).

Joe DeLamielleure (lower) played in the Pro Bowl for five years in a row starting in 1976.

243

BY THE NUMBERS - 1977

TEAM STATISTICS	BILLS	OPP
First downs	246	260
Rushing	93	134
Passing	141	98
Penalty	12	28
Total yards	4,391	4,453
Avg. game	313.6	318.1
Plays	944	922
Avg. play	4.7	4.8
Net rushing yds	1,861	2,405
Avg. game	132.9	171.8
Avg. play	4.1	4.1
Net passing yds	2,530	2,048
Comp/att	221/458	155/316
Sacks/lost	36-273	17-165
Interceptions	24	21
Percentage	48.3	49.1
Punts/avg	83-38.9	73-36.2
Fumbles/lost	36-20	21-12
Penalties/yds	87-866	71-638
Touchdowns	19	39
Extra points	17-19	37-39
Field goals	9-17	14-21
Safeties	1	0
Kick ret./avg	60-20.6	40-20.4
Punt ret./avg	32-11.9	42-14.4

RUSHING	ATT	YDS	AVG	TD
Simpson	126	557	4.4	0
Hooks	128	497	3.9	0
Braxton	113	372	3.3	1
Ferguson	41	279	6.8	2
Collier	31	116	3.7	0
Brown	8	34	4.3	0
Piccone	1	6	6.0	0
Bateman	1	0	0.0	0
Franckowiak	1	0	0.0	0
TOTALS	**450**	**1861**	**4.1**	**3**

PASSING	COMP	ATT	INT	YDS	TD	COMP%	SACKS	RATE
Ferguson	221	457	24	2803	12	48.4	36-273	54.6
Simpson	0	1	0	0	0	00.0	0-0	39.6
TOTALS	**221**	**458**	**24**	**2803**	**12**	**48.3**	**36-273**	**54.8**

KICKING	1-19	20-29	30-39	40-49	50+	TOT	PAT	PTS
Long	0-0	2-2	2-3	3-6	0-0	7-11	13-14	34
O'Donoghue	0-0	1-2	1-2	0-1	0-1	2-6	4-5	10
TOTAL	**0-0**	**3-4**	**3-5**	**3-7**	**0-1**	**9-17**	**17-19**	**44**

PUNTING	NO	AVG	LG	In 20	BL
Bateman	81	39.9	75	14	2
TOTALS	**83**	**38.9**	**75**	**14**	**2**

RECEIVING	CAT	YDS	AVG	TD
Chandler	60	745	12.4	4
Braxton	43	461	10.7	1
Gant	41	646	15.8	2
Piccone	17	240	14.1	2
Hooks	16	195	12.2	0
Simpson	16	138	8.6	0
Kimbrough	10	207	20.7	2
Holland	8	107	13.4	0
Brown	5	20	4.0	1
Collier	3	23	7.7	0
Seymour	2	21	10.5	0
TOTALS	**221**	**2803**	**12.7**	**12**

LEADERS

Kick returns: Moody 30-636 yards, 21.2 avg, 0 TD
Kimbrough 15-346, 23.1, 0 TD

Punt returns: Moody 15-196, 13.1, 1 TD
Kimbrough 16-184, 11.5, 1 TD

Interceptions: Greene 9-144, 16.0, 0 TD
Clark 7-151, 21.6, 0 TD

SCORE BY QUARTERS

BILLS	41	39	33	47	0 -	160
OPP	57	113	81	62	0 -	313

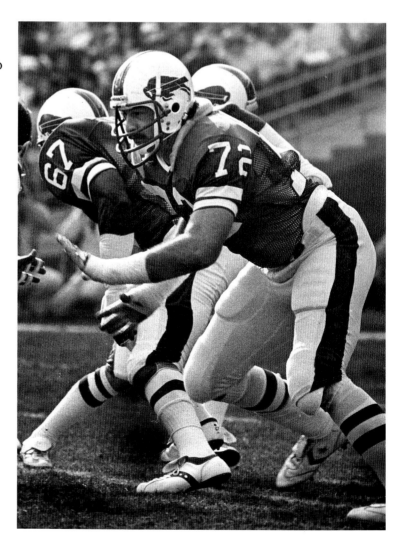

Ken Jones (72) was drafted out of Arkansas State as a defensive end, but was switched to offensive tackle and went on to play 11 years for the Bills.

GAME 1 - Sunday, Sept. 18, 1977 - DOLPHINS 13, BILLS 0

Dolphins	0	3	10	0	-	13
Bills	0	0	0	0	-	0

Attendance at Rich Stadium - 76,097

Mia: FG Yepremian 32, 3:10
Mia: FG Yepremian 37, 9:17
Mia: Bulaich 20 run (Yepremian kick), 9:34

	BUF	MIA
First downs	16	10
Rushing yds	127	96
Passing yds	197	52
Punts-avg	5-46.0	9-36.1
Fumbles-lost	7-3	1-0
Penalties-yds	6-71	1-10

BILLS LEADERS: Rushing - Simpson 21-71, Braxton 11-35, Ferguson 5-19, Hooks 2-2, Bateman 1-0; **Passing** - Ferguson 19-37-1 - 204; **Receiving** - Chandler 5-72, Holland 3-44, Simpson 7-68, Braxton 3-10, Gant 1-10.

DOLPHINS LEADERS: Rushing - Bulaich 14-48, Malone 10-35, Griese 2-1, Davis 6-12; **Passing** - Griese 9-19-0 - 84; **Receiving** - Moore 4-31, Tillman 2-27, Harris 2-26, Bulaich 1-0.

WEEK 1 GAMES

GB 24, NO 20	Phil 13, TB 3
Den 7, St.L 0	Chi 30, Det 20
Oak 24, SD 0	NE 21, KC 17
Clev 13, Cinc 3	Balt 29, Sea 14
NYG 20, Wash 17	Hou 20, NYJ 0
Atl 17, LA 6	Pitt 27, SF 0
Dal 16, Minn 10 (OT)	

NOTES

• For the 15th straight time, Miami walked off the field a winner over the Bills.
• The Bills' defense turned in a great effort, limiting the Dolphins to 148 yards of total offense, but Buffalo's offense was terrible and a critical special teams error led to the only Miami TD.
• Miami's first score came after Freddie Solomon returned a Marv Bateman punt 14 yards and Bob Griese hit Duriel Harris for 19 yards to set up Garo Yepremian's 32-yard field goal.
• Curtis Johnson's interception at the Dolphins 37 started Miami on its second field goal drive. Mario Clark helped position Yepremian with a 36-yard interference penalty on Nat Moore.
• On the ensuing kickoff, Don Nottingham and Wade Bosarge forced rookie Charlie Romes to fumble and Norris Thomas recovered at the Bills 20. On the next play, Norm Bulaich went off right tackle for the touchdown that put away the game.
• Neil O'Donoghue missed field goals from 50 and 41 yards.
• O.J. Simpson ran the ball on 15 of the first 19 first-down situations the Bills faced.

QUOTES

• Jim Ringo: "It was just one of those days, a helluva messed up day out there. You don't belong in this business if you don't put points up on the scoreboard. The defense played excellent and it's a shame that we couldn't score when they held Miami down so well. It was just a horrible day. We felt our defense was ready to complement our offense, but... It's not the end of the season. It's a helluva shock to our football team, but it's not the end of the world."
• Joe Ferguson: "It looks like the same old thing. The receivers dropped the ball, there were a couple of bad calls and we lost the game."
• Miami coach Don Shula: "We had a lot of people around O.J. all the time. We put a lot of emphasis on containment this week in practice. Our defense played very well. They got the ball for the offense several times, but we sputtered. We failed to capitalize on a lot of their mistakes and didn't convert them into points."
• Reggie McKenzie: "They sure came back to haunt us. We made all the crucial mistakes, but you have to give Miami credit, they sure looked a lot better than they did on film. Every time we'd get a drive going, we'd do something to stop it. Everything that always happens to us against Miami started happening. We still have 13 games left. We can't quit."
• O.J. Simpson: "They did a great job of pursuing. We'd run a sweep and there'd be several guys there, you'd go a little further, and there'd be more guys still. We lost it because we made the key mistakes a young football team makes."

GAME 2 - Sunday, Sept. 25, 1977 - BRONCOS 26, BILLS 6

Bills	0	6	0	0	-	6
Broncos	3	7	13	3	-	26

Attendance at Mile High Stadium - 74,897

Den: FG Turner 48, 3:33
Buf: Cornell 22 fumble return (kick failed), 1:39
Den: Morton 1 run (Turner kick), 6:38
Den: Armstrong 1 run (kick failed), 3:49
Den: Odomes 1 pass from Morton (Turner kick), 11:19
Den: FG Turner 26, :58

	BUF	DEN
First downs	8	17
Rushing yds	66	203
Passing yds	63	93
Punts-avg	10-41.3	6-39.3
Fumbles-lost	1-0	2-2
Penalties-yds	6-53	5-60

BILLS LEADERS: Rushing - Simpson 15-43, Braxton 5-7, Ferguson 1-5, Hooks 1- (-3), Brown 2-14; **Passing** - Ferguson 13-28-3 - 111; **Receiving** - Chandler 1-15, Hooks 3-17, Simpson 1-18, Gant 3-24, Braxton 3-13, Holland 2-24.

BRONCOS LEADERS: Rushing - Armstrong 20-96, Keyworth 7-36, Perrin 9-34, Morton 1-5, Lytle 8-31, Moses 1-1; **Passing** - Morton 8-18-0 - 96, Perrin 1-2-0 - 35; **Receiving** - Moses 1-35, Perrin 1-37, Egloff 1-20, Upchurch 1-4, Keyworth 1-6, Odoms 2-18, Dolbin 1-9, Armstrong 1-2.

NOTES

• The Bills managed only 129 yards of total offense in their second straight dreadful outing.
• It was the first time since October of 1971 that Buffalo's offense had been blanked back-to-back.
• O.J. Simpson's wife, Marguerite, gave birth to the couple's third child the morning of the game and he flew to Los Angeles afterward to be with her.
• Linebacker John Skorupan blew out his right knee and was lost for the season. Free agent signee Shane Nelson made a sharp impression with a fumble recovery.
• Rick Upchurch's 28-yard punt return to the Bills 37 set up Jim Turner's 48-yard field goal.
• Early in the second quarter, the Bills went ahead 6-3 when Dan Jilek forced Lonnie Perrin to fumble and Bo Cornell picked up the ball and ran 22 yards for a TD. Neil O'Donoghue missed the extra point.
• Billy Thompson's interception and 38-yard return to the 2 set up Craig Morton's TD that put the Broncos ahead for good.
• After an 11-yard shanked Marv Bateman punt, Otis Armstrong broke a 35-yard run to the 1 and he scored from there to make it 16-6. Later in the third, the Broncos put together their only sustained drive, a 12-play, 82-yard march that was aided by a 23-yard interference penalty on Dwight Harrison. Morton hit Riley Odoms for the TD.
• Upchurch's 37-yard punt return and an ensuing face-mask penalty set up Turner's final field goal.

QUOTES

• Reggie McKenzie: "The total execution is not there and I can't explain it. This is hard to accept and it bothers us because we know we can do better. I feel it's only a matter of time before we bust loose."
• Jim Ringo: "They shut us down good, so they must be a good team. We're supposed to have a good offense, but all day today we were facing second and 10 or 12. We've got a lot of work to do."
• O.J. Simpson: "We are striving for balance on offense so much that we can't do what we always could – move the ball on the ground. The last five years we have never really had problems on offense. I don't know what the reason is now."
• Joe Ferguson: "I can't describe it. Denver definitely had a better defensive team than Miami did. We moved the ball against Miami. To be a great team you have to be able to throw and run. We couldn't run worth a darn today. The flight (home) is going to be short compared to how long the season looks like it's gonna be."
• Denver center Mike Montler: "When I was with Buffalo, we socked it to Denver pretty good (in 1975) and they never forgot it. But what's interesting is they stuck with pretty much the same defensive people they had then. They didn't panic and start trading people like Buffalo."

WEEK 2 GAMES

Minn 9, TB 3	Mia 19, SF 15
LA 20, Phil 0	Wash 10, Atl 6
Cinc 42, Sea 20	Balt 20, NYJ 12
SD 23, KC 7	Det 23, NO 19
Hou 16, GB 10	St.L 16, Chi 13
Oak 16, Pitt 7	Dal 41, NYG 21
Clev 30, NE 27 (OT)	

STANDINGS: SECOND WEEK

AFC EAST	W	L	T	CENTRAL	W	L	T	WEST	W	L	T	NFC EAST	W	L	T	CENTRAL	W	L	T	WEST	W	L	T
Baltimore	2	0	0	Cleveland	2	0	0	Oakland	2	0	0	Dallas	2	0	0	Green Bay	1	1	0	Atlanta	1	1	0
Miami	2	0	0	Houston	2	0	0	Denver	2	0	0	NY Giants	1	1	0	Chicago	1	1	0	LA Rams	1	1	0
New England	1	1	0	Pittsburgh	1	1	0	San Diego	1	1	0	Philadelphia	1	1	0	Minnesota	1	1	0	San Fran	0	2	0
Buffalo	0	2	0	Cincinnati	1	1	0	Kan. City	0	2	0	St. Louis	1	1	0	Detroit	1	1	0	N.Orleans	0	2	0
NY Jets	0	2	0					Seattle	0	2	0	Washington	1	1	0	Tampa Bay	0	2	0				

GAME 3 - Sunday, Oct. 2, 1977 - COLTS 17, BILLS 14

NOTES
• The Bills put up a valiant effort in Baltimore, but fell for the 13th time in a row in the regular season. The loss was Buffalo's fourth in a row to the Colts.
• Buffalo was on the Colts 39, but with no timeouts, helplessly watched the final 12 seconds run out as Mike Barnes and John Dutton employed stall tactics and referee Dick Jorgensen refused to stop the clock. The Bills had thrown over the middle to Lou Piccone, then run to the line to get the next play off, with hopes of trying a tying field goal after that, but never got the chance.
• The Colts took a 7-0 lead as Ron Lee gained 42 yards on an 87-yard march that ended with his TD run.
• The Bills answered late in the first half when Joe Ferguson hit Bob Chandler with a TD pass to cap a 55-yard drive, but the Colts took the lead two minutes later when Marv Bateman's 25-yard punt gave them good field position and Bert Jones fired 26 yards to Fred Scott to set up Toni Linhart's field goal attempt.
• The Bills turned over the ball three times in the third, but only one miscue resulted in Baltimore points when Don McCauley scored on a 15-yard screen pass.
• Buffalo drew within 17-14 in the fourth thanks to a lucky bounce that closed a 10-play, 80-yard drive. Ferguson's pass to the end zone bounced off Colts' defenders Ed Simonini and Tom MacLeod and into the waiting arms of Curtis Brown.

QUOTES
• Colts defensive end Fred Cook with a smile on his face: "I can sympathize with the Bills. But what can you do when everybody isn't set. We tried to get back quickly. Buffalo really surprised us today. That's a good team in the making."
• Reggie McKenzie: "The referee put his foot on the ball and held up play when he should have called timeout. We were lined up and ready to go and there wasn't anything we could do, it was an official's decision. That's what happens when you're a losing team, you get the short end of the stick."
• Joe Ferguson: "Everybody was yelling at the ref to stop the clock. He should have stopped it and he knows it."
• Jim Ringo: "The rules state that a team has to make a bonafide effort to get back to the line of scrimmage. The officials never said anything. They didn't even give us a chance to question them. They just took their ball and went home. We thought we would have time to try a play and then try a field goal."
• O.J. Simpson: "Some of the younger guys might be feeling good, but I've lost too many games to feel good about this. This is not a moral victory. I don't believe in those."

WEEK 3 GAMES
Atl 17, NYG 3	Dal 23, TB 7
NO 42, Chi 24	SD 24, Cinc 3
Wash 24, St.L 14	LA 34, SF 14
Pitt 28, Clev 14	NYJ 30, NE 27
Minn 19, GB 17	Den 24, Sea 13
Det 17, Phil 13	Mia 27, Hou 7
Oak 37, KC 28	

Bills	0 7 0 7 -	14
Colts	0 10 7 0 -	17

Attendance at Memorial Stadium - 49,247

Bal:	R. Lee 9 run (Linhart kick), 2:55
Buf:	Chandler 15 pass from Ferguson (O'Donoghue kick), 12:56
Bal:	FG Linhart 45, 14:56
Bal:	McCauley 15 pass from Jones (Linhart kick), 13:50
Buf:	Brown 12 pass from Ferguson (O'Donoghue kick), 3:04

	BUF	BAL
First downs	18	22
Rushing yds	74	155
Passing yds	228	154
Punts-avg	6-45.7	9-34.1
Fumbles-lost	4-3	4-1
Penalties-yds	5-40	7-55

BILLS LEADERS: Rushing - Simpson 16-52, Braxton 3-13, Ferguson 4-9, Franckowiak 1-0; **Passing** - Ferguson 19-38-2 - 234, Simpson 0-1-0 - 0; **Receiving** - Chandler 7-78, Holland 3-39, Simpson 2-19, Gant 2-49, Seymour 1-10, Kimbrough 1-18, Brown 2-17, Piccone 1-4.

COLTS LEADERS: Rushing - Mitchell 23-90, R. Lee 13-64, McCauley 3-5, Jones 2- (-4); **Passing** - Jones 20-30-0 - 175; **Receiving** - Mitchell 7-32, Chester 3-24, R. Lee 1-8, McCauley 4-32, Scott 4-64, Thompson 1-15.

GAME 4 - Sunday, Oct. 9, 1977 - JETS 24, BILLS 19

NOTES
• O.J. Simpson topped 100 yards for the first time this year and the 40th time in his career.
• Head coach Jim Ringo lost his 13th consecutive game and the Bills lost their 14th straight.
• The Bills had rallied from a 17-7 deficit to tie the game with 5:50 left, but Joe Ferguson fumbled with 2:48 left and Richard Neal recovered at the Bills 22. Two plays later, Clark Gaines ran 14 yards for the go-ahead touchdown.
• After a Buffalo punt, the Jets were unable to move and rather than risk a punt from deep in their own territory into the wind, the Jets opted for an intentional safety. Three plays after the free kick, time ran out for the Bills when they were at the Jets 41.
• The Bills scored on their first possession as O.J. Simpson ran 39 yards on the game's first play to set up Ferguson's TD pass to Lou Piccone. Neil O'Donoghue missed a 39-yard field goal that would have made it 10-0 in the second, and the Bills let down and allowed the Jets to score the next 17 points.
• Todd's TD pass to Wesley Walker tied it, then Pat Leahy made a field goal early in the third. On their next series, Bruce Harper went 55 yards with a screen to set up Jerome Barkum's TD catch.
• Dan Jilek recovered a New York fumble to start the Bills on a 62-yard TD drive capped by Bob Chandler's TD reception and the Bills tied it on O'Donoghue's field goal after Keith Moody recovered a Harper fumble at midfield.

QUOTES
• Joe Ferguson: "It seemed like a good snap, but it just popped out of my hands. I don't think I pulled out on it. We all want to win so bad for Jim. He has a lot of pressure on him and he doesn't deserve it. This has to be my most frustrating day because of the (Ringo) situation."

• Willie Parker, who took the blame for the fumble: "We had 'em and we knew we had 'em. This is the toughest one for me. We're snake bitten right now. I know we're a good team; we believe that."
• Joe DeLamielleure on Jim Ringo's tenuous position: "The coaching isn't to blame for this. I'm a Ringo man and I'm 100 percent behind him. Everything I got out of football I owe to him. He's a helluva coach."
• O.J. Simpson: "I made it clear how I felt last year. I was disturbed that they (the front office) didn't make any moves, but that didn't make any difference. I had hoped we could get off to a good start this year, but we haven't and this is no fun. Ringo is developing young talent for future teams. As for me, I have 26 games to go and then I'm out."

Jets	0 7 10 7 -	24
Bills	7 0 0 12 -	19

Attendance at Rich Stadium - 32,046

Buf:	Piccone 4 pass from Ferguson (O'Donoghue kick), 5:46
NYJ:	Todd 1 run (Leahy kick), 11:43
NYJ:	FG Leahy 35, 8:08
NYJ:	Barkum 5 pass from Todd (Leahy kick), 11:02
Buf:	Chandler 5 pass from Ferguson (O'Donoghue kick), 3:19
Buf:	FG O'Donoghue 24, 9:10
NYJ:	Gaines 14 run (Leahy kick), 12:56
Buf:	Safety, Todd ran out of end zone intentionally, 14:31

	BUF	NYJ
First downs	21	17
Rushing yds	172	172
Passing yds	199	194
Punts-avg	5-42.2	3-37.0
Fumbles-lost	1-1	4-3
Penalties-yds	2-15	5-45

BILLS LEADERS: Rushing - Simpson 23-122, Braxton 3-14, Brown 6-20, Piccone 1-6, Hooks 1-4; **Passing** - Ferguson 18-33-1 - 205; **Receiving** - Chandler 7-98, Simpson 4-21, Piccone 3-46, Gant 2-43, Brown 2- (-3).

JETS LEADERS: Rushing - Gaines 20-94, White 13-47, Harper 7-31, Diggs 1-16, Todd 3- (-16); **Passing** - Todd 10-15-0 - 194; **Receiving** - Walker 4-75, Barkum 3-45, Gaines 2-19, Harper 1-55.

WEEK 4 GAMES
Atl 7, SF 0	Balt 45, Mia 28
Phil 28, NYG 10	Minn 14, Det 7
Cinc 17, GB 7	Wash 10, TB 0
SD 14, NO 0	Dal 30, St.L 24
NE 31, Sea 0	Oak 26, Clev 10
Hou 27, Pitt 10	Den 23, KC 7
Chi 24, LA 23	

STANDINGS: FOURTH WEEK

AFC EAST	W	L	T	CENTRAL	W	L	T	WEST	W	L	T	NFC EAST	W	L	T	CENTRAL	W	L	T	WEST	W	L	T
Baltimore	4	0	0	Houston	3	1	0	Oakland	4	0	0	Dallas	4	0	0	Minnesota	3	1	0	Atlanta	3	1	0
Miami	3	1	0	Cleveland	2	2	0	Denver	4	0	0	Washington	3	1	0	Detroit	2	2	0	LA Rams	2	2	0
New England	2	2	0	Pittsburgh	2	2	0	San Diego	3	1	0	Philadelphia	2	2	0	Chicago	2	2	0	N.Orleans	1	3	0
NY Jets	2	2	0	Cincinnati	2	2	0	Kan. City	0	4	0	St. Louis	1	3	0	Green Bay	1	3	0	San Fran	0	4	0
Buffalo	0	4	0					Seattle	0	4	0	NY Giants	1	3	0	Tampa Bay	0	4	0				

GAME 5 - Sunday, Oct. 16, 1977 - BILLS 3, FALCONS 0

Falcons	0	0	0	0	- 0
Bills	0	3	0	0	- 3

Buf: FG O'Donoghue 30, 10:16

	BUF	ATL
First downs	15	15
Rushing yds	218	114
Passing yds	96	86
Punts-avg	8-31.8	8-42.9
Fumbles-lost	3-2	0-0
Penalties-yds	6-73	6-65

BILLS LEADERS: Rushing - Simpson 23-138, Braxton 18-64, Hooks 1-11, Ferguson 3-5; **Passing** - Ferguson 8-21-0 - 96; **Receiving** - Gant 3-40, Braxton 2-32, Piccone 1-13, Simpson 1-5, Brown 1-6.

FALCONS LEADERS: Rushing - Eley 25-90, Stanback 6-16, Hunter 4-6, Francis 3-3, McQuilken 1- (-1); **Passing** - Hunter 9-29-2 - 95, James 0-1-0 - 0; **Receiving** - Mitchell 4-32, Francis 1-20, Jenkins 2-34, Stanback 1-6, Eley 1-3.

WEEK 5 GAMES

Det 10, GB 6	St.L 21, Phil 17
Balt 17, KC 6	Clev 24, Hou 23
NYG 20, SF 17	Den 30, Oak 7
Dal 34, Wash 16	NE 24, SD 20
LA 14, NO 7	Sea 30, TB 23
Mia 21, NYJ 17	Pitt 20, Cinc 14
Minn 22, Chi 16 (OT)	

NOTES

• The Bills ended their 14-game regular-season losing streak in the lowest-scoring game in team history. It was Jim Ringo's first win as an NFL head coach after 13 defeats.

• O.J. Simpson surpassed 10,000 career rushing yards, but the smallest crowd in Rich Stadium history was onhand to see him pass the milestone.

• The only score of the game came with 4:44 left in the first half when Neil O'Donoghue kicked a 30-yard field goal. John Kimbrough had returned an Atlanta punt 18 yards to the Falcons 35.

• Atlanta was held to 200 yards of total offense and its only scoring threat occurred with 5:21 left in the game when Robert Pennywell blocked a Marv Bateman punt and the Falcons gained possession at the Buffalo 13. Three running plays netted nine yards, and on fourth-and-one, coach Leeman Bennett eschewed the field goal and went for the first down. Quarterback Scott Hunter was stopped short on a rollout by Keith Moody.

• Bob Chandler had a 31-game pass-catching streak snapped.

• It was the Bills' first shutout since Dec. 1, 1974, a 6-0 victory over Baltimore.

• Ringo was mobbed by his players on the field after the game and was presented with a game ball in the locker room by Jim Braxton.

QUOTES

• Jim Ringo: "I walked up that ramp or one like it 13 times with my head down and I died each time. I died 13 times. In a lot of ways we made the same mistakes today we have been making in our four losses, but at least this week the score was different. Sure I was beginning to wonder when we could win one. I was beginning to have doubts. And then when they blocked that punt, I felt like I'd just died. But our defense came to hit today and they showed a lot of people on this team what you have to do to win. It means more to get a win which the defense provided. We've been working since the summer to make our defense respectable."

• Keith Moody on his fourth-down stop: "Both guards pulled out. Doug (Jones) normally takes on one, but he took them both out, turned it back in and got a piece of Hunter. All I had to do was make the tackle. I think they thought they would make it with no problem. If I was them I probably would have gone for it, too."

• Atlanta coach Leeman Bennett: "I made a poor decision (in going for it). I didn't follow my basic philosophy for coaching which is to get points when you can. I thought we could make the first down, maybe even get a touchdown. I sent the play in. All in all, I blew it."

GAME 6 - Sunday, Oct. 23, 1977 - BROWNS 27, BILLS 16

Browns	0	13	7	7	- 27
Bills	7	3	6	0	- 16

Attendance at Rich Stadium - 60,905

Buf: Gant 38 pass from Ferguson (Long kick), 6:07
Cle: FG Cockroft 41, 6:25
Cle: FG Cockroft 27, 12:45
Cle: Warfield 52 pass from Sipe (Cockroft kick), 13:25
Buf: FG Long 41, 14:58
Cle: Miller 6 pass from G. Pruitt (Cockroft kick), 11:55
Buf: Moody 91 punt return (kick failed), 14:56
Cle: Parris 9 pass from Sipe (Cockroft kick), 6:15

	BUF	CLE
First downs	20	26
Rushing yds	162	219
Passing yds	185	127
Punts-avg	5-36.7	5-31.8
Fumbles-lost	2-2	0-0
Penalties-yds	12-139	7-59

BILLS LEADERS: Rushing - Simpson 19-99, Braxton 3-9, Ferguson 3-54; **Passing** - Ferguson 11-29-2 - 199; **Receiving** - Gant 5-111, Piccone 3-52, Chandler 2-27, Braxton 1-9.

BROWNS LEADERS: Rushing - G. Pruitt 21-90, Miller 21-117, Poole 2-7, Sipe 2-0, M. Pruitt 2-5; **Passing** - Sipe 14-22-2 - 143, G. Pruitt 1-2-0 - 6; **Receiving** - Miller 5-20, Rucker 4-46, Parris 2-15, G. Pruitt 2-12, Warfield 1-52, Poole 1-4.

NOTES

• The Bills turned in a miserable effort with 12 penalties and four turnovers. All four turnovers and 108 yards in penalties came in the first half, when Buffalo gained 256 yards yet scored only 10 points.

• The Browns controlled the ball for 22 minutes in the second half, running 41 plays to Buffalo's 19. Over the final 24 minutes, the Bills had possession for 2:47.

• Keith Moody's 91-yard punt return was the longest in Bills' history.

• Cleveland's Thom Darden stopped the Bills first possession with an end zone interception, but the Bills scored on the second series as Joe Ferguson hit Reuben Gant for a TD.

• Moody's 38-yard pass interference helped Cleveland get into position for Don Cockroft's first field goal, and a late-hit penalty on Bo Cornell helped set up his second field goal.

• The Browns took a 13-7 lead late in the first half when Paul Warfield caught a deflected pass that went off Reggie Rucker and Merv Krakau and scored on a 52-yard play.

• The Bills got a Carson Long field goal with two seconds left in the half after O.J. Simpson's 30-yard run and a pass-interference penalty on Gant by Gerald Irons.

• Greg Pruitt's halfback-option TD pass to Cleo Miller capped an 80-yard march. After Moody's punt return made it 20-16, the Browns drove 74 yards to Brian Sipe's TD pass to Gary Parris.

QUOTES

• Joe Ferguson: "Every time we get inside the other team's 20-yard-line, I say to myself 'Damn, don't make the big mistakes.'"

• Jim Ringo: "They just manhandled us (in the second half)."

• O.J. Simpson on the failure to use the running game: "I would think most teams go to what they do best in a tough situation, in a close game. We don't do one thing, we do everything. We're balanced, we do both. We seem to switch back and forth and then we don't do either very well. I'm a runner, I like to carry the ball. I figure the tougher the situation, the more I want to run with the ball. But when you get behind, you have to pass. If the score were different, we could have run on these cats all day. Hey, we ran for almost 3,000 yards in '75 and we still threw 25 touchdown passes."

• Reggie McKenzie: "All I'll say is this; we came out here and pushed them all up and down the field, but once we started throwing the ball around, well, you saw how we did."

• Keith Moody: "On every good punt return, there's 10 guys blocking for you, so you have to give them credit. I reversed field a couple of times and they didn't clip. It was nothing that I planned, it was all instinctive." (On Cleveland's ensuing possession which answered his return): "That was really the crushing blow. I thought that (his return) was going to give us a little spark, but Cleveland came right back and dominated play."

WEEK 6 GAMES

Mia 31, Sea 13	Pitt 27, Hou 10
KC 21, SD 16	Atl 16, Chi 10
NE 17, Balt 3	Oak 28, NYJ 27
St.L 49, NO 31	Dal 16, Phil 10
NYG 17, Wash 6	SF 28, Det 7
Den 24, Cinc 13	GB 13, TB 0
LA 35, Minn 3	

STANDINGS: SIXTH WEEK

AFC EAST	W	L	T	CENTRAL	W	L	T	WEST	W	L	T	NFC EAST	W	L	T	CENTRAL	W	L	T	WEST	W	L	T
Baltimore	5	1	0	Pittsburgh	4	2	0	Denver	6	0	0	Dallas	6	0	0	Minnesota	4	2	0	Atlanta	4	2	0
Miami	5	1	0	Cleveland	4	2	0	Oakland	5	1	0	Washington	3	3	0	Detroit	3	3	0	LA Rams	4	2	0
New England	4	2	0	Houston	3	3	0	San Diego	3	3	0	NY Giants	3	3	0	Chicago	2	4	0	N.Orleans	1	5	0
NY Jets	2	4	0	Cincinnati	2	4	0	Seattle	1	5	0	St. Louis	3	3	0	Green Bay	2	4	0	San Fran	1	5	0
Buffalo	1	5	0					Kan. City	1	5	0	Philadelphia	2	4	0	Tampa Bay	0	6	0				

NOTES

• O.J. Simpson hurt his aching knee and left the game in the first half, but he was unaware of the seriousness of the injury and did not realize that his season and fabulous Bills career was over.

• Seattle set team records for points, margin of victory, yards gained and first downs and handed the Bills perhaps their most embarrassing loss ever.

• Seattle's 559 yards were the most ever gained against the Bills. Jim Zorn had 251 of his 296 yards passing in the first half as Seattle rolled to a 42-3 lead. Seattle scored so quickly and often, Buffalo actually held a four-minute edge in time of possession at the end of the day.

• Carson Long's field goal gave the Bills a brief lead, but Zorn hit Steve Largent with a 31-yard TD pass over Mario Clark and it was all downhill from there. Keith Moody was toasted by Duke Fergerson 1:26 later on a 37-yard scoring strike.

• In the second quarter, Seattle scored four TDs while Joe Ferguson was intercepted three times, Simpson exited the game with his knee injury and Moody botched a kickoff return.

• The Bills took the second-half kickoff, drove 66 yards to the Seattle 20 and turned the ball over on downs. The Seahawks then marched 80 yards to make it 49-3.

QUOTES

• Sherman White: "I just can't believe this has happened to the Buffalo Bills. I will not quit. I still think we have the type of players who will play the Patriots next week head-to-head. I have personal and team goals I still want to reach."

• O.J. Simpson: "The worst thing they (management) could do is relieve him (Jim Ringo). At the end of this year, I will evaluate my situation. I've got a lot of things to talk over with my family."

• Jim Ringo: "It was the longest day of my life. I have no idea what's going to happen."

• Ralph Wilson: "I would hope there won't be a coaching change (caused by Ringo resigning). Jim knows how badly we played. It was one of the worst defeats we've ever suffered. I couldn't see anything good about our team. We played terrible in all departments."

• Bo Cornell: "Humiliating, frustrating and lousy."

• Joe Ferguson: "This kills us. It could have a very detrimental effect, or it could wake us up."

• Seattle quarterback Jim Zorn: "That was pretty exciting out there."

Bills	3 0 7 7 - 17
Seahawks	14 28 7 7 - 56

Attendance at the Kingdome - 61,180

Buf: FG Long 25, 8:25
Sea: Largent 31 pass from Zorn (Leypoldt kick), 10:59
Sea: Fergerson 37 pass from Zorn (Leypoldt kick), 12:25
Sea: Largent 48 pass from Zorn (Leypoldt kick), 5:28
Sea: Zorn 4 run (Leypoldt kick), 6:46
Sea: Smith 13 run (Leypoldt kick), 10:16
Sea: Testerman 10 pass from Zorn (Leypoldt kick), 13:40
Sea: Sims 17 run (Leypoldt kick), 9:18
Buf: Kimbrough 33 pass from Ferguson (Long kick), 13:25
Sea: Hunter 1 run (Leypoldt kick), 7:09
Buf: Ferguson 4 run (Long kick), 11:18

	BUF	SEA
First downs	17	30
Rushing yds	117	226
Passing yds	221	333
Punts-avg	5-35.2	2-36.5
Fumbles-lost	1-0	0-0
Penalties-yds	4-29	4-30

BILLS LEADERS: Rushing - Simpson 9-32, Braxton 10-42, Ferguson 2-11, Hooks 7-32; **Passing** - Ferguson 17-37-3 - 227; **Receiving** - Braxton 7-65, Kimbrough 4-81, Gant 2-33, Chandler 2-29, Piccone 1-12, Simpson 1-7.

SEAHAWKS LEADERS: Rushing - Smith 10-73, Sims 8-58, Hunter 11-56, Testerman 8-31, Zorn 2-8; **Passing** - Zorn 11-23-2 - 296, Myer 4-6-1 - 37; **Receiving** - Largent 4-134, Fergerson 4-113, Testerman 3-33, Smith 1-29, Raible 1-20, Howard 1-10, Sawyer 1- (-6).

WEEK 7 GAMES	
Balt 31, Pitt 21	SD 14, Mia 13
Wash 23, Phil 17	Chi 26, GB 0
Oak 24, Den 14	Clev 44, KC 7
Dal 37, Det 0	Minn 14, Atl 7
NO 27, LA 26	SF 20, TB 10
NE 24, NYJ 13	St.L 28, NYG 0
Cinc 13, Hou 10 (OT)	

NOTES

• The Bills bounced back from the embarrassing Seattle defeat to snap the Patriots' four-game winning streak.

• Roland Hooks, making his first start in place of O.J. Simpson, had career-highs for carries and yards.

• The Bills defense limited the Patriots ground game, No. 1 in the AFC, to 89 yards and picked off four passes, two by Mario Clark. Steve Grogan also was off the mark on a number of throws.

• The Patriots tight end Russ Francis suffered three broken ribs when belted by Steve Freeman in the first quarter.

• The Bills raced to a 14-0 first-quarter lead. Reuben Gant capped a 63-yard drive with a TD catch. Gant had caught a 22-yard pass and Joe Ferguson had scrambled for 24 yards earlier in the drive. The Bills then made it 14-0 as Hooks broke a 66-yard run to set up Jim Braxton's two-yard TD.

• The Patriots got that back 14 seconds later as Raymond Clayborn returned the kickoff for a TD.

• Buffalo's defense controlled the second quarter and Carson Long's field goal made it 17-7 at the half.

• On the second play of the third quarter, Doug Jones intercepted a Steve Grogan pass and went 24 yards for a TD that put the Bills firmly in charge.

QUOTES

• Jim Ringo: "It's attributed to the men. We were living in hell and we wanted to come out of hell."

• Reggie McKenzie: "We walked into the stadium and their fans were laughing at us. They were yelling 'Why'd you even show up' and 'at least give us a decent game.' I told the guys to remember that stuff.

Remember getting laughed at. Have some pride in yourselves. And then we went out and took it to them from the first play."

• Roland Hooks: "I just want to thank everyone on the offensive line. They were telling me all week just to follow them. I did that today and I will continue to do that the rest of the games. They came off the ball so well, all I had to do was run. I really didn't feel the pressure of taking O.J.'s place. I can't explain how I feel but I do feel like I'm part of this team and I never felt that way before."

• Joe Ferguson: "This means more to me and more to the team because we did it without O.J. I'm more involved in the game without him back there and it means that for seven games we have the chance to start building something new. Don't get me wrong, O.J. meant a lot to us. But I think we always sort of were waiting for him to lead us and we never found out about ourselves."

• Joe DeLamielleure: "People have made too much about this O.J. thing. I wish they would just forget it."

• Merv Krakau: "We went out feeling we had nothing to lose and we played like we knew we were capable of playing. With O.J. gone, I expect Joe Ferguson to take over the leadership."

Bills	14 3 7 0 - 24
Patriots	7 0 0 7 - 14

Attendance at Schaefer Stadium - 60,263

Buf: Gant 7 pass from Ferguson (Long kick), 9:13
Buf: Braxton 2 run (Long kick), 14:45
NE: Clayborn 93 kickoff return (Smith kick), 14:59
Buf: FG Long 30, 14:59
Buf: D. Jones 24 interception return (Long kick), :58
NE: Cunningham 10 run (Smith kick), 2:15

	BUF	NE
First downs	21	14
Rushing yds	224	89
Passing yds	175	113
Punts-avg	6-41.3	6-37.5
Fumbles-lost	2-1	1-0
Penalties-yds	10-97	6-40

BILLS LEADERS: Rushing - Hooks 27-155, Braxton 17-38, Ferguson 3-25, Collier 6-6; **Passing** - Ferguson 15-22-1 - 201; **Receiving** - Gant 7-97, Chandler 3-25, Braxton 3-26, Kimbrough 1-42, Seymour 1-11.

PATRIOTS LEADERS: Rushing - Cunningham 14-62, Calhoun 6-22, Forte 3-5, Grogan 1-0; **Passing** - Grogan 9-27-4 - 128; **Receiving** - Cunningham 2-30, Stingley 2-30, Burks 1-15, Chandler 2-30, Forte 1-22, Calhoun 1-1.

WEEK 8 GAMES	
Cinc 10, Clev 7	Det 20, SD 0
KC 20, GB 10	SF 10, Atl 3
Dal 24, NYG 10	Oak 44, Sea 7
Hou 47, Chi 0	St.L 27, Minn 7
LA 31, TB 0	Den 21, Pitt 7
Mia 14, NYJ 10	Phil 28, NO 7
Balt 10, Wash 3	

STANDINGS: EIGHTH WEEK

AFC EAST	W	L	T	CENTRAL	W	L	T	WEST	W	L	T	NFC EAST	W	L	T	CENTRAL	W	L	T	WEST	W	L	T
Baltimore	7	1	0	Cleveland	5	3	0	Denver	7	1	0	Dallas	8	0	0	Minnesota	5	3	0	LA Rams	5	3	0
Miami	6	2	0	Pittsburgh	4	4	0	Oakland	7	1	0	St. Louis	5	3	0	Detroit	4	4	0	Atlanta	4	4	0
New England	5	3	0	Houston	4	4	0	San Diego	4	4	0	Washington	4	4	0	Chicago	3	5	0	San Fran	3	5	0
NY Jets	2	6	0	Cincinnati	4	4	0	Seattle	2	6	0	NY Giants	3	5	0	Green Bay	2	6	0	N.Orleans	2	6	0
Buffalo	2	6	0					Kan. City	2	6	0	Philadelphia	3	5	0	Tampa Bay	0	8	0				

Colts	10	14	7	0	-	31
Bills	7	3	3	0	-	13

Attendance at Rich Stadium - 39,444

Buf: Kimbrough 73 punt return (Long kick), 4:27
Bal: FG Linhart 22, 10:35
Bal: Mitchell 5 run (Linhart kick), 12:51
Bal: Mitchell 13 run (Linhart kick), 3:56
Bal: Leaks 2 run (Linhart kick), 6:00
Buf: FG Long 26, 14:57
Buf: FG Long 45, 2:00
Bal: Jones 7 run (Linhart kick), 9:25

	BUF	BAL
First downs	12	18
Rushing yds	86	145
Passing yds	120	171
Punts-avg	4-43.3	5-32.2
Fumbles-lost	3-2	2-2
Penalties-yds	8-69	5-35

BILLS LEADERS: Rushing - Hooks 13-31, Braxton 2-16, Ferguson 4-39; **Passing** - Ferguson 14-33-3 - 188; **Receiving** - Gant 3-66, Chandler 3-43, Braxton 3-37, Kimbrough 2-18, Hooks 3-24.

COLTS LEADERS: Rushing - Mitchell 21-82, Leaks 14-38, McCauley 8-20, Jones 3-9, Lee 1-0, Troup 1- (-4); **Passing** - Jones 12-23-2 - 180; **Receiving** - McCauley 6-59, Doughty 3-61, Mitchell 3-60.

WEEK 9 GAMES

Sea 17, NYJ 0	LA 24, GB 6
Wash 17, Phil 14	NYG 10, TB 0
Atl 17, Det 6	Oak 34, Hou 29
St.L 24, Dal 17	Mia 17, NE 5
Minn 42, Cinc 10	Den 17, SD 14
Pitt 35, Clev 31	Chi 28, KC 27
SF 10, NO 7 (OT)	

NOTES

• The Colts set a team record with 10 sacks of Joe Ferguson for 68 yards as the Bills couldn't maintain the high from their victory over New England.
• John Dutton had three of the sacks and induced Dave Foley to commit three holding penalties.
• The Bills running game faltered and when forced to throw, the Colts "Sack Pack" dominated the game.
• The Bills got off to a great start when John Kimbrough broke a 73-yard punt return for a TD.
• But three minutes later, Roland Hooks fumbled at the Bills 36 and that led to Toni Linhart's field goal. The Colts then went ahead for good when, after starting a possession at the Bills 40, Bert Jones threw 34 yards to Glenn Doughty to set up Lydell Mitchell's first TD run.
• Buffalo's next three possessions ended in interceptions as Ferguson suffered a brutal day. One of the picks led to Mitchell's 18-yard TD run, the other to Roosevelt Leaks' short TD plunge.
• Carson Long kicked a pair of field goals to get the Bills to within 24-13 in the third, the second one set up by Tony Greene's interception and 47-yard return.
• But the Colts put the game away with a TD drive in the third that frustrated the Bills. Faced with three third-and-long situations, Jones passed all three times to wide-open Don McCauley for first downs and eventually, he scrambled seven yards for the score.

QUOTES

• Jim Ringo: "We didn't play too good."
• Reggie McKenzie: "I guess we laid an egg today. We never got a chance to get our running game in a groove."
• Colts defensive end Fred Cook: "We knew before the game the Bills were going to try to establish control with their 46 play (Roland Hooks sweeping to the right). In the first period we overshifted to the outside to force it in and they only ran that play once. After they found out they couldn't run and went to the pass, I was given the green light to rush the passer. Both John and I got the green light."
• Colts defensive end John Dutton: "Buffalo played right into our hands. It's real easy to just blow in there and play. You can't blame Buffalo's line because it was put in that position."
• Joe Ferguson: "We made some mistakes, got behind and then we had to advertise what we were going to do. It's tough to throw when you have to do it under those circumstances. They would put in a fifth defensive back to take away my receivers and they gave us a big rush. Sure I heard the fans (booing). They have their own opinion and if they want somebody else in there, they have the right to say so."

Patriots	3	0	3	14	-	20
Bills	0	0	7	0	-	7

Attendance at Rich Stadium - 27,598

NE: FG Smith 33, 10:07
NE: FG Smith 25, 10:08
Buf: Braxton 24 pass from Ferguson (Long kick), 13:01
NE: Cunningham 31 run (Smith kick), 2:25
NE: Cunningham 1 run (Smith kick), 8:08

	BUF	NE
First downs	11	19
Rushing yds	126	256
Passing yds	83	73
Punts-avg	6-45.8	3-33.3
Fumbles-lost	1-1	0-0
Penalties-yds	7-75	7-63

BILLS LEADERS: Rushing - Hooks 14-64, Braxton 5-12, Ferguson 5-47, Collier 2-3; **Passing** - Ferguson 10-22-1 - 115; **Receiving** - Gant 2-24, Chandler 2-22, Braxton 3-40, Piccone 2-22, Collier 1-7.

PATRIOTS LEADERS: Rushing - Cunningham 17-69, Calhoun 20-80, Grogan 12-81, Phillips 2-14, Forte 1-1, Ivory 1-1, Morgan 1-10; **Passing** - Grogan 8-17-1 - 73; **Receiving** - Calhoun 3-21, Stingley 2-36, Chandler 2-14, Cunningham 1-2.

WEEK 10 GAMES

Det 16, TB 7	LA 23, SF 10
Pitt 28, Dal 13	Hou 22, Sea 10
St.L 21, Phil 16	Chi 10, Minn 7
Cinc 23, Mia 17	NO 21, Atl 20
Clev 21, NYG 7	SD 12, Oak 7
Den 14, KC 7	Balt 33, NYJ 12
Wash 10, GB 9	

NOTES

• New England's defense, burned by the Bills two weeks earlier, made adjustments while the Bills tried to use the same type of attack. The result was 241 yards in total offense for Buffalo.
• The Patriots also found their ground game, which was missing two weeks ago, as they banged for 256 yards, including 131 in the decisive fourth quarter.
• Ex-Bill Don Calhoun gained 80, but the biggest key was quarterback Steve Grogan running designed bootlegs and keepers to gain 81 yards, 57 in the fourth, when he directed two TD drives.
• John Smith's field goal was the only scoring in the first half, and he added another three-pointer in the third, but Buffalo took a 7-6 lead late in the period when Joe Ferguson, seeing that primary receiver Bob Chandler was covered on a post route, dumped off to Jim Braxton and the fullback powered his way 24 yards into the end zone.
• New England drove right back, though, 76 yards, to take back the lead. Grogan scrambled for 18 yards on a third-and-five play, then Sam Cunningham broke free from Phil Dokes at the line and scampered 31 yards for the score.
• Bob Howard intercepted a pass that bounced off Chandler's hands at the Bills 33 and that set up Cunningham's clinching score. Hooks then broke a 17-yard run on the next series, but lost the ball and the Bills comeback hopes were shattered.
• Ken Jones replaced Dave Foley at right tackle in the second half.

QUOTES

• Joe Ferguson: "We ran the same stuff this time that we did when we beat them last time. It worked then and we thought we would try it again. We just don't have the experience or the speed at wide receiver. Reuben Gant is the fastest that I have. John Kimbrough is fast, he's trying hard and he's going to be a good one, but he's got a lot to learn and he's not what we want right now. I feel sorry for our defense. They played damn well and it must be disheartening to them. I won't blame them for thinking 'Why should we try when the offense is going to give it right back.'"
• Jim Ringo: "They made some adjustments from our first game and kicked the hell out of us. No question Grogan's running had a tremendous effect on the outcome. We just lost containment."
• Joe DeLamielleure: "I know the Bills are going to have a great team one of these days and I know I'm going to be a part of it. It's gonna happen in the next 10 or 12 years. I don't blame the fans (for booing). I wouldn't pay to see this. I'd make some changes, a lot of changes. It's mental now. Everyone is so depressed all the time. We need a change."
• Reggie McKenzie: "We have some crazy fans here. They were getting on us so I pointed to my helmet and said 'You put it on.' They're good fans though, good people. They just want to win."

STANDINGS: TENTH WEEK

AFC EAST	W	L	T	CENTRAL	W	L	T	WEST	W	L	T	NFC EAST	W	L	T	CENTRAL	W	L	T	WEST	W	L	T
Baltimore	9	1	0	Cleveland	6	4	0	Denver	9	1	0	Dallas	8	2	0	Minnesota	6	4	0	LA Rams	7	3	0
Miami	7	3	0	Pittsburgh	6	4	0	Oakland	8	2	0	St. Louis	7	3	0	Detroit	5	5	0	Atlanta	5	5	0
New England	6	4	0	Houston	5	5	0	San Diego	5	5	0	Washington	6	4	0	Chicago	5	5	0	San Fran	4	6	0
NY Jets	2	8	0	Cincinnati	5	5	0	Seattle	3	7	0	NY Giants	4	6	0	Green Bay	2	8	0	N.Orleans	3	7	0
Buffalo	2	8	0					Kan. City	2	8	0	Philadelphia	3	7	0	Tampa Bay	0	10	0				

NOTES

• Mark van Eeghen became the first Raider in team history to top 1,000 yards for the second time.

• O.J. Simpson attended the game and was a guest in the Monday night broadcast booth. He watched the game from Ralph Wilson's private box.

• Raiders receiver Fred Biletnikoff was ejected in the third quarter for bumping an official.

• Buffalo crossed midfield on seven of 10 possessions, the Raiders on nine of 11. The Bills got into Oakland territory three times in the first period, but managed only a Carson Long field goal and fell behind 13-3.

• Ken Stabler fired TD passes of 28 yards to Cliff Branch, who beat Mario Clark, and 44 yards to Biletnikoff, who got past Keith Moody.

• In the second quarter, the Bills stuck close as John Kimbrough beat Willie Brown for a 29-yard TD, but the Raiders regained their 10-point advantage when van Eeghen ran 27 yards to the 3 and Pete Banaszak plowed in two plays later. Late in the half, the Bills ran out the clock rather than try to score even though they had the ball at their own 41.

• Long's second field goal made it 20-13 early in the third, but Oakland put the game away when Stabler beat a blitz and hit Branch for a TD. Recently-signed Mike Collier fumbled at the Bills 20 a few minutes later and Banaszak scored another short TD to make it 34-13.

QUOTES

• Oakland coach John Madden: "Mixed in with the run, we threw some long ones early and that gave them an indication we were ready to go that way. We wanted to let them know we weren't going to go with the run and the short stuff. Once they knew that, they had to be concerned with it and then we were able to mix it up."

• Oakland quarterback Ken Stabler: "I just call the game by the seat of my pants, by feel. I try to keep it balanced."

• Jim Ringo: "They just beat us every way. They blew us out. We felt (Raiders rookie cornerback Neal) Colzie was vulnerable and we tested him. It worked, and it was the only thing that did."

• Joe Ferguson: "The Oakland defense had the biggest bunch of guys I've ever seen. I wish we could have run more, but once again we got behind so early. Looking back on this season, it's been a disaster in what I personally wanted to achieve. But you can learn a lot in adversity, about a lot of things."

WEEK 11 GAMES

Mia 55, St.L 14	Chi 31, Det 14
Minn 13, GB 6	LA 9, Clev 0
Cinc 30, NYG 13	SF 20, NO 17
Atl 17, TB 0	SD 30, Sea 28
Hou 34, KC 20	NE 14, Phil 6
Den 27, Balt 13	Dal 14, Wash 7
Pitt 23, NYJ 20	

Bills	3 7 3 0 - 13
Raiders	13 7 14 0 - 34

Attendance at Oakland-Alameda County Coliseum - 51,558

Oak: Branch 28 pass from Stabler (kick failed), 5:05
Buf: FG Long 33, 8:38
Oak: Biletnikoff 44 pass from Stabler (Mann kick), 9:59
Buf: Kimbrough 20 pass from Ferguson (Long kick), 2:49
Oak: Banaszak 1 run (Mann kick), 5:59
Buf: FG Long 40, 3:41
Oak: Branch 12 pass from Stabler (Mann kick), 6:17
Oak: Banaszak 1 run (Mann kick), 13:21

	BUF	OAK
First downs	18	26
Rushing yds	65	307
Passing yds	239	166
Punts-avg	5-39.4	1-32.0
Fumbles-lost	1-1	2-2
Penalties-yds	7-60	6-82

BILLS LEADERS: Rushing - Hooks 9-29, Braxton 7-21, Collier 3-15; **Receiving** - Gant 2-27, Chandler 9-120, Braxton 3-41, Kimbrough 2-48, Hooks 2-16.

RAIDERS LEADERS: Rushing - van Eeghen 26-143, Davis 14-72, Robiskie 8-42, Banaszak 8-29, Garrett 4-15, Rae 2-7, Stabler 1-0, Ginn 1- (-1); **Passing** - Stabler 7-12-1 - 166, Rae 0-1-1 - 0; **Receiving** - Branch 3-55, Biletnikoff 2-68, Davis 1-38, Casper 1-5.

NOTES

• Just like he did against Oakland, Joe Ferguson threw 25 incomplete passes as the offense sputtered badly against the Redskins in front of a new record low crowd at Rich Stadium.

• It was the smallest home crowd since 1963 and the season's final home attendance of 286,413 was about 27,000 less than in 1972, the Bills' final year at dilapidated War Memorial Stadium.

• Tony Greene intercepted his eighth pass of the season.

• The Bills won every statistical category except the scoreboard. Also, they had three turnovers, missed two field goals and were a meager four-of-15 on third-down conversions.

• Washington's first score was the result of a poor 20-yard punt into the wind by Marv Bateman that rolled dead at the Redskins 47. From there, the Redskins converted three straight third downs and Joe Theismann eventually hit Jean Fugett for the TD with Fugett dragging Doug Jones across the goal line.

• The Bills wasted a great chance to tie when Jim Braxton caught a 16-yard pass to the Redskins 3, but fumbled when he was hit by Mike Curtis and Brad Dusek recovered.

• Ken Houston's interception on Buffalo's next possession killed another threat and the Redskins then drove to Mark Moseley's clinching field goal with 1:43 left.

QUOTES

• Jim Ringo: "It was the same old story. We dropped eight passes, we fumbled at the three-yard-line, we messed up in the kicking game. Hell, what else can I say at this point? I can't catch the ball for them, I can't kick it for them. They call me a lousy coach, but when the receivers drop passes, what can I do, jump out there and catch it for them?"

• Reggie McKenzie: "This game is an indication of how the entire season has gone for us. Like day one. What other adjectives can you use that you haven't already used?"

• Jim Braxton on his fumble: "The pass wasn't supposed to go to me. I was a safety valve. I saw Joe in trouble so I went to an open area where he could find me. I never saw Curtis at all. I spun around and he hit me on the arm."

• Joe Ferguson: "I can't say I'm not happy that it's (the home portion of the schedule) over. It's not easy coming to the stadium knowing the fans are going to boo as soon as you make one mistake. I wouldn't look forward to playing another home game this season. I'll be happy when the season is over. It's been a miserable year."

• Washington tight end Jean Fugett on his TD: "It was a basic play where I ran a quick out and Frank Grant crossed on a post pattern. Both the cornerback and the safety went with Grant."

• Washington quarterback Joe Theismann: "I had to throw to him (Fugett). He was jumping up and down he was so wide open."

Redskins	0 7 0 3 - 10
Bills	0 0 0 0 - 0

Attendance at Rich Stadium - 22,975

Was: Fugett 12 pass from Theismann (Moseley kick), 3:26
Was: FG Moseley 19, 13:17

	BUF	WAS
First downs	19	18
Rushing yds	146	128
Passing yds	180	136
Punts-avg	8-34.0	7-37.1
Fumbles-lost	1-1	3-1
Penalties-yds	4-43	3-30

BILLS LEADERS: Rushing - Hooks 14-49, Braxton 9-32, Collier 8-46, Ferguson 1-19; **Passing** - Ferguson 17-42-2 - 202; **Receiving** - Gant 3-31, Chandler 5-49, Braxton 6-70, Hooks 2-41, Collier 1-11.

REDSKINS LEADERS: Rushing - Harmon 14-46, Thomas 28-89, Theismann 2- (-4), Hill 2- (-3); **Passing** - Theismann 12-28-1 - 150; **Receiving** - Fugett 4-52, Jones 4-45, Thomas 2-28, Buggs 1-15, Harmon 1-10.

WEEK 12 GAMES

NYJ 16, NO 13	Minn 28, SF 27
Pitt 30, Sea 20	LA 20, Oak 14
Dal 24, Phil 14	NYG 27, St.L 7
Cinc 27, KC 7	GB 10, Det 9
Den 24, Hou 14	SD 37, Clev 14
NE 16, Atl 10	Chi 10, TB 0
Mia 17, Balt 6	

STANDINGS: TWELFTH WEEK

AFC EAST	W	L	T	CENTRAL	W	L	T	WEST	W	L	T	NFC EAST	W	L	T	CENTRAL	W	L	T	WEST	W	L	T
Baltimore	9	3	0	Pittsburgh	8	4	0	Denver	11	1	0	Dallas	10	2	0	Minnesota	8	4	0	LA Rams	9	3	0
Miami	9	3	0	Cincinnati	7	5	0	Oakland	9	3	0	St. Louis	7	5	0	Chicago	7	5	0	Atlanta	6	6	0
New England	8	4	0	Houston	6	6	0	San Diego	7	5	0	Washington	7	5	0	Detroit	5	7	0	San Fran	5	7	0
NY Jets	3	9	0	Cleveland	6	6	0	Seattle	3	9	0	NY Giants	5	7	0	Green Bay	3	9	0	N.Orleans	3	9	0
Buffalo	2	10	0					Kan. City	2	10	0	Philadelphia	3	9	0	Tampa Bay	0	12	0				

Bills	0 7 0 7 - 14
Jets	0 3 0 7 - 10

Attendance at Shea Stadium - 31,929

NYJ: FG Leahy 25, :09
Buf: Chandler 5 pass from Ferguson (Long kick), 11:11
NYJ: Walker 9 pass from Todd (Leahy kick), 13:03
Buf: Chandler 11 pass from Ferguson (Long kick), 14:20

	BUF	NYJ
First downs	26	10
Rushing yds	174	57
Passing yds	216	140
Punts-avg	8-30.5	6-32.5
Fumbles-lost	6-2	1-1
Penalties-yds	7-94	3-25

BILLS LEADERS: Rushing - Hooks 26-84, Braxton 13-39, Collier 9-29, Ferguson 5-22; Passing - Ferguson 17-32-1 - 238; Receiving - Gant 3-45, Chandler 7-108, Braxton 4-33, Hooks 2-34, Piccone 1-18.

JETS LEADERS: Rushing - Dierking 8-26, Gaines 12-31, Todd 1-1, Long 1- (-1); Passing - Todd 10-26-3 - 145; Receiving - Gaines 6-68, Walker 2-52, Barkum 1-24, Harper 1-1.

WEEK 13 GAMES

Wash 26, St.L 20	Phil 17, NYG 14
Cinc 17, Pitt 14	Oak 35, Minn 13
Den 17, SD 9	Hou 19, Clev 15
Chi 21, GB 10	NE 14, Mia 10
Det 13, Balt 10	TB 33, NO 14
Sea 34, KC 31	LA 23, Atl 7
Dal 42, SF 35	

NOTES

• The Bills ended a four-game losing streak in thrilling fashion as Joe Ferguson hit Bob Chandler with an 11-yard TD pass with 40 seconds left to play, capping a nine-play, 92-yard drive in just 1:13.
• The Jets had just taken a 10-7 lead 1:17 earlier when Richard Todd fired a nine-yard TD pass to Wesley Walker. New York drove into Buffalo territory six times in the fourth quarter alone, and three times they were stopped by interceptions by Mario Clark, Tony Greene and Doug Jones. But finally, they dented the Bills end zone. Billy Hardee returned a punt 31 yards to the Bills 11 and two plays later, Walker scored when he beat Dwight Harrison to the back corner of the end zone.
• Keith Moody bobbled the ensuing kickoff and was pinned at his own 8 and the Bills seemed doomed. However, Ferguson hit Chandler for 19- and 18-yard gains and he passed 10 yards to Roland Hooks. After a Reuben Gant drop and a miss to Chandler, he hit Lou Piccone for 18 on third-and-10 to the Jets 27. After a Jim Braxton drop, Chandler got open for a 21-yard gain to the 6 and after a five-yard illegal-procedure penalty, Ferguson avoided Burgess Owens on a safety blitz, rolled right and hit Chandler for the winning TD.
• New York's first score, a 25-yard Pat Leahy field goal, came after a Marv Bateman punt was blocked by Ron Mabra and recovered at the Bills 19.
• Ferguson's first TD pass to Chandler capped a 64-yard drive in the second quarter.

QUOTES

• Joe Ferguson: "It was an unbelievable feeling. I shouldn't say we didn't feel we could come back, but you had to wonder. We haven't all year. When they scored, I said to myself 'Damn, we blew another one.' We had 92 yards to go. Chandler just kept getting open. He was beautiful."
• Bob Chandler: "I told Joe before the drive that I felt I could get open on the slant corner pattern. Hardee was playing five yards off me (on the winning TD). He had to respect the quick post and when I cut outside, he had no help. That's putting a cornerback out on an island – all alone. Joe knows me best and might tend to look for me in that situation."
• Jets receiver Wesley Walker: "We were sitting around laughing and joking before the game. Coach Michaels came in and told us to get serious. It's possible we took them too lightly. I know I wasn't as nervous before the game as I was before Pittsburgh or Oakland."
• Jets coach Walt Michaels: "This team has to grow up and be serious. I hope they learned a lesson today. We had a chance to win this game and we messed up."
• Jets linebacker Larry Keller: "They looked like All-World and we looked like All-Gutter."
• Tony Greene: "You can say one thing, the Buffalo Bills are full of thrills."

Bills	0 0 0 14 - 14
Dolphins	7 14 3 7 - 31

Attendance at the Orange Bowl - 39,626

Mia: Moore 7 pass from Griese (Yepremian kick), 2:01
Mia: Solomon 54 pass from Griese (Yepremian kick), 2:14
Mia: Bulaich 3 run (Yepremian kick), 5:11
Mia: FG Yepremian 48, 11:23
Buf: Piccone 11 pass from Ferguson (Long kick), 2:55
Mia: Davis 60 run (Yepremian kick), 11:06
Buf: Ferguson 1 run (Long kick), 14:10

	BUF	MIA
First downs	24	18
Rushing yards	103	238
Passing yards	331	210
Punts-avg	2-46.0	3-34.7
Fumbles-lost	3-1	1-0
Penalties-yds	3-20	6-27

BILLS LEADERS: Rushing - Hooks 13-41, Braxton 7-30, Collier 3-17, Ferguson 3-15; Passing - Ferguson 25-40-3 - 331; Receiving - Gant 3-46, Chandler 7-59, Braxton 5-85, Hooks 4-63, Piccone 5-73, Collier 1-5.

DOLPHINS LEADERS: Rushing - Davis 27-172, Harris 9-23, Bulaich 4-27, Moore 2-16; Passing - Griese 10-14-1 - 210; Receiving - Moore 5-144, Solomon 1-54, Davis 2-16, Bulaich 2- (-4).

NOTES

• The Dolphins missed the playoffs despite the victory because a day later, the Colts beat the Patriots to finish 10-4 and they owned the tiebreaker over Miami. Oakland qualified as the wild card team.
• Bob Griese set a Miami record with 22 TD passes while Nat Moore set a new mark with 12 TD receptions.
• The Bills drove into Miami territory on eight of 11 possessions, racked up 434 yards and 24 first downs, yet still lost by 17 points.
• Moore took a screen pass 67 yards on the second play of the game to set up Miami's first score. The Bills first drive ended when Miami's Tim Foley intercepted a Joe Ferguson pass in the end zone. The pass went through Reuben Gant's hands. Miami then opened the flood gates.
• Freddie Solomon's 54-yard TD reception made it 14-0 and the score ballooned to 21-0 when Norm Bulaich carried in from the 3 after Solomon gained 67 yards on a screen. The Bills were caught blitzing on both long screen passes.
• Down 24-0 in the fourth, Ferguson, who enjoyed his best game in terms of yardage in two years, hit Lou Piccone for a TD. But Gary Davis broke a 60-yard TD run with 4:54 left, offsetting Ferguson's late TD run.

WEEK 14 GAMES

Wash 17, LA 14	Minn 30, Det 21
Balt 30, NE 24	Hou 21, Cinc 16
Dal 14, Den 6	Sea 20, Clev 19
Phil 27, NYJ 0	TB 17, St.L 7
Atl 35, NO 7	GB 16, SF 14
Pitt 10, SD 9	Oak 21, KC 20
Chi 12, NYG 9 (OT)	

QUOTES

• Jim Ringo: "Today's game was like the history of our whole season. We made mistakes at crucial times, the same damn thing all season. It hurts. I'd be foolish to sit here and say it didn't hurt."
• Joe Ferguson on Gant's dropped TD pass that resulted in Foley's interception: "The ball should have been caught. Just about everything we did today was working, but we had too many interceptions, plus a fumble. I thought about asking for a trade earlier in the year, but I don't want to be one of those quarterbacks bouncing all over the league. I want to help build the Bills back into winners."
• Reggie McKenzie: "If they want me back, I'll be back. I'll stay here until I'm agitated enough to leave. They haven't agitated me. They haven't talked contract with me yet even though this is my last year. These people don't do things like that. They wait for people to play out their option year first. I'll tell you, we're a helluva farm team."
• Sherman White: "I think a new coach can come in here and plug the holes with the talent available. I think they made a big mistake playing Phil Dokes as much as they did. I feel I have as much talent as any defensive end in the league."
• Dolphins guard Bob Kuechenberg: "I said some years back that the Bills would never beat us while I'm here. I've been right so far."
• Merv Krakau: "I'm not sure any players want to come back next year and I'm not sure if I want to come back under this situation. We need players and we need a different attitude in the administration. We need a winning attitude from them."

STANDINGS: FOURTEENTH WEEK

AFC EAST	W	L	T	CENTRAL	W	L	T	WEST	W	L	T	NFC EAST	W	L	T	CENTRAL	W	L	T	WEST	W	L	T
Baltimore	10	4	0	Pittsburgh	9	5	0	Denver	12	2	0	Dallas	12	2	0	Minnesota	9	5	0	LA Rams	10	4	0
Miami	10	4	0	Cincinnati	8	6	0	Oakland	11	3	0	Washington	9	5	0	Chicago	9	5	0	Atlanta	7	7	0
New England	9	5	0	Houston	8	6	0	San Diego	7	7	0	St. Louis	7	7	0	Detroit	6	8	0	San Fran	5	9	0
NY Jets	3	11	0	Cleveland	6	8	0	Seattle	5	9	0	NY Giants	5	9	0	Green Bay	4	10	0	N.Orleans	3	11	0
Buffalo	3	11	0					Kan. City	2	12	0	Philadelphia	5	9	0	Tampa Bay	2	12	0				

After winning five **NFC W**est division titles with the **Los Angeles Rams, Chuck Knox** came East to rebuild the **Bills** in 1978. By 1980, Buffalo was champion of the **AFC East**.

At a Glance
1978

Jan. 2 – Stanford coach Bill Walsh had Ralp Wilson to dinner at his home in Palo Alto, Calif., but Walsh didn't think he was in the running for the Bills' head coaching position because he had already gone on record as saying he preferred staying in California.

Jan. 3 – Despite rumors that he was going to Detroit, Monte Clark proclaimed that he was still in the running for the Bills job. "I'm still available," Clark said.

Jan. 5 – A third candidate for the head coaching position, former Denver coach John Ralston, said he was very interested in the Bills' job.

Jan. 11 – In a surprise move, the Bills announced the signing of Los Angeles Rams coach Chuck Knox to a six-year contract worth a reported $200,000 per year. Knox led the Rams to five straight NFC West Division titles. At about the same time, the Lions announced the hiring of Monte Clark.

Jan. 12 – Chuck Knox explained what made him come to Buffalo. "I was impressed with Ralph Wilson and the opportunity he presented me," Knox said. "It's an opportunity to go in and build a solid program. My title is vice president in charge of football operations. I'll be responsible for coaching the team, for supervision of the draft and for trading players." Said Wilson: "Chuck has experienced nothing but success in Los Angeles and we know he is just the man to restore the Bills to prominence in pro football."

Jan. 13 – Joe DeLamielleure expressed glee over the hiring of Knox. "The only bigger shock to me would have been if they had hired Don Shula," he said. "Everybody's just going crazy. He's one of the top football coaches, right up there with John Madden, Shula and Bud Grant. And now we've got him. The encouraging thing to me is that a guy of his stature would come here to Buffalo. He must think there's something here."

Jan. 30 – After meeting with Chuck Knox, O.J. Simpson said he wanted to play at least one more year with Buffalo. His contract was due to expire at the end of 1978.

Feb. 3 – Knox signed three of his Los Angeles assistants to Buffalo contracts. Former Buffalo quarterback Kay Stephenson was named quarterbacks coach, Elijah Pitts was named offensive backfield and special teams coach and Jim Wagstaff, a member of the original 1960 Bills, was hired as defensive backfield coach.

Feb. 7 – Another member of Knox's Los Angeles staff joined the Bills as Tom Catlin (defensive coordinator and linebackers) was hired. Also, Willie Zapalac, who had coached the past two years in St. Louis, was hired as the defensive line coach.

Feb. 28 – Ray Prochaska was hired to coach the offensive line. Also, Norm Pollom was named director of college scouting. Harvey Johnson was demoted to the role of college scout.

March 7 – Free agent Bob Nelson, a major disappointment in Buffalo since he was drafted in the second round in 1975, signed with the Oakland Raiders and the Bills received no compensation. Knox hired Jack Donaldson to be his receivers coach.

March 14 – At the owners meetings in Palm

Springs, the league voted to add a seventh official to crews, the side judge.

March 17 – More changes designed to aid offenses were made. Pass blockers were granted the right to extend their arms and open their hands, and a five-yard contact zone against receivers was established, but once a receiver got out of that zone, no defensive contact was allowed. The owners also voted 26-2 to institute a 15-yard unsportsmanlike penalty to any player deemed by an official to be taunting another player.

March 18 – San Francisco general manager Joe Thomas admitted he had talked to Chuck Knox about the possibility of obtaining O.J. Simpson in a trade. The owners voted to begin experimenting with the use of instant replay in the preseason.

March 23 – Although they denied it, the Bills traded Simpson to San Francisco, but the deal was contingent on Simpson passing his physical.

March 24 – The Simpson trade became official when he passed his physical. The Bills received second- and third-round draft choices in 1978, first- and fourth-round choices in 1979 and a second-round pick in 1980. "We think it's a good deal," Chuck Knox said. "It's good for O.J. because he's getting back to the West Coast and back home, and it gives the Buffalo Bills the opportunity with some high draft choices to get some young football players in the draft. The real test of the deal will come in draft selection. We can't make any mistakes."

March 25 – Most players were ambivalent about Simpson's leaving Buffalo. One Bill said he was glad Simpson was gone and it was believed that many players never forgave Simpson for asking to be traded to a West Coast team in 1976. Joe Ferguson said: "If it'll make him happy, and both teams happy, I guess it's for the best. I hate to see him go because he was such a great player, but we have to start rebuilding somewhere." Joe DeLamielleure said: "I'm a Buffalo Bill and I want what is best for the team. We haven't won with O.J., so now we have to try to win without him."

March 26 – "I'll always be a Buffalo Bill and I'm proud of that," O.J. Simpson said. "Do they call Babe Ruth a Boston Brave or Willie Mays a Met? I think we had more positives in Buffalo than negatives. I just hope they'll remember I always gave my best. My whole adult life I've been a Bill. I don't think any team got along as well or had as much fun as the Bills of 1975. But then politics came (in the front office) and it took the fun out of football for a while."

March 30 – Doug Hafner was hired as director of pro scouting.

April 13 – Tight end Reuben Gant, a disappointing first-round draft choice from 1974, said he wasn't interested in returning to the Bills. The free agent claimed he had offers from Minnesota and Cleveland.

April 15 – Tackle Dave Foley, a member of the Electric Company, announced his retirement.

April 18 – Reuben Gant reconsidered and signed a new contract with the Bills.

April 19 - Tony Greene signed a new contract with the Bills.

April 20 - Steve Moore was hired as a special assignments coordinator, completing Chuck Knox's coaching staff.

May 2 - The Bills, with the fifth pick in the first round, chose O.J. Simpson's replacement, running back Terry Miller from Oklahoma State. The Bills also selected defensive end Scott Hutchinson of

Florida with the second-round pick obtained in the O.J. Simpson trade, and wide receiver Danny Fulton of Nebraska-Omaha with the third-round choice from that trade. Other picks included North Carolina defensive end Dee Hardison (second), Georgia Tech linebacker Lucious Sanford (fourth) and center Will Grant from Kentucky (10th). Houston used the No.1 pick to choose Texas running back Earl Campbell. Other first-round picks included defensive end Art Still by Kansas City (second), wide receiver Wes Chandler by New Orleans (third), offensive tackle Chris Ward by the Jets (fourth), wide receiver James Lofton by Green Bay (sixth) and linebacker Clay Matthews by Cleveland (12th).

May 11 – Kicker Tom Dempsey, who holds the record for the longest field goal in league history of 63 yards, was signed.

May 20 – Mini-camp got off to a rousing start as first-round draft choice Terry Miller signed a series of one-year contracts, making him the richest rookie in team history. The deal was reportedly five years for about $1.2 million.

June 24 – The Bills decided to open up Buffalo Jills tryouts to single women and also lowered the required age from 21 to 18. At Rich Stadium, 127 women showed up for the tryout.

July 4 – The Rolling Stones played before the largest concert crowd in Rich Stadium history, more than 72,000. Other bands on the bill included April Wine, the Atlanta Rhythm Section and Journey.

July 10 – Training camp opened at Niagara University.

July 13 – Chuck Knox fired team physician Dr. Joseph Godfrey. Speculation centered on Godfrey's associate, Dr. Richard Weiss, as his replacement.

July 15 – Veterans reported to camp, but Reggie McKenzie and Mike Kadish didn't show up because of contract disputes.

July 22 – A crowd of about 5,000 turned out at Edinboro (Pa.) State College to watch the Bills beat Cleveland, 18-6, in a rookie scrimmage. Fourth-round pick Lucious Sanford starred.

July 30 – The Bills veterans saw action in a scrimmage against the Browns at Kent State before 21,507 fans. The game ended in a 6-6 tie as Terry Miller scored for Buffalo.

Aug. 3 – Reggie McKenzie reported to camp without a new contract and indicated that he would play out his option and test the market next year.

Aug. 5 – The Bills opened the preseason with a 28-20 loss at Detroit and Joe DeLamielleure suffered a knee injury.

Aug. 6 – Joe DeLamielleure's knee injury wasn't as serious as first expected. It was termed a sprain and he would only miss a few weeks.

Aug. 12 – Cleveland downed the Bills, 20-10, in the preseason home opener before only 23,241 at Rich Stadium as Joe Ferguson suffered a minor knee injury and John Holland suffered a season-ending knee injury. In Oakland, Jack Tatum's vicious tackle paralyzed New England wide receiver Darryl Stingley.

Aug. 13 – It was announced that only 18,084 season tickets were sold, the lowest number since 1963.

Aug. 15 – The Bills Booster Club presented the Bob Kalsu Memorial Plaque to the Pro Football Hall of Fame. Kalsu played for the Bills in 1968 and was the only NFL player killed in Vietnam. Tight end Paul Seymour was traded to Pittsburgh for wide receiver Frank Lewis.

Aug. 19 – In a driving rainstorm at Rich Stadium, Denver defeated the Bills, 23-13, in front of only 18,031 fans. On the bright side, Terry Miller rushed for 77 yards and two TDs.

Aug. 21 – Quarterback Bill Munson, 37, was acquired from San Diego for a future draft choice.

Aug. 24 – A number of Bills holdover veterans were cut including linebacker Bo Cornell and punter Marv Bateman.

Aug. 25 – The Steelers sent Paul Seymour back to the Bills, saying Buffalo wasn't completely honest when discussing the seriousness of his gout condition. Frank Lewis stayed with Buffalo while the teams worked out proper compensation. "I don't think Buffalo was shooting straight with Pittsburgh," Seymour said. "That's the way they operate. They probably used a little deceit."

Aug. 26 – The Bills concluded a winless preseason, losing 30-27 at Minnesota on Rick Danmeier's 43-yard field goal with three seconds left.

Aug. 28 – Dwight Harrison, who began his Bills career in 1972 and ranked fifth on the current team in length of service with the Bills, was traded to Baltimore for a draft choice. He became expendable because second-year pro Charlie Romes showed vast improvement and seven-year veteran Skip Thomas was acquired on waivers from Oakland.

Aug. 29 – Skip Thomas failed his physical and didn't join the Bills. But three Raiders did join the team as kicker Errol Mann, linebacker Randy McClanahan and wide receiver Mike Levenseller were acquired for past considerations. Kicker Tom Dempsey was cut, as was veteran linebacker John Skorupan.

Aug. 30 – Errol Mann refused to report to Buffalo, so the Bills released him and he re-signed with Oakland. The Bills were without a kicker because they had cut Tom Dempsey.

Aug. 31 – Tom Dempsey was re-signed.

Sept. 2 – Holdout Mike Kadish filed a grievance with the Management Council, charging the Bills with failing to bargain in good faith with him; It was announced that both Joe Ferguson and Joe DeLamielleure, out since early in the preseason with knee injuries, would play in the season opener against Pittsburgh.

Sept. 3 – The Bills fell behind, 21-0, to the Steelers and despite a rally sparked by newly-acquired Bill Munson, lost, 28-17, before 64,147 at Rich Stadium.

Sept. 10 – Tom Dempsey's missed extra point proved to be the difference as the Bills lost to the Jets, 21-20, at Rich Stadium.

Sept. 14 – It was revealed that Ralph Wilson turned down an offer from the Los Angeles Memorial Coliseum to move the Bills West. The Rams were planning to move to Anaheim in 1980, leaving the Coliseum vacant.

Sept. 17 – Miami tied a 32-year-old NFL record by beating the Bills for the 17th straight time, 31-24. They now shared the record for one-team domination with Green Bay which once won 17 straight over the Chicago Cardinals from 1937-46.

Sept. 18 – A player-owner relations committee ordered holdout defensive tackle Mike Kadish to report to the Bills.

Sept. 21 – Former Bills linebacker John Tracey died after a short illness in New Jersey. Mike Kadish reported to practice. "It's been a difficult time," he said. "I don't think I'll ever forget the experience. As far as I'm concerned, I'd do it over again, I feel that strongly about it."

Sept. 22 – Offensive tackle Ken Jones, who had been having a terrible time with holding penalties, switched his jersey number from 73 to 72.

Sept. 24 – Chuck Knox won his first game as Bills head coach as Buffalo topped Baltimore, 24-17. Curtis Brown tied a team record with a 102-yard kickoff return for a TD.

Oct. 1 – The Bills erupted for 21 points in a 7:03 span in the second quarter and defeated Marv Levy's Kansas City Chiefs, 28-13, at Rich Stadium.

Oct. 2 – Veteran linebacker Merv Krakau was waived to make room for Mike Kadish on the roster.

Oct. 8 – The two-game winning streak came to an end as the Jets romped past the Bills, 45-14, at Shea Stadium. Kevin Long rushed for 91 yards and three TDs.

Oct. 10 – Jim Braxton was traded to Washington for a future draft choice, and the Redskins then traded him to Miami for running back Benny Malone. "I was never given much of a chance to prove myself under Chuck Knox," Braxton said. "But at least he didn't make me spend the season on the bench. After all these years, it will be tough to leave my friends."

Oct. 15 – The Bills' record in domed stadiums dipped to 0-9 lifetime as Houston handed them a 17-10 defeat at the Astrodome despite an 82-yard punt return TD by Keith Moody.

Oct. 22 – In the second-lowest scoring game in team history, the Bills blanked Cincinnati, 5-0, at Rich Stadium as Tom Dempsey kicked a field goal and Lou Piccone and Curtis Brown trapped punt returner Dennis Law in the end zone for a safety for the only scoring.

Oct. 29 – Cleveland rushed for 309 yards, including 173 by Mike Pruitt, and routed the Bills' 41-20. The Browns totaled 532 yards of offense.

Nov. 5 – Chuck Knox was criticized for a conservative game plan in the Bills 14-10 loss to New England at Rich Stadium.

Nov. 12 – Miami set an NFL record by beating the

Bills for the 18th straight time, but it took a little help from the officials. The Dolphins' 25-24 victory at Rich Stadium was tainted as the Bills were called for 116 yards in penalties, many very questionable. Bills owner Ralph Wilson erupted after the game. "I'm fed up. I'd be embarrassed if I was the head of the officiating crew. The officials stole this game from us. It was disgusting. Pete Rozelle can try to fine me, but I won't pay any fine. He can sue me if he wants, let the league try to sue me."

Nov. 13 – The frustration of the Miami loss spilled over to the next day. "It doesn't eat at me that we lose to Miami, it's the way it came about," Reggie McKenzie said. "Thursday, I imagine the league will call Chuck saying that Roland caught the ball – it was a bad call – a lot of good it's going to do then. But that's show business. We make mistakes, but every time I turn around there's a flag thrown out there."

Nov. 14 – Ralph Wilson issued an apology for storming into the officials dressing room after Sunday's loss to Miami. "I regret the incident in the officials room," he said. "I am willing to admit I was wrong for going in there if they are willing to admit they made an erroneous call on the pass play near the end of the game that very likely cost us the game."

Nov. 17 – It was announced that the league would fine Ralph Wilson $5,000 for his inflammatory remarks. And after saying he wouldn't pay any fine, Wilson relented and said it was more important to "maintain the authority of the commissioner and the integrity of the game than carry the issue any further."

Nov. 19 – The Bills sank to a new low, losing at Tampa Bay, 31-10, the most lopsided Buccaneers victory in the team's brief history.

Nov. 26 – Terry Miller set a Bills rookie rushing record by piling up 208 yards as the Bills ripped the Giants, 41-17, in the home finale at Rich Stadium. Miller's total was the third-best ever by an NFL rookie. Roland Hooks added 115 yards as the Bills

set a team record with 366 yards on the ground.

Nov. 30 – Frustrated because the Bills hadn't cooperated in contract negotiations, Reggie McKenzie said he no longer wished to play in Buffalo once his present contract expired at the end of the year. "I consider myself an optimistic guy and I thought something might get settled. They didn't call me or my lawyer and I don't want them to call now," McKenzie said. "Let me get out. They couldn't settle this six months ago, what makes you think they'll settle it in January?"

Dec. 3 – Kansas City atoned for an earlier loss to Buffalo with a 14-10 victory at Arrowhead Stadium, Marv Levy's fourth win against 10 losses in his rookie season as an NFL coach.

Dec. 10 – New England clinched the AFC East title with a thrilling, come-from-behind 26-24 victory over the Bills at snowy Schaefer Stadium. David Posey kicked a 21-yard field goal with eight seconds left to seal the win.

Dec. 11 – It was announced that offensive tackle Joe Devlin suffered a knee injury against the Patriots and would undergo surgery. Because Cincinnati upset Los Angeles, it assured San Francisco of possessing the worst record in the league and the No. 1 pick in the draft. However, that pick was Buffalo's property thanks to the O.J. Simpson trade.

Dec. 14 – Joe DeLamielleure was selected to the Pro Bowl for the fourth straight year.

Dec. 15 – The Bills selected Curtis Brown as the team's most valuable player.

Dec. 16 – Billy Ehrmann, the brother of Colts defensive tackle Joe Ehrmann, died of a blood disease in a hospital in Baltimore. Both brothers grew up in Buffalo and attended Riverside High School. Joe Ehrmann obviously was excused from the season finale against the Bills.

Dec. 17 – The Bills closed their season with a 24-17 victory at Baltimore as Terry Miller rushed for 123 yards and managed to top 1,000 yards for the season. With the win, the Bills finished at 5-11, as did the Colts, but because of their two-game sweep, the Bills wound up fourth in the AFC East, thus did not receive the easier last-place schedule for 1979.

Dec. 24 – Houston defeated Miami, 17-9, and Atlanta topped Philadelphia, 14-13, in the first wild-card playoff games in league history.

Dec. 30 – Dallas rallied in the second half to knock off Atlanta, 27-20, and Pittsburgh routed Denver, 33-10, in divisional round playoff games.

Dec. 31 – Los Angeles crushed Minnesota, 34-10, while Houston upended New England, 31-14, in the other two divisional playoff games.

Jan. 7, 1979 – Houston turned the ball over nine times and got crushed by Pittsburgh, 34-5, in the AFC Championship Game. Los Angeles turned the ball over seven times and managed only 177 total yards in losing to Dallas, 28-0, in the NFC Championship Game.

Jan. 21, 1979 – In one of the finest Super Bowls ever played, Pittsburgh won its third NFL championship, 35-31, over the Cowboys in front of 78,656 fans at the Orange Bowl. MVP Terry Bradshaw passed for 318 yards and four TDs. Lynn Swann caught seven for 124 yards and a TD and John Stallworth caught three for 115 yards and two TDs.

Jan. 29, 1979 – Roger Staubach threw for 125 yards and the game-winning TD as the NFC beat the AFC in the Pro Bowl, 13-7, at the Los Angeles Coliseum.

By the Numbers - 1978

TEAM STATISTICS	BILLS	OPP
First downs	274	305
Rushing	132	171
Passing	113	104
Penalty	29	30
Total yards	4,630	5,188
Avg. game	289.4	324.3
Plays	974	1,016
Avg. play	4.8	5.1
Net rushing yds	2,381	3,228
Avg. game	148.8	201.8
Avg. play	4.3	4.8
Net passing yds	2,249	1,960
Comp/att	203/388	167/317
Sacks/lost	30-254	22-196
Interceptions	17	14
Percentage	52.3	52.7
Punts/avg	89-37.9	71-36.5
Fumbles/lost	34-17	27-16
Penalties/yds	120-1,103	98-941
Touchdowns	39	46
Extra points	36-39	43-46
Field goals	10-13	11-21
Safeties	1	1
Kick ret./avg	66-19.9	58-20.5
Punt ret./avg	40-9.4	48-9.2

RUSHING	ATT	YDS	AVG	TD
Miller	238	1060	4.5	7
Brown	128	591	4.6	4
Hooks	76	358	4.7	2
D. Johnson	55	222	4.0	2
Ferguson	27	76	2.8	0
Braxton	30	73	2.4	0
Gant	1	14	14.0	0
Jackson	1	-13	-13.0	0
TOTALS	**556**	**2381**	**4.3**	**15**

PASSING	COMP	ATT	INT	YDS	TD	COMP%	SACKS	RATE
Ferguson	175	330	15	2136	16	53.0	29-243	70.5
Munson	24	43	2	328	4	55.8	0-0	91.8
Mays	4	15	0	39	1	26.7	1-11	61.9
TOTALS	**203**	**388**	**17**	**2503**	**21**	**52.3**	**30-254**	**72.2**

KICKING	1-19	20-29	30-39	40-49	50+	TOT	PAT	PTS
Dempsey`	0-0	5-5	4-5	1-3	0-0	10-13	36-39	66

PUNTING	NO	AVG	LG	In 20	BL
Jackson	87	38.8	70	19	2
TOTALS	**89**	**37.9**	**70**	**19**	**2**

RECEIVING	CAT	YDS	AVG	TD
Chandler	44	581	13.2	5
Lewis	41	735	17.9	7
Gant	34	408	12.0	5
Miller	22	246	11.2	0
Brown	18	130	7.2	0
Hooks	15	110	7.3	1
D. Johnson	10	83	8.3	0
Piccone	7	71	10.1	2
Braxton	5	38	7.6	0
Walton	4	66	16.5	1
Willis	2	41	20.5	0
Ferguson	1	-6	-6.0	0
TOTALS	**203**	**2503**	**12.3**	**21**

LEADERS

Kick returns: Brown 17-428 yards, 25.2 avg, 1 TD
Moody 18-371, 20.6, 0 TD

Punt returns: Moody 19-240, 12.6, 1 TD
Piccone 14-88, 6.3, 0 TD

Interceptions: Clark 5-29, 5.8, 0 TD
Nelson 3-69, 23.0, 0 TD
Greene 3-56, 18.7, 0 TD

SCORE BY QUARTERS

BILLS	41	96	43	122	0 -	302
OPP	69	118	89	78	0 -	354

Frank Lewis (left) came to the Bills from the Pittsburgh Steelers in 1978 and led the team in receiving yards (735) and touchdowns (7).

Joe DeLamielleure (opposite page) made his third Pro Bowl appearance in 1978 and established himself as one of the best offensive guards in the NFL.

Steelers	0	14	0	14	-	28
Bills	0	0	0	17	-	17

Attendance at Rich Stadium - 64,147

Pit: Stallworth 28 pass from Bradshaw (Gerela kick), 5:55
Pit: Harris 1 run (Gerela kick), 11:10
Pit: Thornton 2 run (Gerela kick), :48
Buf: Lewis 22 pass from Munson (Dempsey kick), 4:20
Buf: FG Dempsey 32, 8:08
Pit: Bell 15 pass from Bradshaw (Gerela kick), 13:04
Buf: Gant 3 pass from Munson (Dempsey kick), 14:24

	BUF	PIT
First downs	16	21
Rushing yds	100	142
Passing yds	164	217
Punts-avg	6-43.0	4-39.0
Fumbles-lost	0-0	0-0
Penalties-yds	9-62	5-54

BILLS LEADERS: Rushing - Miller 20-60, Braxton 7-9, D. Johnson 2-31; **Passing** - Ferguson 3-10-1 - 20, Munson 10-16-0 - 171; **Receiving** - Miller 6-97, Gant 3-31, Lewis 2-46, Johnson 1-9, Braxton 1-8.

STEELERS LEADERS: Rushing - Harris 27-96, Bleier 6-19, Thornton 7-33, Bradshaw 2- (-4), Moser 1- (-2); **Passing** - Bradshaw 14-19-1 - 217; **Receiving** - Stallworth 3-86, Cunningham 3-70, Harris 3-32, Swann 3-11, Bleier 1-3, Bell 1-15.

NOTES

• The Bills fell behind 21-0, then rallied behind Bill Munson, only to fall short in the season opener.
• Joe Ferguson, out the previous three weeks due to a knee injury, failed to move the team and heard resounding boos and chants of "We Want Munson" and Chuck Knox responded.
• Ferguson's only interception, by Tony Dungy at the Steelers 35, led to the first score. Terry Bradshaw hit John Stallworth, who beat Charlie Romes, for the score on a second-and-14 play.
• A little more than five minutes later, the Steelers capped a 72-yard drive when Franco Harris scored after Stallworth made a 38-yard reception and Lynn Swann a 12-yarder to the 1.
• Jim Braxton was stopped on fourth-and-one at the Steelers 45 late in the third and Pittsburgh marched 55 yards. Sidney Thornton's TD early in the fourth gave the Steelers a 21-0 lead.
• Munson entered, threw an 18-yard pass to Terry Miller on his first play, and later audibled at the line and fired a 22-yard TD pass to ex-Steeler Frank Lewis. Following a punt, Munson drove the Bills to Tom Dempsey's 32-yard field goal.
• But the Steelers iced the game with a nine-play, 73-

WEEK 1 GAMES	
NYG 19, TB 13	Chi 17, St.L 10
SD 24, Sea 20	NO 31, Minn 24
Den 14, Oak 6	Wash 16, NE 14
KC 24, Cinc 23	GB 13, Det 7
NYJ 33, Mia 20	LA 16, Phil 14
Clev 24, SF 7	Atl 20, Hou 14
Dal 38, Balt 0	

yard drive, the key play a 27-yard Bradshaw to Bennie Cunningham pass. Cunningham had caught two passes for 43 yards on the previous scoring drive.

QUOTES

• Joe Ferguson: "How can you help but hear it (the boos). It didn't bother me, especially after last year. The fans are hungry for a win, they can do what they want. I don't have any excuses. What bothers me is we didn't move the ball. If we can win with Bill in there, that's fine with me. I don't doubt my ability. I can throw the ball as well as anyone in the league."
• Chuck Knox: "We'll face next week when it gets here. Joe Ferguson is still our No. 1 quarterback. Much of Joe's problem was that our running game wasn't moving. And let's face it, the Steelers are a great team."
• Tony Greene: "Nothing against Munson, but it's easy to come in when they have the prevent defenses on. Before the game, nobody was saying 'Why isn't Munson starting?'"
• Reggie McKenzie: "Fergy can be a winner, he showed that during the 9-5 seasons. Hey, the man had less than a week to get ready."
• Steelers linebacker Jack Lambert: "Ferguson is a darn good quarterback. When Munson came in, all he had to do was throw to his backs because we were dropping so deep."
• Steelers quarterback Terry Bradshaw: "They shouldn't have started Joe. He hadn't played. I just don't want to see Joe get down. In pro football you've got to be consistent every week, every year, and that's impossible. My advice for him would be to relax, concentrate and block everything else out."

Jets	0	7	7	7	-	21
Bills	0	7	0	13	-	20

Attendance at Rich Stadium - 40,985

Buf: Romes 85 interception return (Dempsey kick), 2:29
NYJ: Barkum 14 pass from Todd (Leahy kick), 13:58
NYJ: Gaffney 36 pass from Todd (Leahy kick), 5:48
Buf: Gant 11 pass from Ferguson (kick failed), :06
Buf: Walton 32 pass from Ferguson (Dempsey kick), 7:26
NYJ: Barkum 3 pass from Todd (Leahy kick), 14:10

	BUF	NYJ
First downs	17	18
Rushing yds	101	117
Passing yds	213	171
Punts-avg	9-32.9	7-31.1
Fumbles-lost	1-0	0-0
Penalties-yds	9-76	4-40

BILLS LEADERS: Rushing - Miller 16-71, Braxton 1-3, D. Johnson 7-35, Ferguson 1- (-8); **Passing** - Ferguson 20-32-1 - 222; **Receiving** - Gant 6-100, Miller 3-18, Johnson 5-28, Lewis 2-10, Walton 2-39, Willis 1-18, Piccone 1-9.

JETS LEADERS: Rushing - Dierking 12-23, Long 14-75, Gaines 3-6, Harper 5-23, Todd 5- (-10); **Passing** - Todd 14-26-2 - 196; **Receiving** - Gaffney 5-108, Walker 2-38, Dierking 2-16, Harper 2-16, Barkum 2-17, Long 1-1.

NOTES

• The Bills fell to 0-2 under Chuck Knox as Tom Dempsey's missed conversion proved to be the difference. Richard Todd shook off a poor game to drive the Jets 77 yards in 11 plays to the winning TD, a three-yard pass to Jerome Barkum with 50 seconds left. Pat Leahy then kicked the PAT.
• The winning drive began with 5:01 remaining and almost never got started as Scott Dierking fumbled on the first play, but managed to recover. Sherman White then sacked Todd for an 11-yard loss, but on third-and-23, Todd hit Wesley Walker for 20, then Dierking made a first down pass reception on fourth-and-three. Later, Walker and Derrick Gaffney made key receptions.
• Charlie Romes opened the scoring when he picked off a Todd pass and raced 85 yards for a TD, the third-longest interception TD return in team history.
• The Jets tied the game when Doug Jones and Mario Clark collided in the end zone, leaving Barkum wide open for a 14-yard TD pass. The drive began after Rusty Jackson's shanked 19-yard punt.
• In the third, with the Jets at the Bills 26, Knox accepted a holding penalty rather than let Leahy attempt a 43-yard field goal, and the move backfired when Todd hit Gaffney for a TD.

WEEK 2 GAMES	
Oak 21, SD 20	Det 15, TB 7
LA 10, Atl 0	Wash 35, Phil 30
GB 28, NO 17	NE 16, St.L 6
Dal 34, NYG 24	Pitt 21, Sea 10
Chi 16, SF 13	Mia 42, Balt 0
Hou 20, KC 17	Min 12, Den 9 (OT)
Clev 13, Cinc 10 (OT)	

• Ferguson drove the Bills 62 yards to Reuben Gant's TD, but Dempsey hit the right upright on the PAT.
• The Bills went ahead with a 92-yard drive capped by Larry Walton's TD reception.

QUOTES

• Tom Dempsey: "I just plain pushed it. No one feels worse than I do. You find the most disappointed fan and multiply it by a thousand times and that's how bad I feel. I let the whole team down."
• Chuck Knox: "We had some calls made by officials who weren't sure what was going on at times. We had some bad bounces, some bad mistakes and failed to capitalize on breaks we got. Ultimately we didn't do enough to win and that leaves me with an empty feeling."
• Joe Ferguson: "After what we've been through the last two years, the people who have been here are going to have to keep their heads up and show leadership. I am worried about the attitude, but we've got the opportunity to see if we're going to be better. A win would have really picked us up. I threw it better than I did last week, but I still made mistakes."
• Jets coach Walt Michaels: "Is there anybody in this room who believes we weren't lucky? The Bills did things today that we did last year, dropping balls, having things happen that you can't explain (like four holding penalties on Ken Jones)."
• Jets tight end Jerome Barkum: "We haven't come back to win like that too much during my career. And I know how the Bills are feeling. We've had days like this. We didn't play too well, but things fell our way during that last drive."

STANDINGS: SECOND WEEK

AFC EAST	W	L	T	CENTRAL	W	L	T	WEST	W	L	T	NFC EAST	W	L	T	CENTRAL	W	L	T	WEST	W	L	T
NY Jets	2	0	0	Pittsburgh	2	0	0	Denver	1	1	0	Dallas	2	0	0	Green Bay	2	0	0	LA Rams	2	0	0
Miami	1	1	0	Cleveland	2	0	0	Kan. City	1	1	0	Washington	2	0	0	Chicago	2	0	0	Atlanta	1	1	0
New England	1	1	0	Houston	1	1	0	San Diego	1	1	0	NY Giants	1	1	0	Minnesota	1	1	0	N.Orleans	1	1	0
Buffalo	0	2	0	Cincinnati	0	2	0	Oakland	1	1	0	St. Louis	0	2	0	Detroit	1	1	0	San Fran	0	2	0
Baltimore	0	2	0					Seattle	0	2	0	Philadelphia	0	2	0	Tampa Bay	0	2	0				

GAME 3 - Sunday, Sept. 17, 1978 - DOLPHINS 31, BILLS 24

NOTES

• The Bills lost to Miami for the 17th straight time, tying an NFL record for most consecutive losses to one team. The Chicago Cardinals lost 17 in a row to Green Bay from 1937-46.
• Miami pounded out 275 rushing yards including 125 by Delvin Williams, who was dealt to Miami by San Francisco when the 49ers acquired O.J. Simpson.
• The Bills trailed 24-17 with 10:30 left and had the ball, but failed to make a first down and punted. The Dolphins then went 78 yards on nine running plays to score the clinching TD.
• Terry Miller and Joe DeLamielleure each missed the second half with injuries.
• A bad snap by Willie Parker sent punter Rusty Jackson scurrying back to his own 7 and he managed a 19-yard punt. Miami took advantage as Leroy Harris scored six plays later to open the scoring.
• Don Strock fumbled a snap and Phil Dokes recovered at the Miami 42 and Buffalo tied the game on Miller's one-yard run. Joe Ferguson hit Frank Lewis twice for 23 and 12 yards.
• Nat Moore's 37-yard catch keyed a 76-yard drive that made it 14-7 at the half.
• After an exchange of field goals, Gary Davis broke a 65-yard TD run.
• Ferguson then threw the longest TD pass of his career, a 92-yarder to Lewis, who beat Norris Thomas with a stop-and-go move. But Miami answered with Williams' 18-yard TD.

QUOTES

• Chuck Knox: "No excuses, no jinxes, no heat, we just got beat. I don't call a bad snap over the punter's head a jinx, or poor tackling and blocking a jinx. Miami's a fine football team, a Super Bowl contender."
• Sherman White on Miami's clinching TD drive: "Maybe it's a sign of immaturity. But we're young and we're getting better."
• Miami quarterback Don Strock on the drive: "It was a good old-fashioned Dolphin drive. We were getting five and six yards a play. It's amazing the ability we have in the backfield. The line is blowing open holes. I can hit holes like that, even with my blazing speed."
• Miami running back Delvin Williams: "That was the best drive we put together all day. We needed the points and we took it right at them. We were getting a lot of one-on-one situations, there wasn't a lot of gang tackling by them. It was a matter of shaking one guy. My TD was the exact same play that Gary Davis scored on."
• Frank Lewis on his TD: "The play was something we had discussed on the sidelines. It looked like they were giving us that pattern, the hook and go. I make a hook move to freeze the defensive back, then try to run by him. It was the longest play I've ever been involved in."

Bills	0	7	3	14	-	24
Dolphins	7	7	10	7	-	31

Attendance at the Orange Bowl - 48,373

Mia: L. Harris 4 run (Yepremian kick), 13:35
Buf: Miller 1 run (Dempsey kick), 8:46
Mia: Tillman 6 pass from Strock (Yepremian kick), 13:06
Mia: FG Yepremian 49, 6:47
Buf: FG Dempsey 46, 9:01
Mia: Davis 65 run (Yepremian kick), 10:38
Buf: Lewis 92 pass from Ferguson (Dempsey kick), 2:33
Mia: Williams 18 run (Yepremian kick), 11:02
Buf: Hooks 4 pass from Ferguson (Dempsey kick), 13:44

	BUF	MIA
First downs	17	17
Rushing yds	128	275
Passing yds	221	88
Punts-avg	6-30.0	4-46.5
Fumbles-lost	1-1	4-1
Penalties-yds	5-47	4-25

BILLS LEADERS: Rushing - Miller 14-44, Braxton 11-32, Hooks 6-35, Johnson 2-6, Ferguson 3-11; **Passing** - Ferguson 14-24-0 - 245; **Receiving** - Walton 1-8, Lewis 5-153, Braxton 4-30, Gant 2-44, Hooks 1-4, Johnson 1-6.

DOLPHINS LEADERS: Rushing - Williams 24-125, L. Harris 8-31, Davis 3-89, Bulaich 7-32, Strock 3- (-4), Moore 1-2; **Passing** - Strock 7-14-0 - 97; **Receiving** - Tillman 2-15, D. Harris 2-18, Moore 3-64.

WEEK 3 GAMES	
LA 27, Dal 14	Phil 24, NO 17
Oak 28, GB 3	Chi 19, Det 0
TB 16, Minn 10	Clev 24, Atl 16
Hou 20, SF 19	Sea 24, NYJ 17
Wash 28, St.L 10	Pitt 28, Cinc 3
Den 27, SD 14	NYG 26, KC 10
Balt 34, NE 27	

GAME 4 - Sunday, Sept. 24, 1978 - BILLS 24, COLTS 17

NOTES

• Curtis Brown tied a team record with a 102-yard kickoff return for a TD to spark the Bills to their first victory under Chuck Knox.
• The Bills enjoyed great field position in the first quarter, starting drives at the Colts 45 and 48 and their own 47. Tom Dempsey wasted the first chance by missing a 41-yard field goal, but the Bills scored two TDs after that.
• The first score was helped by Keith Moody's 12-yard punt return and a 15-yard unsportsmanlike penalty on Wade Griffin. Reuben Gant's 19-yard TD capped a quick 45-yard march, the key being Terry Miller's blitz pick up on the play. On the next series, the Bills went 53 yards. Ferguson scrambled out of the pocket and found Frank Lewis behind Bruce Laird for a TD.
• The Colts tied the game in the second quarter as Roosevelt Leaks caught a TD pass from Bill Troup, playing QB for the injured Bert Jones. Then, Don Hardemann blocked a Rusty Jackson punt and Reese McCall returned it five yards for the TD.
• But the Bills answered with Brown's explosive return, breaking a tackle by McCall along the way.
• The defense forced a punt and the Bills got the ball back with 1:41 left. Ferguson hit Lewis for 34 yards to help set up Dempsey's 21-yard field goal.
• The Colts gained 214 yards in the second half but managed only Toni Linhart's field goal.

QUOTES

• Curtis Brown: "I don't know who the guy was who hit me (McCall) but he tried to take me down with a rolling block instead of getting his arms around me. I bounced outside and saw nothing but clear field. We won and it felt good, and we're going to win a lot more."
• Ben Williams: "They moved the ball pretty well on us, but we came up with the big plays. They made a couple of big runs, but we came back to stop them. That's the mark of a good team."
• Chuck Knox: "It's nice to win, there's no substitute for that, but this one was particularly satisfying. I wanted it for the players. They needed to know the satisfaction of winning."
• Joe Ferguson: "Instead of standing on the sidelines thinking 'Geez, how are we gonna blow this one?' we're thinking about what we can do to win. That's learning how to win and that's important. It looks like it's going to be a weird year. We're right back in the thick of it."
• Colts coach Ted Marchibroda: "The change in the Bills is very obvious. In the past they'd plain beat themselves. They had plenty of chances to do it again today, but they didn't. With all that young talent, they're going to have to be reckoned with as the season wears on."

Colts	0	14	3	0	-	17
Bills	14	10	0	0	-	24

Attendance at Rich Stadium - 55,270

Buf: Gant 19 pass from Ferguson (Dempsey kick), 9:20
Buf: Lewis 29 pass from Ferguson (Dempsey kick), 13:37
Bal: Leaks 17 pass from Troup (Linhart kick), 6:53
Bal: McCall 5 blocked punt return (Linhart kick), 11:59
Buf: Brown 102 kickoff return (Dempsey kick), 12:19
Buf: FG Dempsey 21, 14:57
Bal: FG Linhart 21, 14:53

	BUF	BAL
First downs	12	16
Rushing yds	129	182
Passing yds	118	125
Punts-avg	8-33.9	7-35.1
Fumbles-lost	2-1	1-0
Penalties-yds	5-51	6-60

BILLS LEADERS: Rushing - Miller 25-97, Braxton 9-24, Johnson 1- (-3), Ferguson 6-11; **Passing** - Ferguson 9-14-0 - 154; **Receiving** - Gant 2-31, Walton 1-19, Willis 1-23, Lewis 2-62, Chandler 1-6, Johnson 1-11, Miller 1-2.

COLTS LEADERS: Rushing - R. Lee 14-54, Leaks 1-9, Washington 12-80, Troup 5-17, Hardeman 3-22; **Passing** - Troup 10-27-3 - 134; **Receiving** - Alston 4-49, Leaks 2-28, Washington 2-25, Doughty 1-20, Carr 1-12.

WEEK 4 GAMES	
NO 20, Cinc 18	LA 10, Hou 6
Phil 17, Mia 3	TB 14, Atl 9
Wash 23, NYJ 3	GB 24, SD 3
Sea 28, Det 16	NYG 27, SF 10
Den 23, KC 17 (OT)	NE 21, Oak 14
Dal 21, St.L 12	Min 24, Chi 10
Pitt 15, Clev 9 (OT)	

STANDINGS: FOURTH WEEK

AFC EAST	W	L	T	CENTRAL	W	L	T	WEST	W	L	T	NFC EAST	W	L	T	CENTRAL	W	L	T	WEST	W	L	T
NY Jets	2	2	0	Pittsburgh	4	0	0	Denver	3	1	0	Washington	4	0	0	Chicago	3	1	0	LA Rams	4	0	0
Miami	2	2	0	Cleveland	3	1	0	Oakland	2	2	0	Dallas	3	1	0	Green Bay	3	1	0	N.Orleans	2	2	0
New England	2	2	0	Houston	2	2	0	Seattle	2	2	0	NY Giants	3	1	0	Minnesota	2	2	0	Atlanta	1	3	0
Baltimore	1	3	0	Cincinnati	0	4	0	Kan. City	1	3	0	Philadelphia	2	2	0	Tampa Bay	2	2	0	San Fran	0	4	0
Buffalo	1	3	0					San Diego	1	3	0	St. Louis	0	4	0	Detroit	1	3	0				

GAME 5 - Sunday, Oct. 1, 1978 - BILLS 28, CHIEFS 13

Chiefs	6	0 0 7	-	13
Bills	0	21 7 0	-	28

Attendance at Rich Stadium - 47,310

KC: FG Stenerud 42, 8:41
KC: FG Stenerud 27, 13:40
Buf: Chandler 20 pass from Ferguson (Dempsey kick), 7:08
Buf: Miller 8 run (Dempsey kick), 12:40
Buf: Chandler 22 pass from Ferguson (Dempsey kick), 14:11
Buf: Brown 22 run (Dempsey kick), 10:10
KC: McKnight 41 run (Stenerud kick), 8:44

	BUF	KC
First downs	17	15
Rushing yds	117	238
Passing yds	176	70
Punts-avg	5-41.6	5-37.8
Fumbles-lost	3-2	2-2
Penalties-yds	6-72	4-63

BILLS LEADERS: Rushing - Miller 18-67, Braxton 2-5, Brown 11-43, Hooks 6-11, Johnson 1-(-6), Ferguson 1- (-3); **Passing** - Ferguson 15-18-1 - 210; **Receiving** - Chandler 7-116, Gant 2-14, Lewis 4-74, Miller 1-3, Hooks 1-3.

CHIEFS LEADERS: Rushing - McKnight 7-56, Lane 17-144, Reed 9-29, Livingston 2-7, Morgado 2-7, Marshall 1- (-5); **Passing** - Livingston 2-9-0 - 3, Adams 7-12-0 - 80; **Receiving** - Lane 3-11, White 5-60, Belton 1-12.

NOTES

• The Bills scored three TDs during a 7:03 span of the second quarter and upended Marv Levy's Wing-T Chiefs.
• The Chiefs took a 6-0 first-quarter lead on a pair of Jan Stenerud field goals, the first of which was set up by Dennis Johnson's fumble at the Bills 25.
• Keith Moody's 28-yard punt return to the Chiefs 40 sparked Buffalo's first TD drive. Joe Ferguson completed all four of his passes, two on third down to Bob Chandler. He then hit Chandler for the TD.
• Moody's 22-yard punt return set up the Bills at their own 34 on the next series. Ferguson hit a wide-open Chandler on the right sideline for 44 yards. Two plays later, Terry Miller scored.
• After another punt, the Bills went 63 yards in three plays to Chandler's second TD. The key play was a 46-yard interference penalty on Gary Barbaro to the Chiefs 22. Chandler scored on the next play.
• Ferguson was 11 of 12 for 150 yards in the first half with Chandler catching seven for 116 yards.
• Ferguson set a single-game team record for completion

WEEK 5 GAMES

Mia 24, St.L 10	NE 28, SD 23
Pitt 28, NYJ 17	SF 28, Cin 12
Phil 17, Balt 14	GB 35, Det 14
Atl 23, NYG 20	LA 26, NO 20
Minn 24, TB 7	Den 28, Sea 7
Hou 16, Clev 13	Wash 9, Dal 5
Oak 25, Chi 19 (OT)	

percentage at 83.3 percent.
• A 43-yard pass to Frank Lewis led to Curtis Brown's 22-yard TD run in third quarter.

QUOTES

• Reggie McKenzie: "We've been trying to get some consistency in our running game, but right now, the weapon is the J-Bomb (Ferguson) and we've got to use it. It's his maturity, and look at the receivers we have."
• Joe Ferguson: "This one could have been my best game ever. It was just a matter of taking advantage of what was there. Everything we threw deep was set up by something else before. And you can do things like that when you have receivers like Chandler, Lewis and Gant. I really feel we can win with this offense. And once we get the running game going, this offense is really going to be great. It's a crime he (Chandler) hasn't been to the Pro Bowl; he's as good as anyone in the league."
• Bob Chandler: "I wanted to do something for the coaching staff because it's the best one I've ever had. That's what made this performance gratifying. It's been frustrating (his nagging knee injury) because I hate not to play. I've been kind of a load for four weeks. I had to start earning my salary."
• Chiefs coach Marv Levy: "Let's face it, our offense isn't geared to coming back. And we didn't play well in any area. Buffalo was very well-prepared for us and getting a lead was the best defense they could have had. It (trouble with Bills passing) was a lack of pass rush as much as it was the coverage."

GAME 6 - Sunday, Oct. 8, 1978 - JETS 45, BILLS 14

Bills	7	0 0 7	-	14
Jets	14	21 10 0	-	45

Attendance at Shea Stadium - 44,545

NYJ: Long 5 run (Leahy kick), 7:04
NYJ: Owens 40 interception return (Leahy kick), 9:38
Buf: Gant 16 pass from Ferguson (Dempsey kick), 11:40
NYJ: Long 16 run (Leahy kick), 3:49
NYJ: Long 3 run (Leahy kick), 4:45
NYJ: Harper 82 punt return (Leahy kick), 13:52
NYJ: Gaffney 18 pass from Robinson (Leahy kick), 3:59
NYJ: FG Leahy 36, 8:47
Buf: Chandler 15 pass from Munson (Dempsey kick), 14:32

	BUF	NYJ
First downs	16	18
Rushing yds	137	231
Passing yds	185	47
Punts-avg	5-29.0	4-35.5
Fumbles-lost	2-2	2-1
Penalties-yds	10-78	6-35

BILLS LEADERS: Rushing - Miller 12-39, Johnson 11-59, Brown 7-22, Hooks 5-17; **Passing** - Ferguson 10-24-2 - 140, Munson 2-4-0 - 45; **Receiving** - Miller 4-94, Chandler 1-15, Gant 2-23, Lewis 1-29, Brown 2-13, Hooks 2-11.

JETS LEADERS: Rushing - Long 13-91, Dierking 11-50, Powell 6-31, Gaines 4-18, Harper 3-16, Robinson 3-11, Newton 4-13, Gaffney 1-1; **Passing** - Robinson 4-9-0 - 66, Ryan 0-1-1 - 0; **Receiving** - Barkum 2-41, Gaffney 1-18, Walker 1-7.

WEEK 6 GAMES

SD 23, Den 0	Pitt 31, Atl 7
Dal 24, NYG 3	Balt 30, St.L 17
GB 24, Chi 14	NE 24, Phil 14
Oak 21, Hou 17	Wash 21, Det 19
TB 30, KC 13	LA 27, SF 10
Clev 24, NO 16	Sea 29, Minn 28
Mia 21, Cinc 0	

NOTES

• The Bills turned in a terrible effort with four turnovers and 10 penalties.
• The Jets had minus three yards net passing at halftime yet led, 35-7.
• New York scored on its first possession, then made it 14-0 when Burgess Owens stepped in front of Bob Chandler over the middle and intercepted a Joe Ferguson pass and went 40 yards for a TD.
• Ferguson's 52-yard pass to Terry Miller set up his 16-yard TD toss to Reuben Gant, but then the Jets opened the floodgates in the second quarter and the Bills' mistakes played a key role.
• Larry Keller blocked a Rusty Jackson punt and recovered it at the Bills 30. Three plays later, Kevin Long scored the second of his three TDs. Curtis Brown fumbled the ensuing kickoff and the Jets recovered at the 18. Long scored two plays later. Late in the quarter, Bruce Harper returned a punt 82 yards, the second-longest in Jets history, for a TD and a 35-7 lead.
• New York marched 72 yards to Matt Robinson's TD pass to Derrick Gaffney on its first possession of the second half, ending any hopes of a miracle comeback.
• Jim Braxton spent the day on the bench and Dennis Johnson played fullback.
• The loss was the most lopsided of Knox's six-year head coaching career.
• Lucious Sanford was in on 10 tackles and had two sacks.

QUOTES

• Chuck Knox: "It was just a good, old-fashioned butt-kicking. All I can attribute it to is a complete collapse in every area. We made every mistake there was and that was the poorest exhibition of tackling I've seen in a long time. When you have a young team, you have to expect setbacks along the way. What we have to do is not let one week waste all that work."
• Jets coach Walt Michaels: "What you saw was an

exhibition of aggressive football. It was the kind of football I like to play. I don't mean to belittle Buffalo or anything they did because I'm sure they came prepared to play, but when you play the game aggressively on offense and defense, things will usually go well for you. The team that played aggressively wore green and white."
• Reggie McKenzie: "Man, it was like so many of the beatings we were taking the last two years. The Jets got us down and kept us there. I thought those beatings were behind us."
• Lucious Sanford: "We were ready to play. This was going to be the game that would really start turning our season around."

STANDINGS: SIXTH WEEK

AFC EAST	W	L	T	CENTRAL	W	L	T	WEST	W	L	T	NFC EAST	W	L	T	CENTRAL	W	L	T	WEST	W	L	T
New England	4	2	0	Pittsburgh	6	0	0	Denver	4	2	0	Washington	6	0	0	Green Bay	5	1	0	LA Rams	6	0	0
Miami	4	2	0	Cleveland	4	2	0	Oakland	4	2	0	Dallas	4	2	0	Chicago	3	3	0	N.Orleans	2	4	0
NY Jets	3	3	0	Houston	3	3	0	Seattle	3	3	0	NY Giants	3	3	0	Minnesota	3	3	0	Atlanta	2	4	0
Buffalo	2	4	0	Cincinnati	0	6	0	San Diego	2	4	0	Philadelphia	3	3	0	Tampa Bay	3	3	0	San Fran	1	5	0
Baltimore	2	4	0					Kan. City	1	5	0	St. Louis	0	6	0	Detroit	1	5	0				

GAME 7 - Sunday, Oct. 15, 1978 - OILERS 17, BILLS 10

NOTES
• The Bills' record in domed stadiums fell to 0-9 all-time and their losing streak reached 10 games against Houston. They last beat the Oilers in 1966, when they did it twice.
• Earl Campbell won the battle of the first-round rookie running backs, outgaining Terry Miller, 105-56.
• Curtis Brown fumbled on the first play of the game and Gregg Bingham recovered at the 8. Three plays later, Dan Pastorini threw a TD pass to Rich Caster.
• The Bills drove 77 yards in 14 plays to Tom Dempsey's field goal late in the first quarter, the key play a 31-yard Joe Ferguson-to-Brown pass. Also, Houston was flagged twice for 15-yard personal fouls.
• Keith Moody's 82-yard punt return for a TD gave Buffalo a 10-7 halftime lead. It tied the second-longest in team history, also held by Hagood Clarke in 1968. Moody set the record of 91 yards in 1977 against Cleveland.
• Houston turned around the game in the third. Rusty Jackson punted to the Oilers 3, but the defense allowed a 97-yard, 11-play TD march capped by Rob Carpenter's 18-yard scamper. The drive consumed 6:33 and seemed to suck the life out of the Bills. Pastorini's 32-yard pass to Ken Burrough was a key play, as was his 11-yard pass to Mike Renfro.

QUOTES
• Houston coach Bum Phillips: "From looking at the films, it's hard to believe they're losing."

• Chuck Knox: "We had a good effort, there's no doubt about that. You can't fault the effort. We hit and hustled and scratched and scrapped. But we still made too many mistakes. We were in good shape at halftime, but we had a lot of penalties that wiped out key gains. Once we quit making mistakes, we're going to win."
• Keith Moody: "I really wanted to do it today. I talked to White Shoes (Billy Johnson, his idol). I wanted to let him see me do something instead of me watching him. We had a left return called. I started left, then cut off Lou Piccone's block. After that, it was just a lot of guys running with me. If I had to go another 40 yards, they would have gone the 40 yards with me."
• Oilers running back Rob Carpenter: "We couldn't believe how well-coached they were. I thought they had our playbook. After playing Oakland last week, I can tell you right now that Buffalo hit harder and pursued much harder. We didn't take them lightly. Naturally we're looking ahead to Pittsburgh next week, but we knew how important this game was. I'm in no hurry to play this team again."

WEEK 7 GAMES
Pitt 34, Clev 14	Oak 28, KC 6
GB 45, Sea 28	NYG 17, TB 14
LA 34, Minn 17	NYJ 33, Balt 10
Mia 28, SD 21	NO 14, SF 7
Atl 14, Det 0	NE 10, Cinc 3
Phil 17, Wash 10	Den 16, Chi 7
Dal 24, St.L 21 (OT)	

Bills	3	7	0	0 - 10
Oilers	7	0	7	3 - 17

Attendance at the Astrodome - 47,727

Hou: Caster 4 pass from Pastorini (Fritsch kick), 1:41
Buf: FG Dempsey 33, 14:30
Buf: Moody 82 punt return (Dempsey kick), 8:02
Hou: Carpenter 18 run (Fritsch kick), 13:25
Hou: FG Fritsch 43, 4:51

	BUF	HOU
First downs	15	17
Rushing yds	149	178
Passing yds	80	152
Punts-avg	6-41.2	6-35.0
Fumbles-lost	1-1	1-0
Penalties-yds	7-70	7-80

BILLS LEADERS: **Rushing** - Miller 17-56, Brown 16-58, Ferguson 4-35, Hooks 1-0; **Passing** - Ferguson 9-21-0 - 95, Munson 0-1-0 - 0; **Receiving** - Lewis 2-35, Chandler 2-17, Brown 3-31, Hooks 1-6, Gant 1-6.

OILERS LEADERS: **Rushing** - Campbell 19-105, Carpenter 8-41, Wilson 11-31, Barber 1-1; **Passing** - Pastorini 12-22-0 - 158; **Receiving** - Burrough 3-54, Renfro 3-55, Wilson 1-11, Barber 1-14, Carpenter 1-15, Coleman 1-9, Caster 1-4, Sampson 1- (-4).

GAME 8 - Sunday, Oct. 22, 1978 - BILLS 5, BENGALS 0

NOTES
• In the second-lowest-scoring game in team history, the Bills defense limited winless Cincinnati to 244 yards and knocked Ken Anderson out of the game in the second quarter.
• Tom Dempsey kicked a field goal that capped a seven-play, 35-yard drive that began after Lou Piccone's 10-yard punt return to the Bengals 38. Curtis Brown's 19-yard run was the key play.
• In the fourth, Piccone and Brown trapped Cincinnati punt returner Dennis Law in the end zone for a safety. Law made a huge mistake when he fielded Rusty Jackson's 51-yard punt at the 1 and circled into the end zone, where he was tackled.
• Jackson punted 10 times for 447 yards and dropped five kicks inside the 10-yard-line. He also had a 70-yarder with two minutes left.
• Brown became the first Bills back to top the 100-yard

rushing mark this year.
• Mario Clark had two interceptions, including one at the Bills 11 with 4:45 left in the fourth that cut off Cincinnati's only real scoring threat.
• The Bengals' scoreless streak reached 13 quarters.

QUOTES
• Chuck Knox: "The big thing is to win. I don't care if it's 5-0 or whatever. It wasn't a great offensive show, but it was a helluva defensive effort. And you don't see that kind of punting anymore. Jackson did a great job for us."
• Bengals coach Homer Rice on the safety: "The rule is you stay on the 10 and never go back. Dennis should have known better than to field the ball where he was."
• Curtis Brown on the safety: "Lou came downfield as the end man and he got there before (Law) could get moving. Lou tripped him and I got there just as he was stumbling out, but I jumped on him before he could get out of the end zone."
• Reggie McKenzie on the 17 penalties: "I've seen more flags in our last two games than any other two-game period that I can remember. And I thought last week was flag day. There have been complaints all around the country about all the bad calls, but the officials continue to do it. Winning teams don't get too many calls in games, but here are two teams that are rebuilding."
• Rusty Jackson: "There's a lot of luck involved in a good kick and I just happened to have the ball bouncing right today. Once the ball leaves your foot, you can't control it. I just punted and watched what happened."

Bengals	0	0	0	0 - 0
Bills	0	3	0	2 - 5

Attendance at Rich Stadium - 47,754

Buf: FG Dempsey 20, 2:15
Buf: Safety, Piccone tackled Law in end zone, :53

	BUF	CIN
First downs	12	16
Rushing yds	170	141
Passing yds	56	103
Punts-avg	10-44.7	6-46.0
Fumbles-lost	1-0	2-2
Penalties-yds	10-90	7-61

BILLS LEADERS: **Rushing** - Brown 18-100, Miller 12-46, Ferguson 5-14, Hooks 2-10; **Passing** - Ferguson 12-21-0 - 76; **Receiving** - Chandler 2-22, Gant 3-26, Brown 2-9, Hooks 2-12, Miller 2-2, Lewis 1-5.

BENGALS LEADERS: **Rushing** - Clark 12-44, Griffin 7-31, Elliott 7-7, Anderson 1-16, Johnson 2-19, Davis 3-19, Reaves 1-5; **Passing** - Anderson 0-4-1 - 0, Reaves 13-23-2 - 119; **Receiving** - Curtis 4-31, Brooks 2-33, McInally 3-20, Elliott 1-12, Walker 1-4, Griffin 2-19.

WEEK 8 GAMES
Balt 7, Den 6	NO 10, LA 3
NYJ 23, St.L 10	TB 33, Chi 19
Atl 20, SF 17	NYG 17, Wash 6
Sea 27, Oak 14	Det 31, SD 14
KC 17, Clev 3	NE 33, Mia 24
Minn 21, GB 7	Dal 14, Phil 7
Hou 24, Pitt 17	

STANDINGS: EIGHTH WEEK

AFC EAST	W	L	T	CENTRAL	W	L	T	WEST	W	L	T	NFC EAST	W	L	T	CENTRAL	W	L	T	WEST	W	L	T
New England	6	2	0	Pittsburgh	7	1	0	Denver	5	3	0	Washington	6	2	0	Green Bay	6	2	0	LA Rams	7	1	0
Miami	5	3	0	Houston	5	3	0	Oakland	5	3	0	Dallas	6	2	0	Tampa Bay	4	4	0	N.Orleans	4	4	0
NY Jets	5	3	0	Cleveland	4	4	0	Seattle	4	4	0	NY Giants	5	3	0	Minnesota	4	4	0	Atlanta	4	4	0
Buffalo	3	5	0	Cincinnati	0	8	0	San Diego	2	6	0	Philadelphia	4	4	0	Chicago	3	5	0	San Fran	1	7	0
Baltimore	3	5	0					Kan. City	2	6	0	St. Louis	0	8	0	Detroit	2	6	0				

Bills	0	7	6	7 - 20	
Browns	7	13	14	7 - 41	

Attendance at Cleveland Stadium - 51,409

Cle: Rucker 16 pass from Sipe (Cockroft kick), 12:38
Cle: Hill 15 pass from Sipe (kick failed), 6:22
Buf: Miller 2 run (Dempsey kick), 13:04
Cle: M. Pruitt 1 run (Cockroft kick), 14:40
Cle: Rucker 44 pass from Sipe (Cockroft kick), 8:39
Cle: M. Pruitt 71 run (Cockroft kick), 12:40
Buf: Johnson 1 run (kick failed), 14:35
Cle: Hill 3 pass from Miller (Cockroft kick), 6:23
Buf: Piccone 5 pass from Mays (Dempsey kick), 13:25

	BUF	CLE
First downs	28	28
Rushing yds	82	309
Passing yds	201	223
Punts-avg	4-43.8	2-29.5
Fumbles-lost	4-1	1-1
Penalties-yds	7-64	12-135

BILLS LEADERS: **Rushing** - Brown 7-33, Miller 11-23, Hooks 3-20, Johnson 4-6; **Passing** - Ferguson 13-23-2 - 185, Mays 4-15-0 - 39; **Receiving** - Chandler 7-114, Gant 3-29, Hooks 2-29, Piccone 2-18, Lewis 1-15, Miller 1-10, Brown 1-9.

BROWNS LEADERS: **Rushing** - M. Pruitt 21-173, G. Pruitt 13-87, Hill 6-21, Collins 5-15, Sipe 1-11, Newsome 1-2; **Passing** - Sipe 12-15-0 - 217, Miller 2-2-0 - 17; **Receiving** - Newsome 4-96, Rucker 4-89, Hill 2-18, Logan 1-15, M. Pruitt 1-14, G. Pruitt 2-2.

NOTES

• Cleveland rolled for 532 yards, only 27 fewer than the Bills all-time worst defensive performance, set in 1977 against Seattle. The Browns' 309 yards rushing were only 11 shy of the 320 the Bills allowed the Dallas Texans in 1962.
• Incredibly, both teams recorded 28 first downs.
• Mike Pruitt's 173 rushing yards were the second-most the Bills have allowed, behind only Jim Nance's 185 for the Boston Patriots in 1967.
• Brian Sipe and Mark Miller completed 82.4 percent of their passes, a record against the Bills.
• The Browns scored TDs on five straight possessions. Thom Darden's interception started the Browns on their 67-yard TD march in the first. Darden picked off another Joe Ferguson pass in the second and Cleveland went 81 yards in 11 plays for a 13-0 advantage.
• The Bills pulled to within 13-7 with a 78-yard drive, but Keith Wright returned the kickoff 42 yards and then an interference penalty on Mario Clark in the end zone set up Pruitt's TD run.
• Reggie Rucker caught a 44-yard TD from Sipe, and after a Bills punt, Pruitt broke a 71-yard TD on a third-and-one play.

WEEK 9 GAMES	
Minn 21, Dal 10	GB 9, TB 7
St.L 16, Phil 10	NE 55, NYJ 21
Mia 26, Balt 8	Pitt 27, KC 24
Cinc 28, Hou 13	Wash 38, SF 20
Det 21, Chi 17	SD 27, Oak 23
NO 28, NYG 17	Atl 15, LA 7
Den 20, Sea 17 (OT)	

QUOTES

• Cleveland receiver Reggie Rucker: "All we needed was to be on the field today. We scored almost every time we had the ball."
• Chuck Knox: "There's not much to say, they just whipped us. I don't know what it was, good offense or bad defense. We didn't play well in any area and that's a coach's responsibility."
• Lucious Sanford: "I've said this too many times, but shoot, tackling is just basic and if we aren't ready to go out there and do the basics, we shouldn't be out there."
• Browns running back Mike Pruitt: "This was the opportunity I've been waiting three years for. I'm not really sure it happened. I concentrated a lot harder this week. I just felt the Bills were a team that we could run on. They paid a lot of attention to Greg (Pruitt) and that helped. The 4-3 defense Buffalo uses is easy to block if the line is working and today I had cracks to run through. This is the greatest day of my life."
• Reggie McKenzie: "Hey, after so many blowouts, what else can I say? They got us down, gave us chances to get up, and we never got up. We moved the ball pretty well at times, but let's face it, we have a young defense. And the young defenses are going to get burned. All we need is for the defense to keep it relatively close, but they couldn't do that today."
• Joe Ferguson: "One week the offense moves well and the defense collapses. The next week the defense plays well and the offense stinks. Someday we'll put it together."

Patriots	0	7	7	0 - 14	
Bills	3	0	0	7 - 10	

Attendance at Rich Stadium - 44,897

Buf: FG Dempsey 21, 2:46
NE: Ivory 19 run (Smith kick), 8:12
NE: Ivory 5 run (Smith kick), 3:31
Buf: Chandler 11 pass from Ferguson (Dempsey kick), 13:13

	BUF	NE
First downs	15	20
Rushing yds	140	279
Passing yds	107	40
Punts-avg	4-44.5	3-37.3
Fumbles-lost	2-2	3-2
Penalties-yds	9-75	6-54

BILLS LEADERS: **Rushing** - Brown 13-48, Miller 12-58, Hooks 7-21, Ferguson 2-13; **Passing** - Ferguson 14-23-1 - 114; **Receiving** - Chandler 4-35, Gant 3-26, Lewis 4-34, Miller 1-10, Brown 1-15, Ferguson 1- (-6).
PATRIOTS LEADERS: **Rushing** - Cunningham 13-85, Ivory 16-128, Grogan 5-24, McAlister 2-3, Calhoun 10-39, Wilson 1-0; **Passing** - Grogan 5-17-1 - 65; **Receiving** - Francis 2-26, Morgan 1-20, Cunningham 1-12, Johnson 1-7.

WEEK 10 GAMES	
Minn 17, Det 7	Phil 10, GB 3
Hou 14, Clev 10	Atl 21, SF 10
LA 26, TB 23	St.L 20, NYG 10
SD 22, Cinc 13	Pitt 20, NO 14
Sea 31, Chi 29	Mia 23, Dal 16
Oak 20, KC 10	NYJ 31, Den 28
Balt 21, Wash 17	

NOTES

• The Bills played very conservatively and were criticized for it as the Patriots won their seventh straight.
• Chuck Knox tried to play keep away from the Patriots' offense, which had scored 88 points in its last two games. The Bills ran 34 times, but as usual, penalties stalled some impressive advances.
• Randy McClanahan recovered a muffed punt by Stanley Morgan at the Patriots 20, two minutes into the game. Terry Miller gained 13, but then Buffalo got conservative and picked up only four yards rushing, settling for Tom Dempsey's field goal.
• In the second quarter, Steve Nelson intercepted a Joe Ferguson pass and returned it 24 yards to the Bills 25. Horace Ivory scored three plays later on a 19-yard run.
• On their first possession of the third quarter, the Patriots drove 76 yards in seven plays to another Ivory TD run.
• The Patriots punter Jerrol Wilson dropped a snap at his own 40 and was tackled there, but Curtis Brown fumbled the ball back at the 6.
• In the fourth, Scott Hutchinson recovered a Steve Grogan fumble at the Patriots 33 and Ferguson hit Bob Chandler with an 11-yard TD pass with 1:47 left. The on-sides kick failed, and the Bills dropped to 3-7.

QUOTES

• Joe Ferguson: "We all wanted to open it up, but I don't call the plays. We could have thrown the ball more, but even the way the game went, we could have won." (On settling for Dempsey's field goal early): "That was a big factor. It's a big lift to get an early touchdown. We didn't get a lift from the field goal. We figured if we could keep it tight for two or three quarters, we could open it up and play ball. Our plan was to keep the ball away from them as long as possible. For a quarterback, it was frustrating because there were things I wanted to do."
• Patriots coach Chuck Fairbanks: "I thought Buffalo played well, but we didn't exactly set the world on fire."
• Chuck Knox: "That is a team that scored 55 points last week. We didn't want to give them the ball. Before the game I said they were the best team I have seen this year. I haven't changed my mind. I know it's an old saying, but in the end, we made too many mistakes. Every week the approach changes. We didn't do the same thing against Cleveland that we did against New England. It all depends on the weapons your opponents have. If we had run the ball and won, it would have been a masterful game plan."
• Patriots safety Tim Fox: "Their philosophy was to run and that kind of surprised me because they have a good passing attack."

			STANDINGS: TENTH WEEK																
AFC EAST	**W**	**L**	**T**	**CENTRAL**	**W**	**L**	**T**	**WEST**	**W**	**L**	**T**	**NFC EAST**	**W**	**L**	**T**	**CENTRAL**	**W**	**L**	**T**	**WEST**	**W**	**L**	**T**
New England	8	2	0	Pittsburgh	9	1	0	Denver	6	4	0	Washington	7	3	0	Green Bay	7	3	0	LA Rams	8	2	0
Miami	7	3	0	Houston	6	4	0	Oakland	6	4	0	Dallas	6	4	0	Minnesota	6	4	0	Atlanta	6	4	0
NY Jets	6	4	0	Cleveland	5	5	0	Seattle	5	5	0	NY Giants	5	5	0	Tampa Bay	4	6	0	N.Orleans	5	5	0
Baltimore	4	6	0	Cincinnati	1	9	0	San Diego	4	6	0	Philadelphia	5	5	0	Chicago	3	7	0	San Fran	1	9	0
Buffalo	3	7	0					Kan. City	2	8	0	St. Louis	2	8	0	Detroit	3	7	0				

NOTES

- The Dolphins set an NFL record by beating the Bills for the 18th straight time.
- After the game, Ralph Wilson was furious at the officials whom he claimed "stole the game from us."
- Trailing 25-24 with 1:42 left, the Bills had second-and-six from their 46. Joe Ferguson then passed to Roland Hooks at the 25 and he appeared to make the catch cleanly, but the officials ruled an incomplete pass. After an A.J. Duhe sack, the Bills failed to make a first down and that was it.
- The Dolphins opened the game with a 79-yard drive that was kept alive when the officials failed to rule an obvious fumble by ex-Bill Jim Braxton. Delvin Williams later scored on a 25-yard TD run.
- The Bills answered with a 64-yard drive to Reuben Gant's TD. Williams scored on a 26-yard run and Garo Yepremian added a field goal for a 16-7 lead (Yepremian had two extra points blocked). But Curtis Brown broke a 58-yard TD run to make it 16-14.
- Another break went Miami's way later in the half when Randy McClanahan was nailed for a 36-yard interference call on Andre Tillman and that set up Nat Moore's TD reception.
- Jimmy Cefalo lost a fumble on a punt, and the Bills drove to a field goal that could have been a TD had the officials called an obvious interference by Tim Foley on Gant at the 5.
- After a third-quarter Yepremian field goal, the Bills pulled to within 25-24 on Ferguson's TD pass to Frank Lewis after Randy McClanahan had recovered a Bob Griese fumble at the Miami 35.

QUOTES

- Roland Hooks: "I don't know, it happened so fast. They ruled I didn't catch it so I guess I have to accept that. I thought I caught it. It's been the same all year, we get big gains called back by penalties."
- Bob Chandler: "What's happening I think has a lot to do with the Buffalo Bills not being a good team. The Bills aren't going to achieve parity out there in officiating until they're respected as a football team. It's unbelievable. More calls go against us than for us."
- Chuck Knox: "The guys are busting their rear ends, they work hard week in and week out. It's just frustrating as hell."
- Joe DeLamielleure: "Football is a great game, why don't they let us play it."
- Miami guard Bob Kuechenberg: "Well, that's No. 18. You can't say a Buffalo-Miami game is boring. We've had some of our sweetest victories against the Bills. We take a lot of pride in having never lost to them for so long."
- Miami guard Larry Little: "Eighteen in a row is unbelievable, but it's never easy against the Bills. Every time we play them, we know we've been in a game. I don't have an explanation for the streak except that we've had some luck over the years, more than our share against Buffalo."

WEEK 11 GAMES	
Balt 17, Sea 14	Phil 17, NYJ 9
LA 10, Pitt 7	Det 34, TB 23
Atl 20, NO 17	Minn 17, Chi 14
Dal 42, GB 14	Den 19, Clev 7
St.L 16, SF 10	Hou 21, NE 23
SD 29, KC 23 (OT)	Oak 34, Cinc 21
Wash 16, NYG 13 (OT)	

Dolphins	7	15	3	0 -	25
Bills	7	10	0	7 -	24

Attendance at Rich Stadium - 48,623

Mia: Williams 25 run (Yepremian kick), 5:19
Buf: Gant 5 pass from Ferguson (Dempsey kick), 10:58
Mia: FG Yepremian 47, :04
Mia: Williams 26 run (kick blocked), 4:16
Buf: Brown 58 run (Dempsey kick), 7:02
Mia: N. Moore 16 pass from Griese (kick blocked), 9:44
Buf: FG Dempsey 33, 14:33
Mia: FG Yepremian 24, 7:12
Buf: Lewis 14 pass from Ferguson (Dempsey kick), 11:29

	BUF	MIA
First downs	16	20
Rushing yds	170	193
Passing yds	114	96
Punts-avg	5-31.6	4-30.8
Fumbles-lost	4-2	0-0
Penalties-yds	10-116	5-57

BILLS LEADERS: Rushing - Brown 11-114, Miller 9-17, Hooks 7-39, Ferguson 1-0; **Passing** - Ferguson 15-27-0 - 129; **Receiving** - Chandler 5-52, Gant 2-14, Lewis 4-52, Brown 4-11.

DOLPHINS LEADERS: Rushing - Williams 26-144, Braxton 6-21, Griese 4-4, L. Harris 3-17, Davis 3-7; **Passing** - Griese 13-21-0 - 106; **Receiving** - N. Moore 5-44, Tillman 3-26, D. Harris 2-24, Braxton 1-9, Davis 1-5, Bulaich 1- (-2).

NOTES

- Tampa Bay recorded its most one-sided victory in team history as the Bills fell to 0-5 on the road.
- The Bucs rushed for 204 yards even though Ricky Bell left in the second quarter with a knee injury.
- Joe Ferguson was yanked after the first half when the offense managed only 67 yards, but like Ferguson, Bill Munson was ineffective and he also threw two interceptions.
- The Bucs went 59 yards to score on their first possession and after Cedric Brown's interception at the Bucs 43, ex-Bill Neil O'Donoghue kicked a field goal for a 10-0 halftime lead.
- Two holding penalties on the first possession of the third quarter slowed the Bills, then Munson was intercepted by Jeris White who returned it 23 yards to the Bills 32. Morris Owens then beat Charlie Romes on a post for a 22-yard TD.
- Munson completed five passes on a drive that resulted in Tom Dempsey's field goal, but the Bucs answered after Brown's second interception at the Bucs 49. Mike Rae, playing QB for the injured Doug Williams, hit Jimmie Giles with a 33-yard TD pass for a 24-3 lead.
- After a Dennis Johnson fumble at the Bucs 21, Anthony Davis scored on a three-yard run.

QUOTES

- Joe Ferguson: "I was surprised (that Chuck Knox pulled him). He wanted a change of pace to get something going. I was doing what they (the coaches) were calling."
- Chuck Knox: "I put Munson in to see if we could get things going. We were only down 10-0 at halftime. But it doesn't change Joe Ferguson's status for next week,

he'll be starting. We just played a bad football game. Tampa Bay kicked our butts. I thought we were making improvement, but we went backwards today. We had good practices all week – just like we had against Miami – and we stressed to the players this was strictly a business trip. There's a maturity you have to have in games on the road, not to let things become disconcerted."
- Dee Hardison: "This club just doesn't play well on the road. How can you explain it?"
- Bucs coach John McKay: "It wasn't art, but it was a win. I can't ever remember us winning by a score of 31-10. This might have been our best game ever. I would think it was our best defensive performance because they have a pretty good offense. I don't know why Ferguson went out. That surprised me, although Munson did a pretty good job and he's almost as old as I am."
- Bucs defensive end Lee Roy Selmon: "We did the same things we try to do every week, but I think things worked today because they looked confused at times."
- Bucs linebacker Dave Lewis: "Buffalo didn't seem totally in condition. They looked a little tired, but maybe that's because we (the Bucs defense) weren't out there on the field that much. The offense gave us a lot of rest."

WEEK 12 GAMES	
Dal 27, NO 7	St.L 27, Wash 17
NE 19, NYJ 17	Sea 13, KC 10
Chi 13, Atl 7	Clev 45, Balt 24
Oak 29, Det 17	Phil 19, NYG 17
LA 31, SF 28	Pitt 7, Cinc 6
SD 13, Minn 7	Den 16, GB 3
Hou 35, Mia 30	

Bills	0	0	3	7 -	10
Buccaneers	7	3	7	14 -	31

Attendance at Tampa Stadium - 61,383

TB: Bell 12 run (O'Donoghue kick), 5:36
TB: FG O'Donoghue 28, 9:01
TB: Owens 22 pass from Rae (O'Donoghue kick), 6:00
Buf: FG Dempsey 37, 11:13
TB: Giles 33 pass from Rae (O'Donoghue kick), 2:13
TB: Davis 3 run (O'Donoghue kick), 10:16
Buf: Chandler 9 pass from Munson (Dempsey kick), 12:17

	BUF	TB
First downs	18	20
Rushing yds	79	204
Passing yds	132	107
Punts-avg	5-41.2	4-42.0
Fumbles-lost	1-1	1-1
Penalties-yds	5-55	8-100

BILLS LEADERS: Rushing - Brown 14-44, Miller 7-20, Hooks 3-12, Johnson 2-3; **Passing** - Ferguson 6-16-2 - 47, Munson 12-22-2 - 112; **Receiving** - Gant 4-39, Chandler 6-60, Lewis 1-15, Hooks 2-20, Brown 2-10, Miller 1-3, Piccone 1-11, Johnson 1-1.

BUCCANEERS LEADERS: Rushing - Bell 8-54, Davis 18-73, Rae 4-10, Ragsdale 3-10, Carter 8-34, White 4-23; **Passing** - Rae 7-14-1 - 121; **Receiving** - Owens 3-50, Mucker 2-29, Giles 1-33, Carter 1-9.

STANDINGS: TWELFTH WEEK

AFC EAST	W	L	T	CENTRAL	W	L	T	WEST	W	L	T	NFC EAST	W	L	T	CENTRAL	W	L	T	WEST	W	L	T
New England	9	3	0	Pittsburgh	10	2	0	Denver	8	4	0	Washington	8	4	0	Green Bay	7	5	0	LA Rams	10	2	0
Miami	8	4	0	Houston	8	4	0	Oakland	8	4	0	Dallas	8	4	0	Minnesota	7	5	0	Atlanta	7	5	0
NY Jets	6	6	0	Cleveland	6	6	0	Seattle	6	6	0	Philadelphia	7	5	0	Tampa Bay	5	7	0	N.Orleans	5	7	0
Baltimore	5	7	0	Cincinnati	1	11	0	San Diego	6	6	0	NY Giants	5	7	0	Detroit	4	8	0	San Fran	1	11	0
Buffalo	3	9	0					Kan. City	2	10	0	St. Louis	4	8	0	Chicago	4	8	0				

Giants	7	3	7	0 -	17
Bills	7	0	7	27 -	41

Attendance at Rich Stadium - 28,496

NYG: Dixon 31 pass from Pisarcik (Danelo kick), 5:32
Buf: Brown 1 run (Dempsey kick), 10:48
NYG: FG Danelo 27, 14:08
NYG: Kotar 19 pass from Pisarcik (Danelo kick), 9:06
Buf: Hooks 1 run (Dempsey kick), 11:46
Buf: Brown 1 run (Dempsey kick), 4:58
Buf: Piccone 9 pass from Ferguson (Dempsey kick), 8:40
Buf: Miller 39 run (Dempsey kick), 11:30
Buf: Miller 13 run (kick blocked), 14:51

	BUF	NYG
First downs	27	15
Rushing yds	366	99
Passing yds	99	222
Punts-avg	5-41.2	4-42.0
Fumbles-lost	3-0	0-0
Penalties-yds	6-40	5-57

BILLS LEADERS: **Rushing** - Miller 21-208, Hooks 12-115, Brown 12-31, Johnson 3-12, Ferguson 1-0; **Passing** - Ferguson 9-15-1 - 106; **Receiving** - Chandler 5-75, Piccone 2-24, Miller 2-7.

GIANTS LEADERS: **Rushing** - Hammond 15-60, Csonka 4-10, Kotar 7-15, Pisarcik 2- (-3), Spencer 5-17; **Passing** - Pisarcik 15-24-1 - 230; **Receiving** - Perkins 5-68, Dixon 2-78, Kotar 4-40, Csonka 2-25, Robinson 1-10, Hammond 1-9.

NOTES

• The Bills set a team record with 366 rushing yards as Terry Miller gained 208, a Bills rookie rushing record and the third-best total by a rookie in NFL history.
• The Bills erupted for 27 fourth-quarter points and overcame a 17-7 deficit.
• The Giants were coming off a brutal loss the week before when Joe Pisarcik and Larry Csonka messed up a handoff in the final minute and Philadelphia's Herman Edwards picked up the fumble and raced 26 yards for a stunning, game-winning TD. On the final play of the first half against the Bills, Pisarcik knelt down to kill the clock and the New York writers stood and mockingly applauded.
• The Giants drove 98 yards to Pisarcik's 19-yard TD pass to Doug Kotar in the third quarter for a 17-7 lead and things looked bleak, but Roland Hooks turned the game around on Buffalo's ensuing possession with a 66-yard run to the 1, from where he scored.
• In the fourth, a Joe Ferguson pass was intercepted by Ernie Jones in the end zone, but for once, a call went Buffalo's way as the officials ruled Jones had pushed Miller, giving the Bills a first down. Curtis Brown

WEEK 13 GAMES

Det 17, Den 14	Dal 37, Wash 10
Atl 20, NO 17	KC 23, SD 0
Chi 14, TB 3	Phil 14, St.L 10
NYJ 24, Mia 13	Sea 17, Oak 16
Clev 30, LA 19	NE 35, Balt 14
Pitt 24, SF 7	Hou 17, Cinc 10
GB 10, Minn 10 (OT)	

scored on the next play and the rout was on.
• Lou Piccone caught a TD pass on the next series and Miller scored twice late in the game.

QUOTES

• Giants defensive tackle Gary Jeter: "Terry Miller is the best. He's the best I've played against and that includes Tony Dorsett."
• Terry Miller: "I made a commitment to myself after last week that for the last four games, I was going to let it hang out so next year I could start up where I left off. Sure I was having my doubts, but I am not a give-up type of person. There is extra pressure when you aren't doing what people expect. I was more emotional for this game than I had been since high school. I could tell when the day started off that I felt good. From the very first play, daylight was there. You see the guys like Dorsett get the yardage and you think 'Yeah, someday.' It was great."
• Joe Ferguson on Hooks' 66-yard run: "That was the play that did it. You could just see the offensive line pick up confidence after that. They really had fun out there today.
• Joe DeLamielleure: "You know when the Giants beat us here three years ago, that sent us into a tailspin that we have never recovered from. Maybe this will turn us around in the other direction. I wish more people were here to see us today, but these are the real diehard fans."
• Roland Hooks: "I haven't seen holes like that since I was in high school."

Bills	0	7	3	0 -	10
Chiefs	7	0	7	0 -	14

Attendance at Arrowhead Stadium - 25,781

KC: McKnight 17 run (Stenerud kick), 11:30
Buf: Lewis 40 pass from Ferguson (Dempsey kick), 10:55
Buf: FG Dempsey 22, 10:38
KC: White 3 pass from Livingston (Stenerud kick), 15:00

	BUF	KC
First downs	16	21
Rushing yds	136	241
Passing yds	207	99
Punts-avg	2-24.5	2-27.0
Fumbles-lost	4-2	1-0
Penalties-yds	6-54	8-47

BILLS LEADERS: **Rushing** - Miller 15-57, Hooks 7-19, Brown 10-45, Gant 1-14, Ferguson 1-1; **Passing** - Ferguson 14-25-3 - 207; **Receiving** - Lewis 7-126, Chandler 2-48, Hooks 3-21, Piccone 1-9, Brown 1-3.

CHIEFS LEADERS: **Rushing** - Reed 16-97, McKnight 20-78, Morgado 3-3, Livingston 3-3; **Passing** - Livingston 12-21-1 - 99; **Receiving** - Marshall 3-40, Reed 2-22, Morgado 1-8, White 2-6, McKnight 1-0, Lane 3-23.

WEEK 14 GAMES

GB 17, TB 7	Minn 28, Phil 27
LA 20, NYG 17	NYJ 24, Balt 16
NO 24, SF 13	Sea 47, Clev 24
Den 21, Oak 6	St.L 21, Det 14
Cinc 37, Atl 7	Dal 17, NE 10
Pitt 13, Hou 3	Mia 16, Wash 0
SD 40, Chi 7	

NOTES

• The Bills turned the ball over five times and allowed Marv Levy's Wing-T to rush for 241 yards.
• All three of Joe Ferguson's interceptions came in the fourth quarter, killing comeback efforts. The first two picks came in Bills territory, but the Chiefs failed to capitalize as they punted once and Jan Stenerud had his second field goal of the day blocked, both by Lucious Sanford. The final pick, by Whitney Paul, sealed the Bills' fate with 1:01 remaining.
• Curtis Brown fumbled on the second play of the game at the Bills 23, but Sanford blocked his first field goal.
• Ted McKnight's 17-yard TD run came after a 27-yard Rusty Jackson punt set up the Chiefs at the Bills 42.
• The Bills came back with a 40-yard Ferguson-to-Frank Lewis TD. Lewis also caught a 26-yarder on the drive.
• Tom Dempsey made a 21-yard field goal in the third, but was roughed and Chuck Knox took the points off the board. It looked like a good move as Terry Miller scored on a two-yard run, but Ken Jones was penalized for holding and the Bills eventually settled for Dempsey's 22-yard field goal.
• The Chiefs' winning points came on the final play of the third quarter, as Mike Livingston's TD pass to Walter White capped a 58-yard, eight-play advance.

QUOTES

• Chuck Knox: "You just can't win making the mistakes we made. You can't turn it over the way we did. I even violated an old adage that you don't take points off the board, but we went for the go-ahead touchdown and we get a holding penalty on Miller's apparent TD). It was straight drive blocking (on Miller's apparent TD). In 25 years of coaching I haven't seen many of them (holding penalties) down there. That includes 16 years in the

NFL. I thought we had a chance at the end, then we threw an interception. I can't explain it (Ferguson's sudden fourth-quarter trouble)."
• Chiefs running back Ted McKnight: "We ran inside, outside, around the corner, they just couldn't stop us. The last time up there (in Buffalo), we thought they would be a pushover. They played an excellent game and we weren't ready to play. This time we played with determination."
• Chiefs coach Marv Levy: "We played better because we won, there is no other way to measure it. Our two goal-line stands which forced field goals were as much a key to the game as anything else. And I thought Mike Livingston took control very well. He called every play and he called them better than when I was sending them in the first half."
• Lucious Sanford on his blocks: "Both times were kind of similar. I was just slanting between the upback and the tight end. Coach Pitts saw something a little different in what they were doing on film, so we decided to attack that lane."

AFC EAST	W	L	T	CENTRAL	W	L	T	WEST	W	L	T	NFC EAST	W	L	T	CENTRAL	W	L	T	WEST	W	L	T
New England	10	4	0	Pittsburgh	12	2	0	Denver	9	5	0	Dallas	10	4	0	Green Bay	8	5	1	LA Rams	11	3	0
Miami	9	5	0	Houston	9	5	0	Oakland	8	6	0	Washington	8	6	0	Minnesota	8	5	1	Atlanta	8	6	0
NY Jets	8	6	0	Cleveland	7	7	0	Seattle	8	6	0	Philadelphia	8	6	0	Tampa Bay	5	9	0	N.Orleans	6	8	0
Baltimore	5	9	0	Cincinnati	2	12	0	San Diego	7	7	0	NY Giants	5	9	0	Detroit	5	9	0	San Fran	1	13	0
Buffalo	4	10	0					Kan. City	4	10	0	St. Louis	5	9	0	Chicago	5	9	0				

NOTES

• Chuck Knox's conservative strategy backfired late in the game and New England took advantage to clinch the AFC East division title, their first since the AFL-NFL merger.

• The Bills had taken a 24-21 lead with 4:39 left on Joe Ferguson's 21-yard TD to Frank Lewis, but thanks to a 52-yard Steve Grogan to Stanley Morgan pass, the Patriots were on the Bills 2 within five plays. Sam Cunningham then tried to leap in for a touchdown, but was hit by a group of Bills and fumbled and Tom Graham recovered at the 2 with 2:45 left.

• The Bills failed to get a first down, as Terry Miller was stopped inches shy of the 12-yard-line, and with 1:48 left Knox ordered punter Rusty Jackson to run out of the end zone and take a safety rather than risk a blocked punt. That made it 24-23.

• New England then took possession at the Bills 47 after Stanley Morgan returned Jackson's free kick 17 yards. Grogan needed seven plays to get the Patriots to the Bills 7 before David Posey, replacing the injured John Smith, kicked the winning field goal.

• The Bills opened a 17-7 lead on Miller's 32-yard TD run, but the Patriots got that right back as Horace Ivory returned the kickoff to midfield and Grogan later scored on a scramble.

• Early in the fourth, Tony McGee forced Ferguson to fumble and Ray Hamilton recovered at the Bills 20. Ivory scored on the next play to give the Patriots a 21-17 lead.

QUOTES

• Chuck Knox: "There isn't any regret over the decision. If we give up the two points, we're kicking without pressure. We realized that a field goal could beat us, and we were playing for a win, not a tie. If we get a good kick and good coverage, they still have a way to go. Of course, that didn't work. It's going against the book, but the book doesn't say who the punter is, what the situation is and the fact that Stanley Morgan is back there. We started talking about it right after the first down. It wasn't something that was done on impulse."

• New England guard Sam Adams: "It was a helluva decision. I wouldn't have thought of it, but I'm glad he did."

• New England tight end Russ Francis: "I was a little surprised. We didn't put any pressure on all day and their kicker still didn't kick the ball well without pressure, so what good does a free kick do for you. It seemed kind of strange to me."

• Joe Ferguson: "Everyone was saying go for the first down, we're out of playoff contention and it was only an inch and a half. But you have to have some kind of confidence in your defense. It's a tough decision, he makes it and that's it."

WEEK 15 GAMES	
Pitt 35, Balt 13	Det 45, Minn 14
Den 24, KC 3	Mia 23, Oak 6
Chi 14, GB 0	NYG 17, St.L 10
SF 6, TB 3	Dal 31, Phil 13
Atl 20, Wash 17	Hou 17, NO 13
SD 37, Sea 10	Cinc 20, LA 19
Clev 37, NYJ 34 (OT)	

	1	2	3	4		
Bills	0	10	7	7	-	24
Patriots	0	7	7	12	-	26

Attendance at Schaefer Stadium - 59,598

Buf: Hooks 28 run (Dempsey kick), 1:39
NE: Cunningham 4 run (Posey kick), 8:50
Buf: FG Dempsey 26, 15:00
Buf: Miller 32 run (Dempsey kick), 9:17
NE: Grogan 4 run (Posey kick), 13:22
NE: Ivory 20 run (Posey kick), 6:37
Buf: Lewis 21 pass from Ferguson (Dempsey kick), 10:21
NE: Safety, Jackson ran out of end zone, 13:12
NE: FG Posey 21, 14:52

	BUF	NE
First downs	16	24
Rushing yds	184	249
Passing yds	123	154
Punts-avg	4-32.3	2-20.5
Fumbles-lost	2-1	4-3
Penalties-yds	3-35	2-15

BILLS LEADERS: Rushing - Miller 14-74, Hooks 7-49, Brown 9-53, Johnson 3-17, Ferguson 1-4, Jackson 1- (-13); **Passing** - Ferguson 9-24-1 - 133; **Receiving** - Chandler 1-11, Lewis 4-40, Johnson 1-28, Brown 2-29, Gant 1-25.

PATRIOTS LEADERS: Rushing - Ivory 16-91, Cunningham 19-76, Grogan 8-44, Johnson 8-38; **Passing** - Grogan 13-21-0 - 160; **Receiving** - Morgan 1-52, Ivory 3-16, Cunningham 3-16, Francis 3-38, Westbrook 2-30, Jackson 1-8.

NOTES

• The Bills finished on a winning note, but the victory cost them a chance to play the last-place schedule in 1979. The win was Buffalo's seventh in 19 regular season finales.

• Terry Miller became the first Bills rookie and 10th in NFL history to top 1,000 yards rushing.

• The Bills overcame 13 penalties worth 112 yards and a mere three pass completions by Joe Ferguson as heavy winds made throwing and kicking a real chore.

• The Colts drove 83 yards for their first score and were helped by 30 yards in Bills penalties.

• Lucious Sanford blocked a David Lee punt at the Colts 28 to set up Dennis Johnson's TD run.

• In the third, Ron Graham forced Ron Lee to fumble and Tony Greene recovered at the 50. A few plays later, on third-and-nine from the 39, Ferguson hit Frank Lewis at the 30, Lewis broke ex-Bill Dwight Harrison's tackle and scored to make it 14-7.

• Early in the fourth, Miller followed Reggie McKenzie around end and went 60 yards for a TD, which offset Joe Washington's 26-yard TD pass to Mike Siani 1:50 later. Washington had attempted to run a sweep, but he fumbled. He picked up the ball, saw Bills everywhere, but had the presence of mind to throw downfield to Siani.

• Baltimore's last two possessions ended when Don Hardemann was stopped on fourth-and-one and Greene intercepted a Bill Troup pass.

QUOTES

• Chuck Knox: "We got out of the cellar. It's not much, but it's a step up. We overcame a lot of adversity today. Unlike what we've done most of the year, we didn't let all the adversity make us fold. We were getting killed by penalties and that wind took both teams' passing away. But we finish the year with our first road win

instead of just running for the bus. It will make our winter much shorter."

• Ralph Wilson: "I think Chuck Knox and his staff have done an outstanding job bringing the team together. I think we have a tremendous future."

• Joe DeLamielleure: "I thought we were going to do better than we did, but it's good to win the last one. In the long run, it's going to help us."

• Terry Miller: "I got more confidence as the season wore on and we were able to do some things (on offense) the second half of the year. I think I'm in a good situation. Am I satisfied? You bet."

• Colts coach Ted Marchibroda: "I think the Bills are going to improve next year the way you saw the Jets improve this year. You don't get two automatic wins from those teams anymore."

	1	2	3	4		
Bills	0	7	7	7	-	21
Colts	0	7	0	7	-	14

Attendance at Memorial Stadium - 25,415

Bal: McCauley 1 run (Linhart kick), :05
Buf: Johnson 2 run (Dempsey kick), 8:16
Buf: Lewis 39 pass from Ferguson (Dempsey kick), 3:04
Buf: Miller 60 run (Dempsey kick), 3:30
Bal: Siani 26 pass from Washington (Linhart kick), 5:20

	BUF	BAL
First downs	16	18
Rushing yds	193	139
Passing yds	53	33
Punts-avg	7-33.4	5-29.0
Fumbles-lost	2-1	2-1
Penalties-yds	13-112	8-55

BILLS LEADERS: Rushing - Miller 15-123, Johnson 19-62, Hooks 10-10, Ferguson 1- (-2); **Passing** - Ferguson 3-13-0 - 53; **Receiving** - Lewis 1-39, Hooks 1-4, Chandler 1-10.

COLTS LEADERS: Rushing - Washington 21-70, R. Lee 4-13, McCauley 2-2, Hardeman 17-59, Troup 2- (-5); **Passing** - Troup 4-15-1 - 45, Washington 1-1-0 - 26; **Receiving** - Washington 1-4, Siani 3-54, Hardeman 1-13.

WEEK 16 GAMES	
Pitt 21, Den 17	Chi 14, Wash 10
Sea 23, KC 19	SD 45, Hou 24
Dal 30, NYJ 7	St.L 42, Atl 21
LA 31, GB 14	NO 17, TB 10
Phil 20, NYG 3	Cinc 48, Clev 16
Det 33, SF 14	Oak 27, Minn 20
Mia 23, NE 3	

STANDINGS: SIXTEENTH WEEK

AFC EAST	W	L	T	CENTRAL	W	L	T	WEST	W	L	T	NFC EAST	W	L	T	CENTRAL	W	L	T	WEST	W	L	T
New England	11	5	0	Pittsburgh	14	2	0	Denver	10	6	0	Dallas	12	4	0	Minnesota	8	7	1	LA Rams	12	4	0
Miami	11	5	0	Houston	10	6	0	Oakland	9	7	0	Philadelphia	9	7	0	Green Bay	8	7	1	Atlanta	9	7	0
NY Jets	8	8	0	Cleveland	8	8	0	Seattle	9	7	0	Washington	8	8	0	Chicago	7	9	0	N.Orleans	7	9	0
Buffalo	5	11	0	Cincinnati	4	12	0	San Diego	9	7	0	NY Giants	6	10	0	Detroit	7	9	0	San Fran	2	14	0
Baltimore	5	11	0					Kan. City	4	12	0	St. Louis	6	10	0	Tampa Bay	5	11	0				

At A Glance
1979

Jan. 26 – Bob Lustig, vice-president and general manager of the Bills, said he would be leaving the team to become CEO of a new insurance company that Ralph Wilson was forming in Detroit. Stew Barber was elevated to the newly created position of vice-president in charge of administration, meaning he would assume Lustig's GM duties.

Feb. 1 – Reggie McKenzie, Mike Kadish and Sherman White became free agents when their contracts expired.

Feb. 8 – Former Bills quarterback Tom Flores was named head coach of the Oakland Raiders after John Madden resigned.

Feb. 15 – The Bills formed a scouting combine with Dallas, San Francisco and Seattle. Each team put four scouts into the organization to work full-time. The Bills scouts were Harvey Johnson, Tom Sherman, Elbert Dubenion and Winston Hill.

Feb. 21 – Despite the fact that he had moved to the West Coast to play pro football, O.J. Simpson filed for divorce from his wife Marguerite.

March 1 – WBEN radio reacquired the rights to broadcast Bills games and installed play-by-play man Van Miller and color commentator Stan Barron as its broadcast team. Miller was the voice of the Bills from 1960-71 before WKBW purchased the broadcast rights. WKBW did Bills games for seven years with play-by-play man Al Meltzer and color commentators Rick Azar and Ed Rutkowski.

March 2 – George "Chink" Sengel joined the Bills scouting staff.

March 16 – At the league meetings in Honolulu, NFL owners voted for the elimination of blocking below the waist on kickoffs, punts and field goals. They also ruled out instant replay.

March 18 – With the Bills almost certain to use the No. 1 pick in the draft on Ohio State linebacker Tom Cousineau, worry began to spread around One Bills Drive because Cousineau was considering hiring Howard Slusher as his agent. Slusher gave the Bills huge problems when he represented first- and second-round choices Tom Ruud and Bob Nelson in 1975, keeping them out of camp until right before the season opener.

April 2 – Los Angeles Rams owner Carroll Rosenbloom drowned in Miami Beach. His wife, Georgia, assumed control of the Rams. "I am tremendously saddened," said former Rams coach Chuck Knox. "He gave me the opportunity to be an NFL coach and for that I will always be grateful."

May 3 – As expected, the Bills used the No. 1 pick in the draft to select Ohio State linebacker Tom Cousineau. They also chose Clemson wide receiver Jerry Butler with their own first-round choice, No. 5 overall. Later, the Bills chose Boston College defensive tackle Fred Smerlas (second round), Indiana (Pa.) linebacker Jim Haslett (second), Montana State tackle Jon Borchardt (third), Richmond free safety Jeff Nixon (fourth), Nebraska-Omaha strong safety Rod Kush (fifth) and Kansas State quarterback Dan Manucci (fifth). Elsewhere in the first round, Kansas City chose defensive end Mike Bell (second), Chicago took defensive end Dan Hampton (fourth), Baltimore selected linebacker Barry Krauss (sixth), the Giants took quarterback Phil Simms (seventh), St. Louis took running back O.J. Anderson (eighth), San Diego chose tight end Kellen Winslow (13th) and the Jets took defensive end Marty Lyons (14th).

May 4 – Tom Cousineau, escorted not by Howard Slusher but with New York City lawyer Jim Walsh, met the media at Rich Stadium and indicated he wanted to sign with the Bills quickly. "I anticipate speedy negotiations, there is no reason for me to sit out," he said. "I want to play. I'm going to come in thoroughly prepared to play, in the best shape of my life." Said Walsh: "We expect no problems whatsoever because Tom says he doesn't want to have any problems (signing)."

May 5 – Sizing up the draft, Chuck Knox said: "We feel these are solid football players, but the real test of this draft will come two or three years from now. Smerlas is going to get everybody's attention."

May 9 – The Bills second first-round draft choice, Jerry Butler, wasted no time signing a contract. The Bills said they hoped to have Tom Cousineau signed by mini-camp.

May 16 – The Bills acquired safety Bill Simpson from the Rams for an undisclosed draft choice.

May 20 – Mini-camp opened at Rich Stadium and Tom Cousineau was a no-show. "Not being here hurts him," Chuck Knox said. "If we didn't think it would benefit the players, we wouldn't have them here."

May 26 – Elbert Dubenion, one of only three men in the Bills organization left from 1960, left the team to become a scout with the Miami Dolphins. His departure left scout Harvey Johnson and trainer Ed Abramoski as the only two members of Ralph Wilson's original football staff. Also, scout Tom Sherman was fired, creating a second vacancy in the newly formed scouting combine with Dallas, San Francisco and Seattle.

June 29 – Still unsigned, Tom Cousineau visited with Montreal of the Canadian Football League.

July 8 – Cousineau's agent, Jim Walsh, told a Toronto newspaper: "I think Tom would prefer to play in Montreal (in the CFL). I have no plans to talk to Buffalo, there's nothing to talk about."

July 11 – The Bills acquired another valued member of the Los Angeles Rams defense when linebacker Isiah Robertson came over in exchange for an undisclosed draft choice.

July 15 – Training camp opened at Niagara University.

July 16 – Fred Smerlas agreed to a contract, but Bill Simpson failed his physical and was returned to the Rams. Simpson had a knee problem.

July 17 – Reggie McKenzie, who said near the end of 1978 that he didn't want to play anymore for the Bills, signed a series of one-year contracts that would reportedly pay him more than $100,000 per season. "Now I want to take this team to the Super Bowl," he said. "I think this town would go nuts at a Super Bowl. I want to take us on to glory."

July 19 – Tom Cousineau signed a multi-year contract with Montreal of the CFL, leaving the Bills jilted. "The decision was strictly a business one," Cousineau said. The Bills reportedly had offered Cousineau a five- or six-year pact worth about $1.2 million, which they claimed was the richest offer ever made to an NFL rookie. Cousineau reportedly signed with the Alouettes for four years worth $850,000.

July 21 – Joe DeLamielleure signed a new six-year contract. In the second annual scrimmage at Edinboro, the Bills and Cleveland Browns battled to a 6-6 tie.

July 23 – Mike Kadish, who like Reggie McKenzie indicated at the end of 1978 that he didn't want to play in Buffalo, signed a new contract with the team.

July 27 – Former Bills kicker John Leypoldt arrived at camp prepared to give incumbent Tom Dempsey a challenge. Leypoldt played for New Orleans in 1978.

July 28 – The Bills and Browns battled to a 0-0 tie in a scrimmage at Kent State.

Aug. 4 – The Bills opened the preseason schedule with a 15-7 loss to Super Bowl champion Pittsburgh at Rich Stadium. The Bills used a 3-4 defense for the first time.

Aug. 11 – Detroit pounded the Bills, 34-13, at Rich Stadium.

Aug. 13 – John Leypoldt's bid to return to the Bills ended when he was cut. Also waived was John Holland, who missed all of 1978 with a broken leg.

Aug. 15 – Bob Chandler suffered a separated shoulder in practice and was told he'd be out 7-10 weeks.

Aug. 18 – The Bills fell to 0-3 in the preseason as James Lofton caught a 20-yard TD pass with 15 seconds left to give Green Bay a 7-6 victory at Lambeau Field.

Aug. 22 – Holdout defensive end Sherman White reported to camp.

Aug. 25 – The Bills closed their second straight winless preseason under Chuck Knox with a humbling 48-21 loss in Oakland. Because of the fuel crisis striking the nation, the team flew on its first commercial flight in more than 15 years.

Aug. 27 – Aaren Simpson, the 23-month-old daughter of O.J. Simpson, died in a Los Angeles hospital eight days after she was pulled unconscious

Jerry Butler (left) was the fifth player taken in the first-round of the 1979 draft. In his rookie year, Butler set Bills records for receiving yards (255) and touchdowns (4) in a game against the Jets.

Fred Smerlas (opposite page) was Buffalo's second-round pick in 1979 and he went on to play 11 years and competed in five Pro Bowls.

from a swimming pool.

Aug. 28 – In order to get down to the 45-man roster limit, safety Doug Jones was cut as he lost the battle at strong safety to Steve Freeman.

Sept. 2 – Tom Dempsey missed a 34-yard field goal on the final play, preventing the Bills from beating Miami. The Dolphins escaped with their 19th straight victory over the Bills, 9-7, in front of 69,441 at rain-soaked Rich Stadium, which was deluged by a storm in the fourth quarter.

Sept. 9 – Roland Hooks carried only five times, but scored four touchdowns as the Bills routed Cincinnati, 51-24, at Rich Stadium. Jerry Butler enjoyed his first 100-yard receiving day.

Sept. 14 – Because torrential rains flooded streets around the Buffalo airport, 18 members of the Bills traveling party, including Chuck Knox, missed the team flight to San Diego. They boarded another flight later in the morning.

Sept. 16 – The Bills remained winless on the West Coast since Nov. 24, 1966, a span of 11 games, as San Diego inflicted a 27-19 defeat behind four TDs by Clarence Williams.

Sept. 18 – The Bills auditioned ex-Steeler great Roy Gerela and former Eagle Nick Mike-Mayer as Chuck Knox expressed deep concern over Tom Dempsey's performance.

Sept. 19 – As expected, Tom Dempsey was waived and Knox signed Mike-Mayer to replace him. "It was a tough decision to cut Tom, but it was a decision we had to make for the betterment of the Buffalo Bills," Knox said.

Sept. 23 – Joe Ferguson set a team record with five TD passes and threw for a career-high 367 yards while Jerry Butler caught 10 passes and set team records for yards (255) and TDs (four) as the Bills routed the Jets, 46-31, at Rich Stadium. NBC broadcaster John Brodie said of Butler: "That was

the best single-game performance I've ever seen from a wide receiver. I played 16 years, but I've never seen anything like that."

Sept. 30 – The Bills improved to 3-2, their best start since 1975, as Joe Ferguson topped 300 yards passing for the third time in his career and the first time in back-to-back games in a 31-13 rout of the Colts at Baltimore.

Oct. 7 – Walter Payton rushed for 155 yards on 39 carries and scored the game's only TD on a one-yard swan dive in the fourth quarter as Chicago beat the Bills, 7-0, before 73,383 at Rich Stadium, the largest home crowd since the 1977 season opener against Miami.

Oct. 14 – The Dolphins completed an incredible decade of domination over the Bills, winning 17-7 at the Orange Bowl. It was their 20th straight victory over Buffalo, extending their NFL record.

Oct. 18 – Hall of Famer Johnny Unitas made the following statement on his television show in Baltimore when a caller questioned Colts coach Ted Marchibroda's guts: "I've known Ted a long time. It's wrong to say he doesn't have courage. I think Ted's problem is that he has trouble making decisions. It's his judgment."

Oct. 21 – The Colts came into Rich Stadium and edged the Bills, 14-13, Buffalo's third straight loss.

Oct. 27 – With the new Carrier Dome under construction in Syracuse, the Orangemen played one of their "home" games at Rich Stadium and defeated the University of Miami, 25-15, in front of only about 8,000 fans. Bill Hurley, a St. Joseph's graduate and Buffalo native, rushed for 109 yards and passed for 99 in his return home. Also for Syracuse, kicker Gary Anderson made four field goals and Joe Morris rushed for 124 yards. Miami freshman quarterback Jim Kelly entered the game in the third quarter and threw for one TD and passed for a two-point conversion. He completed seven of 17 passes for 130 yards in the first extended action of his collegiate career. The following week, he started against Penn State and whipped the Nittany Lions at Beaver Stadium, 26-10, and his career took off from there.

Oct. 28 – Down 17-6 after three quarters, the Bills rallied for two fourth-quarter TDs including Joe Ferguson's game-winning seven-yard TD pass to Reuben Gant with 1:25 left as the Bills defeated the struggling Detroit Lions, 20-17, in the Silverdome. After the game, the players awarded the game ball to Detroit native and Bills owner Ralph Wilson and sang him a song: "Hooray for Ralph, Hooray for us, Hooray for Ralph, He's a Horse's Ass!"

Oct. 29 – It was announced that Jerry Butler and Bobby Chandler would be sidelined indefinitely with shoulder injuries, meaning Frank Lewis and Lou Piccone would start.

Nov. 2 – Chandler was placed on injured reserve for what was believed to be the rest of the season. "I'm not going to quit football this way," he said. "By no means am I through being the quality player that I've been."

Nov. 4 – New England forced five Buffalo turnovers and rolled to a 26-6 victory at Rich Stadium. Steve Grogan stunned the Bills with 350 passing yards.

Nov. 11 – With Pat Leahy injured, the Jets signed ex-Colt kicker Toni Linhart. He missed both of his extra point attempts on a rainy day at Shea Stadium and that was the difference in Buffalo's 14-12 victory. Joe Ferguson called his own plays for the first time in his career.

Nov. 18 – Joe Ferguson conducted a 16-play, 81-yard drive that culminated with Mike Collier's one-yard TD run with 3:04 remaining as the Bills beat the Packers, 19-12, at Rich Stadium.

Nov. 21 – Chuck Knox announced that Jeff Nixon would start in place of veteran Tony Greene at free safety against New England. He also announced Frank Lewis would miss the game, but that Jerry Butler would return.

Nov. 25 – Nick Mike-Mayer kicked a 29-yard field goal to give the Bills a 16-13 upset victory over the Patriots at Schaefer Stadium in the first overtime game in club history.

Nov. 26 – Fred Smerlas, who suffered a knee injury at New England, learned that surgery wouldn't be required and his season might not be over.

Nov. 28 – O.J. Simpson was named the NFL's player of the decade by *Pro Football Monthly*.

Dec. 2 – The Bills defense turned in a superb effort, but Jim Turner's 32-yard field goal on the final play of the game gave Denver a 19-16 victory at cold, snowy Rich Stadium. The loss knocked the Bills out of playoff contention. Joe Ferguson set a team record with 27 completions and set a new personal mark with 46 attempts. It was his fifth 300-yard passing game, fourth in '79.

Dec. 8 – O.J. Simpson made it official as he announced his retirement from football effective at the end of the season.

Dec. 9 – The Bills fell below .500 to 7-8 by losing to Minnesota, 10-3, at Metropolitan Stadium, despite a solid defensive performance. Jim Marshall played in his 281st straight game as a Viking and in the final home game of his 20-year career, he recorded a sack.

Dec. 12 – Jerry Butler, Jim Haslett and Fred Smerlas were named to UPI's all-rookie team.

Meanwhile, Joe DeLamielleure was named to the AFC Pro Bowl squad for the fifth straight year. Joe Ferguson, who was the NFL's leading passer through 11 weeks, was left off the team in favor of Dan Fouts and Terry Bradshaw.

Dec. 16 – The Bills closed their season with a real downer, losing their third game in a row, 28-0, to the defending champion Steelers in Pittsburgh. The Steelers needed to win to lock up the AFC Central crown and they dominated, limiting the Bills to 156 yards and eight first downs. Jim Haslett was ejected for stepping on Terry Bradshaw's head after the whistle had blown. In San Francisco, O.J. Simpson made only a token appearance in the 49ers 31-21 loss to Atlanta. In his final NFL game, Simpson gained 12 yards on two carries.

Dec. 17 – Steelers coach Chuck Noll, after reviewing the game film, charged Jim Haslett with deliberately trying to hurt Terry Bradshaw. "It was no question an intentional act," Noll said. Haslett, who told a photographer in the locker room to put his camera away or "I'll break it over you head" calmed down later and actually called the *Pittsburgh Press*. "I didn't want to hurt anybody, especially him (Bradshaw)," Haslett said. "I felt so bad after the game and I didn't know what I should say, so I didn't say anything."

Dec. 21 – Jim Haslett was named defensive rookie of the year by The Associated Press. Haslett's performance certainly made everyone in Buffalo forget about Tom Cousineau.

Dec. 23 – Philadelphia downed Chicago, 27-17, and Houston edged Denver, 13-7, in wild-card playoff games.

Dec. 29 – In the divisional playoffs, Tampa Bay won its first postseason game, edging Philadelphia, 24-17, while Houston nipped San Diego, 17-14.

Dec. 30 – Los Angeles upset Dallas, 21-19, and

Pittsburgh scorched Miami, 34-14, on the second day of the divisional playoffs.

Jan. 6, 1980 – Pittsburgh won its fourth AFC Championship Game in six years, downing arch-rival Houston, 27-13, as the Steel Curtain defense limited Earl Campbell to 15 yards on 17 carries. Los Angeles won its first NFC Championship Game blanking Tampa Bay, 9-0. Frank Corral kicked three field goals and the Rams defense held the Bucs to 177 yards.

Jan. 20, 1980 – Pittsburgh rallied for two fourth-quarter touchdowns and defeated Los Angeles, 31-19, to win its fourth Super Bowl championship in six years. Terry Bradshaw threw for 309 yards and two TDs and won his second consecutive Super Bowl MVP award.

Jan. 27, 1980 – The Pro Bowl was played in Honolulu for the first time and the NFC won for the third year in a row, 37-27, as New Orleans' Chuck Muncie scored twice and was named MVP.

Jim Haslett came out of tiny Indiana (Pa.) University and was named the Defensive Rookie of the Year in 1979 by the Associated Press.

BY THE NUMBERS - 1979

TEAM STATISTICS	BILLS	OPP
First downs	252	273
Rushing	83	137
Passing	147	117
Penalty	22	19
Total yards	4,837	5,011
Avg. game	302.3	313.2
Plays	982	1,022
Avg. play	4.9	4.9
Net rushing yds	1,621	2,481
Avg. game	101.3	155.1
Avg. play	3.4	4.0
Net passing yds	3,216	2,530
Comp/att	241/465	193/382
Sacks/lost	43-387	23-183
Interceptions	15	24
Percentage	51.8	50.5
Punts/avg	96-38.2	92-38.2
Fumbles/lost	32-19	31-17
Penalties/yds	104-887	106-788
Touchdowns	30	34
Extra points	25-30	27-34
Field goals	21-33	16-31
Safeties	0	0
Kick ret./avg	59-19.2	54-21.1
Punt ret./avg	38-8.4	61-9.1

RUSHING	ATT	YDS	AVG	TD
Brown	172	574	3.3	1
Miller	139	484	3.5	1
Hooks	89	320	3.6	6
Collier	34	130	3.8	2
Ferguson	22	68	3.1	1
Powell	10	29	2.9	0
Butler	2	13	6.5	0
Johnson	3	5	1.7	0
Mike-Mayer	1	4	4.0	0
Lewis	2	-6	-3.0	0
TOTALS	**474**	**1621**	**3.4**	**11**

PASSING	COMP	ATT	INT	YDS	TD	COMP%	SACKS	RATE
Ferguson	238	458	15	3572	14	52.0	43-387	74.5
Munson	3	7	0	31	0	42.9	0-0	56.3
TOTALS	**241**	**465**	**15**	**3603**	**14**	**51.8**	**43-387**	**74.2**

KICKING	1-19	20-29	30-39	40-49	50+	TOT	PAT	PTS
Dempsey	1-1	0-0	0-2	0-1	0-0	1-4	8-11	11
Mike-Mayer	0-0	8-8	8-10	4-11	0-0	20-29	17-18	77
TOTALS	**1-1**	**8-8**	**8-12**	**4-12**	**0-0**	**21-33**	**25-29**	**88**

PUNTING	NO	AVG	LG	In 20	BL
Jackson	96	38.2	60	14	0

RECEIVING	CAT	YDS	AVG	TD
Lewis	54	1082	20.0	2
Butler	48	834	17.4	4
Brown	39	401	10.3	3
Piccone	33	556	16.8	2
Hooks	26	254	9.8	0
Gant	19	245	12.9	2
Miller	10	111	11.1	0
Collier	7	43	6.1	0
Shipp	3	43	14.3	1
Fulton	2	34	17.0	0
TOTALS	**241**	**3603**	**15.0**	**14**

LEADERS

Kick returns: Moody 27-556 yards, 20.6 avg, 0 TD
Miller 8-160, 20.0, 0 TD

Punt returns: Moody 38-318, 8.4, 0 TD

Interceptions: Nixon 6-81, 13.5, 0 TD
Clark 5-95, 19.0, 0 TD

SCORE BY QUARTERS

BILLS	21	73	95	76	3 -	268
OPP	54	91	50	84	0 -	279

This missed field goal by **Tom Dempsey** in the 1979 season opener against **Miami** prevented the **Bills** from ending their **NFL-record 18-game losing streak** to the **Dolphins.**

Dolphins	0	0	3 6	- 9
Bills	0	7	0 0	- 7

Attendance at Rich Stadium - 69,441

Buf: Romes 76 blocked field goal return (Dempsey kick), 7:15
Mia: FG von Schamann 34, 8:35 (Dempsey kick), 7:15
Mia: Csonka 1 run (kick failed), 8:31

	BUF	MIA
First downs	5	20
Rushing yds	45	175
Passing yds	76	118
Punts-avg	6-39.6	5-40.2
Fumbles-lost	0-0	0-0
Penalties-yds	2-15	6-50

BILLS LEADERS: Rushing - Brown 9-10, Miller 9-24, Hooks 6-5, Ferguson 1-6; **Passing** - Ferguson 7-13-1 - 85; **Receiving** - Butler 3-32, Lewis 2-48, Gant 1-11, Brown 1-(-6).

DOLPHINS LEADERS: Rushing - Williams 17-52, Csonka 16-87, Davis 7-36; **Passing** - Griese 14-27-1 - 139; **Receiving** - Csonka 4-20, Moore 1-25, Williams 3-22, Hardy 4-41, Cefalo 1-17, Davis 1-14.

WEEK 1 GAMES

TB 31, Det 16	Dal 22, St.L 21
Atl 40, NO 24	Chi 6, GB 3
KC 14, Balt 0	Oak 24, LA 17
Hou 29, Wash 27	Minn 28, SF 22
Den 10, Cinc 0	SD 33, Sea 16
Phil 23, NYG 17	Pit 16, NE 13 OT
Clev 25, NYJ 22 (OT)	

NOTES

• Tom Dempsey missed a 34-yard field goal on the final play and the Bills lost for the 19th straight time to Miami.
• The field was soaked as a monsoon-like rain swept through the stadium starting in the third quarter, but the rain had subsided when Dempsey attempted his kick.
• The Bills' new 3-4 defense played very well in its regular-season debut, but the offense was pathetic with only five first downs and 121 total yards.
• Larry Csonka, returning to the Dolphins after a four-year absence, capped an impressive 14-play, 77-yard march in the fourth that consumed 8:33 while the skies were wide open. Csonka carried seven times for 45 yards on the drive.
• The Bills had taken a 7-0 lead when Sherman White blocked a Uwe von Schamann field goal and Charlie Romes picked up the loose ball and ran 76 yards for a TD in the second quarter.
• The Bills were in position to win when Keith Moody returned a punt 28 yards to the Miami 35 with 1:47 remaining. Terry Miller gained three, then Joe Ferguson hit Reuben Gant for 11. A pair of Curtis Brown runs put the ball on the 18 and set up Dempsey's attempt.
• Jim Haslett made 17 tackles in his NFL debut.

QUOTES

• Tom Dempsey: "This is only the second time it's happened (missing a winning kick on the final play, the first coming in 1973 when he missed against the Bills while playing for the Eagles). It was just a bad kick on my part. It felt good, the snap and hold were good and the weather was not a factor. A kicker's job can depend on one kick and I'm thinking about that right now."
• Dolphins running back Larry Csonka: "It was the same old story. Our offensive line moved them out. I was hoping it would rain because I figured they'd give me the ball more. But for a team that's not too well-known, they have quite a few defensive players who are going to be heard from. In the preseason films, they didn't look too good. I can't remember the names, but I remember the hits."
• Chuck Knox: "Our strategy (at the end) was to play for the field goal. We hadn't scored in 59 minutes so there was no reason to think we'd score one then. If you hold somebody to nine points, you should win. But on that (TD) drive, we let them off the hook. They had a third-and-eight and they made that little sweep (Gary Davis) for the first down. We lost because offensively we didn't move the ball."
• Jim Haslett: "I didn't realize playing Miami was such a big deal around here until the week of the game. The fans started talking and Reggie McKenzie started talking. I made a lot of tackles, but I also made a lot of mistakes. The only time they really hurt us was that one touchdown drive."
• Joe Ferguson on the conservative offense: "I've got a few thoughts on the subject, but I can't talk about it."

Bengals	0	10	7	7	- 24
Bills	0	10	21	20	- 51

Attendance at Rich Stadium - 43,504

Buf: FG Dempsey 18, :51
Cin: Johnson 1 run (Bahr kick), 5:49
Buf: Miller 2 run (Dempsey kick), 9:36
Cin: FG Bahr 24, 13:46
Buf: Hooks 3 run (Dempsey kick), 2:37
Buf: Robertson 23 interception return (Dempsey kick), 10:17
Cin: Brooks 73 pass from Anderson (Bahr kick), 11:41
Buf: Hooks 32 run (Dempsey kick), 12:46
Buf: Hooks 4 run (Dempsey kick), 1:30
Buf: Hooks 28 run (kick blocked), 3:31
Buf: Sanford 3 blocked punt return (Dempsey kick), 4:51
Cin: Thompson 5 run (Bahr kick), 13:06

	BUF	CIN
First downs	23	16
Rushing yds	209	134
Passing yds	246	201
Punts-avg	4-33.3	8-34.3
Fumbles-lost	4-2	1-1
Penalties-yds	3-30	9-67

BILLS LEADERS: Rushing - Brown 14-64, Miller 8-43, Hooks 5-70, Ferguson 1-2, Powell 7-28, Johnson 1-2; **Passing** - Ferguson 16-21-0 - 282; **Receiving** - Butler 7-116, Lewis 2-35, Gant 2-29, Hooks 3-60, Piccone 1-33, Brown 1-9.

BENGALS LEADERS: Rushing - Griffin 12-56, P. Johnson 13-42, Anderson 2-17, Turner 4-10, Alexander 1-4, Thompson 1-5; **Passing** - Anderson 11-22-1 -196, Thompson 2-5-1 - 24; **Receiving** - Brooks 6-156, Griffin 3-31, Alexander 2-13, Bass 1-11, P. Johnson 1-9.

NOTES

• After a terrible opening-day performance, the Bills' offense exploded as Roland Hooks carried five times and scored four touchdowns. He had three career TDs entering the game; Jerry Butler enjoyed his first 100-yard receiving day.
• The Bills gained 258 yards in the first half but managed only a 10-10 tie before scoring 41 second-half points. Charlie Romes stood behind the bench leading the cheers and the crowd responded.
• On the first play of the second half, Isiah Robertson forced Pete Johnson to fumble and Shane Nelson recovered at the Bengals 16. Four plays later, Hooks scored his first TD.
• Robertson then intercepted a Ken Anderson pass and returned it 23 yards for a TD, touching off an incredible 34-point frenzy in about 10 minutes.
• Bill Brooks got behind the Bills secondary for a 73-yard TD to cut the margin to 24-17, but the Bills then took charge. On the first play after the kickoff, Terry Miller ran 25 yards and on the next play, Hooks broke a 32-yard TD run.
• On the next possession, Hooks caught a 42-yard pass which set up his four-yard TD run. Lucious Sanford then intercepted a Jack Thompson pass and returned it 25 yards to the Bengals 33. Two plays later, Hooks scored on a 28-yard gallop. Sanford then finished the rout by blocking a Pat McInally punt and returning it three yards for a TD.

WEEK 2 GAMES

LA 13, Den 9	Clev 27, KC 24
Mia 19, Sea 10	Pitt 38, Hou 7
Dal 21, SF 13	Wash 27, Det 24
St.L 27, NYG 14	Chi 26, Minn 7
GB 28, NO 19	NE 56, NYJ 3
SD 30, Oak 10	Atl 14, Phil 10
B 29, Balt 26 (OT)	

QUOTES

• Roland Hooks: "I learned one thing from watching O.J. Simpson and that's how to follow your blockers. I was playing behind the greatest running back who ever played the game. You can't learn from O.J. because his skills are instinctive. Playing behind him didn't bother me, I was just glad to be on the team. I didn't do anything special today that our other backs couldn't do. I was just in the open so much. The thing that bothers me is I've been here five years and I've played pretty decent, but there's still a lot of people in Buffalo who don't even know who I am."
• Reggie McKenzie: "We wanted to come out smoking, that was our cry as we came out before the game. I saw some O.J. moves out there from Hooks."
• Joe Ferguson: "This may have been the greatest team effort since I've been here. Jerry's the best rookie receiver I've had since I've been here. A lot of guys are scared to go over the middle. You can't coach that. Jerry's moving all the time. After mini-camp, I knew he'd be good."
• Chuck Knox: "We're not as good as the scoreboard indicated, but we're getting better."

STANDINGS: SECOND WEEK

AFC EAST	W	L	T	CENTRAL	W	L	T	WEST	W	L	T	NFC EAST	W	L	T	CENTRAL	W	L	T	WEST	W	L	T
Miami	2	0	0	Pittsburgh	2	0	0	San Diego	2	0	0	Dallas	2	0	0	Tampa Bay	2	0	0	Atlanta	2	0	0
Buffalo	1	1	0	Cleveland	2	0	0	Kan. City	1	1	0	Philadelphia	1	1	0	Chicago	2	0	0	LA Rams	1	1	0
New England	1	1	0	Houston	1	1	0	Denver	1	1	0	Washington	1	1	0	Minnesota	1	1	0	N.Orleans	0	2	0
NY Jets	0	2	0	Cincinnati	0	2	0	Oakland	1	1	0	St. Louis	1	1	0	Green Bay	1	1	0	San Fran	0	2	0
Baltimore	0	2	0					Seattle	0	2	0	NY Giants	0	2	0	Detroit	0	2	0				

NOTES

• Normally an awesome passing team, San Diego churned out 245 rushing yards as Clarence Williams rushed for a career-high 157 yards and four TDs. His four TDs tied the single-game team record set by Lance Alworth in 1968.

• Dan Fouts threw only 13 passes as the Bills took away the aerial game, but paid for it on the ground.

• The temperature soared to 102 degrees during the game.

• The Bills grabbed the early lead as Joe Ferguson hit Frank Lewis for a TD after Willie Parker had recovered a fumbled punt by Mike Fuller at the Chargers 40. Tom Dempsey's PAT was wide.

• The Chargers came back with an 80-yard drive, including 76 on the ground, to take a 7-6 lead, and on their next possession, they went 73 yards to Williams' second TD. Charlie Romes blocked the PAT.

• Late in the half, the Bills began an impressive 80-yard march as Ferguson completed five passes for 57 yards and then scrambled the final 10 yards for the TD with four seconds left. But Dempsey's conversion was wide again, leaving the Bills behind at the half, 13-12.

• The Bills went ahead early in the third as Curtis Brown took a screen pass 84 yards for a TD. But two plays later, Williams used a great block by Charlie Joiner on Tony Greene and broke a 55-yard TD run to make it 20-19 San Diego. The final Williams score culminated an 80-yard march.

QUOTES

• San Diego running back Clarence Williams: "I've been waiting for a chance to run and I got it today. We got the feeling early that we wouldn't have to pass at all. We came out passing on our first series and then we ran on the second. After that, there was no reason to change our tactics. The line did a great job and it was a matter of me running to daylight. The nose guard (Fred Smerlas) was slanting outside a lot and we caught him a few times. I was reading off him on a lot of the runs."

• Chuck Knox: "A lot of people are going to know who Clarence Williams is today, but we made him look awfully good. We did not tackle well at all. We were beaten by a helluva team. You can't ever be pleased when you lose, but we battled our butts off."

• San Diego guard Ed White: "We weren't picking on Smerlas. He has a great future, but he was going against who I consider the best center in the league (Don Macek). We're known for being pretty unpredictable, but today, I think we were true to form. I looked up at the scoreboard and saw our passing stats and I couldn't believe it. I think we surprised them (by running)."

• San Diego coach Don Coryell: "I was impressed with that whole Buffalo club. They're a good football team. Believe me, they're going to win more games than people think."

WEEK 3 GAMES	
Clev 13, Balt 10	Hou 20, KC 6
TB 21, GB 10	Pitt 24, St.L 21
Mia 27, Minn 12	Sea 27, Oak 10
Dal 24, Chi 20	LA 27, SF 24
Phil 26, NO 14	NYJ 31, Det 10
NE 20, Cinc 14	Wash 27, NYG 0
Den 20, Atl 17 (OT)	

Bills	6	6	7	0	-	19
Chargers	7	6	7	7	-	27

Attendance at San Diego Stadium - 50,709

Buf: Lewis 21 pass from Ferguson (kick failed), 5:16
SD: Williams 5 run (Benirschke kick), 10:14
SD: Williams 1 run (kick blocked), 1:34
Buf: Ferguson 10 run (kick failed), 14:56
Buf: Brown 84 pass from Ferguson (Dempsey kick), 5:33
SD: Williams 55 run (Benirschke kick), 6:35
SD: Williams 2 run (Benirschke kick), 3:46

	BUF	SD
First downs	14	18
Rushing yds	59	245
Passing yds	238	94
Punts-avg	7-48.0	6-41.2
Fumbles-lost	1-0	2-1
Penalties-yds	5-45	5-40

BILLS LEADERS: Rushing - Brown 8-11, Miller 8-26, Hooks 4-6, Ferguson 3-18, Johnson 2-3, Lewis 1- (-5); **Passing** - Ferguson 16-29-0 - 257; **Receiving** - Brown 8-157, Lewis 2-36, Hooks 4-43, Gant 1-7, Butler 1-14.

CHARGERS LEADERS: Rushing - C. Williams 18-157, Thomas 13-77, Owens 1-12, Bauer 1-3, Fouts 3- (-4); **Passing** - Fouts 8-13-0 - 100; **Receiving** - Thomas 2-53, Klein 1-6, Joiner 1-9, Winslow 2-19, C. Williams 2-13.

NOTES

• Jerry Butler set a team record for receiving yards and his four TDs tied him with Roland Hooks (earlier in 1979) and O.J. Simpson in (1975). Joe Ferguson set a team mark with his five TD passes and passed for a career-high 367 yards in the rout of New York. Ferguson became the top-rated passer in the NFL with a 119 rating.

• The 497 yards of total offense was a Rich Stadium record, but the Bills' run defense remained porous, averaging 205 yards allowed per game, worst in the NFL.

• The Bills trailed 24-12 late in the first half, but Butler made an amazing play, catching a 75-yard TD pass with one second left on a Hail Mary pass the Bills called the Big Ben.

• Trailing 6-3, the Jets took charge in the second quarter as Tom Newton broke a 51-yard TD run, then capped a 63-yard TD march with a one-yard run. Butler's first TD was answered by Richard Todd's scoring strike to Wesley Walker which capped a quick 80-yard drive. Then came the Big Ben.

• Early in the third, Butler took a pass away from Jets cornerback Johnny Lynn for a 74-yard TD and on the next possession, his nine-yard score ended a 55-yard drive. Just three minutes later, Sherman White decked Todd, who fumbled, and Fred Smerlas returned it 13 yards for a TD.

QUOTES

• Joe Ferguson: "Right now I rate Butler as one of the best receivers we've ever had here. When Bobby Chandler comes back, we'll have to start three receivers because you can't sit Butler or Lewis. It felt good that the fans came out today because it shows me they are starting to believe in us. They picked us up today, especially in the second half." (On the Big Ben): "The play called for Lewis to go high and tip the ball to either Butler or Piccone. We've tried it against three or four teams, but it's never worked."

• Jerry Butler: "I have to thank Joe Ferguson, he's the best quarterback in football. I have come to really look up to him. In my first game here, I was really hurt when the fans booed me because when they boo Joe, I feel they're booing the entire offense." (On the Big Ben): "I've seen it tried on television, but I've never seen it work. I didn't think it was going to work this time."

• Joe DeLamielleure on his feelings before the Big Ben: "I had a feeling we were in trouble. I told the priest (team chaplain John Manion) it's going to be a long day if we don't do something big really quick."

WEEK 4 GAMES	
Mia 31, Chi 16	Det 24, Atl 23
NE 27, SD 21	KC 35, Oak 7
Wash 17, St.L 7	Den 37, Sea 34
TB 21, LA 6	Min 27, GB 21 OT
Phil 17, NYG 13	Pitt 17, Balt 13
NO 30, SF 21	Clev 26, Dal 7
Hou 30, Cinc 27 (OT)	

Jets	3	21	0	7	-	31
Bills	6	13	21	6	-	46

Attendance at Rich Stadium - 68,731

Buf: FG Mike-Mayer 23, 3:56
NYJ: FG Leahy 30, 9:35
Buf: FG Mike-Mayer 29, 13:50
NYJ: Newton 51 run (Leahy kick), :08
NYJ: Newton 1 run (Leahy kick), 5:17
Buf: Butler 5 pass from Ferguson (kick blocked), 9:48
NYJ: Walker 37 pass from Todd (Leahy kick), 11:33
Buf: Butler 75 pass from Ferguson (Mike-Mayer kick), 14:59
Buf: Butler 74 pass from Ferguson (Mike-Mayer kick), 5:29
Buf: Butler 9 pass from Ferguson (Mike-Mayer kick), 9:28
Buf: Smerlas 13 fumble return (Mike-Mayer kick), 12:58
Buf: Shipp 13 pass from Ferguson (kick failed), 11:55
NYJ: Shuler 27 pass from Todd (Leahy kick), 14:59

	BUF	NYJ
First downs	25	22
Rushing yds	149	265
Passing yds	348	151
Punts-avg	3-34.7	2-39.5
Fumbles-lost	1-1	2-1
Penalties-yds	6-60	7-43

BILLS LEADERS: Rushing - Brown 15-73, Miller 12-40, Hooks 10-24, Butler 1-12; **Passing** - Ferguson 19-30-0 - 367; **Receiving** - Butler 10-255, Lewis 3-60, Hooks 2-8, Miller 3-26, Brown 1-5, Shipp 1-13.

JETS LEADERS: Rushing - Newton 8-68, Gaines 13-88, Dierking 17-97, Harper 4-12; **Passing** - Todd 11-21-3 - 168; **Receiving** - Gaffney 2-31, Walker 3-50, Gaines 2-9, Shuler 3-72, Raba 1-6.

STANDINGS: FOURTH WEEK

AFC EAST	W	L	T	CENTRAL	W	L	T	WEST	W	L	T	NFC EAST	W	L	T	CENTRAL	W	L	T	WEST	W	L	T
Miami	4	0	0	Pittsburgh	4	0	0	San Diego	3	1	0	Dallas	3	1	0	Tampa Bay	4	0	0	Atlanta	2	2	0
New England	3	1	0	Cleveland	4	0	0	Denver	3	1	0	Philadelphia	3	1	0	Chicago	2	2	0	LA Rams	2	2	0
Buffalo	2	2	0	Houston	3	1	0	Kan. City	2	2	0	Washington	3	1	0	Minnesota	2	2	0	N.Orleans	1	3	0
NY Jets	1	3	0	Cincinnati	0	4	0	Oakland	1	3	0	St. Louis	1	3	0	Green Bay	1	3	0	San Fran	0	4	0
Baltimore	0	4	0					Seattle	1	3	0	NY Giants	0	4	0	Detroit	1	3	0				

Bills	0 14 17 0 - 31
Colts	3 3 0 7 - 13

Attendance at Memorial Stadium - 31,904

Bal: FG S. Mike-Mayer 20, 9:48
Bal: FG S. Mike-Mayer 33, 1:44
Buf: Hooks 1 run (N. Mike-Mayer kick), 8:07
Buf: Lewis 24 pass from Ferguson (N. Mike-Mayer kick), 14:45
Buf: Piccone 47 pass from Ferguson (N. Mike-Mayer kick), 3:17
Buf: Gant 9 pass from Ferguson (N. Mike-Mayer kick), 8:56
Buf: FG N. Mike-Mayer 41, 12:24
Bal: McCall 4 pass from Landry (S. Mike-Mayer kick), 12:59

	BUF	BAL
First downs	16	18
Rushing yds	66	84
Passing yds	308	265
Punts-avg	6-37.5	5-38.0
Fumbles-lost	1-1	2-1
Penalties-yds	9-85	11-92

BILLS LEADERS: Rushing - Brown 10-15, Miller 4-13, Hooks 11-35, Powell 3-1, Ferguson 2-2; **Passing** - Ferguson 14-23-1 - 317; **Receiving** - Lewis 3-120, Piccone 2-67, Miller 2-49, Butler 3-48, Gant 2-18, Brown 2-15.

COLTS LEADERS: Rushing - Washington 14-37, Leaks 13-25, McCauley 5-14, Landry 4-8; **Passing** - Landry 22-38-1 - 277; **Receiving** - McCall 5-80, Doughty 4-79, McCauley 6-73, Washington 4-27, Leaks 3-18.

WEEK 5 GAMES

LA 21, St.L 0	Hou 31, Clev 10
NO 24, NYG 14	Wash 16, Atl 7
Oak 27, Den 3	Minn 13, Det 10
SD 31, SF 9	Dal 38, Cinc 13
KC 24, Sea 6	TB 17, Chi 13
NYJ 33, Mia 27	Phil 17, Pit 14
GB 27, NE 14	

NOTES

• For the first time in his career, Joe Ferguson had two straight 300-yard passing games.
• This week it was Frank Lewis who took center stage as the Colts doubled Jerry Butler all day.
• The Colts drove into Buffalo territory four times in the first half but scored only six points. In the first 16:44, they ran 30 plays to the Bills' four and out-gained Buffalo, 131-1.
• With the Bills trailing, 6-0, in the second quarter, Lewis caught a 55-yard pass to the 1 from where Roland Hooks scored. A few plays before his catch, Lewis had caught a 75-yard TD pass that was nullified by a holding penalty on Joe Devlin. Lewis then capped an 80-yard drive when he caught a 24-yard TD pass that was deflected by cornerback Doug Nettles with 15 seconds left in the first half. The score came after Terry

Miller toted a Ferguson screen pass 52 yards.
• The Bills made it 21-6 on their first possession of the third as Ferguson hit Lou Piccone with a 47-yard TD.
• Lewis caught a 41-yard pass and Butler made a 21-yard grab to set up Reuben Gant's nine-yard TD later in the third that made it 28-6. Following a Steve Freeman interception, Nick Mike-Mayer capped a 17-point third quarter with a 41-yard field goal.
• The Colts closed the scoring in the fourth on Greg Landry's TD pass to Reese McCall.
• Rain-soaked Colts fans chanted "Good-bye Teddy" to coach Ted Marchibroda as the Colts fell to 0-5.

QUOTES

• Joe Ferguson: "We're not a championship team yet, but we are getting better every week and the team can sense that something good is happening here. We're not a powerhouse by any means, but we're going to be. When Baltimore came out and held the ball, I was worried to death. For a while there, we were afraid we wouldn't be able to use our game plan, but that touchdown to Frank that got called back picked us up. We felt like we could move the ball if our defense could hold them. I'm gaining more confidence in the team, and, I guess, in myself."
• Frank Lewis: "This team is coming on, I can see it happening. It's great being part of a team that's putting it together. Last year we played a lot of close games and finished with a 5-11 record, but I thought with a few breaks we could have been 9-7. I was looking forward to coming back this year."
• Tony Greene: "Most of the guys on the team now don't know about the past. All they know is we're winning and we're making some big plays. Winning solves a lot of problems. It seems every week one of the units is picking the others up."
• Colts coach Ted Marchibroda: "Maybe they're (booing fans) right. I'm in a business where you have to win, but I'll say one thing, we will win."
• Chuck Knox: "It wasn't easy, we had to work for it."

Bears	0 0 0 7 - 7
Bills	0 0 0 0 - 0

Attendance at Rich Stadium - 73,383

Chi: Payton 1 run (Thomas kick), 3:42

	BUF	CHI
First downs	7	15
Rushing yds	64	240
Passing yds	42	18
Punts-avg	9-34.3	8-38.8
Fumbles-lost	2-1	4-2
Penalties-yds	4-40	9-60

BILLS LEADERS: Rushing - Brown 9-7, Miller 6-30, Hooks 6-10, Ferguson 2-16, Butler 1-1; **Passing** - Ferguson 5-21-1 - 50; **Receiving** - Brown 2-11, Piccone 1-23, Butler 1-7, Gant 1-9.

BEARS LEADERS: Rushing - Payton 39-155, Earl 17-74, Deloplaine 4-7, McClendon 1-2, Avellini 1-2; **Passing** - Avellini 4-8-0 - 22; **Receiving** - Earl 2-13, Payton 2-9.

WEEK 6 GAMES

Dal 36, Minn 20	LA 35, NO 7
Den 7, SD 0	Balt 10, NYJ 8
KC 10, Cinc 7	Phil 28, Wash 17
NYG 17, TB 14	Atl 25, GB 7
St.L 24, Hou 17	NE 24, Det 17
Pitt 51, Clev 35	Sea 35, SF 24
Oak 13, Mia 3	

NOTES

• The explosive Bills offense went into hibernation against a tough Bears defense, managing only 106 yards.
• Walter Payton tore through the Bills for 155 yards and scored the only TD in the fourth quarter. On the first play of the fourth, Curtis Brown fumbled and Jerry Muckenstrum recovered at the Bills 13. It took Chicago seven plays to score as Payton flew over a goal-line pile.
• Payton had 100 yards at halftime, but the Bills' defense played better in the second half. His 39 carries were the most ever by a Bills' opponent, breaking the mark of 34 by Boston's Jim Nance.
• Chicago lost two scoring chances in the second quarter as Rochester native Bob Thomas missed a 28-yard field goal and Robin Earl lost a fumble at the Bills 7 to Steve Freeman after being crunched by Jim Haslett and Shane Nelson.
• Bills' receivers dropped eight passes on a rainy afternoon and Joe Ferguson's rating suffered.
• The Bills' only first down of the first half came with four seconds left when Alan Page jumped offside.
• The Bears possessed the ball for 38:19, running 71 plays to Buffalo's 47.
• After the TD, the defense stopped the Bears without a first down twice, but the offense didn't take advantage. Keith Moody's 17-yard punt return to the Bears 35 was wasted and on the next series, the Bills drove to the Chicago 37 and got no further. The Bills never got inside the Bears 35 all day.

QUOTES

• Jerry Butler: "I told Joe 'Don't blame yourself, you got the ball to us.' We dropped it."
• Fred Smerlas on Payton's TD: "All I saw was his feet. I played pretty high, stood my blocker up, and he still flew right over me. We knew Payton was going to run, we just didn't know he was going to fly."
• Bears running back Walter Payton: "I didn't want to jump because linemen usually stay low in goal-line situations, but I wanted the six and jumping was the only way to get in."
• Joe Ferguson: "The weather was a factor because it kept us from taking a few long shots, but the biggest factor was that we always seemed to have bad field position. This is exactly what I meant when I said we would need a running game in order to keep winning."
• Shane Nelson: "When you hold an offense like that to seven points, you have to give yourself a pat on the back. But we can't be happy giving that many rushing yards. A back like Payton puts a lot of pressure on your defense. On any one of those carries, he has the potential to go all the way. I'd like that high jump stick out there to see how high he got."
• Bears cornerback Terry Schmidt: "The score was 7-0, but I think we beat them worse than 7-0. Our defensive coaches (including Buddy Ryan) did a great job."
• Tony Greene: "I think he's (Payton) the greatest back I've seen since O.J."

STANDINGS: SIXTH WEEK

AFC EAST	W	L	T	CENTRAL	W	L	T	WEST	W	L	T	NFC EAST	W	L	T	CENTRAL	W	L	T	WEST	W	L	T
Miami	4	2	0	Pittsburgh	5	1	0	San Diego	4	2	0	Dallas	5	1	0	Tampa Bay	5	1	0	LA Rams	4	2	0
New England	4	2	0	Cleveland	4	2	0	Denver	4	2	0	Philadelphia	5	1	0	Minnesota	3	3	0	Atlanta	3	3	0
Buffalo	3	3	0	Houston	4	2	0	Kan. City	4	2	0	Washington	4	2	0	Chicago	3	3	0	N.Orleans	2	4	0
NY Jets	2	4	0	Cincinnati	0	6	0	Oakland	3	3	0	St. Louis	2	4	0	Green Bay	2	4	0	San Fran	0	6	0
Baltimore	1	5	0					Seattle	2	4	0	NY Giants	1	5	0	Detroit	1	5	0				

NOTES

• The Dolphins beat the Bills for the 20th straight time, all in the 1970s.

• The Bills' offense continued to slump as it had scored only one TD in the last nine quarters.

• Tony Nathan got the Dolphins going with an 86-yard punt return for a TD, the longest punt return in Dolphins history.

• Midway through the second quarter, a 24-yard Rusty Jackson punt set up the Dolphins on the Bills 36 and they needed seven plays to score as Larry Csonka bulled in from the 7. On their next possession, the Dolphins rolled 47 yards on the ground to Uwe von Schamann's field goal and a 17-0 lead.

• Buffalo's only sustained drive of the game came in the third as they went 80 yards in 11 plays. Joe Ferguson completed four passes for 56 yards along the way before Roland Hooks scored.

• In the locker room, some players were openly critical of the offensive game plan and suggested that Ferguson should call his own plays.

• The Dolphins had lost two straight and a Miami radio station conducted a poll that indicated fans preferred Don Strock to Bob Griese by a three-to-one margin.

QUOTES

• Dolphins guard Bob Kuechenberg: "I thought we were in control of the game from the opening snap. We won 17-7, but we could have won 30-7. We just did what we had to do to win. Larry Csonka gives us that old dimension where we have the ability to control the ball for five or six minutes. It's like the early 70's again."

• Dolphins fullback Larry Csonka: "We went into the game feeling we could run on them, that we could get two or three yards any time we needed it."

• Reggie McKenzie: "Let's face it, Joe's been in the league seven years, I think he's qualified to call short-yardage plays. I understand why he (Knox) sends the plays in, it takes some of the heat off Joe."

• Joe Ferguson: "I would have liked to run more play-action passes in the first half. We mixed our plays better in the second half. Last week we just didn't play well. This week we were against a good defensive team."

• Chuck Knox: "Our defense played better in the second half, but you can't spot a team like Miami seven points on an 86-yard punt return and expect to win. And every time I've seen Griese, he's looked great."

• Dolphins safety Tim Foley: "It was a strange game. I felt we were dominating, but I could never get comfortable when I looked at the scoreboard. We got ahead of them early and got them hyper about not making an error and keeping their losing streak going against us."

Bills	0	0	7	0	-	7
Dolphins	7	10	0	0	-	17

Attendance at the Orange Bowl - 45,597

Mia:	Nathan 86 punt return (von Schamann kick), 9:56
Mia:	Csonka 7 run (von Schamann kick), :45
Mia:	FG von Schamann 29, 8:44
Buf:	Hooks 3 run (Mike-Mayer kick), 11:03

	BUF	MIA
First downs	11	14
Rushing yds	70	178
Passing yds	108	101
Punts-avg	5-34.0	3-36.3
Fumbles-lost	2-0	0-0
Penalties-yds	5-25	2-10

BILLS LEADERS: **Rushing** - Brown 8-22, Miller 7-30, Hooks 4-12, Ferguson 1-1, Collier 2-5; **Passing** - Ferguson 11-21-1 - 137; **Receiving** - Lewis 4-59, Butler 2-45, Gant 2-24, Hooks 1-10, Brown 2- (-1).

DOLPHINS LEADERS: **Rushing** - Williams 18-40, Davis 4-48, Csonka 24-90; **Passing** - Griese 7-12-1 - 101; **Receiving** - Harris 2-35, Moore 3-48, Hardy 1-9, Bulaich 1-9.

WEEK 7 GAMES

NYG 32, SF 16	NO 42, TB 14
GB 24, Det 16	Oak 50, Atl 19
NE 27, Chi 7	Cinc 34, Pitt 10
SD 20, Sea 10	Phil 24, St.L 20
Hou 28, Balt 16	Wash 13, Clev 9
Dal 30, LA 6	Den 24, KC 10
NYJ 14, Minn 7	

NOTES

• The last-place Colts upset Buffalo as Bert Jones hit Mack Alston with a four-yard TD pass with 6:05 left to play.

• The Bills allowed five sacks, had four holding penalties and turned the ball over once.

• The defense played well, forcing the Colts to punt eight times without attaining a first down.

• After an Isiah Robertson interception, the Bills moved to the Colts 7, but a holding penalty on Reggie McKenzie and a sack pushed them back and Nick Mike-Mayer wound up missing a 44-yard field goal, his first miss as a Bill.

• Keith Moody fumbled a punt at the Colts 45 in the first and after a 29-yard reception by Joe Washington, Bert Jones eventually scored on a one-yard run for a 7-0 Colts lead.

• The Bills tied it as Joe Ferguson hit Curtis Brown with a TD pass to end an 80-yard drive, keyed by a 36-yard pass to Frank Lewis and a 10-yard interference penalty on Doug Nettles.

• In the fourth, Joe Devlin's holding penalty wiped out a TD pass to Roland Hooks and the Bills settled for a Mike-Mayer field goal. He made a 37-yarder later to make it 13-7.

• But the Colts scored the winner two minutes later, going 80 yards in six plays to Alston's TD. The key play was a 59-yard catch and run by Randy Burke on a play on which Chris Keating blew coverage.

• Down the stretch, Hooks' fumble stopped one series and a fourth-down sack of Ferguson killed the Bills' final possession.

• Robertson finished with an interception, a fumble recovery and two defended passes.

QUOTES

• Chuck Knox: "It's just the same old story. We made too many mistakes. It's like self-destruction. I have no explanation for it."

• Reggie McKenzie: "I didn't dispute it (his holding penalty). It busted up a touchdown. If we convert that opportunity that I messed up, it's a different ballgame. We had a boatload of them (mistakes). The offense played terribly."

• Joe DeLamielleure: "We've lost some games this season, but this is the first time we beat ourselves."

• Joe Ferguson: "The holding penalties hurt more than anything. You just can't make the mistakes we were making today and beat anybody, even Lackawanna High School. Our defense stopped Baltimore almost all day, but we also stopped ourselves."

• Colts defensive end Fred Cook: "Buffalo killed us the last time with their passing game and we were determined to stop it. We didn't take their running game seriously. What we concentrated on most was rushing Ferguson and making his life miserable. I have a lot of respect for Joe Devlin, but I think I beat him a few times today."

Colts	0	7	0	7	-	14
Bills	0	0	7	6	-	13

Attendance at Rich Stadium - 50,581

Bal:	Jones 1 run (S. Mike-Mayer kick), 14:32
Buf:	Brown 21 pass from Ferguson (N. Mike-Mayer kick), 9:38
Buf:	FG N. Mike-Mayer 40, :23
Buf:	FG N. Mike-Mayer 37, 6:55
Bal:	Alston 4 pass from Jones (S. Mike-Mayer kick), 8:55

	BUF	BAL
First downs	20	12
Rushing yds	82	110
Passing yds	242	151
Punts-avg	5-37.2	9-38.2
Fumbles-lost	3-2	1-1
Penalties-yds	6-49	9-50

BILLS LEADERS: **Rushing** - Brown 6-36, Miller 9-24, Hooks 6-14, Ferguson 2-4, Mike-Mayer 1-4; **Passing** - Ferguson 19-39-0 - 284; **Receiving** - Lewis 8-158, Brown 4-51, Hooks 3-29, Butler 1-13, Gant 2-22, Piccone 1-11.

COLTS LEADERS: **Rushing** - Washington 14-49, Hardeman 13-35, McCauley 6-22, Jones 2-4; **Passing** - Jones 8-25-1 - 164; **Receiving** - Alston 3-49, Washington 2-34, Burke 1-59, McCauley 1-16, Hardeman 1-6.

WEEK 8 GAMES

NO 17, Det 7	SD 40, LA 16
Dal 22, St.L 13	Sea 34, Hou 14
NYG 21, KC 17	TB 21, GB 3
Wash 17, Phil 7	NYJ 28, Oak 19
Clev 28, Cinc 27	NE 28, Mia 13
Minn 30, Chi 27	SF 20, Atl 15
Pitt 42, Den 7	

STANDINGS: EIGHTH WEEK

AFC EAST	W	L	T	CENTRAL	W	L	T	WEST	W	L	T	NFC EAST	W	L	T	CENTRAL	W	L	T	WEST	W	L	T
New England	6	2	0	Pittsburgh	6	2	0	San Diego	6	2	0	Dallas	7	1	0	Tampa Bay	6	2	0	LA Rams	4	4	0
Miami	5	3	0	Houston	5	3	0	Denver	5	3	0	Philadelphia	6	2	0	Minnesota	4	4	0	N.Orleans	4	4	0
NY Jets	4	4	0	Cleveland	5	3	0	Kan. City	4	4	0	Washington	6	2	0	Chicago	3	5	0	Atlanta	3	5	0
Buffalo	3	5	0	Cincinnati	1	7	0	Oakland	4	4	0	NY Giants	3	5	0	Green Bay	3	5	0	San Fran	1	7	0
Baltimore	2	6	0					Seattle	3	5	0	St. Louis	2	6	0	Detroit	1	7	0				

Bills	0	0	6	14	- 20
Lions	14	0	3	0	- 17

Attendance at the Silverdome - 61,911

Det:	Scott 5 pass from Komlo (Ricardo kick), 6:49
Det:	King 11 run (Ricardo kick), 14:55
Buf:	FG Mike-Mayer 23, 8:25
Det:	FG Ricardo 40, 13:27
Buf:	FG Mike-Mayer 42, 14:22
Buf:	Brown 3 run (Mike-Mayer kick), 3:23
Buf:	Gant 7 pass from Ferguson (Mike-Mayer kick), 13:35

	BUF	DET
First downs	18	20
Rushing yds	105	208
Passing yds	319	169
Punts-avg	3-43.3	5-45.6
Fumbles-lost	2-1	2-1
Penalties-yds	9-87	5-39

BILLS LEADERS: **Rushing** - Brown 10-52, Miller 5-22, Hooks 5-31; **Passing** - Ferguson 17-35-2 - 339; **Receiving** - Lewis 7-190, Butler 3-41, Brown 3-20, Piccone 2-66, Hooks 1-15, Gant 1-7.

LIONS LEADERS: **Rushing** - Bussey 26-139, Komlo 3-26, Washington 1-24, Gaines 4-12, King 4-10, Thompson 1- (-1), Kane 2- (-2); **Passing** - Komlo 13-17-0 - 138, Swider 1-1-0 - 36; **Receiving** - Scott 4-55, Bussey 4-23, Hill 3-49, Thompson 1-36, Washington 1-10, King 1-1.

NOTES

• The Bills snapped a three-game losing streak by rallying for two fourth-quarter TDs to overcome the pesky Lions. Reuben Gant's seven-yard TD reception with 1:25 left won it.

• Sherman White then blocked Benny Ricardo's 44-yard field goal attempt on the final play of the game.

• Down 17-3 in the third, Joe Ferguson hit Frank Lewis for a 38-yard gain, setting up Nick Mike-Mayer's 42-yard field goal.

• Four minutes later, after Fred Smerlas had recovered a Dexter Bussey fumble at the Bills 42, Curtis Brown scored on a three-yard run. The key play was Ferguson's 49-yard pass to Lou Piccone.

• The winning drive began at the Bills 32 with 2:36 left. Ferguson hit Lewis on fourth-and-five to the 47 with 1:49 left. On the next play, Ferguson scrambled out of the pocket and hit Lewis on a crossing pattern at the Lions 35. Lewis beat ex-Bill Doug Jones and ran all the way to the 7, a 46-yard gain. On the next play, Gant overcame a case of the dropsies and latched on to the winner.

• The Lions jumped to a 14-0 first-quarter lead. The first TD came after punter Larry Swider's 36-yard pass to Leonard Thompson on a fake punt kept an 85-yard drive alive.

• Lewis' 190 yards receiving were a career-high,

Ferguson had his fourth 300-yard passing game, third of '79; Bob Chandler and Jerry Butler both suffered shoulder injuries.

QUOTES

• Joe Ferguson: "If we had lost to Detroit, I would have been seriously worried about how we would have played the rest of the year. A loss would have been very detrimental and I'm not sure how we would have reacted. Frank Lewis played an excellent game. He's consistent, he's hard to beat. You know he's going to be where he's got to be when you need him." (On the long pass to Lewis): "It was the same play I had hit Frank on three times during the game." (On the winning TD): "Reuben had his back to the defender so I knew if I threw it right, the guy would have to interfere with him or not get it. It was a tight throw."

• Isiah Robertson: "A loss would have been devastating, especially because we couldn't have justified it. I think this will be the turning point of our season."

• Chuck Knox: "We made so many foolish mistakes, we dug ourselves a deep hole. I'm happy about the win, but I hope this football team profits from the careless mistakes. This was the Detroit Bowl – and we dedicate this win to Mr. Wilson, who came in breathing fire before the game."

• Frank Lewis: "It was a great game to come back and win. We felt we were playing too good at the end to lose it. We were beating ourselves and everyone was feeling down, but we sucked it up and we came back. The personal stats are fine, and it's nice to be known by people other than your brothers and close friends, but it's still not as satisfying as playing for a champion."

• Reuben Gant: "The way things have been going for me, every catch I make is a big one."

WEEK 9 GAMES	
Oak 45, SD 22	Pitt 14, Dal 3
Clev 38, St.L 20	NO 14, Wash 10
Balt 31, NE 26	TB 12, Minn 10
Den 20, KC 3	Cinc 37, Phil 13
Chi 28, SF 27	NYG 20, LA 14
Mia 27, GB 7	Sea 31, Atl 28
Hou 27, NYJ 24 (OT)	

Patriots	0	6	10	10	- 26
Bills	6	0	0	0	- 6

Attendance at Rich Stadium - 67,935

Buf:	FG Mike-Mayer 39, 5:44
Buf:	FG Mike-Mayer 40, 9:43
NE:	Ivory 6 pass from Grogan (kick failed), 14:55
NE:	FG Smith 33, 5:32
NE:	Morgan 63 pass from Grogan (Smith kick), 9:23
NE:	Morgan 34 pass from Grogan (Smith kick), 8:42
NE:	FG Smith 37, 13:04

	BUF	NE
First downs	15	20
Rushing yds	83	111
Passing yds	181	327
Punts-avg	6-37.7	6-39.7
Fumbles-lost	3-3	3-2
Penalties-yds	10-70	8-75

BILLS LEADERS: **Rushing** - Brown 13-67, Miller 3-9, Hooks 6-7; **Passing** - Ferguson 13-26-2 - 215, Munson 3-7-0 - 31; **Receiving** - Gant 3-57, Lewis 2-35, Brown 3-34, Piccone 4-84, Hooks 4-36.

PATRIOTS LEADERS: **Rushing** - Ivory 14-27, Cunningham 11-19, Grogan 3-15, Morgan 1-6, Tatupu 4-4, Calhoun 4-40; **Passing** - Grogan 19-35-1 - 350; **Receiving** - Morgan 5-158, Jackson 4-69, Ivory 3-21, Westbrook 3-65, Hasselback 3-26, Cunningham 1-11.

NOTES

• Steve Grogan had the second most productive passing day of his career and led a second-half rally that steamrolled the Bills.

• Joe Ferguson was sacked seven times for 65 yards and was knocked out of the game in the fourth quarter with a concussion. The Bills committed five turnovers and 10 penalties in a pitiful performance.

• The Patriots had only 47 yards rushing in the first half against the NFL's worst run defense. The game was tied 6-6 as Nick Mike-Mayer's two field goals offset Horace Ivory's TD run and John Smith's missed PAT.

• Tony Greene's interception led to the first field goal and a drive to the Patriots 23 set up the second. The Bills failed to capitalize later in the first quarter on Fred Smerlas' fumble recovery at the Patriots 24.

• Ivory's TD came with five seconds left in the half, capping a 59-yard drive. Sherman White, who blocked a field goal earlier in the half, blocked the extra point.

• The Patriots realized their running game was going nowhere, so they took to the air in the second half and Grogan tore apart the Bills. Rod Shoate's interception led to the go-ahead field goal and two plays after a Raymond Clayborn interception, Grogan hit Stanley Morgan for a TD as Jeff Nixon missed a tackle.

• Morgan caught a 34-yard TD in the fourth to cap a 70-yard march.

• Lou Piccone, starting for Jerry Butler, had a good day, but the running game lacked.

QUOTES

• Jeff Nixon: "When I come into the game, I'm supposed to do my job. After they catch it, you're supposed to make the tackle. I feel like I'm the biggest one to blame."

• Patriots quarterback Steve Grogan: "I had a terrible warm-up, I couldn't get a feel for the ball and I wasn't even sure I should have started. Then my first pass was intercepted and I thought it was going to be a long afternoon. I really don't expect to have a great day against the Bills' secondary. They have a great secondary, but we hit it with a couple of big plays. Ever since coach (Ron) Erhardt let me call the plays, I've been more relaxed and everyone is more involved in the offense. Take the second touchdown. Stanley told me Tony Greene was playing him tight all day and he could beat him with a pump fake, which is exactly what happened."

• Patriots defensive end Tony McGee: "We knew if we let him (Ferguson) stand back there all day, he'd pick us apart. The No. 1 quarterback in the league poses quite a challenge, but we were all charged up to tackle it."

• Terry Miller on his lack of production: "Sure I'm disappointed, but under the circumstances, when you carry the ball only three or four times a game, there's really no reason for me to be disappointed. I'm just doing what they ask me to do. When my number is called, I feel like's it's now or never for me."

WEEK 10 GAMES	
SD 20, KC 14	St.L 37, Minn 7
NYJ 27, GB 22	Clev 24, Phil 19
Chi 35, Det 7	Atl 17, TB 14
LA 24, Sea 0	Dal 16, NYG 14
Den 10, NO 3	Balt 38, Cinc 28
Oak 23, SF 10	Pitt 38, Wash 7
Hou 9, Mia 6	

STANDINGS: TENTH WEEK																					
AFC EAST	**W**	**L**	**T**	**CENTRAL**	**W**	**L**	**T**	**WEST**	**W**	**L**	**T**	**NFC EAST**	**W**	**L**	**T**	**CENTRAL**	**W**	**L**	**T**	**WEST**	**W**	**L**	**T**
New England	7	3	0	Pittsburgh	8	2	0	San Diego	7	3	0	Dallas	8	2	0	Tampa Bay	7	3	0	N.Orleans	5	5	0
Miami	6	4	0	Houston	7	3	0	Denver	7	3	0	Philadelphia	6	4	0	Chicago	5	5	0	LA Rams	5	5	0
NY Jets	5	5	0	Cleveland	7	3	0	Oakland	6	4	0	Washington	6	4	0	Minnesota	4	6	0	Atlanta	4	6	0
Buffalo	4	6	0	Cincinnati	2	8	0	Kan. City	4	6	0	NY Giants	4	6	0	Green Bay	3	7	0	San Fran	1	9	0
Baltimore	4	6	0					Seattle	4	6	0	St. Louis	3	7	0	Detroit	1	9	0				

GAME 11 - Sunday, Nov. 11, 1979 - BILLS 14, JETS 12

NOTES

• The difference was a pair of failed extra point attempts by Toni Linhart, the ex-Colt kicker who was filling in for the injured Pat Leahy.

• For the first time in his career, Joe Ferguson called his own plays and he was sharp.

• Terry Miller had his best day of the season as Ferguson decided to let him play, unlike Knox who had seemed to lose faith in the former No. 1 pick. The Jets' ground game, averaging 187 yards coming into the game, was limited to 67 by the NFL's worst run defense.

• The Bills took a 7-0 lead on the second possession of the game as they drove 89 yards in 14 plays. They consumed nearly seven minutes and achieved seven first downs before Mike Collier scored.

• The Jets answered with a 54-yard drive as Kevin Long scored after Richard Todd had passed 23 yards to Bruce Harper, but Linhart's PAT was wide and it was 7-6 at halftime.

• In the fourth, the Bills drove to the Jets 4 after Mario Clark's first of two interceptions, but failed to score on four rushes. However, after a short punt, they started a drive at the Jets 36 and three plays later, Curtis Brown made a brilliant one-handed catch, then broke four tackles on the way to a 30-yard TD. The Jets scored with 4:04 left, but Clark's second interception late in the game iced it for the Bills.

QUOTES

• Joe DeLamielleure: "Joe's ready to call his own plays. He was really in command in the huddle. It's funny, though, he acted nervous the night before. Once the game started, he was great. He called a great game."

• Joe Ferguson: "If nobody ever wrote anything about it, it wouldn't have been an issue. But the fans are aware who calls the plays and everyone has an opinion. You have to remember, this is only my second year under Chuck Knox and it takes a while to get to know each other and the system. I'd say the coaches knew what I'd be calling two-thirds of the time. Let's face it, even when the plays were being sent in, I had a pretty good idea what was coming, anyway. You spend all week on a game plan, you know what to call, and when."

• Curtis Brown: "I think it helps our concentration. Before, we were waiting for the plays to come in and had to rush up to the line of scrimmage. With Joe calling them, we had time to line up and get set and Joe had a chance to read the defense."

• Isiah Robertson: "They rushed for 265 yards the first time we played them. When you sit there and watch yourself on film getting blocked and trapped and not playing as well as you should, you take up the challenge. I think guys like Shane Nelson and Jim Haslett grew last week, too. We're growing as a defensive unit."

• Terry Miller: "This by no means is a solution to anything. This game is not going to make me the best running back in the league."

Bills	0	7	0	7 - 14
Jets	0	6	0	6 - 12

Attendance at Shea Stadium - 50,647

Buf: Collier 1 run (Mike-Mayer kick), 5:35
NYJ: Long 1 run (kick failed), 11:06
Buf: Brown 30 pass from Ferguson (Mike-Mayer kick), 3:50
NYJ: Jones 11 pass from Todd (kick failed), 10:56

	BUF	NYJ
First downs	15	16
Rushing yds	138	67
Passing yds	132	170
Punts-avg	6-35.0	5-33.6
Fumbles-lost	1-0	0-0
Penalties-yds	2-20	7-47

BILLS LEADERS: Rushing - Brown 15-51, Miller 24-81, Hooks 2-7, Collier 2-3, Ferguson 1- (-4); **Passing** - Ferguson 11-17-0 - 132; **Receiving** - Piccone 5-64, Brown 2-31, Miller 2-12, Collier 1-19, Lewis 1-6.

JETS LEADERS: Rushing - Gaines 7-27, Dierking 11-18, Harper 4-8, Long 4-6, Todd 1-8; **Passing** - Todd 16-25-3 - 180; **Receiving** - Gaines 4-28, Jones 3-51, Dierking 3-40, Barkum 3-28, Harper 2-29, Gaffney 1-4.

WEEK 11 GAMES

Chi 27, LA 23	Wash 30, St.L 28
NYG 24, Atl 3	Sea 29, Clev 24
Hou 31, Oak 17	TB 16, Det 14
Mia 19, Balt 0	GB 19, Minn 7
Pitt 30, KC 3	NO 31, SF 20
Den 45, NE 10	SD 26, Cinc 24
Phil 31, Dal 21	

GAME 12 - Sunday, Nov. 18, 1979 - BILLS 19, PACKERS 12

NOTES

• The game was tied at 12-12 and Green Bay was driving to the go-ahead score early in the fourth quarter, but Jeff Nixon intercepted a David Whitehurst pass at the Bills 5 and returned it out to the 19. Joe Ferguson then engineered a 16-play, 81-yard drive that consumed nearly 9 1/2 minutes. Mike Collier scored the winning TD with 3:04 left. On the march, an interception by Rich Wingo and his return to the Bills 10 was wiped out by an interference penalty on cornerback Mike McCoy. Also, Joe Devlin covered a Curtis Brown fumble at the Packers 10.

• The Bills overcame 12 penalties, two of which nullified TDs. Brown and Terry Miller enjoyed their best days of the year.

• Green Bay took a 9-6 lead in the second when Whitehurst hit James Lofton with a 34-yard TD on a fourth-and-two play. The Packers had taken possession at the Bills 42 after Wingo recovered a Frank Lewis fumble. Tom Birney missed the PAT, but kicked a field goal before the half ended for a 12-6 lead.

• The Bills drove to Nick Mike-Mayer's third field goal early in the third, then tied the game when Mike-Mayer made a 32-yarder after Nixon forced Paul Coffman to fumble at the Bills 45. Charlie Romes recovered.

• Tony Greene was benched in the second half in favor of Nixon. Frank Lewis suffered a minor knee injury.

QUOTES

• Joe Ferguson: "I was getting a little bit frustrated. I was wondering what we had to do to get a touchdown. Having two touchdowns called back is disgusting and it also has an effect on the defense. They see us marching up and down the field, but when they come out, they look up and see we have no points on the board. It's about time we got some breaks to go our way (the two on the winning drive). It was a lot harder calling plays this week. We had a lot of long-yardage situations and I found myself looking to the sidelines for help. The headaches were bigger."

• Jeff Nixon: "Against New England I didn't play as good as I can, so I told everyone I'd get one for them and I was true to my word. They ran two slants and Lofton was on my side and he ran short. I dropped back to cover the deep back and I just got in front of the guy (Aundra Thompson) at the post. Once Lofton went across, I was just reacting to the quarterback. If I hadn't gotten it, Steve Freeman would have."

• Terry Miller: "It's a good thing Nick was on today. We had lots of chances to get it in and we couldn't. I don't know if it's something we're doing wrong or the defenses are playing well, but we're just not scoring."

• Mario Clark: "The way we figure it, we can win the rest of the games. This is the best record we've had since I've been here. Right now, we feel like we can beat anybody. We feel a little cocky, but not too cocky."

WEEK 12 GAMES

SD 35, Pitt 7	TB 31, NYG 3
KC 24, Oak 21	Sea 38, NO 24
Minn 14, Det 7	Phil 16, St.L 13
Wash 34, Dal 20	Hou 42, Cinc 21
Chi 23, NYJ 13	Den 38, SF 28
NE 50, Balt 21	LA 20, Atl 14
Clev 30, Mia 24 (OT)	

Packers	3	9	0	0 - 12
Bills	3	3	6	7 - 19

Attendance at Rich Stadium - 39,679

GB: FG Birney 25, 8:55
Buf: FG Mike-Mayer 37, 13:02
Buf: FG Mike-Mayer 34, 2:53
GB: Lofton 34 pass from Whitehurst (kick failed), 7:01
GB: FG Birney 32, 14:34
Buf: FG Mike-Mayer 31, 9:37
Buf: FG Mike-Mayer 32, 14:59
Buf: Collier 1 run (Mike-Mayer kick), 11:56

	BUF	GB
First downs	20	14
Rushing yds	187	95
Passing yds	213	195
Punts-avg	3-44.3	3-42.7
Fumbles-lost	3-1	3-2
Penalties-yds	12-113	6-46

BILLS LEADERS: Rushing - Brown 21-93, Miller 15-91, Hooks 1-2, Collier 2-3, Ferguson 2- (-1), Lewis 1- (-1); **Passing** - Ferguson 17-28-0 - 226; **Receiving** - Lewis 6-116, Piccone 7-65, Gant 2-20, Miller 1-7, Fulton 1-18.

PACKERS LEADERS: Rushing - Middleton 7-17, Torkelson 5-15, Simpson 7-15; **Passing** - Whitehurst 13-26-3 - 205; **Receiving** - Coffman 5-73, Lofton 4-112, Torkelson 2-15, Middleton 1-8, Simpson 1- (-3).

STANDINGS: TWELFTH WEEK

AFC EAST	W	L	T	CENTRAL	W	L	T	WEST	W	L	T	NFC EAST	W	L	T	CENTRAL	W	L	T	WEST	W	L	T
New England	8	4	0	Pittsburgh	9	3	0	San Diego	9	3	0	Dallas	8	4	0	Tampa Bay	9	3	0	N.Orleans	6	6	0
Miami	7	5	0	Houston	9	3	0	Denver	9	3	0	Philadelphia	8	4	0	Chicago	7	5	0	LA Rams	6	6	0
Buffalo	6	6	0	Cleveland	8	4	0	Oakland	6	6	0	Washington	8	4	0	Minnesota	5	7	0	Atlanta	4	8	0
NY Jets	5	7	0	Cincinnati	2	10	0	Seattle	6	6	0	NY Giants	5	7	0	Green Bay	4	8	0	San Fran	1	11	0
Baltimore	4	8	0					Kan. City	5	7	0	St. Louis	3	9	0	Detroit	1	11	0				

Bills	0	3	3	7	3 - 16
Patriots	0	3	0	10	0 - 13

Attendance at Schaefer Stadium - 60,991

NE: FG Smith 47, 9:46
Buf: FG Mike-Mayer 29, 14:59
Buf: FG Mike-Mayer 26, 11:33
NE: Grogan 1 run (Smith kick), 1:37
NE: FG Smith 32, 13:35
Buf: Piccone 11 pass from Ferguson (Mike-Mayer kick), 14:49
Buf: FG Mike-Mayer 29, 9:15

	BUF	NE
First downs	18	21
Rushing yds	80	173
Passing yds	201	136
Punts-avg	8-42.9	5-37.4
Fumbles-lost	2-0	1-0
Penalties-yds	6-65	3-15

BILLS LEADERS: Rushing - Brown 15-42, Miller 11-18, Hooks 6-14, Ferguson 1-6; **Passing** - Ferguson 17-33-2 - 235; **Receiving** - Butler 4-95, Gant 2-41, Piccone 5-57, Brown 2-13, Hooks 1-7, Miller 2-6, Fulton 1-16.

PATRIOTS LEADERS: Rushing - Ivory 23-83, Calhoun 20-83, Grogan 5-11, Morgan 1- (-4); **Passing** - Grogan 9-25-4 - 160; **Receiving** - Jackson 4-87, Morgan 1-16, Francis 2-27, Westbrook 1-27, Calhoun 1-3.

NOTES
• Nick Mike-Mayer made a 29-yard field goal to give the Bills the victory in the first overtime game in team history. Joe Ferguson's 51-yard pass to Jerry Butler to the Patriots 12 led to the winning kick. The Bills had gotten the ball in OT when Jim Haslett intercepted Steve Grogan at the Bills 30 on a fourth-and-two play. It was Haslett's second interception of the day.
• The victory was the first for the Bills over a team with a winning record in the Chuck Knox era.
• At 7-6, the Bills moved within one game of first place in the AFC East behind the Patriots and Miami (8-5)
• The Patriots went ahead 10-6 in the fourth as Grogan capped a 66-yard TD drive with a one-yard run, then John Smith tacked on a 32-yard field goal with 2:25 left after Grogan and Harold Jackson had hooked up on a 50-yard pass play.
• But Joe Ferguson maneuvered the Bills 64 yards in six plays in just 1:08 to tie the game. He hit Jerry Butler for a 24-yard gain and Reuben Gant made a diving 19-yard reception. With 11 seconds left, Lou Piccone caught an 11-yard TD pass and Mike-Mayer coolly kicked the conversion.
• Grogan was sacked three times, twice by Sherman White, and he was intercepted four times.

WEEK 13 GAMES	
Hou 30, Dal 24	Det 20, Chi 0
Phil 21, GB 10	Minn 23, TB 22
SD 28, KC 7	NO 37, Atl 6
Mia 28, Balt 24	Oak 14, Den 10
Cinc 34, St.L 28	LA 26, SF 20
NYG 14, Wash 6	Sea 30, NYJ 7
Pitt 33, Clev 30 (OT)	

QUOTES
• Nick Mike-Mayer: "A lot of people try to get themselves up for a big play, but I try to work myself down. On the sidelines I was saying to myself 'Gyugotta' which is a Hungarian word that means take it easy. I treated that kick like just another practice field goal."
• Joe Ferguson on the 51-yard bomb to Butler in OT: "I called the play, but Jerry gave me a big hint on it. He told me 'I can beat this guy (Rick Sanford) deep. So I called it. He's (Sanford) young and that's exactly why we went there. You have to go at the young guys. This was our biggest game in four years. To beat a team of this caliber makes this one big. If we win the next three and New England and Miami lose, we could make the playoffs. It sounds ridiculous, but ... "
• Chuck Knox: "I've been feeling good about a lot of things lately and this goes a helluva long way toward making us a winning team. We beat the leading team in our division, we've won three in a row and the fact that we came back to win in overtime shows a lot of character."
• Reggie McKenzie: "We've got a defense, we actually have a defense."
• Lou Piccone: "I believe in positive thinking because it has kept me going in this league for a long time. I was trying to get guys smiling in the fourth period and saying 'yeah, we're gonna do it, we're gonna win this game.'"
• Sherman White: "We don't wear our T-shirts inside out anymore, we're proud to be Bills."
• Jim Haslett: "We're a good team, and we're young. I waited 17 games for those interceptions. I was going for the all-rookie team, but now I'm going for rookie of the year."

Broncos	3	0	13	3 - 19
Bills	0	10	0	6 - 16

Attendance at Rich Stadium - 37,886

Den: FG Turner 23, 14:15
Buf: Freeman 50 interception return (Mike-Mayer kick), 7:15
Buf: FG Mike-Mayer 28, 14:56
Den: Wright 78 lateral fumble return (pass failed), 5:02
Den: Moses 46 pass from Morton (Turner kick), 9:18
Buf: FG Mike-Mayer 32, :15
Buf: FG Mike-Mayer 34, 13:02
Den: FG Turner 32, 15:00

	BUF	DEN
First downs	19	11
Rushing yds	100	97
Passing yds	298	129
Punts-avg	5-31.6	8-34.5
Fumbles-lost	6-6	5-3
Penalties-yds	7-51	6-69

BILLS LEADERS: Rushing - Brown 16-24, Miller 6-15, Hooks 9-44, Ferguson 4-17; **Passing** - Ferguson 27-46-1 - 316; **Receiving** - Lewis 5-86, Brown 8-62, Piccone 3-60, Butler 5-42, Hooks 4-28, Shipp 1-27, Miller 1-11.

BRONCOS LEADERS: Rushing - Lytle 11-36, Jensen 5-22, Keyworth 5-16, Morton 4-14, Preston 5-9, Canada 2-0; **Passing** - Morton 9-23-1 - 140; **Receiving** - Moses 4-92, Keyworth 2-12, Watson 3-36.

NOTES
• Jim Turner's 32-yard field goal on the final play of the game eliminated the Bills from playoff contention. The Bills turned the ball over seven times, including four fumbles by Curtis Brown.
• Denver took a 3-0 lead after Joe Rizzo intercepted Joe Ferguson at the Bills 17 late in the first quarter and Turner kicked a 23-yard field goal, but the Bills went ahead when Steve Freeman intercepted Craig Morton and went 50 yards for a TD in the second. Nick Mike-Mayer's field goal with four seconds left in the half capped a 69-yard, 10-play drive as Ferguson went six-for-six along the way.
• Brown's fourth fumble was his most costly. The Bills reached the Denver 9 on the first series of the third quarter and Brown lost the handle. Randy Gradishar picked it up at the 14, ran to the 22 and then lateraled to Louis Wright who went the final 78 yards. Denver failed to tie, though, when a bad snap aborted the PAT, so the Bills were still ahead 10-9.
• But four minutes later, Craig Morton hit Haven Moses for a 46-yard TD. The Bills drove right back for a field goal, then after Turner missed a 28-yarder, the Bills drove to Mike-Mayer's third three-pointer that tied it at 16-16 with 1:58 left. The key play was a 24-yard interference penalty on Wright.

WEEK 14 GAMES	
Mia 39, NE 24	Atl 28, SD 26
Chi 14, TB 0	Clev 14, Hou 7
Wash 38, GB 21	Phil 44, Det 7
Dal 28, NYG 7	St.L 13, SF 10
NYJ 30, Balt 17	Pit 37, Cin 17
KC 37, Sea 21	Oak 42, NO 35
LA 27, Minn 21 (OT)	

• After an exchange of punts, the Broncos took over at their 44 with 18 seconds left. Morton hit Steve Watson for 22 to the Bills 34 and Morton called his final timeout with eight seconds left. They bravely ran one play to get the ball closer and it worked as Morton hit Moses on the sideline for 18 yards, even though the Bills knew a sideline pass was Denver's only hope. Turner then kicked the winner.
• Though Chuck Knox wouldn't admit it, Terry Miller was benched for most of the game.
• Ferguson became the first Bills QB in history to top 3,000 yards passing in one season.

QUOTES
• Curtis Brown: "I take the whole game's responsibility on me. I've never had a day like this before. I was fully concentrating, it was just a bad day on my part. Right now I've got a lump in my throat like the world just ended."
• Isiah Robertson on Morton's last two passes: "He just threw two perfect passes. A linebacker on a wide receiver is probably one of the toughest coverages in football and Lucious (Sanford) had him (Watson) covered perfectly, but the guy made a one-in-10 catch."
• Joe Ferguson: "We should have won the game, but when you have seven turnovers, usually you lose by 30 points. It just shows you how the defense stopped them. The thing that is encouraging to me is we never laid down like we have in the past. This team is growing to the point where we can play with anybody."
• Broncos kicker Jim Turner: "I've been there a hundred times before. I've been there three times this season. It should be a rule not to play a game in Buffalo in December."

STANDINGS: FOURTEENTH WEEK

AFC EAST	W	L	T	CENTRAL	W	L	T	WEST	W	L	T	NFC EAST	W	L	T	CENTRAL	W	L	T	WEST	W	L	T
Miami	9	5	0	Pittsburgh	11	3	0	San Diego	10	4	0	Philadelphia	10	4	0	Tampa Bay	9	5	0	LA Rams	8	6	0
New England	8	6	0	Houston	10	4	0	Denver	10	4	0	Dallas	9	5	0	Chicago	8	6	0	N.Orleans	7	7	0
Buffalo	7	7	0	Cleveland	9	5	0	Oakland	8	6	0	Washington	9	5	0	Minnesota	6	8	0	Atlanta	5	9	0
NY Jets	6	8	0	Cincinnati	3	11	0	Seattle	7	7	0	NY Giants	6	8	0	Green Bay	4	10	0	San Fran	1	13	0
Baltimore	4	10	0					Kan. City	6	8	0	St. Louis	4	10	0	Detroit	2	12	0				

NOTES

• The Bills won the battle of the stats, but they turned the ball over twice, had 11 penalties – including three offensive holding calls – allowed four sacks of Joe Ferguson and were forced to punt 10 times. The defense played very well, holding the Vikings to 189 total yards.

• Minnesota's 20-year veteran Jim Marshall, who was playing in his 281st straight game – every game the Vikings have ever played – competed in his final home game and he recorded a sack.

• Joe Ferguson became the Bills' all-time leader in pass completions and he also set a single-season record for completions, but it happened on one of his poorest days of the year.

• The Vikings took a 7-0 lead in the first when Tommy Kramer passed 19 yards to ex-Bill Ahmad Rashad on a third-and-12 play as Jeff Nixon failed to provide double coverage help on the play.

• Rick Danmeier's field goal came after a 32-yard Rusty Jackson punt set up the Vikings at the Bills 36. A roughing-the-passer penalty on Ben Williams moved the ball to the 10.

• In the second half, the Vikes were limited to 78 yards and four first downs, but the Bills' offense continued to sputter. Their only points came on Nick Mike-Mayer's field goal with 4:10 left.

QUOTES

• Joe Ferguson: "I didn't play well today. I was hoping to get by this year without one (bad performance). I kept asking myself 'When is it going to happen?' When you play 20 games, the odds are it'll show up. It's been like this all year where if I'm not having a good day, we're in trouble. We had a lot of passes that were close, but not caught."

• Vikings receiver Ahmad Rashad: "I had the honor and privilege of driving Jim Marshall here to his last game. He

treated it like just another game. I asked him if he wanted me to drive around the stadium a few times for old times sake and he just laughed. He's our spiritual leader and that's not just lip service like it is with so many other so-called spiritual leaders. It's real. He's a remarkable man."

• Jeff Nixon on the TD play to Rashad: "We had him doubled, I had him outside and Steve (Freeman) had him inside. He took Steve to the inside and I just assumed he'd keep going, so when I saw a back open in front of me, I moved up to help Lucious (Sanford). Then I was caught when Rashad went back to the outside. As soon as I saw the ball go over my head, I knew I'd made a mistake. One thing I've learned in this league is when you have a job, you do it and don't worry about helping anyone else."

• Chuck Knox: "We ran 77 plays and couldn't get one big one. Over the course of a game, you should expect a receiver to make a big catch or a running back to make one big run and an offensive lineman to make one big block. But we couldn't even make one big play. That kills me."

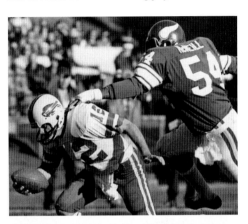

Bills	0	0	0	3	- 3
Vikings	7	3	0	0	- 10

Attendance at Metropolitan Stadium - 42,399

Min: Rashad 19 pass from Kramer (Danmeier kick), 10:50
Min: FG Danmeier 31, 11:35
Buf: FG Mike-Mayer 24, 10:50

	BUF	MIN
First downs	18	12
Rushing yds	105	85
Passing yds	186	104
Punts-avg	10-37.7	10-35.7
Fumbles-lost	0-0	2-0
Penalties-yds	11-86	7-38

BILLS LEADERS: **Rushing** - Collier 10-70, Brown 3-7, Miller 7-5, Hooks 6-23, Ferguson 1-0; **Passing** - Ferguson 18-45-2 - 227; **Receiving** - Lewis 8-111, Butler 5-72, Piccone 1-20, Collier 2-13, Hooks 2-11.

VIKINGS LEADERS: **Rushing** - R. Miller 8-42, Young 11-29, Kramer 6-5, McClanahan 2-5, Brown 1-4; **Passing** - Kramer 12-32-1 - 104; **Receiving** - Rashad 2-31, White 1-19, Miller 3-15, Young 2-15, Voight 1-9, McClanahan 1-9, Tucker 1-6, Brown 1-0.

WEEK 15 GAMES

Dal 24, Phil 17	Sea 28, Den 23
Mia 28, Det 10	NYJ 27, NE 26
Wash 28, Cin 14	Oak 19, Clev 14
SF 23, TB 7	LA 34, Atl 13
Chi 15, GB 14	SD 35, NO 0
St.L 29, NYG 20	KC 10, Balt 7
Hou 20, Pitt 17	

NOTES

• The Bills closed the season with their third straight loss as the Steelers dominated in a game they had to win in order to sew up the AFC Central title for the sixth year in a row.

• Jim Haslett was ejected in the second quarter when officials said he intentionally kicked Terry Bradshaw in the head after a play had been blown dead. It was one of four unsportsmanlike conduct penalties stepped off against Buffalo as the Bills were spirited, but lacked execution.

• Nick Mike-Mayer had a field goal blocked on the Bills' first possession, but Sherman White returned the favor by blocking a Chris Bahr attempt. It was White's seventh blocked kick (one extra point) of the season.

• Lynn Swann capped a 55-yard drive with a 20-yard TD late in the first quarter.

• Two plays after Haslett was tossed, Franco Harris scored to make it 14-0.

• The Steelers took the second-half kickoff and drove 71 yards to Sidney Thornton's TD on a draw, then wrapped it up in the fourth on Harris' 11-yard run to end a 67-yard drive.

QUOTES

• Steelers linebacker Jack Lambert: "As we came off the field, some of the Bills were wondering why we weren't excited to win the division. I don't know why we're not excited. I guess it's because we're expected to win. We had a job to do, we did it, and now we're waiting for the second half of the season (the playoffs). I'll hand it to Buffalo, they played hard in a game where they had nothing riding on the outcome."

• Chuck Knox: "We came ready to play, but we just

weren't good enough."

• Terry Bradshaw on the Haslett play: "I don't know what happened. I'll defend him and say I wasn't kicked. I can't imagine him kicking me. My wig company is going to have to send me a three-quarter inch piece of hair to cover it (his abrasion)."

• Jim Haslett: "I've got nothing to say, ask the referee. They let a couple of things go. They (the Steelers) can do whatever they want out there."

• Joe Ferguson: "We came in here today and found out what it is that championship teams do. We were beaten, outplayed, and maybe we'll learn from it. This game has to make us realize what it takes to be a championship team. We've got to get the running game going next year. It caught up with us the second half of the season. If a team finds out you can't run the ball, there are a lot of things they can do to completely shut off the pass. It made the last three games of the season miserable."

• Joe DeLamielleure: "This doesn't affect the way I feel about the season. I'm going to be fired up next year when I go to camp. We built the most important thing this year with the defense. It takes longer to build a defense than it does an offense. Next year we'll get our offense going and we'll be OK."

WEEK 16 GAMES

NYJ 27, Mia 24	GB 18, Det 13
Phil 26, Hou 20	TB 3, KC 0
Dal 35, Wash 34	Chi 42, St.L 6
NO 29, LA 14	NE 27, Minn 23
Cinc 16, Clev 12	Sea 29, Oak 24
Balt 31, NYG 7	Atl 31, SF 21
SD 17, Den 7	

Bills	0	0	0	0	- 0
Steelers	7	7	7	7	- 28

Attendance at Three Rivers Stadium - 48,002

Pitt: Swann 20 pass from Bradshaw (Bahr kick), 14:59
Pitt: Harris 1 run (Bahr kick), 4:04
Pitt: Thornton 8 run (Bahr kick), 4:41
Pitt: Harris 11 run (Bahr kick), 6:04

	BUF	PIT
First downs	8	24
Rushing yds	78	214
Passing yds	78	201
Punts-avg	10-40.2	4-44.0
Fumbles-lost	1-1	3-2
Penalties-yds	7-56	6-47

BILLS LEADERS: **Rushing** - Collier 16-49, Miller 5-13, Hooks 2-16, Ferguson 1-0; **Passing** - Ferguson 11-31-2 - 103; **Receiving** - Lewis 1-22, Butler 3-54, Piccone 1-6, Shipp 1-3, Collier 4-11, Hooks 1-7.

STEELERS LEADERS: **Rushing** - Harris 21-100, Thornton 10-51, Bleier 2-3, Bradshaw 2-10, Hawthorne 4-9, Kruczek 1-22, Anderson 2-8, Moser 3-11; **Passing** - Bradshaw 14-27-2 - 209; **Receiving** - Cunningham 3-36, Swann 3-61, Stallworth 4-39, Harris 2-18, Thornton 2-55.

STANDINGS: SIXTEENTH WEEK

AFC EAST	W	L	T	CENTRAL	W	L	T	WEST	W	L	T	NFC EAST	W	L	T	CENTRAL	W	L	T	WEST	W	L	T
Miami	10	6	0	Pittsburgh	12	4	0	San Diego	12	4	0	Dallas	11	5	0	Tampa Bay	10	6	0	LA Rams	9	7	0
New England	9	7	0	Houston	11	5	0	Denver	10	6	0	Philadelphia	11	5	0	Chicago	10	6	0	N.Orleans	8	8	0
NY Jets	8	8	0	Cleveland	9	7	0	Seattle	9	7	0	Washington	10	6	0	Minnesota	7	9	0	Atlanta	6	10	0
Buffalo	7	9	0	Cincinnati	4	12	0	Oakland	9	7	0	NY Giants	6	10	0	Green Bay	5	11	0	San Fran	2	14	0
Baltimore	5	11	0					Kan. City	7	9	0	St. Louis	5	11	0	Detroit	2	14	0				

At A Glance
1980

Jan. 2 – Jerry Butler was named AFC rookie of the year by UPI. *The Sporting News* also chose Butler it's AFC rookie of the year.

March 10 – At the league meetings in Palm Springs, the owners voted against Al Davis' proposed transfer of his Oakland Raiders to Los Angeles. "We feel we have a very sound defense and we will prevail," NFL commissioner Pete Rozelle said. Davis wanted to move the Raiders into the Los Angeles Coliseum because the Rams were moving out to Anaheim for the 1980 season.

March 15 – Bob Chandler, who spent almost all of 1979 on the sidelines, said he would welcome a trade to the West Coast. "It's not an ultimatum or anything of the sort, it's just that I'd like to be closer to my family," he said.

April 1 – Equipment manager Tony Marchitte retired after 19 years of working for the team.

April 15 – Joe DeLamielleure said he wanted to be traded. "I just don't enjoy playing under the present situation," DeLamielleure said. "I don't feel I'd be being fair to the Buffalo Bills organization, to Chuck Knox and most important, to myself. I don't enjoy playing for coach Knox or the Bills. I love Buffalo, and I intend to make Buffalo my home should I be traded, but I just don't think I can give 100 percent." DeLamielleure was unhappy with the philosophies of offensive line play being taught and used by Knox and line coach Ray Prochaska.

April 22 – Bob Chandler was traded to the Raiders for linebacker Phil Villapiano. "Several times I didn't think it would work out, and I said fine," Chandler said. "I went up and down a lot on this. I just want to thank Chuck Knox for accomodating me. I asked him to pursue Oakland. The differences we had didn't hinder the deal at all. He put out a sincere effort, which is something done very rarely."

April 23 – Joe Ferguson, who was married earlier in the month, talked about the loss of Chandler and his concern over losing quality players. "There are only a handful of players left who have been with the Bills for the past several years," he said. "I can't help but reflect back to the old days when we lost guys like Ahmad Rashad and J.D. Hill. You look back on that and wonder what's happening. If Joe D is traded, we'll be losing two top-notch players. But at least we're receiving veteran players where in the past, we didn't get anything."

April 24 – Chuck Ziober was hired to replace Tony Marchitte as equipment manager.

April 27 – A report circulated that Joe DeLamielleure would be traded to Detroit. Also, San Francisco's Bill Walsh said he was interested in obtaining the five-time Pro Bowl guard. The Lions and 49ers held the top two picks in the draft.

April 29 – The Bills traded down in the first round of the NFL draft, giving their No. 10 slot to Seattle in exchange for Seattle's 17th position and the Seahawks' third-round choice. The gamble paid off when Knox got his man anyway, North Carolina State offensive lineman Jim Ritcher, who was voted the 1979 Outland Trophy winner as the nation's best lineman. Using a pick from the O.J. Simpson trade two years earlier, the Bills tabbed Auburn running back Joe Cribbs in the second round, then took

Arkansas State quarterback Gene Bradley in their own second-round slot. Also drafted by the Bills were Michigan State tight end Mark Brammer (third round) and with the Seahawks choice in the third, they took Boston College guard John Schmeding. They also chose South Carolina State linebacker Ervin Parker (fourth) and Tennessee-Chattanooga punter Greg Cater (10th). Detroit made running back Billy Sims of Oklahoma the No. 1 choice while the Jets obtained the No. 2 pick from

the 49ers and chose Texas' Lam Jones. Elsewhere, Cincinnati took offensive tackle Anthony Munoz (third), Green Bay chose defensive tackle Bruce Clark (fourth), Baltimore selected running back Curtis Dickey (fifth), the Giants grabbed cornerback Mark Haynes (seventh), Seattle used Buffalo's 10th pick to choose defensive end Jacob Green, New Orleans took guard Stan Brock (12th), Oakland picked quarterback Marc Wilson (16th) and Washington chose wide receiver Art Monk

Joe Cribbs became an instant hit in Buffalo as a rookie in 1980. He was the consensus AFC Rookie of the Year and started in the Pro Bowl. His 1,185 yards rushing were the most ever by a Bills rookie.

(19th).

May 10 – Mini-camp opened at Rich Stadium and Joe DeLamielleure was absent, remaining firm on his demand for a trade.

May 26 – Joe DeLamielleure spoke out in reference to Chuck Knox's failure to trade him, five weeks after his request. "I think Coach Knox is afraid to trade me," he said. "He blew the O.J. Simpson deal and now I think he's afraid to trade me because he might blow it."

May 30 – Fullback Roosevelt Leaks was claimed on waivers from Baltimore and punter Rusty Jackson was released.

June 2 – Jim Ritcher and the Bills agreed to terms and he signed his first pro contract. "I'm going back to Washington tonight (with attorney Richard Bennett) and figure out what to do with the money," Ritcher said. "I'm going to look over some investments and buy a car. Maybe I'll buy a blazer because of all the snow you get here."

June 28 – Jerry Argovitz, the agent for Joe Cribbs, said that his client was interested in going to Canada to play for Montreal.

July 1 – Joe Cribbs decided against the CFL and signed a contract with the Bills.

July 3 – The Bills acquired controversial offensive guard Conrad Dobler from New Orleans for an undisclosed draft choice.

July 20 – Training camp opened at Niagara University, the latest starting date for camp in 12 years.

July 22 – Veteran safety Tony Greene, second on the Bills' all-time interception list with 38, was waived, as was three-year starting center Willie Parker.

July 23 – Joe DeLamielleure indicated that he would not be reporting to camp when veterans were scheduled to come in in two days.

July 25 – Along with DeLamielleure, veterans Sherman White, Mario Clark and Lou Piccone failed to report to camp.

July 26 – The Bills and Browns met in their third annual rookie scrimmage at Edinboro State University and played to a 6-6 tie. Joe Cribbs gained 47 yards on nine carries.

July 28 – O.J. Simpson and Joe DeLamielleuere were named to the NFL's Team of the 70's by the Pro Football Hall of Fame.

July 30 – Defensive lineman Phil Dokes left camp for undisclosed reasons, but the team signed cornerback Mario Clark, thus ending his holdout.

Aug.1 – Veteran wide receiver Ron Jessie was acquired from the Rams for a middle-round choice in the 1981 draft.

Aug. 2 – The agent for Phil Dokes said his client's Bills career, and possibly his football career, likely were over.

Aug. 3 – In front of a Browns Family Day crowd of 26,758 at Kent State, Cleveland edged the Bills, 6-0, in a controlled scrimmage.

Aug. 9 – Philadelphia dumped the Bills, 24-9, in the preseason opener at Rich Stadium.

Aug. 15 – The Bills held what would likely be their final workout at Niagara University. After a 13-year association with the college, the Bills found arrangements no longer could be worked out because the students were coming back earlier and earlier every year. Stew Barber still was actively seeking a new summer home for the Bills.

Aug. 16 – Detroit handed the Bills their 10th straight preseason loss of the Chuck Knox era, 24-17, at the Silverdome, as No.1 draft choice Billy Sims rushed for 78 yards.

Aug. 20 – Lou Piccone ended his holdout and signed.

Aug. 22 – The Bills signed free agents Ken MacAfee, David Humm and Rufus Bess.

Aug. 23 – The Bills beat Green Bay, 14-0, for their first preseason win under Chuck Knox, as the Packers managed only 130 total yards at Rich Stadium.

Aug. 26 – To get to the roster limit of 50, Chuck Knox cut veteran kick returner Keith Moody and newly acquired tight end Ken MacAfee.

Aug. 29 – Houston dealt the Bills a rude 24-7 preseason closing defeat at the Astrodome as Earl Campbell carried 11 times for 109 yards and two TDs.

Aug. 31 – Because a trade wasn't worked out, Joe DeLamielleure had no choice but to rejoin the Bills. He and defensive end Sherman White ended their holdouts and reported to Rich Stadium.

Sept. 1 – After four months of failing to trade Joe DeLamielleure, Chuck Knox completed a deal one day after the veteran guard said he would come back to the team. DeLamielleure was traded to Cleveland for a pair of undisclosed draft choices, believed to be second-rounders in 1981 and '82. "I was shocked, I had given up hope and resigned myself to the fact that I wouldn't be traded," DeLamielleure said. "But to be traded to Cleveland couldn't have made me happier. It's the best place for me to go. It's halfway between Detroit (where he purchased a new home) and Buffalo." Said Chuck Knox: "I'm not relieved at all. What joy can you have from it. What we wanted to do was get it settled today so we could start getting ready for Miami."

Sept. 3 – Knox waived Conrad Dobler and Greg Cater, then brought back both after they cleared waivers, finalizing the roster for the regular season.

Sept. 7 – One of the greatest days in Bills history was enjoyed by a sun-splashed Rich Stadium crowd of 79,598, the third-largest in team history, as the Bills ended their 20-game losing streak to the Miami Dolphins, 17-7. Buffalo overcame seven turnovers and nine penalties along the way. Trailing 7-3 in the fourth, Joe Ferguson passed four yards to Roosevelt Leaks for the go-ahead TD, then Isiah Robertson's interception led to Joe Cribbs' insurance TD. Fans stormed the field and tore down both goal posts, passing one upright all the way up to Ralph Wilson's private box. Fans partied as if the team had won the Super Bowl. "This is the biggest win in the history of the team, 20 years," Wilson said gleefully. "Bigger than the AFL championships. I'll be happy to buy new goal posts."

Sept. 8 – The celebration continued as players expressed awe over what had happened the day before. "I couldn't believe it," said Joe Cribbs of the Bills fans. "I've never seen anything like it. We used to get 84,000 (at Auburn). The way the crowd was yelling, they really picked you up, but what made it different is that they reacted like they had won the game themselves. Hey, I'm 1-0 in the NFL and I've never lost to Miami." Said veteran Phil Villapiano, who played in his first game as a Bill: "I had chills going up and down my spine as soon as I got to the top of the tunnel. It seemed like the old days in Oakland. The people really gave something to the guys and we gave them something."

Sept. 9 – Lost in the hoopla of the Miami conquest were the disgruntled comments of Terry Miller. With Joe Cribbs earning the starting nod and play-ing a starring role against the Dolphins, Miller indicated that he wanted to be traded. "I'm happy for the team, but I'm not happy and apparently they're not happy with me," Miller said. "I hope something can be worked out because it looks like I can't contribute here."

Sept. 14 – The Bills defeated the Jets, 20-10, on the day that O.J. Simpson's No. 32 jersey was retired. Jeff Nixon's 50-yard interception return for a TD was the key. Simpson became the first member of the Bills Wall of Fame. His name would be displayed permananately on the facade below the upper deck. Simpson was impressed with his old team. "Joe Ferguson looks at the top of his game, the line has really improved and the defense is solid," he said. "It looks like the teams we had in 1974 and '75."

Sept. 15 – Reuben Gant, who enjoyed a big day against the Jets, reiterated that he was unhappy about his contract. "I still want to be traded, I haven't changed my mind," he said. "I have been asking to have my contract renegotiated for two years. It's not as if I'm asking for the moon, but I think I'm worth more than I'm getting."

Sept. 20 – Conrad Dobler, Jim Haslett and five other Bills dined at Brennans in New Orleans. Ralph Wilson came over, bought them a bottle of champagne and picked up their tab, which soared to more than $500.

Sept. 21 – Jerry Butler and Frank Lewis combined for 215 yards receiving and two TDs as the Bills rolled to 3-0 by beating New Orleans in the Superdome, 35-26. Joe Ferguson became the Bills' all-time leader in passing yardage, moving past Jack Kemp.

Sept. 28 – The Bills got off to their best start since going 4-0 in 1975 as they rolled past the Oakland Raiders, 24-7, at Rich Stadium. Oakland managed only 179 yards of offense.

Oct. 5 – The Bills went to San Diego and upset the Chargers, 26-24, in a battle of unbeatens. And when Detroit lost to Atlanta, it left the Bills as the NFL's lone remaining unbeaten team. The Bills rallied for 14 fourth-quarter points to overcome San Diego. When the team arrived at the Buffalo airport at 1:46 a.m. Monday morning, about 5,000 fans gathered to welcome them back from San Diego.

Oct. 8 – Veteran safety Bill Simpson was acquired from the Rams. Knox had traded for Simpson in 1979, but he failed his physical and then retired from football. The Bills surrendered a low-round draft choice.

Oct. 12 – The Bills suffered their first loss of the season as Baltimore came to Rich Stadium and pulled a 17-12 upset. The Bills' mistakes doomed them on a cold, windy and wet day.

Oct. 15 – Joe DeLamielleure said that he had no regrets about asking for a trade, even though the Bills were off to such a great start. "I said before I was traded that even if Buffalo went 16-0 this year, I didn't want to play there anymore," he said. "If they make the playoffs this year, I'll be glad for all my friends."

Oct. 16 – The trading deadline passed and Terry Miller was still with the Bills. "I'm not in mourning, I'll just come in and put in my day's work," he said. "I truthfully hope something will happen during the offseason that will be beneficial to both."

Oct. 19 – The Dolphins got back to their winning ways against the Bills, pulling off a 17-14 victory in the Orange Bowl, their 12th in a row over Buffalo in Miami. The Dolphins rushed for 149 yards, including 84 by unsung Terry Robiskie.

Oct. 22 – Both Jeff Nixon and Rod Kush had casts removed from their injured knees and began rehabilitation work, but they wouldn't be back for at least three weeks.

Oct. 26 – The defense turned in a brilliant effort, limiting New England to 148 yards in a 31-13 victory that enabled the Bills to tie the Patriots for first place in the AFC East at 6-2. Gusty winds at Rich Stadium hampered the Patriots far more than the Bills.

Nov. 2 – Atlanta blew out the Bills at Rich, 30-14, thanks to five turnovers and a blocked field goal by Don Smith that turned the game in the Falcons' favor.

Nov. 9 – Frank Lewis caught a 31-yard touchdown pass from Joe Ferguson with six seconds left to give the Bills a thrilling 31-24 victory over the Jets at rain-soaked Shea Stadium. The Bills had blown a 17-0 lead. "We've been losers for a long time, we're just now learning how to win," Joe Ferguson said. "How important was this? It gives us a chance to be division champs and keeps us in the playoff picture. This is something new to us."

Nov. 10 – Jim Haslett and Isiah Robertson got into a fight outside the Pierce Arrow nightclub at about 2 a.m. Haslett suffered a cut finger when Robertson bit him. "There's nothing to talk about, it's personal between me and Haz and it's over and done with," Robertson said.

Nov. 16 – The Bills defense held the Bengals to 213 yards in pitching a 14-0 shutout at Riverfront Stadium. The offense chipped in with a fabulous TD drive in the fourth quarter that ate up 11:59.

Nov. 18 – Disorderly conduct charges against Jim Haslett and Isiah Robertson were dropped in West Seneca town court. "They're pals, I don't expect this to have any effect on our preparation for the Steelers," Chuck Knox said. "Everything will keep going. You guys are going to have to find something else to write about."

Nov. 23 – The Bills posted one of their biggest victories in recent memory, ripping the two-time defending Super Bowl champion Pittsburgh Steelers, 28-13, before the third-largest crowd in Rich Stadium history. After the game, Jim Haslett and Isiah Robertson re-enacted their fight of a couple weeks ago as Haslett stuck his finger in Robertson's mouth and said "Don't bite too hard now, it still hurts."

Nov. 30 – Coming off the high of the Pittsburgh victory, The Bills crashed to earth as host Baltimore inflicted a painful 28-24 defeat. The Bills turned the ball over four times and blew a 14-0 lead.

Dec. 4 – Fred Smerlas was named the NFL's defensive player of the month for November.

Dec. 7 – In another memorable affair at Rich Stadium, the Bills edged the Los Angeles Rams, 10-7, in overtime on Nick Mike-Mayer's 30-yard field goal. After the game, fans refused to leave and called the Bills back for a curtain call. Mike-Mayer, Reggie McKenzie, Jim Haslett, Fred Smerlas, Phil Villapiano, Sherman White, Conrad Dobler and many other Bills returned to the field and danced to the team's theme song, *Talkin' Proud*. Said Dobler: "We came out because these fans are the greatest in the league. That was my first curtain call and I have to confess that I loved it. Loved it to hell. The crowd enthusiasm today was outrageous." Said White: "I said when I came to Buffalo these are the best fans when you win. This used to be a hockey town, but we are making it a football town."

Dec. 14 – With a chance to clinch their first AFC East title since the 1970 merger, the Bills were thrashed at New England, 24-2. Joe Ferguson suffered a sprained left ankle six minutes into the game and could not return to action. Another big crowd greeted the team at the airport upon arrival and Reggie McKenzie told the gathering: "We're going out to San Francisco to kick their ass."

Dec. 15 – Joe Ferguson said his ankle felt better and that he was confident he could play against the 49ers. "I'm very optimistic about it," Chuck Knox said.

Dec. 16 – UPI named Joe Cribbs to its all-rookie team.

Dec. 17 – Joe Cribbs, Fred Smerlas and Jerry Butler were named to the AFC Pro Bowl squad.

Dec. 18 – If Joe Ferguson was unable to play against the 49ers, Conrad Dobler made it perfectly clear that he hoped David Humm played instead of Dan Manucci. He said Manucci had no presence in the pocket and many of the sacks allowed were Manucci's fault. "I timed it on the film and Manucci had 7 1/2 seconds – make that minutes – to get the ball off. After awhile you begin to think 'Maybe it's us, maybe we're not doing our job.' Then you see the films and feel better. And that Manucci has the guts to tell a Boston reporter that his protection broke down."

Dec. 19 – A picture of Joe Montana appeared in *The Buffalo News* with the caption: "Another Ferguson?" San Francisco coach Bill Walsh said: "He's much like Ferguson. They're very similar in ability all the way around. He is as close to Ferguson as any athlete. He (Ferguson) is one of the most stable, consistent quarterbacks in recent years in the NFL."

Dec. 21 – The Bills survived two last-second heaves into the end zone by Joe Montana and defeated the 49ers at muddy Candlestick Park, 18-13, to clinch their first AFC East title. Joe Ferguson toughed it out despite his sore ankle and was the catalyst for the victory. "This is my best one," said Chuck Knox, who won five straight NFC West titles with Los Angeles. "Nobody had us going anywhere. A lot of people picked us for last. We started singing that song (Buffalo's going to the Super Bowl) back in training camp and no one believed that we meant it. But I believed in these guys and they believed in themselves."

Dec. 22 – It was 4 a.m. before the team pulled in to Prior Aviation, but 8,000 fans braved 13-degree cold to welcome the Bills back from San Francisco. "We appreciate what you've done for us, we love you," Chuck Knox said to the fans from the stage of a makeshift bandshell that was erected. Reggie McKenzie recalled what he had said the week before: "I'll reiterate what I told you before. Did we go out there and kick their asses?" Joe Ferguson and Lou Piccone also made brief remarks to the roaring crowd, which swayed to the *Talkin' Proud* theme song.

Dec. 23 – When the San Diego Chargers beat Pittsburgh the night before, New England was eliminated from the playoffs and it meant that the Bills would play either San Diego or Cleveland in their first playoff game. However, the Bills would be on the road regardless of who it was.

Dec. 28 – Oakland ripped Houston, 27-7, in the AFC wild-card game, meaning that Buffalo would have to play at San Diego in the divisional round while Oakland would travel to Cleveland. In the NFC wild-card game, Dallas routed Los Angeles,

34-13.

Dec. 29 – The Bills flew to Vero Beach, Florida, to practice for the week at Dodgertown, the Los Angeles Dodgers spring training base.

Dec. 30 – Joe Cribbs, Reggie McKenzie, Ken Jones, Ben Williams, Jim Haslett and Fred Smerlas were named to the AFC all-star team by UPI.

Dec. 31 – Former Bill and former NBC analyst Paul Maguire, now working for ESPN, said that Isiah Robertson "hasn't done a thing for the best defense in the league. I don't know why he's in there. He's a terrible football player." Robertson replied: "Paul Maguire was a punter, what does he know about football? I laugh at guys like him. He never hit anybody in his life." In a Florida newspaper, Jim Haslett was quoted as saying: "Nobody on the team likes him (Robertson). He's a complete jerk. He's the worst bleeping player on the team. Whenever I see him on the field, I try not to think about him because it just gets me upset." Chuck Knox tried to defuse the situation by saying that Haslett was just teasing.

Jan. 1, 1981 – Haslett said that yes, his remarks were in jest. "Why would I want to start trouble now?" he said. "We've already had it out and we're all right now. I was just trying to make it a little lively, I was messing around with the guy. I went in and apologized to Butch."

Jan. 3, 1981 – Perhaps the most memorable and magical season in Bills history came to an abrupt end as Dan Fouts threw a 50-yard touchdown pass to Ron Smith with 2:08 left to play, lifting the Chargers to a 20-14 playoff victory over the Bills in San Diego. The Bills let a 14-3 halftime lead slip away as Fouts threw for 314 yards and two TDs. In Philadelphia, the Eagles defeated Minnesota, 31-16.

Jan. 4, 1981 – Oakland edged Cleveland, 14-12, as Brian Sipe's pass to the end zone with 41 seconds left was intercepted by Oakland's Mike Davis. Dallas used a 20-point fourth quarter to nip Atlanta, 30-27.

Jan. 11, 1981 – Oakland outgunned San Diego, 34-27, to win the AFC Championship Game, which would have been played in Buffalo had the Bills beaten the Chargers. Jim Plunkett completed 14 of 18 passes for 262 yards and produced three TDs. Philadelphia dominated Dallas, 20-7, to win the NFC Championship Game and qualify for its first Super Bowl. Wilbert Montgomery rushed for 194 yards and one TD.

Jan. 25, 1981 – MVP Jim Plunkett passed for 261 yards and three TDs including two to Cliff Branch and an 80-yarder to Kenny King as the Raiders romped past the Eagles, 27-10, to win Super Bowl XV in the New Orleans Superdome. The Raiders became the first wild-card team to win the championship.

Feb. 1, 1981 – The NFC won the Pro Bowl, 21-7, as Eddie Murray of Detroit kicked four field goals to win the MVP award.

By the Numbers - 1980

TEAM STATISTICS	BILLS	OPP
First downs	317	251
Rushing	134	109
Passing	157	120
Penalty	26	22
Third downs	127-240	91-217
Total yards	4,972	4,101
Avg. game	310.8	256.3
Plays	1,084	952
Avg. play	4.6	4.3
Net rushing yds	2,222	1,819
Avg. game	138.9	113.7
Avg. play	3.7	3.7
Net passing yds	2,750	2,282
Comp/att	262/461	240/433
Sacks/lost	20-186	33-279
Interceptions	19	24
Percentage	56.8	55.4
Punts/avg	74-38.2	82-39.3
Fumbles/lost	36-22	37-20
Penalties/yds	90-731	97-805
Touchdowns	40	31
Extra points	37-40	29-31
Field goals	13-23	15-20
Safeties	2	0
Kick ret./avg	47-17.6	52-20.2
Punt ret./avg	39-6.6	34-6.0

RUSHING	ATT	YDS	AVG	TD
Cribbs	306	1185	3.9	11
Brown	153	559	3.7	3
Leaks	67	219	3.3	2
Hooks	25	118	4.7	1
Ferguson	31	65	2.1	0
Miller	12	35	2.9	0
Manucci	3	29	9.7	0
Butler	1	18	18.0	0
Brammer	1	8	8.0	0
Humm	1	5	5.0	0
Jessie	1	-9	-9.0	0
Cater	2	-10	-5.0	0
TOTALS	**603**	**2222**	**3.7**	**17**

PASSING	COMP	ATT	INT	YDS	TD	COMP%	SACKS	RATE
Ferguson	251	439	18	2805	20	57.2	13-129	74.7
Manucci	5	6	0	64	0	83.3	5-48	111.0
Humm	4	14	1	39	0	28.6	2-9	10.0
Cater	1	1	0	15	0	100.0	0-0	100.0
Cribbs	1	1	0	13	0	100.0	0-0	100.0
TOTALS	**262**	**461**	**19**	**2936**	**20**	**56.8**	**20-186**	**73.2**

KICKING	1-19	20-29	30-39	40-49	50+	TOT	PAT	PTS
Mike-Mayer	0-0	4-4	4-9	5-9	0-1	13-23	37-40	76

PUNTING	NO	AVG	LG	In 20	BL
Cater	73	38.7	61	12	0
TOTALS	**74**	**38.2**	**61**	**12**	**0**

RECEIVING	CAT	YDS	AVG	TD
Butler	57	832	14.6	6
Cribbs	52	415	8.0	1
Lewis	40	648	16.2	6
Brown	27	137	5.1	0
Brammer	26	283	10.9	4
Hooks	23	179	7.8	0
Gant	12	181	15.1	1
Leaks	8	57	7.1	1
Piccone	7	82	11.7	0
Jessie	4	56	14.0	1
Fergerson	3	41	13.7	0
Miller	3	25	8.3	0
TOTALS	**262**	**2936**	**11.2**	**20**

SCORE BY QUARTERS

BILLS	54	104	55	104	3 -	320
OPP	53	87	69	51	0 -	260

DEFENSIVE STATISTICAL LEADERS

TACKLES: Haslett 79 primary - 46 assists - 125 tackles, Nelson 74-35-109, Sanford 75-25-100, Freeman 52-30-82, Robertson 50-26-76, Romes 45-19-64, B. Williams 44-19-63, B. Simpson 33-29-62, Smerlas 35-18-53, Clark 39-10-49, White 25-14-39, Bess 21-5-26, Nixon 18-5-23

SACKS: B. Williams 11, Smerlas 6.5, Sanford 3

FUMBLE RECOVERIES: Clark 3, Kush 3, Sanford 2, Nelson 2, Hutchinson 2

FORCED FUMBLES: Sanford 4, B. Williams 3

INTERCEPTIONS: Freeman 7-107 yards, 15.3 avg., 1 TD; Nixon 5-81, 16.2, 1 TD

SPECIAL TEAMS STATISTICAL LEADERS

KICKOFF RETURNS: Miller 16-303, 18.9, 0 TD; Brown 10-181, 18.1, 0 TD

PUNT RETURNS: Cribbs 29-154, 5.3, 0 TD; Hooks 8-90, 11.3, 0 TD

The Bills defense was ranked No. 1 in the NFL in 1980 as it allowed just 256.3 yards per game. Their performance was the biggest reason why Buffalo won its first AFC East division title.

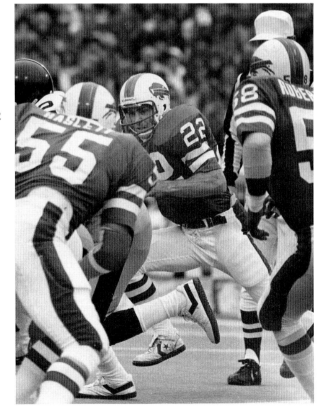

Dolphins	0	0	7	0	-	7	
Bills	0	3	0	14	-	17	

Attendance at Rich Stadium - 79,598

Buf: FG Mike-Mayer 40, 10:30
Mia: Nathan 4 pass from Griese (von Schamann kick), 3:13
Buf: Leaks 4 pass from Ferguson (Mike-Mayer kick), 11:18
Buf: Cribbs 2 run (Mike-Mayer kick), 12:58

	BUF	MIA
First downs	22	13
Rushing yds	144	90
Passing yds	213	110
Punts-avg	2-17.0	5-38.8
Fumbles-lost	4-2	4-2
Penalties-yds	9-44	6-59

BILLS LEADERS: Rushing - Cribbs 18-60, Leaks 7-35, Brown 13-30, Ferguson 4-16, Miller 1-3; **Passing** - Ferguson 20-32-5 - 198, Cater 1-1-0 - 15; **Receiving** - Butler 2-36, Lewis 3-36, Cribbs 9-71, Piccone 2-23, Leaks 2-22, Hooks 1-8, Brown 1-2, Brammer 1-15.

DOLPHINS LEADERS: Rushing - Williams 13-36, Howell 6-43, Nathan 2-11, Griese 1-0; **Passing** - Griese 11-18-2 - 101, Strock 4-8-2 - 38; **Receiving** - Williams 5-32, Harris 3-42, Nathan 3-19, Hardy 2-21, Moore 1-19, Giaquinto 1-6.

WEEK 1 GAMES

NYG 41, St.L 35	TB 17, Cinc 12
Minn 24, Atl 23	Det 41, LA 20
SD 34, Sea 13	Pitt 31, Hou 17
SF 26, NO 23	Phil 27, Den 6
Oak 27, KC 14	NE 34, Clev 17
Balt 17, NYJ 14	Dal 17, Wash 3
GB 12, Chi 6 (OT)	

NOTES

• Ralph Wilson termed it the biggest win in franchise history and no one argued as the Bills overcame seven turnovers and broke their NFL record 20-game losing streak to the Dolphins.
• The third-largest crowd in team history celebrated by tearing down the goal posts.
• The defense held Miami to 200 total yards. Entering the fourth quarter, the Bills trailed 7-3 as Bob Griese threw a TD pass to Tony Nathan. Kim Bokamper had partially blocked a Greg Cater punt, setting up the Dolphins at the Bills 20. Steve Howell ran 17 yards and Nathan scored on the next play.
• But in the fourth, Buffalo drove 68 yards in seven plays and Joe Ferguson hit a well-covered Roosevelt Leaks with a TD pass with 3:42 left. The key play on the march was a 29-yard strike to Jerry Butler to the 11. Glenn Blackwood, who had two interceptions, was beaten on the play.
• Don Strock replaced Bob Griese for the ensuing series. But on first down from the 33, he was intercepted by Isiah Robertson at midfield and Robertson returned it all the way to the 11.
• A five-yard pass to Frank Lewis came up inches short of a first down at the 1 and Chuck Knox opted to go for the score on fourth down. Joe Cribbs dove over the pile and into the end zone and the fans erupted.
• Ferguson shook off a miserable five-interception day.
• Jeff Nixon's interception of Griese led to Nick Mike-Mayer's early field goal.

QUOTES

• Chuck Knox: "It was a great win by a bunch of guys who weren't going to be denied. I don't think I've ever seen a football team come more ready to play. I was proud of Joe Ferguson. I'm proud of all of them because they battled hard to win."
• Joe Ferguson: "Now we've beaten the odds and we know we can beat them. I can think of times in the past where I probably would have blown up. And I'll admit it, I thought 'Here we go again' when they scored early in the third quarter to go ahead 7-3. To me it's better to beat them coming back than to score five touchdowns. This is going to snowball into a good thing."
• Mike Kadish: "That's the way every game should be played. We fought through so much adversity, but we never gave up. It was a superb effort, probably the best defensive effort."
• Reggie McKenzie: "I anticipate a call from O.J. tonight. He'll say 'You suckers finally did it.' Those'll be his exact words."
• Isiah Robertson: "I'm happy for the Bills, but I'm more happy for the fans. I came from an organization (the Rams) where they booed if you were 12-2. These fans have such enthusiasm."
• Dolphins guard Bob Kuechenberg: "A lot of Bills fans felt like they were 0-20. If the shoe was on the other foot, I'd call for work, school and everything else to be closed tomorrow. The fans endured and they deserve a holiday. The streak against Buffalo is something I will stand back 20 years from now and be proud of. It had to end sometime. Maybe I shouldn't have come back from retirement. But this came a week too late for Joe DeLamielleure."

Jets	3	0	0	7	-	10	
Bills	0	10	10	0	-	20	

Attendance at Rich Stadium - 65,315

NYJ: FG Leahy 44, 14:59
Buf: Cribbs 1 run (Mike-Mayer kick), 4:00
Buf: FG Mike-Mayer 47, 14:52
Buf: FG Mike-Mayer 38, 5:31
Buf: Nixon 50 interception return (Mike-Mayer kick), 14:06
NYJ: Gaines 11 pass from Todd (Leahy kick), 14:57

	BUF	NYJ
First downs	22	17
Rushing yds	155	137
Passing yds	207	166
Punts-avg	4-39.8	7-44.3
Fumbles-lost	4-1	0-0
Penalties-yds	4-41	3-23

BILLS LEADERS: Rushing - Cribbs 8-50, Leaks 12-58, Brown 5-21, Ferguson 3-10, Miller 5-12, Jessie 1-(-9), Hooks 2-13; **Passing** - Ferguson 18-29-0 - 207; **Receiving** - Butler 1-20, Piccone 3-43, Gant 4-84, Lewis 3-35, Hooks 2-14, Leaks 3-14, Brown 2-(-3).

JETS LEADERS: Rushing - Gaines 14-94, Dierking 8-32, Harper 2-11, Todd 1-3, Long 1-(-3); **Passing** - Todd 19-34-1 - 168; **Receiving** - Gaines 12-91, J. Jones 2-7, Shuler 1-12, B. Jones 1-16, Walker 1-15, Harper 1-7, Barkum 1-20.

WEEK 2 GAMES

TB 10, LA 9	Chi 22, NO 3
Sea 17, KC 16	Den 41, Dal 20
Det 29, GB 7	Mia 17, Cinc 16
SD 30, Oak 24 (OT)	Pitt 20, Balt 17
Phil 42, Minn 7	Wash 23, NYG 21
Atl 37, NE 21	Hou 16, Clev 7
SF 24, St.L 21 (OT)	

NOTES

• O.J. Simpson's name became the first to be showcased on the Wall of Fame in a halftime ceremony.
• The Jets drove 69 yards on their first possession to a 44-yard Pat Leahy field goal.
• A tight end screen to Reuben Gant turned around the game. The 48-yard gain to the 1 set up Joe Cribbs' one-yard TD plunge on the next play. Then, Joe Ferguson completed four straight passes out of the shotgun formation on the way to Nick Mike-Mayer's field goal late in the half, his longest as a Bill.
• Jeff Nixon's 50-yard interception return for a TD iced the game with one minute left in the third.
• The defense stopped the Jets when it had to all day. The only New York TD came with three seconds left in the game. Knox employed a nickel much of the game and only four of Richard Todd's 19 completions went to wideouts.
• Sherman White replaced Scott Hutchinson early in the game and cemented his spot as the No. 1 right end. Jets LT Chris Ward was called for holding four times, although the Bills accepted only one.

QUOTES

• O.J. Simpson: "I got a little misty before I came out of the tunnel (before the ceremony). I didn't really know how much I missed this uniform and all of you until now. Through your applause and cheers you let me know you appreciated me. I take pride knowing that I have the acceptance and respect of the people in Buffalo."
• Reuben Gant on the tight end screen: "It was a play that might break once a year and the first time we used it, it worked like a charm. We have never run that play since I've been here, so I'm sure it caught them by surprise."
• Joe Ferguson: "We're 2-0 and I think people will start looking our way now. Phil Villapiano and Conrad Dobler talked at the team meeting yesterday and they stressed pride. We're developing pride here, which we'd been lacking. The only way you get it is by winning."
• Jeff Nixon on his interception: "Steve Freeman and I were playing a two-deep zone. Mario Clark held up Wesley Walker real good and I was in position to make the catch. As soon as I caught it, I cut back to the open field instead of going down the sideline. I would have had a touchdown last week against Miami if I had cut back to the middle."
• Conrad Dobler: "This team is made up of people who want to improve. This group isn't made up of 20,000 first-round draft choices who want to be prima donnas. Nobody stands above anyone else. We're all having fun while we're winning. That's all you can ask for."
• Isiah Robertson: "Last year I told Reggie McKenzie and Sherman White that Coach Knox isn't used to losing and that he's bringing in a boat-load of new people this year. Conrad Dobler has come in and fired up the offensive line, Phil Villapiano has made the linebackers play hard."

STANDINGS: SECOND WEEK

AFC EAST	W	L	T	CENTRAL	W	L	T	WEST	W	L	T	NFC EAST	W	L	T	CENTRAL	W	L	T	WEST	W	L	T
Buffalo	2	0	0	Pittsburgh	2	0	0	San Diego	2	0	0	Philadelphia	2	0	0	Tampa Bay	2	0	0	San Fran	2	0	0
New England	1	1	0	Houston	1	1	0	Oakland	1	1	0	Dallas	1	1	0	Detroit	2	0	0	Atlanta	1	1	0
Baltimore	1	1	0	Cleveland	0	2	0	Seattle	1	1	0	NY Giants	1	1	0	Minnesota	1	1	0	N.Orleans	0	2	0
Miami	1	1	0	Cincinnati	0	2	0	Denver	1	1	0	Washington	1	1	0	Green Bay	1	1	0	LA Rams	0	2	0
NY Jets	0	2	0					Kan. City	0	2	0	St. Louis	0	2	0	Chicago	1	1	0				

NOTES

• Joe Ferguson became the Bills' all-time leader in passing yardage as the Bills improved to 3-0.

• The Bills opened the game with a 62-yard scoring drive. But Ferguson was intercepted by Tommy Myers late in the first quarter and Myers returned it 25 yards to the 7. Chuck Muncie scored three plays later.

• The Bills came back with a 12-play, 66-yard march that resulted in Joe Cribbs' TD run. Less than two minutes later, Archie Manning fired a 44-yard TD pass to Ike Harris. Jeff Nixon blocked the PAT.

• Ferguson was intercepted by Jim Kovach which led to Benny Ricardo's field goal for a 16-14 lead. Then the Saints blocked a 51-yard field goal attempt by Nick Mike-Mayer with less than one minute left in the half and after an 18-yard Manning pass to Brooks Williams, Ricardo made a 47-yarder.

• The Bills regained the lead when Lewis caught his second TD, capping a 55-yard march. Later in the third, Ferguson and Jerry Butler combined for a 69-yard gain to the Saints 7 and Ferguson later hit Mark Brammer for

a TD and a 28-19 lead.

• Cribbs capped a seven-minute, 92-yard drive with a TD run that put away the game.

QUOTES

• Joe Ferguson: "This is the best balanced Buffalo team since I've been here. When O.J. was here we ran too much and after he left, we probably passed too much. It's a strange feeling; you don't get it too often in Buffalo. But everything is coming together."

• Fred Smerlas on Chuck Knox: "You have to hand it to him. He kept working and working with a defense which two years ago couldn't stop the run. He stuck with us and the biggest difference this year is that the line has come together. We come down here 2-0, with the third-best defense (points allowed) in the league. They're 0-2, and they're favored. Figure that out. We haven't been on *Monday Night Football* in three years. It seems like nobody wants Buffalo to do well. We're pissed about people not noticing us. Maybe now people will finally believe we're for real."

• Reggie McKenzie: "The Miami game was so important to us in so many ways. It was our proof to ourselves that we have the ingredients to be a good team. We have been doing nothing but getting better since then."

• Chuck Knox: "The thing about this game was we were down 19-14 and things didn't look good. But we came back to win and that shows you something. We ran into a lot of adversity, but the people didn't get down. What impresses me is the way we did it."

WEEK 3 GAMES

Cinc 30, Pitt 28	Det 20, St.L 7
Clev 20, KC 13	Dal 28, TB 17
LA 51, GB 21	Minn 34, Chi 14
SF 37, NYJ 27	Hou 21, Balt 16
SD 30, Den 13	Oak 24, Wash 21
Mia 20, Atl 17	NE 37, Sea 31
Phil 35, NYG 3	

Bills	7	7	7	14 - 35
Saints	0	19	0	7 - 26

Attendance at the Superdome - 51,154

Buf: Lewis 12 pass from Ferguson (Mike-Mayer kick), 5:35
NO: Muncie 1 run (Ricardo kick), :05
Buf: Cribbs 12 run (Mike-Mayer kick), 6:40
NO: Harris 44 pass from Manning (kick blocked), 8:30
NO: FG Ricardo 45, 13:46
NO: FG Ricardo 47, 14:59
Buf: Lewis 18 pass from Ferguson (Mike-Mayer kick), 11:56
Buf: Brammer 2 pass from Ferguson (Mike-Mayer kick), 2:55
Buf: Cribbs 7 run (Mike-Mayer kick), 11:18
NO: Harris 15 pass from Manning (Ricardo kick), 14:23

	BUF	NO
First downs	26	15
Rushing yds	129	38
Passing yds	281	278
Punts-avg	3-43.7	7-40.1
Fumbles-lost	0-0	0-0
Penalties-yds	6-46	6-59

BILLS LEADERS: Rushing - Cribbs 22-89, Leaks 9-25, Brown 3-17, Ferguson 3-(-2); **Passing** - Ferguson 22-31-2 - 295; **Receiving** - Lewis 6-82, Cribbs 6-52, Butler 5-133, Leaks 1-6, Hooks 2-9, Brammer 2-13.

SAINTS LEADERS: Rushing - Muncie 10-22, Galbreath 6-2, Manning 1-14; **Passing** - Manning 24-34-0 - 285; **Receiving** - Williams 6-89, Harris 4-84, Hardy 2-12, Galbreath 6-56, Muncie 2-3, Chandler 4-41.

NOTES

• The Bills' defense dominated the Raiders, limiting them to 179 yards and no points. Oakland's only score came on Lester Hayes' 48-yard interception return. At the half, Oakland had 37 yards.

• After the game, defensive lineman Ken Johnson stood up in the locker room and crooned to a popular disco tune the words "I got a feeling, Buffalo's going to the Super Bowl."

• The Bills had the ball for more than 41 minutes and Joe Cribbs produced 126 yards from scrimmage.

• The Raiders had five turnovers including interceptions by Jeff Nixon and Jim Haslett.

• After a 25-yard punt by Ray Guy, the Bills used nine minutes to drive 81 yards in 16 plays to their first score as Curtis Brown swept around end. The drive included 12 running plays.

• On Oakland's next series, Ben Williams forced Dan Pastorini to fumble and Rod Kush recovered. Five plays later, Cribbs scored.

• Late in the half, Williams sacked Pastorini to force a punt. Guy's second bad kick set the Bills up at the Raiders 48. Using the shotgun, Joe Ferguson moved into position for a Nick Mike-Mayer field goal.

• After Hayes' TD, ex-Bill Bob Chandler caught a 56-yard pass to the Bills 26, but Williams forced Kenny King to fumble and Mario Clark recovered at the 10. Nixon's league-leading fifth interception started the Bills on their last TD drive, a 69-yard march that was keyed by a 42-yard interference on Hayes.

QUOTES

• Mario Clark: "It was a shot in the arm to see if we could play against the best. I was wondering if the teams we had played before were bad offensively, but today we shut down what is potentially a great offensive unit."

• Ken Jones: "We proved we can play with one of the league's best teams."

• Fred Smerlas: "We did everything we wanted to on defense. We shut down their running game, forced Pastorini out of the pocket and sacked him five times. This year, we're a dog facing a cat. We're not afraid anymore."

• Ken Johnson on his song: "That's our victory song this year, our motivator. I started singing it after the Miami game. We hope to sing it 14 more times this season."

• Phil Villapiano on beating his former team: "I worked hard to beat the Raiders. I told my teammates their tendencies and what to expect. I couldn't shut my mouth when I saw things that might work. You can't talk in terms of greatness with this team, but the thing about this team is that they want it. This team wants to win; it wants to be great."

• Chuck Knox: "We've still got a ways to go, but that first half was the best we've ever played."

• Raiders tackle Art Shell: "It wasn't the best pass rush I ever saw, but they certainly did an effective job. When we got behind, they were able to tee off."

Raiders	0	0	7	0 - 7
Bills	7	10	0	7 - 24

Attendance at Rich Stadium - 77,259

Buf: Brown 4 run (Mike-Mayer kick), 14:45
Buf: Cribbs 1 run (Mike-Mayer kick), 3:11
Buf: FG Mike-Mayer 30, 15:00
Oak: Hayes 48 interception return (Bahr kick), 2:06
Buf: Cribbs 21 pass from Ferguson (Mike-Mayer kick), 1:03

	BUF	OAK
First downs	25	12
Rushing yds	165	70
Passing yds	160	109
Punts-avg	4-33.5	3-39.7
Fumbles-lost	1-0	3-3
Penalties-yds	6-68	6-87

BILLS LEADERS: Rushing - Cribbs 30-90, Brown 11-38, Leaks 2-1, Hooks 3-28, Ferguson 3-8; **Passing** - Ferguson 17-22-1 - 175; **Receiving** - Butler 3-49, Lewis 2-23, Gant 2-17, Brown 2-14, Piccone 2-16, Hooks 3-20, Cribbs 3-36.

RAIDERS LEADERS: Rushing - van Eeghen 10-46, King 7-24; **Passing** - Pastorini 10-20-2 - 158; **Receiving** - Casper 4-51, Chandler 3-87, King 2-14, Branch 1-6.

WEEK 4 GAMES

Mia 21, NO 16	LA 28, NYG 7
SD 24, KC 7	Clev 34, TB 27
St.L 24, Phil 14	Balt 35, NYJ 21
Pitt 38, Chi 3	Hou 13, Cinc 10
Atl 20, SF 17	Det 27, Minn 7
Dal 28, GB 7	Sea 14, Wash 0
NE 23, Den 14	

STANDINGS: FOURTH WEEK

AFC EAST	W	L	T	CENTRAL	W	L	T	WEST	W	L	T	NFC EAST	W	L	T	CENTRAL	W	L	T	WEST	W	L	T
Buffalo	4	0	0	Pittsburgh	3	1	0	San Diego	4	0	0	Philadelphia	3	1	0	Detroit	4	0	0	San Fran	3	1	0
New England	3	1	0	Houston	3	1	0	Oakland	2	2	0	Dallas	3	1	0	Tampa Bay	2	2	0	Atlanta	2	2	0
Miami	3	1	0	Cleveland	2	2	0	Seattle	2	2	0	Washington	1	3	0	Minnesota	2	2	0	LA Rams	2	2	0
Baltimore	2	2	0	Cincinnati	1	3	0	Denver	1	3	0	NY Giants	1	3	0	Green Bay	1	3	0	N.Orleans	0	4	0
NY Jets	0	4	0					Kan. City	0	4	0	St. Louis	1	3	0	Chicago	1	3	0				

GAME 5 - Sunday, Oct. 5, 1980 - BILLS 26, CHARGERS 24

| Bills | 3 | 9 | 0 | 14 - 26 |
| Chargers | 7 | 10 | 7 | 0 - 24 |

Attendance at San Diego Stadium - 51,982

Buf: FG Mike-Mayer 48, 4:49
SD: Winslow 4 pass from Fouts (Benirschke kick), 11:56
SD: Jefferson 5 pass from Fouts (Benirschke kick), :04
Buf: FG Mike-Mayer 29, 6:09
Buf: Sanford recovered blocked punt (kick failed), 12:36
SD: FG Benirschke 29, 14:48
SD: Williams 3 run (Benirschke kick), 8:41
Buf: Brammer 9 pass from Ferguson (Mike-Mayer kick), 4:17
Buf: Cribbs 3 run (Mike-Mayer kick), 7:32

	BUF	SD
First downs	14	19
Rushing yds	119	86
Passing yds	83	214
Punts-avg	6-33.2	5-35.8
Fumbles-lost	2-1	5-3
Penalties-yds	1-4	2-15

BILLS LEADERS: Rushing - Cribbs 23-87, Brown 7-21, Leaks 2-9, Hooks 2-3, Miller 1-5, Cater 1-(-1), Ferguson 2-(-5); **Passing** - Ferguson 14-28-0 - 129; **Receiving** - Cribbs 4-16, Butler 3-44, Brammer 3-28, Leaks 1-11, Gant 1-30, Brown 2-0.

CHARGERS LEADERS: Rushing - Muncie 10-37, Cappelletti 10-33, C. Williams 6-15, Fouts 1-1, Partridge 1-0; **Passing** - Fouts 20-35-1 - 220; **Receiving** - Jefferson 7-85, Cappelletti 5-50, Winslow 3-26, Joiner 2-36, C. Williams 2-11, Muncie 1-12.

NOTES

• The Bills moved to the top of the NFL as the only unbeaten team by knocking off San Diego.
• Reserve safety Rod Kush had a heroic game as he blocked one punt, tackled the punter before he could kick on another and recovered two fumbles. But like starter Jeff Nixon, he injured a knee.
• Clarence Williams' third-quarter TD made it 24-12. Kush recovered a fumble on a punt by Mike Fuller at the Chargers 34, but Joe Cribbs was stopped on a fourth-and-one at the 10 and the game looked unwinnable for the Bills. But Kush tackled punter Rick Partridge at the 16 and four plays later Joe Ferguson hit Mark Brammer for a TD on a fourth-and-three from the 9 to pull the Bills within 24-19.
• Jim Haslett then intercepted a Dan Fouts pass and returned it 17 yards to the 21. Three plays later, Cribbs swept around right end for the winning TD.
• Down 7-3 in the second quarter, the Bills got a bad break when Greg Cater failed to get off a punt and was tackled at the Bills 29. Fouts hit John Jefferson for a TD six plays later.
• But Kush blocked a Partridge punt and Lucious Sanford fell on the ball in the end zone. Nick Mike-

WEEK 5 GAMES

Atl 43, Det 28	St.L 40, NO 7
Den 19, Clev 16	KC 31, Oak 17
GB 14, Cinc 9	Phil 24, Wash 14
LA 48, SF 26	Dal 24, NYG 3
NE 21, NYJ 11	Balt 30, Mia 17
Sea 26, Hou 7	Pitt 23, Minn 17
Chi 23, TB 0	

Mayer missed the PAT. Rolf Benirschke's field goal made it 17-12 San Diego at the half.
• It was Buffalo's first win in San Diego since the 1965 AFL Championship Game and first on the West Coast since 1966 when Buffalo won in Oakland.

QUOTES

• Conrad Dobler: "We'll be a team to be reckoned with no matter who we play."
• Rod Kush: "Coming in and out as the nickel back doesn't really get you involved, but I was prepared and I thought I played pretty well." (On special teams plays): "I always played it like I was rushing, but would drop back the first four games. They didn't expect me to come all day and nobody picked me up. That's the greatest game of my life."
• Joe Cribbs: "For a while it looked pretty bleak out there. We were killing ourselves with mistakes, but coach Knox said if we'd just keep playing, they would give up. We felt we were in better condition and on our last drive we knew we could take it to them. We were behind, but that seemed to make us come alive."
• Joe Ferguson: "The kids came through. Brammer came up with two clutch catchs after Reuben went out with a knee injury. Kush came up with big play after big play and Cribbs ran well. That says a lot for Chuck Knox. He's turned things around for us. I can't say enough about him."

GAME 6 - Sunday, Oct. 12, 1980 - COLTS 17, BILLS 12

| Colts | 10 | 7 | 0 | 0 - 17 |
| Bills | 0 | 9 | 0 | 3 - 12 |

Attendance at Rich Stadium - 73,634

Bal: Siani 38 pass from Jones (S. Mike-Mayer kick), 4:06
Bal: FG S. Mike-Mayer 21, 8:30
Buf: Leaks 1 run (kick failed), 8:59
Bal: McCauley 1 run (S. Mike-Mayer kick), 14:13
Buf: FG N. Mike-Mayer 49, 14:58
Buf: FG N. Mike-Mayer 20, 9:07

	BUF	BAL
First downs	24	22
Rushing yds	162	149
Passing yds	201	206
Punts-avg	6-33.3	2-40.0
Fumbles-lost	0-0	3-1
Penalties-yds	10-66	6-34

BILLS LEADERS: Rushing - Cribbs 18-76, Brown 12-56, Leaks 7-17, Ferguson 1-5, Manucci 1-5; **Passing** - Ferguson 17-36-1 - 210; **Receiving** - Butler 4-45, Hooks 4-42, Lewis 3-52, Cribbs 4-42, Gant 2-29.

COLTS LEADERS: Rushing - Washington 22-74, Franklin 13-57, McCauley 3-9, Jones 4-9; **Passing** - Jones 10-21-1 - 206; **Receiving** - Siani 4-91, Carr 3-81, Butler 1-19, Washington 1-6, Franklin 1-9.

WEEK 6 GAMES

Oak 38, SD 24	NYJ 14, Atl 7
Phil 31, NYG 16	Dal 59, SF 14
NE 34, Mia 0	Clev 27, Sea 0
Det 24, NO 13	KC 21, Hou 20
Cinc 17, Pitt 16	Minn 13, Chi 7
LA 21, St.L 13	Den 20, Wash 17
GB 14, TB 14 (OT)	

NOTES

• The Bills suffered their first loss of the season in the wind and rain at Rich Stadium.
• The Colts punted only twice and were never stopped on any possession without at least one first down.
• Greg Cater's 24-yard punt set up the Colts at their own 44 in the first quarter. Six plays later, despite getting leveled by blitzing Jim Haslett, Bert Jones fired a 38-yard TD strike to Mike Siani.
• The Colts made it 10-0 when Steve Mike-Mayer, Nick's brother, kicked a field goal after Cater's 17-yard punt into the wind started the Colts at the Bills 30.
• Buffalo then drove 94 yards in 20 plays, consuming more than 10 minutes. Roosevelt Leaks scored from the 1, but a high snap aborted the extra point attempt.
• The Colts then got a break when Bill Simpson's goal-line interception late in the half was nullified by a questionable illegal-chuck penalty on Lucious Sanford. With a new life, Don McCauley scored.
• Nick Mike-Mayer made a 49-yard field goal, his longest as a Bill, two seconds before halftime.
• The only score of the second half was Nick's 20-yarder with 5:53 left.
• The Bills moved from their 9 to the Colts 39 in the final two minutes, but Ferguson was intercepted in the end zone by Kim Anderson to end the game.

QUOTES

• Joe Ferguson: "We had our chance to win. We moved the ball well, but we hurt ourselves with penalties. The Colts are as good a team as we've faced. Maybe this will relieve some of the pressure. You're always disappointed to lose, but I don't think this game will hurt us much."
• Isiah Robertson on the Sanford penalty: "He (the official) said he didn't know who committed the penalty, just someone in a white jersey. Did he really know what happened?

(Roger) Carr could have tripped over somebody. Some penalties are obvious, but on a call like that, you've got to be sure. It was one of the worst officiated games of my career."
• Bill Simpson on his nullfied interception: "That was big because it would have wiped out a touchdown."
• Colts defensive tackle Mike Barnes on the play of Conrad Dobler: "I really miss my friend Joe D, because I felt challenged. He (Dobler) better hold because I don't think he can block me. He was ridiculous, grabbing and holding on."
• Joe Cribbs: "I didn't think Baltimore was as good as San Diego. I felt we could have run on them all day. We just kept putting ourselves in a hole."
• Conrad Dobler: "All this means is that everyone in the playoffs and in the Super Bowl will have at least one loss. What bothers me is a lot of people are saying 'Oh well, 5-1, nobody thought you'd be in this position.' Fans and the media expected us to lose sometime, you all said so, but there was no reason why we should have."

STANDINGS: SIXTH WEEK

AFC EAST	W	L	T	CENTRAL	W	L	T	WEST	W	L	T	NFC EAST	W	L	T	CENTRAL	W	L	T	WEST	W	L	T
Buffalo	5	1	0	Pittsburgh	4	2	0	San Diego	4	2	0	Philadelphia	5	1	0	Detroit	5	1	0	LA Rams	4	2	0
New England	5	1	0	Houston	3	3	0	Oakland	3	3	0	Dallas	5	1	0	Minnesota	3	3	0	Atlanta	3	3	0
Baltimore	4	2	0	Cleveland	3	3	0	Seattle	3	3	0	St. Louis	2	4	0	Tampa Bay	2	3	1	San Fran	3	3	0
Miami	3	3	0	Cincinnati	2	4	0	Denver	3	3	0	NY Giants	1	5	0	Green Bay	2	3	1	N.Orleans	0	6	0
NY Jets	1	5	0					Kan. City	2	4	0	Washington	1	5	0	Chicago	2	4	0				

NOTES

• The Bills' good fortune against Miami didn't stretch to Florida as the Dolphins beat the Bills for the 12th time in a row in the Orange Bowl. All 17 Miami points were a result of Joe Cribbs' fumbles.

• Just 3:04 into the game, Cribbs was hit by Vern Den Herder, dropped the ball and Don Bessillieu ran 44 yards for a TD. In the second quarter, Bessillieu forced Cribbs to fumble and Glenn Blackwood recovered at the Bills 27. David Woodley hit Nat Moore for a TD eight plays later.

• The Bills pulled to within 14-7 in the third as Bill Simpson forced Terry Robiskie to fumble and Shane Nelson recovered at the Miami 26. Cribbs scored seven plays later on a sweep to the left.

• But later in the third, Cribbs dropped the ball without being hit and Blackwood covered it at the Bills 41. The Dolphins moved into position for a field goal by Uwe von Schamann.

• The Bills missed a chance to get closer early in the fourth, as they failed to recover a muffed punt by Tony Nathan. With 4:43 left, they failed to convert on fourth down, but they got the ball back again and Joe Ferguson engineered a 66-yard TD drive that culminated in Jerry Butler's TD with 1:19 left. When they failed to recover an onside kick, they fell to second place in the the AFC East.

QUOTES

• Joe Cribbs: "I know I can hold on to the ball, I just had a bad game. When I fumbled the first one and they scored, it was on my mind the rest of the game. I think that led to the other fumbles. Everybody fumbles in given situations. The secret is to forget about it. In fact I've already put it out of my mind."

• Miami coach Don Shula: "Anytime you get a defensive score, it helps get the enthusiasm going. That was the play of the game. They came out running, but we did a good job against that. The only time they moved on us was when we were laying back and giving them the short passes."

• Miami defensive end A.J. Duhe: "That (the fumble return) had to knock the wind out of their sails and put it in ours. They came in here with a lot of momentum from all the success they've had, but that play slowed them down pretty good. I felt we outplayed them."

• Reggie McKenzie: "A typical game. It's happened many times before. We had some unfortunate turnovers."

• Chuck Knox: "Anytime you lose three fumbles, you're in trouble. But we can't get down on him, he's been doing a great job for us. It was one of those things."

• Mario Clark: "I would have to say this was our poorest effort of the season."

• Isiah Robertson: "It was the worst game I ever had. No excuse, I just didn't do it. I probably missed more tackles than I ever have."

WEEK 7 GAMES

Sea 27, NYJ 17	NE 37, Balt 21
Clev 26, GB 21	Cinc 14, Minn 0
Wash 23, St.L 0	Phil 17, Dal 10
SD 44, NYG 7	LA 31, SF 17
Atl 41, NO 14	Hou 20, TB 14
KC 23, Den 17	Chi 24, Det 7
Oak 45, Pitt 24	

Bills	0	0	7	7	-	14
Dolphins	7	7	3	0	-	17

Attendance at the Orange Bowl - 41,636

Mia:	Bessillieu 44 fumble return (von Schamann kick), 3:04
Mia:	Moore 3 pass from Woodley (von Schamann kick), 14:38
Buf:	Cribbs 2 run (Mike-Mayer kick), 3:24
Mia:	FG von Schamann 23, 10:16
Buf:	Butler 7 pass from Ferguson (Mike-Mayer kick), 13:41

	BUF	MIA
First downs	18	15
Rushing yds	68	149
Passing yds	221	83
Punts-avg	6-43.2	5-43.8
Fumbles-lost	4-3	3-2
Penalties-yds	8-54	6-48

BILLS LEADERS: Rushing - Cribbs 14-38, Brown 6-17, Miller 1-5, Ferguson 2-8; **Passing** - Ferguson 24-42-0 - 221; **Receiving** - Cribbs 6-33, Gant 1-10, Lewis 4-71, Brown 3-19, Brammer 1-7, Butler 5-52, Miller 2-20, Hooks 2-9.

DOLPHINS LEADERS: Rushing - Williams 16-31, Robiskie 18-84, Woodley 9-31, Nathan 1-3; **Passing** - Woodley 11-17-1 - 93; **Receiving** - Rose 2-17, Moore 4-39, Nathan 1-9, Williams 3-22, Harris 1-6.

NOTES

• The Bills pulled even with the Pats at 6-2 to tie for first in the AFC East as the defense limited New England to 148 yards and eight first downs on a day when winds gusted regularly at 30 mph. Every point in the game was scored with the wind.

• Joe Cribbs enjoyed the first 100-yard rushing game of his career. It was a first for the Bills since '78.

• The Bills went ahead 7-3 in the second, driving 55 yards to Joe Ferguson's TD pass to Frank Lewis. On the march, Ferguson completed a 25-yard pass to Lewis and an 18-yarder to Cribbs.

• The Bills made it 14-3 with an excellent two-minute drill that ended with Ferguson's 13-yard TD to Lewis.

• The Pats pulled to within 14-10 with a four-play, 69-yard drive. Steve Grogan hit Harold Jackson for 22 yards before hitting Russ Francis with a 25-yard TD pass.

• After Bill Matthews intercepted a poor Ferguson pass at the Bills 17, the defense held and John Smith made a field goal that cut the Bills lead to 14-13.

• Curtis Brown lost a fumble at the Pats 20 to kill a drive, but Steve Freeman got it back when he intercepted Grogan and the Bills capitalized with a Nick Mike-Mayer field goal.

• Greg Cater's wind-aided 54-yard punt rolled dead at the 2 and when the Pats couldn't move, punter Mike Hubach got off an eight-yard punt into the wind to the Pats 16. Two plays later, Cribbs scored.

• The final TD by Cribbs came after a Charlie Romes' interception.

QUOTES

• Conrad Dobler: "I was glad to see Joe get his 100. He really wanted it. He came back to prove to everybody in Buffalo that he truly is a pro."

• Joe Ferguson: "It was just beautiful to see Joe run the way he did; that really takes a lot of pressure off me. We were able to run against them and we had success with short passes. Our defense did a great job in getting us the ball. This wasn't the worst wind I've seen here, it was the second-worst (to a Jets game in 1973). We do have an advantage in that we practice in the wind all the time and we're more used to it."

• Joe Cribbs: "Reg and Conrad just told me to forget about the past and concentrate on doing my best against the Patriots. The offensive line was psyched. They all wanted me to go out and have a good game and they certainly blocked that way."

• Chuck Knox: "Outside of one punt, Cater had an excellent day and that was one of the keys to the game. There is enough evidence to state we are making progress in our ambitions to become a competitive team, but eight games do not make a season."

• Pats punter Mike Humbach: "I came out before the game and saw a plane flying above the stadium. It was strange because it was hardly moving. I just said 'Damn.'"

WEEK 8 GAMES

Clev 27, Pitt 26	Dal 42, SD 31
Den 14, NYG 9	GB 16, Minn 3
TB 24, SF 23	Oak 33, Sea 14
Wash 22, NO 14	Phil 17, Chi 14
KC 20, Det 17	Atl 13, LA 10
Hou 23, Cinc 3	NYJ 17, Mia 14
St.L 17, Balt 10	

Patriots	3	0	10	0	-	13
Bills	0	14	0	17	-	31

Attendance at Rich Stadium - 75,092

NE:	FG Smith 41, 6:58
Buf:	Lewis 14 pass from Ferguson (Mike-Mayer kick), 9:18
Buf:	Lewis 12 pass from Ferguson (Mike-Mayer kick), 14:24
NE:	Francis 25 pass from Grogan (Smith kick), 5:32
NE:	FG Smith 32, 6:45
Buf:	FG Mike-Mayer 23, 1:23
Buf:	Cribbs 16 run (Mike-Mayer kick), 5:18
Buf:	Cribbs 5 run (Mike-Mayer kick), 13:00

	BUF	NE
First downs	21	8
Rushing yds	181	39
Passing yds	176	109
Punts-avg	7-36.1	8-28.1
Fumbles-lost	1-1	1-0
Penalties-yds	5-49	6-40

BILLS LEADERS: Rushing - Cribbs 30-118, Brown 11-30, Leaks 6-21, Hooks 2-14, Ferguson 1-(-2); **Passing** - Ferguson 12-28-2 - 176; **Receiving** - Cribbs 3-41, Lewis 5-80, Brown 2-27, Brammer 1-21, Hooks 1-7.

PATRIOTS LEADERS: Rushing - Calhoun 8-24, Ivory 5-7, Grogan 1-4, V. Ferguson 3-4; **Passing** - Grogan 13-29-4 - 138; **Receiving** - Calhoun 2-11, Francis 2-32, Morgan 1-19, Jackson 1-20, V. Ferguson 1-6, Foreman 1-1, Ivory 3-31, Johnson 1-7, Tatupu 1-11.

STANDINGS: EIGHTH WEEK

AFC EAST	W	L	T	CENTRAL	W	L	T	WEST	W	L	T	NFC EAST	W	L	T	CENTRAL	W	L	T	WEST	W	L	T
New England	6	2	0	Cleveland	5	3	0	San Diego	5	3	0	Philadelphia	7	1	0	Detroit	5	3	0	LA Rams	5	3	0
Buffalo	6	2	0	Houston	5	3	0	Oakland	5	3	0	Dallas	6	2	0	Green Bay	3	4	1	Atlanta	5	3	0
Baltimore	4	4	0	Pittsburgh	4	4	0	Seattle	4	4	0	St. Louis	3	5	0	Tampa Bay	3	4	1	San Fran	3	5	0
Miami	4	4	0	Cincinnati	3	5	0	Denver	4	4	0	Washington	3	5	0	Minnesota	3	5	0	N.Orleans	0	8	0
NY Jets	2	6	0					Kan. City	4	4	0	NY Giants	1	7	0	Chicago	3	5	0				

Falcons	0	10	10	10	-	30
Bills	7	7	0	0	-	14

Attendance at Rich Stadium - 57,959

Buf: Lewis 11 pass from Ferguson (Mike-Mayer kick), 8:19
Buf: Cribbs 13 run (Mike-Mayer kick), :09
Atl: FG Mazzetti 28, 14:19
Atl: Miller 16 pass from Bartkowski (Mazzetti kick), 14:38
Atl: Cain 1 run (Mazzetti kick), 10:49
Atl: FG Mazzetti 50, 14:45
Atl: FG Mazzetti 44, 9:47
Atl: Cain 1 run (Mazzetti kick), 12:20

	BUF	ATL
First downs	20	19
Rushing yds	94	150
Passing yds	270	183
Punts-avg	4-33.8	4-38.8
Fumbles-lost	4-2	1-0
Penalties-yds	4-30	7-48

BILLS LEADERS: Rushing - Cribbs 16-31, Brown 7-39, Leaks 1-2, Butler 1-18, Ferguson 3-2, Hooks 1-2; **Receiving** - Butler 9-122, Jessie 1-20, Lewis 4-68, Cribbs 3-27, Gant 1-9, Fergerson 1-14, Brown 1-10.

FALCONS LEADERS: Rushing - Cain 18-59, Andrews 20-87, Bartkowski 4-4; **Passing** - Bartkowski 13-24-3 - 193; **Receiving** - Andrews 2-30, Cain 2-18, Jenkins 4-79, Francis 3-44, Miller 1-16, Jackson 1-6.

NOTES

• In a battle of division leaders, the Bills were in control until late in the first half when the Falcons blocked a field goal and turned the game in their favor.
• Don Smith blocked a 37-yard attempt by Nick Mike-Mayer with 1:50 left and Tom Pridemore returned it to the Bills 47. The Falcons drove to a Tim Mazzetti field goal to cut the deficit to 14-3.
• Instead of sitting on the lead, the Bills tried to move after the kickoff. But Joe Ferguson's first pass was picked off by Al Richardson and returned 20 yards to the Bills 16. On the next play, Steve Bartkowski hit Junior Miller for a TD with 22 seconds left in the half.
• The Falcons continued to surge in the third as William Andrews gained 69 of the 72 yards on the go-ahead TD drive.
• After a Bills punt, Mazzetti kicked a 50-yard field goal for a 20-14 lead.
• Joe Cribbs fumbled a punt in the fourth and Tony Daykin recovered at the Falcons 38 to seriously hurt the Buffalo comeback effort. Mazzetti kicked a field goal and a few plays later, Jim Laughlin intercepted Ferguson

WEEK 9 GAMES	
Hou 20, Den 16	Dal 27, St.L 24
TB 30, NYG 13	Minn 39, Wash 14
Oak 16, Mia 10	Phil 27, Sea 20
NE 34, NYJ 21	LA 45, NO 31
Pitt 22, GB 20	SD 31, Cinc 14
Balt 31, KC 24	Det 17, SF 13
Clev 27, Chi 21	

and returned it to the 15. That led to Lynn Cain's second TD to wrap it up.

QUOTES

• Bill Simpson: "Down 21 points, they probably would have folded their tents and gone home, I've seen them do it many times. Fourteen points isn't a lot in this league, but with another touchdown or the field goal, it's a different story."
• Chuck Knox: "For 28 minutes, we looked like a pretty good football team. Obviously it would have been 17-0 at the half, it would have been a different game. Hey, we might have fumbled on the attempt (on fourth down) or gotten the first down, then tried a pass which could have been picked off and returned for a touchdown." (On not sitting on the lead): "We had three timeouts and we figured we could use them to get into field goal range."
• Joe Ferguson: "It (going for field goal) was a tough call to make. Everyone has to honor the call. Everyone in the stadium wanted to go for the first down and I did, too. But the man wanted three points and if I was in his shoes, I'd have done the same thing. We were a little down at halftime, but mostly shocked."
• Jim Haslett: "It boils down to the fact that they rammed the ball down our throats when they had to. This is pro football, you're not going to shut people down like we've been doing."
• Isiah Robertson: "What we learned is you can't ever afford to let up. When you get someone down, bury them."

Bills	10	7	7	7	-	31
Jets	0	10	0	14	-	24

Attendance at Shea Stadium - 45,677

Buf: Brammer 6 pass from Ferguson (Mike-Mayer kick), 9:22
Buf: FG Mike-Mayer 30, 13:15
Buf: Brammer 3 pass from Ferguson (Mike-Mayer kick), :14
NYJ: Todd 1 run (Leahy kick), 12:36
NYJ: FG Leahy 33, 14:59
Buf: Leaks 1 run (Mike-Mayer kick), 7:02
NYJ: Gaffney 9 pass from Todd (Leahy kick), 3:06
NYJ: Dierking 2 run (Leahy kick), 10:50
Buf: Lewis 31 pass from Ferguson (Mike-Mayer kick), 14:54

	BUF	NYJ
First downs	17	18
Rushing yds	147	103
Passing yds	127	164
Punts-avg	6-40.5	4-43.0
Fumbles-lost	0-0	5-3
Penalties-yds	6-64	7-34

BILLS LEADERS: Rushing - Cribbs 17-59, Brown 14-49, Leaks 3-8, Hooks 1-10, Brammer 1-8, Ferguson 2-13; **Passing** - Ferguson 16-28-0 - 140; **Receiving** - Brammer 5-48, Lewis 2-39, Butler 4-35, Brown 2-14, Hooks 1-3, Cribbs 2-1.

JETS LEADERS: Rushing - Dierking 12-39, Harper 5-24, Todd 6-23, Long 5-9, Newton 1-8; **Passing** - Todd 17-27-1 - 171; **Receiving** - J. Jones 3-68, Harper 5-45, Gaffney 2-28, Long 4-24, Newton 2-4, Dierking 1-2.

WEEK 10 GAMES	
NYG 38, Dal 35	Den 20, SD 13
Chi 35, Wash21	Oak 28, Cinc 17
Mia 35, LA 14	Minn 34, Det 0
GB 23, SF 16	Phil 34, NO 21
Clev 28, Balt 27	Pitt 24, TB 21
KC 31, Sea 30	Hou 38, NE 34
Atl 33, St.L 27 (OT)	

NOTES

• The Bills blew a 17-0 lead and needed Frank Lewis' 31-yard TD reception with six seconds left to win.
• The Jets tied the game at 24 by driving 47 yards in 11 plays to Scott Dierking's TD plunge.
• After an exchange of punts, with Joe Cribbs returning the Jets punt 15 yards to the Jets 48, Joe Ferguson hit Mark Brammer for 17 yards to the 31. Ferguson called his final timeout with 12 seconds remaining. Lewis then beat Donald Dykes on a corner route for the winning TD.
• The Bills held the ball nearly 14 minutes in the first quarter, which was played in a downpour. Brammer's first score capped a 17-play, 66-yard drive. After Jim Haslett recovered a Richard Todd fumble at the Jets 28, Nick Mike-Mayer made it 10-0.
• Brammer's second TD came after Chris Keating recovered Gerald Carter's fumble on the ensuing kickoff.
• But the Jets rallied as Todd scored after a 59-yard march. Then the Jets got the ball late in the half and a 21-yard interference penalty on Mario Clark enabled Pat Leahy to kick a field goal with one second left.
• The teams exchanged touchdowns before the Jets drove to Dierking's game-tying score. The Bills had a TD called back as Clark's interception TD return was nullified by a facemask call on Ben Williams.

QUOTES

• Joe Ferguson on the game-winning TD pass: "Three things came up on the sidelines. First it was 'Let's go for the field goal.' Another was to try to get 10 more yards and the last one was 'Let's go for it all and see what happens. Maybe we'll get an interference or a catch or at least an incompletion that would stop the clock.' I watched Frank all the way. The corner looked like he was going to play him inside. Frank went inside, then he broke it outside and there was no one playing deep. It was a great move and all I had to do was get the ball to him."
• Frank Lewis: "The line had to give him good protection because I had to take it a little deeper than usual. I knew

we had to get into the end zone and Joe put it out there perfectly."
• Conrad Dobler: "I'm glad it all happened like this. This will be a great learning experience for everyone. Unless you do it, you don't know it can be done. All these young people here now know the game isn't over until the final gun. It should have been a blowout, but it wasn't. This is the best defense I've ever been associated with, though."
• Jets cornerback Donald Dykes: "Surprised? Yeah I was surprised when I heard the call for man coverage. There were 12 seconds left, they have no timeouts left and we call man coverage? If we were in a zone, I wouldn't have been put in that situation. I saw him (Lewis) slip and I prayed he'd drop the ball, but he didn't."

STANDINGS: TENTH WEEK

AFC EAST	W	L	T	CENTRAL	W	L	T	WEST	W	L	T	NFC EAST	W	L	T	CENTRAL	W	L	T	WEST	W	L	T
New England	7	3	0	Cleveland	7	3	0	Oakland	7	3	0	Philadelphia	9	1	0	Detroit	6	4	0	Atlanta	7	3	0
Buffalo	7	3	0	Houston	7	3	0	San Diego	6	4	0	Dallas	7	3	0	Minnesota	5	5	0	LA Rams	6	4	0
Baltimore	5	5	0	Pittsburgh	6	4	0	Denver	5	5	0	St. Louis	3	7	0	Tampa Bay	4	5	1	San Fran	3	7	0
Miami	5	5	0	Cincinnati	3	7	0	Kan. City	5	5	0	Washington	3	7	0	Green Bay	4	5	1	N.Orleans	0	10	0
NY Jets	2	8	0					Seattle	4	6	0	NY Giants	2	8	0	Chicago	4	6	0				

GAME 11 - Sunday, Nov. 16, 1980 - BILLS 14, BENGALS 0

NOTES

• The defense recorded four sacks and numerous hurries in pitching a shutout against the Bengals. Starting QB Ken Anderson was knocked out of the game shortly before halftime on a sack by Sherman White.

• The Bills moved into first in the AFC East as New England lost to Los Angeles.

• Reggie McKenzie started his 127th straight game, breaking the old team record set by Al Bemiller.

• Cincinnati threatened to score only twice. In the second quarter, the Bengals recovered a Joe Cribbs fumble and they got to the Bills 13, but Charlie Romes intercepted an Anderson pass in the end zone. Midway through the third, backup QB Jack Thompson scrambled to the Bills 25, but Lucious Sanford forced a fumble and Mario Clark recovered.

• After Romes' interception, the Bills drove 80 yards in 11 plays to Joe Ferguson's TD pass to Jerry Butler. Curtis Brown had a 20-yard run and Butler caught a 17-yard pass that bounced off two Bengals.

• In the fourth, the Bills embarked on an incredible 18-play, 79-yard drive that consumed 11:59. They ran 13 times and Butler made a great catch for 15 yards to the Bengals 16. Roland Hooks eventually scored to clinch the game.

QUOTES

• Chuck Knox: "These are the types of games you have to win. The defense was outstanding all afternoon and the offense struggled, but it came alive when we needed it to. I can't remember seeing a 12-minute drive like that. It's very, very unusual."

• Jim Haslett: "It was the best team effort we've had all year. We only had three or four mental breakdowns all day."

• Bill Simpson: "This came at an opportune time. Lately we've been getting points, but we've been giving up points, too. The defense is learning to believe in itself. We say we're No. 1 in the league; now we have to show it. We did a pretty good job of it today."

• Joe Ferguson: "The defense won this one. The offense wasn't playing up to its capabilities, so the defense came through. And the great thing about our defense is that there are guys who are only in their second, third or fourth years. It's still young. We're in first place, we've got a real good shot now, but anything can happen in five games."

• Fred Smerlas: "It's funny, but a few years ago nobody associated defense with Buffalo. But then Chuck Knox went out and got some defensive players and kind of woke up some of the guys who were already here. Now, we're No. 1."

• Reggie McKenzie: "We've got people taking a lot of pride in being Buffalo Bills."

• Bengals coach Forrest Gregg: "We were playing the best defense in the AFC and believe me, that position is well-deserved. It was tough for us to move the ball on them. We just didn't do anything offensively."

Bills	0	7	0	7 -	14
Bengals	0	0	0	0 -	0

Attendance at Riverfront Stadium - 40,836

Buf: Butler 16 pass from Ferguson (Mike-Mayer kick), 6:49
Buf: Hooks 5 run (Mike-Mayer kick), 12:05

	BUF	CIN
First downs	22	9
Rushing yds	137	89
Passing yds	169	124
Punts-avg	3-41.7	7-45.9
Fumbles-lost	2-2	1-1
Penalties-yds	5-32	12-93

BILLS LEADERS: Rushing - Hooks 13-46, Cribbs 6-11, Brown 13-64, Leaks 5-9, Miller 4-10, Ferguson 2- (-3); **Passing** - Ferguson 15-24-2 - 169; **Receiving** - Brammer 3-31, Brown 3-12, Butler 4-66, Lewis 2-32, Hooks 2-17, Cribbs 1-11.

BENGALS LEADERS: Rushing - Alexander 12-41, Griffin 4-13, Turner 4-12, Montgomery 1-12, Thompson 1-11; **Passing** - Anderson 11-19-1 - 95, Thompson 4-9-0 - 64; **Receiving** - Curtis 4-50, McInally 1-19, Turner 2-5, Ross 4-51, Alexander 3-5, Kreider 1-29.

WEEK 11 GAMES

Phil 24, Wash 0	LA 17, NE 14
Den 31, NYJ 24	Dal 31, St.L 21
Mia 17, SF 13	Balt 10, Det 9
Hou 10, Chi 6	Atl 31, NO 13
Minn 38, TB 30	SD 20, KC 7
Pitt 16, Clev 13	NYG 27, GB 21
Oak 19, Sea 17	

GAME 12 - Sunday, Nov. 23, 1980 - BILLS 28, STEELERS 13

NOTES

• The Bills won a huge game in front of the third-largest crowd in Rich Stadium history, many of them Steelers fans who made the trip and saw their team limited to 239 yards and two-of-11 on third downs.

• Joe Ferguson's second pass was intercepted by Robin Cole and returned to the 2 from where Franco Harris scored, but Ferguson bounced back later in the quarter. He hit Frank Lewis for 29, then threw a 29-yard TD to Jerry Butler who made a circus catch in the end zone over Mel Blount to cap a nine-play, 76-yard drive.

• In the second, Butler made a great catch at the Steelers 11 for 24 yards, then beat Blount for a 10-yard TD.

• The Steelers pulled within 14-10 by halftime as Terry Bradshaw directed a nine-play, 61-yard drive that led to Matt Bahr's field goal. The key plays were his 20-yard pass to Harris and a 21-yarder to Lynn Swann.

• Curtis Brown ran 79 yards with a short pass, but the play was called back on a penalty to Conrad Dobler. Unfazed, the Bills still went on to move 86 yards as Brown ran 34 yards for the TD.

• The clinching score came in the fourth as Mark Brammer went 36 yards with a tight-end-screen pass to the Steelers 10 to set up Reuben Gant's TD reception, capping an eight-play, 70-yard possession.

QUOTES

• Fred Smerlas: "This team can go the distance. There's nothing this team can't do. We gave two games away and had one bad game. We could easily be 11-1. As it is, we're 9-3 and we're smoking. This team beat San Diego, Oakland, New England and Pittsburgh. Who's left to beat?"

• Steelers defensive tackle Mean Joe Greene: "It's the first time we've been whipped and not given one away.

They beat us across the board. Nobody ever has an off day when they play us."

• Steelers defensive end Dwight White: "This game had to be a great confidence-builder for the Bills, but then they have every reason to be confident after today."

• Bill Simpson: "From now on, nobody is going to bully us around. Now we have something under our belts which will always give us something to fall back on. I knew we were capable of this type of effort, but there's a difference between being capable and doing it."

• Steelers quarterback Terry Bradshaw: "It was an emotional game and I was enjoying myself. It was the type of game I like to play in, but unfortunately we weren't able to match up against them and we couldn't keep our defense off the field."

• Chuck Knox: "He (Ferguson) shook off the interceptions and kept hitting those key passes for us in the first half and kept our offense cooking in the second half. I was also real happy with the way our defense hung in there. It's awful tough to push Bradshaw with a three-man line, but we were able to go back there and get him. And we had such good coverage downfield."

• Joe Ferguson: "This is the most satisfying win I've ever had. We were extremely high for the game all week – the most spirit I've ever seen around here. And we showed people across the country that we are a real good team. I think we might have woke some people up today."

Steelers	7	3	0	3 -	13
Bills	7	7	7	7 -	28

Attendance at Rich Stadium - 79,659

Pit: Harris 2 run (Bahr kick), 3:43
Buf: Butler 29 pass from Ferguson (Mike-Mayer kick), 10:54
Buf: Butler 10 pass from Ferguson (Mike-Mayer kick), 8:52
Pit: FG Bahr 36, 15:00
Buf: Brown 34 run (Mike-Mayer kick), 9:51
Buf: Gant 2 pass from Ferguson (Mike-Mayer kick), 2:37
Pit: FG Bahr 42, 7:28

	BUF	PIT
First downs	23	16
Rushing yds	178	84
Passing yds	201	155
Punts-avg	5-45.2	6-40.8
Fumbles-lost	1-1	3-1
Penalties-yds	4-23	9-65

BILLS LEADERS: Rushing - Cribbs 24-110, Brown 14-66, Ferguson 2-2; **Passing** - Ferguson 16-28-1 - 212; **Receiving** - Butler 3-63, Lewis 1-29, Cribbs 2-17, Brammer 4-57, Fergerson 1-19, Gant 1-2, Leaks 1-4, Jessie 1-17, Brown 2-4.

STEELERS LEADERS: Rushing - Harris 12-57, Bleier 3-11, Thornton 2- (-3), Bradshaw 3-17, Stoudt 1-2; **Passing** - Bradshaw 17-31-0 - 155, Stoudt 3-4-0 - 28; **Receiving** - Grossman 4-42, Bleier 3-14, Smith 1-10, Swann 4-70, Harris 7-42, Thornton 1-5.

WEEK 12 GAMES

GB 25, Minn 13	SD 27, Mia 24 OT
Dal 14, Wash 10	Atl 28, Chi 17
KC 21, St.L 13	Den 36, Sea 20
SF 12, NYG 0	Det 24, TB 10
Phil 10, Oak 7	Clev 31, Cinc 7
NE 47, Balt 21	LA 27, NO 7
NYJ 31, Hou 28 (OT)	

STANDINGS: TWELFTH WEEK

AFC EAST	W	L	T	CENTRAL	W	L	T	WEST	W	L	T	NFC EAST	W	L	T	CENTRAL	W	L	T	WEST	W	L	T
Buffalo	9	3	0	Houston	8	4	0	Oakland	8	4	0	Philadelphia	11	1	0	Detroit	7	5	0	Atlanta	9	3	0
New England	8	4	0	Cleveland	8	4	0	San Diego	8	4	0	Dallas	9	3	0	Minnesota	6	6	0	LA Rams	8	4	0
Baltimore	6	6	0	Pittsburgh	7	5	0	Denver	7	5	0	St. Louis	3	9	0	Green Bay	5	6	1	San Fran	4	8	0
Miami	6	6	0	Cincinnati	3	9	0	Kan. City	6	6	0	Washington	3	9	0	Tampa Bay	4	7	1	N.Orleans	0	12	0
NY Jets	3	9	0					Seattle	4	8	0	NY Giants	3	9	0	Chicago	4	8	0				

Bills	7	7	3	7	-	24
Colts	0	14	7	7	-	28

Attendance at Memorial Stadium - 36,184

Buf: Cribbs 2 run (N. Mike-Mayer kick), 10:32
Buf: Jessie 12 pass from Ferguson (N. Mike-Mayer kick), 8:59
Bal: Landry 6 run (S. Mike-Mayer kick), 11:28
Bal: R. Butler 8 pass from Landry (S. Mike-Mayer kick), 13:48
Bal: Dickey 18 run (S. Mike-Mayer kick), 6:21
Buf: FG N. Mike-Mayer 40, 11:27
Bal: Dickey 3 run (S. Mike-Mayer kick), 13:04
Buf: J. Butler 7 pass from Ferguson (N. Mike-Mayer kick), 14:16

	BUF	BAL
First downs	24	14
Rushing yds	120	113
Passing yds	164	88
Punts-avg	4-38.8	6-37.8
Fumbles-lost	3-3	1-1
Penalties-yds	5-36	8-71

BILLS LEADERS: **Rushing** - Cribbs 24-98, Brown 10-20, Leaks 4-7, Hooks 1-2, Cater 1- (-9), Ferguson 1-2; **Passing** - Ferguson 16-27-1 - 151, Cribbs 1-1-0 - 13; **Receiving** - Butler 6-68, Cribbs 4-39, Brammer 2-22, Hooks 2-18, Brown 2-5, Jessie 1-12.

COLTS LEADERS: **Rushing** - Dickey 17-61, Washington 2-14, Franklin 12-32, Landry 6-12, Sims 2-2, Carr 1- (-8); **Passing** - Landry 8-24-2 - 88; **Receiving** - R. Butler 2-30, Dickey 2-25, Franklin 2-16, McCauley 1-9, Burke 1-8.

NOTES

• The Bills blew a 14-0 lead as miscues led to all 28 Baltimore points, including three crucial breakdowns on special teams.

• In the first quarter, Ben Williams recovered Curtis Dickey's fumble at the Colts 2 and one play later, Joe Cribbs scored. Then, the Bills drove 88 yards in 17 plays to make it 14-0 as Joe Ferguson hit Ron Jessie for a TD. Cribbs had two key runs and completed a 13-yard option pass to Jerry Butler on the drive.

• But things began falling apart late in the second quarter. Cribbs fumbled a punt at his 18. Four plays later, Greg Landry, playing for the injured Bert Jones, scored on a six-yard keeper.

• Roland Hooks fumbled the ensuing kickoff, but the Bills defense held. However, when the offense failed to move, punter Greg Cater mishandled a snap and was tackled at the 8 by Derrick Hatchett. Landry beat a blitz by hitting Ray Butler for a TD with Charlie Romes in one-on-one coverage to tie.

• In the third, Lyle Blackwood intercepted Ferguson to stop a drive. The Colts turned around and drove 79 yards to the go-ahead TD, an 18-yard run by Dickey. Dickey also had an 18-yard reception along the way.

• Sherman White intercepted a tipped pass to set up

WEEK 13 GAMES

Dal 51, Sea 7	Atl 10, Wash 6
St.L 23, NYG 7	Clev 17, Hou 14
Cinc 20, KC 6	Minn 23, NO 20
SD 22, Phil 21	Pitt 23, Mia 10
TB 20, GB 17	LA 38, NYJ 13
SF 21, NE 17	Oak 9, Den 3
Chi 23, Det 17 (OT)	

Nick Mike-Mayer's field goal. But the Colts made it 28-17 with 1:56 left as Dickey scored after Cribbs fumbled another punt at the Bills 45.

• The Bills got a late score on Jerry Butler's TD reception, but failed to recover the on-sides kick.

QUOTES

• Greg Cater: "Coach Knox said special teams should win at least three games a year and lose none. On the that snap, I guess it sailed a little bit, but I should have caught it."

• Joe Ferguson: "I've been telling people we could end up 9-7 and be in third or fourth place. We haven't been thinking about that, but now we're going to have to rise up and play. I don't think the Colts or Greg Landry beat us, we beat ourselves."

• Chuck Knox: "I can't ever remember five turnovers on special teams (he was counting a blocked field goal and Cater's mishandled snap). You're just not going to win making those mistakes."

• Fred Smerlas: "We had to try hard to give it away to the Colts. In every game we've lost, we've given it away and beat ourselves. They didn't have Bert Jones and they still won."

• Reggie McKenzie: "Damn, I'm mad. We had it right in our hands. Zip, zip, we're up 14 points and the Colts looked like they were ready to throw in the towel. We could have run them out of town. And then just as quickly, we gave it right back to them. Pfft, just like that it was gone. In the old days we were expected to throw away games like today. We used to have a losing syndrome, but that changed this year. Maybe our problem now is some young players think we have the division title wrapped up."

Rams	0	0	7	0	0	-	7
Bills	0	0	7	0	3	-	10

Attendance at Rich Stadium - 77,133

Buf: Freeman 47 interception return (Mike-Mayer kick), 2:54
LA: Guman 3 run (Mike-Mayer kick), 13:24
Buf: FG Mike-Mayer 30, 5:14

	BUF	LA
First downs	15	14
Rushing yds	150	181
Passing yds	122	34
Punts-avg	5-42.4	8-37.1
Fumbles-lost	4-2	2-2
Penalties-yds	4-62	5-49

BILLS LEADERS: **Rushing** - Cribbs 26-83, Brown 12-45, Leaks 4-14, Ferguson 1-8; **Passing** - Ferguson 10-25-0 - 138; **Receiving** - Lewis 4-87, Butler 1-22, Brammer 1-14, Brown 2-5, Hooks 1-4, Cribbs 1-6.

RAMS LEADERS: **Rushing** - Bryant 17-61, Peacock 6-27, Guman 18-87, Haden 1-6; **Passing** - Haden 5-16-1 - 41, Ferragamo 3-7-0 - 20; **Receiving** - Peacock 1-5, Bryant 1-11, Waddy 1-19, Hicks 2-12, Miller 1-18, Guman 2- (-4).

WEEK 14 GAMES

Hou 6, Pitt 0	Wash 40, SD 17
St.L 24, Det 23	Atl 20, Phil 17
Clev 17, NYJ 14	Cinc 34, Balt 33
Minn 21, TB 10	Chi 61, GB 7
Dal 19, Oak 13	KC 31, Den 14
NYG 27, Sea 21	Mia 16, NE 13 OT
SF 38, NO 35 (OT)	

NOTES

• Nick Mike-Mayer's 30-yard field goal through the rain and fog in OT gave the Bills another memorable victory in what was becoming a very memorable season.

• The defense turned in a great game, holding Vince Ferragamo and Pat Haden to 34 yards passing.

• Chuck Knox, known for being conservative, made two decisions that almost haunted his team. Twice he disdained field goal attempts to go for first downs, and both times the Bills failed. The first one came in the third quarter, when Roosevelt Leaks fumbled into the end zone. The second came with 5:30 left and the Bills at the Rams 8. Rather than kick the go-ahead field goal, Knox went for it. Joe Cribbs was stopped.

• The Bills took a 7-0 lead when Steve Freeman ran 47 yards for a TD with an interception of Haden. Haden had replaced Ferragamo, who was injured in the second quarter.

• The Rams tied the game in the third with a 14-play, 80-yard drive after Leaks' fumble was recovered by Nolan Cromwell. Mike Guman had two key runs and Mario Clark was penalized for holding on the drive.

• The Rams won the toss in OT but couldn't move and punted to the Bills 34. Joe Ferguson converted two third downs, then hit Frank Lewis for 30 yards to set up Mike-Mayer's winning kick.

QUOTES

• Ben Williams: "Coach Knox deserves the game ball. They didn't want him in Los Angeles, but we want him in Buffalo because he's a great man. We knew what type of defense they had and that our offense might have trouble moving the ball, so we had to play a little tougher."

• Chuck Knox: "They battled, they scratched. This was about as much intensity as I've seen on a football field. These guys wanted to win so damn bad it almost brought tears to my eyes. It was very satisfying because it was the Rams. A game like today, it was what football's all about."

• Nick Mike-Mayer: "That last kick saved an otherwise miserable day for me. It was an easy chance to come back and redeem myself (he missed a pair of 38-yarders). All I saw was a 30-yarder in front of me and a chance to give the guys a rest."

• Joe Cribbs: "We had a lot of things that didn't go our way, but we hung in there and battled and that shows you the character of this team."

• Shane Nelson: "The attitude on the sideline was 'However long it takes to win, we will.' We didn't care if we had to play until Thursday."

• Steve Freeman: "Ferragamo likes to throw the long ball and when Haden came in, we knew he liked the intermediate routes to the backs and to the Y (tight end). He was looking right at the Y. I just stepped up and had a clean shot at the ball with nobody in front of me. I've scored three times and the last two, we lost the game. When they scored, I was getting a little nervous."

STANDINGS: FOURTEENTH WEEK

AFC EAST	W	L	T	CENTRAL	W	L	T	WEST	W	L	T	NFC EAST	W	L	T	CENTRAL	W	L	T	WEST	W	L	T
Buffalo	10	4	0	Cleveland	10	4	0	Oakland	9	5	0	Philadelphia	11	3	0	Minnesota	8	6	0	Atlanta	11	3	0
New England	8	6	0	Houston	9	5	0	San Diego	9	5	0	Dallas	11	3	0	Detroit	7	7	0	LA Rams	9	5	0
Baltimore	7	7	0	Pittsburgh	8	6	0	Denver	7	7	0	St. Louis	5	9	0	Chicago	6	8	0	San Fran	6	8	0
Miami	7	7	0	Cincinnati	5	9	0	Kan. City	7	7	0	Washington	4	10	0	Tampa Bay	5	8	1	N.Orleans	0	14	0
NY Jets	3	11	0					Seattle	4	10	0	NY Giants	4	10	0	Green Bay	5	8	1				

NOTES

• With a chance to clinch the AFC East, the Bills failed as Joe Ferguson went down with a left ankle sprain and the offense sputtered behind Dan Manucci and David Humm.

• Curtis Brown was tackled at the 2 on the opening kickoff. The Bills failed to move and punted to the 41. The Pats needed only six plays to take a 7-0 lead as Vagas Ferguson scored.

• Ferguson was hurt on the next series, and the Bills were doomed. Joe Cribbs missed an audible and wasn't in position to take a handoff, so Ferguson scrambled and was hit by Mike Hawkins.

• The Pats drove 80 yards in 15 plays for a second-quarter TD on Russ Francis' 15-yard reception.

• Matt Cavanaugh, playing for Steve Grogan, threw his second TD pass in the third quarter to Andy Johnson as the Pats took the second-half kickoff and drove 75 yards to make it 21-0.

• The Bills' only points came when Rufus Bess tackled Pats punter Mike Hubach for a safety after a bad snap. The Pats got a field goal from John Smith to close the scoring.

• The Bills line had allowed only 12 sacks in 14 games, but the Pats got eight.

QUOTES

• Reggie McKenzie: "I thought 'No, not Joe. Not our No. 1 quarterback.' He's the one guy we can't afford to lose. We're going to beat San Francisco and win the division, then all of this howling by the fans here today won't mean a thing."

• Bill Simpson: "When you lose your quarterback, it shakes the whole team. It's still in our hands. We have the luxury of a one-game lead over New England. We shall return from San Francisco with a victory."

• Joe Ferguson: "I'd like to think that I could have made a difference today, but they were a fired up football team. There's a lot of pain and soreness. The doctors say if the healing process goes as normal, I should be able to play Sunday."

• Pats linebacker Steve Nelson: "I have a lot of respect for Ferguson, he's having a great year. But I don't think it would have mattered today who the quarterback was the way our defensive line was coming off the ball and our coverage made it tough."

• Steve Freeman: "They just ran the ball down our throats. We couldn't stop them. They were ready to play today. We couldn't slow them down."

• Shane Nelson: "We didn't get beat by the New Orleans Saints, we got beat by a good team."

• Dan Manucci: "I felt good; it was fun being out there. I'm disappointed we didn't move the ball better, but I don't think that's a reflection on me. I was a little rusty."

• Chuck Knox: "It was a bad day from the opening kickoff. We didn't do much right."

WEEK 15 GAMES

SD 21, Sea 14	Wash 16, NYG 13
Atl 35, SF 10	NO 21, NYJ 20
Pitt 21, KC 16	Phil 17, St.L 3
Det 27, TB 14	Oak 24, Den 21
Hou 22, GB 3	Min 28, Clev 23
Mia 24, Balt 14	LA 38, Dal 14
Cinc 17, Chi 14 (OT)	

Bills	0 0 2 0 -	2
Patriots	7 7 7 3 -	24

Attendance at Schaefer Stadium - 58,324

NE: V. Ferguson 9 run (Smith kick), 6:12
NE: Francis 5 pass from Cavanaugh (Smith kick), 13:45
NE: A. Johnson 13 pass from Cavanaugh (Smith kick), 5:34
Buf: Safety, Simpson, Bess tackled Hubach in end zone, 13:36
NE: FG Smith 27, 4:39

	BUF	NE
First downs	8	21
Rushing yds	101	195
Passing yds	53	129
Punts-avg	5-40.0	1-28.0
Fumbles-lost	4-2	1-0
Penalties-yds	7-63	3-20

BILLS LEADERS: **Rushing** - Cribbs 12-50, Brown 6-19, Leaks 1-3, Manucci 2-24, Humm 1-5; **Passing** - Ferguson 2-2-0 - 12, Manucci 5-6-0 - 64, Humm 4-14-1 - 39; **Receiving** - Butler 4-43, Brown 2-26, Hooks 1-22, Fergerson 1-8, Jessie 1-7, Miller 1-5, Cribbs 1-4.

PATRIOTS LEADERS: **Rushing** - V. Ferguson 20-81, Calhoun 9-27, Cavanaugh 6-44, Tatupu 8-22, Clark 2-19, Ivory 1-2, Hubach 1-0; **Passing** - Cavanaugh 12-19-2 - 136; **Receiving** - Francis 4-49, Calhoun 2-8, Jackson 1-26, Westbrook 1-21, Johnson 1-13, Ivory 1-10, Morgan 1-6, V. Ferguson 1-3.

NOTES

• The Bills won the AFC East for the first time since the 1970 merger with a thrilling victory in the mud.

• Joe Montana's two Hail Mary passes into the end zone in the final nine seconds fell incomplete.

• Joe Ferguson went all the way despite his sprained ankle and gave the team a huge leadership lift.

• Down 18-13 in the fourth, the 49ers drove to the Bills 8, but Lucious Sanford forced Earl Cooper to fumble and Mario Clark recovered to preserve the Bills lead.

• Joe Cribbs gained a season-high 128 yards, including a 48-yard run on the first play of the game. Eventually, Ferguson hit Jerry Butler for a TD as Butler made a leaping catch just inbounds. A high snap aborted the extra point, but that didn't matter when Ray Wersching missed the PAT after the 49ers' first TD. Cooper's TD run was questionable because he fumbled just as he got to the goal line.

• Roland Hooks' 17-yard punt return to the Bills 43 started a 57-yard drive that ended nine plays later on Curtis Brown's TD run for a 13-6 halftime lead.

• The 49ers tied it early in the third as Cooper broke a 47-yard run to the 4 and Montana hit Eason Ramson with a two-yard TD. The Bills then got a break when Frank Lewis interfered on a long pass, but the call went against 49ers' cornerback Gerard Williams for 35 yards. Nick Mike-Mayer then kicked a field goal.

• The final score came when a bad center snap sailed over 49er's punter Jim Miller and into the end zone where Ken Johnson tackled him for a safety.

• The Bills overcame the loss of Shane Nelson, who broke his wrist. Phil Villapiano stepped in.

QUOTES

• 49ers wide receiver Fred Solomon: "They were beatable, damn right they were. If we had played any kind of game, we would have come out winners instead of them."

• 49ers running back Lenvil Elliott: "They're nowhere near some of the other teams we've played this season. I was more impressed with Atlanta, L.A., New England and Dallas."

• Joe Ferguson on Montana's Hail Mary passes: "I didn't even watch. I just kept pacing up and down in front of the bench and listened to the crowd reaction. I didn't realize until the ankle injury what I mean to these guys. Maybe it was just peer pressure or maybe they were just 'BSing' me. The line told me 'Don't worry, we'll protect you.'" (About the lean years): "I was thinking about it all during the week. All the misery we went through for four or five years was worth it. We learned a lot going through those hardships."

• Reggie McKenzie: "Just to be called champs. It's been such a long time."

• Conrad Dobler: "There's no comparison because the other ones (with St. Louis) are just memories. This gives me another chance to go to the Super Bowl."

• Ralph Wilson speaking to the team: "You win the big ones. You're the champs."

WEEK 16 GAMES

NYJ 24, Mia 17	Chi 14, TB 13
Clev 27, Cinc 24	Oak 33, NYG 17
Den 25, Sea 17	Dal 35, Phil 27
NE 38, NO 27	KC 38, Balt 28
Hou 20, Minn 16	Det 24, GB 3
Wash 31, St.L 7	SD 26, Pitt 17
LA 20, Atl 17 (OT)	

Bills	6 7 5 0 -	18
49ers	6 0 7 0 -	13

Attendance at Candlestick Park - 37,476

Buf: Butler 10 pass from Ferguson (kick failed), 4:41
SF: Cooper 4 run (kick failed), 8:46
Buf: Brown 4 run (Mike-Mayer kick), 5:59
SF: Ramson 2 pass from Montana (Wersching kick), 3:40
Buf: FG Mike-Mayer 25, 9:27
Buf: Safety, Johnson tackled Miller in end zone, 13:22

	BUF	SF
First downs	16	19
Rushing yds	165	146
Passing yds	102	152
Punts-avg	4-40.8	4-43.5
Fumbles-lost	2-2	4-1
Penalties-yds	4-49	5-60

BILLS LEADERS: **Rushing** - Cribbs 18-128, Brown 9-27, Leaks 4-10, Ferguson 1-0; **Passing** - Ferguson 12-20-0 - 102; **Receiving** - Butler 3-34, Brammer 3-27, Cribbs 3-19, Lewis 1-14, Hooks 1-6, Brown 1-2.

49ERS LEADERS: **Rushing** - Cooper 15-90, Elliott 12-47, Solomon 1-9, Miller 1-0; **Passing** - Montana 25-36-0 - 163; **Receiving** - Elliott 8-66, Cooper 6-28, Clark 4-37, Solomon 4-14, Ramson 3-18.

STANDINGS: SIXTEENTH WEEK

AFC EAST	W	L	T	CENTRAL	W	L	T	WEST	W	L	T	NFC EAST	W	L	T	CENTRAL	W	L	T	WEST	W	L	T
Buffalo	11	5	0	Cleveland	11	5	0	San Diego	11	5	0	Philadelphia	12	4	0	Minnesota	9	7	0	Atlanta	12	4	0
New England	10	6	0	Houston	11	5	0	Oakland	11	5	0	Dallas	12	4	0	Detroit	9	7	0	LA Rams	11	5	0
Miami	8	8	0	Pittsburgh	9	7	0	Kan. City	8	8	0	Washington	6	10	0	Chicago	7	9	0	San Fran	6	10	0
Baltimore	7	9	0	Cincinnati	6	10	0	Denver	8	8	0	St. Louis	5	11	0	Tampa Bay	5	10	1	N.Orleans	1	15	0
NY Jets	4	12	0					Seattle	4	12	0	NY Giants	4	12	0	Green Bay	5	10	1				

Bills	0 14 0 0	-	14
Chargers	3 0 7 10	-	20

Attendance at San Diego Stadium - 52,028

SD: FG Benirschke 22, 11:16
Buf: Leaks 1 run (Mike-Mayer kick), :44
Buf: Lewis 9 pass from Ferguson (Mike-Mayer kick), 14:44
SD: Joiner 9 pass from Fouts (Benirschke kick), 1:34
SD: FG Benirschke 22, :51
SD: Smith 50 pass from Fouts (Benirschke kick), 12:52

	BUF	SD
First downs	17	21
Rushing yds	97	96
Passing yds	147	301
Punts-avg	6-44.5	4-27.8
Fumbles-lost	0-0	3-2
Penalties-yds	5-40	6-66

BILLS LEADERS: **Rushing** - Cribbs 18-53, Brown 9-17, Leaks 4-6, Manucci 2-21; **Passing** - Ferguson 15-29-3 - 180, Manucci 0-1-0 - 0; **Receiving** - Butler 2-19, Brammer 4-62, Cribbs 4-36, Lewis 3-45, Hooks 1-1, Leaks 1-17; **Punt returns** - Hooks 2-13; **Kickoff returns** - Solomon 5-84.

CHARGERS LEADERS: **Rushing** - Muncie 18-80, Thomas 5-22, Fouts 2- (-6); **Passing** - Fouts 22-37-1 - 314; **Receiving** - Jefferson 7-102, Muncie 6-53, Joiner 4-83, Smith 1-50, McCrary 2-19, Winslow 1-5, Thomas 1-2; **Punt returns** - Fuller 3-29; **Kickoff returns** - Bauer 2-39, Duncan 1-11.

NOTES

• In their first playoff game since 1974, the Bills lost a heartbreaker when Dan Fouts threw a 50-yard TD pass to little-known Ron Smith with 2:08 remaining for the winning points.

• Smith had caught only four passes all season and this was the longest TD pass against the Bills all year. It was a third-and-10 play and Smith ran a quick post as the Bills played a nickel defense and blitzed both linebackers, Isiah Robertson and Lucious Sanford. Safety Bill Simpson was one-on-one with Smith and he was beaten cleanly. Steve Freeman's man, fullback Mike Thomas, stayed in to block, so Freeman later admitted he should have been able to get over and help on the post.

• Oddly, the nickel defense with the linebackers blitzing had worked much of the day.

• The Bills still had one last chance as Joe Ferguson hit Frank Lewis for 18 yards to the Bills 48, but on the next play, Glen Edwards intercepted a bomb intended for Jerry Butler.

• While Smith's thunderbolt killed the Bills, a play on Buffalo's first series of the game hurt nearly as much. Ferguson re-injured his sprained left ankle and was hobbled all day.

• With Ferguson unable to move effectively, he was sacked three times and threw three interceptions. During the season, he was sacked an NFL-low 20 times.

• Ferguson was hurt on the fifth play of the game, but Dan Manucci managed to drive the Bills to the San Diego 27 on their first possession. Nick Mike-Mayer then missed a 44-yard field goal, hitting the upright.

• The Chargers took the ball and drove 69 yards in 12 plays. Fouts completed six of seven passes for 47 yards, but the Bills defense stiffened and the Chargers settled for Rolf Benirschke's field goal.

• The Bills answered that with a 72-yard march in 12 plays, keyed by a 37-yard pass interference penalty against Ray Preston. Roosevelt Leaks scored on a one-yard plunge.

• The Chargers again drove on the Bills, all the way to the 25, but Benirschke missed a field goal.

• The defense made a big play in the second quarter to get the Bills rolling again. Charlie Romes leveled Charlie Joiner after a completion at the Chargers 35, forcing a fumble which Bill Simpson recovered at the 33 with 1:48 left in the half.

• Ferguson hit Lewis for an 18-yard gain to the 11, then found Lewis open deep in the end zone for the TD and a 14-3 lead.

• The Chargers took the second-half kickoff and motored

70 yards in four plays to pull within 14-10. Chuck Muncie ran for 18 yards, then Joiner beat Mario Clark one-on-one for a 45-yard gain to the 7. Two plays later, Fouts fired a laser to Joiner in the end zone for the TD.

• Lou Piccone blocked a San Diego punt to give the Bills possession at the Chargers 38 midway through the third, but Edwards interecepted Ferguson at the 9 to kill the threat.

• On the Bills next possession, a 40-yard pass to Lewis to the Chargers 21 was wiped out by a holding penalty on Ken Jones. After Buffalo punted, the Chargers moved 45 yards in eight plays to Benirschke's field goal. The Chargers reached the 1, but an illegal motion penalty pushed them back to the 6 and the Bills defense held and forced the field goal attempt early in the fourth that made it 14-13.

• Simpson thwarted another foray into Bills territory when he intercepted a pass at the 7 that bounced off Smith's hands.

• With just over six minutes left, Scott Hutchinson forced punt returner Mike Fuller to fumble at the Chargers 39 and Ken Johnson recovered. The Bills had a chance to put away the game, but Joe Cribbs was stopped on third-and-one and Mike-Mayer was short on a 49-yard field goal attempt.

• Fouts then hit John Jefferson for 17 yards and on a second-and-10 play from the 50, Charlie Romes nearly intercepted a pass intended for Jefferson. On the next play, Smith scored.

QUOTES

• Bill Simpson: "We had a dog on, it was man-to-man and I just got beat. He had the same route on me earlier in the game and I broke it up. He ran a corner route just before that and I intercepted it. That's life in the NFL, I guess."

• Steve Freeman: "I had to cover the back (Thomas) and when he blocked, I started to free up. I had to wait until then. I tried to get my depth and broke just underneath the ball. I came so close. You can't blame Billy all alone. I missed the ball by a hair. They're the toughest team in the league to defend."

• San Diego quarterback Dan Fouts: "As soon as I saw the blitz, I knew where I was going. We couldn't force anything deep. We had to wait and wait and wait and hit them at the right moment. Buffalo's a tough team. Some people say they're overrated, but they do a lot of things well. The statistics don't lie, they are the top-rated defense in the league."

• San Diego wide receiver Ron Smith: "This was nice, but it's only No. 2. No. 1 was the one I caught against Dallas to put the Rams in the Super Bowl last year. This

one was a regular man-to-man post. I saw the middle of the field open and took advantage of it. Their defense was rotating toward Jefferson and that left me one-on-one with the safety."

• Chuck Knox: "They handled it (the loss) with class. I'm very, very proud of them. They battled a team that many had picked to go to the Super Bowl. They came a long way this year when nobody thought they would. It was my most enjoyable year in coaching. I felt we had eight or nine chances where individual players could come up with a big play and we just didn't make them. We make one of those here or there and we could have won. All losses are tough to take, but this was the toughest to come along so far. And I'm so proud of the way Joe played today. You saw Ferguson out there. He gave a courageous performance today. If you don't understand that, then you don't understand sports. I'm so proud of that guy just for playing."

• Joe Ferguson: "The longer the game went on, the more it was hurting. They had to tape it pretty tight, and I think that had a lot to do with the pain. It felt like it did against New England. I couldn't set up like I normally do. I was throwing off my back foot. I couldn't move. If the pass rush was good, I couldn't get out of the way. This loss really hurts. We have a lot of young people who had high hopes, but there is a bright future also because we are young. I know we had a great season, but all I can think about now is the bad things. I'm just dejected."

• Jerry Butler on the last Edwards interception: "It was my fault. I should have made the move outside. I was trying to hold inside position as long as I could, then I couldn't get my feet planted right to make the move. One more step and I might have caught the ball or at least broken it up."

• Reggie McKenzie: "I've never seen the enthusiasm so high. We had some breaks, but we didn't cash in. A couple of times I really thought we were going to win."

• Conrad Dobler: "I kept telling the guys the team that makes the least amount of mistakes will win in the playoffs. We were beaten today by a damn good team, but we had a multitude of opportunities and we didn't take care of them. As I said the other day, the best team would win and they were the best team today."

• Shane Nelson: "We've overcome so much this year. It just so happened that we got beat. We fought 'em, we got a taste of the honey. We'll be back."

• Ralph Wilson: "All I can say is that I'm really proud of the way this team played. I'm optimistic, I've got to be. One of the San Diego people told me afterwards that the Chargers were lucky they didn't have to play against a two-legged quarterback."

Jerry Butler (80) and Frank Lewis could only hang their heads as the Bills lost a playoff heartbreaker to the San Diego Chargers, 20-14.

At A Glance
1981

Jan. 5 – Chuck Knox was named NFL coach of the year by The Associated Press. *The Sporting News* also picked Knox its top coach.

Jan. 7 – The Associated Press ignored the Bills as no Buffalo players made the first or second All-Pro teams. Elijah Pitts's son, Ron, a senior at Orchard Park High School, was named New York State player of the year.

Jan. 8 – Detroit's Billy Sims edged Joe Cribbs for AP offensive rookie of the year.

Jan. 14 – Joe Cribbs was named AFC rookie of the year by UPI.

Jan. 25 – Offensive backfield and special teams coach Elijah Pitts was offered the offensive backfield coaching position for the Houston Oilers.

Jan. 26 – Defensive line coach Willie Zapalac resigned to take a position on Bum Phillips' staff in New Orleans.

Jan. 31 – Former Bills head coach and offensive line coach Jim Ringo earned induction into the Pro Football Hall of Fame.

Feb. 3 – Elijah Pitts decided to accept the Oilers' offensive backfield coaching position.

Feb. 6 – Scouting director Norm Pollom's 36-year-old wife, Janis, died of a brain anuerism.

Feb. 9 – Defensive backfield coach Jim Wagstaff resigned to take the same position with San Diego.

Feb. 12 – Tom Catlin was promoted to assistant head coach.

Feb. 13 – New York Giants defensive coordinator Ralph Hawkins was hired to coach the defensive backfield. Hawkins coached in Buffalo from 1969-71.

Feb. 24 – Jim Carmody was hired to coach the defensive line.

March 6 – Knox completed his staff by hiring Chick Harris to coach the offensive backfield.

March 19 – It was announced that the Bills were in discussions with Fredonia State College about a possible training camp site.

April 7 – The NFL schedule was released and the Bills were slated for four national TV games, including two Monday night appearances and a special Thursday night affair.

April 8 – The Bills made it official, signing a contract to hold their training camp at Fredonia State.

April 18 – Jim Haslett was arrested in Pittsburgh and charged with shoving an officer who had pulled over the car he was riding in as a passenger after the driver had run a stop light. The charges later were dropped.

April 28 – The Bills swung a draft-day deal as they swapped first-round positions with Oakland (23rd for 28th) and picked up an extra third-round choice. With their first-round pick, they chose Penn State fullback Booker Moore. They also chose LSU defensive back Chris Williams and Auburn wide receiver Byron Franklin (second round), Texas A&M wide receiver Mike Mosley and South Carolina State defensive end Robert Geathers (third), Millersville (Pa.) running back Robb Riddick (ninth) and Western Colorado offensive tackle Justin Cross (10th). New Orleans chose running back George Rogers No. 1 overall, the Giants took linebacker Lawrence Taylor (second), running back Freeman McNeil went third to the Jets, Seattle picked safety Kenny Easley (fourth), San Francisco

selected safety Ronnie Lott (eighth), Miami took running back David Overstreet (13th), safety Dennis Smith went to Denver (15th), offensive tackle Brian Holloway went to New England (19th) and Cleveland grabbed cornerback Hanford Dixon (22nd), a player the Bills had hoped to draft.

April 29 – The Bills defended their draft, despite the fact that they had chances to pick Florida wide receiver Cris Collinsworth and Pitt linebacker Rickey Jackson.

April 30 – Chuck Knox admitted he had begun searching for a deal for Tom Cousineau, the linebacker whom the Bills made the No. 1 overall pick in the 1979 draft, then were shunned when he went to Montreal of the CFL. The Bills still owned his NFL rights and Knox said that rather than sign him when his Montreal contract was up, he now wanted to trade Cousineau.

May 5 – Another first-round disappointment, running back Terry Miller, was traded to Cleveland for a pair of draft choices. "I'm very excited," Miller said. "I was beginning to get a little depressed waiting." Said Knox: "I think Terry Miller is a fine football player. I think he'll be a good football player someplace else."

May 8 – Mini-camp opened at Rich Stadium. Jim Ritcher, the No. 1 choice in 1980 who rarely played in '80, worked at guard instead of center. Free agent Joe Devlin decided to skip the mini-camp.

June 3 – The county legislature was asked to pay the bill – more than $500,000 – to replace the aging artificial turf at Rich Stadium.

June 5 – First-round choice Booker Moore signed his first pro contract.

June 18 – The Bills thought they had acquired L.A. veteran linebacker Hacksaw Reynolds, but at the last minute, Reynolds signed with San Francisco. "Sure I was disappointed because he told me our financial package was acceptable," said Stew Barber, the Bills vice-president for administration.

June 30 – Jim Haslet filed unfair labor practice charges against the Bills with the National Labor Relations Board, claiming that the team failed to negotiate in good faith with his agent, Greg Lustig.

July 14 – Buffalo's problems with first-round draft choices struck in an unusual way as Booker Moore was diagnosed as having contracted Guillain-Barre Syndrome, a rare disease that affects the nervous system.

July 19 – With banners strung all over town welcoming the Bills, the team opened its first training camp at Fredonia State.

July 23 – Fred Smerlas and Joe Devlin agreed to new contracts, meaning they would arrive on time when veterans were due to report to camp the next day.

July 24 – Jim Haslett and Mario Clark were the only veterans not to report on time to camp.

July 25 – Cleveland's rookies outplayed the Bills' group despite a 6-6 tie at Edinboro State University, but Buffalo's Robb Riddick had an impressive debut with 47 yards rushing.

July 28 – The Bills signed running back Lawrence McCutcheon, the former Rams star.

Aug. 1 – A crowd estimated at about 6,000 came to Fredonia and watched the Bills beat Green Bay, 12-6, in a scrimmage.

Aug. 3 – Joe Ferguson signed a new six-year contract, reportedly worth an average of $400,000 per season.

Aug. 8 – The Bills opened the exhibition season

with a 21-14 loss on the new turf at Rich Stadium.

Aug. 10 – Mario Clark reported to camp and signed a new contract. Jim Haslett showed up at practice, although his contract situation was still up in the air.

Aug. 15 – Cleveland handed the Bills a 13-10 defeat at Rich.

Aug. 22 – Playing the Browns for the third time this summer, the Bills traveled to Cleveland and pounded them, 31-20.

Aug. 27 – The Bills picked quarterback Matt Robinson off waivers from Denver for $100 to back up Joe Ferguson.

Aug. 28 – In a surprising turn of events, Jim Haslett signed a two-year deal with the Bills, dropped his labor suit with the NLRB and fired his agent, Greg Lustig. In San Diego, the Bills downed the Chargers, 30-24, in their preseason finale.

Sept. 1 – The Bills got down to the roster limit by cutting Reuben Gant, David Humm, Dan Manucci, Lou Piccone and Greg Cater. Piccone and Cater cleared waivers and were re-signed.

Sept. 6 – The Bills opened the regular season with a superb 31-0 blowout of the Jets at Rich Stadium. Joe Ferguson passed for 254 yards and two TDs and the defense held the Jets to eight first downs. "I've never seen an opener like that," safety Bill Simpson said. "Not a whole lot of things went wrong. It'll be hard to find any mistakes."

Sept. 8 – Quarterback Dan Pastorini, who was released by Oakland, was in Buffalo for a tryout.

Sept. 13 – The Bills went into Memorial Stadium and rocked Baltimore, 35-3, as Joe Ferguson pitched for 261 yards and four TDs.

Sept. 17 – Playing in front of the *Monday Night Football* crew on a special Thursday night telecast, the Bills were outplayed at Rich Stadium, 20-14, by defending NFC champion Philadelphia. Lackawanna native Ron Jaworski passed for 240 yards for the Eagles.

Sept. 21 – Shane Nelson, who suffered a knee injury against Philadelphia, wasn't sure if he'd be able to play against the Bengals.

Sept. 27 – Cincinnati pulled off an upset at Riverfront Stadium, beating the Bills in overtime, 27-24, on Jim Breech's 28-yard field goal. It was the first overtime loss in team history.

Oct. 4 – The Bills snapped their two-game skid with a 23-17 victory over the Colts at Rich Stadium as Joe Cribbs rushed for a career-high 159 yards.

Oct. 12 – The unbeaten (4-0-1) Miami Dolphins strutted into Rich Stadium and got waxed by the Bills, 31-21, on *Monday Night Football*. Joe Ferguson passed for 221 yards and three TDs in the first half as the Bills opened a 31-7 lead.

Oct. 15 – Reggie McKenzie's team-record streak of 140 consecutive starts came to an end when he was put on the injured reserve list because of the knee injury he suffered against Miami. Jon Borchardt was slated to replace him. In the meantime, the Bills acquired guard Tom Lynch from Seattle for a draft choice.

Oct. 18 – The Bills were flat after their big victory over Miami and got pummeled in Shea Stadium by the Jets, 33-14. New York rushed for 200 yards.

Oct. 20 – Reggie McKenzie underwent knee surgery in Boston and indicated he would be out for the rest of the season. Lawrence McCutcheon also had knee surgery in Los Angeles and he, too, was told he'd be out for the year.

Oct. 25 – The Bills defense held Denver to 161 total yards, including just 44 in the second half, and

Nick Mike-Mayer provided all the points in a 9-7 victory at Rich Stadium. Mike-Mayer made a 36-yarder with one second left to play. Two years earlier, Denver's Jim Turner kicked the winning field goal for Denver on the game's final play in a 19-16 Broncos win at Rich.

Nov. 1 – Joe Cribbs caught three TD passes and totaled 248 yards rushing and receiving as the Bills downed Cleveland, 22-13, at Rich Stadium.

Nov. 2 – An arthogram performed on Shane Nelson's knee indicated he would miss at least six weeks.

Nov. 9 – Dallas stretched its home-field winning streak to 14 games by whipping the Bills, 27-14, in a Monday Night game. Dallas scored 20 points in the third quarter to blow it open. During the game, Conrad Dobler and Chuck Knox got into a heated argument on the sideline when Knox yanked Dobler from the game for a pair of leg-whipping penalties. After the game in the locker room, the two argued again. "I was aware that Buffalo was a first-half team," Dallas' Too Tall Jones said. "They just folded."

Nov. 11 – Conrad Dobler denied that he told John Dutton he played dirty because he was a cripple. "That's an emphatic lie," Dobler raged. "He said to me 'You can't block your mother.' I said 'That isn't saying much about you, is it? People say I'm crippled and you can't even beat a cripple, so what the hell are you in the game for?' He had two assists. I shut him out, why shouldn't he be crying? I would never apologize to anyone for anything I've done. Never, never."

Nov. 13 – Chuck Knox made a difficult decision as he announced the benching of Conrad Dobler. The news was crushing for Dobler because the Bills were playing in St. Louis against the Cardinals, for whom Dobler played for six years. Knox said second-year man Jim Ritcher would get his first NFL start. "I wasn't given a reason," Dobler said. "The embarrassing thing is here we are playing the Cardinals and I'm not even going to play. This has never happened to me before."

Nov. 14 – Chuck Knox explained his benching of Dobler. "We did it because I felt we needed a change," he said.

Nov. 15 – The Bills played a dreadful game in losing at Busch Stadium, 24-0, to the Cardinals. Joe Ferguson threw four interceptions for the second game in a row. O.J. Anderson rushed for 177 yards, the second-highest total ever yielded by the Bills. Jim Nance of Boston gained 185 in 1967.

Nov. 19 – Chuck Knox announced that Phil Villapiano would start for Chris Keating, who had been filling in for injured Shane Nelson. Also, Roosevelt Leaks would replace fumble-prone Curtis Brown at fullback and Roland Hooks would spell injured Joe Cribbs (bruised ribs) against the Patriots.

Nov. 22 – In one of the wildest Bills victories ever, Joe Ferguson completed a 36-yard Hail Mary pass to Roland Hooks in the end zone with five seconds left to play, giving Buffalo a 20-17 victory over New England at Rich Stadium, which was about one-fourth full when the play occurred.

Nov. 29 – The Bills topped Washington and rookie coach Joe Gibbs, 21-14, at Rich Stadium. Roland Hooks filled in for injured Joe Cribbs and gained 109 yards rushing and scored twice.

Dec. 6 – San Diego totaled 482 yards, including 343 passing by Dan Fouts, but the Bills rallied four times to pull off a 28-27 victory at Jack Murphy

Stadium. They clinched it when Rufus Bess recovered Chuck Muncie's fumble at the Bills 26 with 1:52 left.

Dec. 10 – Police came to One Bills Drive to speak to Lucious Sanford about allegations from a woman who said he raped her three days earlier. The detectives read Sanford his rights, but vice-president for administration Stew Barber intervened, summoned Bills attorney Ralph Halpern and Sanford was not arrested. The investigation continued and two weeks later, a black man who had been passing himself off as Sanford, was arrested and charged with the rape. He had been pretending to be Sanford for more than a year. "I just hope the guys don't think I'm troubled by this thing that has been hanging over my head," Sanford said.

Dec. 13 – The Bills traveled to New England and downed the Patriots, 19-10, for their fourth straight win to clinch at least a wild-card playoff berth. Shane Nelson returned to the lineup, but re-injured his knee in the first quarter and did not return.

Dec. 15 – The Bills left for Vero Beach, Fla. to practice at Dodgertown for three days before the Miami game, rather than work in the snow and cold in Buffalo.

Dec. 17 – Frank Lewis, Fred Smerlas and Joe Cribbs were voted to the AFC Pro Bowl team, Lewis as a starter. It was Lewis' first selection in 11 years in the league.

Dec. 19 – In a nationally-televised Saturday afternoon season finale, the Bills blew their chance to win their second straight AFC East division title, losing to Miami, 16-6. The Dolphins won the division and earned a week off while the Bills were forced to play in the wild-card round the following week. The loss was Buffalo's 13th in a row at the

Orange Bowl.

Dec. 20 – The Jets defeated Green Bay, 28-3, assuring them of hosting a wild-card playoff game against the Bills at Shea Stadium.

Dec. 21 – Jim Haslett had this reaction when he learned the Bills would be playing the Jets: "I hate the New York Jets, I hate Shea Stadium, I hate New York City, I hate those fans, I hate those uniforms, I hate Walt Michaels. There's no place I hate more than that place. They're the dirtiest team in football. They call you names all the time. The last time we were there, Tom Newton spit right in my face. Believe me, he'll pay for that this time."

Dec. 22 – Chuck Knox indicated that he would likely start Jon Borchardt in place of Conrad Dobler at right guard because Knox, while he wouldn't say it publicly, was concerned that Dobler had become a marked man by officials. Dobler was called for three penalties against Miami including a hold that on replays, appeared to be a bad call.

Dec. 27 – The Bills stormed to a 24-0 lead at Shea Stadium, then hung on for dear life as Bill Simpson's goal-line interception with two seconds left preserved a thrilling 31-27 victory over the Jets in the wild-card playoff round. In Philadelphia, the Giants upset the Eagles, 27-21, in the NFC wild-card game.

Dec. 30 – Cleveland Browns owner Art Modell said that he was seriously interested in trading to get the rights to Tom Cousineau when the Bills' season concluded. Cousineau expressed interest in going to Cleveland.

Jan. 2, 1982 – In one of the greatest games in NFL history, San Diego outlasted Miami at the Orange Bowl, 41-38, in overtime in an AFC divisional round game. The teams combined to break 11 NFL playoff records including a 433-yard passing day by Dan Fouts. The teams combined for 1,036 yards. Dallas routed Tampa Bay, 38-0, in an NFC divisional game.

Jan. 3, 1982 – One year to the day of their heartbreaking loss to San Diego in the 1980 playoffs, the Bills lost another gut-wrencher, 28-21, at Cincinnati. Driving for the potential tying TD, the Bills had a first-down completion at the Bengals 14 wiped out by a delay-of-game penalty. On fourth down, they failed to convert and the Bengals wrapped up the victory. In San Francisco, the 49ers rolled past the Giants, 38-24, as Joe Montana passed for 304 yards and two TDs.

Jan. 10, 1982 – Cincinnati defeated San Diego, 27-7, in front of 46,302 fans at Riverfront Stadium who braved the coldest day in NFL history. The temperature was minus nine degrees and the wind-chill was minus 59 degrees. San Francisco won the NFC Championship at Candlestick Park, 28-27, as Joe Montana lofted a six-yard touchdown pass to the leaping Dwight Clark in the back of the end zone, capping an 89-yard drive in the final five minutes. Montana passed for 286 yards and three TDs.

Jan. 24, 1982 – San Francisco capped its brilliant rebound from back-to-back 2-14 seasons just two years ago by edging Cincinnati, 26-21, in Super Bowl XVI at the Silverdome, the first Super Bowl game held in a cold-weather city. MVP Joe Montana passed for 157 yards and one TD and also scored a rushing TD while Ray Wersching kicked four field goals.

Jan. 31, 1982 - Nick Lowery's 23-yard field goal with six seconds left won the Pro Bowl for the AFC, 16-13.

BY THE NUMBERS - 1981

TEAM STATISTICS	BILLS	OPP
First downs	315	298
Rushing	127	113
Passing	163	154
Penalty	25	31
Third downs	94-217	72-218
Total yards	5,640	4,945
Avg. game	352.5	309.1
Plays	1,043	1,037
Avg. play	5.4	4.8
Net rushing yds	2,125	2,075
Avg. game	132.8	129.7
Avg. play	4.1	4.0
Net passing yds	3,515	2,870
Comp/att	253/503	267/474
Sacks/lost	16-146	47-373
Interceptions	20	19
Percentage	50.3	56.3
Punts/avg	80-39.7	77-42.0
Fumbles/lost	33-18	38-17
Penalties/yds	114-1001	93-690
Touchdowns	38	30
Extra points	37-37	30-30
Field goals	14-24	22-26
Safeties	2	0
Kick ret./avg	57-19.0	61-20.8
Punt ret./avg	35-8.3	34-6.5

RUSHING	ATT	YDS	AVG	TD
Cribbs	257	1097	4.3	3
Leaks	91	357	3.9	6
Hooks	51	250	4.9	3
Brown	62	226	3.6	0
McCutcheon	34	138	4.1	0
Ferguson	20	29	1.5	1
Riddick	3	29	9.7	0
Brammer	2	17	8.5	0
Butler	1	1	1.0	0
Robinson	1	-2	-2.0	0
Kush	1	-6	-6.0	0
Franklin	1	-11	-11.0	0
TOTALS	524	2125	4.1	13

PASSING	COMP	ATT	INT	YDS	TD	COMP%	SACKS	RATE
Ferguson	252	498	20	3652	24	50.6	15-137	74.1
Cribbs	1	1	0	9	1	100.0	0-0	100.0
Robinson	0	2	0	0	0	00.0	1-9	19.8
Leaks	0	1	0	0	0	00.0	0-0	39.6
Mike-Mayer	0	1	0	0	0	00.0	0-0	39.6
TOTALS	253	503	20	3661	25	50.3	16-146	74.3

RECEIVING	CAT	YDS	AVG	TD
Lewis	70	1244	17.8	4
Butler	55	842	15.3	8
Cribbs	40	603	15.1	7
Brammer	33	365	11.1	2
Jessie	15	200	13.3	0
Hooks	10	140	14.0	2
Leaks	7	51	7.3	0
Brown	7	46	6.6	1
Piccone	5	65	13.0	0
McCutcheon	5	40	8.0	0
Barnett	4	36	9.0	1
Franklin	2	29	14.5	0
TOTALS	253	3661	14.5	25

KICKING	1-19	20-29	30-39	40-49	50+	TOT	PAT	PTS
Mike-Mayer	0-0	4-6	5-7	5-10	0-1	14-24	37-37	79
Team	0-0	0-0	0-0	0-0	0-0	0-0	0-1	0

PUNTING	NO	AVG	LG	In 20	BL
Cater	80	39.7	71	16	0

SCORE BY QUARTERS

BILLS	78	124	66	43	0 -	311
OPP	44	81	67	81	3 -	276

DEFENSIVE STATISTICAL LEADERS

TACKLES: Freeman 81 primary -55 assists - 136 total, Haslett 82-53-135, Sanford 78-39-118, B. Simpson 57-56-113, Nelson 56-27-83, B. Williams 51-31-82, Robertson 51-30-81, Romes 54-20-74, Smerlas 44-29-73, White 31-32-63, Clark 45-11-56, Villapiano 29-13-42, Kush 23-14-37

SACKS: B. Williams 10.5, White 8, K. Johnson 8, Kush 5.5, Nelson 3

FUMBLE RECOVERIES: Kush 3, Haslett 2

FORCED FUMBLES: Sanford 5, Nelson 3, Freeman 2, Romes 2

INTERCEPTIONS: Clark 5-142 yards, 28.4 avg, 0 TD; Romes 4-113, 28.3, 0 TD; Simpson 4-42, 10.5, 0 TD

SPECIAL TEAMS STATISTICAL LEADERS

KICKOFF RETURNS: Franklin 21-436, 20.8, 0 TD; Riddick 14-257, 18.4, 0 TD

PUNT RETURNS: Hooks 17-142, 8.4, 0 TD; Piccone 9-57, 6.3, 0 TD

Robb Riddick (right) was one of the Bills' small-college finds out of Millersville State.

Jim Haslett (opposite page) wraps up Philadelphia quarterback Ron Jaworski, who is a native of Lackawanna.

NOTES

• The Bills played an almost flawless season opener with 418 yards, 242 in the second half.
• The defense, rated No. 1 in 1980, picked up where it left off, limiting the Jets to eight first downs and allowed them to cross midfield only four times.
• The Jets began their first possession at the Bills 47, but the first of Chris Ward's three holding penalties and Lucious Sanford's sack of Richard Todd drove them backwards. It never got any better.
• Joe Devlin's holding penalty wiped out a Joe Cribbs TD and the Bills settled for Nick Mike-Mayer's field goal in the first quarter. They increased the lead to 10-0 in the second when Joe Cribbs caught a TD pass.
• The Bills blew open the game with a 21-point third quarter. Mario Clark intercepted a Todd pass and returned it 45 yards to the Jets 17. Two plays later, Joe Ferguson hit wide-open Jerry Butler on a slant. A few minutes later, the defense stopped the Jets on fourth down and the offense thanked them as Frank Lewis made a 31-yard reception to set up Cribbs' 14-yard TD run.
• Ferguson's 46-yard pass to Butler led to Roosevelt Leaks' short TD run.

QUOTES

• Fred Smerlas: "We can't let our heads get out of proportion. The key for us was to start off like we ended last year, play the tight defense we can play. This was such a fun game for everyone. When the offense scores 31 points and the defense doesn't give up any, that's how it should be, right? And let's not forget the special teams, they constantly kept the Jets in poor field position."

• Joe Ferguson: "We were doing all right (in the first half), moving the ball up and down the field, but it was like three or four years ago where we weren't scoring." (On the TD pass to Cribbs): "It was a special play put in just for Joe. We tried to isolate him on the linebacker (Ron Crosby) and he just ran right by him. This was a tougher ballgame than the score indicates."
• Conrad Dobler: "We started off a little slow and if somebody had said we'd win by 31 points, I'd have thought they were crazy. But in the second half the defense kept giving us great field position and we capitalized. Last year, we didn't always do that."
• Reggie McKenzie: "We were sharp, it was a good opening day. I think it had a lot to do with the way the coach brought us along in training camp. Joe Ferguson was right, and what else can you say about the defense?"
• Chuck Knox: "It's a good way to get started, but the one thing you learn in this league is yesterday is history. I'm quite satisfied, no question. The guys played hard, but we made a lot of mistakes with penalties and techniques."
• Jim Haslett: "We looked good today, but we'll get better."
• Ralph Wilson: "That's as perfect a game as I've ever seen one of my teams play."

WEEK 1 GAMES

TB 21, Minn 13	KC 37, Pitt 33
Phil 24, NYG 10	Balt 29, NE 28
GB 16, Chi 9	Mia 20, St.L 7
Cinc 27, Sea 21	Dal 26, Wash 10
Hou 27, LA 20	Det 24, SF 17
Atl 27, NO 0	Den 9, Oak 7
SD 44, Clev 24	

Jets	0	0	0	0 -	0
Bills	3	7	21	0 -	31

Attendance at Rich Stadium - 79,754

Buf: FG Mike-Mayer 21, 14:55
Buf: Cribbs 28 pass from Ferguson (Mike-Mayer kick), 13:17
Buf: Butler 19 pass from Ferguson (Mike-Mayer kick), 2:30
Buf: Cribbs 14 run (Mike-Mayer kick), 6:31
Buf: Leaks 1 run (Mike-Mayer kick), 14:18

	BUF	NYJ
First downs	25	8
Rushing yds	182	102
Passing yds	236	129
Punts-avg	5-47.6	8-39.1
Fumbles-lost	1-0	3-0
Penalties-yds	10-84	9-100

BILLS LEADERS: Rushing - Cribbs 15-61, Leaks 12-36, Brown 7-19, Brammer 1-6, Hooks 7-40, McCutcheon 2-20; **Passing** - Ferguson 15-24-1 - 254; **Receiving** - Butler 6-123, Lewis 5-87, Cribbs 1-28, Brown 1-6, Jessie 1-0, Brammer 1-10.

JETS LEADERS: Rushing - Dierking 3-13, Todd 6-32, Long 3-12, McNeil 3-16, Harper 2-3, Newton 3-7, Augustyniak 4-12, Lewis 1-7; **Passing** - Todd 16-25-2 - 138; **Receiving** - Gaffney 2-33, Walker 3-40, Dierking 2-12, Barkum 3-25, Harper 3-11, Long 3-17.

NOTES

• Joe Ferguson threw for 239 yards and three TDs in the first half alone as the Bills rolled.
• The Colts managed only 147 yards and Bert Jones was knocked out of the game in the first half. The defense came up with three turnovers and five sacks.
• The Bills scored on their first possession as Cribbs made a nice over-the-shoulder TD reception.
• The Bills began to sputter, though, as the second drive reached the 21, but a holding penalty on Conrad Dobler and a missed field goal by Nick Mike-Mayer killed it. The third series ended in Ed Smith's interception. A Joe Cribbs fumble at the Bills 38 led to Baltimore's only score, a field goal by Mike Wood that made it 7-3.
• However, two quick TDs late in the second quarter turned it around. Jerry Butler made a brilliant play for a 54-yard catch-and-run TD. After forcing a punt, the Bills drove 43 yards in six plays to Mark Brammer's TD reception. A 28-yard pass to Frank Lewis set it up.
• Greg Landry replaced Jones in the second half and his first pass was intercepted by Charlie Romes and returned 35 yards to the 4. Ferguson then hit Buster Barnett for a TD. The final score, Roland Hooks' TD run, capped a 55-yard drive in which Chuck Knox lifted Ferguson and played Matt Robinson.
• Ferguson set a new team record with his 18th 250-yard passing game.

QUOTES

• Colts coach Mike McCormack: "There's not much to say. They whipped us in every way, especially on the line of scrimmage. They played defense the way you're supposed to play it."
• Conrad Dobler: "I know it's against his (Knox) phi-

losophy, but we're going to get a 50-pointer. I've played so many years (in St. Louis and New Orleans) seeing the scoreboard get lit up, but I've never seen 50. I've always wanted to play in one of those games. And this is the first time in my life I've played on a team with a defense."
• Joe Cribbs: "All we have to do is run the routes correctly and Joe will put the ball in there. He's in complete control and our offense has become explosive. Sure we like to have ball control, but it's always nice to strike quickly when the defense gets you the ball. Our defense is so outstanding, we don't even have to score a lot of points."
• Shane Nelson: "After what (Randy) McMillan and (Curtis) Dickey did to New England last week (226 yards rushing combined), we thought we could show people something if we stopped them. They looked like they got a little frustrated out there."
• Joe Ferguson: "I didn't think I played worth a crap. I threw bad passes, I was intercepted, I didn't play a very good game. And we won."
• Colts linebacker Ed Smith: "I don't think we took them as seriously as we should. I don't think we thought they were as good as they are. I know I didn't. I do now."

WEEK 2 GAMES

Mia 30, Pitt 10	NO 23, LA 17
Atl 31, GB 17	Dal 30, St.L 17
KC 19, TB 10	SF 28, Chi 17
Sea 13, Den 10	SD 28, Det 23
NYG 17, Wash 7	Hou 9, Clev 3
Cinc 31, NYJ 30	Phil 13, NE 3
Oak 36, Minn 10	

Bills	7	14	7	7 -	35
Colts	0	3	0	0 -	3

Attendance at Memorial Stadium - 44,950

Buf: Cribbs 33 pass from Ferguson (Mike-Mayer kick), 3:39
Bal: FG Wood 22, 7:40
Buf: Butler 54 pass from Ferguson (Mike-Mayer kick), 11:24
Buf: Brammer 5 pass from Ferguson (Mike-Mayer kick), 14:43
Buf: Barnett 3 pass from Ferguson (Mike-Mayer kick), 9:48
Buf: Hooks 5 run (Mike-Mayer kick), 5:33

	BUF	BAL
First downs	26	11
Rushing yds	169	73
Passing yds	261	74
Punts-avg	3-47.7	6-43.3
Fumbles-lost	2-2	3-1
Penalties-yds	9-65	1-5

BILLS LEADERS: Rushing - Cribbs 17-66, Brown 9-47, McCutcheon 2-8, Hooks 6-30, Leaks 3-11, Robinson 1- (-2), Ferguson 1-9; **Passing** - Ferguson 16-28-1 - 261; **Receiving** - Butler 3-74, Lewis 4-82, Cribbs 3-46, Brammer 4-55, McCutcheon 1-1, Barnett 1-3.

COLTS LEADERS: Rushing - McMillan 10-29, Dickey 14-35, Dixon 1- (-2), Landry 1-11; **Passing** - Jones 5-11-1 - 30, Landry 7-17-1 - 90; **Receiving** - Dickey 3-30, R. Butler 1-11, McMillan 3-25, Carr 4-50, McCauley 1-4.

STANDINGS: SECOND WEEK

AFC EAST	W	L	T	CENTRAL	W	L	T	WEST	W	L	T	NFC EAST	W	L	T	CENTRAL	W	L	T	WEST	W	L	T
Buffalo	2	0	0	Cincinnati	2	0	0	San Diego	2	0	0	Dallas	2	0	0	Tampa Bay	1	1	0	Atlanta	2	0	0
Miami	2	0	0	Houston	2	0	0	Kan. City	2	0	0	Philadelphia	2	0	0	Green Bay	1	1	0	San Fran	1	1	0
Baltimore	1	1	0	Pittsburgh	0	2	0	Denver	1	1	0	NY Giants	1	1	0	Detroit	1	1	0	N.Orleans	1	1	0
New England	0	2	0	Cleveland	0	2	0	Oakland	1	1	0	St. Louis	0	2	0	Minnesota	0	2	0	LA Rams	0	2	0
NY Jets	0	2	0					Seattle	1	1	0	Washington	0	2	0	Chicago	0	2	0				

Eagles	7	3	7	3	- 20
Bills	0	14	0	0	- 14

Attendance at Rich Stadium - 78,331

Phi: Krepfle 1 pass from Jaworski (Franklin kick), 10:06
Buf: Cribbs 4 run (Mike-Mayer kick), :55
Phi: FG Franklin 29, 6:10
Buf: Lewis 20 pass from Ferguson (Mike-Mayer kick), 12:56
Phi: Carmichael 15 pass from Jaworski (Franklin kick), 4:10
Phi: FG Franklin 46, 11:20

	BUF	PHI
First downs	17	24
Rushing yds	90	160
Passing yds	187	236
Punts-avg	4-41.0	3-38.7
Fumbles-lost	1-1	3-2
Penalties-yds	4-35	10-65

BILLS LEADERS: Rushing - Cribbs 22-63, Brown 2-6, McCutcheon 5-18, Leaks 1-4, Ferguson 1- (-1); **Passing** - Ferguson 14-30-2 - 187; **Receiving** - Butler 3-28, Lewis 7-108, Brown 1-7, Jessie 1-6, Cribbs 1-26, Brammer 1-12.

EAGLES LEADERS: Rushing - Montgomery 27-125, Harrington 9-25, Giammona 1-3, LeMaster 1-7; **Passing** - Jaworski 20-32-1 - 240; **Receiving** - Montgomery 3-54, Carmichael 4-61, Smith 5-64, Harrington 4-11, Krepfle 2-26, Parker 2-24.

NOTES

• Playing in a special Thursday night game on ABC, the Bills weren't able to match up with Wilbert Montgomery, who rushed for 125 yards.
• Nick Mike-Mayer missed a 20-yard field goal early in the fourth that would have tied it at 17-17.
• The Eagles' drive for an insurance field goal was aided by Buffalo's failure to make big plays. Mario Clark dropped an interception that would have been an easy TD and Fred Smerlas failed to hold on to a fumble by Perry Harrington at the Bills 43. On the next play, Sherman White's roughing-the-passer penalty kept the march alive and Tony Franklin eventually made a 46-yarder for a 20-14 lead.
• The Eagles drove 76 yards in 12 plays to Ron Jaworski's TD pass to Keith Krepfle in the first.
• The Bills tied it on Joe Cribbs' TD run after Ervin Parker recovered Wally Henry's fumble on a punt return at the Bills 37. The Eagles came back on their next possession to get Franklin's 29-yard field goal.
• Max Runager's shanked 27-yard punt set up the Bills at the Eagles 47 and they moved in for the go-ahead score as Joe Ferguson hit Frank Lewis for a TD. But on that drive, Jerry Butler got poked in the eye and didn't return.

WEEK 3 GAMES

Minn 26, Det 24	Clev 20, Cinc 17
Den 28, Balt 10	St.L 40, Wash 30
Mia 16, Hou 10	SD 42, KC 31
LA 35, GB 23	Atl 34, SF 17
Pitt 38, NYJ 10	Oak 20, Sea 10
Chi 28, TB 17	NYG 20, NO 17
Dal 35, NE 21	

• The Eagles took the lead for good when Jaworski hit Harold Carmichael with a TD pass to cap a 66-yard march.

QUOTES

• Nick Mike-Mayer on his short miss: "I just looked up at the last minute."
• Ken Jones: "That miss took a little steam out of us. It should have been made, it was only a chip shot. So it did set us back."
• Chuck Knox: "I would have liked to have had those three points, but in a game like this, there's a lot of things you can reflect on. You don't end up looking at one play. We just couldn't get it done tonight. They executed better than we did."
• Eagles coach Dick Vermeil: "We were healthy and able to do some things we weren't able to in the first two games. This was a helluva football game to win in this atmosphere. This is a great football city. This shows us that we have the makings of a championship football team. All they (the Bills) can do is get better after this game. We may be a little more mature than Buffalo. We're six years into our program and maybe it told tonight."
• Joe Ferguson: "They outplayed us in every phase of the game. We both had the same amount of time to prepare. Preparation doesn't mean anything if you don't execute."
• Eagles quarterback Ron Jaworski: "We didn't catch them on a bad day. We got more of a test of mental toughness and physical toughness than any game we'll play this year. I'm a Bills fan, I hope they win their next 13 games. I sat up in the old Rockpile for five or six years all by myself watching them when I was a kid."
• Jim Haslett: "It's only one game, there's 13 more to go."

Bills	0	14	0	10	0	- 24
Bengals	0	10	0	14	3	- 27

Attendance at Riverfront Stadium - 46,418

Cin: Collinsworth 13 pass from Anderson (Breech kick), 1:56
Buf: Lewis 9 pass from Ferguson (Mike-Mayer kick), 7:06
Buf: Brammer 4 pass from Ferguson (Mike-Mayer kick), 13:49
Cin: FG Breech 23, 15:00
Buf: Lewis 5 pass from Ferguson (Mike-Mayer kick), :11
Cin: Kreider 16 pass from Anderson (Breech kick), 3:14
Cin: Kreider 16 pass from Anderson (Breech kick), 13:07
Buf: FG Mike-Mayer 40, 14:59
Cin: FG Breech 28, 9:33

	BUF	CIN
First downs	25	30
Rushing yds	102	113
Passing yds	287	316
Punts-avg	4-43.8	3-55.7
Fumbles-lost	2-1	3-2
Penalties-yds	9-55	6-49

BILLS LEADERS: Rushing - Cribbs 18-48, Leaks 7-37, McCutcheon 3-7, Hooks 2-10; **Passing** - Ferguson 25-45-0 - 287, Mike-Mayer 0-1-0 - 0; **Receiving** - Lewis 8-132, Jessie 4-37, Butler 1-26, Cribbs 7-54, Brammer 3-26, McCutcheon 2-12.

BENGALS LEADERS: Rushing - Johnson 22-85, Anderson 2-21, Alexander 5-1, Griffin 2-6; **Passing** - Anderson 28-40-0 - 328; **Receiving** - Collinsworth 10-111, Kreider 4-75, Ross 1-17, Alexander 1-13, Griffin 3-21, Johnson 3-29, Curtis 2-18, Hargrove 1-0, McInally 2-21, Verser 1-23.

NOTES

• The Bills suffered their first overtime loss in team history.
• The Bengals rolled up 429 yards against the Bills defense, including 316 net passing yards. Ken Anderson completed 28 passes, including 10 to rookie Cris Collinsworth.
• Nick Mike-Mayer forced OT with a 40-yard field goal with one second left.
• The Bills won the toss in OT and drove to the Bengals 39, but Roosevelt Leaks was stopped on third-and-one and Buffalo punted into the end zone. Anderson hit Collinsworth for 23 yards, then hit Pat McInally for 12 on a third-down play. Six plays and a penalty later, Breech kicked the winner.
• The Bills first drive of the game stalled at the 3, but Matt Robinson failed to hold a snap on a field goal attempt and the Bengals took over. They then proceeded to march 97 yards in 18 plays.
• The Bills countered with a 59-yard march to tie, then went ahead 14-7 on Joe Ferguson's TD pass to Mark Brammer after Rod Kush recovered a fumbled punt by Mike Fuller at the Bengals 15.
• Breech made a field goal on the final play of the first half. After a scoreless third, the Bills took a 21-10 lead early in the fourth as Ferguson hit Frank Lewis for his

WEEK 4 GAMES

Phil 36, Wash 13	Dal 18, NYG 10
Det 16, Oak 0	SF 21, NO 14
Minn 30, GB 13	KC 20, Sea 14
Den 42, SD 24	TB 20, St.L 10
Clev 28, Atl 17	NYJ 33, Hou 17
Mia 31, Balt 28	LA 24, Chi 7
Pitt 27, NE 21	

second TD of the game to cap an 80-yard drive.
• Anderson completed four of six passes on an 84-yard march that ended in his TD pass to Steve Kreider. Then, starting from his own 9 with 5:20 left, Anderson went five-for-five including a TD pass to Kreider.

QUOTES

• Bengals coach Forrest Gregg: "Anderson played under a great deal of pressure which our fans put him under. I don't think anybody could play a better game than he played today. I don't see how anyone can boo him now."
• Joe Ferguson on the play Leaks was stopped on in OT: "It's a play we'd run all day and it worked every time. There's nothing I would have done any differently."
• Chuck Knox: "We were beaten in every phase. We didn't execute, we made too many mistakes and you can't expect to win doing that." (On his decision to punt after Leaks was stopped): "We had just lost a yard, so if we go for the first down and don't make it, they have the ball at their 40. Obviously we were hoping to punt the ball deep in their territory (it went into the end zone). I still say it was the safe thing to do. I'd do the same thing again."
• Conrad Dobler: "So, what do we do? Quit? Not this team. We're a good team, we'll regroup and we'll be back. Who's to say we can't go 12-0 the rest of the season. This team won't fold, there's too many good athletes here. We didn't get beat today, we gave this game away."
• Jim Haslett: "I don't think the enthusiasm was there this week. We realize it's not the end of the world. Oakland lost three early ones last year and went on to win the Super Bowl."

STANDINGS: FOURTH WEEK

AFC EAST	W	L	T	CENTRAL	W	L	T	WEST	W	L	T	NFC EAST	W	L	T	CENTRAL	W	L	T	WEST	W	L	T
Miami	4	0	0	Cincinnati	3	1	0	San Diego	3	1	0	Dallas	4	0	0	Tampa Bay	2	2	0	Atlanta	3	1	0
Buffalo	2	2	0	Houston	2	2	0	Kan. City	3	1	0	Philadelphia	4	0	0	Minnesota	2	2	0	San Fran	2	2	0
Baltimore	1	3	0	Pittsburgh	2	2	0	Denver	3	1	0	NY Giants	2	2	0	Detroit	2	2	0	LA Rams	2	2	0
NY Jets	1	3	0	Cleveland	2	2	0	Oakland	2	2	0	St. Louis	1	3	0	Green Bay	1	3	0	N.Orleans	1	3	0
New England	0	4	0					Seattle	1	3	0	Washington	0	4	0	Chicago	1	3	0				

NOTES

• Joe Cribbs rushed for a career-high 159 yards and the Bills snapped a two-game losing streak.
• Mike Garrett's 31-yard punt set up the Bills at the Colts 44 early in the first. Cribbs broke a 28-yard run before Joe Ferguson fired a TD pass to Jerry Butler. On their ensuing series, the Bills marched 80 yards in nine plays with Cribbs' 30-yard run and Butler's 23-yard reception the key plays that led to Roosevelt Leaks' one-yard plunge.
• The teams exchanged field goals in the middle two periods, but the Colts pulled within 17-10 early in the fourth as Bert Jones found Roger Carr in the end zone. On the next series, Cribbs broke a 19-yard run that led to Nick Mike-Mayer's second field goal.
• The defense stopped the Colts on fourth down at the 49 and that resulted in Mike-Mayer's third field goal.
• The Colts scored with nine seconds left to cap an 87-yard march.

QUOTES

• Joe Ferguson: "I don't think our confidence level ever went down. We just knew we didn't play too well last week. It was a pressure game for us, a must game. I was a little off all game, but there's no doubt the running game won the game for us. That and the defense. We had all the ingredients that go into a good running game."
• Fred Smerlas: "Everyone knew we weren't hustling against Cincinnati and we lost a game we did nothing to win. All we have to do is hustle and want to win and we can beat anybody. Today everyone was hustling and sticking."
• Joe Cribbs: "The offensive line probably executed its best all year. We had the holes and I thank them for that. We just wanted to win, that was it. For the past couple of weeks the press and the fans have been on our backs saying we weren't doing the job. Now they'll have to find something else to pick on because the running game is back."
• Jim Haslett: "We were 100 percent better than last week, but we're still not up to par."
• Colts defensive tackle Mike Barnes on his feud with Conrad Dobler: "What do you want me to say, that he cheats? Yeah, frankly, he does cheat. It's very easy to stunt a defensive charge when you tug on a guy's facemask."
• Conrad Dobler: "Listen, I've never been held by the facemask by an individual more than by Barnes. I've faced Barnes three times and twice he didn't finish the game. I know I'm a heckuva lot smarter than Barnes, he didn't get hurt, he just didn't finish the game. Can you imagine that. He didn't finish and I did and he's playing against a cripple. I promised Phil (Villapiano) and the other guys that he wouldn't finish."

WEEK 5 GAMES

SF 30, Wash 17	St.L 20, Dal 17
GB 27, NYG 14	Den 17, Oak 0
LA 27, Clev 16	Pitt 20, NO 6
Minn 24, Chi 21	NE 33, KC 17
SD 24, Sea 10	Hou 17, Cinc 10
TB 28, Det 10	Phil 16, Atl 13
Mia 28, NYJ 28 (OT)	

Colts	0	3	0	14	-	17
Bills	14	0	3	6	-	23

Attendance at Rich Stadium - 77,811

Buf: J. Butler 16 pass from Ferguson (Mike-Mayer kick), 4:14
Buf: Leaks 1 run (Mike-Mayer kick), 9:39
Bal: FG Wood 32, :16
Buf: FG Mike-Mayer 34, 13:20
Bal: Carr 6 pass from Jones (Wood kick), :48
Buf: FG Mike-Mayer 44, 4:07
Buf: FG Mike-Mayer 45, 10:28
Bal: R. Butler 14 pass from Jones (Wood kick), 14:51

	BUF	BAL
First downs	22	23
Rushing yds	229	133
Passing yds	137	245
Punts-avg	3-42.3	5-31.2
Fumbles-lost	3-0	2-1
Penalties-yds	7-49	10-55

BILLS LEADERS: Rushing - Cribbs 17-159, Leaks 3-7, McCutcheon 15-64, Ferguson 1- (-1); **Passing** - Ferguson 14-29-1 - 148; **Receiving** - Lewis 2-16, J. Butler 4-73, McCutcheon 2-27, Cribbs 3-20, Brammer 3-12.

COLTS LEADERS: Rushing - Dickey 10-78, Franklin 12-36, McMillan 1-1, Dixon 6-20, Jones 2- (-2); **Passing** - Jones 22-36-1 - 275; **Receiving** - Dickey 3-80, Burke 1-11, McCall 1-6, Dixon 2-24, McCauley 5-21, Franklin 3-14, R. Butler 3-75, Carr 4-44.

NOTES

• The Bills beat Miami for the second year in a row at home, taking a 31-7 lead at halftime on *Monday Night Football*. It snapped a five-game losing streak on MNF dating to the 1974 season opener.
• Joe Ferguson threw for 338 yards, the third-highest total of his career. He had 221 by halftime.
• Ferguson completed three passes for 40 yards on the first series leading to a Nick Mike-Mayer field goal.
• Isiah Robertson intercepted a Don Strock pass and returned it 15 yards to the Miami 28. On the next play, Ferguson hit Jerry Butler for a TD and a 10-0 lead.
• At the start of the second quarter, the Bills went on a 13-play, 80-yard drive that consumed 8:11 and culminated in Roosevelt Leaks' TD run.
• Fulton Walker returned the ensuing kickoff 90 yards for a TD, but that was only a speed bump for the Bills as one minute later, Joe Cribbs got open over the middle and took a Ferguson pass 65 yards for a TD. Shane Nelson then intercepted a Strock pass and returned it to the 39. Three plays later, Ferguson hit Butler for another TD and a 31-7 lead.
• The Dolphins put together two 87-yard scoring drives in the second half, but it wasn't nearly enough.

QUOTES

• Reggie McKenzie: "Last year was the most satisfying. We came of age as a team and you could see that on the field tonight. Joe was fantastic."
• Frank Lewis: "The first half had to be one of the best we've ever played."
• Joe Ferguson: "I suppose five years from now somebody will be calling me that (underrated). I wasn't hit but twice all night. That's fantastic protection. Also, we got good play-calling from the coaches upstairs. Some of the plays called were designed for defenses Miami was in and we hit them just right. I've been here nine years and that's only the second time we've beaten them. I do get up a little more for them, sometimes I get too high. I think the Thursday night game here against Philadelphia helped us. A lot of guys on this team never played a night game. We were looser than we were that night. We found out it's not such a big deal."
• Sherman White: "In the first half, we were a great team. In the second half, we were a good team."
• Phil Villapiano: "There are moments when we're a great team. It's a mystery why we can't sustain it. We were ahead of Cincinnati 21-10 and then we went to sleep. Great teams don't do that. But when we're hot like we were tonight, forget it."
• Miami coach Don Shula: "It's disturbing because we gave up so much cheap stuff that got us behind. We can't let them catch balls that should be knocked down. Our defense didn't make a play all night long. Ferguson had a great night and they were well-prepared."

Dolphins	0	7	7	7	-	21
Bills	10	21	0	0	-	31

Attendance at Rich Stadium - 78,576

Buf: FG Mike-Mayer 37, 7:05
Buf: Butler 28 pass from Ferguson (Mike-Mayer kick), 13:46
Buf: Leaks 1 run (Mike-Mayer kick), 9:59
Mia: Walker 90 kickoff return (von Schamann kick), 10:18
Buf: Cribbs 65 pass from Ferguson (Mike-Mayer kick), 11:18
Buf: Butler 25 pass from Ferguson (Mike-Mayer kick), 13:06
Mia: Nathan 12 run (von Schamann kick), 12:03
Mia: Rose 4 pass from Strock (von Schamann kick), 14:50

	BUF	MIA
First downs	22	22
Rushing yds	116	99
Passing yds	338	225
Punts-avg	4-35.0	4-44.0
Fumbles-lost	4-1	1-0
Penalties-yds	9-69	3-15

BILLS LEADERS: Rushing - Cribbs 16-60, Leaks 9-37, McCutcheon 7-21, Ferguson 1- (-2); **Passing** - Ferguson 20-29-0 - 338; **Receiving** - Lewis 5-106, Butler 5-82, Brammer 4-46, Cribbs 3-66, Barnett 1-7, Jessie 2-31.

DOLPHINS LEADERS: Rushing - Franklin 9-31, Nathan 8-59, Strock 1-9; **Passing** - Strock 26-44-4 - 245; **Receiving** - Moore 6-39, Nathan 2-13, Lee 2-20, Harris 6-92, Cefalo 3-34, Vigorito 1-1, Rose 5-41, Giaquinto 1-5.

WEEK 6 GAMES

Hou 35, Sea 17	KC 27, Oak 0
Phil 31, NO 14	Wash 24, Chi 7
NYG 34, St.L 14	Pit 13, Clev 7
NYJ 28, NE 24	Minn 33, SD 31
Cin 41, Balt 17	SF 45, Dal 14
LA 37, Atl 35	Den 27, Det 21
TB 21, GB 10	

STANDINGS: SIXTH WEEK

AFC EAST	W	L	T	CENTRAL	W	L	T	WEST	W	L	T	NFC EAST	W	L	T	CENTRAL	W	L	T	WEST	W	L	T
Miami	4	1	1	Cincinnati	4	2	0	Denver	5	1	0	Philadelphia	6	0	0	Tampa Bay	4	2	0	LA Rams	4	2	0
Buffalo	4	2	0	Houston	4	2	0	San Diego	4	2	0	Dallas	4	2	0	Minnesota	4	2	0	San Fran	4	2	0
NY Jets	2	3	1	Pittsburgh	4	2	0	Kan. City	4	2	0	NY Giants	3	3	0	Detroit	2	4	0	Atlanta	3	3	0
Baltimore	1	5	0	Cleveland	2	4	0	Oakland	2	4	0	St. Louis	2	4	0	Green Bay	2	4	0	N.Orleans	1	5	0
New England	1	5	0					Seattle	1	5	0	Washington	1	5	0	Chicago	1	5	0				

Bills	0	7	7	0 -	14
Jets	6	0	21	6 -	33

Attendance at Shea Stadium - 54,607

NYJ: FG Leahy 24, 10:08
NYJ: FG Leahy 29, 13:34
Buf: Lewis 23 pass from Ferguson (Mike-Mayer kick), 5:40
NYJ: Harper 29 run (Leahy kick), 6:09
NYJ: Barkum 19 pass from Todd (Leahy kick), 11:59
Buf: Butler 67 pass from Ferguson (Mike-Mayer kick), 12:34
NYJ: B. Jones 61 fumble return (Leahy kick), 13:35
NYJ: FG Leahy 39, 2:43
NYJ: FG Leahy 22, 10:39

	BUF	NYJ
First downs	14	21
Rushing yds	46	200
Passing yds	242	174
Punts-avg	4-42.5	1-49.0
Fumbles-lost	3-1	3-1
Penalties-yds	4-47	4-20

BILLS LEADERS: Rushing - Cribbs 9-44, Leaks 1- (-1), Brown 5-5, Ferguson 1- (-2); **Passing** - Ferguson 15-34-2 - 250, Robinson 0-2-0 - 0; **Receiving** - Lewis 6-109, Butler 3-78, Brammer 3-36, Franklin 1-13, Cribbs 1-7, Jessie 1-7.

JETS LEADERS: Rushing - Augustyniak 20-80, Harper 7-40, Todd 3-33, Dierking 8-26, Newton 1-13, Long 3-8, Ramsey 1-0; **Passing** - Todd 17-27-0 - 190; **Receiving** - Barkum 5-66, Harper 3-33, Walker 2-17, Gaffney 1-17, Augustyniak 3-16, Dierking 1-14, B. Jones 1-14, L. Jones 1-13.

NOTES
• The Jets atoned for a season-opening rout in Buffalo by taking advantage of a flat Bills effort.
• Nick Mike-Mayer missed a first-quarter field goal and the Jets took possession and drove to Pat Leahy's first field goal. Joe Ferguson then was intercepted by Greg Buttle who returned it to the Bills 21. That led to Leahy's second field goal.
• The Bills marched 95 yards in 12 plays to take the lead. Joe Cribbs had two key runs and Ferguson hit Frank Lewis for 19 before passing 23 yards to Lewis for the TD.
• The Bills blew it open in the third. Mark Brammer fumbled at the Jets 39. New York turned around and drove 61 yards to take the lead for good on Richard Todd's 29-yard TD pass to Bruce Harper.
• After a Bills punt, the Jets moved 68 yards to Jerome Barkum's TD reception.
• The Bills answered that score quickly as Ferguson fired a 67-yard TD pass to Jerry Butler.
• The Jets then got a huge break. Shane Nelson forced Mike Augustyniak to fumble, but after Ben Williams kicked the ball forward, Bobby Jones picked it up for New York and ran 61 yards for a TD.
• Leahy kicked two field goals in the fourth, one after Johnny Lynn intercepted Ferguson.

WEEK 7 GAMES	
Mia 13, Wash 10	KC 28, Den 14
Cinc 34, Pitt 7	NE 38, Hou 10
Oak 18, TB 16	SF 13, GB 3
Atl 41, St.L 20	SD 43, Balt 14
Minn 35, Phil 23	Clev 20, NO 17
Dal 29, LA 17	NYG 32, Sea 0
Det 48, Chi 17	

• The Bills ran only twice for five yards in the second half.
• Shane Nelson was in on 16 tackles.

QUOTES
• Chuck Knox: "It was a frustrating afternoon and the Jets had a lot to do with it."
• Joe Ferguson: "If we had recovered (Augustyniak's fumble), we would have been right back in the game. Early on we ran successfully, but then they shut us down. They were so much more improved than the first time we played them."
• Jets quarterback Richard Todd: "We just gave them a little of what they gave us the first time."
• Shane Nelson: "Our intensity is there, but more or less on a roller coaster. One week it's here, one week it's not. Last year we had it every week. We're not maintaining it. They wanted it more than we did. A team that plays enthusiastically makes the breaks for themselves. I thought we'd get that fumble and we'd have a good shot at taking it in. But they got to the ball first and they didn't get lucky. They just outplayed us. We knew they'd be fired up after the way we beat them. You could sense they really believe in each other."
• Fred Smerlas: "We're not playing up to our capabilities. We're making a ton of mistakes and blowing assignments. But it's not the end of the world. We caught a team on a roll. We'll be all right. The Jets are a good team that happened to play great today."

Broncos	0	7	0	0 -	7
Bills	0	3	3	3 -	9

Attendance at Rich Stadium - 77,757

Den: Watson 36 pass from Morton (Steinfort kick), 13:45
Buf: FG Mike-Mayer 41, 15:00
Buf: FG Mike-Mayer 46, 10:39
Buf: FG Mike-Mayer 36, 14:59

	BUF	DEN
First downs	17	10
Rushing yds	119	64
Passing yds	204	97
Punts-avg	9-46.9	12-44.3
Fumbles-lost	1-1	0-0
Penalties-yds	7-78	4-30

BILLS LEADERS: Rushing - Cribbs 24-123, Brown 2-1, Butler 1-1, Leaks 1-0, Kush 1- (-6); **Passing** - Ferguson 21-42-1 - 223; **Receiving** - Lewis 6-90, Brammer 4-28, Jessie 1-24, Brown 4-24, Cribbs 2-15, Piccone 2-26, Franklin 1-16, Butler 1-0.

BRONCOS LEADERS: Rushing - Preston 11-26, Parros 10-22, Reed 2-11, Upchurch 1-5; **Passing** - Morton 10-25-0 - 151; **Receiving** - Watson 4-91, Parros 1-9, Preston 2-3, Odoms 2-21, Egloff 1-27.

WEEK 8 GAMES	
SF 20, LA 17	St.L 30, Minn 17
Phil 20, TB 10	NO 17, Cinc 7
Chi 20, SD 17 (OT)	Wash 24, NE 22
Det 31, GB 27	Sea 19, NYJ 3
Dal 28, Mia 27	Clev 42, Balt 28
KC 28, Oak 17	Pitt 26, Hou 13
NYG 27, Atl 24 (OT)	

NOTES
• Nick Mike-Mayer provided all nine points, including the winning field goal with one second left.
• Denver had only two first downs and 44 yards of offense in the second half. Craig Morton, who entered the game 4-0 vs. the Bills lifetime, was sacked seven times, including 2 1/2 by Rod Kush and three by Ken Johnson.
• Morton hit Steve Watson for a 36-yard TD late in the first half. A few plays earlier, he hit Watson for a 38-yard gain. The Bills struck back as Joe Ferguson hit Frank Lewis for gains of 13 and 17 yards to position Mike-Mayer for a 41-yard field goal on the final play of the first half.
• In the third, Roland Hooks' 26-yard punt return set up the Bills at their own 40. The drive stalled and Chuck Knox, faced with a 51-yard attempt, opted to punt. However, the Broncos went offsides and Knox sent Mike-Mayer onto the field. He barely cleared the crossbar from 46 yards, into the wind.
• The winning drive began at the Bills 30 after a Denver punt with 3:01 left. With 1:52 left, Ferguson found Lewis for 17 yards and a first down at the Denver 35. Joe Cribbs, who produced his fifth career 100-yard rushing game, broke a 13-yarder and then a run to the middle set the stage for Mike-Mayer.

QUOTES
• Rod Kush: "Last year we were the top defensive team in the league. This year they were No. 1, but I think we proved that maybe that's where we belong. I'd say this game sticks out more than the San Diego game (last year) because I'm still healthy. We put that (dime defense) in in the third or fourth game and I was happy because I hadn't been playing that much."
• Denver coach Dan Reeves: "We played well enough on defense to win. It's tough to lose a game when you don't give up a touchdown. We played great defense except for the drives at the end of each half. It's frustrating as hell. He's (Chuck Knox) got more guts than I've got. I would have tried to score the touchdown (at the end, rather than attempt a field goal). I guess that's what you learn being in the league so long. He obviously has a lot of confidence in his kicker."
• Nick Mike-Mayer: "You always have to be confident when you go out there that you're going to make it. I don't think of the situation. I do my stretching and I concentrate on the mental things."
• Joe Ferguson: "I couldn't watch the kick. I watched a woman in the stands and decided to let her and the fans tell me the story. When she jumped up and down, I knew we had it. I could see the playoffs on that foot."
• Shane Nelson: "We seem to play our best defensive football when our backs are against the wall. The games we've lost are games we were supposed to win. But in the 'must' games, we've played well."
• Fred Smerlas: "I think maybe we had too much success too fast last year and we weren't prepared to play as well as we had to. Today, we had our best defensive effort of the year."

STANDINGS: EIGHTH WEEK

AFC EAST	W	L	T	CENTRAL	W	L	T	WEST	W	L	T	NFC EAST	W	L	T	CENTRAL	W	L	T	WEST	W	L	T
Miami	5	2	1	Cincinnati	5	3	0	Kan. City	6	2	0	Philadelphia	7	1	0	Minnesota	5	3	0	San Fran	6	2	0
Buffalo	5	3	0	Pittsburgh	5	3	0	San Diego	5	3	0	Dallas	6	2	0	Tampa Bay	4	4	0	LA Rams	4	4	0
NY Jets	3	4	1	Houston	4	4	0	Denver	5	3	0	NY Giants	5	3	0	Detroit	4	4	0	Atlanta	4	4	0
New England	2	6	0	Cleveland	4	4	0	Oakland	3	5	0	St. Louis	3	5	0	Green Bay	2	6	0	N.Orleans	2	6	0
Baltimore	1	7	0					Seattle	2	6	0	Washington	2	6	0	Chicago	2	6	0				

NOTES

• Joe Cribbs totaled 248 yards rushing and receiving and caught three TD passes. Cribbs' 163 receiving yards were the second-highest in team history for a back. Wray Carlton had 177 in 1960.

• Shane Nelson suffered a knee injury that would sideline him for five or six weeks. Even without Nelson, the defense had a great day holding the high-powered Browns offense to 211 yards. The Bills recorded six sacks and intercepted three passes by Brian Sipe. They also knocked him out of the game on three occasions.

• The offense piled up a season-high 469 yards, but suffered five turnovers.

• Cribbs' first TD came from the shotgun on a third-down play. He streaked down the left sideline and beat rookie cornerback Hanford Dixon. A high snap foiled the extra point attempt.

• His second TD came when he victimized linebacker Don Goode on a corner route to the end zone.

• The Browns got a Matt Bahr field goal before the half ended, then got another in the third after a Cribbs fumble set up the Browns at their own 37.

• The Bills got a safety late in the third when Paul McDonald, in while Sipe was recovering from another sack, grounded the ball intentionally in the end zone while being tackled by Sherman White.

• After the free kick, Cribbs fumbled at the Bills 21, but Bill Simpson then intercepted Sipe at the 9.

• After Sipe hit Ozzie Newsome for a TD early in the fourth, a drive that was aided by a 36-yard interference penalty on Rufus Bess, Cribbs got his final TD on a 60-yarder as he beat Clay Matthews.

QUOTES

• Joe Cribbs on his last TD: "The play before, he (Matthews) pushed me when I was already out of bounds. Stuff like that happens in the heat of the game, but I felt that was a little uncalled for. I was one-on-one with him on the next play and Joe just laid the ball in there." (On his fumbles): "We all make mistakes. The main thing is not to let the mistakes keep you from winning and we didn't because the defense made some big plays when it had to."

• Joe Ferguson: "We went into the game thinking we could hit our running backs out of the backfield if we got the coverages we were expecting."

• Browns linebacker Clay Matthews: "I don't think there's another back in the league used on deep patterns like Cribbs is used by Buffalo. To be honest, it doesn't take a lot of God-given talent to run straight downfield, just speed."

• Fred Smerlas on getting his first sack: "Every day in practice, Conrad Dobler would go up to me and say 'We have one thing in common, I don't give up any sacks and you don't have any.'"

• Ben Williams, who also got his first two sacks: "The fact that I didn't have any really messed me up. I was thinking about it all the time, I could be eating dinner and start thinking about it. I haven't had the same year with sacks that I did last year."

WEEK 9 GAMES	
Cinc 34, Hou 21	Dal 17, Phil 14
TB 20, Chi 10	NYJ 26, NYG 7
GB 34, Sea 24	Wash 42, St.L 21
SD 22, KC 20	Mia 27, Balt 10
Atl 41, NO 10	LA 20, Det 13
Oak 27, NE 17	SF 17, Pitt 14
Den 19, Minn 17	

Browns	0	3	7	-	**13**
Bills	6	7	2	7	-	**22**

Attendance at Rich Stadium - 78,266

Buf: Cribbs 58 pass from Ferguson (kick failed), 12:05
Buf: Cribbs 15 pass from Ferguson (Mike-Mayer kick), 4:31
Cle: FG Bahr 36, 11:49
Cle: FG Bahr 39, 10:18
Buf: Safety, White tackled McDonald in end zone, 12:43
Cle: Newsome 12 pass from Sipe (Bahr kick), 5:19
Buf: Cribbs 60 pass from Ferguson (Mike-Mayer kick), 7:23

	BUF	CLE
First downs	21	12
Rushing yds	172	71
Passing yds	297	140
Punts-avg	6-38.7	8-45.0
Fumbles-lost	4-4	2-0
Penalties-yds	8-125	5-30

BILLS LEADERS: Rushing - Cribbs 23-85, Brown 14-58, Leaks 3-15, Hooks 2-4, Ferguson 1-(-1), Brammer 1-11; **Passing** - Ferguson 14-30-1 - 297; **Receiving** - Lewis 5-97, Cribbs 5-163, Butler 3-29, Hooks 1-8.

BROWNS LEADERS: Rushing - M. Pruitt 13-39, White 2-4, G. Pruitt 3-22, Sipe 2-6; **Passing** - Sipe 14-37-3 - 199, McDonald 0-1-0 - 0; **Receiving** - Newsome 3-52, G. Pruitt 2-19, Feacher 2-62, M. Pruitt 4-20, C. Miller 1-16, Rucker 1-11, Logan 1-19.

NOTES

• The Bills were in control just before halftime, but Joe Ferguson threw an interception to Michael Downs that prevented them from building on a 14-7 lead. Then, Tony Dorsett took a short Danny White swing pass on the first play of the second half and went 73 yards to tie the game. The Cowboys scored 20 points in the third quarter and won easily.

• Three plays after the kickoff following Dorsett's TD, Everson Walls intercepted Ferguson and returned it 19 yards to the Bills 44. Two plays later, on a flea-flicker, White hit Tony Hill for a 37-yard TD. Too Tall Jones then deflected a Ferguson pass and D.D. Lewis intercepted to set up a Rafael Septien field goal. Late in the third, Septien capped a 67-yard drive with a field goal.

• Things got ugly in the fourth as Conrad Dobler wiped out a 23-yard pass completion when he was caught leg-whipping John Dutton.

• The Bills took a 7-0 lead early on Jerry Butler's 16-yard TD on a third-and-four play. Frank Lewis made a 30-yard reception to set up Butler's TD.

• Dallas got that back as White passed to Doug Cosbie for a score. It shouldn't have happened, though, as two Bill Simpson interceptions on the drive were nullified by penalties.

• The Bills regained the lead as Joe Cribbs threw a nine-yard TD to Curtis Brown on an option pass. That was set up by 38- and 26-yard receptions by Butler on the 76-yard drive.

QUOTES

• Chuck Knox: "I'd say we were hurt by the interception at the end of the half. We were down there close looking at seven or at least three and they come up with an interception."

• Cowboys coach Tom Landry on that interception: "He (Ferguson) was down, although we didn't touch him. If he wants to throw the ball from that position, that's fine with me. That and the Dorsett play really took the wind out of them. That broke their concentration and got things going for us."

• Joe Ferguson on the interception: "I lost my dadgum shoe as I was moving out. I probably shouldn't have thrown it. We had some ridiculous penalties. You can't have that and have a winning team. Some people won't like me saying that, but that's tough."

• Cowboys quarterback Danny White: "Buffalo, in the first half, was the hardest team for us to move on all year. They are also the most physical. But Miami, while not as physical, is a lot smarter team than Buffalo. They don't take those dumb penalties."

• Cowboys linebacker D.D. Lewis: "Coach Landry told us to keep our poise. We know Buffalo plays rough and sometimes a little dirty."

• Cowboys defensive end John Dutton: "I've never played against anyone like him (Dobler) and I hope I never do again. He leg-whipped, kicked, punched. After the game he said to me he had to play that way because he's a cripple. I told him 'Why don't you get out of the game?'"

WEEK 10 GAMES	
Sea 24, Pitt 21	Phil 52, St.L 10
Chi 16, KC 13 (OT)	Hou 17, Oak 16
Mia 30, NE 27 (OT)	NO 21, LA 13
Wash 33, Det 31	Cinc 40, SD 17
GB 26, NYG 24	NYJ 41, Balt 14
Minn 25, TB 10	SF 17, Atl 14
Den 23, Clev 20 (OT)	

Bills	7	7	0	0	-	**14**
Cowboys	7	0	20	0	-	**27**

Attendance at Texas Stadium - 62,583

Buf: Butler 16 pass from Ferguson (Mike-Mayer kick), 4:17
Dal: Cosbie 12 pass from White (Septien kick), 12:55
Buf: Brown 9 pass from Cribbs (Mike-Mayer kick), :57
Dal: Dorsett 73 pass from White (Septien kick), :21
Dal: Hill 37 pass from White (Septien kick), 2:41
Dal: FG Septien 47, 6:17
Dal: FG Septien 31, 14:26

	BUF	DAL
First downs	18	21
Rushing yds	58	196
Passing yds	307	202
Punts-avg	7-35.1	4-43.3
Fumbles-lost	3-1	3-2
Penalties-yds	10-89	7-50

BILLS LEADERS: Rushing - Cribbs 8-19, Brown 8-39; **Passing** - Ferguson 19-42-4 - 301, Cribbs 1-1-0 - 9; **Receiving** - Butler 8-118, Lewis 4-72, Brammer 3-38, Cribbs 3-29, Jessie 1-44, Brown 1-9.
COWBOYS LEADERS: Rushing - Dorsett 28-117, Springs 13-65, Newsome 1-7, White 4-5, Newhouse 1-2; **Passing** - White 9-17-1 - 219; **Receiving** - Cosbie 3-54, Dorsett 1-73, Hill 1-37, Pearson 1-14, Springs 1-5, DuPree 2-36.

STANDINGS: TENTH WEEK

AFC EAST	W	L	T	CENTRAL	W	L	T	WEST	W	L	T	NFC EAST	W	L	T	CENTRAL	W	L	T	WEST	W	L	T
Miami	7	2	1	Cincinnati	7	3	0	Denver	7	3	0	Philadelphia	8	2	0	Minnesota	6	4	0	San Fran	8	2	0
Buffalo	6	4	0	Pittsburgh	5	5	0	San Diego	6	4	0	Dallas	8	2	0	Tampa Bay	5	5	0	LA Rams	5	5	0
NY Jets	5	4	1	Houston	5	5	0	Kan. City	6	4	0	NY Giants	5	5	0	Detroit	4	6	0	Atlanta	5	5	0
New England	2	8	0	Cleveland	4	6	0	Oakland	4	6	0	Washington	4	6	0	Green Bay	4	6	0	N.Orleans	3	7	0
Baltimore	1	9	0					Seattle	3	7	0	St. Louis	3	7	0	Chicago	3	7	0				

Bills	0	0	0	-	0
Cardinals	3	7	0	14 -	24

Attendance at Busch Stadium - 46,214

St.L: FG O'Donoghue 35, 5:43
St.L: Mitchell 2 pass from Lomax (O'Donoghue kick), 3:05
St.L: Anderson 18 run (O'Donoghue kick), 2:02
St.L: Anderson 8 run (O'Donoghue kick), 12:29

	BUF	ST.L
First downs	17	22
Rushing yds	85	258
Passing yds	226	80
Punts-avg	3-45.0	3-33.7
Fumbles-lost	2-2	1-0
Penalties-yds	7-70	6-45

BILLS LEADERS: Rushing - Cribbs 14-55, Brown 3-13, Ferguson 1-13, Hooks 1-4; **Passing** - Ferguson 21-37-4 - 233; **Receiving** - Butler 6-65, Lewis 3-51, Brammer 5-73, Cribbs 2-8, Hooks 1-7, Barnett 1-10, Leaks 1-0, Jessie 2-19.

CARDINALS LEADERS: Rushing - Anderson 27-177, Morris 7-25, Mitchell 3-31, Lomax 3-15, Green 1-10; **Passing** - Lomax 13-23-1 - 102; **Receiving** - Gray 2-36, Anderson 3-9, Tilley 2-25, Mitchell 2-11, Harrell 2-8, Green 1-9, Morris 1-4.

WEEK 11 GAMES

Det 27, Dal 24	Den 24, TB 7
Oak 33, Mia 17	KC 23, Hou 10
Clev 15, SF 12	Cinc 24, LA 10
Minn 20, NO 10	GB 21, Chi 17
NYJ 17, NE 6	Pitt 34, Atl 20
Sea 44, SD 23	Phil 38, Balt 13
Wash 30, NYG 27 (OT)	

NOTES

• Joe Ferguson threw four interceptions for the second week in a row. The loss dropped Buffalo to third in the AFC East. Ferguson did surpass 20,000 career passing yards, the 30th NFL player to do it.
• The Cardinals had allowed a league-worst 303 points entering the game.
• O.J. Anderson rushed for 177 yards, the second-highest yield by a Bills defense behind only Jim Nance's 185 for Boston in 1967.
• Curtis Brown stopped the Bills' first drive with a fumble at the St. Louis 30, recovered by Ken Greene.
• Neil Lomax hit Mel Gray for 28 yards to set up Neil O'Donoghue's field goal.
• The Cards drove 75 yards in seven plays in the second quarter to make it 10-0 on Stump Mitchell's two-yard TD reception. Anderson had a 20-yard run and Chris Keating a 15-yard personal-foul penalty in the march.
• The Bills blew another scoring chance late in the half when Greene intercepted Ferguson in the end zone. Brown fumbled at the Cards 21 on the opening possession of the second half, then Roy Green intercepted Ferguson in the end zone later in the third.
• Greene's second interception and 47-yard return to the Bills 22 set up Anderson's 18-yard TD two plays later. After a Bills fake punt was stopped, the Cards drove 56 yards to the final score.

QUOTES

• Phil Villapiano: "I'm very disappointed. You're allowed to have a couple of games like this, but usually they happen in the early going. This is the stretch drive. Good teams win during this time and losing teams don't. During this period you shouldn't need anybody to spur you on. We need those second efforts and intimidating hits. That's Bills football."
• Joe Ferguson: "This puts us on the edge of a hole. We can't afford to lose another game. This was one of the most disappointing losses I've gone through. I've been there before. I threw the ball, I take the blame for them (interceptions)."
• Fred Smerlas on O.J. Anderson: "He's as quick as Tony Dorsett and as big as Earl Campbell. You try tackling that. He had us running all over the place."
• Jim Haslett: "I don't see how we can go from our best to our worst in two weeks. This was, by far, the best total team losing effort I've seen. I'm baffled. We played so well against Denver and Cleveland and I thought we were more than ready for the stretch run. Now, I don't know. It wasn't a case of singling out one or two players. Everybody played bad." (On Anderson): "He's the best back I've ever faced because he's so big and so damn quick."
• Chuck Knox: "We have no excuses; we did not play well offensively or defensively. I can't remember the last time we were outplayed this badly. I wouldn't say we have trouble with NFC East teams or any team in particular. When you don't play well and you have as many turnovers and mistakes as we had, you're not going to beat anybody."

Patriots	7	0	3	7 -	17
Bills	3	10	0	7 -	20

Attendance at Rich Stadium - 71,593

Buf: FG Mike-Mayer 28, 5:47
NE: Morgan 56 pass from Johnson (Smith kick), 12:45
Buf: FG Mike-Mayer 23, 5:32
Buf: Hooks 11 pass from Ferguson (Mike-Mayer kick), 7:40
NE: FG Smith 43, 7:13
NE: Hasselback 5 pass from Cavanaugh (Smith kick), 13:04
Buf: Hooks 36 pass from Ferguson (Mike-Mayer kick), 14:55

	BUF	NE
First downs	19	11
Rushing yds	185	116
Passing yds	249	181
Punts-avg	5-34.6	5-50.4
Fumbles-lost	2-1	3-2
Penalties-yds	2-20	4-33

BILLS LEADERS: Rushing - Cribbs 10-32, Leaks 19-92, Hooks 13-45, Ferguson 1-16; **Passing** - Ferguson 15-34-1 - 258; **Receiving** - Hooks 6-111, Lewis 4-84, Brammer 1-19, Butler 3-39, Leaks 1-5.

PATRIOTS LEADERS: Rushing - Cunningham 18-57, Collins 4-5, Ferguson 14-59, Tatupu 1- (-1), Johnson 1- (-4); **Passing** - Cavanaugh 6-12-0 - 133, Johnson 1-1-0 - 56; **Receiving** - Morgan 3-141, Cunningham 1-7, Hasselback 3-41.

WEEK 12 GAMES

TB 37, GB 3	NO 27, Hou 24
SD 55, Oak 21	Cinc 38, Den 21
Pitt 32, Clev 10	St.L 35, Balt 24
NYJ 16, Mia 15	KC 40, Sea 13
SF 33, LA 31	NYG 20, Phil 10
Det 23, Chi 7	Dal 24, Wash 10
Atl 31, Minn 30	

NOTES

• Joe Ferguson completed a 36-yard prayer to Roland Hooks with five seconds left to give the Bills an improbable victory. The Bills began their winning drive on their 27 with 35 seconds left and no timeouts. On first down, Hooks made a brilliant diving catch for a 37-yard gain. Ferguson then threw the ball out of bounds to stop the clock with 12 seconds left. He called the Big Ben play where Hooks, Jerry Butler and Frank Lewis line up on the right side, run to the end zone and Ferguson throws the ball up for grabs. There were also six Patriots in the end zone. Linebacker Mike Hawkins got a hand on the ball and Hooks gathered in the deflection.
• The Pats had taken a 17-13 lead with 1:56 left when Matt Cavanaugh threw a five-yard TD pass to Don Hasselback, one play after Mario Clark slipped, allowing Stanley Morgan to catch a 65-yard pass.
• Ferguson then was intercepted by Rick Sanford, but the Bills defense prevented a first down and forced the Pats to punt, giving Ferguson one more chance.
• The Bills took a 3-0 lead on the first series on Nick Mike-Mayer's field goal after Roosevelt Leaks broke a 31-yard run. But after Mike-Mayer missed a field goal, the Pats went ahead on Andy Johnson's halfback-option 56-yard TD pass to Morgan. Morgan also caught a 20-yard pass in that series.
• John Smith missed a field goal in the second quarter and the Bills drove back to a Mike-Mayer field goal.
• Sherman White recovered a Tony Collins fumble at the Pats 33. Six plays later, Hooks caught an 11-yard TD pass from Ferguson for a 13-7 halftime lead.
• Hooks was in the game full-time because Joe Cribbs had been knocked out in the second quarter. Leaks enjoyed the best day of his career. Conrad Dobler replaced Jim Ritcher on the first series and stayed in.

QUOTES

• Roland Hooks: "Frank Lewis is the jumper in the middle. He tries to bat the ball to either me or Jerry Butler. I just happened to be in the right place at the right time. All I was thinking was 'Don't drop it.' I couldn't believe it, it was like what was going on wasn't real."
• Joe Ferguson: "I could see the whole season going down the drain. We had to hit two plays and one of them had to be far enough so we could try the Big Ben. That (Hooks' 37-yard reception) was the key catch of the day. Without that one, we wouldn't have had a chance for the last one."
• Patriots coach Ron Erhardt: "I don't believe it. I can't believe this happened to us."
• Patriots tight end Don Hasselback: "I thought there was a chance that we were going to win, but then again, this is New England and if it can happen, it will happen to us."
• Chuck Knox: "Luck is the residue of design. We had some luck, but a little luck is necessary to be consistent winners in the NFL. Frank was up higher in the air than anyone else, but it was actually Hawkins who tipped it to Roland."
• Patriots linebacker Mike Hawkins: "I'll see that play in my sleep all night. Plays like that have killed us all year."

STANDINGS: TWELFTH WEEK

AFC EAST	W	L	T	CENTRAL	W	L	T	WEST	W	L	T	NFC EAST	W	L	T	CENTRAL	W	L	T	WEST	W	L	T
Miami	7	4	1	Cincinnati	9	3	0	Denver	8	4	0	Philadelphia	9	3	0	Minnesota	7	5	0	San Fran	9	3	0
NY Jets	7	4	1	Pittsburgh	7	5	0	Kan. City	8	4	0	Dallas	9	3	0	Tampa Bay	6	6	0	Atlanta	6	6	0
Buffalo	7	5	0	Houston	5	7	0	San Diego	7	5	0	NY Giants	6	6	0	Detroit	6	6	0	LA Rams	5	7	0
New England	2	10	0	Cleveland	5	7	0	Oakland	5	7	0	Washington	5	7	0	Green Bay	5	7	0	N.Orleans	4	8	0
Baltimore	1	11	0					Seattle	4	8	0	St. Louis	5	7	0	Chicago	3	9	0				

NOTES

• Roland Hooks subbed for the injured Joe Cribbs and rushed for 109 yards and scored twice.

• The defense had a big day, causing five turnovers, overcoming a bad day by Joe Ferguson.

• The Bills drove 77 yards to score on their first possession as Ferguson hit Hooks for the TD. The Redskins marched right back to the Bills 32, but Bill Simpson recovered a fumble by Joe Washington.

• In the second quarter, Mike Humiston stuffed John Riggins on a fourth-and-inches play. The Bills punted, but a few minutes later, Mario Clark intercepted a Joe Theismann pass at the Redskins 37. Five plays later, Hooks scored.

• The Redskins answered that with a 71-yard drive to Riggins' TD run. The Redskins tied the game with 11 seconds left in the half as Theismann fired a TD pass to Art Monk after completing back-to-back 16- and 20-yard passes to Washington.

• In the third, Mike Nelms fumbled a punt and Rod Kush recovered at the Redskins 26. Two plays later, Hooks went 18 yards up the middle for the winning score.

• In the fourth, Sherman White stripped Theismann at the Bills 5 and Fred Smerlas recovered. With six minutes left, Jeff Nixon forced Theismann to fumble on a blitz and Rod Kush recovered at the Redskins 35.

QUOTES

• Jim Haslett: "How many big plays did we have? Five. Well, we had a goal last night to have at least three. We hadn't done that since the Cleveland game."

• Roland Hooks: "I liked it better when I was anonymous. Some guys like to be recognized in the press, but I don't really like it. I just did my job and the line got out on their men and gave us some running room. Next week Joe Cribbs will be back and I'll go back to returning punts and kickoffs."

• Redskins running back Joe Washington on the Bills defense: "They are tough. I'm sore, tired and beat up. Everytime you have the ball, they will stick you but good."

• Phil Villapiano: "You'll get those turnovers if you work your butt off. They come about when guys are hustling to the ball. We hadn't been doing that."

• Joe Ferguson: "The throwing game wasn't there. Washington had excellent coverage. I don't think I ever threw 18 more frustrating passes. I don't feel real good about the way we played. We should have had two more touchdowns, but we turned the ball over. We can't do that and win on the road the next three weeks."

• Rod Kush: "We have a new shot of life and it's coming from the young guys. They know we can play now."

• Redskins coach Joe Gibbs: "There were too many things for us to overcome today."

WEEK 13 GAMES	
Det 27, KC 10	Dal 10, Chi 9
TB 31, NO 14	Pitt 24, LA 0
SF 17, NYG 10	SD 34, Den 17
Oak 32, Sea 31	Cinc 41, Clev 21
NYJ 25, Balt 0	Atl 31, Hou 27
GB 35, Minn 23	St.L 27, NE 20
Mia 13, Phil 10	

Redskins	0	14	0	0	-	14
Bills	7	7	7	0	-	21

Attendance at Rich Stadium - 59,624

Buf: Butler 21 pass from Ferguson (Mike-Mayer kick), 4:40
Buf: Hooks 4 run (Mike-Mayer kick), 6:50
Was: Riggins 2 run (Moseley kick), 12:52
Was: Monk 25 pass from Theismann (Moseley kick), 14:49
Buf: Hooks 18 run (Mike-Mayer kick), 3:34

	BUF	WAS
First downs	18	19
Rushing yds	188	91
Passing yds	41	202
Punts-avg	5-35.4	3-41.0
Fumbles-lost	3-2	5-4
Penalties-yds	5-40	9-80

BILLS LEADERS: Rushing - Hooks 19-109, Leaks 13-50, Riddick 3-29, Ferguson 4-0; **Passing** - Ferguson 6-18-0 - 76; **Receiving** - Butler 3-38, Lewis 1-13, Jessie 1-15, Brammer 1-10.

REDSKINS LEADERS: Rushing - Washington 16-69, Riggins 7-6, Theismann 4-16; **Passing** - Theismann 22-34-1 - 220; **Receiving** - Warren 4-38, Seay 4-55, Monk 6-60, Washington 7-64, Metcalf 1-3.

NOTES

• In one of their most inspired performances in recent memory, the Bills rallied four times to defeat the Chargers, despite big days by Dan Fouts and Chuck Muncie.

• The Chargers had a chance to win, but Muncie was hit by Steve Freeman and fumbled and Rufus Bess recovered at the Bills 26 with 1:52 remaining. A few minutes earlier, the Chargers had driven to the Bills 35 but Muncie was stopped on fourth-and-two by Charlie Romes and Mario Clark.

• Muncie tied an NFL record by scoring his 19th rushing TD in the first, but the Bills tied the game after Clark's interception and 53-yard return to the Chargers 25. Joe Ferguson scored on a keeper.

• Fouts bounced back with a 17-yard TD pass to Wes Chandler to cap an 83-yard drive, but again the Bills came back as Ferguson hit Frank Lewis for 21 and Joe Cribbs for 19 to set up Roosevelt Leaks' TD run.

• Kellen Winslow turned a harmless pass in the flat into a 67-yard TD 55 seconds before halftime. A flag was thrown because the Bills were offsides, and Romes mistakenly thought the play was dead.

• The Bills took the second-half kickoff and Cribbs went 48 yards with a pass to set up Leaks' second TD plunge.

• After a San Diego field goal, Lewis caught passes of 33 and 21 yards, leading to Cribbs' go-ahead TD. Rolf Benirschke's second field goal in the fourth closed the scoring.

• Lewis set a team record for receiving yards in a season, breaking Elbert Dubenion's 1964 record.

QUOTES

• Chuck Knox: "Now that was a football game. I told you we'd come in here and battle them. They felt confidence all week. We had a pretty good idea we were going to win the game. This was a great game against a great team. You can't just shut down San Diego, you hang in there and play tough. This is what football is all about."

• Frank Lewis: "I had the feeling that Joe said to himself 'I'm going to go out there and do my own job and not worry about anyone else. I'm just gonna play as well as I can.' It was a different Ferguson. He was loose and I thought he had a different attitude today."

• Fred Smerlas: "Their offense is just so good, they have so much talent that you can't let one big gain get you down. You have to keep hitting them, wearing them down and hope they turn it over. Hey, we held them to six points in the second half."

• Chargers linebacker Linden King: "I'll tell you, they've got more people that talk crap on that team. I'm not impressed. They weren't physical. Coach Knox said they were going to kick our ass from sideline to sideline. But they weren't hitting. You can tell if you should have won a game and they know they shouldn't have won that game. What they don't want is to play us again."

WEEK 14 GAMES	
Hou 17, Clev 13	Den 16, KC 13
SF 21, Cinc 3	TB 24, Atl 23
Dal 37, Balt 13	NYG 10, LA 7
Mia 24, NE 14	St.L 30, NO 3
Sea 27, NYJ 23	GB 31, Det 17
Chi 10, Minn 9	Wash 15, Phil 13
Oak 30, Pitt 27	

Bills	7	7	14	0	-	28
Chargers	7	14	3	3	-	27

Attendance at Jack Murphy Stadium - 51,488

SD: Muncie 9 run (Benirschke kick), 3:22
Buf: Ferguson 3 run (Mike-Mayer kick), 13:06
SD: Chandler 17 pass from Fouts (Benirschke kick), 3:42
Buf: Leaks 9 run (Mike-Mayer kick), 6:24
SD: Winslow 67 pass from Fouts (Benirschke kick), 14:05
Buf: Leaks 1 run (Mike-Mayer kick), 3:54
SD: FG Benirschke 29, 7:13
Buf: Cribbs 1 run (Mike-Mayer kick), 11:23
SD: FG Benirschke 27, :49

	BUF	SD
First downs	19	28
Rushing yds	84	145
Passing yds	234	337
Punts-avg	7-37.0	4-33.3
Fumbles-lost	0-0	3-1
Penalties-yds	9-88	8-78

BILLS LEADERS: Rushing - Cribbs 14-35, Leaks 8-28, Brown 5-20, Hooks 1-8, Ferguson 5-4, Franklin 1- (-11); **Passing** - Ferguson 13-29-0 - 248; **Receiving** - Butler 2-19, Lewis 5-113, Cribbs 2-67, Piccone 2-24, Barnett 1-16, Leaks 1-9.

CHARGERS LEADERS: Rushing - Muncie 22-119, Cappelletti 3-21, Chandler 1-4, Brooks 3-3, Fouts 3- (-2); **Passing** - Fouts 28-42-1 - 343; **Receiving** - Joiner 7-106, Winslow 6-126, Chandler 7-60, Muncie 6-36, Brooks 3-9, Scales 1-6.

STANDINGS: FOURTEENTH WEEK

AFC EAST	W	L	T	CENTRAL	W	L	T	WEST	W	L	T	NFC EAST	W	L	T	CENTRAL	W	L	T	WEST	W	L	T
Miami	9	4	1	Cincinnati	10	4	0	Denver	9	5	0	Dallas	11	3	0	Tampa Bay	8	6	0	San Fran	11	3	0
Buffalo	9	5	0	Pittsburgh	8	6	0	Kan. City	8	6	0	Philadelphia	9	5	0	Minnesota	7	7	0	Atlanta	7	7	0
NY Jets	8	5	1	Houston	6	8	0	San Diego	8	6	0	NY Giants	7	7	0	Detroit	7	7	0	LA Rams	5	9	0
New England	2	12	0	Cleveland	5	9	0	Oakland	7	7	0	St. Louis	7	7	0	Green Bay	7	7	0	N.Orleans	4	10	0
Baltimore	1	13	0					Seattle	5	9	0	Washington	6	8	0	Chicago	4	10	0				

Bills	14	3	2	0	-	19
Patriots	0	7	0	3	-	10

Attendance at Schaefer Stadium - 42,549

Buf: Leaks 5 run (Mike-Mayer kick), 3:23
Buf: Cribbs 39 pass from Ferguson (Mike-Mayer kick), 10:25
NE: V. Ferguson 19 run (Smith kick), 3:35
Buf: FG Mike-Mayer 29, 14:11
Buf: Safety, Williams tackled Cavanaugh in end zone, 10:33
NE: FG Smith 42, 2:05

	BUF	NE
First downs	20	16
Rushing yds	192	97
Passing yds	137	107
Punts-avg	6-31.2	3-44.0
Fumbles-lost	1-0	1-0
Penalties-yds	6-48	3-15

BILLS LEADERS: Rushing - Cribbs 33-153, Leaks 5-24, Brown 7-18, Ferguson 2- (-3); **Passing** - Ferguson 10-18-0 - 151; **Receiving** - Butler 4-50, Lewis 1-25, Cribbs 3-48, Jessie 1-17, Leaks 1-11.

PATRIOTS LEADERS: Rushing - Collins 9-13, Cunningham 11-42, V. Ferguson 7-42; **Passing** - Cavanaugh 6-13-0 - 51, Owen 6-14-1 - 82, Johnson 0-1-0 - 0; **Receiving** - Jackson 5-47, Morgan 1-9, Dawson 2-22, Collins 1-8, V. Ferguson 1-20, Westbrook 2-27.

NOTES
• The Bills clinched at least a wild-card berth by getting past the pesky Patriots.
• Shane Nelson returned to the lineup but reinjured his knee in the first quarter and failed to come back.
• The Bills led 17-7 at the half, then possessed the ball for 18:33 in the second half to keep the Patriots from rallying. Mario Clark's interception with 4:03 left was the last time the Pats touched the ball.
• The Bills scored on their first two possessions. Charlie Romes intercepted a halfback-option pass by Andy Johnson on the game's second play and returned it 25 yards to the Bills 49. Eight plays later, including a 25-yard run by Joe Cribbs, Roosevelt Leaks scored on a short run. After a Pats punt, the Bills drove 81 yards in eight plays with Joe Ferguson throwing a 39-yard TD pass to Cribbs for a 14-0 advantage.
• The Pats drove 62 yards to get within 14-7 when Vagas Ferguson broke a 19-yard TD run.
• The Bills stopped the Pats on downs on the next series, then drove 58 yards to Nick Mike-Mayer's field goal. The key play was a 30-yard pass to Jerry Butler.
• In the third, Greg Cater pinned the Pats back to the 5 with a punt. two plays later, Ben Williams sacked Matt Cavanaugh in the end zone for a safety. The Pats closed the scoring on a John Smith field goal.

WEEK 15 GAMES
Det 45, Minn 7	NYJ 14, Clev 13
Dal 21, Phil 10	Cinc 17, Pitt 10
Mia 17, KC 7	SD 24, TB 23
NYG 20, St.L 10	Chi 23, Oak 6
GB 35, NO 7	Wash 38, Balt 14
Den 23, Sea 13	SF 28, Hou 6
LA 21, Atl 16	

QUOTES
• Bill Simpson: "They don't ask you how, they ask you how many (wins). This feels great. We worked like dogs the last four weeks to get to this spot. We deserve to be here."
• Jim Haslett: "It wasn't like last week, but it was enough to win. We didn't get as emotionally involved as last week. We got up 14 and we had a little emotional letdown. I think New England just said 'Let's not get blown out.'"
• Joe Ferguson: "We're in the playoffs and we're winning games, but we seem to be missing that little something. I don't know what it is, but I'll tell you what, if we ever find it, we're gonna win the whole thing. I think when we got up today, we kind of slacked off and didn't play as hard as we could. Fortunately we got some big plays later in the game. I really felt that people wrote us off after those two losses to Dallas and St. Louis. But we got together as a team and resolved to win five in a row. Well, we've got four in a row. That first New England game really brought us together. We were spreading apart. Thank goodness for another chance. A lot of maturity came to us after that game."
• Ben Williams: "We all knew we had to win this game. Now we can go down to Miami, play as hard as we can and relax. The pressure's off."
• Fred Smerlas: "That's a tough team, it's amazing that they've only won two games. They played today like they were going to the playoffs."
• Joe Cribbs: "Last year I was grateful we made the playoffs, but I was looking forward to the end of the season. I had kind of played myself out at the end of the season. I wasn't as excited as I am now."

Bills	0	3	0	3	-	6
Dolphins	7	3	3	3	-	16

Attendance at the Orange Bowl - 72,956

Mia: Vigorito 7 pass from Woodley (von Schamann kick), 7:38
Mia: FG von Schamann 22, 9:00
Buf: FG Mike-Mayer 31, 13:59
Mia: FG von Schamann 30, 8:43
Buf: FG Mike-Mayer 36, 5:51
Mia: FG von Schamann 33, 12:45

	BUF	MIA
First downs	15	18
Rushing yds	111	157
Passing yds	129	125
Punts-avg	5-37.4	5-39.0
Fumbles-lost	1-1	1-1
Penalties-yds	6-39	4-20

BILLS LEADERS: Rushing - Cribbs 19-94, Leaks 6-17; **Passing** - Ferguson 14-29-2 - 140, Leaks 0-1-0 - 0; **Receiving** - Cribbs 4-26, Lewis 4-59, Leaks 3-26, Piccone 1-15, Hooks 2-14.

DOLPHINS LEADERS: Rushing - Franklin 15-49, Woodley 15-52, Vigorito 4-29, Hill 13-27; **Passing** - Woodley 10-21-0 - 137, Hill 1-1-0 - 14; **Receiving** - Rose 3-69, Hardy 3-55, Harris 1-6, Hill 1-2, Moore 1-5, Cefalo 1-7, Vigorito 1-7.

WEEK 16 GAMES
NYJ 28, GB 3	TB 20, Det 17
Phil 38, St.L 0	Cinc 30, Atl 28
SF 21, NO 17	Chi 35, Den 24
Sea 42, Clev 21	Hou 21, Pitt 20
KC 10, Minn 6	Wash 30, LA 7
Balt 23, NE 21	SD 23, Oak 10
NYG 13, Dal 10 (OT)	

NOTES
• In a showdown for the AFC East division title, the Bills were outplayed and lost their 13th straight game at the Orange Bowl. The loss meant the Bills would have to play in the wild-card round.
• Miami controlled the ball for 13 more minutes than the Bills in the second half.
• The Dolphins took a 7-0 lead in the first quarter as Tommy Vigorito caught a seven-yard TD pass from David Woodley to cap a 58-yard drive. Woodley converted two third downs with keepers.
• Nick Mike-Mayer hit the left upright with a 27-yard field goal later in the first.
• After a near Buffalo TD, the Bills punted and Miami moved to Uwe von Schamann's 23-yard field goal. Woodley scrambled for 18 yards and hit tight end Joe Rose for a 33-yard gain.
• The Bills answered with a Mike-Mayer field goal to cap a 66-yard drive. Frank Lewis had a 27-yard catch.
• Joe Cribbs broke a 14-yard run in the third, but fumbled at the end and Bob Baumhower recovered at the Miami 21. The Dolphins then drove to another von Schamann field goal as Bruce Hardy made three catches.
• Woodley's fumble at the Miami 42 was recovered by Mario Clark and that led to a Mike-Mayer field goal, but Miami then embarked on a drive that consumed nearly seven minutes and ended in von Schamann's third field goal.
• Lewis set the Bills' single-season record for receptions with 70, breaking Bill Miller's 1963 mark, and Ferguson set the team mark for passing yards in a season (3,652), breaking his 1979 record.

QUOTES
• Charlie Romes: "We just lost the AFC East today, we're still in the playoffs. We just have to regroup."
• Jim Haslett: "We have to look at things realistically. I feel awfully proud. We came from 6-5 to 10-6 and we can look ahead to the rest of the year now. It's a one-game elimination series now."
• Joe Cribbs: "I think the fact that we knew we could lose took a little bit out of the game. It made us more soft than we're accustomed to. We just didn't play well."
• Joe Ferguson: "We had our chances. It's unfortunate, but it just didn't happen. The game is over, we've got to forget about it and start thinking about the playoffs."
• Phil Villapiano: "David Woodley reminded me a lot of Terry Bradshaw a few years ago. You think you have their offense stopped and his running becomes an offense all by itself."
• Jeff Nixon: "I think we play better after a loss sometimes. The season is starting right now. Sure we wanted to have homefield advantage but sometimes that can work against you. You have that extra week off and it's holiday time and it would be easy to get distracted. Now we know we have to get right back to work."

STANDINGS: SIXTEENTH WEEK

AFC EAST	W	L	T	CENTRAL	W	L	T	WEST	W	L	T	NFC EAST	W	L	T	CENTRAL	W	L	T	WEST	W	L	T
Miami	11	4	1	Cincinnati	12	4	0	San Diego	10	6	0	Dallas	12	4	0	Tampa Bay	9	7	0	San Fran	13	3	0
NY Jets	10	5	1	Pittsburgh	8	8	0	Denver	10	6	0	Philadelphia	10	6	0	Detroit	8	8	0	Atlanta	7	9	0
Buffalo	10	6	0	Houston	7	9	0	Kan. City	9	7	0	NY Giants	9	7	0	Green Bay	8	8	0	LA Rams	6	10	0
New England	2	14	0	Cleveland	5	11	0	Oakland	7	9	0	Washington	8	8	0	Minnesota	7	9	0	N.Orleans	4	12	0
Baltimore	2	14	0					Seattle	6	10	0	St. Louis	7	9	0	Chicago	6	10	0				

NOTES

• The Bills won their first playoff game since the 1965 AFL Championship Game as they raced to a 24-0 second-quarter lead, then held off a furious New York rally.

• Bill Simpson's goal-line interception of a Richard Todd pass intended for Derrick Gaffney with two seconds left sealed the victory and sent the Bills to Cincinnati next week for a divisional game.

• It was an ironic twist because Simpson was the man who was beaten by Ron Smith for the game-winning touchdown with 2:08 to play in last year's divisional round playoff game at San Diego.

• By early in the second quarter, it certainly didn't appear there would be any late heroics needed in this game. On the opening kickoff, Ervin Parker forced Bruce Harper to fumble and Charlie Romes picked up the loose ball and ran 26 yards for a touchdown and a quick 7-0 lead.

• A few minutes later, Wesley Walker dropped a sure TD pass and the Jets wound up punting. The Bills then needed only three plays to move 66 yards as Joe Ferguson threw a 50-yard TD pass to Frank Lewis. Lewis had found a seam in the Jets zone between Donald Dykes and Ken Schroy.

• Rufus Bess then picked off a Todd pass and returned it 49 yards to set up Nick Mike-Mayer's 29-yard field goal and it was 17-0 just 10:24 into the game.

• Early in the second quarter, Phil Villapiano stopped a Jets threat with an interception and the Bills proceeded to drive 59 yards to Ferguson's 26-yard TD pass to Lewis. Joe Cribbs' 28-yard reception was the key play on the five-play drive.

• The Jets finally showed some life on the ensuing possession. Mickey Shuler, who hadn't caught a pass in the regular season but was playing in place of injured tight end Jerome Barkum, caught a 30-yard TD pass on a post pattern to cap a four-play, 53-yard advance.

• Ferguson then got greedy and tried to build on the lead. He was intercepted by Greg Buttle who returned it 29 yards to the Bills 14. The Buffalo defense held and forced a Pat Leahy field goal.

• Still, with a 24-10 halftime lead, the Bills appeared to be in control, especially after they escaped the third quarter with the Jets trimming just three points off the lead. Buttle's second interception gave the Jets possession and they drove to the Bills 8 before stalling. Leahy kicked a 19-yard field goal to make it 24-13.

• Another interception of Ferguson, this one by Dykes, was neutralized by an interception by Simpson. Jerry Holmes then hijacked Ferguson for the fourth time, but the Jets failed to capitalize and punted. On the next play, Cribbs took a pitchout, scooted around right end and went 45 yards for the touchdown that seemingly should have killed the Jets. It was 31-13 with 10:16 left.

• But Todd needed only 2:46 to move the Jets 80 yards in eight plays to his 30-yard TD pass to Bobby Jones. The Bills went three-and-out, and Todd engineered a seven-play, 58-yard drive that ended with Kevin Long's one-yard TD run, cutting the deficit to 31-27. Fred Smerlas had sacked Todd on the first play of the possession and on the second, Mario Clark intercepted Todd. But the pick was nullified by an interference call on Clark against Gaffney, giving the Jets an automatic first down. Four straight completions led to Long's run with 3:44 remaining.

• The Bills went three-and-out again and punted and Todd stalked back onto the field starting at his own 20 with 2:36 left and two timeouts still in reserve.

• On the first play, Todd threw 29 yards to Shuler. He then fired a 26-yard strike to Gaffney. A couple plays later, faced with third-and-12 from the 27, Todd was intercepted by Steve Freeman, but again, a penalty on Clark, this time for holding, nullified the pick and gave New York an automatic first down. Later a seven-yard pass to Scott Dierking produced a first down at the Bills 11. An incompletion in the end zone to Shuler stopped the clock with 10 seconds left. Todd then tried to hit Gaffney four yards deep in the end zone, but Simpson intervened and saved the day for the Bills.

• The Bills defense registered five sacks while New York's famed Sack Exchange, led by Joe Klecko and Mark Gastineau, sacked Ferguson only twice.

• The Jets' 71 yards rushing was their second-lowest total of the season; Fred Smerlas had eight tackles and two sacks in perhaps his best game of the year.

QUOTES

• Bill Simpson: "People made more of that play (the winning TD pass by the Chargers last year) than I ever did. I made other mistakes and good plays in that game that people don't remember. But people remember the big plays at the end of a game and I'm just glad they're going to be remembering this one instead of the other one. I just read Todd's eyes and saw he was coming to Gaffney. I just stepped in front of him and the ball was right there. It was a hard-fought victory and a credit to our defense that we never gave up. We're one step farther than we were last year. I think that's important, especially for the younger players, that we've made some progress. I kept thinking about training camp and how far we had come since then. I knew we had to hang on."

• Jets receiver Derrick Gaffney: "It was right there, but Simpson made a helluva play to get it. He came out of nowhere. I thought it was a touchdown. If he had missed it, it would have been six points."

• Jets quarterback Richard Todd: "It was a great comeback, we just didn't finish it. The last play was just a bad read on my part. If I had seen Simpson, I would have thrown the ball out of bounds. I would have liked another chance."

• Jets guard Randy Rasmussen: "For a while there it was like the old Joe Namath days. We would come to the line every time knowing we were going to pass. The fans knew we were going to pass, the defense knew we were going to pass and there was nothing they could do about it. I never saw the play (the interception) but I knew by the silence that it was over."

• Jets linebacker Greg Buttle: "I don't feel like talking, I feel like throwing up."

• Joe Ferguson: "If we'd have lost this game, I'd have taken responsibility myself. I threw some bad intercep-

tions out there. I started out great and wound up out the back door. The trouble was we were using the same plays that we used in the first half and they were reading them."

• Charlie Romes on his fumble return: "I am the safety on the kickoff. My job is to not let anybody get outside. I saw the ball pop loose and it bounced right to me."

• Rod Kush: "We didn't have time to get scared. They just kept coming after us. Thank God for Charlie's kick-off return, although that seems like five days ago."

• Fred Smerlas: "Who is the Sack Exchange? We can rush the passer, too. I saw him (Jets center Joe Fields) after the game and said 'You're a great center' and he said 'Not today.'"

• Will Grant: "The New York Sack Exchange fell in New York. I thought whoever won the line battle would win the game. They got two sacks and we must have passed 40 times (actually 36). I think we won the battle. We wanted to try and redirect Gastineau. We put him on his back."

• Joe Devlin on Gastineau: "I have a lot of respect for him, he gave me more than my hands full. As an offensive lineman all I get (for reward) is the final score and that's all that counts."

• Ben Williams: "I knew we were going to win. But I didn't know."

Bills	17	7	0	7	- 31
Jets	0	10	3	14	- 27

Attendance at Shea Stadium - 57,050

Buf: Romes 26 fumble return (Mike-Mayer kick), :16
Buf: Lewis 50 pass from Ferguson (Mike-Mayer kick), 7:03
Buf: FG Mike-Mayer 29, 10:24
Buf: Lewis 26 pass from Ferguson (Mike-Mayer kick), 9:58
NYJ: Shuler 30 pass from Todd (Leahy kick), 12:13
NYJ: FG Leahy 26, 14:17
NYJ: FG Leahy 19, 9:38
Buf: Cribbs 45 run (Mike-Mayer kick), 4:44
NYJ: B. Jones 30 pass from Todd (Leahy kick), 7:46
NYJ: Long 1 run (Leahy kick), 11:16

	BUF	NYJ
First downs	15	23
Rushing yds	91	71
Passing yds	230	348
Punts-avg	4-43.8	4-33.0
Fumbles-lost	1-0	3-1
Penalties-yds	8-62	6-55

BILLS LEADERS: **Rushing** - Cribbs 14-83, Leaks 6-12, Ferguson 2- (-4); **Passing** - Ferguson 17-34-4 - 268; **Receiving** - Lewis 7-158, Cribbs 4-64, Leaks 3-23, Brammer 2-17, Butler 1-6; **Kickoff returns** - Brown 1-27, Riddick 4-73, Villapiano 1-1; **Punt returns** - Riddick 1-6, Piccone 1-5.

JETS LEADERS: **Rushing** - McNeil 12-32, Long 8-28, Todd 2-11; **Passing** - Todd 28-50-4 - 377; **Receiving** - Shuler 6-116, B. Jones 4-64, Barkum 2-41, Gaffney 4-64, Dierking 7-52, Harper 1-4, Newton 1-12, Walker 3-24; **Kickoff returns** - Harper 4-82, Sohn 1-28; **Punt returns** - Harper 3-31.

Frank Lewis had a great day in Buffalo's 31-27 wild-card playoff victory against the New York Jets. It was Buffalo's first post-season triumph since 1965.

Bills	0	7	7	7	- 21
Bengals	14	0	7	7	- 28

Attendance at Riverfront Stadium - 55,420

Cin: Alexander 4 run (Breech kick), 6:04
Cin: Johnson 1 run (Breech kick), 12:20
Buf: Cribbs 1 run (Mike-Mayer kick), 14:40
Buf: Cribbs 44 run (Mike-Mayer kick), 4:37
Cin: Alexander 20 run (Breech kick), 8:04
Buf: Butler 21 pass from Ferguson (Mike-Mayer kick), :08
Cin: Collinsworth 16 pass from Anderson (Breech kick), 4:21

	BUF	CIN
First downs	21	22
Rushing yds	134	136
Passing yds	202	169
Punts-avg	3-42.0	4-44.5
Fumbles-lost	0-0	0-0
Penalties-yds	6-56	5-44

BILLS LEADERS: Rushing - Cribbs 15-90, Leaks 3-12, Hooks 9-30, Brown 1-2; **Passing** - Ferguson 15-31-2 - 202; **Receiving** - Butler 4-98, Brammer 3-23, Lewis 3-38, Leaks 2-16, Jessie 1-12, Hooks 2-15; **Kickoff returns** - Riddick 4-68, Brown 1-14; **Punt returns** - Riddick 2-8.

BENGALS LEADERS: Rushing - Alexander 13-72, Johnson 17-45, Anderson 2-15, Griffin 1-4; **Passing** - Anderson 14-21-0 - 192; **Receiving** - Johnson 3-23, Ross 6-71, Curtis 1-22, Alexander 1-10, Collinsworth 2-24, Kreider 1-42; **Kickoff returns** - Verser 4-94; **Punt returns** - Fuller 1-2.

NOTES

• The Bills' season came to a heartbreaking conclusion and predictably, a penalty played a huge role in the outcome. With 2:58 left, the Bills had driven to the Cincinnati 20 and were poised to tie the game and force overtime after Joe Ferguson hit Lou Piccone for six yards on a fourth-and-three play. However, a flag was thrown just as the ball was snapped and the Bills were charged with a delay of game penalty, nullifying the first down and creating a fourth-and-eight. Ferguson then overthrew an open Roland Hooks in the end zone and the Bengals rejoiced, having earned the right to host the AFC Championship Game next week.

• Incredibly, the Bills had called timeout before the play to discuss their call. But Piccone and Ron Jessie weren't sent onto the field until 14 seconds were left on the 30-second play clock. Mark Brammer and Curtis Brown then ran to the sidelines. Chuck Knox said that substitution was made to try and confuse the Bengals.

• Cincinnati raced to a 14-0 lead in the first quarter and seemed on its way to a blowout, much like the Bills thought they were in for an easy day last week in New York.

• Mike Fuller's 27-yard punt return set up the Bengals at the Buffalo 41 on their first possession. Seven plays later, Charles Alexander scored on a four-yard TD run.

• Later in the first, Ken Riley's diving interception gave the Bengals the ball at the Bills 48. This time it took eight plays to position Pete Johnson for a one-yard TD run.

• The Bengals almost made it three possessions and three scores, driving to the Bills 9. But Ken Johnson sacked Ken Anderson on third down and Robb Riddick then blocked Jim Breech's 33-yard field goal attempt. The Bills were revived and they drove to the Bengals 28 early in the second quarter, but Ferguson tried to hit Roosevelt Leaks with a pass and was intercepted by Bo Harris.

• Late in the second, Ferguson lofted a perfect pass to Jerry Butler for a 54-yard gain to the Bengals 10. That resulted in Joe Cribbs' one-yard dive into the end zone 20 seconds before halftime.

• Early in the third, Cribbs sped around left end, broke two tackles and went 44 yards for the tying touchdown. However, David Verser returned the ensuing kickoff 40 yards and Mario Clark was nailed with a questionable 18-yard interference penalty. Eventually, Alexander weaved his way through the middle for a 20-yard TD run and a 21-14 Cincinnati lead.

• On the next series, the Bills lost Cribbs to a bruised knee.

However, they ate up the final 6:46 of the third quarter and scored on the first play of the fourth when Ferguson hit Butler with a 21-yard TD pass. The 14-play, 79-yard drive was keyed by Cribbs' replacement, Roland Hooks, who powered for 25 critical yards.

• But once again, the Bengals had an answer. They drove 78 yards in nine plays with Anderson passing 16 yards to Cris Collinsworth for the winning touchdown on a third-and-10 play with 10:39 remaining. The key play was a 42-yard pass to Steve Kreider that started out as a simple 10-yarder on a third-and-one call.

• The Bills began their final possession from their own 30 with five minutes left. Butler made a 17-yard catch and the Bills were awarded 15 more yards when Jim Leclair hit Butler late. Two more completions to Hooks and Mark Brammer left the Bills with second-and-three at the 20. But Hooks was stopped for no gain and Ferguson threw an incompletion before the fateful penalty.

• The victory was the first for the Bengals in the postseason.

QUOTES

• Joe Ferguson: "It's hard to accept because of the way we lost a chance to tie. You can blame me, you can blame the sidelines. We just didn't get the play off in time, that's all. I think we broke the huddle with 11 seconds left, which usually is enough time for us to get a play off. There was a lot of crowd noise and I had to slow my cadence, but usually you can feel when you're getting close to running out of time. I didn't sense it at the time, nor did anybody in the huddle. I didn't see any flag or hear any whistle until the play was over." (On the fourth-down overthrow to Hooks): "They double-covered the wide receivers and the tight end was covered. That meant the middle was open, that was the place to go with the ball. I tried to throw it over the linebacker (Bo Harris) hoping Roland could make an over-the-shoulder catch." (On his performance): "I thought I played pretty well, I tried my best, that's all I can do. I think we showed some character today. We were fighting them from the very start just to stay in the game. We had to overcome a lot of adversity just to be in the playoffs. I've said this before but I don't think our team has played as well as we could. Maybe this is a learning experience that will make us a better team next year."

• Chuck Knox: "We have made changes like that a lot of times this year. You try to keep the defense guessing. We just didn't get it done."

• Bengals linebacker Reggie Williams: "They were trying to play a waiting game, trying to confuse us. They were waiting to see what defense we were in and then they tried to get their people in. They waited too long."

• Jim Haslett: "At first we didn't play real physical like we wanted to. Cinci really came at us hard. We could have gotten blown away, but we fought back. I just think we started playing defense a little too late."

• Mario Clark on his interference penalty: "That's two weeks in a row there have been very questionable calls against me that could have turned the game around. When the ball is in the air, two people have a right to go after it. I can't remember the last time I got the benefit of the doubt. It's a game of offense, but let us play. He (Anderson) had a fine day. He was going to the right guys at the right time."

• Bengals coach Forrest Gregg: "The Bills were keying on Pete Johnson and that's why Alexander was so successful."

• Bengals running back Charles Alexander: "When you're in a playoff game, you tend to give a little more effort. This team has never won a playoff game and we talked about that during the week, about how important it was for all of us to give everything we had."

• Phil Villapiano: "You start to get numb to all the road games. After a while you start to get used to playing away from home just as you'd get used to driving your car to work everyday. I don't think anyone would have beaten us in Buffalo. You'd always like to be home. Sometimes the crowd can make the refs lean a certain way on a call. I was looking forward to a lot more. I would have liked to have gone all the way, but I've been around the league a long time and I've seen better teams than this one lose."

• Fred Smerlas: "They were so fired up because of the crowd and because they got an early turnover. It was tough for awhile. They were taking what we were giving them, bing, bing, bing, nice and deliberate and they had that guy Anderson back there hitting everything in sight. We had some lapses. We'd stop them on first down and then they'd get eight yards on second down. They'd make a perfect pass or we'd miss a tackle. It was like the Fairy Godmother wasn't with us. Two years in a row we've turned into pumpkins. Now we're still waiting for Prince Charming."

• Jerry Butler: "The only thing I can say is usually when I have a big game, we usually lose. I wish I could have contributed a lot more the whole season but I guess you play the role you're dealt."

• Frank Lewis: "It could have been worse. We could have never gotten here."

• Steve Freeman: "I don't know about the rest of the guys, but I'm going to go home (to Texas), jump on a tractor and go to work."

A t A G lance
1982

Jan. 19 – Defensive line coach Jim Carmody resigned to accept the head coaching job at Southern Mississippi.

Jan. 27 – Scouting director Norm Pollom said that 1981 first-round draft choice Booker Moore was completely recovered from Guillain-Barre Syndrome, which sidelined him the entire 1981 season.

Feb. 4 – A new professional football league, to be called the United States Football League, was rumored to be in the works.

Feb. 20 – NFLPA executive director Ed Garvey said that the centerpiece of his argument for a new collective bargaining agreement would be 55 percent control of gross revenues. Reggie McKenzie, the Bills player rep from 1974-78, disagreed with the plan.

Feb. 24 – George Dyer was hired as defensive line coach.

Eugene Marve came out of Saginaw Valley State in 1982 and made a surprisingly quick transition to the NFL and was a mainstay at inside linebacker during the mid-80's. Marve was second on the team in tackles during his rookie year.

March 1 – Tom Cousineau cut his ties with the Montreal Alouettes and became a free agent. The Bills retained his rights and could match any offer he received in order to keep him.

March 10 – The Bills indicated they wouldn't invite Conrad Dobler to training camp and expected him to retire.

March 22 – At the league meetings in Phoenix, the owners agreed to the richest TV contract in history, a five-year, $2 billion deal.

March 24 – The owners threatened a training camp lockout of the players. "If they have the right to strike, we have the right to lock out," said Jack Donlan, the executive director of the Management Council. Said NFLPA head Ed Garvey: "We're in for a helluva fight and we're ready for it."

April 19 – The Houston Oilers presented Tom Cousineau a five-year contract offer worth $3.5 million, including a $1 million signing bonus. It would make him the highest-paid player in the NFL. The Bills had three options: They could match the offer and sign him themselves; they could match the offer, then trade him to another team; or not match and get nothing in return for him.

April 21 – Chuck Knox reiterated that he would love to sign Cousineau, but it was Ralph Wilson's decision, not his.

April 24 – The Bills matched Houston's offer, then turned around and traded Cousineau to the Browns for a package of draft choices, including the Browns' first-round choice in the upcoming draft. "I was shocked by Houston's offer," Ralph Wilson said. "It was way out of line. I thought if it was anything reasonable, he would be playing for the Bills." Chuck Knox expressed disappointment that the team had lost Cousineau.

April 27 – The Bills were slated to pick 21st in the first round of the draft, but traded up two spots in order to choose Clemson wide receiver Perry Tuttle. The Bills swapped places in the first round with Denver and the Broncos got Buffalo's fourth-round choice. The Bills also selected San Diego State quarterback Matt Kofler (second), Saginaw Valley State linebacker Eugene Marve (third), Carson-Newman running back Van Williams (fourth) and Syracuse kicker Gary Anderson (seventh). New England made defensive end Kenneth Sims the No. 1 overall pick. Baltimore chose linebacker Johnnie Cooks (second) and quarterback Art Schlichter (fifth), Cleveland grabbed linebacker Chip Banks (fourth), Chicago took quarterback Jim McMahon (sixth), Houston took offensive lineman Mike Munchak (ninth), Atlanta selected running back Gerald Riggs (10th), Oakland tabbed running back Marcus Allen (11th), St. Louis took offensive lineman Luis Sharpe (18th), Philadelphia grabbed wide receiver Mike Quick (22nd), Green Bay took offensive lineman Ron Hallstrom (24th) and Miami selected offensive lineman Roy Foster (26th).

April 28 – On the second day of the draft, the Bills traded their fifth-round pick to Washington for eight-time Pro Bowl cornerback Lemar Parrish.

April 30 – Conrad Dobler had *Dallas Morning News* columnist Frank Luksa announce that he would not be playing football in 1982, but that he hoped to resume his career the following year. Chuck Knox was attending the Kentucky Derby and did not comment.

May 7 – A jury in Los Angeles ruled in favor of Raiders owner Al Davis in his suit against the NFL, which had tried to block his proposed move of the franchise to Los Angeles. Davis announced he would move the team into the Los Angeles Coliseum. NFL commissioner Pete Rozelle indicated he would fight all the way to the Supreme Court. Bills owner Ralph Wilson was disappointed by the ruling. "If our constitution and bylaws aren't legal, we have nothing. Just reflect on Buffalo. We have 15 years to go on our lease. That's a long way off, but we, or whoever owns the team at that time, could just pick up and move when the lease is up. I don't think that's right."

May 11 – The U.S. Football League announced plans to begin play in the spring of 1983.

May 13 – Minicamp opened at Rich Stadium and Joe Cribbs failed to report, insisting that the Bills renegotiate his contract. "Joe told me 'If they don't want to pay me, I'll do something else,'" said Cribbs' agent, Dr. Jerry Argovitz. "There's no doubt in my mind that he means it." Cribbs earned about $120,000 in 1981.

May 18 – Joe Cribbs expressed his desire to leave the Bills if a new contract could not be worked out. "If we can't get things worked out, then hopefully, they'll send me somewhere else," he said. "I'm sure some other teams would want my talent and would be willing to pay me what I deserve."

May 19 – First-round draft choice Perry Tuttle signed his first pro contract, but it was announced that second-round choice Matt Kofler likely would be lost to Calgary of the CFL.

May 25 – In a reversal of popular opinion, Matt Kofler decided to sign with the Bills for what was described as "first-round money."

June 3 – It was announced that Joe Cribbs would be asking for $1 million in salary, signing bonus and benefits for the 1982 season.

June 16 – Joe Cribbs indicated that he would consider playing in the fledgling USFL if his contract demands were not met by the Bills. "It's a possibility," Cribbs said. "I don't know how strong that league will be, but they signed a big television contract. That might be an option I would explore."

June 17 – The latest Bill to express dissatisfaction over his contract was Jerry Butler, who threatened to sit out 1982 if his deal wasn't renegotiated. "The way I've been treated, I really don't think the Bills care about me," he said. "They don't respect my ability. It's a bum contract, and they know it. It's not costing them anything to have me on the team. With the amount of money deferred, I'm getting no interest and I can't borrow against it or invest in things. I'm on a tight budget."

June 18 – Quarterback Joe Ferguson, the highest-paid Bill, said the team wasn't willing to pay for a championship squad. "It's just an indication they are not 100 percent willing to pay for a winning football team," Ferguson said of the contract disputes concerning Joe Cribbs and Jerry Butler and the trade of Tom Cousineau.

June 19 – NFL commissioner Pete Rozelle admitted that drugs were a problem in the NFL. Former player Carl Eller, a paid drug consultant to the NFL, said he believed 15 percent of the players in the league were "problem users" of cocaine. Mike Barnes, a free agent from the Colts who had numerous run-ins with ex-Bill Conrad Dobler, signed a free agent contract to play for the Bills.

July 15 – The collective bargaining agreement officially expired, but the Management Council said it would not lock training camps.

July 20 – Joe Cribbs said he would not report to training camp unless the Bills met his demand for a salary of at least $400,000 per season. "Joe Cribbs is a fine player, but if a player signs a contract, he should live up to it," Ralph Wilson said.

July 25 – Training camp opened at Fredonia State for rookies and free agent signees.

July 26 – Joe Ferguson said he feared an NFL players strike. He also said "The Buffalo Bills cannot win the Super Bowl without Joe Cribbs and Jerry Butler. They are two Pro Bowl-caliber players whom we have to have in camp."

July 29 – Joe Cribbs said he would skip training camp. "I feel I'm young enough to sit out the season if I have to." He also said that if he did play for Buffalo, he would give a half-hearted effort. "If they are going to pay me only 25 percent of what I'm worth, I'm only going to give 25 percent of my ability. That's my last line of defense."

July 30 – Veterans reported to camp and Joe Cribbs and Jerry Butler were no-shows.

July 31 – The Bills won their annual rookie scrimmage at Edinboro State, 12-0, over the Cleveland Browns. Fullback Booker Moore, the 1981 first-round choice, said it felt good to get hit for real for the first time in two years.

Aug. 7 – The Bills traveled to Green Bay and beat the Packers, 6-0, in a scrimmage at Lambeau Field.

Aug. 12 – Joe Cribbs' agent, Dr. Jerry Argovitz, said the Bills fans were to blame for his client's situation because "they are the ones who keep supporting a team that doesn't want to give them the best product it can. They are foolish enough to keep paying for tickets no matter what kind of team Ralph Wilson puts on the field. Wilson must think the fans are paying to see him sit in his luxury box."

Aug. 14 – The Bills beat Dallas, 14-10, in the preseason opener at Texas Stadium, as Matt Robinson threw a TD pass to Arthur Whittington with 39 seconds left. The teams shook hands at midfield before the game to show their union solidarity.

Aug. 19 – Ralph Halpern, the Bills vice-president and general counsel, said that Joe Cribbs could not become a free agent if individual negotiations didn't resume.

Aug. 21 – The Bills lost their preseason home opener to Chicago, 21-14. Rich Stadium fans booed the pregame handshakes by the two teams.

Aug. 23 – Joe Cribbs declared himself a free agent, but league officials warned that teams should not put in bids for him because he was still under contract to the Bills.

Aug. 25 – Contract talks broke off between the Management Council and the Players' Association and a strike became a serious reality.

Aug. 26 – Jim Joseph, the majority owner of the Arizona USFL franchise, said that Chuck Knox nearly became head coach and general manager of his team. Joseph said that Knox would have taken over the team after the 1983 NFL season. Knox denied the story.

Aug. 27 – The Bills defeated Washington, 20-14, at RFK Stadium as Joe Ferguson threw two TD passes. Gary Anderson fell to zero-for-three on preseason field goal attempts.

Aug. 29 – In what appeared to be a softening of his stance, Joe Cribbs said he would rejoin the Bills if they promised to renegotiate his contract.

Sept. 3 – Jerry Butler ended his holdout and reported to the team. "I was crying some inside when I came through the tunnel (before taking the field for his first practice)," Butler said. "I came to the conclusion that this was the best thing for me to do at this time. I still consider myself a pro football player by profession." It was reported that Butler's salary was adjusted from about $80,000 to $200,000 per season.

Sept. 4 – The Bills closed their preseason with a 13-10 victory over the Lions at Rich Stadium. Nick Mike-Mayer kicked the winning field goal with 1:35 left after rookie Gary Anderson had missed a 38-yarder in the second quarter.

Sept. 6 – Ten-year veteran defensive lineman Mike Kadish was among the players cut as the Bills pared the roster to 45. Also released were Gary Anderson, Lemar Parrish and Rufus Bess.

Sept. 8 – Joe Cribbs reportedly was going to end his holdout, then changed his mind when a Bills offer dated Aug. 25 was pulled back by the club. "I won't prostitute myself," Cribbs said. "I don't care if my career goes down the tubes."

Sept. 9 – NFL players decided against striking before the regular-season opener Sunday, but did not rule out a future walkout.

Sept. 12 – The Bills opened the regular season with a 14-9 victory over Marv Levy's Kansas City Chiefs before a sun-baked crowd of 79,383 at Rich Stadium. Without Joe Cribbs in the lineup, the Bills rushed for 101 yards, but Jerry Butler proved his worth with six catches and the winning TD reception in the second quarter.

Sept. 15 – The players decided they would go on strike Tuesday, Sept. 21, barring a breakthrough in negotiations over the weekend.

Sept. 16 – In a special Thursday night game on ABC, the Bills rallied from a 19-0 first-half deficit to pull off a 23-22 victory over Minnesota at Rich Stadium. It was their first win ever over the Vikings. Joe Ferguson passed for 330 yards and three TDs.

Sept. 17 – A number of Bills expressed their frustration concerning the impending strike. "Why can't somebody get off his butt and get the thing solved?" Isiah Robertson said. "It's sad that we can't get together. It doesn't say much for our country if we can't even settle something like this. But I think the players around the NFL are 99 2/3 percent unified. The handshakes and all that have helped solidarity, but a strike would be very hard for me to take. The guys I feel sorry for are the workers, the vendors here, the people who work here (at the stadium). I always have considered myself a fans' player and I feel sorry for them if a strike comes. The fans can be a bunch of jerks sometimes, but they deserve to see games."

Sept. 18 – Joe Ferguson expressed his anger this way: "I hope this (comment) goes around the world. I hope the owners get off their high horses and I hope the union will get off its high horse and settle this thing. There has to be a happy medium somewhere."

Sept. 20 – Green Bay defeated the Giants, 27-19, and immediately after the game, the players' strike officially began. "I think this will spur both sides," Green Bay wide receiver James Lofton said. "There'll be more urgency now. There didn't seem to be any over the weekend."

Sept. 21 – The Bills cut placekicker Nick Mike-Mayer and signed former Dallas kicker Efren Herrera. Eight-time Pro Bowl cornerback Lemar Parrish, who was a late training camp cut, was re-signed. Jack Donlan said that if enough players ignored the strike, free agents and rookies could be brought in to bolster rosters and the games could go on. He also said the owners were planning legal action to stop the players from staging their planned cable-televised, union-sponsored all-star games.

Sept. 22 – Rod Kush said the Bills were firmly in support of the strike. "I think we are a solid team, one of the most solid in the league. I don't think one person on this team voted against the strike. We're hoping it won't last long, we're hoping this isn't going to be a lost season."

Sept. 23 – The first NFL game was canceled because of the strike. Atlanta was supposed to play in Kansas City on ABC, so the network aired the movie *The Cheap Detective* instead.

Sept. 26 – Representatives of the Management Council and Players' Association met in New York and the players refused to budge on their demand of being guaranteed a wage scale, even when the owners offered a guaranteed $1.6 billion. While most NFL stadiums were empty on the first Sunday of the strike, Rich Stadium was packed as more than 70,000 fans attended a concert by The Who.

Sept. 27 – Chuck Knox said that despite the strike, his staff was still busy at work studying the Patriots, who were scheduled to visit Rich Stadium on Oct. 3. "We don't know what will happen, but we have to be ready," he said. "They might settle this thing Wednesday or Thursday and all of a sudden say 'Let's play.' The uncertainty of not knowing whether or not you're working for nothing is a problem." In Dallas, Shane Nelson underwent knee surgery to repair his anterior cruciate ligament and speculation was that his career was over.

Sept. 29 – The Bills held their first informal practice at Erie Community College South. A total of 41 players showed up for the workout, including disgruntled holdout running back Joe Cribbs. "I am not officially back," Cribbs said. "As long as the guys are working out without coaches or management, I don't feel like I'm giving in." Reggie McKenzie said he was glad Cribbs decided to come in. "We accomplished something the owner, the general manager and the owner's lawyer couldn't do. We got Joe Cribbs to practice." Cribbs was convinced to come to Buffalo by Phil Villapiano who told him "You're on strike, we're on strike, at least work out with us." Lou Piccone, the Bills player rep, was not disappointed that eight players didn't show up. "The guys are here because they want to be here," Piccone said. "We can't make anyone do anything."

Oct. 2 – The two sides had been meeting, but talks broke off again with no word on when they might resume. Jack Donlan of the Management Council said: "We're at a terrible impasse. We've asked them every way we know how for mediation. We obviously need a third party."

Oct. 7 – Ed Garvey, the leader of the Players' Association, said the season would not be canceled. "When the owners figure out how much money they're losing from the strike, how much it's costing them not to play the games, that is when they'll start to negotiate."

Oct. 11 – The two sides met in Washington with federal mediator Kay McMurray with the intention of choosing a mediator to help reach an agreement. NFL commissioner Pete Rozelle said the season would have to be at least 12 games long to be considered credible.

Oct. 12 – San Francisco attorney Sam Kagel was named as the mediator and his first order of business was to get both sides to stop talking to the media. NBC decided that it would not air Canadian Football League games in place of NFL games on Sundays because the ratings were terrible.

Oct. 17 – The Players' Association conducted the first of two weekend all-star games. Ten Bills – Jim Ritcher, Jon Borchardt, Lou Piccone, Greg Cater, Fred Smerlas, Jim Haslett, Ken Johnson, Tim Vogler, Bill Simpson and Sherman White –played for the American Conference East squad, which lost to the National Conference East, 23-22. Washington's Mark Moseley kicked the game-winning field goal with 1:01 left to play. The game was played before a sparse crowd of 8,760 at RFK Stadium in Washington.

Oct. 18 – The second all-star game was played in front of 5,331 at the Los Angeles Coliseum and the American Conference West downed the National Conference West, 31-27. Turner Broadcasting System televised both games on its Superstation, but lost an estimated $800,000 on the two telecasts.

Oct. 19 – The Management Council withdrew its offer of a $1.6 billion package, saying that the offer was no longer valid because the owners had lost substantial amounts of money due to the strike.

Oct. 20 – A U.S. Court of Appeals reversed a lower court decision and ruled that NFL teams may bring lawsuits in state courts to stop striking players from participating in union-sponsored all-star games. Ed Garvey said that all 18 remaining planned all-star games would likely be canceled as a result.

Oct. 24 – The 28 player reps met in Washington

and voted unanimously to continue support of the union.

Oct. 25 – Jerry Jones, publisher of *The Drugstore List Draft Ratings*, a draftnik publication, speculated that the Bills might choose University of Pittsburgh quarterback Dan Marino in the first round of the 1983 draft because Joe Ferguson was in "the twilight years of his career."

Oct. 26 – The sixth weekend of games was officially called off by the owners and commissioner Pete Rozelle said that perhaps a season with less than 12 games might still work. Some of the Bills began to question the strike. "At first we were real solid, we had a lot of unity and everyone was sticking together," rookie Perry Tuttle said. "Now, everyone is going their own way, back home and all, and it seems like that unity is dwindling. I think if the camps opened, a lot of the Bills would go back."

Oct. 27 – Joe Ferguson expressed his dissatisfaction with the strike. "I'm thinking about next year," he said. "No matter what management says or what the union says, this season is over. I'm mad at the Management Council because it hasn't bargained in good faith, I'm mad at the union for asking for ridiculous things. To ask 1,500 players to quit for the whole season just doesn't make any sense. We should go in there and play and let them negotiate."

Oct. 29 – The union filed an unfair labor practice charge with the NLRB against the owners, saying Jack Donlan and Raiders owner Al Davis tried to bargain directly with striking players.

Oct. 30 – Talks resumed in New York after a one-week stalemate.

Oct. 31 – The owners offered a $1.28 billion package which seemed to spark hope.

Nov. 3 – The owners called off the seventh weekend of games.

Nov. 5 – Angered by the union's inability to budge,

the owners' representatives almost walked out of negotiations, but mediator Sam Kagel stopped them.

Nov. 7 – Sam Kagel returned to his home in San Francisco, unable to bring the sides together.

Nov. 12 – The Bills met and about 25 players showed up. Their support for the strike had dwindled. It was reported that the Bills were one of eight teams that no longer backed the union, but assistant player rep Mark Brammer denied that charge. Steve Freeman left the meeting angry and told a reporter: "Tell everyone in this town I'm not in the union. I don't want anything to do with those people." Said Jeff Nixon: "There are a lot of emotions right now. Things are getting tense."

Nov. 14 – The owners made what they said would be their final offer, four years at $1.313 billion.

Nov. 16 – The end of the 57-day strike came when the two sides agreed on a five-year deal worth $1.6 billion, about $1.28 billion for 1983-86 and $300 million for the shortened 1982 season. The minimum salary structure was $30,000 in 1982, $40,000 in '83 and '84 and $50,000 in '85 and '86. As far as wage scale, it was determined that $30,000 would be the minimum for rookies in '82, increasing by $10,000 for each year of service to a maximum of $200,000 for an 18-year player. In '83 and '84, it would be $40,000, increasing by $10,000 for each year of service and the minimum would be $50,000 in '85 and '86. It was determined that the original schedule would be used and pick up with games this weekend. That would leave a nine-game season with the top eight teams in each conference qualifying for the playoffs and being seeded by record. Joe Ferguson said: "I can't blame the fans if they stay away."

Nov. 17 – Joe Cribbs took his physical and seemed ready to come back to work, but then he stormed out of Rich Stadium frustrated because an agreement

still hadn't been reached on his contract. "What they are asking for just doesn't make sense," said vice-president of administration Stew Barber. "Basically there is no change, we're still poles apart." The Bills held their first practice and Chuck Knox was pleased. "It was football all the way," he said. "Our No. 1 concern is conditioning and of course, No. 2 is Miami. It's a short time to get ready, but it's the hand we've been dealt and we'll do the best we can."

Nov. 18 – The latest snag in the Joe Cribbs situation was that his agent, Dr. Jerry Argovitz, was not an approved agent by the NFLPA. In the new collective bargaining agreement, a clause was included that stated all agents must be approved by the union and Argovitz wasn't. Stew Barber realized the problem and broke off talks, which further infuriated Cribbs.

Nov. 19 – Finally, Cribbs joined the team and participated in his first workout. "I'll finish out this season under my old contract because I think that's best for my career, but I definitely won't come in next year if I don't get a new contract. Naturally, it'll take more money to sign me than it would have this year."

Nov. 21 – The NFL season resumed and Miami earned a 9-7 victory over the Bills at Rich Stadium as Uwe von Schamann kicked three field goals. The Bills turned over the ball seven times.

Nov. 22 – Fred Smerlas was disappointed in the crowd for the Miami game, the smallest since 1979. "The people weren't behind us as much as usual," he said. "We have to have that when we play at home."

Nov. 23 – Linebacker Shane Nelson acknowledged that his football career probably was over due to a chronic knee injury. "There's a very outside shot of me ever playing football again," he said. "The doctors were very up front with me and they told me I probably couldn't play again."

Nov. 24 – With the return of Joe Cribbs, running back Arthur Whittington was cut.

Nov. 28 – The Bills set an all-time record by allowing only 88 yards in defeating Baltimore, 20-0, before the smallest Rich Stadium crowd since Nov. 26, 1978.

Nov. 29 – Jim Haslett underwent knee surgery and was expected to be out at least two weeks.

Dec. 5 – For the third week in a row, the Bills played in rain, only this time the grass field at Milwaukee County Stadium turned to mud and five turnovers were costly in a 33-21 loss to Green Bay.

Dec. 6 – Joe Ferguson accepted blame for the Bills' offensive struggles. "There have been some bad throws, some dropped passes, some incorrect routes run in those games, a combination of things, but mostly it's been my fault," he said. "I have to take the blame for most of it, but three rainy games haven't helped." Ferguson reportedly lost $150,000 in salary during the strike and he admitted his outlook on the game was altered. "I made a big mistake getting so involved in the strike. Instead of just letting it go and not worrying about it, it got to a point where I was wondering if I'd still have a job."

Dec. 10 – A judge in California ordered the Raiders to return to Oakland for the 1983 season, using the eminent domain principle that could allow the city of Oakland to take control of the team from Al Davis.

Dec. 12 – The Bills turned in another brilliant defensive performance, limiting Pittsburgh to 94 yards, including minus-2 passing for Terry Bradshaw, in a 13-0 victory at Rich Stadium.

Dec. 19 – The Bills' playoff aspirations suffered a serious blow with a 24-23 loss at Tampa Bay as

Roosevelt Leaks fumbled at the Bucs' 18 with 36 seconds left.

Dec. 20 – The Bills traveled to Vero Beach, Fla. where they were going to practice for a week at Dodgertown leading up to the Miami game. "Let's put it this way, it's the bottom of the ninth, the bases are loaded, there's two outs and a full count. That's where we are right now," Isiah Robertson said. Said Chuck Knox: "We have to get our act together fast."

Dec. 28 – The Bills blew a 10-0 first-quarter lead and lost at the Orange Bowl to Miami, 27-10, putting them in a must-win situation in the season finale at New England. The win was the 200th of Don Shula's coaching career with the Dolphins.

Dec. 29 – Recognizing the do-or-die meaning of the upcoming New England game, Joe Ferguson said: "We have one more chance at it. If we don't get it (playoff berth), then we don't deserve it."

Jan. 2, 1983 – The Bills closed the season with a three-game losing streak, all on the road, as New England earned a 30-19 victory at Schaefer Stadium and eliminated Buffalo from the playoff tournament.

Jan. 8, 1983 – The NFL's unique, strike-imposed playoff tournament began with first-round games. Washington beat Detroit, 31-7, Green Bay routed St. Louis, 41-16, Miami beat New England, 28-13, and the Raiders downed Denver, 27-10.

Jan. 9, 1983 – The rest of the first round was completed as Minnesota rallied to top Atlanta, 30-24, Dallas defeated Tampa Bay, 30-17, San Diego overcame Pittsburgh on two Kellen Winslow TDs in the fourth quarter, 31-28, and the Jets ripped Cincinnati, 44-17.

Jan. 15, 1983 – In second-round action, Washington downed Minnesota, 21-7, and the Jets

upset the Raiders, 17-14.

Jan. 16, 1983 – Miami blew out San Diego, 34-13, and Dallas outlasted Green Bay, 37-26.

Jan. 23, 1983 – In the NFC Championship Game, Washington knocked off arch-rival Dallas, 31-17, as John Riggins carried 36 times for 140 yards and scored two TDs. Miami won the AFC Championship Game, 14-0, over the Jets, as linebacker A.J. Duhe intercepted three passes and returned one of them for a touchdown in the fourth quarter in the rain-soaked Orange Bowl.

Jan. 30, 1983 – MVP John Riggins set Super Bowl records with 38 rushes for 166 yards and his 43-yard TD run was the longest in the game's history as Washington defeated Miami, 27-17, to win Super Bowl XVII at the Rose Bowl.

Feb. 6, 1983 – The NFC rallied for a 20-19 victory in the Pro Bowl as Danny White hit John Jefferson with the winning TD pass with 31 seconds left.

Jim Ritcher (51) moved into a more prominent role on the offensive line in 1982. He and Ken Jones (72) anchored the left side, protecting quarterback Joe Ferguson's blind side.

305

BY THE NUMBERS - 1982

TEAM STATISTICS	BILLS	OPP
First downs	180	151
Rushing	83	64
Passing	84	72
Penalty	13	15
Third downs	57-129	34-112
Total yards	2,927	2,334
Avg. game	325.2	259.3
Plays	604	536
Avg. play	4.8	4.4
Net rushing yds	1,371	1,034
Avg. game	172.9	114.9
Avg. play	4.3	3.9
Net passing yds	1,556	1,300
Comp/att	149/273	114/256
Sacks/lost	12-115	12-82
Interceptions	17	13
Percentage	54.6	44.5
Punts/avg	35-37.9	44-39.3
Fumbles/lost	23-9	14-8
Penalties/yds	69-582	49-395
Touchdowns	18	15
Extra points	15-17	14-15
Field goals	9-18	16-20
Safeties	0	1
Kick ret./avg	36-22.0	34-17.8
Punt ret./avg	26-4.6	10-3.0

SCORE BY QUARTERS

BILLS	26	68	19	37	0 -	150
OPP	14	57	36	47	0 -	154

RUSHING	ATT	YDS	AVG	TD
Cribbs	134	633	4.7	3
Leaks	97	405	4.2	5
Brown	41	187	4.6	0
Ferguson	16	46	2.9	1
Moore	16	38	2.4	0
Hooks	5	23	4.6	0
Kofler	2	21	10.5	0
Whittington	7	15	2.2	0
Holt	1	3	3.0	0
TOTALS	**319**	**1371**	**4.3**	**9**

PASSING	COMP	ATT	INT	YDS	TD	COMP%	SACKS	RATE
Ferguson	144	264	16	1597	7	54.5	11-105	56.3
Robinson	5	8	0	74	1	62.5	1-10	132.0
Cribbs	0	1	1	0	0	00.0	0-0	39.6
TOTALS	**149**	**273**	**17**	**1671**	**8**	**54.6**	**12-115**	**57.3**

KICKING	1-19	20-29	30-39	40-49	50+	TOT	PAT	PTS
Herrera	2-2	0-1	2-4	4-7	0-0	8-14	11-12	35
Mike-Mayer	0-0	1-2	0-0	0-2	0-0	1-4	4-5	7
TOTALS	**2-2**	**1-3**	**2-4**	**4-9**	**0-0**	**9-18**	**15-17**	**42**

PUNTING	NO	AVG	LG	In 20	BL
Cater	35	37.9	61	13	0

RECEIVING	CAT	YDS	AVG	TD
Lewis	28	443	15.8	2
Butler	26	336	12.9	4
Brammer	25	225	9.0	2
Cribbs	13	99	7.6	0
Leaks	13	91	7.0	0
Piccone	12	140	11.7	0
Mosley	9	96	10.7	0
Tuttle	7	107	15.3	0
Brown	6	38	6.3	0
Holt	4	45	11.3	0
Barnett	4	39	9.8	0
Moore	1	8	8.0	0
Haslett	1	4	4.0	0
TOTALS	**149**	**1671**	**11.2**	**8**

DEFENSIVE STATISTICAL LEADERS

TACKLES: B. Simpson 44 primary - 21 assists - 65 total, Marve 42-21-63, Freeman 41-21-62, Romes 35-13-48, Robertson 26-20-46, B. Williams 30-16-46, Haslett 31-14-45, Smerlas 23-21-44, Parker 26-14-40, Keating 27-9-36, White 27-8-35, Clark 27-3-30, Kush 17-11-28

SACKS: White 4, B. Williams 4, Smerlas 2,

FUMBLE RECOVERIES: Smerlas 2, Marve 1, B. Williams 1, Freeman 1, Parker 1, Clark 1, Sanford 1

FORCED FUMBLES: Marve 2, Romes 2

INTERCEPTIONS: Simpson 4-45 yards, 11.3 avg., 0 TD; Freeman 3-27, 9.0, 0 TD

SPECIAL TEAMS STATISTICAL LEADERS

KICKOFF RETURNS: Mosley 18-487, 27.1, 0 TD; Holt 7-156, 22.3, 0 TD

PUNT RETURNS: Mosley 11-51, 5.5, 0 TD; Holt 10-45, 4.5, 0 TD

Frank Lewis led the Bills in receptions and receiving yards during the strike-shortened 1982 season.

GAME 1 - Sunday, Sept. 12, 1982 - BILLS 14, CHIEFS 9

Chiefs	3	3	0	3	-	9
Bills	7	7	0	0	-	14

Attendance at Rich Stadium - 79,383

KC: FG Lowery 39, 3:27
Buf: Lewis 20 pass from Ferguson (Mike-Mayer kick), 11:23
KC: FG Lowery 47, 3:05
Buf: Butler 6 pass from Ferguson (Mike-Mayer kick), 14:23
KC: FG Lowery 42, 5:12

	BUF	KC
First downs	17	17
Rushing yds	101	104
Passing yds	158	125
Punts-avg	6-41.0	4-36.8
Fumbles-lost	2-0	1-1
Penalties-yds	8-68	2-15

BILLS LEADERS: **Rushing** - Brown 13-50, Leaks 7-25, Whittington 6-13, Moore 3-4, Ferguson 5-9; **Passing** - Ferguson 18-31-0 - 166; **Receiving** - Butler 6-51, Mosley 1-5, Brammer 2-15, Lewis 3-58, Tuttle 2-35, Brown 1-3, Piccone 1-6, Leaks 2-13.

CHIEFS LEADERS: **Rushing** - Delaney 13-38, B. Jackson 12-53, Bledsoe 3-9, Kenney 1-4; **Passing** - Kenney 14-30-1 - 149; **Receiving** - Carson 4-26, Marshall 5-69, Delaney 1-4, Hancock 1-15, Rome 1-9, B. Jackson 1-13, Scott 1-13.

NOTES

• The Bills opened the season without Joe Cribbs in the backfield, but still defeated Marv Levy's Chiefs.
• The Chiefs drove 59 yards on their opening possession to Nick Lowery's first field goal, the key play a 24-yard interference call against Charlie Romes.
• The Bills then ate up the next 7:47, moving 81 yards in 16 plays to Joe Ferguson's TD pass to Frank Lewis. Ferguson converted four third downs with passes, including a 12-yarder to Jerry Butler and the TD pass to Lewis, which came on third-and-10.
• The Chiefs answered that with a 14-play, 54-yard drive that netted Lowery's second field goal. Billy Jackson gained two yards on fourth-and-one from the Bills 29.
• The Bills took a 14-6 halftime lead as Ferguson executed the two-minute offense to perfection. He needed only 1:16 to go 52 yards in eight plays before hitting Butler for a TD. He hit Butler for 20 yards and Perry Tuttle for 26 on a third-and-15. But the biggest play was an illegal-contact penalty on Lloyd Burruss that wiped out a Gary Spani interception.
• The Chiefs pulled within 14-9 in the fourth on another Lowery field goal.

WEEK 1 GAMES

LAR 23, SF 17	Clev 21, Sea 7
Mia 45, NYJ 28	St.L 21, NO 7
GB 35, Rams 23	NE 24, Balt 13
Atl 16, NYG 14	Minn 17, TB 10
SD 23, Den 3	Det 17, Chi 10
Cinc 27, Hou 6	Pitt 36, Dal 28
Wash 37, Phil 34 (OT)	

• Shane Nelson reinjured his knee that had forced him to miss the entire preseason and much of 1981.

QUOTES

• Chuck Knox: "What we had was precisely the kind of game we expected. The football was tough and hard-nosed. Butler certainly proved what a player of that magnitude can do even when he hasn't been in camp but a few days."
• Jerry Butler: "I'm always setting goals, but after Coach Knox told me I would start, I wanted to show him that he didn't make a mistake. He's a players' coach and that's what makes him a winning coach. I had to make them (teammates) forget about what happened and I felt if I went out and did well, they'd forget about the negative things and think about the positive things. The holdout was something that I had to do for Jerry Butler. I feel great being here because I feel like I'm needed."
• Joe Ferguson on Butler: "Here's a guy who misses our entire training camp and they are double-teaming him. That says a lot about what he can do for us and it really opened things up for the other guys."
• Reggie McKenzie on Butler: "He made the difference today. He's a good football player who you have to take care of monetarily."
• Chiefs coach Marv Levy: "The whole gist of the game was our inability to stop Ferguson in the first half. We put him in third-down situations, but he'd get out of it. I have a lot of respect for that young man. They did an excellent job of ball control in the second half."
• Shane Nelson on his troublesome knee: "I have a very big decision to make."

GAME 2 - Thursday, Sept. 16, 1982 - BILLS 23, VIKINGS 22

Vikings	2	17	3	0	-	22
Bills	0	7	6	10	-	23

Attendance at Rich Stadium - 77,753

Min: Safety: Mullaney tackled Moore in end zone, 13:47
Min: Bruer 22 pass from Kramer (Danmeier kick), 2:04
Min: Bruer 2 pass from Kramer (Danmeier kick), 5:41
Min: FG Danmeier 43, 12:39
Buf: Lewis 6 pass from Ferguson (Mike-Mayer kick), 14:46
Buf: Butler 4 pass from Ferguson (kick failed), 2:44
Min: FG Danmeier 42, 7:33
Buf: FG Mike-Mayer 21, :02
Buf: Butler 11 pass from Ferguson (Mike-Mayer kick), 12:12

	BUF	MIN
First downs	26	22
Rushing yds	134	113
Passing yds	317	258
Punts-avg	5-34.6	7-32.1
Fumbles-lost	5-1	0-0
Penalties-yds	9-88	15-117

BILLS LEADERS: **Rushing** - Leaks 13-82, Brown 12-54, Whittington 1-2, Moore 2-(-4), Ferguson 2-0; **Passing** - Ferguson 25-45-1 - 330; **Receiving** - Lewis 4-82, Brown 4-32, Brammer 5-53, Leaks 2-22, Mosley 2-21, Butler 7-111, Tuttle 1-9.

VIKINGS LEADERS: **Rushing** - Brown 12-93, Nelson 3-10, Young 1-2, Kramer 1-8; **Passing** - Kramer 20-46-1 - 265; **Receiving** - White 9-142, Senser 3-27, Nelson 2-38, Bruer 2-24, Lewis 1-14, LeCount 2-28, Brown 1-(-8).

NOTES

• The Bills rallied from a 19-0 deficit to pull off a thrilling victory in the final game before the strike.
• Joe Ferguson enjoyed his third straight 300-yard passing game on ABC nighttime telecasts.
• Minnesota was called for a team-record 15 penalties.
• The Bills possessed the ball for 20 minutes, 12 seconds in the second half, including 4:49 on the game-winning eight-play, 94-yard march that ended on Ferguson's TD pass to Jerry Butler. Frank Lewis made a 39-yard reception on third-and-one from the Bills 15 to keep the drive alive.
• Nick Mike-Mayer missed his third field goal attempt of the season early in the game, then Bill Simpson stopped a Vikings drive with an interception. After a Greg Coleman punt pinned the Bills back to their own 4, Minnesota took a 2-0 lead late in the first quarter when Mark Mullaney trapped Booker Moore in the end zone. After the free kick, Tommy Kramer hit Sammy White for 24 yards on a third-and-18 play to help set up his 22-yard TD pass to Bob Bruer.
• Bruer caught another TD pass after Greg Cater's shanked punt gave the Vikings the ball at the Bills 38. Arthur Whittington then fumbled on the next series and the Vikings drove to Rick Danmeier's field goal.
• Down 19-0, the Bills got a key TD when Ferguson hit Lewis 14 seconds before the half to cap a 69-yard drive.

WEEK 2 GAMES

Den 24, SF 21	Det 19, Rams 14
Hou 23, Sea 21	KC 19, SD 12
Phil 24, Clev 21	LAR 38, Atl 14
Wash 21, TB 13	Mia 24, Balt 20
Dal 24, St.L 7	NO 10, Chi 0
NYJ 31, NE 7	GB 27, NYG 19
Pitt 26, Cinc 20 (OT)	

The Bills drove 81 yards after the second-half kickoff to Butler's first TD. All seven of his catches came in the second half. Mike-Mayer continued his struggles, missing the PAT.
• After an exchange of field goals, Buffalo's coming after a 76-yard drive that consumed 7:20, the Bills put together the winning march.

QUOTES

• Joe Ferguson on the third-and-one pass to Lewis: "Frank had the option to run a post or a corner. He made a good run and I laid the ball up and he made a great catch. I think that was the biggest play of the game. I was a little surprised when the play came in, but they were expecting a run." (On the fourth-and-one gamble from their own 30 during the drive to Mike-Mayer's field goal): "I was surprised at that call with that much time left. You know how conservative Coach Knox is. When he called it I said 'Geez!'" (On the play of Curtis Brown): "He worked all offseason on catching the ball and that really tells me something about him. He made some really big catches."
• Curtis Brown: "This is the best I've ever felt here. I don't want to alibi, but I haven't been healthy at any time. It's tough to hang on to the ball when you're not physically right. I didn't have a good season (in 1981) and I know it. This is the best Buffalo team I've ever been on."
• Chuck Knox: "I was proud of the way we came back after making all those mistakes." (On his two gambling play calls): "We felt we needed to come up with some big plays."

STANDINGS: SECOND WEEK

AFC EAST	W	L	T	CENTRAL	W	L	T	WEST	W	L	T	NFC EAST	W	L	T	CENTRAL	W	L	T	WEST	W	L	T
Buffalo	2	0	0	Pittsburgh	2	0	0	Raiders	2	0	0	Washington	2	0	0	Green Bay	2	0	0	Atlanta	1	1	0
Miami	2	0	0	Cincinnati	1	1	0	San Diego	1	1	0	St. Louis	1	1	0	Detroit	2	0	0	N.Orleans	1	1	0
New England	1	1	0	Cleveland	1	1	0	Denver	1	1	0	Dallas	1	1	0	Minnesota	1	1	0	LA Rams	0	2	0
NY Jets	1	1	0	Houston	1	1	0	Kan. City	1	1	0	Philadelphia	1	1	0	Tampa Bay	0	2	0	San Fran	0	2	0
Baltimore	0	2	0					Seattle	0	2	0	NY Giants	0	2	0	Chicago	0	2	0				

NOTES

• It was a sloppy return to the NFL season for the Bills as they turned over the ball seven times including five interceptions for Joe Ferguson on a cold, rainy day.
• Joe Cribbs' return to action was marred when he threw an interception on a halfback-option pass from the Miami 11 in the third quarter. A.J. Duhe intercepted the pass intended for Roosevelt Leaks, killing a scoring threat, which proved critical at the end.
• Glen Kozlowski picked off Ferguson and returned it 36 yards to the Bills 49, leading to Uwe von Schamann's first field goal.
• Mike Mosley returned the kickoff 66 yards to the Miami 34 and eight plays later, Cribbs fumbled while trying to dive over the middle. The ball bounded free, but Ferguson picked it up at the 6 and ran into the end zone. New kicker Efren Herrera converted for a 7-3 lead.
• Miami answered with an eight-play, 58-yard drive that was keyed by David Woodley's 44-yard pass to Nat Moore. The Bills' defense held and von Schamann kicked his second field goal.
• Two Bills possessions ended in interceptions before the half, but newly-acquired Lemar Parrish saved Buffalo after the second pick, which was made by Gerald Small and returned to the Bills 15. Parrish intercepted Woodley three plays later.
• Robert Holt lost a fumble on a reverse early in the fourth. Kozlowski recovered and returned it 30 yards to the 12, setting up von Schamann's winner.

QUOTES

• Joe Cribbs on his interception: "It's a great play when it works, when it doesn't, it's bad. When I threw the ball, Rosey was open, but the ball hung up there long enough for Duhe to intercept it." (On his return): "Maybe the Dolphins expected me not to be in good shape, but throughout my holdout I worked out every day. I really thought I'd play half of what I played, but once we started moving the ball, Coach Knox decided to keep me in there." (On his fumble at the goal line): "I thought the play should have been blown dead because I was stopped, but the way things worked, maybe we should put that in our playbook."
• Chuck Knox: "The turnovers killed us. We controlled the game, we just gave them the ball too many times. Our defense held and held all day. We held them without a touchdown and you don't do that against Miami very often."
• Isiah Robertson: "We had the opportunity to score 25 or 30 points. And all we needed was three more."
• Joe Ferguson: "I don't think I was rusty, I threw during the strike. I just misread some coverages and there was the weather factor. The interceptions were my fault. I felt good, I felt prepared. But it will take two weeks to completely get back to normal. But there are no excuses."

Dolphins	0	6	0	3 -	9
Bills	0	7	0	0 -	7

Attendance at Rich Stadium - 52,945

Mia: FG von Schamann 42, :34
Buf: Ferguson 1 fumble run (Herrera kick), 5:12
Mia: FG von Schamann 29, 7:25
Mia: FG von Schamann 21, 1:51

	BUF	MIA
First downs	18	13
Rushing yds	132	122
Passing yds	126	127
Punts-avg	3-39.3	5-37.4
Fumbles-lost	2-1	1-0
Penalties-yds	9-64	4-30

BILLS LEADERS: Rushing - Cribbs 21-74, Leaks 7-30, Brown 4-18, Ferguson 1-7, Holt 1-3; **Passing** - Ferguson 12-28-5 - 140, Cribbs 0-1-1 - 0; **Receiving** - Lewis 4-50, Brammer 2-35, Butler 2-17, Mosley 1-7, Holt 1-23, Leaks 1-3, Piccone 1-5.

DOLPHINS LEADERS: Rushing - Franklin 17-77, Nathan 10-17, Woodley 1-29, Vigorito 2-8, Strock 2-(-9); **Passing** - Woodley 6-16-1 - 79, Strock 6-13-1 - 48; **Receiving** - Rose 3-58, Harris 3-18, Vigorito 2-11, Moore 1-6, Lee 1-5, Hardy 1-19, Cefalo 1-10.

WEEK 3 GAMES

GB 26, Minn 7	SF 31, St.L 20
NO 27, KC 17	Pitt 24, Hou 10
NYJ 37, Balt 10	Clev 10, NE 7
Dal 14, TB 9	Wash 27, NYG 17
Cinc 18, Phil 14	Sea 17, Den 10
Atl 34, Rams 17	Chi 20, Det 17
LAR 28, SD 24	

NOTES

• The smallest crowd at Rich Stadium since 28,496 watched the Bills play Atlanta on November 26, 1978, saw the defense turn in a record performance on another rainy day. The 88 yards were the fewest Buffalo ever had allowed, as were the 38 offensive plays the Colts ran.
• Jim Haslett injured his left knee and faced surgery.
• Roosevelt Leaks carried a career-high 22 times.
• The Bills took a 3-0 lead in the first as Efren Herrera capped a nine-play, 30-yard drive.
• It became 10-0 in the second when Buffalo went 69 yards in 10 plays to Leaks' first one-yard TD. Joe Ferguson hit Frank Lewis on back-to-back plays for 18 and 14 yards and Leaks gained 25 yards on six carries during the drive.
• Isiah Robertson forced Zachary Dixon to fumble and Sherman White recovered at the Colts 26 with 1:19 left in the half. Derrick Hatchett was called for interference on Lewis in the end zone putting the ball on the 1. Leaks scored two plays later.
• Herrera missed a field goal in the third and had another foiled due to a bad snap.
• The final score came on a field goal in the fourth after the Bills took possession at the Colts 43 after a punt.

QUOTES

• Joe Ferguson on the running game: "That's what we wanted to do. The coaches came into this game with three gameplans because the Colts are young and unpredictable. The weather was part of it because it's tough to pass in the rain. We knew early we wanted to run and it worked."
• Chuck Knox: "When you don't turn the ball over in the rain, you have something to be happy about."
• Roosevelt Leaks: "I guess I'm lucky to be out of there (Baltimore). The people up front blocking were the key. I took my time running and picking the holes. My performance was nothing personal against Baltimore, we just needed a big effort from everybody."
• Ken Jones: "We established the line of scrimmage early and once you do that, why change? This game really helped our line get our timing back and with such a short season, we'll need it for the stretch."
• Sherman White: "This was the greatest defensive effort I've ever been associated with. We were just ready today and the coaches had us prepared."
• Colts quarterback Mike Pagel: "We thought they had some weaknesses we could exploit, but we just didn't execute."
• Ralph Wilson on the small attendance: "It's going to take some time. It's going to take longer than baseball because the momentum is gone."

Colts	0	0	0 -	0	
Bills	3	14	0	3 -	20

Attendance at Rich Stadium - 33,985

Buf: FG Herrera 47, 14:41
Buf: Leaks 1 run (Herrera kick), 7:27
Buf: Leaks 1 run (Herrera kick), 14:40
Buf: FG Herrera 41, 6:24

	BUF	BAL
First downs	21	6
Rushing yds	245	36
Passing yds	67	52
Punts-avg	4-42.3	7-44.3
Fumbles-lost	0-0	1-1
Penalties-yds	10-79	5-72

BILLS LEADERS: Rushing - Cribbs 20-94, Leaks 22-90, Moore 9-38, Ferguson 1-7, Hooks 4-16; **Passing** - Ferguson 6-16-0 - 63, Robinson 1-1-0 - 4; **Receiving** - Brammer 2-19, Mosley 1-7, Lewis 2-32, Piccone 1-5, Haslett 1-4.

COLTS LEADERS: Rushing - Dixon 5-13, McMillan 8-16, Franklin 3-7, Dickey 3-0, Pagel 1-0; **Passing** - Pagel 3-17-0 - 62; **Receiving** - Bouza 1-13, Dixon 1-24, Dickey 1-25.

WEEK 4 GAMES

Dal 31, Clev 14	NYG 13, Det 6
St.L 23, Atl 20	Wash 13, Phil 9
Sea 16, Pitt 0	NYJ 15, GB 13
Rams 20, KC 14	Minn 35, Chi 7
NE 29, Hou 21	NO 23, SF 20
SD 30, Den 20	Cinc 31, LAR 17
TB 23, Mia 17	

STANDINGS: FOURTH WEEK

AFC EAST	W	L	T	CENTRAL	W	L	T	WEST	W	L	T	NFC EAST	W	L	T	CENTRAL	W	L	T	WEST	W	L	T
Miami	3	1	0	Pittsburgh	3	1	0	Raiders	3	1	0	Washington	4	0	0	Green Bay	3	1	0	N.Orleans	3	1	0
Buffalo	3	1	0	Cincinnati	3	1	0	San Diego	2	2	0	Dallas	3	1	0	Detroit	2	2	0	Atlanta	2	2	0
NY Jets	3	1	0	Cleveland	2	2	0	Seattle	2	2	0	St. Louis	2	2	0	Minnesota	2	2	0	San Fran	1	3	0
New England	2	2	0	Houston	1	3	0	Kan. City	1	3	0	Philadelphia	1	3	0	Chicago	1	3	0	LA Rams	1	3	0
Baltimore	0	4	0					Denver	1	3	0	NY Giants	1	3	0	Tampa Bay	1	3	0				

Bills	0	7	0	14 -	21
Packers	6	7	7	13 -	33

Attendance at Milwaukee County Stadium - 46,655

GB: FG Stenerud 33, 1:32
GB: FG Stenerud 25, 5:50
Buf: Cribbs 1 run (Herrera kick), 8:25
GB: Rogers fumble recovery in end zone (Stenerud kick), 12:06
GB: Ivery 1 run (Stenerud kick), 6:21
GB: Thompson 23 pass from Dickey (Stenerud kick), 2:36
GB: FG Stenerud 31, 4:03
Buf: Brammer 8 pass from Ferguson (Herrera kick), 9:03
GB: FG Stenerud 42, 11:59
Buf: Brammer 6 pass from Robinson (Herrera kick), 13:31

	BUF	GB
First downs	22	19
Rushing yds	142	106
Passing yds	194	195
Punts-avg	1-42.0	0-0
Fumbles-lost	5-3	4-2
Penalties-yds	3-42	4-25

BILLS LEADERS: Rushing - Cribbs 14-61, Leaks 9-36, Brown 10-45, Ferguson 1-0; **Passing** - Ferguson 14-29-2 - 134, Robinson 4-7-0 - 70; **Receiving** - Lewis 3-57, Mosley 3-51, Cribbs 2-16, Piccone 1-18, Tuttle 1-12, Holt 1-5, Leaks 4-26, Brammer 3-19.

PACKERS LEADERS: Rushing - Ivery 13-18, Ellis 11-18, Rodgers 5-28, Dickey 2-0, Lofton 1-30, Jensen 2-5, Huckleby 1-7; **Passing** - Dickey 14-23-1 - 195; **Receiving** - Ellis 3-31, Ivery 2-18, Lofton 3-42, Epps 2-26, Jefferson 3-55, Thompson 1-23.

NOTES
• The Bills again were sloppy, turning over the ball five times in the mud at Milwaukee.
• Ted McKnight fumbled the opening kickoff and that led to a Jan Stenerud field goal. On the first play after the kickoff, Joe Cribbs fumbled, but recovered. Two plays later, he fumbled again and Mo Harvey recovered and that led to another Stenerud field goal.
• Cribbs recovered his own fumble on the next possession, but then Ferguson was intercepted. This time, Stenerud missed from 22 yards. Late in the first, Curtis Brown lost a fumble at the Bills 49, but Chris Keating intercepted Lynn Dickey to get the ball back and end a horrible quarter.
• The Bills drove 58 yards in 16 plays, consuming 9:06 to take a 7-6 lead. Cribbs scored on fourth-and-goal from the 1 after Roosevelt Leaks and Brown had been stopped from the 1.
• The Packers took a 13-7 lead when Gerry Ellis fumbled. The ball was batted into the end zone by James Lofton and was recovered by Del Rodgers for a TD. The Bills had a chance for a field goal, but holder Matt Robinson bobbled the snap and Efren Herrera's 26-yard attempt was blocked.
• The Packers drove 60 yards in 11 plays after the second-half kickoff to Eddie Lee Ivery's TD.

WEEK 5 GAMES	
SF 30, Rams 24	Dal 24, Wash 10
Chi 26, NE 13	Pitt 35, KC 14
LAR 28, Sea 23	Mia 22, Minn 14
Atl 34, Den 27	Cin 20, Balt 17
TB 13, NO 10	St.L 23, Phil 20
NYG 17, Hou 14	SD 30, Clev 13
NYJ 28, Det 13	

• After another Herrera miss, Green Bay drove 80 yards in 10 plays to Dickey's TD pass to John Thompson. Two plays after the kickoff, Mark Lee intercepted Ferguson and returned it 40 yards to the 15, setting up Stenerud's third field goal.
• Ivery's fumble, recovered at the Packers 25 by Fred Smerlas, set up Ferguson's TD pass to Mark Brammer, and after Stenerud made another field goal following the on-sides kick, the Bills drove 60 yards in the final minutes to Robinson's TD pass to Brammer.

QUOTES
• Chuck Knox: "We didn't hold on to the ball and we didn't handle the mud very well. We work on ball security constantly. Every Saturday we hold wet-ball drills, something not too many other teams do. We work on it, but we didn't do it today."
• Joe Ferguson: "The ball was slick and the footing on the wet ground made it even tougher to move around. This doesn't mean I'm in a slump. If you think I am, I have to disagree."
• Packers coach Bart Starr: "It was a great win. I saw Chuck Knox after the game and told him we were delighted with the win, but I wish it had come at anyone's expense but his because he's such a classy guy."

Steelers	0	0	0	0 -	0
Bills	0	10	3	0 -	13

Attendance at Rich Stadium - 58,391

Buf: Leaks 1 run (Herrera kick), 7:49
Buf: FG Herrera 34, 13:05
Buf: FG Herrera 19, 8:36

	BUF	PIT
First downs	20	6
Rushing yds	184	96
Passing yds	155	-2
Punts-avg	5-29.6	9-38.7
Fumbles-lost	2-0	1-1
Penalties-yds	6-45	7-47

BILLS LEADERS: Rushing - Cribbs 30-143, Leaks 15-43, Ferguson 1-(-2); **Passing** - Ferguson 14-29-2 - 163; **Receiving** - Butler 5-70, Holt 1-10, Tuttle 3-51, Barnett 1-6, Piccone 1-22, Mosley 1-5, Brammer 1-1, Cribbs 1-(-2).

STEELERS LEADERS: Rushing - Harris 13-52, Hawthorne 3-21, Pollard 2-5, Stoudt 3-15, Davis 1-3; **Passing** - Bradshaw 2-13-2 - 3, Stoudt 2-10-1 - 29; **Receiving** - Swann 2-29, Smith 1-6, Harris 1-(-3).

WEEK 6 GAMES	
NYG 23, Phil 7	SD 41, SF 37
NYJ 32, TB 17	LAR 21, KC 16
NE 3, Mia 0	Sea 20, Chi 14
Wash 12, St.L 7	Det 30, GB 10
Minn 13, Balt 10	Atl 35, NO 0
Den 27, Rams 24	Cinc 23, Clev 10
Dal 37, Hou 7	

NOTES
• The Bills turned in their second straight brilliant defensive performance at home. The Steelers gained only 94 yards, the second-lowest total the Bills have allowed, behind the 88 gained by the Colts two weeks earlier.
• The Steelers' minus-2 passing yards were an all-time low for a Bills opponent, as was the one passing first down. The Bills registered five sacks and forced the benching of Terry Bradshaw.
• The Steelers were two-for-14 on third downs and committed four turnovers on a cold, snowy day.
• Bill Simpson intercepted Bradshaw on the first series of the game, but Efren Herrera missed a field goal.
• Herrera missed another attempt on the Bills' next possession. The Bills' third series began at the Steelers 30 after Jim Ritcher partially blocked a punt, but Dwayne Woodruff intercepted Joe Ferguson at the 2.
• The Bills drove 78 yards in 13 plays to Roosevelt Leaks' TD run, which came on third-and-goal from the 1. Along the way, Ferguson completed three passes to Jerry Butler for 43 yards.
• After a Pittsburgh punt, the Bills moved 40 yards to a 34-yard Herrera field goal. Ferguson hit Lou Piccone for 22 yards on third down to the Steelers 16.
• After Fred Smerlas recovered a Bradshaw fumble, Woodruff made another interception at the 2 to kill a threat with 1:01 left in the half. At halftime, the Bills held a 190-12 lead in yards, 13-1 in first downs.
• Charlie Romes' interception and eight-yard return to the Steelers 32 set up Herrera's second field goal. Leaks was stopped on third-and-goal from the 1.
• Cliff Stoudt replaced Bradshaw, but he was equally ineffective.

QUOTES
• Isiah Robertson: "That was the greatest defensive effort I've ever seen any team play, anywhere. It was our finest ever. The Buffalo Bills proved we are a championship-caliber football team today. It was a game we had to have with those three road games coming up. But this team hasn't jelled yet. If you like what you saw today, keep watching."
• Steelers coach Chuck Noll: "This game was like being in a foxhole in Vietnam. All defense, no offense, at least from us. Buffalo had their backs against the wall and they beat us. We didn't execute at all."
• Chuck Knox: "We certainly played better this week. We played hard and with more emotion."
• Reggie McKenzie: "For me, this game is like Michigan-Michigan State. Playing against Pittsburgh is our rivalry game here because so many of their fans come up here to see the game. During our meeting, I told the guys to get fired up because this was our big game of the year."
• Joe Ferguson: "This team plays better when there is emotion in this locker room and we didn't have any the last three weeks. We still have our backs against the wall because we have to win at least two of our last three, but we sure made some progress today."

STANDINGS: SIXTH WEEK

AFC EAST	W	L	T	CENTRAL	W	L	T	WEST	W	L	T	NFC EAST	W	L	T	CENTRAL	W	L	T	WEST	W	L	T
NY Jets	5	1	0	Cincinnati	5	1	0	Raiders	5	1	0	Washington	5	1	0	Green Bay	4	2	0	Atlanta	4	2	0
Miami	4	2	0	Pittsburgh	4	2	0	San Diego	4	2	0	Dallas	5	1	0	Detroit	3	3	0	N.Orleans	3	3	0
Buffalo	4	2	0	Cleveland	2	4	0	Seattle	3	3	0	St. Louis	3	3	0	Minnesota	3	3	0	San Fran	2	4	0
New England	3	3	0	Houston	1	5	0	Denver	2	4	0	NY Giants	3	3	0	Chicago	2	4	0	LA Rams	1	5	0
Baltimore	0	6	0					Kan. City	1	5	0	Philadelphia	1	5	0	Tampa Bay	2	4	0				

NOTES

• The Bills suffered a pivotal loss as Roosevelt Leaks fumbled at the Bucs 18 with 36 seconds left. The Bills were trying to set up the winning field goal. Lee Roy Selmon caused the fumble, Cedric Brown recovered.
• Of course, the game would have been tied, but Efren Herrera missed the PAT after the Bills' first TD. It came on their opening possession, a Leaks run that capped a 39-yard drive after Mike Mosley returned the opening kickoff 50 yards.
• The Bucs drove 88 yards in the second quarter to Doug Williams' TD pass to Melvin Carter.
• The Bills answered with a 49-yard Herrera field goal with one minute left in the half, but Williams completed a third-and-10 pass to Kevin House, then a pass-interference penalty positioned Bill Capece for a 27-yard field goal on the final play of the half for a 10-9 Tampa Bay lead.
• Bill Simpson's interception early in the third led to Leaks' second TD, but the Bucs came right back with a 77-yard drive to Gordon Jones' TD reception. The key play was a 42-yard pass to House.
• The Bucs drove 51 yards to Carver's TD run early in the fourth. Carver broke numerous tackles.
• Ferguson was intercepted on the next series, but the defense held and forced a punt. From there, Ferguson completed six of seven passes for 60 yards, then scrambled twice for the final 20 yards and a TD.
• The defense forced a punt, and the Bills began their final drive at their 45 with 2:44 left. After two first downs, Leaks ran 16 yards to the 18, but fumbled on the next play.

QUOTES

• Roosevelt Leaks: "Selmon made a helluva play, man, to come from the other side. He hit nothing but ball. I thought I had it wrapped up. With 30 seconds left, you just hold on tight. All I know is I saw the ball go and I thought 'I hope we get it.'"
• Chuck Knox: "We wanted to give the ball to our most secure ball carrier. It's a basic play. We wanted to run up the middle and kick a field goal."
• Joe Ferguson: "Anybody would have fumbled in that situation, Selmon put his helmet right on the ball. We've got a mature football team. We have a lot of veterans who know how to come back. It'll be a sad Christmas this week, but it'll make us prepare that much more for Miami."
• Reggie McKenzie: "We had a whole lot of opportunities. We missed an extra point we shouldn't have, we fumbled a few times and we had interceptions. A lot of people are at fault. That's why you call it a team. You can say maybe we would have won if Rosey hadn't fumbled, but what if we would have missed the (ensuing) field goal? I'm going to sit here and be sorrowful for a while. This one hurts because we were so damn close. I can still see that ball rolling on the grass. I'll see that ball for a long time. Now, we've got a helluva fight (for the playoffs)."

WEEK 7 GAMES

LAR 37, Rams 31	Mia 20, NYJ 19
NE 16, Sea 0	Wash 15, NYG 14
Atl 17, SF 7	KC 37, Den 16
St.L 10, Chi 7	Dal 24, NO 7
Minn 34, Det 31	Clev 10, Pitt 9
Phil 35, Hou 14	SD 50, Cinc 34
GB 20, Balt 20 (OT)	

Bills	6	3	7	7 - 23
Buccaneers	0	10	7	7 - 24

Attendance at Tampa Stadium - 62,510

Buf:	Leaks 8 run (kick failed), 2:08
TB:	Carver 2 pass from Williams (Capece kick), 10:24
Buf:	FG Herrera 49, 14:00
TB:	FG Capece 27, 15:00
Buf:	Leaks 3 run (Herrera kick), 6:03
TB:	Jones 2 pass from Williams (Capece kick), 10:44
TB:	Carver 13 run (Capece kick), 1:00
Buf:	Ferguson 10 run (Herrera kick), 10:55

	BUF	TB
First downs	21	22
Rushing yds	166	138
Passing yds	152	204
Punts-avg	2-40.5	3-45.3
Fumbles-lost	3-2	2-1
Penalties-yds	6-60	3-44

BILLS LEADERS: Rushing - Cribbs 13-49, Leaks 13-62, Ferguson 3-23, Brown 2-20, Kofler 1-12; **Passing** - Ferguson 17-25-3 - 168; **Receiving** - Butler 3-42, Brammer 3-22, Cribbs 4-16, Leaks 3-17, Piccone 2-38, Barnett 1-22, Lewis 1-11.

BUCCANEERS LEADERS: Rushing - Carver 20-89, Wilder 8-25, Williams 7-24; **Passing** - Williams 20-36-3 - 204; **Receiving** - House 4-69, Wilder 9-58, Giles 2-31, Jones 2-28, Obradovich 1-7, Carver 1-2, Carter 1-9.

NOTES

• The Bills blew a 10-0 first-quarter lead and remained winless at the Orange Bowl (0-15-1) since 1966.
• Joe Cribbs ran 62 yards for a TD on the Bills' first offensive play, the longest run of his NFL career.
• Four plays after the kickoff, Isiah Robertson forced a Tony Nathan fumble which Steve Freeman recovered at the 50. The Bills moved to the 25 but stalled and lined up for a field goal. Holder Matt Kofler bobbled the snap, but then ran nine yards to the 16 for a first down. Again, Miami held and Efren Herrera kicked a field goal to make it 10-0.
• Freeman intercepted David Woodley at the 4 to kill a drive and the Bills drove into Miami territory, but Herrera missed a 48-yard attempt. Miami then woke up and went 70 yards to Nathan's TD leap that was set up by Woodley's 39-yard pass to Jimmy Cefalo to the 1 in the second quarter.
• Miami tied it on its first possession of the third on Uwe von Schamann's field goal, with the key play a 23-yard pass to Nat Moore. A few minutes later, Robert Holt muffed a punt at the 2 which Ron Hester recovered. Two plays later, Andra Franklin plowed in for a TD to make it 17-10.
• Two plays after the kickoff, Lyle Blackwood intercepted Joe Ferguson and returned it 20 yards to the Bills 20. That led to another von Schamann field goal.
• Early in the fourth, Bob Baumhower sacked Ferguson, forced a fumble and Glenn Blackwood recovered at the Bills 6. Two plays later, Franklin scored again.
• The victory was the 200th of Don Shula's career in Miami.
• Eugene Marve was in on 13 tackles for the Bills, Ben Williams was in on 12.

QUOTES

• Chuck Knox: "It's a very disappointing loss. I take as much blame as anyone, it's my fault. There's a lot of reasons for a lot of things that have gone wrong. We just didn't get it done offensively, we played a very sloppy game. The defense tried to keep us in it. We have to come back next week and beat New England to get in the playoffs." (On Holt's muffed punt): "We have gone over it and over it that when your feet are on the 10, you let the ball go over your head. He's heard us say that many, many times."
• Joe Ferguson: "Nothing worked. We put in a lot of new plays and a lot of shifting, but they adjusted very well. That's the sign of a good team. If I knew what was wrong, I'd tell you. We just got beat by a good team. I have played Miami too many times, I knew they could come back (from 10-0 deficit). Yeah, I'm frustrated. We should be unbeaten and we're 4-4."
• Phil Villapiano: "I don't think we are capable of winning if we continue to play like this. I've never seen the Buffalo Bills this way in such a big game."
• Joe Cribbs on Holt's muff: "I hate to point to any one thing, but that fumble changed the momentum. Guys were hanging their heads after that."

WEEK 8 GAMES

St.L 24, NYG 21	GB 38, Atl 7
Phil 24, Dal 20	Clev 20, Hou 14
Cinc 24, Sea 10	Chi 34, Rams 26
SF 26, KC 13	TB 23, Det 21
SD 44, Balt 26	LAR 27, Den 10
Wash 27, NO 10	NYJ 42, Minn 14
Pitt 37, NE 14	

Bills	10	0	0	0 - 10
Dolphins	0	7	13	7 - 27

Attendance at the Orange Bowl - 73,924

Buf:	Cribbs 62 run (Herrera kick), 2:05
Buf:	FG Herrera 33, 10:44
Mia:	Nathan 1 run (von Schamann kick), 8:12
Mia:	FG von Schamann 35, 4:23
Mia:	Franklin 2 run (von Schamann kick), 8:17
Mia:	FG von Schamann 30, 13:14
Mia:	Franklin 6 run (von Schamann kick), 6:02

	BUF	MIA
First downs	17	17
Rushing yds	138	161
Passing yds	163	81
Punts-avg	4-40.5	5-46.0
Fumbles-lost	2-2	3-2
Penalties-yds	12-97	7-60

BILLS LEADERS: Rushing - Cribbs 19-108, Leaks 6-21, Kofler 1-9, Moore 2-0; **Passing** - Ferguson 21-33-2 - 199; **Receiving** - Lewis 4-60, Cribbs 4-36, Brammer 3-22, Piccone 4-32, Barnett 2-11, Butler 2-23, Holt 1-7, Moore 1-8.

DOLPHINS LEADERS: Rushing - Nathan 9-48, Franklin 21-62, Woodley 3-17, Diana 4-21, D. Harris 1-13; **Passing** - Woodley 7-18-1 - 88; **Receiving** - Nathan 2-15, D. Harris 1-9, Cefalo 2-40, Moore 2-24.

STANDINGS: EIGHTH WEEK

AFC EAST	W	L	T	CENTRAL	W	L	T	WEST	W	L	T	NFC EAST	W	L	T	CENTRAL	W	L	T	WEST	W	L	T
NY Jets	6	2	0	Cincinnati	6	2	0	Raiders	7	1	0	Washington	7	1	0	Green Bay	5	2	1	Atlanta	5	3	0
Miami	6	2	0	Pittsburgh	5	3	0	San Diego	6	2	0	Dallas	6	2	0	Minnesota	4	4	0	N.Orleans	3	5	0
Buffalo	4	4	0	Cleveland	4	4	0	Seattle	3	5	0	St. Louis	5	3	0	Tampa Bay	4	4	0	San Fran	3	5	0
New England	4	4	0	Houston	1	7	0	Denver	2	6	0	NY Giants	3	5	0	Detroit	3	5	0	LA Rams	1	7	0
Baltimore	0	7	1					Kan. City	2	6	0	Philadelphia	3	5	0	Chicago	3	5	0				

Bills	0	13	3	3 -	19
Patriots	3	7	6	14 -	30

Attendance at Schaefer Stadium - 36,218

NE: FG Smith 42, 4:05
Buf: Cribbs 14 run (Herrera kick), 12:02
Buf: Butler 22 pass from Ferguson (kick failed), 14:03
NE: Bradshaw 11 pass from Grogan (Smith kick), 14:52
NE: Toler 33 pass from Grogan (kick failed), 2:56
Buf: FG Herrera 46, 5:26
NE: Collins 1 run (Smith kick), 1:29
Buf: FG Herrera 25, 2:46
NE: Hasselback 2 pass from Grogan (Smith kick), 8:11

	BUF	NE
First downs	17	29
Rushing yds	129	158
Passing yds	224	260
Punts-avg	5-37.8	4-36.8
Fumbles-lost	2-0	1-0
Penalties-yds	5-34	2-10

BILLS LEADERS: **Rushing** - Cribbs 17-104, Leaks 5-16, Hooks 1-7, Ferguson 2-2; **Passing** - Ferguson 17-28-1 - 234; **Receiving** - Lewis 7-113, Brammer 4-39, Cribbs 2-33, Butler 1-22, Piccone 1-14, Leaks 1-10, Brown 1-3.

PATRIOTS LEADERS: **Rushing** - Van Eeghen 16-73, Collins 15-36, Tatupu 6-33, Grogan 2-18, Weathers 1-(-2); **Passing** - Grogan 20-34-1 - 260; **Receiving** - Morgan 7-141, Hasselback 5-17, Dawson 3-41, Toler 1-33, Bradshaw 1-11, Van Eeghen 1-9, Jones 1-5, Collins 1-3.

NOTES

• The Bills were eliminated from the playoff tournament.
• The Bills' defense, which was rated No. 1 in the NFL before the game, had a bad day allowing 29 first downs and 418 total yards. Eugene Marve had a great day as he was in on 16 tackles.
• Greg Cater's 27-yard punt after Buffalo's first possession gave the Pats the ball at the Bills 47, and they drove to John Smith's field goal for a quick 3-0 lead.
• The Bills went ahead in the second as Steve Freeman intercepted Steve Grogan at the Bills 37. Joe Ferguson hit Frank Lewis for 17- and 32-yard gains and Joe Cribbs went the final 14 yards for the TD.
• After a punt, the Bills scored again as Jerry Butler made a leaping catch in the end zone 1:03 before the end of the half. Ferguson completed all five of his passes, but Matt Kofler bobbled the snap, foiling the PAT.
• Grogan hit Stanley Morgan for a 45-yard gain with 16 seconds left and after a timeout, hit Morris Bradshaw for a TD with eight seconds left in the half to make it 13-10.
• The Pats took the second-half kickoff and scored in five plays on Ken Toler's TD reception. But Smith missed the PAT. That allowed the Bills to tie the game

WEEK 9 GAMES	
Wash 28, St.L 0	Sea 13, Den 11
Cinc 35, Hou 27	NO 35, Atl 6
Det 27, GB 24	NYG 26, Phil 24
Pitt 37, Clev 21	KC 37, NYJ 13
Mia 34, Balt 7	LAR 41, SD 34
Rams 21, SF 20	Minn 31, Dal 27
TB 26, Chi 23 (OT)	

on Efren Herrera's field goal on the ensuing series. Cribbs caught a 31-yard pass and Mark Brammer recovered a Cribbs fumble to keep the possession alive.
• Mike Haynes' interception and 26-yard return to the Bills 12 set up Tony Collins' TD.
• Cribbs then broke a 48-yard run to the 17, but the Bills were faced with fourth-and-inches near the 7 and elected to kick a field goal to pull within 23-19. The Pats then took the kickoff and drove 74 yards to Don Hasselback's TD reception and the Bills were two scores down with 6:49 left. After a punt, the Pats ate up the final 6:12 as the Bills' defense couldn't get the ball back.

QUOTES

• Fred Smerlas: "A lot of guys are glad it's over. Money problems, holdouts, the strike. It was a big mess all year. I'm just glad this mess is over."
• Frank Lewis: "The story of this season for us was we had a little here, a little there, but we could never put it all together."
• Chuck Knox: "Give them credit, they played better than us and we just couldn't make the big plays when we had to. We had problems on defense. We expected them to pass, but we had some missed coverages and we couldn't get any pressure on Grogan. They had to punt once in the second half and it went out of bounds at the 1. That's how things have gone for us all season."
• Pats running back Tony Collins on the Bills decision to kick the field goal in the fourth: "I really thought they'd go for the first down. That gave us a good feeling because we knew we could control the ball on them. It showed the Bills weren't too sure of their offense."

STANDINGS: NINTH WEEK

AFC EAST	W	L	T	CENTRAL	W	L	T	WEST	W	L	T	NFC EAST	W	L	T	CENTRAL	W	L	T	WEST	W	L	T
Miami	7	2	0	Cincinnati	7	2	0	Raiders	8	1	0	Washington	8	1	0	Green Bay	5	3	1	Atlanta	5	4	0
NY Jets	6	3	0	Pittsburgh	6	3	0	San Diego	6	3	0	Dallas	6	3	0	Minnesota	5	4	0	N.Orleans	4	5	0
New England	5	4	0	Cleveland	4	5	0	Seattle	4	5	0	St. Louis	5	4	0	Tampa Bay	5	4	0	San Fran	3	6	0
Buffalo	4	5	0	Houston	1	8	0	Kan. City	3	6	0	NY Giants	4	5	0	Detroit	4	5	0	LA Rams	2	7	0
Baltimore	0	8	1					Denver	2	7	0	Philadelphia	3	6	0	Chicago	3	6	0				

The Bills faltered late in the season and by losing their final game at New England, they failed to make the playoffs. Here Ben Williams gets to Steve Grogan too late to prevent a completed pass.

At A Glance
1983

Jan. 3 – It was a busy day in the locker room as the Bills packed their belongings following the disappointing end to the 1982 season. Isiah Robertson and Bill Simpson said they likely would retire. Frank Lewis indicated he'd be looking for a big raise in 1983, Joe Cribbs reiterated that he wouldn't be back unless he got a huge raise and he also said he still desired a trade more than anything else. And Fred Smerlas said he was considering taking a one-year leave of absence from football in 1983. "I think I am going to take this year off, a sabbatical from football," he said. "The wear and tear on my body has been too much, plus I'm not getting paid what I'm worth, so I think I'll take the year off. I'm only 25 and I'd like to play 10 years in the league. So even if I took a year off, I'd still only be 32 if I'd play 10 years. I may go back to college and finish my degree or travel cross country with my friends while we're still young."

Jan. 4 – Chuck Knox said the 1982 season was the toughest of his 10-year head coaching career in the NFL. With a year left on his contract, he said he would finish it out, but was uncertain if he wanted to stay in Buffalo beyond that. "There are a lot of things Mr. Wilson and I need to talk about," Knox said. "I like Buffalo, but really, there's a thing where, well, you can't always stay where you'd like to live. I can't say now, I just don't know. We are a better team than we were five years ago. We built a solid organization where nothing existed before. We've become competitive, which I promised. To take the shambles that existed before we came here and win a division title in three years ... Well, maybe we did it too soon." In Kansas City, the Chiefs fired head coach Marv Levy.

Jan. 5 – Dr. Jerry Argovitz, Joe Cribbs' agent, said if his client wasn't traded, he'd have no choice but to play for the Bills in 1983. "We will do whatever we can to get Joe out of Buffalo, but the Bills still own him," Argovitz said. "My advice to Joe was to get an offseason job because I feel the Bills will stay on the same road in our negotiation attempts with them."

Jan. 25 – Chuck Knox resigned as head coach of the Bills. Jim Haslett said "This stinks." Fred Smerlas said "I want to get out of here. I figured this was coming. Management has no rapport with its people and it doesn't care about having a winner in Buffalo. This team is going to fall and it's going to fall next year because there will be too much resentment toward management. I don't want to be part of a losing program." The players were obviously bitter toward Ralph Wilson, whom they felt didn't help Knox build a winning team, which is what caused Knox to turn sour. "I love Coach Knox and I would go through a wall for him," said Will Grant. "If he's going, then I want out and I safely feel the majority of players also feel that way. I think Chuck had it up to his eyeballs with everything that was going on around here."

Jan. 26 – Chuck Knox accepted the head coaching position with the Seattle Seahawks. Meanwhile, defensive coordinator Tom Catlin met with Ralph Wilson in Detroit about the vacant Bills job. In Alabama, an entire state weeped at the news of Bear Bryant's sudden death.

Jan. 27 – Tom Catlin indicated that he wanted the

Linebacker Darryl Talley was a second-round pick in the 1983 draft out of West Virginia. After struggling in the early part of his career, Talley blossomed into a Pro Bowl performer when Walt Corey became the team's defensive coordinator in 1987.

Bills job, but he also said he had been in contact with other teams. Wilson reportedly was planning on talking to Dallas assistant Ernie Stautner, former Chiefs coach Marv Levy and former Atlanta coach Leeman Bennett.

Jan. 31 – Quarterback coach Kay Stephenson emerged as the leading candidate to replace Knox as Tom Catlin withdrew his name from consideration, citing personal reasons.

Feb. 1 – Kay Stephenson was named the new head coach of the Bills. "Loyalty to the organization is a high priority with me," Ralph Wilson said. Wilson said the only other candidate he interviewed was Marv Levy. "Kay has been productive while he's been a player for us (1968) and as an assistant and I think he will give us an exciting, competitive team. I believe he's the best man for the job." Said Stephenson: "You would have to be naive not to be aware of the grumblings that have gone on recently around here. I have talked at length with Ralph and I am impressed by his commitment to continue to bring an outstanding football team to Buffalo. I don't think there's going to be a morale problem with our players. I think these players are going to take this thing and run with it."

Feb. 2 – Players continued to express their dissatisfaction with recent events. "I went to the press conference and almost cried when I heard Kay say that Wilson was committed to having a winning team in Buffalo," Jon Borchardt said. "We'll see if

he's committed or not." Said Fred Smerlas: "Kay is going in with a handicap, like a swimmer with handcuffs."

Feb. 3 – Kay Stephenson said he never sought the head coaching job and was surprised to get a call. "My feeling and hope was that Tom (Catlin) would get the job," he said. "Ralph never explained his reasons for selecting me. All of my stuff was in boxes and my bags were packed. I was ready to go somewhere. Then Ralph Wilson called me and told me to fly to Detroit on Friday. I stayed at his house, came back here Saturday, then was told to fly back to Detroit Monday. I got home that night and my wife said I wouldn't believe all the speculation that was going on. She said the Bills were going to call a press conference the next morning and I told her I guess that meant they were going to hire somebody else. I got home and about 45 minutes later, Ralph called and offered me the job."

Feb. 7 – Fred Smerlas asked to be traded.

Feb. 8 – Bills assistant coaches Ray Prochaska, George Dyer, Tom Catlin, Steve Moore, Ralph Hawkins and Chick Harris all joined Chuck Knox on his staff in Seattle.

Feb. 15 – Chuck Knox had a few final remarks. "I'm gone, I'm out of there and I'm happy where I'm at," he said. When told that Wilson was happy when Kay Stephenson mentioned he would open up the offense a little more, Knox said: "He (Wilson) can say what he wants. The same people who called the plays when we won a division championship in 1980 were calling the plays last year. Kay was there last year and he called the majority of the passing plays." Don Lawrence was hired as defensive line coach, becoming the first assistant hired by Stephenson.

Feb. 18 – Miller McCalmon, the only holdover from Chuck Knox's staff, was hired as special teams coach.

Feb. 21 – Jerry Glanville was hired as defensive backfield coach.

March 4 – Perry Moss was hired as an offensive assistant.

March 6 – The rebellious U.S. Football League opened play and its biggest star, Herschel Walker of the New Jersey Generals, was held to 65 yards rushing in a 20-15 loss to the Los Angeles Express in front of 34,002 at the Coliseum.

March 7 – Milt Jackson was hired as receivers coach.

March 14 – Stew Barber, the vice-president for administration, was fired. Fred Smerlas said Barber's abrasive personality made it difficult for many players to get along with him. "This happened for the good of the Bills because Stew was not the man for the job," Smerlas said. "He has a hard personality, he's short with people and he put up a wall between the club and players before negotiations even started."

March 15 – Andy MacDonald was named offensive backfield coach.

March 16 – Fred Smerlas and Jim Haslett reportedly got identical three-year, $1 million offers from the Boston Breakers of the USFL. "I like Buffalo and I like playing here, but I want to make some money, too," Haslett said. "I don't see it happening in Buffalo." Said Smerlas: "I think any player has to listen. The idea is to make money playing football. I'm just going to ask the Bills to let me out of my option year." Smerlas said he would play this year for the Bills, for the Breakers in the spring and summer of 1984, then with the Bills in 1984 before leaving for Boston full-time. "They're (Smerlas and Haslett) like college kids," said the players' agent, Jack Mula. "They want to play football, but they want to feel like they're wanted and they want to play for an organization that wants to win. I think it's obvious they aren't happy in Buffalo or they wouldn't be interested in moving to the USFL."

March 21 – NFL commissioner Pete Rozelle said the league lost about $200 million in revenues because of the 57-day player strike in 1982.

March 22 – Pat McGroder was promoted to executive vice-president and Norm Pollom was promoted to vice-president for player personnel.

April 25 – Bill Simpson officially announced his retirement.

April 26 – The Bills came away from the first day of the college draft thrilled with what they had accomplished. With their own first-round pick, No. 12 overall, they chose Notre Dame tight end Tony Hunter. Two picks later, using a choice obtained from Cleveland in the Tom Cousineau trade, they selected University of Miami quarterback Jim Kelly. Kelly watched the draft on ESPN with his parents at the Akron, Ohio, home of attorney Ken Weinberger and wasn't too thrilled with being picked by the Bills. Buffalo also selected West Virginia linebacker Darryl Talley in the second round and Louisiana Tech linebacker Trey Junkin (fourth). The Baltimore Colts, despite his claim that he would never play for the Colts, selected quarter-

back John Elway No. 1 overall while the Rams picked running back Eric Dickerson (second), Seattle chose running back Curt Warner (third), Denver took offensive tackle Chris Hinton (fourth), Chicago chose offensive tackle Jimbo Covert (sixth), Kansas City selected quarterback Todd Blackledge (seventh), Houston grabbed offensive lineman Bruce Matthews (ninth), New England took quarterback Tony Eason (15th), St. Louis chose safety Leonard Smith (17th), Chicago tabbed wide receiver Willie Gault (18th), Minnesota took safety Joey Browner (19th), San Diego selected cornerback Gill Byrd (22nd), Dallas grabbed defensive end Jim Jeffcoat (23rd), the Jets drafted quarterback Ken O'Brien (24th), Miami took quarterback Dan Marino (27th) and Washington took cornerback Darrell Green (28th). It was one of the most talent-laden first rounds in NFL history. Meanwhile, Pat McGroder said the team was close to reaching an agreement with disgruntled Joe Cribbs. The offer was reportedly for four years at about $1.9 million in total salary.

April 27 – Kay Stephenson said "We had an excellent draft. It would be awfully tough for me to throw cold water on this draft. Neither Norm nor I thought we'd get Darryl in the second round." About Jim Kelly, Stephenson said: "What's nice is we have Joe Ferguson and we don't have to subject a guy to the rigors of the NFL, to throw Kelly into the heat of the battle. If you give a guy a chance to mature at quarterback, he has a better chance of becoming a good player."

May 2 – Threatening to play baseball in the Yankees organization if he wasn't traded, John Elway forced Baltimore to deal him to Denver for the Broncos' first-round choice, Chris Hinton, their No. 1 choice in 1984 and backup quarterback Mark Herrmann.

May 3 – Jim Kelly, Tony Hunter and Darryl Talley attended a luncheon at the Aud Club, and it was reported that Kelly was listening to offers from the USFL's Chicago Blitz. He had visited the Blitz and spoke with coach George Allen a few days earlier. "This is what I've always wanted, the chance to play in the NFL," Kelly said. "But I was very impressed with coach Allen and the whole organization. If I had been drafted by a team like Arizona or Birmingham or a team that doesn't have a professional organization, I wouldn't even think about it. But Chicago will be on par with the NFL in a few years. They made a good point in telling me in Chicago I can do more endorsements and get more media attention than I would in Buffalo. And I think I can play there sooner." Isiah Robertson officially announced his retirement while the Bills announced they had waived Lemar Parrish and Matt Robinson. With Robertson out, that appeared to open the door for Talley to compete for a starting job immediately. "Everybody always complains about the weather here," Talley said. "Well, when you grow up in Cleveland ... I'm happy to be here. What I've seen of Buffalo's defense is that it's very aggressive and I'm aggressive, I like to mix it up."

May 11 – The Bills opened their first minicamp with Kay Stephenson in charge, but Joe Cribbs and Fred Smerlas were absent. Despite reports that a contract settlement was imminent, Cribbs still hadn't signed a new deal and his agent, Dr. Jerry Argovitz, said the "gulf between Joe and the team is as wide as ever. Joe will definitely honor his contract and play for Buffalo this year, but with the options open to Joe – including the new league – he

has to think about his future."

May 13 – Tony Hunter's agent, Robert Bennett, told him to leave mini-camp because negotiations with the Bills "were going nowhere." Hunter flew home to Cincinnati without informing anyone in the organization he was leaving. The Chicago Blitz, who also drafted Hunter, increased their offer.

May 18 – Joe Cribbs said there was a good chance he'd be leaving the Bills after the season, saying he would sign a future services contract with the new USFL team that would be granted to his agent, Dr. Jerry Argovitz. "I'm not saying it definitely will happen, but things are not working out with Buffalo and this looks like a good opportunity for me," Cribbs said. If he did sign, he would play this year for the Bills, then join the Houston Gamblers in 1984. Ralph Wilson's reaction was one of disappointment. "When Joe Cribbs left Pat McGroder last week, the two men shook hands and Joe said everything was worked out. If a man shakes hands and says you have a deal, then says later you don't have a deal, there's something unethical about that."

May 26 – The Bills reportedly offered Jim Kelly a four-year contract worth $2 million, and Kelly's agent Greg Lustig said "If that's it, we won't accept it. That's in the ballpark of what we expected from the Bills."

May 27 – Kelly said he would put off deciding his football future for at least a week. Pat McGroder said Greg Lustig told him the Bills had a heckuva chance of signing Kelly.

May 28 – Greg Lustig said Chicago was offering "sweeteners" which included a radio show, TV show, a lakefront apartment and a "quality of life that Buffalo cannot offer. Let's face it, the Bills can't change the fact that they're in Buffalo." Kelly's father, Joe, said: "I know the decision is his, but I hope it's the NFL. That's all he's ever talked about. And Buffalo's so close for us to drive to. I can't understand what's changed his mind. The NFL is all he's ever dreamed about."

June 6 – On the day he was supposed to announce where he would play pro football, Jim Kelly postponed his decision because the USFL gave Kelly permission to negotiate and sign with any team in the league, despite the fact that the Blitz held his territorial rights. Blitz general manager Bruce Allen said he wanted Kelly in the USFL, even if he didn't play for Chicago. The Blitz would expect some type of compensation, though.

June 9 – And the winner was ... The Houston Gamblers of the USFL. Owner Jerry Argovitz signed Jim Kelly to a four-year contract that was reportedly worth between $4 and $5 million, making him the league's second-highest player behind Herschel Walker. "There are risks in doing what I'm doing, but I made up my mind," Kelly said. "Everybody has to take a risk once in a while. I'm happy I did it and I won't regret it. I always wanted to play in the NFL, but right now, the USFL is the same as the NFL. It's a business now. I did what my agent and I believed to be best for me and my career." The Blitz procured four choices in the 1984 draft as compensation.

June 14 – Darryl Talley signed a four-year contract worth about $1 million with the Bills.

June 16 – The Bills other first-round choice, Tony Hunter, signed a contract worth a reported $1.7 million, making him the highest-paid tight end in the NFL and the second-highest paid Bill behind Joe Ferguson.

June 28 – Reggie McKenzie, the senior member

313

of the Bills, was traded to Seattle for an undisclosed draft choice because he didn't fit into the team's future plans. "I have no bad feelings about being traded," McKenzie said. "I will always be grateful to this town and this team for what they did for me. But I still think I can play three more seasons, so I'm happy to have this chance to join Chuck and continue my career."

July 2 – Joe Cribbs ended his 18-month feud with the Bills and signed a personal services contract with the Birmingham Stallions of the USFL. Cribbs said he would play out his contract with the Bills, then join the Stallions in the spring of 1984. "This really is a great day for me, I'm back down in the South where I belong," Cribbs said. Kay Stephenson said: "Joe still owes us an additional year and we expect him to report to training camp with the rest of the veterans and give the Bills 100 percent effort."

July 17 – Bobby Hebert was named MVP as he led the Michigan Panthers to a 24-22 victory over the Philadelphia Stars in the first USFL championship game at Denver's Mile High Stadium.

July 18 – Rookies and non-veterans reported to Fredonia for the start of Kay Stephenson's first training camp as head coach of the Bills.

July 20 – Fred Smerlas' agent, Jack Mula, said there was hope that his client would report to camp on time if he got deferred money now. "I want the money now, or I'm taking a vacation," Smerlas said. Said Mula: "We're ready to talk and I think the thing will be OK."

July 21 – Sherman White, who had announced his retirement after the 1982 season, changed his mind and signed a one-year contract. "I thought about it and I realized I still wanted to play football," he said.

July 23 – The Bills' and Browns' rookies played to a 6-6 tie in the annual scrimmage at Edinboro State.

July 24 – Veterans were due to report, but Fred Smerlas and Charlie Romes didn't show up, both due to contract disputes.

July 25 – Linebacker Shane Nelson announced his retirement because of a chronic knee injury. "After consulting with the doctor who performed the surgery (Dr. Patrick Evans of Dallas) and with the team physician Dr. Weiss, I have decided to retire. The physical demands of the game and the chances of injury are too great."

July 28 – It was reported that the Chicago Blitz would offer Jim Haslett a four-year contract worth $1.6 million starting in 1984. "All I can say is that if I signed with the Blitz, I'd make more money in one day than I did all last season with the Bills," Haslett said. "The thing is, I don't want to leave Buffalo and I don't want to ask Ralph Wilson to break the bank."

July 31 – The Bills and Browns played to another 6-6 tie in a scrimmage at Edinboro.

Aug. 6 – Bills quarterbacks threw five interceptions in a 27-17 loss at Soldier Field to the Bears in the preseason opener.

Aug. 8 – Fred Smerlas ended his holdout and reported to training camp.

Aug. 9 – Harvey Johnson, an original member of the Bills organization and the team's head coach on two occasions, died of a heart attack at his doctor's office in Bridgeton, N.J. He was 64.

Aug. 13 – After losing to Cleveland, 27-10, in the preseason home opener at Rich Stadium, the Bills traded wide receiver Lou Piccone to San Diego for

cornerback Mike Williams. The Bills also lost Jim Haslett for an unknown period due to a knee injury.

Aug. 17 – Curtis Brown was traded to the Pittsburgh Steelers for a draft choice.

Aug. 18 – Lou Piccone failed his physical with the Chargers, but the trade stood up and Buffalo kept Mike Williams because provisions weren't made to nullify the deal.

Aug. 20 – Right tackle Joe Devlin suffered a broken ankle during the Bills 17-16 victory over Detroit at the Silverdome. Joe Ferguson threw a 12-yard TD pass to Robb Riddick with two seconds left.

Aug. 21 – Joe Devlin underwent surgery to repair his ankle and was lost for the season.

Aug. 23 – Curtis Brown was waived by the Steelers, who therefore did not have to give the Bills the draft choice that was agreed upon in the trade.

Aug. 24 – Charlie Romes ended his holdout, reported to camp and practiced for the first time.

Aug. 27 – The Bills lost their preseason finale at Rich Stadium, 27-19, to Washington.

Sept. 4 – Miami's Uwe von Schamann made four field goals while Fred Steinfort missed three for the Bills in a 12-0 loss to the Dolphins in the season opener at Rich Stadium.

Sept. 7 – Jim Haslett ended speculation he was leaving for the USFL, as he signed a two-year contract with the Bills worth an estimated $550,000. However, he remained sidelined with a knee injury.

Sept. 11 – The Bills traveled to Cincinnati and defeated the Bengals, 10-6. The defense stopped Charles Alexander on fourth-and-one from the 2 with 1:58 left to play, preserving the victory.

Sept. 13 – Fred Steinfort was released and Joe Danelo was signed.

Sept. 18 – The offense broke out of its funk as Joe Cribbs scored three TDs in a 28-23 victory over the Colts at Rich Stadium.

Sept. 25 – Joe Cribbs rushed for a career-high 166 yards and the Bills beat Houston, 30-13, at Rich. It was their first victory over the Oilers since 1966, breaking a 10-game losing streak which had been the longest in the NFL by one team over another. In Pittsburgh, while the Steelers were losing to New England, Franco Harris moved past O.J. Simpson into second place on the all-time NFL rushing list.

Oct. 3 – The Bills were blown out by the Jets, 34-10, in front of a record Rich Stadium crowd of 79,933 and a *Monday Night Football* audience. On the telecast, O.J. Simpson said of the Joe Cribbs situation: "It seems to happen every year. How many times can you tell the players it's an unfortunate thing? I hope it doesn't happen, but if Cribbs leaves, it will have a negative affect on the team and be damaging to the city. It's one thing not signing rookies, but it's another not signing a proven player like Cribbs. It just wasn't handled the right way."

Oct. 5 – Miami coach Don Shula announced that rookie quarterback Dan Marino would make his first NFL start against the Bills. "We're just not putting points on the board," Shula said. "I feel a change is necessary, but by no means do I blame David (Woodley) for all of our offensive failure."

Oct. 9 – The Bills finally exorcised all of their demons against Miami as they beat the Dolphins at the Orange Bowl for the first time since 1966, 38-35 in overtime. Joe Cribbs' one-yard TD reception with 23 seconds left tied it and Joe Danelo's 36-yard field goal with 1:02 left in OT won the game. Joe Ferguson set team records for completions (38), attempts (55) and yards (419), and he tied his own

team mark with five TD passes. The teams combined for 59 first downs, 971 yards and nine TD passes. Dan Marino completed 19 of 29 passes for 322 yards in his first NFL start. "What a day," said Kay Stephenson. "To play like that against the team with the No.1-rated defense. It was Fergy's biggest game."

Oct. 10 – Terry Bledsoe, the assistant general manager for the New York Giants, was reportedly in line to become the Bills GM in 1984.

Oct. 11 – Rod Kush underwent arthroscopic knee surgery and his place on the roster was filled by Buffalo native and former star Syracuse quarterback Bill Hurley. Hurley had been playing with the Saints before getting waived.

Oct. 16 – The Bills routed Baltimore, 30-7, at Memorial Stadium to take over first place in the AFC East at 5-2. Joe Cribbs rushed for 105 yards and scored once.

Oct. 23 – On a rainy day at Rich, New England dismantled the Bills, 31-0. Joe Ferguson completed only 15 of 38 passes and suffered three interceptions, all by Roland James in the fourth quarter that resulted in 17 of New England's 24 fourth-quarter points.

Oct. 24 – Ahmad Rashad was the guest at the Quarterback Club luncheon and he said with a laugh: "If Kay Stephenson was here and throwing the ball as much as he is now, I would have never left. When I was here, they kept handing off to a guy ... what was his name? Simpson."

Oct. 30 – The Bills nearly blew a 27-7 lead in the fourth quarter and had to survive three last-gasp passes into the end zone before their 27-21 victory over New Orleans at Rich Stadium was secure.

Nov. 2 – It was determined Jerry Butler would need arthroscopic knee surgery and would miss the rest of the season. Mike Mosley was inserted as the starter. Kay Stephenson also said free safety Chris Williams would be benched with Steve Freeman moving to free and Mike Kennedy starting at strong safety. Williams, a cornerback, had been playing free safety in place of injured Rod Kush.

Nov. 6 – Joe Ferguson set a Bills record by playing in his 150th game, but it was not a happy day as the Bills lost at New England, 21-7, and Ferguson threw four interceptions.

Nov. 7 – Responding to Joe Cribbs' comment that the Bills weren't running enough, Kay Stephenson said: "It's more happenstance than anything else, it's certainly not by design. If anybody's to blame, it's me. But you don't always do what you set out to do in a game."

Nov. 13 – In their final visit to Shea Stadium, the Bills defeated the Jets, 24-17, as Joe Cribbs caught a 33-yard TD pass with 22 seconds left.

Nov. 14 – Jerry Butler underwent knee surgery in East Lansing, Mich.

Nov. 16 – Hall of Famer Jim Brown, 47, said he would consider coming out of retirement if Franco Harris broke his all-time career rushing record. When he heard the comment, Ervin Parker said: "Tell Jimmy Brown that if he comes out here Sunday, I'll knock him on his butt. Tell him I'll knock him back into retirement. This is a man's game, not an old man's game."

Nov. 17 – Mike Mosley suffered a season-ending knee injury in practice. His place on the roster was taken by Jim Haslett, who was finally ready to play after missing all season with a knee injury. The media didn't see Mosley's injury because thanks to Raider paranoia, Kay Stephenson closed practice to

Kay Stephenson was promoted to head coach before the 1983 season, succeeding Chuck Knox. Stephenson guided the Bills to an 8-8 record his first year.

the media for the first time all season.

Nov. 20 – The Bills rallied from a 24-3 deficit behind Matt Kofler to tie the Raiders, but Chris Bahr killed the comeback with a game-winning 36-yard field goal on the final play for a 27-24 Raiders victory at Rich Stadium. The game featured seven personal foul penalties, five against the Raiders. "Both teams seemed to have the same kind of demeanor," Raiders linebacker Matt Millen said. "There wasn't much talk, just a lot of swinging."

Nov. 27 – The injury-depleted Bills were no match for the Rams in Los Angeles during a 41-17 loss. The Bills were without Jerry Butler, Frank Lewis, Mark Brammer and Justin Cross on offense. Eric Dickerson outrushed Joe Cribbs, 125-40.

Nov. 28 – Angered by a lack of playing time, Jim Haslett vented his frustration. "I might as well have been talking to a wall," he said of a conversation he had with Kay Stephenson. "I think I should be playing. It's a job, I got hurt on the job, I came back and I should be playing." Haslett refused to take over for Chris Keating in the final two minutes against the Rams. Since returning to action against the Raiders, Haslett had played only on special teams.

Dec. 4 – Joe Cribbs set career highs for carries (36) and yards (185) as the Bills downed the Chiefs at Kansas City, 14-9, keeping their playoff hopes alive.

Dec. 10 – The Bills named Terry Bledsoe as their new general manager effective Jan. 1, 1984. He was given the duties that Pat McGroder had assumed the previous nine months on an interim basis after Stew Barber was fired. "I feel very good about the rest of my life," McGroder said, obviously happy that he wouldn't have to deal with player negotiations anymore. "The past nine months haven't been the best

of my life."

Dec. 11 – In Joe Montana's first visit to Rich Stadium, he and the 49ers virtually extinguished Buffalo's playoff hopes with a 23-10 victory before only 38,039. Montana completed 18 of 28 passes for 218 yards and one TD.

Dec. 13 – Jerry Butler admitted that he was concerned his career could be over because of his knee injury. "I don't want to go out of the game this way, out the back door," he said. "But there's some concern. The Good Lord willing, I'll be able to play again."

Dec. 14 – The Bills dropped a plan to build a restaurant at Rich Stadium and instead decided to build 18 new luxury suites in the administration building at a cost of about $490,000.

Dec. 15 – Fred Smerlas and Joe Cribbs were voted to the Pro Bowl, Smerlas as a starter.

Dec. 18 – The Falcons controlled the ball for 37 minutes in a dominating 31-14 victory over the Bills at Atlanta-Fulton County Stadium. In Joe Cribbs' last game as a Bill, he rushed for 22 yards on seven carries.

Dec. 19 – Facing the reality next season of playing without Joe Cribbs, Joe Ferguson said: "Joe's going to be sorely missed. It could force us to make some big changes in our offense. He's a lot of our offense."

Dec. 20 – Joe Cribbs and Fred Smerlas were named to the UPI all-AFC team.

Dec. 21 – The Bills coaching staff was chosen to coach the North squad in the Jan. 14 Senior Bowl in Mobile, Ala.

Dec. 24 – Under Chuck Knox, Seattle won its first playoff game ever, 31-7 over Denver in the AFC wild-card game at the Kingdome.

Dec. 26 – The Los Angeles Rams surprised Dallas, 24-17, in the NFC wild-card game.

Dec. 31 – Seattle shocked Miami at the Orange Bowl, 27-20, in an AFC divisional round game. San Francisco survived Detroit, 24-23, in an NFC divisional game.

Jan. 1, 1984 – The Los Angeles Raiders pounded Pittsburgh, 38-10, in the second AFC divisional round game while in the NFC, Washington embarrassed the Rams, 51-7.

Jan. 8, 1984 – The Raiders outgained Seattle 401-167 and Marcus Allen rushed for 154 yards in Los Angeles' 30-14 romp in the AFC Championship Game at the Coliseum. Washington won the NFC Championship Game, 24-21, over San Francisco, as Mark Moseley kicked a 25-yard field goal with 40 seconds left after Joe Montana had thrown three TD passes in the fourth quarter to forge a tie.

Jan. 22, 1984 – Marcus Allen rushed for a Super Bowl record 191 yards on 20 carries and won the MVP as the Raiders posted the most lopsided Super Bowl victory ever, 38-9 over Washington, before 72,920 at Tampa Stadium.

Jan. 29, 1984 – The NFC won the Pro Bowl for the sixth time in seven years with a 45-3 rout. Washington's Joe Theismann completed 21 of 27 passes for 242 yards and three TDs and was named MVP.

BY THE NUMBERS - 1983

TEAM STATISTICS	BILLS	OPP
First downs	309	332
Rushing	100	148
Passing	171	148
Penalty	38	36
Third downs	70-208	81-219
Total yards	4,823	5,809
Avg. game	301.4	363.1
Plays	1,023	1,078
Avg. play	4.7	5.4
Net rushing yds	1,736	2,503
Avg. game	108.5	156.4
Avg. play	4.2	4.4
Net passing yds	3,087	3,306
Comp/att	317/571	286/480
Sacks/lost	37-351	32-247
Interceptions	28	13
Percentage	55.5	59.6
Punts/avg	89-39.7	78-42.9
Fumbles/lost	24-12	32-18
Penalties/yds	144-1094	128-1298
Touchdowns	36	39
Extra points	34-36	39-39
Field goals	11-26	26-39
Safeties	0	0
Kick ret./avg	64-21.3	53-17.9
Punt ret./avg	44-5.5	42-9.6

RUSHING	ATT	YDS	AVG	TD
Cribbs	263	1131	4.3	3
Moore	60	275	4.6	0
Leaks	58	157	2.7	1
Ferguson	20	88	4.4	0
Hunter	2	28	14.0	0
Kofler	4	25	6.3	0
Riddick	4	18	4.5	0
Williams	3	11	3.7	0
Franklin	1	3	3.0	0
TOTALS	**415**	**1736**	**4.2**	**4**

RECEIVING	CAT	YDS	AVG	TD
Cribbs	57	524	9.2	7
Lewis	36	486	13.5	3
Hunter	36	402	11.2	3
Butler	36	385	10.7	3
Moore	34	199	5.9	1
Franklin	30	452	15.1	4
Brammer	25	215	8.6	2
Tuttle	17	261	15.4	3
Mosley	14	180	12.9	3
Dawkins	11	123	11.2	1
Barnett	10	94	9.4	0
Leaks	8	74	9.3	0
Riddick	3	43	14.3	0
TOTALS	**317**	**3438**	**10.8**	**30**

PASSING	COMP	ATT	INT	YDS	TD	COMP%	SACKS	RATE
Ferguson	281	508	25	2995	26	55.3	27-266	69.3
Kofler	35	61	3	440	4	57.4	10-85	81.3
Cribbs	1	2	0	3	0	50.0	0-0	56.3
TOTALS	**317**	**571**	**28**	**3438**	**30**	**55.5**	**37-351**	**70.5**

KICKING	1-19	20-29	30-39	40-49	50+	TOT	PAT	PTS
Danelo	0-0	2-4	5-6	3-6	0-4	10-20	33-35	63
Steinfort	0-0	1-1	0-2	0-3	0-0	1-6	1-1	4
TOTALS	**0-0**	**3-5**	**5-8**	**3-9**	**0-4**	**11-26**	**34-36**	**67**

PUNTING	NO	AVG	LG	In 20	BL
Cater	89	39.7	60	24	0

SCORE BY QUARTERS

BILLS	28 87 55 110	3 - 283
OPP	29 108 92 122	0 - 351

DEFENSIVE STATISTICAL LEADERS

TACKLES: Marve 136 primary - 64 assists - 200 total, Keating 109-56-165, Freeman 72-70-142, Parker 82-38-120, B. Williams 70-33-103, Smerlas 55-32-87, Kennedy 35-24-59, White 34-14-48, K. Johnson 29-14-43, Talley 26-13-39, Kilson 23-7-30

SACKS: B. Williams 10, Smerlas 6, Talley 5, Parker 4, White 3

FUMBLE RECOVERIES: Kilson 3, B. Williams 2, Freeman 2

FORCED FUMBLES: Keating 1

INTERCEPTIONS: Freeman 3-40 yards, 13.3 avg., 0 TD; C. Williams 3-6, 2.0, 0 TD

SPECIAL TEAMS STATISTICAL LEADERS

KICKOFF RETURNS: Mosley 9-236, 26.2, 0 TD; Williams 25-550, 22.0, 0 TD

PUNT RETURNS: Riddick 42-241, 5.7, 0 TD

Booker Moore (34) missed his rookie year in 1981 because of a rare nerve disease, then played sparingly in 1982. In 1983, he made a bigger contribution and here, he celebrates his first **NFL** touchdown with Jerry Butler.

NOTES

• Uwe von Schamann made four field goals, Fred Steinfort missed three for the Bills in Kay Stephenson's head coaching debut. Miami improved to 28-6-1 all-time vs. the Bills. The shutout was the 14th in Bills' history.

• Starters Justin Cross and Jim Ritcher were benched in the fourth, replaced by Tom Lynch and Tim Vogler.

• Ben Williams made eight tackles, three quarterback sacks and one fumble recovery.

• The Dolphins recorded six sacks, including four by Doug Betters totaling 37 yards.

• Glenn Blackwood's interception set up the Dolphins at the Bills 34 and led to the first field goal.

• Tommy Vigorito's 62-yard punt return to the Bills 11 set up the second field goal.

• Steinfort's first attempt was blocked by Earnest Rhone with 1:42 left in the first half. Williams recovered a David Woodley fumble at the Bills 42 with 12 seconds left and two Ferguson passes to Jerry Butler for 14 and 19 yards positioned Steinfort for a 43-yarder with two seconds left.

• Von Schamann capped a 56-yard drive in the third, and Steinfort missed his third kick later in the quarter.

• Lyle Blackwood's interception and return to the Bills 36 set up the final field goal.

QUOTES

• Charlie Romes: "It hurts for the defense to play as well as we did and still we get no points. Things clicked at first for the offense, then they kind of slowed up."

• Miami kicker Uwe von Schamann: "Kickers are looked upon as a last resort on offense, but I don't think it should necessarily be that way. I wish they would use the kicker as an offensive player. You know, on third-and-six or third-and-seven from the 35-yard-line. Too many times I have seen the quarterback get sacked to take us out of field goal range or seen the ball intercepted."

• Fred Steinfort: "When you miss a field goal, the next time you go out to try another, the last thing you better be thinking about is the last one you missed. The ones I missed today were not because of one another. I missed them one at a time."

• Kay Stephenson: "If anyone's to blame, it's me. We just didn't have a good gameplan. From the offensive standpoint and on special teams, we just had some breakdowns. We scouted ourselves in preseason and found we had thrown a lot. We didn't want to give Miami any tendencies to tie into, so what we tried to do was line up in passing formations and then run the ball."

• Miami defensive tackle Doug Betters: "If you get Fergy under the gun early, he'll hear footsteps and get gun-shy. One reason I had so much success was that Joe (Devlin) wasn't there today. His replacement (Cross) is not in Joe's league. Give credit to our defensive backs, they had the receivers covered all day."

• Miami coach Don Shula: "The defense bailed us out today. I was disappointed in our offense, but give credit to Buffalo's defense. I've always had great respect for their defense. The last two times we've come in here, we haven't scored a touchdown and yet we have two wins."

Dolphins	0	6	3	3	-	12
Bills	0	0	0	0	-	0

Attendance at Rich Stadium - 78,715

Mia: FG von Schamann, 33, :03
Mia: FG von Schamann, 23, 3:29
Mia: FG von Schamann, 36, 5:39
Mia: FG von Schamann, 50, :40

	BUF	MIA
First downs	14	13
Rushing yds	86	151
Passing yds	172	26
Punts-avg	8-37.1	7-43.0
Fumbles-lost	1-0	1-1
Penalties-yds	8-55	1-5

BILLS LEADERS: Rushing - Cribbs 16-76, Leaks 5-10; **Passing** - Ferguson 21-36-2 - 233; **Receiving** - Butler 7-99, Cribbs 7-60, Hunter 2-12, Brammer 2-13, Franklin 1-36, Leaks 2-13.

DOLPHINS LEADERS: Rushing - Nathan 11-44, Franklin 18-75, Overstreet 4-15, Woodley 1-9, Bennett 2-8; **Passing** - Woodley 8-22-0 - 40, Nathan 1-1-0 - 6; **Receiving** - Nathan 6-29, Vigorito 1-7, Woodley 1-6, Bennett 1-4.

WEEK 1 GAMES

Phil 22, SF 17	Atl 20, Chi 17
Balt 29, NE 23	Den 14, Pitt 10
Det 11, TB 0	GB 41, Hou 38
LAR 20, Cinc 10	Rams 16, NYG 6
Minn 27, Clev 21	NYJ 41, SD 29
NO 28, St.L 17	KC 17, Sea 13
Dal 31, Wash 30	

NOTES

• Eugene Marve, Rod Kush and Steve Freeman combined to stop Charles Alexander on a fourth-and-one run from the 2 with 1:58 left, securing the first victory of Kay Stephenson's head coaching career.

• Turk Schonert replaced Ken Anderson, who was injured in the third quarter, at QB for the Bengals.

• Jim Breech missed a 44-yard field goal on the Bengals opening possession. After an exchange of punts, the Bills drove 82 yards in 16 plays to Fred Steinfort's 28-yard field goal.

• After Steinfort missed a 45-yarder with 1:10 left in the half, two defensive penalties against the Bills helped set up Breech's 30-yarder to tie it at 3-3.

• The Bills took the second-half kickoff and drove 81 yards in 12 plays to their first TD of the season, Joe Ferguson's pass to Jerry Butler.

• Late in the third, the Bills couldn't move out from their 6. Greg Cater's weak 32-yard punt gave the Bengals the ball at the Bills 38, but three plays totaled three yards and Breech kicked a field goal.

• Steinfort missed a 45-yarder with 8:59 left and the Bengals began their final drive. Schonert completed four of seven passes, including a 26-yarder to Steve Kreider, who beat Gary Thompson, on third-and-six, for a first down at the Bills 4. However, Alexander was stopped for no gain, Schonert missed a pass, Alexander gained three and then he was stuffed on fourth down.

QUOTES

• Eugene Marve: "Oh heck, there must have been six of us who hit him (Alexander). I might have hit him first, I don't know. Actually, we all hit him. Call it a team tackle."

• Fred Smerlas: "Their line didn't get any movement at all. But our job as interior linemen is to plug the holes and get penetration. That's what we were trying to do. I was dead tired, but I fired ahead as hard as I could."

• Rod Kush: "We gathered as a team during the time-out and said 'This is the game guys. This is it, let's not let it get away.'"

• Gary Thompson on Kreider's catch: "I was thinking 'Oh God, don't let them score.' I felt like a million dollars when we stopped him (Alexander)."

• Bengals receiver Cris Collinsworth on the Bengals offense: "It was like playing a good round of golf and not making any putts."

• Joe Cribbs: "I think we have an offense that is going to score. But it's frustrating to get so close so many times and come up with no points. We should get points every time we cross the 50."

• Fred Steinfort: "It's very disheartening. I felt good before the game, I didn't feel any pressure."

• Joe Ferguson on Steinfort: "He's going to have to improve in a hurry."

Bills	0	3	7	0	-	10
Bengals	0	3	0	3	-	6

Attendance at Riverfront Stadium- 46,839

Buf: FG Steinfort 28, 4:19
Cin: FG Breech 30, 15:00
Buf: Butler 14 pass from Ferguson (Steinfort kick), 5:07
Cin: FG Breech 47, :04

	BUF	CIN
First downs	21	15
Rushing yds	110	80
Passing yds	157	201
Punts-avg	3-37.3	3-43.3
Fumbles-lost	1-0	1-0
Penalties-yds	9-63	8-85

BILLS LEADERS: Rushing - Cribbs 20-83, Leaks 7-29, Ferguson 4-(-2); **Passing** - Ferguson 21-33-0 - 175, Cribbs 1-1-0 - 3; **Receiving** - Butler 6-52, Cribbs 3-31, Hunter 5-31, Leaks 2-20, Franklin 3-23, Moore 3-21.

BENGALS LEADERS: Rushing - Alexander 17-58, Wilson 5-16, Schonert 1-4, Tate 2-2; **Passing** - Anderson 9-12-0 - 117, Schonert 7-13-0 - 84; **Receiving** - Ross 4-58, Harris 2-21, Curtis 1-11, Tate 2-19, Wilson 1-5, Verser 1-22, Kreider 3-40, Collinsworth 2-25.

WEEK 2 GAMES

SF 48, Minn 17	Clev 31, Det 26
Dal 34, St.L 17	Den 17, Balt 10
LAR 20, Hou 6	Mia 34, NE 24
Rams 30, NO 27	NYG 16, Atl 13
Pitt 25, GB 21	Sea 17, NYJ 10
Chi 17, TB 10	Wash 23, Phil 13
SD 17, KC 14	

STANDINGS: SECOND WEEK

AFC EAST	W	L	T	CENTRAL	W	L	T	WEST	W	L	T	NFC EAST	W	L	T	CENTRAL	W	L	T	WEST	W	L	T
Miami	2	0	0	Cleveland	1	1	0	Raiders	2	0	0	Dallas	2	0	0	Minnesota	1	1	0	LA Rams	2	0	0
NY Jets	1	1	0	Pittsburgh	1	1	0	Denver	2	0	0	Philadelphia	1	1	0	Green Bay	1	1	0	Atlanta	1	1	0
Baltimore	1	1	0	Cincinnati	0	2	0	Kan. City	1	1	0	NY Giants	1	1	0	Detroit	1	1	0	N.Orleans	1	1	0
Buffalo	1	1	0	Houston	0	2	0	San Diego	1	1	0	Washington	1	1	0	Chicago	1	1	0	San Fran	1	1	0
New England	0	2	0					Seattle	1	1	0	St. Louis	0	2	0	Tampa Bay	0	2	0				

Colts	6	3	7	7 - 23
Bills	0	7	7	14 - 28

Attendance at Rich Stadium - 40,937

Bal: FG Allegre 28, 6:10
Bal: FG Allegre 49, 14:44
Buf: Cribbs 3 pass from Ferguson (Danelo kick), 10:08
Bal: FG Allegre 45, 14:37
Buf: Cribbs 1 run (Danelo kick), 3:19
Bal: Dickey 72 pass from Pagel (Allegre kick), 6:09
Buf: Lewis 27 pass from Ferguson (Danelo kick), 1:47
Bal: Dickey 33 run (Allegre kick), 4:40
Buf: Cribbs 2 pass from Ferguson (Danelo kick), 10:06

	BUF	BAL
First downs	27	17
Rushing yds	145	147
Passing yds	177	225
Punts-avg	5-42.2	5-52.2
Fumbles-lost	2-0	1-1
Penalties-yds	6-45	15-153

BILLS LEADERS: **Rushing** - Cribbs 24-82, Leaks 2-4, Moore 12-53, Ferguson 4-6; **Passing** - Ferguson 18-27-0 - 189; **Receiving** - Butler 2-21, Cribbs 3-14, Hunter 4-47, Leaks 2-19, Brammer 3-37, Lewis 3-48, Moore 1-3.

COLTS LEADERS: **Rushing** - Dickey 18-80, McMillan 10-39, Pagel 2-27, N. Williams 1-1; **Passing** - Pagel 12-26-0 - 235; **Receiving** - Dickey 2-79, Porter 2-47, Henry 3-36, Sherwin 2-41, Bouza 1-22, McMillan 2-10.

NOTES

• Chris Keating recovered a Mike Pagel fumble at the Colts 14 with 5:54 left. Three plays later, Joe Ferguson threw a game-winning TD pass to Joe Cribbs.

• The Colts had taken a 6-0 lead in the first on two Raul Allegre field goals. The Bills went ahead 7-6 with a 67-yard, 11-play drive in the second quarter capped by a Ferguson TD pass to Cribbs. The Bills were aided by a pass-interference penalty on third-and-seven from their own 46 against Kendall Williams. But the Colts regained the lead on Allegre's third field goal with 23 seconds left in the first half.

• Cribbs' TD run capped the opening drive in the third, but 2:50 later, Curtis Dickey took a short pass on third-and-six and went 72 yards for a TD, breaking tackles by Gary Thompson and Len Walterscheid. It was the first TD allowed this season and snapped a streak of 18 TD-less quarters for the defense at home.

• Ferguson capped an 80-yard drive early in the fourth with a TD pass to Frank Lewis, who made a leaping catch.

• The Colts regained the lead on the ensuing possession as Dickey broke a 33-yard TD run.

• The Bills punted to the Colts 16, but Pagel bobbled a snap and Keating recovered. Cribbs gained four yards

WEEK 3 GAMES	
Clev 17, Cinc 7	Atl 30, Det 14
Wash 27, KC 12	GB 27, Rams 24
Minn 19, TB 16	Dal 28, NYG 13
NE 23, NYJ 13	Phil 13, Den 10
Pitt 40, Hou 28	Sea 34, SD 31
SF 42, St.L 27	LAR 27, Mia 14
NO 34, Chi 31 (OT)	

and Barry Krauss was flagged for a personal foul, moving the ball to the 2. Cribbs scored two plays later.

• The Colts punted on the next series and never saw the ball again as the Bills killed the final 4:02.

QUOTES

• Kay Stephenson: "We made some big plays today when we had to. The defense played well overall. There were some breakdowns, but they got it done when they had to."

• Fred Smerlas: "A lot of our so-called problems on defense were caused by Baltimore. This is the best Baltimore team I've played since I've been here."

• Colts QB Mike Pagel on his fumble: "I took the snap and stopped and then remembered I forgot the ball."

• Colts coach Frank Kush on his team's penalties: "We just kill ourselves in more ways than one. On that one play, Krauss said someone (Will Grant) spit in his face and he retaliated. Well, that's silly to do because the second guy always gets caught. Those penalties are stupid, foolish, asinine. Inexperience has nothing to do with it, we're still making idiotic mistakes."

• Will Grant: "We (the offensive linemen) had a meeting last night and said 'Hey, Fergy's banged up, so we gotta protect him.'"

• Ben Williams: "Were we lucky? Luck is the residue of design. We won, that's the only thing that matters."

Oilers	3	3	7	0 - 13
Bills	7	6	3	14 - 30

Attendance at Rich Stadium - 60,070

Hou: FG Kempf 31, 10:51
Buf: Cribbs 1 run (Danelo kick), 14:24
Buf: Butler 7 pass from Ferguson (kick failed), 12:38
Hou: FG Kempf 26, 14:40
Hou: Campbell 1 run (Kempf kick), 8:29
Buf: FG Danelo 48, 12:34
Buf: Lewis 19 pass from Ferguson (Danelo kick), 6:18
Buf: Kilson 87 fumble return (Danelo kick), 14:22

	BUF	HOU
First downs	21	23
Rushing yds	228	181
Passing yds	105	201
Punts-avg	4-29.3	5-43.2
Fumbles-lost	1-1	2-2
Penalties-yds	7-59	6-50

BILLS LEADERS: **Rushing** - Cribbs 22-166, Moore 10-62; **Passing** - Ferguson 11-22-1 - 127; **Receiving** - Hunter 3-34, Lewis 3-38, Butler 3-37, Brammer 1-11, Moore 1-7.

OILERS LEADERS: **Rushing** - Campbell 30-142, Moriarty 5-25, Walls 1-14, Craft 1-0; **Passing** - Nielsen 19-29-0 - 251; **Receiving** - Smith 11-147, Campbell 2-29, Walls 2-31, McCloskey 3-40, Edwards 1-4.

NOTES

• The Bills posted their first victory over the Oilers since 1966, breaking a 10-game losing streak. The loss was the 11th straight in the regular season for Houston dating back to 1982.

• Joe Cribbs' 166 yards rushing were a career-high.

• Phil Villapiano suffered a season-ending, and probably career-ending, knee injury in the third.

• Earl Campbell carried all seven plays for 27 yards as the Oilers took a 3-0 lead on Florian Kempf's field goal in the first, but the Bills answered with an eight-play, 76-yard drive that ended on Cribbs' TD dive.

• It became 13-3 later in the second as the Bills moved 80 yards in 10 plays to Joe Ferguson's TD pass to Jerry Butler. Earlier, Butler had caught a 23-yard pass and Booker Moore gained 21 yards. A bad snap foiled the PAT.

• Robb Riddick fumbled a punt late in the second and Mike Holston recovered at the Bills 38. Eight plays later, Kempf kicked a field goal 20 seconds before halftime.

• The Oilers took the second-half kickoff and moved 68 yards in 14 plays, consuming 8:29, to Campbell's one-yard TD run on fourth-and-goal. Earlier in the march, Campbell gained 10 on fourth-and-one from the Bills 31.

WEEK 4 GAMES	
SF 24, Atl 20	Balt 22, Chi 19
Cinc 23, TB 17	Clev 30, SD 24
Minn 20, Det 17	Mia 14, KC 6
LAR 22, Den 7	NYJ 27, Rams 24
NE 28, Pitt 23	Dal 21, NO 20
Wash 27, Sea 17	St.L 14, Phil 11
NYG 27, GB 3	

• The Bills responded with a 57-yard drive to Joe Danelo's first field goal as a Bill.

• After a punt, the Bills drove 80 yards in 10 plays to Ferguson's TD pass to Frank Lewis.

• The scoring was finalized when Ben Williams forced Gifford Nielsen to fumble and Dave Kilson returned it 87 yards for a TD with 38 seconds left.

QUOTES

• Ralph Wilson: "All I know is that anytime Joe Cribbs touches the football, he's a threat to take it all the way. I don't worry about records, all I know is he's a great player."

• Kay Stephenson: "We're very happy winning three straight. It wasn't pretty, but a win is a win. The important thing we're all cognizant of is the fact that we have to play better."

• Fred Smerlas: "Earl Campbell is one big Excedrin headache. I'm wondering how he's still alive after all these years. He's a big tough guy who takes a lot of hits, but keeps on ticking."

• Steve Freeman: "He's (Campbell) a big refrigerator of a running back."

• Oilers running back Earl Campbell: "I had a chance to play in the same house O.J. Simpson played in. All I thought about in the final minutes was that he was in the same situation when he played here (losing all the time) and he didn't quit."

• Joe Cribbs: "With Booker running really well, that took a lot of heat off me. The Oilers couldn't just key on me. That made it easier to get a lot of those yards."

STANDINGS: FOURTH WEEK

AFC EAST	W	L	T	CENTRAL	W	L	T	WEST	W	L	T	NFC EAST	W	L	T	CENTRAL	W	L	T	WEST	W	L	T
Miami	3	1	0	Cleveland	3	1	0	Raiders	4	0	0	Dallas	4	0	0	Minnesota	3	1	0	San Fran	3	1	0
Buffalo	3	1	0	Pittsburgh	2	2	0	Denver	2	2	0	Washington	3	1	0	Green Bay	2	2	0	N.Orleans	2	2	0
Baltimore	2	2	0	Cincinnati	1	3	0	Seattle	2	2	0	Philadelphia	2	2	0	Detroit	1	3	0	LA Rams	2	2	0
NY Jets	2	2	0	Houston	0	4	0	San Diego	1	3	0	NY Giants	2	2	0	Chicago	1	3	0	Atlanta	2	2	0
New England	2	2	0					Kan. City	1	3	0	St. Louis	1	3	0	Tampa Bay	0	4	0				

NOTES

• The Bills' three-game winning streak ended as the Jets erupted for 20 points in the final 20 minutes.

• Joe Ferguson suffered a slight concussion and left the game in the third quarter. The Jets had seven sacks.

• Bobby Jackson's interception at the Bills 29 led to the Jets' first TD. Richard Todd completed three straight passes, the last to Bruce Harper for a 7-0 lead.

• Pat Leahy, who missed a 38-yard field goal in the first quarter, made a 19-yarder in the third to make it 10-0. The key play was a 19-yard pass to Scott Dierking on third-and-one from the Bills 40.

• On the ensuing possession, things began to fall apart. Joe Cribbs killed a threat by fumbling at the Jets 1. New York drove to midfield, then punted and the ball was downed at the Bills 1. On the first play, Cribbs fumbled again when hit by Bob Crable and Mark Gastineau recovered in the end zone.

• Joe Danelo made a field goal on the first play of the fourth, but the Jets made it 24-3 just 38 seconds later as Harper broke a 23-yard run and Todd hit Johnny Hector with a 22-yard TD pass.

• After Justin Cross recovered a fumble on a punt by Mike Harmon, Matt Kofler threw a TD pass to Cribbs, but the Jets again came right back with a 59-yard drive to Dierking's TD. Leahy later added a field goal after Kofler was intercepted by Greg Buttle.

• A crowd of 79,933 was a Bills record and the largest crowd to see an NFL game thus far in 1983.

QUOTES

• Jets defensive end Mark Gastineau: "I think we wanted to show who we are. I think we showed people something tonight. Bob Crable gets the cigar, he made the hit on Cribbs that got me the touchdown. It (fans booing) doesn't bother me when they boo. In the long run, I think people wish they had someone on their team doing the same thing (sack dances). It gives the fans something to get excited about. If they were just sitting around, it would be a pretty dull place, right? If the fans get excited, that's good."

• Joe Cribbs on the Gastineau TD: "I don't even remember what happened. All I know is that somebody hit me awfully hard and I felt like I came down on my head."

• Fred Smerlas: "That's what I call a butt-warming. They did anything they wanted."

• Sherman White: "It was a total disaster. Even our special teams played badly. What gets me is they didn't do anything new or anything we didn't expect. But what they did, they did well."

• Kay Stephenson: "When a man hits the floor, he gets up. We're a team of men and we'll get back up. I'm not discouraged about this club. Credit the Jets, they beat us fair and square."

• Joe Ferguson: "Overall we didn't play up to par. Why wouldn't we on a night like that with the crowd, the electricity, I don't know. Maybe it was the Monday Night Football frights. We've got a lot of young ballplayers on this team."

Jets	0	7	10	17	-	34
Bills	0	0	0	10	-	10

Attendance at Rich Stadium - 79,933

NYJ: Harper 11 pass from Todd (Leahy kick), 6:00
NYJ: FG Leahy 19, 3:15
NYJ: Gastineau fumble recovery in end zone (Leahy kick), 11:35
Buf: FG Danelo 38, :03
NYJ: Hector 22 pass from Todd (Leahy kick), :41
Buf: Cribbs 12 pass from Kofler (Danelo kick), 5:10
NYJ: Dierking 1 run (Leahy kick), 9:10
NYJ: FG Leahy 42, 12:55

	BUF	NYJ
First downs	16	24
Rushing yds	65	210
Passing yds	151	201
Punts-avg	6-42.2	4-49.5
Fumbles-lost	3-2	1-1
Penalties-yds	7-55	13-132

BILLS LEADERS: Rushing - Cribbs 13-28, Moore 3-(-1), Ferguson 2-31, Kofler 1-7; **Passing** - Ferguson 13-20-2 - 100, Kofler 12-21-1 - 104; **Receiving** - Cribbs 9-74, Hunter 3-40, Brammer 4-29, Lewis 3-32, Franklin 3-23, Riddick 1-4, Butler 1-2, Moore 1-0.

JETS LEADERS: Rushing - Crutchfield 20-84, Harper 9-118, Todd 6-3, Augustyniak 1-3, Hector 1-1, Dierking 1-1; **Passing** - Todd 20-31-1 - 221; **Receiving** - Walker 3-24, Crutchfield 3-23, Jones 2-33, Harper 3-26, Barkum 3-43, Hector 2-33, Augustyniak 1-7, Dierking 2-25, Shuler 1-7.

WEEK 5 GAMES

Chi 31, Den 14	NO 17, Mia 7
Bal 34, Cin 31	Dal 37, Min 24
Rams 21, Det 10	Pit 17, Hou 10
Wash 37, LAR 35	SD 41, NYG 34
Phil 28, Atl 24	KC 38, St.L 14
SF 33, NE 13	GB 55, TB 14
Sea 24, Clev 9	

NOTES

• The Bills won in the Orange Bowl for the first time since 1966, spoiling the NFL starting debut of Dan Marino.

• Joe Ferguson set team records for attempts, completions and passing yards and tied the mark for TD passes. It was the Bills' first 400-yard passing game in team history.

• Down 28-21, Marino led a 77-yard march that ended on his TD pass to Nat Moore.

• The Dolphins then took their only lead as Ferguson suffered his only interception, by Fulton Walker with 6:38 left. The Dolphins covered 45 yards in eight plays with Mark Clayton making his first NFL TD reception with 3:32 left.

• The Bills then drove 80 yards in 13 plays to tie it. On third-and-16 from his own 23, Ferguson hit Byron Franklin for 21 yards leading to the two-minute warning. He then hit Perry Tuttle for 19, Jerry Butler for 12 and Joe Cribbs for seven. On third-and-three from the 18, he found Mark Brammer for 10. After two incompletions, he hit Joe Cribbs for seven yards, setting up fourth-and-goal from the 1. He then hit Cribbs on the right side of the end zone for the score and Joe Danelo made the extra point to tie.

• Uwe von Schamann missed a 52-yard field goal early in OT, then missed a 43-yarder. After that, Ferguson hit Mike Mosley on third-and-10 for a 35-yard gain to the Miami 29. Three runs later, Danelo kicked the game-winning 36-yard field goal, touching off a wild celebration by the Bills.

QUOTES

• Joe Ferguson: "I couldn't look (at Danelo's winning kick). I told Rosey Leaks to tell me what happened. I feel as good as I've ever felt. It's taken me 11 years to win here in Miami and it's a great win for us. This is something I really wanted to do before I got out of football. It really hasn't sunk in yet what we did against the Dolphins because you just don't do that. It was the most emotional game I've ever played in. I'm happy for everybody, especially Joe Ferguson."

• Joe Danelo: "When Mosley made that catch, I turned to Fred Smerlas and said 'That's the break we needed.' I wanted to have one chance in overtime, because that's all you get."

• Mike Mosley: "They put me in because all the receivers were getting tired. When coach said 'You're in' I couldn't believe it. I didn't think I'd play at all."

• Kay Stephenson: "We had to call timeout to familiarize Mike with what he was doing. He played Frank Lewis' position and we had to tell him where to go and what to do."

• Miami coach Don Shula: "Ferguson just played so well, he had all the answers."

• Miami QB Dan Marino: "I have to feel good about what happened for me out there."

Bills	7	7	7	14	3	-	38
Dolphins	0	7	14	14	0	-	35

Attendance at the Orange Bowl - 59,948

Buf: Franklin 9 pass from Ferguson (Danelo kick), 14:44
Buf: Franklin 30 pass from Ferguson (Danelo kick), 3:43
Mia: Bennett 1 run (von Schamann kick), 10:14
Mia: Duper 63 pass from Marino (von Schamann kick), 5:57
Buf: B. Moore 11 pass from Ferguson (Danelo kick), 8:18
Mia: Duper 48 pass from Clayton (von Schamann kick), 12:04
Buf: Cribbs 4 pass from Ferguson (Danelo kick), 1:42
Mia: N. Moore 2 pass from Marino (von Schamann kick), 7:25
Mia: Clayton 14 pass from Marino (von Schamann kick), 11:54
Buf: Cribbs 1 run (Danelo kick), 14:37
Buf: FG Danelo 36, 13:58

	BUF	MIA
First downs	28	31
Rushing yds	76	153
Passing yds	407	335
Punts-avg	5-38.6	4-42.3
Fumbles-lost	2-1	3-0
Penalties-yds	15-104	4-52

BILLS LEADERS: Rushing - Cribbs 11-49, Moore 4-6, Leaks 8-21; **Passing** - Ferguson 38-55-2 - 419; **Receiving** - Butler 9-89, Lewis 5-61, Cribbs 9-93, Barnett 2-12, Franklin 3-59, Moore 4-25, Tuttle 2-22, Brammer 3-23, Mosley 1-35.

DOLPHINS LEADERS: Rushing - A. Franklin 17-65, Nathan 8-28, Overstreet 8-24, Bennett 6-40, Marino 4- (-4); **Passing** - Marino 19-29-2 - 322, Clayton 1-1-0 - 48; **Receiving** - Duper 7-202, Clayton 2-53, Nathan 5-57, D. Johnson 2-15, N. Moore 3-35, Bennett 1-8.

WEEK 6 GAMES

Den 26, Hou 14	Det 38, GB 14
LAR 21, KC 20	Rams 10, SF 7
Minn 23, Chi 14	Balt 12, NE 7
NO 19, Atl 17	Clev 10, NYJ 7
Phil 17, NYG 13	SD 28, Sea 21
Dal 27, TB 24	Pit 24, Cin 14
Wash 38, St.L 14	

STANDINGS: SIXTH WEEK

AFC EAST	W	L	T	CENTRAL	W	L	T	WEST	W	L	T	NFC EAST	W	L	T	CENTRAL	W	L	T	WEST	W	L	T
Buffalo	4	2	0	Cleveland	4	2	0	Raiders	5	1	0	Dallas	6	0	0	Minnesota	4	2	0	San Fran	4	2	0
Baltimore	4	2	0	Pittsburgh	4	2	0	Seattle	3	3	0	Washington	5	1	0	Green Bay	3	3	0	N.Orleans	4	2	0
Miami	3	3	0	Cincinnati	1	5	0	Denver	3	3	0	Philadelphia	4	2	0	Chicago	2	4	0	LA Rams	4	2	0
NY Jets	3	3	0	Houston	0	6	0	San Diego	3	3	0	NY Giants	2	4	0	Detroit	2	4	0	Atlanta	2	4	0
New England	2	4	0					Kan. City	2	4	0	St. Louis	1	5	0	Tampa Bay	0	6	0				

Bills	7	17	3	3	-	30
Colts	7	0	0	0	-	7

Attendance at Memorial Stadium - 38,565

Bal: R. Butler 52 pass from Pagel (Allegre kick), 9:54
Buf: Cribbs 14 pass from Ferguson (Danelo kick), 12:43
Buf: Brammer 4 pass from Ferguson (Danelo kick), 1:51
Buf: Lewis 20 pass from Ferguson (Danelo kick), 4:57
Buf: FG Danelo 23, 14:55
Buf: FG Danelo 40, 8:20
Buf: FG Danelo 30, :52

	BUF	BAL
First downs	23	13
Rushing yds	171	211
Passing yds	230	73
Punts-avg	4-45.3	5-42.0
Fumbles-lost	0-0	1-1
Penalties-yds	4-45	8-72

BILLS LEADERS: Rushing - Cribbs 19-105, Leaks 10-25, Moore 6-23, Riddick 4-18; **Passing** - Ferguson 21-30-0 - 230, Kofler 0-1-0 - 0; **Receiving** - Butler 3-33, Lewis 5-72, Cribbs 4-50, Brammer 6-54, Franklin 1-9, Tuttle 1-8, Moore 1-4.

COLTS LEADERS: Rushing - Dickey 8-68, McMillan 8-31, Pagel 5-67, Reed 2-27, Moore 4-11, Williams 3-7; **Passing** - Pagel 2-10-2 - 73, Reed 6-10-1 - 34; **Receiving** - Sherwin 2-29, R. Butler 1-52, Bouza 2-24, Williams 1-7, Porter 1-3, Moore 1-(-8).

NOTES

• The Bills moved into sole possession of first in the AFC East, winning their second straight on the road.
• Randy McMillan, hit by Sherman White, fumbled through the end zone to kill the Colts' first possession. The Bills punted, and the Colts got the TD they deserved. Mike Pagel handed to McMillan who pitched back to Pagel. Pagel then hit Ray Butler with a 52-yard TD pass, beating Chris Williams.
• The Bills answered with an eight-play, 73-yard drive leading to Joe Cribbs' TD catch. The key play was an 11-yard pass to Mark Brammer and an additional 15-yard penalty for roughing Ferguson.
• On the next possession, the Bills went 53 yards in five plays to Brammer's TD reception. Ferguson hit Cribbs for 23 and Jerry Butler for 19 on back-to-back plays.
• Chris Williams' interception at the Colts 38 led to Ferguson's TD pass to Frank Lewis and a 21-7 lead. After each team missed a field goal, the Bills drove 75 yards in 13 plays to Joe Danelo's 23-yarder with five seconds left in the half. The key play was Roosevelt Leaks' three-yard run on fourth-and-one from the Colts 35.
• Danelo kicked two field goals for the only scoring in the second half.

QUOTES

• Joe Ferguson: "I think we're not nearly as conservative as we were under Chuck Knox. Basically our plays are the same ones we ran last year. But under Kay, the play-calling has been different. Kay gives you the chance to do so much with the football. Maybe Chuck didn't have confidence in me last year, I don't know. But this year has been a lot of fun for me. We're moving a lot of different people, people with a lot of speed, into the secondary very quickly. That's putting tremendous pressure on the defenses. And Joe Cribbs can do anything. For his size, he blocks so well and he catches the ball and runs the ball."
• Joe Cribbs: "Last year, Fergy had such a bad year. I think he really wanted to come in this year and really get his game back together." (About the USFL): "The USFL is something that will come about at the end of the season. I don't even think about it, I just want to relish this victory. I like contributing as much as I can to the Buffalo Bills in any way I can."
• Fred Smerlas: "After the (McMillan) fumble, the defense came to the sidelines and we all started screaming at each other. We were mad at ourselves for letting them go that far. We decided right then and there to make them go the long route for the rest of the game."
• Colts coach Frank Kush: "We played a very fine football team today. They dominated us. They are the best team in the division. They're in first place and you have to give them credit. Joe Ferguson was remarkable. Between his passing and our inept secondary play, we didn't stand a chance."

Patriots	0	7	0	24	-	31
Bills	0	0	0	0	-	0

Attendance at Rich Stadium - 60,424

NE: Ramsey 35 pass from Grogan (Steinfort kick), 13:07
NE: Ramsey 2 pass from Grogan (Steinfort kick), :54
NE: Collins 50 run (Steinfort kick), 4:57
NE: FG Steinfort 22, 10:11
NE: van Eeghen 2 run (Steinfort kick), 13:55

	BUF	NE
First downs	14	21
Rushing yds	93	200
Passing yds	199	244
Punts-avg	8-40.5	7-46.4
Fumbles-lost	2-0	3-0
Penalties-yds	5-35	7-51

BILLS LEADERS: Rushing - Cribbs 12-30, Moore 6-51, Ferguson 1-12; **Passing** - Ferguson 15-38-3 - 188, Kofler 2-6-0 - 22; **Receiving** - Butler 3-26, Lewis 7-116, Tuttle 3-47, Brammer 1-19, Moore 1-(-4), Cribbs 1-6.

PATRIOTS LEADERS: Rushing - Collins 23-147, Weathers 5-13, van Eeghen 8-20, Grogan 3-10, Tatupu 4-10; **Passing** - Grogan 17-29-0 - 251; **Receiving** - Collins 4-45, Morgan 4-74, Ramsey 3-41, Weathers 4-47, Starring 1-44, Williams 1-0.

NOTES

• The Bills' offense took the day off and the Pats scored 24 points in the fourth quarter for the victory, thanks mainly to ball-hawking Roland James who made three interceptions within seven minutes in the fourth.
• The first 11 possessions of the game ended in punts until the Pats drove 94 yards in 10 plays to Steve Grogan's 35-yard TD pass to Derrick Ramsey late in the second quarter. Mario Clark's holding penalty on third down kept the drive alive, giving the Pats an automatic first down. Before the half ended, each team missed a long field goal attempt.
• Joe Danelo missed a 47-yard attempt early in the third. After an exchange of punts, the Pats used 5:59 to drive 81 yards in 12 plays to Ramsey's second TD reception early in the fourth.
• A few minutes later, James intercepted Joe Ferguson at midfield. On the next play, Tony Collins broke a 50-yard TD run. On the first play after the kickoff, James picked Ferguson again at the Bills 37. Nine plays later, ex-Bill Fred Steinfort made a field goal. Then James intercepted and returned it 17 yards to the Pats 47. Five plays later, Mark van Eeghen plunged in to make it 31-0.

QUOTES

• Joe Ferguson: "It was our turn to blow it today and we blew it. We just got outplayed on offense. I'd rather say I felt like I cost us this game than say something I shouldn't about other people and other people's mistakes. I just have to face the fact that when I don't have a good day, we don't do well. I knew the types of performances I'd had (against Miami and Baltimore) don't happen every week. I just had a bad day. Our receivers have done a good job, I can't complain about them. We'll bounce back. We've just got to turn the page."
• Fred Smerlas: "When the offense isn't rolling, you've got to have big plays on defense. One hand washes the other, but today, both hands stayed dirty."
• Pats running back Tony Collins: "I'm happy about the outcome of the game, what I did was secondary. The victory is what counts."
• Pats safety Roland James: "Coming into the game, I couldn't even imagine shutting them out, not a team like that. I just can't believe it. On the first one, I was just in the right position. The second one was almost the same way. The third one, Rick Sanford was also there and either one of us could have gotten it."
• Kay Stephenson: "Maybe we expected the magic to happen for us again. It didn't happen. I thought we were ready to play, but we failed to take charge of the game early and missed some opportunities."

STANDINGS: EIGHTH WEEK

AFC EAST	W	L	T	CENTRAL	W	L	T	WEST	W	L	T	NFC EAST	W	L	T	CENTRAL	W	L	T	WEST	W	L	T
Buffalo	5	3	0	Pittsburgh	6	2	0	Raiders	6	2	0	Dallas	7	1	0	Minnesota	6	2	0	San Fran	6	2	0
Miami	5	3	0	Cleveland	4	4	0	Denver	5	3	0	Washington	6	2	0	Green Bay	4	4	0	LA Rams	5	3	0
Baltimore	4	4	0	Cincinnati	2	6	0	Seattle	4	4	0	Philadelphia	4	4	0	Detroit	3	5	0	N.Orleans	5	3	0
New England	4	4	0	Houston	0	8	0	Kan. City	4	4	0	NY Giants	2	5	1	Chicago	3	5	0	Atlanta	3	5	0
NY Jets	3	5	0					San Diego	3	5	0	St. Louis	2	5	1	Tampa Bay	0	8	0				

GAME 9 - Sunday, Oct. 30, 1983 - BILLS 27, SAINTS 21

NOTES

• The Bills nearly blew a 27-7 lead in the fourth quarter. The game wasn't secure until the last of three passes into the end zone from the 39 by Saints QB Dave Wilson fell incomplete.

• Joe Ferguson bounced back from the Pats game to throw four TD passes and the Bills had no turnovers.

• Ferguson hit Jerry Butler for a TD on the first possession to cap an 80-yard drive.

• Charlie Romes intercepted Ken Stabler at the Bills 34. Five plays later, Tony Hunter toted a tight end screen 40 yards for his first NFL touchdown.

• The Saints punted on their next series and the Bills went 60 yards in nine plays to Ferguson's TD pass to Mike Mosley. Mosley had replaced Butler, who suffered a knee injury earlier on the drive. The PAT failed.

• The Saints retaliated with a 57-yard drive that led to Wilson's TD pass to Mike Tice. Wilson took over for Stabler, who was injured on a hit by Lucious Sanford late in the first quarter.

• Mosley caught his second TD late in the third. Gary Thompson tackled Russell Erxleben short of a first down on a fake punt to give the Bills the ball at their 45. Three Saints penalties contributed 25 yards and Mosley had a 23-yard catch.

• But the Saints came alive in the fourth. Wilson hit Hoby Brenner for a TD, and after a Bills punt, Wilson completed five passes including a TD to Tyrone Young. The Saints forced a Greg Cater punt with 1:10 left and Wilson hit Lindsay Scott for 25 to the 39 with 30 seconds left. Wilson then launched a pass into the end zone to Eugene Goodlow, who was open, but Steve Freeman made a diving breakup to save the game. Wilson's next two heaves also fell incomplete as the clock ran out.

QUOTES

• Mike Mosley: "I was sick to my stomach thinking they had a chance to win after the way we played in the first half. It would have been the biggest letdown ever if we had lost this game."

• Steve Freeman: "I saw their quarterback looking deep, then I saw the receiver squatting in the end zone ready to get it. You can tell by a receiver's eyes when the ball is coming. When I saw them getting bigger, I figured it was coming and I'd better stick out my hand and see what happens."

• Saints receiver Eugene Goodlow: "I thought there should have been a flag for faceguarding. He lucked out on that one. He was a good two or three yards from me and all I was thinking about was keeping my eyes on the ball and making the catch. I didn't think he had a chance for it."

• Tony Hunter: "I was waiting for that first touchdown. Now they should come easier. The first one is always the toughest."

• Saints coach Bum Phillips: "They got the lead and might have sat on it a bit and that gave us a chance to come back. The people got their money's worth."

• Fred Smerlas: "We nearly gave it to them. If we had lost, it would have been a sin."

WEEK 9 GAMES	
Dal 38, NYG 20	Balt 22, Phil 21
Det 38, Chi 17	Clev 25, Hou 19
Cinc 34, GB 14	Den 27, KC 24
Atl 24, NE 13	Mia 30, Rams 14
NYJ 27, SF 13	St.L 41, Minn 31
Sea 34, LAR 21	Pitt 17, TB 12
Wash 27, SD 24	

Saints	0 7 0 14 -	21
Bills	7 13 7 0 -	27

Attendance at Rich Stadium - 49,413

Buf: Butler 15 pass from Ferguson (Danelo kick), 10:54
Buf: Hunter 40 pass from Ferguson (Danelo kick), 1:46
Buf: Mosley 22 pass from Ferguson (kick failed), 9:01
NO: Tice 12 pass from Wilson (Andersen kick), 13:03
Buf: Mosley 8 pass from Ferguson (Danelo kick), 14:41
NO: Brenner 2 pass from Wilson (Andersen kick), 7:27
NO: Young 5 pass from Wilson (Andersen kick), 11:26

	BUF	NO
First downs	22	20
Rushing yds	132	133
Passing yds	169	256
Punts-avg	7-36.7	4-43.0
Fumbles-lost	0-0	1-1
Penalties-yds	10-95	9-90

BILLS LEADERS: Rushing - Cribbs 26-84, Moore 1-5, Ferguson 1-7, Leaks 9-36; **Passing** - Ferguson 13-25-0 - 173, Kofler 1-1-0 - 11; **Receiving** - Butler 2-26, Lewis 1-9, Mosley 5-59, Franklin 1-11, Brammer 1-16, Hunter 4-63.

SAINTS LEADERS: Rushing - G. Rogers 21-114, Gajan 5-18, Erxleben 1-1, T. Rogers 1-0, Wilson 1-0; **Passing** - Stabler 4-6-1 - 47, Wilson 19-31-1 - 209; **Receiving** - Groth 3-45, Brenner 4-35, G. Rogers 4-28, Duckett 1-11, Tice 2-17, Goodlow 2-30, Gajan 3-24, Young 3-41, Scott 1-25.

GAME 10 - Sunday, Nov. 6, 1983 - PATRIOTS 21, BILLS 7

NOTES

• Playing in his team record 150th game, Joe Ferguson threw four interceptions.

• The teams exchanged two punts and one turnover each in the first quarter, but after Rick Sanford's interception of Ferguson, the Pats drove 57 yards in five plays to Tony Collins' TD.

• Another Ferguson interception on the next series was nullified when David Kilson recovered Mark van Eeghen's fumble, but Joe Danelo then missed a 24-yard field goal. From there, the Pats moved 80 yards to Steve Grogan's first TD pass to Clarence Weathers as Kilson and Steve Freeman collided on the play.

• Lucious Sanford's interception at the Pats 22 with 1:05 left was wasted. The Bills got to the 1 but three runs failed and on fourth down, Ferguson threw incomplete in the end zone with six seconds left.

• After a Greg Cater punt, the Pats made it 21-0 as Weathers beat Chris Williams and hauled in a 58-yard TD.

• Ferguson threw two more interceptions in the third and the Bills punted four times before finally scoring with 4:01 left. Charlie Romes intercepted Grogan and returned it 27 yards to the 18. Ferguson took advantage, passing one yard to Mark Brammer.

• Julius Dawkins had a 45-yard TD pass in the second quarter wiped out when he was called for interference.

• Eugene Marve was in on 12 tackles.

QUOTES

• Joe Ferguson on his failure to score late in the first half: "I thought all the plays were good, I felt we could get in on any of those four plays. But it was a situation where New England just stopped us. It's frustrating not to get in. But with 30 minutes and we're just two touchdowns down, that shouldn't be enough to beat anybody. It shouldn't have been a factor, but it was today."

• Patriots coach Ron Meyer: "The goal-line stand was big because it set up the overall development of the rest of the game. If they knocked it in, then a lot of things could have happened in the second half and self-doubt could have crept in for us. What we try to do against Buffalo is get them in a one-dimensional offense. We try to take away Cribbs, Leaks and Moore and make Ferguson throw. If he's hot, I have a lot of explaining to do. I thought the turning point was the first drive of the second half when we held them. If they had scored, it would have been 14-7. Instead, we forced them to punt and we came right back with a score to make it 21-0."

• Kay Stephenson: "I don't think we were destroyed by not scoring at that time. I don't think it was extremely costly. With Joe, you can get back in the ballgame very quickly."

• Joe Cribbs: "I think some of my talents are being overlooked. For the past couple of weeks we just haven't run the ball as much as I would have liked. I feel like I'm one of the best running backs in the league and I just wish we'd run more."

WEEK 10 GAMES	
NO 27, Atl 10	Balt 17, NYJ 14
Rams 21, Chi 14	Cinc 55, Hou 14
GB 35, Clev 21	Sea 27, Den 19
LAR 28, KC 20	Mia 20, SF 17
Dal 27, Phil 20	Wash 45, St.L 7
Pitt 26, SD 3	TB 17, Minn 12
Det 15, NYG 9	

Bills	0 0 0 7 -	7
Patriots	0 14 7 0 -	21

Attendance at Sullivan Stadium - 42,604

NE: Collins 4 run (Steinfort kick), 2:09
NE: C. Weathers 40 pass from Grogan (Steinfort kick), 12:38
NE: C. Weathers 58 pass from Grogan (Steinfort kick), 6:18
Buf: Brammer 1 pass from Ferguson (Danelo kick), 10:59

	BUF	NE
First downs	20	19
Rushing yds	77	199
Passing yds	186	251
Punts-avg	7-45.0	6-39.7
Fumbles-lost	0-0	4-2
Penalties-yds	10-92	10-139

BILLS LEADERS: Rushing - Cribbs 9-39, Moore 5-38, Leaks 3-0; **Passing** - Ferguson 20-48-4 - 199; **Receiving** - Mosley 5-52, Lewis 5-57, Hunter 2-29, Moore 4-29, Brammer 2-9, Franklin 1-14, Dawkins 1-9.

PATRIOTS LEADERS: Rushing - Collins 21-100, van Eeghen 12-55, Morgan 1-13, Grogan 1-9, Tatupu 6-22; **Passing** - Grogan 15-28-2 - 251; **Receiving** - C. Weathers 2-98, Morgan 4-67, Ramsey 3-37, Collins 2-20, van Eeghen 2-31, Tatupu 1-6, Grogan 1-(-8).

STANDINGS: TENTH WEEK

AFC EAST	W	L	T	CENTRAL	W	L	T	WEST	W	L	T	NFC EAST	W	L	T	CENTRAL	W	L	T	WEST	W	L	T
Miami	7	3	0	Pittsburgh	8	2	0	Raiders	7	3	0	Dallas	9	1	0	Minnesota	6	4	0	San Fran	6	4	0
Buffalo	6	4	0	Cleveland	5	5	0	Denver	6	4	0	Washington	8	2	0	Green Bay	5	5	0	LA Rams	6	4	0
Baltimore	6	4	0	Cincinnati	4	6	0	Seattle	6	4	0	Philadelphia	4	6	0	Detroit	5	5	0	N.Orleans	6	4	0
New England	5	5	0	Houston	0	10	0	Kan. City	4	6	0	St. Louis	3	6	1	Chicago	3	7	0	Atlanta	4	6	0
NY Jets	4	6	0					San Diego	3	7	0	NY Giants	2	7	1	Tampa Bay	1	9	0				

GAME 11 - Sunday, Nov. 13, 1983 - BILLS 24, JETS 17

Bills	0	0	14	10	-	24
Jets	0	14	3	0	-	17

Attendance at Shea Stadium - 48,513

NYJ: Crutchfield 1 run (Leahy kick), 13:48
NYJ: Lynn 42 interception return (Leahy kick), 14:30
Buf: Mosley 10 pass from Ferguson (Danelo kick), 7:26
Buf: Franklin 19 pass from Ferguson (Danelo kick), 10:08
NYJ: FG Leahy 48, 13:56
Buf: FG Danelo 30, 6:28
Buf: Cribbs 33 pass from Ferguson (Danelo kick), 14:38

	BUF	NYJ
First downs	20	18
Rushing yds	69	89
Passing yds	245	236
Punts-avg	7-38.4	6-41.2
Fumbles-lost	1-1	3-2
Penalties-yds	15-110	8-123

BILLS LEADERS: Rushing - Cribbs 13-33, Hunter 1-24, Moore 5-5, Ferguson 1-7; **Passing** - Ferguson 24-41-1 - 262, Kofler 1-3-0 - 11; **Receiving** - Cribbs 7-82, Hunter 6-57, Lewis 3-45, Mosley 3-34, Leaks 2-22, Franklin 2-21, Moore 1-8, Brammer 1-4.

JETS LEADERS: Rushing - Harper 13-42, Crutchfield 10-41, Dierking 5-6; **Passing** - Todd 25-36-1 - 245; **Receiving** - Harper 10-102, Dierking 3-16, Crutchfield 3-15, L. Jones 2-37, Gaffney 2-32, Walker 1-8.

NOTES
• The Bills won in their final visit to Shea Stadium as Joe Cribbs caught the winning TD pass with 22 seconds left. The Bills got the ball at their 25 with 1:17 left. Joe Ferguson hit Cribbs for 13 on third-and-three, then fired a 22-yard pass to Frank Lewis to the Jets 33 with 29 seconds left. On the next play, Cribbs ran a corner route and beat linebacker Lance Mehl.
• In the first quarter, the Bills failed on a fake field goal, then the Jets Pat Leahy missed a 52-yarder.
• In the second quarter, Leahy missed a 49-yarder, and after Tony Hunter fumbled at the Bills 41, the defense got the ball back when Chris Keating intercepted Richard Todd. The Bills had to punt, though, and the Jets then drove 71 yards to Dwayne Crutchfield's TD, one play after Todd's 33-yard pass to Bruce Harper.
• Johnny Lynn then intercepted a Ferguson pass intended for Hunter and went 42 yards for a TD.
• After a Fred Smerlas emotional halftime speech, the Bills responded with a 72-yard drive to Mike Mosley's TD midway through the third. When Joey Lumpkin recovered a fumble on the ensuing kickoff at the 25, the Bills went in to tie the score. First, they overcame two holding penalties thanks to a 29-yard pass interference penalty on Bobby Jackson at the 2. Then, Ferguson was

WEEK 11 GAMES
KC 20, Cinc 15	SD 24, Dal 23
LAR 22, Den 20	Hou 27, Det 17
GB 29, Minn 21	NE 17, Mia 6
SF 27, NO 0	Chi 17, Phil 14
Clev 20, TB 0	Pitt 24, Balt 13
Wash 33, NYG 17	St.L 33, Sea 28
Rams 36, Atl 13	

sacked by Marty Lyons for a loss of 17. But on the next play, Ferguson hit Byron Franklin for the TD.
• The Jets answered with a Leahy field goal, but Joe Danelo matched that in the fourth.
• Keating stopped a Jets drive at the Bills 30 by forcing Crutchfield to fumble and Ken Johnson recovered. The teams then exchanged punts before the Bills' winning drive.

QUOTES
• Joe Cribbs: "I think I owed myself something because I was having a pretty bad game. Fergy and I talked about the play. We had run it before and I was open, but he didn't have time to throw. He told me if the free safety (Darrol Ray) fell off, he'd lay it out there."
• Fred Smerlas on his halftime speech: "It was 14-0 and it should have been 0-0. We were giving the game away and I just tried to get the guys fired up. In my own fashion, I tried to be a catalyst. I was yelling and it caught on. We found a new life. This is the hardest I've seen the Bills hit on defense all year."
• Chris Keating: "To be honest, we were ticked off. Being down 14 points at halftime didn't seem right. We kept after them. Now we have to keep doing that week in and week out."
• Kay Stephenson: "Today was a good example of why you don't take a Joe Ferguson out of a game. Joe is one of the great quarterbacks in the NFL. I'm sure there are some people who felt he should have been benched after the first half. He showed why you don't do that."
• Ervin Parker: "This was the most critical game we've played all season. It was bigger than the win in Miami. If we had lost this game, we would have been out of the playoffs. This is the turning point in our season."

GAME 12 - Sunday, Nov. 20, 1983 - RAIDERS 27, BILLS 24

Raiders	7	3	7	10	-	27
Bills	0	3	0	21	-	24

Attendance at Rich Stadium - 72,393

LAR: Hawkins 2 run (Bahr kick), 7:10
Buf: FG Danelo 48, 10:56
LAR: FG Bahr 41, 13:50
LAR: Allen 4 run (Bahr kick), 6:08
LAR: Christensen 15 pass from Plunkett (Bahr kick), 4:05
Buf: Hunter 23 pass from Kofler (Danelo kick), 6:06
Buf: Cribbs 1 run (Danelo kick), 9:05
Buf: Tuttle 28 pass from Kofler (Danelo kick), 10:19
LAR: FG Bahr 36, 15:00

	BUF	LAR
First downs	15	27
Rushing yds	68	169
Passing yds	116	232
Punts-avg	7-38.4	3-37.7
Fumbles-lost	1-1	4-3
Penalties-yds	6-35	13-117

BILLS LEADERS: Rushing - Cribbs 10-9, Williams 3-11, Leaks 6-16, Ferguson 1-17, Kofler 2-15; **Passing** - Ferguson 3-6-0 - 18, Kofler 9-14-2 - 128, Cribbs 0-1-0 - 0; **Receiving** - Cribbs 3-12, Hunter 2-48, Lewis 1-8, Dawkins 3-30, Franklin 2-20, Tuttle 1-28.

RAIDERS LEADERS: Rushing - Allen 26-89, King 7-46, Hawkins 8-15, Pruitt 3-29, Guy 1-(-10); **Passing** - Plunkett 24-32-0 - 232; **Receiving** - Branch 4-47, Allen 8-68, Barnwell 2-15, Christensen 7-86, Hawkins 2-15, King 1-1.

NOTES
• Matt Kofler, taking over for Joe Ferguson, who was knocked out with a concussion, directed a marvelous rally in the fourth as the Bills came back from a 24-3 deficit to tie. But Chris Bahr kicked the game-winning field goal on the final play after Jim Plunkett executed a perfect winning drive.
• The Bills trailed 10-3 at the half and that became 17-3 in the third when Marcus Allen scored on four-yard run to cap a 62-yard drive which began with Lester Hayes' interception of Kofler.
• Early in the fourth after a punt, LA drove 54 yards to Todd Christensen's TD reception and the game appeared to be over. But a 14-yard pass to Byron Franklin and subsequent 15-yard penalty put the Bills at the LA 36. Two plays later, Kofler found Tony Hunter for a TD.
• Joey Lumpkin then tackled punter Ray Guy at the 8 and four plays later on fourth-and-goal, Joe Cribbs dove in for a TD to make it 24-17. Then, two Raiders failed to field the kickoff and Darryl Caldwell recovered for the Bills at the 23. Four plays later, on fourth-and-15 from the 28, Kofler hit Perry Tuttle, who beat Hayes and Van McElroy, for a TD and the stadium nearly exploded. However, Plunkett methodically mixed passes and runs during a 13-play, 65-yard drive to the winning field goal.

WEEK 12 GAMES
Mia 37, Balt 0	Chi 27, TB 0
Clev 30, NE 0	Det 23, GB 20
Cinc 38, Hou 10	Dal 41, KC 21
NYG 23, Phil 0	Minn 17, Pitt 14
St.L 44, SD 14	Atl 28, SF 24
Den 38, Sea 27	Wash 42, Rams 20
NYJ 31, NO 28	

QUOTES
• Ervin Parker: "We gave them the game. They ran nickel and dime plays on that last drive and took what we gave them. It was that simple."
• Matt Kofler: "Everyone in the whole world knows the Raiders win these types of games. It's their trademark." (On his performance): "You want to prove to people you can play. That's what you're here for. I think I proved we can still move the ball whether Fergy's in there or not. But it would have been much sweeter if we would have won. As I keep playing, I seem to gain more confidence."
• Fred Smerlas: "When they came out for that final drive, the expressions on their faces were the same as they were when they were ahead 24-3. They didn't lose their composure. It was like they just made up their minds they were going to drive for the winning field goal."
• Raiders owner Al Davis: "I think every game we play is mean-tempered. I don't know about (our) intimidation, but I think their coaches got uptight the week before the game (Stephenson closed practice to the media the week before the game)."
• Raiders coach Tom Flores: "We have a reputation as an intimidating team. I don't know how we got that reputation, but teams seem to be ready for us because of it."
• Raiders QB Jim Plunkett: "A lot of things went their way in the last few minutes, but you've got to be able to come back in a situation like that."

STANDINGS: TWELFTH WEEK

AFC EAST	W	L	T	CENTRAL	W	L	T	WEST	W	L	T	NFC EAST	W	L	T	CENTRAL	W	L	T	WEST	W	L	T
Miami	8	4	0	Pittsburgh	9	3	0	Raiders	9	3	0	Dallas	10	2	0	Minnesota	7	5	0	San Fran	7	5	0
Buffalo	7	5	0	Cleveland	7	5	0	Denver	7	5	0	Washington	10	2	0	Green Bay	6	6	0	LA Rams	7	5	0
Baltimore	6	6	0	Cincinnati	5	7	0	Seattle	6	6	0	St. Louis	5	6	1	Detroit	6	6	0	N.Orleans	6	6	0
New England	6	6	0	Houston	1	11	0	Kan. City	5	7	0	Philadelphia	4	8	0	Chicago	5	7	0	Atlanta	5	7	0
NY Jets	5	7	0					San Diego	4	8	0	NY Giants	3	8	1	Tampa Bay	1	11	0				

NOTES

• Joe Ferguson threw five second-half interceptions as the Bills lost two in a row for the first time this season.
• The Bills were within 24-17 after Joe Danelo's field goal early in the fourth, but the Rams scored the final 17.
• George Farmer caught a 45-yard TD pass from Vince Ferragamo in the second quarter. After the Bills answered with Ferguson's TD pass to Tony Hunter to cap a 90-yard march, the Rams answered with a 76-yard drive to Ferragamo's TD pass to Preston Dennard.
• In the third, Henry Ellard's 18-yard punt return set up the Rams at the Bills 39 and they eventually scored on Eric Dickerson's TD run. But again the Bills came back as a 25-yard pass interference penalty on Eric Harris led to Ferguson's 43-yard TD pass to Bryon Franklin on the next play.
• Harris' interception led to a Mike Lansford field goal, but Danelo answered that on the first play of the fourth after Van Williams had recovered Ellard's fumble on a punt return at the Rams 6.

• Here, the Rams took control. Dickerson had a TD called back on a holding penalty, but on the next play, Dennard caught a TD pass. Johnnie Johnson picked off Ferguson, setting up a Lansford field goal and Johnson then returned another pick 60 yards for the final score.

QUOTES

• Eugene Marve: "This is a game we really wanted and one we really needed for the playoffs and we disappointed ourselves. We just did a lot of things wrong."
• Joe Cribbs: "We panicked with our play-calling. We were giving up too early. We were in the position we wanted to be in coming out in the second half. But we were just putting it up long the whole second half. We were down by seven points, that's no time to start throwing it long. You think of certain teams in the league and you think of certain styles. But we don't have a style. We've been up and down, sporadic. I don't know why we don't have a style, but I know it's been a minus for us."
• Joe Ferguson: "What do you want? (to a reporter). Yeah, we lost, but that was the extent of it. Yeah, they (interceptions) were my fault. I threw them, didn't I."
• Ben Williams on Dickerson: "He's in a class by himself. But today goes to show you that they have other weapons."
• Mario Clark: "You're so conscious of Dickerson, you take one step up as a defensive back and that one step can make the difference in a touchdown."

WEEK 13 GAMES	
Det 45, Pitt 3	Dal 35, St.L 17
SD 31, Den 7	Clev 41, Balt 23
Atl 47, GB 41	TB 33, Hou 24
NO 17, Minn 16	NYJ 26, NE 3
LAR 27, NYG 12	Wash 28, Phil 24
Chi 13, SF 3	Mia 38, Cinc 14
Sea 51, KC 48 (OT)	

Bills	0	7	7	3 - 17
Rams	0	14	10	17 - 41

Attendance at Anaheim Stadium - 48,246

LA: Farmer 45 pass from Ferragamo (Lansford kick), 5:41
Buf: Hunter 15 pass from Ferguson (Danelo kick), 10:58
LA: Dennard 11 pass from Ferragamo (Lansford kick), 14:01
LA: Dickerson 2 run (Lansford kick), 7:39
Buf: Franklin 43 pass from Ferguson (Danelo kick), 8:19
LA: FG Lansford 37, 12:09
Buf: FG Danelo 20, :03
LA: Dennard 15 pass from Ferragamo (Lansford kick), 5:23
LA: FG Lansford 49, 12:58
LA: Johnson 60 interception return (Lansford kick), 13:23

	BUF	LA
First downs	22	24
Rushing yds	74	153
Passing yds	271	202
Punts-avg	5-36.6	5-42.6
Fumbles-lost	1-0	1-1
Penalties-yds	7-56	11-79

BILLS LEADERS: **Rushing** - Cribbs 10-40, Moore 4-25, Leaks 1-3, Kofler 1-3, Franklin 1-3; **Passing** - Ferguson 20-44-5 - 233, Kofler 2-5-0 - 39; **Receiving** - Cribbs 2-13, Hunter 3-36, Dawkins 3-25, Moore 8-63, Franklin 4-106, Barnett 1-5, Riddick 1-24.

RAMS LEADERS: **Rushing** - Dickerson 32-125, Guman 2-18, Redden 2-12, Kemp 1-(-2); **Passing** - Ferragamo 18-31-0 - 206; **Receiving** - Hill 3-26, Barber 5-65, Dennard 4-40, Farmer 4-61, Dickerson 1-1, Guman 1-13.

NOTES

• Joe Cribbs set career highs for carries and yards as the Bills kept their playoff hopes alive. He also lost two fumbles, but went over 1,000 yards for the third time in four NFL seasons.
• The Chiefs held the ball for 10:50 in the first quarter, but Nick Lowery missed a field goal so the game was scoreless. After the miss, the Bills drove 76 yards in eight plays to Joe Ferguson's TD pass to Perry Tuttle. Ferguson hit Byron Franklin for 26- and 13-yard gains along the way.
• The Chiefs answered with a Lowery field goal, with the key play Bill Kenney's 20-yard pass to Carlos Carson.
• Ferguson was intercepted by Gary Green at the Bills 29 with 2:55 left in the half, but the Chiefs failed to score on six plays inside the 8, including four from the 1 after a holding penalty on Mario Clark.
• The Chiefs got another Lowery field goal on the first possession of the third, but early in the fourth, Mike Kennedy intercepted a Kenney pass intended for Ed Beckman and returned it 22 yards for a TD. It was his first NFL interception and the Bills' first TD on an interception since Bill Simpson's Dec. 7, 1980.
• After an exchange of punts, the Chiefs got the third Lowery field goal with 4:47 left.
• Chris Williams stopped the final KC threat with an interception with 1:08 left.
• Eugene Marve was in on 17 tackles and the Bills had three sacks.

QUOTES

• Joe Cribbs: "It was strange. I went to sleep after the Auburn-Alabama game thinking about the great day Bo Jackson had. I had a dream that I was back at Auburn. I don't know who I was playing, but when I woke up, I knew I had carried 33 times for 303 yards. We felt if the Chiefs had any weaknesses, it was against the run. We felt it was going to be vital to start out with a good running game. In some games, we've started out sluggish and gotten away from it. Last week against the Rams, we went away from it. I'm kind of a sensitive guy and I notice a lot of things. I really felt we weren't giving the running game a chance."
• Kay Stephenson: "Joe Cribbs played the way I expect him to play. He is no doubt one of the finest backs in the NFL. He knew we would concentrate on the run today and he got himself ready."
• Mike Kennedy: "It's something I've always dreamed about. I only had to run about 20 yards but it felt like 100. All I did was aim for the orange marker at the goal line. I've never done anything like that in my life, not even in college. But I've always dreamed that I could do it and I was glad it was today when we really needed a win."
• Chris Keating: "We realized 'Hey, this is it, it's not time to be tired or to feel sorry for yourself. We had to come up big because of the playoffs.' We had our backs against the wall. Our attitude was we're not going to let the Chiefs do anything."
• Chiefs coach John Mackovich on the Bills' goal line stand: "That series changed the complexion of the game quite a bit."

Bills	0	7	0	7 - 14
Chiefs	0	3	3	3 - 9

Attendance at Arrowhead Stadium - 27,104

Buf: Tuttle 17 pass from Ferguson (Danelo kick), 3:33
KC: FG Lowery 48, 6:15
KC: FG Lowery 25, 7:30
Buf: Kennedy 22 interception return (Danelo kick), 1:50
KC: FG Lowery 42, 10:13

	BUF	KC
First downs	16	23
Rushing yds	188	57
Passing yds	76	284
Punts-avg	5-43.3	4-42.0
Fumbles-lost	4-2	0-0
Penalties-yds	12-61	3-35

BILLS LEADERS: **Rushing** - Cribbs 36-185, Hunter 1-4, Moore 1-4, Ferguson 2- (-5); **Passing** - Ferguson 6-15-1 - 76; **Receiving** - Franklin 2-39, Tuttle 2-32, Hunter 2-5.
CHIEFS LEADERS: **Rushing** - Brown 13-39, Jackson 4-15, Thomas 1-2, Scott 1-1; **Passing** - Kenney 22-43-2 - 306; **Receiving** - Marshall 1-23, Brown 5-57, Hancock 1-11, Thomas 6-60, Carson 3-65, Beckman 2-24, Scott 1-5, Paige 2-48, Smith 1-13.

WEEK 14 GAMES	
LAR 42, SD 10	Wash 37, Atl 21
GB 31, Chi 28	Cinc 23, Pitt 10
Den 27, Clev 6	Dal 35, Sea 10
Mia 24, Hou 17	Phil 13, Rams 9
NE 7, NO 0	NYJ 10, Balt 6
St.L 10, NYG 6	SF 35, TB 21
Det 13, Minn 2	

STANDINGS: FOURTEENTH WEEK

AFC EAST	W	L	T	CENTRAL	W	L	T	WEST	W	L	T	NFC EAST	W	L	T	CENTRAL	W	L	T	WEST	W	L	T
Miami	10	4	0	Pittsburgh	9	5	0	Raiders	11	3	0	Dallas	12	2	0	Detroit	8	6	0	LA Rams	8	6	0
Buffalo	8	6	0	Cleveland	8	6	0	Denver	8	6	0	Washington	12	2	0	Minnesota	7	7	0	San Fran	8	6	0
New England	7	7	0	Cincinnati	6	8	0	Seattle	7	7	0	St. Louis	6	7	1	Green Bay	7	7	0	N.Orleans	7	7	0
NY Jets	7	7	0	Houston	1	13	0	Kan. City	5	9	0	Philadelphia	5	9	0	Chicago	6	8	0	Atlanta	6	8	0
Baltimore	6	8	0					San Diego	5	9	0	NY Giants	3	10	1	Tampa Bay	2	12	0				

49ers	3	3	14	3 - 23
Bills	0	10	0	0 - 10

Attendance at Rich Stadium - 38,039

SF: FG Wersching 37, 13:26
Buf: Leaks 1 run (Danelo kick), 3:42
SF: FG Wersching 29, 11:52
Buf: FG Danelo 33, 14:54
SF: Craig 4 pass from Montana (Wersching kick), 4:33
SF: Tyler 1 run (Wersching kick), 10:32
SF: FG Wersching 30, 8:30

	BUF	SF
First downs	16	19
Rushing yds	120	127
Passing yds	183	183
Punts-avg	4-41.3	5-35.4
Fumbles-lost	3-2	2-1
Penalties-yds	8-60	5-45

BILLS LEADERS: **Rushing** - Cribbs 15-100, Moore 3-4, Leaks 4-7, Ferguson 2-9; **Passing** - Ferguson 23-35-3 - 194; **Receiving** - Moore 6-24, Barnett 5-58, Tuttle 2-21, Franklin 4-45, Cribbs 6-46.

49ERS LEADERS: **Rushing** - Tyler 16-63, Craig 15-47, Montana 4-14, Solomon 1-3, Ring 1-0; **Passing** - Montana 18-28-0 - 218; **Receiving** - Clark 5-71, Francis 3-41, Solomon 2-29, Moore 4-52, Ramson 1-10, Craig 2-10, Tyler 1-5.

NOTES

• The Bills' playoff hopes virtually were crushed as Joe Montana won in his first visit to Rich.
• Ronnie Lott's interception at the 49ers 22 killed a Bills drive in the first. Montana drove his team 48 yards to Ray Wersching's field goal.
• On the ensuing drive, the Bills moved 73 yards in eight plays to Roosevelt Leaks' TD. The key play was a 45-yard run by Joe Cribbs and Joe Ferguson's 11-yard pass to Perry Tuttle on third-and-two to the 6.
• After a Joe Danelo field goal was blocked, the 49ers drove to Wersching's second field goal. But the Bills got that back with an 11-play, 65-yard march in the final 3:02 to Danelo's 33-yarder. Ferguson completed all nine passes he attempted.
• The game turned in San Francisco's favor when Richard Blackmore forced Robb Riddick to fumble the second-half kickoff and Danny Bunz recovered at the Bills 41. Seven plays later, Montana hit Roger Craig for the go-ahead TD.
• After Greg Cater was forced to punt from his end zone, the 49ers went 50 yards in seven plays to Wendell Tyler's TD run. Montana had hit Dwight Clark for 25 yards on the first play.
• Danelo missed a 38-yard attempt early in the fourth and Wersching made a 30-yarder after Dana McLemore returned a punt 43 yards to the Bills 21.
• To make the playoffs, the Bills needed to beat Atlanta, Cleveland had to lose to Pittsburgh and New England and Seattle had to play to a tie.

QUOTES

• Jon Borchardt: "All we can do is play well at Atlanta. I think Pittsburgh would beat Cleveland, but that tie isn't going to happen."
• Mark Brammer: "I don't know what the odds are of a tie, but let's put it this way, things looked more optimistic for us at other points this year."
• Robb Riddick on his fumble: "I got stood up, somebody (Blackmore) snuck around the back of me, grabbed the ball and pulled it out. It was just a good, heads-up play by their coverage team. And it was just human error on my part because the ball wasn't held as tightly as I could have held it. I could see the end zone, it was just me and the kicker, and then the guy pulled the ball out. What was the feeling after it happened? Just emptiness."
• Fred Smerlas on Riddick's fumble: "When that happened, we all went flat. we shouldn't have let it bother us, but for some reason it did. We gave them an early Christmas. That fumble just killed us. It was the biggest turning point in any game I've played since I've been here."
• Kay Stephenson: "There were some things in this game that were almost impossible to overcome. We made some big, big mistakes. But we didn't have one guy who didn't give everything he had. We've overcome a lot this season and I'm proud of this team."

WEEK 15 GAMES

Mia 31, Atl 24	Pitt 34, NYJ 7
Den 21, Balt 19	Chi 19, Minn 13
St.L 34, LAR 24	Sea 17, NYG 12
Wash 31, Dal 10	NE 21, Rams 7
Hou 34, Clev 27	Cinc 17, Det 9
SD 41, KC 38	NO 20, Phil 17
GB 12, TB 9	

Bills	0	7	0	7 - 14
Falcons	3	14	7	7 - 31

Attendance at Atlanta-Fulton County Stadium - 31,015

Atl: FG Luckhurst 40, 9:07
Atl: Cox 7 pass from Bartkowski (Luckhurst kick), :04
Atl: Andrews 10 run (Luckhurst kick), 11:33
Buf: Tuttle 13 pass from Ferguson (Danelo kick), 14:26
Atl: Andrews 1 run (Luckhurst kick), 6:46
Atl: Andrews 6 pass from Bartkowski (Luckhurst kick), 10:37
Buf: Dawkins 28 pass from Kofler (Danelo kick), 14:16

	BUF	ATL
First downs	14	25
Rushing yds	34	243
Passing yds	243	151
Punts-avg	6-42.3	5-41.3
Fumbles-lost	2-2	4-2
Penalties-yds	15-123	8-80

BILLS LEADERS: **Rushing** - Cribbs 7-22, Leaks 3-6, Ferguson 2-6; **Passing** - Ferguson 14-33-2 - 179, Kofler 8-10-0 - 125; **Receiving** - Tuttle 6-103, Franklin 3-46, Moore 3-19, Cribbs 3-43, Dawkins 4-59, Barnett 2-19, Riddick 1-15.

FALCONS LEADERS: **Rushing** - Andrews 28-158, Riggs 9-61, Johnson 2-11, Bartkowski 1-10, Cain 1-3; **Passing** - Bartkowski 20-32-0 - 157; **Receiving** - Andrews 7-49, Cox 3-21, Johnson 5-44, Robinson 2-15, Hodge 1-5, Bailey 1-14, Miller 1-9.

NOTES

• Joe Cribbs' days as a Bill came to an end on a downer as Atlanta's ball-control offense held the ball for 37 minutes and never let the Bills' offense get in sync.
• The Bills were penalized 15 times and finished the season as the league's most penalized team (number and yards).
• The tone of the game was set early as Steve Freeman recovered a William Andrews fumble at the Falcons 12. The Bills then committed three penalties worth 25 yards and Joe Danelo wound up missing a 45-yard field goal.
• The Falcons then moved 48 yards to Mick Luckhurst's field goal.
• Perry Tuttle's fumble after a catch was recovered by Mike Pitts at the Bills 46 and that led to Steve Bartkowski's TD pass to Arthur Cox.
• Darryl Talley recovered a fumble at the Falcons 26, but Ferguson threw an interception.
• On the next series, a Cribbs fumble led to Andrews' TD run and a 17-0 Atlanta lead.
• The Bills got that score back by driving 50 yards in the final 1:29 of the half to Tuttle's TD, enabling Ferguson to set a single-season team TD pass record (26). He also finished with a career-high 25 picks.
• But Atlanta went 89 yards after the second-half kickoff to Andrews' second TD and the Bills were dead.
• Andrews' third TD came in the fourth, and the Bills closed the scoring with a 79-yard drive to Matt Kofler's TD pass to Julius Dawkins.

QUOTES

• Joe Cribbs: "I think I was up for the game. I don't think the attitude of everyone on our team was good, though. I think a lot of players were looking forward to the end of the season and going home. I just wanted to end four years with a big game. The way I think about it, that was my last game as a Buffalo Bill."
• Falcons defensive end Mike Pitts: "I guess Buffalo didn't think they'd have to play that hard to beat us."
• Kay Stephenson: "An awful lot of players played extremely hard, but we just made too many mistakes. We didn't start with any excuses and we won't finish with any."
• Joe Ferguson: "We didn't play well, we didn't concentrate and our penalties reflected that. Hopefully we can correct that in the future. Today and the whole season was very frustrating for a lot of players."
• Fred Smerlas: "People don't come to watch the ref throw yellow flags. I was so frustrated, I can imagine how frustrated the fans must have been. I wish the refs would have watched the plays instead of the individual players. It was ridiculous."

WEEK 16 GAMES

Mia 34, NYJ 14	Min 20, Cinc 14
KC 48, Den 17	Wash 31, NYG 22
Chi 23, GB 21	Balt 20, Hou 10
Rams 26, NO 24	Sea 24, NE 6
LAR 30, SD 14	St.L 31, Phil 7
Det 23, TB 20	Clev 30, Pit 17
SF 42, Dal 17	

STANDINGS: SIXTEENTH WEEK

AFC EAST	W	L	T	CENTRAL	W	L	T	WEST	W	L	T	NFC EAST	W	L	T	CENTRAL	W	L	T	WEST	W	L	T
Miami	12	4	0	Pittsburgh	10	6	0	Raiders	12	4	0	Washington	14	2	0	Detroit	9	7	0	San Fran	10	6	0
Buffalo	8	8	0	Cleveland	9	7	0	Denver	9	7	0	Dallas	12	4	0	Green Bay	8	8	0	LA Rams	9	7	0
New England	8	8	0	Cincinnati	7	9	0	Seattle	9	7	0	St. Louis	8	7	1	Minnesota	8	8	0	N.Orleans	8	8	0
NY Jets	7	9	0	Houston	2	14	0	San Diego	6	10	0	Philadelphia	5	11	0	Chicago	8	8	0	Atlanta	7	9	0
Baltimore	7	9	0					Kan. City	6	10	0	NY Giants	3	12	1	Tampa Bay	2	14	0				

At A Glance
1984

Jan. 6 – Steve Freeman was named to *The Sporting News* all-pro team.

Jan. 18 – The Bills said they would seek a preliminary injunction that would take Joe Cribbs out of the Birmingham Stallions training camp until the court ruled on the validity of a right-of-first-refusal clause in his contract.

Jan. 23 – The Stallions opened their training camp in Birmingham without Cribbs.

Jan. 25 – The Bills' proposed injunction against Cribbs was denied by U.S. District Judge John T. Elfvin, but Cribbs couldn't report to Birmingham until after he represented the Bills in the Pro Bowl on Jan. 29.

Jan. 29 – An NFL study showed that the Bills led the NFL in man-games lost to injury in 1983, a total of 192. The next-highest figure was 160 games lost by the Minnesota Vikings.

Jan. 30 – Jerry Glanville resigned as Bills secondary coach to become the defensive coordinator of the Houston Oilers.

Feb. 1 – Jim Kelly talked about trying to learn the run-and-shoot offense of the Houston Gamblers. "I'm real comfortable with the things we're doing," he said. "I'd never done the sprint out before. I've never done anything but be a dropback passer. But they felt I was a good enough athlete to change."

Feb. 2 – Former Bills vice-president for administration Stew Barber testified in court that Joe Cribbs had agreed to the Bills' right-of-first-refusal clause in his contract.

Feb. 3 – Cribbs began practicing with the Stallions.

Feb. 8 – Joe Cribbs' former agent, Dr. Jerry Argovitz, now the owner of the USFL's Houston Gamblers, testified on behalf of Cribbs for four hours.

Feb. 20 – Testimony in the Cribbs trial ended and Judge John T. Elfvin began deliberating his decision.

Feb. 24 – Elfvin ruled that Cribbs could play for the Stallions, ending his Buffalo career. "The Bills have not sustained the burden of showing that the language in the contract that was entered into with Cribbs in 1980 means something other than what it said." Cribbs said: "When you say Buffalo, that means two things to me – the city and the Buffalo Bills management. I have nothing but fond memories of the city and the fans. I had some great moments there and I was very close with my teammates and coaches. But I had some problems with management. We didn't exactly see eye-to-eye and the scars are there to see."

Feb. 25 – Monte Kiffin was hired as linebackers coach. Offensive assistant Al Sandahl left to become Syracuse University's quarterbacks coach.

Feb. 26 – Joe Cribbs made his USFL debut and gained only 52 yards on 16 carries as the Stallions lost at home to New Jersey, 17-6.

March 2 – The Bills named John Becker as tight ends coach and for the first time in seven years hired a full-time strength and conditioning coach, John Speros.

March 3 – NFL owners said they would not oppose a proposal by Colts owner Robert Irsay to move his team to Indianapolis.

March 20 – It was reported that the Bills' involvement in a four-team scouting combine with Dallas, Seattle and San Francisco would be coming to an end. An 11-man group headed by Bum Bright and Tex Schramm bought the Dallas Cowboys for $55 million.

March 21 – Patrick Bowlen purchased the Denver Broncos.

March 28 – Robert Irsay packed up the Colts' belongings in the middle of the night and moved his team to Indianapolis.

April 19 – Steve Young, who signed a $40 million contract to play for the Los Angeles Express of the USFL, said he expected the USFL to fold "because two leagues can't exist."

April 24 – The NFL said it planned to conduct a special draft of USFL players who would have been eligible for the regular draft May 1 but who already had signed with USFL teams.

April 27 – The Bills announced their Silver Anniversary team: Jack Kemp, O.J. Simpson, Cookie Gilchrist, Elbert Dubenion, Bob Chandler, Ernie Warlick, Joe Devlin, Billy Shaw, Al Bemiller, Reggie McKenzie, Stew Barber, Paul Maguire, Fred Smerlas, Tom Sestak, Ben Williams, Ron McDole, John Tracey, Jim Haslett, Mike Stratton, Robert James, Butch Byrd, George Saimes, Steve Freeman and Pete Gogolak.

April 28 – The Bills revealed their new helmet, the same charging Buffalo, but now laid over a red helmet instead of white.

April 30 – Bob Zeman left the Bills staff to join the Raiders. The team hired Pete Carroll to coach the defensive backfield and promoted Don Lawrence to defensive coordinator.

May 1 – The Bills traded first-round draft positions with Miami, moving from 14th to 26th and also received two third-round picks. The Bills then selected Notre Dame running back Greg Bell with their choice. Miami chose linebacker Jackie Shipp in the Bills' old No. 14 slot. Also chosen by the Bills were San Jose St. wide receiver Eric Richardson (second), Miami cornerback Rodney Bellinger (third), San Diego St. defensive lineman Sean McNanie (third), Miami fullback Speedy Neal (third), Illinois wide receiver Mitchell Brookins (fourth) and Northwestern punter John Kidd (fifth). Around the league, New England chose wide receiver Irving Fryar (first), Houston took offensive guard Dean Steinkuhler (second), the Giants selected linebacker Carl Banks (third), Philadelphia chose wide receiver Kenny Jackson (fourth), Kansas City grabbed nose tackle Bill Maas (fifth), Chicago took linebacker Wilbur Marshall (11th), Minnesota selected defensive end Keith Millard (13th), Cleveland grabbed defensive back Don Rogers (18th) and Pittsburgh picked wide receiver Louis Lipps (23rd).

May 2 – The Bills said Greg Bell's ankle injury suffered during his senior year at Notre Dame did not concern them, nor did his choice of agent Greg Lustig to represent him. Lustig was the man who spirited Jim Kelly away to the USFL.

May 7 – While the Bills top draft choices met at a Quarterback Club luncheon, Greg Lustig said: "I don't think there's any question we're going to get top dollar for Greg. And if there's competition (from the USFL), the price is going up."

May 8 – Joe Cribbs walked out on the Birmingham Stallions in a contract dispute, demanding that his salary be doubled. The club in turn filed a $20 million lawsuit against him.

May 16 – The Bills began their annual mini-camp at Rich Stadium.

May 23 – Joe Cribbs returned to the Stallions and the team dropped its lawsuit.

May 30 – Frank Lewis announced his retirement.

May 31 – Sherman White was released and was unhappy about it. "I'm kind of disappointed with the way they handled the situation," he said of receiving a letter from GM Terry Bledsoe informing him of his fate. "I don't think they handled it with any taste or class."

June 5 – The Bills chose Dwight Drane, Darryl Hart and Don Corbin in a special supplemental draft.

June 24 – Birmingham finished with a 14-4 regular season record and Joe Cribbs won the USFL rushing title with 1,467 yards on 227 carries.

July 2 – Jim Kelly was named the USFL's player of the year after compiling nine 300-yard passing games and throwing for 5,219 yards and a single-season pro football record 44 touchdowns for the Houston Gamblers. Upon receiving the award, Kelly said: "I cried when Buffalo drafted me (in the 1983 draft). Well, maybe I didn't cry, but it wasn't one of the greatest things that happened in my life. You

Ralph Wilson wasn't sure his team would survive three or four years in the old AFL, but in 1984, he and the Bills celebrated their Silver Anniversary season. Unfortunately the Bills slumped to 2-14.

can't be a great quarterback in snow and 30 mph winds." Bills management wasn't pleased by his statements. "I think it's unfortunate that a moment of considerable personal triumph for him turned into a little bit of an unfortunate statement," said Bills general manager Terry Bledsoe. "And I suspect he may feel the same way when he reads it in the papers. He's a talented player and I look forward to the possibility of him being here one day." Said Kay Stephenson: "I don't think anyone should speak first-hand about an organization or place until they've had first-hand experience. Personally, I think Jim Kelly would have liked Buffalo if he'd have come here."

July 14 – Training camp opened for rookies and free agents at Fredonia. First-round draft choice Greg Bell, mired in contract negotiations, did not report. In the second USFL championship, Philadelphia, led by coach Jim Mora, defeated Arizona, 23-3.

July 15 – Rookie free agent Terry Morehead failed his physical and was released by the Bills. He became so angry that he smashed two picture windows in the lobby of Fredonia State's Grissom Hall. No charges were filed.

July 16 – The Bills traded Mario Clark, their starting left cornerback since 1976, to San Francisco for a fourth-round draft pick in 1985.

July 22 – The Bills defeated Cleveland, 12-0, in the annual rookie scrimmage at Edinboro University.

July 24 – Bills veterans reported to training camp and for the first time in many years, there were no holdouts. Upon arriving, Fred Smerlas signed a four-year contract worth $2 million. First-round draft choice Greg Bell ended his one-week holdout by signing a four-year deal worth about $1.74 million. Gov. Mario Cuomo visited the Bills camp and spent the afternoon with owner Ralph Wilson watching practice wearing a Bills No. 1 jersey and a team cap.

July 28 – The Bills traveled to Cleveland Stadium and beat the Browns in a controlled scrimmage, 16-10, as Robb Riddick and Van Williams combined for 118 yards rushing.

Aug. 1 – With Frank Lewis retired and Jerry Butler

expected to miss the season with a knee injury, the Bills traded for a veteran wide receiver, acquiring Preston Dennard from the Rams for a fifth-round draft choice in 1985. The Bills also waived starting outside linebacker Ervin Parker, apparently clearing the way for Darryl Talley to move in, and traded cornerback Chris Williams to the Rams for an undisclosed draft choice.

Aug. 2 – Bill Polian was hired as director of pro personnel.

Aug. 4 – Chuck Knox's Seattle Seahawks beat the Bills, 7-3, in the preseason opener at the Kingdome. Greg Bell debuted with 26 yards on five carries.

Aug. 11 – The Bills opened their home preseason schedule with a 23-13 victory over New England as Greg Bell gained 55 yards and Joe Danelo made three field goals.

Aug. 13 – It was determined that safety Jeff Nixon would need a second year of rehabilitation on his injured knee, so he was placed on the injured reserve list.

Aug. 14 – Terry Bledsoe confirmed that the Bills would build a new indoor practice facility at Rich Stadium, an air-inflated bubble.

Aug. 18 – Detroit handed the Bills a 17-12 loss at Rich Stadium before only 19,659.

Aug. 21 – The Bills traded their first-round draft choice from 1982, wide receiver Perry Tuttle, to Tampa Bay for a seventh-round draft choice. Also, fullback Roosevelt Leaks was waived.

Aug. 22 – USFL owners decided to switch their 1986 season to the fall in an effort to go head-to-head with the NFL. The league planned to play in the spring of 1985.

Aug. 26 – The Bills closed preseason with a horrible performance, a 38-7 loss to Chicago at the Hoosier Dome in Indianapolis.

Aug. 27 – Among the Bills final cuts were punter Greg Cater and running back Roland Hooks.

Aug. 29 – Kay Stephenson announced that rookie Greg Bell would start the season opener against New England. Stephenson defended quarterback Joe Ferguson and took exception to recent criticism he had received. "I think the booing of Joe Ferguson has reached epidemic proportions," he said. "I think

it's bad, very bad. I would hope that our fans would come to the stadium and get behind anybody we put on the field. It's reached drastic proportions and it's not good for our football team."

Sept. 2 – New England spoiled the Bills' season opener, 21-17, before only 48,528 at Rich Stadium. The Bills trailed 21-0 in the second quarter, but rallied in the second half to make it close. Greg Bell gained 19 yards on 12 carries in his less-than-auspicious NFL debut.

Sept. 9 – Joe Ferguson suffered a bruised and bloodied nose, but the damage to the Bills was even worse as they were routed in St. Louis, 37-7. Buffalo gained only 171 yards and nine first downs. "When was the last time we played a game like that?" Ralph Wilson wondered after the game.

Sept. 10 – Joe Ferguson's nose was determined to be not broken, so he was cleared to play against Miami. Cornerback Rodney Bellinger wasn't as lucky. His neck injury would sideline him 8-10 weeks.

Sept. 17 – Miami beat the Bills, 21-17, before 65,455 at Rich Stadium and a *Monday Night Football* audience. Dan Marino completed 26 of 35 passes for 296 yards and three TDs.

Sept. 19 – The Bills acquired veteran cornerback Brian Carpenter from Washington for a 12th-round draft pick in 1985. To make room, Marco Tongue was waived.

Sept. 20 – Strong safety Martin Bayless was claimed off waivers from St. Louis and Len Walterscheid was waived.

Sept. 22 – Kay Stephenson responded to a comment made by O.J. Simpson on the *Monday Night Football* telecast. Simpson said that Stephenson had "taken a relaxed approach. I think it's been a mistake. It's time he got a little tougher and stressed discipline more. This team is in disarray." Said Stephenson: "We probably have one of the best disciplined teams in the NFL. We've probably worked harder than 90 percent of the teams in the league. I've never been associated with a team that has worked as hard as this one." Said Charlie Romes: "Simpson was out of order saying those remarks. We worked our butts off in camp. He's got no right saying that kind of stuff. That ABC stuff has gone to his head."

Sept. 23 – Joe Ferguson had one of his best days ever before suffering a severely sprained right ankle during the Bills' fourth straight loss, 28-26, to the Jets at Rich Stadium. "Joe Ferguson has played better this season than he ever has in the last 11 years," gushed Ralph Wilson. Wilson was asked what he did when Ferguson got hurt. "I went and drank some wine. I've never had a drink during a game in 25 years of owning this team, but I had a few sips of wine then."

Sept. 24 – Kay Stephenson said he would complain formally to the NFL about the officiating in the Jets game, the main issue being Wesley Walker's first TD, which replays showed shouldn't have been a touchdown because he failed to get both feet inbounds.

Sept. 25 – Kay Stephenson said that if Joe Ferguson couldn't play against the Colts in Indianapolis, Joe Dufek would start at quarterback rather than Matt Kofler.

Sept. 26 – O.J. Simpson defended his remarks during the Dolphins' telecast. "Once you're losing, you're sensitive about everything," he said. "It's ironic to me that if there was any (national) criticism of me in the game, it was because I cheered for Buffalo too much. It hurt me to hear the criticism of the players. It bothers me that the only place I was criticized was the town I was cheering for."

Sept. 30 – Joe Ferguson, who was tied for the NFL's longest consecutive quarterback starting streak with Philadelphia's Ron Jaworski at 107, didn't play as the Bills met the Colts in the Hoosier Dome for the first time and lost, 31-17. Joe Dufek got the start and threw for 205 yards while Greg Bell enjoyed his first 100-yard rushing game, gaining 144 in the loss.

Oct. 2 – Talking about the decline of NFL ratings on the networks, CBS executive producer Terry O'Neill said: "It's oversaturation of football. I've never seen a year with such a difference between the good and bad teams. And it's not just bad teams, they're unwatchable. I don't know how anybody can watch the Buffalo Bills. You tell me how it's possible to care about Green Bay or Tampa Bay or the Bengals."

Oct. 7 – The Bills fell to 0-6 and saw their regular-season losing streak reach eight in a 27-17 loss to Philadelphia in front of only 37,755 at Rich Stadium. Joe Ferguson missed his second straight game, Joe Dufek suffered an ankle injury and Matt Kofler had to finish at quarterback.

Oct. 9 – Cornerback Lawrence Johnson was obtained from Cleveland for a draft choice and Lucious Smith was waived.

Oct. 10 – Joe Ferguson returned to practice and seemed likely to play against Seattle. Meanwhile, defensive coordinator Don Lawrence responded to criticism he had been receiving. "I've been in this business long enough to know that if you don't win, there will be criticism," he said. "Whether it's justified or not doesn't make any difference. We've just got to keep working at it. People don't want to hear excuses, so why give any?"

Oct. 12 – Former Bill Reggie McKenzie took a shot at the Bills and their struggles when he said: "When you keep sweeping things under the rug, something is going to start to smell. I'm like O.J., I'm pulling for those people when we're not playing them. I don't like to see them 0-6, but at the present time, a fact is a fact."

Oct. 14 – Seattle jumped to a 17-0 first-quarter lead thanks to special teams breakdowns by Buffalo. The Bills never recovered in a 31-28 loss to the Seahawks at the Kingdome.

Oct. 16 – Receiver Robert Holt failed a physical exam and was released.

Oct. 17 – The USFL filed a $1.32 billion lawsuit against the NFL, accusing the NFL of involvement "in a conspiracy" to destroy the USFL through a monopoly on players, stadium leases and television contracts.

Oct. 21 – Denver raced to a 23-0 halftime lead and rested John Elway in the second half in rolling past the Bills, 37-7. The 31,204 fans at Rich Stadium started singing "Good-bye Kay, we're glad to see you go."

Oct. 24 – Ralph Wilson defended Kay Stephenson: "As far as I'm concerned, it's time for the players to start rallying around Kay and winning a few games. I hope they'll surprise me one day and win a game." Said center Will Grant: "He's right. It's time for people to start blocking, tackling, catching balls. The worst thing that could happen to us would be to change coaches in midstream."

Oct. 28 – The Bills dropped to 0-9 and lost their 11th straight regular season game, a 38-7 disaster to Miami in the Orange Bowl. The Dolphins amassed 493 total yards of offense.

Oct. 30 – Joe Danelo was waived and ex-Rams

kicker Chuck Nelson was signed.

Nov. 4 – Earnest Byner picked up Willis Adams' fumble and raced 55 yards for the winning touchdown with 7:32 left to play, giving Cleveland a 13-10 victory over the Bills at rainy Rich Stadium.

Nov. 5 – The Supreme Court ruled that the NFL could not block future franchise shifts, saying that power violated antitrust laws. But the ruling did not prevent new rules being drawn up to limit franchise shifts. Statistics showed that the Bills offensive line had been penalized 28 times in 10 games for holding or illegal use of hands, Ken Jones leading the way with nine.

Nov. 11 – New England scored 28 second-half points and ran away from the Bills, 38-10, at Sullivan Stadium. Joe Ferguson and Matt Kofler combined to complete just 13 of 48 passes.

Nov. 18 – Greg Bell ran 85 yards for a touchdown on the first play of the game and Buffalo won its first game of the year, stunning Dallas, 14-3, in front of a sellout Rich Stadium crowd. Bell gained a career-high 206 yards.

Nov. 25 – While the Bills were getting pasted by the Redskins, 41-14, in Washington, it was reported that University of Washington coach Don James had been offered the Bills head coaching position starting in 1985, but that he turned it down. Joe Theismann completed 26 of 33 passes for 311 yards and two TDs for the Redskins. In San Diego, Charlie Joiner set a new NFL record for career receptions, breaking Charley Taylor's mark.

Nov. 26 – After Don James allegedly turned down the Bills' head coaching job, it was reported that Illinois coach Mike White had been offered the job. General Manager Terry Bledsoe denied an offer was made.

Nov. 27 – Buffalo radio legend Stan Barron died at Erie County Medical Center of cancer. The longtime Bills' color analyst had remained in the booth through 1983, but his illness sidelined him in 1984. Kay Stephenson announced that for the first time in his career, Joe Ferguson was being benched and Joe Dufek would start against the Colts.

Dec. 2 – The Bills scored 21 points in the first quarter behind new starting quarterback Joe Dufek, then held off the Colts, 21-15, at Rich Stadium, in front of 20,693, the smallest crowd in Rich Stadium history.

Dec. 3 – Lou Saban expressed interest in coaching the Bills for a third time if Ralph Wilson wanted him.

Dec. 8 – A report indicated that former Browns coach Sam Rutigliano was the likely candidate to become the Bills' new head coach, although the Bills denied the report.

Dec. 9 – Joe Dufek suffered a difficult day as the Bills played the Jets for the first time in Giants Stadium and lost, 21-17. Tony Paige scored the winning TD in the fourth quarter. In Los Angeles, Eric Dickerson surpassed O.J. Simpson's single-season rushing record, gaining 215 yards against Houston to give him 2,007 for the year. It did come in the 15th game, whereas Simpson rushed for 2,003 yards in 14 games in 1973.

Dec. 11 – Jim Kelly, responding to a report from Buffalo where Ralph Wilson was wondering when Kelly would be available to the Bills, said: "Are you crazy? That's a typical NFL rumor. I'm not available and there's no problem with my contract."

Dec. 12 – For the first time since 1971, the Bills placed no one on the AFC Pro Bowl squad.

Dec. 16 – The Bills played a brutal run-for-the-bus finale, losing 52-21 in Cincinnati. Ex-Bill Sam Wyche completed his first year as a head coach by

leading the Bengals to an 8-8 record after an 0-5 start.

Dec. 17 – Kay Stephenson turned 40 years old, and the Bills didn't present him with a pink slip as expected. Instead, Stephenson sounded as if he wouldn't be fired. "I told our team that at this time next year, I expect this football team to be in the playoffs," he said. "There's no question we will get this turned around and be a potent football team."

Dec. 20 – Sam Rutigliano's name was dropped as a possible candidate to become the Bills new head coach and speculation was that Kay Stephenson would remain.

Dec. 22 – The defending Super Bowl champion Raiders lost the AFC wild-card game to Seattle, 13-7.

Dec. 23 – The Giants defeated the Rams, 16-13, in the NFC wild-card game.

Dec. 27 – Offensive line coach Jim Niblack resigned to take a similar position with Orlando of the USFL.

Dec. 28 – UPI named Greg Bell to its all-rookie team.

Dec. 29 – A *Buffalo News* fans poll indicated that 72 percent of those who responded said the Bills should use the No. 1 pick in the 1985 draft to pick Boston College quarterback Doug Flutie. Another 16 percent said they should draft someone else, and of the "others" Virginia Tech defensive end Bruce Smith was the second favorite choice behind Pitt offensive tackle Bill Fralic.

Dec. 29 – Miami ripped Seattle, 31-10, and San Francisco got past the Giants, 21-10, as the divisional playoff round began.

Dec. 30 – In the other two divisional round games, Pittsburgh downed Denver, 24-17, and Chicago won its first playoff game since 1963, beating Washington, 23-19.

Jan. 6, 1985 – Dan Marino threw for an AFC Championship Game record 421 yards and had four TD passes as Miami routed Pittsburgh, 45-28, at the Orange Bowl. In the NFC Championship Game at Candlestick Park, the 49ers blanked the Bears, 23-0, as Ray Wersching kicked three field goals and Joe Montana passed for 233 yards and one TD.

Jan. 20, 1985 – San Francisco won its second Super Bowl title in four years, routing the Dolphins, 38-16, at Stanford Stadium. MVP Joe Montana passed for a Super Bowl record 331 yards and three TDs and Roger Craig set a Super Bowl record by scoring three TDs.

Jan. 27, 1985 – Art Still of Kansas City returned a fumble 83 yards for a TD to lift the AFC to a 22-14 victory in the Pro Bowl at Aloha Stadium.

By the Numbers - 1984

TEAM STATISTICS

TEAM STATISTICS	BILLS	OPP
First downs	263	345
Rushing	98	134
Passing	149	186
Penalty	16	25
Third downs	86-243	87-203
Total yards	4,341	5,582
Avg. game	271.3	348.9
Plays	1,046	1,052
Avg. play	4.2	5.3
Net rushing yds	1,643	2,106
Avg. game	102.7	131.6
Avg. play	4.1	4.0
Net passing yds	2,698	3,476
Comp/att	298/588	300/495
Sacks/lost	60-554	26-191
Interceptions	30	16
Percentage	50.7	60.6
Punts/avg	90-41.1	72-39.1
Fumbles/lost	31-14	36-21
Penalties/yds	121-997	87-734
Touchdowns	31	56
Extra points	31-31	56-56
Field goals	11-21	20-28
Safeties	0	1
Kick ret./avg	76-18.7	44-21.8
Punt ret./avg	33-9.0	52-11.5

RUSHING

RUSHING	ATT	YDS	AVG	TD
Bell	262	1100	4.2	7
Neal	49	175	3.6	1
Ferguson	19	102	5.4	0
Moore	24	84	3.5	0
Kofler	10	80	8.0	0
Williams	18	51	2.8	0
Brookins	2	27	13.5	0
Dufek	9	22	2.4	1
Hunter	1	6	6.0	0
Riddick	3	3	1.0	0
Franklin	1	-7	-7.0	0
TOTALS	**398**	**1643**	**4.1**	**9**

PASSING

PASSING	COMP	ATT	INT	YDS	TD	COMP%	SACKS	RATE
Ferguson	191	344	17	1991	12	55.5	35-357	63.5
Dufek	74	150	8	829	4	49.3	10-86	52.9
Kofler	33	93	5	432	2	35.5	15-111	35.8
Mosley	0	1	0	0	0	00.0	0-0	39.6
TOTALS	**298**	**588**	**30**	**3252**	**18**	**50.7**	**60-554**	**56.3**

KICKING

KICKING	1-19	20-29	30-39	40-49	50+	TOT	PAT	PTS
Danelo	0-0	5-5	2-4	0-4	1-3	8-16	17-17	41
Nelson	0-0	0-0	1-2	2-3	0-0	3-5	14-14	23
TOTALS	**0-0**	**5-5**	**3-6**	**2-7**	**1-3**	**11-21**	**31-31**	**64**

PUNTING

PUNTING	NO	AVG	LG	In 20	BL
Kidd	88	42.0	63	16	2

RECEIVING

RECEIVING	CAT	YDS	AVG	TD
Franklin	69	862	12.5	4
Bell	34	277	8.1	1
Hunter	33	331	10.0	2
Moore	33	172	5.2	0
Dennard	30	417	13.9	7
Riddick	23	276	12.0	0
Dawkins	21	295	14.0	2
Brookins	18	318	17.7	1
Neal	9	76	8.4	0
Barnett	8	67	8.4	0
Brammer	7	49	7.0	0
Williams	5	46	9.2	1
Mosley	4	38	9.5	0
White	4	28	7.0	0
TOTALS	**298**	**3252**	**10.9**	**18**

SCORE BY QUARTERS

BILLS	66	57	64	63	0 -	250
OPP	13	148	72	121	0 -	454

DEFENSIVE STATISTICAL LEADERS

TACKLES: Marve 135 primary - 53 assists - 188 total, Haslett 100-48-148, Freeman 64-47-111, D. Wilson 47-46-93, K. Johnson 55-35-90, Talley 64-25-89, Romes 40-42-82, B. Williams 40-37-77, Keating 45-18-63, Smerlas 32-30-62, Sanford 39-14-53, Kush 23-25-48, Carpenter 26-9-35

SACKS: Talley 5, Haslett 3.5, K. Johnson 3.5, McNanie 3, B. Williams 2, Freeman 2, Smerlas 2, Kush 2

FUMBLE RECOVERIES: Marve 3, Haslett 3, Smerlas 2, Sanford 2, Carpenter 2

FORCED FUMBLES: Marve 1, Freeman 1, Talley 1, Romes 1, Smerlas 1, Kush 1, Bellinger 1

INTERCEPTIONS: Romes 5-130 yards, 26.0 avg., 0 TD; Freeman 3-45, 15.0, 0 TD; Carpenter 3-11, 3.7, 0 TD

SPECIAL TEAMS STATISTICAL LEADERS

KICKOFF RETURNS: V. Williams 39-820, 21.0, 0 TD; Wilson 34-576, 16.9, 0 TD

PUNT RETURNS: Wilson 33-297, 9.0, 1 TD

GAME 1 - Sunday, Sept. 2, 1984 - PATRIOTS 21, BILLS 17

Patriots	14	7	0	0 -	21
Bills	0	3	7	7 -	17

Attendance at Rich Stadium - 48,528

NE: Starring 65 pass from Grogan (Franklin kick), :51
NE: Ramsey 3 pass from Grogan (Franklin kick), 7:57
NE: Collins 4 run (Franklin kick), 7:11
Buf: FG Danelo 27, 11:43
Buf: Dennard 8 pass from Ferguson (Danelo kick), 9:39
Buf: Hunter 9 pass from Ferguson (Danelo kick), 10:54

	BUF	NE
First downs	24	16
Rushing yds	94	102
Passing yds	232	213
Punts-avg	3-44.7	4-42.3
Fumbles-lost	3-1	1-1
Penalties-yds	4-35	7-43
Poss. time	34:08	25:52

BILLS LEADERS: Rushing - Bell 12-29, Neal 2-2, Ferguson 3-15, Moore 4-26, Williams 7-16, Hunter 1-6; **Passing** - Ferguson 27-40-0 - 263; **Receiving** - Franklin 10-96, Hunter 5-58, Moore 2-13, Dennard 2-15, Dawkins 2-16, Brookins 3-30, Neal 3-35.

PATRIOTS LEADERS: Rushing - Collins 21-83, Tatupu 5-23, Grogan 3-(-4); **Passing** - Grogan 12-22-1 - 227; **Receiving** - Jones 4-71, Starring 3-105, Collins 2-24, Ramsey 2-13, Dawson 1-14.

NOTES

• The Bills dropped the season opener as the Patriots grabbed a 21-0 lead, then hung on in front of the smallest opening-day crowd to see the Bills in Rich Stadium history.
• Greg Bell had a rough NFL debut and sat out the second half, but Byron Franklin had a big afternoon.
• On the second play of the game, Steve Grogan fired a 65-yard TD pass to Stephen Starring.
• The Bills punted, then the Pats drove 60 yards in nine plays to Grogan's TD pass to Derrick Ramsey. Tony Collins gained 34 yards on six carries on the drive.
• Joe Danelo missed a 45-yard field goal in the second quarter and the Pats proceeded to drive 72 yards in eight plays to Collins' TD run. The key play was Grogan's third-and-seven pass to Collins for 19 to the Bills 40, then his 35-yard strike to Starring to the 4.
• The Bills got on the board with Danelo's field goal after Charlie Romes' interception at the Pats 28.
• Early in the third, after an exchange of punts, the Bills moved 78 yards in 12 plays with Joe Ferguson hitting Preston Dennard for the TD. Ferguson was eight-for-10 for 74 yards on the drive.
• The Bills got to the Pats 9 early in the fourth, but Franklin lost a fumble to Roland James. The Pats gave it

WEEK 1 GAMES

Atl 36, NO 28	Den 20, Cinc 17
KC 37, Pitt 27	LAR 24, Hou 14
NYJ 23, Ind 14	Mia 35, Wash 17
GB 24, St.L 23	NYG 28, Phil 27
SD 42, Minn 13	SF 30, Det 27
Chi 34, TB 14	Sea 33, Clev 0
Dal 20, Rams 13	

back on Ken Johnson's recovery of a Grogan fumble and the Bills went 44 yards in eight plays to pull within 21-17. Booker Moore broke a 21-yard run to the 20 and Ferguson threw 12 yards to Franklin on fourth-and-11. Two plays later, he found Tony Hunter for the TD. The Pats then consumed the final 3:55.

QUOTES

• Fred Smerlas on the slow start: "If you guys had been writing the script, it would have been a 70-0 final."
• Kay Stephenson: "I'm very proud of our team. We're a very young team with many people who never lined up in an NFL game before. They had to come down a hard road and that's tough. New England took us out of our gameplan very early. Without Joe Ferguson doing the job he did today, we could have been in real trouble."
• Patriots running back Tony Collins: "I guess we don't have that killer instinct yet. We know Buffalo is no pushover team, but maybe we got a little slack when we got the lead."
• Ralph Wilson: "I was disappointed with the way our defense played in the first half, we have a better defense than that. But we've got a lot of young players. They could have folded up and lost 55-0. Overall I'm encouraged. We didn't expect, with the young fellows, to come out and roll over people. It's going to take time, maybe a half season. We have to be patient."
• Joe Ferguson: "I think our players are down and will be for a couple of days. I was proud of the way we came back. I just wish our defense hadn't given up those early scores and the offense hadn't made those errors. You've got to be aware of the fans early. I went out there the first time and heard a loud roar. I didn't think it was going to be favorable. The fans were enthusiastic and great."

GAME 2 - Sunday, Sept. 9, 1984 - CARDINALS 37, BILLS 7

Bills	0	0	7	0 -	7
Cardinals	17	7	7	6 -	37

Attendance at Busch Stadium - 35,785

St.L: FG O'Donoghue 23, 4:50
St.L: Green 4 pass from Lomax (O'Donoghue kick), 7:37
St.L: Anderson 4 pass from Lomax (O'Donoghue kick), 13:26
St.L: Anderson 2 run (O'Donoghue kick), 14:15
St.L: Mitchell 1 run (O'Donoghue kick), 7:04
Buf: Dennard 22 pass from Ferguson (Danelo kick), 12:08
St.L: FG O'Donoghue 21, 2:32
St.L: FG O'Donoghue 52, 10:53

	BUF	ST.L
First downs	9	28
Rushing yds	54	221
Passing yds	117	265
Punts-avg	6-35.8	1-36.0
Fumbles-lost	0-0	0-0
Penalties-yds	7-42	7-55
Poss. time	17:17	42:43

BILLS LEADERS: Rushing - Bell 4-3, Ferguson 1-15, Kofler 2-30, Williams 1-6; **Passing** - Ferguson 12-21-2 - 144, Kofler 1-11-1 - 4; **Receiving** - Franklin 2-9, Hunter 4-50, Moore 1-6, Dennard 1-22, Dawkins 2-47, Brookins 2-8, Williams 1-6.
CARDINALS LEADERS: Rushing - Anderson 20-83, Mitchell 11-62, Love 6-34, Ferrell 5-31, Lomax 1-6, McIvor 3-5; **Passing** - Lomax 21-29-0 - 265, McIvor 0-4-0 - 0; **Receiving** - Tilley 5-79, Anderson 5-15, Green 3-51, Marsh 3-72, Mack 2-31, Ferrell 2-8, Harrell 1-9.

WEEK 2 GAMES

Pitt 23, NYJ 17	NYG 28, Dal 7
Rams 20, Clev 17	Ind 35, Hou 21
Chi 27, Den 0	Det 27, Atl 24
LAR 28, GB 7	KC 27, Cinc 22
Phil 19, Minn 17	Mia 28, NE 7
Sea 31, SD 17	NO 17, TB 13
SF 37, Wash 31	

NOTES

• The Bills were manhandled by the Cardinals, managing just 171 yards and nine first downs.
• Joe Ferguson suffered a bad bloody nose when he was sacked by Al Baker in the fourth quarter.
• New cornerback Rod Hill broke his ankle on the opening kickoff, which was returned 39 yards by Stump Mitchell and led to a field goal.
• Mitchell returned John Kidd's first punt 39 yards to the Bills 20 and two plays later, Neil Lomax hit Roy Green for a TD. On the next series, Art Plunkett blocked a Joe Danelo field goal and the Cards proceeded to drive 65 yards in eight plays to O.J. Anderson's TD reception. Lomax hit Cedric Mack for 22 yards and Pat Tilley for 26 on the drive, which gave the Cards a 17-0 lead.
• The Cards drove 83 yards in 10 plays in the second quarter as Anderson scored on a two-yard run. On third-and-13 at the Bills 27, Lomax found Green for a 31-yard gain.
• The score became 31-0 in the third as Mitchell capped a 58-yard drive after a short Kidd punt.
• The Bills scored when Ferguson hit Preston Dennard for a TD. Ferguson had a 15-yard scramble and also hit Julius Dawkins for 37 yards to the Cards 22. Neil O'Donoghue had two fourth-quarter field goals.

QUOTES

• Kay Stephenson: "We got beat physically, mentally, every way you can get beat. They did anything they wanted. They came out and executed and we ended up flat. We didn't get too many at-bats."
• Fred Smerlas: "Our defense couldn't stop them, our special teams put us in bad field position all day and our offense couldn't move the ball. Anytime those three things happen to you, you're in trouble."
• Cards defensive end Al Baker on Ferguson's injury: "His face hit the turf. They say this turf is supposed to be softer than last year's, but if you ask Joe I don't think he'd agree. He got real bloody. Is there a fine for bleeding on the field? Thank goodness it wasn't Joe's throwing arm. Now he might just be a little uglier, like all us defensive linemen."
• Chris Keating: "As far as special teams go, we've just got to get guys who want to fly to the ball. If they aren't playing regularly (on offense or defense), they've got to contribute on special teams and that hasn't been yet this season. Some guys have to wake up and realize that's part of football. I'm not going to point at anybody else, I'll include myself."
• Cards quarterback Neil Lomax: "This reminded me of those great Portland State days. Everything worked. I had a lot of fun out there."

STANDINGS: SECOND WEEK

AFC EAST	W	L	T	CENTRAL	W	L	T	WEST	W	L	T	NFC EAST	W	L	T	CENTRAL	W	L	T	WEST	W	L	T
Miami	2	0	0	Pittsburgh	1	1	0	Raiders	2	0	0	NY Giants	2	0	0	Chicago	2	0	0	San Fran	2	0	0
NY Jets	1	1	0	Cincinnati	0	2	0	Kan. City	2	0	0	Dallas	1	1	0	Green Bay	1	1	0	Atlanta	1	1	0
New England	1	1	0	Cleveland	0	2	0	Seattle	2	0	0	Philadelphia	1	1	0	Detroit	1	1	0	N.Orleans	1	1	0
Indianapolis	1	1	0	Houston	0	2	0	San Diego	1	1	0	St. Louis	1	1	0	Tampa Bay	0	2	0	LA Rams	1	1	0
Buffalo	0	2	0					Denver	1	1	0	Washington	0	2	0	Minnesota	0	2	0				

GAME 3 - Monday, Sept. 17, 1984 - DOLPHINS 21, BILLS 17

NOTES

• The Bills dug themselves another deep hole, then rallied to make it close.

• Uwe von Schamann missed a 38-yard field goal on the first possession, but the Bills failed to move and punted. The Dolphins drove 62 yards in eight plays to Dan Marino's TD pass to Mark Duper. Marino hit Woody Bennett for 23 and Mark Clayton for 22 along the way.

• In the second, Joe Danelo had a 47-yard field goal blocked by Bob Baumhower. Miami then moved 52 yards in eight plays to Marino's TD pass to Clayton. Three Bennett runs picked up first downs.

• Steve Freeman recovered a Tony Nathan fumble at the Miami 22 with 1:16 left, but after Joe Ferguson's 18-yard pass to Buster Barnett, Fergy was sacked for a loss of 12 and Joe Danelo made a 33-yard field goal with five seconds left.

• Miami scored on its first possession of the third as Marino threw a TD pass to Nat Moore.

• The Bills answered with a 13-play, 80-yard drive to Speedy Neal's first NFL TD. Lyle Blackwood's 23-yard interference penalty in the end zone put the ball on the 1.

• Ferguson wasted a Freeman interception by fumbling at the Miami 25, with Doug Betters recovering. Miami gave it back when Darryl Talley forced Jimmy Cefalo to fumble at the Bills 21 and Marco Tongue recovered. The Bills then launched a 79-yard, nine-play drive to Ferguson's 37-yard TD pass to Julius Dawkins. Neal converted on fourth-and-one and Ferguson threw 24 yards to Byron Franklin along the way.

QUOTES

• Kay Stephenson: "Marino got rid of the ball and made big plays when many other quarterbacks would have been on the ground, I assure you."

• Ben Williams: "Miami, *Monday Night Football*, the butt-whipping we took last week, we had enough reasons to play the way we did (fired up). It was probably the best game we played as a team all year. We were just a little short. But we lost to a pretty good team, so you can't hang your head about it. We knew we had to put pressure on Marino. We've got a good secondary, but someone of Marino's caliber can pick them apart. I believe it's (emotion) here to stay. It's got to be. It isn't something you can just turn on and off."

• Miami coach Don Shula: "I don't know of anyone ever who has been more advanced than Marino. He's the first quarterback ever to be picked to start the Pro Bowl in his rookie season (last year) and I think that says it all. He has been outstanding from day one; he never seemed awed or intimidated. This was one tough football game. I had a feeling right from the start that Buffalo would be ready to play. They didn't resemble the team we've seen on film the last two weeks."

WEEK 3 GAMES

Minn 27, Atl 20	Chi 9, GB 7
NYJ 43, Cinc 23	Den 24, Cle 14
TB 21, Det 17	SD 31, Hou 14
Pitt 24, Rams 14	LAR 22, KC 20
Wash 30, NYG 14	SF 30, NO 20
Dal 23, Phil 17	NE 38, Sea 23
St.L 34, Ind 33	

Dolphins	7 7 7 0 -	21
Bills	0 3 7 7 -	17

Attendance at Rich Stadium - 65,455

Mia:	Duper 11 pass from Marino (von Schamann kick), 12:51
Mia:	Clayton 12 pass from Marino (von Schamann kick), 9:56
Buf:	FG Danelo 33, 14:55
Mia:	N. Moore 1 pass from Marino (von Schamann kick), 4:33
Buf:	Neal 1 run (Danelo kick), 11:03
Buf:	Dawkins 37 pass from Ferguson (Danelo kick), 5:40

	BUF	MIA
First downs	16	23
Rushing yds	68	79
Passing yds	228	289
Punts-avg	4-40.0	2-35.7
Fumbles-lost	4-2	4-2
Penalties-yds	9-70	5-43
Poss. time	27:02	32:58

BILLS LEADERS: Rushing - Neal 12-34, Ferguson 2-28, Moore 1-1, Williams 4-5; **Passing** - Ferguson 23-38-0 - 259; **Receiving** - Franklin 7-92, Bell 1-8, Moore 2-10, Dennard 1-6, Dawkins 3-51, Neal 3-21, Williams 3-39, Barnett 2-26, White 1-6.

DOLPHINS LEADERS: Rushing - Nathan 12-27, Bennett 16-56, Marino 5-(-4); **Passing** - Marino 26-35-1 - 296; **Receiving** - Jensen 2-18, Rose 1-18, Johnson 3-44, Duper 5-68, Clayton 2-34, Cefalo 4-52, Nathan 4-24, Moore 4-29, Hardy 1-9.

GAME 4 - Sunday, Sept. 23, 1984 - JETS 28, BILLS 26

NOTES

• Joe Ferguson suffered a severely sprained right ankle when he was sacked by Joe Klecko with 2:49 left and the Bills at their 38 and trying to pull out the game after Eugene Marve had recovered a Tony Paige fumble. Matt Kofler entered and promptly was intercepted by Ken Schroy with 2:33 left.

• The defense got the ball back with 1:04 left, but Kofler threw three incompletions in four plays.

• The Bills took their first lead of the season as Joe Danelo made a first-quarter field goal. On the next series, Ferguson threw a 43-yard pass to Mitchell Brookins to set up his one-yard TD pass to Van Williams.

• The defense then forced a punt, but the Jets ran a fake from the Bills 24 and Paige went 23 yards on the final play of the first quarter. Paige scored three plays later on a two-yard run and the momentum shifted.

• The Jets drove 48 yards in seven plays to Ryan's TD pass to Wesley Walker.

• Then, one play after a Bills punt, Walker caught a 44-yard TD pass, beating Lucious Smith.

• Each team missed a field goal before the half ended, Danelo missing from 40 yards.

• He atoned by making three field goals in the third, but the Bills were frustrated by not scoring a TD, especially on their third possession when they reached the 4. Ferguson was four-of-10 on those three series on plays inside the red zone.

• Lucious Sanford forced and recovered a Freeman McNeil fumble at the Bills 30 early in the fourth, but the Bills didn't capitalize and the Jets came back with Ryan's 35-yard TD pass to Walker.

• The Bills matched it with Ferguson's TD pass to Brookins to cap a 68-yard march.

QUOTES

• Fred Smerlas: "We're playing good ball, we don't deserve to be 0-4."

• Jim Haslett: "What do we have to do to win? When are we going to get a call?"

• Jets quarterback Pat Ryan: "The fake punt was the big play. They had us stopped, but then we caught them with the fake and were able to score, then we got two more touchdowns."

• Kay Stephenson on the fake punt: "You bet it was a good play to call, and we should have been more ready for a play like that at that time. The wind was in his face, in our territory. It was a perfect place to call it and it worked. It gave them a lot of impetus right there. Our problems are obvious. Any time you continually have new players you're going to have a problem with continuity. You're not going to be able to utilize your entire defensive strategy."

WEEK 4 GAMES

Sea 38, Chi 9	Mia 44, Ind 7
Dal 20, GB 6	Atl 42, Hou 10
Den 21, KC 0	Rams 24, Cinc 14
Minn 29, Det 28	Clev 20, Pitt 10
NO 34, St.L 24	SF 21, Phil 9
NYG 17, TB 14	Wash 25, NE 10
LAR 33, SD 30	

Jets	0 21 0 7 -	28
Bills	10 0 9 7 -	26

Attendance at Rich Stadium - 48,330

Buf:	FG Danelo 52, 6:20
Buf:	Williams 1 pass from Ferguson (Danelo kick), 10:21
NYJ:	Paige 2 run (Leahy kick), 1:31
NYJ:	Walker 12 pass from Ryan (Leahy kick), 5:15
NYJ:	Walker 44 pass from Ryan (Leahy kick), 8:23
Buf:	FG Danelo 36, 2:35
Buf:	FG Danelo 27, 7:57
Buf:	FG Danelo 20, 14:14
NYJ:	Walker 35 pass from Ryan (Leahy kick), 8:56
Buf:	Dawkins 31 pass from Ferguson (Danelo kick), 11:02

	BUF	NYJ
First downs	24	23
Rushing yds	87	143
Passing yds	304	248
Punts-avg	4-40.0	4-30.8
Fumbles-lost	2-0	3-2
Penalties-yds	10-83	4-25
Poss. time	30:57	29:03

BILLS LEADERS: Rushing - Bell 11-45, Ferguson 1-2, Moore 4-10, Kofler 1-3, Williams 3-11, Brookins 1-16; **Passing** - Ferguson 31-46-0 - 340, Kofler 0-5-1 - 0; **Receiving** - Franklin 5-55, Bell 1-10, Moore 9-41, Dennard 1-10, Riddick 3-67, Dawkins 3-56, Brookins 3-64, Neal 1-4, Williams 1-1, Barnett 4-32.

JETS LEADERS: Rushing - McNeil 24-112, Paige 5-31, Harper 2-0, Ryan 2-0; **Passing** - Ryan 17-26-1 - 248; **Receiving** - Walker 7-128, Gaffney 3-50, McNeil 2-17, Shuler 2-26, Dennison 2-14, Harper 1-13.

STANDINGS: FOURTH WEEK

AFC EAST	W	L	T	CENTRAL	W	L	T	WEST	W	L	T	NFC EAST	W	L	T	CENTRAL	W	L	T	WEST	W	L	T
Miami	4	0	0	Pittsburgh	2	2	0	Raiders	4	0	0	NY Giants	3	1	0	Chicago	3	1	0	San Fran	4	0	0
NY Jets	3	1	0	Cleveland	1	3	0	Seattle	3	1	0	Dallas	3	1	0	Minnesota	2	2	0	Atlanta	2	2	0
New England	2	2	0	Cincinnati	0	4	0	Denver	3	1	0	St. Louis	2	2	0	Detroit	1	3	0	N.Orleans	2	2	0
Indianapolis	1	3	0	Houston	0	4	0	San Diego	2	2	0	Washington	2	2	0	Tampa Bay	1	3	0	LA Rams	2	2	0
Buffalo	0	4	0					Kan. City	2	2	0	Philadelphia	1	3	0	Green Bay	1	3	0				

Bills	0	10	7	0 - 17	
Colts	7	3	7	14 - 31	

Attendance at the Hoosier Dome - 60,032

Ind: R. Butler 7 pass from Pagel (Biasucci kick), 8:19
Buf: FG Danelo 23, 2:02
Buf: Dufek 11 run (Danelo kick), 7:05
Ind: FG Biasucci 43, 14:57
Buf: Dennard 4 pass from Dufek (Danelo kick), 6:07
Ind: McMillan 10 run (Biasucci kick), 13:37
Ind: McMillan 31 run (Biasuci kick), 5:24
Ind: Kafentzis 59 interception return (Biasucci kick), 8:22

	BUF	IND
First downs	23	21
Rushing yds	175	188
Passing yds	173	142
Punts-avg	5-50.0	5-46.6
Fumbles-lost	0-0	1-1
Penalties-yds	7-55	7-45
Poss. time	34:32	25:28

BILLS LEADERS: Rushing - Bell 29-144, Neal 9-24, Dufek 2-7; **Passing** - Dufek 15-30-3 - 204; **Receiving** - Franklin 5-91, Dennard 3-37, Dawkins 2-27, Brookins 2-32, Brammer 3-17.

COLTS LEADERS: Rushing - McMillan 16-114, Dickey 14-72, Pagel 3-9, Smith 1-(-7); **Passing** - Pagel 14-23-0 - 152; **Receiving** - Butler 6-60, Porter 4-47, McMillan 2-28, Young 1-9, Dickey 1-8.

NOTES

• Joe Dufek made his first NFL start and played respectably. Meanwhile Greg Bell had his first 100-yard rushing game, but it wasn't enough as the Bills lost in their first meeting with the Colts in Indianapolis.
• The Bills led 17-10 in the third when the defense folded. After Terry Daniel's interception, the Colts drove 67 yards to tie on Randy McMillan's 10-yard run up the middle. On the ensuing possession, they drove 96 yards in just seven plays to take the lead. Curtis Dickey got them out of a hole with a 30-yard run on the first play and he later had a 15-yard run before McMillan's 31-yard TD run on a draw.
• Dufek then tried to hit Byron Franklin on a second-and-18 play, but Mark Kafentzis picked it off and ran 59 yards for the clinching TD with 6:38 left to play. At least five Bills could have made the tackle.
• The Colts took a 7-0 lead as Mike Pagel hit Ray Butler for the TD to cap a 76-yard march. But after Dean Biasucci missed a 53-yard field goal, Joe Danelo made a 23-yarder.
• The Bills then went ahead as Dufek ran 11 yards for a TD to cap a 75-yard march that was keyed by Dufek's 54-yard pass to Franklin to the Colts 21. Biasucci tied it before the half ended after a bad snap by Justin Cross aborted a 41-yard Danelo attempt.
• Jim Haslett recovered Larry Anderson's fumbled punt

WEEK 5 GAMES

SF 14, Atl 5	KC 10, Clev 6
Dal 23, Chi 14	SD 27, Det 24
TB 30, GB 27	Den 16, LAR 13
NE 28, NYJ 21	Mia 36, St.L 28
NO 27, Hou 10	Rams 33, NYG 12
Sea 20, Minn 12	Wash 20, Phil 0
Pitt 38, Cinc 17	

in the third at the Colts 29 and Dufek hit Preston Dennard for the go-ahead TD, but then the defense caved in. McMillan gained 110 yards in the second half.

QUOTES

• Will Grant on Daniel's interception that led to the tying TD: "I hate to say this, but they were ready to fold their tents before that interception. We were handling them on the line and they didn't want any part of us. But all of a sudden they got that interception and it gave them a lift. They went from a deflated balloon to one that was over-filled."
• Joe Dufek: "I think I will get better every week. I'm just happy to play because it's the only way to get better. I can't do it sitting on the bench. Hey, you're going to make a couple of mistakes, the key is to cut them down. I had butterflies before the game, but they went away."
• Greg Bell about finally filling Joe Cribbs' shoes: "That's over with; Cribbs is in the USFL. Besides, Cribbs is smaller than I am, so I don't think I'd be able to fit into his shoes. It feels great to go over 100 yards. The linemen and I have been waiting for this day. I think we performed the way we've expected to since the start of the season."
• Charlie Romes: "We shouldn't lose to a team like the Colts. To lose to a team we should have beaten, that's just terrible."
• Colts coach Frank Kush: "We were just pathetic (in the first half). In the second half we changed our blocking and decided to go straight up."
• Rod Kush: "What a horrible second half. They must have talked to McMillan and Dickey extensively at halftime because they just ran like crazy. They're two good backs, but there were wide-open holes to run through and a lot of missed tackles by us."

Eagles	7	10	3	7 - 27	
Bills	7	3	0	7 - 17	

Attendance at Rich Stadium - 37,555

Buf: Bell 12 run (Danelo kick), 8:14
Phi: Woodruff 15 pass from Jaworski (McFadden kick), 13:33
Buf: FG Danelo 27, 5:50
Phi: Kab 4 pass from Jaworski (McFadden kick), 14:11
Phi: FG McFadden 36, 14:58
Phi: FG McFadden 22, 13:27
Buf: Bell 3 run (Danelo kick), 2:42
Phi: Jaworski 1 run (McFadden kick), 10:59

	BUF	PHI
First downs	20	23
Rushing yds	128	111
Passing yds	150	228
Punts-avg	4-48.8	6-37.0
Fumbles-lost	3-1	1-0
Penalties-yds	7-61	9-92
Poss. time	26:51	33:09

BILLS LEADERS: Rushing - Bell 20-77, Moore 2-11, Kofler 2-22, Dufek 4-18; **Passing** - Dufek 4-12-0 - 49, Kofler 10-26-1 - 134; **Receiving** - Franklin 4-71, Bell 4-49, Dennard 3-36, Dawkins 1-7, Brookins 1-14, Brammer 1-6.

EAGLES LEADERS: Rushing - Montgomery 13-67, Oliver 7-26, Williams 8-17, Jaworski 2-1; **Passing** - Jaworski 24-38-0 - 234; **Receiving** - Montgomery 6-45, Spagnola 5-68, Jackson 5-65, Woodruff 4-39, Oliver 2-4, Williams 1-9, Kab 1-4.

NOTES

• Joe Ferguson missed his second straight game. Joe Dufek was injured in the second quarter and Matt Kofler had to finish the Bills' sixth consecutive loss.
• The Bills scored on their opening possession, driving 63 yards to Greg Bell's TD, but the Eagles answered with a 73-yard march to Ron Jaworski's TD pass to Tony Woodruff.
• The Bills took the kickoff and drove 70 yards in 19 plays, but Julius Dawkins dropped a sure TD pass and they settled for Joe Danelo's field goal.
• After an exchange of punts, the Eagles took the lead as Jaworski hit Vyto Kab for a TD. Bell then fumbled one play after the kickoff with 34 seconds left in the half and Paul McFadden made a field goal.
• In the third, after Danelo missed a 52-yarder, the Eagles marched 60 yards to McFadden's field goal.
• In the fourth, Mike Horan's punt from the end zone was returned to the Philadelphia 36 by Donald Wilson. On third-and-four, Wes Hopkins was nailed for a 24-yard pass-interference penalty at the six. Two plays later, Bell scored.
• After an exchange of punts, the Eagles drove 65 yards to the clinching touchdown, the key play a 32-yard pass to Mickey Spagnola and a subsequent personal foul on

WEEK 6 GAMES

Atl 30, Rams 28	Den 28, Det 7
Cinc 13, Hou 3	Mia 31, Pitt 7
TB 35, Minn 31	NE 17, Clev 16
Chi 20, NO 7	NYJ 17, KC 16
St.L 31, Dal 20	SD 34, GB 28
LAR 28, Sea 14	Wash 35, Ind 7
SF 31, NYG 10	

Wilson that put the ball at the 14.
• In trying to rally, Danelo missed a 30-yard field goal and Kofler threw an interception.

QUOTES

• Fred Smerlas: "If we have to give somebody a flying drop kick in the face before the game to get them going, let's do it. I've been on a losing team before, and it's not something I cherish. We've had hard times here before, but 0-6 is ridiculous. There's no excuses, we have to win. That's what we're in the NFL for. That's what makes it all go round. The same chemistry won for us in the past, but it's not now."
• Kay Stephenson: "Anytime you lose the quarterback that you prepared for the week you get hurt some, but that's not meant to be an excuse, you still have to play to win. I'm not going to get into a panic situation because panic breeds disaster. It gets hot in the kitchen, but that's part of it. That's to be expected. You have to gear yourself to handle it."
• Ken Jones: "It seems that when things go bad, everything seems to fall out of the cupboard. But you can't just lay down and die. Maybe if we keep trying, things will go our way."
• Julius Dawkins: "I feel a big responsibility for the loss. If I had caught the ball, 14-7 is a big difference from 10-7. I was about as wide open as you can get; I just misjudged the ball and dropped it. No excuses for it."
• Joe Dufek: "What ticks me off is I can't tell you what a difference it was from last Sunday. I felt good, more relaxed, I was scanning the field much better. It's frustrating to have an opportunity and not take advantage of it."

STANDINGS: SIXTH WEEK

AFC EAST	W	L	T	CENTRAL	W	L	T	WEST	W	L	T	NFC EAST	W	L	T	CENTRAL	W	L	T	WEST	W	L	T
Miami	6	0	0	Pittsburgh	3	3	0	Raiders	5	1	0	Dallas	4	2	0	Chicago	4	2	0	San Fran	6	0	0
NY Jets	4	2	0	Cleveland	1	5	0	Denver	5	1	0	Washington	4	2	0	Tampa Bay	3	3	0	LA Rams	3	3	0
New England	4	2	0	Cincinnati	1	5	0	Seattle	4	2	0	NY Giants	3	3	0	Minnesota	2	4	0	N.Orleans	3	3	0
Indianapolis	2	4	0	Houston	0	6	0	San Diego	4	2	0	St. Louis	3	3	0	Detroit	1	5	0	Atlanta	3	3	0
Buffalo	0	6	0					Kan. City	3	3	0	Philadelphia	2	4	0	Green Bay	1	5	0				

NOTES

• Joe Ferguson returned to action, but two blocked punts in the first quarter led to two Seattle touchdowns and the Bills never recovered.

• Steve Freeman set a new Bills record by playing in his 141st consecutive game.

• The defense actually played pretty well, limiting the Seahawks to 41 yards rushing on 22 attempts, including four yards by newly acquired Franco Harris, leaving him 211 shy of Jim Brown's record.

• Joe Danelo missed a 33-yard field goal on the Bills' first possession. When the second possession failed, Fredd Young blocked John Kidd's punt and the Seahawks took over at the Bills 5, leading to Dave Krieg's TD pass to Daryl Turner. On the next series, Byron Walker blocked Kidd's punt and the Seahawks recovered at the 9, leading to Krieg's TD pass to Steve Largent. One play after the kickoff, Greg Bell fumbled and Bruce Scholtz recovered at the 12, setting up Norm Johnson's field goal and a 17-0 lead.

• The Bills battled back in the second quarter as Freeman stripped Krieg and Lucious Sanford returned the fumble for a TD. Donald Wilson then took a punt back 65 yards for a TD after first fumbling the catch.

• Eric Lane's TD early in the third was keyed by a 29-yard Krieg pass to Turner, but the Bills answered with an 83-yard drive to Ferguson's 50-yard TD pass to Byron Franklin. It was keyed by a third-and-11 pass to Preston Dennard for 18 yards.

• The Bills then went ahead on Ferguson's TD pass to Dennard, after Ferguson had hit Dennard for 48 yards on third-and-14 to the Seahawks 39. But 3:03 later, Krieg hit Largent for the winner as Charlie Romes fell down and the Bills were caught in a blitz, so no one was there to help Romes.

QUOTES

• Seattle coach Chuck Knox: "The Buffalo Bills did a heckuva job. They came in here and battled. They don't deserve to be 0-7."

• Kay Stephenson: "I haven't and won't dwell on what's happened in the past. I can't tell you what an 0-7 team feels like. We just have to get ready for next week."

• Joe Ferguson: "We're 0-7, but we're not really down. Outside of the St. Louis game, we've been in every game. I think we're better than our record."

• Charlie Romes on Largent's winning TD: "I knew what the play was going to be. I had read the route pretty good. We were ready to make the break together, but my feet got caught in his and I just fell down. It's one of those plays you always remember."

• Donald Wilson: "I always think I'm going to break one. When I saw Talley out in front of me, I was pretty sure I was going to go all the way."

• John Kidd on the punt rush: "We worked against it all week. I don't know where the rush came from, I think it was just a basic rush. They just came hard to the outside with good athletes."

WEEK 7 GAMES

St.L 38, Chi 21	NE 20, Cinc 14
Phil 16, Ind 7	Wash 34, Dal 14
Mia 28, Hou 10	LAR 23, Minn 20
NYJ 24, Clev 20	Pitt 20, SF 17
KC 31, SD 13	Det 13, TB 7
NYG 19, Atl 7	Rams 28, NO 10
Den 17, GB 14	

Bills	0 14 7 7	-	28
Seahawks	17 0 7 7	-	31

Attendance at the Kingdome - 59,034

Sea:	Turner 4 pass from Krieg (Johnson kick), 10:54
Sea:	Largent 10 pass from Krieg (Johnson kick), 13:00
Sea:	FG Johnson 25, 15:00
Buf:	Sanford 46 fumble return (Danelo kick), 12:11
Buf:	Wilson 65 punt return (Danelo kick), 13:33
Sea:	Lane 1 run (Johnson kick), 3:18
Buf:	Franklin 50 pass from Ferguson (Danelo kick), 8:50
Buf:	Dennard 3 pass from Ferguson (Danelo kick), 3:50
Sea:	Largent 51 pass from Krieg (Johnson kick), 6:53

	BUF	SEA
First downs	19	15
Rushing yds	142	41
Passing yds	214	197
Punts-avg	4-17.3	6-39.0
Fumbles-lost	3-2	2-1
Penalties-yds	13-99	7-60
Poss. time	35:13	24:47

BILLS LEADERS: Rushing - Bell 28-113, Neal 3-25, Moore 2-7, Ferguson 2-(-3); **Passing** - Ferguson 14-32-2 - 227; **Receiving** - Franklin 3-73, Bell 6-66, Dennard 3-69, Neal 1-8, White 1-11.

SEAHAWKS LEADERS: Rushing - Lane 6-21, Morris 8-12, Harris 3-4, Krieg 3-3, Hughes 2-1; **Passing** - Krieg 17-29-2 - 231; **Receiving** - Largent 5-106, Turner 4-50, Lane 4-22, Metzelaars 1-25, Doornink 1-15, Hughes 1-10, Morris 1-3.

NOTES

• The Bills reached the halfway point winless as they fell behind 23-0 in the first half.

• Joe Ferguson topped 4,000 career passing attempts, but he left the game in the third quarter when his ankle swelled. His counterpart, John Elway, played only the first half.

• There was a scary moment in the third when Donald Wilson crushed Denver receiver Clint Sampson on a pass over the middle. Sampson lay motionless for 15 minutes. Luckily, he regained feeling and was okay.

• Steve Foley's interception and 24-yard return to the Bills 47 set up Rich Karlis' first field goal.

• Two series later, Steve Busick intercepted Ferguson and returned it 16 yards to the Bills 35, leading to Elway's TD pass to Clarence Kay.

• The Bills punted on the next series and two plays later, Elway hit Steve Watson for a 52-yard TD.

• Denver drove 53 yards to Karlis' second field goal 31 seconds before halftime. Then Ferguson fumbled one play after the kickoff. Darren Comeaux recovered and Karlis kicked another field goal.

• In the third, with Gary Kubiak at QB, Denver drove 80 yards in eight plays to Kubiak's TD run.

• Comeaux intercepted Matt Kofler in the fourth to set up Kubiak's TD pass to Sammy Winder. The Bills broke the shutout on the first play after the kickoff as Mitchell Brookins caught a 70-yard TD bomb.

QUOTES

• Kay Stephenson: "Well, we were beaten, beaten soundly by a good football team, outplayed, out-coached, beaten. It was that simple. Joe still couldn't move very well on the ankle and we were getting a lot

of pressure back there. We felt we were taking a chance on the rest of the year by leaving him in there. He was taking a helluva beating." (About fans singing to him): "I knew something was going on, but I was thinking about the game. If it (his firing) happens, it happens. I don't ask Ralph Wilson what he's thinking. I don't have time to do anything but prepare for the next game. If I worry about it, we don't have a chance to be prepared."

• Terry Bledsoe: "Kay's the coach. He's the same guy who was 8-8 last year with a flock of injuries."

• Charlie Romes: "You can't control the crowd. I just hope Kay fights through it."

• Donald Wilson: "I was just hoping I didn't break his (Sampson's) neck or he had some kind of permanent damage. I know football is a contact sport, but I'm not out there trying to disable anyone. I've hit a lot of guys close to that kind of force, but the results were never like that. That's what I thought about (Jack Tatum's paralyzing hit on Darryl Stingley in 1978) when I didn't see him move. As soon as I get out of here, I'm going to the hospital to see how he is."

WEEK 8 GAMES

Chi 44, TB 9	Cinc 12, Clev 9
Det 16, Minn 14	NYJ 28, KC 7
LAR 44, SD 37	Mia 44, NE 24
Phil 24, NYG 10	Ind 17, Pitt 16
SF 34, Hou 21	Sea 30, GB 24
Rams 24, Atl 10	St.L 26, Wash 24
Dal 30, NO 27 (OT)	

Broncos	3 20 7 7	-	37
Bills	0 0 0 7	-	7

Attendance at Rich Stadium - 31,204

Den:	FG Karlis 45, 6:15
Den:	Kay 3 pass from Elway (Karlis kick), :32
Den:	Watson 52 pass from Elway (Karlis kick), 2:30
Den:	FG Karlis 45, 14:29
Den:	FG Karlis 40, 14:56
Den:	Kubiak 3 run (Karlis kick), 9:39
Den:	Winder 14 pass from Kubiak (Karlis kick), 7:23
Buf:	Brookins 70 pass from Kofler (Danelo kick), 7:42

	BUF	DEN
First downs	10	24
Rushing yds	71	107
Passing yds	155	231
Punts-avg	9-44.8	8-37.1
Fumbles-lost	1-1	3-0
Penalties-yds	10-95	2-15
Poss. time	26:57	33:03

BILLS LEADERS: Rushing - Bell 9-28, Neal 4-16, Kofler 3-28, Ferguson 1-1, Williams 1-5, Franklin 1-(-7); **Passing** - Ferguson 9-19-2 - 77, Kofler 8-13-2 - 132; **Receiving** - Franklin 5-64, Bell 7-54, Dennard 1-4, Brookins 1-70, Neal 1-8, Barnett 2-9.

BRONCOS LEADERS: Rushing - Winder 15-65, Parros 6-19, Elway 1-0, Kubiak 4-19, Willhite 1-4; **Passing** - Elway 12-23-0 - 148, Kubiak 8-16-0 - 97, Willhite 1-1-0 - 17; **Receiving** - Watson 5-89, Johnson 4-47, Winder 4-32, Wright 3-41, Kay 3-29, Kubiak 1-20, Willhite 1-4.

STANDINGS: EIGHTH WEEK

AFC EAST	W	L	T	CENTRAL	W	L	T	WEST	W	L	T	NFC EAST	W	L	T	CENTRAL	W	L	T	WEST	W	L	T
Miami	8	0	0	Pittsburgh	4	4	0	Raiders	7	1	0	Washington	5	3	0	Chicago	5	3	0	San Fran	7	1	0
NY Jets	6	2	0	Cincinnati	2	6	0	Denver	7	1	0	Dallas	5	3	0	Tampa Bay	3	5	0	LA Rams	5	3	0
New England	5	3	0	Cleveland	1	7	0	Seattle	6	2	0	St. Louis	5	3	0	Detroit	3	5	0	N.Orleans	3	5	0
Indianapolis	3	5	0	Houston	0	8	0	San Diego	4	4	0	NY Giants	4	4	0	Minnesota	2	6	0	Atlanta	3	5	0
Buffalo	0	8	0					Kan. City	4	4	0	Philadelphia	4	4	0	Green Bay	1	7	0				

Bills	0 0 0 7 - 7
Dolphins	**7 17 0 14 - 38**

Attendance at the Orange Bowl - 58,824

Mia: Clayton 7 pass from Marino (von Schamann kick), 11:42
Mia: D. Johnson 10 pass from Marino (von Schamann kick), :07
Mia: FG von Schamann 22, 7:05
Mia: Clayton 65 pass from Marino (von Schamann kick), 12:27
Mia: Bennett 1 run (von Schamann kick), :41
Mia: P. Johnson 1 run (von Schamann kick), 11:34
Buf: Dennard 5 pass from Kofler (Danelo kick), 13:38

	BUF	MIA
First downs	15	28
Rushing yds	103	191
Passing yds	170	302
Punts-avg	6-43.2	2-39.5
Fumbles-lost	4-3	0-0
Penalties-yds	7-55	2-20
Poss. time	27:23	32:37

BILLS LEADERS: Rushing - Bell 10-62, Neal 3-12, Ferguson 1-20, Moore 1-3, Riddick 1-6; **Passing** - Ferguson 20-30-1 - 136, Kofler 7-10-0 - 75; **Receiving** - Franklin 4-23, Hunter 4-27, Moore 4-15, Dennard 8-72, Riddick 6-61, Brookins 1-13.

DOLPHINS LEADERS: Rushing - Carter 12-93, Nathan 3-40, P. Johnson 9-30, Bennett 6-21, Marino 1-7; **Passing** - Marino 19-28-3 - 282, Strock 3-4-0 - 24; **Receiving** - Duper 5-74, Clayton 3-106, Moore 5-38, Nathan 3-35, D. Johnson 2-10, Hardy 2-31, Carter 1-4, Cefalo 1-8.

NOTES
• The Bills dropped to 0-9 with a listless performance as the Dolphins gained 493 yards.
• Dan Marino, who suffered the first three-interception game of his career but who also set new Miami single-season passing yardage record, completed four passes for 77 yards on Miami's first TD drive, which ended with his TD pass to Mark Clayton.
• A bad John Kidd punt and a 20-yard return by Mike Kozlowski set up the Dolphins at the Bills 47 on the next series. Marino threw a TD pass to Dan Johnson three plays later.
• Charlie Romes intercepted a Marino pass and returned it 55 yards to the Miami 11, but Ferguson was sacked by Mike Charles and lost a fumble to Bob Baumhower. On the next possession, the Bills reached the Miami 17, but Ferguson was sacked and Joe Danelo then missed a field goal.
• Marino's 34-yard strike to Clayton set up Uwe von Schamann's field goal. Then Marino's 65-yard TD pass to Clayton broke open the game 2:33 before the half ended.
• Fulton Walker's 33-yard punt return in the fourth led to Woody Bennett's TD. Then, with Don Strock at QB, Miami drove 68 yards in 12 plays to Pete Johnson's

TD.
• The Bills broke the shutout when Matt Kofler directed a 75-yard drive, capping it with a TD pass to Preston Dennard with 1:22 left.

QUOTES
• Fred Smerlas: "Marino's playing like someone from outer space. Marino is a phenomenon. Without Marino, they have a good offense. With Marino, they have a phenomenal offense. He throws the ball so quickly, it's futile trying to get to him. If he continues like that, he'll be in the Hall of Fame in his third year. You can't stop the Miami Dolphins, you have to outscore them."
• Kay Stephenson: "I thought coming into the ballgame we were going to play a very good ballgame. I was very optimistic, although I'm always optimistic. Miami just took it to us and took the game away early. They're an awesome team right now. We had turnovers, mistakes and whatnot, but give Miami credit."
• Miami coach Don Shula: "We thought Buffalo could be dangerous coming in here because they had gotten some of their injured people back like Haslett and Hunter. But we just didn't give them a chance to get in the game by playing defense and getting into the end zone early."
• Matt Kofler: "Joe's not 100 percent, but a good sign is he did get right back up after a few of the shots he took out there. He is getting better."

WEEK 9 GAMES
Pit 35, Atl 10	Cinc 31, Hou 13
Dal 22, Ind 3	Den 22, LAR 19
GB 41, Det 9	Chi 16, Minn 7
NO 16, Clev 14	NE 30, NYJ 20
St.L 34, Phil 14	SF 33, Rams 0
KC 24, TB 20	NYG 37, Wash 13
Sea 24, SD 0	

Browns	3 3 0 7 - 13
Bills	0 7 3 0 - 10

Attendance at Rich Stadium - 33,343

Cle: FG Bahr 28, 11:10
Buf: Keating 34 fumble return (Nelson kick), 13:13
Cle: FG Bahr 36, 14:55
Buf: FG Nelson 42, 7:18
Cle: Byner 55 fumble recovery (Bahr kick), 7:28

	BUF	CLE
First downs	13	16
Rushing yds	106	211
Passing yds	77	73
Punts-avg	4-40.5	3-40.3
Fumbles-lost	1-0	4-2
Penalties-yds	7-58	8-95
Poss. time	31:21	28:39

BILLS LEADERS: Rushing - Bell 20-82, Neal 5-17, Ferguson 1-(-2), Moore 1-1, Williams 1-8; **Passing** - Ferguson 16-24-2 - 110; **Receiving** - Franklin 1-9, Bell 6-27, Hunter 3-14, Moore 1-7, Riddick 1-7, Dawkins 3-38, White 1-8.

BROWNS LEADERS: Rushing - Green 29-156, Byner 9-58, McDonald 5-(-3); **Passing** - McDonald 7-18-1 - 86; **Receiving** - Newsome 4-53, Harris 2-20, Adams 1-13.

WEEK 10 GAMES
SF 23, Cinc 17	GB 23, NO 13
Pitt 35, Hou 7	Sea 45, KC 0
Chi 17, LAR 6	Rams 16, St.L 13
Mia 31, NYJ 17	Den 26, NE 19
NYG 19, Dal 7	SD 38, Ind 10
Minn 27, TB 24	Wash 27, Atl 14
Det 23, Phil 23 (OT)	

NOTES
• The teams brought a combined record of 1-17 into the game and on a rainy day, the Bills stumbled a little more than the Browns. Earnest Byner picked up a fumble by the Browns' Willis Adams and ran 55 yards for the winning TD. Adams had caught a pass from Paul McDonald on third-and-20, then was hit by Lawrence Johnson, but the ball popped right into Byner's hands.
• Al Gross stopped the Bills' first drive by intercepting Joe Ferguson. The Browns then drove 28 yards to Matt Bahr's field goal.
• Chuck Nelson missed his first field goal attempt as a Bill, from 38 yards in the second quarter.
• After an exchange of interceptions, the Browns were at the Bills 46, but Darryl Talley sacked McDonald, forced him to fumble, and Chris Keating picked it up and went 34 yards for a TD.
• After the kickoff, the Browns moved 61 yards to Bahr's second field goal with five seconds left. Byner had a 20-yard run and McDonald hit Duriel Harris for 13 on third-and-one from the Browns 49.
• In the third, Jim Haslett recovered a Boyce Green fumble at the Browns 17. But Tony Hunter lost seven yards on a tight end screen, necessitating a Nelson field goal from 42 yards.
• After four punts, the Browns took over at their own 28, then picked up a first down on third-and-18 when Ozzie Newsome made a 22-yard catch. After a holding call on Mike Babb, Byner made the winning play.
• The Bills couldn't move on the ensuing possession and the Browns ate up the final 4:16.

QUOTES
• Kay Stephenson on Byner's run: "To be honest with you, I couldn't believe it. I could not believe it. But it happened and it looked to be a legitimate bad break for us."
• Jim Haslett: "We've lost every way imaginable now. We shouldn't have lost that game."
• Lawrence Johnson: "When you make a guy fumble, you think you're doing a good job. It was unbelievable. I saw Adams was having trouble handling the ball and I was close enough to get there and sort of pull it out. I didn't know if it was a catch and a fumble or an incomplete pass. Then you see a guy pick it up and run with it, what can you say?"
• Browns running back Earnest Byner: "I saw Willis was having trouble and I just kept running down the sideline. It was automatic, really. I bobbled the ball at first. I guess I was a little nervous when I first picked it up. I was looking around to see if anyone was near me, but I didn't see anybody."
• Ralph Wilson: "Things just aren't going our way this year. I think they were hustling, trying. I was in the locker room before the game and they were excited and ready to play. I feel for the coaching staff, I feel for the players, because a lot of them have been playing hard, and I feel for the fans. But you know what? We'll pull a rally off, whether it's this year or next year. Things turn around."

STANDINGS: TENTH WEEK

AFC EAST	W	L	T	CENTRAL	W	L	T	WEST	W	L	T	NFC EAST	W	L	T	CENTRAL	W	L	T	WEST	W	L	T
Miami	10	0	0	Pittsburgh	6	4	0	Denver	9	1	0	Dallas	6	4	0	Chicago	7	3	0	San Fran	9	1	0
NY Jets	6	4	0	Cincinnati	3	7	0	Seattle	8	2	0	St. Louis	6	4	0	Detroit	3	6	1	LA Rams	6	4	0
New England	6	4	0	Cleveland	2	8	0	Raiders	7	3	0	Washington	6	4	0	Tampa Bay	3	7	0	N.Orleans	4	6	0
Indianapolis	3	7	0	Houston	0	10	0	Kan. City	5	5	0	NY Giants	6	4	0	Minnesota	3	7	0	Atlanta	3	7	0
Buffalo	0	10	0					San Diego	5	5	0	Philadelphia	4	5	1	Green Bay	3	7	0				

NOTES

• The Bills dropped to 0-11 and lost their 13th straight game dating back to 1983.

• Joe Ferguson and Matt Kofler were 13 of 48 combined with three interceptions and eight sacks.

• The Bills played decent football early in the game. On third-and-nine, Ferguson hit Preston Dennard with a 68-yard TD pass 9:11 into the first quarter. The Pats tied it in the second quarter after Ronnie Lippett's interception. Tony Eason fired a TD pass to Cedric Jones. The teams exchanged field goals and then the critical portion of the game occurred.

• Chuck Nelson missed a 43-yard field goal in the third. After an exchange of punts, the Pats took over at their own 49. Brian Carpenter was called for a 35-yard pass-interference penalty on Jones in the end zone, and Tony Collins scored on the next play for a 17-10 lead. The Bills never recovered.

• On the next series, the Bills punted and Irving Fryar returned it 28 yards to the Bills 35. Three plays later, Collins scored again.

• Lippett intercepted Ferguson early in the fourth, leading to Eason's TD pass to Stanley Morgan. Later, the Bills were stopped on downs at their own 20. Four plays later, Eason hit Jones for the final TD.

QUOTES

• Brian Carpenter: "There wasn't any contact. The official said I hit him in the back, but I was behind him and the ball was underthrown. When I got up, I saw the flag. He (Jones) thought the flag was on him and later on, he said I didn't hit him. I was really upset. The officials have to be looking to make those calls on us."

• Kay Stephenson: "I thought Carpenter made as good a play as he possibly could have. It took some steam out of us. You get into that witch-hunt syndrome or snake-bitten theory and wonder what's going to happen next. All I know is every time there's a close call, it goes against us. We're having problems not only making the big plays, but the not-so-difficult, ordinary plays. I don't expect people on every down to go out and make the difficult play, but you do expect a certain number of plays to be made in a ball game. We've stopped making progress and quite frankly, it's been disastrous."

• Fred Smerlas: "The officials are supposed to control the game, not dictate it. Where's the consistency?"

• Joe Ferguson: "I just played bad. No other reasons, no excuses."

WEEK 11 GAMES	
Rams 29, Chi 13	Ind 9, NYJ 5
Dal 24, St.L 17	Den 16, SD 13
Wash 28, Det 14	Hou 17, KC 16
GB 45, Minn 17	NO 17, Atl 13
TB 20, NYG 17	Mia 24, Phil 23
Cinc 22, Pitt 20	SF 41, Clev 7
Sea 17, LAR 14	

Bills	7	0	3	0	- 10
Patriots	0	10	14	14	- 38

Attendance at Sullivan Stadium - 43,313

Buf:	Dennard 68 pass from Ferguson (Nelson kick), 9:11
NE:	Jones 17 pass from Eason (Franklin kick), 3:03
NE:	FG Franklin 21, 14:27
Buf:	FG Nelson 34, 3:23
NE:	Collins 1 run (Franklin kick), 12:10
NE:	Collins 1 run (Franklin kick), 15:00
NE:	Morgan 24 pass from Eason (Franklin kick), 5:45
NE:	Jones 7 pass from Eason (Franklin kick), 12:51

	BUF	NE
First downs	12	21
Rushing yds	77	68
Passing yds	112	210
Punts-avg	6-46.2	7-40.7
Fumbles-lost	3-1	1-1
Penalties-yds	4-60	3-20
Poss. time	25:06	34:54

BILLS LEADERS: Rushing - Bell 15-63, Ferguson 2-10, Kofler 1-4; **Passing** - Ferguson 9-29-3 - 142, Kofler 4-19-0 - 64; **Receiving** - Franklin 2-36, Hunter 3-47, Moore 1-5, Dennard 2-73, Riddick 2-28, White 1-3, Brammer 2-14.

PATRIOTS LEADERS: Rushing - James 23-55, Eason 6-12, Collins 4-1; **Passing** - Eason 23-34-2 - 227; **Receiving** - James 6-30, Morgan 5-68, Jones 5-49, Ramsey 3-33, Dawson 1-18, Hawthorne 1-15, Starring 1-11, Robinson 1-3.

NOTES

• The Bills pulled off a shocking upset to post their first win of the year. Greg Bell broke an 85-yard TD run on the game's first play and went on to rush for a career-high 206 yards.

• Jack Kemp's name was installed on the Wall of Fame at halftime, joining O.J. Simpson.

• It was the Bills' first victory over the Cowboys.

• The game was the first road non-sellout for the Cowboys in 43 games as the Bills were 833 tickets shy of a sellout.

• The Bills carried Kay Stephenson off the field on their shoulders.

• The Bills could have made it 10-0 in the first as Donald Wilson returned a punt 34 yards to the Dallas 21, but a bad snap aborted a field goal attempt. On the next series, Joe Azelby partially blocked a Danny White punt and the Bills took over at the Dallas 34, but Joe Ferguson was intercepted on the next play by Eugene Lockhart, who returned it 32 yards to the Bills 40. That led to Rafael Septien's field goal.

• Rod Kush and Brian Carpenter stopped Dallas possessions in the second quarter with interceptions.

• After the teams traded two punts each, the Bills began a drive at their 30. On third-and-15, Ferguson hit Byron Franklin for 21 yards to the 46. Six plays later, he threw a TD pass to Bell.

• Dallas had the ball for 3:15 in the fourth quarter and couldn't catch up.

QUOTES

• Dallas coach Tom Landry: "It was somewhat embarrassing, but it's always embarrassing when you lose. It was not one of our better hours."

• Dallas running back Tony Dorsett: "I'm totally embarrassed. I just can't believe it. It's embarrassment at its best and I can't believe there's one player in this locker room who doesn't feel the same way. They're 0-11 and they beat the Dallas Cowboys."

• Jim Haslett: "This was like the old days. Don Lawrence called a great game, he has the last three weeks, just like Tom Catlin used to. We have 13 rookies on this team who have never tasted what winning is like in the NFL."

• Charlie Romes: "This is one game we can always remember. Everybody was against us. People didn't come to see us, they came to see the Dallas Cowboys. Now we're going to have a party."

• Greg Bell: "We won a game, that's what I'm most happy about. The funny thing is, before the game I told Booker Moore that I had a dream that I broke a long run the length of the field for a touchdown on the first play of the game. Booker looked at me and said 'I had the same dream, now let's go make it happen.' They had lined up in a 6-1 defense. We had seen in films that if we could break the line of scrimmage, only the middle linebacker was there and after that, there was nobody left to make the tackle."

• Kay Stephenson: "I don't think too many teams could have gone through what we've gone through this year and come back and won like we did today."

Cowboys	0	3	0	0	- 3
Bills	7	0	0	7	- 14

Attendance at Rich Stadium - 74,391

Buf:	Bell 85 run (Nelson kick), :21
Dal:	FG Septien 20, :47
Buf:	Bell 3 pass from Ferguson (Nelson kick), 3:12

	BUF	DAL
First downs	14	19
Rushing yds	203	78
Passing yds	104	219
Punts-avg	8-43.5	6-32.5
Fumbles-lost	1-0	2-1
Penalties-yds	4-58	5-55
Poss. time	29:22	30:38

BILLS LEADERS: Rushing - Bell 27-206, Moore 3-3, Ferguson 2-(-4), Riddick 1-(-2); **Passing** - Ferguson 13-29-2 - 117, Kofler 0-1-0 - 0; **Receiving** - Franklin 6-55, Bell 2-12, Moore 2-14, Riddick 1-13, Brammer 1-12, Brookins 1-11.

COWBOYS LEADERS: Rushing - Dorsett 17-70, Newsome 3-10, Springs 2-(-3), Jones 1-2, Hogeboom 1-(-1); **Passing** - Hogeboom 22-45-2 - 242, Renfro 0-1-1 - 0; **Receiving** - Hill 4-35, Renfro 2-28, Dorsett 5-29, Cosbie 6-92, Springs 2-15, Jones 1-9, Newsome 2-34.

WEEK 12 GAMES	
Clev 23, Atl 7	Chi 16, Det 14
LAR 17, KC 7	GB 31, Rams 6
SD 34, Mia 28	Den 42, Minn 21
NE 50, Ind 17	Hou 31, NYJ 20
NYG 16, St.L 10	Sea 26, Cinc 6
SF 24, TB 17	Phil 16, Wash 10
NO 27, Pitt 24	

STANDINGS: TWELFTH WEEK

AFC EAST	W	L	T	CENTRAL	W	L	T	WEST	W	L	T	NFC EAST	W	L	T	CENTRAL	W	L	T	WEST	W	L	T
Miami	11	1	0	Pittsburgh	6	6	0	Denver	11	1	0	Dallas	7	5	0	Chicago	8	4	0	San Fran	11	1	0
New England	8	4	0	Cincinnati	4	8	0	Seattle	10	2	0	Washington	7	5	0	Green Bay	5	7	0	LA Rams	7	5	0
NY Jets	6	6	0	Cleveland	3	9	0	Raiders	8	4	0	NY Giants	7	5	0	Tampa Bay	4	8	0	N.Orleans	6	6	0
Indianapolis	4	8	0	Houston	2	10	0	San Diego	6	6	0	St. Louis	6	6	0	Detroit	3	8	1	Atlanta	3	9	0
Buffalo	1	11	0					Kan. City	5	7	0	Philadelphia	5	6	1	Minnesota	3	9	0				

Bills	0 7 7 0 - 14
Redskins	17 10 7 7 - 41

Attendance at RFK Stadium - 51,513

Was: Monk 11 pass from Theismann (Moseley kick), 3:28
Was: FG Moseley 38, 7:31
Was: Riggins 2 run (Moseley kick), 11:31
Was: Brown 18 pass from Theismann (Moseley kick), :57
Buf: Franklin 8 pass from Ferguson (Nelson kick), 9:14
Was: FG Moseley 51, 14:59
Buf: Dennard 36 pass from Ferguson (Nelson kick), 1:55
Was: Dean 11 interception return (Moseley kick), 9:35
Was: Wonsley 3 run (Moseley kick), 9:57

	BUF	WAS
First downs	13	27
Rushing yds	85	116
Passing yds	86	305
Punts-avg	5-44.0	1-49.0
Fumbles-lost	2-1	4-2
Penalties-yds	7-45	3-25
Poss. time	23:37	36:23

BILLS LEADERS: Rushing - Bell 13-53, Neal 3-13, Ferguson 2-13, Moore 2-6; **Passing** - Ferguson 11-26-2 - 124, Kofler 3-8-0 - 23; **Receiving** - Franklin 3-20, Moore 2-8, Dennard 3-45, Riddick 3-41, Mosley 3-33.

REDSKINS LEADERS: Rushing - Griffin 25-92, Moore 2-8, Wonsley 5-7, Riggins 3-6, Theismann 4-3; **Passing** - Theismann 26-33-1 - 311; **Receiving** - Monk 11-104, Muhammed 4-97, Brown 4-68, Didier 4-26, Griffin 1-8, Moore 1-6, Riggins 1-2.

NOTES
• Art Monk set a single-season Redskins record for catches on his way to a brilliant performance against the Bills. The Redskins jumped to a 17-0 lead and never looked back.
• Mike Nelms' 20-yard punt return started the Redskins' first series at the Bills 39. Five plays later, Joe Theismann hit Monk for a TD. Mark Moseley then kicked a field goal after the Redskins started the next possession at their own 47 after a punt. Finally, Curtis Jordan intercepted a Joe Ferguson pass and returned it to the Bills 38, leading the way for John Riggins' TD run and a 17-0 lead.
• In the second quarter, Theismann fired a 52-yard pass to Calvin Muhammad to set up his TD pass to Charlie Brown.
• The Bills answered with a 15-play, 54-yard drive that led to Ferguson's TD pass to Byron Franklin. Fergy had a 15-yard scramble and 15 yards were tacked on when Darryl Grant speared him, moving the ball to the 25.
• The Bills were stopped on downs at the Redskins 32 and Theismann maneuvered his team to Moseley's field goal on the final play of the half for a 27-7 advantage.
• Rick Kane fumbled the second-half kickoff and Brian Carpenter recovered at the 36, setting up Ferguson's

WEEK 13 GAMES	
Det 31, GB 28	Dal 20, NE 17
Cinc 35, Atl 14	Chi 34, Minn 3
LAR 21, Ind 7	Clev 27, Hou 10
NYG 28, KC 27	Rams 34, TB 33
Pitt 52, SD 21	SF 35, NO 3
Sea 27, Den 24	Mia 28, NYJ 17
St.L 17, Phil 16	

TD pass to Preston Dennard.
• Later in the third, Darryl Talley intercepted Theismann at the 2 to kill a drive, but Vernon Dean then picked off a Ferguson pass and ran 11 yards for a TD. The Redskins added a TD in the fourth by George Wonsley, capping a short 42-yard drive after a John Kidd punt.

QUOTES
• Washington quarterback Joe Theismann: "We've got our missiles back. Today we played the kind of football we're capable of. We can play even better than this. Art's healthy this year, he's quicker and he's gotten better. He's been our mainstay. I'll tell you, the potential of Art Monk hasn't been seen yet."
• Kay Stephenson: "Their offense was especially hot today. I'd have to say that's the best offensive team that we've played this year, although it would be tough to choose between Washington and the Miami Dolphins."
• Washington safety Curtis Jordan (on his interception): "I think Fergy would agree it wasn't one of his better throws. He's always forcing the ball. Guys like him and Kenny Stabler who have strong arms will try to throw the ball in there no matter what. It's the Gunslinger's Syndrome. But I also know he doesn't have any pass protection. It was terrible. I've followed Joe since his college days and I've always thought he was a great, great quarterback who always played on teams where he didn't have anything around him."

Colts	0 9 3 3 - 15
Bills	21 0 0 0 - 21

Attendance at Rich Stadium - 20,693

Buf: Bell 7 run (Nelson kick), 4:11
Buf: Hunter 18 pass from Dufek (Nelson kick), 12:21
Buf: Franklin 64 pass from Dufek (Nelson kick), 15:00
Ind: Safety, Humiston tackled Wilson in end zone, 1:07
Ind: Middleton 14 pass from Schlichter (Allegre kick), 13:14
Ind: FG Allegre 28, 5:51
Ind: FG Allegre 21, 5:12

	BUF	IND
First downs	15	13
Rushing yds	104	116
Passing yds	155	125
Punts-avg	7-38.6	8-47.4
Fumbles-lost	2-1	3-3
Penalties-yds	9-65	9-69
Poss. time	33:07	26:53

BILLS LEADERS: Rushing - Bell 30-83, Neal 6-25, Brookins 1-11, Kofler 1-(-7), Dufek 2-(-7), Riddick 1-(-1); **Passing** - Dufek 11-22-1 - 164; **Receiving** - Franklin 3-82, Bell 2-11, Hunter 4-51, Dennard 1-15, Mosley 1-5.

COLTS LEADERS: Rushing - Moore 7-35, McMillan 7-30, Schlichter 5-21, Wonsley 7-21, Middleton 5-9; **Passing** - Schlichter 11-28-1 - 135; **Receiving** - Butler 2-28, Porter 2-16, Bouza 2-20, Middleton 2-26, Sherwin 1-25, Henry 2-20.

NOTES
• The Bills raced to a 21-0 first-quarter lead, then had to hold on for their second victory of the season.
• Joe Dufek started in place of the benched Joe Ferguson and had an effective day.
• Steve Freeman's consecutive games played streak ended at 147 because of a quadriceps injury.
• The game was played in front of the smallest crowd in Rich Stadium history.
• Art Schlichter fumbled the snap on the third play of the game and Fred Smerlas recovered at the Colts 35. Five plays later, Greg Bell scored on third-and-two from the 7.
• After a Rohn Stark punt, the Bills drove 89 yards in 10 plays to Dufek's TD pass to Tony Hunter. The drive was kept alive when Johnnie Cooks' interception was nullified by a roughing-the-passer penalty on Vernon Maxwell.
• On the next possession, Dufek connected with Byron Franklin on a 64-yard TD on the last play of the quarter when cornerback Preston Davis fell down.
• Donald Wilson made an awful mistake a few minutes later, fielding a Rohn Stark punt at the 1, then getting caught in the end zone by Mike Humiston for a safety.
• Late in the half, the Colts drove 37 yards after a short

WEEK 14 GAMES	
Wash 31, Minn 17	Dal 26, Phil 10
Cinc 20, Clev 17	KC 16, Den 13
Sea 38, Det 17	LAR 45, Mia 34
Rams 34, NO 21	NYG 20, NYJ 10
Hou 23, Pitt 20	St.L 33, NE 10
SF 35, Atl 17	GB 27, TB 14
SD 20, Chi 7	

John Kidd punt to Schlichter's TD pass to Frank Middleton.
• The Colts got a Raul Allegre field goal on the first series of the second half. Then a promising Bills drive died with a Dufek interception by Terry Daniel at the 5.
• Wilson fumbled a punt at the Bills 16, but the defense held and forced an Allegre field goal early in the fourth.
• The last Colts chance died when Larry Anderson muffed a punt with 1:45 left. Joe Azelby recovered.

QUOTES
• Joe Dufek: "I'm just happy for the win. It wasn't very artistic, but we won. I didn't throw the ball as well (in the second half) as I did in the first half. I didn't seem to be getting any zip on it. The defense bailed us out in the second half."
• Colts coach Frank Kush: "The first half was a disaster. But it's just typical of the kind of season we've had. We gave up 21 points on mistakes."
• Kay Stephenson: "I think Joe played with a lot of enthusiasm and a lot of confidence and savvy. We didn't expect Joe to go out there and set the world on fire and we obviously tried to protect that situation as best we could."
• Tony Hunter on his TD: "This made me feel like a football player again instead of someone just standing by. He (Dufek) told me the tight end could be a very big asset to the offense and if I got open, he'd get the ball to me. So I was optimistic. It helps, as far as giving me incentive to get out there and know if I get open, I'll get the football."

STANDINGS: FOURTEENTH WEEK																								
AFC EAST	W	L	T	CENTRAL	W	L	T	WEST	W	L	T	NFC EAST	W	L	T	CENTRAL	W	L	T	WEST	W	L	T	
Miami	12	2	0	Pittsburgh	7	7	0	Seattle	12	2	0	Dallas	9	5	0	Chicago	9	5	0	San Fran	13	1	0
New England	8	6	0	Cincinnati	6	8	0	Denver	11	3	0	Washington	9	5	0	Green Bay	6	8	0	LA Rams	9	5	0
NY Jets	6	8	0	Cleveland	4	10	0	Raiders	10	4	0	NY Giants	9	5	0	Detroit	4	9	1	N.Orleans	6	8	0
Indianapolis	4	10	0	Houston	3	11	0	San Diego	7	7	0	St. Louis	8	6	0	Tampa Bay	4	10	0	Atlanta	3	11	0
Buffalo	2	12	0					Kan. City	6	8	0	Philadelphia	5	8	1	Minnesota	3	11	0				

NOTES

• Joe Dufek had a rough time against the Jets defense, producing only 222 yards. He was just four of 16 for 25 yards in the second half, and the Bills managed only three first downs and 43 total yards in the final 30 minutes. The Jets snapped their six-game losing streak.
• Greg Bell topped 1,000 yards rushing for the season.
• The Bills broke on top in the first quarter when Stan David blocked a Chuck Ramsey punt and returned it 36 yards for a TD. However, Bobby Humphrey returned the ensuing kickoff 59 yards to the Bills 26 to set up Cedric Minter's TD run that tied the game at 7-7.
• The Bills drove 80 yards in 13 plays, consuming 8:28 to take the lead on Bell's TD run. The key play was a third-and-seven Dufek completion to Julius Dawkins for 28 yards to the New York 19.
• Mitchell Brookins' 46-yard reception late in the half set up Chuck Nelson's field goal.
• Late in the third, Wesley Walker beat Charlie Romes for a 39-yard TD reception.
• Two series later, after an 18-yard punt return by Minter, the Jets drove 40 yards in five plays to Tony Paige's game-winning TD run. The key plays were a 30-yard pass to Mickey Shuler, then a personal foul on Romes that gave the Jets a first down at the 4.
• Van Williams returned the ensuing kickoff 54 yards to the Jets 44, but Dufek threw three incompletions.
• Buffalo got the ball back once more, but after getting two first downs, was forced to punt.

QUOTES

• Jim Haslett: "I thought the defense played pretty well, we came up with some big plays. It was just a frustrating day. The special teams kept giving them good field position and the offense couldn't move the ball. We were on the field an awful lot in the second half."
• Joe Dufek: "I've got to be the home run hitter on this team. I didn't hit one out today. The game plan in the second half was fine. The quarterback's got to execute, and I didn't. I learned a valuable lesson and that was that I have to keep my poise and stand tough in the face of blitzes. Today, they got me. Next time, I've got to burn them."
• Defensive backfield coach Pete Carroll on Romes' personal foul penalty: "I'm really disappointed that Charlie's frustration came out at that time. He's been around long enough to know better. But he was just so frustrated because he got beat by Walker the same way when we lost to them last time. It was unfortunate because up to that time, Charlie was having a great game, probably his best of the year."
• Greg Bell: "A thousand doesn't mean anything after a game like this. We can't end the season the same way next week. We've got to find out what's wrong with this offense. This is not going to be a pleasant plane ride home."

WEEK 15 GAMES	
SF 51, Minn 7	TB 23, Atl 6
Cinc 24, NO 21	Pitt 23, Clev 20
GB 20, Chi 14	Rams 27, Hou 16
Mia 35, Ind 17	Phil 27, NE 17
St.L 31, NYG 21	Den 16, SD 13
KC 34, Sea 7	Wash 30, Dal 28
LAR 24, Det 3	

Bills	7	10	0	0	-	17
Jets	7	0	7	7	-	21

Attendance at Giants Stadium - 45,378

Buf: David 36 blocked punt return (Nelson kick), 9:57
NYJ: Minter 6 run (Leahy kick), 14:39
Buf: Bell 3 run (Nelson kick), 8:11
Buf: FG Nelson 47, 13:52
NYJ: Walker 39 pass from O'Brien (Leahy kick), 14:21
NYJ: Paige 3 run (Leahy kick), 4:13

	BUF	NYJ
First downs	11	21
Rushing yds	82	140
Passing yds	140	203
Punts-avg	9-36.4	6-34.3
Fumbles-lost	2-1	3-3
Penalties-yds	6-41	4-20
Poss. time	27:34	32:26

BILLS LEADERS: Rushing - Bell 18-54, Neal 2-7, Moore 3-17, Dufek 1-4; **Passing** - Dufek 14-34-2 - 162; **Receiving** - Franklin 2-18, Bell 1-9, Hunter 7-39, Riddick 1-8, Dawkins 1-28, Brookins 2-60.

JETS LEADERS: Rushing - Hector 20-73, Minter 14-58, Paige 3-9, O'Brien 2-0; **Passing** - O'Brien 17-31-1 - 217; **Receiving** - Shuler 6-54, Jones 5-85, Walker 2-47, Dennison 2-23, Minter 1-11, Paige 1-(-3).

NOTES

• The Bills closed a dismal 2-14 season with a horrendous performance as the Bengals scored 31 straight points during one stretch. They improved to 8-8 under rookie head coach Sam Wyche.
• Joe Dufek set career highs for attempts, completions and yards, but had two interceptions returned for TDs before Joe Ferguson relieved, making what likely would be his final appearance as a Bill.
• The Bills, who lost 14 games in one season for the first time, drove 77 yards to score first on Greg Bell's TD run, but the Bengals scored the next 31 points.
• Mike Martin's 32-yard punt return led to the Bengals' first score, and the Bills began a slow death.
• Cris Collinsworth's 27-yard catch to the 1 set up Larry Kinnebrew's TD and a 14-7 lead.
• The Bengals drove 56 and 81 yards for TDs later in the second quarter.
• Martin's 41-yard kickoff return set up Jim Breech's field goal early in the third and after the Bills answered with an 86-yard drive to Dufek's TD pass to Byron Franklin, Stanford Jennings capped an 80-yard Bengals march with a 20-yard TD run to make it 38-14.
• John Simmons and James Griffin then returned interceptions for TDs 2:03 apart.
• The Bills final TD came on Bell's TD run that capped a 69-yard march.

QUOTES

• Rod Kush: "We have a lot of talent. It's going to take something special to get it all together, though. Whether it's Kay or somebody else, I don't know."
• Ben Williams: "I don't call this a season, this is more like a nightmare."
• Fred Smerlas: "It was more like something out of *The Twilight Zone* by Rod Serling. Did they make the announcement (of Stephenson's expected firing)? Sure we expect it to happen, only someone crazy would think it's not going to happen."
• Kay Stephenson on his future: "I haven't talked to Ralph Wilson or anybody about anything. Listen, I haven't given that (resigning) any thought. All I'm interested in for this football team is coming back and being the kind of team we can be, with a few changes."
• Terry Bledsoe: "I feel very much empathy for Kay for what he's gone through. I don't like to see this happening to a good friend of mine. Come to think of it, I don't like to see it happening to me, either."
• Chris Keating: "This was a fitting end to our season."

WEEK 16 GAMES	
SF 19, Rams 16	Den 31, Sea 14
NO 10, NYG 3	Chi 30, Det 13
Clev 27, Hou 20	NE 16, Ind 10
GB 38, Minn 14	KC 42, SD 21
TB 41, NYJ 21	Atl 26, Phil 10
Pitt 13, LAR 7	Mia 28, Dal 21
Wash 29, St.L 27	

Bills	7	0	7	7	-	21
Bengals	7	21	3	21	-	52

Attendance at Riverfront Stadium - 55,771

Buf: Bell 5 run (Nelson kick), 4:06
Cin: Collinsworth 12 pass from Anderson (Breech kick), 8:06
Cin: Kinnebrew 1 run (Breech kick), 3:06
Cin: Holman 11 pass from Anderson (Breech kick), 7:36
Cin: Kreider 11 pass from Anderson (Breech kick), 14:22
Cin: FG Breech 36, 5:20
Buf: Franklin 16 pass from Dufek (Nelson kick), 12:57
Cin: Jennings 20 run (Breech kick), 3:26
Cin: Simmons 43 interception return (Breech kick), 9:10
Cin: Griffin 57 interception return (Breech kick), 11:06
Buf: Bell 1 run (Nelson kick), 14:46

	BUF	CIN
First downs	25	27
Rushing yds	64	201
Passing yds	281	218
Punts-avg	6-41.0	3-35.6
Fumbles-lost	0-0	4-2
Penalties-yds	10-75	5-52
Poss. time	29:05	30:55

BILLS LEADERS: Rushing - Bell 16-58, Ferguson 1-7, Moore 1-(-1); **Passing** - Ferguson 6-10-1 - 52, Dufek 30-47-2 - 250; **Receiving** - Franklin 7-68, Bell 4-31, Hunter 3-45, Moore 9-53, Dennard 1-13, Riddick 6-51, Dawkins 4-25, Brookins 2-16.

BENGALS LEADERS: Rushing - Kinnebrew 14-65, Brooks 7-52, Jennings 5-42, Anderson 1-12, Alexander 6-26, Farley 1-1, Verser 1-3, Esiason 1-0; **Passing** - Anderson 17-23-0 - 206, Esiason 3-5-0 - 21; **Receiving** - Kreider 5-49, Collinsworth 3-62, Martin 3-40, Brooks 2-23, Holman 2-13, Jennings 2-13, M. Harris 1-14, Curtis 1-7, Kinnebrew 1-6.

STANDINGS: SIXTEENTH WEEK

AFC EAST	W	L	T	CENTRAL	W	L	T	WEST	W	L	T	NFC EAST	W	L	T	CENTRAL	W	L	T	WEST	W	L	T
Miami	14	2	0	Pittsburgh	9	7	0	Denver	13	3	0	Washington	11	5	0	Chicago	10	6	0	San Fran	15	1	0
New England	9	7	0	Cincinnati	8	8	0	Seattle	12	4	0	NY Giants	9	7	0	Green Bay	8	8	0	LA Rams	10	6	0
NY Jets	7	9	0	Cleveland	5	11	0	Raiders	11	5	0	Dallas	9	7	0	Tampa Bay	6	10	0	N.Orleans	7	9	0
Indianapolis	4	12	0	Houston	3	13	0	Kan. City	8	8	0	St. Louis	9	7	0	Detroit	4	11	1	Atlanta	4	12	0
Buffalo	2	14	0					San Diego	7	9	0	Philadelphia	6	9	1	Minnesota	3	13	0				

At A Glance
1985

Jan. 9 – Ralph Wilson announced that Kay Stephenson would remain as head coach of the team. "I feel good about the situation," Stephenson said. "If I didn't, then I wouldn't want it to work the way it did."

Jan. 11 – The Bills announced that five assistants – defensive coordinator Don Lawrence, special teams coach Miller McCalmon, defensive backfield coach Pete Carroll, receivers coach Milt Jackson and tight ends coach Perry Moss – were leaving the team, although none were believed to be leaving on their own free will. Kay Stephenson said that he would be looking to hire an offensive coordinator, duties he held the past two seasons.

Jan. 17 – Greg Bell was named the Seagram Sports Award 1984 Rookie of the Year.

Jan. 19 – Hank Bullough was hired as defensive coordinator and assistant head coach. He had been the Bengals defensive coordinator and helped them get to Super Bowl XVI.

Jan. 22 – O.J. Simpson, Roger Staubach, Joe Namath, Pete Rozelle and old-timer Frank Gatski were named to the Pro Football Hall of Fame. Simpson thus became the first Bill enshrined.

Jan. 23 – Greg Bell was named to the Pro Bowl to replace injured Freeman McNeil.

Jan. 25 – Doug Flutie, whom the Bills were courting as a possible No. 1 draft choice, signed with the USFL's New Jersey Generals.

Jan. 28 – Former Bills head coach and offensive line coach Jim Ringo rejoined the Bills coaching staff as offensive coordinator as well as offensive line coach. Ringo left Buffalo after the 1977 season.

Feb. 1 – Interviewed in Houston, Jim Kelly reiterated his disdain for playing in Buffalo. "If Buffalo were my last option, I would go there, but every quarterback wants to play in warm weather," he said. "Of all the places that should have a domed stadium, it's Buffalo. If Buffalo plans on getting anybody, if you ever want a chance of having a winning team, tell Ralph Wilson he's going to have to spend some money."

Feb. 4 – Quarterbacks coach John Becker resigned.

Feb. 5 – Running backs coach Andy MacDonald became the eighth assistant coach to leave the Bills.

Feb. 7 – Terry Bledsoe suffered a heart attack. In his absence, the Bills said director of pro personnel Bill Polian, director of college scouting Norm Pollom and his assistant, Bruce Nicholas, would share contract matters.

Feb. 11 – At the Dunlop Pro-Am Awards Dinner, New York Giants quarterback Phil Simms said the perfect quarterback for Rich Stadium would be Jim Kelly, because he had the arm strength to throw the ball in cold and windy Orchard Park. "Kelly's a stud," Simms said.

Feb. 12 – Kay Dalton was hired as quarterbacks coach. Dalton was on the Bills staff in 1977 under Jim Ringo, coaching the receivers.

Feb. 14 – Bob Leahy was hired as receivers coach and Art Asselta was named tight ends

Bruce Smith was jumping for joy when the Bills made him the first player chosen in the 1985 draft. The defensive end from Virginia Tech struggled early, but came on at the end of the season and recorded 6 1/2 sacks.

coach. The Bills announced that Virginia Tech defensive end Bruce Smith was the player they wanted to select with the No. 1 overall choice in the draft. "Right now, there is only one player we are negotiating with, and that's Bruce Smith," said director of pro personnel Bill Polian. Said Smith: "Playing in the NFL has always been a dream of mine, and it's a dream I don't want to let go. I'm looking forward to playing in the NFL and showing what I can do."

Feb. 15 – Ardell Wiegandt was hired as defensive line coach.

Feb. 19 – Elijah Pitts was named running backs coach, returning to the Bills, where he served under Chuck Knox from 1978-80. Bruce Smith, in Seattle to accept the Outland Trophy award, said he was giving the Bills one week to come up with an acceptable offer, or he was going to sign with the USFL's Baltimore Stars.

Feb. 21 – Dick Moseley was hired as defensive backfield coach.

Feb. 22 – The Bills reached a tentative agreement with Bruce Smith, said to be four years worth $2.6 million. "When you're the first player taken in the draft, there are a lot of eyes on you," Smith said. "People are going to look to you and up at you to set an example. I'm going to have to carry myself in a manner that people respect."

Feb. 24 – Jim Kelly passed for a pro football record 574 yards and threw five TD passes as the

Houston Gamblers rallied from a 33-13 deficit and beat the Los Angeles Express, 34-33, at the Coliseum.

Feb. 26 – Ex-Bills linebacker Shane Nelson came out of retirement and signed with San Diego.

Feb. 28 – Bruce Smith signed his first pro contract. "I think in time I can get them (fans) excited about me," Smith said. "The Buffalo fans really support their team. It's a great place to play. The pro game is a passing game and you need somebody to stop the pass. That's my game." Said Kay Stephenson of the man who recorded 46 sacks in four years at Virginia Tech: "I think impact is an overused word, but I think it's the right adjective to use when describing Bruce Smith. We feel he can be an impact player in his first year. We feel we have the No. 1 player in all of college football, not just defensive end."

March 19 – The Bills offered Dieter Brock, quarterback of the Hamilton Tiger-Cats of the CFL, a four-year, $1.8 million contract.

March 26 – Dieter Brock turned down the Bills and signed with the Rams.

April 23 – Commissioner Pete Rozelle gave University of Miami quarterback Bernie Kosar the option of applying for the regular college draft, or the supplemental draft. When he chose the supplemental draft, the Bills traded their No. 1 supplemental pick to Cleveland so that the

Browns could choose Kosar. In return, the Bills got linebacker Chip Banks, Cleveland's third-round pick in the regular draft, plus the Browns' No. 1 and No. 6 choices in the 1986 draft. By exercising their choice in the supplemental draft, the Bills lost their own first-round spot in the regular 1986 draft.

April 26 – The Bills traded offensive lineman Jon Borchardt to Seattle for a future draft choice.

April 30 – Chip Banks refused to report to Buffalo, so a provision in the Bernie Kosar deal allowed the Bills to send Banks back to Cleveland for the Browns' first-round choice in the draft, No. 7 overall. Once that was done, the Bills traded the pick and a fourth-rounder in 1986 to Green Bay, for the Packers first-round choice (14th overall) and second-round pick in this draft. With that first-round pick, they chose Memphis State cornerback Derrick Burroughs. Later, the Bills chose Nebraska offensive lineman Mark Traynowicz and Jackson State wide receiver Chris Burkett in the second round, Maryland quarterback Frank Reich and Utah State linebacker Hal Garner in the third round, Kutztown State wide receiver Andre Reed and SMU offensive tackle Dale Hellestrae in the fourth, Texas A&M wide receiver Jimmy Teal (fifth), Utah State defensive lineman Mike Hamby (sixth), and Elijah Pitts' son, UCLA cornerback Ron Pitts (seventh). Around the league, Atlanta chose offensive lineman Bill Fralic (second), Houston took defensive lineman Ray Childress (third), Minnesota selected linebacker Chris Doleman (fourth), Indianapolis chose linebacker Duane Bickett (fifth), Detroit took offensive tackle Lomas Brown (sixth), Green Bay chose offensive tackle Ken Ruettgers (seventh), the Jets grabbed wide receiver Al Toon (10th), San Diego selected offensive lineman Jim Lachey (12th), Cincinnati took wide receiver Eddie Brown (13th), San Francisco tapped wide receiver Jerry Rice (16th), Chicago took defensive tackle William Perry (22nd), Denver chose running back Steve Sewell (26th) and Miami chose running back Lorenzo Hampton (27th). Late in the evening, the Bills announced they had traded quarterback Joe Ferguson to the Lions for a future draft choice. Ferguson ended his career as the team's all-time leader in seasons played (12), games (168), and was among the leaders in every major passing category including career attempts (4,166), completions (2,188), yards (27,590), touchdowns (181) and interceptions (190). "I would have liked to have left on a winning note," Ferguson said. "That's my biggest regret. The fans will always wonder if I was the right quarterback for this team in recent years. I want to be remembered as a guy who tried."

May 1 – John Bassett, owner of the Tampa Bay Bandits, said he already had signed Derrick Burroughs to a personal services contract. Burroughs denied the story.

May 2 – Derrick Burroughs' agent, Harold Daniels, said his client did have a contract offer from John Bassett and that the Bills had two weeks to come up with a better offer.

May 15 – Minicamp opened at Rich Stadium and first-round choice Derrick Burroughs said "this is where I want to be" even though an agreement still hadn't been reached.

May 16 – Fred Smerlas' first impression of Bruce Smith was this: "The guy looks like he's carrying a little too much weight, but then you watch him move on the field and you change your mind."

May 17 – Derrick Burroughs signed a four-year contract worth about $1.75 million with the Bills.

May 22 – Vince Ferragamo tried out for the Bills and after his workout, he said: "They can look to me for leadership. I'll lead this team. I'll run the show."

May 24 – Former Bills assistant coach Andy MacDonald, who left the team three months earlier, died of a heart attack while jogging in Ludington, Mich. He was 55.

May 26 – Jim Kelly suffered a season-ending knee injury playing for the Houston Gamblers in the USFL. That ended any speculation that he could join the Bills for the 1985 season.

May 30 – Bruce Smith wrote a check for Virginia Tech in the amount of $50,000 for a football scholarship to be named in his honor.

June 7 – Elbert Dubenion returned to the Bills as an area scout. He had been a scout with the Bills from 1968-79 before leaving to go to the Miami Dolphins as a scout and later as assistant personnel director.

June 16 – Tony Marchitte, the Bills' equipment manager for 19 years before retiring in 1980, died after a two-year bout with lung cancer. He was 72.

July 5 – Bob Ferguson joined the Bills as assistant director of player personnel, replacing Bruce Nicholas who resigned in April to be become a salesman. Also, Rusty Jones joined the team as strength and conditioning coach, replacing Jim Speros, who resigned in order to join a management firm.

July 6 – It was reported that Jim Kelly had softened his anti-Buffalo stance, saying that if the price was right, he would play in Buffalo. The Buffalo talk surfaced after the Gamblers were eliminated from the USFL playoffs and they had failed to pay their players for the final week of the regular season. Jerry Argovitz was known to be trying to sell the team.

July 10 – The Bills reportedly broke off trade talks with the Rams for Vince Ferragamo.

July 14 – The final USFL championship game was won by Baltimore over Oakland.

July 18 – The Bills acquired quarterback Vince Ferragamo and a third-round draft choice in 1986 from the Rams for tight end Tony Hunter. "We're sorry we had to deal Tony, but you have to give up a good player to get one," said general manager Terry Bledsoe.

July 19 – Training camp opened at Fredonia with veterans and rookies reporting. Joe Cribbs said he wanted to return to the Bills and the Birmingham Stallions said they would allow him to go. To become a free agent, Cribbs would have to buy out the remainder of his Stallions contract, about $750,000.

July 21 – The Bills conducted their first training camp practice and Jerry Butler was on the field for the first time in 21 months. "I'm like a kid at Christmas," he said. The only unsigned veterans were Steve Freeman and Chris Keating, and thus they were not in Fredonia. Of first-round pick Bruce Smith, Kay Stephenson said: "He's still got some weight to lose. We would like to see him a few pounds lighter (he weighed 280)."

Also missing from camp were rookies Frank Reich and Chris Burkett.

July 27 – The Bills beat the Browns, 6-0, in their annual rookie scrimmage at Edinboro State University. The Bills improved to 4-0-4 against the Browns in the scrimmage series.

July 29 – Dick Jauron joined the Bills coaching staff as a defensive assistant.

Aug. 1 – Rookie holdout quarterback Frank Reich signed his first contract and reported to camp. Also, veteran Steve Freeman ended his holdout, leaving only Chris Keating unsigned.

Aug. 3 – Cleveland beat the Bills, 16-13, in a controlled scrimmage in front of 16,237 at Rich Stadium who were not charged for admission or parking. In Canton, Ohio, O.J. Simpson officially was inducted into the Pro Football Hall of Fame.

Aug. 9 – The Bills played to a 10-10 tie with the Lions at the Silverdome. Rochester native Mike Johnston missed a 44-yard field goal in OT that would have won it for the Bills. Joe Ferguson completed five of six passes for 51 yards and drove Detroit to a second-quarter field goal in his first appearance against the Bills. Bruce Smith recorded three sacks.

Aug. 14 – The Bills traded quarterback Matt Kofler to Indianapolis for a future draft pick.

Aug. 16 – A deal that would have brought tight end Dan Ross to Buffalo fell through.

Aug. 17 – The Bills traveled to the Orange Bowl and lost to Miami, 27-17.

Aug. 19 – Chris Keating ended his holdout and reported to camp. The Bills reduced their roster to the 60-man limit by cutting 13 players including kicker Chuck Nelson, apparently opening the door for former USFL kicker Scott Norwood to claim the job. "I'll just look to put a little consistency in it," Norwood said of the Bills' sorry placekicking situation the past few years.

Aug. 20 – Byron Franklin, the team's leading receiver in 1984, was traded to Seattle for tight end Pete Metzelaars. Later in the day, wide receiver Preston Dennard was traded to Green Bay for a future draft choice, and the Bills shipped a draft choice to Atlanta for defensive lineman Don Smith.

Aug. 23 – Joe Cribbs held a press conference in Buffalo and said the chances of him returning to the Bills were slim after a failure to reach an agreement with management earlier that day. So he asked for a trade, preferably to Miami or Seattle. "I've given up hope of playing here," he said. "I'd like to, but I have to be realistic. If they had won 13 or 14 games, I could understand the hard stance."

Aug. 24 – In the only preseason game scheduled for Rich Stadium, the Bills lost to Cleveland, 31-28. Vince Ferragamo appeared to take the lead from Joe Dufek in the quarterback derby. He completed 14 of 22 passes for 183 yards.

Aug. 28 – The Bills acquired linebacker Anthony Dickerson from Dallas for a conditional draft pick. The team then waived seven-year veteran linebacker Chris Keating.

Aug. 31 – The Bills closed the preseason the same way they did in 1984, losing in embarrassing fashion to the Chicago Bears, this time 45-14 at Soldier Field.

Sept. 3 – Angered by his team's shoddy loss to the Bears, Ralph Wilson flew to Buffalo asking plenty of questions. "We have to be patient, but my patience is wearing thin," he said. "I don't think some of our players are playing as well as they can play, or did play a couple years ago. This team is going to have to play better, or we'll get new players."

Sept. 4 – It was announced that rookies Andre Reed and Bruce Smith would start the season opener against San Diego, as would Vince Ferragamo. Also, the Bills said they would honor Patrick McGroder on their Wall of Fame, joining O.J. Simpson and Jack Kemp.

Sept. 8 – Vince Ferragamo threw for 371 yards in his Bills debut, but San Diego beat Buffalo, 14-9, before 67,597 at Rich Stadium. Scott Norwood provided all the Bills points with three field goals in his Bills debut, while Bruce Smith made six tackles and Andre Reed caught three passes for 35 yards.

Sept. 10 – Bruce Mathison, the former backup to Dan Fouts at San Diego, came to Rich Stadium for a tryout and was given the backup quarterback job. Joe Dufek then was waived. "I am very bitter with Kay Stephenson," Dufek said after learning of his release. "He told me he didn't feel my accuracy throwing the ball was what he was looking for. He said he didn't feel I would be able to lead the club effectively if something were to happen to Vince. I don't think that's true. I feel very confident in my ability."

Sept. 15 – Freeman McNeil rushed for a Jets' single-game record of 192 yards as New York routed the Bills, 42-3, at Giants Stadium in one of Buffalo's worst performances ever. It was their worst loss since a 43-0 shellacking against the Baltimore Colts in 1971.

Sept. 16 – The Bills signed a pair of players who were waived by Cleveland: Former Bills star Joe DeLamielleure and fullback Mike Pruitt. "I'm glad to be back," DeLamielleure said. "I had a job in the real world lined up. I didn't think I'd be playing football again." Justin Cross broke his left arm against the Jets, leaving the Bills thin on the line.

Sept. 18 – After just two pro starts, Bruce Smith was benched in favor of veteran Don Smith in a move designed to help the run defense. "I just had a bad day at the office," Bruce Smith said. "I'm disappointed in myself. It has taken me a little more time to adjust to the pro running backs. I was surprised, though, that they didn't stick with me longer. But I'll be back."

Sept. 22 – The members of the 1964-65 AFL Championship teams were honored, but they saw the current Bills fall to 0-3 at Rich Stadium as Irving Fryar returned a punt 85 yards for a touchdown and New England pulled out a 17-14 victory.

Sept. 24 – Tight end Mark Brammer was waived off the injured reserve list.

Sept. 29 – The Bills rallied from a 20-3 deficit to tie the game in the fourth quarter, but Ted Brown's TD run with 2:57 left won it for

Minnesota, 27-20. At halftime, Patrick McGroder had his name unveiled on the Wall of Fame and O.J. Simpson was presented his Hall of Fame ring. Jim Kelly was in attendance, witnessing his first Bills game live. "I just came to watch the game," Kelly said. "I met Mr. Wilson for the first time. We didn't talk about anything, except how nice the weather was and how he wished his team would win. No business, this was a pleasure trip."

Oct. 1 – Time ran out for Kay Stephenson as Ralph Wilson fired him and promoted Hank Bullough to head coach. "I don't want to speak for Mr. Wilson," said Terry Bledsoe, "but I think he felt the franchise was in jeopardy and that a change had to be made for the sake of the franchise. We were in what I felt was a tailspin that we couldn't get out of." Said Bullough: "I'm not Kay Stephenson. I'll be doing some things my own way. I don't have a magic wand. If I did, I would have given it to Kay and let him wave it."

Oct. 2 – Kay Stephenson broke his one-day silence. "I accept the consequences. Ralph Wilson feels he has to do what's best for the organization and that's a decision you have to respect. I have no complaints with anyone, no hard feelings whatsoever."

Oct. 4 – The Bills admitted they had auditioned TCU running back Kenneth Davis and were interested in him. Davis was suspended two weeks earlier for having accepted money from a TCU booster. He was trying to get the NFL to conduct a special supplemental draft so he could play in the NFL this season. He would have been eligible for the 1986 draft.

Oct. 6 – Hank Bullough's debut as Bills head coach was a debacle as the Colts dealt Buffalo a 49-17 loss at the Hoosier Dome.

Oct. 9 – Hank Bullough announced lineup changes for Sunday's game in New England. Center Will Grant was benched, with Tim Vogler moving to center and Joe DeLamielleure moving in at right guard; Bruce Smith would take over for Don Smith at defensive end; Darryl Talley

was being benched in favor of Lucious Sanford, and Derrick Burroughs was replacing Rod Hill at cornerback.

Oct. 11 – Joe Cribbs agreed to the Bills final offer and returned to his old team. The deal was worth a reported $2 million over four years. "I want to play football," Cribbs said. "That's what I'm gonna do. Everyone seems to be glad that I'm back, so that's a positive sign."

Oct. 13 – The Bills went to Sullivan Stadium and lost to New England, 14-3, as they were outgained 400-162 and were two-for-12 on third down conversions. For the first time in team history, only one player ran the ball as Greg Bell carried on all 23 Bills rushing plays. Bob Ryan wrote in the *Boston Globe* that the Patriots "didn't beat a professional football team, they beat, well, er, a glorified open date. The Buffalo Bills are to a professional football team what Cheez-Its are to haute cuisine."

Oct. 20 – The Bills got their first victory of the season and the first of Hank Bullough's career, avenging their embarrassing loss to the Colts two weeks earlier with a 21-9 victory at Rich Stadium. Joe Cribbs started in his first game back for the Bills and rushed for 41 yards, but fumbled twice, then decided not to speak to the media afterwards.

Oct. 21 – Mike Pruitt was cut one month after he had been signed and the team picked up running back Anthony Steels off waivers to fill the roster spot. The Bills also waived tight end Buster Barnett off the injured reserve list.

Oct. 27 – The Bills blew a 17-0 lead, allowing the Eagles to score 21 fourth-quarter points and Philadelphia hung on for a 21-17 victory at Veterans Stadium.

Nov. 3 – For the second week in a row, the Bills blew an early lead, this time 10-0, and lost to Cincinnati, 23-17, at Rich Stadium.

Nov. 5 – Paul Maguire observed on ESPN: "Vince Ferragamo is having a terrible year. If the Bills had a quarterback in here, they would have

Former Bills great Elbert Dubenion found Andre Reed at Kutztown State in Pennsylvania and suggested the Bills draft him. Since then Reed has broken virtually every Bills receiving record, many of which were held by Dubenion.

won three or four games. Ferragamo just can't throw. I don't know whether he can't read a defense or his arm is gone or there's something he isn't telling anybody, but he just can't throw."

Nov. 10 – Bruce Mathison made the first start of his NFL career and completed 11 of 22 passes for 121 yards to lead the Bills to a 20-0 victory over Houston before only 21,831 at Rich Stadium. The defense held the Oilers to 142 yards and knocked Warren Moon out of the game.

Nov. 17 – Bruce Mathison couldn't do it two weeks in a row as the Bills lost their 14th straight road game, 17-7, to the Browns and Bernie Kosar. Kosar relied on Cleveland's running game, but did throw one TD pass.

Nov. 21 – Joe Cribbs, who had strung strips of athletic tape in front of his locker stall with a sign that read "Buffalo Prison" removed those, but put up a new sign atop his stall: "My bars are gone, but I'm not. Yet!" Cribbs, who maintained his policy of not speaking to the media, let his agent, Louis Burrell, talk for him. "He's a prisoner of the system, that makes him a prisoner of the team," Burrell said. "Joe told the Bills they needed more than him to make them a competitive team this year. But because of their own self-centeredness, regardless of where they needed help, they were going to keep Joe. The general manager said to me: 'Louis, the Bills may not want Joe Cribbs, but because he's Joe Cribbs, we don't want anyone else to have him.'"

Nov. 24 – On a cold, windy day at Rich Stadium, the Dolphins had to tone down their dynamic passing game and used a ball-control running attack to beat the Bills, 23-14.

Nov. 26 – Joe DeLamielleure announced his retirement effective immediately. "In all fairness to the Bills, they've got some young guys they want to look at for next year," he said. "And I was going to retire after this season anyway. My sticking around was putting Hank and Jim Ringo in an awkward position. It's just easier for everyone if I retire. If we were going to the playoffs, I'd stay around and be glad to help, but at this point, I think I'm a hindrance."

Dec. 1 – Bruce Mathison threw four interceptions against his old team and the Bills were routed in San Diego, 40-7.

Dec. 2 – Ralph Wilson said that "if we field a winning, contending, interesting team, we'll have crowds of 80,000 again. I have no doubt. We just have to field a better product." Of Hank Bullough, Wilson said: "I think he's done an outstanding job. I think he's going to be a very good head coach. He's very straight-forward and he knows the game."

Dec. 3 – The Bills waived quarterback Vince Ferragamo. "We don't have the major portion of our end of the trade, so I think you would have to say it was a bad decision," Terry Bledsoe said of the trade of Tony Hunter to the Rams for Ferragamo. "We thought he could give us the kind of effective quarterback that we felt we needed. For whatever reason, we didn't get it. Of course I'm disappointed." Hank Bullough hired Jim Valek as his administrative assistant.

Dec. 4 – With Vince Ferragamo gone, rookie Frank Reich hoped he would get the chance to play. "I don't know if I'll get the chance, but I'll be ready," Reich said. "I'm dying to play. I'm not used to sitting on the bench. It's tough for any-

body, especially at this level because everybody was big-time on his team in college. I don't enjoy it, but if somebody else can do a better job, he should be in there."

Dec. 8 – Ken O'Brien passed for 370 yards and three TDs, including a 96-yarder to Wesley Walker, as the Jets downed the Bills, 27-7, at Rich Stadium. Hank Bullough delivered his classic malapropos when he described Walker's TD as the play that "took the sail out of our winds."

Dec. 15 – The Bills blew a 21-0 second-quarter lead and lost at Pittsburgh, 30-24, when Walter Abercrombie scored on a two-yard run with 47 seconds left to play. It was the Steelers greatest comeback ever.

Dec. 18 – Joe Ferguson talked about the Bills' predicament at quarterback without him. "I'm not going to lie about it," he said. "Deep down there is vindication. I'm human. I just hope now they realize it wasn't just me. We'll never know, but I personally feel I could have done a better job than those other two guys."

Dec. 19 – For the second year in a row, no Bills were voted to the AFC Pro Bowl squad.

Dec. 22 – The Bills closed their second straight 2-14 season with a miserable 28-0 loss at the Orange Bowl to the Dolphins. The win clinched the AFC East title for Miami. The Bills turned the ball over six times.

Dec. 23 – General manager Terry Bledsoe was fired in a somewhat surprising development. "I wouldn't say whether I deserve this fate or not. Looking back, I think we achieved some things here. I'm grateful to Ralph Wilson for giving me a chance and I feel bad that we're not going to be able to achieve more." Wilson said in a statement that he felt the Bills "need to go in a new direction and I have asked Terry to step aside to give us that opportunity."

Dec. 28 – New England defeated the Jets, 26-14, in the AFC wild-card game.

Dec. 29 – The Giants downed San Francisco, 17-3, in the NFC wild-card game.

Dec. 30 – The Bills named Bill Polian as their new general manager, replacing Terry Bledsoe,

and Bill Munson was promoted to assistant general manager. "It was the last thing in the world that I expected," Polian said. "I was extremely surprised and obviously flattered. It took some thinking on my part for it to sink in. I'm not sure my feet are on the ground yet. I must admit I accept this with mixed emotions. I replace a man I respect highly and consider a friend, but I look forward to the challenge. I know the NFL well, I know its players, I think I'm prepared for the job."

Dec. 31 – Hank Bullough hired Herb Paterra to be his defensive coordinator, freeing Bullough to concentrate on head coaching duties. Paterra played for the Bills in 1963-64.

Jan. 4, 1986 – The Rams blanked Dallas, 20-0, and Miami rallied from a 21-3 deficit to beat Cleveland, 24-21, in the first two divisional round playoff games.

Jan. 5, 1986 – New England surprised the Raiders in Los Angeles, 27-20, and Chicago blanked the Giants, 21-0, in the other two divisional round games.

Jan. 12, 1986 – New England became the third team to qualify for the Super Bowl as a wild-card team, knocking off Miami in the AFC Championship Game at the Orange Bowl, 31-14. New England converted four of its six takeaways into 24 points. It was the Patriots first win in Miami since 1966. The Bears rolled past the Rams, 24-0, in the NFC Championship Game, their second straight playoff shutout.

Jan. 26, 1986 – Chicago scored a Super Bowl record 46 points and routed the Patriots, 46-10, in Super Bowl XX at the Superdome. It was the largest margin of victory in Super Bowl history and it was the Bears first title since 1963. Richard Dent became only the fourth defender to be named MVP as he had 1 1/2 sacks, while Jim McMahon threw for 256 yards and scored two rushing TDs.

Feb. 2, 1986 – MVP Phil Simms of the Giants threw three TD passes in the second half to rally the NFC to a 28-24 victory in the Pro Bowl at Aloha Stadium. Simms passed for 212 yards.

BY THE NUMBERS - 1985

TEAM STATISTICS	BILLS	OPP
First downs	256	320
Rushing	86	142
Passing	151	159
Penalty	19	19
Third downs	68-208	100-226
Total yards	4,595	5,540
Avg. game	287.2	346.3
Plays	971	1,071
Avg. play	4.7	5.2
Net rushing yds	1,611	2,462
Avg. game	100.7	153.9
Avg. play	3.9	4.3
Net passing yds	2,984	3,078
Comp/att	263/517	265/477
Sacks/lost	42-347	25-223
Interceptions	31	20
Percentage	50.9	55.6
Punts/avg.	92-41.5	81-40.5
Fumbles/lost	36-21	36-15
Penalties/yds	132-965	107-870
Touchdowns	23	50
Extra points	23-23	45-50
Field goals	13-17	12-15
Safeties	0	0
Kick ret./avg	68-19.6	41-19.5
Punt ret./avg	38-7.7	49-8.9

SCORE BY QUARTERS

BILLS	58	63	41	38	0 -	200
OPP	51	144	78	108	0 -	381

DEFENSIVE STATISTICAL LEADERS

TACKLES: Haslett 85 primary - 58 assists - 143 total, Marve 56-51-107, Freeman 54-32-86, Romes 47-28-75, Frazier 49-24-73, Bayless 46-26-72, Talley 46-20-66, D. Wilson 40-24-64, Sanford 42-18-60, Williams 34-26-60, B. Smith 36-17-53, Smerlas 22-14-36, L. Johnson 21-10-31

SACKS: B. Smith 6.5, D. Smith 3, McNanie 3, Talley 2, Sanford 2, Perryman 2

FUMBLE RECOVERIES: B. Smith 4, D. Smith 2, Haslett 2

FORCED FUMBLES: Perryman 2

INTERCEPTIONS: Romes 7-56 yards, 8.0 avg., 0 TD; Bellinger 2-64, 32.0, 0 TD; D. Wilson 2-23, 11.5, 0 TD; Hill 2-17, 8.5, 0 TD; Bayless 2-10, 5.0, 0 TD; Burroughs 2-7, 3.5, 0 TD

SPECIAL TEAMS STATISTICAL LEADERS

KICKOFF RETURNS: D. Wilson 22-465, 21.1, 0 TD; Steels 20-338, 16.9, 0 TD

PUNT RETURNS: Wilson 16-161, 10.1, 0 TD; Hill 16-120, 7.5, 0 TD

RUSHING	ATT	YDS	AVG	TD
Bell	223	883	4.0	8
Cribbs	122	399	3.3	1
Mathison	27	231	8.6	1
Steels	4	26	6.5	0
Pruitt	7	24	3.4	0
Moore	15	23	1.5	1
Ferragamo	8	15	1.9	1
Hutchison	2	11	5.5	0
B. Smith	1	0	0.0	0
Reed	3	-1	-0.3	1
TOTALS	**412**	**1611**	**3.9**	**13**

PASSING	COMP	ATT	INT	YDS	TD	COMP%	SACKS	RATE
Ferragamo	149	287	17	1677	5	51.9	19-135	50.8
Mathison	113	228	14	1635	4	49.6	22-203	53.5
Reich	1	1	0	19	0	100.0	0-0	118.8
Bell	0	1	0	0	0	00.0	0-0	39.6
Kidd	0	0	0	0	0	00.0	1-9	0.0
TOTALS	**263**	**517**	**31**	**3331**	**9**	**50.9**	**42-347**	**52.1**

KICKING	1-19	20-29	30-39	40-49	50+	TOT	PAT	PTS
Norwood	0-0	7-8	2-4	4-5	0-0	13-17	23-23	62

PUNTING	NO	AVG	LG	In 20	BL
Kidd	92	41.5	67	33	0

RECEIVING	CAT	YDS	AVG	TD
Bell	58	576	9.9	1
Reed	48	637	13.3	4
Butler	41	770	18.8	2
Ramson	37	369	10.0	1
Burkett	21	371	17.7	0
Cribbs	18	142	7.9	0
Richardson	12	201	16.8	0
Metzelaars	12	80	6.7	1
Moore	7	44	6.3	0
Brookins	3	71	23.7	0
Norris	2	30	15.0	0
Steels	2	9	4.5	0
Teal	1	24	24.0	0
Williams	1	7	7.0	0
TOTALS	**263**	**3331**	**12.7**	**9**

Chargers	7	7	0	0	-	14
Bills	3	6	0	0	-	9

Attendance at Rich Stadium - 67,597

SD: Adams 1 run (Benirschke kick), 4:12
Buf: FG Norwood 27, 13:20
Buf: FG Norwood 34, :48
SD: Sievers 30 pass from Fouts (Benirschke kick), 5:42
Buf: FG Norwood 29, 11:55

	BUF	SD
First downs	19	17
Rushing yds	84	100
Passing yds	371	208
Punts-avg	5-39.8	7-46.0
Fumbles-lost	1-1	2-1
Penalties-yds	7-50	1-37
Poss. time	33:43	26:17

BILLS LEADERS: Rushing - Bell 23-79, Moore 1-0, Reed 1-5; **Passing** - Ferragamo 31-46-2 - 377; **Receiving** - Bell 13-80, Reed 3-35, Butler 4-140, Ramson 3-7, Burkett 1-10, Richardson 1-18, Metzelaars 3-25, Brookins 1-46, Moore 1-9, Williams 1-7.

CHARGERS LEADERS: Rushing - Adams 16-49, Spencer 9-41, Fouts 3-7, Steels 3-7, James 1-(-4); **Passing** - Fouts 16-29-1 - 218; **Receiving** - James 3-23, Chandler 2-41, Joiner 4-62, Spencer 1-6, Sievers 3-50, Johnson 1-12, Holohan 1-12, Adams 1-12.

NOTES

• The Bills lost their season opener despite three field goals by newcomer Scott Norwood and solid rookie debuts by Andre Reed and Bruce Smith.
• The Chargers scored on their opening possession, driving 70 yards in nine plays to Curtis Adams' TD run. Dan Fouts completed passes of 11 yards to Lionel James, 22 to Wes Chandler and 16 to Charlie Joiner.
• Later in the first, the Bills moved 60 yards in 10 plays to Norwood's first field goal, the key play a 41-yard pass to Jerry Butler, his first reception since 1983.
• After a punt, the Bills got another field goal as a 37-yard pass-interference penalty on Danny Walters put the ball at the Chargers 17.
• After an exchange of punts, the Chargers needed only three plays to go 46 yards as Fouts hit Eric Sievers with a 30-yard TD pass. Don Wilson missed a tackle that allowed Sievers to go all the way.
• The Bills answered with Norwood's third field goal to cap a 59-yard march. Greg Bell took a screen for 18 yards and on the next play, Butler made a 48-yard reception to the Chargers 7.
• In the third, Fouts lost a fumble at the Bills 13 to kill a drive, but Eason Ramson lost a fumble at the Chargers 11 to kill a Bills threat. Later, Ferragamo was intercepted by Mike Green.
• The game ended with Eric Richardson failing to get out of bounds at the Chargers 24.
• Bruce Smith was in on six tackles while Jim Haslett led the way with 13.

QUOTES

• Vince Ferragamo: "We moved the ball well, but we had breakdowns that prevented us from getting into the end zone. I guess we'll have to get our big plays to go 100 yards instead of 40. It's going to come, everybody is going to see it. We're on the road to bouncing back."
• Chargers coach Don Coryell: "All in all, I'm just happy to get out of this town alive. We had a great defensive effort, but I wasn't very happy with our offense."
• Kay Stephenson: "Our people played their hearts out against a very talented team, but I am displeased about the scoreboard and not getting the ball in the end zone. The turnovers in the second half were disappointing and they may have cost us some points."
• Jerry Butler: "I just thank God for the opportunity to go out and do what I did today."
• Hank Bullough: "I was surprised we didn't get more fumbles. We were massaging them pretty good today. We will have a defense that creates turnovers. If you keep hustling and hitting, eventually things will fall into place. I was real proud of the guys, they worked hard, but we just came up short."
• Bruce Smith: "When you put pressure on a quarterback, that makes him worry a lot. He has to make hasty decisions that he doesn't want to make. We did a number of things to Fouts that made him jittery and worry a lot."

WEEK 1 GAMES	
Rams 20, Den 16	Det 28, Atl 27
NE 26, GB 20	Pitt 45, Ind 3
KC 47, NO 27	Hou 26, Mia 23
LAR 31, NYJ 0	NYG 21, Phil 0
St.L 27, Clev 24	Minn 28, SF 21
Sea 28, Cinc 24	Chi 38, TB 28
Dal 44, Wash 14	

Bills	3	0	0	0	-	3
Jets	0	21	14	7	-	42

Attendance at Giants Stadium - 63,449

Buf: FG Norwood 32, 10:52
NYJ: McNeil 6 run (Leahy kick), :09
NYJ: Sohn 7 pass from O'Brien (Leahy kick), 4:26
NYJ: McNeil 13 run (Leahy kick), 10:23
NYJ: Paige 2 pass from O'Brien (Leahy kick), 1:27
NYJ: Glenn 15 interception return (Leahy kick), 11:24
NYJ: Paige 2 run (Leahy kick), 4:01

	BUF	NYJ
First downs	16	27
Rushing yds	82	288
Passing yds	188	244
Punts-avg	5-40.6	4-45.3
Fumbles-lost	2-1	1-0
Penalties-yds	14-82	13-99
Poss. time	23:09	36:51

BILLS LEADERS: Rushing - Bell 11-52, Mathison 1-22, Moore 2-8; **Passing** - Ferragamo 16-30-4 - 150, Mathison 5-13-0 - 72; **Receiving** - Bell 3-29, Reed 2-21, Butler 1-4, Ramson 4-69, Burkett 1-8, Richardson 4-58, Metzelaars 3-20, Moore 3-13.

JETS LEADERS: Rushing - McNeil 18-192, Hector 6-43, Paige 7-13, Minter 5-13, Barber 5-24, O'Brien 1-3; **Passing** - O'Brien 16-24-0 - 181, Ryan 4-6-0 - 76; **Receiving** - Sohn 6-56, Shuler 4-40, Toon 3-67, McNeil 3-35, Townsell 1-35, Minter 1-13, Barber 1-9, Paige 1-2.

NOTES

• The Bills turned in one of their worst performances ever, allowing 532 total yards, including a Jets' record 192 yards rushing by Freeman McNeil. It was the Bills' worst loss since 1971.
• McNeil's total was the largest ever against the Bills. The Bills remained without a TD for two games.
• Scott Norwood's field goal gave Buffalo the early 3-0 lead, but even that was a disappointment as an illegal procedure penalty wiped out a TD pass to Chris Burkett, forcing the field goal. It was one of four penalties on the offensive line during the drive.
• The Jets took the kickoff and drove 92 yards in nine plays to McNeil's first TD run.
• Don Wilson fumbled a punt at his 12. Two plays later, Ken O'Brien hit Kurt Sohn for a TD.
• After another punt, O'Brien completed five of six passes during a 67-yard drive to McNeil's second TD.
• The Jets needed just 1:33 to move 86 yards after the second-half kickoff, as McNeil broke a 69-yard run that led to O'Brien's TD pass to Tony Paige for a 28-3 lead.
• Kerry Glenn returned a Vince Ferragamo interception for a TD late in the third. Early in the fourth, backup QB Pat Ryan hit Al Toon for 50 yards to set up Paige's TD run.
• The offensive line was penalized five times for 40 yards and allowed four sacks.
• In the third quarter, Ralph Wilson instructed Kay Stephenson to remove Greg Bell and Ferragamo to protect them from possible injury.

QUOTES

• Ralph Wilson: "We have a few very good players, and the rest can't play in the NFL. The head coach? Did the head coach drop those passes or miss those tackles?"
• Fred Smerlas: "Kay Stephenson had nothing to do with it. When you get your butt kicked, it has to do with yourselves. What the heck does Kay have to do with someone getting blown off the ball? The fault lies with the players. The coaches gave us a good gameplan, we just stunk."
• Kay Stephenson: "It was a very, very poor effort. We didn't block, we didn't tackle, we didn't catch the ball. They really got after us." (About Wilson's directive to remove Ferragamo and Bell): "We were going to do that anyway. Ralph has never interfered in a game. That was a very logical concern. I wouldn't classify it as interference."
• Ben Williams: "Anytime you play against a great back like McNeil, you have to play the run, but obviously we didn't stop him today. The defense as a whole didn't play well. When you give up 42 points, that pretty much speaks for itself."
• Jets running back Freeman McNeil: "Mr. Hess (Jets owner Leon) came over to me prior to the game and said 'I want 200 yards from you today.' He laughed, but I didn't know if he was serious. I didn't panic, but I did keep it in the back of my mind. I guess you could say he gave me something to think about."

WEEK 2 GAMES	
KC 36, LAR 20	SF 35, Atl 16
St.L 41, Cinc 27	Det 26, Dal 21
Wash 16, Hou 13	Mia 30, Ind 13
Rams 17, Phil 6	Minn 31, TB 16
Chi 20, NE 7	Den 34, NO 23
GB 23, NYG 20	Sea 49, SD 35
Clev 17, Pitt 7	

STANDINGS: SECOND WEEK

AFC EAST	W	L	T	CENTRAL	W	L	T	WEST	W	L	T	NFC EAST	W	L	T	CENTRAL	W	L	T	WEST	W	L	T
New England	1	1	0	Houston	1	1	0	Kan. City	2	0	0	St. Louis	2	0	0	Chicago	2	0	0	LA Rams	2	0	0
NY Jets	1	1	0	Pittsburgh	1	1	0	Seattle	2	0	0	NY Giants	1	1	0	Minnesota	2	0	0	San Fran	1	1	0
Miami	1	1	0	Cleveland	1	1	0	Raiders	1	1	0	Dallas	1	1	0	Detroit	2	0	0	N.Orleans	0	2	0
Buffalo	0	2	0	Cincinnati	0	2	0	San Diego	1	1	0	Washington	1	1	0	Green Bay	1	1	0	Atlanta	0	2	0
Indianapolis	0	2	0					Denver	1	1	0	Philadelphia	0	2	0	Tampa Bay	0	2	0				

NOTES

• The game was winnable, but Irving Fryar's punt return in the third was the backbreaker. On the play before, Don Wilson was penalized for being downfield illegally. Fryar had been tackled at the 14.

• The Pats drove 57 yards to Tony Franklin's field goal in the first quarter. Fryar made a 26-yard reception and after a holding penalty, Tony Collins took a screen pass 17 yards to the 28.

• The Bills took the lead early in the second quarter, driving 70 yards to Greg Bell's TD reception. Vince Ferragamo was four-for-four for 58 yards on the march, including a 24-yard strike to Eric Richardson.

• The Pats got that back on the next series as Stephen Starring returned the kickoff 53 yards to the Bills 37. Six plays later, Craig James threw a halfback option TD pass to Collins.

• Late in the third, Charlie Romes recovered a Collins fumble at the Pats 33. On the next play, Bell faked an option pass and ran 15 yards. Then on the next play, Andre Reed caught his first NFL TD pass.

• The Bills punted on the next two series, then the Pats ran out the final 5:19, gaining four first downs.

• The Bills honored their 1964 and '65 AFL Championship teams at halftime. Coach Lou Saban was onhand as well as Cookie Gilchrist, Tom Sestak, Billy Shaw, Mike Stratton, Elbert Dubenion, Stew Barber, Butch Byrd, Ed Rutkowski, Ron McDole, Tom Day, Wray Carlton, George Saimes and others.

QUOTES

• Ralph Wilson: "As far as the coaching situation is concerned, Kay's the football coach and he's doing the best job he can. He doesn't need my vote of confidence. Kay's my head coach."

• Don Wilson on his fatal penalty: "Normally, I have a guy rushing in on me, so I don't get down there that quickly. But on that play, no one was coming in on my side so I had clear sailing. It was an aggressive mistake. My job is to get down there and make the tackle."

• Pats receiver Irving Fryar: "You don't give people a second chance in the NFL or you get burned. The funny thing is I sprained my ankle on the first punt and was coming off the field. When I saw the flag, my ankle healed."

• Kay Stephenson: "I've said it before that the penalty situation is atrocious and I have to take the blame. Mistakes killed us and we had some problems with special teams. We let them return the punt all the way after a mistake and we let them return a kickoff a long way. I think we played with much more emotion and intensity."

• Vince Ferragamo: "It brings tears to your eyes. You work so hard and just come up short."

• Will Grant: "I feel worse this week than I did last week."

• Fred Smerlas: "It was a pretty even game. Our defense pretty much kept their offense under control and vice-versa. The difference was special teams."

WEEK 3 GAMES

Chi 33, Minn 24	Dal 20, Clev 7
Den 44, Atl 28	Ind 14, Det 6
Pitt 20, Hou 0	Mia 31, KC 0
NYJ 24, GB 3	Phil 19, Wash 6
NYG 27, St.L 17	SD 44, Cinc 41
SF 34, LAR 10	NO 20, TB 13
Rams 35, Sea 24	

Patriots	3 7 7 0	- 17
Bills	0 7 0 7	- 14

Attendance at Rich Stadium - 40,334

NE: FG Franklin 32, 10:18
Buf: Bell 16 pass from Ferragamo (Norwood kick), 8:16
NE: Collins 5 pass from James (Franklin kick), 10:32
NE: Fryar 85 punt return (Franklin kick), 5:32
Buf: Reed 18 pass from Ferragamo (Norwood kick), :04

	BUF	NE
First downs	16	14
Rushing yds	55	122
Passing yds	251	105
Punts-avg	9-45.8	7-48.7
Fumbles-lost	1-0	2-1
Penalties-yds	10-80	4-34
Poss. time	28:54	31:06

BILLS LEADERS: Rushing - Bell 12-55, Pruitt 5-15, Ferragamo 2-5, Reed 1-(-20); **Passing** - Ferragamo 23-39-1 - 251; **Receiving** - Bell 6-35, Reed 5-59, Butler 1-19, Ramson 3-34, Burkett 1-10, Richardson 2-45, Metzelaars 3-24, Brookins 2-25.

PATRIOTS LEADERS: Rushing - Collins 8-25, James 18-69, Weathers 6-15, Tatupu 4-15, Fryar 2-3, Eason 2-(-5); **Passing** - Eason 12-21-1 - 100, James 1-1-0 - 5; **Receiving** - Ramsey 5-39, Fryar 2-33, Collins 4-23, Dawson 1-8, Starring 1-2.

NOTES

• Jim Kelly watched the Bills for the first time in person from a luxury box at Rich Stadium.

• He saw them rally from a 20-3 halftime deficit to tie the game, only to see the Vikings come back for the victory when Ted Brown capped a 58-yard drive by scoring on the old "Statue of Liberty" play.

• The Vikings drove 55 yards in the first quarter to Tommy Kramer's TD pass to Leo Lewis.

• Charlie Romes' interception early in the second quarter set up the Bills at the Minnesota 40, but Vince Ferragamo was intercepted by Tim Newton, who rumbled 63 yards to the Bills 17. Two plays later, Kramer hit Brown for the TD. Don Smith blocked Jan Stenerud's extra point.

• Mitchell Brookins returned the ensuing kickoff 36 yards to the 44 and the Bills moved 24 yards to a Scott Norwood field goal. The Vikings then went 80 yards in six plays with Anthony Carter making a 43-yard TD catch. Kramer had scrambled 19 yards on the previous play, a third-and-nine situation.

• Bruce Smith's second sack of the half prevented the Vikings from trying a late field goal.

• The Bills took the second-half kickoff and went 66 yards in 16 plays, using 7:58 to get another Norwood field goal. After the Vikings went three-and-out, Rod Hill returned the punt 17 yards to the Minnesota 45 and the Bills needed only five plays to get Ferragamo's TD sneak to make it 20-13.

• The Bills stopped the Vikes on fourth-and two at their 37, then turned around and drove 63 yards to tie game on Greg Bell's fourth-and-goal dive. The key play was a 28-yard pass to Eason Ramson.

• Buster Rhymes returned the kickoff 32 yards to the 42, and Brown later scored the winning TD.

QUOTES

• Vikings offensive coordinator Jerry Burns on the Statue play: "That play's been around a thousand years. We used it in sandlot games when I was a kid and I'm ancient."

• Kay Stephenson: "That was something they had to dig out of the archives. I think our coaches did a good job of digging up everything Minnesota would come up with. You can't prepare for everything the Vikings have ever done."

• Bruce Smith: "I didn't know what to think. It was a play we weren't expecting. I got blocked and when I saw him (Brown), it was too late." (On recording his first two NFL sacks): "I anticipated it happening a lot sooner than this game."

• Greg Bell on Jim Kelly: "There's nothing I can say that will make him come here. We're friends, we played against each other in college and we worked together at Jack Lambert's football camp in the summer. He knows he can be a force for us, but he's in the USFL."

• Eugene Marve: "We've got to look at the positive side. We've played three close games that could have gone either way."

• Don Smith: "That's all nice that we didn't quit at halftime and came back, but the bottom line is that we didn't win, and that's what the fans come out for."

WEEK 4 GAMES

Clev 21, SD 7	Dal 17, Hou 10
St.L 43, GB 28	NYJ 25, Ind 20
LAR 35, NE 20	Mia 30, Den 26
NO 20, SF 17	NYG 16, Phil 10
KC 28, Sea 7	Det 30, TB 9
Chi 45, Wash 10	Rams 17, Atl 6
Cinc 37, Pitt 24	

Vikings	7 13 0 7	- 27
Bills	0 3 10 7	- 20

Attendance at Rich Stadium - 45,667

Min: Lewis 10 pass from Kramer (Stenerud kick), 7:23
Min: Brown 15 pass from Kramer (kick blocked), 5:07
Buf: FG Norwood 49, 8:17
Min: Carter 43 pass from Kramer (Stenerud kick), 11:21
Buf: FG Norwood 28, 7:50
Buf: Ferragamo 1 run (Norwood kick), 13:18
Buf: Bell 1 run (Norwood kick), 6:15
Min: Brown 22 run (Stenerud kick), 12:03

	BUF	MIN
First downs	20	19
Rushing yds	115	171
Passing yds	162	167
Punts-avg	4-40.8	4-44.8
Fumbles-lost	0-0	1-0
Penalties-yds	7-55	11-78
Poss. time	31:58	28:02

BILLS LEADERS: Rushing - Bell 24-92, Pruitt 2-9, Ferragamo 3-3, Hutchison 2-11; **Passing** - Ferragamo 18-33-2 -173; **Receiving** - Bell 7-61, Reed 1-8, Butler 5-52, Ramson 4-48, Metzelaars 1-4.

VIKINGS LEADERS: Rushing - Brown 13-80, Nelson 15-69, Rice 4-12, Kramer 2-10; **Passing** - Kramer 15-23-1 - 205; **Receiving** - Jordan 5-74, Carter 3-57, Rice 1-6, Jones 1-6, Lewis 2-25, Brown 2-29, Carroll 1-8.

STANDINGS: FOURTH WEEK

AFC EAST	W	L	T	CENTRAL	W	L	T	WEST	W	L	T	NFC EAST	W	L	T	CENTRAL	W	L	T	WEST	W	L	T
Miami	3	1	0	Pittsburgh	2	2	0	Kan. City	3	1	0	St. Louis	3	1	0	Chicago	4	0	0	LA Rams	4	0	0
NY Jets	3	1	0	Cleveland	2	2	0	Seattle	2	2	0	NY Giants	3	1	0	Minnesota	3	1	0	San Fran	2	2	0
New England	2	2	0	Houston	1	3	0	Denver	2	2	0	Dallas	3	1	0	Detroit	3	1	0	N.Orleans	2	2	0
Indianapolis	1	3	0	Cincinnati	1	3	0	San Diego	2	2	0	Washington	1	3	0	Green Bay	1	3	0	Atlanta	0	4	0
Buffalo	0	4	0					Raiders	2	2	0	Philadelphia	1	3	0	Tampa Bay	0	4	0				

Bills	7	3	0	7 -	17
Colts	7	21	14	7 -	49

Attendance at the Hoosier Dome - 60,003

Buf: Bell 18 run (Norwood kick), 6:46
Ind: Pagel 2 run (Allegre kick), 11:26
Ind: Wonsley 7 run (Allegre kick), :07
Buf: FG Norwood 45, 6:33
Ind: Wonsley 3 run (Allegre kick), 11:54
Ind: Butler 18 pass from Pagel (Allegre kick), 14:54
Ind: McMillan 6 run (Allegre kick), 6:59
Ind: Young 28 fumble return (Allegre kick), 7:39
Ind: McMillan 2 run (Allegre kick), 2:19
Buf: Reed 10 pass from Ferragamo (Norwood kick), 6:07

	BUF	IND
First downs	15	28
Rushing yds	68	281
Passing yds	184	183
Punts-avg	5-37.6	3-45.0
Fumbles-lost	2-1	0-0
Penalties-yds	8-54	7-60
Poss. time	23:52	36:08

BILLS LEADERS: Rushing - Bell 17-62, Mathison 1-1; **Passing** - Ferragamo 12-29-2 - 174, Mathison 2-6-0 - 28; **Receiving** - Reed 5-57, Butler 6-95, Ramson 1-22, Burkett 1-16, Norris 1-12.

COLTS LEADERS: Rushing - McMillan 20-112, Bentley 17-100, Gill 5-37, Wonsley 5-28, Pagel 2-4; **Passing** - Pagel 14-25-1 - 183; **Receiving** - Butler 3-49, Bouza 2-40, Martin 2-42, McMillan 2-10, Boyer 1-14, Beach 1-9, Bentley 3-19.

WEEK 5 GAMES

Chi 27, TB 19	Dal 30, NYG 29
GB 43, Det 10	Den 31, Hou 20
LAR 19, KC 10	Rams 13, Minn 10
Clev 24, NE 20	NYJ 29, Cinc 20
NO 23, Phil 21	Mia 24, Pitt 20
Sea 26, SD 21	SF 38, Atl 17
Wash 27, St.L 10	

NOTES

• The Bills were awful in Hank Bullough's debut, allowing two Colts runners to gain 100 yards.
• It was the Bills 11th straight loss on the road dating to December of 1983 in Kansas City.
• The Bills took an early lead on Greg Bell's TD run after Charlie Romes' interception.
• The Colts tied it on the ensuing series as a pass interference call on Rod Hill and a 24-yard run by Albert Bentley led to Mike Pagel's keeper for the TD.
• Barry Krauss intercepted Vince Ferragamo at the Bills 43 and that resulted in George Wonsley's first TD run. The Bills came right back to make it 14-10 on Scott Norwood's field goal.
• The Bills then fell apart. Vince Ferragamo threw a bad interception to Duane Bickett, who returned it to the 3 and Wonsley scored from there. The Colts then moved 85 yards in eight plays, taking just 1:25 to score the killer touchdown on Pagel's pass to Ray Butler with six seconds left in the half.
• The Colts took the second-half kickoff and went 80 yards in 13 plays to Randy McMillan's TD. Forty seconds later, Anthony Young returned Ferragamo's fumble 20 yards for a TD.
• The teams traded TDs in the fourth, the Bills scoring on Andre Reed's TD reception.

QUOTES

• Hank Bullough: "If I had an indication this was going to happen, we wouldn't have shown up. I would have rather paid a fine to the NFL than go through this embarrassment. What I told them after the game is not printable. What kind of question is that? What would you have said to them after a performance like that? It was horrible. The only way we can go is up. Indianapolis has a great running game, but we made it look as good as anyone can."
• Bruce Smith: "Something's wrong here. I'm getting chewed out all the time, which I don't think is right. It really messes up a person. I think I'm playing to avoid being cussed out, instead of going out there and trying to do things right. It seems like it's the first thing that I'm concerned about, it's very distracting. I thought I did some things right out there, maybe I'm wrong, maybe it is my fault. Maybe I alone am the reason for the loss. It's like a parent yelling at a child all the time. After awhile it doesn't do any good, it just ruins you."
• Vince Ferragamo: "It's embarrassing to go someplace and get your clock cleaned. We really didn't play inspired football."
• Colts quarterback Mike Pagel: "What a great feeling. That's the first time since I've been here that we've been on the winning end of a score like that."

Bills	0	3	0	0 -	3
Patriots	0	0	7	7 -	14

Attendance at Sullivan Stadium - 40,462

Buf: FG Norwood 47, 8:21
NE: Fryar 16 pass from Grogan (Franklin kick), 3:40
NE: Clayborn 27 interception return (Franklin kick), 6:48

	BUF	NE
First downs	13	18
Rushing yds	72	82
Passing yds	90	318
Punts-avg	8-35.1	6-38.2
Fumbles-lost	3-2	3-2
Penalties-yds	8-76	9-87
Poss. time	27:44	32:16

BILLS LEADERS: Rushing - Bell 23-72; **Passing** - Ferragamo 12-31-2 - 114; **Receiving** - Bell 6-28, Reed 1-10, Butler 1-12, Ramson 1-10, Burkett 2-36, Norris 1-18.

PATRIOTS LEADERS: Rushing - Collins 5-24, Tatupu 6-37, Weathers 5-15, James 7-6, Eason 1-0; **Passing** - Eason 8-16-2 - 65, Grogan 15-19-0 - 282; **Receiving** - Jones 1-21, Starring 1-16, Fryar 6-132, James 5-79, Morgan 4-60, Collins 4-19, Tatupu 1-15, Weathers 1-5.

WEEK 6 GAMES

Sea 30, Atl 26	Chi 26, SF 10
Clev 21, Hou 6	Den 15, Ind 10
Wash 24, Det 3	SD 31, KC 20
Rams 31, TB 27	GB 20, Minn 17
LAR 23, NO 13	Cinc 35, NYG 30
Phil 30, St.L 7	Dal 27, Pitt 13
NYJ 23, Mia 7	

NOTES

• The Bills were two-for-12 on third downs and gained just 162 yards on offense with four turnovers.
• For the first time in team history, only one player was credited with any rushes as Greg Bell carried on all 23 Bills running plays.
• Joe DeLamielleure was penalized three times for 30 yards and was back on the bench late in the first half with Tim Vogler moving back to guard and Will Grant returning to center.
• Scott Norwood's field goal gave the Bills the lead in the second quarter. It was his eighth straight success, a new club record. Charlie Romes' interception gave the Bills the ball at the Pats 23, but an ineligible-man-downfield penalty on Ken Jones wiped out an Eason Ramson pass reception at the 5 and pushed the ball back to the 30. When the Bills couldn't get a first down, Norwood made his kick.
• Bruce Smith's sack knocked Tony Eason out of the game in the second quarter.
• Steve Grogan replaced Eason and lost a fumble to Jim Haslett at the Pats 28, but the Bills wound up punting.
• The Pats went ahead in the third as they moved 80 yards in eight plays after the second-half kickoff. Grogan hit Irving Fryar for 21 and 16 yards, then threw 16 yards for a TD to Fryar.
• The Pats put the game away with 8:12 left when Raymond Clayborn intercepted a Vince Ferragamo pass intended for Andre Reed and ran 27 yards for a TD.

QUOTES

• Pats coach Raymond Berry: "Without a doubt, the performance of Steve Grogan turned us around today. He came into a tough situation and really lifted the football team."
• Hank Bullough on Ferragamo: "Football's a little different than baseball. A great pitcher can get knocked out of the box and you don't worry about him. But you always think about a quarterback's confidence. Vinnie is an old veteran. You hope he can work his way out of it. Vinnie isn't blocking, so you can't blame the (four) sacks on him. If I pulled Vinnie, maybe I should have pulled the entire offensive line."
• Vince Feragamo: "It certainly wasn't one of my better days. I was trying; I don't ever give up. There were just some times where I tried to get the ball downfield when I should have waited a little bit. I got caught up in what they (the Patriots) were doing instead of taking it to them and making it work. I gave them a touchdown. That was the turning point of the game. It was a quick pass and Ray read the pattern right. What I should have done was thrown to the opposite side of the field."
• Pats cornerback Raymond Clayborn: "He (Ferragamo) throws the ball where they designate him to throw it, and he looks where they tell him to throw the ball."

AFC EAST	W	L	T	CENTRAL	W	L	T	WEST	W	L	T	NFC EAST	W	L	T	CENTRAL	W	L	T	WEST	W	L	T
NY Jets	5	1	0	Cleveland	4	2	0	Raiders	4	2	0	Dallas	5	1	0	Chicago	6	0	0	LA Rams	6	0	0
Miami	4	2	0	Pittsburgh	2	4	0	Seattle	4	2	0	NY Giants	3	3	0	Minnesota	3	3	0	San Fran	3	3	0
New England	3	3	0	Cincinnati	2	4	0	Denver	4	2	0	St. Louis	3	3	0	Detroit	3	3	0	N.Orleans	3	3	0
Indianapolis	2	4	0	Houston	1	5	0	Kan. City	3	3	0	Washington	3	3	0	Green Bay	3	3	0	Atlanta	0	6	0
Buffalo	0	6	0					San Diego	3	3	0	Philadelphia	2	4	0	Tampa Bay	0	6	0				

NOTES

• The Bills snapped their eight-game regular-season losing streak and gave Hank Bullough his first head coaching victory, while avenging an embarrassing loss to the Colts two weeks earlier.

• In his first game back with the Bills, Joe Cribbs started, but fumbled twice.

• The offense managed only 183 yards, but the defense allowed only 191.

• The Bills scored on their first possession, driving 61 yards in eight plays to Greg Bell's first TD, the key block being thrown by Cribbs. Bell had a 17-yard run earlier.

• The Colts got Raul Allegre's first field goal later in the first quarter after Bruce Smith threw George Wonsley for an eight-yard loss on a sweep.

• Martin Bayless intercepted Mike Pagel at the Bills 13 in the second quarter , but on the next play, Cribbs fumbled and Preston Davis recovered. The defense held and forced the second Allegre field goal.

• After the kickoff, the Bills drove 80 yards in 10 plays to Bell's second TD with 17 seconds left in the half. Bell made a 20-yard reception and a personal foul penalty on Byron Smith cost the Colts 15 yards.

• Allegre's third field goal early in the third came after Ferragamo was intercepted by Fredd Young.

• Early in the fourth, Dean Prater blocked a Rohn Stark punt and Sean McNanie ran it to the 3. On the next play, Ferragamo hit Pete Metzelaars for his first TD reception as a Bill.

• Eugene Marve recovered a fumble and Rodney Bellinger had an interception later in the fourth.

• Cribbs decided not to speak to the media after the game.

QUOTES

• Bruce Smith: "There ain't no feeling like winning. It's the sweetest feeling I know."

• Dean Prater: "The tackle gave me a shove on the punt and then he let me go. I think he figured since I was a big guy rushing from the outside, I wouldn't get there in time. I didn't think I had a good chance of blocking it, either, but I put my hand up and the ball hit it."

• Hank Bullough: "I'm sure the Colts coaching staff had a tough time convincing their team that they were in for a tough battle this week. Every week is a new game. The important thing to remember is the helmet goes on the field every week, but the head has to be in it."

• Fred Smerlas: "That first Colts game was a transition for Hank. He only had three days to get ready. Let's face it, we were embarrassed. It's like you writing a column and having bad spelling and grammar. Now, he's brought the players together and we're starting to have some continuity. He's a lot like Chuck Knox, kind of a feisty guy, but he looks out for his players and brings out the best in them."

• Greg Bell on Joe Cribbs: "It opened up the whole offense. With me and Joe, it puts a little diversification in our offense. The last few weeks, teams were probably keying on Greg Bell and doing a good job of it. In the two-back, they don't know which one of us is going to break the long run. It was a good move going to the two-back, a good change."

Colts	3 3 3 0 - 9
Bills	7 7 0 7 - 21

Attendance at Rich Stadium - 28,430

Buf: Bell 7 run (Norwood kick), 4:09
Ind: FG Allegre 41, 12:55
Ind: FG Allegre 27, 10:09
Buf: Bell 1 run (Norwood kick), 14:43
Ind: FG Allegre 38, 4:21
Buf: Metzelaars 3 pass from Ferragamo (Norwood kick), 2:30

	BUF	IND
First downs	13	14
Rushing yds	121	126
Passing yds	61	65
Punts-avg	8-44.1	8-43.0
Fumbles-lost	2-2	4-1
Penalties-yds	6-60	6-50
Poss. time	27:18	32:42

BILLS LEADERS: Rushing - Bell 22-80, Cribbs 13-41; **Passing** - Ferragamo 8-20-1 - 85; **Receiving** - Bell 2-46, Reed 1-4, Butler 2-20, Cribbs 2-12, Metzelaars 1-3.

COLTS LEADERS: Rushing - McMillan 16-46, Wonsley 12-31, Pagel 7-38, Dickey 3-11; **Passing** - Pagel 7-22-2 - 78; **Receiving** - Bouza 4-55, Wonsley 1-7, Beach 2-16.

WEEK 7 GAMES

Hou 44, Cinc 7	Phil 16, Dal 14
LAR 21, Clev 20	Rams 16, KC 0
Atl 31, NO 24	NE 20, NYJ 13
Minn 21, SD 17	Pitt 23, St.L 10
Det 23, SF 21	Den 13, Sea 10
Mia 41, TB 38	NYG 17, Wash 3
Chi 23, GB 7	

NOTES

• The Bills collapsed in the fourth quarter, blowing a 17-0 lead to lose their 13th straight game on the road.

• Greg Bell and Joe Cribbs combined for 252 yards gained from scrimmage.

• The Bills took a 7-0 lead in the first quarter as Andre Reed scored on a 14-yard reverse to cap a 53-yard drive. Jerry Butler made a 21-yard reception along the way.

• In the second quarter, the Bills drove 73 yards in nine plays to Scott Norwood's field goal. Bell had 28- and 17-yard pass receptions, but two holding penalties forced them to settle for a field goal.

• In the third, James Perryman sacked Ron Jaworski, forced him to fumble and Don Smith recovered at Eagles 28. Six plays later, Vince Ferragamo hit Reed for a TD.

• The collapse began late in the third. The Bills had third-and-one at the Eagles 23. Joe Cribbs and Greg Bell came out, Booker Moore went in and was stopped for no gain. Rather than kick a field goal, Hank Bullough went for it and Ferragamo was stopped. The Eagles then drove 77 yards in 11 plays to Jaworski's TD run. Jaworski completed a 36-yard pass to Ron Johnson.

• Just 1:50 later, Wes Hopkins intercepted Ferragamo and went 24 yards for a TD.

• Jaworski then engineered the game-winning seven-play, 87-yard drive, culminating in his 32-yard TD strike to Mike Quick who backpedaled the final 10 yards into the end zone with 1:55 left.

QUOTES

• Martin Bayless: "It was very distasteful. We worked so hard and then to end up like that. More than the Eagles playing hard, we let them come back. We let them get great field position and we let them make great plays. Then the fans got back into the game and the momentum shifted."

• Fred Smerlas: "We had this game the whole way. We lost this game, we didn't get beat."

• Bruce Smith: "We played maybe 48 or 50 minutes of good football. That's not good enough. You need 60 minutes to win." (On the final TD drive): "There was no way in the world I thought they were going to climb out of that hole and move the ball down the field against us. No way."

• Derrick Burroughs on Quick's TD: "The play was my fault totally. I reacted kind of slow. It looked like the ball was going to hit Steve (Freeman) in the head, but it somehow got between us. You have to give Jaworski credit, he really zipped it in there."

• Eagles QB Ron Jaworski: "I looked up at the scoreboard in the fourth quarter and I didn't think our chances were very good. I might have thought differently if we had been moving the ball before, but we hadn't. The Bills did an awful lot of things to confuse us."

• Hank Bullough on going for it on fourth down: "There'll be a lot of controversial plays, I hope, during my career. People better get used to that, because I'm going to be going for it. If I feel the situation is right, I'll go for it. I don't mind people second-guessing me."

WEEK 8 GAMES

Dal 24, Atl 10	Den 30, KC 10
Ind 37, GB 10	Hou 20, St.L 10
Det 31, Mia 21	Chi 27, Minn 9
NE 32, TB 14	NYG 21, NO 13
Cinc 26, Pitt 21	SF 28, Rams 14
NYJ 17, Sea 14	Wash 14, Clev 7
LAR 34, SD 21	

Bills	7 3 7 0 - 17
Eagles	0 0 0 21 - 21

Attendance at Veterans Stadium - 60,987

Buf: Reed 14 run (Norwood kick), 8:41
Buf: FG Norwood 26, 2:15
Buf: Reed 7 pass from Ferragamo (Norwood kick), 5:57
Phi: Jaworski 3 run (McFadden kick), 2:50
Phi: Hopkins 24 interception return (McFadden kick), 4:40
Phi: Quick 32 pass from Jaworski (McFadden kick), 13:05

	BUF	PHI
First downs	17	16
Rushing yds	128	38
Passing yds	211	237
Punts-avg	5-46.6	6-40.0
Fumbles-lost	1-0	1-1
Penalties-yds	9-61	4-30
Poss. time	33:17	26:43

BILLS LEADERS: Rushing - Bell 12-45, Cribbs 13-68, Ferragamo 2-2, Moore 1-(-1), Reed 1-14; **Passing** - Ferragamo 22-36-2 - 219; **Receiving** - Bell 6-71, Reed 3-20, Butler 2-35, Ramson 2-15, Cribbs 7-58, Richardson 2-20.

EAGLES LEADERS: Rushing - E. Jackson 9-31, Haddix 3-6, Jaworski 3-1; **Passing** - Jaworski 21-42-0 - 258; **Receiving** - Quick 8-117, Haddix 4-36, Johnson 3-57, K. Jackson 3-22, Spagnola 2-18, Hunter 1-8.

STANDINGS: EIGHTH WEEK

AFC EAST	W	L	T	CENTRAL	W	L	T	WEST	W	L	T	NFC EAST	W	L	T	CENTRAL	W	L	T	WEST	W	L	T
NY Jets	6	2	0	Cleveland	4	4	0	Raiders	6	2	0	Dallas	6	2	0	Chicago	8	0	0	LA Rams	7	1	0
Miami	5	3	0	Pittsburgh	3	5	0	Denver	6	2	0	NY Giants	5	3	0	Detroit	5	3	0	San Fran	4	4	0
New England	5	3	0	Cincinnati	3	5	0	Seattle	4	4	0	Philadelphia	4	4	0	Minnesota	4	4	0	N.Orleans	3	5	0
Indianapolis	3	5	0	Houston	3	5	0	Kan. City	3	5	0	Washington	4	4	0	Green Bay	3	5	0	Atlanta	1	7	0
Buffalo	1	7	0					San Diego	3	5	0	St. Louis	3	5	0	Tampa Bay	0	8	0				

GAME 9 - Sunday, Nov. 3, 1985 - BENGALS 23, BILLS 17

Bengals	0	6	7	10	- 23
Bills	7	3	0	7	- 17

Attendance at Rich Stadium - 25,640

Buf: Bell 14 run (Norwood kick), 8:45
Buf: FG Norwood 43, 2:15
Cin: Brown 68 pass from Esiason (kick blocked), 11:22
Cin: Harris 22 pass from Esiason (Breech kick), 8:03
Cin: Kinnebrew 2 run (Breech kick), 6:22
Cin: FG Breech 31, 8:30
Buf: Ramson 5 pass from Mathison (Norwood kick), 14:58

	BUF	CIN
First downs	16	21
Rushing yds	95	207
Passing yds	173	182
Punts-avg	4-41.3	3-40.0
Fumbles-lost	1-1	2-1
Penalties-yds	5-30	4-28
Poss. time	19:23	40:37

BILLS LEADERS: Rushing - Bell 10-40, Cribbs 8-39, Mathison 2-16; **Passing** - Ferragamo 7-23-1 - 134, Mathison 5-10-1 - 63, Bell 0-1-0 - 0; **Receiving** - Cribbs 2-24, Butler 2-21, Ramson 4-40, Bell 3-82, Burkett 1-30.

BENGALS LEADERS: Rushing - Brooks 13-52, Kinnebrew 30-128, Alexander 3-15, Jennings 4-9, Esiason 3-3; **Passing** - Esiason 11-21-1 - 193, Kreider 1-1-0 - 1; **Receiving** - Holman 4-34, Harris 2-34, Brown 2-90, Alexander 1-15, Munoz 1-1, Brooks 2-20.

NOTES
• The Bills blew a 10-0 lead and Hank Bullough lost to the Bengals and the defense that he built.
• The Bengals possessed the ball for 40:37 on a cold, rainy day that was suited for the running game.
• Bruce Smith recovered a Larry Kinnebrew fumble at the Bengals 31 early in the first quarter. Five plays later, Tim Vogler's block paved the way for Greg Bell's TD run. Jerry Butler had an 11-yard catch on third-and-nine.
• Late in the first, ex-Bengal Guy Frazier intercepted Boomer Esiason at the Bills 44. Joe Cribbs then broke a 23-yard run that set up Scott Norwood's field goal.
• On the next series, Bell went 45 yards with a short pass, but Norwood missed a 27-yard field goal.
• The Bengals then struck six plays later as Esiason hit Eddie Brown with a 68-yard TD. Brown outjumped Derrick Burroughs for the ball at the Bills 20. Sean McNanie blocked the PAT.
• The Bengals took the lead on their first possession of the third, driving 91 yards in 12 plays to Esiason's TD pass to M.L. Harris. Kinnebrew carried five times for 28 yards and James Brooks had a 12-yard reception.
• After a Bills punt, the Bengals moved 65 yards in 14 plays to Kinnebrew's TD. Kinnebrew carried 11 times for 38 yards during the drive. Anthony Steels then fum-

WEEK 9 GAMES
Chi 16, GB 10   Pitt 10, Clev 9
SD 30, Den 10   Minn 16, Det 13
Hou 23, KC 20   Sea 33, LAR 3
NE 17, Mia 13   Rams 28, NO 10
NYJ 35, Ind 17   SF 24, Phil 13
NYG 22, TB 20   Wash 44, Atl 10
St.L 21, Dal 10

bled the ensuing kickoff and Robert Jackson recovered at the Bills 13, which led to Breech's field goal and a 23-10 lead.
• Bruce Mathison replaced Vince Ferragamo, but his second pass was intercepted by Jackson. On the final series, Mathison drove the Bills 80 yards in 12 plays to Eason Ramson's TD catch with two seconds left.

QUOTES
• Bengals running back Larry Kinnebrew: "They said it was going to be cold and rainy for the game. My kind of weather. I knew I had better get plenty of sleep because Sunday was going to be a very busy day. I think I'm always difficult to tackle, but even moreso on a wet day like this because the defensive guys can't plant. I had a lot of people sliding off me."
• Bruce Smith: "The man (Kinnebrew) isn't easy to bring down. You know what it's like? It's like trying to bring me down. You need two, three, four guys every time. I weigh 282. If I was carrying the ball, do you think one guy would be bringing me down? And they have one of the biggest lines in the NFL."
• Hank Bullough: "We met an excellent, well-coached football team today. I thought we had a chance to beat them, but we had to control their fullback better. The turning point was their ability to control the ball in the third quarter." (On benching Ferragamo): "I'm not going to make that decision (who will start next week) until game time. I'd say we're having trouble with the passing game. But when the quarterback doesn't look good, it can be for a helluva lot of reasons. Sometimes you don't have a chance and sometimes guys aren't getting open. If I do replace him, hell, it's nothing new. Every quarterback gets replaced at one time or another. It's not like we're putting him in Russia."

GAME 10 - Sunday, Nov. 10, 1985 - BILLS 20, OILERS 0

Oilers	0	0	0	0	- 0
Bills	10	0	10	0	- 20

Attendance at Rich Stadium - 21,831

Buf: FG Norwood 24, 8:04
Buf: Bell 2 run (Norwood kick), 13:14
Buf: FG Norwood 23, 3:18
Buf: Mathison 5 run (Norwood kick), 8:24

	BUF	HOU
First downs	18	7
Rushing yds	147	111
Passing yds	60	31
Punts-avg	7-41.1	6-30.2
Fumbles-lost	3-2	4-3
Penalties-yds	8-46	11-74
Poss. time	39:04	20:56

BILLS LEADERS: Rushing - Bell 11-43, Cribbs 23-41, Mathison 5-57, Moore 4-6; **Passing** - Mathison 11-22-0 - 121; **Receiving** - Reed 4-64, Ramson 5-43, Cribbs 1-5, Moore 1-9.

OILERS LEADERS: Rushing - Moriarty 13-49, Woolfolk 7-39, Johnson 1-0, Luck 3-24, Moon 1-(-1); **Passing** - Moon 3-14-3 - 22, Luck 3-7-0 - 18; **Receiving** - Hill 1-9, Woolfolk 3-13, Dressel 1-12, T. Smith 1-6.

WEEK 10 GAMES
Phil 23, Atl 17   Cinc 27, Clev 10
Dal 13, Wash 7   Chi 24, Det 3
GB 27, Minn 17   NE 34, Ind 15
SD 40, LAR 34   NYG 24, Rams 19
Mia 21, NYJ 17   Pitt 36, KC 28
TB 16, St.L 0   Sea 27, NO 3
Den 17, SF 16

NOTES
• The defense posted its first shutout since Dec. 12, 1982, when it blanked Pittsburgh.
• Bruce Mathison made his first start at QB since 1982 while he was in college.
• Mathison's 57 yards rushing were the second-most by a Bills QB in team history. M.C. Reynolds ran for 65 in a 1961 game against San Diego.
• Warren Moon suffered through a miserable passing performance on a rainy day. He threw three interceptions and was benched in the third quarter in favor of Oliver Luck, who fared no better.
• Anthony Steels fumbled the opening kickoff and Patrick Allen recovered for the Oilers at the 31. But three plays later, Moon was intercepted in the end zone by Charlie Romes.
• The Bills couldn't move, but Chuck Donaldson muffed John Kidd's punt and Steve Maidlow recovered at the Oilers 14. Scott Norwood capitalized with his first field goal.
• Later in the first quarter, the Bills drove 51 yards in five plays to Greg Bell's TD run, the key play a 26-yard Mathison pass to Andre Reed.
• The teams traded punts and turnovers in the second, then on the second play of the third quarter, Fred Smerlas recovered Larry Moriarity's fumble at the Oilers 25. Mathison scrambled 22 yards to the 3, but two penalties pushed the Bills back and Norwood kicked his second field goal.
• On the first play after the kickoff, Derrick Burroughs intercepted Moon and returned it to the Oilers 33. Eight plays later, Mathison ran it in for the TD from the 5 to make it 20-0.
• Dean Prater partially blocked a punt and Sean

McNanie forced Luck to fumble, but the Bills wasted both opportunities. In the fourth, the Bills used 9:42 on one possession, but didn't score.

QUOTES
• Bruce Mathison: "I'm not going to take this and blow it out of proportion. I'm not going to say I'm going to be the next great quarterback in Buffalo. It's one game and we'll see what happens down the road. I wasn't great, but I wasn't bad. I was excited, I wasn't real nervous or worried. I just wanted to play and to try to make things happen."
• Hank Bullough: "The players have been working very hard, the coaches have been working hard. We needed this victory really bad, we really did." (On Mathison): "I liked the way he took charge. That's not to say that Vince didn't, but a young quarterback getting his first start is often more worried about his own responsibility than the people around him. And he wasn't exactly playing with a stacked deck out there. We had Tim Vogler, Jim Ritcher and Greg Bell all get hurt."
• Andre Reed on Mathison: "He had some fire. He told us to be quiet and do our jobs."
• Derrick Burroughs: "I don't think Moon ever adjusted to the cold. I'm sure by halftime he was wishing he was back in sunny Houston. We were red-hot and they were freezing. Heck, I'll take rotten weather all the time if it works out to our advantage like this."

STANDINGS: TENTH WEEK

AFC EAST	W	L	T	CENTRAL	W	L	T	WEST	W	L	T	NFC EAST	W	L	T	CENTRAL	W	L	T	WEST	W	L	T
NY Jets	7	3	0	Cincinnati	5	5	0	Denver	7	3	0	Dallas	7	3	0	Chicago	10	0	0	LA Rams	8	2	0
New England	7	3	0	Pittsburgh	5	5	0	Raiders	6	4	0	NY Giants	7	3	0	Detroit	5	5	0	San Fran	5	5	0
Miami	6	4	0	Cleveland	4	6	0	Seattle	6	4	0	Washington	5	5	0	Minnesota	5	5	0	N.Orleans	3	7	0
Indianapolis	3	7	0	Houston	4	6	0	San Diego	5	5	0	Philadelphia	5	5	0	Green Bay	4	6	0	Atlanta	1	9	0
Buffalo	2	8	0					Kan. City	3	7	0	St. Louis	4	6	0	Tampa Bay	1	9	0				

NOTES

• In his first game against the Bills, Bernie Kosar did little through the air. But the Browns' powerful running game keyed the victory. The Browns snapped their four-game losing streak.

• Greg Bell wasn't supposed to play because of a knee injury, but he had to in the fourth when Joe Cribbs got hurt. Bell was missed as the Bills rushed for only 55 yards.

• The Browns scored on their first possession as Matt Bahr made a 40-yard field goal. But the Bills took the kickoff and went 73 yards in 13 plays with Booker Moore scoring the first rushing TD of his four-year NFL career. The key plays were Bruce Mathison's 18-yard pass to Andre Reed, and a 21-yarder to Chris Burkett.

• After a scoreless second quarter, thanks to Cribbs' fumble at the Browns 13 with 39 seconds left, the Browns got a huge break in the third and scored the go-ahead points. Ben Williams was charged with running into punter Jeff Gossett, which gave the Browns a first down with six minutes left in the quarter. They went on to complete a nine-play, 55-yard drive when Earnest Byner scored on a four-yard run.

• In the fourth, Frank Minnifield intercepted Mathison at the Bills 41. The Browns then drove to Kosar's TD pass to Ozzie Newsome with 2:11 remaining. The key was Byner's run for 17 on a third-and-10 play.

• Jim Haslett and Steve Freeman led the defense with 10 tackles each.

• John Kidd had a good day punting. He dropped two kicks inside the 20, giving him an NFL-leading 28.

QUOTES

• Ben Williams on his penalty: "I was on the ground and he (Gossett) stepped on me and fell over. It was a judgement call and I thought it was a bad call. Roughing the kicker is when you run into him when his foot is in the air. That's my interpretation of the rule. Once the referee drops the flag, it doesn't do any good to argue. Six million people saw him drop the flag, you didn't think he was going to pick it up and put it back in his pocket, did you? I told him to write me an 'I'm sorry' note when he reviewed the films."

• Fred Smerlas: "I told him (referee Chuck Heberling) some bad things about his family. It was a lousy call. The guy should have been called for illegally kicking Benny." (On the performance overall): "Our younger people might be spending too much time jumping up and down saying 'We're winning, we're winning' rather than saying 'We've got them down, now we're going to keep them down and win.'"

• Hank Bullough: "I'd like to get them to call games at the half, but I can't convince them to do it. You're not going to run much against the Browns, you're going to have to get the ball moving through the air. Bruce made some bad decisions at the end."

• Bruce Mathison: "Anytime the offense doesn't put the ball in the end zone, you have to look at the quarterback. I had a couple of crummy throws and the ones at the end were just plain dumb. I'm disappointed in myself. We had a chance of winning this one."

Bills	7 0 0 0 - 7
Browns	3 0 7 7 - 17

Attendance at Cleveland Stadium - 50,764

Cle: FG Bahr 40, 3:55
Buf: Moore 1 run (Norwood kick), 11:47
Cle: Byner 4 run (Bahr kick), 12:07
Cle: Newsome 11 pass from Kosar (Bahr kick), 12:49

	BUF	CLE
First downs	13	17
Rushing yds	55	201
Passing yds	162	93
Punts-avg	7-45.7	6-42.5
Fumbles-lost	2-1	2-1
Penalties-yds	6-44	9-62
Poss. time	27:07	32:53

BILLS LEADERS: Rushing - Bell 1-0, Cribbs 18-52, Mathison 2-2, Moore 2-2; **Passing** - Mathison 15-30-2 - 177; **Receiving** - Reed 2-41, Butler 3-37, Ramson 4-31, Burkett 4-58, Metzelaars 1-4, Moore 1-6.

BROWNS LEADERS: Rushing - Byner 15-109, Mack 21-94, Kosar 1-(-2); **Passing** - Kosar 12-25-0 - 103; **Receiving** - Byner 4-20, Brennan 3-48, Newsome 3-17, Mack 1-6, Weathers 1-12.

WEEK 11 GAMES

Chi 44, Dal 0	LAR 17, Cinc 6
SF 31, KC 3	Atl 30, Rams 14
Mia 34, Ind 20	Det 41, Minn 21
NE 20, Sea 13	GB 38, NO 14
Pitt 30, Hou 7	Phil 24, St.L 14
Den 30, SD 24	NYJ 62, TB 24
Wash 23, NYG 21	

NOTES

• With cold, windy conditions, Dan Marino turned to the short passing game and a ball-control running game to beat the Bills. The Dolphins possessed the ball for 35:12 and piled up 28 first downs.

• Miami scored on its first possession as Marino was five-for-five for 34 yards including a TD pass to Ron Davenport during a 10-play, 59-yard drive.

• Charlie Romes intercepted Marino at the Bills 3 to kill a threat in the second quarter, but after the Bills punted, Miami moved 48 yards in seven plays to Marino's TD pass to Dan Johnson.

• The Bills took the kickoff and drove 78 yards in 11 plays to Andre Reed's TD reception with 59 seconds left in the half. Bruce Mathison was four-for-five and also scrambled twice for 29 yards.

• On the first series of the third, Miami got to the Bills 26, but Eugene Marve stopped Davenport on fourth-and-one. Four plays later, Mathison hit Jerry Butler for a 60-yard TD, beating cornerback Don McNeal. It was Butler's first TD reception since Oct. 30, 1983 against New Orleans.

• Late in the third, Don Wilson muffed a punt and Joe Carter recovered for Miami at the Bills 11. Marino threw three straight incompletions, so Fuad Reveiz kicked the go-ahead field goal.

• On the next series, Scott Norwood missed a 47-yard field goal. Two plays later, Lawrence Johnson intercepted Marino at the Bills 40, but the Bills had to punt. Miami then drove 81 yards in nine plays to Tony Nathan's clinching TD run.

QUOTES

• Jerry Butler: "The Dolphins just seem to have a way of winning."

• Bruce Smith: "What it all boils down to is we beat ourselves again. There are key plays in every game, plays that turn things around, and I thought we made enough of those to win the game. Things just always seem to go wrong for us after we make big plays."

• Don Wilson on his muffed punt return: "The wind was gusting and I was trying to judge where it was going to drift. It sailed to my left and went through my hands. I didn't think I'd have any problems fair-catching the ball despite the wind. I just missed the ball."

• Charlie Romes: "Stopping the run in the second half is a problem we've been having and until we can do it, it's going to keep being a tough year."

• Hank Bullough: "Miami played well, but I think we helped them as much as they helped themselves. We're not a good enough football team to overcome ourselves and our opponents. Their plan was to control the ball on offense and keep their defense off the field. They did a good job of it, too. Unfortunately, we weren't able to do the same thing." (On Wilson's muff): "I don't think that put us flat. We held 'em there and then we came back out and didn't get a first down. That hurt us. When you look at it, holding them to three points should have been a mental lift."

• Miami coach Don Shula: "I have a lot of respect for Hank and his defense. He has been one of the great defensive coaches and I'm happy to see he has the opportunity to be a head coach."

Dolphins	7 7 3 6 - 23
Bills	0 7 7 0 - 14

Attendance at Rich Stadium - 50,474

Mia: Davenport 7 pass from Marino (Reveiz kick), 6:29
Mia: Johnson 15 pass from Marino (Reveiz kick), 8:53
Buf: Reed 11 pass from Mathison (Norwood kick), 14:05
Buf: Butler 60 pass from Mathison (Norwood kick), 7:05
Mia: FG Reveiz 22, 13:18
Mia: Nathan 4 run (kick failed), 9:03

	BUF	MIA
First downs	12	28
Rushing yds	94	172
Passing yds	161	216
Punts-avg	7-39.7	3-30.0
Fumbles-lost	2-1	1-0
Penalties-yds	6-30	5-41
Poss. time	24:48	35:12

BILLS LEADERS: Rushing - Bell 16-52, Mathison 3-42; **Passing** - Mathison 15-28-0 - 196; **Receiving** - Burkett 2-21, Reed 6-68, Cribbs 1-7, Ramson 1-4, Butler 3-87, Bell 2-9.

DOLPHINS LEADERS: Rushing - Bennett 10-59, Hampton 6-11, Davenport 9-26, Nathan 14-77, Marino 2-(-1); **Passing** - Marino 22-31-2 - 233; **Receiving** - Davenport 4-23, Hardy 3-28, Clayton 5-60, Nathan 2-10, Bennett 1-16, Moore 1-10, Johnson 1-15, Duper 4-57, Rose 1-14.

WEEK 12 GAMES

Chi 36, Atl 0	Clev 24, Cin 6
LAR 31, Den 28	Rams 34, GB 17
KC 20, Ind 7	NO 30, Minn 23
NYJ 16, NE 13 (OT)	Dal 34, Phil 17
NYG 34, St.L 3	Hou 37, SD 35
Wash 30, Pitt 23	SF 19, Sea 6
TB 19, Det 16 (OT)	

STANDINGS: TWELFTH WEEK

AFC EAST	W	L	T	CENTRAL	W	L	T	WEST	W	L	T	NFC EAST	W	L	T	CENTRAL	W	L	T	WEST	W	L	T
NY Jets	9	3	0	Pittsburgh	6	6	0	Denver	8	4	0	Dallas	8	4	0	Chicago	12	0	0	LA Rams	9	3	0
New England	8	4	0	Cleveland	6	6	0	Raiders	8	4	0	NY Giants	8	4	0	Detroit	6	6	0	San Fran	7	5	0
Miami	8	4	0	Cincinnati	5	7	0	Seattle	6	6	0	Washington	7	5	0	Minnesota	5	7	0	N.Orleans	4	8	0
Indianapolis	3	9	0	Houston	5	7	0	San Diego	5	7	0	Philadelphia	6	6	0	Green Bay	5	7	0	Atlanta	2	10	0
Buffalo	2	10	0					Kan. City	4	8	0	St. Louis	4	8	0	Tampa Bay	2	10	0				

Bills	0	7	0	0 -	7
Chargers	7	17	10	6 -	40

Attendance at Jack Murphy Stadium - 45,487

SD: Joiner 38 pass from Fouts (Thomas kick), 13:14
SD: FG Thomas 24, 1:04
SD: Hendy 75 interception return (Thomas kick), 6:23
SD: Spencer 1 run (Thomas kick), 13:03
Buf: Cribbs 2 run (Norwood kick), 14:18
SD: FG Thomas 28, 6:24
SD: Sievers 23 pass from Fouts (Thomas kick), 13:56
SD: Holohan 13 pass from Fouts (kick failed), 3:59

	BUF	SD
First downs	21	21
Rushing yds	109	96
Passing yds	238	274
Punts-avg	4-43.0	3-27.7
Fumbles-lost	2-1	4-1
Penalties-yds	4-45	4-40
Poss. time	29:44	30:16

BILLS LEADERS: Rushing - Bell 7-22, Cribbs 14-57, Mathison 4-22, Steels 1-4, Moore 2-4; **Passing** - Mathison 18-36-4 - 271; **Receiving** - Bell 1-11, Reed 6-103, Butler 2-61, Ramson 4-38, Burkett 2-37, Cribbs 1-8, Moore 1-7, Steels 1-6.

CHARGERS LEADERS: Rushing - Anderson 9-37, McGee 3-11, Spencer 12-47, James 2-7, Fouts 2-(-3); **Passing** - Fouts 21-36-2 - 261, Herrmann 2-3-0 - 13; **Receiving** - Holohan 7-75, Chandler 2-32, Joiner 3-65, Anderson 3-10, Winslow 1-17, James 4-34, Sievers 2-38, McGee 1-3.

WEEK 13 GAMES

Det 31, NYJ 20	Dal 35, St.L 17
Clev 35, NYG 33	Den 31, Pitt 23
Cinc 45, Hou 27	Sea 24, KC 6
LAR 34, Atl 24	NO 29, Rams 3
Minn 28, Phil 23	NE 38, Ind 31
SF 35, Wash 8	GB 21, TB 0
Mia 38, Mia 24	

NOTES

• Bruce Mathison threw four interceptions against his former team and San Diego dealt the Bills their 15th straight road defeat. Mathison threw for 216 yards in the first half, but the Chargers led 24-7.
• Andre Reed enjoyed his first 100-yard receiving day in the NFL.
• In two games against the NFL's worst defense, the Bills totaled 802 yards, but scored only 16 points.
• Mathison's first interception, by Gill Byrd, killed a scoring chance and set the Chargers off on a 61-yard drive that ended with Dan Fouts hitting Charlie Joiner for a TD.
• In the second quarter, John Hendy intercepted Mathison and returned it to the 11, leading to Bob Thomas' field goal. The Bills took the kickoff and moved into Chargers territory, but Jerry Butler dropped a TD pass and Scott Norwood then missed a field goal.
• On the next series, the Bills again drove, but Hendy picked off another pass and went 75 yards for a TD.
• San Diego marched 59 yards to make it 24-0 on Tim Spencer's TD. The Bills finally answered with an 87-yard hurry-up march. Chris Burkett made a 29-yard catch and Butler a 36-yarder which set up Joe Cribbs' TD run. On that play, Bruce Smith lined up as a fullback and served as the lead blocker.

• The Chargers scored on their first three possessions of the second half. First, they consumed 6:15 to get a Thomas field goal. Then, Earl Wilson sacked Mathison on a fourth-down play and the Chargers drove 58 yards to Fouts' TD pass to Eric Sievers. Finally, in the fourth, Fouts hit Pete Holohan for 22 and 12 yards, then threw to the tight end for the TD that closed the scoring.

QUOTES

• Hank Bullough on Mathison: "We're going to have to live and die with him until he gets some experience. Turnovers are the last thing you want to have against a team like San Diego." (On using Smith at fullback): "We felt Bruce could give us some push at the hole. I don't know if he got any push, but there was a hole there. We just put it in this week."
• Bruce Smith on playing fullback: "I was thrilled. It was just a lead play where I lead Joe through the hole. I'll do anything and play any position to help this football team."
• Bruce Mathison: "Maybe I was a little too revved up. I wanted to come back here and prove that they were wrong in releasing me. I wanted to throw for 400 yards and five touchdowns. Every game is a learning experience and it seems like every week is getting tougher and tougher. I knew some of their personnel, but I didn't know anything about (Hendy). Their defense is tough to figure out. If we limit the turnovers and the dropped passes, we're in that game."
• Chargers cornerback John Hendy on his interceptions: "The first one I just stumbled into. I had inside coverage and the receiver came inside. On the second one, he (Mathison) called the same audible he called in an earlier series. I figured it would be the same play."

Jets	0	21	0	6 -	27
Bills	0	0	7	0 -	7

Attendance at Rich Stadium - 23,122

NYJ: Shuler 20 pass from O'Brien (Leahy kick), :52
NYJ: Walker 96 pass from O'Brien (Leahy kick), 3:28
NYJ: Hector 12 run (Leahy kick), 9:31
Buf: Bell 8 run (Norwood kick), 12:10
NYJ: Shuler 2 pass from O'Brien (kick blocked), 13:45

	BUF	NYJ
First downs	22	24
Rushing yds	86	118
Passing yds	350	367
Punts-avg	5-38.4	6-39.3
Fumbles-lost	3-2	2-1
Penalties-yds	7-69	7-58
Poss. time	30:26	29:34

BILLS LEADERS: Rushing - Bell 6-16, Cribbs 10-40, Mathison 3-26, Moore 3-4, B. Smith 1-0; **Passing** - Mathison 22-39-2 - 357, Reich 1-1-0 - 19; **Receiving** - Butler 5-91, Bell 4-48, Reed 5-82, Burkett 5-127, Cribbs 4-28.

JETS LEADERS: Rushing - McNeil 27-92, Hector 4-21, O'Brien 4-4, Paige 1-1; **Passing** - O'Brien 25-40-1 - 370; **Receiving** - Walker 4-129, Shuler 8-88, Klever 2-32, Paige 2-17, Toon 3-29, McNeil 4-36, Sohn 1-16, Hector 1-23.

WEEK 14 GAMES

KC 38, Atl 10	Sea 31, Clev 13
Cinc 50, Dal 24	NE 23, Det 6
Chi 17, Ind 10	Mia 34, GB 24
St.L 28, NO 16	NYG 35, Hou 14
SD 54, Pitt 44	Minn 26, TB 7
Wash 17, Phil 12	Rams 27, SF 20
LAR 17, Den 14 (OT)	

NOTES

• The Jets scored 21 points in the second quarter, including a 96-yard TD pass to Wesley Walker.
• Mark Gastineau recovered Booker Moore's fumble late in the first quarter. The Jets then drove 63 yards in nine plays to Ken O'Brien's TD pass to Mickey Shuler.
• The Bills went three-and-out, including a third-and-one carry by Bruce Smith that was stuffed for no gain by Kyle Clifton and Barry Bennett. John Kidd's 56-yard punt and a holding penalty on the Jets pinned them back at the 4. But on first down, Walker blew past Don Wilson, ran a streak pattern and caught a 96-yard TD pass. He ran untouched to the end zone for the longest TD pass in Jets history.
• After another punt, it became 21-0 when the Jets drove 75 yards to Johnny Hector's TD run on a third-and-nine play from the 12. It was the Jets third third-down conversion of the series.
• Before the half ended, each team blew a chance as Scott Norwood missed a 37-yard field goal and O'Brien was intercepted at the Bills 22 by Rod Hill.
• On the first series of the second half, back-to-back 23-yard passes by Bruce Mathison to Andre Reed got the Bills to the 1, but Mathison fumbled a snap and Charles Jackson recovered for the Jets.
• The Bills drove to the 4 on the next series, but Kerry Glenn intercepted Mathison in the end zone.
• Late in the third, the Bills finally produced a score as Chris Burkett made catches of 38 and 26 yards to set up Greg Bell's TD run.
• The Jets final TD came late in the game, Shuler's second TD reception.

QUOTES

• Hank Bullough on the Walker TD: "I think that second touchdown they scored kind of took the sail out of our winds."
• Rod Hill on the Walker TD: "It was a blown assignment. I'm not going to mention who did it (Wilson), but someone should have slowed him (Walker) down at the line. The guys started getting their heads down when it was 14-0. That's not good. You've got to keep fighting. This is a game of making plays. But every week, we're blowing assignments and not making the plays."
• Jets receiver Wesley Walker: "I just ran straight up the field. We caught them in the right defense."
• Bruce Mathison: "We had no trouble moving the ball from the 20 to the 10, in fact sometimes it was easy. But when we got to the 10, it seemed like there was a big steel wall there. No matter what we tried, it didn't work. Something always seemed to happen."

STANDINGS: FOURTEENTH WEEK

AFC EAST	W	L	T	CENTRAL	W	L	T	WEST	W	L	T	NFC EAST	W	L	T	CENTRAL	W	L	T	WEST	W	L	T
NY Jets	10	4	0	Cleveland	7	7	0	Raiders	10	4	0	Dallas	9	5	0	Chicago	13	1	0	LA Rams	10	4	0
New England	10	4	0	Cincinnati	7	7	0	Denver	9	5	0	NY Giants	9	5	0	Detroit	7	7	0	San Fran	8	6	0
Miami	10	4	0	Pittsburgh	6	8	0	Seattle	8	6	0	Washington	8	6	0	Minnesota	7	7	0	N.Orleans	5	9	0
Indianapolis	3	11	0	Houston	5	9	0	San Diego	7	7	0	Philadelphia	6	8	0	Green Bay	6	8	0	Atlanta	2	12	0
Buffalo	2	12	0					Kan. City	5	9	0	St. Louis	5	9	0	Tampa Bay	2	12	0				

GAME 15 - Sunday, Dec. 15, 1985 - STEELERS 30, BILLS 24

NOTES

• The Bills blew a 21-0 second-quarter lead and lost when Walter Abercrombie scored with 47 seconds left. It was the Steelers greatest comeback in team history and it came in front of the smallest crowd to ever watch a regular-season game at Three Rivers Stadium.
• The Bills knocked out the Steelers' starting QB David Woodley and backup Mark Malone in the first quarter.
• Greg Bell scored on the first play of the game. After a Steelers punt, Bruce Mathison hit Jerry Butler for a TD early in the second quarter. The Bills made it 21-0 just 3:47 later when Louis Lipps fumbled and Don Wilson picked it up and ran 61 yards for a TD.
• The Steelers began their comeback 1:26 later when Lipps caught a TD pass from Scott Campbell. Frank Pollard had a 22-yard run and Bruce Smith was nailed for a 15-yard roughing the passer penalty.
• Gary Dunn then recovered a Joe Cribbs fumble at the Bills 37 and eight plays later, Pollard scored.
• The Steelers moved 65 yards in 12 plays after the second-half kickoff to set up Gary Anderson's field goal. Pittsburgh then got another field goal 4:23 later after Robin Cole recovered Greg Bell's fumble to make it 21-20.
• Scott Norwood's field goal capped a 74-yard drive early in the fourth.
• Anderson's third field goal 4:25 later came after Campbell fumbled 20 yards behind the line but recovered and threw a 16-yard completion to Pollard to the Bills 12.
• The Steelers began their winning drive at their 29. On the first play, Lipps made a 51-yard reception. Then on third-and-nine, Pollard ran 15 yards on a draw to the 10. On third-and-goal from the 2, Abercrombie scored the winner.

QUOTES

• Greg Bell: "We just don't know how to finish things off. We have problems with those final 10 minutes of games."
• Hank Bullough on rotating Bell and Cribbs despite Bell gaining 112 yards in the first quarter: "We're going to play both our backs. Both Bell and Cribbs (fumbled). I don't look at yardage, I look at the number of times a guy puts the ball on the ground. Besides, 77 came on one run. Give credit to the Steelers for coming back. We have to quit beating ourselves. But we proved we could play with the big boys."
• Don Wilson: "After all that has gone wrong for me individually this season, it was good to see something finally go right. Too bad it didn't come in a win."
• Steelers coach Chuck Noll: "The big thing was Scott's performance. He did an excellent job under trying circumstances. He made some mistakes, but he came up with some big plays."

WEEK 15 GAMES

Chi 19, NYJ 6	Den 14, KC 13
Wash 27, Cinc 24	GB 26, Det 23
Clev 28, Hou 21	Ind 31, TB 23
Atl 14, Minn 13	Dal 28, NYG 21
SD 20, Phil 14	Rams 46, St.L 14
SF 31, NO 19	LAR 13, Sea 3
Mia 30, NE 27	

Bills	7	14	0	3 -	24
Steelers	0	14	6	10 -	30

Attendance at Three Rivers Stadium - 35,953

Buf: Bell 77 run (Norwood kick), :25
Buf: Butler 33 pass from Mathison (Norwood kick), 3:28
Buf: Wilson 61 fumble return (Norwood kick), 7:15
Pit: Lipps 13 pass from Campbell (Anderson kick), 8:31
Pit: Pollard 4 run (Anderson kick), 14:05
Pit: FG Anderson 26, 5:13
Pit: FG Anderson 31, 9:36
Buf: FG Norwood 24, 6:07
Pit: FG Anderson 45, 10:32
Pit: Abercrombie 2 run (Anderson kick), 14:13

	BUF	PIT
First downs	14	25
Rushing yds	189	170
Passing yds	134	264
Punts-avg	4-36.8	4-35.0
Fumbles-lost	6-3	4-1
Penalties-yds	8-60	5-45
Poss. time	27:12	32:48

BILLS LEADERS: Rushing - Bell 19-123, Cribbs 9-13, Mathison 4-31, Steels 3-22; **Passing** - Mathison 10-20-2 - 162; **Receiving** - Butler 3-51, Bell 2-12, Reed 1-21, Burkett 1-18, Richardson 3-60.

STEELERS LEADERS: Rushing - Pollard 16-82, Abercrombie 15-71, Campbell 2-2, Woodley 1-12, Spencer 1-2, Lipps 1-1; **Passing** - Malone 2-7-0 - 21, Campbell 18-38-2 - 275; **Receiving** - Lipps 4-116, Pollard 3-39, Stallworth 3-37, Abercrombie 3-34, Gothard 3-34, Thompson 1-18, Sweeney 3-18.

GAME 16 - Sunday, Dec. 22, 1985 - DOLPHINS 28, BILLS 0

NOTES

• The Bills concluded their second consecutive 2-14 season with a horrific 28-0 loss to Miami that clinched the AFC East title for the Dolphins.
• Buffalo suffered six turnovers. Derrick Burroughs and Mark Duper were ejected for fighting.
• Miami drove 76 yards in 11 plays for the first score, Dan Marino's TD pass to Bruce Hardy. Marino was four-of-six for 50 yards on the drive.
• In the second quarter, Hardy caught a five-yard TD pass to cap a 32-yard drive which started with Jackie Shipp's interception of a Bruce Mathison pass. Marino

hit Mark Clayton for 23 yards to the 9.
• After a scoreless third, the Dolphins put it away in the fourth. Bill Barnett recovered a Mathison fumble at the 26. Six plays later, Tony Nathan scored. Just 5:11 later, Ron Davenport scored after the Dolphins had stopped the Bills on fourth down at the Buffalo 43.
• The Bills failed on fourth-and-one from the 2 in the second quarter. After moving to a first-and-goal from the 8 in the third, Mathison threw an end zone interception to William Judson.
• In the third, Jim Haslett made his first interception since 1980, but after returning it 45 yards, fumbled and Miami's Steve Clark recovered.

QUOTES

• Hank Bullough: "I thought we could beat them if we played errorless, flawless football. Obviously we didn't do that. This was probably our worst game for penalties, and Bruce had an off day throwing the ball. I wish next season was starting tomorrow."
• Jim Haslett: "This was our whole season in a nutshell." (On his interception and fumble): "I knew (Nat) Moore was behind me because the ball was supposed to go to him. After I was running I figured he was closing in. Then I heard my teammates yelling and I tried to lateral and that's when Moore hit me."
• Miami quarterback Dan Marino: "We didn't play as well as we could have."
• Miami coach Don Shula: "We wanted to do it (win the division) ourselves and we got the opportunity. We wanted the bye next week. Buffalo has shown a tendency to play well, and we saw that on film."
• Bruce Mathison: "The penalties were due to a lack of concentration. I was as frustrated as I could be. I forced some things that shouldn't have been forced."

Bills	0	0	0	0 -	0
Dolphins	7	7	0	14 -	28

Attendance at the Orange Bowl - 65,686

Mia: Hardy 19 pass from Marino (Reveiz kick), 6:56
Mia: Hardy 5 pass from Marino (Reveiz kick), 8:59
Mia: Nathan 1 run (Reveiz kick), 6:13
Mia: Davenport 13 run (Reveiz kick), 11:24

	BUF	MIA
First downs	11	24
Rushing yds	111	179
Passing yds	188	129
Punts-avg	4-44.8	5-41.6
Fumbles-lost	5-3	3-1
Penalties-yds	19-123	7-47
Poss. time	26:01	33:59

BILLS LEADERS: Rushing - Bell 9-50, Cribbs 14-48, Mathison 3-13; **Passing** - Mathison 10-24-3 - 188; **Receiving** - Bell 3-64, Reed 3-44, Butler 1-45, Ramson 1-8, Steels 1-3, Teal 1-24.

DOLPHINS LEADERS: Rushing - Davenport 6-57, Nathan 11-54, Bennett 8-31, Carter 5-17, Moore 1-11, Marino 2-4, Hampton 3-11, Strock 2-(-6); **Passing** - Marino 15-24-1 - 136, Strock 1-2-0 - 9; **Receiving** - Nathan 6-45, Hardy 5-52, Clayton 1-23, Moore 1-11, Vigorito 1-9, Carter 1-3, Davenport 1-2.

WEEK 16 GAMES

Den 27, Sea 24	NYG 28, Pitt 10
Wash 27, St.L 16	Atl 16, NO 10
Chi 37, Det 17	NE 34, Cinc 23
NYJ 37, Clev 10	SF 31, Dal 16
GB 20, TB 17	Ind 34, Hou 16
Phil 37, Minn 35	KC 38, SD 34
LAR 16, Rams 6	

STANDINGS: SIXTEENTH WEEK

AFC EAST	W	L	T	CENTRAL	W	L	T	WEST	W	L	T	NFC EAST	W	L	T	CENTRAL	W	L	T	WEST	W	L	T
Miami	12	4	0	Cleveland	8	8	0	Raiders	12	4	0	Dallas	10	6	0	Chicago	15	1	0	LA Rams	11	5	0
New England	11	5	0	Cincinnati	7	9	0	Denver	11	5	0	NY Giants	10	6	0	Green Bay	8	8	0	San Fran	10	6	0
NY Jets	11	5	0	Pittsburgh	7	9	0	Seattle	8	8	0	Washington	10	6	0	Minnesota	7	9	0	N.Orleans	5	11	0
Indianapolis	5	11	0	Houston	5	11	0	San Diego	8	8	0	Philadelphia	7	9	0	Detroit	7	9	0	Atlanta	4	12	0
Buffalo	2	14	0					Kan. City	6	10	0	St. Louis	5	11	0	Tampa Bay	2	14	0				

A_t A G_{lance}
1986

Jan. 3 – Cincinnati receivers coach Bruce Coslet said the Bills offered him their offensive coordinator position.

Jan. 6 – Coslet turned down the Bills. "Bruce is a good young coach and I wanted to see if he would come work for me," Hank Bullough said. "We worked together in Cincinnati. I'd have liked to have him come aboard, but I understand his situation. He's with a contending team, his wife is from Cincinnati, and he's lived there a long time now."

Jan. 15 – Patrick McGroder died after a short illness in Scottsdale, Ariz. The Bills' senior executive vice-president was 81.

Jan. 22 – Hank Bullough fired quarterbacks coach Kay Dalton and tight ends coach Art Asselta. "Both of them did a good job, but I'm just trying to get my own people in," Bullough said.

Feb. 5 – Jim Kelly admitted that the Los Angeles Raiders had inquired about his services should he sever ties with the USFL. "I've always loved the Raiders, I've always wanted to play with them, but Buffalo has my rights for one more year," Kelly said. The Raiders denied any discussions had taken place because they could be charged with tampering.

Feb. 19 – Ted Cottrell was hired as defensive line coach, replacing Ardell Wiegandt, who was switched to coaching outside linebackers. The inside linebackers would be tutored by defensive coordinator Herb Paterra.

Feb. 20 – The New Jersey Generals and Houston Gamblers merged into one team in the USFL, to be based in New Jersey and to be owned by Donald Trump. The move was hailed by USFL commissioner Harry Usher, who said his league would not fold, despite popular opinion.

Feb. 26 – Hank Bullough shuffled his coaching staff again. He hired Joe Faragalli as tight ends coach, offensive coordinator Jim Ringo had those duties cut in half as he was placed in charge of the running game while receivers coach Bob Leahy was put in charge of the passing game. Also, running backs coach Elijah Pitts was given the added position of special teams coordinator.

March 3 – Joe Daniels was hired as receivers coach, replacing the promoted Bob Leahy.

March 10 – Commissioner Pete Rozelle took a hard-line approach on the NFL's battle against drugs, opting for a random drug-testing program.

March 11 – The owners, at their annual winter meetings in Palm Springs, approved the use of instant replay starting with the 1986 season, with a review in 1987. Also, the owners voted to ban players from wearing equipment with personal messages.

March 18 – The NFL Players' Association announced a new drug prevention program that included random drug-testing, but Pete Rozelle didn't think it was strict enough.

April 14 – Joe Cribbs' agent, Louis Burrell, said his client was ready to go to war with the Bills. "We've got our war hats on," Burrell said. "If Joe has to go to training camp with the Bills, he's going to wear a t-shirt that says 'This means war!' He can't play for that club. He's as serious as a man in the hospital with a heart attack."

April 15 – Joe Cribbs fired Burrell because of his remarks the day before, which were published in

USA Today. "I called coach Bullough right away after I read what Louis said," Cribbs said. "I told him I didn't have anything to do with it."

April 16 – The first AFC East coaches conference was held at the Buffalo Hilton. Don Shula, Raymond Berry, Rod Dowhower, Joe Walton and Hank Bullough spoke to the media and discussed a variety of subjects, most notably the NFL's drug problem. Hank Bullough's quips, however, stole the show. When asked how he would rebuild the Bills, Bullough said: "Through the draft, free agents and the waiver wire, and Don said he'd let us have his quarterback (Dan Marino)."

April 23 – Norm Pollom, the vice-president for player personnel, said he would be leaving the Bills after the college draft.

April 24 – A federal judge refused to void the NFL's contracts with the three major TV networks,

saying the USFL hadn't proven that the contracts violated federal antitrust laws.

April 29 – The Bills wound up with two first-round picks in the draft. With the 16th choice overall, a spot obtained in 1985 from Cleveland, the Bills chose Iowa running back Ronnie Harmon. They then traded their second- and third-round spots for San Francisco's first-pound pick, No. 20 overall, and chose Vanderbilt offensive lineman Will Wolford. They also chose South Carolina offensive lineman Leonard Burton (third), Mississippi Valley State fullback Carl Byrum (fifth), Georgia Tech defensive lineman Mark Pike (seventh), Michigan State tight end Butch Rolle (seventh) and Notre Dame linebacker Tony Furjanic (eighth). Around the league, Tampa Bay made running back Bo Jackson the first pick, Atlanta chose defensive lineman Tony Casillas

Jim Kelly's arrival in 1986 not only gave the Bills the marquee player they needed, but it gave the fans renewed hope that the team could reverse the terrible slump that produced back-to-back 2-14 seasons.

(second), Houston grabbed quarterback Jim Everett (third), Indianapolis selected defensive lineman Jon Hand (fourth), New Orleans took offensive lineman and Buffalo native Jim Dombrowski (sixth), San Diego took defensive end Leslie O'Neal (eighth), Philadelphia chose fullback Keith Byars (10th), Cincinnati took linebacker Joe Kelly (11th), Detroit picked quarterback Chuck Long (12th), Seattle took fullback John L. Williams (15th), Atlanta selected Syracuse defensive lineman Tim Green (17th), Dallas picked wide receiver Mike Sherrard (18th), the Giants picked defensive lineman Eric Dorsey (19th), Cincinnati took wide receiver Tim McGee (21st) and Chicago grabbed running back Neal Anderson (27th).

April 30 – Because the Bills drafted a running back in the first round, Joe Cribbs said he assumed he'd be shipped out. "I'm the logical choice, they can't play all three of us," he said, referring to himself, Greg Bell and newcomer Ronnie Harmon. Bell said the selection of Harmon "was very surprising. I don't know what's going on in the front office. My ideas were for us to get a lot of weight with that pick, like a fullback or a lineman."

May 9 – The Bills opened their mini-camp at Rich Stadium. Frank Reich proclaimed that he was ready to become the teams' No. 1 quarterback. "I'm here to play," he said. "Right now, Bruce (Mathison) is No. 1, but I don't think anybody has a lock on any position." Ralph Wilson met with area businessmen to see if they would support his team. The season ticket count of 19,031 in 1985 was the lowest in the NFL and at the time of the mini-camp, only between 13-14,000 season tickets had been sold.

May 10 – The Bills took their mini-camp to Fairport High School in an effort to reach out to the Rochester market. Norm Pollom indicated that he wouldn't be leaving the team as he had originally planned. "I'm leaning toward staying," he said.

May 11 – A new feature of the Bills' mini-camp was an open practice at the stadium and about 8,000 fans turned out on a warm, sunny Mothers Day.

May 12 – The USFL's $1.7 billion antitrust suit against the NFL went to trial in Manhattan.

May 31 – Norm Pollom signed a new contract to remain the team's vice-president for player personnel.

June 9 – Speculation was that the NFL was losing in the antitrust trial against the USFL and that up to six USFL teams might be merged into the NFL.

June 11 – Eddie Abramoski, the only trainer the Bills had ever had, was inducted into the National Athletic Trainers Association Hall of Fame.

June 17 – The Bills signed former Colts quarterback Art Schlichter to a free-agent contract. Schlichter was making a comeback after being suspended in 1983 for gambling.

June 18 – Jerry Foran was named the Bills first director of marketing and sales.

July 4 – Bob Dylan and The Grateful Dead highlighted a Fourth of July rock concert at Rich Stadium.

July 7 – Convinced the owners and players wouldn't be able to negotiate a viable drug program, Pete Rozelle made good on his threat to institute a league-wide random drug-testing policy. He also hired Dr. Forest Tennant to coordinate the testing.

July 9 – Hank Bullough said that the heat would be on linebacker Darryl Talley to make something happen in training camp. "I think it's a key year for Darryl," Bullough said. "He's got to make hay this year. I'm sure he was disappointed in the year he

had last year. He didn't have a good year. He has to play better, he has to make some plays this year."

July 16 – Veteran center Will Grant was waived.

July 18 – Fullback Booker Moore was waived as training camp opened at Fredonia State. A number of players were missing including first-round picks Ronnie Harmon and Will Wolford. Bruce Smith showed up 25 pounds lighter than he was at mini-camp, weighing 273.

July 21 – In a *Sports Illustrated* story, Jim Kelly said that with the merger of the Gamblers and Generals into one team, thus pairing him with Herschel Walker, the new Generals' offense would be unstoppable. "With my receivers and Herschel, we could score 35 points on the Chicago Bears. No question."

July 22 – Public relations director Budd Thalman announced he would be leaving the team to become the associate athletic director at Penn State, effective Aug. 15.

July 25 – With the signing of two rookies and tight end Eason Ramson, the Bills were down to five unsigned players: Ronnie Harmon, Will Wolford, Reggie Bynum, Jim Ritcher and Justin Cross.

July 26 – Cleveland beat the Bills for the first time in the nine-year history of the annual rookie scrimmage at Edinboro University, 12-0.

July 28 – Former Bills fullback Jim Braxton died after a lengthy bout with cancer

July 29 – After an 11-week trial in U.S. District Court in Manhattan, a jury awarded the USFL $1, which was trebled to $3, in its $1.7 billion antitrust suit against the NFL. The jury rejected all of the USFL's television-related claims, which were the heart of the case. The decision thrust the USFL into grave danger of extinction

July 30 – Jim Ritcher ended his holdout and signed a new contract.

July 31 – About 500 mourners, including many ex-teammates, paid their final respects to Jim Braxton. Among the pallbearers were O.J. Simpson, Tony Greene, Reggie McKenzie, Bob Chandler, Joe DeLamielleure, Paul Seymour, Curtis Brown and Lou Piccone.

Aug. 2 – The Bills held an intrasquad scrimmage at Rich Stadium in front of about 8,000 fans.

Aug. 4 – USFL commissioner Harry Usher said his league was not folding, only suspending operations until 1987. According to one of Jim Kelly's agents, A.J. Faigin, this allowed his client to begin negotiations with the Bills. "He has a clause in his contract which requires them to play," Faigin said. "If they fail to play, Jim is free from his obligations. We may have to go to court, which we would if we had to." Said Kelly: "I can call the Bills. I'll talk to Ralph Wilson and see what we can do. For the right money, I'll go."

Aug. 6 – Donald Trump said he would allow Kelly to go to the NFL if he wanted.

Aug. 9 – The Bills opened their preseason schedule with a 19-17 loss to the Browns at Cleveland.

Aug. 11 – Denny Lynch was hired as director of public relations, replacing Budd Thalman. The NFL announced that more than 600 USFL players were now available to NFL teams, but about 30 players –including Jim Kelly – who had personal service contracts with USFL interests had to be cleared by their teams, the USFL office and then the NFL office before beginning negotiations with NFL clubs.

Aug. 12 – Both first-round draft choices, Ronnie

Harmon and Will Wolford, signed their first pro contracts. Both signed four-year deals worth about $1.4 million each. Justin Cross became the final veteran to report to camp.

Aug. 14 – Finally, negotiations between the Bills and Jim Kelly began in New York City.

Aug. 16 – Art Schlichter had a shaky game as the Bills lost in Houston, 23-20. Earlier in the day, it was reported that Jim Kelly, who watched the game with Ralph Wilson, was seeking a contract worth $2 million per season.

Aug. 18 – Jim Kelly signed a five-year, $1.75 million contract with the Bills after intense negotiations in Houston, making him the highest-paid player in the NFL. Bills director of marketing Jerry Foran said the Bills' season ticket count could soar as high as 35,000 because of the signing. Kelly flew to Buffalo later in the day and received an incredible hero's welcome from the city. Fans lined the route from the airport to downtown waving at his limo and holding signs welcoming him. During a huge press conference at the Buffalo Hilton – which was televised live locally – Kelly received a call from New York Gov. Mario Cuomo and Kelly said: "Who knows? Maybe I'll be able to take this team to the Super Bowl and get a call from the President next." He then told the gathering: "I can't promise you a Super Bowl, because you're only as good as the people they put around you. If I can get some help, I definitely think we can take this team to a championship." In another move, the Bills signed former New Jersey Generals center Kent Hull.

Aug. 19 – Joe Cribbs finally was granted his wish to be traded as the Bills dealt him to San Francisco for two future draft choices. Art Schlichter was waived and veteran Ben Williams announced his retirement. Williams finished as the Bills all-time leader in sacks with 51 and was third in games played (150). Jim Kelly reported to Fredonia and participated in the afternoon workout. "I felt pretty comfortable, but I have to get used to the guys," Kelly said. Lines were long at the Bills' ticket office at Rich Stadium. Jerry Foran announced that more than 1,600 season tickets had been sold in the 24 hours since Kelly's signing.

Aug. 20 – Jim Kelly, who had said playing behind the Bills offensive line would "take years off my career" before he signed with the team, admitted to being surprised by their talent. "The offensive line doesn't look as bad as I thought in the beginning," he said.

Aug. 23 – The Bills ended an eight-game preseason winless streak dating to 1984 as they beat the Chiefs in Kansas City, 13-6. The only TD came on Ron Pitts' 76-yard interception return. Jim Kelly did not play in the game.

Aug. 26 - Bruce Mathison, who finished 1985 as the starting quarterback, was one of seven players waived. Another was safety and punt returner Don Wilson. Hank Bullough announced that Jim Kelly would make his debut against the defending Super Bowl champion Chicago Bears in the preseason finale at Notre Dame Stadium.

Aug. 30 – Jim Kelly made an average debut for the Bills in the preseason finale at Notre Dame as the Bills lost to Chicago, 31-17. Kelly completed five of nine passes for 60 yards and had two sure TD passes dropped. "He looked great out there," wide receiver Andre Reed said. "Imagine how good he'll be once he gets a few more passes under his belt. He'll be totally awesome." Frank Reich got the start and he guided the Bills to a 14-0 lead before the

Bears rallied. There was bad news, however, as Jim Haslett suffered a broken leg and likely would miss the season.

Sept. 2 – Kicker Scott Norwood was waived and when he cleared waivers, was re-signed. The team announced that 28,225 season tickets had been sold, the highest number since 1982 and about 9,000 more than in 1985.

Sept. 7 – Before a sellout crowd of 79,951 at Rich Stadium, the Jim Kelly Era began and while the Bills lost to the Jets, 28-24, Kelly showed that the Bills would be much-improved. He completed 20 of 33 passes for 292 yards and three TDs. "With Kelly, you always feel like you've got a chance," Ralph Wilson said. "He's exciting and boy, he's tough."

Sept. 8 – Film review confirmed that Jim Kelly played a great game despite being in Buffalo only three weeks. "He was just outstanding," said quarterbacks coach Bob Leahy. "Jim's a fun kid. As far as personality, he's the closest thing to (Terry) Bradshaw I've seen. Jim doesn't run as well, but he may be a more accurate passer than Terry was, and he probably has a little better touch. He certainly has All-Pro potential."

Sept. 9 – The Bills signed former USFL safety Dwight Drane, whom they had selected in a special USFL player draft in 1984.

Sept. 14 – The Bills blew a 10-point lead in the final 5:19 and lost in overtime to Cincinnati, 36-33, on Jim Breech's 20-yard field goal. Jim Kelly passed for 228 yards, but threw his first two NFL interceptions.

Sept. 15 – Hank Bullough charged someone in the Western New York media with letting out team secrets. Bullough read a pregame report in the *Cincinnati Enquirer* the day of the game that said the Bills would probably move Bruce Smith to different spots on the defensive line to free him up from double-team blocking. Bullough said he nearly threw up when he read it, because he felt the Bengals were able to adjust when they saw that and it had a factor in the game. "I don't know who did it (relayed the information to the *Enquirer*), but the guy probably doesn't sleep very well at night," he said. "I wouldn't stop you guys from watching practice because that's your livelihood, but I'm going to find out who did this and get his name out over the news wires."

Sept. 16 – Bullough softened his stance on the spy theory. "I'm kind of hot-headed at times when I read things," Bullough said. "I've been thinking about it and I don't think we have a spy in the media. I'd venture to say that it probably happened by accident. But if someone tells me an hour before the game, 'Hey, the other team's going to blitz 60 times on you' I'll guarantee you we'll be on the blackboard trying to figure out what we're going to do. I don't know if that report helped the Bengals, but there's the possibility that it did."

Sept. 17 – The Bills signed free agent linebacker Ray Bentley, who had been cut by Tampa Bay. Greg Bell said he wasn't pleased sharing time at halfback with Robb Riddick. "I feel I'm in a position where I have to have a good year, not just for the team, but for my own morale," Bell said. "Right now, I feel I could carry the ball 30 times a game." Said Hank Bullough: "Competition is the name of the game. If a guy can't stand the competition, he's got a problem. Right now, Riddick is a good back. It's a nice situation to have."

Sept. 21 – The Bills ended their eight-game regular season losing streak and Jim Kelly got his first

career NFL victory in a 17-10 win over St. Louis at Rich Stadium.

Sept. 28 – The Bills dropped a 20-17 decision at Rich to Kansas City as Jim Kelly left the game briefly with a forearm injury and returned to throw three interceptions.

Sept. 29 – Jim Kelly said he'd appreciate his teammates fighting for him, meaning that no one reciprocated after Tim Cofield flattened him and injured his forearm the day before. "I would like to see somebody protect me," Kelly said. "When I was with the Gamblers anytime anybody did something around me or my receivers, the offensive line would be in their face. It felt good. Sometimes the linemen don't see what's going on because it happens after the play, maybe that's why they didn't do anything."

Oct. 5 – Mickey Shuler caught a game-winning 36-yard touchdown pass from Ken O'Brien with 57 seconds left to play and the Jets survived a scare from the Bills at Giants Stadium, 14-13. In the second quarter, Marty Lyons was penalized for roughing Jim Kelly and referee Ben Dreith explained over the PA system that Lyons was "giving him the business down there."

Oct. 10 – In a 1985 issue of *Sport* magazine, Kelly had this to say about Dan Marino: "When Marino looks over his shoulder, he sees me. If I were in the NFL, I would be on all the magazine covers instead of Marino." Marino's response during a conference call to the Buffalo media was: "If you have confidence in your own abilities, you don't really have to tell anybody you can do this or that. There really isn't any need for him to keep telling everybody. With him in the NFL, it will be fun to see how good he does. For his sake, I hope he's as successful as he says he's going to be."

Oct. 12 – In their first head-to-head meeting, Dan Marino passed for 337 yards and outgunned Jim Kelly as the Dolphins beat the Bills in 89-degree heat at the Orange Bowl, 27-14. It was Buffalo's last appearance in the old stadium, as they finished 2-18-1 lifetime there.

Oct. 13 – O.J. Simpson was asked about the similarities between his rookie season in Buffalo in 1969 and Kelly's in 1986: "I guess they (the fans) thought I should turn things around all by myself when I got to Buffalo, just as they expect it from Kelly," Simpson said. "Just change the name Simpson to Kelly in all your old stories and you can save a lot of time. It takes more than one person. You have to have other good players, you have to have management doing things right. You have to have strength all through your organization. A lot of quarterbacks can look good playing for Don Shula or Bill Walsh."

Oct. 19 – Ronnie Harmon made his first contribution to the team, filling in for injured Greg Bell and Robb Riddick and rushing for 86 yards as the Bills downed Indianapolis, 24-13, at Rich Stadium.

Oct. 21 – Ray Bentley, who was waived a few days earlier, was re-signed and Guy Frazier was waived.

Oct. 26 – New England came to Rich Stadium and brutally battered Jim Kelly in a 23-3 victory. Kelly was sacked five times, knocked down at least 10 other times and came out of the game with eight minutes left

Oct. 27 – Ralph Wilson expressed his displeasure with the loss to New England: "I'm very frustrated. I'm concerned with the performance. It could go into personnel, it could go into coaching, it could go

into everything that makes up a football team. We're going to investigate the whole situation and hopefully we can come up with the right answers."

Nov. 2 – Robb Riddick dropped Jim Kelly's pass at the goal line on the final play of the game and the Bills dropped their 21st straight road game, 34-28, at Tampa Bay. Kelly threw for 342 yards and three TDs and nearly completed a comeback from 20-0 halftime deficit.

Nov. 3 – Ralph Wilson fired Hank Bullough and replaced him with Marv Levy, former coach of the Kansas City Chiefs. "It's important that the fans understand that we want to make progress," general manager Bill Polian said. "We also know we're not going to the Super Bowl this year, and maybe not next year. But it's important that the progress and the momentum that we've established moves forward, and we're confident Marv Levy's the man who can do that. We feel he'll be able to step in, give the direction that's necessary and start moving this team forward." Said Bullough: "I don't leave on a sad note, I have no bitter feelings toward any of the players."

Nov. 4 – The players discussed Hank Bullough's firing. "I'm sorry to see Hank leave," Jim Kelly said, "but for the team, I think it's a step in the right direction. Everybody is going to have to pull together now. It's going to be hard for him (Levy) and be real hard on us. I think this is going to have a positive effect on the team and bring added enthusiasm." Said Fred Smerlas: "Hank really tried, but something was missing." Levy, who was staying at the Sheraton Hotel, got lost driving to the stadium for his first day of work and turned a 15-minute ride into a 100-minute ordeal. Kelly taped an appearance on NBC's *Late Night with David Letterman*, but because of election day, the episode would not air for two weeks.

Nov. 5 – While Marv Levy was conducting his first practice as head coach, Ralph Wilson admitted that he had decided to fire Hank Bullough the previous Thursday. "The outcome of the (Tampa Bay) game had nothing to do with it," he said. "I thought if we didn't make the change, we'd lose the community. After the way the community and the fans have responded (positively), I figured we owed them something – more than we've shown. The business community and the fans have gone all-out for this team this year. So this was a calculated decision between myself, Bill Polian and (executive vice-president) Dave Olsen. Levy said he spent much of the previous two days watching film and talking to the players and coaches. He hinted his first priority would be shoring up the woeful special teams. Levy had been George Allen's special teams coach with Washington when the Redskins played in Super Bowl VII against Miami.

Nov. 8 – Steve Tasker was acquired on waivers from Houston and was put on the active roster for the Steelers game the next day.

Nov. 9 – Marv Levy was a winner in his Bills' head coaching debut as Buffalo downed Pittsburgh, 16-12, at windy Rich Stadium. The Bills rushed for 172 yards. Ray Bentley made eight tackles in his first start as a Bill.

Nov. 16 – Dan Marino completed 39 of 54 passes for 404 yards and two of his four TD passes came in the fourth quarter as Miami beat the Bills, 34-24, before 76,474 at Rich Stadium. His 39 completions were a record against the Bills and the passing yardage was the most ever at Rich. Jerry Butler suffered a shattered right ankle while catching a second-quarter touchdown pass.

Nov. 21 – Talking about Marv Levy and Hank Bullough, Bruce Smith said: "The difference between those   two is like night and day. There's a big change in attitude around here. We're so much more relaxed. I think a lot of people are very happy."

Nov. 23 – The Bills lost their 22nd in a row on the road as Tony Eason hit Greg Baty with a 13-yard TD pass with 1:40 left to play for a 22-19 victory at Sullivan Stadium.

Nov. 30 – The Bills ended their 22-game road losing streak by upsetting Marv Levy's former team, the Kansas City Chiefs, 17-14. The Bills, whose last road win also was in Kansas City on Dec. 4, 1983, avoided tying the all-time NFL road record for futility, 23 games by the Oilers from 1981-84.

Dec. 7 – In Buffalo's home season finale, played on a rainy day, Cleveland defeated the Bills, 21-17. The Bills finished with their fourth-highest season attendance ever, 531,813. Their average jumped 28,583 per game from 1985.

Dec. 14 – Indianapolis, which had lost 13 games

in a row before beating Atlanta a week earlier, won its second in a row, downing the Bills, 24-14. It was Buffalo's third straight loss in the Hoosier Dome.

Dec. 17 – Pro Bowl nominations were announced and Bruce Smith reacted angrily when he learned he had been left off the AFC team, as were all the Bills. Smith was named an alternate behind Howie Long, Rulon Jones and Jacob Green. "I'm disappointed, I really expected to make it," Smith said. "I thought I played well enough to make the Pro Bowl without leaving any questions in the mind of anybody I had played against this year."

Dec. 20 – In talking about Jim Kelly, Marv Levy said: "Jim Kelly has probably had a better rookie season than any quarterback in history."

Dec. 21 – The Bills closed the season with an uninspired performance in a 16-7 loss to Houston in the Astrodome. The loss clinched the third pick in the 1987 draft.

Dec. 22 – Marv Levy hired Bobby Ross to be the Bills' quarterbacks coach and fired six assistant coaches left from Hank Bullough's staff: Quarterbacks coach Bob Leahy, Joe Daniels

(receivers), Herb Paterra (defensive coordinator), Ardell Wiegandt (outside linebackers), Dick Moseley (defensive backfield) and Jim Valek (administrative assistant). Levy retained Elijah Pitts (running backs, special teams), Jim Ringo (offensive line, running game) and Ted Cottrell (defensive line). "I felt the staff worked hard, but I have other staff plans in mind," Levy said. Said Ross: "I feel like I'm walking into a very good situation. What offensive coach wouldn't look forward to working with a young quarterback with Jim Kelly's potential?"

Dec. 23 – Marv Levy said he didn't want to waste time improving the Bills. "We want to get good fast," Levy said. "I have a problem with people who talk about rebuilding for the future. Teams that take that approach find they are still rebuilding five years later, 10 years later, 20 years later."

Dec. 28 – The Jets romped past Kansas City, 35-15, in the AFC wild-card game, while Washington downed the Rams, 19-7, in the NFC wild-card game.

Dec. 30 – Marv Levy announced the hiring of two assistant coaches: Dick Roach (defensive backfield) and Chuck Dickerson (special assistant to the head coach) and also announced that Bob Ferguson had been promoted to director of pro personnel.

Jan. 3, 1987 – Mark Moseley's field goal lifted Cleveland to a 23-20 overtime victory over the Jets, while Washington whipped the defending Super Bowl champion Bears, 27-13, in divisional round games.

Jan. 4, 1987 – In the other two divisional round games, Denver held off New England, 22-17, and the Giants annihilated San Francisco, 49-3, knocking Joe Montana out of the game in the process.

Jan. 11, 1987 – In a memorable AFC Championship Game, John Elway directed a brilliant 15-play, 98-yard drive that resulted in his five-yard TD pass to Mark Jackson with 37 seconds left, and Denver went on to beat Cleveland, 23-20, in overtime on Rich Karlis' field goal. The Giants blanked Washington, 17-0, in the NFC Championship game, as Joe Morris rushed for 87 yards and scored once.

Jan. 25, 1987 – The Giants crushed Denver, 39-20, in Super Bowl XXI at the Rose Bowl, as MVP Phil Simms completed 22 of 25 passes for 268 yards and three TDs.

Feb. 1, 1987 – In the lowest-scoring Pro Bowl ever, the AFC posted a 10-6 victory, despite four sacks by MVP Reggie White.

Marv Levy replaced Hank Bullough as head coach in early November and although the Bills were just 2-5 after he took over, it was obvious Levy had the club moving in the right direction.

BY THE NUMBERS - 1986

TEAM STATISTICS	BILLS	OPP
First downs	291	334
Rushing	101	100
Passing	152	204
Penalty	38	30
Third downs	60-185	79-216
Total yards	5,017	5,523
Avg. game	313.6	345.2
Plays	963	1,071
Avg. play	5.2	5.2
Net rushing yds	1,654	1,721
Avg. game	103.4	107.6
Avg. play	3.9	3.7
Net passing yds	3,363	3,802
Comp/att	294/499	343/570
Sacks/lost	45-334	36-267
Interceptions	19	10
Percentage	58.9	60.2
Punts/avg	75-40.4	83-38.1
Fumbles/lost	40-20	19-8
Penalties/yds	121-878	128-1098
Touchdowns	34	40
Extra points	32-34	38-40
Field goals	17-27	22-33
Safeties	0	2
Kick ret./avg	55-19.5	56-20.7
Punt ret./avg	32-7.7	32-8.1

RUSHING	ATT	YDS	AVG	TD
Riddick	150	632	4.2	4
Bell	90	377	4.2	4
Kelly	41	199	4.9	0
Harmon	54	172	3.2	0
Byrum	38	156	4.1	0
Moore	33	104	3.2	1
Wilkins	3	18	6.0	0
King	4	10	2.5	0
Kidd	1	0	0.0	0
Reich	1	0	0.0	0
Broughton	1	-6	-6.0	0
Reed	3	-8	-2.7	0
TOTALS	**419**	**1654**	**3.9**	**9**

PASSING	COMP	ATT	INT	YDS	TD	COMP%	SACKS	RATE
Kelly	285	480	17	3593	22	59.4	43-330	83.3
Reich	9	19	2	104	0	47.4	2-4	24.8
TOTALS	**294**	**499**	**19**	**3697**	**22**	**58.9**	**45-334**	**80.9**

RECEIVING	CAT	YDS	AVG	TD
Reed	53	739	13.9	7
Metzelaars	49	485	9.9	3
Riddick	49	468	9.6	1
Burkett	34	778	22.9	4
Moore	23	184	8.0	0
Harmon	22	185	8.4	1
Butler	15	302	20.1	2
Byrum	13	104	8.0	1
Bell	12	142	11.8	2
Wilkins	8	74	9.3	0
Teal	6	60	10.0	1
Rolle	4	56	14.0	0
Broughton	3	71	23.7	0
Richardson	3	49	16.3	0
TOTALS	**294**	**3697**	**12.6**	**22**

KICKING	1-19	20-29	30-39	40-49	50+	TOT	PAT	PTS
Norwood	1-1	6-6	7-7	3-8	0-5	17-27	32-34	83

PUNTING	NO	AVG	LG	In 20	BL
Kidd	75	40.4	57	14	0

SCORE BY QUARTERS

BILLS	51	87	71	78	0 -	287
OPP	70	91	69	115	3 -	348

DEFENSIVE STATISTICAL LEADERS

TACKLES: Marve 85 primary - 72 assists - 157 total, Talley 68-44-112, Freeman 60-42-102, Bayless 67-34-101, Romes 48-26-74, Sanford 39-27-66, Bentley 42-21-63, B. Smith 36-27-63, Bellinger 45-13-58, McNanie 30-26-56, Cumby 20-30-50, Smerlas 28-21-49, Frazier 20-24-44, Drane 30-9-39

SACKS: B. Smith 15, McNanie 6.5, Talley 3, Marve 2.5, Smerlas 2,

FUMBLE RECOVERIES: Bellinger 2, Talley 1, Romes 1, McNanie 1, Cumby 1, Frazier 1, Hamby 1

FORCED FUMBLES: B. Smith 3, McNanie 2

INTERCEPTIONS: Romes 4-23 yards, 5.8 avg., 0 TD; Burroughs 2-49, 24.5, 0 TD

SPECIAL TEAMS STATISTICAL LEADERS

KICKOFF RETURNS: Harmon 18-321, 17.8, 0 TD; Broughton 11-243, 22.1, 0 TD

PUNT RETURNS: Pitts 18-194, 10.8, 1 TD; Broughton 12-53, 4.4, 0 TD

Jets	7	7	0	14 -	28
Bills	7	3	0	14 -	24

Attendance at Rich Stadium - 79,951

Buf: Bell 1 pass from Kelly (Norwood kick), 6:05
NYJ: Paige 2 run (Leahy kick), 9:43
NYJ: Toon 46 pass from O'Brien (Leahy kick), 11:59
Buf: FG Norwood 19, 14:55
Buf: Reed 55 pass from Kelly (Norwood kick), 1:00
NYJ: Hector 1 run (Leahy kick), 5:02
NYJ: Walker 71 pass from O'Brien (Leahy kick), 9:36
Buf: Metzelaars 4 pass from Kelly (Norwood kick), 11:05

	BUF	NYJ
First downs	19	19
Rushing yds	79	103
Passing yds	289	287
Punts-avg	7-40.7	8-34.8
Fumbles-lost	3-2	1-0
Penalties-yds	10-57	10-76
Poss. time	29:47	30:13

BILLS LEADERS: **Rushing** - Riddick 4-19, Bell 17-44, Kelly 3-8, Moore 4-8; **Passing** - Kelly 20-33-0 - 292; **Receiving** - Reed 5-95, Metzelaars 4-46, Riddick 3-26, Moore 1-3, Butler 3-70, Bell 3-38, Burkett 1-14.

JETS LEADERS: **Rushing** - McNeil 21-72, Hector 7-25, Paige 3-6, O'Brien 1-0; **Passing** - O'Brien 18-25-0 - 318; **Receiving** - Toon 6-119, Paige 4-46, Walker 3-93, McNeil 2-35, Shuler 2-17, Klever 1-8.

NOTES
• Jim Kelly made a marvelous debut, even though the Bills lost to the Jets for the fifth straight time in front of the largest crowd in Rich Stadium history. One banner read: "Jim Kelly is God."
• After a Jets punt, Kelly drove the Bills 53 yards in nine plays to his first NFL TD pass, a one-yarder to Greg Bell. His first two completions were passes of 13 and eight yards to Pete Metzelaars.
• On the ensuing series, the Jets punted again, but Walter Broughton muffed it and Tom Baldwin recovered at the 15. Freeman McNeil ran 12 yards, then Tony Paige scored the tying TD.
• Ricky Moore's fumble at the Jets 27 killed a threat early in the second quarter, and the Jets took the lead later in the second on Ken O'Brien's bomb to Al Toon. Toon beat Charlie Romes in man-to-man coverage.
• The Bills answered with an 11-play, 67-yard drive to Scott Norwood's field goal.
• The teams exchanged three punts in the scoreless third before the Bills took the lead early in the fourth on Kelly's 55-yard TD strike to Andre Reed. Kelly beat a blitz. However, the Jets came back with a 64-yard march to Johnny Hector's go-ahead score and tacked on another TD 4:34 later when Wesley Walker took a short pass on the sideline and went all the way when Derrick Burroughs

WEEK 1 GAMES	
Atl 31, NO 10	KC 24, Cinc 14
Chi 41, Clev 31	Det 13, Minn 10
Hou 31, GB 3	NE 33, Ind 3
Den 38, LAR 36	Rams 16, St.L 10
SD 50, Mia 28	Wash 41, Phil 14
Sea 30, Pitt 0	SF 31, TB 7
Dal 31, NYG 28	

gambled on the pick and lost.
• Robb Riddick returned the kickoff 44 yards to the 47 and Kelly hit Jerry Butler for 28 yards on the first play. After two incompletions, he found Metzelaars for 21, then threw a TD pass to Metzelaars to pull Buffalo within 28-24, but the Jets consumed the final 3:46.

QUOTES
• Jets coach Joe Walton on Kelly: "I'm glad to get out of here with a win. He is going to be a star in this league. I'm glad we only have to play Buffalo twice."
• Jets defensive end Mark Gastineau: "I'd compare him right up there with Marino, Fouts, any of the great quarterbacks you can think of. He's great, and the Bills are vastly improved."
• Jim Kelly: "No one in the world wanted to win this game more than I did. I had chills up and down my spine, but to tell you the truth, I was more nervous in some USFL games than I was out there today. I felt pretty comfortable. On a scale of one-to-10, I'd say I was probably a seven today. After the films, it'll probably be a six. I've never been on a losing team and I don't plan on starting now. I told everyone in the locker room to keep your heads up high. We played a good team today, but we're definitely going to win some games this year. Everybody just has to stick together." (On not getting ball at the end of the game): "Everybody was pumped up and we wanted to get a chance to run our two-minute offense and score. I was confident we'd get another shot."
• Hank Bullough: "Jim Kelly is human. No one can learn the playbook in three weeks, but he's learning fast. For crying out loud, I don't even know all our plays. But he makes plays."
• Pete Metzelaars: "He (Kelly) did some amazing things out there."

Bills	3	6	17	7	0 -	33
Bengals	7	14	0	12	3 -	36

Attendance at Riverfront Stadium - 52,714

Cin: Kinnebrew 11 run (Breech kick), 4:19
Buf: FG Norwood 20, 10:01
Cin: Brown 35 pass from Esiason (Breech kick), 3:15
Buf: Riddick 6 run (kick failed), 9:10
Cin: Brown 17 pass from Esiason (Breech kick), 14:18
Buf: FG Norwood 44, 5:17
Buf: Bell 9 run (Norwood kick), 10:51
Buf: Burkett 84 pass from Kelly (Norwood kick), 14:06
Cin: Safety, Kidd ran out of end zone, 3:04
Buf: Metzelaars fumble recovery in end zone (Norwood kick), 8:33
Cin: FG Breech 51, 9:41
Cin: Esiason 2 run (Breech kick), 14:38
Cin: FG Breech 20, :56

	BUF	CIN
First downs	20	22
Rushing yds	171	165
Passing yds	207	247
Punts-avg	4-39.7	5-33.8
Fumbles-lost	5-0	3-2
Penalties-yds	5-37	5-50
Poss. time	29:11	31:45

BILLS LEADERS: **Rushing** - Riddick 11-53, Bell 13-94, Byrum 1-5, Moore 7-15, Reed 1-4, Kelly 2-0; **Passing** - Kelly 13-22-2 - 228; **Receiving** - Reed 1-19, Metzelaars 4-36, Burkett 1-84, Moore 2-14, Butler 1-53, Byrum 2-16, Bell 2-6.

BENGALS LEADERS: **Rushing** - Kinnebrew 13-69, Brooks 8-29, Esiason 7-34, Johnson 5-25, McGee 1-8; **Passing** - Esiason 17-29-1 - 259; **Receiving** - Holman 7-81, Collinsworth 4-89, Brown 3-71, Brooks 1-9, Kattus 1-6, Kinnebrew 1-3.

NOTES
• The Bills blew a 10-point lead in the final 5:19, then lost in overtime.
• Jim Kelly's 84-yard TD pass to Chris Burkett tied for the fifth-longest in team history.
• The Bengals drove 74 yards on their opening possession to Larry Kinnebrew's TD, but the Bills pulled to within 7-3 after Darryl Talley's first NFL interception and 47-yard return to the 5.
• A short John Kidd punt set up the Bengals at the Bills 45 and Boomer Esiason hit Eddie Brown for the TD.
• The Bills answered with an 11-play, 59-yard drive which ended on Robb Riddick's run, but Scott Norwood missed the PAT. Leo Barker then intercepted Kelly and returned it to the Bills 20. Two plays later, Esiason found Brown again for a TD and a 21-9 halftime lead.
• The Bills then took control in the third. Greg Bell's 42-yard run set up a Norwood field goal on Buffalo's first possession. Then, a 25-yard pass-interference penalty against Louis Breeden on Andre Reed and a 53-yard pass to Jerry Butler led to Greg Bell's TD run. Finally, one play after a punt, Kelly hit Burkett for the go-ahead score. Burkett was five yards behind cornerback Ray Horton, who bit on a play-action fake.
• Early in the fourth, John Kidd was forced to take a safety after a bad snap by Dale Hellestrae.
• Fred Smerlas then forced Kinnebrew to fumble, Charlie Romes recovered and the Bills moved 60 yards. Bell broke

WEEK 2 GAMES	
NE 20, NYJ 6	Clev 23, Hou 20
Dal 31, Det 7	Mia 30, Ind 10
NO 24, GB 10	Wash 10, LAR 6
Sea 23, KC 17	Minn 23, TB 10
Chi 13, Phil 10	Atl 33, St.L 13
NYG 20, SD 7	Rams 16, SF 13
Den 21, Pitt 10	

a 33-yard run, then Riddick fumbled into the end zone, but Pete Metzelaars recovered for the TD.
• The Bengals got a field goal from Breech, then drove 74 yards in 11 plays to the tying TD pass to Cris Collinsworth with 22 seconds left. Carl Zander then intercepted Kelly on the first play of OT and Breech kicked the winning field goal.

QUOTES
• Jim Kelly on the OT interception: "I just misread the coverage. I've still got a lot to learn, but when you score 33 points and lose, it hurts, no doubt it hurts. We were up 10, but deep down I was thinking things were going too good. Then when we had to have it at the end, I threw the interception. What can I say, that's football. We will win, I'll tell you that. Watch out, Buffalo Bills football is coming."
• Hank Bullough: "We've got to get better on defense. We aren't going to get 24 and 33 every time out. Some teams are still going to shut us down."
• Fred Smerlas: "No one's down. It's not like they were pounding us. We were more angry than frustrated."

AFC EAST	W	L	T	CENTRAL	W	L	T	WEST	W	L	T	NFC EAST	W	L	T	CENTRAL	W	L	T	WEST	W	L	T
New England	2	0	0	Houston	1	1	0	Denver	2	0	0	Dallas	2	0	0	Chicago	2	0	0	Atlanta	2	0	0
NY Jets	1	1	0	Cincinnati	1	1	0	Seattle	2	0	0	Washington	2	0	0	Detroit	1	1	0	LA Rams	2	0	0
Miami	1	1	0	Cleveland	1	1	0	Kan. City	1	1	0	NY Giants	1	1	0	Minnesota	1	1	0	San Fran	1	1	0
Buffalo	0	2	0	Pittsburgh	0	2	0	San Diego	1	1	0	St. Louis	0	2	0	Green Bay	0	2	0	N.Orleans	1	1	0
Indianapolis	0	2	0					Raiders	0	2	0	Philadelphia	0	2	0	Tampa Bay	0	2	0				

GAME 3 - Sunday, Sept. 21, 1986 - BILLS 17, CARDINALS 10

NOTES

• The Bills snapped their eight-game regular-season losing streak and Jim Kelly got his first NFL victory, although he did it in unusual fashion. Kelly threw only 10 passes. The fewest he ever threw in a USFL game was 23 on three occasions. This was only the second time in 32 pro games that Kelly failed to top 200 yards passing.

• The Cardinals possessed the ball for 37:14 and outgained the Bills 381-176.

• After John Lee missed a field goal for the Cards, the Bills drove 51 yards to Scott Norwood's field goal as Kelly threw a 51-yard flea-flicker to Chris Burkett.

• On the first play after the kickoff, Sean McNanie sacked Neil Lomax, forced him to fumble and Guy Frazier recovered at the Cards 26. On fourth-and-one from the 2, Kelly threw an incompletion, but was roughed by Freddie Joe Nunn and the Bills had an automatic first down at the 1. Ricky Moore scored on the next play.

• Lee missed another field goal on the final play of the first half, but the Cards drove 53 yards on the opening possession of the second half and Lee made a 27-yarder. Lomax was five-for-seven for 37 yards on the drive.

• Early in the fourth, the Bills completed a 72-yard drive on Greg Bell's TD. Bell carried six times for 32 yards and Kelly hit Gary Wilkins for 26 yards on third-and-four from the Cards 36.

• Lomax hit four straight passes for 73 yards on the TD drive late in the fourth, capped by a 19-yarder to Vai Sikahema, then Lionel Washington recovered the onside kick at the Cards 49 with 59 seconds left, but after a 12-yard pass to J.T. Smith, Lomax threw four straight incompletions.

QUOTES

• Fred Smerlas on the Cards final possession: "I've seen too many things happen to this team. Especially after the last two years, you can't take anything for granted around here. Everyone was kind of numb. We had let the last two games slip away and that's in the back of your mind. After they got the one touchdown, I didn't even unbuckle my chin strap. After the last two years, you expect teams to make those plays (recover the onside kick). It was good that the defense got a chance to redeem itself. Everybody has been knocking our defense."

• Jim Kelly: "How many passes did I throw? Ten? No way. That's got to be an all-time low for me. I hope I never do that again. But hey, a win is a win. I'm a team player. If I throw 10 times every week and we win every game, I'll take that."

• Hank Bullough: "We wanted to run. You can't win in this league without running the ball. I'm a firm believer in that. I know some people have criticized me for that, but I've been coaching a lot longer than they have."

• Joe Devlin: "Maybe we played better in the first two games, but psychologically, we needed a lift. It was frustrating to play well enough to win the first two games and to have lost."

Cardinals	0	0	3	7 -	10
Bills	0	10	0	7 -	17

Attendance at Rich Stadium - 65,762

Buf: FG Norwood 35, 2:13
Buf: Moore 2 run (Norwood kick), 6:35
St.L: FG Lee 37, 5:31
Buf: Bell 6 run (Norwood kick), 2:04
St.L: Sikahema 19 pass from Lomax (Lee kick), 14:02

	BUF	St. L
First downs	10	25
Rushing yds	94	122
Passing yds	82	259
Punts-avg	5-49.0	2-32.0
Fumbles-lost	4-1	2-1
Penalties yds	6-33	7-52
Poss. time	22:46	37:14

BILLS LEADERS: Rushing - Riddick 2-7, Bell 20-79, Byrum 2-11, Moore 1-2, Kidd 1-0, Kelly 3-(-5); **Passing** - Kelly 6-10-0 - 105; **Receiving** - Metzelaars 1-10, Burkett 2-59, Moore 2-10, Wilkins 1-26.

CARDINALS LEADERS: Rushing - Ferrell 11-71, Mitchell 8-46, Anderson 7-5; **Passing** - Lomax 27-47-0 - 263; **Receiving** - Smith 6-58, Marsh 5-49, Ferrell 5-28, Mitchell 4-22, Sikahema 3-59, Holman 2-34, Anderson 2-13.

WEEK 3 GAMES

Cinc 30, Clev 13	Atl 37, Dal 35
Den 33, Phil 7	KC 27, Hou 13
Rams 24, Ind 7	NYJ 51, Mia 45
SF 26, NO 17	NYG 14, LAR 9
Minn 31, Pitt 7	Sea 38, NE 31
TB 24, Det 20	Wash 30, SD 27
Chi 25, GB 12	

GAME 4 - Sunday, Sept. 28, 1986 - CHIEFS 20, BILLS 17

NOTES

• The Bills dropped to 1-3 as Jim Kelly threw three interceptions. While he was out for a brief time, Frank Reich and Robb Riddick combined to fumble at the Chiefs 1, killing a scoring threat.

• Steve Freeman played in his 169th game, setting a new Bills record.

• Greg Bell sat out the game with a pulled groin and Riddick had his career-best game.

• The Bills scored quickly as Riddick broke a 41-yard TD run up the middle on a third-and-10 play.

• The Chiefs came back with a 75-yard drive to a Nick Lowery field goal.

• The Bills answered by moving to the Chiefs 2 when Kelly fired a 12-yard pass to Andre Reed, but Tim Cofield leveled him after the throw and knocked Kelly out of the game. Two plays later, Riddick and Reich lost the ball and Lloyd Burruss recovered at the 6.

• Later in the second quarter, Dino Hackett intercepted Kelly at the Chiefs 47 and KC needed just five plays before Todd Blackledge hit Stephone Paige for a TD.

• On the first possession of the second half, the Chiefs got to the 13, but Martin Bayless intercepted Boyce Green's halfback option pass in the end zone. The Bills then drove 80 yards in nine plays to Kelly's TD pass to Ronnie Harmon, Harmon's first NFL TD. Kelly was five-of-six for 68 yards on the drive.

• On the next series, the Bills drove 68 yards in 13 plays to Scott Norwood's field goal.

• The Chiefs responded by going 72 yards in 13 plays to Blackledge's TD pass to Paul Coffman with 4:18 left. On the first play after the kickoff, Deron Cherry intercepted Kelly at the Bills 45. Six plays later, Lowery kicked the game-winning field goal. Kelly was intercepted on the final play of the game, too.

QUOTES

• Jim Kelly: "I'm just getting tired of it. We have a good

team if everyone pulls together, not only the players. There's no doubt they want to win, but we've got to have everyone telling the players 'You're good, you can play.' We need to start building a more positive atmosphere around here. I've always been on teams that think positive, think about winning. If you think you're a loser, you'll play like a loser. We should be 4-0."

• Hank Bullough: "We had a chance to put it away, but Kelly got hurt and then we had the mix-up on the 1-yard-line. That was the biggest turnover of the game."

• Frank Reich: "That turnover (Riddick's fumble) made it a totally different game. The quarterback has to make sure the ball is in his stomach."

• Robb Riddick: "I saw the pileup at the line and I jumped too soon. I was trying to get into the end zone and I got there before he (Reich) was ready. The ball hit my hip."

• Chiefs linebacker Tim Cofield, who was charged with laying a cheap shot on Kelly: "I wasn't trying to hurt him. I don't go out there trying to be a dirty player. I was just trying to do my job, to get to him and make him throw a bad pass. Nobody blocked me on that play."

Chiefs	3	7	0	10 -	20
Bills	7	0	7	3 -	17

Attendance at Rich Stadium - 67,555

Buf: Riddick 41 run (Norwood kick), 3:54
KC: FG Lowery 24, 10:57
KC: Paige 26 pass from Blackledge (Lowery kick), 13:37
Buf: Harmon 14 pass from Kelly (Norwood kick), 7:51
Buf: FG Norwood 32, 2:21
KC: Coffman 1 pass from Blackledge (Lowery kick), 10:42
KC: FG Lowery 46, 13:53

	BUF	KC
First downs	24	20
Rushing yds	97	126
Passing yds	269	201
Punts-avg	2-42.5	4-38.5
Fumbles-lost	1-1	0-0
Penalties-yds	5-36	7-44
Poss. time	26:32	33:28

BILLS LEADERS: Rushing - Riddick 13-79, Harmon 2-13, Moore 4-5, Reich 1-0; **Passing** - Kelly 24-38-3 - 291, Reich 0-1-0 - 0; **Receiving** - Reed 5-55, Metzelaars 5-58, Riddick 5-67, Burkett 3-57, Moore 3-23, Harmon 1-14, Butler 1-5, Byrum 1-12.

CHIEFS LEADERS: Rushing - Green 9-52, Pruitt 10-49, Smith 6-12, Heard 5-10, Blackledge 1-3; **Passing** - Blackledge 17-27-0 - 210, Green 0-1-0 - 0, Marshall 0-1-0 - 0; **Receiving** - Paige 3-85, Hancock 3-56, Coffman 3-15, Smith 2-12, Pruitt 2-11, Heard 1-9, Hayes 1-8, Marshall 1-6, Arnold 1-8.

WEEK 4 GAMES

Atl 23, TB 20	Chi 44, Cinc 7
Clev 24, Det 21	Minn 42, GB 7
Phil 34, Rams 20	Den 27, NE 20
NYG 20, NO 17	NYJ 26, Ind 7
Pitt 22, Hou 16	LAR 17, SD 13
SF 31, Mia 16	Wash 19, Sea 14
Dal 31, St.L 7	

STANDINGS: FOURTH WEEK

AFC EAST	W	L	T	CENTRAL	W	L	T	WEST	W	L	T	NFC EAST	W	L	T	CENTRAL	W	L	T	WEST	W	L	T
NY Jets	3	1	0	Cincinnati	2	2	0	Denver	4	0	0	Washington	4	0	0	Chicago	4	0	0	Atlanta	4	0	0
New England	2	2	0	Cleveland	2	2	0	Seattle	3	1	0	Dallas	3	1	0	Minnesota	3	1	0	LA Rams	3	1	0
Miami	1	3	0	Houston	1	3	0	Kan. City	3	1	0	NY Giants	3	1	0	Detroit	1	3	0	San Fran	3	1	0
Buffalo	1	3	0	Pittsburgh	1	3	0	San Diego	1	3	0	Philadelphia	1	3	0	Tampa Bay	1	3	0	N.Orleans	1	3	0
Indianapolis	0	4	0					Raiders	1	3	0	St. Louis	0	4	0	Green Bay	0	4	0				

| Bills | 0 | 7 | 3 | 3 | - | 13 |
| Jets | 0 | 7 | 0 | 7 | - | 14 |

Attendance at Giants Stadium - 69,504

NYJ: Toon 4 pass from O'Brien (Leahy kick), 13:34
Buf: Bell 40 pass from Kelly (Norwood kick), 14:24
Buf: FG Norwood 23, 12:59
Buf: FG Norwood 32, 4:10
NYJ: Shuler 36 pass from O'Brien (Leahy kick), 14:03

	BUF	NYJ
First downs	16	20
Rushing yds	126	110
Passing yds	194	272
Punts-avg	7-42.0	7-43.3
Fumbles lost	1-0	1-0
Penalties-yds	11-89	11-90
Poss. time	33:01	26:59

BILLS LEADERS: Rushing - Bell 16-58, Kelly 3-30, Moore 9-38; **Passing** - Kelly 18-35-1 - 211; **Receiving** - Reed 3-17, Metzelaars 1-2, Riddick 3-28, Burkett 1-27, Moore 6-67, Bell 4-70.

JETS LEADERS: Rushing - Hector 18-117, Paige 2-1, O'Brien 1-0, Sohn 1-(-3), Ryan 3-(-5); **Passing** - O'Brien 29-39-1 - 288; **Receiving** - Toon 10-86, Shuler 6-68, Hector 9-100, Walker 2-22, Klever 2-12.

WEEK 5 GAMES

Cinc 34, GB 28	Clev 27, Pitt 24
Den 29, Dal 14	Det 24, Hou 13
SF 35, Ind 14	LAR 24, KC 17
NE 34, Mia 7	Chi 23, Minn 0
NYG 13, St.L 6	Phil 16, Atl 0
Rams 26, TB 20	Wash 14, NO 6
Sea 33, SD 7	

NOTES

• The Jets drove 80 yards in five plays to the winning TD as Ken O'Brien hit Mickey Shuler with a 36-yard TD pass with 57 seconds left. Earlier on the drive he hit Wesley Walker for 12 and Johnny Hector for 19.
• Hank Bullough's record as a head coach slipped to 3-14.
• Greg Bell returned to the lineup and had a good game, while Bruce Smith recorded two sacks.
• The game was scoreless until there was 1:26 left in the half when the Jets capped a 57-yard drive on O'Brien's TD pass to Al Toon. But the Bills took the kickoff and moved 80 yards in six plays to Jim Kelly's TD pass to Bell. Bell had a 14-yard run and Marty Lyons was penalized 15 yards for roughing Kelly.
• The Bills used 12:01 of the third quarter on one drive, an 89-yard, 17-play monster that led to Scott Norwood's first field goal. In the fourth, O'Brien's streak of 15 straight completions ended when Derrick Burroughs intercepted

him and returned it 41 yards to the Jets 32. But the Bills only managed Norwood's second field goal as Chris Burkett failed to get both feet inbounds in the end zone on a third-down pass play.
• The Bills' defense held on fourth down on the next series, and the offense got the ball with 5:31 left. After getting two first downs, the Bills were forced to punt and the Jets moved to the winning TD.

QUOTES

• Charlie Romes on how Shuler got wide open on the TD: "We just didn't have a safety in the post area, that's all."
• Steve Freeman: "I knew what the call was, I was making it. The call wasn't late coming in from the sideline. I yelled out the coverage, it's easy to do in practice, but sometimes you don't hear it with 80,000 people yelling."
• Hank Bullough: "There's no such thing as a snakebit team. I think you make your own breaks. They (the defense) all got the call except one guy (Martin Bayless). It's just a combination of a lot of things. It's one guy, then it's another guy. Things happen fast in ballgames and sometimes guys don't react to them. If there was one thing you could put your finger on, you'd tape it up to the bulletin board and say 'That's it, it's solved.' Every loss hurts, especially the ones we've had this year."
• Bruce Smith: "It's miscommunication in every respect. Miscommunication between players, coaches, everybody. Quitting is the last thing on our minds."
• Fred Smerlas: "I'm numb. I thought we were going to win the game. The way we had been playing defense, I figured there was no way they were going to drive 80 yards on us in the last two minutes."
• Jim Kelly: "I don't think I've ever played harder in a game in my life. The team did, too. We wanted to win this game so badly. I looked up in the sky and said 'God, why us? Why does this always happen to us?' We deserved to win the game."

| Bills | 7 | 0 | 0 | 7 | - | 14 |
| Dolphins | 3 | 7 | 10 | 7 | - | 27 |

Attendance at the Orange Bowl - 49,467

Mia: FG Reveiz 22, 6:07
Buf: Bell 1 run (Norwood kick), 12:45
Mia: Duper 30 pass from Marino (Reveiz kck), 13:57
Mia: FG Reveiz 36, 2:22
Mia: Hampton 4 run (Reveiz kick), 7:10
Mia: Hampton 1 run (Reveiz kick), 7:15
Buf: Reed 6 pass from Kelly (Norwood kick), 11:57

	BUF	MIA
First downs	18	27
Rushing yds	108	119
Passing yds	197	328
Punts-avg	1-34.0	0-0
Fumbles-lost	2-2	2-2
Penalties-yds	7-54	1-5
Poss. time	27:21	32:39

BILLS LEADERS: Rushing - Bell 11-48, Riddick 8-47, Kelly 3-13, Moore 2-6, Byrum 1-1, Broughton 1-(-6), Harmon 2-(-1); **Passing** - Kelly 20-28-2 - 218; **Receiving** - Reed 1-6, Metzelaars 3-25, Riddick 7-82, Burkett 1-12, Moore 1-6, Harmon 2-20, Bell 1-6, Rolle 3-48, Wilkins 1-13.

DOLPHINS LEADERS: Rushing - Hampton 17-64, Nathan 4-27, Bennett 5-23, Davenport 2-5, Marino 1-0; **Passing** - Marino 24-41-1 - 337; **Receiving** - Clayton 3-73, Pruitt 3-62, Nathan 3-47, Duper 3-46, Johnson 3-34, Hampton 3-30, Hardy 3-15, Jensen 2-11, Moore 1-19.

NOTES

• The Bills had trouble coping with the 89-degree heat. Dan Marino outgunned Jim Kelly in their first head-to-head meeting. The Bills lost for the 20th time in a row on the road.
• The game featured only one punt, only the fifth such game in NFL history.
• The game was the Bills last in the Orange Bowl. They finished 2-18-1 all-time in the stadium.
• It was Kelly's first game in the Orange Bowl since he starred there for the University of Miami.
• Miami took a 3-0 lead on the first possession on a Fuad Reveiz field goal. Six minutes later, the Bills went ahead as Eugene Marve stripped Bruce Hardy and George Cumby returned the fumble 38 yards to the Miami 14. Greg Bell scored six plays later
• The TD pass to Mark Duper came three plays after Robb Riddick's fumble was recovered by Jerome Foster.
• In the third, Donovan Rose intercepted Kelly and returned it 27 yards to the Bills 34, leading to a Reveiz field goal. Less than five minutes later, Miami drove 67 yards in five plays to Lorenzo Hampton's TD run. The key play was a 39-yard pass to Mark Clayton to the Bills 28.

WEEK 6 GAMES

Chi 20, Hou 7	Den 31, SD 14
Det 21, GB 14	Clev 20, KC 7
Atl 26, Rams 14	Minn 27, SF 24
NO 17, Ind 14	NYJ 31, NE 24
NYG 35, Phil 3	St.L 30, TB 19
LAR 14, Sea 10	Dal 30, Wash 6
Cinc 24, Pitt 22	

• Hampton's one-yard TD run in the fourth capped a 12-play, 76-yard drive.
• The Bills scored late on Kelly's TD pass to Andre Reed after a 12-play, 76-yard march.

QUOTES

• Hank Bullough: "That (Riddick's fumble in the second quarter) was probably the turning point of the game. Miami was the better team today. We were outplayed and outcoached. We had a lot to do with losing the ballgame."
• Fred Smerlas: "I can't wait until they build that new stadium. They can have this place. When he's (Marino) on like he was today, there isn't a quarterback even close. When he's clicking you don't have a prayer."
• Miami quarterback Dan Marino: "I didn't see this as a duel between me and Kelly. I was just looking for a win to get us back on track."
• Jim Kelly: "I've never been 1-5 in my life. After you're 1-5, you try to find things to say, but you can't say anything because we haven't done anything lately. I just hope everybody pulls behind me and starts thinking like me. As far as I'm concerned, I'm not going to let up. I can't say what everyone else is doing. I didn't really think anything about Miami or the Orange Bowl. I just wanted to come back here and win. We couldn't get our receivers deep like we wanted them because they were playing corner roll. They had the corners up tight on us, which wasn't giving us the outside. That's why we had to go underneath. As a quarterback, there's things you want to say, but you can't. We had a game plan, but there were things we had to do and we didn't."

STANDINGS: SIXTH WEEK

AFC EAST	W	L	T	CENTRAL	W	L	T	WEST	W	L	T	NFC EAST	W	L	T	CENTRAL	W	L	T	WEST	W	L	T
NY Jets	5	1	0	Cincinnati	4	2	0	Denver	6	0	0	Washington	5	1	0	Chicago	6	0	0	Atlanta	5	1	0
New England	3	3	0	Cleveland	4	2	0	Seattle	4	2	0	NY Giants	5	1	0	Minnesota	4	2	0	LA Rams	4	2	0
Miami	2	4	0	Houston	1	5	0	Kan. City	3	3	0	Dallas	4	2	0	Detroit	3	3	0	San Fran	4	2	0
Buffalo	1	5	0	Pittsburgh	1	5	0	Raiders	3	3	0	Philadelphia	2	4	0	Tampa Bay	1	5	0	N.Orleans	2	4	0
Indianapolis	0	6	0					San Diego	1	5	0	St. Louis	1	5	0	Green Bay	0	6	0				

NOTES

• The Bills ended their three-game losing streak as Ronnie Harmon stepped in for the injured Greg Bell and Robb Riddick and contributed to the victory. Bell missed the game with a groin injury, Riddick broke a bone in his wrist in the third quarter.

• Another rookie, Rodney Bellinger gave the Bills the early lead by scooping up Randy McMillan's fumble and returning it for a TD. The Colts had been pinned back by John Kidd's punt to the 4.

• Dean Biasucci missed a 37-yard field goal on the next series, but Jim Kelly was intercepted four plays later by Duane Bickett and Biasucci atoned with a 46-yarder.

• The Bills turned around and drove 61 yards to Scott Norwood's field goal with Harmon making a 14-yard run on third-and-eight at the Bills 35 to keep the drive moving.

• The Colts answered with another Biasucci field goal, but the Bills then drove 73 yards in seven plays to Kelly's TD pass to Andre Reed. Kelly completed all six of his passes for 67 yards on the march.

• Charlie Romes stopped the Colts on the first possession of the second half with an interception, but Riddick fumbled on the next play. The Colts then drove 39 yards to Jack Trudeau's TD pass to Bill Brooks.

• Late in the third, Kelly hit Walter Broughton for 57 yards, then was roughed by Bickett for a 15-yard penalty. On the next play, he hit Reed for the clinching TD.

• The Bills defense stopped the Colts twice on fourth down in the fourth quarter to secure the victory.

• Hank Bullough revealed afterward that he had been trapped in an elevator two hours before the game.

QUOTES

• Ralph Wilson: "Everybody was losing patience with Hank except me. I called Hank last Friday – it happened to be my birthday – and told him he had given me a wonderful birthday present. He's taking all the heat in Buffalo and they're finally off my back for a while."

• Hank Bullough: "I'm very proud of our guys. They hung in there when there have been some adverse conditions. People say we don't have togetherness. We have togetherness." (On Harmon): "The young kid had to go in there and carry the load. He made some mistakes, but he played good enough for us to be a winner. He ran the wrong way a few times, but he ran the right way, too." (On getting stuck in the elevator): "They said 'Who is it? and I said 'What the hell difference does it make? Do you have to be President Reagan to get out of here?'"

• Rodney Bellinger: "That was the biggest play I ever made in my whole football career. I saw the ball pop out. Nobody seemed to notice it but me and I thought to myself 'Don't fall on it, pick it up.'"

WEEK 7 GAMES

Minn 23, Chi 7	Dal 17, Phil 14
Rams 14, Det 10	GB 17, Clev 14
Cinc 31, Hou 28	LAR 30, Mia 28
NE 34, Pitt 0	Sea 17, NYG 12
Wash 28, St.L 21	KC 42, SD 41
NO 38, TB 7	NYJ 22, Den 10
Atl 10, SF 10 (OT)	

Colts	3	3	7	0	-	13
Bills	7	10	7	0	-	24

Attendance at Rich Stadium - 50,050

Buf: Bellinger 15 fumble return (Norwood kick), 2:54
Ind: FG Biasucci 46, 12:43
Buf: FG Norwood 37, 1:33
Ind: FG Biasucci 44, 6:54
Buf: Reed 6 pass from Kelly (Norwood kick), 10:45
Ind: Brooks 18 pass from Trudeau (Biasucci kick), 6:00
Buf: Reed 13 pass from Kelly (Norwood kick), 14:10

	BUF	IND
First downs	21	20
Rushing yds	121	130
Passing yds	243	167
Punts-avg	2-23.0	3-45.7
Fumbles-lost	4-1	1-1
Penalties-yds	8-69	13-151
Poss. time	26:24	33:36

BILLS LEADERS: Rushing - Bell 5-24, Kelly 2-2, Harmon 15-86, Moore 3-9; **Passing** - Kelly 20-31-2 - 252; **Receiving** - Reed 3-33, Metzelaars 1-2, Riddick 2-17, Burkett 6-76, Moore 1-8, Harmon 2-15, Butler 2-30, Broughton 3-71.

COLTS LEADERS: Rushing - McMillan 13-47, Bentley 7-51, Trudeau 1-0, Gill 4-25, Wonsley 3-7; **Passing** - Trudeau 19-41-1 - 175; **Receiving** - McMillan 4-27, Bouza 7-69, Brooks 5-76, Wonsley 1-2, Beach 1-3, Bentley 1-(-2).

NOTES

• New England dominated on the line of scrimmage, sacking Jim Kelly five times (3 1/2 by Andre Tippett) and knocking him down at least 10 other times. Kelly came out with eight minutes remaining.

• A prophetic sign read: "Kelly needs less PATS on his back".

• The Pats scored the first time they had the ball, driving 57 yards to Craig James' TD.

• Early in the second, the Pats drove 68 yards to Tony Franklin's field goal, the key play a 23-yard scramble by Tony Eason.

• A few minutes later, Kelly was intercepted by Johnny Rembert at the 4. Rembert ran 37 yards before lateraling to Tippett who went 32 more. Three plays later, Robert Weathers scored.

• Late in the half, Scott Norwood missed a 53-yard field goal, but on the next play, Rodney Bellinger recovered Tony Collins' fumble at the Pats 31. The threat died when Fred Marion intercepted Kelly at the 1.

• In the third, following a Franklin miss, the Bills drove 66 yards to Norwood's field goal. Kelly was sacked by Brent Williams, but on third-and-20, Raymond Clayborn was nailed for a 47-yard interference penalty to the 11.

• The Pats answered that with a Franklin field goal, the key play a 24-yard pass to Stephen Starring.

• In the fourth, Frank Reich was intercepted twice by Ronnie Lippett, the second one setting up Franklin's last field goal on the final play of the game.

QUOTES

• Jim Kelly: "They put pressure on me all day long. As a quarterback you try not to look at the guys coming at you. Today, it was awfully hard not to notice them. I tried to throw (after suffering a twisted back), but it just hurt really bad. I said 'What's the use going out there if I'm not going to be able to throw and give the team 100 percent. This is probably the worst I've ever felt." (On the post-game speech delivered by Ralph Wilson): "He said he's going to get down to the bottom of what's wrong. He said we looked like we were unorganized."

• Fred Smerlas on Ralph Wilson: "I think he's as bewildered as the players are. He's really worked hard putting together a good team. He went out and got Jim Kelly, he streamlined the front office. He's put a lot of money into improving this team, and he hasn't seen any return on his investment. I think we have a lot of guys who are flustered and need to air things out. When you're losing, things fester. We have to get them out in the open."

• Hank Bullough: "We got beat offensively, defensively and in coaching. We put our defense in some tough situations, and on offense, we didn't score when we got down there. Kelly didn't have one of his better games and I think he'd be the first one to admit it. I thought our pass protection was pretty good at the start, but when you have to do it on every down, we're not very good at it."

Patriots	7	10	3	3	-	23
Bills	0	0	3	0	-	3

Attendance at Rich Stadium - 77,808

NE: C. James 2 run (Franklin kick), 2:24
NE: FG Franklin 31, 3:53
NE: Weathers 16 run (Franklin kick), 8:28
Buf: FG Norwood 26, 9:26
NE: FG Franklin 27, 14:54
NE: FG Franklin 26, 15:00

	BUF	NE
First downs	16	20
Rushing yds	77	125
Passing yds	147	173
Punts-avg	5-41.6	4-46.5
Fumbles-lost	1-0	1-1
Penalties-yds	8-50	8-97
Poss. time	26:49	33:11

BILLS LEADERS: Rushing - Kelly 4-29, Harmon 16-39, Byrum 1-2, Moore 2-7; **Passing** - Kelly 13-26-2 - 166, Reich 2-8-2 - 15; **Receiving** - Metzelaars 3-26, Burkett 2-33, Moore 4-30, Harmon 3-36, Butler 2-24, Richardson 1-32.

PATRIOTS LEADERS: Rushing - Eason 4-55, Weathers 6-30, Collins 9-23, James 15-13, Tatupu 5-4; **Passing** - Eason 17-26-0 - 206; **Receiving** - Hawthorne 4-26, Morgan 3-49, Fryar 3-47, Collins 3-36, Starring 1-24, Tatupu 1-10, Baty 1-8, Scott 1-6.

WEEK 8 GAMES

Rams 14, Atl 7	Pitt 30, Cinc 9
Clev 23, Minn 20	Chi 13, Det 7
LAR 28, Hou 17	Mia 17, Ind 13
NYJ 28, NO 23	Dal 37, St.L 6
Phil 23, SD 7	SF 31, GB 17
Den 20, Sea 13	KC 27, TB 20
NYG 27, Wash 20	

STANDINGS: EIGHTH WEEK

AFC EAST	W	L	T	CENTRAL	W	L	T	WEST	W	L	T	NFC EAST	W	L	T	CENTRAL	W	L	T	WEST	W	L	T
NY Jets	7	1	0	Cincinnati	5	3	0	Denver	7	1	0	Washington	6	2	0	Chicago	7	1	0	LA Rams	6	2	0
New England	5	3	0	Cleveland	5	3	0	Seattle	5	3	0	NY Giants	6	2	0	Minnesota	5	3	0	Atlanta	5	2	1
Miami	3	5	0	Pittsburgh	2	6	0	Kan. City	5	3	0	Dallas	6	2	0	Detroit	3	5	0	San Fran	5	2	1
Buffalo	2	6	0	Houston	1	7	0	Raiders	5	3	0	Philadelphia	3	5	0	Tampa Bay	1	7	0	N.Orleans	3	5	0
Indianapolis	0	8	0					San Diego	1	7	0	St. Louis	1	7	0	Green Bay	1	7	0				

Bills	0	0	14	14	-	28
Buccaneers	10	10	0	14	-	34

Attendance at Tampa Stadium - 32,806

TB: FG Igwebuike 49, 8:49
TB: Franklin fumble recovery in end zone (Igwebuike kick), 9:00
TB: FG Igwebuike 26, 10:28
TB: Young 2 run (Igwebuike kick), 10:45
Buf: Metzelaars 1 pass from Kelly (Norwood kick), 7:37
Buf: Metzelaars 44 pass from Kelly (Norwood kick), 14:43
TB: Young 1 run (Igwebuike kick), 2:54
Buf: Pitts 49 punt return (Norwood kick), 7:28
TB: Wilder 45 run (Igwebuike kick), 8:33
Buf: Butler 9 pass from Kelly (Norwood kick), 11:40

	BUF	TB
First downs	23	20
Rushing yds	79	135
Passing yds	324	171
Punts-avg	4-35.8	4-36.8
Fumbles-lost	4-3	1-0
Penalties-yds	12-102	8-102
Poss. time	27:48	32:12

BILLS LEADERS: Rushing - Riddick 10-35, Kelly 5-42, Harmon 4-2; **Passing** - Kelly 29-39-0 - 342; **Receiving** - Reed 3-38, Metzelaars 7-113, Riddick 7-50, Harmon 6-45, Butler 3-71, Richardson 2-17.
BUCCANEERS LEADERS: Rushing - Wilder 20-97, Young 7-32, Wonsley 4-11, Carter 1-(-5); **Passing** - Young 14-24-0 - 193; **Receiving** - Wilder 5-50, Magee 4-52, Bell 3-23, Carter 1-45, Harris 1-23.

WEEK 9 GAMES

NE 25, Atl 17	Cinc 24, Det 17
Clev 24, Ind 9	NYG 17, Dal 14
Den 21, LAR 10	Pitt 27, GB 3
Mia 28, Hou 7	KC 24, SD 23
NYJ 38, Sea 7	NO 23, SF 10
St.L 13, Phil 10	Rams 20, Chi 17
Wash 44, Minn 38 (OT)	

NOTES

• The Bills fell behind, 20-0, at the half, then rallied and could have won had Robb Riddick not dropped Jim Kelly's pass at the goal line on the final play of the game.
• Riddick was wearing a cast to protect a broken bone in his left wrist. He caught seven passes in the game.
• The Bucs took a 10-0 lead in the first quarter as Donald Igwebuike made a field goal, then Pat Franklin recovered a muffed kickoff in the end zone by Ron Pitts for a touchdown 11 seconds later.
• Riddick's fumble, recovered by Bob Nelson at the Bills 31 led to another Igwebuike field goal in the second quarter. Seventeen seconds later, after Rod Jones recovered Walter Broughton's fumble of the ensuing kickoff at the 2, Steve Young scored on a keeper to make it 20-0.
• The Bills began their comeback in the third, driving 85 yards to Kelly's TD pass to Pete Metzelaars, the key play an interference call on Vito McKeever that gave the Bills a first down at the 5.
• Later in the third, the Bills drove 93 yards, as Metzelaars caught a 44-yard TD pass.
• Young hit Gerald Carter for 45 yards, then Derrick Burroughs was called for interference in the end zone to set up Young's second TD run early in the fourth for a 27-14 lead. But the Bills got the points back five minutes later on Pitts' 49-yard punt return TD.
• The Bucs applied the killer 1:05 later when James Wilder broke a 45-yard TD run. But 3:07 later, Kelly found Jerry Butler for a TD to cap a 68-yard drive, 20 of the yards coming on two scrambles.
• Igwebuike missed a 48-yard field goal with 1:28 left. Kelly then hit Butler for 47 yards to the 8. After a five-yard pass to Eric Richardson, three straight incompletions ended the game.

QUOTES

• Jim Kelly: "It makes you so mad. You take the team down the field and on the last play, the ball goes through a guys hands. I'm not blaming Robb. We shouldn't have been in that position anyway. When I looked up at the scoreboard (when down 20-0), I thought about the last time I played against Steve Young in the USFL. I told our guys we came back in LA, I'm not going to give up. I knew we could come back. Sometime, the breaks are going to go our way. Maybe He (God) has something special planned for us."
• Robb Riddick: "It hit me right in the hands and just went right on through. I should have had it. As a little kid you always realize that if the ball hits your hands you should have it. It was just one of those situations. I think it hit the cast, but I had been catching the ball."

Steelers	0	0	12	0	-	12
Bills	6	7	0	3	-	16

Attendance at Rich Stadium - 72,000

Buf: Reed 3 pass from Kelly (kick failed), 8:45
Buf: Riddick 5 run (Norwood kick), 11:54
Pit: Jackson 5 run (kick failed), :16
Pit: Thompson 11 pass from Malone (kick failed), 4:49
Buf: FG Norwood 29, 4:42

	BUF	PIT
First downs	18	11
Rushing yds	172	53
Passing yds	76	132
Punts-avg	7-33.4	10-37.0
Fumbles-lost	2-1	1-0
Penalties-yds	7-40	15-100
Poss. time	36:08	23:52

BILLS LEADERS: Rushing - Riddick 125-108, Byrum 11-40, Moore 1-14, Kelly 2-7, Harmon 3-3; **Passing** - Kelly 11-22-0 - 95; **Receiving** - Reed 3-34, Moore 3-23, Riddick 2-15, Metzelaars 1-10, Butler 1-9, Byrum 1-4.

STEELERS LEADERS: Rushing - Abercrombie 10-29, Jackson 8-24; **Passing** - Malone 18-36-1 - 142; **Receiving** - Abercrombie 5-28, Gothard 4-29, Erenberg 3-25, Sweeney 2-26, Thompson 2-18, Jackson 2-16.

NOTES

• The Bills won in Marv Levy's debut as they overcame wind gusts of up to 40 mph.
• Robb Riddick enjoyed the first 100-yard rushing game of his career.
• The Bills took the wind in the first quarter and held the Steelers to five yards offense while taking a 6-0 lead with a 49-yard drive following a 27-yard Harry Newsome punt. Jim Kelly hit Andre Reed for the TD on third-and-goal. The PAT was no good after the wind blew the snap off course.
• In the second quarter, the Bills made it 13-0, driving 71 yards in seven plays without throwing a pass. Riddick had five carries for 50 yards, including a 26-yard run, then a five-yard TD burst.
• The Steelers rallied with the wind in the third. Eric Richardson fumbled the second-half kickoff and Mike Merriweather recovered at the 5. On the next play, Earnest Jackson scored. The PAT snap was fumbled.
• On the next series, the Bills had to punt and John Kidd managed a five-yarder to the Bills 29. Four plays later, Mark Malone hit Weegie Thompson for a TD, but again, holder Newsome mishandled the snap.
• The teams traded punts twice, and the Steelers made a mistake on their second punt by not calling timeout before the third quarter ended. Into the wind on the first play of the fourth, Newsome punted just 20 yards to the Steelers 48. The Bills then drove 36 yards to Scott Norwood's field goal with Kelly throwing just one pass. The key play was Merriweather's offside penalty that gave the Bills a first down at the Steelers 20.
• The Steelers got to the Bills 29 but Rodney Bellinger intercepted Mark Malone at the goal line on the last play.

QUOTES

• Marv Levy: "Our players and coaches had their eye on the target early in the week despite the unsettling aspects of having a new coach. Their minds were on the Steelers, not me. I didn't call the plays, I left that to Bob Leahy. You try instead to promote philosophical ideas. The goal was to get them to be unselfish and rely on the other players. Winning didn't need to be the goal. Winning will come if you do the other things."
• Kent Hull: "I've seen hurricanes in Mississippi with less velocity than that. I told the offensive line that we've got to open some holes if we want to win this game."
• Jim Kelly on Levy: "He's not a rah-rah kind of guy, but he says the right thing at the right time. I'll tell you what, he's a smart man. It's a new atmosphere around here now. We're not in meetings 10 hours a day. We were physically and mentally drained. We get to relax, enjoy ourselves a little bit. Football is fun around here again."
• Robb Riddick: "We did almost anything we wanted today because we controlled the line of scrimmage. I think the wind had a lot to do with it (his performance). What happened last week happened. I didn't think about it this whole game. We joked about it in practice. Jim would throw me a pass and if I caught it, he'd say 'Why didn't you do that last week?'"

WEEK 10 GAMES

Chi 23, TB 3	Hou 32, Cinc 28
LAR 17, Dal 13	NO 6, Rams 0
Minn 24, Det 10	NE 30, Ind 21
NYG 17, Phil 14	NYJ 28, Atl 14
SF 43, St.L 17	SD 9, Den 3
KC 27, Sea 7	Wash 16, GB 7
Clev 26, Mia 16	

STANDINGS: TENTH WEEK

AFC EAST	W	L	T	CENTRAL	W	L	T	WEST	W	L	T	NFC EAST	W	L	T	CENTRAL	W	L	T	WEST	W	L	T
NY Jets	9	1	0	Cleveland	7	3	0	Denver	8	2	0	Washington	8	2	0	Chicago	8	2	0	LA Rams	7	3	0
New England	7	3	0	Cincinnati	6	4	0	Kan. City	7	3	0	NY Giants	8	2	0	Minnesota	6	4	0	San Fran	6	3	1
Miami	4	6	0	Pittsburgh	3	7	0	Raiders	6	4	0	Dallas	6	4	0	Detroit	3	7	0	Atlanta	5	4	1
Buffalo	3	7	0	Houston	2	8	0	Seattle	5	5	0	Philadelphia	3	7	0	Tampa Bay	2	8	0	N.Orleans	5	5	0
Indianapolis	0	10	0					San Diego	2	8	0	St. Louis	2	8	0	Green Bay	1	9	0				

GAME 11 - Sunday, Nov. 16, 1986 - DOLPHINS 34, BILLS 24

Dolphins	0	10	10	14	- 34
Bills	7	14	3	0	- 24

Attendance at Rich Stadium - 72,474

Buf: Byrum 10 pass from Kelly (Norwood kick), 9:31
Mia: Davenport 19 pass from Marino (Reveiz kick), :58
Buf: Riddick 11 run (Norwood kick), 11:21
Buf: Butler 25 pass from Kelly (Norwood kick), 14:39
Mia: FG Reveiz 52, 15:00
Mia: FG Reveiz 36, 8:12
Mia: Duper 27 pass from Marino (Reveiz kick), 10:29
Buf: FG Norwood 39, 14:50
Mia: Johnson 4 pass from Marino (Reveiz kick), 3:05
Mia: Hampton 2 pass from Marino (Reveiz kick), 7:56

	BUF	MIA
First downs	14	29
Rushing yds	80	85
Passing yds	181	389
Punts-avg	6-47.7	4-43.0
Fumbles-lost	1-1	0-0
Penalties-yds	7-55	5-64
Poss. time	19:53	40:07

BILLS LEADERS: Rushing - Byrum 6-33, Kelly 2-25, Riddick 8-23, Harmon 1-(-1); **Passing** - Kelly 17-33-0 - 189; **Receiving** - Reed 3-51, Byrum 4-39, Harmon 3-30, Metzelaars 3-26, Butler 2-40, Riddick 2-3.
DOLPHINS LEADERS: Rushing - Hampton 11-45, Davenport 10-29, Nathan 1-14, Bennett 1-0, Marino 1-(-3); **Passing** - Marino 39-54-0 - 404; **Receiving** - Hampton 9-48, Duper 7-109, Moore 4-22, Hardy 7-50, Clayton 3-70, Davenport 3-35, Nathan 2-22, Johnson 2-11, Pruitt 1-24, Bennett 1-13.

WEEK 11 GAMES

Chi 13, Atl 10	LAR 27, Clev 24
Dal 24, SD 21	Det 13, Phil 11
Pitt 21, Hou 10	NYJ 31, Ind 16
Den 38, KC 17	NE 30, Rams 28
NYG 22, Minn 20	NO 16, St.L 7
Cinc 34, Sea 7	GB 31, TB 7
Wash 14, SF 6	

NOTES

• Dan Marino outgunned Jim Kelly in a shootout as the Dolphins beat the Bills for the sixth straight time and handed Marv Levy his first loss as Bills head coach. Marino's 39 completions were the most ever against the Bills. The Dolphins scored two TDs in the fourth to pull out the victory.
• Jerry Butler suffered a broken right ankle catching a second-quarter TD pass.
• Bruce Smith raised his sack total to 10 in 11 games, Ray Bentley led the way with 10 tackles.
• The Bills drove 84 yards in 11 plays to Kelly's TD pass to Carl Byrum in the first quarter.
• Miami got that back early in the second quarter with a 67-yard drive to Ron Davenport's TD reception.
• Fred Smerlas blocked a field goal attempt on the next Miami possession and Steve Freeman returned it 33 yards to the Miami 41. Eight plays later, Robb Riddick scored.
• The Bills made it 21-7 on the next series, going 72 yards to Butler's costly TD catch, but Marino's 15-yard pass to Tony Nathan with 11 seconds left and an unsportsmanlike conduct penalty on Lucious Sanford moved the ball to the Bills 35. Fuad Reveiz made a 52-yard field goal as the half ended.
• Reveiz made a 36-yarder to cap a 65-yard drive early in the third. Two plays after the kickoff, Riddick fumbled and Paul Lankford recovered at the Bills 36, leading to Marino's TD pass to Mark Duper.
• Kelly's 30-yard pass to Chris Burkett set up Scott Norwood's field goal late in the third, but the Dolphins answered with a 67-yard drive to Marino's go-ahead TD pass to Dan Johnson. After a Bills punt, Miami went 83 yards in 10 plays to Lorenzo Hampton's TD reception. The Bills punted again and the Dolphins killed the final 6:05, getting four first downs.

QUOTES

• Fred Smerlas: "The headline writers will have an easy time with this one. Just call it the Dan Marino Show. I thought we could rattle him. He sometimes gets impatient when you take the deep stuff away from him. But he kept his poise today. It's a sign of maturity."
• Sean McNanie: "Marino is a lethal weapon. They should put a license on him."
• Jim Kelly on Sanford's penalty right before the half: "When we got to the locker room, there was a bunch of people ticked off. When you have a stupid penalty like that, it sort of takes your enthusiasm away. That really hurt. You want to go in with the advantage, not them."
• Marv Levy: "One of my jobs is to help this team get over the hump, to realize it can win in the second half. Confidence builds slowly, but once you get there, confidence breeds confidence."

GAME 12 - Sunday, Nov. 23, 1986 - PATRIOTS 22, BILLS 19

Bills	0	3	3	13	- 19
Patriots	9	6	0	7	- 22

Attendance at Sullivan Stadium - 60,455

NE: Safety: Kelly fumbled out of end zone, :17
NE: C. James 4 run (Franklin kick), 2:53
NE: FG Franklin 37, 2:53
NE: FG Franklin 47, 10:55
Buf: FG Norwood 48, 14:56
Buf: FG Norwood 34, 6:25
Buf: FG Norwood 33, 2:00
Buf: FG Norwood 28, 9:37
Buf: Riddick 31 pass from Kelly (Norwood kick), 12:10
NE: Baty 13 pass from Eason (Franklin kick), 13:20

	BUF	NE
First downs	13	17
Rushing yds	49	68
Passing yds	192	193
Punts-avg	6-37.3	10-34.5
Fumbles-lost	3-1	2-0
Penalties-yds	9-65	5-35
Poss. time	26:30	33:30

BILLS LEADERS: Rushing - Byrum 6-24, Riddick 12-21, Kelly 1-8, Reed 1-(-4); **Passing** - Kelly 22-32-1 - 250; **Receiving** - Riddick 6-95, Reed 5-65, Metzelaars 4-25, Byrum 4-30, Burkett 1-19, Teal 1-11, Wilkins 1-5.
PATRIOTS LEADERS: Rushing - James 15-33, Eason 6-25, Collins 7-9, Tatupu 2-1; **Passing** - Eason 24-33-1 - 229, James 0-1-0 - 0; **Receiving** - Collins 8-84, James 6-32, Baty 4-36, Morgan 3-45, Starring 1-13, Fryar 1-10, Tatupu 1-9.

NOTES

• The Bills rallied from a 15-0 deficit to take 19-15 lead with 2:50 left, only to see the Pats drive 60 yards in five plays to Tony Eason's TD pass to Greg Baty with 1:40 left.
• Jim Kelly was sacked six times and killed the final Buffalo chance by throwing an interception.
• On the second play of the game, Larry McGrew sacked Kelly, forcing a fumble which Don Blackmon kicked through the end zone for a safety.
• Midway through the first quarter, after a short John Kidd punt, the Pats drove 30 yards to Craig James' TD.
• Eason's 22-yard scramble keyed a march that led to Tony Franklin's first field goal. Franklin made another, his 14th in a row, later in the second quarter.
• Steve Tasker blocked a Rich Camarillo punt with 28 seconds left in the half and Hal Garner recovered at the Pats 22. Scott Norwood kicked his first field goal with four seconds left.
• Norwood then kicked three field goals to get the Bills within 15-12. The first one capped a 44-yard drive, the second came after the Bills reached the 11 but couldn't punch it in, and the third came after Fred Smerlas' inter-

WEEK 12 GAMES

SF 20, Atl 0	Wash 41, Dal 14
NYG 19, Den 16	Det 38, TB 17
Chi 12, GB 10	Hou 31, Ind 17
St.L 23, KC 14	Cinc 24, Minn 20
Rams 26, NO 13	Sea 24, Phil 20
LAR 37, SD 31 (OT)	Mia 45, NYJ 3
Clev 37, Pitt 31 (OT)	

ception at the Pats 17. The Bills then took the lead as Sean McNanie sacked Eason to force a punt. Kelly hit Robb Riddick for 29 yards on first down, then hit Riddick for a 31-yard TD.
• But Stephen Starring returned the ensuing kickoff 34 yards to the 40. Tony Collins then made three receptions in a row, the last on third down for 15 yards. Eason then hit Stanley Morgan for 24 and on the next play, found Baty for the winning TD.
• From the Pats 44, Kelly saw his streak of 104 passes without an interception ended by Ronnie Lippett.

QUOTES

• Pats coach Raymond Berry: "Buffalo didn't disappoint us, did they? Our philosophy all week was they were a fine, hustling football team with an outstanding quarterback and we knew we'd be in for a long, hard day. And that's exactly what happened."
• Fred Smerlas reacting to criticism of the defense by Jim Kelly: "I don't read what Kelly says in the papers, but sometimes you have to check your own laundry. He's right in saying you've got to get the ball back to score, but you've got to score when you get it back. I realize he's getting a little flustered. He wants to win bad and he's not used to being in this situation. Sometimes out of frustration, people say things they don't mean. It wasn't a case of our defense folding up, it was a case of Tony Eason making some great plays. He's come a long way."
• Marv Levy: "I told them I don't want anyone feeling good about this game. I don't want them castigating themselves, but I don't want them looking to rationalize."

STANDINGS: TWELFTH WEEK

AFC EAST	W	L	T	CENTRAL	W	L	T	WEST	W	L	T	NFC EAST	W	L	T	CENTRAL	W	L	T	WEST	W	L	T
NY Jets	10	2	0	Cleveland	8	4	0	Denver	9	3	0	Washington	10	2	0	Chicago	10	2	0	LA Rams	8	4	0
New England	9	3	0	Cincinnati	8	4	0	Raiders	8	4	0	NY Giants	10	2	0	Minnesota	6	6	0	San Fran	7	4	1
Miami	6	6	0	Pittsburgh	4	8	0	Kan. City	7	5	0	Dallas	7	5	0	Detroit	5	7	0	N.Orleans	6	6	0
Buffalo	3	9	0	Houston	3	9	0	Seattle	6	6	0	Philadelphia	3	9	0	Tampa Bay	2	10	0	Atlanta	5	6	1
Indianapolis	0	12	0					San Diego	2	10	0	St. Louis	3	9	0	Green Bay	2	10	0				

Bills	0	10	7	0 -	17
Chiefs	7	0	0	7 -	14

Attendance at Arrowhead Stadium - 31,492

KC: Paige 12 pass from Kenney (Lowery kick), 7:47
Buf: FG Norwood 47, :09
Buf: Reed 9 pass from Kelly (Norwood kick), 8:53
Buf: Reed 10 pass from Kelly (Norwood kick), 6:12
KC: Heard 1 run (Lowery kick), 10:26

	BUF	KC
First downs	25	26
Rushing yds	164	73
Passing yds	172	273
Punts-avg	5-32.8	4-40.0
Fumbles-lost	1-1	1-0
Penalties-yds	11-87	9-62
Poss. time	33:26	26:34

BILLS LEADERS: Rushing - Riddick 27-118, Byrum 10-40, Harmon 1-8, Kelly 1-(-2); **Passing** - Kelly 17-34-1 - 190; **Receiving** - Reed 7-95, Riddick 4-33, Metzelaars 3-15, Burkett 2-44, Byrum 1-3.

CHIEFS LEADERS: Rushing - Pruitt 9-23, Heard 4-22, Green 4-17, Kenney 2-9, Moriarty 2-2; **Passing** - Kenney 25-50-3 - 286; **Receiving** - Paige 9-119, Marshall 4-86, Green 3-19, Smith 3-18, Coffman 2-15, Arnold 2-11, Moriarty 1-19, Heard 1-(-1).

NOTES
• The Bills avoided tying Houston's NFL record for consecutive road losses as they ended their 22-game road losing streak. Their last road win also was in Kansas City on Dec. 4, 1983.
• Robb Riddick gained a career-high 118 yards.
• The Chiefs drove 83 yards in 12 plays to take the lead in the first quarter. Bill Kenney hit Stephone Paige for three separate 12-yard gains, including the TD, and also threw 26 yards to Henry Marshall.
• The Bills took the kickoff and moved 55 yards in 14 plays to Scott Norwood's field goal. The Bills were stopped, but Bill Maas was penalized for running into punter John Kidd, giving the Bills a first down. Robb Riddick had a 12-yard run and Jim Kelly hit Andre Reed for 12 yards.
• After Nick Lowery missed a 41-yard field goal, the Bills drove 77 yards in 10 plays to Kelly's TD pass to Reed. The keys were a 29-yard pass to Chris Burkett and a personal foul penalty on the Chiefs.
• In the third, the Bills drove 66 yards in 11 plays to Reed's second TD reception.
• At the end of the third, Charlie Romes made an end zone interception to kill a scoring chance.
• The Chiefs drew within 17-14 with an 80-yard drive in the fourth, capped by Herman Heard's TD, then Pete

WEEK 13 GAMES	
GB 44, Det 40	Sea 31, Dal 14
Atl 20, Mia 14	Den 34, Cinc 28
Clev 13, Hou 10	Rams 17, NYJ 3
NE 21, NO 20	Chi 13, Pit 10 (OT)
Minn 45, TB 13	Wash 20, St.L 17
SD 17, Ind 3	NYG 21, SF 17
Phil 33, LAR 27 (OT)	

Metzelaars fumbled right after the kickoff at the Bills 39, Kevin Ross recovering. However, Romes made another end zone interception.
• The Chiefs got the ball back with 1:51 left after a 23-yard Kidd punt. Starting from their 34, they moved to the Bills 26, but Kenney threw three incompletions and Lowery missed a 44-yarder with 19 seconds left.

QUOTES
• Robb Riddick, watching Lowery's last-second attempt: "I was saying to myself 'Oh no, this can't be happening to us again.' I just couldn't believe a team could be cursed like this. I then looked to the sky and said 'Give us a miracle, please.' I guess somebody up there finally listened to me."
• Marv Levy on his reaction after Metzelaars' fumble: "After the fumble, I pulled Fred Smerlas aside and told him 'This is just the chance now for our guys to show what they're made of.' On the next play, we intercepted. Romes did it all. Maybe this one had a little extra meaning to it (for him), hopefully not for the wrong reasons. At least we don't have to read about that streak and grapple with that this week. But really, every game is important and the most important win is the one you got today."
• Fred Smerlas: "I'm ticked off because it was harder than it should have been."
• Jim Kelly: "We weren't playing against 11 today, we were playing against 12. That was the worst officiating I've ever seen in my life. We didn't get one call."
• Chiefs quarterback Bill Kenney: "They played completely different than they did the first time. Marv's a good organizational coach and it shows. You could see they had a much more aggressive style, both on offense and defense."

Browns	7	7	7	0 -	21
Bills	0	3	7	7 -	17

Attendance at Rich Stadium - 42,213

Cle: Mack 1 run (Moseley kick), 10:09
Buf: FG Norwood 22, 10:47
Cle: Mack 1 run (Moseley kick), 12:09
Buf: Burkett 75 pass from Kelly (Norwood kick), :21
Cle: Brennan 11 pass from Kosar (Moseley kick), 10:10
Buf: Teal 4 pass from Kelly (Norwood kick), 14:00

	BUF	CLE
First downs	17	21
Rushing yds	83	141
Passing yds	308	230
Punts-avg	5-45.8	8-36.4
Fumbles-lost	3-3	2-1
Penalties-yds	8-46	8-55
Poss. time	26:01	33:59

BILLS LEADERS: Rushing - Riddick 14-54, Kelly 6-23, Wilkins 1-5, Harmon 1-1; **Passing** - Kelly 20-39-0 - 315; **Receiving** - Metzelaars 4-54, Teal 4-40, Burkett 3-122, Reed 3-51, Riddick 3-20, Harmon 1-11, Wilkins 2-17.

BROWNS LEADERS: Rushing - Mack 16-65, Dickey 13-65, Fontenot 3-13, Everett 1-2, Kosar 4-(-4); **Passing** - Kosar 18-33-0 - 240; **Receiving** - Brennan 4-66, Fontenot 4-55, Newsome 4-48, Dickey 2-13, Mack 1-23, Weathers 1-16, Slaughter 1-15, Langhorne 1-4.

NOTES
• The Bills lost their home season finale at rainy Rich Stadium as the fans angered Jim Kelly by throwing snowballs at the team during the game. The Bills had three turnovers, a missed field goal, costly penalties, dropped passes and were hurt by poor field position thanks to Browns punter Jeff Gossett.
• Pete Metzelaars set a new record for receptions by a Bills tight end, breaking Reuben Gant's mark of 41 set in 1977.
• The Browns opened the scoring after Robb Riddick and Gary Wilkins collided, with Riddick fumbling and Mike Johnson recovering at the Bills 38. Kevin Mack dove into the end zone eight plays later.
• Sean McNanie recovered a fumble caused by a bad handoff by Bernie Kosar at the Browns 39 and Scott Norwood capitalized with a field goal, but the Browns needed just six plays to overcome that, going 73 yards to Mack's second touchdown. Kosar hit Ozzie Newsome for 22 and Curtis Dickey had a 32-yard run.
• On the first play of the second half, Kelly fired a 75-yard TD pass to Chris Burkett.
• The Bills started the next two possessions at their 6 and 11 and failed to make a first down. The Browns finally took advantage late in the third, driving 44 yards to Kosar's TD pass to Brian Brennan. The drive was

WEEK 14 GAMES	
Cinc 31, NE 7	Rams 29, Dal 10
KC 37, Den 10	Pitt 27, Det 17
SD 27, Hou 0	Ind 28, Atl 23
Mia 31, NO 20	Minn 32, GB 6
NYG 24, Wash 14	SF 24, NYJ 10
Chi 48, TB 14	Sea 37, LAR 0
Phil 10, St.L 10 (OT)	

kept alive when Ray Bentley dropped an interception.
• Early in the fourth, Butch Rolle jumped offside on fourth-and-one, forcing a field goal attempt that Norwood missed. They later got to the 18, but after three incompletions, Kent Hull's bad snap on fourth down was recovered by Sam Clancy. The Bills got the ball back with 2:39 left and Kelly hit four straight passes, including a TD to Jimmy Teal with 1:00 left, but Newsome recovered the onside kick to clinch it.

QUOTES
• Browns coach Marty Schottenheimer: "It wasn't artistic, but we aren't particularly interested in whether they are or not."
• Marv Levy: "People are complaining that they (Browns) are just squeaking them out, but that's what the good teams do. It's like a baseball team that wins a lot of one-run games. What hurt us the most was our terrible field position. It seemed like we were starting from our 10 every time."
• Chris Burkett on his TD: "I was supposed to be the decoy. I went deep and that's supposed to clear things up underneath for Andre. But the backs went after Andre and left me all alone."
• Butch Rolle on his penalty: "I was over-anxious. It was going to be a run to my side and I got over-anxious and jumped. I felt really bad after we tried the field goal and missed."
• Jim Kelly on the fans: "We're fighting our butts off and people are doing that. I don't know if they were Cleveland fans or what, but it pissed me off. We don't need that. I thought I threw the ball well with it being wet, but you'll have to talk to the receivers (about the many drops). I wasn't out there trying to catch it. I can't do everything."

STANDINGS: FOURTEENTH WEEK

AFC EAST	W	L	T	CENTRAL	W	L	T	WEST	W	L	T	NFC EAST	W	L	T	CENTRAL	W	L	T	WEST	W	L	T
NY Jets	10	4	0	Cleveland	10	4	0	Denver	10	4	0	NY Giants	12	2	0	Chicago	12	2	0	LA Rams	10	4	0
New England	10	4	0	Cincinnati	9	5	0	Raiders	8	6	0	Washington	11	3	0	Minnesota	8	6	0	San Fran	8	5	1
Miami	7	7	0	Pittsburgh	5	9	0	Kan. City	8	6	0	Dallas	7	7	0	Detroit	5	9	0	Atlanta	6	7	1
Buffalo	4	10	0	Houston	3	11	0	Seattle	8	6	0	Philadelphia	4	9	1	Green Bay	3	11	0	N.Orleans	6	8	0
Indianapolis	1	13	0					San Diego	4	10	0	St. Louis	3	10	1	Tampa Bay	2	12	0				

NOTES

• The Bills lost for the third year in a row at the Hoosier Dome as the Colts won their second in a row under new coach Ron Meyer after losing their first 13 games of the season under Rod Dowhower.
• The Bills trailed 17-14 and forced a punt with 1:30 left, but the ball caromed off Eric Richardson's foot and John Holt recovered at the Bills 24. Gary Hogeboom then threw a 15-yard TD pass to Pat Beach with 30 seconds left to preserve the victory.
• Jim Kelly was knocked out of the game for more than a quarter with a mild concussion.
• Kelly hit Chris Burkett with a 42-yard TD pass in the first quarter and threw a 70-yarder to Burkett to the Colts 12 in the second quarter. But Dwight Hicks' interception killed that chance. Later, Kelly was nailed by Donnell Thompson and left the game. Frank Reich entered and directed an impressive 92-yard, 10-play drive to Greg Bell's TD. The key was a 37-yard pass to Andre Reed.
• The Colts tied it in the third. They took the second-half kickoff and consumed 8:28 on a 14-play, 75-yard drive, culminating in Hogeboom's one-yard run. The drive was kept alive when Sean McNanie was called for pass interference in the end zone on fourth-and-goal from the 2, giving the Colts a first down.
• Nesby Glasgow then recovered a Reed fumble at midfield and after George Wonsley went 31 yards with a short pass to the 8, Hogeboom threw a one-yard TD to Tim Sherwin.
• Dean Biasucci kicked the go-ahead field goal in the fourth. With Kelly back, the Bills drove to the Colts 28, but Scott Norwood a missed field goal with two minutes left, setting up Richardson's gaffe.

QUOTES

• Ron Pitts on Richardson's fumble: "I saw right away that there was no way I was going to get to the ball, so I figured I'd stay away and let them down it. I screamed to Eric to be careful, but it was no use. It was so loud in there, he wouldn't have been able to hear me."
• Eric Richardson: "That's a tough situation to be in. You are expected to block your man, but you are also expected to be aware of where the ball is. Sometimes it's hard to do both."
• Fred Smerlas on Richardson's fumble: "You can't really call that a fluke play because a fluke is something that doesn't happen very often. Those kind of plays have become commonplace around here in recent years."
• Andre Reed: "We weren't aware that Indianapolis was capable of making big plays. We were kind of going on what they had done in the past."
• Marv Levy: "I don't think it was so much that they made adjustments, they just came out (in the second half) and played better and we didn't play as well. I think we got away from the run there in the third. They had just used eight minutes and we came back and threw, threw, threw."
• Jim Kelly: "I'm embarrassed that we lost to Indianapolis. I mean, you jump up 14-0 and you can't hold the lead? We only got the ball three times in the second half. That's unbelievable."

WEEK 15 GAMES	
Pitt 45, NYJ 24	Den 31, Wash 30
Clev 34, Cinc 3	GB 21, TB 7
KC 20, LAR 7	Hou 23, Minn 10
NO 14, Atl 9	NYG 27, St.L 7
SF 29, NE 24	Sea 34, SD 24
Phil 23, Dal 21	Chi 16, Det 13
Mia 37, Rams 31 (OT)	

Bills	7 7 0 0 - 14
Colts	0 0 14 10 - 24

Attendance at the Hoosier Dome - 52,783

Buf: Burkett 42 pass from Kelly (Norwood kick), 12:08
Buf: Bell 1 run (Norwood kick), 10:45
Ind: Hogeboom 1 run (Biasucci kick), 8:28
Ind: Sherwin 1 pass from Hogeboom (Biasucci kick), 14:40
Ind: FG Biasucci 52, 7:48
Ind: Beach 15 pass from Hogeboom (Biasucci kick), 14:30

	BUF	IND
First downs	18	21
Rushing yds	94	79
Passing yds	264	296
Punts-avg	4-45.3	4-49.0
Fumbles-lost	2-2	0-0
Penalties-yds	3-17	7-40
Poss. time	25:48	34:12

BILLS LEADERS: Rushing - Bell 13-54, Riddick 6-27, Wilkins 2-13, Kelly 1-5, Harmon 1-(-5); **Passing** - Kelly 11-19-1 - 188, Reich 7-10-0 - 89; **Receiving** - Reed 6-87, Burkett 5-145, Bell 2-22, Riddick 2-2, Teal 1-9, Metzelaars 1-6, Wilkins 1-6.

COLTS LEADERS: Rushing - Wonsley 9-35, McMillan 15-33, Brooks 2-7, Bentley 3-3, Hogeboom 1-1; **Passing** - Hogeboom 23-33-0 - 318; **Receiving** - Bouza 7-79, McMillan 4-77, Wonsley 3-45, Boyer 3-38, Beach 3-33, Brooks 2-45, Sherwin 1-1.

NOTES

• The Bills closed the season with a lackluster effort, giving Marv Levy a 2-5 record since taking over.
• It was the sixth year in a row that the Bills lost their season finale.
• Greg Bell didn't play and Ronnie Harmon and Robb Riddick both left early with injuries.
• Jim Kelly set season team records for completions (285) and completion percentage (59.4).
• The defense failed to come up with a turnover, so the Bills best drive start was their own 30.
• The Oilers drove 65 yards in five plays to Allen Pinkett's TD run. Warren Moon completed passes of 36 and 13 yards to Ernest Givins along the way.
• In the second quarter, Charlie Romes' pass interference penalty gave the Oilers a first down at the 11 and that resulted in a field goal by Tony Zendejas, but the Bills drove 80 yards in eight plays to Kelly's TD pass to Chris Burkett. Kelly completed four passes to Andre Reed for 53 yards, including a 38-yarder to the 13.
• In the third, the Bills were moving when Reed fumbled and Steve Brown returned it 38 yards to the Bills 34, setting up Zendejas' field goal for a 13-7 lead.
• John Grimsley sacked Kelly later in the third, forcing a fumble to end a drive.
• In the fourth, Moon hit Drew Hill for 35 yards to the 7 to set up Zendejas' final field goal.

QUOTES

• Marv Levy: "I've emphasized the importance of turnovers to our team. I used Kansas City as an example. They have the 28th-ranked offense in the league and now they are in the playoffs because they are first in the league in takeaways. You cannot be a good club if you don't take the ball away. We've got to get the ball in the other team's territory. That means turnovers and the kicking game. We didn't have much of that. It's time to switch gears. I know which players can be developed and which I think can't. I have a considerable running start. We need field position changers, guys who can cause turnovers and make something happen on special teams."
• Fred Smerlas on Levy's plead for turnovers: "I don't know what it is. We certainly put some licks on people. We just don't seem to have the guys in the right place when the ball's loose."
• Jim Kelly: "I didn't have a training camp coming into this season, but I'll have one next year and I'll be ready when the season starts. From the start, we didn't catch the football. Then I fumbled and overthrew a lot of receivers in this game. The year's finally through. I can sit back and rest my body. It did take a beating."
• Andre Reed: "I came into this season just trying to better myself and I have. When you get more catches than you did the year before, you can't really say it wasn't worth it. You have to get better every year."

WEEK 16 GAMES	
SF 24, Rams 14	Sea 41, Den 16
NYG 55, GB 24	Atl 20, Det 6
Chi 24, Dal 10	Ind 30, LAR 24
KC 24, Pitt 19	Minn 33, NO 17
Cinc 52, NYJ 21	Clev 47, SD 17
St.L 21, TB 17	Wash 21, Phil 14
NE 34, Mia 27	

Bills	0 7 0 0 - 7
Oilers	7 3 3 3 - 16

Attendance at the Astrodome - 31,409

Hou: Pinkett 1 run (Zendejas kick), 10:43
Hou: FG Zendejas 26, 11:10
Buf: Burkett 12 pass from Kelly (Norwood kick), 14:06
Hou: FG Zendejas 51, 10:08
Hou: FG Zendejas 22, 4:58

	BUF	HOU
First downs	19	16
Rushing yds	60	87
Passing yds	218	191
Punts-avg	5-42.8	6-31.7
Fumbles-lost	3-1	2-0
Penalties-yds	5-51	9-65
Poss. time	31:28	28:32

BILLS LEADERS: Rushing - Harmon 8-27, Riddick 5-17, Kelly 3-14, King 4-10, Reed 1-(-8); **Passing** - Kelly 24-39-1 - 261; **Receiving** - Reed 5-93, Burkett 6-86, Metzelaars 4-31, Riddick 3-30, Harmon 4-14, Wilkins 2-7.

OILERS LEADERS: Rushing - Pinkett 17-46, Moon 6-16, Banks 3-13, Givins 1-8, Edwards 1-3, Oliver 1-1; **Passing** - Moon 14-29-0 - 208; **Receiving** - Hill 5-114, Givins 2-49, Banks 3-27, Pinkett 3-20, Oliver 1- (-2)

STANDINGS: SIXTEENTH WEEK

AFC EAST	W	L	T	CENTRAL	W	L	T	WEST	W	L	T	NFC EAST	W	L	T	CENTRAL	W	L	T	WEST	W	L	T
New England	11	5	0	Cleveland	12	4	0	Denver	11	5	0	NY Giants	14	2	0	Chicago	14	2	0	San Fran	10	5	1
NY Jets	10	6	0	Cincinnati	10	6	0	Kan. City	10	6	0	Washington	12	4	0	Minnesota	9	7	0	LA Rams	10	6	0
Miami	8	8	0	Pittsburgh	6	10	0	Seattle	10	6	0	Dallas	7	9	0	Detroit	5	11	0	Atlanta	7	8	1
Buffalo	4	12	0	Houston	5	11	0	Raiders	8	8	0	Philadelphia	5	10	1	Green Bay	4	12	0	N.Orleans	7	9	0
Indianapolis	3	13	0					San Diego	4	12	0	St. Louis	4	11	1	Tampa Bay	2	14	0				

At A Glance
1987

Jan. 5 – The Bills released recently hired assistant coach Bobby Ross from his contract to allow him to take the vacant head coaching position at Georgia Tech. "Bobby and I had an agreement that if he had an offer from another professional team to become a head coach, we would release him," Marv Levy said. "I said 'Now this doesn't include colleges' and he said 'No, it does not.' So I was taken aback by his decision."

Jan. 7 – Marv Levy offered Walt Corey the defensive coordinator's position with the Bills.

Jan. 10 – Kansas City assistant Frank Gansz, who was rumored to be coming to Buffalo as passing game coordinator and quarterbacks coach, was hired as the Chiefs head coach, replacing the fired John Mackovic. Walt Corey also was in line for the head coaching position and when he didn't get it, he said: "I don't think my pride will allow me to stay. Right now, I'm more of a Bill than I am a Chief." However, because he and the Chiefs staff were coaching in the Jan. 17 Senior Bowl, he refused to announce if he had accepted the Bills defensive coordinator position.

Jan. 13 – Walt Corey decided against waiting and signed with the Bills while he was in Mobile, Ala. for the Senior Bowl. He planned to finish his duties, then join the Bills. "He's a superior coach," Marv Levy, who was in Mobile to scout, said of Corey. "He's great fundamentally, he gets the best out of people. And he's a fine person."

Jan. 14 – Ralph Wilson vowed that he would be more heavily involved in the draft. "If we make a mistake this year," he said, citing the Bills' difficulties with first-round draft choices through the years, "it's going to be my mistake because I'm going to know who we're picking. And I could make a lot of mistakes and still be ahead of the averages. Right now, I like (Oklahoma linebacker Brian) Bosworth. I think he's a terrific player. If he can tackle, he can wear any haircut he wants. He can wear a wig if he likes."

Jan. 16 – Marv Levy completed his coaching staff as he announced the hiring of Ted Marchibroda as passing game coordinator and quarterbacks coach, Ted Tollner as receivers coach and Bruce DeHaven as special teams coach. "Ted Marchibroda is a good teacher," Levy said. "He believes in balance between the pass and run, which is very important. I think he's going to accelerate Jim Kelly's progress."

Jan. 17 – Will Wolford was named to UPI's all-rookie team.

Jan. 31 – After attending the scouting combine in Indianapolis, Colts coach Ron Meyer said he was leaning toward taking Alabama linebacker Cornelius Bennett with the second overall choice in the first round, rather than Brian Bosworth. Bennett said: "Whoever wants Cornelius Bennett, Cornelius Bennett wants them. I just want to play in the NFL and do my best to make that team a winner." Meanwhile, Bills GM Bill Polian expressed disappointment that Penn State linebacker Shane Conlan didn't work out at the combine. The Bills owned the third choice. "From my perspective, the only disappointment was Conlan," Polian said. "We'd seen the others at all-star games where we hadn't had an opportunity to see Conlan. I don't know that that will affect his draft status. It just means that we've got to do more work on him."

Feb. 7 – Ex-Bills kicker John Leypoldt died of a heart attack at St. Joseph Intercommunity Hospital in Cheektowaga. He was 40.

Feb. 8 – A survey of NFL salaries showed that the Bills ranked 19th in the league in average base salary at $165,731 per player. Jim Kelly was the highest-paid player in the NFL in 1986 at $3 million counting bonus money.

March 2 – With 12-year veteran safety Steve Freeman reportedly not in the Bills' future plans, speculation centered on Purdue defensive back Rod Woodson as the Bills' No.1 choice in the upcoming draft.

March 11 – Steve Freeman was traded to Minnesota for what was called past considerations, but in reality, the Bills got nothing and just gave Freeman away as a favor to the player.

March 12 – New York agent Norby Walters admitted that he and his partner, Lloyd Bloom, paid college athletes before their eligibility had expired. One of the athletes was Bills running back Ronnie Harmon while Harmon was a senior at Iowa. Walters announced he was filing a $500,000 breach of contract lawsuit against Harmon.

March 19 – At the league meetings in Hawaii, instant replay survived a narrow vote for at least one more year thanks to Ralph Wilson. Wilson originally was going to vote no, but was talked out of it by commissioner Pete Rozelle.

March 21 – Jack Donlan, the chief negotiator for the Management Council, predicted trouble if the NFLPA insisted on unfettered free agency in the upcoming collective bargaining agreement talks. The CBA was due to expire Aug. 31.

April 3 – Former star defensive lineman Tom Sestak died of a heart attack at Columbus Hospital. He was 51. The Bills said they were planning on announcing that Sestak's name was going to be added to the Wall of Fame at Rich Stadium this season.

April 7 – Tom Sestak's funeral was held in East Aurora and former Bills teammates Paul Maguire, Ron McDole, Gene Sykes, Tom Day, Ed Rutkowski, Joe O'Donnell and Booker Edgerson served as pallbearers.

April 27 – The Bills took a draft day gamble, trading their No. 3 pick to Houston for the Oilers No. 8 slot and a second-round choice (No. 36 overall). All along, the Bills wanted Shane Conlan and they still were able to get him with the eighth pick. They then traded up in the second round, swapping places with Tampa Bay and giving the Bucs their fourth-round choice in order to secure Wisconsin cornerback Nate Odomes. Later in the second round, they got Texas Tech cornerback Roland Mitchell. The Bills also chose Benedictine fullback Jamie Mueller (third), Jackson St. defensive end Leon Seals (fourth), Jacksonville St. tight end Keith McKeller (ninth) and Alabama A&M offensive tackle Howard Ballard (11th). Around the league, Tampa Bay took quarterback Vinny Testaverde (first), Indianapolis selected linebacker Cornelius Bennett (second), Houston chose running back Alonzo Highsmith (third), Green Bay chose running back Brent Fullwood (fourth), Cleveland took linebacker Mike Junkin (fifth), St. Louis grabbed quarterback Kelly Stouffer (sixth), Detroit selected defensive end Reggie Rogers (seventh), Philadelphia took defensive tackle Jerome Brown (ninth), Pittsburgh took cornerback Rod Woodson (10th), Atlanta drafted quarterback Chris Miller (13th), Houston grabbed wide receiver Haywood Jeffires (20th), the Jets took fullback Roger Vick (21st), San Francisco selected offensive lineman Harris Barton (22nd), New England took offensive tackle Bruce Armstrong (23rd), San Diego opted for tight end Rod Bernstine (24th), Chicago took quarterback Jim Harbaugh (26th), Denver went for wide receiver Ricky Nattiel (27th) and the Giants took wide receiver Mark Ingram (28th).

April 29 – Marv Levy said that Shane Conlan would have one of the outside linebacker jobs to lose in training camp. "When I was with Kansas City, we drafted Art Still and lined him up at defensive end from day one," Levy said. "As we are going to do the same thing with Shane. As I've said, we want to get good in a hurry. We were more certain that Shane could start immediately (as opposed to Rod Woodson, on whom the Bills passed)."

April 30 – The Bills released Lucious Sanford, ending his 10-year career with the team.

May 11 – John Butler was hired as the Bills' new director of player personnel and college scouting, replacing Norm Pollom who had indicated before the draft that he was leaving the team. Marv Levy announced that he had hired Chuck Lester as a defensive assistant.

May 15 – The Bills opened minicamp at Rich Stadium. Ten of the Bills' 11 draft choices were on hand. Howard Ballard, the 11th-round pick, announced that he would remain in school and use his final year of college eligibility.

May 17 – The Bills conducted an open practice to conclude minicamp. On select-a-seat day, more than 600 season tickets were sold as more than 11,000 fans attended.

May 28 – Scout Elbert Dubenion left the Bills, frustrated because he wasn't elevated to player personnel director. He accepted a scouting position with the Atlanta Falcons.

June 8 – Jim Kelly hosted his first Celebrity Shoot-out golf tournament at Wanakah Country Club. Among the players in town were quarterbacks Bernie Kosar, Dan Marino, Boomer Esiason, Vinny Testaverde, Pat Ryan and Jack Trudeau.

June 10 – Jim Kelly donned 1920s gangster clothes in Niagara Square for the shooting of his Machine Gun Kelly poster.

June 21 – Ray Bentley was involved in a car accident in Michigan in which a 66-year-old woman died. He was charged with vehicular homicide.

June 22 – A.J. Smith was added to the Bills scouting department, replacing Elbert Dubenion.

July 5 – The Bills made their first contract offer to Shane Conlan, four years worth $1.05 million.

July 13 – Cornerback Charlie Romes was traded to Kansas City for a low 1988 draft choice.

July 22 – The Bills signed second-round pick Nate Odomes, as well as ninth-rounder Keith McKeller and free agent offensive lineman Mitch Frerotte.

July 23 – Training camp, the first for Marv Levy and Jim Kelly, opened at Fredonia without first-round pick Shane Conlan. Levy expressed his

Darryl Talley, shown here chasing down Doug Flutie endured a difficult start to his NFL career, but he persevered and when Marv Levy became head coach in 1986, Talley's career blossomed. He has become one of the best players in franchise history.

anger toward Conlan's agent, Brett Senior, for refusing to negotiate until he knew what Brian Bosworth (Seattle) and Cornelius Bennett (Indianapolis) were going to get. "He's holding Shane Conlan hostage for Brian Bosworth and Cornelius Bennett," Levy said. "He's being very unfair to his client." The most recent Bills offer was $1.25 million for four years, but Senior was holding out for at least $3 million.

July 30 – Veterans were due to report to camp, but Bruce Smith, Martin Bayless and Darryl Talley failed to show. Smith was at home because his father had a heart attack while Bayless and Talley were holding out in contract disputes.

July 31 – Darryl Talley signed a new contract.

Aug. 4 – Bruce Smith reported to training camp with his body fat percentage down to 7.5 percent.

Aug. 6 – Bruce Smith was arrested and charged with punching a bouncer at Mickey Rats Bar on Main St. in Buffalo the night before, then, after meeting with Marv Levy, skipped the morning practice. It was thought he returned home to Norfolk, Va. to be with his father, but he showed up at the afternoon practice and took out his anger on his teammates. He even got into a verbal shouting match with Jim Kelly after he had knocked down backup quarterback Frank Reich.

Aug. 7 – Martin Bayless came to terms, leaving only Shane Conlan unsigned. The Bills told Brett Senior his deadline to get Conlan in was Aug. 8. The Bills final offer was three years at $1.7 million

Aug. 8 – The Browns beat the Bills, 12-6, before about 9,000 fans in the annual rookie scrimmage at Edinboro University. Jim Kelly directed the Bills only scoring drive. Bill Polian extended the deadline for Shane Conlan to sign to Aug. 9

Aug. 9 – Shane Conlan abided by Bill Polian's deadline and ended his holdout, signing a contract worth about $1.7 million for three years. "I'm disgusted with the way the entire negotiation process has taken place this year," Polian said. "It's been awful. I think the agents this year have been absolutely without morals, without scruples and

absolutely avaricious beyond belief." Said Conlan of his holdout: "In terms of money, it was worth it, but not in practice time that I missed."

Aug. 10 – Shane Conlan participated in his first practice, an interesting session that saw Will Wolford get moved from right guard, where he started throughout his rookie season, to the difficult left tackle position which Ken Jones had held down since 1978. Tim Vogler was moved in at right guard.

Aug. 15 – The Bills lost their preseason opener in Atlanta, 19-14, as the Falcons rallied for 10 points in the fourth quarter. In Miami, the Dolphins played their first game in Joe Robbie Stadium against the Bears. That game served as the first NFL broadcast by ESPN.

Aug. 22 – Frank Reich's TD pass to Bob Williams with 28 seconds left gave the Bills a 7-3 victory over the Raiders in Los Angeles.

Aug. 26 – Martin Bayless was traded to San Diego for cornerback Wayne Davis. Mark Murphy, a former Clarence resident who went on to play in the NFL and was now an assistant to Gene Upshaw in the NFLPA, visited the Bills training camp and informed the players that the threat of a strike was very real when the CBA expired Aug. 31. The union already had filed a 60-day strike notice which would go into effect Sept. 15.

Aug. 29 – The Bills traveled to Kansas City and were pummeled by the Chiefs, 34-14.

Aug. 30 – The NFL owners announced that if the players decided to go on strike, they would continue their season, finding the best players available to fill out rosters. "I find it impossible to believe they can play games if we strike," NFLPA executive director Gene Upshaw said.

Aug. 31 – The Bills acquired wide receiver Trumaine Johnson from San Diego for rookie third-round pick David Brandon.

Sept. 4 – The Bills closed their preseason with a 34-20 loss to the Dolphins in Joe Robbie Stadium as Miami rookie Troy Stradford returned a kickoff

83 yards for a TD.

Sept. 6 – The Bills released veterans Jim Haslett and Ken Jones, Jerry Butler was placed on injured reserve and Don Smith was traded to Atlanta for a low-round draft pick in 1988. Haslett said he knew the Bills were trying to build from the bottom, but said he was "shocked" to be released.

Sept. 8 – The Bills signed two linebackers, Scott Radecic and John Kaiser.

Sept. 13 – The Jets beat the Bills, 31-28, in front of 76,718 at Rich Stadium, in the season opener. Bob Crable's interception set up the clinching touchdown for New York with 2:58 left.

Sept. 18 – With another strike looming, Fred Smerlas said of Management Council negotiator Jack Donlan: "He's the one whose urine should be analyzed." Smerlas also predicted that if the owners decided to use scab players as replacements, the games wouldn't draw fans. "You couldn't get me to attend one of those scab games for all the tea in China. I'll be right in front of that ticket office telling people not to waste their money."

Sept. 20 – Jim Kelly rallied the Bills to victory for the first time in his career, producing 10 fourth-quarter points as Buffalo overcame Houston, 34-30, at Rich Stadium. After the game, players addressed the likelihood of a strike in two days and the Bills were dreading the thought of a walkout. "It's like a cloud ... impending doom," Fred Smerlas said. "Here we are, feeling like we can get over a hurdle on the football field, but we can't get over a hurdle in the conference rooms." Said Bruce Smith: "I hope we don't strike because I think the team is on a roll. This (beating Houston) was a giant step forward. Right now, this team can't afford a strike."

Sept. 21 – Reluctantly, the Bills voted to honor the union's plan to strike. "We are going to back the strike," said Joe Devlin, who organized the team meeting along with Fred Smerlas. "We don't want to strike. We're here to play football, but it seems like our backs are against the wall. We've got to do everything to keep together." The Jets beat New England, 43-24, on *Monday Night Football*, and after the game, the NFL players went on strike.

Sept. 22 – Players cleared out their lockers and the management began assembling a team of replacement players. Jim Kelly, getting into his gold Corvette, said: "I might be driving a Volkswagen later." Kelly stood to lose $100,000 per week. Players' Union leader Gene Upshaw met with Management Council negotiator Jack Donlan for 90 minutes to discuss the primary reason for the strike – unfettered free agency – but nothing was resolved.

Sept. 23 – The Bills formed a picket line at Rich Stadium hoping to confront replacement players. None showed up, so about 20 players, led by Joe Devlin and Fred Smerlas, went to the McKinley Park Inn where the new players were headquartered. They found cornerback John Armstrong and cornered him in a video game room. Devlin held a large black Labrador on a leash and Greg Bell teased Armstrong by telling the dog to "sic him, sic him." Smerlas then warned Armstrong, who had been cut by the Bills in training camp, that trouble lied ahead for any scabs who reported to the Bills' camp in 1988. The Bills were asked to leave the motel and did so before Hamburg police arrived.

Sept. 24 – The NFL officially called off the upcoming weekend games, wiping out Buffalo's game at Dallas. It also announced that the season would resume Oct. 4 with scab players representing the NFL teams. The Bills held a voluntary workout at the University of Buffalo's Amherst campus, then went to Rich Stadium to harass the scab players as they arrived for their first practice. The Bills shouted obscenities at the scabs. Some name players around the league, such as Mark Gastineau of the Jets, Randy White of the Cowboys, Marc Wilson of the Raiders and Leonard Smith of the Cardinals bucked the strike and rejoined their teams, but all the Bills remained unified.

Sept. 25 – Bills owner Ralph Wilson predicted a long strike, similar to the one that lasted 57 days in 1982. "They're not going to get it," Wilson said of the players' demand for free agency. "I could not vote for that. If we had that, some of the best players, after their contracts expired, would go to the warm-weather climates. Forget Buffalo. You won't have a team." Meanwhile, Jim Kelly skipped the team's workout at UB. Kelly said free agency wasn't worth striking over.

Sept. 27 – NFL stadiums were dark as the weekend games were canceled.

Sept. 28 – The Bills got nasty on the picket line in front of Rich Stadium. About 30 players gathered to greet the bus transporting the scab players. The Bills forced the bus to a halt, then began pelting it with eggs while shouting obscenities.

Sept. 29 – Fred Smerlas, Joe Devlin, Jim Ritcher and John Kidd attended a regional meeting in Elizabeth, N.J. to hear from Gene Upshaw on the progress of the negotiations. "The general feel from the meeting is that it looks like it's going to be a long strike," Smerlas said glumly.

Sept. 30 – Ex-Bills Jim Haslett and Ken Jones joined the Jets replacement team. Smerlas, perhaps Haslett's best friend, called him a scab. Devlin said: "I love Jonesy like a brother and it hurt me. I'm just sorry it turned out that way."

Oct. 1 – A report in the Rochester *Times-Union* said the Bills had voted en masse to cross the picket line, but the players denied it. "That's totally inaccurate," said Fred Smerlas. "I wonder what the guy who wrote that was smoking? There was no vote taken."

Oct. 4 – With NFL veteran quarterback Gary Hogeboom giving the Colts a huge advantage, Indianapolis' replacement team outclassed the Bills, 47-6, before 9,860 fans at Rich Stadium. Hogeboom tied the Colts record for TD passes in a game with five. Fortunately, coach Ron Meyer had the common sense to take Hogeboom out early in the second half, thus protecting the Colts passing record of 401 yards set by Johnny Unitas. About 20 of the real Bills gathered to protest the arrival of fans to the game, including Jim Kelly, then they went to Delaware Park and mingled with fans and signed autographs.

Oct. 5 – Marv Levy told two players on the Bills' injured reserve list not to come back to work. "We would rather see our team come in as a group," Levy said. "It's difficult for me, as a coach, to say that. There's only one thing that's important to me and that's to win. But by the same token, I'm having to think here about what will be best for us down the line."

Oct. 7 – Fullback Carl Byrum and cornerback Durwood Roquemore became the first two Bills to cross the picket line. "There's going to be 43 lock-

ers and two scab lockers when we come back to work," said Sean McNanie. Said Fred Smerlas: "I feel they've really alienated themselves from the team."

Oct. 10 – The Management Council passed a rule that would allow teams to have an unlimited inactive roster, therefore preventing the bad teams from improving via the waiver wire. "There is no help out there, absolutely none," Marv Levy said.

Oct. 11 – The Counterfeit Bills turned the ball over five times at rain-soaked Sullivan Stadium and lost to the Patriots, 14-7.

Oct. 14 – Robb Riddick, Mike Hamby and rookies Leon Seals and Keith McKeller broke the picket line, as did more than 100 players league-wide, including Lawrence Taylor of the Giants, whom the Bills were scheduled to play next. The players arrived at Rich Stadium just before the 1 p.m. deadline for being eligible to play on the weekend.

Oct. 15 – Gene Upshaw called off the players strike after 24 days, but the regular players were locked out of the weekend games because they didn't come in before 1 p.m. Wednesday. That meant a third week of scab games for the league. With the collapsing of the ranks, Upshaw called off the strike and filed an antitrust suit against the NFL in a federal court in Minneapolis.

Oct. 17 – The Bills agreed to accept per diem pay to begin working out in preparation for the following week's game against Miami, assuring general manager Bill Polian they would return to work.

Oct. 18 – In one of the most memorable games in Bills history, the Counterfeit Bills went out in a blaze of glory, defeating the Lawrence Taylor-led Giants in overtime, 6-3. Orchard Park's Todd Schlopy ended the mistake-laden comedy show with his second field goal. Taylor had five tackles, two sacks, numerous pressures and even played a few downs on offense as a tight end.

Oct. 19 – The real Bills returned to work and they admitted they were rooting for their replacements the day before. "I was pulling for 'em awfully hard to win because we needed the win to keep our playoff hopes alive," Jim Ritcher said. "If anyone can pick up where they left off, we should be able to because I think out of all the teams, we probably had as many people practicing every day during the strike. We had practices in '82 and they weren't anywhere near as productive as these were." Robb Riddick blasted Jim Kelly for Kelly's comments on CBS' NFL Today the day before when Kelly questioned whether the offensive line would block for Carl Byrum. "They're just stupid," Riddick said of Kelly's remarks. "I really hope he wasn't serious." The Bills kept 15 scab players on their roster and waived the rest.

Oct. 23 – It was reported that the Bills were interested in acquiring Eric Dickerson from the Rams. Dickerson said he was adamant about wanting out of Los Angeles.

Oct. 25 – The Bills made their first regular season appearance at Joe Robbie Stadium a memorable one, beating the Dolphins in overtime, 34-31, after trailing 21-3 at halftime. Jim Kelly outpassed Dan Marino, 359-303 and Scott Norwood kicked the game-winning field goal. "This is the type of game that can make a football team," Ralph Wilson said. "I've been bringing my friends to Miami for years and they say after the game, 'Maybe next year.'"

Oct. 26 – Reflecting on the Miami victory, Jim

Kelly said: "Sunday's game was definitely a big one for me and it was one of my best, especially after last year when we lost so many close games. When you're down 21-0, it's hard to think too positive. But I knew we could score, because I knew the receivers were getting open." Said Marv Levy of Kelly: "It never ceases to amaze me that the guy never ceases to amaze me. He's always had confidence, but there's no question that confidence becomes deep-rooted when you experience success."

Oct. 28 – Greg Bell was informed he wouldn't be activated for Sunday's game against Washington and said he sensed that his days as a Bill were nearing an end. "The way I look at it, I'm like cattle about to get slaughtered," Bell said. "I've been practicing for two weeks and feeling pretty good. I could be ready to play this weekend, no problem."

Oct. 31 – The Bills made one of the biggest trades in team history when they acquired the rights to holdout rookie linebacker Cornelius Bennett of Indianapolis. The Bills gave up a first-round draft choice in 1988, first- and second-round picks in 1989 and running back Greg Bell. The Colts then sent that entire package, plus their own first- and second-round picks in '88 and a second-rounder in '89 and running back Owen Gill to the Los Angeles Rams for Eric Dickerson. The Bills then signed Bennett to a five-year contract worth $3.875 million. "It's great to be here, I'm glad to be a part of it," Bennett said. "I said all along any team that I ended up with I'd be happy with. Now, I can do what I like best, play football." Said Bill Polian: "Right off, Bennett is our No. 1 choice (for 1988). If he does for us what we think he'll do, we would be picking in the middle of the first round or higher up the next year. Who knows who we'd get? As it turns out, we get Bennett a year ahead of time."

Nov. 1 – The luster of the Miami victory and the Bennett trade wore off quickly as Washington came to Rich Stadium and whipped the Bills, 27-7. The Bills rushed for just 21 yards.

Nov. 2 – Walt Corey saw Cornelius Bennett on the field for the first time in a non-contact, no-pads workout, but still was impressed. "The guy's got some great quickness," Corey said.

Nov. 4 – Cornelius Bennett participated in his first full practice and Marv Levy said he would start Sunday against Denver with Shane Conlan moving to the inside and Ray Bentley taking a seat on the bench.

Nov. 5 – Greg Bell had this to say of his trade to Los Angeles: "My heart was really pumping. I was really excited. In my mind, it was like going from an ice box, frozen in captivity, to seeing Annette Funicello in a California movie. All I can think now is that they'll miss me. You hear players say they wouldn't like to go to Buffalo and people look at it as a joke, but in a lot of guys' minds it's true. No one wants to go there. The economy is oppressed, it looks like there's a dark cloud over the city."

Nov. 6 – Paul Maguire, talking about his deceased ex-teammate, Tom Sestak, whose name was set to be affixed to the Bills' Wall of Fame at halftime of the Denver game, said: "Many people, especially the younger ones, don't know who Tom Sestak was or how great he was. But talk to his teammates or the guys who played against him in the AFL. Talk to Lenny Dawson or Joe Namath.

365

They'll tell you the truth. Tom Sestak was the greatest defensive tackle to play the game. Ever. He'd be the best even if he was playing today." Said Billy Shaw: "When you played against Tom in practice, you either got better or you retired."

Nov. 7 – With a strong wind hampering John Elway, the Bills upset the defending AFC champion Broncos at Rich Stadium, 21-14. Buffalo blocked two punts which resulted in safeties. In his first game as a Bill, Cornelius Bennett did not start, but he played frequently and was given solely pass rushing duties. On his first play late in the first quarter, he pressured Elway and forced an incompletion. "He's as good as anyone," Elway said of Bennett. "With Smith on one side and Bennett on the other, Buffalo is awfully tough."

Nov. 8 – Upon film review, Marv Levy was stunned by Bennett's performance, which included three tackles, one sack and two pressures. "I can't imagine somebody with three days practice, 10 months off from football, having the impact he had," Levy said.

Nov. 13 – Robb Riddick was placed on the injured list due to a fractured collarbone suffered against Denver.

Nov. 14 – Scott Norwood missed a pair of field goals that could have made a difference as the Bills lost at Cleveland, 27-21. Bernie Kosar passed for 346 yards and two TDs.

Nov. 21 – Shane Conlan was in on 12 tackles and Cornelius Bennett and Bruce Smith split three sacks as the defense keyed a 17-14 victory over the Jets at the Meadowlands.

Nov. 25 – Free agent rookie cornerback Kirby Jackson was signed.

Nov. 28 – The Bills defense turned in a superb performance, intercepting Dan Marino three times, holding Miami to 23 rushing yards and shutting out the Dolphins, 27-0, at Rich Stadium. It was the first time in 30 games Marino didn't throw a TD pass.

Dec. 2 – Bruce Smith was involved in a one-car accident on the New York State Thruway, totaling his Mercedes. Smith said he swerved on icy roads to avoid an animal that had run onto the road. "It was almost like seeing death pass before your eyes," Smith said. "I guess the Lord was on my side. A car can be replaced. You can't replace a person's life."

Dec. 6 – Oft-maligned Raiders quarterback Marc Wilson passed for 337 yards and three TDs to lead Los Angeles to a 34-21 victory over the Bills at the Coliseum. The loss overshadowed Andre Reed's best day as a Bill with 153 receiving yards.

Dec. 9 – Colts coach Ron Meyer called Jim Kelly "the absolutely best there is, and that's saying a mouthful with the tremendous talent at quarterback in the league."

Dec. 13 – Playing in their first big game since 1982, the Bills turned in one of their best efforts of the season and crushed the Colts, 27-3, for their first victory ever in the Hoosier Dome. Eric Dickerson was held to 19 yards on 11 carries.

Dec. 20 – On a gloomy day at Rich Stadium, the Bills had a chance to win the AFC East title for the first time since 1980. Instead, their 13-7 loss to New England and subsequent wins by the Colts and Dolphins knocked Buffalo out of the playoff race entirely. Jim Kelly completed less than 50 percent of his passes for the first time as a pro in the NFL or USFL. Later that night, Kelly got into

a scuffle in a West Seneca nightclub with a woman who threw a drink in his face after she claimed he insulted her.

Dec. 22 – Former Bill Dudley Meredith died of a heart attack in Jacksonville, Fla. He was 52.

Dec. 23 – Bruce Smith and Steve Tasker were named to the AFC Pro Bowl squad. The team was upset that Joe Devlin and Fred Smerlas didn't get picked. Jim Kelly finished third behind Dan Marino and John Elway.

Dec. 27 – Cornelius Bennett played one of the best defensive games in Bills history, recording 16 tackles, three forced fumbles and four sacks worth 34 yards in losses, but the Bills lost their season finale at Veterans Stadium to the Eagles, 17-7.

Dec. 28 – Bruce Smith was named first-team All-Pro by The Associated Press and Shane Conlan made the second team. Conlan was also named defensive rookie of the year by AP.

Dec. 30 – Reggie White of Philadelphia was named defensive player of the year by AP and Bruce Smith finished second in the balloting.

Jan. 3, 1988 – Tony Zendejas' overtime field goal lifted Houston to a 23-20 victory over Seattle in the AFC wild-card game while Minnesota crushed New Orleans, 44-10, in the NFC wild-card game. It was the Saints first postseason game.

Jan. 9, 1988 – Cleveland defeated Indianapolis, 38-21, and Minnesota surprised San Francisco, 36-24, on the first day of divisional round games.

Jan. 10, 1988 – Denver routed Houston, 34-10, and Washington edged Chicago, 21-17, on the second day of divisional play.

Jan. 17, 1988 – For the second year in a row, Denver broke Cleveland's hearts, posting a 38-33 victory, this time at Mile High Stadium, in the AFC Championship Game. The Browns were driving for the winning score, but Earnest Byner fumbled at the Denver 3 with 1:05 left and Jeremiah Castille recovered for the Broncos. Bernie Kosar passed for an AFC title game record of 356 yards. In the NFC Championship Game, Washington defeated Minnesota, 17-10, as Doug Williams threw two TD passes.

Jan. 31, 1988 – Washington scored 35 points in the second quarter as Doug Williams threw four TD passes and the Redskins routed Denver, 42-10, in Super Bowl XXII at Jack Murphy Stadium in San Diego. Williams passed for a Super Bowl record 340 yards and won the MVP award.

Feb. 7, 1988 – Bruce Smith had five tackles and two sacks to win the MVP award as the AFC won the Pro Bowl, 15-6, at Aloha Stadium. Jim Kelly scored the game's only TD on a one-yard run.

Bruce Smith dropped his body weight and fat percentage before the 1987 season and the results were dynamic as he enjoyed his best season to date, even though the NFL strike cost him four games.

BY THE NUMBERS - 1987

TEAM STATISTICS	BILLS	OPP
First downs	294	297
Rushing	111	114
Passing	151	162
Penalty	32	21
Third downs	77-208	82-220
Fourth downs	8-19	10-18
Time of poss	28:41	31:19
Total yards	4,741	4,906
Avg. game	316.1	327.1
Plays	1,018	1,022
Avg. play	4.7	4.8
Net rushing yds	1,840	2,052
Avg. game	122.7	136.8
Avg. play	4.0	3.8
Net passing yds	2,901	2,854
Comp/att	292/516	249/447
Sacks/lost	37-345	34-267
Interceptions	19	17
Percentage	56.6	55.7
Punts/avg.	83-38.2	88-36.7
Fumbles/lost	41-24	37-14
Penalties/yds	94-762	103-840
Touchdowns	33	37
Extra points	32-33	36-37
Field goals	12-20	15-20
Safeties	2	1
Kick ret./avg	45-19.4	43-15.8
Punt ret./avg	31-7.5	35-5.1

RUSHING	ATT	YDS	AVG	TD
Harmon	116	485	4.2	2
Mueller	82	354	4.3	2
Byrum	66	280	4.2	0
Riddick	59	221	3.7	5
R. Porter	47	177	3.8	0
Kelly	29	133	4.6	0
Bell	14	60	4.3	0
Shepherd	12	42	3.5	0
King	9	28	3.1	0
Williams	9	25	2.8	0
Partridge	1	13	13.0	0
Totten	12	11	0.9	0
Manucci	4	6	1.5	0
McClure	2	4	2.0	0
Reed	1	1	1.0	0
K. Porter	2	0	0.0	0
TOTALS	465	1840	4.0	9

RECEIVING	CAT	YDS	AVG	TD
Reed	57	752	13.2	5
Burkett	56	765	13.7	4
Harmon	56	477	8.5	2
Metzelaars	28	290	10.4	0
T. Johnson	15	186	12.4	2
Riddick	15	96	6.4	3
M. Brown	9	120	13.3	1
Gaines	9	115	12.8	0
McKeller	9	80	8.9	0
R. Porter	9	70	7.8	0
Broughton	5	90	18.0	1
McFadden	4	41	10.3	1
Bell	4	37	9.3	0
Byrum	3	23	7.7	0
Mueller	3	13	4.3	0
Bynum	2	24	12.0	0
Rolle	2	6	3.0	2
Kelly	1	35	35.0	0
Chetti	1	9	9.0	0
Belk	1	7	7.0	0
Williams	1	5	5.0	0
King	1	3	3.0	0
Shepherd	1	2	2.0	0
TOTALS	292	3246	11.1	21

PASSING	COMP	ATT	INT	YDS	TD	COMP%	SACKS	RATE
Kelly	250	419	11	2798	19	59.7	27-239	83.8
McClure	20	38	3	181	0	52.6	2-17	32.9
Totten	13	33	2	155	2	39.4	5-62	49.4
Manucci	7	21	2	68	0	33.3	3-27	3.8
Riddick	1	1	0	35	0	100.0	0-0	118.8
Miller	1	3	1	9	0	33.3	0-0	2.8
Kidd	0	1	0	0	0	00.0	0-0	39.6
TOTALS	292	516	19	3246	21	56.6	37-345	73.7

KICKING	1-19	20-29	30-39	40-49	50+	TOT	PAT	PTS
Norwood	0-0	3-4	4-6	3-5	0-0	10-15	31-31	61
Schlopy	0-0	1-1	1-3	0-1	0-0	2-5	1-2	7
TOTALS	0-0	4-5	5-9	3-6	0-0	12-20	32-33	68

PUNTING	NO	AVG	LG	In 20	BL
Kidd	64	39.0	67	20	0
Partridge	19	37.7	52	3	1
TOTALS	83	38.2	67	23	1

SCORE BY QUARTERS

BILLS	17	86	51	110	6 -	270
OPP	54	113	77	61	0 -	305

DEFENSIVE STATISTICAL LEADERS

TACKLES: Conlan 72 primary - 42 assists - 114 total tackles, Radecic 56-25-81, Talley 52-27-79, B. Smith 60-18-78, Bennett 54-15-69, Kelso 42-27-69, Smerlas 31-18-49, Burroughs 41-6-47, Odomes 32-10-42, McNanie 31-8-39, Bentley 22-13-35, Seals 17-14-31, Drane 24-6-30, Pitts 22-6-28

SACKS: B. Smith 12, Bennett 8.5, Seals 3.5, McNanie 2.5, Armstrong 2

QB PRESSURES: B. Smith 17, Conlan 9, Bennett 7, Smerlas 5, Seals 5

FUMBLE RECOVERIES: Radecic 2, B. Smith 2, Kaiser 2, Walters 2

FORCED FUMBLES: Bennett 5, Tasker 3, B. Smith 3

INTERCEPTIONS: Kelso 6-25 yards, 4.2 avg, 0 TD; Pitts 3-19, 6.3, 0 TD

SPECIAL TEAMS STATISTICAL LEADERS

KICKOFF RETURNS: Tasker 11-197, 17.9, 0 TD; R. Porter 8-219, 27.4, 0 TD

PUNT RETURNS: Pitts 23-149, 6.5, 0 TD; McFadden 8-83, 10.4, 0 TD

TACKLES: Kaiser 23, Tasker 20, Prater 12, Bentley 10, Furjanic 9, Radecic 9, Mitchell 8, Mueller 8

GAME 1 - Sunday, Sept. 13, 1987 - JETS 31, BILLS 28

Jets	0	14	3	14	- 31
Bills	0	7	7	14	- 28

Attendance at Rich Stadium - 76,718

Buf: T. Johnson 26 pass from Kelly (Norwood kick), 3:13
NYJ: Walker 55 pass from O'Brien (Leahy kick), 11:47
NYJ: Shuler 4 pass from O'Brien (Leahy kick), 14:34
NYJ: FG Leahy 29, 8:46
Buf: Burkett 6 pass from Kelly (Norwood kick), 12:33
NYJ: Hector 2 run (Leahy kick), 3:01
Buf: Riddick 2 run (Norwood kick), 5:18
NYJ: Hector 1 run (Leahy kick), 12:02
Buf: Riddick 1 pass from Kelly (Norwood kick), 13:44

	BUF	NYJ
First downs	23	26
Rushing yds	67	133
Passing yds	292	261
Punts-avg	5-46.8	5-41.2
Fumbles-lost	0-0	0-0
Penalties-yds	5-42	15-103
Poss. time	21:57	38:03

BILLS LEADERS: Rushing - Bell 10-39, Riddick 2-18, Byrum 3-9, Reed 1-1; **Passing** - Kelly 25-42-1 - 305; **Receiving** - Reed 4-37, Bell 4-37, Harmon 5-51, Metzelaars 4-37, T. Johnson 3-63, Burkett 3-47, Riddick 2-3, Byrum 1-20.

JETS LEADERS: Rushing - McNeil 21-68, Vick 12-34, Faaola 2-11, Hector 4-9, O'Brien 4-7, Jennings 1-4; **Passing** - O'Brien 24-35-1 - 266; **Receiving** - Toon 6-59, Shuler 7-63, Walker 4-91, Hector 4-51, McNeil 2-3, Sohn 1-(-1).

NOTES

• The Bills lost their season opener as Jim Kelly's only interception led to the deciding TD.
• Shane Conlan was in on nine tackles in his NFL debut. Sean McNanie had nine tackles and two sacks.
• The Bills drove 62 yards to take the lead early in the second quarter on Kelly's TD pass to newcomer Trumaine Johnson.
• The Jets tied it on Ken O'Brien's bomb to Wesley Walker, then went ahead with an eight-play, 62-yard drive in the final 1:52 of the half as O'Brien hit Mickey Shuler for the TD. O'Brien was six of seven on the drive.
• New York took the second-half kickoff and went 64 yards in 15 plays to Pat Leahy's field goal, but the Bills took the ensuing kickoff and moved 80 yards in 10 plays to Chris Burkett's TD reception.
• The Jets answered with a 72-yard drive to Johnny Hector's TD run, but again the Bills responded with a 69-yard march that used just 2:06 as Russell Carter was flagged for a 28-yard interference call, putting the ball on the 2 from where Robb Riddick scored to make it 24-21 Jets.
• The defense held and the Jets punted to the end zone. But with 4:24 left, Kelly's first-down pass was batted into the

WEEK 1 GAMES

TB 48, Atl 10	NO 28, Clev 21
St.L 24, Dal 13	Minn 34, Det 19
LAR 20, GB 0	Hou 20, Rams 16
NE 28, Mia 21	Wash 34, Phil 24
KC 20, SD 16	Pitt 30, SF 17
Den 40, Sea 17	Cinc 23, Ind 21
Chi 34, NYG 19	

air and intercepted by Bob Crable who returned it to the 4. Four plays later, on fourth-and-goal, Hector dove in for a TD with 2:58 left. Kelly marched the Bills 71 yards in eight plays to his TD pass to Riddick with 1:16 left, but the Jets recovered the onside kick and killed the clock.

QUOTES

• Jim Kelly on the interception: "One out of about every 1,000 passes I throw will be tipped straight into the air and right into the guy's hands. I wish it would never happen, but it's a play we had called. It's one of my favorite plays, but they came up and caught it. They must have watched a lot of film on it because we do run it very well and they were ready for it."
• Jets linebacker Bob Crable: "I was just looking to bat the ball in the air. We both went up for it, but I had better position than he (Kelly) did and these gifted hands caught the ball."
• Shane Conlan: "I made some plays and I missed some. I'm still thinking a lot out there and it's not really smooth. Once I get the fluid motion, the mental part of the game down, I think I'll do a lot better. I didn't feel that much pressure. We've got Eugene Marve, Ray Bentley and Darryl Talley out there so they're taking the load off me."
• Marv Levy: "We scored 28 points, that's normally enough to win."
• Chris Burkett: "We played good, but I'm tired of playing good and losing. We've got to start playing good and winning."
• Bruce Smith: "I'm an optimist. This is something to build on, but at the same time it's a loss and I don't feel good about it."
• Fred Smerlas: "We must have given away 15 games like this the last two years."

GAME 2 - Sunday, Sept. 20, 1987 - BILLS 34, OILERS 30

Oilers	3	14	3	10	- 30
Bills	3	10	0	21	- 34

Attendance at Rich Stadium - 56,534

Buf: FG Norwood 45, 4:23
Hou: FG Zendejas 52, 11:59
Hou: Hill 2 pass from Moon (Zendejas kick), 1:54
Buf: FG Norwood 38, 5:28
Hou: Rozier 8 run (Zendejas kick), 11:07
Buf: Riddick 11 pass from Kelly (Norwood kick), 14:54
Hou: FG Zendejas 27, 11:06
Buf: Reed 9 pass from Kelly (Norwood kick), 6:23
Hou: Givins 12 pass from Moon (Zendejas kick), 8:23
Hou: FG Zendejas 30, 10:02
Buf: Riddick 2 run (Norwood kick), 11:29
Buf: Harmon 10 pass from Kelly (Norwood kick), 14:03

	BUF	HOU
First downs	30	19
Rushing yds	135	197
Passing yds	248	130
Punts-avg	5-32.6	6-39.0
Fumbles-lost	1-0	2-0
Penalties-yds	7-55	10-113
Poss. time	29:58	30:02

BILLS LEADERS: Rushing - Mueller 9-47, Harmon 12-46, Bell 4-21, Riddick 3-11, Kelly 3-11; **Passing** - Kelly 26-43-2 - 293; **Receiving** - Harmon 8-82, Burkett 7-115, Reed 6-62, Riddick 4-30, Metzelaars 1-4.
OILERS LEADERS: Rushing - Rozier 29-150, Wallace 4-31, Pinkett 3-16, Moon 1-0; **Passing** - Moon 13-27-1 - 142; **Receiving** - Givins 5-66, Hill 4-48, Rozier 3-3, Williams 1-25.

WEEK 2 GAMES

Dal 16, NYG 14	LAR 27, Det 7
Sea 43, KC 14	Mia 23, Ind 10
Minn 21, Rams 16	Phil 27, NO 17
Clev 34, Pitt 10	SD 28, St.L 24
SF 27, Cinc 26	Chi 20, TB 3
Atl 21, Wash 20	NYJ 43, NE 24
Den 17, GB 17 (OT)	

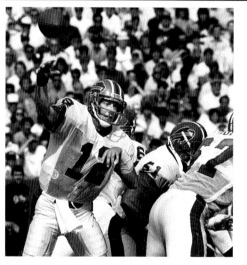

NOTES

• Jim Kelly produced the first fourth-quarter comeback of his career, rallying the Bills from 10 points down with two late scores. The Bills scored three TDs in the final 8:37.
• Bruce Smith and Darryl Talley were ejected in the third for fighting. Houston lost only Doug Williams.
• The Bills took the opening kickoff and drove to a Scott Norwood field goal, but Keith Bostic's interception of Kelly set up Tony Zendejas' tying field goal.
• Houston went ahead early in the second quarter on Warren Moon's TD pass to Drew Hill. But the Bills came back with another Norwood field goal, set up by Kelly's 47-yard bomb to Chris Burkett.
• The Oilers drove 71 yards on the ensuing possession to Mike Rozier's TD. But the Bills scored before the half ended on Robb Riddick's TD reception, capping a 75-

yard march. Burkett had two catches for 40 yards.
• Zendejas kicked a field goal in the third, but the Bills tied the game early in the fourth on Kelly's TD pass to Andre Reed. Reed had a 14-yard catch and a subsequent unsportsmanlike penalty on Steve Brown was tacked on.
• The Oilers needed just five plays to go 82 yards to Ernest Givins' TD, and on the first play after the kickoff, Jeff Donaldson intercepted Kelly, setting up Zendejas' field goal and a 30-20 Houston lead.
• However, the Bills went 80 yards in five plays to Riddick's TD. The keys were a personal foul penalty on Doug Smith and a 33-yard interference on Audrey McMillan.
• The Oilers then went three-and-out and punted to the Bills 46. Kelly took the field with 2:23 left and needed only 1:32 to go 54 yards. Kelly was four-of-six for 44 yards including the TD to Ronnie Harmon.

QUOTES

• Jim Kelly: "I know all the reporters probably said 'Oh no, not this again, Jim Kelly threw an interception in the fourth quarter.' I wanted the chance to come back and be able to put the ball in the end zone and win it. I didn't want a field goal for the tie, I wanted to win it. In my heart and soul, I wanted to show the fans, the reporters and the Bills that Jim Kelly has a winning spirit. You just have to learn to fight back."
• Fred Smerlas: "He certainly got the albatross off from around his neck today. That's why they pay quarterbacks like Kelly and Marino $1 million a year. They can win the game for you."
• Andre Reed: "He was the Kelly he should be, the leader he should be. He was taking charge in the huddle."
• Marv Levy: "Tom Landry could never win the big one, either, until he won four or five Super Bowls (two actually) when his team got better."

STANDINGS: SECOND WEEK

AFC EAST	W	L	T	CENTRAL	W	L	T	WEST	W	L	T	NFC EAST	W	L	T	CENTRAL	W	L	T	WEST	W	L	T
NY Jets	2	0	0	Houston	1	1	0	Raiders	2	0	0	St. Louis	1	1	0	Chicago	2	0	0	N.Orleans	1	1	0
New England	1	1	0	Cincinnati	1	1	0	Denver	1	0	1	Washington	1	1	0	Minnesota	2	0	0	Atlanta	1	1	0
Miami	1	1	0	Pittsburgh	1	1	0	Kan. City	1	1	0	Philadelphia	1	1	0	Tampa Bay	1	1	0	San Fran	1	1	0
Buffalo	1	1	0	Cleveland	1	1	0	Seattle	1	1	0	Dallas	1	1	0	Green Bay	0	1	1	LA Rams	0	2	0
Indianapolis	0	2	0					San Diego	1	1	0	NY Giants	0	2	0	Detroit	0	2	0				

NOTES

• Led by NFL veteran Gary Hogeboom, who defied the strike, the Colts dominated the Bills in the first replacement game since the strike was called.
• Ex-Bill Dan Manucci was the Bills' starting quarterback, joined in the backfield by Johnny Shepherd and Bruce King. The receivers were Thad McFadden and Sheldon Gaines.
• Hogeboom threw two TD passes to another regular Colts player, Walter Murray, then hit Joe Jones and James Noble for scores as the Colts took a 28-0 halftime lead.
• Noble caught another TD in the third before Hogeboom was lifted.
• The Colts made it 37-0 when safety Jim Perryman, the third regular Colts player, blocked a Rick Partridge punt and then tackled Buffalo's Steve Clark, who recovered the ball in the end zone.
• The Colts added 10 more points before the third quarter ended to make it 47-0.
• Willie Totten, who became famous for setting a Division I-AA record for touchdown passes at Mississippi Valley State, most of them to Jerry Rice, replaced Manucci at quarterback in the fourth and after John Armstrong, the player the real Bills had threatened the week before, blocked a punt to give the Bills the ball at the 8, Totten hit Marc Brown for a TD. Todd Schlopy, the kicker from Orchard Park, had the PAT blocked.
• The loss was the second-worst in team history, behind only a 43-0 loss to Baltimore in 1971.
• Attendance was the second-smallest in team history. Only 8,876 saw the Bills play Oakland in 1960 at War Memorial.

QUOTES

• Marv Levy: "We knew it was very possible we'd be beaten very badly. I feel most disappointed for the members of my coaching staff who worked very hard, perhaps the hardest week of work we've had since we came here. We went out there knowing we weren't a very good team, but we wanted to invent a new adage: May the worst team win. It just didn't work out. We didn't do a lot of planning for it (assembling a replacement team in case of a strike). One option was to bring a lot of players to camp, but we elected not to for a very important reason – we have a young team and there were certain players we wanted to develop and give repetitions. Can we improve? Sure, how's 40-17?"
• Ralph Wilson: "You saw the game, there's no use in my making any comments."
• Bill Polian: "The difference was they had three guys who had been in camp nine weeks. We had none. That's the key to winning during the strike. The teams with the most guys crossing the picket line. The people I feel sorry for are our coaches. They worked their butts off for the better part of nine weeks to turn this program around and then they have to be subjected to something like this. It's ridiculous."

WEEK 3 GAMES	
Chi 35, Phil 3	Clev 20, NE 10
Dal 38, NYJ 24	GB 23, Minn 16
Hou 40, Den 10	LAR 35, KC 17
NO 37, Rams 10	Sea 24, Mia 20
Pitt 28, Atl 12	Wash 28, St.L 21
SD 10, Cinc 9	TB 31, Det 27
SF 41, NYG 21	

Colts	7	21	19	0 - 47
Bills	0	0	0	6 - 6

Attendance at Rich Stadium - 9,860

Ind: Murray 37 pass from Hogeboom (Jordan kick), 12:12
Ind: Murray 11 pass from Hogeboom (Jordan kick), 7:56
Ind: Jones 4 pass from Hogeboom (Jordan kick), 13:22
Ind: Noble 18 pass from Hogeboom (Jordan kick), 14:42
Ind: Noble 18 pass from Hogeboom (Jordan kick), :50
Ind: Safety: Perryman blocked punt in end zone, 2:30
Ind: FG Jordan 36, 7:09
Ind: G. Brown 18 run (Jordan kick), 10:10
Buf: M. Brown 8 pass from Totten (kick blocked), 6:08

	BUF	IND
First downs	14	28
Rushing yds	81	166
Passing yds	82	297
Punts-avg	7-27.6	3-20.3
Fumbles-lost	7-4	3-2
Penalties-yds	10-70	5-30
Poss. time	28:16	31:44

BILLS LEADERS: Rushing - Shepherd 7-38, Williams 8-22, Manucci 3-10, King 5-9, Totten 5-2; **Passing** - Manucci 7-20-2 - 68, Totten 4-12-0 - 71, Miller 1-3-1 - 9; **Receiving** - Gaines 6-98, McFadden 3-28, Chetti 1-9, M. Brown 1-8, Williams 1-5.
COLTS LEADERS: Rushing - Banks 16-69, G. Brown 6-38, McLemore 17-58, Nugent 2-1; **Passing** - Hogeboom 17-25-0 - 259, McLemore 3-5-0 - 47; **Receiving** - Murray 7-161, Noble 4-50, Banks 3-27, Jones 2-17, McLemore 1-4, Hawthorne 1-14, Kearse 1-21, Bryant 1-12.

NOTES

• The Bills' scab team fell to 0-2 thanks to five turnovers, ruining a pretty solid defensive showing.
• The Patriots took the lead in the first, driving 76 yards in 10 plays with Rochester native Bob Bleier at quarterback. Carl Woods capped the drive with a four-yard TD run.
• The Bills appeared to get a break early in the second quarter. After a bad snap on a punt, Rick Partridge ran for 13 yards and a first down, and a 15-yard roughing penalty moved the ball to the Pats 45. But on the next play, Willie Totten threw an interception. The Bills had only 63 yards at halftime.
• Carl Byrum, one of two regular Bills playing, fumbled on the first possession of the third, but the Pats failed to move. But one play after the punt, Totten fumbled the

snap and the Pats recovered at the Bills 19. Four plays later, Bleier scored on a sneak for a 14-0 lead.
• The Bills' only score came early in the fourth. Scott Watters blocked a Pats punt and Chip Nuzzo recovered at the Pats 16. Two plays later, Totten hit Thad McFadden for the TD.
• The Bills had three chances to tie after that, but wasted every one. After an interception, the Bills were forced to punt. Later, Will Cokely partially blocked a punt, giving the Bills the ball at the Pats 32, but Totten was sacked and lost a fumble. Finally, after a punt, Totten drove the Bills from their own 28 to the Pats 22, but he was sacked on the final play of the game and was unable to stop the clock.

QUOTES

• Marv Levy: "The players tried and I give them credit for that. They played with spirit and I admire them for that. We felt our best chance was to try and run and control the ball, try to get field position and wait for them (the Patriots) to make mistakes. If we would have had a better running game, it would have been a different outcome."
• Special teams coach Bruce DeHaven on the blocked punts: "What helped is their protection scheme is similar to ours. I know what's hard for me to block. We got in a lot of work on special teams this week. The only thing we didn't get to was techniques."
• Bills linebacker Bob LeBlanc: "We were much better prepared. The coaches really worked hard with us this week. We had three new secondary coverages and we had seven different blitzes. Last week we had one blitz and no stunts. We just took them on head on."

Bills	0	0	0	7 - 7
Patriots	7	0	7	0 - 14

Attendance at Sullivan Stadium - 11,878

NE: Woods 4 run (Franklin kick), 8:34
NE: Bleier 1 run (Franklin kick), 6:36
Buf: McFadden 13 pass from Totten (Schlopy kick), 3:03

	BUF	NE
First downs	14	15
Rushing yds	107	213
Passing yds	61	43
Punts-avg	6-40.0	9-34.6
Fumbles-lost	7-3	2-0
Penalties-yds	5-40	3-26
Poss. time	25:40	34:20

BILLS LEADERS: Rushing - Byrum 19-59, King 4-19, Partridge 1-13, Totten 7-9, Shepherd 5-4, Williams 1-3; **Passing** - Totten 9-21-2 - 84; **Receiving** - Brown 2-44, Gaines 2-19, McFadden 1-13, Belk 1-7, King 1-3, Shepherd 1-2, Byrum 1- (-4).
PATRIOTS LEADERS: Rushing - LeBlanc 35-146, Hansen 13-43, Woods 3-20, McSwain 2-3, Bleier 2-1; **Passing** - Bleier 4-13-1 - 43; **Receiving** - Linne 3-32, Frain 1-11.

WEEK 4 GAMES	
SF 25, Atl 17	Cinc 17, Sea 10
Hou 15, Clev 10	Mia 42, KC 0
Chi 27, Minn 7	St.L 24, NO 19
Ind 6, NYJ 0	Dal 41, Phil 22
Rams 31, Pitt 21	SD 17, TB 13
Wash 38, NYG 12	Den 30, LAR 14
Det 19, GB 16 (OT)	

STANDINGS: FOURTH WEEK

AFC EAST	W	L	T	CENTRAL	W	L	T	WEST	W	L	T	NFC EAST	W	L	T	CENTRAL	W	L	T	WEST	W	L	T
NY Jets	2	2	0	Houston	3	1	0	Raiders	3	1	0	Dallas	3	1	0	Chicago	4	0	0	San Fran	3	1	0
New England	2	2	0	Cleveland	2	2	0	San Diego	3	1	0	Washington	3	1	0	Minnesota	2	2	0	N.Orleans	2	2	0
Miami	2	2	0	Pittsburgh	2	2	0	Denver	2	1	1	St. Louis	2	2	0	Tampa Bay	2	2	0	Atlanta	1	3	0
Indianapolis	2	2	0	Cincinnati	2	2	0	Seattle	2	2	0	Philadelphia	1	3	0	Green Bay	1	2	1	LA Rams	1	3	0
Buffalo	1	3	0					Kan. City	1	3	0	NY Giants	0	4	0	Detroit	1	3	0				

GAME 5 - Sunday, Oct. 18, 1987 - BILLS 6, GIANTS 3 (OT)

Giants	0 0 0 3 0	- 3
Bills	0 0 0 3 3	- 6

Attendance at Rich Stadium - 15,737

NYG: FG Benyola 22, 5:12
Buf: FG Schlopy 31, 11:57
Buf: FG Schlopy 27, 14:41

	BUF	NYG
First downs	22	19
Rushing yds	167	128
Passing yds	164	180
Punts-avg	6-40.8	10-34.5
Fumbles-lost	5-4	4-0
Penalties-yds	11-113	15-145
Poss. time	41:26	33:15

BILLS LEADERS: Rushing - Byrum 25-139, Riddick 11-29, McClure 2-4, Porter 1-(-1), Manucci 1-(-4); **Passing** - McClure 20-38-3 - 181, Manucci 0-1-0 - 0; **Receiving** - McKeller 9-80, M. Brown 6-68, Bynum 2-24, Riddick 2-11, Gaines 1-(-2).

GIANTS LEADERS: Rushing - Dirico 20-79, Williams 11-41, Park 2-6, Covington 2-2, Rutledge 1-0; **Passing** - Rutledge 17-46-2 - 203; **Receiving** - Lovelady 5-59, McGowan 3-48, Williams 2-10, Bennett 2-31, Dirico 2-22, Covington 1-9, Park 1-6, Smith 1-18.

NOTES

• The counterfeit Bills did the real Bills a huge favor, improving the team's record to 2-3 with a memorable victory on Todd Schlopy's overtime field goal.

• The game was perhaps the most comical in team history as mistakes reigned. The teams combined for nine fumbles (four lost, all by the Bills), five interceptions, 26 penalties for 258 yards, five missed field goals and 48 incomplete passes.

• The win was the Bills' fourth in overtime in their history and only the second regular-season OT game in the 15-year history of Rich Stadium.

• Schlopy made a 25-yard field goal in the second, but it was nullified by an illegal procedure penalty and he then missed from 30.

• In the fourth, George Benyola missed a field goal for the Giants, but on the next play, Robb Riddick lost a fumble and the Giants recovered. Benyola then made a 22-yarder.

• The Bills answered with a 56-yard drive, led by quarterback Brian McClure, to Schlopy's tying field goal.

WEEK 5 GAMES

Clev 34, Cinc 0	Den 26, KC 17
Pitt 21, Ind 7	Atl 24, Rams 20
NE 21, Hou 7	NO 19, Chi 17
NYJ 37, Mia 31 (OT)	SF 34, St.L 28
SD 23, LAR 17	Sea 37, Det 14
TB 20, Minn 10	Wash 13, Dal 7
GB 16, Phil 10 (OT)	

McClure was four-for-four on the drive.

• Carl Byrum fumbled and the Giants recovered at the Bills 22 with 16 seconds left, but Benyola missed a field goal to force overtime.

• Schlopy missed a 28-yarder on the Bills' first possession of OT. Later, Steve Clark intercepted Jeff Rutledge and returned it 23 yards to the Bills 40. Nine plays later, Schlopy kicked the winner.

QUOTES

• Todd Schlopy: "I can honestly say, my whole life, I've thought about just such an occasion as right now. It's an awesome feeling. I grew up in this town, I grew up on the Buffalo Bills. I knew every Buffalo kicker and what they were doing through my whole life. I remember Pete Gogalak when I was a kid and John Leypoldt and Nick Mike-Mayer."

• Giants linebacker Lawrence Taylor: "During the game, he (Bills tackle Rick Schulte) would hold me, throw me down and when I would try to get up, he'd knock me down again. He got on my nerves and I came up swinging and I started to concentrate on him. It was frustrating, especially when you don't see any flags, but you should expect that in a game like this."

• Marv Levy: "We're not too bad off. The win was tremendously important to us from the standpoint of still being in it. These games do count. This game was probably unique. There were a lot of mistakes and a lot of opportunities on both sides were squandered."

GAME 6 - Sunday, Oct. 25, 1987 - BILLS 34, DOLPHINS 31 (OT)

Bills	0 3 14 14 3	- 34
Dolphins	14 7 0 10 0	- 31

Attendance at Joe Robbie Stadium - 61,295

Mia: Duper 5 pass from Marino (Reveiz kick), 6:19
Mia: Pruitt 25 pass from Marino (Reveiz kick), 11:13
Mia: Hardy 2 pass from Marino (Reveiz kick), 8:33
Buf: FG Norwood 41, 14:59
Buf: Riddick 1 run (Norwood kick), 8:11
Buf: Burkett 14 pass from Kelly (Norwood kick), 13:43
Mia: FG Reveiz 46, 3:02
Buf: Riddick 1 run (Norwood kick), 7:47
Buf: Riddick 17 pass from Kelly (Norwood kick), 10:56
Mia: Clayton 12 pass from Marino (Reveiz kick), 13:57
Buf: FG Norwood 27, 4:12

	BUF	MIA
First downs	29	21
Rushing yds	144	70
Passing yds	330	296
Punts-avg	3-38.3	3-34.3
Fumbles-lost	1-0	3-2
Penalties-yds	8-55	6-40
Poss. time	37:25	26:47

BILLS LEADERS: Rushing - Riddick 18-66, Harmon 12-45, Kelly 4-21, Byrum 3-5, Mueller 2-7; **Passing** - Kelly 29-39-0 - 359; **Receiving** - Burkett 9-130, Metzelaars 6-85, Harmon 5-43, Riddick 5-38, Reed 4-63.

DOLPHINS LEADERS: Rushing - Hampton 13-52, Bennett 3-9, Stradford 3-5, Clayton 1-4; **Passing** - Marino 24-36-0 - 303; **Receiving** - Clayton 6-81, Stradford 6-72, Duper 4-45, Jensen 3-36, Pruitt 2-45, Hardy 2-6, Hampton 1-18.

WEEK 6 GAMES

Hou 37, Atl 33	Chi 27, TB 26
Pitt 23, Cinc 20	Phil 37, Dal 20
GB 34, Det 33	SD 42, KC 21
Ind 30, NE 16	Wash 17, NYJ 16
NYG 30, St.L 7	SF 24, NO 22
Sea 35, LAR 13	Minn 34, Den 27
Clev 30, Rams 17	

NOTES

• The Bills trailed 21-3 at halftime, but rallied for only their third victory ever in Miami. The game was Buffalo's first regular-season appearance at Joe Robbie Stadium.

• The Dolphins drove 72 and 64 yards on their first two possessions to open a 14-0 lead as Dan Marino threw TD passes to Mark Duper and James Pruitt. Marino was seven of 10 for 80 yards on the two drives.

• Early in the second quarter, Miami went 83 yards in 10 plays to Marino's TD pass to Bruce Hardy.

• The Bills finally got on the board as Scott Norwood capped a 16-play, 58-yard drive with a field goal one second before the half ended. Kelly was seven-of-nine for 63 yards as the Bills overcame a penalty and sack.

• Norwood missed a field goal on the first series of the third, but after a Miami punt, the Bills drove 67 yards to Robb Riddick's TD. Chris Burkett's 33-yard catch was the key play. After another Miami punt, the Bills went 45 yards to Burkett's TD reception. Burkett had a 16-yard reception on third-and-10.

• Early in the fourth, Fuad Reveiz made a field goal, but the Bills tied the game when Riddick scored midway through the fourth. The TD was set up when Steve Tasker forced Scott Schwedes to fumble a punt and Adam Lingner recovered at the 32. Ray Bentley then forced Schwedes to fumble the ensuing kickoff and Scott Radecic recovered at the 33. Five plays later, Kelly hit Riddick for a TD on third-and-five for a 31-24 lead.

• The Dolphins took possession with 4:04 left and Marino drove them 80 yards in 11 plays to his TD pass to Clayton with 1:08 left. On the play before the TD, Marino hit Duper for 17 on fourth-and-ten.

• The Bills won the OT toss and wasted no time, driving 65 yards to Norwood's winning field goal.

QUOTES

• Bill Polian: "This was a turning point win for this franchise. What are the odds of coming back to win after spotting Dan Marino a 21-0 lead? In previous years if we

had gotten down that deep against a team like this, the game would have ended up 48-0."

• Jim Kelly: "I don't know if this was my best game ever, but I'll tell you what, it's awfully sweet. I wouldn't trade this for anything. I prayed so much before that coin flip. I didn't want Marino to get the ball first."

• Marv Levy: "The point in the game when it began to swing our way was when we began to have success running the ball. Until we could run and pass, we didn't have a chance."

• Joe Devlin: "Thank God I called tails (on the coin flip). We were on strike, but when we came back, we wanted to come back and win. The only way to do that was to practice, run and lift weights."

• Miami coach Don Shula: "There's no other way to say it: We caved in as a team."

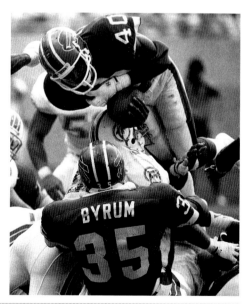

STANDINGS: SIXTH WEEK

AFC EAST	W	L	T	CENTRAL	W	L	T	WEST	W	L	T	NFC EAST	W	L	T	CENTRAL	W	L	T	WEST	W	L	T
NY Jets	3	3	0	Houston	4	2	0	San Diego	5	1	0	Washington	5	1	0	Chicago	5	1	0	San Fran	5	1	0
New England	3	3	0	Cleveland	4	2	0	Seattle	4	2	0	Dallas	3	3	0	Green Bay	3	2	1	N.Orleans	3	3	0
Buffalo	3	3	0	Pittsburgh	4	2	0	Denver	3	2	1	St. Louis	2	4	0	Minnesota	3	3	0	Atlanta	2	4	0
Indianapolis	3	3	0	Cincinnati	2	4	0	Raiders	3	3	0	Philadelphia	2	4	0	Tampa Bay	3	3	0	LA Rams	1	5	0
Miami	2	4	0					Kan. City	1	5	0	NY Giants	1	5	0	Detroit	1	5	0				

NOTES

• The Redskins dominated the Bills, outrushing them 299-21.

• Jim Kelly did manage to tie Joe Ferguson's record for consecutive games with a TD pass (12).

• Inside linebacker Eugene Marve was replaced in the starting lineup by Scott Radecic, who had eight tackles.

• The Redskins drove to an Ali Haji-Shiekh field goal on the first possession of the game.

• Late in the first quarter, Jay Schroeder threw a 51-yard pass to Gary Clark, setting up his TD pass to Kelvin Bryant early in the second for a 10-0 lead.

• On the next series, Monte Coleman intercepted Kelly at the 7 and returned to the Redskins 35. Eight plays later, Schroeder scored on a bootleg on a third-and-one play.

• Late in the half, Dwight Drane sacked Schroeder and appeared to force a fumble which Sean McNanie returned for a TD, but after instant replay, officials' call of the sack and no fumble was upheld.

• On the third play of the third quarter, Todd Bowles intercepted Kelly and returned it 24 yards to the Bills 41. Seven plays later, Schroeder threw another TD pass to Bryant.

• After a Bills punt, the Redskins moved 51 yards in 11 plays to Haji-Sheikh's field goal.

• The Bills' only score came on the first play of the fourth, following Radecic's recovery of a Bryant fumble at the Redskins 35 which was forced by Leon Seals. Kelly hit Andre Reed for 29 yards, but then was sacked for a loss of 11 by Dexter Manley. On the next play, he found Reed for the TD.

QUOTES

• Redskins coach Joe Gibbs: "That was the best we've played in a long time. I think we played as good as we can play. It was just our day and the guys played great."

• Redskins defensive end Charles Mann: "Because their run wasn't getting anywhere, we were able to tee off on Kelly. We were always in his face, rattling him."

• Jim Kelly: "Their whole defense was coming at us. They just had a good defensive scheme. For every pass protection we had, they had a guy coming where we weren't going to be. To say the least, this was an old-fashioned butt-whipping."

• Dwight Drane on the non-fumble: "I was shocked, I think everybody was. I thought it was a touchdown for us, no question about it. We were all celebrating, but when they called it back, that broke the celebration."

• Marv Levy: "To win, you have to be able to run and stop the run. I was afraid coming into the game that their strength would be directed at our weaknesses." (On the non-fumble): "Instant replay is a total failure and a waste of time. Ninety percent of the time after a review, they will state that the whistle had blown. You've got to rise above things like that, but we're not good enough, compared to the Redskins, that we can let those opportunities slip away."

• Ralph Wilson: "They just manhandled us. That's one of the best teams in the league and we don't have the players to compete with them yet."

WEEK 7 GAMES

Den 34, Det 0	Hou 31, Cinc 29
Ind 19, NYJ 14	Chi 31, KC 28
NE 26, LAR 23	Sea 28, Minn 17
NO 38, Atl 0	Mia 35, Pitt 24
Phil 28, St.L 23	SF 31, Rams 10
TB 23, GB 17	Dal 33, NYG 24
SD 27, Clev 24 (OT)	

Redskins	3	14	10	0	-	27
Bills	0	0	0	7	-	7

Attendance at Rich Stadium - 71,640

Wash: FG Haji-Sheikh 30, 4:15
Wash: Bryant 12 pass from Schroeder (Haji-Sheikh kick), :07
Wash: Schroeder 13 run (Haji-Sheikh kick), 7:54
Wash: Bryant 7 pass from Schroeder (Haji-Sheikh kick), 4:58
Wash: FG Haji-Sheikh 33, 12:31
Buf: Reed 17 pass from Kelly (Norwood kick), :03

	BUF	WASH
First downs	14	24
Rushing yds	21	299
Passing yds	259	107
Punts-avg	5-41.6	5-44.4
Fumbles-lost	2-1	2-1
Penalties-yds	7-55	6-45
Poss. time	19:02	40:58

BILLS LEADERS: **Rushing** - Riddick 6-19, Kelly 2-3, Byrum 2-(-1); **Passing** - Kelly 25-43-3 - 292; **Receiving** - Reed 8-108, Harmon 6-70, Burkett 5-55, T. Johnson 4-41, Metzelaars 2-18.

REDSKINS LEADERS: **Rushing** - Rogers 30-125, Smith 7-54, Monk 3-54, Bryant 9-46, Schroeder 3-15, Griffin 1-5; **Passing** - Schroeder 11-18-0 - 132; **Receiving** - Monk 5-38, Clark 2-72, Bryant 3-19, Rogers 1-3.

NOTES

• The Bills pulled the upset on a windy day that hampered John Elway's passing skills.

• Cornelius Bennett did not start as expected, but he played mostly in passing situations and was turned loose to rush Elway. On his first play, he pressured Elway and forced an incompletion.

• The Bills first two possessions ended in turnovers, but the defense forced two Denver punts. On the third series, the Bills drove 64 yards in 10 plays to Jim Kelly's TD pass to Andre Reed early in the second quarter.

• Midway through the second, Robb Riddick blocked a Mike Horan punt through the end zone for a safety.

• After an exchange of punts, the Bills moved 75 yards in 10 plays to Riddick's TD run.

• The defense then held on three downs and forced a Horan punt with seven seconds left in the half. This time, Steve Tasker broke through and blocked it through the end zone for the second safety and an 18-0 halftime lead.

• The Bills took the second-half kickoff and drove 68 yards to Scott Norwood's field goal. They converted twice on third down. Also, Kelly hit Ronnie Harmon with a 17-yard pass to the 14.

• Denver answered three plays after the kickoff. Elway hit Vance Johnson for gains of 15 and 51 yards, setting up Sammy Winder's TD sweep.

• After seven straight punts, Denver put together a 15-play, 90-yard drive culminating in Elway's TD pass to Johnson. Then, Tasker fumbled the ensuing kickoff and Marc Munford recovered at the 11. However, Bruce Smith forced Winder to fumble two plays later and Nate Odomes recovered. The Bills then ate up four minutes and when the Broncos got the ball back, Bennett had a sack and Dwight Drane recovered a fumble by Clarence Kay with 22 seconds left.

QUOTES

• Bruce Smith on Winder's fumble: "We needed a big play. Somebody had to make it and I didn't want to wait around for anybody else. I read draw play and just reacted. Last year I didn't get the publicity I deserved. All I can do is keep playing and I'll definitely get it."

• Marv Levy: "Bruce is recognized by the coaches and by many of the media, but I don't know if you know how outstanding this guy is. He's something else. He's a great defensive end, the best I've been around. Art Still (Kansas City) was a good one, but Bruce has a better surge." (On the key to the win): "It doesn't matter if it's the Rose Bowl with the flowers blooming or here with the wind howling and the snow falling, you have to run the ball to win. I told them 'Do you know who you just beat? You beat a team that was just in the Super Bowl.'"

• Kent Hull: "We felt with the horses we had in the backfield and the horses we have in the line, we felt we could have a little stampede. And we wanted to keep Mr. Elway off the field."

• Joe Devlin: "I don't believe we're world-beaters, but if we work hard and persevere, we can beat any team in the league."

• Broncos quarterback John Elway: "As soon as I walked out of the tunnel, I caught one of those gusts of wind and it just stopped me cold."

WEEK 8 GAMES

Clev 38, Atl 3	Chi 26, GB 24
Det 27, Dal 17	SF 27, Hou 20
Minn 31, LAR 20	Mia 20, Cinc 14
NO 31, Rams 14	Pitt 17, KC 16
SD 16, Ind 13	St.L 31, TB 28
NYG 17, NE 10	Phil 31, Wash 27
NYJ 30, Sea 14	

Broncos	0	0	7	7	-	14
Bills	0	18	3	0	-	21

Attendance at Rich Stadium - 63,698

Buf: Reed 9 pass from Kelly (Norwood kick), 3:23
Buf: Safety: Riddick blocked punt through end zone, 6:50
Buf: Riddick 1 run (Norwood kick), 14:51
Buf: Safety: Tasker blocked punt through end zone, 15:00
Buf: FG Norwood 30, 7:50
Den: Winder 6 run (Karlis kick), 9:27
Den: V. Johnson 15 pass from Elway (Karlis kick), 9:10

	BUF	DEN
First downs	25	12
Rushing yds	258	76
Passing yds	170	139
Punts-avg	7-39.1	9-30.8
Fumbles-lost	4-2	2-2
Penalties-yds	6-47	7-45
Poss. time	37:37	22:23

BILLS LEADERS: **Rushing** - Riddick 19-78, Mueller 9-65, Harmon 18-60, Byrum 6-38, Kelly 6-17; **Passing** - Kelly 14-23-1 - 135, Riddick 1-1-0 - 35; **Receiving** - Reed 5-60, Harmon 3-27, Burkett 2-21, Riddick 2-14, Metzelaars 2-13, Kelly 1-35.

BRONCOS LEADERS: **Rushing** - Winder 12-40, Sewell 6-24, Elway 3-9, Lang 1-3; **Passing** - Elway 13-30-0 163; **Receiving** - Johnson 5-95, Kay 4-38, Nattiel 2-22, Lang 2-8.

STANDINGS: EIGHTH WEEK

AFC EAST	W	L	T	CENTRAL	W	L	T	WEST	W	L	T	NFC EAST	W	L	T	CENTRAL	W	L	T	WEST	W	L	T
Indianapolis	4	4	0	Houston	5	3	0	San Diego	7	1	0	Washington	6	2	0	Chicago	7	1	0	San Fran	7	1	0
New England	4	4	0	Cleveland	5	3	0	Seattle	5	3	0	Dallas	4	4	0	Tampa Bay	4	4	0	N.Orleans	5	3	0
Buffalo	4	4	0	Pittsburgh	5	3	0	Denver	4	3	1	Philadelphia	4	4	0	Minnesota	4	4	0	Atlanta	2	6	0
NY Jets	4	4	0	Cincinnati	2	6	0	Raiders	3	5	0	St. Louis	3	5	0	Green Bay	3	4	1	LA Rams	1	7	0
Miami	4	4	0					Kan. City	1	7	0	NY Giants	2	6	0	Detroit	2	6	0				

Bills	7	0	0	14	- 21
Browns	3	14	7	3	- 27

Attendance at Cleveland Stadium - 78,409

Clev: FG Jaeger 22, 8:50
Buf: Kelso 56 fumble return (Norwood kick), 13:09
Clev: Ellis 27 fumble return (Jaeger kick), :19
Clev: Langhorne 15 pass from Kosar (Jaeger kick), 6:51
Clev: Slaughter 52 pass from Kosar (Jaeger kick), 2:46
Clev: FG Jaeger 40, 2:07
Buf: Burkett 13 pass from Kelly (Norwood kick), 4:00
Buf: Reed 10 pass from Kelly (Norwood kick), 14:08

	BUF	CLE
First downs	17	24
Rushing yds	61	84
Passing yds	206	337
Punts-avg	3-39.3	1-45.0
Fumbles-lost	2-2	2-2
Penalties-yds	6-70	10-90
Poss. time	24:19	35:41

BILLS LEADERS: Rushing - Byrum 3-13, Kelly 4-42, Mueller 5-4, Harmon 6-2, K. Porter 2-0; **Passing** - Kelly 22-35-0 - 222; **Receiving** - Reed 4-36, Burkett 6-91, Harmon 6-52, T. Johnson 2-24, Metzelaars 3-15, R. Porter 1-4.

BROWNS LEADERS: Rushing - Mack 17-48, Byner 10-21, McNeil 1-17, Kosar 3-(-2); **Passing** - Kosar 24-34-1 346; **Receiving** - Newsome 3-70, Slaughter 4-78, Byner 6-64, Mack 4-46, Langhorne 2-25, Tennell 1-24, Brennan 2-15, Weathers 1-14, McNeil 1-10.

NOTES
• The Bills played poorly early in the game and a late rally couldn't overcome the 27-7 deficit.
• Jim Kelly operated out of the two-minute offense for most of the fourth quarter and was effective.
• The Browns drove 69 yards on their first possession to Jeff Jaeger's field goal. On their second series, Bruce Smith forced Kevin Mack to fumble, Mark Kelso picked it up and ran for the go-ahead TD.
• On the first play of the second quarter, Derrick Burroughs intercepted Bernie Kosar at the Bills 24, but on the next play, Frank Minnifield forced Pete Metzelaars to fumble, Ray Ellis picked it up and ran for a TD.
• Scott Norwood missed a 38-yard field goal, and the Browns turned around and drove 79 yards to Kosar's TD pass to Reggie Langhorne. The key play was a 36-yard interference penalty on Nate Odomes.
• Norwood then missed from 36 yards before the half ended.
• The Browns took the second-half kickoff and on the sixth play, Kosar caught the Bills in a safety blitz and threw a 52-yard TD pass to Webster Slaughter for a 24-7 advantage.
• Late in the third, Metzelaars lost another fumble to kill a drive. It led to Jaeger's second field goal.
• Turning to the hurry-up offense, Kelly completed seven straight passes on a 64-yard march to Chris Burkett's TD reception. Late in the game, Kelly was four-of-seven including a TD pass to Andre Reed with 52 seconds left, capping a 59-yard drive. However, the Browns recovered the onside kick.

QUOTES
• Scott Norwood on the bad Cleveland field: "I had a terrible pregame warmup. I didn't handle the conditions very well today. I didn't expect it to be as bad as it was, but I should have been able to make adjustments. You have to rise above it and concentrate a little harder. I knew that Jim had the capability to stage a comeback, I was just hoping he could score enough points to make up for my mistakes."
• Jim Kelly: "I don't think we were outplayed badly. We had a couple of missed field goals, a couple of fumbles that were the difference. A play here, a play there. I was praying so hard that we'd get that onside kick. Cleveland's a very good team, but I feel we could have beaten them if we had one more shot. I feel like we just ran out of time."
• Marv Levy: "There was the six points. Both kicks were inside 40 and you count on making those. I don't think the field had anything to do with it. It never bothered Lou Groza. Did we miss Robb Riddick? In my mind, yes, we missed his running ability."
• Fred Smerlas on Bernie Kosar: "The guy just nickel-and-dimes you to death. He takes that short drop so you can't get one of those pin-your-ears-back rushes on him. He just keeps hitting you with that short stuff and then every so often he'll catch you with a bomb."

WEEK 9 GAMES	
Cinc 16, Atl 10	Wash 20, Det 13
Sea 24, GB 13	Hou 23, Pitt 3
Ind 40, Mia 21	Minn 23, TB 17
Rams 27, St.L 24	NO 26, SF 24
NYG 20, Phil 17	NYJ 16, KC 9
SD 16, LAR 14	Den 31, Chi 29
Dal 23, NE 17 (OT)	

Bills	0	7	10	0	- 17
Jets	0	7	0	7	- 14

Attendance at Giants Stadium - 58,407

NYJ: Shuler 32 pass from O'Brien (Leahy kick), 7:10
Buf: Broughton 25 pass from Kelly (Norwood kick), 10:08
Buf: Mueller 2 run (Norwood kick), 5:49
Buf: FG Norwood 42, 11:43
NYJ: Sohn 4 pass from O'Brien (Leahy kick), 14:03

	BUF	NYJ
First downs	15	21
Rushing yds	127	126
Passing yds	204	192
Punts-avg	7-31.6	7-40.7
Fumbles-lost	1-0	1-0
Penalties-yds	2-15	6-38
Poss. time	29:32	30:28

BILLS LEADERS: Rushing - Harmon 9-61, R. Porter 12-42, Mueller 7-20, Kelly 1-3, Byrum 2-1; **Passing** - Kelly 21-33-1 - 214; **Receiving** - Reed 4-21, R. Porter 4-30, Burkett 4-35, Broughton 3-67, Harmon 2-19, Metzelaars 2-16, T. Johnson 2-26.

JETS LEADERS: Rushing - McNeil 20-103, Vick 3-12, O'Brien 4-8, Faaola 1-4, Hector 1-1, Townsell 1-(-2); **Passing** - O'Brien 18-40-1 - 225; **Receiving** - Shuler 5-68, Toon 4-54, McNeil 2-26, Townsell 2-16, Sohn 2-35, Klever 1-11, Vick 1-7, Hector 1-8.

NOTES
• The Bills' defense turned in a strong game led by Shane Conlan, Cornelius Bennett and Bruce Smith. Those three combined for 23 tackles and three sacks. Smith played despite having the flu.
• Jim Kelly threw a TD pass for the 15th straight game, extending his team record.
• Ricky Porter, who played for the Bills' replacement team, stepped in and performed well.
• The AFC East standings, incredibly, became all even with every team at 5-5.
• Pat Leahy missed a 44-yard field goal in the first quarter, and the Bills' first scoring threat ended with a Kelly interception. The Jets then drove 79 yards in 13 plays to Ken O'Brien's TD pass to Mickey Shuler.
• Midway through the second, Dave Jennings shanked a 19-yard punt, giving the Bills the ball at the Jets 29. Three plays later, Kelly hit Walter Broughton for a TD on third-and-six from the 25.
• The Bills took the second-half kickoff and drove 68 yards to Jamie Mueller's TD plunge. Trumaine Johnson's 19-yard reception on third-and-six from the Jets 47 was the key play.
• After a punt, the Bills moved 46 yards in seven plays to a Scott Norwood field goal. Kelly hit Broughton for 32 yards on third-and-eight from the Bills 29.

• In the fourth, the Jets pulled to within 17-14 by driving 78 yards in 15 plays to O'Brien's TD pass to Kurt Sohn, which was tipped by Bennett, with 57 seconds left. Ron Pitts then recovered the onside kick.

QUOTES
• Bruce Smith on a game he plays with Cornelius Bennett: "First one to the quarterback wins. It's a lot of fun. We were more in tune and comfortable working together. When Cornelius first got here, he didn't know the moves of the guys he was playing next to. That's something you have to get comfortable with in time. I was weak and I started getting the shivers. Somehow or another, I managed to stay in there. If I could play that way every time I'm sick, I'll start getting sick more often."
• Fred Smerlas: "This is the most talented defense we've had since I've been here. People can't single block our down linemen. I think we have one of the best defensive lines in the league. And the scary thing is they're just going to get better."
• Marv Levy: "Our players know they are not playing out of their league. Their confidence is growing. We played awfully good defense. We got a good pass rush and obviously got some good coverage which forced O'Brien to hold the ball a little longer. We haven't stressed winning the division because it distracts you from the target. If we win the rest of our games, we'll win the division. We've got to concentrate on who we play next."
• Jim Kelly: "Ronnie Harmon's a fine back, but he's an outside runner. We needed somebody to hit the hole quick, like Robb, and that's what Ricky does."

WEEK 10 GAMES	
Minn 24, Atl 13	Clev 40, Hou 7
Den 23, LAR 17	Chi 30, Det 10
GB 23, KC 3	NE 24, Ind 0
NO 23, NYG 14	Pitt 30, Cinc 16
Sea 34, SD 3	St.L 31, Phil 19
SF 24, TB 10	Mia 20, Dal 14
Rams 30, Wash 26	

STANDINGS: TENTH WEEK

AFC EAST	W	L	T	CENTRAL	W	L	T	WEST	W	L	T	NFC EAST	W	L	T	CENTRAL	W	L	T	WEST	W	L	T
Indianapolis	5	5	0	Cleveland	7	3	0	San Diego	8	2	0	Washington	7	3	0	Chicago	8	2	0	San Fran	8	2	0
NY Jets	5	5	0	Houston	6	4	0	Seattle	7	3	0	Dallas	5	5	0	Minnesota	6	4	0	N.Orleans	7	3	0
Buffalo	5	5	0	Pittsburgh	6	4	0	Denver	6	3	1	Philadelphia	4	6	0	Green Bay	4	5	1	LA Rams	3	7	0
New England	5	5	0	Cincinnati	3	7	0	Raiders	3	7	0	St. Louis	4	6	0	Tampa Bay	4	6	0	Atlanta	2	8	0
Miami	5	5	0					Kan. City	1	9	0	NY Giants	3	7	0	Detroit	2	8	0				

GAME 11 - Sunday, Nov. 29, 1987 - BILLS 27, DOLPHINS 0

NOTES

• The Bills' defense was brilliant, pitching its first shutout against Miami since the Dolphins lost, 3-0, in the famous snowplow game at New England on Dec. 20, 1982. Dan Marino was held without a TD pass for the first time in 30 games, ending the NFL's second-longest streak in history.

• It was the Bills first shutout since Nov. 10, 1985 against Houston and the most lopsided victory since a 35-3 win over the Colts in 1981. It completed the first Bills sweep of Miami since '66, the Dolphins' first AFL year.

• Andre Reed caught two passes for 47 yards as the Bills drove 85 yards in six plays to Jamie Mueller's TD early in the second quarter. Mueller was making his first NFL start.

• On the next series, Scott Radecic intercepted Marino and the Bills drove 56 yards in 11 plays to Jim Kelly's TD pass to Butch Rolle. Mueller converted two third-and-one situations with plunges.

• After a 77-yard Reggie Roby punt, the Bills drove 97 yards in seven plays to make it 21-0 late in the second. On the final three plays, Ronnie Harmon ran for 19, Kelly hit Reed for 40, then threw 22 yards to Chris Burkett for the TD. Kelly was 10-of-11 for 145 yards at the half.

• On the fourth play of the third, Mark Kelso intercepted Marino and that led to a Scott Norwood field goal.

• In the fourth, Derrick Burroughs intercepted Marino and the Bills went 54 yards in 10 plays to Norwood's second field goal. Don Strock replaced Marino on the next series, but the Dolphins couldn't score.

QUOTES

• Miami linebacker Jackie Shipp: "Buffalo is an improved team, but there's still a stigma about losing to Buffalo."

• Marv Levy: "Not in my wildest dreams did I think we'd come away with a shutout. The biggest thing we overcame was that 77-yard punt. All we have to do there is fumble and they go in and it's 14-7. The whole momentum could have swung, but then we go 97 yards for a touchdown."

• Sean McNanie on Dan Marino: "You could just see it (frustration) in his eyes."

• Fred Smerlas: "As you could see today, the interior guys, myself and Sean, were in Marino's face every play. When that happens, he has to come out of there and you have Bruce and Cornelius on the outside. It's a tough way to make a living. And our DBs came out whacking guys. That throws their patterns off." (On Shipp's comment): "It's the same old crap we've had to put up with the past several years. People in other parts of the country think we're still a bunch of cellar-dwellers. Well, we're not. It's no longer an embarrassing thing to lose to us."

• Miami coach Don Shula: "My disappointment is that we didn't compete in a game that meant so much. Instead, we were dominated. It was complete domination. The only highlight for us was Reggie Roby's punting and when your punting is the only highlight, you know you're in trouble."

• Jim Kelly: "Our offensive line was awesome. They were blowing people off the ball, giving me all the time in the world. And Ronnie Harmon ran the way we thought he could."

Dolphins	0	0	0	0 -	0
Bills	0	21	3	3 -	27

Attendance at Rich Stadium - 68,055

Buf: Mueller 5 run (Norwood kick), :09
Buf: Rolle 3 pass from Kelly (Norwood kick), 9:02
Buf: Burkett 22 pass from Kelly (Norwood kick), 13:58
Buf: FG Norwood 39, 4:59
Buf: FG Norwood 28, 7:04

	BUF	MIA
First downs	21	13
Rushing yds	229	23
Passing yds	217	206
Punts-avg	4-42.0	5-48.2
Fumbles-lost	1-0	4-0
Penalties-yds	8-65	4-30
Poss. time	35:58	24:02

BILLS LEADERS: Rushing - Harmon 23-119, R. Porter 14-67, Mueller 8-32, Kelly 2-11; **Passing** - Kelly 15-21-0 - 217; **Receiving** - Reed 4-96, Burkett 3-62, Metzelaars 3-40, Harmon 3-20, Rolle 1-3, Mueller 1-(-4).

DOLPHINS LEADERS: Rushing - Stadford 15-23, Marino 1-0; **Passing** - Marino 13-28-3 - 165, Strock 7-14-0 - 49; **Receiving** - Jensen 6-34, Davenport 3-41, Stradford 3-38, Pruitt 3-36, Duper 2-19, Clayton 2-33, Hampton 1-13.

WEEK 11 GAMES

KC 27, Det 20	Min 44, Dal 38 OT
Den 31, SD 17	Chi 23, GB 10
Ind 51, Hou 27	NO 20, Pitt 15
Wash 23, NYG 19	NYJ 27, Cinc 20
St.L 34, Atl 21	Rams 35, TB 3
SF 38, Clev 24	LAR 37, Sea 14
Phil 34, NE 31 (OT)	

GAME 12 - Sunday, Dec. 6, 1987 - RAIDERS 34, BILLS 21

NOTES

• The Bills were so concerned about Bo Jackson and Marcus Allen, they forgot about Marc Wilson.

• Andre Reed had his best day as a Bill with 153 receiving yards.

• James Lofton had his best day since joining the Raiders at the start of the season.

• Los Angeles scored on its first possession, driving 80 yards in 11 plays to Wilson's TD pass to Bo Jackson.

• On the next series, they drove to Chris Bahr's field goal. The key play was Jackson's 23-yard reception.

• After a Bahr miss early in the second quarter, the Bills drove 74 yards in 11 plays to Ronnie Harmon's TD. Kelly was six-of-seven on the drive including a 26-yarder to Ricky Porter.

• Bahr made a field goal on the next series, but the Bills needed just four plays to take a 14-13 lead. Kelly hit Chris Burkett for 35 and Reed for 37 on back-to-back plays, leading to the TD to Butch Rolle.

• In the third, the Raiders took control. On the third play, Lofton caught a 41-yard TD pass and after a Bills punt, Los Angeles drove 77 yards in 13 plays to Allen's TD run. Allen carried six times for 30 yards.

• The Bills then had their second four-play, 80-yard march. Kelly hit Reed for 38, Burkett for nine and Pete Metzelaars for 25 before Harmon swept in from the 8 to make it 27-21.

• Early in the fourth, the Bills drove to the Raiders 36 but were stopped on fourth-and-two. After an exchange of punts, Los Angeles went 68 yards in eight plays to the clinching TD, Wilson's pass to Dokie Williams with 2:38 left to play.

QUOTES

• Bruce Smith on Wilson: "I take my hat off to him. We didn't harass him like we did other quarterbacks. He had time and he used it well. And when you have runners like

that, you keep your pass rush honest. You have to do more reading than attacking."

• Marv Levy: "We just didn't make very many big plays. We had a blocked field goal, but that was the only big play defensively. We just didn't play well at all. I feared the Raiders. They're better than they were when they were losing. We had trouble stopping them today. After we forged ahead 14-13, I think our team may have had the feeling 'we've got this thing under control now' and not remembering how good the Raiders are."

• Shane Conlan: "He (Wilson) picked our defense apart. It's tough because most of the time we were only rushing three guys and they have five linemen and a back kept in to block."

• Jim Kelly: "They controlled the ball and kept our offense off the field. We didn't get enough pressure on Wilson. When a quarterback has five or six seconds back there, he's going to complete some. God almighty I'd like to have that much time – and sometimes I do."

Bills	0	14	7	0 -	21
Raiders	10	3	14	7 -	34

Attendance at the Coliseum - 43,143

LAR: Jackson 14 pass from Wilson (Bahr kick), 9:05
LAR: FG Bahr 22, 13:45
Buf: Harmon 8 run (Norwood kick), 6:26
LAR: FG Bahr 33, 11:43
Buf: Rolle 3 pass from Kelly (Norwood kick), 13:44
LAR: Lofton 41 pass from Wilson (Bahr kick), 1:34
LAR: Allen 2 run (Bahr kick), 8:08
Buf: Harmon 8 run (Norwood kick), 10:23
LAR: Williams 23 pass from Wilson (Bahr kick), 12:22

	BUF	LAR
First downs	19	29
Rushing yds	84	144
Passing yds	303	350
Punts-avg	4-46.0	3-42.3
Fumbles-lost	1-1	0-0
Penalties-yds	4-25	2-25
Poss. time	25:12	34:48

BILLS LEADERS: Rushing - Harmon 8-37, Mueller 6-28, R. Porter 3-14, Byrum 1-4, Kelly 3-1; **Passing** - Kelly 22-36-0 - 315; **Receiving** - Reed 7-153, Burkett 6-66, Harmon 3-26, Metzelaars 2-33, R. Porter 2-28, Johnson 1-6, Rolle 1-3.

RAIDERS LEADERS: Rushing - Jackson 19-78, Allen 15-47, Mueller 2-10, Wilson 2-6, Strachan 1-2, Lofton 1-1; **Passing** - Wilson 21-32-0 - 337, Allen 1-1-0 - 23; **Receiving** - Lofton 6-132, Allen 5-58, Jackson 4-59, Christensen 3-62, Williams 2-36, Junkin 1-8, Mueller 1-5.

WEEK 12 GAMES

Atl 21, Dal 10	Ind 9, Clev 7
Rams 37, Det 16	Den 31, NE 20
SF 23, GB 12	Cin 30, KC 27 (OT)
Hou 33, SD 18	Pitt 13, Sea 9
NO 44, TB 34	Wash 34, St.L 17
Chi 30, Minn 24	Mia 37, NYJ 28
NYG 23, Phil 20 (OT)	

STANDINGS: TWELFTH WEEK

AFC EAST	W	L	T	CENTRAL	W	L	T	WEST	W	L	T	NFC EAST	W	L	T	CENTRAL	W	L	T	WEST	W	L	T
Indianapolis	7	5	0	Cleveland	7	5	0	Denver	8	3	1	Washington	9	3	0	Chicago	10	2	0	San Fran	10	2	0
Buffalo	6	6	0	Houston	7	5	0	San Diego	8	4	0	Dallas	5	7	0	Minnesota	7	5	0	N.Orleans	9	3	0
NY Jets	6	6	0	Pittsburgh	7	5	0	Seattle	7	5	0	Philadelphia	5	7	0	Green Bay	4	7	1	LA Rams	5	7	0
Miami	6	6	0	Cincinnati	4	8	0	Raiders	5	7	0	St. Louis	5	7	0	Tampa Bay	4	8	0	Atlanta	3	9	0
New England	5	7	0					Kan. City	2	10	0	NY Giants	4	8	0	Detroit	2	10	0				

Bills	7	6	0	14	-	27
Colts	0	3	0	0	-	3

Attendance at the Hoosier Dome - 60,253

Buf: Harmon 12 pass from Kelly (Norwood kick), 7:11
Buf: FG Norwood 39, 1:17
Ind: FG Biasucci 30, 6:53
Buf: FG Norwood 25, 13:03
Buf: Johnson 8 pass from Kelly (Norwood kick), 5:22
Buf: B. Smith recovered fumble (Norwood kick), 13:49

	BUF	IND
First downs	25	9
Rushing yds	218	33
Passing yds	167	97
Punts-avg	6-37.5	8-40.9
Fumbles-lost	4-4	5-2
Penalties-yds	5-45	4-25
Poss. time	39:08	20:52

BILLS LEADERS: **Rushing** - Harmon 18-85, Mueller 15-81, R. Porter 14-46, Kelly 2-6; **Passing** - Kelly 18-34-0 - 167, Kidd 0-1-0 - 0; **Receiving** - Burkett 4-62, Johnson 3-26, Reed 3-41, Harmon 3-10, Metzelaars 2-9, Mueller 2-17, R. Porter 1-2.

COLTS LEADERS: **Rushing** - Dickerson 11-19, Wonsley 2-14, Trudeau 2-1, Bentley 2-(-1); **Passing** - Trudeau 6-15-2 - 78, Salisbury 8-12-2 - 68; **Receiving** - Brooks 5-55, Bouza 2-18, Dickerson 2-31, Bentley 2-17, Wonsley 2-14, Beach 1-11.

WEEK 13 GAMES

Rams 33, Atl 0	Clev 38, Cin 24
Wash 24, Dal 20	Det 20, TB 10
NO 24, Hou 10	KC 16, LAR 10
Mia 28, Phil 10	GB 16, Minn 10
St.L 27, NYG 24	NE 42, NYJ 20
Pitt 20, SD 16	Sea 28, Den 21
SF 41, Chi 0	

NOTES

• Bruce Smith led a great defensive effort with 2 1/2 sacks, a forced fumble and a fumble recovery for his first NFL TD as the Bills moved into the driver's seat for the division title.
• The Bills had a season-high four interceptions and limited the Colts to 130 net yards.
• The victory was the first for the Bills in the Hoosier Dome. One key was holding Eric Dickerson in check.
• On the opening kickoff, offensive line coach Jim Ringo suffered a broken left leg when a player crashed into him on the sidelines. After getting treatment and a brace, he coached the rest of the game.
• The Bills took the opening kickoff and drove 75 yards in 13 plays to Jim Kelly's TD pass to Ronnie Harmon. It was Kelly's 18th straight game with at least one TD pass.
• After Rohn Stark shanked a 26-yard punt, the Bills drove 25 yards to a Scott Norwood field goal.
• The teams combined for seven turnovers in less than two minutes after that. Dean Biasucci kicked a field goal for the Colts after Jamie Mueller's fumble at the Colts 21.
• The Bills answered with a six-minute, 69-yard drive to another Norwood field goal for a 13-3 lead.
• Late in the third, Tony Furjanic forced Bill Brooks to fumble a punt and John Kaiser recovered at the Colts 30. But Pete Metzelaars gave it back with a fumble.
• After a punt, the Bills put the game away with a 56-yard march to Kelly's TD pass to Trumaine Johnson.
• On the next three Colts series', Mark Kelso and Ron Pitts made interceptions and Smith sacked Sean Salisbury and recovered his fumble for a TD with 1:11 left to play.

QUOTES

• Cornelius Bennett: "We're in the driver's seat. We're going to win it."
• Bruce Smith: "The key was stopping Dickerson. We knew if we stopped him, we could rattle Trudeau."
• Colts running back Eric Dickerson: "It wasn't just one guy, it was 11 guys swarming on me on every play. Give them credit, they just lined up and beat us. There weren't any holes."
• Marv Levy: "The best part was how our defense played after we didn't capitalize on some of the advantages they gave us. Our defense could have let down after some of the mistakes our offense made, but instead, they played harder. We've got to fight for our life every week."
• Colts coach Ron Meyer: "I'm not sure the resurrection of Johnny Unitas would have helped us today. We're not dead, but we're wounded."
• Kent Hull: "If you look at it realistically, this was the first of our playoff games. If we don't win, we don't go. And we're going to take next week as a playoff game. We knew all along we were a playoff-quality team. We overcame some adversity today."
• Ralph Wilson: "About a month ago I sensed that we had a team that was coming together. You don't beat teams like Miami, Denver and the Colts without something going right."

Patriots	7	6	0	0	-	13
Bills	0	0	7	0	-	7

Attendance at Rich Stadium - 74,945

NE: Jones 7 pass from Grogan (Franklin kick), 9:44
NE: Dupard 36 run (kick failed), 13:09
Buf: McNanie 14 fumble return (Norwood kick), 7:53

	BUF	NE
First downs	12	15
Rushing yds	84	150
Passing yds	64	85
Punts-avg	6-45.7	6-32.5
Fumbles-lost	2-1	4-1
Penalties-yds	5-25	2-10
Poss. time	24:13	35:47

BILLS LEADERS: **Rushing** - Mueller 14-37, Kelly 2-19, Harmon 6-15, Byrum 2-13; **Passing** - Kelly 13-31-1 - 125; **Receiving** - Reed 4-19, Harmon 3-42, Burkett 3-31, Metzelaars 1-20, Byrum 1-7, R. Porter 1-6.

PATRIOTS LEADERS: **Rushing** - Dupard 31-78, Perryman 8-42, Fryar 1-16, Tatupu 1-9, Grogan 5-4, Collins 1-1; **Passing** - Grogan 9-15-2 - 85; **Receiving** - Jones 4-57, Collins 3-21, Dawson 2-7.

WEEK 14 GAMES

NYG 20, GB 10	Den 20, KC 17
Clev 24, LAR 17	Ind 20, SD 7
Minn 17, Det 14	NO 41, Cinc 24
Phil 38, NYJ 27	Hou 24, Pitt 16
St.L 31, TB 14	SF 35, Atl 7
Sea 34, Chi 21	Mia 23, Wash 21
Dal 29, Rams 21	

NOTES

• The Bills not only blew a chance to win the AFC East, but the loss knocked them out of the playoff picture.
• Jim Kelly suffered his worst day as a pro, completing less than 50 percent of his passes for the first time in his pro career, a span of 64 games dating back to his University of Miami days.
• Kelly also failed to throw a TD pass for the first time in 18 games and he was sacked five times.
• Winds that gusted to 40 mph were a large reason for his misery, but the Pats played great defense.
• The Pats scored on their first possession, driving 83 yards in 11 plays to Steve Grogan's TD pass to Cedric Jones. Jones caught three passes for 30 yards on the drive and the Bills had three penalties.
• Late in the first quarter, a Ron Pitts' interception gave the Bills the ball at the Pats 16. But on the first play of the second, Ronnie Harmon fumbled a pitchout and the wind affected the ball. Steve Nelson recovered for the Pats.
• After an exchange of punts, the Pats drove 80 yards in 14 plays to Reggie Dupard's 36-yard TD run. Dupard started right, then reversed field to the left and sped into the end zone. The PAT was wide left.
• Midway through the third, Scott Radecic forced Dupard to fumble. Sean McNanie picked up the ball and ran 14 yards for a TD.
• Early in the fourth, the Bills drove to the Pats 4, but stalled when Kelly's fourth-and-three pass to Andre Reed in the end zone fell incomplete. Two plays later, Mark Kelso intercepted Grogan at the Pats 43, but four plays later, Kelly was intercepted by Fred Marion at the goal line. After a punt, the Bills got the ball back at their own 20 with 1:53 left, but Kelly was sacked twice and failed to complete a pass.

QUOTES

• Jim Kelly: "I'm going to take the blame for this one, I didn't have one of my better games. This is probably the hardest loss for me to swallow because I knew it was in our hands and it was just a matter of getting the ball in the end zone. It wasn't the greatest throwing conditions, but Grogan had to do the same thing. The defense did one heckuva job, the offense just couldn't get it going. And when we did, we didn't get it in the end zone. It's hard."
• Fred Smerlas: "We had it right in our hands and we let it get away."
• Marv Levy: "I don't think you win because you have more experience or that you've been there before. You go out and play the game. They played better than we did."
• Kent Hull: "We were coming off a big win in Indianapolis, the stadium was packed, a playoff spot was riding on this game. Everybody expected a big party. Don't blame him (Kelly). We didn't exactly give him good protection. It's not easy when you get sacked five times. I don't know how to explain it other than they stuffed us pretty good. Tippett and Nelson are loads."
• Sean McNanie: "It goes up in smoke pretty fast. This was the biggest football game I've ever been in and the most frustrating feeling I've experienced after a game."
• Joe Devlin: "The opportunity is gone and it's hard to accept. It just hurts."

STANDINGS: FOURTEENTH WEEK

AFC EAST	W	L	T	CENTRAL	W	L	T	WEST	W	L	T	NFC EAST	W	L	T	CENTRAL	W	L	T	WEST	W	L	T
Indianapolis	8	6	0	Cleveland	9	5	0	Denver	9	4	1	Washington	10	4	0	Chicago	10	4	0	San Fran	12	2	0
Miami	8	6	0	Pittsburgh	8	6	0	Seattle	9	5	0	St. Louis	7	7	0	Minnesota	8	6	0	N.Orleans	11	3	0
Buffalo	7	7	0	Houston	8	6	0	San Diego	8	6	0	Philadelphia	6	8	0	Green Bay	5	8	1	LA Rams	6	8	0
New England	7	7	0	Cincinnati	4	10	0	Raiders	5	9	0	Dallas	6	8	0	Tampa Bay	4	10	0	Atlanta	3	11	0
NY Jets	6	8	0					Kan. City	3	11	0	NY Giants	5	9	0	Detroit	3	11	0				

NOTES

• Cornelius Bennett had 16 tackles, four sacks and forced three fumbles, but it wasn't enough as the Bills missed posting their first winning record since 1981.

• The Bills lost their season finale for the seventh year in a row.

• Jim Kelly had his second straight poor game despite playing against the worst pass defense in the league.

• Reggie White had two sacks for the Eagles and finished the season with 21, one short of the NFL record.

• The Bills forced turnovers on the Eagles first two possessions, but failed to capitalize.

• Early in the second quarter, Kelly was intercepted by Byron Evans at the Bills 39, setting up Paul McFadden's field goal. After a Bills punt, Randall Cunningham hit Keith Byars for 30 yards, scrambled for 23 yards, then hit Anthony Toney for an 18-yard TD and a 10-0 lead.

• Late in the half, Bennett forced Cunningham to fumble and Bruce Smith recovered at the Eagles 43, but Kelly was intercepted at the 14 by Andre Waters with 15 seconds left in the half.

• The Eagles scored on their first possession of the third, driving 90 yards in 11 plays to Toney's TD run. Byars carried five times for 53 yards on the drive.

• The Bills only score came midway through the fourth when they drove 66 yards in six plays to Kelly's TD pass to Andre Reed. Ron Pitts later fumbled a punt, preventing the Bills from mounting a comeback.

QUOTES

• Marv Levy: "Believe it or not, I'm more disappointed by the way we played today than we played last week. We just didn't play well enough. If you want to be able to win, you have to be able to run and stop the run. We didn't do either. We had no less to play for than the Eagles, we just looked like we had less to play for. I'm disappointed that somehow we didn't appeal to the pride of the players. I thought we would find out something about their self-esteem. We had a chance to walk away winners. Now we can't."

• Jim Kelly: "Some players came to give 100 percent and there were players who were looking to go home. Those players know who they are. I don't think I played that bad a game. We had too many dropped passes and sometimes I didn't get the ball to my receivers. It's a game I'd rather forget about."

• Cornelius Bennett: "If you lose, it doesn't matter how good you play. You still didn't do enough to win. I guess I was in the right place at the right time. I always play hard, that's just what happens when you play hard. It was a tough one to lose because we were going for a winning season." (On Randall Cunningham): "He's awfully good. He reminds me of a black John Elway."

• Eagles safety Andre Waters on Kelly: "He's had problems with the zone defense, so we played more zone than we normally play. It's difficult for him to read zones. We saw films of the New England game

WEEK 15 GAMES

Clev 19, Pitt 13	Chi 6, LAR 3
Hou 21, Cinc 17	NO 33, GB 24
Dal 21, St.L 16	NYG 20, NYJ 7
Det 30, Atl 13	Den 24, SD 0
KC 41, Sea 20	Ind 24, TB 6
SF 48, Rams 0	NE 24, Mia 10
Wash 27, Minn 24 (OT)	

Bills	0 0 0 7 -	7
Eagles	0 10 7 0 -	17

Attendance at Veterans Stadium - 57,547

Phil: FG McFadden 39, 6:09
Phil: Toney 18 pass from Cunningham (McFadden kick), 11:46
Phil: Toney 2 run (McFadden kick), 8:51
Buf: Reed 4 pass from Kelly (Norwood kick), 8:07

	BUF	PHIL
First downs	14	22
Rushing yds	57	210
Passing yds	134	134
Punts-avg	9-34.6	7-35.9
Fumbles-lost	3-2	3-2
Penalties-yds	5-40	7-65
Poss. time	19:28	40:32

BILLS LEADERS: Rushing - Mueller 7-33, Harmon 4-15, R. Porter 3-9; **Passing** - Kelly 20-39-2 - 154; **Receiving** - Reed 5-46, Harmon 9-35, Burkett 4-50, Broughton 2-23.

EAGLES LEADERS: Rushing - Byars 23-102, Toney 15-48, Cunningham 10-46, Jackson 2-10, Haddix 2-4; **Passing** - Cunningham 16-21-1 - 177; **Receiving** - Toney 5-46, Spagnola 3-24, Byars 2-37, Quick 2-18, Jackson 1-26, Garrity 1-13, Carter 1-10, Tautalatasi 1-3.

STANDINGS: FIFTEENTH WEEK

AFC EAST	W	L	T	CENTRAL	W	L	T	WEST	W	L	T	NFC EAST	W	L	T	CENTRAL	W	L	T	WEST	W	L	T
Indianapolis	9	6	0	Cleveland	10	5	0	Denver	10	4	1	Washington	11	4	0	Chicago	11	4	0	San Fran	13	2	0
Miami	8	7	0	Houston	9	6	0	Seattle	9	6	0	St. Louis	7	8	0	Minnesota	8	7	0	N.Orleans	12	3	0
New England	8	7	0	Pittsburgh	8	7	0	San Diego	8	7	0	Philadelphia	7	8	0	Green Bay	5	9	1	LA Rams	6	9	0
Buffalo	7	8	0	Cincinnati	4	11	0	Raiders	5	10	0	Dallas	7	8	0	Tampa Bay	4	11	0	Atlanta	3	12	0
NY Jets	6	9	0					Kan. City	4	11	0	NY Giants	6	9	0	Detroit	4	11	0				

Cornelius Bennett, shown here against the Colts, played the game of his life in the season finale against Philadelphia.

At A Glance
1988

Jan. 6 – Jim Kelly announced he would conduct a celebrity football camp at St. Bonaventure in the summer.

Jan. 7 – Bruce Smith was named the 1987 AFC defensive player of the year by UPI.

Jan. 18 – Shane Conlan, Cornelius Bennett and Nate Odomes were all named to the UPI all-rookie team.

Jan. 20 – Jim Kelly was named to the AFC Pro Bowl squad to replace the injured Dan Marino. Elijah Pitts interviewed for the vacant Green Bay head coaching position.

Jan. 26 – Shane Conlan was named rookie of the year by the Pro Football Writers of America.

Feb. 8 – Coming off his MVP performance in the Pro Bowl, Bruce Smith said he wanted to become the highest-paid defensive player in the NFL. "Who's the highest-paid defensive player in the league?" Smith asked. When told it was Lawrence Taylor at $1.1 million, Smith said, "I want to be paid

Thurman Thomas, after being shunned by every team in the first-round of the 1988 draft, burst on the scene and began to exact his revenge with a solid rookie season as the Bills advanced to the AFC Championship game.

higher than he is."

March 6 – Erie County Executive Dennis Gorski said in an interview with Vic Carucci of *The Buffalo News* that he would be in no hurry to renegotiate the Rich Stadium lease between the county and the Bills because he would be too busy with waterfront development. He also indicated that if the Bills left town, Buffalo would be able to attract another franchise.

March 8 – While Dennis Gorski was meeting with Bill Polian to smooth over the rough edges created by his comments on the stadium lease, Marv Levy was putting ex-Bills quarterback Joe Ferguson through a 40-minute workout in the practice bubble. The 37-year-old Ferguson was visiting NFL teams in hopes of getting someone to sign him because his two-year contract with Detroit had expired.

March 10 – In a unanimous 3-0 decision, the second circuit court of appeals in New York upheld the verdict of the jury in July of 1986 in the USFL's antitrust suit against the NFL.

March 15 – At the league meetings in Phoenix, the owners approved Cardinals' owner Bill Bidwill's proposed shift of his franchise from St. Louis to Phoenix.

March 16 – Ralph Wilson voted against retaining instant replay, but only four other owners followed suit, so instant replay survived another year. Also, a 45-second clock was voted in to replace the 30-second clock between plays.

March 28 – The Bills signed their 11th-round draft choice from 1987, offensive tackle Howard Ballard. Ballard decided to use his final year of college eligibility rather than join the Bills in 1987.

April 1 – The Bills announced they wouldn't re-sign quarterback Joe Ferguson.

April 7 – At the annual AFC East coaches press conference, this year in Miami, Don Shula said the Bills would be the team to beat in the division in 1988.

April 24 – Without a first round pick in the draft, the Bills had to wait until the second round, the 40th choice overall, before choosing Oklahoma State running back Thurman Thomas. They also chose Central Florida receiver Bernard Ford (third), Texas safety John Hagy (eighth), Central Missouri St. defensive lineman Jeff Wright (eighth), North Carolina linebacker Carlton Bailey (ninth) and Florida State cornerback Martin Mayhew (10th). Around the league, Atlanta chose linebacker Aundray Bruce (first), Kansas City chose defensive end Neil Smith (second), Detroit chose cornerback Bennie Blades (third), Tampa Bay selected offensive lineman Paul Gruber (fourth), the Raiders chose wide receiver Tim Brown (sixth), Green Bay took wide receiver Sterling Sharpe (seventh), the Jets drafted offensive lineman Dave Cadigan (eighth), the Raiders went for cornerback Terry McDaniel (ninth), the Giants took offensive lineman Eric Moore (tenth), Dallas chose wide receiver Michael Irvin (11th), Philadelphia chose tight end Keith Jackson (13th), the Rams took running back Gaston Green (14th), San Diego selected wide receiver Anthony Miller (15th), Miami picked linebacker Eric Kumerow (16th), New England took running back John Stephens (17th), Minnesota picked offensive guard Randall McDaniel (19th), the Rams chose wide receiver Aaron Cox (20th), Houston took running back Lorenzo White (22nd), Chicago chose fullback Brad Muster (23rd) and New Orleans opted for fullback Craig Heyward (24th).

April 25 – Thurman Thomas, who suffered a serious knee injury before his junior season of 1986, said his knee was fine and that the Bills and their fans shouldn't be worried. "The condition of my knee is going to be asked throughout the rest of my career," Thomas said. "I have all the confidence in the world in my knee. I don't even worry about it." Chris Berman of ESPN said of Thomas: "If he plays five or six years, he has a chance to go to the Super Bowl."

April 27 – Ray Bentley was found innocent of negligent homicide charges stemming from a car accident he was involved in in June of 1987. "To say the least, it's a great relief," he said.

May 13 – The Bills minicamp opened at Rich Stadium and the top two draft picks, Thurman Thomas and Bernard Ford, looked impressive. Jim Kelly sat out all workouts because he was undergoing treatment on his sore throwing elbow. Bruce Smith showed up and renewed his demand of a new contract. The team also announced that they would withhold a decision on the future of wide receiver Jerry Butler until training camp. Butler had been out of action since November of 1986 when he broke his right ankle and had undergone four operations since.

May 15 – Minicamp concluded with an open practice at Rich Stadium in front of about 12,000 fans.

With the select-a-seat program in full swing, Jerry Foran said season ticket sales were closing in on 36,000.

June 13 – The Bills traded linebacker Eugene Marve to Tampa Bay for a 1989 draft choice.

June 23 – Defensive end Art Still was acquired from Kansas City for a future draft choice, reuniting him with Marv Levy and Walt Corey. "When you enjoy working for certain people, and they enjoy you being their employee, you're going to be more productive," Still said.

July 7 – In an effort to prove to fans that Jim Kelly's throwing elbow was healthy, Kelly put on a 20-minute workout in front of the media at Rich Stadium.

July 9 – Jim Kelly suffered a sprained ankle at a promotional event near Boston and was expected to miss the early part of training camp.

July 11 – U.S. District Court Judge David Doty refused to grant about 300 players unrestricted free agency. Doty said unrestricted free agency could destroy the competitive balance of the NFL.

July 14 – Thurman Thomas signed his first pro contract.

July 16 – The Bills opened training camp at Fredonia State.

July 20 – The veterans were required to report to training camp and Fred Smerlas, Joe Devlin, Jim Ritcher and Butch Rolle failed to show up. Neither did Jerry Butler, and it was expected Butler would announce his retirement.

July 21 – Fred Smerlas signed a new three-year contract worth about $2 million and reported to camp. Butch Rolle also signed a new deal, leaving only Jim Ritcher and Joe Devlin unsigned. As expected, the Bills waived Jerry Butler and while he hoped to hook on with another team, that occurrence was viewed as highly unlikely.

July 25 – Jim Ritcher and Joe Devlin both signed new contracts and reported to camp.

July 30 – The Bills tied Cleveland, 6-6, in the annual rookie scrimmage at Edinboro University. Thurman Thomas made a nice debut, but one player who looked very impressive was rookie nose tackle Jeff Wright.

Aug. 2 – Jim Kelly announced he was firing his agents, Greg Lustig and A.J. Faigin, and said he was contemplating legal action against them for misrepresenting him. He hired Dan Trevino as his new lawyer and put his brother, Dan Kelly, in charge of Jim Kelly Enterprises.

Aug. 4 – The Bills opened the preseason schedule with a 13-9 loss to Houston in the Astrodome. Playing in his hometown, Thurman Thomas rushed for 34 yards.

Aug. 5 – Robb Riddick was one of seven NFL players suspended for one month because they tested positive for drug abuse. The others were Washington's Dexter Manley, Greg Townsend of the Raiders, Kevin Gogan of Dallas, Doug Dubose of San Francisco, Denver's Richard Reed and Atlanta's Pat Saindon.

Aug. 13 – The Bills were beaten by Cincinnati, 24-13, in the lone home preseason game despite Scott Norwood's 54-yard field goal.

Aug. 18 – Cornelius Bennett said of fellow second-year linebacker Brian Bosworth of Seattle: "I think he might as well give up football and go into acting because that's all he does. People go to the stadium just to see Bosworth's hair or listen to him run his mouth. I think I'm the better ballplayer."

Aug. 19 – The Bills were whipped by the Seahawks, 30-13, at the Kingdome. Jim Kelly made his first appearance of the preseason and completed 12 of 19 passes for 126 yards.

Aug. 22 – Sean McNanie was traded to Phoenix and Mark Traynowicz was dealt to Seattle in separate trades for future draft choices. Traynowicz later returned to the Bills.

Aug. 25 – The Bills closed the preseason with a 14-7 victory over Tampa Bay in Nashville, Tenn. Jim Kelly suffered a mild re-sprain of his right ankle.

Aug. 31 – Robb Riddick and the other players around the league who were suspended for 30 days for testing positive for drug abuse, were allowed to rejoin their teams two days early.

Sept. 2 – In a stunning development, Bruce Smith was suspended 30 days for drug abuse by the NFL, meaning he would miss the first four games of the season. Lawrence Taylor of the New York Giants also was suspended. "This obviously is a sad announcement and it points clearly to all of us the danger that drugs present to our society," Bill Polian said. "We spoke with Bruce and he's in complete agreement with the treatment." Marv Levy said Leon Seals likely would start in Smith's place.

Sept. 4 – Thurman Thomas rushed for 86 yards and scored a TD in his NFL debut as the Bills beat Minnesota, 13-10, for their first season-opening victory since 1982.

Sept. 5 – In the early morning the day after the Vikings game, Andre Reed and Darryl Talley were arrested after a fight in No-Names, an Elmwood Ave. bar. Reed's brother and sister also were involved in the fracas. Asked for a comment, Marv Levy said: "I don't think we have a team that has a problem with anti-social behavior. I think an overwhelming majority of our players are good citizens most of the time."

Sept. 11 – Scott Norwood's third field goal of the game with 3:12 left lifted Buffalo to a 9-6 victory over Miami at Rich Stadium, the Bills third straight win over the Dolphins.

Sept. 13 – Bill Polian told the Quarterback Club luncheon: "I don't think we have anything to crow about. I know the coaches feel the same way. We can play a lot better in all three phases of the game – offense, defense and special teams – than we have so far. We have to guard against getting too high or too low."

Sept. 15 – The Bills called a press conference so that Jim Kelly could refute rumors that he was about to be suspended for drug abuse. "If all the rumors about me were true, they'd have my picture in the post office like Jesse James," Kelly said angrily. "It's just unbelievable. I can't believe I'm even up here having to explain anything. I've never done drugs and I'll take a test anytime someone wants me to." Equally upset over the rumors were Marv Levy and Bill Polian.

Sept. 18 – Scott Norwood's field goal with 11 seconds left capped a 10-point fourth-quarter rally that lifted the Bills to a 16-14 victory over New England at Sullivan Stadium. It was Buffalo's first win over the Patriots since 1981, snapping an 11-game losing streak.

Sept. 20 – The Bills acquired veteran strong safety Leonard Smith from the Cardinals in exchange for cornerback Roland Mitchell and a future draft pick.

Sept. 25 – Scott Norwood tied a club record with five field goals as the Bills rolled past Pittsburgh, 36-28, at Rich Stadium. Norwood stretched his streak of consecutive made field goals to a team-record 12.

Sept. 26 – Joe Devlin refused to get excited about the Bills' 4-0 start. "So we've won four games – big deal," he said. "We're not living in a dream world. We haven't done anything yet."

Sept. 27 – Bruce Smith and four other players including Lawrence Taylor were reinstated after serving 30-day suspensions for drug abuse. "I saw the Bruce that I know – an upbeat guy who wants to get back and be a part of this team and wants to do his best," Bill Polian said after meeting with Smith privately.

Sept. 28 – Bruce Smith met the media for the first time after practice. "It was a difficult time for me," he said of his suspension. "I would like to apologize to my family, my friends, my teammates and the fans. I'm going to continue therapy. I think I'm going to turn this around and use it as a positive. I'm going to prosper from it."

Oct. 1 – Bruce Smith was activated, meaning he would start against Chicago, and Leonard Smith was named starter at strong safety, his first start as a Bill.

Oct. 2 – The Bills' four-game winning streak came crashing to a halt as Chicago laid a 24-3 whipping on them at Soldier Field. The Bills were held to an all-time record low of zero yards rushing.

Oct. 9 – The Bills fell behind 17-0 and were booed robustly at halftime by the Rich Stadium crowd, but they rallied for 34-23 victory over the Colts as Jim Kelly passed for 315 yards and three TDs.

Oct. 13 – At a press conference at Rich Stadium, Jerry Butler officially announced his retirement from football when no teams came calling for his services.

Oct. 14 – Cornelius Bennett told New York sports writers on a conference call that he considered himself the best outside linebacker in the NFL. "Yes, I do," he said. "The reason is because I'm Cornelius Bennett. If I said anything else, I'd be degrading myself."

Oct. 17 – The Bills made their first appearance on *Monday Night Football* in four years a rousing success, ripping the Jets, 37-14, at the Meadowlands as Jim Kelly threw for 261 yards and three TDs in the first half and finished with 302 yards passing.

Oct. 23 – For the second time this season, Scott Norwood beat New England with a late field goal, this time a 33-yarder at Rich Stadium with 13 seconds left for a 23-20 victory. "The turning point was when we lost to Chicago," Jim Kelly said. "We realized 'Hey, we're not as good as people think we are.' Then we went back to work."

Oct. 30 – Depew native Don Majkowski received a rude welcome home from the Bills defense as Cornelius Bennett sacked him 2 1/2 times and Mark Kelso returned an interception 78 yards for a TD during a 28-0 romp. Thurman Thomas rushed for 116 yards, his first NFL game over the century mark.

Oct. 31 – After going more than a year without a player rep since John Kidd resigned in July of 1987, the Bills elected co-reps in Fred Smerlas and Joe Devlin.

Nov. 1 – Jim Kelly, Fred Smerlas, Andre Reed, Kent Hull and Cornelius Bennett posed for the Kelly's Heroes poster to help promote the war against drugs. The poster was shot at the Masten Ave. Armory.

Nov. 6 – The Bills yielded only 145 total yards and posted their first win ever against the Seahawks, 13-3, at the Kingdome.

Nov. 9 – The Bills were hit for the third time by a 30-day drug suspension as linebacker Hal Garner tested positive for drug abuse. "My first reaction was one of not just disappointment but anger toward Hal because he knew the consequences," Marv Levy

Jeff Wright (91, left) didn't get a lot of playing time during his rookie season in 1988, but the little time he got, he made great use of with five sacks.

Fred Smerlas (opposite page) celebrates his blocked field goal in the closing seconds against the New York Jets which forced overtime. The Bills then won the game in the extra period to clinch the AFC East division title.

said.

Nov. 14 – The Bills beat Miami for the fourth straight time, 31-6, in a Monday nighter at Joe Robbie Stadium. It was the first time in the series history that Buffalo had accomplished that feat. Buffalo won the first three games the teams ever played in 1966 and '67, then lost 20 in a row during the 70s. Thurman Thomas missed the game, but the defense again was superb, intercepting Dan Marino three times.

Nov. 20 – Fred Smerlas blocked Pat Leahy's 40-yard field goal with 19 seconds left in regulation, then Scott Norwood kicked a winning field goal 3:47 into the extra session as the Bills beat the Jets, 9-6, and clinched their first AFC East title since 1980. Fans poured onto the field, tore down the goal posts and passed one of the uprights up to Ralph Wilson's luxury box. "It used to be that fans threw programs at me, now they're asking me to sign them," Wilson said. "I've been around football for a long time, but this has been the greatest turnaround I've ever seen. There's no comparison between this team and 1980. The 1980 team got better gradually. This just happened. Two years ago, this team was 4-12."

Nov. 21 – The tearing down of the goal posts cost the Bills $19,000, and while Bill Polian said it was exciting and that the fans deserved to celebrate and let out some pent up frustration, he warned that he didn't want a repeat if the Bills played at home during the playoffs.

Nov. 27 – Clearly flat after the emotion of the week before, the Bills fell behind 21-0 and went on to lose at Cincinnati, 35-21, as Bengals torched the NFL's No. 1 defense for 455 yards. Comedian Bill Murray appeared on NBC's *NFL Live* and joked: "Buffalo's living in a dream world. They've had a good season, but I think they should concentrate on getting the salt out of the streets."

Dec. 4 – The Bills suffered a humbling and damaging loss to Tampa Bay, 10-5, as they rushed for only 39 yards.

Dec. 7 – Hal Garner returned from his drug suspension.

Dec. 11 – The Bills snapped their two-game losing streak with a 37-21 victory over the Los Angeles

Raiders in the coldest game ever played in Buffalo. The temperature was 11 degrees with a windchill of 14 below zero. The crowd of 77,348 enabled the Bills to set an all-time single-season NFL attendance record of 622,793.

Dec. 14 – Six Bills were named to the AFC's Pro Bowl squad, including Fred Smerlas for a team record-tying fifth time. The others were Bruce Smith, Kent Hull, Cornelius Bennett, Shane Conlan and Scott Norwood. Smith, Bennett, Conlan and Norwood were named starters.

Dec. 18 – With home-field advantage and the chance to set a new team record for most regular season victories on the line, the Bills lost to Indianapolis in the dreaded Hoosier Dome, 17-14. The Bills' 1-3 finish enabled Cincinnati to claim homefield advantage through the playoffs.

Dec. 19 – During the taping of a TV show in Rochester called *The Buffalo Bills Football Show*, Robb Riddick took a shot at Jim Kelly, saying he "wasn't happy with the quarterback situation" and complained that Kelly didn't throw enough to the running backs. "I just don't feel that Jim is doing the job that he's paid to do," Riddick said.

Dec. 22 – Although Robb Riddick retracted his statements and Jim Kelly said he wasn't bothered by them, Marv Levy expressed his anger concerning Riddick's comments. "It's always a foolish thing for a player to publicly assess his teammates," Levy said. "Usually he's wrong, as in this case. Players, if they talk to the media, are going to say some things they wish they hadn't said."

Dec. 23 – Bruce Smith, Cornelius Bennett and Scott Norwood were named to The Associated Press All-Pro team.

Dec. 24 – Houston defeated Cleveland, 24-23, to win the AFC wild-card game and set up their playoff game against the Bills.

Dec. 26 – Minnesota downed the Rams, 28-17, in the NFC wild-card game.

Dec. 27 – A pep rally was held in front of the Rath building downtown for the team. Bill Polian urged fans to cheer as loud as they could when the Oilers had the ball so that Rich Stadium could be called the House of Noise.

Dec. 31 – Cincinnati defeated Seattle, 21-13, and

Chicago beat Philadelphia at foggy Soldier Field, 20-12, on the first day of divisional round play.

Jan. 1, 1989 – The Bills' special teams blocked two kicks and the defense forced two turnovers in the fourth quarter as the Bills defeated Houston, 17-10, in the first playoff game in Buffalo since Jan. 1, 1967, when the Bills lost the AFL Championship Game to Kansas City. In the NFC, San Francisco routed Minnesota, 34-9.

Jan. 4, 1989 – Marv Levy said that Cincinnati's no-huddle offense bordered on the illegal because the Bengals kept 12 or 13 men on the field to confuse defenses before getting down to 11 just before the snap. Sam Wyche denied the charge. The week before, Seattle tried to slow the no-huddle down by faking injuries.

Jan. 5, 1989 – Injured linebacker Shane Conlan, who had missed four of the previous five games with a sprained arch, said he would play against the Bengals.

Jan. 8, 1989 – The Bills went against one of Marv Levy's pet philosophies: "Don't play dumb and don't play dirty." They were dumb and dirty in a 21-10 AFC Championship Game loss at Cincinnati. Derrick Burroughs was ejected in the third quarter as he committed one of four personal foul penalties Buffalo was responsible for. Shane Conlan returned to the lineup, but the defense was hurt by an injury to Bruce Smith which slowed him down considerably. In the NFC Championship Game, Joe Montana threw for 288 yards and three TDs as San Francisco routed the Bears in Chicago, 28-3.

Jan. 22, 1989 – Joe Montana directed an 11-play, 92-yard drive in the final three minutes and capped it with a 10-yard TD pass to John Taylor with 34 seconds remaining, giving San Francisco a thrilling 20-16 victory over Cincinnati in Super Bowl XXIII at Miami's Joe Robbie Stadium. Montana threw for a Super Bowl-record 357 yards while MVP Jerry Rice caught 11 passes for a Super Bowl-record 215 yards.

Jan. 29, 1989 – The NFC routed the AFC, 34-3, in the Pro Bowl at Aloha Stadium as Scott Norwood provided the AFC's only points. Randall Cunningham was named MVP.

By the Numbers - 1988

TEAM STATISTICS	BILLS	OPP
First downs	313	299
Rushing	137	114
Passing	161	146
Penalty	15	39
Third downs	88-207	69-192
Fourth downs	9-13	6-17
Time of poss	29:54	30:06
Total yards	5,315	4,578
Avg. game	332.2	286.1
Plays	1,012	971
Avg. play	5.3	4.7
Net rushing yds	2,133	1,854
Avg. game	133.3	115.9
Avg. play	4.0	3.9
Net passing yds	3,182	2,724
Comp/att	271/454	250/448
Sacks/lost	30-229	46-322
Interceptions	17	15
Percentage	59.7	55.8
Punts/avg	62-39.5	75-39.7
Fumbles/lost	26-16	28-17
Penalties/yds	109-824	90-713
Touchdowns	33	29
Extra points	33-33	27-29
Field goals	32-37	12-24
Safeties	1	0
Kick ret./avg	50-18.7	69-16.2
Punt ret./avg	26-5.8	36-6.2

RUSHING	ATT	YDS	AVG	TD
Thomas	207	881	4.3	2
Riddick	111	438	3.9	12
Mueller	81	296	3.7	0
Harmon	57	212	3.7	1
Kelly	35	154	4.4	0
Byrum	28	91	3.3	0
Reed	6	64	10.7	0
Reich	3	-3	-1.0	0
TOTALS	**528**	**2133**	**4.0**	**15**

RECEIVING	CAT	YDS	AVG	TD
Reed	71	968	13.6	6
T. Johnson	37	514	13.9	0
Harmon	37	427	11.5	3
Metzelaars	33	438	13.3	1
Riddick	30	282	9.4	1
Burkett	23	354	15.4	1
Thomas	18	208	11.6	0
F. Johnson	9	170	18.9	1
Mueller	8	42	5.3	0
Rolle	2	3	1.5	2
Byrum	2	0	0.0	0
Kelly	1	5	5.0	0
TOTALS	**271**	**3411**	**12.6**	**15**

PASSING	COMP	ATT	INT	YDS	TD	COMP%	SACKS	RATE
Kelly	269	452	17	3380	15	59.5	30-229	78.2
Riddick	2	2	0	31	0	100.0	0-0	118.8
TOTALS	**271**	**454**	**17**	**3411**	**15**	**59.7**	**30-229**	**78.5**

KICKING	1-19	20-29	30-39	40-49	50+	TOT	PAT	PTS
Norwood	1-1	10-10	15-16	6-9	0-1	32-37	33-33	129

PUNTING	NO	AVG	LG	In 20	BL
Kidd	62	39.5	60	13	0

SCORE BY QUARTERS

BILLS	71	83	81	91	3 -	329
OPP	44	104	27	62	0 -	237

DEFENSIVE STATISTICAL LEADERS

TACKLES: Bentley 68 primary - 54 assists - 122 total tackles, Bennett 85-18-103, Conlan 60-24-84, Still 58-21-79, L. Smith 55-20-75, Talley 46-27-73, Kelso 48-24-72, Radecic 37-20-57, B. Smith 39-17-56, Smerlas 42-12-54, Seals 38-9-47, Odomes 39-5-44, Burroughs 32-7-39, Drane 17-7-24

SACKS: B. Smith 11, Bennett 9.5, Still 6, Wright 5, Smerlas 4, Talley 2.5, Seals 2-5, Conlan 1.5, Radecic 1.5

FUMBLE RECOVERIES: Bennett 3, Seals 3, Radecic 2

FORCED FUMBLES: Bennett 3, B. Smith 3, Still 2, Talley 2

INTERCEPTIONS: Kelso 7-180 yards, 25.7 avg, 1 TD; Bennett 2-30, 15.0, 0 TD

SPECIAL TEAMS STATISTICAL LEADERS

KICKOFF RETURNS: Tucker 15-310, 20.7, 0 TD; F. Johnson 14-250, 17.9, 0 TD

PUNT RETURNS: F. Johnson 16-72, 4.5, 0 TD; Tucker 10-80, 8.0, 0 TD

TACKLES: Rolle 22, Pike 20, Tasker 17, Garner 17, Radecic 16, W. Davis 15, McKeller 10, Graham 9, Drane 9, Cocroft 8, Prater 7, Bailey 6, Wright 6, Mueller 6, Hellestrae 6

Vikings	0	3	0	7 -	10
Bills	10	0	0	3 -	13

Attendance at Rich Stadium - 76,783

Buf: FG Norwood 27, 3:31
Buf: Thomas 5 run (Norwood kick), 14:47
Min: FG Nelson 30, 13:55
Buf: FG Norwood 26, 3:22
Min: Rice 2 run (Nelson kick), 10:22

	BUF	MIN
First downs	18	21
Rushing yds	114	130
Passing yds	196	170
Punts-avg	5-44.0	5-44.2
Fumbles-lost	1-0	2-1
Penalties-yds	1-5	4-25
Poss. time	28:56	31:04

BILLS LEADERS: Rushing - Thomas 18-86, Kelly 5-21, Riddick 1-5, Mueller 2-3, Reed 1-(-1); **Passing** - Kelly 17-31-1 - 204; **Receiving** - Reed 8-78, Metzelaars 2-43, Burkett 2-37, Thomas 2-27, Mueller 2-19, Harmon 1-0.

VIKINGS LEADERS: Rushing - Nelson 10-50, Fenney 8-28, Wilson 4-24, Anderson 4-18, Carter 1-11, Rice 4-(-1), Scribner 1-0; **Passing** - Wilson 19-33-1 - 204; **Receiving** - Anderson 5-44, Jordan 3-55, Carter 3-30, Fenney 2-27, Lewis 1-10, Mularkey 1-8, Rice 1-9, Nelson 2-(-2), Jones 1-23.

NOTES
• Even without Bruce Smith, the Bills recorded six sacks and posted their first victory in a season opener since 1982.
• Thurman Thomas enjoyed a productive NFL debut while Art Still's Bills' debut featured 2 1/2 sacks. Leon Seals was in on eight tackles replacing Smith.
• Cornelius Bennett intercepted Wade Wilson on the third play of the game. The Bills then drove 47 yards to Scott Norwood's field goal. Norwood missed a 42-yarder on the next possession, then the Bills drove 61 yards in six plays on their third possession to Thomas' first NFL TD.
• Jim Kelly was intercepted early in the second quarter by Reggie Rutland and the Vikings proceeded to move 66 yards in 14 plays to Chuck Nelson's field goal.
• Early in the fourth, Vikings punter Bucky Scribner dropped a snap and was tackled by Robb Riddick at the Minnesota 11, setting up Norwood's second field goal.
• The Vikings answered with a 13-play, 74-yard drive to Allen Rice's TD. The drive was kept alive when Wilson hit Hassan Jones for 23 yards on fourth-and-two from the 40, and Alfred Anderson converted a fourth-and-one from the 8.

WEEK 1 GAMES
Det 31, Atl 17	Clev 6, KC 3
Pitt 24, Dal 21	Hou 17, Ind 14
Rams 34, GB 7	Chi 34, Mia 7
NE 28, NYJ 3	Phil 41, TB 14
Cinc 21, Phoe 14	LAR 24, SD 13
SF 34, NO 33	Sea 21, Den 14
NYG 27, Wash 20	

• After an exchange of punts, the Bills got the ball at their own 26 with 1:58 left and ran out the clock as Thomas broke a 28-yard run for a crucial first down.

QUOTES
• Walt Corey: "There's no greater feeling as a coach than to put in a game plan and then have your players implement it just the way you designed it. Every so often you have a day where everything is in sync. Today was one of those days."
• Fred Smerlas on Leon Seals: "I was going to say something to Leon, but when I saw the smoke coming out of his ears, I knew he was ready."
• Leon Seals: "I felt like everyone was behind me. The fans, my teammates, the coaches. They were all in my corner. I was really pumped up."
• Thurman Thomas on being nervous: "You should have seen me before the game. I was just sitting here thinking 'This is going to be my first NFL game.' I'm always nervous before a game, thinking about something. And then they announced me and it all went away once the game started."
• Marv Levy on Thomas: "Were we surprised by him? No. We have seen a lot of good signs in him. We wouldn't have put him in the game at the beginning if we didn't think he was a player with ability, but you don't find out until now."
• Jim Kelly on Thomas: "We haven't had that around here for a long time. It's nice to be able to run wide. On the touchdown, he was patient, stayed behind Ritcher, then made his cut."
• Art Still: "This was a total defensive effort, no one player stood out."

Dolphins	3	0	3	0 -	6
Bills	0	3	0	6 -	9

Attendance at Rich Stadium - 79,520

Mia: FG Reveiz 31, 13:03
Buf: FG Norwood 41, 6:54
Mia: FG Reveiz 27, 12:08
Buf: FG Norwood 35, 3:32
Buf: FG Norwood 28, 11:48

	BUF	MIA
First downs	15	16
Rushing yds	104	115
Passing yds	215	219
Punts-avg	2-40.5	4-31.3
Fumbles-lost	3-3	4-2
Penalties-yds	3-30	4-35
Poss. time	27:57	32:03

BILLS LEADERS: Rushing - Thomas 21-74, Kelly 4-16, Mueller 2-6, Harmon 1-6, Riddick 2-2; **Passing** - Kelly 15-24-1 - 231; **Receiving** - Reed 8-122, Thomas 3-57, Metzelaars 2-39, T. Johnson 2-13.

DOLPHINS LEADERS: Rushing - Stradford 15-48, Bennett 7-23, Hampton 5-23, Jensen 2-21, Marino 1-0; **Passing** - Marino 22-34-0 - 221; **Receiving** - Stradford 7-44, Clayton 5-60, Duper 4-55, Jensen 2-21, Pruitt 1-19, Edmunds 1-10, Hardy 1-8, Bennett 1-4.

WEEK 2 GAMES
Chi 17, Ind 13	Cinc 28, Phil 24
Rams 17, Det 10	Sea 31, KC 10
Hou 38, LAR 35	Minn 36, NE 6
NO 29, Atl 21	NYJ 23, Clev 3
Wash 30, Pitt 29	Den 34, SD 3
SF 20, NYG 17	TB 13, GB 10
Dal 17, Phoe 14	

NOTES
• The Bills beat the Dolphins for the third straight time, tying their longest win streak ever against Miami.
• Jim Kelly was sick in the days leading up to the game and almost didn't play.
• Don Shula fell to 0-2 for the first time since the 1969 season with Baltimore.
• On the Bills' sixth offensive play, Jim Kelly was intercepted by William Judson at the Miami 49. From there, Miami drove 37 yards to Fuad Reveiz's first field goal.
• Early in the second quarter, Art Still sacked Dan Marino, forced a fumble and Scott Radecic recovered at the Miami 39. That led to Scott Norwood's first field goal.
• Miami reached the Bills 22 on the next series, but Cornelius Bennett forced Woody Bennett to fumble and Leon Seals recovered. On the next play, Kelly hit Andre Reed for 30, but Reed lost a fumble just before the half ended. The Bills had only three first downs and 83 yards at the half.
• On the first three plays of the second half, Kelly completed passes of 23 and 11 yards to Reed and 34 to Thurman Thomas, but after getting to the 7, Paul Lankford sacked Kelly, forced a fumble and John Offerdahl recovered. The next Bills series also ended with Offerdahl recovering a fumble by Trumaine Johnson at the Bills 27. That led to Reveiz's second field goal.
• The Bills took the kickoff and drove 64 yards to Norwood's tying field goal early in the fourth.
• After Reveiz missed a 50-yarder, the Bills moved 50 yards to Norwood's winning 28-yarder with 3:12 left. The key plays were a 24-yard pass to Reed and a 22-yarder to Pete Metzelaars.
• Miami drove to the Bills 35, but Marino threw incomplete on fourth-and-two with 37 seconds left.

QUOTES
• Walt Corey: "When you do a good job against Dan Marino, you have to feel good."
• Marv Levy about the offense: "We've been struggling, but the opposition has, too. Miami has a much-improved defense. Our defense played pretty well, particularly when they had to. What our defense did best all day was come up and tackle on short receptions."
• Fred Smerlas: "Those teams, particularly the '80 and '81 teams, won a lot on emotion. I think this is a different team, a better defense. Last week we won on emotion against Minnesota, but today we came out a little flat. But after a while, we woke up."
• Andre Reed on his focus for the game: "That was a test for me, to put (the nightclub incident) out of my mind and see how I would do. I couldn't worry about that. I had a football game to play, and I don't think I let it affect me. I had a good week of practice." (About his 16 catches in two games): "We have so many guys on this team who can make things happen. The ball just happens to be coming to me."

AFC EAST	W	L	T	CENTRAL	W	L	T	WEST	W	L	T	NFC EAST	W	L	T	CENTRAL	W	L	T	WEST	W	L	T
Buffalo	2	0	0	Houston	2	0	0	Seattle	2	0	0	NY Giants	1	1	0	Chicago	2	0	0	San Fran	2	0	0
New England	1	1	0	Cincinnati	2	0	0	Raiders	1	1	0	Philadelphia	1	1	0	Detroit	1	1	0	LA Rams	2	0	0
NY Jets	1	1	0	Pittsburgh	1	1	0	Denver	1	1	0	Washington	1	1	0	Tampa Bay	1	1	0	N.Orleans	1	1	0
Indianapolis	0	2	0	Cleveland	1	1	0	Kan. City	0	2	0	Dallas	1	1	0	Minnesota	1	1	0	Atlanta	0	2	0
Miami	0	2	0					San Diego	0	2	0	Phoenix	0	2	0	Green Bay	0	2	0				

NOTES

• The Bills snapped their 11-game losing streak to the Pats that stretched back to 1981.

• Nate Odomes made his first NFL interception, Jeff Wright his first NFL sack.

• Fred Marion had both Pats interceptions, giving him 19 for his career, six against the Bills.

• Marion's first pick came at the Pats 2, killing a drive early in the second quarter. But on the next play, Odomes forced Robert Perryman to fumble and Shane Conlan recovered, leading to a Scott Norwood field goal.

• Odomes made his interception two plays after the kickoff, but the Bills punted. The Pats then drove 90 yards in 12 plays to Cedric Jones' 41-yard TD reception. Jones beat Derrick Burroughs.

• Marion's second pick came with 38 seconds left in the half at the Bills 43. Grogan then completed all four of his passes, including a 19-yard TD to Stanley Morgan 11 seconds before halftime for a 14-3 lead.

• The Bills drove 51 yards to Norwood's second field goal on their only possession of the third.

• Early in the fourth, the Bills went 66 yards in 10 plays to Robb Riddick's TD catch. The key plays were a 22-yard pass to Pete Metzelaars, a third-and-seven pass for seven to Ronnie Harmon and a 16-yarder to Chris Burkett.

• The Pats then were hurt by a holding penalty on Willie Scott, which nullified a first down with 3:07 left.

• After the Pats had to punt, the Bills began their winning drive at their own 48 with 1:50 left. Kelly hit Harmon for 14 and Andre Reed for seven. Riddick and Harmon then ran for four each and Kelly spiked the ball at the 23 with 16 seconds left to set up Norwood's game-winning 41-yarder.

QUOTES

• Jim Kelly on the last drive: "Our goal was to get the ball to the 30. I told the guys to make sure they got out of bounds and get as much yardage as possible." (On the TD pass to Riddick): "They were coming with an all-out blitz but we knew they would be. We had Robb isolated one-on-one with a linebacker (Johnny Rembert). I just said to myself 'Hurry and make your cut, Robb' and he did. We struggled in the first half, but we have winners in this locker room."

• Scott Norwood: "I may not look like I'm excited, but I am. I just don't believe in jumping up and down. I believe a kicker has to stay on an even keel. He can't get too high when he makes one and he can't get too low when he misses. I had a super warm-up and I felt confident. With about six minutes left I visualized being down there kicking the winning field goal."

• Fred Smerlas on Steve Grogan: "Grogan may need a wheelchair to get around, but he can still get by on smarts. One of these decades he's going to retire." (On the team's attitude): "The attitude in the locker room is totally different than any time since I've been here. At halftime, there wasn't disappointment, only anger. It was 'We shouldn't have let them score, let's come back and win this.' We were so fired up, I thought we were going to knock the lockers over. It was enough to excite even an old gentleman like me."

• Marv Levy on Kelly: "Jim had an outstanding second half. He's able to rise above things."

Bills	0	3	3	10 - 16
Patriots	0	14	0	0 - 14

Attendance at Sullivan Stadium - 55,945

Buf: FG Norwood 38, 2:45
NE: Jones 41 pass from Grogan (Garcia kick), 10:54
NE: Morgan 19 pass from Grogan (Garcia kick), 14:49
Buf: FG Norwood 44, 11:58
Buf: Riddick 3 run (Norwood kick), 5:45
Buf: FG Norwood 41, 14:49

	BUF	NE
First downs	18	14
Rushing yds	105	105
Passing yds	149	159
Punts-avg	5-45.0	6-38.7
Fumbles-lost	0-0	1-1
Penalties-yds	4-39	5-50
Poss. time	33:11	26:49

BILLS LEADERS: Rushing - Thomas 17-55, Kelly 4-18, Mueller 3-8, Harmon 2-8, Riddick 3-16; **Passing** - Kelly 21-33-2 - 170; **Receiving** - Harmon 5-48, Thomas 5-37, Metzelaars 3-32, Burkett 2-24, Reed 2-13, Mueller 2-5, T. Johnson 1-8, Riddick 1-3.

PATRIOTS LEADERS: Rushing - Stephens 24-81, Perryman 7-23, Dupard 1-1; **Passing** - Grogan 14-20-2 - 195; **Receiving** - C. James 3-57, Fryar 3-25, Dupard 3-17, Jones 2-59, Morgan 1-19, Perryman 1-10, Scott 1-8.

WEEK 3 GAMES

Atl 34, SF 17	Cinc 17, Pitt 12
KC 20, Den 13	Mia 24, GB 17
NYJ 45, Hou 3	Rams 22, LAR 17
Minn 31, Chi 7	NO 22, Det 14
NYG 12, Dal 10	Wash 17, Phil 10
Phoe 30, TB 24	SD 17, Sea 6
Clev 23, Ind 17	

NOTES

• Once again, the Bills offense had trouble getting the ball in the end zone, so Scott Norwood bailed them out, tying a team record with five field goals. With 12 successes in a row, he set a new team mark.

• Ronnie Harmon set a career-high with 94 yards receiving.

• On the second play of the game, Bubby Brister fumbled the snap and Derrick Burroughs recovered at the Steelers 14. After a holding penalty, Jim Kelly threw a 24-yard TD pass to Chris Burkett, but instant replay overturned the call as Burkett didn't get both feet in. Norwood eventually kicked a field goal.

• On the next series, the Bills drove 67 yards to Kelly's 26-yard TD pass to Burkett.

• After a punt, Kelly lost a fumble and David Little recovered at the Bills 29. Seven plays later, Brister scored on a keeper. Robb Riddick then lost a fumble, but the defense held and Hal Garner blocked Harry Newsome's punt out of bounds at the Steelers 25, leading to a Norwood field goal.

• The Steelers took the kickoff and drove 80 yards to Brister's go-ahead TD pass to Walter Williams.

• Kelly was intercepted in the end zone 44 seconds before halftime, but Wayne Davis intercepted Brister at the 43 with 28 seconds left. Kelly hit Harmon for 22, setting up another Norwood kick.

• The Bills took the second-half kickoff and drove 81 yards in 14 plays to Riddick's TD run for a 23-14 lead.

• On the ensuing series, Steve Tasker blocked a punt and Riddick picked up the loose ball and scored.

• Late in the third, Darryl Talley recovered an Earnest Jackson fumble at the 28, leading to a field goal.

• Early in the fourth, Mark Kelso's interception set up Norwood's final field goal.

• The Steelers drove 73 yards to a TD, then recovered the onside kick and scored again. They recovered a second onside kick with 1:26 left, but Brister was intercepted by Kelso.

QUOTES

• Kent Hull: "The superstars get a lot of credit, but you can't forget the supporting cast. You need a lot of role players to win championships. I've never been on a team like this. Of course, I've never been 4-0 in my career, either. We just seem to do what we need to do to win. This game is a good indication of how complete this team is."

• Scott Norwood: "I think the reason for the groove is good kicking weather and getting lots of opportunities. It's tough to maintain a groove when you don't kick for a couple weeks."

• Mark Kelso on the crazy finish: "It was starting to get a little hairy there for a minute. It had been a bizarre game and we didn't want it to have a bizarre ending."

Steelers	0	14	0	14 - 28
Bills	10	6	14	6 - 36

Attendance at Rich Stadium - 78,735

Buf: FG Norwood 38, 1:54
Buf: Burkett 26 pass from Kelly (Norwood kick), 7:43
Pit: Brister 1 run (Anderson kick), :52
Buf: FG Norwood 39, 7:01
Pit: Williams 5 pass from Brister (Anderson kick), 11:27
Buf: FG Norwood 39, 14:55
Buf: Riddick 1 run (Norwood kick), 7:19
Buf: Riddick 5 blocked punt return (Norwood kick), 9:40
Buf: FG Norwood 48, :57
Buf: FG Norwood 49, 9:31
Pit: Brister 1 run (Anderson kick), 13:01
Pit: Thompson 42 pass from Brister (Anderson kick), 13:30

	BUF	PIT
First downs	22	25
Rushing yds	116	94
Passing yds	282	314
Punts-avg	1-31.0	4-22.0
Fumbles-lost	2-2	3-2
Penalties-yds	6-40	6-40
Poss. time	30:01	29:59

BILLS LEADERS: Rushing - Thomas 16-49, Harmon 7-36, Mueller 3-22, Riddick 7-9, Byrum 2-1, Kelly 2-(-1); **Passing** - Kelly 20-32-1 - 288; **Receiving** - Harmon 5-94, Metzelaars 4-51, Reed 3-48, Burkett 3-44, T. Johnson 2-20, Riddick 1-26, Mueller 1-3, Thomas 1-2.

STEELERS LEADERS: Rushing - Williams 8-35, Hoge 4-31, Jackson 8-25, Brister 3-2, Stone 1-1; **Passing** - Brister 22-36-3 - 330; **Receiving** - Thompson 4-118, Gothard 4-54, Hoge 4-34, Lipps 2-43, Lockett 2-30, Carter 2-25, Jackson 2-21, Williams 2-5.

WEEK 4 GAMES

Dal 26, Atl 20	Chi 24, GB 6
Cinc 24, Clev 17	Rams 45, NYG 31
Ind 15, Mia 13	Hou 31, NE 6
NYJ 17, Det 10	SD 24, KC 23
Minn 23, Phil 21	SF 38, Sea 7
Phoe 30, Wash 21	NO 13, TB 9
LAR 30, Den 27 (OT)	

STANDINGS: FOURTH WEEK

AFC EAST	W	L	T	CENTRAL	W	L	T	WEST	W	L	T	NFC EAST	W	L	T	CENTRAL	W	L	T	WEST	W	L	T
Buffalo	4	0	0	Cincinnati	4	0	0	Seattle	2	2	0	NY Giants	2	2	0	Chicago	3	1	0	LA Rams	4	0	0
NY Jets	3	1	0	Houston	3	1	0	Raiders	2	2	0	Washington	2	2	0	Minnesota	3	1	0	San Fran	3	1	0
New England	1	3	0	Cleveland	2	2	0	San Diego	2	2	0	Phoenix	2	2	0	Tampa Bay	1	3	0	N.Orleans	3	1	0
Miami	1	3	0	Pittsburgh	1	3	0	Kan. City	1	3	0	Dallas	2	2	0	Detroit	1	3	0	Atlanta	1	3	0
Indianapolis	1	3	0					Denver	1	3	0	Philadelphia	1	3	0	Green Bay	0	4	0				

Bills	3	0	0	0	-	3
Bears	7	17	0	0	-	24

Attendance at Soldier Field - 62,793

Chi:	Moorehead 4 pass from McMahon (Butler kick), 10:50
Buf:	FG Norwood 28, 14:37
Chi:	Morris 63 pass from McMahon (Butler kick), 1:42
Chi:	FG Butler 22, 8:42
Chi:	Gentry 58 run (Butler kick), 12:45

	BUF	CHI
First downs	13	22
Rushing yds	0	163
Passing yds	218	260
Punts-avg	6-35.5	2-26.5
Fumbles-lost	1-0	1-1
Penalties-yds	9-85	5-35
Poss. time	21:21	38:39

BILLS LEADERS: **Rushing** - Thomas 5-12, Mueller 2-8, Kelly 2-4, Harmon 1-(-24); **Passing** - Kelly 20-37-1 - 274; **Receiving** - Reed 7-98, Harmon 5-67, Burkett 3-40, Metzelaars 2-22, T. Johnson 2-14, Thomas 1-33.

BEARS LEADERS: **Rushing** - Gentry 2-64, Muster 6-25, Anderson 15-24, McMahon 3-24, Sanders 4-14, Suhey 6-9, Davis 1-3; **Passing** - McMahon 20-27-1 - 260; **Receiving** - McKinnon 7-97, Gentry 5-56, Thornton 2-19, Suhey 2-8, Morris 1-63, Muster 1-10, Moorehead 1-4, Anderson 1-3.

NOTES
• The Bills were held to a team-record low of zero yards rushing and saw their four-game winning streak end.
• Shane Conlan suffered a foot injury, but it was not a fracture as was first feared.
• In his return to action, Bruce Smith had two tackles, one sack and one batted down pass.
• The Bears possessed the ball for 38:39 while the defense sacked Jim Kelly six times for 56 yards.
• The Bills stopped the Bears on fourth-and-one at the 16 on the first series, but Chicago drove 55 yards on the next possession to Jim McMahon's TD pass to Emory Moorehead. The drive was kept alive when Mark Kelso's interception was nullified by an illegal-contact penalty on Nate Odomes.
• The Bills answered with a 67-yard march to a Scott Norwood field goal, the key play being a 33-yard pass to Thurman Thomas to the Bears 13.
• Just five plays after the kickoff, Ron Morris caught a 63-yard TD pass on a throw that was intended for Dennis Gentry. That gave Chicago a 14-3 lead.
• Kevin Butler capped a 56-yard drive on the next possession with a field goal.
• Late in the second quarter, David Tate intercepted Kelly at the Bears 42. On the next play, Gentry took a handoff on a reverse to the right and scooted 58 yards for the killing TD.

WEEK 5 GAMES	
Cinc 45, LAR 21	Clev 23, Pitt 9
Den 12, SD 0	SF 20, Det 13
TB 27, GB 24	Phil 32, Hou 23
NE 21, Ind 17	Mia 24, Minn 7
Phoe 41, Rams 27	NYG 24, Wash 23
Sea 31, Atl 20	NO 20, Dal 17
KC 17, NYJ 17 (OT)	

• With 47 seconds left in the half, Norwood's streak of 13 straight field goals ended with a miss.
• The Bills only possession of the third ended when on fourth-and-one from the 14, Mike Singletary tackled Ronnie Harmon for a 24-yard loss. In the fourth, the Bears ate up the final 8:10 of the game with one drive.

QUOTES
• Kent Hull: "Maybe the coaches won't force us to look at the film of this game. Maybe they'll just burn it. There's nobody to blame but the five guys up front."
• Mark Kelso on his nullified interception: "We had avoided those kinds of mistakes in earlier games. You're playing with fire when you give Chicago extra opportunities."
• Marv Levy: "Was this a watershed game? I don't think so. You've got 16 games in a season and this was just one of them. I don't see any long-term ramifications from this. I wouldn't have thought there would be even if we had won. Like Duffy Daugherty used to say, 'If you don't learn anything from losing, there's no sense in losing.' We lost this game in every area. This wasn't one of those cases where we beat ourselves, they just plain beat us."
• Jim Kelly: "I have to be careful what I say. The Chicago Bears are a very good team and beat us soundly today. But I also know what a good team the Buffalo Bills are and we'll be back. We weren't going to go 16-0. Over the course of the season, you're going to lose a few games."
• Joe Devlin: "It might be a bit of a sobering experience. I've been saying right along that we're not that good a football team. I believe in our team very strongly, but then again, we're not world-beaters. Maybe it's good that this happened at this point in the season."

Colts	10	7	3	3	-	23
Bills	0	7	14	13	-	34

Attendance at Rich Stadium - 76,018

Ind:	FG Biasucci 31, 3:47
Ind:	Chandler 1 run (Biasucci kick), 12:18
Ind:	Verdin 39 pass from Hogeboom (Biasucci kick), 5:44
Buf:	Harmon 26 pass from Kelly (Norwood kick), 14:09
Buf:	Reed 16 pass from Kelly (Norwood kick), 5:32
Ind:	FG Biasucci 40, 9:38
Buf:	Reed 12 pass from Kelly (Norwood kick), 10:46
Ind:	FG Biasucci 22, 1:53
Buf:	FG Norwood 45, 5:48
Buf:	FG Norwood 19, 7:55
Buf:	Riddick 1 run (Norwood kick), 13:03

	BUF	IND
First downs	25	25
Rushing yds	141	67
Passing yds	315	241
Punts-avg	2-26.5	3-38.0
Fumbles-lost	3-2	2-1
Penalties-yds	9-86	2-15
Poss. time	31:22	28:38

BILLS LEADERS: **Rushing** - Mueller 15-70, Thomas 13-48, Kelly 4-14, Riddick 3-9; **Passing** - Kelly 21-39-1 - 315; **Receiving** - Reed 7-124, Burkett 4-74, Harmon 3-36, Metzelaars 3-36, Riddick 3-30, T. Johnson 1-15.

COLTS LEADERS: **Rushing** - Dickerson 18-66, Bentley 2-7, Chandler 1-1, Hogeboom 1-(-7); **Passing** - Chandler 7-11-0 - 71, Hogeboom 15-32-2 - 202; **Receiving** - Brooks 4-69, Beach 4-33, Bentley 4-32, Dickerson 3-12, Verdin 2-66, Bouza 2-33, Boyer 2-16, Bellini 1-12.

NOTES
• The fans booed the Bills as they fell behind 17-0 before rallying for the victory.
• The Colts drove to a field goal on their first possession of the game, then Barry Krauss intercepted a Jim Kelly pass at the Colts 39 and Indy needed 10 plays to score on Chris Chandler's QB sneak.
• Early in the second quarter, the Colts marched 77 yards in six plays with Gary Hogeboom at QB for the injured Chandler. He hit Clarence Verdin for 27 yards, then threw a 39-yard TD pass to Verdin for a 17-0 lead.
• The Bills got the lift they needed late in the half. After Rohn Stark's punt rolled dead at the 2 with 2:08 left, Kelly completed five of six passes, covering the 98 yards in 1:17. He hit Chris Burkett for 34 yards and on the next play, found Ronnie Harmon for a 26-yard TD.
• On the first possession of the third, the Bills drove 64 yards in 11 plays to Andre Reed's TD reception as Kelly beat a blitz. Thurman Thomas had a 22-yard run on the drive.
• On the next series, Sherman Cocroft intercepted Hogeboom, but Jamie Mueller fumbled it right back and that led to a Dean Biasucci field goal for a 20-14 Colts lead.
• On the first play after the kickoff, Reed made a 58-

WEEK 6 GAMES	
Chi 24, Det 7	Den 16, SF 13 (OT)
Hou 7, KC 6	Rams 33, Atl 0
Mia 24, LAR 14	GB 45, NE 3
NO 23, SD 17	Cinc 36, NYJ 19
Sea 16, Cleve 10	Phoe 31, Pitt 14
Minn 14, TB 13	Wash 35, Dal 17
Phil 24, NYG 13	

yard reception which set up his seven-yard TD catch.
• Another Mueller fumble on the second play of the fourth at the Bills 15 resulted in a Biasucci field goal.
• The Bills got that back, driving 47 yards to Scott Norwood's go-ahead field goal. Then, three plays after the kickoff, Bruce Smith forced Hogeboom to fumble, Cornelius Bennett recovered and Norwood made another field goal for a 27-23 advantage. Hogeboom was intercepted by Leonard Smith and the Bills clinched the game when Riddick scored to cap a 44-yard drive.

QUOTES
• Marv Levy: "I told Jim Kelly he came of age as an NFL quarterback – he got booed by the home fans. I really believe there might be 10 percent of the people who wallow in failure. I told the players 'Don't stamp all of the fans up there by saying that the fans are booing because most of them are for you and they want you to do well.'"
• Jim Kelly: "We've been in this situation before. It's just a matter of everybody staying with me. Kent Hull told me 'We're with you, we're gonna stay with you.' One of the big factors is that I had time to throw." (About the booing): "We have a job to do, to win a championship. You want to win it for the fans, too. But you need backing. I don't think we deserved what we got."
• Pete Metzelaars: "This was a bigger win than most people realize. Chicago had beaten us pretty handily and our confidence was reeling a bit. I guess we silenced a few of the critics."

STANDINGS: SIXTH WEEK

AFC EAST	W	L	T	CENTRAL	W	L	T	WEST	W	L	T	NFC EAST	W	L	T	CENTRAL	W	L	T	WEST	W	L	T
Buffalo	5	1	0	Cincinnati	6	0	0	Seattle	4	2	0	Phoenix	4	2	0	Chicago	5	1	0	LA Rams	5	1	0
NY Jets	3	2	1	Houston	4	2	0	Denver	3	3	0	NY Giants	3	3	0	Minnesota	4	2	0	N.Orleans	5	1	0
Miami	3	3	0	Cleveland	3	3	0	San Diego	2	4	0	Washington	3	3	0	Tampa Bay	2	4	0	San Fran	4	2	0
New England	2	4	0	Pittsburgh	1	5	0	Raiders	2	4	0	Philadelphia	3	3	0	Detroit	1	5	0	Atlanta	1	5	0
Indianapolis	1	5	0					Kan. City	1	4	1	Dallas	2	4	0	Green Bay	1	5	0				

NOTES

• Jim Kelly passed for 261 yards and three TDs in the first half as the Bills made their first *Monday Night Football* appearance in four years a big success. They improved their Monday night record to 4-9. It was Buffalo's first win on Monday since Oct. 12, 1981, and its initial Monday win on the road.

• The Jets managed 10 first downs, only one via the rush. The Bills possessed the ball for 39:54.

• Bruce Smith had 2 1/2 sacks, Leonard Smith was in on seven tackles and had one sack on a blitz.

• The Bills went 59 yards in 11 plays on their first possession to get a Scott Norwood field goal.

• After a punt, Kelly hit Andre Reed on the first play for a 65-yard TD.

• After another punt, the Bills took a 17-0 lead, needing just three plays to get Flip Johnson's 66-yard TD on a pass that was deflected near midfield by Carl Howard and into Johnson's hands.

• Early in the second quarter, Robb Riddick capped a 46-yard drive with a TD plunge. The Jets came back, going 76 yards in eight plays to Johnny Hector's TD run, but the Bills answered with a 70-yard march to Reed's second TD catch. Reed also had 13- and 10-yard receptions during the possession.

• Mark Kelso's interception on the Jets first offensive play of the third led to a Norwood field goal.

• Late in the third, Erik McMillan picked off a Kelly pass intended for Pete Metzelaars and ran for a TD.

• Jeff Wright's fumble recovery in the fourth set up Norwood's final field goal.

QUOTES

• Marv Levy: "We had some fortunate things happen to us early and Jim Kelly was very hot early. This was a big win, but it's only seven games into the season; more than half of it is left. We're standing and gazing."

• Jim Kelly: "I guess this shows the world we're for real." (On Andre Reed): "He's been a great receiver all along. He just doesn't get the notoriety some of the other receivers get. But after tonight, I think he quieted some people down. This was a big night for some of our younger players who had never played on Monday night. Heck, Jim Kelly had never played on Monday night. We wanted to prove that we can play with anybody in the league and I think we proved it."

• Andre Reed: "Even in the pregame warm-up we looked sharp. I think we came out higher than they did at the start and we took a bite out of them early. They (the coaches) kept telling us not to celebrate so much, but I'm thinking 'Forget that, this is prime time. I'm waving to all my friends at home.'"

• Bruce Smith about his first Monday night game: "I was so wound up, I kept walking in and out of the locker room. Finally, for something to do, I called my parents and told them I loved them. They tried all kinds of schemes on me, a couple times, three guys were blocking me."

WEEK 7 GAMES

Den 30, Atl 14	Chi 17, Dal 7
NE 27, Cinc 21	NYG 30, Det 10
GB 34, Minn 14	Hou 34, Pitt 14
LAR 27, KC 17	NO 20, Sea 19
Clev 19, Phil 3	Wash 33, Phoe 17
Mia 31, SD 28	SF 24, Rams 21
Ind 35, TB 31	

Bills	17 14 3 3 - 37
Jets	0 7 7 0 - 14

Attendance at Giants Stadium - 70,218

Buf: FG Norwood 30, 7:12
Buf: Reed 65 pass from Kelly (Norwood kick), 9:11
Buf: F. Johnson 66 pass from Kelly (Norwood kick), 11:55
Buf: Riddick 1 run (Norwood kick), :44
NYJ: Hector 1 run (Leahy kick), 5:25
Buf: Reed 16 pass from Kelly (Norwood kick), 11:42
Buf: FG Norwood 34, 6:28
NYJ: McMillan 40 interception return (Leahy kick), 14:54
Buf: FG Norwood 28, 11:12

	BUF	NYJ
First downs	24	10
Rushing yds	135	45
Passing yds	292	154
Punts-avg	3-32.7	6-43.0
Fumbles-lost	2-0	1-1
Penalties-yds	4-25	6-47
Poss. time	39:54	20:06

BILLS LEADERS: Rushing - Thomas 11-43, Byrum 13-31, Riddick 7-30, Harmon 6-15, Mueller 5-12, Kelly 1-6, Reich 2-(-2); **Passing** - Kelly 16-27-1 - 302; **Receiving** - Reed 7-132, Metzelaars 3-40, F. Johnson 2-75, T. Johnson 2-32, Harmon 1-14, Riddick 1-9.

JETS LEADERS: Rushing - McNeil 7-23, Vick 2-11, Hector 4-11; **Passing** - O'Brien 18-30-1 - 191; **Receiving** - Dunn 6-67, Griggs 6-55, Toon 4-49, Hector 1-11, McNeil 1-9.

NOTES

• Scott Norwood beat the Pats for the second time this season with a late field goal.

• Meanwhile, his counterpart, rookie Teddy Garcia, missed three field goals.

• The Pats averaged only 3.7 yards per offensive play, 2.6 per pass play.

• Garcia's first miss came after Andre Tippett forced Jim Kelly to fumble at the Bills 20.

• One play after the miss, Fred Marion recovered a Ronnie Harmon fumble at the Bills 34. Five plays later, Doug Flutie hit Irving Fryar for a TD.

• The Bills responded by driving 69 yards on the ensuing series to Robb Riddick's TD. Thurman Thomas carried seven times for 55 yards along the way as the Bills never threw a pass.

• On the next series, the Bills traveled 43 yards to a Norwood field goal.

• The Pats then punted, but Errol Tucker muffed it at the Bills 11 and Marvin Allen recovered. On the next play, John Stephens scored to give the Pats a 13-10 lead as a bad snap ruined the PAT.

• Norwood tied it after Trumaine Johnson made a 17-yard catch and Andre Reed ran 36 on a reverse.

• Garcia then missed a 52-yard attempt on the final play of the half. On the Pats' first possession of the third, his 39-yarder was blocked by Howard Ballard. Kelly then drove the Bills 75 yards in six plays. Johnson caught a 49-yard pass before Kelly hit Pete Metzelaars for the TD.

• Raymond Clayborn's interception at the Bills 34 was cashed in when Robert Perryman scored. The Bills contributed four penalties during the sequence.

• However, the Bills took possession with 6:54 left and used all but the final 13 seconds of the game to set up the winning kick. The key plays were Johnson's 21-yard catch, Kelly's 15-yard scramble on third-and-six from the Bills 41, Riddick's two-yard gain on fourth-and-one from the Pats 35 and Carl Byrum's 11-yard run to the 22.

QUOTES

• Kent Hull: "I couldn't believe that we were still in the game after all the turnovers we committed in the first half. We were fortunate."

• Fred Smerlas on the Pats taunting of Norwood before the winning kick: "They were wasting their time because the kid doesn't get rattled. The guy has nerves of steel. He'd be perfect for a bombing mission."

• Marv Levy: "We did some things today that you're not going to do very often and still win. But I feel good that we were able to rise above them."

• Jim Kelly: "This win was special because of the way we did it, against a good team. I've never played very well against them. They've given me problems, especially Fred Marion. Before the game, coach Levy reminded us that they had won the last five games at Rich Stadium. We've been ending a lot of streaks lately. This is just another step."

WEEK 8 GAMES

Clev 29, Phoe 21	Phil 24, Dal 23
Pitt 39, Den 21	Det 7, KC 6
Cinc 44, Hou 21	Ind 16, SD 0
NO 20, LAR 6	Minn 49, TB 20
NYG 23, Atl 16	NYJ 44, Mia 30
Rams 31, Sea 10	Wash 20, GB 17
Chi 10, SF 9	

Patriots	7 6 0 7 - 20
Bills	7 6 7 3 - 23

Attendance at Rich Stadium - 76,824

NE: Fryar 12 pass from Flutie (Garcia kick), 7:18
Buf: Riddick 1 run (Norwood kick), 11:50
Buf: FG Norwood 30, 3:04
NE: Stephens 11 run (kick failed), 4:26
Buf: FG Norwood 35, 10:07
Buf: Metzelaars 10 pass from Kelly (Norwood kick), 13:51
NE: Perryman 1 run (Garcia kick), 7:52
Buf: FG Norwood 33, 14:47

	BUF	NE
First downs	18	22
Rushing yds	190	176
Passing yds	149	47
Punts-avg	2-40.5	5-38.2
Fumbles-lost	3-3	0-0
Penalties-yds	9-58	5-45
Poss. time	29:24	30:36

BILLS LEADERS: Rushing - Thomas 20-84, Reed 1-36, Kelly 3-27, Byrum 6-22, Harmon 2-12, Riddick 4-9; **Passing** - Kelly 12-18-1 - 165; **Receiving** - T. Johnson 6-132, Harmon 1-20, Metzelaars 1-10, Reed 1-3, Thomas 1-2, Riddick 1-1, Byrum 1-(-3).

PATRIOTS LEADERS: Rushing - Stephens 25-134, Dupard 9-18, Perryman 6-16, Flutie 1-9, Tatupu 1-(-1); **Passing** - Flutie 5-16-0 - 58; **Receiving** - Dawson 1-18, Stephens 1-16, Fryar 1-12, Morgan 1-8, Dupard 1-4.

STANDINGS: EIGHTH WEEK

AFC EAST	W	L	T	CENTRAL	W	L	T	WEST	W	L	T	NFC EAST	W	L	T	CENTRAL	W	L	T	WEST	W	L	T
Buffalo	7	1	0	Cincinnati	7	1	0	Seattle	4	4	0	Washington	5	3	0	Chicago	7	1	0	N.Orleans	7	1	0
NY Jets	4	3	1	Houston	5	3	0	Denver	4	4	0	NY Giants	5	3	0	Minnesota	5	3	0	LA Rams	6	2	0
Miami	4	4	0	Cleveland	5	3	0	Raiders	3	5	0	Phoenix	4	4	0	Tampa Bay	2	6	0	San Fran	5	3	0
New England	3	5	0	Pittsburgh	2	6	0	San Diego	2	6	0	Philadelphia	4	4	0	Green Bay	2	6	0	Atlanta	1	7	0
Indianapolis	3	5	0					Kan. City	1	6	1	Dallas	2	6	0	Detroit	2	6	0				

Packers	0	0	0	0	- 0
Bills	7	7	7	7	- 28

Attendance at Rich Stadium - 79,176

Buf: Riddick 2 run (Norwood kick), 13:41
Buf: Rolle 1 pass from Kelly (Norwood kick), 13:55
Buf: Kelso 78 interception return (Norwood kick), 2:59
Buf: Seals 7 fumble return (Norwood kick), 13:44

	BUF	GB
First downs	18	10
Rushing yds	195	77
Passing yds	66	54
Punts-avg	7-32.7	9-42.4
Fumbles-lost	2-1	5-3
Penalties-yds	8-50	3-29
Poss. time	33:33	26:27

BILLS LEADERS: Rushing - Thomas 23-116, Mueller 9-34, Harmon 9-23, Riddick 6-12, Byrum 1-9, Kelly 1-1; **Passing** - Kelly 10-14-2 - 80; **Receiving** - Reed 2-26, Metzelaars 3-17, Thomas 2-13, T. Johnson 1-17, Mueller 1-6, Rolle 1-1.
PACKERS LEADERS: Rushing - Fullwood 7-41, Woodside 6-16, Majkowski 2-12, Mason 4-10, Caruth 1-(-2); **Passing** - Majkowsi 11-29-1 - 93; **Receiving** - West 3-39, Woodside 3-21, Kemp 2-17, Fullwood 2-7, Caruth 1-9.

WEEK 9 GAMES

Atl 27, Phil 24	NE 30, Chi 7
Clev 23, Cinc 16	LAR 17, KC 10
Rams 12, NO 10	Mia 17, TB 14
SF 24, Minn 21	Phoe 16, Dal 10
NYJ 24, Pitt 20	Sea 17, SD 14
Hou 41, Wash 17	Ind 55, Den 23
NYG 13, Det 10 (OT)	

NOTES

• The Bills dominated the Packers, ruining Green Bay quarterback and Depew native Don Majkowski's homecoming. Majkowski was sacked six times, 2 1/2 times by Cornelius Bennett.
• Through three quarters, the Packers had minus-4 yards net passing on a very cold day.
• Thurman Thomas topped 100 yards rushing for the first time in his NFL career.
• The Bills tied a team record with their sixth straight sellout at Rich, tying the marks of 1974, '81.
• The Bills scored twice on defense for the first time since Sept. 9, 1979 against Cincinnati.
• A 27-yard Don Bracken punt gave the Bills the ball at the Packers 29 late in the first quarter and they needed just six plays to score on Robb Riddick's third-down run.
• Jim Kelly was intercepted at the Packers 10 by Clarence native Mark Murphy, but a Bruce Smith sack forced Bracken to punt from the end zone and the Bills took over at the Green Bay 39. Eight plays later, Kelly hit Butch Rolle for a TD. The key play was a 16-yard run by Thomas to the 2.
• On the Pats second play of the third quarter, Bruce Smith got pressure on Majkowski and Mark Kelso picked off his hurried pass and weaved his way 78 yards for a TD.
• Late in the game, Mark Pike forced Paul Ott Carruth to fumble. Leon Seals picked it up and ran seven yards for a touchdown.

QUOTES

• Green Bay quarterback Don Majkowski: "It would have been a lot nicer to come home and have a little better showing. It just goes that way. You have to compliment their defense. Once you fall behind, it's pretty tough because they have some talented defensive linemen."
• Shane Conlan on Majkowski: "We never gave the kid a chance. People were in his face all the time."
• Fred Smerlas on Majkowski: "The Polish rifle had a lot of pressure on him. We were in his face every play. At one point he said 'Where are you coming from?' and I told him 'Stay in one place so I can catch you.' I think our defense is as good as anybody's."
• Kent Hull: "We told Scott (Norwood) to take the week off. We told him he had hogged the headlines enough already. It was time for someone else to get some pub."
• Mark Kelso: "Bruce (Smith) came up to me and said 'I want half that interception and half that touchdown. I'd be happy to give it to him. In fact the whole defensive line deserves it. They make my job so much easier."
• Thurman Thomas: "As the season goes on, I think I get better and stronger with each game. I felt good from the start of the game. During the week we felt we could run on Green Bay and our offensive line went out there and did a great job. The last three or four weeks we've been pounding everybody with the running game."

Bills	3	7	0	3	- 13
Seahawks	0	3	0	0	- 3

Attendance at the Kingdome - 61,074

Buf: FG Norwood 27, 11:23
Sea: FG Johnson 41, 8:36
Buf: Riddick 1 run (Norwood kick), 13:03
Buf: FG Norwood 23, 12:22

	BUF	SEA
First downs	18	10
Rushing yds	142	72
Passing yds	194	73
Punts-avg	5-45.8	7-46.9
Fumbles-lost	1-1	3-1
Penalties-yds	11-78	6-64
Poss. time	34:45	25:15

BILLS LEADERS: Rushing - Riddick 18-75, Thomas 6-21, Mueller 4-15, Byrum 2-14, Reed 1-10, Harmon 4-9, Kelly 2- (-2); **Passing** - Kelly 16-25-1 - 180, Riddick 1-1-0 - 26; **Receiving** - T. Johnson 5-52, F. Johnson 3-51, Reed 3-39, Riddick 3-34, Metzelaars 1-21, Mueller 1-6, Byrum 1-3.

SEAHAWKS LEADERS: Rushing - Warner 11-33, Williams 5-33, Kemp 1-6, Stouffer 3-0; **Passing** - Stouffer 10-22-1 - 105, Kemp 0-1-0 - 0; **Receiving** - Williams 4-18, Tice 3-22, Largent 2-56, Blades 1-9.

WEEK 10 GAMES

NYG 29, Dal 21	Minn 44, Det 17
Atl 20, GB 0	Den 17, KC 11
Phil 30, Rams 24	NE 21, Mia 10
Wash 27, NO 24	Ind 38, NYJ 14
Cinc 42, Pitt 7	Phoe 24, SF 23
Chi 28, TB 10	LAR 13, SD 3
Hou 24, Cleve 17	

NOTES

• The Bills beat Seattle for the first time and now owned at least one victory against every NFL team.
• Seattle entered the game 34-12 at home under ex-Bills coach Chuck Knox.
• The Bills' defense gave up just 145 yards, recorded four sacks for 32 yards and forced two turnovers. Seattle was just one-of-10 on third-down conversions. Bruce Smith had two of the sacks, both on third downs.
• Thurman Thomas was forced to the sidelines late in the first quarter with a shin bruise.
• The Bills drove 61 yards in 14 plays on their first possession to Scott Norwood's field goal.
• The Seahawks tied it in the second quarter, driving 47 yards in eight plays to Norm Johnson's field goal. They overcame an unsportsmanlike conduct penalty on Ron Mattes that put them in a first-and-25 hole. Mattes cheap-shotted Bruce Smith. Steve Largent caught a 38-yard pass on third-and-18, moving the ball to the Bills 40.
• The Bills answered with a 73-yard drive in 10 plays with Robb Riddick diving in for a TD. Riddick threw a 26-yard option pass to Flip Johnson on third-and-four, moving the ball to the Seattle 41. Riddick caught a third-and-two pass for three yards to give the Bills first-and-goal at the 1.
• Flip Johnson fumbled a punt at the Bills 39 late in the third, but Fred Smerlas stopped Kelly Stouffer on a fourth-and-one sneak from the 30. Kelly then was intercepted by Paul Moyer, but the defense held again.
• The Bills were forced to punt, but the ball bounced off Nesby Glasgow's foot and Ray Bentley recovered at the Seahawks 32, leading to Norwood's clinching field goal.

QUOTES

• Fred Smerlas: "We're 9-1. I've been 1-9 before, but never 9-1. I don't know what to say. All I know is I wouldn't want to play against our defense, especially when we've got a team in a must-throw situation. I don't think many people thought we were going to fly out here and beat Seattle. All the experts said we have five of our last seven on the road and we're going to fall apart. So I guess this victory sums up their intelligence."
• Seahawks coach Chuck Knox: "I said going in I thought they were the best team in the NFL and they did nothing to change my mind. We didn't have a chance."
• Marv Levy: "They (the defense) played magnificently again. There's not enough I can say about them. They rose up time and time again, especially when we had some disappointments."
• Kent Hull: "It seems like every week there's somebody saying that we're overrated or not as good as our record. But that kind of talk just fuels the fire. Every week there's something else to prove. Eventually, we'll demand respect."
• Jim Kelly: "Coach Levy keeps telling us the mark of a championship team is the ability to win on the road and we're proving we can do it. This is when it helps to have a really good defense (when the offense struggles). Not too many people thought we'd be in this position at this point. But this team has pulled together. We're fighting hard."

STANDINGS: TENTH WEEK

AFC EAST	W	L	T	CENTRAL	W	L	T	WEST	W	L	T	NFC EAST	W	L	T	CENTRAL	W	L	T	WEST	W	L	T
Buffalo	9	1	0	Cincinnati	8	2	0	Seattle	5	5	0	NY Giants	7	3	0	Chicago	8	2	0	N.Orleans	7	3	0
NY Jets	5	4	1	Houston	7	3	0	Denver	5	5	0	Phoenix	6	4	0	Minnesota	6	4	0	LA Rams	7	3	0
Miami	5	5	0	Cleveland	6	4	0	Raiders	5	5	0	Washington	6	4	0	Tampa Bay	2	8	0	San Fran	6	4	0
New England	5	5	0	Pittsburgh	2	8	0	San Diego	2	8	0	Philadelphia	5	5	0	Green Bay	2	8	0	Atlanta	3	7	0
Indianapolis	5	5	0					Kan. City	1	8	1	Dallas	2	8	0	Detroit	2	8	0				

GAME 11 - Monday, Nov. 14, 1988 - BILLS 31, DOLPHINS 6

NOTES

• The Bills extended their winning streak against Miami to four games, a first in the series history for them.

• Thurman Thomas sat out the game with a bruised shin, but Ronnie Harmon and Robb Riddick scored two TDs each as they shared the halfback position. The victory was the 50th of Marv Levy's NFL career.

• Buffalo was an incredible 14-of-17 on third down, an 82 percent conversion rate.

• The Bills took the opening kickoff and moved 71 yards in 13 plays to Jim Kelly's TD pass to Harmon. Riddick converted three third-down situations, two on runs, one on an 18-yard pass reception.

• Early in the second quarter, Miami reached the Bills 6, but Art Still stopped Woody Bennett on fourth-and-two. The Bills then drove 81 yards in 13 plays to a Scott Norwood field goal. Kelly completed two third-down passes on the drive.

• Miami answered with a 91-yard drive to Dan Marino's TD pass to Mark Clayton. Miami never faced a third-down situation as Marino completed five-of-seven passes.

• The Bills went 80 yards in 11 plays on the first series in the third as Riddick scored on third-and-one. Kelly scrambled for 13 on third-and-six and a roughing penalty tacked on 15 more yards.

• On the first play after the kickoff, Cornelius Bennett intercepted Marino and returned it 30 yards to the 17. After Jamie Mueller converted on a third-and-one, Harmon scored on a six-yard run for a 24-6 lead.

• Three plays after the kickoff, Mark Kelso intercepted Marino and returned it 25 yards to the Bills 46. The Bills moved 54 yards in nine plays to Riddick's diving TD.

QUOTES

• Marv Levy: "I'm proud of the way our team played against a team that puts you under a lot of pressure. I would never have guessed we would have come away with this kind of a margin. If we played again tomorrow, I would expect it to be much closer. They're a better team than the score showed. Even when it was 31-6, I felt tense as hell with Marino out there."

• Fred Smerlas: "When we're off, we win close games. When we're on, we kill teams."

• Robb Riddick: "They used to own us, now we own them. We (he and Harmon) knew it was going to be a busy night when Thurman tested his leg and couldn't go. We were ready. After all, four legs are better than two. When you get the ball and you've already got two or three yards, that helps."

• Miami offensive tackle Ronnie Lee: "We used to go out and kick these guys all over the field. This is just a bad feeling."

• Miami quarterback Dan Marino: "They have a great team and great people. They play a very basic defense, they just come after you. They do basic things, but they do them well."

• Miami coach Don Shula: "I thought at halftime we could still win the game. It's a big disappointment, it's a game we felt we needed to have."

WEEK 11 GAMES

Chi 34, Wash 14	KC 31, Cinc 28
Den 30, Clev 7	Sea 27, Hou 24
Ind 20, GB 13	LAR 9, SF 3
NE 14, NYJ 13	NO 14, Rams 10
Phoe 24, NYG 17	Phil 27, Pitt 26
SD 10, Atl 7	TB 23, Det 20
Minn 43, Dal 3	

Bills	7	3	14	7	- 31
Dolphins	0	6	0	0	- 6

Attendance at Joe Robbie Stadium - 67,091

Buf:	Harmon 16 pass from Kelly (Norwood kick), 5:46
Buf:	FG Norwood 30, 8:51
Mia:	Clayton 4 pass from Marino (kick failed), 13:24
Buf:	Riddick 1 run (Norwood kick), 9:27
Buf:	Harmon 6 run (Norwood kick), 11:58
Buf:	Riddick 1 run (Norwood kick), 3:16

	BUF	MIA
First downs	27	15
Rushing yds	205	33
Passing yds	211	224
Punts-avg	2-45.5	3-48.3
Fumbles-lost	1-0	0-0
Penalties-yds	8-64	10-79
Poss. time	36:43	23:17

BILLS LEADERS: Rushing - Riddick 16-77, Harmon 16-67, Kelly 2-23, Mueller 6-21, Byrum 3-10, Reed 1-8, Reich 1(-1); **Passing** - Kelly 18-26-0 - 211; **Receiving** - Reed 5-65, Riddick 5-48, Harmon 4-37, Burkett 2-34, T. Johnson 1-20, Metzelaars 1-7.

DOLPHINS LEADERS: Rushing - Hampton 8-19, Davenport 3-12, Jensen 1-2, Bennett 1-0; **Passing** - Marino 19-30-3 - 224; **Receiving** - Clayton 5-45, Jensen 4-46, Edmunds 2-32, Banks 2-32, Davenport 2-31, Duper 1-13, Bennett 1-12, Stradford 1-9, Hampton 1-4.

GAME 12 - Sunday, Nov. 20, 1988 - BILLS 9, JETS 6 (OT)

NOTES

• The Bills clinched their first AFC East title since 1980 when Scott Norwood kicked the winning field goal in OT. Norwood became the first Bill to top 100 points in one season since O.J. Simpson in 1975.

• Jim Kelly was intercepted by James Hasty at the Jets 2 on the first possession and the Jets turned around and drove 92 yards in 10 plays to Pat Leahy's first field goal.

• The teams traded punts the rest of the half until Norwood missed from 47 yards one second before the end of the half.

• The Bills took the second-half kickoff and drove 64 yards to a Norwood field goal. Rich Miano's interference penalty and a 15-yard Robb Riddick run were the key plays.

• The Bills drove 64 yards in 12 plays bridging the third and fourth quarters to Norwood's go-ahead field goal. Riddick carried six times for 36 yards and Pete Metzelaars made an 18-yard reception.

• The Jets tied it quickly, going 52 yards in nine plays on the ensuing series. After an exchange of punts, and one play after a 35-yard pass to Metzelaars, Thurman Thomas fumbled and Scott Mersereau recovered at the Jets 30. New York then moved to the Bills 23, setting up Leahy for a winning attempt. However, Fred Smerlas blocked it, forcing OT.

• The Jets won the toss, but on the second play of OT, Derrick Burroughs forced Roger Vick to fumble and Cornelius Bennett recovered at the Jets 32. Riddick ran four times for 20 yards to set up the winning kick.

QUOTES

• Kent Hull on Leahy's potential winning kick: "I knew this guy had one heck of a leg. I knew he never missed from inside the 40. I couldn't bear to watch. It looked like a chip shot and I figured no way he was going to miss. Freddie looked like Michael Jordan on that one. When he made that block, I knew there was no way we were going

to lose." (About the fans' celebration): "These folks are a hungry bunch. They've taken a lot of crap over the years. I'm happy for them."

• Fred Smerlas: "The field goal before, they left a little gap on my side. I figured if I turned sideways a little bit, I could squeeze through and maybe get the ball. I had a strange feeling we were going to block it. It's just something about this team. A few years ago we would have blocked it and they would have picked it up and run for a touchdown. But times have changed for the Buffalo Bills. It's like we're a team of destiny."

• Marv Levy: "We got some inspired play from guys when we really needed it. We are in the playoffs now. We won a game today and if I can, permit me a little bit of hyperbole: We have liberated Paris, but it's 600 miles to Berlin."

• Darryl Talley: "What do they call it, pandemonium? This was fan-demonium. It was fun."

• Cornelius Bennett: "Like Tony the Tiger, everything is grrreat."

• Bill Polian: "You could see this building at the end of last season and then in training camp. But this has still been a remarkable performance."

Jets	0	3	0	3	0	- 6
Bills	0	0	3	3	3	- 9

Attendance at Rich Stadium - 78,389

NYJ:	FG Leahy 23, 2:19
Buf:	FG Norwood 25, 5:38
Buf:	FG Norwood 26, 3:04
NYJ:	FG Leahy 40, 6:36
Buf:	FG Norwood 30, 3:47

	BUF	NYJ
First downs	20	16
Rushing yds	229	140
Passing yds	112	119
Punts-avg	4-39.5	6-42.5
Fumbles-lost	2-1	2-1
Penalties-yds	7-55	9-61
Poss. time	34:47	29:00

BILLS LEADERS: Rushing - Riddick 18-103, Thomas 17-88, Kelly 1-17, Reed 2-11, Byrum 1-4, Mueller 2-3, Harmon 3-3; **Passing** - Kelly 8-18-1 - 115, Riddick 1-1-0 - 5; **Receiving** - Reed 5-56, Metzelaars 3-59, Kelly 1-5.

JETS LEADERS: Rushing - McNeil 12-61, Hector 12-59, Vick 6-21, Ryan 1-(-1); **Passing** - Ryan 10-23-0 - 130; **Receiving** - Toon 5-56, Walker 2-43, McNeil 2-18, Shuler 1-13.

WEEK 12 GAMES

Atl 12, Rams 6	Chi 27, TB 15
Cinc 38, Dal 24	NO 42, Den 0
Det 19, GB 9	Minn 12, Ind 3
Hou 38, Phoe 20	Clev 27, Pitt 7
SD 38, Rams 24	KC 27, Sea 24
NE 6, Mia 3	SF 37, Wash 21
Phil 23, NYG 17 (OT)	

STANDINGS: TWELFTH WEEK

AFC EAST	W	L	T	CENTRAL	W	L	T	WEST	W	L	T	NFC EAST	W	L	T	CENTRAL	W	L	T	WEST	W	L	T
Buffalo	11	1	0	Cincinnati	9	3	0	Seattle	6	6	0	NY Giants	7	5	0	Chicago	10	2	0	N.Orleans	9	3	0
New England	7	5	0	Houston	8	4	0	Denver	6	6	0	Phoenix	7	5	0	Minnesota	8	4	0	LA Rams	7	5	0
Indianapolis	6	6	0	Cleveland	7	5	0	Raiders	6	6	0	Philadelphia	7	5	0	Tampa Bay	3	9	0	San Fran	7	5	0
NY Jets	5	6	1	Pittsburgh	2	10	0	San Diego	4	8	0	Washington	6	6	0	Detroit	3	9	0	Atlanta	4	8	0
Miami	5	7	0					Kan. City	3	8	1	Dallas	2	10	0	Green Bay	2	10	0				

Bills	0	7	7	7	- 21
Bengals	7	14	7	7	- 35

Attendance at Riverfront Stadium - 58,672

Cin: Brooks 3 run (Breech kick), 12:07
Cin: Brooks 13 pass from Esiason (Breech kick), :58
Cin: Woods 2 run (Breech kick), 12:24
Buf: Riddick 1 run (Norwood kick), 13:53
Cin: Woods 1 run (Breech kick), 9:56
Buf: Harmon 9 pass from Kelly (Norwood kick), 12:18
Buf: Riddick 1 run (Norwood kick), :51
Cin: Woods 2 run (Breech kick), 12:41

	BUF	CIN
First downs	21	34
Rushing yds	110	232
Passing yds	243	223
Punts-avg	2-44.5	2-42.5
Fumbles-lost	2-2	1-0
Penalties-yds	5-36	6-55
Poss. time	18:39	41:21

BILLS LEADERS: Rushing - Thomas 10-71, Riddick 6-30, Harmon 1-7, Mueller 1-2; **Passing** - Kelly 24-35-2 - 265; **Receiving** - Harmon 8-94, Riddick 7-57, Reed 4-53, T. Johnson 4-50, Burkett 1-11.

BENGALS LEADERS: Rushing - Woods 26-129, Brooks 22-93, Esiason 2-9, Jennings 2-1; **Passing** - Esiason 18-25-0 - 238; **Receiving** - Woods 5-38, McGee 3-52, Holman 3-41, Brooks 3-21, Brown 2-41, Hillary 1-31, Riggs 1-14.

NOTES

• The Bills came out flat and the NFL's No. 1 defense allowed season-highs in points and yards (455).
• The Bengals possessed the ball for 41:21 and were nine-of-14 on third downs. The Bengals 34 first downs tied the record for the most ever allowed by the Bills. The Bengals set the original record in a 1975 game.
• The Bills stopped the Bengals on fourth-and-goal from the 1 on the first series, but after the Bills punted, the Bengals moved 40 yards in five plays to James Brooks' TD run.
• The Bengals then went 63 yards in five plays on the next series to Brooks' TD reception. The key play was a 29-yard Boomer Esiason pass to Eddie Brown.
• Two plays after the kickoff, Thurman Thomas lost a fumble to Tim Krumrie. Jim Breech then missed a field goal, but seven plays later, Rickey Dixon intercepted Kelly at the Bengals 35. Cincy then went 65 yards in 11 plays, 10 of them runs, and Ickey Woods capped the march with a TD run.
• Kelly drove Buffalo 80 yards in eight plays to Robb Riddick's TD run, but the momentum was wasted early in the third. Kelly was intercepted by David Fulcher in the end zone and the Bengals proceeded to drive 80 yards in 11 plays to Woods' second TD run. Esiason completed two third-down passes along the way.

WEEK 13 GAMES	
Minn 23, Det 0	Hou 25, Dal 17
Clev 17, Wash 3	Chi 16, GB 0
Pitt 16, KC 10	Den 35, Rams 24
NYJ 38, Mia 24	Ind 24, NE 21
Phil 31, Phoe 21	SF 48, SD 10
Atl 17, TB 10	NYG 13, NO 12
Sea 35, LAR 27	

• Buffalo answered with a 68-yard march to Kelly's TD pass to Ronnie Harmon. Harmon caught four passes for 41 yards on the drive. The Bills then pulled to within 28-21 when Kelly hit Andre Reed for 34 yards to the 1, setting up Riddick's TD dive. After a punt, the Bills reached the Bengals 44, but Riddick fumbled after catching a pass and Lewis Billups recovered. The Bengals then drove 65 yards in 15 plays, using 9:24 to get the clinching TD on Woods' third TD run.

QUOTES

• Pete Metzelaars: "It's not an easy place to play, especially when you're turning the ball over four times and not forcing any turnovers of your own against an offense that's that good."
• Bengals coach Sam Wyche: "I don't think I've ever been around a team that has as good a chance to make it to the Super Bowl as this one. I haven't been around a team that has the wherewithal this team does to do what they want with the ball offensively. The home-field advantage continues to be apparent. We'd like to play them again, and we'd very much like to be the host. They had to battle more than just the Cincinnati Bengals players."
• Bengals center Bruce Kozerski: "In the middle of the third quarter, the Bills had a look on them like 'I can't believe this is happening.' It was like they were saying 'We've only lost one game and people just don't score points on us like this.'"
• Marv Levy: "That was quite a display of offense by Cincinnati. I don't think we were flat. That's kind of one of those throwaway terms when you don't play well enough. Maybe we haven't seen a team this good. This is far and away the best offensive team we've played."

Bills	0	0	2	3	- 5
Buccaneers	0	10	0	0	- 10

Attendance at Tampa Stadium - 49,498

TB: FG Carney 29, 6:23
TB: Testaverde 4 run (Carney kick), 13:19
Buf: Safety: B. Smith tackled Testaverde, 4:00
Buf: FG Norwood 30, 1:27

	BUF	TB
First downs	16	19
Rushing yds	39	110
Passing yds	234	143
Punts-avg	5-43.2	5-32.0
Fumbles-lost	1-0	0-0
Penalties-yds	12-100	10-66
Poss. time	25:02	34:58

BILLS LEADERS: Rushing - Mueller 3-16, Riddick 8-16, Harmon 1-6, Thomas 7-1; **Passing** - Kelly 23-40-2 - 249; **Receiving** - Riddick 6-53, T. Johnson 4-63, Burkett 4-62, Metzelaars 4-35, Reed 2-12, Thomas 1-11, F. Johnson 1-8, Harmon 1-5.

BUCCANEERS LEADERS: Rushing - Howard 16-50, J. Smith 1-23, D. Smith 1-15, Goode 9-15, Testaverde 5-8, Tate 3-(-1); **Passing** - Testaverde 12-29-0 - 156; **Receiving** - D. Smith 3-17, Hall 3-32, Carrier 2-42, Howard 2-26, Parks 1-22, J. Smith 1-17.

WEEK 14 GAMES	
Clev 24, Dal 21	LAR 21, Den 20
Det 30, GB 14	Ind 31, Mia 28
Minn 45, NO 3	KC 38, NYJ 34
NYG 44, Phoe 7	Cinc 27, SD 10
SF 13, Atl 3	NE 13, Sea 7
Wash 20, Phil 19	Pitt 37, Hou 34
Rams 23, Chi 3	

NOTES

• The Bills rushed for just 39 yards and saw their home-field advantage hopes for the playoffs take a serious blow with a loss to the lowly Buccaneers.
• The teams exchanged three punts each in the first quarter before the Bucs finally broke the drought with a 14-play, 85-yard march to John Carney's field goal.
• After the Bills' fourth straight punt, the Bucs moved 66 yards in six plays to Vinny Testaverde's TD run. Testaverde completed three-of-four passes for 56 yards on the drive.
• The Bills had 80 yards and four first downs in the first half.
• On the first series of the third, Jim Kelly was intercepted at the 2. But two plays later, Bruce Smith tackled Testaverde for a safety, cutting the deficit to 10-2.
• After a free kick, the Bills drove to the 1, but Robb Riddick was stopped on fourth-and-goal.
• The Bucs punted and the Bills moved 42 yards to Scott Norwood's field goal early in the fourth.
• The Bucs used 10 minutes on the next series, but Smith blocked Carney's field goal, giving the Bills one last chance. They drove to the Bucs 25 with 51 seconds left, but Kelly was intercepted by Mark Robinson.

QUOTES

• Marv Levy: "Maybe our team didn't respect them enough, but I saw no disdain or flippant attitude. There was a lot of talk about 'You guys are going to the Super Bowl' and we still had four or five games left to play."
• Jim Kelly: "It's like we weren't here. I don't know if we thought we could just show up and win, but we sure didn't play the way the Buffalo Bills are capable of playing. Maybe we took a win for granted because we were playing Tampa Bay. All I know is they were ready to play and we weren't. We deserved to lose today, but I know we're

mature enough to come back."
• Fred Smerlas: "It's not the end of the world, we're in the playoffs. We have to keep our composure and continuity. You guys make too much out of a loss. We're 11-3, not 3-11."
• Leonard Smith: "We better hunker down and realize we have to get some momentum going for the playoffs or our season is going to go down the tubes. If we keep playing like this, the only way we're going to go to the Super Bowl is if we pay our way."
• Art Still: "I think we're getting too far ahead of ourselves. We made the playoffs so early that maybe we started looking forward to the postseason about four weeks too soon."
• Chris Burkett: "We had numerous chances to put this game away and we didn't. I don't mean to take away anything from Tampa Bay, but we can't play much worse than this."

STANDINGS: FOURTEENTH WEEK

AFC EAST	W	L	T	CENTRAL	W	L	T	WEST	W	L	T	NFC EAST	W	L	T	CENTRAL	W	L	T	WEST	W	L	T
Buffalo	11	3	0	Cincinnati	11	3	0	Seattle	7	7	0	NY Giants	9	5	0	Chicago	11	3	0	N.Orleans	9	5	0
New England	8	6	0	Houston	9	5	0	Denver	7	7	0	Philadelphia	8	6	0	Minnesota	10	4	0	San Fran	9	5	0
Indianapolis	8	6	0	Cleveland	9	5	0	Raiders	7	7	0	Phoenix	7	7	0	Tampa Bay	4	10	0	LA Rams	8	6	0
NY Jets	6	7	1	Pittsburgh	4	10	0	Kan. City	4	9	1	Washington	7	7	0	Detroit	4	10	0	Atlanta	5	9	0
Miami	5	9	0					San Diego	4	10	0	Dallas	2	12	0	Green Bay	2	12	0				

NOTES

• The Bills moved into the driver's seat in the race for home-field advantage throughout the playoffs.

• The game was the coldest to date ever played in Buffalo with a temperature of 11 and a windchill of minus 14.

• The Bills set a new NFL single-season attendance record of 622,793, winning all eight home games.

• The Bills drove 80 yards in 15 plays on their first possession to Robb Riddick's TD dive.

• The Raiders answered with a 71-yard drive to Steve Smith's TD run. Wayne Davis' holding penalty nullified a Mark Kelso interception to keep the drive alive.

• Ronnie Harmon returned the kickoff 37 yards to the 49. Four plays later, Thurman Thomas broke a TD run.

• The Raiders moved to the Bills 24, but Bruce Smith forced Schroeder to fumble and Art Still recovered. The offense did nothing, but on the next series, Still forced Schroeder to fumble and Fred Smerlas recovered. This time, it resulted in a Scott Norwood field goal.

• Norwood made another field goal late in the half.

• The Bills punted to open the third, but Tim Brown muffed John Kidd's 60-yard kick at the 11 and Sherman Cocroft recovered. Riddick then scored on fourth-and-one from the 2 for a 27-7 lead.

• The Raiders reached the Bills 5 on their next possession, but Schroeder threw an incompletion on fourth down.

• After a punt, Schroeder hit Brown with a TD pass, but the Bills got that back with a 63-yard drive to Butch Rolle's TD reception. Jamie Mueller carried four times for 25 yards.

• The Raiders scored five plays after the kickoff on a TD pass to Steve Smith. Norwood closed the scoring with a field goal to cap a 60-yard march in which the Bills converted two third downs.

QUOTES

• Fred Smerlas on the fans: "Give them as much credit as the players. This is a small market and they set the attendance record. That's pretty amazing. There are a lot of blue-collar people who spend their hard-earned money to support this team. It really pumps you up."

• Thurman Thomas: "We embarrassed ourselves against Tampa Bay. All week long the backs and the linemen talked about redeeming ourselves. Embarrassment is a powerful motive. I don't think they (the Raiders) were too pumped up about coming in here in this kind of weather before this kind of crowd."

• Marv Levy: "You can analyze all you want, but if you win the turnover battle, you'll win about 93 percent of your games. I don't care what the other stats say."

| Raiders | 7 | 0 | 7 | 7 | - 21 |
| Bills | 7 | 13 | 7 | 10 | - 37 |

Attendance at Rich Stadium - 78,348

Buf: Riddick 1 run (Norwood kick), 8:28
LAR: Smith 1 run (Bahr kick), 14:22
Buf: Thomas 37 run (Norwood kick), :56
Buf: FG Norwood 30, 7:01
Buf: FG Norwood 30, 15:00
Buf: Riddick 2 run (Norwood kick), 2:26
LAR: Brown 43 pass from Schroeder (Bahr kick), 13:35
Buf: Rolle 2 pass from Kelly (Norwood kick), 4:04
LAR: Smith 6 pass from Schroeder (Bahr kick), 7:45
Buf: FG Norwood 22, 13:09

	BUF	LAR
First downs	24	17
Rushing yds	255	111
Passing yds	112	207
Punts-avg	5-36.8	3-37.7
Fumbles-lost	1-0	3-3
Penalties-yds	5-31	5-32
Poss. time	33:30	26:30

BILLS LEADERS: Rushing - Thomas 14-106, Mueller 18-61, Harmon 4-44, Riddick 11-44, Kelly 1-0; **Passing** - Kelly 11-24-0 - 128; **Receiving** - T. Johnson 4-53, F. Johnson 3-36, Burkett 2-28, Thomas 1-9, Rolle 1-2.
RAIDERS LEADERS: Rushing - Jackson 12-64, Allen 11-37, Schroeder 3-7, Smith 3-3; **Passing** - Schroeder 14-24-0 - 227; **Receiving** - Smith 4-13, Brown 3-90, Allen 3-31, Lofton 1-57, Fernandez 1-26, Parker 1-7, Mueller 1-3.

WEEK 15 GAMES

NYJ 34, Ind 16	Phil 23, Phoe 17
Rams 22, Atl 7	Hou 41, Cinc 6
Dal 24, Wash 17	Chi 13, Det 12
NYG 28, KC 12	GB 18, Minn 10
SF 30, NO 17	SD 20, Pitt 14
Sea 42, Den 14	Mia 38, Clev 31
NE 10, TB 7 (OT)	

NOTES

• The Bills blew a chance to clinch home-field advantage throughout the playoffs, losing at the Hoosier Dome for the fourth time in five appearances. They also failed to set a new team record for wins.

• Shane Conlan missed his fourth straight game, Fred Smerlas was hurt on the first play and Art Still also left the game. In their places were Scott Radecic, Jeff Wright and Leon Seals.

• Ronnie Harmon fumbled the opening kickoff and kicker Dean Biasucci recovered at the Bills 36. Biasucci then kicked a 52-yard field goal to give the Colts a quick lead.

• After punting on their first three possessions, the Bills moved 52 yards in seven plays to Jim Kelly's TD pass to Andre Reed with 1:07 left in the half.

• In the third, John Kidd pinned the Colts back to their own 3. When the defense held, the Bills took over at the Colts 37 and needed just five plays to get Reed's second TD reception for a 14-3 lead early in the fourth.

• But the Colts rallied, driving 80 yards in 17 plays to Gary Hogeboom's third-down TD pass to Matt Bouza. The Colts accumulated seven first downs on the drive.

• After Indy's defense forced a punt, Hogeboom took over at his own 25 with 3:19 left to play. He ran for six, Eric Dickerson went for 11, Bouza made a 19-yard reception and Dickerson ran for 14 to the Bills 25 with 1:57 left. On third-and-seven Albert Bentley ran a draw for 10 and a delay penalty on the Bills moved the ball to the 7. Hogeboom then hit Bentley for the winning TD pass with 1:18 left.

• Kelly then completed only two of five passes, was forced to scramble twice and finally was sacked on fourth-and-15 from the Bills 49 to end the game. One play before, Robb Riddick's catch for a first down was wiped out by an illegal procedure penalty on Dale Hellestrae.

QUOTES

• Andre Reed: "It's too bad. We played hard and we seemed to have things under control when we went up 14-3. But they came storming back in the final quarter. It's not like we went out there not to win. We didn't have a lackluster performance. They just got fired up and they won."

• Marv Levy: "The buzz words we've been using all week were 'home-field advantage' but it doesn't do you any good unless you win the first one. I'm not making light of this loss, but there's no sense dealing with the ifs and self-castigation. We have to put this behind us. I would have preferred winning, but now I have to put my eye on the next one. This was an important game, but not terminal. The next one we have to win."

• Jim Kelly: "We're up 14-3 with six minutes to play and it looks like we're going to win the game. You figure the only thing that's going to keep you from going to the Super Bowl is not having the home-field advantage. There were some guys who weren't as disappointed as others. I think there were a few of the guys who didn't play as much. I looked at this game as a must-win."

WEEK 16 GAMES

Den 21, NE 10	Cinc 20, Wash 17
NO 10, Atl 9	TB 21, Det 10
GB 26, Phoe 17	Clev 28, Hou 23
SD 24, KC 13	Pitt 40, Mia 24
NYJ 27, NYG 21	Phil 23, Dal 7
Sea 43, LAR 37	Rams 36, SF 16
Minn 28, Chi 27	

| Bills | 0 | 7 | 0 | 7 | - 14 |
| Colts | 3 | 0 | 0 | 14 | - 17 |

Attendance at the Hoosier Dome - 59,908

Ind: FG Biasucci 52, 2:10
Buf: Reed 23 pass from Kelly (Norwood kick), 13:53
Buf: Reed 6 pass from Kelly (Norwood kick), 2:00
Ind: Bouza 3 pass from Hogeboom (Biasucci kick), 9:28
Ind: Bentley 7 pass from Hogeboom (Biasucci kick), 13:42

	BUF	IND
First downs	14	25
Rushing yds	53	184
Passing yds	195	117
Punts-avg	6-42.2	5-45.4
Fumbles-lost	1-1	0-0
Penalties-yds	8-42	4-35
Poss. time	21:18	38:42

BILLS LEADERS: Rushing - Thomas 9-27, Mueller 6-15, Kelly 3-10, Riddick 1-1; **Passing** - Kelly 17-29-0 - 204; **Receiving** - Reed 7-99, Harmon 3-13, T. Johnson 2-25, Riddick 2-21, Metzelaars 1-26, Thomas 1-17, Mueller 1-3.

COLTS LEADERS: Rushing - Dickerson 36-166, Bentley 1-10, Chandler 4-8, Hogeboom 3-5, Verdin 1-5; **Passing** - Hogeboom 10-15-0 - 89, Chandler 4-11-0 - 52; **Receiving** - Brooks 4-52, Dickerson 3-28, Beach 3-22, Bouza 2-22, Bentley 2-17.

STANDINGS: SIXTEENTH WEEK

AFC EAST	W	L	T	CENTRAL	W	L	T	WEST	W	L	T	NFC EAST	W	L	T	CENTRAL	W	L	T	WEST	W	L	T
Buffalo	12	4	0	Cincinnati	12	4	0	Seattle	9	7	0	Philadelphia	10	6	0	Chicago	12	4	0	San Fran	10	6	0
New England	9	7	0	Houston	10	6	0	Denver	8	8	0	NY Giants	10	6	0	Minnesota	11	5	0	LA Rams	10	6	0
Indianapolis	9	7	0	Cleveland	10	6	0	Raiders	7	9	0	Phoenix	7	9	0	Tampa Bay	5	11	0	N.Orleans	10	6	0
NY Jets	8	7	1	Pittsburgh	5	11	0	San Diego	6	10	0	Washington	7	9	0	Detroit	4	12	0	Atlanta	5	11	0
Miami	6	10	0					Kan. City	4	11	1	Dallas	3	13	0	Green Bay	4	12	0				

Oilers	0 3 0 7 -	10
Bills	0 7 7 3 -	17

Attendance at Rich Stadium - 79,532

Buf: Riddick 1 run (Norwood kick), 4:25
Hou: FG Zendejas 35, 10:28
Buf: Thomas 11 run (Norwood kick), 12:02
Buf: FG Norwood 27, 3:25
Hou: Rozier 1 run (Zendejas kick), 9:48

	BUF	HOU
First downs	18	20
Rushing yds	135	125
Passing yds	237	226
Punts-avg	4-39.3	6-37.2
Fumbles-lost	1-0	5-2
Penalties-yds	8-57	8-60
Poss. time	28:53	31:07

BUFFALO TACKLES: Talley 7, Still 7, L. Smith 6, Odomes 5, Davis 4, Bentley 4, Bennett 3, Kelso 3, Radecic 3, Pike 2, B. Smith 2.

HOUSTON TACKLES: Grimsley 9, Brown 9, R. Johnson 7, Jones 3, Childress 3, Donaldson 3, Bryant 2, Lyles 2, A. Smith 2, Caston 2, Fuller 2.

BILLS LEADERS: **Rushing** - Thomas 7-75, Mueller 7-24, Kelly 3-18, Riddick 9-12, Harmon 1-7, Byrum 1-0, Reed 1-(-1); **Passing** - Kelly 19-33-1 - 244; **Receiving** - Reed 6-91, Harmon 5-58, Burkett 3-55, T. Johnson 3-31, Metzelaars 1-7, Mueller 1-2; **Kickoff returns** - Tucker 2-40, Harmon 1-17; **Punt returns** - Tucker 4-56.

OILERS LEADERS: **Rushing** - Highsmith 5-57, Rozier 13-44, Moon 5-11, Pinkett 3-13; **Passing** - Moon 17-33-1 - 240; **Receiving** - Jeffires 5-78, Hill 4-62, Harris 2-44, Pinkett 2-21, Highsmith 2-3, Givins 1-23, Duncan 1-9; **Kickoff returns** - Tillman 2-31, White 2-27; **Punt returns** - Duncan 1-6.

NOTES

• The Bills played a home playoff game for the first time since Jan. 1, 1967, when they lost the AFL Championship Game to Kansas City at War Memorial Stadium.
• It was the first playoff game ever at Rich Stadium and only the third ever played in Buffalo.
• The game was played in unusually balmy 35-degree January weather.
• On the night before the game, special teams coach Bruce DeHaven handed out envelopes with single dollar bills in each to his special teams players. On the back of each dollar, DeHaven wrote: "Special teams wins championships." The Bills blocked a punt and a field goal, limited the Oilers to 64 yards on five kickoff and punt returns, and helped the Bills attain an average drive start of their own 43-yard-line compared to the 21 for Houston.
• Jim Kelly's 19 completions were a single-game Bills playoff record.
• The Oilers went three-and-out on their opening possession, while the Bills moved into position – thanks to two Houston penalties – for a Scott Norwood field goal attempt, but he was short from 50 yards.
• The Oilers again went three-and-out and the Bills took possession at their own 26. A 20-yard pass to Chris Burkett was reduced to five yards after an unsportsmanlike penalty on Ronnie Harmon, but Burkett made a nineyard reception on third-and-three to overcome the penalty. Moments later, Thurman Thomas broke a 40-yard run to the Oilers 2. However, on fourth-and-one from the 3, the Bills elected to go for it and Kelly threw incomplete in the end zone to Pete Metzelaars.
• The Oilers managed two first downs, but again had to punt. This time, Leonard Smith blocked Greg Montgomery's kick and the Bills took over at the Houston 46. Kelly hit Trumaine Johnson on back-to-back plays for 19 and nine yards, then Thomas ripped off a 16-yard run to the 3. Two Robb Riddick runs produced the first score of the game.
• Houston answered with an 11-play, 71-yard drive to Tony Zendejas' field goal. Steve Tasker had tackled Lorenzo White at the 11 on the kickoff, but Warren Moon got the Oilers out of the hole with a 21-yard pass

to Drew Hill on third-and-eight. Two more Moon completions and Alonzo Highsmith's 31-yard run on a draw put the ball on the Bills 18, but the defense stiffened to force the field goal.
• The Bills went three-and-out, and the Oilers took possession with 2:46 left in the half. On back-to-back plays, Moon fired 27 yards to Haywood Jeffires and 23 to Ernest Givins, putting the ball at the Bills 25. But Moon's third-down pass fell incomplete and Cornelius Bennett then blocked Zendejas' 38-yard field goal attempt with 19 seconds left in the half.
• The Oilers held a 202-187 lead in yardage at the half.
• On the fourth play of the third quarter, Tracey Eaton intercepted Kelly at the Bills 47. Highsmith gained 17 on a draw, Mike Rozier gained two, then Rozier gained eight and Bennett was flagged for a personal foul, moving the ball to the 10. Here, two Rozier runs went for six yards. Then after Moon's incomplete third-down pass was nullified by Bruce Smith's offside penalty, Moon threw a bad option pitch to Rozier and the play lost 12 yards. Zendejas then yanked a 31-yard attempt wide to the left.
• The teams traded two punts, giving the Bills possession at their 41 with 4:30 left in the third. Kelly hit Burkett for 26 yards, threw to Harmon for two and after an incompletion set up a third-and-eight, Kelly scrambled 10 yards and also received a five-yard facemask that moved the ball to the 11. On the next play, Thomas scored off right tackle to cap a six-play, 59-yard drive.
• After a punt, the Bills took over at their 43. On the first play, Kelly hit Andre Reed for a 53-yard gain to the 4. Three Riddick runs pushed the ball to the 1 as the third quarter ended. On fourth-and-goal, Riddick was stuffed by John Grimsley, killing the threat.
• However, two plays later, Mark Kelso picked off a pass intended for Givins and returned 28 yards to the 18. It was the Bills first interception since their victory in Miami on Nov. 14. Three runs failed, so Norwood kicked a 27-yard field goal for a 17-3 lead with 11:35 left.
• Two plays after the kickoff, Bennett forced Jeffires to fumble and Derrick Burroughs recovered at the Oilers 23, but the Bills failed to make a first down and Norwood then missed a 36-yard attempt.
• Houston proceeded to drive 80 yards in nine plays to Rozier's TD plunge. Moon was four-for-four on the drive for 65 yards and a pass-interference on Burroughs in the end zone on third-and-goal from the 6 gave Houston an automatic first down.
• The Bills took over with 5:03 left and Kelly threw a gutsy 13-yard pass to Harmon on the first play. Then two snaps later he threw to Reed for eight and another first down. A holding penalty on Jim Ritcher foiled the series and John Kidd was forced to punt with two minutes left. Curtis Duncan fielded it at the Oilers 15, but Tasker forced him to fumble, Ray Bentley recovered, and the Bills then ran out the remaining 1:45 to win the game.

QUOTES

• Ralph Wilson, refusing to look ahead to the Super Bowl in Miami: "All I can see on the map is that city (Cincinnati) in Ohio. I'm going to savor this win for a day or two and then I'm going to concentrate on Cincinnati. All that stuff about the team possibly collapsing was a bunch of baloney. We just had a momentary letdown at the end of the season. Today we played like we did when we went 11-1."
• Marv Levy: "The crowd did a great job and now I think that ought to be the end of it (referring to the fact that now the Bills had to go to Cincinnati). Next week it shouldn't happen." (On the Bills' two failures on fourth-down inside the Oilers 5): "The first one was my call. We initially thought we would go for the field goal and we saw that the quarter was ending so we had time to think about it, so we called a pass play and they defended it well. The second time they just beat us to the draw down near the goal line." (On the defense): "I thought it would take a great effort to shut down their running game and we did a pretty good job. They broke one or two sprint draws, but that was it."
• Kent Hull on those short-yardage mishaps: "In order to beat Cincinnati, we're going to have to put the ball in the

end zone when we get down that far. We felt like we should have scored 40 points today. And in order for us to beat Cincinnati, we're going to have to put up more points on the board than we did today. We're going to have to take advantage of every opportunity we get." (On the emotion of their first playoff game): "I'll tell you what, somebody opened the door about an hour before the game and we could hear the people screaming. That got us fired up. You had to calm yourself back down, especially if you were on offense."
• Oilers coach Jerry Glanville: "The turning point of the game was when we muffed that option down there, missed the touchdown and then missed the field goal. And I thought we still had a chance to win, but unfortunately we muffed the punt return. Unfortunately, a very good football team isn't going to play anymore this season."
• Bruce Smith: "The pressure was on the defense and we responded to it. I knew we were going to have to make some big plays and do what was necessary for us to win the ballgame."
• Jim Kelly: "When I first came to Buffalo my goal was to take the team to the Super Bowl in three years. When they said the (Super Bowl) game was to be in Miami, I figured 'What better place to go?'" (On Robb Riddick's critical comments): "It happens. It got me fired up. I heard everybody saying that Jim Kelly wasn't a good quarterback. I know what I'm capable of doing, but I have to have time to throw. We've heard the complaints the last four games that we were too conservative. We knew what we were doing, we were saving it for the playoffs."
• Bruce DeHaven on his dollar bill ploy: "It was a special game so I figured I'd do something special to sell it a little bit, to motivate them. You get extra money in the playoffs, so I figured I'd give them a little extra. From the way they played, I guess it worked."
• Steve Tasker: "We take a lot of pride in what we do even though we don't get the publicity that the offense and the defense get. We realize that we can set the tempo for both our offense and defense by the plays we make and the field position we give them. It made us feel good that Bruce did what he did the night before the game. Coaches tend to be too analytical, too tied up with X's and O's. It's nice to see a coach become emotionally involved."
• Cornelius Bennett: "The coaches decided to let me do my thing. They wanted me to do a lot of rushing. I've been waiting to do this kind of thing all season. I knew I could do it and I think I proved that today. Our defense had another great game. People say that defense wins championships and I think we're on the way to proving that. We're 60 minutes away from the Super Bowl and the team realizes it's going to be a tough 60 minutes. We'll have a good week of practice, but right now, we're going out to celebrate this win. "
• Fred Smerlas on the matchup with Cincinnati: "We both feel we're the best two teams in the AFC. Now we'll find out who's the best, period."

Bills	0	10	0	0	-	10
Bengals	7	7	0	7	-	21

Attendance at Riverfront Stadium - 59,747

Cin: Woods 1 run (Breech kick), 13:09
Buf: Reed 9 pass from Kelly (Norwood kick), 1:39
Cin: Brooks 10 pass from Esiason (Breech kick), 12:39
Buf: FG Norwood 39, 14:38
Cin: Woods 1 run (Breech kick), :04

	BUF	CIN
First downs	10	23
Rushing yds	45	175
Passing yds	136	74
Punts-avg	6-45.1	6-36.8
Fumbles-lost	0-0	2-0
Penalties-yds	5-50	4-45
Poss. time	20:31	39:29

BUFFALO TACKLES: Talley 11, Still 9, Bentley 9, L. Smith 6, Bennett 5, B. Smith 5, Burroughs 4, Odomes 4, Conlan 4, Radecic 4, Kelso 3.

CINCINNATI TACKLES: Krumrie 6, White 5, Thomas 4, Bussey 3, Barker 3, Fulcher 3, Horton 3, Wilcots 3, Williams 3, Buck 2, Zander 2, Dixon 2.

BILLS LEADERS: **Rushing** - Mueller 8-21, Kelly 2-10, Thomas 4-6, Riddick 1-4, Byrum 1-3, Harmon 1-1; **Passing** - Kelly 14-30-3 - 163; **Receiving** - Reed 5-55, Riddick 3-28, Harmon 3-18, T. Johnson 2-48, Metzelaars 1-14; **Kickoff returns** - Harmon 2-45, Tucker 1-12; **Punt returns** - Tucker 1-2.

BENGALS LEADERS: **Rushing** - Woods 29-102, Wilson 5-29, Esiason 7-26, Jennings 2-12, Brooks 7-6; **Passing** - Esiason 11-20-2 - 94; **Receiving** - Holman 4-38, Brooks 2-21, Riggs 2-16, McGee 2-14, Collinsworth 1-5; **Kickoff returns** - Jennings 1-19, Hillary 2-11; **Punt returns** - Hillary 2-24, Dixon 1-0.

NOTES

• For the second time in franchise history, the Bills narrowly missed going to the Super Bowl. The first time occurred when they lost the AFL title game to Kansas City in 1967 and therefore didn't get to play Green Bay in Super Bowl I.

• The Bengals possessed the ball for 39:29 and the Bills were 0-for-10 on third down.

• The Bills were nailed with four personal fouls, none more damaging than Derrick Burroughs' cheap shot on Bengals receiver Tim McGee late in the third quarter. The play gave the Bengals an automatic first down at the 4 and set up their clinching TD. Burroughs also was ejected for arguing the call.

• Bruce Smith recorded three sacks in the first quarter, though one was nullified by a penalty on Smith for grabbing Boomer Esiason's facemask. However, with 3:58 left in the quarter, he was hit in the right thigh accidentally by Darryl Talley, suffered a deep bruise and was slowed the rest of the game.

• In the locker room after the game, Joe Devlin and Errol Tucker got into a heated exchange.

• Both teams started shaky. The Bengals went three-and-out after the opening kickoff with Smith sacking Esiason. But three plays after the punt, Lewis Billups intercepted Jim Kelly at the Bengals 37. Cincinnati got a break when a second Smith sack and Esiason's fumble were nullified by an offside penalty on Fred Smerlas. The Bengals eventually drove to the Bills 17, but Ray Bentley intercepted Esiason at the 5.

• The teams traded punts, with the Bills taking possession at their own 9. But on the first play, Kelly was intercepted by Eric Thomas, giving the Bengals the ball at the Bills 19. After a penalty and a two-yard loss by Ickey Woods, Esiason hit Rodney Holman for 21 yards to the 5. Two plays later, Woods scored.

• The Bills responded immediately, driving 56 yards in

six plays to Andre Reed's TD. Ronnie Harmon's 22-yard kickoff return to the 44 gave the Bills an excellent drive start. Thurman Thomas gained two, then Kelly hit Reed for 9 and 18 yards to the Bengals 27. Jamie Mueller lost 4, but Kelly fired a 22-yard strike to Trumaine Johnson and then hit Reed for a TD on the next play early in the second quarter.

• After a punt, the Bills took over at their 25. Kelly hit Reed for six and 13 yards, Mueller ran for 13 and Kelly found Pete Metzelaars for 14 to the Bengals 29. The drive stalled and Scott Norwood missed a 43-yard field goal.

• The Bengals turned around and drove 76 yards in 11 plays to take a 14-7 lead. Woods had a 12-yard run, Stanford Jennings gained eight on a third-and-four play from the 44, then Woods broke a 16-yard run to the Bills 32. Four more running plays followed before Esiason found James Brooks for the TD.

• The Bills caught a break with 1:02 left in the half as Mark Kelso intercepted Esiason and returned it 25 yards to the Bengals 29. Norwood then made a 39-yard field goal with 22 seconds left in half.

• The Bengals held a 154-128 yardage edge at the half thanks to 99 rushing yards.

• The teams combined for five punts in the third, but the Bengals won the field position battle. Lee Johnson's second punt, a 58-yarder, was downed at the Bills 1. When Buffalo failed to get a first down, John Kidd's 49-yard punt was returned 15 yards by Ira Hillary to the Bills 39.

• The Bengals quickly were faced with fourth-and-four at the 33. Sam Wyche called for a fake punt and Stanley Wilson ran six yards for the first down. Woods then gained eight on third-and-one, moving the ball to the 10. Here came one of the key plays of the game. After Esiason hit Holman for five, Woods was thrown for a three-yard loss by Conlan to bring up a third-and-goal from the 8. However, the play was nullified when Burroughs threw a forearm at McGee, drawing a personal foul penalty. After arguing vehemently, he was thrown

out of the game. Given a first-and-goal at the 4, Woods ran for three, then scored on the first play of the fourth quarter for a 21-10 lead.
• Riddick's personal foul on the ensuing kickoff forced the Bills to start from their 13 and they went three-and-out.
• After a Bengals punt, the Bills began a drive at their 23 with 10:01 left. Kelly hit, in succession, Riddick for six, Johnson for 26, Harmon for six, Riddick for eight and Riddick for four, giving the Bills a first down at the 17. But Kelly then threw three incompletions and his fourth-down pass to Harmon in the end zone was intercepted by David Fulcher with 8:07 left.
• The Bills never saw the ball again as Cincinnati ate up the rest of the clock, getting four first downs, including three third-down conversions along the way.

QUOTES
• Marv Levy: "The crowd didn't bother us a bit. You could hear a pin drop in here compared to Rich Stadium last week. The Bengals played well enough to win and deserved to win and I think they will make a great representative in the Super Bowl. Walking in (after the game), I thought about what I'd like to say to the players and the media. That's a very disappointed team in that locker room. We've been together every day since July. I just told them that I still loved them. I'm not going to come in here and say this guy did this bad or that guy did that bad. We played a team that deserved to win and to tell you the truth, they were the stronger team today." (On Burroughs' ejection): "I didn't actually see the play, but I saw what was going on (Burroughs arguing) and I told another player to go calm him down. The referee (Gene Barth) came over and said he hit him (McGee) straight in the face and the rules require an ejection. I couldn't argue. We had a good chance to stop that drive and force a field goal." (On Errol Tucker's decision to let Lee Johnson's punt roll dead at the 1): "I guess he misjudged it. He decided to get away from it. That one really hurt."
• Mark Kelso on the Burroughs play: "McGee was trying to cut him all day long, which is not illegal, but I guess it's kind of an unwritten rule. They were going at it all day. To their receivers' credit, they block well. Unfortunately, from a defensive back's standpoint, they like to cut, come down and take someone's leg out. Derrick said McGee gave him an elbow and he just retaliated. Unfortunately, they always catch the second guy."
• Kent Hull: "It's going to take a long, long time to forget about this one. The frustrating thing is we played as hard as we can, but I don't think we played as well as we can. The things we did to win 13 games this year, we didn't do today. It's really disheartening."
• Bruce Smith: "Offensively, we struggled. You can only stop them for so long. I don't think we did the things offensively to keep the defense off the field." (On his injury): "I was in a groove. But when I went down, I was about 80 percent and it slowed my pass rush tremendously."
• Ray Bentley: "We lost the battle of field position. They had us backed up all day."
• Mark Pike on the fake punt: "They just took us by surprise. Linebackers had to go down and play linemen positions and receivers lined up at cornerback. It confused us. It was a good call."
• Jim Kelly: "You can't score points when you get the ball on the 2- and 3-yard-line and come in with a two-tight end offense. I'm not saying anything about the play-calling. It's just that when you have field position like that, you can't open up your offense. We wanted to, but we never had the opportunity because they had us backed up the whole second half. We got beat by a good Cincinnati club, we're a young team and you should be seeing a lot more of us in the playoffs in the years to come. People haven't heard the end of the Bills."
• Bengals cornerback Lewis Billups: "I think what really made us want to play better was when we saw the HBO special and Bruce Smith was talking all that nonsense about what they were gonna do to us. Plus the respect that we didn't get defensive-wise this year. We just wanted to go out and prove a point."
• Darryl Talley: "You can't say it was a great season. You can't say it's great unless you get where you're going."

The Bengals gave Jim Kelly a rough time, sacking him three times and intercepting three of his passes.

At A Glance
1989

Jan. 9 – Derrick Burroughs publicly apologized for his outburst and ejection from the AFC Championship Game. Bruce Smith stated again that he wanted to become the highest-paid defensive player in the league and indicated that he would be willing to leave Buffalo if that's what it took. "I want to talk to some other teams," he said. On his weekly television show, Jim Kelly criticized Ronnie Harmon for dropping too many passes during the season.

Jan. 10 – The *Buffalo News* reported that the Bills had hired detectives to monitor Bruce Smith for three weeks in November of 1988 because they were concerned about his association with a suspected drug dealer. Bill Polian denied the story, but Hamburg police chief Matthew Czerwiec said the detectives came from his department.

Jan. 11 – Marv Levy endorsed Elijah Pitts for any head coaching opportunities around the league. "Somebody ought to take a look at Elijah Pitts," Levy said. The Bills signed four free agents including fullback Larry Kinnebrew and offensive lineman Mitch Frerotte.

Jan. 17 – Marv Levy was named the NFL's coach of the year by *The Sporting News*.

Jan. 18 – Andre Reed was added to the AFC's Pro Bowl squad when Houston's Drew Hill pulled out with a neck injury.

Jan. 23 – One day after losing the Super Bowl, Boomer Esiason decided to pull out of the Pro Bowl. Dan Marino had already pulled out, so Jim Kelly was invited to play in the game and AFC coach Marv Levy wasn't too happy. "My feeling is Esiason should be here, and if he isn't, Marino should be here," Levy said. Levy was concerned about exposing his own quarterback to more contact.

Jan. 25 – Marv Levy and Jim Kelly got their wish as Kelly was allowed to skip the Pro Bowl because of tendinitis in his right shoulder and elbow. He was replaced by Seattle's Dave Krieg. "It's an honor to come here and I want to play, but I don't want to take a chance," Kelly said. When hearing of Kelly's injury, Fred Smerlas said: "He must have hurt his shoulder putting his helmet on."

Feb. 1 – All 28 teams had to submit a list of 37 protected players to the league office under the new Plan B free agency system. All other players were considered unconditional free agents. Among the Bills unprotected players were Joe Devlin, Steve Tasker, Trumaine Johnson, Tim Vogler, Carl Byrum, Robb Riddick, Frank Reich, Hal Garner, Martin Mayhew, Dwight Drane and John Kidd. "If I had my way, I'd like to see all of them come back," Marv Levy said.

Feb. 6 – Offensive coordinator and offensive line coach Jim Ringo retired from coaching, ending a 21-year career which had followed a 15-year Hall of Fame playing career. One of the key reasons for his retirement was the broken leg he suffered in 1987, which he said was preventing him from doing his job properly. In Rochester, Jim Kelly was presented with the Rochester Press-Radio Club's Sports Personality of the Year award.

Feb. 9 – Tom Bresnahan, the Phoenix Cardinals offensive line coach, was hired to replace Jim Ringo in that capacity with the Bills.

Feb. 13 – Receivers coach Ted Tollner resigned to accept the offensive coordinator position with the San Diego Chargers.

Feb. 16 – The Bills said they were interested in signing Plan B free agent quarterback Gary Hogeboom of the Colts.

Feb. 23 – The Bills lost their first player to Plan B free agency when Dale Hellestrae signed with the Raiders. The team hired Nick Nicolau as receivers coach, replacing Ted Tollner.

Feb. 24 – Ralph Wilson admitted he made a mistake in voting to approve the new Plan B free agency system. "Nobody in the league likes this plan," he said. "It's causing havoc and it's going to have to be changed or amended because it can destroy the league. Whoever has the most money will have the best team."

March 1 – The Bills signed two Plan B players, offensive linemen John Davis from Houston and Caesar Rentie of Chicago. They also announced that Scott Berchtold was hired as manager of media relations, replacing Dave Senko who left to become associate athletic director and director of sports information at the University of Washington.

March 3 – The Bills signed their third Plan B free agent, running back Kenneth Davis from the Packers.

March 7 – The Bills lost cornerback Martin Mayhew to the Redskins through Plan B.

March 16 – Adam Lingner became the Bills fourth Plan B free agent to be signed.

March 22 – *The Sporting News* announced that Bill Polian was its choice for NFL Executive of the Year. In a surprise announcement at the league meetings in Palm Springs, Pete Rozelle said he was retiring effective immediately. Lamar Hunt and Wellington Mara said a six-man search committee, which would include Ralph Wilson, would be formed to find Rozelle's successor.

March 23 – The owners voted to reduce training camp rosters to a maximum of 80 players, and instant replay was retained once again by a vote of 24-4.

March 24 – It was confirmed that the Denver Broncos offered Bruce Smith a five-year contract worth $7.5 million, meaning the Bills had one week to either match the offer sheet or lose Smith and get two first-round draft choices from the Broncos as compensation. Smith had turned down a contract offer from the Bills worth $1 million per season.

March 25 – Raiders owner Al Davis questioned whether the Bills' rapid rise during 1988 could be taken seriously. "When you talk about the rise of the Bills, with no disrespect, they have risen this high many times before," Davis said. "I've seen certain organizations have a good year or two and then all of a sudden they can't sustain it. When I talk about staying on top, I'm talking over a period of years, four, five, six years."

March 27 – Bruce Smith said the Bills would be wise not to match the Broncos offer and let him go to Denver. "I don't appreciate some of the things that have happened," Smith said. "I think it's in my best interest to go to another team, money or no money."

March 28 – The Bills decided to match Denver's $7.5 million contract offer for Bruce Smith, making the defensive end the second highest-paid Bill behind Jim Kelly. "I'm happy and excited to be back, but we have to iron out a few things," Smith said, referring to the reports that the Bills had him followed by detectives in November of 1988.

April 1 – The Plan B free agency period ended and 229 players changed teams during the two-month signing period.

April 4 – Fred Smerlas discussed the possibility of a trade with Bill Polian because the team was considering making Jeff Wright its starting nose tackle. "Fred Smerlas is in our plans," Polian said. "He's a valuable and productive member of this team. If we didn't feel that way, we wouldn't have protected him."

April 18 – Jerry Jones purchased the majority interest of the Dallas Cowboys from Bum Bright. Former Cowboys' GM Tex Schramm was named president of the NFL's new international football endeavor, the World League of American Football.

April 23 – With their first- and second-round draft choices gone in the 1987 trade for Cornelius Bennett, the Bills had to wait until the third round, with the 82nd pick overall, to select Chadron State wide receiver Don Beebe. They later chose Richmond cornerback Brian Jordan (seventh), USC cornerback Chris Hale (seventh) and Tulane linebacker Richard Harvey (11th). Dallas, with Jerry Jones and new coach Jimmy Johnson at the controls, made UCLA quarterback Troy Aikman the first pick overall. Green Bay selected offensive lineman Tony Mandarich (second), Detroit chose running back Barry Sanders (third), Kansas City picked linebacker Derrick Thomas (fourth), Atlanta went for cornerback Deion Sanders (fifth), Tampa Bay chose linebacker Broderick Thomas (sixth), Pittsburgh took running back Tim Worley (seventh), San Diego went for defensive lineman Burt Grossman (eighth), Miami picked running back Sammie Smith (ninth), Chicago chose cornerback Donnell Woolford (11th) and defensive lineman Trace Armstrong (12th), Cleveland picked running back Eric Metcalf (13th), the Jets chose defensive lineman Jeff Lageman (14th), Seattle chose offensive lineman Andy Heck (15th), New England chose wide receiver Hart Lee Dykes (16th), the Giants took offensive lineman Brian Williams (18th), New Orleans selected defensive lineman Wayne Martin (19th), Denver selected safety Steve Atwater (20th), the Colts chose wide receiver Andre Rison (22nd), Miami picked safety Louis Oliver (25th) and the Rams took running back Cleveland Gary (26th with the Bills' first-round pick). With the Bills second-round pick, the Rams chose cornerback Darryl Henley.

April 26 – Jim Kelly filed a $58 million lawsuit against his former agents, Greg Lustig, Ken Weinberger and A.J. Faigin, for alleged improprieties in the handling of his business affairs. "The allegations he has made are totally false," said Lustig. "As far as we're concerned, it's merely an attempt to avoid paying several hundred thousand dollars in fees that he owes us."

May 5 – Marv Levy's contract was extended through 1992. "Marv can coach here as long as he wants, as far as I'm concerned," Ralph Wilson said.

May 8 – Don Beebe signed his first pro contract.

May 11 – The Bills opened mini-camp at Rich Stadium. The only player not present was wide receiver Chris Burkett who refused to attend because of a contract dispute.

May 13 – Bill Polian's contract was extended through the 1992 season. "As far as I'm concerned, Bill Polian has done so much for the Buffalo Bills, he can stay in Buffalo as long as he wants," Ralph Wilson said.

June 7 – Bob Ferguson was promoted to assistant general manager/director of pro personnel, John Butler was promoted to director of player personnel and A.J. Smith became the new assistant director for college scouting. Also, Bill Munson was bumped up to assistant general manager/business operations and Jim Overdorf became business manager.

July 3 – Nate Odomes pleaded no contest to a marijuana possession charge in Wisconsin and was placed on six months probation.

July 13 – Bill Polian said that he doubted the Bills could match their 12-4 record of 1988. "I should be very excited about this year – I was last year and I wasn't alone – but this year I'm apprehensive," Polian said.

July 19 – Training camp opened at Fredonia State and Kent Hull, Derrick Burroughs and Darryl Talley failed to report on time because they hadn't signed new contracts.

July 28 – The Bills beat Cleveland, 6-0, in the annual rookie scrimmage at Edinboro University. There was a flap between the school and teams because in advertising for the event, Edinboro said the teams would be using some of their veteran players as well.

Aug. 5 – The Bills opened their preseason by losing, 31-6, to the Redskins, in the annual Hall of Fame Game in Canton, Ohio. "Our goal was to play everybody and we did that," Marv Levy said. "What was disappointing was that no one stood out."

Aug. 10 – Kent Hull ended his holdout, signed a new contract and participated in his first practice.

Aug. 11 – Derrick Burroughs and Darryl Talley ended their holdouts and reported to camp. Burroughs practiced, while Talley signed his new deal and sat out the practices.

Aug. 12 – Green Bay rookie offensive lineman Tony Mandarich, who still hadn't reported to the Packers camp, talked about possibly playing against the Bills and Bruce Smith in an upcoming exhibition game. "I'm human and I've seen the best get knocked on their butt, but Bruce Smith isn't going to be the one to knock me on my butt," he said. "If anyone does, I'm sure it will be Reggie White (of Philadelphia), not Bruce Smith. Reggie White is 10 times better than Bruce Smith." Said Smith: "I'm just looking forward to the day that I can shut his mouth. I hope they trade him to a team that we play twice a year."

Aug. 13 – Cincinnati beat the Bills, 24-20, on Eric Ball's TD with 57 seconds remaining. The winning score was set up by a pass-interference penalty on rookie Chris Hale.

Aug. 19 – The Bills beat the Saints, 10-7, in the only home preseason game in front of 48,512 fans at Rich Stadium.

Aug. 21 – Ralph Wilson said the Bills would not play games at Rich Stadium after 1998 when the stadium lease with the county expired. "When it was built, it was a great stadium, an ideal stadium, but things change," Wilson said, referring to a power outage before the Saints game that nearly caused postponement of the game.

Aug. 26 – The Bills lost to Green Bay, 27-24, in Madison, Wisc. Tony Mandarich did not play, so he was unable to back up his brash talk about Bruce Smith.

Aug. 29 – Sean Doctor, Tom Doctor and Matt Jaworski, all players who grew up in Western New York and were trying to fulfill dreams by playing for the Bills, tested positive for steroids and were suspended for 30 days.

Sept. 1 – Robb Riddick's season came to an end when he suffered a serious knee injury during the Bills 36-17 loss to Atlanta at the Gator Bowl in Jacksonville, Fla.

Sept. 6 – Miami's Mark Duper predicted a Dolphins victory in the season opener at Joe Robbie Stadium. "We're going to kick their butts, you wait and see," Duper said. "I guarantee it." Steve Tasker replied: "Don't write a check with your mouth that your body can't cash."

Sept. 10 – Jim Kelly scored on a daring two-yard run on the final play of the game to cap a rally from an 11-point deficit in the final six minutes, giving the Bills a thrilling 27-24 victory over Miami in the season opener at Joe Robbie Stadium. Kelly was 10 of 12 for 129 yards on the final two series, which he operated in a no-huddle mode and called his own plays. Larry Felser, who had covered the team for its entire history, said it was the greatest finish in the team's 30 years of existence.

Sept. 18 – The Bills opened their home season on *Monday Night Football,* but fell behind 21-0 and lost to Denver, 28-14, as they suffered four turnovers and a safety. During the game, Jim Kelly and Chris Burkett got into a heated argument on the sidelines. At halftime, Ralph Wilson's name was unveiled on the Bills' Wall of Fame. "If it wasn't for Ralph, none of this would be taking place," Bill Polian said. "We would not have a franchise in Western New York."

Sept. 20 – Chris Burkett learned he was being replaced in the starting lineup by Flip Johnson, so he stormed out of the locker room apparently intent on quitting the team.

Sept. 21 – Burkett was waived by the Bills and he signed a contract with the New York Jets. "Kelly is a good athlete and he's one of the top quarterbacks in the NFL, but sometimes it was tough communicating with him," Burkett said.

Sept. 24 – In one of their most memorable wins ever, the Bills outgunned the Oilers in overtime, 47-41, for their first win in the Astrodome since 1966. Jim Kelly passed for 363 yards and five TDs, including the game-winner in OT to Andre Reed. Derrick Burroughs suffered a neck injury and was taken from the field on a stretcher.

Sept. 25 – Burroughs was placed on the injured reserve list and his career was in jeopardy because tests revealed he had a narrowing of the spinal canal which could cause him paralysis.

Sept. 26 – Seven-time Pro Bowl wide receiver James Lofton was signed as a free agent from the Raiders.

Oct. 1 – The Bills defense, off to a shaky start, had its best game, limiting the Patriots to 279 yards in a 31-10 victory at Rich Stadium.

Oct. 8 – Jim Kelly suffered a separated left shoulder when he was sacked by Jon Hand and the Bills were routed in Indianapolis, 37-14. Kelly was having the worst game of his NFL career when he was injured in the third quarter.

Oct. 9 – Jim Kelly created a stir when he publicly chastised right tackle Howard Ballard for missing a block on Jon Hand that resulted in his injury. "It should have never happened," Kelly said. "He (Hand) should have been blocked. Watching film, I don't know what Howard was thinking. It seemed like he was looking outside to see if a guy blitzed or something and not at the guy over him (Hand). I think four of our five positions (on the line) are very solid. I don't even need to tell you guys what position they might have to make a change in. I can't stand up here and say they should or shouldn't do it. I don't make those decisions, but something has to happen." Told of Kelly's remarks, Ballard said: "I'm sorry Jim got hurt, but there's nothing I can do about it now. I just got beat at that particular time. I missed the block in pass protection." Joe Devlin defended Ballard: "Everyone knows Jim Kelly is an intense competitor and he doesn't like to lose and I'm sure he doesn't like getting injured. However, I don't think it's anybody's place, myself included, to ever point the finger at one individual because football is a team-oriented sport. The team has to always, always come first. Everybody makes mistakes."

Oct. 10 – Ex-Bills running back Greg Bell, who was preparing for his return to Rich Stadium as a member of the Los Angeles Rams, fired some shots at his former team. "I'm going to love playing against Fred (Smerlas) because Fred's going to have to watch his butt the whole game," Bell began. "He's an average player who, when he's surrounded by great players, they beef his status up a lot. Jim Haslett and Smerlas were just red-necks. They were prejudiced guys. The fact that a young black man came in making a great deal of money, driving a red Ferrari, dressing out of this world, they were offended by that." Of Marv Levy, Bell said: "I think he's more of a con artist than a coach. Everybody uses that Harvard graduate garbage. I mean, who cares? Harvard graduates don't help you win on the football field. He's no engineer of the game." Smerlas responded by saying: "Tinker is a stinker. He said I was a racist, but none of the black guys on the team liked him either. He got into fights with Derrick (Burroughs), Robb (Riddick), me, Haz, everybody."

Oct. 11 – There were more responses to Greg Bell's comments. "When the guy was here, I didn't like him and I don't like him now," said Ray Bentley. "He'll be lumped up after the game." Said Smerlas: "He's a great talent, but he's running on empty. This is irritating people, especially with this racist stuff. Calling me a racist is far from the truth. Everybody knows what Greg was like." Bills GM Bill Polian said he was concerned, not so much about Jim Kelly's injury or Greg Bell's remarks, but with the state of the Bills' focus. "I really believe we've misplaced our personality," he said. "I think not only last Sunday but the last five weeks, we may have lost our focus a little bit."

Oct. 12 – Jim Kelly spoke to his teammates and apologized to Howard Ballard for publicly blaming him for his injury. "Jim addressed the squad today and, in essence at least, apologized and did so to Howard also," Marv Levy said. "Were Jim's remarks unfortunate? Yes. Did I talk to him about it? Yes. Do I dislike Jim or am I angry with him now? Hell no. I love Jim Kelly and I love Howard Ballard."

Oct. 13 – Former 49ers coach and current NBC football analyst Bill Walsh criticized Bruce Smith. "He can be, or he is already, a great player. But he doesn't want anything to do with the run. He outpositions himself on almost every play and doesn't read the blocks. It's a real problem for him. His pass rush is outstanding, but with the run, he doesn't play through a blocker and get to the ball."

Don Beebe was Buffalo's first draft choice in 1989, but he wasn't chosen until the third round because the Bills had forfeited their first two choices in the 1987 Cornelius Bennett trade. Beebe's blazing speed opened up the Bills deep passing game. He averaged 18.6 yards per reception as a rookie.

Oct. 16 – One of the most tumultuous weeks in Bills history came to a stunningly exciting end when Frank Reich rallied the Bills in the fourth quarter to a 23-20 victory over the previously unbeaten Los Angeles Rams in front of 76,231 fans and a *Monday Night Football* audience. "We want our players to remember how hard they had to work to win this game," Marv Levy said.

Oct. 22 – The Bills rushed 52 times for 204 yards and crushed the Jets at Rich Stadium, 34-3.

Oct. 23 – Assistant coaches Tom Bresnahan and Nick Nicolau were involved in a scuffle in one of the Bills' meeting rooms while watching film of the victory over the Jets. Reports indicated that Nicolau bloodied Bresnahan's chin with an upper-cut, then got Bresnahan in a headlock and rammed his head through a wall. Bresnahan wore a turban around his head during the players' meetings and a light practice later in the day. "The coaches didn't tell me about it, or they don't want to tell me about it, and I'm not going to ask," Marv Levy said. "Coaches have arguments all the time. I know Tom and Nick are close friends, their wives are close friends. They lived together for four or five months in the off-season in an apartment."

Oct. 25 – The Dolphins refused to give credit to the Bills for their come-from-behind victory in the season opener. "We're not going to win it in the last minute," Fred Banks said referring to the rematch at Rich Stadium. "We're going to win it big." Said Troy Stradford: "Buffalo's getting lucky right now." In talking about the Bills victory over Los Angeles, William Judson said: "It's a shame Buffalo could get away with a victory like that, but we've seen them do that before."

Oct. 26 – Paul Tagliabue was chosen to succeed Pete Rozelle as NFL commissioner during a three-day meeting in Cleveland.

Oct. 29 – The Dolphins couldn't back up the talk on the field as Buffalo crushed them, 31-17, before a record crowd of 80,208 at Rich Stadium. Both Thurman Thomas and Larry Kinnebrew topped 100 yards rushing, the sixth time in Bills history that had occurred, and Jeff Wright sacked Dan Marino, ending an NFL record string of 19 games and 759 pass attempts in which Marino hadn't been sacked.

Nov. 1 – Jim Kelly participated in his first full practice since suffering a separated left shoulder Oct. 8 and chances were good that he would start against Atlanta.

Nov. 5 – The Falcons stunned the Bills at Atlanta-Fulton County Stadium, 30-28, on Paul McFadden's 50-yard field goal with two seconds left, capping another game with a wild finish. Jim Kelly was sharp in his return, completing 17 of 22 passes for 231 yards and two TDs. Paul Tagliabue officially began his term as NFL commissioner.

Nov. 12 – Shane Conlan returned to the lineup for the first time since suffering a knee injury against Denver and he helped the Bills rout the Colts, 30-7, at Rich Stadium.

Nov. 15 – Derrick Burroughs, in a tearful press conference at Rich Stadium, announced that he was retiring from football on the advice of team physician Richard Weiss as well as a Philadelphia-based neurologist. "I've always loved being a Bill," he said. "I'm going to miss a lot of the guys. In the off-season I might decide that I might try to come back and maybe I won't. Maybe I might just feel that it's too much of a risk." Said Bill Polian: "I want him to come back to alumni functions walking on his own two feet. I don't want him coming back in a wheelchair."

Nov. 19 – New England scored 20 points in the final 7:45 of the game and overcame the Bills, 33-24, at Foxboro Stadium. The Bills turned the ball over six times and lost Cornelius Bennett on the first play of the game to a knee injury. "This loss better fire us up with Cincinnati coming in next week," Jim Ritcher said.

Nov. 26 – The Bills pounded Cincinnati, 24-7, at Rich Stadium, as Thurman Thomas rushed for 100 yards and Jim Kelly passed for three TDs. The Bills avenged last year's AFC Championship Game loss.

Dec. 4 – John L. Williams ran 51 yards for a touchdown with a short pass with 5:38 left to play and Seattle upset the Bills, 17-16, in the Kingdome.

Dec. 5 – While taping a cable TV show in Rochester with Darryl Talley, Thurman Thomas took a pot shot at Jim Kelly. Talley was asked by a fan in the audience which position needed to be upgraded and before Talley could answer, Thomas said: "Quarterback."

Dec. 6 – Jim Kelly expressed frustration over the play-calling by the coaches. "We run on first down, we run on second down and we throw on third down," he said. "The offense is kind of predictable. They (the Seahawks) knew what we were running, they were ready for us. After the game, some of their players told us they knew where we were going. It's not just the players on the field, it goes into the coaching staff, too."

Dec. 7 – Phil Dokes, the Bills' first-round draft choice in 1977, died of heart failure in Jacksonville, Ark. at the age of 34.

Dec. 10 – The Bills suffered a damaging loss in their home season finale, falling to New Orleans, 22-19, on a cold, snowy day. John Fourcade, starting his first NFL non-strike game, led the Saints to victory. "Eisenhower said 'Morale is built by victory in battle' and I agree," Marv Levy said.

Dec. 11 – At the Monday Quarterback Club luncheon, Bill Polian, angered by a question from radio personality Art Wander, fired this response: "Jim Kelly's still the quarterback, Ted Marchibroda's still the offensive coordinator and Marv Levy's still the head coach and if you don't like it, get out of town. I'm not going to stand up here and point fingers and blame anyone. We ain't changing players and we ain't changing coaches. Not only do we like them, but we believe in them 1,000 percent."

Dec. 12 – Thurman Thomas, appearing on *Sports Line* with Paul Maguire, stood by his remark made a week before about quarterback being the position that needed to be upgraded on the team. Thomas criticized Jim Kelly for his public chastising of a number of players. He then said Kelly's last two games were terrible and implied that Kelly is quick to point the finger at teammates when things go

Jim Kelly and Thurman Thomas endured some tough times during 1989, but both players enjoyed productive years and they led the Bills to another AFC East division title.

wrong, but is slow to take blame himself. Meanwhile, Bill Polian apologized for his outburst at the Quarterback Club, but only because callers to the talk shows interpreted his remarks as being directed at them, the fans. Polian said he was telling a few critical members of the media to "get out of town."

Dec. 13 – Thurman Thomas admitted he "said a few things I shouldn't have said" about Jim Kelly, but then tried to explain his diatribe the previous night on Maguire's show. "Hey, how would he like it if somebody said something bad about him? How would he feel? I don't want people to think I'm a bad person, but I feel it was a chance to let everyone know – not only myself – but how the players feel about Jim saying stuff about Chris Burkett and Ronnie Harmon last year and Howard (Ballard) this year. We all discussed this. A lot of the players feel that way and none of them say anything. It was probably the wrong thing to say, but nobody's taking it in a bad way. I think we're closer together as a result. I get along with Jim, and that's the end of that." Kelly refused comment.

Dec. 14 – Thurman Thomas and Jim Kelly read prepared statements at a joint news conference, apologizing for statements they had made. Kelly began: "I made – we all made – statements which were construed as being critical of certain players and teammates. I'm sorry that it happened, I really am. I like all my teammates. I want them to succeed just like everybody does. I want our team to succeed and I know the only way is by our whole team pulling together as individuals and everybody doing what they're supposed to." Thomas then took his turn: "On any team there are different personalities. We're not always in agreement on

everything that happens on and off the field. One thing we do all agree on is that for the Bills to succeed, all of us – Jim and myself in particular – have to be united in a desire to win. I can assure you that we are. I said some things that I shouldn't have said this week and I'm sorry about that. Both Jim and I and the rest of our teammates would like to put this behind us and get on with the job at hand and that's beating the San Francisco 49ers and then making the playoffs. And we will have no further comment." The final phrase revealed that the two players would not speak to the media for the rest of the season. Bill Polian said the two players were told to read the statements because "the general consensus was that it needed to be done. It's behind us."

Dec. 15 – Fred Smerlas defended Kelly for his forthright nature. "That's his style, Jim has to be Jim. If he thinks a guy broke down at tackle and he wants to say it, that's what he should say."

Dec. 17 – Knowing Miami had lost earlier in the day, the Bills took the field at Candlestick Park knowing a victory would clinch the AFC East. However, even with Joe Montana sitting out with a rib injury and Steve Young playing in his place, the 49ers defeated the Bills, 21-10, Buffalo's third loss in a row.

Dec. 19 – Cornelius Bennett, out for all but one play of the last five games, indicated he would be ready to start in the all-important regular season finale against the Jets. "We've missed him in our pass rush," Marv Levy said. Meanwhile, Ray Bentley was ruled out with a knee injury.

Dec. 20 – Andre Reed, Bruce Smith, Shane Conlan, Thurman Thomas and Kent Hull were named to the AFC's Pro Bowl squad while Darryl Talley was snubbed. Conlan made it despite miss-

ing six games with a knee injury. Smith and Reed were voted to be starters.

Dec. 21 – Bill Polian was named to the prestigious NFL Competition Committee, a seven-man consortium considered the most powerful group in the league because they establish and oversee the modification of rules. Also on the committee were Jim Finks, George Young, Tom Flores, Don Shula, Paul Brown and Marty Schottenheimer.

Dec. 23 – The Bills ended their three-game losing streak in robust fashion, pounding the Jets, 37-0, before only 21,148 freezing fans at Giants Stadium. The victory, the most lopsided in Bills' history, clinched Buffalo's second straight AFC East division title.

Dec. 25 – Joe Devlin accused some of his teammates of not playing as hard as they could have during the season and he accused management of operating under a double standard, treating the teams' superstars with a different set of rules. "When we win, we all win and when we lose, we all lose," he said. "Unfortunately there are those around here who don't see it that way. That's why this is not a team. I keep hearing this bull in the media about the Bills needing a team leader. Well, I've been leading my butt off for the last several years, but when the troops don't listen, if people don't go out and play, then you're not going to win. We knew we had a decent team, but I knew it wasn't as great as everybody built it up to be."

Dec. 27 – After first indicating that they would head south to Vero Beach, Fla. to practice in warm weather, the Bills changed their minds and decided to stay home. "We've done enough traveling," Marv Levy said.

Dec. 28 – Larry Kinnebrew was arrested and charged with assault for his part in a fight at the Ramada Renaissance Hotel.

Dec. 31 - Pittsburgh beat Houston in overtime, 26-23, and Los Angeles defeated Philadelphia, 21-7, in the wild-card playoff games.

Jan. 6, 1990 – The Bills season came to a crashing halt when Clay Matthews intercepted Jim Kelly at the 1-yard-line with three seconds left, enabling Cleveland to escape with a 34-30 divisional round playoff victory at Cleveland Stadium. Ronnie Harmon dropped what would have been a touchdown pass on the play before Matthews' interception. In an NFC divisional game, San Francisco routed Minnesota, 41-13.

Jan. 7, 1990 – Denver edged Pittsburgh, 24-23, and the Rams upset the Giants in overtime, 19-13, on Flipper Anderson's TD reception.

Jan. 14, 1990 – John Elway passed for an AFC Championship Game record 385 yards and three TDs as Denver advanced to its third Super Bowl in four years with a 37-21 victory over Cleveland. In the NFC Championship Game, San Francisco crushed the Rams, 30-3, as Joe Montana completed 26 of 30 passes for 262 yards and two TDs.

Jan. 28, 1990 – San Francisco set Super Bowl records for points and margin of victory as it annihilated Denver, 55-10, in Super Bowl XXIV at the Superdome. Joe Montana won the MVP for a record third time as he threw for 297 yards and a Super Bowl record five TDs including three to Jerry Rice, who caught seven passes for 148 yards.

Feb. 4, 1990 – The NFC held off the AFC, 27-21, in the Pro Bowl at Aloha Stadium. MVP Jerry Gray of the Rams returned an interception 51 yards for a TD and made seven tackles.

BY THE NUMBERS - 1989

TEAM STATISTICS	BILLS	OPP
First downs	334	299
Rushing	136	117
Passing	177	156
Penalty	21	26
Third downs	86-203	75-213
Fourth downs	4-8	7-15
Time of poss	30:12	29:48
Total yards	5,853	5,046
Avg. game	365.8	315.4
Plays	1,045	1,030
Avg. play	5.6	4.9
Net rushing yds	2,264	1,840
Avg. game	141.5	115.0
Avg. play	4.3	3.8
Net passing yds	3,589	3,206
Comp/att	281/478	255/508
Sacks/lost	35-242	38-289
Interceptions	20	23
Percentage	58.8	50.2
Punts/avg	67-38.3	75-38.3
Fumbles/lost	30-21	31-13
Penalties/yds	103-831	87-616
Touchdowns	49	34
Extra points	46-48	33-34
Field goals	23-30	26-37
Safeties	0	1
Kick ret./avg	53-20.0	75-15.8
Punt ret./avg	33-9.1	25-9.1

RUSHING	ATT	YDS	AVG	TD
Thomas	298	1244	4.2	6
Kinnebrew	131	533	4.1	6
K. Davis	29	149	5.1	1
Kelly	29	137	4.7	2
Harmon	17	99	5.8	0
Mueller	16	44	2.8	0
Reed	2	31	15.5	0
Reich	9	30	3.3	0
Gelbaugh	1	-3	-3.0	0
TOTALS	**532**	**2264**	**4.3**	**15**

PASSING	COMP	ATT	INT	YDS	TD	COMP%	SACKS	RATE
Kelly	228	391	18	3130	25	58.3	30-216	86.2
Reich	53	87	2	701	7	60.9	4-24	103.7
F. Johnson	0	0	0	0	0	00.0	1-2	00.0
TOTALS	**281**	**478**	**20**	**3831**	**32**	**58.8**	**35-242**	**89.3**

KICKING	1-19	20-29	30-39	40-49	50+	TOT	PAT	PTS
Norwood	0-0	5-6	8-9	10-15	0-0	23-30	46-47	115

PUNTING	NO	AVG	LG	In 20	BL
Kidd	65	39.4	60	15	2

RECEIVING	CAT	YDS	AVG	TD
Reed	88	1312	14.9	9
Thomas	60	669	11.2	6
Harmon	29	363	12.5	4
F. Johnson	25	303	12.1	1
McKeller	20	341	17.1	2
Metzelaars	18	179	9.9	2
Beebe	17	317	18.6	2
Lofton	8	166	20.8	3
K. Davis	6	92	15.3	2
Kinnebrew	5	60	12.0	0
Burkett	3	20	6.7	0
Mueller	1	8	8.0	0
Rolle	1	1	1.0	1
TOTALS	**281**	**3831**	**13.6**	**32**

SCORE BY QUARTERS

BILLS	59	117	92	135	6 -	409
OPP	62	44	88	123	0 -	317

DEFENSIVE STATISTICAL LEADERS

TACKLES: L. Smith 76 primary - 23 assists - 99 total, Bentley 69-28-97, Talley 70-27-97, B. Smith 66-22-88, Radecic 54-23-77, Bennett 43-11-54, Kelso 43-10-53, Still 36-15-51, Conlan 37-13-50, Odomes 42-4-46, Seals 29-11-40, Jackson 34-3-37, Smerlas 23-8-31, Bailey 16-11-27

SACKS: B. Smith 13, Talley 6, Bennett 5.5, Seals 4, Wright 3, Radecic 1.5

FUMBLE RECOVERIES: L. Smith 2, Bennett 2, Kelso 2, Wright 2

FORCED FUMBLES: L. Smith 3, Odomes 3, Bentley 2, Radecic 2, Still 2

INTERCEPTIONS: Kelso 6-101 yards, 16.8 avg., 0 TD; Odomes 5-20, 4.0, 0 TD

SPECIAL TEAMS STATISTICAL LEADERS

KICKOFF RETURNS: Harmon 18-409 yards, 22.7 avg., 0 TD; Beebe 16-353, 22.1, 0 TD

PUNT RETURNS: Sutton 26-231, 8.9, 0 TD; Tucker 6-63, 10.5, 0 TD

TACKLES: Pike 29, Bailey 29, Tasker 27, Hale 20, Rolle 19, Mueller 14, Monger 13, D. Smith 12, Sutton 11, Drane 11, Hagy 9, Jackson 6, Radecic 5, Lingner 4, McKeller 3

When Jim Kelly missed three games due to a separated shoulder, Frank Reich stepped in and won every one.

GAME 1 - Sunday, Sept. 10, 1989 - BILLS 27, DOLPHINS 24

Bills	3	0	10	14	-	27
Dolphins	0	10	7	7	-	24

Attendance at Joe Robbie Stadium - 54,541

Buf: FG Norwood 34, 12:26
Mia: Stradford 1 run (Stoyanovich kick), 9:12
Mia: FG Stoyanovich 29, 14:57
Buf: Kinnebrew 2 run (Norwood kick), 3:02
Mia: Logan blocked punt recovery (Stoyanovich kick), 7:57
Buf: FG Norwood 37, 2:49
Mia: A. Brown 8 pass from Marino (Stoyanovich kick), 9:43
Buf: F. Johnson 26 pass from Kelly (Norwood kick), 12:10
Buf: Kelly 2 run (Norwood kick), 15:00

	BUF	MIA
First downs	27	21
Rushing yds	141	68
Passing yds	226	255
Punts-avg	5-38.4	4-39.0
Fumbles-lost	2-2	3-2
Penalties-yds	7-65	8-67
Poss. time	29:18	30:42

BILLS LEADERS: **Rushing** - Thomas 13-94, Mueller 5-18, Harmon 4-17, Kinnebrew 4-10, Kelly 1-2; **Passing** - Kelly 25-40-0 - 265; **Receiving** - Reed 6-58, Thomas 8-65, Harmon 4-55, Johnson 3-60, Burkett 2-14, Mueller 1-8, Metzelaars 1-5.
DOLPHINS LEADERS: **Rushing** - Stradford 12-43, Davenport 2-4, T. Brown 2-2, Hampton 6-19, Marino 1-0; **Passing** - Marino 25-38-2 - 255; **Receiving** - Edmunds 5-58, T. Brown 5-57, A. Brown 4-58, Duper 2-30, Jensen 2-27, Stradford 2-7, Banks 1-11, Hardy 1-2, Hampton 3-5.

WEEK 1 GAMES

Chi 17, Cinc 14	Clev 51, Pitt 0
NO 28, Dal 0	Minn 38, Hou 7
Den 34, KC 20	Rams 31, Atl 21
NE 27, NYJ 24	Phoe 16, Det 13
LAR 40, SD 14	SF 30, Ind 24
Phil 31, Sea 7	TB 23, GB 21
NYG 27, Wash 24	

NOTES

• Jim Kelly capped a fourth-quarter rally by running two yards for the winning TD on the final play of the game.
• The Bills remained unbeaten in Joe Robbie Stadium (3-0) and beat Miami for the fifth straight time.
• The Bills drove 82 yards in 16 plays on their first possession to a Scott Norwood field goal.
• Miami took the lead early in the second quarter on Troy Stradford's TD run, capping a 71-yard drive.
• Andre Reed fumbled at the Miami 6 and Rodney Thomas returned it 39 yards with 32 seconds left. Then, a pass-interference call on Nate Odomes put the ball at the 11 and Pete Stoyanovich made a 29-yard field goal for a 10-3 halftime lead.
• Early in the third, Odomes forced Stradford to fumble and Cornelius Bennett recovered at the 2. On the next play, Larry Kinnebrew scored to tie the game.
• On the next series, John Kidd's punt from the end zone was blocked by Jim Jensen and recovered in the end zone for a TD by Marc Logan. The Bills answered with a 52-yard drive to a Norwood field goal.
• The teams combined for three turnovers on the first five snaps of the fourth before the Dolphins put together a 12-play, 73-yard drive to Dan Marino's third-down TD pass to Andre Brown for a 24-13 lead with 5:17 left.
• The Bills got that back in just 2:27 as Kelly completed five straight passes for 82 yards including a TD to Flip Johnson. Odomes then made his second interception of the game on a third-and-10 play and returned it three yards to the Bills 49 with 1:44 left. Kelly completed three passes, moving the ball to the Miami 30, then hit Thurman Thomas for 11 on third-and-five. He then hit Andre Reed for 15 to the 4 and Kelly quickly grounded the ball with two seconds left. An offsides penalty on Brian Socchia nullified the spike and moved the ball to the 2. Kelly then dropped to pass, but decided to run and just beat Louis Oliver to the goal line for his first NFL rushing TD in 45 career games.

QUOTES

• Jim Kelly: "I took the snap, took one step back and started running. I knew I only had a couple of yards to go and I was hoping I was going to make it because I knew if I didn't, boy, I'd be hearing about it the rest of my career. Nate Odomes, thanks for the opportunity. It was supposed to be a pass to the fullback in the flat, but I knew it wasn't going to be open right from what I saw at the beginning."
• Marv Levy: "You're probably wondering when I first thought we had the game wrapped up. The guy (Kelly) is a winner, that's what he does. Maybe he's not pretty or doesn't rack up the big numbers, but he knows how to win."
• Jim Ritcher on Kelly: "On that last drive, he was a general out there. There was no doubts in our minds that we were going to make it."

GAME 2 - Monday, Sept. 18, 1989 - BRONCOS 28, BILLS 14

Broncos	5	13	3	7	-	28
Bills	0	0	7	7	-	14

Attendance at Rich Stadium - 78,176

Den: Safety: Brooks tackled Mueller in end zone, 8:31
Den: FG Treadwell 22, 12:45
Den: FG Treadwell 33, 1:24
Den: Johnson 9 pass from Elway (Treadwell kick), 6:54
Den: FG Treadwell 46, 15:00
Den: FG Treadwell 24, 8:00
Buf: Kinnebrew 1 run (Norwood kick), 11:37
Buf: Harmon 33 pass from Kelly (Norwood kick), :27
Den: Humphrey 5 run (Treadwell kick), 11:05

	BUF	DEN
First downs	29	26
Rushing yds	94	201
Passing yds	319	181
Punts-avg	3-35.0	5-38.0
Fumbles-lost	2-1	2-0
Penalties-yds	8-66	10-71
Poss. time	26:02	33:58

BILLS LEADERS: **Rushing** - Thomas 11-38, Mueller 3-6, Kelly 5-51, Kinnebrew 2-0, Harmon 1-(-1); **Passing** - Kelly 26-44-3 - 298, Reich 2-2-0 - 42; **Receiving** - Reed 13-157, K. Davis 3-55, Harmon 3-47, Thomas 3-30, Johnson 3-23, Kinnebrew 1-14, Metzelaars 1-8, Burkett 1-6.
BRONCOS LEADERS: **Rushing** - Humphrey 10-76, Winder 23-65, Elway 3-33, Jackson 3-15, Alexander 4-12; **Passing** - Elway 15-28-2 - 207, Johnson 0-1-0 - 0; **Receiving** - Johnson 5-51, Alexander 4-40, Sewell 2-66, Jackson 2-18, Young 1-26, Winder 1-6.

WEEK 2 GAMES

Atl 27, Dal 21	NYG 24, Det 14
Hou 34, SD 27	Rams 31, Ind 17
KC 24, LAR 19	Mia 24, NE 10
Chi 38, Minn 7	GB 35, NO 34
Clev 38, NYJ 24	Phoe 34, Sea 24
Phil 42, Wash 37	SF 20, TB 16
Cinc 41, Pitt 10	

NOTES

• The Bills fell behind 21-0 midway through the third and never recovered, losing at Rich for the first time since 1987. Jim Kelly and Chris Burkett got into a heated argument on the sidelines during the game.
• Shane Conlan suffered a knee injury when Clarence Kay blocked him low, an apparent cheap shot.
• Nate Odomes stopped a Denver threat with an interception at the 1, but on the next play, Jamie Mueller was tackled by Michael Brooks for a safety. After the free kick, the Broncos drove to a David Treadwell field goal. After the Bills went three-and-out, Treadwell capped a 41-yard drive with another field goal.
• On the next series, Kelly was intercepted by Wymon Henderson. Five plays and 64 yards later, John Elway passed for a TD to Vance Johnson for a 15-0 midway through the second quarter.
• Scott Norwood missed a 43-yard field goal, and after Randy Robbins recovered an Andre Reed fumble at the Denver 41, the Broncos got into position for a Treadwell field goal and an 18-0 halftime lead.
• Tyrone Braxton intercepted Kelly on the Bills first series of the third leading to Treadwell's fourth field goal.
• The Bills finally sustained a drive, moving 77 yards in nine plays plus three Denver penalties to Larry Kinnebrew's TD plunge. The key play was a third-down illegal-contact penalty on Mark Haynes.
• After a punt, the Bills drove 66 yards to Kelly's TD pass to Ronnie Harmon.
• Mark Kelso then intercepted Elway and returned it to the Bills 31, but Buffalo punted after Harmon dropped a sure TD pass. Denver then drove 86 yards to the clinching score. Elway hit Johnson for 25 yards on third-and-11 from his own 13, then scrambled for 31 yards to the 5 to set up Bobby Humphrey's TD.

QUOTES

• Marv Levy: "We're not going to win because we're good guys or because we know how to pull them out or because we kick a field goal like last year. We're going to win by playing better than we did last year because we had some good fortune. We earned a lot of that good fortune and we have to do it again. We did some dumb, dirty things and gave them some gifts."
• Andre Reed: "Maybe we needed something like this to bring us down to earth."
• Jim Kelly, lobbying for more use of the shotgun: "I don't want to get myself in trouble, but we came out in it in the second half and scored 14 points and moved the ball real well. Maybe we should surprise somebody and come out in the gun." (On the safety): "Those two points really seemed to throw us off."
• Denver coach Dan Reeves: "It was encouraging to see Buffalo go to the shotgun in the third quarter. We felt we had to stop the run and we did."
• Denver quarterback John Elway on the final drive: "Doubts? Yeah, I don't mind saying so. We had to get the momentum back and we did it with that drive."

STANDINGS: SECOND WEEK

AFC EAST	W	L	T	CENTRAL	W	L	T	WEST	W	L	T	NFC EAST	W	L	T	CENTRAL	W	L	T	WEST	W	L	T
Buffalo	1	1	0	Cleveland	2	0	0	Denver	2	0	0	NY Giants	2	0	0	Chicago	2	0	0	San Fran	2	0	0
New England	1	1	0	Cincinnati	1	1	0	Raiders	1	1	0	Philadelphia	2	0	0	Minnesota	1	1	0	LA Rams	2	0	0
Miami	1	1	0	Houston	1	1	0	Kan. City	1	1	0	Phoenix	2	0	0	Tampa Bay	1	1	0	N.Orleans	1	1	0
NY Jets	0	2	0	Pittsburgh	0	2	0	Seattle	0	2	0	Dallas	0	2	0	Green Bay	1	1	0	Atlanta	1	1	0
Indianapolis	0	2	0					San Diego	0	2	0	Washington	0	2	0	Detroit	0	2	0				

NOTES

• Jim Kelly threw for an NFL career-high 363 yards and five TDs as the Bills won in the Astrodome for the first time since 1966. The five TD passes tied the team record held by Joe Ferguson.

• The Bills got a Scott Norwood field goal on their first possession, and after the Oilers took the lead, Leonard Smith's interception at the Houston 23 led to Kelly's TD pass to Thurman Thomas.

• Early in the second quarter, Mark Kelso's interception and 43-yard return set up a Norwood field goal.

• The Oilers drove 81 yards in 18 plays to a Tony Zendejas field goal. During the drive, Derrick Burroughs was taken off the field on a stretcher with a neck injury.

• On the final play of the half, Darryl Talley blocked a field goal and Kelso returned it for a TD.

• On the first series of the third, Kelly hit Don Beebe for a TD on third-and-eight from the 37 for a 27-10 lead.

• The Oilers got that back by driving 75 yards to Alonzo Highsmith's TD. Then Bubba McDowell blocked a

John Kidd punt and Cris Dishman returned it for a TD to make it 27-24.

• Two plays after the kickoff, Andre Reed caught a 78-yard TD pass, the longest of his career, but Warren Moon hit Ernest Givins for a TD just eight plays later. On the next series, Steve Brown intercepted Kelly, returned it to the Bills 7 and Lorenzo White scored to give the Oilers a 38-34 lead.

• The Bills answered with an 83-yard drive to Kelly's TD pass to Thurman Thomas, but the Oilers tied the game on the final play of regulation. The Oilers won the toss in OT and got to the 20, but Zendejas missed a field goal. The Bills then marched 80 yards in seven plays to Reed's winning score.

QUOTES

• Jim Kelly: "I don't think anyone's going to say that our defense always wins games for us because that's a bunch of bull. I love when I can't remember which touchdown I threw."

• Marv Levy: "When my coaching days are over, this is one victory I'll always remember. To keep coming back and overcome a lot of things that went wrong meant a great deal to us. And Jim was just magnificent. He has rallied us so many times, I'm starting to lose count."

• Fred Smerlas: "You've got two of the best quarterbacks playing at the top of their game; you're going to have a lot of points scored. Those guys put on a show that should be bottled."

WEEK 3 GAMES	
Ind 13, Atl 9	Chi 47, Det 27
Rams 41, GB 38	SD 21, KC 6
Den 31, LAR 27	TB 20, NO 10
Pitt 27, Minn 14	NYJ 40, Mia 33
NYG 35, Phoe 7	SF 38, Phil 28
Sea 24, NE 3	Wash 30, Dal 7
Cinc 21, Clev 14	

Bills	10	10	7	14	6 - 47
Oilers	7	3	14	17	0 - 41

Attendance at the Astrodome - 57,278

Buf: FG Norwood 43, 3:01
Hou: Moon 1 run (Zendejas kick), 7:48
Buf: Thomas 6 pass from Kelly (Norwood kick), 14:50
Buf: FG Norwood 26, 3:47
Hou: FG Zendejas 26, 14:03
Buf: Kelso 76 blocked field goal return (Norwood kick), 15:00
Buf: Beebe 63 pass from Kelly (Norwood kick), 6:12
Hou: Highsmith 4 run (Zendejas kick), 11:01
Hou: Dishman 7 blocked punt return (Zendejas kick), 14:33
Buf: Reed 78 pass from Kelly (Norwood kick), :10
Hou: Givins 26 pass from Moon (Zendejas kick), 5:28
Hou: White 1 run (Zendejas kick), 10:20
Buf: Thomas 26 pass from Kelly (Norwood kick), 13:08
Hou: FG Zendejas 52, 14:57
Buf: Reed 28 pass from Kelly (No PAT attempt), 8:42

	BUF	HOU
First downs	23	33
Rushing yds	112	128
Passing yds	337	311
Punts-avg	3-28.3	1-55.0
Fumbles-lost	1-0	1-0
Penalties-yds	13-84	10-59
Poss. time	25:31	43:11

BILLS LEADERS: Rushing - Thomas 12-58, Kelly 3-43, Kinnebrew 9-11; **Passing** - Kelly 17-29-1 - 363; **Receiving** - Reed 5-135, Johnson 5-86, Thomas 3-37, Metzelaars 2-36, Beebe 1-63, McKeller 1-6.
OILERS LEADERS: Rushing - Highsmith 14-55, Moon 5-36, Pinkett 12-26, White 8-11; **Passing** - Moon 28-42-2 - 338; **Receiving** - Duncan 6-69, Jeffires 6-57, Givins 4-65, Highsmith 4-47, Hill 3-58, Pinkett 2-13, Harris 1-13, White 1-11, Mrosko 1-5.

NOTES

• The Bills defense had its best game as the Pats were just four-of-16 on third down.

• Pete Metzelaars set a new team record for career receptions by a tight end.

• Larry Kinnebrew missed a team meeting and practice the day before the game and was suspended for the game.

• After the Pats took a 3-0 lead, the Bills drove 72 yards in seven plays to Thurman Thomas' TD run. The score was set up when Kelly scrambled out of the pocket and threw 36 yards to Andre Reed who made a great catch at the 18. In the second quarter, after a punt pinned them at the 18, the Bills got a break when Raymond Clayborn was flagged for a 43-yard interference penalty. On the next play, Keith McKeller got wide open along the sideline and took in a 39-yard TD pass untouched.

• The Pats went three-and-out and the Bills then went 61 yards in six plays to Pete Metzelaars' TD reception. The score was set up by Reed's 33-yard catch and run. Scott Norwood's field goal closed the first half.

• After the teams traded two punts, the Pats drove 80 yards in 12 plays to Doug Flutie's TD pass to Cedric Jones. Flutie was five-of-seven for 67 yards and had two scrambles for 14 yards.

• Three plays after the kickoff, Thomas was wide open on a streak and caught a 74-yard TD pass.

• The Pats drove inside the Bills 20 twice after that, but were stopped on fourth down both times.

QUOTES

• Jim Kelly: "We've caught the scoring bug and I love

it. I want to beat somebody 45-0. I'd like to see the defense shut them out and us score a lot of points and let Frank Reich take some snaps. Even up 31-10 I was a little worried because the Patriots never give up. I told the team during the week that we had to come right out and dominate on offense and defense and we did that."

• Thurman Thomas on his TD reception: "It's a play we always work on. I run toward the sideline and Andre Reed cuts across the middle. It's like a pick play. We wiped two of their guys out, that's why I was so wide open."

• Bruce Smith: "I'm tired, I'm dehydrated and I don't have any legs and I owe that to Doug Flutie. Anytime you get to somebody as elusive as him, it gives you a great deal of satisfaction."

• Ray Bentley: "This game seemed closer than the final score. Out on the field you felt like if you made one mistake, we'd be in trouble."

• Marv Levy: "This was probably the toughest 31-10 win I've ever been through."

• Pats quarterback Doug Flutie: "I was frustrated. I've been throwing well in practice and I wanted to go out there and fire it, but it just wasn't happening."

WEEK 4 GAMES	
GB 23, Atl 21	Cinc 21, KC 17
Clev 16, Den 13	Ind 17, NYJ 10
Rams 13, SF 12	Hou 39, Mia 10
NYG 30, Dal 13	Pitt 23, Det 3
SD 24, Phoe 13	Sea 24, LAR 20
Minn 17, TB 3	Wash 16, NO 14
Chi 27, Phil 13	

Patriots	3	0	7	0 - 10
Bills	7	17	0	7 - 31

Attendance at Rich Stadium - 78,921

NE: FG Davis 35, 10:26
Buf: Thomas 4 run (Norwood kick), 14:29
Buf: McKeller 39 pass from Kelly (Norwood kick), 6:40
Buf: Metzelaars 8 pass from Kelly (Norwood kick), 10:08
Buf: FG Norwood 36, 14:59
NE: Jones 20 pass from Flutie (Davis kick), 13:14
Buf: Thomas 74 pass from Kelly (Norwood kick), :10

	BUF	NE
First downs	16	17
Rushing yds	115	124
Passing yds	256	155
Punts-avg	6-44.2	6-41.2
Fumbles-lost	2-1	0-0
Penalties-yds	7-55	5-68
Poss. time	26:36	33:24

BILLS LEADERS: Rushing - Thomas 21-105, Davis 3-7, Mueller 1-2, Harmon 2-2, Kelly 4-(-1); **Passing** - Kelly 12-17-0 - 278; **Receiving** - Reed 4-114, Thomas 4-99, Metzelaars 3-26, McKeller 1-39.

PATRIOTS LEADERS: Rushing - Perryman 15-68, Flutie 7-43, Dupard 7-11, Allen 1-2; **Passing** - Flutie 15-41-1 - 176; **Receiving** - Jones 4-48, Dawson 3-28, Morgan 2-27, Perryman 2-13, Dykes 1-29, Martin 1-19, Sievers 1-9, Dupard 1-3.

STANDINGS: FOURTH WEEK																				
AFC EAST	**W**	**L**	**T**	**CENTRAL**	**W**	**L**	**T**	**WEST**	**W**	**L**	**T**	**NFC EAST**	**W**	**L**	**T**	**CENTRAL**	**W**	**L**	**T**	**WEST**	**W**	**L**	**T**
Buffalo	3	1	0	Cleveland	3	1	0	Denver	3	1	0	NY Giants	4	0	0	Chicago	4	0	0	LA Rams	4	0	0
Indianapolis	2	2	0	Cincinnati	3	1	0	San Diego	2	2	0	Philadelphia	2	2	0	Tampa Bay	2	2	0	San Fran	3	1	0
Miami	1	3	0	Houston	2	2	0	Seattle	2	2	0	Phoenix	2	2	0	Minnesota	2	2	0	N.Orleans	1	3	0
NY Jets	1	3	0	Pittsburgh	2	2	0	Raiders	1	3	0	Washington	2	2	0	Green Bay	2	2	0	Atlanta	1	3	0
New England	1	3	0					Kan. City	1	3	0	Dallas	0	4	0	Detroit	0	4	0				

Bills	0	0	7	7 - 14
Colts	14	6	3	14 - 37

Attendance at the Hoosier Dome - 58,890

Ind: Dickerson 1 run (Biasucci kick), 7:16
Ind: Trudeau 1 run (Biasucci kick), 12:07
Ind: FG Biasucci 32, 12:48
Ind: FG Biasucci 46, 14:34
Ind: FG Biasucci 25, 2:47
Buf: Reed 16 pass from Kelly (Norwood kick), 11:16
Ind: Dickerson 4 run (Biasucci kick), 3:46
Buf: Davis 17 pass from Reich (Norwood kick), 9:54
Ind: Taylor 80 interception return (Biasucci kick), 12:22

	BUF	IND
First downs	25	20
Rushing yds	71	153
Passing yds	353	177
Punts-avg	2-51.0	4-38.5
Fumbles-lost	5-3	2-0
Penalties-yds	4-34	1-10
Poss. time	23:13	36:47

BILLS LEADERS: Rushing - Thomas 12-53, Harmon 1-14, Kelly 2-6, Davis 2-(-2); **Passing** - Kelly 20-32-3 - 216, Reich 11-19-1 - 177; **Receiving** - Reed 7-75, Harmon 8-75, Thomas 6-81, Beebe 4-67, Johnson 4-67, Davis 1-17, McKeller 1-11.

COLTS LEADERS: Rushing - Dickerson 22-92, Bentley 10-56, Trudeau 6-4, Verdin 1-1; **Passing** - Trudeau 13-24-1 - 193; **Receiving** - Brooks 5-111, Rison 4-47, Verdin 2-22, Bentley 1-7, Beach 1-6.

NOTES

• Once again, the Hoosier Dome was a House of Horrors for the Bills as they lost for the fifth time in six visits there and lost Jim Kelly to a separated left shoulder when Howard Ballard missed a block and allowed Jon Hand to level Kelly. Interestingly, the play occurred on the Bills' first TD.

• The Colts took the opening kickoff and drove 76 yards in 14 plays to Eric Dickerson's TD run.

• Four plays after the kickoff, Fredd Young sacked Kelly, forced a fumble and Donnell Thompson recovered at the Bills 36. Five plays later, Jack Trudeau scored on a sneak for a 14-0 lead.

• In the second quarter, Duane Bickett intercepted Kelly at the Colts 23 and that resulted in a Dean Biasucci field goal. The key play was a 40-yard pass to Bill Brooks. On the next series, Keith Taylor intercepted Kelly at midfield with 1:15 left in the half and that led to another Biasucci field goal.

• On the third play of the second half, Bruce Plummer picked off Kelly and Biasucci made his third field goal.

• Scott Norwood missed a 40-yard field goal on the next possession, but after a Colts punt, the Bills drove 63 yards in eight plays to Kelly's TD pass to Andre Reed. However, Kelly was hurt on the play.

• The Colts matched that with a 67-yard drive in 10

WEEK 5 GAMES

Rams 26, Atl 14	TB 42, Chi 35
Cinc 26, Pitt 16	GB 31, Dal 13
Minn 24, Det 17	NE 23, Hou 13
KC 20, Sea 16	SF 24, NO 20
Phil 21, NYG 19	Wash 30, Phoe 28
Den 16, SD 10	LAR 14, NYJ 7
Mia 13, Clev 10 (OT)	

plays to Dickerson's second TD.

• Frank Reich lost a fumble to end his first series, but then directed an eight-play, 74-yard march that culminated in his TD pass to Kenneth Davis, Davis' first TD reception in the NFL.

• The final score came when Taylor picked off Reich and went 80 yards for a TD with 2:38 left.

QUOTES

• Bruce Smith: "They jumped out on us so quick and took the momentum."

• Marv Levy: "I talked to Jim after the game and he said it wasn't a cheap shot. He's disappointed. He understood this type of thing can happen, but he's very disappointed and so are all of us. I thought our line played well enough. When you get into a position where you have to pass block on every down, good things aren't going to happen. We're behind this team now, we're chasing them. We may be tied, but they've won the head-to-head and they won it convincingly. We didn't do any of the things you have to do to win."

• Fred Smerlas: "I've seen him (Kelly) wince in pain before, but when I saw him holding his arm, I knew it couldn't be good."

• Colts defensive end Jon Hand: "I wasn't trying to hurt him. I thought he still had the ball. I figured for sure Jim would get right back up. He did every other time I hit him. We had pressure coming up and down the line. He was getting hit all day."

• Cornelius Bennett: "Edit this any way you want, but they kicked our asses."

• Kent Hull: "Their 2-2 record was deceiving. They had lost to two of the best teams (49ers and Rams) in the league. We knew this wouldn't be easy."

Rams	7	0	3	10 - 20
Bills	0	6	0	17 - 23

Attendance at Rich Stadium - 76,231

LA: McGee 3 pass from Everett (Lansford kick), 9:58
Buf: FG Norwood 38, 10:50
Buf: FG Norwood 47, 14:04
LA: FG Lansford 34, 12:04
Buf: FG Norwood 40, :51
LA: FG Lansford 36, 5:59
Buf: Thomas 1 run (Norwood kick), 12:37
LA: Anderson 78 pass from Everett (Lansford kick), 13:38
Buf: Reed 8 pass from Reich (Norwood kick), 14:44

	BUF	LA
First downs	17	15
Rushing yds	134	59
Passing yds	214	207
Punts-avg	6-36.0	7-37.3
Fumbles-lost	4-3	5-1
Penalties-yds	7-69	4-30
Poss. time	29:31	30:29

BILLS LEADERS: Rushing - Thomas 24-105, Kinnebrew 4-16, Harmon 2-12, Reich 1-1; **Passing** - Reich 21-37-1 - 214; **Receiving** - Reed 8-106, Thomas 9-67, McKeller 2-21, Harmon 1-14, Metzelaars 1-6.

RAMS LEADERS: Rushing - Bell 21-44, Delpino 4-6, Brown 2-5, Everett 3-4; **Passing** - Everett 15-36-1 - 219; **Receiving** - Ellard 4-70, Holohan 3-19, Anderson 2-87, Cox 2-20, McGee 2-13, Johnson 1-6, Delpino 1-4.

NOTES

• Frank Reich rallied the Bills in the fourth quarter to an upset over the previously unbeaten Rams on *Monday Night Football*. Reich was 10-of-11 for 132 yards in the final 8:50, producing two TDs.

• It was Reich's first NFL start. Linebacker Carlton Bailey saw extended time after Ray Bentley was injured. Bailey led the Bills with nine tackles. Bruce Smith had five tackles and two sacks.

• Reich was intercepted by Jerry Gray on the first series. The Rams had to punt, but Mickey Sutton muffed it and Richard Brown recovered at the Bills 16 and that led to Jim Everett's TD pass to Buford McGee.

• The Bills failed to make a first down on four of their next six possessions, but they managed two field goals. Art Still forced Greg Bell to fumble and Jeff Wright recovered at the Rams 20, leading to the first Scott Norwood field goal. Late in the second quarter, the Bills began a drive at the Rams 49 after a punt. Thurman Thomas' third-and-one conversion helped set up Norwood's second field goal.

• Midway through the third, the Rams drove 56 yards to a Mike Lansford field goal for a 10-6 lead, but the Bills answered with a 52-yard drive to Norwood's third field goal. Lansford responded with a 36-yarder as the Rams converted two third downs, one coming on

WEEK 6 GAMES

Det 17, TB 16	Minn 26, GB 14
Hou 33, Chi 28	Den 14, Ind 3
LAR 20, KC 14	Mia 20, Cinc 13
Atl 16, NE 15	NO 29, NYJ 14
SF 31, Dal 14	Phil 17, Phoe 5
Sea 17, SD 16	Pitt 17, Cinc 7
NYG 20, Wash 17	

Sutton's interference penalty on third-and-13.

• Reich then drove the Bills 86 yards in 10 plays to his TD pass to Thomas. Reich was sacked by Brett Faryniarz on third down, but Bill Hawkins was called for defensive holding, giving the Bills a first down.

• The Rams went four-and-out as Everett's fourth-down pass to Henry Ellard fell incomplete and the Bills appeared to have the game won. But two plays later, Thomas fumbled and Michael Stewart recovered at the Rams 22. On the next play, Flipper Anderson caught a 78-yard TD pass.

• The Bills took possession at their 36 with 1:17 left. On the first play, Andre Reed caught a short pass but fumbled and Kent Hull saved the day by recovering. On third-and-six, Thomas caught a 17-yard pass to the Rams 40 with 40 seconds left. Reich then hit Thomas for six and 15, Ronnie Harmon for 14 and finally Reed for the eight-yard TD with 16 seconds left.

QUOTES

• Frank Reich: "I was discouraged (about the slow start) but I never really doubted we were going to win the game. We had a few problems early in the game, it took me awhile to get going. I just said to myself 'Frank, hang in there.'" (About crying after the winning TD pass): "I was a pretty happy camper and that was the only way I could express how I felt. Those were tears of joy, tears of knowing that after five years, my prayers were answered."

• Andre Reed on Reich: "A lot of people doubted him coming in, they didn't think he could do anything, they didn't even think he could throw the ball. I think he proved something to the fans of Buffalo and he proved something to this team – that we can count on him."

STANDINGS: SIXTH WEEK

AFC EAST	W	L	T	CENTRAL	W	L	T	WEST	W	L	T	NFC EAST	W	L	T	CENTRAL	W	L	T	WEST	W	L	T
Buffalo	4	2	0	Cincinnati	4	2	0	Denver	5	1	0	NY Giants	5	1	0	Chicago	4	2	0	LA Rams	5	1	0
Indianapolis	3	3	0	Cleveland	3	3	0	Raiders	3	3	0	Philadelphia	4	2	0	Minnesota	4	2	0	San Fran	5	1	0
Miami	3	3	0	Houston	3	3	0	Seattle	3	3	0	Washington	3	3	0	Tampa Bay	3	3	0	N.Orleans	2	4	0
New England	2	4	0	Pittsburgh	3	3	0	San Diego	2	4	0	Phoenix	2	4	0	Green Bay	3	3	0	Atlanta	2	4	0
NY Jets	1	5	0					Kan. City	2	4	0	Dallas	0	6	0	Detroit	1	5	0				

NOTES

• No heroics were needed this time as the running game crushed the Jets and Frank Reich had a limited role in the victory. The Bills had season highs for rushing attempts (52) and yards (204) on a windy day.
• Bruce Smith had six tackles and three sacks worth 21 yards, becoming the team's all-time sack leader (52).
• The Bills were nine-of-17 on third down; the Jets were two-of-12 and managed just 154 total yards.
• Scott Norwood missed a field goal on the first possession, but made a 38-yarder on the next try.
• After the Jets third straight punt in the first quarter, the Bills drove 79 yards in 13 plays. The drive was kept alive when the Jets were caught with 12 men on the field during a Bills punt, giving the Bills a first down.
• On the next series, the Bills moved 56 yards to Norwood's second field goal. Larry Kinnebrew had 30 yards on seven carries during the march. Pat Leahy missed a 52-yard field goal at the end of the half.
• Mickey Sutton's interception early in the third set up Reich's TD pass to Andre Reed three plays later.
• Leahy made a field goal late in the third. Early in the fourth, Scott Radecic forced Freeman McNeil to fumble, Leonard Smith recovered at the Jets 17 and Ronnie Harmon made a brilliant one-handed TD catch.
• Joe Prokop then shanked a 15-yard wind-blown punt and the Bills took over at the Jets 25. Five plays later, Reich found Kenneth Davis for the TD.

QUOTES

• Marv Levy on Reich: "He played as if he experienced a lot of value from last week's performance. I think his total concentration was on the game and not on having to prove something. Overall, he performed excellently, especially in the face of a tough wind."
• Kent Hull on Reich: "I saw a lot of Jim Kelly out there today. Whether he was scrambling for yardage, holding the ball to the last possible second before he passed or reading the blitzes, Frank played like Jim. I think a lot of times we took for granted the things Jim did. And subconsciously, we're more intent on making the running game work with Frank in there."
• Thurman Thomas on Reich: "He was a different quarterback than he was last week."
• Frank Reich: "I concentrated on starting this game better than last week. I didn't have butterflies until this morning. Before the Rams game, I was pretty much nervous all week. If we had lost today, people would have forgotten the Rams game pretty quickly. I know my role on this team, it's backup quarterback. I have a long way to go before even thinking about fighting Jim Kelly, who has done it so well for so long, for a starting job."
• Larry Kinnebrew: "When I felt that wind whipping against me in warmups, I thought it was going to be a busy day for Thurman. That was running weather out there. It was nice to contribute."
• Bruce Smith: "If someone is going to go out there and single block me, I don't think that's fair to the offensive lineman. I can't be single-blocked."

WEEK 7 GAMES	
Phoe 34, Atl 20	KC 36, Dal 28
Mia 23, GB 20	Ind 23, Cinc 12
Phil 10, LAR 7	Minn 20, Det 7
SF 37, NE 20	NO 40, Rams 21
NYG 20, SD 13	Hou 27, Pitt 0
Wash 32, TB 28	Clev 27, Chi 7
Den 24, Sea 21 (OT)	

Jets	0	0	3	0 - 3
Bills	3	10	7	14 - 34

Attendance at Rich Stadium - 76,811

Buf: FG Norwood 38, 9:05
Buf: Thomas 3 run (Norwood kick), 1:43
Buf: FG Norwood 27, 12:26
Buf: Reed 20 pass from Reich (Norwood kick), 7:08
NYJ: FG Leahy 41, 14:44
Buf: Harmon 12 pass from Reich (Norwood kick), 6:18
Buf: Davis 7 pass from Reich (Norwood kick), 9:38

	BUF	NYJ
First downs	22	9
Rushing yds	204	39
Passing yds	139	115
Punts-avg	3-41.3	6-26.7
Fumbles-lost	0-0	2-2
Penalties-yds	5-40	9-65
Poss. time	42:53	17:07

BILLS LEADERS: Rushing - Kinnebrew 17-77, Thomas 20-49, Reich 5-32, Davis 7-31, Harmon 1-13, Mueller 1-5, Gelbaugh 1-(-3); **Passing** - Reich 13-20-0 - 145; **Receiving** - Reed 5-58, Metzelaars 4-41, McKeller 1-20, Harmon 1-12, Davis 1-7, Johnson 1-7.

JETS LEADERS: Rushing - McNeil 5-22, Hector 5-15, Vick 1-2, Malone 1-0; **Passing** - O'Brien 11-29-1 - 140, Malone 2-2-0 - 13; **Receiving** - Burkett 3-42, Shuler 3-34, Townsell 2-33, Hector 2-21, McNeil 2-18, Vick 1-5.

NOTES

• A record Rich Stadium crowd watched the Bills dominate the Dolphins. Thurman Thomas and Larry Kinnebrew both topped 100 yards as the Dolphins allowed the second-highest rushing total in their history. It was the sixth time in Bills history two backs had rushed for 100 yards in the same game.
• Andre Reed saw his team record-tying streak of consecutive games catching a pass snapped at 42, leaving him tied with Elbert Dubenion. Frank Reich threw only nine passes in the game.
• Jeff Wright sacked Dan Marino, ending an NFL record 19-game (759 pass attempts) sackless streak.
• It was Buffalo's sixth straight win over Miami and Reich's third straight win as a starter.
• The Dolphins used the first 6:27 to drive to a Pete Stoyanovich field goal, but the Bills used the next 8:26 to go ahead, driving 76 yards in 15 plays to Kinnebrew's TD run. Reich threw only one pass, a third-and-three completion to Thomas for seven yards.
• Five plays after the kickoff, Bruce Smith pressured Marino into throwing an interception to Cornelius Bennett at the Miami 42. Four plays later, Thomas broke a 30-yard TD run.
• Late in the second quarter after a punt, Reich threw a first-down 63-yard TD pass to Don Beebe.
• Miami scored on its first possession of the third. Starting from the 8, Marino hit Ferrell Edmunds for 30 and a personal foul penalty on Smith tacked on 15 more yards. Marino then hit Mark Clayton for a TD.
• Reich then lost a fumble at the Miami 43, but the defense forced a punt.
• The Bills iced the game in the fourth as Scott Norwood made a field goal and Kirby Jackson returned a Marino interception for a TD. Scott Secules took over for Marino late and hit Andre Brown for a TD.

QUOTES

• Miami linebacker Barry Krauss: "They kept pounding on us and pounding on us. It was a real basic offense. They just lined up and said 'Try to stop us.' They kicked our butts."
• Miami coach Don Shula: "Marino did not have time to take a deep breath. And it seemed like whenever we tried to get the running game going, they had penetration. Kinnebrew and Thomas had great days. It was a disappointment to come up here and get handled like that."
• Frank Reich on the Bills' first possession: "I think that pretty much set the tone for the day. We never intended to run as much as we did coming into the game, but when we saw the way the offensive line was blocking and the way Thurman and Larry were running, we decided to stick with it. It's been a very good three weeks. I was just another spoke in the wheel. My main thought was that when Jim came back, we'd still be in first place and we're still there."
• Jeff Wright on his sack: "Once I beat him (Jeff Uhlenhake), everything moved kind of slow. I was thinking so many thoughts at one time. I was just hoping I could get him before he got it off. I fantasized about doing it, but realistically I didn't think I'd be the one because I only play about half the time. He knew someday someone was going to get him. I'm glad it was me."

WEEK 8 GAMES	
NO 20, Atl 13	GB 23, Det 20
Clev 28, Hou 17	Pitt 23, KC 17
Chi 20, Rams 10	Phil 28, Den 24
Phoe 19, Dal 10	Sea 10, SD 7
SF 23, NYJ 10	Cinc 56, TB 23
LAR 37, Wash 24	NYG 24, Minn 14
NE 23, Ind 20 (OT)	

Dolphins	3	0	7	7 - 17
Bills	0	21	0	10 - 31

Attendance at Rich Stadium - 80,208

Mia: FG Stoyanovich 45, 6:27
Buf: Kinnebrew 1 run (Norwood kick), :02
Buf: Thomas 30 run (Norwood kick), 5:55
Buf: Beebe 63 pass from Reich (Norwood kick), 13:21
Mia: Clayton 44 pass from Marino (Stoyanovich kick), 7:41
Buf: FG Norwood 45, 4:38
Buf: Jackson 40 interception return (Norwood kick), 12:00
Mia: A. Brown 44 pass from Secules (Stoyanovich kick), 13:10

	BUF	MIA
First downs	18	19
Rushing yds	280	65
Passing yds	114	348
Punts-avg	5-35.2	4-45.3
Fumbles-lost	1-1	0-0
Penalties-yds	8-70	5-29
Poss. time	34:41	25:19

BILLS LEADERS: Rushing - Thomas 27-148, Kinnebrew 21-121, Harmon 1-2, Davis 2-9; **Passing** - Reich 6-9-0 - 123; **Receiving** - Thomas 2-21, McKeller 2-36, Beebe 1-63, Johnson 1-3.

DOLPHINS LEADERS: Rushing - Davenport 2-12, Smith 15-36, Secules 1-17; **Passing** - Marino 20-36-3 - 255, Secules 6-11-0 - 109; **Receiving** - A. Brown 5-105, Jensen 3-19, Duper 4-30, Clayton 7-122, Smith 1-12, Banks 4-39, Edmunds 1-30, Davenport 1-7.

STANDINGS: EIGHTH WEEK

AFC EAST	W	L	T	CENTRAL	W	L	T	WEST	W	L	T	NFC EAST	W	L	T	CENTRAL	W	L	T	WEST	W	L	T
Buffalo	6	2	0	Cincinnati	5	3	0	Denver	6	2	0	NY Giants	7	1	0	Minnesota	5	3	0	San Fran	7	1	0
Indianapolis	4	4	0	Cleveland	5	3	0	Raiders	4	4	0	Philadelphia	6	2	0	Chicago	5	3	0	LA Rams	5	3	0
Miami	4	4	0	Houston	4	4	0	Seattle	4	4	0	Washington	4	4	0	Green Bay	4	4	0	N.Orleans	4	4	0
New England	3	5	0	Pittsburgh	4	4	0	Kan. City	3	5	0	Phoenix	4	4	0	Tampa Bay	3	5	0	Atlanta	2	6	0
NY Jets	1	7	0					San Diego	2	6	0	Dallas	0	8	0	Detroit	1	7	0				

NOTES

• Jim Kelly returned to the lineup and played well, but the Bills were beaten by Paul McFadden's 50-yard field goal with two seconds left.

• Cornerback Deion Sanders made his debut at wide receiver for the Falcons, but did not catch a pass.

• Kelly's 52-yard pass to Andre Reed set up a six-yard TD pass to James Lofton in the first quarter, capping a 70-yard drive. It was Lofton's first catch as a Bill and the 600th of his NFL career.

• McFadden gave a hint of things to come, kicking a 54-yarder in the second quarter.

• On the third play of the second half, Elbert Shelley intercepted Kelly and returned it 25 yards to the 6, setting up Keith Jones' TD run. But four plays after the kickoff, Kelly hit Keith McKeller for a TD. He had passed 21 yards to McKeller, 29 to Reed and Thurman Thomas had a 29-yard run.

• The Falcons needed just four plays to retake the lead. Chris Miller hit Stacy Bailey for 41, setting up his TD pass to Floyd Dixon to cap a quick 78-yard march.

• Robert Moore then recovered a Thomas fumble at the Bills 11, setting up a McFadden field goal.

• The Bills answered with a nine-play, 71-yard drive to Thomas' TD. The key plays were a Scott Case interference on third down and a 21-yard pass to McKeller.

• In the fourth, the Falcons began a drive with 3:12 left and moved 61 yards in seven plays to Jones' TD, but Don Beebe returned the ensuing kickoff 85 yards to the 8 and Larry Kinnebrew scored with 29 seconds left.

• However, Miller hit Bailey for 41 yards as Bailey out-jumped Nate Odomes, to set up the winning kick.

QUOTES

• Darryl Talley: "The game is still 60 minutes long and the Falcons used every second. It was just one of those things. You can't blame it on one area, a lot of things went wrong."

• Jim Kelly: "We had a chance to build a little cushion between us and the rest of the division. Now, the race is tightening up again and we have our work cut out for us. I didn't feel rusty at all and it felt good to finally throw."

• Kent Hull: "They deserved to win. We brought the best out in them. Look at their record, it isn't very good, but they've lost a lot of them close. It's a team that has talent. You don't think it's over at that point (Kinnebrew's TD), but you feel pretty damn good. You realize the odds of a team coming back with no time-outs and 30 seconds left aren't very good."

• Don Beebe on his kickoff return: "We had returned right all day, so coach DeHaven decided to change things up and called a middle return. I knew Sanders was behind me. Anytime he's on the field you know he's there. When I got to the 30-yard-line, I was sucking gas. I got some tremendous blocks from Jamie Mueller, Carlton Bailey, Dwight Drane. All I had to do was run."

WEEK 9 GAMES	
GB 14, Chi 13	LAR 28, Cinc 7
Clev 42, TB 31	Hou 35, Det 31
Mia 19, Ind 13	NYG 20, Phoe 13
NYJ 27, NE 26	SD 20, Phil 17
Den 34, Pitt 7	KC 20, Sea 10
Dal 13, Wash 3	SF 31, NO 13
Minn 23, Rams 21 (OT)	

Bills	7	0	14	7 -	28
Falcons	0	3	17	10 -	30

Attendance at Atlanta-Fulton County Stadium - 45,267

Buf: Lofton 6 pass from Kelly (Norwood kick), 13:18
Atl: FG McFadden 54, 10:13
Atl: Jones 1 run (McFadden kick), 2:43
Buf: McKeller 11 pass from Kelly (Norwood kick), 5:06
Atl: Dixon 26 pass from Miller (McFadden kick), 6:14
Atl: FG McFadden 26, 7:52
Buf: Thomas 2 run (Norwood kick), 12:44
Atl: Jones 3 run (McFadden kick), 13:38
Buf: Kinnebrew 1 run (Norwood kick), 14:31
Atl: FG McFadden 50, 14:58

	BUF	ATL
First downs	19	20
Rushing yds	118	127
Passing yds	211	213
Punts-avg	5-44.6	5-44.4
Fumbles-lost	2-1	0-0
Penalties-yds	9-81	6-44
Poss. time	30:55	29:05

BILLS LEADERS: Rushing - Thomas 21-95, Kinnebrew 8-24, Kelly 2-(-1); **Passing** - Kelly 17-22-1 - 231; **Receiving** - Reed 5-100, Johnson 4-29, McKeller 3-55, Lofton 2-16, Kinnebrew 1-17, Thomas 1-9, Beebe 1-5.

FALCONS LEADERS: Rushing - Settle 22-83, Jones 11-32, Miller 1-7, Lang 3-5; **Passing** - Miller 10-23-0 - 220; **Receiving** - Bailey 3-93, Dixon 3-60, Jones 3-50, Settle 1-17.

NOTES

• Jon Hand sacked Jim Kelly, but Kelly survived and the Bills rolled to their eighth straight non-strike home victory over the Colts. The game was the Bills' 15th straight sellout.

• Shane Conlan returned to the lineup for the first time since the Denver game. He made one tackle.

• Mark Pike forced James Pruitt to fumble the opening kickoff and Mickey Sutton recovered at the Colts 22. Four plays later, Kelly hit Thurman Thomas for a TD.

• Five plays after the kickoff, Leonard Smith recovered an Eric Dickerson fumble at the 50 and that led to Scott Norwood's field goal. On the first play after the kick-off, Dickerson fumbled again with Cornelius Bennett recovering at the 35. That set up another Norwood field goal.

• Early in the second quarter, Andre Reed's 32-yard TD reception capped a seven-play, 61-yard drive.

• The Bills began a drive with 2:50 left in the half and they used 2:42 to go 84 yards in 12 plays to Reed's second TD reception, a third-down throw from the 3. The key play was a 27-yard pass to Keith McKeller.

• The Bills ate up the first 8:15 of the third, but Norwood missed a field goal.

• Early in the fourth, Norwood atoned with his third field goal, capping a 36-yard drive.

• The Colts' only score came when Dickerson fumbled into the end zone and Randy Dixon recovered for a TD.

QUOTES

• Ted Marchibroda: "What we've done since the beginning of the year is gone on the attack much more. We are not afraid to go for the big play."

• Jim Kelly on Andre Reed: "Andre has always been an excellent receiver, but I think this year he's developing into a big-play receiver."

• Marv Levy on the running attack: "It's nice when you can put two backs in the backfield who can carry the football. It certainly takes the pressure off the other. Larry, since four or five games after the start of the season, has become more prominent. He has been a tremendous asset to us. If he gets stopped at the line, he is just as likely to work his way into the open. He has a good bit of nimbleness. He has done a pretty good job of controlling his weight, but if he could get down to 245, he might do for us some of the things Christian Okoye does for Kansas City."

• Colts coach Ron Meyer on the early fumbles: "It was devastating, just devastating. All that and Buffalo had the wind. All of a sudden you're 13 points down and you feel fortunate that's all you're down if you can believe that."

• Colts tackle Chris Hinton: "We beat them pretty good in Indianapolis and they wanted revenge and to separate themselves from the rest of the pack in the AFC East. The one way to do that was to beat us and they accomplished it."

• Steve Tasker: "They beat us so badly the first time, we had something to prove to ourselves. We felt it was a very big game for us."

Colts	0	0	0	7 -	7
Bills	13	14	0	3 -	30

Attendance at Rich Stadium - 79,256

Buf: Thomas 8 pass from Kelly (Norwood kick), 2:12
Buf: FG Norwood 42, 7:28
Buf: FG Norwood 40, 10:34
Buf: Reed 32 pass from Kelly (Norwood kick), 5:54
Buf: Reed 3 pass from Kelly (Norwood kick), 14:52
Buf: FG Norwood 32, 3:58
Ind: Dixon recovered fumble in end zone (Biasucci kick), 6:13

	BUF	IND
First downs	26	13
Rushing yds	232	86
Passing yds	161	103
Punts-avg	4-41.5	6-38.3
Fumbles-lost	1-0	4-3
Penalties-yds	5-30	3-15
Poss. time	41:14	18:46

BILLS LEADERS: Rushing - Thomas 29-127, Davis 7-59, Kinnebrew 9-38, Mueller 4-9, Kelly 2-(-1); **Passing** - Kelly 14-30-0 - 172; **Receiving** - Reed 6-76, McKeller 3-41, Thomas 2-21, Johnson 1-14, Beebe 1-12, Kinnebrew 1-8.
COLTS LEADERS: Rushing - Dickerson 19-79, Verdin 1-7; **Passing** - Ramsey 12-27-0 - 125; **Receiving** - Rison 4-81, Brooks 2-15, Dickerson 2-8, Boyer 2-7, Beach 1-7, Bentley 1-7.

WEEK 10 GAMES	
SF 45, Atl 3	Chi 20, Pitt 0
Clev 17, Sea 7	Phoe 24, Dal 20
Den 16, KC 13	Det 31, GB 22
Mia 31, NYJ 23	Minn 24, TB 10
NO 28, NE 24	Rams 31, NYG 10
SD 14, LAR 12	Wash 10, Phil 3
Hou 26, Cinc 24	

STANDINGS: TENTH WEEK

AFC EAST	W	L	T	CENTRAL	W	L	T	WEST	W	L	T	NFC EAST	W	L	T	CENTRAL	W	L	T	WEST	W	L	T
Buffalo	7	3	0	Cleveland	7	3	0	Denver	8	2	0	NY Giants	8	2	0	Minnesota	7	3	0	San Fran	9	1	0
Miami	6	4	0	Houston	6	4	0	Raiders	5	5	0	Philadelphia	6	4	0	Chicago	6	4	0	LA Rams	6	4	0
Indianapolis	4	6	0	Cincinnati	5	5	0	Seattle	4	6	0	Washington	5	5	0	Green Bay	5	5	0	N.Orleans	5	5	0
New England	3	7	0	Pittsburgh	4	6	0	Kan. City	4	6	0	Phoenix	5	5	0	Tampa Bay	3	7	0	Atlanta	3	7	0
NY Jets	2	8	0					San Diego	4	6	0	Dallas	1	9	0	Detroit	2	8	0				

NOTES

• The Bills turned over the ball six times and allowed the Patriots to score 20 points in the final 7:45.
• Steve Grogan improved his career starting record against the Bills to 13-6.
• John Stephens became the first back to top 100 yards rushing against the Bills in 1989.
• The Bills drove 60 yards in 12 plays to Thurman Thomas' TD run on the first possession.
• The Pats took a 13-10 lead in the third, driving 75 two Jason Staurovsky field goals in the second. The first came after Larry McGrew recovered Thomas' fumble at the Bills 16. The second came when Don Beebe fumbled the ensuing kickoff.
• Scott Norwood missed a 24-yarder, but atoned with a 31-yarder before the half ended.
• The Pats took a 13-10 lead in the third, driving 75 yards to Patrick Egu's TD. The Pats ran all 11 plays.
• The Bills wasted a threat when Brent Williams sacked Kelly and forced a fumble at the Pats 21, but Mark Kelso recovered Hart Lee Dykes' fumble three plays later at the Bills 47. On the next play, Kelly hit James Lofton for 47 yards setting up Larry Kinnebrew's TD run on the first play of the fourth quarter.
• Carlton Bailey then intercepted Grogan at the Pats 39. Five plays later, Kelly fired a TD to Thomas.
• Three plays after the kickoff, Grogan hit Dykes for a TD. After a punt, the Pats drove 63 yards to a Staurovsky field goal to get within 24-23. Then, on the first play after the kickoff, Maurice Hurst intercepted Kelly and ran it in for a TD. And on the next series, Gary Jeter sacked Kelly, forced a fumble and Johnny Rembert recovered to set up Staurovsky's clinching field goal.

QUOTES

• Marv Levy: "I didn't feel that that edge of concentration was there while we were preparing for New England. I told them about it, and I didn't like it. We ain't so hot. When we went up 24-13, we started to pack up the equipment bags."
• Fred Smerlas: "We can't afford to slip up anymore. If we do we might be watching the playoffs on television."
• Jim Kelly on Hurst's interception: "It was just a miscommunication between me and James. I thought he was going to hook in and he hooked outside. It was a timing pattern and I just threw to where he wasn't. It wasn't James' fault, their guy just happened to be in the right place. This one is really hard to swallow. Maybe we're not as good as we think we are."
• Shane Conlan: "To have them run the ball on us like that was very upsetting. They just shoved it down our throats. I don't know what it is when we play on the road. It's got to be a mental thing because we're just not the same team. We're the same team, it's the same players. Hopefully we'll snap out of it."

WEEK 11 GAMES	
Cinc 42, Det 7	GB 21, SF 17
Hou 23, LAR 7	Mia 17, Dal 14
Phil 10, Minn 9	NO 26, Atl 17
Rams 37, Phoe 14	Pitt 20, SD 17
NYG 15, Sea 3	TB 32, Chi 31
Ind 27, NYJ 10	Den 14, Wash 10
KC 10, Clev 10 (OT)	

Bills	7	3	0	14	-	24
Patriots	0	6	7	20	-	33

Attendance at Sullivan Stadium - 49,663

Buf: Thomas 3 run (Norwood kick), 9:52
NE: FG Staurovsky 34, 4:28
NE: FG Staurovsky 24, 7:56
Buf: FG Norwood 31, 14:25
NE: Egu 15 run (Staurovsky kick), 9:23
Buf: Kinnebrew 1 run (Norwood kick), :02
Buf: Thomas 25 pass from Kelly (Norwood kick), 6:14
NE: Dykes 14 pass from Grogan (Staurovsky kick), 7:15
NE: FG Staurovsky 34, 11:54
NE: Hurst 16 interception return (Staurovsky kick), 12:11
NE: FG Staurovsky 38, 14:47

	BUF	NE
First downs	24	20
Rushing yds	84	192
Passing yds	340	167
Punts-avg	4-34.0	4-33.3
Fumbles-lost	4-4	3-1
Penalties-yds	8-89	6-33
Poss. time	30:50	29:10

BILLS LEADERS: Rushing - Thomas 22-73, Kinnebrew 5-10, Kelly 1-1; **Passing** - Kelly 21-41-2 - 356; **Receiving** - Reed 6-107, Thomas 6-98, Beebe 4-49, Lofton 2-58, Harmon 1-22, McKeller 1-15, Metzelaars 1-7.

PATRIOTS LEADERS: Rushing - Stephens 23-126, Perryman 13-48, Egu 2-18; **Passing** - Grogan 12-26-3 - 167; **Receiving** - Stephens 4-76, Dykes 3-53, James 3-25, Sievers 2-13.

NOTES

• The Bills avenged their AFC Championship Game loss to the Bengals with an impressive victory.
• Marv Levy fired up the team the night before the game by showing them a tape of the Bengals celebrating that victory. It was the Bills first win over Cincinnati since 1983, a span of four games.
• Andre Reed went over 1,000 yards receiving, the first Bill since Frank Lewis in 1981 to do it.
• Darryl Talley recorded the 500th tackle of his career. James Lofton started his first game as a Bill.
• Scott Norwood passed O.J. Simpson and became the team's all-time leading scorer.
• Shane Conlan intercepted Boomer Esiason at the Bills 21 to stop the first possession. The Bills then drove 73 yards in 17 plays to a Norwood field goal, converting three third downs along the way.
• Two plays after the kickoff, James Brooks fumbled, but two plays later, Larry Kinnebrew gave it back.
• Midway through the second quarter, Jim Kelly hit Andre Reed for a TD. Thurman Thomas had runs of 14 and 19 yards on the six-play, 56-yard drive. On the final play of the half, a Jim Breech field goal was nullified by a false start penalty and because the play was an untimed down, the Bengals couldn't rekick. It was learned later that officials made an error and the Bengals should have gotten a second chance.
• On the second play of the second half, Ray Bentley forced Brooks to fumble and Mark Kelso recovered at the Bengals 34. Three plays later, Ronnie Harmon made a 42-yard TD reception on third-and-eight.
• The Bengals got that back, driving 73 yards in 11 plays to Stanford Jennings' TD run. Esiason completed a 20-yard pass to Tim McGee on fourth-and-six from the Bills 31.

• The Bills put away the game with a 10-play, 72-yard drive to Butch Rolle's TD catch. Don Beebe caught a third-and eight pass and Thomas recovered his own fumble to keep the drive going.

QUOTES

• Bruce Smith on watching the tape of the Bengals: "It was a total package of them shooting their mouths off. This is the NFL, you don't run off at the mouth. You've got to be smarter than that. We were so fired up, we could have played them in street clothes."
• Fred Smerlas on the tape: "Everyone was pretty emotional. It was the most excited I've ever seen the guys before a game. I mean they were all pumped up. Everyone started growling."
• Bengals quarterback Boomer Esiason on the disallowed field goal: "It's a no-win situation. If they give us the three points, there's 80,000 looking for that guy's (referee Red Cashion) car. If he doesn't give us the points, there's only 55 guys looking for his car. You have to remember that turnabout is fair play. We had them twice in Cincinnati last year and they've been anxiously awaiting this game. They are awfully tough at home."
• Kent Hull: "It's too bad we can't play inspired football like this all the time."
• Marv Levy: "Our players bounced back, played magnificently, played their hearts out and deserved to win today. It was a very big win for us."

Bengals	0	0	7	0	-	7
Bills	3	7	7	7	-	24

Attendance at Rich Stadium - 80,074

Buf: FG Norwood 24, 10:31
Buf: Reed 19 pass from Kelly (Norwood kick), 7:56
Buf: Harmon 42 pass from Kelly (Norwood kick), 1:41
Cin: Jennings 5 run (Breech kick), 11:05
Buf: Rolle 1 pass from Kelly (Norwood kick), 4:05

	BUF	CIN
First downs	18	16
Rushing yds	228	165
Passing yds	117	133
Punts-avg	4-35.0	4-36.0
Fumbles-lost	3-2	3-2
Penalties-yds	5-35	3-15
Poss. time	34:39	25:21

BILLS LEADERS: Rushing - Thomas 26-100, Kinnebrew 15-66, Harmon 2-12, Reed 1-23, Kelly 1-15, Davis 2-12; **Passing** - Kelly 10-15-0 - 123; **Receiving** - Thomas 3-30, Johnson 2-8, Harmon 1-42, Reed 1-19, Davis 1-13, Beebe 1-10, Rolle 1-1.
BENGALS LEADERS: Rushing - Brooks 20-105, Taylor 2-22, Esiason 4-18, McGee 1-11, Jennings 3-9; **Passing** - Esiason 11-26-1 - 136; **Receiving** - McGee 5-89, Riggs 2-16, Jennings 1-14, Holman 1-11, Hillary 1-6, Brown 1-0.

WEEK 12 GAMES	
Det 13, Clev 10	Phil 27, Dal 0
NYJ 27, Atl 7	Wash 38, Chi 14
KC 34, Hou 0	GB 20, Minn 19
LAR 24, NE 21	Pitt 34, Mia 14
Ind 10, SD 6	Den 41, Sea 14
TB 14, Phoe 13	SF 34, NYG 24
Rams 20, NO 17 (OT)	

STANDINGS: TWELFTH WEEK

AFC EAST	W	L	T	CENTRAL	W	L	T	WEST	W	L	T	NFC EAST	W	L	T	CENTRAL	W	L	T	WEST	W	L	T
Buffalo	8	4	0	Cleveland	7	4	1	Denver	10	2	0	NY Giants	9	3	0	Minnesota	7	5	0	San Fran	10	2	0
Miami	7	5	0	Houston	7	5	0	Raiders	6	6	0	Philadelphia	8	4	0	Green Bay	7	5	0	LA Rams	8	4	0
Indianapolis	6	6	0	Cincinnati	6	6	0	Kan. City	5	6	1	Washington	6	6	0	Chicago	6	6	0	N.Orleans	6	6	0
New England	4	8	0	Pittsburgh	6	6	0	Seattle	4	8	0	Phoenix	5	7	0	Tampa Bay	5	7	0	Atlanta	3	9	0
NY Jets	3	9	0					San Diego	4	8	0	Dallas	1	11	0	Detroit	3	9	0				

GAME 13 - Monday, Dec. 4, 1989 - SEAHAWKS 17, BILLS 16

Bills	0	10	6	0	-	16
Seahawks	10	0	0	7	-	17

Attendance at the Kingdome - 57,682

Sea: FG Johnson 29, 3:56
Sea: Warner 1 run (Largent run), 8:04
Buf: Reed 61 pass from Kelly (Norwood kick), 2:08
Buf: FG Norwood 32, 13:52
Buf: FG Norwood 40, 2:47
Buf: FG Norwood 43, 8:20
Sea: Williams 51 pass from Krieg (Johnson kick), 9:22

	BUF	SEA
First downs	11	22
Rushing yds	97	78
Passing yds	135	277
Punts-avg	6-41.3	5-38.8
Fumbles-lost	1-1	2-0
Penalties-yds	6-36	2-15
Poss. time	26:14	33:44

BILLS LEADERS: **Rushing** - Thomas 21-79, Kinnebrew 6-14, Kelly 2-4; **Passing** - Kelly 10-23-1 - 144; **Receiving** - Reed 2-77, McKeller 2-26, Kinnebrew 2-21, Lofton 1-10, Harmon 1-6, Metzelaars 1-6, Thomas 1-(-2).

SEAHAWKS LEADERS: **Rushing** - Warner 16-57, Williams 10-23, Rodriquez 1-0, Krieg 2-(-2); **Passing** - Krieg 20-40-2 - 298; **Receiving** - Williams 5-80, Blades 5-66, Warner 5-55, Clark 2-14, McNeal 1-48, Largent 1-24, Skansi 1-11.

NOTES

• The Bills suffered another road loss to an inferior team as John L. Williams scored with 5:38 left and Jim Kelly, suffering a terrible performance, couldn't engineer a comeback.
• Andre Reed became the Bills' all-time leading receiver, passing Elbert Dubenion (296 catches).
• The Bills' record on *Monday Night Football* fell to 6-11.
• Seattle grabbed a quick 10-0 lead in the first 8:04 of the game. Norm Johnson made a field goal to cap the opening possession. After a Bills punt, Dave Krieg threw 48 yards to Travis McNeal, setting up Curt Warner's one-yard TD that capped a six-play, 63-yard possession. A bad snap aborted the PAT kick, but holder Steve Largent was able to run in the ball for the conversion.
• Nate Odomes' interception later in the first quarter went for naught, but early in the second quarter, Reed caught a short pass, broke three tackles and sprinted to the end zone to complete a 61-yard play.
• The Bills got a break later in the second when Harper Le Bel's snap sailed over punter Ruben Rodriquez' head. Rodriquez fell on the ball at the Seattle 10. But the Bills couldn't get a TD and settled for a field goal.
• Art Still intercepted Krieg in the third and that resulted

in Scott Norwood's second field goal.
• A short Rodriquez punt gave the Bills a drive start at the Seattle 43 and Norwood made his third field goal.
• Mickey Sutton's 26-yard punt return to the Seattle 48 was wasted when Norwood missed a 48-yard field goal with 6:02 left. Three plays later, Williams scored the winning TD.
• The Bills next series ended when Larry Kinnebrew fumbled after catching a pass and M.L. Johnson recovered for Seattle. The Seahawks ran out the final 3:57, earning three first downs.

QUOTES

• Seahawks coach Chuck Knox: "You must make plays to win football games and we made some plays. We've played hard all year, but we hadn't been making plays."
• Pete Metzelaars: "We should have won this stupid game. We let them hang in there, then boom, we never put them away. Of course we're concerned. There's no excuse for playing the way we do on the road. You tell us."
• Ray Bentley: "It's the same old story, we're our own worst enemy."
• Jim Kelly: "We have to execute better. It doesn't matter where you play, you've got to get the job done. Tonight, we played like crap. This game was sitting there for us on a silver platter. I deserve a lot of the blame. The defense gave us good field position and we didn't capitalize."
• Fred Smerlas: "There's no way in the world we should lose a game like that. You can't have guys throw dink passes for big plays. We have to go for the jugular when we get teams down. We've got the knife at their throat and we let them get away."

WEEK 13 GAMES

Cinc 21, Clev 0	GB 17, TB 16
Hou 23, Pitt 16	NE 22, Ind 16
Rams 35, Dal 31	KC 26, Mia 21
Det 21, NO 14	NYJ 20, SD 17
Phil 24, NYG 17	SF 23, Atl 10
Wash 29, Phoe 10	Minn 27, Chi 16
LAR 16, Den 13 (OT)	

GAME 14 - Sunday, Dec. 10, 1989 - SAINTS 22, BILLS 19

Saints	13	3	3	3	-	22
Bills	0	12	7	0	-	19

Attendance at Rich Stadium - 70,037

NO: Tice 12 pass from Fourcade (kick failed), 2:18
NO: Hilliard 54 pass from Fourcade (Andersen kick), 9:00
Buf: Lofton 42 pass from Kelly (kick blocked), :05
NO: FG Andersen 31, 4:18
Buf: FG Norwood 43, 7:30
Buf: FG Norwood 48, 14:52
Buf: Metzelaars 2 pass from Kelly (Norwood kick), :47
NO: FG Andersen 26, 4:58
NO: FG Andersen 22, 13:07

	BUF	NO
First downs	16	21
Rushing yds	75	149
Passing yds	204	287
Punts-avg	4-33.0	2-39.5
Fumbles-lost	1-1	2-1
Penalties-yds	2-15	4-25
Poss. time	25:47	34:13

BILLS LEADERS: **Rushing** - Thomas 16-40, Kinnebrew 7-27, Kelly 1-8, Davis 1-0; **Passing** - Kelly 17-35-3 - 211; **Receiving** - Reed 4-35, Thomas 4-51, McKeller 2-40, Harmon 2-15, Metzelaars 2-14, Lofton 1-42, Beebe 1-8, Johnson 1-6.
SAINTS LEADERS: **Rushing** - Hilliard 32-97, Jordan 4-34, Fourcade 4-14, Heyward 1-4; **Passing** - Fourcade 15-27-1 - 302; **Receiving** - E. Martin 4-100, Perriman 4-96, Hilliard 3-55, Tice 2-20, Hill 1-23, Brenner 1-8.

WEEK 14 GAMES

Minn 43, Atl 17	Phil 20, Dal 10
Det 27, Chi 17	KC 21, GB 3
NYG 14, Den 7	LAR 16, Phoe 14
Pitt 13, NYJ 0	Wash 26, SD 21
Sea 24, Cinc 17	Hou 20, TB 17
Mia 31, NE 10	SF 30, Rams 27
Ind 23, Clev 17 (OT)	

NOTES

• John Fourcade, starting his first NFL non-strike game, killed the Bills on a snowy day that hindered Buffalo's offense far more than the supposed warm-weather Saints.
• The Bills' streak of 16 straight home sellouts ended.
• Scott Norwood missed a PAT, his first after 118 straight successes.
• Cornelius Bennett missed his third straight game due to a knee injury suffered against the Pats.
• Pat Swilling intercepted Jim Kelly on the second play of the game and returned it to the 11. Fourcade then hit Mike Tice for a TD on a third-and-11 play. A mishandled snap foiled the PAT.
• On the next series, Rickey Jackson sacked Kelly, forced a fumble and James Geathers recovered at the Saints 33. Five plays later, Fourcade scrambled out of the pocket, then found Dalton Hilliard who went 54 yards for the TD and a 13-0 lead.
• On the first play of the second quarter, Kelly hit James Lofton for a TD, but the PAT was blocked. The Saints answered with an eight-play, 54-yard drive to Morten Andersen's field goal. The key play was a 34-yard pass to Eric Martin.
• The Bills got that back on the ensuing series, moving into position for Scott Norwood's field goal.
• After an Andersen miss from the 41, the Bills pulled to within 16-12 with eight seconds left in the half on a Norwood field goal. Kelly misfired on five of his last six passes as the drive stalled.
• Gene Atkins muffed the second-half kickoff and Mickey Sutton recovered at the 2, setting up Pete Metzelaars' TD reception. but the Saints came right back to tie on an Andersen field goal, the key play a 33-yard pass to Brett Perriman to the Bills 11.
• Nate Odomes' interception and Leon Seals' fumble recovery were wasted as the offense failed to move. After Seals' play, Toi Cook intercepted Kelly at the Saints 15.

New Orleans then drove 81 yards in 14 plays to Andersen's winning field goal with 1:53 left. Fourcade hit Martin for 26 on third-and-12.
• Two plays after the kickoff, Brett Maxie intercepted Kelly to kill any rally possibility.

QUOTES

• Marv Levy: "I think this loss was devastating. It was a chance to come within the magic number of one, whatever that is, to win the division. It's a defeat, not a surrender. And no, we're not changing quarterbacks."
• Leon Seals: "Right now, I'm just at the lowest. I don't think I can get any lower."
• Jim Kelly: "I don't know what's wrong. I don't have the answers."
• Saints safety Brett Maxie on Kelly: "Something we noticed watching film on this guy is that once he wants a receiver, he goes to him the whole way. He doesn't look you off. I think it's a big fault of his."

STANDINGS: FOURTEENTH WEEK

AFC EAST	W	L	T	CENTRAL	W	L	T	WEST	W	L	T	NFC EAST	W	L	T	CENTRAL	W	L	T	WEST	W	L	T
Buffalo	8	6	0	Houston	9	5	0	Denver	10	4	0	NY Giants	10	4	0	Minnesota	9	5	0	San Fran	12	2	0
Miami	8	6	0	Cleveland	7	6	1	Raiders	8	6	0	Philadelphia	10	4	0	Green Bay	8	6	0	LA Rams	9	5	0
Indianapolis	7	7	0	Cincinnati	7	7	0	Kan. City	7	6	1	Washington	8	6	0	Chicago	6	8	0	N.Orleans	7	7	0
New England	5	9	0	Pittsburgh	7	7	0	Seattle	6	8	0	Phoenix	5	9	0	Tampa Bay	5	9	0	Atlanta	3	11	0
NY Jets	4	10	0					San Diego	4	10	0	Dallas	1	13	0	Detroit	5	9	0				

GAME 15 - Sunday, Dec. 17, 1989 - 49ERS 21, BILLS 10

NOTES

• Knowing Miami had lost earlier in the day, the Bills had a chance to clinch the AFC East, but a 21-point explosion in a 5:40 span bridging the third and fourth quarters carried the 49ers to victory.

• Joe Montana sat out the game with a rib injury and Steve Young was adequate in his place.

• It was the Bills fifth road loss in a row. In those five games, the Bills had 21 turnovers.

• Mark Kelso's end zone interception in the first quarter ended a 49er possession. The Bills then marched 75 yards in eight plays to Scott Norwood's field goal. Andre Reed caught a 37-yard pass, James Lofton a 15-yarder and Larry Kinnebrew carried three times for 18 yards on the drive.

• In the second quarter, a 29-yard pass to Jerry Rice put the 49ers on the Bills 20, but sacks by Scott Radecic and Darryl Talley pushed the 49ers out of field goal range.

• The game turned quickly in the third. The 49ers drove from their 1 to the Bills 34 before Kelso stopped the series with an interception at the 10. But three plays later, Bill Romanowski intercepted Jim Kelly and returned it to the 23. Four running plays later, Roger Craig scored.

• Keith DeLong then forced Ronnie Harmon to fumble the ensuing kickoff and Antonio Goss recovered at the Bills 46. Seven plays later, Young ran in from the 2 for a 14-3 lead.

• Three plays after the kickoff, a Kelly pass bounced off Reed's hands and Ronnie Lott intercepted and returned it 28 yards to the 8. On the first play, Young hit Rice in the corner of the end zone for a TD.

• The Bills answered that with a 13-play, 78-yard drive to Kelly's TD run. Kelly completed seven straight passes for 56 yards, then hit Reed for seven on fourth-and-four from the 16.

• After a punt, the Bills wasted a chance when Don Griffin forced Reed to fumble. Mike Walter recovered.

QUOTES

• Marv Levy: "We still control our own fate. We find out next week if we're going to be division champs or not. Do they (his players) deserve the title? If they win next week, they're deserving. Is there some other team that you think is more deserving? I think our team is drowning in analysis. What I'm trying to do is lift that off our team. I'm up to here with analysis." (About Kelly's performance and slump): "I have no explanations."

• Pete Metzelaars: "The playoffs start on Saturday for the Buffalo Bills. We've got to go out and play the Jets like it's our last game."

• Fred Smerlas: "We go out there and give them Christmas gifts before it's Christmas. It's stupid. We deserve to lose."

• Thurman Thomas: "We played as a unit and we haven't been playing like that for a few weeks. For a team that's had as much controversy as we've had lately, this is a great relief. I don't think you're going to hear anymore about finger pointing."

• Ray Bentley: "We're not discouraged, we're excited. It's a one-game season now. We lost today, but I think we came away feeling very positive about ourselves."

Bills	3	0	0	7 - 10
49ers	0	0	7	14 - 21

Attendance at Candlestick Park - 60,927

Buf: FG Norwood 23, 13:46
SF: Craig 1 run (Cofer kick), 12:07
SF: Young 2 run (Cofer kick), 1:30
SF: Rice 8 pass from Young (Cofer kick), 2:47
Buf: Kelly 1 run (Norwood kick), 7:11

	BUF	SF
First downs	16	18
Rushing yds	46	149
Passing yds	255	134
Punts-avg	5-34.6	5-37.0
Fumbles-lost	2-2	0-0
Penalties-yds	4-28	3-25
Poss. time	24:21	35:39

BILLS LEADERS: Rushing - Kinnebrew 8-29, Kelly 4-10, Thomas 6-7; **Passing** - Kelly 26-42-3 - 265; **Receiving** - Reed 10-115, Thomas 8-62, Harmon 4-33, Beebe 3-40, Lofton 1-15.

49ERS LEADERS: Rushing - Craig 25-105, Flagler 8-23, Rathman 2-13, Henderson 3-10, Young 5- (-2); **Passing** - Young 9-19-2 - 166; **Receiving** - Rice 3-46, Rathman 2-38, Taylor 2-30, Henderson 1-40, Craig 1-12.

WEEK 15 GAMES

NYG 15, Dal 0	Den 37, Phoe 0
GB 40, Chi 28	Cinc 61, Hou 7
Ind 42, Mia 13	Rams 38, NYJ 14
SD 20, KC 13	Det 33, TB 7
Wash 31, Atl 30	Sea 23, LAR 17
NO 30, Phil 20	Pitt 28, NE 10
Clev 23, Minn 17 (OT)	

GAME 16 - Saturday, Dec. 23, 1989 - BILLS 37, JETS 0

NOTES

• The Bills turned in a dominating performance when they needed it most and clinched the AFC East.

• It was the most lopsided victory in Bills history and earned them a playoff date with Cleveland.

• Andre Reed finished with single-season team records for receptions (88) and yards (1,312).

• The crowd was the smallest to see a Jets game since the Bills beat the Jets before 5,826 at the Polo Grounds in 1963.

• On their first possession, the Bills drove 76 yards in 15 plays to a Scott Norwood field goal. Jim Kelly completed two third-down passes and Larry Kinnebrew carried four times for 20 yards.

• Pat Leahy had a 29-yard field goal blocked by Darryl Talley early in the second quarter. Three plays later, Kelly was intercepted by Alex Gordon, but four plays after that, Jeff Wright recovered a Tony Eason fumble. Keith McKeller's 31-yard reception then keyed a seven-play, 62-yard drive to Kinnebrew's TD.

• Kelly hit James Lofton for a TD early in the third, but holder John Kidd fumbled the snap and the PAT missed.

• After another Jets punt, the Bills drove 88 yards in nine plays to Ronnie Harmon's TD reception on third-and-10. Thurman Thomas had an 18-yard run and Reed gained eight on a third-and-seven reverse.

• On the first play after the kickoff, Cornelius Bennett intercepted Eason, setting up Thomas' TD run.

• The final score came after a 12-play, 85-yard drive as Kenneth Davis broke free for a TD run.

QUOTES

• Ralph Wilson: "I warned people before the season that it wasn't going to be easy, but it's difficult to convince passionate fans of that. People want you to win all 16 games and that just doesn't happen."

• Bruce Smith: "We didn't do a pretty job of winning it, but we did and that's all that matters."

• Kent Hull: "We needed to go out and beat up badly on somebody to get our confidence back."

• Andre Reed on Jim Kelly: "Sometimes things don't go well for him, but he's the type of person who can shake adversity off. I think he's back to making big plays. A lot of people started counting us out after we lost three games in a row. I think the character of this team showed today."

• Marv Levy: "We've been in first place for 32 straight weeks. Sometimes it's hard to please people. We've won two straight division championships, something that hasn't been done here since the 1960s. I think this team deserves a lot of credit. They won a division championship by earning it all the way."

• Darryl Talley: "I didn't want to sit home during the holidays saying 'Wow, we let a golden opportunity slip away.' Anytime you have a team where people expect so much out of you, when guys falter or stumble, those people say 'Wait a minute, I thought you were supposed to be world-beaters.' Everybody loses sight of everything then."

Bills	3	7	20	7 - 37
Jets	0	0	0	0 - 0

Attendance at Giants Stadium - 21,148

Buf: FG Norwood 26, 10:34
Buf: Kinnebrew 1 run (Norwood kick), 13:53
Buf: Lofton 25 pass from Kelly (kick failed), 4:11
Buf: Harmon 25 pass from Kelly (Norwood kick), 10:21
Buf: Thomas 3 run (Norwood kick), 14:21
Buf: Davis 17 run (Norwood kick), 12:16

	BUF	NYJ
First downs	28	11
Rushing yds	233	54
Passing yds	208	146
Punts-avg	2-40.5	7-39.9
Fumbles-lost	0-0	2-1
Penalties-yds	4-30	6-40
Poss. time	35:53	24:07

BILLS LEADERS: Rushing - Kinnebrew 17-91, Thomas 17-73, Davis 5-33, Harmon 3-28, Reich 3-(-3), Reed 1-8, Mueller 1-3, Kelly 1-0; **Passing** - Kelly 13-21-1 - 208; **Receiving** - Reed 6-80, Harmon 3-42, Metzelaars 2-30, McKeller 1-31, Lofton 1-25.

JETS LEADERS: Rushing - Hector 7-27, Vick 6-27, Eason 1-0; **Passing** - Eason 12-22-1 - 125, Mackey 4-10-0 51; **Receiving** - Toon 6-67, Townsell 2-35, Vick 2-13, Epps 1-18, Burkett 1-15, Hector 1-11, Dressel 1-8, Neubert 1-7, Brown 1-2.

WEEK 16 GAMES

Wash 29, Sea 0	Clev 24, Hou 20
SF 26, Chi 0	SD 19, Den 16
Det 31, Atl 24	GB 20, Dal 10
NO 41, Ind 6	KC 27, Mia 24
NYG 34, LAR 17	Rams 24, NE 20
Pitt 31, TB 22	Phil 31, Phoe 14
Minn 29, Cinc 21	

STANDINGS: SIXTEENTH WEEK

AFC EAST	W	L	T	CENTRAL	W	L	T	WEST	W	L	T	NFC EAST	W	L	T	CENTRAL	W	L	T	WEST	W	L	T
Buffalo	9	7	0	Cleveland	9	6	1	Denver	11	5	0	NY Giants	12	4	0	Minnesota	10	6	0	San Fran	14	2	0
Miami	8	8	0	Houston	9	7	0	Kan. City	8	7	1	Philadelphia	11	5	0	Green Bay	10	6	0	LA Rams	11	5	0
Indianapolis	8	8	0	Pittsburgh	9	7	0	Raiders	8	8	0	Washington	10	6	0	Detroit	7	9	0	N.Orleans	9	7	0
New England	5	11	0	Cincinnati	8	8	0	Seattle	7	9	0	Phoenix	5	11	0	Chicago	6	10	0	Atlanta	3	13	0
NY Jets	4	12	0					San Diego	6	10	0	Dallas	1	15	0	Tampa Bay	5	11	0				

403

Bills	7	7	7	9 -	30
Browns	3	14	14	3 -	34

Attendance at Cleveland Stadium - 77,706

Buf: Reed 72 pass from Kelly (Norwood kick), 9:56
Cle: FG Bahr 45, 14:12
Cle: Slaughter 52 pass from Kosar (Bahr kick), 4:33
Buf: Lofton 33 pass from Kelly (Norwood kick), 7:12
Cle: Middleton 3 pass from Kosar (Bahr kick), 14:54
Cle: Slaughter 44 pass from Kosar (Bahr kick), 4:21
Buf: Thomas 6 pass from Kelly (Norwood kick), 10:22
Cle: Metcalf 90 kickoff return (Bahr kick), 10:37
Buf: FG Norwood 30, 1:08
Cle: FG Bahr 47, 8:10
Buf: Thomas 3 pass from Kelly (kick failed), 11:00

	BUF	CLE
First downs	25	18
Rushing yds	49	90
Passing yds	404	235
Punts-avg	3-41.3	3-37.7
Fumbles-lost	2-1	1-1
Penalties-yds	6-35	5-30
Poss. time	25:44	34:16

BUFFALO TACKLES: Conlan 11, Radecic 9, B. Smith 5, Drane 4, Smerlas 4, Talley 4, Kelso 4, Bennett 3, Still 2, Jackson 2, Hagy 2.
CLEVELAND TACKLES: Gash 9, Matthews 8, Johnson 7, Dixon 7, Perry 6, Grayson 5, Wright 5, Baker 3, Hairston 3, Minnifield 2, Lyons 2.

BILLS LEADERS: Rushing - Thomas 10-27, Kinnebrew 7-17, Kelly 1-5; **Passing** - Kelly 28-54-2 - 405; **Receiving** - Thomas 13-150, Reed 6-115, Harmon 4-50, Lofton 3-66, Beebe 1-17, Kinnebrew 1-7; **Kickoff returns** - Beebe 2-53, Harmon 3-52; **Punt returns** - Sutton 1-4.
BROWNS LEADERS: Rushing - Mack 12-62, Redden 6-13, Tillman 1-8, Manoa 3-6, Metcalf 4-2, Langhorne 1-0, Kosar 3-(-1); **Passing** - Kosar 20-29-0 - 251; **Receiving** - Langhorne 6-48, Newsome 4-35, Slaughter 3-114, Middleton 3-12, Mack 2-19, Brennan 1-15, Metcalf 1-8; **Kickoff returns** - Metcalf 4-159, Oliphant 2-21; **Punt returns** - McNeil 1-0.

NOTES

• The Bills suffered a heartbreaking wild-card playoff loss as Clay Matthews' interception at the 1-yard-line with two seconds left to play prevented a come-from-behind victory.
• On the play before, Ronnie Harmon dropped what would have been a sure TD pass.
• Thurman Thomas tied an NFL playoff record previously held by San Diego's Kellen Winslow as he caught 13 passes. He totaled 150 yards receiving, including 123 on 11 second-half receptions.
• Jim Kelly compiled the first 400-yard passing game of his NFL career and he set Buffalo playoff records for attempts (54), completions (28), yards (405) and TD passes (four). It could have been better, but he was hindered by nine dropped passes.
• The Bills set team single-game playoff records for first downs (24), passing first downs (20), total yards (453), total plays (73), net passing (404), and most points allowed on defense (34).
• Thomas and Andre Reed became the first Bills duo to top 100 yards receiving in the same playoff game.
• Don Beebe endured a scary moment when he was upended in the second quarter and landed on his head like a pogo stick. He walked off the injury after staying on the ground for a few minutes.
• The Bills opened the game using the shotgun formation, used plenty of three-receiver sets and used a no-huddle offense for almost the entire fourth quarter with Kelly calling his own plays.
• Leonard Smith and Ray Bentley missed the game due to injuries. Dwight Drane and Scott Radecic started.
• Eric Metcalf's 90-yard kickoff return, against the NFL's No. 1-ranked kickoff coverage team, was the Browns' first post-season TD kick return ever.
• The Bills punted on their first series. The Browns then drove to the Bills 28, but Matt Bahr missed a 45-yard field goal. Two plays later, Andre Reed turned a quick slant into a 72-yard TD pass.
• The Browns answered with a 10-play, 39-yard drive to Bahr's 45-yard field goal.
• After a Bills punt, Cleveland took the lead as Bernie

Kosar hit Webster Slaughter, who beat Nate Odomes, for a 52-yard TD on third-and-14. An offsides penalty on Darryl Talley had kept the drive alive.
• Five plays after the kickoff, James Lofton caught a 33-yard TD pass to give the Bills a 14-10 lead.
• The teams traded punts with the Browns getting the ball at their own 45 with 4:53 left in the half. Kosar hit Reggie Langhorne for nine on third-and-eight from the 47. Kevin Mack added runs of 15 and 12 yards and on first-and-goal from the 3, Kosar flipped a TD pass to a wide open Ron Middleton after a great play-fake.
• On the Bills' third play of the third, Mark Harper intercepted Kelly at the Bills 46. Three plays later on third-and-eight, the Bills blew a coverage and Slaughter was all alone for a 44-yard TD pass.
• The Bills got to the Browns 40 before Larry Kinnebrew lost a fumble to Felix Wright. But on the next play, Mark Kelso recovered a Mack fumble at the Browns 21. Kelly hit Thomas for 15 yards to the 4 on a third-and-eight play and then Thomas caught a TD pass to get the Bills to within 24-21.
• Metcalf then ripped right through the middle for his 90-yard kickoff return.
• The Bills drove 68 yards in 11 plays to Norwood's field goal early in the fourth, the key play a 27-yard reception by Thomas on third-and-10 that put the ball on the Browns 21.
• Cleveland responded with an 11-play, 38-yard march to Bahr's 47-yard field goal for a 34-24 lead with 6:50 left. But the Bills refused to quit. Kelly completed seven of eight passes (including his last six) on a 77-yard march that culminated in his three-yard TD pass to Thomas. Thomas caught five of the passes for 43 yards and Harmon caught two for 34. However, the poor field condition caused Norwood to miss the extra point, which prevented the Bills from pulling within a field goal and affected their strategy.
• The defense held on three plays, including Darryl Talley's sack of Kosar, and Brian Wagner's 36-yard punt went out of bounds at the Bills 26 with 2:41 left.
• Kelly hit Harmon for nine and seven to get to the two-minute warning. After three incompletions created fourth-and-10, Kelly fired a 17-yard bullet to Beebe to the Browns 41 with 1:16 left. A nine-yard Thomas reception was sandwiched between two incompletions and on fourth-and-one, Kelly hit Reed for 10 to the 22. Kelly then spiked the ball with 34 seconds left. After an incompletion brought up third-and-10, he hit Thomas for 11 to the 11 and he quickly spiked the ball again with 14 seconds remaining. Then came the ill-fated pass to Harmon in the left corner of the end zone. Harmon beat Hanford Dixon, but short-armed the pass and it bounced off his hands. On the next play, Kelly tried to hit Thomas at the goal line, but Matthews intervened.

QUOTES

• Thurman Thomas: "I'd rather lose a game 34-0 because when you lose like that, you know you never had a chance, but we had a chance. It really hurts to lose a close game like this." (On the final interception): "I thought I was open for a second. Jim read the coverage before the snap, which a quarterback is supposed to do, and he thought I'd be open. Give Matthews credit, he made a great play." (On a comment Ronnie Harmon made to him in the huddle after Harmon dropped the TD pass): "Ronnie said 'If he (Kelly) had looked at me a little bit quicker' he would have scored because he was wide open. Jim looked a little bit too long the other way and by the time he looked (Harmon) was almost out of the end zone. I thought Jim played a great game."
• Browns linebacker Clay Matthews: "They had been going to him (Thomas) so I kind of figured they were going to do it again."
• Browns coach Bud Carson on the Bills offense: "That's the best game plan I've seen all year (from the Bills). They did an outstanding job of coming in here with a completely different mixture. They surprised us, caught us off guard. I don't think I've been around a football team that's played as poorly defensively as we did today. But I want to say again, the Bills' game plan was the best I've seen all year."
• Scott Norwood on the missed extra point: "The field was icy and hard and my cleats weren't digging in. That area of the field was the toughest. I compensated the best

I could. I shortened my steps to the ball. It worked out well during the pregame and then during the game up until that particular kick."
• Jim Kelly, who refused to talk to the media, when asked to do so: "No! I'm not talking. How many times have I got to say it. That makes 30 guys who have asked me. Geez!"
• Will Wolford on Kelly: "I thought he played brilliantly." (On Kelly's frame of mind before the final drive): "What did I see? I saw the same Jim Kelly I've always seen. There's a look of confidence, a look of a man ready to play his game. There wasn't a whole lot to say in the huddle. We knew what we had to do."
• Jim Ritcher on the final drive: "I thought it was going to be another Miami. Jim was real confident, he was in charge. Like always, the general leading us down the field."
• Fred Smerlas on Kelly: "He would have thrown for 600 yards if we hadn't dropped all those passes. I had my eyes closed on the final play. I figured if the crowd had booed, we scored and if they cheered, it was over." (On his future): "The big Greek's not going to dance forever, he's 32 years old, has been in the NFL 11 seasons at a position that has chewed up and spit out a lot of players in half the time. So this might have been my last dance. Maybe it was Art Still's and Joe Devlin's last shot, too."
• Marv Levy on Kelly: "He didn't have anything to prove to me. I think the expectations (of fans and media) are too great. He's not going to succeed on every pass, every game. Jim Kelly, to me, is an outstanding quarterback with a big heart. I thought he performed extremely well. If we had won the game, he might have received more credit than he deserved because the whole team played pretty well, particularly the offensive line which did a good job pass protecting against a good pass-rushing team." (On Metcalf's return): "That might have been the biggest play in a game of big plays. When we scored and they turned around and took that touchdown away from us, they got the momentum back."
• Steve Tasker: "Special teams are a definite difference in games like this. Teams are scouted so well and game plans so well-developed so when you can get breaks like those (Metcalf's return, Norwood's missed extra point), it really helps. We knew Metcalf was a great returner and we just didn't stay in our lanes well enough to cover on that play. That was definitely the play that broke the game for them and I'm disappointed it happened against our special teams."
• Darryl Talley: "It's going to take a long time to get over this one. You work your tail off for six months to get a chance to go to the Super Bowl. To get this close and lose, it's pretty tough to take."

At A Glance
1990

Jan. 7 – Fred Smerlas reflected on the tumultuous 1989 season by saying: "The guys who come in here now are guaranteed money. What do they have to care about? When we began playing, we got guaranteed crap. And as money changes, people change. There are just no tough guys around anymore. No matter what happens to me and Joe (Devlin), I think we can feel good about knowing we've been through the good times and the bad times here. We loved the Buffalo Bills. The guys who come in here now don't give a damn about anything."

Jan. 8 – Art Still packed up his belongings and walked out of Rich Stadium likely for the last time. He said he was upset about his decreased playing time during the season and accused Marv Levy of having a double standard in dealing with team members. "I don't think I have a future here," he said. "I don't want to come back to the environment I just came out of. In my 12 years of playing, I was never in a situation where you're in for two series and out for two. All season it's been bugging me. I always thought Marv was a pretty straight-up guy. If there was a problem, it should have been brought to my attention. But he said things behind my back. If you're going to have rules, they should be for everybody."

Jan. 11 – In his post-season press conference, Marv Levy indicated that he wanted the Bills' locker room closed to the media in 1990. "Nobody (in other professions) lets people into their workplace everyday to sample the mood of their workers," Levy explained. "I really feel we prepare better when other people aren't in there." Levy also pointed to four areas the team had to improve on for 1990: Pass rush (sacks were down to 38 from 46 in 1988), takeaway/giveaway ratio (Bills were -5), blocked kicks and kickoffs. Also, Levy said he still had high regard for Art Still and felt bad that Still said what he said.

Jan. 30 – Joe Devlin and Art Still were informed that they wouldn't be re-signed by the Bills.

Feb. 1 – The Bills released their list of unprotected players who would be eligible to sign with other teams during the Plan B free agency period and the big names were Joe Devlin, Art Still, Fred Smerlas, Ronnie Harmon, Derrick Burroughs, Richard Harvey, Flip Johnson, John Kidd, James Lofton, Steve Tasker, Robb Riddick and Tim Vogler.

Feb. 3 – It was reported that Jim Kelly would be signing a contract extension for six years at about $20 million.

Feb. 16 – The NFL announced that it would allow juniors to enter the collegiate draft.

Feb. 22 – Defensive line coach Ted Cottrell resigned to accept the same job with the Phoenix Cardinals.

Feb. 23 – Marv Levy promoted tight ends coach Chuck Dickerson to defensive line coach, replacing Ted Cottrell. He also hired Don Lawrence, a former Bills defensive coordinator, as his offensive quality control/tight ends coach.

Feb. 27 – The NFL announced it would play its 16-game schedule over a 17-week period in 1990 and 1991, affording each team a bye week. It also would eliminate the off week between the confer-

Emotions ran high during the AFC Championship rout over the Raiders as the United States entered the Persian Gulf War during the week leading up to the game.

ence championship games and the Super Bowl.

March 1 – The NFL decided to revise its playoff format, allowing one extra wild-card team in each conference to make the playoffs.

March 12 – At the league meetings in Orlando, Fla., the owners ratified new TV contracts with ABC, NBC, CBS and ESPN and also signed a four-year deal with cable network TNT. The contracts totaled a record $3.6 billion. Also, instant replay survived again, but by the minimum 21-7 vote.

March 13 – Ralph Wilson said that he wanted to become more involved with the day-to-day operation of the Bills. "As I get older, I want to sell off some of the other businesses we've had scattered across the country to try to pull back and restructure," he said. "We're just in too many things. Thirty years ago, it was different. Now, I want to have a little more fun." Wilson and his fellow owners voted for changes to speed up the games, the two most important being reducing the play clock from 30 to 25 seconds and restarting the clock when a player goes out of bounds as soon as the ball is spotted, except for the last two minutes of the first half and the last five minutes of the fourth quarter.

March 14 – Popular punter John Kidd couldn't turn down a $225,000 per year offer from San

Diego and signed with the Chargers, leaving the Bills without a punter.

March 23 – Jim Kelly became the highest-paid player in the NFL, signing a contract worth just over $3 million per season, running through the 1996 season. San Diego signed Ronnie Harmon as a Plan B free agent and New England inked Richard Harvey. WGR radio in Buffalo was awarded the Bills' broadcast rights for four years, beating out WBEN which had owned the rights for all but seven of the team's first 30 years, including the previous 11.

March 27 – The Bills signed their first Plan B free agent, punter Rick Tuten from the Eagles.

March 28 – Fred Smerlas accepted a one-year contract worth $850,000 with San Francisco, thus ending his standout 11-year career with the Bills. "I will always have Buffalo Bills blood in me," Smerlas said. "It's a sad turn of events. My wife's crying, I've been crying. We don't want to leave Buffalo. It really hasn't settled in. It's still hard to believe that I'm no longer a Buffalo Bill. I always wanted it to end with me helping bring a Super Bowl championship to Buffalo."

March 29 – The Bills filled the void created by the loss of Ronnie Harmon by signing Plan B free agent running back Don Smith from Tampa Bay.

April 1 – The Plan B free agency signing period

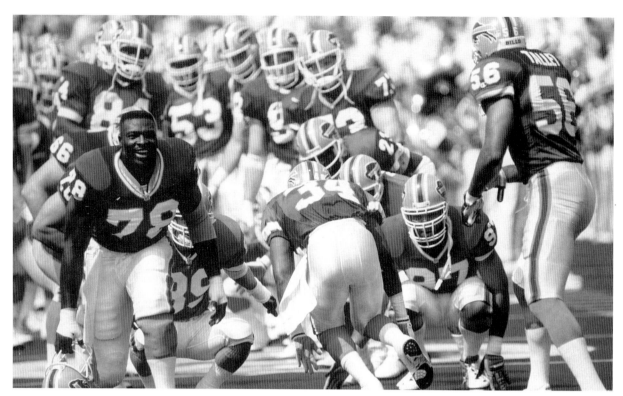

Coming off a heartbreaking playoff loss to Cleveland at the end of 1989, the Bills put their troubles behind them and stormed through their 1990 schedule as a unified team.

ended with 184 players having changed teams.

April 16 – Glenn Deadmond joined the coaching staff as an assistant linebackers coach.

April 22 – The Bills used their No. 1 draft choice, 16th overall, to select Fresno St. cornerback J.D. Williams. They also chose Louisville fullback Carwell Gardner (second), Arizona offensive lineman Glenn Parker (third), LSU running back Eddie Fuller (fourth), UCLA linebacker Marvcus Patton (eighth), UCLA nose tackle Mike Lodish (10th) and NW Louisiana wide receiver Al Edwards (11th). Around the league, Indianapolis acquired the top pick overall from Atlanta in exchange for Andre Rison and Chris Hinton and chose quarterback Jeff George, the Jets took running back Blair Thomas (second), Seattle picked nose tackle Cortez Kennedy (third), Tampa Bay opted for linebacker Keith McCants (fourth), San Diego selected linebacker Junior Seau (fifth), Chicago grabbed safety Mark Carrier (sixth), Detroit picked quarterback Andre Ware (seventh), New England took linebacker Chris Singleton (eighth) and defensive end Ray Agnew (10th), Miami chose offensive tackle Richmond Webb (ninth), the Raiders picked defensive end Anthony Smith (11th), Cincinnati chose linebacker James Francis (12th), New Orleans picked linebacker Renaldo Turnbull (14th), Houston picked linebacker Lamar Lathon (15th), Dallas grabbed running back Emmitt Smith (17th), Green Bay chose linebacker Tony Bennett (18th) and fullback Darrell Thompson (19th), Pittsburgh picked tight end Eric Green (21st), the Giants picked running back Rodney Hampton (24th) and San Francisco opted for running back Dexter Carter (25th).

May 14 – It was reported in *The Buffalo News* by Vic Carucci that Bill Polian, in an unprecedented move, sent a letter to all 12 of the Bills draft picks, advising them that the team was not going to pay any more money on rookies this year than it did in 1989. The letter also included an opening contract offer. "Last year was obscene, and I am not going to go beyond obscene," Polian said. "I've just had

it. The idea that there should be an increase every year and we should accept it is lunacy."

May 16 – The Bills opened minicamp at Rich Stadium.

May 17 – Obviously impressed by the relief performance Frank Reich turned in during 1989, the team signed him to a new five-year deal worth about $500,000 per season.

May 19 – Mini-camp ended with an open workout at Rich Stadium. Afterward, Ralph Wilson said he agreed with Bill Polian's stance on paying rookies. "We think they are getting out of hand and we mean to hold the line on rookie signings," he said. "If a fellow doesn't sign and report to training camp, I don't want him."

July 2 – Fred Smerlas was roasted at the Ramada Renaissance Hotel.

July 5 – Ralph Wilson stated again that the Bills would be needing a new stadium, preferably a dome, when their Rich Stadium lease ran out in 1997. The team postponed a study on the stadium issue to 1991 because the county was too busy with the Buffalo Bisons' bid for a National League franchise, the Buffalo Sabres request for a new arena and the proposal to lure the 1993 World University Games to Buffalo.

July 26 – Andre Reed signed a six-year contract extension worth about $7.5 million, but talks broke down between Bill Polian and the agents for three other stars – Thurman Thomas, Shane Conlan and Will Wolford. The team also announced the signing of rookies J.D. Williams, Glenn Parker, Marvcus Patton and Mike Lodish.

July 27 – Training camp opened at Fredonia State and 11 players failed to report on time, including Thurman Thomas, Shane Conlan and Will Wolford. Because Thomas and Conlan had existing contracts, the Bills could fine them $1,500 for every day of camp they missed.

July 28 – Five of the players who failed to report on time signed deals including veterans Keith McKeller and Kirby Jackson and rookie Carwell Gardner.

July 31 – Safety John Hagy ended his holdout and reported to camp. Meanwhile, Shane Conlan's agent, Ralph Cindrich, expressed concern over the negotiations with Bill Polian. "Buffalo's not the same organization it was last year," he said. "I've done dozens of deals up there in the last four years and I've never seen one with as much emotion as this one. In the past, the negotiations were always on a higher plane. This is a difficult one. There are at least 15 other linebackers who, on the average, would make more than Shane if he were to accept the Bills' offer."

Aug. 2 – After applying for reinstatement to the NFL, Hal Garner was signed by the Bills. He had retired before the 1989 season.

Aug. 4 – Because they weren't going to meet the Cleveland Browns in their annual scrimmage at Edinboro University, the Bills hosted Washington in a scrimmage at Rich Stadium. A crowd of 20,831, paying $3 per ticket, was onhand to see the Redskins win, 27-16. Rookie Marvcus Patton angered Redskins' coach Joe Gibbs when he leveled quarterback Jeff Rutledge during the final 10-play series, injuring the quarterback. There was a no-contact rule in effect for quarterbacks.

Aug. 6 – Butch Rolle ended his holdout and reported to camp.

Aug. 7 – Leonard Burton, slated to start at right guard, suffered a knee sprain that would sideline him until at least midseason, while left guard Jim Ritcher underwent shoulder surgery, sidelining him at least three weeks. With Will Wolford still holding out, the Bills had only two starters in the offensive line, Kent Hull and Howard Ballard. Rookie Glenn Parker was moved to left tackle, Mitch Frerotte to left guard and John Davis to right guard.

Aug. 9 – Bill Polian indicated that negotiations between him and the agents for Thurman Thomas, Shane Conlan and Will Wolford were at the stage where "It's time to move on." And Marv Levy said: "If you have to play without somebody, you do. I'm at the point where I say we may have to play without them."

Aug. 11 – Bill Polian charged agents across the country with collusion, saying none of them were negotiating with NFL teams in an effort to drive salaries up.

Aug. 13 – The Bills opened the preseason at Rich Stadium on ABC's *Monday Night Football* and lost to the New York Giants, 20-6. The Bills announced a season ticket count of 46,037, representing the first decline (47,865 were sold in 1989) since the 1985 season.

Aug. 17 – The Bills traveled to Detroit and lost to the Lions at the Silverdome, 24-13. Earlier in the day, Bill Polian said of Dr. Charles Tucker, the agent for Thurman Thomas: "The man is a charlatan and a fraud. I don't think we can do business with this man. I don't see us signing Thurman Thomas under these circumstances."

Aug. 20 – When told of Bill Polian's remarks, Dr. Charles Tucker replied: "I think he's worse, and he's a liar. I think he's a real punk for saying those things. He hasn't dealt fairly with me. He's acting like a little girl would, running around saying those things."

Aug. 21 – Rookie Eddie Fuller talked about his father, Donald Fuller, an army sergeant stationed in Frankfurt, Germany who was on call and could be summoned at any time to bolster the United States' military effort in Kuwait. "I watch TV everyday and see how it's progressing," he said of the Persian Gulf crisis. "I'm not worried at this point, but I'd be worried if he actually goes."

Aug. 23 – After Thurman Thomas called Bill Polian himself the day before, Thomas, Polian and Dr. Charles Tucker met face-to-face at Rich Stadium, but an agreement could not be worked out.

Aug. 24 – Shane Conlan ended his holdout at 29 days and agreed to a new contract worth just under $1 million per year, making him one of the highest-paid inside linebackers in the NFL.

Aug. 25 – The Bills lost their third straight preseason game, 28-23, to New Orleans at the Superdome. Bill Polian rescinded contract offers that were tendered to Thurman Thomas ($1 million per year over four years) and Will Wolford (three years at $700,000 per year).

Aug. 27 – Thurman Thomas ended his holdout and agreed to a two-year extension worth $1 million per season, taking him through the 1993 season. "I didn't care how long it took," Thomas said of the night-time meeting with Polian and his agent, Dr. Charles Tucker. "I wasn't leaving until we got it done. This was the last day. The terms are great for me. I think I've proven myself over the last two years so I could get this deal."

Aug. 28 – Will Wolford ended his holdout and signed for three years worth $750,000 per year.

Aug. 29 – Fred Smerlas' entertaining autobiography, *By a Nose, The Off-Center Life of Football's Funniest Lineman*, written with Vic Carucci, hit the bookstores.

Aug. 30 – The Bills ended their preseason winless, thanks to a terrible 35-7 loss in Columbia, S.C. to the Bears. "I'm sick and humiliated about how our team played," Marv Levy said angrily. "I apologize to the people here in South Carolina, to Buffalo Bills fans and it damn well isn't going to happen again."

Sept. 4 – One of the Bills moves designed to cut the roster to 47 backfired when waived linebacker Scott Radecic was claimed by the Colts. The Bills were hoping to re-sign Radecic. In all, 11 new faces made the final roster, including eight rookies.

Sept. 6 – After missing the final month of training camp, Darryl Talley and Jim Ritcher were both expected to start the season opener against the Colts. Indianapolis planned to start rookie Jeff George at quarterback, the No. 1 overall pick in the draft.

Sept. 9 – The Bills opened the season with a 26-10 victory over Indianapolis in front of 78,899 at Rich Stadium, as Jim Kelly completed 28 of 37 passes for 283 yards. Cornelius Bennett knocked rookie Jeff George out of the game in the fourth quarter with a vicious open-field hit. Butch Rolle's TD reception was the Bills 1,000th TD in team history and the ball was presented to Ralph Wilson in the locker room after the game.

Sept. 10 – Marv Levy said the Bills would use the no-huddle attack "from time to time, but it will not be our method of operation." Kelly relayed an anecdote from the game Sunday concerning the no-huddle offense: "When we came off the field, the offensive line said 'We're not going to do that again, are we?' and I said, 'No, I think we'll take a break.'"

Sept. 11 – It was reported that Marv Levy had formed a players committee to serve as a liaison between the players and the coaches as a way to deal with internal problems. The group consisted of Jim Kelly, Thurman Thomas, Kent Hull, James Lofton, Pete Metzelaars, Bruce Smith, Mark Kelso, Darryl Talley and Cornelius Bennett.

Sept. 16 – Miami snapped its six-game losing streak to the Bills with a 30-7 rout. It was the Bills first regular-season loss at Joe Robbie Stadium since it opened in 1987. Bruce Smith angrily confronted Marv Levy on the sidelines midway through the fourth quarter when Levy began pulling regulars out of the game with the Bills trailing 30-7.

Sept. 17 – Marv Levy doled out a $500 fine to Bruce Smith for his remarks after the game and also fined Leonard Smith, Nate Odomes and Kirby Jackson $100 each for refusing to leave the field when Levy called for them to. Levy then engaged in a dispute with *Buffalo News* writer Vic Carucci over Carucci's interpretation of Smith's quote "I know I wouldn't have come out." Carucci inferred that Smith was taking a shot at Jim Kelly for adhering to Levy's wish to take him out. "I think some of the things in the story like 'in an apparent swipe at Jim Kelly' I think was a journalistic low blow. He didn't say he was taking a swipe at Jim Kelly, the writer did. I hope the quote was accurate because he's (Smith) been fined heavily for his remarks." Carucci then played the tape for Levy and the coach replied: "The discipline stands. I listened to the tape, but there was never any mention of Kelly. And as far as Bruce not coming out, oh yes he would if we took him out." On his Rochester-based radio show, Smith denied criticizing Kelly "and to a certain degree, I wasn't criticizing coach Levy. I think he's an excellent coach."

Sept. 18 – Fullback Larry Kinnebrew was waived and his place on the roster was taken by punter Rick Tuten, who had been waived at the end of the preseason. Tuten was to replace John Nies as the punter, but Nies was retained for his kickoff ability. "He (Kinnebrew) did some good things and had some good games for us last year," Marv Levy said, "but he was a year older and maybe we didn't see the same explosiveness off the ball as even a year ago."

Sept. 20 – O.J. Simpson came to Buffalo to do interviews for NBC Sports and was stonewalled by the team. "I'm their only Hall of Famer and I openly root for the Bills every week on network television," Simpson said, "but they wouldn't allow me to talk to the players. The coach wouldn't be interviewed, the general manager wouldn't be interviewed. A coach and general manager who won't talk on network television. Isn't that unprecedented." Polian finally relented, but an NBC producer said he made Simpson wait in his office for more than an hour while he went out to run. And Jim Kelly finally agreed only after Simpson agreed to appear at the taping of Kelly's TV show.

Sept. 22 – Ralph Wilson said he was fed up with his team's bickering image. "I'm not putting up with it anymore," he said. "I'm not going to stand for it and I told Marv to tell the players that. The next one of them that goes shooting off his mouth and disrupts the team will be suspended. And if they don't like that, we'll get rid of them. I'm sick of all this nonsense."

Sept. 24 – Thurman Thomas rushed for a career-high 214 yards and the Bills got back on the winning track with a 30-7 romp over the Jets at the Meadowlands on *Monday Night Football*. Thomas' total was the second-highest in the history of *MNF*, with Bo Jackson's 221 yards against Seattle in 1987 the No. 1 all-time rushing game. It was the Bills' first 200-yard rushing game since Greg Bell did it in 1984.

Sept. 25 – Marv Levy expressed anger over what he perceived as the media's continued attempt to create his team's bickering image. "Last week a guy said something and he was disciplined for it," Levy said. "What that has to do with the Bills' unity befuddles me. It was an attempt to stir up the ashes from last year when there was evidence of that (bickering)." Jim Kelly said of the Jets game: "We didn't have anything to prove to anybody in Buffalo, to any newspaper in Buffalo, we just had to go out and prove to ourselves that we could play football. It was never Bickering Bills this year. We know as soon as we lose, someone is going to say 'Oh, there goes the Bills again.'"

Sept. 26 – Bill Polian said that free safety Mark Kelso was not suffering from chronic concussions but from migraine syndrome and that his playing career was not in jeopardy.

Sept. 27 – O.J. Simpson talked about the Bills while in town to do interviews. "They certainly have some outstanding individuals here. As far as that superstar caliber player, Buffalo probably has more than any other AFC team. Talent is very important, but now they have to start playing like they don't have talent. Start playing like the underdog and if they do that, they'll turn it around. This team will be in the playoffs vying for the Super Bowl."

Sept. 30 – The Bills exploded for 20 points in a 77-second span in the fourth quarter and overcame Denver, 29-28, before a frenzied sellout crowd at Rich Stadium. "In all my years, I've never seen a game change like that," Ralph Wilson said. "That rapidly from almost a certain defeat to victory. I was standing there thinking this kick was going to put us away and then we blocked it."

Oct. 1 – Punter/kickoff specialist John Nies was waived and free agent cornerback David Pool was signed. Marv Levy reflected on the Denver victory, saying: "I told our team a lot of people will say, not unjustified, that you were lucky. But I'll tell you one thing, the only way you get lucky is if you don't quit. I think we were very fortunate to win."

Oct. 4 – Addressing the situation in New England where *Boston Herald* reporter Lisa Olson was allegedly sexually harassed in the Patriots locker room, the Bills said they had an open-door policy toward women in the locker room, "As far as I'm concerned, it's a non-issue," Marv Levy said. "It's been established by the league for some years now that accredited women – media – are welcome in the locker room."

Oct. 7 – For the second week in a row, the Bills rallied in spectacular fashion, scoring 24 points in a 6:03 span during the fourth quarter to beat the Raiders, 38-24. The game was played on Sunday night in front of TNT cable cameras and the second-largest crowd in Rich Stadium history (80,076).

Oct. 9 – For the second week in a row, Cornelius Bennett was named AFC defensive player of the week.

Oct. 10 – With his team off because of the new bye weeks in the schedule, Marv Levy said he wouldn't spend Sunday watching games on TV. "I'm going to get out into the country," he said. "It's funny, you know, I don't even know what autumn is like. I come to the stadium and it's dark. I go home and it's dark. It'll be nice to see what autumn is like."

Oct. 21 – For the third game in a row, the Bills rallied in the fourth quarter at home to win, this time 30-27 over the Jets as Jamie Mueller caught a 14-yard TD pass from Jim Kelly with 19 seconds remaining.

Oct. 22 – One day after beating the Jets, Bruce Smith said New York played dirty, especially tight end Mark Boyer who chopped him at the knees. The two tangled in the tunnel leading to the dressing rooms after the game. "We do not play dirty," Jets coach Bruce Coslet said. "We'll block you, but we won't try to hurt you. It's a tough game, this game called NFL football. You don't hear us complaining in the locker room or wanting to fight people in the tunnel."

Oct. 28 – The Bills won their fifth straight game, routing New England, 27-10, at Foxboro as Thurman Thomas shook off his bruised knee and rushed for 136 yards and one TD.

Nov. 4 – The Bills avenged their heartbreaking playoff loss to the Browns with a dazzling 42-0 blowout in Cleveland. Darryl Talley, playing in his hometown, returned an interception for his first NFL TD in the fourth quarter to cap the rout.

Nov. 11 – Despite a howling wind that produced bitter temperatures, the Bills rolled up 45 points in a 45-14 rout of Phoenix at Rich Stadium, their seventh straight win. "The wind was so strong, it almost knocked guys off their feet," said Cards punter Rich Camarillo.

Nov. 18 – New England gave the Bills a great fight before succumbing, 14-0 at Rich Stadium, as J.D. Williams preserved a 7-0 lead with an end zone interception with 1:51 left. Thurman Thomas ripped a career-best 80-yard TD run on the next play. "The fiction has been created that you're going to run over every team, but it's just that, fiction," Bill Polian said.

Nov. 26 – The Bills' eight-game winning streak came to an end as Houston posted a 27-24 *Monday Night Football* victory in the Astrodome. The Oilers outgained the Bills, 411-289.

Nov. 28 – ABC announcer Al Michaels said that

despite the Bills loss to Houston, "I think Buffalo is capable of winning the Super Bowl. I think the road to the Super Bowl will probably go through Buffalo."

Nov. 29 – Bruce Smith got back on his soap box preaching about chop blocks. "I don't care what it takes. If it takes me chasing the guy home after the game's over, running behind him while he's in his car, I'll do it," he said. With the Eagles coming into town, it was an appropriate topic because *The National* sports daily listed three Philadelphia players among the 10 dirtiest in the league, including the man Smith would be facing, left tackle Ron Heller.

Dec. 2 – The Bills played the first quarter in the no-huddle mode, their longest stretch to date, and scored 24 points, then held on for a 30-23 victory over the Eagles at Rich Stadium. Jim Kelly was eight-for-eight for 229 yards and three TDs in the first quarter.

Dec. 5 – Free agent cornerback Clifford Hicks was signed to shore up the injury-depleted secondary.

Dec. 9 – The Bills clinched a playoff berth with a 31-7 romp over Indianapolis at the Hoosier Dome. Andre Reed became the all-time Bills leader in touchdown receptions, breaking Elbert Dubenion's team record.

Dec. 10 – Jim Kelly expressed his pleasure over the Bills fast starts the previous two weeks thanks to opening games in the hurry-up, no-huddle offense. "I really feel comfortable in it," Kelly said. "Coach always leaves it up in the air whether we're going to use it. But now I feel that he has the confidence, not only in myself, but in the people around me, that we will get in the right position and we will execute the way it should be done."

Dec. 12 – Bruce Smith caused a stir that made the New York tabloids sing when he proclaimed that he was the best defensive player in the NFL, not Lawrence Taylor of the Giants. "Over the last 10 years, he has probably been the most dominant player in the league, but I think I've taken it up above him," Smith said. "I can't take anything away from Lawrence, I've admired him for so many years. He's a friend of mine. But right now, it's time to give credit to somebody who deserves it. It would be an injustice if I don't get the MVP." Taylor had no reply, but his teammate, cornerback Mark Collins, did: "How many times has he (Smith) been to the Pro Bowl? When you go to the Pro Bowl nine years in a row, then you can start comparing yourself to the greats."

Dec. 13 – Marv Levy reflected on the last time the Bills played the Giants. It was Oct. 18, 1987, and the Bills replacement players beat the Giants in overtime, 6-3, during the players strike. "I remember that game well, I will for the rest of my life," Levy said. "I think it was the worst game ever played in the National Football League."

Dec. 15 – The starting quarterbacks for both teams, Jim Kelly and Phil Simms, suffered injuries and Frank Reich outpointed Jeff Hostetler, 17-13, to give the Bills a huge morale boost on a cold, misty day at Giants Stadium.

Dec. 17 – An MRI revealed that Jim Kelly injured the medial collateral ligament in his left knee and would be out three to four weeks. Meanwhile, the Bills began rallying around Frank Reich with the AFC East division showdown against Miami on the horizon. "Frank is the ideal backup quarterback," Ted Marchibroda said. "He's the type of kid

who is always ready to play every week. And the backup quarterback is supposed to win when the No. 1 guy gets hurt." It was learned that Will Wolford suffered a sprained knee and that he could return for the Dolphins game.

Dec. 18 – Jim Kelly held a press conference and expressed his dismay over having to miss the biggest game of the season. "I wanted to be a part of it," he said. "It's a game that not only the 47 players on this team but the whole community has been looking forward to. This is the type of game that everybody dreams about and now I'll be watching from the sidelines. It hurts. Everybody has confidence in Frank that he can do it. I know he can do it."

Dec. 19 – Eight Bills were named to the AFC's Pro Bowl squad, but Darryl Talley was again omitted. Thurman Thomas, Andre Reed, Bruce Smith, Kent Hull and Steve Tasker were chosen as starters while Jim Kelly, Cornelius Bennett and Shane Conlan were selected as backups.

Dec. 23 – Frank Reich completed 15 of 21 passes for 234 yards and two TDs and Thurman Thomas rushed for 154 yards to lift the Bills to a convincing 24-14 victory over the Dolphins, clinching their third straight AFC East division title. A record crowd of 80,235 was onhand and many stormed the field after the game and tore down the goal posts. The 13th regular-season victory set a new team record.

Dec. 30 – With home-field advantage wrapped up in the playoffs, the Bills emptied their bench during a 29-14 loss to the Redskins at RFK Stadium. Thurman Thomas carried five times for zero yards and thus did not win the rushing title, losing by seven yards to Detroit's Barry Sanders. Bruce Smith finished with 19 sacks, three shy of Mark Gastineau's record and one behind NFL leader Derrick Thomas of Kansas City.

Dec. 31 – Marv Levy's mentor, George Allen, died at the age of 72.

Jan. 3, 1991 – Bruce Smith, Thurman Thomas and Kent Hull were named to The Associated Press All-Pro first team.

Jan. 5, 1991 – Miami rallied for 14 fourth-quarter points and defeated Kansas City, 17-16, in an AFC wild-card game. In an NFC wild-card game, Washington downed Philadelphia, 20-6.

Jan. 6, 1991 – In the other AFC wild-card game, Cincinnati routed Houston, 41-14, meaning that Miami would be Buffalo's divisional round opponent. In the NFC, Chicago handled New Orleans, 16-6.

Jan. 7, 1991 – The Bills team physician Richard Weiss went on record as saying that Jim Kelly would be able to play against the Dolphins in the Bills' playoff opener coming up on Saturday. "He'll play, I'm sure," Weiss said. "He's right on schedule, there's no reason to think anything else."

Jan. 8, 1991 – Jim Kelly backed off a bit from what Dr. Weiss had said the day before and indicated that the decision on whether he would play or not would ultimately be made by him. "If I feel I'm ready to play, I'll play," Kelly said. "It doesn't matter what the doctor says. If I don't feel I'm ready to play and he says I can, I'm not playing."

Jan. 9, 1991 – Bruce Smith was named The Associated Press' NFL Defensive Player of the Year. *The National* sports daily named Smith its NFL MVP and UPI picked him as its AFC defensive player of the year. Jim Kelly was apprehensive about his availability after taking part in his first

practice. "Dr. Weiss isn't inside my body and he can't feel what my knee feels like," he said. "If I can go, I'll go, but I'm not going to play if I feel it's going to hinder me for the rest of my career."

Jan. 10, 1991 – It was announced that Mark Kelso would start at free safety against the Dolphins, a move that angered John Hagy. Hagy had been playing in Kelso's place for three-quarters of the season.

Jan. 12, 1991 – Jim Kelly returned to action with a vengeance, completing 19 of 29 passes for 339 yards and three TDs as the Bills outlasted the Dolphins, 44-34, in the highest scoring non-overtime playoff game in NFL history. A crowd of 77,087 was onhand for the game, which was played in light snow that coated the field for part of the game. Thurman Thomas rushed for 117 yards. In the first NFC divisional round game, San Francisco defeated Washington, 28-10.

Jan. 13, 1991 – In the other AFC divisional game, Bo Jackson suffered a hip injury, but the Raiders still earned a trip to Buffalo by beating Cincinnati, 20-10. In the NFC, the Giants routed Chicago, 31-3.

Jan. 16, 1991 – The United States and its allies went to war with Iraq as hundreds of planes unleashed a massive attack on targets in Iraq and occupied Kuwait. The start of the war immediately cast doubt on whether the NFL would play its upcoming conference championship games.

Jan. 17, 1991 – Commissioner Paul Tagliabue addressed the Persian Gulf situation: "We're going to monitor the events in the Middle East right up until kickoff Sunday. And if the networks believe the events in the gulf are so dramatic or so significant that they should go to an all-news format, then we would not play our games."

Jan. 18, 1991 – Will Wolford was added to the AFC Pro Bowl squad when Cincinnati's Anthony Munoz pulled out with an injury. He was the ninth

Bill to be placed on the team.

Jan. 19, 1991 – A downtown pep rally was canceled and members of the Bills organization attended a church service with mayor Jimmy Griffin and County Executive Dennis Gorski to pray for the men and women fighting in the Persian Gulf war.

Jan. 20, 1991 – In a shocking display, the Bills crushed the Raiders, 51-3, to win the AFC Championship Game in front of a record crowd of 80,324 at Rich Stadium. The Bills thus qualified for their first Super Bowl, thanks to a 41-point first-half explosion. During the first quarter, NBC broke away from the game because Iraq had fired missiles at Saudi Arabia. In the NFC Championship Game, Lawrence Taylor recovered Roger Craig's fumble, setting up Matt Bahr's game-winning 42-yard field goal as time expired, giving the Giants a 15-13 upset victory over San Francisco at Candlestick Park.

Jan. 21, 1991 – The Bills flew to Tampa and were in jovial moods when they de-planed. "Everybody's excited and really happy to be here – the Super Bowl," Shane Conlan said. Bruce Smith and Cornelius Bennett got off the plane saying: "Showtime, it's showtime."

Jan. 22, 1991 – Marv Levy caused a flap when he failed to show up for the media day session at Tampa Stadium. Attendance was mandatory, but Levy explained he got wrapped up in game-planning, then the driver who was going to take him to the stadium got lost on the way. "I understand people are disturbed and I feel badly," Levy said. During the Giants media session, Lawrence Taylor conceded that Bruce Smith was the best defensive player in the NFL.

Jan. 23, 1991 – Darryl Talley finally made it to the Pro Bowl when he was added to the AFC squad by coach Art Shell as a need player. "I'm extremely honored and elated that coach Shell thought that much of me," Talley said. "Evidently I'm not pop-

ular with my peers." Marv Levy apologized for skipping the first media session, but said: "I've been coaching 40 years and this is the game I've been preparing for all my life. I'm not going to cut a corner on it."

Jan. 25, 1991 – In his mass press conference, NFL commissioner Paul Tagliabue promised the stadium would be heavily secured, but he did not know what it would take to postpone the game. "We've looked at two types of contingencies," Tagliabue said. "One would be if there was activity here in Tampa, the other would be events in the Middle East. We don't have any set of rules. We'll just make the best business judgement when we see what's happening Sunday."

Jan. 27, 1991 – In one of the most exciting Super Bowls ever played, Scott Norwood's 47-yard field goal sailed wide right with four seconds left and the Bills lost to the New York Giants, 20-19, at Tampa Stadium. The game was an emotional one, starting with a stirring National Anthem sung by Whitney Houston, flag-waving fans in the stands, and the climactic finish. Thurman Thomas rushed for 131 yards, but O.J. Anderson, who gained 102, was named the MVP.

Feb. 3, 1991 – Jim Kelly's TD pass to Ernest Givins in the fourth quarter lifted the AFC to a 23-21 victory in the Pro Bowl at Aloha Stadium. Kelly completed 13 of 19 passes for 210 yards to win the MVP award, Bruce Smith recorded three sacks and a blocked field goal and Andre Reed had four catches for 80 yards.

It is the moment that will live in infamy in Buffalo: Scott Norwood's missed 47-yard field goal prevented the Bills from winning Super Bowl XXV in Tampa Stadium.

BY THE NUMBERS - 1990

TEAM STATISTICS	BILLS	OPP
First downs	302	288
Rushing	123	105
Passing	161	159
Penalty	18	24
Third downs	82-186	89-208
Fourth downs	5-11	10-19
Avg. time of poss	28:39	31:21
Total yards	5,276	4,607
Avg. game	329.8	287.9
Plays	931	981
Avg. play	5.7	4.7
Net rushing yds	2,080	1,808
Avg. game	130.0	113.0
Avg. play	4.3	3.7
Net passing yds	3,196	2,799
Comp/att	263/425	254/455
Sacks/lost	27-208	43-326
Interceptions	11	18
Percentage	61.9	55.8
Punts/avg	58-39.3	66-38.2
Fumbles/lost	17-10	33-17
Penalties/yds	92-683	107-839
Touchdowns	53	30
Extra points	50-53	29-30
Field goals	20-29	18-24
Safeties	0	0
Kick ret./avg	51-20.4	73-15.5
Punt ret./avg	25-7.1	31-8.1

RUSHING	ATT	YDS	AVG	TD
Thomas	271	1297	4.8	11
Davis	64	302	4.7	4
Mueller	59	207	3.5	2
D. Smith	20	82	4.1	2
Kelly	22	63	2.9	0
Gardner	15	41	2.7	0
Reich	15	24	1.6	0
Beebe	1	23	23.0	0
Reed	3	23	7.7	0
Kinnebrew	9	18	2.0	1
TOTALS	479	2080	4.3	20

RECEIVING	CAT	YDS	AVG	TD
Reed	71	945	13.3	8
Thomas	49	532	10.9	2
Lofton	35	712	20.3	4
McKeller	34	464	13.6	5
D. Smith	21	225	10.7	0
Mueller	16	106	6.6	1
Beebe	11	221	20.1	1
Metzelaars	10	60	6.0	1
K. Davis	9	78	8.7	1
Rolle	3	6	2.0	3
Tasker	2	44	22.0	2
Edwards	2	11	5.5	0
TOTALS	263	3404	12.9	28

PASSING	COMP	ATT	INT	YDS	TD	COMP%	SACKS	RATE
Kelly	219	346	9	2829	24	63.3	20-158	101.2
Reich	36	63	0	469	2	57.1	6-41	91.3
Gilbert	8	15	2	106	2	53.3	1-9	76.0
D. Smith	0	1	0	0	0	00.0	0-0	00.0
TOTALS	263	425	11	3404	28	61.9	27-208	98.2

KICKING	1-19	20-29	30-39	40-49	50+	TOT	PAT	PTS
Norwood	0-0	9-11	5-8	6-10	0-0	20-29	50-52	110

PUNTING	NO	AVG	LG	In 20	BL
Tuten	53	39.8	55	12	0
Nies	5	34.8	39	0	0
TOTALS	58	39.3	55	12	0

Despite their Super Bowl XXV loss, the Bills returned to Buffalo heroes, as more than 20,000 fans attended a rally downtown in Niagara Square the day after the game.

SCORE BY QUARTERS

BILLS	83	116	69	160	0 -	428
OPP	55	74	72	62	0 -	263

DEFENSIVE STATISTICAL LEADERS

TACKLES: Talley 79 primary - 44 assists - 123 total, B. Smith 82-19-101, L. Smith 65-33-98, Bennett 71-25-96, Conlan 72-21-93, Seals 73-19-92, Wright 51-25-76, Bentley 44-31-75, Bailey 38-19-57, Odomes 31-11-42, Williams 29-9-38, Jackson 22-5-27, Hagy 19-2-21, Kelso 10-9-19

SACKS: B. Smith 19, Wright 5, Talley 4, Bennett 4, Seals 4, Lodish 2, Bailey 2

FUMBLE RECOVERIES: Odomes 3, Bennett 2, Seals 2

FORCED FUMBLES: B. Smith 4, L. Smith 3, Bennett 3, Odomes 2

INTERCEPTIONS: Jackson 3-16 yards, 5.3 avg., 0 TD; Talley 2-60, 30.0, 1 TD; L. Smith 2-39, 19.5, 1 TD; Hagy 2-23, 11.5, 0 TD; Kelso 2-0, 0.0, 0 TD, Williams 2-0, 0.0, 0 TD

SPECIAL TEAMS STATISTICAL LEADERS

KICKOFF RETURNS: D. Smith 32-643 yards, 20.1 avg, 0 TD; Edwards 11-256, 23.3, 0 TD

PUNT RETURNS: Edwards 14-92, 6.6, 0 TD; Hale 10-76, 7.6, 0 TD

TACKLES: Pike 36, Rolle 29, Patton 27, Tasker 25, Bailey 18, Mueller 16, Baldinger 12, Garner 11, Hale 10, Edwards 9, Drane 7, D. Smith 6, Monger 6, Williams 5, Norwood 5

GAME 1 - Sunday, Sept. 9, 1990 - BILLS 26, COLTS 10

NOTES

• The Bills won their season opener for the third year in a row as Thurman Thomas had 145 yards from scrimmage despite missing all of camp. Rookie Glenn Parker started at left tackle over Will Wolford.

• Cornelius Bennett knocked rookie QB Jeff George out of the game in the fourth with a vicious tackle.

• Eric Dickerson did not play due to a hamstring injury.

• The Bills opened the game in a no-huddle offense and drove 78 yards in 15 plays to a Scott Norwood field goal. Jim Kelly completed all nine of his passes, four to Keith McKeller for 45 yards.

• The Colts answered with a 14-play, 69-yard drive to a Dean Biasucci field goal, as George completed four-of-six passes for 53 yards. The Colts had a first-and-goal from the 6, but the Bills' defense held.

• Three plays after Norwood missed a field goal, Bruce Smith sacked George, forced a fumble and Leon Seals recovered at the Colts 22. Five plays later, Kelly hit Butch Rolle for a TD. It was the 1,000th TD in Bills history and it was Rolle's sixth straight reception that had resulted in a TD.

• The Colts went three-and-out and then rookie J.D. Williams blocked Rohn Stark's punt. The Bills took over at the Colts 19. That resulted in Norwood's second field goal.

• Norwood made his third field goal with eight seconds left in the half after the Bills took over at the Colts 43 following a punt. Kelly hit Don Smith for 17 yards to the Indy 19.

• The Colts took the second-half kickoff and drove 67 yards in 10 plays to George's first NFL TD pass, a 25-yarder to Stanley Morgan. George was four-of-six for 67 yards on the march.

• Each team missed a field goal, and the Bills drove 34 yards after a punt to another Norwood field goal.

• Three plays after the kickoff, Mark Kelso intercepted Jack Trudeau and the Bills then marched 67 yards to Thomas' TD. Thomas had a 29-yard breakaway and Andre Reed a 16-yard catch.

QUOTES

• Bruce Smith on Jeff George: "I had my reservations about him, but I don't anymore. I think he's going to be a super quarterback. The kid showed an awful lot of poise. We went after him pretty good and the kid hung in there."

• Ted Marchibroda on the use of the no-huddle: "We wanted to continue what we started in Cleveland last year. Thank goodness it worked, it got us off to a great start. The thing is, Jim Kelly does it so well and has confidence in it."

• Jim Kelly: "That was my kind of football. It's something you haven't seen that much before but Ted has confidence in me and the receivers and the offensive line so it probably won't be the last time you'll see it. I've been telling you guys for three weeks that I felt good. I get almost all the reps in practice and that's really all you need."

• Kent Hull on the no-huddle: "We were tired, but they were more tired because everything on defense is reaction and it takes more out of you, so I felt that was to our advantage."

Colts	3	0	7	0	-	10
Bills	3	13	0	10	-	26

Attendance at Rich Stadium - 78,899

Buf: FG Norwood 29, 6:56
Ind: FG Biasucci 24, 14:48
Buf: Rolle 3 pass from Kelly (Norwood kick), 9:46
Buf: FG Norwood 31, 13:02
Buf: FG Norwood 37, 14:52
Ind: Morgan 25 pass from George (Biasucci kick), 5:22
Buf: FG Norwood 47, 8:24
Buf: Thomas 6 run (Norwood kick), 13:23

	BUF	IND
First downs	24	15
Rushing yds	100	56
Passing yds	283	173
Punts-avg	0-0	3-23.7
Fumbles-lost	2-1	2-1
Penalties-yds	5-30	5-40
Poss. time	33:46	26:14

BILLS LEADERS: Rushing - Thomas 20-84, Kinnebrew 6-17, Kelly 1-0, Reich 1-(-1); **Passing** - Kelly 28-37-0 - 283; **Receiving** - McKeller 7-78, Reed 5-62, Thomas 9-61, Lofton 4-53, D. Smith 2-26, Rolle 1-3.

COLTS LEADERS: Rushing - Bentley 15-50, Trudeau 1-3, Clark 1-3; **Passing** - George 13-24-1 - 160, Trudeau 6-11-1 - 38; **Receiving** - Morgan 2-47, Brooks 3-46, Hester 3-38, Bentley 5-31, Johnson 3-16, Clark 2-15, Beach 1-5.

WEEK 1 GAMES

LAR 14, Den 9	Atl 47, Hou 27
GB 36, Rams 24	Mia 27, NE 24
KC 24, Minn 21	Cinc 25, NYJ 20
Wash 31, Phoe 0	Clev 13, Pitt 3
Dal 17, SD 14	Chi 17, Sea 14
TB 38, Det 21	NYG 27, Phil 20
SF 13, NO 12	

GAME 2 - Sunday, Sept. 16, 1990 - DOLPHINS 30, BILLS 7

NOTES

• The Bills suffered their first regular-season loss at Joe Robbie and had their six-game winning streak over Miami snapped. The victory was the 200th of Don Shula's Dolphin career.

• After not having to punt against the Colts, rookie John Nies punted five times and averaged 34.8 yards.

• The Bills were knocked out of first place in the AFC East for the first time since the end of the 1987 season.

• The Bills drove to the Miami 29 on their first possession, but Larry Kinnebrew was stopped on fourth-and-one.

• Miami then moved 71 yards in 15 plays to Sammie Smith's TD on the first play of the second quarter. Dan Marino completed six of seven passes for 51 yards.

• On the next series, John Offerdahl forced Pete Metzelaars to fumble and Alfred Oglesby recovered at the Bills 36. That led to a Pete Stoyanovich field goal. The key play was a 23-yard pass to Fred Banks.

• Two plays after the kickoff, Louis Oliver intercepted Kelly at the Bills 24 leading to a field goal. Stoyanovich made his third field goal with two seconds left in the half after a short Nies punt.

• Early in the third, David Griggs forced Thurman Thomas to fumble and Jeff Cross recovered at the 49. Nine plays later, Smith scored on third-and-goal from the 1.

• A 32-yard Nies punt gave Miami the ball at the Bills 45. Five plays later, Marino hit Tony Paige for a TD on a bootleg rollout. Marino had hit Banks for 10 on third-and-seven from the 32.

• The Bills drove 70 yards in 10 plays in the fourth to their only score, Kinnebrew's TD plunge.

QUOTES

• Bruce Smith about Levy pulling starters: "We just quit. I know I wouldn't have come out."

• Marv Levy: "We put in Frank (Reich) to get some work. We figured we would be exposing Jim to injury for a minuscule

opportunity to win the game at that time." (About the game): "They did everything right. It certainly hurt to miss the fourth-and-one in the first quarter, then follow with a couple of turnovers."

• Darryl Talley: "He's the coach, he did what he thought was best."

• Andre Reed: "Turnovers took the momentum out of anything we were doing. After our first drive, our offense wasn't on the field very long. This is the NFL, we've got to play like we did against the Colts every week. Nobody's going to lay down for you."

• Thurman Thomas: "Hell, they beat us 20 games in a row (in the 70s). What did you expect? We can't win every damn game we play against them. The streak has to end sometime."

• Miami cornerback Tim McKyer: "It was easy."

• Miami tight end Jim Jensen: "What six-game losing streak? There's a lot of hatred between the teams. Especially when they say they owned us last year. We haven't forgotten that and we went out there and kicked their butts today. It was a great feeling. Today we owned the Bills."

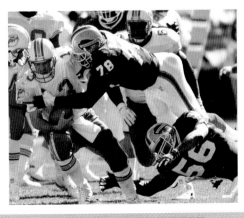

Bills	0	0	0	7	-	7
Dolphins	0	16	7	7	-	30

Attendance at Joe Robbie Stadium - 68,142

Mia: Smith 2 run (Stoyanovich kick), :04
Mia: FG Stoyanovich 23, 4:34
Mia: FG Stoyanovich 29, 9:17
Mia: FG Stoyanovich 48, 14:58
Mia: Smith 1 run (Stoyanovich kick), 10:18
Mia: Paige 17 pass from Marino (Stoyanovich kick), :07
Buf: Kinnebrew 1 run (Norwood kick), 3:15

	BUF	MIA
First downs	12	19
Rushing yds	44	128
Passing yds	161	177
Punts-avg	5-34.8	4-43.3
Fumbles-lost	2-2	4-1
Penalties-yds	4-35	6-50
Poss. time	20:52	39:08

BILLS LEADERS: Rushing - Thomas 8-23, Kelly 1-12, Mueller 3-8, Kinnebrew 3-1; **Passing** - Kelly 14-23-1 - 140, Reich 5-12-0 - 34; **Receiving** - Reed 5-42, D. Smith 4-42, Thomas 4-37, Lofton 2-37, Davis 2-9, Beebe 1-6, Metzelaars 1-1.

DOLPHINS LEADERS: Rushing - Smith 18-56, Logan 7-42, Paige 8-16, Higgs 2-11, Banks 1-3, Jensen 1-2, Secules 1-(-2); **Passing** - Marino 18-26-0 - 177; **Receiving** - Clayton 3-41, Paige 3-34, Banks 2-33, Duper 1-13, Edmunds 2-12, Martin 1-11, Jensen 2-9, Smith 1-9, Logan 2-12, Stradford 1-3.

WEEK 2 GAMES

Det 21, Atl 14	Chi 31, GB 13
Cinc 21, SD 16	NYJ 24, Clev 21
LAR 17, Sea 13	Rams 35, TB 14
NE 16, Ind 14	Minn 32, NO 3
NYG 28, Dal 7	Phoe 23, Phil 21
SF 26, Wash 13	Pitt 20, Hou 9
Den 24, KC 23	

STANDINGS: SECOND WEEK

AFC EAST	W	L	T	CENTRAL	W	L	T	WEST	W	L	T	NFC EAST	W	L	T	CENTRAL	W	L	T	WEST	W	L	T
Miami	2	0	0	Cincinnati	2	0	0	Raiders	2	0	0	NY Giants	2	0	0	Chicago	2	0	0	San Fran	2	0	0
Buffalo	1	1	0	Cleveland	1	1	0	Kan. City	1	1	0	Washington	1	1	0	Green Bay	1	1	0	Atlanta	1	1	0
New England	1	1	0	Pittsburgh	1	1	0	Denver	1	1	0	Dallas	1	1	0	Tampa Bay	1	1	0	LA Rams	1	1	0
NY Jets	1	1	0	Houston	0	2	0	Seattle	0	2	0	Phoenix	1	1	0	Detroit	1	1	0	N.Orleans	0	2	0
Indianapolis	0	2	0					San Diego	0	2	0	Philadelphia	0	2	0	Minnesota	1	1	0				

Bills	7 13 3 7 - 30
Jets	7 0 0 0 - 7

Attendance at Giants Stadium - 69,927

NYJ: Baxter 1 run (Leahy kick), 7:15
Buf: Davis 1 run (Norwood kick), 11:04
Buf: Rolle 2 pass from Kelly (Norwood kick), 4:48
Buf: FG Norwood 48, 11:55
Buf: FG Norwood 42, 15:00
Buf: FG Norwood 27, 10:10
Buf: McKeller 6 pass from Kelly (Norwood kick), 8:26

	BUF	NYJ
First downs	23	17
Rushing yds	292	124
Passing yds	159	125
Punts-avg	4-32.8	6-42.8
Fumbles-lost	0-0	3-2
Penalties-yds	7-86	7-55
Poss. time	30:49	29:11

BILLS LEADERS: Rushing - Thomas 18-214, Davis 7-31, Mueller 8-42, D. Smith 1-3, Kelly 1-2; **Passing** - Kelly 16-26-1 - 174; **Receiving** - McKeller 3-60, Reed 3-47, D. Smith 3-26, Thomas 3-5, Lofton 1-20, Metzelaars 1-8, Mueller 1-6, Rolle 1-2.

JETS LEADERS: Rushing - Baxter 7-36, B. Thomas 6-31, McNeil 3-21, Hector 10-24, O'Brien 3-12; **Passing** - O'Brien 15-30-0 - 153; **Receiving** - Moore 3-41, Burkett 4-39, Townsell 2-29, Toon 2-17, Boyer 2-20, Dressel 1-5, Thomas 1-2.

NOTES

• Thurman Thomas rushed for a career-high 214 yards. It was the first 200-yard rushing game for the Bills since Greg Bell in 1984 and was the second-highest rushing total on *Monday Night Football*. Only Bo Jackson of the Raiders with 221 yards against Seattle in 1987 was better.
• The rushing total was highest since the Bills gained 366 against the Giants in 1978.
• Bruce Smith had six tackles, two sacks and two forced fumbles while Leonard Smith had 11 tackles.
• Will Wolford was forced out in the second quarter and rookie Glenn Parker filled in admirably.
• Brad Baxter scored on the Jets' first possession after a 29-yard interference penalty on J.D. Williams gave them first-and-goal at the 1. The drive was 75 yards in eight plays.
• The Bills answered with a seven-play, 76-yard drive to Kenneth Davis' TD. Jim Kelly hit Keith McKeller for 43 yards to the Jets 1. Earlier he hit James Lofton for 20 on second-and-17 from the Jets 28.
• On the first play after a Jets punt, Thomas ripped off a career-long 60-yard run, but Scott Norwood had a 24-yard field goal blocked. After another Jets punt, Kelly hit Andre Reed for 24 and Jamie Mueller broke a 20-yard run to set up Kelly's TD pass to Butch Rolle, Rolle's sev-enth straight TD catch.
• Bruce Smith forced Johnny Hector to fumble and Nate Odomes recovered at the Jets 30, to set up a field goal. And after a punt, the Bills took possession with 1:49 left in the half. They moved 44 yards in eight plays to another Norwood field goal. Thomas had 146 yards at the half.
• The Bills drove to Norwood's third field goal early in the third. In the fourth, Cornelius Bennett forced Ken O'Brien to fumble and Chris Hale recovered at the 12, and three plays later, Keith McKeller caught a TD pass.

QUOTES

• Thurman Thomas: "I wasn't even thinking about it (O.J. Simpson's team rushing record of 273 yards). At this level, you can't go out and embarrass a team like that. The game was put away and there was no sense going out there and getting hurt. If we would've lost this game, there's no telling what would have happened. The team probably would have exploded and we probably would be bickering. But we came out with fire in our eyes. If we play like this every week, I don't think any team in the NFL can beat us."
• Bruce Smith: "We wanted to come back and show that this team is a unit."
• Kent Hull: "We were embarrassed and humiliated last week, but there really wasn't anything said about it. Everybody knew what happened. I think people just decided it was time to start playing football. We just ran the old counter. Everybody runs the counter."
• Marv Levy: "Our players were aware of being on *Monday Night Football*. We're back to where we played a good game."
• Jets coach Bruce Coslet: "Their running game is unstoppable when we can't tackle or fill gaps. No team should be able to manhandle us like that."

WEEK 3 GAMES

SF 19, Atl 13	Wash 19, Dal 15
Hou 24, Ind 10	KC 17, GB 3
NYG 20, Mia 3	Chi 19, Minn 16
Cinc 41, NE 7	Phil 27, Rams 21
NO 28, Phoe 7	LAR 20, Pitt 3
SD 24, Clev 14	TB 23, Det 20
Den 34, Sea 31 (OT)	

Broncos	7 7 7 7 - 28
Bills	0 3 6 20 - 29

Attendance at Rich Stadium - 74,393

Den: Humphrey 1 run (Treadwell kick), 6:50
Den: Sewell 2 run (Treadwell kick), 13:03
Buf: FG Norwood 37, 14:54
Buf: D. Smith 12 run (kick failed), 7:07
Den: Winder 3 run (Treadwell kick), 10:17
Buf: Bennett 80 blocked field goal return (Norwood kick), 4:33
Buf: L. Smith 39 interception return (kick failed), 5:33
Buf: Davis 2 run (Norwood kick), 5:50
Den: Nattiel 7 pass from Elway (Treadwell kick), 13:35

	BUF	DEN
First downs	15	28
Rushing yds	64	208
Passing yds	133	202
Punts-avg	4-35.0	3-37.3
Fumbles-lost	3-2	3-3
Penalties-yds	4-33	8-60
Poss. time	25:11	34:49

BILLS LEADERS: Rushing - Thomas 13-36, D. Smith 3-18, Kelly 5-6, Mueller 2-2, Davis 1-2; **Passing** - Kelly 18-34-1 - 167; **Receiving** - Lofton 4-57, Thomas 4-25, Mueller 3-6, Reed 2-35, D. Smith 3-30, Edwards 1-5, Metzelaars 1-9.

BRONCOS LEADERS: Rushing - Humphrey 34-177, Elway 4-21, Sewell 3-8, Winder 5-2; **Passing** - Elway 15-28-2 - 221; **Receiving** - Nattiel 4-62, Johnson 3-56, Winder 2-30, Mobley 1-5, Sewell 3-51, Humphrey 1-3, Jackson 1-14.

NOTES

• In one of the best comebacks in team history, the Bills scored 20 points in a 77-second span in the second half.
• The Bills, who improved to 16-2 at home over the last two-plus seasons, were dominated in the game.
• Bruce Smith had two sacks, two tipped passes; Darryl Talley had 13 tackles.
• The Broncos drove 80 yards in 12 plays on their first possession to Bobby Humphrey's TD.
• After an exchange of fumbles, the Broncos drove into field goal range, but Talley blocked it in the second quarter.
• With 3:09 left in the half, Steve Atwater intercepted Jim Kelly and returned it to the Bills 30. John Elway hit Vance Johnson for 25 and two plays later, Steve Sewell scored.
• The Bills took the kickoff and moved 53 yards in 12 plays to a Scott Norwood field goal.
• Early in the third, Smith sacked Elway, forced a fumble and Talley recovered at the Denver 10. Three plays later, on third-and-12, Kelly audibled to a direct snap and Don Smith scored. A fumbled snap aborted the PAT.
• On the first play after a Denver punt, Thurman Thomas fumbled and Elliott Smith recovered at the Bills 19. Two plays later, Sammy Winder scored for a 21-9 lead.

• The Broncos then drove to the Bills 6 early in the fourth, but David Treadwell's field goal was blocked by Nate Odomes and Cornelius Bennett returned it 80 yards for a TD. Two plays after the kickoff, Leon Seals tipped an Elway pass, Leonard Smith intercepted and returned it 39 yards for a TD. Norwood missed the PAT, leaving the score 22-21 Bills. An illegal-block penalty on the kickoff pushed the Broncos back to their 5 and on the first play, Elway fumbled the snap and Bennett recovered. Kenneth Davis scored on the next play.
• After Norwood missed a field goal with 3:37 left, the Broncos drove 70 yards in 10 plays to Elway's TD pass to Ricky Nattiel, but the Bills recovered the onside kick with 1:23 left and ran out the clock.

QUOTES

• Marv Levy: "I told our players if you don't quit, sometimes you get lucky. That prevailed. We look for them to make plays in a situation where you tend to want to sag."
• Cornelius Bennett: "It was my best game in a long time. This is to show all those who doubted Cornelius Bennett. You can knock me down, kick me, but don't ever count me out. I had a long struggle due to injuries. I think I've had a great season. This is for everybody who wanted to ship my butt out of here."
• Kent Hull: "That team (the Bills 1988 squad) always found a way to win. It was always 'Never say die.' I think that's what this team is doing now. That feeling came back today."
• Denver coach Dan Reeves: "It was just one of those crazy games. If you're around long enough, you'll see everything. We just couldn't deliver the knockout punch. But if anybody tells me they were more physical than we were, they weren't watching the same game."

WEEK 4 GAMES

LAR 24, Chi 10	KC 34, Clev 0
NYG 31, Dal 17	GB 24, Det 21
Ind 24, Phil 23	Hou 17, SD 7
Mia 28, Pitt 6	NYJ 37, NE 13
Wash 38, Phoe 10	Sea 31, Cin 16
TB 23, Minn 20 (OT)	
SF, Rams, Atl, NO all had bye weeks	

STANDINGS: FOURTH WEEK

AFC EAST	W	L	T	CENTRAL	W	L	T	WEST	W	L	T	NFC EAST	W	L	T	CENTRAL	W	L	T	WEST	W	L	T
Miami	3	1	0	Cincinnati	3	1	0	Raiders	4	0	0	NY Giants	4	0	0	Chicago	3	1	0	San Fran	3	0	0
Buffalo	3	1	0	Houston	2	2	0	Kan. City	3	1	0	Washington	3	1	0	Tampa Bay	3	1	0	Atlanta	1	2	0
NY Jets	2	2	0	Pittsburgh	1	3	0	Denver	2	2	0	Dallas	1	3	0	Green Bay	2	2	0	LA Rams	1	2	0
New England	1	3	0	Cleveland	1	3	0	San Diego	1	3	0	Phoenix	1	3	0	Detroit	1	3	0	N.Orleans	1	2	0
Indianapolis	1	3	0					Seattle	1	3	0	Philadelphia	1	3	0	Minnesota	1	3	0				

NOTES

• For the second straight week, the Bills put on a huge rally by scoring 24 points in a 6:03 span of the fourth.
• The crowd was the second-largest in Rich Stadium history and the Sunday night game was telecast on TNT.
• Free safety Mark Kelso suffered a broken left ankle late in the game and would be out 10-12 weeks.
• Cornelius Bennett had two sacks for 19 yards and Darryl Talley had 10 tackles.
• The Raiders drove 69 yards to Jay Schroeder's TD pass to Willie Gault in the first quarter, but the Bills tied it in the second quarter when Chris Hale recovered Tim Brown's fumble on a punt at the Raiders 15, forced by Steve Tasker. Three plays later, Jim Kelly hit Andre Reed for a TD. Kelly was intercepted by Eddie Anderson with 1:32 left. Anderson returned 31 yards to the 2, but the defense held, forcing a Jeff Jaeger field goal.
• In the third, Los Angeles drove 47 yards in 11 plays to Marcus Allen's TD, but the Bills answered as Kelly hit Keith McKeller for a TD. During the 78-yard drive, he also hit James Lofton for 23.
• Los Angeles got that back, moving 69 yards to Steve Smith's TD reception, but the Bills then began their rally. Five plays after the kickoff, Kelly hit Lofton for a 42-yard TD to make it 24-21.
• Los Angeles went three-and-out and Tasker blocked a punt which J.D. Williams picked up and scored.
• Three plays after the kickoff, Bennett sacked Schroeder, forced a fumble and recovered it, leading to Scott Norwood's field goal. Then, Nate Odomes stole the ball from Willie Gault and ran for a TD.

QUOTES

• Darryl Talley: "When the clock strikes four (fourth quarter), everybody's eyes light up, tails go up and we just come out of the woodwork."
• Nate Odomes: "When it gets to the fourth quarter, everyone starts looking in each other's eyes and you can just feel the intensity."
• James Lofton: "We knew what we were up against. The Raiders have a hard-nosed defense and an explosive offense. But mystique does not mean you win every game."
• Steve Tasker on his block: "You always feel like you can block a kick. J.D. got in there real quick and (Jeff) Gossett saw him and turned and kicked the ball right into me."
• Marv Levy: "Billy Conn beat the crap out of Joe Louis for 12 rounds and then Louis knocked him out in the 13th. Those plays (blocked kicks) aren't luck. Steve and James spend a lot of time looking at film. We work hard on blocking kicks. If you quit, you'll never get one. This was a very big win, but losing Mark took some of the joy out of it."
• Kent Hull: "We were struggling a long time and the crowd stayed with us. Sometimes when you get behind they start booing, but there was none of that."
• Raiders defensive end Greg Townsend: "They're a good team, but there was a little luck involved. They didn't play football with us on the line, they beat us on fluke plays."

WEEK 5 GAMES	
Det 34, Minn 27	Ind 23, KC 19
Atl 28, NO 27	Mia 20, NYJ 16
Pitt 36, SD 14	SF 24, Hou 21
Sea 33, NE 20	Dal 14, TB 10
Clev 30, Den 29	Chi 27, GB 13
Cinc 34, Rams 31 (OT)	
NYG, Wash, Phil, Phoe had bye weeks	

Raiders	7	3	7	7	- 24
Bills	0	7	7	24	- 38

Attendance at Rich Stadium - 80,076

LAR: Gault 11 pass from Schroeder (Jaeger kick), 11:25
Buf: Reed 13 pass from Kelly (Norwood kick), 10:51
LAR: FG Jaeger 19, 15:00
LAR: Allen 9 run (Jaeger kick), 9:16
Buf: McKeller 15 pass from Kelly (Norwood kick), 13:03
LAR: Smith 4 pass from Schroeder (Jaeger kick), 4:25
Buf: Lofton 42 pass from Kelly (Norwood kick), 6:23
Buf: Williams 38 blocked punt return (Norwood kick), 8:08
Buf: FG Norwood 23, 10:53
Buf: Odomes 49 fumble return (Norwood kick), 12:26

	BUF	LAR
First downs	14	22
Rushing yds	98	122
Passing yds	182	225
Punts-avg	3-40.3	3-19.3
Fumbles-lost	0-0	4-3
Penalties-yds	6-32	7-55
Poss. time	20:46	39:14

BILLS LEADERS: Rushing - Thomas 15-67, Mueller 3-21, Davis 2-4, Kelly 2-6; **Passing** - Kelly 13-21-2 - 182, D. Smith 0-1-0 - 0; **Receiving** - Thomas 4-47, Reed 6-55, Lofton 2-65, McKeller 1-15.

RAIDERS LEADERS: Rushing - Allen 20-71, Smith 7-32, Bell 10-19; **Passing** - Schroeder 17-29-1 - 244; **Receiving** - Fernandez 8-134, Allen 2-16, Gault 6-90, Smith 1-4.

NOTES

• The Bills executed their third straight fourth-quarter rally as Jamie Mueller caught the winning TD pass.
• Thurman Thomas hurt his knee early and missed most of the game. John Hagy started for Mark Kelso at free safety, Hagy's first NFL start. Bruce Smith had another two-sack game.
• The teams traded punts early, then the Jets drove 63 yards to Freeman McNeil's TD run. Two plays after the kickoff, Erik McMillan intercepted Jim Kelly at the Bills 30 and that led to Mark Boyer's TD catch.
• The Bills responded with a 64-yard march to Kelly's TD pass to Andre Reed, but the Jets came back with a 71-yard drive to Ken O'Brien's TD to Al Toon on second-and-12 from the 19. Toon also had a 17-yard catch.
• Again, the Bills answered with a seven-play, 77-yard drive to Reed's second TD catch, which was set up by his 26-yard run on a reverse on a third-and-14 from the Bills 35. Kelly followed that with a 25-yard pass to James Lofton.
• After a punt, the Bills closed the half with a Scott Norwood field goal to get within 21-17.
• The Jets moved 81 yards on their first possession of the second half to Pat Leahy's field goal. But Kelly needed just three passes worth 91 yards to tie the game. He hit Reed for 12 and 19 and Lofton for a 60-yard TD.
• Kirby Jackson's interception early in the fourth was wasted when Norwood missed a 24-yard field goal. The Jets then drove 72 yards in 12 plays to a Leahy field goal with 2:46 left.
• The Bills took over at their 29. Don Smith converted third-and-one, then Kelly completed three passes to put the ball at the Jets 29 with 1:06 left. On third-and-10, he found Reed for 13. After a one-yard loss on a pass to Mueller, he found Mueller alone in the end zone for the winning TD.

QUOTES

• Jamie Mueller: "This is the last thing I ever expected. But when you get the opportunity, you have to make the best of it. I'm blocking weak side and looking for one of the linebackers to come. They both dropped off, so I just find an open area so if Jim needs help or is in a scramble, I try to get in the open field so he can throw to me. And that's what he did."
• Marv Levy: "Today, Jamie caught the one he worked the whole off-season for. You wouldn't know by looking at me that I'm 31 years old. They've gained confidence from doing it (coming from behind to win). You have to win games like that if you want (to go to the Super Bowl)."
• Jim Kelly: "We can't rely on a comeback every week to win. One of these weeks we're going to come out and you're going to see offense, defense and special teams and we're going to blow somebody out. But until we do, a win's a win."

WEEK 6 GAMES	
NO 25, Cle 20	TB 26, GB 14
Phoe 20, Dal 3	KC 43, Det 24
Hou 48, Cinc 17	NYG 24, Wash 20
Pitt 34, Den 17	SD 38, NYJ 3
SF 45, Atl 35	LAR 24, Sea 17
Chi 38, Rams 9	Phil 32, Min 24
Buf, Mia, Ind, NE had bye weeks	

WEEK 7 GAMES	
Mia 17, NE 10	Rams 44, Atl 24
Dal 17, TB 13	Den 27, Ind 17
Sea 19, KC 7	LAR 24, SD 9
Hou 23, NO 10	Wash 13, Phil 7
SF 27, Pitt 7	NYG 20, Phoe 19
Cinc 34, Clev 13	
Chi, Minn, Det, GB had bye weeks	

Jets	7	14	3	3	- 27
Bills	0	17	7	6	- 30

Attendance at Rich Stadium - 79,002

NYJ: McNeil 5 run (Leahy kick), 9:39
NYJ: Boyer 1 pass from O'Brien (Leahy kick), :03
Buf: Reed 19 pass from Kelly (Norwood kick), 4:11
NYJ: Toon 19 pass from O'Brien (Leahy kick), 9:36
Buf: Reed 14 pass from Kelly (Norwood kick), 13:04
Buf: FG Norwood 29, 14:38
NYJ: FG Leahy 28, 7:33
Buf: Lofton 60 pass from Kelly (Norwood kick), 8:42
NYJ: FG Leahy 25, 12:14
Buf: Mueller 14 pass from Kelly (kick failed), 14:41

	BUF	NYJ
First downs	24	23
Rushing yds	129	150
Passing yds	276	192
Punts-avg	3-47.0	3-49.7
Fumbles-lost	0-0	1-0
Penalties-yds	9-61	10-61
Poss. time	22:58	37:02

BILLS LEADERS: Rushing - Thomas 2-5, Mueller 6-17, Kelly 3-21, Davis 7-31, D. Smith 2-17, Reed 2-38; **Passing** - Kelly 19-32-1 - 297; **Receiving** - Mueller 3-43, Reed 8-116, Lofton 3-99, Davis 2-23, Metzelaars 2-17, D. Smith 1-(-1).

JETS LEADERS: Rushing - McNeil 12-48, Hector 13-44, B. Thomas 8-28, Baxter 4-10, O'Brien 1-2, Prokop 1-8, Mathis 1-10; **Passing** - O'Brien 14-28-1 - 210; **Receiving** - Moore 3-46, Toon 5-98, Boyer 3-19, Mathis 2-37, McNeil 1-10.

STANDINGS: SEVENTH WEEK

AFC EAST	W	L	T	CENTRAL	W	L	T	WEST	W	L	T	NFC EAST	W	L	T	CENTRAL	W	L	T	WEST	W	L	T
Miami	5	1	0	Cincinnati	5	2	0	Raiders	6	1	0	NY Giants	6	0	0	Chicago	5	1	0	San Fran	6	0	0
Buffalo	5	1	0	Houston	4	3	0	Kan. City	4	3	0	Washington	4	2	0	Tampa Bay	4	3	0	Atlanta	2	4	0
Indianapolis	2	4	0	Pittsburgh	3	4	0	Denver	3	4	0	Dallas	3	4	0	Green Bay	2	4	0	LA Rams	2	4	0
NY Jets	2	5	0	Cleveland	2	5	0	Seattle	3	4	0	Phoenix	2	4	0	Detroit	2	4	0	N.Orleans	2	4	0
New England	1	5	0					San Diego	2	5	0	Philadelphia	2	4	0	Minnesota	1	5	0				

Bills	7	7	13	0	- 27
Patriots	0	3	0	7	- 10

Attendance at Foxboro Stadium - 51,959

Buf: D. Smith 1 run (Norwood kick), 8:45
Buf: Thomas 3 run (Norwood kick), 7:56
NE: FG Staurovsky 32, 14:48
Buf: FG Norwood 35, 6:08
Buf: FG Norwood 35, 10:21
Buf: McKeller 20 pass from Kelly (Norwood kick), 14:37
NE: Martin 19 pass from Grogan (Staurovsky kick), 3:19

	BUF	NE
First downs	19	17
Rushing yds	161	108
Passing yds	192	154
Punts-avg	2-33.5	4-40.8
Fumbles-lost	1-0	1-1
Penalties-yds	5-25	4-34
Poss. time	31:55	28:05

BILLS LEADERS: Rushing - Thomas 22-136, Mueller 9-30, Kelly 2-(-2), D. Smith 2-(-3); **Passing** - Kelly 14-20-0 - 208; **Receiving** - McKeller 5-72, Reed 4-41, Lofton 3-75, Beebe 1-11, Thomas 1-9.

PATRIOTS LEADERS: Rushing - Stephens 19-93, Perryman 3-11, Adams 1-4, Grogan 1-0; **Passing** - Grogan 15-31-2 - 180; **Receiving** - Perryman 3-21, Fryar 2-49, Adams 2-34, Jones 2-28, Stephens 2-9, Martin 1-19, Cook 1-10, Mowatt 1-6, McMurtry 1-4.

WEEK 8 GAMES

Chi 31, Phoe 21	SF 20, Clev 17
Det 27, NO 10	Mia 27, Ind 7
GB 24, Minn 10	NYJ 17, Hou 12
Phil 21, Dal 20	SD 41, TB 10
NYG 21, Wash 10	Atl 38, Cinc 17
Pitt 41, Rams 10	
Byes: LAR, Den, Sea, KC	

NOTES

• The Bills won their fifth straight and remained tied with Miami for first in the AFC East.
• Thurman Thomas shook off his bruised knee and enjoyed a big running day.
• Leonard Smith led the defense with 11 tackles.
• Steve Grogan was asked to sign a document indicating he had received a letter from a neurosurgeon advising him not to play football again because of a spine injury. He signed.
• The Bills drove 68 yards in 12 plays on their first series to Don Smith's TD run.
• The Pats' ensuing drive reached the Bills 5, but Nate Odomes intercepted Grogan in the end zone.
• In the second quarter, the Bills went 90 yards in eight plays to Thomas' TD run. Jim Kelly hit James Lofton for a 52-yard gain on third-and-nine, moving the ball to the Pats 14.
• The Pats drove 54 yards to a Jason Staurovsky field goal at the end of the half with Grogan converting a third-and-14 with a 32-yard pass to Irving Fryar, and a third-and-four with a five-yard pass to Cedric Jones.
• The Bills put away the game in the third. After a Scott Norwood field goal, Grogan fumbled the snap two plays after the kickoff and Ray Bentley recovered at the Pats 40, leading to another field goal.
• After a punt, the Bills moved 70 yards to Kelly's TD pass to Keith McKeller. On the seven-play drive, Thomas carried five times for 46 yards. The Pats scored in the fourth on a TD pass to Sammy Martin.

QUOTES

• Bruce Smith: "I've been saying all year that we need to jump up on people early so we can get after people and have some fun."
• Thurman Thomas: "I thought we could do anything we wanted against them, run all day against them. Or we could have passed all day. When you have a great quarterback, you can do that. I think we're getting the killer instinct. Last year we came here and lost and everything went downhill for us after that. As a team, we felt this was a must-win. We couldn't let a 1-5 team beat us. To be champions, you have to beat teams like New England. If we keep winning on the road, we'll be sitting pretty. I don't look at it as winning five in a row, I look at it as playing well every week."
• Jim Kelly: "We always seem to let them get back in the game, but not this time. We mixed it up pretty well and when I have time to throw, I can complete 70 percent of my passes."
• Leon Seals on fearing he could hurt Grogan: "I low-keyed it a lot. I'm just going to be honest about it. I wasn't going in there for the kill. It's a touchy situation because as a defensive lineman, you're taught to go in there and rip a person's head off, but in this situation, you have to kind of low-key it. You have to have respect for a guy like that. A couple of us talked about it before the game and everybody said 'I hope I'm not the one to go in and hit him and have him stay down. If I get a sack, I hope he gets back up.' To deliver that kind of hit, it's going to be something you'd have to live with the rest of your life."

Bills	7	7	7	21	- 42
Browns	0	0	0	0	- 0

Attendance at Cleveland Stadium - 79,780

Buf: Thomas 3 run (Norwood kick), 7:15
Buf: Thomas 11 run (Norwood kick), 1:54
Buf: Mueller 1 run (Norwood kick), 3:16
Buf: Thomas 11 pass from Kelly (Norwood kick), 3:04
Buf: Davis 3 run (Norwood kick), 10:28
Buf: Talley 60 interception return (Norwood kick), 12:29

	BUF	CLE
First downs	24	10
Rushing yds	102	43
Passing yds	208	191
Punts-avg	3-34.3	6-36.5
Fumbles-lost	2-0	3-0
Penalties-yds	4-30	13-87
Poss. time	34:56	25:04

BILLS LEADERS: Rushing - Thomas 17-58, Mueller 8-21, Reed 1-(-15), Davis 7-41, Gardner 2-0, Reich 3-(-3); **Passing** - Kelly 14-19-0 - 200, Reich 1-1-0 - 16; **Receiving** - Reed 7-122, McKeller 1-7, Mueller 1-6, Thomas 5-65, Davis 1-16.
BROWNS LEADERS: Rushing - Mack 11-37, Hoard 2-8, Metcalf 1-(-1), Pagel 3-(-1), Slaughter 1-(-5), Gainer 2-5; **Passing** - Pagel 16-38-2 - 195; **Receiving** - Slaughter 2-27, Brennan 5-85, Metcalf 4-34, Newsome 3-40, Mack 1-3, Hoard 1-6.

WEEK 9 GAMES

Pitt 21, Atl 9	Chi 26, TB 6
NYJ 24, Dal 9	Rams 17, Hou 13
KC 9, LAR 7	Phil 48, NE 20
NO 21, Cinc 7	Mia 23, Phoe 3
SD 31, Sea 14	SF 24, GB 20
Minn 27, Den 22	NYG 24, Ind 7
Wash 41, Det 38 (OT)	

NOTES

• The Bills avenged their 1989 playoff loss with an impressive rout, highlighted by Darryl Talley scoring his first NFL TD on an interception while playing in his hometown. For the Browns, it was the worst home loss ever.
• The Bills won their sixth straight and snapped a five-game losing streak to the Browns. They last beat the Browns in '81.
• Browns coach Bud Carson benched Bernie Kosar and started Mike Pagel and he was terrible.
• Nearly 20,000 fans from Buffalo made the trip and were in a raucous mood throughout the game.
• The Bills drove 57 yards on their first possession to Thurman Thomas' TD run. Andre Reed caught two passes for 26 yards and recovered his own fumble to keep the drive alive.
• Chris Hale's 25-yard punt return put the Bills at the Browns 41. Seven plays later Thomas scored his second TD.
• Shane Conlan blocked a Jerry Kauric field goal, then Kauric had a field goal aborted because of a bad snap. Scott Norwood missed from 42 yards with three seconds left in the half.
• On the fourth play of the second half, Andre Reed made a brilliant 43-yard catch-and-run to set up Jamie Mueller's TD, which capped an 80-yard, six-play drive for a 21-0 lead.
• Talley intercepted Pagel at the Bills 13 to kill a drive in the third, and the Bills rolled in the fourth.
• They drove 53 yards to Jim Kelly's TD pass to Thomas. After a punt, they went 50 yards in nine plays to Kenneth Davis' TD with Frank Reich in the game. Reich hit Davis for 16 on a third-and-15 play.
• Talley then wrapped it up with his 60-yard TD return of a bad Pagel pass.

QUOTES

• Jim Kelly on the revenge factor: "There was nothing anybody could say or do that was going to make us change the way we took this game. Coming into this game, we were fired up. We remember last year. There was no payback or anything like that, but we wanted to come out with a big win and we did."
• Darryl Talley: "Overall, this may have been our best game defensively. Everybody was making tackles. But it was not an easy game. Today, we played as well as we did in '88. It was gratifying for me. You always want to play well when you come home."
• Thurman Thomas: "Right now, we're playing as well as any team in the league. It's kind of amazing because they had allowed only 20 points to San Francisco, but our guys accepted the challenge."
• Marv Levy: "Our whole team played very well today. It's one of those games where something doesn't jump right out at you because we played a good game overall. Our team was aware they had to play hard to win."
• Cleveland coach Bud Carson: "At the end it got embarrassing. It's an embarrassing loss for me and for this football team. It was about as frustrating as it can get. We did all the things that losers do."

STANDINGS: NINTH WEEK

AFC EAST	W	L	T	CENTRAL	W	L	T	WEST	W	L	T	NFC EAST	W	L	T	CENTRAL	W	L	T	WEST	W	L	T
Miami	7	1	0	Cincinnati	5	4	0	Raiders	6	2	0	NY Giants	8	0	0	Chicago	7	1	0	San Fran	8	0	0
Buffalo	7	1	0	Pittsburgh	5	4	0	Kan. City	5	3	0	Washington	5	3	0	Tampa Bay	4	5	0	Atlanta	3	5	0
NY Jets	4	5	0	Houston	4	5	0	San Diego	4	5	0	Philadelphia	4	4	0	Green Bay	3	5	0	LA Rams	3	5	0
Indianapolis	2	6	0	Cleveland	2	7	0	Seattle	3	5	0	Dallas	3	6	0	Detroit	3	5	0	N.Orleans	3	5	0
New England	1	7	0					Denver	3	5	0	Phoenix	2	6	0	Minnesota	2	6	0				

GAME 9 - Sunday, Nov. 11, 1990 - BILLS 45, CARDINALS 14

NOTES

• The Bills won their seventh in a row on a bitter day with winds howling up to 30 mph.
• All 59 points were scored with the wind, which blew toward the tunnel end.
• The Bills increased their fourth-quarter scoring production to 119 points. The Cards had 117 points overall to this point.
• On the first series of the game, Jim Kelly was blindsided by Cedric Mack who recovered a fumble and returned it to the Bills 7, setting up Johnny Johnson's TD run.
• The Bills tied it early in the second quarter with a 75-yard drive to Keith McKeller's TD reception.
• The Cards went three-and-out and a wind gust made punter Rich Camarillo drop the snap. Steve Tasker recovered at the Cards 6. That led to Butch Rolle's TD, his eighth straight scoring reception.
• The Bills got the ball with 57 seconds left in the half. A pass to Jamie Mueller lost two, but rather than sit on the ball, Kelly threw a 49-yard pass to Don Beebe, then fired a 24-yard TD pass to Tasker on the next play. It was Tasker's first reception and first TD since joining the Bills in 1986. He was in the game because Andre Reed had suffered an ankle injury and Beebe left the field after his long catch.
• Tim McDonald recovered a Beebe fumble in the third to set up Timm Rosenbach's TD pass to Ernie Jones.
• Scott Norwood made a field goal on the first play of the fourth, and John Hagy intercepted Rosenbach on the first play after the kickoff, leading to Beebe's TD reception on the next play. One play after the kickoff, Leonard Smith forced Johnson to fumble and Leon Seals recovered at the Cards 28. Mueller scored seven plays later, and Kenneth Davis scored late in the game after a pair of 12-yard Camarillo punts.

QUOTES

• Steve Tasker on his TD: "It was six years in the making I guess. It hasn't been my role to catch passes, but I was glad that when I got in there, I was able to make it work. If a guy like me gets in there and drops the ball, he might not see the field again." (On his recovery on the punt snap): "The wind kind of blew the ball away from him. I really didn't cause anything. Here's a guy having a Pro Bowl kind of year and he has something like that happen. Into the wind, we were just letting him kick. How far was the ball going to go?"
• Cards safety Tim McDonald: "You can have this whole city. Whenever we come in November or December, it'll be too soon."
• Marv Levy: "With this weather, you had to score when you had the wind. Even though you live here and play and practice here, it isn't easy to play in that kind of weather. We've always felt we had good depth and today some of those people showed why we have confidence in them."
• Thurman Thomas: "Right now, we're doing everything right. We didn't let the weather bother us. We just did our jobs."
• Jim Kelly: "This was Bills weather. Playing in this weather is fun, when you're ahead."

WEEK 10 GAMES

Chi 30, Atl 24	SD 19, Den 7
GB 29, LAR 16	Ind 13, NE 10
Mia 17, NYJ 3	Minn 17, Det 7
NYG 31, Rams 7	Sea 17, KC 16
NO 35, Atl 7	SF 24, Dal 6
Phil 28, Wash 14	
Cinc, Clev, Hou, Pitt had bye weeks	

Cardinals	7	0	7	0 -	14
Bills	0	21	0	24 -	45

Attendance at Rich Stadium - 74,904

Pho: Johnson 1 run (Del Greco kick), 4:44
Buf: McKeller 2 pass from Kelly (Norwood kick), 2:13
Buf: Rolle 1 pass from Kelly (Norwood kick), 5:35
Buf: Tasker 24 pass from Kelly (Norwood kick), 14:49
Pho: Jones 29 pass from Rosenbach (Del Greco kick), 7:18
Buf: FG Norwood 25, :03
Buf: Beebe 11 pass from Kelly (Norwood kick), :37
Buf: Mueller 1 run (Norwood kick), 4:17
Buf: Davis 13 run (Norwood kick), 14:43

	BUF	PHO
First downs	20	11
Rushing yds	211	81
Passing yds	149	46
Punts-avg	2-43.5	4-24.5
Fumbles-lost	2-1	4-3
Penalties-yds	5-40	3-35
Poss. time	38:02	21:58

BILLS LEADERS: Rushing - Thomas 26-112, D. Smith 3-24, Mueller 2-1, Davis 12-47, Gardner 7-28, Reich 1-(-1); **Passing** - Kelly 11-16-1 - 165; **Receiving** - McKeller 2-40, D. Smith 1-15, Metzelaars 1-4, Rolle 1-1, Lofton 2-23, Tasker 1-24, Beebe 2-60, Mueller 1-(-2).

CARDINALS LEADERS: Rushing - Johnson 20-66, Thompson 6-21, Rosenbach 2-5, Camarillo 1-(-11); **Passing** - Rosenbach 5-10-1 - 74; **Receiving** - Jorden 1-4, Green 1-21, Reeves 1-11, Jones 2-38.

GAME 10 - Sunday, Nov. 18, 1990 - BILLS 14, PATRIOTS 0

NOTES

• The Bills worked hard against the lowly Pats for their eighth straight win. J.D. Williams, who was making his first NFL start because Kirby Jackson was out with a hamstring injury, made an end zone interception with 1:51 left that preserved the lead. Thurman Thomas then ran for a career-long 80-yard TD on the next play.
• Thomas' 165 yards were his second-best output and put him over 3,000 career rushing yards.
• Cornelius Bennett had 11 tackles and one of the Bills' four sacks.
• The Bills drove 65 yards in nine plays to Thomas' TD run on their first possession of the game. Thomas carried seven times for 36 yards and Jim Kelly threw passes of four yards to Keith McKeller and 25 to Andre Reed.
• Early in the second quarter, the Pats drove to first-and-goal at the Bills 6. It became fourth-and-goal at the 1 and Ray Bentley stuffed Marvin Allen. The Bills drove 87 yards from there, but Scott Norwood blew a field goal.
• The teams combined for seven straight punts until the Pats took possession with 4:05 left in the game. Marc Wilson completed four passes and had the Pats at the Bills 38, but Williams intercepted his pass to Irving Fryar. Thomas then broke his clinching run.

QUOTES

• Marv Levy: "It was every bit as tough as I thought it might be. We weren't flat, we weren't anything. They went down to the last minutes of the game without turning the ball over, that's why the game didn't go differently. We didn't turn the ball over or we would have been in big trouble. They played hard, they played sound and they knew us a little better."
• Ray Bentley on his key fourth-down stop: "Before the down, we were alerting ourselves to watch the play-action pass. But once they came out of the huddle, you could see it in their eyes, they were going to try and run

the lead play. Shane (Conlan) said three guys hit him, so I better have made the play. No one touched me so I shot right up in the gap when the guard pulled."
• J.D. Williams: "I knew they were going to try to come after me because I'm the rookie out there. There wasn't much time on the clock so their best chance was to go deep and they tried for me because I'm a rookie. I was nervous for awhile, but I wasn't nervous then. You always want to make the play, but you're always thinking 'Don't get beat deep.'"
• Thurman Thomas: "This type of game really helps us because we're not going to score 30 points every game and I hope people realize that."
• Jim Kelly: "Sometimes the offense has to shine and put points on the board, sometimes the defense has to shut the opponent down. The defense rose to the occasion and won this game."
• Kent Hull: "We're not going to sneak up on anyone anymore. Everybody in the NFL knows we're a quality team. They come ready to play and when it's a 1-8 team, sometimes they're even more dangerous. You wound a dog and put him in the corner, he'll bite you when you stick your hand out. We knew this wasn't going to be easy. You better believe it's a relief."

Patriots	0	0	0	0 -	0
Bills	7	0	0	7 -	14

Attendance at Rich Stadium - 74,720

Buf: Thomas 5 run (Norwood kick), 8:24
Buf: Thomas 80 run (Norwood kick), 13:22

	BUF	NE
First downs	14	18
Rushing yds	209	90
Passing yds	67	196
Punts-avg	6-38.7	7-36.6
Fumbles-lost	0-0	1-0
Penalties-yds	7-71	4-30
Poss. time	25:30	34:30

BILLS LEADERS: Rushing - Thomas 22-165, Beebe 1-23, Kelly 3-13, Mueller 4-8; **Passing** - Kelly 5-15-0 - 79; **Receiving** - Mueller 1-4, Reed 3-70, Thomas 1-5.

PATRIOTS LEADERS: Rushing - Allen 16-57, Tatupu 4-12, Stephens 10-22, Adams 1-0, Fryar 1-(-1); **Passing** - Wilson 21-33-2 - 234; **Receiving** - Fryar 7-85, Adams 4-53, McMurtry 2-25, Mowatt 1-10, Cook 4-47, Stephens 2-9, Jones 1-5.

WEEK 11 GAMES

Dal 24, Rams 21	NYG 20, Det 0
GB 24, Phoe 21	Hou 35, Clev 23
Minn 24, Sea 21	Wash 31, NO 17
Ind 17, NYJ 14	Phil 24, Atl 23
KC 27, SD 10	SF 31, TB 7
Cinc 27, Pitt 3	LAR 13, Mia 10
Chi 16, Den 13 (OT)	

STANDINGS: ELEVENTH WEEK

AFC EAST	W	L	T	CENTRAL	W	L	T	WEST	W	L	T	NFC EAST	W	L	T	CENTRAL	W	L	T	WEST	W	L	T
Buffalo	9	1	0	Cincinnati	6	4	0	Raiders	7	3	0	NY Giants	10	0	0	Chicago	9	1	0	San Fran	10	0	0
Miami	8	2	0	Pittsburgh	5	5	0	Kan. City	6	4	0	Washington	6	4	0	Green Bay	5	5	0	N.Orleans	4	6	0
Indianapolis	4	6	0	Houston	5	5	0	San Diego	5	6	0	Philadelphia	6	4	0	Minnesota	4	6	0	LA Rams	3	7	0
NY Jets	4	7	0	Cleveland	2	8	0	Seattle	4	6	0	Dallas	4	7	0	Tampa Bay	4	7	0	Atlanta	3	7	0
New England	1	9	0					Denver	3	7	0	Phoenix	2	8	0	Detroit	3	7	0				

Bills	7 7 3 7 - 24
Oilers	7 6 7 7 - 27

Attendance at the Astrodome - 60,130

Hou: Jeffires 37 pass from Moon (Garcia kick), 3:18
Buf: Metzelaars 1 pass from Kelly (Norwood kick), 12:29
Hou: FG Garcia 25, 2:18
Hou: FG Garcia 36, 11:53
Buf: McKeller 12 pass from Kelly (Norwood kick), 14:20
Buf: FG Norwood 43, 6:57
Hou: White 1 run (Garcia kick), 11:46
Hou: Harris 3 pass from Moon (Garcia kick), 7:39
Buf: Thomas 1 run (Norwood kick), 11:31

	BUF	HOU
First downs	24	21
Rushing yds	79	128
Passing yds	210	283
Punts-avg	2-34.5	0-0
Fumbles-lost	0-0	1-1
Penalties-yds	3-15	9-66
Poss. time	30:01	29:59

BILLS LEADERS: Rushing - Thomas 15-54, Mueller 3-3, D. Smith 3-11, Davis 2-9, Kelly 1-2; **Passing** - Kelly 23-34-1 - 224; **Receiving** - Reed 6-54, Thomas 4-32, Lofton 3-35, D. Smith 4-71, Metzelaars 1-1, Mueller 3-8, McKeller 2-23.

OILERS LEADERS: Rushing - White 18-125, Moon 7-4, Pinkett 2-1, Jones 1-(-2); **Passing** - Moon 16-22-0 - 300; **Receiving** - White 5-89, Jeffires 1-37, Givins 3-69, Hill 6-102, Harris 1-3.

NOTES

• The Bills were concerned with the run-and-shoot passing of Warren Moon and played a dime defense all night, but it was Lorenzo White who hurt them the most as their eight-game winning streak ended.
• Andre Reed surpassed 5,000 career receiving yards; Bruce Smith had two more sacks.
• The Oilers scored on the fifth play of the game as Haywood Jeffires caught a TD pass to cap a 74-yard march.
• The Bills matched it with a fourth-and-goal TD pass to Pete Metzelaars to cap a 15-play, 75-yard drive.
• White had runs of 12, 22 and 10 yards to set up a Teddy Garcia field goal on the next series.
• The teams exchanged turnovers before Garcia kicked another field goal, set up by a 16-yard run by White and a 29-yard screen pass to White. But the Bills took the halftime lead as Keith McKeller caught a TD pass to end a nine-play, 65-yard drive with 40 seconds left in the half. Kelly was six-of-eight for 59 yards.
• Scott Norwood made a field goal on the first series of the third, but the Oilers moved 79 yards in seven plays to take a 20-17 lead on White's TD run. The key play was a 48-yard Warren Moon pass to Drew Hill to the 1.
• After a Bills punt, the Oilers drove 88 yards in 14 plays

WEEK 12 GAMES	
Det 40, Den 27	Dal 27, Wash 17
NO 10, Atl 7	Minn 41, Chi 13
Ind 34, Cinc 20	KC 27, LAR 24
Rams 28, SF 17	Mia 30, Clev 13
Phoe 34, NE 14	Phil 31, NYG 13
Pitt 24, NYJ 7	GB 20, TB 10
Sea 13, SD 10 (OT)	

to Moon's third-and-goal TD pass to Leonard Harris. Ernest Givins had a 22-yard catch, and White a 16-yard run and a 28-yard pass reception.
• The Bills answered with a 10-play, 76-yard drive to Thurman Thomas' TD run. Don Smith caught passes for 39 and 15 yards. However, the Oilers ran out the final 3:29, converting two third downs.

QUOTES

• Bruce Smith: "When you're No. 1, everyone's knocking at your door. We just didn't come through tonight. We really didn't change our scheme up, but that's the coaches' decision. Whatever they call, we have to make it work. We're not going to fold our tents, though."
• Darryl Talley: "It's just one out of 16. To be a true champ, you have to pick your chin up."
• Nate Odomes: "Let them come to Buffalo on a nice snowy day and see what the run-and-shoot can do."
• Walt Corey: "It's called run-and-shoot for a purpose. It's not the shoot-and-shoot. You have to stop the run. They beat us; they played a superior game and we didn't do enough to stop them. I can't give you one reason to hang your hat on. We tried everything."
• Houston running back Lorenzo White: "Coach (Jack) Pardee told me I was going to be in the game a lot. He said he wanted to run the ball tonight. With the run-and-shoot, if you run the ball well, it makes a big difference."
• Marv Levy: "We knew they'd get their yardage, but we hoped to force a mistake or two more than we did. Moon really handled himself well."
• Thurman Thomas: "We were ready to go (if they had gotten the ball back). In the hurry-up, they couldn't stop us. No doubt in my mind we would've scored again."

Eagles	0 16 7 0 - 23
Bills	24 0 3 3 - 30

Attendance at Rich Stadium - 79,320

Buf: Lofton 63 pass from Kelly (Norwood kick), :45
Buf: FG Norwood 43, 6:31
Buf: Reed 56 pass from Kelly (Norwood kick), 8:47
Buf: Thomas 4 pass from Kelly (Norwood kick), 13:37
Phi: K. Jackson 18 pass from Cunningham (kick failed), 4:26
Phi: FG Ruzek 32, 12:17
Phi: Barnett 95 pass from Cunningham (Ruzek kick), 14:06
Phi: Byars 1 pass from Cunningham (Ruzek kick), 5:32
Buf: FG Norwood 21, 11:28
Buf: FG Norwood 45, :11

	BUF	PHI
First downs	13	19
Rushing yds	59	176
Passing yds	334	181
Punts-avg	5-45.2	6-35-5
Fumbles-lost	0-0	2-1
Penalties-yds	6-57	10-65
Poss. time	26:44	33:16

BILLS LEADERS: Rushing - Thomas 21-53, Davis 2-1, Kelly 1-3, Mueller 1-2; **Passing** - Kelly 19-32-1 - 334; **Receiving** - Lofton 5-174, Reed 7-95, McKeller 1-4, Thomas 2-39, Davis 2-8, Mueller 1-11, Metzelaars 1-3.

EAGLES LEADERS: Rushing - Sherman 11-70, Byars 4-13, Cunningham 7-71, Toney 7-18, Sanders 1-1, Feagles 1-3; **Passing** - Cunningham 15-25-1 - 231; **Receiving** - Byars 5-39, K. Jackson 6-64, Barnett 2-112, Williams 1-13, Sherman 1-3.

NOTES

• The Bills operated from the no-huddle offense throughout the first quarter and rolled to a 24-0 lead as Jim Kelly completed eight-of-eight passes for 229 yards and three TDs.
• Thurman Thomas passed 1,000 yards in rushing, James Lofton moved into third on the all-time NFL receiving yardage list at 11,889 and Andre Reed tied Elbert Dubenion's team TD reception record (35).
• Kelly hit Lofton for a TD on the second play of the game. After an Eagles punt, the Bills drove 39 yards to a Scott Norwood field goal. The Eagles went three-and-out and two plays after the punt, Reed caught a TD pass.
• Another Eagles punt gave the Bills the ball at their 16. On third-and-two, Lofton got loose for a 71-yard reception, setting up Kelly's four-yard TD pass to Thomas for an incredible 24-0 lead.
• The Eagles began their comeback in the second quarter, driving 73 yards in four plays to Randall Cunningham's TD pass to Keith Jackson. The key play was Cunningham's 51-yard run on a scramble. Roger Ruzek missed the PAT.
• After a Bills punt, the Eagles drove 53 yards to a Ruzek field goal. Another Rick Tuten punt, a 52-yarder, pinned the Eagles at their 9, but on third-and-14 from the 5, Cunningham escaped Bruce Smith in the end zone and fired a 95-yard TD pass to Fred Barnett,

WEEK 13 GAMES	
TB 23, Atl 17	Cinc 16, Pitt 12
KC 37, NE 7	Phoe 20, Ind 17
LAR 23, Den 20	Rams 38, Clev 23
Dal 17, NO 13	Wash 42, Mia 20
Minn 23, GB 7	SD 38, NYJ 17
SF 7, NYG 3	Chi 23, Det 17 (OT)
Sea 13, Hou 10 (OT)	

the second-longest TD pass ever against the Bills.
• The Eagles took the second-half kickoff and moved 77 yards in 12 plays to Keith Byars' TD catch. The key was pass interference on Leonard Smith on third-and-10 from the Bills 18. The Bills responded with a 74-yard march to a Norwood field goal, the key a 35-yard pass to Thomas.
• Late in the third, Ray Bentley intercepted Cunningham at the Eagles 27, setting up the final field goal.
• Steve Tasker blocked a Jeff Feagles punt, giving the Bills the ball at the 49 with 8:57 left. Kelly was intercepted by Seth Joyner, but Joyner fumbled and James Lofton recovered. The Bills then ran out all but the final 17 seconds of the game.

QUOTES

• Will Wolford: "The start was great, but look up at the scoreboard and it's still the first quarter. We almost scored too quickly. We didn't take any time off the clock."
• Marv Levy: "I want to express admiration for our team because usually if you've got a lead like that and it fritters away, most of the time teams will go and lose. Our players didn't. They kept playing hard and as a result won the game when it came down to crunch time. I'm proud." (About the no-huddle): "We hoped to get some hits and long runs against their blitz and we did."
• Jim Kelly: "We knew there were some individuals who said we couldn't win in December. We wanted to shut a few people up, shove it down their throats. We knew we could win. We know our talent. I had time, the receivers ran the patterns and the ball was thrown well."
• Eagles coach Buddy Ryan: "They came out fired up, but we didn't throw up our skirts."

STANDINGS: THIRTEENTH WEEK

AFC EAST	W	L	T	CENTRAL	W	L	T	WEST	W	L	T	NFC EAST	W	L	T	CENTRAL	W	L	T	WEST	W	L	T
Buffalo	10	2	0	Cincinnati	7	5	0	Raiders	8	4	0	NY Giants	10	2	0	Chicago	10	2	0	San Fran	11	1	0
Miami	9	3	0	Pittsburgh	6	6	0	Kan. City	8	4	0	Philadelphia	7	5	0	Green Bay	6	6	0	N.Orleans	5	7	0
Indianapolis	5	7	0	Houston	6	6	0	Seattle	6	6	0	Washington	7	5	0	Minnesota	6	6	0	LA Rams	5	7	0
NY Jets	4	9	0	Cleveland	2	10	0	San Diego	6	7	0	Dallas	6	7	0	Tampa Bay	5	8	0	Atlanta	3	9	0
New England	1	11	0					Denver	3	9	0	Phoenix	4	8	0	Detroit	4	8	0				

NOTES

• The Bills clinched a playoff berth and remained one game ahead of Miami in the AFC East race.
• Andre Reed surpassed Elbert Dubenion's team mark for TD receptions (35) with his ninth two-TD game.
• Bruce Smith had a single-game career-high of four sacks worth 33 yards, had nine tackles and one tipped pass.
• The Bills drove 66 yards in seven plays to Reed's record-breaking TD, a 34-yard pass. The key play was a 12-yard pass to James Lofton on third-and-nine from the Colts 42.
• On the ensuing series, Kirby Jackson intercepted Jeff George at the Colts 37. Four plays later, Jim Kelly hit Reed for his second TD. He hit Reed for 12 and Keith McKeller for 18 before the TD.
• Another scoring chance died when Don Smith lost a fumble at the 2 late in the first quarter.
• John Hagy's interception early in the second quarter was wasted. But midway through the second, the Bills marched 64 yards in 11 plays to Thurman Thomas' TD run. The Colts had 57 yards at the half.
• Clarence Verdin's 20-yard punt return started the Colts on a 45-yard drive in the third to George's TD run.
• The Bills responded with a 73-yard drive in seven plays to a Scott Norwood field goal, set up by Thomas' 63-yard catch-and-run of a short Kelly pass.
• Newcomer Clifford Hicks tipped a pass that Leon Seals intercepted late in the third, setting up Thomas' 23-yard TD run that closed the scoring in the Bills second win ever at the Hoosier Dome.

QUOTES

• Colts running back Eric Dickerson: "Buffalo is a great team; we were no match for them. I was listening to the jokes all week that we could man up with them. We can't man up with those guys. They could have run up the score as much as they wanted. They were very tactful about not running it up." (On Jeff George): "He's going to be a good quarterback, but if we don't start protecting him, he's going to end up in a hospital as a cripple."
• Bruce Smith: "I think he (George) was a little rattled. If you get constant pressure on any quarterback, he's going to wonder where it's coming from. On one, he saw me coming and he said 'Oh (expletive).' Ray Donaldson told me after the game they were supposed to double me on every play but apparently they got screwed up on their blocking schemes. They got kind of confused and the way I've been coming off the ball, by the time the second guy got over, it was too late, I was already back there."
• Marv Levy: "You get the same speech every week about Bruce Smith. He just seems to get better and better and he's still improving. I'm glad he's wearing a Buffalo Bills helmet and jersey. Today's win is the best because it's now, it's fresh. We had a lot of players play well."
• Andre Reed on breaking Dubenion's record: "He was one of the guys instrumental in getting me up to Buffalo. Supposedly I was a diamond in the rough. You've got to have a lot of things working for you for that to happen. The line has to protect, Kelly has to get his reads. I just try to go out and do the best I can and when it comes to me, I'm going to make the catch."

Bills	14	7	3	7 - 31
Colts	0	0	7	0 - 7

Attendance at the Hoosier Dome - 53,268

Buf: Reed 34 pass from Kelly (Norwood kick), 4:46
Buf: Reed 7 pass from Kelly (Norwood kick), 7:39
Buf: Thomas 5 run (Norwood kick), 11:53
Ind: George 1 run (Biasucci kick), 8:05
Buf: FG Norwood 25, 11:25
Buf: Thomas 23 run (Norwood kick), 2:08

	BUF	IND
First downs	23	12
Rushing yds	161	75
Passing yds	247	52
Punts-avg	4-48.0	6-45-5
Fumbles-lost	1-1	0-0
Penalties-yds	4-35	4-25
Poss. time	32:12	27:48

BILLS LEADERS: Rushing - Thomas 16-76, Davis 10-57, Mueller 3-16, Gardner 4-12, D. Smith 1-1, Reich 1-(-1); **Passing** - Kelly 18-26-0 - 261; **Receiving** - Reed 7-95, Thomas 4-91, McKeller 2-27, Lofton 2-23, Beebe 1-14, D. Smith 2-11.

COLTS LEADERS: Rushing - Bentley 8-40, Dickerson 12-33, George 2-2; **Passing** - George 13-25-3 - 93; **Receiving** - Bentley 5-30, Hester 3-28, Brooks 4-25, Beach 1-10.

WEEK 14 GAMES

Wash 10, Chi 9	Hou 58, Clev 14
KC 31, Den 20	NYG 23, Minn 15
Pitt 24, NE 3	NO 24, Rams 20
Phoe 24, Atl 13	Sea 20, GB 14
LAR 38, Det 31	Mia 23, Phil 20 (OT)
SF 20, Cinc 17 (OT)	

Dal, TB, NYJ, SD had bye weeks

NOTES

• The Bills' season appeared to go up in flames early in the second quarter when Jim Kelly suffered what looked like a serious left knee injury and Will Wolford hurt his right knee on the same play.
• The Bills had a 14-7 lead at the time. Frank Reich came on and preserved the victory.
• The Giants lost Phil Simms for the season with a sprained arch and Jeff Hostetler replaced him.
• Ray Bentley suffered a torn biceps muscle, but played virtually one-armed and made 14 tackles.
• New York took the opening kickoff and drove 71 yards in 11 plays, using 7:02 to take the lead on O.J. Anderson's TD run on fourth-and-goal from the 1. The Giants ran on 10 of 11 plays.
• The Bills answered with a no-huddle six-play, 74-yard march to Andre Reed's TD reception. Thurman Thomas took a screen 48 yards to set up the score.
• After a New York punt, the Bills drove 78 yards in 11 plays, again in the no-huddle, to Thomas' TD run. Kelly was four-of-five and Don Smith converted a fourth-and-one from the Giants 15.
• The Giants got a Matt Bahr field goal and on the ensuing series, Kelly and Wolford were injured.
• On the first possession of the third, the Giants drove 76 yards in six plays to a Bahr field goal, but lost Simms.
• Reich answered with a nine-play, 55-yard drive to a Scott Norwood field goal on the first play of the fourth, also operating in the no-huddle. He hit Don Beebe three times for 56 yards, including a 43-yarder on second-and-19.
• The teams punted six straight series with the Giants starting a possession at their 43 with 1:04 left. They got to the Bills 26, but Hostetler threw four straight incompletions and the Bills escaped with the win.

QUOTES

• Kent Hull on Reich: "When he was in last year, we had this little saying. I'd look at him and I'd say 'Let's do it.' Today he came in and looked at me and said 'Let's do it.' Jim Kelly is our leader. A team has to reach for something extra when it loses its leader. We had to show we could respond to adversity."
• Marv Levy: "Frank didn't take a snap all week because it was a short week and we felt we had to give Jim as much as we could to get him ready. Frank is always prepared, he studies extremely well and I give him high marks. He went against a great defensive team and he engineered what we had to do."
• Frank Reich: "When I came in, I looked up at the scoreboard and saw we were ahead by four. I've always felt our defense is good enough where as long as we don't turn the ball over, it's going to be hard for another team to drive and score on them. So my first thought was just go out and move the sticks and don't make any mistakes."
• Will Wolford: "Carl Banks hit me on the knee. When I got hit, I reared backwards to try and get my knee out and apparently I fell on Jim's knee. I had no idea Jim was hurt because at that time, I couldn't hear anything. I thought I was done."

Bills	7	7	0	3 - 17
Giants	7	3	3	0 - 13

Attendance at Giants Stadium - 66,893

NYG: Anderson 1 run (Bahr kick), 7:02
Buf: Reed 6 pass from Kelly (Norwood kick), 8:30
Buf: Thomas 2 run (Norwood kick), :51
NYG: FG Bahr 23, 9:04
NYG: FG Bahr 22, 10:53
Buf: FG Norwood 29, :04

	BUF	NYG
First downs	13	20
Rushing yds	65	157
Passing yds	199	156
Punts-avg	6-38.7	6-43-2
Fumbles-lost	0-0	4-0
Penalties-yds	8-52	4-39
Poss. time	22:01	37:59

BILLS LEADERS: Rushing - Thomas 21-60, Kelly 1-5, D. Smith 1-1, Reich 1-(-1); **Passing** - Kelly 7-11-0 - 115, Reich 8-15-0 - 97; **Receiving** - McKeller 4-37, Reed 4-54, Thomas 4-65, Beebe 3-56.

GIANTS LEADERS: Rushing - Hampton 21-105, Hostetler 5-23, Tillman 6-17, Meggett 2-6, Anderson 5-0, Carthon 3-6; **Passing** - Simms 6-10-0 - 59, Hostetler 9-16-0 - 97; **Receiving** - Hampton 5-27, Baker 4-56, Cross 2-35, Meggett 2-16, Manuel 1-15, Ingram 1-7.

WEEK 15 GAMES

Wash 25, NE 10	Clev 13, Atl 10
LAR 24, Cinc 7	Phil 31, GB 0
Hou 27, KC 10	Ind 29, NYJ 21
TB 26, Minn 13	Dal 41, Phoe 10
Pitt 9, NO 6	Den 20, SD 10
Mia 24, Sea 17	Det 38, Chi 21
SF 26, Rams 10	

STANDINGS: FIFTEENTH WEEK

AFC EAST	W	L	T	CENTRAL	W	L	T	WEST	W	L	T	NFC EAST	W	L	T	CENTRAL	W	L	T	WEST	W	L	T
Buffalo	12	2	0	Houston	8	6	0	Raiders	10	4	0	NY Giants	11	3	0	Chicago	10	4	0	San Fran	13	1	0
Miami	11	3	0	Pittsburgh	8	6	0	Kan. City	9	5	0	Washington	9	5	0	Green Bay	6	8	0	N.Orleans	6	8	0
Indianapolis	6	8	0	Cincinnati	7	7	0	Seattle	7	7	0	Philadelphia	8	6	0	Minnesota	6	8	0	LA Rams	5	9	0
NY Jets	4	10	0	Cleveland	3	11	0	San Diego	6	8	0	Dallas	7	7	0	Tampa Bay	6	8	0	Atlanta	3	11	0
New England	1	13	0					Denver	4	10	0	Phoenix	5	9	0	Detroit	5	9	0				

Dolphins	0	0	7	7 -	14
Bills	0	7	10	7 -	24

Attendance at Rich Stadium - 80,235

Buf: Lofton 7 pass from Reich (Norwood kick), 8:04
Buf: Reed 11 pass from Reich (Norwood kick), 3:09
Mia: Duper 30 pass from Marino (Stoyanovich kick), 4:16
Buf: FG Norwood 21, 8:35
Buf: Thomas 13 run (Norwood kick), 1:48
Mia: Clayton 11 pass from Marino (Stoyanovich kick), 14:00

	BUF	MIA
First downs	25	20
Rushing yds	206	35
Passing yds	223	274
Punts-avg	4-42.8	4-43.8
Fumbles-lost	1-0	1-1
Penalties-yds	14-95	5-33
Poss. time	36:41	23:19

BILLS LEADERS: Rushing - Thomas 30-154, Reich 6-13, Davis 8-30, D. Smith 3-9; **Passing** - Reich 15-21-0 - 234; **Receiving** - Thomas 2-29, Beebe 3-74, Lofton 3-32, Reed 4-57, McKeller 2-33, Davis 1-9.

DOLPHINS LEADERS: Rushing - S. Smith 9-28, Logan 3-7; **Passing** - Marino 24-43-1 - 287; **Receiving** - Clayton 8-108, Duper 3-47, Edmunds 1-22, Stradford 1-4, Jensen 6-42, Martin 2-19, S. Smith 1-5, Pruitt 2-40.

NOTES

• The Bills clinched their third straight AFC East title and assured themselves home-field advantage in the playoffs, winning the showdown over the Dolphins before a record crowd.
• Fans rushed the field and tore down the goal posts after the game.
• Don Beebe suffered a broken leg on the final play of the third quarter and was lost for the season.
• Dan Marino was sacked three times, the most he'd gone down in one game since 1988 vs. the Colts.
• On the first series of the game, Brian Sochia forced Frank Reich to fumble and Jeff Cross recovered at the Miami 23, but the defense forced a punt.
• Early in the second quarter, Pete Stoyanovich missed a 28-yard field goal. The Bills then proceeded to drive 80 yards in 13 plays to Reich's TD pass to James Lofton. The Bills overcame two holding penalties on Kent Hull as Reich was six-of-seven for 66 yards.
• Before the half ended, Clifford Hicks stopped a Miami threat with an interception at the 7.
• Marc Logan fumbled the second-half kickoff and Carlton Bailey recovered at the Miami 32. Six plays later, Andre Reed caught a TD for a 14-0 lead. But three plays after the kickoff, Marino hit Mark Duper for a TD.
• Reich answered with a 43-yard pass to Beebe to set up Scott Norwood's field goal.

WEEK 16 GAMES

Det 24, GB 17	LAR 28, Minn 17
Chi 27, TB 14	Ind 35, Wash 28
KC 24, SD 21	Pitt 35, Clev 0
NYJ 42, NE 7	Cinc 40, Hou 20
Sea 17, Den 12	NO 13, SF 10
Phil 17, Dal 3	NYG 24, Phoe 21
Atl 20, Rams 13	

• After a punt, the Bills drove 76 yards in 13 plays to Thomas' clinching TD. He carried the final seven plays for 46 yards. Marino capped an 88-yard drive with a TD pass to Mark Clayton with one minute left.

QUOTES

• Thurman Thomas: "I think we could have run the ball anywhere we wanted to. You've been hearing a lot of things about Jim being gone and the offense not being as effective as when Jim was in there, but today, Frank did everything right. Like Marv and Ted said, we weren't going to change anything. We ran the ball effectively and when Frank had to throw, he did a helluva job."
• Jim Ritcher: "It's going to be sweet playing the playoffs here."
• Miami defensive end Cliff Odom: "The road to the Super Bowl comes through Buffalo. The series is tied 1-1 and I'll tell you something, it will be continued. The rubber game is yet to come. It's not over yet."
• Miami cornerback Tim McKyer: "They brought it to another level. We got beat by a better football team today. I know a better team when I see one and I saw one today. Reich stepped up and showed what kind of quarterback he is."
• Frank Reich: "It didn't hurt playing behind one of the best offensive lines in football. He says 'Ask and you shall receive.' I asked and I received. I told Jim before the game I'm not going to try to be the hero. I'm just trying to go out and get this thing back in Jim's hands."
• Marv Levy: "We feel wonderful, but this isn't our ultimate goal. This was the most butterflies I had before an event since I was in the second grade play for the PTA. I was a tree."
• Miami quarterback Dan Marino: "We controlled them in Miami and they did it to us here."

Bills	0	0	7	7 -	14
Redskins	3	6	3	17 -	29

Attendance at RFK Stadium - 52,397

Was: FG Lohmiller 37, 4:11
Was: FG Lohmiller 24, 1:19
Was: FG Lohmiller 19, 14:00
Buf: Davis 13 pass from Gilbert (Norwood kick), 3:59
Was: FG Lohmiller 43, 10:35
Was: FG Lohmiller 32, 3:26
Was: Riggs 3 run (Lohmiller kick), 8:43
Was: Hobbs 18 pass from Rypien (Lohmiller kick), 12:29
Buf: Tasker 20 pass from Gilbert (Norwood kick), 13:38

	BUF	WAS
First downs	15	16
Rushing yds	105	127
Passing yds	168	172
Punts-avg	5-37.8	1-35-0
Fumbles-lost	3-2	0-0
Penalties-yds	3-22	5-63
Poss. time	26:01	33:59

BILLS LEADERS: Rushing - Thomas 5-0, Mueller 7-36, Davis 6-49, Reich 2-18, Gardner 2-1, D. Smith 1-1; **Passing** - Reich 7-14-0 - 88, Gilbert 8-15-2 - 106; **Receiving** - Lofton 1-19, Tasker 1-20, McKeller 4-68, Thomas 2-22, D. Smith 1-5, Mueller 2-24, Edwards 1-6, Davis 1-13, Metzelaars 2-17.

REDSKINS LEADERS: Rushing - Byner 11-34, Dupard 3-11, Monk 1-9, Riggs 16-67, Rypien 4-3, Mitchell 1-3; **Passing** - Rypien 16-26-1 - 172; **Receiving** - Monk 6-61, Clark 2-6, Sanders 2-32, Warren 1-13, Howard 2-19, Riggs 1-18, Mitchell 1-5, Hobbs 1-18.

NOTES

• The Bills used their regulars only briefly because they had the home-field advantage wrapped up.
• The only injury was a mild knee sprain for Leon Seals, and he was expected to be okay.
• Free safety Mark Kelso returned to action for the first time since suffering a broken ankle vs. the Raiders on Oct. 7. He didn't start, but he played much of the game.
• Chip Lohmiller gave the Redskins a 3-0 lead on their first series.
• Keith McKeller lost a fumble on the ensuing series, but the Bills defense held on downs at their 16.
• Tim Johnson recovered Thurman Thomas' fumble at the Bills 40, setting up Lohmiller's second field goal.
• The Redskins drove 78 yards in nine plays to Lohmiller's third field goal late in the second quarter.
• On the third play of the third, Leonard Smith intercepted Mark Rypien at the Bills 38. Gale Gilbert, seeing his first regular-season action since 1986, drove the Bills 59 yards to his TD pass to Kenneth Davis.
• Washington answered with another Lohmiller field goal and after a punt, he made his fifth field goal early in the fourth. On the ensuing possession, Alvin Walton intercepted Gilbert and returned it 61 yards to the Bills 6, setting up Gerald Riggs' TD and a 22-7 lead.

WEEK 17 GAMES

KC 21, Chi 10	Phil 23, Phoe 21
Atl 26, Dal 7	Cinc 21, Clev 14
Sea 30, Det 10	Den 22, GB 13
Mia 23, Ind 17	NYG 13, NE 10
NYJ 16, TB 14	LAR 17, SD 12
SF 20, Minn 17	Hou 34, Pitt 14
NO 20, Rams 17	

• Three plays after the kickoff, ex-Bill Martin Mayhew intercepted a pass at the Bills 32 and that led to Rypien's TD pass to Stephen Hobbs. The Bills answered with that with Gilbert's TD pass to Steve Tasker that capped a quick five-play, 76-yard drive with 1:22 left to play.

QUOTES

• Gale Gilbert: "I actually felt pretty good, I just wish I hadn't thrown the darn interceptions. The first one, I didn't pick up Walton. I let it go and felt I had him beat, but he came out of nowhere. The second one was just a bad throw."
• Jim Ritcher: "Hopefully this loss will turn into something positive. We know now we're not infallible. We're going to have to play tough football to beat teams like Washington. We're going to be seeing teams like this in the playoffs."
• Marv Levy: "We would have liked to have won the game, sure. But for me, particularly if Leon is OK, I feel very good that we came out healthy. I'm glad we could get playing time for the players who needed it. The effort was fine. Our defense stopped four drives, stiffened and forced field goals."
• Thurman Thomas on not winning the rushing title: "It meant more to my offensive line than it did to me. The most important thing for me right now is my health and how far we can go in the playoffs."

STANDINGS: SEVENTEENTH WEEK

AFC EAST	W	L	T	CENTRAL	W	L	T	WEST	W	L	T	NFC EAST	W	L	T	CENTRAL	W	L	T	WEST	W	L	T
Buffalo	13	3	0	Cincinnati	9	7	0	Raiders	12	4	0	NY Giants	13	3	0	Chicago	11	5	0	San Fran	14	2	0
Miami	12	4	0	Houston	9	7	0	Kan. City	11	5	0	Washington	10	6	0	Green Bay	6	10	0	N.Orleans	8	8	0
Indianapolis	7	9	0	Pittsburgh	9	7	0	Seattle	9	7	0	Philadelphia	10	6	0	Minnesota	6	10	0	LA Rams	5	11	0
NY Jets	6	10	0	Cleveland	3	13	0	San Diego	6	10	0	Dallas	7	9	0	Tampa Bay	6	10	0	Atlanta	5	11	0
New England	1	15	0					Denver	5	11	0	Phoenix	5	11	0	Detroit	6	10	0				

Dolphins	3	14	3	13 -	34
Bills	13	14	3	14 -	44

Attendance at Rich Stadium - 77,087

Buf: Reed 40 pass from Kelly (Norwood kick), 1:54
Mia: FG Stoyanovich 49, 8:00
Buf: FG Norwood 24, 10:11
Buf: FG Norwood 22, 14:09
Buf: Thomas 5 run (Norwood kick), 2:56
Mia: Duper 64 pass from Marino (Stoyanovich kick), 5:06
Buf: Lofton 13 pass from Kelly (Norwood kick), 9:49
Mia: Marino 2 run (Stoyanovich kick), 14:39
Mia: FG Stoyanovich 22, 4:57
Buf: FG Norwood 28, 13:22
Mia: Foster 2 pass from Marino (Stoyanovich kick), :55
Buf: Thomas 5 run (Norwood kick), 4:32
Buf: Reed 26 pass from Kelly (Norwood kick), 5:08
Mia: Martin 8 pass from Marino (Stoyanovich kick), 13:45

	BUF	MIA
First downs	24	24
Rushing yds	154	107
Passing yds	339	323
Punts-avg	1-47.0	2-40-0
Fumbles-lost	3-1	2-1
Penalties-yds	4-30	4-32
Poss. time	27:34	32:26

BUFFALO TACKLES: Conlan 11, L. Smith 10, Bennett 6, Talley 6, Bentley 4, Wright 3, Hicks 3, B. Smith 3, Seals 3, Jackson 2.

MIAMI TACKLES: Green 8, Odom 7, Williams 6, Lankford 5, Reichenbach 5, Lee 5, McKyer 4, Griggs 3, Glenn 2, Brown 2, Oglesby 2, Turner 2.

BILLS LEADERS: Rushing - Thomas 32-117, Kelly 5-37; **Passing** - Kelly 19-29-1 - 339; **Receiving** - Lofton 7-149, Reed 4-122, Thomas 3-38, McKeller 3-15, Edwards 1-12, Davis 1-3; **Kickoff returns** - D. Smith 3-51, Edwards 2-51, Rolle 1-14; **Punt returns** - Edwards 2-17.

DOLPHINS LEADERS: Rushing - S. Smith 21-99, Logan 5-6, Marino 1-2; **Passing** - Marino 23-49-2 - 323; **Receiving** - Duper 3-113, Martin 4-44, Logan 2-8, Edmunds 3-21, S. Smith 1-9, Clayton 4-82, Paige 1-6, Foster 1-2, Jensen 4-38; **Kickoff returns** - Logan 8-138, Adams 1-13; **Punt returns** - Clayton 1-3.

NOTES

• The Bills and Dolphins played the highest-scoring non-overtime game in playoff history on a day where light snow fell, coating the field for parts of the game.

• Jim Kelly returned to the lineup and had a brilliant game, as did Andre Reed and James Lofton, as the Bills played almost the entire game in the no-huddle offense.

• Mark Kelso started for the first time since the Raiders game on Oct. 7 and Kirby Jackson started ahead of rookie cornerback J.D. Williams.

• The Bills beat Miami for the fifth straight time in Buffalo, eighth of nine times overall.

• The Dolphins played without star linebacker John Offerdahl, who sat out with a foot injury.

• The Bills lost rookie special teams player Marvcus Patton on the opening kickoff with a broken ankle.

• The Bills took the opening kickoff and on the first play, Kelly hit Reed for 20 to the 44. On the next play, Thurman Thomas fumbled, but Keith McKeller recovered. Thomas then broke a 14-yard run and after Thomas was stuffed for no gain, Reed beat Louis Oliver for a 40-yard TD just 1:54 into the game.

• The Dolphins drove 40 yards in 10 plays to a Pete Stoyanovich field goal, but the Bills answered with a six-play, 57-yard advance to a Scott Norwood field goal as Lofton made a 44-yard reception to the Miami 12.

• Three plays after the kickoff, Darryl Talley tipped a Dan Marino pass and Nate Odomes intercepted at the Miami 38. On third-and-six from the 34, Kelly scrambled for 16 yards, fumbled, and Kent Hull recovered. Six plays later, Norwood kicked his second field goal for a 13-3 lead.

• Miami punted on the ensuing series and the Bills then went 67 yards in five plays to Thomas' TD run. On third-and-two from the Miami 48, Reed got free for a 43-yard reception to the 5.

• But four plays after the kickoff, Marino fired a 64-yard TD pass to Mark Duper.

• The Bills responded with an 11-play, 68-yard drive to Lofton's TD catch. Lofton had a 19-yard reception, Thomas converted a third-and-one play and Reed caught a 13-yard pass on fourth-and-three from the Miami 32.

• The Dolphins punted on the ensuing series, but Al Edwards fumbled and Reggie Roby recovered at the Bills 47 with 1:41 left in the half. On fourth-and-five from the 42, Marino hit Duper for 38 yards with 49 seconds left. On third-and-goal from the 2, Marino scored on a two-yard run.

• The Bills outgained Miami 300-181 in the first half. Kelly had 222 yards passing.

• The Dolphins took the second-half kickoff and moved to a Stoyanovich field goal. Mark Clayton had a 29-yard reception on the first play and Sammie Smith had a 17-yard run.

• Three plays after the kickoff, Lofton made a 31-yard catch at the Miami 27, but Jarvis Williams intercepted

Kelly two plays later at the 2. The Bills got the ball right back when Kelso intercepted Marino at the Dolphins 48 and the Bills drove 37 yards to another Norwood field goal.

• Back came the Dolphins to Marino's TD pass to guard Roy Foster on a linemen eligible play, but Buffalo responded with a 10-play, 63-yard march to Thomas' second TD run. Lofton had a 21-yard catch, McKeller caught a five-yarder on fourth-and-two from the Miami 34 and a holding penalty on Tim McKyer gave the Bills a first down at the 11.

• Hal Garner forced Marc Logan to fumble the ensuing kickoff and Norwood recovered at the 29. Two plays later, Reed got open for a 26-yard TD and a 44-27 lead.

• Marino capped a 15-play, 91-yard drive with a TD pass to Tony Martin with 1:15 left.

QUOTES

• Bruce Smith: "I want to tell you what gave us some extra incentive, what inspired us even more than playing. We got a tape of a TV interview that a couple of guys in Miami did. I guess they didn't expect we'd get the tape, but we got it and it really fired us up. Keith Sims said Cornelius Bennett and I were soft, that they could run the ball over us, and that they were going to single-block me all day. It ticked us off and embarrassed us. I mean, every time we play this team, they provoke us. Every time we play them, they feel we shouldn't win. We have a world of respect for the Miami Dolphins, but in turn they don't give it back to us. At one point in the first quarter, I told him (Sims) 'If you're gonna talk trash, you better be able to back it up.' But he didn't say anything. This guy hasn't been in the league a year, yet he's going to talk about us the way he did?"

• Miami guard Keith Sims: "I said Cornelius was soft against the run, but I never said Bruce Smith was soft. Bruce Smith is a great player. What I said was we'd be better off running at Bruce Smith than away from him because of his pursuit. If you run away from him, you can't double-team him. I had no idea it would come to something like this."

• Nate Odomes: "Early in the game the weather wasn't really a factor, but somewhere in the second quarter it started to snow really good and that's when the traction left."

• Marv Levy: "We had planned to start in the no-huddle and, as long as we had so much success, we stayed with it." (On playing Kelly): "For the people who say 'Why didn't you wait one more week?' medically he was cleared to play. Now it's up to Jim to say 'I feel good, I'm ready to go.' Wait one more week? Is he going to be less rusty?"

• Jim Kelly: "We went with what we thought we could do best. The key to our offense is to mix it up. With all the weapons we have on offense, you can do things like that. With the weather conditions the way they were, it was going to take a little time for the receivers to get into their patterns and the offensive line did a heckuva job. It was probably the best I've ever seen them play. They gave me the time to throw and that was a key to a lot of plays. All five of them deserve a big hand. We knew the Miami Dolphins didn't get here by being sloppy, we knew we were going to have to score some points because they have a lot of weapons on offense like we do. You don't want to tell your defense that, but we knew this was going to be a battle." (On his knee): "Like I said, I could wait until the Super Bowl and it still wouldn't be 100 percent."

• Andre Reed: "We'd seen it on film all week (that Oliver would be covering Reed in a three-receiver set) and knew we could exploit it. On a drier field, we could have exploited it even more."

• Thurman Thomas: "I felt we could score on them at anytime, that's how much confidence we had in ourselves. I was kind of ticked off. I really don't think Miami gives us the respect we deserve because of the way they shoot off

their mouths saying they didn't play well the last time. I think they played pretty damn well today and we kicked their butts. We kind of kept them off balance with the hurry-up. We've been doing it all season. There was no reason to stop."

• Kent Hull on the no-huddle: "With the success we were having, why change? The one time we didn't use it and did get real conservative, we wound up punting and it was the only time we punted all day. Everybody talks about how you should run the ball in bad weather, but it's a misconception, unless it's really windy. It's so much easier to pass protect and for the receivers to run their routes. It's much harder to run the football because the backs have to make cuts and it's also harder for the defensive backs to cover the receivers." (On Kelly): "There was never any doubt in my mind that he'd play. He's our tough competitor, our leader."

• Ted Marchibroda on the no-huddle: "My first year here, we were down by two TDs against Houston with four minutes to play and Jim brought us back. Now last year, there were three times when we had to score the last two times we had the ball to win – the Rams, Miami and Houston. So I said to myself 'If it's so successful at the end of the half and at the end of games, why would it not be successful during the regular course of the game?' So we opened with it against Indianapolis and it's been going ever since."

• Miami coach Don Shula: "Marino got us back in the ballgame running the offense and we had things going when we got within three. We felt if we could stop them and get the ball back, we'd have a shot at winning. It was the kind of day where they put the ball up and we just didn't make the plays. We tried to mix up the blitz and play coverage and do anything to try to slow them down, but we couldn't. Buffalo has an outstanding team and they're going to be tough to beat. They're AFC East so I'll support them."

Raiders	3	0	0	0	- 3
Bills	21	20	0	10	- 51

Attendance at Rich Stadium - 80,324

Buf: Lofton 13 pass from Kelly (Norwood kick), 3:30
LAR: FG Jaeger 41, 5:49
Buf: Thomas 12 run (Norwood kick), 6:59
Buf: Talley 27 interception return (Norwood kick), 11:51
Buf: Davis 1 run (kick blocked), 5:58
Buf: Davis 3 run (Norwood kick), 11:42
Buf: Lofton 8 pass from Kelly (Norwood kick), 13:54
Buf: Davis 1 run (Norwood kick), :02
Buf: FG Norwood 39, 2:47

	BUF	LAR
First downs	30	21
Rushing yds	202	151
Passing yds	300	169
Punts-avg	2-37.5	3-40-3
Fumbles-lost	3-0	1-1
Penalties-yds	6-32	2-28
Poss. time	31:35	28:25

BILLS LEADERS: Rushing - Thomas 25-138, Kelly 2-12, Davis 10-21, D. Smith 3-3, Mueller 3-6, Gardner 1-23, Reich 2-(-1); **Passing** - Kelly 17-23-1 - 300; **Receiving** - Lofton 5-113, Reed 2-29, Thomas 5-61, McKeller 3-44, Tasker 2-53; **Kickoff returns** - D. Smith 1-11, Edwards 1-19; **Punt returns** - Edwards 1-12, Odomes 1-18.

RAIDERS LEADERS: Rushing - Allen 10-26, S. Smith 4-19, Schroeder 4-33, McCallum 1-4, Bell 5-36, Evans 4-33; **Passing** - Schroeder 13-31-5 - 150, Evans 2-8-1 - 26; **Receiving** - Fernandez 4-57, Gault 2-32, Horton 3-25, T. Brown 2-17, Allen 2-19, Bell 2-26; **Kickoff returns** - Holland 6-60, R. Brown 3-59; **Punt returns** - T. Brown 1-5, Patterson 1-17.

BUFFALO TACKLES: Bailey 7, Conlan 6, Talley 5, L. Smith 5, Jackson 4, Williams 3, Hicks 3, Odomes 3, Seals 3, Bennett 3, Wright 3, Bentley 2

LOS ANGELES TACKLES: Anderson 9, Ellison 7, Robinson 7, Golic 6, Harden 6, Wallace 5, Townsend 5, Washington 4, Lewis 4, McDaniel 2, Long 2

NOTES

• The Bills turned in one of the most stunning performances in team history, embarrassing the Raiders in the AFC Championship Game, thus earning a trip to Super Bowl XXV in Tampa.
• The Bills tied the scoring record for the AFC/AFL Championship Game (51 by San Diego in 1963) and posted the second-most lopsided victory in a playoff game (Chicago beat Washington, 73-0, in 1941). The 41 first-half points was a new postseason record. In all, the teams combined to break 18 Championship Game records, including Jim Kelly's 73.9 completion percentage and the Bills' 30 first downs.
• A couple of times during the game, NBC broke away to coverage of the Persian Gulf War as Iraq attacked Saudi Arabia and the U.S. fought off Scuds with Patriot missiles.
• Ralph Wilson was presented the game ball after he was awarded the Lamar Hunt trophy in the locker room.
• Many fans came to the stadium with American flags and displayed them in support of the troops
• Leon Seals' mother died of cancer the night before the game.
• Bruce Smith was held without a sack for the fifth straight game.
• Bills assistant coach Chuck Lester told play-by-play announcer Van Miller before the game: "It's going to be a blowout."
• The Bills took the opening kickoff and no-huddled their way 75 yards in nine plays to Jim Kelly's TD pass to James Lofton. Kelly had fumbled the snap, but got the ball back and hit Lofton over the middle. Kelly was six-of-six for 65 yards on the drive.
• On the ensuing possession, the Raiders drove to a Jeff Jaeger field goal as Jay Schroeder completed back-to-back 26-yard passes to Mervyn Fernandez and Willie Gault.
• Two plays after the kickoff, Kelly hit Lofton for 41 yards to the Los Angeles 23 and two plays later, Thurman Thomas scored.
• After a Los Angeles punt, Kelly was intercepted by Gary

Lewis at the Los Angeles 20. But three plays later, Schroeder tried to hit Tim Brown, but was forced to throw early by Bruce Smith. Darryl Talley intercepted and returned it 27 yards for a key TD.
• The Raiders punted on the next series and the Bills drove 57 yards in 13 plays to Kenneth Davis' first TD. Scott Norwood's PAT was blocked by Scott Davis. Jamie Holland muffed the kickoff and Jamie Mueller recovered at the Raiders 30, but Norwood missed a field goal.
• Again, Los Angeles couldn't move, punted, and the Bills began a seven-play, 80-yard drive to Davis' second TD. The key play was a 44-yard pass to Steve Tasker to the Raiders 3.
• One play after the kickoff, Schroeder was intercepted by Nate Odomes who returned it to the Bills 39. Five plays later, Kelly hit Lofton for 33 yards, then on the next play, threw a TD pass to Lofton.
• At the half, the Bills held a 23-8 edge in first downs, a 387-148 edge in yards. Thomas had 109 yards rushing, Kelly 247 passing.
• Los Angeles' first possession of the third was ended by a Mark Kelso interception, the second was thwarted by a Leonard Smith interception. After Smith's pick, the Bills drove 78 yards in nine plays to Davis' third TD run on the first play of the fourth quarter. Kelly completed two passes to convert third-down situations.
• Two plays after the kickoff, Talley intercepted Schroeder, setting up a Norwood field goal.
• Vince Evans replaced Schroeder and he moved Los Angeles to the Bills 11, but Buffalo held on downs.
• On Los Angeles' final possession, Ray Bentley intercepted Evans, Buffalo's sixth pick of the day and seventh forced turnover.

QUOTES

• Ralph Wilson: "I've been to almost every Super Bowl and every time I'm there, I daydream. When the players would run out on the field, electricity would fill the stadium and I'd think 'Boy, wouldn't it be great if someday the Bills were able to run out of that tunnel on a Super Bowl Sunday.' I'm a little shell-shocked by the tremendous performance the team put on today. This is probably the best

performance the Bills have ever had. Anything in the last 31 years that didn't go the right way, it was all turned around today." (About the backdrop of the war): "Jack Kemp called me three days ago and told me the troops over there wanted the games to be played, and that's why the league has gone ahead with them. I was happy to hear the fans chant (U.S.A, U.S.A.) because we are all thinking about the brave men and women over in the Gulf showing courage and resolve."
• Kent Hull after reading a placard on the locker room wall that said "We Peak Next Week": "I think that sums it up. I've seen a lot of happier locker rooms in my career after a big win. I think the reason for that was that this team knows that it's got another task ahead of it. Everybody is happy of course, but there's more jubilation ahead. It was a big celebration, but it didn't last long. This is just another step on the way to succeeding in our goal." (On the game): "We felt the Raiders posed a bigger threat to us than anybody else we played this year. I wouldn't have ever dreamed in a fantasy that we would score that many points."
• Ray Bentley, who had a different view of the post-game locker room: "It was bedlam. Everybody was just out of their minds. It was chaos. Guys were running, screaming, banging heads, kissing. In fact I was a little embarrassed by some of the kissing that was going on."
• Marv Levy: "I made the point to them that this is not our goal, to go to the Super Bowl. Our goal is to stay focused for another week, and we want to be winners. This is a great thrill, but as I keep saying, we have one more river to cross. It's not time to sit back and reflect on this."
• Jim Kelly: "The object is to win (the Super Bowl), not to just show up. A lot of teams get the chance, but 20 years down the road, I don't want people to say 'Oh, Buffalo was in it ... But.' We still have one more river to cross. I remember in high school, all 25 guys on our team used to dream about it (playing in the Super Bowl). I was always a Steelers fan. Seeing Terry Bradshaw, Franco Harris, Lynn Swann and those guys playing in a Super Bowl, I'd say 'Maybe I'll get a chance.' Well, my chance has come." (About the game): "Not in my wildest dreams did I think we'd score 51 points against these guys. When you have as many weapons as I do and you have the time to throw, that's what it's all about. Overall, we showed what it takes. It doesn't take just one guy behind the center, it takes 10 other people on the offensive unit. We were always one step ahead of them."
• Raiders defensive end Howie Long: "If they play like they did today, there's nobody who's going to beat them. Plain and simple. We knew they were going to go with the no-huddle. We were prepared for it. I don't think anyone can stop it."
• Raiders linebacker Jerry Robinson: "It's sad, depressing, the embarrassment is there. There's a lot of those things."
• Darryl Talley: "In order to be rated among the best and receive the accolades, you have to show up in a big game. This was the only game in town today. The whole nation was watching. I thought about the bad years here. You'd go out in public and people would be snickering and laughing at you behind your back. I just tried to play as hard as I could during those times and I hoped eventually that better times would come."
• Carlton Bailey, whose father was in the Persian Gulf: "They told me the game was being televised in Saudi Arabia and hopefully he had an opportunity to watch the game. I was going to do whatever it took – sacrificing my body, knocking myself out – to put that extra edge in there for my Pops. And hopefully I made him proud."
• Pete Metzelaars comparing football to the war: "We have to realize what we're doing here is not that big a deal. It is to some people, but we're not talking about losing our lives. We're just out there playing a game."

Bills	3	9	0	7 -	19
Giants	3	7	7	3 -	20

Attendance at Tampa Stadium - 73,813

NYG: FG M. Bahr 28, 7:46
Buf: FG Norwood 23, 9:09
Buf: D. Smith 1 run (Norwood kick), 2:30
Buf: Safety: B. Smith tackled Hostetler, 6:33
NYG: Baker 14 pass from Hostetler (M. Bahr kick), 14:35
NYG: Anderson 1 run (M. Bahr kick), 9:29
Buf: Thomas 31 run (Norwood kick), :08
NYG: FG M. Bahr 21, 7:40

	BUF	NYG
First downs	18	24
Rushing yds	166	172
Passing yds	205	214
Punts-avg	6-38.8	4-43-8
Fumbles-lost	0-0	0-0
Penalties-yds	6-35	5-31
Poss. time	19:27	40:33

BILLS LEADERS: Rushing - Thomas 15-135, Davis 2-4, Mueller 1-3, D. Smith 1-1, Kelly 6-23; **Passing** - Kelly 18-30-0 - 212; **Receiving** - Reed 8-62, Lofton 1-61, Thomas 5-55, McKeller 2-11, Davis 2-23; **Kickoff returns** - D. Smith 4-66, Edwards 2-48; **Punt returns** - None.

GIANTS LEADERS: Rushing - Anderson 21-102, Meggett 9-48, Carthon 3-12, Hostetler 6-10; **Passing** - Hostetler 20-32-0 - 222; **Receiving** - Cross 4-39, Ingram 5-74, Bavaro 5-50, Baker 2-31, Anderson 1-7, Meggett 2-18, Carthon 1-3; **Kickoff returns** - Meggett 2-26, Duerson 1-22; **Punt returns** - Meggett 2-37.

BUFFALO TACKLES: L. Smith 8, Conlan 8, Wright 7, Kelso 6, Seals 5, Odomes 5, Bennett 5, Bentley 4, Talley 4, B. Smith 3, Bailey 3, Jackson 3.

NEW YORK TACKLES: Howard 7, Reasons 6, Collins 6, Thompson 4, Jackson 4, Banks 4, Walls 3, Johnson 3, Taylor 2, Marshall 2, Guyton 2.

NOTES

• The Bills became the seventh straight victim of the NFC in its domination of the Super Bowl.

• This was the closest Super Bowl ever and former NFL commissioner Pete Rozelle, who celebrated the game's 25th anniversary, said it was "the best Super Bowl ever."

• With the Persian Gulf War raging in the Middle East, the game served as a terrific diversion. Many of the troops watched the game in the middle of the night in Saudi Arabia and Kuwait.

• Apache helicopters were stationed at Tampa Stadium, in case anything went wrong. All fans and media had to endure thorough body searches through metal detectors before entering the stadium.

• Whitney Houston sang an inspiring, emotional version of the *Star Spangled Banner* which was punctuated by a fly-over by four F-16 fighter jets.

• The game was the first in Super Bowl history to be played without a turnover.

• The Giants' time of possession of 40:33 was a Super Bowl record.

• The Giants converted nine of 16 third downs, none more important than Mark Ingram's 14-yard catch on third-and-13 from the Bills 32 early in the third. It kept alive New York's go-ahead TD drive, which lasted a Super Bowl record 9:29. Ingram broke at least five tackles on the play.

• Giants running back O.J. Anderson was named MVP, but Thurman Thomas outplayed him. The Bills lost for the first time when Thomas gained 100 yards rushing. They had been 14-0.

• James Lofton and Andre Reed combined for one catch worth four yards in the second half.

• Bruce Smith's safety in the second quarter was the fifth in Super Bowl history.

QUOTES

• Scott Norwood: "I'm disappointed at the way it turned out, but I know I have my teammates behind me. I realize what a big opportunity this was. I'm sure it will never get to a point where I'll ever forget it. It's something I know I'll carry with me into the future. I know I had a good plant and I hit the ball solidly. I kept my head down on it, but I saw the ball wasn't drawing like normal. It stayed out there. I've kicked enough footballs to know, and it was an empty feeling watching it hang out there. That's a kick that I've made. I let a lot of people down. This is a tough emotion for me to deal with. Every swing of the leg is critical."

• Marv Levy on Norwood: "He's got nothing to be ashamed of. He's won a lot of games for us. We know those things happen and we all still love him. Sure you feel a tremendous sinking feeling with all of your team, but we hope to make more appearances and come out on top. I'm not being flippant about the fact, 'Oh well, we lost.' It hurts bad, but you can't agonize too long about it because you can't change it." (On the keys): "I think what they did best was maintain possession on offense. That made a big difference. The drive they had at the start of the second half was some drive. A team with a strong running game that can maintain control of the ball is not easy to beat. When you run the no-huddle, you don't have a lot of possession time and when you don't score, you get rid of the ball fast. Every offense has its advantages and maybe one of the disadvantages of that approach manifested itself today because of the offense the Giants have. We missed some tackles and overall, we probably weren't as sharp as the last two weeks, but we played a team which I think is better."

• Bruce Smith: "Regardless of all that (Giants possession time), we missed tackles and that really hurt us. One point is a pretty bad way to lose. We made it here with 47 guys, we're not going to put any blame anywhere. We're not going to point fingers. When we lose, we lose as a team, it's not one person's fault. We all went down fighting."

• Kent Hull about the field goal: "The disappointing thing was that we shouldn't have been in that position to begin with. We had the opportunity to make plays and we didn't do it. Everything that got us here we didn't do today. We had dropped passes, we had confusion on the offensive line. It didn't come down to the kick, we had trouble before that."

• Ray Bentley: "To say it's disappointing is an understatement, but life goes on, it's just a football game. I'll go home to my wife and kids, so I'll be happy."

• Thurman Thomas: "The important thing is we got a taste of the Super Bowl. Even though we lost, now we know what it takes to get here. I think the way we played today shows that things are looking better and better for us next year. I'm sure next year there will be a lot of believers in the Buffalo Bills because we had a lot of doubters coming into this year."

• Jim Kelly: "It came down to the last kick, and the Super Bowl is supposed to be played that way. If you want to write a Super Bowl script, this is probably what you have to write." (On the missed kick): "It was never meant to be. You know it hurts. Scotty has won so many games for us, so you can't blame him. I knew we were going to have to get the ball to the 30 because I know Scotty can kick from the 50 and in. It's just a matter of him hitting a good one and this time, he didn't. We shouldn't have been in that situation, though." (On the final drive): "I told the guys 'This is what champions are made of, let's play like it and let's be the one.' We knew it was a matter of taking our time, not trying to make the big play right away. We got into field goal position which is really all you can ask for and like I said, it just wasn't meant to be. The Giants played great on defense. They held us to 19 points and not many teams have done that. I think offensively we stopped ourselves in the first half with dropped passes, penalties and I had some misreads, but give the Giants defense credit."

• Giants coach Bill Parcells: "I realized a long time ago that God is playing some of these games and he was on our side today. I think both teams were valiant. They call us predictable and conservative, but I know one thing, power wins football games. It's not always the fanciest way, but it can win games." (On the keys to victory): "The drive at the end of the first half was very important and then we took about 10 minutes off the clock in the third quarter to go ahead. Then it was a seesaw game and in the end, the seesaw was a little short for them." (On O.J. Anderson): "He's going to Canton. I don't see how they can keep the kid out. He's got over 10,000 yards in his career and anyone who watched him today knows he can still do it."

• Giants cornerback Mark Collins: "We wanted to hit them (Bills receivers). When they crossed over the middle, whether they caught the ball or not, we wanted to hit them. A couple of times Andre Reed had a chance to catch the ball and he just dropped it. I'd like to say it was because of the linebackers and safeties hitting him earlier. They made him pay for his catches earlier."

421

STARTING LINEUPS

BILLS OFFENSE: QB - Jim Kelly; RB - Thurman Thomas, Jamie Mueller; WR - Andre Reed, James Lofton; TE - Keith McKeller; OL - Kent Hull, Will Wolford, Howard Ballard, Jim Ritcher, John Davis.
DEFENSE: DL - Bruce Smith, Leon Seals, Jeff Wright; LB - Cornelius Bennett, Darryl Talley, Shane Conlan, Ray Bentley; DB - Nate Odomes, Kirby Jackson, Mark Kelso, Leonard Smith.

GIANTS OFFENSE: QB - Jeff Hostetler; RB - O.J. Anderson, Maurice Carthon; WR - Mark Ingram, Stephen Baker; TE - Mark Bavaro; OL - Jumbo Elliott, Doug Riesenberg, William Roberts, Eric Moore, Bart Oates.
DEFENSE: DL - Eric Dorsey, Erik Howard, Leonard Marshall; LB - Carl Banks, Lawrence Taylor, Steve DeOssie, Pepper Johnson; DB - Mark Collins, Everson Walls, Greg Jackson, Myron Guyton.

SUPER BOWL XXV PLAY-BY-PLAY

FIRST QUARTER

Bills win toss, elect to receive.
New York's Matt Bahr kicks off to Buffalo 14, D. Smith return 20 yards (tackle by M. Bahr).

BILLS 14:52
1-10-B34 - Kelly incomplete pass to Reed; 2-10-B34 - Kelly pass to Reed, 4, (G. Jackson); 3-6-B38 - Kelly pass to Reed, 5, (G. Jackson, Howard); 4-1-B43 - Tuten punt 46, Meggett return 20.

GIANTS 13:29
1-10-N31 - Buffalo penalty, offsides, Talley, 5; 1-5-N36 - Meggett runs right, 4, (Bennett); 2-1-N40 - Carthon runs to middle, 3, (Bentley); 1-10-N43 - Hostetler pass to Cross, 13, (L. Smith); 1-10-B44 - Meggett runs left, 10 (L. Smith, Kelso); 1-10-B34 - Hostetler incomplete pass to Bavaro; 2-10-B34 - Meggett runs left, 3, (Conlan); 3-7-B31 - Hostetler pass to Ingram, 16, (Talley); 1-10-B15 - Anderson runs right, 3, (Conlan); 2-7-B12 - Hostetler runs right, 1, (Seals); 3-6-B11 - Hostetler incomplete pass in end zone to Ingram; 4-6-B11 - Bahr 28 FIELD GOAL. Drive: 11 plays, 58 yards, Time of Possession 6:15. Time of score: 7:46. **New York 3, Buffalo 0**

Bahr kicks off to Buffalo 5, D. Smith return 24, (Rouson).
BILLS 7:04
1-10-B29 - Thomas runs to middle, 2, (Thompson); 2-8-B31 - Kelly deep pass to Lofton, tipped by P. Williams, 61, (Walls); 1-G-N8 - Kelly incomplete pass to McKeller; 2-G-N8 - Thomas runs left, 3, (Howard); 3-G-N5 - Kelly incomplete pass to Thomas; 4-G-N5 - Norwood 23 FIELD GOAL. Drive: 6 plays, 66 yards, TOP 1:23. Time of score: 9:09. **New York 3, Buffalo 3.**

Norwood kicks off to end zone for touchback.
GIANTS 5:45
1-10-N20 - Anderson runs left, 5, (B. Smith); 2-5-N25 - Hostetler runs left, 5, (Bennett); 1-10-N30 - Meggett runs right, 3, (Talley, Wright); 2-7-N33 - Hostetler pass to Baker, 17, (Kelso); 1-10-50 - Anderson runs to middle, 4, (Seals); 2-6-B46 - Hostetler incomplete pass to Baker; 3-6-B46 - Hostetler incomplete pass to Meggett; 4-6-B46 - Landeta punt 46, touchback.

BILLS 1:57
1-10-B20 - Thomas runs left, 3, (Howard); 2-7-B23 - Kelly pass to Reed, 11, (Thompson); 1-10-B34 - Kelly pass to Reed, 4, (Thompson); 2-6-B38 - Buffalo penalty, false start, Ritcher, -5; 2-11-B33 - Kelly pass to Reed, 20, (Collins, Walls); 1-10-N47 - Thomas runs left, 6, (Reasons).

SECOND QUARTER

2-4-N41 - Kelly pass to Thomas, 13, (Banks); 1-10-N28 - Davis runs right, 3, (Howard); 2-7-N25 - Kelly pass to Reed, 9, (Collins); 1-10-N16 - Thomas runs left, 3, (Washington); 2-7-N13 - Kelly pass to McKeller, 5, (Guyton), New York penalty, personal foul, 4; 1-G-N4 - Mueller runs to middle, 3, (Taylor); 2-G-N1 - D. Smith dives right, 1, TOUCHDOWN. Norwood PAT. Drive: 12 plays, 80 yards, TOP 4:27. Time of score: 2:30. **Buffalo 10, New York 3.**

Norwood kicks off to New York 10, Duerson return 22, (Tasker).
GIANTS 12:21
1-10-N32 - Hostetler runs left, 2, (Odomes); 2-8-N34 - Anderson runs left, 2, (Wright); 3-6-N36 - Hostetler incomplete pass to Kyles; 4-6-N38 - Landeta punt 37, Edwards fair catch.

BILLS 10:52
1-10-B27 - Thomas runs left, 14, (Walls); 1-10-B41 - Thomas runs left, 4, (P. Johnson); 2-6-B45 - Kelly incomplete pass to Reed; 3-6-B45 - New York penalty, encroachment, Howard, 5; 3-1-50 - Kelly incomplete pass to Reed; 4-1-50 - Tuten punt 43, Meggett fair catch.

GIANTS 9:38
1-10-N7 - Hostetler pass to Anderson, 7, (K. Jackson); 2-3-N14 - New York penalty, holding, Oates, -7; 2-10-N7 - Hostetler sacked in end zone by B. Smith for SAFETY. Time of score: 6:33. **Buffalo 12, New York 3.** Buffalo penalty, excessive celebration, -5, assessed on free kick.

Landeta free kick from 25, 60 yards, Edwards return 15 (Rouson).
BILLS 8:18
1-10-B30 - Kelly incomplete pass to Reed; 2-10-B30 - Kelly incomplete pass to McKeller; 3-10-B30 - Kelly incomplete pass to McKeller; 4-10-B30 - Tuten punt 47, Meggett fair catch.

GIANTS 7:53
1-10-N23 - Anderson runs left, 3, (Wright); 2-7-N26 - Anderson runs left, 4, (Baldinger); 3-3-N30 - Hostetler incomplete pass, batted down by Seals; 4-3-N30 - Landeta punt 54, Edwards fair catch.

BILLS 6:19
1-10-B16 - Thomas runs right, 18, (Guyton); 1-10-B34 - Thomas runs right, 4, (Howard, Banks); 2-6-B38 - Kelly pass to Thomas, 10, (Collins); 1-10-B48 - Kelly pass to Thomas, 8, (G. Jackson); 2-2-N44 - Kelly incomplete deep pass to Lofton; 3-2-N44 - Buffalo penalty, false start, Wolford, -5; 3-7-N49 - Kelly pass to Reed, 5, (Banks); 4-2-N44 - Tuten punt 31, Meggett fair catch.

GIANTS 3:49
1-10-N13 - Hostetler pass to Bavaro, 6, (Conlan); 2-4-N19 - Anderson runs left, 18, (Kelso); 1-10-N37 - Hostetler pass to Ingram, 22, (Odomes); 1-10-B41 - Meggett runs left, 17, (L. Smith, Kelso); 1-10-B24 (1:55) - Hostetler incomplete pass to Carthon; 2-10-B24 - Hostetler pass to Carthon, 3, (Conlan), New York timeout, 1:13; 3-7-B21 - Hostetler pass to Cross, 7, (Bennett); 1-10-B14 (:39) - Hostetler incomplete pass, batted down by Bennett; 2-10-B14 - Hostetler incomplete pass to Baker; 3-10-B14 (:30) - Hostetler pass to Baker, 14, TOUCHDOWN. Bahr PAT. Drive: 10 plays, 87 yards, TOP 3:24. Time of score: 14:35. **Buffalo 12, New York 10.**

Bahr kicks off to Buffalo 4, D. Smith, fumbles, recovers, returns 9.
BILLS :20
1-10-B13 - Kelly kneels down to end half, -1.

HALFTIME STATS

	BUF	NY
First downs	10	11
Rushing yds	63	87
Passing yds	155	98
Punts-avg	4-41.8	3-45.7
Fumbles-lost	0-0	0-0
Penalties-yds	4-20	3-16
Poss. time	12:04	17:56

RUSHING: **Buf:** Thomas 9-57, Davis 1-3, Mueller 1-3, Smith 1-1, Kelly 1-(-1)
NY: Anderson 7-39, Meggett 5-37, Hostetler 3-8, Carthon 1-3

PASSING: **Buf:** Kelly 12-21-0 - 155
NY: Hostetler 9-18-0 - 105

RECEIVING: **Buf:** Reed 7-58, Thomas 3-31, Lofton 1-61, McKeller 1-5.
NY: Cross 2-20, Ingram 2-38, Baker 2-31, Anderson 1-7, Bavaro 1-6, Carthon 1-3

THIRD QUARTER

Norwood kicks off to New York 9, Meggett return 16 (Gardner).
GIANTS 14:51
1-10-N25 - Hostetler incomplete pass to Cross; 2-10-N25 - New York penalty, false start, Kratch, -5; 2-15-N20 - Hostetler pass to Meggett, 7, (Odomes); 3-8-N27 - Hostetler pass to Meggett, 11, (Odomes); 1-10-N38 - Meggett runs left, 4, (Bentley); 2-6-N42 - Anderson runs right, 5, (Seals, Bentley); 1-10-N47 - Anderson runs left, 24, (Kelso, Bennett); 1-10-B29 - Carthon runs left, 5, (Wright); 2-5-B24 - New York penalty, holding, Bavaro, -10; 2-15-B34 - Hostetler runs to middle, 2, (Wright); 3-13-B32 - Hostetler pass to Ingram, 14, (Williams); 1-10-B18 - Anderson runs to middle, 5, (Lodish); 2-5-B13 - Meggett runs right, 1, (K. Jackson, Bennett); 3-4-B12 - Hostetler pass to Cross, 9, (L. Smith); 1-G-B3 - Anderson runs to middle, 2, (L. Smith); 2-G-B1 - Anderson runs left, 1, TOUCHDOWN. Bahr PAT. Drive: 14 plays, 75 yards, TOP 9:29. Time of score: 9:29. **New York 17, Buffalo 12.**

Bahr kicks off to Buffalo 7, Edwards return 33 (Bahr).
BILLS 5:21
1-10-B40 - Thomas runs left, 8, (Taylor); 2-2-B48 - Kelly runs to middle, 5, (G. Jackson); 1-10-N47 - Thomas runs right, 2, (Reasons); 2-8-N45 - Buffalo penalty, offensive interference, Reed, -10; 2-18-B45 - Kelly incomplete pass to Edwards; 3-18-B45 - Kelly sacked by Marshall, -7; 4-25-B38 - Tuten punt 20, out of bounds.

GIANTS 3:42
1-10-N42 - Hostetler pass to Cross, 10, (Odomes); 1-10-B48 - Buffalo penalty, holding, Odomes, 5; 1-10-B43 - Anderson runs right, 0, (Conlan); 2-10-B43 - Hostetler sacked by Wright, -1; 3-11-B44 - Hostetler pass to Ingram, 9, (L. Smith); 4-2-B35 - Anderson runs left, -2, (B. Smith).

BILLS 1:19
1-10-B37 - Kelly pass to Thomas, 9, (Howard); 2-1-B46 - Kelly pass to K. Davis, 4, (Reasons); 1-10-50 - Kelly pass to K. Davis 19, (Reasons, P. Williams).

Marv Levy didn't win the coach of the year award, but most Buffalo fans thought he deserved it.

FOURTH QUARTER

1-10-N31 - Thomas runs to middle, 31, TOUCHDOWN. Norwood PAT. Drive: 4 plays, 63 yards, TOP 1:27. Time of score: :08. **Buffalo 19, New York 17.**

Norwood kicks off to New York 13, Meggett return 10 (Mueller).
GIANTS 14:43
1-10-N23 - Anderson runs to middle, 3, (Seals); 2-7-N26 - Hostetler incomplete pass to Ingram; 3-7-N26 - Hostetler pass to Bavaro, 17, (Conlan); 1-10-N43 - Anderson runs right, 7, (K. Jackson); 2-3-50 - Carthon runs to middle, 4, (Baldinger); 1-10-B46 - Hostetler pass to Bavaro, 19, (L. Smith); 1-10-B27 - Hostetler pass to Ingram, 13, (L. Smith); 1-10-B14 - Anderson runs left, 4, (Drane, Talley); 2-6-B10 - Hostetler pass to Bavaro, 1, (Conlan); New York timeout; 3-5-B9 - Meggett runs right, 6, (Bentley); 1-G-B3 - Anderson runs left, -4, (Wright); 2-G-B7 - Anderson runs to middle, 4, (Bailey); 3-G-B3 - Hostetler incomplete pass to Anderson, batted down by Bennett; 4-G-B3 - Bahr 21 FIELD GOAL. Drive: 14 plays, 74 yards, TOP 7:32. Time of score: 7:40. **New York 20, Buffalo 19.**

Bahr kicks off to Buffalo 7, D. Smith return 13 (R. Brown).
BILLS 7:11
1-10-B20 - Thomas runs right, 4, (Collins); 2-6-B24 - Kelly pass to Thomas, 15, (Collins); 1-10-B39 - Kelly runs right, 1, (P. Johnson); 2-9-B40 - K. Davis runs left, 1, (Marshall); 3-8-B41 - Kelly incomplete pass to Edwards; 4-8-B41 - Tuten punt 46, Meggett return 17 (Tasker).

GIANTS 5:25
1-10-N30 - Anderson runs left, 5, (Bailey, Talley); 2-5-N35 - Anderson runs to middle, 9, (Conlan, Bailey); 1-10-N44 - Meggett runs right, 0 (Lodish), Buffalo timeout; 2-10-N44 - Hostetler pass to Bavaro, 7, (Kelso), New York timeout; 3-3-B49 - Hostetler runs to middle, 1, (Seals), Buffalo timeout; 4-2-B48 - Landeta punt 38, Edwards fair catch.

BILLS 2:16
1-10-B10 - Kelly scrambles to middle, 8, (P. Johnson); 2-2-B18 (2:00) - Kelly scrambles to middle, 1, (Howard); 3-1-B19 (1:48) - Thomas runs left, 22, (Banks); 1-10-B41 (1:20) - Kelly pass to Reed, 4, (Reasons); 2-6-B45 (1:02) - Kelly scrambles right, 9, (Reasons), Buffalo timeout; 1-10-N46 (:48) - Kelly pass to McKeller, 6, (Thompson), play halted at :29 for replay review; 2-4-N40 - Thomas runs right, 11, (Collins); 1-10-N29 (:09) - Kelly spikes ball to stop clock; 2-10-N29 (:08) - Norwood 47 field goal, no good, wide right.

GIANTS :04
1-10-N 30 - Hostetler kneels to end game. FINAL: **New York 20, Buffalo 19**

At A Glance
1991

Jan. 28 – A crowd estimated at 20,000 attended a welcome home rally for the Bills and they chanted "We want Scott, We want Scott" until Scott Norwood came to the microphone. "I've got to tell you that we're struggling with this right now," Norwood said as his voice cracked. "I know I've never felt more love than I do right now. We all realize the sun's going to come up tomorrow and we're going to start preparing this football team. I'm dedicating next season to the fans of Buffalo."

Jan. 29 – The TV ratings for Super Bowl XXV were the second-lowest in 17 years, but that was attributed mainly to the Persian Gulf War and because both teams were from one area, New York.

Jan. 30 – At his annual post-season press conference, Marv Levy indicated that the Bills needed to get physically stronger on defense and that on offense, he would likely stick with the no-huddle approach.

Feb. 1 – The Bills released their list of unprotected Plan B free agents and it included Ray Bentley, Dwight Drane, Mitch Frerotte, Hal Garner, John Hagy, Chris Hale, Clifford Hicks, James Lofton, Scott Norwood, Robb Riddick, Don Smith, Leonard Smith and Rick Tuten.

Feb. 5 – The Touchdown Club of Washington, D.C. named Marv Levy it's AFC coach of the year and Jim Kelly it's AFC player of the year.

Feb. 19 – Bill Polian said even though ex-Bill Fred Smerlas had expressed interest in returning to Buffalo, he would not sign him.

Feb. 26 – The Bills signed defensive end Reggie Rogers, a 1987 first-round draft choice of the Detroit Lions who was released from a Michigan prison on Feb. 6 after serving 12 1/2 months for negligent homicide. In October of 1988, Rogers ran a red light and crashed into another vehicle, killing three teenagers. "He's had a lot of tragedy in his life, but we don't believe tragedy in a person's life precludes him from being part of the team," Bill Polian said. "We do believe everybody deserves a second chance and we believe he's deserving of it."

Feb. 27 – Commissioner Paul Tagliabue named Neal Austrian to the newly created position of President of the NFL.

March 3 – Because he wasn't getting many nibbles on the free agent market, Leonard Smith told Bill Polian that he would return to the Bills.

March 4 – It was reported that Marv Levy signed a three-year contract extension, estimated to be worth $500,000 per year.

March 7 – Robb Riddick, who was unable to come back from a serious knee injury suffered before the 1989 season, announced his retirement.

March 12 – The formation of the NFL Quarterback Club was announced, with Jim Kelly one of the 11 quarterbacks participating.

March 19 – Once again, by the minimum 21-7 vote, instant replay survived at the league meetings in Hawaii. Also, the owners decided to pull the 1993 Super Bowl out of Phoenix because the state of Arizona did not observe the Martin Luther King Jr. holiday.

March 23 – The NFL launched the World League of American Football, the first weekly sports league to operate on two continents. In the first game ever played, the London Monarchs defeated the Frankfurt

Galaxy in Germany, 24-11, with former Bills back-up quarterback Stan Gelbaugh throwing a 96-yard touchdown pass for London. New York Knights owner Robert F.X. Sillerman said: "I'm going to make a wild statement. Twenty years from now, we'll be here and people will be talking about whether the top draft pick will go to us or the NFL. Our television revenue will be greater than the NFL's." Ex-Bills coach Kay Stephenson was the head coach of the Sacramento Surge and his team beat Raleigh-Durham, 9-3.

March 26 – Safety John Hagy became the first Bill to leave via Plan B, signing with the Houston Oilers. "I want to be a starting free safety and that wasn't going to happen in Buffalo," said Hagy.

March 27 – With the artificial turf ripped out of Rich Stadium to make room for a new carpet, it was announced that the old turf would be sold in pieces in an assortment of Bills memorabilia.

March 28 – Leon Seals said he was "insulted" that the Bills signed defensive end Reggie Rogers. "I've always been a team player, and this is how you get rewarded, you get slapped in the face," he said. "If the Bills want to invest that kind of time and everything else in Reggie Rogers, then don't hold Leon Seals back at the same time. Either trade him or let him go because I know for a fact there are 27 other teams I can go in and start for, no questions asked."

April 1 – The Bills lost running back Don Smith to Miami through Plan B. In all, 139 players changed teams during the two-month signing period. The Bills signed two, safety Brett Tucker from Houston and linebacker David Bavaro from Phoenix.

April 7 – Linebacker Ray Bentley, left unprotected in Plan B but who went unsigned by another team, was given a two-year contract worth just over $1 million.

April 15 – It was announced that the Philadelphia Eagles would play the Bills in London's Wembley Stadium on July 28 as part of the American Bowl series.

April 21 – The Bills chose Illinois defensive back Henry Jones with their first-round pick, 26th overall. They also selected North Dakota St. defensive end Phil Hansen (second), Pittsburg St. defensive back Darryl Wren (third), wide receiver Brad Lamb from Anderson (eighth) and Northern Michigan linebacker Mark Maddox (ninth). Dallas made defensive tackle Russell Maryland the No. 1 pick and later chose wide receiver Alvin Harper (12th), Cleveland chose safety Eric Turner (second), Atlanta picked cornerback Bruce Pickens (third), Denver chose linebacker Mike Croel (fourth), the Rams picked cornerback Todd Lyght (fifth), Phoenix picked defensive end Eric Swann (sixth), Tampa Bay opted for offensive tackle Charles McRae (seventh), Philadelphia picked offensive tackle Antoine Davis (eighth), San Diego picked cornerback Stanley Richard (ninth), Detroit chose wide receiver Herman Moore (10th), New England selected offensive tackle Pat Harlow (11th) and running back Leonard Russell (14th), Seattle picked quarterback Dan McGwire (16th), Kansas City chose running back Harvey Williams (21st), Chicago picked offensive guard Stan Thomas (22nd), Miami picked wide receiver Randal Hill (23rd), the Raiders took quarterback Todd Marinovich (24th), San Francisco picked defensive tackle Ted Washington (25th) and the Giants picked fullback Jarrod Bunch (27th).

May 3 – Mini-camp opened at Rich Stadium.

May 4 – Bill Polian's contract was extended two years through 1994 at an estimated $500,000 per

year.

June 18 – It was reported that Thurman Thomas donated $125,000 to his alma mater, Oklahoma State, and urged other players to give back to their schools.

July 13 – Darryl Talley said he was embarrassed by the offer the Bills put on the table in renegotiating his contract, which had one year left, and said he had no alternative but to hold out. "He's (Bill Polian) always said he's going to pay for production," Talley said. "I've produced, but now he doesn't want to pay me. I can't figure that out."

July 14 – Training camp opened at Fredonia State and Talley did not show up. Neither did Jamie Mueller, Jim Ritcher, Nate Odomes and first-round pick Henry Jones, all embroiled in contract difficulties. However, Mueller and Ritcher signed new contracts in the evening and officially reported.

July 17 – The Bills didn't want him, but ex-Bill Fred Smerlas hooked on with his hometown New England Patriots for one year.

July 18 – Nate Odomes agreed to a new contract and reported to camp.

July 20 – The negotiations with Darryl Talley and Henry Jones continued to be stalemated and Bill Polian said "There's nothing to talk about." Bruce Smith was given permission to leave camp and go to Alabama to see Dr. James Andrews, a renowned orthopedic surgeon, regarding his surgically repaired knee.

July 22 – Bruce Smith underwent arthroscopic surgery on his left knee in Alabama and it was learned that he might miss the first two weeks of the regular season. The Bills departed for London, England to begin preparations for their American Bowl game against the Eagles.

July 25 – The Bills announced that Jim Kelly wouldn't play against the Eagles because of a pulled hamstring suffered on the second day of training camp that had slowed him ever since.

July 28 – The Bills defeated Philadelphia, 17-13, in front of 50,474 at Wembley Stadium as Gale Gilbert completed 12 of 20 passes for 117 yards.

July 31 – Bruce Smith returned to Fredonia and said "With God on my side, we'll get this done. It's possible that I might miss the first two games, then again it's very possible that I could be out there for the first game of the season."

Aug. 1 – Henry Jones' agent, Jim Steiner, asked the Bills to trade the No. 1 pick. "I doubt Henry Jones will ever play for the Buffalo Bills," Steiner said. "Nor do they believe he can. Under those conditions, I don't know how anybody can bargain in good faith."

Aug. 5 – The Bills traveled to Giants Stadium and lost to the Giants, 23-17, in a rematch of Super Bowl XXV. Jim Kelly was supposed to play, but ended up sitting out the game because of his sore hamstring.

Aug. 6 – The Bills announced they had set an all-time team record for season-ticket sales with 54,604. The old record was 54,182 in 1974.

Aug. 10 – In the home preseason opener at Rich Stadium, 51,813 saw the Bills edge Detroit, 21-16, as Jim Kelly made his summer debut and threw a TD pass in one quarter of work.

Aug. 11 – Ex-Bill and current NBC sportscaster Paul Maguire suffered a heart attack and was listed in critical condition at Buffalo General Hospital.

Aug. 12 – Offensive tackle Howard Ballard agreed to a three-year contract extension that would pay him about $600,000 per year. Bill Polian indicated that because Henry Jones had missed so much of camp, he would not be able to help the Bills in 1991. "There's no realistic possibility that he can contribute at the championship level this year," Polian said.

Aug. 14 – Bill Polian withdrew his latest contract offer to Henry Jones. "I know there are people there who want him, it just appears that Bill Polian isn't one of them," Jones' agent, Jim Steiner said.

Aug. 17 – The Bills traveled to Madison, Wisc. and lost to Green Bay, 35-24, at the University of Wisconsin. Jim Kelly suffered a sprained ankle in

the first quarter. It was determined that serious damage was averted and he was expected back to practice in a week.

Aug. 19 – Bill Polian closed off talks with Darryl Talley when Talley's agent, Vern Sharbaugh, rejected what Polian called his "best and final" contract offer. "The door is closed, there really is nothing to talk about anymore," Polian said.

Aug. 20 – It was determined that Jamie Mueller was suffering from a nerve problem in his upper back that was causing numbness in his left arm and

fingers. His career was cast in jeopardy. Punter Rick Tuten was waived, meaning Chris Mohr had won the punting job, and Scott Norwood survived a battle with Bjorn Nittmo for the placekicking job.

Aug. 21 – Center Kent Hull signed a three-year contract extension worth about $850,000 per year, making him one of the highest-paid offensive linemen in the NFL.

Aug. 23 – Jamie Mueller was ruled out of the preseason finale against Chicago and was told to see a nerve specialist. Henry Jones' agent, Jim Steiner, said talks had re-opened with Bill Polian.

Aug. 24 – The Bears pounded the Bills, 30-13, in the preseason finale at Soldier Field.

Aug. 26 – Darryl Talley ended his holdout and signed a two-year contract extension, but agreed to play 1991 under terms of his old contract, meaning he would make around $600,000. "Enough's enough, I'm coming in because I want to play football," Talley said.

Aug. 27 – In getting the roster down to the regular-season limit of 47, Jamie Mueller was placed on the injured reserve list, further evidence that his career could be over. It also looked doubtful that Bruce Smith would play in the season opener against Miami.

Aug. 28 – Henry Jones came to Buffalo and signed a four-year contract worth about $600,000 per season including a $900,000 signing bonus. "It's a long time coming," Jones said, "but I knew it would eventually happen. I had some anxiety at times, but I felt I dealt with it pretty well." Jim Kelly pronounced himself fit for the Dolphins' game.

Sept. 1 – The Bills opened the season with an exciting 35-31 shootout victory over Miami, their ninth win over the Dolphins in the last 10 meetings. Jim Kelly set a regular-season career-high with 381 passing yards and the Bills set a team record for total offense (583 yards). The Dolphins' offensive line arrived at the stadium in a limo, which ticked Thurman Thomas off. "It goes to show you that maybe they were a little too cocky," he said. "At first I thought it was someone important like Bruce Smith because he wasn't playing in the game."

Sept. 2 – With Jeff Wright out half the season, the Bills re-signed nose tackle Odell Haggins, whom they had cut during training camp.

Sept. 3 – Andre Reed used his big game against Miami to sound off against critics who said he had been intimidated during the Super Bowl loss to the Giants. "I'm just tired of people saying things they know nothing about," he said. "That stuff is garbage and people who know me know that. You're not perfect all the time, you're not going to catch every pass."

Sept. 5 – Bill Polian said of Thurman Thomas: "It's a privilege to watch him work. He's going to become one of the NFL's all-time greats."

Sept. 8 – The Bills produced their second-highest scoring output in team history in a 52-34 romp over Pittsburgh at Rich Stadium. Jim Kelly set a team record with six TD passes, including four to Don Beebe. Kelly also set a regular-season personal record with 31 completions.

Sept. 10 – Kicker Brad Daluiso was signed to be the Bills' kickoff and long field goal specialist.

Sept. 12 – Former 49ers coach and current NBC sportscaster Bill Walsh said the Bills' no-huddle offense was "in the spectacular category. Are we talking about the greatest offense ever? I don't know, we have to wait and see what happens over 16 games. But yes, no question, I'm very impressed."

Sept. 15 – The Bills rallied for a 23-20 victory over

Henry Jones (upper) and Phil Hansen (lower) were Buffalo's first two choices in the 1991 draft and by late in the season, were making key contributions to the Bills run to a second straight Super Bowl appearance.

the Jets at the Meadowlands as Jim Kelly hit Thurman Thomas with a 15-yard TD pass with 4:14 left. Thomas tied the team record for pass receptions in a single game with 13.

Sept. 16 – Marv Levy charged the Jets with feigning injuries in an effort to slow down the no-huddle offense. "Sometimes there's poetic justice," he said. "We had a point very late in the game where both Thurman Thomas and James Lofton were shaken up and out of the game. One of their guys took a dive and stayed down for a long time. During that period of time, Thurman and James were out and we thought they'd be out for awhile, but they felt better and went back in." Lofton caught the pivotal fourth-down pass on the winning drive and Thomas caught the winning TD pass.

Sept. 17 – Jets coach Bruce Coslet called Marv Levy an "over-officious jerk" and told Bill Polian to "shove it" after the Bills' front office charged the Jets with feigning injuries. Coslet referred to the 1988 AFC Championship Game when Levy threatened to feign injuries in order to slow down Cincinnati's no-huddle when Coslet was offensive coordinator. "He's a little hypocritical," Coslet said. "He threatened to feign injuries like Seattle did. Now whose integrity is being questioned? What a joke, nobody faked injuries. I'm to a point where I'm tired of taking crap from this guy. It's like he has a vendetta against me or something." Jeff Lageman called Levy "an idiot. They win the game and they complain. They're just crying because they didn't get their 500 yards and they're no longer the unstoppable Bills."

Sept. 18 – Levy attempted to defuse the situation by saying he was misinterpreted. "I said if they were feigning injuries, it was poetic justice," Levy said. Thurman Thomas was named AFC offensive player of the week, meaning a Bill had won the award three weeks in a row, a new record.

Sept. 22 – Keith McKeller's 29-yard TD reception with 5:21 left enabled the Bills to pull out a tough 17-10 victory over the Buccaneers, their first win at Tampa Stadium in six games dating back to 1976, including their heartbreaking Super Bowl XXV loss last January.

Sept. 23 – A television reporter asked Marv Levy to comment on a rumor that Bruce Smith was rehabbing for a drug problem and not a knee injury and Levy erupted in anger. "No, there's nothing to clear and I resent you bringing it up," Levy roared in a rare show of emotion off the field. "It's wrong of you to bring it up. Do you have anything substantial, anything? Why do you bring it up, because some other jerk brought it up who has nothing substantial? You've got some damn nerve bringing it up."

Sept. 25 – Bruce Smith practiced for the first time since undergoing arthroscopic knee surgery on July 22, but his status for the showdown against the unbeaten Bears was unknown.

Sept. 26 – Bill Polian held a press conference to publicly put to rest any rumors about Bruce Smith's involvement with drugs. "We're not denying anything, because there's nothing to deny," Polian said tersely. "They are lies and I brand the people who promulgate it as liars. And I'm talking about a very small group."

Sept. 29 – The Bills treated the largest crowd in Rich Stadium history (80,366) by defeating the Bears, 35-20, in a battle of unbeaten teams. Jim Kelly shook off a poor start to throw for 303 yards and three TDs including a key momentum-swinging 33-yarder to Al Edwards late in the first half.

Sept. 30 – During a meeting with the press in Chicago, Bears coach Mike Ditka downplayed the Bills' victory. "The Redskins and the Saints are the two best teams in the NFL and the Lions are probably the third-best," Ditka said. "I'm going to be in a lot of trouble, but I'm an NFC guy, I can't get too excited about the AFC. The Saints and Redskins have better defenses than the Bills."

Oct. 6 – Due to an accumulation of fluid, Bruce Smith was ruled out of the Monday night game in Kansas City.

Oct. 7 – Kansas City clobbered the Bills, 33-6, in an embarrassing Monday night affair at noisy Arrowhead Stadium. Jim Kelly was sacked six times, four by Derrick Thomas, and lost three of the Bills five fumbles as the offensive line was hampered by the raucous crowd.

Oct. 8 – In the aftermath of their worst defeat in a non-strike game since a 28-0 season-ending loss to Miami in 1985, the Bills vowed they would rebound. "We'll be all right," Shane Conlan said. "We lost last year to Miami (30-7) and we came back pretty strong. We'll see what kind of character this team has this week."

Oct. 10 – Bruce Smith returned to Alabama for further tests on his left knee and his availability for the upcoming Colts game was in serious doubt.

Oct. 12 – Bruce Smith was placed on the injured reserve list, meaning he would have to sit out a minimum of four weeks. Reggie Rogers was activated to take his place, meaning he would be playing in his first regular-season game since 1988.

Oct. 13 – The Bills routed the Colts, 42-6, at Rich Stadium, even though Jim Kelly missed the second half with a concussion. Thurman Thomas and Kenneth Davis both topped 100 yards rushing, the 10th time two Bills backs had done that in the same game.

Oct. 14 – The timing couldn't be better considering the concussion he suffered the day before as Jim Kelly flew to New York to tape a commercial for Nuprin. "I remembered being hit and the next thing I remember is leaving the parking lot in (his parents) the motor home," Kelly said. "The guys were giving it to me pretty good about how I was acting in the huddle. But I think they spiced it up a little bit."

Oct. 21 – Jim Kelly shook off three interceptions on the Bills first three possessions and went on to throw for five TDs and a regular-season career-high 392 yards as the Bills romped past winless Cincinnati, 35-16, in a Monday night game at Rich Stadium.

Oct. 22 – Bill Polian expressed doubt that any of the Bills apologized to Bengals coach Sam Wyche for the officiating which Wyche said was one-sided in Buffalo's favor. "We're not in the habit of apologizing for things we can't control," Polian said. "Let him name names, I'd be interested to know who they are. It would be out of character for any of our players to apologize about anything, much less officiating." Marv Levy said his response when he heard Wyche's comment was to "laugh heartily. It doesn't make any sense to me. I think he was speaking out of frustration."

Oct. 30 – Andre Reed expressed concern over his recent lack of production. "It just seems like the last few games, my number hasn't been called as often," he said. "It's obvious to the media, it's obvious to everybody, but I can't start a controversy because, right away, then I'm selfish and all that and I don't want that."

Oct. 31 – The Reggie Rogers experiment ended

when the Bills waived him to make room for Jeff Wright, who was scheduled to make his return against New England.

Nov. 3 – On a cold, blustery day, the Bills survived four turnovers and a shoddy performance to beat New England at Rich Stadium, 22-17, in their first game after their bye week.

Nov. 10 – James Lofton had a big day against his former team with six catches for 114 yards as the Bills downed the Packers at Milwaukee, 34-24.

Nov. 13 – The Bills shared some reaction to Magic Johnson's announcement that he was retiring from the Los Angeles Lakers because he had tested positive for HIV. "I hate for this to happen to a great person like Magic," Thurman Thomas said. "But it has caused everyone to wake up and realize it could happen to anyone." Said Darryl Talley: "I think it opened a lot of eyes. A lot of single guys are saying 'Wow, I better settle down, maybe I better find myself a wife.'"

Nov. 17 – Detroit Lions offensive guard Mike Utley was paralyzed after suffering a spine injury while making a block. "That hit home big time," Bills center Kent Hull said. "It's just a tragic, freak thing. It makes you think, but I don't think it's something you can try to prevent. The way he got hurt has happened to me 100 times."

Nov. 18 – The Bills won at Joe Robbie Stadium for the fourth time in five visits, routing the Dolphins on *Monday Night Football*, 41-27. Jim Kelly threw three TD passes and Thurman Thomas rushed for 135 yards. Cornelius Bennett had a sack, forced fumble, recovery and TD return all in one play in the second quarter that turned the game the Bills' way.

Nov. 24 – The Bills turned in a dreadful performance in losing to the Patriots at Foxboro Stadium on a gray, misty day, 16-13. The special teams blocked four kicks, but the offense turned the ball over five times, including an NFL career-high four interceptions by Jim Kelly. "I don't think this loss hurt them," Pats coach Dick MacPherson said. "We all wish the Buffalo Bills, champions of our conference, the best of luck the rest of the way since we don't see them the rest of the season. They played like gentleman. I think they are genuinely happy for us."

Nov. 27 – Bruce Smith practiced for the first time since playing in the Bears game Sept. 29 and it was expected he would return to play against the Jets.

Dec. 1 – The Bills clinched their fourth straight AFC East division title, and for the third time, the Jets were the victims as Buffalo posted a 24-13 victory at Rich Stadium. Bruce Smith returned to the lineup and had six tackles and his first sack of the season. "This was probably the hardest one to come by, in terms of all the injuries and adversity we had to overcome to get here," Bill Polian said. "But there are other goals ahead, other challenges and mountains to climb. We'll enjoy this tonight, but all we did was assure ourselves a place in the playoffs, nothing more."

Dec. 2 – Bruce Smith spoke out about the hate mail he had received during his rehabilitation from knee surgery. "I've been busting my butt like I never have before and it still was the negative things in the mail I received – even in my home mailbox – that kind of inspired me," he said. "I couldn't believe some of the things they said about me. It had gotten to the point where I stopped reading my fan mail. There were so many cheap shots on TV and things of that nature."

Dec. 3 – Marv Levy talked about a conversation he had with Bruce Smith prior to the Jets game. "I told him 'Ya know, I see some apprehension in you and I'm going to make a guess on what the apprehension is about and it's not your knee,'" Levy said. "He kind of smiled and I said, 'You're afraid you won't look like Bruce Smith and you've got too much pride to not want to look like that.' I told him, 'We don't expect you to.' He's not where he would be on the top, but he'll come on strong. He gave us a lift, he made a difference."

Dec. 4 – John Davis underwent major reconstructive surgery and it was announced he would miss at least one calendar year.

Dec. 8 – Scott Norwood shook off three missed field goals and a blown extra point to kick the game-winning field goal in overtime as the Bills rallied from a 27-14 fourth-quarter deficit to beat the Raiders in Los Angeles, 30-27. Jim Kelly passed for 347 yards in front of the largest crowd ever to see the Raiders play in Los Angeles, 85,081. "It was the strangest game I've ever been associated with," said Shane Conlan.

Dec. 9 – Despite Scott Norwood's problems against the Raiders, Marv Levy refused to get down on his kicker. "No," Levy said when asked if he would be changing kickers. "It hasn't been discussed within our staff. It's only been discussed outside our staff and we know more than the people outside our staff know."

Dec. 15 – Thurman Thomas, James Lofton and Steve Tasker all suffered ankle injuries during the Bills 35-7 rout of the Colts in Indianapolis. Thomas' hopes of winning the NFL rushing title took a severe blow when he was hurt in the first quarter.

Dec. 16 – Thurman Thomas denied a rumor that said he was going to give each of the offensive linemen $10,000 if he won the NFL rushing title. "I always give my offensive linemen something at the end of the year, but not $10,000," Thomas said with a chuckle. Thomas did admit he was frustrated getting hurt and watching Kenneth Davis racking up 90 yards against the weak Colts. Thomas said he wanted to play most of the final game even though it meant nothing because he wanted a chance to go

head-to-head with Detroit's Barry Sanders and win the rushing crown. Thomas even went so far as to say "It might be one of those situations where we say 'The hell with Marv, we're going for the record.'"

Dec. 17 – Marv Levy spoke with Thurman Thomas and made it clear that he would decide who played and for how long against the Lions. "From the conversations I've been having with Marv, I'd say it was Marv's (decision)," Thomas said. "I guess I just got caught up in the hype of going against Barry. I was kind of running off at the mouth on that thing and not thinking too much as to what kind of head coach I have and that he's going to bring me down to reality."

Dec. 18 – It was announced that James Lofton had suffered a sprained instep against the Colts and he likely would be out for three weeks. The Pro Bowl nominations were announced and Jim Ritcher was the big story, making the AFC team for the first time in his 13-year career. Darryl Talley was voted by his peers onto the team for the first time as well. They were joined by Jim Kelly, Thurman Thomas, Andre Reed, James Lofton, Cornelius Bennett and Steve Tasker. Kelly, Reed, Thomas, Bennett and Tasker all were named starters.

Dec. 20 – It was announced that Thurman Thomas and Jim Kelly would sit out the season finale against the Lions, meaning Thomas had no chance of winning the rushing crown.

Dec. 22 – The Bills, with many of their starters out or playing limited roles, saw their 17-game Rich Stadium winning streak end as Detroit beat them, 17-14, in overtime. Barry Sanders rushed for 108 yards, but he lost the rushing title to Dallas' Emmitt Smith, who gained 160 yards against Atlanta. Thurman Thomas, however, won his third straight yards gained from scrimmage title even though he played half a quarter in the last two games.

Dec. 23 – NFL commissioner Paul Tagliabue said of the Bills record-setting fans: "It speaks well of the unique interest and relationship that the Bills' fans have with the Bills. It has always been a great football area, and to do this (set a new attendance record)

as often as they've done it ranks the Bills' fans among the top of the league."

Dec. 24 – Jim Kelly, Thurman Thomas and Kent Hull were named to the AP All-Pro team.

Dec. 28 – In the first AFC wild-card game, Kansas City edged the Raiders, 10-6, while in the NFC, Atlanta upset New Orleans, 27-20.

Dec. 29 – On the second day of wild-card play, Dallas knocked off Chicago, 17-13, and Houston beat the Jets, 17-10, meaning Kansas City would be Buffalo's divisional round opponent.

Dec. 30 – Thurman Thomas was named the AP's offensive player of the year as well as its overall NFL MVP. "I guess I had a convincing season," Thomas said. "The awards that are starting to come in now, I look back and it sure beats getting a rushing title, I'll tell you that."

Dec. 31 – Kansas City cornerback Kevin Ross said of the Bills: "They want their shot, they got us. They want us, they got us. We'll be there. They won't embarrass us, we've got a team that won't be embarrassed."

Jan. 1, 1992 – Derrick Thomas was perturbed that the national media was discounting the Chiefs because they were playing at Rich Stadium. "From what I hear, nobody in the country is giving us a chance," he said. "That's great. It means either a lot of people are going to be right or a lot of people are going to look stupid."

Jan. 2, 1992 – It was reported that the Indianapolis Colts regarded Bills' offensive coordinator Ted Marchibroda their No. 1 candidate for their vacant head coaching position, but because the Bills were still in the playoffs, they could not make contact with him.

Jan. 4, 1992 – Washington defeated Atlanta, 24-7, and Denver edged Houston, 26-24, on the first day of divisional round play.

Jan. 5, 1992 – Jim Kelly threw three TD passes, Thurman Thomas rushed for 100 yards and the defense intercepted four passes during a 37-14 blowout of Kansas City in the AFC divisional round, sending the Bills into the AFC Championship Game

The Bills won 17 straight games at Rich Stadium in 1990 and 1991, proving how important home-field advantage in the NFL really is.

The Bills began using the no-huddle offense in 1990, but with Ted Marchibroda's tutelage, Jim Kelly turned it into an art form in 1991, as the Bills were virtually unstoppable.

Also, assistant coach Chuck Dickerson made some remarks about the Redskins offensive line, the Hogs, that the Hogs didn't take kindly to.

Jan. 23, 1992 – Thurman Thomas took the podium in front of hundreds of reporters to apologize for skipping the previous day's media session. He explained that he thought he was to appear on the main podium at 8:30 and when no one came to get him by 8:45, he got upset and left. He attributed the whole affair to a misunderstanding. He then responded to questions concerning Ted Marchibroda's comment about Jim Kelly being the Michael Jordan of the offense. "I think I am, but I guess we have two Michael Jordans on this team, me and Jim I guess," he said. "It's not being cocky or arrogant. I've got a lot of confidence in my abilities and it's my understanding that Michael Jordan is that way. I want the football, especially when the game is on the line." Thomas then dispelled any rumors about internal fighting on the Bills. "People want to bring back the Bickering Bills, but that's not the case. On this team, we just have a lot of people who want to speak their mind."

Jan. 24, 1992 – Marv Levy refused to pose with the Vince Lombardi trophy following his final press conference. "Last year when I posed, I was told the picture would be used only if we won the game and I've seen it published, so I'd rather not take it, I think it would be a little presumptuous," he explained. The Bills continued to make news in the press as Bruce Smith, complaining about what he perceived was a lack of respect for the Bills, said: "I truly believe that the Redskins don't think we have any other players on defense other than myself and Corny (Cornelius Bennett). I'm going to have a helluva game, especially if they try to go one-on-one with Jim Lachey on me." In response, Washington coach Joe Gibbs said: "I usually tell the guys, 'Don't help somebody get ready to play us. Don't make a comment that would hurt the team. Just use common sense.'"

Jan. 25, 1992 – Thurman Thomas was named the NFL's Miller Lite Player of the Year.

Jan. 26, 1992 – Thurman Thomas misplaced his helmet and missed the first two plays of the game and things never got any better for the Bills as they were thrashed, 37-24, in Super Bowl XXVI by the Washington Redskins in front of 63,130 at the Metrodome in Minneapolis. The Redskins rolled up 417 yards of offense and MVP Mark Rypien completed 18 of 33 passes for 292 yards and two TDs. Washington's defense intercepted Jim Kelly four times, sacked him five times, and gave him a concussion that knocked him out briefly. Thomas was held to 13 yards on 10 carries. Kelly threw a Super Bowl record and career-high 58 passes.

Feb. 2, 1992 – San Francisco's Jerry Rice caught a game-winning TD pass from Atlanta's Chris Miller with 4:04 left, giving the NFC a 21-15 victory in the Pro Bowl at Aloha Stadium. Jim Kelly threw a first-quarter TD pass to Miami's Mark Clayton. Dallas' Michael Irvin caught eight passes for 125 yards and was named the MVP.

for the third time in four years. In the NFC, Detroit manhandled Dallas, 38-6.

Jan. 7, 1992 – Ted Marchibroda admitted that if the Indianapolis Colts wanted him, he'd like to be their head coach. "I think every assistant coach wants to eventually be the head guy," he said.

Jan. 8, 1992 – It was announced that Mitch Frerotte would make his first NFL start at right guard in place of Glenn Parker, who suffered a knee injury against Kansas City.

Jan. 12, 1992 – Jeff Wright deflected a John Elway pass in the third quarter which Carlton Bailey intercepted and returned 11 yards for the Bills only touchdown in a tense 10-7 AFC Championship Game victory over the Denver Broncos at Rich Stadium. The Bills offense was frustrated, managing a season-low 213 yards. In the NFC Championship Game, Washington routed Detroit, 41-10, as Mark Rypien threw for 228 yards and two TDs.

Jan. 13, 1992 – The Bills remarked how impressive the Redskins NFC Championship Game victory over Detroit was. "I don't see a lot of weaknesses," Kent Hull lamented. Leonard Smith reported to the team meeting in the morning with an extremely sore knee and it was unknown what the problem was.

Jan. 20, 1992 – After a week of mild workouts, something they couldn't do in their first trip to the Super Bowl when there wasn't a two-week break between the championship games and the Super Bowl, the Bills arrived in Minneapolis with a large part of their gameplan already installed. "We're happy to be here," Marv Levy said. "We had a good week in Buffalo getting our plans in place and we're here to take part in the excitement." There was bad news, though. Leonard Smith could barely walk when he got off the plane. An infection had settled into his knee after the Denver game and had gotten progressively worse during the previous week. He made a turn for the better on the weekend, but experienced problems during the plane ride from Buffalo.

Jan. 21, 1992 – Bruce Smith used Media Day at the Metrodome to air his grievances over the hate mail he received during the season while he was recovering from knee surgery. Later, while speaking to hordes of reporters, he suggested he might ask for a trade in the offseason. "It's a good possibility," he said. "Too many things have happened (mainly the hate mail) that I just can't forget. That's just one thing that irritates me and haunts me. I'm not saying that would have anything to do with this team, this is a wonderful team." In an interview, offensive coordinator Ted Marchibroda said that Jim Kelly was the "Michael Jordan of the offense."

Jan. 22, 1992 – Thurman Thomas became the second Bill in as many days to become a big news story. Reportedly upset that Jim Kelly and Bruce Smith had received much of the attention thus far, the NFL's MVP skipped the mandatory morning media session at the team's St. Paul hotel. Meanwhile, Marv Levy reacted to Bruce Smith's comments from the day before. "We're not going to trade Bruce Smith, flat out no," Levy said. "Bruce has received some letters from bigots. He also has received a flood of letters from people in Buffalo and Western New York decrying that type of letter, bolstering and boosting him. And I'll tell you what I'm going to tell Bruce. 'Don't let a bigot or two chase you out of town. You're a bigger man than they are. You don't have a problem, that guy has a problem.'"

By the Numbers - 1991

TEAM STATISTICS	BILLS	OPP
First downs	359	335
Rushing	128	138
Passing	208	166
Penalty	23	31
Third downs	90-191	74-218
Fourth downs	4-12	8-20
Avg. time of poss	26:04	33:56
Total yards	6,252	5,458
Avg. game	390.8	341.1
Plays	1,056	1,086
Avg. play	5.9	5.0
Net rushing yds	2,381	2,044
Avg. game	148.8	127.8
Avg. play	4.7	3.9
Net passing yds	3,871	3,414
Comp/att	332/516	299/536
Sacks/lost	35-269	31-246
Interceptions	19	23
Percentage	64.3	55.8
Punts/avg	54-38.6	70-39.1
Fumbles/lost	25-16	26-14
Penalties/yds	114-870	109-933
Touchdowns	58	34
Extra points	56-58	33-34
Field goals	18-29	27-35
Safeties	0	0
Kick ret./avg	52-18.7	62-20.4
Punt ret./avg	26-10.8	15-3.5

RUSHING	ATT	YDS	AVG	TD
Thomas	288	1407	4.9	7
Davis	129	624	4.8	4
Gardner	42	146	3.5	4
Reed	12	136	11.3	0
Kelly	20	45	2.3	1
Edwards	1	17	17.0	0
Reich	13	6	0.5	0
TOTALS	**505**	**2381**	**4.7**	**16**

RECEIVING	CAT	YDS	AVG	TD
Reed	81	1113	13.7	10
Thomas	62	631	10.2	5
Lofton	57	1072	18.8	8
McKeller	44	434	9.9	3
Beebe	32	414	12.9	6
Edwards	22	228	10.4	1
K. Davis	20	118	5.9	1
Metzelaars	5	54	10.8	2
Gardner	3	20	6.7	0
Rolle	3	10	3.3	2
Tasker	2	39	19.5	1
Alexander	1	7	7.0	0
TOTALS	**332**	**4140**	**12.5**	**39**

PASSING	COMP	ATT	INT	YDS	TD	COMP%	SACKS	RATE
Kelly	304	474	17	3844	33	64.1	31-227	97.6
Reich	27	41	2	305	6	65.9	4-42	107.6
Mohr	1	1	0	-9	0	100.0	0-0	79.2
TOTALS	**332**	**516**	**19**	**4140**	**39**	**64.3**	**35-269**	**99.0**

KICKING	1-19	20-29	30-39	40-49	50+	TOT	PAT	PTS
Norwood	1-1	7-8	3-7	5-9	2-4	18-29	56-58	110

PUNTING	NO	AVG	LG	In 20	BL
Mohr	54	38.6	58	12	0

SCORE BY QUARTERS

BILLS	82	130	106	137	3 -	458
OPP	40	87	92	96	3 -	318

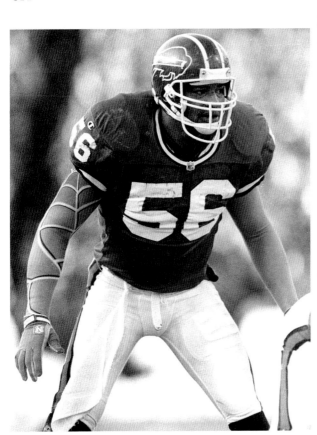

DEFENSIVE STATISTICAL LEADERS

TACKLES: Conlan 82 primary - 40 assists - 122 total, Talley 89-28-117, Bennett 84-23-107, L. Smith 70-24-94, Bailey 61-32-93, Odomes 71-5-76, Kelso 58-12-70, Seals 41-22-63, Jackson 51-5-56, Bentley 32-16-48, Hansen 29-11-40, Lodish 28-9-37, Wright 22-11-33, B. Smith 13-5-18

SACKS: Bennett 9, Wright 6, Talley 4, Hansen 2, L. Smith 2, B. Smith 1.5, Lodish 1.5

FUMBLE RECOVERIES: Kelso 3, Bennett 2, Conlan 2, Talley 2

FORCED FUMBLES: Bennett 4, Talley 4, Hansen 2

INTERCEPTIONS: Odomes 5-120 yards, 24.0 avg., 1 TD; Talley 5-45, 9.0, 0 TD

SPECIAL TEAMS STATISTICAL LEADERS

KICKOFF RETURNS: Edwards 31-623 yards, 20.1 avg., 1 TD; Fuller 8-125, 15.6, 0 TD

PUNT RETURNS: Hicks 12-203, 16.9, 0 TD; Edwards 13-69, 5.3, 0 TD

TACKLES: Tasker 26, Garner 19, Bentley 16, Gardner 14, Jones 13, Pike 13, Hicks 10, Rolle 10, K. Davis 9, Patton 8, Drane 3, Norwood 3, Lingner 3, Hansen 2

NOTES

• The Bills broke their all-time record for most yards in a game with 583 in a wild season-opening victory, breaking the mark of 565 set against Houston on Oct. 11, 1964.

• Thurman Thomas became the first Bill to top 100 yards rushing and receiving in one game. Jim Kelly set a career-high for passing yards in a regular-season game. The previous best was 363 against the Oilers in '89.

• The Bills converted on nine of 11 third-down situations.

• Jeff Wright suffered a knee injury in the third quarter that would keep him out until midseason. Bruce Smith missed the game and Mike Lodish started. Rookie Phil Hansen entered when Wright was hurt.

• Scott Norwood missed a 25-yard field goal on the first series. Four plays later, Dan Marino hit Mark Clayton for a TD. The Bills next series ended when Louis Oliver intercepted Kelly. Miami then drove 65 yards in 10 plays to Mark Higgs' TD run for a 14-0 lead.

• The Bills then went 86 yards in eight plays to Andre Reed's 54-yard TD catch. The Bills had 244 yards at the half, but only seven points.

• Charlie Baumann's field goal capped a 67-yard second-half opening drive, then the Bills took control.

• They drove 80 yards to Frank Reich's TD pass to Butch Rolle. Kelly was hurt during the drive, but Reich completed both of his passes, including a 13-yarder to James Lofton on third-and-10 at the Miami 21.

• After a punt, Kelly led a six-play, 80-yard march, hitting Thomas with a 50-yard TD pass.

• Don Beebe's fumble on the next series was recovered by T.J. Turner at the Bills 44. Marino needed only seven plays to regain a 24-21 lead, hitting Clayton for a TD.

• Six plays after the kickoff, Carwell Gardner scored.

Mark Kelso then recovered Higgs' fumble at the Bills 45, leading to Thomas' TD run. Reed caught two passes for 30 yards along the way.

• Marino hit Mark Duper for a TD on the next series, but the Bills ran out the final 2:23.

QUOTES

• Marv Levy on Kelly: "If there's a tougher quarterback in the league, I don't know who it is. He's a tough son of a gun and he heals fast, although I've never seen him heal that fast."

• Jim Kelly: "It's going to take a lot more than a bum ankle to keep me out. If I can take the field, this is my club. I'm going to do it. I'm not going to stand up here and say I'm a hero, but I know what kind of football player I am and I know what my offensive line and the other players on the team expect of me."

• Thurman Thomas: "At halftime I was just sitting at my locker by myself, the rest of the offensive players and coaches were on the other side. I think they knew I was kinda mad. I didn't say anything to anyone. I knew they knew that whenever I touched the ball a lot against the Dolphins, we usually won. So I figured I'd get it more in the second half. At least I hoped so."

Dolphins	7	7	3	14 - 31
Bills	0	7	14	14 - 35

Attendance at Rich Stadium - 80,252

Mia: Clayton 43 pass from Marino (Baumann kick), 6:04
Mia: Higgs 3 run (Baumann kick), 2:39
Buf: Reed 54 pass from Kelly (Norwood kick), 6:15
Mia: FG Baumann 21, 3:59
Buf: Rolle 3 pass from Reich (Norwood kick), 8:13
Buf: Thomas 50 pass from Kelly (Norwood kick), 12:50
Mia: Clayton 5 pass from Marino (Baumann kick), 3:15
Buf: Gardner 1 run (Norwood kick), 9:02
Buf: Thomas 7 run (Norwood kick), 11:05
Mia: Duper 3 pass from Marino (Baumann kick), 12:28

	BUF	MIA
First downs	33	23
Rushing yds	186	146
Passing yds	397	250
Punts-avg	1-17.0	3-46.0
Fumbles-lost	1-1	1-1
Penalties-yds	8-55	6-35
Poss. time	29:00	31:00

BILLS LEADERS: **Rushing** - Thomas 25-165, Gardner 5-12, Kelly 2-4, K. Davis 1-5; **Passing** - Kelly 29-39-1 - 381, Reich 2-2-0 - 16; **Receiving** - Reed 11-154, Thomas 8-103, Lofton 5-77, Beebe 5-55, Gardner 1-5, Rolle 1-3.

DOLPHINS LEADERS: **Rushing** - Higgs 30-146; **Passing** - Marino 17-28-0 - 267; **Receiving** - Clayton 6-138, Duper 5-67, Paige 3-20, Henry 2-17, Banks 1-25.

WEEK 1 GAMES

KC 14, Atl 3	Den 45, Cinc 14
Dal 26, Clev 14	Hou 47, LAR 17
Chi 10, Minn 6	NE 16, Ind 7
Phil 20, GB 3	Phoe 24, Rams 14
Pitt 26, SD 20	NO 27, Sea 24
NYJ 16, TB 13	Wash 45, Det 0
NYG 16, SF 14	

NOTES

• The Bills erupted for their second-highest point total in team history in routing the Steelers.

• Don Beebe tied a club record for receiving TDs previously set by Jerry Butler in 1979 vs. the Jets.

• Jim Kelly set a team record for TD passes in one game and set a personal record for completions.

• Andre Reed set a team record with his 17th 100-yard receiving game and also caught his 400th pass.

• The scoring barrage began on the Bills' second series when Kelly hit James Lofton for a TD. Then, after Gary Anderson missed a 50-yard field goal, the Bills drove 34 yards to Scott Norwood's 50-yarder.

• After an Anderson field goal early in the second quarter, the Bills went 80 yards in 10 plays to Beebe's first TD.

• After a punt, Reed caught a 32-yard pass and Beebe capped a 63-yard drive with his second TD reception.

• Five plays after the kickoff, Barry Foster broke a 56-yard TD run to get the Steelers to within 24-10.

• The Bills took the second-half kickoff and drove 80 yards to Reed's TD on a third-and-15 play.

• The Steelers got that back with Warren Williams' TD, then Bryan Hinkle returned a Kelly interception for a TD. Later, Rod Woodson's interception set up an Anderson

field goal.

• The Bills then scored 21 points in a 4:41 span of the fourth, highlighted by Nate Odomes' interception for a TD.

QUOTES

• Don Beebe: "Wow, this is unbelievable. I feel like the President. They left me one-on-one a lot and Jim saw me open and got me the ball. Jim is the best quarterback in the league as far as seeing the whole field. He showed that today. If we can stay away from injury and we keep executing, I don't think we can be stopped. It's like a runaway train. You can just see it in the DBs eyes, it's like 'Who's coming next?' I would hate to play defense against us."

• Jim Kelly: "I ran out of plays. It got to a point where it was 'What do I call now?' One of Carlton Bailey's buddies played for them and he said they thought they were going to shut our passing game down. They said they looked like they had exactly what they needed to shut us down. It just goes to show what kind of receivers we have. It's not the system, it's execution."

• Kent Hull: "I think they (Kelly and the coaches) were drawing plays on the ground. A lot of times he'd call a play and then he'd yell something like 'Hey Beebe, run this.'"

• Steelers cornerback Rod Woodson: "They made us look like little kids out there. They come out with that no-huddle, or whatever they call it, and it really winds the defense. I was tired."

Steelers	0	10	17	7 - 34
Bills	10	14	7	21 - 52

Attendance at Rich Stadium - 79,545

Buf: Lofton 53 pass from Kelly (Norwood kick), 6:18
Buf: FG Norwood 50, 11:33
Pit: FG Anderson 25, :07
Buf: Beebe 34 pass from Kelly (Norwood kick), 3:46
Buf: Beebe 14 pass from Kelly (Norwood kick), 8:03
Pit: Foster 56 run (Anderson kick), 10:54
Buf: Reed 15 pass from Kelly (Norwood kick), 3:47
Pit: W. Williams 1 run (Anderson kick), 6:52
Pit: Hinkle 57 interception return (Anderson kick), 8:49
Pit: FG Anderson 27, 13:44
Buf: Beebe 11 pass from Kelly (Norwood kick), 1:51
Buf: Beebe 4 pass from Kelly (Norwood kick), 7:03
Buf: Odomes 32 interception return (Norwood kick), 7:48
Pit: Hoge 1 run (Anderson kick), 9:42

	BUF	PIT
First downs	31	14
Rushing yds	194	152
Passing yds	343	113
Punts-avg	2-32.0	6-36.3
Fumbles-lost	1-1	0-0
Penalties-yds	5-53	9-63
Poss. time	33:06	26:54

BILLS LEADERS: **Rushing** - Thomas 15-107, K. Davis 17-56, Reed 1-11, Gardner 6-21, Reich 1-(-1); **Passing** - Kelly 31-43-2 - 363; **Receiving** - Beebe 10-112, Reed 9-118, Lofton 4-78, Thomas 4-35, McKeller 2-22, Metzelaars 1-1, K. Davis 1-(-3).

STEELERS LEADERS: **Rushing** - Foster 9-121, Hoge 10-32, W. Williams 4-(-1); **Passing** - Brister 15-29-1 - 134; **Receiving** - Hoge 4-26, Mularkey 3-42, Green 3-31, Lipps 3-29, W. Williams 2-6.

WEEK 2 GAMES

Chi 21, TB 20	Clev 20, NE 0
LAR 16, Den 13	Det 23, GB 14
Mia 17, Ind 6	Rams 19, NYG 13
Minn 20, Atl 19	NO 17, KC 10
Sea 20, NYJ 13	Phoe 26, Phil 10
SF 34, SD 14	Hou 30, Cinc 7
Wash 33, Dal 31	

STANDINGS: SECOND WEEK

AFC EAST	W	L	T	CENTRAL	W	L	T	WEST	W	L	T	NFC EAST	W	L	T	CENTRAL	W	L	T	WEST	W	L	T
Buffalo	2	0	0	Houston	2	0	0	Denver	1	1	0	Phoenix	2	0	0	Chicago	2	0	0	N.Orleans	2	0	0
New England	1	1	0	Pittsburgh	1	1	0	Kan. City	1	1	0	Washington	2	0	0	Detroit	1	1	0	LA Rams	1	1	0
NY Jets	1	1	0	Cleveland	1	1	0	Raiders	1	1	0	Dallas	1	1	0	Minnesota	1	1	0	San Fran	1	1	0
Miami	1	1	0	Cincinnati	0	2	0	Seattle	1	1	0	Philadelphia	1	1	0	Green Bay	0	2	0	Atlanta	0	2	0
Indianapolis	0	2	0					San Diego	0	2	0	NY Giants	1	1	0	Tampa Bay	0	2	0				

GAME 3 - Sunday, Sept. 15, 1991 - BILLS 23, JETS 20

Bills	0	10	6	7 - 23
Jets	0	10	7	3 - 20

Attendance at Giants Stadium - 65,309

NYJ: McNeil 1 run (Leahy kick), :43
Buf: FG Norwood 52, 2:54
NYJ: FG Leahy 32, 7:08
Buf: Reed 7 pass from Kelly (Norwood kick), 14:11
Buf: FG Norwood 25, 2:25
NYJ: B. Thomas 5 pass from O'Brien (Leahy kick), 9:36
Buf: FG Norwood 44, 12:36
NYJ: FG Leahy 39, 3:12
Buf: Thomas 15 pass from Kelly (Norwood kick), 10:46

	BUF	NYJ
First downs	22	25
Rushing yds	64	168
Passing yds	240	220
Punts-avg	2-45.5	4-41.3
Fumbles-lost	1-1	4-1
Penalties-yds	6-60	8-104
Poss. time	19:25	40:35

BILLS LEADERS: **Rushing** - Thomas 11-62, K. Davis 1-1, Gardner 1-4, Kelly 2-(-3); **Passing** - Kelly 27-37-1 - 275; **Receiving** - Thomas 13-112, Lofton 5-79, McKeller 3-41, Reed 3-26, K. Davis 2-5, Beebe 1-12.

JETS LEADERS: **Rushing** - Hector 12-69, B. Thomas 12-42, McNeil 8-42, Baxter 5-15; **Passing** - O'Brien 21-35-1 - 237, Taylor 1-1-0 - (-2); **Receiving** - Toon 8-89, Moore 5-94, B. Thomas 4-24, Dressel 2-16, Baxter 1-7, Mathis 1-7, Hector 1- (-2).

NOTES

• Thurman Thomas tied a club record for most receptions in one game and made a dazzling grab of the game-winning TD pass over the middle as the Bills beat the Jets for the eighth straight time.
• James Lofton moved into second place on the all-time NFL receiving yardage list past Charlie Joiner.
• Kyle Clifton killed the Bills' opening possession with an interception at the Jets 21.
• Later in the first quarter, the Jets embarked on a 15-play, 85-yard drive that consumed 8:08 before Freeman McNeil scored on third-and-goal from the 1 early in the second quarter. The Jets converted three third downs on the march.
• Scott Norwood made a career-best 52-yard field goal, tying a team record, on the ensuing series. But Pat Leahy countered with a 32-yarder.
• After an exchange of punts, the Bills went 80 yards in six plays to Andre Reed's TD. The key was a 39-yard interference call on Tony Stargell at the Jets 41.
• J.D. Williams intercepted Ken O'Brien in the end zone late in the half to kill the threat.
• On the third play of the second half, Mike Lodish sacked O'Brien, forced a fumble and Phil Hansen

WEEK 3 GAMES

Atl 13, SD 10	Clev 14, Cinc 13
LAR 16, Ind 0	Det 17, Mia 13
Pitt 20, NE 6	Chi 20, NYG 17
Phil 24, Dal 0	Wash 34, Phoe 0
Minn 17, SF 14	Den 16, Sea 10
GB 15, TB 13	NO 24, Rams 7
Hou 17, KC 7	

recovered at the Jets 16, setting up Norwood's second field goal for a 13-10 lead. The Jets then drove 80 yards in 11 plays to Blair Thomas' TD reception.
• Norwood answered with his third field goal. But on the next series, Thurman Thomas lost a fumble, which resulted in another Leahy field goal.
• The Bills began their winning drive at the Jets 49 with 7:11 left. James Lofton made a 20-yard catch, then made a 10-yard reception on fourth-and-six from the Jets 30. Thomas caught the winner two plays later.
• The Jets drove to the Bills 34, but Leahy missed a 51-yard attempt with 16 seconds left.

QUOTES

• Jim Kelly: "Everybody is talking so much about stopping our offense, but it takes physical talent and they matched up pretty well. Give them credit."
• Cornelius Bennett: "We got away with one today. Those guys played well enough to beat us."
• James Lofton on his key fourth-down catch: "It's just one of those plays that you hear the announcers talk about where the receiver needs to go a couple yards in front of the sticks, turn, catch the ball and hope he doesn't end up short of the first down. Heck, we were scared. We didn't play as well as we would've liked."
• Thurman Thomas: "We were lucky today, but show me a team that doesn't need a little luck during the course of the season. We're not going to score 50 points every game."
• Marv Levy: "If there's an expectancy that we're going to wallop everyone, you're wrong. We're going to have a lot of games like this where we'll have to come from behind."

GAME 4 - Sunday, Sept. 22, 1991 - BILLS 17, BUCCANEERS 10

Bills	7	0	3	7 - 17
Buccaneers	0	0	7	3 - 10

Attendance at Tampa Stadium - 57,323

Buf: Gardner 1 run (Norwood kick), 9:27
TB: Cobb 1 run (Christie kick), 8:09
Buf: FG Norwood 33, 14:52
TB: FG Christie 19, 6:59
Buf: McKeller 29 pass from Kelly (Norwood kick), 9:39

	BUF	TB
First downs	19	22
Rushing yds	120	138
Passing yds	301	165
Punts-avg	3-40.7	6-41.3
Fumbles-lost	3-1	0-0
Penalties-yds	6-50	5-45
Poss. time	20:48	39:12

BILLS LEADERS: **Rushing** - Thomas 17-54, Reed 2-61, Gardner 6-5; **Passing** - Kelly 20-35-1 - 322; **Receiving** - Lofton 5-90, Beebe 5-76, Reed 3-69, McKeller 3-38, Thomas 2-19, Tasker 1-19, Gardner 1-11.

BUCCANEERS LEADERS: **Rushing** - Cobb 21-70, Anderson 13-29, Wilson 3-24, Chandler 4-13, Testaverde 1-2; **Passing** - Chandler 15-27-1 - 137, Testaverde 3-10-0 - 48; **Receiving** - B. Hill 5-46, E. Thomas 4-55, Carrier 3-36, Dawsey 2-29, Wilson 2-7, Drewery 1-8, Anderson 1-4.

WEEK 4 GAMES

NYG 13, Clev 10	Det 33, Ind 24
Mia 16, GB 13	NE 24, Hou 20
Atl 21, LAR 17	SF 27, Rams 10
NO 26, Minn 0	Phil 23, Pitt 14
Den 27, SD 19	KC 20, Sea 13
Wash 34, Cinc 27	Dal 17, Phoe 9
Chi 19, NYJ 13 (OT)	

NOTES

• The Bills struggled against the winless Buccaneers, but won for the first time at Tampa Stadium in the last six visits, including Super Bowl XXV, as Keith McKeller caught the game-winning TD pass.
• Because of injuries, the Bills had to start Mike Lodish and Mark Pike on the defensive line, then lost cornerback J.D. Williams and offensive guard John Davis to knee injuries during the game.
• Cornelius Bennett had a big game with eight tackles and two sacks.
• Carwell Gardner fumbled on the Bills first offensive play at their 17. But Pike blocked Steve Christie's 39-yard field goal attempt. The Bills took over at the 21 and used nine plays before Gardner redeemed himself by scoring on a one-yard run. Gardner caught an 11-yard pass on third-and-six from the Bills 25 and James Lofton hauled in a 40-yard pass on third-and-nine from the Bills 37.
• Scott Norwood was wide right from the 36 in the second quarter, the same goal post he missed in the Super Bowl.
• Midway through the third, the Bucs drove 70 yards in 10 plays to Reggie Cobb's TD run. The drive was directed by Chris Chandler, who had replaced the injured Vinny Testaverde.
• The Bills drove to the Bucs 5 on the next series, but Gardner was stopped on fourth-and-one. However, Nate Odomes intercepted Chandler five plays later, setting up Norwood's 33-yard field goal.
• The Bucs responded with a 13-play, 68-yard drive to Christie's tying field goal. The Bills defense stopped Cobb twice from inside the 2, forcing the field goal.
• Jim Kelly then directed the six-play, 76-yard winning drive, hitting three passes for 49 yards.
• The Bucs then drove to the Bills 8 with eight seconds left, but Leonard Smith tackled Lawrence Dawsey inbounds to keep the clock running. Chandler spiked the ball to stop the clock with two seconds left, then threw incomplete into the end zone to end the game.

QUOTES

• Jim Kelly: "Let's pack our bags and get out of here (referring to Tampa Stadium). I'm just glad to get this one over with. We moved the ball well, we just couldn't get it in the end zone. We could have blown it open, but I missed some passes that I should have hit."
• Nate Odomes: "A lot of people get the impression we're just a Bruce Smith-Cornelius Bennett-Shane Conlan defense, but that's not how it is. There's a lot of capable guys on the field who can go in there and win a game for us."
• Marv Levy: "I was very proud of the defense. Even when some things went wrong, those guys kept hanging in."
• Leonard Smith: "We knew we were going to be in a dogfight. It was just a matter of us believing in ourselves. On the last drive, we were just trying to keep their receivers in front of us. We figured if we made them work for everything, they might not have enough time."
• Darryl Talley: "Let's put it this way. The skin on my teeth is getting awfully thin."

STANDINGS: FOURTH WEEK

AFC EAST	W	L	T	CENTRAL	W	L	T	WEST	W	L	T	NFC EAST	W	L	T	CENTRAL	W	L	T	WEST	W	L	T
Buffalo	4	0	0	Houston	3	1	0	Denver	3	1	0	Washington	4	0	0	Chicago	4	0	0	N.Orleans	4	0	0
New England	2	2	0	Pittsburgh	2	2	0	Raiders	2	2	0	Philadelphia	3	1	0	Detroit	3	1	0	Atlanta	2	2	0
Miami	2	2	0	Cleveland	2	2	0	Kan. City	2	2	0	Phoenix	2	2	0	Minnesota	2	2	0	San Fran	2	2	0
NY Jets	1	3	0	Cincinnati	0	4	0	Seattle	1	3	0	Dallas	2	2	0	Green Bay	1	3	0	LA Rams	1	3	0
Indianapolis	0	4	0					San Diego	0	4	0	NY Giants	2	2	0	Tampa Bay	0	4	0				

NOTES

• The Bills improved to 5-0 in front of a new Rich Stadium record crowd that saw James Lofton move into fourth place on the all-time NFL receptions list, going past Ozzie Newsome.

• Bruce Smith played his first game of the season, but clearly was hampered. He had one tackle.

• The Bills started slowly on offense. Scott Norwood missed a 49-yard field goal and then the Bills got a break when Mark Carrier's 43-yard interception TD return was nullified by a penalty.

• The Bears offense also was sluggish, but Kevin Butler capped a 15-play, 65-yard drive with a field goal.

• After a third Bills punt, the Bears thought they had a TD, but Neal Anderson's 17-yard run was nullified by a penalty, so they settled for Butler's second field goal in the second quarter.

• An exchange of punts gave the Bills the ball at their 15 with 1:59 left. Kelly hit Al Edwards for 11 on third-and-five from the 40. Then after a sack, Kelly hit Edwards for a TD on a third-and-16 play.

• The Bills took the second-half kickoff and moved 91 yards in 12 plays. The score came when Carwell Gardner was stopped on fourth-and-goal from the 1, but fumbled into the end zone and recovered his own muff.

• The Bears went three-and-out and Maury Buford's 26-yard punt carried only to the Bears 35. The Bills scored seven plays later when Butch Rolle caught his 10th consecutive TD pass, dating back to 1987.

• Anderson scored early in the fourth, but on the first play after the kickoff, Lofton caught a 77-yard TD.

• On the first play after the kickoff, Kirby Jackson intercepted Jim Harbaugh at the Bears 38, leading to Thomas'

TD run. Mark Green capped the scoring for the Bears.

QUOTES

• Jim Kelly on the TD pass to Al Edwards: "It was one of those plays Frank (Reich) and I put in last week. We talked to coach Marchibroda and we decided to get that put in and it wound up working."

• Al Edwards: "When we came out of the huddle, Jim said 'Give me a good nine route' and I said, 'Wow, this must be the play.' I just put it on myself to beat the guy (Donnell Woolford). I pushed him up about 15 yards and gave him a move to the outside and he bit."

• Kent Hull on Carwell Gardner's fumble into the end zone: "I saw it there, but I couldn't do anything about it, I had about 380 pounds laying on me. I still say good teams are lucky."

• Thurman Thomas: "We really came out flat in the first half, but our defense played well and gave us the opportunity to get things rolling after halftime."

• Bruce Smith on his return: "I felt I could be a positive influence. I certainly thought I'd be able to accomplish something. It's not like I haven't been busting my butt to get back out there."

WEEK 5 GAMES

Rams 23, GB 21	Sea 31, Ind 3
KC 14, SD 13	NYJ 41, Mia 23
Phoe 24, NE 10	NO 27, Atl 6
Dal 21, NYG 16	LAR 12, SF 6
Det 31, TB 3	Den 13, Minn 6
Wash 23, Phil 20	
Pitt, Cinc, Clev, Hou had bye weeks	

Bears	**0**	**6**	**0**	**14**	**- 20**
Bills	**0**	**7**	**14**	**14**	**- 35**

Attendance at Rich Stadium - 80,366

Chi:	FG Butler 28, 3:42
Chi:	FG Butler 42, 10:12
Buf:	Edwards 33 pass from Kelly (Norwood kick), 14:48
Buf:	Gardner fumble recovery in end zone, (Norwood kick), 6:05
Buf:	Rolle 2 pass from Kelly (Norwood kick), 10:14
Chi:	Anderson 2 run (Butler kick), 6:15
Buf:	Lofton 77 pass from Kelly (Norwood kick), 6:37
Buf:	Thomas 10 run (Norwood kick), 9:10
Chi:	Green 1 run (Butler kick), 14:20

	BUF	CHI
First downs	21	20
Rushing yds	141	84
Passing yds	280	269
Punts-avg	7-32.6	8-33.3
Fumbles-lost	2-1	0-0
Penalties-yds	7-43	12-89
Poss. time	25:13	34:47

BILLS LEADERS: Rushing - Thomas 25-117, K. Davis 5-25, Gardner 2-0, Kelly 1-0, Reich 1-(-1); **Passing** - Kelly 19-29-0 - 303; **Receiving** - Lofton 4-122, Reed 4-33, McKeller 3-40, Thomas 3-40, Edwards 2-44, Beebe 2-22, Rolle 1-2.

BEARS LEADERS: Rushing - Anderson 19-54, Harbaugh 3-16, Rouse 3-7, Morgan 1-2, Green 2-5; **Passing** - Harbaugh 17-35-1 - 203, Willis 5-7-0 - 66; **Receiving** - Davis 5-51, Thornton 1-25, Anderson 5-63, Rouse 2-14, Morgan 3-36, Waddle 3-31, Morris 2-34, Green 1-15.

NOTES

• In one of their worst performances in recent memory, the Bills were embarrassed on *Monday Night Football* as the Chiefs forced five fumbles and sacked Jim Kelly six times, including four by Derrick Thomas.

• The loud crowd gave the Bills' offensive line fits, which was the biggest reason for the sacks.

• The Chiefs had two 100-yard rushers in the same game for the fifth time in team history, the first since 1975.

• The Chiefs' 54 rushing attempts were their most since 1979. The Bills Monday record fell to 7-13.

• The game began ominously when Harvey Williams returned the opening kickoff 38 yards and a personal foul on Carwell Gardner moved the ball to the Bills 46. The Chiefs wound up with a Nick Lowery field goal.

• The Bills stopped the next Kansas City possession when Nate Odomes recovered Jonathan Hayes' fumble and returned it to the Bills 31, but Kelly was sacked by Bill Maas and lost a fumble at his own 23. That set up Pete Holohan's TD reception on third-and-goal from the 1.

• Scott Norwood kicked two field goals on the next two possessions, the second set up when Mike Lodish forced

Christian Okoye to fumble and Leonard Smith recovered at the Chiefs 31.

• Before the half ended, the Chiefs drove 57 yards to Lowery's second field goal, then Lowery made another in the third for a 16-6 lead. Two plays after the kickoff, Lonnie Marts forced Thurman Thomas to fumble and Kevin Ross recovered and returned it to the Bills 17, setting up Okoye's first TD run.

• On the first play after the kickoff, Derrick Thomas sacked Kelly and Dan Saleaumua recovered his fumble at the 10, leading to Okoye's second TD run and a 30-6 lead.

• Early in the fourth, another Derrick Thomas sack and a forced fumble was recovered by Neil Smith, setting up Lowery's fourth field goal which capped a 15-play, 59-yard drive.

QUOTES

• Marv Levy: "I hope we're not as bad as we showed tonight. This was just a total team loss. We were manhandled. It hurts to have someone run over you like they did tonight."

• Jim Kelly: "We gave them enough gifts to last until Christmas."

• Will Wolford on Derrick Thomas: "He's very good, what else can I say? Hindsight is 20-20, but I would have loved to have had some help. That second half, you saw it, it was pretty bad. I felt naked, but he's a great player. I'm not the first person this has happened to."

• Shane Conlan: "We didn't think we'd get manhandled. Okoye is a great running back. He's a load. He's 260 and I'm 228, so I'm going to have trouble stopping him. We all had trouble stopping him. Once he gets moving, forget it. We didn't meet the challenge."

• Mike Lodish: "I'm sure the boys in the (ABC) booth didn't have a lot of good things to say about our defense. We've been struggling all year against the run and the Chiefs certainly overpowered us tonight."

Bills	**0**	**6**	**0**	**0**	**- 6**
Chiefs	**3**	**10**	**17**	**3**	**- 33**

Attendance at Arrowhead Stadium - 76,120

KC:	FG Lowery 41, 2:30
KC:	Holohan 1 pass from Deberg (Lowery kick), :44
Buf:	FG Norwood 44, 8:15
Buf:	FG Norwood 25, 10:54
KC:	FG Lowery 40, 15:00
KC:	FG Lowery 24, 10:39
KC:	Okoye 5 run (Lowery kick), 12:08
KC:	Okoye 2 run (Lowery kick), 14:06
KC:	FG Lowery 22, 10:58

	BUF	KC
First downs	11	26
Rushing yds	65	247
Passing yds	146	150
Punts-avg	3-45.7	1-22.0
Fumbles-lost	5-5	3-2
Penalties-yds	7-65	3-25
Poss. time	15:54	44:06

BILLS LEADERS: Rushing - T. Thomas 13-51, K. Davis 1-14; **Passing** - Kelly 17-23-0 - 189; **Receiving** - Thomas 4-24, Beebe 3-54, McKeller 3-18, Reed 5-84, Lofton 1-11, K. Davis 1-(-2).

CHIEFS LEADERS: Rushing - Okoye 29-130, Williams 20-103, Word 5-14; **Passing** - DeBerg 16-23-0 - 150; **Receiving** - R. Thomas 4-55, Holohan 2-8, F. Jones 1-20, Barnett 2-16, B. Jones 4-24, McNair 2-11, Hayes 1-16.

WEEK 6 GAMES

Dal 20, GB 17	Hou 42, Den 14
Mia 20, NE 10	Det 24, Minn 20
NYJ 17, Clev 14	TB 14, Phil 13
NYG 9, Phoe 9	SD 21, LAR 13
Sea 13, Cinc 7	Wash 20, Chi 7
Pitt 21, Ind 3	
NO, Rams, SF, Atl had bye weeks	

STANDINGS: SIXTH WEEK

AFC EAST	W	L	T	CENTRAL	W	L	T	WEST	W	L	T	NFC EAST	W	L	T	CENTRAL	W	L	T	WEST	W	L	T
Buffalo	5	1	0	Houston	4	1	0	Denver	4	2	0	Washington	6	0	0	Detroit	5	1	0	N.Orleans	5	0	0
NY Jets	3	3	0	Pittsburgh	3	2	0	Kan. City	4	2	0	Dallas	4	2	0	Chicago	4	2	0	Atlanta	2	3	0
Miami	3	3	0	Cleveland	2	3	0	Raiders	3	3	0	Phoenix	3	3	0	Minnesota	2	4	0	San Fran	2	3	0
New England	2	4	0	Cincinnati	0	5	0	Seattle	3	3	0	Philadelphia	3	3	0	Green Bay	1	5	0	LA Rams	2	3	0
Indianapolis	0	6	0					San Diego	1	5	0	NY Giants	3	3	0	Tampa Bay	1	5	0				

Colts	0	6	0	0	-	6
Bills	14	14	7	7	-	42

Attendance at Rich Stadium - 79,015

Buf: Thomas 14 run (Norwood kick), 1:18
Buf: Gardner 3 run (Norwood kick), 7:02
Ind: FG Biasucci 26, 1:56
Ind: FG Biasucci 29, 5:49
Buf: Thomas 7 run (Norwood kick), 9:13
Buf: McKeller 5 pass from Reich (Norwood kick), 14:12
Buf: Lofton 11 pass from Reich (Norwood kick), 5:27
Buf: K. Davis 78 run (Norwood kick), :16

	BUF	IND
First downs	22	20
Rushing yds	276	66
Passing yds	120	174
Punts-avg	1-47.0	2-35.5
Fumbles-lost	2-1	1-1
Penalties-yds	8-56	10-93
Poss. time	25:11	34:49

BILLS LEADERS: Rushing - Thomas 20-117, K. Davis 9-108, Gardner 7-48, Kelly 2-3; **Passing** - Kelly 3-5-0 - 44, Reich 6-7-1 - 76; **Receiving** - Lofton 2-22, Thomas 1-26, McKeller 3-34, Reed 2-34, Gardner 1-4.

COLTS LEADERS: Rushing - Clark 19-44, Johnson 4-11, Perkins 1-4, Manoa 5-7; **Passing** - George 22-33-1 - 168, Trudeau 1-4-1 - 11; **Receiving** - Hester 5-59, Clark 6-31, Brooks 1-14, Mrosko 5-42, Johnson 4-14, Verdin 2-19.

WEEK 7 GAMES

Dal 35, Cinc 23	Wash 42, Clev 17
Hou 23, NYJ 20	KC 42, Mia 7
NO 13, Phil 6	Minn 34, Phoe 7
Rams 30, SD 24	Atl 39, SF 34
LAR 23, Sea 20 OT	NYG 23, Pitt 20

NE, Den, GB, TB, Chi, Det had bye weeks

NOTES

• The Bills bounced back from their first defeat with an easy rout as Thurman Thomas and Kenneth Davis each topped 100 yards rushing, the 10th time the Bills had accomplished that feat.

• Davis' 78-yard TD run in the fourth was his career long and was the longest in the NFL in 1991.

• Jim Kelly was knocked out of the game with a concussion late in the first half and Frank Reich finished.

• On the third play of the game, Phil Hansen forced Ken Clark to fumble and Shane Conlan recovered at the Indy 14. Thomas scored on the next play. After a Colts punt, the Bills drove 62 yards in nine plays to Carwell Gardner's TD run, which was set up by a 26-yard pass to Thomas to the 4.

• The Colts answered with a drive that reached the Bills 1, but ended with a Dean Biasucci field goal. The Colts ran six plays from inside the 3 and failed to get into the end zone.

• Don Beebe fumbled the ensuing kickoff and John Baylor recovered for Indy, setting up a field goal.

• The Bills then drove 71 yards in eight plays as Thomas followed Howard Ballard into the end zone. Thomas carried six times for 51 yards on the drive.

• Late in the half, Kelly was knocked silly, but stayed in the game and didn't know where he was. After two plays, Frank Reich replaced him and wound up hitting Keith McKeller for a TD on a third-and-five play.

• The Bills took the second-half kickoff and drove 76 yards in nine plays to Reich's TD pass to James Lofton.

• The Colts then used more than eight minutes to drive to the Bills 16, but lost the ball on downs.

• Davis broke his 78-yard TD run early in the fourth to close the scoring.

QUOTES

• Kent Hull on Kelly's injury: "Jim got up and you could tell something was wrong. He said 'God, that hurt.' As we kept going, he got a little worse. He couldn't

remember anything. Then, around the two-minute warning he said to Will, 'Are we still in the no-huddle?' He's gonna have to watch films a little closer to see what he missed." (On Reich replacing Kelly): "Nobody is more prepared than Frank. He is constantly studying. There wasn't a bit of dropoff. Nothing changed."

• Frank Reich on Kelly: "When he came to the sideline, you could tell he wasn't very coherent. When I told him one of our most basic running plays and he said 'What's that?' that kind of gave me an indication he didn't know what was going on."

• Thurman Thomas: "We have to take our hat off to the offensive line because coming after a game like Kansas City where they didn't perform the way they'd like to, coming into this game they wanted to prove a point and they did."

• Colts linebacker Scott Radecic: "That's the worst part about this whole day, that they didn't do anything tricky or fancy. They just came out and hammered us and we didn't respond."

Bengals	3	0	10	3	-	16
Bills	0	14	14	7	-	35

Attendance at Rich Stadium - 80,131

Cin: FG Breech 32, 7:14
Buf: Lofton 74 pass from Kelly (Norwood kick), :09
Buf: Metzelaars 51 pass from Kelly (Norwood kick), 11:55
Cin: E. Brown 19 pass from Esiason (Breech kick), 3:30
Buf: Lofton 48 pass from Kelly (Norwood kick), 4:47
Cin: FG L. Johnson 53, 10:46
Buf: Reed 24 pass from Kelly (Norwood kick), 12:41
Cin: FG Breech 42, 2:43
Buf: Thomas 5 pass from Kelly (Norwood kick), 10:09

	BUF	CIN
First downs	19	24
Rushing yds	95	187
Passing yds	392	224
Punts-avg	1-25.0	2-45.5
Fumbles-lost	1-0	1-1
Penalties-yds	7-56	12-105
Poss. time	22:39	37:21

BILLS LEADERS: Rushing - Thomas 14-63, Gardner 5-19, Kelly 3-12, K. Davis 1-2, Reed 1-1, Reich 3-(-2); **Passing** - Kelly 18-27-3 - 392; **Receiving** - Lofton 8-220, Reed 5-80, Thomas 3-24, McKeller 1-17, Metzelaars 1-51.
BENGALS LEADERS: Rushing - Green 26-141, Brooks 7-45, Woods 3-(-1), Esiason 1-2; **Passing** - Esiason 13-21-1 - 149, Wilhelm 9-13-0 - 80, L. Johnson 1-1-0 - 3; **Receiving** - E. Brown 5-69, Rembert 3-33, Holman 2-7, McGee 6-67, Brooks 3-27, Riggs 1-4, Woods 1-16, Taylor 2-9.

NOTES

• Jim Kelly overcame three first-quarter interceptions and went on to set a new career regular-season passing record with 392 yards in a wild Monday Night affair. He also set a new team mark with his fifth 300-yard passing game of the season, breaking Joe Ferguson's record of four set in 1979.

• James Lofton's 220 yards receiving were his career-high and the third-highest in Bills history.

• It was the first time the Bills attracted three crowds of 80,000 or more in the same season.

• Bengals coach Sam Wyche lost his composure and ran into the end zone to protest Lofton's TD catch in the third quarter. He also berated an assistant coach, got into an on-field fracas when Boomer Esiason was leveled by Leonard Smith in the fourth and also argued with fans after the game.

• Kelly was intercepted by Ricky Dixon, Leo Barker and James Francis, but all the Bengals could get was one Jim Breech field goal. Another Breech attempt was faked and Cornelius Bennett stuffed the play.

• Kelly hit Lofton for a 74-yard TD on the first play of the second quarter. Later, he hit Pete Metzelaars for a

WEEK 8 GAMES

Chi 10, GB 0	Phoe 16, Atl 10
SF 35, Det 3	Hou 17, Mia 13
Den 19, KC 16	LAR 20, Rams 17
NYJ 17, Ind 6	Sea 27, Pitt 7
NO 23, TB 7	NE 26, Min 23 OT
Clev 30, SD 24 OT	

Wash, Dal, NYG, Phil had bye weeks

51-yard TD on a third-and-one play, Metzelaars' longest reception of his career.

• The Bengals drove 69 yards with the second-half kickoff to Esiason's TD pass to Eddie Brown, but Lofton got that back four plays later. Wyche argued that Lofton interfered with Richard Fain on the play.

• Lee Johnson answered with a 53-yard field goal, but six plays after the kickoff, Andre Reed caught a TD.

• After a Breech field goal, the Bills drove 90 yards in 12 plays to Thurman Thomas' TD reception.

QUOTES

• Marv Levy: "I felt more than at anytime this season it was a very full team victory."

• Jim Kelly on his start: "You just have to forget about it, only I had to forget three times. The best thing I could do was go back out there and throw the ball. We knew we'd have to pass to beat them."

• Bengals coach Sam Wyche: "We weren't out of control, we reacted to some poor officiating calls, in our opinion. We were out of control for seconds while we watched what we thought were several unfair calls. You can't win with officiating like this. I hope the league will do a thorough job studying and investigating this film. I must have had a half dozen Bills come over and apologize to me, saying 'Sam, I'm sorry, that wasn't a fair shot.' I think people would like to bring the whole house down and point out everything that they suspect might be wrong with me, but my shrink says I've got eight or 10 good years left of semi-normal living. And my job is not at stake, I can tell you that I'm not going to be fired."

STANDINGS: EIGHTH WEEK

AFC EAST	W	L	T	CENTRAL	W	L	T	WEST	W	L	T	NFC EAST	W	L	T	CENTRAL	W	L	T	WEST	W	L	T
Buffalo	7	1	0	Houston	6	1	0	Denver	5	2	0	Washington	7	0	0	Detroit	5	2	0	N.Orleans	7	0	0
NY Jets	4	4	0	Pittsburgh	3	4	0	Kan. City	5	3	0	Dallas	5	2	0	Chicago	5	2	0	Atlanta	3	4	0
New England	3	4	0	Cleveland	3	4	0	Raiders	5	3	0	NY Giants	4	3	0	Minnesota	3	5	0	LA Rams	3	4	0
Miami	3	5	0	Cincinnati	0	7	0	Seattle	4	4	0	Phoenix	4	4	0	Green Bay	1	6	0	San Fran	3	4	0
Indianapolis	0	8	0					San Diego	1	7	0	Philadelphia	3	4	0	Tampa Bay	1	6	0				

NOTES

• Thurman Thomas carried a career-high 32 times as the Bills struggled past the Patriots. Thomas also surpassed 6,000 career yards gained from scrimmage on a cold, windy day.

• Andre Reed recorded his 18th 100-yard receiving game and he topped 6,000 career receiving yards.

• Shawn McCarthy had a wind-aided 93-yard punt in the third, the longest ever against the Bills.

• Coming off a bye week, the Bills were sluggish with four turnovers and were fortunate to be playing the Pats.

• The Bills drove to Scott Norwood's field goal on the first possession, but after Cornelius Bennett recovered a Leonard Russell fumble on the ensuing series, Norwood missed from 47 yards.

• The Bills were sharp in the second quarter after a 67-yard McCarthy punt was downed at the 3 as they drove 94 yards to another Norwood field goal. Thomas carried six times for 50 yards and caught a 32-yard pass to the Pats 8. The Pats answered with a 46-yard march to a Jason Staurovsky field goal.

• The Bills took the second-half kickoff and needed only five plays to get Jim Kelly's TD pass to Don Beebe, the key play a 55-yard pass to Reed.

• Late in the third, Al Edwards muffed a punt and Ivory Joe Hunter recovered at the Bills 16. Three plays later, Russell scored to make it 13-10. The Bills responded with a 46-yard drive to a Norwood field goal. Then two plays after the kickoff, Nate Odomes forced Irving Fryar to fumble and Shane Conlan recovered at the Pats 24, leading to Thomas' TD run three plays later. Garin Veris blocked the PAT, leaving the score 22-10.

• Edwards then muffed his second punt and Chris

Gannon recovered at the Bills 40. Eight plays later, Russell scored. The Pats got the ball back with 46 seconds left, but Darryl Talley made an interception .

QUOTES

• Pats coach Dick MacPherson: "It's very disappointing for us to keep playing and coming so close without coming up with the banana."

• Kent Hull: "I can remember times when this team wouldn't have overcome those things and we would have lost this game. But this team knows how to win, we know what we have to do."

• Al Edwards: "I think after that first one (the 93-yard punt that he let roll), I was tentative every time I went out there. I'm relieved we won the game, but it doesn't mend the wounds. I had a bad game. I should have just got away from the ball and not tried to field it."

WEEK 9 GAMES

Chi 20, NO 7	Hou 35, Cinc 3
Det 34, Dal 10	Den 9, NE 6
Atl 31, Rams 14	Minn 28, Phoe 0
Sea 20, SD 9	Clev 17, Pitt 14
SF 23, Phil 7	Wash 17, NYG 13
KC 24, LAR 21	GB 27, TB 0
Buf, NYJ, Ind, Mia had bye weeks	

WEEK 10 GAMES

Chi 20, Det 10	Cinc 23, Clev 21
NYJ 19, GB 16 OT	Mia 10, Ind 6
NO 24, Rams 17	Dal 27, Phoe 7
Atl 17, SF 14	Minn 28, TB 13
Den 20, Pitt 13	Phil 30, NYG 7
Wash 16, Hou 13 (OT)	
KC, LAR, SD, Sea had bye weeks	

Patriots		0 3 7 7 - 17
Bills		3 3 7 9 - 22

Attendance at Rich Stadium - 78,278

Buf:	FG Norwood 19, 3:38
Buf:	FG Norwood 21, 11:48
NE:	FG Staurovsky 36, 14:53
Buf:	Beebe 13 pass from Kelly (Norwood kick), 1:56
NE:	Russell 1 run (Staurovsky kick), 15:00
Buf:	FG Norwood 42, 3:30
Buf:	Thomas 15 run (kick blocked), 5:48
NE:	Russell 3 run (Staurovsky kick), 10:24

	BUF	NE
First downs	20	17
Rushing yds	153	122
Passing yds	235	143
Punts-avg	2-50.0	5-51.2
Fumbles-lost	2-2	3-2
Penalties-yds	7-56	8-56
Poss. time	29:34	30:26

BILLS LEADERS: Rushing - Thomas 32-126, Gardner 2-12, K. Davis 4-13, Kelly 3-2; **Passing** - Kelly 14-28-2 - 237; **Receiving** - Reed 5-121, McKeller 4-38, Lofton 1-6, Beebe 2-29, Thomas 1-32, K. Davis 1-11.

PATRIOTS LEADERS: Rushing - Russell 27-106, Hunter 3-12, Stephens 1-4; **Passing** - Millen 14-30-1 - 177; **Receiving** - Fryar 5-73, Coates 4-41, Hunter 2-16, McMurtry 1-40, Russell 2-7.

NOTES

• The Bills played only their second game in Milwaukee and won their first (the only previous visit was in 1982).

• James Lofton had a big day against his former teammates as the Bills AFC East lead jumped to four games.

• After trading punts, the Packers drove 42 yards to Vince Workman's TD in the first quarter. The Bills punted twice more before finally driving 50 yards in 10 plays to Andre Reed's TD catch early in the second quarter.

• The Packers drove to the Bills 7 on the ensuing possession, but settled for a Chris Jacke field goal.

• The Bills then moved 80 yards to Don Beebe's TD catch. Lofton had a 24-yard catch and Chuck Cecil was nailed with a personal foul, making it a 39-yard play.

• The Bills took the second-half kickoff and went 78 yards in seven plays to Thomas' TD. The keys were Beebe's 20-yard reception on third-and-nine and a 28-yard interference penalty on Roland Mitchell to the Packers 5.

• After an exchange of punts, Mike Tomczak hit Sterling Sharpe for a 58-yard TD, but the Bills drove 51 yards to a Scott Norwood field goal. The key was a 17-yard Lofton reception on third-and-seven at the Packers 44.

• On the first play of the fourth, Cornelius Bennett ruined a potential tying TD drive by the Packers. First, he nailed Sharpe for a 15-yard loss on a reverse, then sacked Tomczak on the next play, forcing a punt.

• The Bills then drove 75 yards in 12 plays to Kelly's keeper. This time, Lofton had a 19-yard catch on third-and-15 from the Bills 19 and a 29-yard grab to the Packers 12. Leonard Smith's interception led to another Norwood field goal, then the Packers drove 78 yards to Jackie Harris' TD catch.

QUOTES

• Darryl Talley: "Everyone had to play well in order for us to pull this one out and everyone did."

• Marv Levy: "Well, we have a four-game lead with six to play, so we haven't wrapped up anything yet. I thought we started slow, but our players came back well enough to win. That's why it's a 60-minute game. James was magnificent. He had a great game and it was a very appropriate place for him to do it, and maybe it spurred him on."

• Jim Kelly: "James had his average day, which is awesome. We knew the Packers would be aggressive on defense and we knew there would be times they would stop us or slow us down, but patience is a big thing, especially in our offense."

• James Lofton: "I don't know if there's added satisfaction. When I look across the line, there's just a handful of guys who are left (on the Packers). I miss some of the people here, but I'm glad the way my career has turned out. The minute you start looking for an extra incentive angle, you aren't concentrating on your job. It's not about me against the Packers."

WEEK 11 GAMES

Wash 56, Atl 17	TB 30, Det 21
Ind 28, NYJ 27	KC 27, Rams 20
LAR 17, Den 16	NYG 21, Phoe 14
NO 10, SF 3	Phil 32, Clev 30
SD 17, Sea 14	Chi 34, Minn 17
Hou 26, Dal 23 OT	Mia 30, NE 20
Pitt 33, Cinc 27 OT	

Bills		0 14 10 10 - 34
Packers		7 3 7 7 - 24

Attendance at Milwaukee County Stadium - 52,175

GB:	Workman 1 run (Jacke kick), 9:49
Buf:	Reed 6 pass from Kelly (Norwood kick), 4:03
GB:	FG Jacke 25, 11:11
Buf:	Beebe 12 pass from Kelly (Norwood kick), 13:12
Buf:	Thomas 5 run (Norwood kick), 2:17
GB:	Sharpe 58 pass from Tomczak (Jacke kick), 6:42
Buf:	FG Norwood 38, 11:13
Buf:	Kelly 1 run (Norwood kick), 5:34
Buf:	FG Norwood 21, 13:02
GB:	Harris 1 pass from Tomczak (Jacke kick), 14:22

	BUF	GB
First downs	27	23
Rushing yds	147	84
Passing yds	223	197
Punts-avg	4-42.5	5-39.0
Fumbles-lost	1-0	2-0
Penalties-yds	8-55	5-73
Poss. time	28:22	31:38

BILLS LEADERS: Rushing - Thomas 24-106, Gardner 1-1, Kelly 3-11, K. Davis 5-19, Reed 2-7, Reich 2-3; **Passing** - Kelly 17-35-0 - 232, Reich 0-1-0 - 0; **Receiving** - Reed 4-32, Lofton 6-114, Thomas 3-40, Beebe 2-32, K. Davis 1-6, McKeller 1-8.

PACKERS LEADERS: Rushing - Thompson 13-60, Woodside 6-34, Workman 2-2, Tomczak 1-3, Sharpe 1-(-15); **Passing** - Tomczak 23-38-2 - 317; **Receiving** - Sharpe 8-133, Workman 4-11, Harris 2-19, Woodside 1-8, Thompson 1-3, Query 1-26, West 2-39, Kemp 2-48, Weathers 2-30.

STANDINGS: ELEVENTH WEEK

AFC EAST	W	L	T	CENTRAL	W	L	T	WEST	W	L	T	NFC EAST	W	L	T	CENTRAL	W	L	T	WEST	W	L	T
Buffalo	9	1	0	Houston	8	2	0	Denver	7	3	0	Washington	10	0	0	Chicago	8	2	0	N.Orleans	9	1	0
NY Jets	5	5	0	Cleveland	4	6	0	Kan. City	7	3	0	Dallas	6	4	0	Detroit	6	4	0	Atlanta	5	5	0
Miami	5	5	0	Pittsburgh	4	6	0	Raiders	6	4	0	NY Giants	5	5	0	Minnesota	5	6	0	San Fran	4	6	0
New England	3	7	0	Cincinnati	1	9	0	Seattle	5	5	0	Philadelphia	5	5	0	Green Bay	2	8	0	LA Rams	3	7	0
Indianapolis	1	9	0					San Diego	2	8	0	Phoenix	4	7	0	Tampa Bay	2	8	0				

GAME 11 - Monday, Nov. 18, 1991 - BILLS 41, DOLPHINS 27

Bills	10	10	14	7 -	41
Dolphins	3	10	7	7 -	27

Attendance at Joe Robbie Stadium - 71,062

Mia: FG Stoyanovich 33, 4:42
Buf: Thomas 10 pass from Kelly (Norwood kick), 7:55
Buf: FG Norwood 42, 14:43
Mia: S. Smith 1 run (Stoyanovich kick), 5:27
Buf: Bennett 6 fumble return (Norwood kick), 8:45
Buf: FG Norwood 21, 11:33
Mia: FG Stoyanovich 28, 14:17
Buf: Reed 5 pass from Kelly (Norwood kick), 2:58
Buf: Thomas 1 run (Norwood kick), 11:03
Mia: Baty 1 pass from Marino (Stoyanovich kick), 14:31
Buf: Reed 23 pass from Kelly (Norwood kick), 8:18
Mia: Martin 8 pass from Marino (Stoyanovich kick), 10:48

	BUF	MIA
First downs	27	25
Rushing yds	262	75
Passing yds	171	317
Punts-avg	4-38.5	1-62.0
Fumbles-lost	1-0	4-3
Penalties-yds	8-62	2-25
Poss. time	35:23	24:37

BILLS LEADERS: Rushing - Thomas 23-135, K. Davis 25-98, Reed 1-19, Kelly 1-10; **Passing** - Kelly 20-28-0 - 185; **Receiving** - Reed 8-80, Beebe 2-22, Thomas 3-40, K. Davis 3-20, McKeller 2-11, Lofton 2-12.
DOLPHINS LEADERS: Rushing - S. Smith 14-64, Marino 2-9, Craver 1-2; **Passing** - Marino 23-42-2 - 326; **Receiving** - Duper 5-96, Martin 3-48, Clayton 6-90, Paige 2-17, Baty 3-30, Jensen 2-27, Banks 1-11, Craver 1-7.

NOTES

• The Bills beat Miami for the 10th time in the last 11 meetings in impressive fashion on Monday night.
• Thurman Thomas topped 1,000 yards for the third straight season, only the 21st player in NFL history to do it, and he also moved past Joe Cribbs into second place on the Bills' all-time rushing list.
• Don Beebe suffered a broken collarbone and was expected to be out at least until the playoffs.
• Miami got a Pete Stoyanovich field goal on its first possession, but the Bills drove 83 yards in 11 plays to Jim Kelly's TD pass to Thomas. Earlier, Thomas had a 22-yard catch on third-and-three from the Bills 24.
• On the next series, the Bills marched 65 yards to a Scott Norwood field goal, but Miami responded with a 10-play 81-yard drive to Sammie Smith's TD dive. The key play was a 28-yard pass to Mark Clayton.
• After a Bills punt, Cornelius Bennett turned the game Buffalo's way. On third-and-10 from the Miami 15, he sacked Dan Marino and forced a fumble, which he picked up and ran six yards for the go-ahead TD.
• On the first play after the kickoff, Kirby Jackson intercepted Marino, setting up another Norwood field goal.
• Marino engineered a 69-yard drive to a Stoyanovich field goal before the half ended, but the Bills regained the momentum when Mark Pike forced Aaron Craver to fumble the second-half kickoff and Carwell Gardner recovered at the Miami 27. That resulted in Jim Kelly's TD pass to Andre Reed.
• Darryl Talley's interception started the Bills on a 72-yard drive to Thomas' TD run for a 34-13 lead.
• Marino directed 73- and 80-yard TD drives, but in between, the Bills went 89 yards in 15 plays, eating up 8:47 before Kelly hit Reed for the TD.

QUOTES

• Cornelius Bennett on his TD: "On that particular play, I had my mind made up that no matter how many guys blocked me, I was going to get in and get a sack. Of course I didn't know I was going to cause a fumble, recover it and score a touchdown. Watching film this week, I knew he (tackle Mark Dennis) was a little slow coming off the corner, so I figured I could beat him."
• Kent Hull on the second-half kickoff fumble: "We said at halftime the biggest series for our defense would be that opening drive of the second half. Instead, we get the ball and we scored. At that point, they're playing catch-up and the clock is against them."
• Thurman Thomas on his demonstrative spike after his first TD: "I hate Miami, but it wasn't for them, it was for their fans. They were taunting me to do something, so I did a couple things. That's really not my style, but it was an important game."

WEEK 12 GAMES

Chi 31, Ind 17	Phil 17, Cinc 10
NYG 22, Dal 9	Den 24, KC 20
Det 21, Rams 10	Minn 35, GB 21
SD 24, NO 21	NYJ 28, NE 21
SF 14, Phoe 10	LAR 31, Sea 7
Atl 43, TB 7	Wash 41, Pitt 14
Hou 28, Clev 24	

GAME 12 - Sunday, Nov. 24, 1991 - PATRIOTS 16, BILLS 13

Bills	3	7	3	0 -	13
Patriots	0	9	0	7 -	16

Attendance at Foxboro Stadium - 47,053

Buf: FG Norwood 23, 7:09
Buf: Thomas 10 pass from Kelly (Norwood kick), 1:11
NE: FG Baumann 46, 5:31
NE: Fryar 50 pass from Millen (kick blocked), 14:33
Buf: FG Norwood 29, 13:31
NE: Millen 2 run (Baumann kick), 1:51

	BUF	NE
First downs	20	18
Rushing yds	140	82
Passing yds	168	230
Punts-avg	5-34.6	5-29.8
Fumbles-lost	1-1	0-0
Penalties-yds	1-6	3-17
Poss. time	25:43	34:17

BILLS LEADERS: Rushing - Thomas 25-89, K. Davis 4-51; **Passing** - Kelly 26-44-4 - 204; **Receiving** - Reed 7-63, Thomas 6-27, K. Davis 3-17, Edwards 4-36, Lofton 1-12, McKeller 5-49.

PATRIOTS LEADERS: Rushing - Russell 19-69, Hunter 1-2, Stephens 5-9, Millen 5-2; **Passing** - Millen 20-39-2 - 263; McCarthy 1-1-0 - 11; **Receiving** - Fryar 6-134, Cook 7-69, Stephens 3-14, Timpson 1-19, McMurtry 3-27, Coates 1-11.

WEEK 13 GAMES

Dal 24, Wash 21	Sea 13, Den 10
Pitt 26, Hou 14	Det 34, Minn 14
GB 14, Ind 10	Clev 20, KC 15
LAR 38, Cinc 14	NYG 21, TB 14
NYJ 24, SD 3	Phil 34, Phoe 14
Atl 23, NO 20 OT	SF 33, Rams 10
Mia 16, Chi 13 OT	

NOTES

• The Bills suffered a shocking loss at New England even though they blocked four kicks.
• Jim Kelly was forced to throw a career-high-tying 44 passes and suffered a career-high four interceptions as he played with sore ribs.
• Offensive guard John Davis suffered a serious season-ending knee injury in the third quarter.
• After J.D. Williams blocked a Charlie Baumann field goal, the Bills drove 59 yards to a Scott Norwood field goal. The key play was an 11-yard pass to Al Edwards on third-and-five from the Pats 21.
• Late in the first quarter, Steve Tasker blocked a Shawn McCarthy punt and Butch Rolle recovered at the Pats 31, which set up Kelly's TD pass to Thurman Thomas on the fourth play of the second quarter.
• The Pats answered with a 44-yard drive to a Baumann field goal. Kelly was intercepted by Maurice Hurst at the Pats 22 on the next series, but Darryl Talley intercepted Hugh Millen at the Bills 23.
• Kelly gave it right back as Hurst intercepted again at the 50. On the next play, Millen hit Irving Fryar behind Nate Odomes for a 50-yard TD. Jeff Wright blocked the PAT.
• Early in the third, Tasker stopped a fake punt short of a first down at the Bills 35, but two plays later, James Lofton lost a fumble. Late in the third, Kenneth Davis' 27-yard run set up a Norwood field goal.
• The Pats answered with a 10-play, 65-yard drive to the go-ahead Millen TD run. Fryar had a 34-yard catch.
• Baumann had a 32-yard field goal blocked by Leon Seals with 2:27 left. The Bills reached the Pats 41, but Kelly was sacked by Brent Williams on third down and his fourth-down pass to Lofton was incomplete.

QUOTES

• Jim Kelly: "We stunk up the Northeast. We didn't play Buffalo Bills football. When you score only 13 points, something's up. We had breakdowns by myself, the whole offensive unit. We weren't making plays and you can't win when you're turning the ball over."
• Marv Levy: "I've never been in a game where we block four kicks and don't win. We had a somewhat off day on offense. Sometimes a .400 hitter goes 0-for-4. We just didn't put it in the end zone and we didn't play well enough to win and they did."
• Jeff Wright: "You saw it unfold and it was a little depressing. But it's no big deal. We've played well all year, we just came up a little short. Nobody's hanging their heads."
• Pats nose tackle Fred Smerlas: "When I was in Buffalo, I could never figure out why Kelly had so many problems against the Patriots. He always looked confused against them. Now that I've been around here I know it's because of Fred Marion."
• Pats defensive end Brent Williams on a remark James Lofton had made after the first meeting: "He said after the game up there that we were just happy to have been close to them. I didn't appreciate that. We're happy now because we should have beaten them up there. To say we were happy just to be close shows a lot of arrogance. It was a joke."

STANDING: THIRTEENTH WEEK

AFC EAST	W	L	T	CENTRAL	W	L	T	WEST	W	L	T	NFC EAST	W	L	T	CENTRAL	W	L	T	WEST	W	L	T
Buffalo	10	2	0	Houston	9	3	0	Denver	8	4	0	Washington	11	1	0	Chicago	9	3	0	N.Orleans	9	3	0
NY Jets	7	5	0	Cleveland	5	7	0	Raiders	8	4	0	Dallas	7	5	0	Detroit	8	4	0	Atlanta	7	5	0
Miami	6	6	0	Pittsburgh	5	7	0	Kan. City	7	5	0	NY Giants	7	5	0	Minnesota	6	7	0	San Fran	6	6	0
New England	4	8	0	Cincinnati	1	11	0	Seattle	6	6	0	Philadelphia	7	5	0	Green Bay	3	9	0	LA Rams	3	9	0
Indianapolis	1	11	0					San Diego	3	9	0	Phoenix	4	9	0	Tampa Bay	2	10	0				

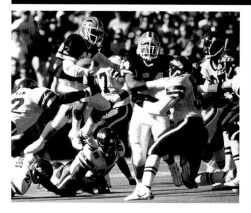

NOTES

• The Bills clinched their fourth straight AFC East division title. It was the third time the Jets were the victim.
• Jim Kelly established a new team record for TD passes in a season (28) and Thurman Thomas became the team's all-time leader in career pass receptions for a running back.
• Bruce Smith returned to the lineup and had six tackles and his first sack of the season.
• On the fourth play of the game, ex-Bill Chris Burkett pressured punter Chris Mohr into throwing a pass that Pete Metzelaars caught for a nine-yard loss, giving the Jets possession at the Bills 24. Three Brad Baxter runs put the ball in the end zone.
• Late in the first quarter, Brian Washington recovered a Thomas fumble at the Jets 6 to kill a drive. But three plays later, Mark Kelso intercepted Ken O'Brien at the Jets 27, leading to Andre Reed's tying TD reception.
• In the second quarter, the Jets drove 81 yards to a Pat Leahy field goal. On the first play after the kickoff, Kelly was sacked by Jeff Lageman. He fumbled with

James Hasty recovering at the Bills 14. Two plays later, O'Brien was intercepted by Kirby Jackson at the 6. The Bills then drove 80 yards to the tying field goal.
• After a Jets punt in the third, the Bills drove 57 yards to Kenneth Davis' third-down TD run. The drive was kept alive when Scott Mersereau roughed Kelly after a third-down pass fell incomplete.
• Erik McMillan's interception of Kelly and 28-yard return to the 6 set up a Leahy field goal as the defense put up an excellent goal-line stand.
• The teams traded two punts, then Hasty intercepted Kelly at the Jets 14. New York drove to the Bills 7, but Darryl Talley (eight tackles) forced Rob Moore to fumble and Mark Kelso recovered. The Bills then marched 93 yards in nine plays to James Lofton's clinching 27-yard TD reception on a third-and-17 play.

QUOTES

• Marv Levy on Darryl Talley: "Darryl deserved one of the game balls, but as a captain, he was giving them out."
• Darryl Talley on Rob Moore's fumble: "He was running a crossing route. I saw him catch the ball and just started running after him. Then I just tried to put my head on the ball and it came out. I couldn't find it for a second and the next thing I knew, Mark was standing there holding it. It's the kind of play that someone has to step up and make." (On not keeping a game ball for himself): "I wouldn't do that, it's against my character. The other guys (Kirby Jackson and Leonard Smith) played well, they deserved them."
• Bruce Smith on Talley: "I said it two years ago that Darryl is the most consistent linebacker in the league and I'll never stop saying it."
• Mark Kelso: "There were three really big plays in this game. One was Kirby's interception in the end zone, another was Darryl causing that fumble, and James Lofton's big touchdown."

Jets	7	3	3	0	-	13
Bills	7	3	7	7	-	24

Attendance at Rich Stadium - 80,243

NYJ: Baxter 3 run (Leahy kick), 3:02
Buf: Reed 16 pass from Kelly (Norwood kick), 13:58
NYJ: FG Leahy 19, 11:59
Buf: FG Norwood 31, 14:56
Buf: K. Davis 4 run (Norwood kick), 5:38
NYJ: FG Leahy 23, 9:53
Buf: Lofton 27 pass from Kelly (Norwood kick), 11:39

	BUF	NYJ
First downs	24	20
Rushing yds	152	121
Passing yds	242	172
Punts-avg	5-43.0	6-34.3
Fumbles-lost	4-2	1-1
Penalties-yds	11-76	7-56
Poss. time	24:32	35:28

BILLS LEADERS: **Rushing** - Thomas 23-124, K. Davis 5-13, Reed 3-15; **Passing** - Kelly 21-38-2 - 251, Mohr 1-1-0 -(-9); **Receiving** - Thomas 4-33, Edwards 9-78, Lofton 5-109, McKeller 2-15, Reed 1-16, Metzelaars 1-(-9).
JETS LEADERS: **Rushing** - B. Thomas 15-52, Baxter 13-48, Hector 2-5, McNeil 1-4, Taylor 1-13, O'Brien 1-(-1); **Passing** - O'Brien 14-28-2 - 171, Taylor 2-3-0 - 21; **Receiving** - Toon 3-62, Boyer 2-41, Dressel 2-12, McNeil 2-9, Moore 3-32, B.Thomas 1-7, Baxter 2-17, Burkett 1-12.

WEEK 14 GAMES

Det 16, Chi 6	Dal 20, Pitt 10
Clev 31, Ind 0	Atl 35, GB 31
KC 19, Sea 6	Den 20, NE 3
SF 38, NO 24	Cinc 27, NYG 24
Mia 33, TB 14	Wash 27, Rams 6
LAR 19, SD 7	Phil 13, Hou 6
Phoe, Minn had bye weeks	

NOTES

• Scott Norwood overcame three missed field goals and a mixed extra point to kick the winning field goal in OT to give the Bills a memorable come-from-behind victory. The Bills set the team mark for TD passes in one season.
• Jim Kelly set regular-season personal records for attempts and completions in one game.
• James Lofton went over 1,000 yards receiving for the season, becoming the oldest player ever to do so.
• Jim Ritcher played in his 182nd game as a Bill, second all-time behind Joe Devlin (197).
• The Raiders grabbed a quick 10-0 lead as Jeff Jaeger kicked a field goal, then Jay Schroeder hit Tim Brown with a 78-yard TD pass. But Al Edwards returned the ensuing kickoff for a TD, the Bills first since Curtis Brown did it on Sept. 24, 1978.
• Los Angeles drove 80 yards in 13 plays to get that back on Nick Bell's TD run.
• Late in the second quarter, Clifford Hicks returned a punt 59 yards to the Los Angeles 33, setting up Keith McKeller's TD reception three plays later. But Jaeger made a field goal on the final play of the half.
• Los Angeles moved 75 yards on the first possession of the third to Marcus Allen's TD for a 27-14 lead.
• Norwood then missed 49- and 32-yard field goals and Kelly threw an interception early in the fourth, wasting a chance provided by Darryl Talley's fumble recovery at the Los Angeles 28.
• However, after a punt, Kelly drove the Bills 67 yards to Kenneth Davis' TD run, with the key a 19-yard pass to Lofton on third-and-10. Norwood missed the PAT. Los Angeles went three-and-out and the Bills took over at

their 36 with 2:36 left. Kelly hit Andre Reed for 20 on fourth-and-one from the Los Angeles 29, then hit Lofton for a TD and Norwood tied the game with the conversion.
• Mark Kelso intercepted Schroeder on the second play of OT and Reed made a 31-yard reception to the Los Angeles 33 to set up the winning field goal.

QUOTES

• Thurman Thomas: "If he (Norwood) would have missed that one (in overtime), I would have dropped him from the plane somewhere over Minnesota or North Dakota."
• Marv Levy: "I was very proud of the way our team hung in there." (On Norwood): "I'd be lying if I said I didn't think about using (Brad) Daluiso."
• Scott Norwood: "Today was the roughest day I've had kicking the ball since I started. You have to consider the bottom line. I'm happy that we won the game, I struggled longer than I should have, but I came back and made the last one. I'm lucky to have the teammates that I have. They were coming up to me even before the final kick and saying they believed in me. Jim Kelly came up and said 'You're going to get another chance.' I just kicked it (the winner) more aggressively. I knew it was good as soon as I hit it."

Bills	7	7	0	13	3	- 30
Raiders	10	10	7	0	0	- 27

Attendance at the Coliseum - 85,081

LAR: FG Jaeger 19, 9:07
LAR: Brown 78 pass from Schroeder (Jaeger kick), 13:30
Buf: Edwards 91 kickoff return (Norwood kick), 13:47
LAR: Bell 12 run (Jaeger kick), 4:50
Buf: McKeller 9 pass from Kelly (Norwood kick), 14:10
LAR: FG Jaeger 28, 15:00
LAR: Allen 1 run (Jaeger kick), 7:42
Buf: K. Davis 1 run (kick failed), 10:54
Buf: Lofton 9 pass from Kelly (Norwood kick), 14:00
Buf: FG Norwood 42, 10:18

	BUF	LAR
First downs	25	18
Rushing yds	79	136
Passing yds	330	250
Punts-avg	4-40.3	6-46.7
Fumbles-lost	0-0	3-1
Penalties-yds	10-57	5-50
Poss. time	26:27	36:07

BILLS LEADERS: **Rushing** - Thomas 15-57, Kelly 1-10, K. Davis 4-12, Gardner 3-2; **Passing** - Kelly 33-52-1 - 347; **Receiving** - McKeller 10-57, Thomas 7-76, Reed 8-107, Edwards 3-35, Lofton 5-72.

RAIDERS LEADERS: **Rushing** - Craig 9-38, Bell 15-36, Allen 16-57, Smith 1-2, Schroeder 4-3; **Passing** - Schroeder 11-21-2 - 252; **Receiving** - Horton 2-29, Brown 2-106, Fernandez 2-75, Allen 3-38, Gault 1-6, Smith 1-(-2).

WEEK 15 GAMES

Atl 31, Rams 14	Den 17, Clev 7
Chi 27, GB 13	Dal 23, NO 14
Det 34, NYJ 20	Phil 19, NYG 14
Hou 31, Pitt 6	KC 20, SD 17 OT
SF 24, Sea 22	Minn 26, TB 24
Wash 20, Phoe 14	Mia 37, Cinc 13
NE 23, Ind 17 OT	

STANDINGS: FIFTEENTH WEEK

AFC EAST	W	L	T	CENTRAL	W	L	T	WEST	W	L	T	NFC EAST	W	L	T	CENTRAL	W	L	T	WEST	W	L	T
Buffalo	12	2	0	Houston	10	4	0	Denver	10	4	0	Washington	13	1	0	Chicago	10	4	0	Atlanta	9	5	0
Miami	8	6	0	Cleveland	6	8	0	Raiders	9	5	0	Dallas	9	5	0	Detroit	10	4	0	N.Orleans	9	5	0
NY Jets	7	7	0	Pittsburgh	5	9	0	Kan. City	9	5	0	Philadelphia	9	5	0	Minnesota	7	7	0	San Fran	8	6	0
New England	5	9	0	Cincinnati	2	12	0	Seattle	6	8	0	NY Giants	7	7	0	Green Bay	3	11	0	LA Rams	3	11	0
Indianapolis	1	13	0					San Diego	3	11	0	Phoenix	4	10	0	Tampa Bay	2	12	0				

Bills	21	7	0	7 - 35
Colts	0	0	0	7 - 7

Attendance at the Hoosier Dome - 48,286

Buf: K. Davis 1 run (Norwood kick), 5:04
Buf: Lofton 11 pass from Kelly (Norwood kick), 11:41
Buf: K. Davis 14 pass from Kelly (Norwood kick), 14:44
Buf: Reed 23 pass from Kelly (Norwood kick), 10:13
Ind: Manoa 1 run (Biasucci kick), 2:58
Buf: Metzelaars 4 pass from Reich (Norwood kick), 8:37

	BUF	IND
First downs	23	18
Rushing yds	156	133
Passing yds	159	195
Punts-avg	4-46.8	4-42.0
Fumbles-lost	0-0	1-0
Penalties-yds	4-47	7-42
Poss. time	26:23	33:37

BILLS LEADERS: Rushing - Thomas 6-34, K. Davis 22-90, Reed 2-22, Edwards 1-17, Gardner 1-0, Kelly 2-(-4), Reich 3-(-3); **Passing** - Kelly 9-11-0 - 119, Reich 4-6-0 - 47; **Receiving** - Reed 4-65, Lofton 3-48, Edwards 2-16, K. Davis 3-33, Metzelaars 1-4.

COLTS LEADERS: Rushing - Clark 21-74, Manoa 6-68, Huffman 1-(-8), Herrmann 1-(-1); **Passing** - George 7-11-0 - 83, Herrmann 11-19-3 - 137, Hilger 0-1-0 - 0; **Receiving** - Clark 3-15, Hester 5-77, Huffman 3-14, Verdin 1-28, Brooks 4-45, Beach 1-26, Mrosko 1-15.

NOTES
• The Bills clinched home-field advantage throughout the playoffs with a workmanlike victory.
• The Bills set a team defensive record with their sixth straight game with at least two interceptions.
• Thurman Thomas suffered a slightly sprained ankle in the first quarter and sat out the rest of the game.
• The Bills wasted no time putting this one away, considering their past troubles in the Hoosier Dome. On their opening possession, they drove 80 yards in 11 plays to Kenneth Davis' TD, but lost Thomas.
• After a Colts punt, the Bills drove 96 yards in 10 plays to Jim Kelly's TD pass to James Lofton.
• The Colts went three-and-out and Clifford Hicks returned the punt 55 yards to the Colts 17, leading to Kelly's TD pass to Davis three plays later. The Bills had 13 first downs in the first quarter and never faced a third down.
• The Colts drove to the Bills 9 early in the second quarter, but turned over the ball on downs when Bruce Smith batted down a fourth-down pass. After trading punts, the Bills drove 41 yards in five plays to Andre Reed's TD catch.
• Nate Odomes' interception at the Bills 9 killed a drive late in the half. Then in the third, the Bills stopped the Colts

WEEK 16 GAMES	
Chi 27, TB 0	SF 28, KC 14
Det 21, GB 17	Dal 25, Phil 13
SD 38, Mia 30	Hou 17, Clev 14
NE 6, NYJ 3	Minn 20, Rams 14
Atl 26, Sea 13	Dal 25, Phil 13
NO 27, LAR 0	Den 24, Phoe 19
Wash 34, NYG 17	

on downs at the 8 and Darryl Talley's interception stopped the next series.
• The Colts finally broke through with a 78-yard drive in the fourth. Tim Manoa broke a 44-yard run, then scored from the 1. The Bills answered with an 82-yard march led by Frank Reich. He hit Pete Metzelaars for the TD.

QUOTES
• Ray Bentley: "I'm glad it turned out the way it did because you always like to win your own championships. We achieved the home-field advantage without help and that's important to us. Over the years we've learned our lessons and we know we can't take anyone lightly."
• Marv Levy: "Everything clicked, we were hot. I'm real proud that our team came out and realized even though they were a favored team, they had to play hard to win. The right to play at home is something you strive for."
• Thurman Thomas: "I've always had troubles with my ankles in high school and college, but I'll be ready to play next week. I looked at the stats and I'm like 33 or 35 yards behind Barry (Sanders of Detroit in the rushing race). Right now, me and the defense are already negotiating. They hold him to a certain amount of yards and I'll treat them to a nice gift, too. I was talking to Kelly on the sidelines and I said 'The only reason you have three touchdown passes is because I'm out of there and you're trying to pad your stats for the rest of the year.'"
• Colts safety Keith Taylor: "We got thoroughly dominated in all places of the game. They did what they wanted to do. If they wanted to run right, they ran right. If they wanted to run left, they ran left."

Lions	0	0	0	14	3 - 17
Bills	0	7	0	7	0 - 14

Attendance at Rich Stadium - 78,059

Buf: Reed 7 pass from Reich (Norwood kick), 1:18
Det: Sanders 1 run (Murray kick), 2:27
Det: S. White 18 interception return (Murray kick), 9:41
Buf: Tasker 20 pass from Reich (Norwood kick), 12:27
Det: FG Murray 21, 4:23

	BUF	DET
First downs	14	22
Rushing yds	151	111
Passing yds	124	245
Punts-avg	6-32.3	6-34.2
Fumbles-lost	0-0	2-1
Penalties-yds	11-70	6-50
Poss. time	32:23	32:00

BILLS LEADERS: Rushing - K. Davis 25-118, Gardner 5-23, Reich 3-10; **Passing** - Reich 15-25-1 - 166; **Receiving** - McKeller 2-46, Reed 2-31, K. Davis 5-31, Metzelaars 1-7, Alexander 1-7, Edwards 2-19, Rolle 1-5, Tasker 1-20.

LIONS LEADERS: Rushing - Sanders 26-108, Kramer 5-3; **Passing** - Kramer 17-36-2 - 251; **Receiving** - Farr 1-28, Perriman 5-44, Green 2-47, Sanders 3-53, Moore 2-25, Clark 4-54.

WEEK 17 GAMES	
GB 27, Minn 7	NYG 24, Hou 20
Dal 31, Atl 27	Pitt 17, Clev 10
Den 17, SD 14	TB 17, Ind 3
KC 27, LAR 21	Cinc 29, NE 7
NO 27, Phoe 3	Phil 24, Wash 22
Sea 23, Rams 9	SF 52, Chi 14
NYJ 23, Mia 20 (OT)	

NOTES
• With home-field clinched, the Bills rested many starters and saw their 17-game home winning streak snapped. Thurman Thomas didn't play, averting a showdown with Barry Sanders, but he still led the NFL in yards gained from scrimmage for the third straight year. Jim Kelly and James Lofton also sat out.
• The Lions clinched the NFC Central with the victory in front of a crowd that enabled the Bills to break their own NFL single-season attendance record (635,889). The Bills slipped to 8-3 all-time in overtime.
• The Bills finished the season with new team records for points (458), TDs (58), TD passes (39), PATs (56), first downs (360), total offense (6,252 yards), completions (382) and net passing (3,871).
• Andre Reed's TD reception was his 10th of the season, tying the team mark shared by Elbert Dubenion (1964) and Bob Chandler (1976).
• The Bills put up a superb goal-line stand in the first quarter, stopping three straight Erik Kramer plunges from the 1.
• Kenneth Davis carried seven straight times for 64 yards to get out of that hole, then Frank Reich hit Reed for 24 and eventually threw a seven-yard TD pass to Reed to cap a 10-play, 99-yard drive.
• In the third, Darryl Talley's interception at the 50 was wasted when Scott Norwood missed a field goal.
• The Lions tied the game early in the fourth as Sanders capped an 85-yard drive with a TD run.
• Stan White then intercepted Reich and returned it for a TD with 5:19 left, but Cornelius Bennett forced Sanders to fumble and Talley recovered at the Lions 20 with 2:38 remaining. On the next play, Reich hit Steve Tasker for the tying TD. The Lions reached the Bills 13, but Eddie Murray missed a 30-yard field goal.
• The Lions won the OT coin toss and seven plays later, Murray atoned by kicking the winner.

QUOTES
• Jeff Wright: "Sure we wanted to win, but we want to go to the Super Bowl. That's the ultimate goal. We don't care

about this game. There's no remorse."
• Marv Levy: "We didn't play some players very much, but our players played hard. I think it would be an insult to our players (to say they didn't give an all-out effort). They're only satisfied when they win. But our first priority was we couldn't play players who we felt were risky. Chicago can still win their division by winning their game."
• Bill Polian: "We did the very best we could, it went into overtime. Anybody who doubts our effort today didn't see the football game. We gave an honest effort. I was with the commissioner all day (Friday) and he didn't say anything about it (the Bills plan to rest starters even though the Lions were still battling for a playoff position)."
• Steve Tasker on his TD: "We came out of the huddle and there was a little delay and they showed their defense and Frank was right on top of it. We huddled back up and changed the play and it was a perfect call for the defense they had called. They had a linebacker over me and the guy ran with me and I was able to get by him."

STANDINGS: SEVENTEENTH WEEK

AFC EAST	W	L	T	CENTRAL	W	L	T	WEST	W	L	T	NFC EAST	W	L	T	CENTRAL	W	L	T	WEST	W	L	T
Buffalo	13	3	0	Houston	11	5	0	Denver	12	4	0	Washington	14	2	0	Detroit	12	4	0	N.Orleans	11	5	0
NY Jets	8	8	0	Pittsburgh	7	9	0	Kan. City	10	6	0	Dallas	11	5	0	Chicago	11	5	0	Atlanta	10	6	0
Miami	8	8	0	Cleveland	6	10	0	Raiders	9	7	0	Philadelphia	10	6	0	Minnesota	8	8	0	San Fran	10	6	0
New England	6	10	0	Cincinnati	3	13	0	Seattle	7	9	0	NY Giants	8	8	0	Green Bay	4	12	0	LA Rams	3	13	0
Indianapolis	1	15	0					San Diego	4	12	0	Phoenix	4	12	0	Tampa Bay	2	14	0				

Chiefs	0	0	7	7 -	14
Bills	7	10	7	13 -	37

Attendance at Rich Stadium - 80,182

Buf: Reed 25 pass from Kelly (Norwood kick), 14:08
Buf: Reed 53 pass from Kelly (Norwood kick), 4:25
Buf: FG Norwood 33, 14:58
Buf: Lofton 10 pass from Kelly (Norwood kick), 3:07
KC: Word 3 run (Lowery kick), 11:52
Buf: FG Norwood 20, 4:06
Buf: FG Norwood 47, 5:52
Buf: K. Davis 5 run (Norwood kick), 10:03
KC: F. Jones 20 pass from Vlasic (Lowery kick), 12:53

	BUF	KC
First downs	29	14
Rushing yds	180	77
Passing yds	268	136
Punts-avg	3-33.3	7-40.3
Fumbles-lost	0-0	3-0
Penalties-yds	6-40	10-59
Poss. time	34:09	25:51

BUFFALO TACKLES: Talley 7, Bennett 6, Bailey 6, Seals 5, Wright 4, Conlan 4, L. Smith 3, Odomes 3, K. Jackson 3, Kelso 2, B. Smith 1.

KANSAS CITY TACKLES: Randle 12, Cherry 10, Marts 9, Ross 7, Burruss 7, N. Smith 6, Sims 5, Thomas 4, Saleaumua 4, Everett 3, Pearson 2, Maas 2.

BILLS LEADERS: Rushing - T. Thomas 22-100, K. Davis 19-75, Reed 1-6, Kelly 1-2, Reich 3-(-3); **Passing** - Kelly 23-35-3 - 273; **Receiving** - McKeller 5-34, Reed 4-100, Lofton 3-34, Beebe 6-77, T. Thomas 4-21, Edwards 1-7; **Kickoff returns** - Edwards 1-24; **Punt returns** - Hicks 3-32.

CHIEFS LEADERS: Rushing - Word 15-50, Williams 8-24, McNair 1-3; **Passing** - Deberg 5-9-0 - 22, Vlasic 9-20-4 - 124; **Receiving** - McNair 5-52, F. Jones 3-31, Birden 2-19, Barnett 1-20, Hayes 1-21, R. Thomas 1-1, B. Jones 1-2; **Kickoff returns** - Williams 3-48; **Punt returns** - Stradford 1-11.

NOTES

• The Bills avenged their embarrassing Monday night defeat earlier in the season with a convincing romp over Kansas City as Thurman Thomas posted his fourth straight postseason 100-yard rushing game, second-most in NFL history behind the six in a row by Washington's John Riggins.
• James Lofton and Don Beebe returned to the lineup and Lofton caught a TD pass.
• Chiefs QB Steve DeBerg was knocked out of the game with a thumb injury in the second quarter. Mark Vlasic replaced him and threw four interceptions.
• On the negative side, four offensive linemen suffered injuries. Kent Hull, Will Wolford and Jim Ritcher all hurt their ankles and Glenn Parker twisted his knee. The severity was unknown after the game.
• In the last three playoff games at Rich, the Bills offense averaged 44 points and 481 yards while the defense had intercepted 12 passes and limited teams to 51 points, only 17 points in the last two games.
• The teams traded punts twice before the Bills broke the ice with an eight-play, 80-yard drive that ended in Jim Kelly's 25-yard TD pass to Andre Reed, who beat Jayice Pearson one-on-one on a corner route. Kelly was five-for-five for 65 yards, including a 19-yard strike to Beebe on third-and-seven from the Chiefs 49.
• The Chiefs went three-and-out and punted, but Kelly was intercepted by Eric Everett at the Chiefs 40. The defense again forced a three-and-out and Clifford Hicks returned Bryan Barker's punt 16 yards to the 31.
• From there, Kelly audibled again when he saw Pearson one-on-one with Reed. Reed ran a fly and left Pearson in his wake as he caught a 53-yard TD pass down the middle.
• On the next series, Deberg was injured. Vlasic came in, but the Chiefs had to punt. Deron Cherry intercepted Kelly on the ensuing possession at the Chiefs 15 with 2:51 left in the first half, but again, the Chiefs went three-and-out and the Bills took possession at their 45 with 1:39 left.
• Kevin Ross could have turned the game around, but he dropped an interception on the left sideline that would have been a sure TD. The Bills eventually moved into position for a 33-yard Scott Norwood field goal with two seconds left for a 17-0 halftime lead.
• On the first play of the third quarter, Harvey Williams fumbled, but Jonathan Hayes recovered. On the next play, Vlasic was intercepted by Kirby Jackson at the KC

36 after Cornelius Bennett had tipped the pass.
• On third-and-five from the 10, Kelly hit Lofton for the TD that, in effect, put the game away.
• Jackson's second interception midway through the third went for naught when Lonnie Marts picked off Kelly two plays later and returned it to the Bills 43. Vlasic then hit Tim Barnett for 20 and Hayes for 21, setting up Barry Word's TD run.
• Buffalo answered with a 14-play, 68-yard march to Norwood's second field goal. The drive was kept alive when Kenneth Davis converted a fourth-and-one from the Chiefs 40 on the second play of the fourth quarter.
• Two plays after the kickoff, Leonard Smith intercepted Vlasic at the Kansas City 31, leading to Norwood's third field goal. On the first play after the kickoff, Clifford Hicks made an interception at the Kansas City 33. Frank Reich came in to play QB and he handed off to Davis six straight plays until he scored.
• Vlasic directed an eight-play, 75-yard drive to the game's final score, his TD pass to Fred Jones.

QUOTES

• Marv Levy: "Our defense played exceptionally well today. I'd have to say it was their best performance of the season. There was a heightened degree of preparation and awareness. Because of the playoffs, they know how potent Kansas City's running game was and how much we had been handled by them the last time. I just think they played their responsibilities without much error."
• Darryl Talley: "The last time we played the Kansas City Chiefs, we learned one thing: If you don't play physical against them and hit up in the holes as linebackers and linemen, they're just going to run the ball down your throat. They are a big, strong, physical football team. The ultimate goal is to get to the next level. We have gotten to the next level and now we have to go out and prepare for the Denver Broncos and let the marbles fall where they may."
• Jeff Wright: "I think we did a darn good job of stuffing them."
• Jim Kelly: "This game, it was just a matter of getting time to throw. One thing we had to do today was go deep on them and make sure we loosened them up some and make them respect our long ball. We respect the defensive backs from Kansas City, but I had a lot of confidence in my receivers that, with the speed they have, we could beat them deep."

• Leonard Smith: "The key was what happened on Monday night. They dominated that game and we didn't want that to happen again. I don't think it was so much revenge, it was just going out and getting respect. We left there with no respect."
• Cornelius Bennett: "I think they were a little too overconfident and not giving us enough credit. I think we've been the no-respect team in the league for four or five years. People say we're just lucky, but we've been in the championship game two years in a row. Sure it's annoying, but we keep it quiet and go out and prove it on the field. We're 14-3 and in the championship game, if they want to keep saying it, we're just going to smile about it. During the week, everyone was talking about Bruce and Jeff would be back (they missed the earlier game in Kansas City) but nobody mentioned my name or Darryl's and both of us had great games. I was thinking 'Damn, what about me?' Like always, I just let my playing do the talking, but my feelings were a little hurt."
• Kent Hull on Thurman Thomas and Kelly: "I think both Jim and Thurman (are the MVPs). I don't know how far this offense would go without either of them. We certainly don't want to find out if we can win in the playoffs without either one of them."
• Andre Reed on his two TDs: "Jim saw something out there and it was just perfect. It was my job to just beat my guy and go to the post and he threw a perfect pass. The first one was pretty much the same thing. I'm not going to say we suckered them, but maybe we showed them something they hadn't seen before. I don't think they expected that (Reed running deep as opposed to Beebe or Lofton)."
• Assistant coach Chuck Dickerson: "I told them (his defensive linemen) 'Remember when you were eight years old and you went out on the back porch and a bully was standing in the grass and he told you to come on down because he wanted to kick your ass?' You knew if you went down there off that porch, then, by God, you had better answer the bell. Today, we answered the bell."

Broncos	0	0	0	7 -	7
Bills	0	0	7	3 -	10

Attendance at Rich Stadium - 80,272

Buf: Bailey 11 interception return (Norwood kick), 9:32
Buf: FG Norwood 44, 10:42
Den: Kubiak 3 run (Treadwell kick), 13:17

	BUF	DEN
First downs	12	20
Rushing yds	104	81
Passing yds	109	223
Punts-avg	8-38.0	6-43.7
Fumbles-lost	0-0	4-1
Penalties-yds	6-35	4-20
Poss. time	25:07	34:53

BUFFALO TACKLES: Bennett 9, L. Smith 9, Bailey 7, Talley 6, Seals 6, B. Smith 5, Wright 4, Conlan 3, Kelso 3, Jackson 3, Odomes 2, Williams 2.

DENVER TACKLES: Brooks 7, Fletcher 7, Mecklenburg 6, Kragen 6 Atwater 6, Powers 6, D. Smith 4, Holmes 3, Braxton 2, Dimry 2, Sochia 2.

BILLS LEADERS: **Rushing** - Thomas 26-72, K. Davis 6-7, Reed 1-16, Kelly 2-9; **Passing** - Kelly 13-25-2 - 117; **Receiving** - McKeller 3-39, Reed 2-19, Lofton 1-11, K. Davis 2-13, Thomas 3-15, Beebe 1-6, Metzelaars 1-14; **Kickoff returns** - Edwards 1-24; **Punt returns** - None.

BRONCOS LEADERS: **Rushing** - Green 19-53, Kubiak 3-22, Sewell 4-3, Elway 4-10, V. Johnson 2-(-7); **Passing** - Elway 11-21-1 - 121, Kubiak 11-21-0 - 136; **Receiving** - Sharpe 3-40, Sewell 7-78, V. Johnson 8-104, Young 3-25, Nattiel 1-10; **Kickoff returns** - Montgomery 2-34, Russell 1-15; **Punt returns** - V. Johnson 3-36.

NOTES

• The Denver defense turned in a great game, frustrating the no-huddle offense and holding the Bills to a season-low passing total, but the Bills' defense rose to the occasion to lift the team to its second straight AFC Championship.
• Buffalo's defense produced four sacks and knocked John Elway out of the game in the fourth quarter. Elway suffered a bruised right thigh on a hit by Leon Seals on the first series of the third quarter, and while he played the rest of the quarter, he was too immobile and Denver coach Dan Reeves inserted Gary Kubiak.
• Denver crossed midfield on 10 of its 14 possessions, but scored only once.
• Chris Mohr's eight punts in the game tied the team play-off record shared by Daryle Lamonica (1963) and Paul Maguire (1967).
• Thurman Thomas saw his streak of 100-yard playoff games end at four.
• The Bills improved to 34-3, counting playoffs, in the last four seasons at Rich Stadium.
• The teams punted twice each to start the game, then Jim Kelly was intercepted by Greg Kragen on a pass that was tipped by Ron Holmes at the line and fell into Kragen's arms at the Bills 29. However, Denver failed to make a first down and David Treadwell missed a 47-yard field goal.
• Kirby Jackson had an apparent interception early in the second quarter, but the replay official reversed the call, so Denver retained possession. The Bills held, but on fourth-and-four at the Bills 31, Jeff Wright went offsides, giving Denver a first down. Again, the drive stalled and Treadwell hit the right upright with a 42-yard attempt.
• After a Bills punt, Elway hit Steve Sewell for 26 yards to set up Treadwell's 37-yard attempt, and he hit the right upright again with 5:52 left in the first half.
• Neither team threatened the rest of the half. The Bills had three first downs and 58 yards at halftime.
• On the first series of the third, Mike Horan blasted a wind-blown 76-yard punt, pinning the Bills at their 5.
• They failed to get a first down and the Broncos took over at the Bills 49, but the defense refused to budge and forced a punt. The Bills finally moved on offense, advancing to the Broncos 26, but Tyrone Braxton intercepted Kelly and returned it out to the 19.

• This set the stage for the play of the game. After an incompletion, Elway tried to throw a middle screen to Sewell, but Wright saw it coming, dropped off his pass rush, tipped the ball into the air and Carlton Bailey came down with it and ran 11 yards for a touchdown.
• After an exchange of punts, Kubiak, playing his final NFL game, replaced Elway and he drove the Broncos to the Bills 33, but his fourth-and-11 pass to Michael Young came up one yard short of a first down as Clifford Hicks made the tackle.
• Three plays later, Kelly hit Keith McKeller for 25 yards on a third-and-five from the 29. After a 10-yard pass to Don Beebe, Thomas ran three times to get the ball to the 26 and Scott Norwood kicked a pressure-packed 44-yard field goal to make it 10-0 with 4:18 left to play.
• Kubiak then marched Denver 85 yards in eight plays to its only score. After his 11-yard scramble, he hit Vance Johnson on three straight plays for 24, seven and four yards to the Bills 43. After an offsides penalty on Mike Lodish, he hit Johnson for gains of 23 yards to the 11 and eight to the 3, then scored on a keeper with 1:43 remaining.
• The Broncos' Steve Atwater then recovered the onside kick at the Denver 49. But on the first play, Sewell caught a short pass, was stripped by Jackson and Jackson recovered the loose ball at the Bills 44. Buffalo then ran out the clock.

QUOTES

• Darryl Talley on the performance of the defense: "Surprise, surprise, surprise."
• Jeff Wright: "Defense wins championships and we were a big part of it today. The offense carried us all season, we just paid them back." (On his deflected pass): "They had run the play earlier in the game and they have a tendency to repeat a lot of plays, so I knew they'd probably be coming back to it and when they did, I reacted. I got through and I saw him (Elway) keep backpedaling, so I knew something was funny so I figured it was going to be another middle screen."
• Carlton Bailey on the interception: "I didn't recognize the tip right away. I heard it, then looked up and saw the ball. All I could think of was 'If I drop this ball, I'm never going to hear the end of it when I show up at the meeting Monday morning.' We used to have this linebacker called Mongo (Matt Monger) and he couldn't catch a cold. If I dropped it, they would have been calling me Mongo the rest of my life."
• Cornelius Bennett: "We tease Carlton about having the worst hands on the team. Now, he has great hands." (About returning to the Super Bowl): "We have some

unfinished business. Last year we were excited about going to the Super Bowl. This time we know what to expect leading up to the game. It (losing) was a tough pill to swallow."
• Marv Levy on Bennett's performance: "I told Cornelius in the locker room 'Remember last week when I told you that was the finest game you ever played? I was wrong, today is.' (On returning to the Super Bowl): "We didn't start out in training camp saying 'We're going back to the Super Bowl.' I think that's too big a bite for any team to take. We just felt the best way to get back would be to play for every week's game. We've done that and now we're going back."
• Kirby Jackson on his saving fumble recovery: "I had underneath coverage and they threw it short and I just focused on the ball. I knew I had stripped it, but I couldn't find it. I think it was meant for me to get that ball. I don't think I get the respect that I deserve, but I think these last two games will bring attention to me. We've (the defense) gotten a lot of criticism this season, but we came together today. Defense wins championships? Well, I guess this is what they mean."
• Jim Kelly: "Everyone always says when the offense doesn't move, 'What was your problem?' There wasn't any problem, it's just that they played one helluva defense. They came at us. They blitzed us a few times and we didn't pick up the sight adjustments. If we had seen them a couple of times, we might have had big plays, but we missed them. I take my hat off to them." (About the Super Bowl): "Last year's Super Bowl lingered in our minds – four, five, six months – and I didn't like that. We have the chance to go back and not many teams get a second opportunity. We have our second opportunity. Now it's a matter of us capitalizing on it."
• Kent Hull: "I've never been around a team that finds so many ways to win a football game. You can't coach it, and it's not bred. It's just a growing process. On this team, each individual player complements the other."
• Thurman Thomas on his thoughts after the onside kick: "I don't know what I was thinking. I remember thinking that I wanted the ball, but I was standing there watching the defense. Then I was thinking the defense had been coming up with big plays all game long."
• James Lofton: "This was a draining game. The defense put forth a lot of effort in stopping them and the offense put forth a lot of energy in wondering when we were going to do something. There's a great deal of satisfaction in what we've accomplished, but we realize there's another step. Hopefully, we'll be ready to take that."
• Will Wolford: "There's a lot of good that should come out of this. Last year we beat Los Angeles 51-3 and everyone in the country said 'Oh, the Bills are unbeatable.' That's just not true in football. This week they'll say 'Well, the offense got shut down, but they pulled one out on defense.' I like that. Our defense received little or no respect this year and the guys have been playing like they're on a mission to earn some respect. Secondly, it's the old cliché that defense wins championships. I certainly hope so, because we're bringing a pretty good one to Minneapolis."
• Denver coach Dan Reeves: "I'm very disappointed. It was a game of complete domination by our defense against the No. 1 offense in the NFL. The way we played in the first half would have won most games. We just didn't get the job done offensively. I had no idea the noise would be as loud as it was, and it was a factor."
• Bill Polian: "We have one more river to cross. When you go (to the Super Bowl) and come up short, you understand how heart-rending it is. So while there's joy today, and justifiably so, we know there is another game to play, an even bigger one than the one we played today."

Redskins	0	17	14	6 -	37
Bills	0	0	10	14 -	24

Attendance at the Metrodome - 63,130

Wash: FG Lohmiller 34, 1:58
Wash: Byner 10 pass from Rypien (Lohmiller kick), 5:06
Wash: Riggs 1 run (Lohmiller kick), 7:43
Wash: Riggs 2 run (Lohmiller kick), :16
Buf: FG Norwood 21, 3:01
Buf: Thomas 1 run (Norwood kick), 9:02
Wash: Clark 30 pass from Rypien (Lohmiller kick), 13:36
Wash: FG Lohmiller 25, :06
Wash: FG Lohmiller 39, 3:24
Buf: Metzelaars 2 pass from Kelly (Norwood kick), 9:01
Buf: Beebe 4 pass from Kelly (Norwood kick), 11:05

	BUF	WASH
First downs	25	24
Rushing yds	43	125
Passing yds	240	292
Punts-avg	6-35.0	4-37.5
Fumbles-lost	6-1	1-0
Penalties-yds	6-50	5-82
Poss. time	26:17	33:43

BUFFALO TACKLES: Bailey 11, Talley 8, Bennett 7, Kelso 6, Seals 6, Jackson 5, Odomes 4, Drane 4, Bentley 3, Wright 3, B. Smith 2, Garner 2.

WASHINGTON TACKLES: Marshall 11, Stokes 6, Mayhew 5, Collins 5, T. Johnson 5, Edwards 4, Gouveia 4, Mays 4, Geathers 3, Green 2.

BILLS LEADERS: Rushing - Thomas 10-13, K. Davis 4-17, Kelly 3-16, Lofton 1-(-3); **Passing** - Kelly 28-58-4 - 275, Reich 1-1-0 - 11; **Receiving** - Lofton 7-92, Reed 5-34, McKeller 2-29, Thomas 4-27, Beebe 4-61, Edwards 1-11, K. Davis 4-38, Metzelaars 1-2, Kelly 1-(-8); **Kickoff returns** - Edwards 4-77; **Punt returns** - Hicks 3-9.

REDSKINS LEADERS: Rushing - Ervins 13-72, Byner 14-49, Riggs 5-7, Rutledge 1-0, Rypien 6-(-4), Sanders 1-1; **Passing** - Rypien 18-33-1 - 292; **Receiving** - Clark 7-114, Monk 7-113, Byner 3-24, Sanders 1-41; **Kickoff returns** - Mitchell 1-16; **Punt returns** - None.

NOTES

• The Bills joined Denver and Minnesota as the only teams to lose in back-to-back Super Bowls.
• The AFC suffered its eighth straight Super Bowl loss.
• Jim Kelly threw a Super Bowl record 58 passes, breaking the mark of 50 set by Dan Marino in 1984.
• The teams combined to set records for the most points in the third quarter (24), fewest rushing yards (168) and most passes thrown (92). The Bills set the mark for passing first downs (18).
• Mark Rypien was named MVP and he had help from Art Monk and Gary Clark who combined for 14 catches for 227 yards.
• Washington's Wilbur Marshall had 11 tackles, one sack and two forced fumbles.
• Instant replay reversed an apparent first-quarter TD pass to Art Monk.
• Andre Reed lost his cool just before halftime when he thought he had been interfered with by Brad Edwards. When no flag was thrown, he threw his helmet and was penalized for unsportsmanlike conduct, knocking the Bills out of field goal range. Edwards had two interceptions and five pass breakups.
• Leon Seals said after the game that he wanted out of Buffalo because he felt he had been mistreated by the front office.
• Shane Conlan left the game less than six minutes in when he suffered a knee injury.
• Leonard Smith could not play because of an infected knee, so Dwight Drane was forced to start.

QUOTES

• Jim Kelly: "You only get so many chances. I'll be 32 next month. Time's running out on me. From the neck down, the whole second half is kind of fuzzy to me. I can remember part of the game, but not all of it. The part I can remember, I didn't like. I'm sure it'll come back if I ever watch this game film – which I doubt I ever will. Sometimes I had an open man and didn't hit him, sometimes there were balls that we didn't catch and sometimes blocks slipped away. We were just outplayed today. This is hard to take because we have such a good team. We've come a long way. You hate to say 'There's always next year.' You get tired of saying that."
• Thurman Thomas: "I don't feel like I was getting the ball enough. I wanted the ball a lot more. We weren't running the plays we ran in practice. I worked my butt off in practice and then I hardly get the ball in the game. One of the reasons we were so ineffective is because we kept running up the middle. They bunched up and stopped us. I know the running game wasn't working, but you can't get away from it. That's what got us here. I thought we should have run some plays outside, maybe that would have loosened

things up. We've got the talent to win the Super Bowl, but once we get here we just don't do it. We're falling in the category of Denver and Minnesota. We play well during the regular season, but when we get to the Super Bowl, we don't play well. In order for us to get respect, you have to win games like this." (About losing his helmet): "I couldn't find it, I didn't know where it was. For some reason, somebody moved it. I was very upset. The first two plays were running plays and I wasn't in there to get it." (On the distractions during the week): "What I said, what Bruce said, didn't have any effect. We're going to speak our minds. Ever since I've been in this league, I haven't been afraid to speak my mind."
• Redskins linebacker Wilbur Marshall: "Thurman gave us more incentive to try and stop him. He's the best, or at least he said he was the best. You just can't say that when you've got a bunch of rowdy guys on the other side of the ball. We took him out of the game, totally."
• Redskins defensive end Charles Mann: "We don't have a lot of guys shooting their mouths off. I think the Buffalo Bills have some characters on their team, about six or seven guys who think they're it. They think they're in Hollywood."
• Bruce Smith responding to Mann: "Charles Mann has a big mouth. We have players on this team that choose to speak their minds. They're grown men. Are we allowed to speak our minds? Does that mean we're in Hollywood?" (About the game): "It's very disappointing. I truly don't believe this has happened. I don't think it will hit me until I walk out of this stadium. We said before the game we wanted to make some history, but we made it the wrong damn way."
• Nate Odomes: "We were competitive at different times, but in certain situations we weren't. You have to look at yourself in the mirror and say 'I didn't play the ballgame that I was capable of playing.' We finished 15-4 the last two seasons and that's not good enough for Buffalo. I think, once again, you have to go back to the drawing board and decide what you want to do. Are we gonna be a loser, or do we want to win everything?" (About the pregame distractions): "We're a football team, we're a family. What we do in our locker room is our business. We have guys with personalities that are deep. I don't think we have guys bickering to the point where it takes away from our play on the football field."
• Marv Levy: "I can't remember a loss more difficult than today's. Overall, we played a team that was better and they showed it. Defeat is always bitter. It's quiet in that (locker) room, very somber. We wanted this game very badly. We'll come down the road again and we'll come home with a win. Despite everything that went wrong in the first half, our players scrapped. Both teams started out, it looked to me, a little tight. They made some big plays

finally in the second quarter and put points on the board." (On Thomas' missing helmet): "I was disturbed he didn't have his helmet but it did not affect the game one iota."
• Kent Hull: "We certainly expected a lot more than what we showed today. It got embarrassing at times. We didn't execute very well and we played a great football team and that's what happens. In the NFL, I guarantee you if you're minus two in the takeaway/giveaway in a game, you're going to lose 90 percent of the time. I don't know what we were, minus four or five. It's pretty hard to win a football game when you turn the ball over."
• Leon Seals: "We can go into training camp with our heads high because this is one game. There are 26 other teams that are probably crying to get to this point. We don't have anything to be embarrassed about, other than we came here and stunk the place up."
• Darryl Talley: "All I'll think about for the next six months is this game. It'll drum at me and pick at me the whole time."
• Redskins center Jeff Bostic on comments made by Chuck Dickerson earlier in the week about the Hogs: "Chuck Dickerson gave us a great motivating speech. Let's see, he said I was an ugly guy and just like the other ugly guys, I probably ate grease. He said Joe (Jacoby) slobbered a lot and that he was a Neanderthal man. And he called Jim Lachey a 310-pound ballerina who should wear a tutu. He made embarrassing remarks about all of us. We didn't appreciate those comments and it fired us up. I wonder what he thinks about us now?"
• Redskins tackle Joe Jacoby: "We take pride in our group and he was making fun of us on national television all week. He really didn't pay us much respect for what we've done. The guys were really upset. We came out to prove something and I think we did. They were here to talk a good game, we were here to play a good game."

STARTING LINEUPS

BILLS OFFENSE: QB - Jim Kelly; RB - Kenneth Davis; WR - Andre Reed, James Lofton; TE - Pete Metzelaars, Keith McKeller; OL - Kent Hull, Will Wolford, Howard Ballard, Jim Ritcher, Glenn Parker.
DEFENSE: DL - Bruce Smith, Leon Seals, Jeff Wright; LB - Cornelius Bennett, Darryl Talley, Shane Conlan, Carlton Bailey; DB - Nate Odomes, Kirby Jackson, Mark Kelso, Dwight Drane.

REDSKINS OFFENSE: QB - Mark Rypien; RB - Earnest Byner; WR - Gary Clark, Art Monk; TE - Ron Middleton, Don Warren; OL - Jim Lachey, Raleigh McKenzie, Jeff Bostic, Mark Schlereth, Joe Jacoby.
DEFENSE: DL - Charles Mann, Erik Williams, Tim Johnson, Fred Stokes; LB - Wilbur Marshall, Kurt Gouveia, Andre Collins; DB - Martin Mayhew, Darrell Green, Danny Copeland, Brad Edwards.

SUPER BOWL XXVI PLAY-BY-PLAY

FIRST QUARTER

Redskins win toss, elect to receive.
Buffalo's Brad Daluiso kicks off before officials signal, re-kick is ordered. Daluiso kicks off through end zone, touchback.
REDSKINS 15:00
1-10-W20 - Byner runs left, 2, (tackled by B. Smith, Seals); 2-8-W22 - Rypien pass to Clark, 4, (Jackson); 3-4-W26 - Rypien incomplete pass; 4-4-W26 - Goodburn punt 33, no return.

BILLS 13:12
1-10-B41 - K. Davis runs left, 1, (Stokes, Marshall); 2-9-B42 - Kelly runs right, 4, (Marshall, Stokes); 3-5-B46 - Kelly sacked by Geathers, -10; 4-15-B36 - Mohr punt 53, Mitchell fair catch.

REDSKINS 11:38
1-10-W11 - Rypien pass to Monk, 12, (Odomes); 1-10-W23 - Rypien pass to Monk, 17, (Bennett); 1-10-W40 - Byner runs left, 8, (Kelso); 2-2-W48 - Byner runs left, 4, (Seals); 1-10-B48 - Byner runs left, -4, (Bennett, Talley). Conlan injures knee, leaves game with 9:07 left; 2-14-W48 - Rypien incomplete pass to Clark; 3-14-W48 - Rypien pass to Monk, 19, (Williams); 1-10-B33 - Rypien pass to Monk, 31, (Kelso); 1-G-B2 - Riggs runs right, 0, (Bentley, Bennett); 2-G-B2 - Riggs runs to middle, 0, (Bentley, Wright); 3-G-B2 - Rypien pass to Monk for TD, but instant replay official reverses call, incomplete pass; 4-G-2 - Rutledge fumbles snap on field goal attempt, recovers at 14.

BILLS 5:46
1-10-B14 - Kelly pass for Reed intercepted by Edwards at 33, return 21.

REDSKINS 5:38
1-10-B12 - Ervins runs right, 0, (Jackson); 2-10-B12 - Sanders reverse right, 1, (Jackson); 3-9-B11 - Rypien pass tipped at line by Wright, intercepted by Jackson at 7, return 4.

BILLS 4:02
1-10-B11 - Thomas runs to middle, 3, (Collins); 2-7-B14 - Kelly pass to Reed, 12, (Gouveia, Marshall); 1-10-B26 - Thomas runs to middle, 2, (Coleman); 2-8-B28 - Kelly incomplete pass to Thomas; 3-8-B28 - Kelly pass to Lofton, 18, (Edwards); 1-10-B46 - Thomas runs right, 2, (Gouveia, T. Johnson); 2-8-B48 - Lofton reverse left, -3, (Stokes); 3-11-B45 - Kelly runs to middle, 3, (Marshall); 4-8-B48 - Mohr punt 33, out of bounds.

REDSKINS :42
1-10-W19 - Rypien pass to Byner, 4, (Bailey).

SECOND QUARTER

2-6-W23 - Byner runs left, 19, (Kelso); 1-10-W42 - Rypien pass to Sanders, 41, (Kelso); 1-10-B17 - Washington penalty, holding, Bostic, -10; 1-20-B27 - Rypien pass to Byner, 10, (Talley); 2-10-B17 - Rypien incomplete pass in end zone to Sanders; 3-10-B17 - Rypien incomplete pass to Clark; 4-10-B17 - Lohmiller 34 FIELD GOAL. Drive: 7 plays, 64 yards, Time of possession 2:40. Time of score: 1:58 elapsed. **Washington 3, Buffalo 0.**

Lohmiller kicks off to Buffalo 5, Edwards return 24 (Lohmiller).
BILLS 13:02
1-10-B29 - Thomas runs right, -1, (Collins, T. Johnson); 2-11-B28 - Kelly incomplete pass to Reed; 3-11-B28 - Kelly incomplete pass to Edwards; 4-11-B28 - Mohr punt 23, out of bounds.

REDSKINS 12:06
1-10-W49 - Rypien pass to Clark, 16, (Odomes); 1-10-B35 - Byner runs left, 6, (Bailey, Talley); 2-4-B29 - Rypien pass to Monk, 8, (Odomes); 1-10-B21 - Buffalo penalty, Bennett, roughing the passer, 10; 1-10-B11 - Byner runs right, 1, (Seals); 2-9-B10 - Rypien pass to Byner, 10 TOUCHDOWN. Lohmiller PAT. Drive: 5 plays, 51 yards, TOP 2:12. Time of score: 5:06. **Washington 10, Buffalo 0.**

Lohmiller kicks off to Buffalo 3, Edwards return 11 (Hoage).
BILLS 9:54
1-10-B14 - Kelly incomplete pass to Lofton; 2-10-B14 - Kelly pass to Lofton intercepted by Green at W45, no return.

REDSKINS 9:35
1-10-W45 - Buffalo penalty, Jackson, illegal contact, 5; 1-10-50 - Ervins runs right, 1, (Bentley, Seals); 2-9-B49 - Rypien incomplete pass to Clark; 3-9-B49 - Rypien pass to Clark, 34, (Jackson); 1-10-B15 - Ervins runs left, 14, (Odomes, Kelso); 1-G-B1 - Riggs runs right, 1 TOUCHDOWN. Lohmiller PAT. Drive: 5 plays, 55 yards, TOP 2:18. Time of score: 7:43. **Washington 17, Buffalo 0.**

Lohmiller kicks off to end zone, touchback.
BILLS 7:17
1-10-B20 - Kelly pass to Reed, 6, (Collins); 2-4-B26 - Thomas runs to middle, 1, (Williams); 3-3-B27 - Kelly pass to Lofton, 12, (Mays); 1-10-B39 - Kelly pass to Reed, 8, fumble out of bounds, (Marshall); 2-2-B47 - Thomas runs left, -4, (Collins); 3-6-B43 - Kelly incomplete pass to McKeller; 4-6-B43 - Mohr punt 43, Mitchell fair catch.

REDSKINS 5:02
1-10-W14 - Ervins runs right, 8, (Bailey); 2-2-W22 - Ervins runs to middle, 0, (Bennett); 3-2-B22 - Rypien incomplete pass to Monk; 4-2-W22 - Goodburn punt 45, Hicks return 7, (Hobbs).

BILLS 3:47
1-10-B40 - Kelly pass to Reed, 4, (Mayhew); 2-6-B44 - Kelly incomplete pass to Lofton; 3-6-B44 - Kelly pass to McKeller, 8, (S. Johnson, Mays); 1-10-W48 - Kelly pass to Lofton, 10, (Mays); 1-10-W38 - Kelly incomplete pass to McKeller; 2-10-W38 - Kelly sacked by Buck, -11, 2:00 warning; 3-21-W49 - Kelly incomplete pass to Lofton; 4-21-W49 - Mohr punt 48, downed at 1 by Tasker.

REDSKINS 1:46
1-10-W1 - Rypien runs to middle, 2, (Talley), Buffalo timeout 1:41; 2-8-W3 - Byner runs middle, -2, (Wright), Buffalo timeout 1:32; 3-10-W1 - Rypien incomplete pass to Orr; 4-10-W1 - Goodburn punt 42, Hicks return 2 (Hobbs).

BILLS 1:16
1-10-W41 - Kelly pass to McKeller, 21, (Edwards), :53; 1-10-W20 - Kelly incomplete pass to Beebe, :48; 2-10-W20 - Kelly sacked by Marshall, -8, fumble recovered by Ballard, :34; 3-18-W28 - Kelly incomplete pass to Reed. Edwards made contact, no call, Reed penalized for unsportsmanlike conduct, -15, :29; 4-33-W43 - Mohr punt 10, no return. Rypien kneels to end half, -1.

HALFTIME STATISTICS

	BUF	WASH
First downs	6	15
Rushing yds	8	60
Passing yds	70	206
Punts-avg	3-29.0	3-40.0
Fumbles-lost	3-0	1-0
Penalties-yds	6-35	1-10
Poss. time	11:33	18:27

RUSHING: **Buf:** Thomas 6-3, K. Davis 1-1, Kelly 2-7, Lofton 1-(-3).
Wash: Byner 10-42, Riggs 3-1, Rutledge 1-0, Ervins 3-15 Sanders 1-1, Rypien 2-1.

PASSING: **Buf:** Kelly 9-21-2 - 99
Wash: Rypien 12-21-1 - 206.

RECEIVING: **Buf:** Reed 4-30, Lofton 3-40, McKeller 2-29
Wash: Clark 3-54, Monk 5-87, Byner 3-24, Sanders 1-41.

THIRD QUARTER

Lohmiller kicks off to end zone, touchback.
BILLS 15:00
1-10-B20 - Kelly pass to McKeller intercepted by Gouveia at B25, return 23 (Thomas).

REDSKINS 14:47
1-G-B2 - Riggs runs left, 2 TOUCHDOWN. Lohmiller PAT. Buffalo penalty, offsides, Williams (assessed on kickoff) Drive: 1 play, 2 yards, TOP :03. Time of score :16. **Washington 24, Buffalo 0.**

Lohmiller kicks off through end zone, touchback.
BILLS 14:44
1-10-B20 - Kelly pass to Thomas, 8, (Gouveia); 2-2-B28 - Kelly pass to Reed, 4, (Gouveia); 1-10-B32 - Kelly incomplete pass to Reed; 2-10-B32 - Kelly incomplete pass to Lofton; 3-10-B32 - Kelly pass to Lofton, 14, (Mayhew, Edwards); 1-10-B46 - Kelly incomplete pass to Lofton; 2-10-B46 - Kelly pass to Beebe, 43, (Edwards); 1-10-W11 - Kelly pass to Thomas, 8, (Collins); 2-2-W3 - Kelly incomplete pass to Beebe in end zone; 3-2-W3 - Kelly incomplete pass to Lofton in end zone; 4-2-W3 - Norwood 21 FIELD GOAL. Drive: 11 plays, 77 yards, TOP 2:45. Time of score: 3:01. **Washington 24, Buffalo 3.**

Daluiso kicks off through end zone, touchback.
REDSKINS 11:59
1-10-W20 - Byner runs left, 4, (Garner); 2-6-W24 - Byner runs right, 6, (Bennett, Bailey); 1-10-W30 - Byner runs right, 0, (Garner, Seals); 2-10-W30 - Rypien pass to Monk, 9, (Talley); 3-1-W39 - Byner runs left, -3, (Talley); 4-4-W36 - Goodburn punt 20, out of bounds.

BILLS 8:17
1-10-B44 - Kelly pass to Lofton, 11, out of bounds; 1-10-W45 - Kelly pass to Beebe, 9, (T. Johnson); 2-1-W36 - Thomas runs to middle, 6, (Stokes, Marshall); 1-10-W30 - Kelly incomplete pass to Lofton in end zone, Washington penalty, interference, Mayhew; 1-G-W1 - Thomas runs to middle, 0, (Caldwell, Mann); 2-G-W1 - K. Davis runs to middle, 0, (Geathers); 3-G-W1 - Thomas runs left, 1 TOUCHDOWN. Norwood PAT. Drive: 6 plays, 56 yards, TOP 2:19. Time of score: 9:02. **Washington 24, Buffalo 10.**

Daluiso kicks off to 5, Mitchell return 16 (H. Jones).
REDSKINS 5:58
1-10-W21 - Rypien pass to Clark, 6, (Drane); 2-4-W27 - Rypien incomplete pass to Clark; 3-4-W27 - Rypien pass to Clark, 10, (Bailey); 1-10-W37 - Ervins runs to middle, 6, (Talley, Seals); 2-4-W43 - Rypien pass to Clark, 14, (Talley); 1-10-B43 - Ervins runs right, 8, (Bailey, Drane); 2-2-B35 - Ervins runs right, 1, (B. Smith); 3-1-B34 - Riggs runs right, 4, (Bailey); 1-10-B30 - Rypien incomplete pass to Sanders; 2-10-B30 - Rypien incomplete pass to Clark; 3-10-B30 - Rypien pass to Clark, 30 TOUCHDOWN. Lohmiller PAT. Buffalo penalty, offsides, Bennett (assessed on kickoff). Drive: 11 plays, 79 yards, TOP 4:34. Time of score: 13:36. **Washington 31, Buffalo 10.**

Lohmiller kicks off through end zone, touchback.
BILLS 1:24
1-10-B20 - Kelly pass to Lofton, 10, out of bounds; 1-10-B30 - Kelly pass batted in air by Stokes, caught by Kelly, -8, (Stokes); 2-18-B22 - Kelly sacked by Mays, -8, fumbles, Stokes recovers at 14.

REDSKINS :51
1-10-B14 - Washington penalty, holding, McKenzie, -10; 1-20-B24 - Rypien incomplete pass to Byner; 2-20-B24 - Rypien pass to Monk, 17, (Drane, Bailey).

FOURTH QUARTER

3-3-B7 - Rypien incomplete pass to Byner; 4-3-B7 - Lohmiller 25 FIELD GOAL. Drive: 4 plays, 7 yards, TOP, :57. Time of score: :06. **Washington 34, Buffalo 10.**

Lohmiller kicks off to 3, Edwards return 21 (Caldwell).
BILLS 14:54
1-10-B24 - Kelly sacked by Stokes, -9; 2-19-B15 - Kelly incomplete pass to Beebe; 3-19-B15 - Kelly pass to Beebe intercepted by Edwards at W32, return 35.

REDSKINS 14:06
1-10-B33 - Ervin runs right, 14, (Jackson); 1-10-B19 - Ervins runs right, -3, (Bennett); 2-13-B22 - Ervins runs right, 0, (Wright); 3-13-B22 - Rypien pass incomplete, tipped by B. Smith; 4-13-B22 - Lohmiller 39 FIELD GOAL. Drive: 5 plays, 11 yards, TOP 2:30. Time of score: 3:24. **Washington 37, Buffalo 10.**

Lohmiller kicks off to goal line, Edwards return 21 (Mayhew).
BILLS 11:36
1-10-B21 - Kelly runs right, 9, injured on play, (Mayhew), Reich in at QB; 2-1-B30 - Buffalo penalty, holding, Hull, -10, Kelly returns; 2-11-B20 - Kelly incomplete pass, Washington penalty, personal foul, Mays, 15; 1-10-B36 - Kelly pass to Thomas, 4, (Marshall); 2-6-B40 - Kelly pass to Beebe, 5, (Marshall); 3-1-B45 - Thomas runs left, 3, (Geathers, T. Johnson); 1-10-B48 - Kelly pass to Lofton, 17, (Green); 1-10-W35 - Kelly pass to Edwards, 11, out of bounds; 1-10-W24 - Kelly pass to Thomas, 7, (Mayhew); 2-3-W17 - Kelly incomplete pass to Lofton in end zone; 3-3-W17 - Kelly incomplete pass to Reed; 4-3-W17 - Kelly pass to K. Davis, 6, (Marshall); 1-10-W11 - Kelly pass to K. Davis, 9, (Hoage); 2-1-W2 - Kelly incomplete pass to Beebe in end zone; 3-1-W2 - Kelly pass to Metzelaars, 2 TOUCHDOWN. Norwood PAT. Drive: 15 plays, 79 yards, TOP 5:37. Time of score: 9:01. **Washington 37, Buffalo 17.**

Norwood onside kick, Bailey recovers for Buffalo at 50.
BILLS 5:59
1-10-50 - Kelly pass to K. Davis 12, (Green); 1-10-W38 - Kelly incomplete pass to Reed; 2-10-W38 - Kelly incomplete pass to K. Davis; 3-10-W38 - Kelly incomplete pass, Washington penalty, interference, Mays, 18; 1-10-W20 - Kelly fumbles snap, recovers, throws incomplete; 2-10-W20 - K. Davis runs to middle, 13, (Marshall); 1-G-W7 - Davis runs to middle, 3, (T. Johnson); 2-G-W4 - Kelly incomplete pass to K. Davis; 3-G-W4 - Kelly incomplete pass to Metzelaars; 4-G-W4 - Kelly pass to Beebe, 4 TOUCHDOWN. Norwood PAT. Drive: 9 plays, 50 yards, TOP 2:04. Time of score: 11:05. **Washington 37, Buffalo 24.**

Norwood onside kickoff, recovered by Hoage for Washington at 50.
REDSKINS 3:55
1-10-50 - Ervins runs right, 21, (Drane); 1-10-B29 - Ervins runs left, 1, (Bennett), Buffalo timeout 2:54; 2-9-B28 - Ervins runs right, 7, (Bailey, Kelso), Buffalo timeout, 2:38; 3-2-B21 - Ervins runs right, 2, (Bailey), 2:00 warning; 1-10-B19 - Rypien kneels, -1, Buffalo timeout 1:56; 2-11-B20 - Rypien kneels, -1; 3-12-B21 - Rypien kneels, -2.

BILLS :25
1-10-B24 - Reich pass to K. Davis, 11, (Mayhew). Game ends. FINAL: **Washington 37, Buffalo 24.**

At A Glance
1992

Jan. 27 – For the second year in a row, fans welcomed home the Bills at Niagara Square, although the crowd was much smaller, estimated at about 10,000.

Jan. 28 – Ted Marchibroda resigned as offensive coordinator of the Bills and was hired as head coach of the Indianapolis Colts. Marchibroda said he wasn't sad to leave Buffalo because he wanted to become a head coach, something he had done for the Colts in the mid-70s.

Jan. 29 – Defensive line coach Chuck Dickerson was fired, speculation arose that offensive line coach Tom Bresnahan would be promoted to offensive coordinator and receivers coach Nick Nicolau, upon hearing that he would likely be bypassed in favor of Bresnahan, resigned and agreed to become offensive coordinator under Ted Marchibroda in Indianapolis.

Jan. 30 – The Bills received permission from the Pittsburgh Steelers to interview Mean Joe Greene for their vacant defensive line coaching position. The Bills also said they were interested in Miami line coach Dan Sekanovich.

Jan. 31 – Marv Levy chose Dan Sekanovich to be his defensive line coach over Joe Greene. Also, Tom Bresnahan was officially named offensive coordinator while running backs coach Elijah Pitts was given the added title of assistant head coach.

Feb. 1 – Among the players left unprotected in the Plan B free agency period were Steve Tasker, Scott Norwood, Ray Bentley, Leonard Smith, Jim Ritcher, Butch Rolle, Mark Pike, Hal Garner and John Davis.

Feb. 2 – Thurman Thomas, in Hawaii for the Pro Bowl, reacting to all the coaching changes and the negative publicity he was receiving back in Buffalo, questioned whether he would be back with the Bills in 1992. "I'm not saying I'll be one of those changes, but if things continue to be like they are, I'd have to see about going somewhere else," he said. "Ever since the Super Bowl, I've been in contact with people back in Buffalo. There have been a lot of things written about me, about how I should have kept my mouth shut, I should have done this or done that."

Feb. 3 – Jim Shofner was named quarterbacks coach, filling a void that was created when Ted Marchibroda left. At his annual postseason press conference, Marv Levy shared blame with general manager Bill Polian for the unsavory comments made by Bruce Smith, Thurman Thomas, Leon Seals and assistant coach Chuck Dickerson in Minneapolis. "Their pronouncements are something we don't approve of and they hurt themselves more than our football team," Levy said. "It is not an accurate reflection of the Buffalo Bills. I talked to the team very strongly about just playing football."

Feb. 4 – Charlie Joiner was hired as receivers coach, replacing Nick Nicolau, completing the 1992 coaching staff.

Feb. 5 – Plan B free agent placekicker Steve Christie was signed to a four-year, $2.3 million contract, indicating that the Bills' all-time leading scorer, Scott Norwood, wouldn't be back with the team.

Feb. 7 – Dallas signed Buffalo kickoff specialist Brad Daluiso in Plan B.

March 7 - Tight end Butch Rolle, who had caught 10 passes in the last five years, all for touchdowns, was signed by Phoenix as a Plan B free agent.

March 16 – At the league meetings in Phoenix, Ralph Wilson said: "Instead of just welcoming them (the players at training camp), I'm going to welcome them by saying 'Now listen you fellas, let's act like professionals, huh? I thought it (some players' behavior at the Super Bowl) was kind of ridiculous."

March 17 – Bill Polian was presented the trophy for being named NFL executive of the year for 1991 by *The Sporting News*, the second time he had won the award.

March 18 – After a seven-year stint, The owners finally voted against using instant replay to aid in officiating. They voted 17-11, thus not gaining the necessary 21 votes.

March 23 – Ray Bentley signed with the Cincinnati Bengals as a Plan B free agent, the third Bill to leave via Plan B.

April 1 – The Plan B free agency period came to an end with 166 players changing teams.

April 26 – The Bills used their first-round draft choice, No. 27 overall, to select Arizona offensive lineman John Fina. They also chose Texas defensive tackle James Patton (second), Penn State linebacker Keith Goganious (third), UCLA safety Matt Darby (fifth), Nebraska fullback Nate Turner (sixth), Eastern Washington safety Kurt Schulz (seventh), Stanford wide receiver Chris Walsh (ninth) and Toledo tight end Vince Marrow (11th). Indianapolis used the first two picks in the draft to select defensive end Steve Emtman and linebacker Quentin Coryatt, the Rams picked defensive lineman Sean Gilbert (third), Washington chose wide receiver Desmond Howard (fourth), Green Bay picked cornerback Terrell Buckley (fifth), Cincinnati went for quarterback David Klingler (sixth), Miami chose cornerback Troy Vincent (seventh) and linebacker Marco Coleman (12th), Atlanta picked offensive tackle Bob Whitfield (eighth), Cleveland chose fullback Tommy Vardell (ninth), New England picked offensive lineman Eugene Chung (13th), the Giants chose tight end Derek Brown (14th), the Jets selected tight end Johnny Mitchell (15th), the Raiders opted for defensive lineman Chester McGlockton (16th), Dallas took cornerback Kevin Smith (17th), San Francisco picked safety Dana Hall (18th), Kansas City picked cornerback Dale Carter (20th), Denver picked quarterback Tommy Maddox (25th) and Detroit chose defensive lineman Robert Porcher (26th).

April 30 – Leonard Smith reported to mini-camp on crutches after undergoing surgery on his infected left knee three months earlier.

May 1 – Scott Norwood said he figured his days as a Bill were numbered with Steve Christie on the roster. "It's obvious, the writing is on the wall as to which direction they're going to go," he said. "It doesn't take a deep thinker to figure it out."

May 11 – St. Louis businessman James Orthwein purchased controlling interest in the New England Patriots.

May 19 – The NFL's expansion committee narrowed its list of prospective cities to five – Baltimore, St. Louis, Memphis, Jacksonville and Charlotte.

June 8 – Scott Norwood was waived by the Bills, ending his Buffalo career as the team's all-time leading scorer (670 points on 133-of-184 field goals and 271-of-278 extra points). "They made a deci-

sion (to sign Steve Christie) and the biggest thing is they backed it with a lot of money, in terms of the good-sized bonus and salary they gave to Steve," Norwood said.

July 20 – First-round draft choice John Fina signed his first pro contract.

July 23 – Training camp opened at Fredonia State and Marv Levy announced that Bruce Smith would go on the physically-unable-to-perform list so that he could slowly work his knee back into shape. Veteran strong safety Leonard Smith was waived and said he planned to sue the Bills for releasing him when he wasn't healthy enough to try out for other teams. Smith's knee infection never healed properly and he wouldn't have been able to participate in training camp.

July 24 – Cornelius Bennett, Keith McKeller, Leon Seals, Kirby Jackson and Kenneth Davis all missed the first practice of camp because they all were unsigned.

July 29 – Kenneth Davis ended his holdout and signed a three-year contract.

July 30 – Thurman Thomas revealed that he had kept a list of writers who wrote negative things about him after the Super Bowl and vowed not to talk to any of them.

Aug. 1 – The Bills returned to Edinboro University for the first time since 1989 to play a rookie scrimmage, but Cleveland wasn't the opponent. The Pittsburgh Steelers replaced the Browns and defeated the Bills, 6-0, in front of 10,521 fans.

Aug. 3 – Offensive coordinator and line coach Tom Bresnahan suffered a broken left arm when Kenneth Davis accidentally ran into him during a drill.

Aug. 5 – Leon Seals ended his holdout and signed a one-year contract.

Aug. 8 – The Bills returned to the site of their Super Bowl XXVI loss, the Metrodome, and lost their preseason opener to the Vikings, 24-3.

Aug. 13 – Bruce Smith traveled to Vail, Col. to have his knee checked by U.S. ski team surgeon Dr. Richard Steadman and he was cleared to begin practice. Nickel back and punt returner Clifford Hicks suffered a broken leg that would keep him out for the first few weeks of the regular season.

Aug. 17 – It took nearly four hours as 31 penalties were called, but the Bills prevailed over Detroit, 30-24, in the lone home preseason game in front of 56,622 and a national TV audience.

Aug. 24 – The Bills traveled to Kansas City for another Monday night exhibition and got trounced, 35-0. Quarterbacks and offensive tackles for both teams experimented with radio transmitters in their helmets aimed at helping communication in noisy stadiums.

Aug. 26 – Fullback Jamie Mueller, who missed all of 1991, was cut and said he planned to file a grievance because he felt the herniated disc in his back was a football-related injury while the Bills said it wasn't.

Aug. 28 – The Bills closed the preseason with an impressive 27-21 victory over the Falcons in the new Georgia Dome as Bruce Smith saw his first live action and came through feeling good.

Aug. 31 – Linebacker Cornelius Bennett ended his holdout when he was given a three-year deal worth a reported $2 million per year, making him the NFL's highest-paid defensive player. Veteran safety Dwight Drane was one of the final roster cuts.

Sept. 1 – Leon Seals was traded to Philadelphia for a 1993 draft choice, meaning that Phil Hansen

In his first year as a starter in 1992, Henry Jones intercepted eight passes and his 263 interception return yards were a new Bills record.

would be the starting left defensive end.

Sept. 2 – Keith McKeller and Kirby Jackson both ended their holdouts and signed two-year contracts.

Sept. 6 – The Bills opened the season with a 40-7 romp over the Los Angeles Rams, spoiling Chuck Knox's first game as Rams head coach. James Lofton caught six passes for 56 yards to become the all-time NFL leader in receiving yards, breaking Steve Largent's record of 13,089 yards. In his first NFL start, Henry Jones made two interceptions.

Sept. 8 – It was determined that tight end Keith McKeller would require surgery on his injured knee and would be out until at least midseason. Rob Awalt was signed to replace him.

Sept. 13 – It was one of the wildest shootouts in Bills history and when the dust settled at Candlestick Park, the Bills had earned a terrific 34-31 victory over the 49ers. For the first time in NFL history, there were no punts attempted in a game. "I thought Jackie Joyner-Kersee and Carl Lewis were going to come into the game before it was over," an excited Bill Polian said. "It looked like the four-by-100-meter relay."

Sept. 14 – Defensive coordinator Walt Corey reviewed the film of his defense's horrendous performance against the 49ers and he counted 24 missed tackles as the Bills allowed a record 598 yards. "The tackling was horrible," he said. "It's hard to believe from one week to the next how big a downfall there was."

Sept. 17 – Disappointed by slow progress in contract talks with the Bills, Jeff Wright spoke out. "I've given them my all, everything I've had, and they're treating me wrong," he said. "It's a matter of respect and they don't respect me."

Sept. 20 – In Ted Marchibroda's return to Buffalo as Colts head coach, his former team routed his new

team, 38-0, as Henry Jones returned two interceptions for touchdowns and the defense pitched its first shutout since 1990. It was the Bills largest regular-season margin of victory in Rich Stadium history.

Sept. 24 – Former Bills fullback Jamie Mueller officially filed a lawsuit against the team in State Supreme Court, alleging the team breached its contract when it placed him on waivers Aug. 26. Mueller said he was seeking the $275,000 his contract called for in 1992 plus moving expenses for him and his family to return to their permanent residence in Overland Park, Kansas. The Bills said they wouldn't bid on any of the four players who were made unrestricted free agents by Judge David Doty in Minneapolis. The players were Keith Jackson, Webster Slaughter, D.J. Dozier and Garin Veris.

Sept. 27 – The Bills scored 35 points in the second half and cruised to a 41-7 romp over New England at Foxboro Stadium as James Lofton scored two TDs and Andre Reed set a personal career-high with 168 yards receiving.

Sept. 28 – The Bills cut nose tackle Gary Baldinger and signed former Pittsburgh Steelers defensive end Keith Willis. The arch-rival Dolphins made a key move, signing unrestricted free agent tight end Keith Jackson. He was expected to see action against the Bills.

Oct. 4 – Keith Jackson made a dynamic Dolphins debut, scoring a touchdown during Miami's shocking 37-10 rout of the Bills at Rich Stadium. Louis Oliver intercepted three Jim Kelly passes and returned one of them 103 yards for a touchdown. It was the fifth-worst loss for the Bills at Rich.

Oct. 7 – Marv Levy, upset by his defensive backfield's play in the first five games, said: "I think we

have to make it a little less fun for the receivers to catch the ball."

Oct. 11 – The Bills suffered a second straight defeat for the first time since 1989 as the Raiders laid a 20-3 whipping on them at the Coliseum. In their last eight quarters, the Bills had only one TD, but had seven turnovers.

Oct. 19 – Almost one year after suffering a serious knee injury, offensive guard John Davis participated in his first full practice. Tight end Keith McKeller, injured in the season opener against the Rams, and wide receiver Don Beebe also practiced as the Bills got back to work after their bye week.

Oct. 21 – Marv Levy said he was surprised by the fans' reaction to the Bills' two-game losing streak. "Some of the fans impress me as if they might have been ready to surrender the day after Pearl Harbor," he said. "I was always a great fan and I felt bad when my team didn't win, but I never felt this almost anger when my team lost. I'm not a commenter on society, but it bothers me that this is a more pessimistic nation than it was 20 years ago. Regardless of how bad the fans are hurting, none of them are hurting close to what our players and coaching staff are."

Oct. 26 – The Bills returned from a long layoff a bit rusty, but pulled it together at the end and beat the Jets, 24-20, on Jim Kelly's TD pass to Thurman Thomas with 51 seconds left to play. It was their 10th straight win over New York and came on *Monday Night Football*. "It was a great win," Shane Conlan said. "If we had lost, we wouldn't have been able to show our faces in Buffalo."

Oct. 27 – During the Jets game, New York quarterback Browning Nagle inferred that Bruce Smith tried to hurt him during a first-quarter scuffle in which Nagle suffered a sprained left foot. "My conscience is clear," Smith said. "It was nothing illegal. I would never try to hurt anyone. That's the worst kind of player." Smith then said that he was the one who received the cheap shot when Jets offensive tackle Irv Eatman piled on top of him during the melee.

Nov. 1 – The Bills handed the Patriots their eighth straight loss, a 16-7 decision at Rich Stadium, after New England had claimed a 7-0 halftime lead.

Nov. 8 – The Bills managed 31 first downs, the second-most in team history. Thurman Thomas set a personal high with 37 carries and gained 155 yards in a 28-20 victory over Pittsburgh.

Nov. 10 – Thurman Thomas said he was misquoted in the recent issue of *Sport* magazine. In an interview with William Ladson, Thomas was quoted as saying that he was a prime target of the media because he's "Barry Bonds, Jose Canseco and Charles Barkley rolled into one. I'm the biggest hit in the NFL." Thomas responded by saying: "Sometimes I say a lot of crazy things, but I never said I was the biggest hit in the NFL."

Nov. 11 – Marv Levy said he hoped the NFL never adopted the two-point conversion. "The two-point rule would be cheap points," he said.

Nov. 16 – The Bills sacked Dan Marino four times and took over first place in the AFC East with an inspired 26-20 *Monday Night Football* victory at Joe Robbie Stadium.

Nov. 18 – The Bills asked Erie County for permission to build 22 new luxury boxes at the scoreboard end of Rich Stadium.

Nov. 22 – The Bills raced to a 35-0 lead in the first 16 minutes of the game and cruised to a 41-14 victory over Atlanta at Rich Stadium. Jim Ritcher became the team's all-time leader in games played with 198. Kenneth Davis ran for a career-high 181 yards.

Nov. 29 – Jack Trudeau passed for 337 yards and Charles Arbuckle caught nine passes for 106 yards as the Colts stunned the Bills in overtime at the Hoosier Dome, 16-13. At the Meadowlands, New York Jets defensive lineman Dennis Byrd was left paralyzed after colliding with teammate Scott Mersereau during the Jets loss to Kansas City.

Nov. 30 – The Bills reacted to Dennis Byrd's situation with sympathy and compassion. "No matter who it happens to around the league, whether it's your worst rival and bitter enemy, everybody's heart goes out to the guy because it's a league-wide ripple effect," Steve Tasker said. "Everybody in the league feels for him and says a prayer."

Dec. 6 – Brian Washington returned a Jim Kelly interception 23 yards for the game-winning touchdown with 1:41 left as the Jets capped an emotionally-charged week with a shocking 24-17 upset of the Bills at Rich Stadium, snapping their 10-game losing streak to Buffalo. Paralyzed Dennis Byrd told his teammates "My eyes will be on every one of you in the fourth quarter." Said Jets defensive end Marvin Washington: "I wish Dennis were here actually playing so he could have the feeling we have beating Buffalo."

Dec. 12 – The Bills snapped their two-game losing streak with a solid 27-17 victory over Denver at Rich Stadium. The team honored its fans by putting the 12th Man on the wall of the administration building. Mark Kelso had a team-record-tying three interceptions and Marv Levy became the all-time leader in coaching victories for a Bills coach.

Dec. 15 – It was revealed that Bruce Smith had suffered a cracked rib against the Broncos and it appeared doubtful he could play against the Saints in New Orleans.

Dec. 16 – Andre Reed, who had seen his pass catching production drop dramatically throughout the season, expressed concern over not seeing the ball. "It's very frustrating," he said. "It's ridiculous. I'm the kind of guy, I don't say much, but when it's this obvious, my pride is hurt."

Dec. 20 – The Bills turned in a gutty performance and rallied to defeat New Orleans at the Superdome, 20-16. Thurman Thomas rushed for 115 yards and the defense, playing without Bruce Smith, limited the Saints to 28 yards and two first downs in the second half.

Dec. 23 – Nine Bills were selected to play in the Pro Bowl. Chosen to start were Thurman Thomas, Bruce Smith, Howard Ballard, Henry Jones and Steve Tasker while Jim Kelly, Andre Reed, Cornelius Bennett and Will Wolford were selected as reserves.

Dec. 24 – A Houston victory over the Bills in the season finale would mean the Oilers might have to come back to Buffalo the following week to play in the wild-card game. This didn't appear to concern Houston receiver Ernest Givins who said: "We're going to kick Buffalo's ass here, and if we have to, we'll go up there and kick their ass. Everyone's going to know that after we beat Buffalo twice that the Houston Oilers are for real."

Dec. 27 – The Bills were crushed by the Oilers, 27-3, thus costing them their fifth straight AFC East title and home-field advantage throughout the playoffs. Miami won the AFC East based on its better record against AFC foes (9-3 compared to 7-5 for the Bills). In the process, Jim Kelly suffered a right

knee injury and his status for the playoffs was in doubt.

Dec. 28 – Tests on Jim Kelly's injured knee revealed a sprain and the Bills ruled him out of the playoff opener against Houston.

Jan. 2, 1993 – San Diego blanked Kansas City, 17-0, and Washington ripped Minnesota, 24-7, on the first day of wild-card play.

Jan. 3, 1993 – The Bills pulled off the greatest comeback in NFL history as they rallied from a 35-3 deficit 1:41 into the third quarter and defeated the Oilers, 41-38, in overtime, in an AFC wild-card game at Rich Stadium. "This is one in a lifetime," Ralph Wilson said. "Naturally when you're down by as much as we were, you just hope you score a couple times and make it respectable. You never expect a team to come back the way the Bills did today. Anybody who does is dreaming." The Bills performed this miracle without Jim Kelly or Cornelius Bennett, and Thurman Thomas missed the second half with a hip pointer. Frank Reich threw for 289 yards and four TDs including three in a row to Andre Reed in a span of 16:33 before Steve Christie kicked the winning field goal 3:06 into overtime. In New Orleans, Philadelphia scored 26 fourth-quarter points and overcame the Saints, 36-20, in the other NFC wild-card game. The Saints remained the only team in the NFL that never had won a playoff game.

Jan. 4, 1993 – Frank Reich, after a day of reflection, still couldn't believe what he had done the day before. "I guess there have been a couple of times when my wife and I would look at each other and say 'Did that really happen?'" he said. "We just kind of shake our heads in awe of the game."

Jan. 6, 1993 – The NFL and lawyers for the players reached settlements on various lawsuits and agreed to a seven-year collective bargaining agreement that included unrestricted free agency and a salary cap. The league had not had a labor agreement since 1987.

Jan. 9, 1993 – Bills traveled to Pittsburgh for a divisional round game, their first road playoff game since the 1989 season, and thrashed the Steelers, 24-3. Buffalo did not turn the ball over while the Steelers lost it three times. Frank Reich wasn't heroic, but he didn't have to be. The Bills' victory snapped a streak of 15 straight playoff games in the AFC that had been won by the home team dating back to 1989. In San Francisco, the 49ers prevented Washington from defending its Super Bowl title by eliminating the Redskins, 20-13.

Jan. 10, 1993 – Dallas crushed Philadelphia, 34-10, and Miami routed San Diego, 31-0, on the second day of divisional round playoffs.

Jan. 11, 1993 – Jim Kelly said he would be able to play in the AFC Championship Game against the Dolphins in Miami. "Without a doubt, I'm taking the approach that I'm playing," Kelly said.

Jan. 17, 1993 – The Bills strutted into Joe Robbie Stadium, where they had had so much success, and mauled the Dolphins, 29-10, to win the AFC Championship Game and advance to their third straight Super Bowl. Jim Kelly returned to action and threw for 177 yards, Thurman Thomas rushed for 96 yards, Steve Christie kicked an NFL playoff record-tying five field goals and the defense forced five Miami turnovers. At San Francisco, the Dallas Cowboys won the NFC Championship Game with a 30-20 victory over the 49ers as Troy Aikman passed for 322 yards and two TDs.

Jan. 19, 1993 – In an effort to turn off the rumor

mill, the Dallas Cowboys allowed defensive coordinator Dave Wannstedt to sign a contract to become the head coach of the Chicago Bears after the Super Bowl. "It was inevitable that he would become the head coach and when it became obvious, I wanted it done," Cowboys coach Jimmy Johnson explained.

Jan. 20, 1993 – The Bills seemed to relish their role as seven-point underdogs to the young Cowboys. "We've had to go the hard road all through the playoffs, so it will be even sweeter if we win it that way as underdogs," said Jeff Wright.

Jan. 24, 1993 – The Bills arrived in Los Angeles to begin Super Bowl XXVII preparations. Players revealed that Marv Levy had warned them to avoid controversies when speaking to the media as to prevent the type of circus atmosphere that permeated their visit to Minneapolis for last year's Super Bowl.

Jan. 25, 1993 – The Bills held their first practice at USC and Nate Odomes learned that he had been added to the AFC Pro Bowl team because San Diego's Gill Byrd had to pull out with an injury.

Jan. 26, 1993 – Media Day at Dodger Stadium was held and Thurman Thomas confronted the horde of questions about his missing helmet from last year's Super Bowl head on and with a sense of humor. "I have to look at it with a sense of humor," he said. "I think it's wrong, but people will judge me on the helmet thing the rest of my career. I don't think it's fair, but there's nothing I can do about it."

Jan. 27, 1993 – A report circulated that Darryl Talley had gotten into a fight with Magic Johnson's bodyguard, Anthony Pitts, at the posh Los Angeles nightclub, The Roxbury Cafe. Talley said "nothing really happened." Several Cowboys players claimed they witnessed the fight. Said affable guard Nate Newton: "The music was loud, the ladies was flirtin' and everybody was having a good time. It all happened so fast. Some saw blood, some didn't."

Jan. 28, 1993 – Thurman Thomas was the featured podium speaker during the Bills' media session at their Los Angeles hotel, and he came armed with miniature Bills helmets to pass out to reporters, making light of his helmet caper from the year before.

Jan. 31, 1993 – The Bills became the first team in NFL history to lose three Super Bowls in a row, and they did it in humiliating fashion, turning the ball over nine times in a 52-17 loss to the Cowboys in front of 98,374 at the Rose Bowl and a worldwide TV audience including more than 133 million in the U.S. alone. That made it the 10th most-watched televised sporting event in history. Jim Kelly reinjured his knee in the second quarter and left the game with the Bills trailing 14-7. Shortly thereafter, Buffalo collapsed and Dallas pounced on the opportunity to turn the game into a rout. "I'm not going to go outside and slit my throat," Ralph Wilson said. "We had an enjoyable season. We overcame a lot of things. This wasn't fun to watch, but these things happen in football. The better team won. That's life."

Feb. 7, 1993 – Steve Tasker blocked a field goal, recovered a fumble and made four special teams tackles to earn the MVP award as the AFC won the Pro Bowl, 23-20, in overtime. Nick Lowery of Kansas City kicked the winning field goal.

445

BY THE NUMBERS - 1992

TEAM STATISTICS	BILLS	OPP
First downs	350	278
Rushing	133	77
Passing	192	185
Penalty	25	16
Third downs	80-202	84-218
Fourth downs	4-10	7-14
Avg. time of poss	28:10	31:50
Total yards	5,893	4,604
Avg. game	368.3	287.8
Plays	1,087	991
Avg. play	5.4	4.6
Net rushing yds	2,436	1,395
Avg. game	152.3	87.2
Avg. play	4.4	3.3
Net passing yds	3,457	3,209
Comp/att	293/509	305/520
Sacks/lost	29-221	44-351
Interceptions	21	23
Percentage	57.6	58.7
Punts/avg	60-42.2	79-43.9
Fumbles/lost	31-17	29-12
Penalties/yds	103-775	118-933
Touchdowns	44	31
Extra points	43-44	31-31
Field goals	24-30	22-30
Safeties	1	0
Kick ret./avg	41-18.6	60-20.3
Punt ret./avg	43-10.8	22-8.4

RUSHING	ATT	YDS	AVG	TD
Thomas	312	1487	4.8	9
Davis	139	613	4.4	6
Gardner	40	166	4.2	2
Reed	8	65	8.1	0
Kelly	31	53	1.7	1
Fuller	6	39	6.5	0
Mohr	1	11	11.0	0
Tasker	1	9	9.0	0
Edwards	1	8	8.0	0
Beebe	1	-6	-6.0	0
Reich	9	-9	-1.0	0
TOTALS	**549**	**2436**	**4.4**	**18**

RECEIVING	CAT	YDS	AVG	TD
Reed	65	913	14.0	3
Thomas	58	626	10.8	3
Lofton	51	786	15.4	6
Beebe	33	554	16.8	2
Metzelaars	30	298	9.9	6
K. Davis	15	80	5.3	0
McKeller	14	110	7.9	0
Lamb	7	139	19.9	0
Gardner	7	67	9.6	0
Awalt	4	34	8.5	0
Edwards	2	25	12.5	0
Tasker	2	24	12.0	0
Fuller	2	17	8.5	0
Frerotte	2	4	2.0	2
Fina	1	1	1.0	1
TOTALS	**293**	**3678**	**12.6**	**23**

PASSING	COMP	ATT	INT	YDS	TD	COMP%	SACKS	RATE
Kelly	269	462	19	3457	23	58.2	20-145	81.2
Reich	24	47	2	221	0	51.1	9-76	46.5
TOTALS	**293**	**509**	**21**	**3678**	**23**	**57.6**	**29-221**	**78.0**

KICKING	1-19	20-29	30-39	40-49	50+	TOT	PAT	PTS
Christie	2-2	9-9	3-6	7-8	3-5	24-30	43-44	115

PUNTING	NO	AVG	LG	In 20	BL
Mohr	60	42.2	61	13	0

SCORE BY QUARTERS

BILLS	77	118	105	81	0	-	381
OPP	46	101	72	61	3	-	283

DEFENSIVE STATISTICAL LEADERS

TACKLES: Talley 73 primary - 33 assists - 106 total; Jones 75-17-92, B. Smith 66-23-89, Conlan 61-21-82, Bennett 61-20-81, Wright 51-19-70, Bailey 44-21-65, Hansen 47-17-64, Odomes 53-10-63, Jackson 42-6-48, Williams 37-2-39, Kelso 24-13-37, M. Patton 20-5-25, Maddox 17-7-24

SACKS: B. Smith 14, Hansen 8, Wright 5.5, Talley 4, Bennett 4, M. Patton 2, Conlan 2

FUMBLE RECOVERIES: Bennett 3, Jones 2, Wright 1, Lodish 1, Schulz 1, Odomes 1

FORCED FUMBLES: B. Smith 3, Talley 2, Jones 2, Bennett 2

INTERCEPTIONS: Jones 8-263 yards, 32.9 avg., 2 TD; Kelso 7-21, 3.0, 0 TD; Odomes 5-19, 3.8, 0 TD

SPECIAL TEAMS STATISTICAL LEADERS

KICKOFF RETURNS: Edwards 12-274 yards, 22.8 avg., 0 TD; K. Davis 14-251, 17.9, 0 TD

PUNT RETURNS: Hicks 29-289, 10.0, 0 TD; Hale 14-175, 12.5, 0 TD

TACKLES: Pike 26, Maddox 19, Tasker 19, Gardner 16, Hale 16, M. Patton 13, Harvey 8, Hicks 8, Darby 7, Schulz 6, Williams 5, Goganious 5, K. Davis 4, Fina 4, Lingner 4

GAME 1 - Sunday, Sept. 6, 1992 - BILLS 40, RAMS 7

NOTES

• Thurman Thomas became the sixth Bill in team history to score four TDs in one game as the Bills rolled.
• James Lofton became the all-time NFL receiving yardage leader, breaking Steve Largent's record of 13,089.
• Chuck Knox, starting his second term as Rams coach, suffered his worst NFL loss.
• Bruce Smith showed he was back in shape with two sacks, seven tackles and two batted-down passes.
• TE Keith McKeller, who had just signed a new contract earlier in the week, suffered a knee injury.
• Magic Johnson was on hand for the game and spent time on the Bills sideline and in the locker room afterward.
• The Bills took the lead on the second possession of the game, driving 55 yards in nine plays to Jim Kelly's third-and-10 TD pass to Thomas. After a Los Angeles punt, the Bills drove 57 yards to Thomas' second TD.
• Early in the second quarter, Henry Jones, making his first NFL start at strong safety, intercepted a Jim Everett pass and returned it 67 yards to the Rams 8. Thomas scored on the first play, but a holding penalty wiped it out. Two plays later, he scored again.
• Later in the second quarter, Kelly was intercepted by Anthony Newman at the Bills 12. One play later, Everett hit Robert Delpino for the Rams' only score. The Bills got that back seven plays after the kickoff as Kelly hit offensive lineman Mitch Frerotte with a two-yard TD pass for a 27-7 halftime lead.
• Nate Odomes' second interception of the day on the second play of the third led to Thomas' fourth TD on a third-and-nine play.
• Jones' second pick late in the third set up Steve Christie's first field goal as a Bill early in the fourth.

• Christie later capped a 45-yard drive with a 38-yarder.

QUOTES

• Jim Kelly, referring sarcastically to doubters who said the Bills would falter after their second straight Super Bowl loss: "I'm sure there are a few people who are disappointed that the Buffalo Bills won the way we did because there are some people out there who were saying we were going to crumble. We have too many great athletes on this team to roll over."
• Rams head coach Chuck Knox: "We fought hard, but we just weren't good enough."
• Marv Levy on Thurman Thomas: "It was the usual, Thurman had another outstanding day. It was a vintage Thurman Thomas performance."
• James Lofton on setting the record: "Words really can't describe it. I'm really happy, it was neat to get it and to get it in front of this crowd in the home opener was fantastic. I had about 100 people come into town for the game, friends from elementary school, high school, college, former teammates from college, from the Packers and Raiders, friends and relatives. I'm sitting there thinking I can't pay for all these people to go to San Francisco (next week)."

WEEK 1 GAMES	
Chi 27, Det 24	KC 24, SD 10
Phil 15, NO 13	Atl 20, NYJ 17
TB 23, Phoe 7	Pitt 29, Hou 24
SF 31, NYG 14	Den 17, LAR 13
Dal 23, Wash 10	Min 23, GB 20 OT
Cinc 21, Sea 3	Ind 14, Clev 3
NE at Mia, ppd (hurricane)	

Rams	0	7	0	0	-	7
Bills	14	13	7	6	-	40

Attendance at Rich Stadium - 79,001

Buf: Thomas 10 pass from Kelly (Christie kick), 7:25
Buf: Thomas 1 run (Christie kick), 13:39
Buf: Thomas 6 run (Christie kick), 3:56
LA: Delpino 12 pass from Everett (Zendejas kick), 11:54
Buf: Frerotte 2 pass from Kelly (kick failed), 14:31
Buf: Thomas 10 run (Christie kick), 3:08
Buf: FG Christie 49, 1:19
Buf: FG Christie 38, 8:38

	BUF	LA
First downs	23	15
Rushing yds	207	66
Passing yds	156	149
Punts-avg	4-42.3	6-42.5
Fumbles-lost	2-0	2-0
Penalties-yds	12-75	7-60
Poss. time	29:49	30:11

BILLS LEADERS: **Rushing** - Thomas 22-103, K. Davis 5-44, Gardner 5-36, Reed 1-24, Kelly 1-0; **Passing** - Kelly 13-19-1 - 106, Reich 6-11-0 - 59; **Receiving** - Lofton 6-56, Thomas 3-33, Metzelaars 1-5, Beebe 1-6, K. Davis 2-13, Reed 2-29, McKeller 1-8, Frerotte 1-2, Gardner 2-13.

RAMS LEADERS: **Rushing** - Gary 9-24, Delpino 9-30, Stradford 3-12, Pagel 1-0; **Passing** - Everett 18-35-4 - 160, Pagel 1-3-0 - 10; **Receiving** - Delpino 5-46, Cox 2-25, Anderson 3-30, Ellard 2-8, Price 3-26, Chadwick 1-7, Gary 3-28.

GAME 2 - Sunday, Sept. 13, 1992 - BILLS 34, 49ERS 31

NOTES

• The Bills produced a huge victory in one of the wildest NFL games ever. The teams combined for 1,086 yards of offense, a new record for a Bills game and it was the fourth-highest total in NFL history.
• For the first time in NFL history, no punts were attempted by either team.
• In setting a new regular-season career high for passing yards in a single game, Jim Kelly became the first Bills QB to top 400 yards. Kelly also surpassed 20,000 yards passing for his career.
• Steve Young also threw for more than 400, making it the third game in history where two QBs topped 400.
• The 49ers' 598 yards offense were a team record and were the most ever allowed by the Bills. San Francisco did it for the most part without Jerry Rice, who was injured in the first quarter.
• The Bills opened in a four-receiver set, giving Steve Tasker his first NFL start.
• Tim Harris' recovery of a Kelly fumble in the first quarter led to Young's TD pass to Odessa Turner. That started a scoring frenzy in which the teams scored on eight straight possessions.
• The Bills got a Steve Christie field goal, but the 49ers went 80 yards to Tom Rathman's TD run.
• The Bills drove 73 yards to Kelly's TD pass to Thurman Thomas. Thomas had made a 24-yard catch on third-and-10. Mike Cofer and Christie traded field goals, and the 49ers closed the half by driving 80 yards in seven plays to John Taylor's TD reception with 11 seconds left.
• The Bills took the second-half kickoff and marched 80 yards in five plays with Pete Metzelaars catching a 53-yard TD pass, the longest of his career. Bruce Smith then forced Keith Henderson to fumble and Cornelius Bennett recovered at the Bills 40. Kelly hit Metzelaars for a TD five plays later for a 27-24 lead.
• The teams traded fumbles before Young hit Taylor with a 54-yard TD pass to regain the lead late in the third.

• After an exchange of interceptions, Kelly drove the Bills 72 yards in 12 plays to Thomas' winning TD run. On the play before, Kelly hit James Lofton for eight on fourth-and-four.
• Cofer missed a 47-yard tying field goal attempt with 54 seconds left.

QUOTES

• Thurman Thomas: "People say we don't play well on the road and that we don't play well on grass, but we won. This was great. One of the best wins we've had since I've been here."
• Nate Odomes: "You saw two of the finest offensive teams on the field today, and two not very good defensive teams."
• Darryl Talley: "I think both teams were a little delirious. It's a shame anyone has to come out on the losing end because both teams laid it out today."

WEEK 2 GAMES	
Wash 24, Atl 17	NO 28, Chi 6
Dal 34, NYG 28	TB 31, GB 3
Hou 20, Ind 10	Det 31, Minn 17
Rams 14, NE 0	Pitt 27, NYJ 10
Den 21, SD 13	KC 26, Sea 7
Phil 31, Phoe 14	Mia 27, Clev 23
Cinc 24, LAR 21 (OT)	

Bills	3	10	14	7	-	34
49ers	7	17	7	0	-	31

Attendance at Candlestick Park - 64,053

SF: Turner 23 pass from Young (Cofer kick), 11:34
Buf: FG Christie 41, 14:42
SF: Rathman 2 run (Cofer kick), 3:17
Buf: Thomas 20 pass from Kelly (Christie kick), 5:25
SF: FG Cofer 24, 8:07
Buf: FG Christie 28, 12:29
SF: Taylor 7 pass from Young (Cofer kick), 14:49
Buf: Metzelaars 53 pass from Kelly (Christie kick), 2:27
Buf: Metzelaars 24 pass from Kelly (Christie kick), 8:09
SF: Taylor 54 pass from Young (Cofer kick), 14:54
Buf: Thomas 11 run (Christie kick), 11:56

	BUF	SF
First downs	25	26
Rushing yds	107	159
Passing yds	381	439
Punts-avg	0-0	0-0
Fumbles-lost	2-2	4-2
Penalties-yds	2-10	5-51
Poss. time	26:22	33:38

BILLS LEADERS: **Rushing** - Thomas 19-85, K. Davis 5-11, Kelly 7-8, Fuller 1-3, Gardner 1-0; **Passing** - Kelly 22-33-1 - 403; **Receiving** - Reed 10-144, Metzelaars 4-113, Thomas 4-94, Lofton 3-39, Beebe 1-13.

49ERS LEADERS: **Rushing** - Watters 16-83, Young 7-50, Rathman 5-20, Henderson 2-6; **Passing** - Young 26-37-1 - 449; **Receiving** - Sherrard 6-159, Taylor 5-112, Rice 3-26, Rathman 5-37, Watters 4-22, Turner 2-80, Williams 1-13.

STANDINGS: SECOND WEEK

AFC EAST	W	L	T	CENTRAL	W	L	T	WEST	W	L	T	NFC EAST	W	L	T	CENTRAL	W	L	T	WEST	W	L	T
Buffalo	2	0	0	Cincinnati	2	0	0	Denver	2	0	0	Dallas	2	0	0	Tampa Bay	2	0	0	N.Orleans	1	1	0
Miami	1	0	0	Pittsburgh	2	0	0	Kan. City	2	0	0	Philadelphia	2	0	0	Chicago	1	1	0	Atlanta	1	1	0
Indianapolis	1	1	0	Houston	1	1	0	Raiders	0	2	0	Washington	1	1	0	Minnesota	1	1	0	San Fran	1	1	0
New England	0	1	0	Cleveland	0	2	0	Seattle	0	2	0	NY Giants	0	2	0	Detroit	1	1	0	LA Rams	1	1	0
NY Jets	0	2	0					San Diego	0	2	0	Phoenix	0	2	0	Green Bay	0	2	0				

447

Colts	0	0	0	0 -	0
Bills	7	3	14	14 -	38

Attendance at Rich Stadium - 77,781

Buf: Metzelaars 1 pass from Kelly (Christie kick), 14:27
Buf: FG Christie 52, 14:41
Buf: Gardner 1 run (Christie kick), 4:38
Buf: Jones 23 interception return (Christie kick), 7:43
Buf: Fina 1 pass from Kelly (Christie kick), 3:28
Buf: Jones 82 interception return (Christie kick), 9:25

	BUF	IND
First downs	24	9
Rushing yds	169	37
Passing yds	211	103
Punts-avg	3-34.7	8-50.0
Fumbles-lost	3-2	4-0
Penalties-yds	7-44	11-82
Poss. time	30:48	29:12

BILLS LEADERS: Rushing - Thomas 14-42, K. Davis 12-64, Kelly 2-3, Gardner 5-19, Reed 2-17, Fuller 3-27, Reich 3-(-3); **Passing** - Kelly 17-27-0 - 211; **Receiving** - Reed 5-77, Metzelaars 6-53, Thomas 2-29, K. Davis 1-15, Lamb 2-36, Fina 1-1.
COLTS LEADERS: Rushing - Culver 14-14, Johnson 5-13, Tupa 2-10, Trudeau 3-0; **Passing** - Trudeau 6-14-2 - 78, Tupa 7-12-1 - 64; **Receiving** - Cash 3-37, Brooks 2-20, Hester 3-42, Culver 2-12, Johnson 3-31.

WEEK 3 GAMES

GB 24, Cinc 23	Clev 28, LAR 16
Phil 30, Den 0	Wash 13, Det 10
Mia 26, Rams 10	NO 10, Atl 7
Dal 31, Phoe 20	Pitt 23, SD 6
SF 31, NYJ 14	Sea 10, NE 6
Minn 26, TB 20	NYG 27, Chi 14
Hou 23, KC 20 (OT)	

NOTES

• The Bills posted the largest regular-season margin of victory in Rich Stadium history.
• It was their first shutout since a 42-0 pounding of Cleveland and the margin of victory ranked second only to that game all-time.
• Henry Jones became the first Bill to return two interceptions for TDs in the same game.
• Bruce Smith had 11 tackles, three sacks and two pressures, though Jeff George didn't play.
• Thurman Thomas lost a fumble on the Bills' first series, but Dean Biasucci missed a field goal. The Bills then drove 69 yards in 11 plays to Pete Metzelaars' TD reception. Thomas caught a 17-yard pass on third-and-13 from the Bills 42.
• Steve Christie missed a 39-yard field goal after a J.D. Williams interception, but Christie made a team-record-tying 52-yarder late in the half.
• The Bills took the second-half kickoff and drove 77 yards in 10 plays to Carwell Gardner's TD.
• After an exchange of punts, Jack Trudeau's pass deflected off Rodney Culver's hands and Jones intercepted and ran 23 yards for the TD to make it 24-0.
• Following a punt, the Bills drove 78 yards in 12 plays to John Fina's first NFL TD on a tackle-eligible play. Jones then made his second interception and returned it 82 yards for a TD.

QUOTES

• Marv Levy on Bruce Smith: "That's just Bruce. Dr. (Richard) Steadman told me 'Don't expect him to be what he was for four or five weeks.' Well, I can hardly wait. I think maybe we forget how he was (before his knee injury). That's the way he plays." (On the defense): "I think our defense was a bit embarrassed by the fact their tackling was so shoddy in the 49ers game. They were determined to go out and play a strong game. They gave the offense a chance to fail on a series or two until it got going."
• Colts tackle Zefross Moss on Smith: "He's the greatest defensive linemen to ever play the game."
• Shane Conlan on Smith: "He makes our job so boring. Both Carlton (Bailey) and I and Cornelius (Bennett) were making some great reads and we'd come in thinking we were going to make a big play and he's already got the guy. He's incredible, he was going right by them. (Colts center) Ray Donaldson was just shaking his head smiling and I said, 'He does that to everybody.'"
• Henry Jones: "I feel good about it, but it's only the third game of the season."

Bills	3	3	21	14 -	41
Patriots	0	0	0	7 -	7

Attendance at Foxboro Stadium - 52,527

Buf: FG Christie 42, 12:54
Buf: FG Christie 30, 13:06
Buf: Lofton 29 pass from Kelly (Christie kick), 3:55
Buf: Thomas 1 run (Christie kick), 8:56
Buf: Reed 45 pass from Kelly (Christie kick), 12:13
Buf: Lofton 22 pass from Kelly (Christie kick), 1:13
Buf: Lodish 18 fumble return (Christie kick), 1:57
NE: Cook 4 pass from Millen (Baumann kick), 6:19

	BUF	NE
First downs	23	16
Rushing yds	182	69
Passing yds	308	196
Punts-avg	1-39.0	4-43.5
Fumbles-lost	2-1	2-2
Penalties-yds	6-43	11-75
Poss. time	30:01	29:59

BILLS LEADERS: Rushing - Thomas 18-120, K. Davis 10-39, Kelly 1-1, Gardner 5-17, Fuller 2-9, Reich 4-(-4); **Passing** - Kelly 15-20-0 - 308; **Receiving** - Reed 9-168, Lofton 4-113, Thomas 2-27.
PATRIOTS LEADERS: Rushing - Russell 18-59, Millen 5-13, Vaughn 1-0, Stephens 1-(-3); **Passing** - Millen 24-33-1 - 202; **Receiving** - McMurtry 7-69, Coates 4-31, Cook 7-60, Stephens 1-9, Fryar 3-29, Timpson 1-7, Russell 1-(-3).

NOTES

• The Bills improved to 4-0. Their 153 points were the most in team history during the first four games.
• Andre Reed set a career-high for receiving yards in one game and Reed and James Lofton became the 10th Bills tandem to have 100-yard receiving games in the same game.
• On the first possession, the Bills converted three third-downs and drove 72 yards in 15 plays to Steve Christie's first field goal.
• In the second quarter, Darryl Talley stopped Leonard Russell on fourth-and-one at the Bills 25. On the next play, Thurman Thomas broke a 31-yard run, then Jim Kelly hit Reed for 27. The Pats stiffened and forced a field goal.
• The Bills took the second-half kickoff and drove 84 yards in eight plays to Lofton's first TD.
• The Pats went three-and-out and after the punt, the Bills moved 68 yards in six plays to Thomas' TD run. The key play was Lofton's 50-yard reception over Maurice Hurst to the Pats 4.
• The Pats again went three-and-out and five plays after a punt, Reed caught a 45-yard TD.
• Late in the third, Mark Kelso intercepted Hugh Millen at the Pats 41. Five plays later, Lofton caught his second

WEEK 4 GAMES

Minn 42, Cinc 7	Rams 18, NYJ 10
GB 17, Pitt 3	Hou 27, SD 0
TB 27, Det 23	SF 16, NO 10
KC 27, LAR 7	Den 12, Clev 0
Chi 41, Atl 31	Mia 19, Sea 17
Phil, Dal, Wash, NYG, Phoe, Ind had bye weeks	

TD. Two plays after the kickoff, Millen fumbled a shot-gun snap and Mike Lodish picked it up and ran for his first NFL TD.
• The Pats broke the shutout with an 11-play, 80-yard drive to Millen's TD pass to Marv Cook.

QUOTES

• Will Wolford: "If we did have a phobia about New England, I hope it's buried now."
• Jim Shofner: "I think Jim (Kelly) was outstanding today. He was very accurate with his passes, he took what they gave us. Then we got them on the run, forcing them to take some gambles and that's how we got some big plays."
• Jim Kelly: "The good thing about myself this week is I totally blocked out of my mind that we were playing the Patriots and I said it was just another game on our schedule. You start getting into what has happened in the past and you'll take one step back. This is one where I concentrated on the game at hand. The things that usually kill us are mistakes and turnovers and we did a good job on that today. You have to be patient against everybody. Teams know about our offense and are going to come after us, but sooner or later we're going to put it in the end zone. I have to say great things about the offensive line. No sacks, they gave me time to complete those big ones, plus Thurman was over 100 yards."
• Kent Hull on the slow start: "We had the ball three times in the first half and we had two field goals and a turnover. And we weren't too happy we had to kick those field goals."
• Patriots nose tackle Fred Smerlas: "The first half we controlled the game, but we didn't put any points on the board. The only way to beat them is to establish your running game and keep their offense off the field."

STANDINGS: FOURTH WEEK

AFC EAST	W	L	T	CENTRAL	W	L	T	WEST	W	L	T	NFC EAST	W	L	T	CENTRAL	W	L	T	WEST	W	L	T
Buffalo	4	0	0	Pittsburgh	3	1	0	Denver	3	1	0	Dallas	3	0	0	Tampa Bay	3	1	0	San Fran	3	1	0
Miami	3	0	0	Houston	3	1	0	Kan. City	3	1	0	Philadelphia	3	0	0	Minnesota	3	1	0	N.Orleans	2	2	0
Indianapolis	1	2	0	Cincinnati	2	2	0	Seattle	1	3	0	Washington	2	1	0	Chicago	2	2	0	LA Rams	2	2	0
New England	0	3	0	Cleveland	1	3	0	Raiders	0	4	0	NY Giants	1	2	0	Green Bay	2	2	0	Atlanta	1	3	0
NY Jets	0	4	0					San Diego	0	4	0	Phoenix	0	3	0	Detroit	1	3	0				

NOTES

• For the first time in 36 in-season weeks, the Bills were not in first, or sharing first, in the AFC East.

• The loss was the fifth-worst all-time for the Bills at Rich Stadium and came in front of a new record crowd.

• All-Pro tight end Keith Jackson made his Miami debut after signing as a free agent earlier in the week and he contributed a TD. On defense, safety Louis Oliver had three interceptions and had an NFL record-tying 103-yard interception return for a TD in Miami's first win at Rich since 1986.

• The teams traded punts on the first two possessions, with Clifford Hicks returning Miami's punt 22 yards to the Bills 48. The Bills then drove 30 yards in six plays to a Steve Christie field goal.

• Pete Stoyanovich capped a 66-yard drive on the ensuing possession with the tying field goal.

• In the second quarter, Oliver's first interception at the Bills 38 set up Dan Marino's TD pass to Jackson.

• On the next series, J.B. Brown intercepted Kelly and returned it 48 yards to the Bills 34 setting up Marino's TD pass to Tony Paige. The Bills answered with a superb two-minute drill, moving 80 yards in 10 plays in just 1:10 before Kelly hit Andre Reed for a TD on a third-and-10 play to make it 17-10.

• Miami regained control by taking the second-half kickoff and driving 82 yards in 13 plays to Bobby Humphrey's TD. Marino converted on third-and-19, third-and-10 and the TD came on third-and-nine.

• The Bills drove to the Miami 5, but on third-and-goal, Oliver stepped in front of Thurman Thomas and ran down the left sideline all the way to the end zone for the game-breaking touchdown.

• Stoyanovich tacked on two more field goals, the second coming after Thomas' fumble.

QUOTES

• Darryl Talley: "Mama said there'd be days like these."

• Kent Hull: "We've been here before. A couple years ago we took a pretty good thrashing in Miami. That was a wakeup call for this team. I won't say we were complacent or arrogant about today. This football team knows it's good. It's a veteran team that knows how to respond. I think we'll respond."

• Miami receiver Mark Clayton on teasing the fans: "Oh boy, I had a ball with them. Those are the same fans who have been there the last six years giving it to me and it was my turn to give it back to them. I had a blast. It's been a long time coming."

• Miami coach Don Shula: "Louis Oliver, needless to say, got the game ball defensively."

• Jim Kelly: "What can you say? When you play a game like today, there's no excuses. We got our butts kicked. You have to look at this as just one defeat. We're still 4-1 and there are many more games to go. I'm not going to crawl into my shell, I'm going to come back and keep firing at them."

WEEK 5 GAMES	
Minn 21, Chi 20	Atl 24, GB 10
Ind 24, TB 14	Den 20, KC 19
SF 27, Rams 24	NO 13, Det 7
LAR 13, NYG 10	SD 17, Sea 6
Phoe 27, Wash 21	NYJ 30, NE 21
Phil 31, Dal 7	
Cinc, Clev, Pitt, Hou had bye weeks	

Dolphins	3 14 17 3 - 37
Bills	3 7 0 0 - 10

Attendance at Rich Stadium - 80,368

Buf: FG Christie 40, 10:08
Mia: FG Stoyanovich 30, 15:00
Mia: Jackson 24 pass from Marino (Stoyanovich kick), 7:21
Mia: Paige 5 pass from Marino (Stoyanovich kick), 13:05
Buf: Reed 16 pass from Kelly (Christie kick), 14:15
Mia: Humphrey 9 pass from Marino (Stoyanovich kick), 5:37
Mia: Oliver 103 interception return (Stoyanovich kick), 10:22
Mia: FG Stoyanovich 43, 14:06
Mia: FG Stoyanovich 34, 5:41

	BUF	MIA
First downs	26	20
Rushing yds	63	80
Passing yds	337	282
Punts-avg	4-40.0	4-36.3
Fumbles-lost	2-1	0-0
Penalties-yds	4-35	11-80
Poss. time	27:53	32:07

BILLS LEADERS: Rushing - Thomas 11-33, Gardner 2-5, K. Davis 6-19, Tasker 1-9, Kelly 1-4, Reed 1-(-7); **Passing** - Kelly 25-48-4 - 306, Reich 6-10-0 - 59; **Receiving** - Reed 6-94, Metzelaars 2-14, Lofton 6-84, Thomas 9-83, Lamb 3-39, Awalt 4-34, Tasker 1-17.

DOLPHINS LEADERS: Rushing - Higgs 15-37, Humphrey 4-22, Saxon 1-0, Marino 2-13, Craver 3-9, Mitchell 1-(-1); **Passing** - Marino 21-33-1 - 282; **Receiving** - Paige 3-35, Humphrey 6-72, Clayton 4-56, Jackson 4-64, Banks 1-6, Martin 2-47, Duper 1-2.

NOTES

• The Bills lost their second in a row, their first two-game losing streak since 1989.

• Jim Kelly became the first Bills QB to throw for 300 yards in three straight games and Andre Reed went over 7,000 career receiving yards.

• Los Angeles drove to the Bills 13 on the first possession, but Henry Jones killed the threat with an interception.

• The Bills missed Kent Hull who played the first series, then had to come out because of a sore hamstring.

• The Bills punted and Los Angeles then drove 50 yards in six plays to Todd Marinovich's TD pass to Eric Dickerson. The key play was Willie Gault's 31-yard reception to the Bills 8.

• The Bills answered with an impressive 17-play, 83-yard march to Steve Christie's field goal. The Bills had been forced to punt after three plays, but after Elvis Patterson rushed Chris Mohr and forced him to abort the punt, Mohr ran 11 yards for a first down at the Bills 21. Kelly then completed five of six passes.

• The Raiders needed only six plays after the kickoff to make it 14-3 as Tim Brown caught a 52-yard TD pass on a third-and-eight play. Earlier on third-and-eight, Marinovich hit Mervyn Fernandez for 21 yards.

• On the ensuing series, Terry McDaniel intercepted Kelly at the Los Angeles 15 and returned it 46 yards to set up Jeff Jaeger's first field goal.

• Christie had a 36-yard field goal blocked by Nolan Harrison with 1:17 left in the first half.

• In the third, Anthony Smith sacked Kelly, forced a fumble and Greg Townsend recovered at the Bills 25, leading to Jaeger's second field goal.

• Early in the fourth, the Bills got to the Raiders 15, but Kelly was sacked back to the 31 and Christie then missed a 49-yard field goal. On their last two possessions, the Bills got to the Los Angeles 35 and 16 and both times gave up the ball on downs.

QUOTES

• Jim Kelly: "Believe me – I'm speaking from the heart – don't count us out. Offensively we can move the ball, we're just not getting it in the end zone. We have to find out the reason why. When you can't get the running game going and you have to pass every down, it makes it tough."

• Thurman Thomas on the two-game losing streak: "It has been the offense's fault. We've gotten down in there (in scoring position) and we've self-destructed. It's not a wakeup call. We got our asses whipped the last two weeks, all right. You can't explain it. We lost two in a row, so what are you going to say, that we're going to lose two more in a row? We're too good of a team to panic. We're 4-2 right now, so what. We have a lot of talent on this team and I'm sure we'll bounce back. We have 10 more games and we stand a good chance of winning all 10 of those."

• Marv Levy: "Sure there's a glumness and there should be. But there's no helmet-kicking or locker-slamming, but there is a glumness and they feel it. They're extremely disappointed and they ought to be. I am, too. We dug a hole and we mean to get out of it. We were disgusted, disappointed, but I don't feel they were listless, I don't have that feeling."

Bills	0 3 0 0 - 3
Raiders	7 10 3 0 - 20

Attendance at the Coliseum - 52,287

LAR: Dickerson 2 pass from Marinovich (Jaeger kick), 9:59
Buf: FG Christie 25, 2:27
LAR: Brown 52 pass from Marinovich (Jaeger kick), 4:35
LAR: FG Jaeger 45, 10:15
LAR: FG Jaeger 36, 9:12

	BUF	LAR
First downs	22	16
Rushing yds	92	92
Passing yds	258	156
Punts-avg	5-49.6	6-40.8
Fumbles-lost	1-1	1-1
Penalties-yds	8-92	5-55
Poss. time	30:59	29:01

BILLS LEADERS: Rushing - Thomas 16-52, Gardner 1-0, K. Davis 9-30, Kelly 2-(-1), Mohr 1-11; **Passing** - Kelly 26-45-1 - 302; **Receiving** - Reed 6-85, Thomas 3-27, Metzelaars 6-41, Lamb 2-64, Lofton 5-72, K. Davis 2-(-4), Fuller 2-17.

RAIDERS LEADERS: Rushing - Dickerson 16-52, Allen 10-37, Smith 3-4, Marinovich 2-(-1); **Passing** - Marinovich 11-21-1 - 188; **Receiving** - Brown 1-52, Dickerson 2-11, Gault 2-47, Fernandez 1-21, Allen 1-11, Horton 1-22, Smith 2-15, Glover 1-9.

WEEK 6 GAMES	
Mia 21, Atl 17	Hou 38, Cinc 24
KC 24, Phil 17	NYG 31, Phoe 21
Clev 17, Pitt 9	SF 24, NE 12
Dal 27, Sea 0	NO 13, Rams 10
Ind 6, NYJ 3 OT	Wash 34, Den 3
Minn, Chi, TB, GB, Det, SD had bye weeks	

STANDINGS: SIXTH WEEK

AFC EAST	W	L	T	CENTRAL	W	L	T	WEST	W	L	T	NFC EAST	W	L	T	CENTRAL	W	L	T	WEST	W	L	T
Miami	5	0	0	Houston	4	1	0	Denver	4	2	0	Philadelphia	4	1	0	Minnesota	4	1	0	San Fran	5	1	0
Buffalo	4	2	0	Pittsburgh	3	2	0	Kan. City	4	2	0	Dallas	4	1	0	Tampa Bay	3	2	0	N.Orleans	4	2	0
Indianapolis	3	2	0	Cincinnati	2	3	0	Raiders	2	4	0	Washington	3	2	0	Chicago	2	3	0	LA Rams	2	4	0
NY Jets	1	5	0	Cleveland	2	3	0	San Diego	1	4	0	NY Giants	2	3	0	Green Bay	2	3	0	Atlanta	2	4	0
New England	0	5	0					Seattle	1	5	0	Phoenix	1	4	0	Detroit	1	4	0				

| Bills | 0 14 3 7 - 24 |
| Jets | 3 3 7 7 - 20 |

Attendance at Giants Stadium - 68,181

NYJ: FG Blanchard 42, 13:28
Buf: K. Davis 2 run (Christie kick), :54
NYJ: FG Blanchard 40, 11:58
Buf: Lofton 16 pass from Kelly (Christie kick), 14:42
NYJ: Chaffey 1 run (Blanchard kick), 9:04
Buf: FG Christie 33, 14:08
NYJ: Baxter 1 run (Blanchard kick), 13:10
Buf: Thomas 12 pass from Kelly (Christie kick), 14:09

	BUF	NYJ
First downs	21	22
Rushing yds	165	142
Passing yds	208	184
Punts-avg	6-36.7	4-49.3
Fumbles-lost	2-1	0-0
Penalties-yds	9-77	6-50
Poss. time	21:36	38:24

BILLS LEADERS: **Rushing** - T. Thomas 21-142, K. Davis 4-22, Kelly 1-4, Gardner 1-3, Beebe 1-(-6); **Passing** - Kelly 15-29-1 - 226; **Receiving** - Reed 3-55, Beebe 6-106, Lofton 2-27, T. Thomas 3-22, Gardner 1-16.

JETS LEADERS: **Rushing** - B. Thomas 20-88, Chaffey 2-30, Baxter 9-24, Nagle 2-0; **Passing** - Nagle 19-32-2 - 167, O'Brien 3-5-0 - 37; **Receiving** - Moore 7-80, Toon 3-18, Boyer 4-23, B. Thomas 2-15, Mitchell 1-18, Mathis 1-17, Whisenhunt 1-10, Baxter 1-8, Burkett 1-6, Chaffey 1-9.

WEEK 7 GAMES

Minn 31, Det 14	SF 56, Atl 17
Clev 17, GB 6	Den 27, Hou 21
Dal 17, KC 10	LAR 19, Sea 0
Mia 38, NE 17	NO 30, Phoe 21
Rams 38, NYG 17	Wash 16, Phil 12
SD 34, Ind 14	Chi 31, TB 14
Pitt 20, Cinc 0	Buf, NYJ had bye weeks

NOTES

• The Bills beat the Jets for the 10th straight time, rallying on Jim Kelly's TD pass to Thurman Thomas with 51 seconds left. It was the second straight year a late TD pass to Thomas won a game at the Meadowlands.
• Darryl Talley set a new team record by playing in his 156th straight game, breaking Fred Smerlas' record of 155 straight games (1979-89).
• On their second possession, the Jets marched 40 yards in 13 plays to a Cary Blanchard field goal.
• The Bills answered with a six-play, 65-yard drive to Kenneth Davis' TD dive. The key plays were a 37-yard pass to Andre Reed and a 19-yard run by Thomas. The teams traded four punts before Blanchard kicked his second field goal. Late in the half, each team came up with an interception, Buffalo's by Nate Odomes with 55 seconds left. Kelly then hit Don Beebe for 15 and 18 yards to the Jets 29, Thomas ran for 13 and Kelly then fired a 16-yard TD pass to James Lofton with 18 seconds left in the half.
• The Jets drove 84 yards in 10 plays on their first series of the third quarter to Pat Chaffey's TD run.
• The Bills came back with a 49-yard advance to a Steve Christie field goal.
• Early in the fourth, Reed lost a fumble, but Henry Jones got the ball back on an interception.
• The Jets took the lead with 1:50 left. J.D. Williams was called for a 44-yard pass-interference penalty putting the ball at the 1 and Brad Baxter scored on the next play.
• The Bills began their winning drive at their own 25.

WEEK 8 GAMES

Chi 30, GB 10	Hou 26, Cinc 10
Clev 19, NE 17	Dal 28, LAR 13
SD 24, Den 21	Det 38, TB 7
Ind 31, Mia 20	Phil 7, Phoe 3
NYG 23, Sea 10	Wash 15, Minn 13
Pitt 27, KC 3	SF, Atl, Rams, NO had bye weeks.

Kelly was sacked by Marvin Washington on the first play, but he hit Beebe for 34 on the next snap. On third-and-10, he hit Beebe for 19 to the Jets 30 with 1:01 left. Thomas ran for 18 and on the next play, caught the TD pass over the middle.

QUOTES

• Marv Levy on Kelly: "You get that look in that guy's eyes. I could see he had his work cut out for him, but he believed in himself and the guys he had with him."
• Jim Kelly: "When it comes down to it, when you have to make the big play, you make it. I just said 'Guys, I know we can do it, let's put it all together.'"
• Jets tackle Irv Eatman: "I know they were lucky to get out of here with a win. We kicked their butts, but we didn't get more points than they did."

| Patriots | 0 7 0 0 - 7 |
| Bills | 0 0 9 7 - 16 |

Attendance at Rich Stadium - 78,268

NE: V. Brown 25 fumble return (Baumann kick), 13:37
Buf: Metzelaars 3 pass from Kelly (Christie kick), 10:18
Buf: Safety: McCarthy tackled in end zone by Hale, 12:26
Buf: Lofton 13 pass from Kelly (Christie kick), 9:55

	BUF	NE
First downs	20	14
Rushing yds	89	69
Passing yds	199	127
Punts-avg	5-37.2	5-34.0
Fumbles-lost	2-1	4-2
Penalties	5-35	9-66
Poss. time	30:06	29:54

BILLS LEADERS: **Rushing** - Thomas 12-29, K. Davis 16-41, Gardner 2-10, Kelly 4-9; **Passing** - Kelly 22-33-2 - 205; **Receiving** - Reed 2-22, Thomas 5-45, Metzelaars 3-17, K. Davis 6-44, Lofton 4-51, Beebe 2-26.

PATRIOTS LEADERS: **Rushing** - Russell 15-40, Vaughn 5-15, Stephens 2-9, Hodson 1-6, Turner 1-(-1), McCarthy 1-0; **Passing** - Hodson 17-26-1 - 171; **Receiving** - Stephens 2-16, McMurtry 4-36, Cook 6-57, Timpson 2-18, Russell 1-7, Fryar 2-37.

NOTES

• The Bills pulled even in the AFC East with Miami when the Dolphins lost to the Jets, but it was a tough day against the winless Patriots who held a 7-0 halftime lead.
• Cornelius Bennett had eight tackles, 2 1/2 sacks and forced a fumble.
• The offense remained in a slump and struggled against the lowly Patriots, but the defense had a big day as the Bills beat the Pats for the eighth time in the last 10 meetings.
• The teams punted on the first eight possessions of the game before, with 1:23 left in the half, Dwayne Sabb forced Thurman Thomas to fumble, Vincent Brown scooped the ball up and ran 25 yards for a TD. As the Bills left the field at halftime, fans booed, angering Jim Kelly.
• The defense stopped the Pats on the first series of the third, and the offense finally advanced the ball as Kelly engineered a 13-play, 74-yard drive to his TD pass to Pete Metzelaars. Thomas fumbled on the second play, but Glenn Parker recovered. Later, Kelly scrambled for eight on third-and-six, he hit Don Beebe for 12 on third-and-two and he hit Andre Reed for 13 on third-and-six from the Pats 17. The Bills also saw a 32-yard Kenneth Davis run wiped out by a penalty on Keith McKeller. Davis then caught a 22-yard pass.

WEEK 9 GAMES

GB 27, Det 13	Cinc 30, Clev 10
SD 26, Ind 0	Pitt 21, Hou 20
NYJ 26, Mia 14	Atl 30, Rams 28
Phoe 24, SF 14	Dal 20, Phil 10
NO 23, TB 21	NYG 24, Wash 7
Minn 38, Chi 1	
Den, LAR, Sea, KC had bye weeks	

• The Pats were pinned back to their 11 on the kickoff. The Bills defense held in three plays, then Pats punter Shawn McCarthy dropped the snap in the end zone and was tackled by Chris Hale for a safety.
• The next three series ended in interceptions, the last by New England's Randy Robbins who returned it to the Bills 25 with 12:49 left. The Pats reached the 13, but Bennett sacked Tommy Hodson, forced a fumble and Jeff Wright recovered at the 27.
• From there, the Bills put the game away by driving 73 yards in 10 plays to Kelly's TD pass to James Lofton on a third-and-one play. Bills also converted two other third downs along the way.

QUOTES

• Thurman Thomas: "I really don't know what all the fuss is about. We're not scoring 40 points a game but we're 6-2 and we're tied for the division lead. What more can you ask for? If we have to win ugly all the time, we have to win ugly all the time."
• Jim Kelly about the booing: "Sure it ticked me off and it ticked a lot of other guys off, too. We're out there doing our best but as soon as something bad happens, here we go, people boo. Well, we're playing for ourselves this year. This was one of those games where when the final seconds ticked off and you're on top, you go home and say 'I'm glad that one's over.'"
• Jeff Wright on the defense: "I wouldn't say it was one of our better efforts, we've had two goose eggs this year, but we held up the offense for a while when they needed it." (On his key fumble recovery): "When we came in at halftime, we said we have to get the ball, we have to make a big play, and Cornelius came through. He stripped the ball and I just landed on it."

STANDINGS: NINTH WEEK

AFC EAST	W	L	T	CENTRAL	W	L	T	WEST	W	L	T	NFC EAST	W	L	T	CENTRAL	W	L	T	WEST	W	L	T
Miami	6	2	0	Pittsburgh	6	2	0	Denver	5	3	0	Dallas	7	1	0	Minnesota	6	2	0	San Fran	6	2	0
Buffalo	6	2	0	Houston	5	3	0	Kan. City	4	4	0	Philadelphia	5	3	0	Chicago	4	4	0	N.Orleans	6	2	0
Indianapolis	4	4	0	Cleveland	4	4	0	San Diego	4	4	0	Washington	5	3	0	Tampa Bay	3	5	0	LA Rams	3	5	0
NY Jets	2	6	0	Cincinnati	3	5	0	Raiders	3	5	0	NY Giants	4	4	0	Green Bay	3	5	0	Atlanta	3	5	0
New England	0	8	0					Seattle	1	7	0	Phoenix	2	6	0	Detroit	2	6	0				

NOTES

• The Bills beat the Steelers for the fourth straight time and sixth in the last seven meetings.

• Mitch Frerotte caught his second TD pass on the lineman-eligible play. The last lineman to catch two TD passes in one year was Cincinnati's Anthony Munoz in 1986.

• The Bills' 31 first downs tied for the second-highest total in club history.

• Thurman Thomas set a career-high with 37 carries.

• The Bills drove to the Steelers 18 on the first series of the game, but Andre Reed lost a fumble. The Steelers punted, then the Bills moved 60 yards in nine plays to James Lofton's TD reception.

• After the Steelers got a Gary Anderson field goal, the Bills drove 82 yards in 11 plays to Frerotte's TD reception. Thomas carried four times for 35 yards on the march.

• The Steelers went three-and-out and the Bills went 49 yards in seven plays to Thomas' TD run. The key play was Jim Kelly's 13-yard pass to Don Beebe on third-and-10.

• Anderson made his second field goal on the last play of the first half after Hardy Nickerson had returned a Kelly fumble 44 yards with eight seconds left. The Steelers then took the second-half kickoff and drove 54 yards to Neil O'Donnell's TD pass to Ernie Mills.

• But the Bills regained momentum with a seven-play, 80-yard march as Lofton hauled in a TD pass.

• In the fourth, the Bills chewed up the final 8:04 as Thomas carried 11 times for 52 yards.

QUOTES

• Thurman Thomas: "One of the things we said at the hotel Saturday night was that we've been kind of slow with the no-huddle, it's not the old no-huddle that we used to run. We wanted to come out today and pick up the tempo and see what happens."

• Jim Kelly: "We showed the old Bills offense. Our tempo seemed to slack off and we said we had to get back to where we were before. I was worrying too much about getting into the right play instead of just going out there and playing football."

• Tom Bresnahan: "It comes down to our people. We have outstanding athletes and if all eight cylinders are firing, our guys are going to make plays."

• Walt Corey on the defensive performance: "They (the steelers) came out the first half and I don't think they thought we were for real or we were as physical as they were. This is a game of attitude. Whoever has the best attitude, finishes every down and runs to the ball is going to win. Two good teams played today and the better team won."

• Bruce Smith on stopping the Steelers running game: "Last year we were so maligned as far as defense against the run. We had key injuries and we were 27th overall (in defense). I think we definitely made a statement today."

WEEK 10 GAMES

Clev 24, Hou 14	Dal 37, Det 3
NYG 27, GB 7	Phil 31, LAR 10
Mia 28, Ind 0	Minn 35, TB 7
NO 31, NE 14	Den 27, NYJ 16
Phoe 20, Rams 14	KC 16, SD 14
Wash 16, Sea 3	Cinc 31, Chi 28
SF 41, Atl 3	

Steelers	0 6 14 0	- 20
Bills	7 14 7 0	- 28

Attendance at Rich Stadium - 80,294

Buf: Lofton 22 pass from Kelly (Christie kick), 9:03
Pit: FG Anderson 28, :11
Buf: Frerotte 2 pass from Kelly (Christie kick), 4:50
Buf: Thomas 1 run (Christie kick), 10:01
Pit: FG Anderson 49, 15:00
Pit: Mills 12 pass from O'Donnell (Anderson kick), 4:31
Buf: Lofton 45 pass from Kelly (Christie kick), 7:17
Pit: Hoge 11 pass from O'Donnell (Anderson kick), 14:30

	BUF	PIT
First downs	31	16
Rushing yds	174	86
Passing yds	284	147
Punts-avg	2-29.5	5-48.0
Fumbles-lost	3-2	1-0
Penalties-yds	7-60	10-73
Poss. time	32:32	27:28

BILLS LEADERS: Rushing - Thomas 37-155, K. Davis 4-16, Kelly 3-3; **Passing** - Kelly 26-33-0 - 290; **Receiving** - Beebe 8-101, McKeller 5-59, Thomas 4-30, Lofton 3-79, Reed 2-2, Frerotte 1-2, Metzelaars 1-6, K. Davis 1-4, Tasker 1-7.

STEELERS LEADERS: Rushing - Foster 22-77, Thompson 2-8, Hoge 1-1; **Passing** - O'Donnell 15-24-0 - 159, Foster 0-1-0 - 0; **Receiving** - Green 4-41, Hoge 2-18, Foster 4-36, Thompson 1-8, Davenport 3-44, Mills 1-12.

NOTES

• The Bills won at Joe Robbie for the fifth time in six tries and Marv Levy recorded his 100th career NFL win.

• Steve Christie's 54-yard field goal was a club record.

• Henry Jones broke Tom Janik's record for interception return yardage in a single season.

• The Dolphins rushed for 30 yards in driving to Greg Baty's TD reception on their first possession of the game. They managed just 34 more yards on the ground the rest of the way.

• The Bills answered that TD with Christie's first field goal, capping a 71-yard march. The key plays were a 21-yard interference on J.B. Brown and Andre Reed's 17-yard catch on the next play to the Miami 12.

• The Dolphins responded with a 66-yard drive to Mark Clayton's TD catch for a 14-3 lead early in the second quarter.

• Christie's 54-yarder on the ensuing possession seemed to turn the tide. Miami went three-and-out and the Bills then drove 83 yards in 11 plays to Kenneth Davis' TD run on third-and-two.

• Pete Stoyanovich made a field goal late in the half and Christie had a 53-yarder blocked.

• The Bills took the lead on their first possession of the third as Davis capped a 46-yard drive.

• Four plays after the kickoff, Darryl Talley forced Mark Higgs to fumble and Cornelius Bennett recovered at the Bills 44 and that led to Christie's third field goal.

• Jones then intercepted Marino and returned it 22 yards to the Miami 18 setting up Christie's fourth kick.

• Stoyanovich missed from 35 in the fourth, then made a 50-yarder, but the Bills ran out the final 4:04 as Thurman Thomas gained five yards on third-and-four with 2:00 left that kept the ball away from Marino.

QUOTES

• Jim Ritcher: "I really felt this was the biggest regular-season game that I might have ever played in my 13 years

in the league. The beating we took up in Buffalo weighed heavily on our minds. It may have even hurt our performance the next week when we lost to the Raiders because all we could think about was coming back and playing these guys."

• Marv Levy on Thurman Thomas' third-down run: "Thurman Thomas has had a lot of great runs, but none greater than that one on third-and-four. That allowed us to run out the last two minutes."

• Thurman Thomas: "That was the biggest run of my career. I don't care if I ever win a rushing title, those four yards were the biggest of my career. It was a matter of who wanted it more. They knew I was going to get the ball, but they still had to stop me."

• Kent Hull: "It's as big a win as we've had this year. A loss could have been devastating."

• Darryl Talley on the pass rush: "It's a very, very rare situation to get Marino in. He's been the least sacked quarterback in the NFL. It's a credit to our defensive backs."

Bills	3 10 13 0	- 26
Dolphins	7 10 0 3	- 20

Attendance at Joe Robbie Stadium - 70,629

Mia: Baty 1 pass from Marino (Stoyanovich kick), 8:37
Buf: FG Christie 26, 12:54
Mia: Clayton 19 pass from Marino (Stoyanovich kick), 2:30
Buf: FG Christie 54, 5:49
Buf: K. Davis 5 run (Christie kick), 11:40
Mia: FG Stoyanovich 21, 14:18
Buf: K. Davis 1 run (Christie kick), 5:44
Buf: FG Christie 23, 11:43
Buf: FG Christie 19, 14:49
Mia: FG Stoyanovich 50, 10:56

	BUF	MIA
First downs	26	20
Rushing yds	111	64
Passing yds	212	286
Punts-avg	2-51.0	2-46.0
Fumbles-lost	0-0	1-1
Penalties-yds	5-24	10-99
Poss. time	27:33	32:27

BILLS LEADERS: Rushing - Thomas 22-73, K. Davis 9-27, Kelly 2-(-2), Gardner 2-4, Reed 1-9; **Passing** - Kelly 19-32-0 - 212; **Receiving** - Thomas 6-66, McKeller 2-11, Reed 3-38, Beebe 3-37, Lofton 3-37, Metzelaars 2-8, Gardner 1-8.

DOLPHINS LEADERS: Rushing - Higgs 12-34, Humphrey 7-30; **Passing** - Marino 22-33-1 - 321; **Receiving** - Duper 5-100, Jackson 5-36, Higgs 1-21, Baty 1-1, Paige 2-22, Clayton 5-98, Humphrey 3-43.

WEEK 11 GAMES

TB 20, Chi 17	NYJ 17, Cinc 14
Hou 17, Minn 13	Pitt 17, Det 14
Rams 27, Dal 23	GB 27, Phil 24
SF 21, NO 20	Atl 20, Phoe 17
SD 14, Clev 13	LAR 20, Sea 3
KC 35, Wash 16	Den 27, NYG 13
NE 37, Ind 34 (OT)	

STANDINGS: ELEVENTH WEEK

AFC EAST	W	L	T	CENTRAL	W	L	T	WEST	W	L	T	NFC EAST	W	L	T	CENTRAL	W	L	T	WEST	W	L	T
Buffalo	8	2	0	Pittsburgh	7	3	0	Denver	7	3	0	Dallas	8	2	0	Minnesota	7	3	0	San Fran	8	2	0
Miami	7	3	0	Houston	6	4	0	Kan. City	6	4	0	Philadelphia	6	4	0	Chicago	4	6	0	N.Orleans	7	3	0
Indianapolis	4	6	0	Cleveland	5	5	0	San Diego	5	5	0	Washington	6	4	0	Tampa Bay	4	6	0	LA Rams	4	6	0
NY Jets	3	7	0	Cincinnati	4	6	0	Raiders	4	6	0	NY Giants	5	5	0	Green Bay	4	6	0	Atlanta	4	6	0
New England	3	7	0					Seattle	1	9	0	Phoenix	3	7	0	Detroit	2	8	0				

Falcons	0	7	0	7	-	14
Bills	28	10	0	3	-	41

Attendance at Rich Stadium - 80,004

Buf: Gardner 2 run (Christie kick), 4:00
Buf: Metzelaars 3 pass from Kelly (Christie kick), 8:11
Buf: Reed 15 pass from Kelly (Christie kick), 10:25
Buf: K. Davis 1 run (Christie kick), 14:33
Buf: K. Davis 64 run (Christie kick), 1:02
Buf: FG Christie 47, 14:33
Atl: Sanders 73 kickoff return (Johnson kick), 14:48
Buf: FG Christie 18, 3:09
Atl: D. Hill 1 pass from Wilson (Johnson kick), 13:54

	BUF	ATL
First downs	19	11
Rushing yds	315	46
Passing yds	97	128
Punts-avg	3-41.3	7-42.4
Fumbles-lost	1-0	0-0
Penalties-yds	6-54	5-30
Poss. time	30:57	29:03

BILLS LEADERS: Rushing - Thomas 13-103, K. Davis 20-181, Kelly 1-(-1), Gardner 8-34, Reich 2-(-2); **Passing** - Kelly 7-15-1 - 93, Reich 1-2-0 - 4; **Receiving** - Reed 4-70, Metzelaars 1-3, McKeller 1-3, Gardner 1-17, K. Davis 1-4.

FALCONS LEADERS: Rushing - K. Jones 10-23, T. Smith 2-5, Broussard 4-8, Pegram 2-10, Wilson 1-0; **Passing** - Wilson 9-13-0 - 89, Tolliver 8-23-1 - 47; **Receiving** - D. Hill 5-35, Haynes 1-12, Rison 6-52, Pritchard 3-26, Broussard 1-3, Phillips 1-8.

WEEK 12 GAMES

Dal 16, Phoe 10	Minn 17, Clev 13
LAR 24, Den 0	Det 19, Cinc 13
GB 17, Chi 3	Mia 19, Hou 16
Pitt 30, Ind 14	NE 24, NYJ 3
Phil 47, NYG 34	SF 27, Rams 10
SD 29, TB 14	KC 24, Sea 14
NO 20, Wash 3	

NOTES

• The Bills rushed for 315 yards, the fourth-highest total in team history, in routing the Falcons.
• Kenneth Davis set a career high for rushing yards. He and Thurman Thomas going over 100 yards rushing were the 11th pair in Bills history to achieve that in one game. However, they became the first duo to do it before the first half had ended.
• Jim Ritcher became the Bills all-time leader in games played (198) surpassing Joe Devlin.
• On the opening kickoff, Steve Tasker made a great tackle of Deion Sanders at the Falcons 9 and Atlanta never got out of the hole. They went three-and-out, Clifford Hicks returned the punt 17 yards to the Falcons 44 and five plays later, Carwell Gardner scored.
• The Falcons again went three-and-out and seven plays later, Pete Metzelaars caught a TD pass after Thomas ran 17 yards to the three on third-and-nine.
• Four plays after the kickoff, Henry Jones intercepted a Billy Joe Tolliver pass and returned it 27 yards to the Falcons 20. Two plays later, Kelly hit Andre Reed for a TD.
• The Falcons went three-and-out. The Bills started at Atlanta's 47 and after Thomas ran 44 yards to the 1, Davis scored to make it 28-0, the second-most productive first quarter in Bills history.
• After yet another three-and-out by Atlanta, Davis broke a 64-yard TD run.
• Late in the half, Steve Christie made a field goal, and then the Falcons got on the board. Christie's squib kickoff was fielded by Roman Fortin who lateraled to Tony Smith. Smith then pitched to Sanders and he sped 73 yards, high-stepping the final 15.
• After Nate Odomes blocked a Norm Johnson field goal late in the third, the Bills drove 79 yards in 15 plays to Christie's field goal. The Falcons closed the scoring with 1:06 left on Wade Wilson's TD pass to Drew Hill which capped an 18-play, 93-yard drive against the Bills' second defensive unit.

QUOTES

• Steve Tasker on tackling Sanders: "He got about five feet in the air faster than I could blink. I think it was just lucky that I happened to grab his foot and got enough to pull him down. Anytime Deion gets his hands on the ball, you breathe a little faster. You fight that (letdown) after a big win like we had in Miami, then you come back after a short week and you're playing a team that everybody in the world thinks you should beat. It's important to keep the intensity level very high. I think by today's performance, we got that done."
• Jim Kelly: "Anytime you get the running game going the way it went today, it makes it easy. The offensive line was opening holes that even Jim Kelly could have run through."

Bills	0	3	7	3	0	-	13
Colts	0	3	0	10	3	-	16

Attendance at the Hoosier Dome - 50,221

Ind: FG Biasucci 52, 4:01
Buf: FG Christie 52, 15:00
Buf: Beebe 65 pass from Kelly (Christie kick), 11:06
Buf: FG Christie 44, 3:43
Ind: Culver 4 run (Biasucci kick), 9:06
Ind: FG Biasucci 23, 13:53
Ind: FG Biasucci 40, 3:51

	BUF	IND
First downs	16	22
Rushing yds	136	107
Passing yds	176	305
Punts-avg	6-48.3	5-46.2
Fumbles-lost	0-0	1-0
Penalties-yds	5-35	6-30
Poss. time	22:47	41:04

BILLS LEADERS: Rushing - Thomas 21-102, K. Davis 6-28, Kelly 1-5, Gardner 1-1; **Passing** - Kelly 11-33-2 - 184; **Receiving** - Thomas 3-37, Reed 2-21, Beebe 4-110, McKeller 1-2, Lofton 1-14.

COLTS LEADERS: Rushing - Johnson 13-50, Culver 5-10, Clark 14-45, Trudeau 1-2; **Passing** - Trudeau 26-41-1 - 337; **Receiving** - Langhorne 5-67, Arbuckle 9-106, Johnson 3-34, Hester 6-80, Cash 2-42, Clark 1-8.

WEEK 13 GAMES

Hou 24, Det 21	Dal 30, NYG 3
Clev 27, Chi 14	KC 23, NYJ 7
NO 24, Mia 13	Minn 31, Rams 17
Atl 34, NE 0	SF 20, Phil 14
Wash 41, Phoe 3	Pitt 21, Cinc 9
GB 19, TB 14	SD 27, LAR 3
Sea 16, Den 13 (OT)	

NOTES

• The Bills lost a heartbreaker to the Colts, under new coach and ex-Bills offensive coordinator Ted Marchibroda. It was the Bills' sixth loss in nine visits to the Hoosier Dome.
• Thurman Thomas went over the 1,000-yard rushing mark for the fourth straight year, but for the first time in his career, the Bills lost a regular-season game in which he gained 100 yards rushing. They were 25-0.
• Dean Biasucci broke a scoreless tie with a field goal in the second quarter. On the ensuing series, the Bills' drive ended when Jim Kelly was intercepted by Jason Belser.
• Late in the half, Biasucci missed a 37-yarder. The Bills then used the final 53 seconds to drive 46 yards in nine plays to Steve Christie's tying field goal. Kelly hit Thomas for 18, Don Beebe for 19.
• Biasucci missed from 52 early in the third. After an exchange of punts left the Bills at their own 5, Kelly hit Beebe for gains of 12 and 14, then uncorked a 65-yard bomb to Beebe for the go-ahead TD.

• On the next series, Mark Kelso intercepted Jack Trudeau and the Bills traveled 31 yards in 10 plays to Christie's second field goal.
• The Colts then came alive. Trudeau went six-for-six for 62 yards on a 75-yard march to Rodney Culver's TD.
• Kelly then was intercepted by Tony Stargell who returned it 15 yards to the Bills 34 with 3:01 left. The Colts had first-and-goal at the 2 with two minutes left, but the defense rose up and forced Biasucci's tying field goal, which necessitated overtime.
• The Colts won the toss and drove 56 yards to Biasucci's winning field goal, the key play a 26-yard pass to Jesse Hester.

QUOTES

• Darryl Talley: "On any given Sunday ... I know people think we're blowing smoke when we say that, but when you get down to it, these guys went to college for four or five years, they play in the NFL and they get paid like everyone else. You have to play everybody as hard as you can. Anyone can be beaten. Prime example is today."
• Shane Conlan: "To tell you the truth, the whole team was flat."
• Jim Kelly: "This was one we shouldn't lose, there's no reason for it, but it was just one of those things. During a 16-game schedule, you have to be pumped up every game. The defense played well enough for us to win, but we just didn't put enough points on the board."
• Kent Hull: "We blew an opportunity (because Miami lost) because we certainly feel we have a better team than the Colts. We didn't play like it and we squandered an opportunity."
• Colts linebacker Duane Bickett: "(Defensive coordinator) Rick Venturi has seen the Bills maybe 20 times over his years, he knows what to do. You could see the frustration in their (the Bills) faces. It was as if they were saying 'This isn't supposed to happen to us, it's what's supposed to happen to the Colts.' That fired us up even more."

STANDINGS: THIRTEENTH WEEK

AFC EAST	W	L	T	CENTRAL	W	L	T	WEST	W	L	T	NFC EAST	W	L	T	CENTRAL	W	L	T	WEST	W	L	T
Buffalo	9	3	0	Pittsburgh	9	3	0	Kan. City	8	4	0	Dallas	10	2	0	Minnesota	9	3	0	San Fran	10	2	0
Miami	8	4	0	Houston	7	5	0	Denver	7	5	0	Philadelphia	7	5	0	Green Bay	6	6	0	N.Orleans	9	3	0
Indianapolis	5	7	0	Cleveland	6	6	0	San Diego	7	5	0	Washington	7	5	0	Tampa Bay	4	8	0	Atlanta	5	7	0
NY Jets	3	9	0	Cincinnati	4	8	0	Raiders	5	7	0	NY Giants	5	7	0	Chicago	4	8	0	LA Rams	4	8	0
New England	2	10	0					Seattle	2	10	0	Phoenix	3	9	0	Detroit	3	9	0				

NOTES

• The Bills saw their 10-game winning streak against the Jets come to an end as New York played an inspired game while their teammate, Dennis Byrd, lay paralyzed in a New York hospital.

• Jim Ritcher became the first Bill to appear in 200 games in a Buffalo uniform.

• The game was played in winds of 35 mph with gusts to 45 mph.

• Chris Mohr's 30-yard punt after the first possession set up the Jets at their own 42 and they drove to Cary Blanchard's field goal.

• On the ensuing series, Thurman Thomas broke a 39-yard run to the Jets 17, setting up Steve Christie's tying field goal.

• The Bills drove 84 yards in 10 plays bridging the first and second quarters with Kenneth Davis scoring the TD. Jim Kelly completed third-down passes to Pete Metzelaars and James Lofton. Davis also converted once.

• The Jets took the second-half kickoff and drove 73 yards in 11 plays to the tie game on Brad Baxter's TD.

• Five plays after the kickoff, Davis lost a fumble to Lonnie Young at the Bills 40. The Jets used eight plays before Baxter scored. The key play was a 16-yard pass to Chris Burkett on third-and-six from the 25.

• The Bills tied it with a six-play, 60-yard drive to Metzelaars' TD reception.

• After the teams punted three times, the Bills took possession with 1:53 left at their own 19. On the second play, Brian Washington intercepted a Kelly pass and raced 23 yards for the winning TD.

• Kelly then lost a fumble to Bill Pickel after reaching the Bills 47 with 1:15 left.

QUOTES

• Kent Hull: "I'm shocked. We've lost two games we definitely should have won. The last two weeks I think we let average teams feel like they've just won the Super Bowl. I really can't explain it. Offensively, we just haven't been productive. We're bleeding, but we're not dead."

• Jeff Wright: "Our backs are up against the wall now. It's either we win every game or we might not get where we want to go."

• Darryl Talley: "If you don't play football, you're going to get beat. Teams are really coming out and shooting at us. When you're at the top of the heap, everybody's coming after you."

• Jim Kelly: "It's been put in my hands so many times and I've come through. I'm human just like everybody else, it's not going to happen. I feel like I can go out there and make it happen and it's my job to get the ball in the end zone. Today, it just didn't happen."

• Jets coach Bruce Coslet: "We didn't talk a whole lot about dedicating the game to Dennis. We just knew what we had to do and we went out there and did it against a helluva team."

• Jets receiver Chris Burkett: "I think this week was the bottom of the barrel for us, it was a test, a challenge."

WEEK 14 GAMES

NO 22, Atl 14	Clev 37, Cinc 21
Dal 31, Den 27	GB 38, Det 10
Ind 6, NE 0	LAR 28, KC 7
SF 27, Mia 3	Phil 28, Minn 17
SD 27, Phoe 21	Pitt 20, Sea 14
Rams 31, TB 27	Wash 28, NYG 10
Hou 24, Chi 7	

Jets	3	0	14	7	-	24
Bills	3	7	0	7	-	17

Attendance at Rich Stadium - 75,876

NYJ: FG Blanchard 41, 4:56
Buf: FG Christie 26, 7:04
Buf: K. Davis 6 run (Christie kick), 3:57
NYJ: Baxter 1 run (Blanchard kick), 6:09
NYJ: Baxter 9 run (Blanchard kick), 13:17
Buf: Metzelaars 1 pass from Kelly (Christie kick), 2:23
NYJ: Washington 23 interception return (Blanchard kick), 13:19

	BUF	NYJ
First downs	21	17
Rushing yds	142	127
Passing yds	203	148
Punts-avg	4-34.3	5-41.8
Fumbles-lost	3-2	3-0
Penalties-yds	2-10	5-40
Poss. time	26:43	33:17

BILLS LEADERS: Rushing - T. Thomas 18-116, K. Davis 9-14, Reed 1-14, Gardner 1-(-2); **Passing** - Kelly 20-35-2 - 215, Reich 0-1-0 - 0; **Receiving** - Metzelaars 4-26, Thomas 2-24, Lofton 5-83, Reed 3-40, K. Davis 2-3, McKeller 2-13, Gardner 1-13, Beebe 1-13.

JETS LEADERS: Rushing - Baxter 19-98, Hector 6-6, Chaffey 5-25, Nagle 3-(-2); **Passing** - Nagle 14-22-1 - 176, Blake 0-0-0 - 0; **Receiving** - Burkett 5-64, Mathis 2-22, Moore 4-68, Boyer 1-15, Chaffey 2-7.

NOTES

• Marv Levy became the Bills' all-time leader in coaching victories (71) in the win over Denver.

• Thurman Thomas became the 35th player in NFL history to top 6,000 career yards rushing.

• Mark Kelso's three interceptions tied a club record for one game.

• With John Elway sidelined, the Broncos rotated quarterbacks Tommy Maddox and Shawn Moore.

• On the second play of the game, Cornelius Bennett recovered Moore's fumble at the Denver 23, but Keith McKeller fumbled the ball back to Steve Atwater at the 4.

• Moore then threw two interceptions to Kelso, but the Bills failed to capitalize as they punted once, and Don Beebe lost a fumble to Dennis Smith at the Denver 20.

• The Bills finally broke through in the second quarter as Kelly hit Beebe with a 64-yard TD pass on a flea flicker.

• After a Denver punt, the Bills drove 65 yards in nine plays to Kelly's TD run.

• After a 16-yard punt gave them possession at Denver's 43, the Bills needed only four plays to get Thomas' TD run. Kelly hit James Lofton for 26 yards to the Denver 19.

• Steve Christie's first field goal midway through the third made it 24-0, but the Broncos then rallied for 17 straight points.

• Atwater's interception led to Maddox's TD pass to Shannon Sharpe and after ex-Bill Brad Daluiso recovered his own onside kick, the Broncos got a field goal from David Treadwell.

• The Bills went three-and-out and Denver drove 58 yards to Greg Lewis' TD run, but the Bills regained control with a 62-yard march to Christie's clinching field goal, converting twice on third down.

QUOTES

• Mark Kelso: "If we hadn't won today, I don't know if we would have won the rest of the year. I just think it

would have really crushed morale. I don't know if we would have made the playoffs. But thank God we got a victory today."

• Marv Levy: "The players wanted to win badly, it meant a lot to them, and to a degree, they played a little uptight at times."

• Thurman Thomas: "It was a very important game. People were down on us, saying we didn't have the fire to get back to the Super Bowl or win a tough game. I think today we played with a lot of emotion. The fans were into it. The players were into it."

• Don Beebe on the flea-flicker: "We put it in Friday, but we practiced in the bubble (because of a snowstorm), so we really couldn't throw it. We just kind of went through the motions and got the rhythm down as far as the double reverse and the flea flicker back to Jim. Their safeties fly to the ball, they like to stop the run and we saw that in the AFC Championship Game last year."

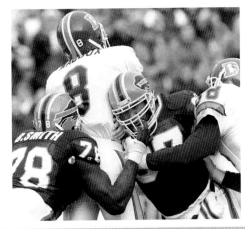

Broncos	0	0	7	10	-	17
Bills	0	21	3	3	-	27

Attendance at Rich Stadium - 71,740

Buf: Beebe 64 pass from Kelly (Christie kick), 7:33
Buf: Kelly 2 run (Christie kick), 13:04
Buf: Thomas 11 run (Christie kick), 14:34
Buf: FG Christie 29, 7:58
Den: Sharpe 1 pass from Maddox (Treadwell kick), 13:54
Den: FG Treadwell 26, 1:35
Den: Lewis 1 run (Treadwell kick), 8:47
Buf: FG Christie 25, 12:56

	BUF	DEN
First downs	17	24
Rushing yds	151	98
Passing yds	210	222
Punts-avg	4-44.3	6-36.3
Fumbles-lost	3-2	3-2
Penalties-yds	10-88	8-49
Poss. time	24:07	35:53

BILLS LEADERS: Rushing - Thomas 26-120, K. Davis 6-9, Reed 1-6, Kelly 4-16; **Passing** - Kelly 13-23-2 - 213; **Receiving** - Beebe 4-104, Thomas 3-39, Lofton 2-45, Reed 1-6, McKeller 2-14, Metzelaars 1-5.
BRONCOS LEADERS: Rushing - Lewis 16-47, Rivers 8-21, Moore 4-15, Maddox 2-15; **Passing** - Maddox 13-28-0 - 122, Moore 10-20-3 - 128; **Receiving** - Jackson 4-38, Sharpe 7-109, Johnson 3-16, Rivers 2-22, Marshall 2-33, Tillman 5-32.

WEEK 15 GAMES

Phoe 19, NYG 0	Atl 35, TB 7
SD 24, Cinc 10	Det 24, Clev 14
Wash 20, Dal 17	KC 27, NE 20
NO 37, Rams 14	Chi 30, Pitt 6
SF 20, Minn 17	GB 16, Hou 14
Mia 20, LAR 7	Ind 10, NYJ 6
Phil 20, Sea 17 (OT)	

STANDINGS: FIFTEENTH WEEK

AFC EAST	W	L	T	CENTRAL	W	L	T	WEST	W	L	T	NFC EAST	W	L	T	CENTRAL	W	L	T	WEST	W	L	T
Buffalo	10	4	0	Pittsburgh	10	4	0	Kan. City	9	5	0	Dallas	11	3	0	Minnesota	9	5	0	San Fran	12	2	0
Miami	9	5	0	Houston	8	6	0	San Diego	9	5	0	Philadelphia	9	5	0	Green Bay	8	6	0	N.Orleans	11	3	0
Indianapolis	7	7	0	Cleveland	7	7	0	Denver	7	7	0	Washington	9	5	0	Chicago	5	9	0	Atlanta	6	8	0
NY Jets	4	10	0	Cincinnati	4	10	0	Raiders	6	8	0	NY Giants	5	9	0	Tampa Bay	4	10	0	LA Rams	5	9	0
New England	2	12	0					Seattle	2	12	0	Phoenix	4	10	0	Detroit	4	10	0				

Bills	3	0	7	10	-	20
Saints	6	7	3	0	-	16

Attendance at the Superdome - 68,591

Buf: FG Christie 25, 3:56
NO: FG Andersen 35, 11:13
NO: FG Andersen 27, 13:11
NO: Small 20 pass from Hebert (Andersen kick), 13:47
Buf: Thomas 6 run (Christie kick), 4:52
NO: FG Andersen 42, 10:58
Buf: Thomas 2 run (Christie kick), 7:41
Buf: FG Christie 29, 11:24

	BUF	NO
First downs	19	12
Rushing yds	181	48
Passing yds	126	157
Punts-avg	7-46.1	7-43.0
Fumbles-lost	3-1	3-2
Penalties-yds	6-39	3-48
Poss. time	30:42	29:18

BILLS LEADERS: Rushing - Thomas 24-115, K. Davis 8-26, Kelly 2-4, Reed 1-2, Gardner 5-34; **Passing** - Kelly 13-28-1 - 135; **Receiving** - Thomas 6-62, Reed 2-19, Beebe 3-38, Lofton 1-11, Edwards 1-5.

SAINTS LEADERS: Rushing - Hilliard 4-16, Heyward 9-19, Dunbar 5-10, Hebert 2-9, Early 1-(-6); **Passing** - Hebert 17-32-1 - 189; **Receiving** - Heyward 3-28, Martin 4-43, Small 4-58, Carroll 1-15, Wainright 1-17, Hilliard 2-16, Early 1-5, Dunbar 1-7.

NOTES

• The Bills played their 500th game in club history and it was a superb road victory without injured Bruce Smith, giving them a 4-0 record over the NFC West.
• The Saints managed just two first downs and 28 yards of offense in the second half even though in addition to Smith, Cornelius Bennett, Shane Conlan and Kirby Jackson were hurt during the game.
• Thurman Thomas became the third player in NFL history to top 2,000 yards from scrimmage two straight years. He also became the fifth player in Bills history to top 300 career points scored.
• Clifford Hicks' 25-yard punt return set up the Bills at the Saints 43 on their first possession of the game and they wound up getting Steve Christie's first field goal. Thomas had a 23-yard pass reception.
• The Saints answered with a 64-yard march to a Morten Andersen field goal. Al Edwards fumbled the ensuing kickoff and Buford Jordan recovered at the Bills 13. The defense forced another Andersen field goal.
• The Bills offense was horrible and couldn't move. After Chris Mohr's fourth punt of the half, the Saints drove 61 yards in seven plays to Bobby Hebert's TD pass to Torrance Small for a 13-3 lead.
• The Bills took the second-half kickoff and went 69

yards in 10 plays to Thomas' TD run. Thomas had a 41-yard run early in the possession and he caught a six-yard pass on third-and-four from the 12.
• Andersen made his third field goal later in the third while Christie missed from 50.
• The Bills drove 85 yards in 10 plays in the fourth to take a 17-16 lead. Kelly was four-of-five for 40 yards. Reginald Jones was called for a 24-yard pass-interference penalty at the 2, setting up Thomas' second TD run.
• Jordan then fumbled the kickoff and Richard Harvey recovered at the Saints 23, setting up a Christie field goal that iced the game with 3:36 left as the Saints couldn't move on two other possessions.

QUOTES

• Jim Kelly: "OK, raise your hand, how many of you (reporters) thought we were going to win this game?" When a few hands went up, he said: "You're a liar, you're a liar, you're a liar."
• Kent Hull: "In a regular-season game, I would say that's probably the best win we've had since we clinched our first division title (in 1988). This was huge because people were counting us out. You turn on the radio shows and they were counting us out and nobody believed in us but ourselves."
• Darryl Talley: "This shows you the character of this football team. I don't think we're as shallow as a lot of people think we are."
• Marv Levy: "I can't remember when I've been more proud of our players. I feel a tremendous sense of pride. It bespeaks the nature and the makeup of the individuals on this team. I think there was a special motivation on their part to overcome the injuries and some of the other obstacles that faced them."

WEEK 16 GAMES

NYG 35, KC 21	SF 21, TB 14
Det 16, Chi 3	Hou 17, Clev 14
GB 28, Rams 13	Minn 6, Pitt 3
Cinc 20, NE 10	Ind 16, Phoe 13
SD 36, LAR 14	Den 10, Sea 6
Mia 19, NYJ 17	Phil 17, Wash 13
Dal 41, Atl 17	

Bills	3	0	0	0	-	3
Oilers	10	10	0	7	-	27

Attendance at the Astrodome - 61,742

Buf: FG Christie 40, 4:47
Hou: FG DelGreco 28, 12:19
Hou: Harris 13 pass from Carlson (DelGreco kick), 14:50
Hou: Jeffires 17 pass from Moon (DelGreco kick), 13:04
Hou: FG DelGreco 18, 15:00
Hou: Brown 1 run (DelGreco kick), 10:11

	BUF	HOU
First downs	17	17
Rushing yds	147	107
Passing yds	90	178
Punts-avg	4-48.0	5-59.2
Fumbles-lost	1-1	0-0
Penalties-yds	9-54	5-35
Poss. time	29:25	30:35

BILLS LEADERS: Rushing - Thomas 18-97, K. Davis 10-37, Gardner 1-5, Edwards 1-8; **Passing** - Kelly 5-9-1 - 47, Reich 11-23-2 - 99; **Receiving** - Lofton 6-75, Reed 5-43, Edwards 1-20, Thomas 3-8, Gardner 1-0.

OILERS LEADERS: Rushing - White 17-66, Carlson 3-18, Brown 8-21, Slaughter 1-2; **Passing** - Carlson 12-19-1 - 105, Moon 6-13-0 - 80; **Receiving** - Jeffires 6-46, Slaughter 4-45, Givins 2-36, Duncan 3-23, White 2-22, Harris 1-13.

WEEK 17 GAMES

LAR 21, Wash 20	NO 20, NYJ 0
Rams 38, Atl 27	Dal 27, Chi 14
KC 42, Den 20	Pitt 23, Clev 13
Minn 27, GB 7	Ind 21, Cinc 17
Phil 20, NYG 13	SD 31, Sea 14
TB 7, Phoe 3	SF 24, Det 6
Mia 16, NE 13 (OT)	

NOTES

• The Bills' loss and Miami's win in New England cost the Bills their fifth consecutive AFC East title. The teams had the same record, but the Dolphins won due to a better AFC record.
• Jim Kelly suffered a knee injury in the second quarter and his availability for the playoffs was in doubt.
• Thurman Thomas set an NFL record by finishing first in yards gained from scrimmage for the fourth straight year. James Lofton tied Bills' assistant coach Charlie Joiner for third on the all-time NFL receiving list with 750 career receptions.
• The Bills took a 3-0 lead as Steve Christie made a field goal to cap their first possession.
• The Oilers answered with a 62-yard drive to Al Del Greco's tying field goal.
• Three plays after the kickoff, Kelly was intercepted by Jerry Gray at the Bills 30 and that set up Cody Carlson's TD pass to Leonard Harris. Carlson started in place of the injured Warren Moon.
• The Bills drove to the Oilers 8, but Kelly was sacked on third down by Ray Childress and hurt his knee. Christie then missed a 33-yard field goal and the Bills unraveled.
• Moon entered the game and directed an impressive 64-yard drive, hitting three-of-four passes including a TD to Haywood Jeffires.
• Frank Reich then was intercepted three plays after the kickoff by Bubba McDowell and he returned it 25 yards to the Bills 33 setting up Del Greco's field goal on the final play of the half for a 20-3 lead.
• The only score of the second half was Gary Brown's TD run.

QUOTES

• Jim Kelly on his first thoughts after the injury: "Why me, why now? It's the same thing I thought about when

we played against the Giants (when he was hurt in 1990). It's disappointing. This year we've been trying to do things the hard way. Maybe in order for us to get to the big one and win it all, we have to go through some tough times and take it that way."
• Frank Reich on the chance to play in the playoffs: "It's exciting. Obviously my first thought is I hope Jim is healthy and ready to go, but if he's not, I'm excited for the opportunity."
• Thurman Thomas: "Our season isn't over and hopefully I can carry the load in the playoffs. There's not a lot of pressure on me, I've been in this situation before. When Kelly has gone down, they've tended to put the load on my shoulders and I've always come through. Last week we won without Bruce and Biscuit and I don't see any reason why we should start to panic right now. We know we can win without Kelly, we've done it before."

STANDINGS: SEVENTEENTH WEEK

AFC EAST	W	L	T	CENTRAL	W	L	T	WEST	W	L	T	NFC EAST	W	L	T	CENTRAL	W	L	T	WEST	W	L	T
Miami	11	5	0	Pittsburgh	11	5	0	San Diego	11	5	0	Dallas	13	3	0	Minnesota	11	5	0	San Fran	14	2	0
Buffalo	11	5	0	Houston	10	6	0	Kan. City	10	6	0	Philadelphia	11	5	0	Green Bay	9	7	0	N.Orleans	12	4	0
Indianapolis	9	7	0	Cleveland	7	9	0	Denver	8	8	0	Washington	9	7	0	Chicago	5	11	0	Atlanta	6	10	0
NY Jets	4	12	0	Cincinnati	5	11	0	Raiders	7	9	0	NY Giants	6	10	0	Detroit	5	11	0	LA Rams	6	10	0
New England	2	14	0					Seattle	2	14	0	Phoenix	4	12	0	Tampa Bay	5	11	0				

NOTES

• Unbelievable is the only word that could accurately describe what took place at Rich Stadium on this cloudy, chilly and breezy day. The Bills pulled off the greatest comeback in NFL history, rallying from a 35-3 deficit to defeat the Oilers in an AFC wild-card playoff game.

• Jim Kelly and Cornelius Bennett did not dress because of injuries and Thurman Thomas missed the second half with a hip pointer, yet the Bills gathered themselves after a horrific start and made history in front of a raucous, stunned crowd.

• The 79 points combined tied for the most in an NFL playoff game, matching the number scored by San Diego and Miami in a 1981 game that also went to overtime.

• Frank Reich, who stepped in for Kelly, tied Kelly's team record for TD passes in a play-off game.

• The Bills remained unbeaten all-time in the postseason at Rich (6-0).

• The Oilers took the opening kickoff and led by Warren Moon, who was starting his first game in more than a month, embarked on a 14-play, 80-yard march. Moon completed six of seven passes for 57 yards including a 32-yard connection with Haywood Jeffires on third-and-eight from the Houston 33. He then hit Jeffires for the TD.

• The Bills came right back, driving 38 yards in 10 plays to Steve Christie's first field goal. Reich hit Andre Reed for 17 on a third-and-five from the Oilers 35.

• The Oilers responded with a 12-play, 80-yard drive as Moon hit Webster Slaughter for a TD. Again, Moon completed six of seven passes along the way including a 23-yarder to Ernest Givins to the Bills 43.

• After the Bills went three-and-out, Lorenzo White gained 10 yards on two carries, Moon fired a 24-yard strike to Givins, White gained two and then Moon hit Curtis Duncan for a 26-yard TD and 21-3 lead.

• The Bills advanced to the Houston 32, but Reich's fourth-and-four pass to Pete Metzelaars fell incomplete.

• Moon took the field with 1:15 left in the half and refused to sit on the lead. He hit five of six passes including four to Jeffires worth 50 yards.

• At the half, Moon had completed 19 of 22 passes for 218 yards and four TDs. The Oilers held advantages in yards (284-79) and first downs (18-5) in a dominating performance.

• On the fourth play of the third quarter, Reich's pass for Keith McKeller went off his hands. Bubba McDowell intercepted and raced down the sideline 58 yards for a TD that seemed to put the game away.

• Al Del Greco squibbed the ensuing kickoff and Mark Maddox recovered at midfield. Ten plays later, Kenneth Davis, in for Thomas, scored behind Jim Ritcher's block.

• Christie then recovered his own onside kick at the Bills 48. Four plays later, Don Beebe got behind the Oilers secondary for a 38-yard TD reception.

• The Oilers went three-and-out and Greg Montgomery's punt traveled only 25 yards to the Bills 41. Reich hit James Lofton for 18 and after a 39-yard pass to Beebe was nullified by a false start on Howard Ballard, Davis ran 19 yards with a screen and then Reich hit Reed on the left side for a TD.

• On the first play after the kickoff, Henry Jones intercepted Moon's pass for Slaughter and returned it 15 yards to the Houston 23. Davis ran twice for five yards, then Reich threw incomplete, bringing up a fourth-and-five from the 18. After calling timeout, Reich fired a TD pass over the middle to Reed to make it 35-31 with two minutes left in the third quarter.

• The teams traded punts, then the Oilers drove to Buffalo's 14. Their drive was kept alive when Carlton Bailey's interception was nullified by a roughing-the-passer penalty on Bruce Smith. The drive stalled and Del Greco came in for a field goal attempt, but the holder, Montgomery, dropped the snap and the Bills took possession at their 26.

• On third-and-four, Davis broke a 35-yard run to the Oilers 33. A few plays later, on third-and-three from the 26, Reich

hit Reed for nine. On the next play, he found Reed for the go-ahead TD to cap a seven-play, 74-yard drive with 3:08 left.

• Moon then moved his team 63 yards in 12 plays to Del Greco's tying field goal. Moon hit Slaughter for 18 yards to the Bills 16 on fourth-and-four.

• The Oilers won the toss and took the ball in OT, but on the third play, Moon overthrew Jeffires and Nate Odomes intercepted at the Houston 35. A facemask penalty against Jeffires moved the ball to the 20. After two Davis runs for six yards, Christie nailed the game-winning field goal from 32 yards.

QUOTES

• Darryl Talley: "Believe, believe, believe. What this shows is that this team has a helluva lot of character."

• Kenneth Davis: "I've never seen anything wilder than this. When we won the AFC Championship (51-3 over the Raiders in 1990) on the way to the first Super Bowl it wasn't this great. This was a very emotional win for us."

• Andre Reed: "Of course it seemed like it was hopeless. Our defense wasn't stopping them. It seemed like they were going to run up and down the field all day on us. But I guess the Oilers got a little lackadaisical out there and it gave us a chance to get the momentum."

• Jim Kelly: "Gale (Gilbert) and I told him before the second half 'Well Frank, you had the greatest comeback in college history (he rallied Maryland from 31-0 down at the half to a 42-40 victory over Miami in 1984), let's see if you can do it in the pros. And he went out and did it. In order to have a comeback like that, you have to make some big plays and I'll tell you, the poise that Frank showed out there, I don't think it can be matched. That was the greatest win I've ever been associated with and I was on the sidelines. It doesn't feel good standing there, but when a guy like Frank pulls through, that's great."

• Frank Reich: "Without question it's the game of my life. I was pretty emotional when I got back to the locker room, I couldn't hold the tears back. Your thought is to take it one play at a time and don't try to force anything. In thinking back to the experience in college, it wasn't any great thing that I did. We only threw 15 times in the second half of that game and we were down 31-0, so I knew it could be done. I never really thought 'Oh, we're out of it.' I still had to go out there. I had thrown some bad passes, but I was seeing the field well. When we scored to make it 35-24 late in the third quarter, that's when I thought it was really within reach."

• Marv Levy on Reich: "Frank is a person of high character. He's a well-rounded family man who's deeply religious. Sometimes the guy who has other things in his life doesn't clutch up. It makes him be able to retain an equilibrium." (On his thoughts at halftime): "I was just thinking this is a humiliating day. Did I still think we had a chance?

	BUF	HOU
First downs	19	27
Rushing yds	98	82
Passing yds	268	347
Punts-avg	2-35.0	2-24.5
Fumbles-lost	0-0	2-0
Penalties-yds	4-30	4-30
Poss. time	25:27	37:39

Oilers	7	21	7	3	0	- 38
Bills	3	0	28	7	3	- 41

Attendance at Rich Stadium - 75,141

Hou: Jeffires 3 pass from Moon (DelGreco kick), 9:09
Buf: FG Christie 36, 13:36
Hou: Slaughter 7 pass from Moon (DelGreco kick), 6:01
Hou: Duncan 26 pass from Moon (DelGreco kick), 10:51
Hou: Jeffires 27 pass from Moon (DelGreco kick), 14:46
Hou: McDowell 58 interception return (DelGreco kick), 1:41
Buf: K. Davis 1 run (Christie kick), 6:08
Buf: Beebe 38 pass from Reich (Christie kick), 7:04
Buf: Reed 26 pass from Reich (Christie kick), 10:19
Buf: Reed 18 pass from Reich (Christie kick), 13:00
Buf: Reed 17 pass from Reich (Christie kick), 11:52
Hou: FG DelGreco 26, 14:48
Buf: FG Christie 32, 3:06

BUFFALO TACKLES: Hansen 10, Talley 7, Kelso 7, Odomes 6, Bailey 5, Williams 5, Conlan 4, Jones 4, B. Smith 3, Patton 3, Wright 2..

HOUSTON TACKLES: A. Smith 7, Robertson 6, Jones 6, Fuller 6 Gray 5, Jackson 4, D. Smith 4, Dishman 3, Robinson 3, McDowell 3, Childress 2..

BILLS LEADERS: Rushing - Thomas 11-26, K. Davis 13-68, Gardner 1-5, Reich 1-(-1); **Passing** - Reich 21-34-1 - 289; **Receiving** - Reed 8-136, Beebe 4-64, K. Davis 2-25, Lofton 2-24, Metzelaars 3-43, Thomas 2-(-3); **Kickoff returns** - K. Davis 2-33, Lamb 1-22; **Punt returns** - None.

OILERS LEADERS: Rushing - White 19-75, Moon 2-7, Montgomery 1-0; **Passing** - Moon 36-50-2 - 371; **Receiving** - Duncan 8-57, Slaughter 8-73, Jeffires 8-98, Givins 9-117, Harris 2-15, White 1-11; **Kickoff returns** - Tillman 1-15, Lewis 1-7, Flannery 1-5, Brown 1-0; **Punt returns** - Slaughter 1-7.

Well, there was a lot of time left so there was a glimmer of hope, but it was about the same chance as you have of winning the New York Lottery. I have to admit it's a tremendous thrill to be part of a game like this."

• Jeff Wright: "We felt as low as we possibly could at half-time. That was as embarrassed as I've ever been on a football field. Marv told us we were going to have to dig down deeper than we had ever dug before. I went up to Ray Childress and he said to me 'I've never seen anything like this.' And his eyes were like bugged out. I told him 'Me either.' I've never witnessed anything like this. It was a great win."

• Steve Christie: "A kicker dreams of an opportunity to be able to kick that last field goal to be able to win it for you. I just can't be more happy than I am right now."

• Oilers cornerback Cris Dishman: "It was the biggest choke in history. Everyone on the team, everyone in the organization, choked. We were outplayed and outcoached in the second half. When we had them down, we should have cut their throats, but we let them breathe and gave them new life. Never in my wildest nightmares did I believe something like this could happen. I think we have to put another word in the English dictionary to describe this loss because devastated doesn't do it. Tell me I'm dreaming and this didn't happen."

• Oilers receiver Ernest Givins: "It's like somebody, somewhere, has a voodoo doll and when the Houston Oilers go on the road to play a playoff game, they start sticking pins in the voodoo doll until there's nothing left of the Houston Oilers."

• Oilers coach Jack Pardee: "It's so disappointing to get in that position and let it get away. We did everything right in the first half and nothing right in the second half. A lot of strange things happened in the second half."

Bills	0	7	7	10	-	24
Steelers	3	0	0	0	-	3

Attendance at Three Rivers Stadium - 60,407

Pit: FG Anderson 38, 7:46
Buf: Frerotte 1 pass from Reich (Christie kick), 13:04
Buf: Lofton 17 pass from Reich (Christie kick), 11:00
Buf: FG Christie 43, 4:47
Buf: Gardner 1 run (Christie kick), 13:04

	BUF	PIT
First downs	19	18
Rushing yds	169	129
Passing yds	156	111
Punts-avg	4-42.3	3-37.3
Fumbles-lost	0-0	4-1
Penalties-yds	4-33	2-23
Poss. time	32:26	27:34

BUFFALO TACKLES: Talley 9, Wright 6, Bennett 5, B. Smith 5, Hansen 5, Kelso 4, Patton 4, Jones 3, Odomes 2, Willis 2, Williams 2, Conlan 2.
PITTSBURGH TACKLES: Shelton 8, J. Williams 8, Hickerson 7, D. Williams 6, D.J. Johnson 5, Lloyd 5, Lake 4, Evans 4, Little 4, Griffin 3.

BILLS LEADERS: Rushing - K. Davis 10-104, Thomas 18-54, Gardner 7-22, Reed 1-(-8), Reich 2-(-3); **Passing** - Reich 16-23-0 - 160; **Receiving** - Beebe 6-72, Thomas 3-25, Lofton 2-29, McKeller 2-22, Metzelaars 2-11, Frerotte 1-1; **Kickoff returns** - K. Davis 1-18, Lamb 1-24; **Punt returns** - None.
STEELERS LEADERS: Rushing - Foster 20-104, O'Donnell 4-26, Thompson 1-3, Royals 1-0, Stone 1-(-4); **Passing** - O'Donnell 15-29-2 - 163; **Receiving** - Mills 8-93, Davenport 3-54, Stone 1-9, Foster 3-7; **Kickoff returns** - Stone 3-65, Thigpen 1-14, Thompson 1-20; **Punt returns** - Woodson 2-14.

NOTES

• Frank Reich wasn't heroic, but he didn't have to be as the Bills drilled the Steelers. It was their first win in the playoffs away from Rich Stadium since Dec. 27, 1981, ending a string of five straight losses (counting Super Bowls).
• The Bills victory snapped a 15-game streak of AFC playoff games that were won by the home team dating to 1989.
• Thurman Thomas was slowed by a bruised shoulder, but Kenneth Davis stepped in and averaged a Bills playoff record 10.4 yards per carry.

• The Bills defense recorded seven sacks of Neil O'Donnell worth 52 yards in losses, including two each by Jeff Wright and ex-Steeler Keith Willis.
• Cornelius Bennett returned to action after missing the previous 2 1/2 games. He played knowing his father had suffered a stroke earlier in the week.
• The crowd at Three Rivers, witnessing the first home playoff game since 1983, was a new stadium record.
• On the Steelers' first possession, they drove 33 yards in nine plays to Gary Anderson's field goal.
• After a Bills punt, Pittsburgh got to the Bills 41, but Nate Odomes intercepted O'Donnell's pass to Ernie Mills. Buffalo failed to move and punted again.
• Later in the second quarter, the Steelers reached the Bills 34, but Bruce Smith sacked O'Donnell, forced a fumble and Phil Hansen recovered at the Bills 41. From there, Reich drove Buffalo 59 yards in nine plays, hitting Mitch Frerotte on a lineman-eligible TD pass, Frerotte's third of the season. Thomas had three runs for 20 yards, Davis had a 14-yard gain and Reich hit Don Beebe for 19 yards.
• J.D. Williams stopped another Pittsburgh drive into Buffalo territory with an interception at the Bills 18 with 58 seconds left in the first half.
• After a Steelers punt to start the third, the Bills took control of the game by driving 80 yards in 13 plays to Reich's TD pass to James Lofton. Reich hit Beebe for nine on third-and-six from the Steelers 34 and also hit Thomas for 11 on third-and-10 from the 25. One play before the TD, Richard Shelton dropped an interception that he would have returned for a TD.
• The Steelers blew a scoring chance late in the third when holder Mark Royals fumbled a snap on a field goal attempt and the Bills took possession at their own 31. Ten plays later, Steve Christie made a 43-yard field goal. The key play was a 23-yard pass to Keith McKeller on third-and-seven from the Bills 34.
• After a punt, the Bills put the game away with an eight-play, 86-yard drive that chewed up 5:20 before Carwell Gardner scored on a short plunge. The Bills ran on every play, including a 41-yard burst by Davis on the first play and another 18-yarder by Davis.

QUOTES

• Frank Reich: "It seems we do play better during adversity. Who knows how to explain it except that we have players who rise to the occasion. There was a lot of pressure this week. I was more nervous for this game because it was on the road and I knew Pittsburgh was awfully good. The crowd noise would be for them. We had a lot to overcome. We can go to the Super Bowl if we play defense like that. They kept us in the game until we got going offensively." (On the TD pass to Frerotte): "I had a feeling that he was going to be open because as I was calling the signals, their whole defense was charging forward."
• Mark Kelso: "I feel we've gotten our confidence back. I don't know that we had it toward the end of the season after we lost those two games (to the Colts and Jets). We have it now. There's a fine line between being good and being so-so and I don't think we had that fine focus at the end of the year. We found that fine line in the second half last week and we carried that into today. I feel like we've reached that plateau where we feel like we're playing really well and we have a lot of confidence in the things we're doing."
• Darryl Talley: "We played one of our best defensive football games. We played total defense."
• Mitch Frerotte on his TD: "Just don't drop it, that's what was going through my mind really. When you're that open you look like an idiot if you drop the ball. I'm showing block first. They think I'm coming to block them. They're putting their heads down and I'm zipping right by them."
• Don Beebe: "Obviously with the two games I had before against Pittsburgh, I thought that hopefully I could have a good game against them. Pittsburgh tries to shut off the middle with their fast linebackers and safeties, so going into the game we did think we could get some outside stuff on 'in' routes and hitches. But we didn't go into the game saying 'We're going to get Don the ball.' I can't believe I've been here four years and I might be in three Super Bowls. That's incredible because some guys play forever and don't even get to the game."
• Steelers running back Barry Foster: "We'd get a couple of plays going and then somebody would break down. They would get a big play on defense – a sack or a loss in the running game – and we just couldn't piece it back together. I saw a lot of our guys really lose control after they scored that second touchdown when they went up 14-3. A lot of our guys didn't bounce back from that."

The Buffalo defense dominated Pittsburgh in the AFC divisional round as the Bills won a road playoff game for the first time since 1981.

NOTES

• The Bills won for the sixth time in seven visits to Joe Robbie Stadium, only this time, the AFC Championship was on the line. With the victory, the Bills qualified for their third straight Super Bowl, tying Miami's record of three straight appearances (1971-73).
• Steve Christie tied an NFL playoff record by making five field goals.
• Jim Kelly returned to action after missing the previous 2 1/2 games with a knee injury.
• The Bills beat Miami for the 12th time in the last 14 games and Marv Levy improved to 12-4 vs. Don Shula.
• The crowd was the largest in Joe Robbie Stadium history.
• By rushing for 182 yards, the Bills produced their third-highest postseason rushing total. Meanwhile, Miami's 33 rushing yards were the lowest ever against the Bills in the playoffs. Miami had just two yards on the ground in the second half.
• The Bills sacked Dan Marino four times, just as they did while winning a game in Miami in November.
• The last AFC team to win two straight road games in the playoffs was New England in 1985.
• The Bills punted after the first series, but got the ball back three plays later when Nate Odomes forced and recovered Fred Banks' fumble at the Miami 25. However, on first down, Kelly was intercepted by J.B. Brown at the 3 and he returned it 32 yards to the 35.
• Four plays later, Bruce Smith sacked Marino, forced him to fumble and Darryl Talley recovered at the Miami 47. Thurman Thomas then broke 24- and 10-yard runs to set up Christie's first field goal.
• The Dolphins answered with a 39-yard drive to Pete Stoyanovich's 51-yard field goal.
• Brad Lamb returned the ensuing kickoff 36 yards and things began to fall apart for Miami. After Kelly hit Andre Reed for nine yards, Bryan Cox roughed Kelly and the 15-yard penalty moved the ball to the Miami 35. Four plays later, Kelly hit Thomas with a 17-yard screen pass for the TD.
• On the first play after the kickoff, Phil Hansen tipped a Marino pass at the line and intercepted it at the Miami 17 and that set up Christie's second field goal for a 13-3 lead.
• The Bills wasted two other scoring chances in the first half. Christie missed a 38-yard field goal and after driving to the Miami 37, Kelly threw an interception to Louis Oliver at the 2 with 52 seconds left.
• At the half, the Bills had outgained Miami, 207-114.
• The Bills put the game away early in the third. Mark Pike forced Mike Williams to fumble the second-half kickoff and Carwell Gardner recovered at the Miami 25. On second down, Thomas fumbled after an 11-yard run and Miami's Marco Coleman recovered, but Don Beebe then stripped Coleman and got the ball back for Buffalo at the 8. Three plays later, Kenneth Davis scored to make it 20-3.
• Miami went three-and-out and the Bills then drove 67 yards in 15 plays, consuming 8:28, to Christie's third field goal. Davis converted a third-and-one from the Bills 39. Lamb caught a 16-yard pass on third-and-five from the Bills 49. Keith McKeller made an 11-yard reception on third-and-five from the Miami 30 and Kelly hit Thomas for 15 yards to the 3 before the Dolphins stiffened and forced a field goal.
• Miami again went three-and-out and the Bills wasted little time getting Christie's fourth field goal. On the first play, Davis took a center screen 30 yards to the Miami 22. He then ran three straight plays for nine yards and Marv Levy elected to kick on the first play of the fourth quarter.
• Marino drove to the Buffalo 12, but he was intercepted by Clifford Hicks who returned it 31 yards.
• On the next series, Miami finally found the end zone, driving 62 yards in seven plays to Mark Duper's TD recep-

tion. Marino was six of nine during the possession.
• The Bills recovered the onside kick, then moved 23 yards to Christie's fifth field goal.

QUOTES

• Marv Levy: "I've never been prouder in all the years I've coached than to be associated with the men on this team. It's been a long road and a hard road. There was a headline (in the *Buffalo News*) prior to the Houston (playoff) game that read, 'Bills Begin Longest Road Today.' I've used that this entire postseason. Today it came through Joe Robbie Stadium." (On Jim Kelly): "I can't think of a quarterback who entered a game like this with so much unfair pressure on him. The denigration of Jim Kelly revolted me. I'm immensely proud of the way he handled the situation. There was never a quarterback controversy, ever, inside the team. If there's anything I'm resentful of, it's the effort that was made to make it an issue when it wasn't."
• Thurman Thomas: "I think this team has matured a lot to where we realize that it's going to take a full effort of 60 minutes to go out and win the Super Bowl. And that's what we plan on doing."
• Mark Kelso: "This is, no question, the sweetest of them all. And the thing that makes it the sweetest is that it was such a team effort. I thank God we've got 47 guys in this room who are willing to put the time in and do the things they need to do to get prepared to play, because you never know when you're going to be called on. The guys who are our so-called stars played great, and the guys who aren't stars rose to the occasion."
• Jim Kelly: "This is our third trip to the Super Bowl, but we still have one more river to cross. This was without a doubt the sweetest victory I've ever been associated with. I just want to thank my teammates for hanging in there with me all week. Every time I needed an encouraging word, they were there for me." (On the controversy over whether he or Frank Reich should start): "It was like in the beginning of the week, I had to apologize for feeling good."
• Kent Hull on Kelly: "Before the game, Jim was his same old self. He was running around the dressing room giving directives: 'Offensive line, you've got to do this, running backs, you've got to do this and wideouts, when we run this route, you've got to do this.' He was very much in command and usually that means he has a lot of confidence." (On going back to the Super Bowl): "I don't want to say this is something we're getting used to because you never want to say that about a Super Bowl. But we know what we're getting into now, so maybe we'll approach it a little differently."

Bills | 3 | 10 | 10 | 6 - 29
Dolphins | 3 | 0 | 0 | 7 - 10

Attendance at Joe Robbie Stadium - 72,703

Buf: FG Christie 21, 9:17
Mia: FG Stoyanovich 51, 13:03
Buf: Thomas 17 pass from Kelly (Christie kick), :40
Buf: FG Christie 33, 2:59
Buf: K. Davis 2 run (Christie kick), 1:58
Buf: FG Christie 21, 11:33
Buf: FG Christie 31, :04
Mia: Duper 15 pass from Marino (Stoyanovich kick), 7:28
Buf: FG Christie 38, 12:23

	BUF	MIA
First downs	20	15
Rushing yds	182	33
Passing yds	176	243
Punts-avg	2-34.5	4-37.0
Fumbles-lost	1-0	4-3
Penalties-yds	3-20	5-40
Poss. time	36:19	23:41

BUFFALO TACKLES: B. Smith 7, Talley 6, Bennett 4, Odomes 4, Hicks 3, Kelso 3, Darby 3, Conlan 3, Jones 2, Jackson 2, Hansen 2.
MIAMI TACKLES: Klingbeil 10, Oliver 10, Griggs 9, Hollier 8, Vincent 7, Cross 6, Cox 5, Braggs 5, Coleman 5, Hobley 4, Grimsley 3.

BILLS LEADERS: **Rushing** - Thomas 20-96, K. Davis 19-61, Kelly 3-4, Reed 2-6, Lamb 1-16, Gardner 3-(-1); **Passing** - Kelly 17-24-2 - 177; **Receiving** - Thomas 5-70, K. Davis 4-52, Reed 3-25, Lofton 2-19, McKeller 1-11, Gardner 1-(-6), Metzelaars 1-6; **Kickoff returns** - Davis 1-23, Lamb 1-36; **Punt returns** - Hicks 1-36.
DOLPHINS LEADERS: **Rushing** - Humphrey 8-22, Craver 2-13, Marino 1-(-2); **Passing** - Marino 22-45-2 - 268; **Receiving** - Jackson 5-71, Humphrey 5-41, Banks 2-18, Clayton 3-32, Duper 2-36, Martin 3-55, Craver 2-15; **Kickoff returns** - Craver 4-48, Williams 3-64; **Punt returns** - Miller 1-14.

• Will Wolford on Kelly: "Everyone knew there was a lot of pressure on Jim this week. If we had lost, no matter how we lost, the finger would have been pointed at him."
• Cornelius Bennett: "The last 10 quarters when it really counted, we played the best football we can play. And our secondary has done a tremendous job in those 10 quarters, which helps us get up in the quarterback's face and make sacks. We've made history twice in a couple of weeks, but we want to make history in two weeks by winning the Super Bowl."
• Shane Conlan: "We knew we were the top team in the AFC. We had some bad luck and lost some games, but talent-wise we knew we had a great team."
• Nate Odomes: "What this win means to me, and I think I can speak for everybody in this locker room, is it means that we have an opportunity to fix what we haven't done yet. We haven't won the big one yet. We can go four or five more times, but if we don't win, 20 or 30 years from now, who's going to remember the Buffalo Bills went to the Super Bowl five or six times?"
• Dolphins coach Don Shula: "The big thing was we weren't able to run with it. We struggled to run every time. They played an outstanding game. That's the kind of team we need to be able to beat to get to our final goal and we weren't able to handle it."
• Dolphins quarterback Dan Marino: "We didn't challenge them at all. That's what makes it so frustrating. We can beat that team for sure, but you can't turn the ball over five times like we did. It's frustrating as a quarterback to stand there and watch them take advantage of all those opportunities."

Nate Odomes and Mark Kelso prevented this Miami pass from being completed. It was a common occurrence during Buffalo's AFC Championship Game victory over the Dolphins.

Bills	7	3	7	0 -	17
Cowboys	14	14	3	21 -	52

Attendance at the Rose Bowl - 98,374

Buf: Thomas 2 run (Christie kick), 5:00
Dal: Novacek 23 pass from Aikman (Elliott kick), 13:24
Dal: Jones 2 fumble return (Elliott kick), 13:39
Buf: FG Christie 21, 11:36
Dal: Irvin 19 pass from Aikman (Elliott kick), 13:06
Dal: Irvin 18 pass from Aikman (Elliott kick), 13:24
Dal: FG Elliott 20, 6:39
Buf: Beebe 40 pass from Reich (Christie kick), 15:00
Dal: Harper 45 pass from Aikman (Elliott kick), 4:56
Dal: E. Smith 10 run (Elliott kick), 6:48
Dal: Norton 9 fumble return (Elliott kick), 7:29

	BUF	DAL
First downs	22	20
Rushing yds	108	137
Passing yds	254	271
Punts-avg	3-45.3	4-32.8
Fumbles-lost	8-5	4-2
Penalties-yds	4-30	8-53
Poss. time	28:48	31:12

BUFFALO TACKLES: Bennett 9, Conlan 8, Talley 6, Patton 5, Jones 5, Williams 5, B. Smith 5, Odomes 4, Wright 3, Hansen 3, Darby 3.
DALLAS TACKLES: Norton 9, Edwards 6, Washington, 6, Maryland 6, Haley 5, Casillas 5, Woodson 4, Lett 3, Everett 3, Holmes 3, Jeffcoat 2.

BILLS LEADERS: Rushing - Thomas 11-19, K. Davis 15-86, Gardner 1-3, Reich 2-0; **Passing** - Kelly 4-7-2 - 82, Reich 18-31-2 - 194; **Receiving** - Reed 8-152, Thomas 4-10, Metzelaars 2-12, Beebe 2-50, Tasker 2-30, K. Davis 3-16, McKeller 1-6; **Kickoff returns** - Lamb 2-49, K. Davis 1-21, Hicks 1-20; **Punt returns** - None.
COWBOYS LEADERS: Rushing - E. Smith 22-108, Aikman 3-28, Gainer 2-1, Johnston 1-0, Beuerlein 1-0; **Passing** - Aikman 22-30-0 - 273; **Receiving** - Irvin 6-114, Novacek 7-72, E. Smith 6-27, Harper 1-45, Johnston 2-15; **Kickoff returns** - K. Martin 4-79; **Punt returns** - K. Martin 3-35.

NOTES

• The Bills became the first team in NFL history to lose three Super Bowls in a row.
• The Cowboys' victory was the third-most lopsided in Super Bowl history.
• Dallas quarterback Troy Aikman won the MVP award for passing for 273 yards and four TDs. It was the 15th time a quarterback had been named the game's MVP.
• Emmitt Smith became the first player in history to win the rushing title and the Super Bowl in the same year.
• Dallas coach Jimmy Johnson became the first to win a national college championship and a Super Bowl.
• Andre Reed had a productive game and he became the all-time leading Super Bowl receiver with 21 catches.
• Dallas made its record sixth appearance in the Super Bowl and won for the third time.
• The 69 points combined made this the highest-scoring Super Bowl ever.
• Dallas also established a record by scoring the two fastest TDs, 15 seconds apart in the second quarter.
• The Bills set Super Bowl records for most fumbles (eight) and fumbles lost (five) in a single game as well as most turnovers (nine). The Cowboys scored 35 points as a result of Bills turnovers.
• Ken Norton Jr.'s hit on Jim Kelly in the second quarter reinjured Kelly's knee and knocked him out of the game for good. Frank Reich entered and wound up tying a Super Bowl record by fumbling three times.
• Don Beebe made the most memorable play of the night when he chased down Leon Lett, who was about to score on a fumble return late in the fourth quarter, and slapped the ball away, preventing the score. The Bills were down 52-17 at the time, but Beebe showed the determination not to quit.

QUOTES

• Marv Levy: "Well, we gave it away nine times and they capitalized I think on five of them for touchdowns. We didn't play well enough and they certainly did. I felt our team came in very motivated and ready to play. They did-

n't appear uptight but they played uptight. Losses are very disappointing and to lose in such a bad way in such a big game adds to the distress you feel." (On whether changes need to be made in personnel): "I don't think so. Anybody that says something like that after any loss is lashing out or looking to place blame on someone." (On Don Beebe's play on Leon Lett): "Here's a game, 52-17, and he has enough pride that he doesn't want the guy to score again."
• Andre Reed: "There's something about this team that's a mystery."
• Shane Conlan on losing three Super Bowls in a row: "They are all disappointing. Because this is the last one, obviously it hurts. But to be embarrassed is pathetic. They played as well as any team we've ever played. You just have to accept it, they beat us badly."
• Bruce Smith: "We've got the talent, but if you don't make the plays, it doesn't mean a damn thing. We knew we were going to make history tonight one way or the other, but we didn't want to make it this way. They all hurt. It's going to be a long off-season."
• Jim Kelly: "Why me, why me? I said early in the week it would come down to turnovers. Unfortunately, I was right. We couldn't beat a college team with that many turnovers. This loss hurts the most because we had worked so hard and overcome so much to get here. Somebody's got to win and somebody's got to lose, I just wish we could see what it feels like to win. We have a lot to be proud of. Everyone counted us out after last year and look what happened this year. We haven't won one yet, but we have a lot to hang our hats on." (On his fourth-and-goal interception in the end zone in the second quarter): "If I get sacked, it's still their ball, so I thought why not take a chance and throw the ball. I saw Pete (Metzelaars), I saw Carwell (Gardner). If I throw the ball out of the end zone, it's their ball."
• James Lofton: "I think they (the Cowboys defense) cheated, I think they had 12 guys out there most of the time. No, they just played good football. They were able to push the pocket, they were able to close on the receivers after we caught the ball. An earthquake over in Santa Monica is the only thing that will stop the Dallas Cowboys."
• Kenneth Davis: "I'm not down and I'm not depressed, I'm just happy we had the opportunity to be here. I think

there are 26 other teams that would have loved to be in this situation. There is no reason for us to be dragging."
• Frank Reich: "It was a very humbling experience. As happy as I felt after the comeback win (against Houston), I feel as disappointed now."
• Darryl Talley on losing three in a row: "It's a gut-wrenching thought, but there's not a whole helluva lot you can do about it. We're a good enough team to get here three consecutive times and to not win once, it's a crying shame."
• Don Beebe: "I just felt coming into this game that we were going to win. The word destiny kind of floated around and I thought we were just destined to win." (On his play on Lett): "I wasn't going to quit. The way I've been taught in high school and college and by Marv Levy is if you can make a play, then make it. I was determined to catch the guy and try to knock the ball out. Then when he started celebrating around the 10-yard-line, I knew I was going to catch him."
• Thurman Thomas: "You're not going to beat a high school team if you have nine turnovers."
• Cowboys coach Jimmy Johnson: "I feel like we had the better team. As for the domination, when you turn the ball over as many times as they did, it just snowballs. Those things are going to happen. We said all year that the best game we were going to play was the last game and we saved the best for last. We felt we might get some turnovers and we've protected the ball pretty well all year so we felt we might have an edge there. There was never any doubt that we would get to this point, but the concern was how long was it going to take."
• Cowboys receiver Michael Irvin: "No, there was never any doubt in my mind."
• Cowboys quarterback Troy Aikman: "This win takes a tremendous amount of weight off my shoulders. No matter what happens in my career now, I can say that I've been with a Super Bowl winner. I worked real hard to not make the game larger than it appeared. This is as great a feeling as I've ever had in my life and I really wish every player could experience this before he's finished playing. Jim's (Kelly) been here three times and hasn't been able to walk away with a win. I really don't know what to say about that. I feel very fortunate I was able to win in my first try."

STARTING LINEUPS

BILLS OFFENSE: QB - Jim Kelly; RB - Thurman Thomas; WR - Andre Reed, Don Beebe, James Lofton; TE - Pete Metzelaars; OL - Will Wolford, Jim Ritcher, Kent Hull, Glenn Parker, Howard Ballard.
DEFENSE: DL - Bruce Smith, Phil Hansen, Jeff Wright; LB - Cornelius Bennett, Darryl Talley, Shane Conlan, Marvcus Patton; DB - Nate Odomes, J.D. Williams, Henry Jones, Mark Kelso.

COWBOYS OFFENSE: QB - Troy Aikman; RB - Emmitt Smith, Daryl Johnston; WR - Michael Irvin, Alvin Harper; TE - Jay Novacek; OL - Mark Tuinei, Nate Newton, Mark Stepnoski, John Gesek, Erik Williams.
DEFENSE: DL - Tony Tolbert, Tony Casillas, Russell Maryland, Charles Haley; LB - Ken Norton, Robert Jones, Vinson Smith; DB - Kevin Smith, Larry Brown, James Washington, Thomas Everett.

SUPER BOWL XXVII PLAY-BY-PLAY

FIRST QUARTER

Bills win toss, elect to receive.
Elliott kicks off to end zone, touchback.
BILLS 15:00
1-10-B20 - Kelly pass to Reed, 14, (tackled by Norton); 1-10-B34 - Thomas runs right, 2, (Maryland); 2-8-B36 - Kelly pass to Thomas, 7, (L. Brown); 3-1-B43 - Kelly sacked by Everett, -2; 4-3-B41 - Mohr punt 45, K. Martin return 1.

COWBOYS 13:19
1-10-D15 - Aikman pass to E. Smith, 0, (Patton); 2-10-D15 - E. Smith runs left, 1, (Talley, Kelso); 3-9-D16 - Aikman incomplete pass to Irvin; 4-9-D16 - Saxon punt is blocked by Tasker, Tasker recovers at D16.

BILLS 11:40
1-10-D16 - Thomas runs left, 9, (Norton); 2-1-D7 - Thomas runs to middle, -2, (Maryland, Gant); 3-3-D9 - Dallas penalty, holding, R. Jones, 4; 1-G-D5 - Thomas runs to middle, 3, (R. Jones, Casillas); 2-G-D2 - Thomas runs right, 2, TOUCH-DOWN. Christie PAT. Drive: 4 plays, 16 yards, Time of possession 1:40. Time of score: 5:00 elapsed. **Buffalo 7, Dallas 0.**

Christie kicks off to D6, K. Martin return 22 (Pike).
COWBOYS 10:00
1-10-D28 - E. Smith runs to middle, 0, (B. Smith, Bennett); 2-10-D28 - Aikman pass to Novacek, 9, (Patton, Conlan); 3-1-D37 - E. Smith runs right, 3, (Wright, Conlan); 1-10-D40 - Dallas penalty, illegal formation, Tuinei, -5; 1-15-D35 - Aikman pass to Johnston, 8, (Williams); 2-7-D43 - Aikman incomplete pass to Novacek; 3-7-D43 - Aikman incomplete pass to K. Martin; 4-7-D43 - Saxon punt 57, touchback.

BILLS 6:21
1-10-B20 - Thomas runs right, -1, (Tolbert, Maryland); 2-11-B19 - Thomas runs right, 0, (Casillas); 3-11-B19 - Buffalo penalty, illegal motion, -5; 3-16-B14 - Dallas penalty, roughing the passer, Lett, 15; 1-10-B29 - Kelly pass for Beebe, intercepted by Washington at D40, return 13 (Metzelaars).

COWBOYS 4:40
1-10-B47 - E. Smith runs to middle, -1, (Wright); 2-11-B48 - Aikman pass to E. Smith, -5, (Patton); 3-16-D47 - Aikman pass to Irvin, 20, (Darby); 1-10-B33 - Aikman scramble right, 2, (Patton); 2-8-B31 - E. Smith runs to middle, 8, (Talley); 1-10-B23 - Aikman pass to Novacek, 23, TOUCHDOWN. Dallas penalty on PAT, holding, Agee, -10; Elliott PAT. Drive: 6 plays, 47 yards, TOP 3:04. Time of score: 13:24. **Buffalo 7, Dallas 7.**

Elliott kicks off to B4, Lamb return 16, (V. Smith), Buffalo penalty, illegal block, Maddox, -10.
BILLS 1:22
1-10-B10 - Kelly sacked by Haley, -8, fumbles, Jones recovers and returns for TOUCHDOWN. Elliott PAT. Time of score: 13:39. **Dallas 14, Buffalo 7.**

Elliott kicks off to B4, Lamb return 28, fumbles, forced by Gant, recovered by Bennett at B42.
BILLS 1:22
1-10-B42 - K. Davis runs to middle, 6, (Norton); 2-4-B48 - K. Davis runs to middle, 8, (Edwards, Norton).

SECOND QUARTER

1-10-D44 - Kelly pass to Reed, 40, (L. Brown); 1-G-D4 - Gardner runs to middle, 3, (Norton, Washington); 2-G-D1 - Thomas runs right, 0, (V. Smith); 3-G-D1 - K. Davis runs to left, 0, (Norton, Washington); 4-G-D1 - Kelly pass for Metzelaars, intercepted in end zone by Everett, touchback.

COWBOYS 11:59
1-10-D20 - E. Smith runs to middle, 2, (Conlan); 2-8-D22 - Aikman pass to Novacek, 11, (Conlan); 1-10-D33 - E. Smith runs right, 3, (Bennett, Jones); 2-7-D36 - Aikman scramble right, 7, (Williams); 1-10-D43 - E. Smith runs left, 0, (Talley, B. Smith); 2-10-D43 - Aikman incomplete pass to Irvin, Dallas timeout, 8:36; 3-10-D43 - Aikman pass to Novacek, 5, (Jones); 4-5-D48 - Saxon punt 37, Hicks fair catch.

BILLS 8:10
1-10-B15 - K. Davis runs left, 7, (Maryland); 2-3-B22 - K. Davis runs right, 4, (Casillas, Edwards); 1-10-B26 - K. Davis runs right, 7, (Haley); 2-3-B33 - Kelly incomplete pass to Reed, Kelly injured knee on play on hit by Norton, Reich in at QB; 3-3-B33 - Reich pass to Metzelaars, 7, (Washington); 1-10-B40 - Reich pass to Reed, 38, (K. Smith); 1-10-D22 - K. Davis runs to middle, 3, (Haley); 2-7-D19 - K. Davis runs right, 7, (Edwards); 1-10-D12 - Thomas runs right, 6, (Washington, Edwards); 2-4-D6 - Reich incomplete pass to Beebe; 3-4-D6 - Dallas penalty, offsides, Haley, 3; 3-1-D3 - Thomas runs left, 0, (Haley, Maryland); 4-1-D3 - Christie 21 FIELD GOAL. Drive: 12 plays, 82 yards, TOP 4:46. Time of score: 11:36. **Dallas 14, Buffalo 10.**

Christie kicks off to D7, K. Martin return 21 (Pike).
COWBOYS 3:15
1-10-D28 - Aikman pass to E. Smith, 6, (Talley); 2-4-D34 - Aikman pass to Novacek, 9, (Bennett, Conlan); 1-10-D43 - Aikman incomplete pass to Johnston, batted down by Talley; 2-10-D43 - E. Smith runs left, 38, (Odomes), official time-out, 1:58; 1-10-B19 - Aikman pass to Irvin, 19, TOUCHDOWN. Elliott PAT. Drive: 5 plays, 72 yards, TOP 1:30. Time of score: 13:06. **Dallas 21, Buffalo 10.**

Elliott kicks off to end zone, touchback.
BILLS 1:54
1-10-B20 - Reich pass to Thomas, -1, Lett forces fumble, J. Jones recovers at B18.

COWBOYS 1:43
1-10-B18 - Aikman pass to Irvin, 18, TOUCHDOWN. Elliott PAT. Drive: 1 play, 18 yards, TOP :07. Time of score: 13:24. **Dallas 28, Buffalo 10.**

Elliott kicks off to end zone, touchback.
BILLS 1:36
1-10-B20 - Reich fumbles snap, K. Davis recovers, -2; 2-12-B18 - Reich pass to Reed, 11, (Woodson); 3-1-B29 - Dallas penalty, offsides, Haley, 5; 1-10-B34 - Reich pass to Beebe intercepted by L. Brown at D28, no return.

COWBOYS :30
1-10-D28 - E. Smith runs to middle, 7, (Bennett); 2-3-D35 - Aikman pass to Irvin, 20, (Jones, Williams); 1-10-B45 - Aikman pass to E. Smith, 5, (Darby). HALF ENDS.

HALFTIME STATISTICS

	BUF	DAL
First downs	12	11
Rushing yds	64	70
Passing yds	127	148
Punts-avg	1-45.0	3-31.3
Fumbles-lost	4-2	1-0
Penalties-yds	2-15	6-42
Poss. time	15:42	14:18

RUSHING:	Buf:	Thomas 10-19, K. Davis 8-42, Gardner 1-3, Reich 1-0
	Dal:	E. Smith 10-61, Aikman 2-9.
PASSING:	Buf:	Kelly 4-7-2 - 82, Reich 4-6-1 - 55.
	Dal:	Aikman 14-19-0 - 148.
RECEIVING:	Buf:	Reed 5-124, Thomas 2-6, Metzelaars 1-7.
	Dal:	Novacek 5-57, Irvin 4-77, Johnston 1-8, E. Smith 4-6.

THIRD QUARTER

Christie kicks off to goal line, K. Martin return 21 (Pike, Goganious).
COWBOYS 15:00
1-10-D21 - E. Smith runs right, 7, (Bennett); 2-3-D28 - E. Smith runs to middle, 11, (Talley, Kelso); 1-10-D39 - Aikman pass to Johnston, 7, (Bennett, Williams); 2-3-D46 - Johnston runs right, 0, (Bennett); 3-3-D46 - Aikman pass to Irvin, 25, (Kelso); 1-10-D29 - E. Smith runs to middle, 7, (Hansen); 2-3-B22 - E. Smith runs to middle, 3, (Wright, Hansen); 1-10-B19 - Aikman pass to Irvin, 12, (Williams); 1-G-B7 - Gainer runs right, 0, (Bennett); 2-G-B7 - Aikman pass to Novacek, 5, (Odomes); 3-G-B2 - Aikman incomplete pass to Novacek; 4-G-B2 - Elliott 20 FIELD GOAL. Drive: 12 plays, 77 yards, TOP 6:39. Time of score: 6:39. **Dallas 31, Buffalo 10.**

Elliott kicks off to B6, K. Davis return 21 (Gainer).
BILLS 8:21
1-10-B27 - Reich incomplete pass to McKeller; 2-10-B27 - Reich pass to Reed, 8, (Casillas, Washington); 3-2-B35 - Reich pass to McKeller, 6, (Norton); 1-10-B41 - Reich pass to Thomas, 0, (Norton); 2-10-B41 - Reich pass to Thomas, 4, (Edwards); 3-6-B45 - Reich incomplete pass to Lofton; 4-6-B45 - Mohr punt 43, K. Martin return 30 (Hale).

COWBOYS 6:00
1-10-D42 - E. Smith runs to middle, 3, (Conlan); 2-7-D45 - Aikman incomplete pass to Novacek; 3-7-D45 - Aikman pass to Novacek, 10, (Odomes); 1-10-B45 - E. Smith runs right, 5, (Hansen, Conlan); 2-5-B40 - E. Smith runs to middle, 3, (Talley, Conlan); 3-2-B37 - E. Smith runs right, -1, (Patton); 4-3-B38 - Aikman incomplete pass to Irvin, batted at line by Patton.

BILLS 2:10
1-10-B39 - K. Davis runs right, 12, (Woodson); 1-10-D49 - Reich pass to Reed, 13, (Everett); 1-10-D36 - K. Davis runs to middle, -4, (Haley); 2-14-D40 - Reich pass to K. Davis, 0, (Edwards); 3-14-D40 - Reich pass to Beebe, 40, TOUCHDOWN. Christie PAT. Drive: 5 plays, 61 yards, TOP 2:10. Time of score: 15:00. **Dallas 31, Buffalo 17.**

FOURTH QUARTER

Christie kicks off to D8, K. Martin return 15 (Maddox).
COWBOYS 14:50
1-10-D23 - Aikman scramble to middle, 19, (Kelso); 1-10-D42 - E. Smith runs to middle, -8, B. Smith forces fumble, Aikman recovers at D30; 2-22-D30 - Aikman pass to E. Smith, 3, (Bennett); 3-19-D33 - Aikman pass to E. Smith, 18, (Darby, Jones); 4-1-B49 - Saxon punt 37, Hicks fumbles, recovers at 12.

BILLS 11:46
1-10-B12 - Thomas runs to middle, 0, (Maryland); 2-10-B12 - Reich incomplete pass to Reed; 3-10-B12 - Reich incomplete pass to Lofton; 4-10-B12 - Mohr punt 48, K. Martin return 4 (Patton).

COWBOYS 10:54
1-10-D44 - E. Smith runs left, 11, (Odomes); 1-10-B45 - Aikman pass to Harper, 45, TOUCHDOWN. Elliott PAT. Drive: 2 plays, 56 yards, TOP :50. Time of score: 4:56. **Dallas 38, Buffalo 17.**

Elliott kicks off to end zone, touchback.
BILLS 9:59
1-10-B20 - Reich incomplete pass to K. Davis; 2-10-B20 - Reich pass to Lofton intercepted by Everett at B30, return 22 (K. Davis).

COWBOYS 9:41
1-G-B8 - E. Smith runs left, 0, (Hansen); 2-G-B8 - Aikman sacked by B. Smith, -2; 3-G-B10 - E. Smith runs left, 10, TOUCHDOWN. Elliott PAT. Drive: 3 plays, 8 yards, TOP 1:29. Time of score: 6:48. **Dallas 45, Buffalo 17.**

Elliott kicks off to end zone, touchback.
BILLS 8:06
1-10-B20 - Reich pass to Reed, 7, (Norton); 2-3-B27 - Buffalo penalty, illegal procedure, Reich, -5; 2-8-B22 - Reich fumbles shotgun snap, K. Norton recovers at B9 and runs for TOUCHDOWN. Elliott PAT. Time of score: 7:29. **Dallas 52, Buffalo 17.**

Elliott kicks off to B5, Hicks return 20 (Pruitt).
BILLS 7:20
1-10-B25 - Reich pass to Tasker, 16, Lett forces fumble, Holmes recovers at B44.

COWBOYS 7:06
1-10-B44 - Beuerlein in at QB. Gainer runs right, 1, (B. Smith); 2-9-B43 - Beuerlein fumbles snap, Hansen recovers at B47.

BILLS 6:14
1-10-B47 - Reich pass to K. Davis, 3, (Horton); 2-7-50 - Reich pass to Tasker, 14, (Everett); 1-10-D36 - Dallas penalty, encroachment, 5; 1-5-D31 - Reich incomplete pass to McKeller; 2-5-D31 - Reich incomplete pass to Tasker; 3-5-D31 - Reich incomplete pass to Lofton; 4-5-D31 - Reich sacked by Jeffcoat, -4, Jeffcoat recovers at D35, runs 64 yards to B1, Beebe catches him from behind, forces fumble that goes through end zone, giving Bills ball at B20.

BILLS 4:42
1-10-B20 - Dallas penalty, interference, Woodson, 6; 1-10-B26 - K. Davis runs left, 5, (Holmes); 2-5-B31 - Buffalo penalty, holding, -10; 2-15-B21 - K. Davis runs right, 2, (Woodson); 3-13-B23 - Reich pass to K. Davis, 13, (Holmes); 1-10-B36 - Reich pass to Beebe, 10, (Woodson); 1-10-B46 - Reich pass to Metzelaars, 5, out of bounds, 2:00; 2-5-D49 - K. Davis runs left, 14, (Holmes); 1-10-D35 - K. Davis runs right, 8, (Holt); 2-2-D27 - K. Davis runs to middle, 7, (Gant); 1-10-D20 - Reich incomplete pass to Lofton, :58; 3-2-D27 - K. Davis runs to middle, 7, (Gant); 1-10-D20 - Reich incomplete pass to Lofton; 2-10-D20 - Reich sacked by Lett, -8, GAME ENDS. FINAL: **Dallas 52, Buffalo 17.**

At A Glance
1993

Feb. 1 – A report circulated in Los Angeles that Marv Levy had suffered a heart attack in the early morning at the Bills hotel, but the rumor was quickly squashed. Later that morning, before boarding the team plane for the return trip to Buffalo, Levy made light of the story by saying: "Maybe I was sick at heart, but that was it."

Feb. 3 – Marv Levy held his annual postseason press conference and he said fans and media should not blame Jim Kelly for the Super Bowl loss to Dallas. "Our team didn't play well and Jim Kelly is part of our team, no better and no worse," Levy said. "I've said it often, too much credit goes to the quarterback when we win and too much criticism goes to him when you lose. I think the expectations of Jim Kelly will never be realized. He could complete 98 percent of his passes and someone would ask why he didn't complete that one pass."

Feb. 4 – In a shocking development, general manager Bill Polian was fired. Polian held a press conference and announced his own dismissal, saying that he and Ralph Wilson had met before the 1992 season and Wilson told him he would not continue as GM after the '92 season. "Just prior to the start of the season, Mr. Wilson and I met in Detroit," Polian explained. "He informed me at that time that he wished to restructure the front office. He reaffirmed that position this week and as a result, I will be leaving the Bills effective today." Of the team that he built, Polian said: "They're a very special group of men. Cherish them, you will not see their like again." Polian also thanked his good friend, Marv Levy, whom he called "my mentor and friend, without whom none of what all of us has achieved would have been possible." The players expressed shock over Polian's firing. "I did not know it was coming," Kent Hull said. "I guess the reason I'm so shocked is the success of the team the past five years. He's basically the man who built the team. If there was going to be changes, I never expected it to start at the top like this."

Feb. 5 – John Butler was promoted to the role of general manager, replacing Bill Polian. Jerry Foran was elevated to vice president of administration. "John is a competent, stable worker," Ralph Wilson said. "I have every confidence in his ability to lead the club and maintain the standard of excellence we have enjoyed for years."

Feb. 6 – Ralph Wilson admitted that his "personal and professional differences" with Bill Polian the last three years led to Polian's firing. Wilson said that the main reason was that Polian could not get along with Jeff Littmann, treasurer of Wilson's Detroit-based company. "They didn't get along very well," Wilson said. "There was some friction there and I just thought it was time to make a change and restructure our front office in Buffalo. The change has nothing to do with football, losing the third straight Super Bowl or anything like that."

Feb. 7 – John Butler talked about his promotion to general manager upon returning from Ralph Wilson's West Palm Beach, Fla. home. "Obviously, I had to feel very, very strongly on commitment," Butler said. "That is of utmost importance to me, having resource availability and everything to keep us tremendously successful and on the same route. I'm really going to be more of a personnel-type general manager than anything. I'll still be scouting talent as much as possible." At the Pro Bowl in Honolulu, Jim Kelly, who sat out the game because of his knee injury, reacted to Bill Polian's firing this way: "We lost the best general manager in football. It's sad to see a guy who's

done so much for us leave. I admire everything Bill has done, not only for the club, but for me personally."

Feb. 10 – John Butler held his first press conference as general manager and said he would not be making sweeping changes in personnel. "We will keep the core of this football team together and always look to improve," he said. "We're not an old football team by any stretch of the imagination. We're an experienced, good football team. One thing I promise you, nobody, and I mean nobody, is going to outwork us to try to get better."

Feb. 11 – According to an NFL Players' Association survey, the Bills had the sixth-highest payroll in the NFL at an average of $564,355 per player.

Feb. 15 – Bob Ferguson resigned as assistant general manager and director of pro personnel to join the Denver Broncos as their director of football operations/player personnel. "It's very hard," he said about leaving Buffalo. "It was a great run. You just hope you can be associated with a team that talented again in your career."

Feb. 17 – Former Bills star linebacker Jim Haslett was named linebackers coach of the Los Angeles Raiders.

Feb. 22 – A.J. Smith was promoted to director of pro personnel, taking over for Bob Ferguson.

Feb. 25 – The Bills decided to name Will Wolford and Jeff Wright as their transition free agents, meaning that under the new free agency system, they retained the right to match any offers those two players received. The team opted not to name a franchise player, who would have been untouchable. By becoming transition players, Wolford and Wright were guaranteed of making at least the average salary of the top 10 players at their position which meant $1.2 million for Wright and $1.1 million for Wolford. The Bills unrestricted free agents were James Lofton, Shane Conlan, Pete Metzelaars, Carlton Bailey, Mitch Frerotte, Clifford Hicks, Rob Awalt, Mark Pike and Adam Lingner.

March 1 – Bill Polian accepted a position in the NFL office in New York with the Management Council. His role was to advise teams on the complex free agency system, which he helped devise.

March 10 – The Bills signed restricted free agent Glenn Parker and unrestricted free agent Adam Lingner to new contracts. Parker was given an enormous two-year deal worth more than $2 million, which provided a sign of what free agency was expected to do to teams' payrolls.

March 22 – Linebacker Carlton Bailey became the first Bill to defect through free agency, signing a gargantuan three-year, $5.25 million contract with the New York Giants. "I'm glad for Carlton, he's a super kid and that's phenomenal money for a guy who came into the league as a ninth-round pick," John Butler said. Said Bailey: "By no means did I want to leave Buffalo, but it's just that I don't know if they were really concerned with having me back. It hurts my heart to leave."

March 23 – Thurman Thomas announced that he was going to hire super-agent Leigh Steinberg to handle his contract negotiations with the Bills.

March 29 – Will Wolford received a blockbuster offer from the Indianapolis Colts, $7.65 million over three years, and the Bills had one week to either match the offer or lose him to the Colts. From the Bills perspective, the Colts were making it very hard to match because of an escalator clause that stipulated that Wolford must be paid a salary equal to his highest-paid offensive teammate in 1993-94 and the highest-paid non-quarterback in 1995. Thus, in order for the Bills to match, they would have to pay him the $2.8 million Jim Kelly makes and possibly whatever salary Thurman Thomas was due to receive in '95, and Thomas was expected to get a huge deal before the

1993 season.

March 31 – The Bills lodged a formal complaint with the Management Council and Players' Association concerning the offer made to Will Wolford. It was decided that an independent arbitrator would decide whether the offer was valid. Meanwhile, the Bills announced that they had signed Colts free agent wide receiver Bill Brooks to a three-year, $3.5 million contract. Also, the Atlanta Falcons decided not to match Buffalo's offer to restricted free agent defensive lineman Oliver Barnett, so Barnett became a member of the Bills.

April 2 – The Will Wolford case was not reviewed by an arbitrator because the NFL said it wanted to solve the matter in-house. The Bills said they would not be able to match the offer unless the NFL forced the Colts to remove the controversial escalator clause.

April 5 – The deadline for the Bills to match the offer sheet for Will Wolford passed because no decision had been made on whether the Colts' offer was valid.

April 7 – Jeff Wright signed an offer sheet from the San Francisco 49ers worth $6 million over four years, leaving the Bills one week to match the contract or lose their starting nose tackle. Wright said he hoped the Bills did not match the offer. "I just feel that it's my turn to move on," he said, obviously still bitter about not having his contract re-done during the 1992 season.

April 8 – Shane Conlan received a three-year, $5.6 million offer from the Los Angeles Rams.

April 10 – Shane Conlan accepted the Rams offer and ended his career with the Bills, the team he grew up following while living in nearby Frewsburg, N.Y. "You hate to lose a player like that," John Butler said. "Unfortunately, the uncertainty of not knowing what's going to happen with the Will Wolford situation and with Jeff Wright signing an offer sheet, that restricted us. I just hate this, so do Marv and Mr. Wilson. Mr. Wilson refuses to let this team break up, but these are very difficult decisions that have to be made."

April 11 – John Butler said that the Bills would match the offer sheet that Jeff Wright signed with San Francisco, meaning they would have to pay him $1.5 million for the next four years. "I'm kind of puzzled why the Bills didn't sign me sooner, but I'm also humored by it," Wright said. "I was upset and angry about it last year, but sometimes patience can reap rewards. In my case, that's what happened."

April 16 – The Will Wolford case remained unsolved because the NFL still hadn't named it's arbitrator. "We're tired of this whole thing," said Wolford's agent, Ralph Cindrich.

April 22 – The Bills lost backup offensive lineman Mitch Frerotte as he signed a free agent contract with the Seattle Seahawks worth about $2 million over three years.

April 23 – The Will Wolford case was finally resolved when arbitrator Arthur Stark ruled that the escalator clause was indeed valid. The Bills, who were angered by the way the hearing was conducted because they couldn't present their case properly, decided they couldn't match the offer, so Wolford became a member of the Indianapolis Colts. "It's definitely like hitting the lottery," Wolford said. "I think I'm more glad that it's over. I definitely have mixed emotions about it, I have a very heavy heart right now."

April 25 – The Bills selected North Carolina cornerback Thomas Smith in the first round of the NFL draft with the 28th overall pick. Also selected were Nebraska defensive lineman John Parrella (second) and Memphis State wide receiver Russell Copeland (fourth). The draft consisted of only eight rounds, down from the usual 12, due to the new collective bargaining agreement. Around the league in the first round, New England selected quarterback Drew Bledsoe No. 1, Seattle took quarterback Rick Mirer (second), Phoenix chose running back Garrison Hearst (third) and offensive lineman Ernest Dye (18th), the Jets opted for linebacker Marvin Jones (fourth), Cincinnati picked defensive lineman John Copeland (fifth), Tampa Bay grabbed defensive lineman Eric Curry (sixth), Chicago chose wide receiver Curtis Conway (seventh), New Orleans took offensive lineman William Roaf (eighth), Atlanta selected offensive lineman Lincoln Kennedy (ninth), the Rams picked fullback Jerome Bettis (10th), Denver went for defensive lineman Dan Williams (11th), the Raiders took safety Patrick Bates (12th), Houston picked offensive lineman Brad Hopkins (13th), Cleveland chose center Steve Everitt (14th), Green Bay took linebacker Wayne Simmons (15th) and safety George Teague (29th), Indianapolis went for wide receiver Sean Dawkins (16th), Washington picked defensive back Tom Carter (17th), Philadelphia picked offensive lineman Lester Holmes (19th) and defensive lineman Leonard Renfro (24th), Minnesota chose running back Robert Smith (21st), Pittsburgh picked cornerback Deon Figures (23rd), Miami chose wide receiver O.J. McDuffie (25th) and San Francisco took defensive linemen Dana Stubblefield (26th) and Todd Kelly (27th).

April 26 – The Bills lost their fifth unrestricted free agent when defensive back/punt returner Clifford Hicks signed with the New York Jets.

April 27 – Marv Levy's contract was extended through the 1996 season. It was reported that Levy was due to earn about $850,000 per season.

April 29 – The Bills announced that they weren't planning on retaining free agent wide receiver James Lofton. "His long career, his talent, his leadership, all that made it difficult," Marv Levy said. "But we weighed everything and it was time to look at the young receivers." Said Lofton: "I was kind of surprised and disappointed because I was looking forward to coming back. I felt I had a pretty good year last year, but they just decided they wanted to go in a different direction."

April 30 – Will Wolford underwent shoulder surgery in Indianapolis and reports indicated he could be out of action until midseason.

May 7 – The Bills opened min-icamp at Rich Stadium and Bruce Smith said that the four-year, $17 million deal that Reggie White signed with Green Bay was the standard by which he would refer to when his contract extension talks with the Bills heated up. "The market's been set," Smith said. "I think it would be embarrassing for the franchise and also embarrassing for me and for the future of my family to accept anything less than what Reggie got."

May 9 – As min-icamp closed, Thurman Thomas, like Bruce Smith about to enter into new contract extension negotiations with the Bills, said he wanted to stay in Buffalo. "I'm real happy here, I have a lot of things going on," he said. "I want to stay here, I haven't made that a secret. I just want to be treated fair. I want to finish my career in Buffalo."

May 25 – The Bills re-signed four players, Pete Metzelaars, Carwell Gardner, Mark Pike and Brad Lamb.

June 11 – Former Bills receiver Jerry Butler was hired by the team to fill the newly-created position of director of player relations and alumni.

June 16 – The Bills paid former fullback Jamie Mueller $90,000 as part of a settlement on his claim that they breached his contract by placing him on waivers in 1992.

July 7 – Bill Polian was honored at a farewell dinner at the Buffalo Hilton.

July 15 – Training camp opened at Fredonia State and Bruce Smith did not show up on time, saying he was discouraged that his contract extension had not been worked out. Smith was subject to a $4,000 per day fine. Thurman Thomas, also seeking an extension, reported on time. The lone unsigned players, first-round draft choice Thomas Smith and veteran Chris Hale, signed contracts and reported on time.

July 16 – Offensive guard John Davis said he wanted the Bills to trade him because he felt the team didn't give him a proper opportunity to win his starting job back last season. He had missed nearly a year with a severe knee injury and when he returned last October, Glenn Parker continued as the starter. "I've asked them to trade me," Davis said. "Let me go somewhere where I can play. Cut me, release me, whatever, I want to go somewhere and have the opportunity to get a starting job and play on a team that respects me a little."

July 19 – Bruce Smith ended his four-day, $16,000 holdout and reported to camp, but he remained upset that a new contract hadn't been worked out. "I'm of the frame of my mind that this will be my last year with the Buffalo Bills unless they can work something out," he said. Rookie second-round draft choice John Parrella left camp and did not tell the coaching staff. He intended on driving home to Grand Island, Nebraska to see his ill father, but he stopped in Toledo, Ohio, called his father and was told to turn around and get back to camp. He arrived back in Fredonia in the evening.

July 21 – Thurman Thomas' agent, Leigh Steinberg, came to an agreement with John Butler on a four-year,

$13.5 million contract extension. "Thurman's been so valuable to this team," Ralph Wilson said. "Without him we wouldn't have made it to three Super Bowls." Said Thomas: "I'm happy that for the rest of my career I'll be a Buffalo Bill. That's something that I wanted. It's a great team, a great organization and a great city to play in." The deal made him the highest-paid running back in the NFL.

July 22 – Bill Polian was given a new position in the NFL office, vice-president of football development. Polian was put in charge of overseeing football-related operations administered by the league including player discipline and game procedures.

July 26 – In a conversation with commissioner Paul Tagliabue, Ralph Wilson asked for draft choice compensation for the loss of free agent Will Wolford. The loophole through which the Bills lost Wolford had since been closed, so Wilson thought he deserved compensation.

July 27 – Bruce Smith and the Bills agreed to a four-year, $13.5 million contract extension, the same deal that Thurman Thomas got. "I started here in 1985 and I want to finish up here," an ecstatic Smith said.

July 30 – The Bills opened the preseason at the Silverdome and lost to Detroit, 14-7. John Fina, the man targeted to replace Will Wolford at left tackle, acquitted himself well in his starting debut.

Aug. 2 – The Bills departed for Berlin, Germany, where they would spend the week preparing for their American Bowl game against the Minnesota Vikings.

Aug. 8 – A crowd of 67,132 at Olympic Stadium, the same place where Jesse Owens won four gold medals in the 1936 Olympics, watched the Vikings defeat Buffalo, 20-6.

Aug. 12 – Just three days after returning from Berlin, the Bills hit the road again, traveling to Kansas City to meet the Chiefs in Joe Montana's first home game as the Chiefs' quarterback. Surprisingly, the Bills put on a terrific preseason performance and routed the Chiefs, 30-7.

Aug. 21 – Tampa Bay blew out the Bills, 32-12, at the Citrus Bowl in Orlando, Fla. The Bills announced that center Kent Hull had undergone a second knee surgery in Vail, Col. and that he would miss at least the first two weeks of the regular season.

Aug. 24 – Marv Levy trimmed the roster to 60 as he cut 18 players including veterans Chris Hale and Keith Willis. He also placed Al Edwards on the season-long injured reserve list.

Aug. 25 – In a move designed to help the Bills deal with the impending salary cap in 1994, the team restructured Jim Kelly's contract, front loading some of the money he was due to receive from 1994-96 to this season. It was reported that Kelly would earn about $4 million in '93 because of the change.

Aug. 27 – In their only home preseason game, the Bills edged Atlanta, 17-16, in front of 51,232 fans who booed loudly when the new *Shout!* theme song was played.

Aug. 29 – It was announced that tight end Keith McKeller would miss the first half of the season due to knee surgery.

Sept. 5 – The Bills opened the regular season with a 38-14 victory over New England in Bill Parcells' first game as Patriots head coach and rookie Drew Bledsoe's first NFL start. The Bills scored 21 fourth-quarter points to blow open a close game, with rookie Russell Copeland returning a punt 47 yards for a TD.

Sept. 7 – Cornerback Kirby Jackson was placed on the season-long injured reserve list and David Pool was signed to take his place on the roster.

Sept. 8 – The Bills announced that Jim Kelly would likely miss the Super Bowl rematch at Texas Stadium against Dallas due to knee swelling. "If I had to play today, I couldn't," Kelly said.

Sept. 9 – Jim Kelly did a 180-degree reversal and said his knee felt much better and he would probably be

able to play against Dallas.

Sept. 12 – Matt Darby's goal-line interception of Troy Aikman with 12 seconds left to play preserved the Bills 13-10 victory in Dallas over the Cowboys. Dallas was without star running back Emmitt Smith, who missed the game due to a contract holdout.

Sept. 15 – Even though the Bills-Dolphins game was more than a week away because both teams had byes, Miami linebacker Bryan Cox started the hype early by saying: "I don't like the Buffalo Bills as a team, I don't like them as people, I don't like the city, I don't like the people in the city, and I don't like their organization. I wouldn't care if any of those people fell off the face of the earth. Some of them think they're so much better than the average person just because they're football players."

Sept. 16 – In response to Bryan Cox's statements, Andre Reed said: "I don't care what he says. If he thinks we like him, he's crazy, too. I don't need to get into a verbal match with him." Said Jeff Wright: "He needs to grow up." Dallas running back Emmitt Smith ended his holdout and signed a contract worth $3.4 million per season, making him the highest-paid running back in the NFL, moving past Thurman Thomas.

Sept. 26 – For the second year in a row, the Dolphins came to Rich Stadium and whipped the Bills, this time 22-13. Dan Marino threw for 282 yards.

Sept. 28 – The NFL fined Miami linebacker Bryan Cox $10,000 for making obscene gestures to fans before the Bills-Dolphins game at Rich Stadium.

Sept. 29 – Marv Levy said that Kent Hull would return to the starting lineup and that John Davis and Glenn Parker would rotate at right guard.

Oct. 3 – Jim Kelly threw an eight-yard TD pass to Pete Metzelaars with 2:27 remaining, giving the Bills a 17-14 victory over the New York Giants in a Sunday night game at Rich Stadium.

Oct. 4 – Ralph Wilson announced a two-year, $23.1 million Rich Stadium renovation project. "This renovation program reaffirms the commitment of the Buffalo Bills in Western New York and lays the foundation for the Bills making their home here well into the 21st century," Wilson said. The project included installation of a Sony Jumbotron scoreboard, the second-largest of its kind in North America behind only the one at Skydome in Toronto. Also, 14 private boxes and two theater-style luxury boxes would be built, restrooms would be added to the upper deck, all parking lots would be paved, a new practice facility would be built and pedestrian bridges across Abbott Road would be erected.

Oct. 10 – Miami quarterback Dan Marino suffered the first major injury of his career, a season-ending Achilles tendon rupture, in the Dolphins' victory over Cleveland.

Oct. 11 – The Houston Oilers returned to Rich Stadium, where they were victims of the greatest comeback in NFL history nine months earlier, but this time the Bills were never in the game as the Bills rolled to a 35-7 Monday night victory. Jim Kelly passed for 247 yards and three TDs.

Oct. 14 – With the salary cap expected to go into effect in 1994, the Bills tried to make room by reworking the contracts of four players – Andre Reed, Don Beebe, Cornelius Bennett and Steve Christie – by moving money they were due to receive next year to this year.

Oct. 21 – The Erie County Legislature approved the $23.1 million Rich Stadium renovation project.

Oct. 24 – The Bills returned from their second bye week and struggled to get past the Jets. A pair of playing streaks came to an end. Jim Ritcher missed the game due to a knee injury, ending his consecutive starts streak at 145. Nate Odomes didn't start for the first time in 110 games because of a shoulder injury, but he did play. Odomes was upset that his starting streak came to an end. "I could've started," he said. "To start

seven years worth of games, it was something I wanted to keep going."

Oct. 26 – The NFL owners voted for Charlotte, N.C. to be one of the two new expansion teams that would join the league in 1995. The team was to be called the Carolina Panthers. However, the owners held off on naming a second franchise.

Nov. 1 – The Bills completed a sweep of the three teams they had lost to in Super Bowls as they defeated Washington, 24-10, in a Monday nighter at Rich Stadium. Thurman Thomas rushed for 129 yards and one TD. Before the game, Elbert Dubenion's name was revealed on the Bills Wall of Fame, the eighth member of the organization to be so honored.

Nov. 7 – The upstart Patriots nearly pulled off a huge upset, but the Bills rallied to tie the game at Foxboro Stadium on Steve Christie's 27-yard field goal with 14 seconds left, then won it, 13-10, on Christie's 32-yarder in overtime.

Nov. 10 – Frank Reich became the sixth player to have his contract restructured, giving him more money this year to save money for the team in 1994 when the salary cap was expected to kick in.

Nov. 15 – The Bills went to Pittsburgh for a Monday night game and got thrashed, 23-0. It was the first time they had been shutout in 133 games dating back to the 1985 season finale, a 28-0 loss to Miami. Thus, it was the first time a Jim Kelly-led Bills team had been blanked.

Nov. 20 – O.J. Simpson and his offensive line, the Electric Company, were honored at a dinner at the Ramada Renaissance Hotel in Cheektowaga on the 20th anniversary of Simpson's 2,003-yard season in 1973. Donnie Green was the only member of the group who was unable to attend.

Nov. 21 – The Bills rebounded from their pounding in Pittsburgh with a 23-9 victory over Indianapolis. Before the game, O.J. Simpson and the offense from the 1973 team were announced to the crowd and honored. "I'm a guy that never liked to look back, but this week I couldn't help it," Simpson said.

Nov. 22 – Jim Kelly announced that he was moving his football camp from St. Bonaventure to Rochester Institute of Technology.

Nov. 25 – On Thanksgiving Day, Dallas' Leon Lett made a grievous error when he tried to recover a loose ball after a blocked field goal at the end of the Dallas-Miami game at icy Texas Stadium. The Dolphins recovered, got to re-kick, and Pete Stoyanovich made a 19-yarder as time ran out, giving Miami a 16-14 victory and a 9-2 record.

Nov. 28 – Joe Montana passed for 208 yards to lead Kansas City to a 23-7 romp over the Bills at noisy Arrowhead Stadium.

Nov. 29 – Marv Levy, growing tired of hearing his players complaining about the gameplans, sent a message to them by telling them in a team meeting to "Say less and play better."

Nov. 30 – The NFL surprisingly selected Jacksonville as the second expansion franchise, bypassing former NFL cities St. Louis and Baltimore. The team was to be called the Jacksonville Jaguars.

Dec. 1 – Jim Kelly expressed concern over the performance of the offense and took his teammates to task. "You see sacks, you see pressures, but a lot of times it's not just the offensive line's fault," he said. "At times, people take plays off. It's something I won't tolerate. My old motto is 'Always running, always alert.' In our offense, you never know if you're going to get the football. In our scheme, the running back can't take a play off, the offensive line can't, the quarterback can't and the receivers can't."

Dec. 5 – Tim Brown caught a 29-yard TD pass from Jeff Hostetler with 4:58 remaining, capping a nine-point fourth quarter rally that produced a 25-24 victory for the Raiders over the Bills at Rich Stadium.

Dec. 6 – After being saddled with back-to-back loss-

es, Marv Levy responded this way: "I know these players will pull together and play hard. The season isn't over by a long shot."

Dec. 8 – Due to injuries suffered against the Raiders, Levy announced that Andre Reed, Jeff Wright, Mark Kelso and Mark Maddox would not start against Philadelphia.

Dec. 9 – Jim Kelly's mother, Alice, suffered a heart attack and was hospitalized in Pittsburgh.

Dec. 12 – The Bills pulled off an incredible 10-7 victory over Philadelphia at Veterans Stadium, rallying for 10 points in the final 3:44 despite playing without Jim Kelly, Andre Reed, Thurman Thomas, Mark Kelso, Jeff Wright and Mark Maddox. After missing three field goals, Steve Christie kicked the winner with 2:18 remaining. "Resilient isn't a word we use loosely," General Manager John Butler said. "Resilient? The definition in the dictionary should say Buffalo Bills."

Dec. 13 – It was announced that Jim Kelly and Thurman Thomas were expected back in time for the upcoming showdown with Miami at Joe Robbie Stadium. Kelly explained why he took himself out of the Eagles game. "I could play with the pain, but when the ankle kept going out, it was time to let Frank go in there," he said. "I couldn't move in the pocket. I said 'Why jeopardize the team?' And I know the kind of ability Frank has. I knew he could do a good job." The Bills got a break when Pittsburgh edged Miami, 21-20, creating a tie atop the AFC East at 9-4.

Dec. 15 – Although Don Shula wouldn't say for sure, it was expected that Scott Mitchell would return to quarterback the Dolphins after missing the previous four games with a separated shoulder. Regardless of whether it was Mitchell or Steve DeBerg, it wasn't going to be Dan Marino, who was out for the year with a ruptured Achilles' tendon. It meant that Marino would be missing his first Miami-Buffalo game since 1983 when he wasn't yet the starter in his rookie season when the Dolphins opened that year with a 12-0 victory over Buffalo. The next time the teams played, Marino made his first NFL start and the Bills beat Miami, 38-35, in overtime, for their first victory in the Orange Bowl since 1966.

Dec. 17 – The Fox network outbid CBS for the rights to NFC football games, paying a record $1.6 billion for four years, meaning that for the first time in 38 years, CBS would be without the NFL starting in 1994.

Dec. 19 – The Bills rolled to a huge 47-34 victory over Miami, their seventh victory in eight tries at Joe Robbie Stadium, and moved into first place in the AFC East as the Dolphins lost their third straight. Jim Kelly returned from his ankle injury and passed for 245 yards. The Bills were 11-of-17 on third downs and the defense forced five turnovers. "You can't always sense what's going to happen in pro football," Ralph Wilson said, "but you could hear a pin drop in this locker room before the game started. When nobody is smiling, nobody is cracking a joke and you can hear people breathe, that means they're really ready to go out there and beat the opponents. You saw what happened."

Dec. 20 – NBC retained the rights to televise AFC games, paying $880 million for four years. ABC would pay $950 million for *Monday Night Football* and some playoff games, and ESPN and TNT were going to pay $450 million each for Sunday night games.

Dec. 21 – Three more players, John Fina, Henry Jones and Marvcus Patton, had their contracts restructured to give them more money this season, saving space for the salary cap in 1994. Since August, the Bills had reworked nine contracts, shaving about $4 million off their 1994 payroll.

Dec. 23 – Darryl Talley and the Bills came to an agreement on a one-year, $2.4 million contract extension, which included an immediate $1 million signing bonus.

Dec. 25 – A Christmas Eve snowstorm dumped more than 20 inches of snow on Rich Stadium. The team offered to pay people $5 an hour to help shovel out the stadium to get it ready for the upcoming Jets game. About 175 people showed up on Christmas Day. The team estimated it would cost about $250,000 to remove the snow.

Dec. 26 – In the coldest game in which the Bills had ever played, 70,817 fans showed up at snowbound Rich Stadium and saw Buffalo clinch the AFC East for the fifth time in six years with a 16-14 victory over the New York Jets. The non-sellout was the first for Buffalo in 25 games, but the temperature was nine degrees and the windchill was minus-28. New York's Cary Blanchard missed three field goals, including a potential game-winning 42-yarder with 53 seconds left to play, while Steve Christie made all three of his attempts. After the game, Marv Levy thanked the people who helped get the stadium ready and recalled what he had said to them the day before. "I told them I hope our team shows as much spunk tomorrow as you're showing right now," he said. "I looked up and had a great admiration for those people. They were a big part of the excitement of the afternoon."

Dec. 28 – Howard Ballard, Nate Odomes, Bruce Smith, Thurman Thomas and Steve Tasker were named starters for the AFC squad in the Pro Bowl while Cornelius Bennett and Andre Reed were chosen as reserves. Despite what he considered his most productive season, Darryl Talley was left off the team.

Dec. 29 – Darryl Talley was left off the Pro Bowl squad, but he was named by the Western New York media as the Bills' player of the year.

Jan. 2, 1994 – With home-field advantage throughout the playoffs on the line, the Bills rolled to a 30-10 victory over Indianapolis in the Hoosier Dome, despite being outgained 402-297.

Jan. 3, 1994 – Bruce Smith was the lone Bill named to the first team Associated Press All-Pro team.

Jan. 7, 1994 – Dan Reeves of the New York Giants was named NFL coach of the year and a number of Bills were disappointed that Marv Levy received no recognition. "Not only was it wrong that he didn't get any votes, but I think he should have won it," Jim Kelly said.

Jan. 8, 1994 – Green Bay rallied to beat Detroit in the Silverdome, 28-24, and Nick Lowery's overtime field goal lifted Kansas City past Pittsburgh, 27-24, on the first day of wild-card playoff action.

Jan. 9, 1994 – The Raiders rolled past Denver, 42-24, earning a trip to Buffalo to meet the Bills, while the Giants stopped Minnesota, 17-10, on the second day of wild-card action.

Jan. 12, 1994 – Former Bills general manager Bill Polian was named general manager of the expansion Carolina Panthers.

Jan. 15, 1994 – The Bills avenged their regular-season loss to the Raiders a month earlier by defeating Los Angeles, 29-23, in the divisional round of the AFC playoffs. It was the coldest game in Bills history with a gametime temperature of zero and a windchill of minus-32. Jim Kelly passed for 287 yards and two TDs. In San Francisco, the 49ers crushed the Giants, 44-3, as Ricky Watters set an NFL playoff record by scoring five TDs. It was the Giants worst playoff loss ever and after the game, Lawrence Taylor announced his retirement.

Jan. 16, 1994 – Joe Montana rallied Kansas City from a 10-0 deficit and beat Houston at the Astrodome, 28-20, ending the Oilers 11-game winning streak. That meant the Chiefs would play in Buffalo for the AFC Championship. In the other NFC divisional game, Dallas overcame Green Bay, 27-17, despite a lackluster performance.

Jan. 19, 1994 – Thurman Thomas ended a six-week media silence and criticized critical media and fans. "When you think about it, half the people who call in and half the people who are watching don't know what the hell they're talking about," he said. "And you guys in the media are like some of the people who call in on the talk shows. You can say you watch football and study it for 30 years, but until you're out there playing the game, you don't know what the hell you're talking about."

Jan. 23, 1994 – The Bills did what no team had ever done in the history of the Super Bowl: By beating the Kansas City Chiefs and Joe Montana, 30-13, the Bills qualified for their fourth consecutive Super Bowl. Miami had reached the game three years in a row in the early 70's. Thurman Thomas set team playoff records for carries (33) and rushing yards (186) and tied a team mark with three TDs. Buffalo tied a team playoff record with 30 first downs. Meanwhile, the defense knocked Montana out of the game early in the third quarter. In the NFC Championship Game, Dallas earned its second straight trip to the Super Bowl with a 38-21 rout of San Francisco as Emmitt Smith produced 173 yards from scrimmage.

Jan. 24, 1994 – Because there was no week off between the conference championships and the Super Bowl, the Bills arrived in Atlanta barely more than 24 hours after their victory over Kansas City.

Jan. 25, 1994 – It took less than a minute for Cornelius Bennett to get perturbed during media day at the Georgia Dome. A reporter asked him if he thought the Bills were going to win and Bennett fired back: "What the hell kind of question is that?" and then repeated that refrain four more times. "No, we're going to lose. To ask me that question is just stupid. Hell yeah I think we're going to win. Do you think we just came here to lose the damn thing? Do you think we came to lose the last three Super Bowls? No, no, OK, so don't ask me that damn question."

Jan. 26, 1994 – Hall of Fame quarterback and four-time Super Bowl winner Terry Bradshaw talked about the Bills' return to the Super Bowl. "Just to get to four in a row is absolutely incredible," Bradshaw said. "I really am kind of in awe about that." (On the Bills being America's sympathy pick to win the game): "I really think the public is feeling sorry for them. They want them to win. Jimmy Johnson rubs many the wrong way because he's perceived as arrogant. The working man, unless you're a Cowboys fan, tends to like the person who's struggled in life. Buffalo fits that bill. If I were them (the Bills), I wouldn't give a rat's fanny about anything. I'd have fun and go out and play. If they lose, so what." (On Jim Kelly): "Kelly's more settled, more focused, maybe not as cocky as he used to be. I really admire what he's doing, he's one of the best. If he loses again, I don't think it will faze him. What the hell, what's one more?"

Jan. 27, 1994 – Bruce Smith said he would skip the Pro Bowl because his father was ill and his wife, Carmen, was due to deliver the couple's first child in early February. Because of rain, the Bills practiced in the Georgia Dome rather than at Georgia Tech. "I was glad for the opportunity to use the site for the game," Marv Levy said.

Jan. 28, 1994 – After not posing with the Vince Lombardi Trophy the previous two years after his final press conference, Marv Levy relented and posed with the hardware.

Jan. 30, 1994 – James Washington returned a Thurman Thomas fumble 46 yards for a touchdown on the third play of the second half to turn the game in Dallas' favor and the Cowboys went on to defeat Buffalo, 30-13, in Super Bowl XXVIII at the Georgia Dome in Atlanta. The Bills extended their NFL record for consecutive losses in a Super Bowl to four. Washington finished with 11 tackles, an interception, a forced fumble and a fumble recovery, but was not named the MVP. That honor went to Emmitt Smith who rushed for 132 yards on 30 carries and scored the go-ahead TD late in the third quarter.

Jan. 31, 1994 – Before leaving for the Atlanta airport for the flight home to Buffalo, Marv Levy said of his team: "I think we'll be remembered well and fondly. However, we aren't putting the remains to rest. I'm not going to give a final eulogy. We are not going to break up the Bills. That would be an overreaction."

Mark Kelso (38) and Mark Maddox helped the Buffalo defense bottle up New England in the 1993 season opener, Bill Parcells' first game as Patriots head coach.

BY THE NUMBERS - 1993

TEAM STATISTICS	BILLS	OPP
First downs	316	331
Rushing	117	114
Passing	176	199
Penalty	23	18
Third downs	98-225	107-235
Fourth downs	5-8	6-18
Avg. time of poss	27:30	32:30
Total yards	5,260	5,554
Avg. game	328.8	347.1
Plays	1,078	1,119
Avg. play	4.9	5.0
Net rushing yds	1,943	1,921
Avg. game	121.4	120.1
Avg. play	3.5	3.8
Net passing yds	3,317	3,633
Comp/att	304/497	323/582
Sacks/lost	31-218	37-256
Interceptions	18	23
Percentage	61.2	55.5
Punts/avg	74-40.4	65-41.8
Fumbles/lost	26-17	35-24
Penalties/yds	94-630	99-681
Touchdowns	37	25
Extra points	36-37	23-25
Field goals	23-32	23-35
Safeties	1	0
Kick ret./avg	45-16.6	43-19.8
Punt ret./avg	33-8.4	29-8.5

RUSHING	ATT	YDS	AVG	TD
Thomas	355	1315	3.7	6
Davis	109	391	3.6	6
Kelly	36	102	2.8	0
Gardner	20	56	2.8	0
Turner	11	36	3.3	0
Brooks	3	30	10.0	0
Reed	9	21	2.3	0
Fina	1	-2	-2.0	0
Reich	6	-6	-1.0	0
TOTALS	**550**	**1943**	**3.5**	**12**

PASSING	COMP	ATT	INT	YDS	TD	COMP%	SACKS	RATE
Kelly	288	470	18	3382	18	61.3	25-171	79.9
Reich	16	26	0	153	2	61.5	6-47	103.5
Thomas	0	1	0	0	0	00.0	0-0	39.6
TOTALS	**304**	**497**	**18**	**3535**	**20**	**61.2**	**31-218**	**81.0**

KICKING	1-19	20-29	30-39	40-49	50+	TOT	PAT	PTS
Christie	0-0	4-5	12-12	6-9	1-6	23-32	36-37	105

PUNTING	NO	AVG	LG	In 20	BL
Mohr	74	40.4	58	19	0

RECEIVING	CAT	YDS	AVG	TD
Metzelaars	68	609	9.0	4
Brooks	60	714	11.9	5
Reed	52	854	16.4	6
Thomas	48	387	8.1	0
Beebe	31	504	16.3	3
K. Davis	21	95	4.5	0
Copeland	13	242	18.6	0
Gardner	4	50	12.5	1
McKeller	3	35	11.7	1
Tasker	2	26	13.0	0
Awalt	2	19	9.5	0
TOTALS	**304**	**3535**	**11.6**	**20**

SCORE BY QUARTERS

BILLS	64	113	51	98	3	-	329
OPP	71	62	67	42	0	-	242

DEFENSIVE STATISTICAL LEADERS

TACKLES: Talley 101 primary - 35 assists - 136 total, M. Patton 76-42-118, B. Smith 87-21-108, Bennett 81-21-102, Jones 67-16-83, Wright 57-22-79, Maddox 34-28-62, Goganious 37-18-55, Kelso 33-21-54, Darby 39-14-53, Odomes 39-8-47, Hansen 31-12-43, Washington 34-7-41, Williams 31-9-40

SACKS: B. Smith 14, Bennett 5, Wright 4.5, Hansen 3.5, Jones 2, Talley 2, Barnett 2

FUMBLE RECOVERIES: M. Patton 3, Washington 2, Williams 2, Talley 2, Maddox 2

FORCED FUMBLES: Talley 4, B. Smith 3, Jones 3, Wright 3, Bennett 2, M. Patton 2, Hansen 2

INTERCEPTIONS: Odomes 9-65 yards, 7.2 avg., 0 TD; Talley 3-74, 24.7, 1 TD; Jones 2-92, 46.0, 1 TD

SPECIAL TEAMS STATISTICAL LEADERS

KICKOFF RETURNS: Copeland 24-436 yards, 18.2 avg., 0 TD; Beebe 10-160, 16.0, 0 TD

PUNT RETURNS: Copeland 31-274, 8.8, 1 TD

TACKLES: Pike 22, Gardner 12, T. Smith 12, Tasker 10, Goganious 9, Harvey 8, Lingner 8, Darby 7, Schulz 7, Brown 6, Maddox 6, M. Patton 6, Fuller 5, Parrella 5, Williams 5

GAME 1 - Sunday, Sept. 5, 1993 - BILLS 38, PATRIOTS 14

Patriots	0	7	7	0	-	14
Bills	0	17	0	21	-	38

Attendance at Rich Stadium - 79,751

Buf: FG Christie 28, 3:21
Buf: Brooks 4 pass from Kelly (Christie kick), 8:51
NE: Coates 54 pass from Bledsoe (Sisson kick), 11:57
Buf: Reed 41 pass from Kelly (Christie kick), 14:04
NE: McMurtry 2 pass from Bledsoe (Sisson kick), 7:28
Buf: Reed 22 pass from Kelly (Christie kick), :04
Buf: Reed 14 pass from Kelly (Christie kick), 3:52
Buf: Copeland 47 punt return (Christie kick), 6:30

	BUF	NE
First downs	20	15
Rushing yds	177	133
Passing yds	157	135
Punts-avg	4-37.0	7-42.6
Fumbles-lost	1-0	4-2
Penalties-yds	5-35	6-30
Poss. time	26:47	33:13

BILLS LEADERS: Rushing - Thomas 24-114, Turner 4-11, Kelly 3-15, Reed 1-15, K. Davis 5-14, Gardner 2-11, Reich 3-(-3); **Passing** - Kelly 13-22-1 - 167; **Receiving** - Reed 6-110, Metzelaars 3-27, Brooks 3-27, Thomas 1-3.

PATRIOTS LEADERS: Rushing - Russell 23-81, Gash 10-44, Bledsoe 3-6, Turner 1-2; **Passing** - Bledsoe 14-30-1 - 148; **Receiving** - Russell 4-20, Coates 1-54, Gash 3-20, Brisby 1-16, McMurtry 3-21, Cook 2-17.

WEEK 1 GAMES

Det 30, Atl 13	Den 26, NYJ 20
GB 36, Rams 6	SF 24, Pitt 13
NYG 26, Chi 20	NO 33, Hou 21
KC 27, TB 3	Clev 27, Cinc 14
Mia 24, Ind 20	LAR 24, Minn 7
SD 18, Sea 12	Phil 23, Phoe 17
Wash 35, Dal 16	

NOTES

• The Bills opened the season by beating the Patriots in Bill Parcells' debut as New England head coach and rookie quarterback Drew Bledsoe's NFL debut.
• John Davis started at center in place of Kent Hull who was recovering from knee surgery.
• Russell Copeland had a punt return for a TD in his NFL debut. It was the Bills first punt return for a TD since Nov. 2, 1986, when Ron Pitts did it against Tampa Bay, one day before Marv Levy became head coach.
• With Mark Clayton no longer in Miami, Jim Kelly and Andre Reed were the No. 1 active TD duo at 47 all-time.
• The first five series ended in punts before the Bills drove 58 yards to a Steve Christie field goal early in the second quarter. The teams then traded turnovers with Cornelius Bennett returning a Leonard Russell fumble 40 yards to set up Kelly's TD pass to Bill Brooks, his first TD as a Bill.
• Bledsoe threw his first NFL TD pass six plays after the kickoff to Ben Coates, but the Bills answered with an eight-play, 80-yard march to Andre Reed's brilliant TD reception on which he broke five tackles.
• The Pats pulled within 17-14 midway through the third by going 61 yards in 14 plays to Greg McMurtry's TD catch. The key play was defensive holding on J.D. Williams on third-and-10 which the gave a Pats first down.
• The Bills broke it open in the fourth. Reed caught his second TD on the first play of the quarter, then Matt Darby forced and recovered a Russell fumble at the Pats 31 and Reed then caught his third TD.
• The Pats went three-and-out and Copeland returned the punt 47 yards for the TD.

QUOTES

• Cornelius Bennett: "The hell with what people say about us, we know we still have a great team here. We're just going to prove it week to week and win those naysayers over again."
• Andre Reed: "Coming out of the blocks like that shows people we still have it. People are always downing us. If we keep our heads on straight, there's nobody out there that can beat us still." (On putting 1992 behind him): "I'm not going to think back to the past. You're not going to be the man every day. It gets frustrating, but if you work through it, things will happen. All I ask for is the opportunity, I'll take care of the rest. I think this staff knows what's up. They know they have to get me the ball as much as they can."
• Marv Levy: "You win 38-14 and it looks easy, but it was a tough struggle for us. It was a game that, to be honest with you, I worried about going in. A lot of ingredients for an upset were there. I think our players understood they would have to earn their victory."
• Jim Kelly on Reed's first TD: "I kept on thinking he was down. I had like three plays go through my head. I said 'OK, he's down, what am I going to run?' Then it was 'OK, he's down the second time' and then it was the third time. Hey, he's tough, that's one of his biggest assets."

GAME 2 - Sunday, Sept. 12, 1993 - BILLS 13, COWBOYS 10

Bills	7	3	0	3	-	13
Cowboys	0	3	0	7	-	10

Attendance at Texas Stadium - 63,226

Buf: Gardner 10 pass from Kelly (Christie kick), 8:41
Buf: FG Christie 48, 6:47
Dal: FG Elliott 43, 14:52
Dal: Williams 5 run (Elliott kick), 8:09
Buf: FG Christie 35, 12:11

	BUF	DAL
First downs	17	23
Rushing yds	100	103
Passing yds	129	290
Punts-avg	7-42.4	5-43.8
Fumbles-lost	1-1	4-2
Penalties-yds	3-20	2-10
Poss. time	26:51	33:09

BILLS LEADERS: Rushing - Thomas 25-75, K. Davis 6-9, Reed 1-9, Turner 2-4, Gardner 1-4, Kelly 3-(-1); **Passing** - Kelly 16-27-1 - 155; **Receiving** - Reed 4-10, Metzelaars 3-26, Brooks 4-56, Thomas 2-8, Beebe 3-26, Gardner 2-23, K. Davis 1-6.

COWBOYS LEADERS: Rushing - Lassic 19-52, Gainer 4-21, Aikman 3-21, Williams 1-5, Johnston 1-4; **Passing** - Aikman 28-45-2 - 297; **Receiving** - Irvin 8-115, Novacek 8-106, Johnston 4-24, Lassic 3-21, Gainer 3-13, Harper 1-13, Williams 1-5.

WEEK 2 GAMES

Minn 10, Chi 7	Ind 9, Cinc 6
NO 34, Atl 31	Phoe 17, Wash 10
NYJ 24, Mia 14	LAR 17, Sea 13
Hou 30, KC 0	Det 19, NE 16 (OT)
Phil 20, GB 17	NYG 23, TB 7
Den 34, SD 17	Rams 27, Pitt 0
Clev 23, SF 13	

NOTES

• The Bills recorded a huge psychological victory, avenging their embarrassing Super Bowl defeat.
• Matt Darby's goal-line interception with 12 seconds left preserved the win.
• Dallas' Emmitt Smith sat out his second straight game due to a contract dispute.
• The temperature of 97 degrees tied the all-time regular season-record for a Bills game.
• Defensive end Phil Hansen suffered a sprained foot and was expected to miss more than a month.
• Nate Odomes' interception at the Bills 37 ended Dallas' first possession. The Bills then drove 63 yards in 12 plays to Carwell Gardner's TD reception. Andre Reed had a 10-yard catch on third-and-five.
• Late in the first quarter, the Bills turned over the ball twice, but Dallas punted once and missed a field goal.
• In the second quarter, J.D. Williams recovered Derrick Lassic's fumble at the Cowboys 37 leading to a Steve Christie field goal, but after an exchange of punts, the Cowboys drove 63 yards in 11 plays to Lin Elliott's field goal just before the half ended. Troy Aikman completed two third-down passes.
• In the third, the teams traded four punts before Elliott missed a 30-yard field goal.
• Early in the fourth, Steve Tasker downed a Chris Mohr punt at the Dallas 2, but Aikman directed a 14-play, 98-yard drive to Kevin Williams' five-yard TD run on a reverse. Aikman was five-of-seven for 70 yards.
• The Bills punted on the ensuing series, but Mark Maddox forced Williams to fumble and Tasker recovered at the Dallas 34. That set up Christie's game-winning field goal with 2:49 left.
• Dallas drove 69 yards in nine plays and had second-and-four at the Bills 11 when Darby made his interception.

QUOTES

• Darryl Talley on Matt Darby's interception: "I could have kissed him."
• Matt Darby: "That was my biggest play, for sure, in pro, college, high school, whatever. The ball got popped in the air and luckily I found it and I got a chance to dive for it. I didn't know they were going to go to (Jay) Novacek, but I had a pretty good idea."
• Marv Levy: "It was a great win – for our team, our whole organization. They wanted this one very badly and to win certainly has special meaning. They were playing such an outstanding team and one that had beaten them badly in the Super Bowl. This wasn't a Super Bowl, but it was a very important game."
• Bruce Smith: "We wanted to prove to ourselves that we're a better football team than the one that played in the Super Bowl. This game means a lot, not only to the players, but to the fans and the management."
• Steve Tasker on his fumble recovery: "That's the way the game is. You make mistakes and you lose. Especially at this level because guys are too good."
• Don Beebe: "It's pretty exciting for the guys. I hate to use the word revenge, but we'd be lying if we said we didn't have a little more incentive to come in and play these guys well."

STANDINGS: SECOND WEEK

AFC EAST	W	L	T	CENTRAL	W	L	T	WEST	W	L	T	NFC EAST	W	L	T	CENTRAL	W	L	T	WEST	W	L	T
Buffalo	2	0	0	Cleveland	2	0	0	Raiders	2	0	0	NY Giants	2	0	0	Detroit	2	0	0	N.Orleans	2	0	0
Miami	1	1	0	Houston	1	1	0	Denver	2	0	0	Philadelphia	2	0	0	Green Bay	1	1	0	San Fran	1	1	0
Indianapolis	1	1	0	Cincinnati	0	2	0	Kan. City	1	1	0	Washington	1	1	0	Minnesota	1	1	0	LA Rams	1	1	0
NY Jets	1	1	0	Pittsburgh	0	2	0	San Diego	1	1	0	Phoenix	1	1	0	Chicago	0	2	0	Atlanta	0	2	0
New England	0	2	0					Seattle	0	2	0	Dallas	0	2	0	Tampa Bay	0	2	0				

NOTES

• The Bills lost at home to Miami for the second year in a row as the Dolphins raced to a 19-0 lead.
• Steve Christie set a Bills record with his 59-yard field goal.
• Center Kent Hull did not start, but he saw his first playing time of the season.
• Dan Marino moved into third place on the all-time NFL passing yardage list.
• Before the game, Bryan Cox responded to fans taunting by sticking up his middle fingers at them.
• Pete Stoyanovich opened the scoring with a field goal to cap Miami's first possession.
• After a second Bills punt, Marino hit Irving Fryar with a TD pass to cap a six-play, 75-yard drive.
• Following the Bills third punt, Marino hit Terry Kirby for 35 yards and on the next play, Marino scored.
• Jim Kelly then was intercepted by Liffort Hobley who returned it to the Bills 15. That set up Stoyanovich's second field goal for 19-0 lead.
• Louis Oliver intercepted Kelly three plays later, but the Dolphins did not capitalize.
• Christie made his first field goal, capping a nine-play, 56-yard drive. Then after a Miami punt, Christie boomed his record field goal on the final play of the half.
• The Dolphins controlled the ball for the first 8:23 of the third to get Stoyanovich's fourth field goal.
• In the fourth, the Bills went 80 yards in 10 plays to Bill Brooks' TD catch. Kelly was six-of-eight for 63 yards.
• The Bills were five-of-16 on third downs and Kelly was sacked three times.

QUOTES

• Bruce Smith: "To put it frankly, we stunk up the place."
• Marv Levy: "You pick it. On the offensive or defensive side of the ball, we didn't do enough to win. We've been able to come back before. Once in a while you have a bad game. We're just very disappointed it happened today when we thought we were ready to play."
• Jeff Wright: "It's a long season, it's only one loss. I'm sure a lot of people have jumped off the bandwagon. We're stubborn people. We're going to win our share."
• Dolphins linebacker Bryan Cox: "Damn this feels good. Of course there was pressure on me, if I didn't play well, I'd look like an idiot. We put a helluva whipping on these guys."

WEEK 3 GAMES	
NO 14, Det 3	Pitt 34, Cinc 7
NYG 20, Rams 10	Phil 34, Wash 31
Sea 17, NE 14	SF 37, Atl 30
Clev 19, LAR 16	SD 18, Hou 17
Dal 17, Phoe 10	KC 15, Den 7
Buf, Ind, Chi, Mia, NYJ, GB, Minn, TB had bye weeks	

WEEK 4 GAMES	
Ind 23, Clev 10	Minn 15, GB 13
Rams 20, Hou 13	Chi 47, TB 17
Det 26, Phoe 20	NO 16, SF 13
Sea 19, Cinc 10	NYJ 45, NE 7
Pitt 45, Atl 17	
Den, KC, LAR, SD, Dal, NYG, Phil, Wash had bye weeks	

Dolphins	16	3	3	0	-	22
Bills	0	6	0	7	-	13

Attendance at Rich Stadium - 79,635

Mia:	FG Stoyanovich 30, 6:45
Mia:	Fryar 36 pass from Marino (kick failed), 10:35
Mia:	Marino 4 run (Stoyanovich kick), 14:56
Mia:	FG Stoyanovich 23, 3:37
Buf:	FG Christie 40, 11:16
Buf:	FG Christie 59, 15:00
Mia:	FG Stoyanovich 24, 8:23
Buf:	Brooks 27 pass from Kelly (Christie kick), 7:37

	BUF	MIA
First downs	16	23
Rushing yds	106	137
Passing yds	176	275
Punts-avg	5-33.2	3-24.3
Fumbles-lost	0-0	2-1
Penalties-yds	4-28	7-75
Poss. time	20:39	39:21

BILLS LEADERS: Rushing - Thomas 12-46, K. Davis 6-32, Kelly 4-33, Reed 1-(-5); **Passing** - Kelly 20-39-0 - 199; **Receiving** - Brooks 6-70, Thomas 3-17, Metzelaars 2-9, Copeland 2-41, K. Davis 4-12, Tasker 2-26, Beebe 1-24.

DOLPHINS LEADERS: Rushing - Higgs 22-77, Byars 8-24, Kirby 9-31, Marino 2-4, Fryar 1-0, Mitchell 1-1; **Passing** - Marino 20-32-1 - 282; **Receiving** - Fryar 7-103, Kirby 6-91, Byars 5-52, Ingram 1-26, Baty 1-10.

NOTES

• The Bills blew a 10-0 first-quarter lead, but rallied to win on Jim Kelly's TD pass to Pete Metzelaars with 2:27 left to play. The Bills were outgained on offense for the third game in a row.
• Ex-Bill Carlton Bailey led the Giants with 13 tackles.
• The teams opened the game by trading punts, then the Bills drove 58 yards to Steve Christie's field goal.
• On the ensuing series, the Giants drove to the Bills 22, but on third-and-one, Phil Simms' pass to Howard Cross was intercepted by Henry Jones and he ran 85 yards for TD, his third TD on TNT Sunday night games.
• In the second quarter after a short Chris Mohr punt from the end zone, the Giants drove 33 yards to Simms' TD pass to Chris Calloway. The score came on a third-and-five play.

• Greg Jackson then intercepted Kelly at the Giants 41 with 4:35 left in the half. New York proceeded to drive 59 yards in nine plays to Mark Jackson's TD reception on third-and-goal from the 2.
• The Bills had only five first downs, 97 yards at the half.
• The Giants turned over the ball twice in the third, but the Bills failed to capitalize.
• Midway through the fourth, Nate Odomes intercepted Simms on third-and-13. The Bills then used 5:20 to drive 73 yards in 11 plays to Metzelaars' winning TD. On the drive, Andre Reed made a diving catch for 20 yards to the New York 29. Two plays before the TD, Thurman Thomas fumbled, but Don Beebe recovered at the 9.

QUOTES

• Jim Kelly on the winning TD pass: "We had a play called, I don't even remember what it was, but then I saw them coming up (to blitz). I started the audible (to a pass to Thurman Thomas), but the play I had called was better against two people coming up the middle, so I knew if they had the middle open, the play to Pete would work." (On the winning drive): "It was real simple. We didn't drop the football, we didn't have any penalties, we didn't make any mistakes. All night we kept shooting ourselves in the foot. Sure it was frustrating."
• Henry Jones on his interception: "It was a short-yardage play and they decided to throw the ball. We had good coverage on the play and he (Simms) threw the ball a little too high. Fortunately I picked it off and there was a convoy down the sideline. I like playing at night. I think it goes back to my high school days. We always played games on Friday nights. All I can say is I've been fortunate in those night games."
• Giants linebacker Lawrence Taylor: "To let a team like Buffalo hang around like we did in the second half, bad things are going to happen. You look at that game and there's no way we should have lost. We controlled both sides of the football."

Giants	0	14	0	0	-	14
Bills	10	0	0	7	-	17

Attendance at Rich Stadium - 79,283

Buf:	FG Christie 24, 6:00
Buf:	Jones 85 interception return (Christie kick), 10:17
NYG:	Calloway 5 pass from Simms (Treadwell kick), 8:45
NYG:	Jackson 2 pass from Simms (Treadwell kick), 14:42
Buf:	Metzelaars 8 pass from Kelly (Christie kick), 12:33

	BUF	NYG
First downs	17	19
Rushing yds	139	146
Passing yds	112	153
Punts-avg	7-40.1	6-42.5
Fumbles-lost	2-1	1-1
Penalties-yds	8-51	9-49
Poss. time	25:44	34:16

BILLS LEADERS: Rushing - Thomas 26-122, K. Davis 5-17, Reed 1-3, Kelly 3-(-3); **Passing** - Kelly 14-25-1 - 142; **Receiving** - Thomas 3-21, Beebe 1-22, Metzelaars 6-44, Brooks 1-14, Reed 3-41.

GIANTS LEADERS: Rushing - Hampton 32-86, Tillman 7-55, Meggett 3-3, Simms 1-2; **Passing** - Simms 12-28-3 - 160; **Receiving** - Hampton 2-16, Meggett 2-37, Sherrard 2-37, Calloway 2-12, Pierce 2-33, McCaffrey 1-23, Jackson 1-2.

WEEK 5 GAMES	
Chi 6, Atl 0	TB 27, Det 10
Dal 36, GB 14	KC 24, LAR 9
Den 35, Ind 9	SF 38, Minn 19
NO 37, Rams 6	Sea 31, SD 14
Phil 35, NYJ 30	Mia 17, Wash 10
Cinc, Clev, Hou, Pitt, Phoe, NE had bye weeks	

STANDINGS: FIFTH WEEK

AFC EAST	W	L	T	CENTRAL	W	L	T	WEST	W	L	T	NFC EAST	W	L	T	CENTRAL	W	L	T	WEST	W	L	T
Buffalo	3	1	0	Cleveland	3	1	0	Kan. City	3	1	0	Philadelphia	4	0	0	Detroit	3	2	0	N.Orleans	5	0	0
Miami	3	1	0	Pittsburgh	2	2	0	Denver	3	1	0	NY Giants	3	1	0	Minnesota	2	2	0	San Fran	3	2	0
Indianapolis	2	2	0	Houston	1	3	0	Seattle	3	2	0	Dallas	2	2	0	Chicago	2	2	0	LA Rams	2	3	0
NY Jets	2	2	0	Cincinnati	0	4	0	Raiders	2	2	0	Washington	1	3	0	Green Bay	1	3	0	Atlanta	0	5	0
New England	0	4	0					San Diego	2	2	0	Phoenix	1	3	0	Tampa Bay	1	3	0				

Oilers	7	0	0	0 -	7
Bills	7	21	0	7 -	35

Attendance at Rich Stadium - 79,613

Buf: Beebe 34 pass from Kelly (Christie kick), 3:10
Hou: Harris 17 pass from Moon (Del Greco kick), 13:52
Buf: Reed 24 pass from Kelly (Christie kick), 1:52
Buf: Reed 39 pass from Kelly (Christie kick), 5:43
Buf: Thomas 7 run (Christie kick), 11:26
Buf: K. Davis 3 run (Christie kick), 10:53

	BUF	HOU
First downs	23	18
Rushing yds	141	84
Passing yds	241	245
Punts-avg	6-35.5	3-49.3
Fumbles-lost	4-1	4-3
Penalties-yds	5-35	12-59
Poss. time	32:08	27:52

BILLS LEADERS: Rushing - Thomas 24-92, K. Davis 16-45, Brooks 1-8, Kelly 1-0, Gardner 1-2, Reed 1-(-4), Reich 2-(-2); **Passing** - Kelly 15-25-0 - 247; **Receiving** - Beebe 3-61, Reed 4-85, Brooks 3-16, Gardner 1-22, Thomas 1-35, Copeland 3-28.

OILERS LEADERS: Rushing - White 12-38, Moon 3-37, Wellman 1-2, Carlson 1-7; **Passing** - Moon 16-25-3 - 177, Carlson 9-15-1 - 95; **Receiving** - White 8-65, Givins 2-31, Harris 2-24, Slaughter 5-45, Jeffires 5-60, Wellman 2-34, Norgard 1-13.

WEEK 6 GAMES

Chi 17, Phil 6	KC 17, Cinc 15
Dal 27, Ind 3	Mia 24, Clev 14
NYG 41, Wash 7	Minn 15, TB 0
Pitt 16, SD 3	NE 23, Phoe 21
LAR 24, NYJ 20	GB 30, Den 27
Atl, Rams, NO, SF, Det, Sea had bye weeks	

NOTES

• The Oilers were unable to avenge their historic wild-card playoff loss to the Bills.
• Houston QB Warren Moon was benched in the third quarter after throwing three interceptions.
• Marvcus Patton had four tackles, one sack, one forced fumble, one recovery and one interception.
• Cornelius Bennett intercepted Moon on the Oilers' fourth play of the game at the Oilers 34. It was the first of Houston's seven turnovers. On the next play, Jim Kelly hit Don Beebe for a TD.
• Five plays after the kickoff, Nate Odomes intercepted Moon, but the Bills ended up punting.
• Late in the first quarter, the Oilers drove 74 yards in 10 plays to Moon's tying TD pass to Leonard Harris. Moon was five-of-eight for 57 yards on the drive.
• The Bills answered with a nine-play, 87-yard drive to Andre Reed's first TD. Thurman Thomas had a 25-yard run. The Oilers went three-and-out and the Bills needed only five plays to go 56 yards to Reed's second TD.
• Two plays after the kickoff, Darryl Talley forced Haywood Jeffires to fumble and Mickey Washington recovered at the Bills 41. The Bills used nine plays to move 59 yards to Thomas' TD run and a 28-7 lead.
• In the third, Bruce Smith sacked Moon, forced him to fumble and Patton recovered. Later, Talley intercepted Moon, but after both turnovers, the Bills failed to move and punted.
• The teams then traded turnovers, and Moon left in favor of Cody Carlson.
• In the fourth, the Bills drove 52 yards in nine plays to Kenneth Davis' TD.

QUOTES

• Jim Kelly: "You're going to struggle at times. That's part of being an offensive unit. But as long as you keep going, sooner or later you're going to get a big one. The defense has just been playing excellent football."
• Marv Levy: "The offense played well and they got some help from the defense with seven takeaways and that makes a helluva difference. On both sides of the ball, we executed our gameplan very well."
• Andre Reed on his two TDs: "We caught them in the right positions on both. Sometimes you win the (blitz) battle, sometimes you lose it."
• Marvcus Patton: "They (the coaches) put me out on the field and said 'Hey, let's make something happen.' They let me go out and play and try to get pressure and I wanted to take advantage of that opportunity. Anytime you get a chance to play without too much responsibility and play to have fun, that's great. Moon's a great quarterback and if you don't put pressure on him, he's going to complete every pass. We knew we had to get to him."
• Houston coach Jack Pardee: "What a mess that was. We stunk up the place."
• Houston quarterback Warren Moon: "I'm thoroughly disgusted and very disappointed. We're running out of

Bills	0	6	7	6 -	19
Jets	7	0	0	3 -	10

Attendance at Giants Stadium - 71,541

NYJ: Baxter 1 run (Blanchard kick), 7:58
Buf: FG Christie 36, 3:17
Buf: FG Christie 33, 14:46
Buf: Talley 61 interception return (Christie kick), 8:28
Buf: FG Christie 22, 2:33
NYJ: FG Blanchard 33, 7:38
Buf: FG Christie 30, 11:13

	BUF	NYJ
First downs	27	15
Rushing yds	197	78
Passing yds	216	159
Punts-avg	1-52.0	3-43.7
Fumbles-lost	1-1	2-2
Penalties-yds	8-58	6-39
Poss. time	37:16	22:44

BILLS LEADERS: Rushing - Thomas 27-117, K. Davis 10-58, Kelly 4-14, Gardner 2-4, Reed 1-4, Turner 1-0; **Passing** - Kelly 22-35-2 - 224; **Receiving** - Thomas 7-67, Reed 5-56, Beebe 4-58, K. Davis 3-12, Metzelaars 2-21, Brooks 1-10.

JETS LEADERS: Rushing - Johnson 11-49, Baxter 6-18, Murrell 2-7, Esiason 2-4; **Passing** - Esiason 14-25-2 - 189; **Receiving** - Mathis 7-93, Burkett 3-25, Mitchell 2-26, Johnson 1-23, Thornton 1-22.

NOTES

• The Bills returned from their second bye week and struggled past the Jets as Darryl Talley made a game-turning interception return for a touchdown in the third quarter.
• Jim Ritcher's streak of 145 consecutive starts ended due to a knee injury suffered against the Oilers. Glenn Parker started at left guard. Nate Odomes had his 110-game consecutive starts streak snapped due to a shoulder injury, but he did play in the game.
• The Jets took the opening kickoff and drove 80 yards in 16 plays to Brad Baxter's TD run. Terance Mathis caught 14- and 13-yard passes on third-and-seven and third-and 10 respectively.
• On their first series of the game, which lingered into the second quarter, the Bills used 21 plays to go 61 yards to Steve Christie's field goal. They converted once on fourth down, twice on third down.
• The teams traded turnovers, then after a Jets punt, the Bills drove 65 yards in 10 plays to Christie's second field goal. Jim Kelly hit Don Beebe twice for 30 yards and Thurman Thomas once for 32.
• The Bills took the second-half kickoff and got to the Jets 7, but Brian Washington intercepted Kelly.
• On the Bills next series, James Hasty intercepted Kelly.

But on the next play, Talley intercepted Boomer Esiason and ran 61 yards down the right sideline for the go-ahead score.
• Early in the fourth, Christie's third field goal capped a 13-play, 81-yard march. Thomas gained 40 yards.
• Cary Blanchard answered with a field goal, and after a Bills punt, the Jets got the ball at their 45 with 5:02 left. But on the first play, Marvcus Patton tipped a pass and Bruce Smith made a diving interception. The Bills then moved to Christie's final field goal.

QUOTES

• Jets safety Brian Washington: "We're not a 2-4 team. We are the best 2-4 team in the NFL, we just have to prove it."
• Jets running back Johnny Johnson: "I know that man-for-man, we're a better team."
• Darryl Talley on his interception: "Before the play we said 'Watch the boot.' I jammed the tight end (Johnny Mitchell) coming off the ball, it was a timing route where Boomer turned around and threw and when I saw the ball coming, I just grabbed it and started running."
• Marv Levy: "Darryl's been a bull worker for our team and he was a deserving guy to do it."

WEEK 7 GAMES

Hou 28, NE 14	Clev 28, Cinc 17
Pitt 37, NO 14	NYG 21, Phil 10
Det 30, Sea 10	Phoe 36, Wash 6
KC 17, SD 14	Dal 26, SF 17
LAR 23, Den 20	Atl 30, Rams 24
Buf, Ind, Mia, NYJ, Chi, GB, Minn, TB had bye weeks	

WEEK 8 GAMES

Atl 26, NO 15	Hou 28, Cinc 12
GB 37, TB 14	Clev 28, Pitt 23
Det 16, Rams 13	SF 28, Phoe 14
Sea 10, NE 9	Mia 41, Ind 27
Minn 19, Chi 12	
Den, LAR, KC, SD, Dal, Wash, Phil, NYG had bye weeks	

STANDINGS: EIGHTH WEEK

AFC EAST	W	L	T	CENTRAL	W	L	T	WEST	W	L	T	NFC EAST	W	L	T	CENTRAL	W	L	T	WEST	W	L	T
Buffalo	5	1	0	Cleveland	5	2	0	Kan. City	5	1	0	NY Giants	5	1	0	Detroit	5	2	0	N.Orleans	5	2	0
Miami	5	1	0	Pittsburgh	4	3	0	Raiders	4	2	0	Dallas	4	2	0	Minnesota	4	2	0	San Fran	4	3	0
Indianapolis	2	4	0	Houston	3	4	0	Seattle	4	3	0	Philadelphia	4	2	0	Chicago	3	3	0	LA Rams	2	5	0
NY Jets	2	4	0	Cincinnati	0	7	0	Denver	3	3	0	Phoenix	2	5	0	Green Bay	3	3	0	Atlanta	2	5	0
New England	1	6	0					San Diego	2	4	0	Washington	1	5	0	Tampa Bay	1	5	0				

NOTES

• The Bills completed a three-game sweep of their Super Bowl conquerors.

• Jim Kelly and Andre Reed hooked up on a TD pass for the 50th time in their careers.

• Bruce Smith recorded the 100th sack of his career, the fifth player to reach the century mark.

• Thurman Thomas fumbled on the fourth play of the game, but the defense forced a Redskins punt. The Bills needed only five plays to go 85 yards with Kelly hitting Reed on a 65-yard TD.

• The Redskins answered with a nine-play, 71-yard march to Reggie Brooks' TD run. Desmond Howard had a 27-yard reception and Mark Rypien hit Ricky Sanders for 14 on third-and-six from the 21.

• The Bills came right back to make it 14-7 with a 12-play, 80-yard drive to Bill Brooks' TD on a third-and-three play. Thomas ran 11 yards to the Redskins 18 on a third-and-10 play.

• The scoring surge continued as Washington took the kick-off and drove 73 yards in 15 plays to Chip Lohmiller's field goal. Art Monk had a 20-yard catch on third-and-five and Howard caught an 11-yard pass. Lohmiller made a 36-yarder but was roughed by Thomas Smith. The Redskins took the points off the board, but again had to settle for a field goal.

• Each QB threw an interception later in the second quarter. In the third, Nate Odomes intercepted Rypien at the Bills 25 and Kelly engineered a 12-play drive to Thomas' TD run. Thomas carried eight times for 41 yards on the march.

• Odomes' second interception at the end of the third in the end zone started the Bills on a 53-yard drive to Steve Christie's field goal that wrapped up the scoring.

QUOTES

• Thurman Thomas: "Sure it's great (beating all three Super Bowl teams), but you wish you could have done it in the last game of the season. But anytime you beat the teams that beat you in the Super Bowl, it's sweet revenge." (On his game-long battle with Redskins safety Brad Edwards): "We were going at it pretty good, but it was in the heat of the battle. He told me after the game he was just trying to get his guys fired up because it's been a frustrating season for them and they're not used to that. But picking on me is the wrong type of guy to be picking on. I get motivated and fired up for things like that."

• Marv Levy: "Our division is our main concern. That's the first priority along the way. I don't think the players in our locker room were making a big issue out of Washington beating us in the Super Bowl two years ago." (On the third-quarter TD drive that resembled NFC-type power football): "That was the one that gave us a big lift. It made it 21-10, it came following an interception when they were moving the ball in the second half. That ensuing drive had to be the one thing that finally put us in position where, if we didn't foul up after that, it said that we were going to win."

Redskins	7	3	0	0	-	10
Bills	14	0	7	3	-	24

Attendance at Rich Stadium - 79,106

Buf: Reed 65 pass from Kelly (Christie kick), 6:00
Wash: R. Brooks 7 run (Lohmiller kick), 10:25
Buf: B. Brooks 11 pass from Kelly (Christie kick), 14:50
Wash: FG Lohmiller 19, 6:36
Buf: Thomas 1 run (Christie kick), 9:33
Buf: FG Christie 45, 3:35

	BUF	WASH
First downs	22	21
Rushing yds	164	140
Passing yds	238	162
Punts-avg	3-42.0	2-40.0
Fumbles-lost	1-1	2-0
Penalties-yds	9-59	5-40
Poss. time	30:08	29:52

BILLS LEADERS: Rushing - Thomas 28-129, K. Davis 6-11, Kelly 3-8, Gardner 5-16; **Passing** - Kelly 18-24-1 - 238; **Receiving** - Reed 7-159, Metzelaars 2-13, B. Brooks 3-37, Copeland 2-18, Thomas 1-1, Awalt 1-10, K. Davis 2-0.

REDSKINS LEADERS: Rushing - R. Brooks 24-117, Byner 4-16, Sanders 1-7; **Passing** - Rypien 15-42-4 - 169; **Receiving** - Sanders 4-37, R. Brooks 3-17, Howard 2-38, Monk 3-42, Wycheck 1-11, Byner 1-20, Middleton 1-4.

WEEK 9 GAMES

GB 17, Chi 3	Mia 30, KC 10
Ind 9, NE 6	TB 31, Atl 24
NYJ 10, NYG 6	Dal 23, Phil 10
NO 20, Phoe 17	SD 30, LAR 23
SF 40, Rams 17	Den 28, Sea 17
Det 30, Minn 27	

Pitt, Clev, Cinc, Hou had bye weeks

NOTES

• The Bills avoided a huge upset by rallying to score 10 points in the final 7:48, then won the game in overtime on Steve Christie's field goal.

• Pete Metzelaars set a single-game career-high with 10 receptions.

• Nate Odomes intercepted his sixth pass of the season to set a new personal best.

• Rookie No. 1 draft choice Drew Bledsoe did not start, but he replaced the injured Scott Secules late in the first half and he had success moving the Pats in the second half.

• The Bills went three-and-out only once in the game, but it was a very quiet 432-yard offensive day.

• Odomes' interception stopped the Pats at the Bills 32 late in the first quarter. Christie then missed a 40-yarder.

• On the next series, Jim Kelly was sacked by Chris Slade and Andre Tippett recovered the fumble at the Bills 29. That threat died when Scott Sisson missed a 28-yard field goal.

• The Pats broke a scoreless tie by driving 73 yards in 14 plays after the second-half kickoff to Leonard Russell's TD run. Russell carried seven times for 39 yards.

• After a Bills punt, the Pats drove 83 yards in 11 plays to Sisson's field goal. Bledsoe hit Vincent Brisby for 17 on a third-and-13 from the Pats 4, then he hit Michael Timpson on the next play for 26.

• The Bills finally broke through with a 15-play, 80-yard drive to Metzelaars' TD. Metzelaars caught four passes on the drive for 29 yards and the Bills converted four times on third down, including on the TD.

• After a Pats punt, the Bills drove to the Pats 27 but Thurman Thomas fumbled and Tippett recovered.

• The Pats punted again and the Bills took over at their 13 with 1:04 left. Kelly hit Bill Brooks for 22 and on the next play, hit Russell Copeland for 56 to the Pats 9. After three incompletions, Christie made his game-tying field goal.

• The Pats won the coin toss and got to the Bills 48, but Cornelius Bennett stopped Russell on fourth-and-one. The Bills got to the Pats 35, but Metzelaars lost a fumble.

• The defense forced a punt and on the first play, Andre Reed caught a 46-yard pass to the Pats 19 to set up the winning field goal.

QUOTES

• Bruce Smith: "We went through the same thing (losing tough games) so I can sympathize with them. It's such a feeling of frustration."

• Andre Reed: "Everytime we come up here, it's always the defense playing better than us (offense). The defense kept us in the game."

• Marv Levy on Jim Kelly: "Jim has pulled a lot of games out. He's never out of a game emotionally or in his belief that he can pull them out."

• Jim Kelly: "One of the keys before the game was to stay patient. Everybody looks at the records and says 'You should blow them out.' When you play the Patriots, it's a battle."

Bills	0	0	0	10	3	-	13
Patriots	0	0	7	3	0	-	10

Attendance at Foxboro Stadium - 54,326

NE: Russell 2 run (Sisson kick), 8:23
NE: FG Sisson 27, 1:27
Buf: Metzelaars 9 pass from Kelly (Christie kick), 7:12
Buf: FG Christie 27, 14:46
Buf: FG Christie 32, 9:22

	BUF	NE
First downs	25	17
Rushing yds	134	187
Passing yds	298	97
Punts-avg	5-40.2	7-43.7
Fumbles-lost	3-3	1-0
Penalties-yds	4-20	4-20
Poss. time	30:43	38:39

BILLS LEADERS: Rushing - Thomas 30-111, K. Davis 3-6, Kelly 4-17; **Passing** - Kelly 29-46-0 - 317; **Receiving** - Metzelaars 10-74, Brooks 7-81, Thomas 5-31, Reed 3-56, Copeland 2-66, Awalt 1-9, K. Davis 1-0.

PATRIOTS LEADERS: Rushing - Russell 25-95, Turner 6-23, Gash 7-21, Croom 3-18, Secules 2-16, Bledsoe 5-14; **Passing** - Bledsoe 8-16-0 - 96, Secules 2-7-1 - 16; **Receiving** - Coates 3-22, Brisby 2-39, Russell 2-18, Turner 2-7, Timpson 1-26.

WEEK 10 GAMES

Den 29, Clev 16	Dal 31, NYG 9
SD 30, Minn 17	Pitt 24, Cinc 16
Hou 24, Sea 14	Det 23, TB 0
LAR 16, Chi 14	NYJ 27, Mia 10
Wash 30, Ind 24	Phoe 16, Phil 3
KC 23, GB 16	

Atl, Rams, SF, NO had bye weeks

STANDINGS: TENTH WEEK

AFC EAST	W	L	T	CENTRAL	W	L	T	WEST	W	L	T	NFC EAST	W	L	T	CENTRAL	W	L	T	WEST	W	L	T
Buffalo	7	1	0	Cleveland	5	3	0	Kan. City	6	2	0	Dallas	6	2	0	Detroit	7	2	0	N.Orleans	6	2	0
Miami	6	2	0	Pittsburgh	5	3	0	Raiders	5	3	0	NY Giants	5	3	0	Minnesota	4	4	0	San Fran	5	3	0
NY Jets	4	4	0	Houston	4	4	0	Denver	5	3	0	Philadelphia	4	4	0	Green Bay	4	4	0	LA Rams	2	6	0
Indianapolis	3	5	0	Cincinnati	0	8	0	San Diego	4	4	0	Phoenix	3	6	0	Chicago	3	5	0	Atlanta	2	6	0
New England	1	8	0					Seattle	4	5	0	Washington	2	6	0	Tampa Bay	2	6	0				

Bills	0	0	0	0 -	0
Steelers	7	3	10	3 -	23

Attendance at Three Rivers Stadium - 60,265

Pitt: Thompson 9 run (Anderson kick), 9:24
Pitt: FG Anderson 37, 5:46
Pitt: Green 1 pass from O'Donnell (Anderson kick), 4:44
Pitt: FG Anderson 19, 12:37
Pitt: FG Anderson 31, 4:27

	BUF	PITT
First downs	9	26
Rushing yds	47	227
Passing yds	110	173
Punts-avg	8-45.8	4-46.8
Fumbles-lost	1-1	0-0
Penalties-yds	5-32	5-55
Poss. time	15:09	44:51

BILLS LEADERS: Rushing - Thomas 13-40, Kelly 1-7; **Passing** - Kelly 7-19-0 - 93, Reich 4-9-0 - 41; **Receiving** - Reed 4-72, Thomas 3-22, Beebe 2-33, Metzelaars 1-4, K. Davis 1-3.

STEELERS LEADERS: Rushing - Thompson 30-108, Hoge 10-64, Foster 5-23, Mills 1-19, Stone 2-8, Cuthbert 1-7, Tomczak 1-(-2); **Passing** - O'Donnell 16-27-0 - 212; **Receiving** - Green 6-69, Graham 3-44, Stone 2-29, Mills 2-16, Thompson 2-16, Cooper 1-38.

WEEK 11 GAMES

GB 19, NO 17	Hou 38, Cinc 3
SF 45, TB 21	Mia 19, Phil 14
Atl 13, Rams 0	NYG 20, Wash 6
KC 31, LAR 20	Dal 20, Phoe 15
Sea 22, Cinc 5	Minn 26, Den 23
NYJ 31, Ind 17	Chi 16, SD 13
Det, NE had bye weeks	

NOTES

• For the first time in 133 games, dating to the 1985 season finale, the Bills were shutout. It was the first time a Jim Kelly Bills team had been blanked.

• Kelly was knocked out of the game late in the second quarter with a concussion and shoulder injury. Andre Reed suffered a broken bone in his left wrist.

• Keith McKeller was activated for the first time this season, but played sparingly.

• The attendance was a regular-season record for Three Rivers Stadium. The attendance record for a playoff game also was set in a game against the Bills the previous January.

• The Steelers lost star running back Barry Foster to a knee injury in the first quarter yet still rushed for 227 yards, the highest total allowed by the Bills thus far this season.

• Pittsburgh converted six of its first seven third downs

and was 10-of-18 for the game.

• The Steelers drove 81 yards in 15 plays on their first possession to Leroy Thompson's TD. Thompson had replaced Foster, who was hurt while dropping a pass.

• In the second quarter, the Steelers drove 35 yards in eight plays to a Gary Anderson field goal.

• The Bills punted after all five of their possessions in the first half.

• The Steelers took the second-half kickoff and moved 70 yards to Eric Green's TD reception.

• After a Bills punt, Pittsburgh went 65 yards to Anderson's second field goal. Mark Kelso intercepted Neil O'Donnell at the 3, but it was nullified by a roughing-the-passer penalty on Oliver Barnett.

• Four plays later, Thurman Thomas fumbled and Kevin Greene recovered. That set up Anderson's final field goal.

QUOTES

• Walt Corey: "I'll tell you what, it was just a good 'ol whupping. They took it to us offensively, defensively and on special teams. I thought we stunk up the joint the whole way. I see everybody sharing the blame. Every now and then this happens, you start thinking you might be better than you really are. You have to get your eyes open."

• Bruce Smith: "They have great players and I'm not just blowing smoke. When I saw them on film, they're a team that really scares you and they proved it."

• Kent Hull: "It hurts your pride, it hurts everything. It seems like every year we get a wakeup call and maybe this was it."

• Steelers cornerback D.J. Johnson: "It shows the whole league we're there now. We're there and you better show us some respect when we come to play you."

Colts	3	3	3	0 -	9
Bills	0	16	7	0 -	23

Attendance at Rich Stadium - 79,101

Ind: FG Biasucci 26, 5:12
Ind: FG Biasucci 22, 3:01
Buf: Safety: Jones tackled George, 7:10
Buf: K. Davis 1 run (Christie kick), 12:25
Buf: Brooks 23 pass from Kelly (Christie kick), 13:05
Ind: FG Biasucci 37, 6:46
Buf: McKeller 13 pass from Kelly (Christie kick), 10:58

	BUF	IND
First downs	21	21
Rushing yds	135	113
Passing yds	268	252
Punts-avg	4-37.8	3-43.3
Fumbles-lost	1-1	2-1
Penalties-yds	7-45	7-55
Poss. time	30:01	29:59

BILLS LEADERS: Rushing - Thomas 27-116, K. Davis 6-17, Turner 1-5, Kelly 2-1, Fina 1-(-2), Reed 1-(-2); **Passing** - Kelly 19-27-1 - 274; **Receiving** - Reed 4-64, Metzelaars 4-37, Thomas 3-48, Brooks 3-67, Beebe 3-42, K. Davis 1-3, McKeller 1-13.

COLTS LEADERS: Rushing - Johnson 18-67, Potts 1-7, Toner 1-6, Culver 6-28, George 3-5; **Passing** - George 21-41-1 - 262; **Receiving** - Hester 7-97, Cash 3-45, Langhorne 7-62, Johnson 3-43, Dawkins 1-15.

NOTES

• The Bills rebounded from their pounding in Pittsburgh on the day O.J. Simpson and the Electric Company were honored on the 20th anniversary of Simpson's 2,003-yard season.

• Jim Kelly had his team record of 75 passes without an interception snapped in the second quarter.

• Keith Goganious made his first NFL start when Mark Maddox was deactivated for the game.

• The Colts took the opening kickoff and drove 56 yards in 12 plays to Dean Biasucci's field goal.

• Late in the first quarter after Steve Christie missed a 55-yarder, the Colts went 59 yards in 12 plays to another Biasucci field goal.

• The Bills responded by driving to the Colts 8, but Ray Buchanan intercepted Kelly at the 2.

• On the next play, Henry Jones blitzed from the right side and sacked Jeff George for a safety which woke up the Bills. After the free kick, they marched 55 yards in 10 plays to Kenneth Davis' TD plunge on fourth-and-goal, taking the lead for good. Thurman Thomas had a 27-yard run.

• Clarence Verdin fumbled the ensuing kickoff after being hit by Richard Harvey and Goganious recovered. Two plays later, Kelly hit ex-Colt Bill Brooks for a TD.

WEEK 12 GAMES

Chi 19, KC 17	NYJ 17, Cinc 12
Atl 27, Dal 14	GB 26, Det 17
Hou 27, Clev 20	Mia 17, NE 13
NYG 7, Phil 3	Den 37, Pitt 13
LAR 12, SD 7	Rams 10, Wash 6
TB 23, Minn 10	SF 42, NO 7
Phoe, Sea had bye weeks	

• On the first possession of the third, Andre Reed fumbled and Jason Belser recovered at the Colts 26. George then directed an 11-play, 54-yard drive to Biasucci's third field goal.

• The Bills answered with a nine-play, 80-yard drive to Keith McKeller's first TD reception in nearly two seasons. Kelly completed five-of-six passes for 47 yards.

• In the fourth, the Colts reached the Bills 7 and the Bills 11 but lost the ball on downs once and Nate Odomes had a pick.

QUOTES

• Kent Hull: "In the first quarter we stumbled around a bit. We made some stupid mistakes and we never got into a rhythm. It was a lot like last Monday night and I think the safety by Henry lifted this football team. It gave us a jolt and woke us up."

• Marv Levy: "The safety turned out to be a 16-point play. I try to impress on our players that a safety can be a nine-point play, but then we got the fumble on the kickoff and it became a 16-point play. We did a great job in red territory. It's hard to sustain a drive. Things change down there. It's harder to click in red territory than it is from farther out."

• Henry Jones on his safety: "We run that play quite often, but usually there's a back picking me up. We were very fortunate they ran something that worked for what we had called. It was a really big play. They had some momentum and the lead and we really needed a big play at that time. He (Jeff George) said to me 'Was that you on the blitz?' I said 'Yeah' and he said 'The tight end (Kerry Cash) was supposed to pick you up.' I said 'Well, that's the way it goes.'"

STANDINGS: TWELFTH WEEK

AFC EAST	W	L	T	CENTRAL	W	L	T	WEST	W	L	T	NFC EAST	W	L	T	CENTRAL	W	L	T	WEST	W	L	T
Buffalo	8	2	0	Pittsburgh	6	4	0	Kan. City	7	3	0	Dallas	7	3	0	Detroit	7	3	0	San Fran	7	3	0
Miami	8	2	0	Houston	6	4	0	Raiders	6	4	0	NY Giants	7	3	0	Green Bay	6	4	0	N.Orleans	6	4	0
NY Jets	6	4	0	Cleveland	5	5	0	Denver	6	4	0	Philadelphia	4	6	0	Minnesota	5	5	0	Atlanta	4	6	0
Indianapolis	3	7	0	Cincinnati	0	10	0	Seattle	5	5	0	Phoenix	3	7	0	Chicago	5	5	0	LA Rams	3	7	0
New England	1	9	0					San Diego	4	6	0	Washington	2	8	0	Tampa Bay	3	7	0				

GAME 11 - Sunday, Nov. 28, 1993 - CHIEFS 23, BILLS 7

NOTES

• Joe Montana, starting only his third game of his career against the Bills, directed a rout at loud Arrowhead Stadium. He was helped by another old veteran and first-year Chief, Marcus Allen. Montana had missed the previous three games with an injury.

• The teams traded punts to open the game, then the Bills drove 80 yards in 13 plays to Kenneth Davis' TD. Jim Kelly hit Bill Brooks for 17 on third-and-nine from their 32 and later hit Brooks on third-and-two.

• Late in the first quarter, Albert Lewis forced Andre Reed to fumble at the Bills 28 and Charles Mincy recovered.

• Four plays later, Allen took a third-and-nine swing pass from Montana and went 18 yards for the TD.

• After a Bills punt, the Chiefs went 55 yards to Nick Lowery's first field goal as Montana was five-of-six.

• The Chiefs got to the Bills 14 later in the second quarter, but Nate Odomes intercepted Montana at the 2. The Bills moved to the Kansas City 33, but Steve Christie missed a 51-yard field goal as the half ended.

• Kansas City took the second-half kickoff and marched 80 yards to Keith Cash's TD. Jonathan Hayes had a 23-yard reception and Odomes was flagged for a 29-yard pass interference in the end zone.

• The Bills' next three possessions ended in a punt and two interceptions, the second pick by Dan Saleaumua which he returned to the Bills 17, setting up Lowery's second field goal.

• The Chiefs drove 50 yards in 13 plays midway through the fourth to Lowery's final field goal.

QUOTES

• Mark Kelso: "We've had three tests and we haven't been successful in any of them. You've got to win the games you're supposed to win and when it's a big game, you're supposed to win some of those, too. Right now, we've got some work to do."

• Kent Hull: "I would say we're concerned, I wouldn't say we're panicking by any means. Who does Kansas City play next week? I don't even know, but they'll probably get beat. They're mentally dead right now. Every time we play somebody, I see it, the fire in their eyes. I think people play us differently than they play anybody else. Pittsburgh was a prime example. Those guys played an exceptional ballgame, almost error-free, and the very next week they played like crap. It's an attitude thing and people say this team (the Bills) has won the AFC the last three years and they get all pumped up and riled up for us. We've been seeing this the last few years. If there's one thing we've learned, it's week after week, if you try to get to that level emotionally, it drains you. It totally drains you."

• Chiefs quarterback Joe Montana: "There were some frustrating times out there today, I don't think I played all that well. But it was good to get back on the field and do things."

• Chiefs coach Marty Schottenheimer: "So people say the AFC is a one-horse race? It wasn't one of Joe's greatest performances, but he certainly made some plays in timely situations."

Bills	7	0	0	0	-	7
Chiefs	7	3	10	3	-	23

Attendance at Arrowhead Stadium - 74,452

Buf: K. Davis 9 run (Christie kick), 10:46
KC: Allen 18 pass from Montana (Lowery kick), 14:48
KC: FG Lowery 30, 7:17
KC: Cash 1 pass from Montana (Lowery kick), 3:42
KC: FG Lowery 22, 12:37
KC: FG Lowery 34, 9:49

	BUF	KC
First downs	17	19
Rushing yds	43	106
Passing yds	213	208
Punts-avg	7-42.9	5-47.0
Fumbles-lost	1-1	2-1
Penalties-yds	8-64	5-20
Poss. time	25:26	34:34

BILLS LEADERS: Rushing - Thomas 15-25, K. Davis 2-9, Kelly 1-9; **Passing** - Kelly 23-36-3 - 214, Reich 5-6-0 - 40; **Receiving** - Metzelaars 10-98, Brooks 6-72, Thomas 6-44, Reed 4-28, Beebe 1-9, K. Davis 1-3.

CHIEFS LEADERS: Rushing - Allen 22-74, Anders 4-10, Stephens 2-10, McNair 2-7, Carter 1-2, Thompson 1-2, Montana 3-1; **Passing** - Montana 18-32-1 - 208; **Receiving** - Birden 5-39, Cash 4-51, Hayes 2-50, Allen 2-28, Barnett 2-10, Jones 1-16, Davis 1-9, Anders 1-5.

WEEK 13 GAMES

NO 17, Minn 14	Atl 17, Clev 14
NYJ 6, NE 0	Cinc 16, LAR 10
GB 13, TB 10	Phil 17, Wash 14
Den 17, Sea 9	SF 35, Rams 10
Hou 23, Pitt 3	NYG 19, Phoe 17
Mia 16, Dal 14	Chi 10, Det 6
SD 31, Ind 0	

GAME 12 - Sunday, Dec. 5, 1993 - RAIDERS 25, BILLS 24

NOTES

• The Bills suffered their second straight loss as the Raiders rallied in the fourth quarter.

• The Bills had planned to use a two-back offense with Nate Turner at fullback, but Turner injured his knee on the opening kickoff and never returned. Andre Reed, Jeff Wright and Mark Kelso also were hurt.

• The defense sacked Jeff Hostetler five times and Darryl Talley had 10 tackles putting him over 100 for the season.

• Thurman Thomas became the eighth player in NFL history to top 1,000 yards rushing five years in a row.

• The Raiders drove to Jeff Jaeger's first field goal on their first possession.

• The Bills punted three times before driving 80 yards in five plays to Thomas' TD run. Pete Metzelaars had a 51-yard catch and run to the Raiders 14 and Greg Townsend was penalized for roughing Kelly.

• Later in the second quarter, Los Angeles moved 72 yards in seven plays to Hostetler's TD run. Tim Brown caught three passes for 42 yards on the drive.

• The Bills answered four plays after the kickoff as Don Beebe caught a 65-yard TD.

• The Raiders took the second-half kickoff and drove 64 yards to Jaeger's second field goal, but the Bills came back with a 63-yard march to Steve Christie's field goal. Beebe had a 24-yard reception.

• The Raiders drove to the third Jaeger field goal late in third after Rocket Ismail's 49-yard kickoff return.

• The Bills seemed to gain control when Thomas scored on the ensuing possession to cap an 80-yard drive, the key being a 34-yard interference penalty on Torin Dorn in the end zone.

• But Terry McDaniel's interception of Kelly and 35-yard return to the 11 set up the fourth Jaeger field goal. Then after a punt, Hostetler hit Nick Bell for 18, James Jett for 10 and then fired the winning 29-yard TD pass to Brown.

• The Bills' final threat ended when Thomas lost a fumble to Eddie Anderson.

QUOTES

• Thurman Thomas on his fumble: "I feel worse than anyone. The coaches called my number in a crucial situation and I didn't come through." (On whether the Bills were mired in controversy): "There's no damn controversy around the Buffalo Bills. Let's get that straight right now. Things weren't working for us, but all you want to talk about is controversy. We're a good team and if you don't like it, you don't have to write about us. There's no Bickering Bills going on here. We're not pointing fingers."

• Marv Levy: "In the moments of greatest disappointment, you find out what you're made of. I've made our players aware that there's a very important part of the season left. We'll go back to work and make some happier moments down the line."

• Jim Kelly: "We'll find out who's behind us and who's not."

Raiders	3	7	6	9	-	25
Bills	0	14	3	7	-	24

Attendance at Rich Stadium - 79,478

LAR: FG Jaeger 37, 7:43
Buf: Thomas 3 run (Christie kick), 5:41
LAR: Hostetler 11 run (Jaeger kick), 12:55
Buf: Beebe 65 pass from Kelly (Christie kick), 14:02
LAR: FG Jaeger 34, 6:46
Buf: FG Christie 36, 10:32
LAR: FG Jaeger 26, 14:38
Buf: Thomas 1 run (Christie kick), 2:48
LAR: FG Jaeger 47, 6:13
LAR: Brown 29 pass from Hostetler (kick blocked), 10:02

	BUF	LAR
First downs	19	25
Rushing yds	91	138
Passing yds	276	261
Punts-avg	5-42.0	3-40.7
Fumbles-lost	3-1	0-0
Penalties-yds	4-23	9-80
Poss. time	22:00	38:00

BILLS LEADERS: Rushing - Thomas 19-74, K. Davis 1-0, Kelly 3-2, Brooks 1-15; **Passing** - Kelly 20-30-1 - 276; **Receiving** - Metzelaars 4-76, Beebe 4-115, Brooks 5-39, Copeland 3-29, Thomas 3-11, Reed 1-6.

RAIDERS LEADERS: Rushing - Robinson 9-56, Bell 16-44, Hostetler 6-39, Smith 5-12, Ismail 1-(-13); **Passing** - Hostetler 18-31-0 - 289; **Receiving** - Brown 10-183, Smith 2-38, Bell 3-38, Jett 1-10, Horton 1-11, Robinson 1-9.

WEEK 14 GAMES

Hou 33, Atl 17	Chi 30, GB 17
Ind 9, NYJ 6	Minn 13, Det 0
Pitt 17, NE 14	Clev 17, NO 13
Wash 23, TB 17	Phoe 38, Rams 10
SD 13, Den 10	NYG 19, Mia 14
KC 31, Sea 16	SF 21, Cinc 8
Dal 23, Phil 17	

STANDINGS: FOURTEENTH WEEK

AFC EAST	W	L	T	CENTRAL	W	L	T	WEST	W	L	T	NFC EAST	W	L	T	CENTRAL	W	L	T	WEST	W	L	T
Miami	9	3	0	Houston	8	4	0	Kan. City	9	3	0	NY Giants	9	3	0	Detroit	7	5	0	San Fran	9	3	0
Buffalo	8	4	0	Pittsburgh	7	5	0	Denver	7	5	0	Dallas	8	4	0	Green Bay	7	5	0	N.Orleans	7	5	0
NY Jets	7	5	0	Cleveland	6	6	0	Raiders	7	5	0	Philadelphia	5	7	0	Chicago	7	5	0	Atlanta	5	7	0
Indianapolis	4	8	0	Cincinnati	1	11	0	San Diego	6	6	0	Phoenix	4	8	0	Minnesota	6	6	0	LA Rams	3	9	0
New England	1	11	0					Seattle	5	7	0	Washington	3	9	0	Tampa Bay	3	9	0				

Bills	0 0 0 10 - 10
Eagles	0 0 7 0 - 7

Attendance at Veterans Stadium - 60,769

Phil: Williams 19 pass from Brister (Bahr kick), 9:43
Buf: Metzelaars 2 pass from Reich (Christie kick), 11:16
Buf: FG Christie 34, 12:42

	BUF	PHIL
First downs	19	21
Rushing yds	101	68
Passing yds	234	298
Punts-avg	3-36.7	5-30.0
Fumbles-lost	2-2	4-4
Penalties-yds	6-40	9-62
Poss. time	29:01	30:59

BILLS LEADERS: Rushing - Thomas 10-31, K. Davis 18-70, Gardner 1-0; **Passing** - Kelly 17-27-2 - 210, Reich 6-10-0 - 42; **Receiving** - Metzelaars 5-59, Brooks 10-90, K. Davis 3-5, Beebe 2-23, Thomas 2-15, Copeland 1-60.

EAGLES LEADERS: Rushing - Sherman 9-37, Walker 9-26, Hebron 2-5; **Passing** - Brister 28-48-0 - 299; **Receiving** - Walker 11-109, Bailey 7-95, Williams 3-40, Hebron 2-17, Lofton 2-7, Bavaro 1-19, Sherman 1-8, Young 1-4.

WEEK 15 GAMES

NYJ 3, Wash 0	Atl 27, SF 24
NE 7, Cinc 2	Hou 19, Clev 17
TB 10, Chi 10	NYG 20, Ind 6
Dal 37, Minn 20	Rams 23, NO 20
Den 27, KC 21	Det 21, Phoe 14
LAR 27, Sea 23	GB 20, SD 13
Pitt 21, Mia 20	

NOTES

• The Bills pulled off a great victory despite playing horribly for 3 1/2 quarters and playing without Andre Reed, Jeff Wright and Mark Kelso, then losing Jim Kelly and Thurman Thomas during the game.

• Steve Christie missed three field goals, but came back to kick the winner with 2:18 left.

• Pete Metzelaars broke his own team record for receptions by a tight end, increasing it to 52.

• Vai Sikahema fumbled the opening kickoff and Thomas Smith recovered at the Eagles 24, but Christie missed from 32 yards.

• Late in the first quarter, Kelly was sacked by Seth Joyner and lost a fumble to Wes Hopkins at the Bills 35, but Matt Bahr missed a 21-yard field goal.

• The Bills drove to the Eagles 6 early in the second quarter, but Kelly was intercepted by Eric Allen in the end zone.

• On the next possession, Christie missed a 29-yarder. Late in the second, Russell Copeland hauled in a 60-yard pass from Kelly to the Eagles 22, but on the next play, Clyde Simmons intercepted Kelly.

• The Bills got to the Eagles 37 on the first possession of the third, but Kenneth Davis lost a fumble.

• After an exchange of punts, the Eagles finally broke the scoreless tie by driving 63 yards in six plays to Bubby Brister's TD pass to Calvin Williams. The key was a 26-yard pass to Herschel Walker.

• Christie missed a 51-yarder on the ensuing possession, during which Kelly was injured. In the fourth, Marvcus Patton forced Heath Sherman to fumble and Mickey Washington recovered at the Bills 29. Frank Reich then directed a 13-play, 71-yard drive to his TD

pass to Metzelaars. The key play was a nine-yard pass to Kenneth Davis on fourth-and-four from the Eagles 37. A 15-yard personal foul on Rich Miano was tacked on. Davis then converted on fourth-and-two from the 5 to set up the TD.

• Carwell Gardner then forced Sikahema to fumble the kickoff and Jerome Henderson recovered at the Eagles 22. The Bills failed to get a first down, but Christie kicked the winning field goal.

• Victor Bailey then caught three passes for 39 yards to give the Eagles a chance to tie, but Bahr missed a 45-yard field goal on the final play of the game.

QUOTES

• Jim Kelly: "One thing about us, we realize what type of players we have and we're never going to give up. We keep falling down, but we keep getting up. Don't count us out."

• Cornelius Bennett: "Had we lost, all hell would have broken loose, no doubt about it. It was in the air already. You could see things blending together to cause trouble. Had we lost, there would have been doubt among us as a team, doubt in the coaches minds, doubt in the front office and even more doubt in the media and with the fans. We showed so much character. Today I think we showed it more than at any time in my career."

• Frank Reich: "This was such a great win for this team. We've undergone some things lately, but we've stayed together and I think this will bring us even closer together."

Bills	9 17 21 0 - 47
Dolphins	7 13 7 7 - 34

Attendance at Joe Robbie Stadium - 71,597

Buf: K. Davis 1 run (kick failed), 4:54
Mia: Ingram 14 pass from Mitchell (Stoyanovich kick), 10:08
Buf: FG Christie 38, 13:40
Mia: FG Stoyanovich 41, 2:56
Mia: Jackson 16 pass from Mitchell (Stoyanovich kick), 4:46
Buf: K. Davis 12 run (Christie kick), 7:59
Buf: FG Christie 32, 13:33
Buf: Washington 27 interception return (Christie kick), 13:41
Mia: FG Stoyanovich 18, 15:00
Buf: Odomes 25 fumble return (Christie kick), :17
Buf: K. Davis 1 run (Christie kick), 2:48
Buf: Beebe 27 pass from Kelly (Christie kick), 5:59
Mia: Kirby 30 pass from DeBerg (Stoyanovich kick), 7:38
Mia: Ingram 7 pass from DeBerg (Stoyanovich kick), 1:34

	BUF	MIA
First downs	28	24
Rushing yds	129	23
Passing yds	245	400
Punts-avg	3-45.3	2-41.5
Fumbles-lost	1-1	2-2
Penalties-yds	9-45	7-40
Poss. time	34:54	25:06

BILLS LEADERS: Rushing - Thomas 26-52, K. Davis 13-64, Brooks 1-7, Gardner 2-5, Reed 1-3, Kelly 1-(-2); **Passing** - Kelly 20-30-1 - 245, Thomas 0-1-0 - 0; **Receiving** - Metzelaars 7-65, Brooks 1-10, Thomas 4-34, Reed 3-65, Beebe 3-49, McKeller 2-22.
DOLPHINS LEADERS: Rushing - Higgs 5-13, Byars 3-8, Kirby 1-6, Mitchell 1-2, Fryar 1-(-6); **Passing** - Mitchell 12-24-2 - 155, DeBerg 20-35-1 - 273; **Receiving** - Kirby 9-148, Ingram 6-80, Fryar 5-59, Jackson 3-42, McDuffie 3-41, Martin 3-38, Byars 2-11, Higgs 1-9.

WEEK 16 GAMES

Den 13, Chi 3	Dal 28, NYJ 7
Wash 30, Atl 17	Hou 26, Pitt 17
Cinc 15, Rams 3	Minn 21, GB 17
NE 20, Clev 17	KC 28, SD 24
SF 55, Det 17	LAR 27, TB 20
Phil 20, Ind 10	NYG 24, NO 14
Phoe 30, Sea 27 (OT)	

NOTES

• The Bills took over first place in the AFC East with a huge victory at Joe Robbie.

• The Bills took the opening kickoff and for the first time in eight games, scored on their first possession, driving 75 yards in 10 plays to Kenneth Davis' TD. Steve Christie missed the extra point.

• The Dolphins answered with a 73-yard march to Mark Ingram's TD reception, but Christie's field goal gave the Bills the lead late in the first quarter. Miami came right back with a Pete Stoyanovich field goal. Then after J.B. Brown intercepted Jim Kelly at the Bills 16, Keith Jackson caught a TD pass two plays later.

• The Bills answered with an 80-yard march to Davis' second TD. Andre Reed had a 32-yard catch on the drive.

• After a Miami punt, the Bills took the lead for good, driving 39 yards to a Christie field goal. One play after the kickoff, Mickey Washington intercepted Scott Mitchell and returned it 27 yards for a TD.

• Stoyanovich made an 18-yard field goal on the final play of the half to make it 26-20 Bills.

• The Bills then exploded for three TDs in the first 5:59 of the third quarter. On the first play after the kickoff, Darryl Talley forced Jackson to fumble and Nate Odomes returned it 25 yards for a TD. Two plays after the kickoff, Matt Darby intercepted Mitchell and returned it 32 yards to the 19. Davis scored his third TD

four plays later. Steve DeBerg replaced Mitchell at QB, but on his fourth play, Keith Byars lost a fumble when hit by Marvcus Patton and Mike Lodish recovered at the Miami 37. Three plays later, Kelly hit Don Beebe for a TD and a 47-20 lead.

• DeBerg stemmed the tide by hitting Terry Kirby with a 30-yard TD four plays after the kickoff.

• Early in the fourth, DeBerg led a 75-yard drive to his TD pass to Mark Ingram, but the Bills' defense turned the Dolphins away on the final two possessions as Odomes had an interception.

QUOTES

• Kent Hull: "You could feel the energy in the locker room. I made a comment last Wednesday that I could feel something around here. You could just tell."

• Andre Reed: "This brought back memories of 1990 and '91. We controlled the line of scrimmage and Jim was making good audibles at the right times. It comes at a good time because you need the offense to be clicking now."

• Miami linebacker Bryan Cox: "We've gone from the penthouse to the outhouse."

STANDINGS: SIXTEENTH WEEK

AFC EAST	W	L	T	CENTRAL	W	L	T	WEST	W	L	T	NFC EAST	W	L	T	CENTRAL	W	L	T	WEST	W	L	T
Buffalo	10	4	0	Houston	10	4	0	Kan. City	10	4	0	NY Giants	11	3	0	Detroit	8	6	0	San Fran	10	4	0
Miami	9	5	0	Pittsburgh	8	6	0	Denver	9	5	0	Dallas	10	4	0	Green Bay	8	6	0	N.Orleans	7	7	0
NY Jets	8	6	0	Cleveland	6	8	0	Raiders	9	5	0	Philadelphia	6	8	0	Chicago	7	7	0	Atlanta	6	8	0
Indianapolis	4	10	0	Cincinnati	2	12	0	San Diego	6	8	0	Phoenix	5	9	0	Minnesota	7	7	0	LA Rams	4	10	0
New England	3	11	0					Seattle	5	9	0	Washington	4	10	0	Tampa Bay	4	10	0				

GAME 15 - Sunday, Dec. 26, 1993 - BILLS 16, JETS 14

NOTES

• This was the first regular-season non-sellout in 25 games, but it also was the coldest game the Bills had ever played in with a temperature of nine degrees and wind-chill of minus 28.

• The Bills clinched the AFC East for the fifth time in six years and for the fourth time, the Jets were the victims.

• Cary Blanchard missed three field goals for New York, including a potential 42-yard game-winner with 53 seconds left. Darryl Talley had eight tackles and made a key fumble recovery for Buffalo.

• The Bills took the opening kickoff and drove 71 yards in 10 plays to Thurman Thomas' TD run. The key plays were Bill Brooks' 16-yard reception and Kenneth Davis had a 28-yard reception to the Jets 2.

• The Jets tied the game later in the first quarter as Johnny Johnson caught a 24-yard TD pass from Boomer Esiason.

• Jim Kelly threw an interception early in the second quarter to Mo Lewis, but on the next play, Talley recovered Esiason's fumble at the Jets 39, setting up Steve Christie's first field goal. Brooks had a 17-yard catch.

• The Jets then drove to the Bills 9, but Blanchard missed from 27 yards. The Bills turned around and drove 62 yards to Christie's second field goal just before the first half ended.

• The Jets took the second-half kickoff and drove 81 yards in 11 plays to Chris Burkett's TD reception.

• On the next possession, Kyle Clifton, who had 17 tackles, intercepted Kelly, but Blanchard missed from 41 yards.

• In the fourth, the Bills drove to the Jets 20 but Carwell Gardner lost a fumble to Clifton.

• After the Jets punted, the Bills took possession at their 33 with 9:18 left. They used 12 plays to go 45 yards, setting up Christie's winning field goal with 3:48 left. The key play was Thomas' 15-yard catch on third-and-11 from the Jets 41.

• Esiason completed five of six passes for 39 yards to move the Jets into field-goal range, but Blanchard missed for the third time.

QUOTES

• Kent Hull: "This is our first steppingstone, it's something we expected to do, win the division. But you can't be too overjubilant. We've still got a lot of work to do."

• Jeff Wright: "We lost the world championship (Super Bowl XXV) on a damn field goal. You just never know when things are going to pan out. You go hard and hope they go your way."

• Steve Christie: "My toes were so numb, I couldn't feel the ball. You know where the ball is, you hope you know where your foot is, and hopefully the two will meet. I knew it was going to be a tough day and unfortunately for Blanchard, it was harder for him than it was for me. But that's our advantage playing at Rich, we're used to the frozen turf."

• Jim Kelly: "This championship is sweet because nobody thought we'd get here. The people in this locker room knew we could do it."

Jets	7	0	7	0 -	14
Bills	7	6	0	3 -	16

Attendance at Rich Stadium - 70,817

Buf: Thomas 2 run (Christie kick), 5:06
NYJ: Johnson 24 pass from Esiason (Blanchard kick), 12:56
Buf: FG Christie 38, 3:06
Buf: FG Christie 36, 14:55
NYJ: Burkett 6 pass from Esiason (Blanchard kick), 7:25
Buf: FG Christie 40, 11:12

	BUF	NYJ
First downs	19	19
Rushing yds	90	120
Passing yds	256	232
Punts-avg	2-36.5	3-38.7
Fumbles-lost	2-1	1-1
Penalties-yds	6-45	6-35
Poss. time	29:50	30:10

BILLS LEADERS: Rushing - Thomas 23-61, K. Davis 7-21, Gardner 3-5, Kelly 3-3; **Passing** - Kelly 20-31-2 - 256; **Receiving** - Metzelaars 4-35, Brooks 5-75, Thomas 3-29, Reed 3-51, Beebe 1-8, Gardner 1-5, K. Davis 3-53.

JETS LEADERS: Rushing - Johnson 16-94, Esiason 5-19, Baxter 2-7, Murrell 2-0; **Passing** - Esiason 22-31-0 - 232; **Receiving** - Johnson 8-81, Burkett 3-18, Baxter 2-17, Mitchell 6-78, Mathis 2-25, Thornton 1-13.

WEEK 17 GAMES

Hou 10, SF 7	Cinc 21, Atl 17
Phoe 17, NYG 6	TB 17, Den 10
Det 20, Chi 14	Phil 37, NO 26
NE 38, Ind 0	Dal 38, Wash 3
GB 28, LAR 0	Clev 42, Rams 14
Sea 16, Pitt 6	Minn 30, KC 10
SD 45, Mia 20	

GAME 16 - Sunday, Jan. 2, 1994 - BILLS 30, COLTS 10

NOTES

• The Bills clinched home-field advantage throughout the playoffs despite being outgained 402-297.

• For the first time since 1985, Andre Reed did not finish the season as the Bills' leader in receptions as Pete Metzelaars (68) and Bill Brooks (60) finished ahead of him.

• Thurman Thomas gained 110 yards, but lost the rushing title and for the first time since 1988, failed to lead the NFL in yards gained from scrimmage. Dallas' Emmitt Smith won both titles.

• The Bills won their season finale for just the second time in eight years under Marv Levy.

• The Bills set a team record with 24 fumble recoveries, and a turnover ratio of plus-12 tied for second-best in team history. The record was plus-14 in 1990. Their 47 take-aways were third-best in team history.

• On the first play of the game, Jeff Wright forced and recovered Anthony Johnson's fumble at the Colts 17, but Thomas lost a fumble through the end zone, giving the Colts the ball back. They drove 78 yards to the 2, but Phil Hansen forced Rodney Culver to fumble in the end zone and Henry Jones recovered.

• The teams traded punts with the Bills taking over at the Colts 45 and that set up a Steve Christie field goal.

• The Colts drove 52 yards in the second quarter to Dean Biasucci's tying field goal, but later in the second, the Bills drove 67 yards in 10 plays to Thomas' TD run on third-and-goal. Ex-Colt Bill Brooks had a 20-yard catch.

• On the Colts first possession of the third, the Bills held on downs at their 42, then turned around and drove to Christie's second field goal. Three plays after the kickoff, Bruce Smith forced Roosevelt Potts to fumble and Mark

Maddox recovered at the Colts 31, setting up Christie's third field goal.

• The Bills put away the game with two quick scores in the fourth. They moved 45 yards in 10 plays to Metzelaars' TD catch. Then on the first play after the kickoff, Nate Odomes caused Reggie Langhorne to fumble and Marvcus Patton recovered at the Colts 31. Frank Reich came in and fired a TD pass to Brooks.

• The Colts answered with a 14-play, 87-yard drive against the Bills' reserves to get Jesse Hester's TD.

QUOTES

• Bruce Smith: "Just like the Wizard of Oz, there's no place like home. That's not saying it's much easier, but I know a lot of teams don't really want to come to Buffalo in the dead middle of winter. The Super Bowl is not on our schedule. We're just thinking about winning."

• Marv Levy: "Our team earned their way all the way. That's the only way to do it."

• Kent Hull: "This is probably bad to say, but we fully expected to win this game. We felt we were superior and we felt like we should win."

• John Davis: "I'm glad we're playing at home, but we haven't done anything yet. We're not going to celebrate until we win the Super Bowl."

Bills	3	7	6	14 -	30
Colts	0	3	0	7 -	10

Attendance at the Hoosier Dome - 43,028

Buf: FG Christie 39, 14:41
Ind: FG Biasucci 22, 5:53
Buf: Thomas 3 run (Christie kick), 14:15
Buf: FG Christie 49, 7:06
Buf: FG Christie 40, 10:32
Buf: Metzelaars 1 pass from Kelly (Christie kick), 1:38
Buf: Brooks 30 pass from Reich (Christie kick), 3:18
Ind: Hester 10 pass from George (Biasucci kick), 8:05

	BUF	IND
First downs	19	25
Rushing yds	149	116
Passing yds	148	286
Punts-avg	4-40.3	4-46.5
Fumbles-lost	1-1	4-4
Penalties-yds	4-30	3-12
Poss. time	27:41	32:19

BILLS LEADERS: Rushing - Thomas 26-110, K. Davis 5-18, Turner 3-16, Gardner 3-9, Kelly 1-(-1), Reed 1-(-2), Reich 1-(-1); **Passing** - Kelly 15-27-0 - 125, Reich 1-1-0 - 30; **Receiving** - Metzelaars 5-21, Reed 4-51, Beebe 3-34, Brooks 2-50, Thomas 1-1, K. Davis 1-(-2).

COLTS LEADERS: Rushing - Potts 14-100, George 1-14, Culver 3-3, Johnson 6-(-1); **Passing** - George 30-48-0 - 330; **Receiving** - Langhorne 9-61, Johnson 6-52, Hester 5-81, Dawkins 2-29, Arbuckle 2-28, Potts 2-20, Culver 1-26, Verdin 1-19, Cash 1-7, Cox 1-7.

WEEK 18 GAMES

Det 30, GB 20	Minn 14, Wash 9
Dal 16, NYG 13 OT	Pitt 16, Clev 9
Phoe 27, Atl 10	KC 34, Sea 24
LAR 33, Den 30 OT	SD 32, TB 17
NO 20, Cinc 13	Hou 24, NYJ 0
NE 33, Mia 27 OT	Rams 20, Chi 6
Phil 37, SF 34	

STANDINGS: EIGHTEENTH WEEK

AFC EAST	W	L	T	CENTRAL	W	L	T	WEST	W	L	T	NFC EAST	W	L	T	CENTRAL	W	L	T	WEST	W	L	T
Buffalo	12	4	0	Houston	12	4	0	Kan. City	11	5	0	Dallas	12	4	0	Detroit	10	6	0	San Fran	10	6	0
Miami	9	7	0	Pittsburgh	9	7	0	Raiders	10	6	0	NY Giants	11	5	0	Green Bay	9	7	0	N.Orleans	8	8	0
NY Jets	8	8	0	Cleveland	7	9	0	Denver	9	7	0	Philadelphia	8	8	0	Minnesota	9	7	0	Atlanta	6	10	0
New England	5	11	0	Cincinnati	3	13	0	San Diego	8	8	0	Phoenix	7	9	0	Chicago	7	9	0	LA Rams	5	11	0
Indianapolis	4	12	0					Seattle	6	10	0	Washington	4	12	0	Tampa Bay	5	11	0				

Raiders	0	17	6	0	- 23
Bills	0	13	9	7	- 29

Attendance at Rich Stadium - 61,923

LAR: FG Jaeger 30, 1:13
Buf: K. Davis 1 run (kick failed), 1:30
LAR: McCallum 1 run (Jaeger kick), 6:50
LAR: McCallum 1 run (Jaeger kick), 13:03
Buf: Thomas 8 run (Christie kick), 14:10
Buf: Brooks 23 pass from Kelly (kick blocked), 11:37
Buf: FG Christie 29, 14:01
LAR: Brown 86 pass from Hostetler (kick failed), 14:30
Buf: Brooks 22 pass from Kelly (Christie kick), 2:55

	BUF	LAR
First downs	25	15
Rushing yds	75	110
Passing yds	280	215
Punts-avg	3-36.3	6-37.0
Fumbles-lost	3-1	2-1
Penalties-yds	2-15	9-77
Poss. time	27:03	32:57

BUFFALO TACKLES: Patton 12, Talley 11, Hansen 7, Wright 7, Maddox 7, Bennett 6, B. Smith 6, Jones 3, Odomes 2, Washington 1, Kelso 1, Goganious 1.
LOS ANGELES TACKLES: Moss 14, M. Jones 13, Anderson 6, Dixon 6, Dorn 4, L. Washington 4, Hoskins 4, Harrison 4, Smith 4, Long 3.

BILLS LEADERS: **Rushing** - Thomas 14-44, K. Davis 11-36, Kelly 5-(-5); **Passing** - Kelly 27-37-0 - 287; **Receiving** - Metzelaars 5-43, Reed 4-53, Brooks 6-96, Thomas 6-48, Beebe 1-9, McKeller 3-21, K. Davis 1-16, Gardner 1-1; **Kickoff returns** - Tasker 1-67, Copeland 2-35, Beebe 1-9; **Punt returns** - Copeland 3-7.
RAIDERS LEADERS: **Rushing** - McCallum 19-56, Montgomery 9-22, Hostetler 5-29, Bell 2-3; **Passing** - Hostetler 14-20-0 - 230; **Receiving** - Brown 5-127, Montgomery 3-26, Horton 2-42, Bell 1-12, McCallum 1-15, Duff 1-5, Jett 1-3; **Kickoff returns** - Ismail 3-51, Gault 2-22, Turk 1-10; **Punt returns** - Brown 3-7.

NOTES

• The Bills avenged their regular-season loss to the Raiders at Rich Stadium, rallying from a 17-6 second-quarter deficit to win the divisional-round game and advance to their fifth AFC Championship in six years.
• The gametime temperature was zero, the windchill was minus 32, making this the coldest game in which the Bills ever had played. An almost constant snow for the previous two weeks made getting the stadium ready a Herculean task for stadium operations, who employed workers the entire time to shovel.
• The game proved to be the last for Raiders great Howie Long, who retired a few weeks later.
• Pete Metzelaars suffered a broken bone and dislocation of a finger on his left hand in the second quarter and did not return to the game.
• Kenneth Davis took over for Thurman Thomas, who went out with a slight concussion in the fourth quarter, and contributed some vital plays as the Bills ran out the final 5:42 of the game.
• The Bills used an eight-man line on defense in the second half, moving strong safety Henry Jones, up and the alignment frustrated the Raiders. Los Angeles managed just one first down and 120 yards in the second half. 86 coming on Tim Brown's TD reception in the third quarter. The Raiders had five possessions in the second half.
• Brown's TD was the longest by the Raiders in the post-season, longest against the Bills in the postseason, and the third-longest in NFL playoff history.
• Steve Tasker's 67-yard kickoff return was the longest in Bills' playoff history.
• A sign in the stadium, playing off Raiders owner Al Davis' favorite refrain of 'Just Win, Baby' read 'Just Freeze, Baby.'
• Los Angeles quarterback Jeff Hostetler lost for the first time in five playoff starts. He beat the Bills in Super Bowl XXV while he was with the Giants.
• The teams traded punts on the first two possessions, then the Raiders moved to the Bills 29, but Jeff Jaeger missed

a 47-yard field goal.
• The Bills then drove to the Raiders 30, but Jim Kelly's fourth-and-one pass to Nate Turner fell incomplete.
• The Raiders broke the scoreless tie early in the second quarter as Jaeger capped an 11-play, 58-yard drive with a field goal. The key play was a second-and-13 pass to Ethan Horton for 36 yards to the Bills 37.
• On the ensuing kickoff, Jaeger hit a line drive that Tasker plucked out of the air at the Bills 32. He then broke up the left sideline and ran all the way to the 1. Davis scored from there, but Steve Christie's extra point was wide right.
• Rocket Ismail returned the kickoff 33 yards to the Raiders 43 and Los Angeles drove 57 yards in eight plays to Napoleon McCallum's TD run. The Raiders never faced a third down.
• On the first play after the kickoff, Metzelaars was hit by Eddie Anderson and fumbled and Terry McDaniel recovered at the Bills 40. Eleven plays later, McCallum scored on fourth-and-goal from the 1 after the Bills had stopped three runs from the 1. Earlier, Hostetler scrambled for 12 on third-and-six from the 13.
• After the kickoff, 1:53 remained in the half. Kelly hit Thomas for 13, Andre Reed for nine, Don Beebe for nine to the Los Angeles 45, then Torin Dorn was called for a 37-yard interference penalty on Reed at the Los Angeles 8. On the next play, Thomas scored behind Kent Hull's block to get the Bills within 17-13.
• The Bills took the second-half kickoff and drove to the Los Angeles 25, but Christie missed a 43-yard field goal.
• Later in the third after a 30-yard Jeff Gossett punt, the Bills started from their 40 and needed only five plays to get Bill Brooks' first TD reception. The extra point was blocked, leaving it 19-17 Bills.
• Two plays after the kickoff, Jeff Wright forced McCallum to fumble and Henry Jones recovered at the Los Angeles 30, setting up Christie's 29-yard field goal for a 22-17 lead.
• J.D. Williams tackled Ismail at the 14, limiting the kick return to six yards, but two plays later, Brown got loose for his 86-yard TD. Jaeger hit the left upright with the extra point, so it was 23-22 Los Angeles.
• The Bills then drove 71 yards in nine plays to Brooks' second TD. Reed had a 19-yard catch and Davis converted on third-and-two from the Raiders 26.
• Los Angeles had the ball for only six plays (not counting two punts) in the fourth quarter. The Bills killed the final 5:42.

QUOTES

• Marv Levy: "It was a helluva game to watch and we played an awful good team that we're gratified and fortunate to beat. You're cold, yes, but you're also into it. You get involved in the excitement of the game. That was warming if nothing else was." (On Jim Kelly): "He's a tough-minded guy. This was his kind of weather, his kind of crowd, his kind of teammates."
• Don Beebe: "Four AFC title games in a row, that's unbelievable, but we don't want it to stop there. Our motto all along has been 'Let's tick 'em all off and go to four (Super Bowls).'"
• John Davis: "We're having fun with all this. Nobody

wants us to be here which makes it all the better. But all we've done is win one more game. We haven't reached our ultimate goal. We have a lot of experience in the playoffs, but most of all, we have a lot of character and character is what's carried us more than anything."
• Kenneth Davis: "We're 13-4 and a lot of people didn't think we'd be there. We had to believe in ourselves and that was a big factor today."
• Kent Hull on Jim Kelly: "It may have been his best game ever. To say it's his best is really saying something because Jim has had so many great games for us through the years. I know the numbers were impressive, but I was more impressed with things that didn't show up in the stats. He was making all the right calls. That audible of his from a pass to a run that resulted in Thurman's touchdown just before the end of the first half was brilliant. So were several of his other calls. He was in complete control. He was like a chess master out there."
• Jim Kelly: "I think our team builds on things, whether it's the revenge factor, whether it's getting even, and I know some of the players on this team build a lot of emotion around it. It can be a lift for us to say 'This team beat us once, but they have to come in and prove they can beat us twice.'" (On the offensive line): "Before the game and all during the course of the week, I kept telling the five guys up front that the key to this game was good pass protection. We thought that these were probably going to be the four toughest guys that we were going to face all year. On both touchdown passes I needed that extra two seconds to throw the football and they gave it to me."
• Bill Brooks on why he was an easier target to throw to: "When you're on the short side, it's an easier throw for the quarterback and it's easier for me because the wind doesn't play tricks with the ball for so long."
• Raiders cornerback Torin Dorn on his first-half interference penalty: "I thought the flag was thrown for offensive interference and they call defensive. That play turned the game, in my mind. It gave them the momentum going into halftime and got the crowd back into it when we should have been up by 11."
• Darryl Talley on Walt Corey's halftime speech: "We weren't playing well defensively and Walt let us know that as soon as we got to the meeting. We played like crap in the first half. He told us 'If we don't play better than this, we're gonna be going home.' The guys just looked at each other and said 'Hey, we've got to make it happen, got to get it done.'"
• Walt Corey on the eight-man front on defense: "We made an adjustment. We had to take a shot at it, and you know what, it worked. That way you have more defenders than they have blockers. You have people in better positions to get to the ball. We played basically the same coverages, only we took Henry and instead of playing him on the tight end side, we put him to the open side and brought him up. If they wanted to run or pass, it didn't change anything. Henry didn't have to move. They were running shallow routes, they didn't even try to throw deep. They didn't do that against Green Bay (during a sub-zero game last month) and I figured they'd be the same here, use a ball-control scheme."

NOTES

• The Bills became the first team in the history of the Super Bowl to reach the championship game four years in a row as they routed Kansas City.

• Thurman Thomas set team playoff records for carries and rushing yards. His 186 yards were the second-most in AFC/AFL Championship Game history behind only the 206 that San Diego's Keith Lincoln gained against Boston in 1963. Thomas also became only the fourth running back in history to top 1,000 yards in career playoff rushing, and his 84 postseason points set a new team mark.

• Andre Reed topped the 1,000-yard receiving mark in the playoffs (1,042) and Jim Kelly surpassed 3,000 career playoff passing yards.

• Bruce Smith extended his own NFL playoff record by recording his 12th sack.

• Kansas City QB Joe Montana was knocked out of the game early in the third quarter with a concussion and never returned.

• It was the Bills eighth straight postseason victory at Rich Stadium and they improved to 49-7 at home (counting playoffs) since the start of the 1988 season.

• Marv Levy became the seventh coach in NFL history to record 10 postseason victories.

• The Bills' 30 first downs tied a team playoff mark and their 17 rushing first downs and 229 yards rushing were new records.

• The Bills improved to 38-3 when Thomas rushes for 100 yards and 21-1 when Kelly isn't sacked.

• A sign in the stadium read: 'Going to Atlanta through Montana.'

• In their four straight AFC title game wins, the Bills defense had allowed 33 points total and intercepted 11 passes while allowing only one TD pass.

• The teams opened the game punting twice each before the Bills put together a six-play, 47-yard march to Thomas' first TD. Russell Copeland's 13-yard punt return set up the Bills at the Chiefs 47, then Reed made a 28-yard reception leading to Thomas' run.

• The Chiefs answered with a 10-play, 51-yard march to Nick Lowery's first field goal. Marcus Allen broke a 24-yard run and Montana completed passes of 11 yards to Keith Cash and 12 yards to Ernie Thompson.

• Bennie Thompson forced Copeland to fumble the ensuing kickoff and Fred Jones recovered at the Bills 24 to set up Lowery's second field goal.

• The Bills responded by driving 80 yards in 14 plays to Thomas' second TD on a third-and-two play. The key play was Thomas' 33-yard burst to the Chiefs 26. On the next play, Kenneth Davis broke a 15-yard run.

• After a Chiefs punt and Copeland's 17-yard return to the Chiefs 46, the Bills drove 41 yards in 10 plays to Steve Christie's field goal. Keith McKeller's seven-yard catch on third-and-six from the Chiefs 42 and Pete Metzelaars' 12-yard catch to the Chiefs 6 were the key plays.

• The Chiefs went three-and-out and the Bills then drove 56 yards in 10 plays to Christie's second field goal that made it 20-6. Reed had a 12-yard catch and Thomas had runs of nine, 10 and 12 yards.

• The Chiefs took possession with 1:56 left in the first half after the kickoff and drove to the Bills 5, but on second down, Montana was intercepted in the end zone by Henry Jones.

• At the half, the Bills held a 263-141 edge in yards and 16-9 advantage in first downs. Thomas had 129 yards rushing at the break and Montana was eight-for-22 for 108 yards.

• On the third play of the third quarter, Montana was sandwiched by Bruce Smith and Jeff Wright and his head hit the turf. He never returned and Dave Krieg finished at quarterback.

• After an exchange of punts, the Chiefs started a drive at their 10 and Krieg led them 90 yards in 14 plays to Allen's TD run. The march consumed 7:18 and Krieg hit J.J. Birden for 26, Willie Davis for 17, Jonathan Hayes for 10, Cash for 19 and Birden for 15 along the way.

• The Bills came back with a 14-play, 79-yard drive to another Christie field goal. Thomas had an 11-yard run, a 15-yard reception and Don Beebe had an 11-yard catch.

• The Chiefs went three-and-out and the Bills then marched 52 yards in eight plays to Thomas' final TD. Thomas carried six times for 41 yards on the clinching drive.

QUOTES

• Chiefs coach Marty Schottenheimer: "What you do is take your hat off to the Buffalo Bills. They were the much better team today. And let me tell you something, if that football team – Buffalo – goes to play (in the Super Bowl) the way they did today, all those 'doomsday' people can pack it away because this is a hell of a team."

• Chiefs quarterback Joe Montana: "It's very difficult to get to the Super Bowl once, let alone as many times as these guys have. That says a lot about that team. I wish them the best." (On his performance): "There were times I had guys open and I just couldn't get the ball to them. They did some stuff to stop us early, but for the most part, it was more me than anything." (On his injury): "I still don't know much about the play. I remember right after that my head hurt. Everything went white for a couple of seconds and there was a real sharp pain in my head. I couldn't remember for most of the third quarter what had even happened let alone what was going on. I was trying to pay attention, but I couldn't even remember what the score was or how they had gotten 20 points."

• Thurman Thomas: "This is our fourth straight AFC Championship, but the job is not over yet. We are 0-3 in Super Bowls and we definitely have to get that monkey off our backs. We don't want to be 0-4, but if we play like we played today, I think we've got a great chance to win in Atlanta." (On his record-breaking day): "This was the best game of my NFL career because it took us to the next level. I was just pumped up. Everytime I touched the ball, the adrenaline was with me. I just can't say enough about my line."

• Marv Levy: "This is the toughest-minded football team that's ever played the game, in my opinion. They are tough-minded and they've shown it over and over. We fought our way back in. It was our best game of the year. It had nothing to do with peaking, it's how we got ready this week that mattered. I know we've won a lot of games in the 90's (58), but we still haven't won the one we want." (On Thomas' performance): "I don't know if I've ever seen him run harder."

• Bruce Smith: "If we didn't gain any respect today, we shut a lot of people up. And that's really what we wanted to do."

• Cornelius Bennett: "In the end, maybe when they're reading us our last rights, then they'll put us in the ranks of the all-time best. We're still a part of history regardless."

• Pete Metzelaars: "Fifteen or 20 years from now, maybe we can say we ranked right up there. It'd sure be nice to win one Super Bowl. We do that, and, well ... But if we don't, we can still say we accomplished an awful lot."

• Jim Kelly on the offensive line: "During the course of the week, I think they heard all the stuff about how good the Chiefs were and we knew they were. We knew what happened the last time we played them – they stopped our running game. Today, we were determined to try to run on them and the offensive line did a helluva job." (On beating Montana): "It was exciting to go out there and win against a great team and a great quarterback, but our goal is the Super Bowl. And our goal is to win, not just show up. He (Montana) told me to 'Go get it' and I said 'I'll give it my best.'"

• Kent Hull: "They were playing a defense that I think was

designed to stop the pass. When we played them in Kansas City, against the same defense, we were unable to audible because of the crowd, which caused us to make some bad plays. I think the defense was vulnerable to the run and with our audible system today, I think we were able to exploit it. We were asked basically just to get Thurman into the secondary. They were playing with one linebacker (Lonnie Marts) for the most part, and if we could get Thurman past him, Thurman was on his own."

• Jeff Wright on Montana's concussion: "He was going down and I hit him up top. He whiplashed his head on the ground. It wasn't pretty. I immediately knew he was hurt. He let out a groan. I've never heard that."

• Henry Jones on his first-half interception: "We had seven guys going (blitzing) and we had a busted coverage on the back (Kimble Anders) coming out of the backfield. Joe just dinked it over the middle. I came off my man (Keith Cash) and was going to try to make the tackle before he (Anders) got to the goal line and I was fortunate to catch the ball. Instead of being down seven and getting the ball after halftime, they don't score."

| Chiefs | 6 | 0 | 7 | 0 | - | 13 |
| Bills | 7 | 13 | 0 | 10 | - | 30 |

Attendance at Rich Stadium - 76,642

Buf:	Thomas 12 run (Christie kick), 8:11
KC:	FG Lowery 31, 12:46
KC:	FG Lowery 31, 14:21
Buf:	Thomas 3 run (Christie kick), 2:58
Buf:	FG Christie 23, 7:58
Buf:	FG Christie 25, 12:59
KC:	Allen 1 run (Lowery kick), 11:54
Buf:	FG Christie 18, 3:05
Buf:	Thomas 3 run (Christie kick), 9:30

	BUF	KC
First downs	30	22
Rushing yds	229	52
Passing yds	160	286
Punts-avg	4-33.3	6-40.8
Fumbles-lost	1-1	1-0
Penalties-yds	2-10	6-29
Poss. time	30:40	29:20

BUFFALO TACKLES: Talley 10, Maddox 9, Patton 5, Wright 4, B. Smith 4, Hansen 4, H. Jones 4, Darby 4, Bennett 3, T. Smith 3, Washington 3, Odomes 3.

KANSAS CITY TACKLES: N. Smith 11, Ross 11, Bayless 8, Marts 7 Lewis 5, Phillips 5, Saleaumua 4, Mincy 4, McDaniels 4, Pickens 3, D. Thomas 3, Rogers 3, Simien 2.

BILLS LEADERS: **Rushing** - Thomas 33-186, K. Davis 10-32, Kelly 2-3, Reed 1-8; **Passing** - Kelly 17-27-0 - 160; **Receiving** - Metzelaars 4-29, Reed 4-49, Brooks 4-34, Thomas 2-22, Beebe 2-19, McKeller 1-7; **Kickoff returns** - Copeland 4-68; **Punt returns** - Copeland 5-70.

CHIEFS LEADERS: **Rushing** - Allen 18-50, Anders 2-1, Montana 1-1; **Passing** - Montana 9-23-1 - 125, Krieg 16-29-1 - 198; **Receiving** - Cash 6-87, W. Davis 5-57, Birden 4-60, Thompson 1-12, Allen 2-36, McNair 2-33, Anders 1-7, Szott 1-6, Hughes 1-11, Hayes 2-14; **Kickoff returns** - Stephens 5-89; **Punt returns** - Hughes 1-11.

Cowboys	6	0	14	10 -	30
Bills	3	10	0	0 -	13

Attendance at the Georgia Dome - 72,817

Dal: FG Murray 41, 2:19
Buf: FG Christie 54, 4:41
Dal: FG Murray 24, 11:05
Buf: Thomas 4 run (Christie kick), 2:34
Buf: FG Christie 28, 15:00
Dal: J. Washington 46 fumble return (Murray kick), :55
Dal: E. Smith 15 run (Murray kick), 6:18
Dal: E. Smith 1 run (Murray kick), 5:10
Dal: FG Murray 20, 12:10

	BUF	DAL
First downs	22	20
Rushing yds	87	137
Passing yds	227	204
Punts-avg	5-37.6	4-43.8
Fumbles-lost	3-2	0-0
Penalties-yds	1-10	6-50
Poss. time	25:31	34:29

BUFFALO TACKLES: Bennett 13, Patton 9, Talley 9, Wright 5, B. Smith 5, Odomes 5, Kelso 4, H. Jones 3, Maddox 3, M. Washington 3, Goganious 2, Lodish 2, Hansen 2, Darby 1, Barnett 1.
DALLAS TACKLES: J. Washington 11, Norton 8, Everett 6, Casillas 6, K. Smith 5, Lett 5, Tolbert 5, Brown 4, Haley 4, J. Jones 3, Woodson 3 Jeffcoat 3, Gant 2, Maryland 2.

BILLS LEADERS: Rushing - Thomas 16-37, K. Davis 9-38, Kelly 2-12; **Passing** - Kelly 31-50-1-260; **Receiving** - Brooks 7-63, Thomas 7-52, Reed 6-75, Beebe 6-60, Metzelaars 1-8, McKeller 1-7, K. Davis 3-(-5); **Kickoff returns** - Copeland 4-82, Beebe 2-62; **Punt returns** - Copeland 1-5.
COWBOYS LEADERS: Rushing - E. Smith 30-132, K. Williams 1-6, Aikman 1-3, Johnston 1-0, Coleman 1-(-3), Kosar 1-(-1); **Passing** - Aikman 19-27-1-207; **Receiving** - Irvin 5-66, Novacek 5-26, E. Smith 4-26, Harper 3-75, Johnston 2-14; **Kickoff returns** - K. Williams 1-50, Gant 1-22; **Punt returns** - K. Williams 1-5.

NOTES

• The Bills suffered their fourth straight loss in the Super Bowl, extending their own NFL futility record. They also became the first major pro sports team to lose their league's championship four years in a row.
• This was the Cowboys' fourth Super Bowl win, tying them with San Francisco and Pittsburgh for the most victories in the Super Bowl. Dallas became the fifth team to win back-to-back Super Bowls.
• Emmitt Smith was named MVP, thus becoming the first player in NFL history to win the rushing title, the Super Bowl and the Super Bowl MVP in the same season.
• Steve Christie's 54-yard field goal was a Super Bowl record.
• Jim Kelly completed a Super Bowl record 31 passes and he became the game's all-time leader in pass attempts (145).
• Andre Reed extended his own Super Bowl record for most pass receptions all-time to 27.
• The NFC stretched its winning streak over the AFC in Super Bowls to 10.
• Thurman Thomas, who set a record by scoring a touchdown in four straight Super Bowls, had another terrible Super Bowl game. In his last three appearances, he had totaled 69 yards in 37 carries.
• For the 28th playoff game in a row, the team that won the turnover battle won the game.
• Pete Metzelaars injured his shoulder in the second quarter and never returned. Phil Hansen hurt his hip in the third and Bruce Smith missed one play with a rib injury and Emmitt Smith scored on that play in the third.
• James Washington, who's fumble return for a TD on the third play of the third quarter turned the game around, finished with 11 tackles, the fumble recovery, a forced fumble and an interception.
• Cornelius Bennett led the Bills with 13 tackles and Jeff Wright had two sacks.
• The Bills were just five-of-17 on third downs, the Cowboys were five-of-13.

QUOTES

• Marv Levy: "They won the turnover battle again today, not as decisively as last year, but that makes a difference. We had three (turnovers) and could only get one and our three led to 17 points. They were just too good for us to succeed." (On James Washington's fumble return): "Devastate? No. They began to move the ball a little after that, but I couldn't see that our team said 'Oh, oh, that's it.' It had a telling effect, there's no question about it. It was a huge play in the game, but the feel I tried to convey was 'It's a bad play, there's 29 minutes left, we're tied, let's go ahead.' Thurman has been the heart and soul of our team. I sure don't castigate him because he fumbled." (On what he said after the game): "I walked around after the game saying 'I don't have any words for you, I just want to shake your hand and I did it with every player. It's disappointment, not devastation. I'll treat it as a lost battle. I'm not ready to throw in the towel."
• Thurman Thomas on his fumbles: "There was no doubt that they were the keys to the ballgame. The second one in the second half, James Washington taking the ball and going in for a touchdown, at that point and time it seemed the momentum switched. The second one turned the entire football game around." (On his reaction to the fumbles): "I was frustrated. Throughout my career I've never been a fumbler. I can't run with two hands around the football, that's not my style. I just did what I normally do and they did a great job of knocking the ball out. Overall I think our team did a great job and I can sit up here and take the blame because I really did change the momentum." (On why he came out of the game after the fumble): "I had cramps in both calves and on my side. I was frustrated that I couldn't get back in there. They went away, but it was kind of too late for me to go back in the game and try to make something happen." (On losing four in a row): "I think with the talent on this team and the quality of players that we have, we should have found some way, some how to win one out of the four. Sure it's frustrating to lose four in a row."
• Jim Kelly: "They came out in the second half and

played well. The first possession we were moving the ball and then the turnover ... When something like that happens, it hurts, and that was a big turning point. I knew that we had to come out and play error-free football in the second half. We gave them a couple of gifts. We have a lot to be proud of, but we have to figure out what it's going to take to win one. We're going to keep going until we get it right. What else can you say? We have to take that long hard road again, but we've been there before. Unfortunately we haven't won the championship, but second place is better than coming in last, I can tell you that much." (On Thomas): "Thurman is really a great running back and I don't know if the fumbles hurt him or what, but Thurman is going to be Thurman. He'll be back. Thurman is a tough character."
• Steve Tasker: "Sometimes you feel like you're beating your head against a wall, but as long as there is a chance for us to come back, we are going to keep fighting."
• Cornelius Bennett: "It's a tough pill to swallow. You bust your butt so much during the season, but it's happening for a reason. Who knows when we get down the line in our lives how big these four losses will actually be in our lives. I look at it as a lesson and I try to learn from it. I think we are still going to be the team to beat next season in the AFC."
• Dallas running back Emmitt Smith: "James Washington's fumble recovery for a touchdown was a big, big plus in this game. Before every game I always talk about the turnovers and James came up with two big turnovers today."
• Dallas safety James Washington: "I had opportunities to showcase my talents today, but if it weren't for Emmitt, we wouldn't be here right now." (On his fumble return): "It seems like I ran forever. You know I'm not the fastest guy in the world, so I have to read my blocks and hopefully, my guys are downfield making plays for me."
• Dallas coach Jimmy Johnson: "We made mistakes in the first half, but in the second half, they made more mistakes than we did. I wasn't as sure this year (about winning). I knew Buffalo was going to be thoroughly prepared for everything we've done. On top of that, I knew they had a driving, burning desire not to lose four in a row." (On Washington's fumble return): "That was large. We felt once we caught up with them, we were going to be fine."
• Dallas defensive end Charles Haley: "The key was the fumble. After that it seemed like they panicked a little bit, went off their game plan."
• Dallas quarterback Troy Aikman: "This one is probably more satisfying. Last year we came in here and there were really no expectations. This year, we've had to deal with the pressure about going back and repeating and winning it all again and it's taken it's toll." (On Jim Kelly): "Jim is a good friend of mine. I wish that every player that plays this game could walk away with a championship ring. It's a special deal. And I hope Jim gets one."

STARTING LINEUPS

BILLS OFFENSE: QB - Jim Kelly; RB - Thurman Thomas; WR - Andre Reed, Bill Brooks, Don Beebe; TE - Pete Metzelaars; OL - John Fina, Glenn Parker, Kent Hull, John Davis, Howard Ballard.

BILLS DEFENSE: DL - Bruce Smith, Phil Hansen, Jeff Wright; LB - Cornelius Bennett, Darryl Talley, Marvcus Patton, Mark Maddox; DB - Mickey Washington, Nate Odomes, Henry Jones, Mark Kelso.

COWBOYS OFFENSE: QB - Troy Aikman; RB - Emmitt Smith, Daryl Johnston; WR - Michael Irvin, Alvin Harper; TE - Jay Novacek; OL - Mark Tuinei, Nate Newton, John Gesek, Kevin Gogan, Erik Williams.

COWBOYS DEFENSE: DL - Charles Haley, Tony Casillas, Tony Tolbert, Leon Lett; LB - Ken Norton Jr., Darrin Smith; DB - Darren Woodson, Kevin Smith, Larry Brown, Thomas Everett, James Washington.

SUPER BOWL XXVIII PLAY-BY-PLAY

1ST QUARTER

Cowboys win toss, elect to receive.
Christie kicks off to D2, Williams return 50, (tackled by Schulz).
COWBOYS 15:00
1-10-B48 - Aikman pass to Irvin, 20, (Odomes, Kelso); 1-10-B28 - Aikman pass to Novacek, 4, (Bennett); 2-6-B24 - E. Smith runs left, 0, (Bennett, B. Smith); 3-6-B24 - Aikman incomplete pass to K. Williams; 4-6-B24 - Murray 41 FIELD GOAL. Drive: 5 plays, 24 yards, Time of possession 2:19. Time of score: 2:19. **Dallas 3, Buffalo 0**.

Murray kicks off to B1, Copeland return 20, (Bates).
BILLS 12:31
1-10-B21 - Thomas runs left, 1, (Lett, Casillas); 2-9-B22 - Kelly pass to Reed, 11, (J. Washington); 1-10-B33 - Thomas runs left, 4, (Haley, Casillas); 2-6-B37 - Kelly pass to Thomas, 24, (Everett); 1-10-D39 - K. Davis runs right, 3, (Norton, Lett); 2-7-D36 - Kelly incomplete pass to Beebe; 3-7-D36 - Kelly incomplete pass to Brooks; 4-7-D36 - Christie 54 FIELD GOAL. Drive: 8 plays, 43 yards, TOP 2:12. Time of score: 4:41. **Dallas 3, Buffalo 3**.

Christie kicks off to end zone, touchback.
COWBOYS 10:14
1-10-D20 - E. Smith runs left, 2, (B. Smith, Bennett); 2-8-D22 - E. Smith runs right, 7, (Patton, Maddox); 3-1-D29 - Dallas penalty, holding, Gesek, -10; 3-11-D19 - Aikman sacked by Wright, -1; 4-12-D18 - Jett punt 41, Copeland fair catch.

BILLS 8:04
1-10-B41 - Kelly pass to Thomas, 7, J. Washington forces fumble, Woodson recovers at 50.

COWBOYS 7:57
1-10-50 - E. Smith runs right, 3, (Maddox, Hansen); 2-7-B47 - Aikman pass to E. Smith, 8, (Patton); 1-10-B39 - Aikman pass to Harper, 24, (Talley); 1-10-B15 - K. Williams reverse right, 6, (M. Washington); 2-4-B9 - Aikman pass to E. Smith, -1, (Patton, Hansen); 3-5-B10 - E. Smith runs right, 3, (Lodish, Talley); 4-2-B7 - Murray 24 FIELD GOAL. Drive: 7 plays, 43 yards, TOP 4:02. Time of score: 11:05. **Dallas 6, Buffalo 3**.

Murray kicks off to end zone, touchback.
BILLS 3:50
1-10-B20 - Thomas runs to middle, 1, (Norton); 2-9-B21 - Kelly pass to Brooks, 5, (K. Smith); 3-4-B26 - Kelly pass to Metzelaars, 8, (Norton, Everett); 1-10-B34 - Thomas runs left, 4, (Brown, Edwards); 2-6-B38 - Kelly pass to Reed, 3, (J. Washington); 3-3-B41 - Kelly incomplete pass to Brooks; 4-3-B41 - Dallas penalty, running into the kicker, D. Thomas, 5; 1-10-B46 - Thomas runs left, 2, (Lett, Tolbert); 2-8-B48 - Kelly pass to Beebe, 9, (Brown); 1-10-D43 - Thomas runs left, -4, (Jeffcoat); 2-14-D47 - Kelly pass to Reed, 13, (J. Washington).

2ND QUARTER

3-1-D34 - K. Davis runs right, 2, (Woodson, Casillas); 1-10-D32 - Kelly pass to Beebe, 7, (K. Smith); 2-3-D25 - K. Davis runs left, 8, (Norton); 1-10-D17 - Thomas runs left, 5, (Maryland); 2-5-D12 - Thomas runs to middle, 2, (Casillas); 3-3-D10 - Kelly pass to Beebe, 6, (Brown); 1-G-D4 - Thomas runs left, 4, TOUCHDOWN. Christie PAT. Drive: 17 plays, 80 yards, TOP 6:29. Time of score: 2:34. **Buffalo 10, Dallas 6**.

Christie kicks off to D1, Gant return 22 (Tasker).
COWBOYS 12:16
1-10-D23 - Aikman pass to Irvin, 15, (H. Jones, Odomes); 1-10-D38 - E. Smith runs to middle, 13, (Kelso); 1-10-B49 - E. Smith runs to middle, 2, (Maddox); 2-8-B47 - Aikman scrambles left, 3, (Bennett); 3-5-B44 - Aikman incomplete pass to Irvin; 4-5-B44 - Jett punt 43, downed by Vanderbeek at the 1.

BILLS 9:32
1-10-B1 - Kelly pass to Reed, 19, (Everett); 1-10-B20 - Thomas runs left, 4, (J. Jones); 2-6-B24 - Kelly pass to Brooks, 8, (J. Washington); 1-10-B32 - Kelly pass to McKeller, 7, (J. Washington); 2-3-B39 - Thomas runs right, 3, (J. Jones, Lett); 1-10-B42 - Kelly pass to Reed, 7, (K. Smith); 2-3-B49 - Kelly pass to Thomas, 5, (Tolbert); 1-10-D46 - Kelly incomplete pass to Beebe; 2-10-D46 - Kelly incomplete pass to Reed; 3-10-D46 - Kelly incomplete pass to Copeland; 4-10-D46 - Mohr punt 45, downed by Tasker at the 1.

COWBOYS 6:15
1-10-D1 - E. Smith runs to middle, 3, (Patton, Bennett); 2-7-D4 - Aikman pass to Irvin, 13, (M. Washington); 1-10-D17 - Aikman incomplete pass to Harper; 2-10-D17 - Aikman pass to Johnston, 11, (Talley); 1-10-D28 - E. Smith runs to middle, 4, (Bennett); 2-6-D32 - Aikman pass to Irvin, 4, (Bennett); 3-2-D36 - Aikman pass to Novacek, 4, (H. Jones); 1-10-D40 - E. Smith runs left, 4, (Wright), official time-out 1:58; 2-6-D44 - Aikman pass to Novacek, 9, (M. Washington); 1-10-B47 - Aikman pass to E. Smith, 10, (Patton); 1-10-B37 - Aikman pass for Irvin, intercepted by Odomes at B12, return 41 to D47.

BILLS 1:03
1-10-D47 - Thomas runs to middle, 1, (Norton), :44; 2-9-D46 - Kelly pass to Thomas, 12, (K. Smith), Buffalo timeout :36; 1-10-D34 - Kelly pass to Reed, 22, (Everett), Buffalo timeout :27; 1-10-D12 - Kelly pass to Thomas, 3, (Woodson); 2-7-D9 - Kelly incomplete pass to McKeller, :17; 3-7-D9 - Kelly pass to Thomas, 0, (D. Smith), Buffalo timeout :02; 4-7-D9 - Christie 28 FIELD GOAL. Drive: 7 plays, 38 yards, TOP 1:03. Time of score: 15:00. **Buffalo 13, Dallas 6**.

HALFTIME STATISTICS

	BUF	DAL
First downs	15	10
Rushing yds	40	50
Passing yds	176	120
Punts-avg	1-45.0	2-42.0
Fumbles-lost	1-1	0-0
Penalties-yds	0-0	2-15
Poss. time	13:18	16:42

RUSHING:	Buf:	Thomas 12-27, K. Davis 3-13.
	Dal:	E. Smith 10-41, Aikman 1-3, K. Williams 1-6.
PASSING:	Buf:	Kelly 19-26-0 - 176.
	Dal:	Aikman 12-16-1 - 121.
RECEIVING:	Buf:	Reed 6-75, Thomas 6-51, Beebe 3-22, Brooks 2-13 Metzelaars 1-8, McKeller 1-7.
	Dal:	Irvin 4-52, Novacek 3-17, E. Smith 3-17, Harper 1-24, Johnston 1-11.

3RD QUARTER

Murray kicks off to B7, Copeland return 21 (D. Thomas).
BILLS 14:51
1-10-B28 - Thomas runs to middle, 6, (J. Washington); 2-4-B34 - Kelly pass to Brooks, 9, (J. Washington); 1-10-B43 - Thomas runs right, 3, Lett forces fumble, J. Washington recovers at 46 and runs for TOUCHDOWN. Dallas penalty, personal foul, Norton, assessed on kickoff. Murray PAT. Time of score: :55. **Dallas 13, Buffalo 13**.

Murray kicks off from D20 to B15, Copeland return 22 (Fishback).
BILLS 14:05
1-10-B37 - Thomas runs to left, 2, (Norton, Haley); 2-8-B39 - Kelly incomplete pass to Reed; 3-8-B39 - Kelly sacked by Jeffcoat, Haley, -13; 4-21-B26 - Mohr punt 38, K. Williams fair catch.

COWBOYS 13:14
1-10-D36 - E. Smith runs right, 9, (Patton); 2-1-D45 - E. Smith runs right, 3, (Patton); 1-10-D48 - E. Smith runs right, 9, (Wright); 2-1-B43 - E. Smith runs left, 7, (Talley); 1-10-B36 - E. Smith runs right, 14, (Talley); 1-10-B22 - E. Smith runs right, 4, (Bennett, Maddox); 2-6-B18 - Aikman pass to Johnston, 3, (Harvey, Lodish); 3-3-B15 - E. Smith runs right, 15, TOUCHDOWN. Murray PAT. Drive: 8 plays, 64 yards, TOP 4:32. Time of score: 6:18. **Dallas 20, Buffalo 13**.

Murray kicks off to B9, Beebe return 28 (Everett).
BILLS 8:30
1-10-B37 - Kelly pass to K. Davis, -8, (Tolbert); 2-18-B29 - K. Davis runs right, 7, (Tolbert); 3-11-B36 - K. Davis runs to middle, 11, (Everett); 1-10-B47 - Kelly incomplete pass to Beebe; 2-10-B47 - Kelly pass to Brooks, 10, (Everett); 1-10-D43 - K. Davis runs left, -3, (Casillas); 2-13-D46 - Kelly incomplete pass to Reed; 3-13-D46 - Kelly incomplete pass to K. Davis; 4-13-D46 - Mohr punt 23, out of bounds.

COWBOYS 6:01
1-10-D23 - E. Smith runs left, 2, (Bennett, Goganious); 2-8-D25 - Aikman pass to Irvin, 14, (Odomes); 1-10-D39 - Aikman pass to Novacek, 5, (Talley); 2-5-D44 - E. Smith runs right, -3, (Goganious); 3-8-D41 - Aikman incomplete pass to E. Smith; 4-8-D41 - Jett punt 43, downed by Gant at B16.

BILLS 3:05
1-10-B16 - Kelly pass to K. Davis, -4, (Woodson); 2-14-B12 - Kelly pass to Beebe, 11, (Norton); 3-3-B23 - K. Davis fumbles, recovers at B23; 4-3-B23 - Mohr punt 52, K. Williams return 5 (Maddox).

COWBOYS 1:20
1-10-D30 - Coleman runs right, -3, (Talley); 2-13-D27 - Aikman incomplete pass to Novacek; 3-13-D27 - Aikman incomplete pass to Novacek; 4-13-D27 - Jett punt 47, Copeland return 5 (Vanderbeek).

BILLS :20
1-10-B31 - Kelly incomplete pass to Reed; 2-10-B31 - K. Davis runs to middle, 4, (Haley).

4TH QUARTER

3-6-B35 - Kelly pass for Beebe, intercepted by J. Washington at B46, return 12 (Fina).

COWBOYS 14:53
1-10-B34 - Dallas penalty, false start, E. Williams, -5; 1-15-B39 - E. Smith runs right, 6, (Barnett); 2-9-B33 - Aikman pass to E. Smith, 9, (Hansen); 1-10-B24 - E. Smith runs right, 4, (B. Smith, Bennett); 2-6-B20 - Aikman sacked by Wright, -2, Dallas timeout 12:20; 3-8-B22 - Aikman pass to Harper, 16, (Odomes); 1-G-B6 - E. Smith runs right, 2, (B. Smith, Kelso); 2-G-B4 - E. Smith runs to middle, 3, (Wright); 3-G-B1 - E. Smith runs right, 0, (Talley); 4-G-B1 - E. Smith runs left, 1, TOUCHDOWN. Murray PAT. Drive: 9 plays, 34 yards, TOP 5:03. Time of score: 5:10. **Dallas 27, Buffalo 13**.

Murray kicks off to B3, Copeland return 19 (Gainer, Bates).
BILLS 9:40
1-10-B22 - Kelly scrambles left, 8, (J. Washington); 2-2-B30 - Kelly pass to Thomas, 1, (Maryland); 3-1-B31 - Kelly runs to middle, 4, (Norton); 1-10-B35 - Kelly pass to Brooks, 1, (J. Washington); 2-9-B36 - Thomas runs left, -1, (J. Jones); 3-10-B35 - Kelly sacked by Jeffcoat, -13; 4-23-B22 - Mohr punt 29, downed by Gardner.

COWBOYS 7:00
1-10-D49 - E. Smith runs right, 5, (Bennett); 2-5-B46 - E. Smith runs to middle, 3, (Talley); 3-2-B43 - Aikman pass to Novacek, 4, (Darby); 1-10-B39 - E. Smith runs right, 3, (Bennett), Dallas timeout 4:17; 2-7-B36 - Aikman incomplete pass to Irvin; 3-7-B36 - Aikman pass to Harper, 35, (Kelso, Odomes), Dallas timeout 3:23; 1-G-B1 - Dallas penalty, false start, Cornish, -5; 1-G-B6 - E. Smith runs left, 5, (Patton), Buffalo timeout 3:16; 2-G-B1 - Johnston runs to middle, 0, (Bennett), Buffalo timeout 3:09; 3-G-B1 - E. Smith runs left, -1, (B. Smith), Buffalo timeout 2:54; 4-G-B2 - Murray 20 FIELD GOAL. Drive: 10 plays, 49 yards, TOP 4:10. Time of score: 12:10. **Dallas 30, Buffalo 13**.

Murray kicks off to goal line, Beebe return 34 (Everett).
BILLS 2:39
1-10-B34 - Kelly pass to Beebe, 18, (Brown); 1-10-D48 - K. Davis direct snap runs right, 6, (Bates); 2-4-D42 - Buffalo penalty, offensive interference, McKeller, -10; 2-14-B48 - Kelly pass to K. Davis, 7, (K. Smith), official timeout 1:58; 3-7-D45 - Kelly incomplete pass to McKeller; 4-7-D45 - Kelly pass to Brooks, 15, (J. Washington); 1-10-D30 - Kelly incomplete pass to K. Davis; 2-10-D30 - Kelly incomplete pass to Beebe; 3-10-D30 - Kelly incomplete pass to Brooks; 4-10-D30 - Kelly pass to Brooks, 15, (Gant); 1-10-D15 - Kelly spikes ball to kill clock, :38; 2-10-D15 - Kelly sacked by Casillas, Tolbert, -7; 3-17-D22 - Kelly incomplete pass to Copeland; 4-17-D22 - Kelly pass to Beebe, 9, (Gant).

COWBOYS :06
1-10-D13 - Kosar kneels down, -1. GAME ENDS. FINAL: **Dallas 30, Buffalo 13**.

BUFFALO BILLS ALL-TIME COACHES ROSTER
1960-1993

NAME	COLLEGE	YEAR (S)
Asselta, Art	Ithaca	1985
Atkins, Bill (d)	Auburn	1972-1975
Ball, Herman	Davis Elkins	1963
Bass, Marvin	William & Mary	1968-71, 1976
Beatty, Bruce	Miami	1977
Becker, John	Cal State-Northridge	1984
Bresnahan, Tom	Holy Cross	1989-1993
Bullough, Hank *	Michigan State	1985-1986
Carmody, Jim	Tulane	1981
Carr, Jim	Morris Harvey	1977
Carroll, Pete	Pacific	1984
Catlin, Tom	Oklahoma	1978-1982
Cavanaugh, Ed	Duke	1972-1976
Celeri, Bob (d)	California	1968
Collier, Joe	Northwestern	1962-65, 66-68
Corey, Walt	Miami	1987-1993
Cottrell, Ted	Delaware Valley	1986-1989
Dalton, Kay	Colorado State	1977, 1985
Daniels, Joe	Slippery Rock	1986
Day, Tom	North Carolina A & T	1971
Deadmond, Glenn	Kent State	1990
DeHaven, Bruce	Southwestern Kansas	1987-1993
Dickerson, Chuck	Illinois	1987-1991
Donaldson, Jack	Ohio State	1978-1982
Dooley, Jim	Miami	1972
Dove, Bob	Notre Dame	1960-1961
Dyer, George	Cal–Santa Barbara	1982
Engelberg, Lewis (d)	East Tennessee	1969-1970
Faragalli, Joe	Villanova	1986
Flores, Tom	Pacific	1971
Gibson, Claude	North Carolina State	1969
Glanville, Jerry	Northern Michigan	1983
Gottfried, Chuck	Illinois	1970-1971
Harris, Chick	Northern Arizona	1981-1982
Hawkins, Ralph	Maryland	1969-71, 81-82
Hunt, Bobby	Auburn	1970-1971
Jackson, Milt	Tulsa	1983-1984
Jauron, Dick	Yale	1985
Johnson, Harvey* (d)	William & Mary	1960-61, 68-71
Joiner, Charlie	Grambling State	1992-1993
Jones, Rusty	Springfield	1985-1993
Jones, Stan	Maryland	1972-1975
Kiffin, Monte	Nebraska	1984-1985
Knox, Chuck *	Juniata	1978-1982
LaRue, Jim	Duke	1976-1977
Lawrence, Don	Notre Dame	1983-84, 1990-93
Leahy, Bob	Emporia State	1985-1986
Lester, Chuck	Oklahoma	1987-1993
Levy, Marv *	Coe	1986-1993
MacDonald, Andy (d)	Central Michigan	1983-1984
Malavasi, Ray (d)	Mississippi State	1969-1970
Marchibroda, Ted	St. Bonaventure	1987-1991
Mazur, John	Notre Dame	1962-1968
McCabe, Richie (d)	Pittsburgh	1966-68, 76-77
McCalmon, Miller	Tulsa	1980-1984
Miller, Bill	Miami	1969
Miller, Bob (Red)	Western Illinois	1962
Moore, Steve	Cal Santa Barbara	1978-1982
Moseley, Dick	Eastern Michigan	1985-1986
Moss, Perry	Illinois	1983-1984
Niblack, Jim	Florida	1983-1984
Nicolau, Nick	Southern Connecticut	1989-1991
O'Connell, Tommy	Illinois	1961
Paterra, Herb	Michigan State	1986
Pitts, Elijah	Philander Smith	1978, 80, 85-93
Prisby, Errol	Cincinnati	1976
Prochaska, Ray	Nebraska	1978-1982
Ramsey, Buster	William & Mary	1960-1961
Rauch, John *	Georgia	1969-1970
Ray, John	Olivet College	1973-1976
Reid, Floyd	Georgia	1960-1961
Ringo, Jim *	Syracuse	1972-77, 85-88
Roach, Dick	Black Hills State	1987-1993
Saban, Lou *	Indiana	1962-65, 72-76
Sandahl, Al	Louisiana College	1983
Sardisco, Tony	Tulane	1968
Sekanovich, Dan	Tennessee	1992-1993
Shaw, Bob	Ohio State	1972-1975
Shofner, Jim	Texas Christian	1992-1993
Smith, Jerry	Wisconsin	1962-1968
Stephenson, Kay *	Florida	1978-82, 83-85
Tollner, Ted	Cal Poly-S.L.O.	1987-1988
Wagstaff, Jim	Idaho State	1978-1980
Wampfler, Jerry	Miami	1976-1977
Wiegandt, Ardell	North Dakota State	1985-1986
Wietecha, Ray	Northwestern	1977
Zapalac, Willie	Texas A & M	1978-1980
Zeman, Bob	Wisconsin	1983

(d) deceased
* denotes head coach

All Time Player Roster

Abramowitz, Dan	WR	Xavier (OH)	1975
Abruzzese, Ray	DB	Alabama	1962-64
Acker, Bill	NT	Texas	1983-84
Adams, Bill	G	Holy Cross	1972-78
Albright, Ira	NT	NE Oklahoma St.	1987
Alexander, Glenn	WR	Grambling	1970
Alexander, Mike	WR	Penn State	1991
Alford, Bruce	K	TX Christian	1968-69
Allen, Doug	LB	Penn State	1974-75
Allen, Jackie	DB	Baylor	1970-71
Alvers, Steve	TE	Miami (FL)	1981
Anderson, Max	RB	Arizona State	1968-70
Anderson, Tim	DB	Ohio State	1976
Andrews, Al	LB	New Mexico	1970-71
Armstrong, John	DB/KR	Richmond	1987
Atkins, Bill	DB	Auburn	1960-63
Auer, Joe	HB	Georgia Tech	1964-65
Awalt, Rob	TE	San Diego St	1992-93
Azelby, Joe	LB	Harvard	1984
Bailey, Bill	FB	Cincinnati	1967
Bailey, Carlton	LB	North Carolina	1988-92
Baker, Art	RB	Syracuse	1961-62
Baker, Mel	WR	Texas Southern	1977
Baldinger, Gary	NT	Wake Forest	1990-92
Ballard, Howard	OL	Alabama A & M	1988-93
Barber, Stew	OT	Penn State	1961-69
Barnett, Buster	TE	Jackson State	1981-84
Barnett, Oliver	DE	Kentucky	1993
Barnett, Robert	E	Baldwin Wallace	1960-66
Bass, Glenn	E	East Carolina	1961-66
Bateman, Marv	K	Utah	1974-77
Bavaro, David	LB	Syracuse	1991
Bayless, Martin	S	Bowling Green	1984-86
Beamer, Tim	S	J.C. Smith	1971
Beard, Tom	C	Michigan State	1972
Becker, Doug	LB	Notre Dame	1978
Beebe, Don	WR	Chadron State	1989-93
Behrman, Dave	C	Michigan State	1963-65
Belk, Veno	TE	Michigan State	1987
Bell, Greg	RB	Notre Dame	1984-87
Bellinger, Rodney	CB	Miami (FL)	1984-86
Bemiller, Al	C	Syracuse	1961-69
Bennett, Cornelius	LB	Alabama	1987-93
Bentley, Ray	LB	Central Mich.	1986-91
Besana, Fred	QB	California	1977
Bess, Gerald	CB	Tuskegee Institute	1987
Bess, Rufus	CB	S. Carolina St.	1980-81
Bivins, Charley	HB	Morris Brown	1967
Blazer, Phil	G	North Carolina	1960
Bock, Joe	C	Virginia	1987
Bohling, Dewey	RB	Hardin-Simmons	1961
Borchardt, Jon	T	Montana State	1979-84
Borden, Nate	E	Indiana	1962
Boyarksy, Jerry	NT	Pittsburgh	1986
Brady, Kerry	K	Hawaii	1989
Brammer, Mark	TE	Michigan State	1980-84
Bravyak, Jack	DE	Temple	1987
Braxton, Hezekiah	HB	Virginia Union	1963
Braxton, Jim	RB	West Virginia	1971-78
Brennan, Mike	OL	Notre Dame	1991
Briscoe, Marlin	WR	Omaha	1969-71
Brodhead, Bob	QB	Duke	1960
Brookins, Mitchell	WR	Illinois	1984-85
Brooks, Bill	WR	Boston University	1993
Brooks, Clifford	DB	Tennessee State	1976
Broughton, Walter	WR	Jacksonville State	1986-88
Brown, Charley	S	Syracuse	1968
Brown, Curtis	RB	Missouri	1977-82
Brown, Fred	HB	Georgia	1961-63
Brown, Marc	WR	Towson State	1987
Brown, Monty	LB	Ferris State	1993
Brown, Tony	OL	Pittsburgh	1987
Brubacker, Richard	E	Ohio State	1960
Bugenhagen, Gary	T	Syracuse	1967
Burkett, Chris	WR	Jackson State	1985-89
Burnett, Bobby	HB	Arkansas	1966-67
Burroughs, Derrick	DB	Memphis State	1985-89
Burton, Leonard	T	South Carolina	1986-89
Butler, Jerry	WR	Clemson	1979-86
Buzynski, Bernie	LB	Holy Cross	1960
Bynum, Reggie	WR	Oregon State	1987
Byrd, George (Butch)	CB	Boston University	1964-70
Byrum, Carl	FB	Mississippi Valley St	1986-88
Cahill, Bill	S	Washington	1973-74
Caldwell, Darryl	OT	Tennessee State	1983
Calhoun, Don	RB	Kansas State	1974-75
Callahan, Bill	S	Pittsburgh	1987
Carey, Richard	DB	Idaho	1990
Campbell, Arnold	DE	Alcorn State	1987
Cannavino, Joe	DB	Ohio State	1962
Cappadonna, Bob	RB	Northeastern	1968
Carpenter, Brian	CB	Michigan	1984
Carlton, Wray	FB	Duke	1960-67
Carr, Levert	T	No. Central Ill	1970-71
Carwell, Larry	S	Iowa State	1973
Catano, Mark	NT	Valdosta State	1986
Cater, Greg	P	Tenn.Chattanooga	1980-83
Celotto, Mario	LB	So. California	1978
Chamberlain, Dan	E	Sacramento St.	1960-61
Chandler, Bob	WR	So. California	1971-79
Chandler, Edgar	LB	Georgia	1968-72
Chapple, Dave	P	Calif. Santa Barbara	1971
Charon, Carl	DB	Michigan State	1962-63
Cheek, Richard	G	Auburn	1970-71
Chelf, Don	G	Iowa	1960-61
Chetti, Joe	FB	C.W. Post	1987
Cheyunski, Jim	LB	Syracuse	1973-74
Christiansen, Bob	TE	UCLA	1972
Christie, Steve	K	William and Mary	1992-93
Christy, Greg	T	Pittsburgh	1985
Clark, Allan	RB	Northern Arizona	1982
Clark, Mario	DB	Oregon	1976-83
Clark, Mike	K	Texas A & M	1972
Clark, Steve	FS	Liberty University	1987
Clarke, Hagood	DB	Florida	1964-68
Cocroft, Sherman	DB	San Jose State	1988
Cofield, Tim	LB	Elizabeth City State	1989
Cokeley, Will	LB	Kansas State	1987
Cole, Linzy	WR	Texas Christian	1972
Coleman, lFred	TE	Northeast Louisiana	1976
Collier, Mike	RB	Morgan State	1977-79
Collins, Greg	LB	Notre Dame	1977
Collins, Jerald	LB	West. Michigan	1969-71
Conlan, Shane	LB	Penn State	1987-92
Copeland, Russell	WR	Memphis State	1993
Cornell, Robert (Bo)	LB	Washington	1973-77
Cornish, Frank	DT	Alcorn A & M	1972
Costa, Dave	DT	Utah	1966-74
Costa, Paul	TE/T	Notre Dame	1965-72
Cowlings, Al	DE	So. California	1970-72
Crafts, Jerry	OL	Louisville	1992-93
Craig, Neal	S	Fisk	1974
Craig, Reggie	WR	Arkansas	1977
Crawford, Hilton	S	Grambling	1969
Cribbs, Joe	RB	Auburn	1980-83,85
Crockett, Bobby	WR	Arkansas	1966-69
Crockett, Monte	E	N. Mexico Highld	1960-62
Croft, Don	DT	Texas-El Paso	1972-75
Cross, Justin	CT	West. State CO	1982-86
Crotty, Jim	DB	Notre Dame	1961-62
Crow, Wayne	HB	California	1962-63
Croyle, Phil	LB	California	1973
Cudzik, Walt	C	Purdue	1964
Cumby, George	LB	Oklahoma	1986
Cunningham, Dick	T	Arkansas	1967-72
Curchin, Jeff	G	Florida State	1972
Daluiso, Brad	K	UCLA	1991
Danelo, Joe	K	Washington State	1983-84
Darby, Matt	S	UCLA	1992-93
Darragh, Dan	QB	William & Mary	1968-70
David, Stan	LB	Texas Tech	1984
Davis, John	T/G	Georgia Tech	1989-93
Davis, Kenneth	RB	Texas Christian	1989-93
Davis, Wayne	CB	Indiana State	1987-89
Dawkins, Julius	WR	Pittsburgh	1983-84
Day, Tom	DE	N.C. A & T	1961-66, 68
DeLamielleure, Joe	G	Michigan St.	1973-79, 85
Delucca, Gerry	T	Middle Tenn. St.	1962-63
Dempsey, Tom	K	Palomar Jr. Coll	1978-79
Dennard, Preston	WR	New Mexico	1984
Denney, Austin	TE	Tennessee	1970-71
Desutter, Wayne	T	Western Illinois	1966
Devleigher, Chuck	DT	Memphis State	1969
Devlin, Joe	T/G	Iowa	1976-82, 84-89
Devlin, Mike	C	Iowa	1993
Dickerson, Anthony	LB	SMU	1985
Discenzo, Tony	T	Michigan State	1960
Dittrich, John	G	Wisconsin	1961
Dobbins, Oliver	DB	Morgan State	1964
Dobler, Conrad	G	Wyoming	1980-81
Dokes, Phil	DE	Oklahoma State	1977-78
Donaldson, Gene	FB	Purdue	1967
Dorow, Al	QB	Michigan State	1962
Dowling, Sean	T	C.W. Post	1987
Drane, Dwight	S	Oklahoma	1986-91
Drungo, Elbert	T	Tennessee State	1978
Dubenion, Elbert	WR	Bluffton	1960-68
Dufek, Joe	QB	Yale	1983-85
Dunaway, Jim	DT	Mississippi	1963-71
Dunstan, Bill	DT	Utah State	1977
Edgerson, Booker	CB	Western Illinois	1962-69
Edwards, Al	WR/KR	N.W. Louisiana St.	1991-2
Edwards, Earl	DE	Wichita State	1973-75
Edwards, Emmett	WR	Kansas	1976
Ehlers, Tom	LB	Kentucky	1978
Enyart, Bill	RB	Oregon State	1969-70
Erlandson, Tom	LB	Washington	1988
Estep, Mike	G	Bowling Green	1987
Farley, Dale	LB	West Virginia	1972-73
Felton, Ralph	LB	Maryland	1961-62
Fergerson, Duke	WR	San Diego State	1980
Ferguson, Charley	TE	Tennessee State	1963-69
Ferguson, Joe	QB	Arkansas	1973-84
Ferragamo, Vince	QB	Nebraska	1985
Fina, John	OL	Arizona	1992-93
Flint, George	G	Arizona State	1962-65, 68
Flint, Judson	S	Memphis State	1983
Flores, Tom	QB	Pacific	1967-69
Foley, Dave	T	Ohio State	1972-77
Ford, Charley	DB	Houston	1975
Ford, Fred	HB	CA Poly (Pomona)	1960
Forsberg, Fred	LB	Washington	1973
Fowler, Wayne	C	Richmond	1970
Fowler, Willmer	HB	Northwestern	1960-61
Francis, Wallace	WR	Ark AM & N	1973-74
Frankowiak, Mike	TE	Central Michigan	1977-78
Franklin, Byron	WR	Auburn	1981, 83-84
Frantz, Jack	C	California	1968
Frazier, Guy	LB	Wyoming	1985-86
Frazier, Wayne	C	Auburn	1967
Freemen, Steve	DB	Mississippi State	1975-86
Frerotte, Mitch	G	Penn State	1987, 90-92
Friday, Larry	S	Mississippi State	1987
Fuller, Eddie	RB	LSU	1991-93
Fulton, Dan	WR	Nebraska-Omaha	1979
Fulton, Ed	G	Maryland	1979
Furjanic, Tony	LB	Notre Dame	1986-87
Gaddis, Bob	WR	Mississippi Valley St.	1976
Gaines, Sheldon	WR	Cal. St (Long Beach)	1987
Gant, Reuben	TE	Oklahoma State	1974-80
Gantt, Jerome	T	No. Carolina Central	1970
Gardner, Carwell	FB	Louisville	1990-93
Garner, Hal	LB	Utah State	1985-88,90-91
Garnett, Scott	NT	Washington	1987
Garror, Leon	S	Alcorn A & M	1972-73
Gelbaugh, Stan	QB	Maryland	1986-89
Gibson, Reuben	RB	Memphis State	1977
Gilbert, Gale	QB	Cal-Berkeley	1989-93
Gilchrist, Cookie	FB	None	1962-64
Gladieux, Bob	RB	Notre Dame	1970
Glosson, Clyde	WR	Texas-El Paso	1970
Goganious, Keith	LB	Penn State	1992-93
Gogolak, Pete	K	Cornell	1964-65
Goode, Irv	G	Kentucky	1972
Goodwin, Doug	FB	Maryland State	1966
Grabosky, Gene	T	Syracuse	1960
Graham, Don	LB	Penn State	1988
Graham, Tom	LB	Oregon	1978
Grant, Wes	DE	UCLA	1971
Grant, Will	C	Kentucky	1978-85, 87
Grate, Willie	TE	So. Carolina State	1969-70
Green, Donnie	T	Purdue	1971-76
Green, John	QB	Chattanooga	1960-61
Green, Van	DB	Shaw	1976
Greene, Doug	DB	Texas A & I	1979-80
Greene, Tony	CB	Maryland	1971-79
Griffith, Brent	OL	Minnesota-Duluth	1990
Gregory, Ben	RB	Nebraska	1968-69
Groman, Bill	E	Heidelberg	1964-65
Guidry, Paul	LB	McNeese State	1966-72
Guthrie, Grant	K	Florida State	1970-71
Hagen, Halvor	T	Weber State	1973-75
Haggins, Odell	NT	Florida State	1991
Hagy, John	DB	Texas	1988-90
Haines, Kris	WR	Notre Dame	1987
Hale, Chris	DB	USC	1989-92
Hamby, Mike	DE	Utah State	1986
Hansen, Phil	DE	No Dakota State	1991-93
Hardison, Dee	DT	North Carolina	1978-80
Harmon, Ronnie	RB	Iowa	1986-89
Harper, Darrell	HB	Michigan	1960
Harris, James	QB	Grambling	1969-71
Harrison, Dwight	DB	Texas A & I	1972-77
Hart, Dick	G	None	1972
Hart, Leo	QB	Duke	1972-73
Harvey, Richard	LB	Tulane	1992-93
Harvey, Waddey	DT	Virginia Tech	1969-70
Haslerig, Clint	RB	Michigan	1974-75
Haslett, Jim	LB	Indiana (PA)	1979-85
Hayman, Gary	RB	Penn State	1974-75
Healy, Don	T	Maryland	1962
Heath, Clayton	RB	Wake Forest	1976
Hellestrae, Dale	T	SMU	1985-88
Henley, Carey	RB	Chattanooga	1962
Hergert, Joe	LB	Florida	1960-61
Hernandez, Scott	NT	Kent State	1987
Henderson, Jerome	DB	Clemson	1993
Herrera, Efren	K	UCLA	1982
Hertwig, Craig	T	Georgia	1978
Hews, Bob	T	Princeton	1971
Hicks, Clifford	DB	Oregon	1993
Higgins, Tom	LB	North Carolina State	1979
Hill, Ike	CB	Catawba	1970-71
Hill, J.D.	WR	Arizona State	1971-75
Hill, Rod	CB	Kentucky State	1984
Hoisington, Al	E	Pasadena City Coll.	1960
Holland, John	WR	Tennessee State	1975-77
Holmes, Mike	WR	Texas Southern	1976
Holt, Robert	WR	Baylor	1982
Hooks, Roland	RB	No Carolina State	1976-82
Howard, Ron	TE	Seattle	1979
Hudlow, Floyd	DB	Arizona	1965
Hudson, Dick	T	Memphis State	1963-68
Hull, Kent	C	Mississippi State	1986-93
Humiston, Mike	LB	Weber State	1981
Humm, David	QB	Nebraska	1980
Hunter, Scott	QB	Alabama	1974
Hunter, Jeff	DE	Albany State	1990
Hunter, Tony	TE	Notre Dame	1983-84
Hurley, Bill	S	Syracuse	1983
Hurston, Chuck	DE	Auburn	1971
Hutchinson, Scott	DE	Florida	1978-80, 83
Hutchison, Anthony	RB	Texas Tech	1985
Ieremia, Mekeli	DE	Brigham Young	1978
Irvin, Darrell	DE	Oklahoma	1980-83
Jackson, Kirby	DB	Mississippi State	1988-92
Jackson, Randy	RB	Wichita State	1972
Jackson, Rusty	P	Louisiana State	1978-79
Jackunas, Frank	C	Detroit	1962
Jacobs, Harry	LB	Bradley	1963-69
Jakowenko, George	K	Syracuse	1976
James, Robert	CB	Fisk	1969-74
Janik, Tom	S	Texas A & I	1965-68
Jarvis, Bruce	C	Washington	1971-74
Jarvis, Ray	WR	Norfolk State	1973
Jenkins, Ed	RB	Holy Cross	1974
Jessie, Ron	WR	Kansas	1980-81
Jeter, Gene	LB	Arkansas A M & N	1967
Jilek, Dan	LB	Michigan	1976-79
Joe, Billy	FB	Villanova	1965
Johnson, Dennis	DT	Delaware	1978
Johnson, Dennis	FB	Mississippi State	1978-79
Johnson, Flip	WR	McNeese State	1988-89
Johnson, Jack	HB	Miami (FL)	1960-61
Johnson, Ken	QB	Colorado	1977
Johnson, Ken	DE	Knoxville Coll	1979-84
Johnson, Lawrence	CB/S	Wisconsin	1984-87
Johnson, Mark	LB	Missouri	1975-76
Johnson, Trumaine	WR	Grambling	1986-87
Jones, Doug	DB	San Fernando Val. St.	1975-78
Jones, Ed	DB	Rutgers	1975
Jones, Greg	RB	UCLA	1970-71
Jones, Henry	DB	Illinois	1991-93
Jones, Ken	DE/OT	Arkansas State	1976-86
Jones, Mike	LB	SUNY Brockport	1987
Jones, Spike	P	Georgia	1971-74
Jones, Steve	RB	Duke	1973-74
Jones, Willie	HB	Purdue	1962
Junkin, Trey	LB	Louisiana Tech	1983-84
Kadish, Mike	DT	Notre Dame	1973-81
Kaiser, John	LB	Arizona	1987
Kalsu, Bob	G	Oklahoma	1968
Kampa, Bob	DT	California	1973-74
Keating, Chris	LB	Maine	1979-84
Keating, Tom	DT	Michigan	1964-65
Kellerman, Ernie	S	Miami (OH)	1973
Kelly, Jim	QB	Miami (FL)	1986-93
Kelso, Mark	S	William & Mary	1986-93
Kemp, Jack	QB	Occidental	1962-69
Kennedy, Mike	S	Toledo	1973
Kern, Don	TE	Arizona State	1986
Kern, Rex	S	Ohio State	1974
Kilson, Dave	CB	Nevada, Reno	1983
Kimbrough, John	WR	St. Cloud State	1977
Kidd, John	P	Northwestern	1984-89
Kingrea, Rick	LB	Tulane	1973
Kinard, Bill	DB	Mississippi	1960
Kindig, Howard	C/DE	Los Angeles State	1967-71
King, Bruce	FB	Purdue	1986
King, Charley	CB	Purdue	1966-67
King, Tony	DB	Findlay	1967
Kinnebrew, Larry	FB	Tennenesse State	1989-90
Kinney, Jeff	RB	Nebraska	1976
Kochman, Roger	HB	Penn State	1963
Koffler, Matt	QB	San Diego State	1982-84
Koy, Ted	LB/TE	Texas	1971-74
Krakau, Merv	LB	Iowa State	1973-78
Kruse, Bob	G	Wayne State	1969
Kubin, Larry	LB	Penn State	1985
Kulbacki, Joe	HB	Purdue	1960
Kush, Rod	SS	Nebraska-Omaha	1980-84
Lamar, Kevin	G	Stanford	1987
Lamb, Brad	WR	Anderson Univ.	1992-93
Lamonica, Daryle	QB	Notre Dame	1963-66
Laraway, Jack	LB	Purdue	1960
Laskey, Bill	LB	Michigan	1965
Laster, Art	T	Maryland State	1970
Lawson, Jerome	CB	Utah	1968
Leaks, Roosevelt	RB	Texas	1980-83
LeBlanc, Bob	LB	Elon College	1970
Ledbetter, Monte	WR	NW Louisiana St.	1967-69
Lee, Ken	LB	Washington	1972
LeMoine, Jim	G	Utah State	1967
Leo, Chuck	G	Indiana	1963
Lettner, Bob	LB	Tennessee	1961
Levenseller, Mike	WR	Washington State	1978
Lewis, Frank	WR	Grambling	1978-83
Lewis, Harold	HB	Houston	1962
Lewis, John	CB	Pittsburgh	1987
Lewis, Richard	LB	Portland State	1973-74
Leypoldt, John	K	None	1971-76
Lincoln, Keith	HB	Washington State	1967-68
Lingner, Adam	C	Illinois	1987, 89-93
Little, John	DT	Oklahoma State	1977
Lloyd, Jeff	DT	West Texas State	1976
Lodish, Mike	NT	UCLA	1990-93
Lofton, James	WR	Stanford	1989-92
Long, Carson	K	Pittsburgh	1977
Louderback, Tom	LB	San Jose State	1962
Loukas, Angelo	G	Northwestern	1969
Loving, Warren	FB	William Penn	1987
Lucas, Richie	QB/HB	Penn State	1960-61
Lumpkin, Joey	LB	Arizona State	1982-83
Lusteg, Booth	K	Connecticut	1966
Lyman, Jeff	LB	Brigham Young	1972
Lynch, Tom	G	Boston College	1981-84
Maddox, Mark	LB	North. Michigan	1992-93
Maguire, Paul	LB/K	The Citadel	1964-70
Maidlow, Steve	LB	Michigan State	1985, 87
Majors, Bill	DB	Tennessee	1961
Manucci, Dan	QB	Kansas State	1979-80, 87
Marangi, Gary	QB	Boston College	1974-76
Marchlewski, Frank	C	Minnesota	1970
Mawrtin, David	CB	Villanova	1987
Marve, Eugene	LB	Saginaw Valley St.	1982-87
Masters, Billy	TE	Louisiana State	1967-69
Mathison, Bruce	QB	Nebraska	1985
Matlock, John	C	Miami	1972
Matsos, Archie	LB	Michigan State	1960-62
Matuszak, Marv	LB	Tulsa	1962-63
Mays, David	QB	Texas Southern	1978
McBath, Mike	DE	Penn State	1968-72
McCabe, Richie	DB	Pittsburgh	1960-61
McCaffrey, Mike	LB	California	1970
McClanahan, Randy	LB	S.W. Louisiana	1978
McClure, Brian	QB	Bowling Green	1987
McConnell, Brian	LB	Michigan State	1973
McCrumbly, John	LB	Texas A & M	1975
McCutcheon, Lawrence	RB	Colorado State	1981
McDermott, Gary	RB	Tulsa	1968
McDole, Ron	DE	Nebraska	1963-70
McDonald, Don	DB	Houston	1961
McFadden, Thad	WR	Wisconsin	1987
McFarland, Jim	TE	Nebraska	1970
McGrail, Joe	NT	Delaware	1987
McGrew, Dan	C	Purdue	1960
McKeller, Keith	TE	Jacksonville State	1987-93
McKenzie, Reggie	G	Michigan	1972-82
McKinley, Bill	LB	Arizona	1971
McKinney, Royce	DB	Kentucky State	1975
McKnight, Ted	RB	Minnesota-Duluth	1982
McMillan, Eddie	CB	Florida State	1978
McMurtry, Chuck	DT	Whittier College	1960-61
McNanie, Sean	DE	San Diego State	1984-87
Means, Dave	DE	S.E. Missouri State	1974
Mercer, Mike	K	No. Arizona	1967-68
Meredith, Dudley	DE	Lamar Tech	1964-68
Merrill, Mark	LB	Minnesota	1983-84
Mesner, Bruce	NT	Maryland	1987
Metzelaars, Pete	TE	Wabash	1985-93
Meyer, Ed	T	W. Texas State	1960
Mike-Mayer, Nick	K	Temple	1979-82
Miller, Bill	E	Miami (FL)	1963
Miller, Mark	QB	Mesa College	1987
Miller, Terry	RB	Oklahoma State	1978-80
Mills, Sullivan	E/DB	Wichita State	1965-66
Minter, Tom	HB	Baylor	1962
Mistler, John	WR	Arizona State	1984
Mitchell, Charley	HB	Washington	1968
Mitchell, Roland	CB	Texas Tech	1987-88
Mohr, Chris	P	Alabama	1991-93
Monger, Matt	LB	Oklahoma State	1989-90
Montler, Mike	C	Colorado	1973-76
Moody, Keith	KR/DB	Syracuse	1976-79
Moore, Booker	FB	Penn State	1982-85
Moore, Leroy	DE	Ft. Valley St.	1960,62-63
Moore, Ricky	FB	Alabama	1986
Morton, Greg	DE	Michigan	1977
Moses, Haven	WR	San Diego State	1968-72
Mosley, Mike	WR	Texas A & M	1982-84
Mosley, Wayne	RB	Alabama A & M	1974
Moss, Roland	RB	Toledo	1970
Muelhaupt, Ed	G	Iowa State	1960-61
Mueller, Jamie	FB	Benedictine Coll.	1987-90
Munson, Bill	QB	Utah State	1978-79
Murdock, Jessie	FB	California Western	1963
Myslinski, Tom	G	Tennessee	1993
Neal, Speedy	FB	Miami (FL)	1984
Nelson, Bob	LB	Nebraska	1975-77
Nelson, Chuck	K	Washington	1984
Nelson, Shane	LB	Baylor	1977-82
Nies, John	P/K	Arizona	1990
Nighswander, Nick	C	Morehead State	1974
Nixon, Jeff	DB	Richmond	1979-82
Norris, Ulysses	TE	Georgia	1984-85
Norwood, Scott	K	James Madison	1985-91
Nunamaker, Julian	DE	Tennessee-Martin	1969-71
Nuzzo, Chip	S	Princeton	1987
O'Connell, Tom	QB	Illinois	1960-61
Odomes, Nate	CB	Wisconsin	1987-93
O'Donnell, Joe	G	Michigan	1964-71
O'Donoghue, Neil	K	Auburn	1977
Ogas, Dave	LB	San Diego State	1969
Okoniewski, Steve	DT	Montana	1972-73
Oldham, Chris	CB	Oregon	1991
Oliver, Frank	DB	Kentucky State	1975
Olson, Harold	T	Clemson	1960-62
Owens, Artie	WR	West Virginia	1980
Palmer, Dick	LB	Kentucky	1972
Palumbo, Sam	C	Notre Dame	1960
Panepinto, Mike	RB	Canisius	1987
Parker, Ervin	LB	So. Carolina State	1980-83
Parker, Glenn	OL	Arizona	1990-93
Parker, Kerry	CB	Grambling	1984
Parker, Willie	C	No. Texas State	1973-79
Parrella, John	DL	Nebraska	1993
Parrish, Lemar	CB	Lincoln	1982
Partridge, Rick	P	Utah	1987
Pate, Lloyd	RB	Cincinnati	1970
Paterra, Herb	LB	Michigan State	1963
Patrick, Wayne	RB	Louisville	1968-72
Patton, Bob	C	Delaware	1976
Patton, James	DL	Texas	1993
Patton, Jerry	DT	Nebraska	1972-73
Patton, Marvcus	LB	UCLA	1990-93
Patulski, Walt	DE	Notre Dame	1972-75
Penchion, Robert	G	Alcorn A & M	1972-73
Perryman, Jim	S	Millikin	1985
Petrich, Bob	DE	West Texas State	1967
Pharr, Tommy	S	Mississippi State	1970
Phillips, Kim	DB	No. Texas State	1990
Piccone, Lou	WR	West Liberty St.	1977-82
Pike, Mark	LB	Georgia Tech	1987-93
Pitts, John	S	Arizona State	1967-73
Pitts, Ron	DB	UCLA	1986-87
Ploeger, Kurt	DE	Gustavus Adolphus	1986
Ply, Bobby	DB	Baylor	1967
Pool, David	DB	Carson-Newman	1990, 93
Porter, Kerry	RB	Washington State	1987
Porter, Ricky	RB	Slippery Rock	1987
Potter, Steve	LB	Virginia	1984
Powell, Art	E	San Jose State	1967
Powell, Darnell	RB	Chattanooga	1976
Powell, Steve	RB	N.E. Missouri St.	1978-79
Prater, Dean	DE	Oklahoma State	1984-88
Prudhomme, Remi	C	LSU	1966-67, 72
Pruitt, Mike	FB	Purdue	1985
Rabb, Warren	QB	LSU	1961-62
Radecic, Scott	LB	Penn State	1987-89
Ramson, Eason	TE	Washington State	1985
Randolph, Al	S	Iowa	1974
Rashad, Ahmad	WR	Oregon	1974-75
Ray, Eddie	RB	Louisiana State	1976
Reed, Andre	WR	Kutztown	1985-93
Reeves, Roy	WR	So. Carolina	1969
Reich, Frank	QB	Maryland	1985-93
Reid, Andy	RB	Georgia	1976
Reilly, Jim	G	Notre Dame	1970-71
Remmert, Dennis	T	Iowa State	1960
Reynolds, M.C.	QB	LSU	1961
Ricardo, Benny	K	San Diego State	1976
Rice, Ken	T	Auburn	1961-63
Richards, Perry	E	Detroit	1961
Richardson, Eric	WR	San Jose State	1985-86
Richardson, Pete	CB	Dayton	1969-71
Richey, Mike	T	No. Carolina	1969
Riddick, Robb	RB	Millersville St.	1981,83-84,86-88
Ridgle, Elston	DE	Nevada-Reno	1989
Ridlehuber, Preston	RB	Georgia	1969
Rissmiller, Ray	T	Georgia	1966
Ritcher, Jim	G	No. Carolina St.	1980-93
Rivera, Hank	DB	Oregon State	1963
Roberson, Bo	E	Cornell	1965
Robertson, Isiah	LB	Southern	1979-82
Robinson, Matt	QB	Georgia	1981-82
Rogers, Reggie	DE	Washington	1991
Rolfe, Butch	TE	Michigan State	1986-91
Romes, Charles	DB	No. Carolina Cent.	1977-86
Roopenian, Mark	NT	Boston College	1982-83
Roquemore, Durwood	S	Texas A & I	1987
Rosdahl, Harrison	DE	Penn State	1964
Rosenmeier, Erik	C	Colgate	1987
Ross, Louis	DE	So. Carolina St.	1971-72
Ross, Willie	FB	Nebraska	1964
Russell, Ben	QB	Louisville	1968
Rutkowski, Charles	E	Ripon	1960
Rutkowski, Ed	QB/WR	Notre Dame	1963-68
Ruud, Tom	LB	Nebraska	1975-77
Rychlec, Tom	E	American Intern.	1960-62
Saidock, Tom	DT	Michigan State	1962
Saimes, George	S	Michigan State	1963-69
Sanford, Lucius	LB	Georgia Tech	1978-86
Saunders, John	S	Toledo	1972
Schaffer, Joe	HB	Tennessee	1960
Schankweiler, Scott	LB	Maryland	1987
Schlopy, Todd	K	Michigan	1987
Schmidt, Bob	C	Minnesota	1966-67
Schmidt, Henry	DT	Southern California	1965
Schnarr, Steve	RB	Otterbein	1975
Schottenheimer, Marty	LB	Pittsburgh	1965-68
Schulte, Rick	OG	Illinois	1987
Schulz, Kurt	S	Eastern Wash.	1992-93
Scott, John	T	Ohio State	1960-61
Seals, Leon	DE	Jackson State	1987-91
Sedlock, Bob	DT	Georgia	1960
Selfridge, Andy	LB	Virginia	1972
Sestak, Tom	DT	McNeese State	1962-68
Seymour, Paul	TE	Michigan	1973-77
Shaw, Billy	G	Georgia Tech	1961-69
Shaw, Dennis	QB	San Diego State	1970-73
Shepherd, Johnny	RB	Livingston Univ.	1987
Sherman, Tom	QB	Penn State	1969
Shipp, Joe	TE	Southern California	1979
Shockley, Bill	HB	West Chester State	1961
Shupe, Mark	C	Arizona State	1987
Silipo, Joe	C	Tulane	1987
Simpson, Bill	FS	Michigan State	1980-82
Simpson, O.J.	RB	South. California	1969-77
Skorupan, John	LB	Penn State	1973-77
Smerlas, Fred	NT	Boston College	1979-89
Smith, Allen	HB	Ft. Valley State	1966-67
Smith, Bobby	HB	North Texas St.	1964-65
Smith, Bruce	DE	Virginia Tech	1985-93
Smith, Carl	FB	Tennessee	1960
Smith, Don	DE	Miami (FL)	1985-86
Smith, Don	RB	Mississippi State	1990
Smith, Joey	WR	Clemson	1990
Smith, Leonard	DB	McNeese State	1988-91
Smith, Lucious	CB	Cal. State-Fullerton	1984
Smith, Marty	DT	Louisville	1976
Smith, Thomas	CB	North Carolina	1993
Smith, Tody	DE	Southern California	1976
Snowden, Cal	DE	Indiana	1971
Solomon, Roland	CB	Utah	1980
Sommer, Don	OT	Texas, El Paso	1987
Sorey, Jim	DT	Texas Southern	1960-62
Spikes, Jack	FB	TCU	1966-67
Staysniak, Joe	OL	Ohio State	1991
Steels, Anthony	KR/RB	Nebraska	1985
Steinfort, Fred	K	Boston College	1983
Stephenson, Kay	QB	Florida	1968
Stone, Don	FB	Arkansas	1965
Stone, Ken	S	Vanderbilt	1973
Stratton, Mike	LB	Tennessee	1962-72
Still, Art	DE	Kentucky	1988-89
Sutton, Mickey	DB/PR	Montana	1989
Switzer, Marvin	DB	Kansas State	1978
Sykes, Gene	DB	LSU	1963-65
Taliaferro, Mike	QB	Illinois	1972
Talley, Darryl	LB	West Virginia	1983-93
Taseff, Carl	DB	John Carroll Univ.	1962
Tasker, Steve	WR/KR	Northwestern	1986-93
Tatarek, Bob	DT	Miami (FL)	1968-72
Taylor, Brian	DB	Oregon State	1991
Teal, Jimmy	WR	Texas A & M	1985-86
Tharpe, Richard	DE	Louisville	1987
Thomas, Ike	DB	Bishop	1975
Thomas, Thurman	RB	Oklahoma State	1988-93
Thompson, Gary	CB	Coll. of Redwoods	1983-84
Thornton, Bubba	WR	Texas Christian	1969
Tongue, Marco	DB	Bowie State	1984
Toomay, Pat	DE	Vanderbilt	1975
Torczon, LaVerne	DE	Nebraska	1960-62
Totten, Willie	QB	Mississippi Valley St.	1987
Tracey, John	LB	Texas A & M	1962-67
Trapp, Richard	WR	Florida	1968
Traynowicz, Mark	G	Nebraska	1985-88
Tucker, Erroll	DB/KR	Utah	1988-89
Turner, Nate	RB	Nebraska	1993
Turner, Vernon	WR	Carson-Newman	1990
Tuten, Rick	P	Florida State	1989
Tuttle, Perry	WR	Clemson	1982-83
Tyler, Maurice	S	Morgan State	1972-73
Valdez, Vernon	DB	San Diego College	1961
Vanvalkenburg, Pete	RB	Brigham Young	1973
Villapiano, Phil	LB	Bowling Green	1980-83
Virkus, Scott	DE	San Francisco C.C.	1983-84
Vogler, Tim	G/T/C	Ohio State	1979-88
Wagstaff, Jim	DB	Idaho State	1960-61
Walczak, Mark	TE	Arizona	1987
Walker, Donnie	DB	Central St. (OH)	1973-74
Walls, Craig	LB	Indiana	1987
Walsh, Chris	WR	Stanford	1992-93
Walterscheid, Len	S	So. Utah State	1983-84
Walton, Larry	WR	Arizona State	1978
Warlick, Ernie	E	No. Carolina Cent.	1962-65
Warner, Charley	DB	Prairie View	1964-66
Washington, Dave	LB	Alcorn State	1972-74
Washington, Mickey	CB	Texas A&M	1993
Washington, Vic	RB	Wyoming	1975-76
Watkins, Larry	FB	Alcorn State	1973-74
Watters, Scott	LB	Wittenberg	1987
Wegert, Ted	HB	None	1960
Wenglikowski, Al	LB	Pittsburgh	1984, 87
West, Willie	DB	Oregon	1962-63
Wheeler, Manch	QB	Maine	1962
White, Craig	WR	Missouri	1984
White, Jan	TE	Ohio State	1971-72
White, Sherman	DE	California	1976-83
Whittington, Arthur	RB	SMU	1982
Wilkins, Gary	FB	Georgia Tech	1986-87
Williams, Ben	DE	Mississippi	1976-85
Williams, Chris	CB	LSU	1982-83
Williams, James	CB	Fresno State	1990-93
Williams, Kevin	CB	Iowa State	1986
Williams, Leonard	RB	Western Carolina	1987
Williams, Van	RB	Carson-Newman	1983-84
Willis, Keith	DE	Northeastern	1992
Willis, Len	WR	Ohio State	1977-79
Wilson, Don	S	No. Carolina St.	1984-85
Wilson, Eric	LB	Maryland	1985
Wilson, Mike	G	Dayton	1971
Winans, Jeff	DT	South. California	1973-75
Winfrey, Stan	RB	Arkansas State	1977
Witt, Billy	DE	North Alabama	1987
Wolff, Wayne	G	Wake Forest	1961
Wolford, Will	G/T	Vanderbilt	1986-92
Word, Roscoe	DB	Jackson State	1976
Wright, Bo	RB	Alabama	1988
Wright, Jeff	NT	Central Missouri	1988-93
Wyatt, Alvin	DB	Bethune-Cookman	1970-73
Wyche, Sam	QB	Furman	1976
Yaccino, John	DB	Pittsburgh	1962
Yeates, Jeff	DT	Boston College	1974-76
Yoho, Mack	DE	Miami (OH)	1960-63
Young, Dave	TE	Purdue	1983
Young, Willie	T	Alcorn State	1971-72
Youngelman, Sid	T	Alabama	1962-63
Zecher, Rich	DT	Utah State	1967
Zelencik, Connie	C	Purdue	1977

About the Author

Sal Maiorana wasn't quite eight years old when his father, Sam, took him for the first time to War Memorial Stadium in Buffalo. On that sunny October day in 1970, O.J. Simpson returned a kickoff 95 yards for a touchdown; Jets quarterback Joe Namath had an equipment problem and his teammates huddled around him to shield him from the crowd while he dropped his pants to get it fixed – "Why are they doing that, dad?" – and the Bills beat New York, 34-31. A love affair with football and the Bills had begun. There had been many Sunday afternoons before that day watching the Bills on television, but it was the first trip to the old Rockpile that captivated the impressionable little boy.

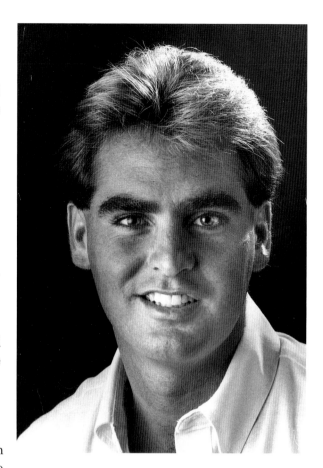

Maiorana was born in Buffalo in 1962, moved to Syracuse when he was five and then to the suburb of Marcellus when he was eight. He attended Bishop Ludden High School in Syracuse, then returned to Buffalo and spent four years at Buffalo State College earning a bachelor of arts degree in journalism in 1984.

He began covering the Bills as a college student in 1982 working part-time for The Associated Press. His first job in the newspaper business was at *The Leader* in Corning, New York and after 20 months, he moved on to the *Democrat and Chronicle* in Rochester in November 1986 where he remains today. Now in his fifth year of covering the Bills – thus fulfilling a dream that was first cultivated while sitting on the hard wooden seats of War Memorial Stadium – Maiorana has seen the Bills play in the Super Bowl in each of his first four years on the beat.

An accomplished golf writer who has covered the U.S. Open and the Ryder Cup, and is a regular correspondent for *Golf World*, *Golf Week*, and *PGA Magazine*, Maiorana's first book was published in May of 1993 by St. Martin's Press Inc., New York, New York. *Through the Green – The Mind and Art of a Professional Golfer* was written with the cooperation of PGA Tour star Davis Love III and provided a unique behind-the-scenes look at life on the pro golf circuit.

Maiorana was the 1993 winner of the Charlie Wagner Sports Writer of the Year Award, presented annually by the Rochester Press-Radio Club. He also was honored as a distinguished citizen in Corning for his work covering area high school sporting events.

Maiorana lives in Walworth, New York with his wife, the former Christine Charlton, and their daughter, Taylor Marie.